THE LITERATURE OF ENGLAND

An Anthology and a History

REVISED SINGLE VOLUME EDITION

by GEORGE K. ANDERSON, *Brown University*

and WILLIAM E. BUCKLER, *New York University*

SCOTT, FORESMAN AND COMPANY

Library of Congress Catalog Card No. 67-21667

Regional offices of Scott, Foresman and Company are located in Atlanta, Dallas,
Glenview, Palo Alto, and Oakland, N.J.

PREFACE

The first edition of The Literature of England appeared in 1936 as the culmination of several years of planning and labor by authors and publishers, who worked together toward a definite objective: the new anthology was to be not just another collection of college readings, but rather a well-articulated interpretation and representation of English civilization as expressed in English literature.

To this fixed end each element of the book—introductory essays outlining the development of English literature, biographical sketches of individual authors, all headnotes, selection of texts, and explanatory footnotes—was considered in terms of the other parts, with a wealth of cross-references, and each item was admitted or excluded only after long deliberation on the part of the authors. Furthermore, each author read critically the work of his associates, and the progress of the book was reviewed at frequent conferences of publishers and authors. As a result, the two finished volumes possessed a true unity, a functional continuity of structure and content.

This particular plan of creating an integrated study of English literature was carried even further in the second edition of 1941. The selection of texts was altered, and the number of these texts was increased to meet the suggestions of teachers. All of the original eight chapters were revised. Since the favorable reception of this new type of anthology had confirmed the faith of the authors and publisher in their original design, the purpose of the book and what the late Professor Lindsay Todd Damon, originally the general editor, used to call its "gross anatomy" remained unchanged. The same plan was deemed sufficient for the third edition of 1947, although certain additions and omissions were effected there in order to take into account contemporary literary developments and trends in the classroom. A particular innovation in the 1947 edition was the material included on the modern scene, presenting the literature of England since 1914 as a new, or ninth, major period of English literature. The process of revision, inclusion, and exclusion of selections and rewriting of introductory chapters and notes was repeated in the later editions of 1958 and 1966, but in the 1966 edition the format was completely changed to allow for the substitution of an ordinary printed page for the old two-column page.

For several years, the authors and publishers had considered bringing out a one-volume edition intended for those general courses in English literature in which the study would cover fewer authors and would call for a closer comprehension of a smaller number of texts. The first such volume, published in 1953, was not a casual abridgment of the two-volume edition, although it was built upon the outlines and followed the same plan of the existing and continuing two-volume work. The nine chapters of the two-volume edition were reduced in number to six by combining the discussions of Old and Middle English literature, of the Renaissance and the Puritan interlude, and of the post-Victorian and twentieth-century literature. Moreover, some new items were added that did not appear in the contents of the two-volume edition until 1966. The introductory headnotes and footnotes, as well as the interchapters, were as usual revised and in most cases shortened. In brief, the book stood on its own as a special contribution to a shorter, more intensive course in English literature from the beginnings to 1950.

In preparing this new version of the one-volume edition, the authors have proceeded with the most thoughtful attention to the wishes of teachers of English literature all over the nation, as expressed in replies to questions put by the publisher. It is no small undertaking to represent adequately in 1300 pages a magnificent literature which has endured and developed for thirteen centuries. No item, however, was omitted which would interfere seriously with the canon of readings preferred by teachers of English literature in this country, though many so-called minor writers represented in the two-volume editions have had to be left out of the one-volume edition. The plays, a feature of the two-volume editions, have been omitted as a general policy, since the inclusion of only two or three plays, in view of space considerations, is meaningless if one is attempting to study the development of the drama. A single exception has been made in the case of Shakespeare's King Lear, because the authors believe that no anthology of English literature can afford to be without a major drama by Shakespeare.

The authors and the publisher take this occasion to thank all friends of the original Literature of England and its later revisions, and especially all who have been helpful in their constructive criticisms and suggestions. Our chief hope for this revised one-volume edition is that as time goes on, it will be thought to merit the acclaim accorded the two-volume editions.

G. K. A.
W. E. B.

CONTENTS

Chapter 1

WARRIOR, PRIEST, AND COMMONER

Chapter 2

THE BRAVE NEW WORLD AND AFTER

Chapter 3

CONVENTION AND REALISM

Chapter 4

REVOLUTION AND ROMANCE

Chapter 5

SCIENCE, DEMOCRACY, AND INDUSTRIALISM

xi

Chapter 6

THE STRUGGLE ON THE DARKLING PLAIN

A NOTE ON THE MAPS AND ILLUSTRATIONS

More and more in scholarly research and in teaching, the art of literature is being studied, not by itself alone, but in relation to other arts. For literature, in so far as it not only reflects the individual author but also holds, "as 'twere, the mirror up to nature," is but one expression of the thought and the taste of the world which produces it. Architecture, painting, music, and, in humbler ways, even dress and decoration, all reveal "the very age and body of the time, his form and pressure." Hence in a book of this kind, which interprets through literature the culture and the life of a people, any illustration must be more than a decorative addition; it must assist the student in peopling the pages of books with men and women in their habits as they lived and in realizing how colorful and many-sided has been the humanity of every age.

To this end, graphic illustrations have been selected that show both the literature and the life of each period of English history as they were seen through the eyes of artists of the time. What are quaintly archaic conventions of medieval literature will, it is hoped, become more enjoyable and meaningful when seen through the archaisms of medieval art. Similarly, the student's understanding will be increased when the richness of Elizabethan poetry is seen as just one expression of Elizabethan life, when the neo-classicism of eighteenth-century verse and prose is paralleled by neo-classical architecture, when the conventions of romantic literature are viewed in relation to the same conventions in other media, when the complexity of more modern literature is seen to be an enlightening commentary upon the growing complexity of modern life. Opposite each chapter opening there is a full page illustration which in some measure symbolizes the age it introduces: for Chapter 1 the medieval street scene, for Chapter 2 the portrait of two prominent young Elizabethans, for Chapter 3 a famous Hogarth scene, for Chapter 4 a Gainsborough genre painting, for Chapters 5 and 6 the contrast of two world's fairs a century apart. Many of the illustrations in these pages are documentary, elucidating the events of the age they represent. A series of parallels running from chapter to chapter—the costume plates, the occupational scenes, the illustrations of sports and pastimes, the architectural sketches, to point out only a few—should make the development of culture and the shifting emphases of taste apparent to the student who wishes to become familiar with the past. In this single-volume edition, by reproducing woodcuts, engravings, and paintings directly, it has been possible also to illustrate the literary selections in contemporary terms, and to incorporate more pictorial material in the text itself.

The maps, too, have been made to serve a useful and an interpretive purpose. Drawn by Mr. Raymond E. Craig, each is carefully executed in a style which is characteristic of the period it represents, and each is based upon an actual map of the time. Further, each symbolizes as far as possible some essential in the world outlook of the period. For example, within the circular shape of a medieval mappamundi a map for Chapter 1 depicts, not the whole medieval world, but the world as the Anglo-Saxons knew it; a second represents medieval England according to Matthew Paris; another in Chapter 2, with its seas full of galleons and whales and serpents, is based on one of Christopher Saxton's maps and brings to mind the deeds of Elizabethan sea dogs and the tales of Elizabethan voyagers; that for Chapter 3 is a map of London because much Restoration and eighteenth-century literature is literature of the town. Those for Chapter 5 emphasize the further growth of Victorian London and its suburbs, and the far-flung Empire of the imperialistic nineteenth century. For the most part the places shown on each map are those which have prominence in the chapter or in the period to which it is attached.

A medieval street scene, from Jean le Tavernier, Chroniques de Charlemagne (Bibliothèque Royale de Belgique), repro-duced in P. Durrieu, La Miniature Flamande, Brussels, 1921.

WARRIOR PRIEST AND COMMONER

From the Anglo-Saxon Invasion to the Accession

of the Tudors, 449-1485

Britain had been known to a few ancient Greek writers as a dim, remote, and altogether mysterious region, but it was only in the time of Julius Caesar that the classical world got direct knowledge of the island. After Caesar's death, nearly a century elapsed before the Roman emperor Claudius led a campaign against the Celtic inhabitants of what is now England and succeeded in establishing the Roman rule in Britain (43 A.D.).

The Romans had little difficulty in colonizing Britain northward into Scotland and in adding their new possession to the growing list of provinces in their mighty empire. They worked the island for whatever resources they could find there and built magnificent roads that have withstood the weight of centuries. But when the huge edifice of the Roman Empire began to crack under the pressure of the Germanic barbarians, this province of Britain, considered the most distant and least important by the government at Rome, was voluntarily left to fend for itself.

The foes of Romanized Britain were, first of all, other Celts—the Irish from the west, and the Scots and Picts from the north. Those, however, who were

At Sutton Hoo in Suffolk was found this buried ship containing what were probably the royal possessions of a seventh-century Anglian king (see below left). The eighty-foot wooden hull had rotted away, leaving its impression in the sand. The picture is used by permission of the British Museum.

This royal helmet, decorated with gold, silver, and garnets, was pieced together from fragments discovered inside the hull of the ship (above) found at Sutton Hoo. It is shown here mounted on a plaster head. The picture was taken for Life by photographer Larry Burrows, copyright by Time, Inc.

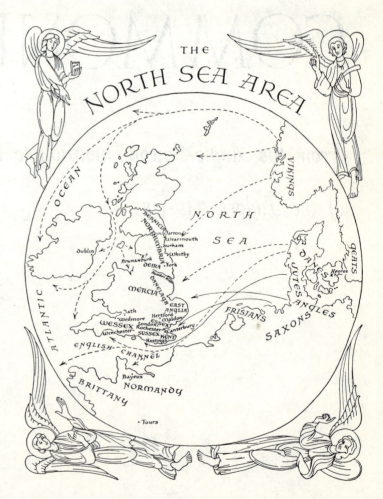

THE NORTH SEA AREA

to submerge the unfortunate remnants of the Roman Empire in Britain were Germanic; their home was eastward across the North Sea, along the shores of the Danish peninsula and on the immediately adjacent coasts of the mainland, perhaps even across the water on the southern tip of the Scandinavian peninsula. They lived near the sea in marshy regions, backed by heavy woodlands, swept by fogs and mists in the spring and autumn and by fierce beating storms in the winter, with but a brief summer to rest them. Their semi-nomadic, semi-settled agricultural society recognized two classes: the *earls*, the ruling class, based originally upon kinship to the founder of the tribe; and the *churls*, the bondmen who traced their ancestry to luckless captives of the tribe. There were also a few *freemen*, who enjoyed a status above that of the churl because they or their ancestors had been freed from bondage as a reward for services rendered to the king. And as for the king, he was in time of war an accepted and revered leader; in time of peace, a wise judge and a generous bestower of gifts and recompenses for the loyal acts of his earls, churls, and freemen.

The tribal social system was simple; justice, for example, was administered in the spirit of "an eye for an eye." Yet a concept of an organization greater than the individual existed, for legal penalties usually took the form of fines of blood money (*wergild*). Only crimes against one's own kin were unforgivable and punishable by death. Each individual's immediate concern, however, was for his daily living—for the strength, the courage, and the weapons needed to overcome an adverse climate, famine, hostile foes, and wild beasts. As a result, the Germanic tribesman's ideal of life came to be embodied in the brave, strong, and loyal warrior and his caste.

When, in the fourth and fifth centuries, the Huns came pouring into Europe, not to be checked until they had penetrated into France, all the Germanic tribes of central and northern Europe felt the pressure, and among them the Angles and the Saxons and the Jutes, from whom the English are descended. The story is told that Vortigern, a king of the Britons, invited some of these restless wanderers to help him protect his Romanized section of Britain against other Celts, outlaws from Scotland and Wales. The Anglo-Saxons, as this marauding horde of Angles, Saxons, and Jutes came to be called, had made occasional raids while the Romans were still occupying Britain. After the half-legendary expedition of the Jutes under Hengest and Horsa (c. 450), the Anglo-Saxons gradually and steadily settled along the eastern British coastline, building temporary quarters here and permanent settlements there, until the whole region that had once been held by the Romans was in the hands of these Germanic invaders. The process was slow; the details—to later generations—often completely obscure; but by about 650 the Anglo-Saxons had England in their possession.

This subjugation of the Britons had been complete and violent; the field was left to the Anglo-Saxon warrior, who, now that he had more territory to live in, was inclined to settle down and enjoy it. But the three major tribes, which by this time had split into seven clearly discernible divisions (the Heptarchy: Bernicia, Deira, Mercia, and East Anglia, formed by the Angles; Wessex and Sussex, by the Saxons; and Kent, by the Jutes), had first to settle among themselves the question of supremacy.

The history of the period from 600 to 850 is the story of the rise and fall of petty kingdoms, with the original seven coalescing into three: Northumbria, Mercia, and Wessex. First Kent, under Ethelbert, stood out as the most important; then Northumbria, from 650 to 750, assumed cultural and political eminence. Mercia in turn dominated until the early ninth century, when Wessex rose to supremacy, only to be threatened by the Danes. At the time of the death of Alfred (899), greatest of the West Saxon kings, the Danish menace had been checked, and the Danes had been restricted to the middle and north of England, in a district known as the Danelagh. But after the death of Edgar (975), who might be called the first king of a united England, there were further Danish invasions and a final Danish triumph (1014)—then a short half-century of disputed successions, a brief return of Anglo-Saxon power, and in the end the Norman Conquest.

All this time it had been to the warrior that the people turned for the solution of their problems. The type of kingdom which the Anglo-Saxon set up in England was the same that the Germanic warrior had known on the Continent. The kingship was a hereditary position subject to the desires of the tribe; the will of the tribe was delegated to the most influential earls and elders, known as the *witan* ("wise men") or the *witenagemot* ("assembly of wise men"), the earliest approach of the Anglo-Saxon to a parliament. The only proviso attached to the election of a new king was that he should be descended from Woden, king of the gods—in Germanic genealogies an easy thing to prove.

Tilling the soil, hunting and fishing and fowling, metal-working, forging, and weaving remained the occupations of the churl, or yeoman, who was bound to the service of an earl, unless he could earn possessions or special favor which would transform him into one of the relatively few freemen, or independent landowners. The churls constituted the subservient multitude, but even less important in the social and political state were women, though they had legal rights. For fighting, by which the destinies of tribes were decided, was very much the business of the earl, "the brave thane of the king."

From an Anglo-Saxon calendar (MS B. M. Cotton Tiberius B, v) come these occupations of the months. Shown here are March (digging and sowing), June (reaping), September (hunting), and December (threshing, winnowing, and storing grain).

The witan—King Pharaoh and his advisers, from MS B. M. Cotton Claudius B, iv (eighth or ninth century).

The Anglo-Saxon, like his descendant, the modern Englishman, was never to lose touch with the warrior's code or with the warrior's stern sense of justice and of law and order. Actually, however, the Anglo-Saxon warrior had known nothing of the world beyond the confines of his narrow little township or county. His eyes and his mind were to be opened slowly by an altogether different type of individual, the priest—so slowly, indeed, that at times one cannot be aware of any advance of thought whatsoever during the entire Old English period.

Although Irish missionaries, under the influence of the great Saint Patrick (372?–460?) had been active in the north of Britain, the great flow of Christianity into England came straight from Rome, when in 597 Pope Gregory the Great sent his emissary Augustine to convert King Ethelbert of Kent. A generation later Northumbria was converted, and, through the Council of Whitby (664), the organization of the Church in England was perfected, and the naming of Theodore of Tarsus as the first Archbishop of Canterbury (668) signalized the event.

The coming of the priests meant, first of all, a new religion wholly opposed to that of the Germanic peoples. Woden (Odin) and Thor, for example, had courage, mighty strength, and a characteristic grim humor, and to the Anglo-Saxon they personified certain natural forces. The Germanic warrior, moreover, had no hope of a future life, save that uncertain future promised him in Valhalla, the home of slain heroes, provided his death came on the battlefield while he was living up to his warrior's code.

The wise man of King Edwin of Northumbria, when he heard the message of the missionary Paulinus, hoped that the new faith of Christianity might bring a more certain promise of the hereafter. His fellow countrymen agreed and embraced the new faith. But there was more to the message of Paulinus than an awakening of faith. Christianity brought a knowledge of Latin and even of Greek, and so the Christianized Anglo-Saxon obtained glimpses of the glorious cultural past of Greece and Rome. He even traveled to Rome and beyond for pilgrimages or for the sake of his own clerical training, thus acquiring slowly and painfully an inner life beyond anything he had hitherto experienced.

The Warrior's Contribution to Literature

No doubt the priest chastened the warrior, but he did not overwhelm him. The beginning of English literature can still be traced to the Heroic Age of the Anglo-Saxons and Danes, while they were still on the Continent. Their political leader was the king, who was surrounded by his retainers, both earl and churl; there would surely be one or more heroes in a given tribe, strong men who embodied most completely the ideals and aspirations of the tribe as a whole, and whose leadership was unquestioned. Since royal birth was not an absolute essential, the throne was not an unusual reward for such heroes.

To celebrate the deeds of the hero, and thereby to perpetuate his name for succeeding generations, was the business of the bard or minstrel, whom the Anglo-Saxons called the *scop*, the entertainer in story and song. Many of these scops were established members of royal courts; others were itinerant. It did not take long for the scop to build up not only a profession, but a tradition for that profession. He soon accumulated a storehouse of epic material and fixed upon a particular method of telling his story—the technique of the heroic epic. And so when Beowulf kills a monster, the folk rejoice and call for a great tribal feast. There the scop composes a lay which, it can be assumed, was partly lyrical but preponderantly narrative. He rises and entertains the guests not only with a new lay about Beowulf's recent feat but also with legends relating the deeds of some great Germanic heroes of the past, such as Siegfried or Siegmund. The audience present is naïve, socially young and intellectually credulous, though having a definite protocol and dignified etiquette; stirring words and rhythm and stimulating imagination will be demanded of the storyteller. Therefore the scop, in a rhythmic chant, no doubt accompanied by a harp, tells the story in alliterative verse, making use of stereotyped phrases, or *formulas*, and since neither he nor his audience is gifted with a transcendent imagination, his poetic flights are moderate and his figures of

her ladies, who pass the mead cup about and then discreetly retire—enjoy the story and then drink more mead.

As time went on, different stories about the same hero were brought together, so that the full-blown heroic epic became a string of separate lays, with the figure of the hero himself serving as the integrating element. After the passing of generations and even centuries, during which the legend circulated entirely by word of mouth, the material eventually came to the knowledge of a gifted poet versed in the traditions of the scop, and this individual poet gave the epic its final form.

Doubtless there were a great many such epics, but there is only one full-length specimen surviving in Old English: *Beowulf* (p. 25), which certainly had its genesis on the Continent, for the story concerns Danes and Swedes and a doubtfully identified tribe called the Geats. The Danes may actually have brought the legend to England, where an Anglo-Saxon poet of great talent shaped it in the form in which it has survived. But Scandinavian or not, Beowulf thoroughly represents the ideal Germanic warrior, whether Norse, German, Anglo-Saxon, or Gothic.

In addition to *Beowulf* there are a few epic fragments left. (*The Fight at Finnsburg* and *Waldhere*). The survival of all of these is accidental: for example, when King Henry VIII of England destroyed the monasteries in the sixteenth century, it was mere good fortune that *Beowulf* was preserved, and bad fortune that hundreds of other manuscripts were lost. But allusions to other works, as in that curious seventh-century piece *Widsith*, are many. In short, the probabilities are

The Bayeux Tapestry is actually a band of linen, 231 feet long and 20 inches wide, embroidered in worsted in eight colors, and representing the conquest of England by the Normans in 1066. This scene shows archers and cavalry against the Saxon shield-wall.

speech confined for the greater part to a simple and elementary metaphor called a "kenning." Descriptive touches are not omitted, and occasionally a lyric note will creep in; but on the whole the scop's lay is straightforward narrative verse on the subject of a great warrior and his deeds, and the audience of earls and princes—with the exception of the queen and

strong that at one time there were extant on the Continent a large number of epics comparable in scope and length and perhaps in excellence to *Beowulf* itself.

Christian writers long after the time of Beowulf's feats continued to make use of the scop's epic tradition, and as late as the tenth century produced two excellent imitations of the battle scenes of the old heroic epic: the vigorous *Battle of Brunanburh*, inserted in *The Anglo-Saxon Chronicle* (p. 9) and celebrating a victory of King Athelstan of Wessex over the Viking Danes in 937; and the noble fragment *The Battle of Maldon*, which recounts a defeat of the Anglo-Saxons at the hands of the Viking Danes in 991.

The materials which made up the warrior's spiritual and emotional store were these—a somber outlook on life, a consciousness of the terrors of the northern winter, a sad but not despairing realization of the transitory nature of human existence, and an acceptance of the cruelty and immensity of the sea, which may well have represented to the Anglo-Saxon warrior the nothingness of the hereafter. The Old English lyric, then, is the direct gift of the fighting earl and his scop; like the epic, it is aristocratic or clerical. An example would be *Deor*, a poem without a single Christian allusion and unquestionably of great age. Divided into rude stanzas, with a refrain, it is the outpouring of a scop's woe at being supplanted in his king's favor by a rival bard. Though filled with epic allusions, it has the form and theme of a lyric.

When the Anglo-Saxons passed from their Heroic and Viking Ages to the Age of Christianity, a deeper lyric note sounded in their poetry, and a genuine feeling for their environment became articulate. The personal lyric, however, remained most uncommon; instead, the prevailing note in Old English lyric poetry is the elegiac—impersonal thoughts on the mutability of fate and the impermanence of life, melancholy and often undeniably poetic in stately alliterative lines. For it is significant that, with the exception of *Deor* and *Wulf and Eadwacer*, the Old English poet used the same alliterative verse form, drew upon the same stock of epithets and kennings, and kept the same poetic style for lyrics as well as epics.

The Priest's Contribution to Literature

For the aristocratic pagan warrior, then, the scop was an accredited spokesman. But since virtually all recorded Old English literature dates from Christian times in England, it was inevitable that all the warrior's literature should come under the scrutiny of the priest, the source of literacy and learning. A heroic epic like *Beowulf*, for instance, would be touched by the hand of the priest. The so-called Beowulf Poet is not identifiable, though it seems obvious that he was a cleric. The two poets of the Old English period who have names—Caedmon and Cynewulf—however shadowy and uncertain their identities may be, were Christian Anglo-Saxons writing in a Christian monastic environment. Their products, steeped in the traditions

of the scop, are what we call the Old English Christian epic.

A Caedmonian cycle of poems—*Genesis*, *Exodus*, *Daniel*, and *Christ and Satan*—belonging to the late seventh or early eighth century has been postulated; there exists also a Cynewulfian cycle, attributed to Cynewulf (750?–825?) and his followers. Four poems —*Juliana*, *Elene*, *Christ*, and *The Fates of the Apostles* —bear Cynewulf's signature in the ancient runic alphabet of the Germanic peoples. Of some half-dozen other poems, most of which seem Cynewulfian rather than Caedmonian, the best known are *Judith* and *The Dream of the Rood*, the scriptural material of which is obvious from the titles.

There are striking passages in many of these poems, particularly in *The Dream of the Rood* and in Cynewulf's *Christ*, and the *Genesis B* in the Caedmonian cycle may just possibly have suggested some passages in Milton's *Paradise Lost*; but all too often the reader will get the impression from these Christian epics that the native fire of the pagan poetry has been smothered under bardic formulas which often trans-

Early eleventh-century masonry is shown in this view of St. Michael's Church, Oxford.

gress the true Christian spirit. Christ, for example, reminds one altogether too often of Beowulf to be veritably Christian; on the other hand, the story of Judith, a forthright and savage Hebrew heroine, reads in places like the conventional Christian saint's life. Nevertheless, for the many virtues in these works— their sincerity, occasional vividness, and massiveness —we can assuredly thank the priest.

Sometimes this Christian Anglo-Saxon poetry will reveal traces of the oriental origins of Christianity, as in *The Phenix*. Or there is *The Bestiary (Physiologus)*, with its amusing "unnatural natural history" of animals; or the rarer sunbursts of classical lore and legend, such as the early romance *Apollonius of Tyre*. The purpose of the cleric in introducing these literary innovations, however, remained didactic, as the significance of the allegory in *The Phenix* or *The Bestiary* and the moralizing tone of *Apollonius of Tyre* make clear. This didactic element, of course, is everywhere in medieval literature—in the midst of an exciting narrative passage in *Beowulf* we may suddenly come upon it; it inspires many of the

arresting *Riddles*; it tinges excellent elegiac verse like *The Wanderer* or *The Seafarer*—an artistic weakness, perhaps, but typical of the Germanic temperament, which is inclined to be introspective and to search for a "message" in literature. As Chaucer once put it:

For seint Paul seith that al that writen is,
To oure doctrine it is ywrite, ywis;
Taketh the fruyt, and lat the chaf be stille.

None of the four important repositories, which include nearly all the poetry of the Anglo-Saxon period—the Beowulf, Junius, and Vercelli Manuscripts, and the famous *Exeter Book*—would be in existence today had it not been for the priest, who, in spite of his preoccupation with Christian doctrine, doubtless carried much of the older pagan literature into his private intellectual life.

The priest remained a teacher, however, and to teach he turned most frequently to the medium of the intellect, prose, the greater part of which before the days of King Alfred of Wessex (849–899) was in Latin. Thus the Venerable Bede (673–735), although born an Englishman, was primarily an international scholar and churchman writing in Latin, and his work is related to vernacular English prose only through King Alfred's translation of his *Ecclesiastical History of the English Nation*.

The most heroic historical figure in the Old English period, Alfred the Great, was also the presiding genius of native Anglo-Saxon prose. Educated carefully by good churchmen, he realized all too clearly the many difficulties which had to be overcome in the business of enlightening his West Saxons. The books which Alfred chose for translation illustrate the essentially wide interests of the man—a work of Platonic philosophy (Boethius' *Consolation of Philosophy*), a book of general knowledge (Orosius' *Compendious History of the World*), a book for the conduct of priestly office (Gregory the Great's *Pastoral Care*), the standard church history of England (Bede's *Ecclesiastical History of the English Nation*), and a typical example of patristic writing (St. Augustine's *Soliloquies*). Alfred's hand in the sponsoring of *The Anglo-Saxon Chronicle*, a year-by-year account of English history, is evident in the wealth of commentary and details of his own wars against the Danes; and throughout the Alfredian works there are many felicitous additions to the original, such as the story of the voyages of Ohthere and Wulfstan in the translation of Orosius or the beautiful introduction to Augustine's *Soliloquies*, which bespeak Alfred as a kindly, intelligent, gifted, and far-seeing shepherd of his people.

Following Alfred there is one other figure that demands brief comment—Aelfric (955?–1025?), the

THE BRITISH ISLES and NORTHERN FRANCE

teaching churchman incarnate. His numerous works are now primarily a matter of interest to the close student of medievalism, but he is also to be remembered because he avoided the simple and unadorned prose style of Alfred and turned to the rhetoric of the Latin monastic tradition, which he may be said to have introduced most effectively into English vernacular prose, and which was full of periodic sentences, with a vocabulary that was rotund and a trifle bombastic. But none of the passages from Aelfric, a writer of limited vision, or from his eleventh-century contemporary Wulfstan (d. 1023), the prophet of calamity in the days of the Danish conquest, can match Alfred's contribution.

Still, all this Christian clothing could not completely cover pagan nakedness. Some of this paganism inherent in Anglo-Saxon folklore survives even today in heathen relics like the Yule log and the mistletoe, in the names of the days of the week, the name of the great Christian spring festival, charms to cure illness or to assist agriculture, books of remedies or "leechdoms"—all of them part and parcel of the older order of divinity. Moreover, except in the purely ecclesiastical literature of orthodox and didactic bias, Old English literature exhibits a chronic uncertainty on one fundamental point of belief. That is the conflict between the Christian God and Wyrd, the pagan goddess of destiny, for in spite of all his teaching, the Englishman has always nursed a secret preference for Wyrd as controller of human destiny. And as it is in his heart, so is it also in his writings.

An Appraisal of Old English Literature

It is easy to be both condescending and unfair in our judgment of English literature before the Norman Conquest. Here is the expression of a people just emerged from the tribal state. Their society is a society of blood and iron, of nobleman and churl, with nothing of modern industry or machine-age civilization. The inferiority of women in the social scene will bother many of us, as will the degree to which the Church assumed control of individual lives and national institutions.

All enthusiasts to the contrary, we must admit the formlessness of this literature, its disturbing tendency to needless and childish repetition, its restricted range as to both subject matter and atmosphere, its deficiency in warmth and sensuous appeal, its poverty in those qualities which we call esthetic: music, soaring imagination, variety, color. So general an admission of weakness would be fatal if we failed to recognize that all such qualities are but relative. A man who sees little of the sun and much of the mists on the wintry northern sea cannot be expected to exhibit familiarity with those manifestations of nature that

Warwick Castle

go with a happier climate. One who has but slight acquaintance with the comforts of luxurious ease cannot be expected to find in his mind or soul compensations for the hard and somber life that has been forced upon him by blind circumstance. It is idle to look for anything in the Anglo-Saxon beyond what he himself experienced.

But the Anglo-Saxon was sincere and earnest—almost aggressive in his earnestness. He took himself and the world about him seriously, and because of a certain native reticence he had his moments of melancholy brooding, active though his external life may have been. His guttural language may not have had much music—no Germanic language is liquid in tone—but it had impressive power and immense virility; his literature may have been formless, but it had mass and sweeping strength. His very naïveté gave him a directness and simplicity of thought that could often strike very deep. His somberness resolved itself into a healthy, active pessimism, and there was more than a little of a grim and rather sardonic humor. If he was intellectually in a childlike state at times, he could nevertheless put his finger upon an eternal verity with all the unshaken conviction of a child. When Scyld Scefing was committed to the flood whence he came, "sorrowful was their heart; mournful their spirit. Men cannot say for a truth—hall-counselors, heroes under heaven—who received that burden."

We are likely to be struck by the tremendous importance in Old English literature of each day's work, the business of eating and drinking and eternal combat. But there was a fierce idealism as well—a conception of honor in oneself and of loyalty to one's leader, a stern fidelity of clan to patriarch—that still pervades the battle poetry. To such simple ideals of courage and trust the Anglo-Saxon was ready to dedicate his life. "Death is better for every man than a life of shame!" cries young Wiglaf to his companions in *Beowulf*. That is the tribesman living up to his code of ethics.

There was the ever-present and mighty sea, dominating the lives of men who lived in dark forebodings of the forces of nature and who saw in them Woden and Thor, or trolls and giants. So these forces appeared to the pagan living in a world of superstition and folklore. But he had struggled too long against the ruthlessness of nature and had been hurt too often not to have built up a defense in a philosophy of fatalism—Wyrd inexorable and unavoidable. In the end, it is apparent that the Anglo-Saxon achieved at least the forms and disciplines, and possibly comprehended the spirit, of Christianity, incongruous as the blend of Woden and Christ may be; and almost all the literature of the Old English period, whether pagan or Christian in origin, has come down to us strained through a Christian filter. We must not lose sight of this cardinal fact, just as we must not lose sight of the fundamental duality, the paganism and Christianity of the Anglo-Saxon mind.

In that fierce and grinding battle of Hastings (1066), this Old English civilization sank in defeat. William the Conqueror, ruling all England with stern and effective hand "by the splendor of God," stands as the harbinger of a new, more varied age. The law, the government, the language, the habits and customs of English society—all were to change. The warrior and the priest were to assume new garments: the warrior was to put on the armor of the knight of chivalry; the churchman was for a time to be decked out in the trappings of the feudal lord. But what the Anglo-Saxon had contributed in this first dim age was in a sense immortal, and so continued to glow steadily amid the scenes of "new men, strange faces, other minds."

Gloucester Cathedral

England After the Norman Conquest

Like every great event of history, the Norman Conquest had its roots embedded deep in the preceding age. Norsemen, checked by the provisions of the Treaty of Wedmore, crossed to France (912), where they established the duchy of Normandy; as time went on, the rulers of the Normans became dukes subservient to the king of France, but remained geographically and ethnically close to England and politically ambitious. It is unnecessary to examine here all the historical details that led a later Duke of Normandy, William by name, to lay claim to the throne of England. Suffice it to say that he had a legal case, and when he was ignored by the English witenagemot, he invaded England with well-disciplined forces, doubly armed with the sanction of Holy Church. His victory made him King of England and opened the island kingdom to a new civilization, more complicated, more advanced in material culture and intellectual outlook, and with far more varied interests than anything which the Anglo-Saxon civilization had offered.

When William the Conqueror landed at Pevensey on that momentous September day in 1066, he slipped while disembarking and fell forward on his hands and knees. With great presence of mind, however, he

Saint George, a woodcut from the Lyfe of Saynt George *by Baptista Spagnuoli, printed by R. Pynson, c. 1515.*

Devils carrying souls to Hell mouth, from R. Rolle, Contemplacyons, *printed by Wynken de Worde, 1506.*

grasped a handful of earth in each fist. This symbolic seizure of land William converted into sober fact; with ruthless force he compelled England to his will, crushing out every sign of opposition, imposing upon the land his Norman law, his Norman government, and where necessary his Norman language. But he brought stability and peace, for, as the saying went, a man could travel with a bag of gold from one end of the kingdom to the other in perfect safety.

The English language fell into low social esteem, and for a century and a half after the battle of Hastings, virtually all literature in England was written in either French or Latin; works in these two languages are actually in the majority until close to 1400. The Englishman of culture, therefore, had to be bilingual. Indeed, for a long time English, as the language of a subject people, was not to be heard in the palace or in the law court, in the university or the church.

The first obvious result of this new Norman order was the rise of feudalism. Every acre of land and every human being in the kingdom belonged in principle henceforth to the king. He distributed the lands of his kingdom, however, among his most important noblemen, who in return owed him money and tangible recompense in the form of military service, either for defense or for aggression. The important noblemen in turn subleased their holdings to lesser noblemen. The ceremony by which all these obligations were acknowledged, that of paying homage and swearing fealty, was sacred and binding without question.

The medieval Church was the greatest of all institutions in the Middle Ages, however, and the Pope, whose spiritual power transcended that of any

This fifteenth-century illustration for the legend of the Holy Grail shows Galahad in the Siege Perilous, from MS B. N., Fr. 120.

sovereign of Christendom, could be called the true overlord of the Western World. In the course of time, the Church became itself a mighty feudal institution in effect, what with its vast property holdings. The Crusades, which began about 1100 and continued for almost two hundred years and which were fostered and supported by the Church, are ample testimony to its power to achieve earthly ends; the coming of missionary friars to England in the thirteenth century and the eventual founding of the universities of Oxford and Cambridge shortly thereafter afford excellent examples of the spiritual and educational influence of the Church.

Nothing is more essential to an understanding of the medieval mind than a recognition of its reliance upon authority as the basis for all thought and action. The Church in its teachings during the Middle Ages tended to emphasize the greater importance of the next world rather than present life; to set the other-worldliness of the Middle Ages against the worldliness of the modern era, or to contrast the deductive method of reasoning of Thomas Aquinas (1225?–1274), the greatest of medieval theologians, with the inductive method of the modern scientific mind, is to appreciate the tremendous gap between the man of the medieval world and the man of the present. Yet human nature then was the same as human nature now; the problems of everyday living had to be met, and there was both humor and vitality in that living.

For a long time after the Norman Conquest there were, as before, but two main social classes: the aristocratic nobleman (ecclesiastical or secular) and the bound serf, or villein. And, as before the Conquest, a commoner could occasionally rise above the masses by accumulating wealth, or by some special service to his feudal lord, in which case he joined the ranks of freemen. The slow but steady growth of trade and industry meant the increase in importance of the town and the development of an industrial middle class that could command certain resources of its own and so was more independent than the villein on the feudal baron's land. The growth of this middle class was extremely gradual, of course, but by the middle of the thirteenth century the class was sufficiently important to form into guilds, or protective associations of the individual crafts, and to raise its voice in the government of the nation. The Great Council or Parliament of 1295, in which both commons and lords were joined, heralded the modern English government.

Although the proclamation of Magna Charta in 1215 represented the first true charter of personal liberty for all Englishmen, it was not until the middle class had definitely asserted itself by 1300 that we can perceive the rising tide of the forces which go to make up our modern world. The Hundred Years' War between England and France, beginning about 1340, based in part upon dynastic ambitions but also upon economic frictions arising from the growth of this English laboring class, showed at once that the English yeoman and freeman were the military superior of the knight on horseback. The Black Death, which ravaged Europe with fearful effect in 1346, 1349, and later, caused a major upheaval in the relations between villein and baron, bred social unrest like the Peasants' Revolt of 1381, and brought precursors of church reform like John Wycliffe (d. 1384). Although a moribund feudalism lasted for generations after the battle of Crécy (1346) and the battle of Poitiers (1349), one can hardly overestimate the importance of the fourteenth century in the building of the modern world.

Supplementing this rise of the industrial middle class was a strong current of nationalism, which was greatly stimulated by the victories of Crécy and Poitiers. The English language, used sporadically in an official way as early as 1265, was by 1385 being taught regularly in the schools in place of French. Culturally, too, the Englishman was asserting himself; in this fourteenth century lived three great writers, Chaucer and the unknown authors of *The Pearl* and of *Piers Plowman*, as well as several less noteworthy literary figures.

It is true that, from the point of view of the English, The Hundred Years' War petered out into anticlimax during the fifteenth century, but more important is the fact that literature and the arts—those great indexes of civilization—languished; and for nearly three quarters of a century after 1400 England appeared to stand still. In this time there are no truly important writers except the Scotsmen William Dunbar (1465?–1530) and Robert Henryson (1425?–1506), and the most vital work done by an Englishman was Malory's *Morte Darthur* (finished in 1469), which looks back to medieval knighthood rather than forward. Within the decade after *Morte Darthur*, however, came the introduction of printing into England. A decade after that came the accession of the Tudor dynasty, with the crowning of Henry VII in 1485; seven years later Columbus came to the New World; near the turn of the century came the humanists (p. 159). The Renaissance, that awakening of knowledge and broadening of horizons, lay just ahead.

The Literature of the Medieval Knight

After the Norman Conquest the role of the Anglo-Saxon warrior came to be filled by the medieval knight, a fighting nobleman who, under the feudal system, was venerated in literature as well as in life. Even as late as Chaucer's day, the knight was accorded the highest rank in society, apart from the select circle at court; it is not surprising, therefore, that the liter-

The Peddler   The Plowman   The Young Child

ature of the knight should be both extensive and influential.

The perennial epic hero, in other words, was now transformed by his changing environment. He became the epic champion of Christianity striving against the thronging hosts of Saracens, or Moslems. There was a further difference: the folk hero had been primarily a patriotic clansman defending his homeland. The medieval knight also fought for his people, but he was in addition a wandering warrior defending his faith and questing in foreign lands for heathens to slay.

Moreover, this knight was not only a warrior but also a lover, for shortly after the beginning of the Crusades, the lady in the story tended to usurp the place which was held in real life by the knight's liege lord; she became a kind of feudal sovereign. Personal service, love, and loyalty to the lady were as rigidly required of the knight as the most sacred fealty to his royal overlord—her will was his law. All this, of course, was in the new fiction rather than in the daily life of the period.

The obvious reason for this startling change in the nature of the epic hero was the larger role that women had come to play in society. This growth in the importance of women was inevitable, but one powerful factor in the process was the cult of the Virgin, which had arisen in the eleventh century. Then again, the first faint glimmer of the Renaissance was partly responsible—Provence, in southern France, developed a literary cult the chief object of which was the revival of love poetry in the manner of the Roman poet Ovid (43 B.C.–17 A.D.). Ovid's ideas were earthly enough, and the songs of the poets of southern France were equally passionate.

Moreover, the minstrel of the Provençal love lyric, the *troubadour*, could lend his song as easily to a love story as to a love lyric. His type of story spread throughout France, thence into Germany and the fruitful literary soil of Spain and Italy, and finally across the Channel to England. Thus the medieval

romance came into being—narratives of love and adventure sung originally in the French vernacular, or "romance" language. The grim folk hero of Anglo-Saxon literature had been transformed, and softened in the transformation. Now he was fully cognizant of the delights of earthly love, but he could when required sublimate this earthly passion into the idealized devotion of a true lover, who would give all to the mistress of his heart. The knight was bound to this woman by oaths of homage and fealty; he could never be unfaithful. Since his high quests for adventure had to be made on horseback, he became the *chivalric* knight (cf. French *cheval*), and his code of conduct became known as the chivalric code.

The surviving romances of the Middle English period are almost always anonymous, but a few *romanciers* on the Continent have real, though obscure, identities. Earlier romances were in verse, possibly chanted or sung to musical accompaniment; later they were in prose, obviously meant to be read. The audience in the earlier period was an assemblage of lords and ladies in gatherings like a banquet or festival or royal entertainment. Women, it should be noted, formed a prominent part of that assemblage.

The romance received a great stimulus in England with the arrival of Eleanor of Aquitaine, who in 1152 became the wife of Henry II of England. It is likely that the first romances composed in England were in French; in fact, most of the medieval romances seem to have had French originals. Although a minstrel may have sung for the benefit of listening English servants, churls, or hirelings as well as the lords and ladies, he adopted the chivalric code, which was, after all, French and therefore of superior prestige and influence.

There were many romances dealing with Germanic materials, such as *King Horn* and other similar pieces (*Havelock the Dane, Guy of Warwick,* etc.), but far more vital and enduring were those of Celtic origin treating of King Arthur and his knights. As for Arthur, the first bare mention of him in literature comes in a

The Old Man

The Agent

The Duchess

chronicle (*Nennius*) of about 800. In the middle of the twelfth century, however, Geoffrey of Monmouth, in his Latin prose chronicle, *A History of the Kings of Britain (Historia Regum Britanniae)*, gives a full account of the career of this invincible ruler of the Britons; the writers following Geoffrey add some details here and there, especially the concept of the Round Table, but most roads of investigation into the origins of Arthurian legends lead sooner or later to Geoffrey's work.

Arthur, a Celtic hero, whose deeds circulated in oral tradition for a long time in both Britain and northern France, has a mysterious and magic birth and a marvelous career at arms; he dies in his last battle; some say he will come again. There is little of the chivalric element in the early Middle English stories about Arthur himself; he is nearer to the epic hero than to the medieval knight of romance, and before long he is eclipsed by his knights of the Round Table.

Among the knights of Celtic origin, there is Gawain, of mythical background, with his strength waxing until noon and then waning, with his white steed and his glorious sword of dazzling rays—the picture of an old sun god; there is Percival, the "male Cinderella," associated clearly with the chivalric tradition; and there is Tristram, the mighty hunter and gifted musician, whose famous love for Isoude is perhaps the peak of attainment in the chivalric love romance. But towering over all is the French Lancelot, the model knight and perfect lover, whose glory is exalted at the expense of both Gawain and Tristram, so that these Celtic rivals later become subordinated and debased.

Of course there were other cycles of medieval romance in addition to the Arthurian. There were particularly stories of Charlemagne and his circle, of Roland and Oliver and their Saracen adversaries, many of whom were converted to Christianity in the romances and became heroes in their own right. There were stories of classical antiquity about Troy, Thebes, and Alexander the Great; and, needless to say, there

The Duke

The King

Scenes from Hans Holbein's Bilder des Todes, 1538.

were many romances which were nothing more than patchwork, composites of historical fact and arrant fantasy, such as accounts of Richard the Lion-Hearted turned cannibal, or of the great Lusignan family of France with a serpent woman among its members.

An attractive type of romance, in briefer form, is seen in the Breton *lai*, which appeared about 1200. The Celtic origin of many of these short narratives

A grotesque dance, a late fifteenth-century engraving by Israhel van Meckenem. Reprinted by courtesy of The Art Institute of Chicago, The Clarence Buckingham Collection.

(some treat of Arthurian figures) gives significance to the name of the type. It is probable that these *lais,* especially those of Marie de France, who flourished, probably in England, about 1200 and who wrote in French, arose beside the more extended romances; if so, these warm, colorful, and poetic narratives in verse stand in relation to the medieval romance as the short story stands to the novel.

Although the English romances preferred a straightforward manner of narration, the French romances, whether written by Frenchmen in France or by Frenchmen in England, were far more sophisticated and gave much time to analyses of motive, to the love psychology of the characters, and to descriptions of dress and armor, of meats for the table, of furnishings for the palace—often to considerable excess. It is no wonder that the fifteenth century preferred the prose versions, for they were much more quick moving. If the battle of Crécy dealt a mortal blow to the feudal system, it also dealt a death thrust at the knight in armor, questing on horseback for adventure and love in a land of make-believe.

Malory's great compilation of Arthurian romance, *Morte Darthur* (1469) contemplated, often with regret, a culture that by Malory's own time was no longer

vital, for Caxton, printing the *Morte Darthur* only half a generation later (1485), can say: "And I, according to my copy, have done set it in imprint, to the intent that noble men may see and learn the noble acts of chivalry, the gentle and virtuous deeds that some knights used in those days, by which they came to honor. . . . And for to pass the time this book shall be pleasant to read in; but for to give faith and belief that all is true that is contained herein, ye be at your liberty." The past tense used by Caxton, as an indication of things long past and out of mind, is most significant.

The Literature of the Medieval Church

"Learn to live as good men, that you may learn to die as good men. . . . Death is to good men the end of all evil, and the gate and entrance to all good. . . . Separate thy spirit from thy body . . . ; go out of this world; go to the land of the living where none die or grow old, that is Paradise. There one learns to live well in wisdom and courtesy, for no villainy enters there. There is the blissful fellowship of God and the angels and saints; there spring up all goodness, beauty, riches, worship, happiness, virtue, love, wisdom, joy without end; there is no hypocrisy, no violence, no flattery, no discord, no hate, no hunger, no thirst, no heat, no cold, no evil, no sorrow, no fear of enemies, but always feasts and the bridals of the King, songs and bliss without end." So wrote Dan Michel in his *The Ayenbite of Inwit* ("The Remorse of Conscience"), a prose homily of about 1340.

Now chivalric "courtesy"—the ideal of good manners, good breeding, noble birth, and Christian virtue —would be acceptable enough to the medieval Church, but the love of Lancelot and Guinevere or of Tristram and Isoude would be considered adulterous and sinful. Yet the Church saw fit to counteract the loose tales of worldly troubadours, not with direct condemnation but with romances of its own inspiration or authorship. The essential difference between a moral romance or "anti-romance" and the older chivalric type lay chiefly in the inclusion in the former of a definite moral, usually rather pointed, but occasionally, if the author was skillful enough, introduced most subtly.

Not every moral romance was written by a cleric, to be sure; the influence of the Church alone was undoubtedly sufficient to produce the type. Witness the complex legend of the Holy Grail, the cup from which Christ was supposed to have drunk at the Last Supper, with its marvelous healing and revitalizing powers; according to tradition it had been brought to England by Joseph of Arimathea, and from England it had later disappeared, to be sought after in the romances by knight after knight. In this Grail cycle, the heroes were given a definite spiritual quest, which turned their minds from the secular pursuits of mere chivalry. Since even Lancelot, as a chivalric lover, failed to retain the perfect virtue needed for the attainer of the Grail, the authors of the Grail legend did the next best thing; they produced a son for Lancelot—Galahad—and had the son achieve the Grail. Galahad is a spiritual idea—absolute purity—personified, and his origin is to be attributed directly to the Church.

Many of the other examples of the moral romance are tedious and overplayed, but one need consider only the beautiful *Sir Gawain and the Green Knight* to realize the occasionally felicitous blend of chivalric and moral. In this romance Gawain is put through a double ordeal which tests not only his courage but also his chastity, and yet the traditional knightly adventure is also present in high degree.

The moral romance could assume an allegorical form; the ancestor of nearly all of these fictional allegories was the French *Roman de la Rose*, written by two authors, both clerics, between the years 1227 and 1267. The first part, by Guillaume de Lorris, has the structure and setting of a typical romance, although the characters are personified abstractions; the second part, by Jean de Meun, is definitely satirical. Chaucer and his followers in the fifteenth century were much indebted to this work; indeed, it is proper to consider the *Roman de la Rose* as one of the most important pieces of literature written during the Middle Ages. The dream vision also occurs frequently throughout medieval literature; it too is often allegorical, and may serve as framework for an extended story or collection thereof. The reader can assume that the dream vision is intended for either didactic or satirical purposes. *Piers Plowman*, Chaucer's *House of Fame*, and *Pearl* are notable instances, and all three works are clearly allegorical.

Often the line between the moral romance, allegorical or otherwise, and the saint's life was very vaguely drawn. For example, the home of the historical Saint George of Cappadocia was near the site of the legendary feat of Perseus, who in Greek mythology slew a dragon that was ravaging the countryside and rescued the fair princess Andromeda; and so Perseus' adventure was transferred to George. Stories of the Virgin, nearly always involving miracles, were numerous. There were literally hundreds of tales told for didactic purposes (*exempla*), usually inserted within a sermon or some longer piece of expository writing. Again, the clerical influence could bring about the adaptation of a piece of folklore like the animal story, or fable, to its educative ends, as with the Middle English *Bestiary*.

The Church, as the fountainhead of all spiritual and intellectual literature during the Middle Ages, was the source of chronicling and historiography. No doubt both William of Malmesbury (1095?–1142?), probably the best of the many able chroniclers of his time, and Geoffrey of Monmouth (1110?–1154?), a free *romancier* who chose the chronicle form, were using the model that Bede had laid down four hundred years before. Again, it is obvious that the Church established the medieval universities, whence emanated all the theological works of the time, arguments, propositions, debates, and catechisms that were designed to clarify by the process of reason man's relationship to God—the great intellectual endeavor which goes under the name of scholasticism.

Lyric poetry inspired by the Church was plentiful throughout the Middle Ages. Some of it glorified the Virgin; some of it was loosely philosophical about the vanity of human wishes contrasted with the radiance of the Heavenly Kingdom. Yet notable Middle English hymns are strangely missing. In the religious poetry written or influenced by only one writer—Richard Rolle (1300?–1349)—do we find the lyric gifts of sweetness, warmth, and music, the *dulcor, calor, et canor* necessary to a great lyricist. The significant hymns are in Latin and are international in their traditions. The comparatively small number of surviving Middle English secular lyrics, such as *Alysoun* or the *Cuckoo Song*, are far more vital.

The flow of orthodox religious teaching through medieval England nevertheless did not proceed without check. The controversial figure of John Wycliffe foreshadowed the Reformation in England. After his studies at Oxford had been completed in 1361, Wycliffe entered upon the career of churchman, in which he had a brilliant rise. Although he had begun his career as an orthodox believer, he gradually came to modify his views on many of the important tenets of Christian faith and was especially incensed by what he considered the worldliness of the medieval Church. He founded an order of "poor priests," itinerant preachers who went about spreading the basic doctrine that the Scriptures were the prime authority and were opposed to, and independent of, ecclesiastical laws and systems. These followers of Wycliffe, known as Lollards (who bore a striking resemblance to some of the Puritan sects of two hundred years later), were eventually suppressed by Henry V in 1415.

Wycliffe's writings, mostly in Latin, comprised many sermons and pamphlets on church policy; some sermons were in English. No doubt his name will always be remembered in English literature for the translation of the Bible, although the exact part Wycliffe played in this translation is rather uncertain. Nicholas of Hereford is believed to have done most of the Old Testament in the earlier version of 1382–1384; John Purvey is the name most closely associated with the later version of about 1400.

Wycliffe, however, was unquestionably the guiding spirit of both versions, even if the later version was not completed until many years after his death in 1384.

The Literature of the Common People

The freeman, the yeoman, and the villein had their stories as well as the knight and the churchman. But these stories, since they belonged to commoners, were not written down until late and, once written down, led a timid and furtive existence. Some of these were nothing more than *exempla,* or tales of worldly wisdom; others, of ribald secular nature, were known as *fabliaux.* Although it is true that most extant *fabliaux* are continental French, it is clear that many were current in the French of medieval England, and doubtless such stories were exceedingly common among the men who built the Pyramids of Egypt. The sex intrigue, in which a wife was adulterous and her husband an object of ridicule (the theme of the foolish cuckold), was the most common plot situation; but the practical joke and the trick of retribution were almost equally frequent. Many of these popular tales, whether moral or satirical, were likely to group themselves into story collections, into which romance material might be introduced. Amusing, likewise, were the popular tales in which the main characters were animals who paraded about as men. The beast story, often dignified into the form of a mock epic (as in the famous cycle of Reynard the Fox), was a very convenient vehicle for popular satire and has a number of links with English folklore.

But the truly indigenous stories of a community—accounts of events of supreme importance to a given locality at some given time—remained in oral tradition for centuries. These now survive as the old popular ballads, many of which had their origins during the Middle English period. A domestic tragedy of the vicinity, a notable case of magic, an exploit by some local hero, perhaps an outlaw like Robin Hood, who had championed the rights of the people against a feudal baron—all this would go to make up the material from which a village Homer would fashion the ballad. Only in the eighteenth century did any considerable collection of these ballads come to light, and only a few included in the famous Percy Manuscript (dating from about 1650) are obviously Middle English—yet Robin Hood's name appears in the lines of *Piers Plowman.*

Of the older folk-ballads, tragic domestic situations and supernatural love affairs, often in combination, form a large part. No doubt many of these "domestic relations" ballads were based on some actual event which has since receded into the mists of antiquity;

many of these folk-ballads, however, originated in the swampland of folk superstition. The later ballads, obviously closer to us in time, are also closer to us in realities—they frequently refer to known historical happenings, such as the border warfare between Englishman and Scotsman. Ballads about actual events great and small go to make up the long list of those produced during the Renaissance and the seventeenth and eighteenth centuries; these were often printed on single sheets called "broadsides" and sold on the streets. And whatever the subject, the popular ballads show the commoner's partiality for music and rhythm and no doubt dancing. These popular ballads were meant to be sung, and many of those surviving have a chorus and marked rhythmic effects which suggest folk dancing.

The secular lyric in the Middle English period is for the most part strictly anonymous. Many of these lyrics have survived in musical settings of abiding value. Such fresh songs are unfortunately but a handful in comparison to the overwhelming number of religious lyrics that have survived. Indeed, it is rather difficult to designate many medieval lyrics as purely secular, for the characteristic medieval distrust of the temporal world colored the thought of virtually all medieval poets. Sometimes, however, the secular lyric turned from emotional expression to satire; in fact, all contemporary criticism of conditions of life was at this time in verse. To run the eye over the titles of some of the typical politically and socially minded songs of the age is to understand at once their complaints and their approvals—they inveigh against Church and State alike, and favor the victims of royal or ecclesiastical tyranny. No further evidence is needed to demonstrate that the common people of England had become articulate. But they developed a literature very slowly; none of the political songs just referred to was written before the fourteenth century.

The Church, the People, and Medieval Drama

The story of English drama from Old English times until the Renaissance is that of a slow replacement of what was entirely sacred and didactic by what was mainly secular and entertaining—even if the shadow of the Church continued to fall faintly upon English plays well through the sixteenth century. The dramatic beginnings within the liturgy of the Church during the tenth century amounted to little more than the introduction into the sacred services, first at Easter and later at Christmas, of a simple acting out (by priests) of familiar episodes, such as the coming of the three Marys to the sepulcher of Jesus at Easter, or the search for the Christ Child by the three shepherds and the three Magi at Christmas. Gradually there crept into these church dramatizations some tendency to change the dignified and sacred mood by presenting characters biblical in name but altogether realistic and contemporary. How these changes came about is not very difficult to explain.

During the Middle Ages the universal principle of human nature that feasting should follow fasting and that holy days should become holidays led to such burlesques of the sacraments and sacred days in the Church calendar as the ordination of the Boy Bishop and the celebration of the Feast of the Ass—to name only two such rebellions against ritual and restraint. Here the same principle combined with another natural tendency, the tendency to indulge in mimetic mockery of typical characters and episodes. As in Greek drama, the sacred and the comic stemmed from the same religious source, but it must be insisted that Greek drama and European drama were entirely independent.

And so the process of secularization went on slowly but certainly, with laymen taking the places of the clergy (who came eventually to disapprove of the practice which they had instituted), with the vernacular replacing the chants in Latin, and with the market place or public square serving as an outdoor stage in place of the church. We have then arrived at that form of medieval drama known as the miracle play or mystery play.

In England the progress of the religious drama was advanced during the thirteenth, fourteenth, and fifteenth centuries by at least two developments in the social structure of the age, one economic and the other ecclesiastical. The first was the notable growth of the towns and the corresponding development in power and importance of the trade guilds. The impulse which the Church gave to the growth of the plays was the establishment of certain festival days, notably, in 1264, of Corpus Christi Day, a movable holiday which fell late in the spring and thus provided a suitable season and occasion for outdoor performances. Just as Chaucer's Canterbury pilgrims did not think it sacrilegious to combine a holy pilgrimage and a spring vacation trip, so, too, the combination at the festival of the Eucharist of a religious and a holiday spirit in the miracle plays was not generally regarded as either irreligious or illogical.

Even before the religious plays had left their Church cradle, they had become more varied in the episodes presented and much freer in their characterizations. Yet dramatized narrative is good drama only by accident, and these miracle plays which eventually appeared presented little in the way of dramatic conflict, rather they tended to satirize contemporary life for purposes of entertainment. Here the commoners made their great contribution to the history of the drama—comedy tending to caricature and horseplay.

This title page from Margarita Philosophica by *Gregorius Reisch, 1503, shows pictorially the medieval curriculum. Wisdom with three heads (representing the natural, rational, and moral instincts) is attended by the trivium (philosophia triceps, or language studies—grammar, rhetoric, logic) and the quadrivium (humanarum rerum or science studies—arithmetic, music, geometry, astronomy), and serves natural philosophy (Aristotle) moral philosophy (Seneca) law and order (Justinian) and theology (St. Gregory, St. Jerome, St. Ambrose).*

Frequently, moreover, certain biblical characters and relationships suggested contemporary parallels; thus in the story of the Deluge (Genesis, Chapters 6–10), Noah's wife is mentioned merely as his companion in the ark, but in the Chester play of the Flood she appears as a village scold, who engages her aged husband in a series of verbal and physical encounters.

Most of the fourteenth- and fifteenth-century miracle plays which have survived in manuscripts belong to what are called cycles, of which there are four important examples: the York, with forty-eight plays; the Wakefield (or Towneley), with thirty-two; the Chester, with twenty-five; and the *Ludus Coventriae* (or Hegge), with forty-three. There are also a few stray individual plays. These cycles reveal that the producers of religious dramas never quite outgrew the original tendency to think of the Easter and Nativity stories as of primary importance; but all these cycles contain also dramatized narratives from the Old Testament, especially from Genesis and Exodus, and also from those parts of the Gospels which do not have solely to do with the birth and death of Jesus. The religious plays performed at the great cathedral center of York are much more somber and restrained than are the freer dramas of Wakefield, the cycle to which the hypothetical Wakefield Master, author of the sprightly *Second Shepherds' Play*, contributed more than one drama.

The actors in the miracle plays were obviously amateurs who were nevertheless paid for their acting and fined for neglect of rehearsals; each play was the business and responsibility of a particular guild. The guild records show also payments for costumes and for stage properties of a simple nature, but there evidently was no apparent attempt to make a historically accurate production, and anachronisms of all sorts abounded. In England, at least in Chester and York, festival performances were played on flat wagons, or "pageants." The program was simple: Early in the morning on a festival day like Corpus Christi the pageant on which the first of the plays in the biblical sequence was to appear was wheeled to the first of a succession of previously selected locations, perhaps the conduit, or town well, of a convenient public square. Having finished its performance, the actors of pageant one would wheel their pageant to location two, and pageant two would move into place in location one. It is obvious that a dramatic performance on an open platform with no curtains would have to be a "multiple stage" performance; that is, the various scenes and episodes would have to appear on the same space with little or no indication of any change of locale. Perhaps this naïve method was not so confusing as it must now appear, for, after all, the scene of action even on a modern stage is actually only that space occupied by the actors who are actively performing and who are thus drawing the attention of the audience entirely to themselves and to their immediate environment.

The miracle plays may reasonably be regarded as the most important of the medieval dramas because of their own qualities and also because of the part they played in the development of the English theater. But there were other types of medieval dramatic production. For example, there were obscure folk plays, whose characters—St. George and the dragon, and Robin Hood and his merry foresters, as well as the motley horde of morris men and sword dancers—belong at best to the borderland of drama, and so may be passed over here.

The morality play, however, is a different matter. It came from the teachings of the clergy, although its true beginnings are most uncertain. Indeed, it may be defined as the dramatic phase of medieval preaching and teaching, for it presents the struggle between the forces of good and of evil for the precious guerdon of man's immortal soul, and it is designed to assist the wavering to keep their feet in the straight and narrow way and out of the "primrose path to the everlasting bonfire." The morality play, originating perhaps in the schools and the universities (though this is still a most debatable point), dates from the first decades of the fifteenth century and lasts for scarcely a hundred years. According to its common formula, man is conceived in sin and born graceless. His mortal career is a struggle from the beginning, for the harassed human race is only a pawn to be moved about between the world, the flesh, and the devil on one side, and the cardinal Christian virtues on the other. The characters in the morality play are abstract virtues or vices. Death usually overtakes the protagonist. Strictly speaking, however, although the action is customarily somber, the morality play is not tragedy, because the soul of mortal man when deserving, though distressed almost to the depths of hell, is in the end judged—and saved.

In spite of the grim subject matter, there is in the morality play much of the comic realism that characterizes the miracle play, for the devils are always lively notwithstanding their baleful designs on the hero. The character of Vice became in time such an amusing rascal that he threatened repeatedly to obscure by his clowning the ethical object of the performance, and he left numerous progeny in the jesters and clowns of Elizabethan drama. The very purpose and nature of the morality play made a clearly defined dramatic conflict inevitable; for, so it is said, the greatest and most dramatic struggle in life and literature is that between good and evil for the possession of man's soul.

Four Great Writers of the Middle English Period

The first of four great writers produced in England between 1350 and the end of the Middle English period is the Pearl Poet, a writer of remarkable talent, probably a churchman and certainly a mystic of vision and depth of soul. (The order of presentation here is purely chronological.) The second, the *Piers Plowman* Poet, embodies the voice of the common people, crying out in prophetic utterance for a better world. The third, Geoffrey Chaucer, one of the three or four greatest of English writers, is the artistic culmination of the age. Finally there is Thomas Malory, fifteenth-century knight and storyteller, a man looking back through rose-tinted glasses, from his vantage point of later days, toward the age of chivalry in bloom, desirous, perhaps, of participation in that golden era, but realizing that such an age would never come again.

Much investigation, and even more speculation, has attempted to identify the gifted writer who composed a group of four poems some time about 1370. Like many other poems written in the north and west of England during the fourteenth century, this group is in alliterative verse imitative of the Old English poetic form. Their style, idiom, dialect, and language all seem to point to a common author, although it has been argued that *Sir Gawain and the Green Knight* is the work of a different author, referred to as the Gawain Poet. Nevertheless, despite ingenious research, convincing final proof of the identity of the author or authors of these four poems is yet to be advanced; it is still not unreasonable to assign all four to a single author, referred to here as the Pearl Poet. It is also relatively safe to assume that this poet had connections with the court of Edward III, that he was very likely a clergyman, but that he was hardly a scholastic theologian.

The first of these four poems is *Pearl*. The elegiac mood of the work is self-evident; the poet has suffered the loss of a little girl. Whether she is related to him or not is uncertain, and thereby hangs much of the dispute as to the identity and profession of the author. Whatever the inspiration, however, *Pearl* can take its place as the first of a distinguished line of English poetic threnodies, more emotionally wrought than most of the elegiac verse in Old English literature. It is a beautiful and impressive example of the dream vision. But the modern reader will regard the theological exposition which occupies the middle portion of the poem as tedious and intrusive, fettering the poetic wings of the author; and even the striking picture of the New Jerusalem at the end of the poem, and the poignant mood of resignation on the part of the man who has suffered a loss can hardly compensate for the difficulty of plodding over all the dreary plains of dogma.

Of the remaining three poems, one already touched upon, *Sir Gawain and the Green Knight* (p. 67), is a moral romance or anti-romance dedicated to the great Welsh sun god and hero, Gawain, and patterns forth the ideal knight, brave and pure. The poem has been called by many the finest of the English medieval romances, although it is far too polished and artistic a performance to be typical. *Patience*, the third poem, is a homily on the virtue described by the title, with Jonah serving as the hero of the accompanying *exemplum*. Finally there is *Purity* (or *Cleanness*), another homily, buttressed by stirring accounts of the fall of the angels, the fall of man, the Deluge, the destruction of Sodom and Gomorrah, and the conquests and ultimate evils of Nebuchadnezzar and Belshazzar, all in contrast to the redemption through Christ and the Virgin. The sweeping

Both of these illustrations are taken from the old manuscript of Sir Gawain and the Green Knight (MS B. M. Cotton Nero A, x, 4). The first shows the beheading game, the second, Gawain and the lady of the castle.

power of this epic poem is certain to remind the reader of the Christian epics of the Caedmonian and Cynewulfian cycles (p. 8); the resounding alliterative verse makes the resemblance all the more striking.

The Pearl Poet, for all his otherworldliness, has an instinctive love for the colorful in natural landscape and for the English countryside at all seasons of the year. There is a certain ruggedness in his scenes that suggests the hill country of the north or the mountainous sections of Wales; a glowing, almost exotic imagination matches this ruggedness. His realistic grasp of medieval court life, however, shows that it is manifestly unfair to call this poet merely a fourteenth-century mystic. He was a man of feeling, of vision, of sincere religious warmth, of quickened imagination, and of sophisticated culture; as such, he stands far apart from the general run of medieval writers.

There are forty-seven extant manuscripts of the huge and formless poem, *Piers Plowman*—a fact which bespeaks an undeniable popularity and impressive significance for a work written before the days of printing. While not highly important as a work of art, the poem is a powerful expression of sincere sympathy and feeling for the lot of the common people, uttered forcefully with a compelling realism that would make itself heard in any age.

From scattered allusions in the many manuscripts, it was assumed for a long time that the poet was William Langland (or Langley), a native of Shropshire; his father perhaps a freeman landholder, or franklin; and he himself later a cleric in the Benedictine establishment of Malvern. Subsequently he came to London and led a vagabondish life through the rest of his days. Possibly he took minor orders in the Church. Born about 1332, he was a contemporary of Chaucer.

Such was the older view of his life. Certain discoveries have been made, however, and certain arguments have been advanced which tend to destroy much of the figure of Langland as he had been previously drawn. There are no less than three separate versions of the poem, known respectively as Text A, Text B, and Text C, and they would seem to cover a period of composition from 1362 to as late as 1398. The three versions differ in many ways, and there is in fact no essential necessity for regarding one man as the author of all three. For that matter, in the course of the three versions more than one man is alluded to as the author.

The chief point to remember is that *Piers Plowman* is far more important than its author. It tells us an intricate story of the Dreamer, Will, who is vouchsafed, in the two later versions, a series of eleven visions peopled by numerous personifications. The humble peasant Piers is first shown striving to lead the wayfarers to Truth, or salvation; later in the poem he is metamorphosed into Christ himself. The aim of the great allegory is to provide the Dreamer with a grasp of the inwardness of Christian truth. There is much in common between the author of *Piers Plowman* and Wycliffe—both base their reforms upon living according to the principles of Christ. But the poem is especially outspoken in its attacks on the parasitism and greed found among churchmen. It is one of the most important English allegories and takes its place as a social document alongside Chaucer's *Canterbury Tales*. Although lacking the order and clarity of Chaucer's artistic conception, it yields nothing to the *Tales* in sincerity and depth of purpose and in power and scope of feeling. It is bitter, devoid of conscious humor, passionate—and memorable.

Chaucer was born in London about 1340; the exact date is uncertain. His entire adult life was one of officialdom; throughout he was a man of affairs at the courts of Edward III and Richard II. He probably suffered some political reverses, it is true, but when he died in 1400, he was clearly in royal favor. He was obviously a man of supreme gifts and a successful one, and must certainly have attained that self-confidence, if not actual complacence, which any self-made man of his abilities, achievements, and environment would be likely to attain.

Witty, shrewd, worldly-wise, kindly, satirical, the trained observer of men and the penetrating reporter of life as he found it, Chaucer shows in addition a narrative skill which for directness, economy, and sustained interest has not been matched by any other English poet. He is, moreover, a graceful lyric poet and a most talented portrait painter; the broad sweeps of his brush in *The Canterbury Tales* and *Troilus and Criseyde* are at once impressionistic and unforgettable. Although often ruthless and bitter in the scourging of fools, hypocrites, and parasites, he can be both tender and sympathetic. At the same time, Chaucer is not a philosopher in the sense that he has a ready system which will solve the complex problems arising out of the conflicts of human beings or the impact of humanity against forces greater than itself. Nor is he a profound mystic like Dante. He is an observer, and he reports with diligence and fidelity. But because he keeps his feet firmly on the ground, he has often been reproached as superficial, facile, lacking in that quality of "high seriousness" which Matthew Arnold, for one, considered indispensable to the truly great writer. The twentieth-century reader may well ignore such criticisms (as he has in large measure done) and instead may appraise for himself one who, by any standard of impartial judgment, must be admitted to a place at the very pinnacle of English literature.

Chaucer's early work is manifestly under the influence of contemporary French poets. To the years before 1372 (the older so-called "French period") can be assigned a great many of his lyrics, such parts of the *Roman de la Rose* as he translated, *The Book of the Duchess* (an elegy on the death of the first wife of his patron John of Gaunt, Duke of Lancaster and son of Edward III). In some degree the works of his "Italian period," from 1372 to about 1385, are inspired by the writings of earlier Italian authors, notably Dante, Petrarch, and Boccaccio, or by the atmosphere of fourteenth-century Italian culture, with which he became acquainted during his official missions to Italy. But in these works of the Italian period it is easy to see Chaucer's highly original genius emerging. *The Parliament of Fowls* is a charming allegorical satire and dream vision; *The House of Fame*, although incomplete, is a more trenchant attack upon gossips, reputations, and rewards for "merit." *The Legend of Good Women* is a collection of short biographies in verse, also incomplete, of famous heroines of classical antiquity—a "mirror" of life held up for all in positions of responsibility to see. The masterpiece of this phase of Chaucer's career, however, is *Troilus and Criseyde*. This magnificent narrative poem, based on a story from the medieval Troy legend, has been termed by many the first psychological novel in English literature because of its insight into human motives and its masterly characterizations. The suave and worldly go-between and the enigmatic Criseyde are remarkable portraits, especially for the Middle Ages, when the analysis of a human soul for other than didactic purposes was virtually unknown. *Troilus and Criseyde* is also interesting historically because it happens to be the finest of all treatments, either as a whole or in part, of the Troy legend in Middle English literature.

The Canterbury Tales, nevertheless, will stand forever as Chaucer's great memorial. The gallery of portraits in the Prologue to this varied collection of stories both popular and artistic would alone have been sufficient to assure its author a high place, and the range and versatility of accomplishment in the tales themselves are a further tribute to his genius. With good reason Dryden (p. 458), the first great modern English literary critic, extolled Chaucer thus:

He must have been a man of a most wonderful comprehensive nature, because, as it has been truly observed of him, he has taken into the compass of his *Canterbury Tales* the various manners and humors (as we now call them) of the whole English nation, in his age. . . . We have our forefathers and great grand-dames all before us, as they were in Chaucer's days . . . for mankind is ever the same, and nothing lost out of Nature, though everything is altered. . . .
—from *Preface to the Fables* (p. 470)

Chaucer is, indeed, more "modern" than nine-

A view of Paris, from Louis de Bruges, Froissart (Bibliothéque Nationale, Paris). *Reproduced in P. Durrieu*, La Miniature Flamande, *Brussels, 1921.*

tenths of the authors studied in traditional courses in English literature. His interest in his characters is a human interest; he is willing to take the world as he finds it, with strong, bracing reality in his concept of it; he is sane, balanced, and yet the consummate artist. But his knowledge is, after all, still that of the medieval world; in his religion he is still devoutly orthodox, no matter how much he may, in anti-clerical fashion, rail against the abuses of his Church. His power to grow beyond his age lies in his coolly appraising humor, his facility of descriptive phrase, his vigorous narrative, his remarkable receptivity to the workings of human nature, and his consequent appeal to the humanity of the ages.

The last outpost of medieval knighthood was Sir Thomas Malory, whose life, from his birth about 1394 until his death in 1471, covered that span of years which was the most barren and uninspired in English literature. Very little is known of his life beyond the possibility that he may have been a raffish member of the gentry who took part in the waning years of the Hundred Years' War, became involved in the fifteenth-century civil conflict in England called the Wars of the Roses, and spent the last twenty years of his life in prison after being convicted of multiple crimes.

Malory cherished the old days of chivalric knighthood, when King Arthur and his Round Table jousted and loved in all courtesy, and when the quest of the Holy Grail was a bright magnet which attracted the best of English knights. Within the pages of a book, the famous *Morte Darthur*, he placed the most complete single version of the Arthurian saga that has been written in English. His sources were, in the main, medieval romances about Arthur and his group, particularly the huge French poems and prose accounts of Lancelot, the Grail, and Tristram. He executed this ambitious project with impressive success. In a simple, almost informal prose style he tells his story; but his simplicity is artful, for he suggests all the pomp and ceremony of the knightly career, all the splendor of the knight's high quests, and all the pathos of the passing of the Round Table. To read the final book of *Morte Darthur* is to become aware of the breaking up of a great social system. The knight was to have brief revivals in subsequent English literature, notably in Spenser (p. 217), but after the seventeenth century had dawned, the knight was laid away until the romantic writers of the early nineteenth century resurrected him. If he was to stand in the pages of Tennyson, of Arnold, and of Swinburne as an ideal, an uneasy ghost amid the disconcerting rush of modern times, it was Malory that enabled the tradition of the chivalric knight to shine, however fitfully, through all the years.

General Considerations of Medieval English Literature

The Middle English period is well named, for it is the bridge between the old age of warrior and priest and the brave, new, and somewhat terrifying era that is our modern age. And yet the Old and Middle English periods should be considered together, for they had much in common, and both are to be placed in opposition to the Modern English period. The old Anglo-Saxon warrior has his descendant in the knight of chivalry. There is the same code of loyalty for the medieval knight as for his epic prototype; but where the epic warrior was faithful to his tribal king, the knight had a threefold loyalty: to his king, to his lady, to his God. The Anglo-Saxon priest is reincarnated in the Middle English churchman, who shares the same feudal outlook as his contemporary knight, and who can assume the armor of the Church militant and fight in the Crusades with Godfrey of Bouillon or Richard the Lion-Hearted. The monastic tradition of the Old English period continues through the Middle English, but broadened by the inevitable increase of knowledge through the centuries. And the people, always occupied with their daily stint of laboring, tilling, and reaping the harvest, led for generations the lives of husbandmen and laborers. In short, much of the Middle English world is merely a widening of the Old English social scene. The roots of much of Middle English literature lie in Old English soil—all the types of medieval literature inspired by the Church, to take but one example, had beginnings earlier than 1066.

Of course the new blood infused after the Norman Conquest was bound to show its effects sooner or later. The greater luxury, the easier ways of life, the intellectual stirrings and realistic outlook, the altered status of women—these and much else were introduced by the Norman. All these qualities and their inevitable consequences—a higher standard of material living—point to the later times, when industry was to mean the growth of towns and the gradual approach of an urban civilization. But for this Middle English period, the Renaissance had not yet come. The worldly had been subordinated however reluctantly to the otherworldly—so far, at least, as teaching was concerned; and until the emphasis in human thought is placed primarily upon the world in which we live rather than upon the world to come, we are not yet within a modern environment, no matter how many Chaucers may rise to charm us with their essential humanity, their poetic genius, or their penetrating observations of the world about them. The Middle English period, even during the ferment of the fourteenth century, is not the Age of Chaucer so much as it is the Age of Piers Plowman.

Beneath all the violence and bloodshed of the Middle Ages, beneath all the filth and ignorance and intolerance and callousness, there still lies a real beauty—the beauty of idealistic thought. It is doubtful whether mankind has since seen that same mystic vision of a New Jerusalem in all its glory or has thrilled to the quest of a Holy Grail which would be a remedy and a healing balm for a suffering world. Nor is it possible to deny the sincerity—ardent, emotional, and unthinking—which actuated the many searchers for the otherworldly in the medieval world. The bigotry that pursued all dissenters, the inhuman cruelty with which Church and State alike took revenge upon their rebels, and the inertia that came upon men's minds because of their too rigid religious training—these it is difficult for a liberal mind to forgive. But it was a vigorous era, as its literature shows, with imagination, feeling, and power. It perpetuated much of the artistic and spiritual traditions of preceding generations; it succeeded in spite of many handicaps in anticipating some of the riches that the future had in store. Above all, it was humanity alive and active, and it has that universal appeal which every great era in human history has for him who cares to seek it out and find it. If one is disposed to reject the Middle English period as unlovely, tyrannical, and blighting, let that one still remember the words of its greatest writer:

Ye knowe eek, that in forme of speche is chaunge
Withinne a thousand yeer; and wordes tho
That hadden prys, now wonder nyce and straunge
Us thinketh hem; and yet they spake hem so,
And spedde as wel in love as men now do. . . .

BEOWULF

Verse translation by Charles W. Kennedy

The only complete epic preserved in Old English survives in a single manuscript (Cotton Vitellius A XV) now lying in the British Museum. It was saved somehow from the destruction that came upon many of the literary treasures of England following the dissolution of the monasteries by Henry VIII in 1536. The manuscript was written in Wessex about the year 1000, but the poem itself was probably composed in Northumbria some time around 725. Historical events described in the poem, such as Hygelac's raid on the Frisians (l. 1751 and note), belong to the early sixth century, but the legendary events are of course much older.

The question of the authorship, single or multiple, has raged since Thorkelin's first edition in 1815. Is it one man, "mindful of saga and lay," who composed the poem as we have it, or did many bards have a hand in the performance, beginning with the bard who celebrated Hygelac's death in 512 or 520? The mosaic quality of Beowulf is apparent from the first reading, but one man, the hypothetical Beowulf Poet, could have put the pieces into place better than several could have done, and the poem is obviously too well integrated to give much support to those believing in multiple authorship, which is always a rather impractical theory.

This Beowulf Poet is little more than a name; the Christian atmosphere in the poem would indicate that he was a churchman—one closely connected with a royal court, familiar with the heroic legends of his race, and expert in the composition of the traditional alliterative poetry. Like many epic poets, he was an admirer of the past; his purpose was to emphasize the established ideals of social and personal conduct by embodying them in the figure of a hero whom his audience could strive to emulate. In fact, one theory has it that Beowulf was written as a poetic book of conduct for princes.

The hero, Beowulf, is a Geat—possibly this could be a Jute of Jutland, but more probably a member of the Old Norse Gautar, a tribe living in what is now southern Sweden, in the Swedish province of Göta-rike. There is every reason to suppose that there was such a tribe and that it had a king Hygelac, whose chief thane, Beowulf, was endowed with extraordinary prowess as a warrior and swimmer. Similar tales were told of heroes before Beowulf, and similar tales were told of later men. In the Norse sagas of the thirteenth century, for instance, which preserve many legends of the Germanic peoples, there are striking parallels to the Grendel story. Parallels of this sort, moreover, are known in general folklore. The Beowulf Poet, clearly familiar with these old traditions, fused them as he wished into the surviving Old English epic.

The figure of the hero Beowulf has dignity and polish, in the sense that he is fully acquainted with the etiquette demanded of a chieftain of his importance. His physical strength, exhibited chiefly in his swimming and his grip, is nothing short of overwhelming. These attributes, then, are Beowulf's peculiar contribution to the epic tradition of Hercules and Siegfried. There is something solid and sure, rather than fiery and brilliant, about his valor; it is not of the impetuous type like Roland's or the Cid's.

Although Beowulf, as an epic, suffers from a comparison with the great poems of Homer, it is nevertheless a work well fitted to stand as the chief monument of Old English literature. Its most obvious flaw, at a first reading, is its seeming laxity of structure, for the Beowulf Poet, like most epic poets, is definitely committed to an episodic manner. Yet a closer reading will demonstrate that the poem possesses a considerable degree of unity, since the character of the hero, summarized in the last sentence of the work, is the one to which all parts of the poem are joined. And in its richness of language, its swift narration, its quality of suggestiveness, its interest in what men think and feel as well as in what they do, and above all in its pictures of brave men struggling against outward foes and inward dreads, and conquering if only in death, Beowulf has genuine claims to greatness.

The alliteration, the free four-beat line with marked caesura or pause in the middle (at the end of the second foot), the absence of rime, and the muscularity of the language are all illustrated in the following lines (1-11) from the poem:

Hwaet! we Gar-Dena   in geardagum,
þeodcyninga   þrym gefrunon,
hu þa aeþelingas   ellen fremedon!
Oft Scyld Scefing   sceaþena þreatum
monegum maegþum   meodosetla ofteah,
egsode eorlas,   syððan aerest wearð
feasceaft funden;   he þaes frofre gebad,
weox under wolcnum,   weorðmyndum þah

oð þaet him aeghwylc   þara ymbsittendra
ofer hronrade   hyran scolde,
gomban gyldan;   þaet waes god cyning!

The pronunciation of the vowels in Old English is generally like that of continental Latin, and the consonants are in the main pronounced as in Modern English. These exceptions should be noted: y represents a sound approximating French u; ae is Modern English a as in hat, cat, man; eo and ea are diphthongs with the stress on the first vowel—among the consonants, c before e and i is probably a ch-sound, otherwise a k; g before e and i is a roughened guttural y, otherwise hard g; sc is probably Modern English sh. All syllables have value, and the accent of a word is normally on the first syllable. ð and þ are symbols for the Modern English th-sounds.

NOTE ON THE OLD ENGLISH LANGUAGE

English is a member of the Anglo-Frisian branch of the West Germanic languages. Its nearest relatives are Frisian, still spoken in the northernmost coastal regions of Holland, and Low German ("Plattdeutsch"), the dialect of northern Germany. As a member of the Germanic language group, English is part of the Indo-European family of languages.

In the period before the Norman Conquest and for a generation or so thereafter, English was highly inflected, even more than Modern German, and it had not made use as yet of its amazing power of borrowing and assimilating foreign words—one of the striking features of Modern English. Its vocabulary was conservative; its grammar complex; its dialectal differences many. During this Old English

period (before 1100) we can recognize four major dialects: the Northumbrian, the Mercian, the West Saxon, and the Kentish. Of these four, Northumbrian and Mercian represent the old dialect of Anglia; West Saxon represents that of Wessex; and Kentish, that of Kent and the original settlement of the Jutes.

Nearly all our remaining monuments of Old English literature were written in the dialect of Wessex (West Saxon), and it is impossible to read this Old English, or Anglo-Saxon, as it is often called, without special training. A comparison of the opening lines of Beowulf with the Modern English translation will serve to illustrate the language hazard which the reader would have to surmount.

The presence of a full inflectional system is a definite distinctive mark of Old English. The inflectional endings begin to weaken and even to disappear during and after the eleventh century. This sloughing-off process was slow; it was not until after 1500 that most of the inflectional endings disappeared. The pronunciation of Old English was based upon the so-called "Continental" quality of the vowels (as in Modern German, for example); some of these vowel sounds had changed their quality by Chaucer's time, and the whole system of long vowels was altered remarkably in the transition to Modern English. There is, therefore, a linguistic reason for the classic division of English literature into Old, Middle, and Modern: Old English (500-1100) being the period of full inflections; Middle English (1100-1500), the period of weakening and disappearing inflectional endings; Modern English (1500 to the present), the period of absence of inflections. The vowel changes just mentioned are also a basic element in the growth of the language through these three stages.

PROLOGUE

The coming and the passing of Scyld, the Danish primeval hero and ancestor of Hrothgar.*

Lo! we have listened to many a lay
Of the Spear-Danes' fame, their splendor of old,
Their mighty princes, and martial deeds!
Many a mead-hall Scyld, son of Sceaf,
Snatched from the forces of savage foes.
From a friendless foundling, feeble and wretched,
He grew to a terror as time brought change.
He throve under heaven in power and pride

Till alien peoples beyond the ocean
Paid toll and tribute. A good king he! . . .   10
    . . . Then his hour struck,
And Scyld passed on to the peace of God.
    As their leader had bidden, whose word was law
In the Scylding realm which he long had ruled,
His loving comrades carried him down
To the shore of ocean; a ring-prowed ship,
Straining at anchor and sheeted with ice,
Rode in the harbor, a prince's pride.
Therein they laid him, their well-loved lord,
Their ring-bestower, in the ship's embrace,   20
The mighty prince at the foot of the mast

The translation of *Beowulf* is reprinted with the permission of Charles W. Kennedy and Oxford University Press.
*Mr. Anderson's translation has been divided into sections and equipped with prose summaries and footnotes by George K. Anderson to meet the conditions of this book. 4. **Scyld, son of Sceaf.** At a time when the Danes were greatly oppressed by their enemies, a ship came mysteriously to their shores, bearing a baby and rich treasures. The baby grew up to lead the Danes victoriously in battle and to establish their dynasty of kings. At his death, he passed away to the great deep whence he had come, probably on the very ship that brought him. Sea burials of this sort were common in Scandinavia from the fourth to the sixth centuries. Scyld's name ("shield") in connection with that of his father Sceaf

("sheaf") suggests a culture god of some sort. 10. **A good king he! . . .** Omitted are some dozen lines treating briefly the career of Scyld's son, and some didactic remarks upon the conduct of a young king. 14. **Scylding.** The Danes are called, for variety's sake, by a number of names: Scyldings, Ingwines, Spear-Danes, Ring-Danes, Victory-Danes, Bright-Danes, East-, West-, North-, and South-Danes. Scyldings, "sons of Scyld," has obvious reference to the name of Scyld, the tribal hero and dynastic progenitor; Ingwines refers to the Danes' claimed descent from Inguaeo, one of the three sons of the first man, Mannus, in Germanic mythology. 37. **To Hrothgar.** Omitted are references to several Danish kings between Scyld and Hrothgar. 52. **Hall of the Hart,** or Heorot; so-called from the antlers with which the gables of the building were

Amid much treasure and many a gem
From far-off lands. No lordlier ship
Have I ever heard of, with weapons heaped,
With battle-armor, with bills and byrnies.
On the ruler's breast lay a royal treasure
As the ship put out on the unknown deep.
With no less adornment they dressed him round,
Or gift of treasure, than once they gave
30 Who launched him first on the lonely sea
While still but a child. A golden standard
They raised above him, high over head,
Let the wave take him on trackless seas.
Mournful their mood and heavy their hearts;
Nor wise man nor warrior knows for a truth
Unto what haven that cargo came.

PART I. BEOWULF AND GRENDEL

1

*Hrothgar, son of Healfdene and king of the
Scyldings, builds a wondrous mead-hall, which he
calls Heorot. The revelry in the hall enrages Grendel,
the evil monster.*

. . . To Hrothgar was granted glory in war,
Success in battle; retainers bold
Obeyed him gladly; his band increased
40 To a mighty host. Then his mind was moved
To have men fashion a high-built hall,
A mightier mead-hall than man had known,
Wherein to portion to old and young
All goodly treasure that God had given,
Save only the folk-land, and lives of men.
His word was published to many a people
Far and wide o'er the ways of earth
To rear a folk-stead richly adorned;
The task was speeded, the time soon came
50 That the famous mead-hall was finished and done.
To distant nations its name was known,
The Hall of the Hart; and the king kept well
His pledge and promise to deal out gifts,
Rings at the banquet. The great hall rose
High and horn-gabled, holding its place
Till the battle-surge of consuming flame
Should swallow it up; the hour was near
That the deadly hate of a daughter's husband
Should kindle to fury and savage feud.
60   Then an evil spirit who dwelt in the darkness
Endured it ill that he heard each day

The din of revelry ring through the hall,
The sound of the harp, and the scop's sweet song.
A skilful bard sang the ancient story
Of man's creation; how the Maker wrought
The shining earth with its circling waters;
In splendor established the sun and moon
As lights to illumine the land of men;
Fairly adorning the fields of earth
With leaves and branches; creating life   70
In every creature that breathes and moves.
So the lordly warriors lived in gladness,
At ease and happy, till a fiend from hell
Began a series of savage crimes.
They called him Grendel, a demon grim
Haunting the fen-lands, holding the moors,
Ranging the wastes, where the wretched wight
Made his lair with the monster kin;
He bore the curse of the seed of Cain
Whereby God punished the grievous guilt   80
Of Abel's murder. Nor ever had Cain
Cause to boast of that deed of blood;

*No building of the Heorot type has survived, but the
chief features of the older tribal halls are preserved in
this eleventh-century Norwegian stave church.*

ornamented. The hart was an age-old symbol of royalty. **56. battle-surge
of consuming flame.** Hrothgar's daughter Freawaru was later married to
Ingeld, prince of the Heathobards, to settle a feud which has long raged
between the two tribes. At the wedding feast the feud again broke out
into war; the men of Ingeld invaded Hrothgar's dominions and burned
Heorot to the ground. This is one of the many allusions to events that
take place before and after the story told in the poem. These allusions
contribute to the sense of unity in the poem as a whole. **60. evil spirit,**
Grendel. The monster is described later (ll. 1075-1080) as in the likeness of a man, only greater in size than any living man. We are not
allowed any closer view of the creature, and barring the fact that he had
a head and shoulder and arm, we can get no clearer idea of his anatomy

than the vague and rather unsatisfactory outline just cited. The belief in
such monsters of legend was undoubtedly fostered by the very real and
material presence of great bears; and, if the legend could be traced back
far enough, to such creatures as saber-toothed tigers and anthropoid apes
of gigantic size. **79. seed of Cain.** Grendel is thought of as descended
from Cain, who, because of the murder of his brother Abel and his
subsequent insolence, was cursed by God to become a wanderer (Genesis
4:10-16). The specific reference here is to the giants mentioned in
Genesis 6:4 ("There were giants in the earth in those days. . . .");
supposedly Grendel was akin to them. **81. Cain . . . blood.** Here, as
frequently elsewhere, is to be noted the characteristic rhetorical device of
litotes, or understatement—an important ingredient of Anglo-Saxon humor.

God banished him far from the fields of men;
Of his blood was begotten an evil brood,
Marauding monsters and menacing trolls,
Goblins and giants who battled with God
A long time. Grimly He gave them reward!

2

*Grendel attacks the hall and devours thirty heroes.
Hrothgar and the Danes are helpless. The slaughter
continues for twelve winters.*

Then at the nightfall the fiend drew near
Where the timbered mead-hall towered on high,
90 To spy how the Danes fared after the feast.
Within the wine-hall he found the warriors
Fast in slumber, forgetting grief,
Forgetting the woe of the world of men.
Grim and greedy the gruesome monster,
Fierce and furious, launched attack,
Slew thirty spearmen asleep in the hall,
Sped away gloating, gripping the spoil,
Dragging the dead men home to his den.
Then in the dawn with the coming of daybreak
100 The war-might of Grendel was widely known.
Mirth was stilled by the sound of weeping;
The wail of the mourner awoke with day.
And the peerless hero, the honored prince,
Weighed down with woe and heavy of heart,
Sat sorely grieving for slaughtered thanes,
As they traced the track of the cursed monster.
From that day onward the deadly feud
Was a long-enduring and loathsome strife.
    Not longer was it than one night later
110 The fiend returning renewed attack
With heart firm-fixed in the hateful war,
Feeling no rue for the grievous wrong.
'Twas easy thereafter to mark the men
Who sought their slumber elsewhere afar,
Found beds in the bowers, since Grendel's hate
Was so baldly blazoned in baleful signs.
He held himself at a safer distance
Who escaped the clutch of the demon's claw.
So Grendel raided and ravaged the realm,
120 One against all, in an evil war
Till the best of buildings was empty and still.
'Twas a weary while! Twelve winters' time
The lord of the Scyldings had suffered woe,
Sore affliction and deep distress.
And the malice of Grendel, in mournful lays,
Was widely sung by the sons of men,
The hateful feud that he fought with Hrothgar—
Year after year of struggle and strife,

An endless scourging, a scorning of peace
With any man of the Danish might.   130
No strength could move him to stay his hand,
Or pay for his murders; the wise knew well
They could hope for no halting of savage assault.
Like a dark death-shadow the ravaging demon,
Night-long prowling the misty moors,
Ensnared the warriors, wary or weak.
No man can say how these shades of hell
Come and go on their grisly rounds. . . .
    Great was the grief of the Scylding leader,
His spirit shaken, while many a lord   140
Gathered in council considering long
In what way brave men best could struggle
Against these terrors of sudden attack.
From time to time in their heathen temples
Paying homage they offered prayer
That the Slayer of souls would send them succor
From all the torment that troubled the folk.
Such was the fashion and such the faith
Of their heathen hearts that they looked to hell,
Not knowing the Maker, the mighty Judge,   150
Nor how to worship the Wielder of glory. . . .

3

*At his home among the Geats, Beowulf hears of
Grendel's deeds, and decides to help Hrothgar. He
prepares his ship and sails with his men to the land
of the Danes. He is greeted by the shore-guard.*

The son of Healfdene was heavy-hearted,
Sorrowfully brooding in sore distress,
Finding no help in a hopeless strife;
Too bitter the struggle that stunned the people,
The long oppression, loathsome and grim.
    Then tales of the terrible deeds of Grendel
Reached Hygelac's thane in his home with the Geats;
Of living strong men he was the strongest,
Fearless and gallant and great of heart.   160
He gave command for a goodly vessel
Fitted and furnished; he fain would sail
Over the swan-road to seek the king
Who suffered so sorely for need of men.
And his bold retainers found little to blame
In his daring venture, dear though he was;
They viewed the omens, and urged him on.
Brave was the band he had gathered about him,
Fourteen stalwarts seasoned and bold,
Seeking the shore where the ship lay waiting,   170
A sea-skilled mariner sighting the landmarks.
Came the hour of boarding; the boat was riding
The waves of the harbor under the hill.

---

123. **lord of the Scyldings,** Hrothgar. 132. **pay for,** i.e., through the payment of blood money. A murderer was required by law to pay this blood money to the relatives of the deceased (as in the case of Ecgtheow, Beowulf's father, as mentioned in l. 406). Grendel, as an uncivilized criminal, did not recognize the law. His whole relation with the Danes is spoken of as a feud, such as that between the Danes and Heathobards (cf. note to l. 56), or between the Geats and the Swedes (cf. note to l. 1924). 138. **grisly rounds.** . . . An obscure passage of a half-dozen lines follows, the general sense of which is that Hrothgar found Heorot to be untenable. 151. **Wielder of glory.** . . . A didactic passage

The eager mariners mounted the prow;
Billows were breaking, sea against sand.
In the ship's hold snugly they stowed their trappings,
Gleaming armor and battle-gear;
Launched the vessel, the well-braced bark,
Seaward bound on a joyous journey.
180 Over breaking billows, with bellying sail
And foamy beak, like a flying bird
The ship sped on, till the next day's sun
Showed sea-cliffs shining, towering hills
And stretching headlands. The sea was crossed,
The voyage ended, the vessel moored.
And the Weder people waded ashore
With clatter of trappings and coats of mail;
Gave thanks to God that His grace had granted
Sea-paths safe for their ocean-journey.
  Then the Scylding coast-guard watched from the
190   sea-cliff
Warriors bearing their shining shields,
Their gleaming war-gear, ashore from the ship.
His mind was puzzled, he wondered much
What men they were. On his good horse mounted,
Hrothgar's thane made haste to the beach,
Boldly brandished his mighty spear
With manful challenge: 'What men are you,
Carrying weapons and clad in steel,
Who thus come driving across the deep
200 On the ocean-lanes in your lofty ship?
Long have I served as the Scylding outpost,
Held watch and ward at the ocean's edge
Lest foreign foemen with hostile fleet
Should come to harry our Danish home,
And never more openly sailed to these shores
Men without password, or leave to land.
I have never laid eyes upon earl on earth
More stalwart and sturdy than one of your troop,
A hero in armor; no hall-thane he
210 Tricked out with weapons, unless looks belie him,
And noble bearing. But now I must know
Your birth and breeding, nor may you come
In cunning stealth upon Danish soil.
You distant-dwellers, you far sea-farers,
Hearken, and ponder words that are plain:
'Tis best you hasten to have me know
Who your kindred and whence you come.'

4

*Beowulf tells the reason for his coming and is guided
to Heorot.*

The lord of the seamen gave swift reply,
The prince of the Weders unlocked his word-hoard:

'We are sprung of a strain of the Geatish stock,   220
Hygelac's comrades and hearth-companions.
My father was famous in many a folk-land,
A leader noble, Ecgtheow his name!
Many a winter went over his head
Before death took him from home and tribe;
Well nigh every wise man remembers him well
Far and wide on the ways of earth.
With loyal purpose we seek your lord,
The prince of your people, great Healfdene's son.
Be kindly of counsel; weighty the cause   230
That leads us to visit the lord of the Danes;
Nor need it be secret, as far as I know!
You know if it's true, as we've heard it told,
That among the Scyldings some secret scather,
Some stealthy demon in dead of night,
With grisly horror and fiendish hate
Is spreading unheard-of havoc and death.
Mayhap I can counsel the good, old king
What way he can master the merciless fiend,
If his coil of evil is ever to end   240
And feverish care grow cooler and fade—
Or else ever after his doom shall be
Distress and sorrow while still there stands
This best of halls on its lofty height.'
  Then from the saddle the coast-guard spoke,
The fearless sentry: 'A seasoned warrior
Must know the difference between words and deeds,
If his wits are with him. I take your word
That your band is loyal to the lord of the Scyldings.
Now go your way with your weapons and armor,   250
And I will guide you; I'll give command
That my good retainers may guard your ship,
Your fresh-tarred floater, from every foe,
And hold it safe in its sandy berth,
Till the curving prow once again shall carry
The loved man home to the land of the Geat.
To hero so gallant shall surely be granted
To come from the swordplay sound and safe.'
  Then the Geats marched on; behind at her mooring,
Fastened at anchor, their broad-beamed boat   260
Safely rode on her swinging cable.
Boar-heads glittered on glistening helmets
Above their cheek-guards, gleaming with gold;
Bright and fire-hardened the boar held watch
Over the column of marching men.
Onward they hurried in eager haste
Till their eyes caught sight of the high-built hall,
Splendid with gold, the seat of the king,
Most stately of structures under the sun;
Its light shone out over many a land.   270
The coast-guard showed them the shining hall,
The home of heroes; made plain the path;

has been omitted. The few lines therein are given over to imprecations upon the heads of those who do not subscribe to the Christian faith. 163. **swan-road,** a notable kenning (simple figure of speech) for "sea." 167. **omens.** The observing of omens, to prophesy the success or failure of the expedition, is an allusion, comparable to that in l. 144, to pagan practices before the coming of Christianity. 186. **Weder.** Evidently this word, signifying "storm," is a nickname of the Geat tribe. 262. **Boar-heads . . . helmets.** The helmets were crested with the images of boars; hence the statement two lines below, "the boar held watch."

Turned his horse; gave tongue to words:
'It is time to leave you! The mighty Lord
In His mercy shield you and hold you safe
In your bold adventure. I'll back to the sea
And hold my watch against hostile horde.'

5

Beowulf and the Geats come to Heorot. They are met by a herald, who announces their arrival to Hrothgar.

The street had paving of colored stone;
The path was plain to the marching men.
280 Bright were their byrnies, hard and hand-linked;
In their shining armor the chain-mail sang
As the troop in their war-gear tramped to the hall.
The sea-weary sailors set down their shields,
Their wide, bright bucklers along the wall,
And sank to the bench. Their byrnies rang.
Their stout spears stood in a stack together
Shod with iron and shaped of ash.
'Twas a well-armed troop! Then a stately warrior
Questioned the strangers about their kin:
290 'Whence come you bearing your burnished shields,
Your steel-gray harness and visored helms,
Your heap of spears? I am Hrothgar's herald,
His servant-thane. I have never seen strangers,
So great a number, of nobler mien.
Not exiles, I ween, but high-minded heroes
In greatness of heart have you sought out Hrothgar.'
Then bold under helmet the hero made answer,
The lord of the Weders, manful of mood,
Mighty of heart: 'We are Hygelac's men,
300 His board-companions; Beowulf is my name.
I will state my mission to Healfdene's son,
The noble leader, your lordly prince,
If he will grant approach to his gracious presence.'
And Wulfgar answered, the Wendel prince,
Renowned for merit in many a land,
For war-might and wisdom: 'I will learn the wish
Of the Scylding leader, the lord of the Danes,
Our honored ruler and giver of rings,
Concerning your mission, and soon report
310 The answer our leader thinks good to give.'
  He swiftly strode to where Hrothgar sat
Old and gray with his earls about him;
Crossed the floor and stood face to face
With the Danish king; he knew courtly custom.
Wulfgar saluted his lord and friend:
'Men from afar have fared to our land

Over ocean's margin—men of the Geats,
Their leader called Beowulf—seeking a boon,
The holding of parley, my prince, with thee.
O gracious Hrothgar, refuse not the favor!   320
In their splendid war-gear they merit well
The esteem of earls; he's a stalwart leader
Who led this troop to the land of the Danes.'

6

Beowulf is welcomed by Hrothgar and tells him how he intends to fight with Grendel.

Hrothgar spoke, the lord of the Scyldings:
'Their leader I knew when he still was a lad.
His father was Ecgtheow; Hrethel the Geat
Gave him in wedlock his only daughter.
Now is their son come, keen for adventure,
Finding his way to a faithful friend.
Sea-faring men who have voyaged to Geatland   330
With gifts of treasure as token of peace,
Say that his hand-grip has thirty men's strength.
God, in His mercy, has sent him to save us—
So springs my hope—from Grendel's assaults.
For his gallant courage I'll load him with gifts!
Make haste now, marshal the men to the hall,
And give them welcome to Danish ground.'
  Then to the door went the well-known warrior,
Spoke from the threshold welcoming words:
'The Danish leader, my lord, declares   340
That he knows your kinship; right welcome you come,
You stout sea-rovers, to Danish soil.
Enter now, in your shining armor
And vizored helmets, to Hrothgar's hall.
But leave your shields and the shafts of slaughter
To wait the issue and weighing of words.'
  Then the bold one rose with his band around him,
A splendid massing of mighty thanes;
A few stood guard as the Geat gave bidding
Over the weapons stacked by the wall.   350
They followed in haste on the heels of their leader
Under Heorot's roof. Full ready and bold
The helmeted warrior strode to the hearth;
Beowulf spoke; his byrnie glittered,
His war-net woven by cunning of smith:
'Hail! King Hrothgar! I am Hygelac's thane,
Hygelac's kinsman. Many a deed
Of honor and daring I've done in my youth.
This business of Grendel was brought to my ears
On my native soil. The sea-farers say   360
This best of buildings, this boasted hall,

---

304. **Wendel,** one of the Vandals, the East-Germanic nation that occupied Spain and northern Africa. 314. **courtly custom.** Note the emphasis placed upon etiquette and correct procedure. 368. **five foes I bound,** etc. We get occasional glimpses, half-obscured, of Beowulf's exploits in his youth; see l. 1735. 383. **scorn . . . sword,** etc. Although Beowulf later learns that a magic spell protects Grendel from attack with sword or spear (ll. 720-724), the hero at this time (cf. also l. 609), is motivated only by chivalry or self-confidence in his desire to meet Grendel

on equal terms. 401. **Wayland,** the Germanic god of the forge. 402. **Fate,** considered as a personified deity presiding over the destinies of man, and in Germanic mythology known as the goddess Wyrd. Compare the three Fates of Greek myth, the "weird sisters" of Shakespeare's *Macbeth,* and the Nornir of Scandinavian mythology. The belief in the power of Wyrd, often expressed in *Beowulf,* is a survival of pagan thought in Christian times. 406. **the greatest of feuds.** The story of Ecgtheow, Beowulf's father, illustrates interesting elements in Germanic law and

Stands dark and deserted when sun is set,
When darkening shadows gather with dusk.
The best of my people, prudent and brave,
Urged me, King Hrothgar, to seek you out;
They had in remembrance my courage and might.
Many had seen me come safe from the conflict,
Bloody from battle; five foes I bound
Of the giant kindred, and crushed their clan.
370 Hard-driven in danger and darkness of night
I slew the nicors that swam the sea,
Avenged the woe they had caused the Weders,
And ended their evil—they needed the lesson!
And now with Grendel, the fearful fiend,
Single-handed I'll settle the strife!
Prince of the Danes, protector of Scyldings,
Lord of nations, and leader of men,
I beg one favor—refuse me not,
Since I come thus faring from far-off lands—
380 That I may alone with my loyal earls,
With this hardy company, cleanse Hart-Hall.
I have heard that the demon in proud disdain
Spurns all weapons; and I too scorn—
May Hygelac's heart have joy of the deed—
To bear my sword, or sheltering shield,
Or yellow buckler, to battle the fiend.
With hand-grip only I'll grapple with Grendel;
Foe against foe I'll fight to the death,
And the one who is taken must trust to God's grace!
390 The demon, I doubt not, is minded to feast
In the hall unaffrighted, as often before,
On the force of the Hrethmen, the folk of the Geats.
No need then to bury the body he mangles!
If death shall call me, he'll carry away
My gory flesh to his fen-retreat
To gorge at leisure and gulp me down,
Soiling the marshes with stains of blood.
There'll be little need longer to care for my body!
If the battle slays me, to Hygelac send
400 This best of corselets that covers my breast,
Heirloom of Hrethel, and Wayland's work,
Finest of byrnies. Fate goes as Fate must!'

7

Hrothgar in his answer speaks of Grendel. A feast in Heorot.

Hrothgar spoke, the lord of the Scyldings:
'Deed of daring and dream of honor
Bring you, friend Beowulf, knowing our need!
Your father once fought the greatest of feuds,

Laid Heatholaf low, of the Wylfing line;
And the folk of the Weders refused him shelter
For fear of revenge. Then he fled to the South-Danes,
The Honor-Scyldings beyond the sea.   410
I was then first governing Danish ground,
As a young lad ruling the spacious realm,
The home-land of warriors. Heorogar was dead,
The son of Healfdene no longer living,
My older brother, and better than I!
Thereafter by payment composing the feud,
O'er the water's ridge I sent to the Wylfing
Ancient treasure; he swore me oaths!
It is sorrow sore to recite to another
The wrongs that Grendel has wrought in the hall,   420
His savage hatred and sudden assaults.
My war-troop is weakened, my hall-band is wasted;
Fate swept them away into Grendel's grip.
But God may easily bring to an end
The ruinous deeds of the ravaging foe.
Full often my warriors over their ale-cups
Boldly boasted, when drunk with beer,
They would bide in the beer-hall the coming of battle,
The fury of Grendel, with flashing swords.
Then in the dawn, when the daylight strengthened,   430
The hall stood reddened and reeking with gore,
Bench-boards wet with the blood of battle;
And I had the fewer of faithful fighters,
Beloved retainers, whom Death had taken.
Sit now at the banquet, unbend your mood,
Speak of great deeds as your heart may spur you!'

Then in the beer-hall were benches made ready
For the Geatish heroes. Noble of heart,
Proud and stalwart, they sat them down
And a beer-thane served them; bore in his hands   440
The patterned ale-cup, pouring the mead,
While the scop's sweet singing was heard in the hall.
There was joy of heroes, a host at ease,
A welcome meeting of Weder and Dane.

8-9

Unferth, a thane of Hrothgar, grows envious of Beowulf. He gives Beowulf the lie, and reminds him of a famous swimming contest he once had with Breca. Beowulf angrily tells the truth about the affair, and discomfits Unferth. Queen Wealhtheow appears. Hrothgar gives the hall over to Beowulf for the night.

Then out spoke Unferth, Ecglaf's son,
Who sat at the feet of the Scylding lord,
Picking a quarrel—for Beowulf's quest,

sociology. When Ecgtheow killed a man belonging to another tribe (the Wylfings), he was in danger of precipitating a feud between that tribe and his own, the Geats. The Geats (or Weders) avoided the feud by exiling Ecgtheow. He sought refuge in the court of Hrothgar, who made it possible for Ecgtheow to rejoin his tribe by paying blood money to the Wylfings (see l. 132). 422. **hall-band,** the retinue of warriors surrounding the king. 427. **boasted, etc.** The "boast" of a warrior was not an instance of conceit, but a means of self-incitement to heroic deeds.

If the boast was not accomplished, the warrior was shamed; and death was preferable to shame. The Germanic custom of boasting—of stating definitely what one intended to do—usually at a feast held on the eve of a great emergency, persisted into later times and is found in some of the earliest chivalric romances.

His bold sea-voyaging, irked him sore;
He bore it ill that any man other
450 In all the earth should ever achieve
More fame under heaven than he himself:
'Are you the Beowulf that strove with Breca
In a swimming match in the open sea,
Both of you wantonly tempting the waves,
Risking your lives on the lonely deep
For a silly boast? No man could dissuade you,
Nor friend nor foe, from the foolhardy venture
Of ocean-swimming; with outstretched arms
You clasped the sea-stream, measured her streets,
460 With plowing shoulders parted the waves.
The sea-flood boiled with its wintry surges,
Seven nights you toiled in the tossing sea;
His strength was the greater, his swimming the
     stronger!
The waves upbore you at break of day
To the stretching beach of the Battle-Raemas;
And Breca departed, beloved of his people,
To the land of the Brondings, the beauteous home,
The stronghold fair, where he governed the folk,
The city and treasure; Beanstan's son
470 Made good his boast to the full against you!
Therefore, I ween, worse fate shall befall,
Stout as you are in the struggle of war,
In deeds of battle, if you dare to abide
Encounter with Grendel at coming of night.'
     Beowulf spoke, the son of Ecgtheow:
'My good friend Unferth, addled with beer
Much have you made of the deeds of Breca!
I count it true that I had more courage,
More strength in swimming than any other man.
480 In our youth we boasted—we were both of us boys—
We would risk our lives in the raging sea.
And we made it good! We gripped in our hands
Naked swords, as we swam in the waves,
Guarding us well from the whales' assault.
In the breaking seas he could not outstrip me,
Nor would I leave him. For five nights long
Side by side we strove in the waters
Till racing combers wrenched us apart,
Freezing squalls, and the falling night,
490 And a bitter north wind's icy blast.
Rough were the waves; the wrath of the sea-fish
Was fiercely roused; but my firm-linked byrnie,
The gold-adorned corselet that covered my breast,
Gave firm defense from the clutching foe.
Down to the bottom a savage sea-beast
Fiercely dragged me and held me fast
In a deadly grip; none the less it was granted me
To pierce the monster with point of steel.
Death swept it away with the swing of my sword.

The grisly sea-beasts again and again   500
Beset me sore; but I served them home
With my faithful blade as was well-befitting.
They failed of their pleasure to feast their fill
Crowding round my corpse on the ocean-bottom!
Bloody with wounds, at the break of day,
They lay on the sea-beach slain with the sword.
No more would they cumber the mariner's course
On the ocean deep. From the east came the sun,
Bright beacon of God, and the seas subsided;
I beheld the headlands, the windy walls.   510
Fate often delivers an undoomed earl
If his spirit be gallant! And so I was granted
To slay with the sword-edge nine of the nicors.
I have never heard tell of more terrible strife
Under dome of heaven in darkness of night,
Nor of man harder pressed on the paths of ocean.
But I freed my life from the grip of the foe
Though spent with the struggle. The billows bore me,
The swirling currents and surging seas,
To the land of the Finns. And little I've heard   520
Of any such valiant adventures from you!
Neither Breca nor you in the press of battle
Ever showed such daring with dripping swords—
Though I boast not of it! But you stained your blade
With blood of your brothers, your closest of kin;
And for that you'll endure damnation in hell,
Sharp as you are! I say for a truth,
Son of Ecglaf, never had Grendel
Wrought such havoc and woe in the hall,
That horrid demon so harried your king,   530
If your heart were as brave as you'd have men think!
But Grendel has found that he never need fear
Revenge from your people, or valiant attack
From the Victor-Scyldings; he takes his toll,
Sparing none of the Danish stock.
He slays and slaughters and works his will
Fearing no hurt at the hands of the Danes!
But soon will I show him the stuff of the Geats,
Their courage in battle and strength in the strife;
Then let him who may go bold to the mead-hall   540
When the next day dawns on the dwellings of men,
And the sun in splendor shines warm from the south.'
Glad of heart was the giver of treasure,
Hoary-headed and hardy in war;
The lordly leader had hope of help
As he listened to Beowulf's bold resolve.
     There was revel of heroes and high carouse,
Their speech was happy; and Hrothgar's queen,
Of gentle manners, in jeweled splendor
Gave courtly greeting to all the guests.   550
The high-born lady first bore the beaker
To the Danish leader, lord of the land,

452. **Breca.** Unferth and Beowulf give two versions of an adventure which was probably the subject of a separate epic lay in the *Beowulf* legend. According to Beowulf, his feat of swimming from southern Sweden to northern Norway was not a contest, but the achieving of a boast that he and Breca, another young warrior, had made in common. Breca is mentioned as an epic hero in *Widsith* (see p. 7). 465. the Battle-Raemas,

probably a tribe whose home was the site of the modern Norwegian Romerike, near Oslo. 520. **Finns**, usually held to be the Lapps, inhabitants of Finmarken, around the North Cape in the northern extremity of Norway, considerably above the Arctic Circle. 525. **blood of your brothers.** Beowulf here retaliates on Unferth by unveiling the story of his past crime, and by accusing him of cowardice. Note the laughter of the

Bade him be blithe at the drinking of beer;
Beloved of his people, the peerless king
Joined in the feasting, had joy of the cup.
Then to all alike went the Helming lady
Bearing the beaker to old and young,
Till the jeweled queen with courtly grace
Paused before Beowulf, proffered the mead.
560 She greeted the Geat and to God gave thanks,
Wise of word, that her wish was granted;
At last she could look to a hero for help,
Comfort in evil. He took the cup,
The hardy warrior, at Wealhtheow's hand
And, eager for battle, uttered his boast;
Beowulf spoke, the son of Ecgtheow:
'I had firm resolve when I set to sea
With my band of earls in my ocean-ship,
Fully to work the will of your people
570 Or fall in the struggle slain by the foe.
I shall either perform deeds fitting an earl
Or meet in this mead-hall the coming of death!'
Then the woman was pleased with the words he uttered,
The Geat-lord's boast; the gold-decked queen
Went in state to sit by her lord.
    In the hall as of old were brave words spoken,
There was noise of revel; happy the host
Till the son of Healfdene would go to his rest.
He knew that the monster would meet in the hall
580 Relentless struggle when light of the sun
Was dusky with gloom of the gathering night,
And shadow-shapes crept in the covering dark,
Dim under heaven. The host arose.
Hrothgar graciously greeted his guest,
Gave rule of the wine-hall, and wished him well,
Praised the warrior in parting words:
'Never to any man, early or late,
Since first I could brandish buckler and sword,
Have I trusted this ale-hall save only to you!
590 Be mindful of glory, show forth your strength,
Keep watch against foe! No wish of your heart
Shall go unfulfilled if you live through the fight.'

10

*Beowulf and his men take over the hall. Grendel
appears.*

    Then Hrothgar withdrew with his host of retainers,
The prince of the Scyldings, seeking his queen,
The bed of his consort. The King of Glory
Had stablished a hall-watch, a guard against Grendel,
Dutifully serving the Danish lord,
The land defending from loathsome fiend.
The Geatish hero put all his hope

In his fearless might and the mercy of God!   600
He stripped from his shoulders the byrnie of steel,
Doffed helmet from head; into hand of thane
Gave inlaid iron, the best of blades;
Bade him keep well the weapons of war.
Beowulf uttered a gallant boast,
The stalwart Geat, ere he sought his bed:
'I count myself nowise weaker in war
Or grapple of battle than Grendel himself.
Therefore I scorn to slay him with sword,
Deal deadly wound, as I well might do!   610
Nothing he knows of a noble fighting,
Of thrusting and hewing and hacking of shield,
Fierce as he is in the fury of war.
In the shades of darkness we'll spurn the sword
If he dares without weapon to do or to die.
And God in His wisdom shall glory assign,
The ruling Lord, as He deems it right.'
Then the bold in battle bowed down to his rest,
Cheek pressed pillow; the peerless thanes
Were stretched in slumber around their lord.   620
Not one had hope of return to his home,
To the stronghold or land where he lived as a boy.
For they knew how death had befallen the Danes,
How many were slain as they slept in the wine-hall.
But the wise Lord wove them fortune in war,
Gave strong support to the Weder people;
They slew their foe by the single strength
Of a hero's courage. The truth is clear,
God rules forever the race of men.
    Then through the shades of enshrouding night   630
The fiend came stealing; the archers slept
Whose duty was holding the horn-decked hall—
Though one was watching—full well they knew
No evil demon could drag them down
To shades under ground if God were not willing.
But the hero watched awaiting the foe,
Abiding in anger the issue of war.

11

*Grendel invades Heorot and kills a Geat. Beowulf
attacks the monster.*

    From the stretching moors, from the misty hollows,
Grendel came creeping, accursed of God,
A murderous ravager minded to snare   640
Spoil of heroes in high-built hall.
Under clouded heavens he held his way
Till there rose before him the high-roofed house,
Wine-hall of warriors gleaming with gold.
Nor was it the first of his fierce assaults
On the home of Hrothgar; but never before

Danish thanes that follows Beowulf's victory in this verbal battle. We can
but wonder that Unferth has such a position of honor at Hrothgar's court
if he were guilty of fratricide. The shedding of a kinsman's blood was an
unforgivable crime among the Germanic peoples. Perhaps this is rather
heavy-handed repartee on Beowulf's part. 564. **Wealhtheow.** Her name
suggests "foreign captive"—"foreign" probably in the sense that she was

from a Celtic (non-Germanic) tribe. Most royal marriages among the
Germanic nations were political; exogamy—marriage outside the tribe—
seems to have been frequent. 576. **as of old,** etc., that is, as in the days
before the coming of Grendel; Beowulf's confidence has communicated
itself to his hosts. 635. **if God were not willing,** etc. God here,
as often in Anglo-Saxon Christian literature, is identified with Wyrd.

Had he found worse fate or hardier hall-thanes!
Storming the building he burst the portal,
Though fastened of iron, with fiendish strength;
650 Forced open the entrance in savage fury
And rushed in rage o'er the shining floor.
A baleful glare from his eyes was gleaming
Most like to a flame. He found in the hall
Many a warrior sealed in slumber,
A host of kinsmen. His heart rejoiced;
The savage monster was minded to sever
Lives from bodies ere break of day,
To feast his fill of the flesh of men.
But he was not fated to glut his greed
660 With more of mankind when the night was ended!
    The hardy kinsman of Hygelac waited
To see how the monster would make his attack.
The demon delayed not, but quickly clutched
A sleeping thane in his swift assault,
Tore him in pieces, bit through the bones,
Gulped the blood, and gobbled the flesh,
Greedily gorged on the lifeless corpse,
The hands and the feet. Then the fiend stepped nearer,
Sprang on the Sea-Geat lying outstretched,
670 Clasping him close with his monstrous claw.
But Beowulf grappled and gripped him hard,
Struggled up on his elbow; the shepherd of sins
Soon found that never before had he felt
In any man other in all the earth
A mightier hand-grip; his mood was humbled,
His courage fled; but he found no escape!
He was fain to be gone; he would flee to the darkness,
The fellowship of devils. Far different his fate
From that which befell him in former days!
680 The hardy hero, Hygelac's kinsman,
Remembered the boast he had made at the banquet;
He sprang to his feet, clutched Grendel fast,
Though fingers were cracking, the fiend pulling free.
The earl pressed after; the monster was minded
To win his freedom and flee to the fens.
He knew that his fingers were fast in the grip
Of a savage foe. Sorry the venture,
The raid that the ravager made on the hall.
    There was din in Heorot. For all the Danes,
690 The city-dwellers, the stalwart Scyldings,
That was a bitter spilling of beer!
The walls resounded, the fight was fierce,
Savage the strife as the warriors struggled.
The wonder was that the lofty wine-hall
Withstood the struggle, nor crashed to earth,
The house so fair; it was firmly fastened
Within and without with iron bands
Cunningly smithied; though men have said
That many a mead-bench gleaming with gold

Sprang from its sill as the warriors strove.   700
The Scylding wise men had never weened
That any ravage could wreck the building,
Firmly fashioned and finished with bone,
Or any cunning compass its fall,
Till the time when the swelter and surge of fire
Should swallow it up in a swirl of flame.
    Continuous tumult filled the hall;
A terror fell on the Danish folk
As they heard through the wall the horrible wailing,
The groans of Grendel, the foe of God   710
Howling his hideous hymn of pain,
The hell-thane shrieking in sore defeat.
He was fast in the grip of the man who was greatest
Of mortal men in the strength of his might,
Who would never rest while the wretch was living,
Counting his life-days a menace to man.

12

Beowulf rips out Grendel's arm and wins the fight.
The monster, mortally wounded, escapes to the fen.

    Many an earl of Beowulf brandished
His ancient iron to guard his lord,
To shelter safely the peerless prince.
They had no knowledge, those daring thanes,   720
When they drew their weapons to hack and hew,
To thrust to the heart, that the sharpest sword,
The choicest iron in all the world,
Could work no harm to the hideous foe.
On every sword he had laid a spell,
On every blade; but a bitter death
Was to be his fate; far was the journey
The monster made to the home of fiends.
    Then he who had wrought such wrong to men,
With grim delight as he warred with God,   730
Soon found that his strength was feeble and failing
In the crushing hold of Hygelac's thane.
Each loathed the other while life should last!
There Grendel suffered a grievous hurt,
A wound in the shoulder, gaping and wide;
Sinews snapped and bone-joints broke,
And Beowulf gained the glory of battle.
Grendel, fated, fled to the fens,
To his joyless dwelling, sick unto death.
He knew in his heart that his hours were numbered,   740
His days at an end. For all the Danes
Their wish was fulfilled in the fall of Grendel.
The stranger from far, the stalwart and strong,
Had purged of evil the hall of Hrothgar,
And cleansed of crime; the heart of the hero
Joyed in the deed his daring had done.

---

661. **kinsman of Hygelac,** Beowulf; he was Hygelac's nephew. 681. **boast . . . banquet.** This refers to Beowulf's previous boast; see l. 605. 724. **no harm . . . hideous foe;** see l. 383 and note. 763. **nicors' pool.** The nicor, or water monster, is a feature of Germanic legendry, and the belief in such creatures survives in our expression "Old Nick" for the devil. 787. **Sigemund.** This summarized lay connects *Beowulf* with

the Norse and German epics of Siegfried, probably the greatest of the Germanic epic heroes. We have seen that cycles of story accruing to these prominent heroes were probably far more numerous than we can imagine from a bare inspection of surviving tales, and no doubt were often inter-related, as the Arthurian stories unquestionably were. Sigemund the Volsung (cf. *Waelsing* in l. 788), was the father of Siegfried (Sigurd,

The lord of the Geats made good to the East-Danes
The boast he had uttered; he ended their ill,
And all the sorrow they suffered long
750 And needs must suffer—a foul offense.
The token was clear when the bold in battle
Laid down the shoulder and dripping claw—
Grendel's arm—in the gabled hall!

13

*Rejoicing of the Danes. They go to follow the track
of the fleeing Grendel. On their return to the Hall of
the Hart, they listen to the tales of the bard.*

When morning came, as they tell the tale,
Many a warrior hastened to hall,
Folk-leaders faring from far and near
Over wide-running ways, to gaze at the wonder,
The trail of the demon. Nor seemed his death
A matter of sorrow to any man
760 Who viewed the tracks of the vanquished monster
As he slunk weary-hearted away from the hall,
Doomed and defeated and marking his flight
With bloody prints to the nicors' pool.
The crimson currents bubbled and heaved
In eddying reaches reddened with gore;
The surges boiled with the fiery blood.
But the monster had sunk from the sight of men.
In that fenny covert the cursed fiend
Not long thereafter laid down his life,
770 His heathen spirit; and hell received him.
    Then all the comrades, the old and young,
The brave of heart, in a blithesome band
Came riding their horses home from the mere.
Beowulf's prowess was praised in song;
And many men stated that south or north,
Over all the world, or between the seas,
Or under the heaven, no hero was greater,
More worthy of rule. But no whit they slighted
The gracious Hrothgar, their good old king.
780 Time and again they galloped their horses,
Racing their roans where the roads seemed fairest;
Time and again a gleeman chanted,
A minstrel mindful of saga and lay.
He wove his words in a winsome pattern,
Hymning the burden of Beowulf's feat,
Clothing the story in skilful verse.
    All tales he had ever heard told he sang of Sige-
        mund's glory,
Deeds of the Waelsing forgotten, his weary roving and
        wars,
Feuds and fighting unknown to men, save Fitela only,

An Anglo-Saxon warrior, MS Cotton Tiberius B, V.

Tales told by uncle to nephew when the two were
        companions,   790
What time they were bosom-comrades in battle and
        bitter strife.
Many of monster blood these two had slain with the
        sword-edge,
Great glory Sigemund gained that lingered long after
        death,
When he daringly slew the dragon that guarded the
        hoard of gold.
Under the ancient rock the warrior ventured alone,
No Fitela fighting beside him; but still it befell
That his firm steel pierced the worm, the point stood
        fast in the wall;
The dragon had died the death! And the hero's daring
Had won the treasure to have and to hold as his heart
        might wish.
Then the Waelsing loaded his sea-boat, laid in the
        breast of the ship   800
Wondrous and shining treasure; the worm dissolved in
        the heat.
Sigemund was strongest of men in his deeds of daring,

Sigurthr, etc.). Fitela (l. 789), the companion of Sigemund's early adventures, was, according to Norse sagas, Sigemund's son by an incestuous relation with his sister (note again the uncle-nephew relationship), and so is analogous to Modred in Arthurian story. Sigemund and Fitela joined to avenge injuries received from the sister's treacherous husband. Sigemund's fight with the dragon (cf. Beowulf's similar fight later in the poem), is not related among his adventures in the Norse saga; but a combat of this sort is among the most famous events in Siegfried's career. The episode in *Beowulf* antedates by several centuries any other version of the story.

Warrior's shield and defender, most famous in days of
    old . . .
    Time and again on their galloping steeds
Over yellow roads they measured the mile-paths;
Morning sun mounted the shining sky
And many a hero strode to the hall,
Stout of heart, to behold the wonder.
The worthy ruler, the warder of treasure,
810 Set out from the bowers with stately train;
The queen with her maidens paced over the mead-path.

14

Hrothgar and his men gaze upon Grendel's arm.

    Then spoke Hrothgar; hasting to hall
He stood at the steps, stared up at the roof
High and gold-gleaming; saw Grendel's hand:
'Thanks be to God for this glorious sight!
I have suffered much evil, much outrage from Grendel,
But the God of glory works wonder on wonder.
I had no hope of a haven from sorrow
While this best of houses stood badged with blood,
820 A woe far-reaching for all the wise
Who weened that they never could hold the hall
Against the assaults of devils and demons.
But now with God's help this hero has compassed
A deed our cunning could no way contrive.
Surely that woman may say with truth,
Who bore this son, if she still be living,
Our ancient God showed favor and grace
On her bringing-forth! . . .'
    Then the nobles gazed at the grisly claw,
830 The fiend's hand fastened by hero's might
On the lofty roof. Most like to steel
Were the hardened nails, the heathen's hand-spurs,
Horrible, monstrous; and many men said
No tempered sword, no excellent iron,
Could have harmed the monster or hacked away
The demon's battle-claw dripping with blood.

15

*A feast is prepared at Heorot. Hrothgar rewards
Beowulf.*

    In joyful haste was Heorot decked
And a willing host of women and men
Gaily dressed and adorned the guest-hall.
840 Splendid hangings with sheen of gold

Shone on the walls, a glorious sight
To eyes that delight to behold such wonders.
The shining building was wholly shattered
Though braced and fastened with iron bands;
Hinges were riven; the roof alone
Remained unharmed when the horrid monster,
Foul with evil, slunk off in flight,
Hopeless of life. . . .
    Soon was the time when the son of Healfdene
Went to the wine-hall; he fain would join   850
With happy heart in the joy of feasting.
I never have heard of a mightier muster
Of proud retainers around their prince.
All at ease they bent to the benches,
Had joy of the banquet; their kinsmen bold,
Hrothgar and Hrothulf, happy of heart,
In the high-built hall drank many a mead-cup.
The hall of Hrothgar was filled with friends;
No treachery yet had troubled the Scyldings.
Upon Beowulf, then, as a token of triumph,   860
Hrothgar bestowed a standard of gold,
A banner embroidered, a byrnie and helm.
In sight of many, a costly sword
Before the hero was borne on high;
Beowulf drank of many a bowl.
No need for shame in the sight of heroes
For gifts so gracious! I never have heard
Of many men dealing in friendlier fashion,
To others on ale-bench, richer rewards,
Four such treasures fretted with gold!   870
On the crest of the helmet a crowning wreath,
Woven of wire-work, warded the head
Lest tempered swordblade, sharp from the file,
Deal deadly wound when the shielded warrior
Went forth to battle against the foe.
Eight horses also with plated headstalls
The lord of heroes bade lead into hall;
On one was a saddle skilfully fashioned
And set with jewels, the battle-seat
Of the king himself, when the son of Healfdene   880
Would fain take part in the play of swords;
Never in fray had his valor failed,
His kingly courage, when corpses were falling.
And the prince of the Ingwines gave all these gifts
To the hand of Beowulf, horses and armor;
Bade him enjoy them! With generous heart
The noble leader, the lord of heroes,
Rewarded the struggle with steeds and with treasure,
So that none can belittle, and none can blame,
Who tells the tale as it truly happened.   890

803. **days of old** . . . Omitted are some twenty lines obscurely sketching the career of Heremod, a villainous king in utter contrast to Beowulf
or Sigemund. Another allusion to Heremod is made later (1. 1437).
828. **On her bringing-forth!** . . . Omitted are two long speeches, the
first by Hrothgar, in which he decides to adopt Beowulf as his son; the
second by Beowulf in acknowledgment of this honor, reviewing his exploit against Grendel. 848. **Hopeless of life** . . . . A few lines of comment on Grendel's spiritual fate have been omitted. 856. **Hrothgar
and Hrothulf,** another allusion to events subsequent to the present
narrative. Hrothulf was the son of Hrothgar's younger brother Halga.

Note once more the uncle-nephew relationship. When Hrothgar grew
old, Hrothulf aided him in his military duties. As is implied in the poem
(ll. 925–938), Wealhtheow feared that Hrothulf would some day dispossess her two sons, the presumptive heirs, and seize the throne for himself. Her fears were evidently realized, although the Norse sagas, in which
Hrothulf (under the name of Hrolf Kraki) is a mighty king, say nothing
about the fate of Hrothgar and his sons. 894. **Gift . . . gold.** Feeling
morally responsible for Grendel's murder of Beowulf's thane (l. 664),
Hrothgar pays Beowulf the blood money; see note to l. 132. 907. **terror
befell them** . . . The bard sings a lay, omitted here, of a bloody fight

Hrothgar gives presents to Beowulf's men.

Then on the ale-bench to each of the earls
Who embarked with Beowulf, sailing the sea-paths,
The lord of princes dealt ancient heirlooms,
Gift of treasure, and guerdon of gold
To requite his slaughter whom Grendel slew,
As he would have slain others, but all-wise God
And the hero's courage had conquered Fate.
The Lord ruled over the lives of men
As He rules them still. Therefore understanding
900 And a prudent spirit are surely best!
He must suffer much of both weal and woe
Who dwells here long in these days of strife.
  Then song and revelry rose in the hall;
Before Healfdene's leader the harp was struck
And hall-joy wakened; the song was sung,
Hrothgar's gleeman rehearsed the lay
Of the sons of Finn when the terror befell them . . .
So the song was sung, the lay recited,
The sound of revelry rose in the hall.
910 Stewards poured wine from wondrous vessels;
And Wealhtheow, wearing a golden crown,
Came forth in state where the two were sitting,
Courteous comrades, uncle and nephew,
Each true to the other in ties of peace.
Unferth, the orator, sat at the feet
Of the lord of the Scyldings; and both showed trust
In his noble mind, though he had no mercy
On kinsmen in swordplay; the Scylding queen spoke:
'My sovereign lord, dispenser of treasure,
920 Drink now of this flagon, have joy of the feast!
Speak to the Geats, O gold-friend of men,
In winning words as is well-befitting;
Be kind to the Geat-men and mindful of gifts
From the gold you have garnered from near and far.
You have taken as son, so many have told me,
This hardy hero. Heorot is cleansed,
The gleaming gift-hall. Rejoice while you may
In lavish bounty, and leave to your kin
People and kingdom when time shall come,
930 Your destined hour, to look on death.
I know the heart of my gracious Hrothulf,
That he'll safely shelter and shield our sons
When you leave this world, if he still is living.
I know he will favor with gracious gifts
These boys of ours, if he bears in mind
The many honors and marks of love

We bestowed upon him while he still was a boy.'
  She turned to the bench where her boys were sitting,
Hrethric and Hrothmund, the sons of heroes,
The youth together; there the good man sat,   940
Beowulf of the Geats, beside the two brothers.

18

The queen gives gifts to Beowulf, and a treasured collar for Hygelac. The feast over, the warriors rest in Heorot.

Then the cup was offered with gracious greeting,
And seemly presents of spiraled gold,
A corselet, and rings, and the goodliest collar
Of all that ever were known on earth.
I have never heard tell of a worthier treasure
In the hoarding of heroes beneath the sky
Since Hama bore off to the shining city
The Brosings' jewel, setting and gems,
Fled from Eormenric's cruel craft   950
And sought the grace of eternal glory.
Hygelac, the Geat, grandson of Swerting
Wore the ring in the last of his raids,
Guarding the spoil under banner in battle,
Defending the treasure. Overtaken by Fate,
In the flush of pride he fought with the Frisians
And met disaster. The mighty prince
Carried the ring o'er the cup of the waves,
The precious jewel, and sank under shield.
Then his body fell into Frankish hands,   960
His woven corselet and jeweled collar,
And weaker warriors plundered the dead
After the carnage and welter of war.
The field of battle was covered with corpses
Of Geats who had fallen, slain by the sword.
  The sound of revelry rose in the hall;
Wealhtheow spoke to the warrior host:
'Take, dear Beowulf, collar and corselet,
Wear these treasures with right good will!
Thrive and prosper and prove your might!   970
Befriend my boys with your kindly counsel;
I will remember and I will repay.
You have earned the undying honor of heroes
In regions reaching as far and wide
As the windy walls that the sea encircles.
May Fate show favor while life shall last!
I wish you wealth to your heart's content;
In your days of glory be good to my sons!
Here each hero is true to other,

---

between the Danes and Frisians. The lay is related to a lost Old English epic, *The Fight at Finnsburg,* of which a short fragment has been preserved. 925. **You have taken, etc.** Wealhtheow, with the nervousness of a fond mother, is afraid that Hrothgar's gratitude may lead him to make Beowulf his actual heir and so cut off his own sons; she tactfully suggests other rewards. 927. **gift-hall,** Heorot, so called because it was the hall wherein the king would reward his warriors "for deeds done" with rings and other objects of value. 948. **Hama, etc.** The story here alluded to is told more clearly in a Norse saga. There we learn that Hama, a follower of Eormenric, historically a king of the East Goths in the fourth century, in legend a cruel tyrant, fled from his lord and took refuge in a monastery ("grace of eternal glory"). In *Beowulf* he is said to have stolen from Eormenric the collar of the Brosings, a famous necklace which, according to Norse legends, belonged originally to the goddess Freyja (who corresponds to Aphrodite, or Venus, in classical mythology). This necklace later came into the possession of Hrothgar, who gave it to Beowulf, who gave it to Hygd (ll. 1725 ff.), who must have given it to Hygelac, her husband, for he lost it in his last, fatal battle.

980 Gentle of spirit, loyal to lord,
Friendly thanes and a folk united,
Wine-cheered warriors who do my will.'
    Then she went to her seat. At the fairest of feasts
Men drank of the wine-cup, knowing not Fate,
Nor the fearful doom that befell the earls
When darkness gathered, and gracious Hrothgar
Sought his dwelling and sank to rest.
A host of heroes guarded the hall
As they oft had done in the days of old.
990 They stripped the benches and spread the floor
With beds and bolsters. But one of the beer-thanes
Bowed to his hall-rest doomed to death.
They set at their heads their shining shields,
Their battle-bucklers; and there on the bench
Above each hero his towering helmet,
His spear and corselet hung close at hand.
It was ever their wont to be ready for war
At home or in field, as it ever befell
That their lord had need. 'Twas a noble race!

19

Grendel's mother comes to avenge her son. She seizes Aeschere in the hall and devours him.

1000   Then they sank to slumber. But one paid dear
For his evening rest, as had often happened
When Grendel haunted the lordly hall
And wrought such ruin, till his end was come,
Death for his sins; it was easily seen,
Though the monster was slain, an avenger survived
Prolonging the feud, though the fiend had perished.
The mother of Grendel, a monstrous hag,
Brooded over her misery, doomed to dwell
In evil waters and icy streams . . .
1010 Rabid and raging his mother resolved
On a dreadful revenge for the death of her son!
    She stole to the hall where the Danes were sleeping,
And horror fell on the host of earls
When the dam of Grendel burst in the door.
But the terror was less as the war-craft is weaker,
A woman's strength, than the might of a man
When the hilted sword, well shaped by the hammer,
The blood-stained iron of tempered edge,
Hews the boar from the foeman's helmet.
1020 Then in the hall was the hard-edged blade,
The stout steel, brandished above the benches;
Seizing their shields men stayed not for helmet
Or ample byrnie, when fear befell.
As soon as discovered, the hag was in haste
To fly to the open, to flee for her life.
One of the warriors she swiftly seized,
Clutched him fast and made off to the fens.
He was of heroes the dearest to Hrothgar,

The best of comrades between two seas;
The warrior brave, the stout-hearted spear-man,   1030
She slew in his sleep. Nor was Beowulf there;
But after the banquet another abode
Had been assigned to the glorious Geat.
There was tumult in Heorot. She tore from its place
The blood-stained claw. Care was renewed!
It was no good bargain when both in turn
Must pay the price with the lives of friends!
    Then the white-haired warrior, the aged king,
Was numb with sorrow, knowing his thane
No longer was living, his dearest man dead.   1040
Beowulf, the brave, was speedily summoned,
Brought to the bower; the noble prince
Came with his comrades at dawn of day
Where the wise king awaited if God would award
Some happier turn in these tidings of woe.
The hero came tramping into the hall
With his chosen band—the boards resounded—
Greeted the leader, the Ingwine lord,
And asked if the night had been peaceful and pleasant.

20

Hrothgar mourns for Aeschere. He tells Beowulf of Grendel's mother and her abode.

Hrothgar spoke, the lord of the Scyldings: 1050
'Ask not of pleasure; pain is renewed
For the Danish people. Aeschere is dead!
Dead is Yrmenlaf's elder brother!
He was my comrade, closest of counselors,
My shoulder-companion as side by side
We fought for our lives in the welter of war,
In the shock of battle when boar-helms crashed.
As an earl should be, a prince without peer,
Such was Aeschere, slain in the hall
By the wandering demon! I know not whither   1060
She fled to shelter, proud of her spoil,
Gorged to the full. She avenged the feud
Wherein yesternight you grappled with Grendel
And savagely slew him because so long
He had hunted and harried the men of my folk.
He fell in the battle and paid with his life.
But now another fierce ravager rises
Avenging her kinsman, and carries it far,
As it seems to many a saddened thane
Who grieves in his heart for his treasure-giver.   1070
This woe weighs heavy! The hand lies still
That once was lavish of all delights.
    Oft in the hall I have heard my people,
Comrades and counselors, telling a tale
Of evil spirits their eyes have sighted,
Two mighty marauders who haunt the moors.
One shape, as clearly as men could see,

1009. **icy streams . . .** There follows a repetition of the statement that Grendel is related to Cain; there is also a résumé, with appropriate Christian remarks, of Grendel's doom. Both have been omitted. 1019. **boar;** see note to l. 262. 1083. **Wild, etc.,** interesting as one

Seemed woman's likeness, and one seemed man,
An outcast wretch of another world,
1080 And huger far than a human form.
Grendel my countrymen called him, not knowing
What monster-brood spawned him, what sire begot.
Wild and lonely the land they live in,
Wind-swept ridges and wolf-retreats,
Dread tracts of fen where the falling torrent
Downward dips into gloom and shadow
Under the dusk of the darkening cliff.
Not far in miles lies the lonely mere
Where trees firm-rooted and hung with frost
1090 Overshroud the wave with shadowing gloom.
And there a portent appears each night,
A flame in the water; no man so wise
Who knows the bound of its bottomless depth.
The heather-stepper, the horned stag,
The antlered hart hard driven by hounds,
Invading that forest in flight from afar
Will turn at bay and die on the brink
Ere ever he'll plunge in that haunted pool.
'Tis an eerie spot! Its tossing spray
1100 Mounts dark to heaven when high winds stir
The driving storm, and the sky is murky,
And with foul weather the heavens weep.
On your arm only rests all our hope!
Not yet have you tempted those terrible reaches,
The region that shelters that sinful wight.
Go if you dare! I will give requital
With ancient treasure and twisted gold,
As I formerly gave in guerdon of battle,
If out of that combat you come alive.'

21

They follow the tracks of Grendel's mother. Beowulf slays a sea-beast.

1110   Beowulf spoke, the son of Ecgtheow:
'Sorrow not, brave one! Better for man
To avenge a friend than much to mourn.
All men must die; let him who may
Win glory ere death. That guerdon is best
For a noble man when his name survives him.
Then let us rise up, O ward of the realm,
And haste us forth to behold the track
Of Grendel's dam. And I give you pledge
She shall not in safety escape to cover,
1120 To earthy cavern, or forest fastness,
Or gulf of ocean, go where she may.
This day with patience endure the burden
Of every woe, as I know you will.'
Up sprang the ancient, gave thanks to God
For the heartening words the hero had spoken.
Quickly a horse was bridled for Hrothgar,

A mettlesome charger with braided mane;
In royal splendor the king rode forth
Mid the trampling tread of a troop of shield-men.
The tracks lay clear where the fiend had fared   1130
Over plain and bottom and woodland path,
Through murky moorland making her way
With the lifeless body, the best of thanes
Who of old with Hrothgar had guarded the hall.
By a narrow path the king pressed on
Through rocky upland and rugged ravine,
A lonely journey, past looming headlands,
The lair of monster and lurking troll.
Tried retainers, a trusty few,
Advanced with Hrothgar to view the ground.   1140
Sudden they came on a dismal covert
Of trees that hung over hoary stone,
Over churning water and blood-stained wave.
Then for the Danes was the woe the deeper,
The sorrow sharper for Scylding earls,
When they first caught sight, on the rocky sea-cliff,
Of slaughtered Aeschere's severed head.
The water boiled in a bloody swirling
With seething gore as the spearmen gazed.
The trumpet sounded a martial strain;   1150
The shield-troop halted. Their eyes beheld
The swimming forms of strange sea-dragons,
Dim serpent shapes in the watery depths,
Sea-beasts sunning on headland slopes;
Snakelike monsters that oft at sunrise
On evil errands scour the sea.
Startled by tumult and trumpet's blare,
Enraged and savage, they swam away;
But one the lord of the Geats brought low,
Stripped of his sea-strength, despoiled of life,   1160
As the bitter bow-bolt pierced his heart.
His watery-speed grew slower, and ceased,
And he floated, caught in the clutch of death.
Then they hauled him in with sharp-hooked boar-
        spears,
By sheer strength grappled and dragged him ashore,
A wondrous wave-beast; and all the array
Gathered to gaze at the grisly guest.
    Beowulf donned his armor for battle,
Heeded not danger; the hand-braided byrnie,
Broad of shoulder and richly bedecked,   1170
Must stand the ordeal of the watery depths.
Well could that corselet defend the frame
Lest hostile thrust should pierce to the heart.
Or blows of battle beat down the life.
A gleaming helmet guarded his head
As he planned his plunge to the depths of the pool
Through the heaving waters—a helm adorned
With lavish inlay and lordly chains,
Ancient work of the weapon-smith
Skilfully fashioned, beset with the boar,   1180

of the earliest pieces of descriptive "landscape" poetry in English literature. 1113. **All men, etc.,** a fine example of the didactic element in
Old English poetry. 1180. **beset . . . boar,** with embossed figures
around the crown of the helmet.

That no blade of battle might bite it through.
Not the least or the worst of his war-equipment
Was the sword the herald of Hrothgar loaned
In his hour of need—Hrunting its name—
An ancient heirloom, trusty and tried;
Its blade was iron, with etched design,
Tempered in blood of many a battle.
Never in fight had it failed the hand
That drew it daring the perils of war,
1190 The rush of the foe. Not the first time then
That its edge must venture on valiant deeds.
But Ecglaf's stalwart son was unmindful
Of words he had spoken while heated with wine,
When he loaned the blade to a better swordsman.
He himself dared not hazard his life
In deeds of note in the watery depths;
And thereby he forfeited honor and fame.
Not so with that other undaunted spirit
After he donned his armor for battle.

22

*Beowulf bids farewell to Hrothgar and dives into the
pool. The monster attacks him. They fight.*

1200 Beowulf spoke, the son of Ecgtheow:
'O gracious ruler, gold-giver to men,
As I now set forth to attempt this feat,
Great son of Healfdene, hold well in mind
The solemn pledge we plighted of old,
That if doing your service I meet my death
You will mark my fall with a father's love.
Protect my kinsmen, my trusty comrades,
If battle take me. And all the treasure
You have heaped on me bestow upon Hygelac,
1210 Hrothgar beloved! The lord of the Geats,
The son of Hrethel, shall see the proof,
Shall know as he gazes on jewels and gold,
That I found an unsparing dispenser of bounty,
And joyed, while I lived, in his generous gifts.
Give back to Unferth the ancient blade,
The sword-edge splendid with curving scrolls,
For either with Hrunting I'll reap rich harvest
Of glorious deeds, or death shall take me.'
After these words the prince of the Weders
1220 Awaited no answer, but turned to the task,
Straightway plunged in the swirling pool.
Nigh unto a day he endured the depths
Ere he first had view of the vast sea-bottom.
Soon she found, who had haunted the flood,
A ravening hag, for a hundred half-years,
Greedy and grim, that a man was groping
In daring search through the sea-troll's home.
Swift she grappled and grasped the warrior

With horrid grip, but could work no harm,
No hurt to his body; the ring-locked byrnie   1230
Cloaked his life from her clutching claw;
Nor could she tear through the tempered mail
With her savage fingers. The she-wolf bore
The ring-prince down through the watery depths
To her den at the bottom; nor could Beowulf draw
His blade for battle, though brave his mood.
Many a sea-beast, strange sea-monsters,
Tasked him hard with their menacing tusks,
Broke his byrnie and smote him sore.
    Then he found himself in a fearsome hall   1240
Where water came not to work him hurt,
But the flood was stayed by the sheltering roof.
There in the glow of firelight gleaming
The hero had view of the huge sea-troll.
He swung his war-sword with all his strength,
Withheld not the blow, and the savage blade
Sang on her head its hymn of hate.
But the bold one found that the battle-flasher
Would bite no longer, nor harm her life.
The sword-edge failed at his sorest need.   1250
Often of old with ease it had suffered
The clash of battle, cleaving the helm,
The fated warrior's woven mail.
That time was first for the treasured blade
That its glory failed in the press of the fray.
But fixed of purpose and firm of mood
Hygelac's earl was mindful of honor;
In wrath, undaunted, he dashed to earth
The jeweled sword with its scrolled design,
The blade of steel; staked all on strength,   1260
On the might of his hand, as a man must do
Who thinks to win in the welter of battle
Enduring glory; he fears not death.
The Geat-prince joyed in the straining struggle,
Stalwart-hearted and stirred to wrath,
Gripped the shoulder of Grendel's dam
And headlong hurled the hag to the ground.
But she quickly clutched him and drew him close,
Countered the onset with savage claw.
The warrior staggered, for all his strength,   1270
Dismayed and shaken and borne to earth.
She knelt upon him and drew her dagger,
With broad bright blade, to avenge her son,
Her only issue. But the corselet's steel
Shielded his breast and sheltered his life
Withstanding entrance of point and edge.
    Then the prince of the Geats would have gone his
        journey,
The son of Ecgtheow, under the ground;
But his sturdy breast-net, his battle-corselet,
Gave him succor, and holy God,   1280
The Lord all-wise, awarded the mastery;
Heaven's Ruler gave right decree.

1183. **herald of Hrothgar,** Unferth, called Ecglaf's son in l. 1192.
Note his changed attitude toward Beowulf. 1184. **Hrunting its name,**
as Arthur's sword was named Excalibur. 1211. **son of Hrethel,** Hygelac.

1216. **sword-edge . . . scrolls,** a reference to the damascened blade.
1249. **harm her life.** The same spell works on the opponents of Grendel's
mother as on the opponents of Grendel himself (note ll. 383-385). 1284.

23

Beowulf suddenly sees a marvelous sword, with which he kills Grendel's dam. He sees Grendel's corpse and cuts off the head. He swims back to his friends, who have been anxiously awaiting him. They all return to Heorot.

Swift the hero sprang to his feet;
Saw mid the war-gear a stately sword,
An ancient war-brand of biting edge,
Choicest of weapons worthy and strong,
The work of giants, a warrior's joy,
So heavy no hand but his own could hold it,
Bear to battle or wield in war.
1290 Then the Scylding warrior, savage and grim,
Seized the ring-hilt and swung the sword,
Struck with fury, despairing of life,
Thrust at the throat, broke through the bone-rings;
The stout blade stabbed through her fated flesh.
She sank in death; the sword was bloody;
The hero joyed in the work of his hand.
The gleaming radiance shimmered and shone
As the candle of heaven shines clear from the sky.
Wrathful and resolute Hygelac's thane
1300 Surveyed the span of the spacious hall;
Grimly gripping the hilted sword
With upraised weapon he turned to the wall.
The blade had failed not the battle-prince;
A full requital he firmly planned
For all the injury Grendel had done
In numberless raids on the Danish race,
When he slew the hearth-companions of Hrothgar,
Devoured fifteen of the Danish folk
Clasped in slumber, and carried away
1310 As many more spearmen, a hideous spoil.
All this the stout-heart had stern requited;
And there before him bereft of life
He saw the broken body of Grendel
Stilled in battle, and stretched in death,
As the struggle in Heorot smote him down.
The corpse sprang wide as he struck the blow,
The hard sword-stroke that severed the head.
Then the tried retainers, who there with Hrothgar
Watched the face of the foaming pool,
1320 Saw that the churning reaches were reddened,
The eddying surges stained with blood.
And the gray, old spearmen spoke of the hero,
Having no hope he would ever return
Crowned with triumph and cheered with spoil.
Many were sure that the savage sea-wolf
Had slain their leader. At last came noon.
The stalwart Scyldings forsook the headland;
Their proud gold-giver departed home.
But the Geats sat grieving and sick in spirit,

Stared at the water with longing eyes,   1330
Having no hope they would ever behold
Their gracious leader and lord again.
Then the great sword, eaten with blood of battle,
Began to soften and waste away
In iron icicles, wonder of wonders,
Melting away most like to ice
When the Father looses the fetters of frost,
Slackens the bondage that binds the wave,
Strong in power of times and seasons;
He is true God! Of the goodly treasures   1340
From the sea-cave Beowulf took but two,
The monster's head and the precious hilt
Blazing with gems; but the blade had melted,
The sword dissolved, in the deadly heat,
The venomous blood of the fallen fiend.
Then he who had compassed the fall of his foes
Came swimming up through the swirling surge.
Cleansed were the currents, the boundless abyss,
Where the evil monster had died the death
And looked her last on this fleeting world.   1350
With sturdy strokes the lord of the seamen
To land came swimming, rejoiced in his spoil,
Had joy of the burden he brought from the depths.
And his mighty thanes came forward to meet him,
Gave thanks to God they were granted to see
Their well-loved leader both sound and safe.
From the stalwart hero his helmet and byrnie
Were quickly loosened; the lake lay still,
Its motionless reaches reddened with blood.
Fain of heart men fared o'er the footpaths,   1360
Measured the ways and the well-known roads.
From the sea-cliff's brim the warriors bore
The head of Grendel, with heavy toil;
Four of the stoutest, with all their strength,
Could hardly carry on swaying spear
Grendel's head to the gold-decked hall.
Swift they strode, the daring and dauntless,
Fourteen Geats, to the Hall of the Hart;
And proud in the midst of his marching men
Their leader measured the path to the mead-hall.   1370
The hero entered, the hardy in battle,
The great in glory, to greet the king;
And Grendel's head by the hair was carried
Across the floor where the feasters drank—
A terrible sight for lord and for lady—
A gruesome vision whereon men gazed!

24-25

Beowulf tells of his adventure. Hrothgar makes an appropriate discourse. Next morning, the Geats prepare to leave.

Beowulf spoke, the son of Ecgtheow:
'O son of Healfdene, lord of the Scyldings!
This sea-spoil wondrous, whereon you stare,
We joyously bring you in token of triumph!   1380

---

stately sword, etc., placed, apparently, among the armor hanging on the wall of the cave. 1317. severed . . . head, to eliminate the ghost and so prevent any later haunting of Heorot. 1328. gold-giver, Hrothgar.

A runic alphabet, inscribed on a sword (c. 700) dredged up from the Thames. From left to right some of the letters, with their usual symbolic signification, are: (1) f (feh, money or goods), (4) a (os, god), (5) r (rad, ride or journey), (7) g (geofu, gift), (8) w (wynn, joy), (12) j (gear, year or harvest), (13) e (eoh, yew or bow).

Barely with life surviving the battle,
The war under water, I wrought the deed
Weary and spent; and death had been swift
Had God not granted His sheltering strength.
My strong-edged Hrunting, stoutest of blades,
Availed me nothing. But God revealed—
Often His arm has aided the friendless—
The fairest of weapons hanging on wall,
An ancient broadsword; I seized the blade,
1390 Slew in the struggle, as fortune availed,
The cavern-warders. But the war-brand old,
The battle-blade with its scrolled design,
Dissolved in the gush of the venomous gore;
The hilt alone I brought from the battle.
The record of ruin, and slaughter of Danes,
These wrongs I avenged, as was fitting and right.
Now I can promise you, prince of the Scyldings,
Henceforth in Heorot rest without rue
For you and your nobles; nor need you dread
1400 Slaughter of follower, stalwart or stripling,
Or death of earl, as of old you did.'
Into the hand of the aged leader,
The gray-haired hero, he gave the hilt,
The work of giants, the wonder of gold.
At the death of the demons the Danish lord
Took in his keeping the cunning craft,
The wondrous marvel, of mighty smiths;
When the world was freed of the ravaging fiend,
The foe of God, and his fearful dam
1410 Marked with murder and badged with blood,
The bound hilt passed to the best of kings
Who ever held scepter beside two seas,
And dealt out treasure in Danish land!
    Hrothgar spoke, beholding the hilt,
The ancient relic whereon was etched
An olden record of struggle and strife,
The flood that ravaged the giant race,
The rushing deluge of ruin and death.
That evil kindred were alien to God,
1420 But the Ruler avenged with the wrath of the deep!
On the hilt-guards, likewise, of gleaming gold
Was rightly carven in cunning runes,
Set forth and blazoned, for whom that blade,
With spiral tooling and twisted hilt,
That fairest of swords, was fashioned and smithied.
Then out spoke Hrothgar, Healfdene's son,
And all the retainers were silent and still:
'Well may he say, whose judgment is just,

Recalling to memory men of the past,
That this earl was born of a better stock!   1430
Your fame, friend Beowulf, is blazoned abroad
Over all wide ways, and to every people.
In manful fashion have you showed your strength,
Your might and wisdom. My word I will keep,
The plighted friendship we formerly pledged.
Long shall you stand as a stay to your people,
A help to heroes, as Heremod was not
To the Honor-Scyldings, to Ecgwela's sons!
Not joy to kindred, but carnage and death,
He wrought as he ruled o'er the race of the Danes.   1440
In savage anger he slew his comrades,
His table-companions, till, lawless and lone,
An odious outcast, he fled from men.
Though God had graced him with gifts of strength,
Over all men exalting him, still in his breast
A bloodthirsty spirit was rooted and strong.
He dealt not rings to the Danes for glory;
His lot was eternal torment of woe,
And lasting affliction. Learn from his fate!
Strive for virtue! I speak for your good;   1450
In the wisdom of age I have told the tale.
  ' 'Tis a wondrous marvel how mighty God
In gracious spirit bestows on men
The gift of wisdom, and goodly lands,
And princely power! He rules over all!
He suffers a man of lordly line
To set his heart on his own desires,
Awards him fullness of worldly joy,
A fair home-land, and the sway of cities,
The wide dominion of many a realm,   1460
An ample kingdom, till, cursed with folly,
The thoughts of his heart take no heed of his end.
He lives in luxury, knowing not want,
Knowing no shadow of sickness or age;
No haunting sorrow darkens his spirit,
No hatred or discord deepens to war;
The world is sweet, to his every desire,
And evil assails not—until in his heart
Pride overpowering gathers and grows!
The warder slumbers, the guard of his spirit;   1470
Too sound is that sleep, too sluggish the weight
Of worldly affairs, too pressing the Foe,
The Archer who looses the arrows of sin.
  'Then is his heart pierced, under his helm,
His soul in his bosom, with bitter dart.
He has no defense for the fierce assaults

1422. **runes,** the ancient Germanic alphabet, derived in large measure from the Greek and Roman, and formed with straight lines to facilitate carving on wood. 1437. **Heremod,** according to one legend, a predecessor of Scyld in the Danish royal line (see note to l. 4); because he misused

his powers, the people suffered, and he himself was finally exiled; see note to l. 803. 1499. **His,** Grendel's. 1519. **raven.** The raven holds the place occupied later by the lark in Shakespeare's song ("Hark! hark! the lark . . ."), as harbinger of day. 1552. **if . . . Hrethric.** Perhaps

Of the loathsome Fiend. What he long has cherished
Seems all too little! In anger and greed
He gives no guerdon of plated rings.
1480 Since God has granted him glory and wealth
He forgets the future, unmindful of Fate.
But it comes to pass in the day appointed
His feeble body withers and fails;
Death descends, and another seizes
His hoarded riches and rashly spends
The princely treasure, imprudent of heart.
Beloved Beowulf, best of warriors,
Avoid such evil and seek the good,
The heavenly wisdom. Beware of pride!
1490 Now for a time you shall feel the fullness
And know the glory of strength, but soon
Sickness or sword shall strip you of might,
Or clutch of fire, or clasp of flood,
Or flight of arrow, or bite of blade,
Or relentless age; or the light of the eye
Shall darken and dim, and death on a sudden,
O lordly ruler, shall lay you low. . . .
But thanks be to God who has spared me to see
His bloody head at the battle's end!
1500 Join now in the banquet; have joy of the feast,
O mighty in battle! And the morrow shall bring
Exchange of treasure in ample store.'
　　Happy of heart the Geat leader hastened,
Took seat at the board as the good king bade.
Once more, as of old, brave heroes made merry
And tumult of revelry rose in the hall.
　　Then dark over men the night shadows deepened;
The host all arose, for Hrothgar was minded,
The gray, old Scylding, to go to his rest.
1510 On Beowulf too, after labor of battle,
Came limitless longing and craving for sleep.
A hall-thane graciously guided the hero,
Weary and worn, to the place prepared,
Serving his wishes and every want
As befitted a mariner come from afar.
The stout-hearted warrior sank to his rest;
The lofty building, splendid and spacious,
Towered above him. His sleep was sound
Till the black-coated raven, blithesome of spirit,
1520 Hailed the coming of Heaven's bliss.
　　Then over the shadows uprose the sun.
The Geats were in haste, and eager of heart
To depart to their people. Beowulf longed
To embark in his boat, to set sail for his home.
The hero tendered the good sword Hrunting
To the son of Ecglaf, bidding him bear
The lovely blade; gave thanks for the loan,
Called it a faithful friend in the fray,
Bitter in battle. The great-hearted hero
1530 Spoke no word in blame of the blade!

Arrayed in war-gear, and ready for sea,
The warriors bestirred them; and, dear to the Danes,
Beowulf sought the high seat of the king.
The gallant in war gave greeting to Hrothgar.

26

Beowulf bids Hrothgar farewell. The old King is moved to tears. Presents are given. The Geats depart.

Beowulf spoke, the son of Ecgtheow:
'It is time at last to tell of our longing!
Our homes are far, and our hearts are fain
To seek again Hygelac over the sea.
You have welcomed us royally, harbored us well
As a man could wish; if I ever can win　　　　1540
Your affection more fully, O leader of heroes,
Swift shall you find me to serve you again!
If ever I learn, o'er the levels of ocean,
That neighboring nations beset you sore,
As in former days when foemen oppressed,
With thanes by the thousand I will hasten to help.
For I know that Hygelac, lord of the Geats,
Prince of the people, though young in years,
Will favor and further by word and deed
That my arm may aid you, and do you honor,　　1550
With stout ash-spear and succor of strength
In the press of need. And if princely Hrethric
Shall purpose to come to the court of the Geats,
He will find there a legion of loyal friends.
That man fares best to a foreign country
Who himself is stalwart and stout of heart.'
　　Hrothgar addressed him, uttered his answer:
'Truly, these words has the Lord of wisdom
Set in your heart, for I never have harkened
To speech so sage from a man so young.　　　1560
You have strength, and prudence, and wisdom of word!
I count it true if it come to pass
That point of spear in the press of battle,
Or deadly sickness, or stroke of sword,
Shall slay your leader, the son of Hrethel,
The prince of your people, and you still live,
The Sea-Geats could have no happier choice
If you would be willing to rule the realm,
As king to hold guard o'er the hoard and the heroes.
The longer I know you, the better I like you,　　1570
Beloved Beowulf! You have brought it to pass
That between our peoples a lasting peace
Shall bind the Geats to the Danish-born;
And strife shall vanish, and war shall cease,
And former feuds, while I rule this realm.
And many a man, in the sharing of treasure,
Shall greet another with goodly gifts
O'er the gannet's bath. And the ring-stemmed ship

following Wealhtheow's hint (l. 934), Beowulf offers to enroll her elder son, the heir, among the Geatish thanes. For a prince to spend a few years in a foreign court was a common Germanic custom; Beowulf himself seems to have enjoyed a similar education. 1578. **gannet's bath,** an interesting kenning for "sea." A gannet is a large, fish-eating bird.

Shall bear over ocean bountiful riches
1580 In pledge of friendship. Our peoples, I know,
Shall be firm united toward foe and friend,
Faultless in all things, in fashion of old.'
   Then the son of Healfdene, shelter of earls,
Bestowed twelve gifts on the hero in hall,
Bade him in safety with bounty of treasure
Seek his dear people, and soon return.
The peerless leader, the Scylding lord,
Kissed the good thane and clasped to his bosom
While tears welled fast from the old man's eyes.
1590 Both chances he weighed in his wise, old heart,
But greatly doubted if ever again
They should meet at council or drinking of mead.
Nor could Hrothgar master—so dear was the man—
His swelling sorrow; a yearning love
For the dauntless hero, deep in his heart,
Burned through his blood. Beowulf, the brave,
Prizing his treasure and proud of the gold,
Turned away, treading the grassy plain.
The ring-stemmed sea-goer, riding at anchor,
1600 Awaited her lord. There was loud acclaim
Of Hrothgar's gifts, as they went their way.
He was a king without failing or fault,
Till old age, master of all mankind,
Stripped him of power and pride of strength.

27-31

*Beowulf rewards the shore-guard with a sword.
The Geats return to their country. They carry their
gifts to the hall where Hygelac and his queen Hygd are
dwelling.*

   Then down to the sea came the band of the brave,
The host of young heroes in harness of war,
In their woven mail; and the coast-warden viewed
The heroes' return, as he heeded their coming!
No uncivil greeting he gave from the sea-cliff
1610 As they strode to ship in their glistening steel;
But rode toward them and called their return
A welcome sight for their Weder kin.
There on the sand the ring-stemmed ship,
The broad-bosomed bark, was loaded with war-gear,
With horses and treasure; the mast towered high
Over the riches of Hrothgar's hoard.
A battle-sword Beowulf gave to the boat-warden
Hilted with gold; and thereafter in hall
He had the more honor because of the heirloom,
1620 The shining treasure. The ship was launched.
Cleaving the combers of open sea

They dropped the shoreline of Denmark astern.
A stretching sea-cloth, a bellying sail,
Was bent on the mast; there was groaning of timbers;
A gale was blowing; the boat drove on.
The foamy-necked plunger plowed through the billows,
The ring-stemmed ship through the breaking seas,
Till at last they sighted the sea-cliffs of Geat-land,
The well-known headlands; and, whipped by the wind,
The boat drove shoreward and beached on the sand. 1630
   Straightway the harbor-watch strode to the seashore;
Long had he watched for the well-loved men,
Scanning the ocean with eager eyes!
The broad-bosomed boat he bound to the shingle
With anchor ropes, lest the rip of the tide
Should wrench from its mooring the comely craft.
   From the good ship Beowulf bade them bear
The precious jewels and plated gold,
The princely treasure. Not long was the path
That led to where Hygelac, son of Hrethel, 1640
The giver of treasure, abode in his home
Hard by the sea-wall, hedged by his thanes.
Spacious the castle, splendid the king
On his high hall-seat; youthful was Hygd,
Wise and well-born—though winters but few
Haereth's daughter had dwelt at court.
She was noble of spirit, not sparing in gifts
Of princely treasure to the people of the Geats. . . .
   Then the hero strode with his stalwart band
Across the stretches of sandy beach, 1650
The wide sea-shingle. The world-candle shone,
The hot sun hasting on high from the south.
      . . . Soon Hygelac heard
Of the landing of Beowulf, bulwark of men,
That his shoulder-companion had come to his court
Sound and safe from the strife of battle.
   The hall was prepared, as the prince gave bidding,
Places made ready for much-traveled men.
And he who came safe from the surges of battle
Sat by the side of the king himself, 1660
Kinsman by kinsman; in courtly speech
His liege lord greeted the loyal thane
With hearty welcome. And Haereth's daughter
Passed through the hall-building pouring the mead,
With courtesy greeting the gathered host,
Bearing the cup to the hands of the heroes.
In friendly fashion in high-built hall
Hygelac questioned his comrade and thane;
For an eager longing burned in his breast
To hear from the Sea-Geats the tale of their travels. 1670
'How did you fare in your far sea-roving,
Beloved Beowulf, in your swift resolve

1648. **the Geats** . . . Omitted is the story of Modthryth, a queen who unlike Hygd, was a shrew and had to be tamed—an old folklore motif—another instance of the habit of the Beowulf Poet to set an unpleasant character against a sympathetic one. 1653. . . . **Soon Hygelac heard.** A few repetitious lines have been omitted. 1692. **battle by night!** . . . Beowulf retells, at considerable length, the story of his fights with the monsters and prophesies that the projected marriage between Hrothgar's daughter Freawaru and Ingeld, a prince of the Heathobards, will not settle the feud between the two tribes, as it was designed to do. See note to l. 56. 1709. **Heorogar,** Hrothgar's elder brother and

his predecessor in the kingship. 1712. **Heoroweard,** Heorogar's son, who had been passed over in the succession. 1725. **necklace,** the collar of the Brosings; see note to l. 948. 1731. **slew** . . . **comrades, etc.,** as did Eormenric, Heremod, and other tyrants; see note to l. 1437. 1746. **hides.** According to the usual estimate, a "hide" (cf. *Hyde Park*) of land came to about 120 modern acres. 1751. **Hygelac, etc.** Hygelac was killed in a raid against the Frisians; see ll. 1900 and 2315. After his death, his wife Hygd offered Beowulf the kingship (l. 1913), but he refused and served as regent during the early years of Hygelac's young son Heardred. When Heardred was slain by the Swedes (the "War-Scylfings" or

To sail to the conflict, the combat in Heorot,
Across the salt waves? Did you soften at all
The sorrows of Hrothgar, the weight of his woe?
Deeply I brooded with burden of care
For I had no faith in this far sea-venture
For one so beloved. Long I implored
That you go not against the murderous monster,
1680 But let the South Danes settle the feud
Themselves with Grendel. To God be thanks
That my eyes behold you unharmed and unhurt.'
　　Beowulf spoke, the son of Ecgtheow:
'My dear lord Hygelac, many have heard
Of that famous grapple 'twixt Grendel and me,
The bitter struggle and strife in the hall
Where he formerly wrought such ruin and wrong,
Such lasting sorrow for Scylding men!
All that I avenged! Not any on earth
1690 Who longest lives of that loathsome brood,
No kin of Grendel cloaked in his crime,
Has cause to boast of that battle by night! . . . .
　　'Then the son of Healfdene, the shelter of earls,
Gave many a treasure to mark the deed.
The good king governed with courtly custom;
In no least way did I lose reward,
The meed of my might; but he gave me treasure,
Healfdene's son, to my heart's desire.
These riches I bring you, ruler of heroes,
1700 And warmly tender with right good will.
Save for you, King Hygelac, few are my kinsmen,
Few are the favors but come from you.'
　　Then he bade men bring the boar-crested headpiece,
The towering helmet, and steel-gray sark,
The splendid war-sword, and spoke this word:
'The good king Hrothgar gave me this gift,
This battle-armor, and first to you
Bade tell the tale of his friendly favor.
He said King Heorogar, lord of the Scyldings,
1710 Long had worn it, but had no wish
To leave the mail to his manful son,
The dauntless Heoroweard, dear though he was!
Well may you wear it! Have joy of it all.'
As I've heard the tale, he followed the trappings
With four bay horses, matched and swift,
Graciously granting possession of both,
The steeds and the wealth. 'Tis the way of a kinsman,
Not weaving in secret the wiles of malice
Nor plotting the fall of a faithful friend.
1720 To his kinsman Hygelac, hardy in war,
The heart of the nephew was trusty and true;
Dear to each was the other's good!
To Hygd, as I've heard it, he presented three horses

Gaily saddled, slender and sleek,
And the gleaming necklace Wealhtheow gave,
A peerless gift from a prince's daughter.
With the gracious guerdon, the goodly jewel,
Her breast thereafter was well bedecked.
　　So the son of Ecgtheow bore himself bravely,
Known for his courage and courteous deeds,　　1730
Strove after honor, slew not his comrades
In drunken brawling; nor brutal his mood.
But the bountiful gifts which the Lord God gave him
He held with a power supreme among men.
He had long been scorned, when the sons of the Geats
Accounted him worthless; the Weder lord
Held him not high among heroes in hall.
Laggard they deemed him, slothful and slack.
But time brought solace for all his ills!
　　Then the battle-bold king, the bulwark of heroes,　1740
Bade bring a battle-sword banded with gold,
The heirloom of Hrethel; no sharper steel,
No lovelier treasure, belonged to the Geats.
He laid the war-blade on Beowulf's lap,
Gave him a hall and a stately seat
And hides seven thousand. Inherited lands
Both held by birth-fee, home and estate.
But one held rule o'er the spacious realm,
And higher therein his order and rank.

PART II. BEOWULF AND THE DRAGON

31 (continued)

*Beowulf later becomes King and reigns for fifty
years. A great dragon, guarding a vast treasure, ravages
the country-side.*

　　It later befell in the years that followed　　1750
After Hygelac sank in the surges of war,
And the sword slew Heardred under his shield
When the Battle-Scylfings, those bitter fighters,
Invaded the land of the victor-folk
Overwhelming Hereric's nephew in war,
That the kingdom came into Beowulf's hand.
For fifty winters he governed it well,
Aged and wise with the wisdom of years,
Till a fire-drake flying in darkness of night
Began to ravage and work his will.　　1760
On the upland heath he guarded a hoard,
A stone barrow lofty. Under it lay
A path concealed from the sight of men.
There a thief broke in on the heathen treasure,
Laid hand on a flagon all fretted with gold,

"Battle-Scylfings" of l. 1753), with whom the Geats had been plunged
into a disastrous feud, Beowulf accepted the throne. 1759. **a fire-drake,
etc.** The story of the treasure and the dragon is somewhat obscure in the
telling. Ages before, a treasure had been buried and protected by a curse
which would fall upon the man who molested it. Nevertheless, it was
found and removed by certain warriors, and passed on through inheritance
to the last survivor of their race. This man buried the treasure in a
mound and barrow; and a dragon, taking up his residence there, guarded
it for the next three hundred years. Then a slave, who had probably
killed a man in his master's household, fled from his master's anger, found

the treasure in the mound, and stole a cup, perhaps to pay the blood
money for his crime. When the cup had purchased his pardon, it was
sent to Beowulf as a present. Meanwhile the dragon, angered by the theft,
spewed out his fiery breath on the countryside and burned Beowulf's
mead hall. 1762. **stone barrow,** a chamber with walls of stone, covered
with earth, with a narrow entrance at its base; see the description here
and in l. 1785. Such mounds were common both in England and in
Scandinavia. This one was situated on a cliff above the sea.

As the dragon discovered, though cozened in sleep
By the pilferer's cunning. The people soon found
That the mood of the dragon was roused to wrath!

32

*The treasure in the barrow and how the dragon came
to guard it. The anger of the dragon.*

Not at all with intent, of his own free will,
1770 Did he ravish the hoard, who committed the wrong;
But in dire distress the thrall of a thane,
A guilty fugitive fleeing the lash,
Forced his way in. There a horror befell him!
Yet the wretched exile escaped from the dragon,
Swift in retreat when the terror arose.
A flagon he took. There, many such treasures
Lay heaped in that earth-hall where the owner of old
Had carefully hidden the precious hoard,
The countless wealth of a princely clan.
1780 Death came upon them in days gone by
And he who lived longest, the last of his line,
Guarding the treasure and grieving for friend,
Deemed it his lot that a little while only
He too might hold that ancient hoard.
A barrow new-built near the ocean billows
Stood cunningly fashioned beneath the cliff;
Into the barrow the ring-warden bore
The princely treasure, the precious trove
Of golden wealth, and these words he spoke:
1790 'Keep thou, O Earth, what men could not keep—
This costly treasure—it came from thee!
Baleful slaughter has swept away,
Death in battle, the last of my blood;
They have lived their lives; they have left the mead-
hall.
Now I have no one to wield the sword,
No one to polish the plated cup,
The precious flagon—the host is fled.
The hard-forged helmet fretted with gold
Shall be stripped of its inlay; the burnishers sleep
1800 Whose charge was to brighten the battle-masks.
Likewise the corselet that countered in war
Mid clashing of bucklers the bite of the sword—
Corselet and warrior decay into dust;
Mailed coat and hero are moveless and still.
No mirth of gleewood, no music of harp,
No good hawk swinging in flight through the hall;
No swift steed stamps in the castle yard;
Death has ravished an ancient race.'
So sad of mood he bemoaned his sorrow,
1810 Lonely and sole survivor of all,

Restless by day and wretched by night
Till the clutch of death caught at his heart.
Then the goodly treasure was found unguarded
By the venomous dragon enveloped in flame,
The old naked night-foe flying in darkness,
Haunting the barrows; a bane that brings
A fearful dread to the dwellers of earth.
His wont is to hunt out a hoard under ground
And guard heathen gold, growing old with the years.
But no whit for that is his fortune more fair! 1820
For three hundred winters this waster of peoples
Held the huge treasure-hall under the earth
Till the robber aroused him to anger and rage,
Stole the rich beaker and bore to his master,
Imploring his lord for a compact of peace.
So the hoard was robbed and its riches plundered;
To the wretch was granted the boon that he begged;
And his liege-lord first had view of the treasure,
The ancient work of the men of old.
Then the worm awakened and war was kindled, 1830
The rush of the monster along the rock,
When the fierce one found the tracks of the foe;
He had stepped too close in his stealthy cunning
To the dragon's head. But a man undoomed
May endure with ease disaster and woe
If he has His favor who wields the world.
Swiftly the fire-drake sought through the plain
The man who wrought him this wrong in his sleep.
Inflamed and savage he circled the mound,
But the waste was deserted—no man was in sight. 1840
The worm's mood was kindled to battle and war;
Time and again he returned to the barrow
Seeking the treasure-cup. Soon he was sure
That a man had plundered the precious gold.
Enraged and restless the hoard-warden waited
The gloom of evening. The guard of the mound
Was swollen with anger; the fierce one resolved
To requite with fire the theft of the cup.
Then the day was sped as the worm desired;
Lurking no longer within his wall 1850
He sallied forth surrounded with fire,
Encircled with flame. For the folk of the land
The beginning was dread as the ending was grievous
That came so quickly upon their lord.

33

*The dragon burns the hall of Beowulf. The old
hero takes measures against him. A word of Beowulf's earlier exploits.*

Then the baleful stranger belched fire and flame,
Burned the bright dwellings—the glow of the blaze

1805. **gleewood**, a kenning for "harp." 1818. **His wont . . . ground,
etc.** Compare the dragon that guards the treasure in the lay of Sigemund
sung by Hrothgar's bard (cf. note to l. 787). Such treasure-guarding
dragons were common in folklore and mythology—for instance, the one
that guarded the Golden Fleece in the story of Jason and the Argonauts.
1906. **Hetware**, Frisians. 1911. **swam . . . land**, another swimming

feat of Beowulf's comparable to his contest with Breca (ll. 452-520).
1924. **over the seas . . . .** Omitted here and elsewhere in the last part
of the poem are references to the complicated feud between the Geats and
the Swedes. The Swedes had invaded Geatland in the reign of Hygelac's
predecessor Haethcyn; Haethcyn was killed in a retributive expedition,
and Hygelac avenged him by killing the Swedish king. After a truce of

Filled hearts with horror. The hostile flier
Was minded to leave there nothing alive.
From near and from far the war of the dragon,
1860 The might of the monster, was widely revealed
So that all could see how the ravaging scather
Hated and humbled the Geatish folk.
Then he hastened back ere the break of dawn
To his secret den and the spoil of gold.
He had compassed the land with a flame of fire,
A blaze of burning; he trusted the wall,
The sheltering mound, and the strength of his might—
But his trust betrayed him! The terrible news
Was brought to Beowulf, told for a truth,
1870 That his home was consumed in the surges of fire,
The goodly dwelling and throne of the Geats.
The heart of the hero was heavy with anguish,
The greatest of sorrows; in his wisdom he weened
He had grievously angered the Lord Everlasting,
Blamefully broken the ancient law.
Dark thoughts stirred in his surging bosom,
Welled in his breast, as was not his wont.
The flame of the dragon had leveled the fortress,
The people's stronghold washed by the wave.
1880 But the king of warriors, prince of the Weders,
Exacted an ample revenge for it all.
The lord of warriors and leader of earls
Bade work him of iron a wondrous shield,
Knowing full well that wood could not serve him
Nor linden defend him against the flame.
The stalwart hero was doomed to suffer
The destined end of his days on earth;
Likewise the worm, though for many a winter
He had held his watch o'er the wealth of the hoard.
1890 The ring-prince scorned to assault the dragon
With a mighty army, or host of men.
He feared not the combat, nor counted of worth
The might of the worm, his courage and craft,
Since often aforetime, beset in the fray,
He had safely issued from many an onset,
Many a combat and, crowned with success,
Purged of evil the hall of Hrothgar
And crushed out Grendel's loathsome kin.
      Nor was that the least of his grim engagements
1900 When Hygelac fell, great Hrethel's son;
When the lord of the people, the prince of the Geats,
Died of his wounds in the welter of battle,
Perished in Friesland, smitten with swords.
Thence Beowulf came by his strength in swimming;
Thirty sets of armor he bore on his back
As he hasted to ocean. The Hetware men
Had no cause to boast of their prowess in battle
When they gathered against him with linden shields.

But few of them ever escaped his assault
Or came back alive to the homes they had left;   1910
So the son of Ecgtheow swam the sea-stretches,
Lonely and sad, to the land of his kin.
Hygd then tendered him kingdom and treasure,
Wealth of riches and royal throne,
For she had no hope with Hygelac dead
That her son could defend the seat of his fathers
From foreign foemen. But even in need,
No whit the more could they move the hero
To be Heardred's 'liege, or lord of the land.
But he fostered Heardred with friendly counsel,   1920
With honor and favor among the folk,
Till he came of age and governed the Geats.
Then the sons of Ohthere fleeing in exile
Sought out Heardred over the sea. . . .

34-35

*Beowulf goes forth, bidding farewell to his thanes.
He shouts aloud, and the dragon comes forth. The
fight begins. It goes hard with Beowulf.*

      . . . So Ecgtheow's son
Had come in safety through all his battles,
His bitter struggles and savage strife,
To the day when he fought with the deadly worm.
With eleven comrades, kindled to rage
The Geat lord went to gaze on the dragon.   1930
Full well he knew how the feud arose,
The fearful affliction; for into his hold
From hand of finder the flagon had come.
The thirteenth man in the hurrying throng
Was the sorrowful captive who caused the feud.
With woeful spirit and all unwilling
Needs must he guide them, for he only knew
Where the earth-hall stood near the breaking billows
Filled with jewels and beaten gold.
The monstrous warden, waiting for battle,   1940
Watched and guarded the hoarded wealth.
No easy bargain for any of men
To seize that treasure! The stalwart king,
Gold-friend of Geats, took seat on the headland,
Hailed his comrades and wished them well.
Sad was his spirit, restless and ready,
And the march of Fate immeasurably near;
Fate that would strike, seek his soul's treasure,
And deal asunder the spirit and flesh.
Not long was his life encased in the body! . . .   1950
      For the last time Beowulf uttered his boast:
'I came in safety through many a conflict

---

some duration the feud was renewed; Hygelac's successor Heardred lost
his life. Beowulf, as king, sent an expedition into the Swedish territories,
gained full revenge, and placed an ally on the Swedish throne. But at
Beowulf's death the trouble seems likely to be renewed (l. 2318 ff.).
1950. **encased in the body!** . . . Beowulf speaks about his youth,
about certain domestic difficulties during the reign of good King Hrethel,
and the accidental killing of one of Hrethel's sons by his youngest son
Haethcyn. He injects a lay of lament for an old father whose son has
been hanged. He winds up this very long digression with many details
of the first conflict between the Swedes and the Geats. This has all
been omitted.

In the days of my youth; and now even yet,
Old as I am, I will fight this feud,
Do manful deeds, if the dire destroyer
Will come from his cavern to meet my sword.'
The king for the last time greeted his comrades,
Bold helmet-bearers and faithful friends:
'I would bear no sword nor weapon to battle
1960 With the evil worm, if I knew how else
I could close with the fiend, as I grappled with Grendel.
From the worm I look for a welling of fire,
A belching of venom, and therefore I bear
Shield and byrnie. Not one foot's space
Will I flee from the monster, the ward of the mound.
It shall fare with us both in the fight at the wall
As Fate shall allot, the lord of mankind.
Though bold in spirit, I make no boast
As I go to fight with the flying serpent.
1970 Clad in your corselets and trappings of war,
By the side of the barrow abide you to see
Which of us twain may best after battle
Survive his wounds. Not yours the adventure,
Nor the mission of any, save mine alone,
To measure his strength with the monstrous dragon
And play the part of a valiant earl.
By deeds of daring I'll gain the gold
Or death in battle shall break your lord.'
    Then the stalwart rose with his shield upon him,
1980 Bold under helmet, bearing his sark
Under the stone-cliff; he trusted the strength
Of his single might. Not so does a coward!
He who survived through many a struggle,
Many a combat and crashing of troops,
Saw where a stone-arch stood by the wall
And a gushing stream broke out from the barrow.
Hot with fire was the flow of its surge,
Nor could any abide near the hoard unburned,
Nor endure its depths, for the flame of the dragon.
1990 Then the lord of the Geats in the grip of his fury
Gave shout of defiance; the strong-heart stormed.
His voice rang out with the rage of battle,
Resounding under the hoary stone.
Hate was aroused; the hoard-warden knew
'Twas the voice of a man. No more was there time
To sue for peace; the breath of the serpent,
A blast of venom, burst from the rock.
The ground resounded; the lord of the Geats
Under the barrow swung up his shield
2000 To face the dragon; the coiling foe
Was gathered to strike in the deadly strife.
The stalwart hero had drawn his sword,
His ancient heirloom of tempered edge;
In the heart of each was fear of the other!
The shelter of kinsmen stood stout of heart
Under towering shield as the great worm coiled;

Clad in his war-gear he waited the rush.
In twisting folds the flame-breathing dragon
Sped to its fate. The shield of the prince
For a lesser while guarded his life and his body   2010
Than heart had hoped. For the first time then
It was not his portion to prosper in war;
Fate did not grant him glory in battle!
Then lifted his arm the lord of the Geats
And smote the worm with his ancient sword
But the brown edge failed as it fell on bone,
And cut less deep than the king had need
In his sore distress. Savage in mood
The ward of the barrow countered the blow
With a blast of fire; wide sprang the flame.   2020
The ruler of Geats had no reason to boast;
His unsheathed iron, his excellent sword,
Had weakened as it should not, had failed in the fight.
It was no easy journey for Ecgtheow's son
To leave this world and against his will
Find elsewhere a dwelling! So every man shall
In the end give over this fleeting life.
    Not long was the lull. Swiftly the battlers
Renewed their grapple. The guard of the hoard
Grew fiercer in fury. His venomous breath   2030
Beat in his breast. Enveloped in flame
The folk-leader suffered a sore distress.
No succoring band of shoulder-companions,
No sons of warriors aided him then
By valor in battle. They fled to the forest
To save their lives; but a sorrowful spirit
Welled in the breast of one of the band.
The call of kinship can never be stilled
In the heart of a man who is trusty and true.

36

*Wiglaf, a young thane, reproaches his comrades. He
goes to help Beowulf. The king's sword is broken, and
he is mortally wounded.*

His name was Wiglaf, Weohstan's son,   2040
A prince of the Scylfings, a peerless thane,
Aelfhere's kinsman; he saw his king
Under his helmet smitten with heat.
He thought of the gifts which his lord had given,
The wealth and the land of the Waegmunding line
And all the folk-rights his father had owned;
Nor could he hold back, but snatched up his buckler,
His linden shield and his ancient sword. . . .
    . . . And Wiglaf, the lad,
Was to face with his lord the first of his battles,   2050
The hazard of war. But his heart did not fail
Nor the blade of his kinsman weaken in war,

2046. **folk-rights.** The Germanic nations or tribes always had a certain amount of land and livestock that was communal property, in addition to the personal property of the individual earl. A trace of this old
custom is seen in the "common" of a typical English village. Each mem-

ber of the tribe had the right to use his share of the common property.
Such a share was known as a "folk-right." 2049. . . . **And Wiglaf,
the lad.** A further reference to the Swedish wars has been omitted.
2057. **bestowed . . . rings.** Rings or other presents, the usual reward for

As the worm soon found when they met in the fight!
  Wiglaf spoke in sorrow of soul,
With bitter reproach rebuking his comrades:
'I remember the time, as we drank in the mead-hall,
When we swore to our lord who bestowed these rings
That we would repay for the war-gear and armor,
The hard swords and helmets, if need like this
2060 Should ever befall him. He chose us out
From all the host for this high adventure,
Deemed us worthy of glorious deeds,
Gave me these treasures, regarded us all
As high-hearted bearers of helmet and spear—
Though our lord himself, the shield of his people,
Thought single-handed to finish this feat,
Since of mortal men his measure was most
Of feats of daring and deeds of fame.
Now is the day that our lord has need
2070 Of the strength and courage of stalwart men.
Let us haste to succor his sore distress
In the horrible heat and the merciless flame.
God knows I had rather the fire should enfold
My body and limbs with my gold-friend and lord.
Shameful it seems that we carry our shields
Back to our homes ere we harry the foe
And ward the life of the Weder king.
Full well I know it is not his due
That he alone, of the host of the Geats,
2080 Should suffer affliction and fall in the fight.
One helmet and sword, one byrnie and shield,
Shall serve for us both in the storm of strife.'
Then Wiglaf dashed through the deadly reek
In his battle-helmet to help his lord.
Brief were his words: 'Beloved Beowulf,
Summon your strength, remember the vow
You made of old in the years of youth
Not to allow your glory to lessen
As long as you lived. With resolute heart,
2090 And dauntless daring, defend your life
With all your force. I fight at your side!'
  Once again the worm, when the words were spoken,
The hideous foe in a horror of flame,
Rushed in rage at the hated men.
Wiglaf's buckler was burned to the boss
In the billows of fire; his byrnie of mail
Gave the young hero no help or defense.
But he stoutly pressed on under shield of his kinsman
When his own was consumed in the scorching flame.
2100 Then the king once more was mindful of glory,
Swung his great sword-blade with all his might
And drove it home on the dragon's head.
But Naegling broke, it failed in the battle,
The blade of Beowulf, ancient and gray.
It was not his lot that edges of iron
Could help him in battle; his hand was too strong,

Overtaxed, I am told, every blade with its blow.
Though he bore a wondrous hard weapon to war,
No whit the better was he thereby!
  A third time then the terrible scather,   2110
The monstrous dragon inflamed with the feud,
Rushed on the king when the opening offered,
Fierce and flaming; fastened its fangs
In Beowulf's throat; he was bloodied with gore;
His life-blood streamed from the welling wound.

37

The fire-drake is killed. Beowulf is left dying.

  As they tell the tale, in the king's sore need
His shoulder-companion showed forth his valor,
His craft and courage, and native strength.
To the head of the dragon he paid no heed,
Though his hand was burned as he helped his king. 2120
A little lower the stalwart struck
At the evil beast, and his blade drove home
Plated and gleaming. The fire began
To lessen and wane. The king of the Weders
Summoned his wits; he drew the dagger
He wore on his corselet, cutting and keen,
And slit asunder the worm with the blow.
So they felled the foe and wrought their revenge;
The kinsmen together had killed the dragon.
So a man should be when the need is bitter!   2130
That was the last fight Beowulf fought;
That was the end of his work in the world.
  The wound which the dragon had dealt him began
To swell and burn; and soon he could feel
The baneful venom inflaming his breast.
The wise, old warrior sank down by the wall
And stared at the work of the giants of old,
The arches of stone and the standing columns
Upholding the ancient earth-hall within.
His loyal thane, the kindest of comrades,   2140
Saw Beowulf bloody and broken in war;
In his hands bore water and bathed his leader,
And loosened the helm from his dear lord's head.
  Beowulf spoke, though his hurt was sore,
The wounds of battle grievous and grim.
Full well he weened that his life was ended,
And all the joy of his years on earth;
That his days were done, and Death most near:
'My armor and sword I would leave to my son
Had Fate but granted, born of my body,   2150
An heir to follow me after I'm gone.
For fifty winters I've ruled this realm,
And never a lord of a neighboring land
Dared strike with terror or seek with sword.

services rendered, were given out by the king of the tribe or nation at
the banquet or feast held in celebration of the deed performed. On less
formal occasions, too, a king would distribute gifts of value among
the chief warriors of his tribe to insure their service to him in the

future. 2103. **Naegling,** Beowulf's sword; see note to l. 1184.
2124. **king of the Weders,** Beowulf. It is interesting to observe
that the dying Beowulf is given the honor of delivering the last blow
in the fight.

In my life I abode by the lot assigned,
Kept well what was mine, courted no quarrels,
Swore no false oaths. And now for all this
Though my hurt is grievous, my heart is glad.
When life leaves body, the Lord of mankind
2160 Cannot lay to my charge the killing of kinsmen!
Go quickly, dear Wiglaf, to gaze on the gold
Beneath the hoar stone. The dragon lies still
In the slumber of death, despoiled of his hoard.
Make haste that my eyes may behold the treasure,
The gleaming jewels, the goodly store,
And, glad of the gold, more peacefully leave
The life and the realm I have ruled so long.'

38

Beowulf looks upon the treasure, and then dies.

Then Weohstan's son, as they tell the tale,
Clad in his corselet and trappings of war,
2170 Hearkened at once to his wounded lord.
Under roof of the barrow he broke his way.
Proud in triumph he stood by the seat,
Saw glittering jewels and gold on the ground,
The den of the dragon, the old dawn-flier,
And all the wonders along the walls.
Great bowls and flagons of bygone men
Lay all unburnished and barren of gems,
Many a helmet ancient and rusted,
Many an arm-ring cunningly wrought.
2180 Treasure and gold, though hid in the ground,
Override man's wishes, hide them who will!
High o'er the hoard he beheld a banner,
Greatest of wonders, woven with skill,
All wrought of gold; its radiance lighted
The vasty ground and the glittering gems.
But no sign of the worm! The sword-edge had slain
   him.
As I've heard the tale, the hero unaided
Rifled those riches of giants of old,
The hoard in the barrow, and heaped in his arms
2190 Beakers and platters, picked what he would
And took the banner, the brightest of signs.
The ancient sword with its edge of iron
Had slain the worm who watched o'er the wealth,
In the midnight flaming, with menace of fire
Protecting the treasure for many a year
Till he died the death. Then Wiglaf departed
In haste returning enriched with spoil.
He feared, and wondered if still he would find
The lord of the Weders alive on the plain,
2200 Broken and weary and smitten with wounds.
With his freight of treasure he found the prince,
His dear lord, bloody and nigh unto death.

With water he bathed him till words broke forth
From the hoard of his heart and, aged and sad,
Beowulf spoke, as he gazed on the gold:
'For this goodly treasure whereon I gaze
I give my thanks to the Lord of all,
To the Prince of glory, Eternal God,
Who granted me grace to gain for my people
Such dower of riches before my death.   2210
I gave my life for this golden hoard.
Heed well the wants, the need of my people;
My hour is come, and my end is near.
Bid warriors build, when they burn my body,
A stately barrow on the headland's height.
It shall be for remembrance among my people
As it towers high on the Cape of the Whale,
And sailors shall know it as Beowulf's Barrow,
Sea-faring mariners driving their ships
Through fogs of ocean from far countries.'   2220
Then the great-hearted king unclasped from his throat
A collar of gold, and gave to his thane;
Gave the young hero his gold-decked helmet,
His ring and his byrnie, and wished him well.
'You are the last of the Waegmunding line.
All my kinsmen, earls in their glory,
Fate has sent to their final doom,
And I must follow.' These words were the last
The old king spoke ere the pyre received him,
The leaping flames of the funeral blaze,   2230
And his breath went forth from his bosom, his soul
Went forth from the flesh, to the joys of the just.

39

Wiglaf reproaches the cowardly retainers.

Then bitter it was for Beowulf's thane
To behold his loved one lying on earth
Suffering sore at the end of life.
The monster that slew him, the dreadful dragon,
Likewise lay broken and brought to his death.
The worm no longer could rule the hoard,
But the hard, sharp sword, the work of the hammer,
Had laid him low; and the winged dragon   2240
Lay stretched near the barrow, broken and still.
No more in the midnight he soared in air,
Disclosing his presence, and proud of his gold;
For he sank to earth by the sword of the king.
But few of mankind, if the tales be true,
Has it prospered much, though mighty in war
And daring in deed, to encounter the breath
Of the venomous worm or plunder his wealth
When the ward of the barrow held watch o'er the
   mound.
Beowulf bartered his life for the treasure;   2250
Both foes had finished this fleeting life.

2180. **Treasure . . . will!** This rather obscure parenthesis seems to
mean, "Gold will bring about the ruin of any man, no matter how carefully it may be hidden." 2288. **land-right,** folk-right; see note to
l. 2046. 2292. **Death . . . shame!** A contrasting viewpoint is held by

Not long was it then till the laggards in battle
Came forth from the forest, ten craven in fight,
Who had dared not face the attack of the foe
In their lord's great need. The shirkers in shame
Came wearing their bucklers and trappings of war
Where the old man lay. They looked upon Wiglaf.
Weary he sat by the side of his leader
Attempting with water to waken his lord.
2260 It availed him little; the wish was vain!
He could not stay his soul upon earth,
Nor one whit alter the will of God.
The Lord ruled over the lives of men
As He rules them still. With a stern rebuke
He reproached the cowards whose courage had failed.
Wiglaf addressed them, Weohstan's son;
Gazed sad of heart on the hateful men:
'Lo! he may say who would speak the truth
That the lord who gave you these goodly rings,
2270 This warlike armor wherein you stand—
When oft on the ale-bench he dealt to his hall-men
Helmet and byrnie, endowing his thanes
With the fairest he found from near or from far—
That he grievously wasted these trappings of war
When battle befell him. The king of the folk
Had no need to boast of his friends in the fight.
But the God of victory granted him strength
To avenge himself with the edge of the sword
When he needed valor. Of little avail
2280 The help I brought in the bitter battle!
Yet still I strove, though beyond my strength,
To aid my kinsman. And ever the weaker
The savage foe when I struck with my sword;
Ever the weaker the welling flame!
Too few defenders surrounded our ruler
When the hour of evil and terror befell.
Now granting of treasure and giving of swords,
Inherited land-right and joy of the home,
Shall cease from your kindred. And each of your clan
2290 Shall fail of his birthright when men from afar
Hear tell of your flight and your dastardly deed.
Death is better for every earl
Than life besmirched with the brand of shame!'

40-42

Beowulf's death is made known to the nation. Words of the messenger. The people go to the scene of the fight.

Then Wiglaf bade tell the tidings of battle
Up over the cliff in the camp of the host
Where the linden-bearers all morning long
Sat wretched in spirit, and ready for both,
The return, or the death, of their dear-loved lord.
Not long did he hide, who rode up the headland,

The news of their sorrow, but spoke before all: 2300
'Our leader lies low, the lord of the Weders,
The king of the Geats, on the couch of death.
He sleeps his last sleep by the deeds of the worm.
The dreadful dragon is stretched beside him
Slain with dagger-wounds. Not by the sword
Could he quell the monster or lay him low.
And Wiglaf is sitting, Weohstan's son,
Bent over Beowulf, living by dead.
Death watch he keeps in sorrow of spirit
Over the bodies of friend and foe. 2310
Now comes peril of war when this news is rumored abroad,
The fall of our king known afar among Frisians and Franks!
For a fierce feud rose with the Franks when Hygelac's warlike host
Invaded the Frisian fields, and the Hetware vanquished the Geats,
Overcame with the weight of their hordes, and Hygelac fell in the fray;
It was not his lot to live on dispensing the spoils of war.
And never since then of the Franks had we favor or friend. . . .
This is the fighting and this the feud,
The bitter hatred, that breeds the dread
Lest the Swedish people should swarm against us 2320
Learning our lord lies lifeless and still.
His was the hand that defended the hoard,
Heroes, and realm against ravaging foe,
By noble counsel and dauntless deed.
Let us go quickly to look on the king
Who brought us treasure, and bear his corpse
To the funeral pyre. The precious hoard
Shall burn with the hero. There lies the heap
Of untold treasure so grimly gained,
Jewels and gems he bought with his blood 2330
At the end of life. All these at the last
The flames shall veil and the brands devour.
No man for remembrance shall take from the treasure,
Nor beauteous maiden adorn her breast
With gleaming jewel; bereft of gold
And tragic-hearted many shall tread
A foreign soil, now their lord has ceased
From laughter and revel and rapture of joy.
Many a spear in the cold of morning
Shall be borne in hand uplifted on high. 2340
No sound of harp shall waken the warrior,
But the dusky raven despoiling the dead
Shall clamor and cry and call to the eagle
What fare he found at the carrion-feast
The while with the wolf he worried the corpses.'
So the stalwart hero had told his tidings,
His fateful message; nor spoke amiss

Falstaff in Shakespeare's *1 Henry IV*, V, i, and also by Richard Steele in his essay "On Duelling," p. 475. **2317. favor or friend . . .**

Omitted are further references to the Geats and their feud with the Swedes. **2342. dusky raven, etc.** Compare *The Twa Corbies*, p. 56.

As to truth or telling. The host arose;
On their woeful way to the Eagles' Ness
2350 They went with tears to behold the wonder.

Beowulf's funeral.

They found the friend, who had dealt them treasure
In former days, on the bed of death,
Stretched out lifeless upon the sand.
The last of the good king's days was gone;
Wondrous the death of the Weder prince!
They had sighted first, where it lay outstretched,
The monstrous wonder, the loathsome worm,
The horrible fire-drake, hideous-hued,
Scorched with the flame. The spread of its length
2360 Was fifty foot-measures! Oft in the night
It sported in air, then sinking to earth
Returned to its den. Now moveless in death
It had seen the last of its earthly lair.
Beside the dragon were bowls and beakers,
Platters lying, and precious swords
Eaten with rust, where the hoard had rested
A thousand winters in the womb of earth.
That boundless treasure of bygone men,
The golden dower, was girt with a spell
2370 So that never a man might ravage the ring-hall
Save as God himself, the Giver of victory—
He is the Shelter and Shield of men—
Might allow such man as seemed to Him meet,
Might grant whom He would, to gather the treasure. . . .
　Then the wise son of Weohstan chose from the host
Seven thanes of the king, the best of the band;
Eight heroes together they hied to the barrow
In under the roof of the fearful foe;
One of the warriors leading the way
2380 Bore in his hand a burning brand.
They cast no lots who should loot the treasure
When they saw unguarded the gold in the hall
Lying there useless; little they scrupled
As quickly they plundered the precious store.
Over the sea-cliff into the ocean
They tumbled the dragon, the deadly worm,
Let the sea-tide swallow the guarder of gold.
Then a wagon was loaded with well-wrought treasure,
A countless number of every kind;
2390 And the aged warrior, the white-haired king,
Was borne on high to the Cape of the Whale.

The Geat folk fashioned a peerless pyre
Hung round with helmets and battle-boards,
With gleaming byrnies as Beowulf bade.
In sorrow of soul they laid on the pyre
Their mighty leader, their well-loved lord.
The warriors kindled the bale on the barrow,
Wakened the greatest of funeral fires.
Dark o'er the blaze the wood-smoke mounted;
The winds were still, and the sound of weeping　2400
Rose with the roar of the surging flame
Till the heat of the fire had broken the body.
With hearts that were heavy they chanted their sorrow,
Singing a dirge for the death of their lord;
And an aged woman with upbound locks
Lamented for Beowulf, wailing in woe.
Over and over she uttered her dread
Of sorrow to come, of bloodshed and slaughter,
Terror of battle, and bondage, and shame.
The smoke of the bale-fire rose to the sky!　2410
　The men of the Weder folk fashioned a mound
Broad and high on the brow of the cliff,
Seen from afar by seafaring men.
Ten days they worked on the warrior's barrow
Inclosing the ash of the funeral flame
With a wall as worthy as wisdom could shape.
They bore to the barrow the rings and the gems,
The wealth of the hoard the heroes had plundered.
The olden treasure they gave to the earth,
The gold to the ground, where it still remains　2420
As useless to men as it was of yore.
Then round the mound rode the brave in battle,
The sons of warriors, twelve in a band,
Bemoaning their sorrow and mourning their king.
They sang their dirge and spoke of the hero
Vaunting his valor and venturous deeds.
So is it proper a man should praise
His friendly lord with a loving heart,
When his soul must forth from the fleeting flesh.
So the folk of the Geats, the friends of his hearth,　2430
Bemoaned the fall of their mighty lord;
Said he was kindest of worldly kings,
Mildest, most gentle, most eager for fame.

POPULAR BALLADS

　The term "popular ballad" has been applied to narrative songs that originated among the people rather than at the courts of kings or in the parlors of the aristocratic or educated.

　The process of ballad-making is many centuries old, and may take place at any time in any nation where the people are unlettered but imaginative. The ballads of England and Scotland lived for hundreds of years in oral tradition; some of them were brought to the New World by emigrants to America. But, as has often been noted, committing these ballads to paper has a curious blighting effect, chiefly because the untutored mind that produces a true popular ballad has difficulty translating it into printed words. To appreciate the full value of a popular ballad, one must hear it sung by an authentic ballad singer.

Of the 305 English and Scottish ballads collected by Child in his great edition, a great many undoubtedly had their origins in the Middle Ages. Yet most of them were not recorded before the mid-seventeenth century in the Percy Manuscript; consequently the language in which they are found is close to Modern English. From the most ancient, Judas (Child, No. 23), to the earliest extant Robin Hood ballad, there is a gap of close to 250 years. And yet Piers Plowman, the important allegorical poem from the latter half of the fourteenth century, refers to "rimes of Robin Hood" so casually that it is possible to assume the currency of these Robin Hood ballads long before 1350.

The problem of the authorship of the older ballads has vexed scholars since Bishop Percy first wrote his memorable Preface to his Reliques of Ancient English Poetry in 1765. Three main schools of thought have subsequently emerged: (1) the ballads were composed by individual authors; (2) the ballads were composed by the community as a whole; (3) the ballads were composed by an individual making, as Kittredge observed: "an improvisation in the presence of a sympathetic company which may even, at times, participate in the process."

The folk-ballad is characterized by the essential narrative element, dialogue, refrains of marked rhythmic or choral value, and repetition, at least of a single word or phrase, and usually of a more subtle nature called "incremental repetition," by which the story is made to "hitch along" through slight variations on a repetitive element. The true folk-ballad is notably objective. The importance of the repetitive elements, the implication of a chorus in the refrain material, the strong suggestion of possible dramatic and choreographic representation in the interchanging dialogue—all these characteristics lend weight to the argument that the folk-ballad is in some sense a communal affair. But one individual probably composed the narrative portions and even acted out the story, while the group, assembled for some special occasion, could have sung the refrain. Improvisation on the part of a few leaders may have helped to advance the composition of the given ballad, but the number of such collaborators would be few, because one must reckon with the practical fact that one person can compose a particular piece better than many. In this sense, then, the third theory mentioned above could account for the origin of the folk-ballad. Song is

assumed for all ballads; choral dancing may have entered into the folk-ballad as well.

On the other hand, many ballads show virtually none of the aforementioned characteristics of the folk-ballad; they are direct narratives in song and verse, often definitely subjective, and to say that they are subjective implies at once an individual originator. Such ballads are called minstrel-ballads; for them the first theory is alone applicable. The minstrel, a bard of the people, familiar with popular taste, probably had some experience at court, and thereby became familiar with romance materials. This would explain why some of these minstrel-ballads are related to the medieval metrical romances (cf. Hind Horn, p. 55). The minstrel probably was responsible for the creation of Robin Hood, the great ballad hero of epic proportions (p. 61); he was probably fighting in the armies of My Lords Douglas and Percy and so created the ballads of border warfare. But however much he may imitate the manner and even the language of the older folk-ballad—even to the point of throwing in a few rhythmic devices in the form of meaningless words and a few faint echoes of incremental repetition—still his work is his own; he has been responsible for the entire ballad. To put Edward (p. 54) beside Robin Hood and Allen-a-Dale (p. 61) is to see at once the essential difference between the two types: folk-ballad and minstrel-ballad.

It is possible to argue that the folk-ballad was composed by individuals with the assistance of the community in varying degrees; the minstrel-ballad, on the other hand, was the work of an individual who catered to the tastes of the people and conformed in a measure to the style of the older folk-ballad. The theory that the community as a whole engaged in ballad-making has been generally discredited; taken literally it would be impossible.

The subject matter of the popular ballads is varied. The folk-ballads are chiefly about mortals of a timeless age, when contact with the supernatural was not in the least out of the way; many, however, deal with personal bereavement or domestic complications or private intrigue. Historical ballads of all kinds, and ballads of the outlaw, are of the minstrel-ballad category (cf. the Robin Hood ballads and Johnie Armstrong, p. 64).

It has been pointed out that musical settings are the rule for all ballads; some of these have actually been recovered from antiquity. Careful usage, however, should limit the term "ballad" to narrative rather than lyric verse set to music, although in the "coronach," or lament, it is difficult to tell whether the narrative or the lyric predominates. Similarly, the ballad often veers toward didactic verse in the ancient type called the riddle-ballad (cf. Riddles Wisely Expounded, p. 54) and toward burlesque verse (as in The Farmer's Curst Wife, p. 66).

Because the ballad was the unwritten product of peasant and commoner, it was not considered highly by scholars and critics until the later eighteenth century when interest in antiquities resulted in the printing of these ancient songs. The romantic writers of the late eighteenth and of the nineteenth century, beginning with Robert Burns (p. 653) and Sir Walter Scott, imitated the ancient ballad. Samuel Taylor Coleridge (p. 711) and Dante Gabriel Rossetti (p. 1090) succeeded brilliantly in capturing the spirit of the minstrel-ballad.

The reader should bear in mind that the ballads in the present selection, although occasionally in Anglo-Scottish dialect, are Modern English in language; most of them, however late their form, are medieval in origin.

RIDDLES WISELY EXPOUNDED

It is a well-known fact that the riddle or enigma is of frequent occurrence in folk literature. It is extremely ancient and remarkably vital; riddle tales, of which this ballad is an illustration, can still be found, in much the same form as the following, among primitive European and Asiatic peoples.

In this ballad we have the customary situation: the devil disguised as a man comes down to try a human, who will be carried away to Hell or general destruction unless he can successfully answer the riddle propounded. Such a theme was often used in medieval times for didactic purposes.

There was a knicht riding frae the east,
  Sing the Cather banks, the bonnie brume,
Wha had been wooing at monie a place,
  And ye may beguile a young thing sune.

He came unto a widow's door,
And speird whare her three dochters were.

The auldest ane's to a washing gane,
The second's to a baking gane.

The youngest ane's to a wedding gane,
10 And it will be nicht or she be hame.

He sat him doun upon a stane,
Till thir three lasses came tripping hame.

The auldest ane's to the bed making,
And the second ane's to the sheet spreading.

The youngest ane was bauld and bricht,
And she was to lye with this unco knicht.

"Gin ye will answer me questions ten,
The morn ye sall be made my ain.

"O what is heigher nor the tree?
20 And what is deeper nor the sea?

"Or what is heavier nor the lead?
And what is better nor the breid?

"O what is whiter nor the milk?
Or what is safter nor the silk?

"Or what is sharper nor a thorn?
Or what is louder nor a horn?

"Or what is greener nor the grass?
Or what is waur nor a woman was?"

"O heaven is higher nor the tree,
And hell is deeper nor the sea.   30

"O sin is heavier nor the lead,
The blessing's better nor the bread.

"The snaw is whiter nor the milk,
And the down is safter nor the silk.

"Hunger is sharper nor a thorn,
And shame is louder nor a horn.

"Poison is greener nor the grass,
And Clootie's waur nor a woman was."

As sune as she the fiend did name,
He flew awa in a blazing flame.

EDWARD

This fine folk-ballad should be studied not only for its story, a characteristic tragedy of the "domestic relations" group of ballads, but also for its structure. The narrative is told in typical bitching fashion through the skillful use of incremental repetition.

"Why dois your brand sae drap wi bluid,
        Edward, Edward,
Why dois your brand sae drap wi bluid,
  And why sae sad gang yee O?"

Riddles Wisely Expounded. 2, 4. **Sing . . . brume; And ye . . . thing sune.** These lines are repeated as refrains in the second and fourth lines, respectively, of each succeeding stanza. 6. **speird,** asked; still common in Anglo-Scottish. 10. **or,** ere, before. 12. **thir,** these; an Old Norse form. 16. **unco,** literally the Old English *un* plus *couth,* "unknown," "strange." It is usually specialized, when used as an adjective, with the connotation of "supernatural." The *unco knicht* is the devil. 17. **Gin,** if. The *g* is pronounced hard. 19. **nor.** We use "than" after comparatives in Modern English. 28. **waur,** worse. 38. **Clootie,** the devil. A *cloot* is the half-hoof of a cloven-footed animal.

"O I hae killed my hauke sae guid,
　　　　Mither, mither,
O I hae killed my hauke sae guid,
　　And I had nae mair bot hee O."

"Your haukis bluid was nevir sae reid,
10　　　　Edward, Edward,
Your haukis bluid was nevir sae reid,
　　My deir son I tell thee O."
"O I hae killed my reid-roan steid,
　　　　Mither, mither,
O I hae killed my reid-roan steid,
　　That erst was sae fair and frie O."

"Your steid was auld, and ye hae gat mair,
　　　　Edward, Edward,
Your steid was auld, and ye hae gat mair,
20　　Sum other dule ye drie O."
"O I hae killed my fadir deir,
　　　　Mither, mither,
O I hae killed my fadir deir,
　　Alas, and wae is mee O!"

"And whatten penance wul ye drie for that,
　　　　Edward, Edward?
And whatten penance wul ye drie for that?
　　My deir son, now tell me O."
"Ile set my feit in yonder boat,
30　　　　Mither, mither,
Ile set my feit in yonder boat,
　　And Ile fare ovir the sea O."

"And what wul ye doe wi your towirs and your ha,
　　　　Edward, Edward?
And what wul ye doe wi your towirs and your ha,
　　That were sae fair to see O?"
"Ile let thame stand tul they doun fa,
　　　　Mither, mither,
Ile let thame stand tul they doun fa,
40　　For here nevir mair maun I bee O."

"And what wul ye leive to your bairns and your wife,
　　　　Edward, Edward?
And what wul ye leive to your bairns and your wife,
　　Whan ye gang ovir the sea O?"
"The warldis room, late them beg thrae life,
　　　　Mither, mither,
The warldis room, late them beg thrae life,
　　For thame nevir mair wul I see O."

"And what wul ye leive to your ain mither deir,
50　　　　Edward, Edward?
And what wul ye leive to your ain mither deir?

My deir son, now tell me O."
"The curse of hell frae me sall ye beir,
　　　　Mither, mither,
The curse of hell frae me sall ye beir,
　　Sic counseils ye gave to me O."

HIND HORN

　　In the medieval romance of King Horn the incident of Horn's return to Rymenhild in the guise of a palmer was an important part of the story, as well as something of a commonplace in medieval romances as a whole. The episode has been detached from the romance and has come into the possession of a ballad-minstrel, who gives it as a story for the yeomen and peasants and commoners. It is supposed that all the ballads having a subject taken from the romances arose in just such a manner, in other words, the romance is the original composition—the ballad is a popularization or vulgarization of the aristocratic fiction. Such a ballad as Hind Horn, in spite of its refrain, is not to be regarded as an indigenous folk-ballad.

In Scotland there was a babie born,
　　Lill lal, etc.
And his name it was called Hind Horn.
　　With a fal lal, etc.

He sent a letter to our king
That he was in love with his daughter Jean.

He's gien to her a silver wand,
With seven living lavrocks sitting thereon.

She's gien to him a diamond ring,
With seven bright diamonds set therein.　　　10

"When this ring grows pale and wan,
You may know by it my love is gane."

One day as he looked his ring upon,
He saw the diamonds pale and wan.

He left the sea and came to land,
And the first that he met was an old beggar man.

"What news, what news?" said young Hind Horn.
"No news, no news," said the old beggar man.

"No news," said the beggar, "no news at a',
But there is a wedding in the king's ha.　　　20

Edward. 8. **mair,** more. 9. **reid,** red. 16. **erst,** once. 20. **dule,** sorrow. 25. **whatten,** what kind of; **drie,** suffer. 33. **ha,** hall. This "satirical legacy," as it is called, is a commonplace of popular literature. 37. **fa,** fall. 45. **thrae,** through.
　Hind Horn. **Hind,** youth, young man; possibly the Old English ad-jective meaning "gracious," "courteous." 4. **With a fal lal, etc.** This verse, with l. 2 (*Lill lal,* etc.), form the fourth and second lines of each succeeding stanza, respectively. 8. **lavrocks,** larks. 16. **beggar man, etc.** In *King Horn* it was a palmer who was met by Horn and asked for news. As here, Horn exchanged clothes and made his way to the hall.

"But there is a wedding in the king's ha,
That has halden these forty days and twa."

"Will ye lend me your begging coat?
And I'll lend you my scarlet cloak.

"Will you lend me your beggar's rung?
And I'll gie you my steed to ride upon.

"Will you lend me your wig o hair,
To cover mine, because it is fair?"

The auld beggar man was bound for the mill,
30 But young Hind Horn for the king's hall.

The auld beggar man was bound for to ride,
But young Hind Horn was bound for the bride.

When he came to the king's gate,
He sought a drink for Hind Horn's sake.

The bride came down with a glass of wine,
When he drank out the glass, and dropt in the ring.

"O got ye this by sea or land?
Or got ye it off a dead man's hand?"

"I got not it by sea, I got it by land,
40 And I got it, madam, out of your own hand."

"O I'll cast off my gowns of brown,
And beg wi you frae town to town.

"O I'll cast off my gowns of red,
And I'll beg wi you to win my bread."

"Ye needna cast off your gowns of brown,
For I'll make you lady o many a town.

"Ye needna cast off your gowns of red,
It's only a sham, the begging o my bread."

The bridegroom he had wedded the bride,
But young Hind Horn he took her to bed.

THE TWA CORBIES

*This ballad combines certain elements of the ani-
mal story with the ballad type; there is also a rather
strong lyric element of lament—the coronach. Particularly effective is the poignant, severe, almost
cynical simplicity with which the lament over the
dead is expressed.*

As I was walking all alane,
I heard twa corbies making a mane;
The tane unto the t'other say,
"Where sall we gang and dine to-day?"

"In behint yon auld fail dyke,
I wot there lies a new slain knight;
And naebody kens that he lies there,
But his hawk, his hound, and lady fair.

"His hound is to the hunting gane,
His hawk to fetch the wild-fowl hame,   10
His lady's ta'en another mate,
So we may mak' our dinner sweet.

"Ye'll sit on his white hause-bane,
And I'll pike out his bonny blue e'en;
Wi' ae lock o' his gowden hair
We'll theek our nest when it grows bare.

"Mony a ane for him makes mane,
But nane sall ken where he is gane;
O'er his white banes, when they are bare,
The wind sall blaw for evermair."

KEMP OWYNE

*The common folklore themes here are (a) the
"loathly lady" and (b) the magic transformation.
Perhaps it could be said that one grows out of the
other. There is, moreover, a test of the knight's
physical courage and endurance. On the magic ring
and belt see notes on lines 27 and 39.*

Her mother died when she was young,
    Which gave her cause to make great moan;
Her father married the warst woman
    That ever lived in Christendom.

She served her with foot and hand,
    In every thing that she could dee,
Till once, in an unlucky time,
    She threw her in ower Craigy's sea.

Says, "Lie you there, dove Isabel,
    And all my sorrows lie with thee;   10
Till Kemp Owyne come ower the sea,
    And borrow you with kisses three,

---

22. **forty days and twa.** Six weeks is an exceptionally long time for
wedding festivities, for the allotted period in the romances was usually
fifteen days. 25. **rung**, staff; cf. the "rung" of a ladder or chair.
The Twa Corbies. Corbies, crows. 2. **mane**, literally a "moan," a
"complaint"; but, in the ballads, generalized to any kind of utterance.
3. **tane**, the one; the excrescent *t* results from the prefixing of the definite
article, which is unaccented and hence blurred in pronunciation. The
same process took place with "the other": *t'other*. 5. **fail dyke**, turf
wall. 13. **hause-bane**, neck bone. 16. **theek**, thatch.
Kemp Owyne. 8. **Craigy's sea**. Although this body of water has not
been identified, there is known a Craigie Wood, a hill south of Perth,
Scotland, on the shores of the River Tay. Possibly, then, Craigy's sea is
the Tay itself. 9. **dove**, a helpless or innocent young woman; so-called,
probably, because the dove is a traditional symbol of helplessness and

Let all the world do what they will,
    Oh borrowed shall you never be!"

Her breath grew strang, her hair grew lang,
    And twisted thrice about the tree,
And all the people, far and near,
    Thought that a savage beast was she.

These news did come to Kemp Owyne,
20   Where he lived, far beyond the sea;
He hasted him to Craigy's sea,
    And on the savage beast looked he.

Her breath was strang, her hair was lang,
    And twisted was about the tree,
And with a swing she came about:
    "Come to Craigy's sea, and kiss with me.

"Here is a royal belt," she cried,
    "That I have found in the green sea;
And while your body it is on,
30   Drawn shall your blood never be;
But if you touch me, tail or fin,
    I vow my belt your death shall be."

He stepped in, gave her a kiss,
    The royal belt he brought him wi;
Her breath was strang, her hair was lang,
    And twisted twice about the tree,
And with a swing she came about:
    "Come to Craigy's sea, and kiss with me.

"Here is a royal ring," she said,
40   "That I have found in the green sea;
And while your finger it is on,
    Drawn shall your blood never be;
But if you touch me, tail or fin,
    I swear my ring your death shall be."

He stepped in, gave her a kiss,
    The royal ring he brought him wi;
Her breath was strang, her hair was lang,
    And twisted ance about the tree,
And with a swing she came about:
50   "Come to Craigy's sea, and kiss with me.

"Here is a royal brand," she said,
    "That I have found in the green sea;
And while your body it is on,
    Drawn shall your blood never be;
But if you touch me, tail or fin,
    I swear my brand your death shall be."

He stepped in, gave her a kiss,
    The royal brand he brought him wi;
Her breath was sweet, her hair grew short,
    And twisted nane about the tree,   60
And smilingly she came about,
    As fair a woman as fair could be.

THOMAS RYMER

This ballad is the best example in English of the story of a mortal man seduced by a fairy queen, the Tannhäuser or Venusberg theme (cf. Wagner's opera).

True Thomas lay oer yon grassy bank,
    And he beheld a ladie gay,
A ladie that was brisk and bold,
    Come riding oer the fernie brae.

Her skirt was of the grass-green silk,
    Her mantel of the velvet fine,
And ilka tett of her horse's mane
    Hung fifty silver bells and nine.

True Thomas he took off his hat,
    And bowed him low down till his knee: 10
"All hail, thou mighty Queen of Heaven!
    For your peer on earth I never did see."

"O no, O no, True Thomas," she says,
    "That name does not belong to me;
I am but the queen of fair Elfland,
    And I'm come here for to visit thee.

"But ye maun go wi me now, Thomas,
    True Thomas, ye maun go wi me,
For ye maun serve me seven years,
    Thro weel or wae as may chance to be."   20

She turned about her milk-white steed,
    And took True Thomas up behind,
And aye wheneer her bridle rang,
    The steed flew swifter than the wind.

For forty days and forty nights
    He wade thro red blude to the knee,
And he saw neither sun nor moon,
    But heard the roaring of the sea.

O they rade on, and further on,
    Until they came to a garden green: 30

innocence. 12. **borrow,** ransom. 27, 39, 51. **belt . . . ring . . . brand.**
These three accouterments are the commonest talismans against wounds.
One would have been enough, but three kisses are required to redeem the
loathly lady, and so three talismans come into the story. For the magic
ring in another use, see *Hind Horn,* p. 55, ll. 9 ff.
    Thomas Rymer. 7. **ilka tett,** each lock; the preposition *from* should
be supplied before *ilka.* 16. **come . . . visit thee.** In the present version

there is a gap in the ballad, but other versions make clear that at this
point the lady granted Thomas her love. 19. **serve me seven years.**
Thomas must serve the traditional period of apprenticeship, so to speak.
His later partaking of food and drink and his intimacy with the Elf
Queen prevent his return even if he had wished it.

"Light down, light down, ye ladie free,
  Some of that fruit let me pull to thee."

"O no, O no, True Thomas," she says,
  "That fruit maun not be touched by thee,
For a' the plagues that are in hell
  Light on the fruit of this countrie.

"But I have a loaf here in my lap,
  Likewise a bottle of claret wine,
And now ere we go farther on,
40 We'll rest a while, and ye may dine."

When he had eaten and drunk his fill,
  "Lay down your head upon my knee,"
The lady sayd, "ere we climb yon hill,
  And I will show you fairlies three.

"O see not ye yon narrow road,
  So thick beset wi thorns and briers?
That is the path of righteousness,
  Tho after it but few enquires.

"And see not ye that braid braid road,
50 That lies across yon lillie leven?
That is the path of wickedness,
  Tho some call it the road to heaven.

"And see not ye that bonny road,
  Which winds about the fernie brae?
That is the road to fair Elfland,
  Where you and I this night maun gae.

"But Thomas, ye maun hold your tongue,
  Whatever you may hear or see,
For gin ae word you should chance to speak,
60 You will neer get back to your ain countrie."

He has gotten a coat of the even cloth,
  And a pair of shoes of velvet green,
And till seven years were past and gone
  True Thomas on earth was never seen.

SIR PATRICK SPENS

In addition to the fine "atmospheric" quality of this ballad, which bespeaks a gifted minstrel author whose talents resembled those of Samuel Coleridge, it is to be noted that this seems to be a historical ballad. It is believed that Sir Patrick Spens, himself difficult to identify, was lost at sea while returning from the expedition (1281) which conducted Margaret, daughter of King Alexander III of Scotland, to her husband, King Eric of Norway.

The king sits in Dunfermline toune
  Drinking the blude-red wine:
"O whar will I get guid sailor,
  To sail this schip of mine?"

Up and spak an eldern knicht,
  Sat at the kings richt kne:
"Sir Patrick Spens is the best sailor
  That sails upon the se."

The king has written a braid letter,
  And signed it wi his hand,   10
And sent it to Sir Patrick Spens,
  Was walking on the sand.

The first line that Sir Patrick red,
  A loud lauch lauched he;
The next line that Sir Patrick red,
  The teir blinded his ee.

"O wha is this has don this deid,
  This ill deid don to me,
To send me out this time o' the yeir,
  To sail upon the se!   20

"Mak hast, mak haste, my mirry men all,
  Our guid schip sails the morne":
"O say na sae, my master deir,
  For I feir a deadlie storme.

"Late late yestreen I saw the new moone,
  Wi the auld moone in hir arme,
And I feir, I feir, my deir master,
  That we will cum to harme."

O our Scots nobles wer richt laith
  To weet their cork-heild schoone;   30
Bot lang owre a' the play wer playd,
  Thair hats they swam aboone.

O lang, lang may their ladies sit,
  Wi thair fans into their hand,
Or eir they se Sir Patrick Spens
  Cum sailing to the land.

O lang, lang may the ladies stand,
  Wi thair gold kems in their hair,
Waiting for thair ain deir lords,
  For they'll se thame na mair.   40

---

34. **fruit . . . touched by thee.** The injunction against touching a certain object, on the penalty of dire and overwhelming disaster (in short, a taboo on touching), reminds one of the classical legend of Pandora and her box, or the Old Testament story of Adam and Eve, and the forbidden tree. 44. **fairlies,** wonders, marvels. 50. **lillie leven,** lovely glade. 64. **True Thomas . . . seen,** because of his intimate association with the fairy queen.

Sir Patrick Spens. 9. **braid,** long, written on a long or broad sheet. 16. **ee,** eye. 25. **Late . . . arme.** The bad omen in such a sight lay in the fact that the new moon was seen late in the evening. The **auld moone in hir arme** is a reference to the semiluminous surface of the moon visible between the horns of the new moon. This phenomenon is due to "earth shine," i.e., a reflection of the light of the earth on the moon. The earth, at the time the moon is new to us, would be full to the inhabitant of the

Haf owre, haf owre to Aberdour,
　　It's fiftie fadom deip,
And thair lies guid Sir Patrick Spens,
　　Wi the Scots lords at his feit.

SWEET WILLIAM'S GHOST

This ballad is, in a sense, the obverse of Thomas
Rymer. *It tells the story of a mortal woman who
rides off with her dead lover and is carried irretrievably to the grave. The demon lover, to be sure, may
not cause the maiden's actual death, but at least he
can do irreparable damage to her soul.*

There came a ghost to Margret's door,
　　With many a grievous groan,
And ay he tirled at the pin,
　　But answer made she none.

"Is that my father Philip,
　　Or is't my brother John?
Or is't my true-love, Willy,
　　From Scotland new come home?"

" 'Tis not thy father Philip,
10　Nor yet thy brother John;
But 'tis thy true-love Willy,
　　From Scotland new come home.

"O sweet Margret, O dear Margret,
　　I pray thee speak to me;
Give me my faith and troth, Margret,
　　As I gave it to thee."

"Thy faith and troth thou's never get,
　　Nor yet will I thee lend,
Till that thou come within my bower,
20　And kiss my cheek and chin."

"If I should come within thy bower,
　　I am no earthly man;
And should I kiss thy rosy lips,
　　Thy days will not be lang.

"O sweet Margret, O dear Margret,
　　I pray thee speak to me;
Give me my faith and troth, Margret,
　　As I gave it to thee."

"Thy faith and troth thou's never get,
30　Nor yet will I thee lend,
Till thou take me to yon kirk,
　　And wed me with a ring."

"My bones are buried in yon kirk-yard,
　　Afar beyond the sea,
And it is but my spirit, Margret,
　　That's now speaking to thee."

She stretched out her lily-white hand,
　　And, for to do her best,
"Hae, there's your faith and troth, Willy,
　　God send your soul good rest."　　　　　　40

Now she has kilted her robes of green
　　A piece below her knee,
And a' the live-lang winter night
　　The dead corp followed she.

"Is there any room at your head, Willy?
　　Or any room at your feet?
Or any room at your side, Willy,
　　Wherein that I may creep?"

"There's no room at my head, Margret,
　　There's no room at my feet;　　　　　　50
There's no room at my side, Margret,
　　My coffin's made so meet."

Then up and crew the red, red cock,
　　And up then crew the gray:
" 'Tis time, 'tis time, my dear Margret,
　　That you were going away."

No more the ghost to Margret said,
　　But, with a grievous groan,
Evanished in a cloud of mist,
　　And left her all alone.　　　　　　60

"O stay, my only true-love, stay!"
　　The constant Margret cry'd;
Wan grew her cheeks, she closed her een,
　　Stretched her soft limbs, and dy'd.

THE WIFE OF USHER'S WELL

Like Sweet William's Ghost, The Wife of Usher's
Well *typifies the common theme of the return of the
dead, but the ghosts in* The Wife of Usher's Well *are
benevolent ghosts. This particular ballad has had a
very long and complicated history and versions of it
have been found in the United States.*

moon. This stanza, in its atmosphere, is reminiscent of Coleridge's *Rime
of the Ancient Mariner,* 11. 263 ff. (p. 714). **30. cork-heild schoone,**
shoes with heels of cork. **31. owre,** ere, before. **35. Or eir,** ere (they)
ever. **41. Haf . . . Aberdour,** halfway on the return journey to Aberdour; that is, halfway home.
　Sweet William's Ghost. 3. **tirled,** rattled at the pin that lifts the
door latch. 39. **Hae,** "Have (it)," "Take (it)"; "Here!" 44. **corp.**

The French word *corps* (body), when borrowed into English, was soon
specialized into *corpse,* a dead body. But in popular belief (popular
etymology), the word *corps* suggested the plural of a hypothetical noun
corp. The same process is seen in *cherry* (from the French *cerise*); or
in *riddle* (from Old English *raedels;* cf. German *Rätsel*).

There lived a wife at Usher's Well,
    And a wealthy wife was she;
She had three stout and stalwart sons,
    And sent them o'er the sea.

They hadna been a week from her,
    A week but barely ane,
When word came to the carline wife
    That her three sons were gane.

They hadna been a week from her,
10 A week but barely three,
When word came to the carline wife
    That her sons she'd never see.

"I wish the wind may never cease,
    Nor fashes in the flood,
Till my three sons come hame to me
    In earthly flesh and blood!"

It fell about the Martinmas,
    When nights are lang and mirk,
The carline wife's three sons came hame,
20 And their hats were o' the birk.

It neither grew in syke nor ditch,
    Nor yet in ony sheugh;
But at the gates o' Paradise
    That birk grew fair eneugh.

"Blow up the fire, my maidens!
    Bring water from the well!
For a' my house shall feast this night,
    Since my three sons are well."

And she has made to them a bed,
30 She's made it large and wide;
And she's ta'en her mantle her about,
    Sat down at the bedside.

Up then crew the red, red cock,
    And up and crew the gray;
The eldest to the youngest said,
    " 'Tis time we were away."

The cock he hadna crawed but once,
    And clapped his wings at a',
When the youngest to the eldest said,
40 "Brother, we must awa'."

"The cock doth craw, the day doth daw,
    The channerin' worm doth chide;
Gin we be missed out o' our place,
    A sair pain we maun bide."

"Lie still, lie still but a little wee while,
    Lie still but if we may;
Gin my mother should miss us when she wakes,
    She'll go mad ere it be day."

"Fare ye weel, my mother dear!
    Fareweel to barn and byre!   50
And fare ye weel, the bonny lass
    That kindles my mother's fire."

BONNY BARBARA ALLAN

Here is the familiar old theme of "lovesickness," this time carried to a fatal conclusion. The maiden, resenting a slight, fancied or otherwise, spurns the man who is dying of love for her. After his death, she dies in sympathy. Few ballads in the entire Child collection have had a greater vitality in America.

It was in and about the Martinmas time,
    When the green leaves were a falling,
That Sir John Graeme, in the West Country,
    Fell in love with Barbara Allan.

He sent his man down through the town,
    To the place where she was dwelling:
"O haste and come to my master dear,
    Gin ye be Barbara Allan."

O hooly, hooly rose she up,
    To the place where he was lying,   10
And when she drew the curtain by,
    "Young man, I think you're dying."

"O it's I'm sick, and very, very sick,
    And 'tis a' for Barbara Allan";
"O the better for me ye's never be,
    Tho your heart's blood were a spilling.

"O dinna ye mind, young man," said she,
    "When ye was in the tavern a drinking,
That ye made the healths gae round and round,
    And slighted Barbara Allan?"   20

He turnd his face unto the wall,
    And death was with him dealing:
"Adieu, adieu, my dear friends all,
    And be kind to Barbara Allan."

And slowly, slowly raise she up,
    And slowly, slowly left him,
And sighing said, she could not stay,
    Since death of life had reft him.

The Wife of Usher's Well. 7. carline, old. 14. fashes, troubles. 17. Martinmas, the feast of St. Martin, November 11. 20. birk, birch. 21. syke, trench. 22. sheugh, furrow. 38. at a', at all. The phrase would mean that the cock had crowed but once and had not yet flapped

his wings; the first cockcrow was supposed to be at 1 A.M. and was the signal for all walking ghosts to return to the graveyard. 50. byre, shed for cattle.
Bonny Barbara Allan. 9. hooly, slowly and softly. 31. jow, stroke

She had not gane a mile but twa,
    When she heard the dead-bell ringing,
And every jow that the dead-bell geid,
    It cry'd "Woe to Barbara Allan!"

"O mother, mother, make my bed!
    O make it soft and narrow!
My love has died for me today,
    I'll die for him tomorrow."

YOUNG WATERS

It is possible that this ballad of an insanely jealous husband was founded upon some event in Scotch history; mention of the "beheading hill" at Stirling seems to confirm it. But it has been shown that the story occurs not only in English and Scotch but in Norse as well.

About Yule, when the wind blew cule,
    And the round tables began,
A there is cum to our king's court
    Mony a well-favord man.

The queen luikt owre the castle-wa,
    Beheld baith dale and down,
And there she saw Young Waters
    Cum riding to the town.

His footmen they did rin before,
    His horsemen rade behind;
And mantel of the burning gowd
    Did keip him frae the wind.

Gowden-graithd his horse before,
    And siller-shod behind;
The horse Young Waters rade upon
    Was fleeter than the wind.

Out then spack a wylie lord,
    Unto the queen said he,
"O tell me wha's the fairest face
    Rides in the company?"

"I've sene lord, and I've sene laird,
    And knights of high degree,
Bot a fairer face than Young Waters
    Mine eyne did never see."

Out then spack the jealous king,
    And an angry man was he:
"O if he had bin twice as fair,
    You micht have excepted me."

"You're neither laird nor lord," she says,
    "Bot the king that wears the crown;
There is not a knight in fair Scotland
    But to thee maun bow down."

For a' that she could do or say,
    Appeased he wad nae bee,
Bot for the words which she had said,
    Young Waters he maun die.

They hae taen Young Waters,
    And put fetters to his feet;
They hae taen Young Waters,
    And thrown him in dungeon deep.

"Aft I have ridden thro Stirling town
    In the wind bot and the weit;
Bot I neir rade thro Stirling town
    Wi fetters at my feet.

"Aft I have ridden thro Stirling town
    In the wind bot and the rain;
Bot I neir rade thro Stirling town
    Neir to return again."

They hae taen to the heiding-hill
    His young son in his craddle
And they hae taen to the heiding-hill
    His horse bot and his saddle.

They hae taen to the heiding-hill
    His lady fair to see,
And for the words the queen had spoke
    Young Waters he did die.

ROBIN HOOD AND ALLEN-A-DALE

As Child, the great authority on the English and Scottish popular ballads, has observed: "Robin Hood is absolutely a creation of the ballad-muse." Attempts to associate him with a historical personage have thus far completely failed. Instead, he is a yeoman, idealized, with a kingly courtesy and courage, the defender of the poor and the champion of womanhood, the avowed enemy of the organized Church. But he is devout and reverent to the Virgin. He is a popular epic figure, and his followers remind one vaguely of the knights of Arthur's Round Table in everyday dress.

The most considerable, and withal the best, treatment of the entire career of Robin Hood is to be found in A Gest of Robyn Hode, a long minstrel-ballad of the late Middle English or early Modern

(of a bell). **geid,** gave (from *gived*).
    Young Waters. 6. **dale and down,** a common alliterative formula in Middle English literature. 9. **rin,** run. 13. **Gowden-graithd,** with gold caparisons and decorations. 14. **siller-shod,** shod with silver. 21. **laird,**

a Scottish landowner, not a knight; about the equivalent of the later English country squire. 42. **bot and,** and also. **weit,** wet. 49. **heiding-hill,** beheading hill; the place of execution at Stirling, Scotland.

English period (c. 1500). So close does A Gest of Robyn Hode come to an epic that it might be called a heroic epic. Although in the later ballads the hero suffers a debasement comparable to that suffered by King Arthur, both Robin Hood and Allen-a-Dale and Robin Hood's Death and Burial show him still in a heroic light.

Come listen to me, you gallants so free,
    All you that loves mirth for to hear,
And I will you tell of a bold outlaw,
    That lived in Nottinghamshire.

As Robin Hood in the forest stood,
    All under the greenwood tree,
There was he ware of a brave young man
    As fine as fine might be.

The youngster was clothed in scarlet red,
10   In scarlet fine and gay,
And he did frisk it over the plain,
    And chanted a roundelay.

As Robin Hood next morning stood,
    Amongst the leaves so gay,
There did he espy the same young man
    Come drooping along the way.

The scarlet he wore the day before,
    It was clean cast away;
And every step he fetcht a sigh,
20   "Alack and a well a day!"

Then stepped forth brave Little John,
    And Nick the miller's son,
Which made the young man bend his bow,
    When as he see them come.

"Stand off, stand off," the young man said,
    "What is your will with me?"
"You must come before our master straight,
    Under yon greenwood tree."

And when he came bold Robin before,
30   Robin asked him courteously,
"O hast thou any money to spare
    For my merry men and me?"

"I have no money," the young man said,
    "But five shillings and a ring;
And that I have kept this seven long years,
    To have it at my wedding.

"Yesterday I should have married a maid,
    But now she is from me tane,

And chosen to be an old knight's delight,
    Whereby my poor heart is slain."   40

"What is thy name?" then said Robin Hood,
    "Come tell me, without any fail."
"By the faith of my body," then said the young man,
    "My name it is Allen-a-Dale."

"What wilt thou give me," said Robin Hood,
    "In ready gold or fee,
To help thee to thy true-love again,
    And deliver her unto thee?"

"I have no money," then quoth the young man,
    "No ready gold nor fee.   50
But I will swear upon a book
    Thy true servant for to be."

"How many miles is it to thy true-love?
    Come tell me without any guile."
"By the faith of my body," then said the young man,
    "It is but five little mile."

Then Robin he hasted over the plain,
    He did neither stint nor lin,
Until he came unto the church
    Where Allin should keep his wedding.   60

"What dost thou do here?" the bishop he said,
    "I prethee now tell to me."
"I am a bold harper," quoth Robin Hood,
    "And the best in the north countrey."

"O welcome, O welcome," the bishop he said,
    "That music best pleaseth me."
"You shall have no music," quoth Robin Hood,
    "Till the bride and the bridegroom I see."

With that came in a wealthy knight,
    Which was both grave and old,   70
And after him a finikin lass,
    Did shine like glistering gold.

"This is no fit match," quoth bold Robin Hood,
    "That you do seem to make here;
For since we are come into the church,
    The bride she shall choose her own dear."

Then Robin Hood put his horn to his mouth,
    And blew blasts two or three;
When four and twenty bowmen bold
    Came leaping over the lea.   80

And when they came into the churchyard,
    Marching all on a row,

Robin Hood and Allen-a-Dale. **12. roundelay,** used here of any joyful song. The technical structure of the roundelay can be disregarded (see *New English Dictionary* on "roundelay"). **44. Allen-a-Dale,** i.e., Allen (who lives) in the dale. **58. stint nor lin,** stop nor cease. **63.**

harper, one of the traditional methods of disguise in the romances and ballads of the Middle Ages; the story is told that Alfred the Great, disguised as a minstrel or harper, visited the camp of Gudrum, the King of the Danes, and gained valuable information. The reader will remember

The first man was Allin-a-Dale,
    To give bold Robin his bow.

"This is thy true-love," Robin he said,
    "Young Allin, as I hear say;
And you shall be married at this same time,
    Before we depart away."

"That shall not be," the bishop he said,
90   "For thy word shall not stand;
They shall be three times askt in the church,
    As the law is of our land."

Robin Hood pulled off the bishop's coat,
    And put it upon Little John;
"By the faith of my body," then Robin said,
    "This cloath doth make thee a man."

When Little John went into the quire,
    The people began for to laugh;
He askt them seven times in the church,
100   Lest three times should not be enough.

"Who gives me this maid?" then said Little John;
    Quoth Robin, "That do I,
And he that doth take her from Allin-a-Dale
    Full dearly he shall her buy."

And thus having ended this merry wedding,
    The bride lookt as fresh as a queen,
And so they returned to the merry greenwood,
    Amongst the leaves so green.

ROBIN HOOD'S DEATH AND BURIAL

*The betrayal of Robin Hood by his cousin is remin-
iscent of the tragic "domestic relations" ballad, where
one relative either kills another or does him a great
wrong.*

When Robin Hood and Little John
    Down a down a down a down
Went oer yon bank of broom,
    Said Robin Hood bold to Little John,
We have shot for many a pound.
    Hey down a down a down a down!

But I am not able to shoot one shot more,
    My broad arrows will not flee;
But I have a cousin lives down below,
10   Please God, she will bleed me.

Now Robin he is to fair Kirkly gone,
    As fast as he can win;

But before he came there, as we do hear,
    He was taken very ill.

And when he came to fair Kirkly-hall,
    He knockd all at the ring,
But none was so ready as his cousin herself
    For to let bold Robin in.

"Will you please to sit down, cousin Robin," she said,
    "And drink some beer with me?"   20
"No, I will neither eat nor drink,
    Till I am blooded by thee."

"Well, I have a room, cousin Robin," she said,
    "Which you did never see,
And if you please to walk therein,
    You blooded by me shall be."

She took him by the lily-white hand,
    And led him to a private room,
And there she blooded bold Robin Hood,
    While one drop of blood would run down.   30

She blooded him in a vein of the arm,
    And locked him up in the room;
There did he bleed all the live-long day,
    Until the next day at noon.

He then bethought him of a casement there,
    Thinking for to get down;
But was so weak he could not leap,
    He could not get him down.

He then bethought him of his bugle-horn,
    Which hung low down to his knee;   40
He set his horn unto his mouth,
    And blew out weak blasts three.

Then Little John, when hearing him,
    As he sat under a tree,
"I fear my master is now near dead,
    He blows so wearily."

Then Little John to fair Kirkly is gone,
    As fast as he can dree;
But when he came to Kirkly-hall,
    He broke locks two or three;   50

Until he came bold Robin to see,
    Then he fell on his knee;
"A boon, a boon," cries Little John,
    "Master, I beg of thee."

"What is that boon," said Robin Hood,
    "Little John, thou begs of me?"

Horn's disguise when he returned to rescue Rymenhild (cf. *Hind Horn*,
p. 55, ll. 16 ff.). 91. **three times . . . church.** The banns must be
proclaimed three Sundays in succession before the marriage.
    Robin Hood's Death and Burial. 3. broom, the plant. 8. broad
arrows, arrows with a forked or barbed head. 48. **dree**, literally
"endure"; to be interpreted here as "be able." Contrast the force of
the word here with *drie* (*Edward*, p. 54, l. 25).

"It is to burn fair Kirkly-hall,
  And all their nunnery."

"Now nay, now nay," quoth Robin Hood,
60   "That boon I'll not grant thee;
I never hurt woman in all my life,
  Nor men in woman's company.

"I never hurt fair maid in all my time,
  Nor at mine end shall it be;
But give me my bent bow in my hand,
  And a broad arrow I'll let flee
And where this arrow is taken up,
  There shall my grave digged be.

"Lay me a green sod under my head,
70   And another at my feet;
And lay my bent bow by my side,
  Which was my music sweet;
And make my grave of gravel and green,
  Which is most right and meet.

"Let me have length and breadth enough,
  With a green sod under my head;
Then they may say, when I am dead
  'Here lies bold Robin Hood.' "

These words they readily granted him,
80   Which did bold Robin please;
And there they buried bold Robin Hood,
  Within the fair Kirkleys.

JOHNIE ARMSTRONG

*The Armstrongs were a powerful Scottish family
living near the border, for many centuries the land
of contention between England and Scotland. John
Armstrong, the hero of this ballad, appeared about
1525. He was a rebel against both the English and
the Scotch, but finally (1530), King James V of Scotland captured Armstrong and had him executed.
The suggestion here is that James got hold of Armstrong through treachery, but such suggestions are
inevitable in the outlaw ballads, where the sympathy
is always with the outlaw.*

There dwelt a man in faire Westmerland,
  Ionnë Armestrong men did him call,
He had nither lands nor rents coming in,
  Yet he kept eight score men in his hall.

He had horse and harness for them all,
  Goodly steeds were all milke-white;

O the golden bands an about their necks,
  And their weapons, they were all alike.

Newes then was brought unto the king
  That there was sicke a won as hee,   10
That livëd lyke a bold out-law,
  And robbëd all the north country.

The king he writt an a letter then,
  A letter which was large and long;
He signëd it with his owne hand,
  And he promised to doe him no wrong.

When this letter came Ionnë untill,
  His heart it was as blythe as birds on the tree:
"Never was I sent for before any king,
  My father, my grandfather, nor none but mee.   20

"And if wee goe the king before,
  I would we went most orderly;
Every man of you shall have his scarlet cloak,
  Laced with silver laces three.

"Every won of you shall have his velvett coat,
  Laced with sillver lace so white;
O the golden bands an about your necks,
  Black hatts, white feathers, all alyke."

By the morrow morninge at ten of the clock,
  Towards Edenburough gon was hee,   30
And with him all his eight score men;
  Good Lord, it was a goodly sight for to see!

When Ionnë came befower the king,
  He fell downe on his knee;
"O pardon, my soveraine leige," he said,
  "O pardon my eight score men and mee!"

"Thou shalt have no pardon, thou traytor strong,
  For thy eight score men nor thee;
For tomorrow morning by ten of the clock,
  Both thou and them shall hang on the gallow-tree." 40

But Ionnë looked over his left shoulder,
  Good Lord, what a grievous look looked hee!
Saying, "Asking grace of a graceles face—
  Why there is none for you nor me."

But Ionnë had a bright sword by his side,
  And it was made of the mettle so free,
That had not the king stept his foot aside,
  He had smitten his head from his faire boddë.

Saying, "Fight on, my merry men all,
  And see that none of you be taine;   50

Johnie Armstrong. 7. **an,** a superfluous word, inserted to fill out the
meter. 10. **sicke a won,** such a one. 17. **untill,** unto. The preposition
is in many cases placed after its object. 65. **young Ionnë Armestrong,**
the son of the outlaw.

For rather then men shall say we were hange'd,
    Let them report how we were slaine."

Then, God wott, faire Eddenburrough rose,
    And so besett poore Ionnë rounde,
That fowerscore and tenn of Ionnës best men
    Lay gasping all upon the ground.

Then like a mad man Ionnë laid about,
    And like a mad man then fought hee,
Untill a falce Scot came Ionnë behinde,
60   And runn him through the faire boddee.

Saying, "Fight on, my merry men all,
    And see that none of you be taine;
For I will stand by and bleed but awhile,
    And than will I come and fight againe."

Newes then was brought to young Ionnë Armestrong,
    As he stood by his nurse's knee,
Who vowed if ere he live'd for to be a man,
    O the treacherous Scots revengd hee'd be.

BONNIE GEORGE CAMPBELL

The ballad is a characteristic example of the cor-onach, or ballad of lament.

Hie upon Hielands,
    And laigh upon Tay,
Bonnie George Campbell
    Rode out on a day.

He saddled, he bridled,
    And gallant rode he,
And hame cam his guid horse,
    But never cam he.

Out cam his mother dear,
10   Greeting fu sair,
And out cam his bonnie bryde,
    Riving her hair.

"The meadow lies green,
    The corn is unshorn,
But Bonnie George Campbell
    Will never return."

Saddled and bridled
    And booted rode he,
A plume in his helmet,
20   A sword at his knee.

But toom cam his saddle,
    All bloody to see,

Oh, hame cam his guid horse,
    But never cam he!

KATHARINE JAFFRAY

This ballad of the border is the obvious source of Scott's Lochinvar *(1808). The situation of the lover carrying the bride away from the bridegroom on their wedding day is something of a commonplace in folklore (see* Robin Hood and Allen-a-Dale, *p. 61).*

There livd a lass in yonder dale,
    And doun in yonder glen, O
And Kathrine Jaffray was her name,
    Well known by many men, O.

Out came the Laird of Lauderdale,
    Out frae the South Countrie,
All for to court this pretty maid,
    Her bridegroom for to be.

He has teld her father and mither baith,
    And a' the rest o' her kin,   10
And has teld the lass hersell,
    And her consent has win.

Then came the Laird of Lochinton,
    Out frae the English border,
All for to court this pretty maid,
    Well mounted in good order.

He's teld her father and mither baith,
    As I hear sindry say,
But he has nae teld the lass hersell,
    Till on her wedding day.   20

When day was set, and friends were met,
    And married to be,
Lord Lauderdale came to the place,
    The bridal for to see.

"O are you come for sport, young man?
    Or are you come for play?
Or are you come for a sight o' our bride,
    Just on her wedding day?"

"I'm nouther come for sport," he says,
    "Nor am I come for play;   30
But if I had one sight o' your bride,
    I'll mount and ride away."

There was a glass of the red wine
    Filld up them atween,

Bonnie George Campbell. 2. **laigh,** low.
Katharine Jaffray. 9. **teld,** stated his position as suitor. **baith,** both. 11. **hersell,** herself. 18. **sindry,** several, many, sundry. 34. **atween,** between. Again the preposition comes after the object.

And ay she drank to Lauderdale,
    Wha her true-love had been.

Then he took her by the milk-white hand,
    And by the grass-green sleeve,
And he mounted her high behind him there,
40   At the bridegroom he askt nae leive.

Then the blude ran down by the Cowden Banks,
    And down by Cowden Braes,
And ay she gard the trumpet sound,
    "O this is foul, foul play!"

Now a' ye that in England are,
    Or are in England born,
Come nere to Scotland to court a lass,
    Or else ye'll get the scorn.

They haik ye up and settle ye by,
50   Till on your wedding day,
And gie ye frogs instead o' fish,
    And play ye foul, foul play.

THE FARMER'S CURST WIFE

The theme of a shrewish, accursed woman who is more than a match for demons themselves is widespread in both Oriental and Occidental folklore.

There was an old farmer in Sussex did dwell,
    (Chorus of whistlers, etc.)

There was an old farmer in Sussex did dwell,
And he had a bad wife, as many knew well.
    (Chorus of whistlers, etc.)

Then Satan came to the old man at the plough:
"One of your family I must have now.

"It is not your eldest son that I crave,
But it is your old wife, and she will I have."

"O welcome, good Satan, with all my heart!
I hope you and she will never more part."

Now Satan has got the old wife on his back,   10
And he lugged her along, like a pedlar's pack.

He trudged away till they came to his hall-gate;
Says he, "Here, take in an old Sussex chap's mate."

O then she did kick the young imps about;
Says one to the other, "Let's try turn her out."

She spied thirteen imps all dancing in chains,
She up with her pattens and beat out their brains.

She knocked the old Satan against the wall;
"Let's turn her out, or she'll murder us all."

Now he's bundled her up on his back amain,   20
And to her old husband he took her again.

"I have been a tormentor the whole of my life,
But I ne'er was tormented so as with your wife."

43. **gard,** made to, caused to. 47. **nere,** never. 49. **They haik . . . ye by,** "They lead you on (keep you in suspense) and then set you aside." 51. **gie,** give. The meaning of the line is, "They give you something you had not expected."
The Farmer's Curst Wife. Compare *Kellyburn Braes* (p. 663).
17. **pattens,** thick-soled wooden shoes.

THE PEARL POET fl. 1370

The resemblances among the four poems in the Middle English Manuscript Cotton Nero A X are so great that they seem to point to a common author. Although it has been argued that the last of the four, reprinted here, is the work of a different author, final proof is yet to be offered, and it is still not unreasonable to assume that all four were written by one man, referred to here as the Pearl Poet, about 1370.

The first of these, Pearl, has already been described (p. 21), as have the second and the third poems, Purity (or Cleanness) and Patience. The last of them in order, Sir Gawain and the Green Knight, has been regarded as the cream of Middle English metrical romances. Instead of the usual manifold adventures that befall the hero, there are only two important events, and they are made to depend upon one another. The entire poem is told with a unity of effect and artistic coloring that are most unusual.

The two central incidents—the beheading incident and the incident of the lady of the castle—test respectively Gawain's physical courage and his fidelity to his word on the one hand and his chastity and moral courage on the other. The ultimate purpose of the romance, therefore, is clearly didactic; Sir Gawain and the Green Knight cannot be considered a true example of the chivalric romance, however thoroughly the Pearl Poet knew the usages of chivalric courtesy and conduct. Rather, the poem is a fine, poetic example of the moral romance (p. 16). Yet Gawain remains human—he flinches quite naturally under the first terrifying blow of the Green Knight's ax, and he does not emerge unscathed from the ordeal of the bed-chamber.

The two incidents are known elsewhere in medieval legendry, but they are combined only in this poem and in two later works closely imitative of Sir Gawain and the Green Knight. The beheading episode is paralleled in a medieval Irish romance, The Feast of Bricriu, even down to the detail of the three strokes aimed at Gawain in the final scene with the Green Knight. The figure of Gawain is a Welsh divinity, and all the important proper names in the story are also Celtic. But it is probable that the Pearl Poet had as his immediate source a French romance based on Celtic legends.

Some have seen in the motto, Evil to him who evil thinks (p. 89), the possibility that Sir Gawain and the Green Knight was written in honor of a particular knightly order, such as the Order of the Garter, of which the French quotation is the motto. One of the later English versions of the story, a fifteenth-century romance called The Green Knight, mentions the Knights of the Bath, but this Order was not in existence at the time of the Pearl Poet. Others have seen in the green color of the knight the badge of spring, and insist that the poem is a spring allegory.

The possibility that Sir Gawain and the Green Knight is a Garter poem is something to be inferred but not to be demonstrated. The presence of the motto might signify merely that the Pearl Poet was a courtier of Edward III, the sovereign who is said to have originated the motto. But all such inferences are playthings for the academic. What is truly important about Sir Gawain and the Green Knight is that it is a superb example of the medieval story-teller's art; it pictures a great romance hero, Gawain, in his best and most attractive moments, before he is debased to make room for the French Lancelot; it is a clear exposition of the ideals of physical and moral integrity demanded of the medieval knight; it combines powerful and vigorous narrative with a deep feeling for nature; it is sophisticated and yet neither cynical nor oversentimental.

The poem is told in four sections, or "fits", the verse form consists of irregular stanzas, which up to the last four lines are in unrimed alliterative verse. The stanzas average about twenty lines, but in each stanza the last five lines are much shorter than the others, and include one "bob" line of a single metrical foot. The opening stanza of the poem is given below, in it the peculiar West Midland dialect of the Pearl Poet is amply illustrated:

Siþen þe sege and þe assaut watȝ sesed at Troye,
þe borȝ brittened and brent to brondeȝ and askeȝ,
þe tulk þat þe trammes of tresoun þer wroȝt
Watȝ tried for his tricherie, þe trewest on erthe:
Hit watȝ Ennias þe athel and his highe kynde,
þat siþen depreced prouinces, and patrounes bicome
Welneȝe of al the wele in the West Iles.
Fro riche Romulus to Rome ricchis hym swyþe,
With gret bobbaunce þat burȝe he biges vpon fyrst,
And neuenes hit his aune nome, as hit now hat;
Ticius to Tuskan and teldes bigynnes,
Langaberde in Lumbardie lyftes vp homes,
And fer ouer þe French flod Felix Brutus
On mony bonkkes ful brode Bretayn he setteȝ
    Wyth wynne,
   Where werre and wrake and wonder
   Bi syþeȝ hatȝ wont þerinne,
   And oft boþe blysse and blunder
   Ful skete hatȝ skyfted synne.

Here, as in the Old English (p. 26), þ is the symbol of the Modern English th-sounds. ȝ is a symbol of several sounds. In the works of the Pearl Poet its use is peculiar: in final position it seems to represent a z-sound, as in brondeȝ and askeȝ ("brands and ashes") in the second line. At the beginning of a word it represents a rather guttural y-sound, and also in the middle of a word before an e or i (cf. burȝe). But in the middle of a word before t it is clearly a spirant sound like the German ch or the Scottish loch (as in wroȝt, "wrought," pronounced here "wrocht").

SIR GAWAIN AND THE GREEN KNIGHT

Prose translation by George K. Anderson

After the siege and assault of Troy, after the city had been shattered and burnt to brands and ashes, and the man who had wrought stratagems of treason had been tried for his trickery—the veriest upon earth—it was Aeneas the noble and his exalted family who then vanquished nations and became sovereigns of well nigh all the lands in the Western Isles. So proud Romulus turned to Rome and with great pomp built that city (and named it with his name, which it bears today); Ticius moved to Tuscany and began

5. **Aeneas the noble.** It was the medieval tradition that Troy had been captured through the machinations of Aeneas. The Trojan prince had concealed from the Greeks the maiden Polyxena, beloved of Achilles; it was Achilles' desire to wed Polyxena that resulted in his being slain by the Trojan prince Paris. As a result of Achilles' death, the siege of Troy, which had been almost brought to an end, was resumed, and the

city was eventually taken. The medieval tradition held that Aeneas was tried by the Greeks for having lured Achilles and was exiled from the city. But in Vergil's *Aeneid*, he was obliged to flee at the sack of Troy. 10. **Ticius . . . Tuscany.** Who Ticius was we do not know. It is altogether likely, however, that Ticius, like Langobard (p. 68, l. 1), was the name of a fictitious descendant of Aeneas.

there his habitation; Langobard in Lombardy raised up homes for himself; and far over the French flood Felix Brutus established on many a shore broad Britain with joy, where wars and waste and wonder by turns have dwelt therein, and often bliss as well as bale have followed one another quickly enow.

And when Britain had been built by this mighty man, brave warriors flourished who loved strife, and many a time they wrought woe. Since that time more 10 wonders have come to pass in this land than in any other of which I have knowledge. But of all the kings of Britain who lived here, Arthur was ever the most gracious, as I have heard tell. And so I desire to make known an adventure that befell in the land (many men consider it a marvel), most surprising even among the many wonders of Arthur's reign. If ye will listen to this lay for a little while, I shall tell it to you straightway, as I heard it told with tongue, and as it has been set forth in story stout and strong, 20 fixed with true letters, as it has long been known in the land.

King Arthur lay at Camelot of a Christmastide, with many a splendid lord, the best men in the world. With him in princely fashion was all the mighty brotherhood of the Round Table. There was many a rich revel and careless joy; there folk tourneyed again and again; the noble knights jousted fairly, then repaired to the court to sing carols. For full fifteen days the feast lasted, with all the food and merriment 30 that man could devise, such riotous glee glorious to hear, sounding forth by day, and lovesome dancing by night. There was good fortune everywhere in halls and chambers among lords and ladies, as they most desired. With all the joy in the world they lived there together: the most famous knights in Christendom and the loveliest ladies that ever lived, and the comeliest king that ever held court. For this fair people was in its youth, the happiest under Heaven; their king the greatest on earth; it would be 40 hard now to name so brave a hero in all the land.

The New Year was so recently come that it had barely arrived. The people on the dais were served double that day. The king had come with all his knights into the hall; the ceremony in the chapel had been brought to a close. Loud were the cries raised by clerks and by others; Noel was celebrated anew and named full often. Gallant men hastened to give their gifts—gave them and asked for them both— admired and talked about the gifts one to another. 50 Ladies laughed aloud, even when they were overlooked (and those that received were not wroth, ye may well believe!). All this revelry they kept until meal-

time. When they had washed, full worthily they went to their seats; the best knights above, as befitted their rank. Then came Guinevere gay, in royal attire, and sat on the dais amid pomp and pleasure. Of fine silk was the seat; above her a canopy of costly Toulouse, hung with tapestries from Tars that were embroidered and embossed with the fairest of gems that could be bought with money and be proved of 60 value. She was the fairest of all to behold; her gray eyes shone; no man could say truthfully that he ever saw one more beautiful.

But Arthur would not eat till all were served; he was so glad in his joy, even as a child; his desire was for an easy life; he could abide neither to lie long nor to sit; his young blood and impetuous brain so worked upon him. And also another habit was fast upon him, which came from his nobility: he would never eat on such a delightful day until some strange 70 kind of wondrous tale had been recounted, some story of mighty marvel, which he could believe, of his ancestors, or of arms and other adventures; or until some strange knight should ask of him that he might join him in a joust and lay his life in jeopardy, life against life, one against another, as fortune might favor them. This was the king's wont when he was holding court, at every high feast among his noble retinue in the hall. And so, fair of face, he was sitting straight in his seat, making great mirth against 80 the New Year.

Thus the valiant king sat there before the high table, talking of light trifles; there good Gawain was seated by Guinevere, and Agravayne à la dure main was sitting on the other side. Both were sons of the King's sister and full courageous knights. Bishop Bawdewyn was at the end of the table; and Ywain, son of Urien, sat eating by himself. These were all worthily served on the dais; and at the lower tables many a valiant retainer. Then in came the first course amid 90 the crackling of trumpets, and many a bright banner waving, the rolling noise of drums with shrill pipes, wild music and melody awakened. Many a heart leaped high at those sounds; dainties were brought forth, full costly meats, abundance of fresh foods, and on so many dishes that it was difficult to find a place before the people to set the silver vessels with their savory viands. Each man took what he liked best; by every two were twelve dishes, good beer and bright wine. 100

Now I will tell you no more about their table-service, for all can understand that there was no lack of good things. For another sound was heard, and a new wonder that folk might well have left their

1. **Langobard,** the traditional ancestor of the Langobardi, or Lombards, a famous Germanic tribe. In myth he is called the great-grandson of Japhet and hence the great-great-grandson of Noah, also the nephew of Brutus (l. 3), a grandson of Aeneas and traditional founder of Britain. 20. **fixed . . . letters.** This phrase probably signifies, "written in alliterative verse." If so, the phrase "long been known in the land" immediately following bespeaks the fact that the alliterative devices had long been recognized in English poetry. 22. **Camelot.** This famous capital of King Arthur's realm was identified by the fifteenth-century romance writer Thomas Malory as Winchester, and this was the usual belief during the later Middle Ages. Another possibility is the town of Colchester; still others are Cadbury (Somersetshire) and Carlisle (Cumberland). But it is suggested by the frequent mention of *Logres* (see p. 73, l. 174, and note) in connection with Camelot that the capital and chief city of

labor to gaze upon. Scarcely had the hum of the banquet dwindled and the first course been served royally in the court, when there rushed in through the hall-door a terrible knight, the greatest in the world as to stature. From neck to loin he was so square and 110 thick-set, and his back and limbs were so long and broad that I think he must have been half giant. Certainly I believe he must have been the tallest of men and the lustiest in size that could ride on horse. His back and breast were sturdy and stout, but his belly and waist were nobly slender; and all his features alike clean-cut. But for his color men stood in wonder, as his semblance appeared clear: he came as a hostile knight, and was green all over.

This man was, indeed, clad all in green; a green 120 cloak clung to his sides, and a simple mantle over it, worthily lined with fur showing clearly and with cloth full clean. Of bright fur, too, was the hood that was thrown back from his locks and lay on his shoulders. Beautifully trimmed was the hem of his coat, and he wore hose of that same green, fastened neatly to the calves of his leg, and clean spurs attached of bright gold, with silken clasps striped most regally, and neat pads under his legs to protect him from galling. All his vesture, in truth, was of pure green, and the 130 ornaments of his belt and fair stones in his girdle, that were nobly arrayed in neat order about his waist and his saddle, on a silk cloth. It would be too tedious to tell of half the adornments that were woven thereon—birds and insects in gay gauds of green, with gold amid them. There were trappings on the neck of his steed and on the crupper; all the ornaments there were of metal and enamel. The stirrups that he stood in were stained green; and the pommel of his saddle, like the stirrups, gleamed and shone with 140 green jewels. The horse that he rode upon, forsooth, was of that same hue, a steed hard to restrain, strong and powerful, in embroidered bridle, full meet for its rider.

Gaily was this knight attired in green, as was the hair of his fine steed. Fair-flowing hair fell over the knight's shoulders; a beard as great as a bush hung over his breast, which, together with his lordly hair on his head, was clipped round about above his elbows, and half his sleeves were clasped in the same 150 manner as is a king's mantle, which encloses the neck. The mane of the horse was curled and twisted with many a knot folded in with gold thread over that fair green; here a twist of hair; there a flash of gold. Both the mane and the tail were tied in like manner and bound around with a band of bright green, decked with precious stones to the very end

of the tail, and tied aloft with a very subtle knot. There many bells of shining gold rang out full bright. Such a horse or such a knight to ride him had never been seen before in that hall by man's eye; he flashed 160 like lightning, so that men who looked upon him said it appeared that no man could survive the stroke of the knight.

But the knight had no helmet nor hauberk, no gorget, nor armor to cover his arms, no spear nor shield to fend or to smite with. Only in his hand he carried a holly-bough, that is greenest when the groves are bare. In the other hand he bore an ax, huge and monstrous, a cruel battle-weapon if one could but describe it. The head of the ax was a full ell long; 170 the grain of green steel and of gold; the blade burnished bright, with a broad edge, as able to shear as the sharpest of razors. The strong man held it set on a stout staff which was braced with iron down to the end of the wood, and all engraved with green in cunning work. A lace was wrapped about it, that was looped over the head and then fastened to the handle; attached to it were costly tassels hanging from buttons of bright green full richly bedecked.

This knight rode in through the entrance of the 180 hall, pushing his way up to the dais, fearing no harm. He saluted never a one, but looked over them all. The first word that he uttered was, "Where is the ruler of this company? Gladly would I see that man with my eyes, and speak with him in very truth." On the knights he cast his glance and swaggered up and down, then stopped still and studied them to see who was the most renowned.

Then there was long looking to gaze upon that knight, for every man marveled what it might mean, 190 that a hero and a horse should have such a hue, as green as grown grass and perhaps greener even than green enamel shining on gold. All that stood there gazed upon him and stepped nearer, with all the wonder in the world, to see who he might be. Many a strange sight had they seen, but never such a one as this; therefore the people thought it a phantasm or faerie. Many were afraid to give him answer, and were astounded at his voice; they sat stone-still in a heavy silence through that noble hall; their talking 200 ceased as if they had been struck with slumber. I believe it was not so much for fear as for courtesy: they would let him whom all should defer to speak himself to that knight.

So Arthur beheld this marvel before his high dais; he greeted the stranger in knightly fashion (never was he rash), and said: "Knight, welcome in truth to this place! My name is Arthur, lord of this hall; light

Arthurian romance was in the southern part of England. 28. sing carols. The "carols" were in reality group dances accompanied by song; originally they were ring dances. 58. Toulouse . . . Tars. Toulouse, a city in southern France, was famous during the Middle Ages for its silk stuffs. Tars is the usual Middle English version of Tharsia, the old name for Turkestan. The cloth imported from Tars was of uncertain material, but was obviously very costly, and is mentioned as synonymous with cloth

of gold. 85. sons . . . sister. Note that Gawain and Arthur have the traditional close epic relationship of nephew to uncle; other examples occur in Beowulf (see p. 30, l. 326). 118. green, etc. Green was a fairy color, hence quite appropriate to this particular knight. Mythologists say, however, that the Green Knight's magic is symbolic of immortal spring.

down, fair sir, and tarry; we shall know later what thy will is." "Nay, so help me," quoth the knight, "He that sits on high; to stay any time in this dwelling was not my errand. But because the renown of this people has been so exalted, because thy castle and thy warriors are esteemed the best and the bravest to ride on steeds under steel harness, the strongest and worthiest of all mankind and proven of excellence in knightly sports—therefore courtesy has flourished here, as I have heard tell; and that has drawn me hither, forsooth, at this time. Ye may be sure by this branch which I bear here that I come in peace and seek no strife. For if I had come in warlike manner with a band beside me—well, I have a hauberk at home and a helmet also; a shield and a sharp spear, shining bright, and other weapons to wield, as I can vouchsafe. But because I desire no war, my garments are softer! If thou art as bold as all men say, thou wilt grant me by rights the sport that I ask." Arthur answered and said: "Sir courteous knight, if thou cravest a mere battle, thou shalt not fail to fight here!"

"Nay," said the knight, "I seek no fight, in faith; about this bench I see naught but beardless children. If I were enclosed in armor upon a lofty steed, there would be no man here to match me, so weak is their strength. And so I crave in this court a Christmas-game, for it is Yule and New Year, and here are many active men. If any one in this hall considers himself so hardy, be his blood so bold or the brain in his head, that he dare strike one stroke for another, I shall give him as a gift this mighty ax, which is heavy enough for him to handle as he pleases; and I will abide the first blow, unarmed as I sit here. If any man be so fierce as to try what I propose, let him leap swiftly upon me, and take his weapon. I quit claim to it; he may keep it as his own. I shall stand his stroke, firm on this floor. If so, thou shalt grant me the right to deal him another, in faith; and yet I shall give him respite for a year and a day. Now hasten, and let us see whether any one here say aught!"

If he had astonished them at first, now all were more silent than ever—all Arthur's followers in the hall, high and low. The warrior on his steed fixed himself in his saddle and rolled his red eyes about most violently, bent his beetling brows, glittering green; he twisted his beard about while he waited for whoever would rise. When none would retort to him, he coughed loudly and spoke to them in loud mockery: "What? Is this Arthur's house, whose fame runs through so many realms? Where is your haughtiness and your conquests, your fierceness and your anger and your mighty words? Now the glory and renown of the Round Table has been overturned by the words of one man; for all fear out of dread, and not a blow seen!" With that he laughed so loud that

it grieved the king; the blood rushed for shame into his fair face; he was as angry as the blast of winter—so were all that were there. The king so brave by nature stepped near to that stern knight, and said: "Knight, by Heaven, thy request is strange; and since thou hast sought folly, thou must in truth find it! I know of no man here that is afraid of thy big words! Give me now thine ax, in God's name, and I shall grant thy boon which thou hast demanded."

Lightly he leaped at the knight and caught at his hand; then fiercely the knight dismounted. Now Arthur has taken the ax and grasped it by the handle and stoutly brandished it, thinking to strike. The sturdy knight towered over the king, higher than any in the house by a head or more; with grisly cheer he stood there and stroked his beard and with an immovable countenance drew aside his coat, no more frightened or dismayed at the king's threatened blows than if some man on the benches had brought him a draught of wine. Then Gawain, who was sitting by the king, leaned toward him and spoke: "I beseech thee now, of a truth, that this affair be mine."

"Would ye, noble lord," said Gawain to the king, "but bid me rise from this bench and stand by you there, that I without discourtesy may leave the table and not displease my liege-lady, I would come to your counsel before your royal court. For it seems to me not seemly, if the truth be known, when such a demand be raised high in your hall, that you should be desirous of taking it upon yourself, while many men so bold are sitting about on the benches—there are not, I hope, men of more precious courage under the heavens, nor better bodies for fighting when strife is lifted up. I know that I am the weakest of them and the feeblest of understanding; and less would be the loss of my life, if the truth were told. Save that you are my uncle there is little to praise in me; I know no virtue in my body save your blood. And since this business is so strange that it is not fitting for you to assume it, and since I have asked it of you first, grant it to me, and if I speak not in comely fashion, let all this court still be without blame." Then the mighty knights all counseled with one accord that the crowned king withdraw and give Gawain the venture.

Then the king commanded the knight to arise; and he rose up full quickly and fixed him fair. Then he knelt down again before the king and grasped the weapon; the king graciously relinquished it to Gawain, and lifted up his hand and gave him God's blessing and was fain to pray that his heart and his hand should both be valiant. "Keep thyself, nephew," said the king, "and set thyself for one blow; if thou hast heard him aright, I think that thou must abide a blow that he will give thee in return." Gawain advanced against the stranger with the ax in his hand; the stranger boldly awaited him, no whit abashed. Then that knight in green said to Sir Gawain: "Let us renew our agreement ere we proceed further. First I ask thee, Sir Knight, what thy name is; thou must tell me truly, so I may trust it." "In good faith," said the good knight, "Gawain I call myself, 120 who offer thee this buffet, whatsoever may befall later. And this time twelvemonth I shall take from thee another, with whatsoever weapon thou wilt, and with none other to help me, none in the world." The other replied: "Sir Gawain, so may I prosper, I am fair and fain to receive the blow that thou shalt direct."

"By God," quoth the Green Knight, "Sir Gawain, it pleases me that I shall take from thy fist what I have asked for here. Thou hast readily rehearsed, 130 correctly indeed, the covenant that I requested of the king; but thou must assure me, knight, by thy troth, that thou shalt seek me thyself, wheresoever thou dost believe I am to be found on the earth, and shalt get for thyself such rewards as thou dealest to me today in the presence of this mighty troop." "Where am I to seek thee," asked Gawain; "where is thy home? I know not where thou dwellest, by Him that made me; nor do I know thy court, O knight, nor thy name. But teach me truly thereto, and tell me 140 thy name, and I shall use all my wits to get myself thither. That I swear of a truth, and by my firm troth." "That is enough on the New Year; we need no more," quoth the warrior in green to Gawain the gracious. "If I tell thee truly, after I have received the stroke, and thou hast struck me in all honor, quickly I will tell thee of my house and my home and mine own name; then thou canst ask my business and keep covenant. And if I waste no speech, so much the better for thee, for thou canst stay longer in thy 150 land, and seek no farther. But enough, take now thy grim weapon and let us see how thou canst strike." "Gladly, sir, forsooth," quoth Gawain, stroking his ax.

The Green Knight quickly made him ready on the ground; he bowed his head a little and uncovered his countenance; his long fair locks he laid over his head and let the naked neck show for the ax. Gawain gripped his weapon and gathered it aloft; his left foot he placed forward on the earth, then let the 160 blade fall quickly on the bare neck. The sharp edge shattered the bones of the stranger, bit through the fair skin and sheared it in two, so that the brown steeled blade ate into the ground. The fair head fell from the neck to earth; many kicked it with their feet as it rolled about; the blood spurted from the body and glistened on the green. Yet the strange warrior never faltered or fell, but stoutly leaped upon sturdy legs, rushed forth and reached out where the warriors were standing, caught up his fair head and 170 lifted it up. Then he turned to his steed, caught the bridle, stepped into the stirrup and mounted; he held

his head by the hair with his hand. And he settled himself in his saddle as calmly as if no accident had befallen him there, although he was headless. He turned his horse about—his ugly body bleeding all the while; many were in terror of him and greatly distrusted the covenant.

For he held up his head in his hand, raising the face toward the most valiant king on the dais. And the head raised its eyelids and looked full about and spoke 180 these words with its mouth, as you may now hear: "Look, Gawain, that thou be ready to go as thou didst promise and seek faithfully, O knight, until thou dost find me, as thou didst promise in this hall in the presence of these knights. Take thy way to the Green Chapel, I charge thee, to get such a blow deservedly as thou hast dealt, to be yielded thee promptly next New Year's Morn. Many men know me as the knight of the Green Chapel; therefore, if thou dost ask to find me, thou wilt never fail. So 190 come, or be called recreant and coward!" Then the stranger turned his bridle and rushed out in a gallop, so that sparks flew up from the hooves of his horse. To what land he went, none there could tell any more than they knew whence he had come. And then? The king and Gawain laughed and joked at that Green Knight; yet it assuredly had been a marvel for those knights to behold.

Then King Arthur was astounded at heart, although he let no hint be given of his wonder, but said aloud 200 to the comely queen in fair speech: "Dear lady, be never dismayed today; such a marvel well becomes Christmastide, when we lack entertainment, laughing or singing, or fair carols sung by knights and ladies. But now I can turn to my food, for I have seen a miracle I can never forget." He looked at Sir Gawain and quickly said: "Now, sir, hang up thine ax; it has hewn enough." So it was placed above the dais, hanging on the back of a seat, where all men could look upon it as a marvel, and by its true 210 evidence tell of the wonder. Then they bowed them to bench, did these warriors together, the king and the good knight, and brave men served them a double portion of all dainties, as was the share of the most valiant—with all manner of meats and minstrelsy as well. In well-being they spent that day on earth, until it came to an end.

Now bethink thee well, Sir Gawain, that thou delay not to seek the harm-fraught adventure which thou hast taken upon thee.   220

2

This beginning of adventures befell Arthur on the New Year, for he yearned to hear of deeds of glory, though his words were few when he sat at his feasts. But now their hands were filled aplenty with grim work. Gawain was glad to begin the game in the

hall, but ye need have no wonder that the end was hard. For though a man be merry in mind when he has had strong drink, a year passes full quickly and never brings again its like; the beginning and the ending accord full seldom. And so this Yule departed, and the year after, and each season in turn followed upon another. After Christmas came crabbed Lent, that tries flesh with fish and simpler foods; then the weather of the world struggles against winter; the cold
10 shrinks away, the clouds uplift themselves; bright pours the rain down in warm showers and falls on the fair fields; flowers peep forth; green are the garments of earth and grove; birds make them ready to build and sing with passion for the solace of soft summer that comes down from the heights. Then bursting blossoms burgeon forth in rich and rank hedgerows, and noble notes enow are heard in the fair woodlands.

After the season of summer with its soft winds,
20 when Zephirus breathes on seeds and grasses—very joyous are the roots that grow thereout—then the moistening dew drips from the leaves, awaiting a blissful glance from the bright sun. But autumn approaches and hardens the seeds, warning them to grow full ripe before winter; in drought he drives the dust in clouds; it whirls aloft over the face of the earth. Angry winds in the heavens wrestle with the sun; leaves drop from the linden and alight on earth; the grass turns gray that once was green. Then all
30 that at first was blooming ripens and rots. So the year passes away into many yesterdays, and winter winds are returned, for which no man need wonder.

When the Michaelmas moon had come with its warnings of winter, Gawain bethought him of his wearisome journey. But he lingered with Arthur until All Souls' Day. And Arthur partook of that feast for the sake of his nephew amid all the rich revel of the Round Table, with knights full courteous and comely ladies. Yet all were in sorrow for the knight Gawain;
40 but nevertheless they spoke of naught but mirth, although many who made there courtly play were joyless. For after the feast, Gawain sadly spoke to his uncle, and mentioned his departure, saying aloud: "Now, liege-lord of my life, I ask your leave. You know the matter of this affair; I need not tell you of the trouble. I am ready unconditionally for the blow; tomorrow I go to seek the man in green, as God will make him known to me." Then gathered together all the best in the castle: Ywain, and Erec,
50 and full many another, Sir Dodinel le Sauvage, the Duke of Clarence, Lancelot, and Lionel, and Lucan the good, Sir Bors and Sir Bedivere, both mighty

men, and many other honorable knights, with Mador de la Port. All this company of the court approached the king to counsel the knight, with care in their hearts. In that hall there was much secret grief pressing at their hearts that so worthy a knight as Gawain should go on that adventure, to endure a grievous blow and not be able to return it with his sword. But the knight kept good cheer and said: 60 "Why should I shrink? What can a man do but try his fate, whether stern or pleasant?"

He dwelt there all that day, and arose in the morning and asked for his arms. They were all brought him. First a royal carpet was stretched over the floor, and great was the gold gear that glittered upon it. The valiant knight stepped thereon, and handled his steel. He was dressed in a doublet of precious silk from Tars, and then in a close hood of crafty design that was lined within with a bright-colored fur. Then they 70 set steel shoes upon the knight's feet; his legs they lapped in steel with ornamented greaves and knee-pieces fastened thereto, brightly polished; about his knees they were riveted with knots of gold. Well-fitting cuisses closed with thongs firmly encased his stout and brawny thighs; then the woven corselet of bright steel rings sewn on a fair stuff they fitted upon the knight; and well-burnished braces on both his arms, with good and gay elbow-pieces, and gloves of mail, and all the goodly gear that would help him 80 in his time of trouble. Thus Gawain stood forth in rich coat of mail, his gold spurs proudly added, girt with a trusty brand, and a silk girdle about his waist.

When he was clad in arms, his war-harness was costly—the smallest latchet or loop gleamed of gold. And harnessed as he was he heard mass celebrated, and made his offering at the high altar. Then he came to the king and his companions of the court, took fairly his leave of lords and ladies; and they kissed him and escorted him forth, committing him to Christ. 90 By that time Gringolet was ready, and girded with a saddle that gleamed full gay with its many gold hangings, richly studded anew for that adventure; the bridle was barred about and braced with bright gold thread; the adornment of the neck-piece and of the sweeping saddle-skirts, the crupper and coverture, all matched the saddle-bow: all were bordered with rich, red-gold buttons that glittered and gleamed like the light of the sun. Then Gawain caught up his helmet and hastily kissed it; that helmet was stoutly braced and 100 stuffed within. It towered high on his head, fastened behind with a light linen kerchief over the aventail, embroidered and bedecked with the best of gems and having a broad silken border and designs of birds:

33. **Michaelmas moon,** the moon which would come to the full about Michaelmas (September 29), hence any time near the coming of autumn. *All Souls' Day* (l. 36) is a celebrated religious holiday of the autumn season. 49. **Ywain . . . Mador de la Port.** It is perhaps unnecessary to give here detailed comment about all the famous names in this catalogue; from the standpoint of Middle English romances, the most im-

portant are Lancelot, Lucan, Bors, and Bedivere. All of these except Lucan participated in the Quest of the Holy Grail. 91. **Gringolet,** with Roland's *Veillantif,* perhaps the most famous steed of medieval legendry. The French form *Guingalet* suggests that he was a Celtic horse, color white (cf. Welsh *gwen,* "white"). 102. **aventail,** the ventail, or movable front of the helmet, sometimes called the "beaver." 116.

preening parrots, turtledoves, and true-loves so closely interwoven as many a maiden in the town had wrought seven years in the making. The circle atop his helmet was of still greater cost; it was a device of diamonds, that were both light and dark.

110 Then they showed him his shield, that was of bright red, with the pentangle painted thereon in pure gold color. He seized it by the baldric and cast it about his neck; it became the knight wondrous fair. And why the pentangle pertained to that noble knight I purpose to tell you, though it delay my story. It is a sign that Solomon set erewhile, as betokening truth; it has its name because it is a figure that has five points, and each line overlaps and is locked in another; ever it is endless, and the English call it 120 everywhere, so I have heard, the "endless knot." Therefore it was fitting for this knight and for his shining arms; for Gawain was known before God as faithful ever in five and many times five various ways, and as refined gold, void of every impurity, and adorned with all virtue in the assemblage. And so this fresh pentangle he bore on shield and coat, the knight truest of speech and noblest of form.

For first he was faultless in his five senses; and the knight had never failed in his five fingers; and 130 all his faith on this earth was in the five wounds that Christ got on the Cross, as the creed tells. And wheresoever this knight was beset in conflict, his earnest thought was in this above all other things: that all his vigor he received from the five joys that the gracious Queen of Heaven had in her Child. For this reason the knight had in the greater part of his shield the image of Our Lady painted, so that, when he looked upon it, his courage could never flag. The fifth five that I find Gawain used were frankness, 140 and fellowship above all; in cleanness and courtesy he was never found wanting; nor in pity that surpasses everything—these virtues five were more firmly wrapped about that hero than about any other. All these, five-fold, forsooth, were linked together in this knight, and each but attached to the other; but they never ended; and were fixed at five points, which never failed. Nor did they ever merge, neither were they ever sundered; everywhere, at all points, they were endless and without a beginning as well. Where- 150 fore on his bright shield this knot was shaped, red-gold upon red; that is the pure pentangle; the people call it so by tradition. Now Sir Gawain was gaily armed; he caught up his lance, and gave them all good-day—he thought, forever.

He smote his steed with the spurs and sprang on his way, so sternly that he struck fire from the stones.

All that saw that seemly sight sighed in their hearts; all folk said truly to each other, in care for that comely knight: "By Christ, it is a pity, that thou, O knight, shouldst be lost, that art of such a pure life! 160 To find his equal in the world, in faith, will not be easy. It would have been wiser to have acted more warily; yonder brave knight should have become a duke; a shining leader of men he is worthy to be, and would have been that more fittingly than cut to pieces or brought low by an elvish man with the pride of arrogance. Whoever knew a king to take such counsel as to put his knights to a venture as a Christmas jest!" Many were the warm tears that were shed when that seemly knight departed from the court that day. But 170 he did not tarry; he went on his way swiftly over many a wild road, as I heard say in the book.

Now the knight was riding through the realm of Logres, Sir Gawain in a good cause, though it seemed to him no sport. Often he lay companionless, alone in the night, nor did he find there the fare that would have pleased him. He had no comrade but his horse, over the woodlands and downs; and there was no one but God with whom he could take counsel. At length he drew full near to North Wales; he kept all the 180 isles of Anglesey on his left and crossed over the fords by the foreland at Holyhead, until he finally passed into the wilderness of Wirral. There dwelt few who loved either God or good men in their hearts. But as Gawain went along, he kept asking folk that he met if they had heard any talk of a green knight anywhere about, or of the Green Chapel. All answered him nay; never in their lives had they seen any such a man of such a green hue. Gawain took strange paths over many an impassable height; 190 full often was his mood to change before he could find the Green Chapel.

Many a cliff he climbed over in strange countries; far away from his friends he rode along as a stranger. At every water-ford and stream that the knight passed he found a foe before him, and one so marvelous and so foul and fierce that it behooved Gawain to fight. It would be too tedious to tell the tenth part of all his adventures; so many wonders befell the knight on his journeyings. Sometimes he fought with 200 dragons and with wolves; sometimes with wild men that lived in the stone-cliffs; with bulls and bears, and sometimes with boars; with giants of the high moorlands who were wont to attack him. Had he not been doughty and stern and a servant of the Lord, doubtless he had been dead, for he was often near to being slain. Yet the fighting troubled him not so much; the winter was worse, when cold clear water was

Solomon . . . erewhile. Solomon's seal consisted of a pentangle, or five-pointed star (cf. l. 114), circumscribed by a circle. The symbol is still to be found in synagogues and in Freemasonry, and is supposed to have originated in the Temple of Solomon. **120. endless knot,** so-called because the interlacing lines are joined in such a way that they are continuous. **134. five joys.** The five joys of the Virgin Mary were usually considered to be the joys in the Annunciation, the Nativity, the Resurrection, the Ascension, and the Assumption, although the list varied slightly with different medieval writers. **174. Logres,** the term applied in Welsh legendry to England south of the River Humber. Since the knight's course is northerly (ll. 180 ff.), it is to be assumed therefore that Camelot is in the southern part of England (see p. 68, l. 22 and note).

shed from the clouds and froze ere it could fall upon the fallow earth. Nearly slain by the sleet he slept in his armor; on more nights than enow on bare rocks, where the cold brook rushed down bubbling from the hill-crest and hung high over his head in hard icicles. Thus in peril and pain and plights full hard, Gawain toiled over the countryside all alone, until Christmas Eve, and on that night he made his prayer to Mary, that she should guide him to some
10 dwelling.

In the morning he rode merrily by a hill into a full deep forest that was fearsome and wild; high hills were on each side of it, and thick woods below them, huge hoary oaks a hundred or more. The hazel and the hawthorn stood there intertwined, with rough ragged moss trailing everywhere and many birds sitting unhappily upon bare twigs, piping piteously for pain of the cold. The knight rode beneath them on Gringolet through many a marsh and quagmire, alone and
20 fearful lest he should not be able to perform the service of our Lord, who on that selfsame night was born of a maiden to allay all our woe. And sighing therefore he said: "I beseech You, Lord, and Mary, that is most mild and precious of mothers, that You grant me some lodging, that I may fittingly hear mass, and Your matins tomorrow. Meekly I ask it and thereto I pray my paternoster and creed." He rode praying and lamented his misdeeds, blessing himself many times and saying: "May the cross of Christ
30 speed me!"

He had not crossed himself, that knight, more than three times before he was aware of a dwelling in the wood surrounded by a moat, above a lawn on a hill, enclosed by many a burly oak-tree that grew about the moat. There was a castle, the comeliest that lord ever possessed, built in a meadow with a park all about it; a spiked palisade closely driven enclosed the trees for more than two miles. The knight saw the castle from one side, as its lights gleamed
40 through the bright oaks. He seized hold of his helmet in joy, and uttered thanks to Jesus and Saint Julian (both are noble), who had courteously made known to him this abode and had hearkened to his prayer. "Now I beseech You yet," quoth the warrior, "that I may have good lodging!" Then he pricked Gringolet with his gilded heels; he rode casually up to the main gate, and came soon to the end of the bridge. The drawbridge had been raised, and the gates were shut fast. The walls were strong; no blast of wind
50 need they fear.

The knight waited on the bank of the deep double ditch that surrounded the place. As he sat on his charger, he saw that the walls were set in the water wondrous deep; and the building towered aloft to a tremendous height. It was of hard hewn stone up to

the corbels, which were adorned under the battlements with excellent taste; many fair watchtowers were placed in between with many well-made loopholes. Never had the knight seen a better barbican. Within he could see the high hall and the tower built 60 with thick cornices; fair turrets marvelously high, with carved capitals, cunningly wrought. He could see chalk-white chimneys on the turreted roofs that shone full white. Many pinnacles were scattered everywhere among the battlements, so thick and white that they seemed to be cut out of paper. The noble knight on his steed thought it all fair enow; he wanted to gain the shelter within, to take lodging in that castle, until pleasant Holy-day had passed. He called, and straightway there came a kindly-faced porter, 70 who stood on the wall, and asked the knight errant in his greeting, what his errand might be.

"Good sir," said Gawain, "wilt thou take my message to the high lord of this house, and crave for me shelter?" "Yea, by Peter," quoth the porter, "truly, I think, O sir knight, you are welcome to stay here while it pleases you." Then the servant went quickly and with him many folk to receive the knight. They let down the great drawbridge, and came forth graciously, and knelt down upon the cold earth, to 80 welcome Gawain as was fitting. They opened for him the broad gate; when it was ready, he bade them rise, and rode over the bridge. Many men held his saddle horse while he dismounted; and bold men enow then stabled his steed. Knights and squires came down to bring the warrior with honor into the hall. When he raised up his helmet, there were many to take it from his hand and serve the gracious knight; his sword and his shield they also received. Then Gawain greeted full graciously each one of the retinue, and praised 90 there many a proud man in order to honor their prince. In his noble armor they escorted him to the hall, where a fair fire on the hearth was briskly burning. Then the lord of the castle came down from his chambers to meet with ceremony the knight in the hall; he said: "You are welcome to do here as it pleases you. What is here is all your own, to have and wield at your will." "Gramercy," said Gawain, "may Christ it requite you." As friends that were fain each one embraced the other. 100

Gawain gazed upon the lord that had greeted him in thus goodly fashion; and thought him a brave warrior who owned the castle—a mighty hero for the nonce, and of high age. Broad and shining was his beard and hued like a beaver; stern and stout was the stride of his stalwart legs. His face was as fierce as fire, but his speech was noble; and he seemed altogether able, so it seemed to Gawain, to be a lord and protector of full valiant men.

The lord led Gawain to a chamber and ordered a 110

retinue to serve his guest in loyal manner. At his bidding came men enow to escort Gawain to a fair bower. There the bedding was royal; the curtains of clean silk and clear gold hems; the counterpanes comely and of fairly embroidered linen. These curtains were run on ropes with red-gold rings; there were tapestries of Toulouse and Tars hung on the walls and carpets underfoot of the same material. There, with many a merry speech, Gawain was relieved of his 120 byrnie and of his bright armor, while alert servants brought him costly garments for him to wear, fair, radiant, and most choice. When he donned these clothes, he saw that they were seemly and fitted him well; the skirts of his mantle flowed gracefully. Truly that hero seemed to outtop all other knights in the fair complexion of his countenance, shining and radiant. It seemed to all that beheld him that Christ had never made a comelier knight. Whatever his origin, they thought that he must be a prince without peer 130 in the field where brave men fight.

Before the fireplace, where a charcoal fire was burning, a chair was placed for Sir Gawain, accoutered with fair cushions and hassocks that were of subtle artistry; and then a simple mantle was offered the knight of a brown samite, richly embroidered, and lined with skins of ermine, and a hood of the same stuff. So Gawain sat him down in that seemly regal chair and warmed himself first of all, and then his mood lightened. Straightway a table was raised up on 140 trestles, covered with a clean cloth that shone clear white; and there were set on that table salt-cellar and napkin and silver spoons. The knight washed at his will and then sat down before his meat. Men enow served him appropriately with several sweet viands, seasoned well, double portions, as it happened, and several kinds of fishes—some baked in bread, some broiled on the fire, some boiled, some in a sauce, savored with spices, with all kinds of subtle devices to please the knight's palate. Gawain called it a feast, 150 full graciously and often, while all the retinue entertained him with gaiety, for they said: "Now take this penance, and it shall be for your amendment." The knight made much mirth of that, for the wine had gone to his head.

Then they questioned Gawain in most temperate fashion, with skilfully chosen questions put to the knight himself, so that he acknowledged in courteous wise the court whence he had come; that noble Arthur the gracious, who was the rich royal king of the Round 160 Table, considered him one of his own knights; that it was Gawain himself who was sitting in that spot, come there on the Christmas, as chance would have it. When the lord heard that he was entertaining that knight, he laughed aloud; it seemed to him glad news indeed. And all the men in the place made great

joy, to be able to appear ready in his presence, for all worth and prowess and pure customs pertained to Gawain's person and had ever been praised. Before all men on earth his virtue had been the greatest. Each man said softly to his comrade: "Now we shall see 170 seemly manners and customs and the blameless terms of courtly talk; what charm lies in speech, we can learn without asking, for we have received in our midst the very father of courtesy. God has given us His goodly grace, forsooth, since He has granted us to have a goodly guest like Gawain, when men sit and sing with pleasure and joy of His birth. The true meaning of simple courtesy this knight will now bring us. I think that he who hears him will learn the subtle speech of love." 180

By that time the dinner was finished and Gawain had risen. It was near nightfall. Chaplains took their way to the chapel; the bells were rung loudly, even as they should be, for the devout evensong of Yule-tide. The lord went thither, and the lady also; she entered into a comely closet; Gawain gaily followed and straightway went thither. The lord caught him by the sleeve and led him to a seat and called him by his name, and told him he was the most welcome person in the world. Gawain thanked him truly, and each saluted 190 the other and sat together in dignity during the time of the service. Then the lady was pleased to look upon the knight; she came forth from her closet with many a fair maiden. But she herself was the fairest of countenance and complexion, of figure and hue and all other charms—even more beautiful than Guinevere, as the knight thought. She passed through the chancel to greet Gawain the gracious; another lady held her by the left hand and was older than she—a dowager, it appeared, with many nobles about her. But the 200 two ladies were unlike in looks; for if the younger was fair, the older was yellow. Rich red was the bloom on the cheeks of the one; rough wrinkled were the cheeks of the other. Kerchiefs with many a lucent pearl adorned the breast and bright throat of the one, and shone more dazzling than snow that falls on the hills. But the other wore on her neck a gorget, wimpling over her pale chin in milk-white folds; her forehead wrapped in silk worked in knots and bordered with trifling decorations. Only the black brows 210 of the dowager were bare, and her two eyes and nose and naked lips—and these were all sour to see and strangely bleared, though one could fairly call her an honorable lady. Her body was short and thick; her buttocks round and broad; far more pleasing to gaze upon was she who walked beside her.

When Gawain saw that gay lady who looked so gracious, he walked towards her, with full permission of the lord. He greeted the elder, bowing full low; but he took the younger lightly in his arms and kissed

was in Wirral has since been abandoned. It is more likely that the Green Knight lived in Cumberland, not far from Carlisle, where many stories of adventure about Arthur and his knights have collected.

41. **Saint Julian,** the patron saint of hospitality. 59. **barbican,** the outer fortification of a castle. 135. **samite,** a silken material.

her in seemly fashion, and spoke to her as became a knight. They hailed him as friend, and he quickly asked to be her servant in truth if it should please her. And so the two ladies escorted him, leading him, while talking, to the hall, before the hearth, and straightway called for spices, which men brought them without stint and right speedily, also good wine to be drunk at this season. The lord sprang to his feet and bade them make merry; he caught off his
10 hood and hung it on a spear, and said he should win the worship thereof who could make most mirth on that Christmas-tide. "And I shall try, by my faith, to contend with the rest, with the help of my friends, before I lose all my raiment!" So with laughing words the lord bestirred him to gladden Sir Gawain that night with games in the hall, until it was time to bid them light the hall. Then Sir Gawain took leave of them and prepared for rest.

On the morrow, when every man calls to mind that
20 Our Lord for our destiny was born to die (joy is breathed into every dwelling in the world for His sake)—so it was there on that day amid many delights. Brave men on the dais were dressed in their best, and there was many a feast and many a cunningly cooked dish. The old dowager sat highest; the lord respectfully was seated beside her. Gawain and the gay lady were together, even in the midst of the board, as the feast was worthily served to each man according to his rank. There were meat
30 and mirth and great joy; it would take me too long to speak thereof, and to describe it I could not though I might try. But I know that Gawain and the lovely lady found great pleasure in each other's company through her sweet words and courteous conversation, her gentle talk free from uncleanness, and her vivacious play charming and pure, fit for a prince. Trumpets and drums and merry piping sounded forth; each man hearkened to his minstrel; and they too hearkened to theirs.
40 High feast they held there that day and the next, and the third day that came in thereafter. The joy on St. John's Day was noble to hear; it was the last of the feast as the folk there intended. The guests were to depart on the gray morning; and so they woke early and drank wine, and danced with vigor to the sound of carols. At last, when it was late, they took their leave, each one departing on his way— that was a brave lord! Gawain gave him good-day; the bold lord took him by the hand, and led him to
50 his own chamber, beside the fireplace, and there he thanked him privately for the great honor that Gawain had bestowed upon him in coming to his castle at that high season, and in adorning his home with his fair countenance. "Surely, sir, while I live, I shall be held the better because Gawain has been my guest at God's own feast." "Gramercy, sir," re-

42. **St. John's Day**, December 27.   155. **trackers**, keepers of the hounds.

plied Gawain, "in good faith, all yours is the honor. May the High King grant it you. I am a knight at your will to do your behest, as I am beholden to you by rights in things both great and small." The 60 lord then endeavored to keep the knight longer; but Gawain answered him that he could nowise tarry.

Then the lord asked him full fairly what stern mission had driven him, at that sacred feast, to depart all alone from his king's court so boldly, ere the holiday's holly had been carried from the town. "Forsooth, sir," quoth Gawain, "you say but the truth; it was a lofty mission and a pressing one that drove me from my home, for I myself am summoned to seek a certain place—I know not where in the world to 70 turn to find it. So help me the Lord, I would give all the land in Logres to find it before New Year's Morn. Therefore, sir, I make this request of you here, that you tell me truly, if you ever heard tell of the Green Chapel or where it stands, or of the knight who keeps it, so green of color? There was established by agreement a compact between us; I must meet that man at that appointed place if I can do so; and of that same New Year there lacks little or no time. I would look on that knight, if God but let me, 80 more gladly, by God's Son, than on any fair sight! Therefore, ywis, by your will, it behooves me to go; I have now but barely three days for the business; I had liefer fall doomed as fail in my errand." Then the lord said, laughing: "Now indeed you must stay; for I shall show you that place by the appointed time, that Green Chapel forsooth. So grieve you no longer. You can take your ease, knight, in your bed till the fourth day; then you can ride on the first of the year and come to the appointed place at mid- 90 morn, to do what you like at that time. Dwell here till New Year's Day; then rise and ride thither. We shall set you on your way; it is not two miles hence."

Then Gawain was full glad, and laughed merrily. "Now I thank you heartily for every thing. Now my quest is achieved; I shall linger here at your service, and do aught else you desire." Then the lord took him and set him beside him; he had the ladies fetched in to please them the better, though they had solace between themselves. The lord for his joy made merry 100 jests, as a man who knew not what to do for his delight. Then he spoke to Gawain, crying aloud: "You have decided to do what I bid you. Will you keep that promise here for the nonce?" "Yea, my lord, forsooth," said Gawain the true, "while I stay in your castle, I shall be obedient to your behests." "Now since you have traveled," said the lord, "from a far-off land, and then watched with me, you have not been refreshed either by rest or by sleep, as I truly perceive. You shall stay in your chamber and 110 lie at your ease tomorrow at mass-tide, and go to meat when you will with my wife. She shall sit with you and console you with her company. Tarry here

until I return home; I shall rise early and go a-hunting."
To all this Gawain agreed, keeping his word as a
gracious man should.

"Yet further," said the lord, "we shall make a
covenant. Whatsoever I win in the wood, it shall be
yours; and whatever fortune you achieve, give it to
120 me in exchange. Good friend, let us so exchange, and
swear it by oath, whether our fortunes, sir knight, be
for better or for worse." "By God," said Gawain the
good, "I agree; and whatever it pleases you to
propose; I shall do thy bidding." "Bring us the wine-
cup; the bargain is made," said the lord of the castle.
They laughed each one; they drank and made merry
and passed the time of day until night, did these
lords and ladies, as it pleased them. Then with gay
talk and many a merry jest they arose and stood and
130 spoke softly, kissed full sweetly, and took leave of
each other. With many a graceful serving-man and
gleaming torches, each knight retired at last to his
bed full soft. But before they went to bed they rehearsed the covenant, for the old lord of the castle
knew well how to make sport.

3

Very early before daybreak the folk rose up; the
guests who would go called their grooms and made
themselves quickly ready; they saddled their steeds
and arranged the harness; set the girths in order, and
140 packed up their bags. The knights dressed themselves
and came forth arrayed for riding; they leaped lightly
to horse, took up their bridles, and each man went on
his way as he pleased. The noble lord of the land
was not the last to prepare for riding, nor the many
men with him. He ate a sop hastily, after he had
heard mass. With a blast of the bugle he fared forth to
the uplands. Before any daylight shone upon earth, he
and his retinue were mounted on their lofty steeds.
Then those huntsmen who knew the sport well coupled
150 their hounds, unclosed the kennel-door, and called
them out. Three blasts were blown gaily on the bugle;
the hounds bayed at the sound, and made a great
racket; and those that were going on the hunt turned
and chastised them—at least a hundred hunters, as I
have been told. The trackers went to their stations
and released the hounds; the forest resounded again
with their lusty blasts.

At the first sound of the hunt the wild things quaked
for fear; deer rushed into the valley; mad with fright
160 they turned back to the heights, but quickly they
were driven back where the huntsmen were stationed,
who shouted lustily. They let the harts pass, with
their high heads and the noble bucks with their broad
antlers, for the brave lord had forbidden that any
man should arouse the male deer in closed season.
The hinds were held back with shouts and commands;
the does were driven with great din into the dells.

There one could see the shooting and falling of
arrows. At each creature that passed under the boughs
in the dell an arrow went winging, which bit deep into 170
the brown deer with broad head. Lo! they darted, then
bled, then died on the heights. The hounds in a rush
followed them swiftly; hunters with loud horns hastened after them, with such a shattering cry that the
cliffs seemed to burst. Whatever wild things escaped
from the hunters were all run down and torn at the
outer ring. Thus were they harmed on the heights, and
pierced at the water; so well did the trackers know
their business, and so great were the greyhounds that
overtook them, that the deer were run down as fast 180
as the hunters could slay them. The lord in joy pressed
ever on, often riding, often dismounting, and passed
the day in bliss. Then came the dark night.

So the lord of the castle sported on the edge of the
linden-woods. But Gawain the good knight lay in his
fair bed, resting, till the daylight gleamed on the walls,
under a coverlet radiant and closely becurtained. And
as he slipped into slumbering, he heard a soft little
noise at his door. So he lifted his head out of the
bedclothes and lifted a little the corner of the bed- 190
curtains, and looked out warily to see what it might
be. It was the lady, most lovely to behold, that closed
the door after her full softly and still, and moved
towards the bed. The knight was ashamed and laid
him down quickly, pretending to sleep. But she stepped
quietly and stole up to his bed, cast up the curtain
and crept within, seating herself softly upon the bedside, and stayed there wondrous long, to see when he
should awaken. A very long time the knight lay there
and considered in his mind what this coming might 200
amount to; he was in great wonder. But finally he said
to himself: "It would be more seemly if I asked her
in words what she wants here." So he awoke and
moved about, and turning towards her unlocked his
eyelids, and pretended to marvel, crossing himself
with his hand, as if to be safer in speech. The lady,
sweet of chin and cheek, looked at him winsomely,
her small lips smiling.

"Good morrow, Sir Gawain," said the fair lady,
"you are a heavy sleeper, since one can enter hither. 210
Now you are taken unawares, but lest you escape
us, I shall bind you in your bed, of that you may be
sure." All laughing, the lady thus fell into jesting.
"Good morrow, fair lady," said Gawain the blithe,
"I will do your will, and that pleases me well. I will
yield me promptly and beseech grace; and that will
be best, I believe, for I needs must do so!" And so he
joked in return with much happy laughter. "But would
you, lovely lady, grant me leave; release your prisoner,
and pray him to rise. I would get up from this bed 220
and array myself. I should then have more comfort
to talk to you better." "Nay, forsooth, fair sir," said
that sweet one, "you shall not rise from your bed; I
shall direct you better. I shall keep you here even

longer, and then talk with my knight which I have captured. For I know well, of a surety, Sir Gawain the noble—whom all the world worships, wheresoever you ride—your honor and courtesy have been graciously praised among lords and ladies and all that are alive. And now you are here, ywis, and we are alone. My lord and his men are far off; other servants in their bed, and my maidens also; the door is drawn and fastened with a strong bolt. And since I have in
10 this house him whom everyone likes, I shall take good care of my time in speech, as long as it lasts. You are welcome to my body, at the wish of your will; it is proper for me, out of courtesy, to be your servant; so I shall be."

"In good faith," quoth Gawain, "it seems unfitting for me—though I am not what you were speaking of—to attain to such an honor as you have just mentioned. I am an unworthy man; I know it myself. By God, I should be glad, if it seemed good to you,
20 to please you with words or with service; verily, it would be pure joy!" "In good faith, Sir Gawain," quoth the fair lady, "the prowess and worth that pleases all other women—if I lacked it, or set it at naught, it were sad courtesy! But there are ladies enow that had liefer now hold a knight in their power, as I hold you here, to dally with the charm of your courteous words, to show them comfort and lighten their cares, than much of the treasure or gold that they possess. But as I love that same Lord who rules
30 the heavens, I have through His grace gotten wholly in my hands that which they all desire." She that was so fair of face made him good cheer; and he with modest speech answered all her sallies.

"Madam," said the happy knight, "Mary requite you, for I have found, in good faith, your frankness noble. Other folk have shown me much courtesy, in truth, but the honor that they have shown me for my poor deserts seems foolish; what is important is the worship of yourself, who know naught but good."
40 "By Mary," said the lady, "it seems to me otherwise; for were I worth all the riches of women alive, and had all the weal of the world in my power, and if I should bargain and choose to get me a lord, then, for the virtues that I have seen in you, Sir Gawain, of beauty, and mildness, and blithe semblance, or have heard of you and consider true—no man in the world would be chosen rather than you!" "Certes, my lady," replied Gawain, "you could have chosen a better; but I am proud of the value that you put on
50 me, and humbly as servant I acknowledge you my sovereign, and am become your knight. Christ requite you." So they talked of many things till mid-morn passed; and ever the lady made as if she loved him, and the knight was cautious and turned the talk aside.

Though she were the brightest of women, the one most in his mind, yet he would show the less love in his bearing, because of the adventure that he sought so near at hand—the blow that must confound him and yet must needs be done. The lady then took her leave, and Sir Gawain straightway granted it. 60

She gave him good-day, and with a laughing glance; but as she stood before him, she astonished him with full stern words: "Now He that speeds fair speech reward you for this disport! But that you are Gawain I sorely mistrust." "Wherefore?" asked the knight, and repeated the question, afraid lest he had failed somehow in his courtesy. But the lady blessed him, and spoke thus: "As good as Gawain is held among men, with courtesy so pure enclosed within him, he could not easily have tarried so long with a lady 70 without asking a kiss out of courtesy, or some token or trifle at the end of the story." Then said Gawain: "Surely; let it be as you will; I shall kiss under orders, as befits a knight who fears lest he displease you. So ask it no more." She came near at those words, and caught him in her arms, bent down in her beauty and kissed the knight. Then they fairly commended each other to Christ; she went out of the door without any sound; and he hastened to rise forthwith. He called to his chamberlain and chose his garments 80 and went forth, when he was ready, blithely to mass. Then he went to his meal that had been graciously kept for him, and made merry with mirth all day until the moon was rising. Never was a knight more fairly lodged; he sat between the two worthy ladies, the older and the younger; in merriment and comfort.

Meanwhile the lord of the castle was occupied with his sport, hunting in holt and heath and chasing the hinds. Such a number he slew, before the sun declined, of does and other deer, that it was a wonder. Then 90 happily they returned in a group at last, and quickly made a quarry of all the killed deer. The best hunters busied themselves with the help of men enow; they gathered the longest grass that they could find and joyfully began to cut up their game, as was their duty. They placed a knife in the deer's breast and tested the fatness; on the poorest of any they found two fingers of fat. Then they slit the stomachs and took out the gullets, flayed them with a sharp knife and then joined the hides together. Then they ripped 100 off the four limbs and rent off the skin; they cut open the belly and took out the entrails; quickly slicing hither and thither they cut off the privy parts. Next they seized on the entrails and speedily parted windpipe from throat, and threw out the lights; they sheared off the shoulders with their sharp knives and tied them together through a little hole to keep the flanks sound. Afterwards they brittled the beast and

---

107. **through a little hole.** George Turberville, whose *The Noble Art of Venerie or Hunting* (1575) is one of the greatest of early authoritative works on the art of hunting, explains the process here alluded to: "And

there (i.e., a little above the elbowe joynt) he rayseth out of the synew or muscle with his knife, and putteth his forefinger of his left hand through under the sayd muscle to hold the leg by." 208. **recheat.**

broke it in two, and going once more to the entrails
110 they rived the whole carcass quickly down to the
crotch, emptied out fat morsels, and truly thereafter
all the tendons and the rib-sheaths they slashed out.
They moved with ease along the backbone, perpendicularly with the haunch, that was joined to the
backbone. They lifted it out all whole and then hewed
it in pieces; some of the flesh they took off for eating,
naming it by name. By the fork of the thighs they
cut out flaps of skin; these they hastened to hew in
two and thus separate from the backbone.
120 Both the head and the throat they cut off then,
and then swiftly sundered the sides from the chine;
the rest they threw into a grove as a reward for the
ravens. Next they pierced each side through by the
ribs and hung them up by the joints in the haunches.
Each man received the reward that pertained to his
station. They fed their hounds on the scraps of the
fair beast; the liver and lights, the fat of the paunch,
and with bread soaked in the blood and scattered
among the scraps. Boldly they sounded the bugle that
130 broke up the hunt; their hounds bayed. Then they
took their trussed booty home, blowing stoutly many
a stirring measure. Before daylight was done, the
troop were all within the comely castle, where Gawain
abode quietly. Amid the warmth of a kindled fire,
the lord had come home, and Gawain met him with all
the joy in the world.

Then the lord had all his retainers gathered together
in the hall; and both the happy ladies joined them with
their maidens. Before all that folk in the hall he had
140 the venison brought in, and called to Gawain in jest
and counted to him all the tails of the beasts and
showed him the glistening fat shorn from the ribs.
"How does this sport please you? Have I not won
praise? Have I not earned hearty thanks for my craft
in the hunt?" "Yea, assuredly," answered Gawain,
"here is the fairest game that I have seen these seven
years in the winter season." "And all I give to you,
Gawain," said the lord, "for by the terms of our
agreement you can claim it as your own." "That is
150 true," said the knight, "I say the same to you, and
this I have honorably won within these walls; and
with as good will I yield it to you." So he clasped
the lord's neck within his arms, and kissed him as
courteously as he might. "Take here my booty; I
gained no more. I vouchsafe it wholly, though it
were greater than this." "It is good," quoth the good
lord, "gramercy therefore. So be it; but were it not
better that you tell me where you won this booty, and
if it were by your own wit?" "That was not our
160 covenant," replied Gawain, "ask me no more; for you
have taken what belongs to you; you can look for no
more." They laughed and made them blithe and spoke

low to each other; straightway they went to a supper
of fresh dainties enow.

And later they sat by the hearth in the chamber.
Men bore them excellent wine more than once. And
still in their jesting they agreed on the morrow to
carry out the same compact that they had made before; for chance might bring it about that their
gains might be different; but what new things they 170
won they would exchange when they met at night
in the presence of the court—such was their covenant.
The night-drink was served amid merriment; and in
friendly wise they took leave of each other at last
and each knight prepared himself for bed. Scarcely
had the cock crowed and cackled but thrice before
the lord of the castle had left his bed and each of his
followers. The meal was served and mass heard
quickly; the retainers turned once more to the wood,
to begin the hunt before day broke. Hunters and 180
horns sounded forth as they passed over the meadows;
the hounds uncoupled ran racing among the thorny
brakes.

Straightway they struck a scent in a field; the
huntsman cheered on the hounds that had first come
upon it; wild shouts were cast forth in a noisy din.
The hounds heard it and hastened up and fell fast
to the chase, forty at once. Then such a yelping
clamor of packing hounds arose that the very rocks
rang out; hunters urged them on with horn and 190
mouth. All came together beside a pool in the woods,
before a rugged crag; in a knot, by a cliff, at the
side of a bluff. There rough boulders had tumbled
in jagged heaps. The huntsmen fared to the finding
and looked about them; the men surrounded the rocky
crag, till they knew for certain that the beast they
had uncovered with their bloodhounds was within
their circle. Then they beat about the bushes and
bade him spring up. Suddenly he rushed fiercely
across the path of the men, a most marvelous boar. 200
Long since he had grown old and departed from his
herd. Surely he was the greatest of wild swine-kind;
and every time he grunted, he caused trouble to
many, for he thrust three to earth at the first rush,
and then raced forth with great speed, without further
injury. Then they hallooed loudly and cried out "Hay!
Hay!" and put their horns to their mouth to blow
the recheat. Great was the rout of men and of hounds
that rushed with boast and noise after the boar to
make the kill. Long he stood at bay, however, and 210
maimed the pack of hounds pressing upon him, hurting them so badly that they most mournfully yowled
and yelled.

The men then turned to shooting; they aimed
their arrows at him and hit him often enow; but
the arrow-heads were blunted by the strength of his
shield-like hide, and the barbs would not bite on his
brow, for the smooth shafts splintered in pieces, and
the arrow-head fell back wherever it struck. But when

Originally the recheat was sounded to call the hounds back from a wrong
scent, but later, as used here, to call the hounds to the hunters or to
urge them on.

the blows of their mighty strokes began to hurt him, then, mad from strife, he rushed upon the huntsmen once more, hurting them sorely wherever he attacked, so that many waxed fearful and drew back a little. But the lord on a swift horse darted after him; like the brave man he was, he swung over the meadow, blowing his horn. He recheated and rode through thick underbrush, ever pursuing this wild boar until the sun sank low.

10   All the day the huntsmen spent in this wise, while our gracious knight lay in his bed, Gawain the noble, at home in rich gear so fair of hue. The lady did not forget, but came in to greet him; full early she was at his side to cheer his mood.

    She came to the curtain and looked at the knight. And Gawain welcomed her fittingly at that time, and she yielded him good morrow, with eager and ready words. Softly she sat down at his side, and laughed much, and with a lovesome look spoke to 20 him thus: "Sir, if you be Gawain, it is a wonder to me—a man that is so turned to God and does not bother with the courtesies of companionship; and if one teaches you how to recognize these courtesies, you cast them forthwith from your mind. You have forgotten promptly what I showed you yesterday, by all the truest tokens of which I have knowledge." "What is that?" asked the knight. "I know, forsooth, nothing of all this; if what you say is true, the blame is all mine." "And yet I taught you of kissing," said 30 the beautiful lady; "wherever a fair face is shown him, it becomes every knight quickly to claim courtly usage." "My dear," said the strong knight, "do away that speech, for that I dare not do, lest I be denied. If I were refused, surely I would be in the wrong if I still proffered a kiss." "My faith," said the sweet woman, "you cannot be denied; you are strong enough to force it with your strength, if it pleased you—if, perchance, any were so churlish as to deny you." "Yea, by God," said Gawain, "your speech is 40 fair; but threats are not profitable in the land where I live; nor any gift that is not given with good will. I am at your command, to kiss you when you please; you may take them when you wish and leave them when it seems the best time." The lady then bent down and kissed his face in comely wise. Much talk they made there of the woes and charms of secret love.

    "I would know from you, sir knight," said the noble lady, "if you will not be angry, what the reason 50 may be that you, so young and so active, as you are at this moment, so courteous and so knightly, as you are known abroad, and choicest of all chivalry and most praised of all in the faithful joys of love and the science of arms—I know not. For to tell all the troubles of a true knight is the beginning, the title, and the text of all works: how ladies for their loyal loves have risked their very lives and endured for

their loved one doleful hours; and how their lovers avenged them by their valor and eased all their care and brought bliss into the bower and raptures all 60 their own. Now you are a knight, fairest of renown in your age; your words and your worship have gone everywhere. Yet I have sat by your side two separate times, and never have I heard you utter any words that pertained to love, small or great. And you, that are so courteous and careful of your promises, should be willing to show a young thing like me some token of true love's craft. Why are you so unlearned who have all men's praise? Is it that you deem me too foolish to listen to your teaching? For shame! I 70 came hither single, and sit beside you to learn from you some skill; come, teach me of your knowledge while my lord is away."

    "In good faith," replied Gawain, "God requite you! Good glee is a great thing; and a wondrous pleasure it is to me that such a beautiful one as you should come hither and bother yourself with so poor a man and pretend that he is your knight with such a sweet countenance; truly it brings me heart's ease! But to take the task upon myself to expound true love, to 80 turn to the stories of love and tales of arms and relate them to you who, I know well, have more skill in the sweet art than a hundred such as I am or ever shall be on the earth where I live—truly, my sweet, it would be manifold folly! I would gladly do your desires as best I can, as I am bound to do, and evermore I will be servant to you, so may God save me!" Thus she tried the knight and tempted him oft to have won him to wrong, whatever else her purpose. But he defended himself so well that no 90 fault appeared and no evil on either side—naught but happiness and jest. They laughed and joked forsooth; at last she kissed him, that fair one, and then took her leave and went her way.

    Then Gawain bestirred him and rose to mass; and then their dinner was prepared and richly served. The knight amused himself with the ladies all day. But the lord of the castle meanwhile rushed over the land in pursuit of the wild boar that went hurtling through the brush and biting the best of his hounds 100 in two. Finally the beast stopped at bay; the bowmen caught up with him and made him, in spite of himself, take to flight again. Many an arrow flew through the air, when those folk gathered. But even the bravest of them the boar made to spring back, until at last he was so wearied that he could run no longer, but with all the haste possible, he hid in a hole in a mound by a rock where the brook ran by. He got the mound over his back and began to dig; the froth foamed at his mouth and dismayed the hunters. He 110 gnashed his white tusks, while the bold hunters that stood near him all exhausted came on toward him. But none yet dared come too near him for fear of harm. He had hurt many before, which all thought was a pity; all the more they were afraid of him and his rending tusks; he was both courageous and frenzied.

But the lord of the castle came up and reined in his steed. Seeing the boar at bay and his men near by, 120 he alighted and left his courser, snatched out his bright brand, and strode forth boldly. Quickly he stalked through the brook to where the fierce creature was standing. The wild beast caught sight of the man with the weapon in his hand. He set his bristles high and snorted so violently that many feared for the lord, lest the monster should crush him. The boar made a lunge at the man; and both knight and swine were thrown in a heap full in the water. But the boar had the worst of it, for the man took good aim when 130 they first met, and plunged the sharp blade fair in the pit of the animal's stomach, driving it up to the hilt, so that the boar's heart was shivered, and snarling he gave up the ghost and was swept down to the water. A hundred hounds leaped upon him and chewed him famously; the hunters dragged him to the bank, and the dogs completed his death.

Then came a notable blowing of many a famous horn, the hallooing of huntsmen on the heights, the baying of the best of hounds, as their masters urged 140 them on—those who were the chief hunters in that dangerous chase. Then a man who was wise in woodcraft began to flay the boar. First he hewed off the head and set it aloft and then rent the shaggy hide along the backbone, snatched out the entrails and burnt them in a fire, later rewarding his hounds with bread mixed therewith. Next he broke out the muscles from the bright broad flanks and removed the heart and lights as was fit and proper. Then he bound the two sides of the beast all whole together 150 and hung the carcass bravely on a stiff strong pole. And then with this boar they came marching home; the boar's head was borne before the huntsman himself —he who had destroyed it in the brook, through the force of his hand so strong. It seemed long to that lord before he caught sight of Gawain in the hall; he called, and Gawain came towards him to receive his reward.

In jesting manner the lord laughed full loud and merry, when he saw Sir Gawain; with kind words he 160 spoke to him. The good ladies were summoned, and the retinue gathered; he showed them the boar's flanks and told them the tale of its largeness and length and fierceness also, and of the fight the wild swine offered in the wood where he had fled. The other knight commended his deeds in comely wise and praised them as great feats and well proving his courage. For such a brawny beast, bold Gawain said, nor such flanks of a boar he had never seen before. Then they felt of the huge head, and the 170 gracious knight praised it, and courteously spoke it so that the lord of the castle might hear. "Now,

Gawain," quoth that good man, "this game is all yours, by a nice covenant and a firm, as you very well know." "That is true," said Gawain, "of a surety; all I have won I shall give back to you, by my troth." He took the lord about the neck and gave him gracious kisses, two of them. "Now we are even," said Gawain, "for this time, in all the covenants that we sealed by law, since I came hither." The lord said: "By Saint Giles; you are the best that I 180 know; you will be rich in a short time if you drive such bargains!"

Then they set up the tables on trestles, cast cloths over them; a clear light shone over the walls, for men had set waxen torches whereby they might serve in the hall. Much noise and laughter rose up therein, about the fire and over the floor, in all manner wise. At the supper and after there were many lovely songs, lays of Christmas-tide and new carols, with all the mirth that a man could imagine. And ever our fair 190 knight sat beside the lady; such a semblant of love she made to Gawain, with still demure countenance to please that stalwart man, that Gawain was all wonder and wroth with himself. But he would not out of courtesy proffer her aught in return, but treated her in all deference, howsoever she might try to twist the words awry. When they had played in the hall as long as it was their will, she called them all to the inner chamber; they turned to the hearth.

And there they drank and dallied and discoursed 200 anew, conversing on a like covenant for the day of New Year's Eve. But Gawain craved leave to depart on the morrow, for it was near to term-time, when he should meet his appointment with the Green Knight. The lord forbade him to go and constrained him to linger and said, "As I am a truthful man, I swear by my troth, that thou shalt reach the Green Chapel and do thy task, sir knight, at the daybreak of the New Year, long before prime. So lie in thy tower, and take thine ease; I shall hunt in the wood and 210 keep the covenant to exchange with thee my winnings, such as I may bring back hither. For I have tried thee twice, and I find thee faithful; now tomorrow will be the third time and the best. Let us make merry while we can, and think of naught but joy. A man can always find misfortune when he so desires!" This Gawain agreed to in courtesy; therefore he tarried. Sweet drink was brought to him, and then they were all lighted to bed. Sir Gawain lay and slept still and soft all night long; the lord of 220 the castle kept to his woodcraft—full early he was all ready.

After mass he and his men had a morsel or two to eat. Fair was the morning, as he called for his mount. All the hunters on horse followed after him: fairly accoutered were their steeds before the hall-gates. Very fair shone the earth to which the frost still clung; all streaked with red the majestic sun rose

on a rack of clouds; soft and clear were the clouds in the heavens. The huntsmen scattered by the woodside; the rocks beneath the boughs of hanging trees echoed to the voice of the hunting-horns. Some came upon the scent of the wily fox, carried often across the path, true to the beast's tricks. A hound cried out threat; the hunter called to him; his fellows joined him, panting hard; they ran forth in a rabble, as was their habit. The fox flitted before them; they
10 espied him straightway; and as they caught sight of him they followed him fast, driving after him savagely with a horrid noise. And the fox tricked and turned through many a rough copse; crossed over and stopped to listen in hedgerows. Finally he leaped a little ditch near one of those hedges and then stole forth quietly by a rugged path, thinking to escape by his wiles from the wood—and from the hounds. Then he came, ere he knew it, to a skilful tracker; indeed, three men at one rush pressed upon the gray little beast
20 together. He drew back quickly and stoutly leaped to one side; in the utmost anguish he turned back to the wood.

Then was it a pleasure indeed to listen to the hounds, when all the hunters had met together in counsel. Such a tumult they made when they caught sight of him once more, as if all the clustering cliffs had crashed down at once. Here the fox was hallooed, when the huntsmen met him; loud was he cried upon with snarling yells. Often was he threatened and called
30 a thief, and ever there were hounds at his tail, so that he could not linger; often was he run at, when he darted out of covert, and often forced back again. But Reynard was wily, and led them low and high, the lord and his huntsmen; now over the mounts, now down, over, and under.

Meanwhile gracious Gawain at home slept most wholesomely, beneath comely coverlets on that cold morning. But the lady for love cared not to sleep, and thus spoil the purpose that was set in her heart. She
40 rose up early, and hurried to Gawain, in a lovely mantle that reached to the ground, furred fine with costly furs, well cared for. No gems wore she on her hair, but the precious stones were all bordering her head-dress, in clusters of twenty. Her beautiful face and her throat she showed all bare, and her breast bare, and her back as well. She came through the chamber door, and closed it after her. Opening a window, she called to Gawain, and thus readily greeted him with cheerful sweet words: "Ah, man, how canst
50 thou sleep, on this morning so clear?" He was in a deep drowse; nevertheless he did hear her.

In a fierce fitful slumber that knight was disturbed, as a man often is in the morning from many bold thoughts. He was dreaming of the destiny that should next day prepare his fate at the Green Chapel, when he was to meet the Green Knight and must abide

190. **spinney,** a thorny hedge.

his buffet without further fight. But when comely Sir Gawain had recovered his wits and awakened from his dreams, he answered the lady in haste. She came towards him laughing in sweet loving manner, 60 bent over his fair face, and featly did kiss him. He welcomed her fondly, with fair good cheer. He saw her so glorious and beautifully attired, so faultless of feature, and so fine of complexion that welling joy warmed his heart. With gentle smiles they fell into mirthful speech, and all was bliss and gaiety and joy that passed between them. They uttered sweet words and exchanged much happiness. Truly, great peril was there for both of them, unless the knight was ware of it!   70

For the princely Gawain was so hard borne down; so tense was the feeling, that it behooved him by need either to take her love on the spot or hatefully refuse it. He cared for his courtesy, lest he be deemed craven, and even more for his honor if he should sin and be a traitor to the lord of the castle. "God forbid!" said the knight, "that shall never happen!" With laughter in love, he turned aside all the special speeches that came from her mouth. Said the lady to the knight: "You should be blamed, if you do not 80 love the life that lies next to you, above all the creatures in the world wounded as she is in heart, unless you have a mistress or true-love that pleases you better, and unless you have pledged faith to that lady, fixed so firm that you will not loosen it. Indeed, that is what I believe. Now I pray you, tell me this truly. For all the love in the world, do not keep the truth a secret, out of guile." The knight replied: "By Saint John," and softly smiled. "In faith, I possess not such a one, nor will I possess one for a time."   90

"That," said the lady, "is the worst thing you could have said; but at least I have been answered, though it is a vexation to me. Now kiss me in courtly wise, and I shall go hence; I can but mourn and weep as a maiden who loves much." Sighing she bent down and gave him a seemly kiss; and then left his embrace and said as she stood beside him: "Now, dear, at our parting give me at least this comfort; yield me some sort of gift, thy glove mayhap, that I may remember the man and lessen my mourning." "Now truly," re- 100 plied Gawain, "I would that I had here the most precious thing I owned, that I might give it you for your love. Forsooth, you have deserved far more reward, and rightly, than I could ever give. But alas, I would then be giving you a keepsake of a love that profited little or nothing. Indeed, it would not be honorable to give you at this time my glove for a recompense, a glove of Gawain, as I am here on an errand the strangest in the world and have with me no retainers bearing bags brimful of precious things. 110 That displeases me greatly, lady, at this time. But every man must fare as he is taken, even for sorrow or ill." "Nay, gracious knight of high honor," said that lovely lawn-clad lady, "though I have naught of yours, yet you shall have something of mine."

She caught up a rich ring worked in red gold with a staring gem standing out of it, that cast beams as dazzling as the bright sun; know ye well, it was of immense worth. But the knight refused it and said forthwith: "I will have no gifts even for good, fair lady, at this time. I have none to offer you, and I will take none." She prayed him eagerly to receive it, and he denied her prayer, and swore firmly by his truth that he would not take it. And she was grieved that he refused it and spoke thus: "If you refuse my ring because it seems to you too costly and you do not wish to be obligated to me, I shall at least give you my girdle that will be a lesser gift." She loosened a lace here and there, which encircled her waist, fastened at her side under the bright mantle. The girdle was of green silk and decorated with gold thread worked about by the fingers; this she offered to the knight and blithely besought him to take it though it were unworthy. But he denied that he would accept in any wise either gold or gift, before God sent him grace to achieve the adventure that he had undertaken there. "And so, I pray you, do not be displeased, and let the matter go, for I can not at all grant your request. I am dearly beholden to you because of your beauty, and will ever be your true servant in hot and cold alike."

"Well, do you refuse this silken piece," then asked the lady, "because it is too simple, as it well seems? Indeed, it seems little, and therefore of less value. But whoever knew the virtues that are hidden therein would appraise it more highly, peradventure. For whatever man is wrapped in this green lace, while he has it tied about him, no hero under the heavens could hew him down; he could not be slain or struck to earth." Truly then Gawain thought, when he pondered in his heart, that it would be a jewel in the jeopardy which had been decreed him when he went to the Green Chapel to receive his blow; might he escape unslain, this were a noble stratagem! So he endured her chiding and suffered her to speak. She carried the girdle to him and offered it to him again. He accepted it, and she handed it over with a good will, and besought him for her sake never to reveal it, but to conceal it faithfully from the lord of the castle. The knight agreed that no wight should know it, for certain, but the two of them. He thanked her again and again, earnestly, with heart and mind. By that time the lady had kissed the gracious knight three times.

Then she took her leave and left him there, for she could not get more pleasure from the knight. When she had gone, Sir Gawain got him ready, rose, and arrayed himself in rich attire, caught up the love-lace which the lady had bestowed upon him, and hid it loyally where he might find it again. Then he took his way fairly to the chapel; there he privily approached a priest and prayed him to forgive his life and teach him better how his soul might be saved when he should go hence. There he was sweetly shriven and confessed his misdeeds both more and less, and besought mercy, and called on the priest for absolution. And he was assoiled in certainty and was made as pure as if Doomsday had been appointed for that morning. And after that he made merry among the noble ladies, with comely carols and all kinds of mirth (as he never had done but that one day with such bliss) even till dark night. Each man had great and marvelous respect for him there and said, of a truth, that he had never been thus joyful before that time, since he had come thither.

Now let Gawain linger in the castle where love had befallen him. But the lord was still abroad, leading his huntsmen. He had destroyed the fox that he had followed long. As he rushed over a spinney to catch sight of the rascal (for he heard the hounds hastening in that direction), Reynard came running through a bushy grove, and all the rabble of hounds in a rush at his heels. The knight saw the wild animal and bided his time, and snatched out his bright sword and struck at the beast. He shrank from the blow and tried to retreat, but a hound seized him before he could reach safety, and they all fell upon him right at the horse's feet and worried him to death with a horrid noise. The lord quickly alighted and caught the fox, raising him quickly out of the mouth of a dog, and holding him high aloft, hallooed loudly. Many a brave hound bayed in return; the hunters all hurried thither with many a horn, recheating aright till they caught sight of their lord. By that time his whole noble retinue had assembled; all that had bugles blew at one and the same time; and those that had no horns hallooed—it was the merriest meet that men ever heard, and the noisiest uproar that was lifted up in jest for Reynard's soul. The hounds had their reward; their heads were stroked and patted; and then they took Reynard and stripped off his coat.

So then they turned homeward, for it was nearly night, blowing most loudly on their mighty horns. The lord at last alighted at his beloved castle; he found fire on the hearth and the knight beside it, Sir Gawain the good, who was fain withal and was having much joy out of love for the ladies. He wore a robe of blue that reached to the earth; his surcoat fitted him well and was beautifully furred; and his hood of the same material hung down to his shoulders, blended with fine linen all about. He met the good lord in the middle of the floor and greeted him in all mirth and said fairly: "Now I shall be the first to fulfill our covenant which we made most happily when there was no lack of wine." So he embraced the lord of the castle and kissed him thrice as carefully

and soberly as he could. "By Christ," said the lord, "you had great fortune in the obtaining of this bargain, if the exchange be good!" "Yea, of the exchange no matter," said the other knight, "since what I owe has been openly paid." "Marry," quoth the lord, "mine is behind, for I have hunted all this day and have got naught but this foul fox-skin—the devil take it—for it is very poor to pay for such precious things as you have given me here—three
10 such kisses so fair." "Enough!" replied Sir Gawain, "I thank you, by the rood!" Then the lord told him, as they were standing there, how the fox was slain.

With mirth and minstrelsy and dainties at their will, they made as merry as any men could, with laughing of the ladies and jests along the board. Gawain and the good lord were both as high-spirited as if the band had gone mad or become over-drunk. Both the men and the retainers joked and jested until
20 the time came when they should depart, when the knights must retire to their beds. Then Gawain the noble humbly took his leave of the lord and thanked him fairly: "For all this happy sojourn that I have had here at this high feast, may the great King repay your worship! I yield myself here as one of yours, if it so please you; now I must needs, as you know, move on the morrow; and you will give me, as you promised, a man to show me the way to the Green Chapel, where God will suffer me to partake on New
30 Year's Day of the destiny decreed me." "In good faith," said the noble lord, "with a good will; all that I ever promised you I shall fulfill with good intent." So he assigned Gawain a servant to set him on his way, and to lead him over the downs, that he might have no trouble in riding through the wood and passing most speedily through the groves. Gawain thanked the lord for the honor he had done him; then the knight took leave of the two noble ladies; with sorrow he kissed them and spoke to them and
40 begged them to have his sincere thanks for everything. And they gave him back a like reply; they commended him to Christ with many cold sighs.

Then Gawain departed from the company in courtesy; each man that he met he thanked for his service and his comfort and his many little pains that he had made for Gawain's sake, to treat him well. And each man was as sorry to part from him as if he had dwelt in the castle forever. Then the servants led him with torches to his chamber and he happily laid
50 down on the bed, to be at rest. Whether he slept soundly I dare not say, for he had much to think about on the morrow, if he would turn his thoughts thereto. Let him lie there still; he was near what he had sought. Now if you will be still a while, I shall tell you what happened.

157. **Hector himself.** The manuscript reads *Hestor*, which occurs in several French romances, but refers without much doubt to the great Trojan hero.

4

Now New Year's Day drew nigh, and the night passed; the day put the darkness to flight, as the Lord had commanded. But stormy weather awakened the world that day; clouds hurled sharp cold down on the earth, hard enow from the north for those who lacked 60 clothing. The snow lay about in heaps and nipped the wild animals of the wood; the howling wind swooped down from on high and piled each valley full of great drifts. Gawain, lying in bed, listened to the storm; though he closed his eyes, full little he had slept; he knew the voice of every cock that had crowed. Quickly he rose ere day broke, for there was light from a lamp that burned in his chamber. He called to his chamberlain who speedily answered him, and bade him fetch his byrnie and saddle his steed. 70 The chamberlain arose and brought the knight's armor, and got Gawain ready in knightly fashion. First he put on his clothes to protect him from the cold, and then his armor that was nobly cared for, his coat of mail and his hauberk, burnished and shining. The rust had been polished away from the ringed mail on his rich byrnie. All was as fresh as at first, and Gawain was fain to thank the chamberlain, for each piece of armor was wiped well and clean—it was the gayest 80 armor from here to Greece. Gawain then called for his steed.

Meanwhile he cast upon himself the proudest garments: his coat with the badge of famous deeds, adorned with precious stones on velvet, the borders worked and embroidered and lined fairly with costly furs. Nor did he forget the girdle, the lady's gift; that, you may be sure, he did not leave behind, for the good it might do him. When he had belted his sword over his round and smooth waist, he wrapped the love-token doubly about him, closely and sweetly 90 folded over his loins, a girdle of green silk that became him very well on the background of royal red cloth, that was gorgeous to behold. But the knight wore the girdle not for its value in treasure or for the glory of its pendants, although they were polished, and although glittering gold-thread gleamed brightly on the ends, but rather to save himself, when it was necessary for him to suffer, to await destruction without fighting back, to guard him against brand or knife. With that the hero, all ready, marched forth quickly, 100 thanking full often the renowned retinue of the lord of the castle.

Then Gringolet the great and strong was ready; he had been lodged with care in a safe place; that proud horse was in good condition for the journey. The knight went up to him and looked on Gringolet's coat, and said soberly to himself, swearing by his truth: "There is a band in this castle that think on honor; joy may they have, and the lord who maintains them; the dear lady, may love befall her all 110

84 *Warrior, Priest, and Commoner*

her life long. Since they for charity cherish a guest and hold honor in their hands, may the Lord, who holds the heavens on high, requite them and all of you! And if I might lead my life anywhere on earth, I would bring you full reward in truth if I could." Then he stepped to the stirrup and bestrode the horse; his servant handed him his shield, and he laid it on his shoulder. He struck Gringolet with his golden spurs, and the steed started to prance on the stones 120 and abide still no longer. His servant was mounted on horse then, bearing Gawain's spear and lance. "This castle I commend to Christ; may He give it ever good chance!"

The drawbridge was let down and the broad gates unbarred and opened on both sides. The knight crossed himself and passed beyond the limits of the castle. He praised the porter, who knelt before the knight, and gave him good-day and commended him to God, that he should pray for Gawain. Then he went on 130 his way, alone with his man, who should show him where to turn to come to that place of woe where he was to receive that rueful blow. They passed by banks and trees with bare boughs; they climbed along cliffs, where the cold clung fast. Naught fell from the heavens, but it was ugly underfoot; mist hovered over the moorlands and dissolved on the mountains. Every hill wore a hat and a huge cloak of haze; the brooks boiled and foamed between their banks, dashed sparkling against the shores where they shelved 140 downwards. Exceeding lonesome was the road as they passed through the wood, until it was the time when the sun should rise on that day of the New Year. They found themselves on a very high hill, covered over with the whitest of snow. The servant riding beside Gawain bade his master halt.

"Well, I have brought you hither, sir knight, this time; and now you are not far from that noted place that you have sought and inquired for so particularly. But I will tell you in truth, since I know you, and 150 you are a knight in the world that I greatly love, that if you follow my counsel you would fare the better. The place to which you proceed is esteemed full perilous. There dwells a creature in that desolation, the worst on earth, for he is brave and stern and loves to strike, and he is greater in size than any man in the world, and his body bigger than those of the best four in Arthur's house or of Hector himself or of any other. He brings it to pass at the Green Chapel that no man can go by that place, be he never 160 so proud in his arms, that this creature does not strike him dead with a blow from his hand. For he is a man without pity and practices no mercy; for be it churl or chaplain that ride by the Chapel, monk or mass-priest, or any other man, it is as pleasant for him to slay them as to pass alive himself. Therefore I say to you, as truly as you are sitting in that saddle, that if you go there, you will be killed. I can counsel you truly, knight, though you had twenty lives to spend. He has lived here full long, and has brought about much violence. Against his terrible 170 blows you cannot defend yourself.

"Therefore, good sir Gawain, let that man alone, and depart some other way, for the sake of Christ. Turn home by some other land, where Christ may speed you; and I shall hie me home again, and promise you, moreover, that I shall swear by God and all His good saints—so help me God and all the saints—oaths enow that I shall faithfully conceal it and never tell tale that you ever took to flight, for fear of the man I described to you."   180

"Gramercy," quoth Gawain, and said in ill humor, "Good fortune for the man who wishes me good; I believe well that thou wouldst conceal my shame loyally! But though thou didst keep my secret ever so truly, and I passed by here, and took to flight out of fear, in the manner you spoke of, I should be a coward knight and could never be forgiven. Therefore I will go on to the Chapel, whatever chance may befall, and tell that fellow there whatever tale I please, be it for weal or for woe, or as fate 190 will be pleased to have it. Though he be a strong knave to control or rule by the rod, still the Lord knows full well how to save His servants."

"Marry," said the retainer, "since thou talkest so much and will take this danger upon thyself, and since it pleases thee to lose thy life, I shall not stop thee. Take here thy helmet on thy head and thy spear in thy hand, and ride down this very path by yonder rocks till thou hast come to the bottom of this rugged valley; then look about a little on thy left hand, and 200 thou shalt see in a grove the very Chapel, and the burly warrior that guards it. Now farewell in God's name, noble Gawain; I would not go with thee for all the gold in the ground, nor bear thee fellowship further on foot through this woodland." With that the man in the wood turned his bridle, hit his horse with his heel as hard as he could, leapt quickly over the land, and left the knight there alone. "By God's self," quoth Gawain, "I shall neither wail nor groan aloud; I am full obedient to God's will, and I have 210 committed myself to him."

Then he spurred on Gringolet, and followed the path, which inclined down through the woods to the edge of a grove. He rode through the rough land right down to the valley, and then looked about him. It was wild country; he saw no sign of a resting-place anywhere about, nothing but towering banks on both sides and rough craggy rocks with jagged stones strewn about. The clouds seemed to him grazed 220 by the cliffs. Then he halted, reigning in his horse for the moment, and changed his gaze now and again, to find the Green Chapel. He saw no such Chapel in any direction, and it seemed strange to him. Then he saw as it were on a rise near by, a

little round mound by a bank, near a stream—near the ford of a stream, indeed, that rushed past. The brook bubbled away as if it were boiling. The knight reigned his steed and came to the mound, gracefully dismounted, and fastened the reins to a linden-branch and his noble horse likewise. Then he turned to the mound and walked about it, debating within himself what it might be. It had an opening in the end and on each side, and was overgrown everywhere with
10 clumps of grass; it was all hollow within, as an old cave, or the crevice of an old crag. He could not tell what it was. "Ah," said the gentle knight, "can this be the Green Chapel? Here the devil may pray his matins at midnight!"

"Now truly," continued Gawain, "it is desolate here. This is an ugly oratory overgrown with herbs; indeed a fitting place for the man clad in green to perform his devotions in devil's worship. In my five wits I feel that it is the fiend that has appointed for me
20 this meeting that he may destroy me here. This is a chapel of mischance, ill fortune befall it; it is the cursedest kirk that ever I came upon!" With his high helmet on his head and his lance in his hand, he wandered up the wall of the rude rocky dwelling. Then he heard from that hill, aloft in a towering rock beyond the brook and above the bank, a wondrous fierce noise. Lo! it echoed about the cliffs so loud that it seemed wild enough to cleave the rocks—as if one were grinding a scythe upon the grindstone. Lo!
30 it whirred and grated like water on a mill-wheel; truly, it rumbled and rang out that it was terrible to hear. Then, "By God!" exclaimed Gawain, "that gear is being prepared, so I think, for the use of the warrior who is to meet me here according to our agreement. But let God do his will. Well, it helps me not a whit even though I lose my life. But no mere sound shall affright me."

Then the brave knight called aloud: "Who dwells in this place, let him hold discourse with me. For
40 now brave Gawain has come hither; if any man would have anything of him now, let him get his business done now or never." "Stay," answered one on the bank above Gawain's head, "and thou shalt have all in haste that I promised thee." Yet for a while the loud noise went on with its jarring sound of whetting before the man appeared. Then he descended from a craggy boulder; he had come out of a cave in the rock, out of some obscure corner, and now stepped forth brandishing a wicked weapon—a Danish ax new
50 burnished, with which to give a mighty blow. The powerful blade bent back in line with the handle; it had been freshly sharpened on a grindstone and was at least four feet wide, no less, and bound to the handle with thongs that shone bright. And the warrior in green was attired as at first as to complexion and

57. **set . . . ground.** The Green Knight was apparently accustomed to use the handle of his ax as a staff when he walked or rested.

limbs, locks, and beard, save that now he walked fair on the ground. He set the handle to the ground and stalked along. When he came to the brookside, he would not wade through, but vaulted over with the help of his ax, and strode along with vigor, fierce 60 and angry in the snow-covered field that stretched far around them. Sir Gawain met the Green Knight without any kind of obeisance; the other said, "Now fair sir, one may trust thee to keep an agreement."

"Gawain," said the Green Knight, "may God protect thee! Truly thou art welcome, knight, to my place; and thou hast timed thy travel as well as a true man could; and thou knowest the covenant drawn up between us: at this time twelvemonth thou didst take what befell thee; and I should on this New 70 Year quickly repay thee. Now we are in this valley verily alone; here are no henchmen to separate us; we may meet as we please. Take thy helmet off thy head, and receive here thy reward; make no more talk now than I offered thee when thou didst strike off my head with one blow." "Nay, by God," replied Gawain, "who didst give me soul; I shall not murmur in ill-will for any mischief that shall be my lot; now settle thyself for the stroke, and I shall stand still and cast no refusal in thy teeth, but let thee do as thou 80 wilt." He stretched forth his neck and bowed, showing his bright skin all bare, and made as if he did not fear, for he would not tremble out of dread.

Then the knight in green got him ready and gathered up the grim weapon to smite Gawain; with all the power in his body he lifted it on high with a mighty feint to slay him. Had the blow fallen as violently as he seemed to intend, Gawain would have been dead from the stroke, doughty as he may have been. But our bold knight caught a glimpse of that ax 90 as it came swishing downward to destroy him there on the hill, and he flinched a little from that sharp iron, moving his shoulders slightly. The Green Knight let the blow swerve and withheld the ax, and then reproved Gawain with many haughty words: "Thou art not Gawain," said the warrior, "who is esteemed so good, who never waxed timid before any band on either hill or dale; and now thou dost shrink for fear before thou dost feel any hurt. Such cowardice I never knew in that knight. Nor did I shrink nor flee, 100 sir knight, when thou didst swing thy stroke over me, nor did I cast any trifling objection in the way there in King Arthur's hall. My head rolled at my feet, and yet I never fled. And thou, ere any harm has befallen thee, art fearful in heart; wherefore I ought to be called the better knight." Said Gawain then: "I flinched once, but I will not do so again; but if my head drops down on the stones, I shall not be able to restore it.

"But, sir knight, by thy faith, hasten and bring me 110 to the point; deal out to me my destiny, and do it out of hand; for I will stand thee a stroke and start no more until thine ax has struck me. Here is my troth!" "Have at thee then," said the Green Knight, and heaved the ax aloft and looked as fierce and grim as if he were beside himself. He aimed a mighty blow, but did not cut Gawain; he held quickly his hand before the weapon could hurt him. Gawain bravely awaited it, and did not flinch in any part of him, but stood as still as a stone or rather the stock of a tree that is fixed in rocky ground with a hundred roots. Then the Green Knight spoke in merry tones: "So now that thou hast thy heart whole, it behooves me to hit. Hold up thy noble hood, that Arthur gave thee, and keep thy neck with this blow, if perchance it survive!" But Gawain in full wrathful anger spoke thus: "Why smite further, thou fierce man; thou hast threatened too long. I believe that thine own heart has grown timid." "Forsooth," retorted the Green Knight, "so boldly thou hast spoken; I will no longer hold back thine adventure. Here it is right now!" So he spread his legs far apart to strike and frowned horribly with lips and brow; it was no marvel that it pleased him little who hoped for no rescue.

Lightly he lifted his ax and let it fall fair, with the cutting edge of the blade against the bare neck. But though he swung mightily, he hurt him no more than before, but nicked him slightly on the side, so that he broke the skin. The sharp blade bit through the flesh and the swelling muscle, so that the bright blood ran over his shoulders and dropped on the ground. And when the knight saw the blood flow on the snow, he sprang forth, swift of foot, more than a spear's length, quickly seized his helmet and set it on his head, threw the fair shield in front of his shoulders, snatched out his bright sword, and spoke fiercely (never since he had been born of his mother had he been so joyous): "Cease, knight, of thy blows; give me no more. I have received a blow in this place without combat; and if thou dost yield me any more, I shall readily repay you and yield you back still more forbidding blows; thou mayest be sure of that! But one stroke is my lot here; the covenant we shaped just so in Arthur's hall. Therefore, sir knight, halt!"

The Green Knight drew off and rested on his ax, setting the shaft on earth, and leaning against the blade. He looked at Sir Gawain, who was in a clearing, and saw how that doughty warrior stood there fearless, armed, and dangerous; in his heart he was pleased. Then in a loud voice he addressed Gawain gaily, and said to the knight in a mighty rumble: "Bold warrior, be not so wroth in the field; no man here has offered thee wrong, nor will do so, except according to the covenant drawn up at the king's court. I promised thee a stroke, and thou hast received it—consider thyself well paid. I release thee of all other claims. If I had been active, peradventure I could have dealt thee a buffet more harshly and have stirred thee to frenzy. First I menaced thee jestingly with a feigned blow, and did not rend thee with a gash or a wound which in justice I should offer thee according to the covenant that we bound on that first night, and that thou faithfully didst hold in keeping with thy faith and troth. All thy gains thou didst yield me, as a good man should. The second blow, sir knight, I gave thee for that morn. Thou didst kiss my lovely wife; those kisses thou didst give to me. For both those days I offered thee here but two mere feints without harm to thee: true man, true return—he need fear no harm. But the third day thou didst fail me, and therefore hadst thou the real blow, though slight.

"For it is my weed that thou are wearing, that same woven girdle; my own wife wove it; I know it well forsooth. Now I know thy kisses, and thy virtues as well, and the wooing of my wife—I brought it all about. I sent her to try thee; in truth I think that thou art the most faultless knight that ever walked on earth. As a pearl among white peas is of more value than they, so is Gawain, in good faith, beside other knights. But yet thou wert lacking in a little, sir, and wert wanting in loyalty; but that was not for any base intrigue or lustful wooing, but because you loved your life. So I blame you the less." Gawain stood for a great while in silent thought, so grieved and angry he trembled within; all the blood from his breast poured into his face, and he shrank back for very shame at what the Green Knight had said. The first words that Gawain spoke were: "Cursed be cowardice and covetousness alike! In you both are villainy and vice that destroys virtue." Then he caught at the knot and loosened the twist and angrily hurled the belt at the Green Knight himself: "Lo! there is the breaking of faith, evil befall it! For fear of thy blow, cowardice taught me to be reconciled with covetousness, to forsake my own nature, which is the generosity and loyalty that pertain to knights. Now I am faulty and false and have been afraid from the beginning; from treachery and untruth both come sorrow and care! I acknowledge to thee once again, sir knight, I have done wrong. Do then thy will; hereafter I shall be more wary."

Then the Green Knight laughed and spoke in friendly manner: "I believe it is all whole now, the hurt that I had. Thou art so cleanly confessed and hast acknowledged thy sins and hast borne open penance through the edge of my weapon, that I esteem thee cleansed of that fault and pure and clean withal as if thou hadst never done ill since the time thou wast born. And I give thee, sir knight, this girdle all gold-hemmed; for it is green like my raiment, Sir Gawain. You can think upon this contest when thou goest forth among great princes of worth; it shall be a pure token of the adventure of the

Green Chapel, as it befell among chivalrous knights. And in this New Year you shall come back to my castle, and we shall revel for the remnant of this high season in mirth and joy." And the Green Knight invited Gawain further and said: "We shall make peace between you and my wife, I ween, for she was your bitter enemy."

"Nay, forsooth," said Gawain, and seized his helmet and doffed it courteously as he thanked the Green 10 Knight, "I have sojourned ill, but may bliss betide you, and may He that dispenses all honor reward you fittingly. Commend me to that noble lady, your comely wife, both to her and to that other lady, both honored, who have thus cleverly beguiled their knight with their trick. But it is no wonder if a man be made a fool of and be brought to sorrow through the wiles of women. For so was Adam beguiled by one, and Solomon by a great many, and Samson also —Delilah dealt him his doom—and David thereafter 20 was deluded by Bathsheba and suffered much woe. All these were brought to disaster by women's wiles; if a knight could love them well and believe them not, it were a great gain! And these were of old the noblest that lived for a time in all worldly prosperity, preeminent among all in the kingdom of the earth, and all bemused by love, all beguiled by women with whom they had dealings. And so if I have now been deceived, I may well be excused.

"But as for your girdle," said Gawain, "God be 30 with you! I will accept it with pleasure, not for the gain of the gold, nor for the silk or samite, nor for the costly pendants, neither for weal nor for worship nor for pride of work; but as a sign of my fault I shall often look upon it. When I ride in pomp, I shall see it as a rebuke to myself for the sin and faintness of crabbed flesh—how likely it is to entice to the desire for evil. And thus when pride shall spur me on in prowess of arms, the sight of this lovely girdle will humble my heart. But one thing I would ask of 40 you, if it displease you not: since you are lord of yonder land, where I have dwelt with you in happiness (may the Lord who upholds the heavens and sits on the high throne ever keep it for you)—what, indeed, is your rightful name? Pray tell me, and I will ask no more." "That I shall truly," said the Green Knight. "I am called Bernlak de Hautdesert in this my home. Morgan le Fay dwells in my house, and through the power and knowledge of clerkly works, well learned in craft, she, the pupil of Merlin, has 50 taken many. For she has long since been the paramour of the excellent magician Merlin, who knows all the knights in Arthur's court. Morgain the goddess is she

called therefore; none has so great haughtiness of spirit that she cannot tame him.

"She sent me in this manner to your joyous hall, to test the pride, if there be pride, that comes from the great renown of the Round Table. She taught me this marvel to take away your wits and to grieve Guinevere and frighten her to death with the fear of the man who spoke in ghostly fashion before the high 60 dais, with his head in his hand. That is she at my home, the dowager lady; she is even thine aunt, Arthur's half-sister, the daughter of the Duchess of Tintagel, on whom great Uther begat Arthur who now is so famous. Therefore I ask thee, sir knight, to come to thine aunt; make merry in my house; my retinue loves thee; and I myself, sir knight, by my faith, I wish thee as well as any man under Heaven, because of thy great devotion to faith." But Gawain shook his head in refusal; he would not 70 return. They embraced and kissed and commended each other to the Prince of Paradise, and parted right there on the cold ground. Gawain on his fair steed turned away boldly to King Arthur's castle; and the knight in bright green turned whither he would.

Through many a wild path now rode Gawain on Gringolet—Gawain who had thus won grace of his life. Often he lodged in a house, and often outside, and had many adventures by the way and vanquished many men, things that I do not intend to recount in 80 this tale. The wound in his neck healed; he bore the shining belt about him, the badge of his fault he wore as a baldric bound at his side, knotted under his left arm, in token of the fact that he had been found remiss; and so he came to Arthur's court, a knight strong and whole. Joy was lifted up in that castle when great Arthur knew that Gawain had come, for he deemed it gain. The king kissed the knight, and the queen also, and many another trusty knight who hurried up to greet him. They asked him of his ad- 90 venture, and he told them all the wondrous happenings—the chance of the chapel, the actions of the Green Knight, the love of the lady, and last of all the girdle. He showed them the scar in his bare neck that he had won from the hands of the Green Knight as a reproach for his lack of loyalty. He suffered torment when he had to tell of that last adventure; he groaned aloud for very grief and shame; the blood rushed into his face in chagrin, but he told of his humiliation. 100

"Lo, my lords and ladies," said knight Gawain, and handled the girdle, "this is the bond of the blame that I bear on my neck; this is the offense and the loss that I have got for myself, the cowardice and

52. **Morgain the goddess.** Morgan le Fay, sister of Arthur, is an evil figure in Arthurian legend. Her hatred of Guinevere is traced to the fact that Morgan had a love affair with a knight, an affair which Guinevere discovered and made known to the court. For this social misadventure Morgan le Fay was banished from Arthur's court. She came eventually under the influence of Merlin, the great magician and necromancer of the Arthurian circle, learned from him the secret of charms and enchantments, and, according to some stories, became his

mistress. Until this relationship with Merlin, her beauty had been startling, but she then became a hag, as in *Sir Gawain and the Green Knight.* 63. **Duchess of Tintagel . . . Arthur.** Arthur's father, Uther Pendragon, had fallen in love with Ygerne or Igern, the Duchess of Tintagel and the wife of Gorlois. Gorlois was slain, and through the help of Merlin, Uther visited Ygerne in the guise of her husband. The child of this union was Arthur.

covetousness that I felt there; this is the token of my disloyalty, in which I was taken; and I must needs wear this as long as I live. For none can hide his fault, but some mishap will reveal it; for if it once has clung to thee, it will never be severed from thee."

110 The king comforted Gawain, and all the court as well, laughing loudly at the whole story. With general accord the lords and the ladies who belonged to the Round Table agreed that each knight of the brotherhood should wear a baldric, a band of bright green as a badge, following Gawain's example. And with this was the renown of the Round Table in accord; and he was honored ever after who wore the badge, as the best book of romance tells the tale.

Thus the adventure of Gawain and the Green 120 Knight befell in Arthur's day, as the book of Brutus bears witness. For since Brutus, that brave knight, first came hither, after the siege and assault of Troy had ceased, forsooth,

> Many adventures herebefore
> Have fallen such as this;
> He that the crown of thorns once bore
> Now bring us to His bliss!   AMEN.

Honi Soit Qui Mal Y Pense.

116. **Round Table in accord, etc.** As suggested in the introductory headnote to *Sir Gawain and the Green Knight,* the poem may have been written as a dedicatory poem in honor of the Knights of the Garter, although the Garter, so far as is known, never used a green collar or band as a badge. The decision of the Round Table here certainly suggests the founding of some order, but the evidence of what particular order is so vague as to be unconvincing. 121. **book of Brutus.** Some of the early legendary chronicles of England were called *Bruts,* or epics of Brutus, notably that by Layamon of about 1200, but none of them contains the story of Gawain and the Green Knight.

PIERS PLOWMAN

Prose translation by George K. Anderson

The authorship of Piers Plowman is a matter for conjecture (p. 22), but it can still be argued that the poem is as much the product of a tradition—the tradition of the commoner and peasant of the later Middle Ages making his voice heard—as it is of a single author.

There are three separate versions of the poem, believed, because of various allusions to contemporary events, to have been written at different times. These three major versions of the poem have been designated as Text A, Text B, and Text C. On the older theory of Langland's life the date of 1362 was suggested for Text A; 1377 for Text B; and 1392-1398 for Text C. Great doubt, however, has lately been thrown upon the dates traditionally assigned to the three texts. Probably the three versions belong to the decade of the 1370's. Until all the very many manuscripts—there are forty-seven extant—have been collated, it will be impossible even to hint at the original text, and much of the question of identity of the author hinges upon this one discovery.

Like many of the poems in fourteenth-century England, Piers Plowman was written in alliterative verse. To illustrate both the metrical form and the language of the poem, the following section—the opening lines of the Prologue—has been subjoined. For the alliteration and meter this passage might be compared with the excerpt from Beowulf (pp. 25-26).

> In a somer seson   whan soft was the sonne,
> I shope me in shroudes   as I a shepe were,
> In habite as an heremite   unholy of workes,
> Went wyde in þis world   wondres to here.
> Ac on a May mornynge   on Malverne hulles,
> Me byfel a ferly   of fairy, me thouȝte;
> I was wery forwandred   and went me to reste
> Under a brode banke   bi a bornes side,
> And as I lay and lened   and loked in þe
>   wateres,
> I slombred in a slepyng,   it sweyved so merye.

(þ, as in Old English, was the symbol for *th;* ȝ represents a spirant sound similar to the German *ch* in *ich, ach.*)

---

1. PROLOGUE—THE FIELD FULL OF FOLK

In a summer season, when soft was the sun, I clothed me in rough clothes as if I were a shepherd, appearing like a hermit unholy of works; I roamed far in this world to hear and see wonders. But on a May morning on Malvern Hills, a marvel befell me—from fairyland, methought: I had wandered until I was weary, and had gone to rest under a broad bank by the side of a brook; and as I lay and idled and

Piers Plowman. 2. **shepherd . . . hermit.** The dress of a rural shepherd in fourteenth-century England would resemble the costume of a hermit. 5. **Malvern Hills,** between Herefordshire and Worcestershire.

For their relation to the possible author, see the introductory note, p. 22. The main action of the poem itself, however, is in London.

looked on the water, I slumbered in a sleeping; it sounded so pleasant.

Then I did dream a marvelous dream: that I was in a wilderness—where, I did not know; and as I looked toward the east, aloft to the sun, I saw a tower on a hillock most splendidly built, and a deep dale beneath, with a dungeon therein, with deep ditches and dark—a dreadful sight. A fair field full of folk I saw lying between, with all manner of men, the humble and the rich, working and wandering as the world required of them. Some put themselves to the plow and played but seldom: in planting and sowing they labored full hard, and won that which wasters expend in their gluttony. And some gave themselves to pride, and dressed them accordingly; in outward show of raiment all decked out they appeared.

To prayers and to penance many did give themselves; all for the love of Our Lord they lived very strictly, in hope to obtain the full bliss of Heaven—such as anchorites and hermits who stay in their cells, and desire not to wander about in the country to indulge their bodies in lecherous living.

And some chose trade, and succeeded right well, as it seems to our sight that such men prosper; and some turned to song, as minstrels use, and got gold with their music, guiltless, I trust. But jesters and jugglers, children of Judas, feign fancies for themselves and make themselves foolish; yet they have their wits when they need them, and can work if they must. What Paul says of them needs here no rehearsing—*Qui turpiloquium loquitur* is the devil's own servant.

Beggars and mendicants were hurrying about, with their bellies and their bags crammed full of bread; telling falsehoods for their food, and fighting at their ale; going to bed in gluttony, as God well knows; and rising with ribaldry, those robber rascals; sleep and sad slothfulness follow them ever.

Pilgrims and palmers in company vowed them to seek Saint James and the saints at Rome. Forth they went on their way with many wise tales and had leave to lie all their life afterwards. I saw some who said that they had sought saints; for each tale that they told, their tongue was tempered to lying more than to tell the truth—so it seemed by their speech.

Hermits in a crowd with their hooked staves went up to Walsingham, and their wenches came with them. All of them were great lubbers tall and strong who hated to work, clothing themselves in copes to be distinguished from others, and clothed like hermits to have their sweet comfort.

Friars saw I there—all the four orders—, who preached to the people with profit to themselves, interpreting the gospel as it seemed good to them, construing it as they would for the profit of their cloth. Many of the master-friars wore what raiment they preferred, walking along together with their money and possessions. For since Love has turned tradesman and eager to shrive lords, many miracles have happened within a few years. Yet if Holy Church and the friars hold not better together, the greatest mischief in the world will mount up fast enow.

There a pardoner was preaching, as if he were a priest, bringing forth a bull with the seals of the bishop, and said he himself could absolve them all of breaking their vows of fasting and then lying about it. Ignorant men believed him entirely and were pleased with his words, coming up kneeling to kiss his bulls. He banged them with his brevet and bleared their eyes, and collected in his charter

3. **marvelous dream, etc.** We have here, in other words, another instance of "vision" literature so popular in the Middle Ages, forming a tradition which is very tenacious. (cf. Bunyan's *Pilgrim's Progress*, p. 368). 6. **hillock.** The word in the original, *toft*, is difficult to translate, since its meaning is very obscure. The context seems to force the meaning "exposed, raised site." The tower is the Abode of Truth, reminding us of the Celestial City in Bunyan's *Pilgrim's Progress*. **deep dale beneath**, i.e., the castle of Care, the dwelling of Falsehood, as explained in an omitted portion of the poem. 8. **field full of folk,** the world. The figure is from Matthew 13:38, "the field is the world," etc. 27. **guiltless, I trust, etc.** Minstrels or troubadours, who played and sang and told stories, had a bad reputation among the conservative, particularly troubadours of the itinerant sort. Doubtless the same objections could be raised against these strolling players that were raised against the friars and pardoners and other parasites of the Church: begging, cheating, immorality, etc. 32. *Qui . . . loquitur,* "who speaks wickedness." This quotation is not found directly in a Pauline epistle, but Ephesians 5:4 and Colossians 3:8 have the same force. 40. **palmers,** pilgrims who had been to the Holy Land and brought back a palm branch. But the term is used almost as a synonym for "wanderer." 41. **Saint James,** the shrine of Saint James at Compostella, Galicia, Spain, was one of the most famous places of pilgrimage in medieval Europe. Cf. Chaucer's Prologue to *The Canterbury Tales,* p. 111, ll. 464–466. 42. **many wise tales,** i.e., tales of their experiences. We cannot fail to see the resemblance to some features of *The Canterbury Tales* in this remark, although the pilgrims here are telling tall stories redounding to their own credit, while Chaucer's pilgrims are telling tales for entertainment and possibly for instruction. Cf. introductory note to *The Canterbury Tales,* p. 102. 49. **Walsingham,** in Norfolk. It was a famous shrine, next in importance to that of St. Thomas at Canterbury (cf. Chaucer's Prologue to *The Canterbury Tales,* p. 104, ll. 15–18, and note). Our Lady of Walsingham was the most visited religious shrine of England. 51. **copes,** mantles, semi-circular in shape, worn by monks. Their use here by hermits is irregular, but was evidently intended by the hermit to impress his ragged asso-ciates with his religiousness. 54. **four orders,** the Carmelites (white friars), the Augustinians (Austin friars), the Dominicans (Jacobins, black friars), and Minorites (gray friars). 60. **Love . . . tradesman,** a fling at the friar's habit of taking money for penance imposed after the hearing of confessions. Moreover, the friars went about the country carrying knives, pins, brooches, to give to women (cf. Chaucer's Prologue to *The Canterbury Tales,* p. 107, ll. 233–234), and their packs resembled peddlers' packs. *Love* here is intended to be the same as "Christian charity." 65. **pardoner.** Pardoners were members of the Church who bore letters of indulgences—and sometimes sold them. They were not supposed to preach; some pardoners actually were laymen. Cf. Chaucer's Prologue to *The Canterbury Tales,* p. 112, l. 543, and note. 66. **bull,** the credentials or license for the pardoner to dispense his pardons or indulgences, with the leaden seal of a Church dignitary attached. From this leaden seal *(bulla),* the whole paper received the name. Usually the word refers to a proclamation by the pope ("papal bull"). 71. **brevet,** his charter or license. 72. **bleared their eyes,** a common colloquial phrase of the time, meaning, "delude, deceive." 83. **pestilence time,** an allusion to the great scourges of the Black Death, which swept through all Europe during the fourteenth century (cf. "Warrior, Priest, and Commoner," p. 13). The three great epidemics—we might more accurately call them pandemics—were in 1348–1349, 1361–1362, and 1369, but the first one was by far the worst and is probably the one referred to here. 84. **license . . . sing.** This method, apparently common enough among parish priests of the age, for securing additional personal income, is mentioned again in Chaucer's Prologue to *The Canterbury Tales,* p. 111, ll. 507–510. Apparently many Church positions were held by the incumbents only as absentees. A priest could have a berth singing "chantries" in St. Paul's Cathedral at London. He received a salary of seven marks a year for singing mass daily for the repose of a particular soul. There were thirty-five such chantries at St. Paul's; and not until 1391 were they restricted to minor canons of the Cathedral only. 85. **simony,** the name given to the purchase or sale of any ecclesiastical office or function or duty; hence to the income derived from such a purchase or sale. The

rings and brooches—thus those fools give their gold to support all those gluttons, and lend it to the good-for-nothings who frequent vice and lechery. Were the bishop a holy man and worth both his ears, his seal would not be sent to deceive the people. But it is not all through the bishop that this young fellow preaches, for the parish priest and the pardoner divide
80 among them the silver that the poor folk of the parish ought to have, were it not for them.

Parsons and parish priests complained to their bishop that their parishes had been poor since pestilence time, desiring a license and leave in London to dwell, and to sing there for simony, for silver is sweet.

Bishops and novices, masters and doctors, who have a cure of souls with Christ's blessing, and a tonsure as a token and sign that they should shrive their
90 parishioners, should preach and pray for them, and feed the poor—they all lie in London during Lent and all seasons. Some serve the king and count his silver in the Exchequer and in Chancery, claiming his debts from wards and ward-meetings, all waifs and strays; and some as servants of great lords and ladies, and instead of stewards they sit and give judgment. Their masses and matins and prayers at all hours are done undevoutly; there is fear as an answer that Christ in consistory shall curse all too many.
100 I had sight of the power that Peter had to keep, to bind and unbind as the book tells us; how he left it with love, as our Lord had commanded, amongst four virtues the best of all virtues ("cardinal" they are called, or the "closing gates"). There Christ is in His kingdom to close and to shut and to open it to them and show the bliss of Heaven. But the cardinals at court who received the name and assumed the power to make a Pope who would hold the power that

Peter held—them I accuse not, for in love and learning the election is fitting, therefore, though I can, I will 110 not speak more of that court.

Then came a king and knighthood behind him; the might of the commons made him the ruler, and then came Common Sense and a train of clerks, to counsel the king and to save the people.

This king with his knighthood and clergy together planned that the commons should look out for themselves. The commons contrived, with the aid of Common Sense, and for the profit of the people ordained the plowmen, to till and to labor, as an honest life 120 demands. The king and the commons, with Common Sense assisting, shaped laws and loyalty, that each man could know his own standing.

Then appeared a lunatic, a lean creature forsooth, who kneeled before the king and said in clerkly wise: "Christ keep thee, Sire King, and thy kingdom also, and grant thee to rule thy land, and loyalty love thee, and for thy righteous ruling be rewarded in Heaven!"

And then in the air on high an angel from Heaven 130 stooped down and spoke in Latin, for ignorant men who should justify themselves can but chatter, not judge, and so suffer and serve—therefore said the angel: *"Sum Rex, sum Princeps, neutrum fortasse deinceps;—O qui iura regis Christi specialia regis, hoc quod agas melius, iustus es, esto pius! Nudum ius a te vestiri vult pietate; qualia vis metere, talia grana sere. Si ius nudatur, nudo de iure metatur; si seritur pietas, de pietate metas!"*

Then a buffoon objected—a glutton of words, and 140 to the angel aloft he answered immediately: *"Dum rex a regere dicatur nomen habere, nomen habet sine re, nisi studet iura tenere."*

And then all the commons cried out verses of

practice was illegitimate, but its currency is amply confirmed by all the important writers of the age in England and abroad. 87. **Bishops . . . doctors.** To be observed throughout *Piers Plowman* is the general assumption by the author that the evils in the Church derived chiefly from the overorganized bureaucracy of the Church on the one hand and the worldly greed shown by its officials on the other. There are, in other words, many points of resemblance between the author of *Piers Plowman* and the figure of John Wycliffe and the Lollards (cf. "Warrior, Priest, and Commoner," p. 17). Masters and doctors are those who have taken degrees in theology at the universities, and so are, by that very fact, qualified to preach and to interpret the Scriptures. 93. **Exchequer,** formerly one of the three courts of law (the King's Bench and the Common Pleas being the other two). The Exchequer passed only upon cases having to do with the collection of revenue. **Chancery,** the supreme court of England, superior to the three courts of law and presided over by the Lord High Chancellor. 94. **waifs and strays,** property without an owner, e.g., strayed cattle. 96. **sit . . . judgment,** i.e., in matters pertaining to the managing of the feudal estate. 98. **there is fear,** it is to be feared. 99. **consistory,** any Church council or assembly of prelates. But here the reference must be to the Judgment Day, with Christ as judge. 101. **the book,** here, as elsewhere in this poem, usually the Bible, although many of the quotations given with this avowed source are not really from the Bible, but from the writings or preachings of some Church father. It is more than likely, however, that the author of *Piers Plowman* refers all religious precepts to the Scriptures. 103. **"cardinal" . . . "closing gates,"** an attempt at translating the Latin *cardinalia,* derived from *cardo,* a hinge. St. Peter, the first head of the Church, deputed the power of the keys to the kingdom of Heaven to the four "gate-opening" or "cardinal" virtues: Prudence, Temperance, Fortitude, and Justice. 106. **cardinals at court,** the College of Cardinals at Rome. 113. **might of the commons.** This rather startling concession shows at least that the author of *Piers Plowman* was writing after the Magna Charta (1215) as a member of the people rather than of the nobility, and very likely was writing during the difficult political unrest following the death of Edward III in 1377,

culminating in the Peasants' Revolt in 1381. 114. **clerks,** first, members of the Church; then, those who could read and write; then, scholars. The last meaning seems to apply here. 118. **with the aid of Common Sense,** that is, with the aid of craftsmen who depended upon common intelligence. 119. **ordained the plowmen.** The usual divisions of Middle English society about 1300 were: (1) king, (2) knights, (3) clergy, (4) commons. The agricultural class (plowmen and serfs) was considered inferior. But the importance of the tiller of the soil was recognized, particularly after the Black Death, with its uncompromising democracy, had tended to level society. Common sense, says the poet, would ordain plowmen in the right to utter their voice in the shaping of the government. 124. **lunatic,** possibly the poet himself, who speaks of himself elsewhere as foolish and raving. We have another instance of that device of the satirist whereby he poses as a fool, or puts his ideas into the mouths of fools or animals. A lunatic is privileged to say strange things and cannot be held accountable for what he says. Note that the lunatic, however, speaks in "clerkly wise"—like a scholar. 131. **spoke in Latin.** The common people who can not understand French or Latin, the languages of the court and the Church, are ignorant and contemptible, and have no right to hear how they may better themselves. Piers is here waxing sarcastic at the snobbery of the Church. 134. *Sum Rex . . . metas!* This appears to be a composition in Latin by the author of the poem, since no definite source can be found. "I am a king; I am a prince; but you may be perhaps neither hereafter. O thou who dost administer the special laws of Christ the King, that you may do it better, be just and merciful. Naked justice would be clothed by thee in mercy; if thou wouldst reap, be sure to sow the seeds. If justice is stripped bare, let it be meted out naked; if mercy is sown, mayest thou reap mercy!" Advice to kings is sufficiently common in medieval literature, and even later. 141. *Dum . . . tenere.* This is apparently a paraphrase of a political song of the time. The sense is: "While a king is said to have the name of king and to rule, he will have the name without the fact, unless he strives to keep the laws."

Latin, to the king's council—let him construe it who will: "*Precepta regis sunt nobis vincula legis.*"

Whereupon there ran out a crowd of rats together, and small mice with them—more than a thousand, and came to a council for their common profit; for a cat from court came when he pleased, and leaped about among them and caught them as he would, and played with them cruelly and pushed them about. "For fear of many things we dare not look about us; and
10 if we complain of his game, he will destroy us, scratch us and claw us and hold us in his clutches, so that we hate life, ere he will let us go. If we could by some plan but withstand his will, we could be lords on high and live at our ease."

A rat of importance, loquacious of tongue, said he had a sovereign remedy for them all: "I have seen men," said he, "in the city of London, bear necklaces bright about their necks, and some cunningly wrought collars. Free as air they go about both in their warrens
20 and in the wastelands, wheresoever they will it, and again they are elsewhere, as I have heard tell. Were there·a bell on their collar, by Jesus, methinks surely men could tell where they went and so run away! And just so," said the rat, "my reason makes clear to me, we should buy a bell of brass or of bright silver, and fasten it to a collar for our own common profit, and hang it on the cat's neck; then we can hear whether he is riding or resting, or running to play. And if he wants sport, then we can see to it,
30 and appear in his presence while he is willing to play; and if he is angry, we can be aware, and shun his path."

All the crowd of rats to this plan gave assent. But though the bell was bought and hung on the necklace, there was no rat in all that crowd, for all the realm of France, who would dare tie on that bell about the cat's neck; no, not bind it to the cat's throat to gain all England. So they thought themselves cowardly, and their counsel feeble, and thought their labor lost,
40 and all their long effort.

But a mouse that knew good, wise, as it seemed to me, moved forward boldly, and stood in their presence, and to that crowd of rats addressed these words: "Even if we killed that cat, yet would come another, to scratch us and our race, though we crept under benches. Therefore I counsel the commons, to let that cat be, and never presume that bell to show him; for I heard my sire say, now seven years passed,

'Where the cat is a kitten, the court is full wretched'; Holy Writ bears that to witness, whosoever will read 50 it: *Vae terrae ubi puer rex est*, etc. Now no man can have rest for us rats at night; but while he catches rabbits, he craves not our carrion, but feeds himself with venison—let us never defame him! For better is a little loss than a long sorrow; confusion among us all though we be without a sinner. For many a man's malt would we mice devour, and you, crowd of rats, would tear men's clothing, were it not for that cat of the court that can leap among you. For if you rats had your will, ye could not govern 60 yourselves. I say for my part," said the mouse, "I foresee so well, that neither cat nor kitten will ever be vexed by my counsel; nor shall there be more talk from me about the collar, which never cost me aught. Yea, though it had cost me my possessions, I would not now acknowledge it, but suffer him to do exactly as he wishes, whether restrained or free—let him catch what he likes. And so every wise man I advise: know well your own standing."

What this dream may portend—ye men that are 70 merry, guess for yourselves, for I dare not, by dear God in Heaven!

Then a hundred folk hovered about in hoods of silk, law-sergeants, it seemed, who served at the bar, pleading the law for pennies or pounds; not once did they loose their lips for love of our Lord. Thou couldst better measure the mist on Malvern Hill than get a mumble from their mouths unless money was shown them.

Barons and burgesses and bondmen also I saw in 80 the multitude, as ye shall hear after. Women—bakers and brewers, weavers of woolens and linens; butchers, tailors, and tinkers, toll-collectors in the markets, masons and miners and many other craftsmen—all kinds of living laborers passed by in groups, such as diggers and delvers, who do work full ill and pass the live-long day with "*Dieu vous sauve, Dame Emme!*"; cooks and their slaveys cried, "Hot pies! hot! good pigs and geese; let's go eat now, let's go!" Taverners followed, saying the same way: "White 90 wine of Osey; red wine of Gascony; from the Rhine and Rochelle, to digest the roast!"

All this saw I sleeping, and seven times more.

[*In the midst of all this confusion, Lady Holy Church appears to the poet and tells him of the*

---

2. **Precepta . . . legis.** "The commands of the king are legal bonds for us." 3. **crowd of rats, etc.** This famous fable of the rats belling the cat seems to have a medieval origin; this version from *Piers Plowman* appears to be the oldest one in English, and no version exists anywhere before the fourteenth century. The rats here represent the middle-class burgesses and more influential men in the Commons; the mice are of less social importance. The cat mentioned is King Edward III, who died in 1377; the kitten is young Richard II, who came to the throne at a very early age. 6. **cat from court,** the king (Edward III). 19. **collars.** Observe the importance of decorative or precious neckwear as a mark of prosperity, as in Old English times. **warrens,** places for keeping animals, enclosures, hutches; hence in keeping with the allegory, "dwellings." 49. **court is full wretched.** A reference to the troublous days of intrigue in the early years of Richard II's reign;

until the death of the monarch there was always more or less unrest at the court, and Richard himself ·passed in a cloud of chicanery and violence. It is difficult, however, to determine whether these lines in the poem are prophetic of a likely event, or merely a comment upon things that have already happened. 51. *Vae . . . rex est,* etc. "Woe to thee, O land, when thy king is a child, and thy princes eat in the morning!"—Ecclesiastes 10:16. The idea, however, is practically proverbial in Early English literature. 55. **confusion . . . sinner.** "if the king died, there would be confusion among us, even though we were without a tyrant." 62. **kitten,** Richard II; cf. 1. 3 and note. 74. **law-sergeants,** legal servants of the king. They were lawyers of at least sixteen years' standing. The judges of the King's Court and the presiding officer of the Exchequer (cf. p. 91, ll. 91–93, and notes) were chosen from their body. Cf. also Chaucer's Prologue to *The*

worldliness of his age, and of the necessity for every Christian man to seek Truth, Faith, and Charity, which will lead to Heaven. The crowd of sinners becomes repentant and determines to seek Truth, but no one can show them the way. Piers Plowman volunteers: he has served Truth for fifty years, and Conscience and Common Sense have shown him the way. There comes a description of the country through which they must pass. Many pilgrims are discouraged. The prophet Piers enjoins them to labor, cultivate their fields, and undergo Hunger and Suffering as a preparation for their journey. Such is the earliest version of the poem (Text A).

Two remarkable episodes of considerable extent are included in this first version, one of which will be given below. The first is the sustained story of Lady Meed (Reward), a rich and noble-appearing lady. Her name, somewhat ambiguous, the poet takes in the sinister sense of undeserved rewards. She is to be married to False, but Theology opposes, and the whole marriage-retinue travels to London, where the question is to be settled by the king's court. Conscience and Reason, the lawyers for Theology, finally persuade the king to break off the match, in spite of the sophistries of False and his shameless bribery of royal officials. False and his followers are forced to flee and take refuge among the Pardoners, the Minstrels, the Merchants, and the Friars—all those whom the poet had attacked in the prologue for dishonesty.

The second episode comes in the course of Reason's sermon before the court, when he invites all sinners to seek the Truth. The Seven Deadly Sins finally are prevailed upon to comply.]

2. THE SHRIVING OF THE SEVEN DEADLY SINS

Then Repentance ran and rehearsed his woe, and made Will to weep water from his eyes.

[1. Pride] Peronell the proud of heart threw herself flat on the ground and lay long before she looked up crying: "Lord, have mercy!" and promising Him who made us all ever to unsew her smock and put on a hair-shirt, to tame her flesh so wild to sin. "Never shall a haughty heart lift me up; I shall hold myself humble, and suffer myself to be slandered, as I never did before. Now I will abase myself and beseech mercy of all that I have hated in my heart." "Repent thee," said Repentance, "as Reason has taught thee, and shrive thyself strictly, and shake off all pride." Then

Pride confessed: "I, Pride, ask penance in patience, for I first and foremost to father and mother have been disobedient (I beseech God for mercy!); I have been disobedient and not abashed as an offense to God and all good men—so great was my pride! Disobedient I was to Holy Church and to them that serve her, adjudging to her evil vices, and inflaming others with my words and my wit to show their evil works, and scorning them and others if I could find a reason, laughing loudly that ignorant men should deem I were witty and wiser than another; scorning and unreasonable to them that demanded reason for my name to be known in all manner wise; putting on airs wheresoever chance offered. To tell any tale I believed myself wiser, in discourse or counsel, than any, learned or ignorant. I was proud of apparel, in my bearing among the people presumptuous in excess, within or without, desiring men should think me rich and clever, as I averred, and living a right life, boasting and bragging with many bold oaths, puffing myself up unto vainest of glory in any undertaking, and so important to myself that, beside all other people, there was none like myself and none so pope-holy; sometimes in one sect, sometimes in another; in all kinds of covetousness contriving how I might be judged a holy one, a hundred times for my profit. I desired that men think my deeds were the best, and my wisdom most searching both of clerks and of others, and strongest in the world, and firmest under my girdle, and the loveliest to look upon, and most pleasing abed. I loved such a life, which no good faith can praise. I was proud of my fine voice, and therefore I sang loudly, and what I gave for praise of God I told all my neighbors, for them to think me holy and charitable. Never was there so bold a beggar to ask and to pray, to tell tales in the taverns and streets. Things that could never be imagined, I swore I saw them and lied by my body and by my life also. Of the works that I did well I take here witness, and say to those who are sitting beside me: 'Lo! if ye believe me not, if ye think I lie, ask of him or of her, and they can tell you what I suffered and saw and at one time had, and what I knew and thought of, and of what kin I came';—all that I wanted men to know, when it redounded to my pride, to be praised among the people, though I seemed but a poor thing: 'Si hominibus placerem, Christi servus non essem. Nemo potest duobus dominis servire.' "

Canterbury Tales, p. 109, ll. 309 ff. 84. craftsmen, tradesmen as well as artisans, and all members of guilds. See "Warrior, Priest, and Commoner," p. 13. 87. Dieu . . . Dame Emme! This seems to be a line or a refrain from some popular song of the time. Later in the poem there is mention of a prostitute named Emme of Shoreditch, a vicinity known for its disreputable character. Unquestionably the song was a "song of the people." 90. Taverners, innkeepers. 91. Osey, a corruption of Alsace. The wine was a sweet, light wine. Gascony, the name of an old province in southwestern France. The wine from this region has been proverbially famous. 92. Rochelle, La Rochelle, France, on the Bay of Biscay, south of the mouth of the Loire. The town was noted for its wine. 95. Will. This seems to be the author of the poem, who refers to himself elsewhere as Will. See, however, note on p. 95, l. 10. 96. Peronell. It may be observed that Peronelle

appears later (p. 98, l. 38) as "of Flanders"; as the name would indicate, she is of French origin. It is noteworthy, too, that Pride is the only one of the Seven Deadly Sins to be represented here by a woman. 100. hair-shirt. Abstinence from food and drink and the wearing of an extremely uncomfortable hair shirt (a garment with the hairs on the inside) twice a week constituted the most common form of penance. 129. pope-holy, hypocritical. 143. by my . . . life also. To invoke one's body and soul was possibly the strongest form of oath next to the invoking of the Savior's body and soul. 152. 'Si . . . essem.' "If I yet pleased men, I should not be the servant of Christ"— Galatians 1:10. 153. 'Nemo . . . servire.' "No man can serve two masters." (Cf. King James Bible, "The Sermon on the Mount," p. 315, l. 174.)

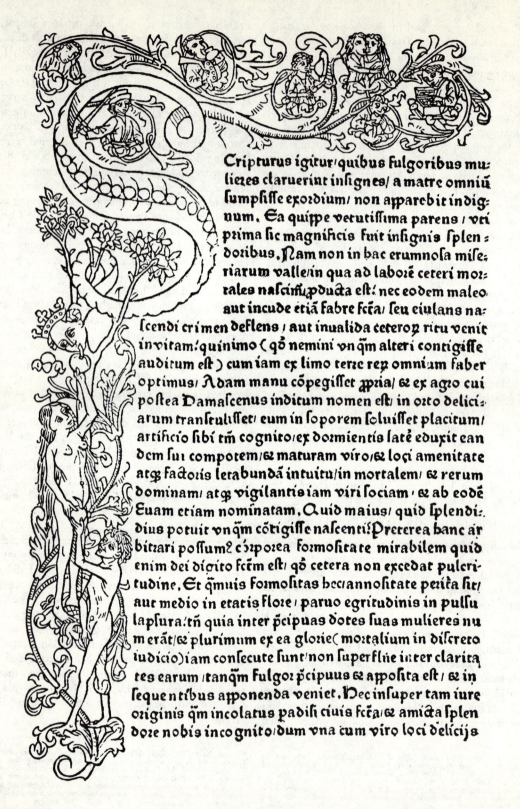

Cripturus igitur quibus fulgoribus mulieres claruerint insignes, a matre omniú sumpsisse exordium, non apparebit indignum. Ea quippe vetutissima parens, vti prima sic magnificis fuit insignis splendoribus. Nam non in hac erumnosa miseriarum valle, in qua ad laborem ceteri mortales nascimur producta est, nec eodem maleo, aut incude etiá fabre ficta, seu eiulans nascendi crimen deflens, aut inualida ceteroz ritu venit inuitam, quinimo (q nemini vnqm alteri contigisse auditum est) cum iam ex limo terre rex omniam faber optimus, Adam manu copegisset ppria, & ex agro cui postea Damascenus inditum nomen est, in orto deliciarum transtulisset, eum in soporem soluisset placitum, artificio sibi tm cognito, ex dormientis late eduxit eandem sui compotem, & maturam viro, & loci amenitate atqz factoris letabundá intuitu, in mortalem, & rerum dominam, atqz vigilantis iam viri sociam, & ab eodé Euam etiam nominatam. Quid maius, quid splendidius potuit vnqm cotigisse nascenti? Preterea hanc ar bitrari possum? corporea formositate mirabilem quid enim dei digito fctm est, q cetera non excedat pulcritudine. Et qmuis formositas hec annositate perita sit, aut medio in etatis flore, paruo egritudinis in pullu lapsura, tn quia inter pcipuas dotes suas mulieres nu m erát, & plurimum ex ea glorie (mortalium in discreto iudicio) iam consecute sunt, non superflue inter claritates earum, tanqm fulgor pcipuus & apposita est, & in sequentibus apponenda veniet. Hec insuper tam iure originis qm incolatus padisi ciuis fcta, & amicta splendore nobis incognito, dum vna cum viro loci delicijs

The seven deadly sins decorate this page from Boccaccio's De Claris Mulieribus, published in Ulm by Johann Zainer in 1473 (from the copy in the Spencer Collection of the New York Public Library). From left to right the sins represented are: Sloth, Wrath, Drunkenness, Pride, Lechery, Gluttony, and Avarice. Usually Envy is represented, Drunkenness and Gluttony being considered one sin, Intemperance.

"Now God of His goodness give thee grace to make amends," said Repentance; and then rose Envy.

[2. Envy] Envy with heavy heart asked for shrift, and cried *"Mea culpa"* and cursed all his enemies. His clothes were of cursing and words of boldness. He shook his fist in wrath; had he wishes that meant deeds, no life should live that came to his realm. Chiding and chattering made his chief livelihood, to blame men behind their back and wish them mis-
10 chance. All that he knew of Will, he told it to Watkin; and what he knew of Watkin he told later to Will, and made foes of friends through his false and fickle tongue. "Through the power of my words and my own foul tricks I have avenged myself oft, or fretted myself within like a pair of sewer's shears, and cursed my fellow-Christian against the teaching of Christ, as clerks tell it in books: *Cuius maledictione os plenum est et amaritudine et dolo; sub lingua eius labor et dolor. Filii hominum, dentes eorum arma et*
20 *sagittae, et lingua eorum gladius acutus.* When I cannot succeed, such melancholy comes over me, that I get cramps, sometimes a heart-attack, or an ague—such my anger!—and sometimes a fever, that takes me for a twelvemonth, until I despise medicine from our Lord, and believe in witchcraft, and say what no clerk can say, nor Christ, so I think, to the cobbler in Southwark. By God, or God's words, or His grace had I never help; but through a charm I had luck and my worldly salvation. For many a year I could
30 not eat as a man ought, for envy and ill will is bad for digestion. Can no sugar nor sweet thing assuage my swellings, nor some toothsome drink drive it from my heart, nor some shame or shrift, unless some one scrape my maw?" "Yea, truly," quoth Repentance, "if thou be right sorry for thy sovereign sin, and beseech God for mercy." "Always I am sorry," said Envy, "I am but seldom otherwise; that makes me so thin, for I cannot have satisfaction, but I am Backbiting's broker, and condemn men's wares often among mer-
40 chants, especially in London. When they sold, and I not, I was ever full ready to lie and to glare on my neighbors, and their works and their words, wheresoever I was settled. Now I repent in my thoughts that ever I did so. Lord! ere I leave life, for love of Thyself, grant me, good Lord, the grace of amending!"

[3. Wrath] Then awoke Wrath, with two pale eyes, and a sniffling nose, biting his lips. "I am Wrath," quoth that fellow, "I will gladly smite with stone or staff and steal upon mine enemy; I bethink me of
50 tricks to slay him with violence. Though I should sit here seven years I could not well tell the harm that I have done with hand and with tongue. Impatient in all penances, complaining, as it were, of God, when His message vexed me or made me angry—thus, sometimes in summer and also in autumn, if I had not the weather I wanted, I charged God with the cause with all manner of angers of which I was able. Among all sorts of men my dwelling may be: with the learned or ignorant, who may be glad to hear harm of some man, forwards or backwards. Friars follow me forth, 60 many a time and oft, and prove very imperfect prelates of Holy Church; yea, the prelates themselves complain of them, for they shrive all their parishes without license or leave; so Wrath lives nearby. So they speak and dispute and despise one another; and beggars as well as barons are often at odds, till I, Wrath, wax and prosper, and walk with them both; thus both may be beggars and live by my spirit, or else all rich and ride about—in any case I, Wrath, have no rest, but must follow these people: my fortune 70 could not be elsewhere.

"I have for aunt a nun and an abbess; she had liefer swoon or die than suffer any pain. I have been cook in her kitchen, and served them in the convent for months and the monks that are with them. I was a maker of pottages for the prioress and other poor, ladies, and made tasty broths of gossip. Dame Joanna was a bastard, and Dame Clarice a knight's daughter, and her father a cuckold; Dame Peronelle a priest's child, and never a prioress! For she had a child in 80 the chapter-house, and was accused at the consistory. So they sit, those sisters together, and dispute, till 'Thou liest!' and 'Thou liest!' be lady of them all. And then I, Wrath, awake and desire to be satisfied. So I cry out and scratch with my sharp nails, and bite and strike and bring out such nasty tricks, that all ladies hate me if they love any virtue. Among wives and widows I am wont to sit enclosed in pews. The parson knows how little I liked Letice at the chancel, for she had her holy bread before I—my 90 temper began to rise. Afterwards, after dinner she and I scolded her friend, and I, Wrath, was aware of it, and angry at them both, till each called the other whore, and off with their clothes, till both their heads were bare and their cheeks all bloody.

"Among monks I can dwell, but many times I shun them, for there are many wicked fellows to spy on my affairs, that is, the prior and sub-prior, and our father the abbot. And if I tell any tales, they gather together, and make me fast Fridays on bread and

4. **Mea culpa.** "My Sin," "My fault." A common formula of the confession, from the Book of Common Prayer. 10. **Will,** probably not the author himself, as on p. 93, l. 95 (see note), but simply a typical masculine name, as is Watkin (Little Walter). 17. **Cuius . . . dolor.** "Whose mouth is full of cursing and deceit and fraud; under his tongue is mischief and vanity."—Psalms 10:7. 19. **Filii . . . acutus.** "Sons of men, whose teeth are spears and arrows, and their tongue a sharp sword."—Psalms 57:4. 26. **the cobbler in Southwark.** Envy's accomplishments in sorcery and black magic are kept, however, from the humble people about him and not spoken of to any clerk or nobleman. Southwark is the suburb of London on the south bank of the Thames, skirting the river from London Bridge eastward to a point about opposite Limehouse. It was an extremely important part of the city in the fourteenth century, since it was the port of entry for nearly all traffic from the south and east of London. The old Kent road ran through it, and for that reason it was the logical place for the Canterbury pilgrims to assemble (cf. Chaucer's Prologue to *The Canterbury Tales,* p. 104, l. 20). 28. **through a charm, etc.** Here is evidence of the persistence of these features of magic, whether beneficent or malevolent, white or black. Such charms, or at least traces of them, can still be found in certain parts of rural England. 81. **chapter-house,** the place for assembly of the governing body of an ecclesistical institution. 94. **heads were bare, etc.,** that is, "I incited them to fighting until they tore out each other's hair."

water. And I am accused in the chapter-house as if I were a child, and flogged on the buttocks with no breeches between. I have no pleasure, believe me, in living among monks, for they eat more fish than meat, and drink feeble ale. But at other times, when wine comes my way, and when I drink late, I have an evil-tasting mouth for five days thereafter. All that I knew of wickedness pertaining to our convent I coughed it up in our cloister, so that all the convent
10 knew it."

"Now repent thee," said Repentance, "and never tell what knowledge thou mayst have of that, by thy face nor by thy speech. And drink not over squeamishly, nor yet too deeply, either, that thy will and thy wits may not turn again to anger. *Esto sobrius*," he said, and absolved him thereafter and bade him pray to God, by His help to amend him.

[4. Lechery] Then said Lechery, "Alas!" and cried to Our Lady, "Lady, bow for me now before thy
20 dear Son, that He may have pity on my rottenness from His pure grace and mercy. And then I shall" (said that rascal) "on Saturdays, for Thy love, drink but with the ducks and dine but once. I, guilty in spirit, before God will shrive me, in my liking for lust and the sins of the body, in words, in clothing, in the expectancy of the eye. Every maid that I met, I made her a sign; some I tasted on the mouth and beneath I did grope till our two lusts were one; to our lust we did go on fasting-days and Fridays and the
30 eve of high feasts, as willingly in Lent as out of Lent, at all times alike—such works with us were never out of season—till we could do no more; then we told merry tales of lust and of paramours, and tempted ourselves through speeches, handling and embracing, and kissing each other back to our sin. Many lewd songs for exciting I framed, and sent out old bawds to win to my will fair women with guile, sometimes by sorcery, and sometimes by sheer force. I lay with the loveliest and never loved them after. When I was old
40 and gray and had lost all my vigor, I took pleasure in laughing at lecherous tales. Now Lord, for thy faith, have mercy on lechers!"

[5. Avarice] Then came Avarice; I cannot describe him, so hungry and hollow did Sir Harvey look. He was beetle-browed and flabby-lipped, with two bleary eyes, and like a leathern purse his cheeks sagged, even more than his chin they shook from age; with his beard all beslobbered like a churl's with bacon juice,

his hood on his head and a lousy hat above it, in a threadbare cloak twelve winters of age. But if a louse 50 could leap, I honestly think, he would not have lingered on that flannel, so threadbare it was. "I have been covetous," said this caitiff, "I acknowledge it here. For some time I served Sim at the Stile, and was bound as his apprentice, to look after his profits. First I learned to lie for a page or two; to weigh out dishonestly was my very first lesson. To Weyhill and Winchester I went to the fair with all kinds of merchandise, as my master commanded. If the grace of deceit had not traveled along with my wares, they 60 would have been unsold for seven years, God help me!

"I went among drapers to learn my primer, to pull the edge of the cloth until its length seemed longer. Among the striped cloths I learned also a lesson, to pierce them with a pack-needle, and fasten them together; I put them in presses and enclosed them therein, till ten yards or twelve really counted thirteen. My wife was a weaver, and made woolen cloth. She spoke to the spinners to spin it thin; the pound weight 70 by which she paid them weighed a quarter more than my steelyard when I weighed it true. I bought her barley; she brewed it to sell; penny-ale and pudding-ale she poured all together for laborers and low folk who lived by themselves. The best ale was in my bedchamber, and whoever tasted it bought it at once, a gallon for a groat, yet no more for good measure, when it came by the cupful—this trick my wife used. Rose the retailer was her right name; she has sold these eleven winters." 80

"Didst thou never repent?" said Repentance, "nor make restitution?" "Yes, once," said Avarice, "I was lodged with a band of merchants; I rose and rifled their bags while they were asleep." "That was a fine restitution," said Repentance, "forsooth, thou shalt hang high for that, here or in Hell! Didst thou ever practice usury in thy time?" "Nay, truly," said Avarice, "save in my youth. I learned among Lombards a lesson, and from Jews, to weigh pence with a weight, and cut down the heaviest, and lend it for 90 the sake of a note, which I thought better and worth more than the money that I loaned other folk. I lent to people who wished to lose a part of each noble, and with Lombards' letters I took gold to Rome; what a man from me borrowed he paid for in time."

"Didst thou ever lend to a lord for the sake of his

---

15. *Esto sobrius*, "be sober." 22. **Saturdays.** Since Saturdays were half holidays, there would be more time for drinking, eating, and general carousing. **drink . . . the ducks,** that is, "drink water only." 30. **high feasts,** important Church holidays. 44. **Sir Harvey look.** "Harvey" seems to have been something of a traditional name for a covetous man. 55. **apprentice.** The system of apprenticeship was based on the principle that a member of a trade or profession—the master—would bind himself to teach another—the apprentice—his trade or profession. The apprentice was equally bound to his master, the whole affair being a kind of indenture, although it was often an oral rather than a written agreement. Ordinarily the apprentice would serve a term of seven years. 57. **Weyhill,** in Hampshire; its annual fair is still famous. 72. **steelyard,** a means of measuring, consisting of a steel scale-beam, weights, and hooks. The article to be weighed is hung on the short end, and the counterweight on the long arm. The point

of balance indicates the weight of the article. 73. **penny-ale . . . pudding-ale.** Penny-ale is common ale costing a penny a gallon. Pudding-ale is the thicker ale, so called from its thick consistency. 77. **groat.** A Low German coin from the trading ports of Holland and northern Germany, notably from Bremen, worth about four silver pennies. 88. **Lombards,** the inhabitants of Lombardy, a region in northern Italy around Milan. They were famous as bankers and brokers during the Middle Ages. Their appearance in England was in connection with papal legates—they were the financial representatives of the pope and notorious in the fourteenth century for their usury. 90. **cut . . . heaviest.** In the Middle Ages, coins were not minted according to standard dimensions, but solely by the weight of gold or silver. Hence it would not be too difficult for an unscrupulous handler of coin to take away some of the metal ("clip or cut down") and pass off the coin as being heavier than it really was. 93. **noble.** A

maintenance?" "Yes," replied Avarice, "I have lent to lords and ladies who never loved me after. I have made many a knight mercer or draper, paying naught
100 for his apprenticeship, not even a pair of gloves. Whoever bargained in my dealings did nothing much later!" "Now truly," said Repentance, "and by the rood, I trust, no executor shall happily possess the silver which thou leavest him, nor will thine heirs, I hope, have joy in what thou didst win. For the pope and all his confessors will lack the power to absolve thee of thy sins without thy restitution; *nunquam dimittitur peccatum, nisi restituatur ablatum.*" "Yea," replied Avarice, "with false words and lying wits I
110 have won all my goods, and with deceit and flattery gathered what I own, adulterated my merchandise, and made a good appearance; the worst was within me— I think that showed clever wits. And if my neighbor had a servant or some beast in addition more valuable than mine, I took many paths; how I might get them was the goal of all my thoughts. And unless I got them some other way, I would finally steal them, or secretly shake my purse and pick open his locks. And if I went to plow, I squeezed his half-acre, to get
120 myself a foot of land or a furrow; of my nearest neighbor I would take what I could. And if I reaped, I would over-reach my land, or tell them who were reaping to seize what they could for me with their sickle; of course I never saw it.

"On holy days in the church, when I heard mass, I never, truly, had the will to pray for my misdeeds; I mourned more for the loss of goods, believe me, than for the sins of my body. Though I did mortal sin, I feared it not so much as when I loaned and thought
130 it lost or far too long overdue. Or if I sent over the sea my servant to Bruges or my apprentice into Prussia to take care of my profits, to bargain with money and make their exchanges—no man could comfort me in the meantime, neither matins nor mass nor other spectacles, nor a penance performed nor a *paternoster* said: my mind was always more on my goods than on the grace of the Lord or his omnipotence. *Ubi thesaurus tuus, ibi est cor teum.*"

"Now truly," said Repentance, "thy way of life
140 makes me pity thee. Were I a friar, in good faith, for all the gold in the earth I would not clothe me with thy linens or repair our church with thy materials or take a bite of food from thy store; if my heart knew for certain that thou wert such as thou hast said, I

should rather starve and die. *Melius est mori quam male vivere.* I trust no faithful friar would sit at thy feast; it were better for me, by our Lord, to live on water-cresses than to have my food and my well-being from the gains of wicked men. *Servus es alterius cum fercula pinguia queris, pane tuo potius vescere,* 150 *liber eris.* Thou art an unnatural creature; I cannot absolve thee until thou hast made, as best thou canst, to all men restitution; for all that possess thy goods (I swear it before God!) will be charged at the Last Judgment to help thee make amends; the priest that receives thy tithes, and none other, I think, would share with thee in purgatory and help pay thy debt, if he knew thou wert such when he received thy offering. If any one think I lie, let him look in the psalter: *Ecce enim veritatem dilexisti.* There he can certainly find 160 out what usury means and what penance the priest shall have, who exults in thy tithes. For a whore with her filthy winnings can pay tithes with more grace than an errant usurer (I swear it before God!) and will come sooner to Heaven, by Christ who made me!"

Then appeared a Welshman in pitiable condition; he was named Evan Yield-again and said: "If I have so much, all that I won in wickedness since I had my five wits—though it ruin my livelihood I will not 170 forbear, each man shall have his ere I go hence. I had rather beg in this life like a good-for-nothing, than live in bliss and lose life and soul."

Robert the robber looked to restore his booty; and since he had not wherewith to do it, he wept full sore; and yet that sinful rascal cried out to Heaven: "Christ who on Calvary didst die on the cross, when Dismas my brother besought thee for grace, thou hadst mercy on that man and didst see fit to remember; so take pity on Robert, who cannot restore and do not expect 180 to win enough, with the craft that I have. Out of thy great mercy I beseech mitigation, condemn me not on Judgment Day because I have done so ill!" What became of this felon I cannot show plain; I know he wept fast; the tears fell from his eyes, and made known his guilt to Christ more than once; crying that he would polish as new Penance his pike-staff, for he had learned the faith once of Latro, Lucifer's aunt.

"By the rood!" said Repentance, "thou art facing 190 toward Heaven, provided it be in thy heart as I have heard on thy tongue. Trust in His great mercy, and

gold coin, worth approximately six shillings and eight pence. 98. **I have made . . . draper,** probably to be taken in the sense, "I have lent money to knights, and when they could not pay, reduced them to commoners." The next sentence explains the allusion, but it must be confessed that the sentence as it stands is not very clear. 107. **nunquam . . . ablatum.** "Never shall a sin be forgiven, unless that is restored which was carried away." The quotation is not from the Scriptures in this case, but is a paraphrase from an epistle of St. Augustine. 118. **shake my purse and pick . . . locks,** that is, persuade his servants through bribery to make accessible the coveted goods. 119. **half-acre,** the usual allotment of land granted a villein under the feudal system (cf. "Warrior, Priest, and Commoner," pp. 12–13). 131. **Bruges,** the city of the Low Countries (in modern Belgium) noted as the center of the Flemish woolen textiles trade. 137. **Ubi . . . teum.** "Where thy treasure is, there is thy heart also." (Cf. the King James Bible, "The

Sermon on the Mount," p. 315.) 145. **Melius . . . vivere.** "Better to die than to live evilly." Cf. the apocryphal Book of Tobit 4:6 for the idea of which this is a paraphrase. 149. **Servus . . . liber eris.** "Thou art the slave of another when thou seekest after dainty dishes; feed rather upon bread of thine own, and thou wilt be a free man." This Latin quotation has no known source. 159. **Ecce . . . dilexisti.** "Lo thou hast loved truth." Cf. Psalms 51:6. 177. **Dismas . . . grace.** The episode of the penitent and impenitent thieves is told in Luke 23:39–43. The names, however, are found only in the apocryphal Gospel of Nicodemus. Dismas' name appears in legend also as Titus; the impenitent thief is Gestas. 188. **Latro,** "a thief." How this name became the name of a particular female fallen angel, the aunt of Lucifer, the author of the poem does not make clear, and one is inclined to think that the relationship is original with the author.

A plowman, from the Luttrell Psalter (c. 1340). "God spede the plowe and sende vs corne ynow."

thou mayst yet be saved. For all the wretchedness of this world and its wicked deeds pass like a spark of fire that falls in the Thames and perishes in a drop of water; so do the sins of all kinds of men who with good will confess them and cry for mercy; they shall never come to Hell. *Omnis iniquitas quoad misericordiam Dei est quasi scintilla in medio maris.* So repent," said Repentance to that foolish usurer, "and keep His mercy in thy mind, and leave all trafficking; for there is no good, in faith, that can be bought with a cake. All that thou didst win thou gottest by deceit; as long as thou livest therewith, thou payest not, but borrowest. And if thou dost not know to whom to restore it all, take it to the bishop and pray him for grace, to dispose of it himself as will be best for thy soul; and he shall answer for thee at the Great Judgment, for thee and for many more, for whom there will be reckonings. What he can teach thee that thou mayst live as a good man, and hold thee from theft—do not forget it."

[6. Gluttony] Now Gluttony arises to go to his shriving, turning to the church to make known his sins. Fasting on a Friday he goes forth by the house of Bet the brewer, who bids him good morrow, and asks him—does the brewing-woman—where he is going.

"To Holy Church," said he, "to hear mass and then sit and be shriven and then sin no more." "I have good ale, friend Gluttony, wilt thou make trial of it?"

"What hast thou," said he, "any hot spices?" "I have pepper and peony-seeds, and a pound of garlic, a farthing's worth of fennel-seed for days of fasting."

So Gluttony went in, and great oaths he uttered. Ciss the seamstress sat on the bench; Watt the warrener and his wife—both drunk; Tom the tinker and two of his working men; Hick the teamster and Hugh the needle-seller; Clarice of Cock's Lane; the clerk of the church; Sir Piers of Pridie, and Peronelle of Flanders; a hayward and a hermit; the hangman at Tyburn; Davie the ditch-digger with a dozen rascals —porters, and pickpockets, and bald-headed tooth-pullers; a fiddler; a rat-catcher; a scavenger from Cheapside; a rope-maker and a riding-knight and Rose the dish-seller; Godfrey of Garlickhithe, and Griffin the Welshman, and second-hand dealers in a mob; though early in the morning they all gave Gluttony a good cheer and good ale for a treat.

Clement the cobbler cast off his cloak and at a new fair announced it for sale. Hick the teamster threw down his hood, and asked Bet the butcher to be on his side. Merchants were called to appraise the goods, so that he who had the hood should not also have the cloak; the better thing, according to the umpires, should make up for the worse. Two rose hastily and conferred together, and appraised the rags alone and apart; there were oaths unnumbered, lest one should get the worse. They could not in all conscience agree, forsooth, till Robin the rope-maker was asked to stand up and was named as an umpire to silence debate. Hick the teamster won the cloak with the understanding that Clement should fill his cup and have the teamster's hood, and consider himself lucky—whoever disagreed with this bargain should stand up at once and greet Sir Gluttony with a gallon of ale.

There was laughing and scowling and "Let go the cup!", bargaining and bibbing began to grow loud; they sat so till vespers rang and loitered about in song, till Gluttony had gulped down a gallon and a gill. His guts began to grumble like two greedy sows . . . He could neither step nor stand until he had seized his staff; then he moved like a minstrel's bitch—now to the side, now to the rear, as he who lays lines to catch fowls. When he got to the door, his eyes dimmed; he stumbled on the threshold and pitched to the ground. Then Clement the cobbler caught him by the waist to lift him up, and got him to his knees. But Gluttony was a large churl and groaned in the lifting, and spewed up a mess into Clement's lap—no hound so hungry in all Herfordshire would lap up that vomit: so unlovely it tasted.

With all the woe in the world his wife and their wench got him to bed after bringing him home; and after all this excess he had a sleeping-stroke. He slept Saturday and Sunday till the sun went to rest. Then he woke pale and wan and wanted a drink; the first word he spoke was "Where is the bowl?" His wife and his conscience reproached him with his shame; he was abashed, that fellow, and made his confession to Repentance right so: "Have pity on me," said he, "Thou Lord that art on high, and on all living creatures! To Thee, God, I, Gluttony, all guilty confess my trespasses with my tongue—I cannot tell how often I have sworn by thy soul and thy sides, and 'So help me, God Almighty,' when there was no need so to swear falsely. And I ate too much at my supper and even at dinner more than my constitution well could digest; and as a dog that eats grass I belched it all up, and lost what might have been spared for others. I cannot speak for shame of the villainy of my foul mouth and my dirty maw. On fasting-days before noon I plied myself with ale out of all reason among ribald men to listen to their ribaldry. For all that, good God, grant me forgiveness,

for all my low living during my lifetime. For I vow to the true God—whether hungry or thirsty, not even fish on Friday will digest in my belly until Abstinence my Aunt has given me leave—she whom I have hated all my life long."

[7. Sloth] Then came Sloth all slobbering with two slimy eyes. "I must sit to be shriven"; said he, "I fear I may nap. I can neither stand nor stoop nor kneel without my stool. Were I brought to my bed, unless my tail-end prompted me, no ringing could raise me until I was ready to dine." *Benedicite* he began with a belch, and then beat his breast, thrashed about, and roared, and finally snored aloud. "Here! awake, man!" said Repentance, "hasten to thy shriving!"

"Should I die this day," said Sloth, "I would be sore adread; I know not my *paternoster* well, as the priest once taught me. But I know rimes of Robin Hood and of Randolph, Earl of Chester, but of Our Lord and Our Lady, the fewest ever. I have vowed forty vows and forgotten them on the morrow; I never performed the penance that the priest laid down for me; when I was truly sorry for these sins I cannot remember. If I ever pray any prayers, unless it be in wrath, what I say with my tongue is ten miles from my heart. I am occupied each day—holy days and others—with idle tales over my ale, or maybe in church; God's pain and His passion are full seldom in my mind. I never visited feeble men nor fettered men in prison; I had rather hear of harlotry or of a falsehood to laugh at, or blame men and ridicule them in unfriendly fashion, than hear all that ever Mark wrote, Matthew, John, or Luke. As for vigils and fasting-days, I can forget them all. I lie in a bed during Lent, my sweetheart in my arms, till matins and mass are over; then I remember the friars. I am not shriven often, unless sickness make me, not twice in ten years; and I have not told the half of it. I have been priest and parson for more than thirty winters; yet I know not to sing *sol-fa*, nor read a saint's life. But I can find a hare in a field or a furrow, and hold a knight's court, and come to accounts with the reeve, though I cannot construe Cato nor read in clerkly wise. If I buy or borrow aught, unless it be tallied, I forget it as quickly; and if any man asks it,

should object, would forfeit another drink to the presiding genius of the feast—in this case, Gluttony. 53. **better thing . . . worse.** Apparently this game of mutual betting did not permit that one man should deprive the other of all his goods. 69. **greedy sows . . .** Omitted here is a passage describing the disastrous effect upon Gluttony of all this swilling. 93. **sworn . . . thy sides,** as pointed out on p. 93, l. 143, to swear by a part of one's body was more discreet than the swearing by some part of the Deity's body. Hard swearing was extremely common in the Middle Ages. 114. **Benedicite,** "bless ye (the Lord)," a mild oath or a familiar opening to a prayer—either one. Here it is the prayer that is meant. 121. **Robin Hood.** See the Robin Hood ballads under "Popular Ballads," p. 53, and the introductory notes, pp. 61 and 63. The allusion in *Piers Plowman* is the first mention of this interesting ballad hero, and we have no more allusions until well into the fifteenth century. It is interesting, further, to see that Sloth, the teller of idle tales, is thoroughly familiar with "rimes of Robin Hood" as early as the later fourteenth century. 122. **Randolph, Earl of Chester.** There were three such personages in English history, but the one who would be most renowned among minstrels or balladmongers would be the third, who was Earl of Chester from 1181 to 1231. He was once besieged by the Welsh in Rhuddlan

Castle and, according to the old legends, was saved by a "rabble of minstrels"—in return he became a prominent patron of minstrelsy in England of the early thirteenth century. 132. **visited . . . prison,** an echo of Matthew 25:43. 145. **hold . . . court.** It would appear that Sloth was often the reeve or steward of the knight's castle, and empowered by the knight to preside over such cases as would come before the knight's local jurisdiction. **accounts with the reeve.** The reeve is mentioned here in his capacity as auditor of a feudal estate. The implication is that Sloth would come to some corrupt financial agreement with the reeve by which some part of the lord's money (the income from the estate, most probably) could be squeezed into Sloth's pockets; the reeve, of course, retaining his share. 146. **Cato.** The reference is not to Cato the famous Roman statesman, but to Dionysius Cato, a name given to the author of a Latin work, probably of about the fourth century, called the *Dionysii Catonis Disticha de Moribus ad Filium*, "The Couplets of Dionysius Cato to His Son on the Subject of Morals." The collection was extremely popular in the Middle Ages, and well illustrates the Anglo-Saxon predilection for didactic epigrams—pithy statements of the laws underlying human nature. 148. **tallied,** kept in account by the system of notches on a stick.

six times or seven, I deny it with oaths; thus I have cheated honest men ten hundred times. And sometimes my servants' wages are behind; it is a pity to hear the reckoning when we read our accounts—with such a wicked disposition my workmen I pay. If any man do me a benefit, or help me in my need, I am unfriendly to courtesy: I cannot understand it. For I have and have had a kind of hawkish habit: I am not lured by love unless something is lying under the
10 thumb. The kindnesses that my fellow-Christians did me in former years—sixty times I, Sloth, have forgotten them since. In speech and in sparing speech I have wasted most of my time; both meat and fish and victuals I kept so long that every man alive would hate to look at it or to smell it—bread, ale, butter, milk, and cheese all wasted on me. In my youth I went about rioting, setting houses afire, and giving myself to no service, and have been a beggar ever since for my foul indolence. *Heu mihi, quod sterilem*
20 *duxi vitam iuvenilem!*"

"Repent thee," said Repentance; and Sloth then swooned, till Vigilate the watchman threw water in his eyes and sprinkled it over his face and cried loudly, saying: "Beware of despair that will betray thee. Say to thyself: 'I am sorry for my sins,' and beat thyself on the breast and pray God for grace; for there is no guilt so great that His goodness is not greater."

Then Sloth sat up, and blessed himself often, and
30 made vows to God against his foul laziness: "No Sunday for seven years, unless sickness prevent me, will I fail to hie me ere the dawn of day to our beloved church, and hear matins and mass as if I were a monk. No ale nor food shall keep me thence till I have heard vespers. I promise it by the rood! . . ."

Then Repentance was ready and commanded them all to kneel. "I shall pray for all sinful men the grace of Our Savior, to be merciful to us all that we may amend all our misdeeds. God, in Thy goodness Thou

didst make the world, and from nothing madest every- 40 thing, and man like Thyself, then didst suffer him to sin—a blight upon us all—all for our benefit, I believe, as ever the book tells us: *O felix culpa! O necessarium peccatum Adae!* For through that sin Thy son was sent to earth, and became man from a maiden, to redeem mankind; and Thou madest Thyself with Thy son our souls' and bodies' leech. *Ego in patre, et pater in me est, et qui videt me, patrem meum videt.* And then in our sight, so it seemed, Thou didst die, on a Friday; in the body of a man Thou didst feel our 50 sorrow. *Captivam duxit captivitatem.* The sun in sadness thereof shone less light for a time, even at noon when it is brightest, at the meal-time of saints. Thou feddest with Thy fresh blood our forefathers in Hell. *Populus qui ambulabat in tenebris, lucem magnam vidit.* The light that leaped from Thee blinded Lucifer and brought Thy blessed thence into the bliss of Heaven. The third day thereafter Thou didst go from our sight. A sinful Mary saw Thee ere Saint Mary Thy mother; and all for the solace of the sinful 60 Thou didst suffer it to be. *Non veni vocare iustos, sed peccatores ad penitentiam.* And all that Mark has told, or Matthew, John, or Luke, all Thy most valiant deeds were done in our sight. *Verbum caro factum est.* And for all that it would appear that we can more surely pray and beseech Thee, if it be Thy will, who art first our Father and of flesh our Brother, and most of all our Savior, for Thou saidst with Thine own tongue that what time we sinful men are sorry for the deeds we have done ill, we shall never be 70 condemned, if we acknowledge them and cry to Christ for mercy. *Quandocumque ingemuerit peccator, omnes iniquitates eius non recordabor amplius.* And for that great mercy, and for the love of Mary Thy mother, take pity on all these rascals who have repented sore, for all the guilt they have done against Thee, O God, in spirit or in deeds."

9. **something . . . under the thumb**, i.e., unless something eatable is held in the hand; the common method of training animals with food as an eventual reward for their efforts. 19. **Heu . . . iuvenilem**, "Woe is me, what a barren life I led as a youth." The origin of this is unknown. 35. **by the rood!** . . . Omitted here is a long exposition by the author on the nature and causes of Sloth and its many branches; also on the evil of flattery, and on the hard-heartedness of the rich. 43. **O felix . . . Adae**, "O blessed guilt, O necessary sin of Adam!" The quotation has been found in the Sarum Missal; there is another allusion to it by Wycliffe, but it has no direct scriptural source. 47. **Ego . . . videt**, "I am in the Father, and the Father is in me; and whosoever sees me, sees my Father," suggested by John 14:9–10 ff. 51. **Captivam duxit captivitatem**, "He led captivity captive"—Ephesians 4:8. 53. **meal-time of saints**, a difficult allusion supposed by most scholars to refer to the time of the crucifixion, when Christ's blood was shed upon the cross, that all might be refreshed and re-

deemed thereby. 54. **forefathers in Hell.** The beautiful verse in Isaiah 9:2—"The people that walked in darkness have seen a great light: they that dwell in the land of the shadow of death, upon them hath the light shined"—was the basis for the story, told later in the apocryphal Gospel of Nicodemus, of how Christ spent the three days between His crucifixion and His resurrection in Hell, redeeming the souls of the patriarchs who had been so unfortunate as to precede Him in time. This is the legend of the "Harrowing of Hell." 55. **Populus . . . vidit.** See the aforementioned verse in Isaiah 9:2. 59. **sinful Mary**, Mary Magdalene, from whom Christ had cast out seven devils; cf. Mark 16:9. 61. **Non . . . penitentiam.** "I am not come to call the righteous, but the sinners to repentance."—Matthew 9:13. 64. **Verbum caro factum est,** "The Word was made flesh."—John 1:14. 72. **Quandocumque . . . amplius,** "Whensoever the sinner may groan, all his iniquities I shall remember no more"—a paraphrase of Jeremiah 31:34.

GEOFFREY CHAUCER c. 1340-1400

The greatest of Middle English writers, Geoffrey Chaucer, was born in London about 1340. His father was a well-to-do burgher, by occupation a wine merchant. The son Geoffrey was first a page to the Countess of Ulster, daughter-in-law of King Edward III, and then served (1359-1360) in the English army in France, where he was taken prisoner (1360), only to be released on payment of a ransom to which the King himself contributed a substantial sum. Chaucer continued at court for some years, meanwhile marrying (1366?) a sister of a future wife of John of Gaunt, Duke of Lancaster and fourth son of Edward III.

About the time of his marriage, Chaucer was probably a secret royal emissary abroad, but it was not until 1372 that his foreign trips brought him to Italy, a land which exerted a strong influence on his later literary work. While negotiating in that year a commercial treaty with Genoa, he was introduced to Italian life and culture firsthand; but that he met either Petrarch (1304-1374) or Boccaccio (1313-1375), the bright stars in the Italian literary firmament of that time, has never been proved. For some twelve years after his return he lived at Aldgate in London and pursued official duties at home and abroad—he was Comptroller of Customs and Subsidy of Wools, Skins, and Hides (later of wines) until 1386, and in addition made other diplomatic journeys to the Continent, once to Flanders and France in 1377, again to France in 1381 and 1387, and certainly a second trip to Italy in 1378.

The remainder of his government service was performed in England. In 1386 he gave up his residence at Aldgate as well as his comptrollerships. Possibly he had been forced out by the influence of the Gloucester faction at the court of young Richard II. He retired to Kent, where he took up for a time the life of a country gentleman, being a justice of the peace in Kent and a Knight of the Shire and Member of Parliament in 1386. His return to political favor is indicated by his appointment as Clerk of the King's Works (1389). This clerkship he gave up in 1391 to become Deputy Forester of the great royal forest of North Petherton, Somersetshire. Since he received no further appointments, although he was granted various royal pensions, it has been inferred by some that he was, during the 1390's, often in financial distress, particularly during the last years of the decade; but there is little true evidence that Chaucer

was ever in serious want, and in any case King Henry IV, before Chaucer's death in October 1400, renewed the royal annuities granted the poet by Richard.

The versatility of Chaucer and the manner in which he illustrates all literary types in the Middle English period have already been discussed (pp. 22-23); so, too, has been the fact that his works fall into three general classifications corresponding roughly to the three thirds of his adult life: (1) the French period (1355?-1370), which saw him writing in the manner of

A portrait of Geoffrey Chaucer from a manuscript of Thomas Hoccleve's Regement of Princes, c. 1411-1412.

contemporary French poets; (2) the Italian period (1370-1385), during which he traveled, made the acquaintance of Italian literature, and followed and acknowledged it in his own work; and (3) the English period (1385-1400), in which he reached full awareness of the English scene and full stature as a literary artist. Such a categorizing is, of course, much too simple; more significant is the fact that the busy Chaucer, whose reading and writing were fitted into spare moments of a crowded official life, was for the age an unusually well-read man; he shows in his works familiarity with Ovid, Virgil, Petrarch, Dante, and many others, and it is almost inconceivable that he did not know Boccaccio's identity, although there is no mention of that Italian writer in Chaucer's work.

Although Troilus and Criseyde (c. 1386) is a true masterpiece, a penetrating psychological novel in verse of a love won and lost, The Canterbury Tales remains the best introduction to Chaucer's work. The masterly gallery of portraits in the Prologue to The Canterbury Tales would alone have made its author famous. The tales themselves are arranged on a "framework" in which a group of people collected for a particular reason spend their time telling stories; many similar collections of narrative will immediately come to mind. Chaucer has taken a setting for his stories fresh from the earth of his native England—some of them are superb realism—and has so skillfully and vividly kept his narrators in action that the account of the pilgrimage to Canterbury is as much of a story as any one of the tales told on the journey.

It is probable that The Canterbury Tales were written between 1386 and 1396 or 1398; some may have been earlier products revised and incorporated into the whole. The project of some 120 stories is only about one-fifth complete. The existing tales are from various sources; Chaucer, like Shakespeare, was gifted at adapting non-original materials to original uses. A few, however, were original. The identity of the characters on the pilgrimage, who constitute a virtual cross section of the society of Chaucer's time, is a fascinating topic for research, inasmuch as a few of them seem to be based on real people. It is more than likely that Chaucer himself did, on some occasion, actually join such a pilgrimage to Canterbury. At any rate, while living in London, he could well have seen many a pilgrimage gather for the journey to the shrine of St. Thomas à Becket at Canterbury, and his reportorial genius would do the rest.

The Prologue, in addition to describing the pilgrims, makes clear the plan of the framework. In the list of twenty-four tales in the collection—of which four are unfinished—virtually every type of medieval fiction is represented; there is even a characteristic medieval sermon (The Parson's Tale) which is not a narrative at all. There is also, in the Rime of Sir Thopas, a delightful burlesque on the medieval romance. In the very incompleteness of the plan lies something typical of the easygoing Chaucer. The stories are allowed to follow a normal narrative course, with the Host (the innkeeper) acting as master of ceremonies and extemporaneous critic. If there is any didactic plan in the arrangement and quality of the stories, as one or two critics have insisted, it is not at all clear; and it should be remarked once and for all that Chaucer as a reformer would by his very breadth of view be pretty much of a failure. It has long been noticed that many of the tales follow quarrels; in other words, that certain tales are grouped together because the people telling them are engaged in a quarrel. Several tales deal with the problem of happiness in married life (the so-called "marriage group").

It is more than likely that Chaucer's purpose was merely to tell his stories for amusement, edification, or satire. He probably had no more express moral purpose in writing The Canterbury Tales than Giovanni Boccaccio had in writing his Decameron nearly a half-century before. Boccaccio's Florentine ladies and gentlemen, sequestered in a villa to escape the ravages of the Black Death in that city, spend ten days telling ten stories a day to pass the irksome and anxious period. In The Canterbury Tales, as in the Decameron, the conversation in the framework may turn upon a certain topic, and stories bearing on that topic will be told; otherwise there is no further didactic plan. The point is immaterial; far more important is the fact that Chaucer's Canterbury Tales holds the mirror up to the life of fourteenth-century England; its characters form a brilliant parade of the colorful society of the age; and the narratives are told with a gusto, a sweep, and an amazing grasp of human experience.

NOTE ON THE MIDDLE ENGLISH LANGUAGE

During the Old English period, the various inflectional endings made use of a variety of vowels. But whatever the vowel had been in Old English, in Middle English it became -e. The reason for this weakening of suffixes was that the accent of a word had become generally fixed upon the first syllable (or the root syllable in verbs), with consequent lack of stress on the final syllable. Thus the Old English sunu ("son"), stanas ("stones"), lufode ("loved") appear in Middle English as sone, stones, luvede or lovede. In certain dialects in the Middle English period and in all dialects after the sixteenth century, the final -e produced by this weakening of suffixes was dropped in pronunciation, although it might be retained in spelling. The occasional change in the pronunciation of vowels in Middle and Modern English has already been mentioned (see also "On Reading Middle English," below).

As a consequence of this leveling of inflectional endings, morphological distinctions (variations in the form of a word by means of which its grammatical functions may be distinguished) began to disappear. There are fewer distinct noun or adjective declensions and verb conjugations in Middle English.

The influence of French culture brought in by the Norman Conquest is not at first so apparent in the English language as one would suppose, although French words begin to appear in the language shortly after 1100. But because there was little vernacular literature before 1200, following the Norman Conquest, it is difficult to generalize. During the thirteenth and particularly the fourteenth century, however, there is a steady and impressive influx of foreign words, mostly French, but some striking Norse and Low German importations as well. The influence of French is also seen in its effect upon English word order (making it different, let us say, from that of Modern German) and on the analytical processes of the language, i.e., the tendency to express an idea by separate words rather than by combining several ideas through the use of suffixes into a single word— compare English I shall have loved with the Latin amavero. But by no stretch of the imagination can it be said that Middle English, even when borrowing most freely, loses its definitely Germanic base.

Middle English literature, unlike that of the Old English period, has survived from all over England. During the earlier half of the Middle English period, however, no single dialect was in general use. Before 1300, one must reckon with considerable dialectal variations and with freedom in spelling, grammar, and syntax. With the increasing importance of towns between 1250 and 1400, the Northern, Southern, and Kentish dialects (which correspond to the Old English Northumbrian, West Saxon, and Kentish dialects respectively) yielded in great measure to Southeast Midland, the dialect of London. In terms of Old English language-geography, the Middle English London dialect is the descendant of West Saxon and East Mercian. Individual forms from any of the other major dialects can be found, however, throughout Middle English; it is from this complex mixture of dialects that standard Modern English has evolved.

It is therefore clear that to the neophyte Middle English, particularly of the earlier medieval period, is nearly as great a linguistic obstacle as Old English. Translations into Modern English are often necessary. But since some Middle English texts are fairly readable even by the modern layman, and since it was felt that some full representation of the language at this time should be made here, the selections from Chaucer have been left in the original. Certain Middle English works of high artistic finish have thus far escaped all attempts to represent them faithfully in modern translation. The present editors have allowed the warm, colorful, almost languorous lines of Chaucer to speak for themselves.

ON READING MIDDLE ENGLISH

Reading Middle English aloud with a fair approximation of the original pronunciation and accent is well worth the effort involved. To do so for Chaucer will be to hear and to appreciate the melody of his lines, as exquisite and as varied as any ever composed in English; to neglect the task is to do him the great injustice of converting his poetry into a series of limping, ugly, ill-balanced units which cannot even be called lines of verse. Even the best modern metrical translation is but a pallid affair when compared with the original. There is no question as to which method of reading will give the reader the more profound and lasting pleasure.

The general principles involved may be briefly stated. All consonants are pronounced, even the g's and k's in words like gnaw and knee. An h or a gh preceding a t, as in niht or laughte, is pronounced like the ch in Modern German ich, or Nacht, depending (as in Modern German) on the quality of the preceding vowel. A similar sound is preserved in Modern Scottish loch. In general, all vowels are also pronounced, including final -e's, which have the sound of the initial vowel in our modern word about (phonetically əbaut). Thus, the word reverence is pronounced as four distinct syllables, re-ve' ren-cë (phonetically, re-və' ren-sə). If you know French or Italian or German, it is enough to say that Chaucer's vowels have the same values as in these languages, except that there is no nasalizing of them before n or m as in the French mon, blanc, parfum and the u's are unrounded like the German u rather than ü. Diphthongs are usually pronounced like the separate vowels that compose them, within the compass of one syllable. Words are accented very much as in Modern English, except that French borrowings are still often given their original French accent. The rhythm of the lines will be a safe guide. Participial nouns ending in -ing(e) have a fairly strong secondary stress on the inflectional syllable: thus gúer-don-ing-e. When the rhythm of a line demands it, the final unaccented -e (or even other final vowels in unaccented words) may be elided with the initial vowel of the next word, as in the phrase time and space (phonetically, 'ti:m and 'spa-sə).

For students unfamiliar with Modern French, German, or Italian, the following table of approximations will serve as guide.

Chaucer's a, when long, is like a in English father;
a, when short, is the same sound shortened, like the vowel in hot;
e, when long, has (a) the quality of the first e in Modern English there, or (b) the quality of the final vowel in the Modern English loan word from the French, fiancée;
e, when short, is like the e in English met;

i, when long, is like the *i* in machine;

i, when short, is like the *i* in sit;

o, when long, is similar (a) to the *o* in English note or (b) to the *o* in born;

o, when short, is like the vowel in dog;

u, when long (though often spelled *ou* or *ow*) is probably like the *oo* in tooth;

u, when short, is pronounced as in English full;

ei (*ey*) and *ai* (*ay*) are both pronounced [aei], somewhat like the Cockney version of day;

au (*aw*) is like *ou* in English house.

The difference between the two long *e*'s and *o*'s in the above table depends upon the etymology of the word as it appears in Old English. The length of vowels can be guessed at on the basis of the length of the vowel in the same word in Modern English, but this is only a tentative basis; again, the etymology of the word must be borne in mind.

It must be insisted that the values and equivalents stated in the table above are merely approximate. Thus in Modern English the vowel of note is not really long o [o:], but the diphthong [ou]. It is useless, however, to harass a beginner with such distinctions.

---

from THE CANTERBURY TALES

PROLOGUE

Whan that Aprille with his shoures soote
The droghte of Marche hath percéd to the roote,
And bathed every veyne in swich licour,
Of which vertu engendred is the flour;
Whan Zephirus eek with his swete breeth
Inspiréd hath in every holt and heeth
The tendre croppes, and the yonge sonne
Hath in the Ram his halfe cours y-ronne,
And smale fowles maken melodye,
10 That slepen al the night with open yë,
(So priketh hem nature in hir corages),
Than longen folk to goon on pilgrimages
(And palmers for to seken straunge strondes)
To ferne halwes, couthe in sondry londes;
And specially, from every shires ende
Of Engelond, to Caunterbury they wende,
The holy blisful martir for to seke,
That hem hath holpen, whan that they were seke.
Bifel that, in that sesoun on a day,
20 In Southwerk at the Tabard as I lay
Redy to wenden on my pilgrimage
To Caunterbury with ful devout corage,
At night was come in-to that hostelrye
Wel nyne and twenty in a companye,
Of sondry folk, by aventure y-falle

In felawshipe, and pilgrims were they alle,
That toward Caunterbury wolden ryde;
The chambres and the stables weren wyde,
And wel we weren esed atte beste.
And shortly, whan the sonne was to reste,   30
So hadde I spoken with hem everichon,
That I was of hir felawshipe anon,
And made forward erly for to ryse,
To take our wey, ther as I yow devyse.
But natheles, whyl I have tyme and space,
Ere that I ferther in this tale pace,
Me thinketh it acordaunt to resoun,
To telle yow al the condicioun
Of ech of hem, so as it semed me,
And whiche they weren, and of what degree;   40
And eek in what array that they were inne:
And at a knight than wol I first biginne.
A KNIGHT ther was, and that a worthy man,
That fro the tyme that he first bigan
To ryden out, he loved chivalrye,
Trouthe and honour, fredom and curteisye.
Ful worthy was he in his lordes werre,
And therto hadde he riden (no man ferre)
As wel in cristendom as hethenesse,
And ever honoured for his worthinesse.   50
At Alisaundre he was, whan it was wonne;
Ful ofte tyme he hadde the bord bigonne
Aboven alle naciouns in Pruce.

Prologue. In *The Canterbury Tales* Chaucer makes use chiefly of (1) the seven-line iambic pentameter stanza (riming *a b a b b c c*) known as the Chaucerian stanza or rime royal, or (2) iambic pentameter riming couplets, as in the selections given here. This iambic pentameter couplet is the "heroic couplet" of neo-classical fame, except that later writers like Dryden and Pope preferred to "close" it to a greater degree; i.e., bring the thought to a more definite conclusion at the end of the second line. 1. **soote,** sweet. 3. **swich,** such. **licour,** moisture. 5. **eek,** also. 6. **holt and heeth.** A *holt* is a cultivated tract, or plantation; *heeth* is the modern "heath." No doubt the combining of these two words in such a phrase is to be attributed in part to the popularity of alliterative formulas in Middle English poetry. 8. **the Ram,** the constellation of Aries, one of the signs of the zodiac. Aries is the spot in the heavens at which the sun is located at the time of the vernal equinox; hence it is the first constellation of the year. (This explains why the sun is called "young" in the preceding line.) 10. **yë,** eye. 11. **corages,** wills, desires. 13. **strondes,** strands, shores. 14. **ferne,** distant. **halwes,** hallowed places, shrines. **couthe,** well-known, famous. 17. **holy . . . seke.** The "holy martyr" is Thomas à Becket, slain (1170) during the course of a Church and Crown dispute. 18. **seke,** sick. Note that this *seke* rimes with *seke* ("seek") in the preceding line. Identical rimes of this sort were not avoided as unharmonious, but were even sought at times, as a kind of forerunner of the play on words so liked during the Elizabethan age. 20. **Southwerk,** the bustling suburb on the south bank of the Thames and the beginning of the old Canterbury Road. **the Tabard.**

A tabard was a short, sleeveless coat, and was used as the "sign" of the inn. There was actually an inn by this name in Southwark during Chaucer's time, and a small public house called by the old name is on the supposed site. 25. **y-falle,** befallen, met with. The prefix *y-* is frequently seen on past participles in Middle English; it is a development of the older form *ge-*, still retained in Modern German. 29. **esed,** entertained, set at ease. **atte beste,** "at the best," in the best possible way. 33. **forward,** agreement. 34. **ther . . . devyse,** "where," or "as I describe it to you." In Chaucer *ther* and *wher* are often interchangeable. 36. **pace,** pass. 37. **acordaunt to resoun,** "according to the right," in keeping with the right thing to do. Cf. the meaning of the Modern French *raison*. But the word may have here the meaning of "order," "arrangement." 48. **ferre,** farther. 51. **Alisaundre, etc.** The Knight is a veteran of many fourteenth-century wars, as enumerated in the following lines. His service is the feudal service to a lord, whose political interests were doubtless many. Indeed, that service, to judge by the places mentioned in his description, must have been in large part the service of King Edward III. Observe that the many expeditions on which he had embarked mark him as a true soldier of fortune, no doubt a mercenary, but always with the backing of a particular feudal prince or lord. Yet Chaucer's treatment of the Knight is always idealistic; no word is said against his character, and he is treated with the utmost respect by the entire company. King Peter of Cyprus, better known as Pierre de Lusignan, a scion of one of the noted chivalric families of France, was a brilliant adventurer, a tireless leader of expeditions for those who "loved chivalrye." One

In Lettow hadde he reysed and in Ruce,
No cristen man so ofte of his degree.
In Gernade at the sege eek hadde he be
Of Algezir, and riden in Belmarye.
At Lyeys was he, and at Satalye,
Whan they were wonne; and in the Grete See
60 At many a noble aryve hadde he be.
At mortal batailles hadde he been fiftene,
And foughten for our feith at Tramissene
In listes thryes, and ay slayn his foo.
This ilke worthy knight hadde been also
Sometyme with the lord of Palatye,
Ageyn another hethen in Turkye:
And everemore he hadde a sovereyn prys,
And though that he were worthy, he was wys,
And of his port as meek as is a mayde.

The Squire

*This picture of the Knight and the following portraits
of the Canterbury pilgrims are based on those in the
Ellesmere Manuscript, now in the Huntington Library.
The woodcuts reproduced here were made by W. H.
Hooper for the Chaucer Society (c. 1880).*

He nevere yet no vileinye ne sayde   • 70
In al his lyf, un-to no maner wight.
He was a verray parfit gentil knight.
But for to tellen yow of his array,
His hors were goode, but he was nat gay.
Of fustian he weréd a gipoun
Al bismoteréd with his habergeoun,
For he was late y-come from his viage,
And wente for to doon his pilgrimage.
    With him there was his sone, a yong SQUYER,
A lovyere, and a lusty bacheler,   80
With lokkes crulle, as they were leyd in presse.
Of twenty yeer of age he was, I gesse.
Of his stature he was of evene lengthe,
And wonderly deliver, and greet of strengthe.
And he had been somtyme in chivachye,
In Flaundres, in Artoys, and Picardye,
And born him wel, as of so litel space,
In hope to stonden in his lady grace.
Embrouded was he, as it were a mede
Al ful of fresshe floures, whyte and rede.   90
Singinge he was, or floytinge, al the day;

of his feats was the capture of Alexandria, Egypt, in 1365. 53. **Pruce,**
Prussia. The Knight had held an honored position at the table (''the
bord bigonne'') as a member of the Teutonic Order of Knights, one
of the great chivalric associations of the Middle Ages and a powerful
preserver of the old Germanic warrior spirit. 54. **Lettow,** Lithuania.
The Lithuanians were converted to Christianity in 1386, largely through
the efforts of the Teutonic Order. If the date of their conversion marked
the earliest possible time at which the Knight could have returned to
England, this would be a valuable means of dating the Prologue.
The conversion, however, was preceded by much campaigning, and
the evidence may not be very convincing. **reysed,** made expeditions.
Ruce, Russia. The Teutonic Order was a powerful buffer between
western Christendom and pagan nations, particularly the Tartars, who
made several incursions into Russia during the Middle Ages. 56.
Gernade . . . Belmarye. There were several raids upon the Moors
in Spain and Morocco during the forties, sixties, and eighties; it is
consequently imposible to tell in which of these the Knight was
involved. *Gernade* is Granada, Spain; *Algezir,* Algeciras; and *Belmarye,*
Benmarin in Morocco. 58. **Lyeys,** Lyas, Armenia, harried by Pierre
de Lusignan in 1367. **Satalye,** Atalia, on the coast of Asia Minor,
captured by Pierre de Lusignan in 1361; Pierre's depredations in the
Mediterranean (''The Grete See'') were too numerous to mention.
60. **aryve,** arrival, disembarkation. Some of the manuscripts, however,
have ''armee,'' which makes better sense. 62. **Tramissene,** Tlemcen
in Algeria; but as in the case of *Belmarye* (l. 57), the allusion is too
vague to help us much; there was fighting along the Moroccan and

Algerian coasts all through the mid-fourteenth century. 65. **Palatye,**
probably Balat in Turkey; the ''lord of Palatye'' was, then, a heathen
allied to Pierre de Lusignan—further evidence of the difference between
a chivalric adventurer like Pierre in the dying days of medieval knighthood, and the chivalric idealist of Arthurian legend; or perhaps it is
merely the difference between fact and romance. But it is difficult to
imagine Sir Lancelot fighting on the same side as a Saracen. 67. **sovereyn
prys,** noble or sovereign worth. *Sovereyn* is here an adjective. 69.
port, bearing. 72. **verray parfit,** true and perfect, not ''very perfect.''
75. **fustian,** a thick cotton cloth. **gipoun,** a tunic. 76. **bismoteréd,**
smutted, marked with dirt. **habergeoun,** hauberk, coat of mail. 79.
Squyer, a young candidate for knighthood. In *The Canterbury Tales*
the squire is the type of the young courtly lover. 81. **crulle,** curled.
85. **chivachye,** cavalry raids; as mentioned here, there must have been
various raids into France during the Hundred Years' War. Chaucer's
own experience qualified him to speak with authority on such subjects. 87. **as . . . space,** considering the short period of time the
Squire had been training for knighthood. 89. **Embrouded,** decorated
with embroidery, but it is barely possible that Chaucer is thinking of
the young man's pink-and-white complexion. **mede,** meadow. 91.
floytinge, playing the flute. The list of accomplishments given in the
description of the Squire represents what was expected of any young
man of breeding.

He was as fresh as is the month of May.
Short was his goune, with sleves longe and wyde.
Wel coude he sitte on hors, and faire ryde.
He coude songes make and wel endyte,
Juste and eek daunce, and wel purtreye and wryte.
So hote he lovede, that by nightertale
He sleep namore than doth a nightingale.
Curteys he was, lowly, and servisable,
100 And carf biforn his fader at the table.
    A YEMAN hadde he, and servaunts namo
At that tyme, for him liste ryde so;
And he was clad in cote and hood of grene;
A sheef of pecok-arwes brighte and kene
Under his belt he bar ful thriftily;
(Wel coude he dresse his takel yemanly:
His arwes drouped noght with fetheres lowe),

The Monk and his hounds

And in his hand he bar a mighty bowe.
A not-heed hadde he, with a broun visage.
110 Of wode-craft wel coude he al the usage.
Upon his arm he bar a gay bracer,
And by his syde a swerd and a bokeler,
And on that other syde a gay daggere,
Harneised wel and sharp as point of spere;
A Cristofre on his brest of silver shene.

An horn he bar, the bawdrik was of grene;
A forster was he, soothly, as I gesse.
    Ther was also a Nonne, a PRIORESSE,
That of hir smyling was ful simple and coy,
Hir gretteste ooth was but by seÿnt Loy;   120
And she was cleped madame Eglentyne.
Ful wel she song the service divyne,
Entuned in hir nose ful semely;
And Frensh she spak ful faire and fetisly,
After the scole of Stratford atte Bowe,
For Frensh of Paris was to hir unknowe.
At mete wel y-taught was she with-alle;
She leet no morsel from hir lippes falle,
Ne wette hir fingres in hir sauce depe.
Wel coude she carie a morsel, and wel kepe,   130
That no drope ne fille up-on hir brest.
In curteisye was set ful muche hir lest.
Hir over lippe wyped she so clene,
That in hir coppe was no ferthing sene
Of grece, whan she dronken hadde hir draughte.
Ful semely after hir mete she raughte,
And sikerly she was of greet disport,
And ful plesaunt, and amiable of port,
And peyned hir to countrefete chere
Of court, and been estatlich of manere,   140
And to ben holden digne of reverence.
But, for to speken of hir conscience,
She was so charitable and so pitous,
She wolde wepe, if that she sawe a mous
Caught in a trappe, if it were deed or bledde.
Of smale houndes had she, that she fedde
With rosted flesh, or milk and wastel breed.
But sore weep she if oon of hem were deed,
Or if men smoot it with a yerde smerte:
And al was conscience and tendre herte.   150
Ful semely hir wimpel pinched was;
Hir nose tretys; hir eyen greye as glas;
Hir mouth ful smal, and ther-to softe and reed;

97. **nightertale,** nighttime. 100. **carf . . . table.** It was a regular duty of a squire to do the carving before a meal. 101. **Yeman,** yeoman. Strictly speaking, he is ranked in military service below the Squire (since he would ordinarily have no pretensions to knighthood), but above a groom. **namo,** no more. 102. **him liste,** it pleased him to. 109. **not-heed,** head with hair cropped short or shaved, also a bullet head. 111. **bracer,** an arm guard worn just above the wrist to protect the archer from the impact of the bowstring. 115. **Cristofre,** an image of St. Christopher, the patron saint of foresters, whose protection the Yeoman desired. 116. **bawdrik,** baldric, the cord or belt from which the horn was slung. 119. **coy,** quiet. 120. **seÿnt Loy,** St. Eloi, or St. Eligius, a minor French saint whose name has been chosen here partly for the sake of the rime, partly for the ladylike sound of his name, and possibly for some other reasons which are now obscure. 124. **fetisly,** neatly. 125. **Stratford atte Bowe,** a nunnery of St. Leonard's in' Bromley, Middlesex, adjoining Stratford-Bow. The implication is then clear; the Prioress spoke the kind of French one would hear in a nunnery of England, not the French of Paris. 134. **ferthing,** bit, trace. 136. **raughte,** reached. 139. **countrefete . . . court,** a satirical

comment on the elegant manners of the Prioress, and possibly her aping of courtly customs. The word *countrefete,* unlike our modern "counterfeit," does not suggest dishonesty or insincerity or falseness, rather merely imitation. 142. **conscience,** sensibility, tender feelings. 143. **pitous,** having pity, tender-hearted. 147. **wastel breed,** a fine, white wheat bread. 151. **pinched,** pleated, fluted. 152. **tretys,** well formed. 159. **gauded . . . grene.** The large beads ("gauds") were covered with green. 161. **a crowned A,** apparently a large A (for "Amor") surmounted by a crown. 164. **chapeleyne,** not "chaplain"; rather a secretary and personal assistant. **Preestes three,** possibly an error on Chaucer's part; three nun's priests would bring the total up to 31, instead of the 29 mentioned in l. 24. One such priest would be required to escort women of the Church, and only one is heard of later. Perhaps the prioress, the nun, and the priest made up the *three* together. 165. **for the maistrye,** "for the mastery (of all others)"; hence, "surpassing all others," then loosely as an adverb, "extremely." 166. **out-rydere,** a monk who had the duty of inspecting the estates and boundaries of a monastery, which were often of considerable extent. 172. **celle,** a subordinate monastery. 173. **seint Maure**

But sikerly she hadde a fair forheed;
It was almost a spanne brood, I trowe;
For, hardily, she was nat undergrowe.
Ful fetis was hir cloke, as I was war.
Of smal coral aboute hir arm she bar
A peire of bedes, gauded al with grene;
160 And ther-on heng a broche of gold ful shene,
On which ther was first write a crowned A,
And after, *Amor vincit omnia.*

    Another NONNE with hir hadde she,
That was hir chapeleyne, and PREESTES three.

    A MONK ther was, a fair for the maistrye,
An out-rydere, that lovede venerye;
A manly man, to been an abbot able.
Ful many a deyntee hors hadde he in stable:
And, whan he rood men mighte his brydel here
170 Ginglen in a whistling wynd as clere,
And eek as loude as doth the chapel-belle
Ther as this lord was keper of the celle.
The reule of seint Maure or of seint Beneit,
By-cause that it was old and som-del streit,
This ilke monk leet olde thinges pace,
And held after the newe world the space.
He yaf nat of that text a pulled hen,
That seith, that hunters been nat holy men;
Ne that a monk, whan he is cloisterlees,
180 Is lykned til a fish that is waterlees;
This is to seyn, a monk out of his cloystre.
But thilke text heeld he nat worth an oystre.
And I seyde his opinion was good.
What sholde he studie, and make hymselven wood,
Upon a book in cloystre alwey to poure,
Or swynken with his handes, and laboure,
As Austyn bit? How shal the world be served?
Lat Austyn have his swynk to him reserved.
Therfore he was a prikasour aright;
190 Grehoundes he hadde, as swift as fowel in flight;
Of prikyng and of huntyng for the hare
Was al his lust, for no cost wolde he spare.
I seigh his sleves y-purfiled at the hond
With grys, and that the fyneste of a lond;
And, for to festne his hood under his chyn,
He hadde of gold y-wroght a ful curious pyn:
A love-knotte in the gretter ende ther was.
His heed was balled, that shoon as any glas,

And eek his face, as it hadde been anoynt.
He was a lord ful fat and in good poynt;   200
Hise eyen stepe, and rollynge in his heed,
That stemed as a forneys of a leed;
His botes souple, his hors in greet estat.
Now certeinly he was a fair prelat;
He was nat pale as a for-pyned goost.
A fat swan loved he best of any roost.
His palfrey was as broun as is a berye.

    A FRERE ther was, a wantown and a merye,
A limitour, a ful solempne man.
In alle the ordres foure is noon that can   210
So muche of daliaunce and fair langage.
He hadde maad ful many a mariage
Of yonge wommen, at his owne cost.
Un-to his ordre he was a noble post.
Ful wel biloved and famulier was he
With frankeleyns over-al in his contree,
And eek with worthy wommen of the toun:
For he had power of confessioun,
As seyde him-self, more than a curat,
For of his ordre he was licentiat.   220
Ful swetely herde he confessioun,
And plesaunt was his absolucioun;
He was an esy man to yeve penaunce
Ther as he wiste to han a good pitaunce;
For unto a povre ordre for to yive
Is signe that a man is wel y-shrive.
For if he yaf, he dorste make avaunt,
He wiste that a man was repentaunt.
For many a man so hard is of his herte,
He may nat wepe al-thogh him sore smerte.   230
Therfore, in stede of weping and preyeres,
Men moot yeve silver to the povre freres.
His tipet was ay farsed ful of knyves
And pinnes, for to yeven faire wyves.
And certeinly he hadde a mery note;
Wel coude he singe and pleyen on a rote.
Of yeddinges he bar utterly the prys.
His nekke whyt was as the flour-de-lys;
There-to he strong was as a champioun.
He knew the tavernes wel in every toun,   240
And everich hostiler and tappestere
Bet than a lazar or a beggestere;
For un-to swich a worthy man as he

---

or of seint Beneit. St. Benedict was the founder of medieval mon-
asticism in western Europe, having established the famous Benedictine
Order in 529. St. Maurus was his follower. 176. the space. The
phrase is probably purely adverbial, and can be translated "meanwhile,"
"for the time" (he held after the new ways). 177. yaf, gave. pulled
hen, plucked hen, another one of the endless symbols for worthless-
ness. 184. What, why? wood, mad, out of his wits. 187. Austyn bit?
Austyn is the shortened form of Augustine, the great Church Father
(354-430). *Bit* is the third person singular present indicative of *bid*,
a contracted form for *biddeth.* 189. prikasour, a hunter on horseback.
191. prikyng, tracking an animal by its footprints (pricks). 194. grys,
an expensive gray fur, possibly of squirrel. 197. love-knotte, any
intertwined pattern. 201. stepe, large, prominent, perhaps bulging
slightly. 202. stemed . . . leed, gleamed like a furnace under a lead
cauldron. 205. for-pyned, tormented, wasted by torture. 208. wantown,
gay. This description of the Friar, however, is full of sly insinuations,
and the probability that he was "wanton" in the later Elizabethan
sense of "sexually irregular" is more than likely to be meant here.
Note ll. 212-213. The Friar, incidentally, is regarded by Chaucer as

a parasite; notice that he was licensed to beg (a mendicant friar)
within certain limits assigned (cf. *limitour*, l. 209). 210. the ordres
foure, Dominicans, Franciscans, Carmelites, and Augustinians. 211.
daliaunce, social conversation, chat; but again, veering into the
chivalric and modern use of the term to mean love caresses. 214. post,
pillar; cf. the modern "pillar of the church." 216. frankeleyns, free
landholders, but not of noble birth. 220. licentiat; i.e., he had
received from his order a license to hear confessions. This practice led
to considerable rivalry between mendicant friars and parish priests. The
friars were accused of granting absolution too easily. 224. pitaunce,
allowance, especially of food, to religious folk. 228. wiste, knew. 233.
tipet, tippet, cape. farsed, stuck through,. stuffed. 237. yeddinges,
songs or ballads, originally in alliterative verse. By Chaucer's time,
however, the term had been generalized to refer to any type of ballad
or song. 241. hostiler, innkeeper. tappestere, female tapster, barmaid.
Note the old feminine -*ster* ending, indicating a feminine noun of
agent, still traceable in many proper names and in the word *spinster.*

Acorded nat, as by his facultee,
To have with seke lazars aqueyntaunce.
It is nat honest, it may nat avaunce
For to delen with no swich poraille,
But al with riche and sellers of vitaille.
And over-al, ther as profit sholde aryse,
250 Curteys he was, and lowly of servyse.
Ther nas no man nowher so vertuous.
He was the beste beggere in his hous;
For thogh a widwe hadde noght a sho,
So plesaunt was his "In principio,"
Yet wolde he have a ferthing, er he wente.
His purchas was wel bettre than his rente.
And rage he coude, as it were right a whelpe.
In love-dayes ther coude he muchel helpe.
For ther he was nat lyk a cloisterer,
260 With a thredbar cope as is a povre scoler,
But he was lyk a maister or a pope.
Of double worsted was his semi-cope,
That rounded as a belle out of the presse.
Somwhat he lipsed, for his wantownesse,
To make his English swete up-on his tonge;
And in his harping, whan that he had songe,
His eyen twinkled in his heed aright,
As doon the sterres in the frosty night.
This worthy limitour was cleped Huberd.
270 A MARCHANT was ther with a forked berd,
In mottelee, and hye on horse he sat,
Up-on his heed a Flaundrish bever hat;
His botes clasped faire and fetisly.
His resons he spak ful solempnely,
Souninge alway th'encrees of his winning.
He wolde the see were kept for any thing
Bitwixe Middelburgh and Orewelle.
Wel coude he in eschaunge sheeldes selle.
This worthy man ful wel his wit bisette;
280 Ther wiste no wight that he was in dette,
So estatly was he of his governaunce,
With his bargaynes, and with his chevisaunce.
For sothe he was a worthy man with-alle,
But sooth to seyn, I noot how men him calle.

The Clerk

A CLERK ther was of Oxenford also,
That un-to logik hadde longe y-go.
As lene was his hors as is a rake,
And he nas nat right fat, I undertake;
But loked holwe, and ther-to soberly.
290 Ful thredbar was his overest courtepy;
For he had geten him yet no benefyce,
Ne was so worldly for to have offyce.
For him was lever have at his beddes heed
Twenty bokes, clad in blak or reed,
Of Aristotle and his philosophye,
Than robes riche, or fithele, or gay sautrye.
But al be that he was a philosophre,
Yet hadde he but litel gold in cofre;
But al that he mighte of his freendes hente,
300 On bokes and on lerninge he it spente,
And bisily gan for the soules preye
Of hem that yaf him wher-with to scoleye.
Of studie took he most cure and most hede.
Noght o word spak he more than was nede,
And that was seyd in forme and reverence,
And short and quik, and ful of hy sentence.
Souninge in moral vertu was his speche,

---

246. **avaunce,** be helpful, advance one; apparently intransitive here.
247. **poraille,** poor folk. 254. *"In principio"*; see the Gospel of John 1:1. 256. **His purchas . . . his rente.** What he picked, up on the side (*his purchas*) amounted to more than his lawful income (*his rente*). The term *purchas* seems always to have had a somewhat sinister connotation in Middle English, applying particularly to what one obtains illegally. 258. **love-dayes,** special days set aside for arbitration of all disputes; the clergy usually took a firm hand in the proceedings. 260. **cope,** cape, cloak. 264. **lipsed,** lisped. 271. **mottelee,** motley, cloth with a figured design, often of more than one color. The material was often used for distinctive liveries among the various guildsmen. 277. **Middelburgh and Orewelle.** *Middelburgh* is a port on the island of Walcheren on the coast of Holland; *Orewelle* is the old port of Orwell, near Harwich, almost directly west of Middelburgh. Here would be, in other words, a direct line for the wool trade between England and the Low Countries. Obviously, then, the Merchant would want this sea path kept open at all costs (*kept for any thing*). 278. **sheeldes,** the French *écu*. This selling of *écus* to Englishmen for profit was distinctly illegal, according to a statute of King Edward III. 281. **estatly,** stately. In other words, the Merchant put up an impressive front. **governaunce,** demeanor. 282. **chevisaunce,** a term referring to borrowing and lending. The word was also used loosely for any illicit income, particularly from usury. Such is its meaning here. 286. **y-go,** gone. Here the verb is to be construed with *unto* in the same line. "To go to logic" would be to study logic. 290. **overest courtepy,** outermost short-coat. 291. **geten . . . benefyce,** been given no religious office. The Clerk is a man of clerical training. 295. **Aristotle . . . philosophye.** The amount of Aristotle's works available through Latin

channels to Englishmen of Chaucer's time could easily have filled twenty volumes, but it is not sensible to assume that Chaucer meant his statement to be taken literally. Indeed, Aristotle was often a convenient representative for all the sages of antiquity. 299. **hente,** get, seize, acquire. 302. **to scoleye,** to go to school, to receive learning. 306. **hy sentence,** lofty thoughts, sentiments, or meaning. 309. **Sergeant of the Lawe,** a legal servant of the king, chosen from barristers of at least sixteen years' standing. Those who were not chosen to serve as judges of the King's Courts or of the Exchequer went about on circuit as justices of the Assize. 310. **parvys,** the porch of St. Paul's in London, where lawyers were accustomed to consult with their clients. 315. **patente,** letters patent from the king, making the appointment as judge. **pleyn commission** refers to the more common certificates of appointment made in the form of letters sealed and addressed to the appointee giving him full jurisdiction. 316. **science,** knowledge (of the law). The Sergeant of the Lawe was clearly more the jurist than the practising attorney. 319. **Al . . . in effect.** "All things were in effect fee simple to him." In other words, he always got property in unrestricted possession (*fee simple*). 320. **purchasing . . . infect,** no defect (*nat . . . infect*) could be found in the title to his possessions. 324. **King William,** William the Conqueror (William I of England), whose passion for orderly codification of the law resulted in the famous Domesday Book. 325. **endyte,** compose, write out (as a legal document). **thing,** a legal document of any sort; in Norse countries this word is still used in the sense of a legal body. 327. **coude,** knew. **by rote,** from its root, from its basic principles. 328. **medlee,** cloth of mixed weave and often of many colors. The official robes of the Sergeant of Lawe had the colors brown and green, and

And gladly wolde he lerne, and gladly teche.

A SERGEANT OF THE LAWE, war and wys,
310 That often hadde been at the parvys,
Ther was also, ful riche of excellence.
Discreet he was, and of greet reverence:
He semed swich, his wordes weren so wyse,
Iustyce he was ful often in assyse,
By patente and by pleyn commissioun;
For his science, and for his heigh renoun
Of fees and robes hadde he many oon.
So greet a purchasour was nowher noon.
Al was fee simple to him in effect,
320 His purchasing mighte nat been infect.
No-wher so bisy a man as he ther nas,
And yet he semed bisier than he was.
In termes hadde he caas and domes alle,
That from the tyme of King William were falle.
Thereto he coude endyte, and make a thing,
Ther coude no wight pinche at his wryting;
And every statut coude he pleyn by rote
He rood but hoomly in a medlee cote
Girt with a ceint of silk, with barres smale;
330 Of his array telle I no lenger tale.

A FRANKELEYN was in his companye;
Whyt was his berd, as is the dayesye.
Of his complexioun he was sangwyn.
Wel loved he by the morwe a sop in wyn.
To liven in delyt was ever his wone,
For he was Epicurus owne sone,
That heeld opinioun, that pleyn delyt
Was verraily felicitee parfyt.
An housholdere, and that a greet, was he;
340 Seynt Iulian he was in his contree.
His breed, his ale, was alwey after oon;
A bettre envyned man was nowher noon.
With-oute bake mete was never his hous,
Of fish and flesh, and that so plentevous,
It snewed in his hous of mete and drinke,
Of alle deyntees that men coude thinke.
After the sondry sesons of the yeer,
So chaunged he his mete and his soper.

Ful many a fat partrich hadde he in mewe,
And many a breem and many a luce in stewe. 350
Wo was his cook, but-if his sauce were
Poynaunt and sharp, and redy al his gere
His table dormant in his halle alway
Stood redy covered al the longe day.
At sessiouns ther was he lord and sire;
Ful ofte tyme he was knight of the shire.
An anlas and a gipser al of silk
Heng at his girdel, whyt as morne milk.
A shirreve hadde he been, and a countour;
Was nowher such a worthy vavasour. 360

AN HABERDASSHER and a CARPENTER,
A WEBBE, a DYERE, and a TAPICER,
Were with us eek, clothed in o liveree,
Of a solempne and greet fraternitee,
Ful fresh and newe hir gere apyked was;
Hir knyves were y-chaped noght with bras,
But al with silver, wroght ful clene and weel.
Hir girdles and hir pouches every-deel.
Wel semed ech of hem a fair burgeys,
To sitten in a yeldhalle on a deys. 370
Everich, for the wisdom that he can,
Was shaply for to been an alderman.
For catel hadde they y-nogh and rente,
And eek hir wyves wolde it wel assente;
And elles certein were they to blame.
It is ful fair to been y-clept "ma dame,"
And goon to vigilyës al bifore,
And have a mantel royalliche y-bore.

A COOK they hadde with hem for the nones,
To boille chiknes with the mary-bones, 380
And poudre-marchant tart, and galingale.
Wel coude he knowe a draughte of London ale.
He coude roste, and sethe, and broille, and frye,
Maken mortreux, and wel bake a pye.
But greet harm was it, as it thoughte me,
That on his shine a mormal hadde he;
For blankmanger, that made he with the beste.

A SHIPMAN was ther, woning fer by weste:
For aught I woot, he was of Dertemouthe.

he wore a sash (ceint, l. 329). 330. **telle . . . tale.** "I shall not tell a longer story." 333. **sangwyn, etc.** According to the older conception of physiology, before Harvey's discovery of the circulation of the blood in 1610, there were four component *humours:* blood, phlegm, bile, and black bile. These humours were held in a kind of harmony or balance, known as the *complexioun.* But in each individual there was a tendency on the part of some one humour to dominate in the *complexioun,* with the result that we hear of sanguine, phlegmatic, bilious, and melancholy *complexiouns* (or temperaments), depending on whether blood, phlegm, bile, or black bile predominated. The Franklin, then, was of sanguine complexion or temperament: blood predominated in his makeup; he was ruddy and a hearty liver. 335. **wone,** wont, habit, custom. 336. **Epicurus owne sone;** in other words, he was an epicure. The philosophy of Epicurus (342?-270 B.C.), which could be interpreted as a definite hedonism, was a little unfairly portrayed as a philosophy of comfortable, pleasurable, opportunistic living for the moment. 340. **Seynt Iulian . . . envyned man.** The Franklin, with his lavish food and drink, was the soul of hospitality, and therefore the patron saint of this friendly quality, like St. Julian himself. 348. **So chaunged . . . soper.** "So did he vary his meals and his supper." 350. **breem,** bream, a fish with arched back. **luce,** pickerel. **stewe,** fish pool. 351. **but-if,** unless. 353. **table dormant,** a table fixed in the floor, instead of being movable, intended for unexpected guests. This would be in keeping with the Franklin's noted hospitality. 355. **sessiouns,** sessions of the local courts, which were presided over by local Justices of the Peace, of which the Franklin was one; he was also a Member of Parliament (knight of the shire). 357. **anlas,** a short, two-edged knife or dagger, sometimes referred to as an *anlace*

today. **gipser,** purse, pouch. 359. **shirreve,** sheriff, king's administrative officer in a county. **countour.** This term is very vague; it might mean "accountant," or it might be a sergeant of the law (cf. note to l. 309). From the mention of the Franklin's position as sheriff, it would seem that "sergeant of the law" is what the word means here; but as to *vavasour,* in the next line, there is very little certainty—perhaps "vassal of vassals" or "important vassal," and so a substantial landholder. 362. **Webbe,** weaver. **Tapicer,** a tapestry maker. 365. **gere apyked,** equipment adorned. 368. **every-deel,** every bit, entirely. 370. **yeldhalle,** guildhall. **deys,** dais, raised platform. In all town-councils the mayor and his aldermen sat on the dais; the common councilors on the floor. 373. **catel,** property in general rather than cattle in particular. To be eligible for the position of municipal alderman, a citizen had to have a certain minimum property; cf. the meaning of the modern *chattel.* 377. **vigilyës.** Each guild had a certain day in the year dedicated to it; in other words, its festival. The *vigilyë* is the celebration held on the eve of the guild's feast day. 379. **for the nones,** "for the once (for that one time)," "for the occasion," but often a rather meaningless intensifying expletive like our "all right." "They had a cook with them for the occasion," however, makes very good sense as it stands. 380. **mary-bones,** marrowbones. 381. **poudre-marchant . . . mortreux,** tarts, sweet Cyperus sauce, and a thick stew-like soup, respectively; the *x* in *mortreux* was probably pronounced as an *s.* 386. **mormal,** an ulcer, a running sore. 387. **blank-manger,** creamed meat stewed with eggs, rice, sugar, and sometimes nuts; cf. the modern *blancmange.*

Geoffrey Chaucer 109

390 He rood up-on a rouncy as he couthe,
In a gowne of falding to the knee.
A daggere hanging on a laas hadde he
Aboute his nekke under his arm adoun.
The hote somer had maad his hewe al broun;
And, certeinly, he was a good felawe.
Ful many a draughte of wyn had he y-drawe
From Burdeux-ward, whyl that the chapman sleep.
Of nyce conscience took he no keep.
If that he faught, and hadde the hyer hond,
400 By water he sente hem hoom to every lond.
But of his craft to rekene wel his tydes,
His stremes and his daungers him bisydes,
His herberwe and his mone, his lodemenage,
Ther nas noon swich from Hulle to Cartage.
Hardy he was, and wys to undertake;
With many a tempest hadde his berd been shake.
He knew wel alle the havenes, as they were,
From Gootlond to the cape of Finistere,
And every cryke in Britayne and in Spayne;
410 His barge y-cleped was the Maudelayne.

    With us ther was a DOCTOUR of PHISYK,

The Doctor

In al this worlde ne was ther noon him lyk
To speke of phisik and of surgerye;
For he was grounded in astronomye.
He kepte his pacient a ful greet del
In houres, by his magik naturel.
Wel coude he fortunen the ascendent
Of his images for his pacient.
He knew the cause of everich maladye,
Were it of hoot or cold, or moiste, or drye,   420
And where engendred, and of what humour;
He was a verray parfit practisour.
The cause y-knowe, and of his harm the roote,
Anon he yaf the seke man his boote.
Ful redy hadde he his apothecaries,
To sende him drogges, and his letuaries,
For ech of hem made other for to winne;
Hir frendschipe nas nat newe to biginne.
Wel knew he th'olde Esculapius,
And Deiscorides, and eek Rufus,   430
Old Ypocras, Haly, and Galien;
Serapion, Razis, and Avicen;
Averrois, Damascien, and Constantyn;
Bernard, and Gatesden, and Gilbertyn.
Of his diete mesurable was he,
For it was of no superfluitee,
But of greet norissing and digestible.
His studie was but litel on the bible.
In sangwin and in pers he clad was al,
Lyned with taffata and with sendal;   440
And yet he was but esy of dispence;
He kepte that he wan in pestilence.
For gold in phisik is a cordial,
Therfor he lovede gold in special.

    A good WYF was ther of bisyde BATHE,
But she was som-del deef, and that was scathe.
Of clooth-making she hadde swiche an haunt,
She passed hem of Ypres and of Gaunt.
In al the parisshe wyf ne was ther noon
That to th' offring bifore hir sholde goon;   450
And if ther dide, certeyn, so wrooth was she,
That she was out of alle charitee.

390. **rouncy.** This word, strangely enough, appears in the equivocal meanings of (a) a broken-down nag, and (b) a good strong horse. The reader can take his choice. **as he couthe,** as best he knew how. The Shipman, a sailor or seafaring man (actually here the captain of a ship), would not be expected to ride like a knight. 391. **falding,** a coarse woolen cloth. 397. **whyl . . . sleep,** "while the merchant napped." The Shipman stole much of the wine which he was carrying for a merchant; he extracted, in other words, some of the cargo which had been entrusted to him. 400. **By water . . . every lond,** presumably the Shipman could turn to piracy and sink his victim's ship and make him walk the plank. 402. **daungers . . . herberwe,** all natural forces controlling navigation and an anchorage. 403. **lodemenage,** pilotage. 404. **Cartage . . . Finistere,** from Cartagena, Spain, to the Baltic and back again to Spain. 414. **astronomye.** The medieval scholar's astronomy is today's astrology, inasmuch as all natural phenomena observable in the heavens were supposed to have direct bearing upon the lives of men. A physician, therefore, would have to be cognizant of the natural laws of astronomy, as they were then understood. Certain times of the day or year, when the celestial bodies were in propitious alignment, were the best for treatment, depending upon the individual patient. 415. **kepte . . . ascendent.** The physician watched *(kepte)* his patient for the times most naturally advantageous to his treatment *(in houres)*. *Magik naturel* is what we would call today the doctor's scientific knowledge; the term was used until the time of Lord Bacon (p. 317), and must always be kept apart from "black magic," which was necromancy, or the arts of the devil. The physician was prepared to observe the degree of the ecliptic (the *ascendent*) rising at any given time, so as to place the patient in an

auspicious course of treatment *(fortunen).* 418. **images,** either representations of the patient (wax or clay figures) or talismans representing the different signs of the zodiac, which any astrological chart will furnish the modern reader. By exposing these images to the firmament on high when there was a favorable ascendant, the physician supposedly worked wonders with the patient's condition. 420. **hoot . . . drye.** There were four elementary qualities, consisting of contrary attributes, which in combinations produced the four elements: (1) cold and dry—earth; (2) hot and moist—air; (3) cold and moist—water; (4) hot and dry—fire. 424. **boote,** remedy. 426. **letuaries,** electuaries, or remedies. 429. **Esculapius, etc.** This is a noteworthy list of the great names in medicine prior to, and contemporaneous with, Chaucer. **Esculapius** (l. 429) is the legendary founder of medicine, according to Greek story. **Deiscorides** (l. 430) was a Greek writer on the *materia medica* of about 50 A.D. **Rufus** (l. 430) was a physician of Ephesus in the second century. **Ypocras** (l. 431) is Hippocrates, the historical founder of Greek medical science, born about 460 B.C. **Haly** is the great Persian doctor Hali ibn el Abbas, who died in 994. **Galien** is Galen, the authority of the second century. **Serapion** (l. 432) is a name belonging to three medical authorities, probably the best known of whom was the Saracen of the late eleventh and early twelfth centuries. **Razis** was the most celebrated physician of ancient Baghdad in the late ninth and early tenth centuries. **Avicen** is Avicenna, the noted Arab philosopher and scientist of the eleventh century, and **Averrois** (l. 433) was his best-known successor among the Arabs of the twelfth century. **Damascien** is doubtful, but two or three figures could qualify for the identity: St. John of Damascus (700?–754?), who was a theologian rather than a scientist, and two ninth-century

Hir coverchiefs ful fyne were of ground;
I dorste swere they weyeden ten pound
That on a Sonday were upon hir heed.
Hir hosen weren of fyn scarlet reed,
Ful streite y-teyd, and shoos ful moiste and newe.
Bold was hir face, and fair, and reed of hewe.
She was a worthy womman al hir lyve,
460 Housbondes at chirche-dore she hadde fyve,
Withouten other companye in youthe;
But thereof nedeth nat to speke as nouthe.
And thryes hadde she been at Jerusalem;
She hadde passed many a straunge streem;
At Rome she hadde been, and at Boloigne,
In Galice at seint Jame, and at Coloigne.
She coude muche of wandring by the weye:
Gat-tothed was she, soothly for to seye.
Up-on an amblere esily she sat,
470 Y-wimpled wel, and on hir heed an hat
As brood as is a bokeler or a targe;
A foot-mantel aboute hir hipes large,
And on hir feet a paire of spores sharpe.
In felawschip wel coude she laughe and carpe.
Of remedyes of love she knew perchaunce,
For she coude of that art the old daunce.

A good man was ther of religioun,
And was a povre PERSOUN of a toun;
But riche he was of holy thoght and werk.
480 He was also a lerned man, a clerk,
That Cristes gospel trewely wolde preche;
His parisshens devoutly wolde he teche.
Benigne he was, and wonder diligent,
And in adversitee ful pacient;
And swich he was y-preved ofte sythes.
Ful looth were him to cursen for his tythes,
But rather wolde he yeven, out of doute,
Un-to his povre parisshens aboute
Of his offring, and eek of his substaunce.
490 He coude in litel thing han suffisaunce.
Wyd was his parisshe, and houses fer a-sonder,
But he ne lafte nat, for reyn ne thonder,
In siknes nor in meschief, to visyte

The ferreste in his parisshe, muche and lyte,
Up-on his feet, and in his hand a staf.
This noble ensample to his sheep he yaf,
That first he wroghte, and afterward he taughte;
Out of the gospel he tho wordes caughte;
And this figure he added eek ther-to,
That if gold ruste, what shal yren do? 500
For if a preest be foul, on whom we truste,
No wonder is a lewed man to ruste;
And shame it is, if a preest take keep,
A shiten shepherde and a clene sheep.
Wel oghte a preest ensample for to yive,
By his clennesse, how that his sheep shold live.
He sette nat his benefice to hyre,
And leet his sheep encombred in the myre,
And ran to London, un-to seÿnt Poules,
To seken him a chaunterie for soules, 510
Or with a bretherhed to been withholde;
But dwelte at hoom, and kepte wel his folde,
So that the wolf ne made it nat miscarie;
He was a shepherde and no mercenarie.
And though he holy were, and vertuous,
He was to sinful man nat despitous,
Ne of his speche daungerous ne digne,
But in his teching discreet and benigne.
To drawen folk to heven by fairnesse
By good ensample, was his bisinesse: 520
But it were any persone obstinat,
What so he were, of heigh or lowe estat,
Him wolde he snibben sharply for the nones.
A bettre preest, I trowe that nowher noon is.
He wayted after no pompe and reverence,
Ne maked him a spyced conscience,
But Cristes lore, and his apostles twelve,
He taughte, but first he folwed it him-selve.

With him ther was a PLOWMAN, was his brother,
That hadde y-lad of dong ful many a fother, 530
A trewe swinker and a good was he,
Livinge in pees and parfit charitee.
God loved he best with al his hole herte
At alle tymes, thogh him gamed or smerte,

doctors from the same city. **Constantyn** is Constantinus Afer of Carthage, who brought much Saracen learning to the great medieval medical center of Salerno, Italy, during the eleventh century. The last three names (l. 434) belong to Englishmen of great influence in the medical world of their day. **Bernard** is Bernard Gordon, professor of medicine at Montpellier, France, about 1300. **Gatesden** was an Oxonian who died in 1361. **Gilbertyn** is Gilbertus Anglicus, who died in the last years of the thirteenth century. 439. **sangwin,** a blood-red cloth. **pers,** a cloth of Persian blue (azure). 441. **esy of dispence,** slow to spend. 442. **pestilence,** not necessarily the Black Death, although such an allusion is certainly possible, but simply any kind of epidemic. It is an interesting fact that Chaucer is notoriously reticent about the great historical events of his time; cf. *The Nun's Priest's Tale*, p. 122, note to l. 574. 446. **som-del,** somewhat. **scathe,** a pity. 447. **swiche an haunt,** such a practice or skill. 453. **coverchiefs,** kerchiefs, literally head-coverings. **ground,** texture. 454. **they weyeden . . . upon hir heed.** The headdress worn by women in England during the fourteenth century was often very heavy. 461. **Withouten other companye,** leaving out, not counting other company. 462. **as nouthe,** "as for now," "at the moment." 466. **seint Jame, etc.** The places mentioned in connection with the Wife of Bath's pilgrimages were the choicest shrines in the Western World. *Seint Jame* is the shrine of St. James (Santiago) of Compostella in Spain. 468. **Gat-tothed,** with teeth set far apart, "gap-toothed," or "gate-toothed." The medieval mind associated this characteristic with sensuality. 472. **foot-mantel,** an outer riding skirt. 474. **carpe,** discourse. 478. **Persoun,** parson, parish priest. 482. **parisshens,** parishioners. 486. **cursen,** to curse, in the sense of excommunicate for nonpayment of tithes. The actual ex-

communication would, of course, have to be pronounced by the local bishop, but the parish priest would be the one to report the offense. Such was the power of the Church in the Middle Ages that excommunication was one of the worst punishments that could be devised for a man, since it meant complete social and spiritual isolation. 490. **han,** a contracted form of *haven,* "to have." 500. **if gold . . . yren do?** This expression is proverbial, particularly in the French didactic romances. 502. **lewed,** ignorant, unlearned; hence a layman. The modern meaning, highly specialized in a moral sense, is comparatively recent. 510. **chaunterie,** a provision whereby a priest was to sing a daily mass for the repose of a soul. There were many such at St. Paul's in London, where the more self-seeking churchmen tried to go, but after 1391 only minor canons of a cathedral were allowed to sing chantries, and so the abuse diminished. The Parson did not leave his charges to hunt for such a position (l. 507). 511. **a bretherhed . . . withholde,** to be retained as a chaplain by a guild—an additional source of income for a worldly priest. 516. **despitous,** spiteful. 517. **daungerous,** here "arrogant" or "arbitrary." **digne,** haughty. 526. **spyced conscience,** oversweetened feelings; in other words, the Parson was not too fastidious in his feelings or in his dealings with his parishioners. 530. **y-lad,** led, pulled. **fother,** load. 531. **swinker,** laborer. 533. **loved . . . him-selve.** This "eleventh" commandment is found expressed most completely in Matthew 22:37–39. 534. **him gamed,** "it rejoiced him." Note the impersonal construction here, as with *smerte* in the same line. The entire phrase, *him gamed or smerte* could be translated "in pleasure or pain"; i.e., "in all circumstances."

And thanne his neighebour right as him-selve.
He wolde thresshe, and ther-to dyke and delve,
For Cristes sake, for every povre wight,
Withouten hyre, if it lay in his might.
His tythes payed he ful faire and wel,
540 Bothe of his propre swink and his catel.
In a tabard he rood upon a mere.

    Ther was also a Reve and a Millere,
A Somnour and a Pardoner also,
A Maunciple, and my-self; ther were namo.

    The MILLER was a stout carl, for the nones,
Ful big he was of braun, and eek of bones;
That proved wel, for over-al ther he cam,
At wrastling he wolde have alwey the ram.
He was short-sholdred, brood, a thikke knarre,
550 Ther nas no dore that he nolde heve of harre,
Or breke it, at a renning, with his heed.
His berd as any sowe or fox was reed,
And ther-to brood, as though it were a spade.
Up-on the cop right of his nose he hade
A werte, and ther-on stood a tuft of heres,
Reed as the bristles of a sowes eres;
His nose-thirles blake were and wyde.
A swerd and bokeler bar he by his syde;
His mouth as greet was as a greet forneys.

The Miller

He was a janglere and a goliardeys, 560
And that was most of sinne and harlotryes.
Wel coude he stelen corn, and tollen thryes,
And yet he hadde a thombe of gold, pardee.
A whyt cote and blew hood wered he.
A baggepype wel coude he blowe and sowne,
And therwithal he broghte us out of towne.

    A gentil MAUNCIPLE was ther of a temple,
Of which achatours mighte take exemple
For to be wyse in bying of vitaille.
For whether that he payde, or took by taille, 570
Algate he wayted so in his achat,
That he was ay biforn and in good stat.
Now is nat that of God a ful fair grace,
That swich a lewed mannes wit shal pace
The wisdom of an heep of lerned men?
Of maistres hadde he mo than thryes ten,
That were of lawe expert and curious;
Of which ther were a doseyn in that hous
Worthy to been stiwardes of rente and lond
Of any lord that is in Engelond, 580
To make him live by his propre good,
In honour dettelees, but he were wood,
Or live as scarsly as him list desire;
And able for to helpen al a shire
In any cas that mighte falle or happe;
And yit this maunciple sette hir aller cappe.

    The REVE was a sclendre colerik man,
His berd was shave as ny as ever he can.
His heer was by his eres round y-shorn.
His top was dokked lyk a preest biforn. 590
Ful longe were his legges, and ful lene,
Y-lyk a staf, ther was no calf y-sene.
Wel coude he kepe a gerner and a binne;
Ther was noon auditour coude on him winne.
Wel wiste he, by the droghte, and by the reyn,
The yeldyng of his seed, and of his greyn.
His lordes sheep, his neet, his dayerye,
His swyn, his hors, his stoor, and his pultrye,
Was hoolly in this reves governing,
And by his covenaunt yaf the rekening, 600
Sin that his lord was twenty yeer of age;
Ther coude no man bringe him in arrerage.
Ther nas baillif, ne herde, ne other hyne,
That he ne knew his sleighte and his covyne,

---

542. **Reve.** This official's duties were many and vague. If the steward (or seneschal) was the manager of a feudal estate, his immediate subordinate would be the bailiff, who would enforce the statutes of the estate and collect taxes, etc. The reeve was apparently subordinate to the bailiff, but in some cases he was superior, as is true of Chaucer's Reeve. Sometimes the reeve was employed chiefly as an auditor. In general, however, his duties were administrative and rarely constabulary. 543. **Pardoner.** Pardoners were distributors of papal indulgences, sometimes for money. In many instances, pardoners were not even ordained clergymen, and were itinerant and consequently irresponsible. Their capacity for dishonesty is unanimously vouched for by the writers of the time. 544. **Maunciple,** the purchasing agent for a college of law or any similar institution, such as an inn of court. **namo,** no more. 548. **At wrastling . . . the ram.** At country fairs, wrestling was one of the favorite sport events, as it was throughout rural sections among the English-speaking peoples. The prize for such a contest was often some livestock, such as a ram or goat. 550. **of harre,** from the hinge. Note the original sense of *of.* 557. **nose-thirles,** "nose-holes," nostrils. 560. **goliar-**

deys, retailer of smutty stories. 562. **tollen thryes,** take toll three times, overcharge. 563. **a thombe of gold,** referring to the skill of the Miller in testing the fineness of flour with his thumb, thereby learning its value. 567. **temple,** possibly the Inner or Middle Temple near the Strand, occupied in Chaucer's time by societies of lawyers. There is a persistent belief that Chaucer may have studied law here at one time. 568. **achatours,** buyers, caterers. 571. **Algate, etc.** Whether the Maunciple did his transactions on a cash or credit (*taille,* l. 570) basis, he always (*algate*) was ahead of the game in his buying (*achat*). 572. **in good stat,** in good financial standing. 577. **curious,** having care for, diligent, skillful. 586. **sette hir aller cappe,** "he set the cap of them all," a slang term of the time for "he made fools of them all." *Aller* is an old genitive plural form. 587. **colerik,** choleric, one in whom the humour *choler* (bile) predominated. See note to l. 333. Such a man would be "hot and dry"—the lean, sallow, nervous type. 597. **neet,** domestic animals, but usually specifying cattle. 598. **stoor,** general possessions, but possibly specialized to "livestock." 602. **bringe him in arrerage,** no man could catch him in arrears; his books were always kept up to the minute.

They were adrad of him, as of the deeth.
His woning was ful fair up-on an heeth,
With grene treës shadwed was his place.
He coude bettre than his lord purchace.
Ful riche he was astored prively,
His lord wel coude he plesen subtilly, 610
To yeve and lene him of his owne good,
And have a thank, and yet a cote, and hood.
In youthe he lerned hadde a good mister;
He was a wel good wrighte, a carpenter.
This reve sat up-on a ful good stot,
That was al pomely grey, and highte Scot.
A long surcote of pers up-on he hade,
And by his syde he bar a rusty blade.
Of Northfolk was this reve, of which I telle,
Bisyde a toun men clepen Baldeswelle. 620
Tukked he was, as is a frere, aboute,
And ever he rood the hindreste of our route.

   A SOMNOUR was ther with us in that place,
That hadde a fyr-reed cherubinnes face,
For sawceflem he was, with eyen narwe.
As hoot he was, and lecherous, as a sparwe;
With scalled browes blake, and piled berd;
Of his visage children were aferd.
Ther nas quik-silver, litarge, ne brimstoon,
Boras, ceruce, ne oille of tartre noon, 630
Ne oynement that wolde clense and byte,
That him mighte helpen of his whelkes whyte,
Ne of the knobbes sittinge on his chekes.
Wel loved he garleek, oynons, and eek lekes,
And for to drinken strong wyn, reed as blood.
Thanne wolde he speke, and crye as he were wood.
And whan that he wel dronken hadde the wyn,
Than wolde he speke no word but Latyn.
A fewe termes hadde he, two or thre,
That he had lerned out of som decree; 640
No wonder is, he herde it al the day;
And eek ye knowen wel, how that a jay
Can clepen "Watte," as well as can the pope.
But who-so coude in other thing him grope,
Thanne hadde he spent al his philosophye;
Ay "Questio quid iuris" wolde he crye.
He was a gentil harlot and a kynde;
A bettre felawe sholde men noght fynde.
He wolde suffre, for a quart of wyn,

The Summoner

A good felawe to have his concubyn 650
A twelf-month, and excuse him atte fulle;
And prively a finch eek coude he pulle.
And if he fond o-wher a good felawe,
He wolde techen him to have non awe,
In swich cas, of the erchedeknes curs,
But-if a mannes soule were in his purs;
For in his purs he sholde y-punisshed be.
"Purs is the erchedeknes helle," seyde he.
But wel I woot he lyed right in dede;
Of cursing oghte ech gilty man him drede— 660
For curs wol slee, right as assoilling saveth—
And also war him of a *significavit*.
In daunger hadde he at his owne gyse
The yonge girles of the diocyse,
And knew hir counseil, and was al hir reed.
A gerland hadde he set up-on his heed,
As greet as it were for an ale-stake;
A bokeler hadde he maad him of a cake.
   With him ther rood a gentil PARDONER
Of Rouncival, his freend and his compeer, 670
That streight was comen fro the court of Rome.
Ful loude he song, "Com hider, love, to me."
This somnour bar to him a stif burdoun,
Was nevere trompe of half so greet a soun.
This pardoner hadde heer as yelow as wex,

603. **herde,** herdsman, shepherd. 604. **he . . . covyne.** The Reeve knew all their tricks *(sleighte)* and their deceits *(covyne)*. 606. **woning,** dwelling. 609. **astored,** provided for. 613. **mister,** profession, occupation (cf. French *métier*). 615. **stot,** stallion. 616. **pomely,** dappled, with spots like an apple. Cf. French *pomme*. **highte,** was named. 620. **Baldeswelle,** Bawdswell in northern Norfolk, the property of the Earl of Pembroke, whom Chaucer may have once served as a deputy. The specific locality mentioned makes us believe that Chaucer had a real person in mind, but the matter is still speculative. 621. **Tukked,** with his coat hitched up behind and held by a girdle. 625. **sawceflem,** pimpled, erupted. The Summoner was suffering from a disease akin to leprosy. 627. **scalled,** scabby. **piled,** scanty, moth-eaten, with hair falling out in patches. 630. **ceruce.** This, like *litarge* in the preceding line, was a compound of lead often used in the treatment of skin diseases. 632. **whelkes,** pustules, blotches. 644. **grope,** question, test. 646. *"Questio quid iuris."* The question (is), what (part) of the law (applies)— apparently a familiar piece of legalistic jargon. 647. **harlot,** rascal, not necessarily limited to the female of the species, as in Modern English. 652. **prively . . . he pulle,** "secretly . . . pluck a finch," a slang phrase of highly indecent nature. 661. **assoilling,** absolution. 662. **significavit.** The opening words of the writ which sent a person to prison following excommunication (the gravest penalty that an ecclesiastical court could impose) were: *Significavit nobis venerabilis pater,* etc.—"The venerable father (the archbishop or papal representative) has made clear to us," etc. 663. **daunger,** power, control. 664. **girles,** young people of either sex. 667. **ale-stake.** As a sign, every inn had a stake projecting horizontally over the door, on which was suspended a hoop (or garland) decorated with ivy leaves— a symbol of festivity. The Summoner's wreath of flowers was not unusual among church people on special occasions, such as an ecclesiastical procession. 670. **Rouncival,** the Hospital of the Blessed Mary of Rouncivalle, near Charing Cross, in London. It was a subordinate convent, or cell, of the great convent of Our Lady of Roncesvalles in Navarre. There are several allusions in Middle English literature to pardoners who made Rouncivalle their headquarters, and all such allusions are satirical. **compeer,** comrade. 673. **stif burdoun,** a strong "burden" or ground melody.

Chaucer

But smothe it heng, as doth a strike of flex;
By ounces henge his lokkes that he hadde,
And there-with he his shuldres overspradde;
But thinne it lay, by colpons oon and oon;
680 But hood, for jolitee, ne wered he noon,
For it was trussed up in his walet.
Him thoughte, he rood al of the newe jet;
Dischevele, save his cappe, he rood al bare.
Swiche glaringe eyen hadde he as an hare.
A vernicle hadde he sowed on his cappe.
His walet lay biforn him in his lappe,
Bret-ful of pardoun come from Rome al hoot.
A voys he hadde as smal as hath a goot.
No berd hadde he, ne never sholde have.
690 As smothe it was as it were late y-shave;
I trowe he were a gelding or a mare.
But of his craft, fro Berwik into Ware,
Ne was ther swich another pardoner.
For in his male he hadde a pilwe-beer,
Which that, he seyde, was our lady veyl:
He sayde, he hadde a gobet of the seyl
That seynt Peter hadde, whan that he wente
Up-on the see, til Jesu Crist him hente.
He hadde a croys of latoun, ful of stones,
700 And in a glas he hadde pigges bones.
But with thise relikes, whan that he fond
A povre person dwelling up-on lond,
Up-on a day he gat him more moneye
Than that the person gat in monthes tweye.
And thus with feyned flaterye and japes,
He made the person and the people his apes.

But trewely to tellen, atte laste,
He was in chirche a noble ecclesiaste.
Wel coude he rede a lessoun or a storie,
But alderbest he song an offertorie;   710
For wel he wiste, whan that song was songe,
He moste preche, and wel affyle his tonge,
To winne silver, as he ful wel coude;
Therefore he song so meriely and loude.
　　Now have I told you shortly, in a clause,
Th'estat, th'array, the nombre, and eek the cause
Why that assembled was this companye
In Southwerk, at this gentil hostelrye,
That highte the Tabard, faste by the Belle.
But now is tyme to yow for to telle   720
How that we baren us that ilke night,
Whan we were in that hostelrye alight.
And after wol I telle of our viage,
And al the remenaunt of our pilgrimage.
But first I pray yow, of your curteisye,
That ye n'arette it nat my vileinye,
Though that I pleynly speke in this matere,
To telle yow hir wordes and hir chere;
Ne thogh I speke hir wordes proprely.
For this ye knowen al-so wel as I,   730
Who-so shal telle a tale after a man,
He moot reherce, as ny as ever he can,
Everich a word, if it be in his charge,
Al speke he never so rudeliche and large;
Or elles he moot telle his tale untrewe,
Or feyne thing, or finde wordes newe.
He may nat spare, al-though he were his brother;
He moot as wel seye o word as another.
Crist spak him-self ful brode in holy writ,
And wel ye woot, no vileinye is it.   740
Eek Plato seith, who-so that can him rede,
The wordes mote be cosin to the dede.
Also I prey yow to foryeve it me,
Al have I nat set folk in hir degree
Here in this tale, as that they sholde stonde;
My wit is short, ye may wel understonde.
　　Greet chere made our hoste us everichon,
And to the soper sette he us anon;
And served us with vitaille at the beste.
Strong was the wyn, and wel to drinke us leste.   750
A semely man our hoste was with-alle
For to han been a marshal in an halle;
A large man he was with eyen stepe,
A fairer burgeys was ther noon in Chepe:

---

676. **strike**, a bunch (of flax). 677. **ounces**, small tufts or bunches. 679. **colpons**, shreds, strips. 685. **vernicle**, a little "Veronica," a copy of the handkerchief which St. Veronica was said to have lent to Christ during the march to Calvary, and which traditionally bore the imprint of his face. 687. **Bret-ful**, brimful. Incidentally, the Pardoner was, in Chaucer's estimation, unique from the north to south of England (Berwick to Ware). 694. **male**, bag. The Modern English "mail" refers to that which is carried in the bag. **pilwe-beer**, pillowcase. 696. **gobet**, piece or fragment. 699. **croys**, cross. **latoun**, latten, an alloy of copper and zinc. 705. **japes**, jests, jokes. 710. **alderbest**, best of all; for *alder-*, see note to l. 586. 719. **the Tabard . . . the Belle**. For the Tabard Inn, and its general location in Southwark, see note to l. 20. The Bell Inn has not been identified certainly, although several inns by that name have been located in

Southwark—none, however, authentically before 1600. 726. **n'arette, etc.**, impute, ascribe. Chaucer's disclaimer here is extremely interesting, since he is deliberately telling the reader or listener of his intention to be as realistic as a reporter should be. 734. **Al**, although. The inverted word order in a clause introduced by this concessive conjunction (*Al speke he* instead of *Al he speke*) is characteristic of Chaucer's syntax. 741. **Plato**. The great Greek philosopher (427?–347 B.C.) and his works were probably known to Chaucer not through the original Greek, but through Latin derivatives, especially Boethius' *Consolation of Philosophy*. 747. **our hoste**. The host, whose description begins with this line, is obviously one of the most important figures in the pilgrimage. He serves as interlocutor and as master of ceremonies, and his reactions to the different stories seem to have been intended by Chaucer as the common-sense

Bold of his speche, and wys, and wel y-taught,
And of manhood him lakkede right naught.
Eek thereto he was right a mery man,
And after soper pleyen he bigan,
And spak of mirthe amonges othere thinges,
760 Whan that we hadde maad our rekeninges;
And seyde thus: "Now, lordinges, trewely,
Ye ben to me right welcome hertely:
For by my trouthe, if that I shal nat lye,
I ne saught this yeer so mery a companye
At ones in this herberwe as is now.
Fayn wolde I doon yow mirthe, wiste I how.
And of a mirthe I am right now bithoght,
To doon yow ese, and it shal coste noght.
  "Ye goon to Caunterbury; God yow spede,
770 The blisful martir quyte yow your mede.
And wel I woot, as ye goon by the weye,
Ye shapen yow to talen and to pleye;
For trewely, confort ne mirthe is noon
To ryde by the weye doumb as a stoon;
And therfore wol I maken yow disport,
As I seyde erst, and doon yow som confort.
And if yow lyketh alle, by oon assent,
Now for to stonden at my jugement,
And for to werken as I shal yow seye,
780 To-morwe, whan ye ryden by the weye,
Now, by my fader soule, that is deed,
But ye be merye, I wol yeve yow myn heed.
Hold up your hond, withouten more speche."
  Our counseil was nat longe for to seche;
Us thoughte it was noght worth to make it wys,
And graunted him withouten more avys,
And bad him seye his verdit, as him leste.
  "Lordinges," quod he, "now herkneth for the beste;
But tak it not, I prey yow, in desdeyn;
790 This is the poynt, to speken short and pleyn,
That ech of yow, to shorte with your weye,
In this viage, shal telle tales tweye,
To Caunterbury-ward, I mene it so,
And hom-ward he shal tellen othere two,
Of aventures that whylom han bifalle.
And which of yow that bereth him best of alle,
That is to seyn, that telleth in this cas
Tales of best sentence and most solas,
Shal have a soper at our aller cost
800 Here in this place, sitting by this post,
Whan that we come agayn fro Caunterbury.
And for to make yow the more mery,

I wol my-selven gladly with yow ryde,
Right at myn owne cost, and be your gyde.
And who-so wol my jugement withseye
Shal paye al that we spenden by the weye.
And if ye vouche-sauf that it be so,
Tel me anon, with-outen wordes mo,
And I wol erly shape me therfore."
  This thing was graunted, and our othes swore   810
With ful glad herte, and preyden him also
That he wold vouche-sauf for to do so,
And that he wolde been our governour,
And of our tales juge and reportour,
And sette a soper at a certeyn prys;
And we wold reuled been in his devys,
In heigh and lowe; and thus, by oon assent,
We been acorded to his jugement
And ther-up-on the wyn was fet anoon;
We dronken, and to reste wente echon,   820
With-outen any lenger taryinge.
  A-morwe, whan that day bigan to springe,
Up roos our host, and was our aller cok,
And gadrede us togidre, alle in a flok,
And forth we riden, a litel more than pas,
Un-to the watering of seint Thomas.
And there our host bigan his hors areste,
And seyde; "Lordinges, herkneth if yow leste.
Ye woot your forward, and I it yow recorde.
If even-song and morwe-song acorde,   830
Lat se now who shal telle the firste tale.
As ever mote I drinke wyn or ale,
Who-so be rebel to my jugement
Shal paye for al that by the weye is spent.
Now draweth cut, er that we ferrer twinne,
He which that hath the shortest shal beginne.
Sire knight," quod he, "my maister and my lord,
Now draweth cut, for that is myn acord.
Cometh neer," quod he, "my lady prioresse;
And ye, sir clerk, lat be your shamfastnesse,   840
Ne studieth noght; ley hond to, every man."
  Anon to drawen every wight bigan,
And shortly for to tellen, as it was,
Were it by aventure, or sort, or cas,
The sothe is this, the cut fil to the knight,
Of which ful blythe and glad was every wight;
And telle he moste his tale, as was resoun,
By forward and by composicioun,
As ye han herd; what nedeth wordes mo?
And whan this gode man saugh it was so,   850

reactions of a typical English middle-class burgeys. His identity with
Henry or Harry Bailly, an innkeeper of Southwark, who appears in
historical documents, has been reasonably well established; certainly
he is the most "historical" member of the group. everichon, every
one. 750. us leste, it pleased us. 754. Chepe, Cheapside, one of
the principal London streets. 758. pleyen, a very vague word, not as
definite even as our modern "play." Here the meaning is simply
"waxed merry," "joked." 770. quyte, requite, reward. mede,
meed, reward. 772. shapen, plan. 776. erst, first. 781. fader soule.
Fader (father) is often undeclined in Middle English. 786. avys,
consideration, argument. 787. verdit, decision. 794. tellen othere
two. This would call for four stories from each pilgrim. Chaucer never
completed this design; he did not actually make the rounds once.
There is evidence that he changed his plan as he progressed in the
collection. 798. solas, amusement, entertainment. 805. withseye,
object to, deny, gainsay. 813. governour, guide and leader. 816.
in his devys, at his direction. 819. fet, fetched. 823. our aller cok,
cock for all of us, our reveille. 826. watering of seint Thomas, a
brook at the second milestone on the Kent road. 835. ferrer twinne,
get farther away (from London). 840. shamfastnesse, not our
"shamefaced," but rather "shyness," "bashfulness," "overmodesty."
844. aventure . . . cas. There is no longer any clear distinction in
the use of these three nouns—all seem to be synonymous here with
"luck" or "chance." 848. By forward . . . composicioun, according to the agreement and the arrangement. 850. saugh, saw.

As he that wys was and obedient
To kepe his forward by his free assent,
He seyde: "Sin I shal beginne the game,
What, welcome be the cut, a Goddes name!
Now lat us ryde, and herkneth what I seye."

    And with that word we riden forth our weye;
And he bigan with right a mery chere
His tale anon, and seyde in this manere.

THE NUN'S PRIEST'S TALE

*The chivalrous Knight, as might be expected, tells
a courtly medieval romance; the coarse and loud-
mouthed Miller tells a ribald, back-stairs fabliau; the
gentle Prioress recites with feminine tenderness and
warmth a story of medieval Christian martyrdom.
And thus it goes, each character in the pilgrimage
tells a story appropriate enough to his occupation,
profession, and character. And so the Nun's Priest,
one of the "preestes three" of line 164 of the Prologue, is presumably a man of vigor and a man of
humor, but he is also a man of God, whose fundamental purpose in life is, after all, to teach.*

*The Nun's Priest's Tale is actually a beast-fable,
with exempla embedded in it. But Chaucer, the observer of humanity, cannot efface himself. The story
becomes a delightful satire on married life through
the shrewd portrayals of the bumbling, pompous
Chauntecleer and the keen but slyly submissive Pertelote.*

A povre widwe, somdel stape in age,
Was whylom dwelling in a narwe cotage,
Bisyde a grove, stonding in a dale.
This widwe, of which I telle yow my tale,
Sin thilke day that she was last a wyf,
In pacience ladde a ful simple lyf,
For litel was hir catel and hir rente;
By housbondrye, of such as God hir sente,
She fond hir-self, and eek hir doghtren two.
10 Three large sowes hadde she, and namo,
Three kyn, and eek a sheep that highte Malle.
Ful sooty was hir bour, and eek hir halle,
In which she eet ful many a sclendre meel.
Of poynaunt sauce hir neded never a deel.
No deyntee morsel passed thurgh hir throte;
Hir dyete was accordant to hir cote.
Repleccioun ne made hir nevere syk;
Attempree dyete was al hir phisyk,
And exercyse, and hertes suffisaunce.

The goute lette hir no-thing for to daunce, 20
N'apoplexye shente nat hir heed;
No wyn ne drank she, neither whyt ne reed;
Hir bord was served most with whyt and blak,
Milk and broun breed, in which she fond no lak,
Seynd bacoun, and somtyme an ey or tweye,
For she was as it were a maner deye.

    A yerd she hadde, enclosed al aboute
With stikkes, and a drye dich with-oute,
In which she hadde a cok, hight Chauntecleer,
In al the land of crowing nas his peer. 30
His vois was merier than the merye orgon
On messe dayes that in the chirche gon;
Wel sikerer was his crowing in his logge,
Than is a clokke, or an abbey orlogge.
By nature knew he ech ascencioun
Of equinoxial in thilke toun;
For whan degrees fiftene were ascended,
Thanne crew he, that it mighte nat ben amended.
His comb was redder than the fyn coral,
And batailed as it were a castel-wal. 40
His bile was blak, and as the jeet it shoon;
Lyk asur were his legges, and his toon;
His nayles whytter than the lilie flour,
And lyk the burned gold was his colour.
This gentil cok hadde in his governaunce
Sevenne hennes, for to doon al his pleasaunce,
Whiche were his sustres and his paramours,
And wonder lyk to him, as of colours.
Of whiche the faireste hewed on hir throte
Was cleped faire damoysele Pertelote. 50

The Nun's Priest

The Nun's Priest's Tale. 1. stape, "stepped," "advanced." **9.
fond,** provided for. **doghtren,** daughters. **11. kyn,** kine, cows. **17.
Repleccioun,** repletion, overeating. **18. Attempree,** temperate, moderate. **21. shente,** injured. **23. whyt and blak,** light and dark ale.
26. deye, dairywoman; cf. the modern surname Day. **30. nas,** "ne"
plus "was" equal "was not." **33. sikerer,** more certain, more de-
pendable. **35. ascencioun of equinoxial.** The *equinoxial* is the great
circle made in the heavens by the extended plane of the earth's equator.
It makes a complete revolution in twenty-four hours; consequently,
fifteen degrees would pass, or "ascend" every hour. In short,
Chauntecleer knew by instinct every hour of the day when it came

around, and proclaimed the arrival of each new hour. **38. it . . .
amended,** it could not be improved upon. **40. batailed,** with battlements (the cock's wattles). **45. governaunce,** control, power. **51.
debonaire,** meek. **55. lith,** limb. **67. drecched,** troubled, afflicted.
73. a-grief, amiss. **74. me mette,** a common impersonal circumlocution
for "I dreamed." **87. douteles,** doubtless, i.e., "never fear." **88.
"Avoy!" "Fie!"** an expression of contemptuous reproach. **herteles,**
"heartless" in the sense of "lacking courage." **101. swevenis . . .
sweven is.** Identical rimes, common enough in modern humorous
verse, were not considered out of place in the serious verse of the
Middle Ages. See note to l. 18 of the Prologue (p. 104). **103.**

Curteys she was, discreet, and debonaire,
And compaignable, and bar hir-self so faire,
Sin thilke day that she was seven night old,
That trewely she hath the herte in hold
Of Chauntecleer loken in every lith,
He loved hir so, that wel him was therwith.
But such a joye was it to here hem singe,
Whan that the brighte sonne gan to springe,
In swete accord, "my lief is faren in londe."
60 For thilke tyme, as I have understonde,
Bestes and briddes coude speke and singe.

    And so bifel, that in a dawenynge,
As Chauntecleer among his wyves alle
Sat on his perche, that was in the halle,
And next him sat this faire Pertelote,
This Chauntecleer gan gronen in his throte,
As man that in his dreem is drecched sore.
And whan that Pertelote thus herde him rore,
She was agast, and seyde, "O herte dere,
70 What eyleth yow, to grone in this manere?
Ye been a verray sleper, fy for shame!"
And he answerde and seyde thus, "Madame,
I pray yow, that ye take it nat a-grief:
By God, me mette I was in swich meschief
Right now, that yet myn herte is sore afright.
Now God," quod he, "my swevene recche aright,
And keep my body out of foul prisoun!
Me mette, how that I romed up and doun
Withinne our yerde, wher-as I saugh a beste,
80 Was lyk an hound, and wolde han maad areste
Upon my body, and wolde han had me deed.
His colour was bitwixe yelwe and reed;
And tipped was his tail, and bothe his eres,
With blak, unlyk the remenant of his heres;
His snowte smal, with glowinge eyen tweye.
Yet of his look for fere almost I deye;
This caused me my groning, douteles.
    "Avoy!" quod she, "fy on yow, herteles!
Allas!" quod she, "for, by that God above,
90 Now han ye lost myn herte and al my love;
I can nat love a coward, by my feith.
For certes, what so any womman seith,
We alle desyren, if it mighte be,
To han housbonds hardy, wyse, and free,
And secree, and no nigard, ne no fool,
Ne him that is agast of every tool,
Ne noon avauntour, by that God above!
How dorste ye seyn for shame unto your love,
That any thing mighte make yow aferd?
100 Have ye no mannes herte, and han a berd?

Allas! and conne ye been agast of swevenis?
No-thing, God wot, but vanitee, in sweven is.
Swevenes engendren of replecciouns
And ofte of fume, and of complecciouns,
Whan humours been to habundant in a wight.
Certes this dreem, which ye han met to-night,
Cometh of the grete superfluitee
Of youre rede *colera*, pardee,
Which causeth folk to dremen in here dremes
Of arwes, and of fyr with rede lemes,   110
Of grete bestes, that they wol hem byte,
Of contek, and of whelpes grete and lyte;
Right as the humour of malencolye
Causeth ful many a man, in sleep, to crye,
For fere of blake beres, or boles blake,
Or elles, blake develes wole hem take.
Of othere humours coude I telle also,
That werken many a man in sleep ful wo;
But I wol passe as lightly as I can.
    "Lo Catoun, which that was so wys a man,   120
Seyde he nat thus, ne do no fors of dremes?
Now, sire," quod she, "whan we flee fro the bemes,
For Goddes love, as tak som laxatyf;
Up peril of my soule, and of my lyf,
I counseille yow the beste, I wol nat lye,
That both of colere, and of malencolye
Ye purge yow; and for ye shul nat tarie,
Though in this toun is noon apotecarie,
I shal my-self to herbes techen yow,
That shul ben for your hele, and for your prow;   130
And in our yerd tho herbes shal I fynde,
The whiche han of hir propretee, by kynde,
To purgen yow binethe, and eek above.
Forget not this, for Goddes owene love!
Ye been ful colerik of compleccioun.
Ware the sonne in his ascencioun
Ne fynde yow nat repleet of humours hote;
And if it do, I dar wel leye a grote,
That ye shul have a fevere terciane,
Or an agu, that may be youre bane.   140
A day or two ye shul have digestyves
Of wormes er ye take your laxatyves,
Of lauriol, centaure, and fumetere,
Or elles of ellebor, that groweth there,
Of catapuce, or of gaytres beryis,
Of erbe yve, growing in our yerd, that mery is;
Pekke hem up right as they growe, and ete hem in.
Be mery, housbond, for your fader kyn!
Dredeth no dreem; I can say yow namore."
    "Madame," quod he, "*graunt mercy of your lore.*   150

---

engendren, have their source in, come about from. replecciouns, overeating. 106. Certes, surely, certainly. 108. rede *colera*. The colera would be bile (yellow bile as distinguished from the other humour, black bile). The belief was held in some quarters that a serious overbalance of one humour in respect to the others would give a corresponding tinge to all objects seen by the patient. Too much bile was supposed to make everything appear red. Cf. 1. 113. 110. lemes, flames. 115. boles, bulls. 120. Catoun, Dionysius Cato. 121. do no fors of, make no account of, attach no importance to. 124. Up, upon, on. 126. colere, choler, bile. malencolye, is, of course, another humour, black bile. 132. by kynde, by nature.

138. leye a grote, wager a groat. The groat was a Low German coin from the trading ports of Holland and North Germany, notably from Bremen, worth about four silver pennies. 140. youre bane. The original meaning of bane is "killer." 143. lauriol, etc. The drugs mentioned in this list include the common cathartics in use during the Middle Ages. Lauriol is the spurge-laurel; centaure, the century-plant, a common remedy for pain in the abdomen; fumetere is fumitory; ellebor, hellebore; catapuce, the caperberry; gaytres beryis, berries of the dogwood; and erbe yve, ground ivy.

But natheless, as touching daun Catoun,
That hath of wisdom such a gret renoun,
Though that he bad no dremes for to drede,
By God, men may in olde bokes rede
Of many a man, more of auctoritee
Than ever Catoun was, so mote I thee,
That al the revers seyn of this sentence,
And han wel founden by experience,
That dremes ben significaciouns,
160 As wel of joye as tribulaciouns
That folk enduren in this lyf present.
Ther nedeth make of this noon argument;
The verray preve sheweth it in dede.
   "Oon of the gretteste auctours that men rede
Seith thus, that whylom two felawes wente
On pilgrimage, in a ful good entente;
And happed so, thay came into a toun,
Wher as ther was swich congregacioun
Of peple, and eek so streit of herbergage,
170 That they ne founde as muche as o cotage,
In which they bothe mighte y-logged be.
Wherfor they mosten, of necessitee,
As for that night, departen compaignye;
And ech of hem goth to his hostelrye,
And took his logging as it wolde falle.
That oon of hem was logged in a stalle,
Fer in a yerd, with oxen of the plough;
That other man was logged wel y-nough,
As was his aventure, or his fortune,
180 That us governeth alle as in commune.
   "And so bifel, that, long er it were day,
This man mette in his bed, ther as he lay,
How that his felawe gan up-on him calle,
And seyde, 'Allas! for in an oxes stalle
This night I shal be mordred ther I lye.
Now help me, dere brother, er I dye;
In alle haste com to me,' he sayde.
This man out of his sleep for fere abrayde;
But whan that he was wakned of his sleep,
190 He turned him, and took of this no keep;
Him thoughte his dreem nas but a vanitee.
Thus twyës in his sleping dremed he.
And atte thridde tyme yet his felawe
Cam, as him thoughte, and seide, 'I am now slawe,
Bihold my blody woundes, depe and wyde!
Arys up erly in the morwe-tyde,
And at the west gate of the toun,' quod he,

'A carte ful of donge ther shaltow see,
In which my body is hid ful prively;
Do thilke carte aresten boldely.
200
My gold caused my mordre, sooth to sayn';
And tolde him every poynt how he was slayn,
With a ful pitous face, pale of hewe.
And truste wel, his dreem he fond ful trewe;
For on the morwe, as sone as it was day,
To his felawes in he took the way;
And whan that he cam to this oxes stalle,
After his felawe he bigan to calle.
   "The hostiler answerde him anon,
And seyde, 'Sire, your felawe is agon,
210
As sone as day he wente out of the toun.'
This man gan fallen in suspecioun,
Remembring on his dremes that he mette,
And forth he goth, no lenger wolde he lette,
Unto the west gate of the toun, and fond
A dong-carte, as it were to donge lond,
That was arrayed in that same wyse
As ye han herd the dede man devyse;
And with an hardy herte he gan to crye
Vengeaunce and justice of this felonye:
220
'My felawe mordred is this same night,
And in this carte he lyth gapinge upright.
I crye out on the ministres,' quod he,
'That sholden kepe and reulen this citee;
Harrow! allas! her lyth my felawe slayn!'
What sholde I more un-to this tale sayn?
The peple out-sterte, and caste the cart to grounde,
And in the middel of the dong they founde
The dede man, that mordred was al newe.
   "O blisful God, that art so just and trewe!
230
Lo, how that thou biwreyest mordre alway!
Mordre wol out, that se we day by day.
Mordre is so wlatsom and abhominable
To God, that is so just and resonable,
That he ne wol nat suffre it heled be;
Though it abyde a yeer, or two, or three,
Mordre wol out, this my conclusioun.
And right anoon, ministres of that toun
Han hent the carter, and so sore him pyned,
And eek the hostiler so sore engyned,
240
That thay biknewe hir wikkednesse anoon,
And were an-hanged by the nekke-boon.
   "Here may men seen that dremes been to drede.
And certes, in the same book I rede,

151. **daun.** Here, as elsewhere, the shortened form of the Latin "dominus" ("lord") used as a title of respect. Cf. the Spanish *Don. Daun Catoun,* then, is "Lord Cato." So Tennyson, in his *Palace of Art,* speaks of "Dan Chaucer," and there is the familiar "Dan Cupid." 157. **sentence,** statement, opinion. 163. **verray preve, etc.** The true test (of the statement) proves it in fact. 169. **streit,** narrow, used here in the sense of "crowded." **herbergage,** lodgings. 173. **departen,** part company. 188. **abrayde,** started up. The word is used of any kind of violent motion. 191. **Him thoughte,** not "he thought" but "it seemed to him," an impersonal construction. The same is true of the more common "methinks," which means "it seems to me." This is not the verb "to think," but the verb seen in the German *es dünkt mir* (it seems to me). 203. **pitous,** pitiable, awakening pity. 206. **in,** inn, lodging. 216. **donge lond,** to cover land with dung. Raw sewage was carried outside the city gates and dumped there. 218. **devyse,** describe. 225. **Harrow! allas!** These two cries of distress are usually found in combination. The

first, "Harrow!" may originally have had some relation to the idea of "harrowing, raking," hence "distressing" (we still speak of a "harrowing" experience), but no doubt that original meaning had long since faded. 233. **wlatsom,** disgusting. 235. **heled,** concealed. 240. **engyned,** put on the rack or on other instruments (engines) of torture. 241. **biknewe,** acknowledged, confessed. 246. **gabbe,** speak idly. It is amusing to see how consistently Chaucer has portrayed Chauntecleer as the pompous, self-important husband. 252. **agayn,** toward, just before. 255. **hem,** them. 256. **oo,** one. 264. **lette,** put off. 271. **vanitees and japes,** follies and jokes. 274. **shal,** shall (be). 275. **sith,** since. 277. **it reweth me,** it rues me, I am sorry—still another in the long list of impersonal constructions. 281. **casuelly,** by accident. 290. **seint Kenelm,** etc. The story is told in one of the many medieval lives of the saints. Kenulphus (Cenwulf), mentioned in l. 291, had a son Kenelm (Cenhelm). Kenulphus was king of Mercia, dying in 821. The boy was only seven years old at the time, and was put under the care of his aunt,

Right in the nexte chapitre after this,
(I gabbe nat, so have I joye or blis,)
Two men that wolde han passed over see,
For certeyn cause, in-to a fer contree,
If that the wind ne hadde been contrarie,
250 That made hem in a citee for to tarie,
That stood ful mery upon an haven-syde.
But on a day, agayn the even-tyde,
The wind gan chaunge, and blew right as hem leste.
Jolif and glad they wente un-to hir reste,
And casten hem ful erly for to saille;
But to that oo man fel a greet mervaille.
That oon of hem, in sleping as he lay,
Him mette a wonder dreem, agayn the day;
Him thoughte a man stood by his beddes syde,
260 And him comaunded, that he sholde abyde,
And seyde him thus, 'If thou to-morwe wende,
Thou shalt be dreynt; my tale is at an ende.'
He wook, and tolde his felawe what he mette,
And preyde him his viage for to lette;
As for that day, he preyde him to abyde.
His felawe, that lay by his beddes syde,
Gan for to laughe, and scorned him ful faste.
'No dreem,' quod he, 'may so myn herte agaste,
That I wol lette for to do my thinges.
270 I sette not a straw by thy dreminges,
For swevenes been but vanitees and japes.
Men dreme al-day of owles or of apes,
And eek of many a mase therwithal;
Men dreme of thing that never was ne shal.
But sith I see that thou wolt heer abyde,
And thus for-sleuthen wilfully thy tyde,
God wot it reweth me; and have good day.'
And thus he took his leve, and wente his way.
But er that he hadde halfe his cours y-seyled,
280 Noot I nat why, ne what mischaunce it eyled,
But casuelly the shippes botme rente,
And ship and man under the water wente
In sighte of othere shippes it byside,
That with hem seyled at the same tyde.
And therfor, faire Pertelote so dere,
By swiche ensamples olde maistow lere,
That no man sholde been to recchelees
Of dremes, for I sey thee, doutelees,
That many a dreem ful sore is for to drede.
290 "Lo, in the lyf of seint Kenelm, I rede,
That was Kenulphus sone, the noble king

Of Mercenrike, how Kenelm mette a thing;
A lyte er he was mordred, on a day,
His mordre in his avisioun he say.
His norice him expounded every del
His sweven, and bad him for to kepe him wel
For traisoun; but he nas but seven yeer old,
And therfore litel tale hath he told
Of any dreem, so holy was his herte.
By God, I hadde lever than my sherte   300
That ye had rad his legende, as have I.
Dame Pertelote, I sey yow trewely,
Macrobeus, that writ th'avisioun
In Affrike of the worthy Cipioun,
Affermeth dremes, and seith that they been
Warning of thinges that men after seen.
"And forther-more, I pray yow loketh wel
In th'olde testament, of Daniel,
If he held dremes any vanitee.
Reed eek of Joseph, and ther shul ye see   310
Wher dremes ben somtyme (I set nat alle)
Warning of thinges that shul after falle.
Loke of Egipt the king, daun Pharao,
His bakere and his boteler also,
Wher they ne felte noon effect in dremes.
Who-so wol seken actes of sondry remes,
May rede of dremes many a wonder thing.
"Lo Cresus, which that was of Lyde king,
Mette he nat that he sat upon a tree,
Which signified he sholde anhanged be?   320
Lo heer Andromacha, Ectores wyf,
That day that Ector sholde lese his lyf,
She dremed on the same night biforn,
How that the lyf of Ector sholde be lorn,
If thilke day he wente in-to bataille;
She warned him, but it mighte nat availle;
He wente for to fighte nathelees,
But he was slayn anoon of Achilles.
But thilke tale is al to long to telle,
And eek it is ny day, I may nat dwelle.   330
Shortly I seye, as for conclusioun,
That I shal han of this avisoun
Adversitee; and I seye forther-more,
That I ne telle of laxatyves no store,
For they ben venimous, I woot it wel;
I hem defye, I love hem nevere a del.
"Now let us speke of mirthe, and stinte al this;
Madame Pertelote, so have I blis,

who conspired to murder him. Before his death the child dreamt that he climbed into a lofty tree; one of his friends came and cut it down; whereupon the boy flew to Heaven as a bird. As a symbol of martyred childhood and innocence, Kenelm was later canonized. 294. **avisioun**, vision, dream. **say**, saw. 298. **tale**, importance. **told**, ascribed, attributed. 303. **Macrobeus**, the "authority" on dreams during the Middle Ages. His accredited importance is hardly fair to another greater writer, Cicero, who, by the way, is probably the "oon of the gretteste auctours" of l. 164, since the tale of the murdered traveler is found in Cicero's *De Divinatione*. Macrobeus, a Latin writer of about 400, made an elaborate commentary on that section of Cicero's *De Republica* known as the "Somnium Scipionis" or "Dream of Scipio," in which commentary there appears a discussion of the various kinds of dreams and their application to human life. It is evident that Macrobeus' work represents an accretion of ancient medical lore and knowledge of dreams. It is worth noting that Macrobeus is more or less a champion of the "portentous" or "premonitory"

interpretation of dreams, as opposed to the physiological interpretation. **th'avisioun . . . Cipioun**, the "Somnium Scipionis" or "Dream of Scipio (Africanus)" just mentioned in the foregoing sentence. 308. **Daniel**, the Old Testament prophet. The passage in the Scriptures relevant to this line is Daniel, Chapter 7. 310. **Joseph**. The manner in which Joseph interpreted dreams is told in Genesis, Chapters 37, 40, 41. The marshaling of authorities (Macrobeus, Daniel, Joseph, and the classical folk) is absolutely typical of the method of reasoning in the Middle Ages. 316. **remes**, realms. 318. **Cresus**. The story is told in *The Romance of the Rose* (p. 17). Cresus, King of Lydia (603?–546 B.C.), was defeated and killed by Cyrus the Great (d.529 B.C.). 321. **Andromacha**, Andromache, the wife of Hector in Homer's *Iliad*. There is nothing in Homer about her dream; it is a fiction of the medieval authors in the development of the Troy legend. 324. **lorn**, lost. 337. **stinte**, cease, stop.

Of o thing God hath sent me large grace;
340 For whan I see the beautee of your face,
Ye ben so scarlet-reed about youre yën,
It maketh al my drede for to dyen;
For, also siker as *In principio,*
Mulier est hominis confusio,
Madame, the sentence of this Latin is—
Womman is mannes joye and al his blis.
For whan I feele anight your softe syde,
Al be it that I may nat on yow ryde,
For that oure perche is maad so narwe, allas!
350 I am so ful of joye and of solas
That I defye bothe sweven and dreem."
And with that word he fley doun fro the beem,
For it was day, and eek his hennes alle;
And with a chuk he gan hem for to calle,
For he had founde a corn, lay in the yerd.
Royal he was, he was namore aferd;
He fethered Pertelote twenty tyme,
And trad as ofte, er that it was pryme.
He loketh as it were a grim leoun,
360 And on his toos he rometh up and doun,
Him deyned not to sette his foot to grounde.
He chukketh, whan he hath a corn y-founde,
And to him rennen thanne his wyves alle.
Thus royal, as a prince is in his halle,
Leve I this Chauntecleer in his pasture;
And after wol I telle his aventure.
    Whan that the month in which the world bigan,
That highte March, whan God first maked man,
Was complet, and [y]-passed were also,
370 Sin March bigan, thritty dayes and two,
Bifel that Chauntecleer, in al his pryde,
His seven wyves walking by his syde,
Caste up his eyen to the brighte sonne,
That in the signe of Taurus hadde y-ronne
Twenty degrees and oon, and somwhat more;
And knew by kynde and by noon other lore,
That it was pryme, and crew with blisful stevene.
"The sonne," he sayde, "is clomben up on hevene
Fourty degrees and oon, and more, y-wis.
380 Madame Pertelote, my worldes blis,
Herkneth thise blisful briddes how they singe,

And see the fresshe floures how they springe;
Ful is myn hert of revel and solas."
But sodeinly him fil a sorweful cas;
For ever the latter ende of joye is wo.
God woot that worldly joye is sone ago;
And if a rethor coude faire endyte,
He in a cronique saufly mighte it write,
As for a sovereyn notabilitee.
Now every wys man, lat him herkne me;   390
This storie is al-so trewe, I undertake,
As is the book of Launcelot de Lake,
That wommen holde in ful gret reverence.
Now wol I torne agayn to my sentence.
    A col-fox, ful of sly iniquitee,
That in the grove hadde woned yeres three,
By heigh imaginacioun forn-cast,
The same night thurgh-out the hegges brast
Into the yerd, ther Chauntecleer the faire
Was wont, and eek his wyves, to repaire;   400
And in a bed of wortes stille he lay,
Til it was passed undern of the day,
Wayting his tyme on Chauntecleer to falle
As gladly doon thise homicydes alle,
That in awayt liggen to mordre men.
O false mordrer lurking in thy den!
O newe Scariot, newe Genilon!
False dissimilour, O Greek Sinon
That broghtest Troye al outrely to sorwe!
O Chauntecleer, acursed be that morwe,   410
That thou into that yerd flough fro the bemes!
Thou were ful wel y-warned by thy dremes,
That thilke day was perilous to thee.
But what that God forwoot mot nedes be,
After the opinioun of certeyn clerkis.
Witnesse on him, that any perfit clerk is,
That in scole is gret altercacioun
In this matere, and greet disputisoun,
And hath ben of an hundred thousand men.
But I ne can not bulte it to the bren,   420
As can the holy doctour Augustyn,
Or Boëce, or the bishop Bradwardyn,
Whether that Goddes worthy forwiting
Streyneth me nedely for to doon a thing,

343. siker, sure. In principio . . . confusio. The quotation begins like the first verse of the Gospel of John or the opening of the Book of Genesis (cf. Prologue to *The Canterbury Tales,* l. 254 and note). The rest (Mulier . . .) means "Woman is man's confusion," and is more or less a proverb of the time. 370. bigan, passed. 374. signe of Taurus, the constellation of Taurus the Bull, the second of the twelve signs of the zodiac, constellations through which the sun must pass in its annual journey through the heavens. Since Aries, or the Ram (see the Prologue to *The Canterbury Tales,* l. 8 and note), is the constellation in which the sun is located at the time of the vernal equinox (March 21–23), a date from which the medieval astronomers began the new year, it is called the first sign of the zodiac. Taurus is the second; the sun would, therefore, be in Taurus from about April 20 to May 20. The reference in the next line to the "twenty-one or more degrees" places the date at early in the month of May. 377. pryme, the first hour of the day (6:00 A.M.), or roughly, from 6:00 to 9:00 in the morning. stevene, voice. 379. y-wis, in truth, surely. Forty-one degrees would be almost half way to the zenith. In May this would be shortly before noon o'clock. 384. sorweful cas, sad event. 386. ago, gone. 388. cronique, chronicle, the type of historical writing most frequently composed during the Middle Ages. 392. Launcelot de Lake, the great chivalric hero of the Arthurian cycle. 397. heigh imaginacioun forn-cast, by divine foreknowledge (imaginacioun) foreordained. 398. brast, burst. 402. undern, morning. The usual hour indicated by this term is nine o'clock in the morning, but it is quite possible that, as in the case of *pryme* (see note to l. 377), the word expresses a two- or three-hour period following the exact original hour. In this analogy, *undern* could mean anywhere from nine o'clock in the morning until noon. 407. Scariot, Judas Iscariot, the disciple who betrayed Christ; see Matthew 26:14–25 and 47–56. Genilon, Ganelon, the traitor in the French epic, *The Song of Roland,* who betrayed Roland's command to the Saracens. 408. Sinon, the man who persuaded the Trojans to admit the wooden horse at Troy, by which plan the city was captured. The story was probably most familiar to medieval readers through Vergil's *Aeneid,* Book II. 418. disputisoun, argument, dispute. 420. I ne . . . bren, "I cannot sift it to the bran," "I cannot analyze the question thoroughly and leave nothing behind but immaterial or irrelevant facts." Chaucer's attitude, here as elsewhere, is that of the superficial and unconcerned spectator, whenever insoluble problems of philosophy happen to get in the way. 422. Boëce, Boethius (475?–524?), whose *Consolation of Philosophy* was one of the works considered by King Alfred as most necessary for the education of his people. In all frankness, it must be allowed that it is extremely difficult to decide what Boethius' position in this problem of Providence v. Free Will really is. His explanation needs further explaining.

(Nedely clepe I simple necessitee);
Or elles, if free choys be graunted me
To do that same thing, or do it noght,
Though God forwoot it, er that it was wroght;
Or if his witing streyneth nevere a del
430 But by necessitee condicionel.
I wol not han to do of swich matere;
My tale is of a cok, as ye may here,
That took his counseil of his wyf, with sorwe,
To walken in the yerd upon that morwe
That he had met the dreem, that I yow tolde.
Wommennes counseils been ful ofte colde;
Wommannes counseil broghte us first to wo,
And made Adam fro paradys to go,
Ther-as he was ful mery, and wel at ese.—
440 But for I noot, to whom it mighte displese,
If I counseil of wommen wolde blame,
Passe over, for I seyde it in my game.
Rede auctours, wher they trete of swich matere,
And what thay seyn of wommen ye may here.
Thise been the cokkes wordes, and nat myne;
I can noon harm of no womman divyne.

Faire in the sond, to bathe hir merily,
Lyth Pertelote, and alle hir sustres by,
Agayn the sonne; and Chauntecleer so free
450 Song merier than the mermayde in the see;
For Phisiologus seith sikerly,
How that they singen wel and merily.
And so bifel that, as he caste his yë,
Among the wortes, on a boterflyë,
He was war of this fox that lay ful lowe.
No-thing ne liste him thanne for to crowe,
But cryde anon, "cok, cok," and up he sterte,
As man that was affrayed in his herte.
For naturelly a beest desyreth flee
460 Fro his contrarie, if he may it see,
Though he never erst had seyn it with his yë.

This Chauntecleer, whan he gan him espyë,
He wolde han fled, but that the fox anon
Seyde, "Gentil sire, allas! wher wol ye gon?
Be ye affrayed of me that am your freend?
Now certes, I were worse than a feend,
If I to yow wolde harm or vileinye.

I am nat come your counseil for t'espye;
But trewely, the cause of my cominge
Was only for to herkne how that ye singe. 470
For trewely ye have as mery a stevene,
As any aungel hath, that is in hevene;
Therwith ye han in musik more felinge
Than hadde Boëce, or any that can singe.
My lord your fader (God his soule blesse!),
And eek your moder, of hir gentilesse,
Han in myn hous y-been, to my gret ese;
And certes, sire, ful fayn wolde I yow plese.
But for men speke of singing, I wol saye,
So mote I brouke wel myn eyen tweye, 480
Save yow, I herde never man so singe,
As dide your fader in the morweninge;
Certes, it was of herte, al that he song.
And for to make his voys the more strong,
He wolde so peyne him, that with both his yën
He moste winke, so loude he wolde cryen,
And stonden on his tiptoon ther-with-al,
And strecche forth his nekke long and smal.
And eek he was of swich discrecioun,
That ther nas no man in no regioun 490
That him in song or wisdom mighte passe.
I have wel rad in daun Burnel the Asse,
Among his vers, how that there was a cok,
For that a preestes sone yaf him a knok
Upon his leg, whyl he was yong and nyce,
He made him for to lese his benefyce.
But certeyn, ther nis no comparisoun
Bitwix the wisdom and discrecioun
Of youre fader, and of his subtiltee.
Now singeth, sire, for seinte Charitee, 500
Let see, conne ye your fader countrefete?"
This Chauntecleer his winges gan to bete,
As man that coude his tresoun nat espye,
So was he ravisshed with his flaterye.

Allas! ye lordes, many a fals flatour
Is in your courtes, and many a losengeour,
That plesen yow wel more, by my feith,
Than he that soothfastnesse unto yow seith.
Redeth Ecclesiaste of flaterye;
Beth war, ye lordes, of hir trecherye. 510

bishop **Bradwardyn**, lecturer at Oxford and Archbishop of Canterbury at the time of his death in 1349. His treatment of the problem was conservative and orthodox—he relied chiefly upon Providence. 424. **Streyneth**, constrains, forces. **nedely**, by necessity, of necessity. 429. **witing**, knowing, knowledge. 430. **necessitee condicionel**, necessity conditioned by God's foreknowledge as contrasted to simple necessity (l. 425), whereby a thing happens because it must happen. 442. **game**, joke, sport. 443. **auctours**, authors and authorities. Once there appears the medieval "love of authority" (*Magister dixit*) motif. 451. **Phisiologus . . . sikerly**. *Sikerly* means *certainly*. The *Phisiologus* is the *Physiologus* or *Latin Bestiary*, a series of didactic poems describing some of the nature and habits of certain animals and drawing Christian allegorical teachings from those characteristics. 460. **contrarie**, opposite. According to medieval belief, every creature or concept had another creature or concept that was its contrary, toward which it felt a natural dislike or fear (dog to cat, bird to snake, love to hate, life to death, etc.). 476. **gentilesse**. The word *gentilesse* has a variety of meanings, which, when blended together, come close to producing the ideal of chivalry either for man or for woman. It is an innate quality which has no reference to social rank or caste, depending rather upon essential nobility of character according to the Christian and knightly codes, courtesy, good breeding, delicacy, tact, and even slenderness and grace of body. All these

come under this one word *gentilesse*. In consequence, no one translation of the word can fit any one occurrence thereof, and the reader must choose for himself. Chaucer wrote a ballade (p. 142) on the subject, and the theme is apparent in *The Wife of Bath's Tale* (p. 137). 480. **So . . . brouke**, another extremely mild oath, of the kind as "So mote I thee" ("So may I prosper") of l. 156. This one means something like "So may I enjoy my eyes!" 488. **smal**, narrow. 492. **daun Burnel the Asse**. There was an Anglo-Latin satirical poem of the late twelfth century by Nigel Wireker called *Burnellus, seu Speculum Stultorum* (*Burnel*, or the *Mirror of Idiots*). The tale is told of a young man named Gundulfus, who was annoyed by a cock. He threw a stone and broke the bird's leg. Later Gundulfus was to be ordained, but the injured cock delayed his crowing so that Gundulfus overslept and lost his benefice, or church living. 501. **countrefete**, imitate and match. As pointed out in the Prologue to *The Canterbury Tales*, l. 139 and note, the word "counterfeit" does not have the meaning of falseness or criminality in Middle English that it has assumed in Modern English. 505. **flatour**. Both this word and *losengeour*, in the next line, signify flatterers. 508. **soothfastnesse**, truth. 509. **Ecclesiaste of flaterye**. The reference is to the apocryphal Book of Ecclesiasticus, not to the poetic Ecclesiastes of the Old Testament. The specific passages in Ecclesiasticus, which are too long to quote here, are Ecclesiasticus 12:10 ff. and 27:26 ff.

Geoffrey Chaucer 121

This Chauntecleer stood hye up-on his toos,
Strecching his nekke, and heeld his eyen cloos,
And gan to crowe loude for the nones;
And daun Russel the fox sterte up at ones,
And by the gargat hente Chauntecleer,
And on his bak toward the wode him beer,
For yet ne was ther no man that him sewed.
O destinee, that mayst nat been eschewed!
Allas, that Chauntecleer fleigh fro the bemes!
520 Allas, his wyf ne roghte nat of dremes!
And on a Friday fil al this meschaunce.
O Venus, that art goddesse of plesaunce,
Sin that thy servant was this Chauntecleer,
And in thy service dide al his poweer,
More for delyt, than world to multiplye,
Why woldestow suffre him on thy day to dye?
O Gaufred, dere mayster soverayn,
That, whan thy worthy king Richard was slayn
With shot, compleynedest his deth so sore,
530 Why ne hadde I now thy sentence and thy lore,
The Friday for to chide, as diden ye?
(For on a Friday soothly slayn was he.)
Than wolde I shewe yow how that I coude pleyne
For Chauntecleres drede, and for his peyne.

  Certes, swich cry ne lamentacioun
Was never of ladies maad, whan Ilioun
Was wonne, and Pirrus with his streite swerd,
Whan he hadde hent king Priam by the berd,
And slayn him (as saith us *Eneydos*),
540 As maden alle the hennes in the clos,
Whan they had seyn of Chauntecleer the sighte.
But sovereynly dame Pertelote shrighte,
Ful louder than dide Hasdrubales wyf,
Whan that hir housbond hadde lost his lyf,
And that the Romayns hadde brend Cartage;
She was so ful of torment and of rage,
That wilfully into the fyr she sterte,
And brende hir-selven with a stedfast herte.
O woful hennes, right so cryden ye,
550 As, whan that Nero brende the citee
Of Rome, cryden senatoures wyves,
For that hir housbondes losten alle hir lyves;
Withouten gilt this Nero hath hem slayn.
Now wol I torne to my tale agayn:

  This sely widwe, and eek hir doghtres two,
Herden thise hennes crye and maken wo,
And out at dores sterten they anoon,
And syen the fox toward the grove goon,
And bar upon his bak the cok away;
560 And cryden, "Out! harrow! and weylaway!
Ha, ha, the fox!" and after him they ran,

And eek with staves many another man;
Ran Colle our dogge, and Talbot, and Gerland,
And Malkin, with a distaf in hir hand;
Ran cow and calf, and eek the verray hogges
So were they fered for berking of the dogges
And shouting of the men and wimmen eke,
They ronne so, hem thoughte hir herte breke.
They yelleden as feendes doon in helle;
The dokes cryden as men wolde hem quelle;   570
The gees for fere flowen over the trees;
Out of the hyve cam the swarm of bees;
So hidous was the noyse, a! *benedicite!*
Certes, he Jakke Straw, and his meynee,
Ne made never shoutes half so shrille,
Whan that they wolden any Fleming kille,
As thilke day was maad upon the fox.
Of bras thay broghten bemes, and of box,
Of horn, of boon, in whiche they blewe and pouped,
And therwithal thay shryked and they houped;   580
It seemed as that heven sholde falle.
Now, gode men, I pray yow herkneth alle!

  Lo, how fortune turneth sodeinly
The hope and pryde eek of hir enemy!
This cok, that lay upon the foxes bak,
In al his drede, un-to the fox he spak,
And seyde, "sire, if that I were as ye,
Yet sholde I seyn (as wis God helpe me):
'Turneth agayn, ye proude cherles alle!
A verray pestilence up-on yow falle!   590
Now am I come un-to this wodes syde,
Maugree your heed, the cok shal heer abyde;
I wol him ete in feith, and that anon.'"
The fox answerde, "in feith, it shal be don"—
And as he spak that word, al sodeinly
This cok brak from his mouth deliverly,
And heighe up-on a tree he fleigh anon.
And whan the fox saugh that he was y-gon,
"Allas!" quod he, "O Chauntecleer, allas!
I have to yow," quod he, "y-doon trespas,   600
In-as-muche as I maked yow aferd,
Whan I yow hente, and broghte out of the yerd;
But, sire, I dide it in no wikke entente;
Com doun, and I shal telle yow what I mente.
I shal seye sooth to yow, God help me so."
"Nay than," quod he, "I shrewe us bothe two,
And first I shrewe my-self, bothe blood and bones,
If thou bigyle me ofter than ones.
Thou shalt namore, thurgh thy flaterye
Do me to singe and winke with myn yë.   610
For he that winketh, whan he sholde see,
Al wilfully, God lat him never thee!"

515. **gargat**, throat. **hente**, seized. 517. **sewed**, pursued, followed.
527. **Gaufred**, Geoffrey de Vinsauf, a writer on the art of poetry.
His major work, the *Poetria Nova*, appeared shortly after the death
of King Richard I (the Lion-Hearted) of England (that is, about
1200). Geoffrey's model for an elegy consists of some lines of
lament on the death of Richard. 533. **pleyne**, complain. 540. **clos**,
yard. 544. **hir housbond . . . lyf**. Hasdrubal was king of Carthage
when the Romans sacked it (146 B.C.). 545. **brend**, burned. 550.
Nero . . . Rome, a reference to the disastrous fire at Rome during
the reign of Nero (37 A.D.–68 A.D.) in the year 64. Traditionally

Nero was supposed to have set the fire himself. 555. **sely**, good,
innocent. 574. **Jakke Straw . . . meynee**. This passage is virtually
the only one in Chaucer's works having reference to an important
event in England during the poet's lifetime. The Peasants' Revolt
of 1381 was featured by a serious demonstration and rioting against
the Flemish who had settled in London and adjacent parts. The competition offered by the Flemish in the wool industry was the chief
reason for the hostile feeling toward them. 578. **bemes**, trumpets.
box, boxwood. 592. **Maugree your heed**, "in spite of you." 596.
deliverly, quickly. 606. **shrewe**, curse. 612. **God . . . thee**, "God let

"Nay," quod the fox, "but God yive him meschaunce,
That is so undiscreet of governaunce,
That jangleth whan he sholde holde his pees."

Lo, swich it is for to be recchelees,
And necligent, and truste on flaterye.
But ye that holden this tale a folye,
As of a fox, or of a cok and hen,
620 Taketh the moralitee, good men.
For seint Paul seith, that al that writen is,
To our doctryne it is y-write, y-wis.
Taketh the fruyt, and lat the chaf be stille.

Now, gode God, if that it be Thy wille,
As seith my Lord, so make us alle good men;
And bringe us to His heighe blisse. Amen.

THE PARDONER'S TALE

*The pilgrims pause beside the road, and the Par-
doner, who has just been asked for a story, partakes of some refreshments in the form of cakes and
ale. Warmed by the drink, he proceeds to a remarkable passage of self-revelation, in which he exposes
the frauds and deceits which he imposes upon the
populace, with his pigs' bones and rags which he
palms off as holy relics. It should be observed that
The Pardoner's Tale, which then follows, begins as
a medieval sermon on the evils of intemperance and
covetousness, in which the narrative proper—the story
of the three roisterers who sought Death and found
him—serves as the usual exemplum.*

*It is not known where Chaucer got this particular
version, but the story itself is a common folk tale
which has been traced back to the Orient; Chaucer
has given it a setting reminiscent of the terrible days
of the Black Death in England of the fourteenth century. The terse style and rushing pace of the narrative combined with its impressive dramatic force make
it one of Chaucer's most notable achievements.*

*When the Pardoner has concluded his gripping tale,
he resumes his harangue and winds it up in a fine
frenzy of oratory; he then has the effrontery to offer
some of his own relics to the pilgrims—for a consideration. He is so misguided as to select the Host
for special attention, and provokes a tremendous outburst from that gentleman which completely silences
him.*

In Flaundres whylom was a companye
Of yonge folk, that haunteden folye,
As ryot, hasard, stewes, and tavernes,
Wher-as, with harpes, lutes, and giternes,

They daunce and pleye at dees bothe day and night,
And ete also and drinken over hir might,
Thurgh which they doon the devel sacrifyse
With-in that develes temple, in curséd wyse,
By superfluitee abhominable;
Hir othes been so grete and so dampnable,   10
That it is grisly for to here hem swere;
Our blisséd Lordes body they to-tere;
Hem thoughte that Jewes rente hym noght ynough,
And ech of hem at otheres synne lough.
And right anon thanne comen tombesteres,
Fetys and smale, and yonge frutesteres,
Syngeres with harpes, baudes, wafereres,
Whiche been the verray develes officeres
To kyndle and blowe the fyr of lecherye,
That is annexed unto glotonye.   20
The hooly writ take I to my witnesse,
That luxurie is in wyn and dronkenesse.

Lo, how that dronken Looth unkyndely
Lay by hise doghtres two unwityngly;
So dronke he was, he nyste what he wroghte.
Herodes, whoso wel the stories soghte,
Whan he of wyn was repleet at his feeste,
Right at his owene table he yaf his heeste
To sleen the Baptist John, ful giltelees.
Senec seith a good word, doutelees;   30
He seith, he kan no difference fynde
Bitwix a man that is out of his mynde,
And a man which that is dronkelewe,
But that woodnesse fallen in a shrewe
Persevereth lenger than dooth dronkenesse.
O glotonye, ful of cursednesse!

The Pardoner

him never prosper," a malediction parallel to the "so mote I thee" of
l. 156. 615. **jangleth,** chatter. 616. **recchelees,** reckless.
    The Pardoner's Tale. 3. **hasard,** gambling, games of chance. 4.
giternes, citherns. 6. **over hir might,** beyond their powers, with
disastrous effect. 12. **body they to-tere, etc.,** reference to the
"tearing" or "rending" of Christ's body through unadvised oaths
like "By God's bones!" "By God's blood!" etc. 16. **frutesteres,**
girls who sell fruit; cf. the "orange girls" of the Restoration period.
This, like **tombesteres** ("dancing girls") in the preceding line, illustrates the feminine noun of agent suffix *-ster.* 17. **wafereres,** sellers
of cakes and wafers (pastry and confectionery). 21. **The hooly writ
. . . dronkenesse.** "And be not drunk with wine, wherein is
excess."—Ephesians 5:18; "Wine is a mocker, strong drink is
raging: and whosoever is deceived thereby is not wise."—Proverbs
20:1. 23. **dronken Looth.** The story of Lot's incest is told in
Genesis 19:30–36. **unkyndely,** unnaturally, against nature. 26.
Herodes . . . heeste. *Yaf his heeste* means "gave his commands."
The story referred to is that of Salome; see Matthew 14:3–12 and
Mark 6:17–29. 30. **Senec,** Seneca (3 B.C.–65 A.D.), the Roman
philosopher and writer of tragedies. 34. **woodnesse,** madness, insanity.

O cause first of oure confusioun!
O original of oure dampnacioun
Til Crist hadde boght us with his blood agayn!
40 Lo, how deere, shortly for to sayn,
Aboght was thilke cursed vileynye!
Corrupt was al this world for glotonye!
Adam oure fader, and his wyf also,
Fro Paradys to labour and to wo
Were dryven for that vice, it is no drede;
For whil that Adam fasted, as I rede,
He was in Paradys, and whan that he
Eet of the fruyt deffended on the tree,
Anon he was out-cast to wo and peyne.
50 O glotonye, on thee wel oghte us pleyne!
O, wiste a man how manye maladyes
Folwen of excesse and of glotonyes,
He wolde been the moore mesurable
Of his diete, sittynge at his table.
Allas! the shorte throte, the tendre mouth
Maketh that est and west and north and south
In erthe, in eir, in water, man to swynke
To gete a glotoun deyntee mete and drynke!
Of this matiere, O Paul! wel kanstow trete,
60 "Mete unto wombe and wombe eek unto mete
Shal God destroyen bothe," as Paulus seith.
Allas, a foul thyng is it, by my feith!
To seye this word, and fouler is the dede,
Whan man so drinketh of the whyte and rede,
That of his throte he maketh his privee,
Thurgh thilke cursed superfluitee.
    The apostel weping seith ful pitously,
"Ther walken many of whiche yow told have I,
I seye it now weping with pitous voys,
70 That they been enemys of Cristes croys,
Of whiche the ende is deeth, wombe is her god."
O wombe! O bely! O stinking cod,
Fulfild of donge and of corrupcioun!
At either ende of thee foul is the soun.
How greet labour and cost is thee to finde!
Thise cokes, how they stampe, and streyne, and grinde,
And turnen substance into accident,
To fulfille al thy likerous talent!
Out of the harde bones knokke they
80 The mary, for they caste noght a-wey
That may go thurgh the golet softe and swote;
Of spicerye of leef, and bark, and rote
Shal been his sauce y-maked by delyt,
To make him yet a newer appetyt.

But certes, he that haunteth swich delyces
Is deed, whyl that he liveth in tho vyces.
    A lecherous thing is wyn, and dronkenesse
Is ful of stryving and of wrecchednesse.
O dronke man, disfigured is thy face,
Sour is thy breeth, foul artow to embrace, 90
And thurgh thy dronke nose semeth the soun
As though thou seydest ay "Sampsoun, Sampsoun!"
And yet, God wot, Sampsoun drank never no wyn.
Thou fallest, as it were a stiked swyn;
Thy tonge is lost, and al thyn honest cure;
For dronkenesse is verray sepulture
Of mannes wit and his discrecioun.
In whom that drinke hath dominacioun,
He can no conseil kepe, it is no drede.
Now kepe yow fro the whyte and fro the rede, 100
And namely, fro the white wyn of Lepe,
That is to selle in Fysshstrete, or in Chepe.
This wyn of Spaigne crepeth subtilly
In othere wynes, growynge faste by,
Of which ther ryseth swich fumositee,
That whan a man hath dronken draughtes three
And weneth that he be at hoom in Chepe,
He is in Spaigne, right at the toune of Lepe,
Nat at the Rochele, ne at Burdeux toun,
And thanne wol he seye "Sampsoun, Sampsoun!" 110
But herkneth, lordes, o word, I yow preye,
That alle the sovereyn actes, dar I seye,
Of victories in the Olde Testament,
Thurgh verray God that is omnipotent,
Were doon in abstinence and in preyere.
Looketh the Bible, and ther ye may it leere.
Looke, Attilla, the grete conquerour,
Deyde in his sleepe, with shame and dishonour,
Bledynge ay at his nose in dronkenesse.
A capitayn sholde lyve in sobrenesse; 120
And over al this avyseth yow right wel,
What was comaunded unto Lamuel,
Nat Samuel, but Lamuel, seye I;
Redeth the Bible and fynde it expresly,
Of wyne-yevyng to hem that han justise.
Namoore of this, for it may wel suffise.
    And now that I have spoken of glotonye,
Now wol I yow deffenden hasardrye.
Hasard is verray moder of lesynges,
And of deceite and cursed forswerynges, 130
Blasphemyng of Crist, manslaughtre and wast also
Of catel and of tyme, and forthermo
It is repreeve and contrarie of honour

---

41. **Aboght,** bought and paid for. 48. **deffended,** forbidden. For
the story, see Genesis, Chapter 3. 57. **swynke,** labor. 68. **Ther
walken . . . her god.** "Meats for the belly (*wombe*), and the belly
for meats: but God shall destroy both it and them."—1 Corinthians
6:13. "For many walk, of whom I have told you often, and now
tell you even weeping, that they are the enemies of the cross of
Christ: whose end is destruction, whose God is their belly," etc. —
Philippians 3:18–19. 72. **cod,** gut, stomach, intestines. 75. **How
greet . . . to finde!** "How great a labor and cost it is to provide
for (*finde*) thee!" 77. **substance into accident.** In the sense peculiar to medieval philosophy the "substance" of a thing is its real
essence; the "accident" comprises the external qualities (color, weight,
shape, etc.). The cooks then will take an edible and labor to change

its "accident" in such a way as to tickle the palate. 95. **honest cure,**
care for one's honor, self-respect. 101. **Lepe . . . Chepe.** *Lepe* is a
town near Cádiz in Spain; Fishstreet (*Fysshstrete*) was a very busy
commercial street near London Bridge. Chaucer's father had been a
wine dealer in the immediate vicinity. Cheapside (*Chepe*) was one of
the principal London streets. 109. **the Rochele,** La Rochelle, France.
Burdeux toun, Bordeaux, France. 117. **Attilla,** the great leader of
the Huns, whose disastrous inroads into western Europe threatened
the foundations of Occidental culture; he died in 453—according to
story—as the result of overdissipation on his wedding night. 122.
Lamuel, Lemuel, whose words against drink are quoted in Proverbs,
Chapter 31. 133. **repreeve . . . honour,** a shame and enemy to
honor. 141. **Stilbon, etc.** The story is told in a late Greek chronicle,

For to ben holde a commune hasardour.
And ever the hyer he is of estaat,
The more is he holden desolaat.
If that a prince useth hasardrye,
In alle governaunce and policye
He is, as by commune opinioun,
140 Y-holde the lasse in reputacioun.

Stilbon, that was a wys embassadour,
Was sent to Corinthe, in ful greet honour,
Fro Lacidomie, to make hir alliaunce.
And whan he cam, him happede, par chaunce,
That alle the grettest that were of that lond,
Pleyinge atte hasard he hem fond.
For which, as sone as it mighte be,
He stal him hoom agayn to his contree,
And seyde, "ther wol I nat lese my name;
150 N' I wol nat take on me so greet defame,
Yow for to allye un-to none hasardours.
Sendeth othere wyse embassadours;
For, by my trouthe, me were lever dye,
Than I yow sholde to hasardours allye.
For ye that been so glorious in honours
Shul nat allyen yow with hasardours
As by my wil, ne as by my tretee."
This wyse philosophre thus seyde he.

Loke eek that, to the king Demetrius
160 The king of Parthes, as the book seith us,
Sente him a paire of dees of gold in scorn,
For he hadde used hasard ther-biforn;
For which he heeld his glorie or his renoun
At no value or reputacioun.
Lordes may finden other maner pley
Honeste y-nough to dryve the day awey.

Now wol I speke of othes false and grete
A word or two, as olde bokes trete.
Gret sweryng is a thyng abhominable
170 And fals sweryng is yet moore reprevable.
The heighe God forbad sweryng at al,
Witnesse on Mathew; but in special
Of sweryng seith the hooly Jeremye,
"Thou shalt seye sooth thyne othes, and nat lye,
And swere in doom, and eek in rightwisnesse,"
But ydel sweryng is a cursednesse.
Bihoold and se, that in the firste table
Of heighe Goddes heestes honurable
How that the seconde heeste of Hym is this:
180 "Take nat my name in ydel or amys."
Lo, rather He forbedeth swich sweryng
Than homycide, or any cursed thyng!

I seye, that as by ordre thus it stondeth,
This knowen that Hise heestes understondeth
How that the seconde heeste of God is that.
And forther-over I wol thee telle al plat,
That vengeance shal nat parten from his hous
That of hise othes is to outrageous—
"By Goddes precious herte and by His nayles,
190 And by the blood of Crist that is in Hayles,
Sevene is my chaunce and thyn is cynk and treye.
By Goddes armes, if thou falsly pleye,
This dagger shal thurghout thyn herte go!"
This fruyt cometh of the bicched bones two,
Forsweryng, ire, falsnesse, homycide!
Now for the love of Crist, that for us dyde,
Lete youre othes bothe grete and smale.
But, sires, now wol I telle forth my tale.

Thise ryotoures three, of whiche I telle,
200 Longe erst er pryme rong of any belle,
Were set hem in a taverne for to drinke;
And as they satte, they herde a belle clinke
Biforn a cors was caried to his grave;
That oon of hem gan callen to his knave,
"Go bet," quod he, "and axe redily,
What cors is this that passeth heer forby;
And look that thou reporte his name wel."
"Sir," quod this boy, "it nedeth never-a-del.
It was me told, er ye cam heer, two houres;
210 He was, pardee, an old felawe of youres;
And sodeynly he was y-slayn to-night,
For-dronke, as he sat on his bench upright;
Ther cam a privee theef, men clepeth Deeth,
That in this contree al the peple sleeth,
And with his spere he smoot his herte atwo,
And wente his wey with-outen wordes mo.
He hath a thousand slayn this pestilence:
And, maister, er ye come in his presence,
Me thinketh that it were necessarie
220 For to be war of swich an adversarie:
Beth redy for to mete him evermore.
Thus taughte me my dame, I sey namore."
"By seinte Marie," seyde this taverner,
"The child seith sooth, for he hath slayn this yeer,
Henne over a myle, within a greet village,
Both man and womman, child and hyne, and page.
I trowe his habitacioun be there;
To been avyséd greet wisdom it were,
Er that he dide a man a dishonour."
230 "Ye, Goddes armes," quod this ryotour,

but the ambassador's name was given as *Chilon*. 159. **Demetrius, etc.**
This story is taken from the same source as that about *Stilbon* (l. 141);
we are uncertain as to which of several kings of Parthia named Demetrius this incident concerns. 172. **Witnesse . . . rightwisnesse.** See
Matthew 5:34 and Jeremiah 4:2. 186. **plat,** flatly. 190. **in Hayles,
etc.** Some of Christ's blood, shed at the time of the Crucifixion, was
believed to be contained in a vessel at Hayles, Gloucestershire. 191.
Sevene . . . treye. This is a clear reference to the game of hazard,
which has a close resemblance to our modern game of craps. Skeat's
quotation from the *English Cyclopaedia* (supplementary volume on the
division of Arts and Sciences) will give the main rules of the game.
The player throwing the dice (the caster) chooses a number (calls
the main) — any number from five to nine, but usually seven. "If

he then throws either seven or eleven, he wins; if he throws aces
(ones) or deuce-ace (two and one) or twelve (sixes), he loses. If he
throws some other number, that number is called the caster's chance
(*chaunce*), and he goes on throwing until either his 'main' or his
'chance' turns up. In the first case he loses; in the second he wins."
Cynk is the number five; *treye* is three. 200. **pryme,** the first hour
of the day (6:00 A.M.); later used for the period between six and
nine in the morning. 208. **never-a-del,** never a bit, not at all.
212. **For-dronke,** very drunk. 225. **Henne,** hence. 226. **hyne,**
servant; specifically, a farm laborer. **page,** boy; also any young man
in attendance or in training for knighthood.

"Is it swich peril with him for to mete?
I shal him seke by wey and eek by strete,
I make avow to Goddes digne bones!
Herkneth, felawes, we three been al ones;
Lat ech of us holde up his hond til other,
And ech of us bicomen otheres brother,
And we wol sleen this false traytour Deeth;
He shal be slayn, which that so many sleeth,
By Goddes dignitee, er it be night."

240 Togidres han thise three her trouthes plight,
To live and dyen ech of hem for other,
As though he were his owene y-boren brother.
And up they sterte al dronken, in this rage,
And forth they goon towardes that village,
Of which the taverner had spoke biforn;
And many a grisly ooth that han they sworn,
And Cristes blesséd body they to-rente—
Deeth shal be deed, if that they may him hente!
    Whan they han goon nat fully half a myle,
250 Right as they wolde han troden over a style,
An old man and a povre with hem mette.
This olde man ful mekely hem grette,
And seyde thus, "Now, lordes, God yow see!"
    The proudest of thise ryotoures three
Answerde agayn, "What? carl, with sory grace,
Why artow al forwrappéd save thy face?
Why livestow so longe in so greet age?"
    This olde man gan loke in his visage,
And seyde thus, "For I ne can nat finde
260 A man, though that I walkéd into Inde,
Neither in citee nor in no village,
That wolde chaunge his youthe for myn age;
And therefore moot I han myn age stille,
As longe time as it is Goddes wille.
Ne deeth, allas! ne wol nat han my lyf;
Thus walke I, lyk a restelees caityf,
And on the ground, which is my modres gate,
I knokke with my staf, bothe erly and late,
And seye, 'Leve moder, leet me in!
270 Lo, how I vanish, flesh, and blood, and skin!
Allas! whan shul my bones been at reste?
Moder, with yow wolde I chaunge my cheste,
That in my chambre longe tyme hath be,
Ye! for an heyre clowt to wrappe me!'
But yet to me she wol nat do that grace,
For which ful pale and welkéd is my face.
    "But, sirs, to yow it is no curteisye
To speken to an old man vileinye,
But he trespasse in worde, or elles in dede.
280 In holy writ ye may your-self wel rede,
'Agayns an old man, hoor upon his heed,
Ye sholde aryse'; wherfor I yeve yow reed,
Ne dooth un-to an old man noon harm now;

Na-more than ye wolde men dide to yow
In age, if that ye so longe abyde;
And God be with yow, wher ye go or ryde.
I moot go thider as I have to go."
"Nay, olde cherl, by God, thou shalt nat so,"
Seyde this other hasardour anon;
"Thou partest nat so lightly, by seint John!   290
Thou spak right now of thilke traitour Deeth,
That in this contree alle our frendes sleeth.
Have heer my trouthe, as thou art his aspye,
Tel wher he is, or thou shalt it abye,
By God, and by the holy sacrament!
For soothly thou art oon of his assent,
To sleen us yonge folk, thou false theef!"
"Now, sirs," quod he, "if that yow be so leef
To finde Deeth, turne up this crokéd wey,
For in that grove I lafte him, by my fey,   300
Under a tree, and ther he wol abyde;
Nat for your boost he wol him no-thing hyde.
See ye that ook? right ther ye shul him finde.
God save yow, that boghte agayn mankinde,
And yow amende!"—thus seyde this olde man.
And everich of thise ryotoures ran,
Til he cam to that tree, and ther they founde
Of florins fyne of golde y-coynéd rounde
Wel ny an eighte busshels, as hem thoughte.
No lenger thanne after Deeth they soughte,   310
But ech of hem so glad was of that sighte,
For that the florins been so faire and brighte,
That doun they sette hem by this precious hord.
The worste of hem he spak the firste word.
    "Brethren," quod he, "tak kepe what I seye;
My wit is greet, though that I bourde and pleye.
This tresor hath Fortune un-to us yiven,
In mirthe and jolitee our lyf to liven,
And lightly as it comth, so wol we spende.
Ey! Goddes precious dignitee! who wende   320
Today, that we sholde han so faire a grace?
But mighte this gold be caried fro this place
Hoom to myn hous, or elles un-to youres—
For wel ye woot that al this gold is oures—
Than were we in heigh felicitee.
But trewely, by daye it may nat be;
Men wolde seyn that we were theves stronge,
And for our owene tresor doon us honge.
This tresor moste y-caried be by nighte
As wysly and as slyly as it mighte.   330
Wherfore I rede that cut among us alle
Be drawe, and lat se wher the cut wol falle;
And he that hath the cut with herte blythe
Shal renne to the toune, and that ful swythe,
And bringe us breed and wyn ful prively.
And two of us shul kepen subtilly

233. digne bones, worthy bones. 234. al ones, all of one mind.
239. dignitee, worthiness, honor. 252. grette, greeted. 256. artow,
art thou? forwrappéd, wrapped up. 276. welkéd, withered. 281.
'Agayns . . . aryse.' "Thou shalt rise up before the hoary head,
and honor the face of the old man," etc.—Leviticus 19:32. 293.
aspye, spy, secret agent. 294. abye, pay for. 298. leef, modern
"lief," glad, eager. 316. bourde, jest, joke. 320. wende, weened,
supposed, expected. 330. slyly, wisely, cleverly. 334. swythe,
quickly; the word is a generally intensifying adverb. 342. fil, fell to.
345. other. The original meaning of this word was always "second";
it was the original ordinal numeral for two. 353. frendes torn, a
friendly turn. 357. conseil, a secret. shrewe, rascal. 383. beye,

This tresor wel; and, if he wol nat tarie,
Whan it is night, we wol this tresor carie
By oon assent, wher-as us thinketh best."
340 That oon of hem the cut broughte in his fest,
And bad hem drawe, and loke wher it wol falle;
And it fil on the yongeste of hem alle;
And forth toward the toun he wente anon.
And al-so sone as that he was gon,
That oon of hem spak thus un-to that other,
"Thou knowest wel thou art my sworne brother,
Thy profit wol I telle thee anon.
Thou woost wel that our felawe is agon;
And heer is gold, and that ful greet plentee,
350 That shal departed been among us three.
But natheles, if I can shape it so
That it departed were among us two,
Hadde I nat doon a frendes torn to thee?"
    That other answerde, "I noot how that may be;
He woot how that the gold is with us tweye,
What shal we doon, what shal we to him seye?"
    "Shal it be conseil?" seyde the firste shrewe,
"And I shal tellen thee, in wordes fewe,
What we shal doon, and bringe it wel aboute."
360   "I graunte," quod that other, "out of doute,
That, by my trouthe, I wol thee nat biwreye."
    "Now," quod the firste, "thou woost wel we be
                                                  tweye,
And two of us shul strenger be than oon.
Look whan that he is set, and right anoon
Arys, as though thou woldest with him pleye;
And I shal ryve him thurgh the sydes tweye
Whyl that thou strogelest with him as in game,
And with thy dagger look thou do the same;
And than shal al this gold departed be,
370 My dere freend, bitwixen me and thee;
Than may we bothe our lustes al fulfille,
And pleye at dees right at our owene wille."
And thus accorded been thise shrewes tweye
To sleen the thridde, as ye han herd me seye.
    This yongest, which that wente un-to the toun,
Ful ofte in herte he rolleth up and doun
The beautee of thise florins newe and brighte.
"O lord!" quod he, "if so were that I mighte
Have al this tresor to my-self allone,
380 Ther is no man that liveth under the trone
Of God, that sholde live so mery as I!"
And atte laste the feend, our enemy,
Putte in his thought that he shold poyson beye,
With which he mighte sleen his felawes tweye;
For-why the feend fond him in swich lyvinge,
That he had leve him to sorwe bringe,
For this was outrely his fulle entente
To sleen hem bothe, and never to repente.

And forth he gooth, no lenger wold he tarie,
Into the toun, un-to a pothecarie,   390
And preyéd him, that he him wolde selle
Some poyson, that he mighte his rattes quelle;
And eek ther was a polcat in his hawe,
That, as he seyde, his capouns hadde y-slawe,
And fayn he wolde wreke him, if he mighte,
On vermin, that destroyéd him by nighte.
    The pothecarie answerde, "And thou shalt have
A thing that, al-so God my soule save,
In al this world ther nis no creature,
That ete or dronke hath of this confiture   400
Noght but the mountance of a corn of whete,
That he ne shal his lyf anon forlete;
Ye, sterve he shal, and that in lasse whyle
Than thou wolt goon a paas nat but a myle;
This poyson is so strong and violent."
    This curséd man hath in his hond y-hent
This poyson in a box, and sith he ran
In-to the nexte strete, un-to a man,
And borwed [of] him large botels three;
And in the two his poyson pouréd he;   410
The thridde he kepte clene for his drinke.
For all the night he shoop him for to swinke
In caryinge of the gold out of that place.
And whan this ryotour, with sory grace,
Had filled with wyn his grete botels three,
To his felawes agayn repaireth he.
    What nedeth it to sermone of it more?
For right as they had cast his deeth bifore,
Right so they han him slayn, and that anon.
And whan that this was doon thus spak that oon, 420
"Now lat us sitte and drinke, and make us merie,
And afterward we wol his body berie."
And with that word it happéd him, par cas,
To take the botel ther the poyson was,
And drank, and yaf his felawe drinke also,
For which anon they storven bothe two.
But certes, I suppose that Avicen
Wroot nevere in no canoun, ne in no fen,
Mo wonder signes of empoisonyng
Than hadde thise wrecches two, er hir endyng.   430
Thus ended been thise homycides two,
And eek the false empoysoner also.
    O cursed synne ful of cursednesse!
O traytours homycide! O wikkednesse!
O glotonye, luxurie, and hasardrye!
Thou blasphemour of Crist, with vileynye,
And othes grete, of usage and of pride,
Allas, mankynde! how may it bitide
That to thy Creatour which that the wroghte,
And with His precious herte-blood thee boghte, 440
Thou art so fals and so unkynde, allas!

buy. 385. For-why, because. 392. quelle, kill. 393. hawe, yard;
the literal meaning is "hedge." 395. wreke him, avenge himself.
400. confiture, concoction, mixture. 402. forlete, leave, abandon,
give up. 403. sterve, die; not specialized to our modern use, "to
die of hunger." 417. What . . . sermone. "Why is it necessary
to make a sermon?" 427. Avicen, the famous Arab philosopher of

the eleventh century, particularly known for his medical studies. 428.
fen, chapter, subdivision; canoun signifies the chapter heading. 434.
traytours, a possessive form serving as an adjective, "traitorous."
441. unkynde, unnatural, monstrous.

Now, goode men, God foryeve yow youre trespas,
And ware yow fro the synne of avarice;
Myn hooly pardoun may yow alle warice,
So that ye offre nobles or sterlynges,
Or elles silver broches, spoones, rynges;
Boweth youre heed under this hooly bulle,
Com up, ye wyves, offreth of youre wolle;
Youre names I entre heer in my rolle anon,
450 Into the blisse of hevene shul ye gon.
I yow assoille by myn heigh power,
Yow that wol offre, as clene and eek as cleer
As ye were born—and lo, sires, thus I preche;
And Jesu Crist, that is oure soules leche,
So graunte yow His pardoun to receyve,
For that is best, I wol yow nat deceyve.

But sires, o word forgat I in my tale,
I have relikes and pardoun in my male
As faire as any man in Engelond,
460 Whiche were me yeven by the popes hond.
If any of yow wole, of devocioun,
Offren and han myn absolucioun,
Com forth anon, and kneleth heere adoun,
And mekely receyveth my pardoun,
Or elles taketh pardoun as ye wende,
Al newe and fressh at every miles ende,
So that ye offren alwey newe and newe
Nobles or pens, whiche that be goode and trewe.
It is an honour to everich that is heer,
470 That ye mowe have a suffisant pardoneer
Tassoille yow, in contree as ye ryde,
For aventures whiche that may bityde.
Paraventure ther may fallen oon or two
Doun of his hors, and breke his nekke atwo.
Look, which a seuretee is it to yow alle
That I am in youre felaweship yfalle,
That may assoille yow, bothe moore and lasse,
Whan that the soule shal fro the body passe.
I rede that oure Hoost heere shal bigynne,
480 For he is moost envoluped in synne.
Com forth, sire Hoost, and offre first anon,
And thou shalt kisse my relikes everychon,
Ye, for a grote, unbokele anon thy purs—

"Nay, nay," quod he, "thanne have I Cristes curs!"
"Lat be," quod he, "it shal nat be, so theech,
Thou woldest make me kisse thyn olde breech,
And swere it were a relyk of a seint,
Though it were with thy fundement depeint!
But, by the croys which that Seint Eleyne fond,
490 I wolde I hadde thy coillons in myn hond
In stide of relikes or of seintuarie.
Lat kutte hem of, I wol thee helpe hem carie
They shul be shryned in an hogges toord!"

This pardoner answerde nat a word;

So wrooth he was, no word ne wolde he seye.
"Now," quod our host, "I wol no lenger pleye
With thee, ne with noon other angry man."
But right anon the worthy Knight bigan,
Whan that he saugh that al the peple lough,
"Na-more of this, for it is right y-nough; 500
Sir Pardoner, be glad and mery of chere;
And ye, sir Host, that been to me so dere,
I prey yow that ye kisse the Pardoner.
And Pardoner, I prey thee, drawe thee neer.
And, as we diden, lat us laughe and pleye."
Anon they kiste, and riden forth hir weye.

THE WIFE OF BATH'S PROLOGUE AND TALE

That hearty animal, the Wife of Bath, introduces the so-called "marriage group" with a most remarkable Prologue, which is in every respect a powerful dramatic monologue of the type made famous five hundred years later by Robert Browning. In this gripping human document, the Wife talks with the utmost frankness about herself (and women in general), as well as about her life with her five husbands; and she explains, further, how by fair means as well as foul, by constant and unremitting aggressiveness and selfish egoism, she clawed her way to a position of "sovereinetee" in her married life. For, in her opinion, a marriage can be "successful" only when the wife can hold complete domination over the husband. As a piece of self-revelation, to say nothing of its devastating satire on women, the Wife of Bath's Prologue cannot be matched in medieval literature.

As for The Wife of Bath's Tale, it is a version of a story known in British literature through a Middle English romance, a popular ballad, and a story from the Confessio Amantis by Chaucer's friend John Gower (1330-1408). Chaucer's immediate source is none of these, and is in fact not known. In this tale there are two celebrated motifs of folklore: that of the loathly lady and that of the riddle. A beautiful woman, turned into a repulsive hag by witchcraft, can be released from the spell only through the devoted and unflinching love of a mortal man. In the riddle motif an individual must answer a riddle on pain of death if he cannot solve it. These two motifs Chaucer has combined into a tale well fit to serve as exemplum to the thesis laid down by the Wife of Bath in her Prologue.

THE WIFE OF BATH'S PROLOGUE

"Experience, though noon auctoritee
Were in this world, is right ynogh for me

444. **warice,** cure. 448. **wolle,** wool. 458. **male,** bag; cf. the Prologue to *The Canterbury Tales,* 1. 694 and note. 471. **Tassoille,** to absolve; the elision is of the preposition *to.* 480. **envoluped,** enveloped. 488. **with . . . depeint,** "daubed with thine own excrement." 489. **croys . . . fond.** St. Helen, the mother of Constantine the Great, was believed to have been the finder of the true Cross. 490.

coillons, cullions, testicles. 499. **lough,** laughed.
The Wife of Bath's Prologue and Tale. 1. **auctoritee,** authority. 7. **If I . . . bee,** "if my marriage to so many could be valid." 10. **Crist . . . Galilee,** as told in John 2:1 ff. 14. **sharp word . . . Samaritan.** For the incident of Christ and the Woman of Samaria, see John 4:6 ff. 26. **glosen,** explain, make commentaries upon. 28.

To speke of wo that is in mariage;
For, lordynges, sith I twelve yeer was of age,
Thonked be God that is eterne on lyve,
Housbondes at chirche dore I have had fyve,—
If I so ofte myghte have ywedded bee,—
And alle were worthy men in hir degree.
But me was toold, certeyn, nat longe agoon is,
10 That sith that Crist ne wente nevere but ones
To weddyng, in the Cane of Galilee,
That by the same ensample taughte he me
That I ne sholde wedded be but ones.
Herkne eek, lo, which a sharp word for the nones,
Biside a welle, Jesus, God and man,
Spak in repreeve of the Samaritan:
'Thou hast yhad fyve housbondes,' quod he,
'And that ilke man that now hath thee
Is noght thyn housbonde,' thus seyde he certeyn.
20 What that he mente therby, I kan nat seyn;
But that I axe, why that the fifthe man
Was noon housbonde to the Samaritan?
How manye myghte she have in mariage?
Yet herde I nevere tellen in myn age
Upon this nombre diffinicioun.
Men may divine and glosen, up and doun,
But wel I woot, expres, withoute lye,
God bad us for to wexe and multiplye;
That gentil text kan I wel understonde.
30 Eek wel I woot, he seyde myn housbonde
Sholde lete fader and mooder, and take to me.
But of no nombre mencion made he,
Of bigamye, or of octogamye;
Why sholde men thanne speke of it vileynye?
  "Lo, heere the wise kyng, daun Salomon;
I trowe he hadde wyves mo than oon.
As wolde God it were leveful unto me
To be refresshed half so ofte as he!
Which yifte of God hadde he for alle his wyves!
40 No man hath swich that in this world alyve is.
God woot, this noble kyng, as to my wit,
The firste nyght had many a myrie fit
With ech of hem, so wel was hym on lyve.
Yblessed be God that I have wedded fyve!
Of whiche I have pyked out the beste,
Bothe of here nether purs and of here cheste.
Diverse scoles maken parfyt clerkes,
And diverse practyk in many sondry werkes
Maketh the werkman parfyt sekirly;
50 Of fyve housbondes scoleying am I.
Welcome the sixte, whan that evere he shal.
For sothe, I wol nat kepe me chaast in al.
Whan myn housbonde is fro the world y-gon,
Som Cristen man shal wedde me anon,
For thanne, th'apostle seith that I am free

The Wife of Bath

To wedde, a Goddes half, wher it liketh me.
He seith that to be wedded is no synne;
Bet is to be wedded than to brynne.
What rekketh me, though folk seye vileynye
Of shrewed Lameth and his bigamye?   60
I woot wel Abraham was an hooly man,
And Jacob eek, as ferforth as I kan;
And ech of hem hadde wyves mo than two,
And many another holy man also.
Wher can ye seye, in any manere age,
That hye God defended mariage
By expres word? I pray yow, telleth me.
Or where comanded he virginitee?
I wot as wel as ye, it is no drede,
Th'apostel, whan he speketh of maydenhede,   70
He seyde that precept thereof hadde he noon.
Men may conseille a womman to been oon,
But conseillyng is no comandement.
He putte it in oure owene juggement;
For hadde God comanded maydenhede,
Thanne hadde he dampned weddyng with the dede.
And certes, if ther were no seed ysowe,
Virginitee, thanne whereof sholde it growe?
Poul dorste nat comanden, atte leeste,
A thyng of which his maister yaf noon heeste. 80
The dart is set up for virginitee:
Cacche whoso may, who renneth best lat see.
  "But this word is nat taken of every wight,
But ther as God lust gyve it of his myght.
I woot wel that th'apostel was a mayde;
But nathelees, though that he wroot and sayde
He wolde that every wight were swich as he,
Al nys but conseil to virginitee.

God . . . multiplye, quoted from Genesis 1:28. 30. **myn housbonde
. . . to me;** see Matthew 19:5. 35. **Salomon, etc.,** as told in
1 Kings 11:3. 50. **scoleying,** schooling. 55. **th'apostle.** Here, as elsewhere in this Prologue, the reference is to St. Paul. The specific passages alluded to are 1 Corinthians 7:9 and 39. 60. **shrewed Lameth,**
accursed Lamech. Lamech (Genesis 4:19–23) was the first bigamist men-

tioned in the Old Testament. 66. **defended,** forbade. 71. **He seyde
. . . noon.** "Now concerning virgins I have no commandment of the
Lord," etc.—1 Corinthians 7:25. 76. **dampned,** damned, condemned.
81. **dart,** the prize in a running contest; it was a kind of spear. 84.
God lust, it pleases God (to). 87. **He . . . as he.** "For I would
that all men were even as myself."—1 Corinthians 7:7.

And for to been a wyf he yaf me leve
90 Of indulgence; so nys it no repreve
To wedde me, if that my make dye,
Withouten excepcion of bigamye.
Al were it good no womman for to touche,—
He mente as in his bed or in his couche;
For peril is, bothe fyr and tow t'assemble:
Ye knowe what this ensample may resemble.
This is al and som, he heeld virginitee
Moore parfit than weddyng in freletee.
Freletee clepe I, but if that he and she
100 Wolde leden al hir lyf in chastitee.

"I graunte it wel, I have noon envie,
Though maydenhede preferre bigamye.
It liketh hem to be clene, body and goost;
Of myn estaat I nyl nat make no boost.
For wel ye knowe, a lord in his houshold,
He hath nat every vessel al of gold;
Somme been of tree, and doon hir lord servyse.
God clepeth folk to hym in sondry wise,
And everich hath of God a propre yifte,
110 Som this, som that, as hym liketh shifte.

"Virginitee is greet perfeccion,
And continence eek with devocion,
But Crist, that of perfeccion is welle,
Bad nat every wight he sholde go selle
Al that he hadde, and gyve it to the poore
And in swich wyse folwe hym and his foore.
He spak to hem that wolde lyve parfitly;
And lordynges, by youre leve, that am nat I.
I wol bestowe the flour of al myn age
120 In the actes and in fruyt of mariage.

"Telle me also, to what conclusion
Were membres maad of generacion,
And for what profit was a wight ywrought?
Trusteth right wel, they were nat maad for nought.
Glose whoso wole, and seye bothe up and doun,
That they were maked for purgacioun
Of uryne, and oure bothe thynges smale
Were eek to knowe a femele from a male,
And for noon oother cause,—sey ye no?
130 The experience woot wel it is nought so.
So that the clerkes be nat with me wrothe,
I sey this, that they maked been for bothe,
This is to seye, for office, and for ese
Of engendrure, ther we nat God displese.
Why sholde men elles in hir bookes sette
That man shal yelde to his wyf hire dette?
Now wherwith sholde he make his paiement,
If he ne used his sely instrument?

Thanne were they maad upon a creature
To purge uryne, and eek for engendrure. 140
"But I seye nought that every wight is holde,
That hath swych harneys as I to yow tolde,
To goon and usen hem in engendrure.
Thanne sholde men take of chastitee no cure.
Crist was a mayde, and shapen as a man
And many a seint, sith that the world bigan;
Yet lyved they evere in parfit chastitee.
I nyl envye no virginitee.
Lat hem be breed of pured whete-seed,
And lat us wyves hoten barley-breed; 150
And yet with barley-breed, Mark telle kan,
Oure Lord Jesu refresshed many a man.
In swich estaat as God hath cleped us
I wol persevere; I nam nat precious.
In wyfhod I wol use myn instrument
As frely as my Makere hath it sent.
If I be daungerous, God yeve me sorwe!
Myn housbonde shal have it bothe eve and morwe,
Whan that hym list come forth and paye his dette.
An housbonde I wol have, I wol nat lette, 160
Which shal be bothe my dettour and my thral,
And have his tribulacioun withal
Upon his flessh, whil that I am his wyf.
I have the power durynge al my lyf
Upon his propre body, and nought he.
Right thus the Apostel tolde it unto me;
And bad oure housbondes for to love us weel.
Al this sentence me liketh every deel—"

Up stirte the Pardoner, and that anon:
"Now, dame," quod he, "by God and by seint John! 170
Ye been a noble prechour in this cas.
I was aboute to wedde a wyf, allas!
What sholde I bye it on my flessh so deere?
Yet hadde I levere wedde no wyf to-yeere!"

"Abyde!" quod she, "my tale is nat bigonne.
Nay, thou shalt drynken of another tonne,
Er that I go, shal savoure wors than ale.
And whan that I have toold thee forth my tale
Of tribulacioun in mariage,
Of which I am expert in al myn age, 180
This is to seyn, myself have been the whippe,—
Than maystow chese wheither thou wolt sippe
Of thilke tonne that I shal abroche.
Be war of it, er thou to ny approche;
For I shal telle ensamples mo than ten.
'Whoso that nyl be war by othere men,
By him shul othere men corrected be.'
The same wordes writeth Ptholomee;

89. **he yaf . . . indulgence.** He said that there was no sin in marry-ing, not excepting the sin of bigamy. 93. **Al,** although. The warning is given in 1 Corinthians 7:1. 99. **but if,** unless. 102. **preferre,** take precedence over, be preferred to. 107. **tree,** wood. 110. **as hym liketh shifte,** as it pleases him to ordain. 116. **foore,** company, disciples. 133. **office,** (physiologica!) functions. 138. **sely,** happy, blessed. 141. **holde,** obligated, bound to. 144. **cure,** care, heed. 149. **pured,** refined. 150. **hoten,** be called. 151. **Mark.** It is actually John; see John 6:9. 154. **precious,** overrefined, finical. 157. **daun-gerous,** too fastidious. 160. **lette,** hesitate, find difficulties. 166. **Apostel tolde it.** See Ephesians 5:25. 173. **bye it,** pay for it. 184.

to, too. 186. **'Whoso'** etc. Although this saying has been attributed to Ptolemy and his *Almagest* (see note to ll. 188–189), it is not actually found there; it seems rather to have been proverbial. 188. **Ptholomee . . . Almageste.** The *Almagest* was the classic treatise on astronomy ascribed to Claudius Ptolemy of Alexandria, who flour-ished in the second century; the name, however, was applied loosely to many works on astronomy and astrology. 193. **praktike,** practice as opposed to theory. 197. **As,** a particle that can be omitted in the reading; note also the superfluous nature of the particle in l. 202. 204. **Unnethe,** with difficulty. 208. **swynke,** labor, work hard. 209. **tolde . . . stoor,** did not consider worth anything. 214. **tolde no deyntee,**

Rede in his Almageste, and take it there."

190 "Dame, I wolde praye yow, if youre wyl it were,"
Seyde this Pardoner, "as ye bigan,
Telle forth youre tale, spareth for no man,
And teche us yonge men of youre praktike."

"Gladly," quod she, "sith it may yow like;
But that I praye to al this compaignye,
If that I speke after my fantasye,
As taketh not agrief of that I seye;
For myn entente is nat but for to pleye.

"Now, sires, now wol I telle forth my tale.—
200 As evere moote I drynken wyn or ale,
I shal seye sooth, tho housbondes that I hadde,
As thre of hem were goode, and two were badde.
The thre were goode men, and riche, and olde;
Unnethe myghte they the statut holde
In which that they were bounded unto me.
Ye woot wel what I meene of this, pardee!
As help me God, I laughe whan I thynke
How pitously a-nyght I made hem swynke!
And, by my fey, I tolde of it no stoor.
210 They had me yeven hir lond and hir tresor;
Me neded nat do lenger diligence
To wynne hir love, or doon hem reverence.
They loved me so wel, by God above,
That I ne tolde no deyntee of hir love.
A wys womman wol bisye hire evere in oon
To gete hire love, ther as she hath noon.
But sith I hadde hem hoolly in myn hond,
And sith they hadde me yeven al hir lond,
What sholde I taken keep hem for to plese,
220 But it were for my profit and myn ese?
I sette hem so a-werke, by my fey,
That many a nyght they songen 'weilawey!'
The bacon was nat fet for hem, I trowe,
That som men han in Essex at Dunmowe.
I governed hem so wel, after my lawe,
That ech of hem ful blisful was and fawe
To brynge me gaye thynges fro the fayre.
They were ful glad whan I spak to hem faire;
For, God it woot, I chidde hem spitously.
230 "Now herkneth how I baar me proprely,
Ye wise wyves, that kan understonde.

"Thus shulde ye speke and bere hem wrong on
honde;
For half so boldely kan ther no man
Swere and lyen, as a womman kan.
I sey nat this by wyves that been wyse,
But if it be whan they hem misavyse.
A wys wyf shal, if that she kan hir good,

Bere hym on honde that the cow is wood,
And take witnesse of hir owene mayde
Of hir assent; but herkneth how I sayde:
240 "'Sire olde kaynard, is this thyn array?
Why is my neighebonres wyf so gay?
She is honoured over al ther she gooth;
I sitte at hoom, I have no thrifty clooth.
What dostow at my neighebonres hous?
Is she so fair? artow so amorous?
What roune ye with oure mayde? Benedicite!
Sire olde lecchour, lat thy japes be!
And if I have a gossib or a freend,
Withouten gilt, thou chidest as a feend,
250 If that I walke or pleye unto his hous!
Thou comest hoom as dronken as a mous,
And prechest on thy bench, with yvel preef!
Thou seyst to me it is a greet meschief
To wedde a povre womman, for costage;
And if that she be riche, of heigh parage,
Thanne seystow that it is a tormentrie
To soffre hire pride and hire malencolie.
And if that she be fair, thou verray knave,
Thou seyst that every holour wol hire have;
260 She may no while in chastitee abyde,
That is assailled upon ech a syde.

"'Thou seyst some folk desiren us for richesse,
Somme for oure shap, and somme for oure fairnesse,
And som for she kan outher synge or daunce,
And som for gentilesse and daliaunce;
Som for hir handes and hir armes smale:
Thus goth al to the devel, by thy tale.
Thou seyst men may nat kepe a castel wal,
It may so long assailled been over al.
270 "'And if that she be foul, thou seyst that she
Coveiteth every man that she may see,
For as a spaynel she wol on hym lepe,
Til that she fynde som man hire to chepe.
Ne noon so grey goos gooth ther in the lake
As, seystow, wol been withoute make.
And seyst it is an hard thyng for to welde
A thyng that no man wole, his thankes, helde.
Thus seistow, lorel, whan thow goost to bedde;
And that no wys man nedeth for to wedde,
280 Ne no man that entendeth unto hevene.
With wilde thonder-dynt and firy levene
Moote thy welked nekke be tobroke!

"'Thou seyst that droppyng houses, and eek smoke,
And chidyng wyves maken men to flee
Out of hir owene hous; a! benedicitee!
What eyleth swich an old man for to chide?

did not consider worth anything. 215. evere in oon, continually.
219. What, Why? 220. But it were, unless it were. 223. bacon . . .
Dunmowe. At the country fair of Dunmowe in Essex, it was the
custom to give a flitch of bacon as a prize to a married couple that
had lived throughout the year in peace and harmony and without
regrets; cf. the phrase "bring home the bacon." 226. fawe, fain, glad.
229. spitously, spitefully, maliciously. 230. proprely, exactly, truly.
232. bere . . . on honde, accuse them falsely, reproach without a
basis. 238. the cow is wood, "the chough is mad." According to
popular English tradition, the chough, a bird of the crow family, was
able to tell a husband if his wife was unfaithful. The wife, according

to the Wife of Bath, should be able to persuade her husband that he
is mistaken in his suspicions. 241. kaynard, old fool, dotard. 244.
thrifty, appearing prosperous. 247. roune, whisper. 249. gossib,
intimate friend. 250. Withouten gilt, although not to blame. 253.
with yvel preef, bad luck to you. 255. costage, expense. 256.
parage, ancestry. 260. holour, lecher, adulterer. 271. foul, ugly,
homely. 274. hire to chepe, to do business with her. 276. make,
mate. 278. his thankes, willingly, voluntarily. helde, hold. 279.
lorel, fool, dolt. 282. levene, lightning. 283. welked, withered.

" 'Thou seyst we wyves wol oure vices hide
Til we be fast, and thanne we wol hem shewe,—
290 Wel may that be a proverbe of a shrewe!
    " 'Thou seist that oxen, asses, hors, and houndes;
They been assayed at diverse stoundes;
Bacyns, lavours, er that men hem bye,
Spoones and stooles, and al swich housbondrye,
And so been pottes, clothes, and array
But folk of wyves maken noon assay,
Til they be wedded; olde dotard shrewe!
And thanne, seistow, we wol oure vices shewe.
    " 'Thou seyst also that it displeseth me
300 But if that thou wolt preyse my beautee,
And but thou poure alwey upon my face.
And clepe me "faire dame" in every place.
And but thou make a feeste on thilke day
That I was born, and make me fressh and gay;
And but thou do to my norice honour,
And to my chamberere withinne my bour,
And to my fadres folk and his allyes,—
Thus seistow, olde barel-ful of lyes!
    " 'And yet of oure apprentice Janekyn,
310 For his crispe heer, shynynge as gold so fyn,
And for he squiereth me bothe up and doun,
Yet hastow caught a fals suspecioun.
I wol him nought, though thou were deed tomorwe!
    " 'But tel me this: why hydestow, with sorwe,
The keyes of thy cheste awey fro me?
It is my good as wel as thyn, pardee!
What, wenestow make an ydiot of oure dame?
Now by that lord that called is Seint Jame,
Thou shalt nat bothe, though thou were wood,
320 Be maister of my body and of my good;
That oon thou shalt forgo, maugree thyne yën.
What helpeth it of me to enquere or spyen?
I trowe thou woldest loke me in thy chiste!
Thou sholdest seye, "Wyf, go wher thee liste;
Taak youre disport, I wol nat leve no talys.
I knowe you for a trewe wyf, dame Alys."
We love no man that taketh kep or charge
Wher that we goon; we wol been at oure large.
    " 'Of alle men yblessed moot he be,
330 The wise astrologien, Daun Ptholome,
That seith this proverbe in his Almageste:
"Of alle men his wysdom is the hyeste,
That rekketh nevere who hath the world in honde."
By this proverbe thou shalt understonde,
Have thou ynough, what thar thee recche or care
How myrily that othere folkes fare?
For, certeyn, olde dotard, by youre leve,
Ye shul have queynte right ynough at eve.
He is to greet a nygard that wolde werne

A man to lighte a candle at his lanterne;   340
He shul have never the lasse light, pardee.
Have thou ynough, thee thar nat pleyne thee.
    " 'Thou seyst also, that if we make us gay
With clothyng, and with precious array,
That it is peril of oure chastitee;
And yet, with sorwe! thou most enforce thee,
And seye thise wordes in the Apostles name:
"In habit maad with chastitee and shame
Ye wommen shul apparaille yow," quod he,
"And nought in tressed heer and gay perree,   350
As perles, ne with gold, ne clothes riche."
After thy text, ne after thy rubriche,
I wol nat wirche as muchel as a gnat.
    " 'Thou seydest this, that I was lyk a cat;
For whoso wolde senge a cattes skyn,
Thanne wolde the cat wel dwellen in his in;
And if the cattes skyn be slyk and gay,
She wol nat dwelle in house half a day,
But forth she wole, er any day be dawed,
To shewe hir skyn, and goon a-caterwawed.   360
This is to seyne, if I be gay, sire shrewe,
I wol renne out, my borel for to shewe.
    " 'Sire olde fool, what helpeth thee to spyen?
Though thou preye Argus with his hundred yën
To be my warde-cors, as he kan best,
In feith, he shal nat kepe me but me lest;
Yet koude I make his berd, so moot I thee!
    " 'Thou seydest eek that ther been thynges three,
The whiche thynges troublen al this erthe,
And that no wight may endure the ferthe.   370
O leeve sire shrewe, Jesu shorte thy lyf!
Yet prechestow and seyst an hateful wyf
Yrekened is for oon of thise meschances.
Been ther none othere maner resemblances
That ye may likne youre parables to,
But if a sely wyf be oon of tho?
    " 'Thou liknest eek wommenes love to helle,
To bareyne lond, ther water may nat dwelle.
Thou liknest it also to wilde fyr;
The moore it brenneth, the moore it hath desir   380
To consume every thing that brent wole be.
Thou seyest, right as wormes shende a tree,
Right so a wyf destroyeth hire housbonde;
This knowe they that been to wyves bonde.'
    "Lordynges, right thus, as ye have understonde,
Baar I stifly myne old housbondes on honde
That thus they seyden in hir dronkenesse;
And al was fals, but that I took witnesse
On Janekyn, and on my nece also.
O Lord! the peyne I dide hem and the wo,   390
Ful giltelees, by Goddes sweete pyne!

---

293. **lavours,** basins. 300. **But if that,** unless. 301. **poure,** pore upon, gaze upon. 305. **norice,** nurse or female attendant. 310. **crispe,** curly. 317. **oure dame,** the mistress of the house; myself, the Wife of Bath. 321. **maugree thyne yën,** "in spite of your eyes"; no matter what. 325. **leve no talys,** believe no tales (gossip). 328. **at oure large,** free to go where we wish. 330. **Ptholome,** etc. See note to ll. 188–189. 335. **what thar thee?** why do you need? 338. **queynte,** private parts. 339. **werne,** refuse. 348. **'In habit . . . riche.'** See

1 Timothy 2:9. 350. **perree,** precious stones. 352. **rubriche,** rubric, title. 353. **I wol . . . gnat,** "I will not do according to your text as much as a gnat is worth." 360. **a-caterwawed,** caterwauling. 362. **borel,** coarse woolen clothes. 364. **Argus,** in classical mythology, a giant having a hundred eyes who was killed by Mercury (Hermes). 365. **warde-cors,** bodyguard. 366. **but me lest,** unless it pleases me. 367. **make his berd,** make a fool of him, outwit him. 376. **sely,** good but wretched. 379. **wilde fyr,** a chemically induced fire not

For as an hors I koude byte and whyne.
I koude pleyne, and yit was in the gilt,
Or elles often tyme hadde I been spilt.
Whoso that first to mille comth, first grynt;
I pleyned first, so was oure werre ystynt.
They were ful glade to excuse hem blyve
Of thyng of which they nevere agilte hir lyve.
   "Of wenches wolde I beren hym on honde,
400 Whan that for syk unnethes myghte he stonde.
Yet tikled it his herte, for that he
Wende that I hadde of hym so greet chiertee!
I swoor that al my walkynge out by nyghte
Was for t'espye wenches that he dighte;
Under that colour hadde I many a myrthe.
For al swich wit is yeven us in oure byrthe;
Deceite, wepyng, spynnyng God hath yive
To wommen kyndely, whil that they may live.
And thus of o thyng I avaunte me,
410 Atte ende I hadde the bettre in ech degree,
By sleighte, or force, or by som maner thyng,
As by continueel murmur or grucchyng.
Namely abedde hadden they meschaunce:
Ther wolde I chide, and do hem no plesaunce;
I wolde no lenger in the bed abyde,
If that I felte his arm over my syde,
Til he had maad his raunson unto me;
Thanne wolde I suffre hym do his nycetee.
And therfore every man this tale I telle,
420 Wynne whoso may, for al is for to selle;
With empty hand men may none haukes lure.
For wynnyng wolde I al his lust endure,
And make me a feyned appetit;
And yet in bacon hadde I nevere delit;
That made me that evere I wolde hem chide.
For though the pope hadde seten hem biside,
I wolde nat spare hem at hir owene bord;
For, by my trouthe, I quitte hem word for word.
As helpe me verray God omnipotent,
430 Thogh I right now sholde make my testament,
I ne owe hem nat a word that it nys quit.
I broghte it so aboute by my wit
That they moste yeve it up, as for the beste,
Or elles hadde we nevere been in reste.
For though he looked as a wood leoun,
Yet sholde he faille of his conclusioun.
   "Thanne wolde I seye, 'Goode lief, taak keep
How mekely looketh Wilkyn, oure sheep!
Com neer, my spouse, lat me ba thy cheke!
440 Ye sholde been al pacient and meke,
And han a sweete spiced conscience,
Sith ye so preche of Jobes pacience.
Suffreth alwey, syn ye so wel kan preche;

And but ye do, certein we shal yow teche
That it is fair to have a wyf in pees.
Oon of us two moste bowen, doutelees;
And sith a man is moore resonable
Than womman is, ye moste been suffrable.
What eyleth yow to grucche thus and grone?
Is it for ye wolde have my queynte allone?   450
Why, taak it al! lo, have it every deel!
Peter! I shrewe yow, but ye love it weel;
For if I wolde selle my *bele chose*,
I koude walke as fressh as is a rose;
But I wol kepe it for youre owene tooth.
Ye be to blame, by God! I sey yow sooth.'
   "Swich manere wordes hadde we on honde.
Now wol I speken of my fourthe housbonde.
   "My fourthe housbonde was a revelour;
This is to seyn, he hadde a paramour;   460
And I was yong and ful of ragerye,
Stibourn and strong, and joly as a pye.
How koude I daunce to an harpe smale,
And synge, ywis, as any nyghtyngale,
Whan I had dronke a draughte of sweete wyn!
Metellius, the foule cherl, the swyn,
That with a staf birafte his wyf hir lyf,
For she drank wyn, though I hadde been his wyf,
He sholde nat han daunted me fro drynke!
And after wyn on Venus moste I thynke,   470
For al so siker as cold engendreth hayl,
A likerous mouth moste han a likerous tayl.
In wommen vinolent is no defence,—
This knowen lecchours by experience.
   "But, Lord Crist! whan that it remembreth me
Upon my yowthe, and on my jolitee,
It tikleth me aboute myn herte roote.
Unto this day it dooth myn herte boote
That I have had my world as in my tyme.
But age, allas! that al wole envenyme,   480
Hath me biraft my beautee and my pith.
Lat go, farewel! the devel go therwith!
The flour is goon, ther is namoore to telle;
The bren, as I best kan, now moste I selle;
But yet to be right myrie wol I fonde.
Now wol I tellen of my fourthe housbonde.
   "I seye, I hadde in herte greet despit
That he of any oother had delit.
But he was quit, by God and by Seint Joce!
I made hym of the same wode a croce;   490
Nat of my body, in no foul manere,
But certeinly, I made folk swich cheere
That in his owene grece I made hym frye
For angre, and for verray jalousye.
By God! in erthe I was his purgatorie,

quenchable by water. 382. **shende,** spoil, ruin. 391. **Goddes sweete pyne,** Christ's blessed Passion. 394. **spilt,** undone, ruined. 395. **grynt,** grinds. 397. **blyve,** quickly. 398. **agilte,** were guilty of. 400. **syk,** sickness; or possibly *for* syk means "very sick." 402. **chiertee,** affection. 404. **dighte,** had intercourse with. 405. **colour,** pretext. 408. **kyndely,** by nature. 413. **Namely,** particularly, especially. 418. **nycetee,** foolishness. 424. **bacon,** a slang term for old meat (hence old men). 428. **quitte,** paid back; so also quit ("paid for") in l. 431.

439. **neer,** nearer. **ba,** buss, kiss lustily. 441. **spiced conscience,** overscrupulous feelings. 452. **Peter!** St. Peter, an oath. 453. *bele chose,* sexual organs. 462. **pye,** magpie. 466. **Metellius, etc.** The story is taken from the works of the Roman writer Valerius Maximus. 473. **vinolent,** full of wine. 484. **bren,** bran. 489. **Joce,** Judocus, a saint of Brittany.

For which I hope his soule be in glorie.
For, God it woot, he sat ful ofte and song,
Whan that his shoo ful bitterly hym wrong.
Ther was no wight, save God and he, that wiste,
500 In many wise, how soore I hym twiste.
He deyde whan I cam fro Jerusalem,
And lith ygrave under the roode beem,
Al is his tombe noght so curyous
As was the sepulcre of hym, Daryus,
Which that Appelles wroghte subtilly;
It nys but wast to burye hym preciously.
Lat hym fare wel, God yeve his soul reste!
He is now in his grave and in his cheste.
    "Now of my fifthe housbonde wol I telle.
510 God lete his soule nevere come in helle!
And yet was he to me the mooste shrewe;
That feele I on my ribbes al by rewe,
And evere shal unto myn endyng day.
But in oure bed he was so fressh and gay,
And therwithal so wel koude he me glose,
Whan that he wolde han my *bele chose*,
That though he hadde me bete on every bon,
He koude wynne agayn my love anon.
I trowe I loved hym best, for that he
520 Was of his love daungerous to me.
We wommen han, if that I shal nat lye,
In this matere a queynte fantasye;
Wayte what thyng we may nat lightly have,
Therafter wol we crie al day and crave.
Forbede us thyng, and that desiren we;
Preesse on us faste, and thanne wol we fle.
With daunger oute we al oure chaffare;
Greet prees at market maketh deere ware,
And to greet cheep is holde at litel prys:
530 This knoweth every womman that is wys.
    "My fifthe housbonde, God his soule blesse!
Which that I took for love, and no richesse,
He som tyme was a clerk of Oxenford,
And hadde left scole, and wente at hom to bord
With my gossib, dwellynge in oure toun;
God have hir soule! hir name was Alisoun.
She knew myn herte, and eek my privetee,
Bet than oure parissh preest, so moot I thee!
To hire biwreyed I my conseil al.
540 For hadde myn housbonde pissed on a wal,
Or doon a thyng that sholde han cost his lyf,
To hire, and to another worthy wyf,

And to my nece, which that I loved weel,
I wolde han toold his conseil every deel.
And so I dide ful often, God it woot,
That made his face ful often reed and hoot
For verray shame, and blamed hymself for he
Had toold to me so greet a pryvetee.
    "And so bifel that ones in a Lente—
So often tymes I to my gossib wente,   550
For evere yet I loved to be gay,
And for to walke in March, Averill, and May,
Fro hous to hous, to heere sondry tales—
That Jankyn clerk, and my gossyb dame Alys,
And I myself, into the feeldes wente.
Myn housbonde was at Londoun al that Lente;
I hadde the bettre layser for to pleye,
And for to see, and eek for to be seye
Of lusty folk. What wiste I wher my grace
Was shapen for to be, or in what place?   560
Therfore I made my visitacions
To vigilies and to processions,
To prechyng eek, and to thise pilgrimages,
To pleyes of miracles, and to mariages,
And wered upon my gaye scarlet gytes.
Thise wormes, ne thise motthes, ne thise mytes,
Upon my peril, frete hem never a deel;
And wostow why? for they were used weel.
    "Now wol I tellen forth what happed me.
I seye that in the feeldes walked we,   570
Til trewely we hadde swich daliance,
This clerk and I, that of my purveiance
I spak to hym and seyde hym how that he,
If I were wydwe, sholde wedde me.
For certeinly, I sey for no bobance,
Yet was I nevere withouten purveiance
Of mariage, n'of othere thynges eek.
I holde a mouses herte nat worth a leek
That hath but oon hole for to sterte to,
And if that faille, thanne is al ydo.   580
    "I bar hym on honde he hadde enchanted me,—
My dame taughte me that soutiltee.
And eek I seyde I mette of hym al nyght,
He wolde han slayn me as I lay upright,
And al my bed was ful of verray blood;
But yet I hope that he shal do me good,
For blood bitokeneth gold, as me was taught.
And al was fals; I dremed of it right naught,
But as I folwed ay my dames loore,

502. **ygrave . . . roode beem,** buried under the rood beam, between the chancel and the nave of the church. 504. **Daryus,** Darius the Great, king of Persia (522–486 B.C.), who overran Greece until he was defeated at the Battle of Marathon (490 B.C.). 505. **Appelles,** a Greek painter of the fourth century B.C. 511. **shrewe,** rascal. 515. **glose,** cajole, flatter (v.). 520. **daungerous,** offish, fastidious. 522. **queynte,** subtle, delicate. 523. **Wayte what,** whatever. 527. **With . . . chaffare.** "In the presence of indifference we will put out all our wares." 529. **cheep,** bargain. 538. **Bet,** better. 539. **biwreyed,** revealed. 548. **pryvetee,** secret. 557. **layser,** leisure. 562. **vigilies,** feasts and entertainments on the eve of feast days. 565. **gytes,** gowns (?). 568. **wostow,** do you know? 572. **purveiance,** foresight. 575. **bobance,** boast. 581. **bar hym on honde,** led him (falsely) to believe. 583. **mette,** dreamt. 584. **upright,** straight. 585. **al my bed . . . blood.** Some critics of a Freudian persuasion have inter-

preted this statement to mean that the Wife of Bath conspired with Jankin to murder her fourth husband (see ll. 573–574), and that the murder was carried out after she had returned from Jerusalem (l. 501), but such a melodramatic tale need not be assumed. After all, the Wife admits she never dreamed as she had said she did (l. 588). 594. **algate,** all the time. 595. **mooten,** must. 598. **undertake,** declare, state openly. 608. **coltes tooth,** a proverbial expression for a lustful disposition. 614. *quoniam,* female sexual organs. 619. **Myn ascendent . . . Mars therinne.** At the time of the Wife of Bath's birth, Taurus, the constellation of the Bull, was rising above the horizon. Taurus is a constellation most favorable to Venus. Mars, in mythology the lover of Venus, made with Venus a most powerful and vigorous combination in respect to planetary influence. 624. **chambre of Venus,** the vulva. 634. **hende,** graceful and gracious. 635. **solempnytee,** pomp and ceremony. 639. **He nolde . . . list.** "He would not stand for what

590 As wel of this as of othere thynges moore.

"But now, sire, lat me see, what shal I seyn?
A ha! by God, I have my tale ageyn.

"Whan that my fourthe housbonde was on beere,
I weep algate, and made sory cheere,
As wyves mooten, for it is usage.
And with my coverchief covered my visage.
But for that I was purveyed of a make,
I wept but smal, and that I undertake.

"To chirche was myn housbonde born a-morwe
600 With neigheboures, that for hym maden sorwe;
And Jankyn, oure clerk! was oon of tho.
As help me God! whan that I saugh hym go
After the beere, me thoughte he hadde a paire
Of legges and of feet so clene and faire
That al myn herte I yaf unto his hoold.
He was, I trowe, a twenty wynter oold,
And I was fourty, if I shal seye sooth;
But yet I hadde alwey a coltes tooth.
Gat-tothed I was, and that bicam me weel;
610 I hadde the prente of seinte Venus seel.
As help me God! I was a lusty oon,
And faire, and riche, and yong, and wel bigon;
And trewely, as myne housbondes tolde me,
I hadde the beste *quoniam* mighte be.
For certes, I am al Venerien
In feelynge, and myn herte is Marcien.
Venus me yaf my lust, my likerousnesse,
And Mars yaf me my sturdy hardynesse;
Myn ascendent was Taur, and Mars therinne.
620 Allas! allas! that evere love was synne!
I folwed ay myn inclinacioun
By vertu of my constellacioun;
That made me I koude nought withdrawe
My chambre of Venus from a good felawe.
Yet have I Martes mark upon my face,
And also in another privee place.
For God so wys be my savacioun,
I ne loved nevere by no discrecioun,
But evere folwede myn appetit.
630 Al were he short, or long, or blak, or whit;
I took no kep, so that he liked me,
How poore he was, ne eek of what degree.

"What sholde I seye? but, at the monthes ende,
This joly clerk, Jankyn, that was so hende,
Hath wedded me with greet solempnytee;
And to hym yaf I al the lond and fee

That evere was me yeven therbifoore.
But afterward repented me ful soore;
He nolde suffre nothyng of my list.
By God! he smoot me ones on the lyst,   640
For that I rente out of his book a leef,
That of the strook myn ere wax al deef.
Stibourn I was as is a leonesse,
And of my tonge a verray jangleresse,
And walke I wolde, as I had doon biforn,
From hous to hous, although he had it sworn;
For which he often tymes wolde preche,
And me of olde Romayn geestes teche;
How he, Symplicius Gallus, lefte his wyf,
And hire forsook for terme of al his lyf,   650
Nought but for open-heveded he hir say
Lookynge out at his dore upon a day.

"Another Romayn tolde he me by name,
That, for his wyf was at a someres game
Withouten his wityng, he forsook hire eke.
And thanne wolde he upon his Bible seke
That ilke proverbe of Ecclesiaste
Where he comandeth, and forbedeth faste,
Man shal nat suffre his wyf go roule aboute.
Thanne wolde he seye right thus, withouten doute: 660

" 'Whoso that buyldeth his hous al of salwes,
And priketh his blynde hors over the falwes,
And suffreth his wyf to go seken halwes,
Is worthy to been hanged on the galwes!'
But al for noght, I sette noght an hawe
Of his proverbes n'of his olde sawe,
Ne I wolde nat of hym corrected be.
I hate hym that my vices telleth me,
And so do mo, God woot, of us than I.
This made hym with me wood al outrely;   670
I nolde noght forbere hym in no cas.

"Now wol I seye yow sooth, by seint Thomas,
Why that I rente out of his book a leef,
For which he smoot me so that I was deef.

"He hadde a book that gladly, nyght and day,
For his desport he wolde rede alway;
He cleped it Valerie and Theofraste,
At which book he lough alwey ful faste.
And eek ther was somtyme a clerk at Rome,
A cardinal, that highte Seint Jerome,   680
That made a book agayn Jovinian;
In which book eek ther was Tertulan,
Crisippus, Trotula, and Helowys,

I wanted." **640. lyst,** ears. **646. sworn,** forbidden. **648. Romayn geestes,** stories of Roman history, hardly the great story collection of the Middle Ages known as the *Gesta Romanorum;* most of the tales told below by the Wife of Bath are derived from Valerius Maximus. So are the tales about Symplicius Gallus (ll. 649 ff.), and *another Romayn* (ll. 653 ff.). **651. open-heveded,** bare-headed. **657. Ecclesiaste,** the apocryphal Book of Ecclesiasticus, not the famous Book of Ecclesiastes in the Old Testament; see, for this particular "proverbe," Ecclesiasticus 22:25. **661.** '**Whoso . . . galwes!**' a proverbial jingle. **662. falwes,** fallow ground. **663. seken halwes,** visit shrines on a pilgrimage. **665. hawe,** the fruit of the hawthorn tree. **676. desport,** amusement. **677. Valerie . . . Theofraste.** Jankin evidently had a manuscript containing, among other items mentioned presently, Walter Map's "Epistle of Valerius to Rufinus, Not to Marry," included in his celebrated Anglo-Latin miscellany, *De Nugis Curialium,* from the

late twelfth century; and the *Liber de Nuptiis* by Theophrastus, concerning whom very little is known unless he is the Greek philosopher 382?–287? B.C. It is evident that Chaucer had become familiar with these works and with the *Epistle Against Jovinian* by St. Jerome (340?–420) before writing the Prologue to *The Wife of Bath's Tale.* See ll. 680–681. **682. Tertulan,** Tertullian, a Christian writer who flourished about 200; he was the author of works on chastity, monogamy, and modesty. **683. Crisippus,** mentioned by St. Jerome in the *Epistle Against Jovinian;* nothing significant is known about him, and he is used here no doubt for "authority" padding. **Trotula,** traditionally a famous female doctor (gynecologist and obstetrician) who taught at the medical center of Salerno, Italy, in the middle of the eleventh century. Some historians, however, do not believe in her historicity. **Helowys,** the wife of the scholiast Abelard of Paris (1079–1142).

That was abbesse nat fer fro Parys;
And eek the Parables of Salomon,
Ovides Art, and bookes many on,
And alle thise were bounden in o volume.
And every nyght and day was his custume,
Whan he hadde leyser and vacacioun
690 From oother worldly occupacioun,
To reden on this book of wikked wyves,
He knew of hem mo legendes and lyves
Than been of goode wyves in the Bible.
For trusteth wel, it is an impossible
That any clerk wol speke good of wyves,
But if it be of hooly seintes lyves,
Ne of noon oother womman never the mo.
Who peyntede the leon, tel me who?
By God! if wommen hadde writen stories,
700 As clerkes han withinne hire oratories,
They wolde han writen of men moore wikkednesse
Than al the mark of Adam may redresse.
The children of Mercurie and of Venus
Been in hir wirkyng ful contrarious;
Mercurie loveth wysdom and science,
And Venus loveth ryot and dispence.
And, for hire diverse disposicioun,
Ech falleth in otheres exaltacioun.
And thus, God woot, Mercurie is desolat
710 In Pisces, wher Venus is exaltat;
And Venus falleth ther Mercurie is reysed.
Therfore no womman of no clerk is preysed.
The clerk, whan he is oold, and may noght do
Of Venus werkes worth his olde sho,
Thanne sit he doun, and writ in his dotage
That wommen kan nat kepe hir mariage!
    "But now to purpos, why I tolde thee
That I was beten for a book, pardee!
Upon a nyght Jankyn, that was oure sire,
720 Redde on his book, as he sat by the fire,
Of Eva first, that for hir wikkednesse
Was al mankynde broght to wrecchednesse,
For which that Jesu Crist hymself was slayn,
That boughte us with his herte blood agayn.
Lo, heere expres of womman may ye fynde,
That womman was the los of al mankynde.
    "Tho redde he me how Sampson loste his heres:
Slepynge, his lemman kitte it with hir sheres;
Thurgh which treson loste he bothe his yën.
730   "Tho redde he me, if that I shal nat lyen,
Of Hercules and of his Dianyre,
That caused hym to sette hymself afyre.

"No thyng forgat he the care and the wo
That Socrates hadde with his wyves two;
How Xantippa caste pisse upon his heed.
This sely man sat stille as he were deed;
He wiped his heed, namoore dorste he seyn,
But 'Er that thonder stynte, comth a reyn!'
    "Of Phasipha, that was the queene of Crete,   740
For shrewednesse, hym thoughte the tale swete;
Fy! spek namoore—it is a grisly thyng—
Of hire horrible lust and hir likyng.
    "Of Clitermystra, for hire lecherye,
That falsly made hire housbonde for to dye,
He redde it with ful good devocioun.
    "He tolde me eek for what occasioun
Amphiorax at Thebes loste his lyf.
Myn housbonde hadde a legende of his wyf,
Eriphilem, that for an ouche of gold
Hath prively unto the Grekes told   750
Wher that hir housbonde hidde hym in a place,
For which he hadde at Thebes sory grace.
    "Of Lyvia tolde he me, and of Lucye:
They bothe made hir housbondes for to dye;
That oon for love, that oother was for hate.
Lyvia hir housbonde, on an even late,
Empoysoned hath, for that she was his fo;
Lucia, likerous, loved hire housbonde so
That, for he sholde alwey upon hir thynke,
She yaf hym swich a manere love-drynke   760
That he was deed er it were by the morwe;
And thus algates housbondes han sorwe.
    "Thanne tolde he me how oon Latumyus
Compleyned unto his fellow Arrius
That in his gardyn growed swich a tree
On which he seyde how that his wyves three
Hanged hemself for herte despitous.
'O leeve brother,' quod this Arrius,
'Yif me a plante of thilke blissed tree,
And in my gardyn planted shal it bee.'   770
    "Of latter date, of wyves hath he red
That somme han slayn hir housbondes in hir bed,
And lete hir lecchour dighte hire al the nyght,
Whan that the corps lay in the floor upright.
And somme han dryve nayles in hir brayn,
Whil that they slepte, and thus they han hem slayn.
Somme han hem yeve poysoun in hire drynke.
He spak moore harm than herte may bithynke;
And therwithal he knew of mo proverbes
Than in this world ther growen gras or herbes.   780
'Bet is,' quod he, 'thyn habitacioun

685. **Parables of Salomon,** the biblical Book of Proverbs. 686. **Art,** the *Ars Amoris* of the Roman poet Ovid (43 B.C.–17? A.D.), which was an authoritative work for the Middle Ages on the subject of love and love making. 698. **Who peyntede the leon, etc.** Since, according to the fable of Aesop, only a man painted the lion, the lion was justified in complaining that the picture must be biased. "Who," inquires the Wife of Bath, "has written about women save men?" 700. **oratories,** chapel or closet for private prayers. 702. **mark of Adam,** likeness of Adam; i.e., men. 703. **children . . . Venus,** men and women born under Mercury and Venus, respectively. If Venus governs love, Mercury governs learning and knowledge. 708. **exaltacioun,** an astrological term for a constellation in which a given planet exerts its greatest influence on mankind. Such an *exaltacioun* means a

dejection (desolation) or weakened influence of a planet of contrary nature in the same constellation. Thus in Pisces, Venus is *exaltat* while Mercury, of contrary nature (since Love and Wisdom do not mix), is *desolat.* 715. **sit,** sitteth, sits. 727. **Sampson, etc.** The account of Samson, as well as that of Hercules and Dianyre (l. 731), is taken from Valerius Maximus. 734. **Socrates, etc.** The stories about Socrates, Pasiphaë, Clytemnestra, and Amphiorax are from St. Jerome (see note to l. 677). 735. **Xantippa,** wife of Socrates. 736. **sely,** wretched and innocent. 739. **Phasipha,** wife of King Minos of Crete, according to classical legend, conceived a violent passion for a bull, by which she gave birth to the monster Minotaur. 753. **Lyvia,** a Roman woman who poisoned Drusus in the reign of the Emperor Tiberius (23 A.D.). **Lucye** was the wife of the great Roman poet Lucretius (96?–55 B.C.);

Be with a leon or a foul dragoun,
Than with a womman usynge for to chyde.'
'Bet is,' quod he, 'hye in the roof abyde,
Than with an angry wyf doun in the hous;
They been so wikked and contrarious,
They haten that hir housbondes loven ay.'
He seyde, 'A womman cast hir shame away,
Whan she cast of hir smok;' and forthermo,
790 'A fair womman, but she be chaast also
Is lyk a gold ryng in a sowes nose.'
Who wolde wene, or who wolde suppose,
The wo that in myn herte was, and pyne?

    "And whan I saugh he wolde nevere fyne
To reden on this cursed book al nyght,
Al sodeynly thre leves have I plyght
Out of his book, right as he radde, and eke
I with my fest so took hym on the cheke
That in oure fyr he fil bakward adoun.
800 And he up stirte as doth a wood leoun,
And with his fest he smoot me on the heed,
That in the floor I lay as I were deed.
And whan he saugh how stille that I lay,
He was agast, and wolde han fled his way,
Til atte laste out of my swogh I breyde.
'O! hastow slayn me, false theef?' I seyde,
'And for my land thus hastow mordred me?
Er I be deed, yet wol I kisse thee.'

    "And neer he cam, and kneled faire adoun,
810 And seyde, 'Deere suster Alisoun,
As help me God! I shal thee nevere smyte.
That I have doon, it is thyself to wyte.
Foryeve it me, and that I thee biseke!'
And yet eftsoones I hitte hym on the cheke,
And seyde, 'Theef, thus muchel am I wreke;
Now wol I dye, I may no lenger speke.'
But atte laste, with muchel care and wo,
We fille acorded by us selven two.
He yaf me al the bridel in myn hond,
820 To han the governance of hous and lond,
And of his tonge, and of his hond also;
And made hym brenne his book anon right tho.
And whan that I hadde geten unto me,
By maistrie, al the soveraynetee,
And that he seyde, 'Myn owene trewe wyf,
Do as thee lyst the terme of al thy lyf;
Keep thyn honour, and keep eek myn estaat—'
After that day we hadden never debaat.
God helpe me so, I was to hym as kynde
830 As any wyf from Denmark unto Ynde,

And also trewe, and so was he to me.
I prey to God, that sit in magestee,
So blesse his soule for his mercy deere.
Now wol I seye my tale, if ye wol heere."

Biholde the wordes bitwene the Somonour and the Frere

    The Frere lough, whan he hadde herd al this;
"Now, dame," quod he, "so have I joye or blis,
This is a long preamble of a tale!"
And whan the Somonour herde the Frere gale,
"Lo," quod the Somonour, "Goddes armes two!
A frere wol entremette hym everemo.   840
Lo, goode men, a flye and eek a frere
Wol falle in every dyssh and eek mateere.
What spekestow of preambulacioun?
What! amble, or trotte, or pees, or go sit doun!
Thou lettest oure disport in this manere."

    "Ye, woltow so, sire Somonour?" quod the Frere;
"Now, by my feith, I shal, er that I go,
Telle of a somonour swich a tale or two,
That alle the folk shal laughen in this place."

    "Now elles, Frere, I bishrewe thy face,"   850
Quod this Somonour, "and I bishrewe me,
But if I telle tales two or thre
Of freres, er I come to Sidyngborne,
That I shal make thyn herte for to morne,
For wel I woot thy pacience is gon."

    Oure Hoste cride, "Pees! and that anon!"
And seyde, "Lat the womman telle hire tale.
Ye fare as folk that dronken been of ale.
Do, dame, telle forth youre tale, and that is best."

    "Al redy, sire," quod she, "right as yow lest,   860
If I have licence of this worthy Frere."

    "Yis, dame," quod he, "tel forth, and I wol heere."

THE WIFE OF BATH'S TALE

    In th' olde dayes of the Kyng Arthour,
Of which that Britons speken greet honour,
Al was this land fulfild of fayeryë.
The elf-queene, with hir joly compaignyë,
Daunced ful ofte in many a grene mede.
This was the olde opinioun, as I rede;
I speke of manye hundred yeres ago.
But now kan no man see none elves mo,   870
For now the grete charitee and prayeres
Of lymytours and other hooly freres,

---

according to tradition she inadvertently poisoned her husband by giving him what she thought was an aphrodisiac. 762. **algates,** always. 763. **Latumyus, etc.** This anecdote comes from Walter Map's *Epistle to Valerius;* it is not known precisely who Latumius was. 772. **somme . . . al the nyght,** evidently the tale of the Matron of Ephesus in a variant form. 775. **somme . . . brayn,** the tale of Jael and Sisera, as told in Judges 4:21. 781. **'Bet is,'** etc., quoted from Ecclesiasticus 25:16. 784. **'Bet is . . . hous,'** quoted from Proverbs 21:9–10. 788. **A womman, etc.,** quoted from St. Jerome; see note to l. 677. 790. **'A fair . . . sowes nose,'** quoted from Proverbs 11:22. 796. **plyght,** plucked, tore out. 800. **stirte,** started, leaped. 805. **swogh,** swoon, faint. 812. **wyte,** blame. 835. **lough,** laughed. 838. **gale,** cry out, exclaim. 839. **Goddes armes two!** "By Christ's two arms!" 840.

entremette, interfere, insert himself. 843. **preambulacioun,** a play on *preamble* (l. 837) and *perambulation.* 845. **lettest,** hinderest. The interchange between Friar and Summoner is preliminary to their "quarrel motif"; the two tell tales on each other after the Wife of Bath has finished her tale. 850. **bishrewe,** curse. 853. **Sidyngborne,** a town some forty miles from London on the old Canterbury road; evidently, then, at this stage the pilgrims were more than halfway along their journey. 862. **"Yis,"** "yes indeed," an emphatic affirmative. 865. **fayeryë,** the great company of fairies. 871. **charitee,** Christian love; the whole passage is bitterly sarcastic. 872. **lymytours,** friars granted licenses to beg within certain territories or limits.

Geoffrey Chaucer 137

That serchen every lond and every streem,
As thikke as motes in the sonne-beem,
Blessynge halles, chambres, kichenes, boures,
Citees, burghes, castels, hye toures,
Thropes, bernes, shipnes, dayeryes—
This maketh that ther been no fayeryës.
For ther as wont to walken was an elf,
880 Ther walketh now the lymytour himself
In undermeles and in morwenynges,
And seyth his matyns and his hooly thinges
As he gooth in his lymytacioun.
Wommen may go now saufly up and doun
In every bussh or under every tree;
Ther is noon oother incubus but he,
And he ne wol doon hem but dishonour.

    And so bifel it that this kyng Arthour
Hadde in his hous a lusty bacheler,
890 That on a day cam ridynge fro ryver;
And happed that, allone as she was born,
He saugh a mayde walkynge hym biforn,
Of which mayde anon, maugree hir heed,
By verray force, he rafte hire maydenhed;
For which oppressioun was swich clamour
And swich pursute unto the kyng Arthour,
That dampned was this knyght for to be deed,
By cours of lawe, and sholde han lost his heed—
Paraventure swich was the statut tho—
900 But that the queene and othere ladyes mo
So longe preyeden the kyng of grace,
Til he his lyf hym graunted in the place,
And yaf hym to the queene, al at hir wille,
To chese wheither she wolde hym save or spille.

    The queene thanketh the kyng with al hir myght,
And after this, thus spak she to the knyght,
Whan that she saugh hir time, upon a day:
"Thou standest yet," quod she, "in swich array
That of thy lyf yet hastow no suretee.
910 I grante thee lyf, if thou kanst tellen me
What thyng is it that wommen moost desiren.
Be war, and keep thy nekke-boon from iren!
And if thou kanst nat tellen it anon,
Yet shal I yeve thee leve for to gon
A twelf-month and a day, to seche and leere
An answere suffisant in this mateere;
And suretee wol I han, er that thou pace,
Thy body for to yelden in this place."
    Wo was this knyght, and sorwefully he siketh;
920 But what! he may nat do al as hym liketh.
And at the laste he chees hym for to wende,
And come agayn, right at the yeres ende,
With swich answere as God wolde hym purveye;

And taketh his leve, and wendeth forth his weye.
    He seeketh every hous and every place
Where as he hopeth for to fynde grace,
To lerne what thyng wommen loven moost;
But he ne coude arryven in no coost
Wher as he myghte fynde in this mateere
Two creatures accordynge in-feere.   930
    Somme seyde wommen loven best richesse,
Somme seyde honour, somme seyde jolynesse,
Somme riche array, somme seyden lust abedde,
And oftetyme to be wydwe and wedde.
Somme seyde that oure hertes been moost esed
Whan that we been yflatered and yplesed.
He gooth ful ny the sothe, I wol nat lye.
A man shal wynne us best with flaterye;
And with attendance, and with bisynesse
Been we ylymed, bothe moore and lesse.   940
    And somme seyen that we loven best
For to be free, and do right as us lest,
And that no man repreve us of our vice,
But seye that we be wise, and no thyng nice.
For trewely ther is noon of us alle,
If any wight wol clawe us on the galle,
That we nel kike, for he seith us sooth.
Assay, and he shal fynde it that so dooth;
For, be we never so vicious withinne,
We wol been holden wise and clene of synne.   950
    And somme seyn that greet delit han we
For to been holden stable, and eek secree,
And in o purpos stedefastly to dwelle,
And nat biwreye thyng that men us telle.
But that tale is nat worth a rake-stele.
Pardee, we wommen konne no thyng hele;
Witnesse on Myda,—wol ye heere the tale?
    Ovyde, amonges othere thynges smale,
Seyde Myda hadde, under his longe heres,
Growinge upon his heed two asses eres,   960
The whiche vice he hydde, as he best myghte,
Ful subtilly from every mannes sighte,
That, save his wyf, there wiste of it namo.
He loved hire moost, and trusted hire also;
He preyede hire that to no creature
She sholde tellen of his disfigure.
    She swoor him, "Nay!", for al this world to wynne,
She nolde do that vileynye or synne,
To make his housbonde han so foul a name.
She sholde nat telle it for hir owene shame.   970
But nathelees, hir thoughte that she dyde,
That she so longe sholde a conseil hyde;
Hir thoughte it swal so soore aboute hir herte
That nedely som word hire moste asterte;

---

875. **boures.** The bour was, strictly speaking, the sleeping quarters of
a medieval castle. 877. **Thropes,** villages, thorps; cf. German *Dorf.*
shipnes, stables, sheds. 881. **undermeles,** afternoon, although *undern*
usually refers to the morning; evidently a contrast with *morwenynges*
is implied here. 886. **incubus . . . dishonour.** In folklore, the incubus, a demoniac spirit that visited mortals in the form of a nightmare,
was likely to impregnate a woman found in the woods; but now the
Friars have chased away the incubi through their prayers and exorcisms,
and the only remaining danger to a woman was violation, since the
Friar would be incapable of impregnating her. 890. **fro ryver,** from

hawking or fowling by the river. 893. **maugree hir heed,** "in spite
of her (head)." 894. **rafte,** took away from her; cf. modern *bereft.*
904. **spille,** destroy. 910. **I grante . . . tellen me,** the so-called
Sphinx motif in folklore. 915. **seche,** seek. **leere,** learn. 928. **in no
coost,** no matter what his expense or effort. 929. **as.** The particle may
be omitted in reading. 930. **in-feere,** together. 940. **ylymed,** limed.
The metaphor is taken from fowling. 946. **clawe us on the galle,** rub
us on a sore spot. 950. **holden,** considered. 952. **secree,** discreet.
955. **rake-stele,** the tooth of a rake. 957. **Myda, etc.** The story is
taken from Ovid's *Metamorphoses* (see l. 988), but Ovid says that

And sith she dorste telle it to no man,
Doun to a mareys faste by she ran—
Til she cam there, hir herte was a-fyre—
And as a bitore bombleth in the myre,
She leyde hir mouth unto the water doun:
980 "Biwreye me nat, thou water, with thy soun,"
Quod she, "to thee I telle it and namo;
Myn housbonde hath longe asses erys two!
Now is myn herte al hool, now is it oute.
I myghte no lenger kepe it, out of doute."
Heere may ye se, though we a tyme abyde,
Yet out it moot; we kan no conseil hyde.
The remenant of the tale if ye wol heere,
Redeth Ovyde, and ther ye may it leere.
    This knyght, of which my tale is specially,
990 Whan that he saugh he myghte nat come thereby,
This is to seye, what wommen love moost,
Withinne his brest ful sorweful was the goost.
But hoom he gooth; he myghte nat sojourne;
The day was come that hoomward moste he tourne.
And in his wey it happed hym to ryde,
In al his care, under a forest syde,
Wher as he saugh upon a daunce go
Of ladyes foure and twenty, and yet mo;
Toward the whiche daunce he drow ful yerne,
1000 In hope that som wysdom sholde he lerne.
But certeinly, er he cam fully there,
Vanisshed was this daunce, he nyste where.
No creature saugh he that bar lyf,
Save on the grene he saugh sittynge a wyf—
A fouler wight ther may no man devyse.
Agayn the knyght this olde wyf gan ryse,
And seyde, "Sire knyght, heer forth ne lith no wey.
Tel me what that ye seken, by youre fey!
Paraventure it may the bettre be;
1010 Thise olde folk kan muchel thyng," quod she.
    "My leeve mooder," quod this knyght, "certeyn
I nam but deed, but if that I kan seyn
What thyng it is that wommen moost desire.
Koude ye me wisse, I wolde wel quite youre hire."
    "Plight me thy trouthe heere in myn hand," quod
    she,
"The nexte thyng that I requere thee,
Thou shalt it do, if it lye in thy myght,
And I wol telle it yow er it be nyght."
    "Have heer my trouthe," quod the knyght, "I
    grante."
1020 "Thanne," quod she, "I dar me wel avante
Thy lyf is sauf; for I wol stonde therby,
Upon my lyf, the queene wol seye as I.
Lat see which is the proudeste of hem alle,

That wereth on a coverchief or a calle,
That dar seye nay of that I shal thee teche.
Lat us go forth, withouten lenger speche."
Tho rowned she a pistel in his ere,
And bad hym to be glad, and have no fere.
    Whan they be comen to the court, this knyght
Seyde he had holde his day, as he hadde hight,   1030
And redy was his answere, as he sayde.
Ful many a noble wyf, and many a mayde,
And many a wydwe, for that they been wise,
The queene hirself sittynge as a justise,
Assembled been, his answere for to heere;
And afterward this knyght was bode appeere.
    To every wight comanded was silence,
And that the knyght sholde telle in audience
What thyng that worldly wommen loven best.
This knyght ne stood nat stille as doth a best,   1040
But to his questioun anon answerde
With manly vois, that al the court it herde:
    "My lige lady, generally," quod he,
"Wommen desiren have sovereynetee
As wel over hir housbonde as hir love,
And for to been in maistrie hym above.
This is youre mooste desir, though ye me kille.
Dooth as yow list; I am heer at youre wille."
In al the court ne was ther wyf, ne mayde,
Ne wydwe, that contraried that he sayde,   1050
But seyden he was worthy han his lyf.
    And with that word up stirte the olde wyf,
Which that the knyght saugh sittynge on the grene;
"Mercy," quod she, "my sovereyn lady queene!
Er that youre court departe, do me right.
I taughte this answere unto the knyght;
For which he plighte me his trouthe there,
The firste thyng that I wolde him requere,
He wolde it do, if it lay in his myght.
Bifore the court thanne preye I thee, sir knyght,"   1060
Quod she, "that thou me take unto thy wyf;
For wel thou woost that I have kept thy lyf.
If I seye fals, sey nay, upon thy fey!"
    This knyght answerde, "Allas! and weylawey!
I woot right wel that swich was my biheste.
For Goddes love, as chees a newe requeste!
Taak al my good, and lat my body go."
    "Nay, thanne," quod she, "I shrewe us bothe two!
For though that I be foul, and oold, and poore,
I nolde for al the metal, ne for oore,   1070
That under erthe is grave, or lith above,
But if thy wyf I were, and eek thy love."
    "My love?" quod he, "nay, my dampnacioun!
Allas! that any of my nacioun

it was Midas' barber who could not keep a secret, not his wife. Possibly
Jankin, the Wife of Bath's fifth husband, had twisted the tale in this
way to suit his thesis of the unreliability of women. 971. **hir thoughte
. . . dyde**, it seemed to her that she would die (if she could not un-
burden herself of her secret). 976. **mareys**, marsh, swamp. 978.
bitore, bittern, a small bird of the heron family (waterfowl). 987.
remenant of the tale. Unfortunately the reeds about the marsh caught
the words up and repeated them in their rustling, so that the whole
world eventually came to know of Midas' secret. 997. **daunce . . .
foure and twenty.** The twenty-four ladies constitute a "fairy ring,"

which is a commonplace of Celtic tales, especially among the Irish. 999.
yerne, eagerly. 1006. **Agayn**, towards. 1010. **kan**, know. 1012. **I
nam but deed**, "I shall be (naught but) dead." **but if**, unless. 1014.
wisse, make to know, inform. 1024. **wereth on**, wears. 1027. **rowned
. . . pistel**, whispered a message. 1030. **holde his day**, kept his appointed day. 1040. **best**, beast, animal. 1066. **as chees**, "choose!"
The *as* may be omitted in the sense. 1074. **nacioun**, probably meaning
"birth" here.

Sholde evere so foule disparaged be!"
But al for nought; the ende is this, that he
Constreyned was, he nedes mooste hire wedde;
And taketh his olde wyf, and gooth to bedde.

Now wolden som men seye, paraventure,
1080 That for my necligence I do no cure
To tellen yow the joye and al th'array
That at the feeste was that ilke day.
To which thyng shortly answeren I shal:
I seye ther nas no joye ne feeste at al;
Ther nas but hevynesse and muche sorwe.
For prively he wedded hire on a morwe,
And al day after hidde hym as an owle,
So wo was hym, his wyf looked so foule.

Greet was the wo the knyght hadde in his thought,
1090 Whan he was with his wyf abedde ybrought;
He walweth and he turneth to and fro.
His olde wyf lay smylynge everemo,
And seyde, "O deere housbonde, *benedicitee!*
Fareth every knyght thus with his wyf as ye?
Is this the lawe of kyng Arthures hous?
Is every knyght of his so dangerous?
I am youre owene love and eek youre wyf;
I am she which that saved hath youre lyf,
And, certes, yet ne dide I yow nevere unright;
1100 Why fare ye thus with me this firste nyght?
Ye faren lik a man had lost his wit.
What is my gilt? For Goddes love, tel me it,
And it shal been amended, if I may."

"Amended?" quod this knyght, "allas! nay, nay!
It wol nat been amended nevere mo.
Thou art so loothly, and so oold also,
And thereto comen of so lough a kynde,
That litel wonder is though I walwe and wynde.
So wolde God myn herte wolde breste!"
1110 "Is this," quod she, "the cause of youre unreste?"
"Ye, certeinly," quod he, "no wonder is."
"Now, sire," quod she, "I koude amende al this,
If that me liste, er it were dayes three,
So wel ye myghte here yow unto me.

"But, for ye speken of swich gentillesse
As is descended out of old richesse,
That therfore sholden ye be gentil men,
Swich arrogance is nat worth an hen.
Looke who that is moost vertuous alway,
1120 Pryvee and apert, and moost entendeth ay
To do the gentil dedes that he kan;
Taak hym for the grettest gentil man.
Crist wole we clayme of hym oure gentilesse,
Nat of oure eldres for hire old richesse.
For though they yeve us al hir heritage,
For which we clayme to been of heigh parage,
Yet may they nat biquethe, for no thyng,

To noon of us hir vertuous lyvyng,
That made hem gentil men ycalled be,
And bad us folwen hem in swich degree.   1130

"Wel kan the wise poete of Florence,
That highte Dant, speken in this sentence.
Lo, in swich maner rym is Dantes tale:
'Ful selde up riseth by his branches smale
Prowesse of man, for God, of his goodnesse,
Wole that of hym we clayme oure gentilesse;'
For of oure eldres may we no thyng clayme
But temporel thyng, that man may hurte and mayme.

"Eek every wight woot this as wel as I,
If gentilesse were planted natureelly   1140
Unto a certeyn lynage doun the lyne,
Pryvee and apert, thanne wolde they nevere fyne
To doon of gentilesse the faire office;
That myghte do no vileynye or vice.

"Taak fyr, and ber it in the derkeste hous
Bitwix this and the mount of Kaukasous,
And lat men shette the dores and go thenne;
Yet wole the fyr as faire lye and brenne
As twenty thousand men myghte it biholde;
His office natureel ay wol it holde,   1150
Up peril of my lyf, til that it dye.

"Heere may ye see wel how that genterye
Is nat annexed to possessioun,
Sith folk ne doon hir operacioun
Alwey, as dooth the fyr, lo, in his kynde.
For, God it woot, men may wel often fynde
A lordes sone do shame and vileynye;
And he that wole han pris of his gentrye,
For he was boren of a gentil hous,
And hadde his eldres noble and vertuous,   1160
And nel hymselven do no gentil dedis,
Ne folwen his gentil auncestre that deed is,
He nys nat gentil, be he duc or erl;
For vileyns synful dedes make a cherl.
For gentilesse nys but renomee
Of thyne ayncestres, for hire heigh bountee,
Which is a strange thyng to thy persone.
Thy gentillesse cometh fro God allone.
Thanne comth oure verray gentillesse of grace;
It was no thyng biquethe us with oure place.   1170

"Thenketh hou noble, as seith Valerius,
Was thilke Tullius Hostilius,
That out of poverte roos to heigh noblesse.
Reedeth Senek, and redeth eek Boece;
Ther shul ye seen expres that it no drede is
That he is gentil that dooth gentil dedes.
And therfore, leeve housbonde, I thus conclude:
Al were it that myne auncestres were rude,
Yet may the hye God, and so hope I,
Grante me grace to lyven vertuously.   1180

1096. dangerous, fussy, overparticular. 1107. lough, low. 1119.
Looke who, whoever. 1132. Dant, etc. The sense of the lines following is paralleled by that in Dante's *Convivio*, iv, 15 ff. 1148. lye,
blaze. 1150. office, function. 1161. nel, will not. 1165. For gentillesse . . . persone, for, so far as your ancestors are concerned, only
the renown of their names contributes to *gentilesse* (i.e., only the
renown that comes from their noble deeds and ideals), and that is a
matter foreign to yourself. Only God can give you true *gentilesse*.
1170. no thyng, not at all. biquethe, bequeathed (the past participle
of the verb). 1174. Senek, Seneca, the Roman philosopher, teacher,
and dramatist (4 B.C.–65 A.D.); the allusion here is to his 17th Epistle.
1182. weyve, avoid, eschew, waive. 1192. al, although. 1198. Juve-

Thanne am I gentil, whan that I bigynne
To lyven vertuously and weyve synne.

"And ther as ye of poverte me repreeve,
The hye God, on whom that we bileeve,
In wilful poverte chees to lyve his lyf.
And certes every man, mayden, or wyf,
May understonde that Jesus, hevene kyng,
Ne wolde nat chese a vicious lyvyng.
Glad poverte is an honest thyng, certeyn;
1190 This wole Senec and othere clerkes seyn.
Whoso that halt hym payd of his poverte,
I holde hym riche, al hadde he nat a sherte.
He that coveiteth is a povre wight,
For he wolde han that is nat in his myght;
But he that noght hath, ne coveiteth have,
Is riche, although ye holde hym but a knave.
Verray poverte, it syngeth proprely;
Juvenal seith of poverte myrily:
'The povre man, whan he gooth by the weye,
1200 Bifore the theves he may synge and pleye.'
Poverte is hateful good and, as I gesse,
A ful greet bryngere out of bisynesse;
A greet amendere eek of sapience
To hym that taketh it in pacience.
Poverte is this, although it seme alenge,
Possessioun that no wight wol chalenge.
Poverte ful ofte, whan a man is lowe,
Maketh his God and eek hymself to knowe.
Poverte a spectacle is, as thynketh me,
1210 Thurgh which he may his verray freendes see.
And therfore, sire, syn that I noght yow greve,
Of my poverte namoore ye me repreve.

"Now, sire, of elde ye repreve me;
And certes, sire, though noon auctoritee
Were in no book, ye gentils of honour
Seyn that men sholde an oold wight doon favour,
And clepe hym fader, for youre gentillesse;
And auctours shal I fynden, as I gesse.

"Now ther ye seye that I am foul and old,
1220 Than drede you nought to been a cokewold;
For filthe and eelde, also mote I thee,
Been grete wardeyns upon chastitee.
But nathelees, syn I knowe youre delit,
I shal fulfille youre worldly appetit.

"Chese now," quod she, "oon of thise thynges
tweye:
To han me foul and old til that I deye,
And be to yow a trewe, humble wyf,
And nevere yow displese in al my lyf;
Or elles ye wol han me yong and fair,
1230 And take youre aventure of the repair
That shal be to youre hous by cause of me,
Or in som other place, may wel be.

Now chese yourselven, wheither that yow liketh."
This knyght avyseth hym and soore siketh,
But atte laste he seyde in this manere:
"My lady and my love, and wyf so deere,
I put me in youre wise governance;
Cheseth youreself which may be moost plesance.
And moost honour to yow and me also.
I do no fors the wheither of the two;   1240
For as yow liketh, it suffiseth me."

"Thanne have I gete of yow maistrie," quod she,
"Syn I may chese and governe as me lest?"

"Ye, certes, wyf," quod he, "I holde it best."

"Kys me," quod she, "we be no lenger wrothe;
For, by my trouthe, I wol be to yow bothe,
This is to seyn, ye, bothe fair and good.
I prey to God, that I moot sterven wood,
But I to yow be also good and trewe
As evere was wyf, syn that the world was newe.   1250
And but I be to-morn as fair to seene
As any lady, emperice, or queene,
That is bitwixe the est and eke the west,
Doth with my lyf and deth right as yow lest.
Cast up the curtyn; looke how that it is."

And whan the knyght saugh verraily al this,
That she so fair was, and so yong therto,
For joye he hente hire in his armes two,
His herte bathed in a bath of blisse.
A thousand tyme a-rewe he gan hire kisse,   1260
And she obeyed hym in every thyng
That myghte doon hym plesaunce or likyng.

And thus they lyve unto hir lyves ende
In parfyt joye; and Jesu Crist us sende
Housbondes meeke, yonge, and fresh abedde,
And grace t'overbyde hem that we wedde;
And eek I praye Jesu shorte hir lyves
That wol nat be governed by hir wyves;
And olde and angry nygardes of dispence,
God sende hem soone verray pestilence!

GENTILESSE

*The subject of nobility, or "gentilesse," is treated
in The Wife of Bath's Tale as well as in the following
ballade. The idea that it is character and not birth that
determines nobility may seem rather radical for the
Middle Ages; but actually this idea was held by many
writers, such as Boethius, Dante, and Jean de Meun,
and has been called an integral part of Christian
democracy. Chaucer evidently drew on all three of
the above-mentioned writers for this poem. Its date is
uncertain.*

nal . . . pleye. Juvenal is an important Roman satirist (60?–140?).
It is not probable that Chaucer could know his works directly, but
sayings from many Roman poets were circulated during the Middle Ages
in anthologies of quotations, or *florilegia*. He might also have picked
up this particular quotation from Dante's quotation of it in the *Convivio*. 1205. **alenge,** wretched, miserable; cf. German *elend.* 1209.
spectacle, looking or reading glass. 1214. **auctoritee,** text of authority. 1220. **cokewold,** cuckold. 1230. **aventure,** chances. 1234.
siketh, sighs. 1248. **sterven wood,** die mad. 1258. **hente,** seized.
1260. **a-rewe,** in a row, in succession. 1266. **t'overbyde,** dominate.

The firste stok, fader of gentilesse—
What man that claymeth gentil for to be,
Must folowe his trace, and alle his wittes dresse
Vertu to sewe, and vyces for to flee.
For unto vertu longeth dignitee,
And noght the revers, saufly dar I deme,
Al were he mytre, croune, or diademe.

This firste stok was ful of rightwisnesse,
Trewe of his word, sobre, pitous, and free,
10 Clene of his goste, and loved besinesse
Ageinst the vyce of slouthe, in honestee;
And, but his heir love vertu, as dide he,
He is noght gentil, thogh he riche seme,
Al were he mytre, croune, or diademe.

Vyce may wel be heir to old richesse;
But ther may no man, as men may wel see,
Bequethe his heir his vertuous noblesse
That is appropred unto no degree,
But to the firste fader in magestee,
20 That maketh him his heir, that can him queme,
Al were he mytre, croune, or diademe.

TRUTH

*Sometimes known as the Balade de Bon Conseyl,
this poem is perhaps the best example of Chaucer's
moral verse. Its philosophy is derived largely from
Boethius' Consolation of Philosophy, and its refrain
echoes the idea in John 8:32: "Ye shall know the
truth, and the truth shall make you free." Legend has
it that the poem was composed on Chaucer's deathbed;
but sober fact throws great doubt upon such a romantic story. It is probable that Chaucer wrote the
ballade to give good counsel to his young friend Sir
Philip de la Vache, who married the daughter of
Chaucer's intimate acquaintance, Sir Lewis Clifford.
The name of de la Vache is seen by most scholars
in the envoy to the poem.*

Fle fro the prees, and dwelle with sothfastnesse;
Suffyce unto thy good, though hit be smal;
For hord hath hate, and clymbing tikelnesse,
Prees hath envye, and wele blent overal;
Savour no more than thee bihove shal;
Werk wel thy-self, that other folk canst rede;
And trouthe shal delivere, hit is no drede.

Tempest thee noght al croked to redresse,
In trust of hir that turneth as a bal;
Gret reste stant in litel besinesse,   10
And eek be war to sporne ageyn an al;
Stryve noght, as doth the crokke with the wal.
Daunte thyself, that dauntest otheres dede;
And trouthe shal delivere, hit is no drede.

That thee is sent, receyve in buxumnesse,
The wrastling for this world axeth a fal.
Her nis non hom, her nis but wildernesse;
Forth, pilgrim, forth! Forth, beste, out of thy stal!
Know thy countree; look up, thank God of al;
Hold the hye-way, and lat thy gost thee lede!   20
And trouthe shal delivere, hit is no drede.

ENVOY

Therefore, thou Vache, leve thyn old wrecchednesse;
Unto the world leve now to be thral;
Crye Him mercy that of His hy goodnesse
Made thee of noght, and in especial
Draw unto Him, and pray in general
For thee, and eek for other, hevenlich mede;
And trouthe shal delivere, hit is no drede.
(1390?)

ENVOY TO BUKTON

*The sharply satirical poem, Envoy to Bukton, was
composed in 1396. It is addressed to either Sir Peter
Bukton, of Holderness in Yorkshire, or to Sir Robert
Bukton, of Goosewold in Suffolk; the evidence seems
to favor the former of the two.*

*Although some have believed that the poem should
not be taken seriously, it is obvious from the effective,
powerful attacks on marriage in The Wife of Bath's
Prologue and The Merchant's Tale, which stay with
the reader after the more conventional treatment of
matrimony in some of Chaucer's other works has been
forgotten, that Chaucer was thoroughly skeptical
about marriage as an institution. The reference to
Friesland (1.23) is hardly a light-hearted, bantering
allusion.*

My maister Bukton, whan of Crist our kyng
Was axed what is trouthe or sothfastnesse,

Gentilesse. 1. **firste stok.** The reference is to Christ or God rather than to Adam. 3. **dresse,** direct prepare. 4. **sewe,** follow. 5. **longeth,** belongs. **dignitee,** worth, honor. 7. **Al,** although. **were,** wear (subjunctive). 12. **but,** unless. 18. **appropred,** made the property of. **degree,** rank. 20. **queme,** please.
Truth. 1. **prees,** press, crowd. **sothfastnesse,** truth, verity. 3. **tikelnesse,** ticklishness, instability. 4. **and . . . overal,** and riches blind (dazzle) one entirely. 5. **Savour,** taste, have relish for. 6. **rede,** advise. The line is a kind of restatement of the familiar "practice what you preach." 7. **hit . . . drede,** there is no doubt. 9. **hir . . . bal.** Fortune, with her mutability, is often pictured as having a wheel or ball. 10. **Gret . . . besinesse,** great peace stands (lies) in little business, or in not being too busy. 11. **sporne . . . al,** to kick against an awl; cf. the old biblical expression of "kicking against the pricks"

(Acts 9:5) as an expression of futile and painful endeavor. 13. **Daunte,** rule, govern. 15. **buxumnesse,** compliance. 16. **The . . . fal,** wrestling for (the sake of) this world is asking for a fall. 20. **gost,** spirit. 22. **Vache.** The word is capitalized by most editors who see in this a reference to Sir Philip de la Vache, mentioned in the headnote above. But there is probably something of a play on words here; Chaucer is picturing man as a lowly beast (1. 18) in a stall; *vache* is the French for "cow." 23. **leve . . . thral.** Cf. p. 921, 11. 83-84 of Browning's A Grammarian's Funeral. 27. **mede,** meed, reward.
Envoy to Bukton. 1. **maister.** If Sir Peter Bukton is the man addressed, as seems likely (see headnote to the poem), the term *maister* would be appropriate because Sir Peter was a lawyer. 2. **Was axed,** etc., referring to the question put to Christ by Pontius Pilate, "What is truth?"—see John 18:38.

He nat a word answerde to that axing,
As who seith, "No man is al trewe," I gesse.
And therfore, though I highte to expresse
The sorwe and wo that is in mariage,
I dar not writen of it no wikkednesse,
Lest I myself falle eft in swich dotage.

I wol nat seyn how that it is the cheyne
10 Of Sathanas, on which he gnaweth evere;
But I dar seyn, were he out of his peyne,
As by his wille he wolde be bounde nevere.
But thilke doted fool that eft hath levere
Ycheyned be than out of prison crepe,
God lete him never fro his wo dissevere,
Ne no man him bewayle, though he wepe!

But yet, lest thow do worse, take a wyf;
Bet is to wedde than brenne in worse wise.

But thow shalt have sorwe on thy flessh, thy lyf,
And been thy wives thral, as seyn thise wise;   20
And yf that hooly writ may nat suffyse,
Experience shal the teche, so may happe,
That the were lever to be take in Frise
Than eft to falle of weddynge in the trappe.

ENVOY

This lytel writ, proverbes, or figure
I sende yow, take kepe of yt, I rede;
Unwys is he that kan no wele endure.
If thow be siker, put thee nat in drede.
The Wyf of Bathe I pray yow that ye rede
Of this matere that we have on honde.   30
God graunte yow your lyf freely to lede
In freedam; for ful hard is to be bonde.

SIR THOMAS MALORY 1394?-1471

If the author of Morte Darthur was indeed the Malory who figures so ingloriously in public record, then the chronicle of his life reads more like that of an incorrigible criminal than a dignified man of letters. He was apparently born about 1394 of a prominent Warwickshire family, served in the last days of the Hundred Years' War, and was a member of Parliament in 1445. But in 1451, he was charged with making a raid upon a monastery occupying land formerly in his possession but taken from him by a prelate who supported a faction opposed to Malory's. Apparently, in these days of civil strife just before the Wars of the Roses, Malory was trying to recover property he thought rightly his. He took matters into his own hands, but was captured, charged with crimes of extortion, robbery, and rape, and was sent to prison, where he seems to have remained the rest of his life.

Malory's one work, so far as is known, was his compilation and arrangement of the various cycles of Arthurian legend, lumped together under the title Morte Darthur, and completed in 1469, while the author was apparently in prison. It is clear that in nearly every case Malory took French versions of the Arthurian stories, condensed them, and rewrote them, giving them a unity by revolving them about the central figure of King Arthur himself. Merlin, Lancelot, Tristram, Gareth, Gawain, and a host of other knights move through the story. Because Malory used French sources, the figure of Lancelot is allowed to rule the early books of Morte Darthur at the expense of the great Celtic hero Gawain, and for the same reason the loves of Lancelot and Guinevere cover many of its pages.

There is another fact of importance to be remembered in reading Morte Darthur. It dwells, more fully than any other work in Middle English literature, upon the quest and attaining of the Holy Grail; it celebrates, in fact, the moral romance as well as the chivalric. No other Arthurian knight has the unblemished record of the moral romance's greatest hero, Galahad. And so when Galahad, the victor in the quest for the Grail (the last great achievement in Arthurian legend), enters into the bliss of the Heavenly Kingdom, a tragic blight falls upon King Arthur and his court. This epic ruin and decay Malory has portrayed in simple yet vivid fashion.

It should be remarked that Malory's Morte Darthur was one of the many works printed by William Caxton (1422?-1491?), who introduced printing into England. Caxton was probably from a family of some importance, for he was apprenticed to Robert Large, one of the richest mercers of London. When Large died in 1449, Caxton was sent to Flanders to complete his apprenticeship. He lived in Bruges for some time and apparently became there a successful merchant and a man of social polish and intellectual interests. Upon his retirement in 1471 he turned to literature. His most ambitious work was his translation of the French writer Lefevre's Recuyel of the Histories of Troye, a compilation of stories about the Trojan War, having much the same relation to the Troy Legend as Malory's Morte Darthur does to the Arthurian romances. The work was completed in 1471.

Caxton then turned to the art of printing, which had been practiced in Europe for about a generation, since the days of John Gutenberg (1410-1468), in fact, Caxton's Recuyel, just mentioned, was the first book printed in the English language (1474). Some time within the next year Caxton moved his press to London, where he printed many beautiful books, beginning with the Dictes and Sayings of the Philosophres (1477) and including among others the first printed editions of Malory's Morte Darthur and Chaucer's Canterbury Tales, both in the year 1485. As printer, translator, and editor, then, Caxton did English literature an inestimable service. Perhaps no single event did so much to bring the Renaissance to England as the establishing of Caxton's press.

---

from MORTE DARTHUR

Book 21

The malcontents Mordred and Agravaine attempt to interest their brothers Gawain, Gareth, and Gaheris in the project of catching Lancelot and Guinevere together, in order that their love intrigue may be made certain to King Arthur. Gawain, Gareth, and Gaheris refuse to do anything against their respected friend Lancelot. But Mordred and Agravaine, in company with many other knights, ambush Lancelot in the queen's apartments. Lancelot fights his way out of the ambush, killing all his opponents save Mordred, but the secret love of Christendom's greatest knight has been discovered, and he must flee. Guinevere is accused of adultery and is to be burnt at the stake. Lancelot, however, rallies about him many of his friends, they make a sudden attack and rescue Guinevere after a fierce battle, carrying her off to Lancelot's great castle, Joyous Gard. In the fight Gaheris and Gareth are inadvertently slain by Lancelot, who did not recognize them, as they were unarmed. This disaster alienates Gawain from Lancelot, and when Arthur is persuaded to summon his forces to avenge himself on Lancelot for thus carrying off the queen, Gawain becomes one of his stanchest supporters.

Arthur besieges Lancelot in Joyous Gard for some time. The Pope finally intercedes and induces Arthur to take Guinevere back. Arthur is even willing to forgive Lancelot, but the irreconcilable Gawain will have none of it. Lancelot deems it expedient to leave the country. He crosses into France, but in the meantime Gawain has persuaded Arthur to take up arms against Lancelot. A great expedition also crosses into France and attacks Lancelot at Benwick (Bayonne). Gawain, against Arthur's wishes, taunts Lancelot into doing battle with him. They meet on more than one occasion. Gawain's peculiar attribute of strength which grows until noonday almost brings about the defeat of Lancelot, but the latter grimly holds his own and finally gives Gawain a blow on the head. While Arthur and his army are attacking Lancelot in France, the dire events with which Book 21 begins are already shaping themselves in England.

CHAPTER 1

How Sir Mordred Presumed and Took on Him to Be King of England, and Would Have Married the Queen, His Uncle's Wife

As Sir Mordred was ruler of all England, he did do make letters as though that they came from beyond the sea, and the letters specified that King Arthur was slain in battle with Sir Launcelot. Wherefore Sir Mordred made a parliament, and called the lords together, and there he made them to choose him king; and so was he crowned at Canterbury, and held a feast there fifteen days; and afterward he drew him unto Winchester, and there he took the Queen Guenever and said plainly that he would wed her which was his 10 uncle's wife and his father's wife. And so he made ready for the feast, and a day prefixed that they should be wedded; wherefore Queen Guenever was passing heavy. But she durst not discover her heart, but spake fair, and agreed to Sir Mordred's will. Then she desired of Sir Mordred for to go to London, to buy all manner of things that longed unto the wedding. And by cause of her fair speech Sir Mordred trusted her well enough and gave her leave to go. And so when she came to London she took the Tower of 20 London, and suddenly in all haste possible she stuffed it with all manner of victual and well garnished it with men, and so kept it. Then when Sir Mordred wist and understood how he was beguiled, he was passing wroth out of measure. And a short tale for to make, he went and laid a mighty siege about the Tower of London, and made many great assaults thereat, and threw many great engines unto them, and shot great guns. But all might not prevail Sir Mordred, for Queen Guenever would never for fair speech nor for foul, would never 30 trust to come in his hands again. Then came the Bishop

---

17. **longed,** belonged, were appropriate to. 36-39. **uncle ... wife.** Arthur supposedly had an incestuous relationship with his sister, Bellicent, from which union was born Mordred, who was at once Arthur's son and nephew. 44. **noise,** spread rumor. 49. **orgulist,** proudest.

of Canterbury, the which was a noble clerk, and an holy man, and thus he said to Sir Mordred: "Sir, what will ye do? will ye first displease God and sithen shame yourself, and all knighthood? Is not King Arthur your uncle, no farther but your mother's brother, and on her himself King Arthur begat you upon his own sister, therefore how may you wed your father's wife? Sir," said the noble clerk, "leave this
40 opinion or I shall curse you with book and bell and candle." "Do thou thy worst," said Sir Mordred, "wit thou well I shall defy thee." "Sir," said the Bishop, "and wit you well I shall not fear me to do that me ought to do. Also where ye noise where my lord Arthur is slain, and that is not so, and therefore ye will make a foul work in this land." "Peace, thou false priest," said Sir Mordred, "for an thou chafe me any more I shall make strike off thy head." So the Bishop departed and did the cursing in the most orgulist wise
50 that might be done. And then Sir Mordred sought the Bishop of Canterbury, for to have slain him. Then the Bishop fled, and took part of his goods with him, and went nigh unto Glastonbury; and there he was as priest hermit in a chapel and lived in poverty and in holy prayers, for well he understood that mischievous war was at hand. Then Sir Mordred sought on Queen Guenever by letters and sondes, and by fair means and foul means, for to have her to come out of the Tower of London; but all this availed not, for she an-
60 swered him shortly, openly and privily, that she had lever slay herself than to be married with him. Then came word to Sir Mordred that King Arthur had araised the siege for Sir Launcelot, and he was coming homeward with a great host, to be avenged upon Sir Mordred; wherefore Sir Mordred made write writs to all the barony of this land, and much people drew to him. For then was the common voice among them that with Arthur was none other life but war and strife, and with Sir Mordred was great joy and bliss. Thus
70 was Sir Arthur depraved, and evil said of. And many there were that King Arthur had made up of nought, and given them lands, might not then say him a good word. Lo, ye all Englishmen, see ye not what a mischief here was! for he that was the most king and knight of the world, and most loved the fellowship of noble knights, and by him they were all upholden, now might not these Englishmen hold them content with him. Lo, thus was the old custom and usage of this land; and also men say that we of this land have not
80 yet lost nor forgotten that custom and usage. Alas, this is a great default of us Englishmen, for there may no thing please us no term. And so fared the people at that time, they were better pleased with Sir Mordred than they were with King Arthur; and much people drew unto Sir Mordred, and said they would abide

with him for better and for worse. And so Sir Mordred drew with a great host to Dover, for there he heard say that Sir Arthur would arrive, and so he thought to beat his own father from his lands; and the most part of all England held with Sir Mordred, the people 90 were so new fangle.

CHAPTER 2

How After that King Arthur Had Tidings, He Returned and Came to Dover, Where Sir Mordred Met Him to Let His Landing, and of the Death of Sir Gawaine

And so as Sir Mordred was at Dover with his host, there came King Arthur with a great navy of ships and galleys and carracks. And there was Sir Mordred ready awaiting upon his landing, to let his own father to land upon the land that he was king over. Then there was launching of great boats and small, and full of noble men of arms; and there was much slaughter of gentle knights, and many a full bold baron was laid full low, on both parties. But King Arthur was 100 so courageous that there might no manner of knights let him to land, and his knights fiercely followed him; and so they landed maugre Sir Mordred and all his power, and put Sir Mordred aback, that he fled and all his people. So when this battle was done, King Arthur let bury his people that were dead. And then was noble Sir Gawaine found in a great boat, lying more than half dead. When Sir Arthur wist that Sir Gawaine was laid so low, he went unto him; and there the king made sorrow out of measure and took Sir 110 Gawaine in his arms, and thrice he there swooned. And then when he awaked, he said: "Alas, Sir Gawaine, my sister's son, here now thou liest, the man in the world that I loved most; and now is my joy gone, for now, my nephew Sir Gawaine, I will discover me unto your person; in Sir Launcelot and you I most had my joy, and mine affiance, and now have I lost my joy of you both; wherefore all mine earthly joy is gone from me." "Mine uncle King Arthur," said Sir Gawaine, "wit you well my death day is come, 120 and all is through mine own hastiness and wilfulness; for I am smitten upon the old wound the which Sir Launcelot gave me, on the which I feel well I must die; and had Sir Launcelot been with you as he was, this unhappy war had never begun; and of all this am I causer, for Sir Launcelot and his blood, through their prowess, held all your cankered enemies in subjection and daunger. And now," said Sir Gawaine, "ye shall miss Sir Launcelot. But alas, I would not accord with him, and therefore," said Sir Gawaine, "I pray 130

53. **Glastonbury,** a town in Somersetshire, England, noted for its famous abbey, where the Holy Grail and the mythical tombs of King Arthur and Queen Guinevere were supposedly located. 57. **sondes,** messengers. 61. **lever,** rather. 63. **araised,** raised, quit. 91. **new**

fangle, fickle, changeable. 94. **carracks,** small, broad, barge-like ships. 95. **let,** prevent. 103. **maugre,** in spite of. 117. **affiance,** trust.

you, fair uncle, that I may have paper, pen, and ink, that I may write to Sir Launcelot a cedle with mine own hands." And then when paper and ink was brought, then Gawaine was set up weakly by King Arthur, for he was shriven a little tofore; and then he wrote thus, as the French book maketh mention: "Unto Sir Launcelot, flower of all noble knights that ever I heard of or saw by my days, I, Sir Gawaine, King Lot's son of Orkney, sister's son unto the noble King Arthur, 10 send thee greeting, and let thee have knowledge that the tenth day of May I was smitten upon the old wound that thou gavest me afore the city of Benwick, and through the same wound that thou gavest me I am come to my death day. And I will that all the world wit, that I, Sir Gawaine, knight of the Table Round, sought my death, and not through thy deserving, but it was mine own seeking; wherefore I beseech thee, Sir Launcelot, to return again unto this realm, and see my tomb, and pray some prayer more or less for my 20 soul. And this same day that I wrote this cedle, I was hurt to the death in the same wound, the which I had of thy hand, Sir Launcelot; for of a more nobler man might I not be slain. Also Sir Launcelot, for all the love that ever was betwixt us, make no tarrying, but come over the sea in all haste, that thou mayst with thy noble knights rescue that noble king that made thee knight, that is my lord Arthur; for he is full straitly bestad with a false traitor, that is my half-brother, Sir Mordred; and he hath let crown him king, 30 and would have wedded my lady Queen Guenever, and so had he done had she not put herself in the Tower of London. And so the tenth day of May last past, my lord Arthur and we all landed upon them at Dover; and there we put that false traitor, Sir Mordred, to flight, and there it misfortuned me to be stricken upon thy stroke. And at the date of this letter was written, but two hours and a half afore my death, written with mine own hand, and so subscribed with part of my heart's blood. And I require thee, most famous knight 40 of the world, that thou wilt see my tomb." And then Sir Gawaine wept, and King Arthur wept; and then they swooned both. And when they awaked both, the king made Sir Gawaine to receive his Saviour. And then Sir Gawaine prayed the king for to send for Sir Launcelot, and to cherish him above all other knights. And so at the hour of noon Sir Gawaine yielded up the spirit; and then the king let inter him in a chapel within Dover Castle; and there yet all men may see the skull of him, and the same wound is seen that Sir 50 Launcelot gave him in battle. Then was it told the king that Sir Mordred had pyghte a new field upon Barham Down. And upon the morn the king rode thither to him, and there was a great battle betwixt them, and much people was slain on both parties; but at the last

Sir Arthur's party stood best, and Sir Mordred and his party fled unto Canterbury.

CHAPTER 3

How After, Sir Gawaine's Ghost Appeared to King Arthur, and Warned Him That He Should Not Fight That Day

And then the king let search all the towns for his knights that were slain, and interred them; and salved them with soft salves that so sore were wounded. Then much people drew unto King Arthur. And then they 60 said that Sir Mordred warred upon King Arthur with wrong. And then King Arthur drew him with his host down by the seaside westward toward Salisbury; and there was a day assigned betwixt King Arthur and Sir Mordred, that they should meet upon a down beside Salisbury, and not far from the seaside; and this day was assigned on a Monday after Trinity Sunday, whereof King Arthur was passing glad, that he might be avenged upon Sir Mordred. Then Sir Mordred araised much people about London, for they of Kent, 70 Southsex, and Surrey, Estsex, and of Southfolk, and of Northfolk, held the most part with Sir Mordred; and many a full noble knight drew unto Sir Mordred and to the king; but they that loved Sir Launcelot drew unto Sir Mordred. So upon Trinity Sunday at night, King Arthur dreamed a wonderful dream, and that was this: that him seemed he sat upon a chaflet in a chair, and the chair was fast to a wheel, and thereupon sat King Arthur in the richest cloth of gold that might be made; and the king thought there was under 80 him, far from him, an hideous deep black water, and therein were all manner of serpents, and worms, and wild beasts, foul and horrible; and suddenly the king thought the wheel turned up so down, and he fell among the serpents, and every beast took him by a limb; and then the king cried as he lay in his bed and slept: "Help!" And then knights, squires, and yeomen awaked the king; and then he was so amazed that he wist not where he was; and then he fell on slumbering again, not sleeping nor thoroughly waking. So the king 90 seemed verily that there came Sir Gawaine unto him with a number of fair ladies with him. And when King Arthur saw him, then he said: "Welcome, my sister's son; I weened thou hadst been dead, and now I see thee on live, much am I beholding unto almighty Jesu. O fair nephew and my sister's son, what be these ladies that hither be come with you?" "Sir," said Sir Gawaine, "all these be ladies for whom I have foughten when I was man living, and all these are those that I did battle for in righteous quarrel; and God hath given 100 them that grace at their great prayer, by cause I did

---

2. **cedle,** schedule, written message. 6. **French book,** one of the numerous French Arthurian romances to which Malory had access for his version. 28. **bestad,** beset. 51. **pyghte,** pitched, prepared. **Barham Down,** section between Canterbury and Folkstone in Kent. 63. **Salis-** bury, a city in Wiltshire, England, about twenty miles from Southampton. 71. **Southsex . . . Northfolk,** archaic forms of the names of the important English counties of *Sussex, Surrey, Essex, Suffolk,*

battle for them, that they should bring me hither unto you: thus much hath God given me leave, for to warn you of your death; for an ye fight as tomorn with Sir Mordred, as ye both have assigned, doubt ye not ye must be slain, and the most part of your people on both parties. And for the great grace and goodness that almighty Jesu hath unto you, and for pity of you, and many more other good men there shall be slain,
110 God hath sent me to you of his special grace, to give you warning that in no wise ye do battle as tomorn, but that ye take a treaty for a month day; and proffer you largely, so as tomorn to be put in a delay. For within a month shall come Sir Launcelot with all his noble knights, and rescue you worshipfully, and slay Sir Mordred, and all that ever will hold with him." Then Sir Gawaine and all the ladies vanished. And anon the king called upon his knights, squires, and yeomen and charged them wightly to fetch his noble lords
120 and wise bishops unto him. And when they were come, the king told them his avision, what Sir Gawaine had told him, and warned him that if he fought on the morn he should be slain. Then the king commanded Sir Lucan the Butler, and his brother Sir Bedivere, with two bishops with them, and charged them in any wise, an they might, "Take a treaty for a month day with Sir Mordred, and spare not, proffer him lands and goods as much as ye think best." So then they departed and came to Sir Mordred, where he had a grim host
130 of an hundred thousand men. And there they entreated Sir Mordred long time; and at the last Sir Mordred was agreed for to have Cornwall and Kent, by Arthur's days: after, all England, after the days of King Arthur.

CHAPTER 4

How by Misadventure of an Adder the Battle Began, Where Mordred Was Slain, and Arthur Hurt to the Death

Then were they condescended that King Arthur and Sir Mordred should meet betwixt both their hosts, and every each of them should bring fourteen persons; and they came with this word unto Arthur. Then said he: "I am glad that this is done"; and so he went into the field. And when Arthur should depart, he warned all
140 his host that an they see any sword drawn: "Look ye come on fiercely, and slay that traitor, Sir Mordred, for I in no wise trust him." In likewise Sir Mordred warned his host that: "An ye see any sword drawn, look that ye come on fiercely, and so slay all that ever before you standeth; for in no wise I will not trust for this treaty, for I know well my father will be avenged on me." And so they met as their appointment was, and so they were agreed and accorded thoroughly; and

wine was fetched, and they drank. Right soon came an adder out of a little heath bush, and it stung a 150 knight on the foot. And when the knight felt him stung, he looked down and saw the adder, and then he drew his sword to slay the adder, and thought of none other harm. And when the host on both parties saw that sword drawn, then they blew beamous, trumpets, and horns, and shouted grimly. And so both hosts dressed them together. And King Arthur took his horse, and said: "Alas this unhappy day!" and so rode to his party. And Sir Mordred in likewise. And never was there seen a more dolefuller battle in no Christian 160 land; for there was but rushing and riding, foining and striking, and many a grim word was there spoken either to other, and many a deadly stroke. But ever King Arthur rode throughout the battle of Sir Mordred many times, and did full nobly as a noble king should, and at all times he fainted never; and Sir Mordred that day put him in devoir, and in great peril. And thus they fought all the long day and never stinted till the noble knights were laid to the cold earth; and ever they fought still till it was near night, and by that 170 time was there an hundred thousand laid dead upon the down. Then was Arthur wood wroth out of measure, when he saw his people so slain from him. Then the king looked about him, and then was he ware, of all his host and of all his good knights, were left no more on live but two knights; that one was Sir Lucan the Butler and his brother Sir Bedivere, and they were full sore wounded. "Jesu mercy," said the king, "where are all my noble knights become? Alas that ever I should see this doleful day, for now," said 180 Arthur, "I am come to mine end. But would to God that I wist where were that traitor Sir Mordred, that hath caused all this mischief." Then was King Arthur ware where Sir Mordred leaned upon his sword among a great heap of dead men. "Now give me my spear," said Arthur unto Sir Lucan, "for yonder I have espied the traitor that all this woe hath wrought." "Sir, let him be," said Sir Lucan, "for he is unhappy; and if ye pass this unhappy day ye shall be right well revenged upon him. Good lord, remember ye of your night's 190 dream, and what the spirit of Sir Gawaine told you this night, yet God of his great goodness hath preserved you hitherto. Therefore, for God's sake, my lord, leave off by this, for blessed be God ye have won the field, for here we be three on live, and with Sir Mordred is none on live; and if ye leave off now this wicked day of destiny is past." "Tide me death, betide me life," saith the king, "now I see him yonder alone he shall never escape mine hands, for at a better avail shall I never have him." "God speed you well," said Sir 200 Bedivere. Then the king gat his spear in both his hands and ran toward Sir Mordred, crying: "Traitor, now is

and *Norfolk*, respectively. 77. **chaflet**, a small platform or dais. 119. **wightly**, valiantly. 134. **condescended**, agreed. 136. **fourteen persons**. A leader and his retinue of fourteen persons is a convention of epic and romance. 140. **An**, if. 155. **beamous**, a kind of trumpet. 161. **foining**, thrusting. 167. **in devoir**, in knightly duty. 172. **wood wroth**, insanely angered.

thy death day come." And when Sir Mordred heard Sir Arthur, he ran until him with his sword drawn in his hand. And there King Arthur smote Sir Mordred under the shield, with a foin of his spear, throughout the body, more than a fathom. And when Sir Mordred felt that he had his death wound, he thrust himself with the might that he had up to the bur of King Arthur's spear. And right so he smote his father Arthur, with his sword holden in both his hands, on the side 10 of the head, that the sword pierced the helmet and the brain pan, and therewithal Sir Mordred fell stark dead to the earth; and the noble Arthur fell in a swoon to the earth, and there he swooned ofttimes. And Sir Lucan the Butler and Sir Bedivere ofttimes heave him up. And so weakly they led him betwixt them both, to a little chapel not far from the seaside. And when the king was there he thought him well eased. Then heard they people cry in the field. "Now go thou, Sir Lucan," said the king, "and do me to wit what betokens that 20 noise in the field." So Sir Lucan departed, for he was grievously wounded in many places. And so as he yede, he saw and hearkened by the moonlight, how that pillers and robbers were come into the field to pill and to rob many a full noble knight of brooches and beads, of many a good ring and of many a rich jewel; and who that were not dead all out, there they slew them for their harness and their riches. When Sir Lucan understood this work, he came to the king as soon as he might and told him all what he had heard and seen. 30 "Therefore by my rede," said Sir Lucan, "it is best that we bring you to some town." "I would it were so," said the king.

CHAPTER 5

How King Arthur Commanded to Cast His Sword Excalibur into the Water, and How He Was Delivered to Ladies in a Barge

"But I may not stand, mine head works so. Ah Sir Launcelot," said King Arthur, "this day have I sore missed thee: alas, that ever I was against thee, for now have I my death, whereof Sir Gawaine me warned in my dream." Then Sir Lucan took up the king the one part, and Sir Bedivere the other part, and in the lifting the king swooned; and Sir Lucan fell in a swoon with 40 the lift, that the part of his guts fell out of his body, and therewith the noble knight's heart brast. And when the king awoke, he beheld Sir Lucan how he lay foaming at the mouth and part of his guts lay at his feet. "Alas," said the king, "this is to me a full heavy sight, to see this noble duke so die for my sake, for he would have holpen me, that had more need of help than I. Alas, he would not complain him, his heart was so set

to help me: now Jesu have mercy upon his soul!" Then Sir Bedivere wept for the death of his brother. "Leave this mourning and weeping," said the king, "for all this 50 will not avail me, for wit thou well an I might live myself, the death of Sir Lucan would grieve me evermore; but my time hieth fast," said the king. "Therefore," said Arthur unto Sir Bedivere, "take thou Excalibur, my good sword, and go with it to yonder water side, and when thou comest there I charge thee throw my sword in that water, and come again and tell me what thou there seest." "My lord," said Bedivere, "your commandment shall be done, and lightly bring you word again." So Sir Bedivere departed, and by the 60 way he beheld that noble sword, that the pommel and the haft was all of precious stones; and then he said to himself: "If I throw this rich sword in the water, thereof shall never come good, but harm and loss." And then Sir Bedivere hid Excalibur under a tree. And so, as soon as he might, he came again unto the king, and said he had been at the water, and had thrown the sword in the water. "What saw thou there?" said the king. "Sir," he said, "I saw nothing but waves and winds." "That is untruly said of thee," said the king, 70 "therefore go thou lightly again and do my commandment; as thou art to me lief and dear, spare not, but throw it in." Then Sir Bedivere returned again, and took the sword in his hand; and then him thought sin and shame to throw away that noble sword, and so efte he hid the sword and returned again, and told to the king that he had been at the water and done his commandment. "What saw thou there?" said the king. "Sir," he said, "I saw nothing but the waters wappe and waves wanne." "Ah, traitor untrue," said King 80 Arthur, "now hast thou betrayed me twice. Who would have weened that thou that hast been to me so lief and dear, and thou art named a noble knight, and would betray me for the richness of the sword. But now go again lightly, for thy long tarrying putteth me in great jeopardy of my life, for I have taken cold. And but if thou do now as I bid thee, if ever I may see thee, I shall slay thee with mine own hands; for thou wouldst for my rich sword see me dead." Then Sir Bedivere departed, and went to the sword, and lightly took it 90 up, and went to the water side; and there he bound the girdle about the hilts, and then he threw the sword as far into the water as he might; and there came an arm and an hand above the water and met it, and caught it, and so shook it thrice and brandished, and then vanished away the hand with the sword in the water. So Sir Bedivere came again to the king, and told him what he saw. "Alas!" said the king, "help me hence, for I dread me I have tarried over long." Then Sir Bedivere took the king upon his back, and so went 100 with him to that water side. And when they were at

---

2. **until**, unto. 21. **yede**, went. 33. **works**, pains. 79-80. **wappe . . . wanne**, lap and ebb. 119. **Avilion**, Avalon, the Celtic abode of the blessed. 132. **flemed**, put to flight. 135. **deeming**, guess, supposition.

158. **Morgan le Fay**, the sorceress sister and lifelong enemy of Arthur, but attending his death as his nearest of kin. 160. **Nimue**. Originally a nymph of the lake, she was insanely loved by the old magician Merlin,

the water side, even fast by the bank hoved a little barge with many fair ladies in it, and among them all was a queen, and all they had black hoods, and all they wept and shrieked when they saw King Arthur. "Now put me into the barge," said the king. And so he did softly; and there received him three queens with great mourning; and so they set them down, and in one of their laps King Arthur laid his head. And then that queen said: "Ah, dear brother, why have ye tarried so long from me? alas, this wound on your head hath caught over-much cold." And so then they rowed from the land, and Sir Bedivere beheld all those ladies go from him. Then Sir Bedivere cried: "Ah my lord Arthur, what shall become of me, now ye go from me and leave me here alone among mine enemies?" "Comfort thyself," said the king, "and do as well as thou mayest, for in me is no trust for to trust in; for I will into the vale of Avilion to heal me of my grievous wound; and if thou hear never more of me, pray for my soul." But ever the queens and ladies wept and shrieked, that it was pity to hear. And as soon as Sir Bedivere had lost the sight of the barge, he wept and wailed, and so took the forest; and so he went all that night, and in the morning he was ware betwixt two holts hoar, of a chapel and an hermitage.

CHAPTER 6

How Sir Bedivere Found Him on the Morrow Dead in an Hermitage, and How He Abode There with the Hermit

Then was Sir Bedivere glad, and thither he went; and when he came into the chapel, he saw where lay an hermit grovelling on all four, there fast by a tomb was new graven. When the hermit saw Sir Bedivere, he knew him well, for he was but little tofore Bishop of Canterbury, that Sir Mordred flemed. "Sir," said Bedivere, "what man is there interred that ye pray so fast for?" "Fair son," said the hermit, "I wot not verily, but by deeming. But this night, at midnight, here came a number of ladies, and brought hither a dead corpse, and prayed me to bury him; and here they offered an hundred tapers, and they gave me an hundred besants." "Alas!" said Sir Bedivere, "that was my lord King Arthur, that here lieth buried in this chapel." Then Sir Bedivere swooned; and when he awoke he prayed the hermit he might abide with him still there, to live with fasting and prayers. "For from hence will I never go," said Sir Bedivere, "by my will, but all the days of my life here to pray for my lord Arthur." "Ye are welcome to me," said the hermit, "for I know ye better than ye ween that I do. Ye are the bold Bedivere, and the full noble duke, Sir Lucan

the Butler, was your brother." Then Sir Bedivere told the hermit all as ye have heard tofore. So there bode Sir Bedivere with the hermit that was tofore Bishop of Canterbury, and there Sir Bedivere put upon him poor clothes and served the hermit full lowly in fasting and in prayers. Thus of Arthur I find never more written in books that he authorised, nor more of the very certainty of his death heard I never read, but thus was he led away in a ship wherein were three queens; that one was King Arthur's sister, Queen Morgan le Fay; the other was the Queen of Northgalis; the third was the Queen of the Waste Lands. Also there was Nimue, the chief lady of the lake, that had wedded Pelleas the good knight; and this lady had done much for King Arthur, for she would never suffer Sir Pelleas to be in no place where he should be in danger of his life; and so he lived to the uttermost of his days with her in great rest. More of the death of King Arthur could I never find, but that ladies brought him to his burials; and such one was buried there, that the hermit bare witness that sometime was Bishop of Canterbury, but yet the hermit knew not in certain that he was verily the body of King Arthur; for this tale Sir Bedivere, knight of the Table Round, made it to be written.

CHAPTER 7

Of the Opinion of Some Men of the Death of King Arthur, and How Queen Guenever Made Her a Nun in Almesbury

Yet some men say in many parts of England that King Arthur is not dead, but had by the will of our Lord Jesu into another place; and men say that he shall come again, and he shall win the holy cross. I will not say it shall be so, but rather I will say, here in this world he changed his life. But many men say that there is written upon his tomb this verse: *Hic jacet Arthurus Rex, quondam Rexque futurus.* Thus leave I here Sir Bedivere with the hermit, that dwelled that time in a chapel beside Glastonbury, and there was his hermitage. And so they lived in their prayers, and fastings, and great abstinence. And when Queen Guenever understood that King Arthur was slain, and all the noble knights, Sir Mordred and all the remnant, then the queen stole away, and five ladies with her, and so she went to Almesbury; and there she let make herself a nun, and ware white clothes and black, and great penance she took, as ever did sinful lady in this land, and never creature could make her merry; but lived in fasting, prayers, and alms-deeds, that all manner of people marveled how virtuously she was changed. Now leave we Queen Guenever in Almesbury, a nun in white clothes and black, and there she was abbess and

whom she lured into a rock and immured there. Nimue seems to have been for a while an associate of the evil-designing Morgan le Fay, but she apparently reformed after her marriage to Pelleas, a young knight.

179-180. **Hic . . . futurus.** Here lies King Arthur, king that was and is to be. 188. **Almesbury,** a town near Salisbury.

ruler as reason would; and turn we from her, and speak we of Sir Launcelot du Lake.

CHAPTER 8

How When Sir Launcelot Heard of the Death of King Arthur, and of Sir Gawaine, and Other Matters, He Came into England

And when he heard in his country that Sir Mordred was crowned king in England, and made war against King Arthur, his own father, and would let him to land in his own land; also it was told Sir Launcelot how that Sir Mordred had laid siege about the Tower of London, by cause the queen would not wed him; then was Sir Launcelot wroth out of measure and said to his
10 kinsmen: "Alas! that double traitor Sir Mordred, now me repenteth that ever he escaped my hands, for much shame hath he done unto my lord Arthur; for all I feel by the doleful letter that my lord Sir Gawaine sent me, on whose soul Jesu have mercy, that my lord Arthur is full hard bestad. Alas!" said Sir Launcelot, "that ever I should live to hear that most noble king that made me knight thus to be overset with his subject in his own realm. And this doleful letter that my lord, Sir Gawaine, hath sent me afore his death, praying
20 me to see his tomb, wit you well his doleful words shall never go from mine heart, for he was a full noble knight as ever was born; and in an unhappy hour was I born that ever I should have that unhap to slay first Sir Gawaine, Sir Gaheris the good knight, and mine own friend Sir Gareth, that full noble knight. Alas, I may say I am unhappy," said Sir Launcelot, "that ever I should do thus unhappily, and, alas, yet might I never have hap to slay that traitor, Sir Mordred." "Leave your complaints," said Sir Bors, "and first revenge
30 you of the death of Sir Gawaine; and it will be well done that ye see Sir Gawaine's tomb, and secondly that ye revenge my lord Arthur, and my lady, Queen Guenever." "I thank you," said Sir Launcelot, "forever ye will my worship." Then they made them ready in all the haste that might be, with ships and galleys, with Sir Launcelot and his host to pass into England. And so he passed over the sea till he came to Dover, and there he landed with seven kings, and the number was hideous to behold. Then Sir Launcelot spered of men of
40 Dover where was King Arthur become. Then the people told him how that he was slain, and Sir Mordred and an hundred thousand died on a day; and how Sir Mordred gave King Arthur there the first battle at his landing, and there was good Sir Gawaine slain; and on the morn Sir Mordred fought with the king upon Barham Down, and there the king put Sir Mordred to the worse. "Alas," said Sir Launcelot, "this is the heav-iest tidings that ever came to me. Now, fair sirs," said Sir Launcelot, "shew me the tomb of Sir Gawaine." And then certain people of the town brought him into 50 the Castle of Dover and shewed him the tomb. Then Sir Launcelot kneeled down and wept, and prayed heartily for his soul. And that night he made a dole, and all they that would come had as much flesh, fish, wine, and ale, and every man and woman had twelve pence, come who would. Thus with his own hand dealt he this money, in a mourning gown; and ever he wept, and prayed them to pray for the soul of Sir Gawaine. And on the morn all the priests and clerks that might be gotten in the country were there, and sang mass of 60 requiem; and there offered first Sir Launcelot, and he offered an hundred pound; and then the seven kings offered forty pound apiece; and also there was a thousand knights, and each of them offered a pound; and the offering dured from morn till night, and Sir Launcelot lay two nights on his tomb in prayers and weeping. Then on the third day Sir Launcelot called the kings, dukes, earls, barons, and knights, and said thus: "My fair lords, I thank you all of your coming into this country with me, but we came too late, and that 70 shall repent me while I live, but against death may no man rebel. But sithen it is so," said Sir Launcelot, "I will myself ride and seek my lady, Queen Guenever, for as I hear say she hath had great pain and much disease; and I heard say that she is fled into the west. Therefore ye all shall abide me here, and but if I come again within fifteen days, then take your ships and your fellowship, and depart into your country, for I will do as I say to you."

CHAPTER 9

How Sir Launcelot Departed to Seek the Queen Guenever, and How He Found Her at Almesbury

Then came Sir Bors de Ganis, and said: "My lord 80 Sir Launcelot, what think ye for to do, now to ride in this realm? wit ye well ye shall find few friends." "Be as be may," said Sir Launcelot, "keep you still here, for I will forth on my journey, and no man nor child shall go with me." So it was no boot to strive, but he departed and rode westerly, and there he sought a seven or eight days; and at the last he came to a nunnery, and then was Queen Guenever ware of Sir Launcelot as he walked in the cloister. And when she saw him there she swooned thrice, that all the ladies and 90 gentlewomen had work enough to hold the queen up. So when she might speak, she called ladies and gentlewomen to her, and said: "Ye marvel, fair ladies, why I make this fare. Truly," she said, "it is for the sight of yonder knight that yonder standeth; wherefore I

---

39. **spered,** asked.   53. **dole,** lamentation, wake.   65. **dured,** lasted.
112. **wrake,** ruin, destruction.   131. **Sangreal,** the Holy Grail.   133-
135. **passed ... son.** Although Lancelot's preëminence would have made

him the logical knight to achieve the Grail, he is ineligible in the eyes of the Church because of his affair with Guinevere. Instead, he is given a son, Galahad, who is to achieve the Grail. Lancelot, although near

pray you all call him to me." When Sir Launcelot was brought to her, then she said to all the ladies: "Through this man and me hath all this war been wrought, and the death of the most noblest knights of the world; for
100 through our love that we have loved together is my most noble lord slain. Therefore, Sir Launcelot, wit thou well I am set in such a plight to get my soul heal; and yet I trust through God's grace that after my death to have a sight of the blessed face of Christ, and at domesday to sit on his right side, for as sinful as ever I was are saints in heaven. Therefore, Sir Launcelot, I require and beseech thee heartily, for all the love that ever was betwixt us, that thou never see me more in the visage; and I command thee, on God's behalf,
110 that thou forsake my company, and to thy kingdom thou turn again, and keep well thy realm from war and wrake; for as well as I have loved thee, mine heart will not serve me to see thee, for through thee and me is the flower of kings and knights destroyed; therefore, Sir Launcelot, go to thy realm, and there take thee a wife, and live with her with joy and bliss; and I pray thee heartily, pray for me to our Lord that I may amend my misliving." "Now, sweet madam," said Sir Launcelot, "would ye that I should now return again
120 unto my country, and there to wed a lady? Nay, madam, wit you well that shall I never do, for I shall never be so false to you of that I have promised; but the same destiny that ye have taken you to, I will take me unto, for to please Jesu, and ever for you I cast me specially to pray." "If thou wilt do so," said the queen, "hold thy promise, but I may never believe but that thou wilt turn to the world again." "Well, madam," said he, "ye say as pleaseth you, yet wist you me never false of my promise, and God defend but I should for-
130 sake the world as ye have done. For in the quest of the Sangreal I had forsaken the vanities of the world had not your lord been. And if I had done so at that time, with my heart, will, and thought, I had passed all the knights that were in the Sangreal except Sir Galahad, my son. And therefore, lady, sithen ye have taken you to perfection, I must needs take me to perfection, of right. For I take record of God, in you I have had mine earthly joy; and if I had found you now so disposed, I had cast to have had you into mine own realm.

CHAPTER 10

How Sir Launcelot Came to the Hermitage Where the Archbishop of Canterbury Was, and How He Took the Habit on Him

140 "But sithen I find you thus disposed, I ensure you faithfully, I will ever take me to penance, and pray while my life lasteth, if I may find any hermit, either

gray or white, that will receive me. Wherefore, madam, I pray you kiss me and never no more." "Nay," said the queen, "that shall I never do, but abstain you from such works"; and they departed. But there was never so hard an hearted man but he would have wept to see the dolor that they made; for there was lamentation as they had been stung with spears; and many times they swooned, and the ladies bare the queen to 150 her chamber. And Sir Launcelot awoke, and went and took his horse, and rode all that day and all night in a forest, weeping. And at the last he was ware of an hermitage and a chapel stood betwixt two cliffs; and then he heard a little bell ring to mass, and thither he rode and alit, and tied his horse to the gate, and heard mass. And he that sang mass was the Bishop of Canterbury. Both the Bishop and Sir Bedivere knew Sir Launcelot, and they spake together after mass. But when Sir Bedivere had told his tale all whole, Sir Launcelot's 160 heart almost brast for sorrow, and Sir Launcelot threw his arms abroad, and said: "Alas! who may trust this world." And then he kneeled down on his knee and prayed the Bishop to shrive him and assoil him. And then he besought the Bishop that he might be his brother. Then the Bishop said: "I will gladly"; and there he put an habit upon Sir Launcelot, and there he served God day and night with prayers and fastings. Thus the great host abode at Dover. And then Sir Lionel took fifteen lords with him and rode to Lon- 170 don to seek Sir Launcelot; and there Sir Lionel was slain and many of his lords. Then Sir Bors de Ganis made the great host for to go home again; and Sir Bors, Sir Ector de Maris, Sir Blamore, Sir Bleoberis, with more other of Sir Launcelot's kin, took on them to ride all England overthwart and endlong, to seek Sir Launcelot. So Sir Bors by fortune rode so long till he came to the same chapel where Sir Launcelot was; and so Sir Bors heard a little bell knell, that rang to mass; and there he alit and heard mass. And when mass was 180 done, the Bishop, Sir Launcelot, and Sir Bedivere came to Sir Bors. And when Sir Bors saw Sir Launcelot in that manner clothing, then he prayed the Bishop that he might be in the same suit. And so there was an habit put upon him, and there he lived in prayers and fasting. And within half a year, there was come Sir Galihud, Sir Galihodin, Sir Blamore, Sir Bleoberis, Sir Villiars, Sir Clarras, and Sir Gahalantine. So all these seven noble knights there abode still. And when they saw Sir Launcelot had taken him to such perfection, 190 they had no list to depart, but took such an habit as he had. Thus they endured in great penance six year; and then Sir Launcelot took the habit of priesthood of the Bishop, and a twelvemonth he sang mass. And there was none of these other knights but they read in books, and holp for to sing mass, and rang bells, and

the Grail, does not have the privilege of seeing it, as do Percival, Bors, and Galahad. **143. gray or white,** anachronistic references to the Franciscans (Gray Friars) and Carmelites (White Friars). **196. holp,** helped.

Sir Thomas Malory 151

did bodily all manner of service. And so their horses went where they would, for they took no regard of no worldly riches. For when they saw Sir Launcelot endure such penance, in prayers and fastings, they took no force what pain they endured, for to see the noblest knight of the world take such abstinence that he waxed full lean. And thus upon a night there came a vision to Sir Launcelot, and charged him, in remission of his sins, to haste him unto Almesbury: "And by then thou
10 come there, thou shalt find Queen Guenever dead. And therefore take thy fellows with thee, and purvey them of an horse bier, and fetch thou the corpse of her, and bury her by her husband, the noble King Arthur." So this advision came to Sir Launcelot thrice in one night.

CHAPTER 11

How Sir Launcelot Went with His Seven Fellows to Almesbury, and Found There Queen Guenever Dead, Whom they Brought to Glastonbury

Then Sir Launcelot rose up or day, and told the hermit. "It were well done," said the hermit, "that ye made you ready, and that you disobey not the advision." Then Sir Launcelot took his seven fellows with him, and on foot they yede from Glastonbury to
20 Almesbury, the which is little more than thirty mile. And thither they came [within two days, for they were weak and feeble to go. And when Sir Launcelot was come] to Almesbury within the nunnery, Queen Guenever died but half an hour afore. And the ladies told Sir Launcelot that Queen Guenever told them all or she passed, that Sir Launcelot had been priest near a twelvemonth, "And hither he cometh as fast as he may to fetch my corpse; and beside my lord, King Arthur, he shall bury me. Wherefore," the
30 queen said in hearing of them all: "I beseech Almighty God that I may never have power to see Sir Launcelot with my worldly eyen"; "and thus," said all the ladies, "was ever her prayer these two days, till she was dead." Then Sir Launcelot saw her visage, but he wept not greatly, but sighed. And so he did all the observance of the service himself, both the dirge at night, and on the morn he sang mass. And there was ordained an horse bier; and so with an hundred torches ever burning about the corpse of the queen, and ever Sir
40 Launcelot with his seven fellows went about the horse bier, singing and reading many an holy orison and frankincense upon the corpse incensed. Thus Sir Launcelot and his seven fellows went on foot from Almesbury unto Glastonbury. And when they were come to the chapel and the hermitage, there she had a dirge, with great devotion. And on the morn the hermit that sometime was Bishop of Canterbury sang the mass of requiem with great devotion. And Sir Launcelot was

the first that offered, and then also his seven fellows. And then she was wrapped in cered cloth of Raines, 50 from the top to the toe, in thirtyfold; and after she was put in a web of lead, and then in a coffin of marble. And when she was put in the earth Sir Launcelot swooned, and lay long still, while the hermit came and awaked him, and said: "Ye be to blame, for ye displease God with such manner of sorrow making." "Truly," said Sir Launcelot, "I trust I do not displease God, for He knoweth mine intent. For my sorrow was not, nor is not, for any rejoicing of sin, but my sorrow may never have end. For when I remember of her 60 beauty, and of her noblesse, that was both with her king and with her, so when I saw his corpse and her corpse so lie together, truly mine heart would not serve to sustain my careful body. Also when I remember me how by my default, mine orgulity, and my pride, that they were both laid full low, that were peerless that ever was living of Christian people, wit you well," said Sir Launcelot, "this remembered, of their kindness and mine unkindness, sank so to mine heart that I might not sustain myself." So the French 70 book maketh mention.

CHAPTER 12

How Sir Launcelot Began to Sicken, and After Died, Whose Body Was Borne to Joyous Gard for to Be Buried

Then Sir Launcelot never after ate but little meat, ne drank, till he was dead. For then he sickened more and more, and dried, and dwined away. For the Bishop nor none of his fellows might not make him to eat, and little he drank, that he was waxen by a cubit shorter than he was, that the people could not know him. For evermore, day and night, he prayed, but sometime he slumbered a broken sleep; ever he was lying groveling on the tomb of King Arthur and Queen 80 Guenever. And there was no comfort that the Bishop, nor Sir Bors, nor none of his fellows, could make him, it availed not. So within six weeks after, Sir Launcelot fell sick, and lay in his bed; and then he sent for the Bishop that there was hermit, and all his true fellows. Then Sir Launcelot said with dreary steven: "Sir Bishop, I pray you give to me all my rites that longeth to a Christian man." "It shall not need you," said the hermit and all his fellows, "it is but heaviness of your blood, ye shall be well mended by the grace of God 90 tomorn." "My fair lords," said Sir Launcelot, "wit you well my careful body will into the earth, I have warning more than now I will say; therefore give me my rites." So when he was houseled and enelid, and had all that a Christian man ought to have, he prayed the Bishop that his fellows might bear his body to

86. **steven,** voice. 94. **houseled and enelid,** given the Eucharist (houseled) and extreme unction. 97. **Alnwick,** a town in Northumber- land. 98. **Bamborough,** a sea town in Northumberland. 116. **dretch- ing of swevens,** confusion of dreams. 188. **favor of makers,** poetic

Joyous Gard. Some men say it was Alnwick, and some men say it was Bamborough. "Howbeit," said Sir Launcelot, "me repenteth sore, but I made mine avow sometime, that in Joyous Gard I would be buried. And by cause of breaking of mine avow, I pray you all, lead me thither." Then there was weeping and wringing of hands among his fellows. So at a season of the night they all went to their beds, for they all lay in one chamber. And so after midnight, against day, the Bishop that was hermit, as he lay in his bed asleep, he fell upon a great laughter. And therewithal the fellowship awoke and came to the Bishop, and asked what he ailed. "Ah, Jesu mercy," said the Bishop, "why did ye awake me? I was never in all my life so merry and so well at ease." "Wherefore?" said Sir Bors. "Truly," said the Bishop, "here was Sir Launcelot with me with more angels than ever I saw men in one day. And I saw the angels heave up Sir Launcelot unto heaven, and the gates of heaven opened against him." "It is but dretching of swevens," said Sir Bors, "for I doubt not Sir Launcelot aileth nothing but good." "It may well be," said the Bishop; "go ye to his bed, and then shall ye prove the sooth." So when Sir Bors and his fellows came to his bed they found him stark dead, and he lay as he had smiled, and the sweetest savor about him that ever they felt. Then was there weeping and wringing of hands, and the greatest dole they made that ever made men. And on the morn the Bishop did his mass of requiem; and after, the Bishop and all the nine knights put Sir Launcelot in the same horse bier that Queen Guenever was laid in tofore that she was buried. And so the Bishop and they all together went with the body of Sir Launcelot daily, till they came to Joyous Gard; and ever they had an hundred torches burning about him. And so within fifteen days they came to Joyous Gard. And there they laid his corpse in the body of the quire, and sang and read many psalters and prayers over him and about him. And ever his visage was laid open and naked, that all folks might behold him. For such was the custom in those days, that all men of worship should so lie with open visage till that they were buried. And right thus as they were at their service, there came Sir Ector de Maris, that had seven years sought all England, Scotland, and Wales, seeking his brother, Sir Launcelot.

CHAPTER 13

How Sir Ector Found Sir Launcelot His Brother Dead, and How Constantine Reigned Next after Arthur, and of the End of This Book.

And when Sir Ector heard such noise and light in the quire of Joyous Gard, he alit and put his horse from him, and came into the quire, and there he saw men sing and weep. And all they knew Sir Ector, but he knew not them. Then went Sir Bors unto Sir Ector, and told him how there lay his brother, Sir Launcelot, dead; and then Sir Ector threw his shield, sword, and helm from him. And when he beheld Sir Launcelot's visage, he fell down in a swoon. And when he waked it were hard any tongue to tell the doleful complaints that he made for his brother. "Ah, Launcelot," he said, "thou were head of all Christian knights, and now I dare say," said Sir Ector, "thou Sir Launcelot, there thou liest, that thou were never matched of earthly knight's hand. And thou were the courteoust knight that ever bare shield. And thou were the truest friend to thy lover that ever bestrad horse. And thou were the truest lover of a sinful man that ever loved woman. And thou were the kindest man that ever struck with sword. And thou were the goodliest person that ever came among press of knights. And thou was the meekest man and the gentlest that ever ate in hall among ladies. And thou were the sternest knight to thy mortal foe that ever put spear in the rest." Then there was weeping and dolor out of measure. Thus they kept Sir Launcelot's corpse on loft fifteen days, and then they buried it with great devotion. And then at leisure they went all with the Bishop of Canterbury to his hermitage, and there they were together more than a month. Then Sir Constantine, that was Sir Cador's son of Cornwall, was chosen king of England. And he was a full noble knight, and worshipfully he ruled this realm. And then this King Constantine sent for the Bishop of Canterbury, for he heard say where he was. And so he was restored unto his Bishopric, and left that hermitage. And Sir Bedivere was there ever still hermit to his life's end. Then Sir Bors de Ganis, Sir Ector de Maris, Sir Gahalantine, Sir Galihud, Sir Galihodin, Sir Blamore, Sir Bleoberis, Sir Villiars le Valiant, Sir Clarras of Clermont, all these knights drew them to their countries. Howbeit King Constantine would have had them with him, but they would not abide in this realm. And there they all lived in their countries as holy men. And some English books make mention that they went never out of England after the death of Sir Launcelot, but that was but favor of makers. For the French book maketh mention, and is authorised, that Sir Bors, Sir Ector, Sir Blamore, and Sir Bleoberis went into the Holy Land thereas Jesu Christ was quick and dead, and anon as they had stablished their lands. For the book saith, so Sir Launcelot commanded them for to do, or ever he passed out of this world. And these four knights did many battles upon the miscreants or Turks. And there they died upon a Good Friday for God's sake.

Here is the end of the book of King Arthur, and of his noble knights of the Round Table, that when they

imagination.
Here, etc., the conventional "retraction," or epilogue, in which the medieval writer confessed his unworthiness and begged for the prayers of his readers.

were whole together there was ever an hundred and forty. And here is the end of the death of Arthur. I pray you all, gentlemen and gentlewomen that readeth this book of Arthur and his knights, from the beginning to the ending, pray for me while I am on live, that God send me good deliverance, and when I am dead, I pray you all pray for my soul. For this book was ended the ninth year of the reign of King Edward the Fourth, by Sir Thomas Maleore, knight, as Jesu help him for his great might, as he is the servant of Jesu both day and night.

Thus endeth this noble and joyous book entitled Le Morte Darthur. Notwithstanding it treateth of the birth, life, and acts of the said King Arthur, of his noble knights of the Round Table, their marvelous enquests and adventures, the achieving of the Sangreal, and in the end the dolorous death and departing out of this world of them all. Which book was reduced into English by Sir Thomas Malory, knight, as afore is said, and by me divided into twenty-one books, chaptered and imprinted, and finished in the abbey Westminster the last day of July the year of our Lord MCCCCLXXXV.

by me divided . . . books, i.e., by Caxton.

The Death of King Arthur—from a painting by Sir Edward Burne-Jones. Historical Pictures Service—Chicago.

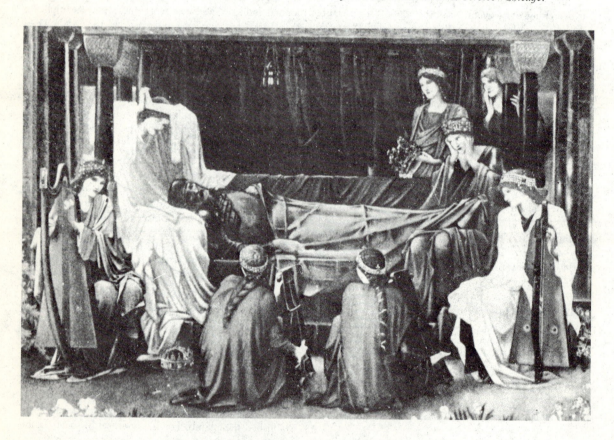

Henry Frederick, Prince of Wales (1594–1612) and Sir John Harington (1592–1614). The portrait was painted about 1603 by an unknown artist. Both of these young men were much interested in literature and patronized authors. John Donne wrote elegies on their untimely deaths. (Courtesy of the Metropolitan Museum of Art)

THE
BRAVE
NEW WORLD
AND AFTER

From the Accession of the Tudors to the

Restoration, 1485-1660

Chapter Two

A sixteenth-century printing office, from an engraving by Joannes Stradanus.

O, wonder!
How many goodly creatures are there here!
How beauteous mankind is! O brave new world,
That has such people in't!
                              —*The Tempest*, V, i.

A wistful pathos attends the passing of every great age, and this note is predominant in Sir Thomas Malory's *Morte Darthur*, the last significant literary record of feudalism and the Middle Ages in England. There is much of the ironic in the circumstance that in 1485, fifteen years after Malory had completed his account of the passing of Arthur, two events occurred which indicated clearly that the changes that Malory deplored had already come. One was the defeat at Bosworth Field of Richard III, which marked the end of the protracted struggles between the royal houses of Lancaster and York and the accession to the throne of "God's captain," Henry VII, the first of the great Tudors. The other was William Caxton's printing of Malory's tale of Arthur and the Round Table. Both of these events are significant of a changing civilization. The defeat of Richard ended the long period of castles and barons and armored knights; and his conqueror, Henry VII, a ruler more mercantile than military, was not the last king of the old world but the first king of the new. Yet even more important than the coming of the Tudors was the coming of the printing press, for if Henry VII stood at the doorway of a new world of exploration, travel, and middle-class expansion, the printing press began the democratization of learning and religion, which differentiates the sixteenth century so sharply from all earlier times.

The sixteenth century was an era of great events in politics, religion, and literature. The reign of Henry VIII (1509–1547) saw the Reformation and the beginnings of the English Renaissance; that of sickly Edward VI (1547–1553) the growth of Protestantism; that of Mary (1553–1558) reaction and persecution; that of Elizabeth (1558–1603) compromise among factions at home, and the climax of the conflict with Spain in the defeat of the Armada in 1588. On Elizabeth's death the dynasty of the strong-willed Tudors came to an end, and the crown passed to the Stuarts when James VI of Scotland became James I of England. His reign was marked by increased ecclesiastical, political, and social stress, and when he died in 1625 he left to his son Charles I an uneasy crown and the troubles that grew into the Civil War. The country was torn asunder; Charles, who believed firmly that

The Sovereign of the Seas, from an engraving by John Payne, 1637.

he was king by divine right, was brought to the block in 1649, the monarchy itself was abolished, and for a time England became a Commonwealth ruled by a military dictator who believed he had been called by the Almighty to be Protector. In such cataclysm the Middle Ages came to an end in England and the new world came into being. The full significance of this change can be appreciated by considering the contrast between the age of the Tudors and that of the Stuarts.

Tudor England: Widening Horizons

If the Tudor world were to be characterized by a single word, that word might be *expansion*. The known world had suddenly grown larger—geographically, politically, economically, and socially, as well as culturally. Old barriers were being swept away, and the age exhibits all the stresses and strains of an era of change. The most obvious phase of expansion was geographical. Henry VII came to the throne just seven years before the discovery of America, and it

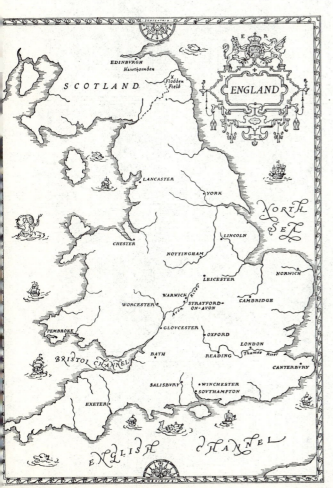

was with his encouragement that the English gave up their vain medieval claims to rights on the Continent and took to the sea. With Henry VII's commission, John and Sebastian Cabot pushed their ships out of the Bristol Channel "to seek out isles, countries, regions, and provinces to the west of England," as well as a passage to Asia. The century that followed was stirred by the discovery of mysterious lands far away, and by the adventures of the daring English sea dogs on uncharted seas. The motives of these undertakings, it must be admitted, were often greed for gain by exploitation and trade, as well as the more lofty spirit of adventure, but whatever the incentives, during Elizabeth's reign Britannia began to rule the waves and to lay the foundations for the far-flung boundaries of an empire. This she did not do without opposition, for on the seas of the Western World the English met the galleons of Spain, and it was not until the destruction of the Spanish Armada in 1588 that the way was cleared for English colonization of the New World. As the star of Spain began to decline, that of the island kingdom rose.

It is not surprising, therefore, that the sea should figure so persistently in all forms of Tudor literature: London was the center of literary England, and London is a seaport. Her waters were afloat with strange vessels laden with the riches of distant countries, and her taverns were crowded with sailors who brought back stirring tales

of the Cannibals that each other eat,
The Anthropophagi, and men whose heads
Do grow beneath their shoulders.
—*Othello*, I, iii.

Prose records of such explorations abound; the new drama is filled with voyages, shipwrecks, storms, and sea fights; and even the poetry of the period expresses the maritime temperament of the English. Elizabethan literature carries the tang of salt air and the exciting odors of tar, cordage, and strange foreign cargoes. If, indeed, it were not known that the English are seafarers, their literature would reveal the fact; and Elizabethan literature would show strikingly their response to the excitement of new seas and new ports.

New Social Conditions

The riches which flowed into England as a result of the widespread exploration and foreign trade helped to create a new social order, that of the wealthy middle class made up mainly of merchants. Although the court and the courtiers formed an essential part of the new English world, England was slowly becoming democratized, and the control was passing from baron to burgher. Evidence of this change appears in

The Brave New World and After 159

An Armorer

A Baker

A Lute-Maker

A Hatter

A Miller

Sixteenth-century occupations are depicted in these woodcuts by Jost Amman for Hans Sachs' Eigentliche Beschreibung Aller Stände, 1568.

The arts and crafts—Agriculture, Metal-Working, Commerce, Architecture, Hunting, Surgery, War. From Bartholomeo a Chesseneo, Catalogus Gloriae Mundi, 1529.

A Bell-Maker

Musicians

A Tudor school, from Queen Mary's Primer of Salisbury Use, Rouen, 1555.

the same elaborateness, the same diversity, and the same pilfering of forms and ideas from all Europe.

Not the least important of the new social trends of the sixteenth century is the new nationalism which sprang up in the reign of Henry VIII and reached its height in that of Elizabeth. Loyalty to the Queen, indeed, meant safety to the kingdom, for there were dangers without and within which threatened both her throne and her people. So it was that the English developed a national pride that expressed itself in chronicle writing, in attacks on the politics, religion, and social manners of European countries, especially Italy and Spain, and, after the defeat of the Spanish Armada in 1588, in a flood of historical plays in which English heroes were glorified. Strange it is, perhaps, that this feeling of national self-sufficiency did little to keep the English from borrowing social and literary ideas from the very countries which they feared and hated most; but their broad vision and rugged common sense refused to condemn the learning and art of those nations with whose political and religious concepts they could not agree.

The New Learning

However ostentatious, stiff-necked, and even ruthless the Tudor sovereigns may appear today, the greatest of them, Henry VIII and Elizabeth, encouraged learning and the arts. Henry's court has been described as "a nest of singing birds," and Henry himself wrote lyrics and composed songs; Elizabeth not only knew Greek and Latin, but also spoke Italian, French, and Spanish with facility. Their pride in their own accomplishments undeniably did much to set a fashion and to inspire the manifold experimentation in all forms of literary art—verse, prose, and drama— which was so characteristic of the sixteenth century.

The Tudor monarchs' love of learning, however, was itself a product of the brave new world of the Renaissance, or the rebirth of learning. The Renaissance had its beginning in Italy in the fifteenth century or earlier, and it came to England with Erasmus in the reign of the first of the Tudors, where it was nourished by a notable group of humanists, of whom Grocyn, More, Colet, and Fisher were the chief. The Renaissance humanist was concerned, as his name implies, with all subjects of human interest. Unlike the "scholar" of the Middle Ages he did not lose himself in speculative philosophy, nor did he follow the law of *magister dixit* that forced him to search for truth in an earlier authority. Thomas Henry Huxley has defined this change from scholasticism to humanism as the transition from the belief that blind faith is a virtue and skepticism a sin to the conviction that unquestioning acceptance is a sin and healthy skepticism a virtue. Thus the otherworldliness of the Middle Ages

the extent to which government offices were falling into the hands of such men as the innkeeper's grandson, Lord Burleigh, who became Elizabeth's most sage adviser. Evidence also appears in the growth of a new aristocracy created out of men knighted, not for defending their sovereign in battle but for lending him money in times of peace, as did the father of Sir Thomas Gresham, founder of the Royal Exchange. Again the literature of the period reflects the change.

The riches which came to Tudor England produced, quite naturally, a display of wealth in living conditions. Although the England of the Tudors and Stuarts had more than her share of poverty, the vagabondage, rags, and roguery were offset by the display of the city and the court. "Goldsmith's Row" in Cheapside set the fashion for frame edifices elaborately carved and decorated, and the interiors of these houses were richly ornamented with French and Flemish tapestries and filled with heavy furniture. The clothing of both men and women was never more ornate and varied— silks, velvets, broadcloths were cut and tailored in dozens of outlandish fashions. If the dress of the citizen was less elaborate than that of the courtier, it was no less substantial in quality. Indeed, the entire period is notable for the variety and the diversity of its social life; and in this respect and in the extent to which it borrowed from its neighbors across the Channel, the social life may be taken as the symbol of the literature of the period which is characterized by

gave way to a very vital concern with the visible world of sense and experience, and the scholars of the new world of thought came gradually to seek for truth in man and nature and not in the *ipse dixits* of those to whom truth had been divinely revealed. Inductive reasoning, therefore, came gradually to supplement and often to replace deductive, and men were as much stimulated by these excursions into new realms of the human mind as by the more concrete explorations into new countries. Patronized by the court and nourished by the great universities of Oxford and Cambridge, the new learning spread rapidly, and scholarship came to be regarded with universal respect and admiration. Creators of English literature drew heavily upon the treasures of Greek and Roman story and literary convention, and Seneca, Plautus, Terence, Vergil, Horace, and Ovid were more frequently copied than were Chaucer and Malory.

Perhaps the most important aspect of the new impulse for learning was, however, the universal quality which it soon acquired. Reading and writing were to be restricted no longer to learned clerks and an occasional nobleman; the very plowboy was to read his Bible with understanding, and even a wool-dealer's son from the country town of Stratford might aspire to write poetry and drama. So new schools were founded, and study spread widely. Such democratization of learning could not have been possible if the tools had not been available, and thus the printing press provided the vital means of disseminating the new learning. Just what a difference in the world of ideas Caxton's introduction of a device for the multiple production of books made, it is difficult to conceive. Before Caxton came, *all* English literature either existed orally or was recorded by hand on manuscripts made with careful

art at great expense and deposited for the most part in the libraries of the monasteries or the castles of noblemen. It is probable that before the first book was printed in England in 1477 not more than two per cent of the English people could either read or write. When Caxton began imitating manuscripts in great numbers, he unloosed what became within a century an avalanche of books, and he who would might read. The result was that while English literature of the Middle Ages was largely that of church and court, the literature after the beginning of the sixteenth century came to be much more universal in its spread, and burgher and craftsman wrote much more frequently and read more widely than it had been possible for them to do in the days of handmade books.

The New Theologies

The intellectual revolt from scholasticism which took the name of humanism had its spiritual counterpart in the rebellion against the Church of Rome, which is called the Reformation. In England there had been earlier rebellions, notably that under Wycliffe and the Lollards, which resulted in the first complete translation of the Bible into English. Wycliffe's reformation failed; the time was not ripe for it, and there could hardly have been any widespread reading of the Bible in English when so few could read and when each copy of the translation had to be made by hand. But what could not be done in the reign of Richard II was accomplished in that of Henry VIII. The impulse to revolt from Rome came, like the new learning, from the Continent, where Martin Luther faced, in 1521, the Diet of Worms and one year later

Wilmecote, an Elizabethan farmhouse.

translated the New Testament out of the original tongues into German. In England the fires of the Reformation were soon blazing; William Tyndale's translation of the New Testament, made at Worms, followed Luther's by only three years (1525); and More, Fisher, and others died for their refusal to subscribe to the Act of Supremacy that established Henry as the head of the Church of England.

The story of the relation of Church and State is matter for history; in a literary record it is the heroic epic of the Bible translations which must be told. Although it is probably not accurate to say with John Richard Green, the historian, that in the days of the Tudors "England became the people of a book, and that book was the Bible," it is true that the nine translations which stretch from Tyndale's New Testament in 1526 to the King James Version in 1611 are all significant, both in their relationship to religion and the state and in their influence on literature. The first complete printed Bible in English, that of Miles Coverdale in 1535, was dedicated to the greatest of the Tudor kings, Henry VIII, and the greatest of all the Bible translations, that of 1611, was dedicated to the first of the Stuarts, James I.

Under Queen Mary, England reverted for a time officially to Catholicism. But Mary's zeal defeated its own ends: the fires that burned the Protestant martyrs at Smithfield served only to strengthen the people's resistance. And Mary's reign was short. With the accession of Elizabeth the tables were turned. Mildly Protestant herself, Elizabeth valued unity in the church as a political, not a spiritual, asset; the extreme traditionalists now went into exile, and the English Protestants exiled under Mary returned home with new zeal from the Continent after contact with

more ruthless reformers. By steering a middle course, going slowly, and pretending at least that nothing final was being done, the government of Elizabeth sought to compromise with faction and faction. But to extremists of either the right or the left, compromise always appears an ignominious surrender, and the Elizabethan settlement satisfied neither the Catholics nor the more severe Protestants. The rebellion against Rome was over at the accession of Elizabeth, but within the Church of England there now arose another conflict, that of Puritanism versus episcopacy, which by the early seventeenth century had gained such momentum that when it turned political and joined forces with an anti-monarchical movement it brought about both civil war and social revolution.

The Molding of Tudor Literature

The current of literature in the Tudor and early Stuart periods flows with such strength and with such bursts, rushes, and spurts from its course that it can hardly be confined to the narrow channel of a brief interpretation. The most that can be done is to indicate some of its sources and something of its general direction.

One of the definite characteristics of Tudor literature is its non-professional quality. Although the invention of the printing press had made possible the unrestricted mechanical duplication of writing, many decades passed before men shook off the medieval conception of literary composition as the recording of ideas and emotions for the relatively few. So courtiers like Wyatt and Surrey (pp. 199-200) continued to write their elegant verses as Chaucer's Squire had done, with no thought that these would ever be read beyond the circle of their immediate acquaintances, and it was not until long after the death of these poets that an enterprising printer garnered the harvest of manuscript and printed it for a curious public. Similarly, although Francis Meres could write in 1598 of Shakespeare's "sugared sonnets among his private friends," not until more than ten years later were these set up in type for all London. Dramas, too, like poetry, usually found their way into print more through the enterprise of the printer than through the ambition of the playwright, and many were not published during the lifetime of their authors.

With the exception, therefore, of the ambitious Robert Greene and one or two others, few writers of the Tudor period attempted to make a living by having their work published. But if there were few who

These weavers' houses in Lavenham date from the sixteenth century.

Examples of Elizabethan costume, from Casper Rutz, Habitus Variarum Orbis Gentium, *1581.*

thought to gain a livelihood from the printer, there were many who hoped to secure position and riches from a patron. The Tudor period was, in fact, an age of patronage—almost feudalistic in the extent to which the man of ambition tried to climb into power by clinging to the doublet of his superior. Much writing that was not purely polemical or designed, like some of the prose romances, for a wide circle of readers, was directed to the individual to whom it was dedicated in the hope that from this patron the writer might receive some gift or preferment. Thus Shakespeare addressed his narrative poems, *Venus and Adonis* and *The Rape of Lucrece,* to the young Earl of Southampton, and Spenser his *Faerie Queene* (p. 219) to Queen Elizabeth herself. It is reasonable to suggest that much of the fulsome compliment of the sonnets, plays, and novels crept in because writers desired the preferment of a patron. For not only in poems like Spenser's *Faerie Queene* and romances like Sidney's *Arcadia,* but also in plays like Lyly's *Endimion,* Peele's *The Arraignment of Paris,* and Shakespeare's *A Midsummer-Night's Dream* and *Macbeth* appear extensively or incidentally those compliments to royalty and nobility that were characteristic of the period.

Patronage was sought, naturally enough, at court rather than in the city, and its very existence in Tudor poetry, prose, and drama discloses the keen interest of the court in literary art. Tudor literature may indeed be divided roughly into that of the courtier and that of the citizen, although such a division would at best be incomplete. It will do, however, as a guide to certain general literary characteristics.

The literature of the court was, on the whole, like the clothes of the courtier, more ornate than that of the city. The courtly author and those who wrote for a courtly audience reflected in their writing the interests, the fashions, even the language of the aristocracy. They indulged in much experimenting, in much borrowing from the Continent, and in much adorning of their lines with "conceits," those oddities and eccentricities of thought and expression that have since become almost exclusively associated with the metaphysical poets. The literature of the court also reflected its intellectual tastes; thus there appear in Tudor literature many adaptations of the Greek and Roman myths, much involved allegory, pastoral convention, medieval philosophy, and literary odds and ends adorning the lines as gems might adorn an Elizabethan bodice. It is doubtful, in fact, whether the literature of any other English period is as word-conscious or as full of pleasing artifice and invention as is that of the Tudor period.

Finally, as might be expected, the literature of the court was, like the courtly literature of the Middle Ages, essentially romantic. It had little to do with reality but presented a world either of the heroic past or of the ideal present, a world peopled with kings and queens, knights and ladies, and courtly gentlemen whose perfect manners furnished "mirrors" for their living counterparts. And just as the Tudors drew their manner of living and their fashions of dress from the Continent, particularly from Italy, so too they gathered much of their literary materials and methods from the same sources. Petrarch gave the model for the sonnet; Boccaccio, Bandello, and Cinthio, countless romantic tales for prose and drama; Ariosto and others, patterns for numerous plays; while Machiavelli supplied political ideas, and Castiglione, a code of conduct. Thus the literary and social channels between Italy and England were kept open in spite of England's religious defection and the numerous attacks by critics like Ascham upon the Italianate Englishmen.

It must not be supposed that the literature of the court did not also concern the citizen of London. He had, however, his own bourgeois tastes that demanded a literary reflection of his own life and interests, and this reflection he got through much prose and drama that contain in their texture more realism than romance and more native stuff than material borrowed from Italy. So Robert Greene and other hucksters of Elizabethan roguery gave him the vicarious thrill of contact with cozeners and vagabonds; Thomas Dekker glorified for him the London craftsman who became Lord Mayor; and in such plays as Thomas Heywood's *The Fair Maid of the West* and *The Four Prentices of London* he might enjoy the spectacle of substantial commoners elevated melodramatically to the stature of knights and adventurers. Such unnatural glorifications of barmaids and prentice lads could hardly go unchallenged by the courtly writers, and one of the most revealing depictions of such bourgeois heroics is the delightful burlesque of the grocer's boy errant in Beaumont and Fletcher's *The Knight of the Burning Pestle*, a satire with all the flavor of Cervantes' *Don Quixote* and Butler's ridicule of the Puritan in *Hudibras*.

The New Poetry, Prose, and Drama

The literature of Renaissance England is characterized by vigorous experiments, richness and fullness of utterance, and infinite variety. The overshadowing figure of William Shakespeare as a dramatist and the vigorous activities of his earlier and later contemporaries in the same literary type combine to obscure the fact that this period presents the fullest and freshest lyrical outburst in the history of English literature. From Wyatt and Surrey to Campion and Jonson runs a stream of song that is full, free, and spontaneous, and so generally diffused that lyrical expression seems almost universal, as though it were the natural language of the people. It may be partly for this reason that poetry did not seem to them an unnatural vehicle of expression in drama, and that some of the most inspired prose of the period, like that of the Bible translations, is so melodious and

rhythmic. It is an age in which "Music and sweet poetry agree."

Lyrics that were written to be sung often have to be detached from the matrix of some play or novel of which they form a part. It is astonishing, indeed, to see to what an extent the dramas are spangled with song; very few of Lyly's or Shakespeare's do not contain singing, and these two playwrights were only following a universal practice. Certain plays, like Shakespeare's *A Midsummer-Night's Dream* and *The Tempest*, had so large a proportion of songs that they are partly operatic. The Tudor English were a singing people; that man of them was ill-trained who could play upon no musical instrument and take no part in an air or a madrigal. And this was true in spite of the musical complexity of the madrigal (see p. 215). Borrowed from the Netherlands and Italy in the fifteenth century, the form became immensely popular in Elizabethan England. The madrigal was usually sung in five or six melodically independent voice parts, un-

A lady of the nobility, a woodcut by Jost Amman, from Gynaeceum, *or The Theater of Women, 1586.*

accompanied and woven into an intricate musical pattern. It is small wonder that in these songs the composers were more honored than the makers of the words.

But the lyric intended to be sung was only one variety of Tudor verse. Wyatt and Surrey introduced into England and later modified the Petrarchan sonnet, thus giving to Sidney, Spenser, Shakespeare, Daniel, and others an accepted stanza for love poems of a reflective type. Surrey experimented also with iambic pentameter blank verse, destined to become the medium for heroic plays. The pastoral mood appeared early and reached its height with Spenser (p. 217). There seems much that is artificial about the convention of classical shepherds and shepherdesses, but, even if this convention was borrowed from Theocritus, Vergil, and Mantuan and suggests in its English dress a translation rather than a native product, the pastoral poem still has the flavor of the outdoor life which the English genuinely loved. It is this love of nature, too, which created so many of the spring songs of the period. Of love songs, conventional and unconventional, there are, of course, many, and of convivial songs not a few. On the reflective side, philosophy and religion claim many poems; in these the depth of feeling is as sincere as the exuberance of the pagan verse. In addition there is heroic and romantic narrative poetry, like the *Faerie Queene*, elaborated and allegorized as it had never been before.

The same variety and spirit of experimentation that characterized Tudor lyrics appeared also in Tudor prose. History, philosophy, and criticism were issued side by side with travels, books of manners, rogue literature, and romances. The sources of inspiration were as varied as the types. The general interest in chronicle records of England's legendary and historical past was increased by the growth of the nationalistic spirit. Interest in the classical past produced Sir Thomas North's translation of Plutarch's *Lives of the Noble Grecians and Romans* (1579), which was much read and provided Shakespeare with source material for his Roman plays. Literary criticism and opinions on education, religion, philosophy, and social life and manners are many, though few possess the crisp, epigrammatic style and the worldly wisdom of the essays of Francis Bacon. Fiction, too, abounds—some of it courtly with its gallery of knights and damsels; some of it pastoral with nobles in the disguise of shepherds and shepherdesses; some of it realistic, celebrating the rascally exploits of rogues or the sterling virtues of good citizens. And in style the range is from the unpretentious narrations of the voyages collected by Richard Hakluyt, to the ornate, intricate, mannered prose of John Lyly's *Euphues*.

But the qualities of richness and variety, and the tendencies to experiment and to borrow that were so characteristic of the poetry and the prose of the Tudor period appeared even more strikingly in the drama. Here was a new art which developed rapidly from mere amateurishness and buffoonery into a great national utterance, a social institution, and an established profession. Between the accession of Elizabeth in 1558 and the closing of the theaters by the Puritan Parliament in 1642, the powerful dramatic current swept upon the stage every variety of material that England and the Continent could furnish. Tragedy, comedy, and history; romance, realism, and satire; classical, medieval, and contemporary stuff—all were poured into the mold of the drama. And the form varied almost as much as the content. To the classical critics the drama—particularly tragedy—was a type of poetry, and its language was the language of verse. To some it was purely a form of diversion; to others it existed solely for moral instruction. To Shakespeare it was the shadow of a shadow; in his plays he held the mirror up to nature and caught the bright reflection of moving men and women. To Ben Jonson it existed to correct the "humors" of society, and his comedies are satires flashing with his keen insights and judgments.

The Tudor Age in Retrospect

Thus, out of eager, enthusiastic ebullience the modern world of England came into being and attained, if not maturity, at least adolescence. The Reformation created the established Church of England, itself a compromise between traditional Catholicism and extreme Protestantism; the Puritan movement represents a rebellion against the conventions and restraints of that established church; the revival of learning brought to England through the Continent not only a contact with the literature of Greece and Rome, but also the impulse for new methods of thought. The literature of the age reflects its diversity, its youthfulness, its unrestraint. The whole era was an age in which young men saw visions and old men dreamed dreams.

Stuart England

If the England of the Tudors had the characteristics of a heroic age, by no stretch of the imagination could the same be said of the England of the Stuarts. Whatever was heroic in the reign of James I was carried over from the period of his predecessors. The life and literature of the Stuart period was still rich and polished; but the impulse to novel experiment had been exhausted, and the freshness and virility had departed. The first of the Stuart kings brought into English life another and a more straitened spirit, and the latter part of his rule and the whole of that of his son and successor, Charles I, show a marked decline

An English great hall from the late Tudor period, 1550–1600, from the Thorne European rooms in miniature, by courtesy of The Art Institute of Chicago.

from "the spacious times of great Elizabeth." Instead of an eager, enthusiastic *outlook* which characterized the Tudor period, in the seventeenth century the attitude was reversed. The nation no longer had the heart or the inclination for any but home affairs. Colonization continued, but the spirit which motivated it was not the Elizabethan spirit of adventure; it was rather dissatisfaction with conditions at home and a willingness to set up a new home, even in the wilderness.

The history of the English people has not, on the whole, been molded by nation-wide party dissensions culminating in armed strife. The war of the barons against John in the early thirteenth century was a revolt of the dominant class against the absolutism of their feudal overlord. The Wat Tyler rebellion in the late fourteenth century was a brief and pathetic outburst of social and economic underlings against arrogant masters. The Wars of the Roses in the fifteenth

Hampton Court Palace, built by Cardinal Wolsey in the early sixteenth cenutry.

These woodcuts showing early seventeenth-century dress accompany The Revolted Lover, *a ballad in the Roxburghe Collection, c. 1630.*

century were the result of a family quarrel for the throne. The English people have the traits of the northern races; they are conservative rather than experimental; cool rather than volatile; long-suffering rather than impatient. Their historical development has been, therefore, evolutionary rather than revolutionary; and only an extraordinarily deep-seated conviction of the justice of their action would lead them to draw the civil sword against their brothers.

The Rise of the Puritans

Because of these English characteristics the Puritan rebellion of the seventeenth century, dividing the nation in civil strife, setting class against class, creed against creed, and neighbor against neighbor, and stamping itself on the literature of the period, is the more significant and remarkable. What were the forces that split the country into Royalists and Puritans? To answer this question, it is necessary to look for the smoldering fire of dissension back in the days of the Tudor Reformation, nearly a hundred years before it burst into the flame of the Great Rebellion.

The English Reformation was a national phase of a European reaction against the Roman Catholic Church. But as is true of all reforms, there could be no general agreement as to the nature, extent, and details of the revolt. The milder rebels thought of the change as

involving only a modification of the older theology and church discipline and ritual. The radical reformers, on the other hand, wanted to cut loose entirely from Catholicism and would have nothing to do with her creeds, her priests, or her church rites. Some wanted their churches governed by the congregation rather than by royally appointed bishops. Hence, their ecclesiastical tenets were not far removed from the growing notion of a constitutional royalty in which the power of the king was dependent upon the will of the governed.

The difference between these groups has been made strikingly clear in Jonathan Swift's allegory, *A Tale of a Tub* (p. 495). In it, the Roman Catholics, the milder Protestant reformers, and the radical reformers are presented respectively in the figures of three brothers, Peter, Martin, and Jack. The three have inherited from their father (Christ) the seamless simple garment of religion pure and undefiled, but Peter, gradually obtaining the ascendancy over his brothers, adorns the cloak with the braid, decorations, and trappings that are the emblems of elaborate ritual. Martin (the Anglican Protestant) restores the garment by carefully removing from it what can be removed without tearing the cloth; but Jack (the radical Protestant) in a blind fury against the decorations destroys the cloak as he rips them off. Swift suggests that the name Jack covers a numerous group of root-and-branch reformers, who were nonconformists in their relation to the milder reformers, the Anglicans. In fact, there arose during the sixteenth and seventeenth centuries in the British Isles several more or less distinct sects of nonconformists, some of which took their names from their leaders, like the Brownists; from their form of government, like the Presbyterians; from some phase of their belief, like the Baptists; or even from the derision of their enemies, like the Quakers, who were accused of trembling in religious ecstasy.

It is difficult to say just when the name *Puritan* was first employed, but it was certainly in use in the early years of Elizabeth's reign. It was given, perhaps derisively, as a generic term to a growing number of men, mostly from the citizen and craftsman classes, who believed that the Anglicans had not gone far enough in their reformation and who were zealously eager to "purify" the church further by increasing the spiritual aspects—the inner life—and decreasing the ritualistic aspects—the outer observances.

One further and very important conception belonging to the period needs to be mentioned. State and church were closely related, and what concerned one concerned the other. The Anglican, or the established, church was the official church of England; the Puritans in general and the various sects of the nonconformists

in particular were therefore in a sense religious rebels. The adherents of the state church were made uneasy by the very existence of the nonconformist groups; and the dissenters, for their part, feared a state-supported tyranny of the established church. Laws to enforce conformity, often made under pressure from the crown and enforced by Anglican bishops, operated to repress the activities of the dissenting ministers and the freedom of belief of their supporters; it was such a law that clapped John Bunyan into the Bedford jail (see p. 368). In Elizabethan England the Puritans, whose strength was then, as well as later, in London, can hardly be said to have formed a political party, although a considerable number of extreme individuals did no doubt see visions of a state church that would lean to Puritanism rather than to Catholicism. Under the Stuarts, however, the Puritans were forced, step by step, into a political alignment against the party of the king. Even with this change of front a large number, including John Milton, never went further than to desire a total separation of church and state, that the clergy might preach to the people uncontrolled by government subventions and political pressures. In Scotland, where that stern reformer, John Knox, had dared to stand up before Queen Mary as did Elijah before Jezebel and denounce her for her sins, Presbyterianism had become a state religion; but when, during the long struggle between King and Parliament it seemed necessary to make Presbyterianism also the state religion of England, there were many among the English nonconformists who resisted the pressure until the Restoration ended the controversy and reestablished firmly the Anglican as the state church.

King, Parliament, and Church

Although the religious background of the Puritan rebellion is important, the more immediate causes of it lay not so much in the days of Queen Elizabeth as in those of James I. When, as James VI of Scotland, he came, in the year 1603, to the English throne as James I, he brought with him the theory of the "divine right of kings," which was contrary to the English conception of the limited power of the ruler. In feudal theory all kings held office by divine right, and in England the theory had many adherents, but no Tudor was unwise enough to insist upon a theory. Even Henry VIII refrained from a desired action once for the confessed reason that "the Commons will not allow it." But with the Stuarts it was different. "The King," declared the seventeenth-century Royalists, "is above the law by his absolute power." To such tyrannical assertions the Parliament declared that "the liberties, franchises, privileges, and jurisdictions of Parliament are the ancient and undoubted birthright and inheritance of the subjects of England." The King stood

Angling, an illustration from Richard Blome's The Gentleman's Recreation, *1686.*

for unquestioning devotion to the crown; the Puritan stood for the law based on established traditions.

In church matters James was equally stubborn. He had seen the Scotch Presbyterians overthrow the episcopacy and establish a church government which paralleled that of the state. In England he confounded Puritanism and Presbyterianism and lived in perpetual fear that the Puritans would establish a religious democracy. "No bishop, no king," was his motto. His method of preventing the catastrophe which he dreaded was to enforce conformity to the ritual of the Church of England. "I will make them conform," said the King after the Hampton Court Conference in 1604, "or I will harry them out of the land." The unrest which his attitude toward Parliament and Puritans caused at home was increased by his unwise foreign policy. His eagerness to form an alliance with Catholic Spain led to his attempt to negotiate a marriage between Prince Charles and the Spanish Infanta. It furthermore caused him to refuse aid to the Protestant Union of German Princes who were eager to go to the assistance of Frederick, king of Bohemia, James' son-in-law, under attack by the Catholic emperor Ferdinand II. The seeds of revolt, therefore, which bore bitter fruit in the Civil War, were sown deep in the soil of James I's absolutism and stubbornness.

Charles I inherited his father's full capacity for arrogant muddling. He was just as extravagant as James had been, and he heaped upon George Villiers, the upstart favorite whom his father had made Duke of Buckingham, riches, power, and distinction that raised the hatred of lord and commoner alike. Charles had his father's thirst for ruling without Parliament, and from 1629 to 1640 no Parliament was convened. To secure the money which his extravagances required, he followed various illegal methods, selling monopolies, imposing customs, forcing taxes and grants. In these tyrannies he had the able assistance of an unscrupulous minister, the Earl of Strafford, whose autocratic policies made him the most hated man in England. What Strafford did to uphold the tyranny and absolutism of Charles in matters of state, Archbishop Laud matched in matters of church. The leanings of Charles were unquestionably away from Protestantism, and he ardently supported Laud's restoration of the abandoned rituals of the Catholic Church. As Charles and Laud seemed to be drawing nearer to Rome, the Puritans saw the fruits of the Reformation lost with the restoration of the rituals and religious symbols which they had long regarded as idolatrous. During the period of no Parliament, from 1629 to 1640, more than twenty thousand Puritans, mostly from the middle classes, immigrated to New England to seek in the wilderness of distant America that freedom which their own country no longer afforded them. But these evidences of dissatisfaction, the protests of John Hampden and other patriots against illegal taxes, and the

resolute revolt of the Scotch Presbyterians against the imposition of the Prayer Book were not enough to open the King's eyes to the dangers of his policies or to do more than increase his determination to rule as an absolute monarch.

In 1638 the Scots promulgated a "National Covenant" against religious changes. Their armed rebellion against the introduction of the Prayer Book and their demand for the right of free assembly and for a Scotch parliament found the King without money to conduct a war against them. In 1640 he was forced, accordingly, to summon a Parliament, but he dissolved it within three weeks. The Parliament which succeeded it in the same year became famous as the "Long Parliament." Its leader was the vigorous patriot John Pym. Like all of the King's earlier Parliaments, it responded to his demands for money by insisting that no taxes would be imposed until the crying grievances of the country had been first redressed. It brought Strafford to trial as chief of the oppressors; and in spite of the King's efforts to save his minister, he was executed on May 12, 1641, on a Bill of Attainder. Strafford's death was followed by the abolition of another instrument of tyranny, the Star Chamber, a secret court for the crown, and by the drawing up in November 1641 of "The Grand Remonstrance," which listed the grievances against Charles and the services to England of the Long Parliament. The King's personal invasion of the House of Commons to arrest the five leaders, Pym, Hampden, Hollis, Strode, and Haselrig, failed because of their earlier withdrawal from their seats. It was a sign, however, of a complete breach, and 1642 found Cavaliers and Puritans engaged in armed conflict.

Cavalier and Puritan

The problem of defining the two factions in the Civil War cannot be resolved by the simple allocation of certain attitudes toward the monarchy: the Cavalier who stood for his king and the Puritan or Roundhead who stood for Parliament. This alignment arose not only from differences in political ideology but also from long-standing religious and social differences.

Puritanism has acquired a strong emotional connotation over the years; its manifestations in colonial New England and Victorian England have drawn attention to its distrust of the arts, its moral intolerance, and its dull utilitarian view of daily life. And in the seventeenth century, the slightest allusion to a Puritan would call up the more disagreeable and absurd aspects of the Puritan community: the dour countenances, the outlandish Hebrew names, the fondness for pietistic cant heavily laced with Biblical quotations, the affected simplicity of dress—all of which aroused the ridicule of many gifted literary exposers. But the more positive strains of Puritanism have left an indelible mark on Anglo-American culture. For example, the habit of tireless spiritual self-inventory established an earnest preoccupation with moral inquiry that had not previously existed or had never before taken root. The Puritans' encouragement of popular study of the Bible indirectly promoted a process of democratization that has continued to the present day. If a common man was capable of interpreting the Gospel by the lights of his own good judgment, without the aid of dogma or clergy, then he might also be able to apply good judgment and the reforming idealism of his religious convictions to the institutions of government under which he lived.

Like the Puritans, the Cavaliers also have been too often reduced to a contemptible stereotype. They were not all profligates and fops, and their Anglicanism was not always an unthinking subscription to a state religion but often a dynamic articulation of naturalized Roman Catholic belief that proved itself receptive, as Puritanism was not, to an open exchange of ideas. Similarly, in supporting Charles, the Cavaliers were not defending tyranny or just trying to save a bygone way of life; many of them wished to see the excesses of the crown checked within the traditional framework of government, and prudently foresaw the repercussions of such radical actions as that which in fact came to pass: regicide and a military coup. In their intelligent conservatism and their unique chivalric integrity, the Cavaliers were perhaps a more attractive group than their adversaries, but they probably did not have so far-reaching and positive effect on subsequent generations of English-speakers as the Puritans. Above all, it was these men—stubborn, colorless,

honest, and often foolish—who redefined not only the structure of the government but even the moral temper of the modern world.

For the first year of the war Charles was everywhere successful. The first skirmish at Edgehill discouraged the raw troops of the Parliamentary army, and Hampden had much difficulty in keeping them from deserting. He was soon afterwards killed at Chalgrove Field in a fight with the cavalry of Prince Rupert of Bavaria, the King's dashing nephew, who had crossed the seas to assist him. In the second year of the war Parliament bought the aid of the Scotch by taking oath to adopt the Presbyterian Covenant. At Marston Moor, July 2, 1644, the forces of Parliament defeated their enemies, largely because of the military brilliance of Oliver Cromwell, and in the following October at Newbury they were again successful.

Soon after Marston Moor, Oliver Cromwell became the acknowledged leader of the Parliamentary forces. His sharpness had brought him to see clearly the reasons for the King's early successes. The first Parliamentary generals, he said, were "afraid to conquer." Eager only to force the King to agree to certain proposed reforms, they never pushed their advantages to the limit. Furthermore, the officers of the Parliamentary armies had been chosen because of their social station or their membership in Parliament and not because of their ability; he would have no social or political distinctions made in the granting of commissions. Finally, the Parliamentary soldiers, drawn largely from the lower and middle classes, could not stand against the dashing horsemen of the Royalists. Cromwell's cure for this condition was to fire his soldiers with religious enthusiasm. He made of their cause a holy war; and the troops prayed before battle and charged to the solemn rhythm of hymns. The "New Model" army, thus born by the infusion of a zealot's spirit into the bodies of tapsters, grocers' clerks, and serving men, was terrifying and invincible. At Naseby on June 14, 1645, it swept the royal forces from the field and ended the war at a blow.

If Charles Stuart had been a man of his word, he might still have saved his throne and his life; but, while carrying on negotiations with both the Parliament and the army, he was plotting to renew the war and was seeking to stir up a Scottish invasion in his favor. It was a foolish and sordid move, for its disclosure convinced Cromwell that only the death of "that man of blood" would save the country. Cromwell defeated a Scotch army overwhelmingly at Preston on August 17, 1648, and the King was seized by

A cavalier: Sir Thomas Urquhart, from an engraving by George Glover, 1641.

a troop of Parliamentary horsemen. But Parliament still refused to press charges against the King; consequently Colonel Pride, an officer in Cromwell's army, purged the House of Commons by expelling about eighty members who favored Charles. "Pride's Purge" occurred on December 6, 1648. The "Rump Parliament" which remained then established a trial court of one hundred and fifty commissioners under John Bradshaw. At first the King refused to plead before this commission or to recognize its authority, and for a time the whole proceedings were at a stalemate. At last, frightened by a rising sympathy for the King, they nevertheless tried, convicted, and condemned him to death without permitting him to make a statement. On January 30, 1649, Charles I was executed as a "tyrant, a traitor, a murderer, and a public enemy."

For the first time in English history the cry of "The King is dead" was not followed by the cry of "Long live the King." The eleven years from 1649 to the restoration of the monarchy in 1660 were astonishing years, for they reveal as perhaps no similar short period in English history does the stability of the English people. The King was dead, and Cromwell was at the head of a powerful army that had brought about the monarch's trial and execution. The Rump Parliament was continued, and a Council of State

consisting of forty-one members created, on May 19, 1649, a "Commonwealth" or "Free State." Under this provisional government Cromwell made a conquest of Ireland, defeated Charles Stuart, son of the late King, at the head of a Scottish army at Worcester; conducted a naval war with Holland; and maintained English prestige on the Continent in numerous diplomatic negotiations. On demand of the army he dissolved the Rump Parliament on April 20, 1653, and in July of the same year the "Praise-God Barebone Parliament" met, taking its popular title from the absurd name of one of its members. By this body Cromwell was made Lord Protector, and the second phase of the Puritan regime came thus to be known as the Protectorate. With his dissolution in January 1655 of the

A lady of the court, an engraving by Wenceslaus Hollar, from Ornatus Muliebris Anglicanus, or The Several Habits of English Women, 1640.

A gentleman of fashion, from an engraving by A. Bosse, mid-seventeenth century.

Parliament of 1654, he became virtually dictator, although until the time of his death, September 3, 1658, he believed that he had been called by the Almighty to his task as Protector. It is not certain that on his deathbed he actually did name his son Richard to succeed him in this high office, but that assumption was made. With the passing of Oliver Cromwell, however, the Puritan power also passed. Richard was a weak man, a mere figurehead, and the people were clamoring for a restoration of the monarchy. Divisions in the army and adroit manipulations by General Monk, who brought his troops from Scotland to London and dictated the convening of a new Parliament with Royalist inclinations, resulted in an invitation to the exiled Stuart prince to return to England as Charles II. He landed at Dover on May 25, 1660, and proceeded to London amid scenes of wild enthusiasm. The brief Puritan interlude was over, and the government of England was once again "by King, Lords, and Commons." But Charles II, the first constitutional monarch, could have no illusions about being king by divine right; he knew he was king by right of Parliament.

Literary Reflections of the Conflict

Any national upheaval which absorbs the interests and activities of all men is certain to stamp itself upon the literary expressions of the times. In the struggle between King and Parliament few authors escaped the Royalist or Puritan label, and much of their writing reflects the spirit of the period if not their actual partisanship. Though not all poetry and prose of the time bear the mark of the struggle, and much, as in every period, is universal in art and in interest, the conflict of Royalist and Roundhead provided a broad background for the literature from 1625 to 1660. It is for this reason that a general knowledge of the causes and results of the Puritan rebellion is a necessary preliminary to an understanding of the literary history of the three and a half decades.

The Puritan period provides a link between the literature of the Elizabethan age and that of the Restoration. Deep into the reign of the first of the Stuarts ran the full, free current of Elizabethan literature. But before the end of his reign elements foreign to the spirit of the Elizabethan and akin to that of the Restoration became apparent; in the reign of Charles I these elements became stronger, until checked, temporarily at least, by Puritan control. A sketch of the literature may well begin, then, with some account of the changes in influence, mood, and form which made the literature of the middle and late seventeenth century different from that of the period preceding.

The most vigorous and important literary form of the late Elizabethan period was the drama. Its importance did not end with the death of Elizabeth in 1603, but continued into the next reign and beyond. Nevertheless, a change and a decline were soon apparent. In the days of Elizabeth various noblemen had sponsored companies of actors, and courtier and commoner alike had patronized the drama. As a consequence, Elizabethan plays offered something to please the tastes of everyone. With the coming of James, however, the companies were taken under royal patronage, actors became Grooms of the Chamber and mere appendages of the Revels Office at court, narrowed in function and interest. Thus drama became more definitely connected with the court than it had been in the time of Elizabeth, and the actors became Royalists by virtue of their positions. It was inevitable, therefore, that in a struggle between King and Parliament the actors should find themselves the target of the Puritans. Actually, Puritan opposition to the stage was already of long standing when Charles I came to the throne in 1625. But in the reign of Charles, Puritan opposition to Cavalier manners and interests extended to further attacks on the stage. On September 2, 1642, the drama was suppressed by act of Parliament.

The poetry of the Elizabethan age was inspired chiefly by Italian authors, but during the reign of the Stuarts, especially after the Restoration, the principal Continental influence was French. This shift is revealed distinctly in the loss of popularity of Petrarch and the growing popularity of the French lyrist Pierre de Ronsard (1525–1585) and his associates of La Pléiade, a group of young French poets who attempted to enrich literature through imitation of the Greek classics. Both Ben Jonson and John Donne, the most influential literary figures of the reigns of James and Charles, turned against the sonnet and introduced into English poetry elements quite different from the limp artificiality and conscious indirectness of much Elizabethan verse. Thus, poetry in the early Stuart period developed new, distinctive qualities.

Of all late Elizabethan poets Jonson and Donne were the best qualified by temperament and art to serve as links between the two periods and to start new impulses in the new age. Both grew up under Elizabethan influences but lived deep into the Stuart period. Both were literary rebels, strong-minded, independent, opposed to the domination of literary traditions and conventions. Both were vigorous, bold, industrious, productive. Neither feared opinion or novelty. These qualities gave their poetry a vitality which was impressive to the apprentice poets of the age of Charles. To the influences of their writing must be added that of their spoken words. Ben Jonson, like Samuel Johnson a century and a half later, was an oral autocrat; Donne was a powerful and popular preacher. Thus the effect of their personalities was added to that of their poems.

Quakers and Quakeresses in Assembly, from Henri Misson's Mémoires et Observations faites par un voyageur en Angleterre [in 1685 and after], 1698. The Society of Friends, derisively called Quakers because they were alleged to tremble with religious ecstasy, was founded by George Fox (1624-1691). The Quakers had no creed, no liturgy, no priesthood, and no sacraments, but emphasized instead meekness and an inward spiritual experience. Women were equal to men.

Finally, in poetry nothing makes clearer the differences between the Elizabethan period and the seventeenth century than a comparison of Spenser's *Faerie Queene* with Milton's *Paradise Lost.* Both are epics, but the former, with its affected archaism, its nostalgic medievalism, its romance and its allegory, is reminiscent of a Tudor building, like Hampton Court Palace, for instance, rambling, startling in its grandeur and in the infinite variety of its ornate detail. The latter, on the other hand, like a classical temple, is more massive, more unified, more formal, less grand but more magnificent.

The prose of the early seventeenth century is not, on the whole, of first importance. Much of it is controversial, as might be expected; much is historical and political. Some is philosophical or antiquarian or both. Almost without exception it is heavy and solid, lacking in brevity, simplicity, and ease of expression. When

Sir Francis Bacon died in 1626, England lost a prose writer much of whose work had been clear in plan and direct and compressed in expression. Five years before his death, *The Anatomy of Melancholy* by Robert Burton (1577–1640) had appeared, a monument of perceptive commentary on the subject of the melancholy "humor" that remains curious, entertaining, and provocative. Sir Thomas Browne's long treatises have now a fascinating quality that comes from both their quaintness and their common sense. Most of Milton's prose is topical and controversial, and little of it is genuinely artistic; his sentences are heavily Ciceronian, and he seems seldom to have paused for breath in thinking or writing. His prose is interesting primarily because it illuminates the character of a great literary figure who was also a political activist. It is the work of the so-called character writers, the elaborate and idiosyncratic studies of Bur-

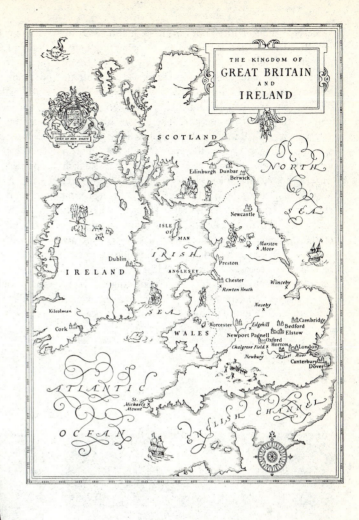

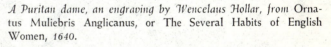

A Puritan dame, an engraving by Wenceslaus Hollar, from Ornatus Muliebris Anglicanus, or The Several Habits of English Women, 1640.

ton and Browne, the idyllic prose of Izaak Walton, and the vigorous allegories of John Bunyan that provide perhaps the most enduringly readable and best-seasoned prose of the period. With these exceptions and a few others, however, the century reveals no thoroughly artistic prose (comparable to that found in the Elizabethan period) before the great satirical and critical writings of John Dryden appeared after the Restoration.

Two Great Puritans

Only two Puritan authors, Milton and Bunyan, belong in the roster of great writers in English literature. John Dryden, Milton's younger contemporary and the greatest literary figure of the Restoration period, attributed to Homer "loftiness of mind," to Vergil "majesty," and to Milton both of these qualities. Of all English writers Milton is the nearest to being prophetic; his learning, his music, his literary skill were fused by a burning, if sometimes narrow, zeal. As a result he is always moral and lofty, always "by the vision splendid. . . on his way attended," often sublime, and even apocalyptic in expression. There is in his poetry little of the realistic and mundane; his flight is never low and common; he is the most bardic of English poets. He is one of that very small band of English spirits who belong, like Homer, Vergil, Dante, and Goethe, not alone to their own nation but to the world. He served his country, his faith, his party, but he transcended them all, and as he himself said, intending "no middle flight," soared above the narrow confines of his nation and his age. The limitations of the Puritan creeds and the political beliefs of the Long Parliament did not keep him from ranging freely in the higher atmosphere of the best that the world had felt, and thought, and said. His literary kinship is with the great writers of all times and places.

John Milton wrote the great Puritan epic; John Bunyan wrote the great Puritan allegory. Bunyan stood apart from his times much more than did Milton; he did not plunge, like Milton, into voluntary service to the Parliamentary cause. Yet he stands, as the greatest prose writer of the period, by the side of Milton, who was the greatest poet. If he had been simply a skillful expositor of Puritan theology, he could have had no secure place in English literature. But such theological doctrines as conviction of sin and salvation through grace he clothes with a narrative form as rugged and moving as appears anywhere in English literature. Bunyan's stories are more than Puritan allegories; they exist in their own narrative right. Bunyan was unlearned save for his deep acquaintance with the Bible, and his prose, unlike Milton's, is therefore not choked with classical constructions and with erudition. He is thoroughly English, and his stories are native, realistic, simple, and rugged. Like Milton he lived in visions; unlike Milton he expressed his visions in mundane terms. Milton was a grand visionary, Bunyan a simple

Satan Calling His Legions. These illustrations by William Blake for Milton's Paradise Lost *are reproduced from the original water colors by permission of the Henry E. Huntington Library and Art Gallery.*

Satan Comes to the Gates of Hell.

one. The Puritan epic and the Puritan allegory are poles apart; they are alike, however, in their high purpose; and against the witty and saucy satires directed against Puritanism in the Restoration period they stand out like granite rocks.

The Puritan Period in Retrospect

Probably in no other period in English history were the political and social changes so varied and so rapid as in the Puritan period. Moved by a firm and unchanging purpose that had its basis not only in a deep, if sometimes narrow, religious faith, but also in a profound sense of righteousness, duty, and justice, the Puritans moved, as Macaulay said, with an unwavering and invincible step until they had trodden down their enemies and established themselves in state and church. But the same uncompromising qualities that won for them a victory over their foes brought about their political downfall. Even before the death of their

stern leader, the reaction against their ways of thought, of life, and of government had set in; and Charles II, the gay, the witty, and the irresponsible son of the king whom they had brought to the bar of justice, returned to an England that cheered for him with as much enthusiasm as, a few brief years before, it had cheered for the Lord Protector.

The return of Charles brought back the traditional English zest for living which had been eclipsed temporarily by Puritan seriousness. It also revived in English literature certain influences which had already been evident before the interregnum. Of these, three are outstanding—the influence of the French, the tendency toward neo-classicism, and the spirit of satire. The period of the Tudors was the period of Italian influence. With James I there was a shift of interest to France, and the marriage of Charles I to a French princess further strengthened England's connections with her nearest Continental neighbor. Thus was begun that relationship in the court, and in literature which reached its height in the reign of the king who returned

Satan Watches Adam and Eve.

Raphael Warns Adam and Eve.

to England from a long exile in his mother's native land. The spirit of neo-classicism had an English source in the influence of Ben Jonson, who developed a new interest in the external forms of Greek and Roman literature. Satire, finally, popular at the courts of James I and Charles I, reached its highest form in the decades following the Restoration, when French wit and the polish and sparkle of the court of an English king bred in France united to produce types of satirical writing that are not, on the whole, so much Anglo-Saxon as Gallic in spirit. The metrical vehicle of these shafts of wit and ridicule was the heroic couplet; and the heroic couplet had, if not its birth, certainly part

of its development, during the Puritan period in the poetry of Edmund Waller.

With the restoration of Charles, Puritanism as a political power died, and its enemies derided it in the sharpest and cleverest Restoration satires, such as Butler's *Hudibras*. As a spiritual force, however, uncompromising toward unrighteousness and injustice, it lived on in English life and literature, checking the excesses of society and of literary license in the reign of Charles II, emerging in the form of Methodism in the eighteenth century, and preaching down immorality and deliberate wrong in the days of the "good queen" Victoria.

Visiting a Prison, from an engraving by Abraham Bosse.

The Dance, from an engraving by Abraham Bosse.

TUDOR PROSE

In an age teeming with controversy of all kinds—social, political, economic, and ecclesiastical—sixteenth-century England reaped the first fruits of printing. Verse no longer predominated, prose tracts expressing every variety of thought came from the presses, and in addition to tracts, there was a considerable amount of imaginative literature as well. Although it is sometimes difficult to draw sharp lines, a subject analysis of English books printed before 1600 reveals that philosophy and religion occupied the minds of men most, then works of pure literature, with government and politics, science, sociology, and history following in order. Moreover, as the century advanced, there was a consciousness about style and the manner in which thought should be expressed that produced not only simple, unaffected prose, but also Ciceronianism and heavily Latinized writing, and such precious, enriched, ornamental, artificial efforts as euphuism, which for all its subtleties has an undeniable vivacity if taken in small doses. The selections which follow illustrate the principal varieties of prose style as well as changing subject matter.

SIR THOMAS MORE 1478-1535

One of the most striking figures at the threshold of the modern world, Sir Thomas More was brought up in the household of Cardinal Morton, Archbishop of Canterbury, and at Oxford sat at the feet of the Greek scholars Grocyn and Linacre. He became an intimate friend of Erasmus, the Dutch humanist who was teaching in England, and was regarded by his contemporaries as one of the most accomplished humanists. But in his home in Chelsea, London, he was no retired scholar. From his election to Parliament at twenty-six until a few years before his death he was the personal friend of Henry VIII and served his monarch on numerous foreign embassies and in varied offices including that of Lord Chancellor, in which he succeeded Cardinal Wolsey in 1529. He died a martyr to his conscience and his faith, for he remained always "the king's good servant, but God's first," and he refused to believe that there were no moral laws higher than those promulgated by Parliament and dictated by an absolute monarch. He went to the block in 1535 rather than subscribe to the Act of Supremacy, which made his temporal ruler head of the Church of England; and like an earlier Thomas, who was crushed between king and conscience and immortalized by his Church and by Geoffrey Chaucer, Sir Thomas More has been canonized as a defender of the faith.

More's most famous literary work is Utopia, written in Latin in 1516 and first translated into English in 1551 by Ralph Robinson, citizen of London. Although More's description of the ideal republic of Nowhere may be compared with Plato's Republic and similar works, Utopia is almost national in its allusions to English social, political, and religious conditions, and personal in criticism of them. In it More makes a noble attack on needless and ruthless warfare and on other social forces that he believed to be destructive, and expresses a religious toleration that he was far from putting into practice in his later uncompromising dealings with Tyndale and "the pestilent sect of Luther." In spite of John Ruskin's condemnation of Utopia as "an infinitely foolish book," it is generally prized by men of all faiths as a noble monument to its age and to an author who was characterized by a contemporary as "a man of singular virtue and of a clear, unspotted conscience." The name Utopian came to be the universal adjective applied to all conceptions of ideal commonwealths.

from UTOPIA

THE SECOND BOOK

Of their living and mutual conversation together

But now will I declare how the citizens use themselves one towards another, what familiar occupying and entertainment there is among the people, and what fashion they use in distributing every thing. First the city consisteth of families, the families most commonly be made of kindreds. For the women, when they be married at a lawful age, they go into their husbands' houses. But the male children with all the whole male offspring continue still in their own family and be governed of the eldest and ancientest father, unless he dote for age, for then the next to

10

him in age is put in his room. But to the intent the prescript number of the citizens should neither decrease, nor above measure increase, it is ordained that no family which in every city be six thousand in the whole, besides them of the country, shall at once have fewer children of the age of fourteen years or thereabout than ten, or more than sixteen, for of children under this age no number can be appointed. This measure or number is easily observed and kept, by putting them that in fuller families be above the number into families of smaller increase. But if chance be that in the whole city the store increase above the just number, therewith they fill up the lack of other cities. But if so be that the multitude throughout the whole island pass and exceed the due number, then they choose out of every city certain citizens, and build up a town under their own laws in the next land where the inhabitants have much waste and unoccupied ground, receiving also of the inhabitants to them, if they will join and dwell with them. They thus joining and dwelling together do easily agree in one fashion of living, and that to the great wealth of both the peoples. For they so bring the matter about by their laws, that the ground which before was neither good nor profitable for the one nor for the other, is now sufficient and fruitful enough for them both. But if the inhabitants of that land will not dwell with them to be ordered by their laws, then they drive them out of those bounds which they have limited, and appointed out for themselves. And if they resist and rebel, then they make war against them. For they count this the most just cause of war, when any people holdeth a piece of ground void and vacant, to no good nor profitable use, keeping other from the use and possession of it, which notwithstanding by the law of nature ought thereof to be nourished and relieved. If any chance do so much diminish the number of any of their cities, that it cannot be filled up again, without the diminishing of the just number of the other cities (which they say chanced but twice since the beginning of the land through a great pestilent plague) then they make up the number with citizens fetched out of their own foreign towns, for they had rather suffer their foreign towns to decay and perish, than any city of their own island to be diminished. But now again to the conversation of the citizens among themselves. The eldest (as I said) ruleth the family. The wives be ministers to their husbands, the children to their parents, and to be short the younger to their elders. Every city is divided into four equal parts. In the midst of every quarter there is a market-place of all manner of things. Thither the works of every family be brought into certain houses. And every kind of thing is laid up in several barns or storehouses. From hence the father of every family, or every householder fetcheth whatsoever he and his have need of, and carrieth it away with him without money, without exchange, without any gage, or pledge. For why should any thing be denied unto him? Seeing there is abundance of all things, and that it is not to be feared, lest any man will ask more than he needeth. For why should it be thought that that man would ask more than enough, which is sure never to lack? Certainly in all kinds of living creatures either fear of lack doth cause covetousness and ravin, or in man only pride, which counteth it a glorious thing to pass and excel other in the superfluous and vain ostentation of things. The which kind of vice among the Utopians can have no place. Next to the market-places that I spake of, stand meat-markets, whither be brought not only all sorts of herbs, and the fruits of trees, with bread, but also fish, and all manner of four-footed beasts, and wild fowl that be man's meat. But first the filthiness and ordure thereof is clean washed away in the running river without the city in places appointed meet for the same purpose. From thence the beasts be brought in killed, and clean washed by the hands of their bondmen. For they permit not their free citizens to accustom themselves to the killing of beasts, through the use whereof they think that clemency, the gentlest affection of our nature, doth by little and little decay and perish. Neither they suffer any thing that is filthy, loathsome, or uncleanly, to be brought into the city, lest the air by the stench thereof infected and corrupt, should cause pestilent diseases. Moreover every street hath certain great large halls set in equal distance one from another, every one known by a several name. In these halls dwell the syphogrants. And to every one of the same halls be appointed thirty families, on either side fifteen. The stewards of every hall at a certain hour come into the meat-markets, where they receive meat according to the number of their halls. But first and chiefly of all, respect is had to the sick, that be cured in the hospitals. For in the circuit of the city, a little without the walls, they have four hospitals, so big, so wide, so ample, and so large, that they may seem four little towns, which were devised of that bigness partly to the intent the sick, be they never so many in number, should not lie too throng or strait, and therefore uneasily and incommodiously, and partly that they which were taken and holden with contagious diseases, such as be wont by infection to creep from one to another, might be laid apart far from the company of the residue. These hospitals be so well appointed, and with all things necessary to health so furnished, and moreover so diligent attendance through the continual presence of cunning physicians is given, that though no man be sent thither against his will, yet

Utopia. 66. **ravin,** ravenousness. 101. **throng or strait,** crowded or limited in space. 131. **of small honesty,** little to one's credit. 152. swathing clothes, swaddling clothes. 154. **let,** hindrance. 183. **wanton,** careless, unrestrained—not necessarily lewd. 199. **honest com-**

notwithstanding there is no sick person in all the city, that had not rather lie there than at home in his own house. When the steward of the sick hath received such meats as the physicians have prescribed, then the best is equally divided among the halls, according to the company of every one, saving that there is had a respect to the prince, the bishop, the tranibores, and to ambassadors and all strangers, if there be any, which be very few and seldom. But they also, when they be there, have certain houses appointed and prepared for them. To these halls at the set hours of dinner and supper cometh all the whole syphogranty or ward, warned by the noise of a brazen trumpet; except such as be sick in the hospitals, or else in their own houses. How be it no man is prohibited or forbid, after the halls be served, to fetch home meat out of the market to his own house, for they know that no man will do it without a cause reasonable. For though no man be prohibited to dine at home, yet no man doth it willingly, because it is counted a point of small honesty. And also it were a folly to take the pain to dress a bad dinner at home, when they may be welcome to good and fine fare so nigh hand at the hall. In this hall all vile service, all slavery, and drudgery, with all laborsome toil and business, is done by bondmen. But the women of every family by course have the office and charge of cookery for seething and dressing the meat, and ordering all things thereto belonging. They sit at three tables or more, according to the number of their company. The men sit upon the bench next the wall, and the women against them on the other side of the table, that if any sudden evil should chance to them, as many times happeneth to women with child, they may rise without trouble or disturbance of anybody, and go thence into the nursery. The nurses sit several alone with their young sucklings in a certain parlor appointed and deputed to the same purpose, never without fire and clean water, nor yet without cradles, that when they will they may lay down the young infants, and at their pleasure take them out of their swathing clothes, and hold them to the fire, and refresh them with play. Every mother is nurse to her own child, unless either death, or sickness be the let. When that chanceth, the wives of the syphogrants quickly provide a nurse. And that is not hard to be done. For they that can do it, do proffer themselves to no service so gladly as to that. Because that there this kind of pity is much praised, and the child that is nourished ever after taketh his nurse for his own natural mother. Also among the nurses sit all the children that be under the age of five years. All the other children of both kinds, as well boys as girls, that be under the age of marriage, do either serve at the tables, or else if they be too young thereto, yet they stand by with marvelous silence. That which is given to them from the table they eat, and other several dinner-time they have none. The syphogrant and his wife sit in the midst of the high table, forasmuch as that is counted the honorablest place, and because from thence all the whole company is in their sight. For that table standeth overthwart the over end of the hall. To them be joined two of the ancientest and eldest. For at every table they sit four at a mess. But if there be a church standing in that syphogranty or ward, then the priest and his wife sitteth with the syphogrant, as chief in the company. On both sides of them sit young men, and next unto them again old men. And thus throughout all the house equal of age be set together, and yet be mixed with unequal ages. This, they say, was ordained, to the intent that the sage gravity and reverence of the elders should keep the younger from wanton license of words and behavior. For as much as nothing can be so secretly spoken or done at the table, but either they that sit on the one side or on the other must needs perceive it. The dishes be not set down in order from the first place, but all the old men (whose places be marked with some special token to be known) be first served of their meat, and then the residue equally. The old men divide their dainties as they think best to the younger that sit on each side of them.

Thus the elders be not defrauded of their due honor, and nevertheless equal commodity cometh to every one. They begin every dinner and supper of reading something that pertaineth to good manners and virtue. But it is short, because no man shall be grieved therewith. Hereof the elders take occasion of honest communication, but neither sad nor unpleasant. How be it they do not spend all the whole dinner-time themselves with long and tedious talks: but they gladly hear also the young men, yea, and do purposely provoke them to talk, to the intent that they may have a proof of every man's wit and towardness, or disposition to virtue, which commonly in the liberty of feasting doth show and utter itself. Their dinners be very short, but their suppers be somewhat longer, because that after dinner followeth labor, after supper sleep and natural rest, which they think to be of more strength and efficacy to wholesome and healthful digestion. No supper is passed without music. Nor their banquets lack no conceits nor junkets. They burn sweet gums and spices for perfumes, and pleasant smells, and sprinkle about sweet ointments and waters, yea, they leave nothing undone that maketh for the cheering of the company. For they be much inclined to this opinion, to think no kind of pleasure forbidden, whereof cometh no harm. Thus therefore and after this sort they live together in the city, but in the country they that dwell alone far from any neighbors, do dine and sup at home in their own houses. For no family there

munication, creditable conversation. 213. conceits, decorations. junkets, delicate foods and desserts.

lacketh any kind of victuals, as from whom cometh all that the citizens eat and live by.

(Latin, 1516; English, 1551)

ROGER ASCHAM 1515-1568

The most notable contributions of Roger Ascham were to English education and English prose style. He was born in Yorkshire and educated at Cambridge, where his proficiency in the classical languages led to his being chosen orator of the University. In 1548 he was appointed tutor to the Princess Elizabeth, and on her accession to the throne ten years later he became attached to her court as Greek preceptor. In the interval he had toured Europe, tutored the unfortunate Lady Jane Grey, and—in spite of his Protestantism—acted as Latin Secretary to Queen Mary. He died two years before the appearance of The Schoolmaster *in 1570.*

Ascham's strong nationalism is evident in his attacks on Italian influences and his defense of English prose. His plan for a more humane and thorough system of education first appears in the Toxophilus (1545), *a treatise on archery in which Ascham adopts the Greek ideal of* mens sana in corpore sano *and advocates instruction in sports. He elaborated this sensible orientation in* The Schoolmaster, *in which he urges, for example, that patience and gentleness in the classroom be substituted for whippings. Although Ascham's sternly Protestant strain and his fervent defense of English culture may seem fanatical today, his philosophy of education was on the whole remarkably enlightened for the period as well as sound and practicable. Moreover, he expressed his opinions with vigor and clarity in a spare, straightforward staple of English prose that diverged significantly from the tendency of such contemporaries as* Lyly *to excessive ornamentation and Latinism.*

from THE SCHOOLMASTER

BOOK I

But I am afraid that over-many of our travelers into Italy do not eschew the way to Circe's Court, but go, and ride, and run, and fly thither; they make great haste to come to her; they make great suit to serve her; yea, I could point out some with my finger,

that never had gone out of England but only to serve Circe in Italy. Vanity and vice and any license to ill living in England was counted stale and rude unto them. And so, being mules and horses before they went, returned very swine and asses home again; yet 10 everywhere very foxes with subtle and busy heads; and where they may, very wolves with cruel malicious hearts. A marvelous monster, which, for filthiness of living, for dullness to learning himself, for wiliness in dealing with others, for malice in hurting without cause, should carry at once, in one body, the belly of a swine, the head of an ass, the brain of a fox, the womb of a wolf. If you think we judge amiss and write too sore against you, hear what the Italian saith of the Englishman, what the master reporteth of the scholar; 20 who uttereth plainly what is taught by him, and what is learned by you, saying "*Inglese Italianato è un diabolo incarnato,*" that is to say, you remain men in shape and fashion, but become devils in life and condition.

This is not the opinion of one for some private spite, but the judgment of all in a common proverb, which riseth of that learning and those manners which you gather in Italy: a good schoolhouse of wholesome doctrine, and worthy masters of commendable scholars, 30 where the master had rather defame himself for his teaching, than not shame his scholar for his learning. A good nature of the master, and fair conditions of the scholars. And now choose you, you Italian Englishmen, whether you will be angry with us for calling you monsters, or with the Italians for calling you devils, or else with your own selves that take so much pains and go so far to make yourselves both. If some yet do not well understand what is an Englishman Italianated, I will plainly tell him. He that by living and traveling 40 in Italy bringeth home into England out of Italy the religion, the learning, the policy, the experience, the manners of Italy. That is to say, for religion, papistry, or worse; for learning, less, commonly, than they carried out with them; for policy, a factious heart, a discoursing head, a mind to meddle in all men's matters; for experience, plenty of new mischiefs never known in England before; for manners, variety of vanities, and change of filthy living.

These be the enchantments of Circe, brought out of 50 Italy to mar men's manners in England; much by example of ill life, but more by precepts of fond books of late translated out of Italian into English, sold in every shop in London, commended by honest titles, the sooner to corrupt honest manners; dedicated overboldly to virtuous and honorable personages, the easier

The Schoolmaster. 2. **Circe's Court.** In Greek legend Circe was the daughter of Helios the sun god and lived on the island of Aeaea, off the coast of Italy. She was an enchantress who turned into animals all men who fell into her power (*Odyssey,* Book X). By analogy Ascham declares that Italy, like Circe, brutalizes Englishmen who go there. 22. "*Inglese Italianato, etc.*" "The Italianate Englishman is a devil incarnate." 52. **fond,** foolish. 60. **Paul's Cross.** An outdoor pulpit in the churchyard of St. Paul's Cathedral in London which was

much used for preaching. 65. **merry books of Italy,** the numerous romantic tales translated from the Italian (see p. 165), and probably a specific allusion to William Painter's *Palace of Pleasure,* which appeared at about the time he was writing *The Schoolmaster.* 66. **Louvain,** a city in the Brabant province of Belgium. The university here, founded in 1423 by John IV, was a great Catholic center celebrated for its magnificent library. 70. **prentice . . . journeyman.** The figure of speech is that of the craft guilds; in these a boy began his training as

to beguile simple and innocent wits. It is pity that those which have authority and charge to allow and disallow books to be printed, be no more circumspect herein than they are. Ten sermons at Paul's Cross do not so much good for moving men to true doctrine, as one of those books do harm with enticing men to ill living. Yea, I say farther, those books tend not so much to corrupt honest living, as they do to subvert true religion. More papists be made by your merry books of Italy than by your earnest books of Louvain. And because our great physicians do wink at the matter, and make no account of this sore, I, though not admitted one of their fellowship, yet having been many years a prentice to God's true religion, and trust to continue a poor journeyman therein all days of my life, for the duty I owe and love I bear both to true doctrine and honest living, though I have no authority to amend the sore myself, yet I will declare my good-will to discover the sore to others.

St. Paul saith that sects and ill opinions be the works of the flesh and fruits of sin. This is spoken no more truly for the doctrine than sensible for the reason. And why? For ill doings breed ill thinkings. And of corrupted manners spring perverted judgments. And how? There be in man two special things: man's will, man's mind. Where will inclineth to goodness, the mind is bent to truth. Where will is carried from goodness to vanity, the mind is soon drawn from truth to false opinion. And so the readiest way to entangle the mind with false doctrine is first to entice the will to wanton living. Therefore, when the busy and open papists abroad could not by their contentious books turn men in England fast enough from truth and right judgment in doctrine, then the subtle and secret papists at home procured bawdy books to be translated out of the Italian tongue, whereby over-many young wills and wits, allured to wantonness, do now boldly contemn all severe books that sound to honesty and godliness.

In our forefathers' time, when papistry, as a standing pool, covered and overflowed all England, few books were read in our tongue, saving certain books of chivalry, as they said, for pastime and pleasure, which, as some say, were made in monasteries by idle monks or wanton canons: as one, for example, *Morte Arthur*, the whole pleasure of which book standeth in two special points—in open manslaughter and bold bawdry. In which book those be counted the noblest knights that do kill most men without any quarrel, and commit foulest adulteries by subtlest shifts: as Sir Launcelot with the wife of King Arthur,

his master; Sir Tristram with the wife of King Mark, his uncle; Sir Lamerock with the wife of King Lot, that was his own aunt. This is good stuff for wise men to laugh at, or honest men to take pleasure at! Yet I know when God's Bible was banished the court, and *Morte Arthur* received into the prince's chamber. What toys the daily reading of such a book may work in the will of a young gentleman or a young maid that liveth wealthily and idly, wise men can judge and honest men do pity. And yet ten *Morte Arthurs* do not the tenth part so much harm as one of these books made in Italy and translated in England. They open not fond and common ways to vice, but such subtle, cunning, new, and diverse shifts to carry young wills to vanity and young wits to mischief, to teach old bawds new schoolpoints, as the simple head of an Englishman is not able to invent, nor never was heard of in England before, yea, when papistry overflowed all. Suffer these books to be read, and they shall soon displace all books of godly learning. For they, carrying the will to vanity and marring good manners, shall easily corrupt the mind with ill opinions and false judgment in doctrine: first, to think ill of all true religion, and at last to think nothing of God himself—one special point that is to be learned in Italy and Italian books. And that which is most to be lamented, and therefore more needful to be looked to, there be more of these ungracious books set out in print within these few months than have been seen in England many score years before. And because our Englishmen made Italians cannot hurt but certain persons and in certain places, therefore these Italian books are made English to bring mischief enough openly and boldly to all states, great and mean, young and old, everywhere.

And thus you see how will enticed to wantonness doth easily allure the mind to false opinions; and how corrupt manners in living breed false judgment in doctrine; how sin and fleshliness bring forth sects and heresies. And, therefore, suffer not vain books to breed vanity in men's wills, if you would have God's truth take root in men's minds.

That Italian that first invented the Italian proverb against our Englishmen Italianated, meant no more their vanity in living than their lewd opinion in religion. For in calling them devils, he carrieth them clean from God; and yet he carrieth them no farther than they willingly go themselves, that is, where they may freely say their minds, to the open contempt of God and all godliness, both in living and doctrine. And how? I will express how, not by a fable of

an apprentice or 'prentice and continued it as a journeyman who traveled from one master craftsman to another to learn their methods. 76. St. Paul. Ascham's original note gives the reference to a single verse (Galatians 5:19); but St. Paul devoted the rest of this chapter to contrasting the fruits of the flesh with those of the spirit. 94. severe, serious, solid, moral. 96. standing pool, stagnant pond—a familiar Elizabethan figure for corruption. 102. *Morte Arthur*, Malory's *Morte Darthur* (see p. 144). 111. Yet I know, etc., is probably an allusion

to Henry VIII, who long opposed translating the Bible into English. 114. toys, wild fancies, foolish ideas. 125. when papistry, etc., i.e., before the Reformation. 136. within these few months, cf. note 1. 65, p. 182. 152. lewd, ignorant. 158. fable, i.e., the fable of Circe; cf. note to 1. 2, p. 182.

Homer, nor by the philosophy of Plato, but by a plain truth of God's Word, sensibly uttered by David thus: "These men, *abominabiles facti in studiis suis*, think verily and sing gladly the verse before, *Dixit insipiens in corde suo, non est Deus*," that is to say, they giving themselves up to vanity, shaking off the motions of grace, driving from them the fear of God, and running headlong into all sin, first lustily contemn God, then scornfully mock his Word, and also spitefully hate and hurt all well-willers thereof. Then they have in more reverence the *Triumphs* of Petrarch than the *Genesis* of Moses. They make more account of Tully's *Offices* than St. Paul's *Epistles*, of a tale in Boccaccio than a story of the Bible. Then they count as fables the holy mysteries of Christian religion. They make Christ and his Gospel only serve civil policy. Then neither religion cometh amiss to them. In time they be promoters of both openly; in place, again, mockers of both privily, as I wrote once in a rude rime:

Now new, now old, now both, now neither,
To serve the world's course, they care not with whether.

For where they dare, in company where they like, they boldly laugh to scorn both protestant and papist. They care for no Scripture; they make no account of general councils; they contemn the consent of the church; they pass for no doctors; they mock the Pope; they rail on Luther; they allow neither side; they like none, but only themselves. The mark they shoot at, the end they look for, the heaven they desire, is only their own present pleasure and private profit; whereby they plainly declare of whose school, of what religion they be, that is, epicures in living and ἄθεοι in doctrine. This last word is no more unknown now to plain Englishmen than the person was unknown some time in England, until some Englishman took pains to fetch that devilish opinion out of Italy. These men thus Italianated abroad cannot abide our godly Italian church at home; they be not of that parish; they be not of that fellowship; they like not that preacher; they hear not his sermons, except sometimes for company they come thither to hear the Italian tongue naturally spoken, not to hear God's doctrine truly preached.

And yet these men in matters of divinity openly pretend a great knowledge, and have privately to themselves a very compendious understanding of all, which, nevertheless, they will utter when and where they list. And that is this: all the mysteries of Moses, the whole law and ceremonies, the Psalms and prophets, Christ and his Gospel, God and the devil, heaven and hell, faith, conscience, sin, death, and all they shortly wrap up, they quickly expound with this one half verse of Horace:
Credat Judaeus Apella.

Yet though in Italy they may freely be of no religion, as they are in England in very deed too, nevertheless, returning home into England, they must countenance the profession of the one or the other, however inwardly they laugh to scorn both. And though for their private matters they can follow, fawn, and flatter noble personages contrary to them in all respects, yet commonly they ally themselves with the worst papists, to whom they be wedded, and do well agree together in three proper opinions: in open contempt of God's Word; in a secret security of sin; and in a bloody desire to have all taken away by sword or burning that be not of their faction. They that do read with an indifferent judgment Pighius and Machiavelli, two indifferent patriarchs of these two religions, do know full well what I say true.

Ye see what manners and doctrine our Englishmen fetch out of Italy. For, finding no other there, they can bring no other hither. And, therefore, many godly and excellent learned Englishmen, not many years ago, did make a better choice, when open cruelty drove them out of this country, to place themselves there where Christ's doctrine, the fear of God, punishment of sin, and discipline of honesty were had in special regard.

I was once in Italy myself; but I thank God my abode there was but nine days. And yet I saw in that little time, in one city, more liberty to sin than ever I heard tell of in our noble city of London in nine years. I saw it was there as free to sin not only without all punishment, but also without any man's marking, as it is free in the city of London to choose without all blame whether a man lust to wear shoe or pantocle. And good cause why; for, being unlike in truth of religion, they must needs be unlike in honesty of living. For blessed be Christ, in our city of London commonly the commandments of God be more diligently taught, and the service of God more reverently used, and that daily in many private men's houses, than they be in Italy once a week in their common churches; where making ceremonies to delight the eye, and vain sounds to please the ear, do quite thrust out of the churches all service of God

2. **David**, Psalm 14:1 (repeated in Psalm 53:1): "The fool hath said in his heart, There is no God. They are corrupt, they have done abominable works, there is none that doeth good." In his Latin quotation Ascham has modified the second part of this verse: "They have been made abominable in *their studies*"; the quotation beginning *Dixit* is, however, translated exactly in the first sentence of the Psalm. 12. **Petrarch**, Italian poet and humanist (1304–1374); famous author of the sonnets to Laura, many of which appeared in his *Trionfi (Triumphs)*; it is probably these love poems that Ascham has in mind. 13. **Tully's**

Offices. Marcus Tullius Cicero (105–43 B.C.), often referred to in English literature as Tully, was a Roman statesman, orator, philosopher, and writer. The *De Officiis*, to which Ascham refers, is a treatise on moral philosophy. 14. **Boccaccio.** Giovanni Boccaccio (1313?–1375) was an Italian writer and humanist, author of the "merry" tales, *The Decameron*, some of which were translated by Painter for his *Palace of Pleasure*. 22. **whether**, which. 34. ἄθεοι, atheists. 39. **Italian . . . home**, a Protestant church in London which conducted services in Italian. 54. **Horace**, Roman satirical poet (65–8 B.C.). The quota-

100 in spirit and truth. Yea, the Lord Mayor of London, being but a civil officer, is commonly, for his time, more diligent in punishing sin, the bent enemy against God and good order, than all the bloody inquisitors in Italy be in seven years. For their care and charge is not to punish sin, not to amend manners, not to purge doctrine, but only to watch and oversee that Christ's true religion set no sure footing where the Pope hath any jurisdiction.

I learned, when I was at Venice, that there it is 110 counted good policy, when there be four or five brethren of one family, one only to marry, and all the rest to welter with as little shame in open lechery as swine do here in the common mire. Yea, there be as fair houses of religion, as great provision, as diligent officers to keep up this misorder, as Bridewell is and all the masters there to keep down misorder. And, therefore, if the Pope himself do not only grant pardons to further these wicked purposes abroad in Italy, but also (although this present Pope 120 in the beginning made some show of misliking thereof) assign both meed and merit to the maintenance of stews and brothel-houses at home in Rome, then let wise men think Italy a safe place for wholesome doctrine and godly manners, and a fit school for young gentlemen of England to be brought up in.

Our Italians bring home with them other faults from Italy, though not so great as this of religion, yet a great deal greater than many good men can well bear. For commonly they come home common con-130 temners of marriage and ready persuaders of all others to the same; not because they love virginity, nor yet because they hate pretty young virgins, but, being free in Italy to go whithersoever lust will carry them, they do not like that law and honesty should be such a bar to their like liberty at home in England. And yet they be the greatest makers of love, the daily dalliers, with such pleasant words, with such smiling and secret countenances, with such signs, tokens, wagers, purposed to be lost before 140 they were purposed to be made, with bargains of wearing colors, flowers, and herbs, to breed occasion of ofter meeting of him and her, and bolder talking of this and that, etc. And although I have seen some, innocent of all ill and staid in all honesty, that have used these things without all harm, without all suspicion of harm, yet these knacks were brought first into England by them that learned them before in Italy in Circe's Court; and how courtly courtesies soever they be counted now, yet, if the meaning and 150 manners of some that do use them were somewhat

amended, it were no great hurt neither to themselves nor to others.

Another property of these our English Italians is to be marvelous singular in all their matters; singular in knowledge, ignorant of nothing; so singular in wisdom (in their own opinion) as scarce they count the best counselor the prince hath comparable with them; common discoursers of all matters; busy searchers of most secret affairs; open flatterers of great men; privy mislikers of good men; fair speakers, 160 with smiling countenances and much courtesy openly to all men; ready backbiters, sore nippers, and spiteful reporters privily of good men. And being brought up in Italy in some free city, as all cities be there, where a man may freely discourse against what he will, against whom he lust, against any prince, against any government, yea, against God himself and his whole religion; where he must be either Guelph or Ghibelline, either French or Spanish, and always compelled to be of some party, of 170 some faction, he shall never be compelled to be of any religion; and if he meddle not over-much with Christ's true religion, he shall have free liberty to embrace all religions, and become, if he lust, at once, without any let or punishment, Jewish, Turkish, papish, and devilish.

A young gentleman thus bred up in this goodly school, to learn the next and ready way to sin, to have a busy head, a factious heart, a talkative tongue, fed with discoursing of factions, led to contemn God 180 and his religion, shall come home into England but very ill taught, either to be an honest man himself, a quiet subject to his prince, or willing to serve God under the obedience of true doctrine, or within the order of honest living.

I know none will be offended with this my general writing, but only such as find themselves guilty privately therein; who shall have good leave to be offended with me, until they begin to amend themselves. I touch not them that be good; and I 190 say too little of them that be not; and so, though not enough for their deserving, yet sufficiently for this time, and more else when if occasion so require. . . .

Learning teacheth more in one year, than experience in twenty; and learning teacheth safely, when experience maketh more miserable than wise. He hazardeth sore, that waxeth wise by experience. An unhappy master is he, that is made cunning by many shipwrecks; a miserable merchant, that is neither

tion, "Let the Jew Apella believe it," is from *Satires*, Bk. i., Sat. 5, l. 100; the phrase is used scornfully to cast doubt on knowledge by suggesting that its truth be attested by a wise man. Cf. the modern "Tell it to the marines." 69. **indifferent**, impartial. 70. **Pighius**, Albert (1490–1542), a Romanist who attacked Calvin for his doctrine concerning predestination and election. **Machiavelli**, Niccolò di Bernardo (1469–1527), Florentine statesman and political writer; author of *Il Principe (The Prince)*, a treatise advising rulers on the control of their subjects; this book had a wide vogue in Tudor England. 90.

pantocle, pantofle, slipper. 115. **Bridewell**, originally a palace in London, donated by Edward VI for a hospital, and later converted into a house of correction. 119. **present Pope**, Pius V (1566–1572). 121. **meed**, reward. 142. **ofter**, oftener. 146. **knacks**, knickknacks, trinkets. 148. **Circe's Court**; see note 1. 2, p. 180. 166. **lust**, please. 169. **Guelph or Ghibelline**, rival parties in medieval Italian politics, supporting respectively the popes and the emperors. 175. **let**, check, impediment, as in "without let or hindrance."

rich nor wise, but after some bankrupts. It is costly wisdom that is bought by experience. We know by experience itself, that it is a marvelous pain, to find out but a short way by long wandering. And surely, he that would prove wise by experience, he may be witty indeed, but even like a swift runner, that runneth fast out of the way, and upon the night, he knoweth not whither. And verily they be fewest in number, that be happy or wise by unlearned experi-10 ence. And look well upon the former life of those few, whether your example be old or young, who without learning have gathered by long experience a little wisdom, and some happiness; and when you do consider, what mischief they have committed, what dangers they have escaped (and yet twenty for one do perish in the adventure), then think well with yourself, whether ye would, that your own son should come to wisdom and happiness by the way of such experience, or no. . . .

20 Erasmus, the honor of learning of all our time, said wisely, "That experience is the common schoolhouse of fools, and ill men. Men of wit, and honesty be otherwise instructed. For there be, that keep them out of fire, and yet was never burned; that beware of water, and yet was never nigh drowning; that hate harlots, and was never at the stews; that abhor falsehood, and never brake promise themselves."

But will ye see a fit similitude of this adventured experience. A father that doth let loose his son to all ex-30 periences, is most like a fond hunter, that letteth slip a whelp to the whole herd; twenty to one, he shall fall upon a rascal, and let go the fair game. Men that hunt so be either ignorant persons, privy stealers, or nightwalkers.

Learning therefore, ye wise fathers, and good bringing up, and not blind and dangerous experience, is the next and readiest way that must lead your children, first to wisdom, and then to worthiness, if ever ye purpose they shall come there.

40 And to say all in short, though I lack authority to give counsel, yet I lack not good will to wish that the youth in England, specially gentlemen, and namely nobility, should be by good bringing up so grounded in judgment of learning, so founded in love of honesty, as when they should be called forth to the execution of great affairs, in service of their Prince and country, they might be able to use, and to order all experiences, were they good, were they bad, and that according to the square, rule, and line, of wisdom, learning, and 50 virtue.

And I do not mean by all this my talk that young gentlemen should always be poring on a book, and by using good studies, should lose honest pleasure, and haunt no good pastime; I mean nothing less. For it is well known that I both like and love, and have always, and do yet still use all exercises and pastimes, that befit for my nature and ability. And beside natural disposition, in judgment also I was never, either stoic in doctrine, or Anabaptist in religion to mislike a merry, pleasant, and playful nature, if no outrage be 60 committed against law, measure, and good order.

Therefore I would wish, that beside some good time fitly appointed, and constantly kept, to increase by reading the knowledge of the tongues, and learning; young gentlemen should use, and delight in all courtly exercises, and gentlemanlike pastimes. And good cause why: For the self same noble city of Athens, justly commended of me before, did wisely, and upon great consideration, appoint the Muses, Apollo, and Pallas, to be patrons of learning to their youth. For the Muses, 70 besides learning, were also ladies of dancing, mirth, and minstrelsy: Apollo was god of shooting, and author of cunning playing upon instruments; Pallas also was lady mistress in wars. Whereby was nothing else meant, but that learning should be always mingled with honest mirth, and comely exercises; and that war also should be governed by learning, and moderated by wisdom; as did well appear in those captains of Athens named by me before, and also in Scipio and Caesar, the two diamonds of Rome. And Pallas was no more feared in 80 wearing Aegida, than she was praised for choosing Olivam; whereby shineth the glory of learning, which thus was governor and mistress in the noble city of Athens, both of war and peace.

Therefore to ride comely, to run fair at the tilt, or ring; to play at all weapons, to shoot fair in bow, or surely in gun; to vault lustily, to run, to leap, to wrestle, to swim; to dance comely, to sing, and to play on instruments cunningly; to hawk, to hunt; to play at tennis, and all pastimes generally, which be joined 90 with labor, used in open place, and on the daylight, containing either some fit exercise for war, or some pleasant pastime for peace, be not only comely and decent, but also very necessary for a courtly gentleman to use.

(1568; 1570)

RICHARD HAKLUYT 1553-1616

Most of the rich records of Elizabethan exploration and adventure would have been lost in manuscript if

20. **Erasmus**, Dutch humanist (1466–1536), who was welcomed to England by More, Colet, Fisher, and other scholars and lectured at Cambridge on Greek. His best work is the *Encomium Moriae (The Praise of Folly)*, 1512. 30. **fond**, foolish. 31. **whelp**, an untrained puppy. 32. **rascal**, in hunting, a lean, ill-conditioned deer. 55. **well known, etc.** In his *Toxophilus*, written some twenty years earlier, Ascham had already advocated physical exercise as an element of edu-

cation. 59. **Anabaptist**, a sect founded in Zurich in 1523 which opposed the doctrines of infant baptism and union of church and state. 81. **Aegida**, the *aegis* or breastplate of Pallas Athena; equipped with serpents and the head of the Gorgon Medusa, it was the symbol of war. 82. **Olivam**, the olive, sacred to Athena and emblem of peace. 94. **a courtly gentleman.** It should be remembered that Ascham was concerned with the instruction of young gentlemen of high birth.

they had not been patriotically and painstakingly collected and published by an anthologist to whom students of the period will be forever indebted. Richard Hakluyt (pronounced Hăk'-loōt) was born about 1553 in London. As a boy he watched the ships come to port from far journeys, and his cousin Richard Hakluyt, a young lawyer, took the pains to give him early lessons in geography which fired his spirit with eagerness to know more about the wonders of the deep. He continued his studies at Oxford, ultimately lectured there on cosmography, and during five years' residence at the English embassy in Paris became increasingly eager to collect the scattered records of English maritime discovery. The accounts which he carefully assembled are alive with the Elizabethan spirit of adventure, they reflect the expanding world of the Tudors and contain the raw stuff from which many an English Odyssey might have been made. Hakluyt was not himself a traveler, and he made his ventures vicariously, but he was moved by the spirit of the age, and his purpose, as may be seen from the following dedicatory letter or preface to his Voyages, was patriotic and lofty. Drayton called him "industrious Hakluyt" (see p. 211, l. 68), and industrious he was, but he was also genuinely inspired, and records in the Voyages glow with much of his high regard for heroic men and noble deeds.

from THE PRINCIPAL NAVIGATIONS,
Voyages, Traffics, and Discoveries of the English Nation, Made by Sea or over Land, to the Remote and Farthest Distant Quarters of the Earth at Any Time within the Compass of These 1500 Years

THE EPISTLE DEDICATORY IN THE FIRST EDITION, 1589

To the Right Honorable Sir Francis Walsingham, Knight, Principal Secretary to Her Majesty, Chancellor of the Duchy of Lancaster, and One of Her Majesty's Most Honorable Privy Council.

Right Honorable: I do remember that being a youth, and one of her Majesty's scholars at Westminster, that fruitful nursery, it was my hap to visit the chamber of Mr. Richard Hakluyt my cousin, a 100 gentleman of the Middle Temple, well-known unto you, at a time when I found lying open upon his board certain books of cosmography, with an universal map. He, seeing me somewhat curious in the view thereof, began to instruct my ignorance, by showing me the division of the earth into three parts after the old account, and

then according to the latter, and better distribution, into more. He pointed with his wand to all the known seas, gulfs, bays, straits, capes, rivers, empires, kingdoms, dukedoms, and territories of each part, with declaration also of their special commodities, and particular wants, which, by the benefit of traffic, and intercourse of merchants, are plentifully supplied. From the map he brought me to the Bible and, turning to the 107th Psalm, directed me to the 23d and 24th verses, where I read that they which go down to the sea in ships and occupy by the great waters, they see the works of the Lord and his wonders in the deep, etc. Which words of the prophet, together with my cousin's discourse (things of high and rare delight to my young nature) took in me so deep an impression that I con- 120 stantly resolved, if ever I were preferred to the University, where better time and more convenient place might be ministered for these studies, I would by God's assistance prosecute that knowledge and kind of literature, the doors whereof (after a sort) were so happily opened before me.

According to which my resolution, when, not long after, I was removed to Christ Church in Oxford, my exercises of duty first performed, I fell to my intended course, and by degrees read over whatsoever printed 130 or written discoveries and voyages I found extant either in the Greek, Latin, Italian, Spanish, Portugal, French, or English languages, and in my public lectures was the first that produced and showed both the old imperfectly composed, and the new lately reformed, maps, globes, spheres, and other instruments of this art for demonstration in the common schools, to the singular pleasure and general contentment of my auditory. In continuance of time, and by reason principally of my insight in this study, I grew familiarly acquainted with 140 the chiefest captains at sea, the greatest merchants, and the best mariners of our nation. By which means having gotten somewhat more than common knowledge, I passed at length the narrow seas into France with Sir Edward Stafford, her Majesty's careful and discreet Ligier, where during my five years' abode with him in his dangerous and chargeable residence in her Highness's service, I both heard in speech and read in books other nations miraculously extolled for their discoveries and notable enterprises by sea, but the English, of all 150 others, for their sluggish security and continual neglect of the like attempts, especially in so long and happy a time of peace, either ignominiously reported or exceedingly condemned; which singular opportunity, if some other people our neighbors had been blessed with, their protestations are often and vehement, they would far otherwise have used. . . . Thus both hearing and

The Principal Navigations. **Sir Francis Walsingham** (1530?–1590), father of Frances Walsingham, wife of Sir Philip Sidney; he served in various offices under Queen Elizabeth. 97. **Westminster,** public school connected with Westminster Abbey. 100. **Middle Temple,** one of the London Inns of Court, or legal societies from which men are admitted to the bar. The Middle Temple derived its name from the Knights Templars, who owned the building. 105. **into three**

parts, i.e., into Europe, Asia, and Africa, before the discovery of America. 118. **the prophet,** King David, referred to as an Old Testament prophet. 133. **my public lectures.** Hakluyt was lecturer on cosmography at Oxford. 146. **Ligier,** a resident ambassador. 147. **chargeable,** responsible.

reading the obloquy of our nation, and finding few or none of our own men able to reply herein, and further, not seeing any man to have care to recommend to the world the industrious labors and painful travels of our countrymen—for stopping the mouths of the reproachers—myself being the last winter returned from France with the honorable the Lady Sheffield, for her passing good behavior highly esteemed in all the French court, determined, notwithstanding all difficulties, to under-
10 take the burden of that work wherein all others pretended either ignorance or lack of leisure or want of sufficient argument, whereas (to speak truly) the huge toil and the small profit to ensue were the chief causes of the refusal. I call the work a burden, in consideration that these voyages lay so dispersed, scattered, and hidden in several hucksters' hands that I now wonder at myself to see how I was able to endure the delays, curiosity, and backwardness of many from whom I was to receive my originals; so that I have just cause
20 to make that complaint of the maliciousness of divers in our time, which Pliny made of the men of his age: *At nos elaborata iis abscondere atque supprimere cupimus, et fraudare vitam etiam alienis bonis,* etc.

To harp no longer upon this string, and to speak a word of that just commendation which our nation do indeed deserve. It cannot be denied but as in all former ages they have been men full of activity, stirrers-abroad, and searchers of the remote parts of the world, so in this most famous and peerless government of her
30 most excellent Majesty, her subjects through the special assistance and blessing of God, in searching the most opposite corners and quarters of the world, and to speak plainly, in compassing the vast globe of the earth more than once, have excelled all the nations and people of the earth. For which of the kings of this land before her Majesty had their banners ever seen in the Caspian Sea? Which of them hath ever dealt with the Emperor of Persia, as her Majesty hath done, and obtained for her merchants large and
40 loving privileges? Who ever saw before this regiment an English Ligier in the stately porch of the Grand Signor at Constantinople? Who ever found English consuls and agents at Tripolis, in Syria, at Aleppo, at Babylon, at Balsara? And which is more, who ever heard of Englishmen at Goa before now? What English ships did heretofore ever anchor in the mighty river of Plate? pass and repass the unpassable (in former opinion) Strait of Magellan, range along the coast of Chili, Peru, and all the backside of Nova
50 Hispania, farther than any Christian ever passed, traverse the mighty breadth of the South Sea, land upon the Luzones in despite of the enemy, enter into alli-

An Astronomer-Geographer, a woodcut by Jost Amman for Hans Sachs' Eigentliche Beschreibung aller Stände (1568).

ance, amity, and traffic with the princes of the Moluccas, and the Isle of Java, double the famous Cape of Bona Speranza, arrive at the Isle of Santa Helena, and, last of all, return home most richly laden with the commodities of China, as the subjects of this now flourishing monarchy have done? . . .

Now whereas I have always noted your wisdom to have had a special care of the honor of her Majesty, the 60 good reputation of our country, and the advancing of navigation, the very walls of this our island, as the oracle is reported to have spoken of the sea forces of Athens; and whereas I acknowledge in all dutiful sort how honorably both by your letter and speech I have been animated in this and other my travels, I see myself bound to make presentment of this work to yourself, as the fruits of your own encouragements, and the manifestation both of my unfeigned service to my prince and country, and of my particular duty to your honor. 70 Which I have done with the less suspicion either of not satisfying the world or of not answering your own expectation, in that, according to your order, it hath passed the sight and partly also the censure of the

21. **Pliny,** the Elder, Roman naturalist (23–79 A.D.). 22. *At nos,* etc., but we are eager to destroy and suppress what they have wrought and to defraud life even of the glories of others. 41. **Grand Signor,** Sultan of Turkey. 44. **Balsara,** Bulsar, seaport in India. 45. **Goa,** port on the Malabar coast, India. 47. **Plate,** Rio de la Plata, estuary between Uruguay and Argentina. 49. **Nova Hispania,** New Spain, Mexico. 51. **South Sea,** old name for the southern Pacific Ocean.

52. **Luzones,** islands of the Malay Archipelago. 54. **Moluccas,** or Spice Islands, between Celebes and New Guinea in the Malay Archipelago. 55. **Cape of Bona Speranza,** Cape of Good Hope, south coast of Africa. **Isle of Santa Helena,** Saint Helena, island in the South Atlantic (Napoleon's place of exile). 56. **return home.** It will be noted that in this single sentence Hakluyt has described a circumnavigation of the earth. 62. **very walls,** ships; the allusion which

learned physician, Mr. Doctor James, a man many ways very notably qualified.

And thus beseeching God, the giver of all true honor and wisdom, to increase both these blessings in you, with continuance of health, strength, happiness, and whatsoever good thing else yourself can wish, I humbly take my leave. London the 17th of November.

Your Honor's most humble always to be commanded,
Richard Hakluyt.

(1589)

JOHN LYLY 1554?-1606

John Lyly was born in Kent in 1554(?). After having taken a degree at Oxford, he appeared at court in 1575, and with that rapidity of development which was characteristic of many of the young writers of the period, he made himself famous at twenty-five by writing Euphues: the Anatomy of Wit. The next year (1580) he issued the sequel, Euphues and his England. Lyly's first drama, Endimion (1591), was written for production by the boy choristers of Savoy Chapel and St. Paul's Cathedral. The Queen encouraged Lyly to aim at the Mastership of the Revels, but although she favored him for a time, and he was a member of the household of Burleigh, her Lord High Treasurer, he never attained to the high office which he sought. He died, an embittered man, in 1606, just three years after the monarch whom he had praised so fulsomely in his dramas.

Never an originator, either in romance or in drama, Lyly was in both forms a notable popularizer; and it was for this reason, no doubt, that the literary style which he most affected was called euphuistic after the hero of his romances, and that he, more than any other dramatist of his time, made comedy fashionable at the court. Gabriel Harvey, cynical contemporary of Lyly, was not altogether incorrect in writing: "Young Euphues but hatched the eggs that his elder friends laid." Lyly certainly did not invent the peculiarly elegant and affected style which has been named after Euphues. Ultimately it may be traced back to the formal balance of Cicero's sentences; its more immediate ancestor, however, was Antonio de Guevara's Dial of Princes, a Spanish book of manners and morals, written in 1529 and translated into English by the industrious Sir Thomas North in 1557. Lyly's prose style is of the court, courtly; it is decorative rather than clear, ornamented rather than direct. It is characterized not only by a careful balance of phrase and clause, but also by

an elaborate interweaving of alliteration and assonance, by antithesis of ideas, by plays on words, and by a most amazing use of similes and metaphors. Finally, it is filled with classical allusions and with quaint references to birds, beasts, and flowers, culled, for the most part, from the pages of Pliny's "unnatural natural history." Something also must be said about the content and mood of the prose romances, for the language is after all only the dress of the ideas. The word euphues is from a Greek word meaning graceful, well-bred; and this etymology indicates at once the author's objective. In writing his two romances Lyly was not concerned with the stories; his objective was to depict in his hero the perfect courtier, the model of good deportment and elegant manners.

As the author of six court comedies, of which Endimion (1591), Alexander and Campaspe (1584), and Midas (1592) are characteristic, Lyly contributed even more to the Elizabethan drama than he did to the development of Elizabethan prose. Indeed, since his dramas were written in prose, the two services united to a certain extent. In drama Lyly was a writer of court comedies, a purveyor to Her Majesty of refined dramatic entertainment. Before Lyly's time comedy was at best crude; its episodes were exaggerated, its characters usually taken from low life, its language rude. Lyly sublimated it. He drew his plots from classical and medieval story; he took his characters from high life; he wrote in the elegant prose that he had already made fashionable in Euphues. Respectable and well-dressed, his comic muse was meet for presentation at court. Lyly is the first writer of high comedy.

from EUPHUES: THE ANATOMY OF WIT

Very pleasant for all Gentlemen to read, and most necessary to remember: wherein are contained the delights that Wit followeth in his youth by the pleasantness of Love, and the happiness he reapeth in age by the perfectness of Wisdom

A COOLING CARD FOR PHILAUTUS AND ALL FOND LOVERS

Musing with myself, being idle, how I might be well employed, friend Philautus, I could find nothing either more fit to continue our friendship, or of greater force to dissolve our folly, than to write a remedy for that which many judge past cure, for love, Philautus, with the which I have been so tormented that I have lost my time, thou so troubled that thou hast forgot reason,

follows is to the prophecy of the Delphic oracle in 490 B.C. that the Athenians would be protected from a Persian attack by their wooden walls, i.e., their fleet (Herodotus, VII, 141).
　Euphues. Greek εὐφυής, well-bred, graceful, an allusion to the model courtliness of the hero. **A Cooling Card . . . Lovers.** In Euphues: the Anatomy of Wit the young Athenian hero visits Naples, where he meets and forms a friendship with the Italian Philautus.

Euphues replaces his friend in the affections of Lucilla but is in turn rejected by the fickle lady for one Curio. In departing for Greece he leaves with Philautus "a certain pamphlet which he terms a cooling card for Philautus, yet generally to be applied to all lovers." A card is a map or plan, more specifically a compass card (cf. Macbeth, I, iii, 17); Shakespeare also uses Lyly's phrase "cooling card" in 1 Henry VI, V, iii, 84.

both so mangled with repulse, inveigled by deceit, and almost murdered by disdain, that I can neither remember our miseries without grief, nor redress our mishaps without groans. How wantonly, yea, and how willingly have we abused our golden time and misspent our gotten treasure! How curious were we to please our lady, how careless to displease our Lord! How devout in serving our goddess, how desperate in forgetting our God! Ah, my Philautus, if the wasting of our money might not dehort us, yet the wounding of our minds should deter us; if reason might nothing persuade us to wisdom, yet shame should provoke us to wit. If Lucilla read this trifle, she will straight proclaim Euphues for a traitor, and, seeing me turn my tippet, will either shut me out for a wrangler, or cast me off for a wiredrawer; either convince me of malice in bewraying their sleights, or condemn me of mischief in arming young men against fleeting minions. And what then? Though Curio be as hot as a toast, yet Euphues is as cold as a clock; though he be a cock of the game, yet Euphues is content to be craven and cry creek; though Curio be old huddle, and twang "ipse, he," yet Euphues had rather shrink in the wetting than waste in the wearing. I know Curio to be steel to the back, standard-bearer in Venus's camp, sworn to the crew, true to the crown, knight marshal to Cupid, and heir apparent to his kingdom. But by that time that he hath eaten but one bushel of salt with Lucilla, he shall taste ten quarters of sorrow in his love; then shall he find for every pint of honey a gallon of gall, for every dram of pleasure an ounce of pain, for every inch of mirth an ell of moan. And yet, Philautus, if there be any man in despair to obtain his purpose, or so obstinate in his opinion that, having lost his freedom by folly, would also lose his life for love, let him repair hither, and he shall reap such profit as will either quench his flames or assuage his fury; either cause him to renounce his lady as most pernicious, or redeem his liberty as most precious. Come, therefore, to me, all ye lovers that have been deceived by fancy, the glass of pestilence, or deluded by women, the gate to perdition; be as earnest to seek a medicine as you were eager to run into a mischief; the earth bringeth forth as well endive to delight the people as hemlock to endanger the patient; as well the rose to distill as the nettle to sting; as well the bee to give honey as the spider to yield poison.

If my lewd life, gentlemen, have given you offense, let my good counsel make amends; if by my folly any be allured to lust, let them by my repentance be drawn to continency. Achilles's spear could as well heal as hurt;

the Scorpion, though he sting, yet he stints the pain; though the herb Nerius poison the sheep, yet is it a remedy to man against poison; though I have infected some by example, yet I hope I shall comfort many by repentance. Whatsoever I speak to men, the same also I speak to women; I mean not to run with the hare and hold with the hound, to carry fire in the one hand and water in the other, neither to flatter men as altogether faultless, neither to fall out with women as altogether guilty; for, as I am not minded to pick a thank with the one, so am I not determined to pick a quarrel with the other; if women be not perverse, they shall reap profit by remedy of pleasure. If Phyllis were now to take counsel, she would not be so foolish to hang herself, neither Dido so fond to die for Aeneas, neither Pasiphaë so monstrous to love a bull, nor Phedra so unnatural to be enamored of her son.

This is, therefore, to admonish all young imps and novices in love not to blow the coals of fancy with desire, but to quench them with disdain. When love tickleth thee, decline it, lest it stifle thee; rather fast than surfeit, rather starve than strive to exceed. Though the beginning of love bring delight, the end bringeth destruction. For, as the first draught of wine doth comfort the stomach, the second inflame the liver, the third fume into the head, so the first sip of love is pleasant, the second perilous, the third pestilent. If thou perceive thyself to be enticed with their wanton glances or allured with their wicked guiles, either enchanted with their beauty or enamored with their bravery, enter with thyself into this meditation: What shall I gain if I obtain my purpose? nay, rather, what shall I lose in winning my pleasure? If my lady yield to be my lover, is it not likely she will be another's leman? and if she be a modest matron, my labor is lost. This, therefore, remaineth; that either I must pine in cares or perish with curses.

If she be chaste, then is she coy; if light, then is she impudent; if a grave matron, who can woo her? if a lewd minion, who would wed her? if one of the Vestal Virgins, they have vowed virginity; if one of Venus's court, they have vowed dishonesty. If I love one that is fair, it will kindle jealousy; if one that is foul, it will convert me into frenzy. If fertile to bear children, my care is increased; if barren, my curse is augmented; if honest, I shall fear her death; if immodest, I shall be weary of her life.

To what end, then, shall I live in love, seeing always it is life more to be feared than death? for all my time wasted in sighs and worn in sobs, for all my treasure spent on jewels and spilled in jollity, what recompense

10. **dehort,** dissuade. 15. **turn my tippet,** to be a "turncoat." 16. **wiredrawer,** a stickler for detail, from the art of drawing wire fine. 21. **cry creek,** admit being beaten. 22. **though . . . he,** though Curio receive her embrace and sing out "I am *ipse*, the man"; cf. *As You Like It,* V, i, 48. 29. **quarters,** eight bushels to the quarter. 32. **ell,** in England forty-five inches. 51. **Achilles's spear . . . hurt.** In Greek legend Telephus, son of Hercules and Auge, was wounded by the spear of Achilles but cured by the same weapon. 64. **Phyllis,** the girl who commits suicide for unrequited love in the pastoral. 66 ff.

Dido, Pasiphaë, and **Phedra,** all women in Greek and Roman legend whose love is tragically misdirected. 69. **imps,** youths. 81. **bravery,** fine dress or display. 85. **leman,** mistress. 92. **Vestal Virgins,** in Roman religion the six virgin priestesses who attended the sacred fire of Vesta, goddess of the hearth. 93. **dishonesty,** unchaste living. 95. **foul,** ugly. 106. **mecock,** perhaps a contraction of meek cock, i.e., henpecked husband. 109. **fond,** foolish. 112. **kind,** thoroughbred. 113. **eiesse,** so printed in the first edition; there have been several unsatisfactory guesses as to its meaning, including *niece,* and *eyas*

shall I reap besides repentance? What other reward shall I have than reproach? What other solace than endless shame? But haply thou wilt say, "If I refuse their courtesy I shall be accounted a mecock, a milksop, taunted and retaunted with check and checkmate, flouted and reflouted with intolerable glee."

110 Alas, fond fool, art thou so pinned to their sleeves that thou regardest more their babble than thine own bliss, more their frumps than thine own welfare? Wilt thou resemble the kind spaniel, which, the more he is beaten the fonder he is, or the foolish eiesse, which will never away? Dost thou not know that women deem none valiant unless he be too venturous?—that they account one a dastard if he be not desperate, a pinchpenny if he be not prodigal; if silent, a sot, if full of words, a fool? Perversely do they always think of their lovers and talk of them scornfully, judging all

120 to be clowns which be no courtiers, and all to be pinglers, that be not coursers.

Seeing therefore the very blossom of love is sour, the bud cannot be sweet. In time prevent danger, lest untimely thou run into a thousand perils. Search the wound while it is green; too late cometh the salve when the sore festereth, and the medicine bringeth double care when the malady is past cure.

Beware of delays. What less than the grain of mustard seed?—in time, almost what thing is greater than

130 the stalk thereof? The slender twig groweth to a stately tree, and that which with the hand might easily have been pulled up will hardly with the ax be hewn down. The least spark, if it be not quenched, will burst into a flame; the least moth in time eateth the thickest cloth; and I have read that, in a short space, there was a town in Spain undermined with conies, in Thessaly with moles, with frogs in France, in Africa with flies. If these silly worms in tract of time overthrow so stately towns, how much more will love, which creepeth

140 secretly into the mind (as the rust doth into the iron and is not perceived), consume the body, yea, and confound the soul. Defer not from hour to day, from day to month, from month to year, and always remain in misery.

He that today is not willing will tomorrow be more willful. But, alas, it is no less common than lamentable to behold the tottering estate of lovers, who think by delays to prevent dangers, with oil to quench fire, with smoke to clear the eyesight. They flatter themselves

150 with a feinting farewell, deferring ever until tomorrow, when as their morrow doth always increase their sorrow. Let neither their amiable countenances, neither their painted protestations, neither their deceitful promises, allure thee to delays. Think this with thyself, that the sweet songs of Calypso were subtle snares to entice Ulysses; that the crab then catcheth the oyster when the sun shineth; that hyena, when she speaketh like a man, deviseth most mischief; that women when they be most pleasant pretend most treachery.

Follow Alexander, which, hearing the commendation 160 and singular comeliness of the wife of Darius, so courageously withstood the assaults of fancy that he would not so much as take a view of her beauty. Imitate Cyrus, a king endued with such continency that he loathed to look on the heavenly hue of Panthea; and, when Araspus told him that she excelled all mortal wights in amiable show, "By so much the more," said Cyrus, "I ought to abstain from her sight; for if I follow thy counsel in going to her, it may be I shall desire to continue with her, and by my light 170 affection neglect my serious affairs." Learn of Romulus to refrain from wine, be it never so delicate; of Agesilaus to despise costly apparel, be it never so curious; of Diogenes to detest women, be they never so comely. He that toucheth pitch shall be defiled; the sore eye infecteth the sound; the society with women breedeth security in the soul, and maketh all the senses senseless. Moreover, take this counsel as an article of thy creed, which I mean to follow as the chief argument of my faith, that idleness is the only 180 nurse and nourisher of sensual appetite, the sole maintenance of youthful affection, the first shaft that Cupid shooteth into the hot liver of a heedless lover. I would to God I were not able to find this for a truth by mine own trial, and I would the example of others' idleness had caused me rather to avoid that fault than experience of mine own folly. How dissolute have I been in striving against good counsel, how resolute in standing in mine own conceit, how forward to wickedness, how froward to wisdom, how wanton 190 with too much cockering, how wayward in hearing correction! Neither was I much unlike these abbey lubbers in my life (though far unlike them in belief) which labored till they were cold, ate till they sweat, and lay in bed till their bones ached. Hereof cometh it, gentlemen, that love creepeth into the mind of privy craft, and keepeth this hold by main courage.

The man being idle, the mind is apt to all uncleanness; the mind being void of exercise, the man is void of honesty. Doth not the rust fret the hardest iron if it 200 be not used? Doth not the moth eat the finest garment if it be not worn? Doth not moss grow on the smoothest stone if it be not stirred? Doth not impiety infect the wisest wit if it be given to idleness? Is not the

(nestling). 121. pinglers. A pingle is a piece of enclosed ground; perhaps, therefore, pinglers are plow horses, as contrasted with coursers. 136. conies, rabbits. 138. silly, simple. 155. Calypso, in Homer's Odyssey (Book V) a sea nymph who detained Ulysses for seven years in her island home. 159. pretend, intend. 160. Alexander . . . Darius. Alexander the Great (356–323 B.C.) was the Macedonian king who captured Darius, king of Persia, and his family. 164. Cyrus, Persian king, who captured Panthea, wife of Abradatas, king of Susa, but refused to visit her lest he might fall victim to her

charms. 171. Romulus, traditional founder of Rome, drank milk instead of wine, according to Pliny. 173. Agesilaus, a fourth-century king of Sparta, dressed simply. 174. Diogenes, the cynic, a Greek philosopher of the sixth century B.C., was notably austere. 175. He . . . defiled, from Ecclesiasticus 13:1; quoted by Falstaff in 1 Henry IV, II, iv, 455, in a passage which is a parody of Lyly's style. 191. cockering, pampering. 192. abbey lubbers, an allusion to idle monks and pensioners.

standing water sooner frozen than the running stream? Is not he that sitteth more subject to sleep than he that walketh? Doth not common experience make this common unto us, that the fattest ground bringeth forth nothing but weeds if it be not well tilled, that the sharpest wit inclineth only to wickedness if it be not exercised? Is it not true which Seneca reporteth, that as too much bending breaketh the bow, so too much remission spoileth the mind? Besides this, immoderate sleep, immodest play, unsatiable swilling of wine doth so weaken the senses and bewitch the soul that before we feel the motion of love, we are resolved into lust. Eschew idleness, my Philautus, so shalt thou easily unbend the bow and quench the brands of Cupid. Love gives place to labor; labor, and thou shalt never love. Cupid is a crafty child, following those at an inch that study pleasure, and flying those swiftly that take pains. Bend thy mind to the law, whereby thou mayest have understanding of old and ancient customs; defend thy clients; enrich thy coffers; and carry credit in thy country. If law seem loathsome unto thee, search the secrets of physic, whereby thou mayest know the hidden natures of herbs; whereby thou mayest gather profit to thy purse and pleasure to thy mind. What can be more exquisite in human affairs than for every fever, be it never so hot, for every palsy, be it never so cold, for every infection, be it never so strange, to give a remedy? The old verse standeth as yet in his old virtue: That Galen giveth goods, Justinian honors. If thou be so nice that thou canst no way brook the practice of physic, or so unwise that thou wilt not beat thy brains about the institutes of the law, confer all thy study, all thy time, all thy treasure to the attaining of the sacred and sincere knowledge of divinity; by this mayest thou bridle thine incontinency, rein thine affections, restrain thy lust. Here shalt thou behold, as it were in a glass, that all the glory of man is as the grass; that all things under heaven are but vain; that our life is but a shadow, a warfare, a pilgrimage, a vapor, a bubble, a blast; of such shortness that David saith it is but a span long; of such sharpness that Job noteth it replenished with all miseries; of such uncertainty that we are no sooner born but we are subject to death; the one foot no sooner on the ground but the other ready to slip into the grave. Here shalt thou find ease for thy burden of sin, comfort for the conscience pined with vanity, mercy for thine offenses by the martyrdom of thy sweet Saviour. By this thou shalt be able to instruct those that be weak, to confute those that be obstinate, to confound those that be erroneous, to confirm the faithful, to comfort the desperate, to cut off the presumptuous, to save thine own soul by thy sure

faith, and edify the hearts of many by thy sound doctrine. If this seem too strait a diet for thy straining disease, or too holy a profession for so hollow a person, then employ thyself to martial feats, to jousts, to tourneys, yea, to all torments, rather than to loiter in love and spend thy life in the laps of ladies; what more monstrous can there be than to see a young man abuse those gifts to his own shame which God hath given him for his own preferment? What greater infamy than to confer the sharp wit to the making of lewd sonnets, to the idolatrous worshiping of their ladies, to the vain delights of fancy, to all kind of vice, as it were against kind and course of nature? Is it not folly to show wit to women, which are neither able nor willing to receive fruit thereof? Does thou not know that the tree Silvacenda beareth no fruit in Pharos? That the Persian trees in Rhodes do only wax green but never bring forth apple?

That amomus and nardus will only grow in India, balsamum only in Syria; that in Rhodes no eagle will build her nest, no owl live in Crete, no wit spring in the will of women? Mortify, therefore, thy affections, and force not nature against nature to strive in vain. Go into the country, look to thy grounds, yoke thine oxen, follow thy plow, graft thy trees, behold thy cattle, and devise with thyself how the increase of them may increase thy profit. In autumn pull thine apples, in summer ply thy harvest, in the spring trim thy gardens, in the winter, thy woods, and thus, beginning to delight to be a good husband, thou shalt begin to detest to be in love with an idle housewife; when profit shall begin to fill thy purse with gold, then pleasure shall have no force to defile thy mind with love. For honest recreation after thy toil, use hunting or hawking; either rouse the deer, or unperch the pheasant; so shalt thou root out the remembrance of thy former love, and repent thee of thy foolish lust. And, although thy sweetheart bind thee by oath always to hold a candle at her shrine, and to offer thy devotion to thine own destruction, yet go, run, fly into the country; neither water thou thy plants, in that thou departest from thy pigsny, neither stand in a mammering whether it be best to depart or not; but by how much the more thou art unwilling to go, by so much the more hasten thy steps, neither feign for thyself any sleeveless excuse whereby thou mayest tarry. Neither let rain nor thunder, neither lightning nor tempest, stay thy journey; and reckon not with thyself how many miles thou hast gone—that showeth weariness; but how many thou hast to go—that proveth manliness. But foolish and frantic lovers will deem my precepts hard, and esteem my persuasions haggard, I must of force confess that it is a corrosive

7. **Seneca** (4 B.C.?–65 A.D.), Roman philosopher. 29. **Galen** (130–200?), Greek physician. **Justinian** (the First, 527–565), emperor of Constantinople and author of a legal code. 38. **as the grass**, Psalm 103:15. 41. **span long**, Psalm 90:10. 42. **Job noteth**, see Job, Chapters 3, 6, 7. 47. **pined**, tormented. 70. **Pharos**, an island in the Bay of Alexandria, once the site of a famous lighthouse. **Rhodes**, an island in the eastern Mediterranean, once the site of a statue of Apollo known as the Colossus of Rhodes. 83. **husband**, husbandman, farmer. 95. **pigsny**, pig's eye, a playful term of endearment. 96. **mammering**, wavering state of indecision. 106. **haggard**, untamed,

to the stomach of a lover, but a comfort to a godly liver to run through a thousand pikes to escape ten thousand perils. Sour potions bring sound health; sharp purgations make short diseases; and the medicine, the more bitter it is, the more better it is in working. To heal the body we try physic, search cunning, prove sorcery, venture through fire and water, leaving nothing unsought that may be gotten for money, be it never so much or procured by any means, be they never so unlawful. How much more ought we to hazard all things for the safeguard of mind, and quiet of conscience! And, certes, easier will the remedy be when the reason is espied; do you not know the nature of women, which is grounded only upon extremities?

Do they think any man to delight in them unless he dote on them? Any to be zealous except they be jealous? Any to be fervent in case he be not furious? If he be cleanly, then term they him proud; if mean in apparel, a sloven; if tall, a longis; if short, a dwarf; if bold, blunt; if shamefaced, a coward; insomuch as they have neither mean in their frumps, nor measure in their folly. But at the first the ox wieldeth not the yoke, nor the colt the snaffle, nor the lover good counsel; yet time causeth the one to bend his neck, the other to open his mouth, and should enforce the third to yield his right to reason. Lay before thine eyes the slights and deceits of thy lady, her snatching in jest and keeping in earnest, her perjury, her impiety, the countenance she showeth to thee of course, the love she beareth to others of zeal, her open malice, her dissembled mischief.

O, I would in repeating their vices thou couldst be as eloquent as in remembering them thou oughtst to be penitent. Be she never so comely, call her counterfeit; be she never so straight, think her crooked. And wrest all parts of her body to the worst, be she never so worthy. If she be well set, then call her a boss; if slender, a hazel twig; if nutbrown, as black as a coal; if well colored, a painted wall; if she be pleasant, then is she a wanton; if sullen, a clown; if honest, then is she coy; if impudent, a harlot.

Search every vein and sinew of their disposition; if she have no sight in descant, desire her to chant it; if no cunning to dance, request her to trip it; if no skill in music, proffer her the lute; if an ill gait, then walk with her; if rude in speech, talk with her; if she be jag-toothed, tell her some merry jest to make her laugh; if pink-eyed, some doleful history to cause her weep: in the one her grinning will show her deformed; in the other her whining, like a pig half roasted.

It is a world to see how commonly we are blinded with the collusions of women, and more enticed by their ornaments being artificial than their proportion being natural. I loathe almost to think on their ointments and apothecary drugs, the sleeking of their faces, and all their slibber sauces which bring queasiness to the stomach and disquiet to the mind.

Take from them their periwigs, their paintings, their jewels, their rolls, their bolsterings, and thou shalt soon perceive that a woman is the least part of herself. When they be once robbed of their robes, then will they appear so odious, so ugly, so monstrous, that thou wilt rather think them serpents than saints; and so like hags that thou wilt fear rather to be enchanted than enamored. Look in their closets, and there shalt thou find an apothecary's shop of sweet confections, a surgeon's box of sundry salves, a pedlar's pack of new fangles. Besides all this, their shadows, their spots, their lawns, their lyfkies, their ruffs, their rings, show them rather cardinals' courtesans than modest matrons, and more carnally affected than moved in conscience. If every one of these things severally be not of force to move thee, yet all of them jointly shall mortify thee.

Moreover, to make thee the more stronger to strive against these sirens, and more subtle to deceive these tame serpents, my counsel is that thou have more strings to thy bow than one; it is safe riding at two anchors; a fire divided in twain burneth slower; a fountain running into many rivers is of less force; the mind enamored on two women is less affected with desire and less infected with despair: one love expelleth another, and the remembrance of the latter quencheth the concupiscence of the first.

Yet, if thou be so weak, being bewitched with their wiles that thou hast neither will to eschew nor wit to avoid their company, if thou be either so wicked that thou wilt not, or so wedded that thou canst not abstain from their glances, yet at the least dissemble thy grief. If thou be as hot as the mount Etna, feign thyself as cold as the hill Caucasus; carry two faces in one hood; cover thy flaming fancy with feigned ashes; show thyself sound when thou art rotten; let thy hue be merry when thy heart is melancholy; bear a pleasant countenance with a pined conscience, a painted sheath with a leaden dagger. Thus, dissembling thy grief, thou mayest recure thy disease. Love creepeth in by stealth, and by stealth slideth away.

If she break promise with thee in the night, or absent herself in the day, seem thou careless, and then will she be careful; if thou languish, then will she be lavish of her honor, yea, and of the other strange beast, her honesty. Stand thou on thy pantofles, and she will veil bonnet. Lie thou aloof, and she will seize on the lure; if thou pass by her door and be called back, either seem deaf and not to hear, or desperate, and not to care. Fly the places, the parlors, the portals wherein thou hast been conversant with thy lady; yea, Philautus, shun the street where Lucilla doth dwell, lest the sight of her window renew the sum of thy sorrow.

Yet, although I would have thee precise in keeping these precepts, yet would I have thee to avoid solitariness—that breeds melancholy; melancholy, mad-
10 ness; madness, mischief and utter desolation. Have ever some faithful fere with whom thou mayest communicate thy counsels: some Pylades to encourage Orestes, some Damon to release Pythias, some Scipio to recure Laelius. Phyllis in wandering the woods hanged herself; Asiarchus, forsaking company, spoiled himself with his own bodkin; Biarus, a Roman, more wise than fortunate, being alone, destroyed himself with a potsherd. Beware solitariness. But, although I would have thee use company for thy
20 recreation, yet would I have thee always to leave the company of those that accompany thy lady; yea, if she have any jewel of thine in her custody, rather lose it than go for it, lest in seeking to recover a trifle thou renew thine old trouble. Be not curious to curl thy hair, nor careful to be neat in thine apparel; be not prodigal of thy gold nor precise in thy going; be not like the Englishman, which preferreth every strange fashion before the use of his country; be thou dissolute, lest thy lady think thee foolish in framing
30 thyself to every fashion for her sake. Believe not their oaths and solemn protestations. their exorcisms and conjurations, their tears which they have at commandment, their alluring looks, their treading on the toe, their unsavory toys.

Let everyone loathe his lady and be ashamed to be her servant. It is riches and ease that nourisheth affection; it is play, wine, and wantonness that feedeth a lover as fat as a fool; refrain from all such meats as shall provoke thine appetite to lust, and all such
40 means as may allure thy mind to folly. Take clear water for strong wine, brown bread for fine manchet, beef and brewis for quails and partridge; for ease, labor; for pleasure, pain; for surfeiting, hunger; for sleep, watching; for the fellowship of ladies, the company of philosophers. If thou say to me, "Physician, heal thyself," I answer that I am meetly well purged of that disease; and yet was I never more willing to cure myself than to comfort my friend. And, seeing the cause that made in me so cold a devotion should
50 make in thee also as frozen a desire, I hope thou wilt be as ready to provide a salve as thou wast hasty

in seeking a sore. And yet, Philautus, I would not that all women should take pepper in the nose, in that I have disclosed the legerdemains of a few, for well I know none will wince unless she be galled, neither any be offended unless she be guilty. Therefore I earnestly desire thee that thou show this cooling card to none except thou show also this my defense to them all. For, although I weigh nothing the ill will of light housewives, yet would I be loath 60 to lose the good will of honest matrons. Thus, being ready to go to Athens, and ready there to entertain thee whensoever thou shalt repair thither, I bid thee farewell, and fly women.

Thine ever,

Euphues.

(1579)

ROBERT GREENE 1560?-1592

Bohemian artists who live dissolutely, work furiously, and burn out early are always fascinating. Of such men Elizabethan England produced more than her share; of the brilliant group that made the last decades of Elizabeth's reign notable none was more bohemian than Robert Greene. Greene was characteristically Elizabethan in the contrasting elements of his character: he was a scholar and a vagabond, a sinner and somewhat of a Puritan, raw and unrestrained in experience but frequently charming and delicate in his interpretations of life. Of all the "University Wits" he had the most extensive university training for Oxford and Cambridge both conferred M. A. degrees upon him. His first university contact was with Cambridge, where he went at an early age from his birthplace in Norwich. After having taken his first degree, he traveled in Italy and Spain, where, according to his own confession, he "saw and practised such villainy as is abominable to declare." Returning to London, Greene spent the third and last decade of his short life in vagabonding and furious writing. He died as he had lived, in squalor and disrepute, with only strangers at his bedside.

Of all the miscellaneous writers of his time Greene was the most miscellaneous, and, unlike many of his contemporaries, he seems to have been equally gifted in prose, verse, and drama, for he earned for himself a definite place in each of these fields. By temperament and inclination he was a realist, but he wrote excellent romances, and in his dramas realism and romanticism are intermingled. Undoubtedly the best of Greene is to

11. **fere,** companion. 12. **Pylades . . . Orestes.** These and the ones following are classical examples of male friendships. 14. **Phyllis.** See p. 188, l. 64; she and the two following are examples of characters driven to self-destruction through loneliness; Lyly seems to have invented Asiarchus and Biarus. 16. **bodkin,** a small dagger. 29. **dissolute,** i.e., carelessly attired. 34. **toys,** trifles, tricks. 36. **servant,** lover. 41. **manchet,** fine white bread. 42. **brewis,** the broth from boiling salted beef. 53. **take pepper in the nose,** be offended. 55. **wince . . . galled.** Cf. *Hamlet,* III, ii, 251; *galled* means chafed by

rubbing. 59. **defense.** Following the *Cooling Card,* lest the author be "mistaken of purpose" or "misconstrued of malice," there is a defense of women which completely cancels and nullifies this tirade. 60. **light,** wanton, unchaste.

Discovery, disclosure, exposé. **Cosenage,** fraud. 67. **cony-catching,** cheating, swindling. A cony is a rabbit and hence a dupe, simpleton, easy victim. In some of the early woodcuts which illustrated these pamphlets the cony-catcher is appropriately represented as a weasel. 68. **setter,** thieves' cant for the rogue who hunts the victims and brings

be found in his semi-autobiographical tracts and in his "cony-catching" pamphlets, in which the repentant bohemian reveals the roguery of the companions of his unregenerate days, the rascals and vagabonds of the London thoroughfares. Greene's exposé is, however, flavored with the suggestion that he bought his knowledge of the seamy side of London life with his own sin.

from A NOTABLE DISCOVERY OF COSENAGE

THE ART OF CONY-CATCHING

There be requisite effectually to act the art of cony-catching three several parties: the setter, the verser, and the barnacle. The nature of the setter is to draw
70 any person familiarly to drink with him, which person they call the cony, and their method is according to the man they aim at; if a gentleman, merchant, or apprentice, the cony is the more easily caught, in that they are soon induced to play, and therefore I omit the circumstance which they use in catching of them. And for because the poor country farmer or yeoman is the mark which they most of all shoot at, who they know comes not empty to the term, I will discover the means they put in practice to bring in some
80 honest, simple and ignorant men to their purpose.

The cony-catchers, appareled like honest civil gentlemen, or good fellows, with a smooth face, as if butter would not melt in their mouths, after dinner when the clients are come from Westminster Hall and are at leisure to walk up and down Paul's, Fleet-street, Holborn, the Strand, and such common haunted places, where these cosening companions attend only to spy out a prey; who as soon as they see a plain country fellow well and cleanly appareled,
90 either in a coat of homespun russet, or of frieze, as the time requires, and a side pouch at his side, "There is a cony," saith one.

At that word out flies the setter, and overtaking the man, begins to salute him thus: "Sir, God save you, you are welcome to London, how doth all our good friends in the country, I hope they be all in health?"

The countryman seeing a man so courteous he knows not, half in a brown study at this strange salu-
100 tation, perhaps makes him this answer: "Sir, all our friends in the country are well, thanks be to God, but truly I know you not, you must pardon me."

"Why, sir," saith the setter, guessing by his tongue

what countryman he is, "are you not such a countryman?"

If he say yes, then he creeps upon him closely. If he say no, then straight the setter comes over him thus: "In good sooth, sir, I know you by your face and have been in your company before; I pray you, if without offence, let me crave your name, and the 110 place of your abode."

The simple man straight tells him where he dwells, his name, and who be his next neighbors, and what gentlemen dwell about him.

After he hath learned all of him, then he comes over his fallows kindly: "Sir, though I have been somewhat bold to be inquisitive of your name, yet hold me excused, for I took you for a friend of mine; but since by mistaking I have made you slack your business, we'll drink a quart of wine, or a pot of ale, 120 together."

If the fool be so ready as to go, then the cony is caught; but if he smack the setter, and smells a rat by his clawing, and will not drink with him, then away goes the setter, and discourseth to the verser the name of the man, the parish he dwells in, and what gentlemen are his near neighbors. With that away

This woodcut from the title page of A Notable Discovery of Cosenage *shows the cony holding the cards. On either side are stoops of wine.*

them in. The functions of the verser and the barnacle appear later. 78. **term,** the stated period, usually four times a year, during which the London law courts were in session; these drew many countrymen to the city. 84. **Westminster Hall,** the public hall in the west end of London in which the court held its sessions. 85. **Paul's,** St. Paul's Cathedral in the heart of London; its broad nave was a popular promenade. The other names are those of prominent London thoroughfares. 91. **time,** i.e., the season. *Frieze* was woolen cloth, *russet* of lighter weight texture, but both were homespun and so marked out the countryman from his city brother. **side pouch,** his pocketbook, worn attached to the belt. 103. **tongue,** dialect, by which the cheat could determine his victim's native shire. 116. **fallows,** plowed land; the figure suggests that having given his victim a preliminary plowing, the rogue cultivates him further. 119. **slack,** neglect. 123. **smack,** detect by smelling; cf. the phrase following. 125. **verser,** cardsharper—as appears later.

goes he, and crossing the man at some turning, meets him full in the face, and greets him thus:

"What, goodman Barton, how fare all our friends about you? You are well met, I have the wine for you, you are welcome to town."

The poor countryman, hearing himself named by a man he knows not, marvels, and answers that he knows him not, and craves pardon.

"Not me, goodman Barton, have you forgot me? 10 Why, I am such a man's kinsman, your neighbor not far off; how doth this or that good gentleman my friend? Good Lord, that I should be out of your remembrance! I have been at your house divers times."

"Indeed, sir," saith the farmer, "are you such a man's kinsman? Surely, sir, if you had not challenged acquaintance of me, I should never have known you. I have clean forgot you, but I know the good gentleman your cousin well, he is my very good neighbor."

20 "And for his sake," saith the verser, "we'll drink afore we part."

Haply the man thanks him, and to the wine or ale they go. Then ere they part, they make him a cony, and so ferret-claw him at cards that they leave him as bare of money as an ape of a tail.

Thus have the filthy fellows their subtle fetches to draw on poor men to fall into their cosening practises. Thus like consuming moths of the commonwealth they prey upon the ignorance of such plain 30 souls as measure all by their own honesty, not regarding either conscience or the fatal revenge that's threatened for such idle and licentious persons, but do employ all their wits to overthrow such as with their handy-thrift satisfy their hearty thirst, they preferring cosenage before labor, and choosing an idle practice before any honest form of good living.

Well, to the method again of taking up their conies. If the poor countryman smoke them still, and will not stoop unto either of their lures, then one, either 40 the verser, or the setter, or some of their crew, for there is a general fraternity betwixt them, steppeth before the cony as he goeth, and letteth drop twelve pence in the highway, that of force the cony must see it. The countryman, spying the shilling, maketh not dainty, for *quis nisi mentis inops oblatum respuit aurum*, but stoopeth very mannerly and taketh it up. Then one of the cony-catchers behind crieth half part, and so challengeth half of his finding. The countryman, content, offereth to change the money. 50 "Nay faith, friend," saith the verser, "'tis ill luck to keep found money; we'll go spend it in a pottle of wine"—or in a breakfast, dinner, or supper, as the time of day requires.

If the cony say he will not, then answers the verser,

"Spend my part." If still the cony refuse, he taketh half and away.

If they spy the countryman to be of a having and covetous mind, then have they a further policy to draw him on; another that knoweth the place of his abode meeteth him and saith, "Sir, well met, I have 60 run hastily to overtake you. I pray you, dwell you not in Darbyshire, in such a village?"

"Yes, marry, do I, friend," saith the cony.

Then replies the verser, "Truly, sir, I have a suit to you, I am going out of town, and must send a letter to the parson of your parish. You shall not refuse to do a stranger such a favor as to carry it him. Haply, as men may in time meet, it may lie in my lot to do you as good a turn; and for your pains I will give you twelve pence."   70

The poor cony in mere simplicity saith, "Sir, I'll do so much for you with all my heart; where is your letter?"

"I have it not, good sir, ready written, but may I entreat you to step into some tavern or alehouse? We'll drink the while, and I will write but a line or two."

At this the cony stoops, and for greediness of the money, and upon courtesy, goes with the setter into the tavern. As they walk, they meet the verser, and 80 then they all three go into the tavern together.

See, gentlemen, what great logicians these cony-catchers be, that have such rhetorical persuasions to induce the poor countryman to his confusion, and what variety of villainy they have to strip the poor farmer of his money.

Well, imagine the cony is in the tavern, then sits down the verser and saith to the setter, "What, sirra! Wilt thou give me a quart of wine, or shall I give thee one?" "We'll drink a pint," saith the setter, "and 90 play a game of cards for it, respecting more the sport than the loss." "Content," quoth the verser, "go call for a pair." And while he is gone to fetch them, he saith to the cony, "You shall see me fetch over my young master for a quart of wine finely. But this you must do for me; when I cut the cards, as I will not cut above five off, mark then, of all the greatest pack, which is undermost, and when I bid you call a card for me, name that, and you shall see we'll make him pay for a quart of wine straight."   100

"Truly," saith the cony, "I am no great player at cards, and I do not well understand your meaning."

"Why," saith he, "it is thus: I will play at mumchance, or decoy, that he shall shuffle the cards and I will cut. Now either of us must call a card; you shall cut for me, and he for himself, and whose card comes first wins. Therefore, when I have cut the cards, then mark the nethermost of the greatest heap,

24. ferret-claw. A ferret is a weasel trained to hunt rabbits or conies. 26. fetches, tricks. 45. *quis nisi*, etc. Nobody is so weak of mind that he will spurn proffered money. 51. pottle, pot or tankard; orig-inally a liquid measure equal to two quarts. 64. verser. Greene meant to write *setter*; see ll. 79–80 below. 93. a pair, a pack; called *pair* because the cards belonged together in a set. 103. mum-chance,

that I set upon the cards which I cut off, and always call that for me."

"Oh, now," saith the cony, "I understand you. Let me alone, I warrant I'll fit your turn."

With that in comes the setter with his cards, and asketh at what game they shall play. "Why," saith the verser, "at a new game called mum-chance, that hath no policy nor knavery, but plain as a pike-staff. You shall shuffle and I'll cut, you shall call a card, and this honest man, a stranger almost to us both, shall call another for me, and which of our cards comes first shall win." "Content," saith the setter, "for that's but mere hazard." And so he shuffles the cards, and the verser cuts off some four cards, and then taking up the heap to set upon them giveth the cony a glance of the bottom card of that heap, and saith, "Now, sir, call for me."

The cony, to blind the setter's eyes, asketh as though he were not made privy to the game, "What shall I cut?"

"What card?" saith the verser. "Why, what you will, either heart, spade, club, or diamond, coat-card or other."

"Oh, is it so?" saith the cony. "Why, then, you shall have the four of hearts"—which was the card he had a glance of.

"And," saith the setter (holding the cards in his hand and turning up the uppermost card, as if he knew not well the game), "I'll have the knave of trumps." "Nay," saith the verser, "there is no trump, you may call what card you will." Then saith he, "I'll have the ten of spades." With that he draws, and the four of hearts comes first. "Well," saith the setter, "'tis but hazard, mine might have come as well as yours, five is up, I fear not the set." So they shuffle and cut, but the verser wins.

"Well," saith the setter, "no butter will cleave on my bread. What, not one draught among five? Drawer, a fresh pint! I'll have another bout with you.—But, sir, I believe," saith he to the cony, "you see some card, that it goes so cross on my side."

"I?" saith the cony, "Nay, I hope you think not so of me; 'tis but hazard and chance, for I am but a mere stranger unto the game. As I am an honest man, I never saw it before."

Thus this simple cony closeth up smoothly to take the verser's part, only for greediness to have him win the wine. "Well," answers the setter, "then I'll have one cast more." And to it they go, but he loseth all, and beginneth to chafe in this manner: "Were it not," quoth he, "that I care not for a quart of wine, I could swear as many oaths for anger as there be hairs on my head. Why should not my luck be as good as yours, and fortune favor me as well as

you? What, not one called card in ten cuts? I'll forswear the game forever."

"What, chafe not, man," saith the verser. "Seeing we have your quart of wine, I'll show you the game." And with that discourseth all to him, as if he knew it not. The setter, as simply as if the knave were ignorant, saith, "Aye, marry, I think so! You must needs win, when he knows what card to call. I might have played long enough before I had got a set."

"Truly," says the cony, "'tis a pretty game, for 'tis not possible for him to lose that cuts the cards. I warrant the other that shuffles may lose Saint Peter's cope if he had it. Well, I'll carry this home with me into the country, and win many a pot of ale with it."

"A fresh pint!" saith the verser. "And then we'll away. But seeing, sir, you are going homeward, I'll learn you a trick worth the noting, that you shall win many a pot with in the winter nights."

With that he culls out the four knaves, and pricks one in the top, one in the midst, and one in the bottom. "Now, sir," saith he, "you see these three knaves apparently; thrust them down with your hand, and cut where you will, and though they be so far asunder I'll make them all come together."

"I pray you, let's see that trick," saith the cony. "Methinks it should be impossible."

So the verser draws, and all the three knaves come in one heap. This he doth once or twice, then the cony wonders at it and offers him a pint of wine to teach it him. "Nay," saith the verser. "I'll do it for thanks; and therefore mark me where you have taken out the four knaves, lay two together above and draw up one of them that it may be seen, then prick the other in the midst and the third in the bottom, so when any cuts, cut he never so warily, three knaves must of force come together, for the bottom knave is cut to lie upon both the upper knaves."

"Aye, marry," saith the setter, "but then the three knaves you showed come not together."

"Truth," saith the verser. "But one among a thousand mark not that; it requires a quick eye, a sharp wit, and a reaching head to spy at the first."

"Now gramercy, sir, for this trick," saith the cony. "I'll domineer with this amongst my neighbors."

Thus doth the verser and the setter feign friendship to the cony, offering him no show of cosenage, nor once to draw him in for a pint of wine, the more to shadow their villainy.

But now begins the sport. As thus they sit tippling, comes the barnacle and thrusts open the door, looking into the room where they are, and as one bashful steppeth back again and saith, "I cry you mercy, gentlemen, I thought a friend of mine had been here. Pardon my boldness." "No harm," saith the verser.

---

a gambling game played silently. 104. **decoy**, a fashionable card game. 109. **set**, bet, wager. 116. **policy**, trick. 130. **coat-card**, face card. 143. **five is up . . . set**, i.e., with five cuts agreed upon, he still hopes to win the wager. 167. **discourseth**, discloses, reveals. 179. **learn**. In the sixteenth and seventeenth centuries this was correct for *teach*. 181. **pricks**, thrusts. 205. **gramercy**, many thanks.

This woodcut from Greene's A Disputation Between a He Cony-Catcher and a She Cony-Catcher *(1592) appropriately represents the cony-catcher as a weasel.*

"I pray you drink a cup of wine with us, and welcome." So in comes the barnacle, and taking the cup drinks to the cony, and then saith, "What, at cards, gentlemen? Were it not I should be offensive to the company, I would play for a pint till my friend come that I look for." "Why, sir," saith the verser, "if you will sit down you shall be taken up for a quart of wine." "With all my heart," saith the barnacle. "What will you play at, primero, primo visto, sant, one and 10 thirty, new cut, or what shall be the game?" "Sir," saith the verser, "I am but an ignorant man at cards, and I see you have them at your fingers' end. I will play with you at a game wherein can be no deceit; it is called mum-chance at cards, and it is thus: you shall shuffle the cards, and I will cut, you shall call one, and this honest country yeoman shall call a card for me, and which of our cards comes first shall win. Here you see is no deceit, and this I'll play."

"No, truly," saith the cony, "methinks there can be 20 no great craft in this."

"Well," saith the barnacle, "for a pint of wine have at you." So they play as before, five up, and the verser wins.

"This is hard luck," saith the barnacle, "and I believe the honest man spies some card in the bottom; and therefore I'll make this, always to prick the bottom card." "Content," saith the verser, and the cony to cloak the matter saith, "Sir, you offer me injury to think that I can call a card, when I neither touch them, shuffle, cut, nor draw them." "Ah, sir," 30 saith the barnacle, "give losers leave to speak."

Well, to it they go again, and then the barnacle, knowing the game best, by chopping a card wins two of the five, but lets the verser win the set; then in a chafe he sweareth 'tis but his ill luck, and he can see no deceit in it, and therefore he will play twelve pence a cut.

The verser is content, and wins twos or threes of the barnacle, whereat he chafes, and saith, "I came hither in an ill hour; but I will win my money again, 40 or lose all in my purse."

With that he draws out a purse with some three or four pounds and claps it on the board. The verser asketh the cony secretly by signs if he will be his half; he says, "Aye," and straight seeks for his purse. Well, the barnacle shuffles the cards thoroughly, and the verser cuts as before. The barnacle when he hath drawn one card saith, "I'll either win something or lose something, therefore I'll vie and revie every card at my pleasure, till either yours or mine come out, 50 and therefore twelve pence upon this card, my card comes first for twelve pence." "No," saith the verser. "Aye," saith the cony, "and I durst hold twelve pence more." "Why, I hold you," saith the barnacle, and so they vie and revie till some ten shillings be on the stake; and then next comes forth the verser's card, that the cony called, and so the barnacle loseth.

Well, this flesheth the cony; the sweetness of gain maketh him frolic, and no man is more ready to vie and revie than he. Thus for three or four times the 60 barnacle loseth; at last, to whet on the cony, he striketh his chopped card, and winneth a goodly stake. "Away with the witch!" cries the barnacle. "I hope the cards will turn at last."

"Aye, much!" thinketh the cony. " 'Twas but a chance that you asked so right, to ask one of the five that was cut off. I am sure there was forty to one on my side, and I'll have you on the lurch anon." So still they vie and revie, and for once that the barnacle wins, the cony gets five. 70

At last when they mean to shave the cony clean of all his coin, the barnacle chafeth, and upon a pawn borroweth some money of the tapster and swears he will vie it to the uttermost. Then thus he chops his card to cross-bite the cony. He first looks on the bottom card, and shuffles often, but still keeping that bottom card which he knows to be uppermost; then sets he down the cards, and the verser to encourage the cony cut off but three cards, whereof the barnacle's card must needs be the uppermost. 80

---

9. **primero, etc.**, card games popular at the time. 22. **five up**, as earlier, the number of points needed to win. 26. **prick**, choose. 33. **chopping**, changing. 49. **vie and revie**, wager and raise the wager.

58. **flesheth**, arouses (by giving a taste of blood). 72. **pawn**, pledge. 75. **cross-bite**, cheat.

Then shows he the bottom card of the other heap cut off, to the cony, and sets it upon the barnacle's card which he knows, so that of force the card that was laid uppermost must come first; and then the barnacle calls that card. They draw a card, and then the barnacle vies and the countryman vies upon him; for this is the law, as often as one vies or revies, the other must see it, else he loseth the stake. Well, at last the barnacle plies it so that perhaps he vies more money 90 than the cony hath in his purse. The cony upon this, knowing his card is the third or fourth card, and that he hath forty to one against the barnacle, pawns his rings if he have any, his sword, his cloak, or else what he hath about him, to maintain the vie, and when he laughs in his sleeve, thinking he hath fleeced the barnacle of all, then the barnacle's card comes forth, and strikes such a cold humor unto his heart that he sits as a man in a trance, not knowing what to do, and sighing while his heart is ready to 100 break, thinking on the money that he hath lost.

Perhaps the man is very simple and patient, and, whatsoever he thinks, for fear goes his way quiet with his loss, while the cony-catchers laugh and divide the spoil, and being out of the doors, poor man, goes to his lodging with a heavy heart, pensive and sorrowful, but too late, for perhaps his state did depend on that money, and so he, his wife, his children, and his family are brought to extreme misery.

Another, perhaps more hardy and subtle, smokes the cony-catchers, and smelleth cosenage, and saith 110 they shall not have his money so; but they answer him with braves, and though he bring them before an officer, yet the knaves are so favored that the man never recovers his money, and yet he is let slip unpunished.

Thus are the poor conies robbed by these baseminded caterpillars; thus are serving men oft enticed to play and lose all; thus are prentices induced to be conies, and so are cosened of their masters' money; yea, young gentlemen, merchants, and others, 120 are fetched in by these damnable rakehells, a plague as ill as hell, which is, present loss of money, and ensuing misery. A lamentable case in England, when such vipers are suffered to breed and are not cut off with the sword of justice. . . .
(1591)

88. **see,** meet the bet—a term still used in poker. 106. **his state did depend,** i.e., he needed the money to meet a mortgage or other payment on his property. 109. **smokes,** detects. 112. **braves,** defiances. 114. **he,** i.e., the rogue.

SONGS AND SONNETS

SIR THOMAS WYATT 1503-1542

Sir Thomas Wyatt, and his younger friend, Henry Howard, Earl of Surrey, have so much in common that they are always spoken of together. They were the first English patricians to write lyric poetry, and they did much to establish the tradition of courtly concern with art and letters which prevailed to the end of the Stuart rule. Both traveled abroad, and both brought back and interpreted to England the charm and the beauty of the Italian Renaissance. They were literary experimenters, introducing terza rima, the sonnet, and blank verse into English. It was Surrey who gave the Italian sonnet the structure of three quatrains and a couplet which ultimately acquired the name of the greatest poet who employed it—William Shakespeare. Both poets suffered under the despotic Henry VIII.

Wyatt was imprisoned in the Tower for suspected adultery with Anne Boleyn, but died a natural death. Surrey was executed on a charge of treason—before he was thirty.

THE LOVER COMPLAINETH THE UNKINDNESS OF HIS LOVE

My lute, awake! Perform the last
Labor that thou and I shall waste,
And end that I have now begun;
For when this song is sung and past,
  My lute, be still, for I have done.

As to be heard where ear is none,
As led to grave in marble stone,
My song may pierce her heart as soon.

The Lover . . . Love. 5. **lute,** a stringed musical instrument of wood, with a pear-shaped body and a long fretted stem, popular in Tudor times; used here as the symbol of the poet's song. 7. **As led.** Structurally, the first two lines should follow the third.

Should we then sigh or sing or moan?
10   No! No! my lute, for I have done.

The rocks do not so cruelly
Repulse the waves continually
As she my suit and affection.
So that I am past remedy,
   Whereby my lute and I have done.

Proud of the spoil that thou hast got
Of simple hearts, thorough love's shot;
By whom, unkind, thou hast them won,
Think not he hath his bow forgot,
20   Although my lute and I have done.

Vengeance shall fall on thy disdain
That makest but game on earnest pain.
Think not alone under the sun
Unquit to cause thy lovers plain,
   Although my lute and I have done.

Perchance thee lie withered and old
The winter nights that are so cold,
Plaining in vain unto the moon.
Thy wishes then dare not be told.
30   Care then who list, for I have done.

And then may chance thee to repent
The time that thou hast lost and spent,
To cause thy lovers sigh and swoon.
Then shalt thou know beauty but lent,
   And wish and want as I have done.

Now cease, my lute. This is the last
Labor that thou and I shall waste,
And ended is that we begun.
Now is this song both sung and past;
   My lute, be still, for I have done.
(1557)

THE LOVER COMPARETH HIS STATE
TO A SHIP IN PERILOUS STORM
TOSSED ON THE SEA

My galley chargéd with forgetfulness
Thorough sharp seas, in winter nights doth pass,
'Tween rock and rock; and eke my foe, alas,
That is my lord, steereth with cruelness,
And every hour, a thought in readiness,
As though that death were light in such a case.

An endless wind doth tear the sail apace
Of forcéd sighs, and trusty fearfulness.
A rain of tears, a cloud of dark disdain
Hath done the wearied cords great hinderance,   10
Wreathéd with error, and with ignorance.
The stars be hid that led me to this pain;
Drowned is reason that should be my comfort,
And I remain, despairing of the port.
(1557)

HENRY HOWARD, EARL OF SURREY
1517?-1547

OF THE DEATH OF SIR [THOMAS] W[YATT]

W. resteth here, that quick could never rest;
Whose heavenly gifts, increaséd by disdain,
And virtue sank the deeper in his breast;
Such profit he by envy could obtain.
A head where wisdom mysteries did frame;
Whose hammers beat still in that lively brain
As on a stithe where that some work of fame
Was daily wrought to turn to Britain's gain.
A visage stern and mild, where both did grow,
Vice to condemn, in virtue to rejoice;   10
Amid great storms, whom grace assuréd so
To live upright and smile at fortune's choice.
A hand that taught what might be said in rime;
That reft Chaucer the glory of his wit:
A mark, the which (unperfected, for time)
Some may approach, but never none shall hit.
A tongue that served in foreign realms his king;
Whose courteous talk to virtue did enflame
Each noble heart; a worthy guide to bring
Our English youth by travail unto fame.   20
An eye whose judgment none affect could blind,
Friends to allure, and foes to reconcile;
Whose piercing look did represent a mind
With virtue fraught, reposéd, void of guile.
A heart where dread was never so imprest,
To hide the thought that might the truth advance;
In neither fortune lost, nor yet represt,
To swell in wealth, or yield unto mischance.
A valiant corse, where force and beauty met;
Happy, alas, too happy, but for foes!   30
Lived, and ran the race that Nature set:
Of manhood's shape, where she the mold did lose.
But to the heavens that simple soul is fled,
Which left with such as covet Christ to know
Witness of faith that never shall be dead,
Sent for our health, but not receivéd so.

---

24. **Unquit**, unpunished. **plain** (noun), plaint, lament.
   Of the Death . . . W. 1. **quick**, alive. 2. **disdain**, i.e., of *vice*;
see l. 10. 7. **stithe**, stithy, anvil. 21. **none affect**, no influence. 29.
corse, body—not necessarily a corpse. 38. **ghost**, here, as elsewhere

in Tudor literature, the spirit, or immortal part of man with no necessary suggestion of its reappearance on earth.
   Description . . . Lover. 1. **soote**, sweet. 4. **turtle**, turtledove,
used in lyric poetry as the symbol of love. 6. **hung his old head,**

Thus for our guilt, this jewel have we lost;
The earth his bones, the heavens possess his ghost!
(1557)

DESCRIPTION OF SPRING WHEREIN EACH THING RENEWS, SAVE ONLY THE LOVER

The soote season that bud and bloom forth brings,
With green hath clad the hill and eke the vale;
The nightingale with feathers new she sings;
The turtle to her mate hath told her tale:
Summer is come, for every spray now springs;
The hart hath hung his old head on the pale;
The buck in brake his winter coat he flings;
The fishes float with new repairéd scale;
The adder all her slough away she slings;
10 The swift swallow pursueth the flies smale;
The busy bee her honey now she mings.
Winter is worn, that was the flowers' bale:
And thus I see among these pleasant things
Each care decays, and yet my sorrow springs!
(1557)

BEAUTY

Brittle beauty, that nature made so frail,
Whereof the gift is small, and short the season,
Flowering today, tomorrow apt to fail,
Tickle treasure abhorréd of reason,
Dangerous to deal with, vain, of none avail,
Costly in keeping, passed not worth two peason,
Slipper in sliding as is an ealé's tail,
Hard to attain, once gotten not geason,
Jewel of jeopardy that peril doth assail,
10 False and untrue, enticéd oft to treason,
Enemy to youth: that most may I bewail.
Ah, bitter sweet! infecting as the poison,
Thou farest as fruit that with the frost is taken:
Today ready ripe, tomorrow all to-shaken.
(1557)

COMPLAINT OF A LOVER REBUKED

Love, that doth reign and live within my thought,
And build his seat within my captive breast,
Clad in the arms wherein with me he fought,
Oft in my face he doth his banner rest.
But she that taught me love, and suffer pain,
My doubtful hope and eke my hot desire
With shamefast look to shadow and refrain,

Her smiling grace converteth straight to ire.
And coward Love then to the heart apace
Taketh his flight, where he doth lurk and plain   10
His purpose lost, and dare not show his face.
For my lord's guilt thus faultless bide I pain.
Yet from my lord shall not my foot remove;
Sweet is the death that taketh end by love.
(1557)

VOW TO LOVE FAITHFULLY HOWSOEVER HE BE REWARDED

Set me whereas the sun doth parch the green
Or where his beams do not dissolve the ice;
In temperate heat, where he is felt and seen;
In presence prest of people, mad or wise;
Set me in high, or yet in low degree;
In longest night, or in the longest day;
In clearest sky, or where clouds thickest be;
In lusty youth, or when my hairs are gray:
Set me in heaven, in earth, or else in hell;
In hill, or dale, or in the foaming flood;   10
Thrall, or at large, alive whereso I dwell;
Sick or in health, in evil fame or good;
Hers will I be, and only with this thought
Content myself, although my chance be naught.
(1557)

THE MEANS TO ATTAIN HAPPY LIFE

Martial, the things that do attain
    The happy life be these, I find:
The riches left, not got with pain;
    The fruitful ground, the quiet mind;

The equal friend; no grudge, no strife;
    No charge of rule, nor governance;
Without disease, the healthful life;
    The household of continuance;

The mean diet, no delicate fare;
    True wisdom joined with simpleness;   10
The night dischargéd of all care,
    Where wine the wit may not oppress.

The faithful wife, without debate;
    Such sleeps as may beguile the night;
Contented with thine own estate,
    Ne wish for death, ne fear his might.
(1557)

---

i.e., shed his old horns. Similarly in ll. 7 and 9 respectively, the loss of the old fur and the old skin are alluded to. 10. **smale**, small. 11. **mings**, for *mengs*, mixes or mingles.
Beauty. 4. **Tickle**, unstable, insecure. 6. **peason**, obsolete plural of pea. 8. **geason**, rare. 14. **to-shaken**, shaken to pieces.
The Means . . . Life. 1. **Martial**, Roman satirical poet of the first century A.D.; this poem is a translation of his *Epigrams*, Book X, number 47. 13. **debate**, wrangling, strife. 16. **Ne . . . ne**, not . . . nor.

ANONYMOUS

BACK AND SIDE GO BARE

CHORUS

Back and side go bare, go bare,
   Both foot and hand go cold;
But, belly, God send thee good ale enough,
   Whether it be new or old.

I cannot eat but little meat,
   My stomach is not good;
But sure I think that I can drink
   With him that wears a hood.
Though I go bare, take ye no care,
10   I am nothing a-cold;
I stuff my skin so full within
   Of jolly good ale and old.

I love no roast but a nutbrown toast,
   And a crab laid in the fire;
A little bread shall do me stead,
   Much bread I not desire.
No frost nor snow, no wind, I trow,
   Can hurt me if I would,
I am so wrapped and thoroughly lapped
20   Of jolly good ale and old.

And Tib my wife, that as her life
   Loveth well good ale to seek,
Full oft drinks she, till ye may see
   The tears run down her cheek.
Then doth she trowl to me the bowl,
   Even as a maltworm should,
And saith "Sweetheart, I have take my part
   Of this jolly good ale and old."

Now let them drink till they nod and wink,
30   Even as good fellows should do;
They shall not miss to have the bliss
   Good ale doth bring men to.
And all poor souls that have scoured bowls,
   Or have them lustily trowled,
God save the lives of them and their wives,
   Whether they be young or old.
(1553?)

MAIDS AND WIDOWS

If ever I marry, I'll marry a maid;
To marry a widow, I am sore afraid;

For maids they are simple, and never will grutch,
But widows full oft, as they say, know too much.

A maid is so sweet, and so gentle of kind,
That a maid is the wife I will choose to my mind.
A widow is froward, and never will yield;
Or if such there be, you will meet them but seeld.

A maid ne'er complaineth, do what so you will;
But what you mean well, a widow takes ill.   10
A widow will make you a drudge and a slave,
And, cost ne'er so much, she will ever go brave.

A maid is so modest, she seemeth a rose
When it first beginneth the bud to unclose;
But a widow full-blowen full often deceives,
And the next wind that bloweth shakes down all her
   leaves.

The widows be lovely, I never gainsay,
But too well all their beauty they know to display;
But a maid hath so great hidden beauty in store,
She can spare to a widow, yet never be poor.   20

Then, if ever I marry, give me a fresh maid,
If to marry with any I be not afraid;
But to marry with any, it asketh much care;
And some bachelors hold they are best as they are.
(?)

MY FLOCKS FEED NOT

My flocks feed not, my ewes breed not,
My rams speed not, all is amiss;
Love is dying, faith's defying,
Heart's renying, causer of this.
All my merry jigs are quite forgot,
All my lady's love is lost, God wot;

Where her faith was firmly fixed in love,
There a nay is placed without remove.
   One silly cross wrought all my loss;
   O frowning Fortune, curséd fickle dame!   10
   For now I see inconstancy
   More in women than in men remain.

In black mourn I, all fears scorn I,
Love hath forlorn me, living in thrall.
Heart is bleeding, all help needing,
Oh cruel speeding fraughted with gall!
My shepherd's pipe can sound no deal;

Back and Side Go Bare. This lively drinking song was printed at the beginning of Act II of *Gammer Gurton's Needle* (composed c. 1553); however, it probably had an earlier existence. 5. **meat,** as usual, food in general. 8. **him . . . hood,** a friar. 14. **crab,** crabapple, roasted and put into ale to give it flavor. 25. **trowl,** troll, pass around. 26. **maltworm,** a good consumer of malt drinks; cf. bookworm. 29. **wink,** close their eyes. 33. **scoured,** emptied (of ale).

Maids and Widows. 3. **grutch,** grudge, murmur. 8. **seeld,** seldom. 12. **brave,** overdressed.
My Flocks Feed Not. This pastoral complaint has been doubtfully assigned to Richard Barnfield (1574?–1627). 4. **renying,** renaying, renouncing. 9. **silly cross,** simple thwarting of my purpose. 14. **forlorn,** deserted. 17. **shepherd's pipe,** the usual symbol for pastoral song. **deal,** part, whit. 18. **wether's bell,** the bell tied about the neck of

My wether's bell rings doleful knell;
My curtal dog, that wont to have played,
20 Plays not at all but seems afraid;
    With sighs so deep procures to weep,
    In howling wise, to see my doleful plight;
    How sighs resound through heartless ground,
    Like a thousand vanquished men in bloody fight.

Clear wells spring not, sweet birds sing not,
Green plants bring not forth their dye;
Herds stand weeping, flocks all sleeping,
Nymphs back peeping fearfully.
All the pleasure known to us poor swains,
30 All our merry meetings on the plains,
All our evening sport from us is fled,
All our love is lost, for Love is dead.
    Farewell, sweet lass, thy like ne'er was
    For a sweet content, the cause of all my moan;
    Poor Corydon must live alone,
    Other help for him I see that there is none.
(?)

CRABBED AGE AND YOUTH

Crabbed Age and Youth
Cannot live together:
Youth is full of pleasance,
Age is full of care;
Youth like summer morn,
Age like winter weather;
Youth like summer brave,
Age like winter bare.
Youth is full of sport,
10 Age's breath is short;
Youth is nimble, Age is lame;
Youth is hot and bold,
Age is weak and cold;
Youth is wild, and Age is tame.
Age, I do abhor thee;
Youth, I do adore thee;
O my Love, my Love is young!
Age, I do defy thee.
O sweet shepherd, hie thee!
For methinks thou stay'st too long.
(1599)

SIR EDWARD DYER 1550?-1607

Sir Edward Dyer was a member of Sir Philip Sidney's Areopagus, an association of scholars and poets,

and was introduced by the Earl of Leicester at Elizabeth's court.

MY MIND TO ME A KINGDOM IS

My mind to me a kingdom is;
    Such present joys therein I find
That it excels all other bliss
    That earth affords or grows by kind.
Though much I want which most would have,
Yet still my mind forbids to crave.

No princely pomp, no wealthy store,
    No force to win the victory,
No wily wit to salve a sore,
    No shape to feed a loving eye;   10
To none of these I yield as thrall—
For why? My mind doth serve for all.

I see how plenty surfeits oft,
    And hasty climbers soon do fall;
I see that those which are aloft
    Mishap doth threaten most of all;
They get with toil, they keep with fear—
Such cares my mind could never bear.

Content to live, this is my stay;
    I seek no more than may suffice;   20
I press to bear no haughty sway;
    Look, what I lack my mind supplies.
Lo, thus I triumph like a king,
Content with that my mind doth bring.

Some have too much, yet still do crave;
    I little have, and seek no more.
They are but poor, though much they have,
    And I am rich with little store.
They poor, I rich; they beg, I give;
They lack, I leave; they pine, I live.   30

I laugh not at another's loss;
    I grudge not at another's pain;
No worldly waves my mind can toss;
    My state at one doth still remain.
I fear no foe, I fawn no friend;
I loathe not life, nor dread my end.

Some weigh their pleasure by their lust,
    Their wisdom by their rage of will;
Their treasure is their only trust;
    A cloakéd craft their store of skill.   40

the leader of the flock to guide the sheep. 19. **curtal dog,** curtailed dog, i.e., one with a docked tail. 21. **procures,** contrives. 26. **dye,** color. 35. **Corydon,** one of the many conventional names for shepherd swains; here it is given to the speaker.
    Crabbed Age and Youth. Like many Elizabethan lyrics this is suggestive of the medieval *debat*' or literary argument. It first appeared in *The Passionate Pilgrim* (1599), a miscellany published with

Shakespeare's name on the title page.
    My Mind to Me a Kingdom Is. This poem, the most famous of Dyer's lyrics, expresses that ideal of the union of scholarship and poetry which was characteristic of the period. 32. **grudge,** grieve. 34. **state,** condition, situation.

But all the pleasure that I find
Is to maintain a quiet mind.

My wealth is health and perfect ease;
   My conscience clear my chief defense;
I neither seek by bribes to please,
   Nor by deceit to breed offense,
Thus do I live; thus will I die;
Would all did so as well as I!
(1588)

CHRISTOPHER MARLOWE 1564-1593

   Christopher Marlowe was the greatest playwright before Shakespeare. His "mighty line" of blank verse, as well as his lofty purpose and high seriousness, became famous. His best plays are Dr. Faustus, The Jew of Malta, *and* Edward II.

THE PASSIONATE SHEPHERD TO HIS LOVE

Come live with me and be my Love,
And we will all the pleasures prove
That hills and valleys, dales and fields,
Or woods or steepy mountain yields.

And we will sit upon the rocks,
And see the shepherds feed their flocks
By shallow rivers, to whose falls
Melodious birds sing madrigals.

And I will make thee beds of roses
10 And a thousand fragrant posies;
A cap of flowers, and a kirtle
Embroidered all with leaves of myrtle;

A gown made of the finest wool
Which from our pretty lambs we pull;
Fair-linéd slippers for the cold,
With buckles of the purest gold;

A belt of straw and ivy buds
With coral clasps and amber studs—
And if these pleasures may thee move,
20 Come live with me and be my Love.

The shepherd swains shall dance and sing
For thy delight each May morning—

If these delights thy mind may move,
Then live with me and be my Love.
(1599)

SIR WALTER RALEIGH 1552?-1618

   Sir Walter Raleigh was a courtier, a statesman, a soldier, and a noted explorer, as well as a poet and a writer of excellent prose. He was Elizabeth's favorite, but he incurred the enmity of King James, and in 1618 was executed on an old unproved charge of treason. The real grievance was that his men had committed piracy against Spain on an expedition to Guiana.

THE NYMPH'S REPLY TO THE SHEPHERD

If all the world and love were young,
And truth in every shepherd's tongue,
These pretty pleasures might me move,
To live with thee and be thy love.

But time drives flocks from field to fold,
When rivers rage, and rocks grow cold;
And Philomel becometh dumb;
The rest complains of cares to come.

The flowers do fade, and wanton fields
To wayward Winter reckoning yields;   10
A honey tongue, a heart of gall,
Is fancy's spring, but sorrow's fall.

Thy gowns, thy shoes, thy bed of roses,
Thy cap, thy kirtle, and thy posies,
Soon break, soon wither, soon forgotten,
In folly ripe, in reason rotten.

Thy belt of straw and ivy buds,
Thy coral clasps and amber studs,
All these in me no means can move,
To come to thee and be thy love.   20

But could youth last, and love still breed,
Had joys no date, nor age no need,
Then these delights my mind might move,
To live with thee and be thy love.
(1599)

The Passionate Shepherd to His Love. This pastoral lyric appeared in *England's Helicon.* 11. kirtle, gown.
The Nymph's . . . Shepherd. 7. Philomel, the nightingale; the allusion is to the legend that Philomela was a maiden whose tongue was cut out by Tereus, her sister Procne's husband, in order that she might not reveal his mistreatment of her.
His Pilgrimage. The poem is characterized by an almost medieval use of allegory and concrete imagery to express abstract concepts. **1. scallop-shell.** Pilgrims returning from Palestine wore on their caps shells from beaches made holy by scriptural story. 3. **scrip,** bag, wallet, used by pilgrims as a receptacle for food. 7. **Blood.** The allusion is to the crucifixion. **balmer,** anointer—with ceremonial balms. 21. **rags of clay,** bodies. 25. **suckets,** sweetmeats, dainties. 38. **forged,** fabricated, bribed to make a false charge. 40. **king's attorney,** the

HIS PILGRIMAGE

Give me my scallop-shell of quiet,
  My staff of faith to walk upon,
My scrip of joy, immortal diet,
  My bottle of salvation,
My gown of glory, hope's true gage;
And thus I'll take my pilgrimage.

Blood must be my body's balmer;
  No other balm will there be given;
Whilst my soul, like a quiet palmer,
10 Traveleth toward the land of heaven,
Over the silver mountains,
Where spring the nectar fountains.
      There will I kiss
      The bowl of bliss,
And drink mine everlasting fill
Upon every milken hill.
My soul will be a-dry before;
But, after, it will thirst no more.

Then by that happy, blissful day
20 More peaceful pilgrims I shall see,
That have cast off their rags of clay,
  A walk appareled fresh like me.
      I'll take them first,
      To quench their thirst
And taste of nectar suckets,
      At those clear wells
      Where sweetness dwells,
Drawn up by saints in crystal buckets.

  And when our bottles and all we
30 Are filled with immortality,
  Then the blessed paths we'll travel,
Strowed with rubies thick as gravel;
Ceilings of diamonds, sapphire floors,
High walls of coral, and pearly bowers.

  From thence to heaven's bribeless hall,
Where no corrupted voices brawl;
No conscience molten into gold;
No forged accuser bought or sold;
No cause deferred, no vain-spent journey,
40 For there Christ is the king's attorney,
Who pleads for all, without degrees,
And he hath angels but no fees.
  And when the grand twelve million jury
Of our sins, with direful fury,
Against our souls black verdicts give,
Christ pleads his death; and then we live.

Be Thou my speaker, taintless pleader!
Unblotted lawyer! true proceeder!
Thou giv'st salvation, even for alms,
Not with a bribéd lawyer's palms.   50
  And this is mine eternal plea
To Him that made heaven and earth and sea:
That since my flesh must die so soon,
And want a head to dine next noon,
Just at the stroke, when my veins start and spread,
Set on my soul an everlasting head!
Then am I ready, like a palmer fit,
To tread those blest paths, which before I writ.

Of death and judgment, heaven and hell,
Who oft doth think, must needs die well.
(c. 1603; 1651)

SIR WALTER RALEIGH THE NIGHT BEFORE HIS DEATH

Even such is time, that takes in trust
  Our youth, our joys, our all we have,
And pays us but with earth and dust;
  Who, in the dark and silent grave,
When we have wandered all our ways,
Shuts up the story of our days.
But from this earth, this grave, this dust,
My God shall raise me up, I trust!
(1618)

JOHN LYLY 1554?-1606

APELLES' SONG

Cupid and my Campaspe played
At cards for kisses; Cupid paid.
He stakes his quiver, bows and arrows,
His mother's doves and team of sparrows;
Loses them too; then down he throws
The coral of his lip, the rose
Growing on's cheek (but none knows how);
With these, the crystal of his brow,
And then the dimple of his chin;
All these did my Campaspe win.   10
At last he set her both his eyes;
She won, and Cupid blind did rise.
O Love, has she done this to thee?
What shall, alas! become of me?
(1584)

lawyer for the state; here the king is the symbol for God. **42. angels,** a pun on the word; the angel was a gold coin worth from six to ten shillings. **44. sins . . . verdicts give.** Human sins, as in medieval religious literature, are here personified. **53. my flesh . . . want a head.** Raleigh probably wrote the poem while a prisoner and under sentence of death by beheading for a plot against James I.
  John Lyly. See p. 189. *Apelles' Song,* from *Alexander and*

Campaspe (1584). Apelles was employed by Alexander to paint a portrait of the fair captive Campaspe. The youth fell in love with her; and Alexander's magnanimity so overcame his jealous anger that he yielded Campaspe to Apelles. **4. mother's,** Aphrodite's; doves and sparrows were her symbolical birds.

SERVANTS' SONG

GRANICUS. O for a bowl of fat canary,
Rich Palermo, sparkling sherry,
Some nectar else from Juno's dairy:
O these draughts would make us merry!

PSYLLUS. O for a wench! (I deal in faces,
And in other daintier things,)
Tickled am I with her embraces,—
Fine dancing in such fairy rings.

MANES. O for a plump fat leg of mutton,
10 Veal, lamb, capon, pig, and coney!
None is happy but a glutton;
None an ass but who wants money.

CHORUS. Wines, indeed, and girls are good,
But brave victuals feast the blood:
For wenches, wine, and lusty cheer,
Jove would leap down to surfeit here.
(1584)

THOMAS LODGE 1558?-1625

Thomas Lodge was the prodigal son of a Lord Mayor of London, one of the "University Wits," and a miscellaneous writer of pamphlets, plays, poems, and romances. The most famous of these is Rosalynde: Euphues' Golden Legacy (1590), upon which Shakespeare founded As You Like It. The following poem is one of Lodge's most graceful lyrics.

ROSALYNDE'S MADRIGAL

Love in my bosom like a bee
Doth suck his sweet:
Now with his wings he plays with me,
Now with his feet.
Within mine eyes he makes his nest,
His bed amidst my tender breast;
My kisses are his daily feast,
And yet he robs me of my rest.
Ah, wanton, will ye?

10 And if I sleep, then percheth he
With pretty flight,
And makes his pillow of my knee
The livelong night.
Strike I my lute, he tunes the string,
He music plays if so I sing,

He lends me every lovely thing,
Yet cruel he my heart doth sting.
Whist, wanton, still ye!

Else I with roses every day
Will whip you hence,   20
And bind you, when you long to play,
For your offence;
I'll shut mine eyes to keep you in,
I'll make you fast it for your sin,
I'll count your power not worth a pin,
Alas, what hereby shall I win,
If he gainsay me?

What if I beat the wanton boy
With many a rod?
He will repay me with annoy,   30
Because a God.
Then sit thou safely on my knee,
And let thy bower my bosom be;
Lurk in mine eyes, I like of thee.
O Cupid, so thou pity me,
Spare not, but play thee.
(1590)

SIR PHILIP SIDNEY 1554-1586

Sir Philip Sidney was courtier, soldier, scholar, poet, and perfect Elizabethan knight; he was in the breadth of his accomplishments the fullest incarnation of the Renaissance ideal. Even during his brief life he became a legend, and the most admired of Elizabeth's courtiers. He crowned his life with glory by joining his uncle, the Earl of Leicester, in a military expedition to the Low Countries, where he died of wounds at Zutphen.

Sidney's Arcadia (written c. 1580) is a pastoral romance, written to amuse his sister, Mary, Countess of Pembroke. Astrophel and Stella, published in 1591, is a sequence of love sonnets, usually thought to be autobiographical, alluding either to an unhappy love affair with Penelope Devereux, who married Lord Rich, or addressed to Frances Walsingham, whom Sidney married in 1583.

from ARCADIA

SONG

Ring out your bells, let mourning shows be spread;
For Love is dead.

Servants' Song, from *Alexander and Campaspe*, a typical three-part song in which each singer sings a stanza, and all sing the chorus. 1. **fat canary**, rich wine from the Canary Islands, characterized by its

sweetness. 2. **Palermo**, wine from Palermo, Sicily. 10. **coney**, rabbit. *Rosalynde's Madrigal.* 18. **Whist**, be quiet. *Arcadia.* 8. **franzy**, frenzy, hysteria. 10. **Good . . . us**, the

All Love is dead, infected
With plague of deep disdain;
  Worth as naught worth rejected,
And Faith fair scorn doth gain.
  From so ungrateful fancy,
  From such a female franzy,
  From them that use men thus,
10 Good Lord, deliver us!

Weep, neighbors, weep; do you not hear it said
    That Love is dead?
  His death-bed, peacock's folly;
  His winding-sheet is shame;
  His will, false-seeming holy;
  His sole exec'tor, blame.
  From so ungrateful fancy,
  From such a female franzy,
  From them that use men thus,
20 Good Lord, deliver us!

Let dirge be sung, and trentals rightly read,
    For Love is dead;
  Sir Wrong his tomb ordaineth
My mistress' marble heart,
  Which epitaph containeth,
  "Her eyes were once his dart."
  From so ungrateful fancy,
  From such a female franzy,
  From them that use men thus,
30 Good Lord, deliver us!

Alas, I lie. Rage hath this error bred;
    Love is not dead;
  Love is not dead, but sleepeth
In her unmatchéd mind,
  Where she his counsel keepeth,
Till due deserts she find.
  Therefore from so vile fancy,
  To call such wit a franzy,
  Who Love can temper thus,
  Good Lord, deliver us!
  (1590)

HEART EXCHANGE

My true love hath my heart, and I have his,
By just exchange, one for the other giv'n:
I hold his dear, and mine he cannot misse:
There never was a bargain better driv'n.

His heart in me keeps me and him in one,
My heart in him his thoughts and senses guides:
He loves my heart, for once it was his own:
I cherish his, because in me it bides.

His heart his wound received from my sight:
My heart was wounded with his wounded heart.   10
For as from me on him his hurt did light:
So still me thought in me his heart did smart:
  Both equal hurt, in his change sought our bliss:
  My true Love hath my heart, and I have his.
(1590)

from ASTROPHEL AND STELLA

1

Loving in truth, and fain in verse my love to show,
That she, dear she, might take some pleasure of my
    pain,
Pleasure might cause her read, reading might make
    her know,
Knowledge might pity win, and pity grace obtain,
I sought fit words to paint the blackest face of woe,
Studying inventions fine, her wits to entertain.
Oft turning others' leaves, to see if thence would flow
Some fresh and fruitful showers upon my sunburnt
    brain.
But words came halting forth, wanting Invention's stay;
Invention, Nature's child, fled step-dame Study's
    blows;   10
And others' feet still seemed but strangers in my way.
Thus great with child to speak, and helpless in my
    throes,
Biting my truant pen, beating myself for spite:
"Fool!" said my Muse to me, "look in thy heart,
    and write."

31

With how sad steps, O Moon, thou climb'st the skies!
How silently, and with how wan a face!
What, may it be that even in heavenly place
That busy archer his sharp arrows tries?
Sure, if that long-with-love-acquainted eyes
Can judge of love, thou feel'st a lover's case.
I read it in thy looks; thy languished grace,
To me that feel the like, thy state descries.
Then, even of fellowship, O Moon, tell me,
Is constant love deemed there but want of wit?   10
Are beauties there as proud as here they be?
Do they above love to be loved, and yet
Those lovers scorn whom that love doth possess?
Do they call virtue there ungratefulness?

39

Come, Sleep! O Sleep, the certain knot of peace,
The baiting-place of wit, the balm of woe,

---

response in the litany. 13. **peacock's folly**, pride. 21. **trentals**, a series of thirty masses for the dead.
  Astrophel and Stella. The words mean *star-lover* and *star*; they are poetic names respectively for Sidney and the lady addressed.
  Sonnet 31. 4. **busy archer**, Cupid.
  Sonnet 39. 2. **baiting-place**, place of refreshment.

The poor man's wealth, the prisoner's release,
The indifferent judge between the high and low;
With shield of proof shield me from out the prease
Of those fierce darts Despair at me doth throw;
Oh make in me those civil wars to cease.
I will good tribute pay, if thou do so.
Take thou of me smooth pillows, sweetest bed,
10 A chamber deaf to noise and blind to light,
A rosy garland and a weary head;
And if these things, as being thine by right,
Move not thy heavy grace, thou shalt in me,
Livelier than elsewhere, Stella's image see.

41

Having this day my horse, my hand, my lance
Guided so well that I obtain'd the prize,
Both by the judgment of the English eyes
And of some sent from that sweet enemy France;
Horsemen my skill in horsemanship advance,
Town folks my strength; a daintier judge applies
His praise to slight which from good use doth rise;
Some lucky wits impute it but to chance;
Others, because of both sides I do take
10 My blood from them who did excell in this,
Think Nature me a man-at-arms did make.
How far they shot awry! The true cause is,
Stella look'd on, and from her heav'nly face
Sent forth thy beams which made so fair my race.

50

Stella, the fullness of my thoughts of thee
Cannot be stayed within my panting breast,
But they do swell and struggle forth of me
Till that in words thy figure be expressed;
And yet, as soon as they so forméd be,
According to my lord Love's own behest,
With sad eyes I their weak proportion see
To portrait that which in this world is best.
So that I cannot choose but write my mind,
10 And cannot choose but put out what I write,
While these poor babes their death in birth do find;
And now my pen these lines had dashéd quite
But that they stopped his fury from the same
Because their fore-front bare sweet Stella's name.
(1591)

GEORGE PEELE 1558?-1597?

George Peele, a writer of plays and verses, was one of the first Elizabethans to give a lyrical quality to drama. Of his plays the most famous is The Old Wives' Tale (published in 1595), a satire on romantic drama of the period and the main source of Milton's Comus.

FAIR AND FAIR

OENONE.
 Fair and fair, and twice so fair,
  As fair as any may be;
 The fairest shepherd on our green,
  A love for any lady.
PARIS.
 Fair and fair, and twice so fair,
  As fair as any may be;
 Thy love is fair for thee alone,
  And for no other lady.
OENONE.
 My love is fair, my love is gay,
 As fresh as bin the flowers in May, 10
 And of my love my roundelay,
 My merry, merry, merry roundelay,
  Concludes with Cupid's curse—
 "They that do change old love for new,
 Pray gods they change for worse!"
AMBO SIMUL.
 They that do change old love for new,
  Pray gods they change for worse!
OENONE.
 Fair and fair, etc.
PARIS.
 Fair and fair, etc.
 Thy love is fair, etc. 20
OENONE.
 My love can pipe, my love can sing,
 My love can many a pretty thing,
 And of his lovely praises ring
 My merry, merry, merry roundelay,
  Amen to Cupid's curse—
 "They that do change," etc.
PARIS.
 They that do change, etc.
AMBO.
 Fair and fair, etc.
(1584)

A FAREWELL TO ARMS

(To Queen Elizabeth)

His golden locks Time hath to silver turned;
 O Time too swift, O swiftness never ceasing!

---

5. **prease,** press, crowd.
 Fair and Fair, is a song from *The Arraignment of Paris,* a court drama characterized by fulsome compliments to Queen Elizabeth. In Greek legend Oenone is the nymph of Mt. Ida who was deserted by Paris when Aphrodite gave him Helen, wife of Menelaus, in return for his award to her of the golden apple. 16. *Ambo Simul,* both together. **They, etc.** The allusion is to Paris' desertion of Oenone for Helen.
 A Farewell to Arms. 10. **Age his,** Age's. 18. **beadsman,** one

His youth 'gainst time and age hath ever spurned,
  But spurned in vain; youth waneth by increasing.
Beauty, strength, youth, are flowers but fading seen;
Duty, faith, love, are roots, and ever green.

His helmet now shall make a hive for bees;
  And, lovers' sonnets turned to holy psalms,
A man-at-arms must now serve on his knees,
10 And feed on prayers, which are Age his alms.
But though from court to cottage he depart,
His saint is sure of his unspotted heart.

And when he saddest sits in homely cell,
  He'll teach his swains this carol for a song—
"Blest be the hearts that wish my sovereign well,
  Curst be the souls that think her any wrong."
Goddess, allow this aged man his right
To be your beadsman now that was your knight.
(1597)

ROBERT GREENE 1560?-1592

SEPHESTIA'S SONG TO HER CHILD

Weep not, my wanton, smile upon my knee;
When thou art old there's grief enough for thee.
  Mother's wag, pretty boy,
  Father's sorrow, father's joy;
  When thy father first did see
  Such a boy by him and me,
  He was glad, I was woe;
  Fortune changéd made him so,
  When he left his pretty boy
10 Last his sorrow, first his joy.

Weep not, my wanton, smile upon my knee;
When thou art old, there's grief enough for thee.
  Streaming tears that never stint,
  Like pearl-drops from a flint,
  Fell by course from his eyes,
  That one another's place supplies;
  Thus he grieved in every part,
  Tears of blood fell from his heart,
  When he left his pretty boy,
20 Father's sorrow, father's joy.

Weep not, my wanton, smile upon my knee;
When thou art old, there's grief enough for thee.
  The wanton smiled, father wept,
  Mother cried, baby leapt;
  More he crowed, more he cried,
  Nature could not sorrow hide.

He must go, he must kiss
Child and mother, baby bless,
For he left his pretty boy,
  Father's sorrow, father's joy.   30
Weep not, my wanton, smile upon my knee;
When thou art old, there's grief enough for thee.
(1589)

SWEET ARE THE THOUGHTS THAT
SAVOR OF CONTENT

Sweet are the thoughts that savor of content;
  The quiet mind is richer than a crown;
Sweet are the nights in careless slumber spent;
  The poor estate scorns fortune's angry frown.
Such sweet content, such minds, such sleep, such
    bliss,
Beggars enjoy, when princes oft do miss.

The homely house that harbors quiet rest;
  The cottage that affords no pride nor care;
The mean that 'grees with country music best;
  The sweet consort of mirth and music's fare;   10
Obscuréd life sets down a type of bliss:
A mind content both crown and kingdom is.
(1591)

SAMUEL DANIEL 1562-1619

Samuel Daniel was a miscellaneous writer best known for his epic poem, Civil Wars between the Two Houses of York and Lancaster. *The first four books appeared in 1595, and the complete work of eight books in 1609. He is also known for his sonnet sequence* Delia, *inspired chiefly by Tasso.*

from DELIA

25

False Hope prolongs my ever certain grief,
Traitor to me, and faithful to my love;
A thousand times it promised me relief,
Yet never any true effect I prove.
Oft when I find in her no truth at all
I banish her and blame her treachery,
Yet soon again I must her back recall,
As one that dies without her company.
Thus often as I chase my hope from me,
Straightway she hastes her unto Delia's eyes;   10

who counts his beads or prays, especially for another.
  Robert Greene. See note, p. 194. **Sephestia's Song,** from the prose romance of *Menaphon;* Sephestia sings it while separated from her husband and being cared for by the shepherd Menaphon. **1. my**

wanton, my pet.
  Sweet Are the Thoughts, sung by Maesia in *Farewell to Folly,* a prose tract. **10. consort,** union, harmony.

Fed with some pleasing look there shall she be,
And so sent back, and thus my fortune lies.
Looks feed my hope, Hope fosters me in vain;
Hopes are unsure, when certain is my pain.
(1592)

54

Care-charmer Sleep, son of the sable Night,
Brother to Death, in silent darkness born:
Relieve my languish, and restore the light,
With dark forgetting of my care return.
And let the day be time enough to mourn
The shipwreck of my ill-adventured youth;
Let waking eyes suffice to wail their scorn,
Without the torment of the night's untruth.
Cease, dreams, the images of day desires,
10 To model forth the passions of the morrow;
Never let rising sun approve you liars,
To add more grief to aggravate my sorrow.
Still let me sleep, embracing clouds in vain,
And never wake to feel the day's disdain.
(1592)

55

Let others sing of knights and paladins
In agéd accents and untimely words,
Paint shadows in imaginary lines,
Which well the reach of their high wits records;
But I must sing of thee, and those fair eyes
Authentic shall my verse in time to come,
When yet the unborn shall say, "Lo where she lies,
Whose beauty made him speak that else was dumb."
These are the arks, the trophies, I erect
10 That fortify thy name against old age;
And these thy sacred virtues must protect
Against the dark and Time's consuming rage.
Though the error of my youth in them appear,
Suffice they show I lived and loved thee dear.
(1592)

THOMAS DEKKER 1570?-1641?

Born and brought up in London, which he calls
"thou beautifullest daughter of the two united monarchies," Thomas Dekker was a free-lance journalist
who wrote miscellaneous prose, verse, and drama, and
remains one of the most warm-hearted of the Elizabethans. Few actual facts of his life have been recorded—a squalid jail sentence for debt, a quarrel
with the vitriolic Jonson, a long duel with his pen
pitted against the bailiff. His very birth and death
dates are known only by conjecture. But Dekker was
a mild man, and the purveyor to later generations of
the most varied and vivid pictures of the times.

SWEET CONTENT

Art thou poor, yet hast thou golden slumbers?
　　　　O sweet content!
Art thou rich, yet is thy mind perplexed?
　　　　O punishment!
Dost thou laugh to see how fools are vexed
To add to golden numbers golden numbers?
　　O sweet content! O sweet, O sweet content!

Work apace, apace, apace, apace,
Honest labor bears a lovely face;
Then hey nonny nonny—hey nonny nonny!　　　　10

Canst drink the waters of the crispéd spring?
　　　　O sweet content!
Swim'st thou in wealth, yet sink'st in thine own tears?
　　　　O punishment!
Then he that patiently want's burden bears,
No burden bears, but is a king, a king!
　　O sweet content! O sweet, O sweet content!

Work apace, apace, apace, apace,
Honest labor bears a lovely face;
Then hey nonny nonny—hey nonny nonny!
(c. 1599; 1603)

MICHAEL DRAYTON 1563-1631

Michael Drayton was a miscellaneous writer of historical and religious verse and of odes and lyrics. His
sonnet sequence Idea's Mirror was probably addressed
to Anne, daughter of Sir Henry Goodere, who had
befriended the poet.

TO THE VIRGINIAN VOYAGE

You brave heroic minds,
Worthy your country's name,
　　That honor still pursue,
　　Go and subdue!
Whilst loitering hinds
Lurk here at home with shame.

Britons, you stay too long;
Quickly aboard bestow you!
    And with a merry gale
10 Swell your stretched sail,
With vows as strong
As the winds that blow you!

Your course securely steer;
West-and-by-south forth keep!
    Rocks, lee shores, nor shoals,
    When Eolus scowls,
You need not fear,
So absolute the deep.

And, cheerfully at sea,
20 Success you still entice,
    To get the pearl and gold;
    And ours to hold,
Virginia,
Earth's only Paradise,

Where Nature hath in store
Fowl, venison, and fish;
    And the fruitful'st soil—
    Without your toil,
Three harvests more,
30 All greater than your wish.

And the ambitious vine
Crowns with his purple mass
    The cedar reaching high
    To kiss the sky,
The cypress, pine,
And useful sassafras.

To whom the Golden Age
Still Nature's laws doth give;
    Nor other cares attend,
40   But them to defend
From winter's rage,
That long there doth not live.

When as the luscious smell
Of that delicious land,
    Above the seas that flows,
    The clear wind throws,
Your hearts to swell,
Approaching the dear strand,

In kenning of the shore
50 (Thanks to God first given!)
    O you, the happiest men,
    Be frolic then!

Let cannons roar,
Frightening the wide heaven!

And in regions far,
Such heroes bring ye forth
    As those from whom we came!
    And plant our name
Under that star
Not known unto our North!   60

And where in plenty grows
The laurel everywhere,
    Apollo's sacred tree,
    Your days may see
A poet's brows
To crown, that may sing there.

Thy *Voyages* attend,
Industrious Hakluyt!
    Whose reading shall inflame
    Men to seek fame;   70
And much commend
To after times thy wit.
(1605)

AGINCOURT

Fair stood the wind for France,
When we our sails advance,
Nor now to prove our chance
    Longer will tarry;
But putting to the main,
At Caux, the mouth of Seine,
With all his martial train
    Landed King Harry.

And taking many a fort,
Furnished in warlike sort,   10
Marcheth toward Agincourt
    In happy hour;
Skirmishing, day by day,
With those that stopped his way,
Where the French general lay
    With all his power.

Which, in his height of pride,
King Henry to deride,
His ransom to provide
    To the King sending;   20
Which he neglects the while,
As from a nation vile,
Yet with an angry smile,
    Their fall portending.

---

5. **hinds,** peasants, here used derogatively. 16. **Eolus,** Aeolus, Greek god of the winds. 49. **kenning,** the distance within which land may be recognized from the ship. 67. *Voyages . . . Hakluyt.* Cf. p. 186.
  Agincourt. The battle of Agincourt was won by the English on St. Crispin's Day, October 25, 1415, over a much larger French army. The general on the English side was Henry V, who invaded France to enforce his claims to the French throne. The story of this invasion forms the basis of Shakespeare's *Henry V.* 2. **advance,** raise. 21. **he,** i.e., the French general, D'Albret, Constable of France, killed in the battle. 22. **vile,** base, of small account.

And turning to his men,
Quoth our brave Henry then:
"Though they to one be ten
    Be not amazéd!
Yet have we well begun:
30 Battles so bravely won
Have ever to the sun
    By fame been raiséd.

"And for myself," quoth he,
"This my full rest shall be:
England ne'er mourn for me,
    Nor more esteem me.
Victor I will remain,
Or on this earth lie slain;
Never shall she sustain
40   Loss to redeem me.

"Poitiers and Cressy tell,
When most their pride did swell,
Under our swords they fell;
    No less our skill is,
Than when our grandsire great,
Claiming the regal seat,
By many a warlike feat
    Lopped the French lilies."

The Duke of York so dread
50 The eager vaward led;
With the main, Henry sped
    Amongst his henchmen:
Exeter had the rear,
A braver man not there!
O Lord, how hot they were
    On the false Frenchmen!

They now to fight are gone:
Armor on armor shone;
Drum now to drum did groan,
60   To hear, was wonder;
That, with the cries they make,
The very earth did shake;
Trumpet to trumpet spake,
    Thunder to thunder.

Well it thine age became,
O noble Erpingham,
Which didst the signal aim
    To our hid forces;
When, from a meadow by,
70 Like a storm suddenly,

The English archery
    Struck the French horses.

With Spanish yew so strong,
Arrows a cloth-yard long,
That like to serpents stung,
    Piercing the weather;
None from his fellow starts,
But, playing manly parts,
And like true English hearts,
    Stuck close together.   80

When down their bows they threw
And forth their bilboes drew
And on the French they flew,
    Not one was tardy;
Arms were from shoulders sent,
Scalps to the teeth were rent,
Down the French peasants went:
    Our men were hardy.

This while our noble King,
His broad-sword brandishing,   90
Down the French host did ding,
    As to o'erwhelm it;
And many a deep wound lent,
His arms with blood besprent,
And many a cruel dent
    Bruiséd his helmet.

Gloster, that duke so good,
Next of the royal blood,
For famous England stood
    With his brave brother.   100
Clarence, in steel so bright,
Though but a maiden knight,
Yet in that furious fight
    Scarce such another!

Warwick in blood did wade;
Oxford, the foe invade,
And cruel slaughter made,
    Still as they ran up.
Suffolk his axe did ply;
Beaumont and Willoughby   110
Bare them right doughtily;
    Ferrers, and Fanhope.

Upon Saint Crispin's Day
Fought was this noble fray
Which Fame did not delay
    To England to carry:

O when shall English men
With such acts fill a pen?
Or England breed again
    Such a King Harry!
(1605)

from IDEA'S MIRROR

1

Like an adventurous sea-farer am I,
Who hath some long and dangerous voyage been;
And called to tell of his discovery,
How far he sailed, what countries he had seen,
Proceeding from the port whence he put forth
Shows by his compass how his course he steered,
When east, when west, when south, and when by
    north,
As how the pole to every place was reared,
What capes he doubled, of what continent,
10 The gulfs and straits that strangely he had passed,
Where most becalmed, wherewith foul weather spent,
And on what rocks in peril to be cast.
    Thus, in my love, Time calls me to relate
    My tedious travels and oft-varying fate.
(1619)

3

Many there be excelling in this kind,
Whose well-tricked rimes with all invention swell.
Let each commend as best shall like his mind
Some Sidney, Constable, some Daniel.
That thus their names familiarly I sing
Let none think them disparagéd to be;
Poor men with reverence may speak of a king,
And so may these be spoken of by me.
My wanton verse ne'er keeps one certain stay,
10 But now at hand, then seeks invention far,
And with each little motion runs astray,
Wild, madding, jocund, and irregular.
    Like me that lust, my honest merry rimes
    Nor care for critic nor regard the times.
(1619)

12

As other men, so I myself do muse
Why in this sort I wrest invention so,
And why these giddy metaphors I use,
Leaving the path the greater part do go.

brother. 102. maiden, untried, inexperienced.
    Sonnet 1. 8. pole, etc. The horizon of every place was, seemingly,
raised—by approaching it in the ship.
    Sonnet 3. 1. this kind, i.e., in sonnets. 2. well-tricked, well-
adorned. 4. Sidney, Constable . . . Daniel. For Sidney and Daniel
see respectively p. 206 and p. 209; Henry Constable (1562-1613)
published his sonnet sequence Diana in 1592.
    Sonnet 12. 2. sort, kind, i.e., the sonnet form. 4. greater part,

I will resolve you. I am lunatic,
And ever this in madmen you shall find,
What they last thought on when the brain grew sick
In most distraction keep that still in mind.
Thus talking idly in this bedlam fit,
Reason and I, you must conceive, are twain;   10
'Tis nine years, now, since first I lost my wit.
Bear with me, then, though troubled be my brain.
    With diet and correction men distraught
    (Not too far past) may to their wits be brought.
(1619)

61

Since there's no help, come, let us kiss and part.
Nay, I have done; you get no more of me.
And I am glad, yea, glad with all my heart
That thus so cleanly I myself can free.
Shake hands for ever; cancel all our vows;
And when we meet at any time again,
Be it not seen in either of our brows
That we one jot of former love retain.
Now at the last gasp of Love's latest breath,
When, his pulse failing, Passion speechless lies,   10
When Faith is kneeling by his bed of death,
And Innocence is closing up his eyes—
    Now, if thou wouldst, when all have given him
        over,
    From death to life thou might'st him yet recover.
(1619)

THOMAS CAMPION 1567?-1619

*Thomas Campion was a poet, musician, and critic
who followed the advocates of classical measures in
attacking "the vulgar and inartificial custom of riming," but he was kept from putting his own theories
into practice by his sense of melody. He wrote several
successful court masques, a treatise on music, and
Four Books of Ayres, which contain most of his best
lyrics. Some of his songs he set to music himself.*

MY SWEETEST LESBIA

My sweetest Lesbia, let us live and love,
And though the sager sort our deeds reprove,
Let us not weigh them. Heaven's great lamps do dive
Into their west and straight again revive,
But soon as once set is our little light,
Then must we sleep one ever-during night.

i.e., most other sonnet writers. 11. nine years, an apparent allusion
to the length of his acquaintance with the subject of his sonnets. wit,
senses, judgment, intelligence.
    Lesbia, the name under which the Latin lyric poet Catullus (87-
54? B.C.) celebrated the subject of many of his verses. This poem and
several others reflect the influence upon Campion of Catullus and Horace.

If all would lead their lives in love like me,
Then bloody swords and armor should not be,
No drum nor trumpet peaceful sleeps should **move**,
10 Unless alarm came from the camp of love.
But fools do live, and waste their little light,
And seek with pain their ever-during night.

When timely death my life and fortune ends,
Let not my hearse be vexed with mourning friends,
But let all lovers, rich in triumph, come
And with sweet pastimes grace my happy tomb;
And, Lesbia, close up thou my little light,
And crown with love my ever-during night.
(1601)

THE MAN OF LIFE UPRIGHT

The man of life upright,
   Whose guiltless heart is free
From all dishonest deeds,
   Or thought of vanity,

The man whose silent days
   In harmless joys are spent,
Whom hopes cannot delude,
   Nor sorrow discontent;

That man needs neither towers
10   Nor armor for defense,
Nor secret vaults to fly
   From thunder's violence.

He only can behold
   With unaffrighted eyes
The horrors of the deep
   And terrors of the skies.

Thus, scorning all the cares
   That fate or fortune brings,
He makes the heaven his book,
20   His wisdom heavenly things,

Good thoughts his only friends,
   His wealth a well-spent age,
The earth his sober inn
   And quiet pilgrimage.
(1601)

ROSE-CHEEKED LAURA

Rose-cheeked Laura, come
Sing thou smoothly with thy beauty's

Silent music, either other
   Sweetly gracing.

Lovely forms do flow
From consent divinely framéd;
Heaven is music, and thy beauty's
   Birth is heavenly.

These dull notes we sing
Discords need for helps **to grace them.**   10
Only beauty purely **loving**
   Knows **no discord,**

But still moves delight,
Like clear springs renewed by flowing,
Ever perfect, ever in themselves eternal.
(1602)

JACK AND JOAN

Jack and Joan they think no ill,
But loving live, and merry still;
Do their week-days' work, and **pray**
Devoutly on the holy day;
Skip and trip it on the green,
And help to choose the summer queen;
Lash out, at a country feast,
Their silver penny with the best.

Well can they judge of nappy ale,
And tell at large a winter tale;   10
Climb up to the apple loft
And turn the crabs till they be soft.
Tib is all the father's joy,
And little Tom the mother's boy.
All their pleasure is content;
And care, to pay their yearly rent.

Joan can call by name her cows
And deck her windows with green boughs;
She can wreaths and tutties make,
And trim with plums a bridal cake.   20
Jack knows what brings gain or loss,
And his long flail can stoutly toss,
Makes the hedge, which others break,
And ever thinks what he doth speak.

Now, you courtly dames and knights,
That study only strange delights,
Though you scorn the home-spun gray
And revel in your rich array,
Though your tongues dissemble deep

Jack and Joan. 7. **Lash out,** squander. 9. **nappy,** foaming. 10.
at **large,** at length. 12. **crabs,** crabapples spread to ripen. 19. **tutties,**
nosegays. 23. **Makes,** mends.
Aspatia's Song, sung by the rejected sweetheart of Amintor in

³⁰ And can your heads from danger keep,
  Yet, for all your pomp and train,
  Securer lives the silly swain.
  (1613)

THERE IS A GARDEN IN HER FACE

There is a garden in her face,
  Where roses and white lilies grow,
A heavenly paradise is that place,
  Wherein all pleasant fruits do flow.
There cherries grow, which none may buy
Till "Cherry ripe!" themselves do cry.

Those cherries fairly do enclose
  Of orient pearl a double row;
Which when her lovely laughter shows,
10 They look like rose-buds filled with snow.
Yet them nor peer nor prince can buy,
Till "Cherry ripe!" themselves do cry.

Her eyes like angels watch them still;
  Her brows like bended bows do stand,
Threatening with piercing frowns to kill
  All that attempt with eye or hand
Those sacred cherries to come nigh,
Till "Cherry ripe!" themselves do cry.
(1618)

JOHN FLETCHER 1579-1625

John Fletcher was one of the best dramatists in the reign of James I. He wrote many plays alone, and wrote others in collaboration with Beaumont, Massinger, Rowley, Shakespeare, and other dramatists. His poetry is characterized by an extremely light, easy movement and by a lyrical quality which appears not only in the blank verse of his dramas but especially in the incidental lyrics with which these are adorned.

ASPATIA'S SONG

Lay a garland on my hearse
  Of the dismal yew;
Maidens, willow branches bear;
  Say I diéd true.

My love was false, but I was firm
  From my hour of birth:

Upon my buried body lie
  Lightly, gentle earth!
(1611)

MELANCHOLY

Hence, all you vain delights,
As short as are the nights
  Wherein you spend your folly!
There's naught in this life sweet,
If man were wise to see't,
  But only melancholy;
  O sweetest melancholy!

Welcome, folded arms and fixéd eyes,
A sigh that piercing mortifies,
A look that's fastened to the ground,   10
A tongue chained up without a sound!
Fountain heads and pathless groves,
Places which pale passion loves!
Moonlight walks, when all the fowls
Are warmly housed save bats and owls!
A midnight bell, a parting groan,
These are the sounds we feed upon.
Then stretch our bones in a still gloomy valley;
Nothing's so dainty sweet as lovely melancholy.
(1624)

THE MADRIGAL

The madrigal was originally a pastoral folk song, but the Elizabethan madrigal developed into the most intricate and courtly of part songs for several unaccompanied voices, sometimes as many as five or six, each of which was melodically independent of the others. The Tudor English were a singing people; that man of them was ill-trained who could play no instrument and take no part in singing. Borrowed from the Netherlands and Italy in the fifteenth century, the madrigal and similar songs became immensely popular in Elizabethan England. Most of the better poets at one time or another wrote lyrics which were intended to be set to these elaborate musical patterns, but today the poets are mostly unknown. It is characteristic of the type that the composers should be more honored than the makers of the words.

The selections are arranged chronologically. The musical composer of each and the song book in which it first appeared are cited in the footnotes.

The Maid's Tragedy, II. i.
  Melancholy, from The Nice Valour; with this song compare Milton's

Il Penseroso (p. 381). Here as in Milton's poem, Melancholy means pensive reflection, sober thoughtfulness.

SING WE AND CHANT IT

Sing we and chant it
While love doth grant it.
Not long youth lasteth,
And old age hasteth.
Now is best leisure
To take our pleasure.

All things invite us
Now to delight us.
Hence, care, be packing!
10 No mirth be lacking!
Let spare no treasure
To live in pleasure.

I FOLLOW, LO, THE FOOTING

I follow, lo, the footing
Still of my lovely cruel,
Proud of herself that she is beauty's jewel.

Madrigal singers, a woodcut by Jost Amman for Hans Sachs' Eigentliche Beschreibung aller Stände (1568).

And fast away she flieth

And fast away she flieth,
Love's sweet delight deriding,
In woods and groves sweet Nature's treasure hiding.
Yet cease I not pursuing,
But since I thus have sought her,
Will run me out of breath till I have caught her.

TO SHORTEN WINTER'S SADNESS

To shorten Winter's sadness,
See where the nymphs with gladness
Disguiséd all are coming
Right wantonly a-mumming.

Though masks encloud their beauty,
Yet give the eye her duty.
When heaven is dark it shineth,
And unto love inclineth.

SING WE AT PLEASURE

Sing we at pleasure,
Content is our treasure.
Sweet Love shall keep the ground,
Whilst we his praises sound
All shepherds in a ring
Shall, dancing, ever sing.

LADY, WHEN I BEHOLD

Lady, when I behold the roses sprouting,
Which, clad in damask mantles, deck the arbors,
And then behold your lips where sweet Love harbors,
My eyes presents me with a double doubting.
For, viewing both alike, hardly my mind supposes
Whether the roses be your lips, or your lips the roses.

FAIR PHYLLIS

Fair Phyllis I saw sitting all alone,
Feeding her flocks near to the mountainside.
The shepherds knew not whither she was gone,
But after her lover Amyntas hied.
Up and down he wandered whilst she was missing;
When he found her, O, then they fell a-kissing.

O CARE, THOU WILT DESPATCH ME

O Care, thou wilt despatch me,
If music do not match thee,

Sing We and Chant It, from Thomas Morley's *The First Book of Ballets* (1595).

I Follow, Lo, the Footing, from Thomas Morley's *Canzonets or Little Airs to Five and Six Voices* (1597). 2. **cruel,** adjective used for noun, cruel lady.

To Shorten Winter's Sadness, from Thomas Weelkes' *Ballets and Madrigals* (1598). 3. **Disguiséd all,** the court ladies, addressed as nymphs, were disguised and masked for a court pageant.

Sing We at Pleasure, from Thomas Weelkes' *Ballets and Madrigals* (1598). 3. **Sweet Love . . . ground,** Cupid will hold court.

Lady, When I Behold, from John Wilbye's *The First Set of English Madrigals* (1598). 4. **eyes presents,** frequent Elizabethan grammatical form for "eyes present." 5. **hardly,** with difficulty.

Fair Phyllis, from John Farmer's *The First Set of English Madrigals* (1599).

O Care, Thou Wilt Despatch Me, from Thomas Weelkes' *Madrigals of Five Parts, Apt for the Viols and Voices* (1600). 1. **despatch,** kill. 2. **match,** encounter and overthrow.

So deadly thou dost sting me,
Mirth only help can bring me.

Hence, Care, thou art too cruel,
Come, music, sick man's jewel.
His force had well nigh slain me,
But thou must now sustain me.

LIGHTLY SHE WHIPPED O'ER THE DALES

Lightly she whipped o'er the dales,
　Making the woods proud with her presence;
　　Gently she trod the flowers;
And as they gently kissed her tender feet
The birds in their best language bade her welcome,
Being proud that Oriana heard their song.
　　The clove-foot satyrs singing
　　Made music to the fauns a-dancing,
　　And both together with an emphasis
10　　Sang Oriana's praises,
Whilst the adjoining woods with melody
Did entertain their sweet, sweet harmony.
Then sang the shepherds and nymphs of Diana:
　　Long live fair Oriana.

SISTER, AWAKE

Sister, awake, close not your eyes,
　The day her light discloses;
And the bright morning doth arise
　Out of her bed of roses.
See the clear sun, the world's bright eye,
　In at our window peeping;
Lo, how he blushes to espy

Us idle wenches sleeping.
Therefore awake, make haste I say,
　And let us without staying　　　　　　　　10
All in our gowns of green so gay
　Into the park a-maying.

THERE IS A JEWEL

There is a jewel which no Indian mines
Can buy, no chimic art can counterfeit.
It makes men rich in greatest poverty;
Makes water wine, turns wooden cups to gold,
The homely whistle to sweet music's strain.
　Seldom it comes, to few from Heaven sent,
　That much in little, all in nought, Content.

AH, DEAR HEART

Ah, dear heart, why do you rise?
The light that shines comes from your eyes.
The day breaks not, it is my heart,
To think that you and I must part.
O stay, or else my joys will die
And perish in their infancy.

THE SILVER SWAN

The silver swan, who living had no note,
When death approached unlocked her silent throat;
Leaning her breast against the reedy shore,
Thus sung her first and last, and sung no more;
Farewell, all joys; O death, come close mine eyes;
More geese than swans now live, more fools than
　wise.

Lightly She Whipped o'er the Dales, by John Munday in *The Triumphs of Oriana*—composed by divers authors (1601). This is one of a sequence of madrigals addressed to Queen Elizabeth as Oriana, and all ending with the couplet:
　　"Then sang the shepherds and nymphs of Diana:
　　　Long live fair Oriana."
7. **clove-foot,** cloven-hoofed. **satyrs,** sylvan deities with goat's legs and feet. 8.**fauns,** deities of field and wood with pointed ears and horns.
Sister, Awake, from Thomas Bateson's *The First Set of English Madrigals* (1604). 12. **a-maying,** cf. Robert Herrick's *Corinna's Going*

A-Maying, p. 346.
There Is a Jewel, from John Wilbye's *The Second Set of Madrigals* (1609).
Ah, Dear Heart, from Orlando Gibbons' *The First Set of Madrigals and Motets* (1612). Authorship of this lyric is attributed to John Donne. A *motet* was a musical composition for a sacred text; the madrigals were all secular.
The Silver Swan, from Orlando Gibbons' *The First Set of Madrigals and Motets* (1612). The madrigal gives expression to the familiar belief that swans sing only while dying; the last line is a frequent satirical comparison.

EDMUND SPENSER c. 1552-1599

"The poets' poet": no epithet given to Edmund Spenser by his contemporaries fits him so well as that which Charles Lamb applied to him two centuries later. Lamb's phrase packs into three words both Spenser's limitations and his power. In his own time he was recognized as a new constellation in the firmament of poets, and ever since, he has been regarded as among the greatest. Popular, however, in the sense in which Shakespeare, Burns, and Tennyson are popular, he never was and never can be. For such popularity he is too scholarly, too intricate in his moods, too complex in his allegories, too varied in the expression of his emotions, too detached from life, too austere and remote. On the other hand, there is perhaps no other poet in English literature who possessed a richer variety of those elements which*

make poetry—a fecund fancy, an exquisite ear, an unerring judgment for words that are graphic, vivid, melodious; a sense of rhythm, assonance, alliteration, and other sound effects that gave to the stanza which he created the harmonies that have but echoed in the poetry of those who strove to imitate him. Thus the occasional reader of poetry will not turn first to The Faerie Queene, but the poet and the lover of poetic melody will. In his epithet Charles Lamb was both a recorder and a prophet, for poets before Lamb had drawn from Spenser, and poets since have gone to the same well of inspiration. So the romantic Keats, whose poetry is lyric mood in almost pure distillation, was introduced early to The Faerie Queene and "went through it," his friend Charles Cowden Clarke reported, "as a young horse through a spring meadow ramping," exclaiming in ecstasy at the poetic images and the melody of the stanzas.

Like his friends Sidney and Raleigh, Spenser belonged to the scholarly and courtly traditions in Elizabethan literature. His father was a clothier from a good family, who was apparently residing in London when the poet was born there about 1552. From the Merchant Taylors' School, where Spenser was entered as a sizar, or scholar receiving financial aid, he went to Pembroke Hall, Cambridge, and earned there both the B.A. and the M.A. degrees. The influence of the university upon him is noteworthy. At Cambridge he became steeped in Platonic philosophy, an influence apparent in many of his poems and notably in his Hymne to Beautie. Pembroke Hall, when Spenser was there, was strongly Calvinistic; and this influence appears in The Faerie Queene. Finally, at Cambridge he became the close friend of Gabriel Harvey, a brilliant young scholar and critic only a couple of years older than the poet. No prominent figure in the field of Elizabethan scholarship and literature has been more heartily attacked than has Gabriel Harvey. He has been thoroughly hated for his pedantry, his arrogance, his meddling in the literary labors of others. Perhaps he deserved some of this abuse, for his scholarship was undoubtedly narrowed by pedantry, and his conceit was accompanied by an arrogance that led him to strain at a literary dictatorship which his lack of art did not justify his assuming. Nevertheless, it should not be overlooked that Gabriel Harvey was a productive scholar whose friendships with Sidney, Spenser, and other poets could hardly have survived had he been a mere arrogant pedant. He and Spenser exchanged many letters on literary subjects, and the poet put him into The Shepheardes Calender in the figure of Hobbinol, a shepherd who praises "fayre Elisa," the queen.

Spenser took his M.A. degree in 1576. From Cambridge he seems to have retreated to Lancashire in the north of England for a sojourn of indefinite length among his kinsfolk there. From this period has emerged only one episode in Spenser's life—his love affair with a disdainful Lancashire lady. Her name is unknown, but in his first long poem, The Shepheardes Calender, she appears as Rosalind, the shepherdess who rejects the advances of Colin Clout, the pastoral impersonation of the poet himself. From this connection of the poem with the north country it would seem that some, at least, of the pastoral elements in Spenser's poetry may have come from his Lancashire visit. To this same country girl Spenser addressed his Hymnes in Honor of Love and Beautie, not published until 1596 but undoubtedly written in his youth. The ideas in these abstract poems were all derived from Plato's Symposium indirectly through the Commentary of Marsilio Ficino, an Italian Platonist who lived in the second half of the fifteenth century.

From Lancashire Spenser returned to London to enter the service of the Earl of Leicester, famous as Queen Elizabeth's favorite courtier. Sir Philip Sidney was Leicester's nephew, and it was not long before he and Spenser were firm friends. To him Spenser dedicated The Shepheardes Calender, published in 1579, a tribute much more sincere than Astrophel, a eulogistic poem written too long after Sidney's death. To this dedication Sidney responded in his Apology for Poetry: "The Shepheardes Calender hath much poetry in his eclogues, indeed worthy the reading, if I be not deceived. That same framing of his style to an old rustic language I dare not allow, since neither Theocritus in Greek, Virgil in Latin, nor Sannazaro in Italian did affect it." Thus the poet-critic at once praised the poetry and condemned the archaic language of his friend's pastorals.

When Spenser first made Sidney's acquaintance, the brilliant young nobleman was the leading member of a group of poets and scholars who called themselves the Areopagus. It is not apparent that Spenser was himself a member of this society, but under the influence of Gabriel Harvey he certainly sympathized for a while with its objectives, which were to put into effect the metrical theories expressed by Roger Ascham in The Schoolmaster (p. 182). Ascham believed that the English accentual verse was crude and inartistic and that it should be abandoned completely in favor of the Latin poetical measures. The only fruit of these theories appears in some metrical experimentations in Sidney's Arcadia. Spenser's interest in the theories and Harvey's pressure upon him were not sufficient, fortunately, to overcome his natural instinct for the native English metrical beat and rhythm.

Spenser's association with Lord Leicester may have cost him the preferment at court which the young scholar-courtier hoped to obtain, for Queen Elizabeth's friendly interest in him was not enough to overcome the opposition of Lord Burleigh, Leicester's jealous enemy and the Queen's Lord Treasurer and chief adviser. Failing to get an office in London, Spenser set out for Ireland in 1580 as secretary to Lord Grey de Wilton, Lord Deputy of Ireland. Grey was a zealous Puritan, whose policy in the unhappy island that he was sent to govern was a cruel root-and-branch stamping out of all rebellion. As his secretary, Spenser must have become thoroughly familiar with his chief's theories and practices. Apparently he came to regard them as stern but necessary, for he immortalized Lord Grey as Artegall, the knight-errant of Justice, in Book V of The Faerie Queene, and defended him ardently in his only notable prose writing, View of the Present State of Ireland, written after Grey had been replaced in office, but not published until 1633. Spenser profited by Grey's methods of seizure and repression, for in 1586 he was granted an Irish estate at Kilcolman in Munster, a home made uncomfortable by reason of constant quarrels with his Irish neighbors, but one that gave him, apparently, some opportunity for work on The Faerie Queene.

The Faerie Queene Spenser had begun to write before the publication of The Shepheardes Calender in 1579. Apparently, therefore, the two poetic symbols of shepherd and knight were born together in his mind. In 1583 he wrote from Ireland that work on the poem was progressing, and in 1589, when Raleigh visited him at Kilcolman Castle, Spenser was deep in the allegory and read portions of the poem to his visitor. Raleigh, himself a poet, was delighted. At his insistence Spenser returned to London with him, and in 1590 the first three books of The Faerie Queene were published with a dedication to "The most Mightie and Magnificent Empresse Elizabeth." The fame and the pension which came with the publication of the poem did not bring with them any regular preferment at court, and Spenser's disappointment was expressed in The Tears of the Muses, a lament for the neglected state of poetry, and in Prosopopoia, or, Mother Hubberd's Tale, an allegorical satire of court manners. The year after the publication of the first part of The Faerie Queene Spenser returned to Ireland, recording his return by Colin Clout's Come Home Again, another allegorical attack on court taste. On June 11, 1594, after a prolonged courtship, which is commemorated in his sonnet sequence Amoretti, he married Elizabeth Boyle, an Irish lady of excellent family. His marriage he celebrated in Epithalamion, probably the most lyrical of all his poems. The next year found him again in London to present to her Majesty the second part of The Faerie Queene, published in 1596. On the occasion of this visit he also published his Hymns in Honor of Love and Beautie, which he had written in his youth under the inspiration of his Lancashire Rosalind, and Prothalamion, an espousal poem celebrating the double marriage of the two daughters of the Earl of Worcester at the house of the Earl of Essex. In 1597 he returned to his family at Kilcolman.

Spenser entered again upon what he chose to consider an exile from court with the full intention of completing the remaining books, of his great poem, for of the twelve projected books he had written by 1596 only six and a part of the seventh. The poem was destined to remain a grand fragment. Shortly after his appointment as Sheriff of Cork in 1598, occurred the Irish rebellion under Hugh O'Neill, Earl of Tyrone, and the English colonists in Munster were attacked with all the savage vindictiveness of an outraged people. Spenser and his wife and four children saved themselves by flight, but Kilcolman Castle was captured by the rebels and burned. The newly made sheriff was dispatched to London to make an oral report of the uprising. The grief and exhaustion of his recent experiences, however, brought on a sickness from which he did not have the strength to recover. He died January 16, 1599, and was buried in Westminster Abbey not far from the tomb of Geoffrey Chaucer, the poet to whom he owed most in inspiration and technique.

---

from **THE FAERIE QUEENE**

Spenser's reputation and popularity through the centuries have seesawed up and down in an unprecedented manner, dizzily swinging from one extreme of favor to the other. But while the general reading public has often dismissed him as too precious, he has always exerted a great formative influence on young poets—on Keats, for example, and Tennyson. Certainly Spenser deserves Lamb's accolade "the poet's poet," but it would be rash to conclude that he is therefore unenjoyable or inaccessible to the common reader. After all, his primary appeal, like Chaucer's and Malory's, remains narrative. One must first resuscitate an almost childlike submissiveness to the pace, the matter, and the dramatic immediacy of The Faerie Queene in order to participate pleasurably in the story's slow, involuted unfolding. To be strict, this curious long poem is neither a series of sensuously detailed medieval tableaux nor an unfinished allegorical romance, and the well-known epic resemblance really applies to its superficial architecture alone. How, then, should The Faerie Queene be characterized as a special instance of narrative poetry? In its illogical, dreamlike progression it seems first of all to have certain conceptual affinities, which C. S. Lewis has designated "polyphonic" or "interwoven" in narrative character, with a species of antique myth and medieval tale. The work, moreover, appears incipiently a form of drama; it contains all the stuff of elemental drama—of, say, the morality play—and it stipulates an unmediated, prerational response to the events as they occur. The reader must abandon sophistication and return to that twilight level of consciousness where, in some sense, he literally believes in the wicked magicianship of Archimago much as a child believes in witches, goblins, or bogeys. A powerful imaginative creation like Archimago persistently eludes reduction to the neat interpretive pigeonhole "personification of Hypocrisy." He must be allowed to reinduce a kind of universal childish fear in the mind, the fear of something dreadful and malign lurking there in the darkness for the unwary soul. And so what, then, if he first bustles into a narrative sequence, drops out for a time while Spenser unaccountably becomes involved with some new set of characters and adventures, and at last, just as unaccountably, pops up again? This inconclusive quality of narrative progression, often so maddening to the logic-minded modern reader, is just the point: Archimago, like the devil, must be viewed as a permanent entity of human psychology and primitive experiential apprehension; he is always there, his pranks never concluded.

The same bygone mode of awareness and reaction holds true, of course, for the rest of the poem's parade of grotesques—for that ubiquitous archetypal temptress Duessa, for example, and that basely intentioned male relative of hers, the obsessive Busirane. All Spenser's personalized embodiments of the forces of negation and sensual threat transcend equation with academic abstractions of sin. They are vital symbolic and dramatic distillations from universal experience, not the externally manipulated stick figures of simplistic moral allegory. No individual who has ever been as intensely involved as the Redcrosse Knight with the eternal problem of coping with life—of "finding himself" in the cherished modern cliché—could doubt the profound psychological realism attending his capitulation to the flesh, his subsequent agonies of shame and despair, and his final spiritual rehabilitation. Appropriately, it is also the account of the Redcrosse Knight which may best exemplify one of Spenser's most important themes in The Faerie Queene, the evaluative discrepancy between true and false choice; for it is only when the hero has arduously acquired the capacity for moral insight that he can "see" the real ugliness beneath Duessa's alluring external appearance and deceitful impersonations:

... that witch they disaraid....
. . . .
Ne spared they to strip her naked all.
Then when they had despoiled her tire and call,
Such as she was, their eyes might her behold,
That her misshapen parts did them appall;

A loathly, wrinkled bag, ill favoured, old,
Whose secret filth good manners biddeth not be told.

(I, viii, 46)

After his humiliating captivity under Duessa and the long ritual of purgation, moreover, the Redcrosse Knight can truly apprehend his radiant Una for the first time and appreciate her worth in terms no longer merely theoretical. Through profiting from painful experience he entitles himself not only to her love but to reinstatement in Gloriana's crusade of moral idealism.

Spenser's little allegorical Bildungsroman of the Redcrosse Knight may suggest, in addition, a certain method in the madness of his quixotic narrative windings. He seems, that is, to conceive of time as a continuum in which man is perpetually falling, perpetually reasserting himself, perpetually riding forth to slay more dragons and confront the same old lures in more sophisticated guises. A generative principle of this variety appears to provide the basic curve of action for every book of The Faerie Queene; it accounts, further, for such recurrent staples of "plot" as the dramatically externalized inner conflict or confusion between lust and love (e.g., Duessa versus Una, Acrasia versus Alma) and incarceration in dens of sensuality (e.g., the Bower of Bliss, the House of Busirane). Evidently everyone in this imagined world must learn for himself, the hard way, again and again. It is Spenser's business in The Faerie Queene to give life and individuation to the timeless drama of Everyman's making an exemplum of himself. In doing so he becomes a kind of myth maker, a dealer in symbolic, extratemporal narrative representations of reality. He creates, in the process, a new strain of English verse narrative which blends the total resource of lyricism with an intrinsically dramatic potentiality.

Spenser's introduction of a complex nine-line stanza ending in an alexandrine as his basic metrical unit in The Faerie Queene largely dictates the deep, brooding tone of the poem. It is a stately measure, capable of evoking a whole range of melancholy, or voluptuousness, or dread. Milton, who admired Spenser's overall poetic technique in The Faerie Queene, described it definitively as "sage and solemn tunes."

A LETTER OF THE AUTHORS,

Expounding his whole intention in the course of this worke: which, for that it giveth great light to the reader, for the better understanding is hereunto annexed.

To the Right Noble and Valorous SIR WALTER RALEIGH, KNIGHT;

Lord Wardein of the Stanneryes, and Her Maiesties Liefetenaunt of the County of Cornewayll.

Sir, knowing how doubtfully all allegories may be construed, and this booke of mine which I have entituled the *Faery Queene*, being a continued allegory, or darke conceit, I have thought good, as well for avoyding of gealous opinions and misconstructions, as also for your better light in reading thereof, (being so by you commanded) to discover unto you the generall intention and meaning, which in the whole course thereof I have fashioned, without expressing of any 10 particular purposes, or by accidents therein occasioned. The generall end therefore of all the booke is to fashion a gentleman or noble person in vertuous and gentle discipline: which for that I conceived shoulde be most plausible and pleasing, being coloured with an historicall fiction, the which the most part of men delight to read, rather for variety of matter then for profite of the ensample, I chose the historye of King Arthure, as most fitte for the excellency of his person, being made famous by many men's former workes, and 20 also furthest from the daunger of envy, and suspition of present time. In which I have followed all the antique Poets historicall: first Homere, who in the Persons of Agamemnon and Ulysses hath ensampled a good governour and a vertuous man, the one in his Ilias, the other in his Odysseis; then Virgil, whose like intention was to doe in the person of Aeneas; after him Ariosto comprised them both in his Orlando: and lately Tasso dissevered them againe, and formed both parts in two persons, namely that part which they in 30 Philosophy call Ethice, or vertues of a private man, coloured in his Rinaldo; the other named Politice in his God fredo. By ensample of which excellente poets, I labour to pourtraict in Arthure, before he was king, the image of a brave knight, perfected in the twelve private morall vertues, as Aristotle hath devised; the which is the purpose of these first twelve bookes: which if I finde to be well accepted, I may be perhaps encoraged to frame the other part of polliticke vertues in his person, after that hee came to be king. 40 To some, I know, this methode will seeme displeasaunt, which had rather have good discipline delivered plainly in way of precepts, or sermoned at large, as they use, then thus clowdily enwrapped in Allegoricall devises. But such, me seeme, should be satisfide with the use of these dayes, seeing all things accounted by their showes, and nothing esteemed of, that is not delightfull and pleasing to commune sence. For this cause is Xenophon preferred before Plato, for that the one, in the exquisite depth of his judgement, 50 formed a commune welth, such as it should be; but the other in the person of Cyrus, and the Persians, fashioned a governement, such as might best be: so much more profitable and gratious is doctrine by ensample, then by rule. So haue I laboured to doe in

the person of Arthure: whome I conceive, after his long education by Timon, to whom he was by Merlin delivered to be brought up, so soone as he was borne of the Lady Igrayne, to have seene in a dream or vision the Faery Queene, with whose excellent beauty ravished, he awaking resolved to seeke her out; 60 and so being by Merlin armed, and by Timon throughly instructed, he went to seeke her forth in Faerye land. In that Faery Queene I meane glory in my generall intention, but in my particular I conceive the most excellent and glorious person of our soveraine the Queene, and her kingdome in Faery land. And yet, in some places els, I doe otherwise shadow her. For considering she beareth two persons, the one of a most royall Queene or Empresse, the other of a most vertuous and beautifull Lady, this latter part in some 70 places I doe expresse in Belphoebe, fashioning her name according to your owne excellent conceipt of Cynthia (Phoebe and Cynthia being both names of Diana). So in the person of Prince Arthure I sette forth magnificence in particular, which vertue for that (according to Aristotle and the rest) it is the perfection of all the rest, and conteineth in it them all, therefore in the whole course I mention the deedes of Arthure applyable to that vertue, which I write of in that booke. But of the xii. other vertues, I make xii. 80 other knights the patrones, for the more variety of the history: of which these three bookes contayn three. The first of the knight of the Redcrosse, in whome I expresse holynes: The seconde of Sir Guyon, in whome I sette forth temperaunce: The third of Britomartis, a lady knight, in whome I picture chastity. But, because the beginning of the whole worke seemeth abrupte, and as depending upon other antecedents, it needs that ye know the occasion of these three knights' severall adventures. For the methode of a poet histori- 90 cal is not such, as of an historiographer. For an historiographer discourseth of affayres orderly as they were donne, accounting as well the times as the actions; but a poet thrusteth into the middest, even where it most concerneth him, and there recoursing to the thinges forepaste, and divining of thinges to come, maketh a pleasing analysis of all.

The beginning therefore of my history, if it were to be told by an historiographer, should be the twelfth booke, which is the last; where I devise that the Faery 100 Queene kept her annuall feaste xii. dayes; upon which xii. severall dayes, the occasions of the xii. severall adventures hapned, which, being undertaken by xii. severall knights, are in these xii. books severally handled and discoursed. The first was this. In the beginning of the feast, there presented him selfe a tall clownishe younge man, who, falling before the Queene of Faeries, desired a boone (as the manner then was)

A Letter of the Authors. 10. **by accidents,** incidental matters. 14. **plausible,** acceptable. 50. **commune welth,** commonwealth; the allusion is to Xenophon's *Cyropaedia,* a political romance. 67. **shadow her,** represent her allegorically. 94. **into the middest.** This is the classical theory, expressed in Horace's *Ars Poetica* in the phrase *in medias res.*

which during that feast she might not refuse: which was that hee might have the atchievement of any adventure, which during that feaste should happen: that being graunted, he rested him on the floore, unfitte through his rusticity for a better place. Soone after entred a faire ladye in mourning weedes, riding on a white asse, with a dwarfe behind her leading a warlike steed, that bore the armes of a knight, and his speare in the dwarfes hand. Shee, falling before the
10 Queene of Faeries, complayned that her father and mother, an ancient king and queene, had bene by an huge dragon many years shut up in a brasen castle, who thence suffred them not to yssew; and therefore besought the Faery Queene to assygne her some one of her knights to take on him that exployt. Presently that clownish person, upstarting, desired that adventure: whereat the Queene much wondering, and the lady much gainesaying, yet he earnestly importuned his desire. In the end the lady told him, that unlesse
20 that armour which she brought, would serve him (that is, the armour of a Christian man specified by Saint Paul, vi. Ephes.) that he could not succeed in that enterprise: which being forthwith put upon him, with dewe furnitures thereunto, he seemed the goodliest man in al that company, and was well liked of the lady. And eftesoones taking on him knighthood, and mounting on that straunge courser, he went forth with her on that adventure: where beginneth the first booke, viz.

30 *A gentle knight was pricking on the playne, etc.*

The second day there came in a palmer, bearing an infant with bloody hands, whose parents he complained to have bene slayn by an enchaunteresse called Acrasia; and therefore craved of the Faery Queene, to appoint him some knight to performe that adventure; which being assigned to Sir Guyon, he presently went forth with that same palmer: which is the beginning of the second booke, and the whole subject thereof. The third day there came in a groome, who
40 complained before the Faery Queene, that a vile enchaunter, called Busirane, had in hand a most faire lady, called Amoretta, whom he kept in most grievous torment, because she would not yield him the pleasure of her body. Whereupon Sir Scudamour, the lover of that lady, presently tooke on him that adventure. But being unable to performe it by reason of the hard enchauntments, after long sorrow, in the end met with Britomartis, who succoured him, and reskewed his love.

But by occasion hereof many other adventures are
50 intermedled; but rather as accidents then intendments:

as the love of Britomart, the overthrow of Marinell, the misery of Florimell, the vertuousness of Belphoebe, the lasciviousness of Hellenora, and many the like.

Thus much, Sir, I have briefly overronne, to direct your understanding to the welhead of the history, that from thence gathering the whole intention of the conceit ye may, as in a handfull, gripe al the discourse, which otherwise may happily seeme tedious and confused. So, humbly craving the continuance of your honorable favour towards me, and th'eternall estab- 60 lishment of your happines, I humbly take leave.

23. January, 1589.
Yours most humbly affectionate,
Ed. Spenser

from BOOK I

1

Lo I the man, whose Muse whilome did maske,
As time her taught, in lowly Shepheards weeds,
Am now enforst a far unfitter taske,
For trumpets sterne to chaunge mine Oaten reeds,
And sing of Knights and Ladies gentle deeds;
Whose prayses having slept in silence long,
Me, all too meane, the sacred Muse areeds
To blazon broad emongst her learned throng:
Fierce warres and faithfull loves shall moralize
  my song.

2

Helpe then, O holy Virgin chiefe of nine,   10
Thy weaker Novice to performe thy will,
Lay forth out of thine everlasting scryne
The antique rolles, which there lye hidden still,
Of Faerie knights and fairest *Tanaquill*,
Whom that most noble Briton Prince so long
Sought through the world, and suffered so much ill,
That I must rue his undeserved wrong:
O helpe thou my weake wit, and sharpen my dull tong.

3

And thou most dreaded impe of highest *Jove*,
Faire *Venus* sonne, that with thy cruell dart   20
At that good knight so cunningly didst rove,
That glorious fire it kindled in his hart,
Lay now thy deadly Heben bow apart,
And with thy mother milde come to mine ayde:
Come both, and with you bring triumphant *Mart*,

13. **yssew**, issue. 24. **furnitures**, articles to complete the equipment. 26. **eftesoones**, forthwith. 49. **by occasion**, incidentally. 50. **intendments**, definite plan.
    Book I. 1. **whilome**, formerly. 2. **Shepheards weeds**, allusion to his authorship of *The Shepheardes Calender*. 4. **trumpets . . . reeds**, respectively, the symbols of epic and of pastoral poetry. 7. **sacred Muse**, Clio. **areeds**, appoints. 10. **Virgin . . . nine**, Clio, the

muse of history. 11. **weaker**. The comparative is here used as an intensive, too weak. 12. **scryne**, shrine; here depository for historical rolls. 14. **Tanaquill**, Queen Elizabeth. 15. **Briton Prince**, King Arthur. 19. **impe**, child; the allusion is to Cupid, son of Venus. 21. **rove**, shoot with an arrow; a term in archery. 23. **Heben**, ebony —suggestive of deadliness. 25. **Mart**, Mars, god of war and paramour of Venus. 28. **Goddesse**, Elizabeth, frequently associated in contem-

In loves and gentle jollities arrayd,
After his murdrous spoiles and bloudy rage allayd.

4

And with them eke, O Goddesse heavenly bright,
Mirrour of grace and Majestie divine,
30 Great Lady of the greatest Isle, whose light
Like *Phoebus* lampe throughout the world doth shine,
Shed thy faire beames into my feeble eyne,
And raise my thoughts too humble and too vile,
To thinke of that true glorious type of thine,
The argument of mine afflicted stile:
The which to heare, vouchsafe, O dearest dred a-while.

CANTO I

The Patron of true Holinesse,
  foule Errour doth defeate:
Hypocrisie him to entrappe,
  doth to his home entreate.

1

A Gentle Knight was pricking on the plaine,
Ycladd in mightie armes and silver shielde,
Wherein old dints of deepe wounds did remaine,
The cruell markes of many' a bloudy fielde;
Yet armes till that time did he never wield:
His angry steede did chide his foming bitt,
As much disdayning to the curbe to yield:
Full jolly knight he seemd, and faire did sitt,
As one for knightly giusts and fierce encounters fitt.

2

10 But on his brest a bloudie Crosse he bore,
The deare remembrance of his dying Lord,
For whose sweete sake that glorious badge he wore,
And dead as living ever him ador'd:
Upon his shield the like was also scor'd,
For soveraine hope, which in his helpe he had:
Right faithfull true he was in deede and word,
But of his cheere did seeme too solemne sad;
Yet nothing did he dread, but ever was ydrad.

3

Upon a great adventure he was bond,
20 That greatest *Gloriana* to him gave,
That greatest Glorious Queene of *Faerie* lond,
To winne him worship, and her grace to have,

Which of all earthly things he most did crave;
And ever as he rode, his hart did earne
To prove his puissance in battell brave
Upon his foe, and his new force to learne;
Upon his foe, a Dragon horrible and stearne.

4

A lovely Ladie rode him faire beside,
Upon a lowly Asse more white then snow,
Yet she much whiter, but the same did hide   30
Under a vele, that wimpled was full low,
And over all a blacke stole she did throw,
As one that inly mournd: so was she sad,
And heavie sat upon her palfrey slow:
Seemed in heart some hidden care she had,
And by her in a line a milke white lambe she lad.

5

So pure an innocent, as that same lambe,
She was in life and every vertuous lore,
And by descent from Royall lynage came
Of ancient Kings and Queenes, that had of yore   40
Their scepters stretcht from East to Westerne shore,
And all the world in their subjection held;
Till that infernall feend with foule uprore
Forwasted all their land, and them expeld:
Whom to avenge, she had this Knight from far
  compeld.

6

Behind her farre away a Dwarfe did lag,
That lasie seemd in being ever last,
Or wearied with bearing of her bag
Of needments at his backe. Thus as they past,
The day with cloudes was suddeine overcast,   50
And angry *Jove* an hideous storme of raine
Did poure into his Lemans lap so fast,
That every wight to shrowd it did constrain,
And this faire couple eke to shroud themselves were
  fain.

7

Enforst to seeke some covert nigh at hand,
A shadie grove not far away they spide,
That promist ayde the tempest to withstand:
Whose loftie trees yclad with sommers pride,
Did spred so broad, that heavens light did hide,
Not perceable with power of any starre: 60

porary literature with the goddesses of classical mythology. **31. Phoebus lampe,** the sun. **33. vile,** lowly. **34. glorious . . . thine,**
Gloriana, the Faerie Queene. **35. afflicted stile,** lowly pen. **36.
dearest dred,** direst inspirer of awe. *Canto i.* 1. **pricking,** spurring
forth. 8. **jolly,** bold. 9. **giusts,** jousts. 17. **cheere,** countenance.
18. **ydrad,** dreaded, feared. 24. **earne,** yearn. 27. **Dragon,** Sin. 28.
A lovely Ladie, Una, Spenser's allegorical representation of religious

truth; note that she is introduced in an associative context that recalls
the Virgin Mary. **29. a lowly Asse,** the symbol of humility and suggestive, like the *bloudie Crosse,* of Christ's atonement. **31. wimpled,**
pleated. **32. stole,** a robe. **36. in a line,** by a cord. **46. Dwarfe,**
Prudence. **52. Lemans,** lover's; *Jove* is used here to symbolize the
heavens, and *Lemans lap* the earth. There is also a suggestion here
of the myth of Danae and the shower of gold.

Edmund Spenser 223

And all within were pathes and alleies wide,
With footing worne, and leading inward farre:
Faire harbour that them seemes; so in they entred arre.

8

And foorth they passe, with pleasure forward led,
Joying to heare the birdes sweete harmony,
Which therein shrouded from the tempest dred,
Seemd in their song to scorne the cruell sky.
Much can they prayse the trees so straight and hy,
The sayling Pine, the Cedar proud and tall,
70 The vine-prop Elme, the Poplar never dry,
The builder Oake, sole king of forrests all,
The Aspine good for staves, the Cypresse funerall.

9

The Laurell, meed of mightie Conquerours
And Poets sage, the Firre that weepeth still,
The Willow worne of forlorne Paramours,
The Eugh obedient to the benders will,
The Birch for shaftes, the Sallow for the mill,
The Mirrhe sweete bleeding in the bitter wound,
The warlike Beech, the Ash for nothing ill,
80 The fruitful Olive, and the Platane round,
The carver Holme, the Maple seeldom inward sound.

10

Led with delight, they thus beguile the way,
Untill the blustring storme is overblowne;
When weening to returne, whence they did stray,
They cannot finde that path, which first was showne,
But wander too and fro in wayes unknowne,
Furthest from end then, when they neerest weene,
That makes them doubt, their wits be not their owne:
So many pathes, so many turnings seene,
90 That which of them to take, in diverse doubt they
   been.

11

At last resolving forward still to fare,
Till that some end they finde or in or out,
That path they take, that beaten seemd most bare,
And like to lead the labyrinth about;
Which when by tract they hunted had throughout,
At length it brought them to a hollow cave,
Amid the thickest woods. The Champion stout
Eftsoones dismounted from his courser brave,
And to the Dwarfe a while his needlesse spere he gave.

12

Be well aware, quoth then that Ladie milde,   100
Least suddaine mischiefe ye too rash provoke:
The danger hid, the place unknowne and wilde,
Breedes dreadfull doubts: Oft fire is without smoke,
And perill without show: therefore your stroke
Sir knight with-hold, till further triall made.
Ah Ladie (said he) shame were to revoke
The forward footing for an hidden shade:
Vertue gives her selfe light, through darkenesse for
   to wade.

13

Yea but (quoth she) the perill of this place
I better wot then you, though now too late   110
To wish you backe returne with foule disgrace,
Yet wisedome warnes, whilest foot is in the gate,
To stay the steppe, ere forced to retrate.
This is the wandring wood, this *Errours den*,
A monster vile, whom God and man does hate:
Therefore I read beware. Fly fly (quoth then
The fearefull Dwarfe:) this is no place for living men.

14

But full of fire and greedy hardiment,
The youthfull knight could not for ought be staide,
But forth unto the darksome hole he went,   120
And looked in: his glistring armor made
A litle glooming light, much like a shade,
By which he saw the ugly monster plaine,
Halfe like a serpent horribly displaide,
But the'other halfe did womans shape retaine,
Most lothsom, filthie, foule, and full of vile disdaine.

15

And as she lay upon the durtie ground,
Her huge long taile her den all overspred,
Yet was in knots and many boughtes upwound,
Pointed with mortall sting. Of her there bred   130
A thousand yong ones, which she dayly fed,
Sucking upon her poisonous dugs, eachone
Of sundry shapes, yet all ill favored:
Soone as that uncouth light upon them shone,
Into her mouth they crept, and suddain all were gone.

16

Their dam upstart, out of her den effraide,
And rushed forth, hurling her hideous taile

---

68. **prayse the trees,** etc. In ll. 69-81 Spenser imitates Chaucer's *Parliament of Fowls,* ll. 171-182; but similar conventions appear also in numerous classical and medieval poems. 73. **meed,** reward. 76. **Eugh,** yew. 77. **Sallow,** a species of willow. 80. **Platane,** plane tree. 81. **Holme,** a species of oak. 84. **weening,** supposing. 86. **in wayes unknowne.** The travelers have now become in a sense spiritually disoriented or "lost"; see ll. 114-116. 116. **read,** advise. **Fly fly,** Prudence counsels the knight to take the safe (but dishonorable) course of action. 124. **Halfe . . . serpent,** a lamia-type creature. 129. **boughtes,** coils. 134. **uncouth,** unfamiliar, strange. 136. **effraide,** frightened. 139. **entraile,** coiling. 141. **to point,** completely. 145. **Elfe.** The Redcrosse Knight was of elfin birth. 147. **trenchand,**

About her cursed head, whose folds displaid
Were stretcht now forth at length without entraile.
140 She lookt about, and seeing one in mayle
Armed to point, sought backe to turne againe;
For light she hated as the deadly bale,
Ay wont in desert darknesse to remaine,
Where plaine none might her see, nor she see any
    plaine.

17

Which when the valiant Elfe perceiv'd, he lept
As Lyon fierce upon the flying pray,
And with his trenchand blade her boldly kept
From turning backe, and forced her to stay:
Therewith enrag'd she loudly gan to bray,
150 And turning fierce, her speckled taile advaunst,
Threatning her angry sting, him to dismay:
Who nought aghast, his mightie hand enhaunst:
The stroke down from her head unto her shoulder
    glaunst.

18

Much daunted with that dint, her sence was dazd,
Yet kindling rage, her selfe she gathered round,
And all attonce her beastly body raizd
With doubled forces high above the ground:
Tho wrapping up her wrethed sterne arownd,
Lept fierce upon his shield, and her huge traine
160 All suddenly about his body wound,
That hand or foot to stirre he strove in vaine:
God helpe the man so wrapt in *Errours* endlesse traine.

19

His Lady sad to see his sore constraint,
Cride out, Now, now, Sir knight, shew what ye bee,
Add faith unto your force, and be not faint:
Strangle her, else she sure will strangle thee.
That when he heard, in great perplexitie,
His gall did grate for griefe and high disdaine,
And knitting all his force got one hand free,
170 Wherewith he grypt her gorge with so great paine,
That soone to loose her wicked bands did her
    constraine.

20

Therewith she spewd out of her filthy maw
A floud of poyson horrible and blacke,
Full of great lumpes of flesh and gobbets raw,

Which stunck so vildly, that it forst him slacke
His grasping hold, and from her turne him backe:
Her vomit full of bookes and papers was,
With loathly frogs and toades, which eyes did lacke,
And creeping sought way in the weedy gras:
Her filthy parbreake all the place defiled has.   180

21

As when old father *Nilus* gins to swell
With timely pride above the *Aegyptian* vale,
His fattie waves do fertile slime outwell,
And overflow each plaine and lowly dale:
But when his later spring gins to avale,
Huge heapes of mudd he leaves, wherein there breed
Ten thousand kindes of creatures, partly male
And partly female of his fruitfull seed;
Such ugly monstrous shapes elswhere may no man
    reed.

22

The same so sore annoyed has the knight,   190
That welnigh choked with the deadly stinke,
His forces faile, ne can no longer fight.
Whose corage when the feend perceiv'd to shrinke,
She poured forth out of her hellish sinke
Her fruitfull cursed spawne of serpents small,
Deformed monsters, fowle, and blacke as inke,
Which swarming all about his legs did crall,
And him encombred sore, but could not hurt at all.

23

As gentle Shepheard in sweete even-tide,
When ruddy *Phoebus* gins to welke in west,   200
High on an hill, his flocke to vewen wide,
Markes which do byte their hasty supper best;
A cloud of cumbrous gnattes do him molest,
All striving to infixe their feeble stings,
That from their noyance he no where can rest,
But with his clownish hands their tender wings
He brusheth oft, and oft doth mar their murmurings.

24

Thus ill bestedd, and fearefull more of shame,
Then of the certaine perill he stood in,
Halfe furious unto his foe he came,   210
Resolv'd in minde all suddenly to win,
Or soone to lose, before he once would lin;
And strooke at her with more then manly force,

trenchant, sharp. 152. **enhaunst,** lifted up. 168. **grate,** stir. **griefe,** anger. 170. **gorge,** throat. 174. **gobbets,** lumps. 177. **bookes and papers,** presumably pamphlet 'attacks on English church and state (or just corrupt literature in general). 185. **his . . . avale,** his flood begins to subside. The river Nile is here represented as a river god. Note the associations of fertility and sexuality which pervade the depiction of Error. 189. **reed,** see. 199. **gentle Shepheard, etc.,** a Homeric or epic simile, a long and elaborate comparison; cf. Stanza 21. 200. **welke,** fade, wane. 203. **cumbrous,** harassing. 208. **bestedd,** beset. 212. **lin,** stop. 213. **manly,** human.

That from her body full of filthie sin
He raft her hatefull head without remorse;
A streame of cole black bloud forth gushed from
    her corse.

25

Her scattred brood, soone as their Parent deare
They saw so rudely falling to the ground,
Groning full deadly, all with troublous feare,
220 Gathred themselves about her body round,
Weening their wonted entrance to have found
At her wide mouth: but being there withstood
They flocked all about her bleeding wound,
And sucked up their dying mothers blood,
Making her death their life, and eke her hurt their
    good.

26

That detestable sight him much amazde,
To see th'unkindly Impes of heaven accurst,
Devoure their dam; on whom while so he gazd,
Having all satisfide their bloudy thurst,
230 Their bellies swolne he saw with fulnesse burst,
And bowels gushing forth: well worthy end
Of such as drunke her life, the which them nurst;
Now needeth him no lenger labour spend,
His foes have slaine themselves, with whom he
    should contend.

27

His Ladie seeing all, that chaunst, from farre
Approcht in hast to greet his victorie,
And said, Faire knight, borne under happy starre,
Who see your vanquisht foes before you lye;
Well worthy be you of that Armorie,
240 Wherein ye have great glory wonne this day,
And proov'd your strength on a strong enimie,
Your first adventure: many such I pray,
And henceforth ever wish, that like succeed it may.

28

Then mounted he upon his Steede againe,
And with the Lady backward sought to wend;
That path he kept, which beaten was most plaine,
Ne ever would to any by-way bend,
But still did follow one unto the end,
The which at last out of the wood them brought.
250 So forward on his way (with God to frend)
He passed forth, and new adventure sought;
Long way he travelled, before he heard of ought.

At length they chaunst to meet upon the way
An aged Sire, in long blacke weedes yclad,
His feete all bare, his beard all hoarie gray,
And by his belt his booke he hanging had;
Sober he seemde, and very sagely sad,
And to the ground his eyes were lowly bent,
Simple in shew, and voyde of malice bad,
And all the way he prayed, as he went,   260
And often knockt his brest, as one that did repent.

30

He faire the knight saluted, louting low,
Who faire him quited, as that courteous was:
And after asked him, if he did know
Of straunge adventures, which abroad did pas.
Ah my deare Sonne (quoth he) how should, alas,
Silly old man, that lives in hidden cell,
Bidding his beades all day for his trespas,
Tydings of warre and worldly trouble tell?
With holy father sits not with such things to mell.   270

31

But if of daunger which hereby doth dwell,
And homebred evill ye desire to heare,
Of a straunge man I can you tidings tell,
That wasteth all this countrey farre and neare.
Of such (said he) I chiefly do inquere,
And shall you well reward to shew the place,
In which that wicked wight his dayes doth weare:
For to all knighthood it is foule disgrace,
That such a cursed creature lives so long a space.

32

Far hence (quoth he) in wastfull wildernesse   280
His dwelling is, by which no living wight
May ever passe, but thorough great distresse.
Now (sayd the Lady) draweth toward night,
And well I wote, that of your later fight
Ye all forwearied be: for what so strong,
But wanting rest will also want of might?
The Sunne that measures heaven all day long,
At night doth baite his steedes the *Ocean* waves emong.

33

Then with the Sunne take Sir, your timely rest,
And with new day new worke at once begin: 290
Untroubled night they say gives counsell best.
Right well Sir knight ye have advised bin,
(Quoth then that aged man;) the way to win

---

215. **raft**, bereft. 227. **unkindly**, unnatural. **Impes**, children, brood.
239. **Armorie**, armor (bearing the Christian symbol). 250. **to frend**,
as a friend. 256. **his booke**, his prayer book. 257. **sad**, pensive,
thoughtful. 262. **louting**, bending. 263. **quited**, requited, returned

the salutation. 267. **Silly**, simple. 268. **Bidding**, telling, counting.
270. **With, etc.** It befits not a hermit to meddle with such matters.
285. **forwearied**, exhausted. 288. **baite**, refresh; the allusion is to
the horses of the sun god. 302. **edifyde**, built. 314. **Saintes and**

Is wisely to advise: now day is spent;
Therefore with me ye may take up your In
For this same night. The knight was well content:
So with that godly father to his home they went.

34

A little lowly Hermitage it was,
Downe in a dale, hard by a forests side,
300 Far from resort of people, that did pas
In travell to and froe: a little wyde
There was an holy Chappell edifyde,
Wherein the Hermite dewly wont to say
His holy things each morne and eventyde:
Thereby a Christall streame did gently play,
Which from a sacred fountaine welled forth alway.

35

Arrived there, the little house they fill,
Ne looke for entertainment, where none was:
Rest is their feast, and all things at their will;
310 The noblest mind the best contentment has.
With faire discourse the evening so they pas:
For that old man of pleasing wordes had store,
And well could file his *tongue as* smooth as glas;
He told of Saintes and Popes, and evermore
He strowd an *Ave-Mary* after and before.

36

The drouping Night thus creepeth on them fast,
And the sad humour loading their eye liddes,
As messenger of *Morpheus* on them cast
Sweet slombring deaw, the which to sleepe them
  biddes.
320 Unto their lodgings then his guestes he riddes:
Where when all drownd in deadly sleepe he findes,
He to his study goes, and there amiddes
His Magick bookes and artes of sundry kindes,
He seekes out mighty charmes, to trouble sleepy
  mindes.

37

Then choosing out few wordes most horrible,
(Let none them read) thereof did verses frame,
With which and other spelles like terrible,
He bade awake blacke *Plutoes* griesly Dame,
And cursed heaven, and spake reprochfull shame
330 Of highest God, the Lord of life and light;
A bold bad man, that dar'd to call by name
Great *Gorgon*, Prince of darknesse and dead night,
At which *Cocytus* quakes, and *Styx* is put to flight.

38

And forth he cald out of deepe darkness dred
Legions of Sprights, the which like little flyes
Fluttring about his ever damned hed,
A-waite whereto their service he applyes,
To aide his friends, or fray his enimies:
Of those he chose out two, the falsest twoo,
And fittest for to forge true-seeming lyes; 340
The one of them he gave a message too,
The other by him selfe staide other worke to doo.

39

He making speedy way through spersed ayre,
And through the world of waters wide and deepe,
To *Morpheus* house doth hastily repaire.
Amid the bowels of the earth full steepe,
And low, where dawning day doth never peepe,
His dwelling is; there *Tethys* his wet bed
Doth ever wash, and *Cynthia* still doth steepe
In silver deaw his ever-drouping hed, 350
Whiles sad Night over him her mantle black doth
  spred.

40

Whose double gates he findeth locked fast,
The one faire fram'd of burnisht Yvory,
The other all with silver overcast;
And wakefull dogges before them farre do lye.
Watching to banish Care their enimy,
Who oft is wont to trouble gentle Sleepe.
By them the Sprite doth passe in quietly,
And unto *Morpheus* comes, whom drowned deepe
In drowsie fit he findes: of nothing he takes keepe. 360

41

And more, to lulle him in his slumber soft,
A trickling streame from high rocke tumbling downe
And ever-drizling raine upon the loft,
Mixt with a murmuring winde, much like the sowne
Of swarming Bees, did cast him in a swowne:
No other noyse, nor peoples troublous cryes,
As still are wont t'annoy the walled towne,
Might there be heard: but carelesse Quiet lyes,
Wrapt in eternall silence farre from enemyes.

42

The messenger approaching to him spake, 370
But his waste wordes returned to him in vaine:
So sound he slept, that nought mought him awake.

Popes. The hermit was Archimago, who symbolized hypocrisy. 317.
sad humour, heavy moisture; the theory was that a "dry brain" did
not rest well. 318. **Morpheus,** the god of sleep. 328. **Plutoes
griesly Dame,** Proserpine. 332. **Gorgon,** Demogorgon, a demon of
magic powers. 333. **Cocytus . . . Styx,** rivers in Hades. 338. **fray,**
terrify. 343. **He,** i.e., the messenger of Archimago. 348. **Tethys,**
in Greek myth the wife of Oceanus; here used of the Ocean himself.
349. **Cynthia,** the moon. 363. **loft,** roof.

Then rudely he him thrust, and pusht with paine,
Whereat he gan to stretch: but he againe
Shooke him so hard, that forced him to speake.
As one then in a dreame, whose dryer braine
Is tost with troubled sights and fancies weake,
He mumbled soft, but would not all his silence breake.

43

The Sprite then gan more boldly him to wake,
380 And threatned unto him the dreaded name
Of *Hecate*: whereat he gan to quake,
And lifting up his lumpish head, with blame
Halfe angry asked him, for what he came.
Hither (quoth he) me *Archimago* sent,
He that the stubborne Sprites can wisely tame,
He bids thee to him send for his intent
A fit false dreame, that can delude the sleepers sent.

44

The God obayde, and calling forth straight way
A diverse dreame out of his prison darke,
390 Delivered it to him, and downe did lay
His heavie head, devoide of carefull carke,
Whose sences all were straight benumbd and starke.
He backe returning by the Yvorie dore,
Remounted up as light as chearefull Larke,
And on his litle winges the dreame he bore
In hast unto his Lord, where he him left afore.

45

Who all this while with charmes and hidden artes,
Had made a Lady of that other Spright,
And fram'd of liquid ayre her tender partes
400 So lively, and so like in all mens sight,
That weaker sence it could have ravisht quight:
The maker selfe for all his wondrous witt,
Was nigh beguiled with so goodly sight:
Her all in white he clad, and over it
Cast a blacke stole, most like to seeme for *Una* fit.

46

Now when that ydle dreame was to him brought,
Unto that Elfin knight he bad him fly,
Where he slept soundly void of evill thought,
And with false shewes abuse his fantasy,
410 In sort as he him schooled privily:
And that new creature borne without her dew,
Full of the makers guile, with usage sly
He taught to imitate that Lady trew,
Whose semblance she did carrie under feigned hew.

47

Thus well instructed, to their worke they hast,
And comming where the knight in slomber lay,
The one upon his hardy head him plast,
And made him dreame of loves and lustfull play,
That nigh his manly hart did melt away,
Bathed in wanton blis and wicked joy: 420
Then seemed him his Lady by him lay,
And to him playnd, how that false winged boy
Her chast hart had subdewd, to learne Dame pleasures
  toy.

48

And she her selfe of beautie soveraigne Queene,
Faire *Venus* seemde unto his bed to bring
Her, whom he waking evermore did weene
To be the chastest flowre, that ay did spring
On earthly braunch, the daughter of a king,
Now a loose Leman to vile service bound:
And eke the *Graces* seemed all to sing,   430
Hymen iô Hymen, dauncing all around,
Whilst freshest *Flora* her with Yvie girlond crownd.

49

In this great passion of unwonted lust,
Or wonted feare of doing ought amis,
He started up, as seeming to mistrust
Some secret ill, or hidden foe of his:
Lo there before his face his Lady is,
Under blake stole hyding her bayted hooke,
And as halfe blushing offred him to kis,
With gentle blandishment and lovely looke,   440
Most like that virgin true, which for her knight
  him took.

50

All cleane dismayed to see so uncouth sight,
And halfe enraged at her shamelesse guise,
He thought have slaine her in his fierce despight:
But hasty heat tempring with sufferance wise,
He stayde his hand, and gan himselfe advise
To prove his sense, and tempt her faigned truth.
Wringing her hands in wemens pitteous wise,
Tho can she weepe, to stirre up gentle ruth,
Both for her noble bloud, and for her tender youth.   450

51

And said, Ah Sir, my liege Lord and my love,
Shall I accuse the hidden cruell fate,

---

376. **dryer braine,** See l. 317. 381. **Hecate,** in Greek myth a triple-formed goddess of moon, earth, and underworld, a type of witch. 391. **carefull carke,** worry that is full of care. 393. **Yvorie**

dore, the gate through which false dreams go out; true dreams passed through the Gate of Horn. 410. **In sort as,** etc., according to the method that he had taught him secretly. 411. **without her dew,**

And mightie causes wrought in heaven above,
Or the blind God, that doth me thus amate,
For hoped love to winne me certaine hate?
Yet thus perforce he bids me do, or die.
Die is my dew: yet rew my wretched state
You, whom my hard avenging destinie
Hath made judge of my life or death indifferently.

52

460 Your owne deare sake forst me at first to leave
My Fathers kingdome, There she stopt with teares;
Her swollen hart her speach seemd to bereave,
And then againe begun, My weaker yeares
Captiv'd to fortune and frayle wordly feares,
Fly to your faith for succour and sure ayde:
Let me not dye in languor and long teares.
Why Dame (quoth he) what hath ye thus dismayd?
What frayes ye, that were wont to comfort me affrayd?

53

Love of your selfe, she said, and deare constraint
470 Lets me not sleepe, but wast the wearie night
In secret anguish and unpittied plaint,
Whiles you in carelesse sleepe are drowned quight.
Her doubtfull words made that redoubted knight
Suspect her truth: yet since no untruth he knew,
Her fawning love with foule disdainefull spight
He would not shend, but said, Deare dame I rew,
That for my sake unknowne such griefe unto you grew.

54

Assure your selfe, it fell not all to ground;
For all so deare as life is to my hart,
480 I deeme your love, and hold me to you bound;
Ne let vaine feares procure your needlesse smart,
Where cause is none, but to your rest depart.
Not all content, yet seemd she to appease
Her mournefull plaintes, beguiled of her art,
And fed with words, that could not chuse but please,
So slyding softly forth, she turned as to her ease.

55

Long after lay he musing at her mood,
Much griev'd to thinke that gentle Dame so light,
For whose defence he was to shed his blood.
490 At last dull wearinesse of former fight
Having yrockt a sleepe his irkesome spright,
That troublous dreame gan freshly tosse his braine,
With bowres, and beds, and Ladies deare delight:

But when he saw his labour all was vaine,
With that misformed spright he backe returnd againe.

from BOOK II

Book II of The Faerie Queene concerns Sir Guyon, who represents the ideal of Temperance or Self-Control in the poem's allegorical scheme; he is accompanied by the Palmer, a holy sage. Briefly, Sir Guyon visits the cave of Mammon (i.e., Materialism, Worldliness), captures the carnal enchantress Acrasia, and razes her Bower of Bliss (Canto xii). The knight is saved at a crucial point in these adventures by Prince Arthur, who first dispatches the pagan brothers Cymochles and Pyrocles and at last personally delivers Alma (the Spirit or Pure Soul, Queen of Body Castle and the House of Temperance). On the whole, Book II is more abstract in the nature of its narrative than Book I and more laden with the elaborate, sensuous, descriptive detail which characterizes so much of Spenser's finest poetry.

CANTO XII

In this celebrated episode Sir Guyon, now accompanied by his Palmer once again, arrives at Acrasia's domain of oppressive sensuality—the Bower of Bliss—and destroys it.

Guyon, by Palmers governance,
   passing through perils great,
Doth overthrow the Bowre of blisse,
   and Acrasie defeat.

1

Now gins this goodly frame of Temperance
Fairely to rise, and her adorned hed
To pricke of highest praise forth to advance,
Formerly grounded, and fast setteled
On firme foundation of true bountihed;
And this brave knight, that for that vertue fights,
Now comes to point of that same perilous sted,
Where Pleasure dwelles in sensuall delights,
Mongst thousand dangers, and ten thousand magick
   mights.

2

Two dayes now in that sea he sayled has, 10
Ne ever land beheld, ne living wight,
Ne ought save perill, still as he did pas:
Tho when appeared the third Morrow bright,
Upon the waves to spred her trembling light,

---

unnaturally. **422. playnd,** complained. **431. Hymen, etc.,** chant to Hymen, god of wedlock. **432. Flora,** goddess of flowers. **444. despight,** anger. **445. sufferance,** patience **449. Tho can,** then did.

ruth, pity. **454. blind God,** Cupid. **amate,** subdue. **468. frayes,** frightens. **469. deare,** dire. **476. shend,** blame. **483. appease,** cease.

An hideous roaring farre away they heard,
That all their senses filled with affright,
And streight they saw the raging surges reard
Up to the skyes, that them of drowning made affeard.

3

Said then the Boteman, Palmer stere aright,
20 And keepe an even course; for yonder way
We needes must passe (God do us well acquight,)
That is the *Gulfe of Greedinesse*, they say,
That deepe engorgeth all this worldes pray:
Which having swallowd up excessively,
He soone in vomit up againe doth lay,
And belcheth forth his superfluity,
That all the seas for feare do seeme away to fly.

4

On th'other side an hideous Rocke is pight,
Of mightie *Magnes* stone, whose craggie clift
30 Depending from on high, dreadfull to sight,
Over the waves his rugged armes doth lift,
And threatneth downe to throw his ragged rift
On who so commeth nigh; yet nigh it drawes
All passengers, that none from it can shift:
For whiles they fly that Gulfes devouring jawes,
They on this rock are rent, and sunck in helplesse
  wawes.

5

Forward they passe and strongly he them rowes,
Untill they nigh unto that Gulfe arrive,
Where streame more violent and greedy growes:
40 Then he with all his puissance doth strive
To strike his oares, and mightily doth drive
The hollow vessell through the threatfull wave,
Which gaping wide, to swallow them alive,
In th'huge abysse of his engulfing grave,
Doth rore at them in vaine, and with great terror rave.

6

They passing by, that griesly mouth did see,
Sucking the seas into his entralles deepe,
That seem'd more horrible then hell to bee,
Or that darke dreadfull hole of *Tartare* steepe,
50 Through which the damned ghosts doen often creepe
Backe to the world, bad livers to torment:
But nought that falles into this direfull deepe,
Ne that approcheth nigh the wide descent,
May backe returne, but is condemned to be drent.

7

On th'other side, they saw that perilous Rocke,
Threatning it selfe on them to ruinate,
On whose sharpe clifts the ribs of vessels broke,
And shivered ships, which had bene wrecked late,
Yet stuck, with carkasses exanimate
Of such, as having all their substance spent   60
In wanton joyes, and lustes intemperate,
Did afterwards make shipwracke violent,
Both of their life, and fame for ever fowly blent.

8

For thy, this hight *The Rocke* of vile *Reproch*,
A daungerous and detestable place,
To which nor fish nor fowle did once approch,
But yelling Meawes, with Seagulles hoarse and bace,
And Cormoyrants, with birds of ravenous race,
Which still sate waiting on that wastfull clift,
For spoyle of wretches, whose unhappie cace,   70
After lost credite and consumed thrift,
At last them driven hath to this despairefull drift.

9

The Palmer seeing them in safetie past,
Thus said; Behold th'ensamples in our sights,
Of lustfull luxurie and thriftlesse wast:
What now is left of miserable wights,
Which spent their looser daies in lewd delights,
But shame and sad reproch, here to be red,
By these rent reliques, speaking their ill plights?
Let all that live, hereby be counselled,   80
To shunne *Rocke of Reproch*, and it as death to dred.

10

So forth they rowed, and that *Ferryman*
With his stiffe oares did brush the sea so strong,
That the hoare waters from his frigot ran,
And the light bubbles daunced all along,
Whiles the salt brine out of the billowes sprong.
At last farre off they many Islands spy,
On every side floting the floods emong:
Then said the knight, Loe I the land descry,
Therefore old Syre thy course do thereunto apply.   90

11

That may not be, said then the *Ferryman*
Least we unweeting hap to be fordonne:
For those same Islands, seeming now and than,
Are not firme lande, nor any certein wonne,

Book II, Canto xii. the Bowre of bliss. Cf. the Garden of Adonis, Book III, Canto vi, and the House of Busirance, Book III, Canto xi. 29. **Magnes**, magnet. 54. **drent**, drowned. 56. **ruinate**, wreak ruin.

59. **exanimate**, lifeless. 62. **make shipwracke**, commit suicide. 63. **blent**, darkened. 92. **fordonne**, destroyed. 97. **wandring Islands.** These islands recall the mythological lotus land (see ll. 100-108).

But straggling plots, which to and fro do ronne
In the wide waters: therefore are they hight
The *wandring Islands*. Therefore doe them shonne;
For they have oft drawne many a wandring wight
Into most deadly daunger and distressed plight.

12

100 Yet well they seeme to him, that farre doth vew,
Both faire and fruitfull, and the ground dispred
With grassie greene of delectable hew,
And the tall trees with leaves apparelled,
Are deckt with blossomes dyde in white and red,
That mote the passengers thereto allure;
But whosoever once hath fastened
His foot thereon, may never it recure,
But wandreth ever more uncertein and unsure.

13

As th'Isle of *Delos* whylome men report
110 Amid th' *Aegaean* sea long time did stray,
Ne made for shipping any certaine port,
Till that *Latona* traveiling that way,
Flying from *Junoes* wrath and hard assay,
Of her faire twins was there delivered,
Which afterwards did rule the night and day;
Thenceforth it firmely was established,
And for *Apolloes* honor highly herried.

14

They to him hearken, as beseemeth meete,
And passe on forward: so their way does ly,
120 That one of those same Islands, which doe fleet
In the wide sea, they needes must passen by,
Which seemd so sweet and pleasant to the eye,
That it would tempt a man to touchen there:
Upon the banck they sitting did espy
A daintie damzell, dressing of her heare,
By whom a little skippet floting did appeare.

15

She them espying, loud to them can call,
Bidding them nigher draw unto the shore;
For she had cause to busie them withall;
130 And therewith loudly laught: But nathemore
Would they once turne, but kept on as afore:
Which when she saw, she left her lockes undight,
And running to her boat withouten ore
From the departing land it launched light,
And after them did drive with all her power and might.

16

Whom overtaking, she in merry sort
Them gan to bord, and purpose diversly,
Now faining dalliance and wanton sport,
Now throwing forth lewd words immodestly;
Till that the Palmer gan full bitterly   140
Her to rebuke, for being loose and light
Which not abiding, but more scornefully
Scoffing at him, that did her justly wite.
She turned her bote about, and from them rowed quite.

17

That was the wanton *Phaedria*, which late
Did ferry him over the *Idle lake*:
Whom nought regarding, they kept on their gate,
And all her vaine allurements did forsake,
When them the wary Boateman thus bespake;
Here now behoveth us well to avyse,   150
And of our safetie good heede to take;
For here before a perlous passage lyes,
Where many Mermayds haunt, making false melodies.

18

But by the way, there is a great Quicksand,
And a whirlepoole of hidden jeopardy,
Therefore, Sir Palmer, keepe an even hand;
For twixt them both the narrow way doth ly.
Scarse had he said, when hard at hand they spy
That quicksand nigh with water covered;
But by the checked wave they did descry   160
It plaine, and by the sea discoloured:
It called was the quicksand of *Unthriftyhed*.

19

They passing by, a goodly Ship did see,
Laden from far with precious merchandize,
And bravely furnished, as ship might bee,
Which through great disaventure, or mesprize,
Her selfe had runne into that hazardize;
Whose mariners and merchants with much toyle,
Labour'd in vaine, to have recur'd their prize,
And the rich wares to save from pitteous spoyle,   170
But neither toyle nor travell might her backe recoyle.

20

On th'other side they see that perilous Poole,
That called was the *Whirlepoole of decay*,
In which full many had with haplesse doole
Beene suncke, of whom no memorie did stay:

---

117. **herried**, respected. 120. **fleet**, float. 125. **daintie damzell**, i.e., Phaedria (l. 145), who appears here as a kind of Lorelei or Circe figure. 126. **skippet**, skiff. 150. **avyse**, advise ourselves. 153. **Mer-**mayds, i.e., Sirens. 162. **Unthriftyhed**, heedlessness. 174. **doole**, lament.

Whose circled waters rapt with whirling sway,
Like to a restlesse wheele, still running round,
Did covet, as they passed by that way,
To draw their boate within the utmost bound
180 Of his wide *Labyrinth*, and then to have them dround.

21

But th'heedfull Boateman strongly forth did stretch
His brawnie armes, and all his body straine,
That th'utmost sandy breach they shortly fetch,
Whiles the dred daunger does behind remaine.
Suddeine they see from midst of all the Maine,
The surging waters like a mountaine rise,
And the great sea puft up with proud disdaine,
To swell above the measure of his guise,
As threatning to devoure all, that his powre despise.

22

190 The waves come rolling, and the billowes rore
Outragiously, as they enraged were,
Or wrathfull *Neptune* did them drive before
His whirling charet, for exceeding feare:
For not one puffe of wind there did appeare,
That all the three thereat woxe much afrayd,
Unweeting, what such horrour straunge did reare.
Eftsoones they saw an hideous hoast arrayd,
Of huge Sea monsters, such as living sence dismayd.

23

Most ugly shapes, and horrible aspects,
200 Such as Dame Nature selfe mote feare to see,
Or shame, that ever should so fowle defects
From her most cunning hand escaped bee;
All dreadfull pourtraicts of deformitee:
Spring-headed *Hydraes,* and sea-shouldring Whales,
Great whirlpooles, which all fishes make to flee,
Bright Scolopendraes, arm'd with silver scales,
Mighty *Monoceros,* with immeasured tayles.

24

The dreadfull Fish, that hath deserv'd the name
Of Death, and like him lookes in dreadfull hew,
210 The griesly Wasserman, that makes his game
The flying ships with swiftnesse to pursew,
The horrible Sea-satyre, that doth shew
His fearefull face in time of greatest storme,
Huge *Ziffius,* whom Mariners eschew
No lesse, then rockes, (as travellers informe,)
And greedy *Rosmarines* with visages deforme.

25

All these, and thousand thousands many more,
And more deformed Monsters thousand fold,

With dreadfull noise, and hollow rombling rore,
Came rushing in the fomy waves enrold,   220
Which seem'd to fly for feare, them to behold:
Ne wonder, if these did the knight appall;
For all that here on earth we dreadfull hold,
Be but as bugs to fearen babes withall,
Compared to the creatures in the seas entrall.

26

Feare nought, (then said the Palmer well aviz'd;)
For these same Monsters are not these in deed,
But are into these fearefull shapes disguiz'd
By that same wicked witch, to worke us dreed,
And draw from on this journey to proceede.   230
Tho lifting up his vertuous staffe on hye,
He smote the sea, which calmed was with speed,
And all that dreadfull Armie fast gan flye
Into great *Tethys* bosome, where they hidden lye.

27

Quit from that daunger, forth their course they kept,
And as they went, they heard a ruefull cry
Of one, that wayld and pittifully wept,
That through the sea the resounding plaints did fly:
At last they in an Island did espy
A seemely Maiden, sitting by the shore,   240
That with great sorrow and sad agony,
Seemed some great misfortune to deplore,
And lowd to them for succour called evermore.

28

Which *Guyon* hearing, streight his Palmer bad,
To stere the boate towards that dolefull Mayd,
That he might know, and ease her sorrow sad:
Who him avizing better, to him sayd;
Faire Sir, be not displeasd, if disobayd:
For ill it were to hearken to her cry;
For she is inly nothing ill apayd,   250
But onely womanish fine forgery,
Your stubborne hart t'affect with fraile infirmity.

29

To which when she your courage hath inclind
Through foolish pitty, then her guilefull bayt
She will embosome deeper in your mind,
And for your ruine at the last awayt.
The knight was ruled, and the Boateman strayt
Held on his course with stayed stedfastnesse,
Ne ever shruncke, ne ever sought to bayt
His tyred armes for toylesome wearinesse,   260
But with his oares did sweepe the watry wildernesse.

195. **woxe,** grew. 200. **mote,** might. 204. **Hydraes, etc.,** legendary
monsters. 224. **bugs,** bugbears, bogeys. 262. **sted,** place. 269.

had **continuall trade,** had always lived. 275. **surquedry,** presumption. 288. **In,** inn. 292. **Meane,** middle part (in music). 307.

30

And now they nigh approched to the sted,
Where as those Mermayds dwelt: it was a still
And calmy bay, on th'one side sheltered
With the brode shadow of an hoarie hill,
On th'other side an high rocke toured still,
That twixt them both a pleasaunt port they made,
And did like an halfe Theatre fulfill:
There those five sisters had continuall trade,
270 And usd to bath themselves in that deceiptfull shade.

31

They were faire Ladies, till they fondly striv'd
With th'*Heliconian* maides for maistery;
Of whom they over-comen, were depriv'd
Of their proud beautie, and th'one moyity
Transform'd to fish, for their bold surquedry,
But th'upper halfe their hew retained still,
And their sweet skill in wonted melody;
Which ever after they abusd to ill,
T'allure weake travellers, whom gotten they did kill.

32

280 So now to *Guyon*, as he passed by,
Their pleasaunt tunes they sweetly thus applide;
O thou faire sonne of gentle Faery,
That art in mighty armes most magnifide
Above all knights, that ever battell tride,
O turne thy rudder hither-ward a while:
Here may thy storme-bet vessell safely ride;
This is the Port of rest from troublous toyle,
The worlds sweet In, from paine and wearisome
    turmoyle.

33

With that the rolling sea resounding soft,
290 In his big base them fitly answered,
And on the rocke the waves breaking aloft,
A solemne Meane unto them measured,
The whiles sweet *Zephirus* lowd whisteled
His treble, a straunge kinde of harmony;
Which *Guyons* senses softly tickeled,
That he the boateman bad row easily,
And let him heare some part of their rare melody.

34

But him the Palmer from that vanity,
With temperate advice discounselled,
300 That they it past, and shortly gan descry
The land, to which their course they leveled;

wist, knew. 319. **ill-faste**, ominous, ugly. 340. **ydred**, afraid.

When suddeinly a grosse fog over spred
With his dull vapour all that desert has,
And heavens chearefull face enveloped,
That all things one, and one as nothing was,
And this great universe seemd one confused mas.

35

Thereat they greatly were dismayd, ne wist
How to direct their way in darkenesse wide,
But feard to wander in that wastfull mist,   310
For tombling into mischiefe unespide.
Worse is the daunger hidden, then descride.
Suddeinly an innumerable flight
Of harmefull fowles about them fluttering, cride,
And with their wicked wings them oft did smight,
And sore annoyed, groping in that griesly night.

36

Even all the nation of unfortunate
And fatall birds about them flocked were,
Such as by nature men abhorre and hate,
The ill-faste Owle, deaths dreadfull messengere,
The hoars Night-raven, trump of dolefull drere,   320
The lether-winged Bat, dayes enimy,
The ruefull Strich, still waiting on the bere,
The Whistler shrill, that who so heares, doth dy,
The hellish Harpies, prophets of sad destiny.

37

All those, and all that else does horrour breed,
About them flew, and fild their sayles with feare:
Yet stayd they not, but forward did proceed,
Whiles th'one did row, and th'other stifly steare;
Till that at last the weather gan to cleare,
And the faire land it selfe did plainly show.   330
Said then the Palmer, Lo where does appeare
The sacred soile, where all our perils grow;
Therefore, Sir knight, your ready armes about you
    throw.

38

He hearkned, and his armes about him tooke,
The whiles the nimble boate so well her sped,
That with her crooked keele the land she strooke,
Then forth the noble *Guyon* sallied,
And his sage Palmer, that him governed;
But th'other by his boate behind did stay.
They marched fairly forth, of nought ydred,   340
Both firmely armd for every hard assay,
With constancy and care, gainst daunger and dismay.

Ere long they heard an hideous bellowing
Of many beasts, that roard outrageously,
As if that hungers point, or *Venus* sting
Had them enraged with fell surquedry;
Yet nought they feard, but past on hardily,
Untill they came in vew of those wild beasts:
Who all attonce, gaping full greedily,
350 And rearing fiercely their upstarting crests,
Ran towards, to devoure those unexpected guests.

40

But soone as they approcht with deadly threat,
The Palmer over them his staffe upheld,
His mighty staffe, that could all charmes defeat:
Eftsoones their stubborne courages were queld,
And high advaunced crests downe meekely feld,
In stead of fraying, they them selves did feare,
And trembled, as them passing they beheld:
Such wondrous powre did in that staffe appeare,
360 All monsters to subdew to him, that did it beare.

41

Of that same wood it fram'd was cunningly,
Of which *Caduceus* whilome was made,
Caduceus the rod of *Mercury*,
With which he wonts the *Stygian* realmes invade,
Through ghastly horrour, and eternall shade;
Th' infernall feends with it he can asswage,
And *Orcus* tame, whom nothing can perswade,
And rule the *Furyes*, when they most do rage:
Such vertue in his staffe had eke this Palmer sage.

42

370 Thence passing forth, they shortly do arrive,
Whereas the Bowre of *Blisse* was situate;
A place pickt out by choice of best alive,
That natures worke by art can imitate:
In which what ever in this worldly state
Is sweet, and pleasing unto living sense,
Or that may dayntiest fantasie aggrate,
Was poured forth with plentifull dispence,
And made there to abound with lavish affluence.

43

Goodly it was enclosed round about,
380 Aswell their entred guestes to keepe within,
As those unruly beasts to hold without;
Yet was the fence thereof but weake and thin;
Nought feard their force, that fortilage to win,

But wisedomes powre, and temperaunces might,
By which the mightiest things efforced bin:
And eke the gate was wrought of substaunce light,
Rather for pleasure, then for battery or fight.

44

Yt framed was of precious yvory,
That seemd a worke of admirable wit;
And therein all the famous history   390
Of *Jason* and *Medae* was ywrit;
Her mighty charmes, her furious loving fit,
His goodly conquest of the golden fleece,
His falsed faith, and love too lightly flit,
The wondred *Argo*, which in venturous peece
First through the *Euxine* seas bore all the flowr of
    Greece.

45

Ye might have seene the frothy billowes fry
Under the ship, as thorough them she went,
That seemed the waves were into yvory,
Or yvory into the waves were sent;   400
And other where the snowy substaunce sprent
With vermell, like the boyes bloud therein shed,
A piteous spectacle did represent,
And otherwhiles with gold besprinkeled;
Yt seemd th'enchaunted flame, which did *Creüsa* wed.

46

All this, and more might in that goodly gate
Be red; that ever open stood to all,
Which thither came: but in the Porch there sate
A comely personage of stature tall,
And semblaunce pleasing, more then naturall,   410
That travellers to him seemd to entize;
His looser garment to the ground did fall,
And flew about his heeles in wanton wize,
Not fit for speedy pace, or manly exercize.

47

They in that place him *Genius* did call:
Not that celestiall powre, to whom the care
Of life, and generation of all
That lives, pertaines in charge particulare,
Who wondrous things concerning our welfare,
And straunge phantomes doth let us oft forsee,   420
And oft of secret ill bids us beware:
That is our Selfe, whom though we do not see,
Yet each doth in him selfe it well perceive to bee.

346. **fell**, fierce. 357. **fraying**, causing fright. 376. **aggrate**, please.
383. **fortilage**, fortress. 401. **sprent**, sprayed. 422. **our Selfe**, i.e.,
our conscience or power of reason, our self-knowledge. 431. **Pleasures
porter**, Idleness. 444. **pleasauns**, delight. 462. **gyaunt babe**, the

48

Therefore a God him sage Antiquity
Did wisely make, and good *Agdistes* call:
But this same was to that quite contrary,
The foe of life, that good envyes to all,
That secretly doth us procure to fall,
Through guilefull semblaunts, which he makes us see.
430 He of this Gardin had the governall,
And Pleasures porter was devizd to bee,
Holding a staffe in hand for more formalitee.

49

With diverse flowres he daintily was deckt,
And strowed round about, and by his side
A mighty Mazer bowle of wine was set,
As if it had to him bene sacrifide;
Wherewith all new-come guests he gratifide:
So did he eke Sir *Guyon* passing by:
But he his idle curtesie defide,
440 And overthrew his bowle disdainfully;
And broke his staffe, with which he charmed
      semblants sly.

50

Thus being entred, they behold around
A large and spacious plaine, on every side
Strowed with pleasauns, whose faire grassy ground
Mantled with greene, and goodly beautifide
With all the ornaments of *Floraes* pride,
Wherewith her mother Art, as halfe in scorne
Of niggard Nature, like a pompous bride
Did decke her, and too lavishly adorne,
450 When forth from virgin bowre she comes in
      th'early morne.

51

Thereto the Heavens alwayes Joviall,
Lookt on them lovely, still in stedfast state,
Ne suffred storme nor frost on them to fall,
Their tender buds or leaves to violate,
Nor scorching heat, nor cold intemperate
T'afflict the creatures, which therein did dwell,
But the milde aire with season moderate
Gently attempred, and disposd so well,
That still it breathed forthsweet spirit and holesome
      smell.

52

460 More sweet and holesome, then the pleasaunt hill
Of *Rhodope*, on which the Nimphe, that bore

A gyaunt babe, her selfe for griefe did kill;
Or the Thessalian *Tempe*, where of yore
Faire *Daphne Phoebus* hart with love did gore;
Or *Ida*, where the gods lov'd to repaire,
When ever they their heavenly bowres forlore;
Or sweet *Parnasse*, the haunt of Muses faire;
Or *Eden* selfe, if ought with *Eden* mote compaire.

53

Much wondred *Guyon* at the faire aspect
Of that sweet place, yet suffred no delight   470
To sincke into his sence, nor mind affect,
But passed forth, and lookt still forward right,
Bridling his will, and maistering his might:
Till that he came unto another gate;
No gate, but like one, being goodly dight
With boughes and braunches, which did broad dilate
Their clasping armes, in wanton wreathings intricate.

54

So fashioned a Porch with rare device,
Archt over head with an embracing vine,
Whose bounches hanging downe, seemed to entice   480
All passers by, to tast their lushious wine,
And did themselves into their hands incline,
As freely offering to be gathered:
Some deepe empurpled as the *Hyacint*,
Some as the Rubine, laughing sweetly red,
Some like faire Emeraudes, not yet well ripened.

55

And them amongst, some were of burnisht gold,
So made by art, to beautifie the rest,
Which did themselves emongst the leaves enfold,
As lurking from the vew of covetous guest,   490
That the weake bowes, with so rich load opprest,
Did bow adowne, as over-burdened.
Under that Porch a comely dame did rest,
Clad in faire weedes, but fowle disordered,
And garments loose, that seemd unmeet for womanhed.

56

In her left hand a Cup of gold she held,
And with her right the riper fruit did reach,
Whose sappy liquor, that with fulnesse sweld,
Into her cup she scruzd, with daintie breach
Of her fine fingers, without fowle empeach,   500
That so faire wine-presse made the wine more sweet:
Thereof she used to give to drinke to each,

giant Athos, sired by Neptune. 476. **dilate**, stretch forth. 494.
weedes, clothes. 499. **scruzd**, squeezed. 500. **empeach**, hindrance.

Whom passing by she happened to meet:
It was her guise, all Straungers goodly so to greet.

57

So she to *Guyon* offred it to tast;
Who taking it out of her tender hond.
The cup to ground did violently cast,
That all in peeces it was broken fond,
510 Whereat *Excesse* exceedingly was wroth,
Yet no'te the same amend, ne yet withstond,
But suffered him to passe, all were she loth;
Who nought regarding her displeasure forward goth.

58

There the most daintie Paradise on ground,
It selfe doth offer to his sober eye,
In which all pleasures plenteously abound,
And none does others happinesse envye:
The painted flowres, the trees upshooting hye,
The dales for shade, the hilles for breathing space,
520 The trembling groves, the Christall running by;
And that, which all faire workes doth most aggrace,
The art, which all that wrought, appeared in no place.

59

One would have thought, (so cunningly, the rude,
And scorned parts were mingled with the fine,)
That nature had for wantonesse ensude
Art, and that Art at nature did repine;
So striving each th'other to undermine,
Each did the others worke more beautifie;
So diff'ring both in willes, agreed in fine:
530 So all agreed through sweete diversitie,
This Gardin to adorne with all varietie.

60

And in the midst of all, a fountaine stood,
Of richest substaunce, that on earth might bee,
So pure and shiny, that the silver flood
Through every channell running one might see;
Most goodly it with curious imageree
Was over-wrought, and shapes of naked boyes,
Of which some seemd with lively jollitee,
To fly about, playing their wanton toyes,
540 Whilest others did them selves embay in liquid joyes.

61

And over all, of purest gold was spred,
A trayle of yvie in his native hew:

For the rich mettall was so coloured,
That wight, who did not well avis'd it vew,
Would surely deeme it to be yvie trew:
Low his lascivious armes adown did creepe,
That themselves dipping in the silver dew,
Their fleecy flowres they tenderly did steepe,
Which drops of Christall seemd for wantones to weepe.

62

Infinit streames continually did well   550
Out of this fountaine, sweet and faire to see,
The which into an ample laver fell,
And shortly grew to so great quantitie,
That like a little lake it seemd to bee;
Whose depth exceeded not three cubits hight,
That through the waves one might the bottom see,
All pav'd beneath with Iaspar shining bright,
That seemd the fountaine in that sea did sayle upright.

63

And all the margent round about was set,
With shady Laurell trees, thence to defend   560
The sunny beames, which on the billowes bet,
And those which therein bathed, mote offend.
As *Guyon* hapned by the same to wend,
Two naked Damzelles he therein espyde,
Which therein bathing, seemed to contend,
And wrestle wantonly, ne car'd to hyde,
Their dainty parts from vew of any, which them eyde.

64

Sometimes the one would lift the other quight
Above the waters, and then downe againe
Her plong, as over maistered by might,   570
Where both awhile would covered remaine,
And each the other from to rise restraine;
The whiles their snowy limbes, as through a vele,
So through the Christall waves appeared plaine:
Then suddeinly both would themselves unhele,
And th'amorous sweet spoiles to greedy eyes revele.

65

As that faire Starre, the messenger of morne,
His deawy face out of the sea doth reare:
Or as the *Cyprian* goddesse, newly borne
Of th'Oceans fruitfull froth, did first appeare: 580
Such seemed they, and so their yellow heare
Christalline humour dropped downe apace.
Whom such when *Guyon* saw, he drew him neare,

508. **fond,** found. 510. **Excesse,** the woman's name. 511. **no'te,**
could not. 512. **all,** although. 525. **ensude,** imitated. 526. **repine,**
take offense. 539. **toyes,** frivolous sports. 540. **embay,** bathe. 542.
his, its. 549. **wantones,** wantonness. 552. **laver,** basin. 575. **unhele,**

And somewhat gan relent his earnest pace,
His stubborne brest gan secret pleasaunce to embrace.

66

The wanton Maidens him espying, stood
Gazing a while at his unwonted guise;
Then th'one her selfe low ducked in the flood,
Abasht, that her a straunger did avise:
590 But th'other rather higher did arise,
And her two lilly paps aloft displayd,
And all, that might his melting hart entise
To her delights, she unto him bewrayd:
The rest hid underneath, him more desirous made.

67

With that, the other likewise up arose,
And her faire lockes, which formerly were bownd
Up in one knot, she low adowne did lose:
Which flowing long and thick, her cloth'd arownd,
And th'yvorie in golden mantle gownd:
600 So that faire spectacle from him was reft,
Yet that, which reft it, no lesse faire was fownd:
So hid in lockes and waves from lookers theft,
Nought but her lovely face she for his looking left.

68

Withall she laughed, and she blusht withall,
That blushing to her laughter gave more grace,
And laughter to her blushing, as did fall:
Now when they spide the knight to slacke his pace,
Them to behold, and in his sparkling face
The secret signes of kindled lust appeare,
610 Their wanton meriments they did encreace,
And to him beckned, to approch more neare,
And shewd him many sights, that courage cold could
reare.

69

On which when gazing him the Palmer saw,
He much rebukt those wandring eyes of his,
And counseld well, him forward thence did draw.
Now are they come nigh to the *Bowre of blis*
Of her fond favorites so nam'd amis:
When thus the Palmer; Now Sir, well avise;
For here the end of all our travell is:
620 Here wonnes *Acrasia*, whom we must surprise,
Else she will slip away, and all our drift despise.

70

Eftsoones they heard a most melodious sound,
Of all that mote delight a daintie eare,

Such as attonce might not on living ground,
Save in this Paradise, be heard elsewhere:
Right hard it was, for wight, which did it heare,
To read, what manner musicke that mote bee:
For all that pleasing is to living eare,
Wad there consorted in one harmonee,
Birdes, voyces, instruments, windes, waters, all agree. 630

71

The joyous birdes shrouded in chearefull shade,
Their notes wnto the voyce attempred sweet;
Th' Angelicall soft trembling voyces made
To th'instruments divine respondence meet:
The silver sounding instruments did meet
With the base murmure of the waters fall:
The waters fall with difference discreet,
Now soft, now loud, unto the wind did call:
The gentle warbling wind low answered to all.

72

There, whence that Musick seemed heard to bee,   640
Was the faire Witch her selfe now solacing,
With a new Lover, whom through sorceree
And witchcraft, she from farre did thither bring:
There she had him now layd a slombering,
In secret shade, after long wanton joyes:
Whilst round about them pleasauntly did sing
Many faire Ladies, and lascivious boyes,
That ever mixt their song with light licentious toyes.

73

And all that while, right over him she hong,
With her false eyes fast fixed in his sight,   650
As seeking medicine, whence she was stong,
Or greedily depasturing delight:
And oft inclining downe with kisses light,
For feare of waking him, his lips bedewd,
And through his humid eyes did sucke his spright,
Quite molten into lust and pleasure lewd;
Wherewith she sighed soft, as if his case she rewd.

74

The whiles some one did chaunt this lovely lay:
Ah see, who so faire thing doest faine to see,
In springing flowre the image of thy day;   660
Ah see the Virgin Rose, how sweetly shee
Doth first peepe forth with bashful modestee,
That fairer seemes, the lesse ye see her may;
Lo see soone after, how more bold and free
Her bared bosome she doth broad display;
Loe see soone after, how she fades, and falles away.

uncover. 579. **Cyprian goddesse,** i.e., Venus. 582. **Christalline humour,** clear moisture. 589. **avise,** look at. 612. **courage . . . reare,** excite dormant lust. 620. **wonnes,** dwells. 651. **stong,** stung. 659-675. **Ah see . . . crime,** a lovely, seductive carpe diem lyric.

75

So passeth, in the passing of a day,
Of mortall life the leafe, the bud, the flowre,
Ne more doth flourish after first decay,
670 That earst was sought to decke both bed and bowre,
Of many a Ladie, and many a Paramowre:
Gather therefore the Rose, whilest yet is prime,
For soone comes age, that will her pride deflowre:
Gather the Rose of love, whilest yet is time,
Whilest loving thou mayst loved be with equall crime.

76

He ceast, and then gan all the quire of birdes
Their diverse notes t'attune unto his lay,
As in approvance of his pleasing words.
The constant paire heard all, that he did say,
680 Yet swarved not, but kept their forward way,
Through many covert groves, and thickets close,
In which they creeping did at last display
That wanton Ladie, with her lover lose,
Whose sleepie head she in her lap did soft dispose.

77

Upon a bed of Roses she was layd,
As faint through heat, or dight to pleasant sin,
And was arayd, or rather disarayd,
All in a vele of silke and silver thin,
That hid no whit her alabaster skin,
690 But rather shewd more white, if more might bee:
More subtile web *Arachne* cannot spin,
Nor the fine nets, which oft we woven see
Of scorched deaw, do not in th'aire more lightly flee.

78

Her snowy brest was bare to readie spoyle
Of hungry eies, which n'ote therewith be fild,
And yet through languour of her late sweet toyle,
Few drops, more cleare then Nectar, forth distild,
That like pure Orient perles adowne it trild
And her faire eyes sweet smyling in delight,
700 Moystened their fierie beames, with which she thrild
Fraile harts, yet quenched not; like starry light
Which sparckling on the silent waves, does seeme
more bright.

79

The young man sleeping by her, seemd to bee
Some goodly swayne of honorable place,
That certes it great pittie was to see

Him his nobilitie so foule deface;
A sweet regard, and amiable grace,
Mixed with manly sternnesse did appeare
Yet sleeping, in his well proportioned face,
And on his tender lips the downy heare   710
Did now but freshly spring, and silken blossomes
beare.

80

His warlike armes, the idle instruments
Of sleeping praise, were hong upon a tree,
And his brave shield, full of old moniments,
Was fowly ra'st, that none the signes might see;
Ne for them, ne for honour cared hee,
Ne ought, that did to his advauncement tend,
But in lewd loves, and wastfull luxuree,
His dayes, his goods, his bodie he did spend:
O horrible enchantment, that him so did blend.   720

81

The noble Elfe, and carefull Palmer drew
So nigh them, minding nought, but lustfull game,
That suddein forth they on them rusht, and threw
A subtile net, which onely for the same
The skilfull Palmer formally did frame.
So held them under fast, the whiles the rest
Fled all away for feare of fowler shame.
The faire Enchauntresse, so unwares opprest,
Tryde all her arts, and all her sleights, thence
out to wrest.

82

And eke her lover strove: but all in vaine;   730
For that same net so cunningly was wound,
That neither guile, nor force might it distraine.
They tooke them both, and both them strongly bound
In captive bandes, which there they readie found:
But her in chaines of adamant he tyde;
For nothing else might keepe her safe and sound;
But *Verdant* (so he hight) he soone untyde,
And counsell sage insteed thereof to him applyde.

83

But all those pleasant bowres and Pallace brave,
Guyon broke downe, with rigour pittilesse;   740
Ne ought their goodly workmanship might save
Them from the tempest of his wrathfulnesse,
But that their blisse he turn'd to balefulnesse:
Their groves he feld, their gardins did deface,
Their arbers spoyle, their Cabinets suppresse.

---

670. **earst**, first.   675. **crime**, sin, fault.   683. **lose**, loose.   686.
dight to, prepared for.   715. **ra'st**, erased.   720. **blend**, blind.   725.
formally, skillfully.   737. **Verdant**, so called because of his youth
and comeliness.   746. **race**, raze.   759. **Whylome**, formerly.   761.
According . . . monstruous. The worst of these beasts, because the
basest in mind as a man, was Grille, transformed most aptly into a

Their banket houses burne, their buildings race,
And of the fairest late, now made the fowlest place.

84

Then led they her away, and eke that knight
They with them led, both sorrowfull and sad:
750 The way they came, the same retourn'd they right,
Till they arrived, where they lately had
Charm'd those wild-beasts, that rag'd with furie mad.
Which now awaking, fierce at them gan fly,
As in their mistresse reskew, whom they lad;
But them the Palmer soone did pacify.
Then *Guyon* askt, what meant those beastes,
    which there did ly.

85

Said he, These seeming beasts are men indeed,
Whom this Enchauntresse hath transformed thus,
Whylome her lovers, which her lusts did feed,
760 Now turned into figures hideous,
According to their mindes like monstruous.
Sad end (quoth he) of life intemperate,
And mournefull meed of joyes delicious:
But Palmer, if it mote thee so aggrate,
Let them returned be unto their former state.

86

Streight way he with his vertuous staffe them strooke,
And streight of beasts they comely men became;
Yet being men they did unmanly looke,
And stared ghastly, some for inward shame,
770 And some for wrath, to see their captive Dame:
But one above the rest in speciall,
That had an hog beene late, hight *Grille* by name,
Repined greatly, and did him miscall,
That had from hoggish forme him brought to naturall.

87

Said *Guyon*, See the mind of beastly man,
That hath so soone forgot the excellence
Of his creation, when he life began,
That now he chooseth, with vile difference,
To be a beast, and lacke intelligence.
780 To whom the Palmer thus, The donghill kind
Delights in filth and foule incontinence:
Let *Grill* be *Grill*, and have his hoggish mind,
But let us hence depart, whilest wether serves
    and wind.

hog. 763. **meed,** reward. 773. **Repined,** grieved. **miscall,** abuse;
Grille, who chooses to remain a swine, seems unable to profit from
the lesson of sensual enslavement and degradation as the others have.

from BOOK III

Book *III* of The Faerie Queene has as its heroine
the lady knight Britomart, who represents the virtue
of Chastity; she does not appear in Canto vi. Her
principal feat is the rescue of Amoret (Feminine
Grace, Fidelity) from the wicked magician Busirane
(Illicit Love). In general, Book *III* is most notable for
its passages of elaborate description, such as that of
the Garden of Adonis, which follows. After Stanza 53
of Canto vi, Spenser, with one transitional stanza, returns to other threads of narrative left unresolved in
the rambling, leisurely course of Book *III*.

CANTO VI

The birth of faire Belphoebe and
    of Amoret is told.
The Gardins of Adonis fraught
    with pleasures manifold.

1

Well may I weene, faire Ladies, all this while
Ye wonder, how this noble Damozell
So great perfections did in her compile,
Sith that in salvage forests she did dwell,
So farre from court and royall Citadell,
The great schoolmistresse of all curtesy:
Seemeth that such wild woods should far expell
All civill usage and gentility,
And gentle sprite deforme with rude rusticity.

2

But to this faire *Belphoebe* in her berth   10
The heavens so favourable were and free,
Looking with myld aspect upon the earth,
In th'*Horoscope* of her nativitee,
That all the gifts of grace and chastitee
On her they poured forth of plenteous horne;
Jove laught on *Venus* from his soveraigne see,
And *Phaebus* with faire beames did her adorne,
And all the *Graces* rockt her cradle being borne.

3

Her berth was of the wombe of Morning dew,
And her conception of the joyous Prime,   20
And all her whole creation did her shew
Pure and unspotted from all loathly crime,
That is ingenerate in fleshly slime.
So was this virgin borne, so was she bred,
So was she trayned up from time to time,

Edmund Spenser 239

In all chast vertue, and true bounti-hed
Till to her dew perfection she was ripened.

4

Her mother was the faire *Chrysogonee*,
The daughter of *Amphisa*, who by race
30 A Faerie was, yborne of high degree,
She bore *Belphoebe*, she bore in like cace
Faire *Amoretta* in the second place:
These two were twinnes, and twixt them two did share
The heritage of all celestiall grace,
That all the rest it seem'd they robbed bare
Of bountie, and of beautie, and all vertues rare.

5

It were a goodly storie, to declare,
By what straunge accident faire *Chrysogone*
Conceiv'd these infants, and how them she bare,
40 In this wild forrest wandring all alone,
After she had nine moneths fulfild and gone:
For not as other wemens commune brood,
They were enwombed in the sacred throne
Of her chaste bodie, nor with commune food,
As other wemens babes, they sucked vitall blood.

6

But wondrously they were begot, and bred
Through influence of th'heavens fruitfull ray,
As it in antique bookes is mentioned.
It was upon a Sommers shynie day,
50 When *Titan* faire his beames did display,
In a fresh fountaine, farre from all mens vew,
She bath'd her brest, the boyling heat t' allay;
She bath'd with roses red, and violets blew,
And all the sweetest flowres, that in the forrest grew.

7

Till faint through irkesome wearinesse, adowne
Upon the grassie ground her selfe she layd
To sleepe, the whiles a gentle slombrings wowne
Upon her fell all naked bare displayd;
The sunne-beames bright upon her body playd,
60 Being through former bathing mollifide,
And pierst into her wombe, where they embayd
With so sweet sence and secret power unspide,
That in her pregnant flesh they shortly fructifide.

8

Miraculous may seeme to him, that reades
So straunge ensample of conception;

But reason teacheth that the fruitfull seades
Of all things living, through impression
Of the sunbeames in moyst complexion,
Doe life conceive and quicknd are by kynd:
So after *Nilus* inundation,   70
Infinite shapes of creatures men do fynd,
Informed in the mud, on which the Sunne hath shynd.

9

Great father he of generation
Is rightly cald, th'author of life and light;
And his faire sister for creation
Ministreth matter fit, which tempred right
With heate and humour, breedes the living wight.
So sprong these twinnes in wombe of *Chrysogone*,
Yet wist she nought thereof, but sore affright,
Wondred to see her belly so upblone,   80
Which still increast, till she her terme had full outgone.

10

Whereof conceiving shame and foule disgrace,
Albe her guiltlesse conscience her cleard,
She fled into the wildernesse a space,
Till that unweeldy burden she had reard,
And shund dishonor, which as death she feard:
Where wearie of long travell, downe to rest
Her selfe she set, and comfortably cheard;
There a sad cloud of sleepe her overkest,
And seized every sense with sorrow sore opprest.   90

11

It fortuned, faire *Venus* having lost
Her little sonne, the winged god of love,
Who for some light displeasure, which him crost,
Was from her fled, as flit as ayerie Dove,
And left her blisfull bowre of joy above.
(So from her often he had fled away,
When she for ought him sharpely did reprove,
And wandred in the world in strange aray,
Disguiz'd in thousand shapes, that none might him
    bewray.)

12

Him for to seeke, she left her heavenly hous,   100
The house of goodly formes and faire aspects,
Whence all the world derives the glorious
Features of beautie, and all shapes select,
With which high God his workmanship hath deckt;
And searched every way, through which his wings
Had borne him, or his tract she mote detect:

Book III, Canto vi. 61. **embayd**, bathed. 63. **fructifide**, a kind of symbolic immaculate conception, based on the notion of spontaneous generation, occurs here (see ll. 70-73). 83. **Albe**, although. 99. **bewray**, recognize. 122. **whot**, hot. 157. **unbraste**, unfastened. 161.

She promist kisses sweet, and sweeter things
Unto the man, that of him tydings to her brings.

13

First she him sought in Court, where most he used
110 Whylome to haunt, but there she found him not;
But many there she found, which sore accused
His falsehood, and with foule infamous blot
His cruell deedes and wicked wyles did spot:
Ladies and Lords she every where mote heare
Complayning, how with his empoysned shot
Their wofull harts he wounded had whyle there,
And so had left them languishing twixt hope and feare.

14

She then the Citties sought from gate to gate,
And every one did aske, did he him see;
120 And every one her answerd, that too late
He had him seene, and felt the crueltie
Of his sharpe darts and whot artillerie;
And every one threw forth reproches rife
Of his mischievous deedes, and said, That hee
Was the disturber of all civill life,
The enimy of peace, and author of all strife.

15

Then in the countrey she abroad him sought,
And in the rurall cottages inquired,
Where also many plaints to her were brought,
130 How he their heedlesse harts with love had fyred,
And his false venim through their veines inspyred;
And eke the gentle shepheard swaynes, which sat
Keeping their fleecie flockes, as they were hyred,
She sweetly heard complaine, both how and what
Her sonne had to them doen; yet she did smile thereat.

16

But when in none of all these she him got,
She gan avize, where else he mote him hyde:
At last she her bethought, that she had not
Yet sought the salvage woods and forrests wyde,
140 In which full many lovely Nymphes abyde,
Mongst whom might be, that he did closely lye,
Or that the love of some of them him tyde:
For thy she thither cast her course t'apply,
To search the secret haunts of Dianes company.

17

Shortly unto the wastefull woods she came,
Whereas she found the Goddesse with her crew,

undight, disordered. 185. apayd, rewarded.

After late chace of their embrewed game,
Sitting beside a fountaine in a rew,
Some of them washing with the liquid dew
From off their dainty limbes the dustie sweat,   150
And soyle which did deforme their lively hew;
Others lay shaded from the scorching heat;
The rest upon her person gave attendance great.

18

She having hong upon a bough on high
Her bow and painted quiver, had unlaste
Her silver buskins from her nimble thigh,
And her lancke loynes ungirt, and brests unbraste,
After her heat the breathing cold to taste;
Her golden lockes, that late in tresses bright
Embreaded were for hindring of her haste,   160
Now loose about her shoulders hong undight,
And were with sweet *Ambrosia* all besprinckled light.

19

Soone as she *Venus* saw behind her backe,
She was asham'd to be so loose surprized,
And woxe halfe wroth against her damzels slacke,
That had not her thereof before avized,
But suffred her so carelesly disguized
Be overtaken. Soone her garments loose
Upgath'ring, in her bosome she comprized,
Well as she might, and to the Goddesse rose,   170
Whiles all her Nymphes did like a girlond her enclose.

20

Goodly she gan faire *Cytherea* greet,
And shortly asked her, what cause her brought
Into that wildernesse for her unmeet,
From her sweete bowres, and beds with pleasures
      fraught:
That suddein change she strange adventure thought.
To whom halfe weeping, she thus answered,
That she her dearest sonne *Cupido* sought,
Who in his frowardnesse from her was fled;
That she repented sore, to have him angered.   180

21

Thereat *Diana* gan to smile, in scorne
Of her vaine plaint, and to her scoffing sayd;
Great pittie sure, that ye be so forlorne
Of your gay sonne, that gives ye so good ayd
To your disports: ill mote ye bene apayd.
But she was more engrieved, and replide;
Faire sister, ill beseemes it to upbrayd
A dolefull heart with so disdainfull pride;
The like that mine, may be your paine another tide.

22

190 As you in woods and wanton wildernesse
　Your glory set, to chace the salvage beasts,
　So my delight is all in joyfulnesse,
　In beds, in bowres, in banckets, and in feasts:
　And ill becomes you with your loftie creasts,
　To scorne the joy, that *Jove* is glad to seeke;
　We both are bound to follow heavens beheasts,
　And tend our charges with obeisance meeke:
　Spare, gentle sister, with reproch my paine to eeke.

23

　And tell me, if that ye my sonne have heard,
200 To lurke emongst your Nymphes in secret wize;
　Or keepe their cabins: much I am affeard,
　Least he like one of them him selfe disguize,
　And turne his arrowes to their exercize:
　So may he long himselfe full easie hide:
　For he is faire and fresh in face and guize,
　As any Nymph (let not it be envyde.)
　So saying every Nymph full narrowly she eyde.

24

　But *Phoebe* therewith sore was angered,
　And sharply said: Goe Dame, goe seeke your boy,
210 Where you him lately left, in *Mars* his bed;
　He comes not here, we scorne his foolish joy,
　Ne lend we leisure to his idle toy:
　But if I catch him in this company,
　By *Stygian* lake I vow, whose sad annoy
　The Gods doe dread, he dearely shall abye:
　Ile clip his wanton wings, that he no more shall fly.

25

　Whom when as *Venus* saw so sore displeased,
　She inly sory was, and gan relent,
　What she had said: so her she soone appeased,
220 With sugred words and gentle blandishment,
　Which as a fountaine from her sweet lips went,
　And welled goodly forth, that in short space
　She was well pleasd, and forth her damzels sent,
　Through all the woods, to search from place to place,
　If any tract of him or tydings they mote trace.

26

　To search the God of love, her Nymphes she sent
　Throughout the wandring forrest every where:
　And after them her selfe eke with her went

　To seeke the fugitive, both farre and nere,
　So long they sought, till they arrived were　　　230
　In that same shadie covert, whereas lay
　Faire *Crysogone* in slombry traunce whilere:
　Who in her sleepe (a wondrous thing to say)
　Unwares had borne two babes, as faire as springing
　　　day.

27

　Unwares she them conceiv'd, unwares she bore:
　She bore withouten paine, that she conceived
　Withouten pleasure: ne her need implore
　Lucinaes aide: which when they both perceived,
　They were through wonder nigh of sense bereaved,
　And gazing each on other, nought bespake:　　　240
　At last they both agreed, her seeming grieved
　Out of her heavy swowne not to awake,
　But from her loving side the tender babes to take.

28

　Up they them tooke, each one a babe uptooke,
　And with them carried, to be fostered;
　Dame *Phoebe* to a Nymph her babe betooke,
　To be upbrought in perfect Maydenhed,
　And of her selfe her name *Belphoebe* red:
　But *Venus* hers thence farre away convayd,
　To be upbrought in goodly womanhed,　　　250
　And in her litle loves stead, which was strayd,
　Her *Amoretta* cald, to comfort her dismayd.

29

　She brought her to her joyous Paradize,
　Where most she wonnes, when she on earth does dwel.
　So faire a place, as Nature can devize:
　Whether in *Paphos*, or *Cytheron* hill,
　Or it in *Gnidus* be, I wote not well;
　But well I wote by tryall, that this same
　All other pleasant places doth excell,
　And called is by her lost lovers name,　　　260
　The *Gardin* of *Adonis*, farre renowmd by fame.

30

　In that same Gardin all the goodly flowres,
　Wherewith dame Nature doth her beautifie,
　And decks the girlonds of her paramoures,
　Are fetcht: there is the first seminarie
　Of all things, that are borne to live and die,
　According to their kindes. Long worke it were,
　Here to account the endlesse progenie

---

193. **banckets,** banquets. 198. **eeke,** increase. 236. **that,** because, since. 238. **Lucinaes,** the goddess of childbirth. 254. **wonnes,** re-

sides. 265. **seminarie,** genetic source. 339. **For formes . . . decay.** Here Spenser introduces one of his most recurrent themes, that of

Of all the weedes, that bud and blossome there;
270 But so much as doth need, must needs be counted here.

31

It sited was in fruitfull soyle of old,
And girt in with two walles on either side;
The one of yron, the other of bright gold,
That none might thorough breake, nor overstride:
And double gates it had, which opened wide,
By which both in and out men moten pas;
Th'one faire and fresh, the other old and dride:
Old *Genius* the porter of them was,
Old *Genius*, the which a double nature has.

32

280 He letteth in, he letteth out to wend,
All that to come into the world desire;
A thousand thousand naked babes attend
About him day and night, which doe require,
That he with fleshly weedes would them attire:
Such as him list, such as eternall fate
Ordained hath, he clothes with sinfull mire,
And sendeth forth to live in mortall state,
Till they againe returne backe by the hinder gate.

33

After that they againe returned beene,
290 They in that Gardin planted be againe;
And grow afresh, as they had never seene
Fleshly corruption, nor mortall paine.
Some thousand yeares so doen they there remaine;
And then of him are clad with other hew,
Or sent into the chaungefull world againe,
Till thither they returne, where first they grew:
So like a wheele around they runne from old to new.

34

Ne needs there Gardiner to set, or sow,
To plant or prune: for of their owne accord
300 All things, as they created were, doe grow,
And yet remember well the mightie word,
Which first was spoken by th'Almightie lord,
That bad them to increase and multiply:
Ne doe they need with water of the ford,
Or of the clouds to moysten their roots dry;
For in themselves eternall moisture they imply.

35

Infinite shapes of creatures there are bred,
And uncouth formes, which none yet ever knew,

mutability (i.e., the principle of inevitable change and decay inherent in human affairs).

And every sort is in a sundry bed
Set by it selfe, and ranckt in comely rew: 310
Some fit for reasonable soules t'indew,
Some made for beasts, some made for birds to weare,
And all the fruitfull spawne of fishes hew
In endlesse rancks along enraunged were,
That seem'd the *Ocean* could not containe them there.

36

Daily they grow, and daily forth are sent
Into the world, it to replenish more;
Yet is the stocke not lessened, nor spent,
But still remaines in everlasting store,
As it at first created was of yore. 320
For in the wide wombe of the world there lyes,
In hatefull darkenesse and in deepe horrore,
An huge eternall *Chaos*, which supplyes
The substances of natures fruitfull progenyes.

37

All things from thence doe their first being fetch,
And borrow matter, whereof they are made,
Which when as forme and feature it does ketch,
Becomes a bodie, and doth then invade
The state of life, out of the griesly shade.
That substance is eterne, and bideth so, 330
Ne when the life decayes, and forme does fade,
Doth it consume, and into nothing go,
But chaunged is, and often altred to and fro.

38

The substance is not chaunged, nor altered,
But th'only forme and outward fashion;
For every substance is conditioned
To change her hew, and sundry formes to don,
Meet for her temper and complexion:
For formes are variable and decay,
By course of kind, and by occasion; 340
And that faire flowre of beautie fades away,
As doth the lilly fresh before the sunny ray.

39

Great enimy to it, and to all the rest,
That in the *Gardin* of *Adonis* springs,
Is wicked *Time*, who with his scyth addrest,
Does mow the flowring herbes and goodly things,
And all their glory to the ground downe flings,
Where they doe wither, and are fowly mard:
He flyes about, and with his flaggy wings
Beates downe both leaves and buds without regard, 350
Ne ever pittie may relent his malice hard.

40

Yet pittie often did the gods relent,
To see so faire things mard, and spoyled quight:
And their great mother *Venus* did lament
The losse of her deare brood, her deare delight:
Her hart was pierst with pittie at the sight,
When walking through the Gardin, them she spyde,
Yet no'te she find redresse for such despight.
For all that lives, is subject to that law:
360 All things decay in time, and to their end do draw.

41

But were it not, that *Time* their troubler is,
All that in this delightfull Gardin growes,
Should happie be, and have immortall blis,
For here all plentie, and all pleasure flowes,
And sweet love gentle fits emongst them throwes,
Without fell rancor, or fond gealosie;
Franckly each paramour his leman knowes,
Each bird his mate, ne any does envie
Their goodly meriment, and gay felicitie.

42

370 There is continuall spring, and harvest there
Continuall, both meeting at one time:
For both the boughes doe laughing blossomes beare,
And with fresh colours decke the wanton Prime,
And eke attonce the heavy trees they clime,
Which seeme to labour under their fruits lode:
The whiles the joyous birdes make their pastime
Emongst the shadie leaves, their sweet abode,
And their true loves without suspition tell abrode.

43

Right in the middest of that Paradise,
380 There stood a stately Mount, on whose round top
A gloomy grove of mirtle trees did rise,
Whose shadie boughes sharpe steele did never lop,
Nor wicked beasts their tender buds did crop,
But like a girlond compassed the hight,
And from their fruitfull sides sweet gum did drop,
That all the ground with precious deaw bedight,
Threw forth most dainty odours, and most sweet
   delight.

44

And in the thickest covert of that shade,
There was a pleasant arbour, not by art,
390 But of the trees owne inclination made,
Which knitting their rancke braunches part to part,

With wanton yvie twyne, entrayld athwart,
And Eglantine, and Caprifole emong,
Fashioned above within their inmost part,
The nether *Phoebus* beams could through them throng,
Nor *Aeolus* sharp blast could worke them any wrong.

45

And all about grew every sort of flowre,
To which sad lovers were transformd of yore;
Fresh *Hyacinthus, Phoebus* paramoure,
And dearest love,   400
Foolish *Narcisse,* that likes the watry shore,
Sad *Amaranthus,* made a flowre but late,
Sad *Amaranthus,* in whose purple gore
Me seemes I see *Amintas* wretched fate,
To whom sweet Poets verse hath given endlesse date.

46

There wont faire *Venus* often to enjoy
Her deare *Adonis* joyous company,
And reape sweet pleasure of the wanton boy;
There yet, some say, in secret he does ly,
Lapped in flowres and pretious spycery,   410
By her hid from the world, and from the skill
Of *Stygian* Gods, which doe her love envy;
But she her selfe, when ever that she will,
Possesseth him, and of his sweetnesse takes her fill.

47

And sooth it seemes they say: for he may not
For ever die, and ever buried bee
In balefull night, where all things are forgot;
All be he subject to mortalitie,
Yet is eterne in mutabilitie,
And by succession made perpetuall,   420
Transformed oft, and chaunged diverslie:
For him the Father of all formes they call;
Therefore needs mote he live, that living gives to all.

48

There now he liveth in eternall blis,
Joying his goddesse, and of her enjoyd:
Ne feareth he henceforth that foe of his,
Which with his cruell tuske him deadly cloyd:
For that wilde Bore, the which him once annoyd,
She firmely hath emprisoned for ay,
That her sweet love his malice mote avoyd,   430
In a strong rocky Cave, which is they say,
Hewen underneath that Mount, that none him losen
   may.

---

373. **Prime,** spring. 393. **Caprifole,** honeysuckle. 404. **Amintas,** probably a reference to Sir Philip Sidney. 428. **annoyd,** injured.

442-450. **And his . . . late.** Here Spenser recounts the classical myth of the lovers Cupid and Psyche. 467. **haveour,** behavior.

49

There now he lives in everlasting joy,
With many of the Gods in company,
Which thither haunt, and with the winged boy
Sporting himselfe in safe felicity:
Who when he hath with spoiles and cruelty
Ransackt the world, and in the wofull harts
Of many wretches set his triumphes hye,
440 Thither resorts, and laying his sad darts
Aside, with faire *Adonis* playes his wanton parts.

50

And his true love faire *Psyche* with him playes,
Faire *Psyche* to him lately reconcyld,
After long troubles and unmeet upbrayes,
With which his mother *Venus* her revyld,
And eke himselfe her cruelly exyld:
Bnt now in steadfast love and happy state
She with him lives and hath him borne a chyld,
Pleasure, that doth both gods and men aggrate,
450 *Pleasure*, the daughter of *Cupid* and *Psyche* late.

51

Hither great *Venus* brought this infant faire,
The younger daughter of *Chrysogonee*,
And unto *Psyche* with great trust and care
Committed her, yfostered to bee,
And trained up in true feminitee:
Who no lesse carefully her tendered,
Then her owne daughter *Pleasure*, to whom shee
Made her companion, and her lessoned
In all the lore of love, and goodly womanhead.

52

460 In which when she to perfect ripenesse grew,
Of grace and beautie noble Paragone,
She brought her forth into the worldes vew,
To be th'ensample of true love alone,
And Lodestarre of all chaste affectione,
To all faire Ladies, that doe live on ground.
To Faery court she came, where many one
Admyrd her goodly haveour, and found
His feeble hart wide launched with loves cruell wound.

53

But she to none of them her love did cast,
470 Save to the noble knight Sir *Scudamore*,
To whom her loving hart she linked fast
In faithfull love, t'abide for evermore,
And for his dearest sake endured sore,

Sore trouble of an hainous enimy;
Who her would forced have to have forlore
Her former love, and stedfast loialty,
As ye may elsewhere read that ruefull history.

(1590)

from AMORETTI

Spenser married Elizabeth Boyle on June 11, 1594, after a prolonged courtship. To her he addressed his sonnet sequence and his glorious spousal hymn Epithalamion, which were published together a year after the marriage. The Amoretti consists of eighty-eight sonnets. These are for the most part the conventional tributes to a lady; they contain among other ideas his repeated assertion that he is immortalizing her in his verses. The metrical form is neither Petrarchan nor Shakespearean; like the English sonnet, the fourteen lines are divided into three quatrains and a concluding couplet, but Spenser has linked his quatrains much after the manner of the Spenserian stanza links so that the metrical effect is distinctly individual.

1

Happy ye leaves when as those lilly hands,
    which hold my life in their dead doing might,
    shall handle you and hold in loves soft bands,
    lyke captives trembling at the victors sight.
And happy lines, on which with starry light,
    those lamping eyes will deigne sometimes to look
    and reade the sorrowes of my dying spright,
    written with teares in harts close bleeding book.
And happy rymes bath'd in the sacred brooke,
    of *Helicon* whence she derived is,   10
    when ye behold that Angels blessed looke,
    my soules long lacked foode, my heavens blis.
Leaves, lines, and rymes, seeke her to please alone,
    whom if ye please, I care for other none.

15

Ye tradefull Merchants that with weary toyle,
    do seeke most pretious things to make your gain:
    and both the Indias of their treasures spoile,
    what needeth you to seeke so farre in vaine?
For loe my love doth in her selfe containe
    all this worlds riches that may farre be found,
    if Saphyres, loe her eies be Saphyres plaine,

Sonnet 1.   1. **leaves**, pages of the sonnets.   2. **dead doing**, death-
dealing.   6. **lamping**, shining.   10. *Helicon*, a mountain in Boeotia
sacred to Apollo and the Muses.
Sonnet 15.   3. **Indias**, i.e., both the East and the West Indies.

Spenser reading The Faerie Queene *to Sir Walter Raleigh. Historical Pictures Service—Chicago.*

if Rubies, loe hir lips be Rubies sound:
If Pearles, hir teeth be pearles both pure and round;
10   if Yuorie, her forhead yuory weene;
   if Gold, her locks are finest gold on ground;
   if silver, her faire hands are silver sheene,
But that which fairest is, but few behold,
   her mind adornd with vertues manifold.

16

One day as I unwarily did gaze
   on those fayre eyes my loves immortall light:
   the whiles my stonisht hart stood in amaze,
   through sweet illusion of her lookes delight.
I mote perceive how in her glauncing sight,
   legions of loves with little wings did fly:

darting their deadly arrowes fyry bright,
   at every rash beholder passing by.
One of those archers closely I did spy,
   ayming his arrow at my very hart: 10
   when suddenly with twincle of her eye,
   the Damzell broke his misintended dart.
Had she not so doon, sure I had bene slayne,
   yet as it was, I hardly scap't with paine.

23

Penelope for her *Ulisses* sake,
   deviz'd a Web her wooers to deceave:
   in which the worke that she all day did make
   the same at night she did againe unreave.
Such subtile craft my Damzell doth conceave,
   th' importune suit of my desire to shonne:

Sonnet 16. 5. **mote,** might. 6. **loves,** cupids. 14. **hardly,** barely, with difficulty.
   Sonnet 23. 1. *Penelope,* in Greek legend the faithful wife of Odysseus, or Ulysses. The story of the web is told in the *Odyssey.*

Book II. 4. **unreave,** unravel. 6. **shonne,** shun. 11. **spils,** destroys.
   Sonnet 34. 10. *Helice,* the constellation of the Great Bear.
   Sonnet 70. 1. **loves mighty king,** Cupid. 2. **cote armour,** the tabard of the herald, Spring. 11. **make,** mate. 12. **amearst,** amerced,

for all that I in many dayes doo weave,
  in one short houre I find by her undonne.
So when I thinke to end that I begonne,
10 I must begin and never bring to end:
  for with one looke she spils that long I sponne,
  and with one word my whole yeares work doth rend.
Such labour like the Spyders web I fynd,
  whose fruitlesse worke is broken with least wynd.

34

Lyke as a ship that through the Ocean wyde,
  by conduct of some star doth make her way,
  whenas a storme hath dimd her trusty guyde,
  out of her course doth wander far astray.
So I whose star, that wont with her bright ray,
  me to direct, with cloudes is overcast,
  doe wander now in darknesse and dismay,
  through hidden perils round about me plast.
Yet hope I well, that when this storme is past
10 my *Helice* the lodestar of my lyfe
  will shine again, and looke on me at last,
  with lovely light to cleare my cloudy grief.
Till then I wander carefull comfortlesse,
  in secret sorrow and sad pensivenesse.

70

Fresh spring the herald of loves mighty king,
  in whose cote armour richly are displayd
  all sorts of flowers the which on earth do spring
  in goodly colours gloriously arrayd.
Goe to my love, where she is carelesse layd,
  yet in her winters bowre not well awake:
  tell her the joyous time wil not be staid
  unlesse she doe him by the forelock take.
Bid her therefore her selfe soone ready make,
10 to wayt on love amongst his lovely crew:
  where every one that misseth then her make,
  shall be by him amearst with penance dew.
Make hast therefore sweet love, whilest it is prime,
  for none can call againe the passed time.

74

Most happy letters fram'd by skilfull trade,
  with which that happy name was first desynd:
  the which three times thrise happy hath me made,
  with guifts of body, fortune, and of mind.
The first my being to me gave by kind,
  from mothers womb deriv'd by dew descent,
  the second is my sovereigne Queene most kind,
  that honour and large richesse to me lent.

The third my love, my lives last ornament,
  by whom my spirit out of dust was raysed: 10
  to speake her prayse and glory excellent,
  of all alive most worthy to be praysed.
Ye three Elizabeths for ever live,
  that three such graces did unto me give.

75

One day I wrote her name upon the strand,
  but came the waves and washed it away:
  agayne I wrote it with a second hand,
  but came the tyde, and made my paynes his pray.
Vayne man, sayd she, that doest in vaine assay,
  a mortall thing so to immortalize,
  for I my selve shall lyke to this decay,
  and eek my name bee wyped out lykewize.
Not so, (quod I) let baser things devize
  to dy in dust, but you shall live by fame: 10
  my verse your vertues rare shall eternize,
  and in the hevens wryte your glorious name.
Where whenas death shall all the world subdew,
  our love shall live, and later life renew.

79

Men call you fayre, and you doe credit it,
  for that your selfe ye dayly such doe see:
  but the trew fayre, that is the gentle wit,
  and vertuous mind, is much more praysd of me.
For all the rest, how ever fayre it be,
  shall turne to nought and loose that glorious hew:
  but onely that is permanent and free
  from frayle corruption, that doth flesh ensew.
That is true beautie: that doth argue you
  to be divine and borne of heavenly seed: 10
  deriv'd from that fayre Spirit, from whom al true
  And perfect beauty did at first proceed.
He onely fayre, and what he fayre hath made,
  all other fayre lyke flowres untymely fade.
(1595)

EPITHALAMION

Ye learned sisters which have oftentimes
Beene to me ayding, others to adorne:
Whom ye thought worthy of your gracefull rymes,
That even the greatest did not greatly scorne
To heare theyr names sung in your simple layes,
But joyed in theyr prayse.
And when ye list your owne mishaps to mourne,
Which death, or love, or fortunes wreck did rayse,

  Sonnet 70. 1. **loves mighty king,** Cupid. 2. **cote armour,** the
tabard of the herald, Spring. 11. **make,** mate. 12. **amearst,** amerced,
punished. 13. **prime,** spring. With this sonnet compare Herrick's
To the Virgins to Make Much of Time, p. 345.
  Sonnet 74. 5. **kind,** nature. 8. **lent,** granted, bestowed.
  Sonnet 75. 11. **my verse, etc.,** a common sonnet conceit.

  Sonnet 79. 1. **credit,** believe. 6. **loose,** lose. 11. **fayre Spirit,**
God.
  Epithalamion. 1. **learned sisters,** the nine Muses. 8. **wreck,** vio-
lence.

Your string could soone to sadder tenor turne,
10 And teach the woods and waters to lament
Your dolefull dreriment.
Now lay those sorrowfull complaints aside,
And having all your heads with girland crownd,
Helpe me mine owne loves prayses to resound,
Ne let the same of any be envide:
So Orpheus did for his owne bride,
So I unto my selfe alone will sing,
The woods shall to me answer and my Eccho ring.

Early before the worlds light giving lampe,
20 His golden beame upon the hils doth spred,
Having disperst the nights unchearefull dampe,
Doe ye awake, and with fresh lusty-hed,
Go to the bowre of my beloved love,
My truest turtle dove,
Bid her awake; for Hymen is awake,
And long since ready forth his maske to move,
With his bright Tead that flames with many a flake,
And many a bachelor to waite on him,
In theyr fresh garments trim.
30 Bid her awake therefore and soone her dight,
For lo the wished day is come at last,
That shall for al the paynes and sorrowes past,
Pay to her usury of long delight:
And whylest she doth her dight,
Doe ye to her of joy and solace sing,
That all the woods may answer and your eccho ring.

Bring with you all the Nymphes that you can heare
Both of the rivers and the forrests greene:
And of the sea that neighbours to her neare,
40 Al with gay girlands goodly wel beseene.
And let them also with them bring in hand,
Another gay girland
For my fayre love of lillyes and of roses,
Bound truelove wize with a blew silke riband.
And let them make great store of bridale poses,
And let them eeke bring store of other flowers
To deck the bridale bowers.
And let the ground whereas her foot shall tread,
For feare the stones her tender foot should wrong
50 Be strewed with fragrant flowers all along,
And diapred lyke the discolored mead.
Which done, doe at her chamber dore awayt,
For she will waken strayt,
The whiles doe ye this song unto her sing,
The woods shall to you answer and your Eccho ring.

Ye Nymphes of Mulla which with carefull heed,
The silver scaly trouts doe tend full well,

And greedy pikes which use therein to feed,
(Those trouts and pikes all others doo excell)
And ye likewise which keepe the rushy lake, 60
Where none doo fishes take,
Bynd up the locks the which hang scatterd light,
And in his waters which your mirror make,
Behold your faces as the christall bright,
That when you come whereas my love doth lie,
No blemish she may spie.
And eke ye lightfoot mayds which keepe the deere,
That on the hoary mountayne use to towre,
And the wylde wolves which seeke them to devoure,
With your steele darts doo chace from comming neer, 70
Be also present heere,
To helpe to decke her and to help to sing,
That all the woods may answer and your eccho ring.

Wake, now my love, awake: for it is time,
The Rosy Morne long since left Tithones bed,
All ready to her silver coche to clyme,
And Phoebus gins to shew his glorious hed.
Hark how the cheerefull birds do chaunt theyr laies
And carroll of loves praise.
The merry Larke hir mattins sings aloft, 80
The thrush replyes, the Mavis descant playes,
The Ouzell shrills, the Ruddock warbles soft,
So goodly all agree with sweet consent,
To this dayes merriment.
Ah my deere love why doe ye sleepe thus long,
When meeter were that ye should now awake,
T'awayt the comming of your joyous make,
And hearken to the birds love-learned song,
The deawy leaves among.
For they of joy and pleasance to you sing, 90
That all the woods them answer and theyr eccho ring.

My love is now awake out of her dreame,
And her fayre eyes like stars that dimmed were
With darksome cloud, now shew theyr goodly beams
More bright then Hesperus his head doth rere.
Come now ye damzels, daughters of delight,
Helpe quickly her to dight,
But first come ye fayre houres which were begot
In Jove's sweet paradice, of Day and Night,
Which doe the seasons of the yeare allot, 100
And al that ever in this world is fayre
Doe make and still repayre.
And ye three handmayds of the Cyprian Queene,
The which doe still adorne her beauties pride,
Helpe to addorne my beautifullest bride:
And as ye her array, still throw betweene
Some graces to be seene,

---

16. **Orpheus,** son of Apollo and Calliope. Orpheus went to Hades to recover his dead wife Eurydice, tamed Cerberus, the watchdog of Hades, and with the persuasive power of his music moved Pluto to release Eurydice. But on his return to the world of light, he disobeyed Pluto's injunctions by looking back to see if his wife was following him; consequently he lost her again. 25. **Hymen,** the god of marriage. 26. **maske,** a court entertainment, here in celebration of a wedding.

27. **Tead,** torch, Hymen's symbol. 28. **bachelor,** candidate for knighthood. 30. **dight,** dress. 39. **neighbours . . . neare,** is near neighbor to her; Elizabeth Boyle, to whom the hymn was addressed, lived at Kilcoran on the Bay of Youghal, Cork County. 40. **beseene,** adorned. 51. **diapred,** variegated. 68. **towre,** climb in a spiral. 75. **Tithones,** the beloved of Aurora, who prevailed upon Jupiter to grant him immortality, but failed to ask for eternal youth also. 81. **Mavis,** song

And as ye use to Venus, to her sing,
The whiles the woods shal answer and your eccho ring.

110 Now is my love all ready forth to come,
Let all the virgins therefore well awayt,
And ye fresh boyes that tend upon her groome
Prepare your selves; for he is comming strayt.
Set all your things in seemely good aray
Fit for so joyfull day,
The joyfulst day that ever sunne did see.
Faire Sun, shew forth thy favourable ray,
And let thy lifull heat not fervent be
For feare of burning her sunshyny face,
120 Her beauty to disgrace.
O fayrest Phoebus, father of the Muse,
If ever I did honour thee aright,
Or sing the thing that mote thy mind delight,
Doe not thy servants simple boone refuse,
But let this day let this one day be myne,
Let all the rest be thine.
Then I thy soverayne prayses loud wil sing,
That all the woods shal answer and theyr eccho ring.

Harke how the Minstrels gin to shrill aloud
130 Their merry Musick that resounds from far,
The pipe, the tabor, and the trembling Croud,
That well agree withouten breach or jar.
But most of all the Damzels doe delite,
When they their tymbrels smyte,
And thereunto doe daunce and carrol sweet,
That all the sences they doe ravish quite,
The whyles the boyes run up and downe the street,
Crying aloud with strong confused noyce,
As if it were one voyce.
140 Hymen, iô Hymen, Hymen they do shout,
That even to the heavens theyr shouting shrill
Doth reach, and all the firmament doth fill,
To which the people standing all about,
As in approvance doe thereto applaud
And loud advaunce her laud,
And evermore they Hymen, Hymen sing,
That al the woods them answer and theyr eccho ring.

Loe where she comes along with portly pace
Lyke Phoebe from her chamber of the East,
150 Arysing forth to run her mighty race,
Clad all in white, that seemes a virgin best.
So well it her beseemes that ye would weene
Some angell she had beene.
Her long loose yellow locks lyke golden wyre,
Sprinckled with perle, and perling flowres a tweene,
Doe lyke a golden mantle her attyre,

And being crowned with a girland greene,
Seeme lyke some mayden Queene.
Her modest eyes abashed to behold
So many gazers, as on her do stare,   160
Upon the lowly ground affixed are.
Ne dare lift up her countenance too bold,
But blush to heare her prayses sung so loud,
So farre from being proud.
Nathlesse doe ye still loud her prayses sing.
That all the woods may answer and your eccho ring.

Tell me ye merchants daughters did ye see
So fayre a creature in your towne before,
So sweet, so lovely, and so mild as she,
Adornd with beautyes grace and vertues store,   170
Her goodly eyes lyke Saphyres shining bright,
Her forehead yvory white,
Her cheekes lyke apples which the sun hath rudded,
Her lips lyke cherryes charming men to byte,
Her brest like to a bowle of creame uncrudded,
Her paps lyke lyllies budded,
Her snowie necke lyke to a marble towre,
And all her body like a pallace fayre,
Ascending uppe with many a stately stayre,
To honours seat and chastities sweet bowre.   180
Why stand ye still ye virgins in amaze,
Upon her so to gaze,
Whiles ye forget your former lay to sing,
To which the woods did answer and your eccho ring.

But if ye saw that which no eyes can see,
The inward beauty of her lively spright,
Garnisht with heavenly guifts of high degree,
Much more then would ye wonder at that sight,
And stand astonisht lyke to those which red
Medusaes mazeful hed.   190
There dwels sweet love and constant chastity,
Unspotted fayth and comely womanhood,
Regard of honour and mild modesty,
There vertue raynes as Queene in royal throne,
And giveth lawes alone.
The which the base affections doe obay,
And yeeld theyr services unto her will,
Ne thought of thing uncomely ever may
Thereto approch to tempt her mind to ill.
Had ye once seene these her celestial threasures,   200
And unrevealed pleasures,
Then would ye wonder and her prayses sing,
That al the woods should answer and your eccho ring.

Open the temple gates unto my love,
Open them wide that she may enter in,

thrush. **descant,** an accompanying melody. 82. **Ouzell,** blackbird.
Ruddock, the European robin. 87. **make,** mate. 95. **Hesperus,** the
evening star. 103. **three handmayds,** the three Graces who served
Aphrodite. 108. **as ye use,** as you are accustomed to do. 118. **lifull,**
life-giving. 131. **tabor,** a small drum. **Croud,** crowd, an ancient
Celtic stringed instrument played with a bow. 140. **Hymen, iô Hymen,**
a shout of joy in praise of the god of marriage, used in Latin marriage

songs. 145. **laud,** praise. 148. **portly pace,** dignified step. 149.
Phoebe, the moon. 175. **uncrudded,** uncurdled. 177. **a marble towre.**
With this cf. Song of Solomon 4:4. 189. **red,** saw. 190. **Medusaes**
mazeful hed. The snaky-locked head of the Gorgon turned to stone
all who beheld it. 204. **Open . . . gates.** Again the phrasing is Biblical; cf. Psalms, p. 312, 24:7-10.

And all the postes adorne as doth behove,
And all the pillours deck with girlands trim,
For to recyve this Saynt with honour dew,
That commeth in to you.
210 With trembling steps and humble reverence,
She commeth in, before th'almighties vew,
Of her ye virgins learne obedience,
When so ye come into those holy places,
To humble your proud faces:
Bring her up to th'high altar, that she may
The sacred ceremonies there partake,
The which do endlesse matrimony make,
And let the roring Organs loudly play
The praises of the Lord in lively notes,
220 The whiles with hollow throates
The Choristers the joyous Antheme sing,
That al the woods may answere and their eccho ring.

Behold whiles she before the altar stands
Hearing the holy priest that to her speakes
And blesseth her with his two happy hands,
How the red roses flush up in her cheekes,
And the pure snow with goodly vermill stayne,
Like crimsin dyde in grayne,
That even th'Angels which continually,
230 About the sacred Altare doe remaine,
Forget their service and about her fly,
Ofte peeping in her face that seemes more fayre,
The more they on it stare.
But her sad eyes still fastened on the ground,
Are governed with goodly modesty,
That suffers not one looke to glaunce awry,
Which may let in a little thought unsownd.
Why blush ye love to give to me your hand,
The pledge of all our band?
240 Sing, ye sweet Angels, Alleluya sing,
That all the woods may answere and your eccho ring.

Now al is done; bring home the bride againe,
Bring home the triumph of our victory,
Bring home with you the glory of her gaine,
With joyance bring her and with jollity.
Never had man more joyfull day then this,
Whom heaven would heape with blis.
Make feast therefore now all this live long day,
This day for ever to me holy is,
250 Poure out the wine without restraint or stay,
Poure not by cups, but by the belly full,
Poure out to all that wull,
And sprinkle all the postes and wals with wine,
That they may sweat, and drunken be withall.
Crowne ye God Bacchus with a coronall,
And Hymen also crowne with wreathes of vine,

And let the Graces daunce unto the rest;
For they can doo it best:
The whiles the maydens doe theyr carroll sing,
To which the woods shal answer and theyr eccho ring. 260

Ring ye the bels, ye yong men of the towne,
And leave your wonted labors for this day:
This day is holy; doe ye write it downe,
That ye for ever it remember may.
This day the sunne is in his chiefest hight,
With Barnaby the bright,
From whence declining daily by degrees,
He somewhat loseth of his heat and light,
When once the Crab behind his back he sees.
But for this time it ill ordained was,   270
To chose the longest day in all the yeare,
And shortest night, when longest fitter weare:
Yet never day so long, but late would passe.
Ring ye the bels, to make it weare away,
And bonefiers make all day,
And daunce about them, and about them sing:
That all the woods may answer, and your eccho ring.

Ah when will this long weary day have end,
And lende me leave to come unto my love?
How slowly do the houres theyr numbers spend?   280
How slowly does sad Time his feathers move?
Hast thee O fayrest Planet to thy home
Within the Westerne fome:
Thy tyred steedes long since have need of rest.
Long though it be, at last I see it gloome,
And the bright evening star with golden creast
Appeare out of the East.
Fayre childe of beauty, glorious lampe of love
That all the host of heaven in rankes doost lead,
And guydest lovers through the nightes dread,   290
How chearefully thou lookest from above,
And seemst to laugh atweene thy twinkling light
As joying in the sight
Of these glad many which for joy doe sing,
That all the woods them answer and their eccho ring.

Now ceasse ye damsels your delights forepast;
Enough is it, that all the day was youres:
Now day is doen, and night is nighing fast:
Now bring the Bryde into the brydall boures.
Now night is come, now soone her disaray,   300
And in her bed her lay;
Lay her in lillies and in violets,
And silken courteins over her display,
And odourd sheetes, and Arras coverlets.
Behold how goodly my faire love does ly
In proud humility;

---

227. **vermill**, crimson. 228. **in grayne**, in the grain; i.e., a natural, unmanufactured dye. 234. **sad**, serious. 239. **band**, bond, union. 265. **sunne . . . hight.** June 11, Spenser's wedding day, was, in the old calendar, the summer solstice—the longest day of the year; it was also St. Barnabas' Day. 269. **Crab**, the zodiacal sign of Cancer, whose first point is in the summer solstice. 288. **Fayre childe**, Hesperus, the evening star. 304. **Arras**, tapestry covers woven in Arras, France. 307. **Maia**, one of the Pleiades, or seven daughters of Atlas, who formed a constellation. She became the mother of Hermes by Zeus, who met her in Tempe, a Thessalian valley. 310. **Acidalian brooke**, the outlet

Like unto Maia, when as Jove her tooke,
In Tempe, lying on the flowry gras,
Twixt sleepe and wake, after she weary was,
310 With bathing in the Acidalian brooke.
Now it is night, ye damsels may be gon,
And leave my love alone,
And leave likewise your former lay to sing:
The woods no more shal answere, nor your eccho ring.

Now welcome night, thou night so long expected,
That long daies labour doest at last defray,
And all my cares, which cruell love collected,
Hast sumd in one, and cancelled for aye:
Spread thy broad wing over my love and me,
320 That no man may us see,
And in thy sable mantle us enwrap,
From feare of perrill and foule horror free.
Let no false treason seeke us to entrap,
Nor any dread disquiet once annoy
The safety of our joy:
But let the night be calme and quietsome,
Without tempestuous storms or sad afray:
Lyke as when Jove with fayre Alcmena lay,
When he begot the great Tirynthian groome:
330 Or lyke as when he with thy selfe did lie,
And begot Majesty.
And let the mayds and yongmen cease to sing:
Ne let the woods them answer, nor theyr eccho ring.

Let no lamenting cryes, nor dolefull teares,
Be heard all night within nor yet without:
Ne let false whispers, breeding hidden feares,
Breake gentle sleepe with misconceived dout.
Let no deluding dreames, nor dreadful sights
Make sudden sad affrights;
340 Ne let housefyres, nor lightnings helpelesse harmes,
Ne let the Pouke, nor other evill sprights,
Ne let mischivous witches with theyr charmes,
Ne let hob Goblins, names whose sence we see not,
Fray us with things that be not.
Let not the shriech Oule, nor the Storke be heard:
Nor the night Raven that still deadly yels,
Nor damned ghosts cald up with mighty spels,
Nor griesly vultures make us once affeard:
Ne let th'unpleasant Quyre of Frogs still croking
350 Make us to wish theyr choking.
Let none of these theyr drery accents sing;
Ne let the woods them answer, nor theyr eccho ring.

But let stil Silence trew night watches keepe,
That sacred peace may in assurance rayne,
And tymely sleep, when it is tyme to sleepe,
May poure his limbs forth on your pleasant playne,

The whiles an hundred little winged loves,
Like divers fethered doves,
Shall fly and flutter round about your bed,
And in the secret darke, that none reproves,   360
Their prety stealthes shal worke, and snares shal
    spread
To filch away sweet snatches of delight,
Conceald through covert night.
Ye sonnes of Venus, play your sports at will,
For greedy pleasure, carelesse of your toyes,
Thinks more upon her paradise of joyes,
Then what ye do, albe it good or ill.
All night therefore attend your merry play,
For it will soone be day:
Now none doth hinder you, that say or sing,   370
Ne will the woods now answer, nor your Eccho ring.

Who is the same, which at my window peepes?
Or whose is that faire face, that shines so bright,
Is it not Cinthia, she that never sleepes,
But walkes about high heaven al the night?
O fayrest goddesse, do thou not envy
My love with me to spy:
For thou likewise didst love, though now unthought,
And for a fleece of woll, which privily,
The Latmian shepherd once unto thee brought,   380
His pleasures with thee wrought.
Therefore to us be favorable now;
And sith of wemens labours thou hast charge,
And generation goodly dost enlarge,
Encline thy will t'effect our wishfull vow,
And the chast wombe informe with timely seed,
That may our comfort breed:
Till which we cease our hopefull hap to sing,
Ne let the woods us answere, nor our Eccho ring.

And thou great Juno, which with awful might   390
The lawes of wedlock still dost patronize,
And the religion of the faith first plight
With sacred rites hast taught to solemnize:
And eeke for comfort often called art
Of women in their smart,
Eternally bind thou this lovely band,
And all thy blessings unto us impart.
And thou glad Genius, in whose gentle hand,
The bridale bowre and geniall bed remaine,
Without blemish or staine,   400
And the sweet pleasures of theyr loves delight
With secret ayde dost succour and supply,
Till they bring forth the fruitfull progeny,
Send us the timely fruit of this same night.
And thou fayre Hebe, and thou Hymen free,
Grant that it may so be.

---

of the well Acidalis in Boeotia. 329. **Tirynthian groome,** Hercules;
by Juno's craft he was made subject to Eurystheus. 341. **Pouke,** in
Irish folklore the Pooka, a malicious phantom; cf. Puck (*A Midsummer-
Night's Dream*). 374. **Cinthia,** the moon. 380. **Latmian shepherd,**
Endymion, a lovely shepherd boy from Mount Latmos with whom the
moon goddess fell in love as he slept; Spenser has modified the legend.
388. **hap,** good fortune. 399. **geniall,** nuptial. 405. **Hebe,** goddess
of youth.

Til which we cease your further prayse to sing,
Ne any woods shal answer, nor your Eccho ring.

And ye high heavens, the temple of the gods,
410 In which a thousand torches flaming bright
Doe burne, that to us wretched earthly clods,
In dreadful darknesse lend desired light;
And all ye powers which in the same remayne,
More then we men can fayne,
Poure out your blessings on us plentiously,
And happy influence upon us raine,
That we may raise a large posterity,
Which from the earth, which they may long possesse,
With lasting happinesse,
420 Up to your haughty pallaces may mount,
And for the guerdon of theyr glorious merit
May heavenly tabernacles there inherit,
Of blessed Saints for to increase the count.
So let us rest, sweet love, in hope of this,
And cease till then our tymely joyes to sing,
The woods no more us answer, nor our eccho ring.

Song made in lieu of many ornaments,
With which my love should duly have bene dect,
While cutting off through hasty accidents,
430 Ye would not stay your dew time to expect,
But promist both to recompens,
Be unto her a goodly ornament,
And for short time an endlesse moniment.
(1595)

PROTHALAMION

Calme was the day, and through the trembling ayre
Sweete-breathing Zephyrus did softly play
A gentle spirit, that lightly did delay
Hot Titans beames, which then did glyster fayre;
When I, (whom sullein care,
Through discontent of my long fruitlesse stay
In Princes Court, and expectations vayne
Of idle hopes, which still doe fly away,
Like empty shaddowes, did afflict my brayne,)
10 Walkt forth to ease my payne
Along the shoare of silver streaming Themmes;
Whose rutty Bancke, the which his River hemmes
Was paynted all with variable flowers,
And all the meades adorned with daintie gemmes
Fit to deck maydens bowres,
And crowne their Paramours
Against the Brydale day, which is not long:
    Sweete Themmes! runne softly, till I end my Song.

There, in a Meadow, by the Rivers side,
A Flocke of Nymphes I chaunced to espy,   20
All lovely Daughters of the Flood thereby,
With goodly greenish locks, all loose untyde,
As each had bene a Bryde;
And each had a little wicker basket,
Made of fine twigs, entrayled curiously,
In which they gathered flowers to fill their flasket,
And with fine Fingers crept full feateously
The tender stalkes on hye.
Of every sort, which in that Meadow grew,
They gathered some; the Violet, pallid blew,   30
The little Dazie, that at evening closes,
The virgin Lillie, and the Primrose trew,
With store of vermeil Roses,
To decke their Bridegromes posies
Against the Brydale day, which was not long:
    Sweete Themmes! runne softly, till I end my Song.

With that I saw two Swannes of goodly hewe
Come softly swimming downe along the Lee;
Two fairer Birds I yet did never see;
The snow, which doth the top of Pindus strew,   40
Did never whiter shew,
Nor Jove himselfe, when he a Swan would be,
For love of Leda, whiter did appeare;
Yet Leda was (they say) as white as he,
Yet not so white as these, nor nothing neare;
So purely white they were,
That even the gentle streame, the which them bare,
Seem'd foule to them, and bad his billowes spare
To wet their silken feathers, least they might
Soyle their fayre plumes with water not so fayre,   50
And marre their beauties bright,
That shone as heavens light,
Against their Brydale day, which was not long:
    Sweete Themmes! runne softly, till I end my Song.

Eftsoones the Nymphes, which now had Flowers their
    fill,
Ran all in haste to see that silver brood,
As they came floating on the Christal Flood;
Whom when they sawe, they stood amazed still,
Their wondring eyes to fill;
Them seem'd they never saw a sight so fayre,   60
Of Fowles, so lovely, that they sure did deeme
Them heavenly borne, or to be that same payre
Which through the Skie draw Venus silver Teeme;
For sure they did not seeme
To be begot of any earthly Seede,
But rather Angels, or of Angels breede;
Yet were they bred of Somers-heat, they say,
In sweetest Season, when each Flower and weede

414. fayne, imagine. 421. guerdon, reward. 422. heavenly tabernacles. Cf. John 14:2. 429. hasty accidents. Possibly the marriage
date had been advanced. 433. moniment, monument.
    Prothalamion. A spousal poem written to celebrate the double wed-
ding on the same day of two sisters, Elizabeth and Katherine Somerset,
daughters of the Earl of Worcester, to Henry Guilford and William

Peter. 2. Zephyrus, the west wind. 4. Titans beames, the sun. 8.
still, always. 12. rutty, rooty. 25. entrayled, intertwined. 26.
flasket, a shallow basket. 27. feateously, neatly. 33. vermeil, vermilion. 38. Lee, stream. 40. Pindus, a mountain range in northern
Greece, separating Thessaly from Epirus. 43. Leda, a beautiful girl
to whom Jupiter made love in the form of a swan. 55. Eftsoones,

The earth did fresh aray;
70 So fresh they seem'd as day,
Even as their Brydale day, which was not long:
    Sweete Themmes! runne softly, till I end my Song.

Then forth they all out of their baskets drew
Great store of Flowers, the honor of the field,
That to the sense did fragrant odours yeild,
All which upon those goodly Birds they threw
And all the Waves did strew,
That like old Peneus Waters they did seeme,
When downe along by pleasant Tempes shore,
Scattered with Flowres, through Thessaly they
80   streeme,
That they appeare, through Lillies plenteous store,
Like a Brydes Chamber flore.
Two of those Nymphes, meane while, two Garlands
      bound
Of freshest Flowres which in that Mead they found,
The which presenting all in trim Array,
Their snowie Foreheads therewithall they crownd,
Whilst one did sing this Lay,
Prepar'd against that Day,
Against their Brydale day, which was not long:
90   Sweete Themmes! runne softly, till I end my Song.

"Ye gentle Birdes! the worlds faire ornament,
And heavens glorie, whom this happie hower
Doth leade unto your lovers blisfull bower,
Joy may you have, and gentle hearts content
Of your loves couplement;
And let faire Venus, that is Queene of love,
With her heart-quelling Sonne upon you smile,
Whose smile, they say, hath vertue to remove
All Loves dislike, and friendships faultie guile
100 For ever to assoile.
Let endlesse Peace your steadfast hearts accord,
And blessed Plentie wait upon your bord;
And let your bed with pleasures chaste abound,
That fruitfull issue may to you afford,
Which may your foes confound,
And make your joyes redound
Upon your Brydale day, which is not long:
    Sweete Themmes! runne softly, till I end my Song."

So ended she; and all the rest around
110 To her redoubled that her undersong,
Which said their brydale day should not be long:
And gentle Eccho from the neighbour ground
Their accents did resound.
So forth those joyous Birdes did passe along,
Adowne the Lee, that to them murmurde low,
As he would speake, but that he lackt a tong,

Yet did by signes his glad affection show,
Making his streame run slow.
And all the foule which in his flood did dwell
Gan flock about these twaine, that did excell   120
The rest, as far as Cynthia doth shend
The lesser starres. So they, enranged well,
Did on those two attend,
And their best service lend
Against their wedding day, which was not long:
    Sweete Themmes! runne softly, till I end my Song.

At length they all to mery London came,
To mery London, my most kyndly Nurse,
That to me gave this Lifes first native sourse,
Though from another place I take my name,   130
An house of auncient fame:
There when they came, whereas those bricky towres
The which on Themmes brode aged backe doe ryde,
Where now the studious lawyers have their bowers,
There whylome wont the Templer Knights to byde,
Till they decayd through pride:
Next whereunto there stands a stately place,
Where oft I gayned giftes and goodly grace
Of that great Lord, which therein wont to dwell,
Whose want too well now feeles my freendles case; 140
But ah! here fits not well
Olde woes, but joyes, to tell
Against the Brydale daye, which is not long:
    Sweete Themmes! runne softly, till I end my Song.

Yet therein now doth lodge a noble Peer,
Great Englands glory, and the Worlds wide wonder,
Whose dreadfull name late through all Spaine did
      thunder
And Hercules two pillars standing neere
Did make to quake and feare;
Faire branch of Honor, flower of Chevalrie!   150
That fillest England with thy triumphes fame,
Joy have thou of thy noble victorie,
And endlesse happinesse of thine owne name
That promiseth the same;
That through thy prowesse, and victorious armes,
Thy country may be freed from forraine harmes,
And great Elisaes glorious name may ring
Through all the world, fil'd with thy wide Alarmes,
Which some brave muse may sing
To ages following.   160
Upon the Brydale day, which is not long:
    Sweete Themmes! runne softly, till I end my Song.

From those high Towers this noble Lord issuing,
Like Radiant Hesper, when his golden hayre
In th' Ocean billowes he hath bathed fayre,

forthwith. **64. seeme,** Venus' team of swans; see Ovid *Metamorphoses*
x, 708. **67. Somers-heat,** a pun on Somerset, the family name of the
brides. **78. Peneus,** a river of Thessaly that traverses the Vale of
Tempe, famous for its beauty. **88. against,** in anticipation. **100.
assoile,** absolve. **110. undersong,** refrain. **121. shend,** shame. **139.
Lord,** the Earl of Leicester, Spenser's patron, who died in 1588. **145.**

Peer, the Earl of Essex, who occupied the house after the death of
Leicester. **147. Spaine,** a reference to the Cádiz campaign of 1596
when Essex commanded the ground forces. **148. pillars,** the rocks on
either side of the Strait of Gibraltar. **153. happinesse,** probably a
pun on Essex' family name, Devereux (Fr. *heureux*, happy). **164.
Hesper,** the evening star.

Descended to the Rivers open viewing,
With a great traine ensuing.
Above the rest were goodly to bee seene
Two gentle Knights of lovely face and feature,
170 Beseeming well the bower of anie Queene,
With gifts of wit, and ornaments of nature,
Fit for so goodly stature,

That like the twins of Jove they seem'd in sight,
Which decke the Bauldricke of the Heavens bright;
They two, forth pacing to the Rivers side,
Received those two faire Brides, their Loves delight;
Which at th' appointed tyde,
Each one did make his Bryde
Against their Brydale day, which is not long:
　　Sweete Themmes! runne softly, till I end my Song.
(1596)

169. **Knights,** the grooms.　173. **twins of Jove,** Castor and Pollux, the constellation Gemini.

WILLIAM SHAKESPEARE 1564-1616

The flower of the Renaissance is by general consent William Shakespeare. He was both poet and dramatist; his greatest work was in the field of drama, but his finest lyrics adorn his plays.

Stripped of the traditions and surmises that have grown up around it, William Shakespeare's life was singularly simple and uneventful. He was born of good middle-class stock in the country town of Stratford-upon-Avon in April 1564. Apparently he had the usual grammar school education of the time with its staple of Latin, but nothing positive is known about his education. Like others of his class he married young, and by the time he reached his majority he was the father of three children. His dramatic career began about 1590; in 1594 he became an actor-sharer in the Lord Chamberlain's company, one of the ablest of the theatrical troupes; in 1598 he was mentioned as among the best in both comedy and tragedy for the stage, commended for his "fine-filed phrase," and praised for his poetry, especially for "his sugared sonnets among his private friends." For the Chamberlain's Men, a company which became the King's Men in 1603 at the accession of James, Shakespeare wrote the whole or the major part of thirty-seven plays. Various legal records show him to have been a respected man of property both in London and in Stratford. About 1611 or 1612 he retired to his native city to spend his last days in "ease, retirement, and the conversation of his friends." He died on April 23, 1616, and was buried in the chancel of the Church of the Holy Trinity in Stratford. Many of his plays were published in single editions during his lifetime, and after his death thirty-six of them were collected together in the famous First Folio edition of 1623—fourteen comedies, ten histories, and twelve tragedies.

If genius could be accounted for, it might perhaps be said that Shakespeare's acquaintance with the art of the actor helped him in an understanding of the art of the playwright. But this explanation is not enough; to it must be added an observing mind, a profound sympathetic understanding of life, an acquaintance with all classes of men and women that is reminiscent of Chaucer's, and, above all, a perception of the great constants of human nature which are the same today, tomorrow, and forever, and which represent all people. His genius did not lie in his power of originating plots, for almost all of his stories he borrowed from chronicle, biography, prose tale, or earlier play, but rather in his unerring capacity for seizing upon the dramatic elements and for revealing life in its full richness and movement.

William Shakespeare the dramatist was also William Shakespeare the poet, for he thought of drama as a form of poetry, and his most magnificent verse he put into the mouths of his characters. Furthermore, his songs and lyrics, like those of many of his contemporaries in the drama, are to be found in the matrix of his plays. In addition, however, he became early in his career the author of two long narrative poems, Venus and Adonis and The Rape of Lucrece, and of an extended sonnet sequence. His lyrical poetry may be divided, therefore, into two general groups: first, his independent poems, and second, the songs from the plays. They will be commented upon in this order.

When Shakespeare first went to London (about 1588), he found that advancement for a writer who had no social connections, no influence, and no money lay in securing a rich and noble patron whose favors he might buy with his verses. Such a patron he discovered in the brilliant young Earl of Southampton, and to this courtier—several years the poet's junior—he addressed his first published poems, Venus and Adonis (1593) and The Rape of Lucrece (1594). The poems are narratives which retell in formal stanzas the classical stories of the hapless love of Venus for the beautiful youth Adonis and, by contrast, the wicked rape of the chaste Roman matron Lucrece by the haughty king Tarquin. Actually, the poems are more descriptive than narrative, they present a succession of situations rather than a continuous action and wander in the leisurely manner of the medieval romances through episodes that are pictured rather than told. They seem, indeed, much like metrical tapestries, with suggestions of far-off happenings and characters remote from life and moving like figures in a pattern rather than like creatures of flesh and blood. The stanzas are even more static than those in The Faerie Queene, and they do not possess the rich qualities of melody and sweep that Spenser has given to his great verses.

Did Shakespeare also address the young Earl of Southampton in his long sonnet sequence? Nobody knows, and the whole problem of the sonnets has teased the minds of scholars and of sentimentalists for many decades. The sonnets were not published until 1609, at least ten or fifteen years after they were written, and it is apparent that Shakespeare had no personal connection with their printing. Thomas Thorpe, their publisher, dedicated them to Mr. W. H., "the onlie begetter of these ensuing sonnets," but who he was is not known, although both William, Lord Herbert—later Earl of Pembroke—and Henry Wriothesley, Earl of Southampton have been suggested as the unknown. Out of the maze of all these speculations there stand certain facts: that Shakespeare wrote one hundred fifty-four sonnets during the last decade of the sixteenth century, that of these the first one hundred twenty-six were addressed to a young man, and that the concluding sonnets celebrate the charms of a "dark lady," a disdainful brunette who apparently rewarded with scorn the praises which the poet heaped upon her. The ideas in the sonnets are not novel: he begs for his patron's favor, urges him to marry that his charm and virtue may be perpetuated in his children, expresses his hope that the fame of his patron may live in his verses, asserts that no frown from his noble friend will discourage him, expresses jealousy for a rival poet who is seeking the patron's favor. The form of the sonnets is that of the Elizabethan variation of the Italian—three quatrains with alternate rimes (abab cdcd efef) and a concluding couplet (gg). The thought division follows that of the lines: lament in the quatrains, comfort in the couplet; a question in the quatrains, the answer in the couplet, and similar adjustment of thought and structure. Sometimes the sonnets are linked in a minor sequence of pairs, often, however, they stand alone. Furthermore, they are uneven in merit. Many are quite conventional and artificial, but others express lofty ideas in noble and melodious verse.

The songs from the plays form the main body of Shakespeare's greatest lyrics. The casual reader of the dramas can get little idea of the extent to which they are adorned with music and song. Very few are entirely without lyrics, and others, like A Midsummer-Night's Dream and The Tempest, almost sing themselves from beginning to end. But Shakespeare has not added the songs as pure decoration; in every instance where they appear, they reflect the mood of the play or spring easily and naturally from action and character. Sometimes, as in the "going-out songs," they help to clear the curtainless stage of its figures, sometimes, as in poor Ophelia's mad songs, they reveal tragedy; sometimes they run like an irrepressible ripple throughout the drama, as they do in many of the romantic comedies. No English dramatist had more skill and sensitivity than did Shakespeare in melodizing and sweetening his scenes with song. These must be thought of as sung and sung for a dramatic purpose; they reflect the drama as well as adorn it.

SONNETS

15

When I consider everything that grows
Holds in perfection but a little moment,
That this huge stage presenteth nought but shows
Whereon the stars in secret influence comment;
When I perceive that men as plants increase,
Cheeréd and checked even by the self-same sky,
Vaunt in their youthful sap, at height decrease,
And wear their brave state out of memory—
Then the conceit of this inconstant stay
Sets you most rich in youth before my sight,
10 Where wasteful Time debateth with Decay,
To change your day of youth to sullied night;

And all in war with Time for love of you,
As he takes from you, I engraft you new.

18

Shall I compare thee to a summer's day?
Thou art more lovely and more temperate:
Rough winds do shake the darling buds of May,
And summer's lease hath all too short a date:
Sometime too hot the eye of heaven shines,
And often is his gold complexion dimmed;
And every fair from fair sometime declines,
By chance or nature's changing course untrimmed;
But thy eternal summer shall not fade,
Nor lose possession of that fair thou owest;   10
Nor shall Death brag thou wander'st in his shade,

Sonnet 15. 5. **as,** like. 9. **conceit,** thought, concept. 14. **engraft,** graft, i.e., add by my verse what Time takes from you.

Sonnet 18. 7. **every fair,** every beautiful thing. 8. **untrimmed,** stripped. 10. **owest,** ownest.

When in eternal lines to time thou growest:
   So long as men can breathe, or eyes can see,
   So long lives this, and this gives life to thee.

23

As an unperfect actor on the stage,
Who with his fear is put besides his part,
Or some fierce thing replete with too much rage,
Whose strength's abundance weakens his own heart,
So I, for fear of trust, forget to say
The perfect ceremony of love's rite,
And in mine own love's strength seem to decay,
O'ercharged with burden of mine own love's might.
O, let my books be then the eloquence
10 And dumb presagers of my speaking breast,
Who plead for love, and look for recompense,
More than that tongue that more hath more expressed.
   O, learn to read what silent love hath writ:
   To hear with eyes belongs to love's fine wit.

25

Let those who are in favor with their stars
Of public honor and proud titles boast,
Whilst I, whom fortune of such triumph bars,
Unlooked for joy in that I honor most.
Great princes' favorites their fair leaves spread
But as the marigold at the sun's eye,
And in themselves their pride lies buried,
For at a frown they in their glory die.
The painful warrior famouséd for fight,
10 After a thousand victories once foiled
Is from the book of honor razéd quite,
And all the rest forgot for which he toiled:
   Then happy I, that love and am beloved,
   Where I may not remove nor be removed.

29

When, in disgrace with fortune and men's eyes,
I all alone beweep my outcast state,
And trouble deaf heaven with my bootless cries,
And look upon myself, and curse my fate,
Wishing me like to one more rich in hope,
Featured like him, like him with friends possessed,
Desiring this man's art and that man's scope,
With what I most enjoy contented least;
Yet in these thoughts myself almost despising,
10 Haply I think on thee—and then my state,
Like to the lark at break of day arising
From sullen earth, sings hymns at heaven's gate;

For thy sweet love remembered such wealth brings
That then I scorn to change my state with kings.

30

When to the sessions of sweet silent thought
I summon up remembrance of things past,
I sigh the lack of many a thing I sought,
And with old woes new wail my dear time's waste.
Then can I drown an eye, unused to flow,
For precious friends hid in death's dateless night,
And weep afresh love's long since canceled woe,
And moan the expense of many a vanished sight.
Then can I grieve at grievances foregone,
And heavily from woe to woe tell o'er   10
The sad account of fore-bemoanéd moan,
Which I new pay as if not paid before.
   But if the while I think on thee, dear friend,
   All losses are restored and sorrows end.

32

If thou survive my well-contented day,
When that churl Death my bones with dust shall
    cover,
And shalt by fortune once more re-survey
These poor rude lines of thy deceaséd lover,
Compare them with the bettering of the time,
And though they be outstripped by every pen,
Reserve them for my love, not for their rime,
Exceeded by the height of happier men.
O, then vouchsafe me but this loving thought:
"Had my friend's Muse grown with this growing age, 10
A dearer birth than this his love had brought,
To march in ranks of better equipage:
   But since he died, and poets better prove,
   Theirs for their style I'll read, his for his love."

33

Full many a glorious morning have I seen
Flatter the mountain-tops with sovereign eye,
Kissing with golden face the meadows green,
Gilding pale streams with heavenly alchemy;
Anon permit the basest clouds to ride
With ugly rack on his celestial face,
And from the forlorn world his visage hide,
Stealing unseen to west with this disgrace.
Even so my sun one early morn did shine
With all-triumphant splendor on my brow;   10
But, out, alack! he was but one hour mine,
The region cloud hath masked him from me now.

14. **this,** this sonnet.
   Sonnet 23. 2. **fear . . . part,** i.e., stage fright makes him forget his role.
   Sonnet 25. 1. **in favor with their stars,** born under a lucky star, fortunate. 11. **razéd,** erased, destroyed.
   Sonnet 29. 14. **state,** situation.

Sonnet 30. 6. **dateless,** without date, endless.
   Sonnet 33. 6. **rack,** thin, broken clouds. 14. **stain,** become stained.
   Sonnet 54. 5. **canker-blooms,** the dog rose, or wild rose, which has color but no perfume. 12. **sweet . . . made.** The fragrance of the dead petals is preserved in the rose jar; similarly the memory of the "beauteous and lovely youth" is distilled in the poet's sonnet.

Yet him for this my love no whit disdaineth;
Suns of the world may stain when heaven's sun
    staineth.

54

O, how much more doth beauty beauteous seem
By that sweet ornament which truth doth give!
The rose looks fair, but fairer we it deem
For that sweet odor which doth in it live.
The canker-blooms have full as deep a dye
As the perfuméd tincture of the roses,
Hang on such thorns, and play as wantonly
When summer's breath their maskéd buds discloses;
But, for their virtue only is their show,
10 They live unwooed and unrespected fade,
Die to themselves. Sweet roses do not so;
Of their sweet deaths are sweetest odors made:
    And so of you, beauteous and lovely youth,
    When that shall fade, my verse distills your truth.

55

Not marble, nor the gilded monuments
Of princes, shall outlive this powerful rime;
But you shall shine more bright in these contents
Than unswept stone, besmeared with sluttish time.
When wasteful war shall statues overturn,
And broils root out the work of masonry,
Nor Mars his sword nor war's quick fire shall burn
The living record of your memory.
'Gainst death and all-oblivious enmity
10 Shall you pace forth; your praise shall still find room
Even in the eyes of all posterity
That wear this world out to the ending doom.
    So, till the judgment that yourself arise,
    You live in this, and dwell in lovers' eyes.

60

Like as the waves make towards the pebbled shore,
So do our minutes hasten to their end;
Each changing place with that which goes before,
In sequent toil all forwards do contend.
Nativity, once in the main of light,
Crawls to maturity, wherewith being crowned,
Crooked eclipses 'gainst his glory fight,
And Time that gave doth now his gift confound.
Time doth transfix the flourish set on youth
10 And delves the parallels in beauty's brow,
Feeds on the rarities of nature's truth,
And nothing stands but for his scythe to mow:

And yet to times in hope my verse shall stand,
Praising thy worth, despite his cruel hand.

64

When I have seen by Time's fell hand defaced
The rich-proud cost of outworn buried age;
When sometime lofty towers I see downrazed,
And brass eternal slave to mortal rage;
When I have seen the hungry ocean gain
Advantage on the kingdom of the shore
And the firm soil win of the watery main,
Increasing store with loss and loss with store;
When I have seen such interchange of state,
Or state itself confounded to decay;   10
Ruin hath taught me thus to ruminate,
That Time will come and take my love away.
    This thought is as a death, which cannot choose
    But weep to have that which it fears to lose.

65

Since brass, nor stone, nor earth, nor boundless sea,
But sad mortality o'er-sways their power,
How with this rage shall beauty hold a plea,
Whose action is no stronger than a flower?
O, how shall summer's honey breath hold out
Against the wreckful siege of battering days,
When rocks impregnable are not so stout,
Nor gates of steel so strong, but Time decays?
O fearful meditation! where, alack,
Shall Time's best jewel from Time's chest lie hid? 10
Or what strong hand can hold his swift foot back?
Or who his spoil of beauty can forbid?
    O, none, unless this miracle have might,
    That in black ink my love may still shine bright.

66

Tired with all these, for restful death I cry,
As, to behold desert a beggar born,
And needy nothing trimmed in jollity,
And purest faith unhappily forsworn,
And gilded honor shamefully misplaced,
And maiden virtue rudely strumpeted,
And right perfection wrongfully disgraced,
And strength by limping sway disabled,
And art made tongue-tied by authority,
And folly, doctor-like, controlling skill,   10
And simple truth miscalled simplicity,
And captive good attending captain ill:
    Tired with all these, from these would I be gone,
    Save that, to die, I leave my love alone.

Sonnet 55. 1. Not . . . nor, neither . . . nor. 3. these contents, this sonnet. 7. Nor Mars his, Neither Mars'. 12. the ending doom, the Day of Judgment.
   Sonnet 60. 5. main of light, chief light, the sun. 8. confound, overthrow, destroy. 10. delves the parallels, digs the furrows.
   Sonnet 64. 1. When I have seen, etc. The close interrelation of sonnets 64 and 65 should be noted.
   Sonnet 65. 10. Time's best jewel, beauty. 14. in black ink, the familiar allusion to the power of verse to immortalize.
   Sonnet 66. 1. all these, the injustices listed in the lines that follow.

That time of year thou mayst in me behold
When yellow leaves, or none, or few, do hang
Upon those boughs which shake against the cold,
Bare ruined choirs, where late the sweet birds sang.
In me thou see'st the twilight of such day
As after sunset fadeth in the west,
Which by and by black night doth take away,
Death's second self, that seals up all in rest.
In me thou see'st the glowing of such fire
10 That on the ashes of his youth doth lie,
As the death-bed whereon it must expire,
Consumed with that which it was nourished by.
   This thou perceivest, which makes thy love more
     strong,
   To love that well which thou must leave ere long.

76

Why is my verse so barren of new pride,
So far from variation or quick change?
Why with the time do I not glance aside
To new-found methods and to compounds strange?
Why write I still all one, ever the same,
And keep invention in a noted weed,
That every word doth almost tell my name,
Showing their birth, and where they did proceed?
O! know, sweet love, I always write of you,
10 And you and love are still my argument;
So all my best is dressing old words new,
Spending again what is already spent:
   For as the sun is daily new and old,
   So is my love still telling what is told.

97

How like a winter hath my absence been
From thee, the pleasure of the fleeting year!
What freezings have I felt, what dark days seen!
What old December's bareness everywhere!
And yet this time removed was summer's time;
The teeming autumn, big with rich increase,
Bearing the wanton burden of the prime,
Like widowed wombs after their lords' decease:
Yet this abundant issue seemed to me
10 But hope of orphans and unfathered fruit;
For summer and his pleasures wait on thee,
And, thou away, the very birds are mute;
   Or, if they sing, 'tis with so dull a cheer
   That leaves look pale, dreading the winter's near.

To me, fair friend, you never can be old,
For as you were when first your eye I eyed,
Such seems your beauty still. Three winters cold
Have from the forests shook three summers' pride,
Three beauteous springs to yellow autumn turned
In process of the seasons have I seen,
Three April perfumes in three hot Junes burned,
Since first I saw you fresh, which yet are green,
Ah, yet doth beauty, like a dial-hand,
Steal from his figure, and no pace perceived;   10
So your sweet hue, which methinks still doth stand,
Hath motion, and mine eye may be deceived:
   For fear of which, hear this, thou age unbred:
   Ere you were born was beauty's summer dead.

106

When in the chronicle of wasted time
I see descriptions of the fairest wights,
And beauty making beautiful old rime
In praise of ladies dead and lovely knights,
Then, in the blazon of sweet beauty's best,
Of hand, of foot, of lip, of eye, of brow,
I see their antique pen would have expressed
Even such a beauty as you master now.
So all their praises are but prophecies
Of this our time, all you prefiguring;   10
And, for they looked but with divining eyes,
They had not skill enough your worth to sing.
   For we, which now behold these present days,
   Have eyes to wonder, but lack tongues to praise.

116

Let me not to the marriage of true minds
Admit impediments. Love is not love
Which alters when it alteration finds,
Or bends with the remover to remove.
Oh, no! it is an ever-fixéd mark
That looks on tempests and is never shaken;
It is the star to every wandering bark,
Whose worth's unknown, although his height be
    taken.
Love's not Time's fool, though rosy lips and cheeks
Within his bending sickle's compass come;   10
Love alters not with his brief hours and weeks,
But bears it out even to the edge of doom.
   If this be error and upon me proved,
   I never writ, nor no man ever loved.

Sonnet 76. 1. **pride,** that which creates pride, such as beauty, orna-ment. 6. **noted weed,** familiar garb. 10. **argument,** theme.
Sonnet 97. 5. **this time removed,** the actual season of my separa-tion from you. 7. **the prime,** the spring, or seedtime, of the year.
Sonnet 106. 5. **blazon,** description, especially with a view to display.
Sonnet 116. 10. **compass,** sweep.
Sonnet 119. 1. **Siren,** in Greek mythology one of a group of sea nymphs who enticed mariners to death by their singing; used here as

an adjective, the meaning of which is expressed in lines 3–4. 2. **lim-becks,** short form of *alembic,* an instrument used in chemistry for distilling liquids. 7. **fitted,** forced by paroxysm.
Sonnet 128. 2. **blesséd wood,** the virginal, a small spinet, played, like a piano, by a keyboard; the strings, however, are mechanically plucked, not struck with hammers. 5. **jacks,** the keys.
Sonnet 130. 1. **My mistress' eyes,** etc. This sonnet is a clever satire on the conventional poetic description of a lady. 8. **reeks,** is

258   *The Brave New World and After*

What potions have I drunk of Siren tears,
Distilled from limbecks foul as hell within,
Applying fears to hopes and hopes to fears,
Still losing when I saw myself to win!
What wretched errors hath my heart committed,
Whilst it hath thought itself so blessèd never!
How have mine eyes out of their spheres been fitted,
In the distraction of this madding fever!
O benefit of ill! now I find true
10 That better is by evil still made better;
And ruined love, when it is built anew,
Grows fairer than at first, more strong, far greater.
　　So I return rebuked to my content,
　　And gain by ill thrice more than I have spent.

128

How oft, when thou, my music, music playest,
Upon that blessèd wood whose motion sounds
With thy sweet fingers, when thou gently swayest
The wiry concord that mine ear confounds,
Do I envy those jacks that nimble leap
To kiss the tender inward of thy hand,
Whilst my poor lips, which should that harvest reap,
At the wood's boldness by thee blushing stand!
To be so tickled, they would change their state
10 And situation with those dancing chips,
O'er whom thy fingers walk with gentle gait,
Making deadwood more blest than living lips.
　　Since saucy jacks so happy are in this,
　　Give them thy fingers, me thy lips to kiss.

130

My mistress' eyes are nothing like the sun;
Coral is far more red than her lips' red;
If snow be white, why then her breasts are dun;
If hairs be wires, black wires grow on her head.
I have seen roses damasked, red and white,
But no such roses see I in her cheeks;
And in some perfumes is there more delight
Than in the breath that from my mistress reeks.
I love to hear her speak, yet well I know
10 That music hath a far more pleasing sound;
I grant I never saw a goddess go;
My mistress, when she walks, treads on the ground.
　　And yet, by heaven, I think my love as rare
　　As any she belied with false compare.

Poor soul, the center of my sinful earth—
[My sinful earth] these rebel powers array—
Why dost thou pine within and suffer dearth,
Painting thy outward walls so costly gay?
Why so large cost, having so short a lease,
Dost thou upon thy fading mansions spend?
Shall worms, inheritors of this excess,
Eat up thy charge? Is this thy body's end?
Then, soul, live thou upon thy servant's loss,
And let that pine to aggravate thy store;　　10
Buy terms divine in selling hours of dross;
Within be fed, without be rich no more:
　　So shalt thou feed on Death, that feeds on men,
　　And Death once dead, there's no more dying then.
(Before 1598; 1609)

SONGS FROM THE PLAYS

WHEN ICICLES HANG BY THE WALL

When icicles hang by the wall,
　　And Dick the shepherd blows his nail,
And Tom bears logs into the hall,
　　And milk comes frozen home in pail,
When blood is nipped and ways be foul,
Then nightly sings the staring owl,
"Tu-whit, tu-who!" A merry note,
While greasy Joan doth keel the pot.

When all aloud the wind doth blow,
　　And coughing drowns the parson's saw,　　10
And birds sit brooding in the snow,
　　And Marian's nose looks red and raw,
When roasted crabs hiss in the bowl,
Then nightly sings the staring owl,
"Tu-whit, tu-who!" A merry note,
While greasy Joan doth keel the pot.
(1590-2; 1598)

WHO IS SILVIA?

Who is Silvia? What is she,
　　That all our swains commend her?
Holy, fair, and wise is she;
　　The heaven such grace did lend her,
That she might admirèd be.

Is she kind as she is fair?
　　For beauty lives with kindness.

---

exhaled. 11. go, walk.
　Sonnet 146. 2. **[My sinful earth].** The first words of this line are missing in the first edition of the sonnets and have been variously filled in by scholars; "my sinful earth" means "my mortal clay," "my body." array, clothe. 10. **aggravate,** increase. 12. **Within be fed,** etc. Spiritual food will create immortality and so destroy Death.
　When icicles hang by the wall. Sung as a "going-out song" in *Love's Labour's Lost* (V, ii, 922). In this song Hiems, or Winter, repre-

sented by a clown dressed as an owl, replies to Ver, or Spring, the cuckoo. 2. **blows his nail,** i.e., breathes on his fingers to warm them. 8. **greasy Joan,** the kitchen girl. **keel,** cool by stirring it so that it will not boil over. 10. **saw,** discourse; here, sermon. 13. **roasted crabs,** hot crabapples put into the ale to flavor it.
　Who is Silvia? Sung as a serenade under Silvia's chamber window in *The Two Gentlemen of Verona* (IV, ii, 39).

Love doth to her eyes repair,
   To help him of his blindness;
10 And, being helped, inhabits there.

Then to Silvia let us sing,
   That Silvia is excelling;
She excels each mortal thing
   Upon the dull earth dwelling.
To her let us garlands bring.
(1592-4; 1623)

YOU SPOTTED SNAKES

You spotted snakes with double tongue,
   Thorny hedge-hogs, be not seen;
Newts and blind-worms, do no wrong,
   Come not near our fairy queen.
CHORUS: Philomel, with melody,
Sing in our sweet lullaby:
Lulla, lulla, lullaby; lulla, lulla, lullaby.
Never harm, nor spell, nor charm,
Come our lovely lady nigh;
10 So good night, with lullaby.

Weaving spiders, come not here.
   Hence, you long-legged spinners, hence!
Beetles black, approach not near;
   Worm, nor snail, do no offense.
CHORUS: Philomel, with melody,
Sing in our sweet lullaby:
Lulla, lulla, lullaby; lulla, lulla, lullaby.
Never harm, nor spell, nor charm,
Come our lovely lady nigh;
So good night, with lullaby.

THE OUSEL COCK

The ousel cock so black of hue,
   With orange-tawny bill,
The throstle with his note so true,
   The wren with little quill;

The finch, the sparrow, and the lark,
   The plain-song cuckoo gray,
Whose note full many a man doth mark,
   And dares not answer nay.
(1594?; 1600)

TELL ME WHERE IS FANCY BRED

Tell me where is fancy bred,
Or in the heart, or in the head?

How begot, how nourishéd?
   Reply, reply.
It is engend'red in the eyes,
With gazing fed; and fancy dies
In the cradle where it lies.
Let us all ring fancy's knell;
I'll begin it—Ding, dong, bell.
   Ding, dong, bell.
(1594-6; 1600)

SIGH NO MORE, LADIES

Sigh no more, ladies, sigh no more;
   Men were deceivers ever;
One foot in sea, and one on shore,
   To one thing constant never.
Then sigh not so, but let them go,
   And be you blithe and bonny,
Converting all your sounds of woe
   Into "Hey nonny, nonny!"

Sing no more ditties, sing no moe
   Of dumps so dull and heavy;
The fraud of men was ever so,
   Since summer first was leavy.
Then sigh not so, but let them go,
   And be you blithe and bonny,
Converting all your sounds of woe
   Into "Hey nonny, nonny!"
(1598-1600; 1600)

UNDER THE GREENWOOD TREE

   Under the greenwood tree
   Who loves to lie with me,
   And turn his merry note
   Unto the sweet bird's throat,
Come hither, come hither, come hither!
      Here shall he see
      No enemy
But winter and rough weather.

   Who doth ambition shun,
   And loves to live i' the sun,
   Seeking the food he eats,
   And pleased with what he gets,
Come hither, come hither, come hither!
      Here shall he see
      No enemy
But winter and rough weather.

You spotted snakes with double tongue. Lullaby song to Titania, Queen of the Fairies, sung by members of her train in A Midsummer-Night's Dream (II, ii, 9). .5. **Philomel,** the nightingale.
   The ousel cock so black of hue. Titania is sung asleep by a fairy song; she is awakened in A Midsummer-Night's Dream (III, i, 128) by this song from the raucous throat of the ass-headed Bottom, her monster lover. The ousel cock (he pronounced it woosel-cock) is the

blackbird. 3. **throstle,** thrush. 6. **plain-song,** thematic or based on one subject. Because its name and its note suggested cuckold, its song was "unwelcome to a married ear."
   Tell me where is fancy bred. A song devised by Portia to guide her favorite suitor Bassanio in his choice of the one of three caskets that would bring him her hand in marriage in The Merchant of Venice (III, ii, 63). The suitor is told, in effect, not to judge by appearances,

It was a lover and his lass,
 With a hey, and a ho, and a hey nonino,
That o'er the green corn-field did pass
 In the spring time, the only pretty ring time,
 When birds do sing, hey ding a ding, ding!
 Sweet lovers love the spring.

Between the acres of the rye,
 With a hey, and a ho, and a hey nonino,
These pretty country folks would lie,
10 In spring time, the only pretty ring time,
 When birds do sing, hey ding a ding, ding!
 Sweet lovers love the spring.

This carol they began that hour,
 With a hey, and a ho, and a hey nonino,
How that a life was but a flower
 In spring time, the only pretty ring time,
 When birds do sing, hey ding a ding, ding!
 Sweet lovers love the spring.

And therefore take the present time,
 With a hey, and a ho, and a hey nonino,   20
For love is crownéd with the prime
 In spring time, the only pretty ring time,
 When birds do sing, hey ding a ding, ding!
 Sweet lovers love the spring.

(1599-1600; 1623)

The first setting of "It was a lover and his lass," from the unique copy of Thomas Morley's First Booke of Ayres. Or Little Short Songs, to Sing and Play to the Lute, with the Base Viole (1600), preserved in the Folger Shakespeare Library, Washington. The accompaniment is printed in reverse so that the lutenist-singer and the bass-viol player could sit opposite to one another, with the book between them. Compared with the Shakespearian version, the text offers some interesting verbal and stanzaic variants. There is no evidence, however, that Morley's setting was used in performance, or that Shakespeare was the author of the words.

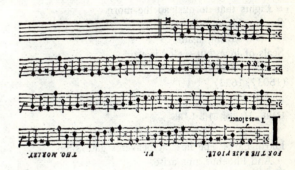

and the *l* and *ed* sounds in the lyric offer a hint to Bassanio that he should choose the leaden casket.

 Sigh no more, ladies, sigh no more. Sung by Balthasar, a singing attendant of Don Pedro in *Much Ado About Nothing* (II, iii, 64). 10. **dumps,** low spirits. The term was applied to mournful songs; cf. the modern "blues."

 Under the greenwood tree. Sung by Amiens, the "singing squire,"

in the train of the banished duke in *As You Like It* (II, v, 1). Its Arcadian philosophy is immediately parodied and reduced to absurdity by the melancholy Jaques.

 It was a lover and his lass. Sung, very appropriately, by two pages to Touchstone, the court jester, and his country sweetheart, Audrey, in *As You Like It* (V, iii, 17). 21. **prime,** spring.

O MISTRESS MINE

O mistress mine, where are you roaming?
O, stay and hear; your true love's coming,
    That can sing both high and low.
Trip no further, pretty sweeting,
Journeys end in lovers meeting,
    Every wise man's son doth know.

What is love? 'Tis not hereafter;
Present mirth hath present laughter;
    What's to come is still unsure.
10 In delay there lies no plenty;
Then come kiss me, sweet and twenty,
    Youth's a stuff will not endure.
(1599-1601; 1623)

TAKE, OH, TAKE THOSE LIPS AWAY

Take, oh, take those lips away,
    That so sweetly were forsworn;
And those eyes, the break of day,
    Lights that do mislead the morn.
But my kisses bring again,
            Bring again;
Seals of love, but sealed in vain,
            Sealed in vain.
(1603?; 1623)

HARK, HARK! THE LARK

Hark, hark! The lark at heaven's gate sings,
    And Phoebus gins arise,
His steeds to water at those springs
    On chaliced flowers that lies;
And winking Mary-buds begin
    To ope their golden eyes.
With every thing that pretty is,
    My lady sweet, arise!
    Arise, arise!

FEAR NO MORE THE HEAT O' THE SUN

Fear no more the heat o' the sun,
    Nor the furious winter's rages;
Thou thy worldly task hast done,
    Home art gone, and ta'en thy wages.
Golden lads and girls all must,
As chimney-sweepers, come to dust.

Fear no more the frown o' the great;
    Thou art past the tyrant's stroke;
Care no more to clothe and eat;
    To thee the reed is as the oak.
The scepter, learning, physic, must   10
All follow this, and come to dust.

Fear no more the lightning-flash,
    Nor the all-dreaded thunder-stone;
Fear not slander, censure rash;
    Thou hast finished joy and moan.
All lovers young, all lovers must
Consign to thee, and come to dust.

No exorciser harm thee!
    Nor no witchcraft charm thee!   20
Ghost unlaid forbear thee!
    Nothing ill come near thee!
Quiet consummation have;
    And renownéd be thy grave!
(1610-1612; 1623)

WHEN DAFFODILS BEGIN TO PEER

When daffodils begin to peer,
    With hey! the doxy over the dale,
Why, then comes in the sweet o' the year;
    For the red blood reigns in the winter's pale.

The white sheet bleaching on the hedge,
    With hey! the sweet birds, oh, how they sing!
Doth set my pugging tooth on edge;
    For a quart of ale is a dish for a king.

The lark, that tirra-lirra chants,
    With hey! with hey! the thrush and the jay,   10
Are summer songs for me and my aunts,
    While we lie tumbling in the hay.

LAWN AS WHITE AS DRIVEN SNOW

Lawn as white as driven snow;
Cypress black as e'er was crow;
Gloves as sweet as damask roses;
Masks for faces and for noses;
Bugle bracelet, necklace amber,
Perfume for a lady's chamber:
Golden quoifs and stomachers,
For the lads to give their dears;
Pins and poking-sticks of steel,

O mistress mine, where are you roaming? Sung by Feste, the clown, to Sir Toby and Sir Andrew Aguecheek in *Twelfth Night* (II, iii, 40).
Take, oh, take those lips away. Sung by "a Boy" to the deserted Mariana at the moated grange in *Measure for Measure* (IV, i, 1).
Hark, hark! The lark. . . . An aubade, or morning serenade, sung to Imogen by Cloten's musicians in *Cymbeline* (II, iii, 21). 4. **chaliced flowers.** The figure is that of the sun drying the dew in the flower cups. 5. **winking Mary-buds**, sleeping marigolds.
Fear no more the heat o' the sun. Sung by Guiderius and Arviragus at the grave of the supposedly dead Imogen in *Cymbeline* (IV, ii, 258).

When daffodils begin to peer. Spring song of Autolycus, rogue and thief in *The Winter's Tale* (IV, iii, 1). 2. **doxy**, thieves' cant for prostitute. 4. **red blood**, etc. The red blood (of spring) has seized control of winter's domains. 7. **pugging**, thieving. *Tooth* is used here as a figure for liking, or taste (cf. "sweet tooth"); Autolycus had a "tooth" for picking up "unconsidered trifles," as he confesses elsewhere. 11. **aunts**, cant for prostitutes.
Lawn as white as driven snow. Sung by Autolycus, disguised as a peddler in *The Winter's Tale* (IV, iv, 220). 2. **Cypress**, crape. 5. **Bugle**, a long bead of black glass. 7. **quoifs**, hoods, caps. 9. **poking-sticks**, metal rods which were used when heated to set the pleats of ruffs.

10 What maids lack from head to heel.
  Come buy of me, come; come buy, come buy;
  Buy, lads, or else your lasses cry;
  Come buy.
  (1610? 1623)

COME UNTO THESE YELLOW SANDS

Come unto these yellow sands,
    And then take hands;
Curtsied when you have, and kissed
    The wild waves whist,
    Foot it featly here and there;
And, sweet sprites, the burthen bear.
        Hark, hark!
(Burden, dispersedly) Bow-wow.
    The watch-dogs bark!
10 (Burden, dispersedly) Bow-wow.
    Hark, hark! I hear
    The strain of strutting chanticleer
    Cry, "Cock-a-diddle-dow!"

FULL FATHOM FIVE

Full fathom five thy father lies:
    Of his bones are coral made;
Those are pearls that were his eyes;
    Nothing of him that doth fade

But doth suffer a sea-change
Into something rich and strange.
Sea-nymphs hourly ring his knell:
                    Ding-dong!
Hark! now I hear them—Ding-dong, bell!

NO MORE DAMS I'LL MAKE FOR FISH

No more dams I'll make for fish;
    Nor fetch in firing
    At requiring;
Nor scrape trencher, nor wash dish:
    'Ban, 'Ban, Ca —Caliban
Has a new master—get a new man.
Freedom, hey-day! hey-day, freedom! freedom, hey-
    day, freedom!

WHERE THE BEE SUCKS

Where the bee sucks, there suck I;
In a cowslip's bell I lie;
There I couch when owls do cry.
On the bat's back I do fly
After summer merrily.
Merrily, merrily, shall I live now
Under the blossom that hangs on the bough.
(1610?; 1623)

Come unto these yellow sands. Sung by Ariel to entice Prince Ferdinand to follow him in *The Tempest* (I, ii, 376). 4. **whist**, be silent. 5. **featly**, nimbly.
Full fathom five thy father lies. Sung by Ariel to Ferdinand in *The Tempest* (I, ii, 396).

No more dams I'll make for fish. Cleverly labeled by Professor Tucker Brooke "Caliban's Marseillaise." He "sings drunkenly" to Stephano and Trinculo in *The Tempest* (II, ii, 184); a contrast to Ariel's song of freedom, "Where the bee sucks" (V, i, 88). Caliban was the earthy gnome; Ariel, the airy spirit of the play.

KING LEAR

For the date of Shakespeare's composition of King Lear all available evidence points to 1605 or 1606, probably shortly after Othello and just before Macbeth. The best basis for the text of the play is the First Folio (1623), published by two members of Shakespeare's company, John Heminges and Henry Condell. It is a condensed acting version which must be supplemented by the apparently uncut First Quarto (1608). Except for its omission of about three hundred lines genuinely Shakespeare's, the Folio text is considered more nearly authoritative.

The shadowy, quasi-divine figure of a king named Lear (Leir) appears first in the mythology of the ancient Britons. Then, in the twelfth century, Geoffrey of Monmouth incorporated this legend into his Historia Regum Britanniae with the attachment of the old folk tale of Lear's three daughters. Shakespeare also seems to have been stimulated by the versions recounted in Holinshed's Chronicles and The Mirror for Magistrates (1574), two of the Elizabethan dramatists' most favored source books, and perhaps, in addition, he was

acquainted with Spenser's Faerie Queene (II, 10) and a popular historical poem, Warner's Albion's England (1586). The main plot of the tragedy, however, is a remarkably free adaptation of an anonymous earlier play with a happy ending, The True Chronicle History of King Lear, while the subplot parallel of Gloucester and his sons takes its germ from an episode in Sidney's Arcadia (II, 10). Shakespeare's foremost wholly original contributions to the narrative stock of the Lear saga include the characters of the Fool, Kent, and Oswald, the madness, and the tragic denouement. But in creating his own King Lear the playwright of course proceeded to subdue this mass of raw situational material to his own techniques of verse drama. Most fundamentally, Shakespeare's treatment of the Lear story reveals a profound governing impulse towards the symbolic or allegorical, an orientation for which there were no antecedents of any consequence.

By the time he began composition of King Lear, probably the most disturbing of his great tragedies, Shakespeare had behind him almost fifteen years of experience in the theater, as both actor and playwright. Although the staple of his dramatic art was then de-

fined, he would continue, as this play notably demonstrates, to experiment within it. The broad movement of the playwright's endless creative reconsideration of technique was to become reflected increasingly by a dense verbal texture, complex overlays of symbol, and, above all, by the persistent internal search for an honest metaphysic of affirmation. These trends of the Shakespearean progression to an integrated medium of stagecraft and poetry are perhaps best exemplified in King Lear. Exhibiting a quality common to all of Shakespeare's finer mature drama, the experience of the play transpires more in the "word" that defines it than in the "act" that simply expresses it, more in the specifically poetic effects of language and figure than in the overall narrative data of circumstance and character. The structure of meaning which Lear suggests, in short, seems to arise from somewhere within its recurrent single veins and intricate networks of imagery. Shakespeare's evident conception of his story as a vehicle for universal allegory appears to have compelled spontaneously a qualifying poetic ambience of this constitution. The patterns that it precipitates should first be solicited in the course of any examination into the final experiential insights propounded by King Lear.

One crucial area of investigation within the play, for example, reposes almost entirely on repetitions of the word "nature" and the scheme of attitudes, nuance, and situational environment in which they occur. What, the characters demand, is the moral nature of the universe, benign or indifferent or malignant? Are the "gods" just, as Edgar asserts (V, iii, 170-171), or are they the "wanton boys" of his blinded father's indictment (IV, i, 36-37)? Still more to the heart of the play's central experience, what is the permanent nature of the shared human condition? Once initiated by Lear's irrevocable question "Who is it that can tell me who I am?" (I, iv, 231), this line of urgent philosophical inquiry leads him from perverse self-will to the agonizing recognition on the heath that mankind, even a king, is no more than a "poor, bare, forked animal" (III, iv, 107-108). Lear achieves compassion and humility much as Gloucester learns submission, through the purgative ordeal of severe spiritual affliction. In the process of confronting the harsher realities and imponderables of human experience, Lear goes mad and thereby acquires wisdom, while Gloucester, in another of the play's many symbolic inversions, acquires a true inner vision only with the loss of his eyesight. Moreover, both these sufferers come to apprehend a certain transcendency, a certain knot of intransigent positive values inherent in human experience which no degree of pain or deed of atrocity can negate. There is, the play affirms, an enduring meaningfulness to such love and loyalty as that displayed by Cordelia, Edgar, the Fool, and Kent. And just as surely, there is a principle of self-consuming destruction inextricable from the rationalized egotism and consciencelessness of the Edmund-Goneril-Regan faction in the Lear universe. Cordelia chiefly represents the bedrock metaphysical affirmation which lies beneath this tragedy's excruciating curve of action; she it is "who redeems nature from the general curse which twain have brought her to" (IV, vi, 206-207).

KING LEAR

DRAMATIS PERSONAE

LEAR, King of Britain.
KING OF FRANCE.
DUKE OF BURGUNDY.
DUKE OF CORNWALL.
DUKE OF ALBANY.
EARL OF KENT.
EARL OF GLOUCESTER.
EDGAR, son to Gloucester.
EDMUND, bastard son to Gloucester.

CURAN, a courtier.
OLD MAN, tenant to Gloucester.
DOCTOR.
LEAR'S FOOL.
OSWALD, steward to Goneril.
A CAPTAIN under Edmund's command.
GENTLEMEN.
A HERALD.
SERVANTS to Cornwall.

GONERIL,
REGAN, } daughters to Lear.
CORDELIA,

KNIGHTS attending on Lear, OFFICERS, MESSENGERS, SOLDIERS, ATTENDANTS.

SCENE: Britain

ACT I

SCENE I King Lear's Palace.

Enter KENT, GLOUCESTER, and EDMUND. KENT and GLOUCESTER converse. EDMUND stands back.

KENT. I thought the King had more affected the Duke of Albany than Cornwall.

GLOU. It did always seem so to us; but now, in the division of the kingdom, it appears not which of the Dukes he values most, for equalities are so weigh'd

Act I, Sc. i. 1. **had more affected**, preferred. 7. **moiety**, half, share. 11. **braz'd**, hardened. 12. **conceive**, understand. Gloucester puns on the double meaning of the word. 24. **whoreson**, bastard. 32. **out**, abroad. 33. **sennet**, notes on a trumpet announcing the approach of the king. 36. **we**, the "royal we." 38. **fast intent**, firm purpose. 41. **crawl**,

that curiosity in neither can make choice of either's moiety.

KENT. Is not this your son, my lord?

GLOU. His breeding, sir, hath been at my charge. I
10 have so often blush'd to acknowledge him that now I
am braz'd to't.

KENT. I cannot conceive you.

GLOU. Sir, this young fellow's mother could; whereupon she grew round-womb'd, and had indeed, sir, a
son for her cradle ere she had a husband for her bed.
Do you smell a fault?

KENT. I cannot wish the fault undone, the issue of
it being so proper.

GLOU. But I have, sir, a son by order of law, some
20 year elder than this, who yet is no dearer in my account. Though this knave came something saucily into
the world before he was sent for, yet was his mother
fair, there was good sport at his making, and the
whoreson must be acknowledged.—Do you know this
noble gentleman, Edmund?

EDM. [Comes forward] No, my lord.

GLOU. My Lord of Kent. Remember him hereafter as
my honourable friend.

EDM. My services to your lordship.

30 KENT. I must love you, and sue to know you better.

EDM. Sir, I shall study deserving.

GLOU. He hath been out nine years, and away he
shall again. [Sound a sennet.] The King is coming.

Enter one bearing a coronet; then LEAR; then the DUKES
OF ALBANY and CORNWALL; next, GONERIL, REGAN,
CORDELIA, with FOLLOWERS.

LEAR. Attend the lords of France and Burgundy,
Gloucester.

GLOU. I shall, my liege.

[Exeunt GLOUCESTER and EDMUND.]

LEAR. Meantime we shall express our darker pur-
pose.
Give me the map there. Know we have divided
In three our kingdom; and 'tis our fast intent
To shake all cares and business from our age,
40 Conferring them on younger strengths while we
Unburthen'd crawl toward death. Our son of Cornwall,
And you, our no less loving son of Albany,
We have this hour a constant will to publish
Our daughters' several dowers, that future strife
May be prevented now. The princes, France and
Burgundy,
Great rivals in our youngest daughter's love,

Long in our court have made their amorous sojourn,
And here are to be answer'd. Tell me, my daughters
(Since now we will divest us both of rule,
Interest of territory, cares of state),   50
Which of you shall we say doth love us most?
That we our largest bounty may extend
Where nature doth with merit challenge. Goneril,
Our eldest-born, speak first.

GON. Sir, I love you more than words can wield the
matter;
Dearer than eyesight, space, and liberty;
Beyond what can be valued, rich or rare;
No less than life, with grace, health, beauty, honour;
As much as child e'er lov'd, or father found;
A love that makes breath poor, and speech unable.   60
Beyond all manner of so much I love you.

COR. [aside] What shall Cordelia speak? Love, and
be silent.

LEAR. Of all these bounds, even from this line to
this,
With shadowy forests and with champains rich'd,
With plenteous rivers and wide-skirted meads,
We make thee lady. To thine and Albany's issue
Be this perpetual.—What says our second daughter,
Our dearest Regan, wife to Cornwall? Speak.

REG. Sir, I am made
Of the selfsame metal that my sister is,   70
And prize me at her worth. In my true heart
I find she names my very deed of love;
Only she comes too short, that I profess
Myself an enemy to all other joys
Which the most precious square of sense possesses,
And find I am alone felicitate
In your dear Highness' love.

COR.   [Aside] Then poor Cordelia!
And yet not so; since I am sure my love's
More richer than my tongue.

LEAR. To thee and thine hereditary ever   80
Remain this ample third of our fair kingdom,
No less in space, validity, and pleasure
Than that conferr'd on Goneril.—Now, our joy,
Although the last, not least; to whose young love
The vines of France and milk of Burgundy
Strive to be interest; what can you say to draw
A third more opulent than your sisters? Speak.

COR. Nothing, my lord.

LEAR. Nothing?

COR. Nothing.   90

LEAR. Nothing can come of nothing. Speak again.

COR. Unhappy that I am, I cannot heave
My heart into my mouth. I love your Majesty
According to my bond; no more nor less.

LEAR. How, how, Cordelia? Mend your speech a little,

indicative of Lear's advanced age. 49. divest. Imagery of divestiture is
of great symbolic significance throughout the course of Lear's subsequent
experience. 55. can . . . matter, can express. 64. champains, fertile
plains. 75. square, criterion, arbiter (a term of measurement in car-
pentry). 76. felicitate, confirmed in happiness. 79. more richer, a
double comparative, common in Elizabethan English. 91. Nothing . . .
nothing. The repetition of the word "nothing" is important in Lear's
pained later realization of his self-deception in this scene. 94. my bond,
as a child should love a father. Lear implicitly claims a godlike exemption from this "bond" of nature when he denies Cordelia as his daughter.

Lest it may mar your fortunes.

COR.   Good my lord,
You have begot me, bred me, lov'd me; I
Return those duties back as are right fit,
Obey you, love you, and most honour you.
100 Why have my sisters husbands, if they say
They love you all? Haply, when I shall wed,
That lord whose hand must take my plight shall carry
Half my love with him, half my care and duty.
Sure I shall never marry like my sisters,
To love my father all.
    LEAR. But goes thy heart with this?
    COR.   Ay, good my lord.
    LEAR. So young, and so untender?
    COR. So young, my lord, and true.
    LEAR. Let it be so! thy truth then be thy dower!
110 For, by the sacred radiance of the sun,
The mysteries of Hecate and the night;
By all the operation of the orbs
From whom we do exist and cease to be;
Here I disclaim all my paternal care,
Propinquity and property of blood,
And as a stranger to my heart and me
Hold thee from this for ever. The barbarous Scythian,
Or he that makes his generation messes
To gorge his appetite, shall to my bosom
120 Be as well neighbour'd, pitied, and reliev'd,
As thou my sometime daughter.
    KENT.   Good my liege—
    LEAR. Peace, Kent!
Come not between the dragon and his wrath.
I lov'd her most, and thought to set my rest
On her kind nursery.—Hence and avoid my sight!—
So be my grave my peace as here I give
Her father's heart from her! Call France! Who stirs?
Call Burgundy! Cornwall and Albany,
With my two daughters' dowers digest this third;
130 Let pride, which she calls plainness, marry her.
I do invest you jointly in my power,
Preëminence, and all the large effects
That troop with majesty. Ourself, by monthly course,
With reservation of an hundred knights,
By you to be sustain'd, shall our abode
Make with you by due turns. Only we still retain
The name, and all th' additions to a king. The sway,
Revenue, execution of the rest,
Beloved sons, be yours; which to confirm,
This coronet part betwixt you.
140 KENT.   Royal Lear,
Whom I have ever honour'd as my king,
Lov'd as my father, as my master follow'd,
As my great patron thought on in my prayers—
    LEAR. The bow is bent and drawn; make from the
        shaft.

KENT. Let it fall rather, though the fork invade
The region of my heart! Be Kent unmannerly
When Lear is mad. What wouldst thou do, old man?
Think'st thou that duty shall have dread to speak
When power to flattery bows? To plainness honour's
    bound
When majesty falls to folly. Reverse thy doom;   150
And in thy best consideration check
This hideous rashness. Answer my life my judgment,
Thy youngest daughter does not love thee least,
Nor are those empty-hearted whose low sound
Reverbs no hollowness.
    LEAR.   Kent, on thy life, no more!
    KENT. My life I never held but as a pawn
To wage against thine enemies; nor fear to lose it,
Thy safety being the motive.
    LEAR.   Out of my sight!
    KENT. See better, Lear, and let me still remain
The true blank of thine eye.   160
    LEAR. Now by Apollo—
    KENT.   Now by Apollo, King,
Thou swear'st thy gods in vain.
    LEAR.   O vassal! miscreant!
                        [Lays his hand on his sword.]
    ALB., CORN. Dear sir, forbear!
    KENT. Do!
Kill thy physician, and the fee bestow
Upon the foul disease. Revoke thy gift,
Or, whilst I can vent clamour from my throat,
I'll tell thee thou dost evil.
    LEAR.   Hear me, recreant!
On thine allegiance, hear me!
Since thou hast sought to make us break our vow—   170
Which we durst never yet—and with strain'd pride
To come between our sentence and our power,—
Which nor our nature nor our place can bear,—
Our potency made good, take thy reward.
Five days we do allot thee for provision
To shield thee from diseases of the world,
And on the sixth to turn thy hated back
Upon our kingdom. If, on the tenth day following,
Thy banish'd trunk be found in our dominions,
The moment is thy death. Away! By Jupiter,   180
This shall not be revok'd.
    KENT. Fare thee well, King. Since thus thou wilt
        appear,
Freedom lives hence, and banishment is here.
[To CORDELIA] The gods to their dear shelter take thee,
        maid,
That justly think'st and hast most rightly said!
[To REGAN and GONERIL] And your large speeches may
        your deeds approve,
That good effects may spring from words of love.
Thus Kent, O princes, bids you all adieu;   [Exit.]

---

102. **plight,** my plighted faith in marriage. 117. **barbarous Scythian.**
Scythians were traditionally believed prone to extreme cruelty. 118.
generation, offspring. **messes,** portions of food. 121. **sometime,** former. 123. **the dragon,** the traditional emblem of the ancient Briton
kings. 134. **an hundred knights.** Goneril and Regan will gradually
cut the number down to "nothing." 144. **The bow . . . the shaft.** My
mind is made up; Look out for yourself. 155. **Reverbs,** reverberates.
160. **The true blank of thine eye,** your adviser most to be trusted.

He'll shape his old course in a country new.

Flourish. Enter GLOUCESTER, *with* FRANCE *and* BUR-
GUNDY; ATTENDANTS.

190   GLOU. Here's France and Burgundy, my noble lord.
    LEAR. My Lord of Burgundy,
We first address toward you, who with this king
Hath rivall'd for our daughter. What in the least
Will you require in present dower with her,
Or cease your quest of love?
    BUR.   Most royal Majesty,
I crave no more than hath your Highness offer'd,
Nor will you tender less.
    LEAR.   Right noble Burgundy,
When she was dear to us, we did hold her so;
But now her price is fall'n. Sir, there she stands.
200 If aught within that little seeming substance,
Or all of it, with our displeasure piec'd,
And nothing more, may fitly like your Grace,
She's there, and she is yours.
    BUR.   I know no answer.
    LEAR. Will you, with those infirmities she owes,
Unfriended, new adopted to our hate,
Dow'r'd with our curse, and stranger'd with our oath,
Take her, or leave her?
    BUR.   Pardon me, royal sir.
Election makes not up on such conditions.
    LEAR. Then leave her, sir; for, by the pow'r that
      made me,
I tell you all her wealth. [*To* FRANCE] For you, great
210   King,
I would not from your love make such a stray
To match you where I hate; therefore beseech you
T' avert your liking a more worthier way
Than on a wretch whom nature is asham'd
Almost t' acknowledge hers.
    FRANCE.   This is most strange,
That she that even but now was your best object,
The argument of your praise, balm of your age,
Most best, most dearest, should in this trice of time
Commit a thing so monstrous to dismantle
220 So many folds of favour. Sure her offence
Must be of such unnatural degree
That monsters it, or your fore-vouch'd affection.
Fall'n into taint; which to believe of her
Must be a faith that reason without miracle
Should never plant in me.
    COR.   I yet beseech your Majesty,
If for I want that glib and oily art
To speak and purpose not, since what I well intend,
I'll do't before I speak—that you make known
It is no vicious blot, murder, or foulness,

No unchaste action or dishonoured step,   230
That hath depriv'd me of your grace and favour;
But even for want of that for which I am richer—
A still-soliciting eye, and such a tongue
As I am glad I have not, though not to have it
Hath lost me in your liking.
    LEAR.   Better thou
Hadst not been born than not t' have pleas'd me better.
    FRANCE. It is but this—a tardiness in nature
Which often leaves the history unspoke
That it intends to do? My Lord of Burgundy,
What say you to the lady? Love's not love   240
When it is mingled with regards that stands
Aloof from th' entire point. Will you have her?
She is herself a dowry.
    BUR.   Royal Lear,
Give but that portion which yourself propos'd,
And here I take Cordelia by the hand,
Duchess of Burgundy.
    LEAR. Nothing! I have sworn; I am firm.
    BUR. I am sorry then you have so lost a father
That you must lose a husband.
    COR.   Peace be with Burgundy!
Since that respects of fortune are his love,   250
I shall not be his wife.
    FRANCE. Fairest Cordelia, that art most rich, being
      poor;
Most choice, forsaken; and most lov'd, despis'd!
Thee and thy virtues here I seize upon.
Be it lawful I take up what's cast away.
Gods, gods! 'tis strange that from their cold'st neglect
My love should kindle to inflam'd respect.
Thy dow'rless daughter, King, thrown to my chance,
Is queen of us, of ours, and our fair France.
Not all the dukes in wat'rish Burgundy   260
Can buy this unpriz'd precious maid of me.
Bid them farewell, Cordelia, though unkind.
Thou losest here, a better where to find.
    LEAR. Thou hast her, France; let her be thine; for we
Have no such daughter, nor shall ever see
That face of hers again. Therefore be gone
Without our grace, our love, our benison.
Come, noble Burgundy.

Flourish. Exeunt LEAR, BURGUNDY, CORNWALL, ALBANY,
GLOUCESTER, *and* ATTENDANTS.

    FRANCE. Bid farewell to your sisters.
    COR. The jewels of our father, with wash'd eyes   270
Cordelia leaves you. I know you what you are;
And, like a sister, am most loath to call
Your faults as they are nam'd. Use well our father.
To your professed bosoms I commit him;
But yet, alas, stood I within his grace,

174. **potency,** royal power. 200. **seeming substance,** merely apparent
reality. 208. **Election . . . conditions.** There is no question of choice
under such unfavorable circumstances. 222. **fore-vouch'd,** previously
declared. 233. **still-soliciting,** always entreating, wheedling. 237. a
tardiness in nature, etc., a reluctance to speak glibly. 267. **benison,**
blessing.

I would prefer him to a better place!
So farewell to you both.

GON. Prescribe not us our duties.

REG.   Let your study
Be to content your lord, who hath receiv'd you
280 At fortune's alms. You have obedience scanted,
And well are worth the want that you have wanted.

COR. Time shall unfold what plighted cunning hides.
Who cover faults, at last shame them derides.
Well may you prosper!

FRANCE.   Come, my fair Cordelia.

[Exeunt FRANCE and CORDELIA.]

GON. Sister, it is not little I have to say of what most
nearly appertains to us both. I think our father will
hence tonight.

REG. That's most certain, and with you; next month
with us.

290 GON. You see how full of changes his age is. The
observation we have made of it hath not been little.
He always lov'd our sister most, and with what poor
judgment he hath now cast her off appears too grossly.

REG. 'Tis the infirmity of his age; yet he hath ever
but slenderly known himself.

GON. The best and soundest of his time hath been
but rash; then must we look to receive from his age,
not alone the imperfections of long-ingraffed condition, but therewithal the unruly waywardness that in-
300 firm and choleric years bring with them.

REG. Such unconstant starts are we like to have from
him as this of Kent's banishment.

GON. There is further compliment of leave-taking
between France and him. Pray you let's hit together.
If our father carry authority with such dispositions as
he bears, this last surrender of his will but offend us.

REG. We shall further think on't.

GON. We must do something, and i' th' heat.

[Exeunt.]

SCENE II *The Earl of Gloucester's Castle.*

Enter EDMUND *with a letter.*

EDM. Thou, Nature, art my goddess; to thy law
My services are bound. Wherefore should I
Stand in the plague of custom, and permit
The curiosity of nations to deprive me,
For that I am some twelve or fourteen moonshines
Lag of a brother? Why bastard? wherefore base?

When my dimensions are as well compact,
My mind as generous, and my shape as true,
As honest madam's issue? Why brand they us
With base? with baseness? bastardy? base, base?   10
Who, in the lusty stealth of nature, take
More composition and fierce quality
Than doth, within a dull, stale, tired bed,
Go to th' creating a whole tribe of fops
Got 'tween asleep and wake? Well then,
Legitimate Edgar, I must have your land.
Our father's love is to the bastard Edmund
As to th' legitimate. Fine word—'legitimate'!
Well, my legitimate, if this letter speed,
And my invention thrive, Edmund the base   20
Shall top th' legitimate. I grow; I prosper.
Now, gods, stand up for bastards!

Enter GLOUCESTER.

GLOU. Kent banish'd thus? and France in choler
parted?
And the King gone to-night? subscrib'd his pow'r?
Confin'd to exhibition? All this done
Upon the gad? Edmund, how now? What news?

EDM. So please your lordship, none.

[Puts up the letter.]

GLOU. Why so earnestly seek you to put up that
letter?

EDM. I know no news, my lord.

GLOU. What paper were you reading?   30

EDM. Nothing, my lord.

GLOU. No? What needed then that terrible dispatch
of it into your pocket? The quality of nothing hath not
such need to hide itself. Let's see. Come, if it be nothing, I shall not need spectacles.

EDM. I beseech you, sir, pardon me. It is a letter
from my brother that I have not all o'er-read; and for
so much as I have perus'd, I find it not fit for your
o'erlooking.

GLOU. Give me the letter, sir.   40

EDM. I shall offend, either to detain or give it. The
contents, as in part I understand them, are to blame.

GLOU. Let's see, let's see!

EDM. I hope, for my brother's justification, he wrote
this but as an essay or taste of my virtue.

GLOU. [*Reads*] 'This policy and reverence of age
makes the world bitter to the best of our times; keeps

<hr>

281. **the want . . . wanted,** the same absence of love you have shown.
293. **grossly,** manifestly. 295. **slenderly known himself.** The narrative crux of the play is progression to self-knowledge. 298. **long-
ingraffed condition,** his ingrained temperament. 301. **starts,** unpredictable freaks of behavior. 303. **compliment,** ceremony. 304. **hit
together,** join in our conduct towards him. 308. **i' th' heat,**
promptly.
Sc. ii. 1-22. **Thou, Nature . . . bastards.** Edmund engages in
witty word play on the words "natural," "base," and "legitimate"
throughout this first self-revealing soliloquy. He is a bastard, i.e., a
"natural" son and younger than Edgar; therefore, he cannot be Gloucester's heir. In asserting Nature to be his goddess, Edmund joins
Goneril and Regan in a philosophy of egotism and uncurbed natural

impulse. 4. **curiosity,** fastidiousness. 5. **moonshines,** months. 7. **my
dimensions,** my bodily construction. 10. **base . . . base.** Edmund's
word trick of repeating "base" and "legitimate" reduces them to meaningless terms. 12. **More composition and fierce quality,** more innate
strength and energy. 19. **speed,** prove successful. 24. **subscrib'd,** resigned. 25. **exhibition,** an allowance from his daughters. 26. **Upon
the gad,** on the spur of the moment. 45. **an essay or taste,** a test.
46-47. **This policy . . . times,** the prevailing social order which upholds
the position of respect and authority of the older generation. 49. **an
idle and fond bondage,** a subservient condition to which it is silly to
submit. Ironically, the letter which Gloucester believes to be Edgar's
contains the philosophy just expressed by Edmund in his soliloquy. 51.
suffer'd, allowed. 63. **character,** handwriting. 74-75. **the father . . .**

our fortunes from us till our oldness cannot relish them. I begin to find an idle and fond bondage in the oppression of aged tyranny, who sways, not as it hath power, but as it suffer'd. Come to me, that of this I may speak more. If our father would sleep till I wak'd him, you should enjoy half his revenue for ever, and live the beloved of your brother,

'EDGAR.'

Hum! Conspiracy? 'Sleep till I wak'd him, you should enjoy half his revenue.' My son Edgar! Had he a hand to write this? a heart and brain to breed it in? When came this to you? Who brought it?

EDM. It was not brought me, my lord: there's the cunning of it. I found it thrown in at the casement of my closet.

GLOU. You know the character to be your brother's?

EDM. If the matter were good, my lord, I durst swear it were his; but in respect of that, I would fain think it were not.

GLOU. It is his.

EDM. It is his hand, my lord; but I hope his heart is not in the contents.

GLOU. Hath he never before sounded you in this business?

EDM. Never, my lord. But I have heard him oft maintain it to be fit that, sons at perfect age, and fathers declining, the father should be as ward to the son, and the son manage his revenue.

GLOU. O villain, villain! His very opinion in the letter! Abhorred villain! Unnatural, detested, brutish villain! worse than brutish! Go, sirrah, seek him. I'll apprehend him. Abominable villain! Where is he?

EDM. I do not well know, my lord. If it shall please you to suspend your indignation against my brother till you can derive from him better testimony of his intent, you should run a certain course; where, if you violently proceed against him, mistaking his purpose, it would make a great gap in your own honour and shake in pieces the heart of his obedience. I dare pawn down my life for him that he hath writ this to feel my affection to your honour, and to no other pretence of danger.

GLOU. Think you so?

EDM. If your honour judge it meet, I will place you where you shall hear us confer of this and by an auricular assurance have your satisfaction, and that without any further delay than this very evening.

GLOU. He cannot be such a monster.

EDM. Nor is not, sure.

GLOU. To his father, that so tenderly and entirely loves him. Heaven and earth! Edmund, seek him out; wind me into him, I pray you; frame the business after your own wisdom. I would unstate myself to be in a due resolution.

EDM. I will seek him, sir, presently; convey the business as I shall find means, and acquaint you withal.

GLOU. These late eclipses in the sun and moon portend no good to us. Though the wisdom of nature can reason it thus and thus, yet nature finds itself scourg'd by the sequent effects. Love cools, friendship falls off, brothers divide. In cities, mutinies; in countries, discord; in palaces, treason; and the bond crack'd 'twixt son and father. This villain of mine comes under the prediction; there's son against father: the King falls from bias of nature; there's father against child. We have see the best of our time. Machinations, hollowness, treachery, and all ruinous disorders follow us disquietly to our graves. Find out this villain, Edmund; it shall lose thee nothing; do it carefully. And the noble and true-hearted Kent banish'd! his offence, honesty! 'Tis strange.   [Exit.]

EDM. This is the excellent foppery of the world, that, when we are sick in fortune, often the surfeit of our own behaviour, we make guilty of our disasters the sun, the moon, and the stars; as if we were villains on necessity; fools by heavenly compulsion; knaves, thieves, and treachers by spherical predominance; drunkards, liars, and adulterers by an enforc'd obedience of planetary influence; and all that we are evil in, by a divine thrusting on. An admirable evasion of whoremaster man, to lay his goatish disposition to the charge of a star! My father compounded with my mother under the Dragon's Tail, and my nativity was under Ursa Major, so that it follows I am rough and lecherous. Fut! I should have been that I am, had the maidenliest star in the firmament twinkled on my bastardizing. Edgar—

Enter EDGAR.

and pat! he comes, like the catastrophe of the old comedy. My cue is villainous melancholy, with a sigh like Tom o' Bedlam. O, these eclipses do portend these divisions! Fa, sol, la, mi.

EDG. How now, brother Edmund? What serious contemplation are you in?

the son, the parallel to the case of Lear with his daughters is evident. Shakespeare uses the subplot of Gloucester and his sons throughout the play in an elucidating counterpoint to Lear's tragic parental experience. 83. run a certain course, proceed without the risk of a misstep. 87. feel, test. 88-89. pretence of danger, intention of harm. 99. wind me into him. Insinuate yourself into his confidence for me. 100-101. I would ... resolution. I would give up my fortune to have my doubts resolved. 104-118. These late eclipses ... 'Tis strange. Gloucester believes these disruptions in the world of nature to have bearing on the recent reversals and general disharmony at court. 105-106. Though the wisdom ... and thus, though scientific examination can find causes. 108. mutinies, rebellions, riots. 112. bias of nature, the natural course of life; the mutually loving relationship between parent and child. 116.

lose thee nothing, a hint that Edmund will be rewarded. 119-134. This is ... Edgar. Edmund the rationalist mocks his father's pious credulity. 119. foppery, foolishness. 120. surfeit, excesses. 124-126. by spherical predominance ... planetary influence, as the result of the predominance of some planet at our birth. 128. whoremaster man. Edmund displays a view of humanity as essentially bestial. goatish, lustful. 132. Fut, nonsense. that I am, what I am. 135. pat, right on time. catastrophe, the event which brings about the denouement of the plot. 136. villainous, extreme. 137. Tom o' Bedlam, colloquial phrase for a vagrant madman, i.e., one no longer confined in Bedlam (Bethlehem Hospital, London). 138. Fa, sol, la, mi. Edmund sings to himself in order to appear oblivious of his brother's approach.

EDM. I am thinking, brother, of a prediction I read this other day, what should follow these eclipses.

EDG. Do you busy yourself with that?

EDM. I promise you, the effects he writes of succeed unhappily: as of unnaturalness between the child and the parent; death, dearth, dissolutions of ancient amities; divisions in state, menaces and maledictions against king and nobles; needless diffidences, banishment of friends, dissipation of cohorts, nuptial 150 breaches, and I know not what.

EDG. How long have you been a sectary astronomical?

EDM. Come, come! When saw you my father last?

EDG. The night gone by.

EDM. Spake you with him?

EDG. Ay, two hours together.

EDM. Parted you in good terms? Found you no displeasure in him by word or countenance?

EDG. None at all.

EDM. Bethink yourself wherein you may have of- 160 fended him; and at my entreaty forbear his presence until some little time hath qualified the heat of his displeasure, which at this instant so rageth in him that with the mischief of your person it would scarcely allay.

EDG. Some villain hath done me wrong.

EDM. That's my fear. I pray you have a continent forbearance till the speed of his rage goes slower; and, as I say, retire with me to my lodging, from whence I will fitly bring you to hear my lord speak. Pray ye, 170 go! There's my key. If you do stir abroad, go arm'd.

EDG. Arm'd, brother?

EDM. Brother, I advise you to the best. Go arm'd. I am no honest man if there be any good meaning toward you. I have told you what I have seen and heard; but faintly, nothing like the image and horror of it. Pray you, away!

EDG. Shall I hear from you anon?

EDM. I do serve you in this business. [*Exit* EDGAR.] A credulous father! and a brother noble, 180 Whose nature is so far from doing harms That he suspects none; on whose foolish honesty My practices ride easy! I see the business. Let me, if not by birth, have lands by wit; All with me's meet that I can fashion fit.   [*Exit.*]

SCENE III *The Duke of Albany's Palace.*

Enter GONERIL *and her steward* OSWALD.

GON. Did my father strike my gentleman for chiding
     of his fool?

OSW. Ay, madam.

GON. By day and night, he wrongs me! Every hour

He flashes into one gross crime or other
That sets us all at odds. I'll not endure it.
His knights grow riotous, and himself upbraids us
On every trifle. When he returns from hunting,
I will not speak with him. Say I am sick.
If you come slack of former services,
You shall do well; the fault of it I'll answer.   10
                              [*Horns within.*]

OSW. He's coming, madam; I hear him.

GON. Put on what weary negligence you please,
You and your fellows. I'd have it come to question.
If he distaste it, let him to our sister,
Whose mind and mine I know in that are one,
Not to be overrul'd. Idle old man,
That still would manage those authorities
That he hath given away! Now, by my life,
Old fools are babes again, and must be us'd
With checks as flatteries, when they are seen abus'd. 20
Remember what I have said.

OSW.   Very well, madam.

GON. And let his knights have colder looks among
     you.
What grows of it, no matter. Advise your fellows so.
I would breed from hence occasions, and I shall,
That I may speak. I'll write straight to my sister
To hold my very course. Prepare for dinner. [*Exeunt.*]

SCENE IV *The Duke of Albany's Palace.*

Enter KENT, *disguised.*

KENT. If but as well I other accents borrow,
That can my speech defuse, my good intent
May carry through itself to that full issue
For which I raz'd my likeness. Now, banish'd Kent,
If thou canst serve where thou dost stand condemn'd.
So may it come, thy master, whom thou lov'st,
Shall find thee full of labours.

Horns within. Enter LEAR, KNIGHTS, *and* ATTENDANTS.

LEAR. Let me not stay a jot for dinner; go get it ready. [*Exit an* ATTENDANT.] How now? What art thou?   10

KENT. A man, sir.

LEAR. What dost thou profess? What wouldst thou with us?

KENT. I do profess to be no less than I seem, to serve him truly that will put me in trust, to love him that is honest, to converse with him that is wise and says little, to fear judgment, to fight when I cannot choose, and to eat no fish.

LEAR. What art thou?

---

144. **effects**, events, fulfillments of the prophecy. 146. **dearth**, famine. 148. **diffidences**, incidents of distrust. 149. **dissipation of cohorts**, breaking up of troops. 151. **sectary astronomical**, a believer in astrology. 163-164. **with ... allay**. His anger would not even be abated by injuring you physically. 166-167. **have a continent forbearance**. Restrain yourself and avoid his presence. 182. **practices**, plots. **business**, undertaking,

outcome. 184. **all with me's ... fit.** Everything is my due which I can obtain by discreet contriving.
    Sc. iii. 4. **crime**, offence. 20. **checks**, rebukes. 24. **occasions**, opportunities (for action).
    Sc. iv. 2. **defuse**, disguise. 4. **raz'd**, erased, disguised. 5. **canst serve**, find employment. 8. **stay a jot**, be kept waiting. 12. **profess.**

KENT. A very honest-hearted fellow, and as poor as the King.

LEAR. If thou be'st as poor for a subject as he's for a king, thou art poor enough. What wouldst thou?

KENT. Service.

LEAR. Who wouldst thou serve?

KENT. You.

LEAR. Dost thou know me, fellow?

KENT. No, sir; but you have that in your countenance which I would fain call master.

LEAR. What's that?

KENT. Authority.

LEAR. What services canst thou do?

KENT. I can keep honest counsel, ride, run, mar a curious tale in telling it and deliver a plain message bluntly. That which ordinary men are fit for, I am qualified in, and the best of me is diligence.

LEAR. How old art thou?

KENT. Not so young, sir, to love a woman for singing, nor so old to dote on her for anything. I have years on my back forty-eight.

LEAR. Follow me; thou shalt serve me. If I like thee no worse after dinner, I will not part from thee yet. Dinner, ho, dinner! Where's my knave? my fool? Go you and call my fool hither.   [*Exit an* ATTENDANT.]

Enter OSWALD *the steward.*

You, you, sirrah, where's my daughter?

OSW. So please you—   [*Exit.*]

LEAR. What says the fellow there? Call the clotpoll back. [*Exit a* KNIGHT.] Where's my fool, ho? I think the world's asleep.

Enter KNIGHT.

How now? Where's that mongrel?

KNIGHT. He says, my lord, your daughter is not well.

LEAR. Why came not the slave back to me when I call'd him?

KNIGHT. Sir, he answered me in the roundest manner, he would not.

LEAR. He would not?

KNIGHT. My lord, I know not what the matter is; but to my judgment your Highness is not entertain'd with that ceremonious affection as you were wont. There's a great abatement of kindness appears as well in the general dependants as in the Duke himself also and your daughter.

LEAR. Ha! say'st thou so?

KNIGHT. I beseech you pardon me, my lord, if I be mistaken; for my duty cannot be silent when I think your Highness wrong'd.

LEAR. Thou but rememb'rest me of mine own conception. I have perceived a most faint neglect of late, which I have rather blamed as mine own jealous curiosity than as a very pretence and purpose of unkindness. I will look further into't. But where's my fool? I have not seen him this two days.

KNIGHT. Since my young lady's going into France, sir, the fool hath much pined away.

LEAR. No more of that; I have noted it well. Go you and tell my daughter I would speak with her. [*Exit* KNIGHT.] Go you, call hither my fool.

[*Exit an* ATTENDANT.]

Enter OSWALD *the steward.*

O, you, sir, you! Come you hither, sir. Who am I, sir?

OSW. My lady's father.

LEAR. 'My lady's father'? My lord's knave! You whoreson dog! you slave! you cur!

OSW. I am none of these, my lord; I beseech your pardon.

LEAR. Do you bandy looks with me, you rascal?

[*Strikes him.*]

OSW. I'll not be strucken, my lord.

KENT. Nor tripp'd neither, you base football player?

[*Trips up his heels.*]

LEAR. I thank thee, fellow. Thou serv'st me, and I'll love thee.

KENT. Come, sir, arise, away! I'll teach you differences. Away, away! If you will measure your lubber's length again, tarry; but away! Go to! Have you wisdom? So.   [*Pushes him out.*]

LEAR. Now, my friendly knave, I thank thee. There's earnest of thy service.   [*Gives money.*]

Enter FOOL.

FOOL. Let me hire him too. Here's my coxcomb.

[*Offers* KENT *his cap.*]

LEAR. How now, my pretty knave? How dost thou?

FOOL. Sirrah, you were best take my coxcomb.

KENT. Why, fool?

FOOL. Why? For taking one's part that's out of favour. Nay, an thou canst not smile as the wind sits, thou'lt catch cold shortly. There, take my coxcomb! Why, this fellow hath banish'd two on's daughters, and did the third a blessing against his will. If thou follow him, thou must needs wear my coxcomb.—How now, nuncle? Would I had two coxcombs and two daughters!

LEAR. Why, my boy?

FOOL. If I gave them all my living, I'ld keep my coxcombs myself. There's mine! beg another of thy daughters.

Lear asks Kent his profession and Kent plays on the word, telling Lear instead what sort of man he professes to be.   18. **eat no fish**, be a Protestant (an anachronism in the supposedly ancient British setting of the play's events).   28. **countenance**, bearing.   34. **curious**, elaborate.   55. **roundest**, most outspoken.   The knight's deference to the king here supports Lear's later exoneration of his retinue from the fabricated charges of Goneril.   70-71. **jealous curiosity**, overly suspicious tendency. 71. **pretence**, intention.   85. **bandy**, exchange.   87. **football player.** Football was then considered a low game.   90. **differences**, distinctions in rank.   103. **on's**, of his.   106. **nuncle**, uncle.

LEAR. Take heed, sirrah—the whip.

FOOL. Truth's a dog must to kennel; he must be whipp'd out, when Lady the brach may stand by th' fire and stink.

LEAR. A pestilent gall to me!

FOOL. Sirrah, I'll teach thee a speech.

LEAR. Do.

FOOL. Mark it, nuncle.

120　Have more than thou showest,
　　Speak less than thou knowest,
　　Lend less than thou owest,
　　Ride more than thou goest,
　　Learn more than thou trowest,
　　Set less than thou throwest;
　　Leave thy drink and thy whore,
　　And keep in-a-door,
　　And thou shalt have more
　　Than two tens to a score.

130　KENT. This is nothing, fool.

FOOL. Then 'tis like the breath of an unfeed lawyer—you gave me nothing for't. Can you make no use of nothing, nuncle?

LEAR. Why, no, boy. Nothing can be made out of nothing.

FOOL. [To KENT] Prithee tell him, so much the rent of his land comes to. He will not believe a fool.

LEAR. A bitter fool!

FOOL. Dost thou know the difference, my boy, be-
140　tween a bitter fool and a sweet fool?

LEAR. No, lad; teach me.

FOOL.

　　That lord that counsell'd thee
　　　To give away thy land,
　　Come place him here by me—
　　　Do thou for him stand.
　　The sweet and bitter fool
　　　Will presently appear;
　　The one in motley here,
　　　The other found out there.

150　LEAR. Dost thou call me fool, boy?

FOOL. All thy other titles thou hast given away; that thou wast born with.

KENT. This is not altogether fool, my lord.

FOOL. No, faith; lords and great men will not let me. If I had a monopoly out, they would have part on't. And ladies too, they will not let me have all the fool to myself; they'll be snatching. Give me an egg, nuncle, and I'll give thee two crowns.

LEAR. What two crowns shall they be?

FOOL. Why, after I have cut the egg i' th' middle 160 and eat up the meat, the two crowns of the egg. When thou clovest thy crown i' th' middle and gav'st away both parts, thou bor'st thine ass on thy back o'er the dirt. Thou hadst little wit in thy bald crown when thou gav'st thy golden one away. If I speak like my-self in this, let him be whipp'd that first finds it so.

[Sings.]

　　Fools had ne'er less grace in a year,
　　　For wise men are grown foppish;
　　They know not how their wits to wear,
　　　Their manners are so apish.　　　　　　170

LEAR. When were you wont to be so full of songs, sirrah?

FOOL. I have us'd it, nuncle, ever since thou mad'st thy daughters thy mother; for when thou gav'st them the rod, and put'st down thine own breeches, [Sings.]

　　Then they for sudden joy did weep,
　　　And I for sorrow sung,
　　That such a king should play bo-peep
　　　And go the fools among.

Prithee, nuncle, keep a schoolmaster that can teach thy 180 fool to lie. I would fain learn to lie.

LEAR. An you lie, sirrah, we'll have you whipp'd.

FOOL. I marvel what kin thou and thy daughters are. They'll have me whipp'd for speaking true; thou'lt have me whipp'd for lying; and sometimes I am whipp'd for holding my peace. I had rather be any kind o' thing than a fool! And yet I would not be thee, nuncle. Thou hast pared thy wit o' both sides and left nothing i' th' middle. Here comes one o' the parings.

Enter GONERIL.

LEAR. How now, daughter? What makes that front- 190 let on? Methinks you are too much o' late i' th' frown.

FOOL. Thou wast a pretty fellow when thou hadst no need to care for her frowning. Now thou art an O without a figure. I am better than thou art now: I am a fool, thou art nothing. [To GONERIL] Yes, forsooth,

---

114. **Lady the brach,** Lady the bitch-hound (equated here with flat-terers). 116. **gall,** irritation. 123. **Ride . . . goest.** Ride more than you travel on foot. 130-133. **This is . . . nuncle,** again, the more broadly relevant repetition of "nothing." 142-145. **That lord . . . stand.** The implication is that Lear was his own foolish adviser in the matter of dividing his kingdom. Upon realizing this folly, ·Lear does become the "bitter fool" of his Fool's riddle. 151. **that thou wast born with,** meaning not only that Lear is "a born fool" by reason of his self-willed character but also that every man has his propensity for such folly or delusion. 155. **monopoly,** royal patent entitling one to be the sole dealer. 158. **two crowns.** The precariousness of Lear's divided kingdom is suggested by the analogy of a cracked eggshell. 162-164. **thou clovest . . . dirt.** You behaved as the man who carried his ass in-stead of having it carry him (proverb). 165-166. **If I speak . . . so.** Do not have me whipped for my frankness, but the one who first realizes that I speak the truth (Lear himself). 167-170. **Fools . . . apish.** The general commentary of the Fool's song is that men who were once wise have changed places with fools. 168. **foppish,** foolish. 170. **apish,** absurd. 173-174. **ever since . . . thy mother,** another inversion in the "natural" scheme of things. 178. **should play bo-peep,** should be so foolish as to hide his true condition. 188-189. **Thou hast . . . i' th' mid-dle.** Lear must now bear the consequences of his error in judgment. 190. **frontlet,** a forehead band; used figuratively. 200. **a sheal'd peascod,** a shelled peapod. The Fool thus underscores the pertinence of his song to Lear's case. 203. **carp,** find fault. 206. **safe,** sure. 208. **put it on,** encourage it. 209-214. **Which . . . proceeding.** The meas-ures which we are forced to take in the public interest might be called shameful under ordinary circumstances but in this instance will be con-

I will hold my tongue. So your face bids me, though
you say nothing. Mum, mum!

        He that keeps nor crust nor crum,
        Weary of all, shall want some.—

200 [*Points at* LEAR] That's a sheal'd peascod.
    GON. Not only, sir, this your all-licens'd fool,
But other of your insolent retinue
Do hourly carp and quarrel, breaking forth
In rank and not-to-be-endured riots. Sir,
I had thought, by making this well known unto you,
To have found a safe redress, but now grow fearful,
By what yourself, too, late have spoke and done,
That you protect this course, and put it on
By your allowance; which if you should, the fault
210 Would not scape censure, nor the redresses sleep,
Which, in the tender of a wholesome weal,
Might in their working do you that offence
Which else were shame, that then necessity
Must call discreet proceeding.
    FOOL. For you know, nuncle,

        The hedge-sparrow fed the cuckoo so long
        That it had it head bit off by it young.

So out went the candle, and we were left darkling.
    LEAR. Are you our daughter?
220   GON. Come, sir,
i would you would make use of that good wisdom
Whereof I know you are fraught, and put away
These dispositions that of late transform you
From what you rightly are.
    FOOL. May not an ass know when the cart draws the
horse? Whoop, Jug, I love thee!
    LEAR. Doth any here know me? This is not Lear.
Doth Lear walk thus? speak thus? Where are his eyes?
Either his notion weakens, his discernings
230 Are lethargied—Ha! waking? 'Tis not so!
Who is it that can tell me who I am?
    FOOL. Lear's shadow.
    LEAR. I would learn that; for, by the marks of sov-
ereignty, knowledge, and reason, I should be false
persuaded I had daughters.
    FOOL. Which they will make an obedient father.
    LEAR. Your name, fair gentlewoman?

    GON. This admiration, sir, is much o' th' savour
Of other your new pranks. I do beseech you
To understand my purposes aright.   240
As you are old and reverend, you should be wise.
Here do you keep a hundred knights and squires;
Men so disorder'd, so debosh'd, and bold
That this our court, infected with their manners,
Shows like a riotous inn. Epicurism and lust
Make it more like a tavern or a brothel
Than a grac'd palace. The shame itself doth speak
For instant remedy. Be then desir'd
By her that else will take the thing she begs
A little to disquantity your train,   250
And the remainder that shall still depend
To be such men as may besort your age,
Which know themselves, and you.
    LEAR.   Darkness and devils!
Saddle my horses! Call my train together!
Degenerate bastard, I'll not trouble thee;
Yet have I left a daughter.
    GON. You strike my people, and your disorder'd
      rabble
Make servants of their betters.

Enter ALBANY.

    LEAR. Woe that too late repents!—O, sir, are you
      come?
Is it your will? Speak, sir!—Prepare my horses.   260
Ingratitude, thou marble-hearted fiend,
More hideous when thou show'st thee in a child
Than the sea-monster!
    ALB.   Pray, sir, be patient.
    LEAR. [*To* GONERIL] Detested kite, thou liest!
My train are men of choice and rarest parts,
That all particulars of duty know
And in the most exact regard support
The worships of their name.—O most small fault,
How ugly didst thou in Cordelia show!
Which, like an engine, wrench'd my frame of nature 270
From the fix'd place; drew from my heart all love
And added to the gall. O Lear, Lear, Lear!
Beat at this gate that let thy folly in [*strikes his head*]
And thy dear judgment out! Go, go, my people.
    ALB. My lord, I am guiltless, as I am ignorant
Of what hath mov'd you.
    LEAR.   It may be so, my lord.

---

sidered prudent. 216-217. **The hedge-sparrow . . . young,** the cuckoo,
which lays its eggs in other birds' nests. 218. **darkling,** in the dark.
Since reason (the "head") no longer avails in this topsy-turvy situation, the Fool implies that some other means to try to understand the
predicament must be found. 223. **dispositions,** capricious moods. 226.
Whoop, Jug, I love thee, an ironic bit of nonsense. 228. **Where are
his eyes?** Lear's question implicates the problem of the general discrepancy between appearance and reality in the play, e.g., between what
the evil sisters first appeared to be and what they actually are. Frequent allusions to the act of seeing by the characters henceforward prepare the audience for the blinding of Gloucester and his paradoxical
acquisition of true insight. 229. **his notion,** his understanding. 231.
Who is it that can tell me who I am? This first profound self-
questioning of Lear and the grim answer of his Fool starts him on his
journey toward the tragic perceptions of the heath sequence. More
broadly, Lear's question raises the basic issues involved in the allegory of
universal human experience which attends his individual history. 233-235.
I would . . . daughters. Lear bitterly enters the play's world of inverted relationships, values, and definitions. 238. **This admiration,** this
pretending to not know who you are. 243. **debosh'd,** debauched.
250. **disquantity,** reduce in number. 252. **besort,** befit. 255. **bastard.** The parallel to Edmund the bastard is reinforced by this curse.
264. **kite,** hawk. 265. **parts,** qualities. 270. **engine,** machine. 270-
271. **wrench'd . . . place.** Lear's first agonized recognition of the consequences of his denial of the "bond" of nature between Cordelia and
himself.

Hear, Nature, hear! dear goddess, hear!
Suspend thy purpose, if thou didst intend
To make this creature fruitful.
280 Into her womb convey sterility;
Dry up in her the organs of increase;
And from her derogate body never spring
A babe to honour her! If she must teem,
Create her child of spleen, that it may live
And be a thwart disnatur'd torment to her.
Let it stamp wrinkles in her brow of youth,
With cadent tears fret channels in her cheeks,
Turn all her mother's pains and benefits
To laughter and contempt, that she may feel
290 How sharper than a serpent's tooth it is
To have a thankless child! Away, away!   [Exit.]
    ALB. Now, gods that we adore, whereof comes this?
    GON. Never afflict yourself to know the cause;
But let his disposition have that scope
That dotage gives it.

Enter LEAR.

    LEAR. What, fifty of my followers at a clap?
Within a fortnight?
    ALB.   What's the matter, sir?
    LEAR. I'll tell thee. [To GONERIL] Life and death! I
am asham'd
That thou hast power to shake my manhood thus;
300 That these hot tears, which break from me perforce,
Should make thee worth them. Blasts and fogs upon
    thee!
Th' untented woundings of a father's curse
Pierce every sense about thee!—Old fond eyes,
Beweep this cause again, I'll pluck ye out,
And cast you, with the waters that you lose,
To temper clay. Yea, is it come to this?
Let it be so. Yet have I left a daughter,
Who I am sure is kind and comfortable.
When she shall hear this of thee, with her nails
310 She'll flay thy wolvish visage. Thou shalt find
That I'll resume the shape which thou dost think
I have cast off for ever; thou shalt, I warrant thee.
        [Exeunt LEAR, KENT, and ATTENDANTS.]
    GON. Do you mark that, my lord?
    ALB. I cannot be so partial, Goneril,
To the great love I bear you—
    GON. Pray you, content.—What, Oswald, ho!
[To the FOOL] You, sir, more knave than fool, after
    your master!
    FOOL. Nuncle Lear, nuncle Lear, tarry! Take the
fool with thee.

A fox, when one has caught her,   320
And such a daughter,
Should sure to the slaughter,
If my cap would buy a halter.
So the fool follows after.   [Exit.]

    GON. This man hath had good counsel! A hundred
    knights?
'Tis politic and safe to let him keep
At point a hundred knights; yes, that on every dream,
Each buzz, each fancy, each complaint, dislike,
He may enguard his dotage with their pow'rs
And hold our lives in mercy.—Oswald, I say!   330
    ALB. Well, you may fear too far.
    GON.   Safer than trust too far.
Let me still take away the harms I fear,
Not fear still to be taken. I know his heart.
What he hath utter'd I have writ my sister.
If she sustain him and his hundred knights,
When I have show'd th' unfitness—

Enter OSWALD the Steward.

                      How now, Oswald?
What, have you writ that letter to my sister?
    OSW. Yes, madam.
    GON. Take you some company, and away to horse!
Inform her full of my particular fear,   340
And thereto add such reasons of your own
As may compact it more. Get you gone,
And hasten your return. [Exit OSWALD.] No, no, my
    lord!
This milky gentleness and course of yours,
Though I condemn it not, yet, under pardon,
You are much more at task for want of wisdom
Than prais'd for harmful mildness.
    ALB. How far your eyes may pierce I cannot tell.
Striving to better, oft we mar what's well.
    GON. Nay then—   [Exeunt.] 350
    ALB. Well, well; th' event.

SCENE V Court before the Duke of Albany's Palace.

Enter LEAR, KENT, and FOOL.

    LEAR. Go you before to Gloucester with these letters.
Acquaint my daughter no further with anything you
know than comes from her demand out of the letter.
If your diligence be not speedy, I shall be there afore
you.
    KENT. I will not sleep, my lord, till I have delivered
your letter.   [Exit.]

277-291. **Hear, Nature, hear . . . away.** Lear's conception of the goddess Nature differs widely from the callous patron deity of conscienceless opportunists which Edmund has invoked (I, ii, 1-22). Lear implores Nature to bestow upon Goneril only the reverse of her usual bounties. Diametrically opposed attitudes towards Nature exist throughout the play. 282. **derogate,** blighted. 284. **child of spleen,** a child of malice and perversity. 285. **a thwart disnatur'd torment,** a perverse, unnatural cause of pain. 287. **cadent,** falling. 290-291. **How sharper . . . child.** Lear curses Goneril much as he earlier curses Cor-

delia, self-pitying and with blind anger; he has yet to accept full responsibility for his own folly. 301. **Blasts and fogs,** commonly believed to be pestilential. 302. **untented woundings,** wounds too deep to be cleansed by a tent (a linen swab). 308. **comfortable,** comforting. 318-319. **Take the fool with thee.** In addition to the literal meaning, the line is a gibe at Lear to take the title of "fool" with him. 323. **halter,** noose. 327. **At point,** fully equipped. 328. **buzz,** rumor. 342. **compact it more,** substantiate it further. 344. **milky gentleness.** Goneril is of the same family of evil female characters in

FOOL. If a man's brains were in's heels, were't not in danger of kibes?

10 LEAR. Ay, boy.

FOOL. Then I prithee be merry. Thy wit shall ne'er go slipshod.

LEAR. Ha, ha, ha!

FOOL. Shalt see thy other daughter will use thee kindly; for though she's as like this as a crab's like an apple, yet I can tell what I can tell.

LEAR. What canst tell, boy?

FOOL. She'll taste as like this as a crab does to a crab. Thou canst tell why one's nose stands i' th' mid-
20 dle on's face?

LEAR. No.

FOOL. Why, to keep one's eyes of either side's nose, that what a man cannot smell out, 'a may spy into.

LEAR. I did her wrong.

FOOL. Canst tell how an oyster makes his shell?

LEAR. No.

FOOL. Nor I neither; but I can tell why a snail has a house.

LEAR. Why?

30 FOOL. Why, to put's head in; not to give it away to his daughters, and leave his horns without a case.

LEAR. I will forget my nature. So kind a father!—Be my horses ready?

FOOL. Thy asses are gone about 'em. The reason why the seven stars are no moe than seven is a pretty reason.

LEAR. Because they are not eight?

FOOL. Yes indeed. Thou wouldst make a good fool.

LEAR. To tak't again perforce! Monster ingratitude!

40 FOOL. If thou wert my fool, nuncle, I'ld have thee beaten for being old before thy time.

LEAR. How's that?

FOOL. Thou shouldst not have been old till thou hadst been wise.

LEAR. O, let me not be mad, not mad, sweet heaven! Keep me in temper; I would not be mad!

Enter a GENTLEMAN.

How now? Are the horses ready?

GENT. Ready, my lord.

LEAR. Come, boy.

FOOL. She that's a maid now, and laughs at my de-
50 parture,

Shall not be a maid long, unless things be cut shorter.
[*Exeunt.*]

ACT II

SCENE I *A court within the Castle of the Earl of Gloucester.*

Enter EDMUND *the Bastard and* CURAN, *meeting.*

EDM. Save thee, Curan.

CUR. And you, sir. I have been with your father, and given him notice that the Duke of Cornwall and Regan his Duchess will be here with him this night.

EDM. How comes that?

CUR. Nay, I know not. You have heard of the news abroad—I mean the whisper'd ones, for they are yet but ear-kissing arguments?

EDM. Not I. Pray you, what are they?

CUR. Have you heard of no likely wars toward 10 'twixt the two Dukes of Cornwall and Albany?

EDM. Not a word.

CUR. You may do, then, in time. Fare you well, sir.
[*Exit.*]

EDM. The Duke be here to-night? The better! best! This weaves itself perforce into my business. My father hath set guard to take my brother; And I have one thing, of a queasy question, Which I must act. Briefness and fortune, work! Brother, a word! Descend! Brother, I say!

Enter EDGAR.

My father watches. O sir, fly this place! 20 Intelligence is given where you are hid. You have now the good advantage of the night. Have you not spoken 'gainst the Duke of Cornwall? He's coming hither; now, i' th' night, i' th' haste, And Regan with him. Have you nothing said Upon his party 'gainst the Duke of Albany? Advise yourself.

EDG.   I am sure on't, not a word.

EDM. I hear my father coming. Pardon me! In cunning I must draw my sword upon you. Draw, seem to defend yourself; now quit you well.— 30 Yield! Come before my father. Light, ho, here! Fly, brother.—Torches, torches!—So farewell.
[*Exit* EDGAR.]

Some blood drawn on me would beget opinion Of my more fierce endeavour. [*Stabs his arm.*] I have seen drunkards
Do more than this in sport.—Father, father!— Stop, stop! No help?

Enter GLOUCESTER, *and* SERVANTS *with torches.*

GLOU. Now, Edmund, where's the villain?

EDM. Here stood he in the dark, his sharp sword out, Mumbling of wicked charms, conjuring the moon To stand 's auspicious mistress.

Shakespeare as Lady Macbeth, who was created slightly later, but lacks her imagination and capacity for remorse. 351. **th' event.** Let us then await the outcome.
Sc. v. 9. **kibes,** chilblains. 12. **slipshod,** in slippers (because of chilblains); i.e., Lear has no wits. 15. **crab,** crabapple. 24. **her,** Cordelia. 32. **So kind a father,** spoken ironically, in self-reproach. 39. **To tak't again perforce,** to resume the title of fool to which he is already entitled. 45. **let me not . . . heaven,** in pained response to the truth of the Fool's reason. Lear's fear that the anguish of his recent discoveries will drive him mad dramatically foreshadows his actual madness on the heath. 50-51. **She . . . shorter,** a piece of clowning addressed to the audience; it marks the end of the first act.
Act II, Sc. i. 7. **ones,** news. 8. **ear-kissing,** whispered. 10. **toward,** in the near future. 17. **of a queasy question,** requiring adroit execution. 30. **quit you well,** put on a good show. 33. **beget opinion,** increase credence. 38-40. **Here . . . mistress.** Edmund adapts the lie to his father's superstition.

GLOU.   But where is he?

EDM. Look, sir, I bleed.

GLOU.   Where is the villain, Edmund?

EDM. Fled this way, sir. When by no means he
could—

GLOU. Pursue him, ho! Go after. [*Exeunt some* SERV-
ANTS.] By no means what?

EDM. Persuade me to the murther of your lordship;
But that I told him the revenging gods
'Gainst parricides did all their thunders bend;
Spoke with how manifold and strong a bond
The child was bound to th' father—sir, in fine,
Seeing how loathly opposite I stood
To his unnatural purpose, in fell motion
With his prepared sword he charges home
My unprovided body, lanch'd mine arm;
But when he saw my best alarum'd spirits,
Bold in the quarrel's right, rous'd to th' encounter,
Or whether gasted by the noise I made,
Full suddenly he fled.

GLOU.   Let him fly far.
Not in this land shall he remain uncaught;
And found—dispatch. The noble Duke my master,
My worthy arch and patron, comes to-night.
By his authority I will proclaim it,
That he which finds him shall deserve our thanks,
Bringing the murderous caitiff to the stake;
He that conceals him, death.

EDM. When I dissuaded him from his intent
And found him pight to do it, with curst speech
I threaten'd to discover him. He replied,
'Thou unpossessing bastard, dost thou think,
If I would stand against thee, would the reposal
Of any trust, virtue, or worth in thee
Make thy words faith'd? No. What I should deny
(As this I would; ay, though thou didst produce
My very character), I'ld turn it all
To thy suggestion, plot, and damned practice;
And thou must make a dullard of the world,
If they not thought the profits of my death
Were very pregnant and potential spurs
To make thee seek it.'

GLOU.   Strong and fast'ned villain!
Would he deny his letter? I never got him.

[*Tucket within.*]

Hark, the Duke's trumpets! I know not why he comes.
All ports I'll bar; the villain shall not scape;
The Duke must grant me that. Besides, his picture
I will send far and near, that all the kingdom

May have due note of him, and of my land,
Loyal and natural boy, I'll work the means
To make thee capable.

Enter CORNWALL, REGAN, *and* ATTENDANTS.

CORN. How now, my noble friend? Since I came
hither
(Which I can call but now) I have heard strange news.

REG. If it be true, all vengeance comes too short
Which can pursue th' offender. How dost, my lord?

GLOU. O madam, my old heart is crack'd, it's
crack'd!

REG. What, did my father's godson seek your life?
He whom my father nam'd? Your Edgar?

GLOU. O lady, lady, shame would have it hid!

REG. Was he not companion with the riotous knights
That tend upon my father?

GLOU. I know not, madam. 'Tis too bad, too bad!

EDM. Yes, madam, he was of that consort.

REG. No marvel then though he were ill affected.
'Tis they have put him on the old man's death,
To have th' expense and waste of his revenues.
I have this present evening from my sister
Been well inform'd of them, and with such cautions
That, if they come to sojourn at my house,
I'll not be there.

CORN.   Nor I, assure thee, Regan.
Edmund, I hear that you have shown your father
A childlike office.

EDM.   'Twas my duty, sir.

GLOU. He did bewray his practice, and receiv'd
This hurt you see, striving to apprehend him.

CORN. Is he pursued?

GLOU.   Ay, my good lord.

CORN. If he be taken, he shall never more
Be fear'd of doing harm. Make your own purpose,
How in my strength you please. For you, Edmund,
Whose virtue and obedience doth this instant
So much commend itself, you shall be ours.
Natures of such deep trust we shall much need;
You we first seize on.

EDM.   I shall serve you, sir,
Truly, however else.

GLOU.   For him I thank your Grace.

CORN. You know not why we came to visit you—

REG. Thus out of season, threading dark-ey'd night.
Occasions, noble Gloucester, of some poise,
Wherein we must have use of your advice.
Our father he hath writ, so hath our sister,

90

100

110

120

45-52. **But that I told him . . . mine arm.** Edmund's sportive blas-
pheming and the zest he displays in active evil-doing throughout this
scene ally him to Shakespeare's other villains of vice-like energy and cool
hypocritical craftiness. He is particularly close to Iago and also resembles Richard III. 50. **fell,** fierce. 52. **unprovided,** undefended.
lanch'd, pierced. 53. **my best alarum'd spirits,** all my best powers
summoned to action. 55. **gasted,** panic-stricken. 58. **dispatch,** kill
him. 59. **arch and patron,** chief patron. 62. **caitiff,** wretch. 65.
pight, determined. **curst,** furious. 71-77. **As this . . . it.** With brazen
self-confidence Edmund describes his own trick of the forged letter in
words supposedly uttered by Edgar. 76. **pregnant and potential,**
ready and powerful. 77. **fast'ned,** hardened. 78. **got him,** begot him.
Here Gloucester, like Lear with Cordelia, revokes his paternity of
Edgar. After 78. **Tucket,** notes on a trumpet. 80. **ports,** seaports. 84.
natural, used with both senses in mind. 85. **capable,** of being my heir
(Gloucester promises to legitimize Edmund by law). 91-92. **What . . .
Edgar.** It is significant that Edgar and Lear are thus closely associated
from the beginning of their respective misfortunes. 100. **expense,** spending. 107. **bewray,** reveal. 115. **Natures . . . need,** an unconscious
irony. 119. **threading,** making our way through. 120. **poise,** im-

Of differences, which I best thought it fit
To answer from our home. The several messengers
From hence attend dispatch. Our good old friend,
Lay comforts to your bosom, and bestow
Your needful counsel to our business,
Which craves the instant use.

GLOU.   I serve you, madam.
Your Graces are right welcome.   [*Exeunt. Flourish.*]

SCENE II *Before Gloucester's Castle.*

Enter KENT *and* OSWALD *the Steward, severally.*

OSW. Good dawning to thee, friend. Art of this
house?

KENT. Ay.

OSW. Where may we set our horses?

KENT. I' th' mire.

OSW. Prithee, if thou lov'st me, tell me.

KENT. I love thee not.

OSW. Why then, I care not for thee.

KENT. If I had thee in Lipsbury Pinfold, I would
10 make thee care for me.

OSW. Why dost thou use me thus? I know thee not.

KENT. Fellow, I know thee.

OSW. What dost thou know me for?

KENT. A knave; a rascal; an eater of broken meats;
a base, proud, shallow, beggarly, three-suited, hundred-
pound, filthy, worsted-stocking knave; a lily-liver'd,
action-taking, whoreson, glass-gazing, superserviceable,
finical rogue; one-trunk-inheriting slave; one that
wouldst be a bawd in way of good service, and art
20 nothing but the composition of a knave, beggar, coward, pander, and the son and heir of a mongrel bitch;
one whom I will beat into clamorous whining, if thou
deny the least syllable of thy addition.

OSW. Why, what a monstrous fellow art thou, thus
to rail on one that's neither known of thee nor knows
thee!

KENT. What a brazen-fac'd varlet art thou, to deny
thou knowest me! Is it two days ago since I beat thee
and tripp'd up thy heels before the King? [*Draws his
30 sword.*] Draw, you rogue! for, though it be night, yet
the moon shines. I'll make a sop o' th' moonshine o'
you. Draw, you whoreson cullionly barbermonger!
draw!

OSW. Away! I have nothing to do with thee.

KENT. Draw, you rascal! You come with letters
against the King, and take Vanity the puppet's part
against the royalty of her father. Draw, you rogue, or
I'll so carbonado your shanks! Draw, you rascal! Come

your ways!

OSW. Help, ho! murther! help!   40

KENT. Strike, you slave! Stand, rogue! Stand, you
neat slave! Strike!   [*Beats him.*]

OSW. Help, ho! murther! murther!

Enter EDMUND, *with his rapier drawn,* GLOUCESTER,
CORNWALL, REGAN, SERVANTS.

EDM. How now? What's the matter? [*Parts them.*]

KENT. With you, goodman boy, an you please!
Come, I'll flesh ye! Come on, young master!

GLOU. Weapons? arms? What's the matter here?

CORN. Keep peace, upon your lives!
He dies that strikes again. What is the matter?

REG. The messengers from our sister and the King.   50

CORN. What is your difference? Speak.

OSW. I am scarce in breath, my lord.

KENT. No marvel, you have so bestirr'd your valour.
You cowardly rascal, nature disclaims in thee; a tailor
made thee.

CORN. Thou art a strange fellow. A tailor make a
man?

KENT. Ay, a tailor, sir. A stonecutter or a painter
could not have made him so ill, though he had been
but two hours at the trade.   60

CORN. Speak yet, how grew your quarrel?

OSW. This ancient ruffian, sir, whose life I have
spar'd at suit of his grey beard—

KENT. Thou whoreson zed! thou unnecessary letter!
My lord, if you'll give me leave, I will tread this unbolted villain into mortar and daub the walls of a jakes
with him. 'Spare my grey beard,' you wagtail?

CORN. Peace, sirrah!
You beastly knave, know you no reverence?

KENT. Yes, sir, but anger hath a privilege.   70

CORN. Why art thou angry?

KENT. That such a slave as this should wear a sword,
Who wears no honesty. Such smiling rogues as these,
Like rats, oft bite the holy cords atwain
Which are too intrinse t' unloose; smooth every passion
That in the natures of their lords rebel,
Bring oil to fire, snow to their colder moods;
Renege, affirm, and turn their halcyon beaks
With every gale and vary of their masters,
Knowing naught (like dogs) but following.   80
A plague upon your epileptic visage!
Smile you my speeches, as I were a fool?
Goose, an I had you upon Sarum Plain,

---

portance. 128. **Which craves the instant use**, requires instant action.
Sc. ii. 9. **in Lipsbury Pinfold**, in my clutches (a pinfold is a pound
for stray livestock). 15. **three-suited**, referring to his menial condition
(a manservant was usually allowed three suits a year). **hundred-
pound**, of very little property. 16. **worsted-stocking**. A gentleman
would wear silk. 17. **action-taking**, litigious. **superserviceable**, ready
to be of use beyond the limits of honorable service. 23. **thy addition**, your itemized bill (of epithets). 31-32. **I'll make . . . o' you**. I'll
pierce you full of holes. 32. **cullionly**, testicular. **barbermonger**,
frequent client of barbers. 36. **Vanity the puppet**, doll representing

the sin of vanity in a puppet morality play. 38. **carbonado**, slash.
41-42. **you neat slave**, you foppish underling. 46. **flesh ye**, initiate you.
65. **unbolted**, thoroughgoing. 66. **jakes**, privy. 67. **wagtail**, a
comically nervous bird. 74. **the holy cords**, the bonds of familial love.
75. **intrinse**, intricate, close. 78. **Renege, affirm**, say "no" or
"yes" according to their masters' moods. **halcyon**, changeable. 79.
gale and vary, varying wind. 81. **epileptic**. Oswald is trying unsuccessfully to smile. 83. **Sarum Plain**, Salisbury Plain, noted for its
geese, and reputed to have been the site of King Arthur's court.

I'ld drive ye crackling home to Camelot.

CORN. What, art thou mad, old fellow?

GLOU. How fell you out? Say that.

KENT. No contraries hold more antipathy
Than I and such a knave.

CORN. Why dost thou call him knave? What is his
fault?

90 KENT. His countenance likes me not.

CORN. No more perchance does mine, or his, or hers.

KENT. Sir, 'tis my occupation to be plain.
I have seen better faces in my time
Than stands on any shoulder that I see
Before me at this instant.

CORN. This is some fellow
Who, having been prais'd for bluntness, doth affect
A saucy roughness, and constrains the garb
Quite from his nature. He cannot flatter, he!
An honest mind and plain—he must speak truth!
100 An they will take it, so; if not, he's plain.
These kind of knaves I know which in this plainness
Harbour more craft and more corrupter ends
Than twenty silly-ducking observants
That stretch their duties nicely.

KENT. Sir, in good faith, in sincere verity,
Under th' allowance of your great aspect,
Whose influence, like the wreath of radiant fire
On flickering Phoebus' front—

CORN. What mean'st by this?

KENT. To go out of my dialect, which you discom-
110 mend so much. I know, sir, I am no flatterer. He that
beguil'd you in a plain accent was a plain knave,
which, for my part, I will not be, though I should win
your displeasure to entreat me to't.

CORN. What was th' offence you gave him?

OSW. I never gave him any.
It pleas'd the King his master very late
To strike at me, upon his misconstruction;
When he, conjunct, and flattering his displeasure,
Tripp'd me behind; being down, insulted, rail'd
120 And put upon him such a deal of man
That worthied him, got praises of the King
For him attempting who was self-subdu'd;
And, in the fleshment of this dread exploit,
Drew on me here again.

KENT. None of these rogues and cowards
But Ajax is their fool.

CORN. Fetch forth the stocks!
You stubborn ancient knave, you reverent braggart,
We'll teach you—

KENT. Sir, I am too old to learn.

Call not your stocks for me. I serve the King;
On whose employment I was sent to you.
You shall do small respect, show too bold malice 130
Against the grace and person of my master,
Stocking his messenger.

CORN. Fetch forth the stocks! As I have life and
honour,
There shall he sit till noon.

REG. Till noon? Till night, my lord, and all night too!

KENT. Why, madam, if I were your father's dog,
You should not use me so.

REG. Sir, being his knave, I will.

CORN. This is a fellow of the selfsame colour
Our sister speaks of. Come, bring away the stocks!
[Stocks brought out.]

GLOU. Let me beseech your Grace not to do so. 140
His fault is much, and the good King his master
Will check him for't. Your purpos'd low correction
Is such as basest and contemn'dest wretches
For pilf'rings and most common trespasses
Are punish'd with. The King must take it ill
That he, so slightly valued in his messenger,
Should have him thus restrain'd.

CORN. I'll answer that.

REG. My sister may receive it much more worse,
To have her gentleman abus'd, assaulted,
For following her affairs. Put in his legs.— 150
[KENT is put in the stocks.]
Come, my good lord, away.
[Exeunt all but GLOUCESTER AND KENT.]

GLOU. I am sorry for thee, friend. 'Tis the Duke's
pleasure,
Whose disposition, all the world well knows,
Will not be rubb'd nor stopp'd. I'll entreat for thee.

KENT. Pray do not, sir. I have watch'd and travell'd
hard.
Some time I shall sleep out, the rest I'll whistle.
A good man's fortune may grow out at heels.
Give you good morrow!

GLOU. The Duke's to blame in this; 'twill be ill
taken. [Exit.]

KENT. Good King, that must approve the common
saw, 160
Thou out of heaven's benediction com'st
To the warm sun!
Approach, thou beacon to this under globe,
That by thy comfortable beams I may
Peruse this letter. Nothing almost sees miracles
But misery. I know 'tis from Cordelia,
Who hath most fortunately been inform'd

90. **likes,** pleases. 97-98. **constrains the garb . . . nature,** pretends to be plain-spoken, contrary to his actual character. 103. **silly-ducking,** obsequiously bowing. 104. **nicely,** punctiliously. 105-108. **Sir, in good faith . . . front.** Kent parodies the extravagant speech of such a servant as Oswald. 117. **upon his misconstruction,** because of his deliberate misinterpretation. 118. **conjunct,** taking the King's part. 121. **That worthied him,** that won honor for him. 122. **For . . . self-subdu'd,** for attacking one who had not resisted. 123. **in the fleshment,** while still in that fierce mood. 125. **Ajax . . . fool.** Even the great warrior Ajax is their inferior; there is also a vulgar pun on jakes (see note to l. 66). 126. **stubborn,** ferocious. 154. **rubb'd,** deterred, obstructed.

155. **watch'd,** gone without sleep. 160. **must approve the common saw,** you are obliged to exemplify the familiar proverb (about a foolish man who left his place in the shade on a hot day to sit in the sun). 165-166. **Nothing . . . misery.** Any relief seems miraculous when conditions have come to such a pass. 168. **obscured course,** plan of action in disguise. 169. **this enormous state,** the monstrous state of the realm. 173. **turn thy wheel.** Kent has in mind the familiar medieval representation of the goddess Fortuna capriciously turning her wheel. A cyclical and somewhat fatalistic view of history is implied.
Sc. iii. 1-21. **I heard . . . nothing am.** Edgar's descent here into the physical misery, defenselessness, and isolation of a mad beggar pre-

Of my obscured course—and [reads] 'shall find time
From this enormous state, seeking to give
170 Losses their remedies'—All weary and o'erwatch'd,
Take vantage, heavy eyes, not to behold
This shameful lodging.
Fortune, good night; smile once more, turn thy wheel.
                                                    [Sleeps.]

SCENE III *The open country.*

Enter EDGAR.

    EDG. I heard myself proclaim'd,
And by the happy hollow of a tree
Escap'd the hunt. No port is free, no place
That guard and most unusual vigilance
Does not attend my taking. Whiles I may scape,
I will preserve myself; and am bethought
To take the basest and most poorest shape
That ever penury, in contempt of man,
Brought near to beast. My face I'll grime with filth,
10 Blanket my loins, elf all my hair in knots,
And with presented nakedness outface
The winds and persecutions of the sky.
The country gives me proof and precedent
Of Bedlam beggars, who, with roaring voices,
Strike in their numb'd and mortified bare arms
Pins, wooden pricks, nails, sprigs of rosemary;
And with this horrible object, from low farms,
Poor pelting villages, sheepcotes, and mills,
Sometime with lunatic bans, sometime with prayers,
20 Enforce their charity. 'Poor Turlygod! poor Tom!'
That's something yet! Edgar I nothing am.   [*Exit.*]

SCENE IV *Before Gloucester's Castle;* KENT *in the stocks.*

Enter LEAR, FOOL, *and* GENTLEMAN.

    LEAR. 'Tis strange that they should so depart from
        home,
And not send back my messenger.
    GENT.   As I learn'd,
The night before there was no purpose in them
Of this remove.
    KENT.   Hail to thee, noble master!
    LEAR. Ha!
Mak'st thou this shame thy pastime?
    KENT.   No, my lord.
    FOOL. Ha, ha! look! he wears cruel garters. Horses
are tied by the head, dogs and bears by th' neck,
monkeys by th' loins, and men by th' legs. When
10 a man's over-lusty at legs, then he wears wooden

nether-stocks.
    LEAR. What's he that hath so much thy place mistook
To set thee here?
    KENT.   It is both he and she—
Your son and daughter.
    LEAR. No.
    KENT. Yes.
    LEAR. No, I say.
    KENT. I say yea.
    LEAR. No, no, they would not!
    KENT. Yes, they have.   20
    LEAR. By Jupiter, I swear no!
    KENT. By Juno, I swear ay!
    LEAR.   They durst not do't;
They would not, could not do't. 'Tis worse than murther
To do upon respect such violent outrage.
Resolve me with all modest haste which way
Thou mightst deserve or they impose this usage,
Coming from us.
    KENT.   My lord, when at their home
I did commend your Highness' letters to them,
Ere I was risen from the place that show'd
My duty kneeling, came there a reeking post,   30
Stew'd in his haste, half breathless, panting forth
From Goneril his mistress salutations;
Deliver'd letters, spite of intermission,
Which presently they read; on whose contents,
They summon'd up their meiny, straight took horse,
Commanded me to follow and attend
The leisure of their answer, gave me cold looks,
And meeting here the other messenger,
Whose welcome I perceiv'd had poison'd mine—
Being the very fellow which of late   40
Display'd so saucily against your Highness—
Having more man than wit about me, drew.
He rais'd the house with loud and coward cries.
Your son and daughter found this trespass worth
The shame which here it suffers.
    FOOL. Winter's not gone yet, if the wild geese fly
that way.

    Fathers that wear rags
        Do make their children blind;
    But fathers that bear bags   50
        Shall see their children kind.
    Fortune, that arrant whore,
    Ne'er turns the key to th' poor.

But for all this, thou shalt have as many dolours for
thy daughters as thou canst tell in a year.

pares the audience for Lear's confrontation on the heath with the harsher realities and imponderables of universal human experience. 8. in contempt of man, as if to demonstrate how contemptible or feeble man is. 10. elf, mat, tangle. 11. outface, confront, defy. 13. proof, example. 15. mortified, deadened, cruelly exposed. 17. object, spectacle. 18. pelting, paltry. 19. bans, curses. 20. Turlygod, perhaps the name of an order of mad beggars in France. 21. Edgar I nothing am. I am no longer Edgar (there is no hope for me as Edgar now, only as Tom). Here again the word "nothing" becomes important as the outlawed Edgar, feigning madness, proceeds onto the heath where Lear will soon join him in the mad suffering of his own exile. There both are

reduced to the essential condition of man, pitiful and bewildered in a grim, unrelenting world of powerful destructive forces.
    Sc. iv. 9. monkeys by th' loins. Monkeys were believed to be lustful. 10. at legs, at wenching. 11. nether-stocks, stockings. 24. upon respect, against the respect due to the king. 25. modest, moderate. 33. spite of intermission, despite interrupting. 35. meiny, household, train. 41. Display'd so saucily, showed himself to be so imprudent. 52-53. Fortune . . . poor, another allusion to the changeability and indifference of Fortune. 54. dolours, griefs (with a pun on "dollars").

William Shakespeare 279

LEAR. O, how this mother swells up toward my
    heart!
Hysterica passio! Down, thou climbing sorrow!
Thy element's below! Where is this daughter?
    KENT. With the Earl, sir, here within.
    LEAR.   Follow me not;
60 Stay here.   [Exit.]
    GENT. Made you no more offence but what you
speak of?
    KENT. None.
How chance the King comes with so small a number?
    FOOL. An thou hadst been set i' th' stocks for that
question, thou'dst well deserv'd it.
    KENT. Why, fool?
    FOOL. We'll set thee to school to an ant, to teach
thee there's no labouring i' th' winter. All that follow
70 their noses are led by their eyes but blind men, and
there's not a nose among twenty but can smell him
that's stinking. Let go thy hold when a great wheel
runs down a hill, lest it break thy neck with following
it; but the great one that goes upward, let him draw
thee after. When a wise man gives thee better counsel,
give me mine again. I would have none but knaves
follow it, since a fool gives it.

        That sir which serves and seeks for gain,
            And follows but for form,
80   Will pack when it begins to rain
            And leave thee in the storm.
        But I will tarry; the fool will stay,
            And let the wise man fly.
        The knave turns fool that runs away;
            The fool no knave, perdy.

    KENT. Where learn'd you this, fool?
    FOOL. Not i' th' stocks, fool.

Enter LEAR and GLOUCESTER.

    LEAR. Deny to speak with me? They are sick? they
    are weary?
They have travell'd all the night? Mere fetches—
90 The images of revolt and flying off!
Fetch me a better answer.
    GLOU.   My dear lord,
You know the fiery quality of the Duke,
How unremovable and fix'd he is
In his own course.
    LEAR. Vengeance! plague! death! confusion!
Fiery? What quality? Why, Gloucester, Gloucester,
I'ld speak with the Duke of Cornwall and his wife.
    GLOU. Well, my good lord, I have inform'd them so.

LEAR. Inform'd them? Dost thou understand me,
    man?
    GLOU. Ay, my good lord.   100
    LEAR. The King would speak with Cornwall; the
    dear father
Would with his daughter speak, commands her service.
Are they inform'd of this? My breath and blood!
Fiery? the fiery Duke? Tell the hot Duke that—
No, but not yet! May be he is not well.
Infirmity doth still neglect all office
Whereto our health is bound. We are not ourselves
When nature, being oppres'd, commands the mind
To suffer with the body. I'll forbear;
And am fallen out with my more headier will,   110
To take the indispos'd and sickly fit
For the sound man.—Death on my state! Wherefore
Should he sit here? This act persuades me
That this remotion of the Duke and her
Is practice only. Give me my servant forth.
Go tell the Duke and 's wife I'ld speak with them—
Now, presently. Bid them come forth and hear me,
Or at their chamber door I'll beat the drum
Till it cry sleep to death.
    GLOU. I would have all well betwixt you. [Exit.] 120
    LEAR. O me, my heart, my rising heart! But down!
    FOOL. Cry to it, nuncle, as the cockney did to the
eels when she put 'em i' th' paste alive. She knapp'd
'em o' th' coxcombs with a stick and cried 'Down,
wantons, down!' 'Twas her brother that, in pure kindness to his horse, buttered his hay.

Enter CORNWALL, REGAN, GLOUCESTER, SERVANTS.

    LEAR. Good morrow to you both.
    CORN.   Hail to your Grace!
                        [KENT *here set at liberty.*]
    REG. I am glad to see your Highness.
    LEAR. Regan, I think you are; I know what reason
I have to think so. If thou shouldst not be glad, 130
I would divorce me from thy mother's tomb,
Sepulchring an adultress. [*To* KENT] O, are you free?
Some other time for that.—Beloved Regan,
Thy sister's naught. O Regan, she hath tied
Sharp-tooth'd unkindness, like a vulture, here!
                        [*Lays his hand on his heart.*]
I can scarce speak to thee. Thou'lt not believe
With how deprav'd a quality—O Regan!
    REG. I pray you, sir, take patience. I have hope
You less know how to value her desert
Than she to scant her duty.
    LEAR.   Say, how is that?   140
    REG. I cannot think my sister in the least

---

56. **this mother**, the "mother" was the colloquial name for *hysterica
passio*, "hysterical suffering"; Lear again feels the imminence of madness.
69-72. **All that follow . . . stinking**, another vivid anticipation of the
blinding of Gloucester. 72. **a great wheel**, Fortune's wheel. 78-85.
That sir . . . perdy. Only a man who is a fool remains loyal when his
master's fortunes have fallen; a wiser man will be selfish and flee.
89. **fetches**, pretexts. 107-112. **Whereto . . . state.** Lear has begun to

be somewhat more patient, less self-willed and rash. 114. **this remotion**,
avoiding me. 123. **knapp'd**, rapped. 125. **her brother**, evidently
another fool of the same breed. 131-132. **I would . . . an adultress.** Lear
suggests that Regan must be a bastard if this unnatural treatment of her
father indicates her true nature (another parallel to Edmund the Bastard
and the disowning of Cordelia and Edgar by their respective duped fathers). 134-135. **O Regan . . . here**, possibly a reference to the torments

280 *The Brave New World and After*

Would fail her obligation. If, sir, perchance
She have restrain'd the riots of your followers,
'Tis on such ground, and to such wholesome end,
As clears her from all blame.
    LEAR. My curses on her!
    REG.   O, sir, you are old!
Nature in you stands on the very verge
Of her confine. You should be rul'd, and led
By some discretion that discerns your state
150 Better than you yourself. Therefore I pray you
That to our sister you do make return;
Say you have wrong'd her, sir.
    LEAR.   Ask her forgiveness?
Do you but mark how this becomes the house:
'Dear daughter, I confess that I am old.   [Kneels.]
Age is unnecessary. On my knees I beg
That you'll vouchsafe me raiment, bed, and food.'
    REG. Good sir, no more! These are unsightly tricks.
Return you to my sister.
    LEAR.   [Rises.] Never, Regan!
She hath abated me of half my train;
160 Look'd black upon me; struck me with her tongue,
Most serpent-like, upon the very heart.
All the stor'd vengeances of heaven fall
On her ingrateful top! Strike her young bones,
You taking airs, with lameness!
    CORN.   Fie, sir, fie!
    LEAR. You nimble lightnings, dart your blinding
      flames
Into her scornful eyes! Infect her beauty,
You fen-suck'd fogs, drawn by the pow'rful sun,
To fall and blast her pride!
    REG. O the blest gods! so will you wish on me
170 When the rash mood is on.
    LEAR. No, Regan, thou shalt never have my curse.
Thy tender-hefted nature shall not give
Thee o'er to harshness. Her eyes are fierce; but thine
Do comfort, and not burn. 'Tis not in thee
To grudge my pleasures, to cut off my train,
To bandy hasty words, to scant my sizes,
And, in conclusion, to oppose the bolt
Against my coming in. Thou better know'st
The offices of nature, bond of childhood,
180 Effects of courtesy, dues of gratitude.
Thy half o' th' kingdom hast thou not forgot,
Wherein I thee endow'd.
    REG.   Good sir, to th' purpose.
                 [Tucket within.]
    LEAR. Who put my man i' th' stocks?
    CORN.   What trumpet's that?
    REG. I know't—my sister's. This approves her letter,
That she would soon be here.

Enter OSWALD *the Steward.*

                  Is your lady come?
    LEAR. This is a slave, whose easy-borrowed pride
Dwells in the fickle grace of her he follows.
Out, varlet, from my sight!
    CORN.   What means your Grace?

Enter GONERIL.

    LEAR. Who stock'd my servant? Regan, I have good
      hope
Thou didst not know on't—Who comes here? O
      heavens!   190
If you do love old men, if your sweet sway
Allow obedience—if yourselves are old,
Make it your cause! Send down, and take my part!
[To GONERIL] Art not asham'd to look upon this
    beard?—
O Regan, wilt thou take her by the hand?
    GON. Why not by th' hand, sir? How have I
    offended?
All's not offence that indiscretion finds
And dotage terms so.
    LEAR.   O sides, you are too tough!
Will you yet hold? How came my man i' th' stocks?
    CORN. I set him there, sir; but his own disorders   200
Deserv'd much less advancement.
    LEAR.   You? Did you?
    REG. I pray you, father, being weak, seem so.
If, till the expiration of your month,
You will return and sojourn with my sister,
Dismissing half your train, come then to me.
I am now from home, and out of that provision
Which shall be needful for your entertainment.
    LEAR. Return to her, and fifty men dismiss'd?
No, rather I abjure all roofs, and choose
To wage against the enmity o' th' air,   210
To be a comrade with the wolf and owl—
Necessity's sharp pinch! Return with her?
Why, the hot-blooded France, that dowerless took
Our youngest born, I could as well be brought
To knee his throne, and, squire-like, pension beg
To keep base life afoot. Return with her?
Persuade me rather to be slave and sumpter
To this detested groom.   [Points at OSWALD.]
    GON.   At your choice, sir.
    LEAR. I prithee, daughter, do not make me mad.
I will not trouble thee, my child; farewell.   220
We'll no more meet, no more see one another.
But yet thou art my flesh, my blood, my daughter;
Or rather a disease that's in my flesh,
Which I must needs call mine. Thou art a boil,

of Prometheus. 147-148. **Nature . . . confine.** You have only a short time
left to live. 155. **Age is unnecessary.** Old people are useless. 162-168.
All . . . pride. Lear again curses Goneril. 172. **tender-hefted,** inclined to
tenderness. 176. **sizes,** allowances. 201. **much less advancement,**
worse treatment. 205. **Dismissing half your train.** This quibbling over
the number of attendants that Lear should be allowed to retain fills the
rest of the scene; his train is finally reduced to zero, "nothing." 209-212.

No, rather I . . . her. This speech reinforces Lear's closeness to the
condition of poor Tom. 217. **sumpter,** packhorse. 222. **But yet thou
art my flesh.** Lear begins to question the rationality of a universe which
nurtures, from the same union, both evil and good children.

A plague sore, an embossed carbuncle
In my corrupted blood. But I'll not chide thee.
Let shame come when it will, I do not call it.
I do not bid the Thunder-bearer shoot
Nor tell tales of thee to high-judging Jove.
230 Mend when thou canst; be better at thy leisure;
I can be patient, I can stay with Regan,
I and my hundred knights.

    REG.   Not altogether so.
I look'd not for you yet, nor am provided
For your fit welcome. Give ear, sir, to my sister;
For those that mingle reason with your passion
Must be content to think you old, and so—
But she knows what she does.

    LEAR.   Is this well spoken?
    REG. I dare avouch it, sir. What, fifty followers?
Is it not well? What should you need of more?
240 Yea, or so many, sith that both charge and danger
Speak 'gainst so great a number? How in one house
Should many people, under two commands,
Hold amity? 'Tis hard; almost impossible.
    GON. Why might not you, my lord, receive attendance
From those that she calls servants, or from mine?
    REG. Why not, my lord? If then they chanc'd to
    slack ye,
We could control them. If you will come to me
(For now I spy a danger), I entreat you
To bring but five-and-twenty. To no more
250 Will I give place or notice.
    LEAR. I gave you all—
    REG.   And in good time you gave it!
    LEAR. Made you my guardians, my depositaries;
But kept a reservation to be followed
With such a number. What, must I come to you
With five-and-twenty, Regan? Said you so?
    REG. And speak't again, my lord. No more with me.
    LEAR. Those wicked creatures yet do look well-
    favour'd
When others are more wicked; not being the worst
Stands in some rank of praise. [To GONERIL] I'll go
    with thee.
260 Thy fifty yet doth double five-and-twenty,
And thou art twice her love.
    GON.   Hear me, my lord.
What need you five-and-twenty, ten, or five,
To follow in a house where twice so many
Have a command to tend you?
    REG.   What need one?
    LEAR. O, reason not the need! Our basest beggars
Are in the poorest thing superfluous.
Allow not nature more than nature needs,
Man's life is cheap as beast's. Thou are a lady:

If only to go warm were gorgeous,
Why, nature needs not what thou gorgeous wear'st,   270
Which scarcely keeps thee warm. But, for true need—
You heavens, give me that patience, patience I need!
You see me here, you gods, a poor old man,
As full of grief as age; wretched in both.
If it be you that stirs these daughters' hearts
Against their father, fool me not so much
To bear it tamely; touch me with noble anger,
And let not women's weapons, water drops,
Stain my man's cheeks! No, you unnatural hags!
I will have such revenges on you both   280
That all the world shall—I will do such things—
What they are yet, I know not; but they shall be
The terrors of the earth! You think I'll weep.
No, I'll not weep.
I have full cause of weeping, but this heart
Shall break into a hundred thousand flaws
Or ere I'll weep. O fool, I shall go mad!
    [Exeunt LEAR, GLOUCESTER, KENT, and FOOL.
          Storm and tempest.]
    CORN. Let us withdraw; 'twill be a storm.
    REG. This house is little; the old man and 's people
Cannot be well bestow'd.   290
    GON. 'Tis his own blame; hath put himself from rest
And must needs taste his folly.
    REG. For his particular, I'll receive him gladly,
But not one follower.
    GON.   So am I purpos'd.
Where is my Lord of Gloucester?
    CORN. Followed the old man forth.

Enter GLOUCESTER.

                  He is return'd.
    GLOU. The King is in high rage.
    CORN.   Whither is he going?
    GLOU. He calls to horse, but will I know not whither.
    CORN. 'Tis best to give him way; he leads himself.
    GON. My lord, entreat him by no means to stay.   300
    GLOU. Alack, the night comes on, and the bleak
    winds
Do sorely ruffle. For many miles about
There's scarce a bush.
    REG.   O, sir, to wilful men
The injuries that they themselves procure
Must be their schoolmasters. Shut up your doors.
He is attended with a desperate train,
And what they may incense him to, being apt
To have his ear abus'd, wisdom bids fear.
    CORN. Shut up your doors, my lord; 'tis a wild night.
My Regan counsels well. Come out o' th' storm.   310
    [Exeunt.]

238. **avouch**, confirm. After 287. **Exeunt . . . tempest.** The stage direction indicates who will remain faithful to Lear throughout the devastating experiences on the heath. The characters left onstage, along with Edmund, compose the evil faction of the play. 302. **ruffle,** rage. 310. **Come out o' th' storm.** Cornwall advocates looking after oneself alone, not becoming involved in the plight of others. The antirationalist characters aligned with Lear practice, in contrast, the "foolish" philosophy of assisting and sharing another's misfortune.

Act III, Sc. i. 6. **main,** land. 10. **his little world of man.** A man is a microcosm in comparison to the macrocosm, the universe. 12. **cub-drawn,** with udders sucked dry by her cubs. 18. **note,** acquaintance, estimation. 19. **Commend,** intrust. **a dear thing,** an important matter. 24. **spies and speculations,** spies. 25. **Intelligent of our state,** informers to our cause. 26. **snuffs,** cases in which they have openly shown antagonism. **packings,** plots. 29. **furnishings,** pretexts. 30. **a power,** troops. 35. **my credit,** your belief in me. 45. **out-wall,**

SCENE I *A Heath. Storm still.*

Enter KENT *and a* GENTLEMAN *at several doors.*

KENT. Who's there, besides foul weather?
GENT. One minded like the weather, most unquietly.
KENT. I know you. Where's the King?
GENT. Contending with the fretful elements;
Bids the wind blow the earth into the sea,
Or swell the curled waters 'bove the main,
That things might change or cease; tears his white hair,
Which the impetuous blasts, with eyeless rage,
Catch in their fury and make nothing of;
10 Strives in his little world of man to outscorn
The to-and-fro-conflicting wind and rain.
This night, wherein the cub-drawn bear would couch,
The lion and the belly-pinched wolf
Keep their fur dry, unbonneted he runs,
And bids what will take all.
    KENT.   But who is with him?
    GENT. None but the fool, who labours to outjest
His heart-struck injuries.
    KENT.   Sir, I do know you,
And dare upon the warrant of my note
Commend a dear thing to you. There is division
20 (Although as yet the face of it be cover'd
With mutual cunning) 'twixt Albany and Cornwall;
Who have (as who have not, that their great stars
Thron'd and set high?) servants, who seem no less,
Which are to France the spies and speculations
Intelligent of our state. What hath been seen,
Either in snuffs and packings of the Dukes,
Or the hard rein which both of them have borne
Against the old kind King, or something deeper,
Whereof, perchance, these are but furnishings—
30 But, true it is, from France there comes a power.
Into this scattered kingdom, who already,
Wise in our negligence, have secret feet
In some of our best ports and are at point
To show their open banner. Now to you:
If on my credit you dare build so far
To make your speed to Dover, you shall find
Some that will thank you, making just report
Of how unnatural and bemadding sorrow
The King hath cause to plain.
40 I am a gentleman of blood and breeding,
And from some knowledge and assurance offer
This office to you.
    GENT. I will talk further with you.
    KENT.   No, do not.
For confirmation that I am much more

Than my out-wall, open this purse and take
What it contains. If you shall see Cordelia
(As fear not but you shall), show her this ring,
And she will tell you who your fellow is
That yet you do not know. Fie on this storm!
I will go seek the King.   50
    GENT. Give me your hand. Have you no more to
      say?
    KENT. Few words, but, to effect, more than all yet:
That, when we have found the King (in which your
    pain
That way, I'll this), he that first lights on him
Holla the other.   [*Exeunt severally.*]

SCENE II *Another part of the heath. Storm still.*

Enter LEAR *and* FOOL.

LEAR. Blow, winds, and crack your cheeks! rage!
    blow!
You cataracts and hurricanoes, spout
Till you have drench'd our steeples, drown'd the cocks!
You sulph'rous and thought-executing fires,
Vaunt-couriers to oak-cleaving thunderbolts,
Singe my white head! And thou, all-shaking thunder,
Strike flat the thick rotundity o' th' world,
Crack Nature's moulds, all germains spill at once,
That make ingrateful man!
    FOOL. O nuncle, court holy water in a dry house is 10
better than this rain water out o' door. Good nuncle,
in, and ask thy daughters' blessing! Here's a night
pities neither wise men nor fools.
    LEAR. Rumble thy bellyful! Spit, fire! spout, rain!
Nor rain, wind, thunder, fire are my daughters.
I tax not you, you elements, with unkindness.
I never gave you kingdom, call'd you children,
You owe me no subscription. Then let fall
Your horrible pleasure. Here I stand your slave,
A poor, infirm, weak, and despis'd old man.   20
But yet I call you servile ministers,
That will with two pernicious daughters join
Your high-engender'd battles 'gainst a head
So old and white as this! O! O! 'tis foul!
    FOOL. He that has a house to put 's head in has a
good headpiece.

        The codpiece that will house
          Before the head has any,
        The head and he shall louse:
          So beggars marry many.   30
        The man that makes his toe
        What he his heart should make

outer appearance. 48. **your fellow,** your associate in serving the King.
53. **pain,** effort.
    Sc. ii. 3. **cocks,** weathercocks. 8. **germains,** seeds. 10. **court holy
water,** colloquial term for flattery, hypocrisy. 18. **subscription,** obedience. 27-30. **The codpiece ... many.** A man who begets children before
he has a house for them will soon become a beggar; many beggars get
married in this fashion. Lear, the Fool suggests, has also behaved, without
forethought (in respect to dividing his kingdom) and consequently finds

himself now in the position of a beggar, unsheltered unless he "begs" his
daughters' favor. 31-34. **The man ... wake,** another allusion to Lear's
folly. Lear too has unnaturally and unwisely reversed his "toe" with
his "heart" and thereby developed a "corn" or a heavy grief which
destroys all serenity.

Shall of a corn cry woe,
And turn his sleep to wake.

For there was never yet fair woman but she made mouths in a glass.

Enter KENT.

LEAR. No, I will be the pattern of all patience;
I will say nothing.
KENT. Who's there?
40 FOOL. Marry, here's grace and a codpiece; that's a wise man and a fool.
KENT. Alas, sir, are you here? Things that love night
Love not such nights as these. The wrathful skies
Gallow the very wanderers of the dark
And make them keep their caves. Since I was man,
Such sheets of fire, such bursts of horrid thunder,
Such groans of roaring wind and rain, I never
Remember to have heard. Man's nature cannot carry
Th' affliction nor the fear.
LEAR.   Let the great gods,
50 That keep this dreadful pudder o'er our heads,
Find out their enemies now. Tremble, thou wretch,
That hast within thee undivulged crimes
Unwhipp'd of justice. Hide thee, thou bloody hand;
Thou perjur'd, and thou simular man of virtue
That art incestuous. Caitiff, in pieces shake
That under covert and convenient seeming
Hast practis'd on man's life. Close pent-up guilts,
Rive your concealing continents, and cry
These dreadful summoners grace. I am a man
More sinn'd against than sinning.
60 KENT.   Alack, bareheaded?
Gracious my lord, hard by here is a hovel;
Some friendship will it lend you 'gainst the tempest.
Repose you there, whilst I to this hard house
(More harder than the stones whereof 'tis rais'd,
Which even but now, demanding after you,
Denied me to come in) return, and force
Their scanted courtesy.
LEAR.   My wits begin to turn.
Come on, my boy. How dost, my boy? Art cold?
I am cold myself. Where is this straw, my fellow?
70 The art of our necessities is strange,
That can make vile things precious. Come, your hovel.
Poor fool and knave, I have one part in my heart
That's sorry yet for thee.
FOOL. [*Sings*]

He that has and a little tiny wit—
With hey, ho, the wind and the rain—
Must make content with his fortunes fit,
For the rain it raineth every day.

LEAR. True, my good boy. Come, bring us to this hovel.

[*Exeunt* LEAR *and* KENT.]
FOOL. This is a brave night to cool a courtesan.
I'll speak a prophecy ere I go: 80

When priests are more in word than matter;
When brewers mar their malt with water;
When nobles are their tailors' tutors,
No heretics burn'd, but wenches' suitors;
When every case in law is right,
No squire in debt nor no poor knight;
When slanders do not live in tongues,
Nor cutpurses come not to throngs;
When usurers tell their gold i' th' field,
And bawds and whores do churches build: 90
Then shall the realm of Albion
Come to great confusion.
Then comes the time, who lives to see't,
That going shall be us'd with feet.

This prophecy Merlin shall make, for I live before his time.   [*Exit.*]

SCENE III *Gloucester's Castle.*

Enter GLOUCESTER *and* EDMUND.

GLOU. Alack, alack, Edmund, I like not this unnatural dealing! When I desir'd their leave that I might pity him, they took from me the use of mine own house, charg'd me on pain of perpetual displeasure neither to speak of him, entreat for him, nor any way sustain him.
EDM. Most savage and unnatural!
GLOU. Go to; say you nothing. There is division betwixt the Dukes, and a worse matter than that. I have received a letter this night—'tis dangerous to be 10 spoken—I have lock'd the letter in my closet. These injuries the King now bears will be revenged home; there's part of a power already footed; we must incline to the King. I will seek him and privily relieve him. Go you and maintain talk with the Duke, that my charity be not of him perceived. If he ask for me, I am ill and

35-36. For there, etc., a bit of the Fool's nonsense. made ... glass, admired herself. 40. grace, a reasonable, honorable man. codpiece, vulgar term for the male genitalia (literally, a front flap on breeches). 44. Gallow, terrify. 48. carry, endure. 50. pudder, turmoil (of the storm). 54. simular, pretended, hypocritical. 56. convenient, conventional. 57. practis'd on, plotted against. 58. Rive, burst, split. concealing continents, means of concealment. 58-59. cry ... grace, ask these arresting officers for mercy. 59-60. I am ... sinning. Lear asserts that he is not guilty; therefore the storm, as the dispenser of divine justice, will not arraign him as well. He has yet to fully recognize his own responsibility for his plight. 70. art, craft, manner. 74. and, a "filler" word, without meaning. 76. Must ... fit, must accept any turn of his fortunes, for such is the nature of life. 78. True. Lear understands

that the Fool's ditty applies to himself. Paradoxically, Lear begins to display a deeper insight into things as well as a deep genuine concern for others (here, for the helpless Fool who has faithfully accompanied him) at the onset of his madness. He acquires wisdom, humility, and compassion only with extreme suffering and being himself reduced to a condition of powerlessness. 79. brave, excellent. 83. tailors' tutors, even greater experts on fashion. 91. Albion, England. 94. That going ... feet, then the world will again be as it should. us'd, performed by. 95. This ... time. Merlin was the magician in King Arthur's court. This comic anachronism in the supposed time of the play's events is intentional.
Sc. iii. 12. home, to the utmost. 13. footed, landed, marching. 14. privily, secretly. 19. toward, imminent. 23. a fair deserving, a deed

gone to bed. Though I die for't, as no less is threat'ned me, the King my old master must be relieved. There is some strange thing toward, Edmund. Pray you be 20 careful. [Exit.]

EDM. This courtesy, forbid thee, shall the Duke
Instantly know, and of that letter too.
This seems a fair deserving, and must draw me
That which my father loses—no less than all.
The younger rises when the old doth fall. [Exit.]

SCENE IV *The heath. Before a hovel. Storm still.*

Enter LEAR, KENT, *and* FOOL.

KENT. Here is the place, my lord; Good my lord,
    enter.
The tyranny of the open night's too rough
For nature to endure.
    LEAR.   Let me alone.
KENT. Good my lord, enter here.
    LEAR.   Wilt break my heart?
KENT. I had rather break mine own. Good my lord,
    enter.
LEAR. Thou think'st 'tis much that this contentious
    storm
Invades us to the skin. So 'tis to thee;
But where the greater malady is fix'd,
The lesser is scarce felt. Thou'dst shun a bear;
10 But if thy flight lay toward the raging sea,
Thou'dst meet the bear i' th' mouth. When the mind's
    free,
The body's delicate. The tempest in my mind
Doth from my senses take all feeling else
Save what beats there. Filial ingratitude!
Is it not as this mouth should tear this hand
For lifting food to't? But I will punish home!
No, I will weep no more. In such a night
To shut me out! Pour on; I will endure.
In such a night as this! O Regan, Goneril!
20 Your old kind father, whose frank heart gave all!
O, that way madness lies; let me shun that!
No more of that.
    KENT.   Good my lord, enter here.
    LEAR. Prithee go in thyself; seek thine own ease.
This tempest will not give me leave to ponder
On things would hurt me more. But I'll go in.
[*To the* FOOL] In, boy; go first.—You houseless poverty—
Nay, get thee in. I'll pray, and then I'll sleep.
                                  [*Exit* FOOL.]
Poor naked wretches, wheresoe'er you are,

That bide the pelting of this pitiless storm,
How shall your houseless heads and unfed sides, 30
Your loop'd and window'd raggedness, defend you
From seasons such as these? O, I have ta'en
Too little care of this! Take physic, pomp;
Expose thyself to feel what wretches feel,
That thou mayst shake the superflux to them
And show the heavens more just.
    EDG. [*Within*] Fathom and half, fathom and half!
Poor Tom!

Enter FOOL *from the hovel.*

FOOL. Come not in here, nuncle, here's a spirit. Help
me, help me! 40
    KENT. Give me thy hand. Who's there?
    FOOL. A spirit, a spirit! He says his name's poor
Tom.
    KENT. What art thou that dost grumble there i' th'
straw? Come forth.

Enter EDGAR *disguised as a madman.*

EDG. Away! the foul fiend follows me! Through the
sharp hawthorn blows the cold wind. Humh! go to thy
cold bed, and warm thee.
    LEAR. Hast thou given all to thy two daughters, and
art thou come to this? 50
    EDG. Who gives anything to poor Tom? whom the
foul fiend hath led through fire and through flame,
through ford and whirlpool, o'er bog and quagmire;
that hath laid knives under his pillow and halters in
his pew, set ratsbane by his porridge, made him proud
of heart, to ride on a bay trotting horse over four-
inch'd bridges, to course his own shadow for a traitor.
Bless thy five wits! Tom's acold. O, do de, do de, do
de. Bless thee from whirlwinds, star-blasting, and
taking! Do poor Tom some charity, whom the foul 60
fiend vexes. There could I have him now—and there—
and there again—and there! [*Storm still.*]
    LEAR. What, have his daughters brought him to this
    pass?
Couldst thou save nothing? Didst thou give 'em all?
    FOOL. Nay, he reserv'd a blanket, else we had been
all sham'd.
    LEAR. Now all the plagues that in the pendulous air
Hang fated o'er men's faults light on thy daughters!
    KENT. He hath no daughters, sir.

---

that will win favor for me (with the Duke). Edmund anticipates that Cornwall will probably execute Gloucester and then reward him with his father's wealth. 24-25. **That which ... fall,** a characteristic Shakespearean rhyme-tag used to close a scene. The Gloucester-Lear parallel appears particularly marked here.
Sc. iv. The extremity of Lear's suffering is again emphasized; his physical and psychological ordeal on the heath appears so intense that he is conceived as undergoing unbearable agony. 11. **free,** untroubled. 14. **beats there,** throbs in my mind and heart. 20. **frank,** generous. 29. **bide,** endure. 31. **loop'd and window'd,** full of holes. 33-36. **Take physic, pomp ... just.** Suffer the misery of the lowly to cure your lack of compassionate understanding. 35. **superflux,** superfluity. 35-36. **That ... just,** so that you may cast off your superfluity, what you do not

absolutely need, and give it to them; God's treatment of humanity will then appear more equitable. 44. **grumble,** whimper. 46-47. **Through ... wind,** what winter means to those without protection from it. It is this kind of first-hand knowledge of the essential human predicament which Lear, the formerly pampered and flattered monarch, must now learn. 49-50. **Hast thou ... this.** Lear perceives his experiential kinship with the shivering young "madman." 51-62. **Who gives ... there.** Edgar describes how the "foul fiend" has variously tempted him to suicide. 59. **star-blasting,** star-shooting (comets). 60. **taking,** infection, disease. 61-62. **There ... and there.** Edgar makes lunges at his demon. 67. **pendulous,** overhanging.

William Shakespeare 285

LEAR. Death, traitor! nothing could have subdu'd
nature
To such a lowness but his unkind daughters.
Is it the fashion that discarded fathers
Should have thus little mercy on their flesh?
Judicious punishment! 'Twas this flesh begot
Those pelican daughters.

EDG. Pillicock sat on Pillicock's Hill.
'Allow, 'allow, loo, loo!

FOOL. This cold night will turn us all to fools and
madmen.

EDG. Take heed o' th' foul fiend; obey thy parents;
keep thy word justly; swear not; commit not with
man's sworn spouse; set not thy sweet heart on proud
array. Tom's acold.

LEAR. What hast thou been?

EDG. A servingman, proud in heart and mind; that
curl'd my hair, wore gloves in my cap; serv'd the lust
of my mistress' heart and did the act of darkness with
her; swore as many oaths as I spake words, and broke
them in the sweet face of heaven; one that slept in
the contriving of lust, and wak'd to do it. Wine lov'd
I deeply, dice dearly; and in woman outparamour'd
the Turk. False of heart, light of ear, bloody of hand;
hog in sloth, fox in stealth, wolf in greediness, dog in
madness, lion in prey. Let not the creaking of shoes
nor the rustling of silks betray thy poor heart to
woman. Keep thy foot out of brothel, thy hand out of
placket, thy pen from lender's book, and defy the foul
fiend. Still through the hawthorn blows the cold wind;
says suum, mun, hey, no, nonny. Dolphin my boy, my
boy, sessa! let him trot by.

[Storm still.]

LEAR. Why, thou wert better in thy grave than to
answer with thy uncover'd body this extremity of the
skies. Is man no more than this? Consider him well.
Thou ow'st the worm no silk, the beast no hide, the
sheep no wool, the cat no perfume. Ha! Here's three
on's are sophisticated! Thou .art the thing itself; unaccommodated man is no more but such a poor, bare,
forked animal as thou art. Off, off, you lendings! Come,
unbutton here.

[Tears at his clothes.]

FOOL. Prithee, nuncle, be contented! 'Tis a naughty
night to swim in. Now a little fire in a wild field were
like an old lecher's heart—a small spark, all the rest
on 's body cold. Look, here comes a walking fire.

Enter GLOUCESTER *with a torch.*

EDG. This is the foul fiend Flibbertigibbet. He begins
at curfew, and walks till the first cock. He gives the
web and the pin, squints the eye, and makes the
harelip; mildews the white wheat, and hurts the poor
creature of earth.

Saint Withold footed thrice the 'old;
He met the nightmare, and her nine fold;   120
    Bid her alight
    And her troth plight,
And aroint thee, witch, aroint thee!

KENT. How fares your Grace?

LEAR. What's he?

KENT. Who's there? What is't you seek?

GLOU. What are you there? Your names?

EDG. Poor Tom, that eats the swimming frog, the
toad, the tadpole, the wall-newt and the water; that in
the fury of his heart, when the foul fiend rages, eats   130
cow-dung for sallets, swallows the old rat and the
ditch-dog, drinks the green mantle of the standing
pool; who is whipp'd from tithing to tithing, and stock-
punish'd and imprison'd; who hath had three suits to
his back, six shirts to his body, horse to ride, and
weapon to wear;

But mice and rats, and such small deer,
Have been Tom's food for seven long year.

Beware my follower. Peace, Smulkin! peace, thou fiend!

GLOU. What, hath your Grace no better company?   140

EDG. The prince of darkness is a gentleman!
Modo he's call'd, and Mahu.

GLOU. Our flesh and blood is grown so vile, my lord,
That it doth hate what gets it.

EDG. Poor Tom's acold.

GLOU. Go in with me. My duty cannot suffer
T' obey in all your daughters' hard commands.
Though their injunction be to bar my doors
And let this tyrannous night take hold upon you,
Yet have I ventur'd to come seek you out   150
And bring you where both fire and food is ready.

LEAR. First let me talk with this philosopher.
What is the cause of thunder?

KENT. Good my lord, take his offer; go into th'
house.

---

73. **thus little mercy on their flesh.** Edgar has pierced his arms as
part of the disguise (II, iii, 14-16). 75. **pelican.** Pelicans were believed
to feed their offspring from their own flesh. The bird was widely used
as a symbol of Christ-like charity. 76. **Pillicock,** Edgar's version of
"pelican." He recites part of an old nursery rhyme. 80-83. **Take heed
. . . acold.** Edgar seems to be trying to recite the Ten Commandments.
But like the Fool's oblique satire, his own supposedly crazed babble
often contains a vein of pointed moral judgment. 86. **gloves in my cap,**
a token of his lady's favor. 85-100. **A servingman . . . trot by.** Edgar
forcefully enumerates some of the moral deviations poisoning the world
of *King Lear:* treachery, self-seeking, animalistic behavior, greed, and so
forth. 92. **light of ear,** given to eavesdropping, spying. 93-94. **hog in
sloth . . . lion in prey.** The seven Deadly Sins were often typified by
such animals. The play generally contains a great deal of animal imagery
in accordance with the savagery of the events. 94. **creaking of shoes.**
Shoes that creaked were fashionable. 97. **placket,** the slit in a woman's

petticoat. 97-98. **defy the foul fiend,** withstand his temptations to evil.
Edgar's repeated allusions to the tormenting familiar spirit that he has
invented for Tom soon accrue more universal relevance; the "fiend"
comes to suggest a principle of spiritual trial or divine retribution inherent in the course of human affairs. 98. **Still . . . wind,** another univer-
salizing symbolic notation on the nature of life and its sterner realities.
99. **suum . . . nonny,** an imitation of the sound of the wind. **Dolphin
my boy,** possibly a line from an old ballad. 100. **sessa.** There he goes.
103. **Is man no more than this?** By now Lear has apprehended Nature's
uncompromising answer to this fundamental question. 105. **the cat,** the
civet cat. 106-107. **unaccommodated man,** unprotected man, man without the artificial trappings and defenses to which he is accustomed. 107-
108. **a poor, bare, forked animal.** Lear recognizes at last that this is the
condition of all humanity. 108. **lendings,** clothes. Lear's speech here and
the act of tearing off his clothes mark one of the play's central perceptions
as well as the climax of its imagery of divestiture. Lear is now "naked"

LEAR. I'll talk a word with this same learned Theban. What is your study?

EDG. How to prevent the fiend and to kill vermin.

LEAR. Let me ask you one word in private.

KENT. Importune him once more to go, my lord. His wits begin t' unsettle.

160 GLOU.   Canst thou blame him?

                                 [Storm still.]

His daughters seek his death. Ah, that good Kent!
He said it would be thus—poor banish'd man!
Thou say'st the King grows mad: I'll tell thee, friend,
I am almost mad myself. I had a son,
Now outlaw'd from my blood. He sought my life
But lately, very late. I lov'd him, friend—
No father his son dearer. True to tell thee,
The grief hath craz'd my wits. What a night's this!
I do beseech your Grace—

LEAR.   O, cry you mercy, sir.

170 Noble philosopher, your company.

EDG. Tom's acold.

GLOU. In, fellow, there, into th' hovel; keep thee warm.

LEAR. Come, let's in all.

KENT.   This way, my lord.

LEAR.   With him!

I will keep still with my philosopher.

KENT. Good my lord, soothe him; let him take the fellow.

GLOU. Take him you on.

KENT. Sirrah, come on; go along with us.

LEAR. Come, good Athenian.

GLOU. No words, no words! hush.

180 EDG. Child Rowland to the dark tower came;
        His word was still,—Fie, foh, and fum!
        I smell the blood of an British man. [Exeunt.]

SCENE V Gloucester's Castle.

Enter CORNWALL and EDMUND.

CORN. I will have my revenge ere I depart his house.

EDM. How, my lord, I may be censured, that nature thus gives way to loyalty, something fears me to think of.

CORN. I now perceive it was not altogether your brother's evil disposition made him seek his death; but a provoking merit, set awork by a reproveable badness in himself.

EDM. How malicious is my fortune that I must repent to be just! This is the letter he spoke of, which 10 approves him an intelligent party to the advantages of France. O heavens! that this treason were not—or not I the detector!

CORN. Go with me to the Duchess.

EDM. If the matter of this paper be certain, you have mighty business in hand.

CORN. True or false, it hath made thee Earl of Gloucester. Seek out where thy father is, that he may be ready for our apprehension.

EDM. [Aside] If I find him comforting the King, it 20 will stuff his suspicion more fully.—I will persever in my course of loyalty, though the conflict be sore between that and my blood.

CORN. I will lay trust upon thee, and thou shalt find a dearer father in my love.   [Exeunt.]

SCENE VI A farmhouse near Gloucester's Castle.

Enter GLOUCESTER, LEAR, KENT, FOOL, and EDGAR.

GLOU. Here is better than the open air; take it thankfully. I will piece out the comfort with what addition I can. I will not be long from you.

KENT. All the power of his wits have given way to his impatience. The gods reward your kindness!

                    [Exit GLOUCESTER.]

EDG. Fraterretto calls me, and tells me Nero is an angler in the lake of darkness. Pray, innocent, and beware the foul fiend.

FOOL. Prithee, nuncle, tell me whether a madman be a gentleman or a yeoman.   10

LEAR. A king, a king!

FOOL. No, he's a yeoman that has a gentleman to his son; for he's a mad yeoman that sees his son a gentleman before him.

LEAR. To have a thousand with red burning spits Come hizzing in upon 'em—

EDG. The foul fiend bites my back.

FOOL. He's mad that trusts in the tameness of a wolf, a horse's health, a boy's love, or a whore's oath.

LEAR. It shall be done; I will arraign them straight. 20 [To EDGAR] Come, sit thou here, most learned justicer.

to universal human experience. 110. naughty, terrible, wicked. 114. Flibbertigibbet, name of a devil. 116. the web and the pin, cataracts of the eye (colloquial expression). 117-118. the poor creature of earth, man. 119-123. Saint . . . thee, an old incantation to ward off the goblin believed to cause nightmares. 119. 'old, wold, plain. 122. her troth plight, give her word (to do no harm). 123. aroint thee. Be gone. 129-130. in the fury of his heart . . . rages. Here again the "fiend" is associated with an avenging fatality or the pangs of conscience. 131. sallets, salads. 132. standing, stagnant. 133. tithing, parish, district. 137. deer, game; an adaptation of a couplet from a popular old romance. 139. my follower, the "foul fiend." Smulkin, name of a devil. 141. The prince of darkness is a gentleman, and therefore suitable company for a king. 142. Modo . . . Mahu, the chief devil, Satan. 144. gets, begets. This play is profoundly about the mystery of generation, especially the question of why some children of the same family are good and others evil. 145. Poor Tom's acold. Edgar's pitiable appearance as Tom and such plaintive cries as these establish the broad allegorical dimension of his character. He embodies the extremes of suffering attendant upon human life. 153. What is the cause of thunder, besides the literal meaning, what provokes divine wrath. 156. study, field of specialization (in philosophy). 175. soothe him, humor him. 178. Athenian. Lear associates the "madman" with the great Greek philosophers. 180. Child Rowland . . . came, a line from an old ballad. "Child" was the title of a candidate for knighthood. 181. word, watchword, motto. The sentence which follows is the Giant's speech in Jack the Giant-Killer. The disjointedness and ominous quality of Edgar's mutterings here provide an appropriate transition for the next scenes, particularly in anticipation of the blinding of Gloucester.
    Sc. v. 3. fears me, frightens me. 11. intelligent party, informant.
    Sc. vi. 6. Fraterretto, name of the devil who informs Edgar of Nero's punishment in hell. 20. It shall . . . straight. Lear proceeds to direct a mock trial of Goneril and Regan. 21. justicer, judge.

[*To the* FOOL] Thou, sapient sir, sit here. Now, you she-foxes!

EDG. Look, where he stands and glares!
Want'st thou eyes at trial, madam?

Come o'er the bourn, Bessy, to me.

FOOL. Her boat hath a leak,
And she must not speak
Why she dares not come over to thee.

EDG. The foul fiend haunts poor Tom in the voice of
30 a nightingale. Hoppedance cries in Tom's belly for two
white herring. Croak not, black angel; I have no food
for thee.

KENT. How do you, sir? Stand you not so amaz'd.
Will you lie down and rest upon the cushions?

LEAR. I'll see their trial first. Bring in their evidence.
[*To* EDGAR] Thou, robed man of justice, take thy place.
[*To the* FOOL] And thou, his yokefellow of equity,
Bench by his side. [*To* KENT] You are o' th' commis-
sion,
Sit you too.

40 EDG. Let us deal justly.

Sleepest or wakest thou, jolly shepherd?
Thy sheep be in the corn;
And for one blast of thy minikin mouth
Thy sheep shall take no harm.

Purr! the cat is gray.

LEAR. Arraign her first. 'Tis Goneril. I here take my
oath before this honourable assembly, she kicked the
poor King her father.

FOOL. Come hither, mistress. Is your name Goneril?

50 LEAR. She cannot deny it.

FOOL. Cry you mercy, I took you for a joint-stool.

LEAR. And here's another, whose warp'd looks pro-
claim
What store her heart is made on. Stop her there!
Arms, arms! sword! fire! Corruption in the place!
False justicer, why hast thou let her 'scape?

EDG. Bless thy five wits!

KENT. O pity! Sir, where is the patience now
That you so oft have boasted to retain?

EDG. [*Aside*] My tears begin to take his part so much
60 They'll mar my counterfeiting.

LEAR. The little dogs and all,
Tray, Blanch, and Sweetheart, see, they bark at me.

EDG. Tom will throw his head at them.
Avaunt, you curs!

Be thy mouth or black or white,
Tooth that poisons if it bite;
Mastiff, greyhound, mongrel grim,
Hound or spaniel, brach or lym,
Bobtail tyke or trundle-tail—
Tom will make them weep and wail;   70
For, with throwing thus my head,
Dogs leap the hatch, and all are fled.

Do 'de, de, de. Sessa! Come, march to wakes and fairs
and market towns. Poor Tom, thy horn is dry.

LEAR. Then let them anatomize Regan. See what
breeds about her heart. Is there any cause in nature
that makes these hard hearts? [*To* EDGAR] You, sir—I
entertain you for one of my hundred; only I do not
like the fashion of your garments. You'll say they are
Persian attire; but let them be chang'd.   80

KENT. Now, good my lord, lie here and rest awhile.

LEAR. Make no noise, make no noise; draw the curtains. So, so, so. We'll go to supper i' th' morning.
So, so, so.

FOOL. And I'll go to bed at noon.

Enter GLOUCESTER.

GLOU. Come hither, friend. Where is the King my
master?

KENT. Here, sir; but trouble him not; his wits are
gone.

GLOU. Good friend, I prithee take him in thy arms.
I have o'erheard a plot of death upon him.
There is a litter ready; lay him in't   90
And drive towards Dover, friend, where thou shalt
meet
Both welcome and protection. Take up thy master.
If thou shouldst dally half an hour, his life,
With thine, and all that offer to defend him,
Stand in assured loss. Take up, take up!
And follow me, that will to some provision
Give thee quick conduct.

KENT.   Oppressed nature sleeps.
This rest might yet have balm'd thy broken senses,
Which, if convenience will not allow,
Stand in hard cure. [*To the* FOOL] Come, help to bear
thy master.   100

23-24. **Look . . . madam.** Edgar bids one of Lear's imaginary defendants
to notice that the "fiend" is a spectator at her hearing. He then woos her
to come over to him to join the devil's faction. 26-28. **Her boat . . .
thee.** The Fool adds that she dare not because she knows her own guilt.
30. **Hoppedance,** a devil's name. 31. **Croak,** rumble (from hunger).
33. **so amaz'd,** so confounded. 43. **minikin,** pretty, little. 45. **the cat,**
a demon in the shape of a cat. 51. **Cry . . . stool,** a conventional
apology for overlooking someone's presence. 53. **store,** substance. 57.
patience, self-control. 61-62. **The little . . . me.** Lear thinks of his household dogs at the palace. 63. **his head.** Another of the play's tensions
between the head and the heart. Regan, for example, demonstrates herself
to be rational but she is nevertheless cruel. Meanwhile, though a madman, poor Tom gallantly promises to protect Lear from the dogs by
the absurd but self-sacrificing gesture of hurling his own "head." 65-72.
Be thy . . . fled. The vicious dogs are implicitly associated with Goneril
and Regan. 68. **lym,** bloodhound. 72. **hatch,** lower part of the two-
part entrance door of a house. 74. **thy horn is dry,** beggar's formula
in asking for a drink. 75-76. **See . . . her heart,** determine the scientific
reason for her cruelty. 76-77. **any cause . . . hearts,** any explanation which
man can fathom for these unaccountable turns of personality towards evil.
78. **entertain,** retain, employ. **my hundred,** the hundred knights originally allotted to Lear. 80. **Persian attire.** Edgar is wearing only a
blanket, perhaps toga-fashion. 82. **curtains.** Lear imagines a splendid
bed. 83. **supper i' th' morning,** suggestive of the play's numerous
reversals of the normal. 100. **Stand in hard cure,** will be difficult to
cure. 101. **Thou must not stay behind.** Symbolically, the wisdom and
experience of the Fool are now part of Lear's character; they have become as if one entity. Moreover, the character of the Fool henceforth
does not reappear in the play nor is his absence ever mentioned (a much-
discussed question in Shakespearian criticism). The playwright's objective

Thou must not stay behind.

GLOU.   Come, come, away!

[*Exeunt all but* EDGAR.]

EDG. When we our betters see bearing our woes,
We scarcely think our miseries our foes.
Who alone suffers suffers most i' th' mind,
Leaving free things and happy shows behind;
But then the mind much sufferance doth o'erskip
When grief hath mates, and bearing fellowship.
How light and portable my pain seems now,
When that which makes me bend makes the King bow,
110 He childed as I fathered! Tom, away!
Mark the high noises, and thyself bewray
When false opinion, whose wrong thought defiles thee,
In thy just proof repeals and reconciles thee.
What will hap more tonight, safe 'scape the King!
Lurk, lurk.   [*Exit.*]

SCENE VII *Gloucester's Castle.*

Enter CORNWALL, REGAN, GONERIL, EDMUND *the Bastard, and* SERVANTS.

CORN. [*To* GONERIL] Post speedily to my lord your
husband, show him this letter. The army of France is
landed.—Seek out the traitor Gloucester.

[*Exeunt some of the* SERVANTS.]

REG. Hang him instantly.

GON. Pluck out his eyes.

CORN. Leave him to my displeasure. Edmund, keep
you our sister company. The revenges we are bound
to take upon your traitorous father are not fit for your
beholding. Advise the Duke where you are going, to a
10 most festinate preparation. We are bound to the like.
Our posts shall be swift and intelligent betwixt us.
Farewell, dear sister; farewell, my Lord of Gloucester.

Enter OSWALD *the Steward.*

How now? Where's the King?

OSW. My Lord of Gloucester hath convey'd him
hence.
Some five or six and thirty of his knights,
Hot questrists after him, met him at gate;
Who, with some other of the lord's dependants,
Are gone with him towards Dover, where they boast
To have well-armed friends.

CORN.   Get horses for your mistress.

20 GON. Farewell, sweet lord, and sister.

CORN. Edmund, farewell.

[*Exeunt* GONERIL, EDMUND, *and* OSWALD.]

Go seek the traitor Gloucester,
Pinion him like a thief, bring him before us.

[*Exeunt other* SERVANTS.]

Though well we may not pass upon his life
Without the form of justice, yet our power
Shall do a court'sy to our wrath, which men
May blame, but not control.

Enter GLOUCESTER, *brought in by two or three.*

Who's there? the traitor?

REG. Ingrateful fox! 'tis he.

CORN. Bind fast his corky arms.

GLOU. What mean your Graces? Good my friends,
consider
You are my guests. Do me no foul play, friends.   30

CORN. Bind him, I say.   [SERVANTS *bind him.*]

REG.   Hard, hard. O filthy traitor!

GLOU. Unmerciful lady as you are, I am none.

CORN. To this chair bind him. Villain, thou shalt
find—   [REGAN *plucks his beard.*]

GLOU. By the kind gods, 'tis most ignobly done
To pluck me by the beard.

REG. So white, and such a traitor!

GLOU.   Naughty lady,
These hairs which thou dost ravish from my chin
Will quicken, and accuse thee. I am your host.
With robber's hands my hospitable favours
You should not ruffle thus. What will you do?   40

CORN. Come, sir, what letters had you late from
France?

REG. Be simple-answer'd, for we know the truth.

CORN. And what confederacy have you with the
traitors
Late footed in the kingdom?

REG. To whose hands have you sent the lunatic
King?
Speak.

GLOU.   I have a letter guessingly set down,
Which came from one that's of a neutral heart,
And not from one oppos'd.

CORN.   Cunning.

REG.   And false.

CORN. Where hast thou sent the King?

GLOU. To Dover.   50

REG. Wherefore to Dover? Wast thou not charg'd at
peril—

in making this bold omission may have been to suggest Lear's symbolic
absorption of the Fool. In addition, Cordelia now returns to Britain
and assumes a good part of the Fool's former dramaturgical function
in relation to Lear; the presence of both the Fool and Cordelia onstage
therefore would have been most awkward. 105. **free**, carefree. **happy
shows**, the appearance of happiness. 107. **bearing**, endurance. 108.
portable, tolerable. 110. **He . . . fathered.** His children are as unnatural as my father. 111. **Mark the high noises.** Pay close attention
to discord in high places. 113. **reconciles thee**, to Gloucester. 114.
safe 'scape the King. May the King escape safely. 115. **Lurk, lurk.**
Meanwhile, remain disguised.
    Sc. vii. 5. **Pluck . . . eyes.** An immediately shocking suggestion which
only Gloucester, knowing Goneril's character, somehow foresees to be
his fate. 10. **most festinate preparation**, the speediest possible mobili-
zation (for war). 16. **questrists**, riders, searchers. Henceforward the

moral universe of the play begins to operate in favor of the oppressed:
the knights ride to join Cordelia, Gloucester's servant is moved to attack
Cornwall, two other servants secretly assist their blinded master, and
so forth. Lear has now expiated his folly; the evil-doers, by their outrage upon Gloucester, have gone too far. Thus the obscurely moral
organism enfolding the world of *Lear* now begins its travail to expel
or scourge the opposing party in their turn. 24. **the form of justice,**
the mere appearance of a fair trial. Gloucester's "trial" contrasts
markedly with Lear's imaginary arraignment of his daughters in the
previous scene. 28. **corky,** withered. 30. **You are my guests.** It was
considered a grave dishonor as well as a crime of the first magnitude to
harm one's host or one's guest. 38. **quicken,** come to life. 51. **at
peril,** under penalty (of death).

William Shakespeare 289

CORN. Wherefore to Dover? Let him first answer
  that.

GLOU. I am tied to th' stake, and I must stand the
  course.

REG. Wherefore to Dover, sir?

GLOU. Because I would not see thy cruel nails
Pluck out his poor old eyes; nor thy fierce sister
In his anointed flesh stick boarish fangs.
The sea, with such a storm as his bare head
In hell-black night endur'd, would have buoy'd up
60 And quench'd the stelled fires.
Yet, poor old heart, he holp the heavens to rain.
If wolves had at thy gate howl'd that stern time,
Thou shouldst have said, 'Good porter, turn the key.'
All cruels else subscrib'd. But I shall see
The winged vengeance overtake such children.

CORN. See't shalt thou never. Fellows, hold the chair.
Upon these eyes of thine I'll set my foot.

GLOU. He that will think to live till he be old,
Give me some help!—O cruel! O ye gods!

70 REG. One side will mock another. Th' other too!

CORN. If you see vengeance—

FIRST SERV.   Hold your hand, my lord!
I have serv'd you ever since I was a child;
But better service have I never done you
Than now to bid you hold.

REG.   How now, you dog?

FIRST SERV. If you did wear a beard upon your chin,
I'd shake it on this quarrel.

REG.   What do you mean?

CORN. My villain!   [Draw and fight.]

FIRST SERV. Nay, then, come on, and take the chance
  of anger.

REG. Give me thy sword. A peasant stand up thus?
          [She takes a sword and runs at him behind.]

FIRST SERV. O, I am slain! My lord, you have one
80   eye left
To see some mischief on him. O!   [He dies.]

CORN. Lest it see more, prevent it. Out, vile jelly!
Where is thy lustre now?

GLOU. All dark and comfortless! Where's my son
  Edmund?
Edmund, enkindle all the sparks of nature
To quit this horrid act.

REG.   Out, treacherous villain!
Thou call'st on him that hates thee. It was he
That made the overture of thy treasons to us;

Who is too good to pity thee.

GLOU. O my follies! Then Edgar was abus'd.   90
Kind gods, forgive me that, and prosper him!

REG. Go thrust him out at gates, and let him smell
His way to Dover.   [Exit one with GLOUCESTER.]
                    How is't, my lord? How look you?

CORN. I have receiv'd a hurt. Follow me, lady.
Turn out that eyeless villain. Throw this slave
Upon the dunghill. Regan, I bleed apace.
Untimely comes this hurt. Give me your arm.
          [Exit CORNWALL, led by REGAN.]

SEC. SERV. I'll never care what wickedness I do,
If this man come to good.

THIRD SERV.   If she live long,
And in the end meet the old course of death,   100
Women will all turn monsters.

SEC. SERV. Let's follow the old Earl, and get the
  bedlam
To lead him where he would. His roguish madness
Allows itself to anything.

THIRD SERV. Go thou. I'll fetch some flax and whites
  of eggs
To apply to his bleeding face. Now heaven help him!
          [Exeunt.]

ACT IV

SCENE I *The heath.*

Enter EDGAR.

EDG. Yet better thus, and known to be contemn'd,
Than still contemn'd and flatter'd. To be worst,
The lowest and most dejected thing of fortune,
Stands still in esperance, lives not in fear.
The lamentable change is from the best;
The worst returns to laughter. Welcome then,
Thou unsubstantial air that I embrace!
The wretch that thou hast blown unto the worst
Owes nothing to thy blasts.

Enter GLOUCESTER, led by an OLD MAN.

                    But who comes here?
My father, poorly led? World, world, O world!   10
But that thy strange mutations make us hate thee,
Life would not yield to age.

OLD MAN.   O my good lord,
I have been your tenant, and your father's tenant,

57. anointed. At coronation the king was consecrated as God's temporal minister. 60. stelled fires, the fires of the stars. 61. he holp the heavens to rain. Lear's suffering mystically brought about a suffusion of divine grace over the realm's troubles (literally, he shed tears). 64. All cruels else subscrib'd. All cruel beasts except yourselves were made mild with the storm. 65. winged vengeance, divine retribution. 69. O ye gods. Gloucester's ejaculation calls upon the supernatural powers presiding over human affairs to dispense justice for this atrocity. Then, as if in answer, a servant dramatically rises to challenge the old man's torturers. Later, Albany interprets the coming forth of this unexpected champion as an act of divine intervention (IV, ii) and he too becomes an avenger for Gloucester. 86. quit, repay. 92-93. let him . . . to Dover. The lower senses in King Lear are aligned with what are usually considered the higher faculties, particularly with perception or insight. Moreover, the characters who most exhibit the ability to reason (Edmund, Goneril) are evil while those who act upon extra-rational humane

instinct (the Fool, Edgar as poor Tom, Gloucester's appalled servants) are most endorsed. Within this symbolic scheme of inversions Lear must go mad before he can be truly sane and Gloucester must be blinded before he can attain a true inner vision of things. 101. Women will all turn monsters, because they will no longer dread vengeance from the gods. 102. the bedlam, the madman (Edgar). 103-104. His roguish madness . . . anything. Since he is known to be mad, he may do anything without fear of being punished for it.
Act IV, Sc. i. 4. Stands still in esperance, continues to admit of hope. Edgar's outlook is characteristically affirmative. 6. The worst . . . laughter. One may expect a return to happiness when one's fortunes have reached their lowest ebb. 8-9. The wretch . . . blasts. The person who has endured the worst possible blows of fortune no longer has a spiritual "debt." 10. My father, poorly led. Gloucester's entrance as the ward of an old man further projects him into the context of Everyman (here, of Everyman at the end of his life's journey). The old man who guides

These fourscore years.

GLOU. Away, get thee away! Good friend, be gone.
Thy comforts can do me no good at all;
Thee they may hurt.

OLD MAN. You cannot see your way.

GLOU. I have no way, and therefore want no eyes;
I stumbled when I saw. Full oft 'tis seen
20 Our means secure us, and our mere defects
Prove our commodities. Ah dear son Edgar,
The food of thy abused father's wrath!
Might I but live to see thee in my touch,
I'ld say I had eyes again!

OLD MAN. How now? Who's there?

EDG. [Aside] O gods! Who is't can say, 'I am at the worst'?
I am worse than e'er I was.

OLD MAN. 'Tis poor mad Tom.

EDG. [Aside] And worse I may be yet. The worst is not
So long as we can say 'This is the worst.'

OLD MAN. Fellow, where goest?

GLOU. Is it a beggarman?

30 OLD MAN. Madman and beggar too.

GLOU. He has some reason, else he could not beg.
I' th' last night's storm I such a fellow saw,
Which made me think a man a worm. My son
Came then into my mind, and yet my mind
Was then scarce friends with him. I have heard more since.
As flies to wanton boys are we to th' gods.
They kill us for their sport.

EDG. [Aside] How should this be?
Bad is the trade that must play fool to sorrow,
Ang'ring itself and others.—Bless thee, master!

GLOU. Is that the naked fellow?

40 OLD MAN. Ay, my lord.

GLOU. Then prithee get thee gone. If for my sake
Thou wilt o'ertake us hence a mile or twain
I' th' way toward Dover, do it for ancient love;
And bring some covering for this naked soul,
Who I'll entreat to lead me.

OLD MAN. Alack, sir, he is mad!

GLOU. 'Tis the time's plague when madmen lead the blind.
Do as I bid thee, or rather do thy pleasure.
Above the rest, be gone.

OLD MAN. I'll bring him the best 'parel that I have,

Come on't what will. [Exit.] 50

GLOU. Sirrah naked fellow—

EDG. Poor Tom's acold. [Aside] I cannot daub it further.

GLOU. Come hither, fellow.

EDG. [Aside] And yet I must.—Bless thy sweet eyes, they bleed.

GLOU. Know'st thou the way to Dover?

EDG. Both stile and gate, horseway and footpath.
Poor Tom hath been scar'd out of his good wits. Bless thee, good man's son, from the foul fiend! Five fiends have been in poor Tom at once: of lust, as Obidicut; Hobbididence, prince of dumbness; Mahu, of stealing; 60 Modo, of murder; Flibbertigibbet, of mopping and mowing, who since possesses chambermaids and waiting women. So, bless thee, master!

GLOU. Here, take this purse, thou whom the heavens' plagues
Have humbled to all strokes. That I am wretched
Makes thee the happier. Heavens, deal so still!
Let the superfluous and lust-dieted man,
That slaves your ordinance, that will not see
Because he does not feel, feel your pow'r quickly;
So distribution should undo excess, 70
And each man have enough. Dost thou know Dover?

EDG. Ay, master.

GLOU. There is a cliff, whose high and bending head
Looks fearfully in the confined deep.
Bring me but to the very brim of it,
And I'll repair the misery thou dost bear
With something rich about me. From that place
I shall no leading need.

EDG. Give me thy arm.
Poor Tom shall lead thee. [Exeunt.]

SCENE II *Before the Duke of Albany's Palace.*

Enter GONERIL *and* EDMUND *the Bastard.*

GON. Welcome, my lord. I marvel our mild husband
Not met us on the way.

Enter OSWALD *the Steward.*

Now, where's your master?

OSW. Madam, within, but never man so chang'd.
I told him of the army that was landed:
He smil'd at it. I told him you were coming:
His answer was, 'The worse.' Of Gloucester's treachery

Gloucester after his ordeal is a kind of symbolic harbinger of death much as the Fool who accompanied Lear onto the heath functioned in part to symbolize an aspect of his master's developing character and experience. 10-12. **World . . . age.** Everyman could commit suicide in view of the seemingly irrational vicissitudes of this life if it were not for the fact that they stir us to anger. 18. **I have no way.** My path in life is at its end. 19-21. **Full oft . . . commodities.** Felicity makes us complacent whereas adversity forces us to contemplate the hard realities of life. 20. **secure us,** make us too comfortable. **defects,** lacks. 21. **commodities,** advantages, benefits. 22. **food,** object. **abused,** deceived. 25. **Who is't . . . I am at the worst.** Edgar now perceives his hopeful attitudes to have become a mockery. He asserts bitterly that there is no bottom to the miseries with which a man can be afflicted; the idea that pain must have an end, he implies, derives only from our inability to imagine infinite suffering. 36-37. **As flies . . . for their sport.** Gloucester seems to suggest that the operation of the universe is irrational

and unjust. However, there is also an implication here to the effect that man may provoke, perhaps even deserve, such treatment from the gods because of his puny, fallible character. 38. **Bad is . . . to sorrow.** Grim are the circumstances which necessitate pretending insanity before one who is in sorrow. 52. **daub,** feign (literally, plaster over). 61-62. **mopping and mowing,** grimacing and making faces. 67. **lust-dieted,** satiated by sexual excess. 68. **slaves your ordinance,** behaves as though the wealth bestowed upon him by the gods did not entail the obligation to employ it charitably. 77-78. **From that place . . . need.** Gloucester expects to die there. 79. **Poor Tom shall lead thee.** The powerful visual impact of this exit—a blind old man being led off by a "madman," his son—intends again to reinforce the substantial layer of allegory evident within the Gloucester-Edgar plot. Here, moreover, Edgar assumes the symbolic role of the Fool's relationship to Lear in his darkest hour.

And of the loyal service of his son
When I inform'd him, then he call'd me sot
And told me I had turn'd the wrong side out.
10 What most he should dislike seems pleasant to him;
What like, offensive.

    GON.   [*To* EDMUND] Then shall you go
      no further.
It is the cowish terror of his spirit,
That dares not undertake. He'll not feel wrongs
Which tie him to an answer. Our wishes on the way
May prove effects. Back, Edmund, to my brother.
Hasten his musters and conduct his pow'rs.
I must change arms at home and give the distaff
Into my husband's hands. This trusty servant
Shall pass between us. Ere long you are like to hear
20 (If you dare venture in your own behalf)
A mistress's command. Wear this.   [*Gives a favour.*]
                    Spare speech.
Decline your head. This kiss, if it durst speak,
Would stretch thy spirits up into the air.
Conceive, and fare thee well.

    EDM. Yours in the ranks of death!   [*Exit.*]
    GON.   My most dear Gloucester!
O, the difference of man and man!
To thee a woman's services are due;
My fool usurps my body.

    OSW.   Madam, here comes my lord.
                    [*Exit.*]
Enter ALBANY.

    GON. I have been worth the whistle.
    ALB.   O Goneril,
30 You are not worth the dust which the rude wind
Blows in your face! I fear your disposition.
That nature which contemns its origin
Cannot be bordered certain in itself.
She that herself will sliver and disbranch
From her material sap, perforce must wither
And come to deadly use.

    GON. No more! The text is foolish.
    ALB. Wisdom and goodness to the vile seem vile;
Filths savour but themselves. What have you done?
40 Tigers, not daughters, what have you perform'd?
A father, and a gracious aged man,
Whose reverence even the head-lugg'd bear would lick,
Most barbarous, most degenerate, have you madded.
Could my good brother suffer you to do it?
A man, a prince, by him so benefited!
If that the heavens do not their visible spirits
Send quickly down to tame these vile offences,
It will come,

Humanity must perforce prey on itself,
Like monsters of the deep.

    GON.   Milk-liver'd man!   50
That bear'st a cheek for blows, a head for wrongs;
Who hast not in thy brows an eye discerning
Thine honour from thy suffering; that not know'st
Fools do those villains pity who are punish'd
Ere they have done their mischief. Where's thy drum?
France spreads his banners in our noiseless land,
With plumed helm thy state begins to threat,
Whiles thou, a moral fool, sit'st still, and criest
'Alack, why does he so?'

    ALB.   See thyself, devil!
Proper deformity seems not in the fiend   60
So horrid as in woman.

    GON.   O vain fool!
    ALB. Thou changed and self-cover'd thing, for shame!
Bemonster not thy feature! Were't my fitness
To let these hands obey my blood,
They are apt enough to dislocate and tear
Thy flesh and bones. Howe'er thou art a fiend,
A woman's shape doth shield thee.

    GON. Marry, your manhood mew!

Enter a GENTLEMAN.

    ALB. What news?
    GENT. O, my good lord, the Duke of Cornwall's
      dead,   70
Slain by his servant, going to put out
The other eye of Gloucester.

    ALB.   Gloucester's eyes?
    GENT. A servant that he bred, thrill'd with remorse,
Oppos'd against the act, bending his sword
To his great master; who, thereat enrag'd,
Flew on him, and amongst them fell'd him dead;
But not without that harmful stroke which since
Hath pluck'd him after.

    ALB.   This shows you are above,
You justicers, that these our nether crimes
So speedily can venge! But O poor Gloucester!   80
Lost he his other eye?

    GENT.   Both, both, my lord.
This letter, madam, craves a speedy answer.
'Tis from your sister.

    GON.   [*Aside*] One way I like this well;
But being widow, and my Gloucester with her,
May all the building in my fancy pluck
Upon my hateful life. Another way
The news is not so tart.—I'll read, and answer. [*Exit.*]

Sc. ii. 12. **cowish**, cowed, cowardly. 15. **May prove effects**, may be fulfilled. 17. **change**, exchange. I must assume the sword and give my husband the distaff (staff used in spinning, the emblem of wifely occupation). 19-24. **Ere long . . . well.** Goneril speaks forwardly and with calculated sexual suggestiveness. 28. **My fool**, my lawful husband, a man fit only to be a jester. Goneril repeatedly calls Albany a fool for his merciful and just disposition. She considers him so, as Albany realizes, because she is too base even to comprehend goodness. Again, the "fools" of the play's universe are its only worthy inhabitants. 29. **worth the whistle**, kept waiting. 31. **fear**, am anxious about.

33. **Cannot be . . . in itself**, can have no certain limits on conduct. 35. **From her material sap**, from her origin, her father; also, from her womanly nature. 37. **text**, of Albany's "sermon." 39. **Filths . . . themselves.** All things taste foul to the filthy (proverb). 42. **head-lugg'd**, dragged along by the head, surly. 63. **Bemonster . . . feature.** Do not allow yourself to be transformed into a monster (by your unnatural acts and these looks of hatred). **Were't my fitness**, if it were right for me to injure a woman, to take justice into my own hands. 68. **your manhood mew**, I say "mew" to your manhood, i.e., I scorn it. 73. **thrill'd with remorse**, aroused by pity. 79. **our nether crimes**,

ALB. Where was his son when they did take his eyes?

GENT. Come with my lady hither.

ALB.   He is not here.

90 GENT. No, my good lord; I met him back again.

ALB. Knows he the wickedness?

GENT. Ay, my good lord. 'Twas he inform'd against
him,
And quit the house on purpose, that their punishment
Might have the freer course.

ALB.   Gloucester, I live
To thank thee for the love thou show'dst the King,
And to revenge thine eyes. Come hither, friend.
Tell me what more thou know'st.   [*Exeunt.*]

SCENE III *The French camp near Dover.*

Enter KENT *and a* GENTLEMAN.

KENT. Why the King of France is so suddenly gone
back know you the reason?

GENT. Something he left imperfect in the state, which
since his coming forth is thought of, which imports to
the kingdom so much fear and danger that his personal return was most required and necessary.

KENT. Who hath he left behind him general?

GENT. The Marshal of France, Monsieur La Far.

KENT. Did your letters pierce the Queen to any
10 demonstration of grief?

GENT. Ay, sir. She took them, read them in my
presence,
And now and then an ample tear trill'd down
Her delicate cheek. It seem'd she was a queen
Over her passion, who, most rebel-like,
Sought to be king o'er her.

KENT.   O, then it mov'd her?

GENT. Not to a rage. Patience and sorrow strove
Who should express her goodliest. You have seen
Sunshine and rain at once: her smiles and tears
Were like, a better way. Those happy smilets
20 That play'd on her ripe lip seem'd not to know
What guests were in her eyes, which parted thence
As pearls from diamonds dropp'd. In brief,
Sorrow would be a rarity most belov'd,
If all could so become it.

KENT.   Made she no verbal question?

GENT. Faith, once or twice she heav'd the name of
father
Pantingly forth, as if it press'd her heart;
Cried 'Sisters, sisters! Shame of ladies! Sisters!
Kent! father! sisters! What, i' th' storm? i' th' night?

Let pity not be believ'd!' There she shook
The holy water from her heavenly eyes,   30
And clamour moisten'd. Then away she started
To deal with grief alone.

KENT.   It is the stars,
The stars above us, govern our conditions;
Else one self mate and mate could not beget
Such different issues. You spoke not with her since?

GENT. No.

KENT. Was this before the King return'd?

GENT.   No, since.

KENT. Well, sir, the poor distressed Lear's i' th'
town;
Who sometime, in his better tune, remembers
What we are come about, and by no means   40
Will yield to see his daughter.

GENT.   Why, good sir?

KENT. A sovereign shame so elbows him; his own
unkindness,
That stripp'd her from his benediction, turn'd her
To foreign casualties, gave her dear rights
To his dog-hearted daughters—these things sting
His mind so venomously that burning shame
Detains him from Cordelia.

GENT.   Alack, poor gentleman!

KENT. Of Albany's and Cornwall's powers you heard
not?

GENT. 'Tis so; they are afoot.

KENT. Well, sir, I'll bring you to our master Lear   50
And leave you to attend him. Some dear cause
Will in concealment wrap me up awhile.
When I am known aright, you shall not grieve
Lending me this acquaintance. I pray you go
Along with me.   [*Exeunt.*]

SCENE IV *The French camp.*

Enter, with Drum and Colours, CORDELIA, DOCTOR, *and*
SOLDIERS.

COR. Alack, 'tis he! Why, he was met even now
As mad as the vex'd sea, singing aloud,
Crown'd with rank fumiter and furrow weeds,
With hardocks, hemlock, nettles, cuckoo flow'rs,
Darnel, and all the idle weeds that grow
In our sustaining corn. A century send forth.
Search every acre in the high-grown field
And bring him to our eye. [*Exit an* OFFICER.] What
can man's wisdom
In the restoring his bereaved sense?
He that helps him take all my outward worth.   10

our crimes on earth.   81. **Both, both.** The stress throughout this interchange on Gloucester's loss of both his eyes also implicates the loss of
both his sons, Edgar outlawed and Edmund a traitor to him.   84-86. **But
being . . . life.** Goneril fears that Regan will entice Edmund into marriage and thus upset her own ambitions, presumably to marry him and
use his services in a campaign to become sole queen of Britain.   87.
tart, disagreeable.   88. **eyes,** the loss of your eyes, your sons.
    Sc. iii. 16. **Not to a rage,** unlike Lear in his violent earlier phase
of character.   19. **a better way,** better than this.   30. **holy water . . .
heavenly eyes.** Cordelia too is implicitly a minister of divine justice.

31. **clamour,** lamentation.   32-35. **It is the stars . . . issues.** It is blind
chance or supernatural manipulation which determines the quality of
our characters.   39. **in his better tune,** during more lucid intervals.
    Sc. iv. 3-5. **fumiter . . . that grow,** names of various weeds (as
opposed, symbolically, to nourishing growths).   6. **corn,** wheat. **century,**
troop of one hundred.   8-9. **What can . . . bereaved sense.** Macbeth's
classic question "Canst thou minister to a mind diseased."

DOCT. There is means, madam.
Our foster nurse of nature is repose,
The which he lacks. That to provoke in him
Are many simples operative, whose power
Will close the eye of anguish.
   COR.   All blest secrets,
All you unpublish'd virtues of the earth,
Spring with my tears! be aidant and remediate
In the good man's distress! Seek, seek for him!
Lest his ungovern'd rage dissolve the life
That wants the means to lead it.

Enter MESSENGER.

20 MESS.   News, madam.
The British pow'rs are marching hitherward.
   COR. 'Tis known before. Our preparation stands
In expectation of them. O dear father,
It is thy business that I go about.
Therefore great France
My mourning and important tears hath pitied.
No blown ambition doth our arms incite,
But love, dear love, and our ag'd father's right.
Soon may I hear and see him!   [*Exeunt.*]

SCENE V *Gloucester's Castle.*

Enter REGAN *and* OSWALD *the Steward.*

   REG. But are my brother's pow'rs set forth?
   OSW.   Ay, madam.
   REG. Himself in person there?
   OSW.   Madam, with much ado.
Your sister is the better soldier.
   REG. Lord Edmund spake not with your lord at
    home?
   OSW. No, madam.
   REG. What might import my sister's letter to him?
   OSW. I know not, lady.
   REG. Faith, he is posted hence on serious matter.
It was great ignorance, Gloucester's eyes being out,
10 To let him live. Where he arrives he moves
All hearts against us. Edmund, I think, is gone,
In pity of his misery, to dispatch
His nighted life; moreover, to descry
The strength o' th' enemy.
   OSW. I must needs after him, madam, with my letter.

   REG. Our troops set forth to-morrow. Stay with us.
The ways are dangerous.
   OSW.   I may not, madam.
My lady charg'd my duty in this business.
   REG. Why should she write to Edmund? Might not
    you
Transport her purposes by word? Belike,   20
Something—I know not what—I'll love thee much—
Let me unseal the letter.
   OSW.   Madam, I had rather—
   REG. I know your lady does not love her husband;
I am sure of that; and at her late being here
She gave strange eliads and most speaking looks
To noble Edmund. I know you are of her bosom.
   OSW. I, madam?
   REG. I speak in understanding. Y'are! I know't.
Therefore I do advise you take this note.
My lord is dead; Edmund and I have talk'd,   30
And more convenient is he for my hand
Than for your lady's. You may gather more.
If you do find him, pray you give him this;
And when your mistress hears thus much from you,
I pray desire her call her wisdom to her.
So farewell.
If you do chance to hear of that blind traitor,
Preferment falls on him that cuts him off.
   OSW. Would I could meet him, madam! I should
    show
What party I do follow.
   REG.   Fare thee well. [*Exeunt.*] 40

SCENE VI *The country near Dover.*

Enter GLOUCESTER, *and* EDGAR *like a Peasant.*

   GLOU. When shall I come to th' top of that same
    hill?
   EDG. You do climb up it now. Look how we labour.
   GLOU. Methinks the ground is even.
   EDG.   Horrible steep.
Hark, do you hear the sea?
   GLOU.   No, truly.
   EDG. Why, then, your other senses grow imperfect
By your eyes' anguish.
   GLOU.   So may it be indeed.
Methinks thy voice is alter'd, and thou speak'st
In better phrase and matter than thou didst.

16. **virtues,** medicinal herbs. 17. **be aidant and remediate,** serve as aids and remedies. Cordelia invokes Nature itself to relieve Lear. 20. **the means,** the sanity; also, the reason for living. **lead.** Both Edgar and Cordelia "lead" their wronged fathers. 26. **important,** importunate. 27-28. **No blown . . . right.** Here the tide of events actively begins its swing to the support of the virtuous people and causes. Pity has been the prime mover of this general moral reorientation in the *Lear* universe. **blown,** proud, selfish.
Sc. v. 2. **With much ado,** as the result of much effort. 9-11. **It was . . . against us.** Again, pity (here, for Gloucester) is the agency of the gathering opposition to Lear's evil daughters and Edmund. 12-13. **In pity of his misery . . . life.** A blatantly hypocritical glossing over of the projected patricide. 20. **Belike,** probably. 25. **eliads,** flirtatious glances. 26. **of her bosom,** in her confidence. 29. **take this note,** consider this hint. 30. **have talk'd,** have come to an understanding. 31. **more convenient,** more fitting. 33. **this,** probably a love token. 38. **Preferment,** advantage, promotion.

Sc. vi. 10. **my garments.** Edgar is no longer dressed as poor Tom. 11-12. **How fearful . . . so low.** Edgar alludes not only to the distance between the "cliff" and the sea but also to the play's great spiritual ordeals that he has witnessed (Gloucester's and Lear's experiences), with despair. He meditates aloud thus morbidly as a stratagem for alleviating his father's state. 13. **choughs,** jackdaws. 14. **gross,** large. 15. **sampire,** samphire, an aromatic relish. It was collected by men lowered down the cliff on ropes, an enterprise which Edgar evidently conceives to be as difficult and perilous as the conduct of life itself. 19. **cock,** cock-boat. 23. **and the deficient sight,** and I, my sight failing me. 38. **quarrel,** question. Gloucester apparently believes that such an attitude would be a greater sin than suicide. However, he has already expressed subversive doubts on the rationality and benevolence of the universe. 42. **conceit,** imagination. 47. **pass,** die. 50. **fathom,** fathoms. **precipitating,** falling headlong. 53. **at each,** placed end to end. 55. **Thy life's a miracle.** Edgar faithfully continues to voice the positive element in human life; he never yields to despair or fatalism.

EDG. Y'are much deceiv'd. In nothing am I chang'd
But in my garments.

GLOU.   Methinks y'are better spoken.

10 EDG. Come on, sir; here's the place. Stand still. How
    fearful
And dizzy 'tis to cast one's eyes so low!
The crows and choughs that wing the midway air
Show scarce so gross as beetles. Halfway down
Hangs one that gathers sampire—dreadful trade!
Methinks he seems no bigger than his head.
The fishermen that walk upon the beach
Appear like mice; and yond tall anchoring bark,
Diminish'd to her cock; her cock, a buoy
20 Almost too small for sight. The murmuring surge
That on th' unnumb'red idle pebble chafes
Cannot be heard so high. I'll look no more,
Lest my brain turn, and the deficient sight
Topple down headlong.

GLOU.   Set me where you stand.

EDG. Give me your hand. You are now within a foot
Of th' extreme verge. For all beneath the moon
Would I not leap upright.

GLOU.   Let go my hand.
Here, friends, 's another purse; in it a jewel
Well worth a poor man's taking. Fairies and gods
30 Prosper it with thee! Go thou further off;
Bid me farewell, and let me hear thee going.

EDG. Now fare ye well, good sir.

GLOU.   With all my heart.

EDG. [Aside] Why I do trifle thus with his despair
Is done to cure it.

GLOU.   O you mighty gods!   [He kneels.]
This world I do renounce, and, in your sights,
Shake patiently my great affliction off.
If I could bear it longer and not fall
To quarrel with your great opposeless wills,
My snuff and loathed part of nature should
40 Burn itself out. If Edgar live, O, bless him!
Now, fellow, fare thee well.

            [He falls forward and swoons.]

EDG.   Gone, sir, farewell.—
And yet I know not how conceit may rob
The treasury of life when life itself
Yields to the theft. Had he been where he thought,
By this had thought been past.—Alive or dead?
Ho you, sir! friend! Hear you, sir? Speak!—
Thus might he pass indeed. Yet he revives.

What are you, sir?

GLOU.   Away, and let me die.

EDG. Hadst thou been aught but gossamer, feathers,
    air,
So many fathom down precipitating,   50
Thou'dst shiver'd like an egg; but thou dost breathe;
Hast heavy substance; bleed'st not; speak'st; art sound.
Ten masts at each make not the altitude
Which thou hast perpendicularly fell.
Thy life's a miracle. Speak yet again.

GLOU. But have I fall'n, or no?

EDG. From the dread summit of this chalky bourn.
Look up a-height. The shrill-gorg'd lark so far
Cannot be seen or heard. Do but look up.

GLOU. Alack, I have no eyes!   60
Is wrechedness depriv'd that benefit
To end itself by death? 'Twas yet some comfort
When misery could beguile the tyrant's rage
And frustrate his proud will.

EDG.   Give me your arm.
Up—so. How is't? Feel you your legs? You stand.

GLOU. Too well, too well.

EDG.   This is above all strangeness.
Upon the crown o' th' cliff what thing was that
Which parted from you?

GLOU.   A poor unfortunate beggar.

EDG. As I stood here below, methought his eyes
Were two full moons; he had a thousand noses,   70
Horns whelk'd and wav'd like the enridged sea.
It was some fiend. Therefore, thou happy father,
Think that the clearest gods, who make them honours
Of men's impossibilities, have preserv'd thee.

GLOU. I do remember now. Henceforth I'll bear
Affliction till it do cry out itself
'Enough, enough,' and die. That thing you speak of,
I took it for a man. Often 'twould say
'The fiend, the fiend'—he led me to that place.

EDG. Bear free and patient thoughts.

Enter LEAR, mad, fantastically dressed with weeds.

                    But who comes here? 80
The safer sense will ne'er accommodate
His master thus.

LEAR. No, they cannot touch me for coining;
I am the King himself.

EDG. O thou side-piercing sight!

---

57. **bourn,** boundary. 63. **beguile,** deceive, elude. As Gloucester laments having been thwarted in the act of ending his own miseries, so Lear at first regrets his restoration to sanity. The spiritual re-ascent of Gloucester and Lear, initiated through the agency of their respective good children, is executed dramaturgically with the most skillful parallelism. Both the fathers undergo a period of profound bitterness, skepticism, and disaffection from life while their two children maintain positions of unconscious philosophical organicism or quasi-religious faith in Nature and exemplify submission to the inscrutable divine will. 67. **what thing.** The unexpected application to Tom o' Bedlam of this neuter noun, reiterated by Gloucester, first casts an aura of some vast, dreadful racial mystery about Edgar's explanation. 69-71. **As I stood . . . sea,** a primordial image of supernatural malignity. 71. **whelk'd,** with wave-like ridges. 72. **some fiend,** recalls poor Tom's outcries about the "foul fiend" who tortures him and, most significant here, persistently tempts him to suicide. Psychologically, the figure represents a timeless inner debate between the positive and the destructive impulses of man's mind

under duress. **father,** title used to address any venerable man, but Edgar evidently finds comfort in thus addressing Gloucester. 73. **clearest,** glorious. 73-74. **who make . . . impossibilities,** carries the proverbial sense of "Man's extremities are God's opportunities." 80. **free,** free from grief, cheerful. **patient.** The virtue of patience is repeatedly enjoined throughout the play. For Lear, in his earlier phase of personality, it connotes restraint, humility, emotional equilibrium, and the like. Later, however, the idea of pious resignation also becomes incorporated into the word. Gloucester's despair and Lear's "rage" are relieved by their final receptivity to this condition of spirit and insight. **Enter Lear, mad.** Cf. Edgar's appearance as poor Tom. In the mad scene which ensues Lear has virtually subsumed the characters of Tom and the Fool; he speaks in their idiom of insanity mixed with disillusioned philosophy and biting satire. 81. **safer sense,** reason. 83. **coining,** counterfeiting money. 85. **side-piercing,** heartbreaking.

LEAR. Nature's above art in that respect. There's your press money. That fellow handles his bow like a crow-keeper. Draw me a clothier's yard. Look, look, a mouse! Peace, peace; this piece of toasted cheese will
90 do't. There's my gauntlet; I'll prove it on a giant. Bring up the brown bills. O, well flown, bird! i' th' clout, i' th' clout! Hewgh! Give the word.

EDG. Sweet marjoram.

LEAR. Pass.

GLOU. I know that voice.

LEAR. Ha! Goneril with a white beard? They flatter'd me like a dog, and told me I had white hairs in my beard ere the black ones were there. To say 'ay' and 'no' to everything I said! 'Ay' and 'no' too was no good
100 divinity. When the rain came to wet me once, and the wind to make me chatter; when the thunder would not peace at my bidding; there I found 'em, there I smelt 'em out. Go to, they are not men o' their words! They told me I was everything. 'Tis a lie—I am not ague-proof.

GLOU. The trick of that voice I do well remember. Is't not the King?

LEAR.   Ay, every inch a king!
When I do stare, see how the subject quakes.
I pardon that man's life. What was thy cause?
110 Adultery?
Thou shalt not die. Die for adultery? No.
The wren goes to't, and the small gilded fly
Does lecher in my sight.
Let copulation thrive; for Gloucester's bastard son
Was kinder to his father than my daughters
Got 'tween the lawful sheets.
To't, luxury, pell-mell! for I lack soldiers.
Behold yond simp'ring dame,
Whose face between her forks presageth snow,
120 That minces virtue, and does shake the head
To hear of pleasure's name.
The fitchew nor the soiled horse goes to't
With a more riotous appetite.
Down from the waist they are Centaurs,
Though women all above.
But to the girdle do the gods inherit,
Beneath is all the fiend's.
There's hell, there's darkness, there's the sulphurous
pit; burning, scalding, stench, consumption. Fie, fie, fie!
130 pah, pah! Give me an ounce of civet, good apothecary,
to sweeten my imagination. There's money for thee.

GLOU. O, let me kiss that hand!

LEAR. Let me wipe it first; it smells of mortality.

GLOU. O ruin'd piece of nature! This great world

Shall so wear out to naught. Dost thou know me?

LEAR. I remember thine eyes well enough. Dost thou squiny at me? No, do thy worst, blind Cupid! I'll not love. Read thou this challenge; mark but the penning of it.

GLOU. Were all the letters suns, I could not see one. 140

EDG. [Aside] I would not take this from report. It is, And my heart breaks at it.

LEAR. Read.

GLOU. What, with the case of eyes?

LEAR. O, ho, are you there with me? No eyes in your head, nor no money in your purse? Your eyes are in a heavy case, your purse in a light. Yet you see how this world goes.

GLOU. I see it feelingly.

LEAR. What, art mad? A man may see how the 150 world goes with no eyes. Look with thine ears. See how yond justice rails upon yond simple thief. Hark in thine ear. Change places and handy-dandy, which is the justice, which is the thief? Thou hast seen a farmer's dog bark at a beggar?

GLOU. Ay, sir.

LEAR. And the creature run from the cur? There thou mightst behold the great image of authority: a dog's obeyed in office.
Thou rascal beadle, hold thy bloody hand!   160
Why dost thou lash that whore? Strip thine own back.
Thou hotly lusts to use her in that kind
For which thou whip'st her. The usurer hangs the
          cozener.
Through tatter'd clothes small vices do appear;
Robes and furr'd gowns hide all. Plate sin with gold,
And the strong lance of justice hurtless breaks;
Arm it in rags, a pygmy's straw does pierce it.
None does offend, none—I say none! I'll able 'em.
Take that of me, my friend, who have the power
To seal th' accuser's lips. Get thee glass eyes   170
And, like a scurvy politician, seem
To see the things thou dost not. Now, now, now, now!
Pull off my boots. Harder, harder! So.

EDG. O, matter and impertinency mix'd!
Reason in madness!

LEAR. If thou wilt weep my fortunes, take my eyes.
I know thee well enough; thy name is Gloucester.
Thou must be patient. We came crying hither;
Thou know'st, the first time that we smell the air
We wawl and cry. I will preach to thee. Mark.   180

GLOU. Alack, alack the day!

LEAR. When we are born, we cry that we are come
To this great stage of fools. This' a good block.

It were a delicate stratagem to shoe
A troop of horse with felt. I'll put 't in proof,
And when I have stol'n upon these sons-in-law,
Then kill, kill, kill, kill, kill, kill!

Enter a GENTLEMAN *with* ATTENDANTS.

GENT. O, here he is! Lay hand upon him.—Sir,
Your most dear daughter—
190 LEAR. No rescue? What, a prisoner? I am even
The natural fool of fortune. Use me well;
You shall have ransom. Let me have a surgeon;
I am cut to th' brains.
GENT.   You shall have anything.
LEAR. No seconds? All myself?
Why, this would make a man a man of salt,
To use his eyes for garden waterpots,
Ay, and laying autumn's dust.
GENT.   Good sir—
LEAR. I will die bravely, like a smug bridegroom.
  What!
I will be jovial. Come, come, I am a king;
200 My masters, know you that?
GENT. You are a royal one, and we obey you.
LEAR. Then there's life in't. Nay, an you get it, you
shall get it by running. Sa, sa, sa, sa!
              [*Exit running.* ATTENDANTS *follow.*]
GENT. A sight most pitiful in the meanest wretch,
Past speaking of in a king! Thou hast one daughter
Who redeems nature from the general curse
Which twain have brought her to.
EDG. Hail, gentle sir.
GENT.   Sir, speed you. What's your will?
EDG. Do you hear aught, sir, of a battle toward?
210   GENT. Most sure and vulgar. Every one hears that
Which can distinguish sound.
EDG.   But, by your favour,
How near's the other army?
GENT. Near and on speedy foot. The main descry
Stands on the hourly thought.
EDG.   I thank you, sir. That's all.
GENT. Though that the Queen on special cause is
    here,
Her army is mov'd on.
EDG.   I thank you, sir.
                              [*Exit* GENTLEMAN.]
GLOU. You ever-gentle gods, take my breath from
    me;
Let not my worser spirit tempt me again

To die before you please!
EDG.   Well pray you, father.
GLOU. Now, good sir, what are you?   220
EDG. A most poor man, made tame to fortune's blows,
Who, by the art of known and feeling sorrows,
Am pregnant to good pity. Give me your hand;
I'll lead you to some biding.
GLOU.   Hearty thanks.
The bounty and the benison of heaven
To boot, and boot!

Enter OSWALD *the Steward.*

OSW.   A proclaim'd prize! Most happy!
That eyeless head of thine was first fram'd flesh
To raise my fortunes. Thou old unhappy traitor,
Briefly thyself remember. The sword is out
That must destroy thee.
GLOU.   Now let thy friendly hand   230
Put strength enough to't.   [EDGAR *interposes.*]
OSW.   Wherefore, bold peasant,
Dar'st thou support a publish'd traitor? Hence!
Lest that th' infection of his fortune take
Like hold on thee. Let go his arm.
EDG. Chill not let go, zir, without vurther 'cagion.
OSW. Let go, slave, or thou diest!
EDG. Good gentleman, go your gait, and let poor voke
pass. An chud ha' bin zwagger'd out of my life, 'twould
not ha' bin zo long as 'tis by a vortnight. Nay, come
not near th' old man. Keep out, che vore ye, or Ise try 240
whether your costard or my ballow be the harder. Chill
be plain with you.
OSW. Out, dunghill!   [*They fight.*]
EDG. Chill pick your teeth, zir. Come! No matter vor
your foins.
                              [OSWALD *falls.*]
OSW. Slave, thou hast slain me. Villain, take my
    purse.
If ever thou wilt thrive, bury my body,
And give the letters which thou find'st about me
To Edmund Earl of Gloucester. Seek him out
Upon the British party. O, untimely death! Death! 250
                                          [*He dies.*]
EDG. I know thee well. A serviceable villain,
As duteous to the vices of thy mistress
As badness would desire.
GLOU.   What, is he dead?
EDG. Sit you down, father; rest you.
Let's see his pockets; these letters that he speaks of
May be my friends. He's dead. I am only sorry
He had no other deathsman. Let us see.

should not arraign or punish another, as Lear did during his reign,
since all are fallible and each equally a sinner in some way; instead, one
should acknowledge his own imperfections and practice forgiveness and pity
towards others. 163. **cozener,** swindler. 164-167. **Through . . . pierce
it.** The lesson of shared essential humanity which Lear learned from the
spectacle of poor Tom's nakedness. 169. **Take that.** He hands Gloucester an imaginary pardon. 174. **impertinency,** incoherence. 182-183. **we
cry . . . stage of fools.** Lear takes the newborn infant's wail to be emblematic of the overall pain of life. 183. **good block,** well-made hat
(nonsense). 185. **put 't in proof,** attempt, test it. 187. **kill . . . kill.**
The weirdly bloodcurdling climax of Lear's harangue on "justice." 191.

The natural fool of fortune, one designed to be a victim of Fortune.
198. **die,** with a pun on the word's sexual meaning. 205-207. **Thou . . .
her to.** The affirmative dimension to the enigma of generation in the play.
210. **vulgar,** generally known. 218. **my worser spirit,** my evil genius,
Edgar's "fiend." 221-223. **A most poor . . . pity.** An apt summation for
the experience of Gloucester and Lear as well. 224. **biding,** refuge, shelter. 229. **Briefly . . . remember.** Recollect your sins, pray. 235. **Chill
. . . 'caigon.** Edgar adopts the rustic southern English dialect. 241. **costard,** head. **ballow,** cudgel. 245. **foins,** thrusts. 257. **deathsman,**
comrade in death.

William Shakespeare **297**

Leave, gentle wax; and, manners, blame us not.
To know our enemies' minds, we'ld rip their hearts;
260 Their papers, is more lawful. [*Reads the letter.*]

    'Let our reciprocal vows be rememb'red. You have many opportunities to cut him off. If your will want not, time and place will be fruitfully offer'd. There is nothing done, if he return the conqueror. Then am I the prisoner, and his bed my jail; from the loathed warmth whereof deliver me, and supply the place for your labour.

      'Your (wife, so I would say) affectionate servant,
                        'GONERIL.'

270 O indistinguish'd space of woman's will!
A plot upon her virtuous husband's life,
And the exchange my brother! Here in the sands
Thee I'll rake up, the post unsanctified
Of murtherous lechers; and in the mature time
With this ungracious paper strike the sight
Of the death-practis'd Duke. For him 'tis well
That of thy death and business I can tell.
    GLOU. The King is mad. How stiff is my vile sense,
That I stand up, and have ingenious feeling
280 Of my huge sorrows! Better I were distract.
So should my thoughts be sever'd from my griefs,
And woes by wrong imaginations lose
The knowledge of themselves. [*A drum afar off.*]
    EDG.   Give me your hand.
Far off methinks I hear the beaten drum.
Come, father, I'll bestow you with a friend. [*Exeunt.*]

SCENE VII *A tent in the French camp.*

Enter CORDELIA, KENT, DOCTOR, *and* GENTLEMAN.

    COR. O thou good Kent, how shall I live and work
To match thy goodness? My life will be short
And every measure fail me.
    KENT. To be acknowledg'd, madam, it o'erpaid.
All my reports go with the modest truth;
Nor more nor clipp'd, but so.
    COR.   Be better suited.
These weeds are memories of those worser hours.
I prithee put them off.
    KENT.   Pardon, dear madam.
Yet to be known shortens my made intent.
10 My boon I make it that you know me not
Till time and I think meet.
    COR. Then be't so, my good lord. [*To the* DOCTOR]
      How does the King?
    DOCT. Madam, sleeps still.

    COR. O you kind gods,
Cure this great breach in his abused nature!
Th' untun'd and jarring senses, O, wind up
Of this child-changed father!
    DOCT.   So please your Majesty
That we may wake the King? He hath slept long.
    COR. Be govern'd by your knowledge, and proceed
I' th' sway of your own will. Is he array'd?   20

Enter LEAR *in a chair carried by* SERVANTS.

    GENT. Ay, madam. In the heaviness of sleep
We put fresh garments on him.
    DOCT. Be by, good madam, when we do awake him.
I doubt not of his temperance.
    COR.   Very well.   [*Music.*]
    DOCT. Please you draw near. Louder the music there!
    COR. O my dear father; restoration hang
Thy medicine on my lips, and let this kiss
Repair those violent harms that my two sisters
Have in thy reverence made!
    KENT.   Kind and dear princess!
    COR. Had you not been their father, these white
      flakes   30
Had challeng'd pity of them. Was this a face
To be oppos'd against the warring winds?
To stand against the deep dread-bolted thunder?
In the most terrible and nimble stroke
Of quick cross lightning? to watch—poor perdu!—
With this thin helm? Mine enemy's dog,
Though he had bit me, should have stood that night
Against my fire; and wast thou fain, poor father,
To hovel thee with swine and rogues forlorn,
In short and musty straw? Alack, alack!   40
'Tis wonder that thy life and wits at once
Had not concluded all.—He wakes. Speak to him.
    DOCT. Madam, do you; 'tis fittest.
    COR. How does my royal lord? How fares your
      Majesty?
    LEAR. You do me wrong to take me out o' th' grave.
Thou art a soul in bliss; but I am bound
Upon a wheel of fire, that mine own tears
Do scald like molten lead.
    COR.   Sir, do you know me?
    LEAR. You are a spirit, I know. When did you die?
    COR. Still, still, far wide!
    DOCT. He's scarce awake. Let him alone awhile.   50
    LEAR. Where have I been? Where am I? Fair
      daylight?
I am mightily abus'd. I should e'en die with pity,
To see another thus. I know not what to say.

I will not swear these are my hands. Let's see.
I feel this pin prick. Would I were assur'd
Of my condition!

    COR.   O, look upon me, sir,
And hold your hands in benediction o'er me.
No, sir, you must not kneel.

    LEAR.   Pray, do not mock me.
60 I am a very foolish fond old man,
Fourscore and upward, not an hour more nor less;
And, to deal plainly,
I fear I am not in my perfect mind.
Methinks I should know you, and know this man;
Yet I am doubtful; for I am mainly ignorant
What place this is; and all the skill I have
Remembers not these garments; nor I know not
Where I did lodge last night. Do not laugh at me;
For (as I am a man) I think this lady
To be my child Cordelia.

70   COR.   And so I am! I am!
    LEAR. Be your tears wet? Yes, faith. I pray weep not.
If you have poison for me, I will drink it.
I know you do not love me; for your sisters
Have, as I do remember, done me wrong.
You have some cause, they have not.

    COR.   No cause, no cause.
    LEAR. Am I in France?

    KENT.   In your own kingdom, sir.
    LEAR. Do not abuse me.

    DOCT. Be comforted, good madam. The great rage
You see is kill'd in him; and yet it is danger
80 To make him even o'er the time he has lost.
Desire him to go in. Trouble him no more
Till further settling.

    COR. Will't please your Highness walk?
    LEAR.   You must bear with me.
Pray you now, forget and forgive. I am old and foolish.
           [Exeunt. Manent KENT and GENTLEMAN.]

    GENT. Holds it true, sir, that the Duke of Cornwall
was so slain?

    KENT. Most certain, sir.

    GENT. Who is conductor of his people?

    KENT. As 'tis said, the bastard son of Gloucester.

90   GENT. They say Edgar, his banish'd son, is with the
Earl of Kent in Germany.

    KENT. Report is changeable. 'Tis time to look about;
the powers of the kingdom approach apace.

    GENT. The arbitrement is like to be bloody. Fare
you well, sir.   [Exit.]

    KENT. My point and period will be throughly
        wrought,
Or well or ill, as this day's battle's fought.   [Exit.]

ACT V

SCENE I *The British camp near Dover.*

Enter, with Drum and Colours, EDMUND, REGAN, GEN-
TLEMAN, *and* SOLDIERS.

    EDM. Know of the Duke if his last purpose hold,
Or whether since he is advis'd by aught
To change the course. He's full of alteration
And self-reproving. Bring his constant pleasure.
                   [Exit an OFFICER.]

    REG. Our sister's man is certainly miscarried
    EDM. 'Tis to be doubted, madam.

    REG.   Now, sweet lord,
You know the goodness I intend upon you.
Tell me—but truly—but then speak the truth—
Do you not love my sister?

    EDM.   In honour'd love.
    REG. But have you never found my brother's way   10
To the forfended place?

    EDM.   That thought abuses you.
    REG. I am doubtful that you have been conjunct
And bosom'd with her, as far as we call hers.

    EDM. No, by mine honour, madam.

    REG. I never shall endure her. Dear my lord,
Be not familiar with her.

    EDM.   Fear me not.
She and the Duke her husband!

Enter, with Drum and Colours, ALBANY, GONERIL,
SOLDIERS.

    GON. [*Aside*] I had rather lose the battle than that
      sister
Should loosen him and me.

    ALB. Our very loving sister, well bemet.   20
Sir, this I hear: the King is come to his daughter,
With others whom the rigour of our state
Forc'd to cry out. Where I could not be honest,
I never yet was valiant. For this business,
It toucheth us as France invades our land,
Not bolds the King, with others whom, I fear,
Most just and heavy causes make oppose.

    EDM. Sir, you speak nobly.

    REG.   Why is this reason'd?

    GON. Combine together 'gainst the enemy;
For these domestic and particular broils   30
Are not the question here.

    ALB.   Let's then determine
With th' ancient of war on our proceeding.

---

fragility are stressed throughout the play. 80. **To make him,** to inform
him of the events of his madness. 83-84. **You must bear with me . . .
foolish.** Lear has now fully acquired humility and forgiveness. His exit
here on Cordelia's arm recalls the poignant last exit of Gloucester with
Edgar. 94. **arbitrement,** decision, outcome. 96-97. **My point . . .
fought.** The completion of my lot in life, for better or worse, depends
on this battle.

    Act V, Sc. i. 4. **constant pleasure,** final determination. 5. **sis-**
ter's man, Oswald. 6. **doubted,** feared. 11. **forfended,** forbidden.
abuses you. You are mistaken. 12. **doubtful,** suspicious. **conjunct,**
united. 16. **Fear me not.** Don't worry about that. 23. **be honest,** act
with conscience. 28. **Why . . . reason'd.** Why bother yourself about the
justice of our cause. 30. **particular,** individual. 32. **th' ancient of
war,** the veterans.

EDM. I shall attend you presently at your tent.
REG. Sister, you'll go with us?
GON. No.
REG. 'Tis most convenient. Pray you go with us.
GON. [Aside] O, ho, I know the riddle.—I will go.
      [As they are going out, enter EDGAR, disguised.]
EDG. If e'er your Grace had speech with man so poor,
Hear me one word.
ALB.   I'll overtake you.—Speak.
      [Exeunt all but ALBANY and EDGAR.]
40 EDG. Before you fight the battle, ope this letter.
If you have victory, let the trumpet sound
For him that brought it. Wretched though I seem,
I can produce a champion that will prove
What is avouched there. If you miscarry,
Your business of the world hath so an end,
And machination ceases. Fortune love you!
ALB. Stay till I have read the letter.
EDG.   I was forbid it.
When time shall serve, let but the herald cry,
And I'll appear again.
50 ALB. Why, fare thee well. I will o'erlook thy paper.
                        [Exit EDGAR.]

Enter EDMUND.

EDM. The enemy's in view; draw up your powers.
Here is the guess of their true strength and forces
By diligent discovery; but your haste
Is now urg'd on you.
ALB.   We will greet the time.   [Exit.]
EDM. To both these sisters have I sworn my love;
Each jealous of the other, as the stung
Are of the adder. Which of them shall I take?
Both? one? or neither? Neither can be enjoy'd,
If both remain alive. To take the widow
60 Exasperates, makes mad her sister Goneril;
And hardly shall I carry out my side,
Her husband being alive. Now then, we'll use
His countenance for the battle, which being done,
Let her who would be rid of him devise
His speedy taking off. As for the mercy
Which he intends to Lear and to Cordelia—
The battle done, and they within our power,
Shall never see his pardon; for my state
Stands on me to defend, not to debate.   [Exit.]

SCENE II A field between the two camps.

Alarum within. Enter, with Drum and Colours, the
Powers of France over the stage, CORDELIA with her
Father in her hand, and exeunt. Enter EDGAR and
GLOUCESTER.

EDG. Here, father, take the shadow of this tree
For your good host. Pray that the right may thrive.
If ever I return to you again,
I'll bring you comfort.
GLOU.   Grace go with you, sir!
                        [Exit EDGAR.]

Alarum and retreat within. Enter EDGAR.

EDG. Away, old man! give me thy hand! away!
King Lear hath lost, he and his daughter ta'en.
Give me thy hand! come on!
GLOU. No further, sir. A man may rot even here.
EDG. What, in ill thoughts again? Men must endure
Their going hence, even as their coming hither;   10
Ripeness is all. Come on.
GLOU.   And that's true too. [Exeunt.]

SCENE III The British camp, near Dover.

Enter, in conquest, with Drum and Colours, EDMUND;
LEAR and CORDELIA as prisoners; SOLDIERS, CAPTAIN.

EDM. Some officers take them away. Good guard
Until their greater pleasures first be known
That are to censure them.
COR.   We are not the first
Who with best meaning have incurr'd the worst.
For thee, oppressed king, am I cast down;
Myself could else outfrown false Fortune's frown.
Shall we not see these daughters and these sisters?
LEAR. No, no, no, no! Come, let's away to prison.
We two alone will sing like birds i' th' cage.
When thou dost ask me blessing, I'll kneel down   10
And ask of thee forgiveness. So we'll live,
And pray, and sing, and tell old tales, and laugh
At gilded butterflies, and hear poor rogues
Talk of court news; and we'll talk with them too—
Who loses and who wins; who's in, who's out—
And take upon 's the mystery of things,
As if we were God's spies; and we'll wear out,
In a wall'd prison, packs and sects of great ones
That ebb and flow by th' moon.

45. **Your business,** your life. 50. **o'erlook,** peruse. 53. **diligent discovery,** careful reconnoitering haste. The rapid movement of events in Act V, the evil characters' frequent adjurations among themselves to make haste, and the accumulation of references to time produce an impression of time's running out on the anti-Lear group and of order about to be restored. 54. **greet the time,** meet the emergency at once. 61. **carry out my side,** win my game (of attempting to be king); possibly a figure from cards. 63. **countenance,** authority, support. 68-69. **my state . . . debate.** The intelligent course for me to follow under the circumstances is to protect myself, not to waste time on weighing the moral issues involved. (Albany has just been scorned for so doing by Edmund's confederates in conscienceless self-seeking.)
  Sc. ii. The two opening stage directions visually reinforce the parallelism between Cordelia and Edgar, Lear and Gloucester. **within,** behind the scenes. The battle is over when Edgar re-enters (a choice specimen

of Shakespeare's later use of classical dramatic condensation). 9-11. **Men . . . Come on.** Appropriately, it is the clear-sighted, affirmative Edgar who utters what may be the play's ultimate experiential formulation or "moral." 11. **Ripeness is all,** our most important consideration in life is to cultivate spiritual preparedness for the death and judgment that shall inevitably overtake us. **And . . . too.** Edgar has succeeded in recalling Gloucester to the state of being that he attained in Act IV (that of enlightened submission before the imponderables of human experience).
  Sc. iii. 2. **greater pleasures,** the wishes of those of higher rank. 3. **censure them,** pass sentence upon them (another of the play's recurrent ironies on "justice"). 13. **gilded butterflies.** Lear's figure suggests that men are actually base and vain or pretentious ("gilded") as well as fragile (like butterflies). **rogues,** wretched people. 16. **mystery,** the elusive larger meanings behind the pain of human experience.

EDM.   Take them away.
20   LEAR. Upon such sacrifices, my Cordelia,
The gods themselves throw incense. Have I caught thee?
He that parts us shall bring a brand from heaven
And fire us hence like foxes. Wipe thine eyes.
The goodyears shall devour 'em, flesh and fell,
Ere they shall make us weep! We'll see 'em starv'd first.
Come.   [Exeunt LEAR and CORDELIA, guarded.]
       EDM.   Come hither, Captain; hark.
Take thou this note [gives a paper]. Go follow them to
       prison.
One step I have advanc'd thee. If thou dost
As this instructs thee, thou dost make thy way
30 To noble fortunes. Know thou this, that men
Are as the time is. To be tender-minded
Does not become a sword. Thy great employment
Will not bear question. Either say thou'lt do't,
Or thrive by other means.
       CAPT.   I'll do't, my lord.
       EDM. About it! and write happy when th' hast done.
Mark—I say, instantly; and carry it so
As I have set it down.
       CAPT. I cannot draw a cart, nor eat dried oats;
If it be man's work, I'll do't.   [Exit.]

Flourish. Enter ALBANY, GONERIL, REGAN, SOLDIERS.

40   ALB. Sir, you have show'd today your valiant strain,
And fortune led you well. You have the captives
Who were the opposites of this day's strife.
We do require them of you, so to use them
As we shall find their merits and our safety
May equally determine.
       EDM.   Sir, I thought it fit
To send the old and miserable King
To some retention and appointed guard;
Whose age has charms in it, whose title more,
To pluck the common bosom on his side
50 And turn our impress'd lances in our eyes
Which do command them. With him I sent the Queen,
My reason all the same; and they are ready
Tomorrow, or at further space, t' appear
Where you shall hold your session. At this time
We sweat and bleed: the friend hath lost his friend;
And the best quarrels, in the heat, are curs'd
By those that feel their sharpness.
The question of Cordelia and her father
Requires a fitter place.

ALB.   Sir, by your patience,
I hold you but a subject of this war,   60
Not as a brother.
       REG.   That's as we list to grace him.
Methinks our pleasure might have been demanded
Ere you had spoke so far. He led our powers,
Bore the commission of my place and person,
The which immediacy may well stand up
And call itself your brother.
       GON.   Not so hot!
In his own grace he doth exalt himself
More than in your addition.
       REG.   In my rights
By me invested, he compeers the best.
       GON. That were the most if he should husband you. 70
       REG. Jesters do oft prove prophets.
       GON.   Holla, holla!
That eye that told you so look'd but asquint.
       REG. Lady, I am not well; else I should answer
From a full-flowing stomach. General,
Take thou my soldiers, prisoners, patrimony;
Dispose of them, of me; the walls are thine.
Witness the world that I create thee here
My lord and master.
       GON.   Mean you to enjoy him?
       ALB. The let-alone lies not in your good will.
       EDM. Nor in thine, lord.
       ALB.   Half-blooded fellow, yes.   80
       REG. [To EDMUND] Let the drum strike, and prove
       my title thine.
       ALB. Stay yet; hear reason. Edmund, I arrest thee
On capital treason; and, in thine attaint,
This gilded serpent [points to GONERIL]. For your claim,
       fair sister,
I bar it in the interest of my wife.
'Tis she is subcontracted to this lord,
And I, her husband, contradict your banes.
If you will marry, make your loves to me;
My lady is bespoke.
       GON.   An interlude!
       ALB. Thou art arm'd, Gloucester. Let the trumpet
       sound.   90
If none appear to prove upon thy person
Thy heinous, manifest, and many treasons,
There is my pledge [throws down a glove]! I'll prove
       it on thy heart,
Ere I taste bread, thou art in nothing less
Than I have here proclaim'd thee.

---

17. **God's,** the only reference to God in the play (the principle of deity or universal law is otherwise generally rendered by the pagan formula of "gods"). 18. **packs and sects,** factions. 19. **by th' moon.** The moon was an emblem of flux and inconstancy. 22. **He . . . heaven.** No human power can ever part us again. Lear's assertion here of the transcendency of their love henceforth over any blows of Fortune or malign human acts continues to have validity even after Cordelia's murder. The positive elements of life in what would otherwise be an unbearably painful and unedifying tragedy are represented throughout this play by its many warm, selfless, personal relationships (Edgar-Gloucester, Lear-Cordelia, the Fool-Kent) and by the numerous instances of basic human goodness or of a compensating system of grace inherent in the universe. 23. **fire us hence,** smoke us from our holes. 24. **The goodyears.** They will eventually be punished by time, fate (literally, the plague). **fell,** skin. 27. **Go follow them.** As commonly occurs in the savage world of

Lear, the moment of affirmation is followed by another unthinkable outrage. 31. **as the time is.** They should be fierce in time of war. 33. **bear question,** admit of discussion, bear moral examination. 39. **man's work,** ironic. It is obviously much more bestial work than that of the cart-horse. 50. **lances . . . eyes.** The image recalls the blinding, as yet unavenged, of Edmund's father. 61. **That's . . . grace him.** That depends on how I wish to honor him. 63-64. **He led . . . person.** Edmund was her immediate representative. 69. **compeers,** equals. 74. **a full-flowing stomach,** furious resentment. 78. **enjoy,** sexually possess. 79. **let-alone,** prohibitive command. 80. **Half-blooded,** illegitimate. 83. **in thine attaint,** as an accomplice. 85-89. **I bar it . . . bespoke,** an elaborate irony. 89. **An interlude.** What a farce.

REG.   Sick, O, sick!

GON. [*Aside*] If not, I'll ne'er trust medicine.

EDM. There's my exchange [*throws down a glove*].
    What in the world he is
That names me traitor, villain-like he lies.
Call by thy trumpet. He that dares approach,
100 On him, on you, who not? I will maintain
My truth and honour firmly.

ALB. A herald, ho!

EDM.   A herald, ho, a herald!

ALB. Trust to thy single virtue; for thy soldiers,
All levied in my name, have in my name
Took their discharge.

REG.   My sickness grows upon me.

ALB. She is not well. Convey her to my tent.

                        [*Exit* REGAN, *led.*]

Enter a HERALD.

Come hither, herald. Let the trumpet sound,
And read out this.

CAPT. Sound, trumpet!   [*A trumpet sounds.*]

110 HER. (*Reads*) 'If any man of quality or degree within
the lists of the army will maintain upon Edmund, supposed Earl of Gloucester, that he is a manifold traitor,
let him appear by the third sound of the trumpet. He
is bold in his defence.'

EDM. Sound!   [*First trumpet.*]

HER. Again!   [*Second trumpet.*]

HER. Again!   [*Third trumpet.*]

                   [*Trumpet answers within.*]

Enter EDGAR, *armed, at the third sound, a Trumpet
before him.*

ALB. Ask him his purposes, why he appears
Upon this call o' th' trumpet.

HER.   What are you?
120 Your name, your quality? and why you answer
This present summons?

EDG.   Know my name is lost;
By treason's tooth bare-gnawn and canker-bit.
Yet am I noble as the adversary
I come to cope.

ALB.   Which is that adversary?

EDG. What's he that speaks for Edmund Earl of
    Gloucester?

EDM. Himself. What say'st thou to him?

EDG.   Draw thy sword,
That, if my speech offend a noble heart,
Thy arm may do thee justice. Here is mine.
Behold, it is the privilege of mine honours,
130 My oath, and my profession. I protest—

Maugre thy strength, youth, place, and eminence,
Despite thy victor sword and fire-new fortune,
Thy valour and thy heart—thou art a traitor;
False to thy gods, thy brother, and thy father;
Conspirant 'gainst this high illustrious prince;
And from th' extremest upward of thy head
To the descent and dust beneath thy foot,
A most toad-spotted traitor. Say thou 'no,'
This sword, this arm, and my best spirits are bent
To prove upon thy heart, whereto I speak,   140
Thou liest.

EDM.   In wisdom I should ask thy name;
But since thy outside looks so fair and warlike,
And that thy tongue some say of breeding breathes,
What safe and nicely I might well delay
By rule of knighthood, I disdain and spurn.
Back do I toss those treasons to thy head;
With the hell-hated lie o'erwhelm thy heart;
Which—for they yet glance by and scarcely bruise—
This sword of mine shall give them instant way
Where they shall rest for ever. Trumpets, speak!   150

                 [*Alarums. Fight.* EDMUND *falls.*]

ALB. Save him, save him!

GON.   This is mere practice, Gloucester.
By th' law of arms thou wast not bound to answer
An unknown opposite. Thou are not vanquish'd,
But cozen'd and beguil'd.

ALB.   Shut your mouth, dame,
Or with this paper shall I stop it.

           [*Shows her her letter to* EDMUND.]

                 [*To* EDMUND] Hold, sir.

[*To* GONERIL] Thou worse than any name, read thine
    own evil.
No tearing, lady! I perceive you know it.

GON. Say if I do—the laws are mine, not thine.
Who can arraign me for't?

ALB.   Most monstrous!
Know'st thou this paper?

GON.   Ask me not what I know.   160

                               [*Exit.*]

ALB. Go after her. She's desperate; govern her.

                         [*Exit an* OFFICER.]

EDM. What you have charg'd me with, that have I
    done,
And more, much more. The time will bring it out.
'Tis past, and so am I.—But what art thou
That hast this fortune on me? If thou'rt noble,
I do forgive thee.

EDG.   Let's exchange charity.
I am no less in blood than thou art, Edmund;
If more, the more th' hast wrong'd me.

96. **medicine**, poison. 103. **virtue**, ability. 122. **canker-bit**, eaten
away by canker. 131. **Maugre**, in spite of. 138. **toad-spotted**, covered
with venomous spots like the toad (a popular notion). 159. **arraign
me**, a ruler cannot be brought to trial. In the broader context of *Lear*
Goneril will of course be "arraigned" by the gods. 161. **govern her**,
restrain her from committing suicide. 163. **much more**. A private reference to the murder of Cordelia that he has commissioned. Edmund
appears coolly talkative throughout the scene because he is stalling for
time, the time the Captain needs to accomplish his mission. Characteris-

tically, Edmund enjoys this final bit of play-acting and takes great vice-
like relish in the perpetration by remote control, as it were, of his
crowning enormity. His later "repentance" thus seems a last fiendish
gesture of blasphemy and exhilarating melodrama; he realizes that the
murder has already been done by that time. 170. **The gods are just.**
Edgar again vindicates divine justice as it has been seen to operate in the
play. 172. **thee he got**, begot you (in adultery). 174. **The wheel**,
Fortune's wheel. **here**, again at the bottom. 181. **nursing**. One learns
a pity in the scheme of *Lear* by feeling or sharing misfortune. 184. **O,**

My name is Edgar and thy father's son.
170 The gods are just, and of our pleasant vices
Make instruments to scourge us.
The dark and vicious place where thee he got
Cost him his eyes.
 EDM.   Th' hast spoken right; 'tis true.
The wheel is come full circle; I am here.
 ALB. Methought thy very gait did prophesy
A royal nobleness. I must embrace thee.
Let sorrow split my heart if ever I
Did hate thee, or thy father!
 EDG.   Worthy prince, I know't.
 ALB. Where have you hid yourself?
180 How have you known the miseries of your father?
 EDG. By nursing them, my lord. List a brief tale;
And when 'tis told, O that my heart would burst!
The bloody proclamation to escape
That follow'd me so near (O, our lives' sweetness!
That with the pain of death would hourly die
Rather than die at once!) taught me to shift
Into a madman's rags, t' assume a semblance
That very dogs disdain'd; and in this habit
Met I my father with his bleeding rings,
190 Their precious stones new lost; became his guide,
Led him, begg'd for him, sav'd him from despair;
Never (O fault!) reveal'd myself unto him
Until some half hour past, when I was arm'd,
Not sure, though hoping of this good success,
I ask'd his blessing, and from first to last
Told him my pilgrimage. But his flaw'd heart
(Alack, too weak the conflict to support!)
'Twixt two extremes of passion, joy and grief,
Burst smilingly.
 EDM.   This speech of yours hath mov'd me,
200 And shall perchance do good; but speak you on;
You look as you had something more to say.
 ALB. If there be more, more woful, hold it in;
For I am almost ready to dissolve,
Hearing of this.
 EDG.   This would have seem'd a period
To such as love not sorrow; but another,
To amplify too much, would make much more,
And top extremity.
Whilst I was big in clamour, came there a man,
Who, having seen me in my worst estate,
210 Shunn'd my abhorr'd society; but then, finding
Who 'twas that so endur'd, with his strong arms
He fastened on my neck, and bellowed out
As he'd burst heaven; threw him on my father;
Told the most piteous tale of Lear and him
That ever ear receiv'd; which in recounting

His grief grew puissant, and the strings of life
Began to crack. Twice then the trumpets sounded,
And there I left him tranc'd.
 ALB.   But who was this?
 EDG. Kent, sir, the banish'd Kent; who in disguise
Followed his enemy king and did him service   220
Improper for a slave.

Enter a GENTLEMAN *with a bloody knife.*

 GENT. Help, help! O, help!
 EDG.   What kind of help?
 ALB.   Speak, man.
 EDG. What means that bloody knife?
 GENT.   'Tis hot, it smokes.
It came even from the heart of—O, she's dead!
 ALB. Who dead? Speak, man.
 GENT. Your lady, sir, your lady! and her sister
By her is poisoned; she hath confess'd it.
 EDM. I was contracted to them both. All three
Now marry in an instant.

Enter KENT.

 EDG.   Here comes Kent.
 ALB. Produce their bodies, be they alive or dead.   230
                [*Exit* GENTLEMAN.]
This judgment of the heavens, that makes us tremble,
Touches us not with pity. O, is this he?
The time will not allow the compliment
That very manners urges.
 KENT.   I am come
To bid my king and master aye good night.
Is he not here?
 ALB.   Great thing of us forgot!
Speak, Edmund, where's the King? and where's
 Cordelia?
   [*The bodies of* GONERIL *and* REGAN *are brought in.*]
Seest thou this object, Kent?
 KENT. Alack, why thus?
 EDM.   Yet, Edmund was belov'd.
The one the other poisoned for my sake,   240
And after slew herself.
 ALB. Even so. Cover their faces.
 EDM. I pant for life. Some good I mean to do,
Despite of mine own nature. Quickly send
(Be brief in't) to the castle; for my writ
Is on the life of Lear and on Cordelia.
Nay, send in time.
 ALB.   Run, run, O, run!
 EDG. To who, my lord? Who has the office? Send
Thy token of reprieve.
 EDM. Well thought on. Take my sword;   250

our lives' sweetness, another affirmation of life. Edgar consistently opposes despair or bitter fatalism and suicide. 196. **pilgrimage.** The occurrence of this term again suggests an allegorical frame of reference.
flaw'd, broken, overburdened. 200. **speak you on.** Edmund continues to
angle for more time. 204. **period,** end. 216. **puissant,** powerful.
221. **Improper for a slave,** unfitting even for a slave, beyond the call
of duty. 223. **'Tis hot,** taken to be a sign or omen testifying that
Goneril was in league with the devil. 228-229. **All ... marry,** are united
in death (an urbane, boastful jest). Edmund's enjoyment of the scene's

dire events and his own wit never flag even though he knows that he
himself is about to die. 233. **compliment,** ceremony. 235. **aye,** forever. 238. **object,** sight. 239-241. **Yet, Edmund ... herself,** a grue-
somely satisfying thought for Edmund the egotist. 244. **mine own nature,**
my natural disposition to be evil (a somewhat deterministic observation in
keeping with his character).

William Shakespeare 303

Give it the Captain.

ALB.   Haste thee for thy life.

                              [*Exit* EDGAR.]

EDM. He hath commission from thy wife and me
To hang Cordelia in the prison and
To lay the blame upon her own despair
That she fordid herself.

ALB. The gods defend her! Bear him hence awhile.

                         [EDMUND *is borne off.*]

Enter LEAR, *with* CORDELIA [*dead*] *in his arms,* EDGAR,
CAPTAIN, *and others following.*

LEAR. Howl, howl, howl, howl! O, you are men of
    stone.
Had I your tongues and eyes, I'ld use them so
That heaven's vault should crack. She's gone for ever!
260 I know when one is dead, and when one lives.
She's dead as earth. Lend me a looking glass.
If that her breath will mist or stain the stone,
Why, then she lives.

KENT.   Is this the promis'd end?

EDG. Or image of that horror?

ALB.   Fall and cease!

LEAR. This feather stirs; she lives! If it be so,
It is a chance which does redeem all sorrows
That ever I have felt.

KENT.   O my good master!

LEAR. Prithee away!

EDG.   'Tis noble Kent, your friend.

LEAR. A plague upon you, murderers, traitors all!
270 I might have sav'd her; now she's gone for ever!
Cordelia, Cordelia! stay a little. Ha!
What is't thou say'st? Her voice was ever soft,
Gentle, and low—an excellent thing in woman.
I kill'd the slave that was a-hanging thee.

CAPT. 'Tis true, my lords, he did.

LEAR.   Did I not, fellow?
I have seen the day, with my good biting falchion
I would have made them skip. I am old now,
And these same crosses spoil me. Who are you?
Mine eyes are not o' th' best. I'll tell you straight.

280 KENT. If fortune brag of two she lov'd and hated,
One of them we behold.

LEAR. This' a dull sight. Are you not Kent?

KENT.   The same—
Your servant Kent. Where is your servant Caius?

LEAR. He's a good fellow, I can tell you that.
He'll strike, and quickly too. He's dead and rotten.

KENT. No, my good lord; I am the very man—

LEAR. I'll see that straight.

KENT. That from your first of difference and decay
Have followed your sad steps.

LEAR.   You're welcome hither.

KENT. Nor no man else! All's cheerless, dark, and
    deadly.   290
Your eldest daughters have fordone themselves,
And desperately are dead.

LEAR.   Ay, so I think.

ALB. He knows not what he says; and vain is it
That we present us to him.

EDG.   Very bootless.

Enter a CAPTAIN.

CAPT. Edmund is dead, my lord.

ALB.   That's but a trifle here.
You lords and noble friends, know our intent.
What comfort to this great decay may come
Shall be applied. For us, we will resign,
During the life of this old Majesty,
To him our absolute power; [*to* EDGAR *and* KENT] you
    to your rights;   300
With boot, and such addition as your honours
Have more than merited.—All friends shall taste
The wages of their virtue, and all foes
The cup of their deservings.—O, see, see!

LEAR. And my poor fool is hang'd! No, no, no life!
Why should a dog, a horse, a rat, have life,
And thou no breath at all? Thou'lt come no more,
Never, never, never, never, never!
Pray you undo this button. Thank you, sir.
Do you see this? Look on her! look! her lips!   310
Look there, look there!   [*He dies.*]

EDG.   He faints! My lord, my lord!

KENT. Break, heart; I prithee break!

EDG.   Look up, my lord.

KENT. Vex not his ghost. O, let him pass! He hates
    him
That would upon the rack of this tough world
Stretch him out longer.

EDG.   He is gone indeed.

KENT. The wonder is, he hath endur'd so long.
He but usurp'd his life.

ALB. Bear them from hence. Our present business
Is general woe. [*To* KENT *and* EDGAR] Friends of my
    soul, you twain
Rule in this realm, and the gor'd state sustain.   320

KENT. I have a journey, sir, shortly to go.
My master calls me; I must not say no.

ALB. The weight of this sad time we must obey,
Speak what we feel, not what we ought to say.
The oldest have borne most; we that are young
Shall never see so much, nor live so long.

                         [*Exeunt with a dead march.*]

(1605; 1623)

255. **fordid**, destroyed. 257. **Howl . . . howl,** another of Lear's eerie primordial shrieks against the unrelenting agony of life in such a universe. 259. **She's gone for ever.** A great many words further emphasizing this burden of finality accrue throughout the scene. 260-261. **I know . . . glass.** The inference is that death and life are virtually interchangeable terms in a world so harsh. 262. **stone,** the mirror's surface. 263. **promis'd end,** Day of Judgment. 264. **image,** exact likeness. **Fall and** cease. Then let the end of all things come. 272. **What . . . say'st.** Lear still labors under the desperate delusion that she may be alive yet. 278. **crosses,** troubles (another possible association with the Passion of Christ). 279. **straight,** in a moment. 280. **If fortune . . . lov'd and hated.** Lear and Cordelia have both experienced the extremes of good and bad fortune. 283. **Caius,** the name Kent used while serving Lear in disguise. 285. **dead and rotten.** Lear now seems to believe that all those who

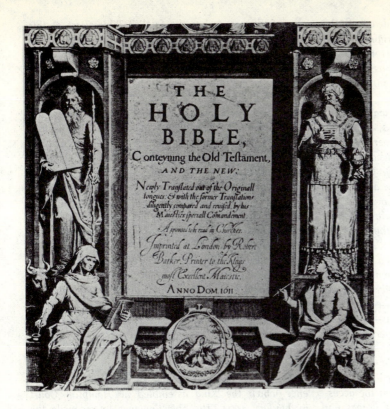

Title page of the King James Bible,
published in 1611.
Historical Pictures Service—Chicago.

THE ENGLISH BIBLE

*As has been already indicated (p. 163), the hub
of the English Reformation was the English Bible.
Under the Protestant dispensation every man might
read the word of God himself, or, if he was illiterate,
he might hear it read in a language which he could
understand. So the English Bible was chained to the
pillars of the churches, and ultimately small and in-
expensive editions came to the family firesides and
to the pockets of individuals. If the English Reformation had been a uniform rebellion against the Roman
Catholic Church, it is conceivable that a correspondingly uniform translation of the Bible might have
resulted. But there was reformation within the Reformation, and the gap, indeed, between Episcopacy
and Presbyterianism seemed at times to be even
greater than that between Episcopacy and Roman
Catholicism. The English Bible tended, therefore, not
only to guide men in the way of life but also in the
doctrines peculiar to one sect or another. So it was*

*that the Puritans at Geneva made their own transla-
tion in 1560, and the Bishops of the Established
Church in England eight years later made another
translation to offset the alarming popularity of the
Geneva version. And the Roman Catholics, for obvious reasons, made their own translation from the
Latin Vulgate. The English translations were made
usually from early Hebrew and Greek manuscripts
and checked carefully against Greek, Latin, Continental, and earlier English translations.*

*A comparison of all these translations gives a fas-
cinating conception of the battle of faiths and doctrines of the period. Here no extended comparison is
possible· a single psalm from the Old Testament has
been chosen, therefore, from six of the leading translations of the period in order that some slight idea of
the variations may be secured. For technical reasons
modern type has been used for all six versions, and
the numerous sidenotes and other interpretations of*

loved him must also be dead. **288. from your first ... decay,** from
the beginning of your decline in fortune. **295. a trifle.** Edmund's death
is hardly sufficient restitution. **297. this great decay,** this ruined king.
305. my poor fool, victim of fortune; my poor darling. There is some
evidence in Elizabethan stage tradition that the same boy actor played
both the roles of the Fool and Cordelia. Moreover, the Fool's disap-
pearance from the action suggestively coincides with the return of

Cordelia. If this doubling of roles was indeed the practice, Lear's cry of
"fool" here would be vastly enlarged in meaning, irony, and stark horror.
309. undo this button, the climax of the imagery of divestiture and
reappareling or rebirth. Lear symbolically leaves the world as naked as
when he was born into it. **310-311. Look ... there.** Lear dies in a state
of delusion. **313. ghost,** departing spirit.

the text according to the doctrinal ideas of the translators have been omitted. The original spellings and usages have, however, been retained. A few words about each translation follows as a supplement to the general treatment in the introductory essay (p. 163).

The first complete Bible in English was that of Miles Coverdale, produced abroad in 1535. Coverdale worked chiefly from German and Latin versions, but his New Testament was much influenced by the earlier work of William Tyndale (1526). Our Bible today owes much to Coverdale for his grace and beauty of phrasing. The Great Bible of 1539, so called because of its size, was a revision of Coverdale's, whence his version of the Psalter passed into the Book of Common Prayer. It was the first Bible "Appointed to be Read in Churches." The Geneva Bible of 1560 was also translated on the Continent by religious refugees. Its popularity arose partly from its small size, its roman type, and its use—for the first time in English biblical translations—of numbers for the verses. Its elaborate notes cover historical and geographical matters and point out the moral lessons to be gathered from the text. It was published in more than one hundred forty editions over a period of eighty-four years, roughly from the accession of Elizabeth to the Civil War. Thus it was not only the Bible of Shakespeare, but that of Cromwell, Milton, Bunyan, and the Pilgrim Fathers as well. The Bishops' Bible of 1568 was translated under the direction of Archbishop Parker by eight bishops and several other scholars in England mainly to replace the authorized "Great Bible" of 1539 but also to counteract the Calvinist trend in the notes of the Geneva Version. In this second purpose it failed, for its size, cost, ornate Gothic type, and uneven quality prevented it from ever becoming popular; so the last edition appeared in 1602, or forty-two years before the last edition of its rival. The Roman Catholic translation of the New Testament was issued at Rheims in 1582, and the Old Testament at Douai in 1609-1610. As with so many of the translations the work was done by religious exiles from England; William Allen directed the translation, and the actual work was done largely by Gregory Martin, an Oxford graduate. The Protestant translations were, of course, not acceptable to the Roman Catholics, and their own translation follows the meaning and the form of St. Jerome's Latin Bible (the Vulgate); thus the Rheims-Douai translation is essentially the Vulgate "in English dress." The version was printed in roman type on a small page. Modern Catholic Bibles in English translation, it may be added, have departed substantially from this Elizabethan version; many are based on the translation of Dr. Richard Challoner (1749-1750).

No other book in English literature has exerted as much influence as has the English Bible. Part of this influence has come, without doubt, from the religious nature of the volume; but religion aside, its effect has been great because of its high merit as a work of literary art. Although drawn from ancient Hebrew and Greek originals and filtered through many translations before the days of Elizabeth and James, the book was made thoroughly English by the inspired craftsmanship of its translators. The nine English translations in the time of the Tudors and James I are an epic of devoted labor. It is the last of the Protestant translations, however, the King James Bible of 1611 (sometimes referred to as the "Authorized Version"), that has come to be regarded as the English Bible. By the middle of the century in which it first appeared, it had displaced the Geneva Version in popularity, and for over three hundred years it has been stamping upon English literature and speech its ideas and its phrases. This result was inevitable. In high seriousness, dignity, power, simplicity, felicity of phrase, and cadence of sentence it is unequaled by any other translation; it has justly been accepted as a great monument not only of the Elizabethan period but of the English people.

The King James Bible had its origin in a conference which the King assembled at Hampton Court in January 1604. His objective was to reconcile the divergent Protestant groups that had been tearing England apart in the reign of Elizabeth. In this he did not succeed. The proposal, however, of Dr. John Reynolds of Oxford that a new translation of the Bible be made which would be acceptable to all religious groups was eagerly adopted; and after some delay, the work was actively begun and pushed to a magnificent conclusion. It was his majesty's suggestion that the translation "bee done by the best learned in both Universities; after them to be reviewed by the Bishops, and the chiefe learned of the Church, from them to be presented to the Privie Counsell, and lastly to be ratified by his Royall Authoritee, and so this whole Church be bound unto it, and none other." The actual work was done by groups of scholars at Westminster, Cambridge, and Oxford, who worked independently and then conferred until they agreed. The Bishops' Bible was used as a guide, but the originals and all earlier translations were diligently consulted. It was inevitable that by this method the inspired work of Tyndale should have formed the basis of the King James Version. The scholars were supported in their labors by ecclesiastical endowments, by the company of stationers, and by the printer, Robert Barker. The translation appeared in 1611, seven years after it had been proposed; within three years it had run through fourteen editions— and after three hundred odd years it still outsells all other English books.

The Bible is not a book but a book of books. History, law, wisdom, biography, poetry, pastoral letters —almost all forms of literature go to the making up of the thirty-nine books of the Old Testament and the twenty-seven of the New. The selections reprinted here represent: in Job, poetry and philosophy; in Psalms, lyric poetry; in Proverbs and Ecclesiastes, poetry and wisdom; in The Birth of Jesus, biography; in The Sermon on the Mount, religious and social philosophy; in The Prodigal Son, a parable; and, finally, in First Corinthians, a pastoral letter of universal significance. Of these the longest—Job —demands fuller comment than the footnotes allow.

The Book of Job has been classified as a drama. Dramatic it is in its situations and almost Aeschylean in its structure and mood. But though Job himself is suggestive of the bound Prometheus, the book is more like a philosophical argument than a drama, an argument in which Job and his three friends, Eliphaz the Temanite, Bildad the Shuhite, and Zophar the Naamathite, debate the ancient problem of the relation of sin and suffering. Job's final act is to ask the Almighty for a solution of the problem, and out of the storm comes the voice of God speaking the magnificent poetry of the last chapters of the book.

THE TWENTY-THIRD PSALM IN SIX TRANSLATIONS

COVERDALE BIBLE, 1535

The Lorde is my shepherde, I can wante nothinge. He fedeth me in a grene pasture, and ledeth me to a fresh water. He quickeneth my soule, and bringeth me forth in the way of rightuousnes for his names sake. Though I shulde walke now in the valley of the shadowe of death, yet I feare no euell, for thou art with me: thy staffe and they shephoke comforte me. Thou preparest a table before me agaynst mine enemies: thou anoyntest my heade with oyle, and fyllest
10 my cuppe full. O let thy louynge kyndnes and mercy folowe me all the dayes of my life, that I maye dwell in the house of the Lorde for euer.

GREAT BIBLE, 1539

The Lorde is my shepherde, therfore can I lack nothing. He shall fede me in a grene pasture, and leade me forth besyde the waters of comforte. He shall conuert my soule, and brynge me forth in the pathes of ryghteousnes for hys names sake. Yee though I walke thorow the valley of the shadow of death, I will feare no euell, for thou art with me: thy
20 rodde and thy staffe comforte me.

Thou shalt prepare a table before me agaynst them that trouble me: thou has anoynted my head with oyle, and my cuppe shal be full.

But thy louynge kyndnes and mercy shall folowe me all the dayes of my lyfe: and I will dwell in the house of the Lord for euer.

GENEVAN BIBLE, 1560

The Lord is my shepherd, I shall not want. He maketh me to rest in grene pasture, and leadeth me by the waters of comforte. He restoreth my soule, and
30 leadeth me in the paths of righteousnes for his Names sake. Yea, thogh I shulde walke through the valley of the shadow of death, I wil feare no euil: for thou

art with me: thy rod and thy staffe, they comforte me. Thou doest prepare a table before me in the sight of mine aduersaries: thou doest anoint mine head with oyle and my cup runneth ouer. Douteles kindenes, and Mercie shal follow me al the dayes of my life, and I shal remaine a long season in the house of the Lord.

BISHOPS' BIBLE, 1568

God is my sheephearde, therfore I can lacke 40 nothyng: he wyll cause me to repose my selfe in pasture full of grasse, and he wyll leade me vnto calme waters.

He wyll conuert my soule: he wyll bring me foorth into the pathes of righteousnesse for his name sake.

Yea though I walke through the valley of the shadow of death, I wyll feare no euyll, for thou art with me, thy rodde and thy staffe be the thynges that do comfort me.

Thou wylt prepare a table before me in the pres- 50 ence of myne aduersaries: thou has annoynted my head with oyle, and my cup shal be brymme full.

Truely felicitie and mercie shal folowe me all the dayes of my life: and I wyll dwell in the house of God for a long tyme.

RHEIMS-DOUAI BIBLE, 1610

Our Lord ruleth me, and nothing shal be wanting to me: in place of pasture there he hath placed me. Vpon the water of refection he hath brought me vp: he hath conuerted my soule. He hath conducted me vpon the pathes of iustice, for his name. For, al- 60 though I shal walke in the middes of the shadow of death, I will not feare euils: because thou art with me. Thy rod and thy staffe: they haue comforted me. Thou has prepared in my sight a table, against them that truble me. Thou hast fatted my head with oyle: and my chalice inebriating how goodlie is it! And thy mercie shal folow me al the dayes of my life: And that I may dwel in the house of our Lord, in longitude of dayes.

The Lord is my shepheard, I shall not want.

He maketh me to lie downe in greene pastures: he leadeth mee beside the still waters.

He restoreth my soule: he leadeth me in the pathes of righteousnes, for his names sake.

Yea though I walke through the valley of the shadowe of death, I will feare no euill: for thou art with me, thy rod and thy staffe, they comfort me.

10 Thou preparest a table before me, in the presence of mine enemies: thou anointest my head with oyle, my cuppe runneth ouer.

Surely goodnes and mercie shall followe me all the daies of my life: and I will dwell in the house of the Lord for euer.

THE LORD ANSWERETH JOB

CHAPTER 38

1 Then the LORD answered Job out of the whirlwind, and said,

2 Who is this that darkeneth counsel by words without knowledge?

3 Gird up now thy loins like a man; for I will 20 demand of thee, and answer thou me.

4 Where wast thou when I laid the foundations of the earth? declare, if thou hast understanding.

5 Who hath laid the measures thereof, if thou knowest? or who hath stretched the line upon it?

6 Whereupon are the foundations thereof fastened? or who laid the corner stone thereof;

7 When the morning stars sang together, and all the sons of God shouted for joy?

8 Or who shut up the sea with doors, when it 30 brake forth, as if it had issued out of the womb?

9 When I made the cloud the garment thereof, and thick darkness a swaddling band for it,

10 And brake up for it my decreed place, and set bars and doors,

11 And said, Hitherto shalt thou come, but no further: and here shall thy proud waves be stayed?

12 Hast thou commanded the morning since thy days; and caused the dayspring to know his place;

13 That it might take hold of the ends of the 40 earth, that the wicked might be shaken out of it?

14 It is turned as clay to the seal; and they stand as a garment.

15 And from the wicked their light is withholden, and the high arm shall be broken.

16 Hast thou entered into the springs of the sea? or hast thou walked in the search of the depth?

17 Have the gates of death been opened unto thee? or hast thou seen the doors of the shadow of death?

18 Hast thou perceived the breadth of the earth? declare if thou knowest it all. 50

19 Where is the way where light dwelleth? and as for darkness, where is the place thereof,

20 That thou shouldest take it to the bound thereof, and that thou shouldest know the paths to the house thereof?

21 Knowest thou it, because thou wast then born? or because the number of thy days is great?

22 Hast thou entered into the treasures of the snow? or hast thou seen the treasures of the hail,

23 Which I have reserved against the time of 60 trouble, against the day of battle and war?

24 By what way is the light parted, which scattereth the east wind upon the earth?

25 Who hath divided a watercourse for the overflowing of waters, or a way for the lightning of thunder;

26 To cause it to rain on the earth, where no man is; on the wilderness, wherein there is no man;

27 To satisfy the desolate and waste ground; and to cause the bud of the tender herb to spring forth? 70

28 Hath the rain a father? or who hath begotten the drops of dew?

29 Out of whose womb came the ice? and the hoary frost of heaven, who hath gendered it?

30 The waters are hid as with a stone, and the face of the deep is frozen.

31 Canst thou bind the sweet influences of Pleiades, or loose the bands of Orion?

32 Canst thou bring forth Mazzaroth in his season? or canst thou guide Arcturus with his sons? 80

33 Knowest thou the ordinances of heaven? canst thou set the dominion thereof in the earth?

34 Canst thou lift up thy voice to the clouds, that abundance of waters may cover thee?

35 Canst thou send lightnings, that they may go, and say unto thee, Here we are?

36 Who hath put wisdom in the inward parts? or who hath given understanding to the heart?

37 Who can number the clouds in wisdom? or who can stay the bottles of heaven, 90

38 When the dust groweth into hardness, and the clods cleave fast together?

39 Wilt thou hunt the prey for the lion? or fill the appetite of the young lions,

40 When they couch in their dens, and abide in the covert to lie in wait?

The Lord Answereth Job, Job 38–42:6. 15. whirlwind, storm, the clouds of which veiled God's glory. 17. Who . . . knowledge; the allusion may be to Elihu, who has been arguing sophomorically and conventionally with Job, or to Job himself, who has dared to set up his own judgment against that of the Almighty. 19. Gird up, etc. Job is challenged to answer some questions relating to God's power. 38. dayspring, dawn. 39. ends of the earth; the allusion is to the gradual spread of light, until it embraces the entire horizon. It is alluded to also as a moral agent which causes the wicked, who hate light, to flee. 41. It . . . seal. As the light spreads, the earth changes its appearance as clay does under a stamp, with all its details becoming sharp and forming a many-colored vestment. 44. high arm, the arm of violence uplifted in the dark. 47. the gates of death. Death is personified here as Sheol, the abode of the dead beneath the seas. 56. then born. The ironic suggestion is made that Job came into being with the creation of light. 58. treasures, treasuries, magazines. 62.

An illustration by William Blake for the book of Job. "When the Morning Stars Sang Together." Reproduced by permission from the original water color in The Pierpont Morgan Library.

41 Who provideth for the raven his food? when his young ones cry unto God, they wander for lack of meat.

CHAPTER 39

100   1 Knowest thou the time when the wild goats of the rock bring forth? or canst thou mark when the hinds do calve?

2 Canst thou number the months *that* they fulfil? or knowest thou the time when they bring forth?

3 They bow themselves, they bring forth their young ones, they cast out their sorrows.

4 Their young ones are in good liking, they grow up with corn; they go forth, and return not unto them.

5 Who hath sent out the wild ass free? or who 110 hath loosed the bands of the wild ass?

light parted; perhaps, how is the light, which appears first in the east, distributed in all directions? 64. overflowing of waters, rain-flood, which follows a channel cut in the heavens. 77. sweet influences, the control which the stars exercise over man's destiny. Pleiades . . . Orion . . . Mazzaroth . . . Arcturus, stars and constellations. 80. his sons, the stars that project from the Great Bear. 87. inward parts . . . heart; since this entire chapter deals with the natural phenomena of the universe, these words may allude to the secret core of nature

rather than to the intelligence of man. 93. the lion. Chapter 39 should logically begin here, for the divine speaker turns at this point from the world of natural phenomena to that of living creatures. 98. they wander; i.e., the parents search for food for their young. 107. in good liking, in good condition. 108. with corn, i.e., in the open fields without man's care. 109. them, the parent animals. 110. wild ass, the frequent symbol in Near Eastern literature of uncontrolled freedom.

6 Whose house I have made the wilderness, and the barren land his dwellings.

7 He scorneth the multitude of the city, neither regardeth he the crying of the driver.

8 The range of the mountains is his pasture, and he searcheth after every green thing.

9 Will the unicorn be willing to serve thee, or abide by thy crib?

10 Canst thou bind the unicorn with his band in the furrow? or will he harrow the valleys after thee?

11 Wilt thou trust him, because his strength is great? or wilt thou leave thy labor to him?

12 Wilt thou believe him, that he will bring home thy seed, and gather it into thy barn?

13 Gavest thou the goodly wings unto the peacocks? or wings and feathers unto the ostrich?

14 Which leaveth her eggs in the earth, and warmeth them in the dust,

15 And forgetteth that the foot may crush them, or that the wild beast may break them.

16 She is hardened against her young ones, as though they were not hers: her labor is in vain without fear;

17 Because God hath deprived her of wisdom, neither hath he imparted to her understanding.

18 What time she lifteth up herself on high, she scorneth the horse and his rider.

19 Hast thou given the horse strength? hast thou clothed his neck with thunder?

20 Canst thou make him afraid as a grasshopper? the glory of his nostrils is terrible.

21 He paweth in the valley, and rejoiceth in his strength: he goeth on to meet the armed men.

22 He mocketh at fear, and is not affrighted; neither turneth he back from the sword.

23 The quiver rattleth against him, the glittering spear and the shield.

24 He swalloweth the ground with fierceness and rage: neither believeth he that it is the sound of the trumpet.

25 He saith among the trumpets, Ha, ha! and he smelleth the battle afar off, the thunder of the captains, and the shouting.

26 Doth the hawk fly by thy wisdom, and stretch her wings toward the south?

27 Doth the eagle mount up at thy command, and make her nest on high?

28 She dwelleth and abideth on the rock, upon the crag of the rock, and the strong place.

29 From thence she seeketh the prey, and her eyes behold afar off.

30 Her young ones also suck up blood: and where the slain are, there is she.

CHAPTER 40

1 Moreover the LORD answered Job, and said,

2 Shall he that contendeth with the Almighty instruct him? he that reproveth God, let him answer it.

3 ¶Then Job answered the LORD, and said,

4 Behold, I am vile; what shall I answer thee? I will lay mine hand upon my mouth.

5 Once have I spoken; but I will not answer: yea, twice; but I will proceed no further.

6 ¶Then answered the LORD unto Job out of the whirlwind, and said,

7 Gird up thy loins now like a man: I will demand of thee, and declare thou unto me.

8 Wilt thou also disannul my judgment? wilt thou condemn me, that thou mayest be righteous?

9 Hast thou an arm like God? or canst thou thunder with a voice like him?

10 Deck thyself now with majesty and excellency; and array thyself with glory and beauty.

11 Cast abroad the rage of thy wrath: and behold every one that is proud, and abase him.

12 Look on every one that is proud, and bring him low; and tread down the wicked in their place.

13 Hide them in the dust together; and bind their faces in secret.

14 Then will I also confess unto thee that thine own right hand can save thee.

15 ¶Behold now behemoth, which I made with thee; he eateth grass as an ox.

16 Lo now, his strength is in his loins, and his force is in the navel of his belly.

17 He moveth his tail like a cedar: the sinews of his stones are wrapped together.

18 His bones are as strong pieces of brass; his bones are like bars of iron.

19 He is the chief of the ways of God: he that made him can make his sword to approach unto him.

20 Surely the mountains bring him forth food, where all the beasts of the field play.

---

7. **unicorn;** not the one-horned beast of medieval folklore, but the wild ox, contrasted here with the domesticated ox. 21. **may break them,** i.e., by trampling on them. 23. **without fear,** i.e., without apprehension for the eggs. 27. **What time,** whenever. **lifteth . . . high,** i.e., in flight. 28. **scorneth,** i.e., she can outrun horse and rider. 30. **thunder.** The allusion is to the shaking of the mane and quivering of the neck. The horse described here is the war horse in battle. 31. **grasshopper,** locust; the allusion is to the horse's bounding. 40. **believeth;** perhaps, he can hardly believe it for joy at the prospect of battle. 42. **Ha, ha!** the snorting of the horse in eager response to the sound of the war trumpets. 43. **thunder of the captains,** the roaring commands of the leaders. 46. **wings . . . south.** The allusion is to the southern migration of the birds at the beginning of the cold season. 59. **Job answered.** Job's answer to God's review of his power is a humble admission of his own lowliness. Then God proceeds to challenge the contender to take the Almighty's place in the universe. 60. **vile,** mean. 62. **Once . . . spoken.** Job refers to what he has said earlier about the Almighty. 63. **proceed no further,** i.e., I will contend with the Almighty no more. 64. **answered the Lord.** God's first address to Job humbled him for his presumption by revealing the omnipotence of the Creator; the second address answers Job's charge that God is unrighteous in his control of the world and particularly in his treatment of him. Job is challenged to assume the Almighty's place. 68. **disannul,** probably, to deny God's righteousness. 77. **in their place,** where they stand. 78. **bind . . . secret,** i.e., imprison them in the house of Death. 82. **behemoth,** probably the hippopotamus, but used here to typify the most monstrous of land creatures. 88. **pieces,** i.e., pipes or rods. 91. **his sword.** The meaning is that the creator

21 He lieth under the shady trees, in the covert of the reed, and fens.

22 The shady trees cover him *with* their shadow; the willows of the brook compass him about.

23 Behold, he drinketh up a river, *and* hasteth not: he trusteth that he can draw up Jordan into his mouth.

24 He taketh it with his eyes: *his* nose pierceth through snares.

CHAPTER 41

1 Canst thou draw out leviathan with a hook? or his tongue with a cord *which* thou lettest down?

2 Canst thou put a hook into his nose? or bore his jaw through with a thorn?

3 Will he make many supplications unto thee? will he speak soft *words* unto thee?

4 Will he make a covenant with thee? wilt thou take him for a servant for ever?

5 Wilt thou play with him as *with* a bird? or wilt thou bind him for thy maidens?

6 Shall the companions make a banquet of him? shall they part him among the merchants?

7 Canst thou fill his skin with barbed irons? or his head with fish spears?

8 Lay thine hand upon him, remember the battle, do no more.

9 Behold, the hope of him is in vain: shall not *one* be cast down even at the sight of him?

10 None *is* so fierce that dare stir him up: who then is able to stand before me?

11 Who hath prevented me, that I should repay *him?* whatsoever *is* under the whole heaven is mine.

12 I will not conceal his parts, nor his power, nor his comely proportion.

13 Who can discover the face of his garment? or who can come *to him* with his double bridle?

14 Who can open the doors of his face? his teeth *are* terrible round about.

15 *His* scales *are his* pride, shut up together *as with* a close seal.

16 One is so near to another, that no air can come between them.

17 They are joined one to another, they stick together, that they cannot be sundered.

18 By his neesings a light doth shine, and his eyes *are* like the eyelids of the morning.

19 Out of his mouth go burning lamps, *and* sparks of fire leap out.

20 Out of his nostrils goeth smoke, as *out* of a seething pot or caldron.

21 His breath kindleth coals, and a flame goeth out of his mouth.

22 In his neck remaineth strength, and sorrow is turned into joy before him.

23 The flakes of his flesh are joined together: they are firm in themselves; they cannot be moved.

24 His heart is as firm as a stone; yea, as hard as a piece of the nether *millstone.*

25 When he raiseth up himself, the mighty are afraid: by reason of breakings they purify themselves.

26 The sword of him that layeth at him cannot hold: the spear, the dart, nor the habergeon.

27 He esteemeth iron as straw, *and* brass as rotten wood.

28 The arrow cannot make him flee: sling stones are turned with him into stubble.

29 Darts are counted as stubble: he laugheth at the shaking of a spear.

30 Sharp stones *are* under him: he spreadeth sharp pointed things upon the mire.

31 He maketh the deep to boil like a pot: he maketh the sea like a pot of ointment.

32 He maketh a path to shine after him; *one* would think the deep *to be* hoary.

33 Upon earth there is not his like, who is made without fear.

34 He beholdeth all high *things:* he *is* a king over all the children of pride.

CHAPTER 42

1 Then Job answered the Lord, and said,

2 I know that thou canst do every *thing,* and *that* no thought can be withholden from thee.

3 Who *is* he that hideth counsel without knowledge? therefore have I uttered that I understood not; things too wonderful for me, which I knew not.

4 Hear, I beseech thee, and I will speak: I will demand of thee, and declare thou unto me.

5 I have heard of thee by the hearing of the ear; but now mine eye seeth thee:

6 Wherefore I abhor *myself,* and repent in dust and ashes.

of this monster can also destroy him. 92. **mountains.** Apparently the suggestion is that behemoth, in seeking food, depastures mountains that would satisfy numerous beasts of the field. 101. **He taketh.** This may suggest the animal's habit of swimming up to his eyes, as though he were drinking with them. 103. **leviathan,** usually interpreted as the crocodile, but the word is sometimes translated *whale.* 106. **thorn,** spike. 114. **part . . . merchants,** i.e., cut him up and sell him as merchandise. 117. **remember . . . more,** i.e., the struggle to capture leviathan will deter you from completing the task. 119. **of him,** i.e., of capturing him. 123. **Who . . . him,** i.e., Who dares to stand before me, who made leviathan? 127. **his garment,** i.e., his scaly coat. 128. **double bridle,** better translated, double coat of mail. 137. **neesings,** sneezings, i.e., his breathing out of spray from his monstrous lungs. 138. **eyelids . . . morning,** i.e., red like the dawn. 139. **burning . . .** **fire.** The allusion is probably to the vapor and spray which he blows into the sunlight as he emerges from the water. 147. **flakes of his flesh, etc.,** i.e., the parts of his body are joined firmly at his neck and joints. 150. **nether *millstone.*** The lower stone which bore all the pressure had to be even harder than the upper one. 152. **by reason . . . themselves,** i.e., because of their fear they are beside themselves. 154. **habergeon,** coat of mail. 161. **he spreadeth . . . mire,** he leaves in the mud where he has been lying the impression of the scales of his belly. 165. **path to shine.** The allusion is to the luminous trail left by his fast swimming. 169. **beholdeth,** looketh boldly on. **high *things,*** great beasts. 170. **children of pride,** proud animals. 174. **hideth counsel;** cf. 38:2. Job confesses that he has spoken without full understanding of God's greatness, and he repents "in dust and ashes."

PSALM 19

To the chief Musician, A Psalm of David.

1 The heavens declare the glory of God; and the firmament showeth his handiwork.

2 Day unto day uttereth speech, and night unto night showeth knowledge.

3 *There is* no speech nor language, *where* their voice is not heard.

4 Their line is gone out through all the earth, and their words to the end of the world. In them hath he set a tabernacle for the sun,

10 5 Which *is* as a bridegroom coming out of his chamber, *and* rejoiceth as a strong man to run a race.

6 His going forth *is* from the end of the heaven, and his circuit unto the ends of it: and there is nothing hid from the heat thereof.

7 The law of the LORD *is* perfect, converting the soul: the testimony of the LORD *is* sure, making wise the simple.

8 The statutes of the LORD *are* right, rejoicing the heart: the commandment of the LORD *is* pure, en-
20 lightening the eyes.

9 The fear of the LORD *is* clean, enduring for ever: the judgments of the LORD *are* true *and* righteous altogether.

10 More to be desired *are they* than gold, yea, than much fine gold: sweeter also than honey and the honeycomb.

11 Moreover by them is thy servant warned: *and* in keeping of them *there is* great reward.

12 Who can understand *his* errors? cleanse thou
30 me from secret *faults.*

13 Keep back thy servant also from presumptuous *sins;* let them not have dominion over me: then shall I be upright, and I shall be innocent from the great transgression.

14 Let the words of my mouth, and the meditation of my heart, be acceptable in thy sight, O LORD, my strength, and my redeemer.

PSALM 24

A Psalm of David.

1 The earth *is* the LORD'S, and the fulness thereof; the world, and they that dwell therein.

40 2 For he hath founded it upon the seas, and established it upon the floods.

3 Who shall ascend into the hill of the LORD? or who shall stand in his holy place?

4 He that hath clean hands, and a pure heart; who hath not lifted up his soul unto vanity, nor sworn deceitfully.

5 He shall receive the blessing from the LORD, and righteousness from the God of his salvation.

6 This *is* the generation of them that seek him, that seek thy face, O Jacob. Selah.   50

7 Lift up your heads, O ye gates; and be ye lifted up, ye everlasting doors; and the King of glory shall come in.

8 Who *is* this King of glory? The LORD strong and mighty, the LORD mighty in battle.

9 Lift up your heads, O ye gates; even lift *them* up, ye everlasting doors; and the King of glory shall come in.

10 Who is this King of glory? The LORD of hosts, he *is* the King of glory. Selah.   60

PSALM 91

1 He that dwelleth in the secret place of the Most High shall abide under the shadow of the Almighty.

2 I will say of the LORD, *He is* my refuge and my fortress: my God; in him will I trust.

3 Surely he shall deliver thee from the snare of the fowler, *and* from the noisome pestilence.

4 He shall cover thee with his feathers, and under his wings shalt thou trust: his truth *shall be thy* shield and buckler.

5 Thou shalt not be afraid for the terror by night; 70 nor for the arrow *that* flieth by day;

6 *Nor* for the pestilence *that* walketh in darkness; nor for the destruction *that* wasteth at noonday.

7 A thousand shall fall at thy side, and ten thousand at thy right hand; *but* it shall not come nigh thee.

8 Only with thine eyes shalt thou behold and see the reward of the wicked.

9 Because thou hast made the LORD, *which is* my refuge, *even* the Most High, thy habitation;

10 There shall no evil befall thee, neither shall any 80 plague come nigh thy dwelling.

11 For he shall give his angels charge over thee, to keep thee in all thy ways.

12 They shall bear thee up in *their* hands, lest thou dash thy foot against a stone.

13 Thou shalt tread upon the lion and adder: the young lion and the dragon shalt thou trample under feet.

14 Because he hath set his love upon me, therefore

Psalm 19. A hymn of praise revealing the orderliness of God's law in the heavens (1–6) and in the heart of man (7–11) with a concluding prayer for guidance (12–14). 5. *where;* omitted in the Revised Version. The meaning is that the spiritual communion of day with day and night with night is silent. 7. **Their line, etc.** Day and night extend their measuring line over the whole earth. 8. **them,** the heavens. 12. **His,** the sun's. 27. **warned;** the chief purpose of God's laws is to warn against sin. 29. **his,** i.e., his own. 31. **presumptuous sins,**

i.e., sins of presumption or pride.

Psalm 24. Anthem sung on the occasion of King David's bringing the ark of God from its exile in the house of Obed-Edom to Jerusalem; cf. 2 Samuel, Chapter 6. The first part of the anthem (1–6) was sung at the foot of the hill upon which the city was built, and the second (7–10) as the ark approached the city gates. 50. **Selah,** a musical direction of some kind, the exact meaning of which is unknown. 52. **everlasting,** ancient. **King of glory;** the Lord was supposed to

90 will I deliver him: I will set him on high, because he hath known my name.

15 He shall call upon me, and I will answer him: I *will be* with him in trouble; I will deliver him, and honor him.

16 With long life will I satisfy him, and show him my salvation.

PSALM 137

1 By the rivers of Babylon, there we sat down, yea, we wept, when we remembered Zion.

2 We hanged our harps upon the willows in the 100 midst thereof.

3 For there they that carried us away captive required of us a song; and they that wasted us *required of us* mirth, *saying,* Sing us *one* of the songs of Zion.

4 How shall we sing the LORD'S song in a strange land?

5 If I forget thee, O Jerusalem, let my right hand forget *her cunning.*

6 If I do not remember thee, let my tongue cleave to the roof of my mouth; if I prefer not Jerusalem 110 above my chief joy.

7 Remember, O LORD, the children of Edom in the day of Jerusalem; who said, Rase *it,* rase *it, even* to the foundation thereof.

8 O daughter of Babylon, who art to be destroyed; happy *shall he be,* that rewardeth thee as thou hast served us.

9 Happy *shall he be,* that taketh and dasheth thy little ones against the stones.

PROVERBS

CHAPTER 8

1 Doth not wisdom cry? and understanding put 120 forth her voice?

2 She standeth in the top of high places, by the way in the places of the paths.

3 She crieth at the gates, at the entry of the city, at the coming in at the doors:

4 Unto you, O men, I call; and my voice *is* to the sons of man.

5 O ye simple, understand wisdom: and, ye fools, be ye of an understanding heart.

6 Hear; for I will speak of excellent things; and the 130 opening of my lips *shall be* right things.

7 For my mouth shall speak truth; and wickedness *is* an abomination to my lips.

8 All the words of my mouth *are* in righteousness; *there is* nothing froward or perverse in them.

9 They *are* all plain to him that understandeth, and right to them that find knowledge.

10 Receive my instruction, and not silver; and knowledge rather than choice gold.

11 For wisdom *is* better than rubies; and all the things that may be desired are not to be compared to 140 it.

12 I wisdom dwell with prudence, and find out knowledge of witty inventions.

13 The fear of the LORD *is* to hate evil: pride, and arrogancy, and the evil way, and the froward mouth, do I hate.

14 Counsel *is* mine, and sound wisdom: I *am* understanding; I have strength.

15 By me kings reign, and princes decree justice.

16 By me princes rule, and nobles, *even* all the 150 judges of the earth.

17 I love them that love me; and those that seek me early shall find me.

18 Riches and honor *are* with me; *yea,* durable riches and righteousness.

19 My fruit *is* better than gold, yea, than fine gold; and my revenue than choice silver.

20 I lead in the way of righteousness, in the midst of the paths of judgment:

21 That I may cause those that love me to inherit 160 substance; and I will fill their treasures.

22 The LORD possessed me in the beginning of his way, before his works of old.

23 I was set up from everlasting, from the beginning, or ever the earth was.

24 When *there were* no depths, I was brought forth; when *there were* no fountains abounding with water.

25 Before the mountains were settled, before the hills was I brought forth: 170

26 While as yet he had not made the earth, nor the fields, nor the highest part of the dust of the world.

27 When he prepared the heavens, I *was* there: when he set a compass upon the face of the depth:

28 When he established the clouds above: when he strengthened the fountains of the deep:

29 When he gave to the sea his decree, that the waters should not pass his commandment: when he appointed the foundations of the earth:

30 Then I was by him, *as* one brought up *with him:* 180 and I was daily *his* delight, rejoicing always before him;

31 Rejoicing in the habitable part of his earth; and my delights *were* with the sons of men.

manifest his presence in the sacred ark; it became, therefore, the symbol of the Almighty.

Psalm 91. A song of thanksgiving and praise for God's protection in time of trouble. 65. **thee;** the psalmist is addressing himself.

Psalm 137. An elegy of exile during the period of captivity in Babylon. 98. **Zion,** a hill in Jerusalem. To exiled Jews it became the symbol of the homeland. 107. **cunning,** i.e., to play the harp. 111. **Edom,** a country south of the Dead Sea; the inhabitants, traditionally descended from Esau, sided with the army of Nebuchadnezzar, king of Babylon, against Judah. The last part of this psalm (7-9) is a vigorous hymn of hate. 112. **day of Jerusalem,** i.e., when Jerusalem is restored.

Proverbs, Chapter 8. This chapter and the preceding one form together one of the most magnificent tributes to wisdom in any literature. In Chapter 8, Wisdom personified is represented as speaking, offering her riches to all men and declaring her divine origin and ancient lineage.

32 Now therefore hearken unto me, O ye children: for blessed *are they that* keep my ways.

33 Hear instruction, and be wise, and refuse it not.

34 Blessed *is* the man that heareth me, watching daily at my gates, waiting at the posts of my doors.

35 For whoso findeth me findeth life, and shall obtain favor of the LORD.

36 But he that sinneth against me wrongeth his own soul: all they that hate me love death.

ECCLESIASTES

CHAPTER 12

10   1 Remember now thy Creator in the days of thy youth, while the evil days come not, nor the years draw nigh, when thou shalt say, I have no pleasure in them;

2 While the sun, or the light, or the moon, or the stars, be not darkened, nor the clouds return after the rain:

3 In the day when the keepers of the house shall tremble, and the strong men shall bow themselves, and the grinders cease because they are few, and those 20 that look out of the windows be darkened,

4 And the doors shall be shut in the streets, when the sound of the grinding is low, and he shall rise up at the voice of the bird, and all the daughters of music shall be brought low;

5 Also *when* they shall be afraid of *that which is* high, and fears *shall be* in the way, and the almond tree shall flourish, and the grasshopper shall be a burden, and desire shall fail: because man goeth to his long home, and the mourners go about the streets:

30   6 Or ever the silver cord be loosed, or the golden bowl be broken, or the pitcher be broken at the fountain, or the wheel broken at the cistern.

7 Then shall the dust return to the earth as it was: and the spirit shall return unto God who gave it.

8 ¶Vanity of vanities, saith the Preacher; all *is* vanity.

9 And moreover, because the. Preacher was wise, he still taught the people knowledge; yea, he gave good heed, and sought out, *and* set in order many proverbs.

40   10 The Preacher sought to find out acceptable words: and *that which was* written *was* upright, *even* words of truth.

11 The words of the wise *are* as goads, and as nails fastened *by* the masters of assemblies, *which* are given from one shepherd.

12 And further, by these, my son, be admonished: of making many books *there is* no end; and much study *is* a weariness of the flesh.

13 ¶Let us hear the conclusion of the whole matter: Fear God, and keep his commandments: for this *is* 50 the whole *duty* of man.

14 For God shall bring every work into judgment, with every secret thing, whether *it be* good, or whether *it be* evil.

THE BIRTH OF JESUS

1 And it came to pass in those days, that there went out a decree from Caesar Augustus, that all the world should be taxed.

2 (*And* this taxing was first made when Cyrenius was governor of Syria.)

3 And all went to be taxed, every one into his own 60 city.

4 And Joseph also went up from Galilee, out of the city of Nazareth, into Judea, unto the city of David, which is called Bethlehem, (because he was of the house and lineage of David,)

5 To be taxed with Mary his espoused wife, being great with child.

6 And so it was, that, while they were there, the days were accomplished that she should be delivered.

7 And she brought forth her firstborn son, and 70 wrapped him in swaddling clothes, and laid him in a manger; because there was no room for them in the inn.

8 And there were in the same country shepherds abiding in the field, keeping watch over their flock by night.

9 And, lo, the angel of the Lord came upon them, and the glory of the Lord shone round about them; and they were sore afraid.

10 And the angel said unto them, Fear not: for, 80 behold, I bring you good tidings of great joy, which shall be to all people.

11 For unto you is born this day in the city of David a Saviour, which is Christ the Lord.

12 And this *shall be* a sign unto you; Ye shall find

Ecclesiastes 12. The Hebrew title of the book is *Koheleth.* The English equivalent is usually given as *Preacher;* actually it should be *Debater,* for Koheleth was the Hebrew philosopher who, arguing pro and con, tried to sound the depths of the mystery of life. Chapter 12 forms the justly famous conclusion of this short wisdom book. It is a poetical lyric on the end of life, with an emphasis on the idea that the fear of God is the whole duty of man. At times the imagery is so startlingly brilliant that it is difficult to interpret. This elegy may be compared to Shakespeare's dirge to Fidele in *Cymbeline,* IV, ii (p. 262). 17. **keepers of the house.** The approach of old age is represented as being like the coming of a storm, which strikes fear in the hearts of the householders, causes the operators of mills to cease work, and the women to draw away from the windows. Allegorically, this is often explained as alluding to the growing infirmities of old age—weakened legs, fewer teeth, dimmed eyes, etc. 21. **doors shall be shut,** a continued allusion to the approaching storm of old age. 22. **rise up . . . bird.** Usually interpreted as referring to the sleeplessness of old age which is disturbed by the early chirping of a bird. 23. **daughters . . . low,** a possible allusion to increasing deafness. 25. **be afraid . . . high;** perhaps, fear to climb because of loss of strength. 26. **almond . . . flourish.** Of this enigmatic phrase there have been dozens of explanations; one might suspect it of alluding to the bitterness of old age were it not for the fact that Jordan almonds are notably sweet. It may allude for this reason to the old man's loss of taste for dainty food; and since the locust was also a delicacy, the same loss of appetite may be suggested by the following phrase "desire shall fail." 28. **his long home;** this has become the proverbial phrase for the grave. 30. **silver cord.** The figures in this verse are symbols of the end of all. The first two probably refer to the failure of the lamp of life and the cord that supported it; the last two to the similar failure of the fountain of life. 35. **Vanity of vanities.** The elegy on old age and death completed, the Debater returns to his general contemplation of the true end of living. 40. **acceptable words,** words that delight. 43. **nails . . . masters, etc.**

the babe wrapped in swaddling clothes, lying in a manger.

13 And suddenly there was with the angel a multitude of the heavenly host praising God, and saying,

90 14 Glory to God in the highest, and on earth peace, good will toward men.

15 And it came to pass, as the angels were gone away from them into heaven, the shepherds said one to another, Let us now go even unto Bethlehem, and see this thing which is come to pass, which the Lord hath made known unto us.

16 And they came with haste, and found Mary and Joseph, and the babe lying in a manger.

17 And when they had seen *it*, they made known
100 abroad the saying which was told them concerning this child.

18 And all they that heard *it* wondered at those things which were told them by the shepherds.

19 But Mary kept all these things, and pondered *them* in her heart.

20 And the shepherds returned, glorifying and praising God for all the things that they had heard and seen, as it was told unto them.

from THE SERMON ON THE MOUNT

1 Take heed that ye do not your alms before men,
110 to be seen of them: otherwise ye have no reward of your Father which is in heaven.

2 Therefore when thou doest *thine* alms, do not sound a trumpet before thee, as the hypocrites do in the synagogues and in the streets, that they may have glory of men. Verily I say unto you, They have their reward.

3 But when thou doest alms, let not thy left hand know what thy right hand doeth:

4 That thine alms may be in secret: and thy
120 Father which seeth in secret himself shall reward thee openly.

5 ¶And when thou prayest, thou shalt not be as the hypocrites *are*: for they love to pray standing in the synagogues and in the corners of the streets, that they may be seen of men. Verily I say unto you, They have their reward.

6 But thou, when thou prayest, enter into thy closet, and when thou hast shut thy door, pray to thy Father which is in secret; and thy Father which seeth in secret shall reward thee openly. 130

7 But when ye pray, use not vain repetitions, as the heathen *do*: for they think that they shall be heard for their much speaking.

8 Be not ye therefore like unto them: for your Father knoweth what things ye have need of, before ye ask him.

9 After this manner therefore pray ye: Our Father which art in heaven, Hallowed be thy name.

10 Thy kingdom come. Thy will be done in earth, as *it is* in heaven. 140

11 Give us this day our daily bread.

12 And forgive us our debts, as we forgive our debtors.

13 And lead us not into temptation, but deliver us from evil: For thine is the kingdom, and the power, and the glory, for ever. Amen.

14 For if ye forgive men their trespasses, your heavenly Father will also forgive you:

15 But if ye forgive not men their trespasses, neither will your Father forgive your trespasses. 150

16 ¶Moreover when ye fast, be not, as the hypocrites, of a sad countenance: for they disfigure their faces, that they may appear unto men to fast. Verily I say unto you, They have their reward.

17 But thou, when thou fastest, anoint thine head, and wash thy face;

18 That thou appear not unto men to fast, but unto thy Father which is in secret: and thy Father which seeth in secret shall reward thee openly.

19 ¶Lay not up for yourselves treasures upon earth, 160 where moth and rust doth corrupt, and where thieves break through and steal:

20 But lay up for yourselves treasures in heaven, where neither moth nor rust doth corrupt, and where thieves do not break through nor steal:

21 For where your treasure is, there will your heart be also.

22 The light of the body is the eye: if therefore thine eye be single, thy whole body shall be full of light. 170

23 But if thine eye be evil, thy whole body shall be full of darkness. If therefore the light that is in thee be darkness, how great *is* that darkness!

24 ¶No man can serve two masters: for either he will hate the one, and love the other; or else he will

More correctly translated by J. M. Powis Smith: "The words of the wise are like goads; and collections which are given by one teacher are like nails driven with a sledge." 47. **many books.** Hebrew teaching was oral; much reading of books was therefore condemned. **The Birth of Jesus,** Luke 2:1–20. This is the more famous and detailed of the two accounts of the birth; the other is in the first two chapters of Matthew. The order of the gospels is: Matthew, Mark, Luke, John; for obvious reasons, however, the story of Jesus' birth is put here before the record of his teachings. 55. **in those days;** the allusion is to the account in Chapter 1 of the birth of John the Baptist and the Annunciation to the Virgin Mary. 56. **Caesar Augustus,** first Roman emperor (ruled 27 B.C.–14 A.D.). **all . . . taxed,** an enrollment or census preliminary to taxation. 58. **Cyrenius . . . Syria.** Judea was not annexed to the Province of Syria until 61 A.D.; but at the time of the birth of Jesus the whole of Palestine was under Roman rule, with Herod only a puppet of Caesar. 60. **to be taxed,** i.e., to register. 90. **Glory . . . men.** According to many ancient manuscripts this should read: Glory to God in the highest and peace on earth to men of good will. 104. **these things,** these words.
The Sermon on the Mount, Matthew, Chapter 6. Jesus' sermon was delivered to his disciples as they gathered around him on a mountain top. The general theme is the Kingdom of Heaven, its subjects, laws, and characteristics. It begins with the beatitudes (5:3–12) and proceeds through a simple but vivid reinterpretation of the spiritual wisdom of the Old Testament. The sermon covers Chapters 5, 6, and 7; of these Chapter 6, containing the Lord's Prayer, has been selected for reprinting. At the conclusion of the sermon "the people were astonished at his doctrine: for he taught them as one having authority, and not as the scribes." 128. **closet,** a private room set aside for prayer. 131. **vain,** useless, mechanical. 142. **debts,** sins; i.e., we may expect God's pardon only in proportion to the forgiveness we have extended to others. 169. **single,** sound, healthy. 171. **evil,** diseased.

hold to the one, and despise the other. Ye cannot serve God and mammon.

25 Therefore I say unto you, Take no thought for your life, what ye shall eat, or what ye shall drink; nor yet for your body, what ye shall put on. Is not the life more than meat, and the body than raiment?

26 Behold the fowls of the air: for they sow not, neither do they reap, nor gather into barns; yet your heavenly Father feedeth them. Are ye not much better than they?

27 Which of you by taking thought can add one cubit unto his stature?

28 And why take ye thought for raiment? Consider the lilies of the field, how they grow; they toil not, neither do they spin:

29 And yet I say unto you, That even Solomon in all his glory was not arrayed like one of these.

30 Wherefore, if God so clothe the grass of the field, which to-day is, and to-morrow is cast into the oven, *shall he* not much more *clothe* you, O ye of little faith?

31 Therefore take no thought, saying, What shall we eat? or, What shall we drink? or, Wherewithal shall we be clothed?

32 (For after all these things do the Gentiles seek:) for your heavenly Father knoweth that ye have need of all these things.

33 But seek ye first the kingdom of God, and his righteousness; and all these things shall be added unto you.

34 Take therefore no thought for the morrow: for the morrow shall take thought for the things of itself. Sufficient unto the day *is* the evil thereof.

THE PRODIGAL SON

11 And he said, A certain man had two sons:

12 And the younger of them said to *his* father, Father, give me the portion of goods that falleth *to me*. And he divided unto them *his* living.

13 And not many days after the younger son gathered all together, and took his journey into a far country, and there wasted his substance with riotous living.

14 And when he had spent all, there arose a mighty famine in that land; and he began to be in want.

15 And he went and joined himself to a citizen of that country; and he sent him into his fields to feed swine.

16 And he would fain have filled his belly with the husks that the swine did eat: and no man gave unto him.

17 And when he came to himself, he said, How many hired servants of my father's have bread enough and to spare, and I perish with hunger!

18 I will arise and go to my father, and will say unto him, Father, I have sinned against heaven, and before thee,

19 And am no more worthy to be called thy son: make me as one of thy hired servants.

20 And he arose, and came to his father. But when he was yet a great way off, his father saw him, and had compassion, and ran, and fell on his neck, and kissed him.

21 And the son said unto him, Father, I have sinned against heaven, and in thy sight, and am no more worthy to be called thy son.

22 But the father said to his servants, Bring forth the best robe, and put *it* on him; and put a ring on his hand, and shoes on *his* feet:

23 And bring hither the fatted calf, and kill *it*; and let us eat, and be merry:

24 For this my son was dead, and is alive again; he was lost, and is found. And they began to be merry.

25 Now his elder son was in the field: and as he came and drew nigh to the house, he heard music and dancing.

26 And he called one of the servants, and asked what these things meant.

27 And he said unto him, Thy brother is come; and thy father hath killed the fatted calf, because he hath received him safe and sound.

28 And he was angry, and would not go in: therefore came his father out, and entreated him.

29 And he answering said to *his* father, Lo, these many years do I serve thee, neither transgressed I at any time thy commandment; and yet thou never gavest me a kid, that I might make merry with my friends:

30 But as soon as this thy son was come, which hath devoured thy living with harlots, thou hast killed for him the fatted calf.

31 And he said unto him, Son, thou art ever with me, and all that I have is thine.

2. **mammon,** wealth. 3. **Take no thought,** i.e., do not be anxious. 12. **cubit,** a linear measure of approximately eighteen inches. **stature.** The reference is probably not to height but, by a figure of speech, to the span of life. 18. **grass,** general term for green herbage. 19. **cast . . . oven,** i.e., dried and burned for fuel. 25. **the Gentiles,** the non-Jewish world; the suggestion is that Jews should have loftier desires than do the heathen. 33. **Sufficient . . . thereof,** i.e., today has its own anxieties; do not borrow distress from the future.
The Prodigal Son, Luke 15:11–32. "All these things spake Jesus unto the multitude in parables; and without a parable spake he not unto them" (Matthew, 13:34). Parables are the most characteristic and frequently used of Jesus' didactic methods; they were, indeed, the natural way of making clear the spiritual truths which were the subjects of his teaching. A parable is an extended comparison in which an abstract concept is expressed in concrete descriptive or narrative

terms. Jesus made man's spiritual and social relationships clear by likening them to simple events and elements in the daily lives of his listeners. Of his numerous parables the story of the prodigal son is one of the most famous; here he expresses God's mercy to a repentant sinner by telling of the forgiveness of an earthly father for a derelict son. Simple, direct, clear; these were the characteristics of all his parables. 36. **the portion of goods.** By law (Deuteronomy 21:17) this would be one third. 48. **husks,** literally, the pods of the carob-tree which were sometimes eaten by the very poor. 66. **robe . . . ring . . . shoes.** These details reveal not only the low state of the prodigal but the willingness of his father to receive him as a son and not as a servant. 68. **kill,** i.e., sacrifice as a thank offering. 81. **angry.** His sin is to be understood as that of self-righteousness; he also needed his father's forgiveness.

32 It was meet that we should make merry, and be glad: for this thy brother was dead, and is alive again; and was lost, and is found.

FIRST CORINTHIANS

CHAPTER 13

1 Though I speak with the tongues of men and of angels, and have not charity, I am become *as* sounding brass, or a tinkling cymbal.

2 And though I have *the gift of* prophecy, and 100 understand all mysteries, and all knowledge; and though I have all faith, so that I could remove mountains, and have not charity, I am nothing.

3 And though I bestow all my goods to feed *the poor,* and though I give my body to be burned, and have not charity, it profiteth me nothing.

4 Charity suffereth long, *and* is kind; charity envieth not; charity vaunteth not itself, is not puffed up,

5 Doth not behave itself unseemly, seeketh not her own, is not easily provoked, thinketh no evil;

6 Rejoiceth not in iniquity, but rejoiceth in the 110 truth;

7 Beareth all things, believeth all things, hopeth all things, endureth all things.

8 Charity never faileth: but whether *there be* prophecies, they shall fail; whether *there be* tongues, they shall cease; whether *there be* knowledge, it shall vanish away.

9 For we know in part, and we prophesy in part.

10 But when that which is perfect is come, then that which is in part shall be done away. 120

11 When I was a child, I spake as a child, I understood as a child, I thought as a child: but when I became a man, I put away childish things.

12 For now we see through a glass, darkly; but then face to face: now I know in part; but then shall I know even as also I am known.

13 And now abideth faith, hope, charity, these three; but the greatest of these *is* charity.

SIR FRANCIS BACON 1561-1626

In 1592, at about the time when Christopher Marlowe was creating in Dr. Faustus a scholar who exchanged his soul for knowledge, a brilliant young philosopher wrote to his kinsman, Lord Burleigh: "I confess that I have as vast contemplative ends as I have moderate civil ends, for I have taken all knowledge to be my province." This bold assertion expressed Francis Bacon's lifelong creed, he was concerned with civil preferment only because a government appointment would make possible an unrestricted devotion to his titanic purpose of surveying all knowledge and reorganizing it for the benefit of mankind. This task he never did complete, but the very fragments of his immense labors have gained for him a secure position as a gigantic intellect and a pioneer in the realms of light. In philosophy it was Bacon's work more than that of any other man which carried Elizabethan thought forward into the Restoration period and beyond.

Francis Bacon was born in London in 1561. His father, Sir Nicholas Bacon, was lord keeper of the great seal, and his older brother, Anthony, had a brilliant political career. Bacon was educated at Cambridge and trained further by a service from 1576-1579 at the English embassy in France. On his return to England he sought a government appointment by petitioning Burleigh, a kinsman on his mother's side of the house, but during Elizabeth's reign preferment was slow in coming—perhaps because of the self-

confident and aggressive manner of his seeking it. Tired of waiting he studied law and was admitted to the bar in 1582. Two years later he became a member of Parliament. In 1597 he became one of the Queen's learned counsels, and on the accession of James I he was appointed one of the King's ordinary counsels. Under James his political advancement was rapid. In 1607 he became solicitor general; in 1613, attorney general; in 1616, privy councilor; in 1617, lord keeper; and in 1618 he reached the height of his political career by becoming lord chancellor. Accompanying these offices were various honors and recognitions; he was knighted—with three hundred others—on the accession of James in 1603; he was created Baron Verulam in 1618, and Viscount St. Albans in 1621. In this same year came his sudden and rapid fall from the pyramid to which he had been raised, for he was accused of having taken bribes, confessed the charge, and was deprived of all his offices, fined heavily, imprisoned, and barred from court and from sitting in Parliament. The imprisonment was short and the fine was mitigated, but never again did he fill a Parliamentary seat. Five years later the aging philosopher stepped from the shelter of his coach in early April to experiment with the preservative qualities of snow; the resulting chill killed him on April 9, 1626.

All of Bacon's high offices and dignities he persisted in regarding as secondary to his literary labors, and these he continued eagerly to the very end, dying almost literally with pen in hand. The list of his productions began with a thin volume of essays published in 1597; a second edition, much enlarged, appeared in 1612, and the final and complete collection came out in 1625, a year before his death. Of his philosophical work The Advancement of Learning was published in 1605, the Novum Organum in 1620, and the De Augmentis Scientiarum in 1623. The Sylva Sylvarum and the New Atlantis (written 1624) were left unfinished. In 1622, the year after his disgrace, he issued the History of Henry VII.

Bacon's piquant essays will long be regarded as the most literary of his writings; certainly they are the most popular. Growing out of his habit of filling memorandum books with digests and observations, and written as a relief from his more serious labors, they provide, nevertheless, a body of concentrated and aphoristic wisdom unequaled in English literature. His style varied in the quarter century covered by the essays; on the whole, however, they display a sense of perspicuity, methodical arrangement, and verbal economy beyond that of any other prose of the period. They are more worldly-wise than spiritual, as practical guides in the conduct of life they are uncannily brilliant and helpful.

Bacon's essays, however, are but chips from his workshop. His massive writings are closely related to his unified plan of life, a plan so bold in conception and so extensive in scope that no one man could have fulfilled it. It was no less than the creation of a great "instauration," or renewal of science. He aimed first to study all existing sciences and all existing methods of acquiring truth; second, to develop a new organon, or scientific method for interpreting nature; and third to reconstruct all knowledge on the basis of the new plan. The language was to be Latin, that the work might be permanent. This ambitious plan was beyond the power of any man, beyond even a Bacon; but the great fragments of it which he did complete are amazing in their penetration and power. His Advancement of Learning is really a prelude to the first part of his plan; and the De Augmentis Scientiarum is an elaboration of it in Latin. The Sylva Sylvarum contributes to his review of the existing state of knowledge. The greatest work connected with the plan of the Instauration is the Novum Organum; it contains the famous analysis of human fallacies that obscure the light of understanding. The New Atlantis, never "perfected," would seem to be a thing apart from the great scheme of writing. Actually it is not. Although it presents an ideal commonwealth, just as does More's Utopia, it differs radically from the Utopia in emphasizing the place in the perfect republic not of government and social institutions but of the light of the intellect. More was hardly a prophet; Bacon was one, for his ideal vision of a Society of Scholars and Scientists laboring together to do as a group what—he had come to realize—no one could do as an individual became a reality in the founding in 1662 of the Royal Society. The spirit of Francis Bacon must have attended the ceremonies of that inauguration.

The ideas of Bacon which emerge in all of his writings reveal him to be a true pioneer of thought and learning. Knowledge by authority he despised, and syllogistic reasoning he condemned as unsound. The establishment of man's empire over nature depends upon knowledge, in his view, and the just and methodical process which leads to sound truth must be inductive, for true knowledge is a knowledge of causes, and experience and observation must precede general truths.

While the pioneering intellect of Bacon is still widely admired, his private moral failure and final disgrace have continued to draw censure. Alexander Pope, for example, considered him "the wisest, brightest, meanest of mankind," a species of fallen angel. Cardinal Newman, in the nineteenth century, deplored Bacon's meagerness of aspiration, viewing the ultimate spiritual deficiency of such a mind as an early argument against the pursuit of knowledge divorced from virtue. Bacon's personal reputation remains unrehabilitated, but he has acquired a well-deserved new laurel, the title of "father of modern technology." To some, in fact, Bacon has become a virtual archetype of the "soulless scientist." The monument of his literary accomplishment cannot, however, be slighted, and it is for his incisive, rather magisterial essays, above all, that Bacon will continue to be reverenced as well as read.

ESSAYS OR COUNSELS—CIVIL AND MORAL

1. OF TRUTH

"What is truth?" said jesting Pilate, and would not stay for an answer. Certainly there be that delight in giddiness, and count it a bondage to fix a belief; affecting free-will in thinking, as well as in acting. And though the sects of philosophers of that kind be gone, yet there remain certain discoursing wits which are of the same veins, though there be not so much blood in them as was in those of the ancients. But it is not only the difficulty and labor which men

---

Essays or Counsels. 1. **Pilate,** Roman procurator of Judea before whom Jesus was tried. Pilate's question was addressed to Jesus, who had just testified that he came into the world to bear witness unto the truth; but the ruler did not wait for Jesus' answer (John 18:37–38). 2. **that,** those who. 3. **giddiness,** lightness of thought. 5. **philosophers . . . kind,** the sceptics, the Greek sophists and members of later philosophical schools who believed that all knowledge is uncertain. 6. **discoursing,** discursive. 13. **One . . . Grecians,** Lucian (120?–200?), Greek satirist. 14. **stand,** halt. 20. **masques . . . triumphs;** the figure alludes to the elaborate court entertainments produced at night. 31. **One of the fathers,** the church father St. Augustine (354–430). 32. **vinum daemonum,** the devil's wine. 44. **creature,** created thing.

take in finding out of truth, nor again that when it is found it imposeth upon men's thoughts, that doth bring lies in favor; but a natural though corrupt love of the lie itself. One of the later school of the Grecians examineth the matter, and is at a stand to think what should be in it, that men should love lies; where neither they make for pleasure, as with poets; nor for advantage, as with the merchant; but for the lie's sake. But I cannot tell; this same truth is a naked and open daylight, that doth not show the masques and mummeries and triumphs of the world, half so stately and daintily as candlelights. Truth may perhaps come to the price of a pearl, that showeth best by day; but it will not rise to the price of a diamond or carbuncle, that showeth best in varied lights. A mixture of a lie doth ever add pleasure. Doth any man doubt, that if there were taken out of men's minds vain opinions, flattering hopes, false valuations, imaginations as one would, and the like, but it would leave the minds of a number of men poor shrunken things, full of melancholy and indisposition, and unpleasing to themselves? One of the fathers, in great severity, called poesy *vinum dae-monum*, because it filleth the imagination, and yet it is but with the shadow of a lie. But it is not the lie that passeth through the mind, but the lie that sinketh in and settleth in it, that doth the hurt, such as we spake of before. But howsoever these things are thus in men's depraved judgments and affections, yet truth, which only doth judge itself, teacheth that the inquiry of truth, which is the love-making or wooing of it, the knowledge of truth, which is the presence of it, and the belief of truth, which is the enjoying of it, is the sovereign good of human nature. The first creature of God, in the works of the days, was the light of the sense; the last was the light of reason; and his sabbath work, ever since, is the illumination of his Spirit. First he breathed light upon the face of the matter or chaos; then he breathed light into the face of man; and still he breathed and inspireth light into the face of his chosen. The poet that beautified the sect that was otherwise inferior to the rest, saith yet excellently well: *It is a pleasure to stand upon the shore, and to see ships tossed upon the sea: a pleasure to stand in the window of a castle, and to see a battle and the adventures thereof below: but no pleasure is comparable to the standing upon the vantage ground of Truth* (a hill not to be commanded, and where the air is always clear and serene), *and to see the errors, and wanderings, and mists, and tempests, in the vale below:* so always that this prospect be with pity, and not with swelling or pride. Certainly, it is heaven

upon earth, to have a man's mind move in charity, rest in providence, and turn upon the poles of truth.

To pass from theological and philosophical truth, to the truth of civil business: it will be acknowledged, even by those that practise it not, that clear and round dealing is the honor of man's nature; and that mixture of falsehood is like alloy in coin of gold and silver; which may make the metal work the better, but it embaseth it. For these winding and crooked courses are the goings of the serpent; which goeth basely upon the belly, and not upon the feet. There is no vice that doth so cover a man with shame as to be found false and perfidious. And therefore Montaigne saith prettily, when he inquired the reason, why the word of the lie should be such a disgrace and such an odious charge? Saith he, *If it be well weighed, to say that a man lieth, is as much to say as that he is brave towards God and a coward towards men. For a lie faces God, and shrinks from man.* Surely the wickedness of falsehood and breach of faith cannot possibly be so highly expressed, as in that it shall be the last peal to call the judgments of God upon the generations of men; it being foretold, that when Christ cometh, *he shall not find faith upon the earth.*
(1625)

5. OF ADVERSITY

It was an high speech of Seneca (after the manner of the Stoics): *That the good things which belong to prosperity are to be wished; but the good things that belong to adversity are to be admired. Bona rerum secundarum optabilia, adversarum mirabilia.* Certainly, if miracles be the command over nature, they appear most in adversity. It is yet a higher speech of his than the other (much too high for a heathen). *It is true greatness to have in one the frailty of a man, and the security of a god. Vere magnum, habere fragilitatem hominis, securitatem dei.* This would have done better in poesy, where transcendences are more allowed. And the poets indeed have been busy with it; for it is in effect the thing which is figured in that strange fiction of the ancient poets, which seemeth not to be without mystery; nay, and to have some approach to the state of a Christian: that *Hercules, when he went to unbind Prometheus* (by whom human nature is represented), *sailed the length of the great ocean in an earthen pot or pitcher:* lively describing Christian resolution, that saileth in the frail bark of the flesh through the waves of the world. But to speak in a mean. The virtue of prosperity is temperance; the virtue of

works of the days, the creation; see Genesis 1:3–26. **51. poet,** Lucretius (96?–55? B.C.), Roman poet; in his *De Rerum Natura (On the Nature of Things)* he ascribed grace to the sect of the Epicureans upon whose philosophy he based his poem. **59. errors,** windings. **61. so,** provided. **76. Montaigne,** French philosopher and essayist (1533–1592). **85. foretold,** Luke 18:8; Jesus' words form a question, not an assertion, as here. **91. admired,** wondered at (Latin, *admiror*). **99. transcendences,** hyperboles, exaggerations. **105. Hercules . . . Prometheus.** In Greek mythology Prometheus was a Titan chained by Zeus to a rock on Mt. Caucasus for stealing fire from the heavens; he was ultimately released by Hercules, son of Zeus and Alcmena. **110. in a mean,** moderately, without exaggeration.

adversity is fortitude; which in morals is the more heroical virtue. Prosperity is the blessing of the Old Testament; adversity is the blessing of the New; which carrieth the greater benediction, and the clearer revelation of God's favor. Yet even in the Old Testament, if you listen to David's harp, you shall hear as many hearse-like airs as carols; and the pencil of the Holy Ghost hath labored more in describing the afflictions of Job than the felicities of Solomon. Prosperity is not without many fears and distastes; and adversity is not without comforts and hopes. We see in needleworks and embroideries, it is more pleasing to have a lively work upon a sad and solemn ground, than to have a dark and melancholy work upon a lightsome ground: judge therefore of the pleasure of the heart by the pleasure of the eye. Certainly virtue is like precious odors, most fragrant when they are incensed or crushed: for prosperity doth best discover vice; but adversity doth best discover virtue.

(1625)

7. OF PARENTS AND CHILDREN

The joys of parents are secret, and so are their griefs and fears: they cannot utter the one, nor they will not utter the other. Children sweeten labors, but they make misfortunes more bitter: they increase the cares of life, but they mitigate the remembrance of death. The perpetuity by generation is common to beasts; but memory, merit, and noble works are proper to men: and surely a man shall see the noblest works and foundations have proceeded from childless men, which have sought to express the images of their minds, where those of their bodies have failed: so the care of posterity is most in them that have no posterity. They that are the first raisers of their houses are most indulgent towards their children; beholding them as the continuance not only of their kind but of their work; and so both children and creatures.

The difference in affection of parents towards their several children is many times unequal, and sometimes unworthy, especially in the mother; as Solomon saith: "A wise son rejoiceth the father, but an ungracious son shames the mother." A man shall see, where there is a house full of children, one or two of the eldest respected, and the youngest made wantons; but in the midst some that are as it were forgotten, who many times nevertheless prove the best. The illiberality of parents in allowance towards their children is an harmful error; makes them base; acquaints them with shifts; makes them sort with mean company; and makes them surfeit more when they come to plenty: and therefore the proof is best, when men keep their authority towards their children, but not their purse. Men have a foolish manner (both parents and schoolmasters and servants) in creating and breeding an emulation between brothers during childhood, which many times sorteth to discord when they are men, and disturbeth families. The Italians make little difference between children and nephews or near kinsfolks; but so they be of the lump, they care not though they pass not through their own body. And, to say truth, in nature it is much a like matter; insomuch that we see a nephew sometimes resembleth an uncle or a kinsman more than his own parents, as the blood happens. Let parents choose betimes the vocations and courses they mean their children should take; for then they are most flexible; and let them not too much apply themselves to the disposition of their children, as thinking they will take best to that which they have most mind to. It is true, that if the affection or aptness of the children be extraordinary, then it is good not to cross it; but generally the precept is good, *Optimum elige, suave et facile illud faciet consuetudo.* Younger brothers are commonly fortunate, but seldom or never where the elder are disinherited.

(1612, 1625)

8. OF MARRIAGE AND SINGLE LIFE

He that hath wife and children hath given hostages to fortune; for they are impediments to great enterprises, either of virtue or mischief. Certainly, the best works, and of greatest merit for the public, have proceeded from the unmarried or childless men, which both in affection and means have married and endowed the public. Yet it were great reason that those that have children should have greatest care of future times; unto which they know they must transmit their dearest pledges. Some there are, who though they lead a single life, yet their thoughts do end with themselves, and account future times impertinences. Nay, there are some other that account wife and children but as bills of charges. Nay more, there are some foolish rich covetous men that take a pride in having no children, because they may be thought so much the richer. For perhaps they have heard some talk: "Such an one is a great rich man," and another except to it: "Yea, but he hath a great charge of children"; as if it were an abatement to his riches. But the most ordinary cause of a single life is liberty; especially in certain self-pleasing and humorous minds, which are so sensible of every restraint, as they will go near to

6. **David's harp**, the Psalms of King David; see p. 312. 13. **sad**, dull, somber. 40. **Solomon saith**, Proverbs 10:1. 44. **wantons**, spoiled darlings. 47. **illiberality . . .** allowance, stinginess in providing for. 49. **sort**, consort, associate. 51. **proof**, experience. 56. **sorteth**, conduceth. 65. **betimes**, early. 70. **affection**, tendency. 73. *Optimum . . . consuetudo*. Choose the best; habit will make it pleasant and easy. 97. **humorous**, whimsical. 114. **exhaust**, exhausted. 119. *Vetulam . . . immortalitati*. He preferred his aged wife to immortality. The allusion is to the passage in the *Odyssey* (Book V) in which Calypso chides her guest with preferring his mortal wife to immortality as guardian of the nymph's home. 127. **quarrel**, difficult decision. 129. **A young man . . . all**, ascribed to Thales, Greek sage of the sixth

think their girdles and garters to be bonds and shackles. Unmarried men are best friends, best masters, best servants; but not always best subjects; for they are light to run away; and almost all fugitives are of that condition. A single life doth well with churchmen; for charity will hardly water the ground where it must first fill a pool. It is indifferent for judges and magistrates; for if they be facile and corrupt, you shall have a servant five times worse than a wife. For soldiers, I find the generals commonly in their hortatives put men in mind of their wives and children; and I think the despising of marriage amongst the Turks maketh the vulgar soldier more base. Certainly wife and children are a kind of discipline of humanity; and single men, though they be many times more charitable, because their means are less exhaust, yet, on the other side, they are more cruel and hard-hearted (good to make severe inquisitors), because their tenderness is not so oft called upon. Grave natures, led by custom, and therefore constant, are commonly loving husbands; as was said of Ulysses, *Vetulam suam praetulit immortalitati.* Chaste women are often proud and froward, as presuming upon the merit of their chastity. It is one of the best bonds both of chastity and obedience in the wife, if she think her husband wise; which she will never do if she find him jealous. Wives are young men's mistresses; companions for middle age; and old men's nurses. So as a man may have a quarrel to marry when he will. But yet he was reputed one of the wise men, that made answer to the question, when a man should marry? "A young man not yet, an elder man not at all." It is often seen that bad husbands have very good wives; whether it be that it raiseth the price of their husband's kindness when it comes; or that the wives take a pride in their patience. But this never fails, if the bad husbands were of their own choosing, against their friends' consent; for then they will be sure to make good their own folly.

(1612, 1625)

10. OF LOVE

The stage is more beholding to love than the life of man. For as to the stage, love is ever matter of comedies, and now and then of tragedies; but in life it doth much mischief; sometimes like a siren, sometimes like a fury. You may observe that amongst all the great and worthy persons (whereof the memory remaineth, either ancient or recent), there is not one that hath been transported to the mad degree of love; which shows that great spirits and great business do keep out this weak passion. You must except, never-

theless, Marcus Antonius, the half partner of the empire of Rome, and Appius Claudius, the decemvir and lawgiver; whereof the former was indeed a voluptuous man, and inordinate; but the latter was an austere and wise man; and therefore it seems (though rarely) that love can find entrance not only into an open heart, but also into a heart well fortified, if watch be not well kept. It is a poor saying of Epicurus, *Satis magnum alter alteri theatrum sumus;* as if man, made for the contemplation of heaven and all noble objects, should do nothing but kneel before a little idol, and make himself subject, though not of the mouth (as beasts are), yet of the eye, which was given him for higher purposes. It is a strange thing to note the excess of this passion, and how it braves the nature and value of things, by this, that the speaking in a perpetual hyperbole is comely in nothing but in love. Neither is it merely in the phrase; for whereas it hath been well said that the arch-flatterer, with whom all the petty flatterers have intelligence, is a man's self, certainly the lover is more. For there was never proud man thought so absurdly well of himself as the lover doth of the person loved; and therefore it was well said, *That it is impossible to love and to be wise.* Neither doth this weakness appear to others only, and not to the party loved, but to the loved most of all, except the love be reciproque. For it is a true rule, that love is ever rewarded either with the reciproque or with an inward and secret contempt. By how much the more men ought to beware of this passion, which loseth not only other things, but itself. As for the other losses, the poet's relation doth well figure them: that he that preferred Helena quitted the gifts of Juno and Pallas. For whosoever esteemeth too much of amorous affection quitteth both riches and wisdom. This passion hath his floods in the very times of weakness; which are great prosperity and great adversity (though this latter hath been less observed); both which times kindle love and make it more fervent, and therefore show it to be the child of folly. They do best, who, if they cannot but admit love, yet make it keep quarter, and sever it wholly from their serious affairs and actions of life; for if it check once with business, it troubleth men's fortunes and maketh men that they can no ways be true to their own ends. I know not how, but martial men are given to love; I think it is but as they are given to wine; for perils commonly ask to be paid in pleasures. There is in man's nature a secret inclination and motion towards love of others, which, if it be not spent upon some one or a few, doth naturally spread itself towards many and maketh men become humane and charitable; as it is seen sometime in friars. Nuptial love maketh mankind; friendly love

and seventh centuries B.C. 148. **Marcus Antonius,** the lover of Cleopatra. 149. **Appius Claudius.** The Roman decemvir plotted to possess Virginia, whose father killed her to save her from the tyrant; the story is told by Livy and by Painter in *The Palace of Pleasure.* 155. **Epicurus,** Greek philosopher (342–270 B.C.) and founder of the school of thought that bears his name. *Satis . . . sumus.* We are a sufficiently great show to one another. 175. **reciproque,** reciprocal. 179. **he that preferred Helena,** Paris. He refused Juno's bribe of riches and Pallas Athene's bribe of wisdom so that he might accept Aphrodite's gift—Helen of Troy. In return Paris gave to Aphrodite the golden apple of Discord. 188. **keep quarter,** keep within bounds. 190. **check,** interfere with.

perfecteth it; but wanton love corrupteth and embaseth it.

(1612, 1625)

11. OF GREAT PLACE

Men in great places are thrice servants: servants of the sovereign or state; servants of fame; and servants of business. So as they have no freedom, neither in their persons, nor in their actions, nor in their times. It is a strange desire, to seek power and to lose liberty; or to seek power over others and to lose power over a man's self. The rising unto place is
10 laborious, and by pains men come to greater pains; and it is sometimes base, and by indignities men come to dignities. The standing is slippery; and the regress is either a downfall, or at least an eclipse, which is a melancholy thing. *Cum non sis qui fueris, non esse cur velis vivere.* Nay, retire men cannot when they would; neither will they when it were reason; but are impatient of privateness, even in age and sickness, which require the shadow: like old townsmen, that will be still sitting at their street door, though thereby they offer
20 age to scorn. Certainly, great persons had need to borrow other men's opinions, to think themselves happy; for if they judge by their own feeling, they cannot find it; but if they think with themselves what other men think of them, and that other men would fain be as they are, then they are happy as it were by report, when perhaps they find the contrary within. For they are the first that find their own griefs, though they be the last that find their own faults. Certainly, men in great fortunes are strangers to themselves, and
30 while they are in the puzzle of business they have no time to tend their health, either of body or mind. *Illi mors gravis incubat, qui notus nimis omnibus, ignotus moritur sibi.* In place there is license to do good and evil; whereof the latter is a curse; for in evil the best condition is not to will, the second not to can. But power to do good is the true and lawful end of aspiring. For good thoughts (though God accept them) yet towards men are little better than good dreams, except they be put in act; and that cannot be
40 without power and place, as the vantage and commanding ground. Merit and good works is the end of man's motion; and conscience of the same is the accomplishment of man's rest. For if a man can be partaker of God's theater, he shall likewise be partaker of God's rest. *Et conversus Deus, ut aspiceret opera quae fecerunt manus suae, vidit quod omnia essent bona nimis,* and then the Sabbath. In the discharge of thy place, set before thee the best examples; for imitation is a globe of precepts. And after a time set before

thee thine own example; and examine thyself strictly, 50 whether thou didst not best at first. Neglect not also the examples of those that have carried themselves ill in the same place; not to set off thyself by taxing their memory, but to direct thyself what to avoid. Reform, therefore, without bravery or scandal of former times and persons; but yet set it down to thyself as well to create good precedents as to follow them. Reduce things to the first institution and observe wherein and how they have degenerate; but yet ask counsel of both times; of the ancient time, what is 60 best; and of the latter time, what is fittest. Seek to make thy course regular, that men may know beforehand what they may expect; but be not too positive and peremptory; and express thyself well when thou digressest from thy rule. Preserve the right of thy place, but stir not questions of jurisdiction; and rather assume thy right in silence and *de facto,* than voice it with claims and challenges. Preserve likewise the rights of inferior places; and think it more honor to direct in chief than to be busy in all. Embrace and invite helps 70 and advices touching the execution of thy place; and do not drive away such as bring thee information as meddlers, but accept of them in good part. The vices of authority are chiefly four: delays, corruption, roughness, and facility. For delays, give easy access; keep times appointed; go through with that which is in hand; and interlace not business but of necessity. For corruption, do not only bind thine own hands or thy servants' hands from taking, but bind the hands of suitors also from offering. For integrity used doth the 80 one; but integrity professed, and with a manifest detestation of bribery, doth the other. And avoid not only the fault, but the suspicion. Whosoever is found variable, and changeth manifestly without manifest cause, giveth suspicion of corruption. Therefore always when thou changest thine opinion or course, profess it plainly and declare it, together with the reasons that move thee to change; and do not think to steal it. A servant or a favorite, if he be inward, and no other apparent cause of esteem, is commonly thought but 90 a by-way to close corruption. For roughness, it is a needless cause of discontent: severity breedeth fear, but roughness breedeth hate. Even reproofs from authority ought to be grave, and not taunting. As for facility, it is worse than bribery. For bribes come but now and then; but if importunity or idle respects lead a man, he shall never be without. As Solomon saith: *To respect persons is not good; for such a man will transgress for a piece of bread.* It is most true that was anciently spoken, *A place showeth the man;* and it 100 showeth some to the better, and some to the worse. *Omnium consensu capax imperii, nisi imperasset,*

14. **Cum . . . vivere.** Since you are not what you were, there is no reason why you should wish to live. (Cicero's *Letters.*) 18. **the shadow,** retreat from active life. 32. **Illi mors . . . sibi.** Death lies heavily on the man who dies too well known to all, but to himself unknown. (Seneca's *Thyestes,* ll. 401–403). 36. **can,** know; cf. *ken.* 42. **conscience,** consciousness. 45. **Et conversus . . . nimis.** And God,

turning back to look upon the works which his hands had made, saw that they were all very good. (Amplified from the Latin Bible, Genesis 1:31). 47. **then the Sabbath.** God "rested on the seventh day from all his work which he had made" (Genesis 2:2). 55. **bravery,** boasting, ostentation. 67. **de facto,** as a matter of fact. 75. **facility,** easy going. 88. **steal,** conceal. 89. **inward,** familiar. 91. **close,** secret. 97.

saith Tacitus of Galba; but of Vespasian he saith, *Solus imperantium Vespasianus mutatus in melius:* though the one was meant of sufficiency, the other of manners and affection. It is an assured sign of a worthy and generous spirit, whom honor amends. For honor is, or should be, the place of virtue; and as in nature things move violently to their place, and calmly in their place; so virtue in ambition is violent, in authority settled and calm. All rising to great place is by a winding stair; and if there be factions, it is good to side a man's self whilst he is in the rising, and to balance himself when he is placed. Use the memory of thy predecessor fairly and tenderly; for if thou dost not, it is a debt will sure be paid when thou art gone. If thou have colleagues, respect them, and rather call them when they look not for it, than exclude them when they have reason to look to be called. Be not too sensible or too remembering of thy place in conversation and private answers to suitors; but let it rather be said, *When he sits in place he is another man.*

(1612, 1625)

18. OF TRAVEL

Travel, in the younger sort, is a part of education; in the elder, a part of experience. He that travelleth into a country before he hath some entrance into the language, goeth to school, and not to travel. That young men travel under some tutor, or grave servant, I allow well; so that he be such a one that hath the language and hath been in the country before; whereby he may be able to tell them what things are worthy to be seen in the country where they go; what acquaintances they are to seek; what exercises or discipline the place yieldeth. For else young men shall go hooded, and look abroad little. It is a strange thing that in sea-voyages, where there is nothing to be seen but sky and sea, men should make diaries, but in land-travel, wherein so much is to be observed, for the most part they omit it; as if chance were fitter to be registered than observation. Let diaries, therefore, be brought in use. The things to be seen and observed are: the courts of princes, specially when they give audience to ambassadors; the courts of justice, while they sit and hear causes, and so of consistories ecclesiastic; the churches and monasteries, with the monuments which are therein extant; the walls and fortifications of cities and towns, and so the havens and harbors; antiquities and ruins; libraries; colleges, disputations, and lectures, where any are; shipping and navies; houses and gardens of state and pleasure, near great cities; armories; arsenals; magazines; exchanges; burses; warehouses; exercises of horsemanship, fencing, training of soldiers, and the like; comedies, such whereunto the better sort of persons do resort; treasuries of jewels and robes; cabinets and rarities; and, to conclude, whatsoever is memorable in the places where they go. After all which the tutors or servants ought to make diligent enquiry. As for triumphs, masques, feasts, weddings, funerals, capital executions, and such shows, men need not to be put in mind of them; yet are they not to be neglected. If you will have a young man to put his travel into a little room, and in short time to gather much, this you must do. First, as was said, he must have some entrance into the language, before he goeth. Then he must have such a servant, or tutor, as knoweth the country, as was likewise said. Let him carry with him also some card or book describing the country where he traveleth; which will be a good key to his enquiry. Let him keep also a diary. Let him not stay long in one city or town; more or less as the place deserveth, but not long; nay, when he stayeth in one city or town, let him change his lodging from one end and part of the town to another; which is a great adamant of acquaintance. Let him sequester himself from the company of his countrymen and diet in such places where there is good company of the nation where he traveleth. Let him, upon his removes from one place to another, procure recommendation to some person of quality residing in the place whither he removeth; that he may use his favor in those things he desireth to see or know. Thus he may abridge his travel with much profit. As for the acquaintance which is to be sought in travel; that which is most of all profitable is acquaintance with the secretaries and employed men of ambassadors; for so in traveling in one country he shall suck the experience of many. Let him also see and visit eminent persons in all kinds, which are of great name abroad; that he may be able to tell how the life agreeth with the fame. For quarrels, they are with care and discretion to be avoided: they are commonly for mistresses, healths, place, and words. And let a man beware how he keepeth company with choleric and quarrelsome persons; for they will engage him into their own quarrels. When a traveler returneth home, let him not leave the countries where he hath traveled altogether behind him, but maintain a correspondence by letters with those of his acquaintance which are of most worth. And let his travel appear rather in his discourse than in his apparel or gesture; and in his discourse, let him be rather advised in his answers than forwards to tell stories; and let it appear that he doth not change his country manners for those of foreign parts, but only

---

To respect persons, etc., to show favoritism; inexactly quoted from Proverbs 28:21. 102. Omnium . . . imperasset. A man whom all would have thought capable of ruling—if he had not (actually) ruled. 103. Tacitus, Roman historian (c. 55–c. 117 A.D.). Vespasian, Roman emperor (69–79 A.D.). Solus . . . melius. Of all emperors Vespasian alone changed for the better. 105. sufficiency, capacity. 124. in the younger sort, among younger persons. 126. entrance into, knowledge of. 129. allow well, approve of. 134. hooded, blindfolded, like a falcon. 144. consistories ecclesiastic, church tribunals. 152. burses, bourses, or exchanges. 167. card, chart, map. 174. adamant, lodestone—to draw new acquaintances. 182. abridge, shorten. 191. healths, drinking of healths. 192. place, precedence, order of priority.

prick in some flowers of that he hath learned abroad into the customs of his own country.

(1625)

42. OF YOUTH AND AGE

A man that is young in years may be old in hours if he have lost no time. But that happeneth rarely. Generally youth is like the first cogitations, not so wise as the second. For there is a youth in thoughts as well as in ages. And yet the invention of young men is more lively than that of old; and imaginations stream into their minds better and, as it were, more 10 divinely. Natures that have much heat, and great and violent desires and perturbations, are not ripe for action till they have passed the meridian of their years, as it was with Julius Caesar and Septimius Severus, of the latter of whom it is said, *Juventutem egit erroribus, imo furoribus, plenam!* And yet he was the ablest emperor almost of all the list. But reposed natures may do well in youth, as it is seen in Augustus Caesar, Cosmos, Duke of Florence, Gaston de Foix, and others. On the other side, heat and 20 vivacity in age is an excellent composition for business. Young men are fitter to invent than to judge, fitter for execution than for counsel, and fitter for new projects than for settled business. For the experience of age, in things that fall within the compass of it, directeth them; but in new things, abuseth them. The errors of young men are the ruin of business; but the errors of aged men amount but to this, that more might have been done, or sooner.

Young men, in the conduct and manage of actions, 30 embrace more than they can hold; stir more than they can quiet; fly to the end, without consideration of the means and degrees; pursue some few principles, which they have chanced upon, absurdly; care not to innovate, which draws unknown inconveniences; use extreme remedies at first; and, that which doubleth all errors, will not acknowledge or retract them, like an unready horse, that will neither stop nor turn. Men of age object too much, consult too long, adventure too little, repent too soon, and seldom 40 drive business home to the full period, but content themselves with a mediocrity of success. Certainly it is good to compound employments of both, for that will be good for the present, because the virtues of either age may correct the defects of both; and good for succession, that young men may be learners, while men in age are actors; and, lastly, good for extern accidents, because authority followeth old men, and favor and popularity youth. But for the moral part perhaps youth will have the preeminence, as age hath for the politic. A certain rabbin 50 upon the text, "Your young men shall see visions, and your old men shall dream dreams," inferreth that young men are admitted nearer to God than old, because vision is a clearer revelation than a dream. And certainly the more a man drinketh of the world the more it intoxicateth; and age doth profit rather in the powers of understanding than in the virtues of the will and affections. There be some have an over-early ripeness in their years, which fadeth betimes; these are, first, such as have brittle wits, 60 the edge whereof is soon turned—such as was Hermogenes, the rhetorician, whose books are exceeding subtle, who afterwards waxed stupid. A second sort is of those that have some natural dispositions, which have better grace in youth than in age, such as is a fluent and luxuriant speech, which becomes youth well, but not age; so Tully saith of Hortensius, *Idem manebat, neque idem decebat.* The third is of such as take too high a strain at the first, and are magnanimous more than tract of years can uphold; 70 as was Scipio Africanus, of whom Livy saith in effect, *Ultima primis cedebant.*

(1612, 1625)

50. OF STUDIES

Studies serve for delight, for ornament, and for ability. Their chief use for delight is in privateness and retiring; for ornament, is in discourse; and for ability, is in the judgment and disposition of business; for expert men can execute, and perhaps judge of particulars, one by one; but the general counsels, and the plots and marshaling of affairs come best from those that are learned. To spend too much time 80 in studies is sloth; to use them too much for ornament is affectation; to make judgment wholly by their rules is the humor of a scholar. They perfect nature, and are perfected by experience; for natural abilities are like natural plants, that need pruning by study; and studies themselves do give forth directions too much at large, except they be bounded in by experience. Crafty men contemn studies, simple men admire them, and wise men use them; for they teach not their own use; but that is a wisdom without 90 them and above them, won by observation. Read not to contradict and confute, nor to believe and take for granted, nor to find talk and discourse, but

13. **Septimius Severus**, Roman emperor (146–211). 14. *Juventutem . . . plenam.* He spent his entire youth in errors, nay, in mad acts (Spartianus: *Vita Severi*). 18. **Cosmos**, Cosimo I de Medici (1519–1574). **Gaston de Foix**, Duke of Nemours, French general (1489–1512). 25. **abuseth**, imposes upon. 29. **manage**, management, control. 33. **care . . . innovate**, i.e., are not careful about beginning new ventures. 37. **unready**, headstrong. 42. **compound employments**, i.e., to employ both old men and young. 47. **extern**, external. 50. **rabbin**, rabbi; Isaac Abrabanel (1437–1508). 51. **Your . . . dreams**, Joel 2:28. 60. **brittle**, unstable, inconstant. 61. **Hermogenes**, Greek rhetorician of the second century A.D. who lost his mind at twenty-five. 67. **Tully**, Cicero. **Hortensius**, Roman orator of the first century B.C. 68. *Idem . . . decebat.* He continued the same, when the same was no longer becoming to him. 71. **Scipio Africanus** (237–183 B.C.), Roman general who defeated Hannibal. **Livy**, Roman historian (59 B.C.–17 A.D.). 72. *Ultima primis cedebant.* His last acts fell below his first. 77. **expert**, experienced. 89. **admire**, wonder at.

to weigh and consider. Some books are to be tasted, others to be swallowed, and some few to be chewed and digested; that is, some books are to be read only in parts; others to be read but not curiously, and some few to be read wholly, and with diligence and attention. Some books also may be read by deputy, and extracts made of them by others; but that would be only in the less important arguments and the meaner sort of books; else distilled books are, like common distilled waters, flashy things. Reading maketh a full man; conference a ready man; and writing an exact man. And, therefore, if a man write little, he had need have a great memory; if he confer little, he had need have a present wit; and if he read little, he had need have much cunning, to seem to know that he doth not. Histories make men wise; poets, witty; the mathematics, subtle; natural philosophy, deep; moral, grave; logic and rhetoric, able to contend: *Abeunt studia in mores!* Nay, there is no stand or impediment in the wit but may be wrought out by fit studies; like as diseases of the body may have appropriate exercises. Bowling is good for the stone and reins, shooting for the lungs and breast, gentle walking for the stomach, riding for the head, and the like. So if a man's wit be wandering, let him study the mathematics; for in demonstrations, if his wit be called away never so little, he must begin again. If his wit be not apt to distinguish or find differences, let him study the schoolmen; for they are *cymini sectores!* If he be not apt to beat over matters, and to call up one thing to prove and illustrate another, let him study the lawyers' cases. So every defect of the mind may have a special receipt.

(1597, 1612, 1625)

97. **curiously,** with much care.   103. **flashy,** tasteless, flat.   108. **that,** that which.   111. *Abeunt . . . mores.* Studies develop into habits

(Ovid's *Heroides*, XV, 83).   115. **stone and reins,** testicles and kidneys.   122. *cymini sectores,* hairsplitters.

DONNE AND THE METAPHYSICAL POETS

The almost paradoxical versatility of the Elizabethan mind is magnificently illustrated by John Donne. Donne's poetry is often in revolt against the conventions of the Elizabethan lyric; like every great poet, Donne is a trail blazer. He is, therefore, cynical, grotesque, abrupt, tender, and rhetorical by turns. His form is often rough and angular; his metrics crabbed and irregular. His imagery shows frequently a high degree of concentration and an amazing originality and ingenuity. In these respects he comes so close to the ideals of twentieth-century poetry that it is scarcely surprising to see him hailed by many present-day critics as a major English poet. Nor is such high praise all a matter of critical fads. Donne has magnificent power and vision; his phraseology is sometimes unforgettable. In his lighter moments, moreover, his lack of sentimentality is refreshing. But his greatest poetic asset is his ability to touch the naked truth, the eternal verity, with a directness and an honesty that strikes the reader with inescapable force, once that reader has truly mastered the secret of the Elizabethan conceit and the involutions of Elizabethan prose style. Whether in prose or in verse, however, Donne is always the poet; and plays on words, antitheses, inversions of word order, and bizarre images cannot conceal the solid gold that lies underneath and can suddenly blaze forth in dazzling light.

Like Ben Jonson (see p. 342), John Donne was extremely influential upon younger poets, some of whom came under the influence of both. In general Jonson's influence was felt principally by the Cavalier lyrists (see below, p. 341), especially Carew and Lovelace, and by those, like Herrick and Waller, who were akin to them; and Donne's influence was felt by the poets of the so-called metaphysical school, the writers of sober, sacred poems, like Herbert, Crashaw, Vaughan, and Traherne. In their use of philosophical conceits, startling ideas, oddments of erudition, and an unusual vocabulary, these men were closely akin to Donne.

"The metaphysical poets" was the term applied by Samuel Johnson—possibly on a hint from Dryden—to that group of lyrists of the Puritan period whose vision was inward rather than outward, upward rather than downward, and who expressed their spiritual experiences and religious emotions in sacred poems that are characterized by subtleties of feeling and expression.

JOHN DONNE 1573-1631

John Donne was the son of a wealthy merchant of London; through his mother he claimed relationship to Sir Thomas More. He was educated at both Oxford and Cambridge but took a degree from neither university because of his Catholic scruples. For a time (1590-1591) he studied law. His father's death soon thereafter left him with a considerable inheritance. The young man was already writing poetry showing great talent; he was celebrated for his wit, for his dashing, almost swashbuckling behavior, for his reckless worldliness. But this recklessness coincided curiously with a period of religious doubt. He ultimately abandoned the Catholic faith, though many of his earlier religious poems were written from the Catholic point of view. By 1593 he had composed many of the pieces in his Divine Poems, as well as the first three of his Satires, the third of which, printed below (p. 332), is an admirable exposition of the situation confronting a man of religious nature in the London of the times, when a choice of religions was becoming more and more a matter of free option.

In 1594 Donne began to travel; he wandered over most of Europe, as was appropriate to a man of his age and worldly means. He was present as a soldier under the Earl of Essex at the taking of Cádiz in 1596 and on the expedition to the Azores in 1597. Possibly he took part in some of the fighting in the Netherlands during this decade. His sojourns in Italy and Spain brought him into the full current of Renaissance literature; indeed, his unusual liking for conceits may have been due to the influence of the Spanish writer Góngora.

The next important event of Donne's life, however, was more romantic than intellectual. As private secretary to Sir Thomas Egerton, he fell in love with the daughter of one of Sir Thomas' guests and secretly married her. The father, Sir George More, lord lieutenant of the Tower, was so angered that he effected Donne's dismissal from the secretaryship and managed to get his luckless son-in-law thrown into prison for a time. When he was released, Donne and his wife, who had been cut off by her intransigent father, would have had a hard time of it, if it had not been for the kindness of Sir Francis Wooley, who offered them a home. There is evidence in his poetry that Donne was devoted to his wife; and yet Izaak Walton (p. 363), his earliest biographer, who as a rule speaks in admiration of Donne, states flatly that the marriage was the great mistake of Donne's life.

In the meantime the poet had found the opportunity to write some more; he finished his Satires and the mystical Of the Progress of the Soul (1601). In the following year a collection of ten sonnets was printed; these, however, along with a great many of his short love poems, belong to indeterminate periods of his young manhood. Also an earlier work, and a startling one, was Biathanatos, a defense of suicide, which was not printed, however, until after his death.

After a considerable amount of spiritual struggle, Donne was persuaded to take holy orders in the Anglican Church, and was known thenceforth for his holy way of life and his intense, passionate religious devotion. It was not until 1615, that he finally took this critical step, but in the years immediately preceding he engaged in anti-Catholic polemical writing, with his prose Pseudo-Martyr (1610) and Ignatius His Conclave (1611). The curious and arresting work of great mystical power, An Anatomy of the World, also appeared in 1611. After Donne had preached before King James I, who was peculiarly devoted to the poet as a man of religion, a new phase is evident in the poet's literary work. Thenceforth he excels as a prose writer, a homiletic artist of great force and intense insight. He was not much interested in a variety of livings in the Church; he preferred to remain for most of his career as Dean of St. Paul's in London, an office which he filled from 1621 until his death and in which he achieved his great reputation as a divine. His collected poems were first printed in 1633; his prose work, comprising especially Juvenilia, Essays in Divinity, Devotions upon Emergent Occasions, his Letters, and more than 150 Sermons, was gathered together and printed in various fragments between 1633 and 1651.

SONG

Go and catch a falling star,
  Get with child a mandrake root,
Tell me where all past years are,
  Or who cleft the devil's foot;
Teach me to hear mermaids singing,
Or to keep off envy's stinging,
    And find
    What wind
Serves to advance an honest mind.

If thou be'st born to strange sights,   10
  Things invisible go see,
Ride ten thousand days and nights
  Till Age snow white hairs on thee;
Thou, when thou return'st, wilt tell me
All strange wonders that befell thee,
    And swear
    No where
Lives a woman true and fair.

If thou find'st one, let me know;
  Such a pilgrimage were sweet.   20
Yet do not; I would not go,
  Though at next door we might meet.
Though she were true when you met her,
And last till you write your letter,

Song. 2. **mandrake**, the mandragora, a European herb with a forked root which was supposed to resemble a human being and to shriek when pulled up.

Yet she
Will be
False, ere I come, to two or three.
(1633)

THE INDIFFERENT

I can love both fair and brown;
Her whom abundance melts, and her whom want
    betrays;
Her who loves loneness best, and her who masks and
    plays;
Her whom the country formed, and whom the town;
Her who believes, and her who tries;
Her who still weeps with spongy eyes,
And her who is dry cork and never cries.
I can love her, and her, and you, and you;
I can love any, so she be not true.

10 Will no other vice content you?
Will it not serve your turn to do as did your mothers?
Or have you all old vices spent and now would find
    out others?
Or doth a fear that men are true torment you?
O we are not, be not you so;
Let me—and do you—twenty know;
Rob me, but bind me not, and let me go.
Must I, who came to travel thorough you,
Grow your fixed subject, because you are true?

Venus heard me sigh this song;
20 And by love's sweetest part, variety, she swore,
She heard not this till now; it should be so no more.
She went, examined, and returned ere long,
And said, "Alas! some two or three
Poor heretics in love there be,
Which think to stablish dangerous constancy.
But I have told them, 'Since you will be true,
You shall be true to them, who're false to you.' "
(1633)

THE ECSTASY

Where, like a pillow on a bed,
    A pregnant bank swelled up, to rest
The violet's reclining head,
    Sat we two, one another's best.
Our hands were firmly cemented
    With a fast balm, which thence did spring,
Our eye-beams twisted, and did thread
    Our eyes, upon one double string;
So t' intergraft our hands, as yet

Was all the means to make us one,   10
    And pictures in our eyes to get
    Was all our propagation.
As 'twixt two equal armies, fate
    Suspends uncertain victory,
Our souls (which to advance their state,
    Were gone out) hung 'twixt her, and me.
And whil'st our souls negotiate there,
    We like sepulchral statues lay;
All day, the same our postures were,
    And we said nothing, all the day.   20
If any, so by love refined
    That he soul's language understood,
And by good love were grown all mind,
    Within convenient distance stood,
He (though he knew not which soul spake,
    Because both meant, both spake the same)
Might thence a new concoction take,
    And part far purer than he came.
This Ecstasy doth unperplex
    (We said) and tell us what we love;   30
We see by this, it was not sex,
    We see, we saw not what did move:
But as all several souls contain
    Mixtures of things, they know not what,
Love, these mixed souls, doth mix again,
    And makes both one, each this and that.
A single violet transplant,
    The strength, the color, and the size,
(All which before was poor, and scant)
    Redoubles still, and multiplies.   40
When love, with one another so
    Interinanimates two souls,
That abler soul, which thence doth flow,
    Defects of loneliness controls.
We then, who are this new soul, know
    Of what we are composed, and made,
For, th' atomies of which we grow,
    Are souls, whom no change can invade.
But O alas, so long, so far
    Our bodies why do we forbear?   50
They are ours, though they are not we; we are
    The intelligences, they the sphere.
We owe them thanks, because they thus,
    Did us, to us, at first convey,
Yielded their forces, sense, to us,
    Nor are dross to us, but allay.
On man heaven's influence works not so,
    But that it first imprints the air,
So soul into the soul may flow,
    Though it to body first repair.   60
As our blood labors to beget
    Spirits, as like souls as it can,
Because such fingers need to knit

That subtle knot, which makes us man:
So must pure lovers' souls descend
   T' affections, and to faculties,
Which sense may reach and apprehend,
   Else a great prince in prison lies.
T' our bodies turn we then, that so
70 Weak men on love revealed may look;
Love's mysteries in souls do grow,
   But yet the body is his book.
And if some lover, such as we,
   Have heard this dialogue of one,
Let him still mark us, he shall see
   Small change, when we're to bodies gone.
(1633)

A HYMN TO GOD THE FATHER

Wilt thou forgive that sin where I begun,
   Which was my sin, though it were done before?
Wilt thou forgive that sin through which I run,
   And do run still, though still I do deplore?
When thou hast done, thou hast not done;
     For I have more.

Wilt thou forgive that sin which I have won
   Others to sin, and made my sins their door?
Wilt thou forgive that sin which I did shun
10 A year or two, but wallowed in a score?
When thou hast done, thou hast not done;
     For I have more.

I have a sin of fear, that when I've spun
   My last thread, I shall perish on the shore;
But swear by thyself that at my death thy Son
   Shall shine as he shines now and heretofore;
And having done that, thou hast done;
     I fear no more.
(1633)

DEATH

Death, be not proud, though some have callèd thee
Mighty and dreadful, for thou art not so;
For those whom thou think'st thou dost overthrow
Die not, poor Death; nor yet canst thou kill me.
From rest and sleep, which but thy picture be,
Much pleasure; then from thee much more must
   flow;
And soonest our best men with thee do go—

Rest of their bones and souls' delivery!
Thou 'rt slave to fate, chance, kings, and desperate
   men,
And dost with poison, war, and sickness dwell;   10
And poppy or charms can make us sleep as well
And better than thy stroke. Why swell'st thou then?
One short sleep past, we wake eternally,
And Death shall be no more: Death, thou shalt die!
(1633)

THE GOOD-MORROW

I wonder by my troth, what thou and I
Did, till we loved? were we not weaned till then?
But sucked on country pleasures, childishly?
Or snorted we in the seven sleepers' den?
'Twas so; but this, all pleasures fancies be.
If ever any beauty I did see,
Which I desired, and got, 'twas but a dream of thee.

And now good-morrow to our waking souls,
Which watch not one another out of fear;
For love, all love of other sights controls,   10
And makes one little room an everywhere.
Let sea-discoverers to new worlds have gone,
Let maps to other, worlds on worlds have shown,
Let us possess one world; each hath one, and is one.

My face in thine eye, thine in mine appears,
And true plain hearts do in the faces rest,
Where can we find two better hemispheres
Without sharp North, without declining West?
What ever dies was not mixed equally;
If our two loves be one, or thou and I   20
Love so alike that none do slacken, none can die.
(1633)

LOVE'S INFINITENESS

If yet I have not all thy love,
Dear, I shall never have it all,
I cannot breathe one other sigh, to move;
Nor can entreat one other tear to fall,
And all my treasure, which should purchase thee,
Sighs, tears, and oaths, and letters I have spent.
Yet no more can be due to me,
Than at the bargain made was meant,
If then thy gift of love were partial,
That some to me, some should to others fall,   10
   Dear, I shall never have thee all.

The Good-Morrow. 4. the seven sleepers' den. According to legend, seven Christian youths from Ephesus fled from the persecution of the Roman Emperor Decius (c. 250) and hid in a cave. The emperor ordered them to be walled up in the cave, but they were miraculously preserved through a deep sleep which lasted 187 years. Like Rip Van Winkle, the Seven were amazed to see the changes that had been wrought during the approximately two centuries of their slumber. **17. two better hemispheres.** Each of the lovers is a whole world to the other. Looking into the other's eyes, each sees a hemisphere reflected, because the whole cannot be reflected. In the next line the references to North and West refer respectively to the traditional *coldness* of the north and the *alteration* represented by the setting sun

Or if then thou gavest me all,
All was but all, which thou hadst then;
But if in thy heart, since, there be or shall,
New love created be, by other men,
Which have their stocks entire, and can in tears,
In sighs, in oaths, and letters outbid me,
This new love may beget new fears,
For, this love was not vowed by thee.
20 And yet it was, thy gift being general,
The ground; thy heart is mine, what ever shall
   Grow there, dear, I should have it all.

Yet I would not have all yet;
He that hath all can have no more,
And since my love doth every day admit
New growth, thou shouldst have new rewards in
   store;
Thou canst not every day give me thy heart,
If thou canst give it, then thou never gavest it:
Love's riddles are, that though thy heart depart,
30 It stays at home, and thou with losing savest it:
But we will have a way more liberal,
Than changing hearts, to join them, so we shall
   Be one, and one another's all.
(1633)

SONG

Sweetest love, I do not go,
   For weariness of thee,
Nor in hope the world can show
   A fitter love for me;
     But since that I
Must die at last, 'tis best,
To use myself in jest
     Thus by feigned deaths to die;

Yesternight the sun went hence,
10   And yet is here today,
He hath no desire nor sense,
   Nor half so short a way:
     Then fear not me,
But believe that I shall make
Speedier journeys, since I take
     More wings and spurs than he.

O how feeble is man's power,
   That if good fortune fall,
Cannot add another hour,
20   Nor a lost hour recall!
     But come bad chance,

And we join to it our strength,
And we teach it art and length,
   Itself o'er us to advance.

When thou sigh'st, thou sigh'st not wind,
   But sigh'st my soul away,
When thou weep'st, unkindly kind,
   My life's blood doth decay.
     It cannot be
That thou lov'st me, as thou say'st,   30
If in thine my life thou waste,
   Thou art the best of me.

Let not thy divining heart
   Forethink me any ill,
Destiny may take thy part,
   And may thy fears fulfill;
     But think that we
Are but turn'd aside to sleep;
They who one another keep
     Alive, ne'er parted be.
(1633)

THE LEGACY

When I died last, and, dear, I die
   As often as from thee I go,
   Though it be but an hour ago,
And lovers' hours be full eternity,
I can remember yet, that I
   Something did say, and something did bestow;
Though I be dead, which sent me, I should be
Mine own executor and legacy.

I heard me say, 'Tell her anon,
   That myself (that is you, not I)   10
   Did kill me, and when I felt me die,
I bid me send my heart, when I was gone,
But I, alas, could there find none,
   When I had ripped me, and searched where hearts
     did lie;
It killed me again, that I, who still was true,
In life, in my last will should cozen you.'

Yet I found something like a heart,
   But colors it, and corners, had,
   It was not good, it was not bad,
It was entire to none, and few had part.   20
As good as could be made by art
   It seemed; and therefore for our losses sad,

in the west. 20. **If . . . die.** If our two loves are one, dissolution is
impossible; this is also true if the loves are two, provided they are
identical. An old theological tenet has it that what is simple, such as
God or the soul, cannot be dissolved; what is compound is likewise
indissoluble, if there is no contrariety of elements in the parts of the
compound (for example, celestial bodies).

Song. This extremely moving lyric was allegedly written before the
poet departed on a brief trip to France; it is addressed to his wife.
   The Legacy. 20. **entire to none.** No one had all of it, and few
had parts of it.

I meant to send this heart instead of mine,
But oh, no man could hold it, for 'twas thine.
(1633)

THE ANNIVERSARY

All kings, and all their favorites,
All glory of honors, beauties, wits,
The sun itself, which makes times, as they pass,
Is elder by a year, now, than it was
When thou and I first one another saw:
All other things to their destruction draw,
    Only our love hath no decay;
This, no tomorrow hath, nor yesterday,
Running it never runs from us away,
10 But truly keeps his first, last, everlasting day.

Two graves must hide thine and my corse,
If one might, death were no divorce.
Alas, as well as other princes, we
(Who prince enough in one another be)
Must leave at last in death, these eyes, and ears,
Oft fed with true oaths, and with sweet salt tears;
    But souls where nothing dwells but love
(All other thoughts being inmates) then shall prove
This, or a love increaséd there above,
20   When bodies to their graves, souls from their graves
    remove.

And then we shall be throughly blest,
But we no more than all the rest;
Here upon earth, we are kings, and none but we
Can be such kings, nor of such subjects be.
Who is so safe as we? where none can do
Treason to us, except one of us two.
    True and false fears let us refrain,
Let us love nobly, and live, and add again
Years and years unto years, till we attain
To write threescore: this is the second of our reign.
(1633)

THE WILL

Before I sigh my last gasp, let me breathe,
Great love, some legacies. Here I bequeath
Mine eyes to Argus, if mine eyes can see,
If they be blind, then, Love, I give them thee;
My tongue to Fame; to ambassadors my ears;
    To women or the sea, my tears.
Thou, Love, hast taught me heretofore
By making me serve her who had twenty more,
That I should give to none but such as had too
    much before.

My constancy I to the planets give;   10
My truth to them who at the court do live;
Mine ingenuity and openness,
To Jesuits; to buffoons my pensiveness;
My silence to any who abroad hath been;
    My money to a Capuchin.
Thou Love taught'st me, by appointing me
To love there where no love received can be,
Only to give to such as have an incapacity.

My faith I give to Roman Catholics;
All my good works unto the schismatics   20
Of Amsterdam; my best civility
And courtship, to an university;
My modesty I give to soldiers bare;
    My patience let gamesters share.
Thou Love taught'st me, by making me
Love her that holds my love disparity,
Only to give to those that count my gifts indignity.

I give my reputation to those
Which were my friends; mine industry to foes;
To schoolmen I bequeath my doubtfulness;   30
My sickness to physicians, or excess;
To Nature, all that I in rhyme have writ;
    And to my company my wit.
Thou Love, by making me adore
Her who begot this love in me before,
Taught'st me to make, as though I gave, when I did
    but restore.

To him for whom the passing-bell next tolls,
I give my physic-books; my written rolls
Of moral counsels, I to Bedlam give;
My brazen medals unto them which live   40
In want of bread; to them which pass among
    All foreigners, mine English tongue.
Thou, Love, by making me love one
Who thinks her friendship a fit portion
For younger lovers, dost my gifts thus disproportion.

Therefore I'll give no more; but I'll undo
The world by dying, because love dies too.
Then all your beauties will be no more worth
Than gold in mines, where none doth draw it
    forth;
And all your graces no more use shall have   50
    Than a sun-dial in a grave.
Thou Love taught'st me, by making me
Love her who doth neglect both me and thee,
To invent, and practice this one way, to annihilate all
    three.

(1633)

The Anniversary. 3. times, seasons.
The Will. 3. Argus, the hundred-eyed dragon of Greek legend. 15.
Capuchin, a mendicant Franciscan friar of an order founded in 1526;
as a group, the Capuchins were notoriously poverty-stricken. 20. schismatics Of Amsterdam, an extremely rigorous Puritan sect. 30. doubtfulness, skepticism. 37. the passing-bell . . . tolls, a favorite theme
in Donne; cf. the excerpt from Devotions upon Emergent Occasions (p.
320). 39. Bedlam, Bethlehem hospital, the madhouse of London.

RENUNCIATION

This is my play's last scene, here heavens appoint
My pilgrimage's last mile; and my race
Idly, yet quickly, run, hath this last pace,
My span's last inch, my minute's latest point,
And gluttonous Death will instantly unjoint
My body, and soul, and I shall sleep a space,
But my ever-waking part shall see that face,
Whose fear already shakes my every joint:
Then, as my soul, to Heaven, her first seat, takes
    flight,
10 And earth-born body, in the earth shall dwell,
So, fall my sins, that all may have their right,
To where they are bred, and would press me, to
    Hell.
Impute me righteous, thus purged of evil,
For thus I leave the world, the flesh, the devil.
(1633)

HIS PICTURE

Here take my picture; though I bid farewell,
Thine, in my heart, where my soul dwells, shall dwell.
'Tis like me now, but I dead, 'twill be more
When we are shadows both, than 'twas before.
When weather-beaten I come back, my hand
Perhaps with rude oars torn, or sunbeams tanned,
My face and breast of haircloth, and my head
With cares' rash sudden storms, being o'er spread,
My body a sack of bones, broken within,
10 And powder's blue stains scattered on my skin;
If rival fools tax thee to have loved a man,
So foul and coarse as, Oh, I may seem then,
This shall say what I was: and thou shalt say,
Do his hurts reach me? doth my worth decay?
Or do they reach his judging mind, that he
Should now love less what he did love to see?
That which in him was fair and delicate,
Was but the milk, which in Love's childish state
Did nurse it: who now is grown strong enough
To feed on that which to disuséd tastes seems tough.
(1633)

ON HIS MISTRESS

By our first strange and fatal interview,
By all desires which thereof did ensue,
By our long starving hopes, by that remorse
Which my words' masculine persuasive force
Begot in thee, and by the memory
Of hurts, which spies and rivals threatened me,

John Donne in his Shroud, from Death's Duel, *1632.*

I calmly beg: but by thy father's wrath,
By all pains which want and divorcement hath,
I conjure thee, and all the oaths which I
And thou have sworn to seal joint constancy,   10
Here I unswear, and overswear them thus,
Thou shalt not love by ways so dangerous.
Temper, O fair Love, love's impetuous rage,
Be my true mistress still, not my feigned page;
I'll go, and, by thy kind leave, leave behind
Thee, only worthy to nurse in my mind,
Thirst to come back; O, if thou die before,
My soul from other lands to thee shall soar.
Thy (else Almighty) beauty cannot move
Rage from the seas, nor thy love teach them love,   20
Nor tame wild Boreas' harshness; thou hast read
How roughly he in pieces shiveréd
Fair Orithea, whom he swore he loved.
Fall ill or good, 'tis madness to have proved
Dangers unurged; feed on this flattery
That absent lovers one in th' other be.
Dissemble nothing, not a boy, nor change
Thy body's habit, nor mind's; be not strange
To thyself only; all will spy in thy face
A blushing womanly discovering grace;   30
Richly clothed apes, are called apes, and as soon
Eclipsed as bright we call the moon the moon.

On His Mistress. 21. *Boreas' . . . Orithea.* In Greek mythology Boreas was the personification of the north wind. He abducted Orithea, daughter of Erechtheus, king of Athens. According to some versions, he lived happily with Orithea at his abode on Mt. Haemus in Thrace; according to others, his violent lovemaking destroyed the maiden.

Men of France, changeable chameleons,
Spittles of diseases, shops of fashions,
Love's fuellers, and the rightest company
Of players, which upon the world's stage be,
Will quickly know thee, and no less, alas!
Th' indifferent Italian, as we pass
His warm land, well content to think thee page,
40 Will hunt thee with such lust, and hideous rage,
As Lot's fair guests were vext. But none of these
Nor spongy, hydroptic Dutch shall thee displease,
If thou stay here. O stay here, for, for thee
England is only a worthy gallery,
To walk in expectation, till from thence
Our greatest King call thee to His presence.
When I am gone, dream me some happiness,
Nor let thy looks our long hid love confess,
Nor praise, nor dispraise me, nor bless nor curse
50 Openly love's force, nor in bed fright thy nurse
With midnight's startings, crying out, 'Oh! oh! oh!
Nurse, O my love is slain, I saw him go
O'er the white Alps alone; I saw him, I,
Assailed, fight, taken, stabbed, bleed, fall, and die.'
Augur me better chance, except dread Jove
Think it enough for me to have had thy love.
(1633)

THE THIRD SATIRE

Kind pity chokes my spleen; brave scorn forbids
Those tears to issue which swell my eyelids;
I must not laugh, nor weep sins, and be wise;
Can railing then cure these worn maladies?
Is not our mistress fair Religion,
As worthy of all our soul's devotion,
As virtue was to the first blinded age?
Are not Heaven's joys as valiant to assuage
Lusts, as earth's honor was to them? Alas,
10 As we do them in means, shall they surpass
Us in the end, and shall thy father's spirit
Meet blind philosophers in Heaven, whose merit
Of strict life may be imputed faith, and hear
Thee, whom he taught so easy ways and near
To follow, damned? O if thou dar'st, fear this;
This fear great courage and high valor is.
Dar'st thou aid mutinous Dutch, and dar'st thou lay
Thee in ships' wooden sepulchers, a prey
To leader's rage, to storms, to shot, to dearth?
20 Dar'st thou dive seas and dungeons of the earth?
Hast thou courageous fire to thaw the ice
Of frozen Norths' discoveries? and thrice
Colder than salamanders, like divine

Children in the oven, fires of Spain, and the line,
Whose countries limbecks to out bodies be,
Canst thou for gain bear? and must every he
Which cries not, 'Goddess!' to thy mistress, draw,
Or eat thy poisonous words? courage of straw!
O desperate coward, wilt thou seem bold, and
To thy foes and his (who made thee to stand 30
Sentinel in his world's garrison) thus yield,
And for forbidden wars leave the appointed field?
Know thy foes: the foul Devil (whom thou
Strivest to please), for hate, not love, would allow
Thee fain, his whole realm to be quit; and as
The world's all parts wither away and pass
So the world's self, thy other loved foe, is
In her decrepit wane; and thou loving this,
Dost love a withered and worn strumpet; last,
Flesh (itself's death) and joys which flesh can taste, 40
Thou lovest; and thy fair goodly soul, which doth
Give this flesh power to taste joy, thou dost loathe.
Seek true Religion. O where? Mirreus,
Thinking her unhoused here, and fled from us,
Seeks her at Rome; there, because he doth know
That she was there a thousand years ago;
He loves her rags so, as we here obey
The state-cloth where the prince sat yesterday.
Crantz to such brave loves will not be enthralled,
But loves her only, who at Geneva is called   50
Religion, plain, simple, sullen, young,
Contemptuous, yet unhandsome; as among
Lecherous humors, there is one that judges
No wenches wholesome, but coarse country drudges.
Graius stays still at home here, and because
Some preachers, vile ambitious bawds, and laws
Still new like fashions, bid him think that she
Which dwells with us, is only perfect, he
Embraceth her, whom his godfather's will
Tender to him, being tender, as wards still   60
Take such wives as their guardians offer, or
Pay values. Careless Phrygius doth abhor
All, because all cannot be good, as one
Knowing some women whores, dares marry none.
Graccus loves all as one, and thinks that so
As women do in divers countries go
In divers habits, yet are still one kind,
So doth, so is Religion; and this blind-
Ness too much light breeds; but unmoved thou
Of force must one, and forced but one allow;   70
And the right; ask thy father which is she,
Let him ask his; though truth and falsehood be
Near twins, yet truth a little elder is;
Be busy to seek her, believe me this,
He's not of none, nor worst, that seeks the best.

34. **Spittles,** hospitals; there may be an unpleasant play on words here. 37. **know,** have sexual intercourse with; cf. the biblical use of this word. 38. **Th' . . . page,** a characteristic slur on the alleged homosex- uality of the Italian dandy. 41. **Lot's . . . vext.** See Genesis, Chapter 19. Lot, living in Sodom, was visited by two angels; as soon as the townspeople heard that Lot was entertaining visitors, they rushed to his house to commit rape on the guests. The angels solved the matter by striking the townspeople with blindness and persuaded Lot to leave

Sodom. 42. **hydroptic,** afflicted with dropsy.
  The Third Satire. 17. **mutinous Dutch,** a reference to the revolt of the Dutch Protestants against their overlord, the King of Spain, a revolt out of which grew the Dutch Republic. The adjective *mutinous* applied here suggests that Donne still had a Catholic viewpoint at the time this poem was written. 24. **Children . . . oven,** an allusion to the Israelites Shadrach, Meshach, and Abednego, who were cast into a fiery furnace by Nebuchadnezzar but were miraculously preserved by

To adore, or scorn an image, or protest,
May all be bad; doubt wisely; in strange way
To stand inquiring right, is not to stray;
To sleep, or run wrong, is. On a huge hill,
80 Cragged and steep, Truth stands, and he that will
Reach her, about must, and about must go;
And what the hill's suddenness resists, win so;
Yet strive so, that before age, Death's twilight,
Thy soul rest, for none can work in that night.
To will, implies delay, therefore now do:
Hard deeds, the body's pains; hard knowledge too
The mind's endeavors reach, and mysteries
Are like the sun, dazzling, yet plain to all eyes.
Keep the truth which thou hast found; men do not
    stand
90 In so ill case here, that God hath with his hand
Signed kings' blank-charters to kill whom they hate,
Nor are they vicars, but hangmen to Fate.
Fool and wretch, wilt thou let thy soul be tied
To Man's laws, by which she shall not be tried
At the last day? Oh, will it then boot thee
To say a Philip, or a Gregory,
A Harry, or a Martin taught thee this?
Is not this excuse for mere contraries,
Equally strong? Cannot both sides say so?
That thou mayest rightly obey power, her bounds
100 know;
Those past, her nature and name is changed; to be
Then humble to her is idolatry.
As streams are, Power is; those blest flowers that
    dwell
At the rough stream's calm head, thrive and do well,
But having left their roots, and themselves given
To the stream's tyrannous rage, alas, are driven
Through mills, and rocks, and woods, and at last,
    almost
Consumed in going, in the sea are lost:
So perish souls, which more choose men's unjust
Power from God claimed, than God Himself to trust.
(1633)

from PARADOXES AND PROBLEMS

A DEFENSE OF WOMEN'S INCONSTANCY

That Women are Inconstant, I with any man confess, but that Inconstancy is a bad quality, I against
any man will maintain: For every thing as it is one
better than another, so is it fuller of change; The
Heavens themselves continually turn, the Stars move,
the Moon changeth; Fire whirleth, Air flyeth, Water

ebbs and flows, the face of the Earth altereth her
looks, time staies not; the Colour that is most light,
will take most dyes: so in Men, they that have the
most reason are the most inalterable in their de- 10
signs, and the darkest or most ignorant, do seldomest
change; therefore Women changing more than Men,
have also more Reason. They cannot be immutable
like stocks, like stones, like the Earths dull Center;
Gold that lieth still, rusteth; Water, corrupteth; Air
that moveth not poisoneth; then why should that
which is the perfection of other things, be imputed
to Women as greatest imperfection? Because thereby
they deceive Men. Are not your wits pleased with
those jests, which cozen your expectation? You can 20
call it pleasure to be beguil'd in troubles, and in the
most excellent toy in the world, you call it Treachery:
I would you had your Mistresses so constant, that
they would never change, no not so much as their
smocks, then should you see what sluttish vertue,
Constancy were. Inconstancy is a most commendable
and cleanly quality, and Women in this quality are
far more absolute than the Heavens, than the Stars,
Moon, or any thing beneath it; for long observation
hath picked certainty out of their mutability. The 30
Learned are so well acquainted with the Stars, Signs,
and Planets, that they make them but Characters, to
read the meaning of the Heaven in his own forehead. Every simple fellow can bespeak the change of
the Moon a great while beforehand: but I would fain
have the learnedest man so skilfull, as to tell when
the simplest Woman meaneth to vary. Learning
affords no rules to know, much less knowledge to rule
the mind of a Woman: For as Philosophy teacheth
us, that Light things do always tend upwards, and 40
heavy things decline downward; Experience teacheth
us otherwise that the disposition of a Light Woman,
is to fall down, the nature of women being contrary
to all Art and Nature. Women are like Flies, which
feed among us at our Table, or Fleas sucking our
very blood, who leave not our most retired places
from their familiarity, yet for all their fellowship will
they never be tamed nor commanded by us. Women
are like the Sun, which is violently carried one way,
yet hath a proper course contrary: so though they, 50
by the mastery of some over-ruling churlish husbands, are forced to his Bias, yet have they a motion
of their own, which their husbands never know of:
It is the nature of nice and fastidious minds to know
things only to be weary of them: Women by their sly
changeableness, and pleasing doubleness, prevent
even the mislike of those, for they can never be so
well known, but that there is still more unknown.

God's intervention; see Daniel, Chapter 3. **line,** the Equator. **36. all
parts,** everywhere. **43. Mirreus,** a name given to a young man of a
particular religious persuasion. _Crantz_ (l. 49), _Graius_ (l. 55), and
Phrygius (l. 62) are other such youths. **81. about must,** must turn
around. **82. win so,** i.e., by turning around or changing plans. **91.
blank-charters,** death warrants left blank, the name of the victim to be
filled in at the convenience of the prosecutor. **96. Philip . . . Martin,**
Philip and _Gregory_ represent worldly Catholicism and ecclesiastical

Catholicism, respectively; _Philip_ is Philip II of Spain, the chief Cath-
olic potentate of the time, and _Gregory_ is the name of several popes—
perhaps Gregory the Great (c. 500) is meant, but more likely either
Gregory XIII or Gregory XIV, who were popes after the Reformation.
Harry is, of course, Henry VIII of England, and _Martin_ is Martin
Luther.
  A Defense . . . Inconstancy. 1. Inconstant, cf. _The Indifferent,_
p. 327.

Every woman is a Science; for he that plods upon a woman all his life long, shall at length find himself short of the knowledge of her: they are born to take down the pride of wit, and ambition of wisdom, making fools wise in the adventuring to win them, wisemen fools in conceit of losing their labours; witty men stark mad, being confounded with their uncertainties. Philosophers write against them for spite, not desert, that having attained to some knowl-
10 edge in all other things, in them only they know nothing, but are merely ignorant: Active and Experienced men rail against them, because they love in their liveless and decrepit age, when all goodness leaves them. These envious Libellers ballad against them, because having nothing in themselves able to deserve their love, they maliciously discommend all they cannot obtain, thinking to make men believe they know much, because they are able to dispraise much, and rage against Inconstancy, when they were
20 never admitted into so much favour as to be forsaken. In mine opinion such men are happy that women are Inconstant, for so may they chance to be beloved of some excellent woman (when it comes to their turn) out of their Inconstancy and mutability, though not out of their own desert. And what reason is there to clog any woman with one man, be he never so singular? Women had rather, and it is far better and more Judicial to enjoy all the virtues in several men, than but some of them in one, for other-
30 wise they lose their taste, like divers sorts of meat minced together in one dish: and to have all excellencies in one man (if it were possible) is Confusion and Diversity. Now who can deny, but such as are obstinately bent to undervalue their worth, are those that have not soul enough to comprehend their excellency, Women being the most excellent Creatures, in that Man is able to subject all things else, and to grow wise in every thing, but still persists a fool in Woman? The greatest Scholar, if he
40 once take a wife, is found so unlearned, that he must begin his Horn-book, and all is by Inconstancy. To conclude therefore; this name of Inconstancy, which hath so much been poisoned with slanders, ought to be changed into variety, for the which the world is so delightful, and a Woman for that the most delightful thing in this world.
(1633, 1659)

from DEVOTIONS UPON EMERGENT OCCASIONS

MEDITATION XVII

The poet, confined to his bed with a serious illness, hears the bells of the church adjoining, and is thereby reminded of death and the transiency of human life.

4. **wit**, minds. 27. **singular**, remarkable.

Perchance he for whom this bell tolls may be so ill, as that he knows not it tolls for him; and perchance I may think myself so much better than I am, as that they who are about me, and see my 50 state, may have caused it to toll for me, and I know not that. The church is catholic, universal, so are all her actions; all that she does belongs to all. When she baptizes a child, that action concerns me; for that child is thereby connected to that head which is my head too, and ingrafted into that body whereof I am a member. And when she buries a man, that action concerns me: all mankind is of one author, and is one volume; when one man dies, one chapter is not torn out of the book, but translated into a better 60 language; and every chapter must be so translated; God employs several translators; some pieces are translated by age, some by sickness, some by war, some by justice; but God's hand is in every translation, and his hand shall bind up all our scattered leaves again for that library where every book shall lie open to one another. As therefore the bell that rings to a sermon calls not upon the preacher only, but upon the congregation to come, so this bell calls us all; but how much more me, who am brought 70 so near the door by this sickness. There was a contention as far as a suit (in which both piety and dignity, religion and estimation, were mingled), which of the religious orders should ring to prayers first in the morning; and it was determined, that they should ring first that rose earliest. If we understand aright the dignity of this bell that tolls for our evening prayer, we would be glad to make it ours by rising early, in that application, that it might be ours as well as his, whose indeed it is. The bell 80 doth toll for him that thinks it doth; and though it intermit again, yet from that minute that that occasion wrought upon him, he is united to God. Who casts not up his eye to the sun when it rises? but who takes off his eye from a comet when that breaks out? Who bends not his ear to any bell which upon any occasion rings? but who can remove it from that bell which is passing a piece of himself out of this world? No man is an island, entire of itself; every man is a piece of the continent, a part 90 of the main. If a clod be washed away by the sea, Europe is the less, as well as if a promontory were, as well as if a manor of thy friend's or of thine own were: any man's death diminishes me, because I am involved in mankind, and therefore never send to know for whom the bell tolls; it tolls for thee. Neither can we call this a begging of misery, or a borrowing of misery, as though we were not miserable enough of ourselves, but must fetch in more from the next house, in taking upon us the misery of our neighbors. 100 Truly it were an excusable covetousness if we did, for affliction is a treasure, and scarce any man hath enough of it. No man hath affliction enough that is not matured and ripened by it, and made fit for God by that affliction. If a man carry treasure in bullion, or in a wedge of gold, and have none coined into current money, his treasure will not defray him as he travels. Tribulation is a treasure in the nature of it, but it is not current money in the use of it, except we get nearer and nearer our home, Heaven, by it. Another man may be sick too, and sick to death, and this affliction may lie in his bowels, as gold in a mine, and be of no use to him; but this bell, that tells me of his affliction, digs out and applies that gold to me: if by this consideration of another's danger I take mine own into contemplation, and so secure myself, by making my recourse to my God, who is our only security.

MEDITATION XVIII

The bell rings out, the pulse thereof is changed; the tolling was a faint and intermitting pulse, upon one side; this stronger, and argues more and better life. His soul is gone out, and as a man who had a lease of one thousand years after the expiration of a short one, or an inheritance after the life of a man in a consumption, he is now entered into the possession of his better estate. His soul is gone, whither? Who saw it come in, or who saw it go out? Nobody; yet everybody is sure he had one, and hath none. If I will ask mere philosophers what the soul is, I shall find amongst them that will tell me, it is nothing but the temperament and harmony, and just and equal composition of the elements in the body, which produces all those faculties which we ascribe to the soul; and so in itself is nothing, no separable substance that overlives the body. They see the soul is nothing else in other creatures, and they affect an impious humility to think as low of man. But if my soul were no more than the soul of a beast, I could not think so; that soul that can reflect upon itself, consider itself, is more than so. If I will ask, not mere philosophers, but mixed men, philosophical divines, how the soul, being a separate substance, enters into man, I shall find some that will tell me, that it is by generation and procreation from parents, because they think it hard to charge the soul with the guiltiness of original sin if the soul were infused into a body in which it must necessarily grow foul, and contract original sin whether it will or no; and I shall find some that will tell me, that it is by immediate infusion from God, because they think it hard to maintain an immortality in such a soul, as should be begotten and derived with the body from mortal parents. If I will ask, not a few men, but almost whole bodies, whole churches, what becomes of the souls of the righteous at the departing thereof from the body, I shall be told by some, that they attend an expiation, a purification in a place of torment; by some, that they attend the fruition of the sight of God in a place of rest, but yet but of expectation; by some, that they pass to an immediate possession of the presence of God. St. Augustine studied the nature of the soul as much as any thing, but the salvation of the soul; and he sent an express messenger to St. Jerome, to consult of some things concerning the soul; but he satisfies himself with this: "Let the departure of my soul to salvation be evident to my faith, and I care the less how dark the entrance of my soul into my body be to my reason." It is the going out, more than the coming in, that concerns us. This soul this bell tells me is gone out, whither? Who shall tell me that? I know not who it is, much less what he was, the condition of the man, and the course of his life, which should tell me whither he is gone, I know not. I was not there in his sickness, nor at his death; I saw not his way nor his end, nor can ask them who did, thereby to conclude or argue whither he is gone. But yet I have one nearer me than all these, mine own charity; I ask that, and that tells me he is gone to everlasting rest, and joy, and glory. I owe him a good opinion; it is but thankful charity in me, because I received benefit and instruction from him when his bell tolled; and I, being made the fitter to pray by that disposition, wherein I was assisted by his occasion, did pray for him; and I pray not without faith; so I do charitably, so I do faithfully believe, that that soul is gone to everlasting rest, and joy, and glory. But for the body, how poor a wretched thing is that? we cannot express it so fast, as it grows worse and worse. That body, which scarce three minutes since was such a house, as that that soul, which made but one step from thence to Heaven, was scarce thoroughly content to leave that for Heaven; that body hath lost the name of a dwelling-house, because none dwells in it, and is making haste to lose the name of a body, and dissolve to putrefaction. Who would not be affected to see a clear and sweet river in the morning, grow a kennel of muddy land-water by noon, and condemned to the saltness of the sea by night? and how lame a picture, how faint a representation is that, of the precipitation of man's body to dissolution? Now all the parts built up, and knit by a lovely soul, now but a statue of clay, and now these limbs melted off, as if that clay were but snow; and now the whole house is but a handful of sand, so much dust, and but a peck of rubbish, so much bone. If he who, as this bell tells me, is gone now, were some excellent artificer, who comes to him for a cloak or a garment now? or for counsel, if he were a lawyer? if a magistrate, for justice? man, before he hath his immortal soul, hath a soul of sense, and a soul of vegetation before that: this immortal soul did not forbid other souls to be in us before, but when this soul departs, it carries all with it; no more vegetation, no more sense. Such a mother-in-law is the earth, in respect of our natural mother; in her womb we grew, and when she was delivered of us, we were planted in some place, in some calling in the world; in the womb of the earth we diminish, and when she is delivered of us, our grave opened for another; we are not transplanted, but transported, our dust blown away with profane dust, with every wind.

(1624)

GEORGE HERBERT 1593-1633

George Herbert, a man of singular purity and fervor, was the most important of the metaphysical poets. He came from the border family of the Herberts, and was born in Montgomery in 1593. Three years later his father died. Herbert was educated at Westminster School and at Trinity College, Cambridge. His brilliance as a student and public speaker won for him the post of university orator when he was only eighteen. In 1626 he became deacon in Lincoln Cathedral, and four years later he was ordained as an Anglican priest and assigned to the rectory of Fulston St. Peter's, Bemerton, Wiltshire. After only three years he died (1633) and was buried under the altar at which he had served with a reverence and devotion that distinguished him throughout England. Herbert's sacred poems, The Temple, were published the year of his death. This collection contains one hundred twenty-nine poems which form together the record of his spiritual experiences— the history of a soul.

THE PEARL

I know the ways of learning, both the head
And pipes that feed the press and make it run;
What reason hath from nature borrowéd,
Or of itself, like a good housewife, spun
In laws and policy; what the stars conspire;
What willing nature speaks, what forced by fire;
Both the old discoveries, and the new-found seas,
The stock and surplus, cause and history;
All these stand open, or I have the keys:
10 Yet I love Thee.

I know the ways of honor, what maintains
The quick returns of courtesy and wit;
In vies of favors whether party gains
When glory swells the heart, and moldeth it
To all expressions, both of hand and eye,

Which on the world a true-love knot may tie,
And bear the bundle wheresoe'er it goes;
How many drams of spirit there must be
To sell my life unto my friends or foes:
Yet I love Thee.   20

I know the ways of pleasure, the sweet strains,
The lullings and the relishes of it;
The propositions of hot blood and brains;
What mirth and music mean; what love and wit
Have done these twenty hundred years and more;
I know the projects of unbridled store;
My stuff is flesh, not brass; my senses live,
And grumble oft that they have more in me
Than he that curbs them, being but one to five:
Yet I love Thee.   30

I know all these, and have them in my hand;
Therefore not seeléd but with open eyes
I fly to Thee, and fully understand
Both the main sale and the commodities;
And at what rate and price I have Thy love,
With all the circumstances that may move.
Yet through the labyrinths, not my groveling wit,
But Thy silk twist let down from heaven to me,
Did both conduct and teach me how by it
To climb to Thee.   40

(1633)

THE QUIP

The merry World did on a day
With his train-bands and mates agree
To meet together where I lay
And all in sport to jeer at me.

First Beauty crept into a rose,
Which when I pluckt not, "Sir," said she,
"Tell me, I pray, whose hands are those?"
But Thou shalt answer, Lord, for me.

Then Money came, and clinking still,
"What tune is this, poor man?" said he;   10
"I heard in Musick you had skill."
But Thou shalt answer, Lord, for me.

Then came brave Glory, puffing by
In silks that whistled, who but he!
He scarce allowed me half an eye.
But Thou shalt answer, Lord, for me.

Then came quick Wit and Conversation,
And he would needs a comfort be,

The Pearl. 6. **forced by fire**, i.e., wrung from nature in the flame of the experimental laboratory. 26. **store**, wealth. 32. **seeléd**, in falconry, blinding a hawk by running through its eyelids threads which were then tied over its head. 38. **twist**, cord.

The Quip. 7. **whose . . . those,** i.e., what are your hands for?
The Collar, the symbol of spiritual restraint; cf. Matthew 11:29: "Take my yoke upon you." 5. **store**, abundance. 6. **still in suit**, always forced to entreat. 26. **wink**, close thy eyes.

And, to be short, make an oration.
20 But Thou shalt answer, Lord, for me.

Yet when the hour of Thy design
To answer these fine things shall come,
Speak not at large; say, I am Thine,
And then they have their answer home.
(1633)

THE COLLAR

I struck the board, and cried, "No more;
    I will abroad!
What! shall I ever sigh and pine?
My lines and life are free; free as the road,
  Loose as the wind, as large as store.
    Shall I be still in suit?
  Have I no harvest but a thorn
  To let me blood, and not restore
What I have lost with cordial fruit?
10   Sure there was wine
  Before my sighs did dry it; there was corn
    Before my tears did drown it;
    Is the year only lost to me?
    Have I no bays to crown it,
No flowers, no garlands gay? all blasted,
    All wasted?
  Not so, my heart, but there is fruit,
    And thou hast hands.
  Recover all thy sigh-blown age
20 On double pleasures; leave thy cold dispute
Of what is fit and not; forsake thy cage,
    Thy rope of sands
Which petty thoughts have made, and made to thee
  Good cable, to enforce and draw,
    And be thy law,
While thou didst wink and wouldst not see.
    Away! take heed;
    I will abroad.
Call in thy death's head there, tie up thy fears;
30   He that forbears
    To suit and serve his need
    Deserves his load."
But as I raved, and grew more fierce and wild
    At every word,
Methought I heard one calling, "Child";
    And I replied, "My Lord."
(1633)

RICHARD CRASHAW 1612?-1649

Richard Crashaw was the most mystical of the metaphysical poets. His father was a Puritan divine in London noted for his violent hatred of Roman Catholics. At Pembroke Hall, Cambridge, where the poet went in 1631 when he was about nineteen, he took a keen interest in ecclesiastical matters. His further interest in the Spanish and Italian mystics fed his own deep strain of mysticism, and after having lost his fellowship at Cambridge in 1644 because of his Royalist and high church leanings, he embraced the Roman Catholic faith. The year 1646 saw him in Paris. Shortly afterwards he became secretary to Cardinal Palotta, governor of Rome. By condemning the corruption of other members of the governor's staff he aroused their resentment and was sent for his own safety to the Church of Our Lady of Loretto. He died almost immediately afterwards, not without its being suspected that his enemies had poisoned him. The first volume of his secular and sacred poems was published in 1646 under the title Steps to the Temple. Sacred Poems, With other Delights of the Muses. *These and later poems were issued in Paris, as* Carmen Deo Nostro, *three years after his death. Crashaw has the distinction of having been the only notable Roman Catholic metaphysical poet in England in the seventeenth century.*

DESCRIPTION OF A RELIGIOUS HOUSE AND CONDITION OF LIFE

(Out of Barclay)

No roofs of gold o'er riotous tables shining,
Whole days and suns devoured with endless dining;
No sails of Tyrian silk proud pavement sweeping,
Nor ivory couches costlier slumbers keeping;
False lights of flaring gems; tumultuous joys;
Halls full of flattering men and frisking boys;
Whate'er false shows of short and slippery good
Mix the mad sons of men in mutual blood.
But walks and unshorn woods; and souls, just so
Unforced and genuine; but no shady though.   10
Our lodgings hard and homely as our fare,
That chaste and cheap, as the few clothes we wear;
Those, coarse and negligent, as the natural locks
Of these loose groves; rough as th' unpolished rocks.
A hasty portion of prescribed sleep;
Obedient slumbers, that can wake and weep,
And sing, and sigh, and work, and sleep again;
Still rolling a round sphere of still-returning pain.
Hands full of hearty labors; pains that pay
And prize themselves; do much, that more they may, 20
And work for work, not wages; let tomorrow's
New drops wash off the sweat of this day's sorrows.
A long and daily-dying life, which breathes

Description of a Religious House and Condition of Life, from *Carmen Deo Nostro* (Song to Our Lord). **Barclay.** Crashaw's poem was adapted from a Latin one beginning "*Non isthic aurata domus*"— "Here no gilt roofs"—which appeared in the *Argenis* of John Barclay (1582-1621), a Scottish satirist and writer of Latin poems. Crashaw translated from medieval Latin many religious poems, including the famous *Dies Irae, Dies Illa*—Judgment Day.

A respiration of reviving deaths.
But neither are there those ignoble stings
That nip the blossom of the World's best things,
And lash Earth-laboring souls.
No cruel guard of diligent cares, that keep
Crown'd woes awake, as things too wise for sleep:
30 But reverent discipline, and religious fear,
And soft obedience, find sweet biding here;
Silence, and sacred rest; peace, and pure joys;
Kind loves keep house, lie close, and make no
   noise;
And room enough for monarchs, while none swells
Beyond the kingdoms of contentful cells.
The self-rememb'ring soul sweetly recovers
Her kindred with the stars; not basely hovers
Below: but meditates her immortal way
Home to the original source of Light and intellectual
   day.
(1652)

WISHES TO HIS SUPPOSED MISTRESS

Whoe'er she be,
That not impossible she,
That shall command my heart and me;

Whe'er she lie,
Locked up from mortal eye,
In shady leaves of destiny:

Till that ripe birth
Of studied fate stand forth
And teach her fair steps to our earth;

10 Till that divine
Idea take a shrine
Of crystal flesh, through which to shine:

Meet you her, my wishes,
Bespeak her to my blisses,
And be ye called, my absent kisses.

I wish her beauty,
That owes not all its duty
To gaudy tire, or glist'ring shoe-tie.

Something more than
20 Taffeta or tissue can,
Or rampant feather, or rich fan.

More than the spoil
Of shop, or silkworm's toil,
Or a bought blush, or a set smile.

A face that's best
By its own beauty drest,
And can alone commend the rest.

A face made up
Out of no other shop
Than what Nature's white hand sets ope.   30

A cheek where youth
And blood, with pen of truth,
Write what the reader sweetly ru'th.

A cheek where grows
More than a morning rose:
Which to no box his being owes.

Lips where all day
A lover's kiss may play,
Yet carry nothing thence away.

Looks that oppress   40
Their richest tires, but dress
Themselves in simple nakedness.

Eyes that displace
The neighbor diamond, and out-face
That sunshine by their own sweet grace.

Tresses that wear
Jewels, but to declare
How much themselves more precious are.

Whose native ray
Can tame the wanton day   50
Of gems, that in their bright shades play.

Each ruby there,
Or pearl that dares appear,
Be its own blush, be its own tear.

A well-tamed heart,
For whose more noble smart
Love may be long choosing a dart.

Eyes that bestow
Full quivers on Love's bow;
Yet pay less arrows than they owe.   60

Smiles that can warm
The blood, yet teach a charm,
That chastity shall take no harm.

Blushes that bin
The burnish of no sin,
Nor flames of aught too hot within.

Wishes to His Supposed Mistress. 2. **she,** a common use of the pronoun for the noun. 4. **lie,** live. 18. **tire,** attire, merely clothes. 20.
tissue, cloth of gold or silver. 30. **ope,** open. 33. **Write . . . ru'th.**
Depict a beauty which makes the beholder suffer the sweet sorrow of
love. 36. **box,** i.e., is not produced by cosmetics. **his,** its. 39. nothing, i.e., no paint or lipstick. 40. **oppress . . . nakedness,** overpower,
outshine the richest dress, and need nothing to adorn them. 57. **dart,**
a weapon powerful enough to reach so well-controlled (well-tamed) a
heart. 60. **owe,** possess, own. 70. **fond . . . flight,** foolish and fleeting. 74. **are,** i.e., that are. 88. **Sidneian showers,** i.e., discourses as

Joys that confess
Virtue their mistress,
And have no other head to dress.

70 Fears, fond and flight
As the coy bride's, when night
First does the longing lover right.

Tears, quickly fled,
And vain, as those are shed
For a dying maidenhead.

Days that need borrow
No part of their good morrow,
From a fore-spent night of sorrow.

Days that in spite
80 Of darkness, by the light
Of a clear mind are day all night.

Nights, sweet as they,
Made short by lovers' play,
Yet long by th' absence of the day.

Life that dares send
A challenge to his end,
And when it comes, say "Welcome, friend."

Sidneian showers
Of sweet discourse, whose powers
90 Can crown old Winter's head with flowers.

Soft silken hours,
Open suns, shady bowers,
'Bove all, nothing within that lowers.

Whate'er delight
Can make Day's forehead bright,
Or give down to the wings of Night.

In her whole frame
Have Nature all the name,
Art and ornament the shame.

100 Her flattery,
Picture and poesy:
Her counsel her own virtue be.

I wish her store
Of worth may leave her poor
Of wishes; and I wish — no more.

Now, if Time knows
That her, whose radiant brows
Weave them a garland of my vows;

Her whose just bays
My future hopes can raise,   110
A trophy to her present praise;

Her that dares be
What these lines wish to see:
I seek no further; it is she.

'Tis she, and here
Lo! I unclothe and clear
My wishes' cloudy character.

May she enjoy it,
Whose merit dare apply it,
But modesty dares still deny it.   120

Such worth as this is,
Shall fix my flying wishes,
And determine them to kisses.

Let her full glory,
My fancies, fly before ye:
Be ye my fictions, but her story.
(1641)

HENRY VAUGHAN 1622?-1695

Henry Vaughan was born, the elder of twin boys, about 1622 at Newton St. Bridget on the Usk. His love for the Welsh mountains entered deeply into his soul and is embodied in his selection of a pen name; the Silurist, he called himself, from the Silures or ancient inhabitants of southern Wales. From Jesus College, Oxford, Vaughan went up to London to study law, but changed his plan of life and devoted himself to the study of medicine. In 1647 he returned to his beloved home on the Usk to live and practice among his own people. Between this date and 1650 he suffered from a prolonged sickness which deepened and strengthened his spiritual nature. His religious as well as his literary guide became "the blessed man Mr. George Herbert" (though Vaughan was only a lad when the older man died), and the link between the two spirits was very close. Vaughan was a true mystic; mysticism is mingled with his inherent love of nature, so that, in a sense, he seems to anticipate Emily Dickinson, the American recluse of two centuries later. Vaughan's sacred poems appeared in 1650 as Silex Scintillans, and his secular verse as Poems (1646) and Thalia Rediviva (1678). Vaughan outlived by many years the other metaphysical poets, not dying until 1695.

gentle and well-bred as those of Sir Philip Sidney. 98. **name**, report, fame. 100. **Her . . . be**, i.e., painting and poetry may flatter her, but her own virtue should be her sole confidant or counselor. 103. **I . . . wishes.** I hope that she may have such an abundance of worth that she will need to wish for little more. 111. **trophy**, monument.

117. **cloudy**, shadowy, secret. 118. **enjoy**, often pronounced in Crashaw's day to rhyme with *apply*. 123. **determine them**, resolve them into. 126. **my . . . story**, my imaginings, but hers in fact.

THE RETREAT

Happy those early days, when I
Shined in my angel-infancy!
Before I understood this place
Appointed for my second race,
Or taught my soul to fancy aught
But a white, celestial thought;
When yet I had not walked above
A mile or two from my first love,
And looking back at that short space,
10 Could see a glimpse of his bright face;
When on some gilded cloud or flower
My gazing soul would dwell an hour,
And in those weaker glories spy
Some shadows of eternity;
Before I taught my tongue to wound
My conscience with a sinful sound,
Or had the black art to dispense,
A several sin to every sense,
But felt through all this fleshly dress
20 Bright shoots of everlastingness.
    O, how I long to travel back,
And tread again that ancient track,
That I might once more reach that plain,
Where first I left my glorious train;
From whence the enlightened spirit sees
That shady city of palm trees.
But ah! my soul with too much stay
Is drunk, and staggers in the way!
Some men a forward motion love,
30 But I by backward steps would move;
And when this dust falls to the urn,
In that state I came, return.
(1650)

THE WORLD

I saw Eternity the other night,
Like a great ring of pure and endless light,
    All calm, as it was bright;
And round beneath it, Time, in hours, days, years,
    Driven by the spheres
Like a vast shadow moved; in which the world
    And all her train were hurled.
The doting lover in his quaintest strain
    Did there complain;
10 Near him, his lute, his fancy, and his flights,
    Wit's sour delights,
With gloves, and knots, the silly snares of pleasure,
    Yet his dear treasure,
All scattered lay, while he his eyes did pour
    Upon a flower.

The darksome statesman, hung with weights and woe,
Like a thick midnight-fog moved there so slow,
    He did not stay, nor go;
Condemning thoughts, like sad eclipses, scowl
    Upon his soul,   20
And clouds of crying witnesses without
    Pursued him with one shout.
Yet digged the mole, and lest his ways be found,
    Worked under ground,
Where he did clutch his prey; but one did see
    That policy;
Churches and altars fed him; perjuries
    Were gnats and flies;
It rained about him blood and tears, but he
    Drank them as free.   30

The fearful miser on a heap of rust
Sat pining all his life there, did scarce trust
    His own hands with the dust,
Yet would not place one piece above, but lives
    In fear of thieves.
Thousands there were as frantic as himself,
    And hugged each one his pelf;
The downright epicure placed heaven in sense,
    And scorned pretense;
While others, slipped into a wide excess,   40
    Said little less;
The weaker sort, slight, trivial wares enslave,
    Who think them brave;
And poor, despiséd Truth sat counting by
    Their victory.

Yet some, who all this while did weep and sing,
And sing and weep, soared up into the ring;
    But most would use no wing.
O fools, said I, thus to prefer dark night
    Before true light!   50
To live in grots and caves, and hate the day
    Because it shows the way,
The way, which from this dead and dark abode
    Leads up to God;
A way where you might tread the sun, and be
    More bright than he!
But, as I did their madness so discuss,
    One whispered thus
"This ring the Bridegroom did for none provide,
    But for his bride."
(1650)

DEPARTED FRIENDS

They are all gone into the world of light!
    And I alone sit lingering here;

The Retreat. 4. second race, earthly existence. With these ideas may be compared those in Wordsworth's Ode on Intimations of Immortality from Recollections of Early Childhood (p. 700). 18. several, separate, different. 26. shady city, the celestial city (heaven).
The World. 10. fancy . . . flights, his love poems.

Their very memory is fair and bright,
   And my sad thoughts doth clear.

It glows and glitters in my cloudy breast,
   Like stars upon some gloomy grove,
Or those faint beams in which this hill is drest,
   After the sun's remove.

I see them walking in an air of glory,
10   Whose light doth trample on my days;
My days, which are at best but dull and hoary,
   Mere glimmering and decays.

O holy Hope! and high Humility,
   High as the heavens above!
These are your walks, and you have showed them me,
   To kindle my cold love.

Dear, beauteous Death! the jewel of the just,
   Shining nowhere but in the dark,
What mysteries do lie beyond thy dust,
20   Could man outlook that mark!

He that hath found some fledged bird's nest, may
   know

At first sight if the bird be flown;
But what fair well or grove he sings in now,
   That is to him unknown.

And yet, as angels in some brighter dreams
   Call to the soul, when man doth sleep,
So some strange thoughts transcend our wonted
      themes,
   And into glory peep.

If a star were confined into a tomb,
   The captive flames must needs burn there,   30
But when the hand that locked her up gives room,
   She'll shine through all the sphere.

O Father of eternal life, and all
   Created glories under thee,
Resume thy spirit from this world of thrall
   Into true liberty.

Either disperse these mists, which blot and fill
   My perspective still as they pass,
Or else remove me hence unto that hill,
   Where I shall need no glass.
(1655)

Departed Friends. 38. **perspective,** telescope. The figure is that of a mortal trying to see heaven through the mists of the world; cf. the similar figure in 1 Corinthians 13:12 (p. 317), where the "glass," however, is a mirror in which the world is dimly reflected.

THE CAVALIER POETS AND THE "SONS OF BEN"

The Stuart monarchs, like Queen Elizabeth, delighted to crowd their courts with witty, versatile, and clever young men, who were useful on diplomatic missions, serviceable—or at least decorative—at court, and graceful and entertaining at all times. At the court of Charles I was a particularly brilliant group of wits and poets, who came to be known in literature, because of their party affiliations, as "the Cavalier Poets." Although each of them had individual characteristics, their verse has many elements in common—grace, ease, elegance, and wit. Most of these poets came at one time or another under the influence of Ben Jonson, but the peculiar qualities of John Donne, who must have known many and influenced more, can be traced in much of their work.

The poets of the "tribe of Ben" form a much more important group than the Cavaliers. Under the leadership of Ben Jonson they created an informal and unnamed Pléiade, and at the Mermaid and the Devil taverns they gathered about him at a banquet of wit that "outdid the frolic wine." These literary feasts were pagan, and the literary dictator who presided was a classicist. His enthusiasms were not, however, for the romantic and ornate Ovid, so popular with the Elizabethans, but rather for Anacreon, the Greek poet who five hundred years before the beginning of the Christian era sang gaily of wine, women, and song. And among the Romans of a much later date Jonson and his "sons" admired the amorous and witty Catullus and the satirical and outspoken Horace. So Jonson infused into the new poets a pagan love for the joys of living in the present and for gathering rosebuds before the frost scatters the leaves. And this joie de vivre was served with the sharp sauce of cynicism and satire, for Jonson was a satirist, and his admiring followers were smart young men, Royalists like himself, who found pleasure in shooting shafts of ridicule—especially if the target was a Puritan.

BEN JONSON 1573-1637

Ben Jonson was a commoner and a blunt outspoken fellow, admired for his honesty and the brilliance of his classical learning rather than for his courtesy and his taste. His father, who was a minister, died when Jonson was a boy, the widow married a bricklayer, and for a time Ben Jonson seems to have followed his stepfather's calling. He attended Westminster School but there is no record of his having gone to either Oxford or Cambridge, yet he "was master of arts in both . . . by their favor, not his study." He acquired his classical knowledge through his own efforts. For a time he served with the troops in the Low Countries, and in 1598 began with Every Man in His Humour a series of epoch-making satirical comedies based upon "the humors" or idiosyncrasies of men. His naturally quarrelsome disposition involved him in numerous controversies, but with the coming of King James, Jonson was in high favor at the court as a writer of masques—elaborate and costly entertainments concocted chiefly of song, dance, and allegorical pageantry. To the last decade of his life belongs his inspiration of the "tribe of Ben" to carry into later decades the richness of his philosophy and his art. Many of Jonson's lyrics are scattered through his plays, others appeared in Epigrams (1616), The Forest (1616), and Underwoods (1640). Jonson is usually considered the first poet laureate by virtue of a pension bestowed on him by James I.

HYMN TO DIANA

Queen and Huntress, chaste and fair,
  Now the sun is laid to sleep,
Seated in thy silver chair
    State in wonted manner keep:
      Hesperus entreats thy light,
      Goddess excellently bright.

Earth, let not thy envious shade
  Dare itself to interpose;
Cynthia's shining orb was made
10 Heaven to clear when day did close:
      Bless us then with wishéd sight,
      Goddess excellently bright.

Lay thy bow of pearl apart
  And thy crystal-shining quiver;

Give unto the flying hart
  Space to breathe, how short soever:
      Thou that mak'st a day of night,
      Goddess excellently bright.

(1600)

SONG: TO CELIA

Come, my Celia, let us prove,
While we can, the sports of love.
Time will not be ours for ever;
He, at length, our good will sever;
Spend not then his gifts in vain.
Suns that set may rise again;
But if once we lose this light,
'T is with us perpetual night.
Why should we defer our joys?
Fame and rumor are but toys.   10
Cannot we delude the eyes
Of a few poor household spies?
Or his easier ears beguile,
Thus removéd by our wile?
'T is no sin love's fruits to steal;
But the sweet theft to reveal,
To be taken, to be seen,
These have crimes accounted been.

(1605)

SONG TO CELIA

Drink to me only with thine eyes,
  And I will pledge with mine;
Or leave a kiss but in the cup,
  And I'll not look for wine.
The thirst that from the soul doth rise
  Doth ask a drink divine;
But might I of Jove's nectar sup,
  I would not change for thine.

I sent thee late a rosy wreath,
  Not so much honoring thee   10
As giving it a hope, that there
  It could not withered be.
But thou thereon didst only breathe,
  And sent'st it back to me;
Since when it grows, and smells, I swear,
  Not of itself, but thee.

(1616)

Hymn to Diana, sung by Hesperus in *Cynthia's Revels,* V, iii.
  Song: to Celia, sung by Volpone in *Volpone,* III, vi. **10. toys,** trifles. **13. his.** The reference is to Celia's husband, Corvino.
  Song to Celia, from *The Forest.*
  Simplex Munditiis, in simple elegance (from Horace's *Odes,* I, v). The song is from *The Silent Woman,* I, i.
  Epitaph on Elizabeth L. H. L. H.; cf. ll. 9–10.
  It Is Not Growing . . . Tree, from *A Pindaric Ode on the Death*

of H. Morison. The Pindaric ode, developed by the Greek poet Pindar (522–443 B.C.), is an elaborate laudatory address divided formally into several divisions. The stanza here is the *Strophe,* or *Turn,* of the third division.
  To the Memory . . . Shakespeare. This tribute was published in the first complete edition of Shakespeare's plays, 1623, where it is the first of four laudatory poems which follow the dedication of the volume to the Earls of Pembroke and Montgomery. **2. ample,** i.e., do I thus

SIMPLEX MUNDITIIS

Still to be neat, still to be drest,
As you were going to a feast;
Still to be powdered, still perfumed;
Lady, it is to be presumed,
Though art's hid causes are not found,
All is not sweet, all is not sound.

Give me a look, give me a face
That makes simplicity a grace;
Robes loosely flowing, hair as free.
10 Such sweet neglect more taketh me
Than all the adulteries of art;
They strike mine eyes, but not my heart.
(1609?; 1616)

EPITAPH ON ELIZABETH L. H.

Would'st thou hear what man can say
In a little? Reader, stay.

Underneath this stone doth lie
As much beauty as could die,
Which in life did harbor give
To more virtue than doth live.

If at all she had a fault,
Leave it buried in this vault.
One name was Elizabeth,
10 The other, let it sleep with death!
Fitter, where it died, to tell,
Than that it lived at all. Farewell!
(1616)

IT IS NOT GROWING LIKE A TREE

It is not growing like a tree
In bulk, doth make men better be;
Or standing long an oak, three hundred year,
To fall a log at last, dry, bald, and sear:
    A lily of a day
    Is fairer far in May;
Although it fall and die that night,
It was the plant and flower of light.
In small proportions we just beauties see,
And in short measures life may perfect be.
(1616)

TO THE MEMORY OF MY BELOVED
MASTER, WILLIAM SHAKESPEARE

To draw no envy, Shakespeare, on thy name,
Am I thus ample to thy book and fame;
While I confess thy writings to be such
As neither man, nor muse, can praise too much.
'Tis true, and all men's suffrage. But these ways
Were not the paths I meant unto thy praise;
For silliest ignorance on these may light,
Which, when it sounds at best, but echoes right;
Or blind affection, which doth ne'er advance
The truth, but gropes, and urgeth all by chance;   10
Or crafty malice might pretend this praise,
And think to ruin, where it seemed to raise.
These are, as some infamous bawd or whore
Should praise a matron. What could hurt her more?
But thou art proof against them, and, indeed,
Above the ill fortune of them, or the need.
I therefore will begin. Soul of the age!
The applause, delight, the wonder of our stage!
My Shakespeare, rise! I will not lodge thee by
Chaucer, or Spenser, or bid Beaumont lie   20
A little further, to make thee a room;
Thou art a monument without a tomb,
And art alive still while thy book doth live
And we have wits to read and praise to give.
That I not mix thee so, my brain excuses,
I mean with great, but disproportioned Muses;
For if I thought my judgment were of years,
I should commit thee surely with thy peers,
And tell how far thou didst our Lyly outshine,
Or sporting Kyd, or Marlowe's mighty line.   30
And though thou hadst small Latin and less Greek,
From thence to honor thee, I would not seek
For names; but call forth thundering Aeschylus,
Euripides, and Sophocles to us;
Pacuvius, Accius, him of Cordova dead,
To life again, to hear thy buskin tread,
And shake a stage; or, when thy socks were on,
Leave thee alone for the comparison
Of all that insolent Greece or haughty Rome
Sent forth, or since did from their ashes come.   40
Triumph, my Britain, thou hast one to show
To whom all scenes of Europe homage owe.
He was not of an age, but for all time!
And all the Muses still were in their prime,
When, like Apollo, he came forth to warm
Our ears, or like a Mercury to charm!
Nature herself was proud of his designs
And joyed to wear the dressing of his lines!

add my poem to your book. 5. **suffrage,** vote. 20. **Chaucer, etc.** Jonson suggests that it is not necessary to Shakespeare's fame that he be buried in Westminster Abbey beside these poets. 29. **Lyly.** See p. 189. 30. **Kyd,** Thomas Kyd (1557?-1595?), early dramatic contemporary of Shakespeare; author of *The Spanish Tragedy* (printed 1594). **Marlowe.** See p. 202. 33. **Aeschylus, Euripides, and Sophocles,** Greek tragic dramatists of the fifth and sixth centuries B.C. 35. **Pacuvius, Accius,** Roman tragic dramatists of the second century B.C. him

of Cordova, Seneca (4 B.C.–65 A.D.), politician, philosopher, and writer of tragedies that influenced Elizabethan drama; he was born in Cordova, Spain. 36. **buskin,** the thick-soled boot used by Greek and Roman tragic actors to increase their stature; thus the symbol of tragedy. The sock, or thin-soled shoe, worn by comic actors became, similarly, the symbol of comedy. 45. **warm,** make glow, thrill. 46. **Mercury,** the Roman messenger of the gods who charmed with his *caduceus,* or rod.

Which were so richly spun, and woven so fit,
50 As, since, she will vouchsafe no other wit.
The merry Greek, tart Aristophanes,
Neat Terence, witty Plautus, now not please,
But antiquated and deserted lie,
As they were not of Nature's family.
Yet must I not give Nature all; thy art,
My gentle Shakespeare, must enjoy a part.
For though the poet's matter nature be,
His art doth give the fashion; and, that he
Who casts to write a living line, must sweat
60 (Such as thine are) and strike the second heat
Upon the Muses' anvil; turn the same
(And himself with it) that he thinks to frame,
Or, for the laurel, he may gain a scorn;
For a good poet's made, as well as born.
And such wert thou! Look how the father's face
Lives in his issue; even so the race
Of Shakespeare's mind and manners brightly shines
In his well turnéd, and true filéd lines;
In each of which he seems to shake a lance,
70 As brandished at the eyes of ignorance.
Sweet Swan of Avon! what a sight it were
To see thee in our waters yet appear,
And make those flights upon the banks of Thames,
That so did take Eliza, and our James!
But stay, I see thee in the hemisphere
Advanced, and made a constellation there!
Shine forth, thou Star of poets, and with rage
Or influence, chide or cheer the drooping stage,
Which, since thy flight from hence, hath mourned
    like night,
And despairs day, but for thy volume's light.
(1623)

ROBERT HERRICK 1591-1674

Robert Herrick, the parish priest of Dean Prior, Devonshire, was the most varied and lyrical member of the "tribe of Ben." To him Jonson was an incarnate inspiration, and the pagan in him was constantly at war with the priest, with a resultant enrichment of his lyrical quality. Herrick's Hesperides is an amazing collection of a great variety of poetic types which exhibit the poet's threefold connections with court, church, and country, and which give full expression to the carpe diem philosophy of "gather ye rosebuds while you may." His Noble Numbers are sincere verses of repentance and of praise in which the country parson, for the time being, eclipses the pagan.

THE ARGUMENT OF HIS BOOK

I sing of brooks, of blossoms, birds, and bowers,
Of April, May, of June and July flowers;
I sing of May-poles, hock-carts, wassails, wakes,
Of bridegrooms, brides, and of their bridal cakes;
I write of youth, of love, and have access
By these to sing of cleanly wantonness;
I sing of dews, of rains, and piece by piece
Of balm, of oil, of spice and ambergris;
I sing of times trans-shifting, and I write
How roses first came red and lilies white; 10
I write of groves, of twilight, and I sing
The Court of Mab, and of the Fairy King;
I write of hell; I sing (and ever shall)
Of heaven, and hope to have it after all.
(1648)

AN ODE FOR BEN JONSON

Ah, Ben!
Say how or when
Shall we, thy guests,
Meet at those lyric feasts,
Made at the Sun,
The Dog, the Triple Tun;
Where we such clusters had,
As made us nobly wild, not mad?
And yet each verse of thine
Out-did the meat, out-did the frolic wine. 10

My Ben!
Or come again,
Or send to us
Thy wit's great overplus;
But teach us yet
Wisely to husband it,
Lest we that talent spend;
And having once brought to an end
That precious stock, the store
Of such a wit the world should have no more.
(1648)

THE NIGHT PIECE, TO JULIA

Her eyes the glow-worm lend thee;
The shooting stars attend thee;
    And the elves also,
    Whose little eyes glow
Like the sparks of fire, befriend thee.

51. Aristophanes, Greek comic dramatist (448?-380? B.C.). **52. Terence . . . Plautus,** Roman comic dramatists respectively of the second and third centuries B.C. **59. casts,** intends; the word also carries out the figure by suggesting metal work. **64. good poet's made,** an allusion to the famous proverb "Poeta nascitur, non fit," "The poet is born, not made." **69. shake a lance,** a pun on "shake spear." **71. Avon,** the river in Warwickshire which flows through Stratford, Shakespeare's native town. **74. Eliza . . . James,** Queen Elizabeth and James I.
    The Argument of His Book. **3. hock-carts,** the last carts loaded at the harvest home festival. Herrick has written a poem entitled *The Hock-Cart.* **wassails,** drinking bouts. **wakes,** parish festivals similar to country fairs. **8. ambergris,** a wax-like secretion in the alimentary canal of the sperm whale, refined and used as perfumery. **12. Mab,**

No will-o'-the-wisp mislight thee,
Nor snake or slow-worm bite thee;
    But on, on thy way
    Not making a stay,
10 Since ghosts there's none to affright thee.

Let not the dark thee cumber;
What though the moon does slumber?
    The stars of the night
    Will lend thee their light
Like tapers clear without number.

Then, Julia, let me woo thee,
Thus, thus to come unto me;
    And when I shall meet
    Thy silv'ry feet,
My soul I'll pour into thee.
(1648)

CHERRY-RIPE

Cherry-ripe, ripe, ripe, I cry,
Full and fair ones; come and buy!
If so be you ask me where
They do grow, I answer, there,
Where my Julia's lips do smile;
There's the land, or cherry-isle,
Whose plantations fully show
All the year where cherries grow.
(1648)

DELIGHT IN DISORDER

A sweet disorder in the dress
Kindles in clothes a wantonness.
A lawn about the shoulders thrown
Into a fine distraction;
An erring lace, which here and there
Enthrals the crimson stomacher;
A cuff neglectful, and thereby
Ribbands to flow confusedly;
A winning wave, deserving note,
10 In the tempestuous petticoat;
A careless shoestring, in whose tie
I see a wild civility;—
Do more bewitch me, than when art
Is too precise in every part.
(1648)

UPON JULIA'S CLOTHES

Whenas in silks my Julia goes,
Then, then, methinks, how sweetly flows
The liquefaction of her clothes.

Next, when I cast mine eyes, and see
That brave vibration, each way free,
Oh, how that glittering taketh me!
(1648)

UPON MISTRESS SUSANNA
SOUTHWELL HER FEET

    Her pretty feet
    Like snails did creep
A little out, and then,
As if they playéd at bo-peep,
    Did soon draw in again.
(1648)

TO DAFFODILS

Fair daffodils, we weep to see
    You haste away so soon;
As yet the early-rising sun
    Has not attained his noon.
        Stay, stay
    Until the hasting day
          Has run
    But to the evensong;
And, having prayed together, we
    Will go with you along.   10

We have short time to stay, as you,
    We have as short a spring;
As quick a growth to meet decay,
    As you, or anything.
        We die
    As your hours do, and dry
        Away
    Like to the summer's rain;
Or as the pearls of morning's dew,
    Ne'er to be found again.
(1648)

TO THE VIRGINS TO MAKE MUCH OF TIME

Gather ye rosebuds while ye may,
    Old Time is still a-flying;

the queen of the fairies; see Shakespeare's *Romeo and Juliet*, I, iv, 53–95.   14. **after all**, i.e., after my life is ended.
    An Ode for Ben Jonson.   4. **those lyric feasts.** See p. 341 of the headnote. The names that follow are those of London taverns.   7. **clusters**, i.e., clusters of grapes, wine.
    The Night Piece, to Julia.   1. **glow-worm**, the wingless females and larvae of a type of European beetle with luminous abdominal seg-

ments.   6. **will-o'-the-wisp**, *ignis fatuus*, light appearing over marshy grounds, which sometimes misleads travelers.   7. **slow-worm**, the blind-worm, incorrectly considered venomous.
    Cherry-Ripe. In his tribute to Julia's lips Herrick has adopted the familiar street cry of the London cherry vendor.
    Delight in Disorder. 5. **erring**, straying, wandering.

And this same flower that smiles today,
  Tomorrow will be dying.

The glorious lamp of heaven, the sun,
  The higher he's a-getting,
The sooner will his race be run,
  And nearer he's to setting.

That age is best which is the first,
10 When youth and blood are warmer;
But being spent, the worse and worst
  Times still succeed the former.

Then be not coy, but use your time,
  And while ye may, go marry;
For, having lost but once your prime,
  You may forever tarry.
(1648)

CORINNA'S GOING A-MAYING

Get up, get up for shame, the blooming morn
Upon her wings presents the god unshorn.
  See how Aurora throws her fair
  Fresh-quilted colors through the air:
  Get up, sweet slug-a-bed, and see
  The dew bespangling herb and tree.
Each flower has wept and bowéd toward the east
Above an hour since: yet you not dressed;
  Nay! not so much as out of bed?
10 When all the birds have matins said
  And sung their thankful hymns, 't is sin,
  Nay, profanation, to keep in,
Whenas a thousand virgins on this day
Spring, sooner than the lark, to fetch in May.

Rise, and put on your foliage, and be seen
To come forth, like the springtime, fresh and green,
  And sweet as Flora. Take no care
  For jewels for your gown or hair:
  Fear not; the leaves will strew
20 Gems in abundance upon you:
Besides, the childhood of the day has kept,
Against you come, some orient pearls unwept;
  Come and receive them while the light
  Hangs on the dew-locks of the night:
  And Titan on the eastern hill
  Retires himself, or else stands still
Till you come forth. Wash, dress, be brief in praying:
Few beads are best when once we go a-Maying.

Come, my Corinna, come; and, coming mark
30 How each field turns a street, each street a park

Made green and trimmed with trees; see how
Devotion gives each house a bough
Or branch: each porch, each door ere this
An ark, a tabernacle is,
Made up of white-thorn, neatly interwove;
As if here were those cooler shades of love.
  Can such delights be in the street
  And open fields and we not see 't?
  Come, we'll abroad; and let's obey
  The proclamation made for May: 40
And sin no more, as we have done, by staying;
But, my Corinna, come, let 's go a-Maying.

There's not a budding boy or girl this day
But is got up, and gone to bring in May.
  A deal of youth, ere this, is come
  Back, and with white-thorn laden home.
  Some have dispatched their cakes and cream
  Before that we have left to dream:
And some have wept, and wooed, and plighted troth,
And chose their priest, ere we can cast off sloth: 50
  Many a green-gown has been given;
  Many a kiss, both odd and even:
  Many a glance too has been sent
  From out the eye, love's firmament;
Many a jest told of the keys betraying
This night, and locks picked, yet we're not a-Maying.

Come, let us go while we are in our prime;
And take the harmless folly of the time.
  We shall grow old apace, and die
  Before we know our liberty.   60
  Our life is short, and our days run
  As fast away as does the sun;
And, as a vapor or a drop of rain,
Once lost, can ne 'er be found again,
  So when or you or I are made
  A fable, song, or fleeting shade,
  All love, all liking, all delight
  Lies drowned with us in endless night.
Then while time serves, and we are but decaying,
Come, my Corinna, come let 's go a-Maying.
(1648)

THE WAKE

Come, Anthea, let us two
Go to feast, as others do.
Tarts and custards, creams and cakes,
Are the junkets still at wakes;
Unto which the tribes resort,

Corinna's Going A-Maying. **A-Maying,** the festival of "bringing in the May" by invading the fields and woods early on the morning of May first and bringing back spring flowers and greens. The poem is a classical pastoral in form and tone. **2. the god unshorn.** Apollo, the sun, is presented by Aurora, the dawn, before he has begun to send out light streamers, his hair. **10. matins,** morning prayer service. **17.**

Flora, goddess of flowers. **25. Titan,** the sun god. **28. Few beads are best.** Each bead on the rosary represents a prayer. **30. turns a street.** The fields are crowded with young people a-Maying. **48. left,** ceased. **51. green-gown . . . given,** i.e., many a dress has been grass-stained because its wearer has been thrown down.
The Wake. **4. junkets,** delicacies. **7. Morris-dancers,** dancers in a

Where the business is the sport.
Morris-dancers thou shalt see;
Marian, too, in pageantry;
And a mimic to devise
10 Many grinning properties.
Players there will be, and those
Base in action as in clothes;
Yet with strutting they will please
The incurious villages.
Near the dying of the day
There will be a cudgel-play,
Where a coxcomb will be broke,
Ere a good word can be spoke;
But the anger ends all here,
20 Drenched in ale or drowned in beer.
Happy rustics, best content
With the cheapest merriment,
And possess no other fear
Than to want the wake next year.
(1648)

THE HAG

The hag is astride
This night for to ride,
The devil and she together;
Through thick and through thin,
Now out, and then in,
Though ne'er so foul be the weather.

A thorn or a burr
She takes for a spur,
With a lash of a bramble she rides now;
10 Through brakes and through briars,
O'er ditches and mires,
She follows the spirit that guides now.

No beast for his food
Dares now range the wood,
But hushed in his lair he lies lurking:
While mischiefs by these,
On land and on seas,
At noon of night are a-working.

The storm will arise
20 And trouble the skies
This night; and, more for the wonder,
The ghost from the tomb
Affrighted shall come,
Called out by the clap of the thunder.
(1648)

country dance, usually performed at May games and festivals by performers disguised as Robin Hood, Maid Marian, and other popular figures; see l. 8. **14. incurious**, uncritical. **16. cudgel-play**, a contest
between players equipped with clubs; much like the Elizabethan quarter-
staff bouts. **24. to want**, not to have. **next year.** The wake was an
annual fair. For a dramatic presentation of a similar holiday see

HIS PRAYER FOR ABSOLUTION

For those my unbaptizéd rimes,
Writ in my wild unhallowed times,
For every sentence, clause, and word,
That 's not inlaid with thee, my Lord
Forgive me, God, and blot each line
Out of my book that is not thine.
But if, 'mongst all, thou find'st here one
Worthy thy benediction,
That one of all the rest shall be
The glory of my work and me.
(1648)

LITANY TO THE HOLY SPIRIT

In the hour of my distress,
When temptations me oppress,
And when I my sins confess,
        Sweet Spirit, comfort me!

When I lie within my bed,
Sick in heart and sick in head,
And with doubts discomforted,
        Sweet Spirit, comfort me!

When the house doth sigh and weep,
And the world is drowned in sleep,   10
Yet mine eyes the watch do keep,
        Sweet Spirit, comfort me!

When the artless doctor sees
No one hope, but of his fees,
And his skill runs on the lees,
        Sweet Spirit, comfort me!

When his potion and his pill,
His, or none, or little skill,
Meet for nothing but to kill,
        Sweet Spirit, comfort me!   20

When the passing bell doth toll,
And the furies in a shoal
Come to fright a parting soul,
        Sweet Spirit, comfort me!

When the tapers now burn blue,
And the comforters are few,
And that number more than true,
        Sweet Spirit, comfort me!

When the priest his last hath prayed,
And I nod to what is said,   30

Jonson's *Bartholomew Fair.*
        The Hag. **18. noon of night**, midnight, the witching hour.
        Litany to the Holy Spirit. **13. artless**, lacking art or skill.

'Cause my speech is now decayed,
    Sweet Spirit, comfort me!

When, God knows, I'm tossed about
Either with despair or doubt;
Yet before the glass be out,
    Sweet Spirit, comfort me!

When the tempter me pursu'th
With the sins of all my youth,
And half damns me with untruth,
    Sweet Spirit, comfort me!

40

When the flames and hellish cries
Fright mine ears and fright mine eyes,
And all terrors me surprise,
    Sweet Spirit, comfort me!

When the Judgment is revealed,
And that opened which was sealed,
When to Thee I have appealed,
    Sweet Spirit, comfort me!
(1648)

THOMAS CAREW 1598?-1639?

Thomas Carew was among the best known of the Cavalier poets. He was an Oxford man who left college without taking a degree. After studying law, he went to Venice as secretary to Sir Dudley Carleton, English ambassador there. The year 1619 found him at the French court. On the accession of Charles I, he was given a court position at the palace of Whitehall as gentleman of the King's privy chamber. He was both a city man and a courtier; he was a member of the "tribe of Ben" and a friend of Suckling.

CELIA SINGING

You that think love can convey,
  No other way
But through the eyes, into the heart
  His fatal dart,
Close up those casements, and but hear
  This siren sing;
  And on the wing
Of her sweet voice it shall appear
That love can enter at the ear.

10 Then unveil your eyes: behold
  The curious mold
Where that voice dwells; and as we know

When the cocks crow
  We freely may
  Gaze on the day,
So may you, when the music's done,
Awake and see the rising sun.
(1640)

DISDAIN RETURNED

He that loves a rosy cheek,
  Or a coral lip admires,
Or from starlike eyes doth seek
  Fuel to maintain his fires,
As old Time makes these decay,
So his flames must waste away.

But a smooth and steadfast mind,
  Gentle thoughts and calm desires,
Hearts with equal love combined,
  Kindle never-dying fires.
Where these are not, I despise
Lovely cheeks or lips or eyes.

10

No tears, Celia, now shall win
  My resolved heart to return;
I have searched thy soul within,
  And find naught but pride and scorn;
I have learned thy arts, and now
  Can disdain as much as thou.
Some power, in my revenge, convey
  That love to her I cast away.
(1640)

SONG

Ask me no more where Jove bestows,
When June is past, the fading rose;
For in your beauty's orient deep
These flowers, as in their causes, sleep.

Ask me no more whither do stray
The golden atoms of the day;
For in pure love heaven did prepare
Those powders to enrich your hair.

Ask me no more whither doth haste
The nightingale when May is past;
For in your sweet, dividing throat
She winters and keeps warm her note.

10

Ask me no more where those stars 'light
That downwards fall in dead of night;

<hr>

35. **the glass,** the hourglass; the figure alludes to the running out of the sands of his life.
Song. 18. **phoenix,** in Greek fable a bird which lived for five hun-

dred years and then burned itself on a funeral pile, fragrant with spices; from the ashes it arose reborn.
On a Girdle. 6. **pale,** enclosure.

For in your eyes they sit, and there
Fixéd become as in their sphere.

Ask me no more if east or west
The phoenix builds her spicy nest;
For unto you at last she flies,
And in your fragrant bosom dies.
(1640)

EDMUND WALLER 1606-1687

Edmund Waller was the most popular lyric poet of his own time, partly because of his persistent use of the comparatively novel distich, or rhymed couplet, which became the accepted meter for heroic poetry in the Restoration period, and partly because of his active share in the struggle between King and Parliament. He was born in Coleshill in 1606, and educated at Eton and King's College, Cambridge. He was an inveterate sitter-in-Parliament, finding his way there before he was twenty and taking an active part in the debates. He maintained a close association with the patriot Hampden, who was his kinsman, and with Pym, leader of the impeachment of Strafford and Laud. But at the outbreak of hostilities he openly favored the king and made himself obnoxious to his Puritan associates. In 1643 he engaged in a plot to secure London for Charles, was arrested, fined heavily, and banished. He was pardoned in 1651, and four years later Cromwell made him commissioner of trade. After the Restoration he again entered Parliament. He died in 1687, two years after Charles II.

In the poems which he wrote to Sacharissa, Waller carried on the tradition of the Elizabethan sonneteers. The object of his metrical addresses was Lady Dorothy Sidney, daughter of Robert, Earl of Leicester. It is quite possible that his regard for the lady was more poetic than genuine; at any rate, she would have none of him, and both of them found other mates after the episode.

ON A GIRDLE

That which her slender waist confined
Shall now my joyful temples bind;
No monarch but would give his crown,
His arms might do what this has done.

It was my heaven's extremest sphere,
The pale which held that lovely deer;
My joy, my grief, my hope, my love,
Did all within this circle move.

A narrow compass, and yet there
Dwelt all that's good and all that's fair;   10
Give me but what this ribband bound,
Take all the rest the sun goes round!
(1645)

GO, LOVELY ROSE!

Go, lovely rose!
Tell her that wastes her time and me,
That now she knows,
When I resemble her to thee,
How sweet and fair she seems to be.

Tell her that's young,
And shuns to have her graces spied,
That hadst thou sprung
In deserts, where no men abide,
Thou must have uncommended died.   10

Small is the worth
Of beauty from the light retired;
Bid her come forth,
Suffer herself to be desired,
And not blush so to be admired.

Then die! that she
The common fate of all things rare
May read in thee;
How small a part of time they share
That are so wondrous sweet and fair!
(1645)

OF THE LAST VERSES IN THE BOOK

When we for age could neither read nor write,
The subject made us able to indite;
The soul, with nobler resolutions decked,
The body stooping, does herself erect.
No mortal parts are requisite to raise
Her that, unbodied, can her Maker praise.
    The seas are quiet when the winds give o'er;
So, calm are we when passions are no more!
For then we know how vain it was to boast
Of fleeting things, so certain to be lost.   10
Clouds of affection from our younger eyes
Conceal that emptiness which age descries.
    The soul's dark cottage, battered and decayed,
Lets in new light through chinks that time has made;
Stronger by weakness, wiser men become,
As they draw near to their eternal home.
Leaving the old, both worlds at once they view,
That stand upon the threshold of the new.
(1690)

Go, Lovely Rose! 4. resemble, liken.
Of the Last Verses in the Book. These verses provide a good
illustration of Waller's use of the closed couplet—a completed thought
expressed in two riming iambic pentameter lines.

SIR JOHN SUCKLING 1609-1642

Sir John Suckling was even more typically a Cavalier lyrist than either Carew or Waller. He was born at Twickenham, near London, and educated at Cambridge and at Gray's Inn. His early years were spent in an adventurous knight-errantry in France and Italy. He was knighted on his return to England. Soon afterwards—in 1631—he went with Charles, Marquis of Hamilton, to participate in the Protestant campaign of Gustavus Adolphus, King of Sweden, against Tilly. In 1639 Suckling took part in the Scottish campaign, and was with the King at the time of the monarch's defeat by Leslie. He sat in the Long Parliament in 1640, but he joined a Royalist plot to make Charles head of the army, was discovered, and was forced to flee to France. Two years later he committed suicide without ever having returned to England.

WHY SO PALE AND WAN, FOND LOVER?

Why so pale and wan, fond lover?
  Prithee, why so pale?
Will, when looking well can't move her,
  Looking ill prevail?
  Prithee, why so pale?

Why so dull and mute, young sinner?
  Prithee, why so mute?
Will, when speaking well can't win her,
  Saying nothing do 't?
10 Prithee, why so mute?

Quit, quit for shame! This will not move,
  This cannot take her.
If of herself she will not love,
  Nothing can make her:
  The devil take her!
(1639)

CONSTANCY

Out upon it, I have loved
  Three whole days together!
And am like to love three more,
  If it prove fair weather.

Time shall molt away his wings
  Ere he shall discover
In the whole wide world again
  Such a constant lover.

But the spite on 't is, no praise
  Is due at all to me: 10
Love with me had made no stays,
  Had it any been but she.

Had it any been but she,
  And that very face,
There had been at least ere this
  A dozen dozen in her place.
(1639)

RICHARD LOVELACE 1618-1658

Richard Lovelace was the eldest son of Sir William Lovelace of Woolwich. He was educated at Charterhouse and at Oxford. Like Suckling, he served in the Scottish campaign of 1639, but he appears not to have taken any very great part in the actual fighting between King and Parliament. In 1642 he was chosen to present to the Long Parliament the petition from Kent for "a restoration of the bishops, liturgy, and common prayer"; as a result he was imprisoned for seven weeks, during which time he wrote his famous lyric to Althea. He served in the French continental wars, and was again imprisoned on his return to England in 1648. His poems were published in the year of the King's execution. After this event he lived quietly in London until his own death in 1658. Lovelace was not definitely a follower of either Jonson or Donne. His poems were more uneven in quality than those of the other Cavalier poets mentioned here, but in the poems to Lucasta and Althea reprinted below he attained a felicity of phrase that has added several lines to the body of popular English quotations.

TO LUCASTA, GOING TO THE WARS

Tell me not, sweet, I am unkind,
  That from the nunnery
Of thy chaste breast and quiet mind
  To war and arms I fly.

True, a new mistress now I chase,
  The first foe in the field;
And with a stronger faith embrace
  A sword, a horse, a shield.

Yet this inconstancy is such
  As thou too shalt adore;   10
I could not love thee, dear, so much,
  Loved I not honor more.
(1649)

Why So Pale and Wan, Fond Lover? 15. The devil take her, a typical echo of Donne's abrupt manner.
To Lucasta, Going to the Wars. Lucasta, Lucy Sacheverell, his

betrothed, to whom he wrote many love poems; on the false report of his death in battle Lucasta married another suitor.
To Althea, from Prison. Lovelace wrote this poem from the Gate-

TO ALTHEA, FROM PRISON

When Love with unconfinéd wings
  Hovers within my gates,
And my divine Althea brings
  To whisper at the grates;
When I lie tangled in her hair
  And fettered to her eye,
The birds that wanton in the air
  Know no such liberty.

When flowing cups run swiftly round
10 With no allaying Thames,
Our careless heads with roses bound,
  Our hearts with loyal flames;
When thirsty grief in wine we steep,
  When healths and draughts go free,
Fishes that tipple in the deep
  Know no such liberty.

When, like committed linnets, I
  With shriller throat will sing
The sweetness, mercy, majesty,
20 And glories of my king;
When I shall voice aloud how good
  He is, how great should be,
Enlargéd winds, that curl the flood,
  Know no such liberty.

Stone walls do not a prison make,
  Nor iron bars a cage;
Minds innocent and quiet take
  That for an hermitage;
If I have freedom in my love
30 And in my soul am free,
Angels alone, that soar above,
  Enjoy such liberty.
(1649)

TO AMARANTHA, THAT SHE WOULD DISHEVEL HER HAIR

Amarantha sweet and fair,
Ah, braid no more that shining hair!
  As my curious hand or eye,
Hovering round thee, let it fly.

Let it fly as unconfined
As its calm ravisher, the wind,
  Who hath left his darling, the East,
To wanton o'er that spicy nest.

Ev'ry tress must be confest:
10 But neatly tangled at the best;

Like a clue of golden thread,
Most excellently raveled.

Do not then wind up that light
In ribbands, and o'er-cloud in night,
  Like the sun in 's early ray;
But shake your head, and scatter day.

See, 'tis broke! within this grove,
The bower and the walks of love,
  Weary lie we down and rest,
And fan each other's panting breast. 20

Here we'll strip and cool our fire,
In cream below, in milk-baths higher:
  And when all wells are drawn dry,
I'll drink a tear out of thine eye.

Which our very joys shall leave,
That sorrows thus we can deceive;
  Or our very sorrows weep,
That joys so ripe so little keep.
(1653)

ABRAHAM COWLEY 1618-1667

Abraham Cowley (pronounced Cooley in his own time) was, like Herrick, an ardent Royalist. He was born in London in 1618 and given his preliminary schooling at Westminster. He went to Trinity College, Cambridge, but lost his fellowship there in 1643 because of his Royalist sympathies. During part of the Civil War he served the Cavalier cause as secretary in France to the Queen and the court in the correspondence with Charles I. In 1656 he occupied the dangerous position of Royalist spy in England. He died seven years after the Restoration. Cowley, like Pope, seems to have "lisped in numbers"; he was only fourteen when his Poeticall Blossomes was published, and only eighteen when his Sylva appeared. His maturer work came out in 1647 under the title of The Mistress. Although he delighted in Horace, he also had an affinity with Donne; he imitated especially Donne's abrupt beginnings and far-fetched similes. His most ambitious work is Davideis, a Sacred Poem of the Troubles of David, composed in decasyllabic couplets and designed to carry the troubles of David through twelve books; only four were actually completed. Cowley also attempted to reproduce the odes of Pindar, the Greek poet of the fifth century B.C. Of Pindar's elaborate metrical system Cowley seems to have had no real understanding. After his usual manner, he intro-

house Prison at Westminster, where he was imprisoned for presenting the "Kentish Petition" to the Long Parliament in 1642. 10. **no allaying Thames,** a typical Cavalier conceit for "undiluted with water."

17. **committed,** caged. 23. **Enlargéd,** free.

duced into these imitations bold figures, "conceits," and artificialities of all sorts in an effort to catch the "enthusiastical manner" of his original. The result was sometimes acceptable verse, but as Pindaric odes Cowley's imitations were distinctly pseudo-classical.

THE GRASSHOPPER

Happy insect, what can be
In happiness compared to thee?
Fed with nourishment divine,
The dewy morning's gentle wine!
Nature waits upon thee still,
And thy verdant cup does fill;
'Tis filled wherever thou dost tread,
Nature's self's thy Ganymede.
Thou dost drink, and dance, and sing,
10 Happier than the happiest king!
All the fields which thou dost see,
All the plants belong to thee;
All the summer hours produce,
Fertile made with early juice.
Man for thee does sow and plow,
Farmer he, and landlord thou!
Thou dost innocently enjoy;
Nor does thy luxury destroy.
The shepherd gladly heareth thee,
20 More harmonious than he.
Thee country hinds with gladness hear,
Prophet of the ripened year!
Thee Phoebus loves, and does inspire;
Phoebus is himself thy sire.
To thee, of all things upon earth,
Life is no longer than thy mirth.
Happy insect! happy thou,
Dost neither age nor winter know;
But when thou'st drunk, and danced, and sung
30 Thy fill, the flowery leaves among,
(Voluptuous and wise withal,
Epicurean animal!)
Sated with thy summer feast,
Thou retir'st to endless rest.
(1656)

THE SWALLOW

Foolish prater, what do'st thou
So early at my window do
With thy tuneless serenade?
Well 't had been, had Tereus made
Thee as dumb as Philomel;

There his knife had done but well.
In thy undiscovered nest
Thou dost all the winter rest,
And dreamest o'er thy summer joys,
Free from the stormy season's noise,   10
Free from th' ill thou'st done to me;
Who disturbs, or seeks out thee?
Had'st thou all the charming notes
Of the wood's poetic throats,
All thy art could never pay
What thou'st ta'en from me away;
Cruel bird, thou'st ta'en away
A dream out of my arms today,
A dream that ne'er must equaled be
By all that waking eyes may see.   20
Thou this damage to repair,
Nothing half so sweet or fair,
Nothing half so good can'st bring,
Though men say, "Thou bring'st the spring."
(1647)

THE WISH

Well then! I now do plainly see
This busy world and I shall ne'er agree.
The very honey of all earthly joy
Does of all meats the soonest cloy;
    And they, methinks, deserve my pity
Who for it can endure the stings,
The crowd and buzz and murmurings,
    Of this great hive, the city.

Ah, yet, ere I descend to the grave
May I a small house and large garden have;   10
And a few friends, and many books, both true,
Both wise, and both delightful, too!
    And since love ne'er will from me flee,
A mistress moderately fair,
And good as guardian angels are,
    Only beloved and loving me.

O fountains! when in you shall I
Myself eased of unpeaceful thoughts espy?
O fields! O woods! when, when shall I be made
The happy tenant of your shade?   20
    Here's the spring-head of pleasure's flood;
Here's wealthy Nature's treasury,
Where all the riches lie that she
    Has coined and stamped for good.

Pride and ambition here
Only in far-fetched metaphors appear;

The Grasshopper, derived from one of the Anacreontics, Greek imitations of the songs of Anacreon, Greek lyrist of the fifth century B.C. 8. Ganymede, in Greek mythology the cupbearer of Jove. 21. hinds, farm servants. 24. Phoebus . . . sire. Phoebus, the god of music, was, by a figure of speech, the ancestor of the singing grasshopper.

The Swallow. Like the preceding poem, this was an imitation of the Anacreontics. 4. Tereus . . . Philomel. In Greek legend Tereus, king of Thrace, ravished his sister-in-law, Philomela, and then cut off her tongue that she might not reveal the outrage. However, she disclosed it to her sister Procne, the king's wife, by weaving the episode into

Here naught but winds can hurtful murmurs scatter,
And naught but Echo flatter.
    The gods, when they descended, hither
30 From heaven did always choose their way;
And therefore we may boldly say
    That 'tis the way, too, thither.

How happy here should I
And one dear She live, and embracing die!
She who is all the world, and can exclude,
In deserts, solitude.
    I should have then this only fear:
Lest men, when they my pleasures see,
Should hither throng to live like me,
    And so make a city here.
(1647)

ANDREW MARVELL 1621-1678

Andrew Marvell was the only Puritan lyrist of the period besides Milton who wrote really distinguished poetry. His affinity is with the writers of sacred verse and the metaphysical poets, rather than with the Cavalier lyrists. In his prose and his poetry the controversial element, as in Milton's work, runs strong and deep, and the Puritan strain in him resisted injustice and wrong.

Marvell was born in 1621. His father was a Church of England parson of the parish of Winestead, but the son displayed an early leaning toward religious non-conformity. From the Hull grammar school he proceeded to Trinity College, Cambridge, where he got an A.B. degree in 1638. In his own time Marvell was noted for his prose rather than for his verse.

TO HIS COY MISTRESS

Had we but world enough, and time,
This coyness, lady, were no crime.
We would sit down, and think which way
To walk, and pass our long love's day.
Thou by the Indian Ganges' side
Shouldst rubies find: I by the tide
Of Humber would complain. I would
Love you ten years before the flood,
And you should, if you please, refuse
10 Till the conversion of the Jews;
My vegetable love should grow
Vaster than empires and more slow;
An hundred years should go to praise

Thine eyes, and on thy forehead gaze;
Two hundred to adore each breast,
But thirty thousand to the rest;
An age at least to every part,
And the last age should show your heart.
For, lady, you deserve this state;
Nor would I love at lower rate.   20

But at my back I always hear
Time's wingéd chariot hurrying near;
And yonder all before us lie
Deserts of vast eternity.
Thy beauty shall no more be found,
Nor in thy marble vault shall sound
My echoing song; then worms shall try
That long preserved virginity;
And your quaint honor turn to dust,
And into ashes all my lust: 30
The grave's a fine and private place,
But none, I think, do there embrace.

Now therefore, while the youthful hue
Sits on thy skin like morning dew,
And while thy willing soul transpires
At every pore with instant fires,
Now let us sport us while we may,
And now, like amorous birds of prey,
Rather at once our time devour
Than languish in his slow-chapped power,   40
Let us roll all our strength and all
Our sweetness up into one ball,
And tear our pleasures with rough strife
Thorough the iron gates of life:
Thus, though we cannot make our sun
Stand still, yet we will make him run.
(c. 1650; 1681)

AN HORATIAN ODE UPON CROMWELL'S RETURN FROM IRELAND

The forward youth that would appear
Must now forsake his muses dear,
    Nor in the shadows sing
    His numbers languishing:

'Tis time to leave the books in dust,
And oil the unused armor's rust,
    Removing from the wall
    The corselet of the hall.

So restless Cromwell would not cease
In the inglorious arts of peace,   10

a piece of tapestry. They avenged themselves by killing Itys, son of Tereus and Procne. Thereupon the gods changed the king into a hoopoe, Philomela into a nightingale, and Procne into a swallow.
    To His Coy Mistress. 7. **Humber,** an estuary in the east coast of England. **complain,** i.e., utter love complaints. 8. **flood,** the biblical

deluge, Genesis, Chapters 6, 7. 29. **quaint,** proud. 40. **slow-chapped,** slowly crushing.

But through adventurous war
Urgéd his active star;

And, like the three-forked lightning, first
Breaking the clouds where it was nursed,
　　Did thorough his own side
　　His fiery way divide;

For 'tis all one to courage high,
The emulous or enemy,
　　And with such to inclose,
20　Is more than to oppose.

Then burning through the air he went,
And palaces and temples rent;
　　And Caesar's head at last
　　Did through his laurels blast.

'Tis madness to resist or blame
The force of angry heaven's flame;
　　And if we would speak true,
　　Much to the man is due,

Who from his private gardens, where
30 He lived reserved and austere,
　　As if his highest plot
　　To plant the bergamot,

Could by industrious valor climb
To ruin the great work of Time,
　　And cast the kingdoms old,
　　Into another mold,

Though Justice against Fate complain,
And plead the ancient rights in vain;
　　But those do hold or break,
40　As men are strong or weak.

Nature, that hateth emptiness,
Allows of penetration less,
　　And therefore must make room
　　Where greater spirits come.

What field of all the civil wars,
Where his were not the deepest scars?
　　And Hampton shows what part
　　He had of wiser art;

Where, twining subtle fears with hope,
50 He wove a net of such a scope
　　That Charles himself might chase
　　To Carisbrooke's narrow case,

That thence the royal actor borne
The tragic scaffold might adorn,
　　While round the arméd bands
　　Did clap their bloody hands.

He nothing common did, or mean,
Upon that memorable scene,
　　But with his keener eye
　　The axe's edge did try;　　　　　　　　　60

Nor called the gods with vulgar spite
To vindicate his helpless right,
　　But bowed his comely head
　　Down, as upon a bed.

This was that memorable hour,
Which first assured the forcéd power;
　　So, when they did design
　　The capitol's first line,

A bleeding head where they begun,
Did fright the architects to run;　　　　　70
　　And yet in that the state
　　Foresaw its happy fate.

And now the Irish are ashamed
To see themselves in one year tamed;
　　So much one man can do,
　　That does both act and know.

They can affirm his praises best,
And have, though overcome, confessed
　　How good he is, how just,
　　And fit for highest trust;　　　　　　80

Nor yet grown stiffer with command,
But still in the republic's hand,
　　How fit he is to sway,
　　That can so well obey!

He to the Commons' feet presents
A kingdom for his first year's rents;
　　And, what he may, forbears
　　His fame, to make it theirs;

And has his sword and spoils ungirt,
To lay them at the public's skirt:　　　　90
　　So when the falcon high
　　Falls heavy from the sky,

She, having killed, no more doth search,
But on the next green bough to perch;

An Horatian Ode . . . Ireland. 16. divide, an allusion to differences which arose in 1647 between the Puritan army and the Puritan
Parliament. Cromwell settled the issues by bringing the army to London. A regiment of cavalry in Hyde Park was an effective persuasive.
23. laurels, i.e., in spite of his crown and
high dignity. 32. bergamot, a kind of pear. Cromwell came from retirement in 1649 to conduct the Irish campaign. 47. Hampton, an allusion to a contemporary belief that Cromwell abetted Charles' flight
from Hampton Court to Carisbrooke Castle in November 1647. It is
here used as an instance of Cromwell's fairness and mercy. 57. He,
Charles I. Although Marvell admired the strong rule of Cromwell, he
pays just tribute to Charles' courage and dignity. 68. capitol's, the
Roman capitol's. Pliny tells the story in his *Natural History*, xxviii,
4. 86. kingdom, i.e., Ireland. Actually the Irish conquest was not

Where, when he first does lure,
The falconer has her sure.

What may not then our isle presume,
While victory his crest does plume?
　　What may not others fear,
100　If thus he crowns each year?

As Caesar, he, ere long, to Gaul,
To Italy a Hannibal,
　　And to all states not free
　　Shall climacteric be.

The Pict no shelter now shall find
Within his parti-colored mind,
　　But, from this valor sad,
　　Shrink underneath the plaid;

Happy if in the tufted brake
110 The English hunter him mistake,
　　Nor lay his hounds in near
　　The Caledonian deer.

But thou, the war's and Fortune's son,
March undefatigably on;
　　And for the least effect,
　　Still keep thy sword erect;

Besides the force it has to fright
The spirit of the shady night,
　　The same arts that did gain
　　A power, must it maintain.
(1650, 1681)

THE GARDEN

How vainly men themselves amaze,
To win the palm, the oak, or bays,
And their incessant labors see
Crowned from some single herb or tree
Whose short and narrow-vergéd shade
Does prudently their toils upbraid,
While all the flowers and trees do close
To weave the garlands of repose!

Fair Quiet, have I found thee here,
10 And Innocence, thy sister dear?
Mistaken long, I sought you then
In busy companies of men.
Your sacred plants, if here below,
Only among the plants will grow;

Society is all but rude
To this delicious solitude.

No white nor red was ever seen
So amorous as this lovely green.
Fond lovers, cruel as their flame,
Cut in these trees their mistress' name.　　20
Little, alas! they know or heed,
How far these beauties hers exceed!
Fair trees! wheres'e'r your barks I wound
No name shall but your own be found.

When we have run our passion's heat,
Love hither makes his best retreat.
The gods, that mortal beauty chase,
Still in a tree did end their race;
Apollo hunted Daphne so,
Only that she might laurel grow;　　30
And Pan did after Syrinx speed,
Not as a nymph, but for a reed.

What wondrous life is this I lead!
Ripe apples drop about my head;
The luscious clusters of the vine
Upon my mouth do crush their wine;
The nectarine, and curious peach,
Into my hands themselves do reach;
Stumbling on melons, as I pass,
Ensnared with flowers, I fall on grass.　　40

Meanwhile the mind, from pleasure less,
Withdraws into its happiness;—
The mind, that ocean where each kind
Does straight its own resemblance find;
Yet it creates, transcending these,
Far other worlds, and other seas,
Annihilating all that's made
To a green thought in a green shade.

Here at the fountain's sliding foot,
Or at some fruit-tree's mossy root,　　50
Casting the body's vest aside,
My soul into the boughs does glide:
There, like a bird, it sits and sings,
Then whets and combs its silver wings,
And, till prepared for longer flight,
Waves in its plumes the various light.

Such was that happy garden-state,
While man there walked without a mate.
After a place so pure and sweet,
What other help could yet be meet!　　60

completed until 1658, and then by Cromwell's successors. **104. climacteric,** a dangerous menace. **105. Pict,** Scot. **106. parti-colored,**
i.e., fickle, an allusion to the many-colored Scottish plaids. Scotland
had supported Charles I, and in 1651 crowned Charles II. Cromwell
was recalled from Ireland because of the threat of a Scottish rebellion.
107. sad, sobered.
　The Garden. 1. amaze, bewilder. **18. amorous,** attractive. **29.**

Apollo . . . Daphne . . . Pan . . . Syrinx. In Greek myth Apollo
pursued Daphne, and Pan, Syrinx. The first nymph was turned into a
laurel bush and the second into a clump of reeds, from which the god
made his "Pan's pipes." **37. curious,** rare, delicate.

The Cavalier Poets and the "Sons of Ben"　　355

But 'twas beyond a mortal's share
To wander solitary there:
Two paradises 'twere in one,
To live in paradise alone.

How well the skilful gardener drew
Of flowers, and herbs, this dial new;
Where, from above, the milder sun
Does through a fragrant zodiac run,
And, as it works, the industrious bee
70 Computes its time as well as we!
How could such sweet and wholesome hours
Be reckoned but with herbs and flowers?
(c. 1650–1652; 1681)

BERMUDAS

Where the remote Bermudas ride
In the ocean's bosom unespied,
From a small boat that rowed along
The listening winds received this song:

"What should we do but sing His praise
That led us through the watery maze
Unto an isle so long unknown,
And yet far kinder than our own?
Where He the huge sea-monsters wracks
10 That lift the deep upon their backs,
He lands us on a grassy stage,

Safe from the storms' and prelates' rage.
He gave us this eternal spring
Which here enamels everything,
And sends the fowls to us in care
On daily visits through the air.
He hangs in shades the orange bright
Like golden lamps in a green night,
And does in the pomegranates close
Jewels more rich than Ormus shows. 20
He makes the figs our mouths to meet
And throws the melons at our feet;
But apples plants of such a price,
No tree could ever bear them twice.
With cedars chosen by His hand
From Lebanon He stores the land;
And makes the hollow seas that roar
Proclaim the ambergris on shore.
He cast (of which we rather boast)
The Gospel's pearl upon our coast; 30
And in these rocks for us did frame
A temple where to sound His name.
Oh, let our voice His praise exalt
Till it arrive at heaven's vault,
Which thence, perhaps, rebounding may
Echo beyond the Mexique bay!"

Thus sung they in the English boat
A holy and a cheerful note;
And all the way, to guide their chime,
With falling oars they kept the time.
(1681)

Bermudas. 9. wracks, wrecks. 20. Ormus, Ormuz, an ancient seaport of Persia noted in the Middle Ages for its riches. 25. cedars . . . Lebanon, i.e., cedars like the famous ones of the Lebanon Mountains in Palestine; see 1 Kings, Chapters 5, 6. 28. ambergris, a wax-like secretion in the alimentary canal of the sperm whale, refined and used as perfumery.

STUART AND COMMONWEALTH PROSE

THE CHARACTER WRITERS

In the sixteenth and seventeenth centuries the rapid growth of London as a great commercial center and the gayety of the Tudor and Stuart courts brought to the crowded metropolis varied and colorful types from the British Isles and from the Continent. The city was thronged with staid citizens, sober statesmen and parliamentarians, Anglican priests and Puritan clergymen, gay and overdressed courtiers, lawyers, actors, students, tradesmen, craftsmen, soldiers, sailors, adventurers, traveling showmen, thieves, cony-catchers, prostitutes, and gutter rats. From the countryside there came up to London to attend the court sessions and to see the sights farmers and villagers from every district. Elizabethan and Stuart London presented an even more varied Vanity Fair than did the London of Chaucer. For descriptive and satirical writers, and for dramatists who liked to crowd their stage with characters, it was a happy hunting ground. So Jonson's figures stepped from the city streets directly upon the stage of his comedy of humours, and Greene (p. 194), Dekker, and others gave a sparkling verbal dress to rogues, vagabonds, and upstart courtiers. From the beginning of the reign of James I to the Restoration of his grandson, character sketching in prose was highly popular, and a considerable group of writers amused themselves and others by such analyses and descriptions. Such sketches vary greatly in mood and form.

Some are largely descriptive, others are analytical. Some present individuals, some types. A great many are deliberately satirical, some are more objective. Taken together they form not only an important species of prose writing but a lively picture of humanity in the seventeenth century.

The chief impulse to character writing came from the time itself. A classical original, however, who greatly influenced a number of writers of this type of prose, was Theophrastus (373-284 B.C.), an Athenian philosopher of the Peripatetic School of Aristotle, whose monitory *Characters* presents thirty generic analyses of ethical types. The English Theophrastians sometimes stick to human qualities in general; more frequently, however, their portraits are more specific in quality. Of the character writers the best known are Sir Thomas Overbury and John Earle, although character writing is found in the work of others.

SIR THOMAS OVERBURY 1581-1613

Sir Thomas Overbury was the center of a cause célèbre. He was tactless enough to oppose the marriage of his friend Lord Rochester, one of James I's numerous favorites, to Lady Essex; as a result he was imprisoned in the Tower and killed by slow poison. Rochester and his wife were acquitted at the trial, but four of their subordinates were executed. To the second edition of Overbury's poem A Wife, first published the year after his death, were added twenty-one characters, some written by him, some, admittedly, by his friends. In these sketches the general Theophrastian style is seasoned by a dash of mockery and by an occasional conversational manner. In one of the characters, "An Excellent Actor," he helped to elevate a profession not highly regarded by the London citizens of the period.

THE CHARACTERS

A MELANCHOLY MAN

Is a strayer from the drove: one that nature made sociable, because she made him man, and a crazed disposition hath altered. Impleasing to all, as all to him; straggling thoughts are his content, they make him dream waking, there's his pleasure. His imagination is never idle, it keeps his mind in a continual motion, as the poise the clock: he winds up his thoughts often, and as often unwinds them; Penelope's web thrives faster. He'll seldom be found without the shade of some grove, in whose bottom a river 10 dwells. He carries a cloud in his face, never fair weather: his outside is framed to his inside, in that he keeps a decorum, both unseemly. Speak to him; he hears with his eyes; ears follow his mind, and that's not at leisure. He thinks business, but never does any: he is all contemplation, no action. He hews and fashions his thoughts, as if he meant them to some purpose; but they prove unprofitable, as a piece of wrought timber to no use. His spirits and the sun are enemies; the sun bright and warm, his 20 humor black and cold: variety of foolish apparitions people his head, they suffer him not to breathe, according to the necessities of nature; which makes him sup up a draught of as much air at once, as would serve at thrice. He denies nature her due in sleep, and over-pays her with watchfulness: nothing pleaseth him long, but that which pleaseth his own fantasies: they are the consuming evils, and evil consumptions that consume him alive. Lastly he is a man only in show, but comes short of the better 30 part; a whole reasonable soul, which is a man's chief preëminence, and sole mark from creatures sensible. (1614)

AN EXCELLENT ACTOR

Whatsoever is commendable to the grave orator is most exquisitely perfect in him, for by a full and significant action of body he charms our attention. Sit in a full theater and you will think you see so many lines drawn from the circumference of so many ears, while the actor is the center. He doth not strive to make nature monstrous; she is often seen in the same scene with him, but neither on stilts nor 40 crutches; and for his voice, 'tis not lower than the prompter, nor louder than the foil or target. By his action he fortifies moral precepts with examples, for what we see him personate we think truly done before us: a man of a deep thought might apprehend the ghost of our ancient heroes walked again, and take him at several times for many of them. He is much affected to painting, and 'tis a question whether that made him an excellent player, or his playing an exquisite painter. He adds grace to the poet's labors, 50 for what in the poet is but ditty, in him is both ditty and music. He entertains us in the best leisure of our life—that is, between meals, the most unfit time either for study or bodily exercise. The flight of hawks and chase of wild beasts, either of them are

The Characters. A Melancholy Man; the pensive scholar was a favorite type in all forms of literature of the period. In drama the most famous example is *Hamlet*; in poetry Milton's *Il Penseroso*. The most extensive analysis of the spirit of melancholy is *The Anatomy of Melancholy* (1621) by Robert Burton (1577-1640), who was himself a sufferer from hypochondria. 3. all to him. Cf. Hamlet's ". . . man delights not me; no, nor woman neither . . ." (*Hamlet*, II, ii, 322-323). 7. poise, weight—which operates the works by force of gravity.

8. Penelope's web. In the *Odyssey*, Penelope, faithful wife of the wandering Odysseus, delays her numerous suitors by promising to marry one after she has completed weaving a web; at night she unravels what she has woven during the day. 21. humor, mood. 42. foil or target, the sword and shield used in stage fighting. 47. several, different. 53. between meals. Elizabethan and Stuart plays were performed in the afternoon.

delights noble; but some think this sport of men the worthier, despite all calumny. All men have been of his occupation; and indeed, what he doth feignedly, that do others essentially. This day one plays a monarch, the next a private person; here one acts a tyrant, on the morrow an exile; a parasite this man tonight, tomorrow a precisian; and so of divers others. I observe, of all men living, a worthy actor in one kind is the strongest motive of affection that can 10 be; for, when he dies, we cannot be persuaded any man can do his parts like him. But, to conclude, I value a worthy actor by the corruption of some few of the quality as I would do gold in the ore—I should not mind the dross, but the purity of the metal.

(1614)

JOHN EARLE 1601?-1665

John Earle wrote his Microcosmographie (1628) at Oxford; these characters reveal the university point of view and are further interesting from the fact that he often deals with simple, colorless characters who are commonplace and have no striking eccentricities.

MICROCOSMOGRAPHIE

A PRETENDER TO LEARNING

Is one that would make all others more fools than himself, for though he know nothing, he would not have the world know so much. He conceits nothing in learning but the opinion, which he seeks to pur-20 chase without it, though he might with less labor cure his ignorance than hide it. He is indeed a kind of scholar-mountebank, and his art our delusion. He is tricked out in all the accoutrements of learning, and at the first encounter none passes better. He is oftener in his study than at his book, and you cannot pleasure him better than to deprehend him: yet he hears you not till the third knock, and then comes out very angry, as interrupted. You find him in his slippers and a pen in his ear, in which formality 30 he was asleep. His table is spread wide with some classic folio, which is as constant to it as the carpet, and hath laid open in the same page this half year. His candle is always a longer sitter-up then himself, and the boast of his window at midnight. He walks much alone in the posture of meditation, and has a book still before his face in the fields. His pocket

is seldom without a Greek Testament or Hebrew Bible, which he opens only in the church, and that when some stander-by looks over. He has his sentences for company, some scatterings of Seneca and 40 Tacitus, which are good upon all occasions. If he read anything in the morning, it comes up all at dinner; and as long as that lasts, the discourse is his. He is a great plagiary of tavern wit, and comes to sermons only that he may talk of Austin. His parcels are the mere scrapings from company, yet he complains at parting what time he has lost. He is wondrously capricious to seem a judgment, and listens with a sour attention to what he understands not. He talks much of Scaliger, and Casaubon, and 50 the Jesuits, and prefers some unheard of Dutch names before them all. He has verses to bring in upon these and these hints, and it shall go hard but he will wind in his opportunity. He is critical in a language he cannot construe, and speaks seldom under Arminius in divinity. His business and retirement and caller-away is his study, and he protests no delight to it comparable. He is a great nomenclator of authors, which he has read in general in the catalogue, and in particular in the title, and goes seldom 60 so far as the dedication. He never talks of anything but learning, and learns all from talking. Three encounters with the same men pump him, and then he only puts in or gravely says nothing. He has taken pains to be an ass, though not to be a scholar, and is at length discovered and laughed at.

(1628)

AN ANTIQUARY

He is a man strangely thrifty of time past, and an enemy indeed to his maw, whence he fetches out many things when they are now all rotten and stinking. He is one that hath that unnatural disease to be 70 enamored of old age and wrinkles, and loves all things (as Dutchmen do cheese), the better for being moldy and worm-eaten. He is of our religion, because we say it is most ancient; and yet a broken statue would almost make him an idolater. A great admirer he is of the rust of old monuments, and reads only those characters where time hath eaten out the letters. He will go you forty miles to see a saint's well or a ruined abbey; and if there be but a cross or stone foot-stool in the way, he'll be considering it so long, 80 till he forget his journey. His estate consists much in shekels, and Roman coins; and he hath more pictures of Caesar than James or Elizabeth. Beggars cozen him with musty things which they have raked from dunghills, and he preserves their rags for pre-

---

7. **precisian,** a formalist; applied in the seventeenth century to Puritans. *Microcosmographie.* 18. **conceits,** conceives. 19. **opinion,** reputation. 26. **deprehend,** catch by surprise. 40. **Seneca,** Roman philosopher and dramatist of the first century. 41. **Tacitus,** Roman historian (55?–120?). 44. **plagiary . . . wit,** thief of scraps of wisdom heard at the tavern. 45. **Austin,** Saint Augustine, Numidian Bishop of Hippo

(354–430), author of *The Confessions,* a spiritual autobiography much quoted by mystics. 50. **Scaliger,** Julius Caesar (1484–1558), an Italian poet, philologist, and critic, author of a Latin treatise on poetics and learned philosophical works. **Casaubon,** Isaac (1559–1614), French Huguenot scholar and theologian who lived in London the last four years of his life. 55. **Arminius,** Jacobus (died 1609), Dutch Prot-

cious relics. He loves no library but where there are more spiders' volumes than authors', and looks with great admiration on the antique work of cobwebs. Printed books he contemns, as a novelty of this latter age, but a manuscript he pores on everlastingly, especially if the cover be all moth-eaten, and the dust make a parenthesis between every syllable. He would give all the books in his study (which are rarities all) for one of the old Roman bindings, or six lines of Tully in his own hand. His chamber is hung commonly with strange beasts' skins, and is a kind of charnel-house of bones extraordinary; and his discourse upon them, if you will hear him, shall last longer. His very attire is that which is the eldest out of fashion and you may pick a criticism out of his breeches. He never looks upon himself till he is gray-haired, and then he is pleased with his own antiquity. His grave does not fright him, for he has been used to sepulchers, and he likes death the better, because it gathers him to his fathers. (1628)

A YOUNG MAN

He is now out of Nature's protection, though not yet able to guide himself; but left loose to the world and fortune, from which the weakness of his childhood preserved him; and now his strength exposes him. He is indeed just of age to be miserable, yet in his own conceit first begins to be happy; and he is happier in this imagination, and his misery not felt is less. He sees yet but the outside of world and men, and conceives them according to their appearing glister, and out of this ignorance believes them. He pursues all vanities for happiness, and enjoys them best in this fancy. His reason serves not to curb, but understand his appetite, and prosecute the motions thereof with a more eager earnestness. Himself is his own temptation, and needs not Satan; and the world will come hereafter. He leaves repentance for gray hairs, and performs it in being covetous. He is mingled with the vices of the age as the fashion and custom, with which he longs to be acquainted; and sins to better his understanding. He conceives his youth as the season of his lust, and the hour wherein he ought to be bad; and because he would not lose his time, spends it. He distastes religion as a sad thing, and is six years elder for a thought of heaven. He scorns and fears, and yet hopes for old age, but dare not imagine it with wrinkles. He loves and hates with the same inflammation; and when the heat is over, is cool alike to friends and enemies. His friendship is seldom so steadfast, but that lust, drink, or anger may overturn it. He offers you his blood today in kindness, and is ready to take yours tomorrow. He does seldom anything which he wishes not to do again, and is only wise after a misfortune. He suffers much for his knowledge, and a great deal of folly it is makes him a wise man. He is free from many vices, by being not grown to the performance, and is only more virtuous out of weakness. Every action is his danger, and every man his ambush. He is a ship without pilot or tackling, and only good fortune may steer him. If he escape this age, he has escaped a tempest, and may live to be a man.
(1628)

SIR THOMAS BROWNE 1605-1682

An eager speculative mind, always raising odd questions and attempting their answers, a genuine interest in scientific truth and a wholesome skepticism toward unproved assertions, a passion for bits of recondite learning, and finally a literary style so curious and quaint that it delighted Charles Lamb a century and a half later, all went into the making of Sir Thomas Browne, one of the distinguished prose writers of the seventeenth century. He was born in London in 1605, the son of a merchant. He graduated from Pembroke College, Oxford, in 1626, took an M.A. degree in 1629, and pursued his medical studies at Montpelier, Padua, and finally at Leyden, where he took a degree in medicine. Returning to England in 1633, he established himself in Yorkshire, but on receiving an M.D. degree from Oxford in 1637, he moved to Norwich, where he lived until his death. He was always a sincere Royalist, but he appears to have taken very little part in the Great Rebellion. After the Restoration, honors were heaped upon him; he was made honorary fellow of the College of Physicians in 1664 and was knighted by Charles II in 1671. He died at Norwich in 1682.

Browne's first book, Religio Medici, was designed, as the title implies, as a defense of the physician against charges of skepticism and irreligion. It was written in 1635 and circulated in manuscript until in 1642 it came into the hands of a piratical printer who published it; the following year the book was reprinted, with added material, under the author's own supervision. This early work exhibits Browne's literary style rather fully: it has a marked prose rhythm, vivid color, subtle conceptions, quaint figures and odd "conceits," a vocabulary so rich in unusual

estant opponent of the theories of Calvin and founder of Arminianism, which refused to hold God responsible for evil. 58. **nomenclator,** one who calls persons by name. 59. **catalogue,** here, list of authors and titles. 63. **pump,** i.e., pump dry, exhaust his knowledge. 64. **puts in,** makes an occasional remark. 68. **maw,** the stomach; used here figuratively of his store of learning. 73. **our religion.** The allusion is probably to Christianity in general. 84. **cozen,** cheat. 95. **Tully,** Cicero, Roman orator, first century B.C. 100. **pick . . . breeches,** i.e., his breeches would serve as a fit subject for antiquarian comment. 111. **conceit,** opinion. 129. **sad,** serious, sober.

words that it frequently breaks over into manufactured ones. At times Browne seems to be a prose Donne. He was one of the most widely read men of his time, and his learning is displayed naturally rather than deliberately. As was characteristic of much of the early prose of the seventeenth century, his sentences are long, heavy, involved; they lack the precision and crispness of most of Bacon's. The skepticism against which Browne defended himself in Religio Medici *appears in full measure in* Pseudodoxia Epidemica *(1646), known also as* Vulgar Errors. *This early exposure of popular fallacies and traditional beliefs has the desultory and choppy quality of a catalogue, in spite of his attempt to make a subject classification of his "errors." In 1658* Hydriotaphia, or Urn Burial *and* The Garden of Cyrus *were published together. Each tract has five chapters. The first is a mournful, solemn, sometimes morbid, treatise on funeral rites and ceremonies; the second deals with the subject of the formal gardens of antiquity, and with the mysteries of the quincunx or symbol for the number five.* Christian Morals, *not published until after his death, had the distinction of being edited in 1756 by Samuel Johnson.*

from HYDRIOTAPHIA, OR URN BURIAL

OF AMBITION AND FAME

Now since these dead bones have already outlasted the living ones of Methuselah, and in a yard under ground, and thin walls of clay, outworn all the strong and specious buildings above it; and quietly rested under the drums and tramplings of three conquests: what prince can promise such diuturnity unto his relics, or might not gladly say,

Sic ego componi versus in ossa velim?

Time, which antiquates antiquities, and hath an art to make dust of all things, hath yet spared these minor monuments.

In vain we hope to be known by open and visible conservatories, when to be unknown was the means of their continuation, and obscurity their protection. If they died by violent hands, and were thrust into their urns, these bones become considerable, and some old philosophers would honor them, whose souls they conceived most pure, which were thus snatched from their bodies, and to retain a stronger propension unto them; whereas they wearily left a languishing corpse, and with faint desires of reunion. If they fell by long and aged decay, yet wrapped up in the bundle of time, they fall into indistinction, and make but one blot with infants. If we begin to die when we live, and long life be but a prolongation of death, our life is a sad composition; we live with death, and die not in a moment. How many pulses made up the life of Methuselah, were work for Archimedes: common counters sum up the life of Moses his man. Our days become considerable, like petty sums, by minute accumulations; where numerous fractions make up but small round numbers; and our days of a span long, make not one little finger.

If the nearness of our last necessity brought a nearer conformity into it, there were a happiness in hoary hairs, and no calamity in half-senses. But the long habit of living indisposeth us for dying: when avarice makes us the sport of death, when even David grew politicly cruel, and Solomon could hardly be said to be the wisest of men. But many are too early old, and before the date of age. Adversity stretcheth our days, misery makes Alcmena's nights, and time hath no wings unto it. But the most tedious being is that which can unwish itself, content to be nothing, or never to have been, which was beyond the malcontent of Job, who cursed not the day of his life, but his nativity; content to have so far been, as to have a title to future being, although he had lived here but in a hidden state of life, and as it were an abortion.

What song the Sirens sang, or what name Achilles assumed when he hid himself among women, though puzzling questions, are not beyond all conjecture. What time the persons of these ossuaries entered the famous nations of the dead, and slept with princes and counselors, might admit a wide solution. But who were the proprietaries of these bones, or what bodies these ashes made up, were a question above antiquarism; not to be resolved by man, nor easily perhaps by spirits, except we consult the provincial guardians, or tutelary observators. Had they made as good provision for their names, as they have done for their relics, they had not so grossly erred in the art of perpetuation. But to subsist in bones, and be but pyramidally extant, is a fallacy in dura-

Hydriotaphia, or Urn Burial. **1. these dead bones.** The allusion is to bones found in some funeral urns dug up near Norfolk; these relics, presumably Roman, occasioned the treatise on urn burial. **2. Methuselah,** the oldest man mentioned in the Bible; he lived nine hundred and sixty-nine years and "begat sons and daughters" (Genesis 5:27). **5. three conquests:** the Roman, Anglo-Saxon, and Norman, unless, because the bones were Roman, Browne alludes to the Danish invasion. **6. diuturnity,** lasting quality. **8. Sic . . . velim.** So might I, when I am turned into bones, wish to be disposed. **20. propension,** propensity, inclination. **29. Archimedes,** Greek mathematician (287?–212 B.C.). **30. Moses his man,** Moses' man. The allusion is to a prayer of Moses (Psalms 90:10): "The days of our years are threescore years and ten"—the "psalmist's span." **43. Alcmena's nights.** In Greek legend the night in which Zeus begot Hercules of Alcmena, wife of Amphitruo, was artificially lengthened. **47. Job . . . nativity;** see Job, Chapter 3. **52. Sirens,** in Greek mythology a group of sea nymphs who attracted mariners to destruction by their sweet singing; the specific allusion is to the episode in the *Odyssey* which tells how Odysseus had them while safely lashed to the mast of his ship. **Achilles.** In the *Iliad* the Greek hero attempted to avoid going to the Trojan War by hiding among the women. **55. ossuaries,** receptacles for human bones. **62. tutelary observators,** guardian spirits. **66. pyramidally,** by the agency of a tombstone. **74. Atropos,** that one of the three Greek Fates who cut the thread of life. **78. meridian,** the zenith. **84. Elias,** Elijah the prophet, who in 1 Kings 21:17–29 prophesied the death of Ahab, King of Israel, and Jezebel, his queen. **Charles**

tion. Vain ashes which in the oblivion of names, persons, times, and sexes, have found unto themselves a fruitless continuation, and only arise unto
70 late posterity, as emblems of mortal vanities, antidotes against pride, vainglory, and madding vices. Pagan vainglories which thought the world might last for ever, had encouragement for ambition, and, finding no *Atropos* unto the immortality of their names, were never damped with the necessity of oblivion. Even old ambitions had the advantage of ours, in the attempts of their vainglories, who acting early, and before the probable meridian of time, have by this time found great accomplishment of their de-
80 signs, whereby the ancient heroes have already outlasted their monuments, and mechanical preservations. But in this latter scene of time, we cannot expect such mummies unto our memories, when ambition may fear the prophecy of Elias, and Charles the Fifth can never hope to live within two Methuselahs of Hector.

And therefore, restless inquietude for the diuturnity of our memories unto present considerations seems a vanity almost out of date, and superan-
90 nuated piece of folly. We cannot hope to live so long in our names, as some have done in their persons. One face of Janus holds no proportion unto the other. 'Tis too late to be ambitious. The great mutations of the world are acted, or time may be too short for our designs. To extend our memories by monuments, whose death we daily pray for, and whose duration we cannot hope, without injury to our expectations in the advent of the last day, were a contradiction to our beliefs. We whose generations are
100 ordained in this setting part of time, are providentially taken off from such imaginations; and, being necessitated to eye the remaining particle of futurity, are naturally constituted unto thoughts of the next world, and cannot excusably decline the consideration of that duration, which maketh pyramids pillars of snow, and all that's past a moment.

Circles and right lines limit and close all bodies, and the mortal right-lined circle must conclude and shut up all. There is no antidote against the opium
110 of time, which temporally considereth all things: our fathers find their graves in our short memories, and sadly tell us how we may be buried in our survivors. Gravestones tell truth scarce forty years. Generations pass while some trees stand, and old families last not three oaks. To be read by bare inscriptions

like many in Gruter, to hope for eternity by enigmatical epithets or first letters of our names, to be studied by antiquaries, who we were, and have new names given us like many of the mummies, are cold consolations unto the students of perpetuity, even 120 by everlasting languages.

To be content that times to come should only know there was such a man, not caring whether they knew more of him, was a frigid ambition in Cardan; disparaging his horoscopal inclination and judgment of himself. Who cares to subsist like Hippocrates's patients, or Achilles's horses in Homer, under naked nominations, without deserts and noble acts, which are the balsam of our memories, the *entelechia* and soul of our subsistences? To be nameless in worthy 130 deeds, exceeds an infamous history. The Canaanitish woman lives more happily without a name, than Herodias with one. And who had not rather have been the good thief, than Pilate?

But the iniquity of oblivion blindly scattereth her poppy, and deals with the memory of men without distinction to merit of perpetuity. Who can but pity the founder of the pyramids? Herostratus lives that burnt the temple of Diana, he is almost lost that built it. Time hath spared the epitaph of Adrian's 140 horse, confounded that of himself. In vain we compute our felicities by the advantage of our good names, since bad have equal durations, and Thersites is like to live as long as Agamemnon. Who knows whether the best of men be known, or whether there be not more remarkable persons forgot, than any that stand remembered in the known account of time? Without the favor of the everlasting register, the first man had been as unknown as the last, and Methuselah's long life had been his only chronicle. 150

Oblivion is not to be hired. The greater part must be content to be as though they had not been, to be found in the register of God, not in the record of man. Twenty-seven names make up the first story, and the recorded names ever since contain not one living century. The number of the dead long exceedeth all that shall live. The night of time far surpasseth the day, and who knows when was the equinox? Every hour adds unto that current arithmetic, which scarce stands one moment. And since 160 death must be the Lucina of life, and even Pagans could doubt, whether thus to live were to die; since our longest sun sets at right descensions, and makes but winter arches, and therefore it cannot be long

the Fifth, Emperor of Germany (1500–1558). 86. **Hector,** Trojan prince and warrior whose deeds are recounted in Homer's *Iliad.* 92. **Janus,** ancient Roman god of gates, doors, and beginnings, represented with two opposite faces. 108. **mortal right-lined circle,** "the character of death" (Browne's note). 116. **Gruter,** or Gruytere, Jan (1560–1627), Dutch critic and scholar, author of a book on inscriptions. 124. **Cardan,** Geronimo (1501–1576), Italian physician, mathematician, and astrologer. 126. **Hippocrates,** Greek physician of the fifth century B.C. 127. **Achilles's horses;** these immortal but unnamed animals appear in the *Iliad.* 129. **entelechia,** actual being, a term from Aristotelian philosophy. 131. **Canaanitish woman.** Jesus healed her daughter (Matthew 15:22–28). 133. **Herodias,** the wicked wife of King Herod who instructed her daughter to demand of the King the head of John

the Baptist as a reward for the girl's dancing. (See Matthew 14:1–12 and Oscar Wilde's drama *Salome.*) 134. **good thief . . . Pilate.** The first was the repentant but unnamed sinner who was one of the two malefactors crucified with Jesus (Luke 23:39–43); the second was the Roman governor who washed his hands of all responsibility for Jesus' execution (Matthew 27:24). 138. **Herostratus . . . Diana.** The temple of Diana of the Ephesians was thus destroyed in 356 B.C. 140. **Adrian** (76–138), Emperor of Rome. 143. **Thersites . . . Agamemnon,** the first a rogue, the second a heroic leader in Homer's *Iliad.* 154. **Twenty-seven . . . story,** the record of the "generations of Adam" who lived before the Flood (Genesis, Chapter 5). 161. **Lucina,** the Roman goddess of childbirth, applied sometimes to Juno.

before we lie down in darkness, and have our light in ashes; since the brother of death daily haunts us with dying mementos, and time that grows old in itself, bids us hope no long duration; diuturnity is a dream and folly of expectation.

Darkness and light divide the course of time, and oblivion shares with memory a great part even of our living beings; we slightly remember our felicities, and the smartest strokes of affliction leave but short 10 smart upon us. Sense endureth no extremities, and sorrows destroy us or themselves. To weep into stones are fables. Afflictions induce callosities; miseries are slippery, or fall like snow upon us, which notwithstanding is no unhappy stupidity. To be ignorant of evils to come, and forgetful of evils past, is a merciful provision in nature, whereby we digest the mixture of our few and evil days, and, our delivered senses not relapsing into cutting remembrances, our sorrows are not kept raw by the edge 20 of repetitions. A great part of antiquity contented their hopes of subsistency with a transmigration of their souls,—a good way to continue their memories, while, having the advantage of plural successions, they could not but act something remarkable in such variety of beings, and enjoying the fame of their passed selves, make accumulation of glory unto their last durations. Others, rather than be lost in the uncomfortable night of nothing, were content to recede into the common being, and make one particle 30 of the public soul of all things, which was no more than to return into their unknown and divine original again. Egyptian ingenuity was more unsatisfied, contriving their bodies in sweet consistencies, to attend the return of their souls. But all was vanity, feeding the wind, and folly. The Egyptian mummies, which Cambyses or time hath spared, avarice now consumeth. Mummy is become merchandise, Mizraim cures wounds, and Pharaoh is sold for balsams.

In vain do individuals hope for immortality, or 40 any patent from oblivion, in preservations below the moon; men have been deceived even in their flatteries, above the sun, and studied conceits to perpetuate their names in heaven. The various cosmography of that part hath already varied the names of contrived constellations; Nimrod is lost in Orion, and Osiris in the Dog-star. While we look for incorruption in the heavens, we find they are but like the earth;—durable in their main bodies, alterable in their parts; whereof, beside comets and new stars, 50 perspectives begin to tell tales, and the spots that wander about the sun, with Phaeton's favor, would make clear conviction.

There is nothing strictly immortal, but immortality. Whatever hath no beginning, may be confident of no end (all others have a dependent being and within the reach of destruction); which is the peculiar of that necessary Essence that cannot destroy itself; and the highest strain of omnipotency, to be so powerfully constituted as not to suffer even from the power of itself. But the sufficiency of Christian immortality 60 frustrates all earthly glory, and the quality of either state after death makes a folly of posthumous memory. God who can only destroy our souls, and hath assured our resurrection, either of our bodies or names hath directly promised no duration. Wherein there is so much of chance, that the boldest expectants have found unhappy frustration; and to hold long subsistence, seems but a scape in oblivion. But man is a noble animal, splendid in ashes, and pompous in the grave, solemnizing nativities and deaths with 70 equal luster, nor omitting ceremonies of bravery in the infamy of his nature.

Life is a pure flame, and we live by an invisible sun within us. A small fire sufficeth for life, great flames seemed too little after death, while men vainly affected precious pyres, and to burn like Sardanapalus; but the wisdom of funeral laws found the folly of prodigal blazes, and reduced undoing fires unto the rule of sober obsequies, wherein few could be so mean as not to provide wood, pitch, a mourner, 80 and an urn.

Five languages secured not the epitaph of Gordianus. The man of God lives longer without a tomb than any by one, invisibly interred by angels, and adjudged to obscurity, though not without some marks directing human discovery. Enoch and Elias, without either tomb or burial, in an anomalous state of being, are the great examples of perpetuity, in their long and living memory, in strict account being still on this side death, and having a late part yet to 90 act upon this stage of earth. If in the decretory term of the world we shall not all die but be changed, according to received translation, the last day will make but few graves; at least quick resurrections will anticipate lasting sepultures. Some graves will be opened before they be quite closed, and Lazarus be no wonder. When many that feared to die, shall groan that they can die but once, the dismal state is the second and living death, when life puts despair on the damned; when men shall wish the coverings 100 of mountains, not of monuments, and annihilation shall be courted.

While some have studied monuments, others have studiously declined them, and some have been so

32. **Egyptian . . . sweet consistencies;** the allusion is to the practice of embalming the dead in spices. 36. **Cambyses,** king of Persia (died 522 B.C.); he conquered Egypt but spared her tombs. 37. **Mummy.** In the Middle Ages mummies were powdered and used for medicine. **Mizraim,** grandson of Noah, whose descendants, according to a biblical record, peopled Egypt (Genesis 10:6–13). 45. **Nimrod . . . Orion,** respectively, legendary Hebrew and Greek hunters. 46. **Osiris,** in Egyptian myth the god of the underworld and of the Nile River. The

rising of Sirius, the Dog Star, synchronized with the beginning of the Nile floods. 50. **perspectives,** telescopes. 51. **Phaeton,** son of Apollo, the sun god; used here for the god himself. 68. **scape,** a chance. 76. **Sardanapalus,** a Persian monarch who, when besieged in Nineveh by the Medes, set fire to his palace and burned himself and his court. The date of the event is uncertain. 82. **Gordianus,** Emperor of Rome in the third century. **man of God,** Moses, of whom it was said in Deuteronomy 34:6 that "no man knoweth of his sepulcher unto this

vainly boisterous, that they durst not acknowledge their graves; wherein Alaricus seems most subtle, who had a river turned to hide his bones at the bottom. Even Sylla, that thought himself safe in his urn, could not prevent revenging tongues, and
110 stones thrown at his monument. Happy are they whom privacy makes innocent, who deal so with men in this world, that they are not afraid to meet them in the next; who, when they die, make no commotion among the dead, and are not touched with that poetical taunt of Isaiah.

Pyramids, arches, obelisks, were but the irregularities of vainglory, and wild enormities of ancient magnanimity. But the most magnanimous resolution rests in the Christian religion, which trampleth upon
120 pride, and sits on the neck of ambition, humbly pursuing that infallible perpetuity, unto which all others must diminish their diameters, and be poorly seen in angles of contingency.

Pious spirits who passed their days in raptures of futurity, made little more of this world than the world that was before it, while they lay obscure in the chaos of preordination, and night of their forebeings. And if any have been so happy as truly to understand Christian annihilation, ecstasies, exolu-
130 tion, liquefaction, transformation, the kiss of the spouse, gustation of God, and ingression into the divine shadow, they have already had an handsome anticipation of heaven; the glory of the world is surely over, and the earth in ashes unto them.

To subsist in lasting monuments, to live in their productions, to exist in their names and predicament of chimeras, was large satisfaction unto old expectations, and made one part of their Elysiums. But all this is nothing in the metaphysics of true belief.
140 To live, indeed, is to be again ourselves, which being not only an hope, but an evidence in noble believers, 'tis all one to lie in St. Innocent's churchyard, as in the sands of Egypt. Ready to be anything, in the ecstasy of being ever, and as content with six foot as the *moles* of Adrianus.

(1658)

IZAAK WALTON 1593-1683

Izaak Walton was born in Stafford in 1593 of yeoman stock. He was apprenticed to an ironmonger in London and became a freeman of that company in 1618. In spite of his vocation his inclinations seem always to have been literary. He knew both Donne and Jonson, and was acquainted, too, with Sir Henry

Wotton and with other poets. He was a Royalist by sympathy, but since he was half a century old when the Great Rebellion broke out, he does not seem to have taken sides very actively with either party. It is characteristic of this quiet man that after the execution of the King, during the years in which Cromwell and his Parliaments were struggling to establish a stable government, Izaak Walton was peacefully writing about fish. To the feverish contestants he gave only one admonition: love virtue, trust in Providence, be quiet, and go a-angling. It was his own peaceful creed.

Walton's admiration for Donne expressed itself in his first book, a biography of the poet written in 1640. To this study he added biographies of Sir Henry Wotton (1651), Richard Hooker (1665), George Herbert (1670), and Robert Sanderson (1678). On all counts, however, his best work is his fisherman's classic, The Complete Angler, the first edition of which appeared in 1653 in an abbreviated form. This charming mixture of learning and wisdom is built on the framework of five days of fishing and quiet conference between Piscator, the fisherman (who is Walton himself), Venator, the hunter, and Auceps, the falconer. Thus three country sports are represented, but the fisherman leads the others and in the end converts them to his quiet form of recreation. From Donne, Walton acquired enough of the trick of introducing the erudite to give his prose a quaint seasoning of learning. But The Complete Angler is characterized by wisdom rather than learning. The style is quiet, natural, simple, naïve, childlike. It harmonizes with the subject matter, fishing, and the country background of peaceful meadows, quiet streams, singing milkmaids, and brook fish breaking the water to snap at the fisherman's flies. Walton has been called "the prose poet of the English countryside," and the epithet exactly suits him.

from THE COMPLETE ANGLER

THE FIRST DAY

A Conference betwixt an Angler, a Falconer, and a Hunter, each commending His Recreation.

CHAPTER 1

PISCATOR, VENATOR, AUCEPS

PISCATOR. You are well overtaken, Gentlemen! A good morning to you both! I have stretched my legs

---

day." 86. **Enoch and Elias.** Genesis 5:24 and 2 Kings 2:1–11 tell respectively of the passage to heaven without dying of Enoch and the prophet Elias or Elijah. 96. **Lazarus,** man raised from the tomb by Jesus (see John, Chapter 11). 106. **Alaricus,** Alaric (370?–410), king of the Visigoths and conqueror of Rome, buried as indicated so that his foes might not dishonor his corpse. 108. **Sylla,** Lucius Cornelius Sulla (138–78 B.C.), Roman general. 115. **taunt of Isaiah;** see Isaiah 14:16 ff. 129. **exolution,** release. 131. **gustation of God,**

the holy communion. This and other terms in this sentence Browne describes in his own note as "terms and phrases characteristic of the speculations of Christian mystics. 136. **predicament of chimeras,** state or condition of ghosts. 138. **Elysiums.** In classical belief the Elysian fields were the dwelling place of happy souls. 142. **St. Innocent's,** "In Paris, where bodies soon consume" (author's note). 145. *moles* **of Adrianus,** a mausoleum built in Rome by the Emperor Hadrian (76–138); it is now called Castel Sant' Angelo.

up Tottenham Hill to overtake you, hoping your business may occasion you towards Ware whither I am going this fine fresh May morning.

VENATOR. Sir, I, for my part, shall almost answer your hopes; for my purpose is to drink my morning's draught at the Thatched House in Hoddesden; and I think not to rest till I come thither, where I have appointed a friend or two to meet me: but for this gentleman that you see with me, I know not how far 10 he intends his journey; he came so lately into my company, that I have scarce had time to ask him the question.

AUCEPS. Sir, I shall by your favor bear you company as far as Theobalds, and there leave you; for then I turn up to a friend's house, who mews a Hawk for me, which I now long to see.

VENATOR. Sir, we are all so happy as to have a fine, fresh, cool morning; and I hope we shall each be the happier in the others' company. And, Gentle- 20 men, that I may not lose yours, I shall either abate or amend my pace to enjoy it, knowing that, as the Italians say, "Good company in a journey makes the way to seem the shorter."

AUCEPS. It may do so, Sir, with the help of good discourse, which, methinks, we may promise from you, that both look and speak so cheerfully: and for my part, I promise you, as an invitation to it, that I will be as free and open-hearted as discretion will allow me to be with strangers.

30 VENATOR. And, Sir, I promise the like.

PISCATOR. I am right glad to hear your answers; and, in confidence you speak the truth, I shall put on a boldness to ask you, Sir, whether business or pleasure caused you to be so early up, and walk so fast? for this other gentleman hath declared he is going to see a hawk, that a friend mews for him.

VENATOR. Sir, mine is a mixture of both, a little business and more pleasure; for I intend this day to do all my business, and then bestow another day or two 40 in hunting the Otter, which a friend, that I go to meet, tells me is much pleasanter than any other chase whatsoever: howsoever, I mean to try it; for tomorrow morning we shall meet a pack of Otter-dogs of noble Mr. Sadler's, upon Amwell Hill, who will be there so early, that they intend to prevent the sunrising.

PISCATOR. Sir, my fortune has answered my desires, and my purpose is to bestow a day or two in helping to destroy some of those villainous vermin: for I hate them perfectly, because they love fish so 50 well, or rather, because they destroy so much; indeed so much, that, in my judgment all men that keep Otter-dogs ought to have pensions from the King, to encourage them to destroy the very breed of those base Otters, they do so much mischief.

VENATOR. But what say you to the Foxes of the Nation, would not you as willingly have them destroyed? for doubtless they do as much mischief as Otters do.

PISCATOR. Oh, Sir, if they do, it is not so much to me and my fraternity, as those base vermin the Otters 60 do.

AUCEPS. Why, Sir, I pray, of what fraternity are you, that you are so angry with the poor Otters?

PISCATOR. I am, Sir, a Brother of the Angle, and therefore an enemy to the Otter: for you are to note, that we Anglers all love one another, and therefore do I hate the Otter both for my own, and their sakes who are of my brotherhood.

VENATOR. And I am a lover of Hounds; I have followed many a pack of dogs many a mile, and heard 70 many merry Huntsmen make sport and scoff at Anglers.

AUCEPS. And I profess myself a Falconer, and have heard many grave, serious men pity them, it is such a heavy, contemptible, dull recreation.

PISCATOR. You know, Gentlemen, it is an easy thing to scoff at any art or recreation; a little wit mixed with ill nature, confidence, and malice, will do it; but though they often venture boldly, yet they are often caught, even in their own trap, according to that 80 of Lucian, the father of the family of Scoffers:

Lucian, well skilled in scoffing, this hath writ,
Friend, that's your folly, which you think your wit:
This you vent oft, void both of wit and fear,
Meaning another, when yourself you jeer.

If to this you add what Solomon says of Scoffers, that they are an abomination to mankind, let him that thinks fit scoff on, and be a Scoffer still; but I account them enemies to me and all that love Virtue and Angling. 90

And for you that have heard many grave, serious men pity Anglers; let me tell you, Sir, there be many men that are by others taken to be serious and grave men, whom we contemn and pity. Men that are taken to be grave, because nature hath made them of a sour complexion; money-getting men, men that spend all their time, first in getting, and next, in anxious care to keep it; men that are condemned to be rich, and then always busy or discontented: for these poor rich-men, we Anglers pity them perfectly, and stand in 100 no need to borrow their thoughts to think ourselves so happy. No, no, Sir, we enjoy a contentedness above the reach of such dispositions, and as the learned and ingenuous Montaigne says, like himself, freely, "When my Cat and I entertain each other with mutual apish tricks, as playing with a garter, who knows but that I make my Cat more sport than she makes me? Shall I conclude her to be simple, that has her time to begin

The Complete Angler. 15. mews, keeps in a cage. 81. Lucian, Greek satirist (120?–200?). 104. Montaigne, French philosopher and essayist (1533–1592). 150. make a catch, sing a round; the catch was sung without musical accompaniment by three or more singers each

or refuse, to play as freely as I myself have? Nay, who knows but that it is a defect of my not understanding her language, for doubtless Cats talk and reason with one another, that we agree no better: and who knows but that she pities me for being no wiser than to play with her, and laughs and censures my folly, for making sport for her, when we two play together?"

Thus freely speaks Montaigne concerning Cats; and I hope I may take as great a liberty to blame any man, and laugh at him too, let him be never so grave, that hath not heard what Anglers can say in the justification of their Art and Recreation; which I may again tell you, is so full of pleasure, that we need not borrow their thoughts, to think ourselves happy. . . .

THE THIRD DAY

On the Nature and Breeding of the Trout, and how to fish for him.

CHAPTER 4

PISCATOR, VENATOR, MILK-WOMAN, MAUDLIN, HOSTESS

. . . [PISCATOR] And now you shall see me try my skill to catch a Trout; and at my next walking, either this evening or tomorrow morning, I will give you direction how you yourself shall fish for him.

VENATOR. Trust me, master, I see now it is a harder matter to catch a Trout than a Chub; for I have put on patience, and followed you these two hours, and not seen a fish stir, neither at your minnow nor your worm.

PISCATOR. Well, scholar, you must endure worse luck sometime, or you will never make a good angler. But what say you now? there is a Trout now, and a good one too, if I can but hold him; and two or three turns more will tire him. Now you see he lies still, and the sleight is to land him: reach me that landing-net. So, Sir, now he is mine own: what say you now, is not this worth all my labor and your patience?

VENATOR. On my word, master, this is a gallant Trout; what shall we do with him?

PISCATOR. Marry, e'en eat him to supper: we'll go to my hostess from whence we came; she told me, as I was going out of door, that my brother Peter, a good angler and a cheerful companion, had sent word he would lodge there tonight, and bring a friend with him. My hostess has two beds, and I know you and I may have the best: we'll rejoice with my brother Peter and his friend, tell tales, or sing ballads, or make a catch, or find some harmless sport to content us, and pass away a little time without offense to God or man.

VENATOR. A match, good master, let's go to that

one of whom "caught" a part in turn. 153. **A match,** i.e., I agree.
197. Kit Marlow ... Sir Walter Raleigh; see pp. 204 ff.

house, for the linen looks white, and smells of lavender, and I long to lie in a pair of sheets that smell so. Let's be going, good master, for I am hungry again with fishing.

PISCATOR. Nay, stay a little, good scholar. I caught my last Trout with a worm; now I will put on a minnow, and try a quarter of an hour about yonder trees for another; and so, walk towards our lodging. Look you, scholar, thereabouts we shall have a bite presently, or not at all. Have with you, Sir: o' my word I have hold of him. Oh! it is a great logger-headed Chub; come, hang him upon that willow twig, and let's be going. But turn out of the way a little, good scholar! toward yonder high honeysuckle hedge; there we'll sit and sing, whilst this shower falls so gently upon the teeming earth, and gives yet a sweeter smell to the lovely flowers that adorn these verdant meadows.

Look! under that broad beech-tree I sat down, when I was last this way a-fishing; and the birds in the adjoining grove seemed to have a friendly contention with an echo, whose dead voice seemed to live in a hollow tree near to the brow of that primrose-hill. There I sat viewing the silver streams glide silently towards their center, the tempestuous sea; yet sometimes opposed by rugged roots and pebble-stones, which broke their waves, and turned them into foam; and sometimes I beguiled time by viewing the harmless lambs; some leaping securely in the cool shade, whilst others sported themselves in the cheerful sun; and saw others craving comfort from the swollen udders of their bleating dams. As I thus sat, these and other sights had so fully possest my soul with content, that I thought, as the poet has happily exprest it,

I was for that time lifted above earth;
And possest joys not promised in my birth.

As I left this place, and entered into the next field, a second pleasure entertained me; 'twas a handsome milk-maid, that had not yet attained so much age and wisdom as to load her mind with any fears of many things that will never be, as too many men too often do; but she cast away all care, and sung like a nightingale. Her voice was good, and the ditty fitted for it; it was that smooth song which was made by Kit Marlow, now at least fifty years ago; and the milk-maid's mother sung an answer to it, which was made by Sir Walter Raleigh, in his younger days. They were old-fashioned poetry, but choicely good; I think much better than the strong lines that are now in fashion in this critical age. Look yonder! on my word, yonder, they both be a-milking again. I will give her the Chub, and persuade them to sing those two songs to us.

God speed you, good woman! I have been a-fishing; and am going to Bleak Hall to my bed; and having caught more fish than will sup myself and my friend, I will bestow this upon you and your daughter, for I use to sell none.

MILK-WOMAN. Marry! God requite you, Sir, and we'll eat it cheerfully. And if you come this way a-fishing two months hence, a grace of God! I'll give you a syllabub of new verjuice, in a new-made hay-cock, for it. And my Maudlin shall sing you one of her best ballads; for she and I both love all anglers, they be such honest, civil, quiet men. In the meantime will
10 you drink a draught of red cow's milk? you shall have it freely.

PISCATOR. No, I thank you; but, I pray, do us a courtesy that shall stand you and your daughter in nothing, and yet we will think ourselves still something in your debt: it is but to sing us a song that was sung by your daughter when I last passed over this meadow, about eight or nine days since.

MILK-WOMAN. What song was it, I pray? Was it, "Come, Shepherds, deck your herds"? or, "As at
20 noon Dulcina rested"? or, "Phillida flouts me"? or, "Chevy Chace"? or, "Johnny Armstrong"? or, "Troy Town"?

PISCATOR. No, it is none of those; it is a Song that your daughter sung the first part, and you sung the answer to it.

MILK-WOMAN. O, I know it now. I learned the first part in my golden age, when I was about the age of my poor daughter; and the latter part, which indeed fits me best now, but two or three years ago, when
30 the cares of the world began to take hold of me: but you shall, God willing, hear them both; and sung as well as we can, for we both love anglers. Come, Maudlin, sing the first part to the gentlemen, with a merry heart; and I'll sing the second when you have done.

THE MILK-MAID'S SONG

Come, live with me, and be my love,
And we will all the pleasures prove,
That valleys, groves, or hills, or fields,
Or woods, and steepy mountains yields;

Where we will sit upon the rocks,
40 And see the shepherds feed our flocks,
By shallow rivers, to whose falls
Melodious birds sing madrigals.

And I will make thee beds of roses;
And, then, a thousand fragrant posies;
A cap of flowers, and a kirtle,
Embroidered all with leaves of myrtle;

A gown made of the finest wool,
Which from our pretty lambs we pull;

Slippers, lined choicely for the cold,
With buckles of the purest gold;   50

A belt of straw and ivy-buds,
With coral clasps, and amber studs.
And if these pleasures may thee move,
Come, live with me, and be my love.

Thy silver dishes, for thy meat,
As precious as the Gods do eat,
Shall, on an ivory table, be
Prepared each day for thee and me.

The shepherd swains shall dance and sing
For thy delight, each May morning.   60
If these delights thy mind may move,
Then live with me, and be my love.

VENATOR. Trust me, master, it is a choice song, and sweetly sung by honest Maudlin. I now see it was not without cause that our good Queen Elizabeth did so often wish herself a milk-maid all the month of May, because they are not troubled with fears and cares, but sing sweetly all the day, and sleep securely all the night: and without doubt, honest, innocent, pretty Maudlin does so. I'll bestow Sir Thomas Overbury's 70 milk-maid's wish upon her, "that she may die in the Spring; and, being dead, may have good store of flowers stuck round about her winding-sheet."

THE MILK-MAID'S MOTHER'S ANSWER

If all the world and love were young,
And truth in every shepherd's tongue,
These pretty pleasures might me move
To live with thee, and be thy love.

But Time drives flocks from field to fold;
When rivers rage, and rocks grow cold;
Then Philomel becometh dumb;   80
And age complains of cares to come.

The flowers do fade, and wanton fields
To wayward winter reckoning yields.
A honey tongue, a heart of gall,
Is fancy's spring but sorrow's fall.

Thy gowns, thy shoes, thy beds of roses,
Thy cap, thy kirtle, and thy posies,
Soon break, soon wither, soon forgotten;
In folly ripe, in reason rotten.

Thy belt of straw, and ivy-buds,   90
Thy coral clasps, and amber studs,

2. use to sell none, do not make a practice of selling any. 6. syllabub
. . . verjuice, sweetened cream beaten to a stiff froth and flavored with
the juice of tart or green fruit. 19. Come, Shepherds, etc., titles of
old pastoral songs and ballads. The Milk-Maid's Song. For notes on

this song and the one that follows see Christopher Marlowe's The
Passionate Shepherd to His Love, p. 204. 70. Sir Thomas Overbury's;
see p. 357. 132. These verses; the allusion is to some poetry which
has just been recited. The section reprinted here is the conclusion of

All these in me no means can move
To come to thee, and be thy love.

What should we talk of dainties, then,
Of better meat than's fit for men?
These are but vain: that's only good
Which God hath blessed, and sent for food.

But could youth last, and love still breed;
Had joys no date, nor age no need;
100 Then those delights my mind might move
To live with thee, and be thy love.

MOTHER. Well! I have done my song. But stay, honest anglers; for I will make Maudlin sing you one short song more. Maudlin! sing that song that you sung last night, when young Coridon the shepherd played so purely on his oaten pipe to you and your cousin Betty.

MAUDLIN. I will, mother.

I married a wife of late,
110 The more's my unhappy fate:
I married her for love,
As my fancy did me move,
And not for a worldly estate:

But oh! the green sickness
Soon changed her likeness;
And all her beauty did fail.
But 'tis not so
With those that go
Thro' frost and snow,
120 As all men know,
And carry the milking-pail.

PISCATOR. Well sung, good woman; I thank you. I'll give you another dish of fish one of these days; and then beg another song of you. Come, scholar! let Maudlin alone: do not you offer to spoil her voice. Look! yonder comes mine hostess, to call us to supper. How now! is my brother Peter come?

HOSTESS. Yes, and a friend with him. They are both glad to hear that you are in these parts; and long to 130 see you; and long to be at supper, for they be very hungry. . . .

THE FIFTH DAY

. . . VENATOR. Well, Master, these verses be worthy to keep a room in every man's memory. I thank you for them; and I thank you for your many instructions, which, God willing, I will not forget. And as St. Austin, in his *Confessions*, commemorates

the kindness of his friend Verecundus, for lending him and his companion a country house, because there they rested and enjoyed themselves, free from the troubles of the world, so, having had the like advantage, 140 both by your conversation and the art you have taught me, I ought ever to do the like; for, indeed, your company and discourse have been so useful and pleasant, that, I may truly say, I have only lived since I enjoyed them and turned angler, and not before. Nevertheless, here I must part with you; here in this now sad place, where I was so happy as first to meet you: but I shall long for the ninth of May; for then I hope again to enjoy your beloved company, at the appointed time and place. And now I wish for some 150 somniferous potion, that might force me to sleep away the intermitted time, which will pass away with me as tediously as it does with men in sorrow; nevertheless I will make it as short as I can, by my hopes and wishes: and, my good Master, I will not forget the doctrine which you told me Socrates taught his scholars, that they should not think to be honored so much for being philosophers, as to honor philosophy by their virtuous lives. You advised me to the like concerning Angling, and I will endeavor to do so; and 160 to live like those many worthy men, of which you made mention in the former part of your discourse. This is my firm resolution. And as a pious man advised his friend, that, to beget mortification, he should frequent churches, and view monuments, and charnel-houses, and then and there consider how many dead bodies time had piled up at the gates of death, so when I would beget content, and increase confidence in the power, and wisdom, and providence of Almighty God, I will walk the meadows, by some gliding stream, and 170 there contemplate the lilies that take no care, and those very many other various little living creatures that are not only created, but fed, man knows not how, by the goodness of the God of Nature, and therefore trust in him. This is my purpose; and so, let everything that hath breath praise the Lord: and let the blessing of St. Peter's Master be with mine.

PISCATOR. And upon all that are lovers of virtue; and dare trust in his providence; and be quiet; and go a Angling. 180
"Study to be quiet."

(1653)

JOHN BUNYAN 1628-1688

John Bunyan was born in Elstow, Bedfordshire, in 1628. He was the son of an artisan, and he himself took to the craft of brazier. At sixteen he was drafted

the book. 136. **St. Austin,** St. Augustine (354–430), Bishop of Hippo, whose *Confessions,* a spiritual autobiography, was much read and quoted in England in the seventeenth century. 171. **lilies, etc.** The allusion is to the words of Jesus; cf. Matthew 6:28 (see p. 316). 177 **St.**

Peter. Simon Peter, one of the disciples of Jesus, was a fisherman; hence the allusion. 181. **"Study to be quiet,"** St. Paul's words from 1 Thessalonians 4:11.

into the Parliamentary army and served from November 1644 to June 1647, at Newport Pagnell under the command of Sir Samuel Luke. At the end of his service in the army, Bunyan returned to his native village, married, and settled down to his craft. Here he took seriously to reading his Bible. "I was never out of the Bible," he wrote later, "either by reading or meditation." Inasmuch as his earlier education had been very scant, the Bible became his textbook, and to it he owes the force, simplicity, rhythm, charm, and other qualities of his own prose.

In 1653 Bunyan joined a Baptist church in Bedford, and shortly afterwards he put to use his natural talents for vivid and vigorous utterances by preaching lay sermons in his own and neighboring churches. Attacks by Quakers, who heckled him as he preached, brought about his first published writing, a controversial tract entitled Some Gospel Truths Opened (1656). The Restoration was unkind to all non-conformists, under the old Conventicle Act they were forbidden to preach and were punished for their own expressions of belief. In the very first year of the return of Charles II, therefore, Bunyan was clapped into the Bedford jail, where he remained for twelve years until the royal declaration of indulgence released him in 1672. So it was that most of his writing was done by the dim light of the prison house. Grace Abounding to the Chief of Sinners (1666), like the Confessions of Augustine and the Apologia pro Vita Sua of Cardinal Newman, is a spiritual autobiography recounting his religious experiences. The Holy City, or the New Jerusalem (1666) followed his reading of the book of Revelation and is a forecast of the glowing description of the celestial city in The Pilgrim's Progress. A Confession of My Faith and a Reason of My Practice, written in 1672 just before his release, was an addition to the record of his spiritual experiences.

On his release from prison under the King's declaration of indulgence which permitted non-conformist ministers to preach, Bunyan was elected pastor of the church in Bedford of which he had been a member for nearly twenty years. This post he held for three years, then the royal indulgence was withdrawn under pressure of the Anglicans, and Bunyan was again cast into prison, this time for six months. During this second term of imprisonment for his faith he produced his masterpiece, The Pilgrim's Progress from This World to That Which Is to Come. The first short form of this allegory was published in 1678; another and enlarged edition appeared later in the same year; and a third and still further enlarged issue came out in the following year. After his release from prison he continued to write. The Life and Death of Mr. Badman, an allegorical story of immense power and reality, which anticipates Defoe in its stark realism, appeared in 1680. The Holy War (1682) is an allegory in which Bunyan made use of his military experiences with the Parliamentary army. He died in 1688.

The popularity of Pilgrim's Progress has been second only to that of the Bible. Not only in England but in Puritan New England it became a universally read classic. "This is the great merit of the book," said Dr. Johnson, "that the most cultivated man cannot find anything to praise more highly, and the child knows nothing more amusing." The influence of the book on American children of the past century appears in Louisa M. Alcott's Little Women (1868). Here the author tells how, on rainy days, the "little women," Meg, Jo, Beth, and Amy, played "Pilgrim's Progress" by climbing, pack on back, from the ground floor of the rambling New England home to the "Heavenly City" in the great attic.

from THE PILGRIM'S PROGRESS

[CHRISTIAN SETS FORTH]

As I walked through the wilderness of this world, I lighted on a certain place where was a Den, and I laid me down in that place to sleep; and, as I slept, I dreamed a dream. I dreamed, and behold I saw a man clothed with rags, standing in a certain place, with his face from his own house, a book in his hand, and a great burden upon his back (Isaiah 64:6; Luke 14:33; Psalms 38:4; Habakkuk 2:2; Acts 16:31). I looked and saw him open the book and read therein; and, as he read, he wept, and trembled; and not being 10 able longer to contain, he brake out with a lamentable cry, saying, "What shall I do?" (Acts 2:37).

In this plight, therefore, he went home and refrained himself as long as he could, that his wife and children should not perceive his distress; but he could not be silent long, because that his trouble increased. Wherefore at length he brake his mind to his wife and children; and thus he began to talk to them. O my dear wife, said he, and you the children of my bowels, I, your dear friend, am in myself undone by reason of 20 a burden that lieth hard upon me; moreover, I am for certain informed that this our city will be burned with fire from heaven, in which fearful overthrow both myself, with thee, my wife, and you my sweet babes, shall miserably come to ruin, except (the which yet I see not) some way of escape can be found, whereby we may be delivered. At this his relations were sore amazed; not for that they believed that what he had said to them was true, but because they thought that some frenzy distemper had 30 got into his head; therefore, it drawing towards night, and they hoping that sleep might settle his

---

The Pilgrim's Progress. 40. **carriages,** bearings, demeanors. 72. **Tophet,** a place in the Valley of Hinnom, near Jerusalem, where human sacrifices by fire were offered to Moloch; hence, the fiery pit, Hell. For Milton's use of the term see p. 391, ll. 392 ff. 84. **wicket-gate,**

Frontispiece to Bunyan's Pilgrim's Progress, *third edition, 1679. This portrait of Bunyan appeared for the first time in the edition of 1679; the lion in his den symbolizes the forces of evil, and the lone figure of the pilgrim with his Bible and load of sin, journeying from the City of Destruction to the Heavenly City, not only illustrates Bunyan's story, but typifies also the English Puritan.*

he began to retire himself to his chamber, to pray for and pity them, and also to condole his own misery; he would also walk solitarily in the fields, sometimes reading, and sometimes praying: and thus for some days he spent his time.

Now, I saw, upon a time, when he was walking in the fields, that he was, as he was wont, reading in his book, and greatly distressed in his mind; and as 50 he read, he burst out, as he had done before, crying, "What shall I do to be saved?"

I saw also that he looked this way and that way, as if he would run; yet he stood still, because, as I perceived, he could not tell which way to go. I looked then, and saw a man named Evangelist coming to him, who asked, Wherefore dost thou cry? (Job 33:23.)

He answered, Sir, I perceive by the book in my hand that I am condemned to die, and after that to 60 come to judgment (Hebrews 9:27), and I find that I am not willing to do the first (Job 16:21), nor able to do the second (Ezekiel 22:14).

Christian no sooner leaves the World but meets
Evangelist, who lovingly him greets
With tidings of another; and doth show
Him how to mount to that from this below.

Then said Evangelist, Why not willing to die, since this life is attended with so many evils? The man answered, Because I fear that this burden that is upon 70 my back will sink me lower than the grave, and I shall fall into Tophet (Isaiah 30:33). And, sir, if I be not fit to go to prison, I am not fit to go to judgment, and from thence to execution; and the thoughts of these things make me cry.

Then said Evangelist, If this be thy condition, why standest thou still? He answered, Because I know not whither to go. Then he gave him a parchment roll, and there was written within, "Flee from the wrath to come" (Matthew 3:7). 80

The man therefore read it, and looking upon Evangelist very carefully, said, Whither must I fly? Then said Evangelist, pointing with his finger over a very wide field, Do you see yonder wicket-gate? (Matthew 7:13, 14.) The man said, No. Then said the other, Do you see yonder shining light? (Psalms 119:105; 2 Peter 1:19.) He said, I think I do. Then said Evangelist, Keep that light in your eye, and go up directly thereto: so shalt thou see the gate; at which when thou knockest it shall be told thee what thou shalt do. So 90 I saw in my dream that the man began to run. Now, he had not run far from his own door, but his wife and children perceiving it, began to cry after him to return; but the man put his fingers in his ears, and ran on, crying, Life, life! eternal life! (Luke 14:26.) So he looked not behind him, but fled towards the middle of the plain (Genesis 19:17). . . .

brains, with all haste they got him to bed. But the night was as troublesome to him as the day; wherefore, instead of sleeping, he spent it in sighs and tears. So, when the morning was come, they would know how he did. He told them, Worse and worse: he also set to talking to them again: but they began to be hardened. They also thought to drive away his distemper 40 by harsh and surly carriages to him; sometimes they would deride, sometimes they would chide, and sometimes they would quite neglect him. Wherefore

a small and narrow gate, usually forming part of a larger gate or door.

But now, in this Valley of Humiliation, poor Christian was hard put to it; for he had gone but a little way, before he espied a foul fiend coming over the field to meet him; his name is Apollyon. Then did Christian begin to be afraid, and to cast in his mind whether to go back or to stand his ground. But he considered again that he had no armor for his back; and therefore thought that to turn the back to him might give him the greater advantage with ease to
10 pierce him with his darts. Therefore he resolved to venture and stand his ground; for, thought he, had I no more in mine eye than the saving of my life, it would be the best way to stand.

So he went on, and Apollyon met him. Now the monster was hideous to behold; he was clothed with scales, like a fish (and they are his pride), he had wings like a dragon, feet like a bear, and out of his belly came fire and smoke, and his mouth was as the mouth of a lion. When he was come up to Christian,
20 he beheld him with a disdainful countenance, and thus began to question with him.

APOL. Whence come you? and whither are you bound?

CHR. I am come from the City of Destruction, which is the place of all evil, and am going to the City of Zion.

APOL. By this I perceive thou art one of my subjects, for all that country is mine, and I am the prince and god of it. How is it, then, that thou hast run away
30 from thy king? Were it not that I hope thou mayest do me more service, I would strike thee now, at one blow, to the ground.

CHR. I was born, indeed, in your dominions, but your service was hard, and your wages such as a man could not live on, "for the wages of sin is death" (Romans 6:23); therefore, when I was come to years, I did as other considerate persons do, look out, if, perhaps, I might mend myself.

APOL. There is no prince that will thus lightly lose
40 his subjects, neither will I as yet lose thee; but since thou complainest of thy service and wages, be content to go back: what our country will afford, I do here promise to give thee.

CHR. But I have let myself to another, even to the King of princes; and how can I, with fairness, go back with thee?

APOL. Thou hast done in this, according to the proverb, "Changed a bad for a worse"; but it is ordinary for those that have professed themselves his servants,
50 after a while to give him the slip, and return again to me. Do thou so too, and all shall be well.

CHR. I have given him my faith, and sworn my allegiance to him; how, then, can I go back from this, and not be hanged as a traitor?

APOL. Thou didst the same to me, and yet I am willing to pass by all, if now thou wilt yet turn again and go back.

CHR. What I promised thee was in my nonage; and, besides, I count the Prince under whose banner now I stand is able to absolve me; yea, and to pardon also 60 what I did as to my compliance with thee; and besides, O thou destroying Apollyon! to speak truth, I like his service, his wages, his servants, his government, his company and country, better than thine; and, therefore, leave off to persuade me further; I am his servant, and I will follow him.

APOL. Consider, again, when thou art in cool blood, what thou art like to meet with in the way that thou goest. Thou knowest that, for the most part, his servants come to an ill end, because they are trans- 70 gressors against me and my ways. How many of them have been put to shameful deaths; and, besides, thou countest his service better than mine, whereas he never came yet from the place where he is to deliver any that served him out of their hands; but as for me, how many times, as all the world very well knows, have I delivered, either by power, or fraud, those that have faithfully served me, from him and his, though taken by them; and so I will deliver thee.

CHR. His forbearing at present to deliver them is 80 on purpose to try their love, whether they will cleave to him to the end; and as for the ill end thou sayest they come to, that is most glorious in their account; for, for present deliverance, they do not much expect it, for they stay for their glory, and then they shall have it, when their Prince comes in his and the glory of the angels.

APOL. Thou hast already been unfaithful in thy service to him; and how dost thou think to receive wages of him? 90

CHR. Wherein, O Apollyon! have I been unfaithful to him?

APOL. Thou didst faint at first setting out, when thou wast almost choked in the Gulf of Despond; thou didst attempt wrong ways to be rid of thy burden, whereas thou shouldest have stayed till thy Prince had taken it off; thou didst sinfully sleep and lose thy choice thing; thou wast, also, almost persuaded to go back, at the sight of the lions; and when thou talkest of thy journey, and of what thou hast heard and seen, thou 100 art inwardly desirous of vain-glory in all that thou sayest or doest.

CHR. All this is true, and much more which thou hast left out; but the Prince whom I serve and honor is merciful, and ready to forgive; but, besides, these infirmities possessed me in thy country, for there I sucked them in; and I have groaned under them,

---

1. **Valley of Humiliation;** the preceding episode recounts how Christian entered the Valley under the guidance of Discretion, Piety, Charity, and Prudence. 44. **let,** entered upon a contract with. 97. **choice thing,** his parchment roll, or certificate, which he lost while he slept.

been sorry for them, and have obtained pardon of my Prince.

110 APOL. Then Apollyon broke out into a grievous rage, saying, I am an enemy to this Prince; I hate his person, his laws, and people; I am come out on purpose to withstand thee.

CHR. Apollyon, beware what you do; for I am in the king's highway, the way of holiness; therefore take heed to yourself.

APOL. Then Apollyon straddled quite over the whole breadth of the way, and said, I am void of fear in this matter: prepare thyself to die; for I swear by my 120 infernal den, that thou shalt go no further; here will I spill thy soul.

And with that he threw a flaming dart at his breast; but Christian had a shield in his hand, with which he caught it, and so prevented the danger of that.

Then did Christian draw, for he saw it was time to bestir him: and Apollyon as fast made at him, throwing darts as thick as hail; by the which, notwithstanding all that Christian could do to avoid it, Apollyon wounded him in his head, his hand, and foot. This made 130 Christian give a little back; Apollyon, therefore, followed his work amain, and Christian again took courage, and resisted as manfully as he could. This sore combat lasted for above half a day, even till Christian was almost quite spent; for you must know that Christian, by reason of his wounds, must needs grow weaker and weaker.

Then Apollyon, espying his opportunity, began to gather up close to Christian, and wrestling with him, gave him a dreadful fall; and with that Christian's 140 sword flew out of his hand. Then said Apollyon, I am sure of thee now. And with that he had almost pressed him to death, so that Christian began to despair of life: but as God would have it, while Apollyon was fetching of his last blow, thereby to make a full end of this good man, Christian nimbly stretched out his hand for his sword, and caught it saying, "Rejoice not against me, O mine enemy: when I fall I shall arise" (Micah 7:8); and with that gave him a deadly thrust, which made him give back, as one that had received his mortal 150 wound. Christian perceiving that, made at him again, saying, "Nay, in all these things we are more than conquerors through him that loved us" (Romans 8:37). And with that Apollyon spread forth his dragon's wings, and sped him away, that Christian for a season saw him no more. (James 4:7.)

In this combat no man can imagine, unless he had seen and heard as I did, what yelling and hideous roaring Apollyon made all the time of the fight—he spake like a dragon; and, on the other side, what sighs 160 and groans burst from Christian's heart. I never saw him all the while give so much as one pleasant look, till he perceived he had wounded Apollyon with his two-

edged sword; then, indeed, he did smile, and look upward; but it was the dreadfulest sight that ever I saw.

A more unequal match can hardly be—
Christian must fight an angel; but you see,
The valiant man by handling Sword and Shield,
Doth make him, though a Dragon, quit the field.

So when the battle was over, Christian said, "I will here give thanks to him that delivered me out of the 170 mouth of the lion, to him that did help me against Apollyon." And so he did, saying—

"Great Beelzebub, the captain of this fiend,
Designed my ruin; therefore to this end
He sent him harnessed out: and he with rage
That hellish was, did fiercely me engage.
But blessed Michael helped me, and I,
By dint of sword, did quickly make him fly.
Therefore to him let me give lasting praise,
And thank and bless his holy name always." . . .   180

[VANITY FAIR]

Then I saw in my dream, that when they were got out of the wilderness, they presently saw a town before them, and the name of that town is Vanity; and at the town there is a fair kept, called Vanity Fair: it is kept all the year long; it beareth the name of Vanity Fair, because the town where it is kept is lighter than vanity; and also because all that is there sold, or that cometh thither, is vanity. As is the saying of the wise, "all that cometh is vanity" (Ecclesiastes 1:2, 14; 2:11, 17; 11:8; Isaiah 51:29).   190

This fair is no new-erected business, but a thing of ancient standing; I will show you the original of it.

Almost five thousand years agone, there were pilgrims walking to the Celestial City, as these two honest persons are: and Beelzebub, Apollyon, and Legion, with their companions, perceiving by the path that the pilgrims made, that their way to the city lay through this town of Vanity, they contrived here to set up a fair; a fair wherein should be sold all sorts of vanity, and that it should last all the year long: 200 therefore at this fair are all such merchandise sold, as houses, lands, trades, places, honors, preferments, titles, countries, kingdoms, lusts, pleasures, and delights of all sorts, as whores, bawds, wives, husbands, children, masters, servants, lives, blood, bodies, souls, silver, gold, pearls, precious stones, and what not.

And, moreover, at this fair there is at all times to be seen juggling, cheats, games, plays, fools, apes, knaves, and rogues, and that of every kind.

Here are to be seen, too, and that for nothing,

---

166. **angel,** a supernatural spirit; here a fiend. 177. **Michael,** archangel who led the heavenly hosts in the fight against Satan. Bunyan has in mind, however, the Michael who fought against the dragon (Revelation 12:7).

thefts, murders, adulteries, false swearers, and that of a blood-red color.

And as in other fairs of less moment, there are the several rows and streets, under their proper names, where such and such wares are vended; so here likewise you have the proper places, rows, streets (viz. countries and kingdoms), where the wares of this fair are soonest to be found. Here is the Britain Row, the French Row, the Italian Row, the Spanish Row, the
10 German Row, where several sorts of vanities are to be sold. But, as in other fairs, some one commodity is as the chief of all the fair, so the ware of Rome and her merchandise is greatly promoted in this fair; only our English nation, with some others, have taken a dislike thereat.

Now, as I said, the way to the Celestial City lies just through this town where this lusty fair is kept; and he that will go to the City, and yet not go through this town, must needs "go out of the world" (1 Corinthians
20 5:10). The Prince of princes himself, when here, went through this town to his own country, and that upon a fair day too; yea, and as I think, it was Beelzebub, the chief lord of this fair, that invited him to buy of his vanities; yea, would have made him lord of the fair, would he but have done him reverence as he went through the town. (Matthew 4:8; Luke 4:5-7.) Yea, because he was such a person of honor, Beelzebub had him from street to street, and showed him all the kingdoms of the world in a little time, that he might,
30 if possible, allure the Blessed One to cheapen and buy some of his vanities; but he had no mind to the merchandise, and therefore left the town, without laying out so much as one farthing upon these vanities. This fair, therefore, is an ancient thing, of long standing, and a very great fair. Now these pilgrims, as I said, must needs go through this fair. Well, so they did: but, behold, even as they entered into the fair, all the people in the fair were moved, and the town itself as it were in a hubbub about them; and that for several reasons:
40 for—

First, The pilgrims were clothed with such kind of raiment as was diverse from the raiment of any that traded in that fair. The people, therefore, of the fair, made a great gazing upon them: some said they were fools, some they were bedlams, and some they are outlandish men. (1 Corinthians 2:7, 8.)

Secondly, And as they wondered at their apparel, so they did likewise at their speech; for few could understand what they said; they naturally spoke the
50 language of Canaan, but they that kept the fair were the men of this world; so that, from one end of the fair to the other, they seemed barbarians each to the other.

Thirdly, But that which did not a little amuse the merchandisers was, that these pilgrims set very light by all their wares; they cared not so much as to look upon them; and if they called upon them to buy, they would put their fingers in their ears, and cry, "Turn away mine eyes from beholding vanity," and look upwards, signifying that their trade and traffic was in 60 heaven. (Psalms 119:37; Philippians 3:19, 20.)

One chanced mockingly, beholding the carriage of the men, to say unto them, What will ye buy? But they, looking gravely upon him, answered, "We buy the truth" (Proverbs 23:23). At that there was an occasion taken to despise the men the more; some mocking, some taunting, some speaking reproachfully, and some calling upon others to smite them. At last things came to a hubbub and great stir in the fair, insomuch that all order was confounded. Now was word 70 presently brought to the great one of the fair, who quickly came down, and deputed some of his most trusty friends to take these men into examination, about whom the fair was almost overturned. So the men were brought to examination; and they that sat upon them, asked them whence they came, whither they went, and what they did there, in such an unusual garb? The men told them that they were pilgrims and strangers in the world, and that they were going to their own country, which was the heavenly Jeru- 80 salem (Hebrews 11:13-16); and that they had given no occasion to the men of the town, nor yet to the merchandisers, thus to abuse them, and to let them in their journey, except it was for that, when one asked them what they would buy, they said they would buy the truth. But they that were appointed to examine them did not believe them to be any other than bedlams and mad, or else such as came to put all things into a confusion in the fair. Therefore they took them and beat them, and besmeared them with dirt, and 90 then put them into the cage, that they might be made a spectacle to all the men of the fair.

Behold Vanity Fair! the Pilgrims there
   Are chained and stand beside:
Even so it was our Lord passed here,
   And on Mount Calvary died. . . .

[GIANT DESPAIR]

Neither could they, with all the skill they had, get again to the stile that night. Wherefore, at last, lighting under a little shelter, they sat down there until the day-break; but, being weary, they fell asleep. Now 100 there was, not far from the place where they lay, a castle called Doubting Castle, the owner whereof was Giant Despair; and it was in his grounds they now were sleeping: wherefore he, getting up in the morning early, and walking up and down in his fields, caught Christian and Hopeful asleep in his grounds. Then,

---

12. **ware of Rome,** an allusion to the Roman Catholic ritual, symbols, etc. 14. **English . . . others;** the reference is to the various Protestant reformations in England and on the Continent. 27. **Beelzebub;** see p.

388, l. 81. 30. **cheapen,** to ask the price of. 46. **outlandish men,** foreigners. 50. **Canaan,** a district in Palestine; applied also to the whole of Palestine. 83. **let,** hinder. 91. **cage,** a cage-like prison in which the

with a grim and surly voice, he bid them awake; and asked them whence they were, and what they did in his grounds. They told him they were pilgrims, and that they had lost their way. Then said the Giant, You have this night trespassed on me, by trampling in and lying on my grounds, therefore you must go along with me. So they were forced to go, because he was stronger than they. They also had but little to say, for they knew themselves in a fault. The Giant, therefore, drove them before him, and put them into his castle, into a very dark dungeon, nasty and stinking to the spirits of these two men. (Psalms 88:18.) Here, then, they lay from Wednesday morning till Saturday night, without one bit of bread, or drop of drink, or light, or any to ask how they did; they were, therefore, here in evil case, and were far from friends and acquaintance. Now in this place Christian had double sorrow, because it was through his unadvised counsel that they were brought into this distress.

The pilgrims now, to gratify the flesh,
Will seek its ease; but oh! how they afresh
Do thereby plunge themselves new griefs into!
Who seek to please the flesh, themselves undo.

Now, Giant Despair had a wife, and her name was Diffidence. So when he was gone to bed, he told his wife what he had done; to wit, that he had taken a couple of prisoners and cast them into his dungeon, for trespassing on his grounds. Then he asked her also what he had best to do further to them. So she asked him what they were, whence they came, and whither they were bound; and he told her. Then she counseled him that when he arose in the morning he should beat them without any mercy. So, when he arose, he getteth him a grievous crab-tree cudgel, and goes down into the dungeon to them, and there first falls to rating of them as if they were dogs, although they never gave him a word of distaste. Then he falls upon them, and beats them fearfully, in such sort, that they were not able to help themselves, or to turn them upon the floor. This done, he withdraws and leaves them, there to condole their misery, and to mourn under their distress. So all that day they spent the time in nothing but sighs and bitter lamentations. The next night, she, talking with her husband about them further, and understanding they were yet alive, did advise him to counsel them to make away themselves. So when morning was come, he goes to them in a surly manner as before, and perceiving them to be very sore with the stripes that he had given them the day before, he told them, that since they were never like to come out of that place, their only way would be forthwith to make an end of themselves, either with knife, halter, or poison, for why, said he, should you choose life, seeing it is attended with so much bitterness? But they desired him to let them go. With that he looked ugly upon them, and, rushing to them, had doubtless made an end of them himself, but that he fell into one of his fits (for he sometimes, in sunshiny weather, fell into fits), and lost for a time the use of his hand; wherefore he withdrew, and left them as before, to consider what to do. Then did the prisoners consult between themselves, whether it was best to take his counsel or no; and thus they began to discourse:—

CHR. Brother, said Christian, what shall we do? The life that we now live is miserable. For my part I know not whether it is best, to live thus, or to die out of hand. "My soul chooseth strangling rather than life," and the grave is more easy for me than this dungeon. (Job 7:15.) Shall we be ruled by the Giant?

HOPE. Indeed, our present condition is dreadful, and death would be far more welcome to me than thus for ever to abide; but yet, let us consider, the Lord of the country to which we are going hath said, Thou shalt do no murder: no, not to another man's person; much more, then, are we forbidden to take his counsel to kill ourselves. Besides, he that kills another can but commit murder upon his body; but for one to kill himself is to kill body and soul at once. And, moreover, my brother, thou talkest of ease in the grave; but hast thou forgotten the hell, whither for certain the murderers go? For "no murderer hath eternal life," etc. And let us consider, again, that all the law is not in the hand of Giant Despair. Others, so far as I can understand, have been taken by him, as well as we; and yet have escaped out of his hand. Who knows, but that God that made the world may cause that Giant Despair may die? or that, at some time or other, he may forget to lock us in? or that he may, in a short time, have another of his fits before us, and may lose the use of his limbs? and if ever that should come to pass again, for my part, I am resolved to pluck up the heart of a man, and to try my utmost to get from under his hand. I was a fool that I did not try to do it before; but, however, my brother, let us be patient, and endure a while. The time may come that may give us a happy release; but let us not be our own murderers. With these words, Hopeful at present did moderate the mind of his brother; so they continued together (in the dark) that day, in their sad and doleful condition.

Well, towards evening, the Giant goes down into the dungeon again, to see if his prisoners had taken his counsel; but when he came there he found them alive; and truly, alive was all; for now, what for want of bread and water, and by reason of the wounds they received when he beat them, they could do little but breathe. But, I say, he found them alive; at which

prisoners were exposed to the gaze and insults of the public. 97. they, i.e., Christian and his companion Hopeful. They had attempted to take an easier way to the gates of the Celestial City by climbing over a stile and going through *By-Path-Meadow*, but soon got into pitfalls and then came to Doubting Castle.

he fell into a grievous rage, and told them that, seeing they had disobeyed his counsel, it should be worse with them than if they had never been born.

At this they trembled greatly, and I think that Christian fell into a swoon; but, coming a little to himself again, they renewed their discourse about the Giant's counsel; and whether yet they had best to take it or no. Now Christian again seemed to be for doing it, but Hopeful made his second reply as followeth:—

HOPE. My brother, said he, remembereth thou not how valiant thou hast been heretofore? Apollyon could not crush thee, nor could all that thou didst hear, or see, or feel, in the Valley of the Shadow of Death. What hardship, terror, and amazement hast thou already gone through! And art thou now nothing but fear! Thou seest that I am in the dungeon with thee, a far weaker man by nature than thou art; also, this Giant has wounded me as well as thee, and hath also cut off the bread and water from my mouth; and with thee I mourn without the light. But let us exercise a little more patience; remember how thou playedst the man at Vanity Fair, and wast neither afraid of the chain, nor cage, nor yet of bloody death. Wherefore let us (at least to avoid the shame, that becomes not a Christian to be found in) bear up with patience as well as we can.

Now, night being come again, and the Giant and his wife being in bed, she asked him concerning the prisoners, and if they had taken his counsel. To which he replied, They are sturdy rogues, they choose rather to bear all hardship, than to make away themselves. Then said she, Take them into the castle-yard to-morrow, and show them the bones and skulls of those that thou hast already despatched, and make them believe, ere a week comes to an end, thou also wilt tear them in pieces, as thou hast done their fellows before them.

So when the morning was come, the Giant goes to them again, and takes them into the castle-yard, and shows them, as his wife had bidden him. These, said he, were pilgrims as you are, once, and they trespassed in my grounds, as you have done; and when I thought fit, I tore them in pieces, and so, within ten days, I will do you. Go, get you down to your den again; and with that he beat them all the way thither. They lay, therefore, all day on Saturday in a lamentable case, as before. Now, when night was come, and when Mrs. Diffidence and her husband, the Giant, were got to bed, they began to renew their discourse of their prisoners; and withal the old Giant wondered, that he could neither by his blows nor his counsel bring them to an end. And with that his wife replied, I fear, said she, that they live in hope that some will come to relieve them,

or that they have picklocks about them, by the means of which they hope to escape. And sayest thou so, my dear? said the Giant; I will, therefore, search them in the morning.

Well, on Saturday, about midnight, they began to pray, and continued in prayer till almost break of day.

Now, a little before it was day, good Christian, as one half amazed, brake out in this passionate speech: What a fool, quoth he, am I, thus to lie in a stinking dungeon, when I may as well walk at liberty! I have a key in my bosom, called Promise, that will, I am persuaded, open any lock in Doubting Castle. Then said Hopeful, That is good news, good brother; pluck it out of thy bosom, and try.

Then Christian pulled it out of his bosom, and began to try at the dungeon door, whose bolt (as he turned the key) gave back, and the door flew open with ease, and Christian and Hopeful both came out. Then he went to the outward door that leads into the castle-yard, and, with his key, opened that door also. After, he went to the iron gate, for that must be opened too; but that lock went damnable hard, yet the key did open it. Then they thrust open the gate to make their escape with speed, but that gate, as it opened, made such a creaking, that it waked Giant Despair, who, hastily rising to pursue his prisoners, felt his limbs to fail, for his fits took him again, so that he could by no means go after them. Then they went on, and came to the King's highway, and so were safe, because they were out of his jurisdiction.

Now, when they were gone over the stile, they began to contrive with themselves what they should do at that stile, to prevent those that should come after, from falling into the hands of Giant Despair. So they consented to erect there a pillar, and to engrave upon the side thereof this sentence—"Over this stile is the way to Doubting Castle, which is kept by Giant Despair, who despiseth the King of the Celestial Country, and seeks to destroy his holy pilgrims." Many, therefore, that followed after, read what was written, and escaped the danger. This done, they sang as follows:—

Out of the way we went, and then we found
What 'twas to tread upon forbidden ground;
And let them that come after have a care,
Lest heedlessness makes them, as we, to fare.
Lest they for trespassing his prisoners are,
Whose castle's Doubting, and whose name's
    Despair. . . .

[THE CELESTIAL CITY]

Now I saw in my dream, that by this time the

---

113. **turtle**, turtledove. 127. **corn**, grain in general. 198. **Enoch and Elijah**. Both went to heaven without dying. The first "walked with

God: and he was not; for God took him" (Genesis 5:24); the second was carried to heaven in a chariot of fire (2 Kings 2:11). 214. **Selah**,

pilgrims were got over the Enchanted Ground, and entering into the country of Beulah, whose air was very sweet and pleasant, the way lying directly through it, they solaced themselves there for a season. (Isaiah 62:4.) Yea, here they heard continually the singing of birds, and saw every day the flowers appear in the earth, and heard the voice of the turtle in the land. (Canticles 2:10-12.) In this country the sun shineth night and day; wherefore this was beyond the Valley of the Shadow of Death, and also out of the reach of Giant Despair, neither could they from this place so much as see Doubting Castle. Here they were within sight of the city they were going to, also here met them some of the inhabitants thereof; for in this land the Shining Ones commonly walked, because it was upon the borders of heaven. In this land also, the contract between the bride and the bridegroom was renewed; yea, here, "As the bridegroom rejoiceth over the bride, so did their God rejoice over them" (Isaiah 62:5). Here they had no want of corn and wine; for in this place they met with abundance of what they had sought for in all their pilgrimage. (Verse 8.) Here they heard voices from out of the city, loud voices, saying, "Say ye to the daughter of Zion, behold, thy salvation cometh! Behold, his reward is with him!" (Verse 11.) Here all the inhabitants of the country called them, "The holy people, The redeemed of the Lord, Sought out," etc. (Verse 12.)

Now, as they walked in this land, they had more rejoicing than in parts more remote from the kingdom to which they were bound; and drawing near to the city, they had yet a more perfect view thereof. It was builded of pearls and precious stones, also the street thereof was paved with gold; so that by reason of the natural glory of the city, and the reflection of the sunbeams upon it, Christian with desire fell sick; Hopeful also had a fit or two of the same disease. Wherefore, here they lay by it a while, crying out, because of their pangs, "If ye find my beloved, tell him that I am sick of love" (Canticles 5:8).

But, being a little strengthened, and better able to bear their sickness, they walked on their way, and came yet nearer and nearer, where were orchards, vineyards, and gardens, and their gates opened into the highway. Now, as they came up to these places, behold the gardener stood in the way, to whom the pilgrims said, Whose goodly vineyards and gardens are these? He answered, They are the King's, and are planted here for his own delight, and also for the solace of pilgrims. So the gardener had them into the vineyards, and bid them refresh themselves with the dainties. (Deuteronomy 23:24.) He also showed them there the King's walks, and the arbors where he delighted to be; and here they tarried and slept.

a word occurring in Psalms; apparently a direction to the musicians, but employed by Bunyan as though it were equivalent to Amen.

Now I beheld in my dream, that they talked more in their sleep at this time than ever they did in all their journey; and being in a muse thereabout, the gardener said even to me, Wherefore musest thou at the matter? It is the nature of the fruit of the grapes of these vineyards to go down so sweetly as to cause the lips of them that are asleep to speak.

So I saw that when they awoke, they addressed themselves to go up to the city; but, as I said, the reflection of the sun upon the city (for "the city was pure gold," Revelation 21:18) was so extremely glorious, that they could not, as yet, with open face behold it, but through an instrument made for that purpose. (2 Corinthians 3:18.) So I saw, that as I went on, there met them two men, in raiment that shone like gold; also their faces shone as the light.

These men asked the pilgrims whence they came; and they told them. They also asked them where they had lodged, what difficulties and dangers, what comforts and pleasures they had met in the way; and they told them. Then said the men that met them, You have but two difficulties more to meet with, and then you are in the city.

Christian then, and his companion, asked the men to go along with them; so they told them they would. But, said they, you must obtain it by your own faith. So I saw in my dream that they went on together, until they came in sight of the gate.

Now, I further saw, that betwixt them and the gate was a river, but there was no bridge to go over: the river was very deep. At the sight, therefore, of this river, the pilgrims were much stunned; but the men that went with them said, You must go through, or you cannot come at the gate.

The pilgrims then began to inquire if there was no other way to the gate; to which they answered, Yes; but there hath not any, save two, to wit, Enoch and Elijah, been permitted to tread that path, since the foundation of the world, nor shall, until the last trumpet shall sound. (1 Corinthians 15:51, 52.) The pilgrims then, especially Christian, began to despond in their minds, and looked this way and that, but no way could be found by them, by which they might escape the river. Then they asked the men if the waters were all of a depth. They said, No; yet they could not help them in that case; for, said they, you shall find it deeper or shallower, as you believe in the King of the place.

They then addressed themselves to the water; and entering, Christian began to sink, and crying out to his good friend Hopeful, he said, I sink in deep waters; the billows go over my head, all his waves go over me! Selah.

Then said the other, Be of good cheer, my brother, I feel the bottom, and it is good. Then said Christian, Ah! my friend, "the sorrows of death have compassed me about"; I shall not see the land that flows with milk and honey; and with that a great darkness and horror fell upon Christian, so that he could not see before him. Also here he in great measure lost his senses, so that he could neither remember, nor orderly talk of any of those sweet refreshments that he had met with in the way of his pilgrimage. But all the words that he spake still tended to discover that he had horror of mind, and heart fears that he should die in that river, and never obtain entrance in at the gate. Here also, as they that stood by perceived, he was much in the troublesome thoughts of the sins that he had committed, both since and before he began to be a pilgrim. It was also observed that he was troubled with apparitions of hobgoblins and evil spirits, for ever and anon he would intimate so much by words. Hopeful, therefore, here had much ado to keep his brother's head above water; yea, sometimes he would be quite gone down, and then, ere a while, he would rise up again half dead. Hopeful also would endeavor to comfort him, saying, Brother, I see the gate, and men standing by to receive us; but Christian would answer, It is you, it is you they wait for; you have been Hopeful ever since I knew you. And so have you, said he to Christian. Ah, brother! said he, surely if I was right he would now arise to help me; but for my sins he hath brought me into the snare, and hath left me. Then said Hopeful, My brother, you have quite forgot the text, where it is said of the wicked, "There are no bands in their death, but their strength is firm. They are not in trouble as other men, neither are they plagued like other men" (Psalms 73:4, 5). These troubles and distresses that you go through in these waters are no sign that God hath forsaken you; but are sent to try you, whether you will call to mind that which heretofore you have received of his goodness, and live upon him in your distresses.

Then I saw in my dream, that Christian was as in a muse a while. To whom also Hopeful added this word, Be of good cheer. Jesus Christ maketh thee whole; and with that Christian brake out with a loud voice, Oh! I see him again, and he tells me, "When thou passest through the waters, I will be with thee; and through the rivers, they shall not overflow thee" (Isaiah 43:2). Then they both took courage, and the enemy was after that as still as a stone, until they were gone over. Christian therefore presently found ground to stand upon, and so it followed that the rest of the river was but shallow. Thus they got over. Now, upon the bank of the river, on the other side, they saw the two shining men again, who there waited for them; wherefore, being come out of the river, they saluted them saying, We are ministering spirits, sent forth to minister for those that shall be heirs of salvation. Thus they went along towards the gate.

Now, now look how the holy pilgrims ride,
Clouds are their Chariots, Angels are their Guide:
Who would not here for him all hazards run,
That thus provides for his when this world's done.

Now you must note that the city stood upon a mighty hill, but the pilgrims went up that hill with ease, because they had these two men to lead them up by the arms; also, they had left their mortal garments behind them in the river, for though they went in with them, they came out without them. They, therefore, went up here with much agility and speed, though the foundation upon which the city was framed was higher than the clouds. They, therefore, went up through the regions of the air, sweetly talking as they went, being comforted, because they safely got over the river, and had such glorious companions to attend them.

The talk they had with the Shining Ones was about the glory of the place; who told them that the beauty and glory of it was inexpressible. There, said they, is the "Mount Zion, the heavenly Jerusalem, the innumerable company of angels, and the spirits of just men made perfect" (Hebrews 12:22-24). You are going now, said they, to the paradise of God, wherein you shall see the tree of life, and eat of the never-fading fruits thereof; and when you come there, you shall have white robes given you, and your walk and talk shall be every day with the King, even all the days of eternity. (Revelation 2:7; 3:4; 22:5.) There you shall not see again such things as you saw when you were in the lower region upon the earth, to wit, sorrow, sickness, affliction, and death, "for the former things are passed away." You are now going to Abraham, to Isaac, and Jacob, and to the prophets—men that God hath taken away from the evil to come, and that are now resting upon their beds, each one walking in his righteousness. (Isaiah 57:1, 2; 65:17.) The men then asked, What must we do in the holy place? To whom it was answered, You must there receive the comforts of all your toil, and have joy for all your sorrow; you must reap what you have sown, even the fruit of all your prayers, and tears, and sufferings for the King by the way. (Galatians 6:7.) In that place you must wear crowns of gold, and enjoy the perpetual sight and vision of the Holy One, for "there you shall see him as he is" (1 John 3:2). There also you shall serve him continually with praise, with shouting, and thanksgiving, whom you desired to serve in the world, though with much difficulty, because of the infirmity of your flesh. There your eyes shall be delighted with seeing, and your ears with hearing the pleasant voice of the Mighty One. There you shall enjoy your friends again, that are gone thither before you; and there you shall with joy receive, even every one that follows into the holy place after you. There also shall you be clothed with glory and majesty, and put into an equipage fit to ride out with the King of glory. When he shall come with the sound of trumpet in the clouds, as upon the wings of the wind, you shall come with him; and when he shall sit upon the throne of judgment, you shall sit by him; yea, and when he shall pass sentence upon all the workers of iniquity, let them be angels or men, you also shall have a voice in that judgment, because they were his and your enemies. (1 Thessalonians 4:13-17; Jude 14; Daniel 7:9, 10; 1 Corinthians 6:2, 3.) Also, when he shall again return to the city, you shall go too, with sound of trumpet, and be ever with him.

Now while they were thus drawing towards the gate, behold a company of the heavenly host came out to meet them; to whom it was said, by the other two Shining Ones, These are the men that have loved our Lord when they were in the world, and that have left all for his holy name; and he hath sent us to fetch them, and we have brought them thus far on their desired journey, that they may go in and look their Redeemer in the face with joy. Then the heavenly host gave a great shout, saying, "Blessed are they which are called unto the marriage supper of the Lamb" (Revelation 19:9.) There came out also at this time to meet them, several of the King's trumpeters, clothed in white and shining raiment, who, with melodious noises, and loud, made even the heavens to echo with their sound. These trumpeters saluted Christian and his fellow with ten thousand welcomes from the world; and this they did with shouting, and sound of trumpet.

This done, they compassed them round on every side; some went before, some behind, and some on the right hand, some on the left (as it were to guard them through the upper regions), continually sounding as they went, with melodious noise, in notes on high: so that the very sight was to them that could behold it, as if heaven itself was come down to meet them. Thus, therefore, they walked on together; and as they walked, ever and anon these trumpeters, even with joyful sound, would, by mixing their music with looks and gestures, still signify to Christian and his brother, how welcome they were into their company, and with what gladness they came to meet them; and now were these two men, as it were, in heaven, before they came at it, being swallowed up with the sight of angels, and with hearing of their melodious notes. Here also they had the city itself in view, and they thought they heard all the bells therein to ring, to welcome them thereto. But above all, the warm and joyful thoughts that they had about their own dwelling there, with such company, and that for ever and ever. Oh, by what tongue or pen can their glorious joy be expressed! And thus they came up to the gate.

Now, when they were come up to the gate, there was written over it in letters of gold, "Blessed are they that do his commandments, that they may have right to the tree of life, and may enter in through the gates into the city" (Revelation 22:14).

Then I saw in my dream, that the Shining Men bid them call at the gate; the which, when they did, some looked from above over the gate, to wit, Enoch, Moses, and Elijah, etc., to whom it was said, These pilgrims are come from the City of Destruction, for the love that they bear to the King of this place; and then the pilgrims gave in unto them each man his certificate, which they had received in the beginning; those, therefore, were carried in to the King, who, when he had read them, said, Where are the men? To whom it was answered, They are standing without the gate. The King then commanded to open the gate, "That the righteous nation," said he, "which keepeth the truth, may enter in" (Isaiah 26:2).

Now I saw in my dream that these two men went in at the gate: and lo, as they entered, they were transfigured, and they had raiment put on that shone like gold. There were also that met them with harps and crowns, and gave them to them—the harps to praise withal, and the crowns in token of honor. Then I heard in my dream that all the bells in the city rang again for joy, and that it was said unto them, "ENTER YE INTO THE JOY OF YOUR LORD." I also heard the men themselves, that they sang with a loud voice, saying, "BLESSING AND HONOR, AND GLORY, AND POWER, BE UNTO HIM THAT SITTETH UPON THE THRONE, AND UNTO THE LAMB, FOR EVER AND EVER" (Revelation 5:13).

Now, just as the gates were opened to let in the men, I looked in after them, and, behold, the City shone like the sun; the streets also were paved with gold, and in them walked many men, with crowns on their heads, palms in their hands, and golden harps to sing praises withal.

There were also of them that had wings, and they answered one another without intermission, saying, "Holy, holy, holy is the Lord" (Revelation 4:8). And after that they shut up the gates; which, when I had seen, I wished myself among them.

Now while I was gazing upon all these things, I turned my head to look back, and saw Ignorance come up to the river side; but he soon got over, and that without half that difficulty which the other two men met with. For it happened that there was then in that place, one Vain-hope, a ferryman, that with his boat helped him over; so he, as the other I saw, did ascend the hill, to come up to the gate, only he came alone; neither did any man meet him with the least encouragement. When he was come up to the gate, he looked up to the writing that was above, and then began to knock, supposing that entrance should have been quickly administered to him; but he was asked

by the men that looked over the top of the gate, Whence came you? and what would you have? He answered, I have eat and drank in the presence of the King, and he has taught in our streets. Then they asked him for his certificate, that they might go in and show it to the King; so he fumbled in his bosom for one, and found none. Then said they, Have you none? But the man answered never a word. So they told the King, but he would not come
10 down to see him, but commanded the two Shining Ones that conducted Christian and Hopeful to the City, to go out and take Ignorance, and bind him hand and foot, and have him away. Then they took him up, and carried him through the air, to the door that I saw in the side of the hill, and put him in there. Then I saw that there was a way to hell, even from the gates of heaven, as well as from the City of Destruction! So I awoke, and behold it was a dream.

(1678)

JOHN MILTON 1608-1674

John Milton's life falls, like the period itself, into three natural divisions—the years before the Great Rebellion, the years from the beginning of the Rebellion to the Restoration, and the years after the Restoration. Milton was born on December 9, 1608, in London. His father was a prosperous lawyer, cultured and musical, who had the generosity and the foresight to give his son a rich, full training. From St. Paul's school and private tutors Milton went to Christ's College, Cambridge, in 1625, the year of the accession of Charles I. Here, after having gained a reputation for being studious, reserved, and sometimes refractory, he took an M.A. degree in 1632. He had seemed destined for Anglican orders, but his growing rebellion against what he regarded as the corruption of the clergy made such a program for him quite impossible; and after leaving Cambridge, therefore, he joined his father in the retirement of Horton, a village twenty miles from London. Here, in the quiet and solitude of the country, he studied and wrote. To the Horton period belong Comus (1634), a masque marked with that peculiar moral elevation that is characteristic of all his writing, Lycidas (1637), and probably L'Allegro and Il Penseroso. In 1635 he was granted an M.A. degree by Oxford. Milton's mother died in April 1637; just a year later he left for the Continent on a prolonged and leisurely journey that took him to Paris, Nice, Genoa, Florence, Venice, and Geneva. At Florence, much to his delight and profit, he met the astronomer Galileo. But the voices prophesying war reached him from home and roused his sense of duty; like Newman two centuries later, he turned homeward that he might share in the struggle for righteousness. With his landing in England in August 1639, the first period of his professional life came to an end.

From a residence in London where he was doing private tutoring Milton issued in 1641 Of Reforma-tion Touching Church Discipline in England, a treatise which indicated clearly on which side of the struggle he stood. In 1643 he married Mary Powell, a girl of seventeen, who apparently found the austere husband of twice her years too impractical and uncompromising; at any rate, she returned to her parents within a month, and Milton saw nothing more of her for two years. But her parents were Royalists, and with the collapse of the King's cause in 1645 Mary returned to her husband. Of this reunion three daughters were born; the mother died at the birth of a fourth child in 1652.

Milton's most direct service to the state came with his appointment in 1649 to the office of Latin secretary to the newly created commission of foreign affairs; here his task was to translate the Latin letters from foreign countries and to write replies in the same language. The tremendous strain upon his eyes which this work occasioned resulted in his becoming totally blind in 1652. He never saw his second wife, Catherine Woodcock, whom he married in 1656, and who died, like Mary Powell, in childbirth. His third wife, Elizabeth Minshull, a young woman of twenty-four when he married her in 1663, survived him by many years. In the year of the battle of Naseby, Milton issued his Poems . . . both English and Latin, Compos'd at several times. Then for twenty years the pamphleteer eclipsed the poet, and no published verse came from his pen. To modern readers the prose is less attractive than the poetry. It is characterized often by animus rather than reason and shows the spirit of controversy rather than that of restraint. It is difficult not to believe that his Doctrine and Discipline of Divorce, written just after Mary Powell had left him, was the product of his personal resentment at her action. His Eikonoklastes (1649) and Defensio pro Populo Anglicano (1651) are arguments in defense of Parliament. The more famous *Areopagitica* (1644) *was an argument before Parliament for the freedom of the press, and it has therefore a more permanent interest than the other tracts of the times. But of all Milton's writing, the prose could be most readily dispensed with. The Restoration marks the end of the second period of his professional life.*

It was not the policy of Charles II to press too severely the punishment of all who had been concerned with his father's death. Thus Milton, though a rebel to the end, escaped a penalty more severe than impoverishment. *The last twelve years of his life—poetically the grandest—he spent in London in Artillery Row on the way to Bunhill Fields. Here he wrote the greatest poem that came out of Puritanism. Paradise Lost was published August 20, 1667; Paradise Regained, a shorter epic that tells the story of Christ's triumph, was issued in 1671. With it was published Samson Agonistes, a poem in the form of a Greek tragedy. This poetic manifesto of the great recalcitrant appeared three years before his death in 1674.*

L'ALLEGRO

Hence, loathéd Melancholy,
  Of Cerberus and blackest Midnight born
In Stygian cave forlorn
  'Mongst horrid shapes, and shrieks, and sights unholy!
Find out some uncouth cell,
  Where brooding Darkness spreads his jealous wings,
And the night-raven sings;
  There, under ebon shades and low-browed rocks,
As ragged as thy locks,
10 In dark Cimmerian desert ever dwell.

But come, thou Goddess fair and free,
In heaven ycleped Euphrosyne,
And by men heart-easing Mirth,
Whom lovely Venus at a birth
With two sister Graces more
To ivy-crownéd Bacchus bore;
Or whether (as some sager sing)
The frolic Wind that breathes the spring,
Zephyr with Aurora playing,
20 As he met her once a-Maying,
There on beds of violets blue,
And fresh-blown roses washed in dew,
Filled her with thee, a daughter fair,
So buxom, blithe, and debonair.
Haste thee, nymph, and bring with thee
Jest, and youthful Jollity,
Quips, and cranks, and wanton wiles,
Nods, and becks, and wreathéd smiles,

Such as hang on Hebe's cheek,
And love to live in dimple sleek; 30
Sport that wrinkled Care derides,
And Laughter holding both his sides,
Come, and trip it as ye go,
On the light fantastic toe;
And in thy right hand lead with thee
The mountain nymph, sweet Liberty;
And, if I give thee honor due,
Mirth, admit me of thy crew,
To live with her, and live with thee,
In unreprovéd pleasures free; 40
To hear the lark begin his flight,
And, singing, startle the dull night,
From his watch-tower in the skies,
Till the dappled dawn doth rise;
Then to come, in spite of sorrow,
And at my window bid good-morrow,
Through the sweet-briar or the vine,
Or the twisted eglantine;
While the cock with lively din,
Scatters the rear of darkness thin; 50
And to the stack, or the barn-door,
Stoutly struts his dames before;
Oft listening how the hounds and horn
Cheerly rouse the slumbering morn,
From the side of some hoar hill,
Through the high wood echoing shrill;
Sometime walking, not unseen,
By hedgerow elms, on hillocks green,
Right against the eastern gate,
Where the great Sun begins his state, 60
Robed in flames and amber light,

L'Allegro, an Italian title meaning "the cheerful man." This poem and *Il Penseroso*—"the contemplative man"—are companion pieces—poetic "characters"—which present two contrasting views of living, respectively that of the social man and that of the retiring, scholarly man. It is idle to speculate with which type Milton identified himself; he was both scholar and lover of man and nature, and the poems were probably both written during his studious retirement at Horton, his father's country place in Buckinghamshire. **2. Cerberus,** in classical mythology the three-headed dog that guarded the gateway to Hades. **3. Stygian,** adjective from Styx, the gloomy river of Hades, over which the shades of the dead were ferried by Charon; cf. *Paradise Lost,* Book II, l. 577 (p. 401). **10. Cimmerian.** In classical cosmography Cimmeria was the land of darkness and mist which lay beyond the ocean stream bounding the world plain; cf. *The Odyssey,* xi, 13–19. **12. ycleped,** named. **Euphrosyne,** one of the three Graces, goddesses of joy and gentleness; the word means "cheerful." **15. two sister Graces,** Aglaia and Thalia. **16. Bacchus,** or Dionysus, the god of wine; the three Graces are usually represented as being the daughters of Zeus and Eurynome. **19. Zephyr . . . Aurora,** respectively the god of the west wind and the goddess of the morn; this account of the birth of Euphrosyne is Milton's invention. **20. a-Maying.** See p. 346. **27. Quips, and cranks,** respectively, witty sayings and quick turns of speech. **28. becks,** beckonings. **29. Hebe,** daughter of Zeus and Hera and cup-bearer to the gods. **31. Sport . . . derides.** In this clause the object of *derides* is *Care.* **36. mountain nymph, sweet Liberty.** Cf. Wordsworth's sonnet, *Thought of a Briton on the Subjugation of Switzerland,* p. 702, l. 2. **45. Then to come,** etc., a somewhat difficult passage that has been variously interpreted. The present editor believes that "to come" is co-ordinate with "to hear," four lines earlier, and that the passage means that L'Allegro, awakened by the lark, comes to his bedroom window and, through the vines that shade it, bids the world a cheerful good morning. **48. eglantine,** another name for sweetbriar, but Milton probably had in mind some twisting vine like the honeysuckle; perhaps the need of a rime determined the choice of a noun.

The clouds in thousand liveries dight;
While the plowman, near at hand,
Whistles o'er the furrowed land,
And the milkmaid singeth blithe,
And the mower whets his scythe,
And every shepherd tells his tale
Under the hawthorne in the dale.
Straight mine eye hath caught new pleasures,
70 Whilst the landskip round it measures:
Russet lawns, and fallows gray,
Where the nibbling flocks do stray;
Mountains on whose barren breast
The laboring clouds do often rest;
Meadows trim with daisies pied;
Shallow brooks, and rivers wide.
Towers and battlements it sees
Bosomed high in tufted trees,
Where perhaps some beauty lies,
80 The cynosure of neighboring eyes.
Hard by, a cottage chimney smokes
From betwixt two agéd oaks,
Where Corydon and Thyrsis met,
Are at their savory dinner set
Of herbs and other country messes,
Which the neat-handed Phyllis dresses;
And then in haste her bower she leaves,
With Thestylis to bind the sheaves;
Or, if the earlier season lead,
90 To the tanned haycock in the mead.
Sometimes, with secure delight,
The upland hamlets will invite,
When the merry bells ring round,
And the jocund rebecks sound
To many a youth and many a maid
Dancing in the checkered shade;
And young and old come forth to play
On a sunshine holiday,
Till the livelong daylight fail;
100 Then to the spicy nut-brown ale,
With stories told of many a feat,
How Faery Mab the junkets eat,
She was pinched and pulled, she said;
And he, by Friar's lantern led,
Tells how the drudging goblin sweat
To earn his cream-bowl duly set,
When, in one night, ere glimpse of morn,

His shadowing flail hath threshed the corn
That ten day-laborers could not end;
Then lies him down the lubber fiend,   110
And, stretched out all the chimney's length,
Basks at the fire his hairy strength,
And crop-full out of doors he flings,
Ere the first cock his matin rings.
Thus done the tales, to bed they creep,
By whispering winds soon lulled asleep.
Towered cities please us then,
And the busy hum of men,
Where throngs of knights and barons bold,
In weeds of peace, high triumphs hold,   120
With store of ladies, whose bright eyes
Rain influence, and judge the prize
Of wit or arms, while both contend
To win her grace whom all commend.
There let Hymen oft appear
In saffron robe, with taper clear,
And pomp, and feast, and revelry,
With mask and antique pageantry;
Such sights as youthful poets dream
On summer eves by haunted stream.   130
Then to the well-trod stage anon,
If Jonson's learnéd sock be on,
Or sweetest Shakespeare, Fancy's child,
Warble his native wood-notes wild.
And ever, against eating cares,
Lap me in soft Lydian airs,
Married to immortal verse,
Such as the meeting soul may pierce
In notes with many a winding bout
Of linkéd sweetness long drawn out,   140
With wanton heed and giddy cunning,
The melting voice through mazes running,
Untwisting all the chains that tie
The hidden soul of harmony;
That Orpheus' self may heave his head
From golden slumber on a bed
Of heaped Elysian flowers, and hear
Such strains as would have won the ear
Of Pluto to have quite set free
His half-regained Eurydice.   150
These delights if thou canst give,
Mirth, with thee I mean to live.
(1632?; 1645)

---

62. **dight,** dressed. 67. **tells his tale.** Inasmuch as the preceding line describes the mower at work, this phrase probably means "counts the number of his sheep" (cf. bank *teller*); it may mean, however, "tells a story" or "courts a maid." 71. **lawns,** grassy fields. 80. **cynosure,** center of attraction; from the constellation of Ursa Minor, toward which, since it contains the North Star, mariners look for fixed direction. 83 ff. **Corydon, Thyrsis, Phyllis, Thestylis,** all conventional names for shepherds and shepherdesses in classical pastoral poetry. 91. **secure,** carefree. 94. **rebecks,** early stringed instruments played with a bow. 102. **Faery Mab,** the English queen of the fairies, described by Mercutio in *Romeo and Juliet,* I, iv, 53–93. **eat,** ate. 103. **She, he,** two of the storytellers. 104. **Friar's lantern,** will-o'-the-wisp, *ignis fatuus;* cf. *A Midsummer-Night's Dream,* II, i, 39. 105. **drudging goblin,** Puck or Robin Goodfellow, the household brownie. 106. **cream-bowl,** the usual fee for the goblin's services. 110. **lubber fiend,** clumsy elf.

117. **Towered cities, etc.** Having described the pleasures which L'Allegro enjoys in the country, the poet gives a contrasting picture of social life in the city. 120. **weeds,** garments. **high triumphs,** elaborate court entertainments such as masques and tournaments. 121. **store of,** many. 122. **Rain influence.** The ladies' eyes are thought of as stars that control the destinies of the contestants. 123. **wit,** intelligence, such as might be displayed in a debate or poetic contest. 125. **Hymen,** the classical god of marriage, frequently personified at noble weddings; cf. *As You Like It,* V, iv, 120 ff. 132. **sock,** the flat-soled shoe worn by Greek and Roman comic actors; hence the symbol of comedy. Jonson's scholarship is expressed in the adjective *learned.* 136. **Lydian airs,** a soft mode in ancient Greek music. 139. **bout,** turn or round. 145. **Orpheus.** In Greek mythology the musician Orpheus followed his wife Eurydice into the halls of Pluto, god of the underworld, and played so sweetly that the god promised to release her if Orpheus did

IL PENSEROSO

Hence, vain deluding Joys,
    The brood of Folly without father bred!
How little you bested,
    Or fill the fixéd mind with all your toys!
Dwell in some idle brain,
    And fancies fond with gaudy shapes possess,
As thick and numberless
    As the gay motes that people the sun-beams,
    Or likest hovering dreams,
10   The fickle pensioners of Morpheus' train.

But, hail! thou Goddess sage and holy!
Hail, divinest Melancholy!
Whose saintly visage is too bright
To hit the sense of human sight,
And therefore to our weaker view
O'erlaid with black, staid Wisdom's hue;
Black, but such as in esteem
Prince Memnon's sister might beseem,
Or that starred Ethiop queen that strove
20 To set her beauty's praise above
The Sea-Nymphs, and their powers offended.
Yet thou art higher far descended;
Thee bright-haired Vesta long of yore
To solitary Saturn bore;
His daughter she; in Saturn's reign
Such mixture was not held a stain.
Oft in glimmering bowers and glades
He met her, and in secret shades
Of woody Ida's inmost grove,
30 Whilst yet there was no fear of Jove.
Come, pensive Nun, devout and pure,
Sober, steadfast, and demure,
All in a robe of darkest grain,
Flowing with majestic train,
And sable stole of cypress lawn
Over thy decent shoulders drawn.
Come; but keep thy wonted state,
With even step, and musing gait,
And looks commercing with the skies,
40 Thy rapt soul sitting in thine eyes;
There, held in holy passion still,
Forget thyself to marble, till
With a sad leaden downward cast

Thou fix them on the earth as fast.
And join with thee calm Peace and Quiet,
Spare Fast, that oft with gods doth diet,
And hears the Muses, in a ring,
Aye round about Jove's altar sing.
And add to these retiréd Leisure,
That in trim gardens takes his pleasure.   50
But first, and chiefest, with thee bring,
Him that yon soars on golden wing,
Guiding the fiery-wheeléd throne,
The cherub Contemplation;
And the mute silence hist along,
'Less Philomel will deign a song,
In her sweetest saddest plight,
Smoothing the rugged brow of Night,
While Cynthia checks her dragon yoke
Gently o'er the accustomed oak.   60
Sweet bird, that shunn'st the noise of folly,
Most musical, most melancholy!
Thee, chantress, oft, the woods among,
I woo, to hear thy even-song;
And, missing thee, I walk unseen
On the dry smooth-shaven green,
To behold the wandering moon
Riding near her highest noon,
Like one that had been led astray
Through the heaven's wide pathless way,   70
And oft, as if her head she bowed,
Stooping through a fleecy cloud.
Oft, on a plat of rising ground,
I hear the far-off curfew sound
Over some wide-watered shore,
Swinging slow with sullen roar;
Or, if the air will not permit,
Some still, removéd place will fit,
Where glowing embers through the room
Teach light to counterfeit a gloom;   80
Far from all resort of mirth,
Save the cricket on the hearth,
Or the bellman's drowsy charm
To bless the doors from nightly harm.
Or let my lamp, at midnight hour,
Be seen in some high lonely tower
Where I may oft outwatch the Bear
With thrice great Hermes, or unsphere
The spirit of Plato, to unfold

---

not look back upon her until both had passed the gates of Hades; the musician, however, broke his promise and so lost his wife again.

    Il Penseroso. See footnote to *L'Allegro*, p. 379; the modern Italian form of the word is *pensieroso.* **3. bested,** profit, avail. **4. toys,** trifles. **6. fond,** foolish. **possess,** possessed. **10. Morpheus,** in classical mythology the god of dreams. **train,** following. **18. Prince Memnon,** in Greek mythology the beautiful black king of the Ethiopians who assisted Priam in the Trojan War. He was the son of Tithonus and Aurora. **beseem,** suit. **19. Ethiop queen,** in classical mythology the beautiful wife of Cepheus, king of the Ethiopians, whose boast that she was more beautiful than the sea nymphs resulted in their sending a sea monster to ravage the country; on her death the gods transformed her into a star. **23. Vesta,** goddess of the hearth, a daughter of Saturn, ancient god of agriculture. **29. Ida's . . . no fear of Jove.** Milton apparently identified Saturn with Cronus, who was overthrown by his son Jove

after the infant god had been concealed from his father and brought up in the caves of Mount Ida in Crete. **33. grain.** The reference is not to the texture but to the dark dye. **35. stole,** a scarf. **cypress lawn,** thin black crape. **36. decent,** seemly. **43. sad,** serious, pensive. **52. Him that yon soars.** Cf. Ezekiel, Chapter 10. **55. hist along,** bring silently. **56. 'Less,** unless. **Philomel,** the nightingale; contrasts with the skylark in *L'Allegro,* l. 41. **57. plight,** mood. **59. Cynthia,** Diana, goddess of the moon. **65. I walk unseen,** contrasts with *L'Allegro,* l. 57. **83. bellman's drowsy charm,** the night watchman's hourly call of "All's well." **87. outwatch the Bear,** sit up all night; the constellation of the Great Bear, or Big Dipper, never sets in England. **88. thrice great Hermes,** Hermes Trismegistus, a mythical king of Egypt and reputed author of scholarly treatises on numerous subjects. **unsphere,** call back from whatever sphere his spirit inhabits.

90 What worlds or what vast regions hold
The immortal mind that hath forsook
Her mansion in this fleshly nook,
And of those demons that are found
In fire, air, flood, or underground,
Whose power hath a true consent,
With planet or with element.
Sometime let gorgeous Tragedy,
In sceptered pall, come sweeping by,
Presenting Thebes, or Pelops' line,
100 Or the tale of Troy divine,
Or what (though rare) of later age
Ennobled hath the buskined stage.
But, O sad virgin! that thy power
Might raise Musaeus from his bower;
Or bid the soul of Orpheus sing
Such notes as, warbled to the string,
Drew iron tears down Pluto's cheek,
And made hell grant what love did seek;
Or call up him that left half told
110 The story of Cambuscan bold,
Of Camball, and of Algarsife,
And who had Canacé to wife
That owned the virtuous ring and glass,
And of the wondrous horse of brass,
On which the Tartar king did ride;
And if aught else great bards beside
In sage and solemn tunes have sung,
Of tourneys, and of trophies hung,
Of forests, and enchantments drear,
120 Where more is meant than meets the ear.
Thus, Night, oft see me in thy pale career,
'Till civil-suited Morn appear,
Not tricked and flounced as she was wont
With the Attic boy to hunt,
But kerchiefed in a comely cloud,
While rocking winds are piping loud;
Or ushered with a shower still,
When the gust hath blown his fill,
Ending on the rustling leaves,
130 With minute-drops from off the eaves.
And, when the sun begins to fling
His flaring beams, me, goddess, bring
To archéd walks of twilight groves,
And shadows brown, that Sylvan loves,
Of pine, or monumental oak,
Where the rude axe with heavéd stroke

Was never heard the nymphs to daunt
Or fright them from their hallowed haunt.
There in close covert by some brook,
Where no profaner eye may look, 140
Hide me from day's garish eye,
While the bee, with honeyed thigh,
That at her flowery work doth sing,
And the waters murmuring,
With such consort as they keep,
Entice the dewy-feathered sleep;
And let some strange mysterious dream
Wave at his wings, in airy stream
Of lively portraiture displayed,
Softly on my eyelids laid. 150
And, as I wake, sweet music breathe
Above, about, or underneath,
Sent by some spirit to mortals good,
Or the unseen Genius of the wood.
But let my due feet never fail
To walk the studious cloister's pale,
And love the high embowéd roof,
With antique pillars massy proof,
And storied windows richly dight,
Casting a dim religious light: 160
There let the pealing organ blow
To the full-voiced choir below
In service high and anthems clear
As may with sweetness, through mine ear,
Dissolve me into ecstasies,
And bring all heaven before mine eyes.
And may at last my weary age
Find out the peaceful hermitage,
The hairy gown and mossy cell,
Where I may sit and rightly spell 170
Of every star that heaven doth shew,
And every herb that sips the dew,
Till old experience do attain
To something like prophetic strain.
These pleasures, Melancholy, give,
And I with thee will choose to live.
(1632?; 1645)

LYCIDAS

*In this Monody the Author bewails a learned
Friend, unfortunately drowned in his passage from*

---

95. **consent,** agreement, harmony. 99. **Thebes,** in Greek legend the capital of Boeotia and the scene of the tragedies of Oedipus, Polynices, and Eteocles. **Pelops' line.** Atreus, Thyestes, Aegisthus, and Agamemnon were all, in Greek legend, descendants of Pelops whose tragic fate came to be presented on the "buskined stage" (see l. 102, and note). 100. **tale of Troy,** the familiar legends of the Trojan War. 102. **buskined stage.** The buskin, or cothurnus, was a thick-soled boot worn by Greek and Roman tragic actors to increase their stature to heroic proportions; the word came to be used, therefore, as a symbol of tragedy. Cf. note on *L'Allegro*, l. 132. 104. **Musaeus,** a Greek poet of about the sixth century, author of a poem on *Hero and Leander*, tragic lovers in Greek legend. 105. **Orpheus.** See *L'Allegro*, note on ll. 145 ff. 109. **him,** Chaucer, who left the *Squire's Tale* unfinished. 110 ff. **Cambuscan** was a king of Tartary; **Camball** and **Algarsife** were his sons, and **Canacé** his daughter. The ring, the mirror, and the brass horse, which had magic properties, were gifts from the king of Arabia. 113. **virtuous,** powerful, potent. 123. **tricked and flounced,**

adorned and plaited. 124. **the Attic boy,** Cephalus, an Athenian (Attic) huntsman beloved of Aurora (Dawn). 130. **minute-drops,** drops that drip slowly. 134. **brown,** dusk. **Sylvan,** Sylvanus, the god of forest glades. 145. **consort,** either companionship or concert, harmony. **they,** seems to refer to "the waters murmuring." 148. **Wave at his wings,** a probable allusion to the misty, wavering uncertainty of dream visions. 151. **sweet music.** Let is understood. 154. **Genius of the wood,** the presiding deity of the locality. 156. **pale,** bounds, enclosure. 159. **storied windows,** sacred stories in stained glass. 170. **spell,** study. 173. **old,** grown old by practice.
Lycidas, an elegy in the form of a pastoral in which the dead poet, Edward King, and the author appear as shepherds. The explanatory headnote was written by Milton. A *Monody* is a funeral song or dirge. 1. **once more.** The allusion is to his having written other poems. 3. **I come to pluck.** The author would gather a laurel wreath to honor his dead friend 11. **to sing,** i.e., how to sing. 15. **Sisters . . . well,** the nine Muses whose home was the Pierian spring near Mt. Olympus

Chester on the Irish Seas, 1637; and by occasion, foretells the ruin of our corrupted Clergy, then in their height. (Milton's note)

Yet once more, O ye laurels, and once more,
Ye myrtles brown, with ivy never sear,
I come to pluck your berries harsh and crude,
And with forced fingers rude
Shatter your leaves before the mellowing year.
Bitter constraint and sad occasion dear
Compels me to disturb your season due;
For Lycidas is dead, dead ere his prime,
Young Lycidas, and hath not left his peer.
10 Who would not sing for Lycidas? He knew
Himself to sing, and build the lofty rime.
He must not float upon his watery bier
Unwept, and welter to the parching wind,
Without the meed of some melodious tear.
  Begin, then, Sisters of the sacred well,
That from beneath the seat of Jove doth spring;
Begin, and somewhat loudly sweep the string.
Hence with denial vain and coy excuse;
So may some gentle muse
20 With lucky words favor my destined urn,
And as he passes turn
And bid fair peace be to my sable shroud!
  For we were nursed upon the selfsame hill,
Fed the same flock, by fountain, shade, and rill;
Together both, ere the high lawns appeared
Under the opening eyelids of the Morn,
We drove afield, and both together heard
What time the gray-fly winds her sultry horn,
Battening our flocks with the fresh dews of night,
30 Oft till the star that rose at evening, bright,
Toward heaven's descent had sloped his westering
    wheel.
Meanwhile the rural ditties were not mute,
Tempered to the oaten flute;
Rough Satyrs danced, and Fauns with cloven heel
From the glad sound would not be absent long;
And old Damoetas loved to hear our song.
  But, oh! the heavy change, now thou art gone,
Now thou art gone, and never must return!
Thee, Shepherd, thee the woods and desert caves,
40 With wild thyme and the gadding vine o'ergrown,
And all their echoes, mourn.
The willows, and the hazel copses green,

Shall now no more be seen
Fanning their joyous leaves to thy soft lays.
As killing as the canker to the rose,
Or taint-worm to the weanling herds that graze,
Or frost to flowers, that their gay wardrobe wear,
When first the white-thorn blows—
Such, Lycidas, thy loss to shepherd's ear.
  Where were ye, Nymphs, when the remorseless
    deep   50
Closed o'er the head of your loved Lycidas?
For neither were ye playing on the steep
Where your old bards, the famous Druids, lie,
Nor on the shaggy top of Mona high,
Nor yet where Deva spreads her wizard stream.
Aye me! I fondly dream
"Had ye been there"—for what could that have done?
What could the Muse herself that Orpheus bore,
The Muse herself, for her enchanting son,
Whom universal nature did lament,   60
When, by the rout that made the hideous roar,
His gory visage down the stream was sent,
Down the swift Hebrus to the Lesbian shore?
  Alas! what boots it with uncessant care
To tend the homely, slighted shepherd's trade,
And strictly meditate the thankless Muse?
Were it not better done as others use,
To sport with Amaryllis in the shade,
Or with the tangles of Neaera's hair?
Fame is the spur that the clear spirit doth raise 70
(That last infirmity of noble mind)
To scorn delights, and live laborious days;
But, the fair guerdon when we hope to find,
And think to burst out into sudden blaze,
Comes the blind Fury with the abhorréd shears,
And slits the thin-spun life. "But not the praise,"
Phoebus replied, and touched my trembling ears;
"Fame is no plant that grows on mortal soil,
Nor in the glistering foil
Set off to the world, nor in broad rumor lies,   80
But lives and spreads aloft by those pure eyes
And perfect witness of all-judging Jove;
As he pronounces lastly on each deed,
Of so much fame in heaven expect thy meed."
  O fountain Arethuse, and thou honored flood,
Smooth-sliding Mincius, crowned with vocal reeds,
That strain I heard was of a higher mood.
But now my oat proceeds,

(the seat of Jove). 20. **lucky**, propitious. **urn**, a figure for death; Milton expresses a hope that on his death some poetic tribute may be paid to him. 23. **nursed . . . hill**, a figure for "attended the same college"—at Cambridge. 29. **Battening**, feeding. 34. **Satyrs . . . Fauns.** In Greek mythology these were minor wood deities; here, perhaps, the allusion is to Milton's fellow students. 36. **Damoetas**, stock name for an older, philosophical shepherd; the allusion may be to a college tutor. 40. **gadding**, rambling. 45. **canker**, a cankerworm. 50. **Nymphs**, the Muses referred to in l. 15. 53. **Druids**, ancient Celtic priests, represented here as having been bardic singers. 54. **Mona**, old Roman name for the Isle of Man or of Anglesey, off the coast of Wales. 55. **Deva**, the river Dee in North Wales; it flows into the Irish Sea. There is another river Dee in Scotland. **wizard**, powerful in its control of the fate of Wales. 58. **Muse . . . Orpheus bore.** Calliope, the Muse of heroic poetry, could not save her son, the musician, from being torn to pieces by the Thracian women who were maddened by his laments for his dead wife Eurydice; they cast his dismembered corpse into the *Hebrus* River, down which it floated to the Isle of *Lesbos*. 64. **what boots it, etc.** What is to be gained by writing poetry? 66. **meditate . . . Muse**, compose a poem which goes unrewarded. 68. **Amaryllis . . . Neaera**, common pastoral names for shepherdesses. 71. **last infirmity**, i.e., the last weakness which the noble mind conquers. 75. **the blind Fury**. In Greek myth the Atropos was the one of the three Fates who cut the thread of life. Milton calls her blind because she does not discriminate, and a *Fury* because of the malignant nature of her function. 77. **touched . . . ears**, a symbolic act; the ear was regarded as the seat of memory. 79. **foil**, tinsel. 85. **Arethuse.** In Greek myth the river god Alpheus pursued the nymph Arethusa under land and sea until they merged in the fountain in Ortygia near Sicily which took her name. Theocritus sang of Arethusa. 86. **Mincius**, a river near Mantua in Italy, the birthplace of Vergil, who sang of the stream. 88. **oat**, for oaten reed, the symbol of pastoral song.

John Milton   383

And listens to the Herald of the Sea
90 That came in Neptune's plea.
He asked the waves, and asked the felon winds,
What hard mishaps hath doomed this gentle swain!
And questioned every gust of rugged wings
That blows from off each beakéd promontory.
They knew not of his story;
And sage Hippotades their answer brings,
That not a blast was from his dungeon strayed;
The air was calm, and on the level brine
Sleek Panope with all her sisters played.
100 It was that fatal and perfidious bark,
Built in the eclipse, and rigged with curses dark,
That sunk so low that sacred head of thine.

Next, Camus, reverend sire, went footing slow,
His mantle hairy, and his bonnet sedge,
Inwrought with figures dim, and on the edge
Like to that sanguine flower inscribed with woe.
"Ah! who hath reft," quoth he, "my dearest pledge?"
Last came, and last did go,
The Pilot of the Galilean Lake;
110 Two massy keys he bore of metals twain
(The golden opes, the iron shuts amain).
He shook his mitered locks, and stern bespake:
"How well could I have spared for thee, young swain,
Enow of such as, for their bellies' sake,
Creep, and intrude, and climb into the fold!
Of other care they little reckoning make
Than how to scramble at the shearers' feast,
And shove away the worthy bidden guest.
Blind mouths! that scarce themselves know how to
hold
120 A sheep-hook, or have learned aught else the least
That to the faithful herdman's art belongs!
What recks it them? What need they? They are sped;
And, when they list, their lean and flashy songs
Grate on their scrannel pipes of wretched straw;
The hungry sheep look up, and are not fed,
But, swoln with wind and the rank mist they draw,
Rot inwardly, and foul contagion spread;
Besides what the grim wolf with privy paw
Daily devours apace, and nothing said.
130 But that two-handed engine at the door

Stands ready to smite once, and smite no more."
Return, Alpheus, the dread voice is past
That shrunk thy streams; return, Sicilian Muse,
And call the vales, and bid them hither cast
Their bells and flowerets of a thousand hues.
Ye valleys low, where the mild whispers use
Of shades, and wanton winds, and gushing brooks,
On whose fresh lap the swart star sparely looks,
Throw hither all your quaint enameled eyes,
That on the green turf suck the honeyed showers, 140
And purple all the ground with vernal flowers.
Bring the rathe primrose that forsaken dies,
The tufted crow-toe, and pale jessamine,
The white pink, and the pansy freaked with jet,
The glowing violet,
The musk-rose, and the well-attired woodbine,
With cowslips wan that hang the pensive head,
And every flower that sad embroidery wears;
Bid amaranthus all his beauty shed,
And daffodillies fill their cups with tears, 150
To strew the laureate hearse where Lycid lies.
For so, to interpose a little ease,
Let our frail thoughts dally with false surmise.
Aye me! Whilst thee the shores and sounding
seas
Wash far away, where'er thy bones are hurled,
Whether beyond the stormy Hebrides,
Where thou perhaps under the whelming tide
Visit'st the bottom of the monstrous world;
Or whether thou, to our moist vows denied,
Sleep'st by the fable of Bellerus old, 160
Where the great Vision of the guarded mount
Looks toward Namancos and Bayona's hold.
Look homeward, Angel, now, and melt with ruth;
And, O ye dolphins, waft the hapless youth.

Weep no more, woeful shepherds, weep no more,
For Lycidas, your sorrow, is not dead,
Sunk though he be beneath the watery floor;
So sinks the day-star in the ocean bed,
And yet anon repairs his drooping head,
And tricks his beams, and with new-spangled ore 170
Flames in the forehead of the morning sky.
So Lycidas sunk low, but mounted high,

89. **Herald of the Sea**, Triton, in Greek myth a sea god represented in art as blowing on a conch shell; hence the epithet *herald*. 90. **Neptune**, in Greek myth the principal god of the sea. 96. **Hippotades**, Aeolus, god of the winds. 99. **Panope . . . sisters**, the Nereids, daughters of the sea god Nereus. 101. **Built in the eclipse**; work done during an eclipse of the moon was regarded as ill-omened. 103. **Camus**, the god of the river Cam; it flows gently past the college "backs" or lawns at Cambridge (the *bridge* over the *Cam*). This is the tribute of the college to its dead graduate. 106. **sanguine . . . woe**, the hyacinth, supposed in Greek myth to have sprung from the blood of the youth Hyacinthus, accidentally killed by Apollo; the markings on the petals resemble the Greek word αἴαῖ, alas. 109. **Pilot of the Galilean Lake**, St. Peter, disciple of Jesus, who was a fisherman on Lake Galilee in Palestine. At this point Milton begins his condemnation of "our corrupted Clergy" of the Anglican Church and his forecast of their ruin. 110. **Two massy keys**. Jesus' words to Peter were: "And I will give unto thee the keys of the kingdom of heaven" (Matthew 16:19). 112. **mitered locks**; as first "Bishop of Rome," he wore the official headdress of the bishop. 114. **Enow**, enough. 119. **Blind mouths!**, a highly compressed and figurative expression for clergy blind to all but greed. 120. **sheep-hook**; the allusion is to the *crosier* or pastoral staff of the bishop, the symbol of his office as shepherd of

God's flock. 122. **sped**, taken care of. 123. **list**, wish. **flashy**, flat, uninspired. 124. **scrannel**, harsh, unmelodious. The entire figure is that of pastoral song; the allusions are, of course, to the thin and empty sermons and teachings of the uninspired clergy. 126. **wind . . . mist**, figure for shallow sermons and false and destructive doctrines. 128. **grim . . . paw**, figure for the Roman Catholic Church engaged in secret proselyting. 130. **two-handed engine**, variously explained as the sword of justice, the ax "laid unto the root of the trees . . . which bringeth not forth good fruit" (Matthew 3:10), and the two Houses of Parliament. Of these agencies for overthrowing the corrupt clergy, the last was the most effective. 132. **Alpheus**, see note, l. 85. 133. **Sicilian Muse**, pastoral poetry. 136. **use**, inhabit. 138. **swart star**, Sirius, the Dog Star; it was supposed to wither vegetation. 142. **rathe**, early. 143. **crow-toe**, crowfoot. 144. **freaked with jet**, striped with black. 151. **laureate**, covered with laurel in honor of the dead poet. 153. **with false surmise**, i.e., with imagining that the body of Lycidas is really present and not floating "upon his watery bier." 160. **Bellerus**; a rocky island, coined by Milton from Bellerium, the Roman name for Land's End. 161. **Vision . . . mount**. Near Land's End is St. Michael's Mount, a rocky island, guarded by the Archangel Michael. 162. **Namancos**, ancient town in Spain opposite St. Michael's Mount and near the Spanish castle of Bayona. 163. **Angel**, St. Michael, who

Through the dear might of Him that walked the
    waves,
Where, other groves and other streams along,
With nectar pure his oozy locks he laves,
And hears the unexpressive nuptial song,
In the blest kingdoms meek of joy and love.
There entertain him all the Saints above,
In solemn troops, and sweet societies,
180 That sing, and singing in their glory move,
And wipe the tears forever from his eyes.
Now, Lycidas, the shepherds weep no more;
Henceforth thou art the Genius of the shore,
In thy large recompense, and shalt be good
To all that wander in that perilous flood.
    Thus sang the uncouth swain to the oaks and rills,
While the still morn went out with sandals gray;
He touched the tender stops of various quills,
With eager thought warbling his Doric lay.
190 And now the sun had stretched out all the hills,
And now was dropped into the western bay.
At last he rose, and twitched his mantle blue;
Tomorrow to fresh woods and pastures new.
(1637)

ON HIS HAVING ARRIVED AT THE
AGE OF TWENTY-THREE

How soon hath Time, the subtle thief of youth,
Stolen on his wing my three and twentieth year!
My hasting days fly on with full career,
But my late spring no bud or blossom shew'th.
Perhaps my semblance might deceive the truth
That I to manhood am arrived so near;
And inward ripeness doth much less appear,
That some more timely-happy spirits endu'th.
Yet be it less or more, or soon or slow,
10 It shall be still in strictest measure even
To that same lot, however mean or high,
Toward which Time leads me, and the will of Heaven;
All is, if I have grace to use it so,
As ever in my great Task-Master's eye.
(1645)

ON SHAKESPEARE

What needs my Shakespeare for his honored bones
The labour of an age in piléd stones?
Or that his hallowed reliques should be hid
Under a star-ypointing pyramid?
Dear son of memory, great heir of fame,
What need'st thou such weak witness of thy name?
Thou in our wonder and astonishment
Hast built thyself a livelong monument.
For whilst, to the shame of slow-endeavoring art
Thy easy numbers flow, and that each heart   10
Hath from the leaves of thy unvalued book
Those Delphic lines with deep impression took,
Then thou, our fancy of itself bereaving,
Dost make *us* marble with too much conceiving,
And so sepúlchred in such pomp dost lie
That kings for such a tomb would wish to die.
(1632)

TO THE LORD GENERAL CROMWELL

ON THE PROPOSALS OF CERTAIN MINISTERS AT THE
COMMITTEE FOR PROPAGATION OF THE GOSPEL

Cromwell, our chief of men, who through a cloud
Not of war only, but detractions rude,
Guided by faith and matchless fortitude,
To peace and truth thy glorious way hast plowed,
And on the neck of crownéd Fortune proud
Hast reared God's trophies, and his work pursued,
While Darwen stream, with blood of Scots imbrued,
And Dunbar field, resounds thy praises loud,
And Worcester's laureate wreath: yet much remains
To conquer still; Peace hath her victories   10
No less renowned than War: new foes arise,
Threatening to bind our souls with secular chains.
Help us to save free conscience from the paw
Of hireling wolves, whose gospel is their maw.
(1652; 1694)

is urged to turn his gaze from Spain to England. 164. **dolphins . . . youth,** an allusion to the Greek legend of the rescue of the bard Arion by dolphins when he was cast overboard by sailors. 168. **day-star,** sun. 170. **tricks,** for tricks out, dresses, adorns. 176. **unexpressive,** inexpressible. **nuptial song,** for the "marriage of the Lamb" (see Revelation 19:7); the lines which follow were suggested by St. John's description of the heavenly city in Revelation. 183. **Genius,** guardian spirit. 184. **In . . . recompense,** as thy reward. 188. **quills,** reeds in his pastoral pipe. 189. **Doric lay,** for pastoral poetry; Greek pastorals were written in the Doric dialect. 192. **twitched,** pulled it about him. 193. **Tomorrow . . . new,** a somewhat obscure allusion to Milton's plan for writing other types of poetry.
    On His Having . . . Twenty-Three. 4. **shew'th,** the pronunciation is indicated by the rime with *youth.* 5. **semblance,** i.e., his youthful appearance. 8. **timely-happy spirits,** persons whose intellectual and spiritual development has an appropriate agreement with their age and physical appearance. 13. **All is, etc.** The general meaning seems to be, to quote from a later poet, "All service ranks alike with God." Compare also the last lines of his sonnet *On His Blindness,* p. 386.
    On Shakespeare. Prefixed to the Second Folio edition of Shakespeare's plays. 1. **What,** why. 4. **star-ypointing,** pointing up to the stars; the **y** shows an artificial and inaccurate use of the old prefix of the past

participle. 11. **unvalued,** invaluable. 12. **Delphic lines,** i.e., prophetic like the Greek oracle at Delphi. 13. **our fancy, etc.** Milton means that our own imagination is so absorbed in Shakespeare's greater power that in our admiration and wonder we are as silent and speechless as marble and thus become his monument.
    To the Lord General Cromwell. Proposals. The proposals were to continue the state support of the clergy, and the sonnet is an appeal to Cromwell, a member of the committee, to oppose the proposals; Cromwell, however, voted for them. 2. **detractions rude,** criticisms directed against him by certain members of the Presbyterian Party who did not approve of Cromwell's religious doctrines. 5. **crownéd Fortune,** possible allusion to Charles I. 7. **Darwen stream,** in Lancashire. Here, at the battle of Preston in 1648, Cromwell defeated the Scottish invaders under Hamilton. 8. **Dunbar field;** here Cromwell defeated the Scotch under Leslie in 1650. 9. **Worcester,** scene of Cromwell's final victory over Prince Charles and his Scottish allies in 1651. Prince Charles later became King Charles II. 12. **secular chains,** the allusion is to the danger of a state control of religion. 14. **hireling wolves . . . maw,** figure for clergy paid by the state and greedy for gain; cf. *Lycidas,* ll. 114–131.

ON THE LATE MASSACRE IN PIEDMONT

Avenge, O Lord, Thy slaughtered saints, whose bones
Lie scattered on the Alpine mountains cold;
Even them who kept Thy truth so pure of old
When all our fathers worshiped stocks and stones,
Forget not: in Thy book record their groans
Who were Thy sheep, and in their ancient fold
Slain by the bloody Piedmontese, that rolled
Mother with infant down the rocks. Their moans
The vales redoubled to the hills, and they
10 To heaven. Their martyred blood and ashes sow
O'er all the Italian fields, where still doth sway
The triple Tyrant, that from these may grow
A hundredfold, who, having learnt Thy way,
Early may fly the Babylonian woe.
(1655; 1673)

ON HIS BLINDNESS

When I consider how my light is spent
Ere half my days in this dark world and wide,
And that one talent which is death to hide
Lodged with me useless, though my soul more bent
To serve therewith my Maker, and present
My true account, lest He returning chide;
"Doth God exact day-labor, light denied?"
I fondly ask. But Patience, to prevent
That murmur, soon replies, "God doth not need
10 Either man's work or his own gifts. Who best
Bear his mild yoke, they serve him best. His state
Is kingly: thousands at his bidding speed,
And post o'er land and ocean without rest;
They also serve who only stand and wait."
(1655?; 1673)

ON HIS DECEASED WIFE

Methought I saw my late espouséd saint
Brought to me like Alcestis from the grave,
Whom Jove's great son to her glad husband gave,
Rescued from death by force though pale and faint.
Mine as whom washed from spot of child-bed taint,
Purification in the old law did save,
And such, as yet once more I trust to have
Full sight of her in Heaven without restraint,
Came vested all in white, pure as her mind.
10 Her face was veiled, yet to my fancied sight,
Love, sweetness, goodness, in her person shined,
So clear, as in no face with more delight.

But O, as to embrace me she inclined,
I waked, she fled, and day brought back my night.
(1658; 1673)

from PARADISE LOST

English literature has two major epics, Beowulf (p. 25) and Paradise Lost. The first is a folk epic, with its roots in popular legend and folkways, and no one knows who assembled in one poem the scattered songs of the hero. The second is an epic of art, the production of one poet, a learned and cultured man who wrote with a purpose and with a full knowledge of generations of literature behind him. His objective is clear; he would "justify the ways of God to men" by showing that Evil in the world came not from a deity who is all loving, all knowing, all powerful, but from a spirit who is the essence of evil, as God is the essence of good.

The plot of Paradise Lost is, in its essentials, as simple as the story of the creation of man and his expulsion from Eden in the first chapters of Genesis. Evil came before man was created, for it was born of pride and rebellion in Heaven itself. The poem tells of this rebellion, of the fall of Satan, the leader, and all his misled hosts, and of his determination never to yield but to fight the Almighty by guile. So he makes an excursion to earth, where newly created man and woman are living in a Paradise of sweet delights. He seduces Eve, the woman, to disobedience against God, and she in turn seduces Adam to the same trespass. They have sinned and are expelled from Eden but comforted with the promise that God's own son will come as their Redeemer. The grand author of their transgression returns in triumph to his evil hosts, but at the very moment of his boasting he and the rest of the rebel angels sink from their upright state to the hissing, crawling forms of serpents.

Stripped of its poetry, the plot is but a skeleton, but about that frame the poet has built an epic that reveals his high seriousness, his theology, his learning, and his poetic art. It is evident that he knew the ancient classical epics of Homer and Vergil, for he has used the epic formulas and devices, the invocation, "the beginning in the midst of things," the "epic throwback" made by putting part of the antecedent action into the mouth of a narrator, the formal roll call of the leaders, the long "Homeric similes," the stock epithets, and the numerous other decorative devices. It is apparent, too, that he knew Dante's Divina Commedia, for in his description of Hell are many echoes

On the Late Massacre in Piedmont. This sonnet is Milton's protest against the killing of the Vaudois, or Waldenses, the oldest Protestant sect in Europe, by the Duke of Savoy for their refusal to embrace the Roman Catholic faith or go into exile. Cromwell's official protest, which was written by Milton as the Latin secretary, was effective in preventing further outrages of the same sort. 12. **The triple Tyrant,** the Pope; the allusion is to the tiara, or triple crown, which he wears.
On His Blindness. 2. **half my days;** Milton was about forty-three

when he became totally blind. 3. **one talent;** the allusion is to Jesus' parable of the talents (Matthew 25:15–30); the "unprofitable servant" was condemned for hiding his one talent in the earth. 8. **fondly,** foolishly. 11. **mild yoke;** allusion to the words of Jesus "my yoke is easy" (Matthew 11:29–30). 12. **thousands,** i.e., of angels.
On His Deceased Wife. 1. **late espouséd saint,** either Mary Powell, Milton's first wife or Catherine Woodcock, his second wife, both of whom died in childbirth (see 1. 5). 2. **Alcestis.** In Greek

of the Inferno of the Italian poet. And it is evident, perhaps most of all, that he knew his Bible, for the lines of the poem are crowded with allusions, not only to Genesis, where the loss of Paradise is told, and to Revelation, where the war in Heaven is reflected rather than detailed, but to innumerable other parts of the book, Old Testament and New. Finally, there went into the poem the influence of his Puritan theology, his belief in God's justice, mercy, and goodness, in the existence of a personal Adversary, and in the creed that included the doctrines of original sin and salvation by the atonement.

But breaking down the poem into the various elements that have gone into the making of it is like plucking a flower to pieces to examine its parts. It should be considered as a whole epic. As an epic poem it has certain definite characteristics, which are usually thought of in connection with it, which differentiate it from the epics of Homer and Virgil. It does not deal with the fortunes of a single hero, like Odysseus and Aeneas. It has, indeed, no hero, for it is only a quibble to insist, as has been done, that Satan is the hero; whatever strength Satan possesses is always used for evil. Like the classical epics it ranges from Heaven to Hell, but unlike them its milieu is in no one country. Its characters are not only not national—for it is not a national epic—but are not even, in a sense, human. The only human beings are Adam and Eve, and they become really human only after their fall has made them creatures of both good and evil impulses. Moreover, many of the figures, as in Spenser's Faerie Queene—which greatly influenced Milton—are allegorical, witness Sin and Death and their dreadful train. But if the characters are not human beings, they have, nevertheless, human characteristics; and the great parliament of fallen angels in Book II, if it is forgotten that they are supernatural beings, might be a session of the Long Parliament. Sprung from a religious purpose and loaded with learning and theology, the poem can have only a very slow action. Matthew Arnold has characterized Homer's epics as rapid. Milton's epic, on the contrary, is not rapid; like Spenser's Faerie Queene it is almost static in places, and even in the parts presenting the most vigorous action, as in the narration of the battles in Heaven in Books V and VI, the movement is slow as compared with similar passages in the Iliad and the Odyssey. A comparison, therefore, of Paradise Lost with the classical epics reveals more essential differences than resemblances.

But in one respect it transcends all other epics. It is grand—the most grand of all English narrative

poems. Milton's own nobility and high seriousness are reflected in his poem, and his purpose of making "no middle flight" he has surely maintained. Part of the loftiness of his epic is in the subject matter and in his purpose; part, however, is in his art and notably in the "Miltonic blank verse." In the Elizabethan age blank verse grew from a series of single lines, independent in metrical structure and often in thought, to a more closely knit group in which structure and thought ran through several lines. It remained for Milton to employ the "blank verse paragraph," a device in which the measure is used with the utmost flexibility and freedom and built into a larger structure, much as in prose a single sentence is articulated with others to form a paragraph. If to this control and flexibility is added the sense of melody of a poet who was also an accomplished organist, the result is one of the most effective metrical instruments in English. Seriousness of purpose, loftiness of thought, and melody of verse have united to give to the English one of the great epics of the world.

BOOK I

THE ARGUMENT

This First Book proposes, first in brief, the whole subject—Man's disobedience, and the loss thereupon of Paradise, wherein he was placed: then touches the prime cause of his fall—the Serpent, or rather Satan in the Serpent; who, revolting from God, and drawing to his side many legions of Angels, was, by the command of God, driven out of Heaven, with all his crew, into the great Deep. Which action passed over, the Poem hastens into the midst of things; presenting Satan, with his Angels, now fallen into Hell—described 10 here not in the Center (for heaven and earth may be supposed as yet not made, certainly not yet accursed), but in a place of utter darkness, fitliest called Chaos. Here Satan, with his Angels lying on the burning lake, thunderstruck and astonished, after a certain space recovers, as from confusion; calls up him who, next in order and dignity, lay by him; they confer of their miserable fall. Satan awakens all his legions, who lay till then in the same manner confounded. They rise: their numbers, array of battle; their chief leaders 20 named, according to the idols known afterwards in Canaan and the countries adjoining. To these Satan directs his speech; comforts them with hope yet of regaining Heaven; but tells them, lastly, of a new world and new kind of creature to be created, according to an ancient prophecy, or report, in Heaven—for

legend Alcestis, devoted wife of King Admetus, offered up her life that her husband might live; she was rescued from the tomb by Hercules, "Jove's great Son," after a struggle with Death for her possession, and restored to her husband. The story was dramatized by Euripides in *Alcestis*, and interpreted by Browning in a "transcription" of the play which forms a part of *Balaustion's Adventure*. 6. **Purification . . . law**; the allusion is to the Hebrew law for women who have borne children (see Leviticus, Chapter 12).

Argument, subject, theme. 9. **into . . . things**, an echo of *in medias res* from Horace's *Ars Poetica*, the critical principle that the epic should begin in the midst of the action and later, by an "epic throwback," recount the antecedent action. This is the plan which Milton follows; Books V and VI, as in the *Odyssey* and the *Aeneid*, put the earliest part of the story into the mouth of a narrator who took part in the action.

*that Angels were long before this visible creation was
the opinion of many ancient Fathers. To find out the
truth of this prophecy, and what to determine thereon,*
30 *he refers to a full council. What his associates thence
attempt. Pandemonium, the palace of Satan, rises,
suddenly built out of the Deep: the infernal Peers
there sit in council.*

Of Man's first disobedience, and the fruit
Of that forbidden tree whose mortal taste
Brought death into the World, and all our woe,
With loss of Eden, till one greater Man
Restore us, and regain the blissful seat,
Sing, Heavenly Muse, that, on the secret top
Of Oreb, or of Sinai, didst inspire
That shepherd who first taught the chosen seed
In the beginning how the heavens and earth
10 Rose out of Chaos: or, if Sion hill
Delight thee more, and Siloa's brook that flowed
Fast by the oracle of God, I thence
Invoke thy aid to my adventurous song,
That with no middle flight intends to soar
Above the Aonian mount, while it pursues
Things unattempted yet in prose or rime.
And chiefly Thou, O Spirit, that dost prefer
Before all temples the upright heart and pure,
Instruct me, for Thou know'st; Thou from the first
20 Wast present, and, with mighty wings outspread,
Dove-like sat'st brooding on the vast Abyss,
And mad'st it pregnant: what in me is dark
Illumine, what is low raise and support;
That, to the highth of this great argument,
I may assert Eternal Providence,
And justify the ways of God to men.

Say first—for Heaven hides nothing from thy view,
Nor the deep tract of Hell—say first what cause
Moved our grand Parents, in that happy state,
30 Favored of Heaven so highly, to fall off
From their Creator, and transgress his will
For one restraint, lords of the World besides.
Who first seduced them to that foul revolt?

The infernal Serpent; he it was whose guile,
Stirred up with envy and revenge, deceived
The mother of mankind, what time his pride
Had cast him out from Heaven, with all his host
Of rebel Angels, by whose aid, aspiring
To set himself in glory above his peers,
40 He trusted to have equaled the Most High,
If he opposed, and with ambitious aim
Against the throne and monarchy of God,
Raised impious war in Heaven and battle proud,

With vain attempt. Him the Almighty Power
Hurled headlong flaming from the ethereal sky,
With hideous ruin and combustion, down
To bottomless perdition, there to dwell
In adamantine chains and penal fire,
Who durst defy the Omnipotent to arms.

Nine times the space that measures day and night 50
To mortal men, he, with his horrid crew,
Lay vanquished, rolling in the fiery gulf,
Confounded, though immortal. But his doom
Reserved him to more wrath; for now the thought
Both of lost happiness and lasting pain
Torments him: round he throws his baleful eyes,
That witnessed huge affliction and dismay,
Mixed with obdurate pride and steadfast hate.
At once, as far as Angel's ken, he views
The dismal situation waste and wild.   60
A dungeon horrible, on all sides round,
As one great furnace flamed; yet from those flames
No light; but rather darkness visible
Served only to discover sights of woe,
Regions of sorrow, doleful shades, where peace
And rest can never dwell, hope never comes
That comes to all, but torture without end
Still urges, and a fiery deluge, fed
With ever-burning sulphur unconsumed.
Such place Eternal Justice had prepared   70
For those rebellious; here their prison ordained
In utter darkness, and their portion set,
As far removed from God and light of Heaven
As from the center thrice to the utmost pole.
Oh, how unlike the place from whence they fell!
There the companions of his fall, o'erwhelmed
With floods and whirlwinds of tempestuous fire,
He soon discerns; and, weltering by his side,
One next himself in power, and next in crime,
Long after known in Palestine, and named   80
BEËLZEBUB. To whom the Arch-Enemy,
And thence in Heaven called SATAN, with bold words
Breaking the horrid silence, thus began:—

"If thou beest he—but Oh, how fallen! how changed
From him!—who, in the happy realms of light,
Clothed with transcendent brightness, didst outshine
Myriads, though bright—if he whom mutual league,
United thoughts and counsels, equal hope
And hazard in the glorious enterprise,
Joined with me once, now misery hath joined   90
In equal ruin; into what pit thou seest
From what highth fallen: so much the stronger proved
He with his thunder: and till then who knew
The force of those dire arms? Yet not for those,

31. *Pandemonium,* literally, (the place) of all demons.
Book I. 6. **Heavenly Muse,** the holy spirit that inspired Moses,
David, and the prophets; by implication Milton contrasts this inspiration with that of the Greek muses. 7. **Oreb,** or Horeb, the mountain
of God on which Jehovah spoke to Moses from the midst of a burning
bush (Exodus, Chapter 3). **Sinai,** the holy mountain in the wilderness
of Sinai at the top of which Moses received from God the laws to
govern the Hebrews (Exodus, Chapter 19). 8. **That shepherd,** Moses,

to whose authorship has been ascribed the book of Genesis, which includes the story of the creation. 10. **Sion hill,** the height upon which
Jerusalem was built. 11. **Siloa's brook,** stream which flowed near
the hill on which the temple was erected in Jerusalem. 15. **Aonian
mount,** Helicon in Boeotia, sacred to the Muses; Milton's inspiration
is higher than that of the classical poets. 17. **Spirit,** the Holy Ghost.
21. **Dove-like:** "And the Holy Ghost descended in a bodily shape
like a dove . . ." (Luke 3:22). **brooding . . . Abyss;** cf. Genesis

Nor what the potent Victor in his rage
Can else inflict, do I repent, or change,
Though changed in outward luster, that fixed mind,
And high disdain from sense of injured merit,
That with the Mightiest raised me to contend,
100 And to the fierce contention brought along
Innumerable force of Spirits armed,
That durst dislike his reign, and, me preferring,
His utmost power with adverse power opposed
In dubious battle on the plains of Heaven,
And shook his throne. What though the field be lost?
All is not lost—the unconquerable will,
And study of revenge, immortal hate,
And courage never to submit or yield:
And what is else not to be overcome.
110 That glory never shall his wrath or might
Extort from me. To bow and sue for grace
With suppliant knee, and deify his power
Who, from the terror of this arm, so late
Doubted his empire—that were low indeed;
That were an ignominy and shame beneath
This downfall; since, by fate, the strength of Gods,
And this empyreal substance, cannot fail;
Since, through experience of this great event,
In arms not worse, in foresight much advanced,
120 We may with more successful hope resolve
To wage by force or guile eternal war,
Irreconcilable to our grand Foe,
Who now triumphs, and in the excess of joy
Sole reigning holds the tyranny of Heaven."

So spake the apostate Angel, though in pain,
Vaunting aloud, but racked with deep despair;
And him thus answered soon his bold compeer:—
"O Prince, O Chief of many thronéd Powers
That led the embattled Seraphim to war
130 Under thy conduct, and, in dreadful deeds
Fearless, endangered Heaven's perpetual King,
And put to proof his high supremacy,
Whether upheld by strength, or chance, or fate!
Too well I see and rue the dire event
That, with sad overthrow and foul defeat,
Hath lost us Heaven, and all this mighty host
In horrible destruction laid thus low,
As far as Gods and Heavenly Essences
Can perish: for the mind and spirit remains
140 Invincible, and vigor soon returns,
Though all our glory extinct, and happy state
Here swallowed up in endless misery.
But what if He our Conqueror (whom I now
Of force believe almighty, since no less
Than such could have o'erpowered such force as ours)

Have left us this our spirit and strength entire,
Strongly to suffer and support our pains,
That we may so suffice his vengeful ire,
Or do him mightier service as his thralls
By right of war, whate'er his business be,   150
Here in the heart of Hell to work in fire,
Or do his errands in the gloomy Deep?
What can it then avail though yet we feel
Strength undiminished, or eternal being
To undergo eternal punishment?"
Whereto with speedy words the Arch-Fiend re-
plied:—
"Fallen Cherub, to be weak is miserable,
Doing or suffering: but of this be sure—
To do aught good never will be our task,
But ever to do ill our sole delight,   160
As being the contrary to His high will
Whom we resist. If then His providence
Out of our evil seek to bring forth good,
Our labor must be to pervert that end,
And out of good still to find means of evil;
Which ofttimes may succeed so as perhaps
Shall grieve him, if I fail not, and disturb
His inmost counsels from their destined aim.
But see! the angry Victor hath recalled
His ministers of vengeance and pursuit   170
Back to the gates of Heaven: the sulphurous hail,
Shot after us in storm, o'erblown hath laid
The fiery surge that from the precipice
Of Heaven received us falling; and the thunder,
Winged with red lightning and impetuous rage,
Perhaps hath spent his shafts, and ceases now
To bellow through the vast and boundless Deep.
Let us not slip the occasion, whether scorn
Or satiate fury yield it from our Foe.
Seest thou yon dreary plain, forlorn and wild,   180
The seat of desolation, void of light,
Save what the glimmering of these livid flames
Casts pale and dreadful? Thither let us tend
From off the tossing of these fiery waves;
There rest, if any rest can harbor there;
And, re-assembling our afflicted powers,
Consult how we may henceforth most offend
Our enemy, our own loss how repair,
How overcome this dire calamity,
What reinforcement we may gain from hope,   190
If not what resolution from despair."
Thus Satan, talking to his nearest mate,
With head uplift above the wave, and eyes
That sparkling blazed; his other parts besides
Prone on the flood, extended long and large,

1:2. 32. **For one restraint,** in respect to one prohibition. 64. **discover,** disclose. 74. **center . . . pole.** For the purposes of his plot Milton followed the Ptolemaic system of cosmography. At the center was the circle of the stellar universe, and at the center of this circle was Earth; around it, each in its own orbit, revolved the planets. Above was Heaven; at the opposite extreme was Hell, cut out of Chaos. The radius of the stellar circle was one third of the distance from Heaven to Hell. 81. **Beëlzebub,** mentioned in 2 Kings, Chapter 1

as Baal-zebub, the god of the Philistine city of Ekron. 82. **Satan, the** Adversary; see Job, Chapter 1. 128. **Powers . . . Seraphim.** Milton follows the celestial hierarchy employed by Dante, *Divina Commedia, Paradiso,* Canto 28. The order is: 1. Seraphim, 2. Cherubim, 3. Thrones, 4. Dominions, 5. Virtues, 6. Powers, 7. Principalities, 8. Archangels, 9. Angels. 144. **Of force,** of necessity, perforce.

Lay floating many a rood, in bulk as huge
As whom the fables name of monstrous size,
Titanian or Earth-born, that warred on Jove,
Briareos or Typhon, whom the den
200 By ancient Tarsus held, or that sea-beast
Leviathan, which God of all his works
Created hugest that swim the ocean-stream.
Him, haply slumbering on the Norway foam,
The pilot of some small night-foundered skiff,
Deeming some island, oft, as seamen tell,
With fixéd anchor in his scaly rind,
Moors by his side under the lee, while night
Invests the sea, and wishéd morn delays.
So stretched out huge in length the Arch-Fiend lay,
210 Chained on the burning lake; nor ever thence
Had risen, or heaved his head, but that the will
And high permission of all-ruling Heaven
Left him at large to his own dark designs,
That with reiterated crimes he might
Heap on himself damnation, while he sought
Evil to others, and enraged might see
How all his malice served but to bring forth
Infinite goodness, grace, and mercy, shewn
On Man by him seduced, but on himself
220 Treble confusion, wrath, and vengeance poured.
  Forthwith upright he rears from off the pool
His mighty stature; on each hand the flames
Driven backward slope their pointing spires, and,
    rolled
In billows, leave i' the midst a horrid vale.
Then with expanded wings he steers his flight
Aloft, incumbent on the dusky air,
That felt unusual weight; till on dry land
He lights—if it were land that ever burned
With solid, as the lake with liquid fire,
230 And such appeared in hue as when the force
Of subterranean wind transports a hill
Torn from Pelorus, or the shattered side
Of thundering Aetna, whose combustible
And fuelled entrails, thence conceiving fire,
Sublimed with mineral fury, aid the winds,
And leave a singéd bottom all involved
With stench and smoke. Such resting found the sole
Of unblest feet. Him followed his next mate;
Both glorying to have escaped the Stygian flood
240 As gods, and by their own recovered strength,
Not by the sufferance of supernal power.
  "Is this the region, this the soil, the clime,"
Said then the lost Archangel, "this the seat
That we must change for Heaven?—this mournful
    gloom

For that celestial light? Be it so, since He
Who now is sovran can dispose and bid
What shall be right: farthest from Him is best,
Whom reason hath equaled, force hath made supreme
Above his equals. Farewell, happy fields,
Where joy for ever dwells! Hail, horrors! hail,   250
Infernal World! and thou, profoundest Hell,
Receive thy new possessor—one who brings
A mind not to be changed by place or time.
The mind is its own place, and in itself
Can make a Heaven of Hell, a Hell of Heaven.
What matter where, if I be still the same,
And what I should be, all but less than he
Whom thunder hath made greater? Here at least
We shall be free; the Almighty hath not built
Here for his envy, will not drive us hence: 260
Here we may reign secure; and, in my choice,
To reign is worth ambition, though in Hell:
Better to reign in Hell than serve in Heaven.
But wherefore let we then our faithful friends,
The associates and co-partners of our loss,
Lie thus astonished on the oblivious pool,
And call them not to share with us their part
In this unhappy mansion, or once more
With rallied arms to try what may be yet
Regained in Heaven, or what more lost in Hell?"   270
  So Satan spake; and him Beëlzebub
Thus answered:—"Leader of those armies bright
Which, but the Omnipotent, none could have foiled!
If once they hear that voice, their liveliest pledge
Of hope in fears and dangers—heard so oft
In worst extremes, and on the perilous edge
Of battle, when it raged, in all assaults
Their surest signal—they will soon resume
New courage and revive, though now they lie
Grovelling and prostrate on yon lake of fire,   280
As we erewhile, astounded and amazed;
No wonder, fallen such a pernicious highth!"
  He scarce had ceased when the superior Fiend
Was moving toward the shore; his ponderous shield,
Ethereal temper, massy, large, and round,
Behind him cast. The broad circumference
Hung on his shoulders like the moon, whose orb
Through optic glass the Tuscan artist views
At evening, from the top of Fesolè,
Or in Valdarno, to descry new lands,   290
Rivers, or mountains, in her spotty globe.
His spear—to equal which the tallest pine
Hewn on Norwegian hills, to be the mast
Of some great ammiral, were but a wand—
He walked with, to support uneasy steps

---

199. **Briareos or Typhon,** in Greek myth, two monsters, the first with
a hundred hands, the second with a hundred fire-breathing heads, who
attempted to overthrow the dynasty of Jove. Typhon lived in Cilicia,
of which Tarsus was the capital. 201. **Leviathan;** see p. 311, l. 10?.
204. **night-foundered,** obliged to furl sail for the night. The fable
alluded to here is a very ancient one which appears, among other places,
in *The Arabian Nights.* 232. **Pelorus,** northeastern promontory of
Sicily near the volcano of Mt. Etna. 288. **optic glass,** telescope.
Tuscan artist, Galileo, Italian astronomer, whom Milton had met at

Florence on his Italian travels; he was a defender of the Copernican
theory of astronomy, which was opposed to the Ptolemaic theory. 289.
Fesolè, the modern Fiesole, a hill near Florence. 290. **Valdarno,** the
valley of the River Arno, in which Florence is situated. 294. **ammiral,**
admiral, the flagship bearing the commander of the fleet. 303. **Vallombrosa,** a valley twenty miles east of Florence. Ancient *Etruria* is now
Tuscany and part of Umbria. 305. **Orion,** in Greek myth a hunter
who became a constellation upon his death; when the constellation rises
late (in November), it is supposed to create storms. 307. **Busiris,** a

Over the burning marle, not like those steps
On Heaven's azure; and the torrid clime
Smote on him sore besides, vaulted with fire.
Nathless he so endured, till on the beach
300 Of that inflaméd sea he stood, and called
His legions—Angel Forms, who lay entranced
Thick as autumnal leaves that strow the brooks
In Vallombrosa, where the Etrurian shades
High over-arched embower; or scattered sedge
Afloat, when with fierce winds Orion armed
Hath vexed the Red-Sea coast, whose waves o'erthrew
Busiris and his Memphian chivalry,
While with perfidious hatred they pursued
The sojourners of Goshen, who beheld
310 From the safe shore their floating carcases
And broken chariot-wheels. So thick bestrown,
Abject and lost, lay these, covering the flood,
Under amazement of their hideous change.
He called so loud that all the hollow deep
Of Hell resounded:—"Princes, Potentates,
Warriors, the Flower of Heaven—once yours; now
        lost,
If such astonishment as this can seize
Eternal Spirits! Or have ye chosen this place
After the toil of battle to repose
320 Your wearied virtue, for the ease you find
To slumber here, as in the vales of Heaven?
Or in this abject posture have ye sworn
To adore the Conqueror, who now beholds
Cherub and Seraph rolling in the flood
With scattered arms and ensigns, till anon
His swift pursuers from Heaven-gates discern
The advantage, and, descending, tread us down
Thus drooping, or with linkéd thunderbolts
Transfix us to the bottom of this gulf?—
330 Awake, arise, or be for ever fallen!"
    They heard, and were abashed, and up they sprung
Upon the wing, as when men wont to watch,
On duty sleeping found by whom they dread,
Rouse and bestir themselves ere well awake.
Nor did they not perceive the evil plight
In which they were, or the fierce pains not feel;
Yet to their General's voice they soon obeyed
Innumerable. As when the potent rod
Of Amram's son, in Egypt's evil day,
340 Waved round the coast, up-called a pitchy cloud
Of locusts, warping on the eastern wind,
That o'er the realm of impious Pharaoh hung
Like Night, and darkened all the land of Nile;
So numberless were those bad Angels seen
Hovering on wing under the cope of Hell,

'Twixt upper, nether, and surrounding fires;
Till, as a signal given, the uplifted spear
Of their great Sultan waving to direct
Their course, in even balance down they light
On the firm brimstone, and fill all the plain: 350
A multitude like which the populous North
Poured never from her frozen loins to pass
Rhene or the Danaw, when her barbarous sons
Came like a deluge on the South, and spread
Beneath Gibraltar to the Libyan sands.
Forthwith, from every squadron and each band,
The heads and leaders thither haste where stood
Their great Commander—godlike Shapes, and Forms
Excelling human; princely Dignities;
And Powers that erst in Heaven sat on thrones,   360
Though of their names in Heavenly records now
Be no memorial, blotted out and rased
By their rebellion from the Books of Life.
Nor had they yet among the sons of Eve
Got them new names, till, wandering o'er the earth,
Through God's high sufferance for the trial of man,
By falsities and lies the greatest part
Of mankind they corrupted to forsake
God their Creator, and the invisible
Glory of Him that made them to transform   370
Oft to the image of a brute, adorned
With gay religions full of pomp and gold,
And devils to adore for deities:
Then were they known to men by various names,
And various idols through the Heathen World.
    Say, Muse, their names then known, who first, who
        last,
Roused from the slumber on that fiery couch,
At their great Emperor's call, as next in worth
Came singly where he stood on the bare strand,
While the promiscuous crowd stood yet aloof.   380
    The chief were those who, from the pit of Hell
Roaming to seek their prey on Earth, durst fix
Their seats, long after, next the seat of God,
Their altars by His altar, gods adored
Among the nations round, and durst abide
Jehovah thundering out of Sion, throned
Between the Cherubim; yea, often placed
Within His sanctuary itself their shrines,
Abominations; and with curséd things
His holy rites and solemn feasts profaned,   390
And with their darkness durst affront His light.
First, *Moloch*, horrid king, besmeared with blood
Of human sacrifice, and parents' tears;
Though, for the noise of drums and timbrels loud,
Their children's cries unheard that passed through fire

mythical king of Egypt; he was not, however, the Pharaoh of the Exodus
(see Exodus, Chapter 14). **309. sojourners of Goshen,** the Hebrews,
who lived, before the Exodus, in a district of northern Egypt called
Goshen (see Genesis 47:27). **339. Amram's son,** Moses; for the
account of the plague of locusts see Exodus 10:12–19. **353. Rhene . . .
Danaw,** respectively, Rhine and Danube. The allusion is to the invasion
of the Roman Empire by the northern tribes in the third and fourth
centuries; they spread westward to Spain and, crossing to Africa, captured Carthage. **376. Say . . . names.** This roll call of leaders may

have been suggested by the naming and numbering of the Greek and
Trojan hosts in Book II of the *Iliad,* Milton gives to his devil chieftains the names of the principal heathen gods. **383. next the seat.**
Milton is alluding to the numerous occasions on which in Hebrew
history, as in the reign of Solomon, shrines to foreign gods were
erected in or near the Temple of Jehovah. **392. Moloch,** fire god worshiped by the sacrifice of infants incinerated in the heated arms of his
statue. He was worshiped by the Ammonites, a tribe dwelling to the
south and east of Palestine (see 1 Kings 11:7).

To his grim idol. Him the Ammonite
Worshiped in Rabba and her watery plain,
In Argob and in Basan, to the stream
Of utmost Arnon. Nor content with such
400 Audacious neighborhood, the wisest heart
Of Solomon he led by fraud to build
His temple right against the temple of God
On that opprobrious hill, and made his grove
The pleasant valley of Hinnom, Tophet thence
And black Gehenna called, the type of Hell.
Next *Chemos*, the obscene dread of Moab's sons,
From Aroar to Nebo and the wild
Of southmost Abarim; in Hesebon
And Horonaim, Seon's realm, beyond
410 The flowery dale of Sibma clad with vines,
And Elealè to the Asphaltic Pool:
Peor his other name, when he enticed
Israel in Sittim, on their march from Nile,
To do him wanton rites, which cost them woe.
Yet thence his lustful orgies he enlarged
Even to that hill of scandal, by the grove
Of Moloch homicide, lust hard by hate,
Till good Josiah drove them thence to Hell.
With these came they who, from the bordering flood
420 Of old Euphrates to the brook that parts
Egypt from Syrian ground had general names
Of *Baalim* and *Ashtaroth*—those male,
These feminine. For Spirits, when they please,
Can either sex assume, or both; so soft
And uncompounded is their essence pure,
Not tied or manacled with joint or limb,
Nor founded on the brittle strength of bones,
Like cumbrous flesh; but, in what shape they choose,
Dilated or condensed, bright or obscure,
430 Can execute their aery purposes,
And works of love or enmity fulfil.
For those the race of Israel oft forsook
Their Living Strength, and unfrequented left
His righteous altar, bowing lowly down
To bestial gods; for which their heads, as low
Bowed down in battle, sunk before the spear
Of despicable foes. With these in troop
Came *Astoreth*, whom the Phoenicians called
Astarte, queen of heaven, with crescent horns;
440 To whose bright image nightly by the moon
Sidonian virgins paid their vows and songs;
In Sion also not unsung, where stood

Her temple on the offensive mountain, built
By that uxorious king whose heart, though large,
Beguiled by fair idolatresses, fell
To idols foul. *Thammuz* came next behind,
Whose annual wound in Lebanon allured
The Syrian damsels to lament his fate
In amorous ditties all a summer's day,
While smooth Adonis from his native rock   450
Ran purple to the sea, supposed with blood
Of Thammuz yearly wounded: the love-tale
Infected Sion's daughters with like heat,
Whose wanton passions in the sacred porch
Ezekiel saw, when, by the vision led,
His eye surveyed the dark idolatries
Of alienated Judah. Next came one
Who mourned in earnest, when the captive ark
Maimed his brute image, head and hands lopt off,
In his own temple, on the grunsel-edge.   460
Where he fell flat and shamed his worshipers:
Dagon his name, sea-monster, upward man
And downward fish; yet had his temple high
Reared in Azotus, dreaded through the coast
Of Palestine, in Gath and Ascalon,
And Accaron and Gaza's frontier bounds.
Him followed *Rimmon*, whose delightful seat
Was fair Damascus, on the fertile banks
Of Abbana and Pharphar, lucid streams.
He also against the house of God was bold: 470
A leper once he lost, and gained a king—
Ahaz, his sottish conqueror, whom he drew
God's altar to disparage and displace
For one of Syrian mode, whereon to burn
His odious offerings, and adore the gods
Whom he had vanquished. After these appeared
A crew who, under names of old renown—
Osiris, Isis, Orus, and their train—
With monstrous shapes and sorceries abused
Fanatic Egypt and her priests to seek   480
Their wandering gods disguised in brutish forms
Rather than human. Nor did Israel scape
The infection, when their borrowed gold composed
The calf in Oreb; and the rebel king
Doubled that sin in Bethel and in Dan,
Likening his Maker to the grazéd ox—
Jehovah, who, in one night, when he passed
From Egypt marching, equalled with one stroke
Both her first-born and all her bleating gods.

397 ff. **Rabba**, capital of Ammon; *Argob, Basan* (for Bashan), and *Arnon* are east of the Jordan River and in the northern sections of Ammon. 403. **opprobrious hill**, the Mount of Olives where Solomon built a shrine to Moloch (see 1 Kings 11:5–7). 404. **Tophet**, probably not the valley itself but a place of sacrifice to Moloch. In *Gehenna*—the Greek name for the Valley of Hinnom—perpetual fires were maintained to burn the city refuse. 406. **Chemos**, god of Moab, another tribe east of the Jordan. 407. **Aroar**, etc., names of towns and mountains in the district of the Jordan River extending south to the Dead Sea—the Asphaltic Pool (so-called because of the bitumen in it). 414. **To do . . . rites**. At Shittim, during the wanderings, thousands of the children of Israel were executed for taking Moabitish wives and worshiping Baal-peor, the god of the Moabites (Numbers, Chapter 25). 416. **hill of scandal**, see l. 403. 418. **Josiah**; see 2 Kings, Chapter 23; the good king of Judah, who restored the worship of Jehovah. 422.

Baalim and Ashtaroth, collective names for manifestations of the sun god and the moon goddess respectively; the individual names Milton gives later. 441. **Sidonian**, from Sidon, a Phoenician city. 444. **uxorious king**, Solomon. 446. **Thammuz**, the Adonis of Greek myth, who was slain by a boar. 447. **annual wound in Lebanon**; the allusion is to the bringing down of the red mud from the Lebanon mountains of northern Palestine in the Adonis River, swollen by spring freshets. 453. **Sion's daughters**, the women of Jerusalem. 455. **Ezekiel saw**; see Ezekiel 8:13 ff. 460. **grunsel-edge**, threshold. 462. **Dagon**, sea god of the Philistines, who dwelt on the coast of Palestine. 464. **Azotus . . . Gaza**, the five chief cities of the Philistines. 467. **Rimmon**, god of Damascus. 471. **A leper . . . king**; see 2 Kings, Chapter 5. 472. **Ahaz**, King of Judah (see 2 Kings, Chapter 16). 481. **brutish forms**: *Osiris*, bull, *Isis*, cow; *Orus*, sun. 484. **The calf in Oreb**; see Exodus, Chapter 32. **the rebel king,**

Belial came last; than whom a Spirit more lewd
Fell not from Heaven, or more gross to love
Vice for itself. To him no temple stood
Or altar smoked; yet who more oft than he
In temples and at altars, when the priest
Turns atheist, as did Eli's sons, who filled
With lust and violence the house of God?
In courts and palaces, he also reigns,
And in luxurious cities, where the noise
Of riot ascends above their loftiest towers,
And injury and outrage; and, when night
Darkens the streets, then wander forth the sons
Of Belial, flown with insolence and wine.
Witness the streets of Sodom, and that night
In Gibeah, where the hospitable door
Exposed a matron, to avoid worse rape.
    These were the prime in order and in might:
The rest were long to tell; though far renowned
The Ionian gods—of Javan's issue held
Gods, yet confessed later than Heaven and Earth,
Their boasted parents;—Titan, Heaven's first-born,
With his enormous brood, and birthright seized
By younger Saturn: he from mightier Jove,
His own and Rhea's son, like measure found;
So Jove usurping reigned. These, first in Crete
And Ida known, thence on the snowy top
Of cold Olympus ruled the middle air,
Their highest heaven; or on the Delphian cliff,
Or in Dodona, and through all the bounds
Of Doric land; or who with Saturn old
Fled over Adria to the Hesperian fields,
And o'er the Celtic roamed the utmost Isles.
    All these and more came flocking; but with looks
Downcast and damp; yet such wherein appeared
Obscure some glimpse of joy to have found their Chief
Not in despair, to have found themselves not lost
In loss itself; which on his countenance cast
Like doubtful hue. But he, his wonted pride
Soon recollecting, with high words, that bore
Semblance of worth, not substance, gently raised
Their fainting courage, and dispelled their fears:
Then straight commands that, at the warlike sound
Of trumpets loud and clarions, be upreared
His mighty standard. That proud honor claimed
Azazel as his right, a Cherub tall:
Who forthwith from the glittering staff unfurled
The imperial ensign; which, full high advanced,

Shone like a meteor streaming to the wind,
With gems and golden luster rich emblazed,
Seraphic arms and trophies; all the while
Sonorous metal blowing martial sounds:
At which the universal host up-sent
A shout that tore Hell's concave, and beyond
Frighted the reign of Chaos and old Night.
All in a moment through the gloom were seen
Ten thousand banners rise into the air,
With orient colors waving: with them rose
A forest huge of spears; and thronging helms
Appeared, and serried shields in thick array
Of depth immeasurable. Anon they move
In perfect phalanx to the Dorian mood
Of flutes and soft recorders—such as raised
To highth of noblest temper heroes old
Arming to battle, and instead of rage
Deliberated valor breathed, firm, and unmoved
With dread of death to flight or foul retreat;
Nor wanting power to mitigate and swage
With solemn touches troubled thoughts, and chase
Anguish and doubt and fear and sorrow and pain
From mortal or immortal minds. Thus they,
Breathing united force with fixéd thought,
Moved on in silence to soft pipes that charmed
Their painful steps o'er the burnt soil. And now
Advanced in view they stand—a horrid front
Of dreadful length and dazzling arms, in guise
Of warriors old, with ordered spear and shield,
Awaiting what command their mighty Chief
Had to impose. He through the arméd files
Darts his experienced eye, and soon traverse
The whole battalion views—their order due,
Their visages and stature as of gods;
Their number last he sums. And now his heart
Distends with pride, and, hardening in his strength,
Glories: for never, since created Man,
Met such embodied force as, named with these,
Could merit more than that small infantry
Warred on by cranes—though all the giant brood
Of Phlegra with the heroic race were joined
That fought at Thebes and Ilium, on each side
Mixed with auxiliar gods; and what resounds
In fable or romance of Uther's son,
Begirt with British and Armoric knights;
And all who since, baptized or infidel,
Jousted in Aspramont, or Montalban,

490 — 500 — 510 — 520 — 530 — 540 — 550 — 560 — 570 — 580

Jeroboam, who rebelled with ten tribes against Rehoboam, son of Solomon, and established the northern kingdom of Israel; his idolatry in the two northern cities is told in 1 Kings 12:28–33. 488. **equalled,** made equal (in death): The allusion is to the tenth plague (see Exodus, Chapter 12). 495. **Eli's sons;** see 1 Samuel 2:12–17; "now the sons of Eli were [the] sons of Belial; they knew not the Lord." 498. **luxurious,** lustful. 502. **flown,** flushed. 503. **Sodom,** the wicked city of the plain, destroyed with its sister city Gomorrah; for the particular episode alluded to see Genesis 19:1–11. 504. **Gibeah;** see Judges, Chapter 19. 508. **Ionian,** Greek. **Javan,** one of the sons of Japheth. 510. **Titan,** son of Heaven (Uranus) and Earth (Gaea). 512. **Saturn,** a Titan who dethroned his father Uranus, and was in turn dethroned by his son Zeus (Jove). 515. **Ida;** according to Greek mythology Zeus was born on Mount Ida and established his regular abode on Mount Olympus. 517. **Delphian cliff,** an oracle of Apollo. 518. **Dodona,** an oracle of Zeus. 519. **Doric,** Greek. 520. **Adria,** the Adriatic. **Hesperian fields;** the allusion is to Italy, where the older dynasty of Greek gods was worshiped by the Romans. 521. **the Celtic,** France and Spain. **utmost Isles,** the islands of Britain. 536. **advanced,** raised. 546. **orient,** bright. 550. **phalanx,** body of troops in close array. **Dorian mood,** stern and suitable for battle. 563. **horrid,** bristling with spears. 568. **traverse,** across. 575. **small infantry.** In classical legend the Pygmies of Ethiopia waged continual war with the cranes who attacked them. 576. **giant brood,** the giants who were defeated by the gods at Phlegra in Macedonia. 578. **Thebes and Ilium.** The battle involving Thebes is "The Seven Against Thebes," and that of Ilium is the Trojan War. 580. **Uther's son,** King Arthur. 581. **Armoric,** Breton. 583. **Aspramont, etc.,** places made famous by exploits of crusaders and heroes of the romances of chivalry.

Damasco, or Marocco, or Trebisond,
Or whom Biserta sent from Afric shore
When Charlemain with all his peerage fell
By Fontarabbia. Thus far these beyond
Compare of mortal prowess, yet observed
Their dread Commander. He, above the rest
590 In shape and gesture proudly eminent,
Stood like a tower. His form had yet not lost
All her original brightness, nor appeared
Less than Archangel ruined, and the excess
Of glory obscured: as when the sun new-risen
Looks through the horizontal misty air
Shorn of his beams, or, from behind the moon,
In dim eclipse, disastrous twilight sheds
On half the nations, and with fear of change
Perplexes monarchs. Darkened so, yet shone
600 Above them all the Archangel: but his face
Deep scars of thunder had intrenched, and care
Sat on his faded cheek, but under brows
Of dauntless courage, and considerate pride
Waiting revenge. Cruel his eye, but cast
Signs of remorse and passion, to behold
The fellows of his crime, the followers rather
(Far other once beheld in bliss), condemned
For ever now to have their lot in pain—
Millions of Spirits for his fault amerced
610 Of Heaven, and from eternal splendors flung
For his revolt—yet faithful how they stood,
Their glory withered; as, when heaven's fire
Hath scathed the forest oaks or mountain pines,
With singéd top their stately growth, though bare,
Stands on the blasted heath. He now prepared
To speak; whereat their doubled ranks they bend
From wing to wing, and half enclose him round
With all his peers: attention held them mute.
Thrice he assayed, and thrice, in spite of scorn,
620 Tears, such as Angels weep, burst forth: at last
Words interwove with sighs found out their way:—
   "O myriads of immortal Spirits! O Powers
Matchless, but with the Almighty!—and that strife
Was not inglorious, though the event was dire,
As this place testifies, and this dire change,
Hateful to utter. But what power of mind,
Foreseeing or presaging, from the depth
Of knowledge past or present, could have feared
How such united force of gods, how such
630 As stood like these, could ever know repulse?
For who can yet believe, though after loss,
That all these puissant legions, whose exile
Hath emptied Heaven, shall fail to re-ascend,
Self-raised, and re-possess their native seat?
For me, be witness all the host of Heaven,
If counsels different, or danger shunned

By me, have lost our hopes. But he who reigns
Monarch in Heaven till then as one secure
Sat on his throne, upheld by old repute,
Consent or custom, and his regal state   640
Put forth at full, but still his strength concealed—
Which tempted our attempt, and wrought our fall.
Henceforth his might we know, and know our own,
So as not either to provoke, or dread
New war provoked: our better part remains,
To work in close design, by fraud or guile,
What force effected not; that he no less
At length from us may find, Who overcomes
By force hath overcome but half his foe.
Space may produce new Worlds; whereof so rife   650
There went a fame in Heaven that He ere long
Intended to create, and therein plant
A generation whom his choice regard
Should favor equal to the Sons of Heaven.
Thither, if but to pry, shall be perhaps
Our first eruption—thither, or elsewhere;
For this infernal pit shall never hold
Celestial Spirits in bondage, nor the Abyss
Long under darkness cover. But these thoughts
Full counsel must mature. Peace is despaired;   660
For who can think submission? War, then, war
Open or understood, must be resolved."
   He spake; and, to confirm his words, outflew
Millions of flaming swords, drawn from the thighs
Of mighty Cherubim; the sudden blaze
Far round illumined Hell. Highly they raged
Against the Highest, and fierce with graspéd arms
Clashed on their sounding shields the din of war,
Hurling defiance toward the vault of Heaven.
   There stood a hill not far, whose grisly top   670
Belched fire and rolling smoke; the rest entire
Shone with a glossy scurf—undoubted sign
That in his womb was hid metallic ore,
The work of sulphur. Thither, winged with speed,
A numerous brigad hastened: as when bands
Of pioneers, with spade and pickax armed,
Forerun the royal camp, to trench a field,
Or cast a rampart. Mammon led them on—
Mammon, the least erected Spirit that fell
From Heaven; for even in Heaven his looks and
    thoughts   680
Were always downward bent, admiring more
The riches of Heaven's pavement, trodden gold,
Than aught divine or holy else enjoyed
In vision beatific. By him first
Men also, and by his suggestion taught,
Ransacked the Center, and with impious hands
Rifled the bowels of their mother Earth
For treasures better hid. Soon had his crew

---

585. **Biserta . . . Charlemain . . . Fontarabbia.** The allusion is to the defeat of Charlemagne and the twelve peers of France as told in the *Chanson de Roland.* 605. **passion,** suffering. 609. **amerced,** punished (by being deprived of Heaven). 651. **fame,** rumor, report. 675. **brigad,** brigade, company. 676. **pioneers,** soldiers detailed to make

entrenchments, lay roads, and do other military engineering; labor battalions. 678. **Mammon,** symbol of riches; "ye cannot serve God and mammon" (Matthew 6:24, p. 316). 686. **The Center;** cf. note l. 74. 690. **admire,** wonder. 694. **Babel;** the allusion is to the building of the Tower of Babel (Genesis 11:1–9). **Memphian kings;** the

Opened into the hill a spacious wound,
690 And digged out ribs of gold. Let none admire
That riches grow in Hell; that soil may best
Deserve the precious bane. And here let those
Who boast in mortal things, and wondering tell
Of Babel, and the works of Memphian kings,
Learn how their greatest monuments of fame,
And strength, and art, are easily outdone
By Spirits reprobate, and in an hour
What in an age they, with incessant toil
And hands innumerable, scarce perform.
700 Nigh on the plain, in many cells prepared,
That underneath had veins of liquid fire
Sluiced from the lake, a second multitude
With wondrous art founded the massy ore,
Severing each kind, and scummed the bullion-dross.
A third as soon had formed within the ground
A various mold, and from the boiling cells
By strange conveyance filled each hollow nook;
As in an organ, from one blast of wind,
To many a row of pipes the sound-board breathes.
710 Anon out of the earth a fabric huge
Rose like an exhalation, with the sound
Of dulcet symphonies and voices sweet—
Built like a temple, where pilasters round
Were set, and Doric pillars overlaid
With golden architrave; nor did there want
Cornice or frieze, with bossy sculptures graven:
The roof was fretted gold. Not Babylon
Nor great Alcairo such magnificence
Equalled in all their glories, to enshrine
720 Belus or Serapis their gods, or seat
Their kings, when Egypt with Assyria strove
In wealth and luxury. The ascending pile
Stood fixed her stately highth; and straight the doors,
Opening their brazen folds, discover, wide
Within, her ample spaces o'er the smooth
And level pavement: from the archéd roof,
Pendent by subtle magic, many a row
Of starry lamps and blazing cressets, fed
With naphtha and asphaltus, yielded light
730 As from a sky. The hasty multitude
Admiring entered; and the work some praise,
And some the architect. His hand was known
In Heaven by many a towered structure high,
Where sceptered Angels held their residence,
And sat as Princes, whom the supreme King
Exalted to such power, and gave to rule,
Each in his hierarchy, the Orders bright.
Nor was his name unheard or unadored
In ancient Greece; and in Ausonian land
740 Men called him Mulciber; and how he fell
From Heaven they fabled, thrown by angry Jove

Sheer o'er the crystal battlements: from morn
To noon he fell, from noon to dewy eve,
A summer's day, and with the setting sun
Dropt from the zenith, like a falling star,
On Lemnos, the Aegean isle. Thus they relate,
Erring; for he with this rebellious rout
Fell long before; nor aught availed him now
To have built in Heaven high towers; nor did he scape
By all his engines, but was headlong sent,   750
With his industrious crew, to build in Hell.
   Meanwhile the wingéd Haralds, by command
Of sovran power, with awful ceremony
And trumpet's sound, throughout the host proclaim
A solemn council forthwith to be held
At Pandemonium, the high capital
Of Satan and his peers. Their summons called
From every band and squaréd regiment
By place or choice the worthiest: they anon
With hundreds and with thousands trooping came   760
Attended. All access was thronged; the gates
And porches wide, but chief the spacious hall
(Though like a covered field, where champions bold
Wont ride in armed, and at the Soldan's chair
Defied the best of Panim chivalry
To mortal combat, or career with lance),
Thick swarmed, both on the ground and in the air,
Brushed with the hiss of rustling wings. As bees
In spring-time, when the Sun with Taurus rides,
Pour forth their populous youth about the hive   770
In clusters; they among fresh dews and flowers
Fly to and fro, or on the smoothéd plank,
The suburb of their straw-built citadel,
New rubbed with balm, expatiate, and confer
Their state-affairs: so thick the aery crowd
Swarmed and were straitened; till, the signal given,
Behold a wonder! They but now who seemed
In bigness to surpass Earth's giant sons,
Now less than smallest dwarfs, in narrow room
Throng numberless—like that pygmean race   780
Beyond the Indian mount; or faery elves,
Whose midnight revels, by a forest-side
Or fountain, some belated peasant sees,
Or dreams he sees, while overhead the Moon
Sits arbitress, and nearer to the Earth
Wheels her pale course: they, on their mirth and dance
Intent, with jocund music charm his ear;
At once with joy and fear his heart rebounds.
Thus incorporeal Spirits to smallest forms
Reduced their shapes immense, and were at large,   790
Though without number still, amidst the hall
Of that infernal court. But far within,

allusion here is to the building of the Pyramids. 718. **Alcairo,** Cairo.
720. **Belus or Serapis,** respectively the Assyrian god Bel and an
Egyptian deity. 728. **cressets,** fire baskets for illumination. 737. **Each
. . . hierarchy;** see l. 128. 739. **Ausonian land,** Italy. 740. **Mulciber,** Vulcan or Hephaestos. 764. **Soldan's,** Sultan's. 765. **Panim,**
paynim, pagan. 769. **Sun with Taurus;** the Sun is in Taurus, the
bull—a sign of the zodiac—April 19–May 20.

John Milton   395

And in their own dimensions like themselves,
The great Seraphic Lords and Cherubim
In close recess and secret conclave sat,
A thousand demi-gods on golden seats,
Frequent and full. After short silence then,
And summons read, the great consult began.

BOOK II

THE ARGUMENT

The consultation begun, Satan debates whether an-
other battle be to be hazarded for the recovery of
Heaven; some advise it, others dissuade. A third pro-
posal is preferred, mentioned before by Satan—to
search the truth of that prophecy or tradition in
Heaven concerning another world, and another kind of
creature, equal, or not much inferior, to themselves,
about this time to be created. Their doubt who shall
be sent on this difficult search: Satan, their chief,
10 *undertakes alone the voyage; is honored and applauded.*
The council thus ended, the rest betake them several
ways and to several employments, as their inclina-
tions lead them, to entertain the time till Satan return.
He passes on his journey to Hell-gates, finds them
shut, and who sat there to guard them; by whom at
length they are opened, and discover to him the great
gulf between Hell and Heaven. With what difficulty
he passes through, directed by Chaos, the Power
of that place, to the sight of this new World which he
sought.

High on a throne of royal state, which far
Outshone the wealth of Ormus and of Ind,
Or where the gorgeous East with richest hand
Showers on her kings barbaric pearl and gold,
Satan exalted sat, by merit raised
To that bad eminence; and, from despair
Thus high uplifted beyond hope, aspires
Beyond thus high, insatiate to pursue
Vain war with Heaven; and, by success untaught,
10 His proud imaginations thus displayed:—
    "Powers and Dominions, Deities of Heaven!—
For, since no deep within her gulf can hold
Immortal vigor, though oppressed and fallen,
I give not Heaven for lost: from this descent
Celestial Virtues rising will appear
More glorious and more dread than from no fall,
And trust themselves to fear no second fate!—
Me though just right, and the fixed laws of Heaven,
Did first create your leader—next, free choice,
20 With what besides in council or in fight
Hath been achieved of merit—yet this loss,
Thus far at least recovered, hath much more
Established in a safe, unenvied throne,

Yielded with full consent. The happier state
In Heaven, which follows dignity, might draw
Envy from each inferior; but who here
Will envy whom the highest place exposes
Foremost to stand against the Thunderer's aim
Your bulwark, and condemns to greatest share
Of endless pain? Where there is, then, no good   30
For which to strive, no strife can grow up there
From faction: for none sure will claim in Hell
Precedence; none whose portion is so small
Of present pain that with ambitious mind
Will covet more! With this advantage, then,
To union, and firm faith, and firm accord,
More than can be in Heaven, we now return
To claim our just inheritance of old,
Surer to prosper than prosperity
Could have assured us; and by what best way,   40
Whether of open war or covert guile,
We now debate. Who can advise may speak."
    He ceased; and next him Moloch, sceptered king,
Stood up—the strongest and the fiercest Spirit
That fought in Heaven, now fiercer by despair.
His trust was with the Eternal to be deemed
Equal in strength, and rather than be less
Cared not to be at all; with that care lost
Went all his fear: of God, or Hell, or worse,
He recked not, and these words thereafter spake:— 50
    "My sentence is for open war. Of wiles,
More unexpert, I boast not: them let those
Contrive who need, or when they need; not now.
For, while they sit contriving, shall the rest—
Millions that stand in arms, and longing wait
The signal to ascend—sit lingering here,
Heaven's fugitives, and for their dwelling-place
Accept this dark opprobrious den of shame,
The prison of His tyranny who reigns
By our delay? No! let us rather choose,   60
Armed with Hell-flames and fury, all at once
O'er Heaven's high towers to force resistless way,
Turning our tortures into horrid arms
Against the Torturer; when, to meet the noise
Of his almighty engine, he shall hear
Infernal thunder, and, for lightning, see
Black fire and horror shot with equal rage
Among his Angels, and his throne itself
Mixed with Tartarean sulphur and strange fire,
His own invented torments. But perhaps   70
The way seems difficult, and steep to scale
With upright wing against a higher foe!
Let such bethink them, if the sleepy drench
Of that forgetful lake benumb not still,
That in our proper motion we ascend
Up to our native seat; descent and fall
To us is adverse. Who but felt of late,
When the fierce foe hung on our broken rear

---

797. **Frequent,** crowded. 798. **consult,** consultation.
    Book II. 2. **Ormus,** for Ormuz, an ancient and very rich commer-
cial city on an island in the Persian Gulf. **Ind,** for India. 9. **success,**

experience. 50. **recked,** cared. 69. **Tartarean,** from Tartarus, in
classic myth the infernal regions and the abode of evil spirits. 75.
our proper motion, i.e., the natural motion for angels, upward. 82.

Insulting, and pursued us through the Deep,
80 With what compulsion and laborious flight
We sunk thus low? The ascent is easy, then;
The event is feared! Should we again provoke
Our stronger, some worse way his wrath may find
To our destruction, if there be in Hell
Fear to be worse destroyed! What can be worse
Than to dwell here, driven out from bliss, condemned
In this abhorréd deep to utter woe;
Where pain of unextinguishable fire
Must exercise us without hope of end
90 The vassals of his anger, when the scourge
Inexorably, and the torturing hour,
Calls us to penance? More destroyed than thus,
We should be quite abolished, and expire.
What fear we then? what doubt we to incense
His utmost ire? which, to the highth enraged,
Will either quite consume us, and reduce
To nothing this essential—happier far
Than miserable to have eternal being!—
Or, if our substance be indeed divine,
100 And cannot cease to be, we are at worst
On this side nothing; and by proof we feel
Our power sufficient to disturb his Heaven,
And with perpetual inroads to alarm,
Though inaccessible, his fatal throne:
Which, if not victory, is yet revenge."
He ended frowning, and his look denounced
Desperate revenge, and battle dangerous
To less than gods. On the other side up rose
Belial, in act more graceful and humane.
110 A fairer person lost not Heaven; he seemed
For dignity composed, and high exploit.
But all was false and hollow; though his tongue
Dropt manna, and could make the worse appear
The better reason, to perplex and dash
Maturest counsels: for his thoughts were low—
To vice industrious, but to nobler deeds
Timorous and slothful. Yet he pleased the ear,
And with persuasive accent thus began:—
"I should be much for open war, O Peers,
120 As not behind in hate, if what was urged
Main reason to persuade immediate war
Did not dissuade me most, and seem to cast
Ominous conjecture on the whole success;
When he who most excels in fact of arms,
In what he counsels and in what excels
Mistrustful, grounds his courage on despair
And utter dissolution, as the scope
Of all his aim, after some dire revenge.
First, what revenge? The towers of Heaven are filled
130 With arméd watch, that render all access
Impregnable: oft on the bordering Deep
Encamp their legions, or with obscure wing
Scout far and wide into the realm of Night,

Scorning surprise. Or, could we break our way
By force, and at our heels all Hell should rise
With blackest insurrection to confound
Heaven's purest light, yet our great Enemy,
All incorruptible, would on his throne
Sit unpolluted, and the ethereal mold,
Incapable of stain, would soon expel   140
Her mischief, and purge off the baser fire,
Victorious. Thus repulsed, our final hope
Is flat despair: we must exasperate
The Almighty Victor to spend all his rage;
And that must end us; that must be our cure—
To be no more. Sad cure! for who would lose,
Though full of pain, this intellectual being,
Those thoughts that wander through eternity,
To perish rather, swallowed up and lost
In the wide womb of uncreated Night,   150
Devoid of sense and motion? And who knows,
Let this be good, whether our angry Foe
Can give it, or will ever? How he can
Is doubtful; that he never will is sure.
Will He, so wise, let loose at once his ire,
Belike through impotence or unaware,
To give his enemies their wish, and end
Them in his anger whom his anger saves
To punish endless? 'Wherefore cease we, then?'
Say they who counsel war; 'we are decreed,   160
Reserved, and destined to eternal woe;
Whatever doing, what can we suffer more,
What can we suffer worse?' Is this, then, worst—
Thus sitting, thus consulting, thus in arms?
What when we fled amain, pursued and strook
With Heaven's afflicting thunder, and besought
The Deep to shelter us? This Hell then seemed
A refuge from those wounds. Or when we lay
Chained on the burning lake? That sure was worse.
What if the breath that kindled those grim fires, 170
Awaked, should blow them into sevenfold rage,
And plunge us in the flames; or from above
Should intermitted vengeance arm again
His red right hand to plague us? What if all
Her stores were opened, and this firmament
Of Hell should spout her cataracts of fire,
Impendent horrors, threatening hideous fall
One day upon our heads; while we perhaps,
Designing or exhorting glorious war,
Caught in a fiery tempest, shall be hurled,   180
Each on his rock transfixed, the sport and prey
Of racking whirlwinds, or for ever sunk
Under yon boiling ocean, wrapt in chains,
There to converse with everlasting groans,
Unrespited, unpitied, unreprieved,
Ages of hopeless end? This would be worse.
War, therefore, open or concealed, alike
My voice dissuades; for what can force or guile

event, outcome. 97. essential, being, substance. 104. fatal, established
by fate. 106. denounced, threatened. 124. fact, deed. 181. Each
. . . transfixed, as Prometheus was chained to a rock on Mt. Caucasus

by Zeus in Greek myth, and as Ajax was split upon a rock by Neptune
in the Trojan War cycle.

With Him, or who deceive His mind, whose eye
Views all things at one view? He from Heaven's

190   highth
All these our motions vain sees and derides,
Not more almighty to resist our might
Than wise to frustrate all our plots and wiles.
Shall we, then, live thus vile—the race of Heaven
Thus trampled, thus expelled, to suffer here
Chains and these torments? Better these than worse,
By my advice; since fate inevitable
Subdues us, and omnipotent decree,
The Victor's will. To suffer, as to do,

200 Our strength is equal; nor the law unjust
That so ordains. This was at first resolved,
If we were wise, against so great a foe
Contending, and so doubtful what might fall.
I laugh when those who at the spear are bold
And venturous, if that fail them, shrink, and fear
What yet they know must follow—to endure
Exile, or ignominy, or bonds, or pain,
The sentence of their conqueror. This is now
Our doom; which if we can sustain and bear,

210 Our Supreme Foe in time may much remit
His anger, and perhaps, thus far removed,
Not mind us not offending, satisfied
With what is punished; whence these raging fires
Will slacken, if his breath stir not their flames.
Our purer essence then will overcome
Their noxious vapor; or, inured, not feel;
Or, changed at length, and to the place conformed
In temper and in nature, will receive
Familiar the fierce heat; and, void of pain,

220 This horror will grow mild, this darkness light;
Besides what hope the never-ending flight
Of future days may bring, what chance, what change
Worth waiting—since our present lot appears
For happy though but ill, for ill not worst,
If we procure not to ourselves more woe."

    Thus Belial, with words clothed in reason's garb,
Counselled ignoble ease and peaceful sloth,
Not peace; and after him thus Mammon spake:—
    "Either to disenthrone the King of Heaven

230 We war, if war be best, or to regain
Our own right lost. Him to unthrone we then
May hope, when everlasting Fate shall yield
To fickle Chance, and Chaos judge the strife.
The former, vain to hope, argues as vain
The latter; for what place can be for us
Within Heaven's bound, unless Heaven's Lord Su-
    preme
We overpower? Suppose he should relent,
And publish grace to all, on promise made
Of new subjection; with what eyes could we

240 Stand in his presence humble, and receive
Strict laws imposed, to celebrate his throne

With warbled hymns, and to his Godhead sing
Forced Hallelujahs, while he lordly sits
Our envied sovran, and his altar breathes
Ambrosial odors and ambrosial flowers,
Our servile offerings? This must be our task
In Heaven, this our delight. How wearisome
Eternity so spent in worship paid
To whom we hate! Let us not then pursue,
By force impossible, by leave obtained   250
Unacceptable, though in Heaven, our state
Of splendid vassalage; but rather seek
Our own good from ourselves, and from our own
Live to ourselves, though in this vast recess,
Free and to none accountable, preferring
Hard liberty before the easy yoke
Of servile pomp. Our greatness will appear
Then most conspicuous when great things of small,
Useful of hurtful, prosperous of adverse,
We can create, and in what place soe'er   260
Thrive under evil, and work ease out of pain
Through labor and endurance. This deep world
Of darkness do we dread? How oft amidst
Thick clouds and dark doth Heaven's all-ruling Sire
Choose to reside, His glory unobscured
And with the majesty of darkness round
Covers His throne, from whence deep thunders roar,
Mustering their rage, and Heaven resembles Hell!
As He our darkness, cannot we His light
Imitate when we please? This desert soil   270
Wants not her hidden luster, gems and gold;
Nor want we skill or art from whence to raise
Magnificence; and what can Heaven show more?
Our torments also may, in length of time,
Become our elements, these piercing fires
As soft as now severe, our temper changed
Into their temper; which must needs remove
The sensible of pain. All things invite
To peaceful counsels, and the settled state
Of order, how in safety best we may   280
Compose our present evils, with regard
Of what we are and where, dismissing quite
All thoughts of war. Ye have what I advise."

    He scarce had finished, when such murmur filled
The assembly as when hollow rocks retain
The sound of blustering winds, which all night long
Had roused the sea, now with hoarse cadence lull
Seafaring men o'erwatched, whose bark by chance,
Or pinnace, anchors in a craggy bay
After the tempest. Such applause was heard   290
As Mammon ended, and his sentence pleased,
Advising peace: for such another field
They dreaded worse than Hell; so much the fear
Of thunder and the sword of Michaël
Wrought still within them; and no less desire
To found this nether empire, which might rise,

---

294. **Michaël**, chief warrior of the heavenly armies; the archangel's battle with Satan is narrated in Book VI. 306. **Atlantean**, like Atlas, in Greek myth a Titan who bore the heavens on his shoulders. 311. **Virtues**, one of the orders in the celestial hierarchy (see note to

By policy and long process of time,
In emulation opposite to Heaven.
Which when Beëlzebub perceived—than whom,
300 Satan except, none higher sat—with grave
Aspect he rose, and in his rising seemed
A pillar of state. Deep on his front engraven
Deliberation sat, and public care;
And princely counsel in his face yet shone,
Majestic, though in ruin. Sage he stood,
With Atlantean shoulders, fit to bear
The weight of mightiest monarchies; his look
Drew audience and attention still as night
Or summer's noontide air, while thus he spake:—
    "Thrones and Imperial Powers, Offspring of
310   Heaven,
Ethereal Virtues! or these titles now
Must we renounce, and, changing style, be called
Princes of Hell? for so the popular vote
Inclines—here to continue, and build up here
A growing empire; doubtless! while we dream,
And know not that the King of Heaven hath doomed
This place our dungeon—not our safe retreat
Beyond his potent arm, to live exempt
From Heaven's high jurisdiction, in new league
320 Banded against his throne, but to remain
In strictest bondage, though thus far removed,
Under the inevitable curb, reserved
His captive multitude. For He, be sure,
In highth or depth, still first and last will reign
Sole king, and of his kingdom lose no part
By our revolt, but over Hell extend
His empire, and with iron scepter rule
Us here, as with his golden those in Heaven.
What sit we then projecting—peace and war?
330 War hath determined us and foiled with loss
Irreparable; terms of peace yet none
Vouchsafed or sought; for what peace will be given
To us enslaved, but custody severe,
And stripes and arbitrary punishment
Inflicted? and what peace can we return,
But, to our power, hostility and hate,
Untamed reluctance, and revenge, though slow,
Yet ever plotting how the Conqueror least
May reap his conquest, and may least rejoice
340 In doing what we most in suffering feel?
Nor will occasion want, nor shall we need
With dangerous expedition to invade
Heaven, whose high walls fear no assault or siege,
Or ambush from the Deep. What if we find
Some easier enterprise? There is a place
(If ancient and prophetic fame in Heaven
Err not)—another World, the happy seat
Of some new race, called Man, about this time
To be created like to us, though less
350 In power and excellence, but favored more

Of Him who rules above; so was His will
Pronounced among the Gods, and by an oath
That shook Heaven's whole circumference confirmed.
Thither let us bend all our thoughts, to learn
What creatures there inhabit, of what mold
Or substance, how endued, and what their power
And where their weakness: how attempted best,
By force or subtlety. Though Heaven be shut,
And Heaven's high Arbitrator sit secure
In His own strength, this place may lie exposed, 360
The utmost border of His kingdom, left
To their defense who hold it: here, perhaps,
Some advantageous act may be achieved
By sudden onset—either with Hell-fire
To waste His whole creation, or possess
All as our own, and drive, as we are driven,
The puny inhabitants; or, if not drive,
Seduce them to our party, that their God
May prove their foe, and with repenting hand
Abolish His own works. This would surpass 370
Common revenge, and interrupt His joy
In our confusion, and our joy upraise
In His disturbance; when His darling sons,
Hurled headlong to partake with us, shall curse
Their frail original, and faded bliss—
Faded so soon! Advise if this be worth
Attempting, or to sit in darkness here
Hatching vain empires." Thus Beëlzebub
Pleaded his devilish counsel—first devised
By Satan, and in part proposed: for whence, 380
But from the author of all ill, could spring
So deep a malice, to confound the race
Of mankind in one root, and Earth with Hell
To mingle and involve, done all to spite
The great Creator? But their spite still serves
His glory to augment. The bold design
Pleased highly those Infernal States, and joy
Sparkled in all their eyes: with full assent
They vote: whereat his speech he thus renews:—
    "Well have ye judged, well ended long debate, 390
Synod of Gods, and, like to what ye are,
Great things resolved, which from the lowest deep
Will once more lift us up, in spite of fate,
Nearer our ancient seat—perhaps in view
Of those bright confines, whence, with neighboring
    arms,
And opportune excursion, we may chance
Re-enter Heaven; or else in some mild zone
Dwell, not unvisited of Heaven's fair light,
Secure, and at the brightening orient beam
Purge off this gloom: the soft delicious air, 400
To heal the scar of these corrosive fires,
Shall breathe her balm. But, first, whom shall we send
In search of this new World? whom shall we find
Sufficient? who shall tempt with wandering feet

Book I, l. 128). 346. **fame,** report. 379. **first devised;** see Book I,
ll. 650 ff. 387. **States,** estates, authorities, as in the modern "three
estates,'' referring to the lords, the clergy, and the commons. 394.
seat, home.

The dark, unbottomed, infinite Abyss,
And through the palpable obscure find out
His uncouth way, or spread his aery flight,
Upborne with indefatigable wings
Over the vast Abrupt, ere he arrive
410 The happy Isle? What strength, what art, can then
Suffice, or what evasion bear him safe
Through the strict senteries and stations thick
Of Angels watching round? Here he had need
All circumspection: and we now no less
Choice in our suffrage; for on whom we send
The weight of all, and our last hope, relies."
    This said, he sat; and expectation held
His look suspense, awaiting who appeared
To second, or oppose, or undertake
420 The perilous attempt. But all sat mute,
Pondering the danger with deep thoughts; and each
In other's countenance read his own dismay,
Astonished. None among the choice and prime
Of those Heaven-warring champions could be found
So hardy as to proffer or accept,
Alone, the dreadful voyage; till, at last,
Satan, whom now transcendent glory raised
Above his fellows, with monarchal pride
Conscious of highest worth, unmoved thus spake:—
430 "O Progeny of Heaven! Empyreal Thrones!
With reason hath deep silence and demur
Seized us, though undismayed. Long is the way
And hard, that out of Hell leads up to Light.
Our prison strong, this huge convex of fire,
Outrageous to devour, immures us round
Ninefold; and gates of burning adamant,
Barred over us, prohibit all egress.
These passed, if any pass, the void profound
Of unessential Night receives him next,
440 Wide-gaping, and with utter loss of being
Threatens him, plunged in that abortive gulf.
If thence he scape, into whatever world,
Or unknown region, what remains him less
Than unknown dangers, and as hard escape?
But I should ill become this throne, O Peers,
And this imperial sovranty, adorned
With splendor, armed with power, if aught proposed
And judged of public moment in the shape
Of difficulty or danger, could deter
450 Me from attempting. Wherefore do I assume
These royalties, and not refuse to reign,
Refusing to accept as great a share
Of hazard as of honor, due alike
To him who reigns, and so much to him due
Of hazard more as he above the rest
High honored sits? Go, therefore, mighty Powers,

Terror of Heaven, though fallen; intend at home,
While here shall be our home, what best may ease
The present misery, and render Hell
More tolerable; if there be cure or charm   460
To respite, or deceive, or slack the pain
Of this ill mansion: intermit no watch
Against a wakeful foe, while I abroad
Through all the coasts of dark destruction seek
Deliverance for us all. This enterprise
None shall partake with me." Thus saying, rose
The Monarch, and prevented all reply;
Prudent lest, from his resolution raised,
Others among the chief might offer now,
Certain to be refused, what erst they feared,   470
And, so refused, might in opinion stand
His rivals, winning cheap the high repute
Which he through hazard huge must earn. But they
Dreaded not more the adventure than his voice
Forbidding; and at once with him they rose.
Their rising all at once was as the sound
Of thunder heard remote. Toward him they bend
With awful reverence prone, and as a God
Extol him equal to the Highest in Heaven.
Nor failed they to express how much they praised 480
That for the general safety he despised
His own: for neither do the Spirits damned
Lose all their virtue; lest bad men should boast
Their specious deeds on earth, which glory excites,
Or close ambition varnished o'er with zeal.
    Thus they their doubtful consultations dark
Ended, rejoicing in their matchless Chief:
As, when from mountain-tops the dusky clouds
Ascending, while the North-wind sleeps, o'erspread
Heaven's cheerful face, the louring element   490
Scowls o'er the darkened landskip snow or shower,
If chance the radiant sun, with farewell sweet,
Extend his evening beam, the fields revive,
The birds their notes renew, and bleating herds
Attest their joy, that hill and valley rings.
O shame to men! Devil with devil damned
Firm concord holds; men only disagree
Of creatures rational, though under hope
Of heavenly grace, and, God proclaiming peace,
Yet live in hatred, enmity, and strife   500
Among themselves, and levy cruel wars
Wasting the earth, each other to destroy:
As if (which might induce us to accord)
Man had not hellish foes enow besides,
That day and night for his destruction wait!
    The Stygian council thus dissolved; and forth
In order came the grand Infernal Peers:
Midst came their mighty Paramount, and seemed

405. **Abyss,** the undefined portion of the cosmic space between Heaven and Hell. 407. **uncouth,** unknown, uncertain. 409. **Abrupt,** the space or gulf in Chaos between Hell and Earth. **arrive,** reach. 439. **unessential,** without essence, formless. 457. **intend,** deliberate, consider. 484. **specious,** showy. 503. **accord,** agreement. 506. **Stygian,** hellish; from Styx, in classic myth a river of the underworld. 508. **Midst,** in

their midst. **Paramount,** chief. 513. **horrent,** bristling. 530. **Olympian . . . Pythian,** athletic meets of ancient Greece. 531. **shun the goal.** The allusion is to the chariot race, in which the driver wheeled as closely as possible to the turning posts. 539. **Typhoean;** see note, Book I, l. 199. 542. **Alcides . . . Lichas.** Hercules, returning with his bride Deianira from one of his successful exploits, slew with a

Alone the antagonist of Heaven, nor less
510 Than Hell's dread Emperor, with pomp supreme,
And god-like imitated state: him round
A globe of fiery Seraphim enclosed
With bright emblazonry, and horrent arms.
Then of their session ended they bid cry
With trumpet's regal sound the great result:
Toward the four winds four speedy Cherubim
Put to their mouths the sounding alchymy,
By herald's voice explained; the hollow Abyss
Heard far and wide, and all the host of Hell
520 With deafening shout returned them loud acclaim.
Thence more at ease their minds, and somewhat raised
By false presumptuous hope, the rangéd Powers
Disband; and, wandering, each his several way
Pursues, as inclination or sad choice
Leads him perplexed, where he may likeliest find
Truce to his restless thoughts and entertain
The irksome hours, till his great Chief return.
Part on the plain, or in the air sublime,
Upon the wing or in swift race contend,
530 As at the Olympian games or Pythian fields;
Part curb their fiery steeds, or shun the goal
With rapid wheels, or fronted brigades form:
As when, to warn proud cities, war appears
Waged in the troubled sky, and armies rush
To battle in the clouds; before each van
Prick forth the aery knights, and couch their spears,
Till thickest legions close; with feats of arms
From either end of heaven the welkin burns.
Others, with vast Typhoean rage, more fell,
540 Rend up both rocks and hills, and ride the air
In whirlwind; Hell scarce holds the wild uproar:—
As when Alcides, from Oechalia crowned
With conquest, felt the envenomed robe, and tore
Through pain up by the roots Thessalian pines,
And Lichas from the top of Oeta threw
Into the Euboic sea. Others, more mild,
Retreated in a silent valley, sing
With notes angelical to many a harp
Their own heroic deeds, and hapless fall
550 By doom of battle, and complain that Fate
Free Virtue should enthrall to Force or Chance.
Their song was partial; but the harmony
(What could it less when Spirits immortal sing?)
Suspended Hell, and took with ravishment
The thronging audience. In discourse more sweet
(For Eloquence the Soul, Song charms the Sense)
Others apart sat on a hill retired,
In thoughts more elevate, and reasoned high
Of Providence, Foreknowledge, Will, and Fate—

Fixed fate, free will, foreknowledge absolute—   560
And found no end, in wandering mazes lost.
Of good and evil much they argued then,
Of happiness and final misery,
Passion and apathy, and glory and shame:
Vain wisdom all, and false philosophy!—
Yet, with a pleasing sorcery, could charm
Pain for a while or anguish, and excite
Fallacious hope, or arm the obduréd breast
With stubborn patience as with triple steel.
Another part, in squadrons and gross bands,   570
On bold adventure to discover wide
That dismal world, if any clime perhaps
Might yield them easier habitation, bend
Four ways their flying march, along the banks
Of four infernal rivers, that disgorge
Into the burning lake their baleful streams—
Abhorréd Styx, the flood of deadly hate;
Sad Acheron of sorrow, black and deep;
Cocytus, named of lamentation loud
Heard on the rueful stream; fierce Phlegeton,   580
Whose waves of torrent fire inflame with rage.
Far off from these, a slow and silent stream,
Lethe, the river of oblivion, rolls
Her watery labyrinth, whereof who drinks
Forthwith his former state and being forgets—
Forgets both joy and grief, pleasure and pain.
Beyond this flood a frozen continent
Lies dark and wild, beat with perpetual storms
Of whirlwind and dire hail, which on firm land
Thaws not, but gathers heap, and ruin seems   590
Of ancient pile; all else deep snow and ice,
A gulf profound as that Serbonian bog
Betwixt Damiata and Mount Casius old,
Where armies whole have sunk: the parching air
Burns frore, and cold performs the effect of fire.
Thither, by harpy-footed Furies haled,
At certain revolutions all the damned
Are brought; and feel by turns the bitter change
Of fierce extremes, extremes by change more fierce,
From beds of raging fire to starve in ice   600
Their soft ethereal warmth, and there to pine
Immovable, infixed, and frozen round
Periods of time—thence hurried back to fire.
They ferry over this Lethean sound
Both to and fro, their sorrow to augment,
And wish and struggle, as they pass, to reach
The tempting stream, with one small drop to lose
In sweet forgetfulness all pain and woe,
All in one moment, and so near the brink;
But Fate withstands, and, to oppose the attempt,   610
Medusa with Gorgonian terror guards

poisoned arrow the centaur Nessus, who attempted to carry her off.
Dying, Nessus told Deianira to give her husband a robe anointed with
his blood. The poison maddened Hercules, and in his rage he threw
his servant Lichas into the sea. 560. free will, foreknowledge; these
concepts were of constant recurrence in Protestant theology, the second
usually under the term predestination. 570. gross, large. 575. four

infernal rivers; these are streams of classical mythology, as in Lethe,
river of oblivion. 592. Serbonian bog, Lake Serbonis, which had the
deceitful appearance of solid ground but was really a dangerous morass.
611. Medusa, in Greek myth the Gorgon with the snaky locks, whose
appearance was so terrible that anyone who looked at her was turned
to stone.

The ford, and of itself the water flies
All taste of living wight, as once it fled
The lip of Tantalus. Thus roving on
In confused march forlorn, the adventurous bands,
With shuddering horror pale, and eyes aghast,
Viewed first their lamentable lot, and found
No rest. Through many a dark and dreary vale
They passed, and many a region dolorous,
620 O'er many a frozen, many a fiery Alp,
Rocks, caves, lakes, fens, bogs, dens, and shades of
death—
A universe of death, which God by curse
Created evil, for evil only good;
Where all life dies, death lives, and Nature breeds,
Perverse, all monstrous, all prodigious things,
Abominable, inutterable, and worse
Than fables yet have feigned or fear conceived,
Gorgons, and Hydras, and Chimaeras dire.
Meanwhile the Adversary of God and Man,
630 Satan, with thoughts inflamed of highest design,
Puts on swift wings, and toward the gates of Hell
Explores his solitary flight: sometimes
He scours the right-hand coast, sometimes the left;
Now shaves with level wing the deep, then soars
Up to the fiery concave towering high.
As when far off at sea a fleet descried
Hangs in the clouds, by equinoctial winds
Close sailing from Bengala, or the isles
Of Ternate and Tidore, whence merchants bring
640 Their spicy drugs; they on the trading flood,
Through the wide Ethiopian to the Cape,
Ply stemming nightly toward the pole: so seemed
Far off the flying Fiend. At last appear
Hell-bounds, high reaching to the horrid roof,
And thrice threefold the gates; three folds were brass,
Three iron, three of adamantine rock,
Impenetrable, impaled with circling fire,
Yet unconsumed. Before the gates there sat
On either side a formidable Shape.
650 The one seemed woman to the waist, and fair,
But ended foul in many a scaly fold,
Voluminous and vast—a serpent armed
With mortal sting. About her middle round
A cry of Hell-hounds never-ceasing barked
With wide Cerberean mouths full loud, and rung
A hideous peal; yet, when they list, would creep,
If aught disturbed their noise, into her womb,
And kennel there; yet there still barked and howled
Within unseen. Far less abhorred than these
660 Vexed Scylla, bathing in the sea that parts
Calabria from the hoarse Trinacrian shore;
Nor uglier follow the night-hag, when, called
In secret, riding through the air she comes,
Lured with the smell of infant blood, to dance

With Lapland witches, while the laboring moon
Eclipses at their charms. The other Shape—
If shape it might be called that shape had none
Distinguishable in member, joint, or limb;
Or substance might be called that shadow seemed,
For each seemed either—black it stood as Night, 670
Fierce as ten Furies, terrible as Hell,
And shook a dreadful dart: what seemed his head
The likeness of a kingly crown had on.
Satan was now at hand, and from his seat
The monster moving onward came as fast
With horrid strides; Hell trembled as he strode.
The undaunted Fiend what this might be admired—
Admired, not feared (God and his Son except,
Created thing naught valued he nor shunned),
And with disdainful look thus first began:— 680
"Whence and what art thou, execrable Shape,
That dar'st, though grim and terrible, advance
Thy miscreated front athwart my way
To yonder gates? Through them I mean to pass,
That be assured, without leave asked of thee.
Retire; or taste thy folly, and learn by proof,
Hell-born, not to contend with Spirits of Heaven."
To whom the Goblin, full of wrath, replied:—
"Art thou that Traitor-Angel, art thou he,
Who first broke peace in Heaven and faith, till then 690
Unbroken, and in proud rebellious arms
Drew after him the third part of Heaven's sons,
Conjured against the Highest—for which both thou
And they, outcast from God, are here condemned
To waste eternal days in woe and pain?
And reckon'st thou thyself with Spirits of Heaven,
Hell-doomed, and breath'st defiance here and scorn,
Where I reign king, and, to enrage thee more,
Thy king and lord? Back to thy punishment,
False fugitive; and to thy speed add wings, 700
Lest with a whip of scorpions I pursue
Thy lingering, or with one stroke of this dart
Strange horror seize thee, and pangs unfelt before."
So spake the grisly Terror, and in shape,
So speaking and so threatening, grew ten fold
More dreadful and deform. On the other side,
Incensed with indignation, Satan stood
Unterrified, and like a comet burned,
That fires the length of Ophiuchus huge
In the arctic sky, and from his horrid hair 710
Shakes pestilence and war. Each at the head
Levelled his deadly aim; their fatal hands
No second stroke intend; and such a frown
Each cast at the other as when two black clouds,
With heaven's artillery fraught, come rattling on
Over the Caspian—then stand front to front
Hovering a space, till winds the signal blow
To join their dark encounter in mid-air.

614. **Tantalus,** a sinner represented in Greek legend as punished in the underworld by the torture of unsatisfied hunger and thirst. 628. **Gorgons . . . Hydras . . . Chimaeras,** monsters of the underworld in Greek myth. 632. **Explores,** pursues uncertainly. 638. **Bengala.**

. . . **Ternate . . . Tidore,** respectively, an arm of the Indian Ocean, and two small islands of the Dutch Indies. 641. **wide Ethiopian,** the Indian Ocean. 655. **Cerberean mouths,** like those of Cerberus, the three-headed hound of hell in classic myth. 660. **Scylla,** a female sea

So frowned the mighty combatants that Hell
720 Grew darker at their frown; so matched they stood;
For never but once more was either like
To meet so great a foe. And now great deeds
Had been achieved, whereof all Hell had rung,
Had not the snaky Sorceress, that sat
Fast by Hell-gate and kept the fatal key,
Risen, and with hideous outcry rushed between.
      "O father, what intends thy hand," she cried,
"Against thy only son? What fury, O son,
Possesses thee to bend that mortal dart
730 Against thy father's head? And know'st for whom?
For Him who sits above, and laughs the while
At thee, ordained his drudge to execute
Whate'er his wrath, which He calls justice, bids—
His wrath, which one day will destroy ye both!"
      She spake, and at her words the hellish Pest
Forbore: then these to her Satan returned:—
      "So strange thy outcry, and thy words so strange
Thou interposest, that my sudden hand,
Prevented, spares to tell thee yet by deeds
740 What it intends, till first I know of thee
What thing thou art, thus double-formed, and why,
In this infernal vale first met, thou callest
Me father, and that phantasm callest my son.
I know thee not, nor ever saw till now
Sight more detestable than him and thee."
      To whom thus the Portress of Hell-gate replied:—
"Hast thou forgot me, then; and do I seem
Now in thine eyes so foul?—once deemed so fair
In Heaven, when at the assembly, and in sight
750 Of all the Seraphim with thee combined
In bold conspiracy against Heaven's King,
All on a sudden miserable pain
Surprised thee, dim thine eyes, and dizzy swum
In darkness, while thy head flames thick and fast
Threw forth, till on the left side opening wide,
Likest to thee in shape and countenance bright,
Then shining heavenly fair, a goddess armed,
Out of thy head I sprung. Amazement seized
All the host of Heaven; back they recoiled afraid
760 At first, and called me *Sin*, and for a sign
Portentous held me; but, familiar grown,
I pleased, and with attractive graces won
The most averse—thee chiefly, who, full oft
Thyself in me thy perfect image viewing,
Becam'st enamored; and such joy thou took'st
With me in secret that my womb conceived
A growing burden. Meanwhile war arose,
And fields were fought in Heaven: wherein remained
(For what could else?) to our Almighty Foe
770 Clear victory; to our part loss and rout
Through all the Empyrean. Down they fell,
Driven headlong from the pitch of Heaven, down

Into this Deep; and in the general fall
I also: at which time this powerful key
Into my hands was given, with charge to keep
These gates for ever shut, which none can pass
Without my opening. Pensive here I sat
Alone; but long I sat not, till my womb,
Pregnant by thee, and now excessive grown,
Prodigious motion felt and rueful throes.   780
At last this odious offspring whom thou seest,
Thine own begotten, breaking violent way,
Tore through my entrails, that, with fear and pain
Distorted, all my nether shape thus grew
Transformed: but he my inbred enemy
Forth issued, brandishing his fatal dart,
Made to destroy. I fled, and cried out *Death!*
Hell trembled at the hideous name, and sighed
From all her caves, and back resounded *Death!*
I fled; but he pursued (though more, it seems,   790
Inflamed with lust than rage), and, swifter far,
Me overtook, his mother, all dismayed,
And, in embraces forcible and foul
Engendering with me, of that rape begot
These yelling monsters, that with ceaseless cry
Surround me, as thou saw'st—hourly conceived
And hourly born, with sorrow infinite
To me: for, when they list, into the womb
That bred them they return, and howl, and gnaw
My bowels, their repast; then, bursting forth   800
Afresh, with conscious terrors vex me round,
That rest or intermission none I find.
Before mine eyes in opposition sits
Grim Death, my son and foe, who sets them on,
And me, his parent, would full soon devour
For want of other prey, but that he knows
His end with mine involved, and knows that I
Should prove a bitter morsel, and his bane,
Whenever that shall be: so Fate pronounced.
But thou, O father, I forewarn thee, shun   810
His deadly arrow; neither vainly hope
To be invulnerable in those bright arms,
Though tempered heavenly; for that mortal dint,
Save He who reigns above, none can resist."
      She finished; and the subtle Fiend his lore
Soon learned, now milder, and thus answered
      smooth:—
      "Dear daughter—since thou claim'st me for thy
      sire,
And my fair son here show'st me, the dear pledge
Of dalliance had with thee in Heaven, and joys
Then sweet, now sad to mention, through dire change 820
Befallen us unforeseen, unthought-of—know,
I come no enemy, but to set free
From out this dark and dismal house of pain
Both him and thee, and all the Heavenly host

---

monster destructive to mariners. She lived in the sea between Italy
and Sicily, opposite the destructive whirlpool Charybdis; to escape
this double danger sailors had to steer carefully. 665. **Lapland**, believed to be the special haunt of witches. 677. **Admired**, wondered.

688. **Goblin**, fiend. 709. **Ophiuchus**, a constellation. 758. **Out of
thy head.** Milton has borrowed this concept from Greek myth in which
Pallas Athene has born by springing full-grown from the head of Zeus.
781. **this odius offspring**, "the wages of sin is death."

Of Spirits that, in our just pretenses armed,
Fell with us from on high. From them I go
This uncouth errand sole, and one for all
Myself expose, with lonely steps to tread
The unfounded Deep, and through the void immense
830 To search, with wandering quest, a place foretold
Should be—and, by concurring signs, ere now
Created vast and round—a place of bliss
In the purlieus of Heaven; and therein placed
A race of upstart creatures, to supply
Perhaps our vacant room, though more removed,
Lest Heaven, surcharged with potent multitude,
Might hap to move new broils. Be this, or aught
Than this more secret, now designed, I haste
To know; and, this once known, shall soon return,
840 And bring ye to the place where thou and Death
Shall dwell at ease, and up and down unseen
Wing silently the buxom air, embalmed
With odors. There ye shall be fed and filled
Immeasurably; all things shall be your prey."
    He ceased; for both seemed highly pleased, and
        Death
Grinned horrible a ghastly smile, to hear
His famine should be filled, and blessed his maw
Destined to that good hour. No less rejoiced
His mother bad, and thus bespake her sire:—
850   "The key of this infernal Pit, but due
And by command of Heaven's all-powerful King,
I keep, by Him forbidden to unlock
These adamantine gates; against all force
Death ready stands to interpose his dart,
Fearless to be o'ermatched by living might.
But what owe I to His commands above,
Who hates me, and hath hither thrust me down
Into this gloom of Tartarus profound,
To sit in hateful office here confined,
860 Inhabitant of Heaven and heavenly-born—
Here in perpetual agony and pain,
With terrors and with clamors compassed round
Of mine own brood, that on my bowels feed?
Thou art my father; thou my author, thou
My being gav'st me; whom should I obey
But thee? whom follow? Thou wilt bring me soon
To that new world of light and bliss, among
The gods who live at ease, where I shall reign
At thy right hand voluptuous, as beseems
870 Thy daughter and thy darling, without end."
    Thus saying, from her side the fatal key,
Sad instrument of all our woe, she took;
And, toward the gate rolling her bestial train,
Forthwith the huge portcullis high up-drew,
Which, but herself, not all the Stygian Powers
Could once have moved; then in the key-hole turns
The intricate wards, and every bolt and bar
Of massy iron or solid rock with ease

Unfastens. On a sudden open fly,
With impetuous recoil and jarring sound,   880
The infernal doors, and on their hinges grate
Harsh thunder, that the lowest bottom shook
Of Erebus. She opened; but to shut
Excelled her power: the gates wide open stood,
That with extended wings a bannered host,
Under spread ensigns marching, might pass through
With horse and chariots ranked in loose array;
So wide they stood, and like a furnace-mouth
Cast forth redounding smoke and ruddy flame.
Before their eyes in sudden view appear   890
The secrets of the hoary Deep—a dark
Illimitable ocean, without bound,
Without dimension; where length, breadth, and
        highth,
And time, and place, are lost; where eldest Night
And Chaos, ancestors of Nature, hold
Eternal anarchy, amidst the noise
Of endless wars, and by confusion stand.
For Hot, Cold, Moist, and Dry, four champions fierce,
Strive here for mastery, and to battle bring
Their embryon atoms: they around the flag   900
Of each his faction, in their several clans,
Light-armed or heavy, sharp, smooth, swift, or slow,
Swarm populous, unnumbered as the sands
Of Barca or Cyrene's torrid soil,
Levied to side with warring winds, and poise
Their lighter wings. To whom these most adhere
He rules a moment: Chaos umpire sits,
And by decision more embroils the fray
By which he reigns: next him, high arbiter,
Chance governs all. Into this wild Abyss,   910
The womb of Nature, and perhaps her grave,
Of neither Sea, nor Shore, nor Air, nor Fire,
But all these in their pregnant causes mixed
Confusedly, and which thus must ever fight,
Unless the Almighty Maker them ordain
His dark materials to create more worlds—
Into this wild Abyss the wary Fiend
Stood on the brink of Hell and looked a while,
Pondering his voyage; for no narrow frith
He had to cross. Nor was his ear less pealed   920
With noises loud and ruinous (to compare
Great things with small) than when Bellona storms
With all her battering engines, bent to rase
Some capital city; or less than if this frame
Of heaven were falling, and these elements
In mutiny had from her axle torn
The steadfast Earth. At last his sail-broad vans
He spreads for flight, and, in the surging smoke
Uplifted, spurns the ground; thence many a league,
As in a cloudy chair, ascending rides   930
Audacious; but, that seat soon failing, meets
A vast vacuity. All unawares,

827. uncouth, unknown. 889. redounding, billowy. 904. Barca
. . . Cyrene, ancient cities of Libya, northern Africa. 922. Bellona,
Roman goddess of war. 927. vans, wings. 939. Syrtis, quicksands off

the north coast of Africa. 943. gryphon, griffon, fabulous monster
with a lion's body and an eagle's wings. 945. Arimaspian, one-eyed
people of Scythia who warred against the griffons to get the gold which

Fluttering his pennons vain, plumb-down he drops
Ten thousand fathom deep, and to this hour
Down had been falling, had not, by ill chance,
The strong rebuff of some tumultuous cloud,
Instinct with fire and niter, hurried him
As many miles aloft. That fury stayed—
Quenched in a boggy Syrtis, neither sea,
940 Nor good dry land—nigh foundered, on he fares,
Treading the crude consistence, half on foot,
Half flying; behoves him now both oar and sail.
As when a gryphon through the wilderness
With wingéd course, o'er hill or moory dale,
Pursues the Arimaspian, who by stealth
Had from his wakeful custody purloined
The guarded gold; so eagerly the Fiend
O'er bog or steep, through strait, rough, dense, or
    rare,
With head, hands, wings, or feet, pursues his way,
950 And swims, or sinks, or wades, or creeps, or flies.
At length a universal hubbub wild
Of stunning sounds, and voices all confused,
Borne through the hollow dark, assaults his ear
With loudest vehemence. Thither he plies
Undaunted, to meet there whatever Power
Or Spirit of the nethermost Abyss
Might in that noise reside, of whom to ask
Which way the nearest coast of darkness lies
Bordering on light; when straight behold the throne
960 Of *Chaos*, and his dark pavilion spread
Wide on the wasteful Deep! With him enthroned
Sat sable-vested *Night*, eldest of things,
The consort of his reign; and by them stood
Orcus and Ades, and the dreaded name
Of Demogorgon; Rumor next, and Chance,
And Tumult, and Confusion, all embroiled,
And Discord with a thousand various mouths.
    To whom Satan, turning boldly, thus:—"Ye Powers
And Spirits of this nethermost Abyss,
970 Chaos and ancient Night, I come no spy
With purpose to explore or to disturb
The secrets of your realm; but, by constraint
Wandering this darksome desert, as my way
Lies through your spacious empire up to light,
Alone and without guide, half lost, I seek,
What readiest path leads where your gloomy bounds
Confine with Heaven; or, if some other place,
From your dominion won, the Ethereal King
Possesses lately, thither to arrive
980 I travel this profound. Direct my course:
Directed, no mean recompense it brings
To your behoof, if I that region lost,
All usurpation thence expelled, reduce
To her original darkness and your sway
(Which is my present journey), and once more
Erect the standard there of ancient Night.

Yours be the advantage all, mine the revenge!"
    Thus Satan; and him thus the Anarch old,
With faltering speech and visage incomposed,
Answered:—"I know thee, stranger, who thou art— 990
That mighty leading Angel, who of late
Made head against Heaven's King, though over-
    thrown.
I saw and heard; for such a numerous host
Fled not in silence through the frighted Deep,
With ruin upon ruin, rout on rout,
Confusion worse confounded; and Heaven-gates
Poured out by millions her victorious bands,
Pursuing. I upon my frontiers here
Keep residence; if all I can will serve
That little which is left so to defend,   1000
Encroached on still through our intestine broils
Weakening the scepter of old Night: first Hell,
Your dungeon, stretching far and wide beneath;
Now lately Heaven and Earth, another world
Hung o'er my realm, linked in a golden chain
To that side Heaven from whence your legions fell!
If that way be your walk, you have not far;
So much the nearer danger. Go, and speed;
Havoc, and spoil, and ruin, are my gain."
    He ceased; and Satan stayed not to reply,   1010
But, glad that now his sea should find a shore,
With fresh alacrity and force renewed
Springs upward, like a pyramid of fire,
Into the wild expanse, and through the shock
Of fighting elements, on all sides round
Environed, wins his way; harder beset
And more endangered than when Argo passed
Through Bosporus betwixt the justling rocks,
Or when Ulysses on the larboard shunned
Charybdis, and by the other Whirlpool steered.   1020
So he with difficulty and labor hard
Moved on. With difficulty and labor he;
But, he once passed, soon after, when Man fell,
Strange alteration! Sin and Death amain,
Following his track (such was the will of Heaven)
Paved after him a broad and beaten way
Over the dark Abyss, whose boiling gulf
Tamely endured a bridge of wondrous length,
From Hell continued, reaching the utmost Orb
Of this frail World; by which the Spirits perverse 1030
With easy intercourse pass to and fro
To tempt or punish mortals, except whom
God and good Angels guard by special grace.
    But now at last the sacred influence
Of light appears, and from the walls of Heaven
Shoots far into the bosom of dim Night
A glimmering dawn. Here Nature first begins
Her farthest verge, and Chaos to retire,
As from her outmost works, a broken foe,
With tumult less and with less hostile din;   1040

the monsters guarded. **964. Orcus,** the personification of the Roman
Lower World. **Ades,** personification of death. **965. Demogorgon,** a
mysterious infernal deity so powerful as to control the fates of gods as

well as of men. **1017. Argo,** Jason's ship in the search for the golden
fleece. **1019. Ulysses . . . Charybdis;** see note, l. 660. **1029. Orb,**
the outermost of the ten spheres which surrounded the earth.

That Satan with less toil, and now with ease,
Wafts on the calmer wave by dubious light,
And, like a weather-beaten vessel, holds
Gladly the port, though shrouds and tackle torn;
Or in the emptier waste, resembling air,
Weighs his spread wings, at leisure to behold
Far off the Empyreal Heaven, extended wide
In circuit, undetermined square or round,
With opal towers and battlements adorned
1050 Of living sapphire, once his native seat,
And, fast by, hanging in a golden chain,
This pendent World, in bigness as a star
Of smallest magnitude close by the moon.
Thither, full-fraught with mischievous revenge,
Accurst, and in a cursed hour, he hies.

BOOK IV

THE ARGUMENT

*Satan, now in prospect of Eden, and nigh the
place where he must now attempt the bold enterprise which he undertook alone against God and
man, falls into many doubts with himself, and many
passions, fear, envy, and despair; but at length confirms himself in evil, journeys on to Paradise, whose
outward prospect and situation is described, over-
leaps the bounds, sits in the shape of a cormorant
on the Tree of Life, as highest in the Garden, to*
10 *look about him. The Garden described; Satan's first
sight of Adam and Eve; his wonder at their excellent
form and happy state, but with resolution to work
their fall; overhears their discourse, thence gathers
that the Tree of Knowledge was forbidden them to
eat of, under penalty of death; and thereon intends
to found his temptation by seducing them to transgress; then leaves them a while, to know further
of their state by some other means. Meanwhile Uriel,
descending on a sunbeam, warns Gabriel, who had*
20 *in charge the gate of Paradise, that some evil spirit
had escaped the deep, and passed at noon by his
sphere, in the shape of a good angel, down to Paradise; discovered after by his furious gestures in the
mount. Gabriel promises to find him ere morning.
Night coming on, Adam and Eve discourse of going
to their rest: their bower described; their evening
worship. Gabriel, drawing forth his bands of night-
watch to walk the round of Paradise, appoints two
strong angels to Adam's bower, lest the evil spirit*
30 *should be there doing some harm to Adam or Eve
sleeping; there they find him at the ear of Eve, tempting her in a dream, and bring him, though unwilling,
to Gabriel; by whom questioned, he scornfully answers, prepares resistance, but hindered by a sign
from Heaven, flies out of Paradise.*

O for that warning voice, which he who saw
The Apocalypse heard cry in Heaven aloud,
Then when the Dragon, put to second rout,
Came furious down to be revenged on men,
"Woe to the inhabitants on Earth!" that now,
While time was, our first parents had been warned
The coming of their secret foe, and scaped,
Haply so scaped, his mortal snare; for now
Satan, now first inflamed with rage, came down,
The tempter ere the accuser of mankind,   10
To wreak on innocent frail man his loss
Of that first battle, and his flight to Hell:
Yet not rejoicing in his speed, though bold,
Far off and fearless, nor with cause to boast,
Begins his dire attempt, which nigh the birth
Now rolling, boils in his tumultuous breast,
And like a devilish engine back recoils
Upon himself; horror and doubt distract
His troubled thoughts, and from the bottom stir
The Hell within him, for within him Hell   20
He brings, and round about him, nor from Hell
One step no more than from himself can fly
By change of place. Now conscience wakes despair
That slumbered, wakes the bitter memory
Of what he was, what is, and what must be
Worse; of worse deeds worse sufferings must ensue.
Sometimes towards Eden which now in his view
Lay pleasant, his grieved look he fixes sad,
Sometimes towards Heaven and the full-blazing sun,
Which now sat high in his meridian tower.   30
Then much revolving, thus in sighs began:
"O thou that with surpassing glory crowned,
Look'st from thy sole dominion like the god
Of this new world; at whose sight all the stars
Hide their diminished heads; to thee I call,
But with no friendly voice, and add thy name,
O sun, to tell thee how I hate thy beams
That bring to my remembrance from what state
I fell, how glorious once above thy sphere;
Till pride and worse ambition threw me down   40
Warring in Heaven against Heaven's matchless King.
Ah wherefore? He deserved no such return
From me, whom he created what I was
In that bright eminence, and with his good
Upbraided none; nor was his service hard.
What could be less than to afford him praise,
The easiest recompense, and pay him thanks,
How due! Yet all his good proved ill in me,
And wrought but malice; lifted up so high
I 'sdained subjection, and thought one step higher   50
Would set me highest, and in a moment quit
The debt immense of endless gratitude,
So burdensome still paying, still to owe;
Forgetful what from him I still received,
And understood not that a grateful mind

Book IV. 1. **he . . . Earth,** St. John the Divine, author of Revelation. The passage alluded to is in Chapter 12. During the war in
heaven, a great red dragon, having seven crowned heads and ten horns,
was cast out by Michaël and his angels, and overcome only by the
blood of the Lamb. 30. **meridian tower,** i.e., it was noon. 50.
sdained, disdained. 53. **still,** ever. 66. **free will,** one of many expressions of this doctrine in *Paradise Lost.* 75. **myself . . . Hell.** Cf.
Marlowe's *Doctor Faustus,* Scene iii. 116. **borrowed visage,** disguise.

By owing owes not, but still pays, at once
Indebted and discharged; what burden then?
O had his powerful destiny ordained
Me some inferior angel, I had stood
60 Then happy; no unbounded hope had raised
Ambition. Yet why not? some other power
As great might have aspired, and me though mean
Drawn to his part; but other powers as great
Fell not, but stand unshaken, from within
Or from without, to all temptations armed.
Hadst thou the same free will and power to stand?
Thou hadst. Whom hast thou then or what to accuse,
But Heaven's free love dealt equally to all?
Be then his love accurst, since love or hate,
70 To me alike, it deals eternal woe.
Nay cursed be thou, since against his thy will
Chose freely what it now so justly rues.
Me miserable! which way shall I fly
Infinite wrath, and infinite despair?
Which way I fly is Hell; myself am Hell;
And in the lowest deep a lower deep
Still threatening to devour me opens wide,
To which the Hell I suffer seems a Heaven.
O then at last relent: is there no place
80 Left for repentance, none for pardon left?
None left but by submission; and that word
Disdain forbids me, and my dread of shame
Among the spirits beneath, whom I seduced
With other promises and other vaunts
Than to submit, boasting I could subdue
The Omnipotent. Ay me, they little know
How dearly I abide that boast so vain,
Under what torments inwardly I groan;
While they adore me on the throne of Hell,
90 With diadem and scepter high advanced,
The lower still I fall, only supreme
In misery; such joy ambition finds.
But say I could repent and could obtain
By act of grace my former state; how soon
Would highth recall high thoughts, how soon unsay
What feigned submission swore: ease would recant
Vows made in pain, as violent and void.
For never can true reconcilement grow
Where wounds of deadly hate have pierced so deep;
100 Which would but lead me to a worse relapse
And heavier fall: so should I purchase dear
Short intermission bought with double smart.
This knows my Punisher; therefore as far
From granting he, as I from begging peace.
All hope excluded thus, behold instead
Of us outcast, exiled, his new delight,
Mankind created, and for him this World.
So farewell hope, and with hope farewell fear,
Farewell remorse! All good to me is lost;
110 Evil, be thou my good; by thee at least

Divided empire with Heaven's King I hold
By thee, and more than half perhaps will reign;
As man ere long, and this new World shall know."
    Thus while he spake, each passion dimmed his face
Thrice changed with pale, ire, envy, and despair,
Which marred his borrowed visage, and betrayed
Him counterfeit, if any eye beheld.
For heavenly minds from such distempers foul
Are ever clear. Whereof he soon aware,
Each perturbation smoothed with outward calm,   120
Artificer of fraud; and was the first
That practised falsehood under saintly show,
Deep malice to conceal, couched with revenge:
Yet not enough had practised to deceive
Uriel once warned, whose eye pursued him down
The way he went, and on the Assyrian mount
Saw him disfigured, more than could befall
Spirit of happy sort: his gestures fierce
He marked and mad demeanor, then alone,
As he supposed, all unobserved, unseen.   130
So on he fares, and to the border comes
Of Eden, where delicious Paradise,
Now nearer, crowns with her enclosure green
As with a rural mound the champaign head
Of a steep wilderness, whose hairy sides
With thicket overgrown, grotesque and wild,
Access denied; and overhead up grew
Insuperable highth of loftiest shade,
Cedar, and pine, and fir, and branching palm,
A sylvan scene, and as the ranks ascend   140
Shade above shade, a woody theater
Of stateliest view. Yet higher than their tops
The verdurous wall of Paradise up sprung;
Which to our general sire gave prospect large
Into his nether empire neighboring round.
And higher than that wall a circling row
Of goodliest trees loaden with fairest fruit,
Blossoms and fruits at once of golden hue,
Appeared, with gay enameled colors mixed;
On which the sun more glad impressed his beams 150
Than in fair evening cloud, or humid bow,
When God hath showered the earth; so lovely seemed
That landscape. And of pure now purer air
Meets his approach, and to the heart inspires
Vernal delight and joy, able to drive
All sadness but despair; now gentle gales
Fanning their odoriferous wings dispense
Native perfumes, and whisper whence they stole
Those balmy spoils. As when to them who sail
Beyond the Cape of Hope, and now are past   160
Mozambic, off at sea north-east winds blow
Sabaean odors from the spicy shore
Of Araby the Blest, with such delay
Well pleased they slack their course, and many a
    league

125. **Uriel,** the sharp-sighted "Regent of the Sun," had been beguiled by Satan, disguised as a lesser angel, and had directed him on his flight to the Earth. 126. **Assyrian mount,** Mount Niphates, where Satan first lighted on his flight. 134. **champaign,** level, open country. 160.

Cape . . . Hope, Cape of Good Hope, on the southernmost tip of Africa. Mozambic (Mozambique) is on the east coast of Africa, opposite Madagascar. 162. **Sabaean,** Arabian.

Cheered with the grateful smell old ocean smiles;
So entertained those odorous sweets the Fiend
Who came their bane, though with them better pleased
Than Asmodëus with the fishy fume,
That drove him, though enamored, from the spouse
170 Of Tobit's son, and with a vengeance sent
From Media post to Egypt, there fast bound.
    Now to the ascent of that steep savage hill
Satan had journeyed on, pensive and slow;
But further way found none, so thick entwined,
As one continued brake, the undergrowth
Of shrubs and tangling bushes had perplexed
All path of man or beast that passed that way.
One gate there only was, and that looked east
On the other side; which when the Arch-Felon saw,
180 Due entrance he disdained, and in contempt,
At one slight bound high overleaped all bound
Of hill or highest wall, and sheer within
Lights on his feet. As when a prowling wolf,
Whom hunger drives to seek new haunt for prey,
Watching where shepherds pen their flocks at eve
In hurdled cotes amid the field secure,
Leaps o'er the fence with ease into the fold;
Or as a thief bent to unhoard the cash
Of some rich burgher, whose substantial doors,
190 Cross-barred and bolted fast, fear no assault,
In at the window climbs, or o'er the tiles:
So clomb this first grand thief into God's fold;
So since into his church lewd hirelings climb.
Thence up he flew, and on the Tree of Life,
The middle tree and highest there that grew,
Sat like a cormorant; yet not true life
Thereby regained, but sat devising death
To them who lived; nor on the virtue thought
Of that life-giving plant, but only used
200 For prospect, what well used had been the pledge
Of immortality. So little knows
Any, but God alone, to value right
The good before him, but perverts best things
To worst abuse, or to their meanest use.
    Beneath him with new wonder now he views
To all delight of human sense exposed
In narrow room Nature's whole wealth, yea more,
A Heaven on Earth, for blissful Paradise
Of God the garden was, by him in the east
210 Of Eden planted; Eden stretched her line
From Auran eastward to the royal towers
Of great Seleucia, built by Grecian kings,
Or where the sons of Eden long before
Dwelt in Telassar. In this pleasant soil

His far more pleasant garden God ordained;
Out of the fertile ground he caused to grow
All trees of noblest kind for sight, smell, taste;
And all amid them stood the Tree of Life,
High eminent, blooming ambrosial fruit
Of vegetable gold; and next to life   220
Our death, the Tree of Knowledge, grew fast by,
Knowledge of good bought dear by knowing ill.
Southward through Eden went a river large,
Nor changed his course, but through the shaggy hill
Passed underneath ingulfed, for God had thrown
That mountain as his garden mold, high raised
Upon the rapid current, which through veins
Of porous earth with kindly thirst up drawn,
Rose a fresh fountain, and with many a rill
Watered the garden; thence united fell   230
Down the steep glade, and met the nether flood,
Which from his darksome passage now appears,
And now divided into four main streams,
Runs diverse, wandering many a famous realm
And country whereof here needs no account;
But rather to tell how, if art could tell,
How from that sapphire fount the crisped brooks,
Rolling on orient pearl and sands of gold,
With mazy error under pendent shades
Ran nectar, visiting each plant, and fed   240
Flowers worthy of Paradise, which not nice art
In beds and curious knots, but Nature boon
Poured forth profuse on hill and dale and plain,
Both where the morning sun first warmly smote
The open field, and where the unpierced shade
Imbrowned the noontide bowers. Thus was this place,
A happy rural seat of various view;
Groves whose rich trees wept odorous gums and balm,
Others whose fruit burnished with golden rind
Hung amiable, Hesperian fables true,   250
If true, here only, and of delicious taste.
Betwixt them lawns, or level downs, and flocks
Grazing the tender herb, were interposed,
Or palmy hillock, or the flowery lap
Of some irriguous valley spread her store,
Flowers of all hue, and without thorn the rose.
Another side, umbrageous grots and caves
Of cool recess, o'er which the mantling vine
Lays forth her purple grape, and gently creeps
Luxuriant; meanwhile murmuring waters fall   260
Down the slope hills, dispersed, or in a lake,
That to the fringed bank with myrtle crowned
Her crystal mirror holds, unite their streams.
The birds their choir apply; airs, vernal airs,

---

168. **Asmodëus,** a fiend who killed in succession all seven of Sarah's husbands. Tobias then married Sarah, and with the aid of Raphael drove Asmodeus to Egypt. The story is told in the apocryphal Book of Tobit. 193. **So . . . climb.** Cf. *Lycidas,* l. 115. 196. **cormorant,** a voracious sea bird. 211. **Auran,** Aram, the ancient name for Syria and Mesopotamia. 212. **Seleucia,** a city on the Syrian coast, port of Antioch. 214. **Telassar;** see 2 Kings 19:12, and Isaiah 37:12. 239. **error,** meandering. 240. **nectar,** a delicious sweet drink. 241. **nice,** fastidious. Paradise was an informal garden. 250. **Hesperian fables,** legends of the Garden of Hesperides, in which grew the golden apples that Gaea gave to Juno when she married Jupiter. The Garden was

surrounded by the sea and guarded by a fearful dragon. One of the labors of Hercules was to secure these apples. 255. **irriguous,** well-watered. 266. **Pan,** god of woods and fields, the personification of Nature. The name Pan means all, everything. 269. **Enna . . . world,** an allusion to the famous myth of the seasons. From the Vale of Enna, where spring reigns eternal, Proserpina was abducted by Dis or Pluto. Her mother, Ceres, the goddess of fertility, sought her daughter the world over. During her search on earth all vegetation died. At last Ceres learned that Proserpina had been carried to Erebus, or Hell, whence she could be returned only if during her stay she had partaken of no food. The girl, however, had been tempted by a shriveled pome-

Breathing the smell of field and grove, attune
The trembling leaves, while universal Pan,
Knit with the Graces and the Hours in dance,
Led on the eternal spring. Not that fair field
270 Of Enna, where Prosérpine gathering flowers,
Herself a fairer flower, by gloomy Dis
Was gathered, which cost Ceres all that pain
To seek her through the world; nor that sweet grove
Of Daphne by Orontes, and the inspired
Castalian spring, might with this Paradise
Of Eden strive; nor that Nyseian isle,
Girt with the river Triton, where old Cham,
Whom Gentiles Ammon call and Libyan Jove,
Hid Amalthea and her florid son
Young Bacchus from his stepdame Rhea's eye;
280 Nor where Abassin kings their issue guard,
Mount Amara, though this by some supposed
True Paradise, under the Ethiop line
By Nilus' head, enclosed with shining rock,
A whole day's journey high, but wide remote
From this Assyrian garden, where the Fiend
Saw undelighted all delight, all kind
Of living creatures new to sight and strange.
    Two of far nobler shape erect and tall,
God-like erect, with native honor clad
290 In naked majesty seemed lords of all,
And worthy seemed, for in their looks divine
The image of their glorious Maker shone,
Truth, wisdom, sanctitude severe and pure,
Severe but in true filial freedom placed;
Whence true authority in men; though both
Not equal, as their sex not equal seemed;
For contemplation he and valor formed,
For softness she and sweet attractive grace;
He for God only, she for God in him.
300 His fair large front and eye sublime declared
Absolute rule; and hyacinthine locks
Round from his parted forelock manly hung
Clustering, but not beneath his shoulders broad:
She as a veil down to the slender waist
Her unadorned golden tresses wore
Disheveled, but in wanton ringlets waved
As the vine curls her tendrils, which implied
Subjection, but required with gentle sway,
And by her yielded, by him best received,
310 Yielded with coy submission, modest pride,
And sweet reluctant amorous delay.
Nor those mysterious parts were then concealed;
Then was not guilty shame; dishonest shame
Of Nature's works, honor dishonorable,

Sin-bred, how have ye troubled all mankind
With shows instead, mere shows of seeming pure,
And banished from man's life his happiest life,
Simplicity and spotless innocence.
So passed they naked on, nor shunned the sight
Of God or angel, for they thought no ill;   320
So hand in hand they passed, the loveliest pair
That ever since in love's embraces met,
Adam the goodliest man of men since born
His sons, the fairest of her daughters Eve.
Under a tuft of shade that on a green
Stood whispering soft, by a fresh fountain side
They sat them down; and after no more toil
Of their sweet gardening labor than sufficed
To recommend cool Zephyr, and made ease
More easy, wholesome thirst and appetite   330
More grateful, to their supper fruits they fell,
Nectarine fruits which the compliant boughs
Yielded them, sidelong as they sat recline
On the soft downy bank damasked with flowers.
The savory pulp they chew, and in the rind
Still as they thirsted scoop the brimming stream;
Nor gentle purpose, nor endearing smiles
Wanted, nor youthful dalliance, as beseems
Fair couple linked in happy nuptial league,
Alone as they. About them frisking played   340
All beasts of the earth, since wild, and of all chase
In wood or wilderness, forest or den;
Sporting the lion ramped, and in his paw
Dandled the kid; bears, tigers, ounces, pards,
Gamboled before them; the unwieldy elephant
To make them mirth used all his might, and wreathed
His lithe proboscis; close the serpent sly
Insinuating, wove with Gordian twine
His braided train, and of his fatal guile
Gave proof unheeded; others on the grass   350
Couched, and now filled with pasture gazing sat,
Or bedward ruminating; for the sun
Declined was hasting now with prone career
To the ocean isles, and in the ascending scale
Of Heaven the stars that usher evening rose:
When Satan still in gaze, as first he stood,
Scarce thus at length failed speech recovered sad:
    "O Hell! what do mine eyes with grief behold!
Into our room of bliss thus high advanced
Creatures of other mold, earth-born perhaps,   360
Not spirits, yet to heavenly spirits bright
Little inferior; whom my thoughts pursue
With wonder, and could love, so lively shines
In them divine resemblance, and such grace

granate brought to her from earth by her wily abductor, and had sucked the sweet pulp from a few seeds. Hence, she was permitted to pass only half of the year with her mother, the rest as queen of Erebus. 273. **Daphne,** loved by Apollo; she fled from his embraces, and at her earnest plea was changed into a laurel, which has since been sacred to Apollo. 274. **Castalian spring,** a spring on Mount Parnassus, sacred to Apollo and the Muses. It was named for Castalia, daughter of Achelous, who plunged into it to escape Apollo. 275. **Nyseian,** Nicene, from Nicea, a town in Bithynia. 277. **Ammon . . . Jove,** Amon, the Hidden; originally an Egyptian deity who corresponds to Jupiter. 278. **Amalthea,** a nymph who nursed the infant Jove. 279. **Bacchus,** son

of Jupiter and Semele. **Rhea,** the Roman *magna mater,* sister-queen with Cronus (Saturn) of Heaven and Earth. She was the mother of Jupiter. 280. **Abassin,** Abyssinian. 281. **Mount Amara,** a place where the Abyssinian kings secluded their sons as a precaution against sedition. 282. **Ethiop line,** equator. 301. **hyacinthine locks,** beautiful hair, like that of Hyacinthus, a youth beloved of Apollo. He was killed accidentally when, in the games, Apollo struck Hyacinthus with a discus. The flower commemorates him; the first hyacinth sprang from his blood. 329. **Zephyr,** the west wind. 344. **ounces,** panthers. 348. **Gordian,** intricate knot, like that tied by Gordius, King of Gordium in Phrygia; and cut by Alexander.

The hand that formed them on their shape hath poured.
Ah gentle pair, ye little think how nigh
Your change approaches, when all these delights
Will vanish and deliver ye to woe,
More woe, the more your taste is now of joy;
370 Happy, but for so happy ill secured
Long to continue, and this high seat your Heaven
Ill fenced for Heaven to keep out such a foe
As now is entered; yet no purposed foe
To you whom I could pity thus forlorn,
Though I unpitied. League with you I seek,
And mutual amity so strait, so close,
That I with you must dwell, or you with me
Henceforth; my dwelling haply may not please,
Like this fair Paradise, your sense, yet such
380 Accept your Maker's work; he gave it me,
Which I as freely give; Hell shall unfold,
To entertain you two, her widest gates,
And send forth all her kings; there will be room,
Not like these narrow limits, to receive
Your numerous offspring; if no better place,
Thank him who puts me loth to this revenge
On you who wrong me not, for him who wronged.
And should I at your harmless innocence
Melt, as I do, yet public reason just,
390 Honor and empire with revenge enlarged
By conquering this new World, compels me now
To do what else though damned I should abhor."
    So spake the Fiend, and with necessity,
The tyrant's plea, excused his devilish deeds.
Then from his lofty stand on that high tree
Down he alights among the sportful herd
Of those four-footed kinds, himself now one,
Now other, as their shape served best his end
Nearer to view his prey, and unespied
400 To mark what of their state he more might learn
By word or action marked. About them round
A lion now he stalks with fiery glare;
Then as a tiger, who by chance hath spied
In some purlieu two gentle fawns at play,
Straight couches close, then rising, changes oft
His couchant watch, as one who chose his ground
Whence rushing he might surest seize them both
Gripped in each paw; when Adam first of men
To first of women, Eve, thus moving speech,
410 Turned him all ear to hear new utterance flow:
    "Sole partner and sole part of all these joys,
Dearer thyself than all, needs must the Power
That made us, and for us this ample World,
Be infinitely good, and of his good
As liberal and free as infinite,
That raised us from the dust and placed us here
In all this happiness, who at his hand
Have nothing merited, nor can perform
Aught whereof he hath need; he who requires

From us no other service than to keep   420
This one, this easy charge, of all the trees
In Paradise that bear delicious fruit
So various, not to taste that only Tree
Of Knowledge, planted by the Tree of Life,
So near grows death to life, whate'er death is,
Some dreadful thing no doubt; for well thou know'st
God hath pronounced it death to taste that Tree,
The only sign of our obedience left
Among so many signs of power and rule
Conferred upon us, and dominion given   430
Over all other creatures that possess
Earth, air, and sea. Then let us not think hard
One easy prohibition, who enjoy
Free leave so large to all things else, and choice
Unlimited of manifold delights;
But let us ever praise him, and extol
His bounty, following our delightful task
To prune these growing plants, and tend these flowers,
Which were it toilsome, yet with thee were sweet."
    To whom thus Eve replied: "O thou for whom   440
And from whom I was formed flesh of thy flesh,
And without whom am to no end, my guide
And head, what thou hast said is just and right.
For we to him indeed all praises owe,
And daily thanks, I chiefly who enjoy
So far the happier lot, enjoying thee
Pre-eminent by so much odds, while thou
Like consort to thyself canst nowhere find.
That day I oft remember, when from sleep
I first awaked, and found myself reposed   450
Under a shade on flowers, much wondering where
And what I was, whence thither brought, and how.
Not distant far from thence a murmuring sound
Of waters issued from a cave and spread
Into a liquid plain, then stood unmoved
Pure as the expanse of Heaven; I thither went
With unexperienced thought, and laid me down
On the green bank, to look into the clear
Smooth lake, that to me seemed another sky.
As I bent down to look, just opposite   460
A shape within the watery gleam appeared
Bending to look on me: I started back,
It started back, but pleased I soon returned,
Pleased it returned as soon with answering looks
Of sympathy and love; there I had fixed
Mine eyes till now, and pined with vain desire,
Had not a voice thus warned me: 'What thou seest,
What there thou seest, fair creature, is thyself,
With thee it came and goes; but follow me,
And I will bring thee where no shadow stays   470
Thy coming, and thy soft embraces, he
Whose image thou art, him thou shalt enjoy
Inseparably thine; to him shalt bear
Multitudes like thyself, and thence be called

376. **strait**, strict. 397. **himself . . . one,** i.e., Satan, for purposes of
disguise, assumed various shapes. 478. **platane,** the Oriental plane tree.

549. **Gabriel,** an archangel, "Chief of the Angelic Guards." 555.
Uriel, see l. 125 and note. 581. **meridian hour,** noon.

Mother of human race.' What could I do
But follow straight, invisibly thus led?
Till I espied thee, fair indeed and tall,
Under a platane; yet methought less fair,
Less winning soft, less amiably mild,
480 Than that smooth watery image; back I turned,
Thou following cried'st aloud, 'Return, fair Eve,
Whom fli'st thou? whom thou fli'st, of him thou art,
His flesh, his bone; to give thee being I lent
Out of my side to thee, nearest my heart,
Substantial life, to have thee by my side
Henceforth an individual solace dear.
Part of my soul I seek thee, and thee claim
My other half.' With that thy gentle hand
Seized mine, I yielded, and from that time see
490 How beauty is excelled by manly grace
And wisdom, which alone is truly fair."
    So spake our general mother, and with eyes
Of conjugal attraction unreproved,
And meek surrender, half embracing leaned
On our first father; half her swelling breast
Naked met his under the flowing gold
Of her loose tresses hid. He in delight
Both of her beauty and submissive charms
Smiled with superior love, as Jupiter
500 On Juno smiles, when he impregns the clouds
That shed May flowers; and pressed her matron lip
With kisses pure. Aside the Devil turned
For envy, yet with jealous leer malign
Eyed them askance, and to himself thus plained:
    "Sight hateful, sight tormenting! thus these two
Imparadised in one another's arms,
The happier Eden, shall enjoy their fill
Of bliss on bliss, while I to Hell am thrust,
Where neither joy nor love, but fierce desire,
510 Among our other torments not the least,
Still unfulfilled with pain of longing pines;
Yet let me not forget what I have gained
From their own mouths. All is not theirs, it seems;
One fatal tree there stands, of Knowledge called,
Forbidden them to taste. Knowledge forbidden?
Suspicious, reasonless. Why should their Lord
Envy them that? can it be sin to know,
Can it be death? and do they only stand
By ignorance, is that their happy state,
520 The proof of their obedience and their faith?
O fair foundation laid whereon to build
Their ruin! Hence I will excite their minds
With more desire to know, and to reject
Envious commands, invented with design
To keep them low whom knowledge might exalt
Equal with gods. Aspiring to be such,
They taste and die; what likelier can ensue?
But first with narrow search I must walk round
This garden, and no corner leave unspied;
530 A chance but chance may lead where I may meet
Some wandering spirit of Heaven, by fountain side,

Or in thick shade retired, from him to draw
What further would be learnt. Live while ye may,
Yet happy pair; enjoy, till I return,
Short pleasures, for long woes are to succeed."
    So saying, his proud step he scornful turned,
But with sly circumspection, and began
Through wood, through waste, o'er hill, o'er dale, his
    roam.
Meanwhile in utmost longitude, where Heaven
With Earth and Ocean meets, the setting sun   540
Slowly descended, and with right aspect
Against the eastern gate of Paradise
Leveled his evening rays. It was a rock
Of alabaster, piled up to the clouds,
Conspicuous far, winding with one ascent
Accessible from Earth, one entrance high;
The rest was craggy cliff, that overhung
Still as it rose, impossible to climb.
Betwixt these rocky pillars Gabriel sat,
Chief of the angelic guards, awaiting night;   550
About him exercised heroic games
The unarmed youth of Heaven, but nigh at hand
Celestial armory, shields, helms, and spears,
Hung high, with diamond flaming and with gold.
Thither came Uriel, gliding through the even
On a sunbeam, swift as a shooting star
In autumn thwarts the night, when vapors fired
Impress the air, and shows the mariner
From what point of his compass to beware
Impetuous winds. He thus began in haste: 560
    "Gabriel, to thee thy course by lot hath given
Charge and strict watch that to this happy place.
No evil thing approach or enter in;
This day at highth of noon came to my sphere
A spirit, zealous, as he seemed, to know
More of the Almighty's works, and chiefly man,
God's latest image. I described his way
Bent all on speed, and marked his airy gait;
But in the mount that lies from Eden north,
Where he first lighted, soon discerned his looks   570
Alien from Heaven, with passions foul obscured.
Mine eye pursued him still, but under shade
Lost sight of him; one of the banished crew
I fear, hath ventured from the deep, to raise
New troubles; him thy care must be to find."
    To whom the winged warrior thus returned:
"Uriel, no wonder if thy perfect sight,
Amid the sun's bright circle where thou sitt'st,
See far and wide. In at this gate none pass
The vigilance here placed, but such as come   580
Well known from Heaven; and since meridian hour
No creature thence. If spirit of other sort,
So minded, have o'erleaped these earthy bounds
On purpose, hard thou know'st it to exclude
Spiritual substance with corporeal bar.
But if within the circuit of these walks,
In whatsoever shape he lurk, of whom

Thou tell'st, by morrow dawning I shall know."
    So promised he, and Uriel to his charge
590 Returned on that bright beam, whose point now raised
Bore him slope downward to the sun now fallen
Beneath the Azores; whether the prime orb,
Incredible how swift, had thither rolled
Diurnal, or this less volúble Earth
By shorter flight to the east, had left him there
Arraying with reflected purple and gold
The clouds that on his western throne attend.
    Now came still evening on, and twilight gray
Had in her sober livery all things clad;
600 Silence accompanied, for beast and bird,
They to their grassy couch, these to their nests
Were slunk, all but the wakeful nightingale;
She all night long her amorous descant sung;
Silence was pleased. Now glowed the firmament
With living sapphires; Hesperus that led
The starry host, rode brightest, till the moon
Rising in clouded majesty, at length
Apparent queen unveiled her peerless light,
And o'er the dark her silver mantle threw;
610   When Adam thus to Eve: "Fair consort, the hour
Of night, and all things now retired to rest
Mind us of like repose, since God hath set
Labor and rest, as day and night to men
Successive, and the timely dew of sleep
Now falling with soft slumbrous weight inclines
Our eyelids; other creatures all day long
Rove idle, unemployed, and less need rest;
Man hath his daily work of body or mind
Appointed, which declares his dignity,
620 And the regard of Heaven on all his ways;
While other animals unactive range,
And of their doings God takes no account.
To-morrow ere fresh morning streak the east
With first approach of light, we must be risen,
And at our pleasant labor, to reform
Yon flowery arbors, yonder alleys green,
Our walks at noon, with branches overgrown,
That mock our scant manuring, and require
More hands than ours to lop their wanton growth.
630 Those blossoms also, and those dropping gums,
That lie bestrown unsightly and unsmooth,
Ask riddance, if we mean to tread with ease;
Meanwhile, as Nature wills, night bids us rest."
    To whom thus Eve with perfect beauty adorned:
"My author and disposer, what thou bidd'st
Unargued I obey; so God ordains.
God is thy law, thou mine; to know no more
Is woman's happiest knowledge and her praise.
With thee conversing I forget all time,
640 All seasons and their change, all please alike.
Sweet is the breath of morn, her rising sweet,

With charm of earliest birds; pleasant the sun
When first on this delightful land he spreads
His orient beams, on herb, tree, fruit, and flower,
Glistering with dew; fragrant the fertile Earth
After soft showers; and sweet the coming on
Of grateful evening mild, then silent night
With this her solemn bird and this fair moon,
And these the gems of Heaven, her starry train:
But neither breath of morn when she ascends   650
With charm of earliest birds, nor rising sun
On this delightful land, nor herb, fruit, flower,
Glistering with dew, nor fragrance after showers,
Nor grateful evening mild, nor silent night
With this her solemn bird, nor walk by moon
Or glittering starlight, without thee is sweet.
But wherefore all night long shine these, for whom
This glorious sight, when sleep hath shut all eyes?"
    To whom our general ancestor replied:
"Daughter of God and man, accomplished Eve,   660
Those have their course to finish, round the Earth,
By morrow evening, and from land to land
In order, though to nations yet unborn,
Ministering light prepared, they set and rise;
Lest total darkness should by night regain
Her old possession, and extinguish life
In nature and all things; which these soft fires
Not only enlighten, but with kindly heat
Of various influence foment and warm,
Temper or nourish, or in part shed down   670
Their stellar virtue on all kinds that grow
On Earth, made hereby apter to receive
Perfection from the sun's more potent ray.
These then, though unbeheld in deep of night,
Shine not in vain, nor think, though men were none,
That Heaven would want spectators, God want praise;
Millions of spiritual creatures walk the Earth
Unseen, both when we wake, and when we sleep:
All these with ceaseless praise his works behold
Both day and night. How often from the steep   680
Of echoing hill or thicket have we heard
Celestial voices to the midnight air,
Sole, or responsive each to other's note,
Singing their great Creator; oft in bands
While they keep watch, or nightly rounding walk,
With heavenly touch of instrumental sounds
In full harmonic number joined, their songs
Divide the night, and lift our thoughts to Heaven."
    Thus talking, hand in hand alone they passed
On to their blissful bower; it was a place   690
Chosen by the sovran Planter, when he framed
All things to man's delightful use; the roof
Of thickest covert was inwoven shade,
Laurel and myrtle, and what higher grew
Of firm and fragrant leaf; on either side

605. **Hesperus,** the evening star, the planet, Venus. 648. **solemn bird,** the nightingale. 704. **worm,** serpent. 707. **Silvanus,** a god presiding over forest glades and ploughed fields. 708. **Faunus,** a god of fields and shepherds. 711. **hymenean,** marriage song. 714. **Pandora.** When Prometheus stole fire from heaven to benefit his creatures, man-

kind, Jupiter planned for man a curse in the shape of a woman. She was Pandora, "the all-gifted," beautiful, charming, talented—every god and goddess contributed something to her perfection. She was brought to earth by Hermes, the messenger of the gods, and presented to Epimetheus, brother of Prometheus, who had cautioned him to beware

Acanthus, and each odorous bushy shrub
Fenced up the verdant wall; each beauteous flower,
Iris all hues, roses, and jessamine
Reared high their flourished heads between, and
     wrought
700 Mosaic; under foot the violet,
Crocus, and hyacinth with rich inlay
Broidered the ground, more colored than with stone
Of costliest emblem. Other creature here,
Beast, bird, insect, or worm durst enter none;
Such was their awe of man. In shadier bower
More sacred and sequestered, though but feigned,
Pan or Silvanus never slept, nor nymph
Nor Faunus haunted. Here in close recess
With flowers, garlands, and sweet-smelling herbs
710 Espoused Eve decked first her nuptial bed,
And heavenly choirs the hymenean sung,
What day the genial angel to our sire
Brought her in naked beauty more adorned,
More lovely than Pandora, whom the gods
Endowed with all their gifts, and O too like
In sad event, when to the unwiser son
Of Japhet brought by Hermes, she ensnared
Mankind with her fair looks, to be avenged
On him who had stole Jove's authentic fire.
720   Thus at their shady lodge arrived, both stood,
Both turned, and under open sky adored
The God that made both sky, air, Earth, and Heaven,
Which they beheld, the moon's resplendent globe
And starry pole: "Thou also mad'st the night,
Maker Omnipotent, and thou the day,
Which we in our appointed work employed
Have finished happy in our mutual help
And mutual love, the crown of all our bliss
Ordained by thee, and this delicious place
730 For us too large, where thy abundance wants
Partakers, and uncropped falls to the ground.
But thou hast promised from us two a race
To fill the Earth, who shall with us extol
Thy goodness infinite, both when we wake,
And when we seek, as now, thy gift of sleep."
    This said unanimous, and other rites
Observing none, but adoration pure
Which God likes best, into their inmost bower
Handed they went; and eased the putting off
740 These troublesome disguises which we wear,
Straight side by side were laid, nor turned, I ween,
Adam from his fair spouse, nor Eve the rites
Mysterious of connubial love refused;
Whatever hypocrites austerely talk
Of purity and place and innocence,
Defaming as impure what God declares
Pure, and commands to some, leaves free to all.
Our Maker bids increase; who bids abstain

But our destroyer, foe to God and man?
Hail, wedded Love, mysterious law, true source   750
Of human offspring, sole propriety
In Paradise of all things common else.
By thee adulterous lust was driven from men
Among the bestial herds to range; by thee,
Founded in reason, loyal, just, and pure,
Relations dear, and all the charities
Of father, son, and brother first were known.
Far be it that I should write thee sin or blame,
Or think thee unbefitting holiest place,
Perpetual fountain of domestic sweets,   760
Whose bed is undefiled and chaste pronounced,
Present or past, as saints and patriarchs used.
Here Love his golden shafts employs, here lights
His constant lamp, and waves his purple wings,
Reigns here and revels; not in the bought smile
Of harlots, loveless, joyless, unendeared,
Casual fruition; nor in court amours,
Mixed dance, or wanton mask, or midnight ball,
Or serenate, which the starved lover sings
To his proud fair, best quitted with disdain.   770
These lulled by nightingales, embracing slept,
And on their naked limbs the flowery roof
Showered roses, which the morn repaired. Sleep on,
Blest pair; and O yet happiest if ye seek
No happier state, and know to know no more.
    Now had night measured with her shadowy cone
Half way up hill this vast sublunar vault,
And from their ivory port the Cherubim
Forth issuing at the accustomed hour stood armed
To their night-watches in warlike parade,   780
When Gabriel to his next in power thus spake:
    "Uzziel, half these draw off, and coast the south
With strictest watch; these other wheel the north;
Our circuit meets full west." As flame they part,
Half wheeling to the shield, half to the spear.
From these, two strong and subtle spirits he called
That near him stood, and gave them thus in charge:
    "Ithuriel and Zephon, with winged speed
Search through this garden; leave unsearched no nook;
But chiefly where those two fair creatures lodge,   790
Now laid perhaps asleep secure of harm.
This evening from the sun's decline arrived
Who tells of some infernal spirit seen
Hitherward bent (who could have thought?) escaped
The bars of Hell, on errand bad no doubt:
Such where ye find, seize fast, and hither bring."
    So saying, on he led his radiant files,
Dazzling the moon; these to the bower direct
In search of whom they sought. Him there they found
Squat like a toad, close at the ear of Eve,   800
Assaying by his devilish art to reach
The organs of her fancy, and with them forge

of Jupiter's wily tricks. In the hand of Pandora was placed a casket she was forbidden to open. Her curiosity overcame her; when she lifted the cover there escaped a thousand ills and diseases to plague mankind. When Pandora hastily closed the lid, only one thing remained in the casket, and that was hope. **716. son . . . Japhet**, Epimetheus.

741 ff. In Milton's paradise the attitude toward sex is obviously far from "puritanical"; love is natural, innocent, holy, and important. Cf. ll. 312 ff. and 492 ff. **782. Uzziel**, an angel next in power to Gabriel.

John Milton 413

Illusions as he list, phantasms and dreams;
Or if, inspiring venom, he might taint
The animal spirits that from pure blood arise
Like gentle breaths from rivers pure, thence raise
At least distempered, discontented thoughts,
Vain hopes, vain aims, inordinate desires
Blown up with high conceits engendering pride.
810 Him thus intent Ithuriel with his spear
Touched lightly; for no falsehood can endure
Touch of celestial temper, but returns
Of force to its own likeness. Up he starts
Discovered and surprised. As when a spark
Lights on a heap of nitrous powder, laid
Fit for the tun some magazine to store
Against a rumored war, the smutty grain
With sudden blaze diffused, inflames the air:
So started up in his own shape the Fiend.
820 Back stepped those two fair angels half amazed
So sudden to behold the grisly king;
Yet thus, unmoved with fear, accost him soon:
    "Which of those rebel spirits adjudged to Hell
Com'st thou, escaped thy prison; and transformed,
Why sat'st thou like an enemy in wait
Here watching at the head of these that sleep?"
    "Know ye not then," said Satan, filled with scorn,
"Know ye not me? Ye knew me once no mate
For you, there sitting where ye durst not soar;
830 Not to know me argues yourselves unknown,
The lowest of your throng; or if ye know,
Why ask ye, and superfluous begin
Your message, like to end as much in vain?"
To whom thus Zephon, answering scorn with scorn:
"Think not, revolted spirit, thy shape the same,
Or undiminished brightness, to be known
As when thou stood'st in Heaven upright and
        pure;
That glory then, when thou no more wast good,
Departed from thee, and thou resemblest now
840 Thy sin and place of doom obscure and foul.
But come, for thou, be sure, shalt give account
To him who sent us, whose charge is to keep
This place inviolable, and these from harm."
    So spake the Cherub, and his grave rebuke,
Severe in youthful beauty, added grace
Invincible. Abashed the Devil stood,
And felt how awful goodness is, and saw
Virtue in her shape how lovely; saw, and pined
His loss; but chiefly to find here observed
850 His luster visibly impaired; yet seemed
Undaunted. "If I must contend," said he,
"Best with the best, the sender not the sent;
Or all at once; more glory will be won,
Or less be lost." "Thy fear," said Zephon bold,
"Will save us trial what the least can do
Single against thee wicked, and thence weak."

The Fiend replied not, overcome with rage;
But like a proud steed reined, went haughty on,
Champing his iron curb. To strive or fly
He held it vain; awe from above had quelled   860
His heart, not else dismayed. Now drew they nigh
The western point, where those half-rounding guards
Just met, and closing stood in squadron joined
Awaiting next command. To whom their chief
Gabriel from the front thus called aloud:
    "O friends, I hear the tread of nimble feet
Hasting this way, and now by glimpse discern
Ithuriel and Zephon through the shade,
And with them comes a third, of regal port,
But faded splendor wan, who by his gait   870
And fierce demeanor seems the Prince of Hell,
Not likely to part hence without contest;
Stand firm, for in his look defiance lours."
    He scarce had ended, when those two approached
And brief related whom they brought, where found,
How busied, in what form and posture couched.
    To whom with stern regard thus Gabriel spake:
"Why hast thou, Satan, broke the bounds prescribed
To thy transgressions, and disturbed the charge
Of others, who approve not to transgress   880
By thy example, but have power and right
To question thy bold entrance on this place;
Employed it seems to violate sleep, and those
Whose dwelling God hath planted here in bliss?"
    To whom thus Satan, with contemptuous brow:
"Gabriel, thou hadst in Heaven the esteem of wise,
And such I held thee; but this question asked
Puts me in doubt. Lives there who loves his pain?
Who would not, finding way, break loose from
        Hell,
Though thither doomed? Thou wouldst thyself, no
        doubt,   890
And boldly venture to whatever place
Farthest from pain, where thou mightst hope to change
Torment with ease, and soonest recompense
Dole with delight, which in this place I sought;
To thee no reason, who know'st only good,
But evil hast not tried. And wilt object
His will who bound us? let him surer bar
His iron gates, if he intends our stay
In that dark durance. Thus much what was asked.
The rest is true, they found me where they say;   900
But that implies not violence or harm."
    Thus he in scorn. The warlike angel moved,
Disdainfully half smiling thus replied:
"O loss of one in Heaven to judge of wise,
Since Satan fell, whom folly overthrew,
And now returns him from his prison scaped,
Gravely in doubt whether to hold them wise
Or not, who ask what boldness brought him hither
Unlicensed from his bounds in Hell prescribed;

---

816. **tun,** barrel, cask. 817. **smutty,** soot colored. 869. **port,** bearing,
appearance. 980. **ported,** held at port, across the chest. 987. **Tener-**
iffe, the largest of the Canary Islands. **Atlas,** a mountain in Lybia
named for the god who supported the heavens. 998. **Astraea . . .**

910 So wise he judges it to fly from pain
However, and to scape his punishment.
So judge thou still, presumptuous, till the wrath,
Which thou incurr'st by flying, meet thy flight
Sevenfold, and scourge that wisdom back to Hell,
Which taught thee yet no better, that no pain
Can equal anger infinite provoked.
But wherefore thou alone? wherefore with thee
Came not all Hell broke loose? is pain to them
Less pain, less to be fled, or thou than they
920 Less hardy to endure? Courageous chief,
The first in flight from pain, hadst thou alleged
To thy deserted host this cause of flight,
Thou surely hadst not come sole fugitive."
　　To which the Fiend thus answered frowning stern:
"Not that I less endure, or shrink from pain,
Insulting angel, well thou know'st I stood
Thy fiercest, when in battle to thy aid
The blasting volleyed thunder made all speed
And seconded thy else not dreaded spear.
930 But still thy words at random, as before,
Argue thy inexperience what behoves,
From hard assays and ill successes past,
A faithful leader, not to hazard all
Through ways of danger by himself untried.
I therefore, I alone first undertook
To wing the desolate abyss, and spy
This new-created World, whereof in Hell
Fame is not silent, here in hope to find
Better abode, and my afflicted powers
940 To settle here on Earth, or in mid-air;
Though for possession put to try once more
What thou and thy gay legions dare against;
Whose easier business were to serve their Lord
High up in Heaven, with songs to hymn his
　　throne,
And practised distances to cringe, not fight."
　　To whom the warrior angel soon replied:
"To say and straight unsay, pretending first
Wise to fly pain, professing next the spy,
Argues no leader but a liar traced,
950 Satan, and couldst thou 'faithful' add? O name,
O sacred name of faithfulness profaned!
Faithful to whom? to thy rebellious crew?
Army of fiends, fit body to fit head;
Was this your discipline and faith engaged,
Your military obedience, to dissolve
Allegiance to the acknowledged Power Supreme?
And thou sly hypocrite, who now wouldst seem
Patron of liberty, who more than thou
Once fawned, and cringed, and servilely adored
960 Heaven's awful Monarch? wherefore but in hope
To dispossess him, and thyself to reign?
But mark what I areed thee now: Avaunt!
Fly thither whence thou fledd'st. If from this hour

Within these hallowed limits thou appear,
Back to the infernal pit I drag thee chained,
And seal thee so, as henceforth not to scorn
The facile gates of Hell too slightly barred."
　　So threatened he, but Satan to no threats
Gave heed, but waxing more in rage replied:
　　"Then when I am thy captive talk of chains, 970
Proud limitary Cherub, but ere then
Far heavier load thyself expect to feel
From my prevailing arm, though Heaven's King
Ride on thy wings, and thou with thy compeers,
Used to the yoke, draw'st his triumphant wheels
In progress through the road of Heaven star-paved."
　　While thus he spake, the angelic squadron bright
Turned fiery red, sharpening in mooned horns
Their phalanx, and began to hem him round
With ported spears, as thick as when a field 980
Of Ceres ripe for harvest waving bends
Her bearded grove of ears, which way the wind
Sways them; the careful ploughman doubting stands
Lest on the threshing-floor his hopeful sheaves
Prove chaff. On the other side Satan alarmed
Collecting all his might dilated stood,
Like Teneriffe or Atlas unremoved:
His stature reached the sky, and on his crest
Sat Horror plumed; nor wanted in his grasp
What seemed both spear and shield. Now dreadful
　　deeds 990
Might have ensued, nor only Paradise
In this commotion, but the starry cope
Of Heaven perhaps, or all the elements
At least had gone to wrack, disturbed and torn
With violence of this conflict, had not soon
The Eternal to prevent such horrid fray
Hung forth in Heaven his golden scales, yet seen
Betwixt Astraea and the Scorpion sign,
Wherein all things created first he weighed,
The pendulous round Earth with balanced air 1000
In counterpoise, now ponders all events,
Battles and realms. In these he put two weights,
The sequel each of parting and of fight;
The latter quick up flew, and kicked the beam;
Which Gabriel spying, thus bespake the Fiend:
　　"Satan, I know thy strength, and thou know'st mine,
Neither our own but given; what folly then
To boast what arms can do, since thine no more
Than Heaven permits, nor mine, though doubled now
To trample thee as mire. For proof look up, 1010
And read thy lot in yon celestial sign
Where thou art weighed, and shown how light, how
　　weak,
If thou resist." The Fiend looked up and knew
His mounted scale aloft: nor more; but fled
Murmuring, and with him fled the shades of night.
(1667)

Scorpion, zodiacal constellations, Virgo and Scorpio. 1000. pendulous
. . . Earth. In Milton's cosmology the Earth hung by a silver chain

from the floor of Heaven.

Southwark Fair, by William Hogarth. The realistic details in the portion of the engraving shown here include a female drummer, a fire-eating mountebank and his merry-andrew, a farthing show, and a player at back sword, mounted on a blind horse and ready to challenge any oncomers.

CONVENTION AND REALISM

From the Restoration to the Death of

Samuel Johnson, 1660-1784

Chapter Three

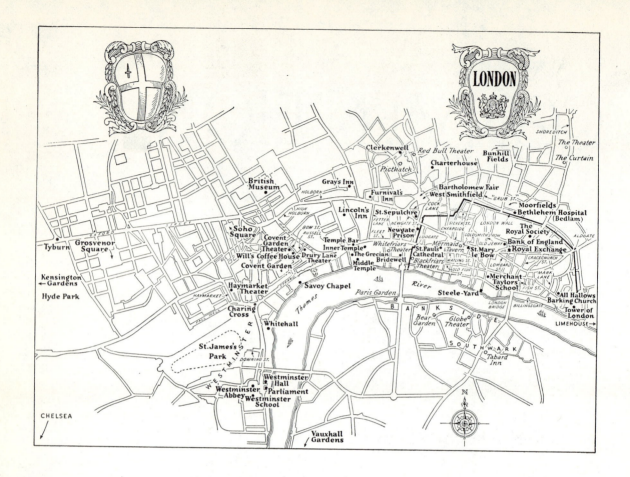

The Neo-Classical Age in England

"May 29, 1660. This day his Majesty Charles II came to London after a sad and long exile and calamitous suffering both of the King and Church, being seventeen years. This was also his birthday, and with a triumph of above 200,000 horse and foot, brandishing their swords and shouting with inexpressible joy; the ways strewed with flowers, the bells ringing, the streets hung with tapestry, fountains running with wine; the Mayor, Alderman, and all the Companies in their liveries, chains of gold and banners; Lords and Nobles clad in cloth of silver, gold, and velvet; the windows and balconies all set with ladies; trumpets, music, and myriads of people flocking, even so far as Rochester, so as they were seven hours in passing the City, even from two in the afternoon till nine at night. I stood in the Strand and beheld it, and blessed God."

So spoke John Evelyn, traveler, intellectual, and author of one of the most valuable diaries in English literature. But this day of the restoration of the Stuarts, after the horror of a civil war and the severe Puritan interlude that was the Commonwealth, meant more to England than a return to the trappings of royalty.

This May day in 1660 marks the beginning of the neo-classical period in English life and thought, a period both rich and distinctive. In its desire to imitate the ways of life known to ancient Greece and Rome, it gave to English literature and art neatness, finish, balance, and a discipline never known before; it laid the foundations and fixed the forms of the modern novel; and it developed a prose style that was clear, well-mannered, dignified, and altogether usable. And it carried further the intellectual assumptions of the Renaissance. During this period, a new faith in the intellect and reason, rather than in the emotions, emerged, and the period gradually lost its esthetic coherence and came to an end as a new interest in the emotional, the mysterious, and the individualistic began to assert itself. Three important events finally terminated the period: the death of Johnson in 1784, the outbreak of the French Revolution in 1789, and the publication of *Lyrical Ballads* in 1798.

Leading scholars now insist that there is no justification for designating these 138 years of English life and literature by the single term "neo-classicism." Rather, the attempt at classicism came in the late seventeenth century, and was followed, during the first half of the eighteenth century, by a period of common

The Great Fire of London, an engraving by Wenceslaus Hollar, in John Leake's An Exact Surveigh of the Streets contained within the Ruins of the City of London, *1669.*

The Church of St. Mary le Bow, rebuilt by Sir Christopher Wren, in the years 1670-1680.

sense. The second half of the century, finally, developed a new sensibility which eventually flowered in the romanticism of the early decades of the nineteenth century.

Literary tags are useful, but it is almost unthinkable that a century and a half of English literature could have a single common denominator. During these crucial years, England witnessed the final triumph of Parliament over King, the colossal expansion of the British Empire, and the coming of an industrial revolution which was to change the face of the landscape, expand the cities, and give a profound shock to traditional habits of thought and life. In addition, at least three generations of writers lived and wrote their serious responses to the shifting pressures of these rapidly changing conditions of life and thought; the assumptions of a Blake at the end of the period are clearly different from the assumptions of a Dryden at the beginning. It is an age which is being rediscovered, and its literature demands a critical and inductive approach.

The Restoration

The restoration of Charles II has given its name to the first of the three major divisions into which the neo-classical age falls. The generation ruled by Charles II and his immediate successors has certain qualities which differentiate it from the generations of the eighteenth century. The most conspicuous feature of the Restoration is its direct antagonism to the Puritan tradition. Charles II was at heart a Catholic and a believer in the divine right of kings, but he had learned, by the tragic death of his father and the disasters of the Civil War, to subordinate his own religious and political instincts, to leave the government largely to his ministers, and to subscribe outwardly to the Church of England. His French background—his mother was French and his exile during

An English salon, or drawing room, of the late Stuart period, 1670-1700, from the Thorne European Rooms in Miniature, by courtesy of The Art Institute of Chicago.

the days of the Commonwealth had been in France—marked him for a life of gaiety. His court in England was brilliant, dissolute, and morally rather calloused; it set correspondingly gay and dissolute standards, and was responsible for witty, sparkling, unprincipled literature. Puritanism was for the moment prostrate and powerless. Within a year or two after Charles' return, the bodies of Cromwell and of other Puritan leaders had been exhumed and exposed to public scorn; the judges who had sentenced Charles I to death were either executed or forced to flee the country. Milton, as an important Puritan official, had been pushed into retirement. The Puritans, nevertheless, while politically in eclipse, were still articulate; the two greatest works of Puritan literature, Milton's *Paradise Lost* and Bunyan's *Pilgrim's Progress,* were printed during the period of the Restoration.

The generally violent reaction against Puritanism, while it survived for some time in literature, had a briefer political life. In 1672 Charles proclaimed a general religious amnesty. But the Church of England, hitting out at its enemies—the Catholics on the one hand and the Puritans and other Protestant dissenters on the other—kept the political broth boiling, something that is easy to explain when one considers to what an extent religious faiths and political parties

were synonymous during the seventeenth century. All through the reign of Charles II, there was disquiet on the part of the people about the succession, especially when it became apparent that the King would not leave any legitimate children, and that, barring accidents, the heir apparent was Charles' brother James, Duke of York, an avowed Catholic. In consequence there were many scares, widespread political and religious incertitude, and more than a little civil bloodshed, notably in the Titus Oates anti-Catholic agitation in 1678 and the Monmouth rebellion of 1681–1685.

As if this internal strife were not enough, England was visited during the reign of Charles II by national calamities and foreign malice. In 1665 came a fearful outbreak of the bubonic plague—the worst since the days of the Black Death in the fourteenth century—and straight upon the heels of the pestilence came the Great Fire of London, which destroyed most of the older city. During this year of wonders (1665-1666), the *Annus Mirabilis* celebrated by the greatest poet of the Restoration, John Dryden (p. 458), came naval war with Holland, the unavoidable collision of two powers with colonial aspirations. The English court did not shine in the leadership of the war, and for a time London was in serious danger from the

Dutch fleet, but the traditional prowess of the English seaman finally brought the war to a moderately successful conclusion. It should be remarked that the foreign prestige of England was at a rather low ebb throughout the Restoration period.

In 1685 Charles II died and was succeeded by the Catholic James II. The Duke of Monmouth, an illegitimate son of Charles II, led a rebellion against James, but was defeated and executed, and once more England saw the melancholy spectacle of religious persecution and bloodshed. Neither James nor his religion was popular in England, and in 1688 the Protestant leaders invited to the throne Mary, the Protestant daughter of James, with her husband William of Orange, a Dutchman of much military skill and champion of the Protestants on the Continent. James II was driven into exile; the result was the "Glorious Revolution" of 1688, by which Parliament became once and for all supreme. James made at least one serious effort to regain his throne and enlisted the help of the French and Irish, but the battle of the Boyne (1690) crushed his hopes; he fled to France, where his son and grandson, the Old and Young Pretenders respectively, made life uneasy for the subsequent English rulers by their efforts to return to the English throne. The followers of James were known as Jacobites; it was not until 1746 that the Jacobite ghost was finally laid.

William and Mary were co-rulers, but William was the driving force in the administration. His reign was marked by the sharp and clear emergence of two great political parties. The Whigs represented most of the important noblemen and the rich businessmen; the Tories were made up largely of the country squires and the clergy—that is, the fundamentally conservative classes. No feature of eighteenth-century history is more clearly discernible than the violence and thoroughness of party strife; the lives of the great men of letters and of the chief thinkers of the time were made or marred as completely by the fortunes of their political associations as in the seventeenth century they had been by their religious beliefs.

Social conditions during most of the neo-classical period were, judged by present-day standards, raw and brutal. Hygiene and sanitation were as yet untouched sciences; disease and filth were always plentiful. The country squire, living in rural backwardness, would have to plan carefully for his trip up to London, for the roads were poor, at times even impassable, and always infested with highwaymen. Transportation by stagecoach was uncomfortable and laborious. Once in London, the visitor would find himself in ill-kept streets, without adequate fire or police protection; it was unsafe to travel about at night on the unlighted, thug-ridden highways and byways. The criminal, living in squalor and grime, was subject to punishment by an appallingly severe penal code; the

A dining room of the English Georgian period (1770-1790), from the Thorne European Rooms in Miniature, courtesy of The Art Institute of Chicago.

An English drawing room of the early Georgian period, c. 1735, from the Thorne European Rooms in Miniature, by courtesy of The Art Institute of Chicago.

theft of a handkerchief was thought as worthy of the death penalty as the murder of a helpless old woman or an infant in arms.

But somehow people lived on, as often as not to a ripe old age, and the nation grew and prospered. If swaggering ruffians like the "Mohawks" endangered life or limb in the streets of London at night, the citizen could well enjoy himself by day in the theater or in recreation centers like St. James' Park or Vauxhall Gardens. He could temper the strain of his business or professional affairs with the society afforded him by the many coffee or chocolate houses of London, which seem to have combined the functions of

"London's Gazette, here"

The merry milkmaid

"Knives or scissors to grind"

lunchroom, saloon, city club, and forum. Individual coffee houses were frequented generally by individual professions or political parties. So the poets and critics went to Will's, the clergy to Truby's, scholars and academicians to The Grecian, Tories to the Cocoa Tree, Whigs to St. James' Coffee House. The human instinct to retail news and gossip and to converse with one's friends found in these coffee houses a natural outlet, and developed them as instruments for enriching the art of conversation. Seldom had there been a period in history when wit and telling phrase joined hand in hand to better effect. The tendency of the coffee houses to develop cliques, while unfortunate for the cause of liberal thought, was nevertheless in keeping with the partisan spirit of the day; in that partisanship, moreover, the issues of the time were clarified. The importance of the coffee house, therefore, as an inaugurator of English journalism is immense, but in a more general way it was no less valuable as the breeding place of eighteenth-century tastes and standards.

Queen Anne and Her Successors

Queen Mary died of smallpox in 1694, and a fall from his horse killed William III in 1702 and brought to the throne his sister-in-law Anne, the second daughter of James II. Her reign is notable for many events that have left their impress upon English letters or English politics. First of all, England was obliged to face the self-seeking schemes of the son of James II, James Edward, known as the Old Pretender, who had won the support of France in his quest after the lost English throne. The political implication of this apparently simple design, and the various dynastic repercussions throughout Europe need not detain us here; but a war broke out between England and France, with various allies attaching themselves to each of the two great antagonists. This war, known as the War of the Spanish Succession, deter-

"Buy my Dutch biscuits"

"Knives, combs, or inkhorns"

"Sweep, sweep"

*This series of figures is from P. Tempest's
The Cries of London, 1711.*

mined that England was to have her own way in the settling of her royal problems; the decisive blows were the victories by the Duke of Marlborough at Blenheim in 1704 and at Ramilles in 1706. Next to be noted is the formal union of England and Scotland, which was brought about in 1707, not without considerable opposition from the Scotch, who were aided and abetted by King Louis XIV of France, still agitating for the Old Pretender. A third feature of Anne's reign was the bitter fight between Whig and Tory. The Tories, under the leadership of Harley and Boling-broke, were in power at the beginning and the end of Anne's reign; but with the death of Anne in 1714, the Whigs got control, drove out Tory officeholders, and turned the lives of men like Swift into channels other than politics.

Anne died without any heirs; her seventeen children had all died in childhood. The succession was thereby opened to controversy, but Parliament had insisted (1701) that the next monarch after Anne must be a Protestant. The only eligible candidate in 1701 was the Grand Duchess Sophia of Hanover, Germany, the aged granddaughter of King James I of England. When Anne died, two months after Sophia, Sophia's son George, a fifty-four-year-old German who could speak no English, became the king of England under the name of George I. He took no interest in the government; nor did his son George II, who reigned from 1727 to 1760. As a result, the task of governing England fell into the hands of the ministers and of Parliament; most prominent among the many gifted prime ministers of the period was Robert Walpole,

Women's Fashions, c. 1760, from Recueil des Planches, Diderot's Encyclopédie, 1762-1767.

Spinning in the Home, mid-eighteenth century, from Recueil des Planches, Diderot's Encyclopédie, 1762-1767.

A Barber Shop, mid-eighteenth century, from Recueil des Planches, Diderot's Encyclopédie, 1762-1767.

premier from 1715 to 1717 and 1721 to 1742, a hard-headed politician but none the less one of talent and ability.

In Scotland some dissatisfaction had arisen over the union with England, and the Young Pretender, son of the Old Pretender, headed a last desperate Jacobite rebellion. But "Bonnie Prince Charlie," as the Young Pretender was called, was crushed by the Duke of Cumberland at the battle of Culloden in 1746, and with him went the last active aspirations of the Stuarts. Thenceforth it was the house of Hanover (changed during the World War of 1914 to the house of Windsor) that was to rule England, by the grace of Parliament and the English people.

On the whole, this period of the triumph of neoclassicism, called sometimes the Queen Anne period or the Augustan age (on the analogy of the golden age of Roman letters, when Vergil, Ovid, and Horace flourished under the patronage of the Emperor Augustus), was fairly settled and undisturbed. The government fell more and more into the hands of the country gentry, who spoke through their representatives in Parliament; the population as a whole appeared to have become a little more observant of their social maladjustments than had previous generations, though very little effort was made to relieve unfavorable conditions. The country as a whole was prosperous, in spite of the disastrous South Sea Bubble panic in 1720. By 1713 England had gained control of the seas. The people were conservatively disposed to the point of complacence.

The Transition to Revolution

After 1740 came various intermittent wars. The most significant were the Seven Years' War (1756–1763), by which England wrested Canada from France, and the expeditions of Clive in India (1756–1760), the importance of which, from the standpoint of the British Empire, was incalculable. George III, who came to the throne in 1760, showed a greater disposition to have a say in the ruling of his country than had his predecessors, but he was a poor statesman. Moreover, the colonial theory of the time, which presupposed that all colonies existed for the good of the mother country, combined with the natural conservatism of the age, irritated the American colonists, and the result was the outbreak of the American Revolution (1776–1783). The complacence of the eighteenth-century Briton was rudely disturbed; he realized that new ideas were in the air— ideas of the equality of man, of the rights of man to what the American Declaration of Independence so aptly phrases as "life, liberty, and the pursuit of happiness." Almost before he was aware, the Englishman of Queen Anne vintage, the apostle of conven-

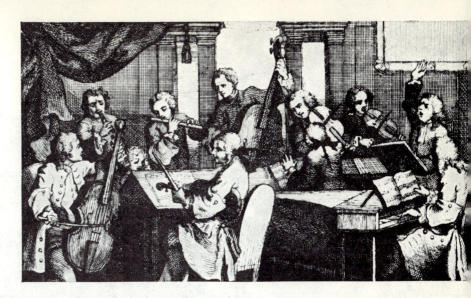

A concert ticket designed by William Hogarth.

tion and realism, had to yield to the young, urgent forces of revolt and romanticism. The year 1776, the time of the American Declaration of Independence, and the year 1789, when the French Revolution broke out, are milestones in human history. The former, because of the constructive possibilities of the Declaration of Independence, is perhaps the more significant. Some other important "revolutionary" dates are 1764, when Hargreaves invented the spinning jenny, and 1769 when James Watt patented the steam engine. But the real effect of these four dates cannot be seen appreciably until the beginning of the next century; but it is obvious that the years from 1750 on were a period of transition to a new order; and nowhere is the transitional nature of the era more apparent than in the literature produced between 1745 and 1780.

The Mold of Neo-Classical Literature

The neo-classical age, in its first stages from 1660 to 1700, stands historically and philosophically as the enemy of Puritanism. The Puritan had been at heart the foe of the Renaissance. It should not be difficult, therefore, to find much in common between the Renaissance and the neo-classical period. As a matter of fact, the neo-classical period is in many ways a continuation of the Renaissance tradition; there are in both periods the same fundamental worldliness, the same worship of classical antiquity, the same intellectual curiosity and inventiveness, the same skepticism. In the individualism of a Machiavelli or a Henry VIII can be seen the independence that characterized the great French philosopher and mathematician Descartes (1596–1650), whose *cogito ergo*

sum ("I think, therefore I exist") is perhaps the fountainhead of all the ideas to be associated with the neo-classical age. Bacon (p. 317), the founder of modern inductive thought, stands behind the whole scientific trend of the seventeenth century, which led in 1662 to the founding of the Royal Society, still the most selective and sought after scientific association of modern times. The Renaissance applauded ingenuity and artful contrivance in poetry; neo-classicism cherished the ideal of perfection of poetic form. The Renaissance was interested in humanity active and alive, particularly among the common people, even of the underworld; the neo-classical age had the power to observe common man, although objectively and rather abstractly.

The differences between the Renaissance and the neo-classical world are equally striking. The Renaissance was an era of enthusiastic expansion, pushing back intellectual and geographical horizons; the neo-classical age was an era of intense concentration, in which man tried to come to terms with the new knowledge he had gained and to give it some kind of order. Out of a desire for order comes a respect for rules, but it would be a mistake to assume that this period succumbed in all areas to a mechanical application of a few strict, accepted rules. From first to last—that is, from John Dryden to Samuel Johnson—there was very clearly a struggle of the best minds of the age to find a sensible accommodation of vigorous native genius and literary propriety. In fact, neo-classicism was rooted in the Renaissance, in the theory and practice of such writers as Ben Jonson. And if the writers of the neo-classical period seem to have sacrificed some of the lyrical spontaneity of the Renaissance, it should be remembered that at the same time they managed to create a profound and polished literature of statement.

The Wren additions to Hampton Court Palace, late seventeenth century.

Respect for convention is very often cited as a characteristic of the neo-classical period. But it should be kept in mind that this convenient handle is valid only if the word "convention" is used with great discrimination. The beribboned and periwigged fashions of society during the Restoration and Augustan days, the punctilious attention to etiquette and good breeding, as in Chesterfield's *Letters* to his son, the well-worn grooves in which city life moved, all so brilliantly described in Pope's *Rape of the Lock* (p. 539), or in Gay's *Trivia*, or in the lighter "society verse" of Matthew Prior (1664–1721)—such manifestations of convention are distinctive enough in their way, but they are not fundamental. The real character of the neo-classical period is to be found in the nature of its art and literature. Here the conventions are rather arbitrary, primarily as a result of the great impact of the Renaissance. The Renaissance had worshiped the genius of the Greek philosopher and scholar Aristotle (384–322 B.C.), whose *Poetics* was for generations without a rival as an authority on literary standards. Derived from this work is the requirement of orderliness, of the three unities in drama—the unity of time, according to which the action of a play should cover not more than a day; the unity of place, which decreed that the scene of a play should take place in one given locality; and, most carefully observed of all, the unity of action, according to which a play should be of one type only, wholly comic or wholly tragic, and should have only one plot. These unities afford a good example of classical rule in literature. The English writers paid less attention than the French did to these unities as a whole, but were likely to insist upon unity of action. More important, however, than any single rule of classical criticism was the creation of a definite spirit in literature through the massed weight of classical tradition, with its sharp critical sense, its intelligence, its bent toward a lofty purpose, its dignity, its love of moderation, and its search after the golden mean—what Pope expressed so admirably in his injunction:

Be not the first by whom the new are tried,
Nor yet the last to lay the old aside.

Such qualities the neo-classical period tried to imitate. But it should be remembered that strict neo-classicism ended with Dryden and that minor figures tend to exhibit the characteristics of a period in gross, unrefined form. Thus, Aristotle's influence was fading by the time of Queen Anne, and men of common sense like Swift and Johnson condemned slavish imitation of classical models. The classical bent, as found in Homer and Vergil, could lead to the effusions of poetasters but also to such a masterpiece as Pope's *Essay on Man* (p. 548). The sense of dignity and decorum in the Greek dramatists or the Latin poet Horace gave the literature of the age a love for the resounding word and the elegant phrase. The tendency was summarized in Johnson's dictum that the business of a poet was to present the general rather than the specific. A characteristic of neo-classical poetic style was to use an adjective of rather vague descriptive powers to qualify an equally general noun, the combined adjective and substantive taking the place of a single concrete word. This, the well-known "epithet" mannerism, resulted in such occasional monstrosities as "finny tribe" for "fish," "leveled tube" for "gun," and "plumy band" for "birds." Even when used with discrimination and taste, these circumlocutions become a striking and unmistakable peculiarity.

Moreover, since dignity can never be achieved without smoothness and finish, the neo-classical poets favored a sonorous and neatly rounded verse form, the heroic, or closed, couplet. This couplet consisted of two riming lines of iambic pentameter verse. The second line of the couplet completed the thought; hence the expression "closed couplet." Of course iambic pentameter couplets were not new; Chaucer had employed them in *The Canterbury Tales* (p. 104) during the fourteenth century; they had been used by Elizabethan poets like Ben Jonson (p. 342) and by his imitators in the seventeenth century. Two of these, John Denham (1615–1669) in his landscape poem *Cooper's Hill* (1642) and Edmund Waller (1606–1687) in his *Poems* of 1645, had made notable use of the form and had done a great deal to popularize it. The second line in the couplets of all these poets, however, did not necessarily complete the thought, but with Denham and Waller the proportion of closed couplets definitely increased. Later the form appeared in the "heroic" plays of Dryden and Otway, whence the name "heroic couplet." By this time the couplet was normally closed, according to the tradition of the French neo-classical writers, among whom Boileau (1636–1711) was the literary arbiter. His *L'Art Poétique* (1674) and Pope's *Essay on Criticism* (p. 533), both stemming from such works as Horace's *Ars Poetica,* and both excellent summations of neo-classical literary standards, should be consulted by every student of the neo-classical period.

The heroic couplet, sharply closed at the end of the second line, was the favorite poetic instrument of the satirists of the time. It satisfied their predilection for symmetry and balance; it provided an effective vehicle for expressing critical insights; it gave them a constant upon which to work poetic variations. The heroic couplet invites rapid reading, but few readers are sufficiently sensitized to its subtle combinations of sound and sense to be able to read it rapidly and well. As a matter of fact, it provides a dominant rhythm against which to measure a marvelous variety of alliteration and assonance, balance and antithesis, pause and forward movement. The heroic couplet furnishes an organic filament tying the poetry of Dryden to the poetry of Johnson. Not until the nineteenth century, with the rise of the romantic movement, did it come to yield its dominance to blank verse.

A Gentleman of the Court (late seventeenth century), from a print by J. Bonnard.

A Lady of Fashion (late seventeenth century), from a print by J. D. de St. Jean.

Such standards of symmetry, balance, grace, and order having been duly established during the second half of the seventeenth century, they persisted as a significant measure of achievement in art—not only literature but music and architecture as well—throughout the eighteenth century. They were touchstones, not of slavish and mechanical imitation—except perhaps among the minor figures—but of informal judgment and practice. Alexander Pope, in dealing with the practice of literature and criticism, put the matter well:

You, then, whose judgment the right course would steer
Know well each ancient's proper character;
His fable, subject, scope in every page;
Religion, country, genius of his age:
Without all these at once before your eyes,
Cavil you may, but never criticise.
Be Homer's works your study and delight,
Read them by day, and meditate by night;
Thence form your judgment, thence your maxims bring,
And trace the Muses upward to their spring.
Still with itself compared, his text peruse;
And let your comment be the Mantuan Muse . . .
Learn hence for ancient rules a just esteem;
To copy nature is to copy them. . . .
—*Essay on Criticism*, I, 118 ff.

From all of this it should be clear that the "proportion just and due" of all great art—the golden moderation of a Horace, for example—was distinctly a contribution by the great ancients. Furthermore, the analysis of life, particularly the sophisticated city life of Athens or Rome, had been, in the hands of an Aristophanes, a Persius, or a Juvenal, an aggressive manifestation of the critical spirit applied to society; this, too, the neo-classical poet attempted, often with brilliant success, as in *The Rape of the Lock*. Indeed, criticism of life was the greatest inspiration of the writers of the time.

Such a critical attitude, of course, implies a restraint of emotion under the disciplining hands of reason. And so one returns again to the statement of Descartes: "I think, therefore I exist." Man is great because he is a rational being; his continued existence depends upon that selfsame characteristic. Once having accepted the Cartesian doctrine, the writers of the high neo-classical period and, more flexibly, their successors in the eighteenth century devoted their best talent to a literature of critical statement in both poetry and prose.

It is still fair to say that the writers of this period were chary of the caprice, eccentricity, and logical chaos to which undisciplined emotion could lead and that they endorsed a reasonable, orderly, realistic approach to life and letters. On the other hand, it is misleading to continue to accept and repeat, out of context, Matthew Arnold's famous statement that the age of Dryden and Pope was a "prosaic" age. The prose of the journalists, diarists, essayists, and novelists of the period was impressive—supple, direct, and excellent; but the poetry was impressive too. The lyric impulse may have waned, but the poetry was, given the intellectual currents of the age, what eighteenth-century poets had to write if, indeed, they were to write poetry at all.

Beside Descartes' "I think, therefore I exist" should be placed a quotation from another great seventeenth-century philosopher. John Locke (1632–1704) preached in his *Essay Concerning Human Understanding* (1690) that truth was to be found "in the contemplation of things themselves." The reason, if turned into literary channels, will come sooner or later to realism, "the contemplation of things" as they are. So it was with the neo-classical writers, who never let their imagination carry them far beyond the realm of probability or verisimilitude; even such a towering achievement of the imagination as Swift's *Gulliver's Travels* (p. 500) exhales a sober air of truth that envelops completely its passionate protest against the evils of the universe. As this mood of realism deepens, the writers give us the sights and smells of everyday London, at first consciously, as in the *Diary* of Samuel Pepys (p. 443); painstakingly and profusely in the work of Daniel Defoe; and then with unfailing truthfulness in the novels of Fielding or Smollett, the glittering measures of Pope, the savage outpourings of Swift, or, in pictorial art, the cruel portraitures of Hogarth.

The net impression left by neo-classical literature is, therefore, one of the realistic wedded to the rational. By temperament it is immensely conservative; whatever the political party governing England, the articulate thinking men were, in the main, Tories. Their outlook on religion is a good case in point. Once the Revolution of 1688 had been settled, the people as a group sank into a comfortable acceptance of the Church of England or of a Puritan creed, but with not too great a zeal for the literal belief in a personal God. Particularly did they abhor in religion the quality of enthusiasm; the very word "enthusiasm" was a reproach, for it indicated to them a silly, emotional, frenzied type of faith. Instead, as a group—actuated by their assured rationalism— they drifted into a belief in an impersonal creating principle that governs all; to this principle they gave the name "God," but a more accurate name would be "originator of natural law." According to this belief, which was called deism, mankind is the creation of an all-powerful God, not anthropomorphic, but the inaugurator of natural laws. In the face of this God the world, including mankind, is completely impotent and can only acquiesce in the realization that God is good, God is great, and God is plenteous in his nature—in fact, all-inclusive, so that further divinity would not be possible, and less divinity would be equally unthinkable. The most ardent neo-classical philosopher, the German Gottfried Leibnitz (1646–1716), came to the conclusion that this was the best of all possible worlds. There were some, notably Jonathan Swift and the Frenchman Voltaire (1694–1778), who disagreed violently with Leibnitz' thesis, but the general opinion of neo-classical thinkers favored Leibniz, and even the famous "Whatever is, is right" of Pope's *Essay on Man* was taken out of context and used in support of this thesis. This philosophy proved to be unsuitable for the more emotional age of the romantic movement which followed, but in the eighteenth century it seemed to find general acceptance among the educated.

The Literature of the Restoration

(1660-1700)

To return for the moment to the first period of the neo-classical age, perhaps the first trait of Restoration literature to strike the casual reader is its anti-Puritan tone. The two most spectacular types of literature produced in this age—the drama and the satire—were encouraged by the court of Charles II. The reckless worldlings surrounding the king "who never said a foolish thing and never did a wise one" were the indispensable patrons of nearly all the important literature written during the Restoration; all plays, and most of the nondramatic poetry and prose between 1660 and 1700, were composed with the aristocratic audience in mind; the tastes of the court, dissolute, gay, unprincipled, and cynically witty, gave the period its peculiar color and largely created the bad moral repute into which the generation fell. In short, Restoration literature represents a violent reaction against Puritanism and is consequently more highly tinted than the literature of the more settled days of thoroughgoing neo-classicism; and yet it is possible to find all the basic strands of neo-classicism in those brilliant and colorful early decades.

The Puritans had closed the theaters in 1642, but not without some profit to all concerned, for the fashions of Elizabethan playwriting had degenerated into cheap melodrama and lurid sensationalism. Plays, masques, and various stage entertainments, such as humorous playlets or "drolls" were performed surreptitiously during the Commonwealth, but the first play sanctioned after the closing of the theaters was Sir William Davenant's *The Siege of Rhodes* (1656), an attempt at opera, a type which was popular throughout the Restoration. Immediately after the Restoration two companies were licensed in London

A doorway in Berkeley Square.

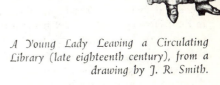

A Young Lady Leaving a Circulating Library (late eighteenth century), from a drawing by J. R. Smith.

—the Duke of York's company under the leadership of Davenant in 1661, and the King's company in 1663. These troupes played revivals of Elizabethan plays, operas, and the characteristic types of Restoration drama: the heroic play, the classical tragedy, and the comedy of manners.

The heroic play had for its aim the portrayal on a heroic scale of conflicts in love and mighty deeds. It was a rather short-lived type and has little interest for the modern reader. Its obvious shortcomings were its bombast and rant, its utter lack of reality, its wordiness, its overcomplication of plot, and its extravagantly exotic atmosphere. On the other hand, its roots were in the plays of Corneille and Racine, it was spectacular and gaudy, and the Restoration applauded it mightily. Samuel Pepys, whose judgments on Elizabethan plays were almost uniformly unfavorable, was delighted by such a play as Dryden's *Indian Queen* (1664), the scene of which was Peru and Mexico in the days of the Conquistadors. The type, however, never recovered from the brilliant burlesque directed against it in *The Rehearsal* (1671), written by the irrepressible George Villiers, Duke of Buckingham, assisted by some other wits, including Samuel Butler.

An heir of the heroic play was the Restoration tragedy. Some tragedies, in fact, had been written by Dryden during the heyday of the heroic play. The classical tragedy had greater realism than the heroic play, and it tended to depart from the riming couplets of the heroic play and adopt the blank verse of the great Elizabethan tragedies. But the neo-classical ideal of dignity frowned upon the inclusion of comic scenes, as in the tragedies of Shakespeare; and the neo-classical unities demanded a greater integration of plot, so that one must look hard to find in a Restoration tragedy a subplot like that in *King Lear*. *All for Love* (1678), Dryden's version of the story of Antony and Cleopatra and his finest play, is also the best example of Restoration tragedy. Next to Dryden in the writing of tragedies comes Thomas Otway (1652–1685), whose plays, notably *Venice Preserved* (1682), are characterized by a searching pathos, not only moving in itself, but interesting as a symptom of the approach of the sentimental, which came to be the bane of the drama after 1700. Less successful was Nathaniel Lee (1653–1692), who frittered away often splendid material, as in *The Rival Queens* (1677), with his incurable rant and frenzied action.

On the whole, Restoration tragedy showed that the grand manner of the Elizabethans had been lost in the course of fifty years. When, on the other hand, one turns to Restoration comedy, one can realize how definitely this type of play was suited to the Restoration temperament, for no period in subsequent English dramatic history has produced such a brilliant series of comedies of manners. The brilliance is of a hard, unfeeling sort, but it nevertheless scintillates in its bold realism, its easy rapier-like dialogue, and its swaggering pace. The ultimate ancestor of Restoration comedy is the "comedy of humors" that Ben Jonson had made famous a half-century before; there is the same tendency to caricature, the same labeling of characters by appropriate surnames, the same inclination to parade those characters over the stage and thereby achieve a series of striking though loosely connected scenes. One should not inquire too closely into the niceties of plot in the Restoration comedies. The action is often rather confused, and the structure of the play is often incoherent. Consequently they make difficult reading as a whole, but go well on the stage—thereby passing the ultimate test of a successful play.

The best writers of Restoration comedy were Sir George Etherege (1634?–1691), William Wycherley (1640–1716), William Congreve (1670–1729), George Farquhar (1678–1707), and Sir John Vanbrugh (1664–

1726). Each of these men has his own peculiarities: "Gentle George" Etherege has the lightest touch; "Brawney" Wycherley is the deepest cutting satirist in the group; William Congreve is the most skilled dramatic technician and the greatest wit; George Farquhar has the best sense of the theater and deals more with the middle class than the aristocracy; and Sir John Vanbrugh—"Honest Van"—inclines rather to farce than to comedy of manners. But all aim at brilliant witty satire of fashionable folly. Their stage is filled with coxcombs, coquettes, men about town, dupes, and fools; their plots are all intrigues; and they are all more or less bawdy in their fun.

From the standpoint of the Puritans, the great middle class, who in their political subjection looked on with a sense of outrage at the freedom of the Restoration stage, the plays of Wycherley or Congreve appeared scandalously immoral. With the inevitable reaction against the excesses of the Restoration came a revulsion against the type of plays being shown. The loudest opening gun in this revolt came in 1698, when Jeremy Collier, a nonjuring clergyman of the period, published his *Short View of the Immorality and Profaneness of the English Stage*. Collier's work is unfair in many ways and silly in others, but it has a case and presents it effectively. It names plays and authors in its accusation and concludes that "nothing has gone further in debauching the age than the stage poets and playhouse." The question raged for a quarter of a century later, but even the plays of Farquhar, coming a bare decade after Collier's blast, have a somewhat greater regard for conventions of morality. The old carelessness of Restoration comedy was being checked; the Restoration itself was coming to a close.

A much more reliable mirror of the irresponsible, carefree life of the Restoration is the incomparable *Diary* of Samuel Pepys (1633–1703). Running from 1660 to 1669, it is a superb picturing of Restoration London, given through the informal and secret jottings of a man who was connected with the admiralty and later one of the most influential men in the government. The theater, St. James' Park, the gossip of the court, the involved, amusing, and pathetic domestic affairs of Samuel Pepys himself, the Great Fire, the plague, the Dutch War, summer days in the country near Cambridge—all are there. Pepys' *Diary* is unique as a personal journal, but there were other diarists, like John Evelyn, and keepers of journals and letter writers extraordinary—all the manifestations of a discursively realistic age.

There were scientific stirrings in this age; the spirit of Francis Bacon lived again. The Royal Society was established in 1662; the grand figure of Sir Isaac Newton (1642–1727) emerges, in his *Principia* (1687), to fix our present-day conceptions of the universe. Most influential in the philosophical literature of the

An Assembly at the Pantheon in the Oxford Road, 1772; from a mezzotint by Richard Earlom after Charles Brandoin.

A Belle, from F. Rivelon, The Rudiments of Genteel Behaviour, *1737.*

day was Locke's *Essay Concerning Human Understanding*, already mentioned. But the dominant figure in the literature of the Restoration, one who entered every field but the scientific and strictly philosophical is that of John Dryden, playwright, poet, satirist, and critic, whose significance is appraised in the headnote to the selections from his work (p. 458). It is impossible to enjoy the neo-classical period without first enjoying Dryden. But he lived in the seventeenth century, and he belongs to the early formative days of the neo-classical period, partaking of their violence and color alike. When he died in 1700, the Restoration had really come to an end.

The Literature of Common Sense

(1700-1745)

The chief figures of English literature from the death of Dryden to the death of Johnson (1784), with the exception of the major novelists and the distin-

guished playwrights Richard Brinsley Sheridan and John Gay, are appraised in the headnotes to the selections from their works in this chapter: Daniel Defoe, Richard Steele and Joseph Addison, Jonathan Swift, Alexander Pope, Samuel Johnson, and Oliver Goldsmith. These appraisals need not be repeated here since they will confront the student in due course. However, a few words on the general character of the first half of the eighteenth century are necessary.

Two important influences of the Restoration did not long survive the turn of the century: the dominance of the Tory Party and the anti-Puritanism which had so significantly controlled the tone of Restoration literature. With the death of Queen Anne, control of the government fell into the hands of the Whigs, who dominated the political scene throughout the rest of the period. And the pamphlet which Jeremy Collier

The Cockpit, by William Hogarth.

had published in 1698 against the Restoration theater, the rebuke which the great Dryden had accepted and which Congreve had but feebly answered, was the first clear indication that the Puritan influence had begun to reassert itself. It had not found its proper leader: John Wesley's Moravian conversion did not come until the 1730's, but a climate was emerging which would enable Wesley's voice to be heard and his influence felt.

In other words, the middle class was becoming uppermost in English life, a class that was growing both large and literate. As the era of the bourgeoisie waxed, the era of the royal patron waned, and the pence of the people began to exert a subtle influence on literature. It became gradually more moral, inevitably more sentimental. Vanbrugh's Lord Foppington was soon to give way to Lillo's George Barnwell, apprentice, and to Fielding's Tom Jones, foundling.

The populace demanded a popular press, and the writers provided it. Thus the periodical, which had begun with news journals like Sir Roger L'Estrange's *Observator* (1681-1687) and newspapers like Henry Muddiman's *London Gazette* (first published as the *Oxford Gazette,* 1665), flourished into Defoe's *Review* (1704); *The Daily Courant* (1702), the first daily journal; *The Tatler* (1709) and *Spectator* (1711) of Addison and Steele; climaxing in *The Gentleman's*

Magazine (1731), credited as the first English magazine in the modern sense. This period, then, deserves full credit for expanding and bringing to a high point of perfection not only the essay itself but also the gathering together of literary material for regular publication to make a periodical.

The periodicals informed, entertained, and instructed. They strove not only to amuse their readers, but also to edify them. But the real literary flower of the period was a moral criticism far more profound than that which came from either the press or the pulpit, for it was the glory of Augustan literature to possess two of the deepest and most dedicated moralists in English: Alexander Pope and Jonathan Swift. And it was through them that the period won its title of the "Age of Common Sense." Each wore a savage mask; each carried the satiric mode to its genuine extremes. The one a disenfranchised Catholic, the other an expatriated Anglican clergyman, they devoted their genius to the colossal effort of urging the world to see things as they in fact are. Pope has been accused of saying, superficially, "Whatever is, is right"; Swift has been accused, with equal superficiality, of saying "Whatever is, is wrong." Both were supremely educated men, and they used a technique of shock which, in their judgments, the times required. But both, rightly read, will be found to have negotiated between the extremes of eccentricity and torpor, speculative reason and dullness, unregulated optimism and despair.

The Literature of Sensibility (1745-1798)

The years from the death of Pope (1744) and Swift (1745) to the publication of *Lyrical Ballads* (1798) have not yet earned for themselves designation as a specific period or age. They are sometimes referred to as the Age of Johnson, but this is only for convenience and is really a misnomer. Johnson towered above the period, but he did not direct its sensibility. He had taken his particular bent before the new period began, and he stands in it like a latter-day giant of common sense. Efforts to characterize these years as a reaction against Augustanism have, as many critics have often pointed out, produced few useful insights: such efforts require making of Augustanism an impossible straw man. Since it was, spiritually, the age, not of Johnson, but of Collins, Young, Christopher Smart, Chatterton, Cowper, Crabbe, Macpherson, Blake, and Burns, the term "pre-romantic" is most commonly used to describe its literary character. A stimulating dissenter from the implications of this point of view—for example, that the "pre-romantics" knew that the Romantic movement was going to succeed them—is Professor Northrop Frye. Professor Frye sees the individually distinctive character of this period as resting on a Longinian, psychological (as distinct from an Aristotelian, esthetic) view of literature. In this view, literature is a process, not a product. In the novel, this view is perfected by Laurence Sterne: "here we are not being led into a story, but into the process of writing a story: we wonder, not what is coming next, but what the author will think of next." In poetry, "the qualities of subconscious association take the lead, and the poetry becomes hypnotically repetitive, oracular, incantatory, dreamlike and in the original sense of the word charming." Fear and pity are present, but not in the Aristotelian sense, for they are without object. Fear without an object is "anxiety," and it lies behind and motivates the Ossian poet, the graveyard poets, the Gothic-horror novelists, and the writers of tragic ballads. Pity without an object "expresses itself as an imaginative animism":

At one end of its range is the apocalyptic exultation of all nature bursting into human life that we have in Smart's *Song to David* and the ninth Night of *The Four Zoas*. Next comes an imaginative sympathy with the kind of folklore that peoples the countryside with elemental spirits, such as we have in Collins, Fergusson, Burns and the Wartons. Next we have the curiously intense awareness of the animal world which (except for some poems of D. H. Lawrence) is unrivalled in this period, and is expressed in some of its best realized writing: in Burns' *To a Mouse*, in Cowper's exquisite snail poem, in Smart's superb lines on his cat Geoffrey, in the famous starling and ass episodes in Sterne, in the opening of Blake's *Auguries of Innocence*. Finally comes the sense of sympathy with man himself, the sense that no one can afford to be indifferent to the fate of anyone else, which underlies the protests against slavery and misery in Cowper, in Crabbe and in Blake's *Songs of Experience*.

This view of the period, whether called pre-romanticism or an age of sensibility, deserves very special attention for several reasons. First, it gives to the period its own center of gravity. Second, it shows the *literary* result of the waning of the Aristotelian influence which has already been remarked upon. Third, it makes clear the differences between the poetry of this period and the poetry of rational, objective statement. Finally, it was with an attack upon sensibility and a return to Aristotle that the Victorians tried to correct their romantic inheritance.

On a more factual, external level, the second half of the eighteenth century witnessed the rise of a new poetry of melancholy—whether of the "graveyard school" as exemplified by Edward Young's *The Complaint: or Night Thoughts on Life, Death, and Immortality* (1742-1746) or of the Penseroso kind (after Milton's prototype) as seen in William Collins' *Ode to Evening* (1747) and Thomas Gray's *Elegy Written in a Country Churchyard* (1750). Concomitant and sympathetic with this new melancholy was an intensified interest in medieval architecture and literature. The former expressed itself in a revival of Gothic-style architecture, the most famous example being Horace Walpole's "little Gothic castle," Strawberry Hill. The most significant medieval literary form to attract wide attention, especially in light of later literary developments, was the ballad, legitimately in Thomas Percy's *Reliques of Ancient English Poetry* (1765) and fraudulently in Thomas Chatterton's "Rowley poems" and James Macpherson's "Ossian poems." The gradual decay of the neoclassic ideals of balance, simplicity, and order was further signaled in the 1750's and 1760's by a lively appreciation of Chinese art and architecture. Finally, through the efforts of such writers as William Collins and Joseph Warton (1722-1800), the poetry of statement began to yield to the poetry of spontaneity, and a new age of lyricism was about to be born.

The Beginnings of the English Novel

Before turning directly to the new kind of literature rising while that of the neo-classical age was declin-

A traffic snarl in a country town at the time of a race—a light traveling coach, a phaeton, and a stagecoach; a colored etching by V. Green after W. Mason, 1789.

ing, one must consider briefly a very important contribution made by that neo-classical age—the modern novel. To define a novel is almost as futile as to define poetry. Most people, however, would agree that a novel is a fictitious narrative having a closely knit plot of some intricacy and characters that approach human reality. It has epic length and scope, but also a definite unity of effect. The plot may be subordinated to the characters (or the characters to the plot), but there is usually some kind of narrative action; and even if the limits of space and time covered are small, the novel has a sweep or a sense of bigness that differentiates it from a tale or a short story.

The modern novel had innumerable ancestors, but it did not really emerge as a well-defined literary form until the eighteenth century. Defoe's *Robinson Crusoe* (1719), sometimes considered the first English novel, is still a classic tale of adventure. This he followed with several other narratives, all about the adventures of some historical or quasi-historical per-

son. Among them *Moll Flanders* (1722) was his most successful.

After Defoe's work came a series of novels from the pens of four gifted men who not only constructed good complex plots, but also created convincing characters and variety of incident. The first is Samuel Richardson (1689-1761), whose *Pamela, or Virtue Rewarded* (1740), *Clarissa Harlowe* (1748), and *Sir Charles Grandison* (1753) gave body and spirit to the novel of characters, and in spite of their leisurely tempo, their effeminacy, and their occasional lapses into sentimentality, did succeed in creating plausible human beings and in reflecting domestic and social manners. Henry Fielding (1707-1754), satirical playwright, journalist, and later justice of the peace, turned to fiction because to him Richardson's morality seemed shallow, overconventional, and commonplace. His *History and Adventures of Joseph Andrews* (1742) began as a burlesque of Richardson's *Pamela*, but it turned out to be a fine comic novel in its own right. An exhilarating humor was Fielding's greatest asset, and *Tom Jones* (1749) is generally considered his masterpiece and one of the greatest novels of all time. It is a picaresque narrative, discursive, but amusing, with an admirably constructed plot, realistic characters, and a wholesome, unsentimentalized philosophy. Fielding is the first to bring character and plot into something resembling equipoise; he clearly broadened the scope of the novel. Tobias Smollett (1721-1771), the third of this group of eighteenth-century novelists, was a harsher critic of humanity. But he continued what Fielding had begun, wrote about the sea and sailors, and created a masterpiece in *Humphry Clinker* (1771). While Richardson, Fielding, and Smollett reflected and interpreted contemporary morals and customs, the last of a group of four, Laurence Sterne (1713-1768) was a novelist of personal eccentricity. His only lengthy work, *The Life and Opinions of Tristram Shandy, Gent.* (9 volumes, 1760-1767) is a miscellany of narrative and reflections of the most whimsical and erratic nature. After the passing of Sterne and Smollett, the novel was affected by a growing sentimentality and an interest in romantic settings, themes, and episodes.

The Ultimate Contribution of the Neo-Classical Age

Between the Renaissance and the neo-classical era events had occurred that considerably altered the English scene. The power of government had shifted from king to Parliament; there had been a thrusting up of middle-class psychology and social ideals; there had developed, also, a markedly greater freedom of thought and scientific advance. But there are many similarities between the Renaissance and the neo-classical age. Together with the brave new age of discovery and the Puritan interlude, the period that produced Dryden, Pope, Swift, Fielding, and Johnson goes to make up the first of the two great historical subdivisions of modern English civilization. A startling new age of social and industrial upheaval was to follow—our present age, in which can be seen various stages: the romantic age, the Victorian era, the periods before and after the World War of 1914. The pattern of this new age, for all its crazy designs, has developed steadily since the coming of the industrial revolution about 1770—a bold contrast to the mannered, orderly scheme of the eighteenth century.

The rotunda at Ranelagh Gardens, from a contemporary print. This building was erected for concerts and became a resort for the fashionable society of the time.

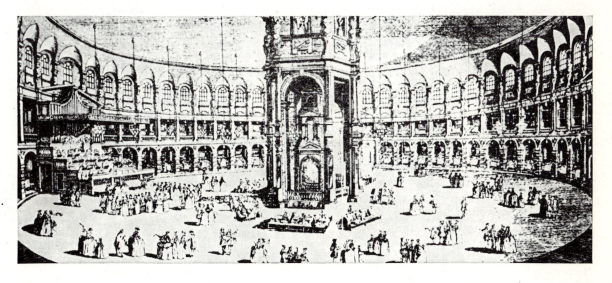

SAMUEL BUTLER 1612-1680

The son of a small farmer of Worcestershire, Samuel Butler was educated in the cathedral school of Worcester and later gained knowledge of law and legal terms while serving in the offices of county magistrates. At the age of seventeen he entered the service of the Countess of Kent, in whose home he had the advantages of an extensive library. Later he lived at Cople Hoo, Bedfordshire, with Sir Samuel Luke, who was a colonel in Cromwell's army and a fanatical Presbyterian. What Butler's function was in Sir Samuel's household is unknown, and how one of Butler's undoubted Royalist tendencies came into the employ of such a Puritan as Sir Samuel is equally obscure. But at Cople Hoo, frequently the open resort of Puritans and politicians who came there for prayer and counsel, Butler had opportunity to observe the actions and the characters of men responsible for the revolution then going on in the country. During 1661 Butler held an appointment as steward of Ludlow Castle but resigned apparently in expectation of a dowry from the rich woman he may have married about that time. Her fortune, however, was afterwards dissipated. Probably because he would not accept any but substantial preferments, Butler suffered many disappointments. His satirical jibes, moreover, the result of an ardent and rather irritable temperament, made him many enemies. He is said to have died in want.

Butler's writings represent the revolt against Puritanism. Chief of these writings is Hudibras, a mock-heroic poem ridiculing the absurd notions and practices of religious sects that were opposed to the monarchy at the time of the Restoration. In the material, in the setting, and in the method of Hudibras Butler shows familiarity with the work of Paul Scarron (1610-1660), a French satirical poet, and with the greatest of all burlesques upon the medieval romance, the Don Quixote of the Spaniard Cervantes (1547-1616). The name of the hero of Hudibras is derived from Spenser's Faerie Queene, II, 2, 17:

> He that made love unto the eldest dame
> Was hight Sir Hudibras, an hardy man,
> Yet not so good of deeds as great of name,
> Which he by many rash adventures wan.

In the poem Butler employs the conventions of chivalric romance; he describes the qualifications and accomplishments of the Puritan knight in great detail, but in a vein of satirical exaggeration. Hudibras' beggarly accoutrements, and those of his squire Ralpho, as they set out on their mission to suppress bear baiting and other popular amusements of the Royalists, are meant to excite contempt for the boastful pretensions of Presbyterians and Independents, the two extremes of the Puritan party. The effects desired are secured by Butler in brilliant fashion by a lively display of sparkling wit, an infinite variety of mock erudition, and the most appropriate use of sprightly short couplets and whimsical rhymes.

The poem was not printed until 1663, when it had become safe to publish anti-Puritan matter. King Charles II rewarded the author with a gift of three hundred pounds and constantly quoted the book, a copy of which he habitually carried in his pocket. Two additional parts were subsequently published in 1664 and 1678, but the poem was not finished. No less than twenty-seven imitations and many spurious versions of Hudibras appeared within a century.

---

from HUDIBRAS

THE ARGUMENT

Sir Hudibras his passing worth,
The manner how he sallied forth,
His arms and equipage, are shown;
His horse's virtues and his own.
Th' adventure of the bear and fiddle
Is sung, but breaks off in the middle.

from PART I, CANTO 1

When civil fury first grew high,
And men fell out, they knew not why;

---

1. **civil fury,** the Civil War in England which established the Commonwealth in 1649. 9. **gospel-trumpeter,** a nonconformist minister. 10. **long-eared rout,** the Puritans, who in church put their hands behind their ears under pretense of hearing the sermon better. The suggested resemblance to a jackass is obvious. 14. **a colonelling,** acting like a colonel. The allusion is to the behavior of the Roundhead army during the early days of the Civil War when there was a lack of centralized generalship, but plenty of warlike activity under Colonel This or Colonel That. 19-20. **blow . . . shoulder-blade.** He submitted only to the king's blow that made him a knight. 22. **chartel,** a written message concerning the terms of a duel. 23. **Great . . . bench, etc.** Butler means to satirize Hudibras not only as a man of war but as a man of peace. 24. **bind o'er as swaddle.** To swaddle is to beat, to cudgel, or to drab. In other words, the knight as a Justice of the Peace in his county could bind over for the Assizes; as a Colonel, he could lay about with his cudgel. 38. **Montaigne . . . cat.** Michel de

When hard words, jealousies, and fears
Set folks together by the ears,
And made them fight, like mad or drunk,
For Dame Religion as for punk;
Whose honesty they all durst swear for,
Though not a man of them know wherefore;
When gospel-trumpeter, surrounded
10 With long-eared rout, to battle sounded;
And pulpit, drum ecclesiastic,
Was beat with fist instead of a stick;
Then did Sir Knight abandon dwelling,
And out he rode a colonelling.
A wight he was, whose very sight would
Entitle him Mirror of Knighthood,
That never bowed his stubborn knee
To anything but chivalry,
Nor put up blow, but that which laid
20 Right Worshipful on shoulder-blade;
Chief of domestic knights and errant,
Either for chartel or for warrant;
Great on the bench, great in the saddle,
That could as well bind o'er as swaddle;
Mighty he was at both of these
And styled of war, as well as peace.
(So some rats, of amphibious nature,
Are either for the land or water.)
But here our authors make a doubt
30 Whether he were more wise or stout.
Some hold the one, and some the other;
But, howsoe'er they make a pother,
The diff'rence was so small, his brain
Outweighed his rage but half a grain;
Which made some take him for a tool
That knaves do work with, called a fool.
For 't has been held by many, that
As Montaigne, playing with his cat,
Complains she thought him but an ass,
40 Much more she would Sir Hudibras;
(For that's the name our valiant knight
To all his challenges did write.)
But they're mistaken very much;
'Tis plain enough he was no such.
We grant, although he had much wit,
H' was very shy of using it,
As being loth to wear it out,
And therefore bore it not about,
Unless on holidays or so,
50 As men their best apparel do.
Beside, 'tis known he could speak Greek
As naturally as pigs squeak;
That Latin was no more difficile,

Than to a blackbird 'tis to whistle.
Being rich in both, he never scanted
His bounty unto such as wanted;
But much of either would afford
To many that had not one word.
For Hebrew roots, although they're found
To flourish most in barren ground,   60
He had such plenty as sufficed
To make some think him circumcised.
And truly so perhaps he was;
'Tis many a pious Christian's case.
    He was in logic a great critic,
Profoundly skilled in analytic;
He could distinguish, and divide
A hair 'twixt south and southwest side;
On either which he would dispute,
Confute, change hands, and still confute.   70
He'd undertake to prove, by force
Of argument, a man's no horse;
He'd prove a buzzard is no fowl,
And that a lord may be an owl;
A calf an alderman, a goose a justice,
And rooks committee-men and trustees.
He'd run in debt by disputation,
And pay with ratiocination.
All this by syllogism, true
In mood and figure he would do.   80
    For rhetoric, he could not ope
His mouth, but out there flew a trope;
And when he happened to break off
I' th' middle of his speech, or cough,
H' had hard words ready to show why,
And tell what rules he did it by;
Else, when with greatest art he spoke,
You'd think he talked like other folk.
For all a rhetorician's rules
Teach nothing but to name his tools.   90
But when he pleased to show't, his speech
In loftiness of sound was rich;
A Babylonish dialect,
Which learnéd pedants much affect;
It was a parti-colored dress
Of patched and piebald languages;
'Twas English cut on Greek and Latin,
Like fustian heretofore on satin;
It had an odd promiscuous tone,
As if h' had talked three parts in one;   100
Which made some think, when he did gabble,
Th' had heard three laborers of Babel,
Or Cerberus himself pronounce
A leash of languages at once.

Montaigne (1553-1592), the noted French essayist, remarked in one of his essays: "When I am playing with my cat, who knows whether she have more sport in dallying with me than I have in gaming with her? We entertain one another with mutual apish tricks; if I have my hour, to begin or to refuse, so hath she hers." 55. **never scanted,** was never stingy (about). 76. **committee-men,** committees that under authority of Parliament had power to fine and to imprison; they often took personal advantage of that power. 83-84. **break off ... cough.** Coughing and hemming were regarded as ornaments of speech during the seventeenth century. 93. **Babylonish dialect,** a confusion of languages; an allusion to the confusion of tongues following the building of the Tower of Babel. 98. **fustian,** originally a stout material of cotton and flax. 103. **Cerberus,** in classical mythology, the sleepless watchdog at the entrance to Hades, usually represented with three heads.

This he as volubly would vent,
As if his stock would ne'er be spent;
And truly, to support that charge,
He had supplies as vast and large;
For he could coin or counterfeit
110 New words with little or no wit;
Words so debased and hard, no stone
Was hard enough to touch them on;
And when with hasty noise he spoke 'em,
The ignorant for current took 'em;
That, had the orator, who once
Did fill his mouth with pebble stones
When he harangued, but known his phrase,
He would have used no other ways.

In mathematics he was greater
120 Than Tycho Brahe or Erra Pater;
For he, by geometric scale,
Could take the size of pots of ale;
Resolve by sines and tangents, straight
If bread or butter wanted weight;
And wisely tell what hour o' th' day
The clock does strike, by algebra.

Besides, he was a shrewd philosopher,
And had read every text and gloss over;
Whate'er the crabbed'st author hath,
130 He understood b' implicit faith;
Whatever sceptic could inquire for,
For every *why* he had a *wherefore*;
Knew more than forty of them do,
As far as words and terms could go;
All which he understood by rote,
And, as occasion served, would quote,
No matter whether right or wrong;
They might be either said or sung.
His notions fitted things so well,
140 That which was which he could not tell,
But oftentimes mistook the one
For th' other, as great clerks have done.
He could reduce all things to acts,
And knew their natures by abstracts;
Where entity and quiddity,
The ghosts of defunct bodies, fly;
Where Truth in person does appear,
Like words congealed in northern air.
He knew what's what, and that's as high
150 As metaphysic wit can fly.

In school-divinity as able
As he that hight Irrefragable;
A second Thomas, or, at once,
To name them all, another Duns;
Profound in all the nominal
And real ways beyond them all;
And, with as delicate a hand,
Could twist as tough a rope of sand;
And weave fine cobwebs, fit for skull
That's empty when the moon is full;   160
Such as take lodgings in a head
That's to be let unfurnishéd.
He could raise scruples dark and nice,
And after solve 'em in a trice;
As if divinity had catched
The itch, on purpose to be scratched;
Or, like a mountebank, did wound
And stab herself with doubts profound,
Only to show with how small pain
The sores of faith are cured again;   170
Although by woeful proof we find
They always leave a scar behind.
He knew the seat of Paradise,
Could tell in what degree it lies,
And, as he was disposed, could prove it
Below the moon, or else above it;
What Adam dreamt of when his bride
Came from her closet in his side;
Whether the devil tempted her
By an High-Dutch interpreter,   180
If either of them had a navel;
Who first made music malleable;
Whether the serpent at the fall
Had cloven feet, or none at all.
All this, without a gloss or comment,
He could unriddle in a moment,
In proper terms, such as men smatter
When they throw out and miss the matter.

For his religion, it was fit
To match his learning and his wit;   190
'Twas Presbyterian true blue;
For he was of that stubborn crew
Of errant saints whom all men grant
To be the true church militant;
Such as do build their faith upon
The holy text of pike and gun;

115. **orator, etc.** Demosthenes (384-322 B.C.), the famous Greek orator, trained himself to speak clearly by the method mentioned in the ensuing lines. 120. **Tycho Brahe,** a noted Danish astronomer (1546-1601). **Erra Pater,** probably a nickname for William Lilly (1602-1681), a well-known English astrologer. 145. **entity and quiddity,** abstract terms of scholastic philosophy. *Entity* is the being of a thing, *quiddity* the reasons for that being; hence, the essential nature. The two words are used by Butler to indicate the hairsplitting propensities of the philosophers of his day, and his remark here is that metaphysical essences are only ghosts of real substances. 148. **congealed . . . air.** There was an old belief that in Nova Zembla, or Greenland, it was so cold that men's words froze in wintertime, not to thaw and be heard until the following spring. 152. **hight Irrefragable,** was called irrefragable, unbreakable, invincible. The allusion is to Alexander Hales, a noted English medieval theologian (?-1245) known as "Doctor Irrefragabilis." 153. **Thomas,** Thomas Aquinas (1225?-1274). The medieval Catholic Church considered him the greatest of theologians during the Middle Ages. 154. **Duns,** Duns

Scotus (1265?-1308), a Scottish philosopher whose teachings were generally opposed to those of Thomas Aquinas, and who was regarded as erratic and undependable by the more conservative elements in the medieval church; whence the word "dunce." 160. **moon is full,** a reference to the popular notion that the full moon aggravated insanity. 163. **nice,** overly particular, mixed also with the idea of obscurity or ignorance. 173. **seat of Paradise.** Butler is ridiculing the many learned treatises of the time which attempted to locate the Garden of Eden. 178. **closet . . . side.** The rib out of which Eve was created was taken from Adam while he was in deep sleep (Genesis, 2:21). 180. **High-Dutch interpreter.** The Dutchman Johannes G. Becanus (1518-1572) held that Dutch was the oldest language in the world and assumed that it was spoken in Paradise. 181. **had a navel.** A painting of Adam and Eve in the king's palace caused much comment in Butler's day because the figures were represented with navels. The common theological argument was that since neither Adam nor Eve had been born of woman, they had no need of the umbilical cord and so had no navels. 182. **made music malleable,** an allusion to the idea that music was

Decide all controversies by
Infallible artillery;
And prove their doctrine orthodox,
200 By apostolic blows and knocks;
Call fire and sword, and desolation,
A godly, thorough reformation,
Which always must be carried on,
And still be doing, never done;
As if religion were intended
For nothing else but to be mended;
A sect whose chief devotion lies
In odd perverse antipathies;
In falling out with that or this,
210 And finding somewhat still amiss;
More peevish, cross, and splenetic,
Than dog distract, or monkey sick;
That with more care keep holy-day
The wrong, than others the right way;
Compound for sins they are inclined to,
By damning those they have no mind to;
Still so perverse and opposite,
As if they worshiped God for spite.
The self-same thing they will abhor
220 One way, and long another for.
Free-will they one way disavow,
Another, nothing else allow:
All piety consists therein
In them, in other men all sin:
Rather than fail, they will defy
That which they love most tenderly;
Quarrel with minced-pies, and disparage
Their best and dearest friend, plum-porridge;
Fat pig and goose itself oppose,
230 And blaspheme custard through the nose.
Th' apostles of this fierce religion,
Like Mahomet's, were ass and widgeon,
To whom our knight, by fast instinct
Of wit and temper, was so linked,
As if hypocrisy and nonsense
Had got th' advowson of his conscience.
   Thus was he gifted, and accoutred,
We mean on th' inside, not the outward:
That next of all we shall discuss;
240 Then listen, Sirs, it follows thus:
His tawny beard was th' equal grace
Both of his wisdom and his face;

In cut and die so like a tile,
A sudden view it would beguile;
The upper part whereof was whey,
The nether orange, mixed with gray.
This hairy meteor did denounce
The fall of scepters and of crowns;
With grisly type did represent
Declining age of government,   250
And tell, with hieroglyphic spade,
Its own grave and the state's were made.
Like Samson's heart-breakers, it grew
In time to make a nation rue;
Though it contributed its own fall,
To wait upon the public downfall;
It was monastic, and did grow
In holy orders by strict vow.
Of rule as sullen and severe,
As that of rigid Cordeliere: 260
'T was bound to suffer persecution,
And martyrdom, with resolution;
T' oppose itself against the hate
And vengeance of th' incenséd state,
In whose defiance it was worn,
Still ready to be pulled and torn,
With red-hot irons to be tortured,
Reviled, and spit upon, and martyred;
Maugre all which 't was to stand fast
As long as monarchy should last;   270
But when the state should hap to reel,
'T was to submit to fatal steel,
And fall, as it was consecrate,
A sacrifice to fall of state,
Whose thread of life the Fatal Sisters
Did twist together with its whiskers,
And twine so close that time should never,
In life or death, their fortunes sever,
But with his rusty sickle mow
Both down together at a blow.   280
So learnéd Taliacotius, from
The brawny part of porter's bum,
Cut supplemental noses, which
Would last as long as parent breech,
But when the date of nock was out,
Off dropt the sympathetic snout.
   His back, or rather burthen, showed
As if it stooped with its own load;

invented by Pythagoras, a Greek philosopher of the fifth century B.C. after he heard the variations of sound made by a blacksmith's hammer on an anvil. 184. **cloven feet . . . all.** Before the curse laid by God upon the serpent, following the seduction of Adam and Eve, the snake was supposed to have had feet like a man. 193. **errant,** here used in a secondary sense derived from the original meaning of "wandering," to signify "rascally," "vagabond," "worthless." The word in this sense is now spelled *arrant.* 207-208. **sect . . . antipathies.** The Presbyterians opposed pastimes and amusements of the people. They differed from the Cavaliers even to the extent of considering it sinful to eat plum porridge or mince pies at Christmas. 221. **Free-will . . . allow.** The Presbyterians held for freedom of the individual conscience and absolute freedom in church rites, but denied the liberty of man's will under the doctrine of predestination. 232. **Mahomet's . . . widgeon.** The ass is the milk-white beast that Mahomet dreamed was to carry him into the presence of God; the *widgeon* ("simpleton") is here used satirically for the pigeon that was trained to eat out of Mahomet's ear to create an impression of delivering inspired messages.

236. **advowson,** ecclesiastical patronage, the right of appointment to a vacant position in the church. 243. **cut . . . tile.** In the time of Charles I (King of England from 1625 to 1649), men wore their beards trimmed in triangular form like an old English tile. 251. **hieroglyphic spade.** The beard, shaped like a spade, was symbolic (*hieroglyphic*) of the grave. 253. **heart-breakers,** curls, usually artificial, worn by both men and women. 260. **Cordeliere,** a strict monastic order in France, so-called from the knotted cord worn by the members about the waist. 275. **Fatal Sisters,** in classical mythology, the Fates—the goddesses Clotho (who held the thread of life), Lachesis (who spun the thread), and Atropos (who cut the thread). 281. **Taliacotius,** an Italian surgeon (1553-1599) known for his treatise on the art of ingrafting noses. Many of his achievements in the field of modern plastic surgery have been regarded with extreme skepticism by later medical scholars. 282. **bum,** buttocks. 285. **nock,** the rump or buttocks. Some critics have seen in this allusion a jibe at Cromwell, who at one time was a brewer. In one of Ben Jonson's masques, there appeared a brewer named Notch.

Woodcut of Puritans and Cavaliers—a study of contrast in seventeenth-century England. Reproduced by permission of The Bettmann Archive.

For as Aeneas bore his sire
290 Upon his shoulders through the fire,
Our knight did bear no less a pack
Of his own buttocks on his back;
Which now had almost got the upper-
Hand of his head, for want of crupper.
To poise this equally, he bore
A paunch of the same bulk before,
Which still he had a special care
To keep well-crammed with thrifty fare,
As white-pot, buttermilk, and curds,
300 Such as a country-house affords;

With other victual, which anon
We further shall dilate upon,
When of his hose we come to treat,
The cup-board where he kept his meat.
    His doublet was of sturdy buff,
And though not sword-, yet cudgel-proof,
Whereby 'twas fitter for his use
Who feared no blows but such as bruise.
    His breeches were of rugged woollen,
And had been at the siege of Bullen;   310
To old King Harry so well known,
Some writers held they were his own.

289-290. **Aeneas ... fire,** told in Vergil's *Aeneid*, Book II. 299. **white-pot,** a famous Devonshire dish, a pudding made of milk, eggs, sugar, and bread. 310. **siege of Bullen,** the siege of Boulogne, France, on July 14, 1544, by King Henry VIII (old *King Harry* of l. 311). 312. **his own,** Hudibras' breeches had once been King Henry VIII's. 314. **ammunition-bread,** pieces of bread carried along for emergencies while a soldier was on the march. 338. **farthingal,** hoopskirt. King Arthur set up a round table to avoid questions of precedence among his knights since there could be no head to a round table. 346. **nuncheons,** afternoon lunches, light repasts. 359. **Toledo trusty.** The city of Toledo in Spain was famous for the manufacture of swords. 370. **exigents,** writs summoning persons to deliver themselves up on penalty

Through they were lined with many a piece
Of ammunition-bread and cheese,
And fat black-puddings, proper food
For warriors that delight in blood.
For, as we said, he always chose
To carry victual in his hose,
That often tempted rats and mice
320 The ammunition to surprise;
And when he put a hand but in
The one or t' other magazine,
They stoutly in defense on 't stood,
And from the wounded foe drew blood;
And till th' were stormed, and beaten out,
Ne're left the fortified redoubt.
And though knights-errant, as some think,
Of old did neither eat nor drink,
Because when thorough deserts vast,
330 And regions desolate, they passed,
Where belly-timber above ground
Or under was not to be found,
Unless they grazed there's not one word
Of their provision on record;
Which made some confidently write,
They had no stomachs but to fight.
'T is false; for Arthur wore in hall
Round-table like a farthingal,
On which, with shirt pulled out behind,
340 And eke before, his good knights dined.
Though 't was no table some suppose,
But a huge pair of round trunk-hose,
In which he carried as much meat
As he and all his knights could eat,
When, laying by their swords and truncheons,
They took their breakfasts or their nuncheons.
But let that pass at present, lest
We should forget where we digrest,
As learnéd authors use, to whom
350 We leave it, and to th' purpose come.
    His puissant sword unto his side,
Near his undaunted heart, was tied,
With basket-hilt that would hold broth,
And serve for fight and dinner both;
In it he melted lead for bullets,
To shoot at foes, and sometimes pullets,
To whom he bore so fell a grutch,
He ne're gave quarter t' any such.
The trenchant blade, Toledo trusty,
360 For want of fighting was grown rusty,
And ate into itself for lack
Of somebody to hew and hack:
The peaceful scabbard where it dwelt,
The rancor of its edge had felt;

For of the lower end two handful
It had devoured, 'twas so manful,
And so much scorned to lurk in case,
As if it durst not show its face.
In many desperate attempts
Of warrants, exigents, contempts,   370
It had appeared with courage bolder
Than Serjeant Bum invading shoulder;
Oft had it ta'en possession,
And pris'ners too, or made them run.
    This sword a dagger had, his page,
That was but little for his age,
And therefore waited on him so,
As dwarfs upon knights-errant do.
It was a serviceable dudgeon,
Either for fighting or for drudging;   380
When it had stabbed, or broke a head,
It would scrape trenchers, or chip bread;
Toast cheese or bacon; though it were
To bait a mouse-trap, 'twould not care;
'Twould make clean shoes, and in the earth
Set leeks and onions, and so forth.
It had been 'prentice to a brewer,
Where this and more it did endure,
But left the trade as many more
Have lately done on the same score.   390
    In th' holsters, at his saddle-bow,
Two agéd pistols he did stow,
Among the surplus of such meat
As in his hose he could not get;
These would inveigle rats with th' scent,
To forage when the cocks were bent,
And sometimes catch 'em with a snap,
As cleverly as th' ablest trap.
They were upon hard duty still,
And every night stood sentinel,   400
To guard the magazine in th' hose
From two-legged and from four-legged foes.
    Thus clad and fortified, Sir Knight
From peaceful home set forth to fight.
But first with nimble active force
He got on th' outside of his horse.
For having but one stirrup tied
T' his saddle on the further side,
It was so short h' had much ado
To reach it with his desp'rate toe;   410
But after many strains and heaves,
He got upon the saddle eaves,
From whence he vaulted into th' seat
With so much vigor, strength, and heat,
That he had almost tumbled over
With his own weight, but did recover

of being outlawed. **contempts,** writs hailing a man into court for contempt of court. 372. **Serjeant Bum ... shoulder.** This is an allusion to the method used by bailiffs in arresting persons by tapping them on the shoulder. The usual hireling of the law was referred to as a "Bum-bailiff," from the word *bum* ("buttocks"), as used in 1. 282; so the name of the sergeant, Bum. 375. **his,** its. Grammatical gender was still used in connection with a few common objects. 379. **dudgeon,** a short sword or dagger. 387. **brewer ... score.** The reference to the brewer is plainly a thrust at Cromwell.

By laying hold on tail and mane,
Which oft he used instead of rein.
   But now we talk of mounting steed,
420 Before we further do proceed,
It doth behove us to say something
Of that which bore our valiant bumkin.
The beast was sturdy, large, and tall,
With mouth of meal and eyes of wall,
I would say eye, for h' had but one,
As most agree, though some say none.
He was well staid, and in his gait,
Preserved a grave, majestic state;
At spur or switch no more he skipped
430 Or mended pace, than Spaniard whipped,
And yet so fiery, he would bound,
As if he grieved to touch the ground;
That Caesar's horse, who, as fame goes,
Had corns upon his feet and toes,
Was not by half so tender-hooft,
Nor trod upon the ground so soft;

And as that beast would kneel and stoop
(Some write) to take his rider up,
So Hudibras his ('tis well known)
Would often do to set him down.   440
We shall not need to say what lack
Of leather was upon his back,
For that was hidden under pad,
And breech of knight, galled full as bad.
His strutting ribs on both sides showed
Like furrows he himself had plowed;
For underneath the skirt of panel,
'Twixt ev'ry two there was a channel.
His graggling tail hung in the dirt,
Which on his rider he would flirt,   450
Still as his tender side he pricked,
With armed heel, or with unarmed, kicked:
For Hudibras wore but one spur,
As wisely knowing could he stir
To active trot one side of 's horse,
Th' other would not hang an arse.

                  (1662; 1663)

422. **bumkin,** "little bum," small buttocks, a term of contempt. 424. **mouth of meal and eyes of wall,** mealy-mouthed and walleyed. 430. **Spaniard whipped.** This is an allusion to a story told, among other places, in Cervantes' *Don Quixote*, Part I, Book 3, Chapter 9. A Spaniard was being forced to run a gauntlet of lashes, but would not hasten his pace to save himself. One of the spectators advised him that the longer he was on his way, the longer he must be under the scourge; and the more haste he made, the sooner he would be out of his pain. "Noble sir," said the Spaniard, "I kiss your hand for your courtesy, but it is below the spirit of a man to run like a dog; if ever it shall be your fortune to fall under the same discipline, you shall have my consent to walk your course at what rate you please yourself; but in the meantime, with your good favor, I shall make bold to use my own liberty." 433. **Caesar's horse ... feet and toes.** The Roman historian Suetonius (of the first century A.D.) tells us that the hooves of Caesar's horses were divided into toes. 437. **kneel and stoop.** Since stirrups were not in use in Caesar's time, horses were taught to stoop to be mounted. 447. **panel,** the pad underneath the saddle.

SAMUEL PEPYS 1633-1703

Samuel Pepys, the son of a London tailor, secured an education at St. Paul's School and at Cambridge University through the help of his kinsman and patron, Sir Edward Montagu, first Earl of Sandwich. Pepys had an early appetite for the activities of important people: as a lad at school, he was an eyewitness of the execution of King Charles I in 1649; as secretary to Montagu, he was with the fleet that brought Charles II back from exile in 1660. Through Montagu's aid Pepys rose from minor government offices to the position of Secretary of the Admiralty. This post he held from 1673 to the Revolution of 1688. With the coming of William III, Pepys was not only removed from office but for a short time was imprisoned because of his sympathies with the descendants of Charles. Released through the influence of powerful friends, he retired to Clapham, where his last years passed quietly.

Pepys left behind him two works: his Memoirs of the Navy (1690) and his Diary. The Diary, surely the most extensive and withal the most revealing document of its kind in English literature, has rendered Pepys, in a sense, immortal. It covers the period from January 1, 1660, to May 31, 1669. Undoubtedly Pepys kept this record not only as a means of preserving the memory of his gayer days, but also as a kind of emotional exhaust. There is much to assure us

that he had not the slightest inkling that it would some day be spread before the eager eyes of the reading public. It was written in shorthand and not deciphered until 1825. The Diary was apparently composed secretly, for Samuel Pepys alone. At the age of thirty-six Pepys was suffering from a fear of blindness, and wrote in the last paragraph of his Diary: "I resolve from this time forward to have it kept by my people in long-hand and must therefore be contented to set down no more than is fit for them and all the world to know."

The entries in the Diary are extremely full and intimate, no matter what Pepys gossips about— his official and family affairs, his flirtations as well as his jealousies; the foibles and scandals of his acquaintances; the theaters, operas, and other amusements of Restoration London; the Dutch War, the plague, the fire of London. Pepys wrote artlessly but with genuine relish, and sympathizing as he did with the glitter of metropolitan life in the days of "good King Charles," he left behind him a document amazing not only for its vitality, but for its supremely human qualities. Informal, racy, full of unconscious humor, the Diary builds up for the reader an unforgettable personality living in an unforgettable period in English history.

---

from THE DIARY

1659-60

Blessed be God, at the end of the last year, I was in very good health, without any sense of my old pain, but upon taking of cold. I lived in Axe Yard, having my wife, and servant Jane, and no other in family than us three.

The condition of the State was thus: viz. the Rump, after being disturbed by my Lord Lambert, was lately returned to sit again. The officers of the Army all forced to yield. Lawson lies still in the river, and Monk
10 is with his army in Scotland. Only my Lord Lambert

is not yet come into the Parliament, nor is it expected that he will, without being forced to it. The new Common Council of the City do speak very high; and had sent to Monk, their sword-bearer, to acquaint him with their desires for a free and full Parliament, which is at present the desires, and the hopes, and the expectations of all: twenty-two of the old secluded members having been at the House-door the last week to demand entrance, but it was denied them; and it is believed that neither they nor the people will be satisfied till the House be filled. My own private condition very handsome, and esteemed rich, but indeed very poor; besides my goods of my house, and my office, which at present is somewhat certain. Mr. Downing master of my office.

---

2. **pain . . . cold.** On March 26, 1658, Pepys had successfully undergone an operation for a gall bladder condition, an illness which had affected several members of his family. Pepys always commemorated the day. 6. **Rump,** the Rump Parliament, the remnant of the Long Parliament, established by the expulsion of the Presbyterian members in 1648, dismissed by force in 1653, and restored briefly in 1659–1660. 7. **Lambert,** John Lambert (1619–1683), a major general in the Parliamentary forces during the Civil War, but condemned as a traitor after the Restoration. He was banished to Guernsey and later to Plymouth Island, where he lived in exile and imprisonment for twenty years. 9. **Lawson,** Sir John Lawson (d. 1665), son of a poor man of Hull. He rose from common seaman to the rank of admiral and distinguished himself during the Protectorate. Nevertheless, he readily supported the restoration of the monarchy. 14. **Monk,** George Monk (1608–1670), afterwards Duke of Albemarle. He helped to restore Charles II to the throne. 17. **secluded,** excluded by the Parliamentarian army in 1647 and 1648. 24. **Downing,** George Downing (c. 1623–1684), of the Exchequer, in whose office Pepys was a clerk.

July 1, 1660 (Lord's day.)—Infinite of business, my heart and head full. Met with Purser Washington, with whom and a lady, a friend of his, I dined at the Bell Tavern in King Street, but the rogue had no more manners than to invite me, and to let me pay my club. This morning come home my fine camlet cloak, with gold buttons, and a silk suit, which cost me much money, and I pray God to make me able to pay for it. In the afternoon to the Abbey, where a good sermon by a stranger, but no Common Prayer yet.

October 11, 1660.— . . . To walk in St. James's Park, where we observed the several engines at work to draw up water, with which sight I was very much pleased. Above all the rest, I liked that which Mr. Greatorex brought, which do carry up the water with a great deal of ease. Here, in the Park, we met with Mr. Salisbury, who took Mr. Creed and me to the Cockpit to see *The Moore of Venice,* which was well done. Burt acted the Moore; by the same token, a very pretty lady that sat by me, called out, to see Desdemona smothered. . . .

October 13, 1660.—I went out to Charing Cross, to see Major-General Harrison hanged, drawn, and quartered; which was done there, he looking as cheerful as any man could do in that condition. He was presently cut down, and his head and heart shown to the people, at which there was great shouts of joy. It is said, that he said that he was sure to come shortly at the right hand of Christ to judge them that now had judged him; and that his wife do expect his coming again. Thus it was my chance to see the King beheaded at White Hall, and to see the first blood shed in revenge for the King at Charing Cross. Setting up shelves in my study.

November 1, 1660.—This morning—Sir W. Pen and I were mounted early, and had very merry discourse all the way, he being very good company. We come to Sir W. Batten's, where he lives like a prince, and we were made very welcome. Among other things, he showed me my Lady's closet, wherein was great store of rarities; as also a chair, which he calls King Harry's chaire, where he that sits down is catched with two irons, that come round about him, which makes good sport. Here dined with us two or three more country gentlemen; among the rest, Mr. Christmas, my old school-fellow, with whom I had much talk. He did remember that I was a great Roundhead when I was a boy, and I was much afraid that he would have remembered the words that I said the day the King was beheaded (that, were I to preach upon him, my text should be—"The memory of the wicked shall rot"); but I found afterwards that he did go away from school before that time. He did make us good sport in imitating Mr. Case, Ash, and Nye, the ministers; but a deadly drinker he is, and grown very fat.

December 25, 1660 (Christmas day.)—To church in the morning, and there saw a wedding in the church, which I have not seen many a day; and the young people so merry one with another! and strange to see what delight we married people have to see these poor fools decoyed into our condition, every man and woman gazing and smiling at them. Here I saw again my beauty Lethulier. Home to look over and settle my papers, both of my accounts private, and those of Tangier, which I have let go so long that it were impossible for any soul, had I died, to understand them, or ever come to good end in them. I hope God will never suffer me to come to that disorder again.

March 23, 1661.—To the Red Bull (where I had not been since plays come up again) . . . up to the tiring-room, where strange the confusion and disorder that there is among them in fitting themselves, especially here, where the clothes are very poor, and the actors but common fellows. At last into the pit, where I think there was not above ten more than myself, and not one hundred in the whole house. And the play, which is called *All's Lost by Lust,* poorly done; and with so much disorder, among others, in the music-room the boy that was to sing a song, not singing it right, his master fell about his ears and beat him so, that it put the whole house in an uproar. . . .

January 1, 1662.—Waking this morning out of my sleep on a sudden, I did with my elbow hit my wife a great blow over her face and neck, which waked her with pain, at which I was sorry, and to sleep again. . . .

March 1, 1662.—My wife and I by coach, first to see my little picture that is a-drawing, and thence to the Opera, and there saw *Romeo and Juliet,* the first time it was ever acted, but it is a play of itself the worst that ever I heard, and the worst acted that ever I saw these people do, and I am resolved to go no more to see the first time of acting, for they were all of them out more or less. . . .

September 30, 1662.—To the Duke's play-house, where we saw *The Duchess of Malfy* well performed, but Betterton and Ianthe [Mrs. Betterton] to admiration. Strange to see how easily my mind do revert to its former practice of loving plays and wine; but this night

2. **Washington,** a friend of Pepys in the Admiralty office. 6. **club,** share of the expenses. **camlet,** a rich material made of silk and camel's hair or wool. 10. **Common Prayer,** its use had been abolished during the Commonwealth. 18. **Cockpit,** a theater in Drury Lane. *Moore of Venice,* Shakespeare's Othello. 19. **Burt,** Nicholas Burt, one of the good Restoration actors. 23. **Harrison,** Thomas Harrison, son of a butcher in Newcastle-under-Lyme, appointed by Cromwell to convey Charles I from Windsor to Whitehall for trial. He also sat as one of the king's judges. 35. **Pen,** an associate and friend of the rising Pepys in the Admiralty office, captain at twenty-one, rear admiral of Ireland at twenty-three, and vice-admiral of England at thirty-two. He was the father of William Penn, founder of Pennsylvania. 38. **Batten,** Commis-

sioner of the Navy. 54. **Case . . . Nye,** royal chaplains. 63. **Lethulier,** wife of a London merchant, and friend of Pepys. 70. **Red Bull,** an old playhouse in St. John street, Clerkenwell. 72. **tiring-room,** dressing room. 78. **All's . . . Lust,** a play by William Rowley (1585?-1642?). 90. **Opera,** Lincoln's Inn Fields Theatre. 96. **Duke's play-house,** Lincoln's Inn Fields Theatre. 97. *The Duchess of Malfy,* a play by John Webster (?-1634). 98. **Betterton,** Thomas Betterton (1635-1710), the greatest of the Restoration actors. 99. **Strange . . . next.** Pepys repeatedly made resolutions to give up seeing plays, or to go only when his wife accompanied him. But he always broke them. 108. **Sandwich,** Sir Edward Montagu, one of the Council of State, and a distant relative of Pepys, who owed his rise in the Admiralty to him. 114. **Mr.**

I have again bound myself to Christmas next. I have also made up this evening my monthly ballance, and find that, notwithstanding the loss of £30 to be paid to the loyall and necessitous cavaliers by act of Parliament, yet I am worth about £680, for which the Lord God be praised. My condition at present is this:—I have long been building, and my house, to my great content, is now almost done. My Lord Sandwich has lately been in the country, and very civil to my wife, 110 and hath himself spent some pains in drawing a plot of some alterations in our house there, which I shall follow as I get money. As for the office, my late industry hath been such, as I am become as high in reputation as any man there, and good hold I have of Mr. Coventry and Sir G. Carteret, which I am resolved, and it is necessary for me, to maintain, by all fair means. Things are all quiet. The late outing of the Presbyterian clergy, by their not renouncing the Covenant as the Act of Parliament commands, is the greatest piece of state 120 now in discourse. But, for ought I see, they are gone out very peaceably, and the people not so much concerned therein as was expected.

October 2, 1662.—At night, hearing that there was a play at the Cockpit, and my Lord Sandwich, who come to town last night, at it, I do go thither, and by very great fortune did follow four or five gentlemen who were carried to a little private door in a wall, and so crept through a narrow place, and come into one of the boxes next the King's, but so as I could not see 130 the King or Queen, but many of the fine ladies, who yet are not really so handsome generally as I used to take them to be, but that they are finely dressed. Then we saw *The Cardinall,* a tragedy I had never seen before, nor is there any great matter in it. The company that come in with me into the box were all Frenchmen, that could speak no English; but, Lord! what sport they made to ask a pretty lady that they got among them, that understood both French and English, to make her tell them what the actors said.

140 December 26, 1662.—Up, my wife to the making of Christmas pies all day, being now pretty well again, and I abroad to several places about some businesses, among others bought a bake-pan in Newgate Market, and sent it home; it cost me 16s. So to Dr. Williams, but he is out of town, then to the Wardrobe. Hither come Mr. Battersby; and we falling into a discourse of a new book of drollery in verse called *Hudebras,* I would needs go find it out, and met with it at the Temple; cost me 2s. 6d. But when I came to read 150 it, it is so silly an abuse of the Presbyter Knight going

to the wars, that I am ashamed of it; and by and by meeting at Mr. Townshend's at dinner, I sold it to him for 18d. Here we dine with many tradesmen that belong to the Wardrobe, but I was weary soon of their company, and broke up dinner as soon as I could, and away, with the greatest reluctancy and dispute (two or three times my reason stopping my sense and I would go back again) within myself, to the Duke's house and saw *The Villain,* which I ought not to do without my wife, but that my time is now out that I did undertake 160 it for. But, Lord! to consider how my natural desire is to pleasure, which God be praised that he has given me the power by my late oaths to curb so well as I have done, and will do again after two or three plays more. Here I was better pleased with the play than I was at first, understanding the design better than I did. Here I saw Gosnell and her sister at a distance, and could have found it in my heart to have accosted them, but thought not prudent. But I watched their going out and found that they came, she, her sister and 170 another woman, alone, without any man, and did go over the fields a foot. I find that I have an inclination to have her come again, though it is most against my interest either of profit or content of mind, other than for their singing. Home on foot, in my way calling at Mr. Rawlinson's and drinking only a cup of ale there. He tells me my uncle has ended his purchase, which cost him £4,500, and how my uncle do express his trouble that he has with his wife's relations; but I understand his great intentions are for the Wights that 180 hang upon him and by whose advice this estate is bought. Thence home, and found my wife busy among her pies, but angry for some saucy words that her maid Jane has given her, which I will not allow of, and therefore will give her warning to be gone. As also we are both displeased for some slight words that Sarah, now at Sir W. Pen's, hath spoke of us, but it is no matter. We shall endeavor to join the lion's skin to the fox's tail. So to my office alone awhile, and then home to my study and supper and bed. Being also 190 vexed at my boy for his staying playing abroad when he is sent of errands, so that I have sent him tonight to see whether their country carrier be in town or no, for I am resolved to keep him no more.

July 13, 1663.— . . . I met the Queen-Mother walking in the Pell Mell, led by my Lord St. Alban's. And finding many coaches at the Gate, I found upon enquiry that the Duchess is brought to bed of a boy; and hearing that the King and Queen are rode abroad with the Ladies of Honor to the Park, and seeing a

Coventry and Sir G. Carteret, associates of Pepys in the Admiralty office. 133. *The Cardinall,* a tragedy by James Shirley (1596-1666). 141. pretty well again. Mrs. Pepys had spent the preceding day in bed. 145. the Wardrobe, the official residence of Pepys' employer, Sir Edward Montagu, Earl of Sandwich. 147. *Hudebras;* a satire on the Puritans by Samuel Butler. The official date of publication of *Hudibras* is 1663, so that it could have been off the press but a few days before Pepys came upon it. 159. *The Villain,* a tragedy by Thomas Porter, an otherwise completely obscure seventeenth-century playwright. 167. Gosnell, Mrs. Pepys' maid, just recently discharged. Pepys speaks elsewhere of her good singing voice, and of the fact that she appeared with some success upon the stage. 187. Sarah, Gosnell's predecessor

in the employ of the Pepys household. Mrs. Pepys, who seems to have been a woman of quick temper—often, it may be said, with cause—had discharged Sarah about a month before the entry in question. 188. join . . . tail, a proverbial expression of the times for patching up matters and making the best of them. 195. Queen-Mother, Queen Henrietta Maria, widow of Charles I and mother of Charles II. She died shortly after, in 1665. 198. Duchess . . . boy. The Duchess of York, wife of James, Duke of York, who later became James II of England, reigning from 1685 to 1688. The boy here referred to was James Stuart, Duke of Cambridge, the second son of James. He lived but a short time, dying in 1667.

great crowd of gallants staying here to see their return,
I also stayed walking up and down. . . . By and by the
King and Queen, who looked in this dress (a white
laced waistcoat and a crimson short petticoat, and her
hair dressed *à la negligence*) mighty pretty; and the
King rode hand in hand with her. Here was also my
Lady Castlemaine rode among the rest of the ladies;
but the King took, methought, no notice of her; nor
when she light, did any body press (as she seemed
10 to expect, and stayed for it) to take her down, but
was taken down by her own gentlemen. She looked
mighty out of humor, and had a yellow plume in her
hat (which all took notice of) and yet is very handsome,
but very melancholy; nor did anybody speak to her,
or she so much as smile or speak to anybody. I followed them up into White Hall, and into the Queen's
presence, where all the ladies walked, talking and fiddling with their hats and feathers, and changing and
trying one another's by one another's heads, and
20 laughing. But it was the finest sight to me, considering
their great beauties, and dress, that ever I did see in
all my life. But, above all, Mrs. Stewart in this dress,
with her hat cocked and a red plume, with her sweet
eye, little Roman nose, and excellent taille, is now the
greatest beauty I ever saw, I think, in my life; and, if
ever woman can, do exceed my Lady Castlemaine, at
least in this dress; nor do I wonder if the King changes,
which I verily believe is the reason of his coldness to
my Lady Castlemaine. . . .

30 January 4, 1664.—I to my Lord Sandwich's lodgings, but he not being up, I to the Duke's chamber,
and there by and by to his closet, where, since his
lady was ill, a little red bed of velvet is brought for him
to lie alone, which is a very pretty one. After doing
business here, I to my Lord's again, and there spoke
with him, and he seems now almost friends again, as
he used to be. Here meeting Mr. Pierce, the surgeon,
he told me, among other Court news, how the Queen
is very well again; and that she speaks now very
40 pretty English, and makes her sense out now and then
with pretty phrases: as among others this is mightily
cried up; that, meaning to say that she did not like
such a horse so well as the rest, he being too prancing
and full of tricks, she said he did make too much vanity.
To the Tennis Court, and there saw the King play at
tennis and others: but to see how the King's play
was extolled, without any cause at all, was a loathsome sight, though sometimes, indeed, he did play very
well, and deserved to be commended; but such open
50 flattery is beastly. Afterwards to St. James's Park,
seeing people play at Pell Mell; where it pleased me
mightily to hear a gallant, lately come from France,

swear at one of his companions for suffering his man,
a spruce blade, to be so saucy as to strike a ball while
his master was playing on the Mall. My wife is mighty
sad to think of her father, who is going into Germany
against the Turkes; but what will become of her
brother I know not. He is so idle, and out of all
capacity, I think, to earn his bread.

January 6, 1664 (Twelfth day.)—This morning I 60
began a practice, which I find, by the ease I do it
with, that I shall continue, it saving me money and
time; that is, to trimme myself with a razer: which
pleases me mightily.

August 7, 1664 (Lord's day.)—My wife telling
me sad stories of the ill, improvident, disquiet, and
sluttish manner, that my father and mother and Pall do
live in the country, which troubles me mightily, and
I must seek to remedy it. Showed my wife, to her
great admiration and joy, Mr. Gauden's present of 70
plate, the two flaggons, which indeed are so noble that
I hardly can think that they are yet mine. I saw several poor creatures carried by, by constables, for
being at a conventicle. They go like lambs, without
any resistance. I would to God they would either
conform, or be more wise, and not be catched!

October 10, 1664.—Sir W. Pen do grow every day
more and more regarded by the Duke, because of his
service heretofore in the Dutch war, which I am confident is by some strong obligations he hath laid upon 80
Mr. Coventry; for Mr. Coventry must needs know that
he is a man of very mean parts, but only a bred seaman. Sat up till past twelve at night, to look over the
account of the collections for the Fishery, and to the
loose and base manner that monies so collected are
disposed of in, would make a man never part with a
penny in that manner; and, above all, the inconvenience
of having a great man, though never so seeming pious
as my Lord Pembroke is. He is too great to be called
to an account, and is abused by his servants, and yet 90
obliged to defend them, for his own sake. This day, by
the blessing of God, my wife and I have been married
nine years: but my head, being full of business, I did
not think of it to keep it in any extraordinary manner.
But bless God for our long lives, and loves, and health
together, which the same God long continue, I wish,
from my very heart!

June 7, 1665.— . . . This day, much against my
will, I did in Drury Lane see two or three houses
marked with a red cross upon the doors, and "Lord 100
have mercy upon us" writ there; which was a sad
sight to me, being the first of the kind, that to my
remembrance, I ever saw. It put me into an ill conception of myself and my smell, so that I was forced to

---

7. **Lady Castlemaine,** Barbara Villiers, Duchess of Cleveland, one of
the better-known mistresses of Charles II. She bore him issue; her rival,
Frances Stuart, mentioned below, seems to have been a temporary infatuation. 24. **taille,** figure. 51. **Pell Mell,** a game in which a boxwood ball was driven through an iron ring suspended at a height in a
long alley. Pall Mall, the fashionable club street in London, was developed from one of these alleys. 67. **Pall,** Paulina, Pepys' sister. 70.

Mr. Gauden, Dennis Gauden, later Sir Dennis, victualler to the Navy.
Pepys was not above taking presents. There was even a proposal that
Paulina Pepys was to be married to one of Mr. Gauden's sons. But Pepys
gave up the idea lest his suspicious enemies misinterpret his motives. 74.
conventicle, a clandestine meeting of nonconformists, probably Quakers.
78. **Duke,** the Duke of York, High Admiral. 89. **Pembroke,** Philip,
fifth Earl of Pembroke (d. 1669). 103. **ill conception . . . smell.**

buy some roll-tobacco to smell to and chaw, which took away the apprehension.

July 26, 1665.—To Greenwich, to the Park, where I heard the King and Duke are come by water this morn from Hampton Court. They asked me several questions. The King mightily pleased with his new buildings there. I followed them to Castle's ship, in building, and there met Sir W. Batten, and thence to Sir G. Carteret's, where all the morning with them; they not having any but the Duke of Monmouth, and Sir W. Killigrew, and one gentleman, and a page more. Great variety of talk, and was often led to speak to the King and Duke. By and by they to dinner, and all to dinner and sat down to the King, saving myself, which, though I could not in modesty expect, yet, God forgive my pride! I was sorry I was there, that Sir W. Batten should say that he could sit down where I could not. The King having dined, he came down, and I went in the barge with him, I sitting at the door. Down to Woolwich, and there I just saw and kissed my wife, and saw some of her painting, which is very curious; and away again to the King, and back again with him in the barge, hearing him and the Duke talk, and seeing and observing their manner of discourse. And, God forgive me! though I admire them with all the duty possible, yet the more a man considers and observes them, the less he finds of difference between them and other men, though, blessed be God! they are both princes of great nobleness and spirits. The Duke of Monmouth is the most skittish leaping gallant that ever I saw, always in action, vaulting, or leaping, or clambering. Sad news of the death of so many in the parish of the plague, forty last night. The bell always going. To the Exchange, where I went up and sat talking with my beauty, Mrs. Batelier, a great while, who is indeed one of the finest women I ever saw in my life. This day poor Robin Shaw at Backewell's died, and Backewell himself now in Flanders. The King himself asked about Shaw, and being told he was dead, said he was very sorry for it. The sickness is got into our parish this week, and is got, indeed, every where; so that I begin to think of setting things in order, which I pray God enable me to put, both as to soul and body.

August 3, 1665.— . . . To the ferry, where I was forced to stay a great while before I could get my horse brought over, and then mounted and rode very finely to Dagenhams; all the way people, citizens, walking to and again to inquire how the plague is in the city this week by the Bill; which by chance, at Greenwich, I had heard was 2020 of the plague, and 3000 and odd of all diseases; but methought it was a sad question to be so often asked me. Coming to

Dagenhams, I there met our company coming out of the house, having stayed as long as they could for me; so I let them go a little before, and went and took leave of my Lady Sandwich, . . . Then down to the buttery, and eat a piece of cold venison pie, and drank and took some bread and cheese in my hand; and so mounted after them, Mr. Marr very kindly staying to lead me the way. . . . [and] telling me how a maid-servant of Mr. John Wright's (who lives thereabouts) falling sick of the plague, she was removed to an out-house, and a nurse appointed to look to her; who, being once absent, the maid got out of the house at the window, and run away. The nurse coming and knocking, and having no answer, believed she was dead, and went and told Mr. Wright so; who and his lady were in great strait what to do to get her buried. At last resolved to go to Burntwood hard by, being in the parish, and there get people to do it. But they would not; so he went home full of trouble, and in the way met the wench walking over the common, which frightened him worse than before; and was forced to send people to take her, which he did; and they got one of the pest coaches and put her into it to carry her to a pest house. And passing in a narrow lane, Sir Anthony Browne, with his brother and some friends in the coach, met this coach with the curtains drawn close. The brother being a young man, and believing there might be some lady in it that would not be seen, and the way being narrow, he thrust his head out of his own into her coach, and to look, and there saw somebody look very ill, and in a sick dress, and stunk mightily; which the coachman also cried out upon. And presently they came up to some people that stood looking after it, and told our gallants that it was a maid of Mr. Wright's carried away sick of the plague; which put the young gentleman into a fright had almost cost him his life, but is now well again. . . .

August 12, 1665.— . . . The people die so, that now it seems they are fain to carry the dead to be buried by daylight, the nights not sufficing to do it in. And my Lord Mayor commands people to be within at nine at night all, as they say, that the sick may have liberty to go abroad for air. There is one also dead out of one of our ships at Deptford, which troubles us mightily; the Providence fire-ship, which was just fitted to go to sea. But they tell me today no more sick on board. And this day W. Bodham tells me that one is dead at Woolwich, not far from the Rope-yard. I am told, too, that a wife of one of the grooms at Court is dead at Salisbury; so that the King and Queen are speedily to be all gone to Milton. God preserve us!

October 16, 1665.— . . . God knows what will

The older theory about the spread of the plague was that the disease was contagious through the smell of the victim. 114. **Duke of Monmouth,** illegitimate son of Charles II. He was then only a lad. 115. **Killigrew,** elder brother of Thomas Killigrew, the playwright. He also wrote verses and plays. 139. **Mrs. Batelier.** Mary Batelier kept a linen draper's shop in the Royal Exchange; she and her brother William are frequently mentioned in the Diary. 141. **Robin Shaw,** an employee of Alderman Backewell. 151. **Dagenhams,** a village about ten miles from London. 201. **fire-ship,** a naval vessel which in action would be loaded with combustibles or explosives and set adrift into the enemy's line.

become of all the King's matters in a little time, for he runs in debt every day, and nothing to pay them looked after. Thence I walked to the Tower; but, Lord! how empty the streets are and melancholy, so many poor sick people in the streets full of sores; and so many sad stories overheard as I walk, everybody talking of his dead, and that man sick, and so many in this place, and so many in that. And they tell me that, in Westminster, there is never a physician and but one apothecary left, all being dead; but that there are great hopes of a great decrease this week; God send it! . . .

August 14, 1666 (Thanksgiving day.)—Comes Mr. Foley and his man with a box of great variety of carpenter's and joyner's tooles, which I had bespoke, which please me mightily, but I will have more. Povy tells me how mad my letter makes my Lord Peterborough, and what a furious letter he hath writ to me in answer, though it is not come yet. This did trouble me; for, though there be no reason, yet to have a nobleman's mouth open against a man, may do a man hurt; so I endeavoured to have found him out and spoke with him, but could not. So to the chapel, and heard a piece of the Dean of Westminster's sermon, and a speciall good anthemne before the King, after sermon. After dinner, with my wife and Mercer to the Beare Garden; where I have not been, I think, of many years, and saw some good sport of the bull's tossing the dogs—one into the very boxes. But it is a very rude and nasty pleasure. We had a great many hectors in the same box with us, and one very fine went into the pit, and played his dog for a wager; which was a strange sport for a gentleman; where they drank wine, and drank Mercer's health first; which I pledged with my hat off. We supped at home, and very merry. And then about nine to Mrs. Mercer's gate, where the fire and boys expected us, and her son had provided abundance of serpents and rockets; and there mighty merry, my Lady Pen and Pegg going thither with us, and Nan Wright, till about twelve at night, flinging our fireworks, and burning one another, and the people over the way. And, at last, our business being most spent, we went into Mrs. Mercer's, and there mighty merry, smutting one another with candle grease and soot, till most of us were like devils. And that being done, then we broke up, and to my house; and there I made them drink, and upstairs we went, and then fell into dancing, W. Batelier dancing well; and dressing, him and I, and one Mr. Banister, who, with my wife, come over also with us, like women; and Mercer put on a suit of Tom's, like a boy, and mighty mirth we had and Mercer danced a jigg; and Nan Wright and my wife and Pegg Pen put on perriwigs. Thus we spent till three or four in the morning, mighty merry; and then departed, and to bed.

September 2, 1666 (Lord's day).—Some of our maids sitting up late last night to get things ready against our feast today, Jane called us up about three in the morning, to tell us of a great fire they saw in the city. So I rose and slipped on my night-gown, and went to her window; and thought it to be on the backside of Marke-lane at the farthest; but, being unused to such fires as followed, I thought it far enough off; and so went to bed again, and to sleep. About seven rose again to dress myself, and there looked out at the window, and saw the fire not so much as it was, and further off. So to my closet to set things to rights, after yesterday's cleaning. By and by Jane comes and tells me that she hears that above 300 houses have been burned down tonight by the fire we saw, and that it is now burning down all Fish Street, by London Bridge. So I made myself ready presently, and walked to the Tower; and there got up upon one of the high places, Sir J. Robinson's little son going up with me; and there I did see the houses at that end of the bridge all on fire, and an infinite great fire on this and the other side the end of the bridge; which, among other people, did trouble me for poor little Michell and our Sarah on the bridge. So down with my heart full of trouble, to the Lieutenant of the Tower, who tells me that it begun this morning in the King's baker's house in Pudding-lane, and that it hath burned St. Magnus's Church and most part of Fish Street already. So I down to the water-side, and there got a boat, and through bridge and there saw a lamentable fire. Poor Michell's house, as far as the Old Swan, already burned that way, and the fire running further, that, in a very little time, it got as far as the Steele-yard, while I was there. Everybody endeavoring to remove their goods, and flinging into the river, or bringing them into lighters that lay off; poor people staying in their houses as long as till the very fire touched them, and then running into boats, or clambering from one pair of stairs, by the water-side, to another. And, among other things, the poor pigeons, I perceive, were loth to leave their houses, but hovered about the windows and balconies, till some of them burned their wings, and fell down. Having stayed, and in an hour's time seen the fire rage every way; and nobody, to my sight, endeavoring to quench it, but to remove their goods, and leave all to the fire, and having seen it get as far as the Steele-yard, and the wind mighty high, and driving it into the city: and everything, after so long a drought, proving combustible, even the very stones of churches; and, among other things, the poor steeple by which pretty Mrs. —— lives, and whereof my old schoolfellow Elborough is parson, taken fire in the very top, and there burned till it fell down; I to White Hall, with a gentleman with me who desired to go off from the Tower, to see the fire, in my boat;

2. **in debt every day.** In an earlier part of this same entry, Pepys had been speaking of the lewd behavior of Charles and his extravagances with his mistresses. 13. **Thanksgiving day,** in honor of a naval victory. 24.

Dean of Westminster, John Dolben, afterwards Archbishop of York. The sermon is in print. 27. **Beare Garden,** an old pleasure resort on Bankside in Southwark. 30. **hectors,** bullies, rowdies. 34. **Mercer,**

to White Hall, and there up to the King's closet in the Chapel, where people come about me, and I did give them an account dismayed them all, and word was carried into the King. So I was called for, and did tell the King and Duke of York what I saw; and, that unless his Majesty did command houses to be pulled down, nothing could stop the fire. They seemed much troubled, and the King commanded me to go to my Lord Mayor from him, and command him to spare no 120 houses, but to pull down before the fire every way. The Duke of York bid me tell him, that if he would have any more soldiers, he shall; and so did my Lord Arlington afterwards, as a great secret. Here meeting with Captain Cocke, I in his coach, which he lent me, and Creed with me to Paul's; and there walked along Watling Street, as well as I could, every creature coming away loaden with goods to save, and, here and there, sick people carried away in beds. Extraordinary good goods carried in carts and on backs. 130 At last met my Lord Mayor in Canning Street, like a man spent, with a handkercher about his neck. To the King's message, he cried like a fainting woman, "Lord! what can I do? I am spent; people will not obey me. I have been pulling down houses; but the fire overtakes us faster than we can do it." That he needed no more soldiers; and that, for himself, he must go and refresh himself, having been up all night. So he left me, and I him, and walked home, seeing people all almost distracted, and no manner of means used to 140 quench the fire. The houses, too, so very thick thereabouts, and full of matter for burning, as pitch and tar, in Thames Street; and warehouses of oil, and wines, and brandy, and other things. Here I saw Mr. Isaake Houblon, the handsome man, prettily dressed and dirty at his door at Dowgate, receiving some of his brothers' things, whose houses were on fire; and, as he says, have been removed twice already; and he doubts, as it soon proved, that they must be, in a little time, removed from his house also, which was a 150 sad consideration. And to see the churches all filling with goods by people who themselves should have been quietly there at this time. By this time, it was about twelve o'clock; and so home, and there find my guests, which was Mr. Wood and his wife Barbary Shelden, and also Mr. Moone; she mighty fine, and her husband, for aught I see, a likely man. But Mr. Moone's design and mine, which was to look over my closet, and please him with the sight thereof, which he hath long desired, was wholly disappointed; for we 160 were in great trouble and disturbance at this fire, not knowing what to think of it. However, we had an extraordinary good dinner, and as merry as at this time we could be. While at dinner, Mrs. Batelier come to enquire after Mr. Woolfe and Stanes, who, it seems, are related to them, whose houses in Fish Street are

all burned, and they in a sad condition. She would not stay in the fright. Soon as dined, I and Moone away, and walked through the city, the streets full of nothing but people and horses and carts loaden with goods, ready to run over one another, and removing goods 170 from one burned house to another. They now removing out of Canning Street, which received goods in the morning, into Lumbard Street, and further; and among others, I now saw my little goldsmith Stokes receiving some friend's goods, whose house itself was burned the day after. We parted at Paul's; he home, and I to Paul's Wharf, where I had appointed a boat to attend me, and took in Mr. Carcasse and his brother, whom I met in the street, and carried them below and above bridge too and again to see the fire, which was now got 180 further, both below and above, and no likelihood of stopping it. Met with the King and Duke of York in their barge, and with them to Queenhithe, and there called Sir Richard Browne to them. Their order was only to pull down houses apace, and so below bridge at the waterside; but little was or could be done, the fire coming upon them so fast. Good hopes there was of stopping it at the Three Cranes above, and at Buttulph's Wharf below bridge, if care be used; but the wind carries it into the city, so as we know not, by the 190 waterside, what it do there. River full of lighters and boats taking in goods, and good goods swimming in the water; and only I observed that hardly one lighter or boat in three that had the goods of a house in, but there was a pair of virginals in it. Having seen as much as I could now, I away to White Hall by appointment, and there walked to St. James's Park; and there met my wife, and Creed, and Wood, and his wife, and walked to my boat; and there upon the water again, and to the fire up and down, it still encreasing, and the wind 200 great. So near the fire as we could for smoke; and all over the Thames, with one's face in the wind, you were almost burned with a shower of fire-drops. This is very true; so as houses were burned by these drops and flakes of fire, three or four, nay, five or six houses, one from another. When we could endure no more upon the water, we to a little ale-house on the Bankside, over against the Three Cranes, and there stayed till it was dark almost and saw the fire grow; and, as it grew darker, appeared more and more; and 210 in corners and upon steeples, and between churches and houses, as far as we could see up the hill of the city, in a most horrid, malicious, bloody flame, not like the fine flame of an ordinary fire. Barbary and her husband away before us. We stayed till, it being darkish, we saw the fire as only one entire arch of fire from this to the other side the bridge, and in a bow up the hill for an arch of above a mile long; it made me weep to see it. The churches, houses, and all on fire, and flaming at once; and a horrid noise the flames

Mrs. Pepys' gentlewoman; she was quite vivacious and could sing. 125. Paul's, St. Paul's Cathedral. 195. virginals, small legless pianos. The name was probably derived from the fact that young ladies included play-

ing upon this instrument as one of their necessary social accomplishments.

made, and the cracking of houses at their ruin. So home with a sad heart, and there find everybody discoursing and lamenting the fire; and poor Tom Hater come with some few of his goods saved out of his house, which was burned upon Fish Street Hill. I invited him to lie at my house, and did receive his goods; but was deceived in his lying there, the news coming every moment of the growth of the fire; so as we were forced to begin to pack up our own goods, and prepare for their removal; and did by moonshine, it being brave, dry, and moonshine and warm weather, carry much of my goods into the garden; and Mr. Hater and I did remove my money and iron chests into my cellar, as thinking that the safest place. And got my bags of gold into my office, ready to carry away, and my chief papers of accounts also there, and my tallies into a box by themselves. So great was our fear, as Sir W. Batten hath carts come out of the country to fetch away his goods this night. We did put Mr. Hater, poor man! to bed a little; but he got but very little rest, so much noise being in my house, taking down of goods.

September 5, 1666.—I lay down in the office again upon W. Hewer's quilt, being mighty weary, and sore in my feet with going till I was hardly able to stand. About two in the morning my wife calls me up, and tells me of new cries of fire, it being come to Barking Church, which is the bottom of our lane. I up; and finding it so, resolved presently to take her away, and did, and took my gold, which was about £2350, W. Hewer and Jane down by Proundy's boat to Woolwich; but, Lord! what a sad sight it was by moonlight, to see the whole city almost on fire, that you might see it plain at Woolwich, as if you were by it. There, when I come, I find the gates shut, but no guard kept at all; which troubled me, because of discourse now begun, that there is plot in it, and that the French had done it. I got the gates open, and to Mr. Shelden's, where I locked up my gold, and charged my wife and W. Hewer never to leave the room without one of them in it, night or day. So back again, by the way seeing my goods well in the lighters at Deptford, and watched well by people. Home, and whereas I expected to have seen our house on fire, it being now about seven o'clock, it was not. But to the fire, and there find greater hopes than I expected; for my confidence of finding our office on fire was such, that I durst not ask anybody how it was with us, till I come and saw it not burned. But, going to the fire, I find, by the blowing up of houses, and the great help given by the workmen out of the King's yards, sent up by Sir W. Pen, there is a good stop given to it, as well as at Marke Lane end as ours; it having only burned the dial of Barking Church, and part of the porch, and was there

quenched. I up to the top of Barking steeple, and there saw the saddest sight of desolation that I ever saw; everywhere great fires, oil-cellars, and brimstone, and other things burning. I became afeard to stay there long, and therefore down again as fast as I could, the fire being spread as far as I could see it; and to Sir W. Pen's, and there eat a piece of cold meat, having eaten nothing since Sunday, but the remains of Sunday's dinner. Here I met with Mr. Young and Whistler; and, having removed all my things, and received good hopes that the fire at our end is stopped, they and I walked into the town, and find Fenchurch Street, Gracious Street, and Lumbard Street all in dust. The Exchange a sad sight, nothing standing there, of all the statues or pillars, but Sir Thomas Gresham's picture in the corner. Walked into Moorfields, our feet ready to burn, walking through the town among the hot coals, and find that full of people, and poor wretches carrying their goods there, and everybody keeping his goods together by themselves; and a great blessing it is to them that it is fair weather for them to keep abroad night and day; drank there, and paid two-pence for a plain penny loaf. Thence homeward, having passed through Cheapside, and Newgate Market, all burned; and seen Anthony Joyce's house in fire; and took up, which I keep by me, a piece of glass of Mercer's Chapel in the street, where much more was, so melted and buckled with the heat of the fire like parchment. I also did see a poor cat taken out of a hole in a chimney, joyning to the wall of the Exchange, with the hair all burned off the body, and yet alive. So home at night, and find there good hopes of saving our office; but great endeavors of watching all night, and having men ready; and so we lodged them in the office, and had drink and bread and cheese for them. And I lay down and slept a good night about midnight; though, when I rose, I heard that there had been a great alarm of French and Dutch being risen, which proved nothing. But it is a strange thing to see how long this time did look since Sunday, having been always full of variety of actions, and little sleep, that it looked like a week or more, and I had forgot almost the day of the week.

September 17, 1666.—Up betimes, and shaved myself after a week's growth: but, Lord! how ugly I was yesterday, and how fine to-day! By water, seeing the City all the way—a sad sight indeed, much fire being still in. Sir W. Coventry was in great pain lest the French fleete should be passed by our fleete, who had notice of them on Saturday, and were preparing to go meet them; but their minds altered, and judged them merchant-men; when, the same day, the Success, Captain Ball, made their whole fleete, and come to Brighthelmstone, and thence at five o'clock afternoon, Saturday, wrote Sir W. Coventry news thereof; so that

---

107. **Brightelmstone,** Brighton on the Sussex coast. 110. **Sir Thomas Clifford,** a gallant naval officer who was knighted for his conduct in a sea fight, 1665. 130. **Mrs. Stewart,** a great beauty of the court, one of Charles II's mistresses, and for a time the rival of Lady Castlemaine.

138. **Nell,** Nell Gwyn, the vivacious actress who rose from the gutter to the palace of Charles II. 148. **Cree Church,** the Church of St. Catherine Cree, one of the few city churches to escape the Fire. It was used by the Lord Mayor and the Corporation after the destruction of

we do much fear our missing them. Here come in and
110 talked with Sir Thomas Clifford, who appears a very
fine gentleman, and much set by at Court for his activity in going to sea, and stoutness every where, and
stirring up and down.

February 14, 1667.— . . . This morning come up to
my wife's bedside, I being up dressing myself, little
Will Mercer to be her Valentine; and brought her
name writ upon blue paper in gold letters, done by
himself, very pretty; and we were both well pleased
with it. But I am also this year my wife's Valentine,
120 and it will cost me £5; but that I must have laid out
if we had not been Valentines.

February 25, 1667.—Lay long in bed, talking with
pleasure with my poor wife, how she used to make
coal fires, and wash my foul clothes with her own hand
for me, poor wretch! in our little room at my Lord
Sandwich's; for which I ought for ever to love and admire her, and do; and persuade myself she would do
the same thing again, if God should reduce us to it.
At my goldsmith's did observe the King's new medall,
130 where, in little, there is Mrs. Stewart's face as well
done as ever I saw anything in my whole life, I think:
and a pretty thing it is, that he should choose her face
to represent Britannia by.

March 2, 1667.— . . . After dinner with my wife
to the King's house to see *The Mayden Queene*, a
new play of Dryden's, mightily commended for the
regularity of it, and the strain and wit; and the truth is,
there is a comical part done by Nell, which is Florimell,
that I never can hope ever to see the like done again
140 by man or woman. The King and Duke of York were at
the play. But so great performance of a comical part
was never, I believe, in the world before as Nell do
this, both as a mad girl, then most and best of all
when she comes in like a young gallant; and hath the
motions and carriage of a spark the most that ever I
saw any man have. It makes me, I confess, admire
her. . . .

August 18, 1667.—To Cree Church, to see it how it
is: but I find no alteration there, as they say there
150 was, for my Lord Mayor and Aldermen to come to
sermon, as they do every Sunday, as they did formerly
to Paul's. There dined with me Mr. Turner and
his daughter Betty. Betty is grown a fine young lady
as to carriage and discourse. We had a good haunch
of venison, powdered and boiled, and a good dinner.
I walked towards White Hall, but, being wearied,
turned into St. Dunstan's Church, where I heard an
able sermon of the minister of the place; and stood by
a pretty, modest maid, whom I did labour to take by
160 the hand; but she would not, but got further and
further from me; and, at last, I could perceive her to
take pins out of her pocket to prick me if I should

touch her again—which, seeing, I did forbear, and
was glad I did spy her design. And then I fell to gaze
upon another pretty maid, in a pew close to me, and
she on me; and I did go about to take her by the
hand, which she suffered a little, and then withdrew.
So the sermon ended, and the church broke up, and
my amours ended also. . . .

October 5, 1667.— . . . To the King's house; and 170
there going in met with Knipp, and she took us up into
the tiring-rooms; and to the women's shift, where Nell
was dressing herself, and was all unready, and is very
pretty, prettier than I thought. And so walked all up
and down the house above, and then below into the
scene-room, and there sat down, and she gave us
fruit; and here I read the questions to Knipp, while
she answered me, through all her part of *Flora's Figarys*,
which was acted today. But, Lord! to see how they
were both painted would make a man mad, and did 180
make me loathe them; and what base company of
men comes among them, and how lewdly they talk!
And how poor the men are in clothes, and yet what a
show they make on the stage by candle-light, is very
observable. But to see how Nell cursed, for having
so few people in the pit, was pretty; the other house
carrying away all the people at the new play, and
is said now-a-days to have generally most company,
as being better players. By and by into the pit, and
there saw the play, which is pretty good, but my belly 190
was full of what I had seen in the house, and so, after
the play done, away home. . . .

September 4, 1668.—At the Office all the morning;
and at noon my wife, and Deb., and Mercer, and W.
Hewer and I to the Fair, and there, at the old house,
did eat a pig, and was pretty merry, but saw no sights,
my wife having a mind to see the play *Bartholomew-
Fair*, with puppets. And it is an excellent play; the
more I see it, the more I love the wit of it; only the
business of abusing the Puritans begins to grow stale, 200
and of no use, they being the people that, at last,
will be found the wisest. And here Knipp come to us,
and sat with us, and thence took coach in two
coaches, and losing one another, my wife, and Knipp,
and I to Hercules Pillars, and there supped, and I
did take from her mouth the words and notes of her
song of "the Larke," which pleases me mightily. And
so set her at home, and away we home, where our
company come before us. This night Knipp tells us
that there is a Spanish woman lately come over, that 210
pretends to sing as well as Mrs. Knight; both of whom
I must endeavour to hear.

May 31, 1669.— . . . And thus ends all that I doubt
I shall ever be able to do with my own eyes in the
keeping of my Journal, I being not able to do it any
longer, having done now so long as to undo my eyes

St. Paul's Cathedral. 155. **powdered,** salted. 171. **Knipp,** an actress
of some promise and considerable sparkle, with whom Pepys carried
on an intermittent flirtation. She is known to have played in sixteen
roles between 1664 and 1678. 178. *Flora's Figarys,* i.e., Flora's Vagar-
ies, a comedy by a young Oxford student, Richard Rhodes. Nell Gwyn
made a great success of the role of Flora in this play. 194. **Deb.,**
Mrs. Pepys' maid. 197. *Bartholomew-Fair,* a comedy by Ben Jonson,
satirizing the Puritans (1614).

Samuel Pepys 451

almost every time that I take a pen in my hand; and, therefore, whatever comes of it, I must forbear: and, therefore, resolve, from this time forward, to have it kept by my people in long-hand, and must be contented to set down no more than is fit for them and all the world to know; or, if there be any thing, I must endeavour to keep a margin in my book open, to add, here and there, a note in short-hand with my own hand.

And so I betake myself to that course, which is almost as much as to see myself go into my grave: for which, and all the discomforts that will accompany my being blind, the good God prepare me! (1825)

DANIEL DEFOE 1659-1731

Daniel Defoe (originally Foe) was born in London of a middle-class family of nonconformists, Puritan in their outlook. Equipped with a good education, he took active part in the political, religious, and economic controversies of his day. He was soldier, trader, journalist, and pamphleteer; in all these various occupations he suffered from abuse and scorn leveled at him by his contemporaries—his spirit of independence alarmed one group; his spirit of moderation irritated others. In view of his Puritan background it is not surprising to see him in close intimacy with the government of William III, the Protestant king who had come to save England from what its inhabitants considered the terrors of popery. Between the years 1695 and 1702 Defoe worked hard for William; he wrote several pamphlets in defense of William's policies and composed The True-Born Englishman (1701), a vigorous satirical poem directed against the national objection to William as a foreigner and against the English insistence upon "purity of blood" as a necessary attribute of leadership. In this same period came his Essay upon Projects (1697-1698), setting forth many of his own views on social and political questions—views that were often extremely liberal for that time. He won a considerable audience among the middle classes; and when he was placed in the pillory, fined, and imprisoned for his hard-bitten satire against the Church of England party, The Shortest Way with Dissenters (1702), he became something of a popular hero.

Upon his release from prison in 1704, Defoe started a journal, The Review, a triweekly newspaper published until 1713. In this he frankly discussed questions of the day and printed reflections upon the morals and manners of contemporary England, in a manner anticipating The Tatler and The Spectator of Steele and Addison (p. 473). The last twenty years of Defoe's career is interesting to the student of literature chiefly because he wrote the stories for which he is best known: Robinson Crusoe (1719), Memoirs of a Cavalier (1720), Captain Singleton (1720), The Fortunes and Misfortunes of Moll Flanders (1772), A Journal of the Plague Year (1772), an excerpt from which is given below; The History of Colonel Jack (1722); Roxana, or The Fortunate Mistress (1724).

Above all, Defoe was a great realist. His pioneering in the foothills of the novel was successful because he was an accurate observer and because he invested all that he wrote with the quality of factual truth. He was a natural reporter, always straightforward, lucid, and vigorous. If occasionally his Puritanism caused him to moralize, he was nevertheless a journalist of keen intelligence and a significant figure to stand at the threshold of the eighteenth century.

---

from AN ESSAY UPON PROJECTS

This Essay is a miscellany of schemes for improving contemporary conditions relating to education, insurance, banking, highways, treatment of seamen, etc. These were favorite topics of discussion during the period, and the ideas advanced by Defoe prove both his versatility and his modernity. Although great interest was being expressed in the education of men, the education of women was attracting only slight attention; and it took considerable courage for a man to advocate, as Defoe did, a type of education for young women that should instruct them in something more than subjects conducive to "plain living and the practice of charity and devotion." In suggesting for women a curriculum of modern studies, the author was notably in advance of his generation. The following selection is a section of the chapter "Of Academies."

THE EDUCATION OF WOMEN

I have often thought of it as one of the most barbarous customs in the world, considering us as a civilized and a Christian country, that we deny the advantages of learning to women. We reproach the sex every day with folly and impertinence, while I am confident, had they the advantages of education equal to us, they would be guilty of less than ourselves.

One would wonder, indeed, how it should happen that women are conversible at all, since they are only beholding to natural parts for all their knowledge. Their youth is spent to teach them to stitch and sew or make baubles. They are taught to read, indeed, and perhaps to write their names or so, and that is the height of a woman's education. And I would but ask any who slight the sex for their understanding, what is a man (a gentleman, I mean) good for that is taught no more?

I need not give instances, or examine the character of a gentleman with a good estate, and of a good family, and with tolerable parts, and examine what figure he makes for want of education.

The soul is placed in the body like a rough diamond, and must be polished, or the luster of it will never appear: and 'tis manifest that as the rational soul distinguishes us from brutes, so education carries on the distinction and makes some less brutish than others. This is too evident to need any demonstration. But why then should women be denied the benefit of instruction? If knowledge and understanding had been useless additions to the sex, God Almighty would never have given them capacities, for He made nothing needless. Besides, I would ask such what they can see in ignorance that they should think it a necessary ornament to a woman? or how much worse is a wise woman than a fool? or what has the woman done to forfeit the privilege of being taught? Does she plague us with her pride and impertinence? Why did we not let her learn, that she might have had more wit? Shall we upbraid women with folly, when 'tis only the error of this inhuman custom that hindered them being made wiser?

The capacities of women are supposed to be greater and their senses quicker than those of the men; and what they might be capable of being bred to is plain from some instances of female wit, which this age is not without; which upbraids us with injustice, and looks as if we denied women the advantages of education for fear they should vie with the men in their improvements.

To remove this objection, and that women might have at least a needful opportunity of education in all sorts of useful learning, I propose the draught of an Academy for that purpose.

I know 'tis dangerous to make public appearances of the sex. They are not either to be confined or exposed; the first will disagree with their inclinations, and the last with their reputations, and therefore it is somewhat difficult; and I doubt a method proposed by an ingenious lady in a little book called *Advice to the Ladies*, would be found impracticable, for, saving my respect to the sex, the levity, which perhaps is a little peculiar to them, at least in their youth, will not bear the restraint; and I am satisfied nothing but the height of bigotry can keep up a nunnery. Women are extravagantly desirous of going to heaven, and will punish their pretty bodies to get thither; but nothing else will do it, and even in that case sometimes it falls out that nature will prevail.

When I talk, therefore, of an academy for women, I mean both the model, the teaching, and the government different from what is proposed by that ingenious lady, for whose proposal I have a very great esteem, and also a great opinion of her wit; different, too, from all sorts of religious confinement, and, above all, from vows of celibacy.

Wherefore the academy I propose should differ but little from public schools, wherein such ladies as were willing to study should have all the advantages of learning suitable to their genius. But since some severities of discipline more than ordinary would be absolutely necessary to preserve the reputation of the house, that persons of quality and fortune might not be afraid to venture their children thither, I shall venture to make a small scheme by way of essay.

The house I would have built in a form by itself, as well as in a place by itself. The building should be of three plain fronts, without any jettings or bearing-work; that the eye might at a glance see from one coign to the other; the gardens walled in the same triangular figure, with a large moat, and but one entrance. When thus every part of the situation was contrived as well as might be for discovery, and to render intriguing dangerous, I would have no guards, no eyes, no spies set over the ladies, but shall expect them to be tried by the principles of honor and strict virtue. . . .

Upon this ground I am persuaded such measures might be taken that the ladies might have all the freedom in the world within their own walls, and yet no intriguing, no indecencies, nor scandalous affairs happen; and in order to this the following customs and laws should be observed in the colleges, of which I would propose one at least in every county in England, and about ten for the city of London.

After the regulation of the form of the building as before:—

1. All the ladies who enter into the house should set their hands to the orders of the house, to signify their consent to submit to them.

2. As no woman should be received but who declared herself willing, and that it was the act of her choice to enter herself, so no person should be confined

An Essay upon Projects. 9. conversible, able to be conversed with. 10. beholding . . . parts, dependent upon nature and instinct. 59. ingenious lady, Mary Astell (1668–1731), an English authoress whose particular interest was the education of women. Her most important contribution to the problem was *A Serious Proposal to the Ladies Wherein a Method Is Offered for the Improvement of Their Minds.* 77. public schools. As used in England, this term applies to one of the several great preparatory schools, such as Rugby or Eton. 79. genius, natural talents and abilities. 84. essay, trial, attempt. 87. jettings or bearing-work. *Jettings* in architecture is an old name for anything jutting out from the perpendicular; *bearing-work* would refer to that part of a wall which bore the weight of such projections. 107. set their hands . . . house, sign their names to the ordinances or bylaws.

Daniel Defoe 453

to continue there a moment longer than the same voluntary choice inclined her.

3. The charges of the house being to be paid by the ladies, everyone that entered should have only this encumbrance, that she should pay for the whole year, though her mind should change as to her continuance.

4. An Act of Parliament should make it felony without clergy for any man to enter by force or fraud into the house, or to solicit any woman, though 10 it were to marry, while she was in the house. And this law would by no means be severe, because any woman who was willing to receive the addresses of a man might discharge herself of the house when she pleased; and, on the contrary, any woman who had occasion, might discharge herself of the impertinent addresses of any person she had an aversion to by entering into the house.

In this house, the persons who enter should be taught all sorts of breeding suitable both to their genius 20 and quality, and in particular, music and dancing, which it would be cruelty to bar the sex of, because they are their darlings; but besides this, they should be taught languages, as particularly French and Italian; and I would venture the injury of giving a woman more tongues than one. They should, as a particular study, be taught all the graces of speech, and all the necessary air of conversation, which our common education is so defective in that I need not expose it. They should be brought to read books, and especially history; and so 30 to read as to make them understand the world, and be able to know and judge of things when they hear of them.

To such whose genius would lead them to it, I would deny no sort of learning; but the chief thing, in general, is to cultivate the understandings of the sex, that they may be capable of all sorts of conversation; that, their parts and judgments being improved, they may be as profitable in their conversation as they are pleasant.

40 Women, in my observation, have little or no difference in them, but as they are or are not distinguished by education. Tempers, indeed, may in some degree influence them, but the main distinguishing part is their breeding.

The whole sex are generally quick and sharp. I believe I may be allowed to say generally so, for you rarely see them lumpish and heavy when they are children, as boys will often be. If a woman be well bred, and taught the proper management of her natural wit, 50 she proves generally very sensible and retentive; and without partiality, a woman of sense and manners is the finest and most delicate part of God's creation, the glory of her Maker, and the great instance of His singular regard to man, His darling creature, to whom He gave the best gift either God could bestow or man

receive. And 'tis the sordidest piece of folly and ingratitude in the world to withhold from the sex the due luster which the advantage of education gives to the natural beauty of their minds.

A woman well bred and well taught, furnished with 60 the additional accomplishments of knowledge and behavior, is a creature without comparison; her society is the emblem of sublimer enjoyments; her person is angelic and her conversation heavenly; she is all softness and sweetness, peace, love, wit, and delight. She is every way suitable to the sublimest wish, and the man that has such a one to his portion has nothing to do but rejoice in her and be thankful.

On the other hand, suppose her to be the very same woman, and rob her of the benefit of education, 70 and it follows thus:

If her temper be good, want of education makes her soft and easy. Her wit, for want of teaching, makes her impertinent and talkative. Her knowledge, for want of judgment and experience, makes her fanciful and whimsical. If her temper be bad, want of breeding makes her worse, and she grows haughty, insolent, and loud. If she be passionate, want of manners makes her termagant and a scold, which is much at one with lunatic. If she be proud, want of discretion (which still 80 is breeding) makes her conceited, fantastic, and ridiculous. And from these she degenerates to be turbulent, clangorous, noisy, nasty, and the devil.

Methinks mankind for their own sakes—since, say what we will of the women, we all think fit at one time or other to be concerned with them—should take some care to breed them up to be suitable and serviceable, if they expected no such thing as delight from them. Bless us! what care do we take to breed up a good horse and to break him well! and what a value 90 do we put upon him when it is done, and all because he should be fit for our use! and why not a woman? Since all her ornaments and beauty without suitable behavior is a cheat in nature, like the false tradesman, who puts the best of his goods uppermost, that the buyer may think the rest are of the same goodness.

Beauty of the body, which is the women's glory, seems to be now unequally bestowed, and Nature, or rather Providence, to lie under some scandal about it, as if 'twas given a woman for a snare to men, and 100 so made a kind of a she-devil of her; because, they say, exquisite beauty is rarely given with wit, more rarely with goodness of temper, and never at all with modesty. And some, pretending to justify the equity of such a distribution, will tell us 'tis the effect of the justice of Providence in dividing particular excellencies among all His creatures, share and share alike, as it were, that all might for something or other be acceptable to one another, else some would be despised.

I think both these notions false, and yet the last, 110

---

8. **without clergy.** In earlier times, it was possible for any member of the clergy, and then somewhat later for anyone who could read or write, when convicted of some capital crime other than treason, to appear before an ecclesiastical rather than a civil court. When discharged from this ecclesiastical court, the accused would suffer a lesser punishment than death, usually whipping or branding or perhaps only heavy fines.

which has the show of respect to Providence, is the worst, for it supposes Providence to be indigent and empty, as if it had not wherewith to furnish all the creatures it had made, but was fain to be parsimonious in its gifts, and distribute them by piecemeal for fear of being exhausted.

If I might venture my opinion against an almost universal notion, I would say most men mistake the proceedings of Providence in this case, and all the world at this day are mistaken in their practice about it. And because the assertion is very bold, I desire to explain myself.

That Almighty First Cause which made us all is certainly the fountain of excellence, as it is of being, and by an invisible influence could have diffused equal qualities and perfections to all the creatures it has made, as the sun does its light, without the least ebb or diminution to Himself, and has given indeed to every individual sufficient to the figure His providence had designed him in the world.

I believe it might be defended if I should say that I do suppose God has given to all mankind equal gifts and capacities in that He has given them all souls equally capable, and that the whole difference in mankind proceeds either from accidental difference in the make of their bodies or from the foolish difference of education.

1. *From Accidental Difference in Bodies.* I would avoid discoursing here of the philosophical position of the soul in the body. But if it be true, as philosophers do affirm, that the understanding and memory is dilated or contracted according to the accidental dimensions of the organ through which 'tis conveyed, then, though God has given a soul as capable to me as another, yet if I have any natural defect in those parts of the body by which the soul should act, I may have the same soul infused as another man, and yet he be a wise man and I a very fool. For example, if a child naturally have a defect in the organ of hearing, so that he could never distinguish any sound, that child shall never be able to speak or read, though it have a soul capable of all the accomplishments in the world. The brain is the center of all the soul's actings, where all the distinguishing faculties of it reside; and 'tis observable a man who has a narrow contracted head, in which there is not room for the due and necessary operations of nature by the brain, is never a man of very great judgment; and that proverb, "A great head and little wit," is not meant by nature, but is a reproof upon sloth, as if one should, by way of wonder, say, "Fie, fie! you that have a great head have but little wit; that's strange! that must certainly be your own fault." From this notion I do believe there is a great matter in the breed of men and women—not that wise men shall always get wise children, but I believe strong and healthy bodies have the wisest children, and sickly, weakly bodies affect

As Defoe uses the sense here, he is practically saying, "to make it a crime without any possible mitigation of the punishment."

the wits as well as the bodies of their children. We are easily persuaded to believe this in the breeds of horses, cocks, dogs, and other creatures, and I believe 'tis as visible in men.

But to come closer to the business, the great distinguishing difference which is seen in the world between men and women is in their education, and this is manifested by comparing it with the difference between one man or woman and another.

And herein it is that I take upon me to make such a bold assertion that all the world are mistaken in their practice about women; for I cannot think that God Almighty ever made them so delicate, so glorious creatures, and furnished them with such charms, so agreeable and so delightful to mankind, with souls capable of the same accomplishments with men, and all to be only stewards of our houses, cooks, and slaves.

Not that I am for exalting the female government in the least; but, in short, I would have men take women for companions, and educate them to be fit for it. A woman of sense and breeding will scorn as much to encroach upon the prerogative of the man as a man of sense will scorn to oppress the weakness of the woman. But if the women's souls were refined and improved by teaching, that word would be lost; to say, the *weakness of the sex* as to judgment, would be nonsense, for ignorance and folly would be no more found among women than men. I remember a passage which I heard from a very fine woman; she had wit and capacity enough, an extraordinary shape and face, and a great fortune, but had been cloistered up all her time, and, for fear of being stolen, had not had the liberty of being taught the common necessary knowledge of women's affairs; and when she came to converse in the world, her natural wit made her so sensible of the want of education that she gave this short reflection on herself—"I am ashamed to talk with my very maids," says she, "for I don't know when they do right or wrong. I had more need go to school than be married."

I need not enlarge on the loss the defect of education is to the sex, nor argue the benefit of the contrary practice; 'tis a thing will be more easily granted than remedied. This chapter is but an essay at the thing, and I refer the practice to those happy days, if ever they shall be, when men shall be wise enough to mend it. (1692; 1697)

from A JOURNAL OF THE PLAGUE YEAR

In 1722 Defoe published, under the title A Journal of the Plague Year, an account of the outbreak of bubonic plague that swept through Western Europe in the 1660's, ravaging England during the summer and fall of 1665. The account by Samuel Pepys (p. 446) was that of an eyewitness and survivor, that by Defoe is, so far as first-hand experience is concerned, entirely fic-

titious. A comparison of Defoe's work with the appropriate pages of Pepys' Diary will be illuminating; although the account of Pepys has the unquestioned authenticity of the first-hand observer, while Defoe's account has a slight artificiality, it is apparent at once that Defoe's imagination achieved a great triumph. His fiction has, in effect, won such a power over fact that it has itself become fact. No work of Defoe's will illustrate better the peculiar qualities of his ability. Though overshadowed by the greater works like Robinson Crusoe or Moll Flanders, the Journal of the Plague Year shows the attention to minute detail, the realism, and the moral bias that Defoe generally exhibits, as well as an occasional veering toward sentimentality, which Defoe as a middle-class Englishman could hardly avoid.

. . . It pleased God that I was still spared, and very hearty and sound in health, but very impatient of being pent up within doors without air, as I had been for fourteen days or thereabouts; and I could not restrain myself, but I would go and carry a letter for my brother to the post-house; then it was, indeed, that I observed a profound silence in the streets. When I came to the post-house, as I went to put in my letter,
10 I saw a man stand in one corner of the yard, and talking to another at a window, and a third had opened a door belonging to the office. In the middle of the yard lay a small leather purse, with two keys hanging at it, with money in it, but nobody would meddle with it. I asked how long it had lain there; the man at the window said it had lain almost an hour, but they had not meddled with it, because they did not know but the person who dropped it might come back to look for it. I had no such need of money, nor was the sum so big that I had any inclination to meddle with it, or to
20 get the money at the hazard it might be attended with, so I seemed to go away, when the man who had opened the door said he would take it up; but so, that if the right owner came for it he should be sure to have it. So he went in and fetched a pail of water, and set it down hard by the purse, then went again and fetched some gunpowder, and cast a good deal of powder upon the purse, and then made a train from that which he had thrown loose upon the purse; the train reached about two yards; after this he goes in a third time, and
30 fetches out a pair of tongs red-hot, and which he had prepared, I suppose, on purpose; and first setting fire to the train of powder, that singed the purse, and also smoked the air sufficiently. But he was not content with that, but he then takes up the purse with the tongs, holding it so long till the tongs burnt through the purse, and then he shook the money out into the pail of water, so he carried it in. The money, as I

remember, was about thirteen shillings, and some smooth groats and brass farthings.

Much about the same time I walked out into the 40 fields toward Bow, for I had a great mind to see how things were managed in the river, and among the ships; and as I had some concern in shipping, I had a notion that it had been one of the best ways of securing one's self from the infection to have retired into a ship; and musing how to satisfy my curiosity in that point, I turned away over the fields, from Bow to Bromley and down to Blackwall, to the stairs that are there for landing or taking water.

Here I saw a poor man walking on the bank or sea- 50 wall, as they call it, by himself. I walked awhile also about, seeing the houses all shut up; at last I fell into some talk, at a distance, with this poor man. First I asked how people did thereabouts. "Alas! sir," says he, "almost desolate, all dead or sick. Here are very few families in this part, or in that village," pointing at Poplar, "where half of them are dead already, and the rest sick." Then he pointing to one house, "They are all dead," said he, "and the house stands open, nobody dares go into it. A poor thief," says he, "ventured in to 60 steal something, but he paid dear for his theft; for he was carried to the churchyard too, last night." Then he pointed to several other houses. "There," says he, "they all are dead, the man and his wife and five children." "There," says he, "they are shut up, you see a watchman at the door; and so of other houses." "Why," says I, "what do you here all alone?" "Why," says he, "I am a poor desolate man; it hath pleased God I am not yet visited, though my family is, and one of my children dead." "How do you mean, then," said I, 70 "that you are not visited?" "Why," says he, "that is my house," pointing to a very little low boarded house, "and there my poor wife and two children live," said he, "if they may be said to live; for my wife and one of the children are visited, but I do not come at them." And with that word I saw the tears run very plentifully down his face; and so they did down mine, too, I assure you.

"But," said I, "why do you not come at them? How can you abandon your own flesh and blood?" "Oh, sir," 80 says he, "the Lord forbid! I do not abandon them, I work for them as much as I am able; and, blessed be the Lord, I keep them from want." And with that I observed he lifted up his eyes to Heaven with a countenance that presently told me I had happened on a man that was no hypocrite, but a serious, religious, good man; and his ejaculation was an expression of thankfulness that, in such a condition as he was in, he should be able to say his family did not want. "Well," says I, "honest man, that is a great mercy, as things 90 go now with the poor. But how do you live, then, and

---

A Journal of the Plague Year. 33. **smoked . . . sufficiently.** The older theory was that the plague was transmitted by bodily exhalations (cf. the extract from Pepys' Diary, p. 446). The gunpowder would permeate the air with its own odor and so drive out the "exhalations" that would make the purse infectious. 39. **groats,** old Dutch coins, worth about fourpence. They were not coined after 1662. 155. **swelling**

how are you kept from the dreadful calamity that is now upon us all?" "Why, sir," says he, "I am a waterman, and there is my boat," says he, "and the boat serves me for a house; I work in it in the day, and I sleep in it in the night, and what I get I lay it down upon that stone," says he, showing me a broad stone on the other side of the street, a good way from the house; "and then," says he, "I halloo and call to them till I make them hear, and they come and fetch it."

"Well, friend," says I, "but how can you get money as a waterman? Does anybody go by water these times?" "Yes, sir," says he, "in the way I am employed there does. Do you see there," says he, "five ships lie at anchor," pointing down the river a good way below the town; "and do you see," says he, "eight or ten ships lie at the chain there, and at anchor yonder?" pointing above the town. "All those ships have families on board, of their merchants and owners, and such like, who have locked themselves up, and live on board, close shut in, for fear of infection; and I tend on them to fetch things for them, carry letters and do what is absolutely necessary, that they may not be obliged to come on shore; and every night I fasten my boat on board one of the ship's boats, and there I sleep by myself, and, blessed be God, I am preserved hitherto."

"Well," said I, "friend, but will they let you come on board after you have been on shore here, when this has been such a terrible place, and so infected as it is?"

"Why, as to that," said he, "I very seldom go up the ship side, but deliver what I bring to their boat, or lie by the side, and they hoist it on board. If I did, I think they are in no danger from me, for I never go into any house on shore, or touch anybody, no, not for my own family; but I fetch provisions for them."

"Nay," says I, "but that may be worse, for you must have those provisions of somebody or other; and since all this part of the town is so infected, it is dangerous so much as to speak with anybody; for the village," said I, "is as it were the beginning of London, though it be at some distance from it."

"That is true," added he, "but you do not understand me right; I do not buy provisions for them here; I row up to Greenwich, and buy fresh meat there, and sometimes I row down the river to Woolwich, and buy there; then I go to single farm houses on the Kentish side, where I am known, and buy fowls, and eggs, and butter, and bring to the ships as they direct me, sometimes one, sometimes the other. I seldom come on shore here; and I came only now to call my wife and hear how my little family do, and give them a little money which I received last night."

"Poor man!" said I, "and how much hast thou gotten for them?"

"I have gotten four shillings," said he, "which is a great sum as things go now with poor men; but they have given me a bag of bread, too, and a salt fish, and some fresh; so all helps out."

"Well," said I, "and have you given it them yet?"

"No," said he, "but I have called, and my wife has answered that she cannot come out yet, but in half an hour she hopes to come, and I am waiting for her. Poor woman!" says he, "she is brought sadly down; she has had a swelling, and it is broke, and I hope she will recover, but I fear the child will die; but it is the Lord!" Here he stopped and wept very much.

"Well, honest friend," said I, "thou hast a sure comforter if thou hast brought thyself to be resigned to the will of God; He is dealing with us all in judgment."

"Oh, sir," says he, "it is infinite mercy if any of us are spared; and who am I to repine?"

"Say'st thou so?" said I, "and how much less is my faith than thine!" And here my heart smote me, suggesting how much better this poor man's foundation was, on which he stayed in the danger, than mine; that he had nowhere to fly; that he had a family to bind him to attendance, which I had not; and mine was mere presumption, his a true dependence and a courage resting on God, and yet that he used all possible caution for his safety.

I turned a little away from the man while these thoughts engaged me; for, indeed, I could no more refrain from tears than he.

At length, after some further talk, the poor woman opened the door and called: "Robert, Robert!" He answered, and bid her stay a few moments, and he would come; so he ran down the common stairs to his boat, and fetched up a sack in which were the provisions he had brought from the ships; and when he returned he hallooed again; then he went to the great stone which he showed me, and emptied the sack, and laid all out, everything by themselves, and then retired; and his wife came with a little boy to fetch them away; and he called and said such a captain had sent such a thing, and such a captain such a thing, and at the end adds: "God has sent it all; give thanks to Him." When the poor woman had taken up all, she was so weak she could not carry it at once in, though the weight was not much neither; so she left the biscuit, which was in a little bag, and left a little boy to watch it till she came again.

"Well, but," says I to him, "did you leave her the four shillings, too, which you said was your week's pay?"

"Yes, yes," said he, "you shall hear her own it." So he calls again, "Rachel, Rachel" (which, it seems, was her name), "did you take up the money?" "Yes,"

. . . **broke.** Bubonic plague is characterized by the swelling of the lymphatic glands. The opinion held by the physicians of the time was that these swellings should somehow be made to open; if they could be poulticed, well and good. "If these swellings could be brought to a head, and to break and run, or, as the surgeons call it, to digest, the patient generally recovered."—*A Journal of the Plague Year.*

said she. "How much was it?" said he. "Four shillings and a groat," said she. "Well, well," says he, "the Lord keep you all"; and so he turned to go away.

As I could not refrain from contributing tears to this man's story, so neither could I refrain my charity for his assistance; so I called him, "Hark thee, friend," said I, "come hither, for I believe thou art in health, that I may venture thee"; so I pulled out my hand, which was in my pocket before, "Here," says I, "go and call thy Rachel once more, and give her a little more comfort from me. God will never forsake a family that trusts in Him as thou dost"; so I gave

him four other shillings, and bade him go lay them on the stone, and call his wife.

I have not words to express the poor man's thankfulness, neither could he express it himself, but by tears running down his face. He called his wife, and told her God had moved the heart of a stranger, upon hearing their condition, to give them all that money; and a great deal more such as that he said to her. The woman, too, made signs of the like thankfulness, as well to Heaven as to me, and joyfully picked it up; and I parted with no money all that year that I thought better bestowed. . . .

(1722)

JOHN DRYDEN 1631-1700

Dryden was born in Northamptonshire of sturdy Puritan and anti-monarchical stock. While attending Westminster School, and later at Trinity College, Cambridge, he attracted attention by his elegiac verses. His first considerable poem, Heroic Stanzas (1659), was written on the death of Cromwell. The next year he wrote Astraea Redux, a panegyric on the return of Charles II, thus, as Dr. Johnson said, "he changed with the nation." It was in this poem that Dryden first showed his mastery of the heroic couplet, the poetic form that was to prevail generally in English literature for nearly a hundred years. After an unsuccessful attempt at tragedy, Dryden wrote several rather commercial comedies, but these plays also proved failures. He produced two heroic plays, The Indian Queen (1664) and The Indian Emperor (1665), both striking successes, partly because of the use of heroic verse and particularly because of the melodramatic qualities and the splendor of the stage spectacle. In 1667 he made himself even better known by his Annus Mirabilis, a poem that describes the great events in English history during the period 1665-1666: the war with Holland, the terrors of the plague, and the Great Fire of London (cf. Pepys' Diary, p. 448). At royal request he was granted the M.A. degree from Cambridge in 1668, and in 1670 was made poet laureate and historiographer to the King.

The use of rime in tragedy had been vigorously attacked as artificial and bombastic, but Dryden ably defended his practice and set forth his critical views in his Essay of Dramatic Poesy (1668), in his prefaces, and in other prose writings. For the next fifteen years, he wrote many plays, but both his satirical comedies and his rather extravagant tragedies met with only spasmodic and indifferent success. He admitted having grown tired of rime in the prologue to

Aurengzebe (1676), his last rimed tragedy. His next dramatic work was All for Love (1678), a powerful version of the story of Antony and Cleopatra, in blank verse; it is probably Dryden's best play.

Some of Dryden's finest talent was expressed in satire. During the political and religious strife of his age, he wrote numerous treatises, chiefly in verse, defending his evolving convictions. Absalom and Achitophel (p. 459), written in 1681, a brilliant satire full of ridicule and invective, attacked those who planned to establish the Duke of Monmouth on the throne. In 1682 came The Medal, directed against the Whigs, MacFlecknoe (p. 462), a witty and exuberant literary satire, and Religio Laici, a defense of the Church of England against its enemies. Three years later Dryden became a Roman Catholic and in 1687 published his most famous religious poem, The Hind and the Panther. In this satire, the hind is the symbol of the Roman Church, persecuted by the panther, the wolf, the bear, the boar, and other animals, representing the Anglicans, the Calvinists, and various other hostile sects. Although Dryden's ecclesiastical and political shifting of position has led to some doubt as to his sincerity, there is no evidence that he was motivated by opportunism. It is hasty and erroneous to consider Dryden a professional turncoat, as has too often been charged. His several changes in politics and religion represent, rather, the outcome of a lifelong habit of philosophical skepticism, a conscientious search after authority in matters of government and private belief, and an increasingly conservative cast of mind; in this general orientation Dryden fits solidly within the tentative, open-minded philosophical tradition of Pyrrho of Elis and Montaigne.

In the last ten to fifteen years of his life Dryden showed a remarkable burst of lyricism, producing the beautiful Song for St. Cecilia's Day (p. 465), Alexander's Feast (p. 466), and the ode To Mrs. Anne Killigrew. Then after the Revolution of 1688 and the exile of King James II, Dryden refused for reasons of conscience to swear allegiance to William and Mary; he thereby lost all pensions and offices, including the laureateship, and was forced back upon his pen for support. He wrote plays, odes, eulogies, criticism, and an epoch-making translation of Vergil as well as numerous translations from various other classical authors. His poetic translations of some of the fables of Ovid, Homer, Boccaccio, and Chaucer appeared with one of Dryden's most significant critical prefaces (p. 470) a few months before his death in 1700. He was buried in Westminster Abbey beside Chaucer and Cowley.

In his old age Dryden was treated with the respect due to the greatest of living English poets, dramatists, and critics; among his admirers were Congreve, Vanbrugh, and Addison (p. 473), but his greatest disciple was Pope. It is no exaggeration to say that Dryden during the 1690's was a literary dictator in England, and his influence was spread posthumously for more than a generation after 1700. So in Will's coffee house during his last years he could pronounce to Swift that he would never become a poet, or be reverenced by Pope, a twelve-year-old aspirant to poetic fame. But Dryden's achievement rests upon a much more solid foundation than mere personality, charming as his seems to have been. First of all, he established the heroic couplet as the fashion for satiric and didactic poetry. As Mark Van Doren has said, Dryden's contribution to the manner of poetry is "the story of a poet who inherited a medium, perfected it by long manipulation, stamped it with his genius, and handed it on. That medium was heroic couplet verse." In addition to his extraordinary accomplishment in poetry, Dryden left a legacy of direct, simple, and lucid prose; he is the first writer in the Modern English period of the language who writes a prose that sounds truly modern. He throws aside the rhetorical conventions of the Elizabethan prose-writers and speaks at once informally, forcefully, and clearly. Dryden's style is sure and urbane, an admirable vehicle for human communication. As Matthew Arnold expressed it, Dryden was "the inaugurator of an age of prose and reason"; he dominated that age and cast his shadow far over the next century.

---

from ABSALOM AND ACHITOPHEL

(FROM PART I)

Si propius stes
Te capiat magis

Absalom and Achitophel, a political satire and allegory, deals with the attempt of Lord Shaftesbury's party (the Whigs) to exclude Charles II's brother James, Duke of York, from the British throne because he was a Roman Catholic, and to set in his place Charles' illegitimate son, James, Duke of Monmouth, a Protestant. Shaftesbury had been deprived of his ministerial office and imprisoned on the charge of high treason. Before the trial was held, Dryden wrote the poem to influence popular opinion, as well as the jury, against the Whig leader, but Shaftesbury was acquitted. The allegorical basis of the satire is the thinly veiled biblical story of King David and his son Absalom (2 Samuel, Chapters 13-18). Monmouth is Absalom; Shaftesbury, the false tempter Achitophel; and Charles II, King David. Dryden supports King Charles and the Tories as he severely lashes the Whigs. His major stylistic achievement in the poem is the blending of an elevated style with a satiric purpose. The Biblical mask enables him, in Browning's phrase, to "tell a truth obliquely."

In pious times, ere priestcraft did begin,
Before polygamy was made a sin;
When man on many multiplied his kind,
Ere one to one was cursedly confined;
When nature prompted, and no law denied
Promiscuous use of concubine and bride;
Then Israel's monarch after Heaven's own heart,
His vigorous warmth did variously impart
To wives and slaves; and, wide as his command,
Scattered his Maker's image through the land.   10
Michal of royal blood, the crown did wear;
A soil ungrateful to the tiller's care:
Not so the rest; for several mothers bore
To godlike David several sons before.
But since like slaves his bed they did ascend,
No true succession could their seed attend.
Of all this numerous progeny was none
So beautiful, so brave, as Absalon:
Whether, inspired by some diviner lust,
His father got him with a greater gust;   20
Or that his conscious destiny made way,
By manly beauty, to imperial sway.
Early in foreign fields he won renown
With kings and states allied to Israel's crown;
In peace the thoughts of war he could remove,
And seemed as he were only born for love.
Whate'er he did, was done with so much ease,

Absalom and Achitophel. Si . . . magis, "the closer you stand, the more it pleases you."—Horace, *The Art of Poetry,* 361. **7. Israel's monarch,** King David, representing Charles II of England; *Israel* is England. **11. Michal,** daughter of Saul and wife of David; she represents Charles II's queen, Catharine of Portugal, who was childless. **13. several mothers . . . before.** The "several mothers" were the many mistresses of Charles II, some of whom were mentioned in the pages of Pepys' *Diary* (p. 446). **18. Absalon,** a variant of **Absalom,** the third son of David; he represents James, Duke of Monmouth, son of Charles II and Lucy Waters. **23. foreign fields . . . crown.** Monmouth commanded the English army against the Dutch in 1672-1674, and against the Scotch in 1675; he served also in a war with France in 1678.

In him alone 'twas natural to please:
His motions all accompanied with grace;
30 And paradise was opened in his face.
With secret joy indulgent David viewed
His youthful image in his son renewed:
To all his wishes nothing he denied;
And made the charming Annabel his bride.
What faults he had (for who from faults is free?)
His father could not or he would not see.
Some warm excesses which the law forbore,
Were construed youth that purged by boiling o'er,
And Amnon's murder, by a specious name,
40 Was called a just revenge for injured fame.
Thus praised and loved the noble youth remained,
While David, undisturbed, in Sion reigned.

But life can never be sincerely blest;
Heaven punishes the bad, and proves the best.
The Jews, a headstrong, moody, murmuring race,
As ever tried th' extent and stretch of grace;
God's pampered people, whom, debauched with ease,
No king could govern, nor no God could please;
(Gods they had tried of every shape and size,
50 That god-smiths could produce, or priests devise);
These Adam-wits, too fortunately free,
Began to dream they wanted liberty;
And when no rule, no precedent was found,
Of men by laws less circumscribed and bound;
They led their wild desires to woods and caves,
And thought that all but savages were slaves.
They who, when Saul was dead, without a blow,
Made foolish Ishbosheth the crown forego;
Who banished David did from Hebron bring,
60 And with a general shout proclaimed him king:
Those very Jews, who, at their very best,
Their humor more than loyalty expressed,
Now wondered why so long they had obeyed
An idol monarch, which their hands had made;
Thought they might ruin him they could create,
Or melt him to that golden calf, a State.
But these were random bolts; no formed design,
Nor interest made the factious crowd to join:
The sober part of Israel, free from stain,
70 Well knew the value of a peaceful reign;
And, looking backward with a wise affright,
Saw seams of wounds, dishonest to the sight:
In contemplation of whose ugly scars
They cursed the memory of civil wars.
The moderate sort of men, thus qualified,

Inclined the balance to the better side;
And David's mildness managed it so well,
The bad found no occasion to rebel.
But when to sin our biased nature leans,
The careful Devil is still at hand with means; 80
And providently pimps for ill desires:
The Good Old Cause, revived, a plot requires.
Plots, true or false, are necessary things,
To raise up commonwealths and ruin kings.

Th' inhabitants of old Jerusalem
Were Jebusites, the town so called from them;
And theirs the native right.
But when the chosen people grew more strong,
The rightful cause at length became the wrong;
And every loss the men of Jebus bore, 90
They still were thought God's enemies the more.
Thus worn and weakened, well or ill content,
Submit they must to David's government:
Impoverished and deprived of all command,
Their taxes doubled as they lost their land;
And, what was harder yet to flesh and blood,
Their gods disgraced, and burned like common wood.
This set the heathen priesthood in a flame;
For priests of all religions are the same:
Of whatsoe'er descent their godhead be, 100
Stock, stone, or other homely pedigree,
In his defense his servants are as bold,
As if he had been born of beaten gold.
The Jewish rabbins, though their enemies,
In this conclude them honest men and wise:
For 'twas their duty, all the learnéd think,
T' espouse his cause, by whom they eat and drink.
From hence began that Plot, the nation's curse,
Bad in itself, but represented worse,
Raised in extremes, and in extremes decried, 110
With oaths affirmed, with dying vows denied,
Not weighed or winnowed by the multitude;
But swallowed in the mass, unchewed and crude.
Some truth there was, but dashed and brewed with lies,
To please the fools, and puzzle all the wise:
Succeeding times did equal folly call,
Believing nothing, or believing all.
Th' Egyptian rites the Jebusites embraced;
Where gods were recommended by their taste.
Such sav'ry deities must needs be good, 120
As served at once for worship and for food.
By force they could not introduce these gods,
For ten to one in former days was odds;

---

34. **Annabel**, Anne Scott, Countess of Buccleuch, a wealthy heiress of Scotland. 39. **Amnon's murder.** Amnon was killed by order of his brother Absalom (cf. 2 Samuel, Chapter 13) because he had ravished his sister Tamar. The reference in Dryden's poem is probably an allusion to a brutal attack by Monmouth's men upon Sir John Coventry, who had criticized the king's amours. 42. **Sion**, London. 45. **The Jews**, the English people. 51. **Adam-wits**, foolish persons who do not know when they are well off, like Adam before his fall. 55. **woods and caves**, the American colonies, settled by the English in the beginning of the seventeenth century. 57. **Saul**, Oliver Cromwell (1599-1658), Lord Protector of the Commonwealth. 58. **Ishbosheth**, son of Saul; he represents Richard Cromwell, son of Oliver Cromwell, who succeeded his father as Lord Protector of the Commonwealth for a few

brief months before the Restoration in 1660. 59. **Hebron**, probably Scotland. Charles II returned to Scotland from Holland in 1649, and was there crowned at Scone in 1651. (It should be remembered that Charles was a Stuart, a member of the royal family of Scotland, and became king of Scotland automatically upon the death of his father, Charles I, in 1649. He was theoretically king of England, too; but the Civil War prevented his making good his claim at the time.) Hebron was the name of the town in which David was anointed king of Israel (cf. 2 Samuel 5:1-3). 74. **civil wars**, the Civil War of the 1640's. 86. **Jebusites**, Roman Catholics. 88. **chosen people**, Protestants. 98. **heathen priesthood**, Catholic priests. 104. **Jewish rabbins**, leading clergymen of the Church of England. 108. **that Plot**, the famous popish plot of 1677-1679. The Jesuits were charged, on doubtful evidence,

So fraud was used (the sacrificer's trade):
Fools are more hard to conquer than persuade.
Their busy teachers mingled with the Jews,
And raked for converts e'en the court and stews:
Which Hebrew priests the more unkindly took,
Because the fleece accompanies the flock.
130 Some thought they God's anointed meant to slay
By guns, invented since full many a day:
Our author swears it not; but who can know
How far the Devil and Jebusites may go?
This Plot, which failed for want of common sense,
Had yet a deep and dangerous consequence:
For, as when raging fevers boil the blood,
The standing lake soon floats into a flood,
And every hostile humor, which before
Slept quiet in its channels, bubbles o'er;
140 So several factions from this first ferment
Work up to foam, and threat the government.
Some by their friends, more by themselves thought
    wise,
Opposed the power to which they could not rise.
Some had in courts been great, and thrown from
    thence,
Like fiends were hardened in impenitence.
Some, by their monarch's fatal mercy, grown
From pardoned rebels kinsmen to the throne,
Were raised in power and public office high;
Strong bands, if bands ungrateful men could tie.

150   Of these the false Achitophel was first;
A name to all succeeding ages curst:
For close designs and crooked counsels fit;
Sagacious, bold, and turbulent of wit;
Restless, unfixed in principles and place;
In power unpleased, impatient of disgrace:
A fiery soul, which, working out its way,
Fretted the pigmy body to decay,
And o'er-informed the tenement of clay.
A daring pilot in extremity;
160 Pleased with the danger, when the waves went high,
He sought the storms; but, for a calm unfit,
Would steer too nigh the sands, to boast his wit.
Great wits are sure to madness near allied,
And thin partitions do their bounds divide;
Else why should he, with wealth and honor blest,
Refuse his age the needful hours of rest?
Punish a body which he could not please;
Bankrupt of life, yet prodigal of ease?
And all to leave what with his toil he won,

To that unfeathered two-legged thing, a son;   170
Got, while his soul did huddled notions try,
And born a shapeless lump, like anarchy.
In friendship false, implacable in hate;
Resolved to ruin or to rule the State.
To compass this the triple bond he broke,
The pillars of the public safety shook;
And fitted Israel for a foreign yoke;
Then seized with fear, yet still affecting fame,
Usurped a patriot's all-atoning name.
So easy still it proves in factious times,   180
With public zeal to cancel private crimes.
How safe is treason, and how sacred ill,
Where none can sin against the people's will!
Where crowds can wink, and no offense be known,
Since in another's guilt they find their own!
Yet fame deserved no enemy can grudge;
The statesman we abhor, but praise the judge.
In Israel's court ne'er sat an Abbethdin
With more discerning eyes, or hands more clean;
Unbribed, unsought, the wretched to redress;   190
Swift of dispatch, and easy of access.
Oh, had he been content to serve the crown,
With virtues only proper to the gown;
Or had the rankness of the soil been freed
From cockle, that oppressed the noble seed;
David for him his tuneful harp had strung,
And Heaven had wanted one immortal song.
But wild ambition loves to slide, not stand,
And fortune's ice prefers to virtue's land.
Achitophel, grown weary to possess   200
A lawful fame, and lazy happiness,
Disdained the golden fruit to gather free,
And lent the crowd his arm to shake the tree.
Now, manifest of crimes contrived long since,
He stood at bold defiance with his prince;
Held up the buckler of the people's cause
Against the crown, and skulked behind the laws.
The wished occasion of the Plot he takes;
Some circumstances finds, but more he makes.
By buzzing emissaries fills the ears   210
Of listening crowds with jealousies and fears
Of arbitrary counsels brought to light,
And proves the king himself a Jebusite.
Weak arguments! which yet he knew full well
Were strong with people easy to rebel.
For, governed by the moon, the giddy Jews
Tread the same track when she the prime renews;
And once in twenty years, their scribes record,

with a conspiracy to overthrow the government and place a Catholic on
the throne, with the aid of France. One consequence of this was a
minor war with France. 118. **Egyptian,** French. These two lines (118–
119) are an attack upon the Roman Catholic doctrine of transubstantia-
tion. 127. **court and stews.** The King was thought to be a Catholic;
some of his mistresses were Catholics, as was also his brother, the Duke
of York, later James II. 128. **Hebrew priests,** clergymen of the Church
of England. 130. **God's anointed,** the King. 150. **Achitophel,** Anthony Ashley Cooper, Earl of Shaftesbury. 152. **close,** secret. 157.
pigmy body. Shaftesbury was small in size. 158. **o'er-informed,** made
his mind too active for his body. 175. **triple bond,** Triple Alliance of
England, Holland, and Sweden against France, made in 1668. Actually
this alliance was not broken by Shaftesbury, as Dryden thought, but by

Charles II in 1670, when he made a secret treaty with the French king.
180. **So easy, etc.** The next dozen lines (180–191) were inserted in the
second edition of the poem (1681), after Shaftesbury had been acquitted
and released. 188. **Abbethdin,** a Jewish officer of the high court of
justice. Shaftesbury was Lord Chancellor (1672–1673); he had also
served as President of the Privy Council. 197. **wanted,** lacked. The
"immortal song" is Dryden's poem. 204. **manifest of,** detected in,
guilty of. 213. **king . . . Jebusite.** Charles II died a Catholic; it has
since been proved that he was one during his reign. 217. **the prime
renews,** becomes new. The implication here is that the people are as
changeable as the moon.

By natural instinct they change their lord.
220 Achitophel still wants a chief, and none
Was found so fit as warlike Absalon:
Not that he wished his greatness to create,
For politicians neither love nor hate,
But, for he knew his title not allowed,
Would keep him still depending on the crowd,
That kingly power, thus ebbing out, might be
Drawn to the dregs of a democracy. . . .

*[In the next three hundred lines (which have been
omitted here) Dryden reviews the events culminating
in the Restoration of Charles II, and marches through
the list of the various political factions and individual
malcontents who were opposed to Charles and his government. He castigates these bitterly. Then he turns
his attention to what he considers Achitophel's artful
seduction of Monmouth and describes in almost Miltonic manner the way in which all these enemies of
Charles linked themselves together under Shaftesbury's
banner. He then proceeds to focus his gaze upon
individual leaders like Zimri (ll. 544 ff.).]*

A numerous host of dreaming saints succeed,
530 Of the true old enthusiastic breed:
'Gainst form and order they their power employ,
Nothing to build, and all things to destroy.
But far more numerous was the herd of such,
Who think too little, and who talk too much.
These, out of mere instinct, they knew not why,
Adored their fathers' God and property;
And, by the same blind benefit of fate,
The Devil and the Jebusite did hate:
Born to be saved, even in their own despite,
540 Because they could not help believing right.
Such were the tools; but a whole Hydra more
Remains, of sprouting heads too long to score.
Some of their chiefs were princes of the land:
In the first rank of these did Zimri stand;
A man so various, that he seemed to be
Not one, but all mankind's epitome:
Stiff in opinions, always in the wrong;
Was everything by starts, and nothing long;
But, in the course of one revolving moon,
550 Was chemist, fiddler, statesman, and buffoon;
Then all for women, painting, riming, drinking,
Besides ten thousand freaks that died in thinking.
Blest madman, who could every hour employ,

With something new to wish, or to enjoy!
Railing and praising were his usual themes;
And both (to show his judgment) in extremes.
So over-violent, or over-civil,
That every man, with him, was God or Devil.
In squand'ring wealth was his peculiar art:
Nothing went unrewarded but desert.   560
Beggared by fools, whom still he found too late,
He had his jest, and they had his estate.
He laughed himself from court; then sought relief
By forming parties, but could ne'er be chief;
For, spite of him, the weight of business fell
On Absalom and wise Achitophel:
Thus, wicked but in will, of means bereft,
He left not faction, but of that was left. . . .
(1681)

MACFLECKNOE

OR, A SATIRE UPON THE TRUE-BLUE PROTESTANT
POET, T. S.

*Thomas Shadwell (1640?-1692), here made the
object of Dryden's satire, was a contemporary poet and
dramatist. He was a Whig and Protestant; Dryden was
a Tory and was to become a Catholic. In spite of
these differences, the two were friends for some time,
but they began to quarrel, first because of literary divergences, and then because of their widely separated
political and religious outlooks. It has long been thought
that when Dryden published* Absalom and Achitophel
and The Medal—*both violent attacks upon Shaftesbury and the Whigs—Shadwell replied in a very
scurrilous poem,* The Medal of John Bayes, *and that
Dryden's counterblast was* MacFlecknoe, *so brilliant
and devastating a piece of personal satire that Shadwell
was overwhelmed. But a reference has been found to*
MacFlecknoe *in a contemporary newspaper of a date
(February 1682) too early to make it likely that the
poem was intended as an answer to* The Medal of John
Bayes. *Besides, there is some doubt that Shadwell
wrote* The Medal of John Bayes. *It is now suggested
that* MacFlecknoe, *an incident in the bad relations of
Dryden and Shadwell, was written perhaps as early as
1678, just after the death of Richard Flecknoe, a feeble
Irish poet. In any case, as a result of Dryden's blistering*

224. title not allowed. Monmouth, of course, was barred from the throne because of his illegitimate birth. **530. enthusiastic.** This word, throughout the Restoration and neo-classical periods, is always a word of reproach. The original meaning, "inspired by a god," "inspired by religious emotion," always connoted to Dryden and his contemporaries the unbalanced, the emotionally violent, the lunatic fringe. **541. Hydra,** in classical mythology, the nine-headed monster of the Lernaean swamps, which was killed by Hercules as one of his twelve labors. As fast as one head was cut off, two grew in its place, until Hercules finally burnt off the heads with a firebrand. **544. Zimri.** George Villiers, Duke of Buckingham (1628-1687). He was one of the authors of *The Rehearsal* (1672), a burlesque drama in which Dryden is ridiculed. Dryden here takes revenge in one of the notable portraits in satirical literature, one that Dryden himself said was worth the whole poem of *Absalom and Achitophel.* Buckingham was one of Charles' ministers, but was dis-

missed in 1674 and joined the opposition. **559. wealth.** After the Restoration, Buckingham's income was twenty thousand pounds a year, an
immense fortune for those days.
    MacFlecknoe. **3. Augustus,** Augustus Caesar, first emperor of Rome,
from 27 B.C. to 14 A.D. He was thirty-two when he became emperor.
25. his goodly fabric. Shadwell was an unusually large man as Shaftesbury had been small (cf. *Absalom and Achitophel,* l. 157). **29.
Heywood and Shirley.** Thomas Heywood, an Elizabethan playwright
(1575-1650), was a prolific author. His masterpiece was the domestic
tragedy *A Woman Killed with Kindness* (performed 1603); but the violent tragedy *The Yorkshire Tragedy,* which was once ascribed to Shakespeare, and the historical drama *Edward IV*—both of which are often assigned to Heywood—are well worth reading. *The Fair Maid of the West*
is also conceded to be his. James Shirley (1596-1666) is far more obscure; his specialties were bloody tragedy and realistic comedy—*The*

satire, Shadwell has actually come to possess the reputation in posterity which this poem gave him. And yet he was far from a fool; his plays, comedies of manners and satires upon contemporary life, are readable and lively.

The name "MacFlecknoe" means "son of Flecknoe." Dryden got his cue from Andrew Marvell (p. 353), who had lampooned Flecknoe in 1645. Flecknoe's attack upon the immorality of the English stage in A Discourse, published 1664, may have aroused Dryden's hostility to the author. At any rate, Dryden represents him, in mock-heroic fashion, as abdicating the throne of dullness in favor of Shadwell. In its harsh invective, its blasting scorn, MacFlecknoe is one of the earliest and one of the most vigorous of a long line of personal satires that reached a peak in the invectives of Pope. In fact, Pope tells us that MacFlecknoe gave him the inspiration for The Dunciad.

All human things are subject to decay,
And when fate summons, monarchs must obey.
This Flecknoe found, who, like Augustus, young
Was called to empire, and had governed long;
In prose and verse was owned, without dispute,
Through all the realms of Nonsense absolute.
This aged prince, now flourishing in peace,
And blessed with issue of a large increase;
Worn out with business, did at length debate
10 To settle the succession of the State;
And, pondering which of all his sons was fit
To reign, and wage immortal war with wit,
Cried; " 'Tis resolved; for nature pleads, that he
Should only rule, who most resembles me.
Sh—— alone my perfect image bears,
Mature in dullness from his tender years:
Sh—— alone, of all my sons, is he
Who stands confirmed in full stupidity.
The rest to some faint meaning make pretense,
20 But Sh—— never deviates into sense.
Some beams of wit on other souls may fall,
Strike through, and make a lucid interval;
But Sh——'s genuine night admits no ray,
His rising fogs prevail upon the day.
Besides, his goodly fabric fills the eye,
And seems designed for thoughtless majesty;
Thoughtless as monarch oaks that shade the plain,
And, spread in solemn state, supinely reign.
Heywood and Shirley were but types of thee,

Thou last great prophet of tautology.   30
Even I, a dunce of more renown than they,
Was sent before but to prepare thy way;
And, coarsely clad in Norwich drugget, came
To teach the nations in thy greater name.
My warbling lute, the lute I whilom strung,
When to King John of Portugal I sung,
Was but the prelude to that glorious day,
When thou on silver Thames didst cut thy way,
With well-timed oars before the royal barge,
Swelled with the pride of thy celestial charge;   40
And big with hymn, commander of a host,
The like was ne'er in Epsom blankets tossed.
Methinks I see the new Arion sail,
The lute still trembling underneath thy nail.
At thy well-sharpened thumb from shore to shore
The treble squeaks for fear, the basses roar;
Echoes from Pissing Alley Sh—— call,
And Sh—— they resound from Aston Hall.
About thy boat the little fishes throng,
As at the morning toast that floats along.   50
Sometimes, as prince of thy harmonious band,
Thou wield'st thy papers in thy threshing hand.
St. André's feet ne'er kept more equal time,
Not e'en the feet of thy own *Psyche's* rime;
Though they in number as in sense excel:
So just, so like tautology, they fell,
That, pale with envy, Singleton forswore
The lute and sword, which he in triumph bore,
And vowed he ne'er would act Villerius more."
Here stopped the good old sire, and wept for joy   60
In silent raptures of the hopeful boy.
All arguments, but most his plays, persuade,
That for anointed dullness he was made.

   Close to the walls which fair Augusta bind
(The fair Augusta much to fears inclined),
An ancient fabric raised t' inform the sight,
There stood of yore, and Barbican it hight:
A watchtower once; but now, so fate ordains,
Of all the pile an empty name remains.
From its old ruins brothel-houses rise,   70
Scenes of lewd loves, and of polluted joys,
Where their vast courts the mother-strumpets
   keep,
And, undisturbed by watch, in silence sleep.
Near these a Nursery erects its head,
Where queens are formed, and future heroes
   bred;

Cardinal (1641) is a favorable example of the first, and *The Lady of Pleasure* (1635) of the second. Indeed, *The Lady of Pleasure* foreshadows much of the Restoration comedy spirit, as seen in the works of Congreve, and particularly of Vanbrugh and Farquhar. Neither Heywood nor Shirley, it may be remarked, were as prolix or dull as Dryden would have them. **33. Norwich drugget,** a coarse woolen or mixed fabric. **36. King John of Portugal.** Flecknoe once visited Portugal and said he had enjoyed the patronage of King John IV (d. 1656). **37. prelude . . . day.** The occasion described by this and the next few lines (37–42) has never been ascertained. It is known, however, that Shadwell was rather gifted in music. **42. Epsom blankets tossed,** a reference to *Epsom Wells* (1673), a play by Shadwell; and to a scene in Shadwell's *The Virtuoso* (1676), in which a character is tossed in a blanket. **43. Arion,** a Greek musician of the eighth century B.C.—another allusion to Shadwell and his musical pretensions. **51. harmonious band . . .**

threshing hand. The implication here is unmistakable that Shadwell's music was of the rustic untutored kind—from the neo-classical point of view such music would be beneath contémpt. **53. St. André,** a popular French dancing master of the day. **54. Psyche,** a rimed opera by Shadwell, produced in 1675. **57. Singleton,** a contemporary opera singer. **59. Villerius,** a general in *The Siege of Rhodes,* an opera by Sir William Davenant (1606–1668). **64. Augusta,** a Roman name for London. Charles II was sometimes called Caesar Augustus. The next line refers to the fact that London had been in fear of "popish" (Catholic) plots. **67. Barbican,** literally an outer fortification. In London it was the name given to the site of an old watchtower, from which a view could be had not only of the city but of the adjacent counties. **74. Nursery,** a theater built in 1664 to train young actors.

Where unfledged actors learn to laugh and cry,
Where infant punks their tender voices try,
And little Maximins the gods defy.
Great Fletcher never treads in buskins here,
80 Nor greater Jonson dares in socks appear;
But gentle Simkin just reception finds
Amidst this monument of vanished minds:
Pure clinches the suburbian Muse affords,
And Panton waging harmless war with words.
Here Flecknoe, as a place to fame well known,
Ambitiously designed his Sh——'s throne;
For ancient Dekker prophesied long since,
That in this pile should reign a mighty prince,
Born for a scourge of wit, and flail of sense;
90 To whom true dullness should some *Psyches* owe,
But worlds of *Misers* from his pen should flow;
Humorists and hypocrites it should produce,
Whole Raymond families, and tribes of Bruce.

Now Empress Fame had published the renown
Of Sh——'s coronation through the town.
Roused by report of Fame, the nations meet,
From near Bunhill, and distant Watling Street.
No Persian carpets spread th' imperial way,
But scattered limbs of mangled poets lay;
100 From dusty shops neglected authors come;
Martyrs of pies, and relics of the bum.
Much Heywood, Shirley, Ogleby there lay,
But loads of Sh—— almost choked the way.
Bilked stationers, for yeomen stood prepared,
And Herringman was captain of the guard.
The hoary prince in majesty appeared,
High on a throne of his own labors reared.
At his right hand our young Ascanius sate,
Rome's other hope, and pillar of the State.
110 His brows thick fogs, instead of glories, grace,
And lambent dullness played around his face.
As Hannibal did to the altars come,
Sworn by his sire a mortal foe to Rome;
So Sh—— swore, nor should his vow be vain,
That he till death true dullness would maintain;
And, in his father's right, and realm's defense,
Ne'er to have peace with wit, nor truce with sense.
The king himself the sacred unction made,
As king by office, and as priest by trade.
120 In his sinister hand, instead of ball,
He placed a mighty mug of potent ale;

Love's Kingdom to his right he did convey,
At once his scepter, and his rule of sway;
Whose righteous lore the prince had practiced young,
And from whose loins recorded *Psyche* sprung.
His temples, last, with poppies were o'erspread,
That nodding seemed to consecrate his head.
Just at that point of time, if fame not lie,
On his left hand twelve reverend owls did fly.
So Romulus, 'tis sung, by Tiber's brook,   130
Presage of sway from twice six vultures took.
Th' admiring throng loud acclamations make,
And omens of his future empire take.
The sire then shook the honors of his head,
And from his brows damps of oblivion shed
Full on the filial dullness: long he stood,
Repelling from his breast, the raging god;
At length burst out in this prophetic mood:
"Heavens bless my son, from Ireland let him reign
To far Barbadoes on the western main;   140
Of his dominion may no end be known,
And greater than his father's be his throne;
Beyond *Love's Kingdom* let him stretch his pen!"
He paused, and all the people cried, "Amen."
Then thus continued he: "My son, advance
Still in new impudence, new ignorance.
Success let others teach, learn thou from me
Pangs without birth, and fruitless industry.
Let *Virtuosos* in five years be writ;
Yet not one thought accuse thy toil of wit.   150
Let gentle George in triumph tread the stage,
Make Dorimant betray, and Loveit rage;
Let Cully, Cockwood, Fopling, charm the pit,
And in their folly show the writer's wit.
Yet still thy fools shall stand in thy defense,
And justify their author's want of sense.
Let 'em be all by thy own model made
Of dullness, and desire no foreign aid;
That they to future ages may be known,
Not copies drawn, but issue of thy own.   160
Nay, let thy men of wit too be the same,
All full of thee, and differing but in name.
But let no alien S—dl—y interpose,
To lard with wit thy hungry *Epsom* prose.
And when false flowers of rhetoric thou wouldst cull,
Trust nature, do not labor to be dull;
But write thy best, and top; and, in each line,

77. **infant punks**, child prostitutes. Restoration slang sometimes referred to actors as "punks," but the reason for the use of the word is all too apparent. 78. **Maximins.** Maximin was a bombastic hero in Dryden's early play, *Tyrannic Love* (1669), in which Nell Gwyn scored a popular success. 79. **Fletcher.** John Fletcher (1579–1625), the noted Elizabethan dramatist, always associated in the mind of the student of English literature with his collaborator Francis Beaumont. 80. **Jonson**, Ben Jonson, famous for his comedies of "humor." The sock, a low shoe or sandal, worn by actors of comedy in ancient Greece and Rome, refers here to the comedies of Jonson. 81. **Simkin**, a contemporary stage clown. 83. **clinches**, puns. **Panton**, Thomas Panton (d. 1685), a noted contemporary wit and punster. 87. **Dekker**, Thomas Dekker (1570?–1641?), well-known Elizabethan dramatist, pamphleteer, and poet (cf. p. 210). 88. **pile**, building. **Misers . . . Bruce.** The *Miser* (1671) and *The Humorist* (1672) were plays by Shadwell. Raymond is a character in *The Humorist*; Bruce, in Shadwell's *The Virtuoso*. 97. **Bunhill . . . Watling Street.** Bunhill and Watling Streets are close together in Old London. Dryden's implication here is that

Shadwell's fame was limited to this very small area; his use of "distant" is therefore pure mockery. 101. **pies . . . bum.** Leaves from discarded books were placed under pies and cakes by bakers; they were also used for toilet paper. 102. **Ogleby**, John Ogleby (1600–1676), an inferior poet and translator of Homer, Vergil, and Aesop. 104. **Bilked stationers**; defrauded or cheated booksellers—there was no sale of the works of poor poets like Shadwell. 105. **Herringman**, Dryden's London publisher. 108. **Ascanius**, Shadwell. In Vergil's *Aeneid*, XII, 168, Ascanius, the son and heir of Aeneas, is called "the other hope of great Rome." 112. **Hannibal**, a great Carthaginian general (247–183 B.C.), who at the age of nine is said to have been compelled by his father to swear eternal hatred for Rome. 120. **sinister**, left. At the coronation ceremony, the king held an orb in his left hand as a symbol of authority over the whole world. 122. **Love's Kingdom**, a pastoral tragicomedy by Flecknoe. 125. **Psyche.** The opera by Shadwell was mentioned above (l. 54); hence the use of the word *recorded*, "reported." 130. **Romulus . . . brook.** Romulus was the legendary founder and first king of Rome. With his twin brother Remus, he was thrown into the Tiber in

Sir Formal's oratory will be thine:
Sir Formal, though unsought, attends thy quill,
170 And does thy northern dedications fill.
Nor let false friends seduce thy mind to fame,
By arrogating Jonson's hostile name.
Let father Flecknoe fire thy mind with praise,
And uncle Ogleby thy envy raise.
Thou art my blood, where Jonson has no part:
What share have we in nature, or in art?
Where did his wit on learning fix a brand,
And rail at arts he did not understand?
Where made he love in Prince Nicander's vein,
180 Or swept the dust in *Psyche's* humble strain?
Where sold he bargains, 'whip-stitch, kiss my arse,'
Promised a play and dwindled to a farce?
When did his Muse from Fletcher scenes purloin,
As thou whole Eth'rege dost transfuse to thine?
But so transfused as oil on water's flow,
His always floats above, thine sinks below.
This is thy province, this thy wondrous way,
New humors to invent for each new play:
This is that boasted bias of thy mind,
190 By which one way, to dullness, 'tis inclined;
Which makes thy writings lean on one side still,
And, in all changes, that way bends thy will.
Nor let thy mountain-belly make pretense
Of likeness; thine's a tympany of sense.
A tun of man in thy large bulk is writ,
But sure thou'rt but a kilderkin of wit.
Like mine, thy gentle numbers feebly creep;
Thy tragic Muse gives smiles, thy comic sleep.
With whate'er gall thou sett'st thyself to write,
200 Thy inoffensive satires never bite.
In thy felonious heart though venom lies,
It does but touch thy Irish pen, and dies.
Thy genius calls thee not to purchase fame
In keen iambics, but mild anagram.
Leave writing plays, and choose for thy command
Some peaceful province in acrostic land.
There thou may'st wings display and altars raise,
And torture one poor word ten thousand ways.
Or, if thou wouldst thy diff'rent talents suit,
210 Set thy own songs, and sing them to thy lute."
    He said: but his last words were scarcely heard;
For Bruce and Longvil had a trap prepared,
And down they sent the yet declaiming bard.

Sinking he left his drugget robe behind,
Borne Upwards by a subterranean wind.
The mantel fell to the young prophet's part,
With double portion of his father's art.   (1682)

A SONG FOR ST. CECILIA'S DAY

St. Cecilia, a Christian martyr of the third century, was the patron saint of music. On St. Cecilia's Day (November 22) it was customary to present an original ode set to music, and Dryden wrote this and the following poem for this purpose. It is instructive to note that this irregular ode was the fond work of a major poet of the neo-classical triumph. Dryden exploits rime, length of line, assonance, and alliteration in the manner of a virtuoso to achieve musical approximation and variety (stanzas 3-6) in a poem built upon the harmony of the universe and the great chain of being.

From harmony, from heavenly harmony,
    This universal frame began:
  When Nature underneath a heap
    Of jarring atoms lay,
  And could not heave her head,
The tuneful voice was heard from high:
    "Arise, ye more than dead."

Then cold and hot and moist and dry
  In order to their stations leap,
    And Music's power obey.   10
From harmony, from heavenly harmony,
    This universal frame began:
    From harmony to harmony
Through all the compass of the notes it ran,
The diapason closing full in Man.

What passion cannot Music raise and quell!
    When Jubal struck the chorded shell,
  His listening brethren stood around,
    And wondering, on their faces fell
  To worship that celestial sound.   20
Less than a god they thought there could not dwell
    Within the hollow of that shell
    That spoke so sweetly and so well.
What passion cannot Music raise and quell!

infancy, but was rescued and suckled by a wolf. According to the ancient story the brothers could not agree on the exact place where Rome was to be built. They decided to resort to augury, and each took his position on his chosen hill. Six vultures flew past Remus, but when Romulus reported that twelve had flown past him, his hill was declared approved. 149. *Virtuosos*, a reference to Shadwell's *Virtuoso* (cf. l. 42 and note), a play on which Shadwell was engaged for five years. 150. **wit**, intelligence. 151. **gentle George**, George Etherege (1635?-1691), a well-known comic dramatist of the Restoration. His three plays: *The Comical Revenge, or Love in a Tub* (1664); *She Would If She Could* (1668); and *The Man of Mode, or Sir Fopling Flutter* (1676) are characteristic Restoration comedies in their sparkling wit, satirical outlook, and bawdy tendencies. *Dorimant, Loveit, Cully*, etc. (ll. 152-153), are characters from his plays. 163. **S—dl—y**, Sir Charles Sedley (1635?-1701), a court poet and wit, who had written the prologue to Shadwell's *Epsom Wells* and probably had helped Shadwell in other plays. 169. **Sir Formal**, Sir Formal Trifle, a character in Shadwell's *Virtuoso*, called "the orator, a florid coxcomb." 170. **northern dedications**, an allusion to Shadwell's dedication of several books to the Duke of Newcastle and members of his family; Newcastle is in northern England. 172. **Jonson's . . . name.** Shadwell had frequently given lavish praise to Ben Jonson as a writer of comedies, and regarded himself as Jonson's successor. Dryden's rather mild praise of Jonson (cf. *Essay of Dramatic Poesy*, p. 451) had irritated Shadwell. 179. **Nicander**, a character in Shadwell's *Psyche*. 181. **whip-stitch**, a contemptuous term for a tailor. Phrases like these are used by Sir Samuel Hearty in Shadwell's *Virtuoso*. 194. **tympany**, inflation, conceit. 196. **kilderkin**, a small cask. 207. **wings . . . raise**, an allusion to the fanciful verse forms of the metaphysical poets; cf. Chaucer's *Prologue* to *The Canterbury Tales*, p. 110, ll. 420 ff. 17. **Jubal**, mentioned in Genesis 4:21 as the "father of all such as handle the harp and organ."

A Song for St. Cecilia's Day. 8. **cold . . . dry**, the qualities of the four elements, according to ancient and medieval natural philosophy and astrology; cf. Chaucer's *Prologue to The Canterbury Tales*, p. 110, ll. 420 ff. 17. **Jubal**, mentioned in Genesis 4:21 as the "father of all such as handle the harp and organ."

The trumpet's loud clangor
    Excites us to arms
With shrill notes of anger
    And mortal alarms.
The double, double, double beat
30   Of the thundering drum
    Cries: "Hark! the foes come;
Charge, charge, 'tis too late to retreat!"

The soft complaining flute
    In dying notes discovers
    The woes of hopeless lovers,
Whose dirge is whispered by the warbling lute.
    Sharp violins proclaim
Their jealous pangs and desperation,
Fury, frantic indignation,
40 Depth of pains, and height of passion,
    For the fair, disdainful dame.

But oh! what art can teach,
What human voice can reach
    The sacred organ's praise?
    Notes inspiring holy love,
Notes that wing their heavenly ways
    To mend the choirs above.
Orpheus could lead the savage race;
And trees unrooted left their place,
50   Sequacious of the lyre;
But bright Cecilia raised the wonder higher:
When to her organ vocal breath was given,
An angel heard, and straight appeared,
    Mistaking earth for heaven.

GRAND CHORUS

As from the power of sacred lays
    The spheres began to move,
And sung the great Creator's praise
    To all the blessed above;
So when the last and dreadful hour
60 This crumbling pageant shall devour,
The trumpet shall be heard on high,
The dead shall live, the living die,
And Music shall untune the sky.
(1687)

ALEXANDER'S FEAST; OR, THE POWER OF MUSIC

AN ODE IN HONOR OF ST. CECILIA'S DAY

*See the introductory note to the preceding poem.
Dryden spoke of this ode as the best of all his poetry
and rejoiced when it received popular approval. It was
praised by Pope in his Essay on Criticism (p. 537).
As the "feast" was a celebration of victory, so the
poem celebrates the power of music over the passions.*

1

'T was at the royal feast, for Persia won
    By Philip's warlike son:
    Aloft in awful state
    The godlike hero sate
      On his imperial throne:
His valiant peers were placed around;
Their brows with roses and with myrtles bound:
    (So should desert in arms be crowned.)
The lovely Thaïs, by his side,
Sate like a blooming Eastern bride   10
In flower of youth and beauty's pride.
      Happy, happy, happy pair!
        None but the brave,
        None but the brave,
    None but the brave deserves the fair.

CHORUS

Happy, happy, happy pair!
    None but the brave,
    None but the brave,
None but the brave deserves the fair.

2

Timotheus, placed on high   20
    Amid the tuneful choir,
With flying fingers touched the lyre:
    The trembling notes ascend the sky,
      And heavenly joys inspire.
    The song began from Jove,
    Who left his blissful seats above,
    (Such is the power of mighty love.)
A dragon's fiery form belied the god:
Sublime on radiant spires he rode,
When he to fair Olympia pressed;   30
    And while he sought her snowy breast:
Then, round her slender waist he curled,
And stamped an image of himself, a sovereign of the
        world.
The listening crowd admire the lofty sound;
"A present deity," they shout around;
"A present deity," the vaulted roofs rebound:
    With ravished ears
    The monarch hears,
    Assumes the god,

---

48. **Orpheus . . . race.** In Greek mythology Orpheus was a Thracian poet and musician whose lyre could charm beasts and move trees and rocks. 50. **Sequacious,** following after. 56. **spheres . . . move.** The ancients believed that the stars made music as they revolved in their spheres; for a burlesque of this idea, cf. Swift's *Gulliver's Travels* (p. 500).

Alexander's Feast. **1. Persia,** etc. The feast celebrates the conquest of Persia by Alexander the Great (356–323 B.C.), son of Philip of Macedon. The decisive battles in this conquest were the Battles of Issus (333 B.C.) and Arbela (331 B.C.). **9. Thaïs,** an Athenian courtesan, who accompanied Alexander into Asia and who was thought to have incited him to fire the Persian palaces at Persepolis. **20. Timotheus,**

Affects to nod,
And seems to shake the spheres.

CHORUS

With ravished ears
The monarch hears,
Assumes the god,
Affects to nod,
And seems to shake the spheres.

3

The praise of Bacchus then the sweet musician sung,
Of Bacchus ever fair and ever young:
The jolly god in triumph comes;
Sound the trumpets; beat the drums;
Flushed with a purple grace
He shows his honest face:
Now give the hautboys breath; he comes, he comes.
Bacchus, ever fair and young,
Drinking joys did first ordain;
Bacchus' blessings are a treasure,
Drinking is the soldier's pleasure;
Rich the treasure,
Sweet the pleasure,
Sweet is pleasure after pain.

CHORUS

Bacchus' blessings are a treasure,
Drinking is the soldier's pleasure;
Rich the treasure,
Sweet the pleasure,
Sweet is pleasure after pain.

4

Soothed with the sound, the king grew vain;
Fought all his battles o'er again;
And thrice he routed all his foes; and thrice he slew the
slain.
The master saw the madness rise;
His glowing cheeks, his ardent eyes;
And, while he heaven and earth defied,
Changed his hand, and checked his pride
He chose a mournful Muse,
Soft pity to infuse:
He sung Darius great and good,
By too severe a fate,
Fallen, fallen, fallen, fallen,
Fallen from his high estate,
And weltering in his blood;

Deserted, at his utmost need,
By those his former bounty fed;
On the bare earth exposed he lies,
With not a friend to close his eyes.
With downcast looks the joyless victor sate,
Revolving in his altered soul
The various turns of chance below;
And, now and then, a sigh he stole;
And tears began to flow.

CHORUS

Revolving in his altered soul
The various turns of chance below;
And, now and then, a sigh he stole;
And tears began to flow.

5

The mighty master smiled to see
That love was in the next degree:
'T was but a kindred sound to move,
For pity melts the mind to love.
Softly sweet, in Lydian measures,
Soon he soothed his soul to pleasures.
"War," he sung, "is toil and trouble;
Honor, but an empty bubble;
Never ending, still beginning,
Fighting still, and still destroying:
If the world be worth thy winning,
Think, O think it worth enjoying;
Lovely Thaïs sits beside thee,
Take the good the gods provide thee."
The many rend the skies with loud applause;
So Love was crowned, but Music won the cause.
The prince, unable to conceal his pain,
Gazed on the fair
Who caused his care,
And sighed and looked, sighed and looked,
Sighed and looked, and sighed again:
At length, with love and wine at once oppressed,
The vanquished victor sunk upon her breast.

CHORUS

The prince, unable to conceal his pain,
Gazed on the fair
Who caused his care,
And sighed and looked, sighed and looked,
Sighed and looked, and sighed again:
At length, with love and wine at once oppressed,
The vanquished victor sunk upon her breast.

Alexander's favorite musician. 28. dragon's fiery form. Jove is represented as having assumed the form of a dragon, in which he wooed Olympias, the mother of Alexander. Alexander, one of the nine worthies of antiquity, was one of the important heroes of the medieval romance. As a romance hero, he partakes of some of the mythical qualities common to Arthur, and there is an interesting parallel in the reputed magical birth of both heroes. 29. radiant spires, coils. 30. Olympia, Olympias, Alexander's mother. 47. Bacchus, the god of wine in classical mythology (Dionysus in the Greek). 53. hautboys, the reed instrument known today as the oboe. 75. Darius, Darius III, emperor of Persia from 336 B.C. until his defeat by Alexander and death in 331 B.C. 97. Lydian measures, sweet and sensuous measures.

Now strike the golden lyre again:
A louder yet, and yet a louder strain.
Break his bands of sleep asunder,
And rouse him, like a rattling peal of thunder.
    Hark, hark, the horrid sound
      Has raised up his head:
      As awaked from the dead,
130   And amazed, he stares around.
"Revenge, revenge!" Timotheus cries,
    "See the Furies arise!
    See the snakes that they rear,
    How they hiss in their hair,
And the sparkles that flash from their eyes!
    Behold a ghastly band,
    Each a torch in his hand!
Those are Grecian ghosts, that in battle were slain,
    And unburied remain
140   Inglorious on the plain:
    Give the vengeance due
    To the valiant crew.
Behold how they toss their torches on high,
    How they point to the Persian abodes,
And glittering temples of their hostile gods!"
The princes applaud, with a furious joy;
And the king seized a flambeau with zeal to destroy;
    Thaïs led the way,
    To light him to his prey,
150 And, like another Helen, fired another Troy.

CHORUS

And the king seized a flambeau with zeal to destroy;
    Thaïs led the way,
    To light him to his prey,
And, like another Helen, fired another Troy.

7

    Thus, long ago,
Ere heaving bellows learned to blow,
    While organs yet were mute;
    Timotheus, to his breathing flute,
    And sounding lyre,
160 Could swell the soul to rage, or kindle soft desire.
    At last, divine Cecilia came,
    Inventress of the vocal frame;
The sweet enthusiast, from her sacred store,
    Enlarged the former narrow bounds,
    And added length to solemn sounds,
With nature's mother wit, and arts unknown before.
    Let old Timotheus yield the prize,

    Or both divide the crown;
He raised a mortal to the skies;
    She drew an angel down.

GRAND CHORUS

    At last, divine Cecilia came,
    Inventress of the vocal frame;
The sweet enthusiast, from her sacred store,
    Enlarged the former narrow bounds,
    And added length to solemn sounds,
With nature's mother wit, and arts unknown before.
    Let old Timotheus yield the prize,
    Or both divide the crown;
He raised a mortal to the skies;
    She drew an angel down.

(1697)

from AN ESSAY OF DRAMATIC POESY

In his literary essays Dryden shows critical acumen and a mastery of vigorous and understandable prose. His work, therefore, is doubly significant; it lays the foundation for a modern prose style and for modern literary criticism. This famous Essay is written in the form of a Ciceronian dialogue, in which four friends discuss the comparative merits of French and English drama. It was once held that each speaker represented a specific historical person, with Dryden as Neander, but these identifications are now less certain; the speakers should be identified not with any individuals but with points of view. The conversation is represented as taking place on a barge in the Thames, within sound of the guns discharged in the naval engagement between England and Holland in June 1665. All London had stopped to listen, and when the sound of the guns died away, the conversation in Dryden's little group, cheered by the prospect of victory, turned to human behavior, then to art, and then to literary standards. In the selection following, Neander (Dryden) is defending the English drama against the French.

". . . I dare boldly affirm these two things of the English drama: First, that we have many plays of ours as regular as any of theirs, and which, besides, have more variety of plot and characters; and secondly, that in most of the irregular plays of Shakespeare or Fletcher (for Ben Jonson's are for the most part regular), there is a more masculine fancy and greater spirit in the writing than there is in any of the French. I could produce, even in Shakespeare's and Fletcher's works,

132. **Furies,** the ancient classical goddesses of vengeance, characterized by hideous features, disgusting habits, and fearful snaky hair. 147. **flambeau,** a flaming torch. 150. **Helen,** wife of Menelaus, king of Sparta, carried off on account of her beauty by Paris, son of Priam, king of Troy. The incident caused the Trojan War, the theme of Homer's epics and of much of Vergil's *Aeneid,* not to mention an important cycle of medieval romance. 162. **vocal frame,** the organ, supposed to have been invented by St. Cecilia, who, because of her virtue and piety, was

said to have been visited by an angel (l. 170). The form of circumlocution seen here in "vocal frame" is characteristic of neo-classical verse, not only in the Latinity of the words, but in the combination of a single adjective ("epithet") with a noun of vague meaning, which combination is an "elegant" way of expressing a very plain and concrete word. So "levelled tube" for "gun"; "finny tribe" for "fish," etc. 163. **enthusiast.** Again, in the literal sense of "inspired by a god," probably not intended by Dryden to have the usual sinister connotation

10 some plays which are almost exactly formed; as *The Merry Wives of Windsor*, and *The Scornful Lady*: but because (generally speaking) Shakespeare, who writ first, did not perfectly observe the laws of comedy, and Fletcher, who came nearer to perfection, yet through carelessness made many faults, I will take the pattern of a perfect play from Ben Jonson, who was a careful and learned observer of the dramatic laws, and from all his comedies I shall select *The Silent Woman*, of which I will make a short examen, 20 according to those rules which the French observe."

As Neander was beginning to examine *The Silent Woman*, Eugenius, earnestly regarding him: "I beseech you, Neander," said he, "gratify the company, and me in particular, so far, as before you speak of the play, to give us a character of the author; and tell us frankly your opinion, whether you do not think all writers, both French and English, ought to give place to him."

"I fear," replied Neander, "that in obeying your commands I shall draw some envy on myself. Besides, 30 in performing them, it will be first necessary to speak somewhat of Shakespeare and Fletcher, his rivals in poesy; and one of them, in my opinion, at least his equal, perhaps his superior.

"To begin, then, with Shakespeare. He was the man who of all modern, and perhaps ancient poets, had the largest and most comprehensive soul. All the images of nature were still present to him, and he drew them, not laboriously, but luckily; when he describes anything, you more than see it, you feel it too. Those who 40 accuse him to have wanted learning, give him the greater commendation: he was naturally learned; he needed not the spectacles of books to read nature; he looked inwards, and found her there. I cannot say he is everywhere alike; were he so, I should do him injury to compare him with the greatest of mankind. He is many times flat, insipid, his comic wit degenerating into clenches, his serious swelling into bombast. But he is always great, when some great occasion is presented to him; no man can say he ever had a fit 50 subject for his wit, and did not then raise himself as high above the rest of poets,

Quantum lenta solent inter viburna cupressi.

The consideration of this made Mr. Hales of Eton say that there was no subject of which any poet ever writ, but he would produce it much better done in Shakespeare; and however others are now generally preferred before him, yet the age wherein he lived, which had contemporaries with him Fletcher and Jonson, never equaled them to him in their esteem: and in the last king's court, when Ben's reputation was at highest, 60 Sir John Suckling, and with him the greater part of the courtiers, set our Shakespeare far above him. . . .

"As for Jonson, to whose character I am now arrived, if we look upon him while he was himself (for his last plays were but his dotages), I think him the most learned and judicious writer which any theater ever had. He was a most severe judge of himself, as well as others. One cannot say he wanted wit, but rather that he was frugal of it. In his words you find little to retrench or alter. Wit, and language, and humor also 70 in some measure, we had before him; but something of art was wanting to the drama, till he came. He managed his strength to more advantage than any who preceded him. You seldom find him making love in any of his scenes, or endeavoring to move the passions; his genius was too sullen and saturnine to do it gracefully, especially when he knew he came after those who had performed both to such an height. Humor was his proper sphere; and in that he delighted most to represent mechanic people. He was deeply conversant 80 in the ancients, both Greek and Latin, and he borrowed boldly from them; there is scarce a poet or historian among the Roman authors of those times, whom he has not translated in *Sejanus* and *Catiline*. But he has done his robberies so openly, that one may see he fears not to be taxed by any law. He invades authors like a monarch; and what would be theft in other poets, is only victory in him. With the spoils of these writers he so represents old Rome to us, in its rites, ceremonies, and customs, that if one of their 90 poets had written either of his tragedies, we had seen less of it than in him. If there was any fault in his language, it was, that he weaved it too closely and laboriously, in his comedies especially; perhaps too, he did a little too much Romanize our tongue, leaving the words which he translated almost as much Latin as he found them, wherein, though he learnedly followed their language, he did not enough comply with the idiom of ours. If I would compare him with Shakespeare, I might acknowledge him the more correct 100 poet, but Shakespeare the greater wit. Shakespeare was the Homer, or father of our dramatic poets; Jonson was the Virgil, the pattern of elaborate writing; I admire him, but I love Shakespeare. To conclude of him; as he has given us the most correct plays, so in the precepts which he has laid down in his *Discoveries*, we have as many and profitable rules for perfecting the stage, as any wherewith the French can furnish us. . . ."
(1668)

of "unbalanced," "insane," etc.
An Essay of Dramatic Poesy. 5. **Fletcher**, John Fletcher, the noted Elizabethan dramatist (see *MacFlecknoe*, p. 464, l. 79, and note). 11. *The Scornful Lady*, a satirical play (1616) by Beaumont and Fletcher. *The Merry Wives of Windsor*, just referred to, is the well-known comedy by Shakespeare. 29. **envy**, ill-feeling, malice. 47. **clenches**, puns. 52. *Quantum . . . cupressi*, "as cypresses tower above low-bending shrubs" (Vergil's *First Eclogue*). 53. **Mr. Hales of Eton**, John Hales (1584-1656), critic and theologian, Greek professor at Oxford, and fellow of Eton College. 60. **last king's**, Charles I's, reigning from 1625 to 1649. 61. **Sir John Suckling**. See p. 350. 80. **mechanic people**, tradespeople, the middle class. 84. *Sejanus, Catiline*, classical tragedies by Jonson, produced in 1603 and 1611, respectively. 86. **taxed**, accused, found fault with. 100. **correct**, following literary rules closely and religiously. 101. **wit**, genius.

from PREFACE TO THE FABLES

Dryden's last volume, published in March 1700,
bore the title Fables, Ancient and Modern. *It consists*
of narratives loosely translated from Homer, Ovid, Boc-
caccio, and Chaucer. The Preface to the volume ranks
with the Essay of Dramatic Poesy *as Dryden's best*
prose work but surpasses the Essay *as an example*
of the author's critical genius. In the Preface,
Dryden "discovered" the first great writer in Eng-
lish poetry, Geoffrey Chaucer, in it, too, he ex-
posed his informal but compelling love of great
literature.

For its compactness, lucidity, and precision, for
its geniality, its ease and dignity, the Preface
ranks as one of the most interesting and impor-
tant documents in the whole range of English prose.

. . . With Ovid ended the golden age of the Roman
tongue; from Chaucer the purity of the English tongue
began. The manners of the poets were not unlike.
Both of them were well-bred, well-natured, amorous,
and libertine, at least in their writings; it may be, also
in their lives. Their studies were the same, philosophy
and philology. Both of them were knowing in astronomy; of which Ovid's books of the *Roman Feasts,* and
Chaucer's *Treatise of the Astrolabe,* are sufficient wit-
10 nesses. But Chaucer was likewise an astrologer, as
were Virgil, Horace, Persius, and Manilius. Both
writ with wonderful facility and clearness; neither
were great inventors: for Ovid only copied the Grecian
fables, and most of Chaucer's stories were taken from
his Italian contemporaries, or their predecessors. Boccaccio his *Decameron* was first published, and from
thence our Englishman has borrowed many of his
Canterbury Tales: yet that of *Palamon and Arcite*
was written, in all probability, by some Italian wit,
20 in a former age, as I shall prove hereafter. The tale of
Griselda was the invention of Petrarch; by him sent to
Boccaccio, from whom it came to Chaucer. *Troilus and*
Cressida was also written by a Lombard author, but

much amplified by our English translator, as well as
beautified; the genius of our countrymen, in general,
being rather to improve an invention than to invent
themselves, as is evident not only in our poetry, but
in many of our manufactures. I find I have anticipated
already, and taken up from Boccaccio before I come
to him: but there is so much less behind; and I am of 30
the temper of most kings, who love to be in debt, are
all for present money, no matter how they pay it afterwards; besides, the nature of a preface is rambling,
never wholly out of the way, nor in it. This I have
learned from the practice of honest Montaigne, and
return at my pleasure to Ovid and Chaucer, of whom
I have little more to say.

Both of them built on the inventions of other men;
yet since Chaucer had something of his own, as *The*
Wife of Bath's Tale, The Cock and the Fox, which I 40
have translated, and some others, I may justly give
our countryman the precedence in that part; since I
can remember nothing of Ovid which was wholly his.
Both of them understood the manners; under which
name I comprehend the passions, and, in a larger
sense, the descriptions of persons, and their very
habits. For an example, I see Baucis and Philemon
as perfectly before me, as if some ancient painter had
drawn them; and all the Pilgrims in *The Canterbury*
Tales, their humors, their features, and the very dress, 50
as distinctly as if I had supped with them at the *Ta-*
bard in Southwark. Yet even there, too, the figures of
Chaucer are much more lively, and set in a better
light; which though I have not time to prove, yet
I appeal to the reader, and am sure he will clear me
from partiality. The thoughts and words remain to be
considered, in the comparison of the two poets, and
I have saved myself one-half of the labor, by owning
that Ovid lived when the Roman tongue was in its
meridian; Chaucer, in the dawning of our language: 60
therefore that part of the comparison stands not on an
equal foot, any more than the diction of Ennius and
Ovid, or of Chaucer and our present English. The
words are given up, as a post not to be defended in our
poet, because he wanted the modern art of fortifying.
The thoughts remain to be considered; and they are to

Preface to the Fables. 7. philology, all studies in literature or
subjects touched by literature, not necessarily language study. **8. Roman**
Feasts, Ovid's *Fasti,* six books of all kinds of antiquarian matter on six
months of the year. **9. Treatise of the Astrolabe,** a textbook by
Chaucer on the use of the astrolabe, an obsolete instrument for measuring the altitudes of celestial bodies. **11. Virgil,** the great Roman poet
(70–19 B.C.), author of the epic *Aeneid,* the pastoral *Eclogues,* and the
didactic *Georgics.* **Horace,** the lyric and satiric poet of imperial Rome
(65–8 B.C.), writer of odes, and fashioner of the form known as the
Horatian ode. **Persius,** a mordant Roman satirist (34–62 A.D.). **Manil-**
ius, an obscure Roman poet about the beginning of the Christian era,
known only for his *Astronomicae,* a didactic poem on the heavens. **16.**
Decameron, the story collection by Giovanni Boccaccio (1313–1375),
mentioned in connection with Chaucer's *Canterbury Tales* (p. 102).
The phrase "Boccaccio his *Decameron*" is a curious grammatical misconception. In Old and Middle English it was possible to render a
possessive case in the following manner: "Enoc his children," "Alfred
his book." From this use, the idea spread that the possessive ending *'s*
(originally *-es*) was actually formed from the possessive pronoun "his,"
and for a considerable time the use of this Middle English expression
survived as a curious archaism. **17. borrowed . . . Canterbury Tales.**
It is reasonably certain that Chaucer was not familiar with the original
of Boccaccio's *Decameron;* the similarity between some of *The Canter-*
bury Tales and some of the stories in the *Decameron* probably arose from

the fact that both Chaucer and Boccaccio were using a common source.
18. Palamon and Arcite, *The Knight's Tale* in *The Canterbury Tales.*
In this instance, Chaucer obviously used much material from Boccaccio's long narrative poem, the *Teseide.* **21. Griselda,** the archetype
of the "patient wife" in medieval story. There are many versions of
the legend in Europe during the Middle Ages; Chaucer's *Clerk's Tale*
in *The Canterbury Tales* is one; Boccaccio's tenth story of the *tenth day*
in the *Decameron* is another, but these two stories are drawn from the
common legend, and have no direct connection with each other. **Pet-**
rarch, the great Italian poet and storyteller, a contemporary of Boccaccio. Chaucer evidently used Petrarch's Latin translation of Boccaccio's
version of the Griselda story. **23. Lombard author.** As pointed" out
(l. 18 and note), Chaucer's source for *The Knight's Tale* was Boccaccio's *Teseide.* **35. Montaigne,** the French essayist (1533–1592), was
a pioneer in the writing of the informal essay in modern European
letters. **40. The Cock and the Fox,** better known as *The Nun's Priest's*
Tale, p. 116. Neither of the stories mentioned was invented by Chaucer.
47. Baucis and Philemon, characters in one of the stories from Ovid's
Metamorphoses—an elderly couple who entertained Jupiter so hospitably
that he transformed their humble cottage into a splendid temple of
which the god made them priest and priestess. They died at the same
hour, as they had requested, and were transformed into trees, whose
boughs intertwined. **51. Tabard in Southwark,** the inn from which the
Canterbury pilgrims set out on their journey (cf. Chaucer's *Prologue to*

be measured only by their propriety; that is, as they flow more or less naturally from the persons described, on such and such occasions. The vulgar judges, which are nine parts in ten of all nations, who call conceits and jingles wit, who see Ovid full of them, and Chaucer altogether without them, will think me little less than mad for preferring the Englishman to the Roman. Yet, with their leave, I must presume to say that the things they admire are only glittering trifles, and so far from being witty, that in a serious poem they are nauseous, because they are unnatural. Would any man, who is ready to die for love, describe his passion like Narcissus? Would he think of *inopem me copia fecit*, and a dozen more of such expressions, poured on the neck of one another, and signifying all the same thing? If this were wit, was this a time to be witty, when the poor wretch was in the agony of death? This is just John Littlewit, in *Bartholomew Fair*, who had a conceit (as he tells you) left him in his misery; a miserable conceit. On these occasions the poet should endeavor to raise pity; but, instead of this, Ovid is tickling you to laugh. Virgil never made use of such machines when he was moving you to commiserate the death of Dido: he would not destroy what he was building. Chaucer makes Arcite violent in his love, and unjust in the pursuit of it; yet, when he came to die, he made him think more reasonably: he repents not of his love, for that had altered his character; but acknowledges the injustice of his proceedings, and resigns Emilia to Palamon. What would Ovid have done on this occasion? He would certainly have made Arcite witty on his deathbed; he had complained he was further off from possession, by being so near, and a thousand such boyisms, which Chaucer rejected as below the dignity of the subject. They who think otherwise, would, by the same reason, prefer Lucan and Ovid to Homer and Virgil, and Martial to all four of them. As for the turn of words, in which Ovid particularly excels all poets, they are sometimes a fault, and sometimes a beauty, as they are used properly or improperly; but in strong passions always to be shunned, because passions are serious, and will admit no playing. The French have a high

value for them; and, I confess, they are often what they call delicate, when they are introduced with judgment; but Chaucer writ with more simplicity, and followed Nature more closely than to use them. I have thus far, to the best of my knowledge, been an upright judge betwixt the parties in competition, not meddling with the design nor the disposition of it; because the design was not their own; and in the disposing of it they were equal. It remains that I say somewhat of Chaucer in particular.

In the first place, as he is the father of English poetry, so I hold him in the same degree of veneration as the Grecians held Homer, or the Romans Virgil. He is a perpetual fountain of good sense; learned in all sciences; and, therefore, speaks properly on all subjects. As he knew what to say, so he knows also when to leave off; a continence which is practiced by few writers, and scarcely by any of the ancients, excepting Virgil and Horace. One of our late great poets is sunk in his reputation, because he could never forgive any conceit which came in his way; but swept like a drag-net, great and small. There was plenty enough, but the dishes were ill sorted; whole pyramids of sweetmeats for boys and women, but little of solid meat for men. All this proceeded not from any want of knowledge, but of judgment. Neither did he want that in discerning the beauties and faults of other poets, but only indulged himself in the luxury of writing; and perhaps knew it was a fault, but hoped the reader would not find it. For this reason, though he must always be thought a great poet, he is no longer esteemed a good writer; and for ten impressions which his works have had in so many successive years, yet at present a hundred books are scarcely purchased once a twelvemonth; for, as my last Lord Rochester said, though somewhat profanely, "Not being of God, he could not stand."

Chaucer followed Nature everywhere, but was never so bold to go beyond her; and there is a great difference of being *poeta* and *nimis poeta*, if we may believe Catullus, as much as betwixt a modest behavior and affectation. The verse of Chaucer, I confess, is not harmonious to us; but 'tis like the eloquence of one whom Tacitus commends, it was *auribus istius temporis*

The Canterbury Tales, p. 104, l. 20). 53. **lively**, lifelike. 62. **Ennius**, an early Roman epic poet (239–169 B.C.). 65. **wanted . . . fortifying**. Dryden is basing his point on the assumption that Middle English per se is inferior to Modern English both as a vehicle of human expression and as an artistic medium. 79. **Narcissus**. The story is told in Ovid's *Metamorphoses*. Narcissus, a beautiful youth, rejected the nymph Echo, because he was infatuated with his own beauty, and spent his time admiring his own reflection in the water. He pined away and was finally changed by the gods into the flower that bears his name. Meanwhile Echo, too, had languished until she became a mere voice. *inopem . . . fecit*, "my wealth has made me poor" (Ovid's *Metamorphoses*, III, 466). 84. *Bartholomew Fair*, one of Ben Jonson's best satirical comedies (1614), a play thronged with a multitude of characters from the London of Jonson's time. It is almost as interesting a cross section of English life as that given in Chaucer's *Prologue to The Canterbury Tales*. 90. **Dido**, the legendary queen of Carthage, who fell in love with Aeneas, and committed suicide when Aeneas left her. The story is told in the *Aeneid*, Book IV. 91. **Arcite**, one of the two young princes vying for the hand of Emilia in Chaucer's *Knight's Tale*. His rival Palamon was the successful suitor. 100. **boyisms**, immature expressions worthy only of a boy. 103. **Lucan**, Marcus Annaeus Lucanus (39–65 A.D.), a Roman epic poet, whose special subject was the Civil War between Caesar and Pompey in 48 B.C.; *Pharsalia* was the name of the poem, which was left unfinished. **Martial**, Marcus Valerius Mar-

tialis (40?–104), a powerful Roman satirist, particularly gifted in the use of epigram. For this very reason he was a favorite source for many neo-classical writers. 104. **turn of words**, the neatly rounded phrase in the proper place; in other words, the instinct for the epigram. 128. **One . . . late great poets**, Abraham Cowley (1618–1667), a distinguished writer of odes but a rather mediocre lyric writer. 144. **Lord Rochester**, John Wilmot, Earl of Rochester (1648–1680), the most famous of the wits at the court of King Charles II as well as the one with the most notorious reputation. He wrote some lyric poetry, distinctly in the Cavalier tradition, and some satires. *A Satire Against Mankind* is usually considered his masterpiece. 148. *poeta . . . poeta*, "a poet—and too much of a poet" (Martial, *Epigrams* III, 44; cf. l. 103 and note). 149. **Catullus**, a Roman lyric poet (84–54 B.C.). 152. *auribus . . . accommodata*, "suited to the ears of that time" (Tacitus' *De Oratoribus*, xxi). Tacitus (55–120) was a celebrated Roman historian and legal orator, particularly interesting to the student of English literature because he has the most complete account, from a contemporary viewpoint, of the Germanic peoples while they were still in the barbaric state. Dryden has really paraphrased the quotation from Tacitus, whose original phrase ran: *auribus iudicum accommodata*, "suited to the ears of judges."

accommodata: they who lived with him, and some time after him, thought it musical; and it continues so, even in our judgment, if compared with the numbers of Lidgate and Gower, his contemporaries; there is the rude sweetness of a Scotch tune in it, which is natural and pleasing, though not perfect. 'Tis true, I cannot go so far as he who published the last edition of him; for he would make us believe the fault is in our ears, and that there were really ten syllables in a verse where we find
10 but nine: but this opinion is not worth confuting; 'tis so gross and obvious an error that common sense (which is a rule in everything but matters of Faith and Revelation) must convince the reader, that equality of numbers, in every verse which we call *heroic*, was either not known, or not always practiced, in Chaucer's age. It were an easy matter to produce some thousands of his verses, which are lame for want of half a foot, and sometimes a whole one, and which no pronunciation can make otherwise. We can only say, that he lived
20 in the infancy of our poetry, and that nothing is brought to perfection at the first. We must be children before we grow men. There was an Ennius, and in process of time a Lucilius, and a Lucretius, before Virgil and Horace; even after Chaucer there was a Spenser, a Harrington, a Fairfax, before Waller and Denham were in being; and our members were in their nonage till these last appeared. I need say little of his parentage, life and fortunes; they are to be found at large in all the editions of his works. He was employed abroad, and
30 favored, by Edward the Third, Richard the Second, and Henry the Fourth, and was poet, as I suppose, to all three of them. In Richard's time, I doubt, he was a little dipped in the rebellion of the Commons; and being brother-in-law to John of Gaunt, it was no wonder if he followed the fortunes of that family; and was well with Henry the Fourth when he had deposed his predecessor. Neither is it to be admired, that Henry, who was a wise as well as a valiant prince, who claimed by succession, and was sensible that his title
40 was not sound, but was rightfully in Mortimer, who had married the heir of York; it was not to be admired,

I say, if that great politician should be pleased to have the greatest wit of those times in his interests, and to be the trumpet of his praises. Augustus had given him the example, by the advice of Maecenas, who recommended Virgil and Horace to him; whose praises helped to make him popular while he was alive, and after his death have made him precious to posterity. As for the religion of our poet, he seems to have some little bias towards the opinions of Wyclif, after John 50 of Gaunt his patron; somewhat of which appears in the tale of *Piers Plowman*: yet I cannot blame him for inveighing so sharply against the vices of the clergy in his age: their pride, their ambition, their pomp, their avarice, their worldly interest, deserved the lashes which he gave them, both in that, and in most of his *Canterbury Tales*. Neither has his contemporary Boccaccio spared them: yet both those poets lived in much esteem with good and holy men in orders; for the scandal which is given by particular priests 60 reflects not on the sacred function. Chaucer's Monk, his Canon, and his Friar, took not from the character of his Good Parson. A satirical poet is the check of the laymen on bad priests. We are only to take care that we involve not the innocent with the guilty in the same condemnation. The good cannot be too much honored, nor the bad too coarsely used; for the corruption of the best becomes the worst. When a clergyman is whipped, his gown is first taken off, by which the dignity of his order is secured. If he be wrongfully 70 accused, he has his action of slander; and 'tis at the poet's peril if he transgress the law. But they will tell us that all kind of satire, though never so well deserved by particular priests, yet brings the whole order into contempt. Is then the peerage of England anything dishonored when a peer suffers for his treason? If he be libeled, or any way defamed, he has his *scandalum magnatum* to punish the offender. They who use this kind of argument seem to be conscious to themselves of somewhat which has deserved the poet's 80 lash, and are less concerned for their public capacity than for their private; at least there is pride at the

4. **Lidgate and Gower.** John Lydgate (1370?–1451?), a follower of Chaucer, was possibly the most voluminous poet that English literature has produced, but one of inferior talent. And yet his was probably the most substantial talent among English poets of the fifteenth century. He made a large collection of the many Troy legends of the Middle Ages, known as the *Troy-Book*; he wrote a series of *Saints' Lives*; and borrowing from Boccaccio's *De Casibus Virorum Illustrium* he wrote *The Fall of Princes*. These are only a few of the many works ascribed to the Lydgate canon. John Gower (1325?–1408), friend of Chaucer, court poet, and scholar, wrote in three languages, Latin, French, and English. His most ambitious work is the *Confessio Amantis*, in English, a story collection belonging to the "framework tradition." 7. **last edition of him.** This was the edition of Chaucer by Thomas Speght, first published in 1598 and reprinted in 1602 and in 1687. Speght's edition was not a perfect printing of Chaucer's text, but Speght himself was right about Chaucer's ten syllables to a line. Dryden did not realize that in Middle English all vowels including final *-e*'s are pronounced. Cf. "On Reading Middle English," p. 103. 14. **heroic . . . age.** As a matter of fact, the *Prologue* to Chaucer's *Canterbury Tales* would have been considered to be written in good heroic couplets had the thought been completed at the end of the second line. 23. **Lucilius,** a Roman satirical poet of the second century B.C. **Lucretius,** a noted Roman poet and philosopher (95–55 B.C.), the proponent of a grandiose and noble conception of the universe based on a kind of "atomic" theory. 24. **Spenser,** Edmund Spenser, cf. p. 217. 25. **Harrington,** Sir John Harrington (1561–1612), the translator of the great Italian Renaissance epic, the *Orlando Furioso* of Ludovico Ariosto (1474–1533). **Fairfax,** Edward Fairfax

(1580–1635), translator of another important Italian Renaissance epic, the *Jerusalem Delivered* of Torquato Tasso (1544–1595). **Waller,** Edmund Waller, the Cavalier poet (cf. p. 349). **Denham,** John Denham (1615–1669). Waller wrote some beautiful lyrics; Denham's chief contribution to English letters was *Cooper's Hill*, a didactic poem with a considerable amount of "landscape" description. But neither Waller nor Denham merit their exalted position here in company with Ariosto, Tasso, Vergil, Horace, or Chaucer. It happened, however, that both Waller and Denham were instrumental in establishing the use of the heroic couplet in true neo-classical style. This fact, coupled with their poetic gifts, was perhaps enough to lift them high in Dryden's eyes. 26. **nonage,** the period in which a person is a minor in the eyes of the law. 32. **doubt,** suspect, hardly "fear," as the word had originally meant. 34. **John of Gaunt,** Duke of Lancaster, son of King Edward III, and both friend and patron to Geoffrey Chaucer. Dryden's guess here as to the political course Chaucer pursued during the 1380's and 1390's, particularly about 1385–1386 is as good as our own, but cf. Chaucer's life (p. 101). 37. **admired,** wondered at. 40. **Mortimer,** Edmund Mortimer, Earl of March, heir presumptive to King Richard II. He had been supported by Richard II but was pushed aside by Henry IV, who seized the throne from Richard in 1399. 45. **Maecenas,** a Roman statesman and a rich patron of letters during the reign of the Emperor Augustus. 50. **Wyclif,** see p. 17. 52. *Piers Plowman,* not the great social document of fourteenth-century England, but *The Plowman's Tale,* another piece belonging to the Piers Plowman tradition, and ascribed for a long time to Chaucer. 77. *scandalum magnatum,* the crime of lèse-majesté, or the defaming of rulers.

bottom of their reasoning. If the faults of men in orders are only to be judged among themselves, they are all in some sort parties; for, since they say the honor of their order is concerned in every member of it, how can we be sure that they will be impartial judges? How far I may be allowed to speak my opinion in this case, I know not; but I am sure a dispute of this nature 90 caused mischief in abundance betwixt a King of England and an Archbishop of Canterbury; one standing up for the laws of his land, and the other for the honor (as he called it) of God's Church; which ended in the murder of the prelate, and in the whipping of his Majesty from post to pillar for his penance. The learned and ingenious Dr. Drake has saved me the labor of inquiring into the esteem and reverence which the priests have had of old; and I would rather extend than diminish any part of it. Yet I must needs say that when 100 a priest provokes me without any occasion given him, I have no reason, unless it be the charity of a Christian, to forgive him; *prior laesit* is justification sufficient in the civil law. If I answer him in his own language, self-defense I am sure must be allowed me; and if I carry it further, even to a sharp recrimination, somewhat may be indulged to human frailty. Yet my resentment has not wrought so far but that I have followed Chaucer, in his character of a holy man, and have enlarged on that subject with some pleasure; reserving to myself 110 the right, if I shall think fit hereafter, to describe another sort of priests, such as are more easily to be found than the Good Parson; such as have given the last blow to Christianity in this age, by a practice so contrary to their doctrine. But this will keep cold till another time. In the meanwhile, I take up Chaucer where I left him.

He must have been a man of a most wonderful comprehensive nature, because, as it has been truly observed of him, he has taken into the compass of his *Canterbury Tales* the various manners and humors 120 (as we now call them) of the whole English nation, in his age. Not a single character has escaped him. All his pilgrims are severally distinguished from each other; and not only in their inclinations, but in their very physiognomies and persons. Baptista Porta could not have described their natures better than by the marks which the poet gives them. The matter and manner of their tales, and of their telling, are so suited to their different educations, humors, and callings, that each of them would be improper in any other mouth. 130 Even the grave and serious characters are distinguished by their several sorts of gravity: their discourses are such as belong to their age, their calling, and their breeding; such as are becoming of them, and of them only. Some of his persons are vicious, and some virtuous; some are unlearned, or (as Chaucer calls them) lewd, and some are learned. Even the ribaldry of the low characters is different: the Reeve, the Miller, and the Cook, are several men, and distinguished from each other as much as the mincing Lady-Prioress and the 140 broad-speaking gap-toothed Wife of Bath. But enough of this; there is such a variety of game springing up before me that I am distracted in my choice, and know not which to follow. 'Tis sufficient to say, according to the proverb, that "Here is God's plenty." We have our forefathers and great grand-dames all before us, as they were in Chaucer's days: their general characters are still remaining in mankind, and even in England, though they are called by other names than those of Monks, and Friars, and Canons, and Lady Abbesses, 150 and Nuns; for mankind is ever the same, and nothing lost out of Nature, though everything is altered. . . .

(1700)

90. **King . . . Canterbury,** an allusion to the famous quarrel between King Henry II of England and Thomas à Becket, Archbishop of Canterbury, which culminated in the assassination of Becket in 1170. 96. **Dr. Drake,** James Drake (1667–1707), who wrote a reply to Jeremy Collier's attack upon the English stage (1698). 102. *prior laesit,* "he struck first," from the prologue to the *Eunuchus,* a comedy by the early Roman playwright, Terence (195?–159 B.C.). 120. **humors,** temperaments, essential mental types. According to the humor theory individual characteristics were determined by the relative proportions in the body of the four chief fluids—blood, phlegm, choler or bile, and melancholy or black bile. 125. **Baptista Porta,** a noted Italian physiognomist (1543–1617). 137. **lewd.** This word, to judge from Dryden's use of it here, has apparently taken on the modern meaning.

JOSEPH ADDISON 1672-1719
RICHARD STEELE 1672-1729

Joseph Addison, the son of a churchman, went to Oxford and then embarked upon a career of letters. He first won the attention of certain leaders in the Whig party, particularly the Earl of Halifax. Although it was a period of partisanship, and a great career was possible for any young man with a gift for political *writing, Addison nevertheless began his creative activity with poems, few of which have been remembered except by students of the period. In 1699, Addison was given the opportunity by his patrons of traveling abroad, presumably to train himself for future diplomatic employment, but the death of King William III in*

1702 brought a temporary eclipse of the Whigs and the cessation of political support to Addison, who now felt a distinct financial pinch. Out of the welter of party strife during the next few years, however, Addison emerged with The Campaign (1704), a poem in praise of the Duke of Marlborough, the hero of the hour for his victories at Blenheim and Ramillies during the War of the Spanish Succession (p. 422). The same year saw the beginning of Addison's active political career, so successful that, in spite of the fluctuating fortunes of the Whigs, who were not given much advantage until the death of Queen Anne in 1714, he eventually gained the post of secretary of state in 1717. His marriage just before to the Countess of Warwick undoubtedly was a powerful aid to this important political attainment. Unfortunately Addison was unable to enjoy his position long, for he was forced to resign on account of ill health and died in 1719.

The name always associated with that of Addison in literary pursuits is that of Richard Steele, who was born at Dublin in the same year as Addison, met Addison in school and went up with him to Oxford. But unlike his more conservative-minded friend, Steele did not wait to take a degree from the university but joined the army—an act for which he was promptly disinherited by his uncle. He remained in the army for some time, though not in active service, and rose to the rank of captain. His pamphlet, The Christian Hero (1701), aroused the admiration of King William III, although its didactic tone irritated one of Steele's military comrades. As a result, a duel was arranged in which Steele dangerously wounded his adversary; he always thereafter opposed dueling and affairs of honor. Indeed, by this time Steele was dedicated to the life of a literary opportunist. He first turned to the stage, and wrote four sentimental comedies which were received with some popularity: The Funeral (1701), The Lying Lover (1703), The Tender Husband (1705), and The Conscious Lovers (1722).

By 1705, therefore, Steele had actually achieved greater success in literature than Addison, who had been trying to sit on the twin chairs of literature and politics at the same time. Nevertheless, it was Addison's preoccupation with political preferment that got Steele his first taste of journalism, for Addison had Steele made official gazetteer (mouthpiece and publicity agent) for the Whigs. The success of the periodical The Gazette, appearing in May 1707, was the first definite indication that the periodical was more useful than the pamphlet for political controversy and exposition. Hard upon the heels of The Gazette came The Tatler, a newspaper not only for party politics but also for social comment, published three times a week. The combination in Steele of political reporter and coffee-house gossip was excellent for the journalistic success of The Tatler; it was for Addison with his greater stylistic dignity and more penetrating critical ability to give the periodical something more than ephemeral journalistic success. As Steele himself said, "I fared like a distressed prince, who calls in a powerful neighbor to his aid; I was undone by my auxiliary; when I had once called him in I could not subsist without dependence on him." Nevertheless, Steele, who was the first editor of The Tatler under the pseudonym of Isaac Bickerstaff, furnished the initiative for most of the essays in The Tatler, and should therefore be given pre-eminence in the founding of the periodical essay in England. Addison followed Steele's lead for the greater part, especially in this their first joint periodical venture.

The Tatler appeared first in 1709. In January 1711, the paper was stopped for financial as well as for political reasons. Two months later, at the suggestion of Addison, a new periodical, The Spectator, made its debut. The chief distinction of The Spectator, as compared with The Tatler, is the presence of the Sir Roger de Coverley papers, a series of sketches of the famous country squire and his circle, the Spectator Club (p. 479) who are not only subjects for individual satire, but also mouthpieces for Addison's and Steele's pithy observations. The conception of Sir Roger and his group was originally Steele's, but Addison gave variety, depth, and a certain satirical bent to the characterization. Most of the essays in The Tatler were by Steele, most of those in The Spectator were by Addison, although the total of both Tatler and Spectator papers would show that Steele was more active than Addison. To both periodicals, moreover, many other writers of the time—notably Swift—contributed scattered articles.

The Spectator ran until December 1712. Its purpose had been definitely stated by Addison (No. 58): "to banish vice and ignorance out of the territories of Great Britain." In undertaking this high project Addison said, "I shall endeavor to enliven morality with wit and to temper wit with morality." The general achievement of The Spectator, as compared with that of The Tatler, was to treat in mildly satirical fashion a greater variety of subjects, and to be, as it were, a mirror of contemporary opinion and comment. The unusual inventiveness of the authors is shown in critical and descriptive papers covering the whole area of ordinary life in eighteenth-century England, whether discovered in pleasant rambles through the countryside, or in genial gossip at coffee houses, taverns, and theaters in town.

The chief glory of The Spectator will always belong to Addison. He was responsible not only for the whimsicalities of Sir Roger de Coverley, but also for the kindly satires upon the corrupt tastes and the ridiculous manners of the period, for literary criticism, including praise of the ballad Chevy Chase and of Paradise Lost, and for vigorous thinking and quiet meditation. Steele, on the other hand, though he never attained the polish of Addison, excelled in personal portraits, in the sentimental, and in the characteristic eighteenth-century didacticism.

Neither Addison nor Steele ever matched subsequently the achievement of The Tatler or The Spectator. Addison, as remarked before, found political opportunity knocking at his door, from which a successor to The Spectator, The Guardian (1713), could not distract him. His only other important work, the classical tragedy Cato (1713), won him much contemporary applause with a political echo, but is really a very commonplace play. Steele, on the other hand, went on in the field of journalism through a series of periodical ventures, most famous of which was The Plebeian, appearing first in 1718, in which he found himself in a position opposed politically to that of Addison. With the coming into power of the Whigs in 1714, Steele profited, but his telling literary work was finished. He could never clear himself of financial difficulties because of his improvident, generous nature. His prestige in the world of letters nevertheless remained great.

What is most important about these two men, gifted so strikingly with such dissimilar gifts, is that they established, in a comparatively short time, the journalistic essay as a significant form of modern writing. Their work has greater variety than Defoe's, and the work of Addison especially provides an excellent example of the neo-classical ideal of a dignified, lucid, and harmonious prose style.

ON DUELLING

(STEELE)

The Tatler, No. 25: Tuesday, June 7, 1709.

Quicquid agunt homines——
——nostri est farrago libelli.—JUVENAL

A letter from a young lady, written in the most passionate terms, wherein she laments the misfortune of a gentleman, her lover, who was lately wounded in a duel, has turned my thoughts to that subject and inclined me to examine into the causes which precipitate men into so fatal a folly. And as it has been proposed to treat of subjects of gallantry in the article from hence and no one point in nature is more proper to be considered by the company who frequent this
10 place than that of duels, it is worth our consideration to examine into this chimerical, groundless humor and to lay every other thought aside, until we have stripped it of all its false pretenses to credit and reputation amongst men.

But I must confess, when I consider what I am going about, and run over in my imagination all the endless crowd of men of honor who will be offended at such a discourse, I am undertaking, methinks, a work worthy an invulnerable hero in romance, rather than a private
20 gentleman with a single rapier: but as I am pretty well acquainted by great opportunities with the nature of man and know of a truth that all men fight against their will, the danger vanishes and resolution rises upon this subject. For this reason, I shall talk very freely on a custom which all men wish exploded, though no man has courage enough to resist it.

But there is one unintelligible word, which I fear will extremely perplex my dissertation and I confess to you I find very hard to explain, which is the term "satisfaction." An honest country gentleman had the 30 misfortune to fall into company with two or three modern men of honor, where he happened to be very ill-treated; and one of the company, being conscious of his offense, sends a note to him in the morning and tells him he was ready to give him satisfaction. "This is fine doing," says the plain fellow; "last night he sent me away cursedly out of humor, and this morning he fancies it would be a satisfaction to be run through the body."

As the matter at present stands, it is not to do hand- 40 some actions denominates a man of honor; it is enough if he dares to defend ill ones. Thus you often see a common sharper in competition with a gentleman of the first rank; though all mankind is convinced that a fighting gamester is only a pickpocket with the courage of a highwayman. One cannot with any patience reflect on the unaccountable jumble of persons and things in this town and nation, which occasions very frequently that a brave man falls by a hand below that of a common hangman and yet his executioner 50 escapes the clutches of the hangman for doing it. I shall, therefore, hereafter consider how the bravest men in other ages and nations have behaved themselves upon such incidents as we decide by combat; and show, from their practice, that this resentment neither has its foundation from true reason or solid fame; but is an imposture, made of cowardice, falsehood, and want of understanding. For this work, a good history of quarrels would be very edifying to the public and I apply myself to the town for particulars and cir- 60 cumstances within their knowledge which may serve to embellish the dissertation with proper cuts. Most of the quarrels I have ever known have proceeded from some valiant coxcomb's persisting in the wrong, to defend some prevailing folly and preserve himself from the ingenuousness of owning a mistake.

By this means it is called "giving a man satisfac-

On Duelling. Quicquid . . . libelli, "Whate'er men do, or say, or think, or dream, Our motley paper seizes as its theme." 8. hence, i.e., from White's Chocolate House, from which this paper, and others on subjects of gallantry, was dated.

tion," to urge your offense against him with your sword; which puts me in mind of Peter's order to the keeper in *The Tale of a Tub:* "if you neglect to do all this, damn you and your generation for ever: and so we bid you heartily farewell." If the contradiction in the very terms of one of our challenges were as well explained and turned into downright English, would it not run after this manner?

"Sir:

10   "Your extraordinary behavior last night and the liberty you were pleased to take with me makes me this morning give you this, to tell you, because you are an ill-bred puppy, I will meet you in Hyde Park an hour hence; and because you want both breeding and humanity, I desire you would come with a pistol in your hand, on horseback, and endeavor to shoot me through the head, to teach you more manners. If you fail of doing me this pleasure, I shall say you are a rascal on every post in town: and so, sir, if you will 20 not injure me more, I shall never forgive what you have done already. Pray, sir, do not fail of getting everything ready; and you will infinitely oblige, Sir, Your most obedient humble servant, etc."

TOM FOLIO

(ADDISON)

The Tatler, No. 158: Thursday, April 13, 1710.

Faciunt nae intelligendo, ut nihil intelligant.

Tom Folio is a broker in learning, employed to get together good editions, and stock the libraries of great men. There is not a sale of books begins until Tom Folio is seen at the door. There is not an auction where his name is not heard, and that too in the very nick of time, in the critical moment, before the last 30 decisive stroke of the hammer. There is not a subscription goes forward in which Tom is not privy to the first rough draught of the proposals; nor a catalogue printed, that doth not come to him wet from the press. He is an universal scholar, so far as the title-page of all authors; knows the manuscripts in which they were discovered, the editions through which they have passed, with the praises or censures which they have received from the several members of the learned world. He has a greater esteem for Aldus and Elzevir, 40 than for Virgil and Horace. If you talk of Herodotus, he breaks out into a panegyric upon Harry Stephens. He thinks he gives you an account of an author, when

he tells you the subject he treats of, the name of the editor, and the year in which it was printed. Or if you draw him into farther particulars, he cries up the goodness of the paper, extols the diligence of the corrector, and is transported with the beauty of the letter. This he looks upon to be sound learning and substantial criticism. As for those who talk of the fineness of style, and the justness of thought, or describe the brightness 50 of any particular passages; nay, though they themselves write in the genius and spirit of the author they admire; Tom looks upon them as men of superficial learning and flashy parts.

I had yesterday morning a visit from this learned *idiot,* for *that* is the light in which I consider every pedant, when I discovered in him some little touches of the coxcomb, which I had not before observed. Being very full of the figure which he makes in the republic of letters, and wonderfully satisfied with his great stock 60 of knowledge, he gave me broad intimations that he did not believe in all points as his forefathers had done. He then communicated to me a thought of a certain author upon a passage of Virgil's account of the dead, which I made the subject of a late paper. This thought hath taken very much among men of Tom's pitch and understanding, though universally exploded by all that know how to construe Virgil, or have any relish of antiquity. Not to trouble my reader with it, I found, upon the whole, that Tom did not believe a future 70 state of rewards and punishments, because Aeneas, at his leaving the empire of the dead, passed through the gate of ivory, and not through that of horn. Knowing that Tom had not sense enough to give up an opinion which he had once received, that I might avoid wrangling, I told him "that Virgil possibly had his oversights as well as another author." "Ah! Mr. Bickerstaff," says he, "you would have another opinion of him, if you would read him in Daniel Heinsius's edition. I have perused him myself several times in that edition," 80 continued he; "and after the strictest and most malicious examination, could find but two faults in him; one of them is in the *Aeneid,* where there are two commas instead of a parenthesis; and another in the third *Georgic,* where you may find a semicolon turned upside down." "Perhaps," said I, "these were not Virgil's faults, but those of the transcriber." "I do not design it," says Tom, "as a reflection on Virgil; on the contrary, I know that all the manuscripts declaim against such a punctuation. Oh! Mr. Bickerstaff," says 90 he, "what would a man give to see one simile of Virgil writ in his own hand?" I asked him which was the simile he meant; but was answered, any simile in

3. *The Tale of a Tub,* by Jonathan Swift, see p. 493.
  Tom Folio. Faciunt . . . intelligant. "While they pretend to know more than others, they really know nothing," from the prologue to Terence's *Andria,* l. 17. 39. **Aldus and Elzevir, etc.** Aldus Manutius (1450?-1515) was a famous Venetian printer of the classics; *Elzevir* was the name of a family of Dutch printers in the early seventeenth century. As for *Virgil* and *Horace,* mentioned in the next line, they are of course the noted Roman poets of the first century B.C. 40. **Herodotus,** a famous Greek historian (484-428 B.C.). 41. **Harry Stephens,**

Henri Estienne (1528-1598), a French printer and scholar of the classics, one of a distinguished family of printers. 65. **late paper,** No. 154 of *The Tatler.* 71. **Aeneas,** the Trojan prince, hero of Vergil's *Aeneid.* The episode alluded to is from the *Aeneid,* Book VI, ll. 893 ff.:

    Two gates the silent house of Sleep adorn;
    Of polished ivory this, that of transparent horn—
    True visions through transparent horn arise;
    Through polished ivory pass deluding lies.
        —translated by Dryden.

Virgil. He then told me all the secret history in the commonwealth of learning; of modern pieces that had the names of ancient authors annexed to them; of all the books that were now writing or printing in the several parts of Europe; of many amendments which are made, and not yet published, and a thousand other
100 particulars, which I would not have my memory burdened with for a Vatican.

At length, being fully persuaded that I thoroughly admired him, and looked upon him as a prodigy of learning, he took his leave. I know several of Tom's class, who are professed admirers of Tasso, without understanding a word of Italian: and one in particular, that carries a *Pastor Fido* in his pocket, in which, I am sure, he is acquainted with no other beauty but the clearness of the character.

110 There is another kind of pedant, who, with all Tom Folio's impertinences, hath greater superstructures and embellishments of Greek and Latin; and is still more insupportable than the other, in the same degree as he is more learned. Of this kind very often are editors, commentators, interpreters, scholiasts, and critics; and, in short, all men of deep learning without common sense. These persons set a greater value on themselves for having found out the meaning of a passage in Greek, than upon the author for having written it;
120 nay, will allow the passage itself not to have any beauty in it, at the same time that they would be considered as the greatest men of the age, for having interpreted it. They will look with contempt on the most beautiful poems that have been composed by any of their contemporaries; but will lock themselves up in their studies for a twelvemonth together, to correct, publish, and expound such trifles of antiquity, as a modern author would be contemned for. Men of the strictest morals, severest lives, and
130 the gravest professions, will write volumes upon an idle sonnet, that is originally in Greek or Latin; give editions of the most immoral authors; and spin out whole pages upon the various readings of a lewd expression. All that can be said in excuse for them is, that their works sufficiently show they have no taste of their authors; and that what they do in this kind, is out of their great learning, and not out of any levity or lasciviousness of temper.

A pedant of this nature is wonderfully well described
140 in six lines of Boileau, with which I shall conclude his character:

Un Pédant enyvré de sa vaine science,
Tout berissé de Grec, tout bouffi d'arrogance,

Et qui de mille auteurs retenus mot pour mot,
Dans sa tête entassés n'a souvent fait qu'un sot,
Croit qu'un livre fait tout, et que sans Aristote
La raison ne voit goute, et le bon sens radote.

Brim-ful of learning see that pedant stride,
Bristling with horrid Greek, and puffed with pride!
A thousand authors he in vain has read, 150
And with their maxims stuffed his empty head;
And thinks that, without Aristotle's rule,
Reason is blind, and common sense a fool.

RECOLLECTIONS OF SORROW

(STEELE)

The Tatler, No. 181: Tuesday, June 6, 1710.

—*Dies, ni fallor, adest, quem semper acerbum,*
Semper honoratum (sic di voluistis), habebo.

There are those among mankind who can enjoy no relish of their being, except the world is made acquainted with all that relates to them, and think everything lost that passes unobserved; but others find a solid delight in stealing by the crowd, and modeling their life after such a manner, as is as much above the approbation as the practice of the vulgar. Life being 160 too short to give instances great enough of true friendship or good-will, some sages have thought it pious to preserve a certain reverence for the *manes* of their deceased friends, and have withdrawn themselves from the rest of the world at certain seasons, to commemorate in their own thoughts such of their acquaintance who have gone before them out of this life: and indeed, when we are advanced in years, there is not a more pleasing entertainment than to recollect in a gloomy moment the many we have parted with that have been 170 dear and agreeable to us, and to cast a melancholy thought or two after those with whom, perhaps, we have indulged ourselves in whole nights of mirth and jollity. With such inclinations in my heart I went to my closet yesterday in the evening, and resolved to be sorrowful; upon which occasion, I could not but look with disdain upon myself, that though all the reasons which I had to lament the loss of many of my friends, are now as forcible as at the moment of their departure, yet did not my heart swell with 180 the same sorrow which I felt at that time; but I could, without tears, reflect upon many pleasing

79. Daniel Heinsius, a noted Dutch classical scholar (1580–1655). His well-known edition of Vergil was published in 1636. **105. Tasso,** Torquato Tasso (1544–1595), the great Italian Renaissance poet, author of *Jerusalem Delivered* (1575), an epic which had considerable influence upon Milton's *Paradise Lost.* **107. Pastor Fido,** an Italian pastoral drama by Guarini (1537–1612), which had much influence upon Elizabethan pastoral dramas, notably Fletcher's *Faithful Shepherdess* (printed in 1610). **109. character,** type. **140. Boileau,** Nicolas Boileau-Despréaux (1636–1711), a French satirist and critic, most important in fixing neo-classical ideals upon French literature of the seventeenth century. **142. Un Pédant . . . radote,** a quotation from Boileau's *Satires,* IV, 5–10. The translation is by Wynne.
Recollections of Sorrow. **Dies . . . habebo,** "And now the rising day renews the year, A day forever sad, forever dear."—from Vergil's *Aeneid,* V, 49-50, translated by Dryden. **163. manes,** the spirit of a dead person.

adventures I have had with some who have long been blended with common earth. Though it is by the benefit of nature that length of time thus blots out the violence of afflictions; yet with tempers too much given to pleasure, it is almost necessary to revive the old places of grief in our memory, and ponder step by step on past life, to lead the mind into that sobriety of thought which poises the heart, and makes it beat with due time, without being quickened with desire, or retarded with despair, from its proper and equal motion. When we wind up a clock that is out of order, to make it go well for the future, we do not immediately set the hand to the present instant but we make it strike the round of all its hours, before it can recover the regularity of its time. "Such," thought I, "shall be my method this evening; and since it is that day of the year which I dedicate to the memory of such in another life as I much delighted in when living, an hour or two shall be sacred to sorrow and their memory, while I run over all the melancholy circumstances of this kind which have occurred to me in my whole life."

The first sense of sorrow I ever knew was upon the death of my father, at which time I was not quite five years of age; but was rather amazed at what all the house meant, than possessed with a real understanding why nobody was willing to play with me. I remember I went into the room where his body lay, and my mother sat weeping alone by it. I had my battledore in my hand, and fell a beating the coffin, and called "Papa"; for I know not how I had some slight idea that he was locked up there. My mother catched me in her arms, and transported beyond all patience of the silent grief she was before in, she almost smothered me in her embrace, and told me in a flood of tears, papa could not hear me, and would play with me no more, for they were going to put him under ground, whence he could never come to us again. She was a very beautiful woman, of a noble spirit, and there was a dignity in her grief amidst all the wildness of her transport, which methought, struck me with an instinct of sorrow, which, before I was sensible of what it was to grieve, seized my very soul, and has made pity the weakness of my heart ever since. The mind in infancy is, methinks, like the body in embryo, and receives impressions so forcible, that they are as hard to be removed by reason, as any mark with which a child is born is to be taken away by any future application. Hence it is that good nature in me is no merit; but having been so frequently overwhelmed with her tears

An eighteenth-century coffee house, from a contemporary French print.

Paris Cher Monsʳ Trolaria

29. **battledore**, a kind of bat, used in the game of battledore and shuttlecock. 60. **We . . . old.** Actually, Steele was only thirty-eight at the time this essay was written. 107. **Garraway's Coffee-house, etc.** The issue of *The Tatler* in which this essay appeared carried an advertisement of the wine intended for the sale alluded to in this sentence. Garraway's Coffee House was the haunt of London merchants.

before I knew the cause of any affliction, or could draw defenses from my own judgment, I imbibed commiseration, remorse, and an unmanly gentleness of mind, which has since ensnared me into ten thousand calamities, and from whence I can reap no advantage, except it be, that in such a humor as I am now in, I can the better indulge myself in the softness of humanity, and enjoy that sweet anxiety which arises from the memory of past afflictions.

60 We that are very old, are better able to remember things which befell us in our distant youth than the passages of later days. For this reason it is, that the companions of my strong and vigorous years present themselves more immediately to me in this office of sorrow. Untimely or unhappy deaths are what we are most apt to lament, so little are we able to make it indifferent when a thing happens, though we know it must happen. Thus we groan under life, and bewail those who are relieved from it. Every object that returns 70 to our imagination raises different passions according to the circumstance of their departure. Who can have lived in an army, and in a serious hour reflect upon the many gay and agreeable men that might long have flourished in the arts of peace, and not join with the imprecations of the fatherless and widow on the tyrant to whose ambition they fell sacrifices? But gallant men who are cut off by the sword move rather our veneration than our pity, and we gather relief enough from their own contempt of death to make it no evil, which 80 was approached with so much cheerfulness, and attended with so much honor. But when we turn our thoughts from the great parts of life on such occasions, and instead of lamenting those who stood ready to give death to those from whom they had the fortune to receive it; I say, when we let our thoughts wander from such noble objects, and consider the havoc which is made among the tender and the innocent, pity enters with an unmixed softness, and possesses all our souls at once.

90 Here (were there words to express such sentiments with proper tenderness) I should record the beauty, innocence, and untimely death, of the first object my eyes ever beheld with love. The beauteous virgin! How ignorantly did she charm, how carelessly excel! O Death! thou hast right to the bold, to the ambitious, to the high, and to the haughty, but why this cruelty to the humble, to the meek, to the undiscerning, to the thoughtless? Nor age, nor business, nor distress can erase the dear image from my imagination. In the same 100 week, I saw her dressed for a ball, and in a shroud. How ill did the habit of Death become the pretty trifler! I still behold the smiling earth——

A large train of disasters were coming on to my memory when my servant knocked at my closet door, and interrupted me with a letter, attended with a hamper of wine, of the same sort with that which is to be put to sale on Thursday next at Garraway's Coffeehouse. Upon the receipt of it, I sent for three of my friends. We are so intimate that we can be company in whatever state of mind we meet, and can entertain 110 each other without expecting always to rejoice. The wine we found to be generous and warming, but with such a heat as moved us rather to be cheerful than frolicsome. It revived the spirits without firing the blood. We commended it till two of the clock this morning, and, having today met a little before dinner, we found that, though we drank two bottles a man, we had much more reason to recollect than forget what had passed the night before.

THE SPECTATOR INTRODUCES HIMSELF TO THE READER

(ADDISON)

The Spectator, No. 1: Thursday, March 1, 1711.

Non fumum ex fulgore, sed ex fumo dare lucem Cogitat, ut speciosa dehinc miracula promat.—HORACE

I have observed that a reader seldom peruses a 120 book with pleasure till he knows whether the writer of it be a black or a fair man, of a mild or choleric disposition, married or a bachelor, with other particulars of the like nature that conduce very much to the right understanding of an author. To gratify this curiosity, which is so natural to a reader, I design this paper and my next as prefatory discourses to my following writings, and shall give some account in them of the several persons that are engaged in this work. As the chief trouble of compiling, digesting, and correcting 130 will fall to my share, I must do myself the justice to open the work with my own history. I was born to a small hereditary estate, which, according to the tradition of the village where it lies, was bounded by the same hedges and ditches in William the Conqueror's time that it is at present, and has been delivered down from father to son whole and entire, without the loss or acquisition of a single field or meadow, during the space of six hundred years. There runs a story in the family that my mother dreamed that she was brought 140 to bed of a judge: whether this might proceed from a lawsuit which was then depending in the family, or my father's being a justice of the peace, I cannot determine; for I am not so vain as to think it presaged any dignity that I should arrive at in my future life, though that was the interpretation which the neighborhood put upon it. The gravity of my behavior at my very first appearance in the world seemed to favor my

---

The Spectator Introduces Himself to the Reader. Non . . . promat, "Not smoke from fire his object is to bring, But fire from smoke, a very different thing," quoted from Horace's *Ars Poetica*, 143–144 in Conington's translation. 122. **choleric,** irritable. In ancient medical lore, a preponderance of bile (*choler*) produced an irascible disposition. 142. **depending,** pending, hanging fire.

mother's dream: for, as she has often told me, I threw away my rattle before I was two months old, and would not make use of my coral till they had taken away the bells from it.

As for the rest of my infancy, there being nothing in it remarkable, I shall pass it over in silence. I find that, during my nonage, I had the reputation of a very sullen youth, but was always a favorite of my schoolmaster, who used to say *that my parts were solid and*
10 *would wear well.* I had not been long at the University before I distinguished myself by a most profound silence; for during the space of eight years, excepting in the public exercises of the college, I scarce uttered the quantity of an hundred words; and indeed do not remember that I ever spoke three sentences together in my whole life. Whilst I was in this learned body, I applied myself with so much diligence to my studies that there are very few celebrated books, either in the learned or the modern tongues, which I am not ac-
20 quainted with.

Upon the death of my father I was resolved to travel into foreign countries, and therefore left the University with the character of an odd, unaccountable fellow, that had a great deal of learning if I would but show it. An insatiable thirst after knowledge carried me into all the countries of Europe in which there was anything new or strange to be seen; nay, to such a degree was my curiosity raised that having read the controversies of some great men concerning the antiquities of Egypt,
30 I made a voyage to Grand Cairo, on purpose to take the measure of a pyramid; and as soon as I had set myself right in that particular, returned to my native country with great satisfaction.

I have passed my latter years in this city, where I am frequently seen in most public places, though there are not above half a dozen of my select friends that know me; of whom my next paper shall give a more particular account. There is no place of general sort wherein I do not often make my appearance; sometimes
40 I am seen thrusting my head into a round of politicians at Will's, and listening with great attention to the narratives that are made in those little circular audiences. Sometimes I smoke a pipe at Child's, and whilst I seem attentive to nothing but *The Postman*, overhear the conversation of every table in the room. I appear on Sunday nights at St. James's Coffee-House, and sometimes join the little committee of politics in the Inner room, as one who comes there to hear and improve. My face is likewise very well known at the
50 Grecian, the Cocoa-Tree, and in the theaters both of Drury Lane and the Haymarket. I have been taken for a merchant upon the Exchange for above these ten years, and sometimes pass for a Jew in the assembly of stock-jobbers at Jonathan's. In short, wherever I see a cluster of people, I always mix with them, though I never open my lips but in my own club.

Thus I live in the world rather as a SPECTATOR of mankind than as one of the species; by which means I have made myself a speculative statesman, soldier,
60 merchant, and artisan, without ever meddling with any practical part in life. I am very well versed in the theory of an husband or a father, and can discern the errors in the economy, business, and diversion of others better than those who are engaged in them; as standers-by discover blots which are apt to escape those who are in the game. I never espoused any party with violence, and am resolved to observe an exact neutrality between the Whigs and Tories, unless I shall be forced to declare myself by the hostilities of either side. In short, I have acted in all the parts of
70 my life as a looker-on, which is the character I intend to preserve in this paper.

I have given the reader just so much of my history and character as to let him see I am not altogether unqualified for the business I have undertaken. As for other particulars in my life and adventures, I shall insert them in following papers as I shall see occasion. In the meantime, when I consider how much I have seen, read, and heard, I began to blame my own taciturnity: and since I have neither time nor inclination
80 to communicate the fullness of my heart in speech, I am resolved to do it in writing, and to print myself out, if possible, before I die. I have been often told by my friends that it is a pity so many useful discoveries which I have made should be in the possession of a silent man. For this reason, therefore, I shall publish a sheetful of thoughts every morning for the benefit of my contemporaries; and if I can in any way contribute to the diversion or improvement of the country in which I live, I shall leave it, when I am summoned out of it,
90 with the secret satisfaction of thinking that I have not lived in vain.

There are three very material points which I have not spoken to in this paper, and which, for several important reasons, I must keep to myself, at least for some time: I mean, an account of my name, my age, and my lodgings. I must confess I would gratify my reader in anything that is reasonable; but, as for these three particulars, though I am sensible they might tend very much to the embellishment of my paper, I
100

41. **Will's.** Most of the coffee houses, such as *Will's*, the *St. James*, the *Grecian*, and the *Cocoa-Tree*, have been described briefly (p. 422). *Child's* (l. 43) was another coffee house frequented by the clergy. *Jonathan's* (l. 54) was used chiefly by brokers and bankers. 44. **The Postman**, a mythical newsletter, intended by Addison to typify all such current news sheets, the forerunners of our modern newspapers. 51. **Drury Lane ... Haymarket**, at this time (1711) the two theaters of London. The *Drury Lane* was first opened in 1663, but was rebuilt after the Great Fire of London (see p. 448) and was reopened in 1674. The *Haymarket* has been equally famous in London theatrical history; but until about 1720 it served more or less as a training ground and annex to the *Drury Lane*. 108. **complexion**, general appearance. 120.

Mr. Buckley, the senior partner of the firm which published *The Spectator*.
The Spectator Club. Haec . . . ore, "Six others or more cry out with one voice," a quotation from the seventh *Satire* (ll. 166–167) of the Roman satirist Juvenal (60–140 A.D.). 144. **Lord Rochester,** John Wilmot, Earl of Rochester (1648–1680), a courtier, man of fashion, and poet, perhaps the most notorious person in the court of Charles II. 145. **Sir George Etherege,** playwright of the Restoration (1635–1691), author of the three striking comedies, *The Comical Revenge, or Love in a Tub* (1664); *She Would If She Could* (1668), of which Pepys said in his *Diary*, "though my wife and I arrived at the house by two o'clock, there were one thousand people put back that could not have room in

cannot yet come to a resolution of communicating them to the public. They would indeed draw me out of that obscurity which I have enjoyed for many years and expose me in public places to several salutes and civilities which have been always very disagreeable to me; for the greatest pain I can suffer is the being talked to and being stared at. It is for this reason, likewise, that I keep my complexion and dress as very great secrets, though it is not impossible but I may make discoveries of both in the progress of the work I have undertaken.

After having been thus particular upon myself, I shall in tomorrow's paper give an account of those gentlemen who are concerned with me in this work; for, as I have before intimated, a plan of it is laid and concerted (as all other matters of importance are) in a club. However, as my friends have engaged me to stand in the front, those who have a mind to correspond with me may direct their letters *To The Spectator, at Mr. Buckley's, in Little Britain.* For I must further acquaint the reader that, though our club meets only on Tuesdays and Thursdays, we have appointed a committee to sit every night for the inspection of all such papers as may contribute to the advancement of the public weal.

THE SPECTATOR CLUB

(STEELE)

The Spectator, No. 2: Friday, March 2, 1711.

——*Haec alii sex
Vel plures uno conclamant ore.*

The first of our society is a gentleman of Worcestershire, of ancient descent, a baronet; his name Sir Roger de Coverley. His great-grandfather was inventor of that famous country-dance which is called after him. All who know that shire are very well acquainted with the parts and merits of Sir Roger. He is a gentleman that is very singular in his behavior, but his singularities proceed from his good sense, and are contradictions to the manners of the world only as he thinks the world is in the wrong. However, this humor creates him no enemies, for he does nothing with sourness of obstinacy; and his being unconfined to modes and forms makes him but the readier and more capable to please and oblige all who know him. When he is in town, he lives in Soho Square. It is said he keeps himself a bachelor by reason he was crossed in love by a perverse, beautiful widow of the next county to him. Before this disappointment, Sir Roger was what you call a fine gentleman, had often supped with my Lord Rochester and Sir George Etherege, fought a duel upon his first coming to town, and kicked Bully Dawson in a public coffee-house for calling him "youngster." But being ill-used by the above-mentioned widow, he was very serious for a year and a half; and though, his temper being naturally jovial, he at last got over it, he grew careless of himself, and never dressed afterward. He continues to wear a coat and doublet of the same cut that were in fashion at the time of his repulse, which, in his merry humors, he tells us, has been in and out twelve times since he first wore it. 'Tis said Sir Roger grew humble in his desires after he had forgot this cruel beauty; but this is looked upon by his friends rather as matter of raillery than truth. He is now in his fifty-sixth year, cheerful, gay, and hearty; keeps a good house in both town and country; a great lover of mankind; but there is such a mirthful cast in his behavior that he is rather beloved than esteemed. His tenants grow rich, his servants look satisfied, all the young women profess love to him, and the young men are glad of his company; when he comes into a house he calls the servants by their names, and talks all the way upstairs to a visit. I must not omit that Sir Roger is a justice of the quorum; that he fills the chair at a quarter-session with great abilities; and, three months ago, gained universal applause by explaining a passage in the Game Act.

The gentleman next in esteem and authority among us is another bachelor, who is a member of the Inner Temple; a man of great probity, wit, and understanding; but he has chosen his place of residence rather to obey the direction of an old humorsome father, than in pursuit of his own inclinations. He was placed there to study the laws of the land, and is the most learned of any of the house in those of the stage. Aristotle and Longinus are much better understood by him than Littleton or Coke. The father sends up, every post, questions relating to marriage-articles, leases, and tenures, in the neighborhood; all which questions he agrees with an attorney to answer and take care of in the lump. He is studying the passions themselves, when he should be inquiring into the debates among men which arise from them. He knows the argument of each of the orations of Demosthenes and Tully, but not one case in the

---

the pit"; and *The Man of Mode, or Sir Fopling Flutter* (1676), which showed Etherege as a master of "gaiety, candor, and foppish wit." Sir Fopling, indeed, was a character much imitated by other playwrights who followed Etherege. 146. **Bully Dawson,** a notorious London sharper of the seventeenth century. 168. **Justice of the quorum,** justice of the peace in a county. 169. **quarter-session,** a meeting of a court every three months. 173. **Inner Temple.** The Inns of Court were voluntary legal societies in London, which had their origin toward the end of the thirteenth century. By the time of Elizabeth, they had become "a whole university, as it were, of students, practicers or pleaders, and judges of the laws of this realm," to quote a writer of the time. The Inns of Court were four in number: Lincoln's Inn, the Inner Temple, the Mid-

dle Temple, and Gray's Inn. 180. **Aristotle and Longinus,** both famous Greek critics whose opinions were held in high esteem during the eighteenth century. Aristotle, "the father of all knowledge," lived from 384 to 322 B.C.; Longinus from 210 to 273 A.D. 181. **Littleton or Coke.** Sir Thomas Littleton (1402–1481) was perhaps the greatest English jurist of the Middle Ages; Sir Edward Coke (1552–1634), who was in his day Lord Chief Justice, wrote a commentary on Littleton's treatise on land tenure. 189. **Demosthenes,** adjudged the greatest of ancient Greek orators (384–322 B.C.). **Tully,** Marcus Tullius Cicero (106–43 B.C.), noted Roman orator, and, for the eighteenth century at least, perhaps the greatest of classical authorities on prose style.

reports of our own courts. No one ever took him for a fool, but none, except his intimate friends, know he has a great deal of wit. This turn makes him at once both disinterested and agreeable; as few of his thoughts are drawn from business, they are most of them fit for conversation. His taste of books is a little too just for the age he lives in; he has read all, but approves of very few. His familiarity with the customs, manners, actions, and writings of the ancients makes him a very
10 delicate observer of what occurs to him in the present world. He is an excellent critic, and the time of the play is his hour of business; exactly at five he passes through New Inn, crosses through Russell Court, and takes a turn at Will's till the play begins; he has his shoes rubbed and his periwig powdered at the barber's as you go into the Rose. It is for the good of the audience when he is at a play, for the actors have an ambition to please him.

The person of next consideration is Sir Andrew
20 Freeport, a merchant of great eminence in the city of London, a person of indefatigable industry, strong reason, and great experience. His notions of trade are noble and generous, and (as every rich man has usually some sly way of jesting which would make no great figure were he not a rich man) he calls the sea the British Common. He is acquainted with commerce in all its parts, and will tell you that it is a stupid and barbarous way to extend dominion by arms; for true power is to be got by arts and industry. He will often
30 argue that if this part of our trade were well cultivated, we should gain from one nation; and if another, from another. I have heard him prove that diligence makes more lasting acquisitions than valor, and that sloth has ruined more nations than the sword. He abounds in several frugal maxims, among which the greatest favorite is, "A penny saved is a penny got." A general trader of good sense is pleasanter company than a general scholar; and Sir Andrew having a natural un- affected eloquence, the perspicuity of his discourse
40 gives the same pleasure that wit would in another man. He has made his fortunes himself, and says that England may be richer than other kingdoms by as plain methods as he himself is richer than other men; though at the same time I can say this of him, that there is not a point in the compass but blows home a ship in which he is an owner.

Next to Sir Andrew in the club-room sits Captain Sentry, a gentleman of great courage, good under- standing, but invincible modesty. He is one of those
50 that deserve very well, but are very awkward at putting their talents within the observation of such as should take notice of them. He was some years a captain, and behaved himself with great gallantry in several

The Spectator Club, an illustration by Francis Hayman for The Spectator, Dublin, 1778.

engagements and at several sieges; but having a small estate of his own, and being next heir to Sir Roger, he has quitted a way of life in which no man can rise suitably to his merit who is not something of a courtier as well as a soldier. I have heard him often lament that in a profession where merit is placed in so conspicuous a view, impudence should get the better of modesty. 60 When he has talked to this purpose I never heard him make a sour expression, but frankly confess that he left the world because he was not fit for it. A strict honesty and an even, regular behavior are in themselves ob- stacles to him that must press through crowds who endeavor at the same end with himself—the favor of a commander. He will, however, in this way of talk, excuse generals for not disposing according to men's desert, or inquiring into it, "For," says he, "that great man who has a mind to help me, has as many to break 70

16. the Rose, a tavern adjoining Drury Lane Theater. 20. city of London, i.e., in the central business district of London. 111. Duke of Monmouth, an illegitimate son of Charles II, greatly admired in Eng- lish society for his manners and graceful dancing. Cf. Dryden's Absalom

and Achitophel (p. 459).
Westminster Abbey. Pallida . . . Plutonia, quoted from Horace's Odes, I, iv, 13 ff:
With equal foot, rich friend, impartial fate

through to come at me as I have to come at him";
therefore he will conclude that the man who would
make a figure, especially in a military way, must get
over all false modesty, and assist his patron against the
importunity of other pretenders by a proper assurance
in his own vindication. He says it is a civil cowardice
to be backward in asserting what you ought to expect,
as it is a military fear to be slow in attacking when it
is your duty. With this candor does the gentleman
80 speak of himself and others. The same frankness runs
through all his conversation. The military part of his
life has furnished him with many adventures, in the
relation of which he is very agreeable to the company;
for he is never overbearing, though accustomed to
command men in the utmost degree below him; nor
ever too obsequious from an habit of obeying men
highly above him.

But that our society may not appear a set of
humorists unacquainted with the gallantries and pleas-
90 ures of the age, we have among us the gallant Will
Honeycomb, a gentleman who, according to his years,
should be in the decline of his life, but having ever
been very careful of his person, and always had a very
easy fortune, time has made but very little impression
either by wrinkles on his forehead or traces in his
brain. His person is well turned and of a good height.
He is very ready at that sort of discourse with which
men usually entertain women. He has all his life
dressed very well, and remembers habits as others
100 do men. He can smile when one speaks to him, and
laughs easily. He knows the history of every mode, and
can inform you from which of the French king's
wenches our wives and daughters had this manner of
curling their hair, that way of placing their hoods;
whose frailty was covered by such a sort of petticoat,
and whose vanity to show her foot made that part of
the dress so short in such a year. In a word, all his conversation and knowledge has been in the female world.
As other men of his age will take notice to you what
110 such a minister said upon such and such an occasion,
he will tell when the Duke of Monmouth danced at
court such a woman was then smitten, another was
taken with him at the head of his troop in the Park.
In all these important relations, he has ever about the
same time received a kind glance or a blow of a fan
from some celebrated beauty, mother of the present
Lord Such-a-one. If you speak of a young commoner
that said a lively thing in the House, he starts up: "He
has good blood in his veins; Tom Mirabell, the rogue,
120 cheated me in that affair; that young fellow's mother
used me more like a dog than any woman I ever made
advances to." This way of talking of his very much
enlivens the conversation among us of a more sedate

turn; and I find there is not one of the company but
myself, who rarely speak at all, but speaks of him as
of that sort of man who is usually called a well-bred,
fine gentleman. To conclude his character, where
women are not concerned, he is an honest, worthy
man.

I cannot tell whether I am to account him whom I 130
am next to speak of as one of our company, for he visits
us but seldom; but when he does, it adds to every
man else a new enjoyment of himself. He is a clergyman, a very philosophic man, of general learning, great
sanctity of life, and the most exact good breeding. He
has the misfortune to be of a very weak constitution,
and consequently cannot accept of such cares and business as preferments in his function would oblige him to;
he is therefore among divines what a chamber-counselor
is among lawyers. The probity of his mind and the 140
integrity of his life create him followers, as being eloquent or loud advances others. He seldom introduces
the subject he speaks upon; but we are so far gone in
years that he observes, when he is among us, an
earnestness to have him fall on some divine topic,
which he always treats with much authority, as one
who has no interest in this world, as one who is hastening to the object of all his wishes and conceives hope
from his decays and infirmities. These are my ordinary
companions.
150

WESTMINSTER ABBEY

(ADDISON)

The Spectator, No. 26: Friday, March 30, 1711.

Pallida mors aequo pulsat pede pauperum tabernas,
  Regnumque turres, O beate Sexti,
Vitae summa brevis spem nos vetat inchoare longam,
  Jam te premet nox, fabulaeque manes,
Et domus exilis Plutonia.

When I am in a serious humor, I very often walk
by myself in Westminster Abbey; where the gloominess
of the place, and the use to which it is applied, with the
solemnity of the building, and the condition of the
people who lie in it, are apt to fill the mind with a kind
of melancholy, or rather thoughtfulness, that is not disagreeable. I yesterday passed a whole afternoon in the
churchyard, the cloisters, and the church, amusing
myself with the tombstones and inscriptions that I met
with in those several regions of the dead. Most of 160
them recorded nothing else of the buried person, but
that he was born upon one day and died upon another:

Knocks at the cottage and the palace-gate
Life's span forbids thee to extend thy cares,
And stretch thy hopes beyond thy years;
Night soon will seize, and you must quickly go

To story'd ghosts, and Pluto's house below.
  —translated by Thomas Creech (d. 1700).

the whole history of his life being comprehended in those two circumstances, that are common to all mankind. I could not but look upon these registers of existence, whether of brass or marble, as a kind of satire upon the departed persons; who had left no other memorial of them, but that they were born and that they died. They put me in mind of several persons mentioned in the battles of heroic poems, who have sounding names given them, for no other reason
10 but that they may be killed, and are celebrated for nothing but being knocked on the head. Γλαῦκόν τε Μέδοντά τε Θερσίλοχόν τε.—Hom. Glaucumque, Medontaque, Thersilochumque.—Virg. The life of these men is finely described in holy writ by "the path of an arrow," which is immediately closed up and lost.

Upon my going into the church, I entertained myself with the digging of a grave; and saw in every shovelful of it that was thrown up, the fragment of a
20 bone or skull intermixt with a kind of fresh moldering earth, that some time or other had a place in the composition of a human body. Upon this I began to consider with myself what innumerable multitudes of people lay confused together under the pavement of that ancient cathedral; how men and women, friends and enemies, priests and soldiers, monks and prebendaries, were crumbled amongst one another and blended together in the same common mass; how beauty, strength, and youth, with old age, weakness,
30 and deformity, lay undistinguished in the same promiscuous heap of matter.

After having thus surveyed this great magazine of mortality, as it were, in the lump, I examined it more particularly by the accounts which I found on several of the monuments which are raised in every quarter of that ancient fabric. Some of them were covered with such extravagant epitaphs that, if it were possible for the dead person to be acquainted with them, he would blush at the praises which his friends have bestowed
40 upon him. There are others so excessively modest that they deliver the character of the person departed in Greek or Hebrew, and by that means are not understood once in a twelvemonth. In the poetical quarter, I found there were poets who had no monuments, and monuments which had no poets. I observed, indeed, that the present war had filled the church with many of these uninhabited monuments, which had been erected to the memory of persons whose bodies were perhaps buried in the plains of Blenheim, or in the
50 bosom of the ocean.

I could not but be very much delighted with several modern epitaphs, which are written with great elegance of expression and justness of thought, and therefore do honor to the living as well as to the dead. As a foreigner is very apt to conceive an idea of the ignorance or politeness of a nation from the turn of their public monuments and inscriptions, they should be submitted to the perusal of men of learning and genius before they are put in execution. Sir Cloudesly Shovel's monument has very often given me great offense: in- 60 stead of the brave rough English Admiral, which was the distinguishing character of that plain gallant man, he is represented on his tomb by the figure of a beau, dressed in a long periwig, and reposing himself upon velvet cushions under a canopy of state. The inscription is answerable to the monument; for instead of celebrating the many remarkable actions he had performed in the service of his country, it acquaints us only with the manner of his death, in which it was impossible for him to reap any honor. The Dutch, whom we are apt 70 to despise for want of genius, show an infinitely greater taste of antiquity and politeness in their buildings and works of this nature than what we meet with in those of our own country. The monuments of their admirals, which have been erected at the public expense, represent them like themselves; and are adorned with rostral crowns and naval ornaments, with beautiful festoons of sea-weed, shells, and coral.

But to return to our subject. I have left the repository of our English kings for the contemplation of 80 another day, when I shall find my mind disposed for so serious an amusement. I know that entertainments of this nature are apt to raise dark and dismal thoughts in timorous minds and gloomy imaginations; but for my own part, though I am always serious, I do not know what it is to be melancholy; and can therefore take a view of nature in her deep and solemn scenes, with the same pleasure as in her most gay and delightful ones. By this means I can improve myself with those objects which others consider with terror. When I 90 look upon the tombs of the great, every emotion of envy dies in me; when I read the epitaphs of the beautiful, every inordinate desire goes out; when I meet with the grief of parents upon a tomb-stone, my heart melts with compassion; when I see the tomb of the parents themselves, I consider the vanity of grieving for those whom we must quickly follow: when I see kings lying by those who deposed them, when I consider rival wits placed side by side, or the holy men that divided the world with their contests and disputes, I reflect with 100 sorrow and astonishment on the little competitions, factions, and debates of mankind. When I read the several dates of the tombs, of some that died yesterday, and some six hundred years ago, I consider that great day when we shall all of us be contemporaries, and make our appearance together.

11. Γλαῦκόν . . . Thersilochumque, names of Greek heroes lost in the Trojan War, as cited by Homer and Vergil. 26. prebendaries, persons who receive the revenues of a cathedral. 46. the present war, the War of the Spanish Succession with France (cf. p. 422). One of the great victories won by the English in this war took place at Blenheim, Bavaria, in 1704 (cf. l. 49). 59. Sir Cloudesly Shovel, a noted British naval leader (1650–1707). 76. rostral, of, or pertaining to, a rostrum.
Party Patches. Qualis . . . maculas, "Like the tigress when, at the

PARTY PATCHES

(ADDISON)

The Spectator, No. 81: Saturday, June 2, 1711.

Qualis ubi audito venantum murmure tigris
Horruit in maculas—

About the middle of last winter I went to see an opera at the theater in the Haymarket, where I could not but take notice of two parties of very fine women, 110 that had placed themselves in the opposite side-boxes, and seemed drawn up in a kind of battle array one against another. After a short survey of them, I found they were patched differently; the faces on one hand being spotted on the right side of the forehead, and those upon the other on the left. I quickly perceived that they cast hostile glances upon one another; and that their patches were placed in those different situations, as party-signals to distinguish friends from foes. In the middle boxes, between these two opposite bodies, were several ladies who patched indifferently 120 on both sides of their faces, and seemed to sit there with no other intention but to see the opera. Upon inquiry I found that the body of Amazons on my right hand were Whigs, and those on my left, Tories; and that those who had placed themselves in the middle boxes were a neutral party, whose faces had not yet declared themselves. These last, however, as I afterwards found, diminished daily, and took their party with one side or the other; insomuch that I observed in several of them, the patches, which 130 were before dispersed equally, are now all gone

The Laughing Audience, an engraving by William Hogarth.

sound of the hunters, spots appear upon her skin," from the *Thebaid,* II, ll. 128–129, an epic by the Roman poet Statius (45–96). 123. **Amazons,** an ancient race of female warriors, famous in literature for their contests with the Greeks. They were alleged by Herodotus to exist in Scythia.

over to the Whig or Tory side of the face. The censorious say that the men, whose hearts are aimed at, are very often the occasions that one part of the face is thus dishonored, and lies under a kind of disgrace, while the other is so much set off and adorned by the owner; and that the patches turn to the right or to the left, according to the principles of the man who is most in favor. But whatever may be the motives of a few fantastical coquettes who do not patch

10 for the public good so much as for their own private advantage, it is certain that there are several women of honor who patch out of principle, and with an eye to the interest of their country. Nay, I am informed that some of them adhere so steadfastly to their party, and are so far from sacrificing their zeal for the public to their passion for any particular person, that in a late draft of marriage articles a lady has stipulated with her husband that, whatever his opinions are, she shall be at liberty to patch on which side she pleases.

20 I must here take notice that Rosalinda, a famous Whig partisan, has most unfortunately a very beautiful mole on the Tory part of her forehead; which, being very conspicuous, has occasioned many mistakes, and given a handle to her enemies to misrepresent her face, as though it had revolted from the Whig interest. But, whatever this natural patch may seem to intimate, it is well known that her notions of government are still the same. This unlucky mole, however, has misled several coxcombs; and like the hanging out of

30 false colors, made some of them converse with Rosalinda in what they thought the spirit of her party, when on a sudden she has given them an unexpected fire, that has sunk them all at once. If Rosalinda is unfortunate in her mole, Nigranilla is as unhappy in a pimple, which forces her, against her inclinations, to patch on the Whig side.

I am told that many virtuous matrons, who formerly have been taught to believe that this artificial spotting of the face was unlawful, are now reconciled by a zeal

40 for their cause, to what they could not be prompted by a concern for their beauty. This way of declaring war upon one another puts me in mind of what is reported of the tigress, that several spots rise in her skin when she is angry, or as Mr. Cowley has imitated the verses that stand as the motto on this paper,

—She swells with angry pride,
And calls forth all her spots on ev'ry side.

When I was in the theater the time above-mentioned, I had the curiosity to count the patches on both sides,

50 and found the Tory patches to be about twenty stronger than the Whig; but to make amends for this small inequality, I the next morning found the whole puppet-show filled with faces spotted after the Whiggish manner. Whether or no the ladies had retreated hither in order to rally their forces I cannot tell; but the next night they came in so great a body to the opera that they outnumbered the enemy.

This account of party patches will, I am afraid, appear improbable to those who live at a distance from the fashionable world; but as it is a distinction of 60 a very singular nature, and what perhaps may never meet with a parallel, I think I should not have discharged the office of a faithful Spectator had I not recorded it.

I have, in former papers, endeavored to expose this party-rage in women, as it only serves to aggravate the hatreds and animosities that reign among men, and in a great measure deprive the fair sex of those peculiar charms with which nature has endowed them.

When the Romans and Sabines were at war, and 70 just upon the point of giving battle, the women, who were allied to both of them, interposed with so many tears and entreaties, that they prevented the mutual slaughter which threatened both parties, and united them together in a firm and lasting peace.

I would recommend this noble example to our British ladies, at a time when their country is torn with so many unnatural divisions, that if they continue, it will be a misfortune to be born in it. The Greeks thought it so improper for women to interest themselves in com- 80 petitions and contentions, that for this reason, among others, they forbade them, under pain of death, to be present at the Olympic games, notwithstanding these were the public diversions of all Greece.

As our English women excel those of all nations in beauty, they should endeavor to outshine them in all other accomplishments proper to the sex, and to distinguish themselves as tender mothers, and faithful wives, rather than as furious partisans. Female virtues are of a domestic turn. The family is the proper prov- 90 ince for private women to shine in. If they must be showing their zeal for the public, let it not be against those who are perhaps of the same family, or at least of the same religion or nation, but against those who are the open, professed, undoubted enemies of their faith, liberty, and country. When the Romans were pressed with a foreign enemy, the ladies voluntarily contributed all their rings and jewels to assist the government under a public exigence, which appeared so laudable an action in the eyes of their country- 100 men, that from thenceforth it was permitted by a law to pronounce public orations at the funeral of a woman in praise of the deceased person, which till that time was peculiar to men. Would our English

46. **She swells . . . side,** from the *Davideis*, III, ll. 403–404, an epic poem by Abraham Cowley (1618–1667). 70. **Romans and Sabines.** The Sabines were an ancient people living in central Italy. Their history is bound up with the early history of the Romans. The story given here is legendary, but may easily have happened. There were at least three

wars between the Romans and Sabines, at widely separated dates; the marriage of Sabine women to Romans supposedly occurred in the first war, shortly after the founding of Rome in the eighth century B.C. 115. **Lacedaemonians,** Spartans. Sparta was the great rival of Athens among the ancient Greek cities. The Peloponnesian War was brought about

ladies, instead of sticking on a patch against those of their own country, show themselves so truly public-spirited as to sacrifice every one her necklace against the common enemy, what decrees ought not to be made in favor of them?

110   Since I am recollecting upon this subject such passages as occur to my memory out of ancient authors, I cannot omit a sentence in the celebrated funeral oration of Pericles, which he made in honor of those brave Athenians that were slain in a fight with the Lacedaemonians. After having addressed himself to the several ranks and orders of his countrymen, and shown them how they should behave themselves in the public cause, he turns to the female part of his audience: "And as for you (says he) I shall advise you in very few
120 words: Aspire only to those virtues that are peculiar to your sex; follow your natural modesty, and think it your greatest commendation not to be talked of one way or other."

A COUNTRY SUNDAY

(ADDISON)

The Spectator, No. 112: Monday, July 9, 1711.

'Αθανάτους μὲν πρῶτα θεοὺς, νόμῳ ὡς διάκειται, Τίμα.
             —PYTHAGORAS

    I am always very well pleased with a country Sunday, and think, if keeping holy the seventh day were only a human institution, it would be the best method that could have been thought of for the polishing and civilizing of mankind. It is certain the country people would soon degenerate into a kind of savages and barbarians
130 were there not such frequent returns of a stated time in which the whole village meet together with their best faces, and in their cleanliest habits, to converse with one another upon indifferent subjects, hear their duties explained to them, and join together in adoration of the Supreme Being. Sunday clears away the rust of the whole week, not only as it refreshes in their minds the notions of religion, but as it puts both the sexes upon appearing in their most agreeable forms, and exerting all such qualities as are apt to give them a
140 figure in the eye of the village. A country fellow distinguishes himself as much in the churchyard as a citizen does upon the 'Change, the whole parish politics being generally discussed in that place either after sermon or before the bell rings.

    My friend Sir Roger, being a good churchman, has beautified the inside of his church with several texts of his own choosing; he has likewise given a handsome pulpit-cloth, and railed in the communion-table at his own expense. He has often told me that, at his coming to his estate, he found his parishioners very irregular; 150 and that, in order to make them kneel and join in the responses, he gave every one of them a hassock and a common-prayer-book, and at the same time employed an itinerant singing-master, who goes about the country for that purpose, to instruct them rightly in the tunes of the Psalms; upon which they now very much value themselves, and indeed outdo most of the country churches that I have ever heard.

    As Sir Roger is landlord to the whole congregation, he keeps them in very good order, and will suffer no- 160 body to sleep in it besides himself; for, if by chance he has been surprised into a short nap at sermon, upon recovering out of it he stands up and looks about him, and if he sees anybody else nodding, either wakes them himself, or sends his servant to them. Several other of the old knight's particularities break out upon these occasions; sometimes he will be lengthening out a verse in the Singing-Psalms half a minute after the rest of the congregation have done with it; sometimes, when he is pleased with the matter of his devotion, he pro- 170 nounces "Amen" three or four times to the same prayer; and sometimes stands up when everybody else is upon their knees, to count the congregation, or see if any of his tenants are missing.

    I was yesterday very much surprised to hear my old friend, in the midst of the service, calling out to one John Matthews to mind what he was about, and not disturb the congregation. This John Matthews, it seems, is remarkable for being an idle fellow, and at that time was kicking his heels for his diversion. This 180 authority of the knight, though exerted in that odd manner which accompanies him in all circumstances of life, has a very good effect upon the parish, who are not polite enough to see anything ridiculous in his behavior; besides that the general good sense and worthiness of his character makes his friends observe these little singularities as foils that rather set off than blemish his good qualities.

    As soon as the sermon is finished, nobody presumes to stir till Sir Roger is gone out of the church. The 190 knight walks down from his seat in the chancel between a double row of his tenants, that stand bowing to him on each side, and every now and then inquires how such an one's wife, or mother, or son, or father do, whom he does not see at church—which is understood as a secret reprimand to the person that is absent.

    The chaplain has often told me that, upon a catechizing day, when Sir Roger had been pleased with

largely by the rivalry of Athens and Sparta, and culminated in the defeat of the Athenians and the capture of their city in 404 B.C. *Pericles* (?–429 B.C.) was the greatest of Athenian rulers; the apex of ancient Greek literature is often alluded to as the Age of Pericles.
A Country Sunday. 'Αθανάτους, etc., "First, in obedience to thy country's rites, worship the immortal gods." 142. *'Change,* the London Stock Exchange, held during the time of Addison and Steele in Jonathan's Coffee House in Change Alley.

a boy that answers well, he has ordered a Bible to be given him next day for his encouragement, and sometimes accompanies it with a flitch of bacon to his mother. Sir Roger has likewise added five pounds a year to the clerk's place; and, that he may encourage the young fellows to make themselves perfect in the church service, has promised, upon the death of the present incumbent, who is very old, to bestow it according to merit.

10 The fair understanding between Sir Roger and his chaplain, and their mutual concurrence in doing good, is the more remarkable because the very next village is famous for the differences and contentions that rise between the parson and the squire, who live in a perpetual state of war. The parson is always preaching at the squire, and the squire, to be revenged on the parson, never comes to church. The squire has made all his tenants atheists and tithe-stealers, while the parson instructs them every Sunday in the dignity of 20 his order, and insinuates to them in almost every sermon that he is a better man than his patron. In short, matters are come to such an extremity that the squire has not said his prayers either in public or in private this half year; and that the parson threatens him, if he does not mend his manners, to pray for him in the face of the whole congregation.

Feuds of this nature, though too frequent in the country, are very fatal to the ordinary people, who are so used to be dazzled with riches that they pay as 30 much deference to the understanding of a man of an estate as of a man of learning; and are very hardly brought to regard any truth, how important soever it may be, that is preached to them, when they know there are several men of five hundred a year who do not believe it.

SIR ROGER AT THE ASSIZES

(ADDISON)

The Spectator, No. 122: Friday, July 20, 1711.

Comes jucundus in via pro vehiculo est.
—PUBL. SYR. FRAG.

A man's first care should be to avoid the reproaches of his own heart; his next, to escape the censures of the world. If the last interferes with the former, it ought to be entirely neglected; but otherwise there cannot 40 be a greater satisfaction to an honest mind than to see those approbations which it gives itself seconded by the applauses of the public. A man is more sure of conduct when the verdict which he passes upon his own be-

havior is thus warranted and confirmed by the opinion of all that know him.

My worthy friend Sir Roger is one of those who is not only at peace within himself, but beloved and esteemed by all about him. He receives a suitable tribute for his universal benevolence to mankind, in the returns of affection and good-will, which are paid him by every 50 one that lives within his neighborhood. I lately met with two or three odd instances of that general respect which is shown to the good old knight. He would needs carry Will Wimble and myself with him to the county assizes. As we were upon the road, Will Wimble joined a couple of plain men who rid before us and conversed with them for some time; during which my friend Sir Roger acquainted me with their characters.

"The first of them," says he, "that has a spaniel by 60 his side is a yeoman of about an hundred pounds a year, an honest man. He is just within the game-act and qualified to kill a hare or a pheasant. He knocks down a dinner with his gun twice or thrice a week; and by that means lives much cheaper than those who have not so good an estate as himself. He would be a good neighbor if he did not destroy so many partridges. In short he is a very sensible man; shoots flying, and has been several times foreman of the petty jury. 70

"That other that rides along with him is Tom Touchy, a fellow famous for 'taking the law' of everybody. There is not one in the town where he lives that he has not sued at a quarter-sessions. The rogue had once the impudence to go to law with the widow. His head is full of costs, damages, and ejectments. He plagued a couple of honest gentlemen so long for a trespass in breaking one of his hedges, till he was forced to sell the ground it enclosed to defray the charges of the prosecution; his father left him fourscore 80 pounds a year; but he has cast and been cast so often that he is not now worth thirty. I suppose he is going upon the old business of the willow tree."

As Sir Roger was giving me this account of Tom Touchy, Will Wimble and his two companions stopped short till we came up to them. After having paid their respects to Sir Roger, Will told him that Mr. Touchy and he must appeal to him upon a dispute that arose between them. Will, it seems, had been giving his fellow-traveler an account of his angling one day in 90 such a hole; when Tom Touchy, instead of hearing out his story, told him that Mr. Such-a-one, if he pleased, might "take the law of him" for fishing in that part of the river. My friend Sir Roger heard them both, upon a round trot; and after having paused some time, told them, with the air of a man who would not give his judgment rashly, that "much might be said on both

---

18. **tithe-stealers,** those who do not pay their tithes. By not paying they may be said to "steal" from the church.
Sir Roger at the Assizes. Comes . . . est, "An agreeable companion upon the road is as good as a coach," quoted from some fragments by

Publius Syrus, a Roman slave poet (fl. 45 B.C.). 62. **within the game-act.** The right to kill game depended upon one's income and social position; this law was in effect until 1831. 68. **shoots flying,** i.e., on the wing. 70. **petty jury,** the jury that sits at a trial in an ordinary civil

sides." They were neither of them dissatisfied with the knight's determination, because neither of them found himself in the wrong by it; upon which we made the best of our way to the assizes.

The court was sat before Sir Roger came; but notwithstanding all the justices had taken their places upon the bench, they made room for the old knight at the head of them; who, for his reputation in the country, took occasion to whisper in the judge's ear, that he was glad his lordship had met with so much good weather in his circuit. I was listening to the proceedings of the court with much attention, and infinitely pleased with that great appearance of solemnity which so properly accompanies such a public administration of our laws; when, after about an hour's sitting, I observed to my great surprise, in the midst of a trial, that my friend Sir Roger was getting up to speak. I was in some pain for him till I found he had acquitted himself of two or three sentences, with a look of much business and great intrepidity.

Upon his first rising the court was hushed, and a general whisper ran among the country people that Sir Roger "was up." The speech he made was so little to the purpose that I shall not trouble my readers with an account of it; and I believe was not so much designed by the knight himself to inform the court as to give him a figure in my eye, and keep up his credit in the country.

I was highly delighted, when the court rose, to see the gentlemen of the country gathering about my old friend and striving who should compliment him most; at the same time that the ordinary people gazed upon him at a distance, not a little admiring his courage, that was not afraid to speak to the judge.

In our return home we met with a very odd accident which I cannot forbear relating, because it shows how desirous all who know Sir Roger are of giving him marks of their esteem. When we were arrived upon the verge of his estate, we stopped at a little inn to rest ourselves and our horses. The man of the house had, it seems, been formerly a servant in the knight's family; and to do honor to his old master, had some time since, unknown to Sir Roger, put him up in a sign-post before the door; so that the knight's head had hung out upon the road about a week before he himself knew anything of the matter. As soon as Sir Roger was acquainted with it, finding that his servant's indiscretion proceeded wholly from affection and good-will, he only told him that he had made him too high a compliment; and when the fellow seemed to think that could hardly be, added with a more decisive look that it was too great an honor for any man under a duke; but told him at the same time that it might be altered with a very few touches and that he himself

would be at the charge of it. Accordingly, they got a painter by the knight's directions to add a pair of whiskers to the face, and by a little aggravation of the features to change it into the *Saracen's Head*. I should not have known this story, had not the inn-keeper, upon Sir Roger's alighting, told him in my hearing, that his honor's head was brought back last night with the alterations that he had ordered to be made in it. Upon this my friend with his usual cheerfulness related the particulars above-mentioned and ordered the head to be brought into the room. I could not forbear discovering greater expressions of mirth than ordinary upon the appearance of this monstrous face, under which, notwithstanding it was made to frown and stare in a most extraordinary manner, I could still discover a distant resemblance of my old friend. Sir Roger, upon seeing me laugh, desired me to tell him truly if I thought it possible for people to know him in that disguise. I at first kept my usual silence; but upon the knight's conjuring me to tell him whether it was not still more like himself than a Saracen, I composed my countenance in the best manner I could, and replied "that much might be said on both sides."

These several adventures, with the knight's behavior in them, gave me as pleasant a day as ever I met with in any of my travels.

A CONSIDERATION OF MILTON'S PARADISE LOST

(ADDISON)

The Spectator, No. 267: Saturday, January 5, 1712.

Cedite, Romani scriptores, cedite Graii.

There is nothing in nature so irksome as general discourses, especially when they turn chiefly upon words. For this reason I shall waive the discussion of that point which was started some years since, whether Milton's *Paradise Lost* may be called an heroic poem. Those who will not give it that title, may call it (if they please) a divine poem. It will be sufficient to its perfection, if it has in it all the beauties of the highest kind of poetry; and as for those who allege it is not an heroic poem, they advance no more to the diminution of it, than if they should say Adam is not Aeneas, nor Eve Helen.

I shall therefore examine it by the rules of epic poetry, and see whether it falls short of the *Iliad* or *Aeneid* in the beauties which are essential to that kind of writing. The first thing to be considered in an epic poem is the fable, which is perfect or imperfect ac-

or criminal case. 75. **the widow,** the object of Sir Roger's affections, frequently referred to in the papers.
   A Consideration . . . Lost. Cedite . . . Graii, "Give place, ye Roman and Greek writers," quoted from the *Elegies* of the Roman poet

Sextus Propertius (50–16 B.C.), II, No. 34, 165. 194. **fable.** Here the word is used to mean the plot or story.

cording as the action which it relates is more or less so. This action should have three qualifications in it. First, it should be but one action. Secondly, it should be an entire action; and, thirdly, it should be a great action. To consider the action of the *Iliad, Aeneid,* and *Paradise Lost,* in these three several lights: Homer, to preserve the unity of his action, hastens into the midst of things, as Horace has observed. Had he gone up to Leda's egg, or begun much later, even at the rape of Helen, or the investing of Troy, it is manifest that the story of the poem would have been a series of several actions. He therefore opens his poem with the discord of his princes and artfully interweaves, in the several succeeding parts of it, an account of everything material which relates to them and had passed before that fatal dissention. After the same manner Aeneas makes his first appearance in the Tyrrhene seas, and within sight of Italy, because the action proposed to be celebrated was that of his settling himself in Latium. But because it was necessary for the reader to know what had happened to him in the taking of Troy, and in the preceding parts of his voyage, Virgil makes his hero relate it by way of episode in the second and third books of the *Aeneid;* the contents of both which books come before those of the first book in the thread of the story, though for preserving this unity of action they follow them in the disposition of the poem. Milton, in imitation of these two great poets, opens his *Paradise Lost* with an infernal council plotting the fall of man, which is the action he proposed to celebrate; and as for those great actions, which preceded, in point of time, the battle of the angels, and the creation of the world, (which would have entirely destroyed the unity of the principal action, had he related them in the same order that they happened) he cast them into the fifth, sixth, and seventh books, by way of episode to this noble poem.

Aristotle himself allows that Homer has nothing to boast of as to the unity of his fable, though at the same time that great critic and philosopher endeavors to palliate this imperfection in the Greek poet by imputing it in some measure to the very nature of an epic poem. Some have been of opinion that the *Aeneid* also labors in this particular, and has episodes which may be looked upon as excrescences rather than as parts of the action. On the contrary, the poem which we have now under our consideration hath no other episodes than such as naturally arise from the subject, and yet is filled with such a multitude of astonishing incidents that it gives us at the same time a pleasure of the greatest variety and of the greatest simplicity; *uniform in its nature, though diversified in the execution.*

I must observe also, that as Virgil, in the poem which was designed to celebrate the original of the Roman empire, has described the birth of its great rival, the Carthaginian commonwealth; Milton, with the like art, in his poem on the fall of man, has related the fall of those angels who are his professed enemies. Besides the many other beauties in such an episode, its running parallel with the great action of the poem hinders it from breaking the unity so much as another episode would have done, that had not so great an affinity with the principal subject. In short, this is the same kind of beauty which the critics admire in the *Spanish Friar,* or the *Double Discovery,* where the two different plots look like counter-parts and copies of one another.

The second qualification required in the action of an epic poem is that it should be an entire action. An action is entire when it is complete in all its parts; or as Aristotle describes it, when it consists of a beginning, a middle, and an end. Nothing should go before it, be intermixed with it, or follow after it, that is not related to it. As, on the contrary, no single step should be omitted in that just and regular process which it must be supposed to take from its original to its consummation. Thus we see the anger of Achilles in its birth, its continuance, and effects; and Aeneas's settlement in Italy carried on through all the oppositions in his way to it both by sea and land. The action in Milton excels (I think) both the former in this particular; we see it contrived in hell, executed upon earth, and punished by heaven. The parts of it are told in the most distinct manner and grow out of one another in the most natural method.

The third qualification of an epic poem is its greatness. The anger of Achilles was of such consequence that it embroiled the kings of Greece, destroyed the heroes of Troy, and engaged all the gods in factions. Aeneas's settlement in Italy produced the Caesars and gave birth to the Roman empire. Milton's subject was still greater than either of the former; it does not determine the fate of single persons or nations; but of a whole species. The united powers of hell are joined together for the destruction of mankind, which they effected in part, and would have completed, had not Omnipotence itself interposed. The principal actors are man in his greatest perfection, and woman in her highest beauty. Their enemies are the fallen angels; the Messiah their friend; and the Almighty their Protector. In short, everything that is great in the whole circle of being, whether within the verge of nature, or out of it, has a proper part assigned it in this admirable poem.

---

8. **Horace has observed,** in his *Ars Poetica.* 9. **Leda's egg.** It has been assumed here that the reader is familiar with the general outline of the narrative in the *Iliad* and the *Aeneid.* The Trojan War, which underlies both epics, had its primary cause in the abduction of Helen by Paris of Troy (l. 10). But the enmity of Greeks and Trojans went further back than this particular episode; Addison implies here that it would be impractical for the epic poet, however, to go too far back in tracing the causes of the conflict. Thus, Helen was born miraculously from an egg delivered by her mother Leda (who had been wooed by Zeus in the disguise of a swan); but it is sufficient to start the epic thread with the actual presence of Helen in the world rather than from her rather startling biogenetic origin. 17. **Tyrrhene seas,** in ancient geography, that part of the Mediterranean off the west coast of Italy. 65. *Spanish . . . Discovery,* a tragedy by John Dryden, produced in 1681.

In poetry, as in architecture, not only the whole, but the principal members, and every part of them, should be great. I will not presume to say, that the book of games in the *Aeneid*, or that in the *Iliad*, are not of this nature; nor to reprehend Virgil's simile of the top, and many other of the same kind in the *Iliad*, as liable to any censure in this particular; but I think we may say, without derogating from those wonderful performances, that there is an unquestionable magnificence in every part of *Paradise Lost*, and indeed a much greater than could have been formed upon any pagan system.

But Aristotle, by the greatness of the action, does not only mean that it should be great in its nature, but also in its duration, or in other words, that it should have a due length in it, as well as what we properly call greatness. The just measure of this kind of magnitude he explains by the following similitude: An animal no bigger than a mite cannot appear perfect to the eye, because the sight takes it in at once and has only a confused idea of the whole, and not a distinct idea of all its parts; if on the contrary, you should suppose an animal of ten thousand furlongs in length, the eye would be so filled with a single part of it that it could not give the mind an idea of the whole. What these animals are to the eye, a very short or a very long action would be to the memory. The first would be, as it were, lost and swallowed up by it, and the other difficult to be contained in it. Homer and Virgil have shown their principal art in this particular; the action of the *Iliad*, and that of the *Aeneid*, were in themselves exceeding short but are so beautifully extended and diversified by the invention of episodes, and the machinery of gods, with the like poetical ornaments, that they make up an agreeable story, sufficient to employ the memory without overcharging it. Milton's action is enriched with such a variety of circumstances that I have taken as much pleasure in reading the contents of his books as in the best invented story I ever met with. It is possible that the traditions on which the *Iliad* and the *Aeneid* were built had more circumstances in them than the history of the fall of man, as it is related in scripture. Besides, it was easier for Homer and Virgil to dash the truth with fiction, as they were in no danger of offending the religion of their country by it. But as for Milton, he had not only a very few circumstances upon which to raise his poem but was also obliged to proceed with the greatest caution in everything that he added out of his own invention. And indeed, notwithstanding all the restraint he was under, he has filled his story with so many surprising incidents, which bear so close an analogy with what is delivered in holy writ, that it is capable of pleasing the most delicate reader without giving offense to the most scrupulous.

The modern critics have collected from several hints in the *Iliad* and *Aeneid* the space of time which is taken up by the action of each of those poems; but as a great part of Milton's story was translated in regions that lie out of the reach of the sun and the sphere of day, it is impossible to gratify the reader with such a calculation, which indeed would be more curious than instructive, none of the critics, either ancient or modern, having laid down rules to circumscribe the action of an epic poem with any determined number of years, days, or hours.

This piece of criticism on Milton's *Paradise Lost* shall be carried on in the following Saturdays' papers.

A YOUNG LADY'S DIARY

(ADDISON)

The Spectator, No. 323: *Tuesday, March 11, 1712.*

Modo vir, modo femina.—OVID

The Journal with which I presented my readers on Tuesday last has brought me in several letters with accounts of many private lives cast into that form. I have the Rake's Journal, the Sot's Journal, the Whoremaster's Journal, and among several others a very curious piece, entitled, The Journal of a Mohock. By these instances I find that the intention of my last Tuesday's paper has been mistaken by many of my readers. I did not design so much to expose vice as idleness, and aimed at those persons who pass away their time rather in trifles and impertinence, than in crimes and immoralities. Offenses of this later kind are not to be dallied with, or treated in so ludicrous a manner. In short, my journal only holds up folly to the light, and shows the disagreeableness of such actions as are indifferent in themselves, and blamable only as they proceed from creatures endowed with reason.

My following correspondent, who calls herself Clarinda, is such a journalist as I require: she seems by her letter to be placed in a modish state of indifference between vice and virtue, and to be susceptible of either, were there proper pains taken with her. Had her journal been filled with gallantries, or such occurrences as had shown her wholly divested of her natural innocence, notwithstanding it might have been more pleasing to the generality of readers, I should not have published it; but as it is only the picture of a life

It ranks with *All for Love* and *Don Sebastian* (1690) as his best serious drama. 170. **This . . . papers.** No fewer than twenty papers on Milton and *Paradise Lost* were published in *The Spectator*.
A Young Lady's Diary. Modo . . . femina, "Sometimes a man, sometimes a woman," quoted from Ovid's *Metamorphoses*, IV, 280. 172. **Journal . . . last.** *Spectator* paper No. 317 was the account of a journal or diary written by a private citizen, "of greater consequence in his own thoughts than in the eye of the world." 177. **Mohock,** or Mohawk, the name given to thugs and hoodlums who infested the streets of London after dark. Sometimes they were referred to as "Hectors," from which our modern English verb *to hector*, meaning *to bully* is derived.

filled with a fashionable kind of gayety and laziness, I shall set down five days of it, as I have received it from the hand of my correspondent.

Dear Mr. Spectator,

You having set your readers an exercise in one of your last week's papers, I have performed mine according to your orders and herewith send it you enclosed. You must know, Mr. Spectator, that I am a maiden lady of a good fortune, who have had several
10 matches offered me for these ten years last past, and have at present warm applications made to me by a very pretty fellow. As I am at my own disposal, I come up to town every winter and pass my time after the manner you will find in the following journal, which I began to write upon the very day after your *Spectator* upon that subject.

TUESDAY *night*. Could not go to sleep till one in the morning for thinking of my journal.

WEDNESDAY. *From eight till ten*. Drank two dishes
20 of chocolate in bed, and fell asleep after them.

From ten to eleven. Eat a slice of bread and butter, drank a dish of bohea, read *The Spectator*.

From eleven to one. At my toilette, tried a new head. Gave orders for Veny to be combed and washed. Mem. I look best in blue.

From one till half an hour after two. Drove to the Change. Cheapened a couple of fans.

Till four. At dinner. Mem. Mr. Froth passed by in his new liveries.
30 *From four to six*. Dressed, paid a visit to old Lady Blithe and her sister, having before heard they were gone out of town that day.

From six to eleven. At basset. Mem. Never set again upon the ace of diamonds.

THURSDAY. *From eleven at night to eight in the morning*. Dreamed that I punted to Mr. Froth.

From eight to ten. Chocolate. Read two acts in *Aurenzebe* a-bed.

From ten to eleven. Tea-table. Sent to borrow Lady
40 Faddle's Cupid for Veny. Read the play-bills. Received a letter from Mr. Froth. Mem. Locked it up in my strong box.

Rest of the morning. Fontange, the tire-woman, her account of my Lady Blithe's wash. Broke a tooth in my little tortoise-shell comb. Sent Frank to know how my Lady Hectic rested after her monkey's leaping out at window. Looked pale. Fontange tells me my glass is not true. Dressed by three.

From three to four. Dinner cold before I sat down.

From four to eleven. Saw company. Mr. Froth's 50 opinion of Milton. His account of the Mohocks. His fancy for a pin-cushion. Picture in the lid of his snuff-box. Old Lady Faddle promises me her woman to cut my hair. Lost five guineas at crimp.

Twelve a clock at night. Went to bed.

FRIDAY. *Eight in the morning*. A-bed. Read over all Mr. Froth's letters. Cupid and Veny.

Ten a clock. Stayed within all day, not at home.

From ten to twelve. In conference with my mantua-maker. Sorted a suit of ribands. Broke my blue china 60 cup.

From twelve to one. Shut myself up in my chamber, practiced Lady Betty Modely's skuttle.

One in the afternoon. Called for my flowered handkerchief. Worked half a violet leaf in it. Eyes ached and head out of order. Threw by my work, and read over the remaining part of *Aurenzebe*.

From three to four. Dined.

From four to twelve. Changed my mind, dressed, went abroad, and played at crimp till midnight. Found 70 Mrs. Spitely at home. Conversation Mrs. Brilliant's necklace false stones. Old Lady Loveday going to be married to a young fellow that is not worth a groat. Miss Prue gone into the country. Tom Towneley has red hair. Mem. Mrs. Spitely whispered in my ear that she had something to tell me about Mr. Froth; I am sure it is not true.

Between twelve and one. Dreamed that Mr. Froth lay at my feet, and called me Indamora.

SATURDAY. Rose at eight a clock in the morning. 80 Sat down to my toilette.

From eight to nine. Shifted a patch for half an hour before I could determine it. Fixed it above my left eyebrow.

From nine to twelve. Drank my tea and dressed.

From twelve to two. At Chapel. A great deal of good company. Mem. The third air in the new opera. Lady Blithe dressed frightfully.

From three to four. Dined. Mrs. Kitty called upon me to go to the opera before I was risen from table. 90

From dinner to six. Drank tea. Turned off a footman for being rude to Veny.

Six a clock. Went to the opera. I did not see Mr. Froth till the beginning of the second act. Mr. Froth talked to a gentleman in a black wig. Bowed to a lady in the front box. Mr. Froth and his friend clapped Nicolini in the third act. Mr. Froth cried out Ancora.

---

22. **bohea**, a kind of tea. 24. **head**, headdress. **Veny**, short for Venice, Clarinda's lap dog (cf. note to l. 40). 25. **Mem**. Here, as elsewhere in this paper, a note indicating "I must remember." 27. **Cheapened**, priced. 33. **basset**, a game of cards somewhat resembling the old game of faro. 36. **punted to**, gambled with, played cards with. 38. **Aurenzebe**, Dryden's heroic play *Aurengzebe* (1676). 40. **Cupid**, a male lap dog, evidently borrowed for studding purposes. 43. **Fontange**. Mademoiselle de Fontange was a famous hairdresser of London, who introduced a new type of headdress that was extremely fashionable. 54. **crimp**, another card game popular in the seventeenth and eighteenth centuries. 59. **mantua**, a woman's loose cloak. 63. **skuttle**, scuttle. Evidently Lady Modely's walk was an affected, hurried kind of walk, and yet one that was deemed worthy of imitation. 73. **groat**, originally a Dutch coin; by the eighteenth century, however, it had the monetary value of fourpence and the figurative value of a mere trifle. 79. **Indamora**, the captive queen in Dryden's *Aurengzebe* (cf. note to l. 38). 83. **determine**, decide where it belonged. 91. **Turned off**, discharged. 97. **Nicolini**, a famous Italian opera singer of that day. **Ancora**, encore.

Mr. Froth led me to my chair. I think he squeezed my hand.

100   *Eleven at night.* Went to bed. Melancholy dreams. Methought Nicolini said he was Mr. Froth.

SUNDAY. Indisposed.

MONDAY. *Eight a clock.* Waked by Miss Kitty. *Aurenzebe* lay upon the chair by me. Kitty repeated without book the eight best lines in the play. Went in our mobs to the dumb man, according to appointment. Told me that my lover's name began with a G. Mem. The conjurer was within a letter of Mr. Froth's name, *etc.*

110   Upon looking back into this my journal, I find that I am at a loss to know whether I pass my time well or ill; and indeed never thought of considering how I did it, before I perused your speculation upon that subject. I scarce find a single action in these five days that I can thoroughly approve of, except the working upon the violet leaf, which I am resolved to finish the first day I am at leisure. As for Mr. Froth and Veny, I did not think they took up so much of my time and thoughts, as I find they do upon my 120 journal. The latter of them I will turn off if you

insist upon it; and if Mr. Froth does not bring matters to a conclusion very suddenly, I will not let my life run away in a dream.

             Your humble servant,
                Clarinda.

To resume one of the morals of my first paper, and to confirm Clarinda in her good inclinations, I would have her consider what a pretty figure she would make among posterity, were the history of her whole life published like these five days of it. I shall conclude 130 my paper with an epitaph written by an uncertain author on Sir Philip Sidney's sister, a lady who seems to have been of a temper very much different from that of Clarinda. The last thought of it is so very noble that I dare say my reader will pardon the quotation.

On the Countess Dowager of Pembroke

> *Underneath this marble hearse*
> *Lies the subject of all verse,*
> *Sidney's sister, Pembroke's mother,*
> *Death, ere thou hast killed another,*   140
> *Fair and learned and good as she,*
> *Time shall throw a dart at thee.*

106. **mobs,** caps or headdresses worn by women and tied under the chin.
131. **uncertain author.** Actually the author of the following verses is generally conceded to be Ben Jonson, the famous Elizabethan dramatist and critic.

JONATHAN SWIFT 1667-1745

   Swift's first experience in life was that of a being dependent upon the charity of another; he was born in Dublin, the posthumous son of a penniless English father. He was supported for a time, rather grudgingly, by his uncle, with the result that young Swift was embittered against all his Irish relations. Eventually he matriculated at Trinity College, Dublin, where his moodiness and discontent made him a poor student. He left the university and became a secretary to Sir William Temple at Moor Park, near London. The young secretary was desperately unhappy under Temple's employment, but was solaced by the friendship of Esther Johnson, a member of the household who was to become the companion of Swift's thoughts

and feelings for thirty years; his series of intimate letters, published later in the century as the Journal to Stella, is addressed to her.

   The years of service to Temple won Swift a certain recognition from King William III, who gave him some promise of a church career. Swift was ordained, and after a delay, he got a living at Kilroot, Ireland (1695), which he soon abandoned to return to his post with Sir William Temple. At this time Swift seriously tried his hand at literature; he produced A Tale of a Tub (published 1704), a prose satire on "corruptions in religion and learning," and The Battle of the Books, his satirical contribution to the question whether the ancients or the moderns were superior as literary figures. Both works were well received, but it is possible that the unpleasant repercussions of A Tale of a Tub at court adversely affected Swift's ecclesiastical career.

When Swift returned to Ireland after the death of Temple in 1699, he carried with him a considerable reputation as a writer of polemic. He had also made the acquaintance of many important literary men of the day: Congreve, Addison, Steele, Pope, Gay, and others. Swift continued to make frequent visits to London and to maintain intercourse with these friends.

In the following years several events of importance occurred in Swift's life. In 1708 he met Esther Vanhomrigh, the "Vanessa" of his poem Cadenus and Vanessa, with whom he had, for fifteen years, an uneven affair of the heart. Perhaps more important, he went over to the Tory side in politics in 1710 and attacked the Whig ministry in The Examiner, which he edited. Swift continued to write numerous effective pamphlets and articles on political and religious questions throughout the first two decades of the eighteenth century; he rose to powerful influence in the state by these writings. In 1713 Swift was appointed Dean of St. Patrick's, Dublin. In the next year Queene Anne died, the Tories were discredited, and Swift's political fortunes sank like a plummet. Disillusioned, he devoted himself increasingly to his church and Ireland. He also joined some of his famous literary friends in founding the satirical Scriblerus Club. In 1724, with the publication of his Drapier's Letters against the debasement of Irish currency, Swift became a national hero to his people; this work, with A Modest Proposal, represents his most effective championing of Irish affairs.

After the publication of his masterpiece, Gulliver's Travels, in 1726, Swift produced little that is notable. He suffered intense aggravation of a chronic illness (Ménière's syndrome—affecting the inner ear and causing physical imbalance, nausea, and deafness) in 1738 and was declared non compos mentis in 1742. He died three years later and was buried by the side of "Stella" in St. Patrick's, Dublin.

Jonathan Swift was one of the great English propagandists—perhaps even the greatest. An especially virulent version of the modern spirit was abroad at the time, and its ultimate tendency was, in Swift's judgment, inimical to the Establishment—to Church and Crown alike. Swift's devotion to the Establishment was both ardent and rational, and he turned a unique combination of emotional intensity and devastating wit upon its enemies. His stroke was, in fact, so hard and its penetration so deep that many readers have attempted to turn Swift's merciless wit back upon him and let him sink out of literature, self-destroyed. Swift has often been called a misanthrope, a hater of mankind. There are two letters which Swift wrote to Alexander Pope in 1725 which put this matter into perspective. In the first, he says:

. . . when you think of the world, give it one lash the more at my Request. I have ever hated all Nations, Professions, and Communities; and all my love is towards Individuals; for instance, I hate the Tribe of Lawyers, Physicians . . . Soldiers, English, Scotch, French, and the rest. But principally I hate and detest that animal called Man, although I heartily love John, Peter, Thomas, and so forth. This is the system upon which I have governed myself many years . . . and so I shall go on until I have done with them. I have got Materials toward a Treatise, proving the falsity of that Definition, Animal rationale and to show that it should be only rationis capax. Upon this great foundation of Misanthropy (although not in Timon's Manner) the whole building of my travels is erected; and I will never have Peace of Mind until all honest Men are of my Opinion. . . .

In the second letter, Swift pursues further his attitude toward man as a rational being:

I tell you after all I do not hate Mankind, it is vous autres who hate them, because you would have them reasonable animals, and are angry at being disappointed: I have always rejected that Definition, and made another of my own.

If one assumes that man is a rational being, Swift argues, and that he will therefore, syllogistically, act in a rational manner, one is doomed to very severe disappointment and is thus in danger of an equally dangerous misanthropy. Swift prefers the view that man is an animal capable of reason, a capability which he may or may not live up to. Further, Swift was constantly repelled by abstract arguments about man and about man as a mere metaphor: Swift was affected by the moral performance of the individual—Tom, Dick, and Harry. Thus it is possible to assert that Swift was not a misanthrope, but a hard-headed and outspoken realist and that his view of man is essentially that of Pope, expressed compellingly in the Essay on Man (p. 549). And it is surely to Swift's credit that he did not, like Timon of Athens, withdraw from the world and vituperate in isolation, as a true misanthrope might. Instead, in the manner of a persistent propagandist, he sought to bring "all honest men" around to his opinion.

Swift's manner of writing, his style, was not such as to win endorsement of his opinions from the faint of heart. His style was never made prolix by a display of "learning or oratory or politeness"; he was determined not to draw the attention of the reader away from the object and to himself by rhetorical flourish; he disdained the sonorous and balanced qualities of the prose of some of his estimable contemporaries. The basic elements in his prose are nouns and verbs. He uses adverbs only to identify specific qualifications, and his adjectives are analytical, not colorful. Swift has himself given us an important clue to his style: "When a Man's Thoughts are clear, the proper-est Words will generally offer themselves first, and his own Judgment will direct him in what Order to place them, so that they may be best understood. In short, that Simplicity, without which no human Performance can arrive to any great Perfection, is no where more eminently useful than in this." The condition: clear thinking, the object: true understanding, the characteristic: simplicity. Swift's writing avoids dullness by a combination of several qualities: his constant use of irony, which jogs the lethargic mind, his persistent concentration on substantial issues, and his employment of a completely functional style, emphasizing the concrete and the immediately intelligible.

A MEDITATION UPON A BROOMSTICK

This essay is a parody of the moralizing Meditations *of Robert Boyle (1627-1691), a famous scientist, commonly regarded as "the father of chemistry."*

This single stick, which you now behold ingloriously lying in that neglected corner, I once knew in a flourishing state in a forest: it was full of sap, full of leaves, and full of boughs; but now, in vain does the busy art of man pretend to vie with nature, by tying that withered bundle of twigs to its sapless trunk; it is now, at best, but the reverse of what it was, a tree turned upside down, the branches on the earth, and the root in the air; it is now handled by every dirty wench, 10 condemned to do her drudgery, and by a capricious kind of fate, destined to make other things clean, and be nasty itself; at length, worn to the stumps in the service of the maids, it is either thrown out of doors, or condemned to the last use, of kindling a fire. When I beheld this, I sighed, and said within myself, *Surely Man is a Broomstick!* Nature sent him into the world strong, and lusty, in a thriving condition, wearing his own hair on his head, the proper branches of this reasoning vegetable, until the ax of intemperance has 20 lopped off his green boughs, and left him a withered trunk; he then flies to art, and puts on a periwig, valuing himself upon an unnatural bundle of hairs (all covered with powder) that never grew on his head;

but now, should this our broomstick pretend to enter the scene, proud of those birchen spoils it never bore, and all covered with dust, though the sweepings of the finest lady's chamber, we should be apt to ridicule and despise its vanity. Partial judges that we are of our own excellencies, and other men's defaults!

But a broomstick, perhaps you will say, is an emblem 30 of a tree standing on its head; and pray what is man, but a topsy-turvy creature, his animal faculties perpetually mounted on his rational, his head where his heels should be, groveling on the earth! And yet, with all his faults, he sets up to be a universal reformer and corrector of abuses, a remover of grievances, rakes into every slut's corner of nature, bringing hidden corruption to the light, and raises a mighty dust where there was none before; sharing deeply all the while in the very same pollutions he pretends to sweep away; his 40 last days are spent in slavery to women, and generally the least deserving; till worn out to the stumps, like his brother's besom, he is either kicked out of doors, or made use of to kindle flames for others to warm themselves by.

(1704)

from A TALE OF A TUB

The name of the work is a seventeenth-century slang phrase for a hoax, a jest, an idle discourse; the author observes that the work is intended to divert the wits, as seamen divert a whale which is attacking their ship by throwing it a tub to play with. A Tale of a Tub is a vivid, realistic, and powerful allegory of the history of the Christian Church and its three great modern branches of Catholicism, Anglicanism, and dissenting Protestantism. Interwoven with the allegory is a chain of provocative essays, or "digressions," as the author calls them, which represent studies of, and attacks upon, the age in general, notably the world of literature, politics, society, and religion.

The opening section, a general introduction, is a criticism of the times in terms of literary and religio-political disputes. The second section, given below, begins the allegorical narrative. The reader learns of the three sons of Christ and how they fell out—how Peter became proud, arrogant, and overworldly; Jack noisy, slovenly, and violent; and Martin self-seeking, vacillating, and often distempered. In the present excerpt it will be sufficient to observe how, under the leadership of Peter, the three brothers became unscrupulous, socially ambitious worldlings. Two of the digressions spoken of above are particularly brilliant—the first of these (Section III) is entitled "A Digression Concerning Critics," and the second (Section VII) "A Digression in Praise of Digressions." No other work of Swift, with the exception of Gulliver's Travels (p. 500), has the hard-hitting force of A Tale of a Tub, nor such a cosmic range of merciless satire.

II

Once upon a time, there was a man who had three sons by one wife, and all at a birth, neither could the midwife tell certainly which was the eldest. Their father died while they were young; and upon his death-bed, calling the lads to him, spoke thus:

"Sons, because I have purchased no estate, nor was born to any, I have long considered of some good legacies to bequeath you; and at last, with much care, as well as expense, have provided each of you (here 10 they are) a new coat. Now, you are to understand that these coats have two virtues contained in them: one is that with good wearing they will last you fresh and sound as long as you live; the other is that they will grow in the same proportion with your bodies, lengthening and widening of themselves, so as to be always fit. Here, let me see them on you before I die. So, very well; pray, children, wear them clean and brush them

often. You will find in my will (here it is) full instructions in every particular concerning the wearing and management of your coats; wherein you must be very 20 exact, to avoid the penalties I have appointed for every transgression or neglect, upon which your future fortunes will entirely depend. I have also commanded in my will that you should live together in one house like brethren and friends, for then you will be sure to thrive and not otherwise."

Here, the story says, this good father died, and the three sons went altogether to seek their fortunes.

I shall not trouble you with recounting what adventures they met for the first seven years; any farther 30 than by taking notice that they carefully observed their father's will and kept their coats in very good order; that they traveled through several countries, encountered a reasonable quantity of giants, and slew certain dragons.

Being now arrived at the proper age for producing themselves, they came up to town and fell in love with the ladies, but especially three, who about that time were in chief reputation; the Duchess d'Argent, Madame de Grands Titres, and the Countess d'Orgueil. 40 On their very first appearance our three adventurers met with a very bad reception; and soon with great sagacity guessing out the reason, they quickly began to improve in the good qualities of the town: they writ, and rallied, and rimed, and sung, and said, and said nothing: they drank, and fought, and whored, and slept, and swore, and took snuff: they went to new plays on the first night, haunted the chocolate-houses, beat the watch, lay on bulks, and got claps: they bilked hackney-coachmen, ran in debt with shopkeepers, and 50 lay with their wives: they killed bailiffs, kicked fiddlers downstairs, ate at Locket's, loitered at Will's: they talked of the drawing-room and never came there: dined with lords they never saw: whispered a duchess, and spoke never a word: exposed the scrawls of their laundress for billetdoux of quality: came ever just from court, and were never seen in it: attended the levee sub dio: got a list of peers by heart in one company, and with great familiarity retailed them in another. Above all, they constantly attended those Committees 60 of Senators, who are silent in the House, and loud in the coffee-house; where they nightly adjourn to chew the cud of politics and are encompassed with a ring of disciples, who lie in wait to catch up their droppings. The three brothers had acquired forty other qualifications of the like stamp, too tedious to

A Tale of a Tub. 1. **man . . . sons.** The man is Christ; the three sons, named later in the work, are Peter (the Catholic Church), Martin (the Church of England), and Jack (all dissenting Protestant sects). *Peter* is named, of course, from St. Peter; *Martin* from Martin Luther; and *Jack* from John Calvin. 6. **purchased,** acquired. 9. **provided . . . coat.** The coats represent the doctrine and faith of Christianity, fitted by the wisdom of the Father to all times, places, and conditions. 18. **my will,** the New Testament. 39. **Duchess . . . d'Orgueil,** the Duchess of Money, Madame of Great Possessions, and the Countess of Pride. They represent respectively covetousness, ambition, and pride, which the early Church fathers considered the most serious of sins. 49. **lay . . . claps,** lay with prostitutes and caught gonorrhea. 52. **Locket's,** a noted

London tavern. **Will's,** a coffee house particularly frequented by poets and literary figures. 57. **levee,** a royal reception given shortly after noon, and intended for men only. 58. *sub dio,* similar to the slang expression, "crashing the gate." 74. **a sect.** The following passage is to be regarded as an incidental satire upon dress and fashion, which lays the foundation for the more specific satire in the next pages. The "philosophy of clothes" indicated here, which was by no means new in the eighteenth century, received notable treatment in the nineteenth century by Thomas Carlyle (1795–1881) in his *Sartor Resartus* (1833–1834). 76. *grand monde,* the world of society. 77. **idol,** a tailor. 82. **superficies,** any flat surface or area. 83. **goose,** the tailor's pressing iron. 85. **Jupiter Capitolinus.** In 390 B.C. the Gauls defeated the Romans and

recount, and by consequence were justly reckoned the most accomplished persons in the town. But all would not suffice, and the ladies aforesaid continued still inflexible. To clear up which difficulty I must, with the reader's good leave and patience, have recourse to some points of weight, which the authors of that age have not sufficiently illustrated.

For about this time it happened a sect arose, whose tenets obtained and spread very far, especially in the *grand monde,* and among everybody of good fashion. They worshiped a sort of idol, who, as their doctrine delivered, did daily create men by a kind of manufactory operation. This idol they placed in the highest parts of the house, on an altar erected about three foot: he was shewn in the posture of a Persian emperor, sitting on a superficies, with his legs interwoven under him. This god had a goose for his ensign, whence it is that some learned men pretend to deduce his original from Jupiter Capitolinus. At his left hand, beneath the altar, Hell seemed to open, and catch at the animals the idol was creating; to prevent which, certain of his priests hourly flung in pieces of the uninformed mass, or substance, and sometimes whole limbs already enlivened, which that horrid gulf insatiably swallowed, terrible to behold. The goose was also held a subaltern divinity or *deus minorum gentium,* before whose shrine was sacrificed that creature, whose hourly food is human gore, and who is in so great renown abroad, for being the delight and favorite of the Aegyptian Cercopithecus. Millions of these animals were cruelly slaughtered every day, to appease the hunger of that consuming deity. The chief idol was also worshiped as the inventor of the yard and the needle; whether as the god of seamen, or on account of certain other mystical attributes, hath not been sufficiently cleared.

The worshipers of this deity had also a system of their belief, which seemed to turn upon the following fundamental. They held the universe to be a large suit of clothes, which invests everything: that the earth is invested by the air; the air is invested by the stars; and the stars are invested by the *primum mobile.* Look on this globe of earth, you will find it to be a very complete and fashionable dress. What is that which some call land, but a fine coat faced with green? or the sea, but a waistcoat of water-tabby? Proceed to the particular works of the creation, you will find how curious a Journeyman Nature hath been, to trim up the vegetable beaux; observe how sparkish a periwig adorns the head of a beech, and what

a fine doublet of white satin is worn by the birch. To conclude from all, what is man himself but a micro-coat, or rather a complete suit of clothes with all its trimmings? As to his body, there can be no dispute; but examine even the acquirements of his mind, you will find them all contribute in their order toward furnishing out an exact dress. To instance no more: is not religion a cloak; honesty a pair of shoes worn out in the dirt; self-love a surtout; vanity a shirt; and conscience a pair of breeches; which, though a cover for lewdness as well as nastiness, is easily slipped down for the service of both?

These *postulata* being admitted, it will follow in due course of reasoning that those beings, which the world calls improperly suits of clothes, are in reality the most refined species of animals; or to proceed higher, that they are rational creatures, or men. For is it not manifest that they live, and move, and talk, and perform all other offices of human life? Are not beauty, and wit, and mien, and breeding, their inseparable properties? In short, we see nothing but them, hear nothing but them. Is it not they who walk the streets, fill up parliament-, coffee-, play-, bawdy-houses? 'Tis true, indeed, that these animals, which are vulgarly called suits of clothes, or dresses, do, according to certain compositions, receive different appellations. If one of them be trimmed up with a gold chain, and a red gown, and a white rod, and a great horse, it is called a Lord-Mayor; if certain ermines and furs be placed in a certain position, we style them a Judge; and so an apt conjunction of lawn and black satin we entitle a Bishop.

Others of these professors, though agreeing in the main system, were yet more refined upon certain branches of it; and held that man was an animal compounded of two dresses, the natural and the celestial suit, which were the body and the soul; that the soul was the outward, and the body the inward clothing; that the latter was *ex traduce,* but the former of daily creation and circumfusion; this last they proved by scripture, because in them we live, and move, and have our being; as likewise by philosophy, because they are all in all, and all in every part. "Besides," said they, "separate these two, and you will find the body to be only a senseless unsavory carcass. By all which it is manifest, that the outward dress must needs be the soul."

To this system of religion were tagged several subaltern doctrines, which were entertained with great

sacked the city of Rome, except for the citadel of the Capitol atop Capitoline Hill. Legend has it that the citadel was rescued from a surprise attack through the uproar raised by geese belonging to the priestesses of Jupiter in a temple on Capitoline Hill. From that time on, the goose was a bird sacred to Jupiter. 92. **deus minorum gentium,** god of the lesser peoples, god of the Gentiles. 95. **Cercopithecus,** the monkey god of ancient Egypt. His favorite food was lice, which fact explains the reference in the preceding line to the creature whose hourly food is human gore. 107. **primum mobile.** According to the old Ptolemaic system of cosmography (which assumed the earth to be at the center of the universe), the heavenly bodies were arranged above and below the earth in concentric circles, corresponding to their orbits. Seven such circles were occupied by the seven planets (the Sun, the Moon, Mercury, Venus, Mars, Jupiter, and Saturn). The eighth sphere was the sphere in which were located all the fixed stars and their constellations. The ninth sphere, or *primum mobile,* was a grand sphere, the motion of which produced motion in all the other spheres, thus explaining—according to the theory—all the movements of celestial bodies. 111. **water-tabby,** wavy silk fabric. 118. **micro-coat,** referring to *microcosm,* or little world—a term in frequent use among eighteenth-century philosophers when alluding to man and his little earthly existence. 124. **surtout,** a close fitting overcoat. 128. **postulata,** things postulated, laid down, or claimed. 154. **ex traduce,** produced by propagation from one body to another.

vogue; as particularly, the faculties of the mind were deduced by the learned among them in this manner; embroidery was sheer wit; gold fringe was agreeable conversation; gold lace was repartee; a huge long periwig was humor; and a coat full of powder was very good raillery; all which required abundance of *finesse* and *delicatesse* to manage with advantage, as well as a strict observance after times and fashions.

I have, with much pains and reading, collected out of ancient authors this short summary of a body of philosophy and divinity, which seems to have been composed by a vein and race of thinking very different from any other systems, either ancient or modern. And it was not merely to entertain or satisfy the reader's curiosity, but rather to give him light into several circumstances of the following story; that knowing the state of disposition and opinions in an age so remote, he may better comprehend those great events, which were the issue of them. I advise, therefore, the courteous reader to peruse with a world of application, again and again, whatever I have written upon this matter. And leaving these broken ends, I carefully gather up the chief thread of my story and proceed.

These opinions, therefore, were so universal, as well as the practices of them, among the refined part of court and town, that our three brother-adventurers, as their circumstances then stood, were strangely at a loss. For, on the one side, the three ladies they addressed themselves to (whom we have named already) were ever at the very top of the fashion and abhorred all that were below it but the breadth of a hair. On the other side, their father's will was very precise, and it was the main precept in it, with the greatest penalties annexed, not to add to, or diminish from, their coats one thread, without a positive command in the will. Now, the coats their father had left them were, 'tis true, of very good cloth, and, besides, so neatly sewn you would swear they were all of a piece; but, at the same time, very plain, and with little or no ornament; and it happened that before they were a month in town, great shoulder-knots came up; straight all the world was shoulder-knots; no approaching the ladies *ruelles* without the *quota* of shoulder-knots. "That fellow," cries one, "has no soul, where is his shoulder-knot?" Our three brethren soon discovered their want by sad experience, meeting in their walks with forty mortifications and indignities. If they went to the play-house, the door-keeper showed them into the twelve-penny gallery. If they called a boat, says a waterman, "I am first sculler." If they stepped to the Rose to take a bottle, the drawer would cry, "Friend, we sell no ale." If they went to visit a lady, a footman met them at the door, with "Pray send up your message." In this unhappy case, they went immediately to consult their father's will, read it over and over, but not a word of the shoulder-knot. What should they do? What temper should they find? Obedience was absolutely necessary, and yet shoulder-knots appeared extremely requisite. After much thought, one of the brothers, who happened to be more book-learned than the other two, said, he had found an expedient. "'Tis true," said he, "there is nothing here in this will, *totidem verbis*, making mention of shoulder-knots; but I dare conjecture we may find them *inclusive*, or *totidem syllabis*." This distinction was immediately approved by all; and so they fell again to examine the will. But their evil star had so directed the matter, that the first syllable was not to be found in the whole writing. Upon which disappointment, he who found the former evasion, took heart and said, "Brothers, there is yet hopes; for though we cannot find them *totidem verbis*, nor *totidem syllabis*, I dare engage we shall make them out, *tertio modo*, or *totidem literis*." This discovery was also highly commended, upon which they fell once more to the scrutiny and picked out "s," "h," "o," "u," "l," "d," "e," "r"; when the same planet, enemy to their repose, had wonderfully contrived that a "k" was not to be found. Here was a weighty difficulty! But the distinguishing brother (for whom we shall hereafter find a name), now his hand was in, proved by a very good argument that "k" was a modern illegitimate letter, unknown to the learned ages, nor anywhere to be found in ancient manuscripts, *Calendae* hath in Q.V.C. been sometimes writ with a "k," but erroneously; for in the best copies it has been ever spelled with a "c." And by consequence it was a gross mistake in our language to spell "*knot*" with a "k"; but that from hence forward he would take care it should be writ with a "c." Upon this all further difficulty vanished; shoulder-knots were made clearly out to be *jure paterno*, and our three gentle-

24. **I . . . proceed.** According to the eighteenth-century editor of *A Tale of a Tub*, William Wotton, whose notes are often very valuable to the reader: "The first part of the tale is the history of Peter; thereby Popery is exposed: everybody knows the Papists have made great additions to Christianity; that, indeed, is the great exception which the Church of England makes against them; accordingly Peter begins his pranks with adding a shoulder-knot to his coat. . . . His description of the cloth of which the coat was made has a farther meaning than the words may seem to import: 'The coats their father had left them were of very good cloth, and, besides, so neatly sewn you would swear it had been all of a piece; but, at the same time, very plain, with little or no ornament.' This is the distinguishing character of the Christian religion: *Christiana religio absoluta et simplex*, was Ammianus Marcellinus's description of it, who was himself a heathen." 43. **shoulder-knots.** These symbolize the introduction of pageantry into the Catholic ritual, and various ornaments of worship, which Swift conceives to be useless and inconvenient, as a huge shoulder knot would be on a coat. 45. *ruelles*, alleys. 52. **"I . . . sculler,"** "I scull only for the ladies and gentlemen of fashion." 53. **Rose,** another well-known and well-frequented London tavern. 65. *totidem verbis*, in so many words. 67. *totidem syllabis*, in so many syllables. Cf. Wotton: "When the Papists cannot find anything which they want in scripture, they go to oral tradition: thus Peter is introduced satisfied with the tedious way of looking for all the letters of any word, which he has occasion for in the Will, when neither the constituent syllables, nor much less the whole word, was there in the end." It is clear that the "more book-learned" brother of l. 63 is Peter. 76. *tertio . . . literis*, in a third way, that is, in so many letters. 86. *Calendae*, the Kalends, or beginning of the Roman month. 87. **Q.V.C.,** an abbreviation of *quibusdam veteribus codicibus*, "in some ancient manuscripts." 94. *jure paterno*, according to the father's (paternal) law. 102. **gold lace.** This probably refers to some new method of forcing or straining the letter of the Scriptures; possibly,

men swaggered with as large and as flaunting ones as the best.

But, as human happiness is of a very short duration, so in those days were human fashions, upon which it entirely depends. Shoulder-knots had their time, and we must now imagine them in their decline; for a certain lord came just from Paris with fifty yards of gold lace upon his coat, exactly trimmed after the court fashion of that month. In two days all mankind appeared closed up in bars of gold lace: whoever durst peep abroad without his compliment of gold lace was as scandalous as a ———, and as ill received among the women. What should our three knights do in this momentous affair? They had sufficiently strained a point already in the affair of the shoulder-knots. Upon recourse to the will, nothing appeared there but *altum silentium*. That of the shoulder-knots was a loose, flying, circumstantial point; but this of gold lace seemed too considerable an alteration without better warrant. It did *aliquo modo essentiae adhaerere*, and therefore required a positive precept. But about this time it fell out that the learned brother aforesaid had read *Aristotelis Dialectica*, and especially that wonderful piece *de Interpretatione*, which has the faculty of teaching its readers to find out a meaning in everything but itself, like commentators on the Revelation, who proceed prophets without understanding a syllable of the text. "Brothers," said he, "you are to be informed that of wills *duo sunt genera*, nuncupatory and scriptory; that to the scriptory will here before us, there is no precept or mention about gold lace, *conceditur*: but, *si idem affirmetur de nuncupatorio, negatur*. For, brothers, if you remember, we heard a fellow say, when we were boys, that he heard my father's man say, that he heard my father say, that he would advise his sons to get gold lace on their coats, as soon as ever they could procure money to buy it." "By G—! That is very true," cries the other; "I remember it perfectly well," said the third. And so without more ado they got the largest gold lace in the parish, and walked about as fine as lords.

Awhile after there came up all in fashion a pretty sort of flame-colored satin for linings; and the mercer brought a pattern of it immediately to our three gentlemen: "An please your worships," said he, "my Lord C——and Sir J. W. had linings out of this very piece last night; it takes wonderfully, and I shall not have a remnant left enough to make my wife a pincushion by tomorrow morning at ten o'clock." Upon this they fell again to rummage the will, because the present case also required a positive precept, the lining being held by orthodox writers to be of the essence of the coat. After long search, they could fix upon nothing to the matter in hand except a short advice of their father's in the will to take care of fire and put out their candles before they went to sleep. This, though a good deal for the purpose, and helping very far toward self-conviction, yet not seeming wholly of force to establish a command; and being resolved to avoid further scruple, as well as future occasion for scandal, says he that was the scholar, "I remember to have read in wills of a codicil annexed, which is indeed a part of the will, and what it contains hath equal authority with the rest. Now, I have been considering of this same will here before us, and I cannot reckon it to be complete for want of such a codicil: I will therefore fasten one in its proper place very dexterously: I have had it by me some time; it was written by a dog-keeper of my grandfather's, and talks a great deal (as good luck would have it) of this very flame-colored satin." The project was immediately approved by the other two; an old parchment scroll was tagged on according to art, in the form of a codicil annexed, and the satin bought and worn.

Next winter a player, hired for the purpose by the corporation of fringe-makers, acted his part in a new comedy, all covered with silver fringe, and, according to the laudable custom, gave rise to that fashion. Upon which the brothers, consulting their father's will: "*Item*, I charge and command my said three sons to wear no sort of silver fringe upon or about their said coats," etc., with a penalty, in case of disobedience, too long here to insert. However, after some pause, the brother so often mentioned for his erudition, who was well skilled in criticisms, had found in a certain author, which he said should be nameless, that the same word, which in the will is called fringe, does also signify a broom-stick and doubtless ought to have the same interpretation in this paragraph. This another of the brothers disliked, because of that epithet silver, which could not, he humbly conceived, in propriety of speech, be reason-

however, it is merely an additional reference to the introduction of what Swift considers gaudy, and unnecessary adornments in the church service. 111. *altum silentium*, a high silence. 114. *aliquo . . . adhaerere*, adhere in some way to the spirit (of the will). 117. *Aristotelis Dialectica*. There are some thirty treatises attributed to Aristotle and known as the *Dialectics*; of these about half are probably his, and the others belong to the Aristotelian tradition. Included in the list of authentic works is the treatise on Interpretations, Dreams, and Prophesying in Sleep, which is the work Swift is probably alluding to here. 123. "Brothers" . . . informed. This refers undoubtedly to the many glosses and interpretations of the Scriptures undertaken by Catholic writers. 124. *duo sunt genera*, there are two kinds. nuncupatory and scriptory, belonging to oral tradition and to the Scriptures, respectively. 126. *conceditur*, it is conceded. 127. *si . . . negatur*, if the same thing is affirmed about the nuncupatory will, it is wrong. 138. satin for linings. Cf. Wotton: "This is purgatory, whereof he speaks more particularly

hereafter; but here, only to shew how scripture was perverted to prove it, which was done by giving equal authority with the *Canon* (of the Old and New Testaments) and the *Apocrypha*, called here a codicil annexed. . . . It is likely the author, in every one of these changes in the brothers' dresses, refers to some particular error in the Church of Rome, though it is not easy, I think, to apply them all; but by this of flame-colored satin, is manifestly meant purgatory; by gold lace may perhaps be understood, the lofty ornaments and plate in the churches; the shoulder-knots and silver fringe are not so obvious, at least to me; but the Indian figures of men, women and children plainly relate to the pictures in the Roman churches, of God like an old man, of the Virgin Mary, and our Saviour as a child." 151. put . . . sleep, that is, to take care of hell; and to achieve that, to subdue, quench, and extinguish lust. 164. dog-keeper . . . grandfather's, possibly referring to Tobit and his dog, found in the Book of Tobit in the Apocrypha. 173. silver fringe, referring evidently to further pomp and circumstance in the church.

ably applied to a broom-stick; but it was replied upon him that this epithet was understood in a mythological and allegorical sense. However, he objected again, why their father should forbid them to wear a broom-stick upon their coats, a caution that seemed unnatural and impertinent; upon which he was taken up short, as one that spoke irreverently of a mystery, which doubtless was very useful and significant but ought not to be overcuriously pried into, or nicely
10 reasoned upon. And, in short, their father's authority being now considerably sunk, this expedient was allowed to serve as a lawful dispensation for wearing their full proportion of silver fringe.

Awhile after was revived an old fashion, long antiquated, of embroidery with Indian figures of men, women, and children. Here they remembered but too well how their father had always abhorred this fashion; that he made several paragraphs on purpose, importing his utter detestation of it, and bestow-
20 ing his everlasting curse to his sons whenever they should wear it. For all this, in a few days they appeared higher in the fashion than anybody else in the town. But they solved the matter by saying that these figures were not at all the same with those that were formerly worn and were meant in the will. Besides, they did not wear them in the sense as forbidden by their father; but as they were in a commendable custom, and of great use to the public. That these rigorous clauses in the will did, therefore, re-
30 quire some allowance and a favorable interpretation, and ought to be understood *cum grano salis*.

But fashions perpetually altering in that age, the scholastic brother grew weary of searching further evasions and solving everlasting contradictions; resolved, therefore, at all hazards, to comply with the modes of the world, they concerted matters together and agreed unanimously to lock up their father's will in a strong box, brought out of Greece or Italy (I have forgot which), and trouble themselves no further
40 to examine it but only refer to its authority whenever they thought fit. In consequence whereof, awhile after it grew a general mode to wear an infinite number of points, most of them tagged with silver: upon which the scholar pronounced *ex cathedra*, that points were absolutely *jure paterno*, as they might very well remember. 'Tis true, indeed, the fashion prescribed somewhat more than were directly named in the will; however, that they, as heirs-general of their father, had power to make and add cer-
50 tain clauses for public emolument, though not deducible, *totidem verbis*, from the letter of the will, or else *multa absurda sequerentur*. This was under-

stood for canonical, and therefore on the following Sunday they came to church all covered with points.

The learned brother, so often mentioned, was reckoned the best scholar in all that, or the next street to it; insomuch as, having run something behindhand with the world, he obtained the favor from a certain lord to receive him into his house and to teach his children. Awhile after the lord died, and he, 60 by long practice of his father's will, found the way of contriving a deed of conveyance of that house to himself and his heirs; upon which he took possession, turned the young squires out, and received his brothers in their stead.

(1704)

from GULLIVER'S TRAVELS

Gulliver's Travels (1726) is the supreme achievement of Swift's literary career. The book takes its place with Robinson Crusoe *and* Huckleberry Finn *as a household necessity which "every schoolboy knows"; like them, it is an adventure book whose profound underlying commentary need not knit the brows of the young; like them, it contains a sustained analysis of the human condition which repeated readings will not exhaust.*

There are four parts to Gulliver's Travels. Parts I and II are companion pieces in the sense that they present Lemuel Gulliver in reversed situations. In Part I, Captain Gulliver is shipwrecked on the coast of Lilliput, where the inhabitants are only six inches tall. Initially enchanted by the ingenuity, humaneness, and esthetic qualities of these diminutive people, the reader soon becomes shocked by the disproportion between their negligible size and their monstrous corruption. Gulliver eventually looks down upon them as the higher orders must look down upon man.

In Part II, reprinted here, the situation is entirely reversed: in Brobdingnag, Gulliver stands dwarf to giants sixty feet in height; here it is he, the European man, who is contemptible. He is morally myopic, and his social and political assumptions gradually emerge as irrational and absurd. The King cries out the sentence: "I cannot but conclude the Bulk of your Natives to be the most pernicious Race of little odious Vermin that Nature ever suffered to crawl upon the surface of the Earth." Gulliver himself establishes the tone of Part II by his fear that the peasant who discovers him may dash him to the ground "as we usually do any little hateful Animal which we have a Mind to

15. **Indian . . . children,** the images of God and the saints, the Virgin Mary, and the infant Christ. 31. *cum grano salis,* with a grain of salt. 38. **strong box . . . Italy.** Cf. Wotton: "The Papists formerly forbade the people use of scripture in a vulgar tongue; Peter therefore locks up his father's will in a strong box brought out of Greece or Italy. Those countries are named because the New Testament is written in Greek,

and the vulgar Latin, which is the authentic edition of the Bible in the Church of Rome, is in the language of ancient Italy." 44. **ex cathedra,** from the (papal) throne. Cf. Wotton: "The popes, in their decretals and bulls, have given their sanction to very many gainful doctrines, which are now received in the Church of Rome, that are not mentioned in scripture, and are unknown to the primitive church." Peter, accord-

destroy." The world of the Brobdingnagians is practical, concrete, simple, and benevolent. And Gulliver sees mankind as an insect might or as we might see ourselves under a huge microscope: cancerous, blotched, coarse, lousy, and nauseous. Thus Swift introduces, in his technique of shock, the bold element of disgust.

The third voyage takes Gulliver to Laputa and to other countries (The Flying Island, Balnibari) whose inhabitants are scholars, scientists, philosophers, inventors, and professors who devote themselves to absurd and pedantic research. This part has been called "a digression on madness"—in government, philosophy, economics, and experimentation. Under the genial metaphor of science, Swift satirizes overreliance on the speculative reason. In this part also we find the race of Struldbrugs, or Immortals, who in their endless and ghastly dotage are the most miserable of beings. Swift here exposes the distressing faults of old age and the folly of desiring an overlong life.

Part IV is probably the most difficult and controversial of all the parts of Gulliver's Travels. Before tackling it, which is recommended, one should remind himself that Gulliver is Gulliver and Swift is Swift. Swift is the author, Gulliver is the narrator and chief actor, with a created character and personality: he is a reliable reporter, not an authoritative commentator or interpreter. After all, Swift very often arranges his situations so as to point up Gulliver's limitations, the limitations of the average good European—partially educated, observant, intelligent to a point, brave, hopeful, and unimaginative. It is through this specific persona that Swift filters the experiences recorded in Gulliver's Travels. Further, one should remind himself that, even in Part IV—so full of "gravity, anger, anxiety, frustration"—there is still the countertension of the comic, principally centered in the Houyhnhnms, the idealized horse-humans. It is Gulliver, not Swift, who looks upon life in Houyhnhnmland as ideal, and Swift does not, like Gulliver, identify the savage Yahoos with man. Swift is critical of stoicism and bestiality alike.

PART II

A VOYAGE TO BROBDINGNAG

CHAPTER I

A great storm described, the long-boat sent to fetch water, the Author goes with it to discover the country. He is left on shore, is seized by one of the natives, and carried to a farmer's house. His reception there, with several accidents that happened there. A description of the inhabitants.

Having been condemned by nature and fortune to an active and restless life, in two months after my return, I again left my native country, and took shipping in the Downs on the 20th day of June, 1702, in the *Adventure*, Captain John Nicholas, a Cornish man, [70] Commander, bound for Surat. We had a very prosperous gale till we arrived at the Cape of Good Hope, where we landed for fresh water, but discovering a leak we unshipped our goods and wintered there; for the Captain falling sick of an ague, we could not leave the Cape till the end of March. We then set sail, and had a good voyage till we passed the Straits of Madagascar; but having got northward of that island, and to about five degrees south latitude, the winds, which in those seas are observed to blow a constant equal [80] gale between the north and west from the beginning of December to the beginning of May, on the 19th of April began to blow with much greater violence, and more westerly than usual, continuing so for twenty days together, during which time we were driven a little to the east of the Molucca Islands, and about three degrees northward of the Line, as our Captain found by an observation he took the 2nd of May, at which time the wind ceased, and it was a perfect calm, whereat I was not a little rejoiced. But he, being a man [90] well experienced in the navigation of those seas, bid us all prepare against a storm, which accordingly happened the day following: for a southern wind, called the southern monsoon, began to set in.

Finding it was likely to overblow, we took in our sprit-sail, and stood by to hand the fore-sail; but making foul weather, we looked the guns were all fast, and handed the mizen. The ship lay very broad off, so we thought it better spooning before the sea, than trying or hulling. We reefed the fore-sail and set [100] him, we hawled aft the fore-sheet; the helm was hard a weather. The ship wore bravely. We belayed the fore-down-hall; but the sail was split, and we hawled down the yard, and got the sail into the ship, and unbound all the things clear of it. It was a very fierce storm; the sea broke strange and dangerous. We hawled off upon the laniard of the whipstaff, and helped the man at helm. We would not get down our top-cast, but let all stand, because she scudded before the sea well, and we knew that the top-mast being [110] aloft, the ship was the wholesomer, and made better way through the sea, seeing we had searoom. When the storm was over, we set fore-sail and main-sail, and brought the ship to. Then we set the mizen, main-top-sail, and the fore-top-sail. Our course was east north-east, the wind was at south-west. We got the starboard tacks aboard, we cast off our weatherbraces and lifts; we set in the lee-braces, and hawled forward by the weather-bowlings, and hawled them tight, and belayed them, and hawled over the mizen tack to windward, and kept her full and by as near as she 10 would lie.

During this storm, which was followed by a strong wind west south-west, we were carried by my computation about five hundred leagues to the east, so that the oldest sailor on board could not tell in what part of the world we were. Our provisions held out well, our ship was staunch, and our crew all in good health; but we lay in the utmost distress for water. We thought it best to hold on the same course, rather than turn more northerly, which might have brought 20 us to the north-west parts of Great Tartary, and into the frozen sea.

On the 16th day of June, 1703, a boy on the top-mast discovered land. On the 17th we came in full view of a great island or continent (for we knew not whether) on the south side whereof was a small neck of land jutting out into the sea, and a creek too shallow to hold a ship of above one hundred tons. We cast anchor within a league of this creek, and our Captain sent a dozen of his men well armed in the 30 long-boat, with vessels for water if any could be found. I desired his leave to go with them, that I might see the country, and make what discoveries I could. When we came to land we saw no river or spring, nor any sign of inhabitants. Our men therefore wandered on the shore to find out some fresh water near the sea, and I walked alone about a mile on the other side, where I observed the country all barren and rocky. I now began to be weary, and seeing nothing to entertain my curiosity, I returned gently down towards the 40 creek; and the sea being full in my view, I saw our men already got into the boat, and rowing for life to the ship. I was going to hollow after them, although it had been to little purpose, when I observed a huge creature walking after them in the sea, as fast as he could: he waded not much deeper than his knees, and took prodigious strides: but our men had the start of him half a league, and the sea thereabouts being full of sharp-pointed rocks, the monster was not able to overtake the boat. This I was afterwards told, for 50 I durst not stay to see the issue of that adventure; but ran as fast as I could the way I first went, and then climbed up a steep hill, which gave me some prospect of the country. I found it fully cultivated; but that which first surprised me was the length of the grass, which in those grounds that seemed to be kept for hay, was about twenty foot high.

I fell into a high road, for so I took it to be, though it served to the inhabitants only as a foot-path through a field of barley. Here I walked on for some time, but could see little on either side, it being now near har- 60 vest, and the corn rising at least forty foot. I was an hour walking to the end of this field, which was fenced in with a hedge of at least one hundred and twenty foot high, and the trees so lofty that I could make no computation of their altitude. There was a stile to pass from this field into the next. It had four steps, and a stone to cross over when you came to the uppermost. It was impossible for me to climb this stile, because every step was six foot high, and the upper stone above twenty. I was endeavouring to find some gap 70 in the hedge, when I discovered one of the inhabitants in the next field, advancing towards the stile, of the same size with him whom I saw in the sea pursuing our boat. He appeared as tall as an ordinary spire-steeple, and took about ten yards at every stride, as near as I could guess. I was struck with the utmost fear and astonishment, and ran to hide myself in the corn, from whence I saw him at the top of the stile, looking back into the next field on the right hand, and heard him call in a voice many degrees louder than 80 a speaking-trumpet: but the noise was so high in the air, that at first I certainly thought it was thunder. Whereupon seven monsters like himself came towards him with reaping-hooks in their hands, each hook about the largeness of six scythes. These people were not so well clad as the first, whose servants or labourers they seemed to be: for, upon some words he spoke, they went to reap the corn in the field where I lay. I kept from them at as great a distance as I could, but was forced to move with extreme difficulty, for the 90 stalks of the corn were sometimes not above a foot distant, so that I could hardly squeeze my body betwixt them. However, I made a shift to go forward till I came to a part of the field where the corn has been laid by the rain and wind. Here it was impossible for me to advance a step; for the stalks were so interwoven that I could not creep through, and the beards of the fallen ears so strong and pointed that they pierced through my clothes into my flesh. At the same time I heard the reapers not above an hundred yards 100 behind me. Being quite dispirited with toil, and wholly overcome by grief and despair, I lay down between two ridges, and heartily wished I might there end my days. I bemoaned my desolate widow, and fatherless children. I lamented my own folly and wilfulness in attempting a second voyage against the advice of all my friends and relations. In this terrible agitation of mind I could not forbear thinking of Lilliput, whose inhabitants looked upon me as the greatest prodigy that ever appeared in the world; where I was able to draw 110 an Imperial Fleet in my hand, and perform those other actions which will be recorded for ever in the chroni-

cles of that empire, while posterity shall hardly believe them, although attested by millions. I reflected what a mortification it must prove to me to appear as inconsiderable in this nation as one single Lilliputian would be among us. But this I conceived was to be the least of my misfortunes: for, as human creatures are observed to be more savage and cruel in propor-
120 tion to their bulk, what could I expect but to be a morsel in the mouth of the first among these enormous barbarians that should happen to seize me? Undoubtedly philosophers are in the right when they tell us, that nothing is great or little otherwise than by comparison. It might have pleased fortune to have let the Lilliputians find some nation, where the people were as diminutive with respect to them, as they were to me. And who knows but that even this prodigious race of mortals might be equally overmatched in some
130 distant part of the world, whereof we have yet no discovery?

Scared and confounded as I was, I could not forbear going on with these reflections, when one of the reapers approaching within ten yards of the ridge where I lay, made me apprehend that with the next step I should be squashed to death under his foot, or cut in two with his reaping-hook. And therefore when he was again about to move, I screamed as loud as fear could make me. Whereupon the huge creature
140 trod short, and looking round under him for some time, at last espied me as I lay on the ground. He considered a while with the caution of one who endeavours to lay hold on a small dangerous animal in such a manner that it shall not be able either to scratch or bite him, as I myself have sometimes done with a weasel in England. At length he ventured to take me up behind by the middle between his forefinger and thumb, and brought me within three yards of his eyes, that he might behold my shape more per-
150 fectly. I guessed his meaning, and my good fortune gave me so much presence of mind, that I resolved not to struggle in the least as he held me in the air about sixty foot from the ground, although he grievously pinched my sides, for fear I should slip through his fingers. All I ventured was to raise my eyes towards the sun, and place my hands together in a supplicating posture, and to speak some words in an humble melancholy tone, suitable to the condition I then was in. For I apprehended every moment that he would dash
160 me against the ground, as we usually do any little hateful animal which we have a mind to destroy. But my good star would have it, that he appeared pleased with my voice and gestures, and began to look upon me as a curiosity, much wondering to hear me pronounce articulate words, although he could not understand them. In the mean time I was not able to forbear groaning and shedding tears, and turning my head towards my sides; letting him know, as well as I could,

how cruelly I was hurt by the pressure of his thumb and finger. He seemed to apprehend my meaning; for, 170 lifting up the lappet of his coat, he put me gently into it, and immediately ran along with me to his master, who was a substantial farmer, and the same person I had first seen in the field.

The farmer having (as I supposed by their talk) received such an account of me as his servant could give him, took a piece of a small straw, about the size of a walking staff, and therewith lifted up the lappets of my coat; which it seems he thought to be some kind of covering that nature had given me. He 180 blew my hairs aside to take a better view of my face. He called his hinds about him, and asked them (as I afterwards learned) whether they had ever seen in the fields any little creature that resembled me. He then placed me softly on the ground upon all four, but I got immediately up, and walked slowly backwards and forwards, to let those people see I had no intent to run away. They all sat down in a circle about me, the better to observe my motions. I pulled off my hat, and made a low bow towards the farmer. I fell 190 on my knees, and lifted up my hands and eyes, and spoke several words as loud as I could: I took a purse of gold out of my pocket, and humbly presented it to him. He received it on the palm of his hand, then applied it close to his eye, to see what it was, and afterwards turned it several times with the point of a pin (which he took out of his sleeve), but could make nothing of it. Whereupon I made a sign that he should place his hand on the ground. I then took the purse, and opening it, poured all the gold into his 200 palm. There were six Spanish pieces of four pistoles each, beside twenty or thirty smaller coins. I saw him wet the tip of his little finger upon his tongue, and take up one of my largest pieces, and then another, but he seemed to be wholly ignorant what they were. He made me a sign to put them again to my purse, and the purse again into my pocket, which after offering to him several times, I thought it best to do.

The farmer by this time was convinced I must be a rational creature. He spoke often to me, but the 210 sound of his voice pierced my ears like that of a watermill, yet his words were articulate enough. I answered as loud as I could, in several languages, and he often laid his ear within two yards of me, but all in vain, for we were wholly unintelligible to each other. He then sent his servants to their work, and taking his handkerchief out of his pocket, he doubled and spread it on his left hand, which he placed flat on the ground, with the palm upwards, making me a sign to step into it, as I could easily do, for it was not above a foot 220 in thickness. I thought it my part to obey, and for fear of falling, laid myself at length upon the handkerchief, with the remainder of which he lapped me up to the head for further security, and in this manner carried me home to his house. There he called his wife, and showed me to her; but she screamed and ran back, as women in England do at the sight of a toad or a spider. However, when she had a while seen my behaviour, and how well I observed the signs her husband made, she was soon reconciled, and by degrees grew extremely tender of me.

It was about twelve at noon, and a servant brought in dinner. It was only one substantial dish of meat 10 (fit for the plain condition of an husbandman) in a dish of about four-and-twenty foot diameter. The company were the farmer and his wife, three children, and an old grandmother. When they were sat down, the farmer placed me at some distance from him on the table, which was thirty foot high from the floor. I was in a terrible fright, and kept as far as I could from the edge for fear of falling. The wife minced a bit of meat, then crumbled some bread on a trencher, and placed it before me. I made her a low bow, took 20 out my knife and fork, and fell to eat, which gave them exceeding delight. The mistress sent her maid for a small dram cup, which held about two gallons, and filled it with drink; I took up the vessel with much difficulty in both hands, and in a most respectful manner drank to her ladyship's health, expressing the words as loud as I could in English, which made the company laugh so heartily that I was almost deafened with the noise. This liquor tasted like a small cyder, and was not unpleasant. Then the master made me 30 a sign to come to his trencher side; but as I walked on the table, being in great surprise all the time, as the indulgent reader will easily conceive and excuse, I happened to stumble against a crust, and fell flat on my face, but received no hurt. I got up immediately, and observing the good people to be in much concern, I took my hat (which I held under my arm out of good manners) and waving it over my head, made three huzzas, to show I had got no mischief by my fall. But advancing forwards toward my master (as 40 I shall henceforth call him), his youngest son who sat next to him, an arch boy of about ten years old, took me up by the legs, and held me so high in the air, that I trembled every limb; but his father snatched me from him, and at the same time gave him such a box on the left ear, as would have felled an European troop of horse to the earth, ordering him to be taken from the table. But being afraid the boy might owe me a spite, and well remembering how mischievous all children among us naturally are to sparrows, rabbits, 50 young kittens, and puppy dogs, I fell on my knees, and pointing to the boy, made my master to understand, as well as I could, that I desired his son might be pardoned. The father complied, and the lad took his seat again; whereupon I went to him and kissed his hand, which my master took, and made him stroke me gently with it.

In the midst of dinner, my mistress's favourite cat leapt into her lap. I heard a noise behind me like that of a dozen stocking-weavers at work; and turning my head, I found it proceeded from the purring of 60 this animal, who seemed to be three times larger than an ox, as I computed by the view of her head, and one of her paws, while her mistress was feeding and stroking her. The fierceness of this creature's countenance altogether discomposed me; though I stood at the farther end of the table, above fifty foot off; and although my mistress held her fast for fear she might give a spring, and seize me in her talons. But it happened there was no danger; for the cat took not the least notice of me when my master placed me within 70 three yards of her. And as I have been always told, and found true by experience in my travels, that flying, or discovering fear before a fierce animal, is a certain way to make it pursue or attack you, so I resolved in this dangerous juncture to show no manner of concern. I walked with intrepidity five or six times before the very head of the cat, and came within half a yard of her; whereupon she drew herself back, as if she were more afraid of me: I had less apprehension concerning the dogs, whereof three or four came into the 80 room, as it is usual in farmers' houses; one of which was a mastiff, equal in bulk to four elephants, and a greyhound, somewhat taller than the mastiff, but not so large.

When dinner was almost done, the nurse came in with a child of a year old in her arms, who immediately spied me, and began a squall that you might have heard from London-Bridge to Chelsea, after the usual oratory of infants, to get me for a plaything. The mother out of pure indulgence took me up, and 90 put me towards the child, who presently seized me by the middle, and got my head in his mouth, where I roared so loud that the urchin was frighted, and let me drop; and I should infallibly have broke my neck if the mother had not held her apron under me. The nurse to quiet her babe made use of a rattle, which was a kind of hollow vessel filled with great stones, and fastened by a cable to the child's waist: but all in vain, so that she was forced to apply the last remedy by giving it suck. I must confess no object ever dis- 100 gusted me so much as the sight of her monstrous breast, which I cannot tell what to compare with, so as to give the curious reader an idea of its bulk, shape and colour. It stood prominent six foot, and could not be less than sixteen in circumference. The nipple was about half the bigness of my head, and the hue both of that and the dug so varified with spots, pimples, and freckles, that nothing could appear more nauseous: for I had a near sight of her, she sitting down the more conveniently to give suck, and I standing on the 110 table. This made me reflect upon the fair skins of our English ladies, who appear so beautiful to us, only because they are of our own size, and their defects not to be seen but through a magnifying glass, where we find by experiment that the smoothest and whitest skins look rough and coarse, and ill-coloured.

I remember when I was at Lilliput, the complexion of those diminutive people appeared to me the fairest in the world; and talking upon this subject with a person of learning there, who was an intimate friend of mine, he said that my face appeared much fairer and smoother when he looked on me from the ground, than it did upon a nearer view when I took him up in my hand and brought him close, which he confessed was at first a very shocking sight. He said he could discover great holes in my skin; that the stumps of my beard were ten times stronger than the bristles of a boar, and my complexion made up of several colours altogether disagreeable: although I must beg leave to say for myself, that I am as fair as most of my sex and country, and very little sunburnt by all my travels. On the other side, discoursing of the ladies in that Emperor's court, he used to tell me, one had freckles, another too wide a mouth, a third too large a nose, nothing of which I was able to distinguish. I confess this reflection was obvious enough; which, however, I could not forbear, lest the reader might think those vast creatures were actually deformed: for I must do them justice to say they are a comely race of people; and particularly the features of my master's countenance, although he were but a farmer, when I beheld him from the height of sixty foot, appeared very well proportioned.

When dinner was done, my master went out to his labourers, and as I could discover by his voice and gesture, gave his wife a strict charge to take care of me. I was very much tired, and disposed to sleep, which my mistress perceiving, she put me on her own bed, and covered me with a clean white handkerchief, but larger and coarser than the main-sail of a man of war.

I slept about two hours, and dreamed I was at home with my wife and children, which aggravated my sorrows when I awaked and found myself alone in a vast room, between two and three hundred foot wide, and above two hundred high, lying in a bed twenty yards wide. My mistress was gone about her household affairs, and had locked me in. The bed was eight yards from the floor. Some natural necessities required me to get down; I durst not presume to call, and if I had, it would have been in vain, with such a voice as mine, at so great a distance as from the room where I lay to the kitchen where the family kept. While I was under these circumstances, two rats crept up the curtains, and ran smelling backwards and forwards on the bed. One of them came up almost to my face, whereupon I rose in a fright, and drew out my hanger to defend myself. These horrible animals had the boldness to attack me on both sides, and one of them held his fore-feet at my collar; but I had the good fortune to rip up his belly before he could do me any mischief. He fell down at my feet, and the other seeing the fate of his comrade, made his escape, but not without one good wound on the back, which I gave him as he fled, and made the blood run trickling from him. After this exploit, I walked gently to and fro on the bed, to recover my breath and loss of spirits. These creatures were of the size of a large mastiff, but infinitely more nimble and fierce, so that if I had taken off my belt before I went to sleep, I must have infallibly been torn to pieces and devoured. I measured the tail of the dead rat, and found it to be two yards long, wanting an inch; but it went against my stomach to drag the carcass off the bed, where it lay still bleeding; I observed it had yet some life, but with a strong slash across the neck, I thoroughly dispatched it.

Soon after my mistress came into the room, who seeing me all bloody, ran and took me up in her hand. I pointed to the dead rat, smiling and making other signs to show I was not hurt, whereat she was extremely rejoiced, calling the maid to take up the dead rat with a pair of tongs, and throw it out of the window. Then she set me on a table, where I showed her my hanger all bloody, and wiping it on the lappet of my coat, returned it to the scabbard. I was pressed to do more than one thing, which another could not do for me, and therefore endeavoured to make my mistress understand that I desired to be set down on the floor; which after she had done, my bashfulness would not suffer me to express myself farther than by pointing to the door, and bowing several times. The good woman with much difficulty at last perceived what I would be at, and taking me up again in her hand, walked into the garden, where she set me down. I went on one side about two hundred yards, and beckoning to her not to look or to follow me, I hid myself between two leaves of sorrel, and there discharged the necessities of nature.

I hope the gentle reader will excuse me for dwelling on these and the like particulars, which however insignificant they may appear to grovelling vulgar minds, yet will certainly help a philosopher to enlarge his thoughts and imagination, and apply them to the benefit of public as well as private life, which was my sole design in presenting this and other accounts of my travels to the world; wherein I have been chiefly studious of truth, without affecting any ornaments of learning or of style. But the whole scene of this voyage made so strong an impression on my mind, and is so deeply fixed in my memory, that in committing it to paper I did not omit one material circumstance: however, upon a strict review, I blotted out several passages of less moment which were in my first copy, for fear of being censured as tedious and trifling, whereof travellers are often, perhaps not without justice, accused.

CHAPTER II

A description of the farmer's daughter. The Author carried to a market-town, and then to the metropolis. The particulars of his journey.

My mistress had a daughter of nine years old, a child of forward parts for her age, very dexterous at her needle, and skilful in dressing her baby. Her mother and she contrived to fit up the baby's cradle for me against night: the cradle was put into a small drawer of a cabinet, and the drawer placed upon a hanging shelf for fear of the rats. This was my bed all 10 the time I stayed with those people, though made more convenient by degrees, as I began to learn their language, and make my wants known. This young girl was so handy, that after I had once or twice pulled off my clothes before her, she was able to dress and undress me, though I never gave her that trouble when she would let me do either myself. She made me seven shirts, and some other linen, of as fine cloth as could be got, which indeed was coarser than sackcloth; and these she constantly washed for me with her own 20 hands. She was likewise my school-mistress to teach me the language: when I pointed to any thing, she told me the name of it in her own tongue, so that in a few days I was able to call for whatever I had a mind to. She was very good-natured, and not above forty foot high, being little for her age. She gave me the name of *Grildrig*, which the family took up, and afterwards the whole kingdom. The word imports what the Latins call *nanunculus*, the Italians *homunceletino*, and the English *mannikin*. To her I chiefly owe my 30 preservation in that country: we never parted while I was there; I called her my *Glumdalclitch*, or little nurse: and I should be guilty of great ingratitude, if I omitted this honourable mention of her care and affection towards me, which I heartily wish it lay in my power to requite as she deserves, instead of being the innocent but unhappy instrument of her disgrace, as I have too much reason to fear.

It now began to be known and talked of in the neighbourhood, that my master had found a strange 40 animal in the field, about the bigness of a *splacknuck*, but exactly shaped in every part like a human creature; which it likewise imitated in all its actions; seemed to speak in a little language of its own, had already learned several words of theirs, went erect upon two legs, was tame and gentle, would come when it was called, do whatever it was bid, had the finest limbs in the world, and a complexion fairer than a nobleman's daughter of three years old. Another farmer

who lived hard by, and was a particular friend of my master, came on a visit on purpose to enquire into the 50 truth of this story. I was immediately produced, and placed upon a table, where I walked as I was commanded, drew my hanger, put it up again, made my reverence to my master's guest, asked him in his own language how he did, and told him he was welcome, just as my little nurse had instructed me. This man who was old and dim-sighted, put on his spectacles to behold me better, at which I could not forbear laughing very heartily, for his eyes appeared like the full moon shining into a chamber at two windows. Our 60 people, who discovered the cause of my mirth, bore me company in laughing, at which the old fellow was fool enough to be angry and out of countenance. He had the character of a great miser, and to my misfortune he well deserved it, by the cursed advice he gave my master to show me as a sight upon a market-day in the next town, which was half an hour's riding, about two and twenty miles from our house. I guessed there was some mischief contriving, when I observed my master and his friend whispering long together, 70 sometimes pointing at me; and my fears made me fancy that I overheard and understood some of their words. But the next morning Glumdalclitch, my little nurse, told me the whole matter, which she had cunningly picked out from her mother. The poor girl laid me on her bosom, and fell a weeping with shame and grief. She apprehended some mischief would happen to me from rude vulgar folks, who might squeeze me to death, or break one of my limbs by taking me in their hands. She had also observed how modest I was 80 in my nature, how nicely I regarded my honour, and what an indignity I should conceive it to be exposed for money as a public spectacle to the meanest of the people. She said, her papa and mamma had promised that Grildrig should be hers, but now she found they meant to serve her as they did last year, when they pretended to give her a lamb, and yet, as soon as it was fat, sold it to a butcher. For my own part, I may truly affirm that I was less concerned than my nurse. I had a strong hope, which never left me, that I should 90 one day recover my liberty; and as to the ignominy of being carried about for a monster, I considered myself to be a perfect stranger in the country, and that such a misfortune could never be charged upon me as a reproach, if ever I should return to England; since the King of Great Britain himself, in my condition, must have undergone the same distress.

My master, pursuant to the advice of his friend, carried me in a box the next market-day to the neighbouring town, and took along with him his little daugh- 100 ter, my nurse, upon a pillion behind him. The box was close on every side, with a little door for me to go in and out, and a few gimlet-holes to let in air. The girl had been so careful to put the quilt of her baby's bed into it, for me to lie down on. However, I was terribly shaken and discomposed in this journey, though it were but of half an hour. For the horse went about forty foot at every step, and trotted so high, that the agitation was equal to the rising and falling of a ship in a great storm, but much more frequent. Our journey was somewhat further than from London to St. Albans. My master alighted at an inn which he used to frequent; and after consulting a while with the innkeeper, and making some necessary preparations, he hired the *Grultrud*, or crier, to give notice through the town of a strange creature to be seen at the Sign of the Green Eagle, not so big as a *splacknuck* (an animal in that country very finely shaped, about six foot long), and in every part of the body resembling an human creature, could speak several words, and perform an hundred diverting tricks.

I was placed upon a table in the largest room of the inn, which might be near three hundred foot square. My little nurse stood on a low stool close to the table, to take care of me, and direct what I should do. My master, to avoid a crowd, would suffer only thirty people at a time to see me. I walked about on the table as the girl commanded: she asked me questions as far as she knew my understanding of the language reached, and I answered them as loud as I could. I turned about several times to the company, paid my humble respects, said they were welcome, and used some other speeches I had been taught. I took up a thimble filled with liquor, which Glumdalclitch had given me for a cup, and drank their health. I drew out my hanger, and flourished with it after the manner of fencers in England. My nurse gave me part of a straw, which I exercised as a pike, having learned the art in my youth. I was that day shown to twelve sets of company, and as often forced to go over again with the same fopperies, till I was half dead with weariness and vexation. For those who had seen me made such wonderful reports, that the people were ready to break down the doors to come in. My master for his own interest would not suffer any one to touch me except my nurse; and, to prevent danger, benches were set round the table at such a distance as put me out of every body's reach. However, an unlucky school-boy aimed a hazel nut directly at my head, which very narrowly missed me; otherwise, it came with so much violence, that it would have infallibly knocked out my brains, for it was almost as large as a small pumpion: but I had the satisfaction to see the young rogue well beaten, and turned out of the room.

My master gave public notice, that he would show me again the next market-day, and in the meantime he prepared a more convenient vehicle for me, which he had reason enough to do; for I was so tired with my first journey, and with entertaining company for eight hours together, that I could hardly stand upon my legs, or speak a word. It was at least three days

Gulliver on display on market day in Brobdingnag. Reproduced by permission of The Bettmann Archive.

before I recovered my strength; and that I might have no rest at home, all the neighbouring gentlemen from an hundred miles round, hearing of my fame, came to see me at my master's own house. There could not be fewer than thirty persons with their wives and children (for the country is very populous); and my master demanded the rate of a full room whenever he showed me at home, although it were only to a single family; so that for some time I had but little ease every day of the week (except Wednesday, which is their Sabbath) although I were not carried to the town.

My master finding how profitable I was likely to be, resolved to carry me to the most considerable cities of the kingdom. Having therefore provided himself with all things necessary for a long journey, and settled his affairs at home, he took leave of his wife, and upon the 17th of August, 1703, about two months after my arrival, we set out for the metropolis, situated near the middle of that empire, and about three thousand miles distance from our house. My master made his daughter Glumdalclitch ride behind him. She carried me on her lap in a box tied about her waist. The girl had lined it on all sides with the softest cloth she could get, well quilted underneath, furnished it with her baby's bed, provided me with linen and other necessities, and made everything as convenient as she could. We had no other company but a boy of the house, who rode after us with the luggage.

My master's design was to show me in all the towns by the way, and to step out of the road for fifty or an hundred miles, to any village or person of quality's house where he might expect custom. We made easy journeys of not above seven or eight score miles a day: for Glumdalclitch, on purpose to spare me, complained she was tired with the trotting of the horse. She often took me out of my box, at my own desire, to give me air, and show me the country, but always held me fast by a leading-string. We passed over five or six rivers many degrees broader and deeper than the Niles or the Ganges; and there was hardly a rivulet so small as the Thames at London-Bridge. We were ten weeks in our journey, and I was shown in eighteen large towns besides many villages and private families.

On the 26th day of October, we arrived at the metropolis, called in their language Lorbrulgrud, or Pride of the Universe. My master took a lodging in the principal street of the city, not far from the royal palace, and put out bills in the usual form, containing an exact description of my person and parts. He hired a large room between three and four hundred foot wide. He provided a table sixty foot in diameter, upon which I was to act my part, and pallisadoed it round three foot from the edge, and as many high, to prevent my falling over. I was shown ten times a day to the wonder and satisfaction of all people. I could now speak the language tolerably well, and perfectly understood every word that was spoken to me. Besides, I had learnt their alphabet, and could make a shift to explain a sentence here and there; for Glumdalclitch had been my instructor while we were at home, and at leisure hours during our journey. She carried a little book in her pocket, not much larger than a Sanson's Atlas; it was a common treatise for the use of young girls, giving a short account of their religion: out of this she taught me my letters, and interpreted the words.

CHAPTER III

The Author sent for to Court. The Queen buys him of his master the farmer, and presents him to the King. He disputes with his Majesty's great scholars. An apartment at Court provided for the Author. He is in high favour with the Queen. He stands up for the honour of his own country. His quarrels with the Queen's dwarf.

The frequent labours I underwent every day made in a few weeks a very considerable change in my health: the more my master got by me, the more insatiable he grew. I had quite lost my stomach, and was almost reduced to a skeleton. The farmer observed it, and concluding I soon must die, resolved to make as good a hand of me as he could. While he was thus reasoning and resolving with himself, a *Slardral*, or Gentleman Usher, came from court, commanding my master to carry me immediately thither for the diversion of the Queen and her ladies. Some of the latter had already been to see me, and reported strange things of my beauty, behaviour, and good sense. Her Majesty and those who attended her were beyond measure delighted with my demeanour. I fell on my knees, and begged the honour of kissing her Imperial foot; but this gracious princess held out her little finger towards me (after I was set on a table), which I embraced in both my arms, and put the tip of it, with the utmost respect, to my lip. She made me some general questions about my country and my travels, which I answered as distinctly and in as few words as I could. She asked whether I would be content to live at court. I bowed down to the board of the table, and humbly answered, that I was my master's slave, but if I were at my own disposal, I should be proud to devote my life to her Majesty's service. She then asked my master whether he were willing to sell me at a good price. He, who apprehended I could not live a month, was ready enough to part with me, and demanded a thousand pieces of gold, which were ordered him on the spot, each piece being about the bigness of eight hundred moidores; but, allowing for the proportion of all things between that country and Europe, and the high price of gold among them, was hardly so great a sum as a thousand guineas would be in England. I then said to the Queen, since I was now her Majesty's most humble creature and vassal, I must beg the favour, that Glumdalclitch, who had always tended me with so much care and kindness, and understood to do it so well, might be admitted into her service, and continue to be my nurse and instructor. Her Majesty agreed to my petition, and easily got the farmer's consent, who was glad enough to have his daughter preferred at court: and the poor girl herself was not able to hide her joy. My late master withdrew, bidding me farewell, and saying he had left me in a good service; to which I replied not a word, only making him a slight bow.

The Queen observed my coldness, and when the farmer was gone out of the apartment, asked me the reason. I made bold to tell her Majesty that I owed no other obligation to my late master, than his not dashing out the brains of a poor harmless creature found by chance in his field; which obligation was amply recompensed by the gain he had made in showing me through half the kingdom, and the price he had now sold me for. That the life I had since led, was laborious enough to kill an animal of ten times my strength. That my health was much impaired by the continual drudgery of entertaining the rabble every hour of the day, and that if my master had not thought my life in danger, her Majesty perhaps would not have got so cheap a bargain. But as I was out of all fear of being ill treated under the protection of so great and good an Empress, the Ornament of Nature, the Darling of the World, the Delight of her Subjects, the Phoenix of the Creation; so I hoped my late master's apprehensions would appear to be groundless, for I already found my spirits to revive by the influence of her most august presence.

This was the sum of my speech, delivered with great improprieties and hesitation; the latter part was altogether framed in the style peculiar to that people, whereof I learned some phrases from Glumdalclitch, while she was carrying me to court.

The Queen giving great allowance for my defectiveness in speaking, was however surprised at so much wit and good sense in so diminutive an animal. She took me in her own hand, and carried me to the King, who was then retired to his cabinet. His Majesty, a prince of much gravity, and austere countenance, not well observing my shape at first view, asked the Queen after a cold manner, how long it was since she grew fond of a *splacknuck*, for such it seems he took me to be, as I lay upon my breast in her Majesty's right hand. But this princess, who hath an infinite deal of wit and humour, set me gently on my feet upon the scrutore,

and commanded me to give his Majesty an account of myself, which I did in a very few words; and Glumdalclitch, who attended at the cabinet door, and could not endure I should be out of her sight, being admitted, confirmed all that had passed from my arrival at her father's house.

The King, although he be as learned a person as any in his dominions, and had been educated in the study of philosophy, and particularly mathematics; yet when he observed my shape exactly, and saw me walk erect, before I began to speak, conceived I might be a piece of clock-work (which is in that country arrived to a very great perfection), contrived by some ingenious artist. But when he heard my voice, and found what I delivered to be regular and rational, he could not conceal his astonishment. He was by no means satisfied with the relation I gave him of the manner I came into his kingdom, but thought it a story concerted between Glumdalclitch and her father, who had taught me a set of words to make me sell at a higher price. Upon this imagination he put several other questions to me, and still received rational answers, no otherwise defective than by a foreign accent, and an imperfect knowledge in the language, with some rustic phrases which I had learned at the farmer's house, and did not suit the polite style of a court.

His Majesty sent for three great scholars who were then in their weekly waiting, according to the custom in that country. These gentlemen, after they had a while examined my shape with much nicety, were of different opinions concerning me. They all agreed that I could not be produced according to the regular laws of nature, because I was not framed with a capacity of preserving my life, either by swiftness, or climbing of trees, or digging holes in the earth. They observed by my teeth, which they viewed with great exactness, that I was a carnivorous animal; yet most quadrupeds being an over-match for me, and field mice, with some others, too nimble, they could not imagine how I should be able to support myself, unless I fed upon snails and other insects, which they offered, by many learned arguments, to evince that I could not possibly do. One of these virtuosi seemed to think that I might be an embryo, or abortive birth. But this opinion was rejected by the other two, who observed my limbs to be perfect and finished, and that I had lived several years, as it was manifest from my beard, the stumps whereof they plainly discovered through a magnifying-glass. They would not allow me to be a dwarf, because my littleness was beyond all degrees of comparison; for the Queen's favourite dwarf, the smallest ever known in that kingdom, was near thirty foot high. After much debate, they concluded unanimously that I was only *relplum scalcath*, which is interpreted literally, *lusus naturae*; a determination exactly agreeable to the modern philosophy of Europe, whose professors, disdaining the old evasion of *occult causes*, whereby the followers of Aristotle endeavour in vain to disguise their ignorance, have invented this wonderful solution of all difficulties, to the unspeakable advancement of human knowledge.

After this decisive conclusion, I entreated to be heard a word or two. I applied myself to the King, and assured his Majesty, that I came from a country which abounded with several millions of both sexes, and of my own stature; where the animals, trees, and houses were all in proportion, and where by consequence I might be as able to defend myself, and to find sustenance, as any of his Majesty's subjects could do here; which I took for a full answer to those gentlemen's arguments. To this they only replied with a smile of contempt, saying, that the farmer had instructed me very well in my lesson. The King, who had a much better understanding, dismissing his learned men, sent for the farmer, who by good fortune was not yet gone out of town. Having therefore first examined him privately, and then confronted him with me and the young girl, his Majesty began to think that what we told him might possibly be true. He desired the Queen to order that a particular care should be taken of me, and was of opinion that Glumdalclitch should still continue in her office of tending me, because he observed we had a great affection for each other. A convenient apartment was provided for her at court: she had a sort of governess appointed to take care of her education, a maid to dress her, and two other servants for menial offices; but the care of me was wholly appropriated to herself. The Queen commanded her own cabinet-maker to contrive a box that might serve me for a bed-chamber, after the model that Glumdalclitch and I should agree upon. This man was a most ingenious artist, and according to my directions, in three weeks finished for me a wooden chamber of sixteen foot square, and twelve high, with sash-windows, a door, and two closets, like a London bed-chamber. The board that made the ceiling was to be lifted up and down by two hinges, to put in a bed ready furnished by her Majesty's upholsterer, which Glumdalclitch took out every day to air, made it with her own hands, and letting it down at night, locked up the roof over me. A nice workman, who was famous for little curiosities, undertook to make me two chairs, with backs and frames, of a substance not unlike ivory, and two tables, with a cabinet to put my things in. The room was quilted on all sides, as well as the floor and the ceiling, to prevent any accident from the carelessness of those who carried me, and to break the force of a jolt when I went in a coach. I desired a lock for my door, to prevent rats and mice from coming in: the smith, after several attempts, made the smallest that ever was seen among them, for I have known a larger at the gate of a gentleman's house in England. I made a shift to keep the key in a pocket of my own, fearing Glumdalclitch might lose it. The Queen likewise ordered the thinnest silks that could be gotten, to make me clothes, not much thicker than an English blanket, very cumbersome till I was accustomed to them. They were after the fashion of the kingdom, partly resembling the Persian, and partly the Chinese, and are a very grave and decent habit.

The Queen became so fond of my company, that she could not dine without me. I had a table placed upon the same at which her Majesty eat, just at her left elbow, and a chair to sit on. Glumdalclitch stood upon a stool on the floor, near my table, to assist and take care of me. I had an entire set of silver dishes and plates, and other necessaries, which, in proportion to those of the Queen, were not much bigger than what I have seen of the same kind in a London toy-shop, for the furniture of a baby-house: these my little nurse kept in her pocket, in a silver box, and gave me at meals as I wanted them, always cleaning them herself. No person dined with the Queen but the two Princesses Royal, the elder sixteen years old, and the younger at that time thirteen and a month. Her Majesty used to put a bit of meat upon one of my dishes, out of which I carved for myself, and her diversion was to see me eat in miniature. For the Queen (who had indeed but a weak stomach) took up at one mouthful, as much as a dozen English farmers could eat at a meal, which to me was for some time a very nauseous sight. She would craunch the wing of a lark, bones and all, between her teeth, although it were nine times as large as that of a full-grown turkey; and put a bit of bread into her mouth, as big as two twelve-penny loaves. She drank out of a golden cup, above a hogshead at a draught. Her knives were twice as long as a scythe set straight upon the handle. The spoons, forks, and other instruments were all in the same proportion. I remember when Glumdalclitch carried me out of curiosity to see some of the tables at court, where ten or a dozen of these enormous knives and forks were lifted up together, I thought I had never till then beheld so terrible a sight.

It is the custom that every Wednesday (which, as I have before observed, was their Sabbath) the King and Queen, with the royal issue of both sexes, dine together in the apartment of his Majesty, to whom I was now become a great favourite; and at these times my little chair and table were placed at his left hand, before one of the salt-cellars. This prince took a pleasure in conversing with me, enquiring into the manners, religion, laws, government, and learning of Europe; wherein I gave him the best account I was able. His apprehension was so clear, and his judgment so exact, that he made very wise reflections and observations upon all I said. But, I confess, that after I had been a little too copious in talking of my own beloved country, of our trade, and wars by sea and land, of our schisms in religion, and parties in the state; the prejudices of his education prevailed so far, that he could not forbear taking me up in his right hand, and stroking me gently with the other, after an hearty fit of laughing, asked me, whether I were a Whig or a Tory. Then turning to his first minister, who waited behind him with a white staff, near as tall as the main-mast of the *Royal Sovereign*, he observed how contemptible a thing was human grandeur, which could be mimicked by such diminutive insects as I: and yet, said he, I dare engage, these creatures have their titles and distinctions of honour, they contrive little nests and burrows, that they call houses and cities; they make a figure in dress and equipage; they love, they fight, they dispute, they cheat, they betray. And thus he continued on, while my colour came and went several times, with indignation to hear our noble country, the mistress of arts and arms, the scourge of France, the arbitress of Europe, the seat of virtue, piety, honour, and truth, the pride and envy of the world, so contemptuously treated.

But as I was not in a condition to resent injuries, so, upon mature thoughts, I began to doubt whether I were injured or no. For, after having been accustomed several months to the sight and converse of this people, and observed every object upon which I cast my eyes, to be of proportionable magnitude, the horror I had first conceived from their bulk and aspect was so far worn off, that if I had then beheld a company of English lords and ladies in their finery and birth-day clothes, acting their several parts in the most courtly manner, of strutting, and bowing, and prating; to say the truth, I should have been strongly tempted to laugh as much at them as the King and his grandees did at me. Neither indeed could I forbear smiling at myself, when the Queen used to place me upon her hand towards a looking-glass, by which both our persons appeared before me in full view together; and there could be nothing more ridiculous than the comparison; so that I really began to imagine myself dwindled many degrees below my usual size.

Nothing angered and mortified me so much as the Queen's dwarf, who being of the lowest stature that was ever in that country (for I verily think he was not full thirty foot high) became insolent at seeing a creature so much beneath him, that he would always affect to swagger and look big as he passed by me in the Queen's antechamber, while I was standing on some table talking with the lords or ladies of the court, and he seldom failed of a smart word or two upon my littleness; against which I could only revenge myself by calling him brother, challenging him to wrestle, and such repartees as are usual in the mouths of court pages. One day at dinner this malicious little cub was so nettled with something I had said to him, that rais-

ing himself upon the frame of her Majesty's chair, he took me up by the middle, as I was sitting down, not thinking any harm, and let me drop in a large silver bowl of cream, and then ran away as fast as he could. I fell over head and ears, and if I had not been a good swimmer, it might have gone very hard with me; for Glumdalclitch in that instant happened to be at the other end of the room, and the Queen was in such a fright that she wanted presence of mind to assist me. But my little nurse ran to my relief, and took me out, after I had swallowed above a quart of cream. I was put to bed; however, I received no other damage than the loss of a suit of clothes, which was utterly spoiled. The dwarf was soundly whipped, and as a farther punishment, forced to drink up the bowl of cream, into which he had thrown me: neither was he ever restored to favour: for, soon after the Queen bestowed him on a lady of high quality, so that I saw him no more, to my very great satisfaction; for I could not tell to what extremity such a malicious urchin might have carried his resentment.

He had before served me a scurvy trick, which set the Queen a laughing, although at the same time she was heartily vexed, and would have immediately cashiered him, if I had not been so generous as to intercede. Her Majesty had taken a marrow-bone upon her plate, and after knocking out the marrow, placed the bone again in the dish erect as it stood before; the dwarf watching his opportunity, while Glumdalclitch was gone to the sideboard, mounted the stool she stood on to take care of me at meals, took me up in both hands, and squeezing my legs together, wedged them into the marrow bone above my waist, where I stuck for some time, and made a very ridiculous figure. I believe it was near a minute before any one knew what was become of me, for I thought it below me to cry out. But, as princes seldom get their meat hot, my legs were not scalded, only my stockings and breeches in a sad condition. The dwarf, at my entreaty, had no other punishment than a sound whipping.

I was frequently rallied by the Queen upon account of my fearfulness, and she used to ask me whether the people of my country were as great cowards as myself. The occasion was this: the kingdom is much pestered with flies in summer; and these odious insects, each of them as big as a Dunstable lark, hardly gave me any rest while I sat at dinner, with their continual humming and buzzing about my ears. They would sometimes alight upon my victuals, and leave their loathsome excrement or spawn behind, which to me was very visible, though not to the natives of that country, whose large optics were not so acute as mine in viewing smaller objects. Sometimes they would fix upon my nose or forehead, where they stung me to the quick, smelling very offensively, and I could easily trace that viscous matter, which our naturalists tell us

enables those creatures to walk with their feet upwards upon a ceiling. I had much ado to defend myself against these detestable animals, and could not forbear starting when they came on my face. It was the common practice of the dwarf to catch a number of these insects in his hand, as schoolboys do among us, and let them out suddenly under my nose, on purpose to frighten me, and divert the Queen. My remedy was to cut them in pieces with my knife as they flew in the air, wherein
10 my dexterity was much admired.

I remember one morning when Glumdalclitch had set me in my box upon a window, as she usually did in fair days to give me air (for I durst not venture to let the box be hung on a nail out the window, as we do with cages in England), after I had lifted up one of my sashes, and sat down at my table to eat a piece of sweet cake for my breakfast, above twenty wasps, allured by the smell, came flying into the room, humming louder than the drones of as many bagpipes.
20 Some of them seized my cake, and carried it piecemeal away, others flew about my head and face, confounding me with the noise, and putting me in the utmost terror of their stings. However I had the courage to rise and draw my hanger, and attack them in the air. I dispatched four of them, but the rest got away, and I presently shut my window. These insects were as large as partridges: I took out their stings, found them an inch and a half long, and as sharp as needles. I carefully preserved them all, and having since shown
30 them with some other curiosities in several parts of Europe; upon my return to England I gave three of them to Gresham College, and kept the fourth for myself.

CHAPTER IV

The country described. A proposal for correcting modern maps. The King's palace, and some account of the metropolis. The Author's way of travelling. The chief temple described.

I now intend to give the reader a short description of this country, as far as I travelled in it, which was not above two thousand miles round Lorbrulgrud the metropolis. For the Queen, whom I always attended, never went further when she accompanied the King in his progresses, and there stayed till his Majesty
40 returned from viewing his frontiers. The whole extent of this prince's dominions reacheth about six thousand miles in length, and from three to five in breadth. From whence I cannot but conclude that our geographers of Europe are in a great error, by supposing nothing but sea between Japan and California; for it was ever my opinion, that there must be a balance of earth to counterpoise the great continent of Tartary; and therefore they ought to correct their maps and

charts, by joining this vast tract of land to the northwest parts of America, wherein I shall be ready to lend 50 them my assistance.

The kingdom is a peninsula, terminated to the northeast by a ridge of mountains thirty miles high, which are altogether impassable by reason of the volcanoes upon the tops. Neither do the most learned know what sort of mortals inhabit beyond those mountains, or whether they be inhabited at all. On the three other sides it is bounded by the ocean. There is not one seaport in the whole kingdom, and those parts of the coasts into which the rivers issue are so full of pointed 60 rocks, and the sea generally so rough, that there is no venturing with the smallest of their boats, so that these people are wholly excluded from any commerce with the rest of the world. But the large rivers are full of vessels, and abound with excellent fish, for they seldom get any from the sea, because the sea-fish are of the same size with those in Europe, and consequently not worth catching; whereby it is manifest, that nature, in the production of plants and animals of so extraordinary a bulk, is wholly confined to this continent, of 70 which I leave the reasons to be determined by philosophers. However, now and then they take a whale that happens to be dashed against the rocks, which the common people feed on heartily. These whales I have known so large that a man could hardly carry one upon his shoulders; and sometimes for curiosity they are brought in hampers to Lorbrulgrud: I saw one of them in a dish at the King's table, which passed for a rarity, but I did not observe he was fond of it; for I think indeed the bigness disgusted him, although 80 I have seen one somewhat larger in Greenland.

The country is well inhabited, for it contains fifty-one cities, near an hundred walled towns, and a great number of villages. To satisfy my curious reader, it may be sufficient to describe Lorbrulgrud. This city stands upon almost two equal parts on each side the river that passes through. It contains above eighty thousand houses, and about six hundred thousand inhabitants. It is in length three *glonglungs* (which make about fifty-four English miles) and two and a half 90 in breadth, as I measured it myself in the royal map made by the King's order, which was laid on the ground on purpose for me, and extended an hundred feet: I paced the diameter and circumference several times bare-foot, and computing by the scale, measured it pretty exactly.

The King's palace is no regular edifice, but an heap of buildings about seven miles round: the chief rooms are generally two hundred and forty foot high, and broad and long in proportion. A coach was allowed to 100 Glumdalclitch and me, wherein her governess frequently took her out to see the town, or go among the shops; and I was always of the party, carried in my box; although the girl at my own desire would often take me out, and hold me in her hand, that I might more conveniently view the houses and the people, as we passed along the streets. I reckoned our coach to be about a square of Westminster-Hall, but not altogether so high; however, I cannot be very 110 exact. One day the governess ordered our coachman to stop at several shops, where the beggars, watching their opportunity, crowded to the sides of the coach, and gave me the most horrible spectacles that ever an European eye beheld. There was a woman with a cancer in her breast, swelled to a monstrous size, full of holes, in two or three of which I could have easily crept, and covered my whole body. There was a fellow with a wen in his neck, larger than five wool-packs, and another with a couple of wooden legs, each about 120 twenty foot high. But the most hateful sight of all was the lice crawling on their clothes. I could see distinctly the limbs of these vermin with my naked eye, much better than those of an European louse through a microscope, and their snouts with which they rooted like swine. They were the first I had ever beheld, and I should have been curious enough to dissect one of them, if I had proper instruments (which I unluckily left behind me in the ship), although indeed the sight was so nauseous, that it perfectly turned my stomach.

130   Besides the large box in which I was usually carried, the Queen ordered a smaller one to be made for me, of about twelve foot square, and ten high, for the convenience of travelling, because the other was somewhat too large for Glumdalclitch's lap, and cumbersome in the coach; it was made by the same artist, whom I directed in the whole contrivance. This travelling closet was an exact square with a window in the middle of three of the squares, and each window was latticed with iron wire on the outside, to prevent accidents 140 in long journeys. On the fourth side, which had no window, two strong staples were fixed, through which the person that carried me, when I had a mind to be on horseback, put in a leathern belt, and buckled it about his waist. This was always the office of some grave trusty servant in whom I could confide, whether I attended the King and Queen in their progresses, or were disposed to see the gardens, or pay a visit to some great lady or minister of state in the court, when Glumdalclitch happened to be out of order: for I soon 150 began to be known and esteemed among the greatest officers, I suppose more upon account of their Majesties' favour, than any merit of my own. In journeys, when I was weary of the coach, a servant on horseback would buckle on my box, and place it on a cushion before him; and there I had a full prospect of the country on three sides from my three windows. I had in this closet a field-bed and a hammock hung from the ceiling, two chairs and a table, neatly screwed to the floor, to prevent being tossed about by the agitation of the horse or the coach. And having been long

used to sea-voyages, those motions, although sometimes very violent, did not much discompose me.

Whenever I had a mind to see the town, it was always in my travelling-closet, which Glumdalclitch held in her lap in a kind of open sedan, after the fashion of the country, borne by four men, and attended by two others in the Queen's livery. The people, who had often heard of me, were very curious to crowd about the sedan, and the girl was complaisant enough to make the bearers stop, and to take me in her 170 hand that I might be more conveniently seen.

I was very desirous to see the chief temple, and particularly the tower belonging to it, which is reckoned the highest in the kingdom. Accordingly one day my nurse carried me thither, but I may truly say I came back disappointed; for the height is not above three thousand foot, reckoning from the ground to the highest pinnacle top; which allowing for the difference between the size of those people, and us in Europe, is no great matter for admiration, nor at all equal in 180 proportion (if I rightly remember) to Salisbury steeple. But, not to detract from a nation to which during my life I shall acknowledge myself extremely obliged, it must be allowed, that whatever this famous tower wants in height is amply made up in beauty and strength. For the walls are near an hundred foot thick, built of hewn stone, whereof each is about forty foot square, and adorned on all sides with statues of Gods and Emperors cut in marble larger than the life, placed in their several niches. I measured a little finger which 190 had fallen down from one of these statues, and lay unperceived among some rubbish, and found it exactly four foot and an inch in length. Glumdalclitch wrapped it up in a handkerchief, and carried it home in her pocket to keep among other trinkets, of which the girl was very fond, as children at her age usually are.

The King's kitchen is indeed a noble building, vaulted at top, and about six hundred foot high. The great oven is not so wide by ten paces as the cupola at St. Paul's: for I measured the latter on purpose after my 200 return. But if I should describe the kitchen-grate, the prodigious pots and kettles, the joints of meat turning on the spits, with many other particulars, perhaps I should be hardly believed; at least a severe critic would be apt to think I enlarged a little, as travellers are often suspected to do. To avoid which censure, I fear I have run too much into the other extreme; and that if this treatise should happen to be translated into the language of Brobdingnag (which is the general name of that kingdom) and transmitted thither, the 210 King and his people would have reason to complain that I had done them an injury by a false and diminutive representation.

His Majesty seldom keeps above six hundred horses in his stables: they are generally from fifty-four to sixty foot high. But when he goes abroad on solemn days, he is attended for state by a militia guard of five hundred horse, which indeed I thought was the most splendid sight that could be ever beheld, till I saw part of his army in battalia, whereof I shall find another occasion to speak.

CHAPTER V

Several adventures that happened to the Author. The execution of a criminal. The Author shows his skill in navigation.

I should have lived happy enough in that country, if my littleness had not exposed me to several ridiculous and troublesome accidents: some of which I shall venture to relate. Glumdalclitch often carried me into 10 the gardens of the court in my smaller box, and would sometimes take me out of it and hold me in her hand, or set me down to walk. I remember, before the dwarf left the Queen, he followed us one day into those gardens, and my nurse having set me down, he and I being close together, near some dwarf apple-trees, I must needs show my wit by a silly allusion between him and the trees, which happens to hold in their language as it doth in ours. Whereupon, the malicious rogue watching his opportunity, when I was 20 walking under one of them, shook it directly over my head, by which a dozen apples, each of them near as large as a Bristol barrel, came tumbling about my ears; one of them hit me on the back as I chanced to stoop, and knocked me down flat on my face, but I received no other hurt, and the dwarf was pardoned at my desire, because I had given the provocation.

Another day Glumdalclitch left me on a smooth grassplot to divert myself while she walked at some distance with her governess. In the meantime there 30 suddenly fell such a violent shower of hail, that I was immediately by the force of it struck to the ground: and when I was down, the hailstones gave me such cruel bangs all over the body, as if I had been pelted with tennis-balls; however I made a shift to creep on all four, and shelter myself by lying flat on my face on the lee-side of a border of lemon thyme, but so bruised from head to foot that I could not go abroad in ten days. Neither is this at all to be wondered at, because nature in that country observing the same 40 proportion through all her operations, a hailstone is near eighteen hundred times as large as one in Europe, which I can assert upon experience, having been so curious to weigh and measure them.

But a more dangerous accident happened to me in the same garden, when my little nurse believing she had put me in a secure place, which I often entreated her to do, that I might enjoy my own thoughts, and having left my box at home to avoid the trouble of carrying it, went to another part of the garden with 50 her governess and some ladies of her acquaintance.

While she was absent, and out of hearing, a small white spaniel belonging to one of the chief gardeners, having got by accident into the garden, happened to range near the place where I lay. The dog following the scent, came directly up, and taking me in his mouth, ran straight to his master, wagging his tail, and set me gently on the ground. By good fortune he had been so well taught, that I was carried between his teeth without the least hurt, or even tearing my clothes. But the poor gardener, who knew me well, and 60 had a great kindness for me, was in a terrible fright. He gently took me up in both his hands, and asked me how I did; but I was so amazed and out of breath, that I could not speak a word. In a few minutes I came to myself, and he carried me safe to my little nurse, who by this time had returned to the place where she left me, and was in cruel agonies when I did not appear, nor answer when she called: she severely reprimanded the gardener on account of his dog. But the thing was hushed up, and never known at court; for 70 the girl was afraid of the Queen's anger, and truly as to myself, I thought it would not be for my reputation that such a story should go about.

This accident absolutely determined Glumdalclitch never to trust me abroad for the future out of her sight. I had been long afraid of this resolution, and therefore concealed from her some little unlucky adventures that happened in those times when I was left by myself. Once a kite hovering over the garden made a stoop at me, and if I had not resolutely drawn my 80 hanger, and run under a thick espalier, he would have certainly carried me away in his talons. Another time walking to the top of a fresh mole-hill, I fell to my neck in the hole through which that animal had cast up the earth, and coined some lie, not worth remembering, to excuse myself for spoiling my clothes. I likewise broke my right shin against the shell of a snail, which I happened to stumble over, as I was walking alone, and thinking on poor England.

I cannot tell whether I were more pleased or morti- 90 fied, to observe in those solitary walks, that the smaller birds did not appear to be at all afraid of me, but would hop about within a yard distance, looking for worms, and other food, with as much indifference and security, as if no creature at all were near them. I remember, a thrush had the confidence to snatch out of my hand, with his bill, a piece of cake that Glumdalclitch had just given me for my breakfast. When I attempted to catch any of these birds, they would boldly turn against me, endeavouring to pick my fingers, 100 which I durst not venture within their reach; and then they would hop back unconcerned, to hunt for worms or snails, as they did before. But one day I took a thick cudgel, and threw it with all my strength so luckily at a linnet, that I knocked him down, and seizing him by the neck with both my hands, ran with him in triumph to my nurse. However, the bird, who had only been stunned, recovering himself, gave me so many boxes with his wings on both sides of my head and body, though I held him at arm's length, and was out of the reach of his claws, that I was twenty times thinking to let him go. But I was soon relieved by one of our servants, who wrung off the bird's neck, and I had him next day for dinner, by the Queen's command. This linnet, as near as I can remember, seemed to be somewhat larger than an English swan.

The Maids of Honour often invited Glumdalclitch to their apartments, and desired she would bring me along with her, on purpose to have the pleasure of seeing and touching me. They would often strip me naked from top to toe, and lay me at full length in their bosoms; wherewith I was much disgusted; because, to say the truth, a very offensive smell came from their skins; which I do not mention or intend to the disadvantage of those excellent ladies, for whom I have all manner of respect; but I conceive that my sense was more acute in proportion to my littleness, and that those illustrious persons were no more disagreeable to their lovers, or to each other, than people of the same quality are with us in England. And, after all, I found their natural smell was much more supportable than when they used perfumes, under which I immediately swooned away. I cannot forget that an intimate friend of mine in Lilliput took the freedom in a warm day, when I had used a good deal of exercise, to complain of a strong smell about me, although I am as little faulty that way as most of my sex: but I suppose his faculty of smelling was as nice with regard to me, as mine was to that of this people. Upon this point, I cannot forbear doing justice to the Queen my mistress, and Glumdalclitch my nurse, whose persons were as sweet as those of any lady in England.

That which gave me most uneasiness among these Maids of Honour (when my nurse carried me to visit them) was to see them use me without any manner of ceremony, like a creature who had no sort of consequence. For they would strip themselves to the skin, and put on their smocks in my presence, while I was placed on their toilet directly before their naked bodies, which, I am sure, to me was very far from being a tempting sight, or from giving me any other emotions than those of horror and disgust. Their skins appeared so coarse and uneven, so variously coloured, when I saw them near, with a mole here and there as broad as a trencher, and hairs hanging from it thicker than packthreads, to say nothing further concerning the rest of their persons. Neither did they at all scruple, while I was by, to discharge what they had drunk, to the quantity of at least two hogsheads, in a vessel that held above three tuns. The handsomest among these Maids of Honour, a pleasant frolicsome girl of sixteen, would sometimes set me astride upon one of her nipples, with many other tricks, wherein the reader will excuse me for not being over particular. But I was so much displeased, that I entreated Glumdalclitch to contrive some excuse for not seeing that young lady any more.

One day a young gentleman, who was nephew to my nurse's governess, came and pressed them both to see an execution. It was of a man who had murdered one of that gentleman's intimate acquaintance. Glumdalclitch was prevailed on to be of the company, very much against her inclination, for she was naturally tender-hearted: and as for myself, although I abhorred such kind of spectacles, yet my curiosity tempted me to see something that I thought must be extraordinary. The malefactor was fixed in a chair upon a scaffold erected for the purpose, and his head cut off at a blow with a sword of about forty foot long. The veins and arteries spouted up such a prodigious quantity of blood, and so high in the air, that the great jet d'eau at Versailles was not equal for the time it lasted; and the head, when it fell on the scaffold floor, gave such a bounce, as made me start, although I were at least half an English mile distant.

The Queen, who often used to hear me talk of my sea-voyages, and took all occasions to divert me when I was melancholy, asked me whether I understood how to handle a sail, or an oar, and whether a little exercise of rowing might not be convenient for my health. I answered, that I understood both very well: for although my proper employment had been to be surgeon or doctor to the ship, yet often, upon a pinch, I was forced to work like a common mariner. But I could not see how this could be done in their country, where the smallest wherry was equal to a first-rate man of war among us, and such a boat as I could manage would never live in any of their rivers. Her Majesty said, if I would contrive a boat, her own joiner should make it, and she would provide a place for me to sail in. The fellow was an ingenious workman, and, by my instructions, in ten days finished a pleasure-boat, with all its tackling, able conveniently to hold eight Europeans. When it was finished, the Queen was so delighted, that she ran with it in her lap to the King, who ordered it to be put in a cistern full of water, with me in it, by way of trial; where I could not manage my two sculls, or little oars, for want of room. But the Queen had before contrived another project. She ordered the joiner to make a wooden trough of three hundred foot long, fifty broad, and eight deep; which being well pitched to prevent leaking, was placed on the floor along the wall, in an outer room of the palace. It had a cock near the bottom to let out the water when it began to grow stale, and two servants could easily fill it in half an hour. Here I often used to row for my own diversion, as well as that of the

Queen and her ladies, who thought themselves well entertained with my skill and agility. Sometimes I would put up my sail, and then my business was only to steer, while the ladies gave me a gale with their fans; and when they were weary, some of the pages would blow my sail forward with their breath, while I showed my art by steering starboard or larboard as I pleased. When I had done, Glumdalclitch always carried my boat into her closet, and hung it on a nail 10 to dry.

In this exercise I once met an accident which had like to have cost me my life: for, one of the pages having put my boat into the trough, the governess, who attended Glumdalclitch, very officiously lifted me up to place me in the boat, but I happened to slip through her fingers, and should have infallibly fallen down forty feet upon the floor, if by the luckiest chance in the world, I had not been stopped by a corking-pin that stuck in the good gentlewoman's stom-20 acher; the head of the pin passed between my shirt and the waistband of my breeches, and thus I was held by the middle in the air till Glumdalclitch ran to my relief.

Another time, one of the servants, whose office it was to fill my trough every third day with fresh water, was so careless to let a huge frog (not perceiving it) slip out of his pail. The frog lay concealed till I was put into my boat, but then seeing a resting-place, climbed up, and made it lean so much on one side, that I was forced to balance it with all my weight on 30 the other, to prevent overturning. When the frog was got in, it hopped at once half the length of the boat, and then over my head, backwards and forwards, daubing my face and clothes with its odious slime. The largeness of its features made it appear the most deformed animal that can be conceived. However, I desired Glumdalclitch to let me deal with it alone. I banged it a good while with one of my sculls, and at last forced it to leap out of the boat.

But the greatest danger I ever underwent in that 40 kingdom, was from a monkey, who belonged to one of the clerks of the kitchen. Glumdalclitch had locked me up in her closet, while she went somewhere upon business, or a visit. The weather being very warm, the closet-window was left open, as well as the windows and the door of my bigger box, in which I usually lived, because of its largeness and conveniency. As I sat quietly meditating at my table, I heard something bounce in at the closet-window, and skip about from one side to the other; whereat, although I were 50 much alarmed, yet I ventured to look out, but not stirring from my seat; and then I saw this frolicsome animal, frisking and leaping up and down, till at last he came to my box, which he seemed to view with great pleasure and curiosity, peeping in at the door and every window. I retreated to the farther corner of my room, or box, but the monkey looking in at every side, put me into such a fright, that I wanted presence of mind to conceal myself under the bed, as I might easily have done. After some time spent in peeping, grinning, and chattering, he at last espied me, and reaching one 60 of his paws in at the door, as a cat does when she plays with a mouse, although I often shifted place to avoid him, he at length seized the lappet of my coat (which being made of that country silk, was very thick and strong) and dragged me out. He took me up in his right fore-foot, and held me as a nurse does a child she is going to suckle, just as I have seen the same sort of creature do with a kitten in Europe: and when I offered to struggle, he squeezed me so hard, that I thought it more prudent to submit. I have good rea- 70 son to believe that he took me for a young one of his own species, by his often stroking my face very gently with his other paw. In these diversions he was interrupted by a noise at the closet door, as if somebody were opening it; whereupon he suddenly leaped up to the window, at which he had come in, and thence upon the leads and gutters, walking upon three legs, and holding me in the fourth, till he clambered up to a roof that was next to ours. I heard Glumdalclitch give a shriek at the moment he was carrying me out. 80 The poor girl was almost distracted: that quarter of the palace was all in an uproar; the servants ran for ladders; the monkey was seen by hundreds in the court, sitting upon the ridge of a building, holding me like a baby in one of his forepaws, and feeding me with the other, by cramming into my mouth some victuals he had squeezed out of the bag on one side of his chaps, and patting me when I would not eat; whereat many of the rabble below could not forbear laughing; neither do I think they justly ought to be 90 blamed, for without question the sight was ridiculous enough to every body but myself. Some of the people threw up stones, hoping to drive the monkey down; but this was strictly forbidden, or else very probably my brains had been dashed out.

The ladders were now applied, and mounted by several men, which the monkey observing, and finding himself almost encompassed; not being able to make speed enough with his three legs, let me drop on a ridge tile, and made his escape. Here I sat for some 100 time, three hundred yards from the ground, expecting every moment to be blown down by the wind, or to fall by my own giddiness, and come tumbling over and over from the ridge to the eaves; but an honest lad, one of my nurse's footmen, climbed up, and putting me into his breeches pocket, brought me down safe.

I was almost choked with the filthy stuff the monkey had crammed down my throat: but my dear little nurse picked it out of my mouth with a small needle, and then I fell a vomiting, which gave me great relief. 110 Yet I was so weak and bruised in the sides with the squeezes given me by this odious animal, that I was forced to keep my bed a fortnight. The King, Queen, and all the court, sent every day to enquire after my health, and her Majesty made me several visits during my sickness. The monkey was killed, and an order made that no such animal should be kept about the palace.

When I attended the King after my recovery, to return him thanks for his favours, he was pleased to rally me a good deal upon this adventure. He asked me what my thoughts and speculations were while I lay in the monkey's paw; how I liked the victuals he gave me; his manner of feeding; and whether the fresh air on the roof had sharpened my stomach. He desired to know what I would have done upon such an occasion in my own country. I told his Majesty, that in Europe we had no monkeys, except such as were brought for curiosities from other places, and so small, that I could deal with a dozen of them together, if they presumed to attack me. And as for that monstrous animal with whom I was so lately engaged (it was indeed as large as an elephant), if my fears had suffered me to think so far as to make use of my hanger (looking fiercely and clapping my hand upon the hilt as I spoke), when he poked his paw into my chamber, perhaps I should have given him such a wound, as would have made him glad to withdraw it with more haste than he put it in. This I delivered in a firm tone, like a person who was jealous lest his courage should be called in question. However, my speech produced nothing else besides a loud laughter, which all the respect due to his Majesty from those about him could not make them contain. This made me reflect how vain an attempt it is for a man to endeavour doing himself honour among those who are out of all degree of equality or comparison with him. And yet I have seen the moral of my own behaviour very frequent in England since my return, where a little contemptible varlet, without the least title to birth, person, wit, or common sense, shall presume to look with importance, and put himself upon a foot with the greatest persons of the kingdom.

I was every day furnishing the court with some ridiculous story: and Glumdalclitch, although she loved me to excess, yet was arch enough to inform the Queen, whenever I committed any folly that she thought would be diverting to her Majesty. The girl, who had been out of order, was carried by her governess to take the air about an hour's distance, or thirty miles from town. They alighted out of the coach near a small foot-path in a field, and Glumdalclitch setting down my travelling-box, I went out of it to walk. There was a cow-dung in the path, and I must needs try my activity by attempting to leap over it. I took a run, but unfortunately jumped short, and found myself just in the middle up to my knees. I waded through with some difficulty, and one of the footmen wiped me as clean as he could with his handkerchief; for I was filthily bemired, and my nurse confined me to my box till we returned home; where the Queen was soon informed of what had passed, and the footmen spread it about the court: so that all the mirth, for some days, was at my expense.

CHAPTER VI

Several contrivances of the Author to please the King and Queen. He shows his skill in music. The King enquires into the state of Europe, which the Author relates to him. The King's observations thereon.

I used to attend the King's levee once or twice a week, and had often seen him under the barber's hand, which indeed was at first very terrible to behold: for the razor was almost twice as long as an ordinary scythe. His Majesty, according to the custom of the country, was only shaved twice a week. I once prevailed on the barber to give me some of the suds or lather, out of which I picked forty or fifty of the strongest stumps of hair. I then took a piece of fine wood, and cut it like the back of a comb, making several holes in it at equal distance with as small a needle as I could get from Glumdalclitch. I fixed in the stumps so artificially, scraping and sloping them with my knife toward the points, that I made a very tolerable comb; which was a seasonable supply, my own being so much broken in the teeth, that it was almost useless: neither did I know any artist in that country so nice and exact, as would undertake to make me another.

And this puts me in mind of an amusement wherein I spent many of my leisure hours. I desired the Queen's woman to save for me the combings of her Majesty's hair, whereof in time I got a good quantity, and consulting with my friend the cabinet-maker, who had received general orders to do little jobs for me, I directed him to make two chair-frames, no larger than those I had in my box, and then to bore little holes with a fine awl around those parts where I designed the backs and seats; through these holes I wove the strongest hairs I could pick out, just after the manner of cane-chairs in England. When they were finished, I made a present of them to her Majesty, who kept them in her cabinet, and used to show them for curiosities, as indeed they were the wonder of every one that beheld them. The Queen would have had me sit upon one of these chairs, but I absolutely refused to obey her, protesting I would rather die a thousand deaths than place a dishonourable part of my body on those precious hairs that once adorned her Majesty's head. Of these hairs (as I had always a mechanical genius) I likewise made a neat little purse about five foot long, with her Majesty's name deciphered in gold letters, which I gave to Glumdalclitch, by the Queen's consent. To say the truth, it was more for show than use, being not of strength to bear the weight of the larger coins, and therefore she kept nothing in it but some little toys that girls are fond of.

The King, who delighted in music, had frequent concerts at court, to which I was sometimes carried, and set in my box on a table to hear them: but the noise was so great, that I could hardly distinguish the tunes. I am confident that all the drums and trumpets of a royal army, beating and sounding together just at your ears, could not equal it. My practice was to have my box removed from the places where the performers sat, as far as I could, then to shut the doors and windows of it, and draw the window curtains; after which I found their music not disagreeable.

I had learned in my youth to play a little upon the spinet. Glumdalclitch kept one in her chamber, and a master attended twice a week to teach her: I call it a spinet, because it somewhat resembled that instrument, and was played upon in the same manner. A fancy came into my head that I would entertain the King and Queen with an English tune upon this instrument. But this appeared extremely difficult: for the spinet was near sixty foot long, each key being almost a foot wide, so that, with my arms extended, I could not reach to above five keys, and to press them down required a good smart stroke with my fist, which would be too great a labour, and to no purpose. The method I contrived was this. I prepared two round sticks about the bigness of common cudgels; they were thicker at one end than the other, and I covered the thicker ends with a piece of mouse's skin, that by rapping on them I might neither damage the tops of the keys, nor interrupt the sound. Before the spinet a bench was placed, about four foot below the keys, and I was put upon the bench. I ran sideling upon it that way and this, as fast as I could, banging the proper keys with my two sticks, and made a shift to play a jig, to the great satisfaction of both their Majesties: but it was the most violent exercise I ever underwent, and yet I could not strike above sixteen keys, nor, consequently, play the bass and treble together, as other artists do; which was a great disadvantage to my performance.

The King, who, as I before observed, was a prince of excellent understanding, would frequently order that I should be brought in my box, and set upon the table in his closet. He would then command me to bring one of my chairs out of the box, and sit down within three yards distance upon the top of the cabinet, which brought me almost to a level with his face. In this manner I had several conversations with him. I one day took the freedom to tell his Majesty, that the contempt he discovered towards Europe, and the rest of the world, did not seem answerable to those excellent qualities of the mind he was master of. That reason did not extend itself with the bulk of the body: on the contrary, we observed in our country, that the tallest persons were usually least provided with it. That among other animals, bees and ants had the reputation of more industry, art and sagacity, than many of the larger kinds. And that, as inconsiderable as he took me to be, I hoped I might live to do his Majesty some signal service. The King heard me with attention, and began to conceive a much better opinion of me than he had ever before. He desired I would give him as exact an account of the government of England as I possibly could; because, as fond as princes commonly are of their own customs (for so he conjectured of other monarchs, by my former discourses), he should be glad to hear of any thing that might deserve imitation.

Imagine with thyself, courteous reader, how often I then wished for the tongue of Demosthenes or Cicero, that might have enabled me to celebrate the praise of my own dear native country in a style equal to its merits and felicity.

I began my discourse by informing his Majesty, that our dominions consisted of two islands, which composed three mighty kingdoms under one sovereign, beside our plantations in America. I dwelt long upon the fertility of our soil, and the temperature of our climate. I then spoke at large upon the constitution of an English Parliament, partly made up of an illustrious body called the House of Peers, persons of the noblest blood, and of the most ancient and ample patrimonies. I described that extraordinary care always taken of their education in arts and arms, to qualify them for being counsellors born to the king and kingdom; to have a share in the legislature; to be members of the highest Court of Judicature, from whence there could be no appeal; and to be champions always ready for the defence of their prince and country, by their valour, conduct, and fidelity. That these were the ornament and bulwark of the kingdom, worthy followers of their most renowned ancestors, whose honour had been the reward of their virtue, from which their posterity were never once known to degenerate. To these were joined several holy persons, as part of that assembly, under the title of Bishops, whose peculiar business it is to take care of religion, and of those who instruct the people therein. These were searched and sought out through the whole nation, by the prince and his wisest counsellors, among such of the priesthood as were most deservedly distinguished by the sanctity of their lives, and the depth of their erudition; who were indeed the spiritual fathers of the clergy and the people.

That the other part of the Parliament consisted of an assembly called the House of Commons, who were all principal gentlemen, freely picked and culled out by the people themselves, for their great abilities and love of their country, to represent the wisdom of the whole nation. And these two bodies make up the most august assembly in Europe, to whom, in conjunction with the prince, the whole legislature is committed.

I then descended to the Courts of Justice, over which the Judges, those venerable sages and interpreters of 120 the law, presided, for determining the disputed rights and properties of men, as well as for the punishment of vice, and protection of innocence. I mentioned the prudent management of our treasury; the valour and achievements of our forces by sea and land. I computed the number of our people, by reckoning how many millions there might be of each religious sect, or political party among us. I did not omit even our sports and pastimes, or any other particular which I thought might redound to the honour of my country. And I 130 finished all with a brief historical account of affairs and events in England for about an hundred years past.

This conversation was not ended under five audiences, each of several hours, and the King heard the whole with great attention, frequently taking notes of what I spoke, as well as memorandums of what questions he intended to ask me.

When I had put an end to these long discourses, his Majesty in a sixth audience consulting his notes, proposed many doubts, queries, and objections, upon every 140 article. He asked what methods were used to cultivate the minds and bodies of our young nobility, and in what kind of business they commonly spent the first and teachable part of their lives. What course was taken to supply that assembly when any noble family became extinct. What qualifications were necessary in those who are to be created new lords: whether the humour of the prince, a sum of money to a court lady, or a prime minister, or a design of strengthening a party opposite to the public interest, ever happened 150 to be motives in those advancements. What share of knowledge these lords had in the laws of their country, and how they came by it, so as to enable them to decide the properties of their fellow-subjects in the last resort. Whether they were always so free from avarice, partialities, or want, that a bribe, or some other sinister view, could have no place among them. Whether those holy lords I spoke of were always promoted to that rank upon account of their knowledge in religious matters, and the sanctity of their lives, had never been 160 compliers with the times, while they were common priests, or slavish prostitute chaplains to some nobleman, whose opinions they continued servilely to follow after they were admitted into that assembly.

He then desired to know what arts were practised in electing those whom I called commoners: whether a stranger with a strong purse might not influence the vulgar voters to choose him before their own landlord, or the most considerable gentleman in the neighbourhood. How it came to pass, that people were so violently bent upon getting into this assembly, which I 170 allowed to be a great trouble and expense, often to the ruin of their families, without any salary or pension: because this appeared such an exalted strain of virtue and public spirit, that his Majesty seemed to doubt it might possibly not be always sincere: and he desired to know whether such zealous gentlemen could have any views of refunding themselves for the charges and trouble they were at, by sacrificing the public good to the designs of a weak and vicious prince in conjunction with a corrupted ministry. He multi- 180 plied his questions, and sifted me thoroughly upon every part of this head, proposing numberless enquiries and objections, which I think it not prudent or convenient to repeat.

Upon what I said in relation to our Courts of Justice, his Majesty desired to be satisfied in several points: and this I was the better able to do, having been formerly almost ruined by a long suit in chancery, which was decreed for me with costs. He asked, what time was usually spent in determining between right and 190 wrong, and what degree of expense. Whether advocates and orators had liberty to plead in causes manifestly known to be unjust, vexatious, or oppressive. Whether party in religion or politics were observed to be of any weight in the scale of justice. Whether those pleading orators were persons educated in the general knowledge of equity, or only in provincial, national, and other local customs. Whether they or their judges had any part in penning those laws which they assumed the liberty of interpreting and glossing 200 upon at their pleasure. Whether they had ever at different times pleaded for and against the same cause, and cited precedents to prove contrary opinions. Whether they were a rich or a poor corporation. Whether they received any pecuniary reward for pleading or delivering their opinions. And particularly, whether they were ever admitted as members in the lower senate.

He fell next upon the management of our treasury; and said, he thought my memory had failed me, be- 210 cause I computed our taxes at about five or six millions a year, and when I came to mention the issues, he found they sometimes amounted to more than double; for the notes he had taken were very particular in this point, because he hoped, as he told me, that the knowledge of our conduct might be useful to him, and he could not be deceived in his calculations. But, if what I told him were true, he was still at a loss how a kingdom could run out of its estate like a private person. He asked me, who were our credi- 220 tors; and where we should find money to pay them. He wondered to hear me talk of such chargeable and expensive wars; that certainly we must be a quarrelsome people, or live among very bad neighbours, and that our generals must needs be richer than our kings. He asked what business we had out of our own islands, unless upon the score of trade or treaty, or to defend the coasts with our fleet. Above all, he was amazed to hear me talk of a mercenary standing army in the midst of peace, and among a free people. He said, if we were governed by our own consent in the persons of our representatives, he could not imagine of whom we were afraid, or against whom we were to fight; and would hear my opinion, whether a private man's house might not better be defended by himself, his children, and family, than by a half dozen rascals picked up at a venture in the streets, for small wages, who might get an hundred times more by cutting their throats.

He laughed at my odd kind of arithmetic (as he was pleased to call it) in reckoning the numbers of our people by a computation drawn from the several sects among us in religion and politics. He said, he knew no reason, why those who entertain opinions prejudicial to the public, should be obliged to change, or should not be obliged to change, or should not be obliged to conceal them. And as it was tyranny in any government to require the first, so it was weakness not to enforce the second: for a man may be allowed to keep poisons in his closet, but not to vend them about for cordials.

He observed, that among the diversions of our nobility and gentry, I had mentioned gaming. He desired to know at what age this entertainment was usually taken up, and when it was laid down; how much of their time it employed; whether it ever went so high as to affect their fortunes; whether mean vicious people, by their dexterity in that art, might not arrive at great riches, and sometimes keep our very nobles in dependence, as well as habituate them to vile companions, wholly take them from the improvement of their minds, and force them, by the losses they have received, to learn and practise that infamous dexterity upon others.

He was perfectly astonished with the historical account I gave him of our affairs during the last century; protesting it was only an heap of conspiracies, rebellions, murders, massacres, revolutions, banishments, the very worst effects that avarice, faction, hypocrisy, perfidiousness, cruelty, rage, madness, hatred, envy, lust, malice, or ambition, could produce.

His Majesty, in another audience, was at the pains to recapitulate the sum of all I had spoken; compared the questions he made with the answers I had given; then taking me into his hands, and stroking me gently, delivered himself in these words, which I shall never forget, nor the manner he spoke them in: My little friend Grildrig, you have made a most admirable panegyric upon your country; you have clearly proved that ignorance, idleness, and vice, are the proper ingredients for qualifying a legislator: that laws are best

explained, interpreted, and applied by those whose interest and abilities lie in perverting, confounding, and eluding them. I observe among you some lines of an institution, which in its original might have been tolerable, but these half erased, and the rest wholly blurred and blotted by corruptions. It doth not appear from all you have said, how any one virtue is required towards the procurement of any one station among you; much less that men are ennobled on account of their virtue, that priests are advanced for their piety or learning, soldiers for their conduct or valour, judges for their integrity, senators for the love of their country, or counsellors for their wisdom. As for yourself (continued the King), who have spent the greatest part of your life in travelling, I am well disposed to hope you may hitherto have escaped many vices of your country. But by what I have gathered from your own relation, and the answers I have with much pains wringed and extorted from you, I cannot but conclude the bulk of your natives to be the most pernicious race of little odious vermin that nature ever suffered to crawl upon the surface of the earth.

CHAPTER VII

The Author's love of his country. He makes a proposal of much advantage to the King, which is rejected. The King's great ignorance in politics. The learning of that country very imperfect and confined. Their laws, and military affairs, and parties in the State.

Nothing but an extreme love of truth could have hindered me from concealing this part of my story. It was in vain to discover my resentments, which were always turned into ridicule; and I was forced to rest with patience while my noble and most beloved country was so injuriously treated. I am heartily sorry as any of my readers can possibly be, that such an occasion was given: but this prince happened to be so curious and inquisitive upon every particular, that it could not consist either with gratitude or good manners to refuse giving him what satisfaction I was able. Yet thus much I may be allowed to say in my own vindication, that I artfully eluded many of his questions, and gave to every point a more favourable turn by many degrees than the strictness of truth would allow. For I have always borne that laudable partiality to my own country, which Dionysius Halicarnassensis with so much justice recommends to an historian: I would hide the frailties and deformities of my political mother, and place her virtues and beauties in the most advantageous light. This was my sincere endeavour in those many discourses I had with that mighty monarch, although it unfortunately failed of success.

But great allowances should be given to a King who lives wholly secluded from the rest of the world, and must therefore be altogether unacquainted with the manners and customs that most prevail in other nations: the want of which knowledge will ever produce many prejudices, and a certain narrowness of thinking, from which we and the politer countries of Europe are wholly exempted. And it would be hard indeed, if so remote a prince's notions of virtue and vice were to be offered as a standard for all mankind.

To confirm what I have now said, and further, to show the miserable effects of a confined education, I shall here insert a passage which will hardly obtain belief. In hopes to ingratiate myself farther into his Majesty's favour, I told him of an invention discovered between three and four hundred years ago, to make a certain powder, into an heap of which the smallest spark of fire falling, would kindle the whole in a moment, although it were as big as a mountain, and make it all fly up in the air together, with a noise and agitation greater than thunder. That a proper quantity of this powder rammed into an hollow tube of brass or iron, according to its bigness, would drive a ball of iron or lead with such violence and speed, as nothing was able to sustain its force. That the largest balls thus discharged, would not only destroy whole ranks of an army at once, but batter the strongest walls to the ground, sink down ships, with a thousand men in each, to the bottom of the sea; and, when linked together by a chain, would cut through masts and rigging, divide hundreds of bodies in the middle, and lay all waste before them. That we often put this powder into large hollow balls of iron, and discharged them by an engine into some city we were besieging, which would rip up the pavements, tear the houses to pieces, burst and throw splinters on every side, dashing out the brains of all who came near. That I knew the ingredients very well, which were cheap, and common; I understood the manner of compounding them, and could direct his workmen how to make those tubes, of a size proportionable to all other things in his Majesty's kingdom, and the largest need not be above an hundred foot long; twenty or thirty of which tubes, charged with the proper quantity of powder and balls, would batter down the walls of the strongest town in his dominions in a few hours, or destroy the whole metropolis, if ever it should pretend to dispute his absolute commands. This I humbly offered to his Majesty, as a small tribute of acknowledgment in return of so many marks that I had received of his royal favour and protection.

The King was struck with horror at the description I had given of those terrible engines, and the proposal I had made. He was amazed how so impotent and grovelling an insect as I (these were his expressions) could maintain such inhuman ideas, and in so familiar a manner as to appear wholly unmoved at all the scenes of blood and desolation, which I had painted as the common effects of those destructive machines, whereof he said, some evil genius, enemy to mankind, must have been the first contriver. As for himself, he protested, that although few things delighted him so much as new discoveries in art or in nature, yet he would rather lose half his kingdom than be privy to such a secret, which he commanded me, as I valued my life, never to mention any more.

A strange effect of narrow principles and short views! that a prince possessed of every quality which procures veneration, love, and esteem; of strong parts, great wisdom, and profound learning, endued with admirable talents for government, and almost adored by his subjects, should from a nice unnecessary scruple, whereof in Europe we can have no conception, let slip an opportunity put into his hands, that would have made him absolute master of the lives, the liberties, and the fortunes of his people. Neither do I say this with the least intention to detract from the many virtues of that excellent King, whose character I am sensible will on this account be very much lessened in the opinion of an English reader: but I take this defect among them to have risen from their ignorance, they not having hitherto reduced politics into a science, as the more acute wits of Europe have done. For, I remember very well, in a discourse one day with the King, when I happened to say there were several thousand books among us written upon the art of government, it gave him (directly contrary to my intention) a very mean opinion of our understandings. He professed both to abominate and despise all mystery, refinement, and intrigue, either in a prince or a minister. He could not tell what I meant by secrets of state, where an enemy or some rival nation were not in the case. He confined the knowledge of governing within very narrow bounds; to common sense and reason, to justice and lenity, to the speedy determination of civil and criminal causes; with some other obvious topics, which are not worth considering. And he gave it for his opinion, that whoever could make two ears of corn, or two blades of grass to grow upon a spot of ground where only one grew before, would deserve better of mankind, and do more essential service to his country, than the whole race of politicians put together.

The learning of this people is very defective, consisting only in morality, history, poetry, and mathematics, wherein they must be allowed to excel. But the last of these is wholly applied to what may be useful in life, to the improvement of agriculture, and all mechanical arts; so that among us it would be little esteemed. And as to ideas, entities, abstractions, and transcendentals, I could never drive the least conception into their heads.

No law of that country must exceed in words the number of letters in their alphabet, which consists only in two and twenty. But, indeed, few of them extend

Gulliver bows to the citizens of Brobdingnag. Reproduced by permission of The Bettmann Archive.

even to that length. They are expressed in the most plain and simple terms, wherein those people are not mercurial enough to discover above one interpretation: and to write a comment upon any law is a capital crime. As to the decision of civil causes, or proceedings against criminals, their precedents are so few, that they have little reason to boast of any extraordinary skill in either.

They have had the art of printing, as well as the
10 Chinese, time out of mind: but their libraries are not very large; for that of the King's, which is reckoned the biggest, doth not amount to above a thousand volumes, placed in a gallery of twelve hundred foot long, from whence I had liberty to borrow what books I pleased. The Queen's joiner had contrived in one of Glumdalclitch's rooms a kind of wooden machine five and twenty foot high, formed like a standing ladder; the steps were each fifty foot long. It was indeed a moveable pair of stairs, the lowest end placed at ten

foot distance from the wall of the chamber. The book 20 I had a mind to read was put up leaning against the wall. I first mounted to the upper step of the ladder, and turning my face towards the book, began at the top of the page, and so walking to the right and left about eight or ten paces, according to the length of the lines, till I had gotten a little below the level of my eyes, and then descending gradually till I came to the bottom: after which I mounted again, and began the other page in the same manner, and so turned over the leaf, which I could easily do with both my 30 hands, for it was as thick and stiff as a pasteboard, and in the largest folios not above eighteen or twenty foot long.

Their style is clear, masculine, and smooth, but not florid, for they avoid nothing more than multiplying unnecessary words, or using various expressions. I have perused many of their books, especially those in history and morality. Among the rest, I was much diverted with a little old treatise, which always lay in Glumdalclitch's bed-chamber, and belonged to her governess, a grave elderly gentlewoman, who dealt in writings of morality and devotion. The book treats of the weakness of human kind, and is in little esteem, except among the women and the vulgar. However, I was curious to see what an author of that country could say upon such a subject. This writer went through all the usual topics of European moralists, showing how diminutive, contemptible, and helpless an animal was man in his own nature; how unable to defend himself from the inclemencies of the air, or the fury of wild beasts: how much he was excelled by one creature in strength, by another in speed, by a third in foresight, by a fourth in industry. He added, that nature was degenerated in these latter declining ages of the world, and could now produce only small abortive births in comparison of those in ancient times. He said, it was very reasonable to think, not only that the species of men were originally much larger, but also, that there must have been giants in former ages, which, as it is asserted by history and tradition, so it hath been confirmed by huge bones and skulls casually dug up in several parts of the kingdom, far exceeding the common dwindled race of man in our days. He argued, that the very laws of nature absolutely required we should have been made in the beginning, of a size more large and robust, not so liable to destruction from every little accident of a tile falling from a house, or a stone cast from the hand of a boy, or of being drowned in a little brook. From this way of reasoning the author drew several moral applications useful in the conduct of life, but needless here to repeat. For my own part, I could not avoid reflecting how universally this talent was spread, of drawing lectures in morality, or indeed rather matter of discontent and repining, from the quarrels we raise with nature. And I believe, upon a strict enquiry, those quarrels might be shown as ill grounded among us, as they are among that people.

As to their military affairs, they boast that the King's army consists of an hundred and seventy-six thousand foot, and thirty-two thousand horse: if that may be called an army which is made up of tradesmen in the several cities, and farmers in the country, whose commanders are only the nobility and gentry, without pay or reward. They are indeed perfect enough in their exercises, and under very good discipline, wherein I saw no great merit; for how should it be otherwise, where every farmer is under the command of his own landlord, and every citizen under that of the principal men in his own city, chosen after the manner of Venice by ballot?

I have often seen the militia of Lorbrulgrud drawn out to exercise in a great field near the city of twenty miles square. They were in all not above twenty-five thousand foot, and six thousand horse; but it was impossible for me to compute their number, considering the space of ground they took up. A cavalier mounted on a large steed, might be about an hundred foot high. I have seen this whole body of horse, upon a word of command, draw their swords at once, and brandish them in the air. Imagination can figure nothing so grand, so surprising, and so astonishing! It looked as if ten thousand flashes of lightning were darting at the same time from every quarter of the sky.

I was curious to know how this prince, to whose dominions there is no access from any other country, came to think of armies, or to teach his people the practice of military discipline. But I was soon informed, both by conversation, and reading their histories. For, in the course of many ages they have been troubled with the same disease to which the whole race of mankind is subject; the nobility often contending for power, the people for liberty, and the King for absolute dominion. All which, however happily tempered by the laws of that kingdom, have been sometimes violated by each of the three parties, and have once or more occasioned civil wars, the last whereof was happily put an end to by this prince's grandfather by a general composition; and the militia, then settled with common consent, hath been ever since kept in the strictest duty.

CHAPTER VIII

The King and Queen make a progress to the frontiers. The Author attends them. The manner in which he leaves the country very particularly related. He returns to England.

I had always a strong impulse that I should some time recover my liberty, though it was impossible to conjecture by what means, or to form any project with the least hope of succeeding. The ship in which I sailed was the first ever known to be driven within sight of that coast, and the King had given strict orders, that if at any time another appeared, it should be taken ashore, and with all its crew and passengers brought in a tumbril to Lorbrulgrud. He was strongly bent to get me a woman of my own size, by whom I might propagate the breed: but I think I should rather have died than undergone the disgrace of leaving a posterity to be kept in cages like tame canary birds, and perhaps, in time, sold about the kingdom to persons of quality for curiosities. I was, indeed, treated with much kindness: I was the favourite of a great King and Queen, and the delight of the whole court, but it was upon such a foot as ill became the dignity of human kind. I could never forget those domestic pledges I had left behind me. I wanted to be among people with whom I could converse upon even terms, and walk about the streets and fields without fear of being trod to death like a frog or a young puppy. But my deliverance came sooner than I expected, and in a manner not very common: the whole story and circumstances of which I shall faithfully relate.

I had now been two years in this country; and about the beginning of the third, Glumdalclitch and I attended the King and Queen in a progress to the south coast of the kingdom. I was carried, as usual, in my travelling-box, which, as I have already described, was a very convenient closet of twelve foot wide. And I had ordered a hammock to be fixed by silken ropes from the four corners at the top, to break the jolts, when a servant carried me before him on horseback, as I sometimes desired, and would often sleep in my hammock while we were upon the road. On the roof of my closet, just over the middle of the hammock, I ordered the joiner to cut out a hole of a foot square, to give me air in hot weather, as I slept; which hole I shut at pleasure with a board that drew backwards and forwards through a groove.

When we came to our journey's end, the King thought proper to pass a few days at a palace he hath near Flanflasnic, a city within eighteen English miles of the seaside. Glumdalclitch and I were much fatigued; I had gotten a small cold, but the poor girl was so ill as to be confined to her chamber. I longed to see the ocean, which must be the only scene of my escape, if ever it should happen. I pretended to be worse than I really was, and desired leave to take the fresh air of the sea, with a page whom I was very fond of, and who had sometimes been trusted with me. I shall never forget with what unwillingness Glumdalclitch consented, nor the strict charge she gave the page to be careful of me, bursting at the same time into a flood of tears, as if she had some foreboding of what was to happen. The boy took me out in my box about half an hour's walk from the palace, towards the rocks on the sea-shore. I ordered him to set me down, and lifting up one of my sashes, cast many a wistful melancholy look towards the sea. I found myself not very well, and told the page that I had a mind to take a nap in my hammock, which I hoped would do me good. I got in, and the boy shut the window close down to keep out the cold. I soon fell asleep, and all I can conjecture is, that while I slept, the page, thinking no danger could happen, went among the rocks to look for birds' eggs, having before observed him from my window searching about, and picking up one or two in the clefts. Be that as it will, I found myself suddenly awaked with a violent pull upon the ring which was fastened at the top of my box for the conveniency of carriage. I felt my box raised very high in the air, and then borne forward with prodigious speed. The first jolt had like to have shaken me out of my hammock, but afterwards the motion was easy enough. I called out several times, as loud as I could raise my voice, but all to no purpose. I looked towards my windows, and could see nothing but the clouds and sky. I heard a noise just over my head like the clapping of wings, and then began to perceive the woeful condition I was in; that some eagle had got the ring of my box in his beak, with an intent to let it fall on a rock like a tortoise in a shell, and then pick out my body, and devour it. For the sagacity and smell of this bird enable him to discover his quarry at a great distance, though better concealed than I could be within a two-inch board.

In a little time I observed the noise and flutter of wings to increase very fast, and my box was tossed up and down, like a sign-post in a windy day. I heard several bangs or buffets, as I thought, given to the eagle (for such I am certain it must have been that held the ring of my box in his beak), and then all on a sudden felt myself falling perpendicularly down for above a minute, but with such incredible swiftness that I almost lost my breath. My fall was stopped by a terrible squash, that sounded louder to my ears than the cataract of Niagara; after which I was quite in the dark for another minute, and then my box began to rise so high that I could see light from the tops of my windows. I now perceived that I was fallen into the sea. My box, by the weight of my body, the goods that were in, and the broad plates of iron fixed for strength at the four corners of the top and bottom, floated about five foot deep in water. I did then, and do now suppose that the eagle which flew away with my box was pursued by two or three others, and forced to let me drop while he was defending himself against the rest, who hoped to share in the prey. The plates of iron fastened at the bottom of the box (for those were the strongest) preserved the balance while it fell, and hindered it from being broken on the surface of the water. Every joint of it was well grooved, and the door did not move on hinges, but up and down like a sash, which kept my closet so tight that very little water came in. I got with much difficulty out of my hammock, having first ventured to draw back the slip-board on the roof already mentioned, contrived on purpose to let in air, for want of which I found myself almost stifled.

How often did I then wish myself with my dear Glumdalclitch, from whom one single hour had so far divided me! And I may say with truth, that in the midst of my own misfortunes I could not forbear lamenting my poor nurse, the grief she would suffer for my loss, the displeasure of the Queen, and the ruin of her fortune. Perhaps many travellers have not been under greater difficulties and distress than I was at this juncture, expecting every moment to see my box dashed in pieces, or at least overset by the first violent blast, or a rising wave. A breach in one single pane of glass would have been immediate death: nor could any thing have preserved the windows, but the strong lattice wires placed on the outside against accidents in travelling. I saw the water ooze in at several crannies, although the leaks were not considerable, and I endeavoured to stop them as well as I could. I was not able to lift up the roof of my closet, which otherwise I certainly should have done, and sat on the top of it, where I might at least preserve myself some hours longer than by being shut up, as I may call it, in the hold. Or, if I escaped these dangers for a day or two, what could I expect but a miserable death of cold and hunger! I was four hours under these circumstances, expecting and indeed wishing every moment to be my last.

I have already told the reader, that there were two strong staples fixed upon that side of my box which had no window, and into which the servant who used to carry me on horseback would put a leathern belt, and buckle it about his waist. Being in this disconsolate state, I heard or at least thought I heard some kind of grating noise on that side of my box where the staples were fixed, and soon after I began to fancy that the box was pulled or towed along in the sea; for I now and then felt a sort of tugging, which made the waves rise near the tops of my windows, leaving me almost in the dark. This gave me some faint hopes of relief, although I was not able to imagine how it could be brought about. I ventured to unscrew one of my chairs, which were always fastened to the floor; and having made a hard shift to screw it down again directly under the slipping-board that I had lately opened, I mounted on the chair, and putting my mouth as near as I could to the hole, I called for help in a loud voice, and in all the languages I understood. I then fastened my handkerchief to a stick I usually carried, and thrusting it up the hole, waved it several times in the air, that if any boat or ship were near, the seamen might conjecture some unhappy mortal to be shut up in the box.

I found no effect from all I could do, but plainly perceived my closet to be moved along; and in the space of an hour, or better, that side of the box where the staples were, and had no window, struck against something that was hard. I apprehended it to be a rock, and found myself tossed more than ever. I plainly heard a noise upon the cover of my closet, like that of a cable, and the grating of it as it passed through the ring. I then found myself hoisted up by degrees at least three foot higher than I was before. Whereupon I again thrust up my stick and handkerchief, calling for help till I was almost hoarse. In return to which, I heard a great shout repeated three times, giving me such transports of joy, as are not to be conceived but by those who feel them. I now heard a trampling over my head, and somebody calling through the hole with a loud voice in the English tongue, If there be any body below, let them speak. I answered, I was an Englishman, drawn by ill fortune into the greatest calamity that ever any creature underwent, and begged, by all that was moving, to be delivered out of the dungeon I was in. The voice replied, I was safe, for my box was fastened to their ship; and the carpenter should immediately come and saw an hole in the cover, large enough to pull me out. I answered, that was needless, and would take up too much time, for there was no more to be done, but let one of the crew put his finger into the ring, and take the box out of the sea into the ship, and so into the captain's cabin. Some of them upon hearing me talk so wildly thought I was mad; others laughed; for indeed it never came into my head that I was now got among people of my own stature and strength. The carpenter came, and in a few minutes sawed a passage about four foot square, then let down a small ladder, upon which I mounted, and from thence was taken into the ship in a very weak condition.

The sailors were all in amazement, and asked me a thousand questions, which I had no inclination to answer. I was equally confounded at the sight of so many pigmies, for such I took them to be, after having so long accustomed my eyes to the monstrous objects I had left. But the Captain, Mr. Thomas Wilcocks, an honest worthy Shropshire man, observing I was ready to faint, took me into his cabin, gave me a cordial to comfort me, and made me turn in upon his own bed, advising me to take a little rest of which I had great need. Before I went to sleep, I gave him to understand that I had some valuable furniture in my box, too good to be lost; a fine hammock, an handsome field-bed, two chairs, a table, and a cabinet: that my closet was hung on all sides, or rather quilted, with silk and cotton: that if he would let one of the crew bring my closet into his cabin, I would open it there before him, and show him my goods. The Captain hearing me utter these absurdities, concluded I was raving: however (I suppose to pacify me), he promised to give order as I desired, and going upon deck sent some of his men down into my closet, from whence (as I afterwards found) they drew up all my goods, and stripped off the quilting; but the chairs, cabinet, and bedstead, being screwed to the floor, were much damaged by the ignorance of the seamen, who tore them up by force. Then they knocked off some of the boards for the use of the ship, and when they had got all they had a mind for, let the hull drop into the sea, which by reason of many breaches made in the bottom and sides, sunk to rights. And indeed I was glad not to have been a spectator of the havoc they made; because I am confident it would have sensibly touched me, by bringing former passages into my mind, which I had rather forget.

I slept some hours, but perpetually disturbed with dreams of the place I had left, and the dangers I had escaped. However, upon waking I found myself much recovered. It was now about eight o'clock at night, and the Captain ordered supper immediately, thinking I had already fasted too long. He entertained me with great kindness, observing me not to look wildly, or talk inconsistently: and when we were left alone, desired I would give him a relation of my travels, and by what accident I came to be set adrift in that monstrous wooden chest. He said, that about twelve o'clock at noon, as he was looking through his glass, he spied it at a distance, and thought it was a sail, which he had a mind to make, being not much out of his course, in hopes of buying some biscuit, his own beginning to fall short. That upon coming nearer, and finding his error, he sent out his long-boat to discover what I was; that his men came back in a fright, swearing they had seen a swimming house. That he laughed at their folly, and went himself in the boat, ordering his men to take a strong cable along with them. That the weather being calm, he rowed round me several times, observed my windows, and the wire lattices that defended them. That he discovered two staples upon one side, which was all of boards, without any passage for light. He then commanded his men to row up to that side, and fastening a cable to one of the staples, ordered them to tow my chest (as he called it) towards the ship. When it was there, he gave directions to fasten another cable to the ring fixed in the cover, and to raise up my chest with pulleys, which all the sailors were not able to do above two or three foot. He said, they saw my stick and handkerchief thrust out of the hole, and concluded that some unhappy man must be shut up in the cavity. I asked whether he or the crew had seen any prodigious birds in the air about the time he first discovered me. To which he answered, that discoursing this matter with the sailors while I was asleep, one of them said he had observed three eagles flying towards the north, but remarked nothing of their being larger than the usual size, which I suppose must be imputed to the great height they were at; and he could not guess the reason of my question. I then asked the Captain how far he reckoned we might be from land; he said, by the best computation he could make, we were at least an hundred leagues. I assured him, that he must be mistaken by almost half, for I had not left the country from whence I came above two hours before I dropt into the sea. Whereupon he began again to think that my brain was disturbed, of which he gave me a hint, and advised me to go to bed in a cabin he had provided. I assured him I was well refreshed with his good entertainment and company, and as much in my senses as ever I was in my life. He then grew serious, and desired to ask me freely whether I were not troubled in mind by the consciousness of some enormous crime, for which I was punished at the command of some prince, by exposing me in that chest, as great criminals in other countries have been forced to sea in a leaky vessel without provisions: for, although he should be sorry to have taken so ill a man into his ship, yet he would engage his word to set me safe on shore in the first port where we arrived. He added, that his suspicions were much increased by some very absurd speeches I had delivered at first to the sailors, and afterwards to himself, in relation to my closet or chest, as well as by my odd looks and behaviour while I was at supper.

I begged his patience to hear me tell my story, which I faithfully did from the last time I left England to the moment he first discovered me. And, as truth always forceth its way into rational minds, so this honest worthy gentleman, who had some tincture of learning, and very good sense, was immediately convinced of my candour and veracity. But further to confirm all I had said, I entreated him to give order that my cabinet should be brought, of which I had the key in my pocket (for he had already informed me how the seamen disposed of my closet). I opened it in his presence, and showed him the small collection of rarities I made in the country from whence I had been so strangely delivered. There was the comb I had contrived out of the stumps of the King's beard, and another of the same materials, but fixed into a paring of her Majesty's thumb-nail, which served for the back. There was a collection of needles and pins from a foot to half a yard long; four wasp-stings, like joiners' tacks; some combings of the Queen's hair; a gold ring which one day she made me a present of in a most obliging manner, taking it from her little finger, and throwing it over my head like a collar. I desired the Captain would please to accept this ring in return of his civilities; which he absolutely refused. I showed him a corn that I had cut off with my own hand, from a maid of honour's toe; it was about the bigness of a Kentish pippin, and grown so hard that when I returned to England, I got it hollowed into a cup, and set in silver. Lastly, I desired him to see the breeches I had then on, which were made of a mouse's skin.

I could force nothing on him but a footman's tooth, which I observed him to examine with great curiosity, and found he had a fancy for it. He received it with abundance of thanks, more than such a trifle could deserve. It was drawn by an unskilful surgeon, in a mistake, from one of Glumdalclitch's men, who was afflicted with the tooth-ache, but it was as sound as any in his head. I got it cleaned, and put it into my cabinet. It was about a foot long, and four inches in diameter.

The Captain was very well satisfied with this plain relation I had given him, and said, he hoped when we returned to England, I would oblige the world by putting it in paper, and making it public. My answer was, that I thought we were already overstocked with books of travels: that nothing could now pass which was not extraordinary; wherein I doubted some authors less consulted truth than their own vanity, or interest, or the diversion of ignorant readers. That my story could contain little besides common events, without those ornamental descriptions of strange plants, trees, birds, and other animals, or of the barbarous customs and idolatry of savage people, with which most writers abound. However, I thanked him for his good opinion, and promised to take the matter into my thoughts.

He said he wondered at one thing very much, which was, to hear me speak so loud, asking me whether the King or Queen of that country were thick of hearing. I told him, it was what I had been used to for above two years past; and that I admired as much at the voices of him and his men, who seemed to me only to whisper, and yet I could hear them well enough. But when I spoke in that country, it was like a man talking in the street to another looking out from the top of a steeple, unless when I was placed on a table, or held in any person's hand. I told him, I had likewise observed another thing, that when I first got into the ship, and the sailors stood all about me, I thought they were the most little contemptible creatures I had ever beheld. For, indeed, while I was in that prince's country, I could never endure to look in a glass after my eyes had been accustomed to such prodigious objects, because the comparison gave me so despicable a conceit of myself. The Captain said, that while we were at supper, he observed me to look at every thing with a sort of wonder, and that I often seemed hardly able to contain my laughter, which he knew not well how to take, but imputed it to some disorder in my brain. I answered, it was very true; and I wondered how I could forbear, when I saw his dishes of the size of a silver three-pence, a leg of pork hardly a mouthful, a cup not so big as a nut-shell; and so I went on, describing the rest of his household-stuff and provisions after the same manner. For, although the Queen had ordered a little equipage of all things necessary for me while I was in her service, yet my ideas were wholly taken up with what I saw on every side of me, and I winked at my own littleness as people do at their own faults. The Captain understood my raillery very well, and merrily replied with the old English proverb, that he doubted my eyes were bigger than my belly, for he did not observe my stomach so good, although I had fasted all day; and continuing in his mirth, protested he would have gladly given an hundred pounds to have seen my closet in the eagle's bill, and afterwards in its fall from so great an height into the sea; which would certainly have been a most astonishing object, worthy to have the description of it transmitted to future ages: and the comparison of Phæton was so obvious, that he could not forbear applying it, although I did not much admire the conceit.

The Captain having been at Tonquin, was in his return to England driven north-eastward to the latitude of 44 degrees, and of longitude 143. But meeting a trade-wind two days after I came on board him, we sailed southward a long time, and coasting New Holland kept our course west-south-west, and then south-south-west till we doubled the Cape of Good Hope. Our voyage was very prosperous, but I shall not trouble the reader with a journal of it. The Captain called in at one or two ports, and sent in his long-boat for provisions and fresh water, but I never went out of the ship till we came into the Downs, which was on the third day of June, 1706, about nine months after my escape. I offered to leave my goods in security for payment of my freight: but the Captain protested he would not receive one farthing. We took kind leave of each other, and I made him promise he would come to see me at my house in Redriff. I hired a horse and guide for five shillings, which I borrowed of the Captain.

As I was on the road, observing the littleness of the houses, the trees, the cattle, and the people, I began to think myself in Lilliput. I was afraid of trampling on every traveller I met, and often called aloud to have them stand out of the way, so that I had like to have gotten one or two broken heads for my impertinence.

When I came to my own house, for which I was forced to enquire, one of the servants opening the door, I bent down to go in (like a goose under a gate) for fear of striking my head. My wife ran out to embrace me, but I stooped lower than her knees, thinking she could otherwise never be able to reach my mouth. My daughter kneeled to ask my blessing, but I could not see her till she arose, having been so long used to stand with my head and eyes erect to above sixty foot; and then I went to take her up with one hand, by the waist. I looked down upon the servants and one or two friends who were in the house, as if they had been pigmies, and I a giant. I told my wife, she had been too thrifty, for I found she had starved herself and her daughter to nothing. In short, I behaved myself so unaccountably, that they were all of the Captain's opinion when he first saw me, and concluded I had lost my wits. This I mention as an instance of the great power of habit and prejudice.

In a little time I and my family and friends came to a right understanding: but my wife protested I should never go to sea any more; although my evil destiny so ordered that she had not power to hinder me, as the reader may know hereafter. In the mean time I here conclude the second part of my unfortunate voyages.

(1726)

A MODEST PROPOSAL

FOR PREVENTING THE CHILDREN OF POOR PEOPLE IN IRELAND FROM BEING A BURDEN TO THEIR PARENTS OR COUNTRY, AND FOR MAKING THEM BENEFICIAL TO THE PUBLIC.

Compared to Swift's trenchant essay The Abolishing of Christianity, A Modest Proposal *is desperately bitter. It is a "sick joke," but Swift was sick at heart over the deplorable condition of Ireland. In the preceding year (1728) he had published two of his numerous pieces on the subject of Irish grievances against England:* A Short View of the State of Ireland *and* On the Present Miserable State of Ireland. *In the former, he dwelt upon the ironic pathos of the fact that although Ireland was favored by nature with a fruitful soil and a mild climate, there was general desolation in the island. England, he said, was receiving all the revenues from Ireland without the slightest return to the Irish: "How long we shall be able to continue the payment I am not in the least certain: one thing I know, that when the hen is starved to death there will be no more golden eggs."*

One of the favorite maxims of economic writers of the period was "people are the riches of a nation." Swift is arguing that this darling maxim of his time applies to Ireland only if cannibalism is permitted. (Elsewhere he accepted the slave trade as an alternative.) This explains the "mask" which Swift wears in the essay: He pretends to be one of the numerous tribe of economic "projectors" offering a "scheme" for solving the problem of poverty in Ireland. The irony becomes ever more bitter as Swift sustains his analytical calculations through a revelation of the brutalizing plight of the Irish people; the despair of a nation is presented through the facile optimism of an economic theorist.

It is a melancholy object to those who walk through this great town, or travel in the country, when they see the streets, the roads, and cabin doors crowded with beggars of the female sex, followed by three, four, or six children, all in rags and importuning every passenger for an alms. These mothers, instead of being able to work for their honest livelihood, are forced to employ all their time in strolling to beg sustenance for their helpless infants; who as they grow up either turn 10 thieves, for want of work, or leave their dear native country to fight for the pretender in Spain, or sell themselves to the Barbados.

I think it is agreed by all parties that this prodigious number of children in the arms, or on the backs, or at the heels of their mothers, and frequently of their fathers, is, in the present deplorable state of the kingdom, a very great additional grievance; and therefore whoever could find out a fair, cheap, and easy method of making these children sound, useful members of the commonwealth would deserve so well of the public as 20 to have his statue set up for a preserver of the nation.

But my intention is very far from being confined to provide only for the children of professed beggars: it is of a much greater extent and shall take in the whole number of infants at a certain age, who are born of parents in effect as little able to support them as those who demand our charity in the streets.

As to my own part, having turned my thoughts for many years upon this important subject and maturely weighed the several schemes of our projectors, I have 30 always found them grossly mistaken in their computation. It is true, a child just dropped from its dam may be supported by her milk for a solar year, with little other nourishment: at most not above the value of two shillings which the mother may certainly get, or the value in scraps, by her lawful occupation of begging; and it is exactly at one year old that I propose to provide for them in such a manner, as, instead of being a charge upon their parents or the parish, or wanting food and raiment for the rest of their lives, they shall, 40 on the contrary, contribute to the feeding and partly to the clothing of many thousands.

There is likewise another great advantage in my scheme, that it will prevent those voluntary abortions and that horrid practice of women murdering their bastard children, alas! too frequent among us, sacrificing the poor innocent babes, I doubt more to avoid the expense than the shame, which would move tears and pity in the most savage and inhuman breast.

The number of souls in this kingdom being usually 50 reckoned one million and a half, of these I calculate there may be about two hundred thousand couple, whose wives are breeders; from which number I subtract thirty thousand couple, who are able to maintain their own children (although I apprehend there cannot be so many, under the present distresses of the kingdom), but this being granted, there will remain an hundred and seventy thousand breeders. I again subtract fifty thousand for those women who miscarry, or whose children die by accident or disease within 60 the year. There only remains one hundred and twenty thousand children of poor parents annually born. The question therefore is, How this number shall be reared and provided for? which, as I have already said, under the present situation of affairs, is utterly impossible

A Modest Proposal. 11. the pretender, James Stuart, son of King James II of England. He laid claim to the throne which his father had lost in the Revolution of 1688 and actually landed in Britain in 1715, but was defeated. He retired to the Continent, where he and his son kept alive the "Jacobite" agitation, and where he intrigued not only with the King of France but with the French puppet sovereigns in Spain.

by all the methods hitherto proposed. For we can neither employ them in handicraft or agriculture; we neither build houses (I mean in the country) nor cultivate land: they can very seldom pick up a livelihood by stealing till they arrive at six years old, except where they are of towardly parts; although I confess they learn the rudiments much earlier; during which time they can, however, be properly looked upon only as probationers; as I have been informed by a principal gentleman in the county of Cavan, who protested to me that he never knew above one or two instances under the age of six, even in a part of the kingdom so renowned for the quickest proficiency in that art.

I am assured by our merchants that a boy or a girl before twelve years old is no salable commodity; and even when they come to this age they will not yield above three pounds, or three pounds and half a crown at most, on the exchange; which cannot turn to account either to the parents or kingdom, the charge of nutriment and rags having been at least four times that value.

I shall now therefore humbly propose my own thoughts, which I hope will not be liable to the least objection.

I have been assured by a very knowing American of my acquaintance in London that a young healthy child well nursed is at a year old a most delicious, nourishing, and wholesome food, whether stewed, roasted, baked, or boiled; and I make no doubt that it will equally serve in a fricassee or a ragout.

I do therefore humbly offer it to public consideration that of the hundred and twenty thousand children already computed, twenty thousand may be reserved for breed, whereof only one-fourth part to be males; which is more than we allow to sheep, black cattle, or swine; and my reason is that these children are seldom the fruits of marriage, a circumstance not much regarded by our savages; therefore one male will be sufficient to serve four females. That the remaining hundred thousand may, at a year old, be offered in sale to the persons of quality and fortune through the kingdom; always advising the mother to let them suck plentifully in the last month, so as to render them plump and fat for a good table. A child will make two dishes at an entertainment for friends; and when the family dines alone, the fore or hind quarter will make a reasonable dish, and seasoned with a little pepper or salt will be very good boiled on the fourth day, especially in winter.

I have reckoned upon a medium that a child just born will weigh twelve pounds, and in a solar year, if tolerably nursed, will increase to twenty-eight pounds.

I grant this food will be somewhat dear, and therefore very proper for landlords, who, as they have already devoured most of the parents, seem to have the best title to the children.

Infant's flesh will be in season throughout the year, but more plentifully in March, and a little before and after: for we are told by a grave author, an eminent French physician, that fish being a prolific diet, there are more children born in Roman Catholic countries about nine months after Lent than at any other season; therefore, reckoning a year after Lent, the markets will be more glutted than usual, because the number of popish infants is at least three to one in this kingdom: and therefore it will have one other collateral advantage, by lessening the number of papists among us.

I have already computed the charge of nursing a beggar's child (in which list I reckon all cottagers, laborers, and four-fifths of the farmers) to be about two shillings per annum, rags included; and I believe no gentleman would repine to give ten shillings for the carcass of a good fat child, which, as I have said, will make four dishes of excellent nutritive meat, when he has only some particular friend or his own family to dine with him. Thus the squire will learn to be a good landlord and grow popular among his tenants; the mother will have eight shillings net profit and be fit for work till she produces another child.

Those who are more thrifty (as I must confess the times require) may flay the carcass; the skin of which artificially dressed will make admirable gloves for ladies and summer boots for fine gentlemen.

As to our city of Dublin, shambles may be appointed for this purpose in the most convenient parts of it, and butchers we may be assured will not be wanting; although I rather recommend buying the children alive and dressing them hot from the knife as we do roasting pigs.

A very worthy person, a true lover of his country, and whose virtues I highly esteem, was lately pleased, in discoursing on this matter, to offer a refinement upon my scheme. He said that many gentlemen of this kingdom, having of late destroyed their deer, he conceived that the want of venison might be well supplied by the bodies of young lads and maidens, not exceeding fourteen years of age nor under twelve; so great a number of both sexes in every country being now ready to starve for want of work and service; and these to be disposed of by their parents, if alive, or otherwise by their nearest relations. But with due deference to so excellent a friend and so deserving a patriot, I cannot be altogether in his sentiments; for as to the males, my American acquaintance assured me from frequent experience that

In 1718, the Spanish statesman Alberoni started an expedition to help the Scottish Jacobites, but the fleet was wrecked on its way from Cádiz. 71. **towardly**, ready to learn. 75. **Cavan**, a county in northern Ireland, bordering the present republic of Eire.

their flesh was generally tough and lean, like that of our schoolboys, by continual exercise, and their taste disagreeable; and to fatten them would not answer the charge. Then as to the females, it would, I think, with humble submission be a loss to the public, because they soon would become breeders themselves: and besides, it is not improbable that some scrupulous people might be apt to censure such a practice (although indeed very unjustly), as a little border-
10 ing upon cruelty; which, I confess, has always been with me the strongest objection against any project, however so well intended.

But in order to justify my friend, he confessed that this expedient was put into his head by the famous Psalmanazar, a native of the island Formosa, who came from thence to London above twenty years ago: and in conversation told my friend that in his country when any young person happened to be put to death, the executioner sold the carcass to
20 persons of quality as a prime dainty; and that in his time the body of a plump girl of fifteen, who was crucified for an attempt to poison the emperor, was sold to his imperial majesty's prime minister of state, and other great mandarins of the court, in joints from the gibbet, at four hundred crowns. Neither indeed can I deny that if the same use were made of several plump young girls in this town, who, without one single groat to their fortunes, cannot stir abroad without a chair, and appear at a playhouse and assem-
30 blies in foreign fineries which they never will pay for, the kingdom would not be the worse.

Some persons of a desponding spirit are in great concern about that vast number of poor people, who are aged, diseased, or maimed; and I have been desired to employ my thoughts, what course may be taken to ease the nation of so grievous an incumbrance. But I am not in the least pain upon that matter, because it is very well known that they are every day dying and rotting, by cold and famine, and
40 filth and vermin, as fast as can be reasonably expected. And as to the young laborers, they are now in almost as hopeful a condition: they cannot get work, and consequently pine away for want of nourishment to a degree that if at any time they are accidentally hired to common labor, they have not strength to perform it; and thus the country and themselves are happily delivered from the evils to come.

I have too long digressed and therefore shall re-
50 turn to my subject. I think the advantages, by the proposal which I have made, are obvious and many, as well as of the highest importance.

For first, as I have already observed, it would greatly lessen the number of papists, with whom we are yearly overrun, being the principal breeders of the nation, as well as our most dangerous enemies; and who stay at home on purpose to deliver the kingdom to the pretender, hoping to take their advantage by the absence of so many good protestants, who have chosen rather to leave their country than stay 60 at home and pay tithes against their conscience to an episcopal curate.

Secondly, the poorer tenants will have something valuable of their own, which by law may be made liable to distress, and help to pay their landlord's rent; their corn and cattle being already seized, and money a thing unknown.

Thirdly, whereas the maintenance of a hundred thousand children, from two years old and upwards, cannot be computed at less than ten shillings a piece 70 per annum, the nation's stock will be thereby increased fifty thousand pounds per annum, beside the profit of a new dish introduced to the tables of all gentlemen of fortune in the kingdom, who have any refinement in taste. And the money will circulate among ourselves, the goods being entirely of our own growth and manufacture.

Fourthly, the constant breeders, beside the gain of eight shillings sterling per annum by the sale of their children, will be rid of the charge of maintaining 80 them after the first year.

Fifthly, this food would likewise bring great custom to taverns: where the vintners will certainly be so prudent as to procure the best receipts for dressing it to perfection, and consequently have their houses frequented by all the fine gentlemen, who justly value themselves upon their knowledge in good eating: and a skilful cook, who understands how to oblige his guests, will contrive to make it as expensive as they please. 90

Sixthly, this would be a great inducement to marriage, which all wise nations have either encouraged by rewards or enforced by laws and penalties. It would increase the care and tenderness of mothers toward their children, when they were sure of a settlement for life to the poor babes, provided in some sort by the public, to their annual profit instead of expense. We should see an honest emulation among the married women, which of them could bring the fattest child to the market. Men would become as 100 fond of their wives during the time of their pregnancy as they are now of their mares in foal, their cows in calf, or sows when they are ready to farrow; nor offer to beat or kick them (as is too frequent a practice) for fear of a miscarriage.

Many other advantages might be enumerated. For instance, the addition of some thousand carcasses in our exportation of barreled beef, the propagation of swine's flesh, and improvement in the art of making good bacon, so much wanted among us by the 110

---

15. **Psalmanazar**, George Psalmanazar (1679?–1763), an imposter, born in France, who pretended to be a Japanese Christian, native of Formosa. His famous *Description of Formosa*, with an introductory "autobiography," appeared in 1704. After a serious illness in 1728, he made a full

great destruction of pigs, too frequent at our tables; which are no way comparable in taste or magnificence to a well-grown, fat, yearling child, which roasted whole will make a considerable figure at a lord mayor's feast, or any other public entertainment. But this and many others I omit, being studious of brevity.

Supposing that one thousand families in this city would be constant customers for infants' flesh, besides others who might have it at merry-meetings, particularly weddings and christenings, I compute that Dublin would take off annually about twenty thousand carcasses; and the rest of the kingdom (where probably they will be sold somewhat cheaper) the remaining eighty thousand.

I can think of no one objection that will possibly be raised against this proposal, unless it should be urged that the number of people will be thereby much lessened in the kingdom. This I freely own, and it was indeed one principal design in offering it to the world. I desire the reader will observe that I calculate my remedy for this one individual kingdom of Ireland, and for no other that ever was, is, or, I think, ever can be upon earth. Therefore let no man talk to me of other expedients: of taxing our absentees at five shillings a pound: of using neither clothes nor household furniture, except what is of our own growth and manufacture: of utterly rejecting the materials and instruments that promote foreign luxury: of curing the expensiveness of pride, vanity, idleness, and gaming in our women: of introducing a vein of parsimony, prudence, and temperance: of learning to love our country, in the want of which we differ even from Laplanders and the inhabitants of Topinamboo: of quitting our animosities and factions, nor acting any longer like the Jews, who were murdering one another at the very moment their city was taken: of being a little cautious not to sell our country and conscience for nothing: of teaching landlords to have at least one degree of mercy toward their tenants: lastly, of putting a spirit of honesty, industry, and skill into our shop-keepers; who, if a resolution could now be taken to buy only our native goods, would immediately unite to cheat and exact upon us in the price, the measure, and the goodness, nor could ever yet be brought to make one fair proposal of just dealing, though often and earnestly invited to it.

Therefore, I repeat, let no man talk to me of these and the like expedients, till he has at least some glimpse of hope that there will be ever some hearty and sincere attempt to put them in practice.

But as to myself, having been wearied out for many years with offering vain, idle, visionary thoughts, and at length utterly despairing of success, I fortunately fell upon this proposal; which, as it is wholly new, so it has something solid and real, of no expense and little trouble, full in our own power, and whereby we can incur no danger in disobliging England. For this kind of commodity will not bear exportation, the flesh being of too tender a consistence to admit a long continuance in salt, although perhaps I could name a country which would be glad to eat up our whole nation without it.

After all, I am not so violently bent upon my own opinion as to reject any offer proposed by wise men, which shall be found equally innocent, cheap, easy, and effectual. But before something of that kind shall be advanced in contradiction to my scheme, and offering a better, I desire the author or authors will be pleased maturely to consider two points. First, as things now stand, how they will be able to find food and raiment for an hundred thousand useless mouths and backs. And secondly, there being a round million of creatures in human figure throughout this kingdom, whose whole subsistence put into a common stock would leave them in debt two millions of pounds sterling, adding those who are beggars by profession to the bulk of farmers, cottagers, and laborers, with their wives and children, who are beggars in effect; I desire those politicians, who dislike my overture, and may perhaps be so bold as to attempt an answer, that they will first ask the parents of these mortals, whether they would not at this day think it a great happiness to have been sold for food at a year old in the manner I prescribe, and thereby have avoided such a perpetual scene of misfortunes as they have since gone through by the oppression of landlords, the impossibility of paying rent without money or trade, the want of common sustenance, with neither house nor clothes to cover them from the inclemencies of the weather, and the most inevitable prospect of entailing the like or greater miseries upon their breed for ever.

I profess, in the sincerity of my heart, that I have not the least personal interest in endeavoring to promote this necessary work, having no other motive than the public good of my country, by advancing our trade, providing for infants, relieving the poor, and giving some pleasure to the rich. I have no children by which I can propose to get a single penny; the youngest being nine years old, and my wife past child-bearing.

(1729)

confession, and lived to be a very useful citizen, the friend of Dr. Johnson.

ALEXANDER POPE 1688-1744

Alexander Pope was born in London on May 21, 1688, the son of a successful London merchant and a Roman Catholic. Two years later he was afflicted by a more serious handicap than his religion, the spinal tuberculosis which left him hunchbacked and fragile for the rest of his life. In 1709 and 1711 young Pope brought himself to the attention of the leading literary men of the age, including Joseph Addison, with the publication of his Pastorals and the Essay on Criticism. He published the first version of The Rape of the Lock, later revised, in 1712 and also established life-long friendships about this time with Swift, Arbuthnot, John Gay, and other outstanding literary figures. When he published Windsor Forest in 1713, Pope consolidated his claim to be the foremost poet of his time. During the next twelve years he was extremely active: he translated and published his controversial edition of the Iliad and the Odyssey which made his fortune, instigated the formation of the Scriblerus Club to satirize abuses of learning, issued the first collected volume of his Works (which included Verses to the Memory of an Unfortunate Lady and Eloisa to Abelard), and published a six-volume edition of Shakespeare. During the same period Pope moved with his parents to Twickenham, on the Thames near London, where he stayed for the rest of his life. In 1728 he published a first, incomplete version of The Dunciad, which was to be revised and enlarged three times before his death, and in the 1730's the Epistle to Dr. Arbuthnot and the Imitations of Horace appeared. The complete Dunciad in four books, with Colley Cibber as the new hero of the dunces, was his last published work; Pope died on May 30, 1744.

The poetry of Pope has been seriously devalued for as much as a century. For this fact, several reasons seem relevant. In the first place, Pope's generation labored on the far side of the romantic "revolution." They took as their central endeavor not the establishment of new forms but the perfection of established forms. Therefore, they were neoclassic in the sense that they (a) accepted as compelling the models and the canons of classical taste and propriety (classic) and (b) they lent their talent and energy to the functional modernization of these models and canons by the tactful application of them to their own times and in their own language (neo). The postrevolutionary generations have developed a penchant for the icono-clastic—in politics, in religion, in philosophy, and in esthetics—and a consequent disdain for tradition. Thus Pope and his "prosaic" contemporaries (to use a phrase from Matthew Arnold) have suffered in critical estimation.

Secondly, the poetry of the nineteenth century was ushered in by means of a singular shift in poetic idiom, a shift explicitly announced in the Preface to the second edition (1800) of Wordsworth's Lyrical Ballads. The nineteenth-century poet went not to example but to nature; he used almost any diction which his subject matter prompted; and he was free to write as he chose as the eighteenth-century poet was not.

The poet of Pope's day wrote "kinds" of poetry—including epic, tragedy in verse, pindaric, elegy, heroic and familiar epistle, pastoral, georgic, occasional verse, translation, and imitation. And his diction, which the nineteenth century dismissed as "poetical," was closely and consciously related to the kind of poem he was trying to write. For example, Pope: "After writing a poem, one should correct it all over, with one single view at a time. Thus for language; if an elegy, 'these lines are very good, but are they not of too heroical a strain?' and so vice versa." Readers of eighteenth-century poetry have increasingly lost sight of the poetic forms among which those poets worked and of the linguistic accommodations to those forms which they took great pains to make. As a result, readers have tended to dismiss eighteenth-century poetry as artificial, stilted, and frozen.

Further, as Wordsworth and his contemporaries ushered in a new idiom, they also effected a fundamental shift in man's attitude toward nature. It is often erroneously held that the eighteenth century essentially ignored nature, an error which Pope's very first volume, Pastorals (1709), contradicts. But it is true that the eighteenth-century poet did not deify nature, that for him nature culminated in man. Thus several generations of readers who have learned from nineteenth-century poetry to look upon nature, picturesquely presented, as instructor and personal physician have read the major poetry of the preceding century without a deeply affective response.

It must be admitted, finally, that some of the less sensitive members of a generation of scholars of eighteenth-century poetry, largely centered in the 1930's and 1940's, betrayed their critical trust and thus contributed to the divorce between the modern reader and the poetry of Pope. They overplayed the waspishness of his character and the personal animosities of his coterie and ignored the fact that their readers go to poetry not for ideas but for experience. They codified and classified and almost interred a century of distinguished literary achievement.

And yet, Alexander Pope was the greatest English poet between Milton and Wordsworth. He attempted with success each of the kinds of poetry acceptable in his day; he led his contemporaries in making concepts of wit, taste, judgment, and genius organic rather than tangential to poetry; he brought the heroic couplet to a new level of concise statement, which made even so concise a writer as Swift envy and admire him: *"When he can in one Couplet fix/More sense than I can do*

in six." In other respects, too, Pope gave new poetic validity to the heroic couplet. In his hands, it never degenerates into the monotone of the metronome. He can turn it to elevated narrative, as in The Rape of the Lock, or he can get from it that Horatian plainspeaking which animates much of the Essay on Criticism. In fact, his mastery of the heroic couplet is so complete that he could even capture realistic conversation, as he does in the Epilogue to the Satires. Finally, Pope could rend from the heroic couplet, through subtle nuances of sound and varied patterns of rhythm and syntax, wholly satisfying and hauntingly memorable statements about the human condition. The classic example is the opening passage of the second epistle of the Essay on Man, reprinted in this selection (p. 548).

---

from AN ESSAY ON CRITICISM

The accommodation of modern literary theory and practice to ancient rule and example is nowhere so well set forth in English as in Pope's Essay. Though written when he was very young, it is the maturest "defense of poetry" his age produced. Its main outlines are not novel, being based on the ideas of Horace and Boileau, but in it Pope does accomplish his own definition of "true wit": "... Nature to advantage dressed,/What oft was thought, but ne'er so well expressed." In Part 1, Pope explores the relationship of "wit" and art in poetry; in Part 2 he exposes "false wit" and in doing so defends literature itself.

1

'Tis hard to say, if greater want of skill
Appear in writing or in judging ill;
But, of the two, less dangerous is the offense
To tire our patience, than mislead our sense.
Some few in that, but numbers err in this,
Ten censure wrong for one who writes amiss;
A fool might once himself alone expose,
Now one in verse makes many more in prose.

'Tis with our judgments as our watches; none
10 Go just alike, yet each believes his own.
In poets as true genius is but rare,
True taste as seldom is the critic's share;
Both must alike from Heaven derive their light,
These born to judge, as well as those to write.
Let such teach others who themselves excel,
And censure freely who have written well.

Authors are partial to their wit, 'tis true,
But are not critics to their judgment too?

Yet if we look more closely, we shall find
Most have the seeds of judgment in their mind: 20
Nature affords at least a glimmering light;
The lines, though touched but faintly, are drawn right.
But as the slightest sketch, if justly traced,
Is by ill-coloring but the more disgraced,
So by false learning is good sense defaced;
Some are bewildered in the maze of schools,
And some made coxcombs nature meant but fools.
In search of wit these lose their common sense,
And then turn critics in their own defense;
Each burns alike, who can, or cannot write, 30
Or with a rival's or an eunuch's spite.
All fools have still an itching to deride,
And fain would be upon the laughing side.
If Maevius scribble in Apollo's spite,
There are who judge still worse than he can write.

Some have at first for wits, then poets passed,
Turned critics next, and proved plain fools at last.
Some neither can for wits nor critics pass,
As heavy mules are neither horse nor ass.
Those half-learned witlings, numerous in our isle, 40
As half-formed insects on the banks of Nile;
Unfinished things, one knows not what to call,
Their generation's so equivocal;
To tell 'em, would a hundred tongues require,
Or one vain wit's, that might a hundred tire.

But you who seek to give and merit fame,
And justly bear a critic's noble name,
Be sure yourself and your own reach to know,

An Essay on Criticism. **34. Maevius,** an inferior Roman poet of the first century. **41. half-formed . . . Nile.** The Nile is noted for its periodic overflowings. Insects forming along its bank are prematurely destroyed.

How far your genius, taste, and learning go;
50 Launch not beyond your depth, but be discreet,
And mark that point where sense and dullness meet.

Nature to all things fixed the limits fit,
And wisely curbed proud man's pretending wit.
As on the land while here the ocean gains,
In other parts it leaves wide sandy plains;
Thus in the soul while memory prevails,
The solid power of understanding fails;
Where beams of warm imagination play,
The memory's soft figures melt away.
60 One science only will one genius fit;
So vast is art, so narrow human wit:
Not only bounded to peculiar arts,
But oft in those confined to single parts.
Like kings we lose the conquests gained before,
By vain ambition still to make them more;
Each might his several province well command,
Would all but stoop to what they understand.

First follow nature, and your judgment frame
By her just standard, which is still the same:
70 Unerring nature, still divinely bright,
One clear, unchanged, and universal light,
Life, force, and beauty, must to all impart,
At once the source, and end, and test of art.
Art from that fund each just supply provides,
Works without show, and without pomp presides:
In some fair body thus the informing soul
With spirits feeds, with vigor fills the whole,
Each motion guides, and every nerve sustains;
Itself unseen, but in the effects, remains.
80 Some, to whom Heaven in wit has been profuse,
Want as much more, to turn it to its use;
For wit and judgment often are at strife,
Though meant each other's aid, like man and wife.
'Tis more to guide than spur the Muse's steed;
Restrain his fury, than provoke his speed;
The wingéd courser, like a generous horse,
Shows most true mettle when you check his course.

Those rules of old discovered, not devised,
Are nature still, but nature methodized;
90 Nature, like liberty, is but restrained
By the same laws which first herself ordained.

Hear how learned Greece her useful rules indites,
When to repress, and when indulge our flights:
High on Parnassus' top her sons she showed,
And pointed out those arduous paths they trod;
Held from afar, aloft, the immortal prize,
And urged the rest by equal steps to rise.

Just precepts thus from great examples given,
She drew from them what they derived from Heaven.
The generous critic fanned the poet's fire,   100
And taught the world with reason to admire.
Then criticism the Muse's handmaid proved,
To dress her charms, and make her more beloved:
But following wits from that intention strayed,
Who could not win the mistress, wooed the maid;
Against the poets their own arms they turned,
Sure to hate most the men from whom they learned.
So modern 'pothecaries, taught the art
By doctor's bills to play the doctor's part,
Bold in the practice of mistaken rules,   110
Prescribe, apply, and call their masters fools.
Some on the leaves of ancient authors prey,
Nor time nor moths e'er spoiled so much as they.
Some dryly plain, without invention's aid,
Write dull receipts, how poems may be made.
These leave the sense, their learning to display,
And those explain the meaning quite away.

You, then, whose judgment the right course would
    steer,
Know well each ancient's proper character;
His fable, subject, scope in every page;   120
Religion, country, genius of his age:
Without all these at once before your eyes,
Cavil you may, but never criticise.
Be Homer's works your study and delight,
Read them by day, and meditate by night;
Thence form your judgment, thence your maxims
    bring,
And trace the Muses upward to their spring.
Still with itself compared, his text peruse;
And let your comment be the Mantuan Muse.

When first young Maro in his boundless mind   130
A work to outlast immortal Rome designed,
Perhaps he seemed above the critic's law,
And but from nature's fountains scorned to draw:
But when to examine every part he came,
Nature and Homer were, he found, the same.
Convinced, amazed, he checks the bold design;
And rules as strict his labored work confine,
As if the Stagirite o'erlooked each line;
Learn hence for ancient rules a just esteem;
To copy nature is to copy them.   140

Some beauties yet no precepts can declare,
For there's a happiness as well as care.
Music resembles poetry; in each
Are nameless graces which no methods teach,
And which a master-hand alone can reach.

53. wit, judgment, intelligence. 94. Parnassus, a mountain range in Greece celebrated as the haunt of the Muses of poetry and music. 115. receipts, recipes. 124. Homer's works . . . delight. The "works" are, of course, the Iliad and the Odyssey. This is a definite and succinct statement by the neo-classicist revealing his veneration for the writers of

Greece and Rome. 129. Mantuan Muse, the great Roman poet Vergil (70–19 B.C.), a native of Mantua, Italy, author of the Aeneid as well as some didactic and lyric verse (the Georgics and Eclogues). His family name was Maro (cf. l. 130). 138. Stagirite, Aristotle (384–322 B.C.), so called from Stagira, his birthplace in Greece. The critical doctrines

If, where the rules not far enough extend,
(Since rules were made but to promote their end)
Some lucky license answer to the full
The intent proposed, that license is a rule.
150 Thus Pegasus, a nearer way to take,
May boldly deviate from the common track;
From vulgar bounds with brave disorder part,
And snatch a grace beyond the reach of art,
Which without passing through the judgment, gains
The heart, and all its end at once attains.
In prospects thus, some objects please our eyes,
Which out of nature's common order rise,
The shapeless rock, or hanging precipice.
Great wits sometimes may gloriously offend,
160 And rise to faults true critics dare not mend.
But though the ancients thus their rules invade,
(As kings dispense with laws themselves have made)
Moderns, beware! or if you must offend
Against the precept, ne'er transgress its end;
Let it be seldom and compelled by need;
And have, at least, their precedent to plead.
The critic else proceeds without remorse,
Seizes your fame, and puts his laws in force.

I know there are, to whose presumptuous thoughts
170 Those freer beauties, even in them, seem faults.
Some figures monstrous and mis-shaped appear,
Considered singly, or beheld too near,
Which, but proportioned to their light or place,
Due distance reconciles to form and grace.
A prudent chief not always must display
His powers in equal ranks, and fair array,
But with the occasion and the place comply,
Conceal his force, nay, seem sometimes to fly.
Those oft are stratagems which errors seem,
180 Nor is it Homer nods, but we that dream.

Still green with bays each ancient altar stands,
Above the reach of sacrilegious hands;
Secure from flames, from envy's fiercer rage,
Destructive war, and all-involving age.
See, from each clime the learned their incense bring!
Hear, in all tongues, consenting paeans ring!
In praise so just let every voice be joined,
And fill the general chorus of mankind.
Hail, bards triumphant! born in happier days;
190 Immortal heirs of universal praise!
Whose honors with increase of ages grow,
As streams roll down, enlarging as they flow;
Nations unborn your mighty names shall sound,
And worlds applaud that must not yet be found!
Oh, may some spark of your celestial fire,
The last, the meanest of your sons inspire,

(That on weak wings, from far, pursues your flights;
Glows while he reads, but trembles as he writes)
To teach vain wits a science little known,
To admire superior sense, and doubt their own!   200

2

Of all the causes which conspire to blind
Man's erring judgment, and misguide the mind,
What the weak head with strongest bias rules,
Is pride, the never-failing vice of fools.
Whatever nature has in worth denied,
She gives in large recruits of needful pride;
For as in bodies, thus in souls, we find
What wants in blood and spirits, swelled with wind:
Pride, where wit fails, steps in to our defense,
And fills up all the mighty void of sense.   210
If once right reason drives that cloud away,
Truth breaks upon us with resistless day.
Trust not yourself; but your defects to know,
Make use of every friend—and every foe.

A little learning is a dangerous thing;
Drink deep, or taste not the Pierian spring:
There shallow draughts intoxicate the brain,
And drinking largely sobers us again.
Fired at first sight with what the Muse imparts,
In fearless youth we tempt the heights of arts,   220
While from the bounded level of our mind,
Short views we take, nor see the lengths behind;
But more advanced, behold with strange surprise
New distant scenes of endless science rise!
So pleased at first the towering Alps we try,
Mount o'er the vales, and seem to tread the sky,
The eternal snows appear already past,
And the first clouds and mountains seem the last;
But, those attained, we tremble to survey
The growing labors of the lengthened way,   230
The increasing prospect tires our wandering eyes,
Hills peep o'er hills, and Alps on Alps arise!
A perfect judge will read each work of wit
With the same spirit that its author writ:
Survey the whole, nor seek slight faults to find
Where nature moves, and rapture warms the mind;
Nor lose, for that malignant dull delight,
The generous pleasure to be charmed with wit.
But in such lays as neither ebb, nor flow,
Correctly cold, and regularly low,   240
That shunning faults, one quiet tenor keep;
We cannot blame indeed, but we may sleep.
In wit, as nature, what affects our hearts
Is not the exactness of peculiar parts;
'Tis not a lip, or eye, we beauty call,

---

of Aristotle were held in high esteem by the English neo-classicists; indeed, his is one of the greatest of all literary and philosophic influences. 150. **Pegasus,** the winged horse of classical mythology that was finally conquered and ridden by Bellerophon. The winged horse is a symbol for poetic inspiration. 169. **there are,** i.e., there are those to whom, etc.

206. **recruits,** supplies. 216. **the Pierian spring.** Pieria, in Thessaly, was considered the birthplace of the Muses. It was believed that the Muses were originally nymphs, spirits who dwelt in forests, brooks, or fountains. To "drink" of the Pierian spring would be to quaff inspiration.

But the joint force and full result of all.
Thus when we view some well-proportioned dome,
(The world's just wonder, and e'en thine, O Rome!)
No single parts unequally surprise,
250 All comes united to the admiring eyes;
No monstrous height, or breadth, or length appear;
The whole at once is bold, and regular.

Whoever thinks a faultless piece to see,
Thinks what ne'er was, nor is, nor e'er shall be.
In every work regard the writer's end,
Since none can compass more than they intend;
And if the means be just, the conduct true,
Applause, in spite of trivial faults, is due;
As men of breeding, sometimes men of wit,
260 To avoid great errors, must the less commit:
Neglect the rules each verbal critic lays,
For not to know some trifles, is a praise.
Most critics, fond of some subservient art,
Still make the whole depend upon a part.
They talk of principles, but notions prize,
And all to one loved folly sacrifice.

Once on a time, La Mancha's knight, they say,
A certain bard encountering on the way,
Discoursed in terms as just, with looks as sage,
270 As e'er could Dennis of the Grecian stage;
Concluding all were desperate sots and fools,
Who durst depart from Aristotle's rules.
Our author, happy in a judge so nice,
Produced his play, and begged the knight's advice;
Made him observe the subject, and the plot,
The manners, passions, unities, what not?
All which, exact to rule, were brought about,
Were but a combat in the lists left out.
"What! leave the combat out?" exclaims the knight;
280 Yes, or we must renounce the Stagirite.
"Not so, by Heaven" (he answers in a rage),
"Knights, squires, and steeds, must enter on the stage."
So vast a throng the stage can ne'er contain.
"Then build a new, or act it in a plain."

Thus critics, of less judgment than caprice,
Curious not knowing, not exact but nice,
Form short ideas; and offend in arts
(As most in manners) by a love to parts.

Some to conceit alone their taste confine,
290 And glittering thoughts struck out at every line;
Pleased with a work where nothing's just or fit;
One glaring chaos and wild heap of wit.

Poets like painters, thus unskilled to trace
The naked nature and the living grace,
With gold and jewels cover every part,
And hide with ornaments their want of art.
True wit is nature to advantage dressed,
What oft was thought, but ne'er so well expressed;
Something, whose truth convinced at sight we find,
That gives us back the image of our mind.   300
As shades more sweetly recommend the light,
So modest plainness sets off sprightly wit.
For works may have more wit than does 'em good,
As bodies perish through excess of blood.

Others for language all their care express,
And value books, as women, men, for dress:
Their praise is still—the style is excellent:
The sense, they humbly take upon content.
Words are like leaves; and where they most abound,
Much fruit of sense beneath is rarely found;   310
False eloquence, like the prismatic glass,
Its gaudy colors spreads on every place;
The face of nature we no more survey,
All glares alike, without distinction gay:
But true expression, like the unchanging sun,
Clears and improves whate'er it shines upon,
It gilds all objects, but it alters none.
Expression is the dress of thought, and still
Appears more decent, as more suitable;
A vile conceit in pompous words expressed,   320
Is like a clown in regal purple dressed:
For different styles with different subjects sort,
As several garbs with country, town, and court.
Some by old words to fame have made pretense,
Ancients in phrase, mere moderns in their sense;
Such labored nothings, in so strange a style,
Amaze the unlearned, and make the learnéd smile.
Unlucky, as Fungoso in the play,
These sparks with awkward vanity display
What the fine gentlemen wore yesterday;   330
And but so mimic ancient wits at best,
As apes our grandsires, in their doublets dressed.
In words, as fashions, the same rule will hold;
Alike fantastic, if too new, or old:
Be not the first by whom the new are tried,
Nor yet the last to lay the old aside.

But most by numbers judge a poet's song;
And smooth or rough, with them, is right or wrong:
In the bright Muse though thousand charms conspire,
Her voice is all these tuneful fools admire;   340
Who haunt Parnassus but to please their ear,

248. wonder . . . Rome, the Cathedral of St. Peter in Rome. 267. La Mancha's knight, Don Quixote, the hero of the celebrated Spanish mock-romance of the same name by Cervantes (1547–1616). 270. Dennis, John Dennis (1657–1734), an English critic and dramatist who had written about Aristotle; he became a lifelong foe of Pope. (Cf. Epistle to Dr. Arbuthnot, p. 560, ll. 270 and 370.) 298. What . . . expressed, a splendid example of the conservative neo-classical ideal in art. 328. Fungoso, a foppish character in Ben Jonson's Every Man Out of His Humor (1599), who unsuccessfully tries to keep up with court fashions.

333. In words . . . aside, another excellent illustration of neo-classical conservatism. 337. numbers, verses. 356. Alexandrine, a line containing twelve syllables, iambic hexameter. The next line (l. 357) is an illustration. The name is derived from the fact that the important French medieval romance on Alexander the Great was written in this meter. 361. Denham . . . Waller, Sir John Denham (1615–1669) and Edmund Waller (1608–1687) were minor seventeenth-century poets, who had been praised as the originators of the closed couplet, which was developed by Dryden and perfected by Pope. 369. The hoarse . . . roar.

Not mend their minds; as some to church repair,
Not for the doctrine, but the music there.
These equal syllables alone require,
Though oft the ear the open vowels tire;
While expletives their feeble aid do join;
And ten low words oft creep in one dull line:
While they ring round the same unvaried chimes,
With sure returns of still expected rimes;
350 Where'er you find "the cooling western breeze,"
In the next line, it "whispers through the trees";
If crystal streams "with pleasing murmurs creep,"
The reader's threatened (not in vain) with "sleep":
Then, at the last and only couplet fraught
With some unmeaning thing they call a thought,
A needless Alexandrine ends the song,
That, like a wounded snake, drags its slow length along.
Leave such to tune their own dull rimes, and know
What's roundly smooth or languishingly slow;
360 And praise the easy vigor of a line,
Where Denham's strength, and Waller's sweetness join.
True ease in writing comes from art, not chance,
As those move easiest who have learned to dance.
'Tis not enough no harshness gives offense,
The sound must seem an echo to the sense:
Soft is the strain when Zephyr gently blows,
And the smooth stream in smoother numbers flows;
But when loud surges lash the sounding shore,
The hoarse, rough verse should like the torrent roar:
370 When Ajax strives some rock's vast weight to throw,
The line too labors, and the words move slow;
Not so, when swift Camilla scours the plain,
Flies o'er the unbending corn, and skims along the main.
Hear how Timotheus' varied lays surprise,
And bid alternate passions fall and rise!
While, at each change, the son of Libyan Jove
Now burns with glory, and then melts with love;
Now his fierce eyes with sparkling fury glow,
Now sighs steal out, and tears begin to flow:
380 Persians and Greeks like turns of nature found,
And the world's victor stood subdued by sound!
The power of music all our hearts allow,
And what Timotheus was, is Dryden now.

Avoid extremes; and shun the fault of such,
Who still are pleased too little or too much,
At every trifle scorn to take offense,
That always shows great pride, or little sense;
Those heads, as stomachs, are not sure the best,
Which nauseate all, and nothing can digest.
390 Yet let not each gay turn thy rapture move,
For fools admire, but men of sense approve:

As things seem large which we through mists descry,
Dullness is ever apt to magnify.

Some foreign writers, some our own despise;
The ancients only, or the moderns prize.
Thus wit, like faith, by each man is applied
To one small sect, and all are damned beside.
Meanly they seek the blessing to confine,
And force that sun but on a part to shine,
Which not alone the southern wit sublimes,   400
But ripens spirits in cold northern climes;
Which from the first has shone on ages past,
Enlights the present, and shall warm the last;
Though each may feel increases and decays,
And see now clearer and now darker days.
Regard not then if wit be old or new,
But blame the false, and value still the true.

Some ne'er advance a judgment of their own,
But catch the spreading notion of the town;
They reason and conclude by precedent,   410
And own stale nonsense which they ne'er invent.
Some judge of authors' names, not works, and then
Nor praise nor blame the writings, but the men.
Of all this servile herd the worst is he
That in proud dullness joins with quality,
A constant critic at the great man's board,
To fetch and carry nonsense for my lord.
What woeful stuff this madrigal would be,
In some starved hackney sonneteer, or me?
But let a lord once own the happy lines,   420
How the wit brightens; how the style refines!
Before his sacred name flies every fault,
And each exalted stanza teems with thought!

The vulgar thus through imitation err;
As oft the learned by being singular;
So much they scorn the crowd, that if the throng
By chance go right, they purposely go wrong;
So schismatics the plain believers quit,
And are but damned for having too much wit.
Some praise at morning what they blame at night;   430
But always think the last opinion right.
A Muse by these is like a mistress used,
This hour she's idolized, the next abused;
While their weak heads like towns unfortified,
'Twixt sense and nonsense daily change their side.
Ask them the cause; they're wiser still, they say;
And still tomorrow's wiser than today.
We think our fathers fools, so wise we grow;
Our wiser sons, no doubt, will think us so.

Pope is here trying to adapt the sound of the line to the sense (onomatopoeia). **370. Ajax . . . Camilla.** *Ajax* is a leading Greek hero in the Trojan War, noted for his great size and strength (cf. Homer's *Iliad*, VII, 265 ff.). *Camilla* is the swift-footed female warrior slain while fighting against the Trojan band in Italy (cf. Vergil's *Aeneid*, VII, 808-811). **374. Timotheus,** the favorite musician of Alexander the Great; cf. Dryden's *Alexander's Feast*, p. 468, ll. 158 ff. **376. son of Libyan Jove,** Alexander the Great (356-323 B.C.), king of Macedon, whom the priests of the Libyan Jupiter saluted as the son of their god. Historically,

of course, Alexander was the son of King Philip of Macedon. There was a particularly powerful cult of Jupiter (Zeus) in Libya, Africa. **391. approve,** test. **419. hackney,** at first a horse for ordinary driving, then figuratively, a drudge of any sort. As applied to a writer, the term means one who writes anything that comes his way in order to live. The combination "hackney writer" has been shortened to "hack writer" or "hack." **428. schismatics,** people who promote schisms, i.e., disbeliefs or divisions in some body, particularly a religious one.

440 Once school-divines this zealous isle o'erspread;
Who knew most Sentences, was deepest read;
Faith, Gospel, all seemed made to be disputed:
And none had sense enough to be confuted:
Scotists and Thomists, now in peace remain,
Amidst their kindred cobwebs in Duck Lane;
If faith itself has different dresses worn,
What wonder modes in wit should take their turn?
Oft, leaving what is natural and fit,
The current folly proves the ready wit;
450 And authors think their reputation safe,
Which lives as long as fools are pleased to laugh.

Some valuing those of their own side of mind,
Still make themselves the measure of mankind:
Fondly we think we honor merit then,
When we but praise ourselves in other men.
Parties in wit attend on those of state,
And public faction doubles private hate.
Pride, malice, folly, against Dryden rose,
In various shapes of parsons, critics, beaus;
460 But sense survived when merry jests were past;
For rising merit will buoy up at last.
Might he return, and bless once more our eyes,
New Blackmores and new Milbourns must arise:
Nay, should great Homer lift his awful head,
Zoilus again would start up from the dead.
Envy will merit, as its shade, pursue;
But like a shadow, proves the substance true;
For envied wit, like Sol eclipsed, makes known
The opposing body's grossness, not its own.
470 When first that sun too powerful beams displays,
It draws up vapors which obscure its rays;
But even those clouds at last adorn its way,
Reflect new glories, and augment the day.

Be thou the first true merit to defend,
His praise is lost, who stays till all commend.
Short is the date, alas, of modern rimes,
And 'tis but just to let them live betimes.
No longer now that golden age appears,
When patriarch-wits survived a thousand years:
480 Now length of fame (our second life) is lost,
And bare threescore is all even that can boast;
Our sons their fathers' failing language see,
And such as Chaucer is, shall Dryden be.
So when the faithful pencil has designed
Some bright idea of the master's mind,
Where a new word leaps out at his command,
And ready nature waits upon his hand;
When the ripe colors soften and unite,
And sweetly melt into just shade and light;

When mellow years their full perfection give, 490
And each bold figure just begins to live,
The treacherous colors the fair art betray,
And all the bright creation fades away!

Unhappy wit, like most mistaken things,
Atones not for that envy which it brings.
In youth alone its empty praise we boast,
But soon the short-lived vanity is lost:
Like some fair flower the early spring supplies,
That gaily blooms, but even in blooming dies.
What is this wit, which must our cares employ? 500
The owner's wife, that other men enjoy;
Then most our trouble still when most admired,
And still the more we give, the more required;
Whose fame with pains we guard, but lose with ease,
Sure some to vex, but never all to please;
'Tis what the vicious fear, the virtuous shun,
By fools 'tis hated, and by knaves undone!

If wit so much from ignorance undergo,
Ah, let not learning too commence its foe!
Of old, those met rewards who could excel, 510
And such were praised who but endeavored well:
Though triumphs were to generals only due,
Crowns were reserved to grace the soldiers too.
Now, they who reach Parnassus' lofty crown,
Employ their pains to spurn some others down;
And while self-love each jealous writer rules,
Contending wits become the sport of fools:
But still the worst with most regret commend,
For each ill author is as bad a friend.
To what base ends, and by what abject ways, 520
Are mortals urged through sacred lust of praise!
Ah, ne'er so dire a thirst of glory boast,
Nor in the critic let the man be lost.
Good-nature and good-sense must ever join;
To err is human, to forgive, divine.

But if in noble minds some dregs remain
Not yet purged off, of spleen and sour disdain;
Discharge that rage on more provoking crimes,
Nor fear a dearth in these flagitious times.
No pardon vile obscenity should find, 530
Though wit and art conspire to move your mind;
But dullness with obscenity must prove
As shameful sure as impotence in love.
In the fat age of pleasure, wealth, and ease,
Sprung the rank weed, and thrived with large increase:
When love was all an easy Monarch's care;
Seldom at council, never in a war:
Jilts ruled the state, and statesmen farces writ;

441. **Sentences,** a reference to the *Book of Sentences,* a collection of religious precepts by Peter Lombard (fl. 1151). 444. **Scotists and Thomists,** disputing followers of Duns Scotus and St. Thomas Aquinas, scholastic philosophers of the thirteenth century. 445. **Duck Lane,** a London street famous for its second-hand bookstores. 463. **Blackmores.** Sir Richard Blackmore (1652–1729), physician and poet, had attacked Pope in *A Satire on Wit.* **Milbourns.** The Reverend Luke Milbourn (1649–1720), poet and translator, had unfavorably criticized Dryden's translation of Vergil. 465. **Zoilus,** a Greek critic of the fourth century B.C., said to have been put to death for attacking Homer. 483. **as Chaucer . . . be.** It is interesting, in view of Dryden's great praise of Chaucer in the *Preface to the Fables* (p. 470), that Pope and his contemporaries regarded Chaucer as obsolete. 529. **flagitious,** corrupt, grossly wicked. 536. **an easy Monarch,** the gay and dissolute Charles II, whose reign, referred to in the next few lines, covers the years 1660–1685. 538. **Jilts,** strumpets. 545. **Socinus,** the name of two Italian

Nay, wits had pensions, and young lords had wit:
540 The fair sat panting at a courtier's play,
And not a mask went unimproved away:
The modest fan was lifted up no more,
And virgins smiled at what they blushed before.
The following license of a foreign reign
Did all the dregs of bold Socinus drain;
Then unbelieving priests reformed the nation,
And taught more pleasant methods of salvation;
Where Heaven's free subjects might their rights dis-
      pute,
Lest God himself should seem too absolute;
550 Pulpits their sacred satire learned to spare,
And vice admired to find a flatterer there!
Encouraged thus, wit's Titans braved the skies,
And the press groaned with licensed blasphemies.
These monsters, critics! with your darts engage,
Here point your thunder, and exhaust your rage!
Yet shun their fault, who, scandalously nice,
Will needs mistake an author into vice;
All seems infected that the infected spy,
As all looks yellow to the jaundiced eye.
(1711)

THE RAPE OF THE LOCK

*This mock epic poem about Lord Petre's playful
clipping of a lock of hair from the head of Arabella
Fermor, a famous beauty of the period, was written
by Pope, at the request of his friend John Caryll, to
heal the quarrel between the two families. It has all
of the characteristics of the elevated epic frame—the
allusions to Homer and Vergil, the "invocation," the
epic similes, the visit to the underworld, the heroic
battle, the clever strategy (Belinda's snuff), and the
deus ex machina ending—but in the interests of comedy they are subjected to a process of diminution:
Pope substitutes a trivial incident for a great action,
a woman for an epic hero, a stolen lock of hair for
the rape of Helen, etc. Everything is made smaller in
size and exquisitely feminine. But the poem is more
than whimsy; without damage to its comic brilliance
it seriously mirrors the "disarray of values" in the
society it describes.*

CANTO 1

What dire offense from amorous causes springs,
What mighty contests rise from trivial things,
I sing— This verse to Caryl, Muse! is due:

This, even Belinda may vouchsafe to view:
Slight is the subject, but not so the praise,
If she inspire, and he approve my lays.

Say what strange motive, goddess! could compel
A well-bred lord to assault a gentle belle?
Oh, say what stranger cause, yet unexplored,
Could make a gentle belle reject a lord? 10
In tasks so bold, can little men engage,
And in soft bosoms dwells such mighty rage?

Sol through white curtains shot a timorous ray,
And oped those eyes that must eclipse the day;
Now lap-dogs give themselves the rousing shake,
And sleepless lovers, just at twelve, awake;
Thrice rung the bell, the slipper knocked the ground,
And the pressed watch returned a silver sound.
Belinda still her downy pillow pressed,
Her guardian sylph prolonged the balmy rest: 20
'Twas he had summoned to her silent bed
The morning dream that hovered o'er her head;
A youth more glittering than a birth-night beau
(That e'en in slumber caused her cheek to glow),
Seemed to her ear his winning lips to lay,
And thus in whispers said, or seemed to say:

"Fairest of mortals, thou distinguished care
Of thousand bright inhabitants of air!
If e'er one vision touched thy infant thought,
Of all the nurse and all the priest have taught 30
Of airy elves by moonlight shadows seen,
The silver token, and the circled green,
Or virgins visited by angel powers,
With golden crowns and wreaths of heavenly flowers;
Hear and believe! thy own importance know,
Nor bound thy narrow views to things below.
Some secret truths, from learned pride concealed,
To maids alone and children are revealed;
What though no credit doubting wits may give?
The fair and innocent shall still believe. 40
Know, then, unnumbered spirits round thee fly,
The light militia of the lower sky:
These, though unseen, are ever on the wing,
Hang o'er the box, and hover round the Ring,
Think what an equipage thou hast in air,
And view with scorn two pages and a chair.
As now your own, our beings were of old,
And once enclosed in woman's beauteous mold;
Thence, by a soft transition, we repair
From earthly vehicles to these of air. 50
Think not, when woman's transient breath is fled,
That all her vanities at once are dead;

theologians, Laelius Socinus (1525-1562) and Faustus Socinus (1539-
1604). They were the forerunners of modern Unitarianism.
      Canto 1. 17. **slipper . . . ground,** knocked for a servant. 18.
pressed . . . sound, a type of watch quite common among the wealthier
in the eighteenth century, in which pressure placed upon the stem would
cause the watch to strike the last hour again. 20. **guardian sylph.** The
sylphs and nymphs, lesser spirits of the air, take the place in this mock-
epic of the gods and goddesses of classical mythology, who stalk through

the pages of Homer and Vergil, giving aid and comfort to their pro-
tégés. 31. **elves . . . seen,** etc. These few lines give a flash of a "romantic" nature that is most unusual in Pope. 44. **box . . . Ring.** The
box is a box at the theater; the Ring is a circular driveway or promenade
in Hyde Park, London.

Succeeding vanities she still regards,
And though she plays no more, o'erlooks the cards.
Her joy in gilded chariots, when alive,
And love of ombre, after death survive.
For when the fair in all their pride expire,
To their first elements their souls retire:
The sprites of fiery termagants in flame
60 Mount up, and take a salamander's name.
Soft yielding minds to water glide away,
And sip, with nymphs, their elemental tea.
The graver prude sinks downward to a gnome,
In search of mischief still on earth to roam.
The light coquettes in sylphs aloft repair,
And sport and flutter in the fields of air.

"Know further yet; whoever fair and chaste
Rejects mankind, is by some sylph embraced;
For spirits, freed from mortal laws, with ease
70 Assume what sexes and what shapes they please.
What guards the purity of melting maids,
In courtly balls, and midnight masquerades,
Safe from the treacherous friend, the daring spark,
The glance by day, the whisper in the dark,
When kind occasion prompts their warm desires,
When music softens, and when dancing fires?
'Tis but their sylph, the wise celestials know,
Though honor is the word with men below.
Some nymphs there are, too conscious of their face,
80 For life predestined to the gnomes' embrace.
These swell their prospects and exalt their pride,
When offers are disdained, and love denied:
Then gay ideas crowd the vacant brain,
While peers, and dukes, and all their sweeping train,
And garters, stars, and coronets appear,
And in soft sounds 'Your Grace' salutes their ear.
'Tis these that early taint the female soul,
Instruct the eyes of young coquettes to roll,
Teach infant cheeks a bidden blush to know,
90 And little hearts to flutter at a beau.

"Oft, when the world imagine women stray,
The sylphs through mystic mazes guide their way,
Through all the giddy circle they pursue,
And old impertinence expel by new.
What tender maid but must a victim fall
To one man's treat, but for another's ball?
When Florio speaks, what virgin could withstand,
If gentle Damon did not squeeze her hand?
With varying vanities, from every part,
100 They shift the moving toyshop of their heart;
Where wigs with wigs, with sword-knots sword-knots
strive,
Beaux banish beaux, and coaches coaches drive.

This erring mortals levity may call;
Oh, blind to truth! the sylphs contrive it all.

"Of these am I, who thy protection claim,
A watchful sprite, and Ariel is my name.
Late, as I ranged the crystal wilds of air,
In the clear mirror of thy ruling star
I saw, alas! some dread event impend,
Ere to the main this morning sun descend, 110
But Heaven reveals not what, or how, or where:
Warned by the sylph, O pious maid, beware!
This to disclose is all thy guardian can:
Beware of all, but most beware of man!"

He said; when Shock, who thought she slept too
long,
Leaped up, and waked his mistress with his tongue.
'Twas then, Belinda, if report say true,
Thy eyes first opened on a billet-doux;
Wounds, charms, and ardors were no sooner read,
But all the vision vanished from thy head. 120

And now, unveiled, the toilet stands displayed,
Each silver vase in mystic order laid.
First, robed in white, the nymph intent adores,
With head uncovered, the cosmetic powers.
A heavenly image in the glass appears.
To that she bends, to that her eyes she rears;
The inferior priestess, at her altar's side,
Trembling begins the sacred rites of pride.
Unnumbered treasures ope at once, and here
The various offerings of the world appear; 130
From each she nicely culls with curious toil,
And decks the goddess with the glittering spoil.
This casket India's glowing gems unlocks,
And all Arabia breathes from yonder box.
The tortoise here and elephant unite,
Transformed to combs, the speckled, and the white.
Here files of pins extend their shining rows,
Puffs, powders, patches, bibles, billets-doux.
Now awful beauty puts on all its arms;
The fair each moment rises in her charms, 140
Repairs her smiles, awakens every grace,
And calls forth all the wonders of her face;
Sees by degrees a purer blush arise,
And keener lightnings quicken in her eyes.
The busy sylphs surround their darling care,
These set the head, and those divide the hair,
Some fold the sleeve, whilst others plait the gown;
And Betty's praised for labors not her own.

CANTO 2

Not with more glories, in the ethereal plain,
The sun first rises o'er the purpled main,

---

56. ombre, a fashionable card game usually played by three people; see
Canto 3, ll. 25 ff. 59. termagants. Termagant was originally a supposed
deity of the Saracens. In the morality plays, in which Termagant appeared, he was always represented as a violent, brawling person. Hence
the term came to be applied to any brawling person, and particularly to
a scolding, shrewish, fiery woman. 60. salamander. It was an old

Than, issuing forth, the rival of his beams
Launched on the bosom of the silver Thames.
Fair nymphs, and well-dressed youths around her
    shone,
But every eye was fixed on her alone.
On her white breast a sparkling cross she wore,
Which Jews might kiss, and infidels adore.
Her lively looks a sprightly mind disclose,
10 Quick as her eyes, and as unfixed as those;
Favors to none, to all she smiles extends;
Oft she rejects, but never once offends.
Bright as the sun, her eyes the gazers strike,
And, like the sun, they shine on all alike.
Yet graceful ease, and sweetness void of pride,
Might hide her faults, if belles had faults to hide;
If to her share some female errors fall,
Look on her face, and you'll forget 'em all.

This nymph, to the destruction of mankind,
20 Nourished two locks, which graceful hung behind
In equal curls, and well conspired to deck
With shining ringlets the smooth ivory neck.
Love in these labyrinths his slaves detains,
And mighty hearts are held in slender chains.
With hairy springes, we the birds betray,
Slight lines of hair surprise the finny prey,
Fair tresses man's imperial race ensnare,
And beauty draws us with a single hair.

The adventurous baron the bright locks admired;
30 He saw, he wished, and to the prize aspired.
Resolved to win, he meditates the way,
By force to ravish, or by fraud betray;
For when success a lover's toil attends,
Few ask, if fraud or force attained his ends.

For this, ere Phoebus rose, he had implored
Propitious Heaven, and every power adored,
But chiefly Love—to Love an altar built,
Of twelve vast French romances, neatly gilt.
There lay three garters, half a pair of gloves;
40 And all the trophies of his former loves;
With tender billets-doux he lights the pyre,
And breathes three amorous sighs to raise the fire.
Then prostrate falls, and begs with ardent eyes
Soon to obtain, and long possess the prize;
The powers gave ear, and granted half his prayer,
The rest, the winds dispersed in empty air.

But now secure the painted vessel glides,
The sunbeams trembling on the floating tides:
While melting music steals upon the sky,
50 And softened sounds along the waters die;
Smooth flow the waves, the zephyrs gently play,

Belinda smiled, and all the world was gay.
All but the sylph—with careful thoughts oppressed,
The impending woe sat heavy on his breast.
He summons straight his denizens of air;
The lucid squadrons round the sails repair:
Soft o'er the shrouds aërial whispers breathe,
That seemed but zephyrs to the train beneath.
Some to the sun their insect wings unfold,
Waft on the breeze, or sink in clouds of gold;   60
Transparent forms, too fine for mortal sight,
Their fluid bodies half dissolved in light.
Loose to the wind their airy garments flew,
Thin glittering textures of the filmy dew,
Dipped in the richest tincture of the skies,
Where light disports in ever-mingling dyes,
While every beam new transient colors flings,
Colors that change whene'er they wave their wings.
Amid the circle, on the gilded mast,
Superior by the head, was Ariel placed;   70
His purple pinions opening to the sun,
He raised his azure wand, and thus begun.

"Ye sylphs and sylphids, to your chief give ear!
Fays, fairies, genii, elves, and demons, hear!
Ye know the spheres, and various tasks assigned
By laws eternal to the aërial kind.
Some in the fields of purest ether play,
And bask and whiten in the blaze of day.
Some guide the course of wandering orbs on high,
Or roll the planets through the boundless sky.   80
Some less refined, beneath the moon's pale light
Pursue the stars that shoot athwart the night,
Or suck the mists in grosser air below,
Or dip their pinions in the painted bow,
Or brew fierce tempests on the wintry main,
Or o'er the glebe distil the kindly rain.
Others on earth o'er human race preside,
Watch all their ways, and all their actions guide:
Of these the chief, the care of nations own,
And guard with arms divine the British throne.   90

"Our humbler province is to tend the fair.
Not a less pleasing, though less glorious care;
To save the powder from too rude a gale,
Nor let the imprisoned essences exhale;
To draw fresh colors from the vernal flowers;
To steal from rainbows ere they drop in showers,
A brighter wash; to curl their waving hairs,
Assist their blushes, and inspire their airs;
Nay, oft in dreams, invention we bestow,
To change a flounce, or add a furbelow.   100

"This day, black omens threat the brightest fair
That e'er deserved a watchful spirit's care;

belief that salamanders could pass unharmed through fire. 97. **Florio**
. . . Damon, traditional names for heroes in the pastoral literature of
the classics, and consequently for young swains in neo-classical writings.

115. **Shock,** Belinda's lap dog. 148. **Betty,** a traditional name for a
personal maid; here, Belinda's.
    Canto 2. 70. **Superior,** above. 100. **furbelow,** frill.

Alexander Pope   541

Some dire disaster, or by force, or slight;
But what, or where, the fates have wrapped in night.
Whether the nymph shall break Diana's law,
Or some frail china jar receive a flaw;
Or stain her honor, or her new brocade;
Forget her prayers, or miss a masquerade;
Or lose her heart, or necklace, at a ball;
110 Or whether Heaven has doomed that Shock must fall.
Haste, then, ye spirits! to your charge repair;
The fluttering fan be Zephyretta's care;
The drops to thee, Brillante, we consign;
And, Momentilla, let the watch be thine;
Do thou, Crispissa, tend her favorite lock;
Ariel himself shall be the guard of Shock.

"To fifty chosen sylphs, of special note,
We trust the important charge, the petticoat:
Oft have we known that seven-fold fence to fail,
120 Though stiff with hoops, and armed with ribs of whale;
Form a strong line about the silver bound,
And guard the wide circumference around.

"Whatever spirit, careless of his charge,
His post neglects, or leaves the fair at large,
Shall feel sharp vengeance soon o'ertake his sins,
Be stopped in vials, or transfixed with pins;
Or plunged in lakes of bitter washes lie,
Or wedged whole ages in a bodkin's eye:
Gums and pomatums shall his flight restrain,
130 While clogged he beats his silken wings in vain;
Or alum styptics with contracting power
Shrink his thin essence like a rivelled flower:
Or, as Ixion fixed, the wretch shall feel
The giddy motion of the whirling mill,
In fumes of burning chocolate shall glow,
And tremble at the sea that froths below!"

He spoke; the spirits from the sails descend;
Some, orb in orb, around the nymph extend;
Some thrid the mazy ringlets of her hair;
140 Some hang upon the pendants of her ear;
With beating hearts the dire event they wait,
Anxious, and trembling for the birth of fate.

CANTO 3

Close by those meads, forever crowned with flowers,
Where Thames with pride surveys his rising towers,
There stands a structure of majestic frame,
Which from the neighboring Hampton takes its name.
Here Britain's statesmen oft the fall foredoom
Of foreign tyrants and of nymphs at home;

Here thou, great Anna! whom three realms obey,
Dost sometimes counsel take—and sometimes tea.

Hither the heroes and the nymphs resort,
To taste awhile the pleasures of a court;   10
In various talk the instructive hours they passed,
Who gave the ball, or paid the visit last;
One speaks the glory of the British queen,
And one describes a charming Indian screen;
A third interprets motions, looks, and eyes;
At every word a reputation dies.
Snuff, or the fan, supply each pause of chat,
With singing, laughing, ogling, and all that.

Meanwhile, declining from the noon of day,
The sun obliquely shoots his burning ray;   20
The hungry judges soon the sentence sign,
And wretches hang that jurymen may dine;
The merchant from the Exchange returns in peace,
And the long labors of the toilet cease.
Belinda now, whom thirst of fame invites,
Burns to encounter two adventurous knights,
At ombre singly to decide their doom;
And swells her breast with conquests yet to come.
Straight the three bands prepare in arms to join,
Each band the number of the sacred nine.   30
Soon as she spreads her hand, the aërial guard
Descend, and sit on each important card:
First, Ariel perched upon a Matadore,
Then each, according to the rank they bore;
For sylphs, yet mindful of their ancient race,
Are, as when women, wondrous fond of place.

Behold, four kings in majesty revered,
With hoary whiskers and a forky beard;
And four fair queens whose hands sustain a flower,
The expressive emblem of their softer power;   40
Four knaves in garbs succinct, a trusty band,
Caps on their heads, and halberts in their hand;
And parti-colored troops, a shining train,
Draw forth to combat on the velvet plain.

The skillful nymph reviews her force with care:
Let spades be trumps! she said, and trumps they were.

Now moved to war her sable Matadores,
In show like leaders of the swarthy Moors.
Spadillio first, unconquerable lord!
Led off two captive trumps, and swept the board.   50
As many more Manillio forced to yield,
And marched a victor from the verdant field.
Him Basto followed, but his fate more hard

105. **Diana's law,** the law of chastity; Diana was the goddess of maidenhood. 129. **Gums . . . pomatums,** perfumed ointments; pomatum
was used particularly for the hair. 132. **rivelled,** withered. 133. **Ixion
fixed.** Ixion was a legendary king who, for making love to Juno, wife of
Jupiter and queen of the gods, was fastened by Jupiter to an endlessly
revolving wheel in Hades. He is described there by Vergil in Book VI
of the *Aeneid.* 139. **thrid,** threaded, passed through.
Canto 3. 3. **structure . . . frame,** Hampton Court, one of the royal

palaces near London. 7. **Anna,** Queen Anne, last of the Stuarts, whose
reign from 1702 to 1714 is noteworthy because she was the first sovereign for whom the term ruler "of England, Scotland, and Wales" was
an absolute reality. England and Scotland had been united politically
in 1707. 8. **tea,** pronounced as French *thé,* to rime with obey. 33.
Matadore, one of the three highest cards in ombre; their names are
given below. *Spadillio* (l. 49) was the ace of spades; *Manillio* (l. 51),
the two of black trumps or the seven of red trumps; *Basto* (l. 53) was

Gained but one trump and one plebeian card.
With his broad saber next, a chief in years,
The hoary majesty of spades appears,
Puts forth one manly leg, to sight revealed,
The rest, his many-colored robe concealed.
The rebel knave, who dares his prince engage,
60 Proves the just victim of his royal rage.
Even mighty Pam, that kings and queens o'erthrew,
And mowed down armies in the fights of Loo,
Sad chance of war! now destitute of aid,
Falls undistinguished by the victor spade!

Thus far both armies to Belinda yield;
Now to the baron fate inclines the field.
His warlike Amazon her host invades,
The imperial consort of the crown of spades,
The clubs black tyrant first her victim died,
70 Spite of his haughty mien, and barbarous pride:
What boots the regal circle on his head,
His giant limbs, in state unwieldy spread;
That long behind he trails his pompous robe,
And of all monarchs only grasps the globe?

The baron now his diamonds pours apace;
The embroidered king who shows but half his face,
And his refulgent queen, with powers combined,
Of broken troops an easy conquest find.
Clubs, diamonds, hearts, in wild disorder seen,
80 With throngs promiscuous strew the level green.
Thus when dispersed a routed army runs,
Of Asia's troops, and Afric's sable sons,
With like confusion different nations fly,
Of various habit, and of various dye,
The pierced battalions disunited fall,
In heaps on heaps; one fate o'erwhelms them all.

The knave of diamonds tries his wily arts,
And wins (oh, shameful chance!) the queen of hearts.
At this the blood the virgin's cheek forsook,
90 A livid paleness spreads o'er all her look;
She sees, and trembles at the approaching ill,
Just in the jaws of ruin, and codille.
And now (as oft in some distempered state)
On one nice trick depends the general fate,
An ace of hearts steps forth; the king unseen
Lurked in her hand, and mourned his captive queen:
He springs to vengeance with an eager pace,
And falls like thunder on the prostrate ace.
The nymph exulting fills with shouts the sky;
100 The walls, the wood, and long canals reply.

Oh, thoughtless mortals! ever blind to fate,
Too soon dejected, and too soon elate.

Sudden, these honors shall be snatched away,
And cursed forever this victorious day.

For lo! the board with cups and spoons is crowned,
The berries crackle, and the mill turns round;
On shining altars of Japan they raise
The silver lamp; the fiery spirits blaze:
From silver spouts the grateful liquors glide,
While China's earth receives the smoking tide: 110
At once they gratify their scent and taste,
And frequent cups prolong the rich repast.
Straight hover round the fair her airy band;
Some, as she sipped, the fuming liquor fanned,
Some o'er her lap their careful plumes displayed,
Trembling, and conscious of the rich brocade.
Coffee (which makes the politician wise,
And see through all things with his half-shut eyes)
Sent up in vapors to the baron's brain
New stratagems the radiant lock to gain. 120
Ah, cease, rash youth! desist ere 'tis too late,
Fear the just gods, and think of Scylla's fate!
Changed to a bird, and sent to flit in air,
She dearly pays for Nisus' injured hair!

But when to mischief mortals bend their will,
How soon they find fit instruments of ill!
Just then Clarissa drew with tempting grace
A two-edged weapon from her shining case;
So ladies in romance assist their knight,
Present the spear, and arm him for the fight. 130
He takes the gift with reverence, and extends
The little engine on his fingers' ends;
This just behind Belinda's neck he spread,
As o'er the fragrant steams she bends her head.
Swift to the lock a thousand sprites repair,
A thousand wings, by turns, blow back her hair;
And thrice they twitched the diamond in her ear;
Thrice she looked back, and thrice the foe drew near.
Just in that instant, anxious Ariel sought
The close recesses of the virgin's thought; 140
As on the nosegay in her breast reclined,
He watched the ideas rising in her mind,
Sudden he viewed, in spite of all her art,
An earthly lover lurking at her heart.
Amazed, confused, he found his power expired,
Resigned to fate, and with a sigh retired.

The peer now spreads the glittering forfex wide,
To inclose the lock; now joins it, to divide.
Even then, before the fatal engine closed,
A wretched sylph too fondly interposed; 150
Fate urged the shears, and cut the sylph in twain,

---

the ace of clubs. **41. succinct**, encircled by a girdle. **42. halberts,** halberds, long-handled, ax-like weapons surmounted by a long point; they were used frequently in the armies of the fifteenth and sixteenth centuries. **61. Pam . . . Loo.** Pam was the jack (knave) of clubs, the highest card in the game of Loo. **92. codille**, failure to take the largest number of tricks. Here, as elsewhere in this poem, Pope makes brilliant use of the device of anticlimax. **94. nice**, possibly in the older sense of "foolish"; probably used here in the sense of "neat, precise, trim."

106. berries . . . mill, coffee beans ground in a hand mill at the table. **107. altars of Japan,** small lacquered tables. **122. Scylla . . . Nisus' . . . hair.** In Greek legend, Scylla, the daughter of King Nisus of Megara, gave to an enemy a lock of her father's hair, on which the safety of the state depended; for this offense she was changed into a bird. She must not be confused with Scylla, the dreadful sea monster whose home was opposite the whirlpool Charybdis in the Straits of Messina. **147. forfex,** shears, scissors.

(But airy substance soon unites again)
The meeting points the sacred hair dissever
From the fair head, forever, and forever!

Then flashed the living lightning from her eyes,
And screams of horror rend the affrighted skies.
Not louder shrieks to pitying Heaven are cast,
When husbands, or when lap-dogs breathe their last;
Or when rich China vessels, fallen from high,
160 In glittering dust and painted fragments lie!

"Let wreaths of triumph now my temples twine,"
(The victor cried); "the glorious prize is mine!
While fish in streams, or birds delight in air,
Or in a coach and six the British fair,
As long as Atalantis shall be read,
Or the small pillow grace a lady's bed,
While visits shall be paid on solemn days,
When numerous wax-lights in bright order blaze,
While nymphs take treats, or assignations give,
170 So long my honor, name, and praise shall live!
What Time would spare, from steel receives its date,
And monuments, like men, submit to fate!
Steel could the labor of the gods destroy,
And strike to dust the imperial towers of Troy;
Steel could the works of mortal pride confound,
And hew triumphal arches to the ground.
What wonder then, fair nymph! thy hairs should feel
The conquering force of unresisted steel?"

CANTO 4

But anxious cares the pensive nymph oppressed,
And secret passions labored in her breast.
Not youthful kings in battle seized alive,
Not scornful virgins who their charms survive,
Not ardent lovers robbed of all their bliss,
Not ancient ladies when refused a kiss,
Not tyrants fierce that unrepenting die,
Not Cynthia when her manteau's pinned awry,
E'er felt such rage, resentment, and despair,
10 As thou, sad virgin, for thy ravished hair.
For, that sad moment, when the sylphs withdrew
And Ariel weeping from Belinda flew,
Umbriel, a dusky, melancholy sprite,
As ever sullied the fair face of light,
Down to the central earth, his proper scene,
Repaired to search the gloomy cave of Spleen.

Swift on his sooty pinions flits the gnome,
And in a vapor reached the dismal dome.
No cheerful breeze this sullen region knows,

"The Prize is Mine!" from Bernard Lintott's edition of
The Rape of the Lock, London, 1714.

The dreaded east is all the wind that blows.   20
Here in a grotto, sheltered close from air,
And screened in shades from day's detested glare,
She sighs forever on her pensive bed,
Pain at her side, and Megrim at her head.
Two handmaids wait the throne, alike in place,
But differing far in figure and in face.
Here stood Ill-nature like an ancient maid,
Her wrinkled form in black and white arrayed;
With store of prayers, for mornings, nights, and noons,
Her hand is filled; her bosom with lampoons.   30

There Affectation, with a sickly mien,
Shows in her cheek the roses of eighteen,

165. Atalantis . . . read. New Atalantis (1709), a popular book of
contemporary scandal and gossip, by Mrs. Mary Manley (1663–1724).
The title of the book is something of a play upon the title of Bacon's
New Atlantis (1624). Bacon's work was an account of a Utopia, or
mythical kingdom, Atlantis; Mrs. Manley's was an account of a woman's
world of gossip named for the "unapproachable, all-powerful" female of
Greek legend, Atalanta.

Canto 4. 1. anxious cares, etc. This and the following lines (2–10)
afford some excellent examples of the neo-classical predilection in style
for the "epithet." It is to be noted that virtually every noun has a
single descriptive adjective in attendance. 8. Cynthia, Diana, the goddess of chastity. manteau, mantle. 24. Megrim, melancholy, depression.
51. pipkin, a small jar. Homer's tripod, a self-moving tripod, described
by Homer in the Iliad, XVIII, 372 ff. 56. spleenwort, maidenhair, an

Practiced to lisp, and hang the head aside,
Faints into airs, and languishes with pride,
On the rich quilt sinks with becoming woe,
Wrapped in a gown, for sickness, and for show.
The fair ones feel such maladies as these,
When each new night-dress gives a new disease.

A constant vapor o'er the palace flies;
40 Strange phantoms rising as the mists arise;
Dreadful, as hermit's dreams in haunted shades,
Or bright, as visions of expiring maids.
Now glaring fiends, and snakes on rolling spires,
Pale specters, gaping tombs, and purple fires:
Now lakes of liquid gold, Elysian scenes,
And crystal domes, and angels in machines.

Unnumbered throngs on every side are seen,
Of bodies changed to various forms by Spleen.
Here living tea-pots stand, one arm held out,
50 One bent; the handle this, and that the spout:
A pipkin there, like Homer's tripod, walks;
Here sighs a jar, and there a goose-pie talks;
Men prove with child, as powerful fancy works,
And maids, turned bottles, call aloud for corks.

Safe passed the gnome through this fantastic band,
A branch of healing spleenwort in his hand.
Then thus addressed the power: "Hail, wayward
        queen!
Who rule the sex, to fifty from fifteen;
Parent of vapors and of female wit,
60 Who give the hysteric, or poetic fit,
On various tempers act by various ways,
Make some take physic, others scribble plays;
Who cause the proud their visits to delay,
And send the godly in a pet to pray.
A nymph there is, that all thy power disdains,
And thousands more in equal mirth maintains.
But oh! if e'er thy gnome could spoil a grace,
Or raise a pimple on a beauteous face,
Like citron-waters matrons' cheeks inflame,
70 Or change complexions at a losing game;
If e'er with airy horns I planted heads,
Of rumpled petticoats, or tumbled beds,
Or caused suspicion when no soul was rude,
Or discomposed the head-dress of a prude,
Or e'er to costive lap-dog gave disease,
Which not the tears of brightest eyes could ease;
Hear me, and touch Belinda with chagrin,
That single act gives half the world the spleen."

The goddess with a discontented air
80 Seems to reject him, though she grants his prayer.

A wondrous bag with both her hands she binds,
Like that where once Ulysses held the winds;
There she collects the force of female lungs,
Sighs, sobs, and passions, and the war of tongues.
A vial next she fills with fainting fears,
Soft sorrows, melting griefs, and flowing tears.
The gnome rejoicing bears her gifts away,
Spreads his black wings, and slowly mounts to day.

Sunk in Thalestris' arms the nymph he found,
Her eyes dejected and her hair unbound.   90
Full o'er their heads, the swelling bag he rent,
And all the furies issued at the vent.
Belinda burns with more than mortal ire,
And fierce Thalestris fans the rising fire.
"O wretched maid!" she spread her hands, and cried,
(While Hampton's echoes, "Wretched maid!" re-
        plied)
"Was it for this you took such constant care
The bodkin, comb, and essence to prepare?
For this your locks in paper durance bound,
For this with torturing irons wreathed around?   100
For this with fillets strained your tender head,
And bravely bore the double loads of lead?
Gods! shall the ravisher display your hair,
While the fops envy, and the ladies stare!
Honor forbid! at whose unrivalled shrine
Ease, pleasure, virtue, all our sex resign.
Methinks already I your tears survey,
Already hear the horrid things they say,
Already see you a degraded toast,
And all your honor in a whisper lost!   110
How shall I, then, your helpless fame defend?
'Twill then be infamy to seem your friend!
And shall this prize, the inestimable prize,
Exposed through crystal to the gazing eyes,
And heightened by the diamond's circling rays,
On that rapacious hand forever blaze?
Sooner shall grass in Hyde Park Circus grow,
And wits take lodgings in the sound of Bow;
Sooner let earth, air, sea, to chaos fall,
Men, monkeys, lap-dogs, parrots, perish all!"   120

She said; then raging to Sir Plume repairs,
And bids her beau demand the precious hairs.
(Sir Plume, of amber snuff-box justly vain,
And the nice conduct of a clouded cane)
With earnest eyes, and round unthinking face,
He first the snuff-box opened, then the case,
And thus broke out—"My lord, why, what the devil?
Z——ds! damn the lock! 'fore Gad, you must be civil!
Plague on't! 'tis past a jest—nay prithee, pox!

---

herb used formerly for the treatment of diseases of the spleen. **59. vapors,** whims. **69. citron-waters,** spirits distilled from citron rind, used
for skin lotions. **71. horns . . . heads,** an allusion to the old belief
that horns were supposed to grow on the heads of husbands with unfaithful wives. **82. Ulysses, etc.** Ulysses, during the course of his
wanderings, visited the island of Aeolus, god of the winds, and took away
a bagful of the various winds to help him in his journey. The story is
told in Homer's *Odyssey,* X, 19 ff. **89. Thalestris,** said to be Mrs.
Morley, friend to Arabella (Belinda) Fermor. **118. sound of Bow,**
within sound of the bells of the church of St. Mary in Bow, near an
unfashionable section of London. **124. clouded cane,** a walking stick
with carvings in the shape of clouds. **128. Z—ds!** "Zounds," a corruption of "God's wounds."

130 Give her the hair," he spoke, and rapped his box.
"It grieves me much," replied the peer again,
"Who speaks so well should ever speak in vain.
But by this lock, this sacred lock, I swear,
(Which never more shall join its parted hair;
Which never more its honors shall renew,
Clipped from the lovely head where late it grew)
That while my nostrils draw the vital air,
This hand, which won it, shall forever wear."
He spoke, and speaking, in proud triumph spread
140 The long-contended honors of her head.

But Umbriel, hateful gnome! forbears not so;
He breaks the vial whence the sorrows flow.
Then see! the nymph in beauteous grief appears,
Her eyes half languishing, half drowned in tears;
On her heaved bosom hung her drooping head,
Which, with a sigh, she raised; and thus she said:

"Forever cursed be this detested day,
Which snatched my best, my favorite curl away!
Happy! ah, ten times happy had I been,
150 If Hampton Court these eyes had never seen!
Yet am not I the first mistaken maid,
By love of courts to numerous ills betrayed.
Oh, had I rather unadmired remained
In some lone isle or distant northern land;
Where the gilt chariot never marks the way,
Where none learn ombre, none e'er taste bohea!
There kept my charms concealed from mortal eye,
Like roses, that in deserts bloom and die.
What moved my mind with youthful lords to roam?
160 Oh, had I stayed, and said my prayers at home!
'Twas this, the morning omens seemed to tell,
Thrice from my trembling hand the patch-box fell;
The tottering china shook without a wind.
Nay, Poll sat mute, and Shock was most unkind!
A sylph, too, warned me of the threats of fate,
In mystic visions, now believed too late!
See the poor remnants of these slighted hairs!
My hands shall rend what e'en thy rapine spares;
These in two sable ringlets taught to break,
170 Once gave new beauties to the snowy neck;
The sister lock now sits uncouth, alone,
And in its fellow's fate foresees its own;
Unfurled it hangs, the fatal shears demands,
And tempts once more, thy sacrilegious hands.
Oh, hadst thou, cruel! been content to seize
Hairs less in sight, or any hairs but these!"

CANTO 5

She said; the pitying audience melt in tears.
But Fate and Jove had stopped the baron's ears.

In vain Thalestris with reproach assails,
For who can move when fair Belinda fails?
Not half so fixed the Trojan could remain,
While Anna begged and Dido raged in vain.
Then grave Clarissa graceful waved her fan;
Silence ensued, and thus the nymph began:

"Say, why are beauties praised and honored most,
The wise man's passion, and the vain man's toast? 10
Why decked with all that land and sea afford,
Why angels called, and angel-like adored?
Why 'round our coaches crowd the white-gloved
    beaux,
Why bows the side-box from its inmost rows?
How vain are all these glories, all our pains,
Unless good sense preserve what beauty gains:
That men may say, when we the front-box grace:
'Behold the first in virtue as in face!'
Oh! if to dance all night, and dress all day,
Charmed the smallpox, or chased old age away;   20
Who would not scorn what housewife's cares produce,
Or who would learn one earthly thing of use?
To patch, nay ogle, might become a saint,
Nor could it sure be such a sin to paint.
But since, alas! frail beauty must decay,
Curled or uncurled, since locks will turn to gray;
Since painted, or not painted, all shall fade,
And she who scorns a man must die a maid;
What then remains but well our power to use,
And keep good humor still what'er we lose?   30
And trust me, dear! good humor can prevail,
When airs, and flights, and screams, and scolding
    fail.
Beauties in vain their pretty eyes may roll;
Charms strike the sight, but merit wins the soul."

So spoke the dame, but no applause ensued;
Belinda frowned, Thalestris called her prude.
"To arms, to arms!" the fierce virago cries,
And swift as lightning to the combat flies.
All side in parties, and begin th' attack;
Fans clap, silks rustle, and tough whale-bones crack; 40
Heroes' and heroines' shouts confusedly rise,
And bass and treble voices strike the skies.
No common weapons in their hands are found,
Like gods they fight, nor dread a mortal wound.

So when bold Homer makes the gods engage,
And heavenly breasts with human passions rage;
'Gainst Pallas, Mars; Latona, Hermes arms;
And all Olympus rings with loud alarms:
Jove's thunder roars, Heaven trembles all around,
Blue Neptune storms, the bellowing deeps resound: 50

---

156. **bohea**, an expensive brand of tea. 162. **patch-box**, a box containing patches of court plaster, which was used to decorate the face. See Addison's *Party Patches*, p. 485.

Canto 5. 5. **Trojan . . . vain.** The "Trojan" is Aeneas, hero of Vergil's *Aeneid*, who on command of Jupiter determined to leave Carthage in spite of the grief and pleas of Queen Dido of Carthage and of her sister Anna (*Aeneid*, IV, 4 ff.). 47. **Pallas . . . Neptune,** Pallas Athena (Minerva), goddess of wisdom and war; *Mars*, god of war; *Latona*, mother of Apollo and goddess of the night; *Hermes* (Mercury), messenger of the gods; *Olympus*, a mountain in Thessaly, the home of the gods; *Neptune*, god of the sea. 53. **sconce**, a bracket in a wall for holding candles. 62. **Dapperwit . . . Sir Fopling.** Dapperwit was the

A mournful glance Sir Fopling upwards cast,
"Those eyes are made so killing"—was his last.
Thus on Meander's flowery margin lies
The expiring swan, and as he sings he dies.

When bold Sir Plume had drawn Clarissa down,
Chloe stepped in and killed him with a frown;
She smiled to see the doughty hero slain,
But, at her smile, the beau revived again.   70
Now Jove suspends his golden scales in air,
Weighs the men's wits against the lady's hair;
The doubtful beam long nods from side to side;
At length the wits mount up, the hairs subside.

See, fierce Belinda on the baron flies,
With more than usual lightning in her eyes;
Nor feared the chief the unequal fight to try,
Who sought no more than on his foe to die.
But this bold lord with manly strength endued,
She with one finger and a thumb subdued;   80
Just where the breath of life his nostrils drew,
A charge of snuff the wily virgin threw;
The gnomes direct, to every atom just,
The pungent grains of titillating dust.
Sudden, with starting tears each eye o'erflows,
And the high dome re-echoes to his nose.

"Now meet thy fate," incensed Belinda cried,
And drew a deadly bodkin from her side.
(The same, his ancient personage to deck,
Her great great grandsire wore about his neck,   90
In three seal-rings; which after, melted down,
Formed a vast buckle for his widow's gown;
Her infant grandame's whistle next it grew,
The bells she jingled, and the whistle blew;
Then in a bodkin graced her mother's hairs,
Which long she wore, and now Belinda wears.)

"Boast not my fall," he cried, "insulting foe!
Thou by some other shalt be laid as low,
Nor think to die dejects my lofty mind;
All that I dread is leaving you behind!   100
Rather than so, ah, let me still survive,
And burn in Cupid's flames—but burn alive."

"Restore the lock!" she cries; and all around
"Restore the lock!" the vaulted roofs rebound
Not fierce Othello in so loud a strain
Roared for the handkerchief that caused his pain.
But see how oft ambitious aims are crossed,
And chiefs contend till all the prize is lost!
The lock, obtained with guilt, and kept with pain,
In every place is sought, but sought in vain: 110

*The Combat of Beaux and Belles, from Bernard Lintott's
edition of* The Rape of the Lock, *London, 1714.*

Earth shakes her nodding towers, the ground gives
   way,
And the pale ghosts start at the flash of day!

Triumphant Umbriel on a sconce's height
Clapped his glad wings, and sat to view the fight:
Propped on their bodkin spears, the sprites survey
The growing combat, or assist the fray.

While through the press enraged Thalestris flies,
And scatters death around from both her eyes,
A beau and witling perished in the throng,
60 One died in metaphor, and one in song.
"O cruel nymph! a living death I bear,"
Cried Dapperwit, and sunk beside his chair.

name of a ludicrous character in *Love in a Wood*, a comedy by William
Wycherley (1640?–1715); Sir Fopling is a nervous character in *The
Man of Mode*, a comedy by Sir George Etherege (1635?–1691?). 65.
Meander . . . lies. The Meander is a river in Asia Minor, often men-
tioned in ancient poetry. It was particularly noted for its extremely wind-
ing course; hence our word "to meander," meaning to wander rather

slowly and aimlessly. 105. **Othello . . . pain.** Suspecting that Desdemona has given a highly prized handkerchief to Cassio, her supposed
lover, Othello asks for it and becomes angry when Desdemona fails to
produce it.

With such a prize no mortal must be blessed,
So Heaven decrees! with Heaven who can contest?

Some thought it mounted to the lunar sphere,
Since all things lost on earth are treasured there.
There heroes' wits are kept in ponderous vases,
And beaux' in snuff-boxes and tweezer cases.
There broken vows and death-bed alms are found,
And lovers' hearts with ends of riband bound,
The courtier's promises, and sick man's prayers,
120 The smiles of harlots, and the tears of heirs,
Cages for gnats, and chains to yoke a flea,
Dried butterflies, and tomes of casuistry.

But trust the Muse—she saw it upward rise,
Though marked by none but quick, poetic eyes:
(So Rome's great founder to the heavens withdrew,
To Proculus alone confessed in view)
A sudden star, it shot through liquid air,
And drew behind a radiant trail of hair.
Not Berenice's locks first rose so bright,
130 The heavens bespangling with disheveled light.
The sylphs behold it kindling as it flies,
And pleased pursue its progress through the skies.

This the beau monde shall from the Mall survey,
And hail with music its propitious ray.
This the blest lover shall for Venus take,
And send up vows from Rosamonda's lake.
This Partridge soon shall view in cloudless skies,
When next he looks through Galileo's eyes;
And hence the egregious wizard shall foredoom
140 The fate of Louis and the fall of Rome.

Then cease, bright nymph! to mourn thy ravished
    hair,
Which adds new glory to the shining sphere!
Not all the tresses that fair head can boast,
Shall draw such envy as the lock you lost.
For, after all the murders of your eye,
When, after millions slain, yourself shall die:
When those fair suns shall set, as set they must,
And all those tresses shall be laid in dust,
This lock, the Muse shall consecrate to fame,
And 'midst the stars inscribe Belinda's name.
(1712, 1714)

from AN ESSAY ON MAN

An Essay on Man is Pope's "theodicy"—that is, a philosophical work which deals with the problem of existence of evil in a world which is, presumably, the creation of a benevolent God. It was written, then, according to Pope's own testimony, for the same reason that Milton wrote Paradise Lost, "to vindicate the ways of God to man." Protestant England in the seventeenth and eighteenth centuries could not rest its view of man's relationship to the universe, to himself, to society, and to happiness on the dogmatic premises of the Catholic Middle Ages. Yet, restless spirits like Voltaire were pressing for a tenable answer. An Essay on Man is a segment of a much more ambitious scheme of Pope's to devote his writing to philosophical and ethical speculations.

The Essay is dedicated to Pope's friend, the deistic philosopher Henry St. John Viscount Bolingbroke, who encouraged him to do the work. In the "Design" to the poem, Pope tells something of his intentions: "This I might have done in prose, but I chose verse, and even rime, for two reasons. The one will appear obvious, that principles, maxims, or precepts so written, both strike the reader more strongly at first, and are more easily retained by him afterwards. The other may seem odd, but it is true, I found I could express them more shortly this way than in prose itself; and nothing is more certain than that much of the force as well as grace of arguments or instructions depends on their conciseness. I was unable to treat this part of my subject more in detail without becoming dry and tedious, or more poetically without sacrificing perspicuity to ornament, without wandering from the precision, or breaking the chain of reasoning. If any man can unite all these without diminution of any of them, I freely confess he will compass a thing above my capacity." Pope's efforts, then, reached toward vividness, memorableness, conciseness, simplicity of style, logical coherence—principal characteristics of a "poetry of statement" which, in English, Pope brought to its highest perfection.

The central thesis of the Essay—the classic statement of eighteenth-century moral and philosophical optimism—is stated in the closing lines of Epistle I, culminating in the maxim, "Whatever is, is right." Pope does not deny the existence of evil in the world but rather asserts its necessity, and when he states or implies that this is "the best of all possible worlds," he asserts not that it is absolutely good but that it is the best conceivable.

122. **tomes of casuistry,** volumes of oversubtle reasoning about conscience and conduct. 125. **Rome's . . . view.** The founder of Rome, Romulus, was carried in a storm to heaven by his father Mars, and was deified by the Romans. To the Roman senator Proculus, Romulus is said to have expressed a wish for deification as Quirinus. The story is told in *From the Founding of the City,* a history of Rome by the Roman Titus

Livius (Livy) (59 B.C.–17 A.D.). 129. **Berenice's . . . bright.** Berenice was an Egyptian queen who dedicated her beautiful hair to Venus, goddess of love, for the safe return of her husband from war. The hair was changed into a comet. There is an astronomical constellation in the Northern Hemisphere known as *Coma Berenicis* (Berenice's hair). 136. **Rosamonda's lake,** a small pond in St. James' Park, London. It was named

The modern reader, with his post-romantic orientation, may sometimes scoff at the seemingly facile or fatuous optimism of such a philosophy. But for all the individuality of Pope's phrasing, his position is not necessarily logically inconsistent with those of such philosophers and moral commentators as St. Thomas Aquinas and Dante. And it is important to remember that between Paradise Lost *and* Wordsworth's Prelude, *there is no poem on religious and moral questions as significant as Pope's* Essay on Man.

EPISTLE 1

Awake, my St. John! leave all meaner things
To low ambition, and the pride of kings.
Let us (since life can little more supply
Than just to look about us and to die)
Expatiate free o'er all this scene of man;
A mighty maze! but not without a plan;
A wild, where weeds and flowers promiscuous shoot;
Or garden, tempting with forbidden fruit.
Together let us beat this ample field,
10 Try what the open, what the covert yield;
The latent tracts, the giddy heights, explore
Of all who blindly creep, or sightless soar;
Eye nature's walks, shoot folly as it flies,
And catch the manners living as they rise;
Laugh where we must, be candid where we can;
But vindicate the ways of God to man.

I. Say first, of God above, or man below,
What can we reason, but from what we know?
Of man, what see we but his station here,
20 From which to reason, or to which refer?
Through worlds unnumbered though the God be
    known,
'Tis ours to trace him only in our own.
He, who through vast immensity can pierce,

See worlds on worlds compose one universe,
Observe how system into system runs,
What other planets circle other suns,
What varied being peoples every star,
May tell why Heaven has made us as we are.
But of this frame the bearings, and the ties,
The strong connections, nice dependencies,   30
Gradations just, has thy pervading soul
Looked through? or can a part contain the whole?
    Is the great chain, that draws all to agree,
And drawn supports, upheld by God, or thee?

II. Presumptuous man! the reason wouldst thou find,
Why formed so weak, so little, and so blind?
First, if thou canst, the harder reason guess,
Why formed no weaker, blinder, and no less?
Ask of thy mother earth, why oaks are made
Taller or stronger than the weeds they shade?   40
Or ask of yonder argent fields above,
Why Jove's satellites are less than Jove?
    Of systems possible, if 'tis confessed
That wisdom infinite must form the best,
Where all must full or not coherent be,
And all that rises, rise in due degree;
Then, in the scale of reasoning life, 'tis plain,
There must be, somewhere, such a rank as man:
And all the question (wrangle e'er so long)
Is only this, if God has placed him wrong?   50
    Respecting man, whatever wrong we call,
May, must be right, as relative to all.
In human works, though labored on with pain,
A thousand movements scarce one purpose gain;
In God's, one single can its end produce;
Yet serves to second too some other use.
So man, who here seems principal alone,
Perhaps acts second to some sphere unknown,
Touches some wheel, or verges to some goal:
'Tis but a part we see, and not a whole.   60
    When the proud steed shall know why man re-
        strains
His fiery course, or drives him o'er the plains:
When the dull ox, why now he breaks the clod,
Is now a victim, and now Egypt's god:
Then shall man's pride and dullness comprehend
His actions', passions', being's, use and end;
Why doing, suffering, checked, impelled; and why
This hour a slave, the next a deity.
    Then say not man's imperfect, Heaven in fault;
Say rather, man's as perfect as he ought: 70
His knowledge measured to his state and place;
His time a moment, and a point his space.
If to be perfect in a certain sphere,
What matter, soon or late, or here or there?

supposedly for Rosamond Clifford, mistress of Henry II, who was king of England from 1154 to 1189. **137. Partridge,** John Partridge (1644–1715), astrologer and almanac-maker, ridiculed by Swift in his Bickerstaff papers; two of Partridge's annual predictions were the downfalls of the King of France and of the Pope. **138. Galileo's eyes,** the telescope, invented by Galileo (1564–1642), Italian astronomer. **140. Rome, the** papacy.
    Epistle 1. **5. Expatiate,** wander. **16. vindicate . . . man,** cf. the purpose of Milton, as expressed in *Paradise Lost,* I, ll. 24 ff., p. 388. **30. nice dependencies,** delicate and intricate interrelations. **41. argent,** silvery. **64. Egypt's god.** The ox was a sacred animal in ancient Egypt.

The blest today is as completely so,
As who began a thousand years ago.

III. Heaven from all creatures hides the book of fate,
All but the page prescribed, their present state:
From brutes what men, from men what spirits know:
80 Or who could suffer being here below?
The lamb thy riot dooms to bleed today,
Had he thy reason, would he skip and play?
Pleased to the last, he crops the flowery food,
And licks the hand just raised to shed his blood.
O blindness to the future! kindly given,
That each may fill the circle marked by Heaven:
Who sees with equal eye, as God of all,
A hero perish, or a sparrow fall,
Atoms or systems into ruin hurled,
90 And now a bubble burst, and now a world.
    Hope humbly then; with trembling pinions soar;
Wait the great teacher death: and God adore.
What future bliss, He gives not thee to know,
But gives that hope to be thy blessing now.
Hope springs eternal in the human breast:
Man never is, but always to be blest:
The soul, uneasy and confined from home,
Rests and expatiates in a life to come.
    Lo, the poor Indian! whose untutored mind
100 Sees God in clouds, or hears him in the wind:
His soul proud science never taught to stray
Far as the solar walk, or Milky Way;
Yet simple nature to his hope has given,
Behind the cloud-topped hill, an humbler heaven;
Some safer world in depth of woods embraced,
Some happier island in the watery waste,
Where slaves once more their native land behold,
No fiends torment, no Christians thirst for gold.
To be, contents his natural desire,
110 He asks no angel's wing, no seraph's fire;
But thinks, admitted to that equal sky,
His faithful dog shall bear him company.

IV. Go, wiser thou! and, in thy scale of sense,
Weigh thy opinion against Providence;
Call imperfection what thou fanciest such,
Say, here He gives too little, there too much:
Destroy all creatures for thy sport or gust,
Yet cry, if man's unhappy, God's unjust;
If man alone ingross not Heaven's high care,
120 Alone made perfect here, immortal there:
Snatch from his hand the balance and the rod,
Re-judge his justice, be the God of God.
In pride, in reasoning pride, our error lies;
All quit their sphere, and rush into the skies.
Pride still is aiming at the blest abodes,

Men would be angels, angels would be Gods.
Aspiring to be Gods, if angels fell,
Aspiring to be angels, men rebel:
And who but wishes to invert the laws
Of order, sins against th' eternal cause.   130

V. Ask for what end the heavenly bodies shine,
Earth for whose use? Pride answers, " 'Tis for mine:
For me kind nature wakes her genial power,
Suckles each herb, and spreads out every flower;
Annual for me, the grape, the rose renew
The juice nectareous, and the balmy dew;
For me, the mine a thousand treasures brings;
For me, health gushes from a thousand springs;
Seas roll to waft me, suns to light me rise;
My foot-stool earth, my canopy the skies."   140
    But errs not nature from his gracious end,
From burning suns when livid deaths descend,
When earthquakes swallow, or when tempests sweep
Towns to one grave, whole nations to the deep?
"No," 'tis replied, "the first Almighty Cause
Acts not by partial, but by general laws;
Th' exceptions few; some change since all began:
And what created perfect?"—Why then man?
If the great end be human happiness,
Then nature deviates; and can man do less?   150
As much that end a constant course requires
Of showers and sunshine, as of man's desires;
As much eternal springs and cloudless skies,
As men forever temperate, calm, and wise.
If plagues or earthquakes break not Heaven's design,
Why then a Borgia, or a Catiline?
Who knows but He, whose hand the lightning forms,
Who heaves old ocean, and who wings the storms;
Pours fierce ambition in a Caesar's mind,
Or turns young Ammon loose to scourge mankind?   160
From pride, from pride, our very reasoning springs;
Account for moral as for natural things:
Why charge we Heaven in those, in these acquit?
In both, to reason right is to submit.
    Better for us, perhaps, it might appear,
Were there all harmony, all virtue here;
That never air or ocean felt the wind;
That never passion discomposed the mind.
But all subsists by elemental strife;
And passions are the elements of life.   170
The general order, since the whole began
Is kept in nature, and is kept in man.

VI. What would this man? Now upward will he soar,
And, little less than angel, would be more;
Now looking downwards, just as grieved appears
To want the strength of bulls, the fur of bears.

99. **poor Indian . . . mind.** Compare this attitude toward the primitive man with that of the romantic writers of the late eighteenth and early nineteenth centuries, particularly the conception of the Indian as a "noble savage." Cf. Chapter 4. 102. **solar walk,** the ecliptic, the path of the sun through the heavens. 111. **equal,** impartial. 117. **gust,**

delight. 156. **Borgia,** Cesare Borgia (1476–1507), Italian cardinal and military leader notorious for his cruelty, violence, and treachery. His father was Alexander VI, pope from 1492 to 1503. **Catiline,** the famous Roman conspirator and archenemy of Cicero, during the first century B.C. 160. **young Ammon,** Alexander the Great, king of Macedon

Made for his use all creatures if he call,
Say what their use, had he the powers of all?
Nature to these, without profusion, kind,
180 The proper organs, proper powers assigned;
Each seeming want compensated of course,
Here with degrees of swiftness, there of force;
All in exact proportion to the state;
Nothing to add, and nothing to abate.
Each beast, each insect, happy in its own:
Is Heaven unkind to man, and man alone?
Shall he alone, whom rational we call,
Be pleased with nothing, if not blessed with all?
 The bliss of man (could pride that blessing find)
190 Is not to act or think beyond mankind;
No powers of body or of soul to share,
But what his nature and his state can bear.
Why has not man a microscopic eye?
For this plain reason, man is not a fly.
Say what the use, were finer optics given,
T' inspect a mite, not comprehend the heaven?
Or touch, if tremblingly alive all o'er,
To smart and agonize at every pore?
Or quick effluvia darting through the brain,
200 Die of a rose in aromatic pain?
If nature thundered in his opening ears,
And stunned him with the music of the spheres,
How would he wish that Heaven had left him still
The whispering zephyr, and the purling rill?
Who finds not Providence all good and wise,
Alike in what it gives, and what denies?

 VII. Far as creation's ample range extends,
The scale of sensual, mental powers ascends:
Mark how it mounts, to man's imperial race,
210 From the green myriads in the peopled grass:
What modes of sight betwixt each wide extreme,
The mole's dim curtain, and the lynx's beam:
Of smell, the headlong lioness between,
And hound sagacious on the tainted green:
Of hearing, from the life that fills the flood,
To that which warbles through the vernal wood:
The spider's touch, how exquisitely fine!
Feels at each thread, and lives along the line:
In the nice bee, what sense so subtly true
220 From poisonous herbs extracts the healing dew?
How instinct varies in the groveling swine,
Compared, half-reasoning elephant, with thine!
'Twixt that, and reason, what a nice barrier,
Forever separate, yet forever near!
Remembrance and reflection how allied;
What thin partitions sense from thought divide:
And middle natures, how they long to join,
Yet never pass th' insuperable line!

Without this just gradation, could they be
Subjected, these to those, or all to thee?   230
The powers of all subdued by thee alone,
Is not thy reason all these powers in one?

 VIII. See, through this air, this ocean, and this earth,
All matter quick, and bursting into birth.
Above, how high progressive life may go!
Around, how wide! how deep extend below!
Vast chain of being! which from God began,
Natures ethereal, human, angel, man,
Beast, bird, fish, insect, what no eye can see,
No glass can reach; from Infinite to thee,   240
From thee to nothing.—On superior powers
Were we to press, inferior might on ours:
Or in the full creation leave a void,
Where, one step broken, the great scale's destroyed:
From nature's chain whatever link you strike,
Tenth or ten-thousandth, breaks the chain alike.
 And, if each system in gradation roll
Alike essential to th' amazing whole,
The least confusion but in one, not all
That system only, but the whole must fall.   250
Let earth unbalanced from her orbit fly,
Planets and suns run lawless through the sky;
Let ruling angels from their spheres be hurled,
Being on being wrecked, and world on world;
Heaven's whole foundations to their center nod,
And nature tremble to the throne of God.
All this dread order break—for whom? for thee?
Vile worm!—O madness! Pride! Impiety!

 IX. What if the foot, ordained the dust to tread,
Or hand, to toil, aspired to be the head?   260
What if the head, the eye, or ear repined
To serve mere engines to the ruling mind?
Just as absurd for any part to claim
To be another, in this general frame:
Just as absurd, to mourn the tasks or pains,
The great directing mind of all ordains.
 All are but parts of one stupendous whole,
Whose body nature is, and God the soul;
That, changed through all, and yet in all the same;
Great in the earth, as in th' ethereal frame;   270
Warms in the sun, refreshes in the breeze,
Glows in the stars, and blossoms in the trees,
Lives through all life, extends through all extent,
Spreads undivided, operates unspent;
Breathes in our soul, informs our mortal part
As full, as perfect, in a hair as heart:
As full, as perfect, in vile man that mourns,
As the rapt Seraph that adores and burns:
To him no high, no low, no great, no small;
He fills, he bounds, connects, and equals all.   280

from 336 through 323 B.C., called the son of Jupiter Ammon; he was in reality the son of King Philip of Macedon (382–336 B.C.). 174. **less than angel,** suggested by the well-known verses: "What is man, that thou art mindful of him? and the son of man, that thou visitest him? For thou hast made him a little lower than the angels, and hast crowned him with glory and honor" (Psalms 8:4–5). 176. **want,** lack. 199. **effluvia,** that which flows out, emanations. 202. **music of the spheres.** The ancients believed that the stars made music as they revolved in their spheres. 219. **nice,** delicate, discriminating.

X. Cease then, nor order imperfection name:
Our proper bliss depends on what we blame.
Know thy own point: This kind, this due degree
Of blindness, weakness, Heaven bestows on thee.
Submit.—In this, or any other sphere,
Secure to be as blessed as thou canst bear:
Safe in the hand of one disposing power,
Or in the natal, or the mortal hour.
All nature is but art, unknown to thee;
290 All chance, direction, which thou canst not see;
All discord, harmony not understood;
All partial evil, universal good:
And, spite of pride, in erring reason's spite,
One truth is clear, *Whatever is, is right.*

EPISTLE 2

Know then thyself, presume not God to scan,
The proper study of mankind is man.
Placed on this isthmus of a middle state,
A being darkly wise and rudely great:
With too much knowledge for the skeptic side,
With too much weakness for the stoic's pride,
He hangs between; in doubt to act, or rest;
In doubt to deem himself a god, or beast;
In doubt his mind or body to prefer;
10 Born but to die, and reasoning but to err;
Alike in ignorance, his reason such,
Whether he thinks too little, or too much:
Chaos of thought and passion, all confused;
Still by himself abused, or disabused;
Created half to rise, and half to fall;
Great lord of all things, yet a prey to all;
Sole judge of truth, in endless error hurled:
The glory, jest, and riddle of the world! . . .
    Go, wondrous creature; mount where science guides,
20 Go, measure earth, weigh air, and state the tides;
Instruct the planets in what orbs to run,
Correct old Time, and regulate the sun;
Go, soar with Plato to th' empyreal sphere,
To the first good, first perfect, and first fair;
Or tread the mazy round his followers trod,
And quitting sense call imitating God;
As eastern priests in giddy circles run,
And turn their heads to imitate the sun.
Go, teach Eternal Wisdom how to rule—
30 Then drop into thyself, and be a fool!
    Superior beings, when of late they saw
A mortal man unfold all nature's law,
Admired such wisdom in an earthly shape,
And showed a Newton, as we show an ape.
    Could he, whose rules the rapid comet bind,
Describe or fix one movement of his mind?

Who saw its fires here rise, and there descend,
Explain his own beginning or his end?
Alas! what wonder! Man's superior part
Unchecked may rise, and climb from art to art; 40
But when his own great work is but begun,
What reason weaves, by passion is undone.
    Trace science, then, with modesty thy guide;
First strip off all her equipage of pride;
Deduct what is but vanity or dress,
Or learning's luxury, or idleness,
Or tricks to show the stretch of human brain,
Mere curious pleasure, or ingenious pain;
Expunge the whole, or lop th' excrescent parts
Of all our vices have created arts; 50
Then see how little the remaining sum,
Which served the past, and must the times to come!

    II. Two principles in human nature reign;
Self-love to urge, and reason to restrain;
Nor this a good, nor that a bad we call,
Each works its end to move or govern all:
And to their proper operation still
Ascribe all good; to their improper, ill.
    Self-love, the spring of motion, acts the soul;
Reason's comparing balance rules the whole. 60
Man, but for that, no action could attend,
And, but for this, were active to no end:
Fixed like a plant on his peculiar spot,
To draw nutrition, propagate, and rot;
Or, meteor-like, flame lawless thro' the void,
Destroying others, by himself destroyed.
    Most strength the moving principle requires;
Active its task, it prompts, impels, inspires:
Sedate and quiet, the comparing lies,
Formed but to check, deliberate, and advise. 70
Self-love still stronger, as its objects nigh;
Reason's at distance and in prospect lie:
That sees immediate good by present sense;
Reason, the future and the consequence.
Thicker than arguments, temptations throng,
At best more watchful this, but that more strong.
The action of the stronger to suspend,
Reason still use, to reason still attend.
Attention, habit, and experience gains;
Each strengthens reason, and self-love restrains. 80
    Let subtle schoolmen teach these friends to fight,
More studious to divide than to unite;
And grace and virtue, sense and reason split,
With all the rash dexterity of wit.
Wits, just like fools, at war about a name,
Have full as oft no meaning, or the same.
Self-love and reason to one end aspire,
Pain their aversion, pleasure their desire;

Epistle 2. **22. regulate the sun.** This refers to the reformation of the calendar, which was undertaken in Europe during the eighteenth century in order to make up the approximately twelve days that had been lost during the course of many centuries through the inaccurate Julian calendar formerly in use. The new Gregorian calendar, however, did not reach England until 1751. **23. Plato . . . sphere.** The *empyreal sphere* was the *primum mobile* (p. 497, l. 107, and note). Bolingbroke, the chief source of the *Essay on Man*, thought little of Plato. **27. eastern . . . run,** an allusion to the whirling dervishes of the Orient. **59. acts,** actuates, moves. **69. comparing.** The word "principle" should be sup-

But greedy that, its object would devour,
90 This taste the honey, and not wound the flower:
Pleasure, or wrong or rightly understood,
Our greatest evil, or our greatest good.

   III. Modes of self-love the passions we may call;
'Tis real good, or seeming, moves them all:
But since not every good we can divide,
And reason bids us for our own provide,
Passions, though selfish, if their means be fair,
List under reason, and deserve her care;
Those that imparted, court a nobler aim,
100 Exalt their kind, and take some virtue's name.
   In lazy apathy let stoics boast
Their virtue fixed: 'tis fixed as in a frost;
Contracted all, retiring to the breast;
But strength of mind is exercise, not rest:
The rising tempest puts in act the soul,
Parts it may ravage, but preserves the whole.
On life's vast ocean diversely we sail,
Reason the card, but passion is the gale;
Nor God alone in the still calm we find,
110 He mounts the storm, and walks upon the wind.
   Passions, like elements, though born to fight,
Yet, mixed and softened, in his work unite:
These 'tis enough to temper and employ;
But what composes man, can man destroy?
Suffice that reason keep to nature's road,
Subject, compound them, follow her and God.
Love, hope, and joy, fair pleasure's smiling train,
Hate, fear, and grief, the family of pain,
These, mixed with art, and to due bounds confined,
120 Make and maintain the balance of the mind:
The lights and shades, whose well-accorded strife
Gives all the strength and color of our life.
   Pleasures are ever in our hands or eyes;
And when in act they cease, in prospect rise:
Present to grasp, and future still to find,
The whole employ of body and of mind.
All spread their charms, but charm not all alike;
On different senses different objects strike;
Hence different passions more or less inflame,
130 As strong or weak the organs of the frame;
And hence one master-passion in the breast,
Like Aaron's serpent, swallows up the rest.
   As man, perhaps, the moment of his breath,
Receives the lurking principle of death;
The young disease, that must subdue at length,
Grows with his growth, and strengthens with his
      strength:
So, cast and mingled with his very frame,
The mind's disease, its ruling passion, came;
Each vital humor which should feed the whole,

Soon flows to this, in body and in soul: 140
Whatever warms the heart, or fills the head,
As the mind opens, and its functions spread,
Imagination plies her dangerous art,
And pours it all upon the peccant part.
Nature its mother, habit is its nurse;
Wit, spirit, faculties, but make it worse;
Reason itself but gives it edge and pow'r,
As Heaven's blest beam turns vinegar more sour.
   We, wretched subjects, though to lawful sway,
In this weak queen some favorite still obey;   150
Ah! if she lend not arms as well as rules,
What can she more than tell us we are fools?
Teach us to mourn our nature, not to mend;
A sharp accuser, but a helpless friend!
Or from a judge turn pleader, to persuade
The choice we make, or justify it made;
Proud of an easy conquest all along,
She but removes weak passions for the strong.
So, when small humors gather to a gout,
The doctor fancies he has driven them out.   160
   Yes, nature's road must ever be preferred;
Reason is here no guide, but still a guard;
'Tis hers to rectify, not overthrow,
And treat this passion more as friend than foe:
A mightier power the strong direction sends,
And several men impels to several ends:
Like varying winds by other passions tossed,
This drives them constant to a certain coast.
Let power or knowledge, gold or glory, please,
Or (oft more strong than all) the love of ease;   170
Through life 'tis followed, even at life's expense;
The merchant's toil, the sage's indolence,
The monk's humility, the hero's pride,
All, all alike find reason on their side.
   Th' Eternal Art, educing good from ill,
Grafts on this passion our best principle:
'Tis thus the mercury of man is fixed,
Strong grows the virtue with his nature mixed;
The dross cements what else were too refined,
And in one interest body acts with mind.   180
   As fruits, ungrateful to the planter's care,
On savage stocks inserted, learn to bear,
The surest virtues thus from passions shoot,
Wild nature's vigor working at the root.
What crops of wit and honesty appear
From spleen, from obstinacy, hate, or fear!
See anger, zeal and fortitude supply;
Even avarice, prudence; sloth, philosophy;
Lust, through some certain strainers well refined,
Is gentle love, and charms all womankind;   190
Envy, to which th' ignoble mind's a slave,
Is emulation in the learned or brave;

plied after "comparing." 108. card, compass chart. 132. Aaron's
serpent. The reference is to Exodus 7:10–12. "And Moses and Aaron
went in unto Pharaoh, and they did so as the Lord had commanded: and
Aaron cast down his rod before Pharaoh, and before his servants, and it
became a serpent. Then Pharaoh also called the wise men and the sor-
cerers: now the magicians of Egypt, they also did in like manner with
their enchantments. For they cast down every man his rod, and they
became serpents: but Aaron's rod swallowed up their rods." 144. peccant, diseased.

Nor virtue, male or female, can we name,
But what will grow on pride, or grow on shame.
    Thus nature gives us (let it check our pride)
The virtue nearest to our vice allied;
Reason the bias turns to good from ill,
And Nero reigns a Titus, if he will.
The fiery soul abhorred in Catiline,
200 In Decius charms, in Curtius is divine:
The same ambition can destroy or save,
And makes a patriot as it makes a knave.

    IV. This light and darkness in our chaos joined,
What shall divide? The God within the mind.
    Extremes in nature equal ends produce,
In man they join to some mysterious use;
Though each by turns the other's bound invade,
As, in some well-wrought picture, light and shade,
And oft so mix, the difference is too nice
210 Where ends the virtue, or begins the vice.
    Fools! who from hence into the notion fall,
That vice or virtue there is none at all.
If white and black blend, soften, and unite
A thousand ways, is there no black or white?
Ask your own heart, and nothing is so plain;
'Tis to mistake them costs the time and pain.

    V. Vice is a monster of so frightful mien,
As to be hated needs but to be seen;
Yet seen too oft, familiar with her face,
220 We first endure, then pity, then embrace.
But where th' extreme of vice, was ne'er agreed:
Ask where 's the north? at York, 'tis on the Tweed;
In Scotland, at the Orcades; and there,
At Greenland, Zembla, or the Lord knows where.
No creature owns it in the first degree,
But thinks his neighbor further gone than he;
Even those who dwell beneath its very zone,
Or never feel the rage, or never own;
What happier natures shrink at with affright
230 The hard inhabitant contends is right.

    VI. Virtuous and vicious every man must be;
Few in th' extreme, but all in the degree:
The rogue and fool by fits is fair and wise;
And even the best, by fits, what they despise.
'Tis but by parts we follow good or ill;
For, vice or virtue, self directs it still;
Each individual seeks a several goal;
But Heaven's great view is one, and that the whole.
That counterworks each folly and caprice;
240 That disappoints th' effect of every vice;
That, happy frailties to all ranks applied,

Shame to the virgin, to the matron pride,
Fear to the statesman, rashness to the chief,
To kings presumption, and to crowds belief:
That, virtue's ends from vanity can raise,
Which seeks no interest, no reward but praise;
And build on wants, and on defects of mind,
The joy, the peace, the glory of mankind.
    Heaven, forming each on other to depend,
A master, or a servant, or a friend,   250
Bids each on other for assistance call,
Till one man's weakness grows the strength of all.
Wants, frailties, passions, closer still ally
The common interest, or endear the tie.
To these we owe true friendship, love sincere,
Each home-felt joy that life inherits here;
Yet from the same we learn, in its decline,
Those joys, those loves, those interests to resign:
Taught half by reason, half by mere decay,
To welcome death, and calmly pass away.   260
    Whate'er the passion—knowledge, fame, or pelf—
Not one will change his neighbor with himself.
The learned is happy nature to explore,
The fool is happy that he knows no more;
The rich is happy in the plenty given,
The poor contents him with the care of Heaven.
See the blind beggar dance, the cripple sing,
The sot a hero, lunatic a king;
The starving chemist in his golden views
Supremely blest, the poet in his Muse.   270
    See some strange comfort every state attend,
And pride bestowed on all, a common friend:
See some fit passion every age supply,
Hope travels through, nor quits us when we die.
    Behold the child, by Nature's kindly law,
Pleased with a rattle, tickled with a straw;
Some livelier plaything gives his youth delight,
A little louder, but as empty quite;
Scarfs, garters, gold, amuse his riper stage,
And beads and prayer-books are the toys of age: 280
Pleased with this bauble still, as that before;
Till tired he sleeps, and life's poor play is o'er.
    Meanwhile Opinion gilds, with varying rays,
Those painted clouds that beautify our days;
Each want of happiness by hope supplied,
And each vacuity of sense by pride:
These build as fast as knowledge can destroy;
In Folly's cup still laughs the bubble joy;
One prospect lost, another still we gain;
And not a vanity is given in vain;   290
Even mean self-love becomes, by force divine,
The scale to measure others' wants by thine.
See, and confess, one comfort still must rise;
'Tis this, *Though man's a fool, yet God is wise!*

---

198. **Nero . . . Titus.** The tyrant becomes a benefactor. Nero (37–68 A.D.), the corrupt, cruel, and perverted Roman emperor; Titus (40–81 A.D.) had a brief but distinguished reign as emperor about a dozen years after Nero. 199. **Catiline**, a famous Roman conspirator (108–62 B.C.), denounced and driven to destruction by Cicero. 200. **Decius**

. . . divine. Publius Decius Mus was consul of Rome in the year 340 B.C. during the war between the Romans and the Samnite-Latins. A vision had informed him that victory would lie on the side whose general should fall in battle. Decius therefore sacrificed himself by rushing recklessly into the thick of the combat. Curtius sacrificed himself similarly in

Convention and Realism

[Epistles 3 and 4 are summarized by the following "arguments" prefixed to all editions of the poem.]

EPISTLE 3

Of the Nature and State of Man with Respect to Society

I. The whole universe one system of society, ver. 7, etc. Nothing made wholly for itself, nor yet wholly for another, ver. 27. The happiness of animals mutual, ver. 49. II. Reason or instinct operate alike to the good of each individual, ver. 79. Reason or instinct operate also to society in all animals, ver. 109. III. How far society carried by instinct, ver. 115. How much farther by reason, ver. 128. IV. Of that which is called the state of nature, ver. 144. Reason instructed by instinct in the invention of arts, ver. 166, and in the forms of society, ver. 176. V. Origin of political societies, ver. 196. Origin of monarchy, ver. 207. Patriarchal government, ver. 212. VI. Origin of true religion and government, from the same principle of love, ver. 231, etc. Origin of superstition and tyranny, from the same principle of fear, ver. 237, etc. The influence of self-love operating to the social and public good, ver. 266. Restoration of true religion and government on their first principle, ver. 285. Mixed government, ver. 288. Various forms of each, and the true end of all, ver. 300, etc.

EPISTLE 4

Of the Nature and State of Man with Respect to Happiness

I. False notions of happiness, philosophical and popular, answered from ver. 19 to 27. II. It is the end of all men, and attainable by all, ver. 29. God intends happiness to be equal; and to be so it must be social, since all particular happiness depends on general, and since he governs by general, not particular, laws, ver. 35. As it is necessary for order, and the peace and welfare of society, that external goods should be unequal, happiness is not made to consist in these, ver. 51. But notwithstanding that inequality, the balance of happiness among mankind is kept even by Providence by the two passions of hope and fear, ver. 70. III. What the happiness of individuals is, as far as is consistent with the constitution of this world; and that the good man has here the advantage, ver. 77. The error of imputing to virtue what are only the calamities of Nature or of Fortune, ver. 94. IV. The folly of expecting that God should alter his general laws in favor of particulars, ver. 121. V. That we are not judges who are good; but that, whoever they are, they must be happiest, ver. 131, etc. VI. That external goods are not the proper rewards, but often inconsistent with, or destructive of virtue, ver. 167. That even these can make no man happy without virtue; instanced in riches, ver. 185. Honors, ver. 193. Nobility, ver. 205. Greatness, ver. 217. Fame, ver. 237. Superior talents, ver. 259, etc. With pictures of human infelicity in men possessed of them all, ver. 269, etc. VII. That virtue only constitutes a happiness whose object is universal, and whose prospect eternal, ver. 309. That the perfection of virtue and happiness consists in a conformity to the order of Providence here, and a resignation to it here and hereafter, ver. 326, etc.

(1733)

THE UNIVERSAL PRAYER

Father of all! in every age,
　In every clime adored,
By saint, by savage, and by sage,
　Jehovah, Jove, or Lord!

Thou Great First Cause, least understood:
　Who all my sense confined
To know but this, that Thou art good,
　And that myself am blind;

Yet gave me, in this dark estate,
　To see the good from ill;　　　　　10
And binding nature fast in fate,
　Left free the human will.

What conscience dictates to be done,
　Or warns me not to do,
This, teach me more than hell to shun,
　That, more than heaven pursue.

What blessings Thy free bounty gives,
　Let me not cast away;
For God is paid when man receives:
　T' enjoy is to obey.　　　　　　20

Yet not to earth's contracted span
　Thy goodness let me bound,
Or think Thee Lord alone of man,
　When thousand worlds are round.

Let not this weak, unknowing hand
　Presume Thy bolts to throw,

362 B.C. A great chasm had appeared in the Roman Forum, and the soothsayers declared that it could be filled only if Rome's greatest treasure were thrown into it. Curtius leaped in, remarking that the greatest treasure of the city was a brave, self-sacrificing citizen. 223. **Orcades,** the old name for the Orkney Islands, off the northeast coast of Scotland. 224. **Zembla,** Nova Zembla, a large uninhabited pair of islands off the northern coast of Russia within the Arctic Circle. 269. **chemist,** alchemist. 279. **garters,** referring to the badge of the Order of the Garter, the highest order in English knighthood.

And deal damnation round the land,
   On each I judge Thy foe.

If I am right, Thy grace impart,
30   Still in the right to stay;
If I am wrong, oh! teach my heart
   To find that better way.

Save me alike from foolish pride,
   Or impious discontent,
At aught Thy wisdom has denied,
   Or aught Thy goodness lent.

Teach me to feel another's woe,
   To hide the fault I see;
That mercy I to others show,
40   That mercy show to me.

Mean though I am, not wholly so,
   Since quickened by Thy breath;
Oh, lead me wheresoe'er I go,
   Through this day's life or death.

This day, be bread and peace my lot:
   All else beneath the sun,
Thou know'st if best bestowed or not,
   And let Thy will be done.

To Thee, whose temple is all space,
50   Whose altar earth, sea, skies,
One chorus let all being raise,
   All nature's incense rise!
(1738)

EPISTLE TO DR. ARBUTHNOT

*Dr. John Arbuthnot (1667-1735), prominent phy-
sician and man of letters, was a life-long friend of Pope.
The poem is a dialogue between the two. The immediate
occasion of the* Epistle *was the publication of the two
poems named in the following Advertisement, the first
written probably by Lady Mary Wortley Montagu and
Lord John Hervey, the second by Hervey. Both these
writers had been previously attacked by Pope in* The
Dunciad *(1728) and in the first Imitation of Horace
(1733). They are here accorded another severe lashing.*

The Epistle to Dr. Arbuthnot *is the most personal of
Pope's poems. In addition to the author's interesting
estimate of himself and his literary position, the poem*
contains satirical portraits of contemporaries done in
matchless style.

ADVERTISEMENT

This paper is a sort of bill of complaint, begun many
years since, and drawn up by snatches, as the several
occasions offered. I had no thoughts of publishing it,
till it pleased some persons of rank and fortune (the
authors of *Verses to the Imitator of Horace,* and of an
*Epistle to a Doctor of Divinity from a Nobleman at
Hampton Court*) to attack, in a very extraordinary
manner, not only my writings (of which, being public,
the public is judge), but my person, morals, and family,
whereof, to those who know me not, a truer information
may be requisite. Being divided between the necessity
to say something of myself and my own laziness to undertake so awkward a task, I thought it the shortest way
to put the last hand to this Epistle. If it have anything
pleasing, it will be that by which I am most desirous
to please, the truth and the sentiment; and if anything
offensive, it will be only to those I am least sorry to
offend, the vicious or the ungenerous.

Many will know their own pictures in it, there being
not a circumstance but what is true; but I have for the
most part spared their names, and they may escape
being laughed at if they please.

I would have some of them know it was owing to the
request of the learned and candid friend to whom it is
inscribed that I make not as free use of theirs as they
have done of mine. However, I shall have this advantage and honor on my side, that whereas, by their
proceeding, any abuse may be directed at any man,
no injury can possibly be done by mine, since a
nameless character can never be found out but by
its truth and likeness.

P. Shut, shut the door, good John! (fatigued, I said),
Tie up the knocker, say I'm sick, I'm dead.
The Dog-star rages! nay 'tis past a doubt,
All Bedlam, or Parnassus, is let out:
Fire in each eye, and papers in each hand,
They rave, recite, and madden round the land.

   What walls can guard me, or what shade can hide?
They pierce my thickets, through my Grot they glide;
By land, by water, they renew the charge;
They stop the chariot, and they board the barge. 10
No place is sacred, not the Church is free;
E'en Sunday shines no Sabbath-day to me;
Then from the Mint walks forth the man of rime,

Happy to catch me just at dinner-time.
   Is there a parson, much bemused in beer,
A maudlin poetess, a riming peer,
A clerk, foredoomed his father's soul to cross,
Who pens a stanza, when he should *engross*?
Is there, who, locked from ink and paper, scrawls
20 With desperate charcoal round his darkened walls?
All fly to Twit'nam, and in humble strain
Apply to me, to keep them mad or vain.
Arthur, whose giddy son neglects the laws,
Imputes to me and my damned works the cause:
Poor Cornus sees his frantic wife elope,

*"Shut, shut the door, good John," an illustration by
Francis Hayman for the* Epistle to Dr. Arbuthnot *in* The
Works of Alexander Pope, *London, 1760.*

And curses wit, and poetry, and Pope.
   Friend to my life (which did not you prolong,
The world had wanted many an idle song),
What drop or nostrum can this plague remove?
Or which must end me, a fool's wrath or love?   30
A dire dilemma! either way I'm sped,
If foes, they write; if friends, they read me dead.
Seized and tied down to judge, how wretched I!
Who can't be silent, and who will not lie.
To laugh, were want of goodness and of grace,
And to be grave, exceeds all power of face.
I sit with sad civility, I read
With honest anguish, and an aching head;
And drop at last, but in unwilling ears,
This saving counsel "Keep your piece nine years."   40
   "Nine years!" cries he, who high in Drury-Lane,
Lulled by soft zephyrs through the broken pane,
Rimes ere he wakes, and prints before term ends,
Obliged by hunger, and request of friends:
"The piece, you think, is incorrect? why, take it,
I'm all submission, what you'd have it, make it."
   Three things another's modest wishes bound,
My friendship, and a prologue, and ten pound.
   Pitholeon sends to me: "You know his Grace,
I want a patron; ask him for a place."   50
Pitholeon libeled me—"but here's a letter
Informs you, sir, 'twas when he knew no better.
Dare you refuse him? Curll invites to dine,
He'll write a *Journal,* or he'll turn divine."
   Bless me! a packet.—"'Tis a stranger sues,
A virgin tragedy, an orphan Muse."
If I dislike it, "Furies, death and rage!"
If I approve, "Commend it to the stage."
There (thank my stars) my whole commission ends,
The players and I are, luckily, no friends,   60
Fired that the house reject him, "'Sdeath, I'll print it,
And shame the fools——Your interest, sir, with
      Lintot!"
Lintot, dull rogue! will think your price too much:
"Not, sir, if you revise it, and retouch."
All my demurs but double his attacks;
At last he whispers, "Do; and we go snacks."
Glad of a quarrel, straight I clap the door,
Sir, let me see your works and you no more.
   'Tis sung, when Midas' ears began to spring
(Midas, a sacred person and a king),   70
His very minister who spied them first,
(Some say his queen) was forced to speak, or burst.
And is not mine, my friend, a sorer case,
When every coxcomb perks them in my face?

and note. 31. **sped,** done for. 40. **"Keep . . . years,"** the advice of
Horace in his *Ars Poetica,* l. 388. 43. **term ends.** The *term* is the
season of the sessions of law courts. 49. **Pitholeon,** "the name of a
foolish poet of Rhodes who pretended much to Greek"—Pope's note.
He represents Leonard Welsted (1688–1747), a prolific writer and joint
author of the libelous *One Epistle,* written in the early 1730's, which
charged Pope with causing a lady's death. In *The Dunciad* (II, 207–
210; III, 169–172), Pope accuses Welsted of squeezing money out of patrons by dedications. 53. **Curll,** Edmund Curll (1675–1747), a piratical
publisher, who did Pope several ill turns. 61. **'Sdeath,** the oath formed

from "God's death!"; cf. "zounds" for "God's wounds" or "'sblood"
for "God's blood." 62. **Lintot,** Bernard Lintot (1675–1736), a publisher of many of Pope's works. 69. **Midas,** a mythological king whose
ears were changed to ass's ears because in a musical contest he gave the
prize to Pan rather than to Apollo. In some accounts it was Midas'
barber who told the secret of his ears; in Chaucer's *Wife of Bath's
Tale* it was the queen.

A. Good friend, forbear! you deal in dangerous things.
I'd never name queens, ministers, or kings;
Keep close to ears, and those let asses prick;
'Tis nothing— P. Nothing? if they bite and kick?
Out with it, *Dunciad!* let the secret pass,
80 That secret to each fool, that he's an ass:
The truth once told (and wherefore should we lie?)
The queen of Midas slept, and so may I.
    You think this cruel? take it for a rule,
No creature smarts so little as a fool.
Let peals of laughter, Codrus! round thee break,
Thou unconcerned canst hear the mighty crack:
Pit, box, and gallery in convulsions hurled,
Thou stand'st unshook amidst a bursting world.
Who shames a scribbler? break one cobweb through,
90 He spins the slight, self-pleasing thread anew:
Destroy his fib or sophistry, in vain;
The creature's at his dirty work again,
Throned in the center of his thin designs,
Proud of a vast extent of flimsy lines!
Whom have I hurt? has poet yet, or peer,
Lost the arched eye-brow, or Parnassian sneer?
And has not Colley still his lord and whore?
His butchers Henley? his freemasons Moore?
Does not one table Bavius still admit?
100 Still to one bishop, Philips seem a wit?
Still Sappho— A. Hold! for God's sake— you'll offend,
No names!—be calm!—learn prudence of a friend!
I too could write, and I am twice as tall;
But foes like these— P. One flatterer's worse than all.
Of all mad creatures, if the learned are right,
It is the slaver kills, and not the bite.
A fool quite angry is quite innocent:
Alas! 'tis ten times worse when they *repent.*
    One dedicates in high heroic prose,
110 And ridicules beyond a hundred foes:
One from all Grub Street will my fame defend,
And, more abusive, calls himself my friend.
This prints my *letters,* that expects a bribe,
And others roar aloud, "Subscribe, subscribe."
    There are, who to my person pay their court:
I cough like Horace, and, though lean, am short,
Ammon's great son one shoulder had too high,

Such Ovid's nose, and "Sir! you have an eye"—
Go on, obliging creatures, make me see
All that disgraced my betters, met in me.   120
Say for my comfort, languishing in bed,
"Just so immortal Maro held his head":
And when I die, be sure you let me know
Great Homer died three thousand years ago.
    Why did I write? what sin to me unknown
Dipped me in ink, my parents', or my own?
As yet a child, nor yet a fool to fame,
I lisped in numbers, for the numbers came.
I left no calling for this idle trade,
No duty broke, no father disobeyed.   130
The Muse but served to ease some friend, not wife,
To help me through this long disease, my life,
To second, Arbuthnot! thy art and care,
And teach the being you preserved, to bear.
    But why then publish? Granville the polite,
And knowing Walsh, would tell me I could write;
Well-natured Garth inflamed with early praise;
And Congreve loved, and Swift endured my lays;
The courtly Talbot, Somers, Sheffield, read;
E'en mitered Rochester would nod the head,   140
And St. John's self (great Dryden's friends before)
With open arms received one poet more.
Happy my studies, when by these approved!
Happier their author, when by these beloved!
From these the world will judge of men and books,
Not from the Burnets, Oldmixons, and Cookes.
    Soft were my numbers; who could take offense,
While pure description held the place of sense?
Like gentle Fanny's was my flowery theme,
A painted mistress, or a purling stream.   150
Yet then did Gildon draw his venal quill;—
I wished the man a dinner, and sat still.
Yet then did Dennis rave in furious fret;
I never answered—I was not in debt.
If want provoked, or madness made them print,
I waged no war with Bedlam or the Mint.
    Did some more sober critic come abroad;
If wrong, I smiled; if right, I kissed the rod.
Pains, reading, study, are their just pretense,
And all they want is spirit, taste, and sense.   160

75. **A.,** John Arbuthnot, the friend of Pope to whom this epistle was addressed (see headnote). In addition to being a physician, he was an eminent mathematician and classical scholar, a prominent Tory politician, and a member of the famous Scriblerus Club, which numbered Pope, Addison, and Swift, among others. 79. **Dunciad,** the masterpiece of personal satire written by Pope in two parts; the *first* appeared in 1728, the *second* in 1743. Cf. p. 532. 85. **Codrus,** a Roman poetaster ridiculed by Vergil; probably a fictitious name applied to poetasters in general. 97. **Colley,** Colley Cibber (1671–1757), actor, dramatist, and poet laureate; for his various attacks upon Pope he was made the hero of the second version of Pope's *Dunciad* (1743). 98. **Henley,** John Henley (1692–1756), an eccentric and pompous London preacher who delivered a lecture before the Butchers Guild of London "in which he lauded the trade extravagantly." **Moore,** James Moore-Smythe, dandy and poetaster, the son of Arthur Moore mentioned in l. 23. 99. **Bavius,** an inferior Roman poet of the first century A.D. 100. **bishop, Philips.** The bishop was Hugh Boulter (1672–1742), Archbishop of Armagh, Ireland, and friend and patron of Ambrose Philips (1675?–1749), Pope's rival in pastoral poetry. 101. **Sappho,** the noted Greek lyric poetess of the seventh century B.C. The allusion here, however, is to Lady Mary Wortley Montagu (1689–1762), one of the most interesting and brilliant women of her time. 111. **Grub Street,** famous as the abode of indigent writers. 113. *letters.* Actually, Pope himself instigated

Edmund Curll's publication of his literary correspondence in 1735, then sought to discredit the publication in order that he might issue an "authentic" edition himself. 117. **Ammon's great son,** Alexander the Great, king of Macedon from 336 to 323 B.C., according to legend the son of Jupiter Ammon; his historical father was King Philip of Macedon (382–336 B.C.). 118. **Ovid,** the Roman didactic, lyric, and narrative poet (43 B.C.–17 A.D.). 122. **Maro,** the family name of Vergil (70–19 B.C.). 135. **Granville,** George Granville (1667–1735), who had urged Pope to publish his *Windsor Forest* in 1713. 136. **Walsh,** William Walsh (1663–1709), friend of both Dryden and Pope. 137. **Garth,** Samuel Garth (1661–1719), physician and man of letters. 138. **Congreve,** William Congreve (1670–1729), one of the most important of Restoration playwrights, author of *The Way of the World* (1700) and *Love for Love* (1695), two brilliant social comedies. **Swift,** see p. 493. 139. **Talbot,** Charles Talbot, Duke of Shrewsbury. **Somers,** John Somers, Lord Chancellor. **Sheffield,** John Sheffield, Duke of Buckingham. All those mentioned in this and the preceding line were prominent statesmen of the time who had encouraged Pope in his early work. 140. **Rochester,** Francis Atterbury (1662–1732), Bishop of Rochester. The miter is the liturgical headdress of a bishop. 141. **St. John,** Henry St. John (1678–1754), Viscount Bolingbroke, the statesman and political writer. It was he who gave Pope not only the encouragement but most of the ideas for his *Essay on Man* (cf. p. 548). 146. **Burnets.** We

Commas and points they set exactly right,
And 'twere a sin to rob them of their mite.
Yet ne'er one sprig of laurel graced these ribalds,
From slashing Bentley down to piddling Tibalds:
Each wight, who reads not, and but scans and spells,
Each word-catcher, that lives on syllables,
E'en such small critics some regard may claim,
Preserved in Milton's or in Shakespeare's name.
Pretty! in amber to observe the forms
170 Of hairs, or straws, or dirt, or grubs, or worms!
The things, we know, are neither rich nor rare,
But wonder how the devil they got there.

    Were others angry: I excused them too;
Well might they rage, I gave them but their due.
A man's true merit 'tis not hard to find;
But each man's secret standard in his mind,
That casting-weight pride adds to emptiness,
This, who can gratify? for who can guess?
The bard whom pilfered pastorals renown,
180 Who turns a Persian tale for half a crown,
Just writes to make his barrenness appear,
And strains, from hard-bound brains, eight lines a year;
He, who still wanting, though he lives on theft,
Steals much, spends little, yet has nothing left:
And he, who now to sense, now nonsense leaning,
Means not, but blunders round about a meaning:
And he, whose fustian's so sublimely bad,
It is not poetry, but prose run mad:
All these, my modest satire bade translate,
190 And owned that nine such poets made a Tate.
How did they fume, and stamp, and roar, and chafe!
And swear, not Addison himself was safe.

    Peace to all such! but were there one whose fires
True genius kindles, and fair fame inspires;
Blessed with each talent and each art to please,
And born to write, converse, and live with ease:
Should such a man, too fond to rule alone,
Bear, like the Turk, no brother near the throne,
View him with scornful, yet with jealous eyes,
200 And hate for arts that caused himself to rise;
Damn with faint praise, assent with civil leer,
And without sneering, teach the rest to sneer;
Willing to wound, and yet afraid to strike,

Just hint a fault, and hesitate dislike;
Alike reserved to blame, or to commend,
A timorous foe, and a suspicious friend;
Dreading e'en fools, by flatterers besieged,
And so obliging, that he ne'er obliged;
Like Cato, give his little senate laws,
And sit attentive to his own applause;   210
While wits and Templars every sentence raise,
And wonder with a foolish face of praise:——
Who but must laugh, if such a man there be?
Who would not weep, if Atticus were he?

    What though my name stood rubric on the walls
Or plastered posts, with claps, in capitals?
Or smoking forth, a hundred hawkers' load,
On wings of winds came flying all abroad?
I sought no homage from the race that write;
I kept, like Asian monarchs, from their sight: 220
Poems I heeded (now be-rimed so long)
No more than thou, great George! a birthday song.
I ne'er with wits or witlings passed my days,
To spread about the itch of verse and praise;
Nor like a puppy, daggled through the town,
To fetch and carry sing-song up and down;
Nor at rehearsals sweat, and mouthed, and cried,
With handkerchief and orange at my side;
But sick of fops, and poetry, and prate,
To Bufo, left the whole Castalian state.   230

    Proud as Apollo on his forkéd hill,
Sat full-blown Bufo, puffed by every quill;
Fed with soft dedication all day long,
Horace and he went hand in hand in song.
His library (where busts of poets dead
And a true Pindar stood without a head),
Received of wits an undistinguished race,
Who first his judgment asked, and then a place:
Much they extolled his pictures, much his seat,
And flattered every day, and some days eat: 240
Till grown more frugal in his riper days,
He paid some bards with port, and some with praise:
To some a dry rehearsal saw assigned,
And others (harder still) he paid in kind.
Dryden alone (what wonder?) came not nigh,
Dryden alone escaped this judging eye:

know nothing about this man except that he was a "writer of secret and scandalous history," to quote Pope's own phrase. **Oldmixons,** John Oldmixon (1673–1742), a contemporary historian and pamphleteer. **Cookes,** Thomas Cooke (1703–1756), who had attacked Pope in a pamphlet in 1725. 149. **Fanny's.** Fanny is a contemptuous reference to Lord Hervey (1696–1743), the *Sporus* of ll. 305 ff. 151. **Gildon,** Charles Gildon (1665–1724), an abusive critic of Pope. 153. **Dennis,** John Dennis (1657–1734), a reputable critic though a favorite object of Pope's satire. 164. **Bentley,** Richard Bentley (1662–1742), noted critic and classical scholar at Cambridge, who published a poor edition of Milton's *Paradise Lost* in 1732. **Tibalds,** Lewis Theobald (1688–1744), minor poet and editor of Shakespeare; for his attack upon Pope's edition of Shakespeare he was made the hero of the first version of Pope's *Dunciad* (1728). 179. **The bard,** Ambrose Philips (cf. l. 100 and note), who translated a book called *Persian Tales.* 190. **Tate,** Nahum Tate (1652–1715), dramatist and poet laureate, known also for his hymn writing. 192. **Addison;** see pp. 473 ff. 193. **were there one, etc.** This characterization of Addison as Atticus (l. 214) is one of the most famous in all satiric literature. It shows Pope at his best and perhaps at his fairest. Obviously Pope and Addison, as two of the leading writers of their day, had many interests in common, but they differed in temperament and politics, so that they finally drifted into mutual distrust. The culmination of their strained relations, this passage in the

Epistle to Dr. Arbuthnot, was printed after Addison's death, although Pope indignantly denied that it had been written when the object of the attack could not answer. 209. **Cato,** a Roman statesman, general, and writer (234–119 B.C.), and hero of Addison's classical tragedy *Cato,* for which Pope had written the prologue. This line (209) is quoted from Pope's Prologue, l. 23. 211. **Templars,** students of the temple, i.e., law students. 214. **Aticus,** a Roman scholar and bookseller of the first century B.C. 215. **rubric,** in red. Names of new books were usually posted in red letters on the walls of the bookshops. 216. **claps,** posters. 225. **daggled,** wet, dirty, and limp; bedraggled. 230. **Bufo,** probably Charles Montagu (1661–1715), Lord Halifax, poet, statesman, and patron of letters; an enemy of Pope. **Castalian state,** the realm of poetry, named from Castalia, a fountain on Mt. Parnassus, supposed to give inspiration to those who drank of it. 231. **forkéd hill.** Apollo was god of both poetry and music. 236. **Pindar,** a famous Greek lyric poet (522?–443? B.C.). It was he who gave his name to the elaborate form of exalted lyric known as the ode; his type, the Pindaric ode was imitated by Ben Jonson (p. 342) and by Thomas Gray (p. 639). Pope is here ridiculing the affectation of antiquarians who often exhibited the headless trunks of statues of Plato, Homer, Pindar, etc.

But still the great have kindness in reserve,
He helped to bury whom he helped to starve.
    May some choice patron bless each gray goose
      quill!
250 May every Bavius have his Bufo still!
So, when a statesman wants a day's defense,
Or envy holds a whole week's war with sense,
Or simple pride for flattery makes demands,
May dunce by dunce be whistled off my hands!
Blessed be the great! for those they take away,
And those they left me; for they left me Gay;
Left me to see neglected genius bloom,
Neglected die, and tell it on his tomb:
Of all thy blameless life the sole return
260 My verse, and Queensbury weeping o'er thy urn.
    Oh, let me live my own, and die so too!
(To live and die is all I have to do)
Maintain a poet's dignity and ease,
And see what friends, and read what books I please;
Above a patron, though I condescend
Sometimes to call a minister my friend.
I was not born for courts or great affairs;
I pay my debts, believe, and say my prayers;
Can sleep without a poem in my head;
270 Nor know, if Dennis be alive or dead.
    Why am I asked what next shall see the light?
Heavens! was I born for nothing but to write?
Has life no joys for me? or (to be grave)
Have I no friend to serve, no soul to save?
"I found him close with Swift"—"Indeed? no doubt"
(Cries prating Balbus), "something will come out."
'Tis all in vain, deny it as I will.
"No, such a genius never can lie still";
And then for mine obligingly mistakes
280 The first lampoon Sir Will or Bubo makes.
Poor guiltless I! and can I choose but smile,
When every coxcomb knows me by my style?
    Cursed be the verse, how well soe'er it flow,
That tends to make one worthy man my foe,
Give virtue scandal, innocence a fear,
Or from the soft-eyed virgin steal a tear!
But he who hurts a harmless neighbor's peace,
Insults fallen worth, or beauty in distress,
Who loves a lie, lame slander helps about,
290 Who writes a libel, or who copies out:
That fop, whose pride affects a patron's name,
Yet absent, wounds an author's honest fame:
Who can your merit selfishly approve,
And show the sense of it without the love;
Who has the vanity to call you friend,
Yet wants the honor, injured, to defend;
Who tells whate'er you think, whate'er you say,

And, if he lie not, must at least betray:
Who to the Dean, and silver bell can swear,
And sees at Canons what was never there;   300
Who reads, but with a lust to misapply,
Make satire a lampoon, and fiction, lie.
A lash like mine no honest man shall dread,
But all such babbling blockheads in his stead.
    Let Sporus tremble— A. What? that thing of silk,
Sporus, that mere white curd of ass's milk!
Satire or sense, alas! can Sporus feel?
Who breaks a butterfly upon a wheel?
P. Yet let me flap this bug with gilded wings,
This painted child of dirt, that stinks and stings;   310
Whose buzz the witty and the fair annoys,
Yet wit ne'er tastes, and beauty ne'er enjoys:
So well-bred spaniels civilly delight
In mumbling of the game they dare not bite.
Eternal smiles his emptiness betray,
As shallow streams run dimpling all the way.
Whether in florid impotence he speaks,
And, as the prompter breathes, the puppet squeaks;
Or at the ear of Eve, familiar toad,
Half froth, half venom, spits himself abroad,   320
In puns, or politics, or tales, or lies,
Or spite, or smut, or rimes, or blasphemies.
His wit all see-saw, between that and this,
Now high, now low, now master up, now miss,
And he himself one vile antithesis.
Amphibious thing! that acting either part,
The trifling head or the corrupted heart,
Fop at the toilet, flatterer at the board,
Now trips a lady, and now struts a lord.
Eve's tempter thus the rabbins have expressed,   330
A cherub's face, a reptile all the rest;
Beauty that shocks you, parts that none will trust;
Wit that can creep, and pride that licks the dust.
    Not fortune's worshiper, nor fashion's fool,
Not lucre's madman, nor ambition's tool,
Not proud, nor servile;—be one poet's praise,
That, if he pleased, he pleased by manly ways:
That flattery, e'en to kings, he held a shame,
And thought a lie in verse or prose the same.
That not in fancy's maze he wandered long,   340
But stooped to truth, and moralized his song:
That not for fame, but virtue's better end,
He stood the furious foe, the timid friend,
The damning critic, half-approving wit,
The coxcomb hit, or fearing to be hit;
Laughed at the loss of friends he never had,
The dull, the proud, the wicked, and the mad;
The distant threats of vengeance on his head,
The blow unfelt, the tear he never shed;

256. **Gay,** John Gay (1685–1732), poet and dramatist praised and befriended by Pope. 260. **Queensbury,** Charles Douglas (1698–1778), Duke of Queensbury, a leader of fashion and patron of letters. Gay died in the house of the Duke and Duchess of Queensbury, who provided his monument in Westminster Abbey. 276. **Balbus,** George Hay, seventh Earl of Kinnoul (d. 1758). 280. **Sir Will,** Sir William Yonge (d. 1755), fop and small poet. King George II called him "stinking Yonge."

Pope was annoyed that verses by Yonge should be taken for his. **Bubo,** George Bubb Doddington (1691–1762), politician and promiscuous patron of letters. 305. **Sporus,** Lord John Hervey, a court favorite; cf. p. 556. In history Sporus was an effeminate favorite at the court of the Roman emperor Nero (37-68 A.D.). The passage on Sporus is one of Pope's most vicious attacks. 330. **rabbins,** Jewish rabbis.

350 The tale revived, the lie so oft o'erthrown,
Th' imputed trash, and dullness not his own;
The morals blackened when the writings 'scape,
The libeled person, and the pictured shape,
Abuse, on all he loved, or loved him, spread,
A friend in exile, or a father dead;
The whisper, that to greatness still too near,
Perhaps, yet vibrates on his Sovereign's ear:—
Welcome for thee, fair virtue! all the past;
For thee, fair virtue! welcome e'en the last!
360   A. But why insult the poor, affront the great?
P. A knave's a knave, to me, in every state:
Alike my scorn, if he succeed or fail.
Sporus at court, or Japhet in a jail,
A hireling scribbler, or a hireling peer,
Knight of the post corrupt, or of the shire;
If on a pillory, or near a throne,
He gain his prince's ear, or lose his own.
  Yet soft by nature, more a dupe than wit,
Sappho can tell you how this man was bit;
370 This dreaded satirist Dennis will confess
Foe to his pride, but friend to his distress:
So humble, he has knocked at Tibbald's door,
Has drunk with Cibber, nay has rimed for Moore.
Full ten years slandered, did he once reply?
Three thousand suns went down on Welsted's lie.
To please a mistress one aspersed his life;
He lashed him not, but let her be his wife.
Let Budgell charge low Grub Street on his quill,
And write whate'er he pleased, except his will;
380 Let the two Curlls of town and court, abuse
His father, mother, body, soul, and muse.
Yet why? that father held it for a rule,
It was a sin to call our neighbor fool;
That harmless mother thought no wife a whore:
Hear this, and spare his family, James Moore!

Unspotted names, and memorable long!
If there be force in virtue, or in song.
  Of gentle blood (part shed in honor's cause,
While yet in Britain honor had applause)
Each parent sprung— A. What fortune, pray?—
    P. Their own,   390
And better got, than Bestia's from the throne.
Born to no pride, inheriting no strife,
Nor marrying discord in a noble wife,
Stranger to civil and religious rage,
The good man walked innoxious through his age.
Nor courts he saw, no suits would ever try,
Nor dared an oath, nor hazarded a lie.
Unlearned, he knew no schoolman's subtle art,
No language, but the language of the heart.
By nature honest, by experience wise,   400
Healthy by temperance, and by exercise;
His life, though long to sickness past unknown,
His death was instant, and without a groan.
O grant me, thus to live, and thus to die!
Who sprung from kings shall know less joy than I.
  O friend! may each domestic bliss be thine!
Be no unpleasing melancholy mine:
Me, let the tender office long engage,
To rock the cradle of reposing age,
With lenient arts extend a mother's breath,   410
Make languor smile, and smooth the bed of death,
Explore the thought, explain the asking eye,
And keep a while one parent from the sky!
On cares like these if length of days attend,
May Heaven, to bless those days, preserve my friend,
Preserve him social, cheerful, and serene,
And just as rich as when he served a queen.
A. Whether that blessing be denied or given,
Thus far was right, the rest belongs to Heaven.
(1734; 1735)

---

363. **Japhet**, Japhet Crooks, a notorious Londoner of Pope's day, imprisoned for forging deeds and wills. 365. **Knight . . . corrupt.** The so-called knights of the post stood by the sheriff's pillars near the courts, ready to testify for pay to anything whatsoever. 375. **Welsted's lie.** For Welsted, see l. 49 and note. The lie was told in 1730. 378. **Budgell**, Eustace Budgell (1686–1737), a relative of Addison and author of thirty-seven of *The Spectator* papers. He was charged with forging a will to his own advantage. 380. **two Curlls.** For Edmund Curll see l. 53, and note. He had a son Henry. Both were unscrupulous publishers.

385. **spare . . . Moore.** Pope had accused Moore's mother of unchastity. 391. **Bestia**, probably the Duke of Marlborough, who was accused of making financial profit from the War of the Spanish Succession, which lasted intermittently from 1701 to 1713. L. Capurnius Besta was a Roman proconsul who in 111 B.C. accepted bribes from Jugurtha, king of Numidia (d. 104 B.C.), which sealed a dishonorable peace between the Roman republic and the wild kingdom of Numidia. 417. **served a queen.** Arbuthnot had been Queen Anne's favorite physician.

JOHNSON AND HIS CIRCLE

  In an age of clubs and coteries, the most brilliant in England was that which surrounded Dr. Samuel Johnson, "the Great Cham of Literature." Known only as The Club, and later as The Literary Club, it had its informal beginnings in 1764, and included among its original members, besides Dr. Johnson: Sir Joshua Reynolds, the famous painter; Edmund Burke, distinguished parliamentarian; Dr. Christopher Nugent, physician; Bennet Langton, classical scholar; Sir John Hawkins, man of letters; Anthony Chamier, government official; Topham Beauclerk, wit; and Oliver Goldsmith, author. Later there were added David Garrick, the actor; Charles James Fox, statesman; Thomas and Joseph Warton, poets and critics; Adam Smith, econo-

mist; Bishop Percy of Dromore, editor of the famous Reliques; Edward Gibbon, historian; Dr. Charles Burney, musician; and James Boswell, man about town and Johnson's biographer. In all there were about thirty-five members. The Club met weekly, or fortnightly, at the Turk's Head in Gerrard Street, Soho, and later at other taverns, and, according to Boswell, they "generally continued their conversation until a pretty late hour." Not all of the members were authors, but they were all interested in literature and good conversationalists about it. Selections from the writings of the most distinguished authors among them follow.

OLIVER GOLDSMITH 1728-1774

Oliver Goldsmith was born in the delightful Athlone country in the center of Ireland. He went off to Dublin in 1744, becoming a sizar (one granted free board) at Trinity College. But he did not apply himself too seriously, and following an entanglement because of the drenching of some bailiffs in the college cistern, he sold his books and ran away to Cork. In 1749, however, he was granted his B.A. degree. His well-meaning uncle then got him a tutorship, but young Oliver escaped from this sentence as soon as possible. In a Dublin gaming house he squandered the fifty pounds given him by the same patient uncle for the purpose of studying law. Goldsmith next made a sally into the field of medicine, which amounted to little more than a gay year in Edinburgh. In 1753 he went to the Continent with one clean shirt and a flute, but the accounts of his three years' rambling there are too artfully touched up by Goldsmith's own jeu d'esprit to be accepted as strictly autobiographical.

Goldsmith returned to London claiming to have a medical degree, but failed to receive a desired medical position and was thus left in poverty. He was forced, like Samuel Johnson before him, to plod away at literary back work, doing editorial work for booksellers. He was a mere literary novice when he undertook to affirm that literary criticism is almost synonymous with literary decadence; a treatise on this topic, called An Enquiry into the Present State of Polite Learning in Europe, appeared in 1759. Goldsmith was at that time contributing regularly to The Bee, a rather nondescript weekly, and his broadening reputation netted him a better living.

The Citizen of the World essays appeared between June 24, 1760, and August 14, 1761. To a newspaper called The Public Ledger Goldsmith had contributed a series of letters supposedly written to friends in the Orient by a Chinese traveler in London, who makes unprejudiced comments on the strange ways of English civilization. In 1762 this series was republished under the title Letters from a Citizen of the World.

Although The Citizen of the World papers eased the pinch of poverty, more catch-penny pamphlets followed from Goldsmith's pen. The Traveller, a philosophical poem, appeared in 1764 and justified Johnson's previous statement that "Goldsmith was one of the first men we now have as an author." The stage was well set for The Vicar of Wakefield (1766), the manuscript of which, as the story goes, Johnson himself took to the publishers to pay Goldsmith's debt to his landlady. The reception of this novel, a story of rational characters which ends on a sentimental note, was favorable; its sweetness and vivacity make it still an attractive book.

The success of The Vicar of Wakefield was matched by that of his collected essays (1767). Then George Coleman produced Goldsmith's comedy The Good-natur'd Man (1768). Two more triumphs followed, The Deserted Village in 1770, and She Stoops to Conquer, written in 1771 but not produced until 1773. The public response to this comedy of manners was most flattering, but the financial returns paid off no more than a mere fraction of Goldsmith's large debts. His sinking health made further effort with the pen absolute drudgery. Retaliation, a masterly series of caricatures, was his last important achievement before his death in 1774.

THE DESERTED VILLAGE

The Deserted Village, like Gray's Elegy, is one of the most genuinely popular poems which the eighteenth century produced. In fact, its tone is that of the pastoral elegy, and its final scene is that of personified "rural Virtues"—Toil, Care, Tenderness, Piety, Loyalty, Love—in a funereal march to the sea. The poem contains, too, an apostrophe to "sweet Poetry"—to be found, in one form or another, in the elegies of Milton, Gray, Tennyson, and Arnold. The several themes of the poem also give it broad popular appeal—a celebration of such homely virtues as sturdy self-reliance, a lamentation over the passing of an era, an indictment of the new age of the tyranny of trade, material luxury, and moral pride. Finally, if one contrasts Goldsmith's use of the heroic couplet with Pope's (say, in An Essay on Man), he will observe that a basic shift has taken place. Pope is sharp, crisp, rapid, and ratiocinative; Goldsmith is slow, suggestive, and sentimental. Many of the characteristic devices of the heroic couplet can still be identified, but they have ceased to claim primary attention, have, as it were, relaxed. Genial sentiment has replaced epigrammatic sophistication; the anxious heart has begun to find poetic expression.

Two fundamental revolutions were taking place in England, the one only a little in advance of the other, which were destined to alter the conditions of ordinary life. The agricultural revolution, greatly accelerated by the Enclosure Acts, was driving people from the land; public lands were being "enclosed" and made part of large private estates. The small farmer, who had tilled public land and grazed his stock in public parks, was driven to the city or across the sea. The Industrial Revolution, which would make England into a nation of factory workers and shopkeepers, was beginning to gain momentum, with the result that England was about to undergo a very rapid and very painful urbanization. As Goldsmith saw, "Sweet Auburn" was soon to be replaced by the vicious slums of London, Birmingham, and Manchester, and it is to his credit that he saw the wave of the future more accurately than did the economic and political theorists of his generation.

Sweet Auburn! loveliest village of the plain,
Where health and plenty cheered the laboring swain,
Where smiling spring its earliest visit paid,
And parting summer's lingering blooms delayed;
Dear lovely bowers of innocence and ease,
Seats of my youth, when every sport could please;
How often have I loitered o'er thy green,
Where humble happiness endeared each scene!
How often have I paused on every charm,
10 The sheltered cot, the cultivated farm,
The never-failing brook, the busy mill,
The decent church that topped the neighboring hill;
The hawthorn bush, with seats beneath the shade,
For talking age and whispering lovers made!
How often have I blessed the coming day,
When toil, remitting, lent its turn to play,
And all the village train, from labor free,
Led up their sports beneath the spreading tree!
While many a pastime circled in the shade,
20 The young contending as the old surveyed;
And many a gambol frolicked o'er the ground,
And sleights of art and feats of strength went round;
And still, as each repeated pleasure tired,
Succeeding sports the mirthful band inspired—
The dancing pair that simply sought renown,
By holding out to tire each other down;
The swain mistrustless of his smutted face,
While secret laughter tittered round the place;
The bashful virgin's side-long looks of love;
30 The matron's glance, that would those looks reprove.
These were thy charms, sweet village! sports like these,
With sweet succession, taught e'en toil to please;

These round thy bowers their cheerful influence shed;
These were thy charms—but all these charms are fled.

Sweet smiling village, loveliest of the lawn,
Thy sports are fled, and all thy charms withdrawn;
Amidst thy bowers the tyrant's hand is seen,
And desolation saddens all thy green;
One only master grasps the whole domain,
And half a tillage stints thy smiling plain.   40
No more thy glassy brook reflects the day,
But, choked with sedges, works its weedy way;
Along thy glades, a solitary guest,
The hollow-sounding bittern guards its nest;
Amidst thy desert walks the lapwing flies,
And tires their echoes with unvaried cries;
Sunk are thy bowers in shapeless ruin all,
And the long grass o'ertops the moldering wall;
And, trembling, shrinking from the spoiler's hand,
Far, far away thy children leave the land.   50

Ill fares the land, to hastening ills a prey,
Where wealth accumulates, and men decay.
Princes and lords may flourish, or may fade;
A breath can make them, as a breath has made,
But a bold peasantry, their country's pride,
When once destroyed, can never be supplied.

A time there was, ere England's griefs began,
When every rood of ground maintained its man;
For him light labor spread her wholesome store,
Just gave what life required, but gave no more: 60
His best companions, innocence and health;
And his best riches, ignorance of wealth.

But times are altered; trade's unfeeling train
Usurp the land, and dispossess the swain;
Along the lawn, where scattered hamlets rose,
Unwieldy wealth and cumbrous pomp repose;
And every want to opulence allied,
And every pang that folly pays to pride.
Those gentle hours that plenty bade to bloom,
Those calm desires that asked but little room,   70
Those healthful sports that graced the peaceful scene,
Lived in each look, and brightened all the green—
These, far departing, seek a kinder shore,
And rural mirth and manners are no more.

Sweet Auburn! parent of the blissful hour,
Thy glades forlorn confess the tyrant's power.
Here, as I take my solitary rounds,
Amidst thy tangling walks and ruined grounds,
And, many a year elapsed, return to view
Where once the cottage stood, the hawthorn grew—   80

The Deserted Village.   1. Sweet Auburn. Auburn may have been suggested by the village of Lissoy, Ireland, Goldsmith's childhood home. But the name "Auburn" is a poetical name, and little else; the village is a typical farm village in southern England.

39. grasps . . . domain. The Enclosure Acts (1760-1774) excluded villagers from the use of grazing grounds formerly held to be common property. 40. stints, restricts to scant allowance.

Remembrance wakes with all her busy train,
Swells at my breast, and turns the past to pain.

In all my wanderings round this world of care,
In all my griefs—and God has given my share—
I still had hopes, my latest hours to crown,
Amidst these humble bowers to lay me down;
To husband out life's taper at the close,
And keep the flame from wasting by repose;
I still had hopes, for pride attends us still,
90 Amidst the swains to show my book-learned skill,
Around my fire an evening group to draw,
And tell of all I felt, and all I saw;
And, as a hare, whom hounds and horns pursue,
Pants to the place from whence at first she flew,
I still had hopes, my long vexations past,
Here to return—and die at home at last.

O blest retirement, friend to life's decline,
Retreats from care, that never must be mine,
How happy he who crowns, in shades like these,
100 A youth of labor with an age of ease;
Who quits a world where strong temptations try,
And, since 'tis hard to combat, learns to fly!
For him no wretches, born to work and weep,
Explore the mine, or tempt the dangerous deep;
No surly porter stands, in guilty state,
To spurn imploring famine from the gate;
But on he moves to meet his latter end,
Angels around befriending virtue's friend;
Bends to the grave with unperceived decay,
110 While resignation gently slopes the way;
And, all his prospects brightening to the last,
His heaven commences ere the world be past!

Sweet was the sound, when oft, at evening's close,
Up yonder hill the village murmur rose.
There, as I passed with careless steps and slow,
The mingled notes came softened from below;
The swain responsive as the milkmaid sung,
The sober herd that lowed to meet their young;
The noisy geese that gabbled o'er the pool,
120 The playful children just let loose from school;
The watch-dog's voice that bayed the whispering wind,
And the loud laugh that spoke the vacant mind;—
These all in sweet confusion sought the shade,
And filled each pause the nightingale had made.
But now the sounds of population fail,
No cheerful murmurs fluctuate in the gale,
No busy steps the grass-grown footway tread,
For all the bloomy flush of life is fled—
All but yon widowed, solitary thing,
130 That feebly bends beside the plashy spring;
She, wretched matron—forced, in age for bread,
To strip the brook with mantling cresses spread,

To pick her wintry faggot from the thorn,
To seek her nightly shed, and weep till morn—
She only left of all the harmless train,
The sad historian of the pensive plain.

Near yonder copse, where once the garden smiled,
And still where many a garden-flower grows wild,
There, where a few torn shrubs the place disclose,
The village preacher's modest mansion rose.   140
A man he was to all the country dear,
And passing rich with forty pounds a year.
Remote from towns he ran his godly race,
Nor e'er had changed, nor wished to change, his place;
Unpracticed he to fawn, or seek for power
By doctrines fashioned to the varying hour;
Far other aims his heart had learned to prize,
More skilled to raise the wretched than to rise.
His house was known to all the vagrant train;
He chid their wanderings, but relieved their pain;   150
The long-remembered beggar was his guest,
Whose beard descending swept his aged breast;
The ruined spendthrift, now no longer proud,
Claimed kindred there, and had his claims allowed;
The broken soldier, kindly bade to stay,
Sat by his fire, and talked the night away;—
Wept o'er his wounds, or, tales of sorrow done,
Shouldered his crutch, and showed how fields were
        won.
Pleased with his guests, the good man learned to glow,
And quite forgot their vices in their woe;   160
Careless their merits or their faults to scan,
His pity gave ere charity began.

Thus to relieve the wretched was his pride,
And e'en his failings leaned to virtue's side;
But in his duty prompt at every call,
He watched and wept, he prayed and felt for all;
And, as a bird each fond endearment tries
To tempt its new-fledged offspring to the skies,
He tried each art, reproved each dull delay,
Allured to brighter worlds, and led the way.   170

Beside the bed where parting life was laid,
And sorrow, guilt, and pain, by turns dismayed,
The reverend champion stood. At his control,
Despair and anguish fled the struggling soul;
Comfort came down the trembling wretch to raise,
And his last faltering accents whispered praise.

At church, with meek and unaffected grace,
His looks adorned the venerable place;
Truth from his lips prevailed with double sway,
And fools, who came to scoff, remained to pray.   180
The service past, around the pious man

---

140. **village preacher.** The original of this portrait may have been either Goldsmith's father or his brother Henry. 210. **gauge,** measure; here, to survey. 221. **nut-brown drafts,** draughts of ale. 232. **twelve**

good rules, rules of conduct printed on cards and meant to be hung on walls. The legend goes that these rules were originally discovered in the rooms of Charles I after his execution. **game of goose,** a dice game

With steady zeal, each honest rustic ran;
E'en children followed, with endearing wile,
And plucked his gown, to share the good man's smile;
His ready smile a parent's warmth expressed;
Their welfare pleased him, and their cares distressed:
To them his heart, his love, his griefs were given,
But all his serious thoughts had rest in heaven.
As some tall cliff that lifts its awful form,
190 Swells from the vale, and midway leaves the storm,
Though round its breast the rolling clouds are spread,
Eternal sunshine settles on its head.

    Beside yon straggling fence that skirts the way,
With blossomed furze unprofitably gay,
There, in his noisy mansion, skilled to rule,
The village master taught his little school.
A man severe he was, and stern to view;
I knew him well, and every truant knew;
Well had the boding tremblers learned to trace
200 The day's disasters in his morning face;
Full well they laughed with counterfeited glee
At all his jokes, for many a joke had he;
Full well the busy whisper, circling round,
Conveyed the dismal tidings when he frowned.
Yet he was kind, or if severe in aught,
The love he bore to learning was in fault.
The village all declared how much he knew;
'Twas certain he could write, and cipher too;
Lands he could measure, terms and tides presage,
210 And e'en the story ran that he could gauge.
In arguing, too, the parson owned his skill,
For e'en though vanquished, he could argue still;
While words of learnéd length and thundering sound
Amazed the gazing rustics ranged around;
And still they gazed, and still the wonder grew,
That one small head could carry all he knew.
But past is all his fame;—the very spot,
Where many a time he triumphed, is forgot.

    Near yonder thorn, that lifts its head on high,
220 Where once the sign-post caught the passing eye,
Low lies that house where nut-brown drafts inspired,
Where gray-beard mirth and smiling toil retired,
Where village statesmen talked with looks profound,
And news much older than their ale went round.
Imagination fondly stoops to trace
The parlor splendors of that festive place;
The whitewashed wall, the nicely-sanded floor,
The varnished clock that clicked behind the door,
The chest, contrived a double debt to pay,
230 A bed by night, a chest of drawers by day,
The pictures placed for ornament and use,
The twelve good rules, the royal game of goose,
The hearth, except when winter chilled the day,

With aspen boughs, and flowers, and fennel, gay;—
While broken teacups, wisely kept for show,
Ranged o'er the chimney, glistened in a row.

    Vain transitory splendors! could not all
Reprieve the tottering mansion from its fall?
Obscure it sinks, nor shall it more impart
An hour's importance to the poor man's heart.   240
Thither no more the peasant shall repair,
To sweet oblivion of his daily care;
No more the farmer's news, the barber's tale,
No more the woodman's ballad shall prevail;
No more the smith his dusky brow shall clear,
Relax his ponderous strength, and lean to hear;
The host himself no longer shall be found
Careful to see the mantling bliss go round;
Nor the coy maid, half willing to be pressed,
Shall kiss the cup to pass it to the rest.   250

    Yes! let the rich deride, the proud disdain,
These simple blessings of the lowly train;
To me more dear, congenial to my heart,
One native charm, than all the gloss of art.
Spontaneous joys, where nature has its play,
The soul adopts, and owns their first-born sway;
Lightly they frolic o'er the vacant mind,
Unenvied, unmolested, unconfined:
But the long pomp, the midnight masquerade,
With all the freaks of wanton wealth arrayed,   260
In these, ere triflers half their wish obtain,
The toiling pleasure sickens into pain;
And, e'en while fashion's brightest arts decoy,
The heart distrusting asks, if this be joy.

    Ye friends to truth, ye statesmen, who survey
The rich man's joys increase, the poor's decay,
'Tis yours to judge how wide the limits stand
Between a splendid and a happy land.
Proud swells the tide with loads of freighted ore,
And shouting folly hails them from her shore;   270
Hoards, e'en beyond the miser's wish, abound,
And rich men flock from all the world around.
Yet count our gains. This wealth is but a name
That leaves our useful products still the same.
Not so the loss. The man of wealth and pride
Takes up a space that many poor supplied;
Space for his lake, his park's extended bounds,
Space for his horses, equipage, and hounds;
The robe that wraps his limbs in silken sloth,
Has robbed the neighboring fields of half their growth; 280
His seat, where solitary sports are seen,
Indignant spurns the cottage from the green;
Around the world each needful product flies,
For all the luxuries the world supplies;

---

of the parchesi type, generally known by the French name *jeu de l'oie.*
250. **kiss . . . rest.** For another statement of this idea, cf. Ben Jonson's

Song to Celia. 282. **spurns,** literally "to kick aside," here in the weaker sense of "displaces."

While thus the land, adorned for pleasure all,
In barren splendor feebly waits the fall.

    As some fair female, unadorned and plain,
Secure to please while youth confirms her reign,
Slights every borrowed charm that dress supplies,
290 Nor shares with art the triumph of her eyes;
But when those charms are past, for charms are frail,
When time advances, and when lovers fail,
She then shines forth, solicitous to bless,
In all the glaring impotence of dress;
Thus fares the land by luxury betrayed;
In nature's simplest charms at first arrayed;—
But verging to decline, its splendors rise,
Its vistas strike, its palaces surprise;
While, scourged by famine, from the smiling land
300 The mournful peasant leads his humble band;
And while he sinks, without one arm to save,
The country blooms—a garden and a grave!

    Where, then, ah! where shall poverty reside,
To 'scape the pressure of contiguous pride?
If to some common's fenceless limits strayed,
He drives his flock to pick the scanty blade,
Those fenceless fields the sons of wealth divide,
And e'en the bare-worn common is denied.

    If to the city sped—what waits him there?
310 To see profusion that he must not share;
To see ten thousand baneful arts combined
To pamper luxury and thin mankind;
To see those joys the sons of pleasure know
Extorted from his fellow-creature's woe;
Here while the courtier glitters in brocade,
There the pale artist plies the sickly trade;
Here while the proud their long-drawn pomps display,
There the black gibbet glooms beside the way;
The dome where pleasure holds her midnight reign,
320 Here, richly decked, admits the gorgeous train;
Tumultuous grandeur crowds the blazing square,
The rattling chariots clash, the torches glare.
Sure scenes like these no troubles e'er annoy!
Sure these denote one universal joy!—
Are these thy serious thoughts?—ah, turn thine eyes
Where the poor houseless shivering female lies;
She once, perhaps, in village plenty blessed,
Has wept at tales of innocence distressed;
Her modest looks the cottage might adorn,
330 Sweet as the primrose peeps beneath the thorn;
Now lost to all, her friends, her virtue, fled,
Near her betrayer's door she lays her head,
And, pinched with cold, and shrinking from the
    shower,
With heavy heart deplores that luckless hour,
When idly first, ambitious of the town,
She left her wheel, and robes of country brown.

The Sad Historian, a wood engraving by John Bewick for
Poems of Goldsmith and Parnell, *London, 1795.*

    Do thine, sweet Auburn, thine, the loveliest train,
Do thy fair tribes participate her pain?
E'en now, perhaps, by cold and hunger led,
At proud men's doors they ask a little bread!   340

    Ah, no. To distant climes, a dreary scene,
Where half the convex world intrudes between,
Through torrid tracts with fainting steps they go,
Where wild Altama murmurs to their woe.
Far different there from all that charmed before,
The various terrors of that horrid shore;
Those blazing suns that dart a downward ray,
And fiercely shed intolerable day;
Those matted woods where birds forget to sing,
But silent bats in drowsy clusters cling;   350
Those poisonous fields, with rank luxuriance crowned,
Where the dark scorpion gathers death around;
Where at each step the stranger fears to wake
The rattling terrors of the vengeful snake;
Where crouching tigers wait their hapless prey,
And savage men more murderous still than they;
While oft in whirls the mad tornado flies,
Mingling the ravaged landscape with the skies.
Far different these from every former scene,
The cooling brook, the grassy-vested green,   360

---

304. **contiguous pride, etc.,** "Where can the poor man live so as to
escape the presence of a domineering rich man?" 308. **common, the**
old "folk-right" or "land-right" of the Anglo-Saxon citizen. 336.
wheel, spinning wheel. 338. **participate,** share. 344. **Altama,** the

The breezy covert of the warbling grove,
That only sheltered thefts of harmless love.

    Good Heaven! what sorrows gloomed that parting
        day,
That called them from their native walks away;
When the poor exiles, every pleasure past,
Hung round their bowers, and fondly looked their last,
And took a long farewell, and wished in vain,
For seats like these beyond the western main;
And shuddering still to face the distant deep,
370 Returned and wept, and still returned to weep!
The good old sire the first prepared to go
To new-found worlds, and wept for others' woe;
But for himself, in conscious virtue brave,
He only wished for worlds beyond the grave.
His lovely daughter, lovelier in her tears,
The fond companion of his helpless years,
Silent went next, neglectful of her charms,
And left a lover's for a father's arms.
With louder plaints the mother spoke her woes,
380 And blessed the cot where every pleasure rose,
And kissed her thoughtless babes with many a tear,
And clasped them close, in sorrow doubly dear;
Whilst her fond husband strove to lend relief
In all the silent manliness of grief.

    O luxury, thou cursed by Heaven's decree,
How ill exchanged are things like these for thee!
How do thy potions, with insidious joy,
Diffuse their pleasures only to destroy!
Kingdoms by thee to sickly greatness grown,
390 Boast of a florid vigor not their own;
At every draft more large and large they grow,
A bloated mass of rank unwieldy woe;
Till sapped their strength, and every part unsound,
Down, down they sink, and spread a ruin round.

    E'en now the devastation is begun,
And half the business of destruction done;
E'en now, methinks, as pondering here I stand,
I see the rural virtues leave the land.
Down where yon anchoring vessel spreads the sail,
400 That idly waiting flaps with every gale,
Downward they move, a melancholy band,
Pass from the shore, and darken all the strand;
Contented toil, and hospitable care,
And kind connubial tenderness are there;
And piety with wishes placed above,
And steady loyalty, and faithful love.

    And thou, sweet Poetry, thou loveliest maid,
Still first to fly where sensual joys invade!
Unfit, in these degenerate times of shame,
410 To catch the heart, or strike for honest fame;

Dear charming nymph, neglected and decried,
My shame in crowds, my solitary pride;
Thou source of all my bliss and all my woe,
That found'st me poor at first, and keep'st me so;
Thou guide by which the nobler arts excel,
Thou nurse of every virtue, fare thee well!
Farewell! and oh! where'er thy voice be tried,
On Torno's cliffs, or Pambamarca's side,
Whether where equinoctial fervors glow,
Or winter wraps the polar world in snow,   420
Still let thy voice, prevailing over time,
Redress the rigors of th' inclement clime;
Aid slighted truth with thy persuasive strain;
Teach erring man to spurn the rage of gain;
Teach him that states, of native strength possessed,
Though very poor, may still be very blest;
That trade's proud empire hastes to swift decay,
As ocean sweeps the labored mole away;
While self-dependent power can time defy,
As rocks resist the billows and the sky.   430
(1770)

SAMUEL JOHNSON 1709-1784

    Samuel Johnson was born in 1709, the son of a bookseller in Lichfield. A childhood attack of scrofula left his health precarious but young Johnson nevertheless performed an extraordinary task in educating himself, chiefly by voracious reading. He entered Oxford in 1728 but had to leave without a degree because of his father's straitened circumstances and death. Johnson published his first work in 1735, a translation of Father Lobo's Voyage to Abyssinia, *and in the same year he married Mrs. Elizabeth Porter, a widow old enough to be his mother; the couple then opened a private school near Lichfield. When the school failed two years later, he set out for London with one of his pupils, the great future actor David Garrick. From 1737 to 1746 Johnson worked doggedly at literary and journalistic projects, especially for* The Gentleman's Magazine; *he published* London, *a satirical poem in imitation of Juvenal, and his* Life of Richard Savage *(1774), which looks forward to the* Lives of the Poets. *The "Plan" of Johnson's ambitious* Dictionary *was issued in 1747 and during the next seven years, with the help of only six assistants, he completed this incomparable work. In 1749 he published* The Vanity of Human Wishes, *his highest achievement in poetry, and his friend Garrick unsuccessfully produced Johnson's classical tragedy* Irene. *During the next ten years he imitated* The Spectator *in* The Rambler *(1750-1752) and* The Idler *(1758-1760), periodical essays on manners, morals, and literature; he also published his* Dic-

Altamaha River in the state of Georgia.   418. **Torno,** the River Tornea (Tana), which flows into the Gulf of Bothnia, at the northern extremity   of Sweden. **Pambamarca,** a mountain near Quito, Ecuador. 419. **equinoctial fervors,** the intense heat of the equator.

tionary (1755), which greatly enhanced his reputation, and Rasselas (1759), a novel composed in a week to enable him to pay his mother's funeral expenses and debts. He finally received a government pension in 1762, which much improved his financial condition. The next year he met Boswell, who became his admiring friend for more than twenty years. In 1765 Johnson published his edition of Shakespeare and also met the Thrales, a wealthy couple who extended him hospitality for eighteen years and with whom he enjoyed abundant intellectual and social intercourse. His life at this time was greatly given to his friends, particularly to the distinguished group of literary and professional men who formed his famous Literary Club. Johnson's last published work, The Lives of the English Poets, appeared in two parts in 1779 and 1781. He died in 1784 and was buried in Westminster Abbey.

There are two Dr. Johnsons, not just one—the Johnson of the "popular tradition" and the Johnson of the "learned tradition." The former was firmly set by Thomas Babington Macaulay in 1831 and has undergone no fundamental change since; it chiefly emphasizes his colorful personal peculiarities. The "learned tradition," the one to which the serious student of literature should look, has undergone change. At the beginning of the nineteenth century, Johnson was considered one of the "most illustrious writers of any age or nation"; at the beginning of the twentieth century, he was hardly thought of as a writer at all: Boswell's vivid Life had "embalmed" him better than he knew. Since that low-water mark, Johnson's reputation as a writer has steadily risen, so that now criticism applauds him, not just as a great conversationalist or as a great eccentric but as a great man of letters.

As a poet, Johnson was neither great nor negligible. His total poetic output was slight, and he worked within a tradition which he did not extend or refresh. Yet Johnson's poems are individually distinctive creations, each with a note of sadness about it, each with a note of acceptance. His most ambitious poem, and his finest, is The Vanity of Human Wishes, and its quality clearly demonstrates that, had Johnson had more leisure, more faith in himself as a poet, and a circle of friends more devoted to the writing of poetry, he could have been a distinguished English poet. The poem is in imitation of Juvenal's tenth satire, and there are inevitable echoes from Pope and Milton in it. It is a laudable example of poetry of statement: the couplets are compact, rhythmically varied, and replete with felicitous sound; the language is muscular and active; the theme is turned around and around and aptly illustrated; the portraits are vivid and dramatic (see ll. 99-120); and the personifications are often well-fleshed actors in this Vanity Fair. It is not great poetry, but it is very impressive.

As a literary critic, Johnson was certainly the greatest of his century, and his stature is not even to be measured against any English critic other than Dryden, Coleridge, and Matthew Arnold. Johnson has come to be valued more as modern readers have come to value practical, rather than theoretical, criticism—that is, criticism brought to specific cases. "[T]he reader may be weary," he said, "though the critick may commend. Works of imagination excel by their allurement and delight; by their power of attracting and detaining the attention. That book is good in vain which the reader throws away. He only is the master who keeps the mind in pleasing captivity; whose pages are perused with eagerness, and in hope of new pleasure are perused again; and whose conclusion is perceived with an eye of sorrow, such as the traveller casts upon departing day." This is criticism of common sense with a healthy respect for the common reader. Besides his native common sense, Johnson had another tremendous asset as a critic: it is probably little exaggeration to say that he had read everything of any literary note published in English. Therefore, though his taste might mislead him, his ignorance could not. Johnson judged because judgment is the business of the literary critic, but he did not follow a particular "school" of thought. He expected of literature the two sustaining qualities of truth to nature and novelty. It is through pleasure that the reader becomes involved in the literary work, and unless that work can give pleasure, however brilliant or profound it may be, it cannot be effective.

In religion and politics, Johnson was an enlightened conservative. The sceptical mind which vitalizes his thoughts on literature is not absent; it has simply been put to new uses. He craved political stability and an ultimate meaning to life. For the former, he looked to the authority of the Crown; for the latter, to the Christian revelation. Thus the Whigs, whose constant effort was to reduce the authority of the Crown, were anathema to Johnson. In religion, Johnson's absolute monarch became the Supreme Authority; the only alternative seemed to be universal chaos. "None would have recourse to an invisible power," he said, "but that all other subjects have eluded their hopes." And so intensely did he feel the need for his "hopes" that he sometimes suffered (how frequently is not known) the dark night of the soul, agonized periods dominated by self-abasement and an intensely personalized fear of God.

Johnson's prose style has been judged "perhaps the greatest of his achievements." Its chief characteristics are directness, balance (words, phrases, clauses), consciously wrought structure (especially the periodic), significant attention to rhythm and sound, occasional use of unusual polysyllabic words, abstract nouns, and that-clauses. The example of "balanced elaboration"

---

30. **madded,** maddened. 42. **brake,** thicket of dense underbrush. 49. **Democritus,** "the laughing philosopher" (fifth century B.C.). 84.

palladium, a statue of Pallas Athena, upon which the safety of Troy was supposed to depend. 97. **weekly libels,** attacks in the weekly

THE VANITY OF HUMAN WISHES

In Imitation of the Tenth Satire of Juvenal

Let Observation, with extensive view,
Survey mankind, from China to Peru;
Remark each anxious toil, each eager strife,
And watch the busy scenes of crowded life;
Then say how hope and fear, desire and hate
O'erspread with snares the clouded maze of fate,
Where wavering man, betrayed by venturous pride
To tread the dreary paths without a guide,
As treacherous phantoms in the mist delude,
10 Shuns fancied ills, or chases airy good;
How rarely Reason guides the stubborn choice,
Rules the bold hand, or prompts the suppliant voice;
How nations sink, by darling schemes oppressed,
When Vengeance listens to the fool's request.
Fate wings with every wish the afflictive dart,
Each gift of nature, and each grace of art;
With fatal heat impetuous courage glows,
With fatal sweetness elocution flows,
Impeachment stops the speaker's powerful breath,
20 And restless fire precipitates on death.
But scarce observed, the knowing and the bold
Fall in the general massacre of gold;
Wide-wasting pest! that rages unconfined,
And crowds with crimes the records of mankind;
For gold his sword the hireling ruffian draws,
For gold the hireling judge distorts the laws;
Wealth heaped on wealth, nor truth nor safety buys,
The dangers gather as the treasures rise.
Let History tell where rival kings command,
30 And dubious title shakes the madded land,
When statutes glean the refuse of the sword,
How much more safe the vassal than the lord,
Low skulks the hind beneath the rage of power,
And leaves the wealthy traitor in the Tower,
Untouched his cottage, and his slumbers sound,
Though Confiscation's vultures hover round.
The needy traveler, serene and gay,
Walks the wild heath, and sings his toil away.
Does envy seize thee? crush the upbraiding joy,
40 Increase his riches and his peace destroy;
New fears in dire vicissitude invade,
The rustling brake alarms, and quivering shade,
Nor light nor darkness bring his pain relief,
One shows the plunder, and one hides the thief.
Yet still one general cry the skies assails,
And gain and grandeur load the tainted gales;
Few know the toiling statesman's fear or care,
The insidious rival and the gaping heir.

Once more, Democritus, arise on earth,
With cheerful wisdom and instructive mirth, 50
See motley life in modern trappings dressed,
And feed with varied fools the eternal jest:
Thou who couldst laugh where Want enchained
    Caprice,
Toil crushed Conceit, and man was of a piece;
Where Wealth unloved without a mourner died;
And scarce a sycophant was fed by Pride;
Where ne'er was known the form of mock debate,
Or seen a new-made mayor's unwieldy state;
Where change of favorites made no change of laws,
And senates heard before they judged a cause; 60
How wouldst thou shake at Britain's modish tribe,
Dart the quick taunt, and edge the piercing gibe?
Attentive truth and nature to descry,
And pierce each scene with philosophic eye,
To thee were solemn toys or empty show
The robes of pleasures and the veils of woe:
All aid the farce, and all thy mirth maintain,
Whose joys are causeless, or whose griefs are vain.
Such was the scorn that filled the sage's mind,
Renewed at every glance on human kind; 70
How just that scorn ere yet thy voice declare,
Search every state, and canvass every prayer.
Unnumbered suppliants crowd Preferment's gate,
Athirst for wealth, and burning to be great;
Delusive Fortune hears the incessant call,
They mount, they shine, evaporate, and fall.
On every stage the foes of peace attend,
Hate dogs their flight, and Insult mocks their end.
Love ends with hope, the sinking statesman's door
Pours in the morning worshiper no more; 80
For growing names the weekly scribbler lies,
To growing wealth the dedicator flies;
From every room descends the painted face,
That hung the bright palladium of the place;
And smoked in kitchens, or in auctions sold,
To better features yields the frame of gold;
For now no more we trace in every line
Heroic worth, benevolence divine:
The form distorted justifies the fall,
And Detestation rids the indignant wall. 90
But will not Britain hear the last appeal,
Sign her foes' doom, or guard her favorites' zeal?
Through Freedom's sons no more remonstrance rings,
Degrading nobles and controlling kings;
Our supple tribes repress their patriot throats,
And ask no questions but the price of votes,
With weekly libels and septennial ale.
Their wish is full to riot and to rail.
In full-blown dignity, see Wolsey stand,
Law in his voice, and fortune in his hand: 100
To him the church, the realm, their powers consign,
Through him the rays of regal bounty shine;

---

newspapers. **septennial ale,** ale given away by politicians at election time, at least every seven years. 99. **Wolsey,** Thomas Cardinal Wolsey

(1475?-1530), Lord Chancellor under Henry VIII.

Cutting silhouettes was a very popular pastime in the eighteenth century. Above are profiles of Garrick and Hogarth, from Samuel Ireland's Graphic Illustrations of Hogarth, 1799.

Or liv'st thou now, with safer pride content,
The wisest justice on the banks of Trent?
For why did Wolsey, near the steeps of fate,
On weak foundations raise the enormous weight?
Why but to sink beneath misfortune's blow,
With louder ruin to the gulfs below?
   What gave great Villiers to the assassin's knife,
And fixed disease on Harley's closing life?   130
What murdered Wentworth, and what exiled Hyde,
By kings protected and to kings allied?
What but their wish indulged in courts to shine,
And power too great to keep or to resign?
   When first the college rolls receive his name,
The young enthusiast quits his ease for fame;
Resistless burns the fever of renown
Caught from the strong contagion of the gown:
O'er Bodley's dome his future labors spread,
And Bacon's mansion trembles o'er his head.   140
Are these thy views? proceed, illustrious youth,
And Virtue guard thee to the throne of Truth!
Yet should thy soul indulge the generous heat,
Till captive Science yields her last retreat;
Should Reason guide thee with her brightest ray,
And pour on misty Doubt resistless day;
Should no false kindness lure to loose delight,
Nor praise relax, nor difficulty fright;
Should tempting Novelty thy cell refrain,
And Sloth effuse her opiate fumes in vain;   150
Should Beauty blunt on fops her fatal dart,
Nor claim the triumph of a lettered heart;
Should no disease thy torpid veins invade,
Nor Melancholy's phantoms haunt thy shade;
Yet hope not life from grief or danger free,
Nor think the doom of man reversed for thee:
Deign on the passing world to turn thine eyes,
And pause a while from letters, to be wise;
There mark what ills the scholar's life assail,
Toil, envy, want, the patron, and the jail.   160
See nations slowly wise, and meanly just,
To buried merit raise the tardy bust.
If dreams yet flatter, once again attend,
Hear Lydiat's life, and Galileo's end.
   Nor deem, when Learning her last prize bestows,
The glittering eminence exempt from foes;
See when the vulgar 'scapes, despised or awed,
Rebellion's vengeful talons seize on Laud.
From meaner minds though smaller fines content,
The plundered palace, or sequestered rent;   170
Marked out by dangerous parts he meets the shock,
And fatal Learning leads him to the block:
Around his tomb let Art and Genius weep,

Turned by his nod the stream of honor flows,
His smile alone security bestows:
Still to new heights his restless wishes tower,
Claim leads to claim, and power advances power;
Till conquest unresisted ceased to please,
And rights submitted, left him none to seize.
At length his sovereign frowns—the train of state
110 Mark the keen glance, and watch the sign to hate.
Where'er he turns, he meets a stranger's eye,
His suppliants scorn him, and his followers fly;
At once is lost the pride of awful state,
The golden canopy, the glittering plate,
The regal palace, the luxurious board,
The liveried army, and the menial lord.
With age, with cares, with maladies oppressed,
He seeks the refuge of monastic rest.
Grief aids disease, remembered folly stings,
120 And his last sighs reproach the faith of kings.
   Speak thou, whose thoughts at humble peace repine,
Shall Wolsey's wealth, with Wolsey's end be thine?

129. **Villiers,** George Villiers (1592-1628), 1st Duke of Buckingham and a royal favorite; he was assassinated. 130. **Harley,** Robert Harley (1661-1724), 1st Earl of Oxford, one of Queen Anne's principal ministers. The year after her death he was imprisoned by the Whigs. 131. **Wentworth,** Thomas Wentworth (1593-1641), 1st Earl of Strafford, and adviser to Charles I. Known as "Black Tom Tyrant," he was executed with Charles' assent in 1641. **Hyde,** Edward Hyde (1609-1674), Earl of Clarendon. He was the father-in-law of James II and Charles

II's principal minister. Impeached in 1667, he fled to France. 139. **Bodley's,** the Bodleian Library at Oxford. 140. **Bacon,** Roger Bacon (1214?-1294), "the founder of English philosophy," was a learned professor at Oxford. Legend held that when a more learned man came to Oxford, Bacon's study would come crashing down. 164. **Lydiat,** Thomas Lydiat (1572-1646), an Oxford scholar who died in want because of his sympathies for the Royalists. **Galileo,** Galileo Galilei (1564-1642), Italian astronomer and physicist imprisoned as a heretic by

But hear his death, ye blockheads, hear and sleep.
    The festal blazes, the triumphal show,
The ravished standard, and the captive foe,
The senate's thanks, the gazette's pompous tale,
With force resistless o'er the brave prevail.
Such bribes the rapid Greek o'er Asia whirled,
180 For such the steady Romans shook the world;
For such in distant lands the Britons shine,
And stain with blood the Danube or the Rhine;
This power has praise that virtue scarce can warm,
Till fame supplies the universal charm.
Yet Reason frowns on War's unequal game,
Where wasted nations raise a single name,
And mortgaged states their grandsires' wreaths regret
From age to age in everlasting debt;
Wreaths which at last the dear-bought right convey
190 To rust on medals, or on stones decay.
    On what foundation stands the warrior's pride,
How just his hopes, let Swedish Charles decide;
A frame of adamant, a soul of fire,
No dangers fright him, and no labors tire;
O'er love, o'er fear, extends his wide domain,
Unconquered lord of pleasure and of pain;
No joys to him pacific scepters yield,
War sounds the trump, he rushes to the field;
Behold surrounding kings their powers combine,
200 And one capitulate, and one resign;
Peace courts his hand, but spreads her charms in vain;
"Think nothing gained," he cries, "till naught remain,
On Moscow's walls till Gothic standards fly,
And all be mine beneath the polar sky."
The march begins in military state,
And nations on his eye suspended wait;
Stern Famine guards the solitary coast,
And Winter barricades the realms of Frost;
He comes, nor want nor cold his course delay—
210 Hide, blushing Glory, hide Pultowa's day:
The vanquished hero leaves his broken bands,
And shows his miseries in distant lands;
Condemned a needy supplicant to wait,
While ladies interpose, and slaves debate.
But did not Chance at length her error mend?
Did no subverted empire mark his end?
Did rival monarchs give the fatal wound?
Or hostile millions press him to the ground?
His fall was destined to a barren strand,
220 A petty fortress, and a dubious hand:
He left the name at which the world grew pale,
To point a moral, or adorn a tale.
    All times their scenes of pompous woes afford,
From Persia's tyrant to Bavaria's lord.

In gay hostility, and barbarous pride,
With half mankind embattled at his side,
Great Xerxes comes to seize the certain prey,
And starves exhausted regions in his way;
Attendant Flattery counts his myriads o'er,
Till counted myriads sooth his pride no more; 230
Fresh praise is tried till madness fires his mind,
The waves he lashes, and enchains the wind;
New powers are claimed, new powers are still bestowed,
Till rude resistance lops the spreading god;
The daring Greeks deride the martial show,
And heap their valleys with the gaudy foe;
The insulted sea with humbler thought he gains,
A single skiff to speed his flight remains;
The encumbered oar scarce leaves the dreaded coast
Through purple billows and a floating host. 240
    The bold Bavarian, in a luckless hour,
Tries the dread summits of Caesarean power,
With unexpected legions bursts away,
And sees defenseless realms receive his sway;
Short sway! fair Austria spreads her mournful charms,
The queen, the beauty, sets the world in arms;
From hill to hill the beacon's rousing blaze
Spreads wide the hope of plunder and of praise;
The fierce Croatian, and the wild Hussar,
With all the sons of ravage crowd the war; 250
The baffled prince, in honor's flattering bloom
Of hasty greatness finds the fatal doom;
His foes' derision, and his subjects' blame,
And steals to death from anguish and from shame.
    Enlarge my life with multitude of days!
In health, in sickness, thus the suppliant prays;
Hides from himself his state, and shuns to know,
That life protracted is protracted woe.
Time hovers o'er, impatient to destroy,
And shuts up all the passages of joy; 260
In vain their gifts the bounteous seasons pour,
The fruit autumnal, and the vernal flower;
With listless eyes the dotard views the store,
He views, and wonders that they please no more;
Now pall the tasteless meats, and joyless wines,
And Luxury with sighs her slave resigns.
Approach, ye minstrels, try the soothing strain,
Diffuse the tuneful lenitives of pain:
No sounds, alas! would touch the impervious ear,
Though dancing mountains witnessed Orpheus near; 270
Nor lute nor lyre his feeble powers attend,
Nor sweeter music of a virtuous friend,
But everlasting dictates crowd his tongue,
Perversely grave, or positively wrong.
The still returning tale, and lingering jest,

the Inquisition. 168. **Laud,** William Laud (1573-1645), Archbishop of Canterbury and a supporter of Charles I against Parliament; he was executed. 179. **the rapid Greek,** Alexander the Great. 192. **Swedish Charles, etc.** Charles XII of Sweden (1682-1718) was ambitious that "all be mine beneath the polar sky." Frederick IV of Denmark capitulated and Augustus II of Poland "resigned" (l. 200). Charles was defeated by the Russians (l. 216) at Pultowa and died in an attack on "a petty fortress" in Norway (ll. 219-220). 224. **Persia's tyrant, etc.** Xerxes,

King of Persia from 485 to 465 B.C., bridged the Hellespont with boats and invaded Greece. At Thermopylae, a narrow pass between the mountains and the sea, a mere handful of Greeks and Spartans resisted for three days the vast army of the Persians (480 B.C.) 241. **bold Bavarian, etc.** Charles Albert, Elector of Bavaria, contested the crown of the Holy Roman Empire with the German archduchess Maria Theresa of Austria, thus causing the War of the Austrian Succession (1740-1748).

Perplex the fawning niece and pampered guest,
While growing hopes scarce awe the gathering sneer,
And scarce a legacy can bribe to hear;
The watchful guests still hint the last offense;
280 The daughter's petulance, the son's expense,
Improve his heady rage with treacherous skill,
And mold his passions till they make his will.

Unnumbered maladies his joints invade,
Lay siege to life and press the dire blockade;
But unextinguished avarice still remains,
And dreaded losses aggravate his pains;
He turns, with anxious heart and crippled hands,
His bonds of debt, and mortgages of lands;
Or views his coffers with suspicious eyes,
290 Unlocks his gold, and counts it till he dies.

But grant, the virtues of a temperate prime
Bless with an age exempt from scorn or crime;
An age that melts with unperceived decay,
And glides in modest innocence away;
Whose peaceful day Benevolence endears,
Whose night congratulating Conscience cheers;
The general favorite as the general friend:
Such age there is, and who shall wish its end?

Yet even on this her load Misfortune flings,
300 To press the weary minutes' flagging wings;
New sorrow rises as the day returns,
A sister sickens, or a daughter mourns.
Now kindred Merit fills the sable bier,
Now lacerated Friendship claims a tear;
Year chases year, decay pursues decay,
Still drops some joy from withering life away;
New forms arise, and different views engage,
Superfluous lags the veteran on the stage,
Till pitying Nature signs the last release,
310 And bids afflicted Worth retire to peace.

But few there are whom hours like these await,
Who set unclouded in the gulfs of Fate.
From Lydia's monarch should the search descend,
By Solon cautioned to regard his end,
In life's last scene what prodigies surprise,
Fears of the brave, and follies of the wise!
From Marlborough's eyes the streams of dotage flow,
And Swift expires a driveler and a show.

The teeming mother, anxious for her race,
320 Begs for each birth the fortune of a face:
Yet Vane could tell what ills from beauty spring;
And Sedley cursed the form that pleased a king.
Ye nymphs of rosy lips and radiant eyes,
Whom Pleasure keeps too busy to be wise,
Whom Joys with soft varieties invite,
By day the frolic, and the dance by night;
Who frown with vanity, who smile with art,
And ask the latest fashion of the heart;
What care, what rules your heedless charms shall save,

Each nymph your rival, and each youth your slave? 330
Against your fame with Fondness Hate combines,
The rival batters, and the lover mines.
With distant voice neglected Virtue calls,
Less heard and less, the faint remonstrance falls;
Tired with contempt, she quits the slippery reign,
And Pride and Prudence take her seat in vain.
In crowd at once, where none the pass defend,
The harmless freedom, and the private friend.
The guardians yield, by force superior plied:
To Interest, Prudence; and to Flattery, Pride. 340
Now Beauty falls betrayed, despised, distressed,
And hissing Infamy proclaims the rest.

Where then shall Hope and Fear their objects find?
Must dull Suspense corrupt the stagnant mind?
Must helpless man, in ignorance sedate,
Roll darkling down the torrent of his fate?
Must no dislike alarm, no wishes rise,
No cries invoke the mercies of the skies?
Inquirer, cease; petitions yet remain,
Which Heaven may hear, nor deem religion vain. 350
Still raise for good the supplicating voice,
But leave to Heaven the measure and the choice.
Safe in His power, whose eyes discern afar
The secret ambush of a specious prayer.
Implore His aid, in His decisions rest,
Secure, what'er He gives, He gives the best.
Yet when the sense of sacred presence fires,
And strong devotion to the skies aspires,
Pour forth thy fervors for a healthful mind,
Obedient passions, and a will resigned; 360
For love, which scarce collective man can fill;
For patience sovereign o'er transmuted ill;
For faith, that panting for a happier seat,
Counts death kind Nature's signal of retreat;
These goods for man the laws of Heaven ordain,
These goods He grants, who grants the power to gain,
With these celestial Wisdom calms the mind,
And makes the happiness she does not find.
(1749)

from THE DICTIONARY

When Johnson defined lexicographer as "a harm-less drudge," he spoke from experience as well as from a sense of humor. The Dictionary occupied his time and thought for eight years or more, but it was a remarkable achievement, since during the period he was busy with much other writing.

As stated in the original "Plan," addressed to Lord Chesterfield, it was Johnson's hope to write "a dictionary by which the pronunciation of our language may be fixed, and its attainment facilitated; by which

313. **Lydia's monarch.** Croesus, last king of Lydia, was the wealthiest of men ("rich as Croesus"). He was warned by the philosopher Solon that a man cannot claim happiness who has not ended his life happily. He lost his kingdom to Cyrus of Persia. 317. **Marlborough.** The 1st Duke of Marlborough, John Churchill (1650-1722), passed from the life of a brilliant soldier to senility. 318. **Swift.** Jonathan Swift died *non compos mentis.* 321. **Vane,** Anne Vane, mistress of the Prince of Wales, son of George II. 322. **Sedley,** Catherine Sedley, mistress of James II.

its purity may be preserved, its use ascertained, and its duration lengthened." Although adhering tenaciously to these fixed standards, Johnson later admitted in the Preface that language is subject to change, yet his work is significant in that it established the criterion of reputable use. The Dictionary, therefore, was meant to aid the writer rather than the reader of the English language. In his ambitious way Johnson set out to include quotations illustrating the proper uses of the words defined. This feature was an innovation in dictionary making and one of priceless value in any survey of the language. In still another feature the Dictionary is a notable work. Johnson excelled in definitions. Sometimes a delicious flavor was given by odd quirks of personal prejudice or humor, or by difficulties encountered in explaining the obvious. With little etymological understanding, he safely relied upon his abundant common sense and his keen, vigorous intellect to carry him through the project. The chief merit of the Dictionary lies in its definitions; not only do they illustrate Johnson's personality but they throw much light upon the eighteenth-century English Tory as well.

dry: desiccative.

dryness: siccity or aridity.

excise: a hateful tax levied upon commodities, and adjudged, not by the common judges of property, but wretches hired by those to whom excise is paid.

Grub Street: the name of a street in London, much inhabited by writers of small histories, *dictionaries*, and temporary poems; whence any mean production is called Grub Street.

10 *hatchet-faced*: an ugly face; such, I suppose, as might be hewn out of a block by a hatchet.

lexicographer: a writer of dictionaries, a harmless

Grub Street: Bookseller and Author, a late eighteenth-century drawing by H. Wigstead.

drudge that busies himself in tracing the original and detailing the significance of words.

network: anything reticulated or decussated at equal distances with interstices between the intersections.

oats: a grain which in England is generally given to horses, but in Scotland supports the people.

patriotism: the last refuge of a scoundrel.

patron: one who countenances, supports, or protects. 20 Commonly a wretch who supports with insolence, and is paid with flattery.

pension: an allowance made to anyone without an equivalent. In England it is generally understood to mean pay given to a state hireling for treason to his country.

pensioner: a slave of state, hired by a stipend to obey his master.

politician: a man of artifice; one deep of contrivance.

Redcoat: a name of contempt for a soldier.   30

thunder: a most bright flame rising on a sudden, moving with great violence, and with a very rapid velocity, through the air, according to any determination, and commonly ending with a loud noise or rattling.

Tory: one who adheres to the ancient constitution of the state, and the apostolical hierarchy of the Church of England, opposed to a Whig.

transpire: to escape from secrecy to notice, a sense lately innovated from France without necessity.   40

Whig: the name of a faction.

willow: a tree worn by forlorn lovers.

(1755)

from THE IDLER

The Idler was a section of The Universal Chronicle, or Weekly Gazette, *a periodical that was started early in 1758 and published on Saturdays. Johnson contributed a series of essays from April 15, 1758, to April 5, 1760. These papers are somewhat shorter than those in* The Rambler *and are lighter in vein. The heavy Latinized diction of the earlier publication has yielded to a simpler and, though still Johnsonian, a more homely English style. There is observable a wider range in both character sketches and subject matter in general.*

MR. MINIM AS CRITIC

The Idler, No. 61: Saturday, June 15, 1759

Mr. Minim had now advanced himself to the zenith of critical reputation; when he was in the pit, every eye in the boxes was fixed upon him; when he

Mr. Minim as Critic. 1. **Mr. Minim.** Dick Minim appears in several of the *Idler* papers; he is something of a critical mouthpiece for Johnson himself.

entered his coffee-house, he was surrounded by circles of candidates, who passed their novitiate of literature under his tuition; his opinion was asked by all who had no opinion of their own, and yet loved to debate and decide; and no composition was supposed to pass in safety to posterity till it had been secured by Minim's approbation.

Minim professes great admiration of the wisdom and munificence by which the academies of the continent were raised, and often wishes for some standard of taste, for some tribunal, to which merit may appeal from caprice, prejudice, and malignity. He has formed a plan for an academy of criticism, where every work of imagination may be read before it is printed, and which shall authoritatively direct the theaters what pieces to receive or reject, to exclude or to revive.

Such an institution would, in Dick's opinion, spread the fame of English literature over Europe, and make London the metropolis of elegance and politeness, the place to which the learned and ingenious of all countries would repair for instruction and improvement, where nothing would any longer be applauded or endured that was not conformed to the nicest rules, and finished with the highest elegance.

Till some happy conjunction of the planets shall dispose our princes or ministers to make themselves immortal by such an academy, Minim contents himself to preside four nights in a week in a critical society selected by himself, where he is heard without contradiction, and whence his judgment is disseminated through the great vulgar and the small.

When he is placed in the chair of criticism, he declares loudly for the noble simplicity of our ancestors, in opposition to the petty refinements, and ornamental luxuriance. Sometimes he is sunk in despair, and perceives false delicacy daily gaining ground, and sometimes brightens his countenance with a gleam of hope, and predicts the revival of the true sublime. He then fulminates his loudest censures against the monkish barbarity of rime; wonders how beings that pretend to reason can be pleased with one line always ending like another; tells how unjustly and unnaturally sense is sacrificed to sound; how often the best thoughts are mangled by the necessity of confining or extending them to the dimensions of a couplet; and rejoices that genius has, in our days, shaken off the shackles which had encumbered it so long. Yet he allows that rime may sometimes be borne, if the lines be often broken, and the pauses judiciously diversified.

From blank verse he makes an easy transition to Milton, whom he produces as an example of the slow advance of lasting reputation. Milton is the only writer in whose books Minim can read forever without weariness. What cause it is that exempts this pleasure from satiety he has long and diligently inquired, and believes it to consist in the perpetual variation of the numbers, by which the ear is gratified and the attention awakened. The lines that are commonly thought rugged and unmusical, he conceives to have been written to temper the melodious luxury of the rest, or to express things by a proper cadence: for he scarcely finds a verse that has not this favorite beauty; he declares that he could shiver in a hot-house when he reads that

The ground
Burns frore, and cold performs th' effect of fire;

and that, when Milton bewails his blindness, the verse,

So thick a drop serene has quenched these orbs,

has, he knows not how, something that strikes him with an obscure sensation like that which he fancies would be felt from the sound of darkness.

Minim is not so confident of his rules of judgment as not very eagerly to catch new light from the name of the author. He is commonly so prudent as to spare those whom he cannot resist, unless, as will sometimes happen, he finds the public combined against them. But a fresh pretender to fame he is strongly inclined to censure, till his own honor requires that he commend him. Till he knows the success of a composition, he intrenches himself in general terms; there are some new thoughts and beautiful passages, but there is likewise much which he would have advised the author to expunge. He has several favorite epithets, of which he has never settled the meaning, but which are very commodiously applied to books which he has not read, or cannot understand. One is *manly*, another is *dry*, another *stiff*, and another *flimsy*; sometimes he discovers delicacy of style, and sometimes meets with *strange expressions*.

He is never so great, or so happy, as when a youth of promising parts is brought to receive his directions for the prosecution of his studies. He then puts on a very serious air; he advises the pupil to read none but the best authors, and, when he finds one congenial to his own mind, to study his beauties, but avoid his faults; and, when he sits down to write, to consider how his favorite author would think at the present time on the present occasion. He exhorts him to catch those moments when he finds his thoughts expanded and his genius exalted, but to take care lest imagination hurry him beyond the bounds of nature. He holds diligence the mother of success; yet enjoins him, with great earnestness, not to read

67. **The . . . fire,** quoted (somewhat inaccurately) from Milton's *Paradise Lost,* II, 594-595 (p. 401). 71. **So . . . orbs,** quoted from Milton's *Paradise Lost,* III, 25.

The Lives . . . Poets. 115. English Poems, L'Allegro (p. 379), Il Penseroso (p. 381), Lycidas (p. 382), etc., as distinguished from earlier poems in Italian and Latin. 138. "lion . . . kid," from *Paradise Lost,*

more than he can digest, and not to confuse his mind by pursuing studies of contrary tendencies. He tells him that every man has his genius and that Cicero could never be a poet. The boy retires illuminated, resolves to follow his genius, and to think how Milton would have thought: and Minim feasts upon his own beneficence till another day brings another pupil.

(1759)

from THE LIVES OF THE ENGLISH POETS

The Lives of the English Poets *grew out of a plan of London booksellers to issue an edition of "all the English poets of reputation from Chaucer to the present day." Johnson, at the age of sixty-seven, was engaged in 1777 to write brief biographical and critical notes to precede the various selections of poetry. The original design, however, was modified as the work of Johnson progressed, and he wrote more copiously than was intended. Confining himself to a century of English poets beginning with Abraham Cowley (1618-67), Johnson completed fifty-two sketches, which were straightway published in ten volumes with the title* Prefaces Biographical and Critical to the Works of the English Poets *(1779, 1781).*

It is a fascinating document: a great man of letters sits down with leisure and without want to have his say on the most abiding love of his life—English poetry. He writes of an era in literature of which he himself is the embodied end—its ally and its gadfly—with sufficient sympathy to give it a fair hearing but with enough scepticism not to be tempted by panegyric. That he despised Lycidas, was harsh with Gray, and was unappreciative of some aspects of the metaphysical poets is relatively unimportant. What is important is that the book exists—the best course available in a watershed century of English poetry.

from MILTON

The English poems, though they make no promises of *Paradise Lost,* have this evidence of genius, that they have a cast original and unborrowed. But their peculiarity is not excellence: if they differ from verses of others, they differ for the worse; for they are too often distinguished by repulsive harshness; the combinations of words are new, but they are not pleasing; the rimes and epithets seem to be laboriously sought, and violently applied.

That in the early parts of his life he wrote with much

care appears from his manuscripts, happily preserved at Cambridge, in which many of his smaller works are found as they were first written, with the subsequent corrections. Such relics show how excellence is acquired; what we hope ever to do with ease, we may learn first to do with diligence.

Those who admire the beauties of this great poet sometimes force their own judgment into false approbation of his little pieces, and prevail upon themselves to think that admirable which is only singular. All that short compositions can commonly attain is neatness and elegance. Milton never learned the art of doing little things with grace; he overlooked the milder excellence of suavity and softness: he was a "lion" that had no skill "in dandling the kid."

One of the poems upon which most praise has been bestowed is *Lycidas,* of which the diction is harsh, the rimes uncertain, and the numbers unpleasing. What beauty there is we must therefore seek in the sentiments and images. It is not to be considered as the effusion of real passion; for passion runs not after remote allusions and obscure opinions. Passion plucks no berries from the myrtle and ivy, nor calls upon Arethuse and Mincius, nor tells of "rough satyrs and fauns with cloven heel." Where there is leisure for fiction there is little grief.

In this poem there is no nature, for there is no truth; there is no art, for there is nothing new. Its form is that of a pastoral, easy, vulgar, and therefore disgusting. Whatever images it can supply are long ago exhausted; and its inherent improbability always forces dissatisfaction on the mind. When Cowley tells of Hervey that they studied together, it is easy to suppose how much he must miss the companion of his labors, and the partner of his discoveries; but what image of tenderness can be excited by these lines!

We drove afield, and both together heard
What time the gray-fly winds her sultry horn,
Battening our flocks with the fresh dews of night.

We know that they never drove afield, and that they had no flocks to batten; and though it be allowed that the representation may be allegorical, the true meaning is so uncertain and remote, that it is never sought because it cannot be known when it is found.

Among the flocks and copses and flowers appear the heathen deities, Jove and Phoebus, Neptune and Aeolus, with a long train of mythological imagery, such as a college easily supplies. Nothing can less display knowledge, or less exercise invention, than to tell how a shepherd has lost his companion, and must now feed his flocks alone, without any judge of his skill in piping; and how one god asks another god what has become of Lycidas, and how neither god can tell.

IV, 343-344 (cf. p. 409). 141. **Lycidas**; cf. p. 382. 148. **rough satyrs**, etc., from *Lycidas,* p. 383, l. 34. 156. **Cowley . . . Hervey.** Abraham Cowley (1618-1667) wrote an elegy on the death of his intimate friend, William Hervey. 161. **We . . . night**, *Lycidas,* ll. 27 ff. 171. **Aeolus**, in classical mythology, god of the winds.

He who thus grieves will excite no sympathy; he who thus praises will confer no honor.

This poem has yet a grosser fault. With these trifling fictions are mingled the most awful and sacred truths, such as ought never to be polluted with such irreverent combinations. The shepherd likewise is now a feeder of sheep, and afterwards an ecclesiastical pastor, a superintendent of a Christian flock. Such equivocations are always unskilful; but here they are indecent, and at
10 least approach to impiety, of which, however, I believe the writer not to have been conscious.

Such is the power of reputation justly acquired, that its blaze drives away the eye from nice examination. Surely no man could have fancied that he read *Lycidas* with pleasure, had he not known its author. . . .

from DRYDEN

Dryden may be properly considered as the father of English criticism, as the writer who first taught us to determine upon principles the merit of composition. Of our former poets, the greatest dramatist wrote without
20 rules, conducted through life and nature by a genius that rarely misled, and rarely deserted him. Of the rest, those who knew the laws of propriety had neglected to teach them.

Two *Arts of English Poetry* were written in the days of Elizabeth by Webb and Puttenham, from which something might be learned, and a few hints had been given by Jonson and Cowley; but Dryden's *Essay on Dramatic Poetry* was the first regular and valuable treatise on the art of writing.
30 He who, having formed his opinions in the present age of English literature, turns back to peruse this dialogue will not perhaps find much increase of knowledge, or much novelty of instruction; but he is to remember that critical principles were then in the hands of a few, who had gathered them partly from the ancients and partly from the Italians and French. The structure of dramatic poems was then not generally understood. Audiences applauded by instinct, and poets perhaps often pleased by chance.
40 A writer who obtains his full purpose loses himself in his own luster. Of an opinion which is no longer doubted, the evidence ceases to be examined. Of an art universally practiced, the first teacher is forgotten. Learning once made popular is no longer learning; it has the appearance of something which we have bestowed upon ourselves, as the dew appears to rise from the field which it refreshes.

To judge rightly of an author, we must transport ourselves to his time, and examine what were the wants

of his contemporaries, and what were his means of sup- 50 plying them. That which is easy at one time was difficult at another. Dryden at least imported his science and gave his country what it wanted before; or rather, he imported only the materials and manufactured them by his own skill.

The dialogue on the drama was one of his first essays of criticism, written when he was yet a timorous candidate for reputation, and therefore labored with that diligence which he might allow himself somewhat to remit when his name gave sanction to his positions, and his 60 awe of the public was abated, partly by custom, and partly by success. It will not be easy to find, in all the opulence of our language, a treatise so artfully variegated with successive representations of opposite probabilities, so enlivened with imagery, so brightened with illustrations. His portraits of the English dramatists are wrought with great spirit and diligence. The account of Shakespeare may stand as a perpetual model of encomiastic criticism; exact without minuteness, and lofty without exaggeration. The praise 70 lavished by Longinus on the attestation of the heroes of Marathon, by Demosthenes, fades away before it. In a few lines is exhibited a character so extensive in its comprehension, and so curious in its limitations, that nothing can be added, diminished or reformed; nor can the editors and admirers of Shakespeare, in all their emulation of reverence, boast of much more than of having diffused and paraphrased this epitome of excellence, of having changed Dryden's gold for baser metal, of lower value though of greater bulk. 80

In this, and in all his other essays on the same subject, the criticism of Dryden is the criticism of a poet; not a dull collection of theorems, nor a rude detection of faults, which perhaps the censor was not able to have committed; but a gay and vigorous dissertation, where delight is mingled with instruction, and where the author proves his right of judgment, by his power of performance.

The different manner and effect with which critical knowledge may be conveyed was perhaps never more 90 clearly exemplified than in the performances of Rymer and Dryden. It was said of a dispute between two mathematicians, "*malim cum Scaligero errare, quam cum Clavio recte sapere*," that *it was more eligible to go wrong with one than right with the other*. A tendency of the same kind every mind must feel at the perusal of Dryden's prefaces and Rymer's discourses. With Dryden we are wandering in quest of Truth, whom we find, if we find her at all, dressed in the graces of elegance, and if we miss her, the labor of 100 the pursuit rewards itself; we are led only through

19. **greatest dramatist**, Shakespeare. 25. **Webb**, William Webbe (b. 1550), author of *Discourse of English Poetrie*, 1586. **Puttenham**, George Puttenham (d. 1590), supposed author of *The Arte of English Poesie*. 27. **Jonson and Cowley**, Ben Jonson (1573–1637) and Abraham Cowley (1618–1667). See pp. 342 and 351. *Essay . . . Poetry*; cf. p. 468. Dryden's *Essay of Dramatic Poesy* was written in 1666. 56. **essays**, attempts. 69. **encomiastic**, laudatory. 71. **Longinus**, celebrated Greek critic and philosopher (c. 210–273 A.D.). 72. **Marathon**, the famous battle between the Greeks and the Persians, 490 B.C. **Demosthenes**, a noted Greek orator of the third century B.C. 91. **Rymer**, Thomas Rymer (1641–1713), critic and archaeologist. He published his *Tragedies of the Last Age Considered* in 1678. He was unfriendly to the plays of Shakespeare. 93. *Scaligero*, Joseph Scaliger (1540–1609), referred to as the greatest scholar of modern times; an eminent Italian Renaissance linguist, philosopher, and mathematician. 129. **Spence . . . Odyssey**, Joseph Spence (1699–1768), English critic; he published his

fragrance and flowers. Rymer, without taking a nearer, takes a rougher way; every step is to be made through thorns and brambles, and Truth, if we meet her, appears repulsive by her mien and ungraceful by her habit. Dryden's criticism has the majesty of a queen; Rymer's has the ferocity of a tyrant.

As he had studied with great diligence the art of poetry, and enlarged or rectified his notions, by ex-
110 perience perpetually increasing, he had his mind stored with principles and observations; he poured out his knowledge with little labor; for of labor, notwith-standing the multiplicity of his productions, there is sufficient reason to suspect that he was not a lover. To write con amore, with fondness for the employment, with perpetual touches and retouches, with unwilling-ness to take leave of his own idea, and an unwearied pursuit of unattainable perfection, was, I think, no part of his character.

120 His criticism may be considered as general or occa-sional. In his general precepts, which depend upon the nature of things and the structure of the human mind, he may doubtless be safely recommended to the con-fidence of the reader; but his occasional and particular positions were sometimes interested, sometimes negli-gent, and sometimes capricious. . . .

He is therefore by no means constant to himself. His defense and desertion of dramatic rime is generally known. Spence, in his remarks on Pope's Odyssey,
130 produces what he thinks an unconquerable quotation from Dryden's preface to the Aeneid, in favor of translating an epic poem into blank verse; but he for-gets that when his author attempted the Iliad, some years afterwards, he departed from his own decision, and translated into rime.

When he has any objection to obviate, or any li-cense to defend, he is not very scrupulous about what he asserts, nor very cautious, if the present purpose be served, not to entangle himself in his own sophistries.
140 But when all arts are exhausted, like other hunted animals, he sometimes stands at bay; when he cannot disown the grossness of one of his plays, he declares that he knows not any law that prescribes morality to a comic poet.

His remarks on ancient or modern writers are not always to be trusted. His parallel of the versification of Ovid with that of Claudian has been very justly censured by Sewell. His comparison of the first line of Virgil with the first of Statius is not happier. Virgil,
150 he says, is soft and gentle, and would have thought Statius mad if he had heard him thundering out

Quae superimposito moles geminata colosso.

Essay on Pope's Odyssey in 1726. 133. some years afterwards. Pope completed his Odyssey in 1726, his Iliad in 1718. Johnson is wrong. 147. Ovid, famous Roman poet (43 B.C.–17 A.D.). Claudian, noted Latin poet (fourth century A.D.). 148. Sewell. George Sewell (d. 1726), a critic of the time of Pope. 149. Statius, Roman poet (first century A.D.), author of the epic Thebais. 152. Quae, etc., "With a colossus on top there is a double weight," from Statius' Silvae, I, 1. 160. Gorbuduc, Gorboduc, the first regular English tragedy, written by

Statius perhaps heats himself, as he proceeds, to exaggerations somewhat hyperbolical; but undoubtedly Virgil would have been too hasty if he had condemned him to straw for one sounding line. Dryden wanted an instance, and the first that occurred was impressed into the service.

What he wishes to say, he says at hazard; he cited Gorbuduc, which he had never seen; gives a false 160 account of Chapman's versification; and discovers, in the preface to his Fables, that he translated the first book of the Iliad without knowing what was in the second.

It will be difficult to prove that Dryden ever made any great advances in literature. As having distinguished himself at Westminster under the tuition of Busby, who advanced his scholars to a height of knowledge very rarely attained in grammar schools, he resided afterwards at Cambridge, it is not to be supposed that 170 his skill in the ancient languages was deficient, com-pared with that of common students; but his scholastic acquisitions seem not proportionate to his oppor-tunities and abilities. He could not, like Milton or Cow-ley, have made his name illustrious merely by his learning. He mentions but few books, and those such as lie in the beaten track of regular study; from which if ever he departs, he is in danger of losing himself in unknown regions.

In his dialogue on the drama, he pronounces with 180 great confidence that the Latin tragedy of Medea is not Ovid's, because it is not sufficiently interesting and pathetic. He might have determined the question upon surer evidence; for it is quoted by Quintilian as the work of Seneca; and the only line which remains of Ovid's play, for one line is left us, is not there to be found. There was therefore no need of the gravity of conjecture, or the discussion of plot or sentiment, to find what was already known upon higher authority than such discussions can ever reach. 190

His literature, though not always free from ostenta-tion, will be commonly found either obvious, and made his own by the art of dressing it; or superficial, which, by what he gives, shows what he wanted; or erroneous, hastily collected, and negligently scattered.

Yet it cannot be said that his genius is ever unpro-vided of matter, or that his fancy languishes in penury of ideas. His works abound with knowledge, and sparkle with illustrations. There is scarcely any science or faculty that does not supply him with occasional 200 images and lucky similitudes; every page discovers a mind very widely acquainted both with art and nature, and in full possession of great stores of intellectual wealth. Of him that knows much, it is natural to sup-

Thomas Norton (1532–1584) and Thomas Sackville (1536–1608). 161. Chapman, George Chapman (1559–1634), poet, dramatist, and trans-lator of Homer. discovers, makes known. On Dryden's Preface to the Fables, cf. p. 470. 167. Busby, Richard Busby (1606-1695), head-master of Westminster School, which Dryden attended. 181. Medea, probably by the Roman tragedian Seneca (3 B.C.–65 A.D.). 184. Quintilian, celebrated Roman rhetorician and teacher of oratory (first century A.D.).

pose that he has read with diligence; yet I rather believe that the knowledge of Dryden was gleaned from accidental intelligence and various conversation, by a quick apprehension, a judicious selection, and a happy memory, a keen appetite of knowledge, and a powerful digestion; by vigilance that permitted nothing to pass without notice, and a habit of reflection that suffered nothing useful to be lost. A mind like Dryden's, always curious, always active, to which every understanding was proud to be associated, and of which everyone solicited the regard, by an ambitious display of himself, had a more pleasant, perhaps a nearer way to knowledge than by the silent progress of solitary reading. I do not suppose that he despised books, or intentionally neglected them; but that he was carried out, by the impetuosity of his genius, to more vivid and speedy instructors; and that his studies were rather desultory and fortuitous than constant and systematical.

It must be confessed that he scarcely ever appears to want book-learning but when he mentions books; and to him may be transferred the praise which he gives his master Charles.

His conversation, wit, and parts,
His knowledge in the noblest useful arts,
Were such, dead authors could not give,
But habitudes of those that live;
Who, lighting him, did greater lights receive,
He drained from all, and all they knew,
His apprehension quick, his judgment true;
That the most learned with shame confess
His knowledge more, his reading only less.

Of all this, however, if the proof be demanded, I will not undertake to give it; the atoms of probability, of which my opinion has been formed, lie scattered over all his works; and by him who thinks the question worth his notice, his works must be perused with very close attention.

Criticism, either didactic or defensive, occupies almost all his prose, except those pages which he has devoted to his patrons; but none of his prefaces were ever thought tedious. They have not the formality of a settled style, in which the first half of a sentence betrays the other. The clauses are never balanced, nor the periods modeled; every word seems to drop by chance, though it falls into its proper place. Nothing is cold or languid; the whole is airy, animated, and vigorous: what is little, is gay; what is great, is splendid. He may be thought to mention himself too frequently; but while he forces himself upon our esteem, we cannot refuse him to stand high in his own. Everything is excused by the play of images and the sprightliness of expression. Though all is easy, nothing is feeble; though all

seems careless, there is nothing harsh; and though since his earlier works more than a century has passed, they have nothing yet uncouth or obsolete.

He who writes much will not easily escape a manner, such a recurrence of particular modes as may be easily noted. Dryden is always "another and the same"; he does not exhibit a second time the same elegances in the same form, nor appears to have any art other than that of expressing with clearness what he thinks with vigor. His style could not easily be imitated, either seriously or ludicrously; for, being always equable and always varied, it has no prominent or discriminative characters. The beauty who is totally free from disproportion of parts and features, cannot be ridiculed by an overcharged resemblance.

From his prose, however, Dryden derives only his accidental and secondary praise; the veneration with which his name is pronounced by every cultivator of English literature is paid to him as he refined the language, improved the sentiments, and tuned the numbers of English Poetry.

After about half a century of forced thoughts and rugged meter, some advances towards nature and harmony had been already made by Waller and Denham; they had shown that long discourses in rime grew more pleasing when they were broken into couplets, and that verse consisted not only in the number but the arrangement of syllables.

But though they did much, who can deny that they left much to do? Their works were not many, nor were their minds of very ample comprehension. More examples of more modes of composition were necessary for the establishment of regularity, and the introduction of propriety in word and thought.

Every language of a learned nation necessarily divides itself into diction scholastic and popular, grave and familiar, elegant and gross; and from a nice distinction of these different parts arises a great part of the beauty of style. But if we except a few minds, the favorites of nature, to whom their own original rectitude was in the place of rules, this delicacy of selection was little known to our authors. Our speech lay before them in a heap of confusion, and every man took for every purpose what chance might offer him.

There was therefore before the time of Dryden no poetical diction, no system of words at once refined from the grossness of domestic use, and free from the harshness of terms appropriated to particular arts. Words too familiar, or too remote, defeat the purpose of a poet. From those sounds which we hear on small or on coarse occasions, we do not easily receive strong impressions, or delightful images; and words to which we are nearly strangers, whenever

22. **Charles,** King Charles II, reigning from 1660 to 1685, whom Dryden praised extravagantly in *Astraea Redux* (1660), an occasional poem inspired by the restoration of the monarchy. 54. **they . . . obsolete.** This sentence is an excellent example of the right judgment of which

Johnson was often capable. So far as Dryden's prose is concerned, posterity has vindicated Johnson's praise. 72. **tuned the numbers,** regularized the meter. Dryden established the closed couplet that had been introduced by Edmund Waller (1606–1687) and Sir John Denham

they occur, draw that attention on themselves which they should transmit to things.

Those happy combinations of words which distinguish poetry from prose had been rarely attempted; we had few elegances or flowers of speech; the roses had not yet been plucked from the bramble, or different colors had not yet been joined to enliven one another.

It may be doubted whether Waller and Denham could have overborne the prejudices which had long prevailed, and which even then were sheltered by the protection of Cowley. The new versification, as it was called, may be considered as owing its establishment to Dryden; from whose time it is apparent that English poetry has had no tendency to relapse to its former savageness. . . .

from POPE

. . . [Pope] professed to have learned his poetry from Dryden, whom, whenever an opportunity was presented, he praised through his whole life with unvaried liberality; and perhaps his character may receive some illustration if he be compared with his master.

Integrity of understanding and nicety of discernment were not allotted in a less proportion to Dryden than to Pope. The rectitude of Dryden's mind was sufficiently shown by the dismission of his poetical prejudices, and the rejection of unnatural thoughts and rugged numbers. But Dryden never desired to apply all the judgment that he had. He wrote, and professed to write, merely for the people; and when he pleased others, he contented himself. He spent no time in struggles to rouse latent powers; he never attempted to make that better which was already good, nor often to mend what he must have known to be faulty. He wrote, as he tells us, with very little consideration; when occasion or necessity called upon him, he poured out what the present moment happened to supply, and, when once it had passed the press, ejected it from his mind; for when he had no pecuniary interest, he had no further solicitude.

Pope was not content to satisfy; he desired to excel, and therefore always endeavored to do his best: he did not court the candor, but dared the judgment of his reader, and, expecting no indulgence from others, he showed none to himself. He examined lines and words with minute and punctilious observation, and retouched every part with indefatigable diligence, till he had left nothing to be forgiven.

For this reason he kept his pieces very long in his hands, while he considered and reconsidered them. The only poems which can be supposed to have been written with such regard to the times as might hasten their publication were the two satires of *Thirty-eight*, of which Dodsley told me that they were brought to him by the author, that they might be fairly copied. "Almost every line," he said, "was then written twice over; I gave him a clean transcript, which he sent some time afterwards to me for the press, with almost every line written twice over a second time."

His declaration that his care for his works ceased at their publication was not strictly true. His parental attention never abandoned them; what he found amiss in the first edition, he silently corrected in those that followed. He appears to have revised the *Iliad*, and freed it from some of its imperfections; and the *Essay on Criticism* received many improvements after its first appearance. It will seldom be found that he altered without adding clearness, elegance, or vigor. Pope had perhaps the judgment of Dryden; but Dryden certainly wanted the diligence of Pope.

In acquired knowledge, the superiority must be allowed to Dryden, whose education was more scholastic, and who before he became an author had been allowed more time for study, with better means of information. His mind has a larger range, and he collects his images and illustrations from a more extensive circumference of science. Dryden knew more of man in his general nature, and Pope in his local manners. The notions of Dryden were formed by comprehensive speculation, and those of Pope by minute attention. There is more dignity in the knowledge of Dryden, and more certainty in that of Pope.

Poetry was not the sole praise of either; for both excelled likewise in prose; but Pope did not borrow his prose from his predecessor. The style of Dryden is capricious and varied; that of Pope is cautious and uniform. Dryden obeys the motions of his own mind; Pope constrains his mind to his own rules of composition. Dryden is sometimes vehement and rapid; Pope is always smooth, uniform, and gentle. Dryden's page is a natural field, rising into inequalities, and diversified by the varied exuberance of abundant vegetation; Pope's is a velvet lawn, shaven by the scythe, and leveled by the roller.

Of genius, that power which constitutes a poet; that quality without which judgment is cold, and knowledge is inert; that energy which collects, combines, amplifies, and animates; the superiority must, with some hesitation, be allowed to Dryden. It is not to be inferred that of this poetical vigor Pope had only a little, because Dryden had more; for every other writer since Milton must give place to Pope; and even of Dryden it must be said, that, if he has brighter paragraphs, he has not better poems. Dryden's performances were always hasty, either excited by some

(1615-1669). 132. **dismission**, laying aside; a typical Johnsonian choice of words. 159. **satires of *Thirty-eight***, the *Epilogue to the Satires*, in two dialogues, written in 1738. The first dialogue was originally entitled *One Thousand Seven Hundred and Thirty-eight*. 160. **Dodsley**, Robert Dodsley (1703-1764), poet, dramatist, and bookseller. 172. *Essay on Criticism*; cf. p. 533.

external occasion, or extorted by domestic necessity; he composed without consideration, and published without correction. What his mind could supply at call, or gather in one excursion, was all that he sought, and all that he gave. The dilatory caution of Pope enabled him to condense his sentiments, to multiply his images, and to accumulate all that study might produce or chance might supply. If the flights of Dryden therefore are higher, Pope continues longer 10 on the wing. If of Dryden's fire the blaze is brighter, of Pope's the heat is more regular and constant. Dryden often surpasses expectation, and Pope never falls below it. Dryden is read with frequent astonishment, and Pope with perpetual delight.

This parallel will, I hope, when it is well considered, be found just; and if the reader should suspect me, as I suspect myself, of some partial fondness for the memory of Dryden, let him not too hastily condemn me; for meditation and inquiry may, 20 perhaps, show him the reasonableness of my determination. . . .
(1779-1781)

LETTERS

TO THE EARL OF CHESTERFIELD

To the Right Honorable
the Earl of Chesterfield

February 7, 1755.

My Lord: I have lately been informed by the proprietor of *The World*, that two papers, in which my *Dictionary* is recommended to the public, were written by your lordship. To be so distinguished is an honor which, being very little accustomed to favors 30 from the great, I know not well how to receive, or in what terms to acknowledge.

When, upon some slight encouragement, I first visited your lordship, I was overpowered, like the rest of mankind, by the enchantment of your address; and I could not forbear to wish that I might boast myself *"Le vainqueur du vainqueur de la terre"*; that I might obtain that regard for which I saw the world contending; but I found my attendance so little encouraged, that neither pride nor modesty would suffer 40 me to continue it. When I had once addressed your lordship in public, I had exhausted all the art of pleasing which a retired and uncourtly scholar can possess. I had done all that I could; and no man is well pleased to have his all neglected, be it ever so little.

Seven years, my lord, have now passed, since I waited in your outward rooms, or was repulsed from your door; during which time I have been pushing on my work through difficulties, of which it is useless to complain, and have brought it at last to the verge 50 of publication, without one act of assistance, one word of encouragement, or one smile of favor. Such treatment I did not expect, for I never had a patron before.

The shepherd in Virgil grew at last acquainted with Love, and found him a native of the rocks.

Is not a patron, my lord, one who looks with unconcern on a man struggling for life in the water, and, when he has reached ground, encumbers him with help? The notice which you have been pleased 60 to take of my labors, had it been early, had been kind; but it has been delayed till I am indifferent, and cannot enjoy it; till I am solitary, and cannot impart it; till I am known, and do not want it. I hope it is no very cynical asperity not to confess obligations where no benefit has been received, or to be unwilling that the public should consider me as owing that to a patron, which Providence has enabled me to do for myself.

Having carried on my work thus far with so little 70 obligation to any favorer of learning, I shall not be disappointed though I should conclude it, if less be possible, with less; for I have been long wakened from that dream of hope, in which I once boasted myself with so much exaltation,
My Lord,
Your Lordship's most humble,
Most obedient servant,

Sam. Johnson

TO JAMES MACPHERSON

Mr. James Macpherson: I received your foolish and 80 impudent letter. Any violence offered me I shall do my best to repel; and what I cannot do for myself the law shall do for me. I hope I shall never be deterred from detecting what I think a cheat, by the menaces of a ruffian.

What would you have me retract? I thought your book an imposture; I think it an imposture still. For this opinion I have given my reasons to the public, which I here dare you to refute. Your rage I defy. Your abilities, since your *Homer*, are not so formi- 90 dable; and what I hear of your morals inclines me to pay regard not to what you shall say, but to what you shall prove. You may print this if you will.

Sam. Johnson

(1775)

Letters. 23. **Chesterfield.** The *prospectus* of Johnson's *Dictionary* was addressed in 1747 to Lord Chesterfield, at that time one of the leading secretaries of state, who gave the design his approval. Chesterfield, however, took little or no notice of Johnson during the seven years that the latter laboriously gave to the task; but when the *Dictionary* was about to be published, Chesterfield attempted to gain Johnson's favor by writing two articles for *The World* strongly praising the work. Not being able to reconcile the long period of neglect with this fulsome praise, Johnson wrote this letter "expressed in civil terms, but such as might show him that I did not mind what he said or wrote, and that I had done with him"—Boswell's *Life of Johnson*, 1791. 25. **proprietor . . . World,** Edward Moore, an old friend of Johnson's. 36. **Le vainqueur,** etc., conqueror of the conqueror of the Earth. 55. **shepherd in Virgil,** *Eclogues,* 8, 43 ff. 80. **James Macpherson** (1736–1796), al-

To the Reverend Dr. Taylor,

Dear Sir: What can be the reason that I hear nothing from you? I hope nothing disables you from writing. What I have seen, and what I have felt, gives me reason to fear everything. Do not omit giving me the 100 comfort of knowing, that after all my losses I have yet a friend left.

I want every comfort. My life is very solitary and very cheerless. Though it has pleased God wonderfully to deliver me from the dropsy, I am yet very weak, and have not passed the door since the 13th of December. I hope for some help from warm weather, which will surely come in time.

I could not have the consent of physicians to go to church yesterday; I therefore received the holy sacra-110 ment at home, in the room where I communicated with dear Mrs. Williams, a little before her death. O! my friend, the approach of death is very dreadful. I am afraid to think on that which I know I cannot avoid. It is vain to look round and round for that help which cannot be had. Yet we hope and hope, and fancy that he who has lived today may live tomorrow. But let us learn to derive our hope only from God.

In the meantime let us be kind to one another. 120 I have no friend now living but you and Mr. Hector, that was the friend of my youth. Do not neglect, dear Sir,

Yours affectionately,

Sam. Johnson

London, Easter Monday,
April 12, 1784.

TO MRS. THRALE

To Mrs. Thrale,

Madam: If I interpret your letter right, you are ignominiously married, if it is yet undone, let us at 130 once talk together. If you have abandoned your children and your religion, God forgive your wickedness; if you have forfeited your Fame, and your country, may your folly do no further mischief.

If the last act is yet to do, I, who have loved you, esteemed you, reverenced you, and served you, I who long thought you the first of humankind, entreat that before your fate is irrevocable, I may once more see you.

I was, I once was, Madam

140 most truly yours,

July 2, 1784.   Sam. Johnson

leged translator of the ancient poems of Ossian—*Fingal*, 1761; *Temora*, 1763; etc. Johnson had publicly questioned Macpherson's honesty and had denied the existence of any originals. Macpherson sent Johnson a challenge; Johnson purchased a stout oak stick and answered in this letter. 90. *Homer*. Macpherson published in 1773 a poor prose translation of Homer's Iliad. 95. **Dr. Taylor**, Dr. John Taylor, Prebendary of Westminster, a schoolfellow and friend of Johnson. 111. **Mrs. Williams**,

PREFACE TO SHAKESPEARE

Johnson's edition of Shakespeare's plays appeared in 1765 with a preface which is considered one of his best pieces of prose. The essay also represents a substantial, and in some ways climactic, contribution to criticism and interpretation of Shakespeare. Three points deserve special attention: the basis of Johnson's attack on the unities; the implicit attack, in his praise of Shakespeare's handling of action, on the fantastic and the accidental; his emphasis, more often associated with the Victorians, on the moralistic qualities of literature.

Shakespeare with his excellencies has likewise faults, and faults sufficient to obscure and overwhelm any other merit. I shall show them in the proportion in which they appear to me, without envious malignity or superstitious veneration. No question can be more innocently discussed than a dead poet's pretensions to renown; and little regard is due to that bigotry which sets candor higher than truth.

His first defect is that to which may be imputed 150 most of the evil in books or in men. He sacrifices virtue to convenience, and is so much more careful to please than to instruct that he seems to write without any moral purpose. From his writings indeed a system of social duty may be selected, for he that thinks reasonably must think morally, but his precepts and axioms drop casually from him; he makes no just distribution of good or evil, nor is always careful to show in the virtuous a disapprobation of the wicked;

Dr. Johnson having tea with the Boswells in James Court, a caricature by Thomas Rowlandson.

Anna Williams, Johnson's friend and companion of many years; she died in 1783. See Boswell's *Life of Johnson*, p. 568, ll. 19 ff. 120. **Mr. Hector**, Edmund Hector, surgeon at Birmingham, schoolfellow and friend of Johnson. 127. **Mrs. Thrale**. After the death of Thrale in 1781, his widow married (1784) Gabriele Piozzi, an Italian music master.

he carries his persons indifferently through right and wrong, and at the close dismisses them without further care, and leaves their examples to operate by chance. This fault the barbarity of his age cannot extenuate; for it is always a writer's duty to make the world better, and justice is a virtue independent on time or place.

The plots are often so loosely formed that a very slight consideration may improve them, and so carelessly pursued that he seems not always fully to comprehend his own design. He omits opportunities of instructing or delighting which the train of his story seems to force upon him, and apparently rejects those exhibitions which would be more affecting for the sake of those which are more easy.

It may be observed that in many of his plays the latter part is evidently neglected. When he found himself near the end of his work, and in view of his reward, he shortened the labor to snatch the profit. He therefore remits his efforts where he should most vigorously exert them, and his catastrophe is improbably produced or imperfectly represented.

He had no regard to distinction of time or place, but gives to one age or nation, without scruple, the customs, institutions, and opinions of another, at the expense not only of likelihood but of possibility. These faults Pope has endeavored, with more zeal than judgment, to transfer to his imagined interpolators. We need not wonder to find Hector quoting Aristotle, when we see the loves of Theseus and Hippolyta combined with the Gothic mythology of fairies. Shakespeare, indeed, was not the only violator of chronology, for in the same age Sidney, who wanted not the advantages of learning, has, in his *Arcadia,* confounded the pastoral with the feudal times, the days of innocence, quiet, and security with those of turbulence, violence, and adventure.

In his comic scenes he is seldom very successful when he engages his characters in reciprocations of smartness and contests of sarcasm; their jests are commonly gross, and their pleasantry licentious; neither his gentlemen nor his ladies have much delicacy, nor are sufficiently distinguished from his clowns by any appearance of refined manners. Whether he represented the real conversation of his time is not easy to determine: the reign of Elizabeth is commonly supposed to have been a time of stateliness, formality, and reserve; yet perhaps the relaxations of that severity were not very elegant. There must, however, have been always some modes of gaiety preferable to others, and a writer ought to choose the best.

In tragedy his performance seems constantly to be worse as his labor is more. The effusions of passion, which exigence forces out, are for the most part striking and energetic; but whenever he solicits his invention, or strains his faculties, the offspring of his throes is tumor, meanness, tediousness, and obscurity.

In narration he affects a disproportionate pomp of diction and a wearisome train of circumlocution, and tells the incident imperfectly in many words which might have been more plainly delivered in few. Narration in dramatic poetry is naturally tedious, as it is unanimated and inactive, and obstructs the progress of the action; it should therefore always be rapid and enlivened by frequent interruption. Shakespeare found it an encumbrance, and instead of lightening it by brevity, endeavored to recommend it by dignity and splendor.

His declamations or set speeches are commonly cold and weak, for his power was the power of nature; when he endeavored, like other tragic writers, to catch opportunities of amplification and, instead of inquiring what the occasion demanded, to show how much his stores of knowledge could supply, he seldom escapes without the pity or resentment of his reader.

It is incident to him to be now and then entangled with an unwieldy sentiment which he cannot well express, and will not reject; he struggles with it awhile, and, if it continues stubborn, comprises it in words such as occur, and leaves it to be disentangled and evolved by those who have more leisure to bestow upon it.

Not that always where the language is intricate the thought is subtle, or the image always great where the line is bulky; the equality of words to things is very often neglected, and trivial sentiments and vulgar ideas disappoint the attention, to which they are recommended by sonorous epithets and swelling figures.

But the admirers of this great poet have most reason to complain when he approaches nearest to his highest excellence, and seems fully resolved to sink them in dejection and mollify them with tender emotions by the fall of greatness, the danger of innocence, or the crosses of love. What he does best, he soon ceases to do. He is not long soft and pathetic without some idle conceit or contemptible equivocation. He no sooner begins to move than he counteracts himself; and terror and pity, as they are rising in the mind, are checked and blasted by sudden frigidity.

A quibble is to Shakespeare what luminous vapors are to the traveler: he follows it at all adventures; it is sure to lead him out of his way, and sure to engulf him in the mire. It has some malignant power over his mind, and its fascinations are irresistible. Whatever be the dignity or profundity of his disquisitions, whether he be enlarging knowledge or exalting affection, whether he be amusing attention with incidents, or enchaining it in suspense, let but a quibble spring up before him, and he leaves his work unfinished. A quibble is the golden apple for which he will always

57. **tumor,** tumidity, pomposity. 100. **quibble,** a pun. 156. **Corneille.** Corneille's *Discourse des trois unités* (1660) was the classic statement.

turn aside from his career or stoop from his elevation. A quibble, poor and barren as it is, gave him such delight that he was content to purchase it by the sacrifice of reason, propriety, and truth. A quibble was to him the fatal Cleopatra for which he lost the world, and was content to lose it.

It will be thought strange that in enumerating the defects of this writer, I have not yet mentioned his neglect of the unities; his violation of those laws which
120 have been instituted and established by the joint authority of poets and critics.

For his other deviations from the art of writing, I resign him to critical justice without making any other demand in his favor than that which must be indulged to all human excellence: that his virtues be rated with his failings. But from the censure which this irregularity may bring upon him I shall, with due reverence to that learning which I must oppose, adventure to try how I can defend him.

130 His histories, being neither tragedies nor comedies, are not subject to any of their laws; nothing more is necessary to all the praise which they expect than that the changes of action be so prepared as to be understood; that the incidents be various and affecting, and the characters consistent, natural, and distinct. No other unity is intended, and therefore none is to be sought.

In his other works, he has well enough preserved the unity of action. He has not, indeed, an intrigue
140 regularly perplexed and regularly unraveled: he does not endeavor to hide his design only to discover it, for this is seldom the order of real events, and Shakespeare is the poet of nature: but his plan has commonly what Aristotle requires, a beginning, a middle, and an end; one event is concatenated with another, and the conclusion follows by easy consequence. There are, perhaps, some incidents that might be spared, as in other poets there is much talk that only fills up time upon the stage; but the general system makes gradual
150 advances, and the end of the play is the end of expectation.

To the unities of time and place he has shown no regard; and perhaps a nearer view of the principles on which they stand will diminish their value and withdraw from them the veneration which, from the time of Corneille, they have very generally received, by discovering that they have given more trouble to the poet than pleasure to the auditor.

The necessity of observing the unities of time and
160 place arises from the supposed necessity of making the drama credible. The critics hold it impossible that an action of months or years can be possibly believed to pass in three hours; or that the spectator can suppose himself to sit in the theater while ambassadors go and return between distant kings, while armies are levied and towns besieged, while an exile wanders and

returns, or till he whom they saw courting his mistress shall lament the untimely fall of his son. The mind revolts from evident falsehood, and fiction loses its force when it departs from the resemblance of reality. 170

From the narrow limitation of time necessarily arises the contraction of place. The spectator who knows that he saw the first act at Alexandria cannot suppose that he sees the next at Rome, at a distance to which not the dragons of Medea could, in so short a time, have transported him; he knows with certainty that he has not changed his place; and he knows that place cannot change itself, that what was a house cannot become a plain, that what was Thebes can never be Persepolis.

Such is the triumphant language with which a critic 180 exults over the misery of an irregular poet, and exults commonly without resistance or reply. It is time, therefore, to tell him by the authority of Shakespeare that he assumes, as an unquestionable principle, a position which, while his breath is forming it into words, his understanding pronounces to be false. It is false that any representation is mistaken for reality; that any dramatic fable in its materiality was ever credible or, for a single moment, was ever credited.

The objection arising from the impossibility of pass- 190 ing the first hour at Alexandria and the next at Rome supposes that when the play opens the spectator really imagines himself at Alexandria, and believes that his walk to the theater has been a voyage to Egypt, and that he lives in the days of Antony and Cleopatra. Surely he that imagines this may imagine more. He that can take the stage at one time for the palace of the Ptolemies may take it in half an hour for the promontory of Actium. Delusion, if delusion be admitted, has no certain limitation; if the spectator can 200 be once persuaded that his old acquaintances are Alexander and Caesar, that a room illuminated with candles is the plain of Pharsalia or the bank of Granicus, he is in a state of elevation above the reach of reason or of truth, and from the heights of empyrean poetry may despise the circumscriptions of terrestrial nature. There is no reason why a mind thus wandering in ecstasy should count the clock, or why an hour should not be a century in that calenture of the brain that can make the stage a field. 210

The truth is that the spectators are always in their senses, and know, from the first act to the last, that the stage is only a stage, and that the players are only players. They came to hear a certain number of lines recited with just gesture and elegant modulation. The lines relate to some action, and an action must be in some place; but the different actions that complete a story may be in places very remote from each other; and where is the absurdity of allowing that space to represent first Athens, and then Sicily, which was al- 220 ways known to be neither Sicily nor Athens but a modern theater?

By supposition, as place is introduced, time may be extended; the time required by the fable elapses, for the most part, between the acts; for, of so much of the action as is represented, the real and poetical duration is the same. If, in the first act, preparations for war against Mithridates are represented to be made in Rome, the event of the war may, without absurdity, be represented, in the catastrophe, as happening in Pontus; we know that there is neither war nor prep-
10 aration for war; we know that we are neither in Rome nor Pontus, that neither Mithridates nor Lucullus are before us. The drama exhibits successive imitations of successive actions; and why may not the second imitation represent an action that happened years after the first, if it be so connected with it that nothing but time can be supposed to intervene? Time is, of all modes of existence, most obsequious to the imagination; a lapse of years is as easily conceived as a passage of hours. In contemplation we easily contract
20 the time of real actions, and therefore willingly permit it to be contracted when we only see their imitation.

It will be asked how the drama moves if it is not credited. It is credited with all the credit due to a drama. It is credited, whenever it moves, as a just picture of a real original; as representing to the auditor what he would himself feel if he were to do or suffer what is there feigned to be suffered or to be done. The reflection that strikes the heart is not that the evils before us are real evils, but that they are evils to
30 which we ourselves may be exposed. If there be any fallacy, it is not that we fancy the players, but that we fancy ourselves, unhappy for a moment; but we rather lament the possibility than suppose the presence of misery, as a mother weeps over her babe when she remembers that death may take it from her. The delight of tragedy proceeds from our consciousness of fiction; if we thought murders and treasons real, they would please no more.

Imitations produce pain or pleasure, not because
40 they are mistaken for realities, but because they bring realities to mind. When the imagination is recreated by a painted landscape, the trees are not supposed capable to give us shade or the fountains coolness; but we consider how we should be pleased with such fountains playing beside us and such woods waving over us. We are agitated in reading the history of *Henry the Fifth*, yet no man takes his book for the field of Agincourt. A dramatic exhibition is a book recited with concomitants that increase or diminish its effect.
50 Familiar comedy is often more powerful on the theater than in the page; imperial tragedy is always less. The humor of Petruchio may be heightened by grimace; but what voice or what gesture can hope to add dignity or force to the soliloquy of Cato?

A play read affects the mind like a play acted. It is therefore evident that the action is not supposed to be real; and it follows that between the acts a longer or shorter time may be allowed to pass, and that no more account of space or duration is to be taken by the auditor of a drama than by the reader 60 of a narrative, before whom may pass in an hour the life of a hero or the revolutions of an empire.

Whether Shakespeare knew the unities and rejected them by design or deviated from them by happy ignorance, it is, I think, impossible to decide and useless to inquire. We may reasonably suppose that, when he rose to notice, he did not want the counsels and admonitions of scholars and critics, and that he at last deliberately persisted in a practice which he might have begun by chance. As nothing is essential to the 70 fable but unity of action, and as the unities of time and place arise evidently from false assumptions, and, by circumscribing the extent of the drama, lessen its variety, I cannot think it much to be lamented that they were not known by him, or not observed: nor, if such another poet could arise, should I very vehemently reproach him that his first act passed at Venice and his next in Cyprus. Such violations of rules merely positive become the comprehensive genius of Shakespeare, and such censures are suitable to the 80 minute and slender criticism of Voltaire.

Non usque adeo permiscuit imis
Longus summa dies, ut non, si voce Metelli
Serventur leges, malint a Caesare tolli.

Yet when I speak thus slightly of dramatic rules, I cannot but recollect how much wit and learning may be produced against me; before such authorities I am afraid to stand: not that I think the present question one of those that are to be decided by mere authority, but because it is to be suspected that these precepts 90 have not been so easily received but for better reasons than I have yet been able to find. The result of my inquiries, in which it would be ludicrous to boast of impartiality, is that the unities of time and place are not essential to a just drama, that though they may sometimes conduce to pleasure, they are always to be sacrificed to the nobler beauties of variety and instruction; and that a play written with nice observation of critical rules is to be contemplated as an elaborate curiosity, as the product of superfluous and ostenta- 100 tious art, by which is shown rather what is possible than what is necessary.

He that without diminution of any other excellence shall preserve all the unities unbroken deserves the like applause with the architect who shall display all the

---

52. **Petruchio**, in Shakespeare's *The Taming of the Shrew*. 54. **Cato**, the title character in a wooden tragedy by Joseph Addison. 82-

84. **Non . . . tolli.** In substance, the laws (rules) would rather be trampled on by a Caesar than sustained by a Metellus (Lucan).

orders of architecture in a citadel without any deduction for its strength; but the principal beauty of a citadel is to exclude the enemy, and the greatest graces of a play are to copy nature and instruct life.
(1765)

JAMES BOSWELL 1740-1795

The modern student of literature has an access to James Boswell denied to six generations of readers. Known to all but the specialist as the author of a solitary if monumental work (even the Journal of a Tour to the Hebrides, *1785, was considered a fragmentary study for* The Life of Samuel Johnson), *Boswell has lately emerged as a substantial literary personage in his own right. In the 1950's alone, six volumes of his* Journals *(for example,* London Journal, *1762-1763;* Boswell in Search of a Wife, *1766-1769) were issued. The time is fast approaching, then, when the man who "embalmed" Dr. Johnson (it is Boswell's own word) will himself be embalmed, though it is unlikely that fate will treat him as kindly as, through him, it treated Dr. Johnson. Boswell's biographer will have as his subject a Scotsman well born enough to have access to the best circles, a man with an insatiable thirst for experience, both savory and unsavory, at once a penetrating and a reflective man, who saw life minutely and ruminated on life objectively, a realistic autobiographer with, for some, a disquieting tendency to tell the literal truth about himself. That, in addition, he wrote the greatest biography in English should not be undervalued simply because it is perhaps easier to evaluate the greatest novel or the greatest poem or the greatest play.*

Boswell made certain fundamental decisions without which Johnson could not have been "seen in this work more completely than any man who has ever lived": (1) he decided that "the extraordinary vigor and vivacity" of Johnson's expressed mind "constituted one of the first features of his character"; (2) he decided to tell the truth—to see his object as he in fact was; (3) he decided to step back as much as possible and let the drama itself come forward; and (4) he decided that he would not exclude details, an indirect form of editorializing, but would present them in all their minute abundance. Behind all these right judgments lies the genuine perception which sustains them—namely, that in the person of Samuel Johnson was embodied the extraordinary concurrence of the power of a man with the power of an age.

from THE LIFE OF SAMUEL JOHNSON, LL.D.

110   To write the Life of him who excelled all mankind in writing the lives of others, and who, whether we consider his extraordinary endowments, or his various works, has been equaled by few in any age, is an arduous, and may be reckoned in me a presumptuous, task.

Had Dr. Johnson written his own life, in conformity with the opinion which he has given, that every man's life may be best written by himself; had he employed in the preservation of his own history, that clearness of narration and elegance of language 120 in which he has embalmed so many eminent persons, the world would probably have had the most perfect example of biography that was ever exhibited. But although he at different times, in a desultory manner, committed to writing many particulars of the progress of his mind and fortunes, he never had persevering diligence enough to form them into a regular composition. Of these memorials a few have been preserved; but the greater part was consigned by him to the flames, a few days before his death.   130

As I had the honor and happiness of enjoying his friendship for upwards of twenty years; as I had the scheme of writing his life constantly in view; as he was well apprised of this circumstance, and from time to time obligingly satisfied my inquiries, by communicating to me the incidents of his early years; as I acquired a facility in recollecting, and was very assiduous in recording, his conversation, of which the extraordinary vigor and vivacity constituted one of the first features of his character; and as I have 140 spared no pains in obtaining materials concerning him, from every quarter where I could discover that they were to be found, and have been favored with the most liberal communications by his friends; I flatter myself that few biographers have entered upon such a work as this, with more advantages; independent of literary abilities, in which I am not vain enough to compare myself with some great names who have gone before me in this kind of writing. . . .

Instead of melting down by materials into one 150 mass, and constantly speaking in my own person, by which I might have appeared to have more merit in the execution of the work, I have resolved to adopt and enlarge upon the excellent plan of Mr. Mason, in his *Memoirs of Gray.* Wherever narrative is necessary to explain, connect, and supply, I furnish it to the best of my abilities; but in the chronological series of Johnson's life, which I trace as distinctly as I can, year by year, I produce, wherever it is in my power, his own minutes, letters or conver- 160 sation, being convinced that this mode is more lively, and will make my readers better acquainted with him, than even most of those were who actually

The Life of Samuel Johnson. 117-118. opinion . . . himself, in Johnson's essay in *The Idler,* No. 84. 155. Mason . . . Gray. William Mason (1724–1797) was a minor poet and a close friend of Thomas Gray. His *Memoirs of Gray* appeared in 1775.

knew him, but could know him only partially; whereas there is here an accumulation of intelligence from various points, by which his character is more fully understood and illustrated.

Indeed I cannot conceive a more perfect mode of writing any man's life, than not only relating all the most important events of it in their order, but interweaving what he privately wrote, and said, and thought; by which mankind are enabled as it were to see him live, and to "live o'er each scene" with him, as he actually advanced through the several stages of his life. Had his other friends been as diligent and ardent as I was, he might have been almost entirely preserved. As it is, I will venture to say that he will be seen in this work more completely than any man who has ever yet lived.

And he will be seen as he really was; for I profess to write, not his panegyric, which must be all praise, but his Life; which, great and good as he was, must not be supposed to be entirely perfect. To be as he

was, is indeed subject of panegyric enough to any man in this state of being; but in every picture there should be shade as well as light, and when I delineate him without reserve, I do what he himself recommended, both by his precept and his example.

"If the biographer writes from personal knowledge, and makes haste to gratify the public curiosity, there is danger lest his interest, his fear, his gratitude, or his tenderness overpower his fidelity, and tempt him to conceal, if not to invent. There are many who think it an act of piety to hide the faults or failings of their friends, even when they can no longer suffer by their detection; we therefore see whole ranks of characters adorned with uniform panegyric, and not to be known from one another but by extrinsic and casual circumstances. 'Let me remember,' says Hale, 'when I find myself inclined to pity a criminal, that there is likewise a pity due to the country.' If we owe regard to the memory of the dead, there is yet

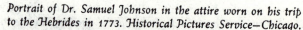

Portrait of Dr. Samuel Johnson in the attire worn on his trip to the Hebrides in 1773. Historical Pictures Service—Chicago.

37. **Hale,** Sir Matthew Hale (1609–1676), an eminent jurist and miscellaneous writer.   41-42. **virtue...truth.** This entire paragraph ("If the biographer," etc.) is quoted from Johnson's own words in *The Rambler,* No. 60.   47-48. **given...occasion,** in Boswell's *Journal of a Tour to the Hebrides,* an account of the journey taken in the company of Johnson, published in 1785.   69. **Julius Caesar,** the great Roman statesman and proconsul (100?–44 B.C.).   70-74. **Apothegms...oracle,** quoted from Book I in *Of the Advancement of Learning* by Sir Francis Bacon.   89. **Mr. Gentleman,** Francis Gentleman (1728–1784), actor, dramatist, and critic.   97. **Mr. Derrick,** Samuel Derrick (1724-1769),

more respect to be paid to knowledge, to virtue and to truth."

What I consider as the peculiar value of the following work, is, the quantity it contains of Johnson's conversation; which is universally acknowledged to have been eminently instructive and entertaining; and of which the specimens that I have given upon a former occasion, have been received with so much approbation, that I have good grounds for supposing that the world will not be indifferent to more ample communications of a similar nature. . . .

Of one thing I am certain, that considering how highly the small portion which we have of the table-talk and other anecdotes of our celebrated writers is valued, and how earnestly it is regretted that we have not more, I am justified in preserving rather too many of Johnson's sayings, than too few; especially as from the diversity of dispositions it cannot be known with certainty beforehand, whether what may seem trifling to some, and perhaps to the collector himself, may not be most agreeable to many; and the greater number that an author can please in any degree, the more pleasure does there arise to a benevolent mind.

To those who are weak enough to think this a degrading task, and the time and labor which have been devoted to it misemployed, I shall content myself with opposing the authority of the greatest man of any age, Julius Caesar, of whom Bacon observes, that "in his book of Apothegms which he collected, we see that he esteemed it more honor to make himself but a pair of tables, to take the wise and pithy words of others, than to have every word of his own to be made an apothegm or an oracle."

Having said thus much by way of introduction, I commit the following pages to the candor of the Public. . . .

Boswell Introduced to Johnson (1763)

This is to me a memorable year; for in it I had the happiness to obtain the acquaintance of that extraordinary man whose memoirs I am now writing; an acquaintance which I shall ever esteem as one of the most fortunate circumstances in my life. Though then but two-and-twenty, I had for several years read his works with delight and instruction, and had the highest reverence for their author, which had grown up in my fancy into a kind of mysterious veneration, by figuring to myself a state of solemn elevated abstraction, in which I supposed him to live in the immense metropolis of London. Mr. Gentleman, a native of Ireland, who passed some years in Scotland as a player, and as an instructor in the English language, a man whose talents and worth were depressed by misfortune, had given me a representation of the figure and manner of DICTIONARY JOHNSON! as he was then generally called; and during my first visit to London, which was for three months in 1760, Mr. Derrick the poet, who was Gentleman's friend and countryman, flattered me with hopes that he would introduce me to Johnson, an honor of which I was very ambitious. But he never found an opportunity. . . .

Mr. Thomas Davies the actor, who then kept a bookseller's shop in Russell Street, Covent Garden, told me that Johnson was very much his friend, and came frequently to his house, where he more than once invited me to meet him; but by some unlucky accident or other he was prevented from coming to us.

Mr. Thomas Davies was a man of good understanding and talents, with the advantage of a liberal education. Though somewhat pompous, he was an entertaining companion; and his literary performances have no inconsiderable share of merit. He was a friendly and very hospitable man. Both he and his wife (who has been celebrated for her beauty), though upon the stage for many years, maintained an uniform decency of character; and Johnson esteemed them, and lived in as easy an intimacy with them as with any family which he used to visit. Mr. Davies recollected several of Johnson's remarkable sayings, and was one of the best of the many imitators of his voice and manner, while relating them. He increased my impatience more and more to see the extraordinary man whose works I highly valued, and whose conversation was reported to be so peculiarly excellent.

At last, on Monday the 16th of May, when I was sitting in Mr. Davies's back-parlor, after having drunk tea with him and Mrs. Davies, Johnson unexpectedly came into the shop; and Mr. Davies having perceived him through the glass door in the room in which we were sitting, advancing towards us, he announced his awful approach to me, somewhat in the manner of an actor in the part of Horatio, when he addresses Hamlet on the appearance of his father's ghost, "Look, my Lord, it comes." I found that I had a very perfect idea of Johnson's figure, from the portrait of him painted by Sir Joshua Reynolds soon after he had published his *Dictionary*, in the attitude of sitting in his easy chair in deep meditation; which was the first picture his friend did for him, which Sir Joshua very kindly presented to me, and from which an engraving has been made for this work. Mr. Davies mentioned my name, and respectfully introduced me to him. I was much agitated; and recollecting his

friend of Johnson and editor of Dryden. 103. **Covent Garden,** a district in London, once occupied by the abbey of St. Peter, Westminster, from which the name is derived (the older form of "convent"). The region is now occupied in part by a great market, and has further fame from the presence of the Covent Garden Theater, built in 1731, and one of the best-known theaters in eighteenth-century London. 128. **shop,** the bookseller's shop mentioned in l. 103. 133-134. **"Look . . . comes,"** from Shakespeare's *Hamlet,* I, iv. 38. 136. **Sir Joshua Reynolds,** the eminent portrait painter (1723–1792). 137. **Dictionary.** Johnson's *Dictionary* was completed in 1755.

prejudice against the Scotch, of which I had heard much, I said to Davies, "Don't tell where I come from."—"From Scotland," cried Davies, roguishly. "Mr. Johnson," said I, "I do indeed come from Scotland, but I cannot help it." I am willing to flatter myself that I meant this as light pleasantry to soothe and conciliate him, and not as an humiliating abasement at the expense of my country. But however that might be, this speech was somewhat unlucky; 10 for with that quickness of wit for which he was so remarkable, he seized the expression "come from Scotland," which I used in the sense of being of that country; and, as if I had said that I had come away from it, or left it, retorted, "That, Sir, I find is what a very great many of your countrymen cannot help." This stroke stunned me a good deal; and when we had sat down, I felt myself not a little embarrassed, and apprehensive of what might come next. He then addressed himself to Davies: "What do you think of 20 Garrick? He has refused me an order for the play for Miss Williams, because he knows the house will be full, and that an order would be worth three shillings." Eager to take any opening to get into conversation with him, I ventured to say, "O, Sir, I cannot think Mr. Garrick would grudge such a trifle to you." "Sir," said he, with a stern look, "I have known David Garrick longer than you have done; and I know no right you have to talk to me on the subject." Perhaps I deserved this check; for it was rather pre-30 sumptuous in me, an entire stranger, to express any doubt of the justice of his animadversion upon his old acquaintance and pupil. I now felt myself much mortified, and began to think that the hope which I had long indulged of obtaining his acquaintance was blasted. And, in truth, had not my ardor been uncommonly strong, and my resolution uncommonly persevering, so rough a reception might have deterred me forever from making any further attempts. Fortunately, however, I remained upon the field not 40 wholly discomfited; and was soon rewarded by hearing some of his conversation. . . .

I was highly pleased with the extraordinary vigor of his conversation, and regretted that I was drawn away from it by an engagement at another place. I had, for a part of the evening, been left alone with him, and had ventured to make an observation now and then, which he received very civilly; so that I was satisfied that though there was a roughness in his manner, there was no ill-nature in his disposition. Davies 50 followed me to the door, and when I complained to him a little of the hard blows which the great man

had given me, he kindly took upon him to console me by saying, "Don't be uneasy. I can see he likes you very well."

Boswell's First Call on Johnson (1763)

A few days afterwards I called on Davies, and asked him if he thought I might take the liberty of waiting on Mr. Johnson at his chambers in the Temple. He said I certainly might, and that Mr. Johnson would take it as a compliment. So on Tuesday the 24th of May, after having been enlivened by the 60 witty sallies of Messieurs Thornton, Wilkes, Churchill, and Lloyd, with whom I had passed the morning, I boldly repaired to Johnson. His chambers were on the first floor of No. 1, Inner-Temple-lane, and I entered them with an impression given me by the Reverend Dr. Blair, of Edinburgh, who had been introduced to him not long before, and described his having "found the Giant in his den"; an expression which, when I came to be pretty well acquainted with Johnson, I repeated to him, and he was diverted 70 at this picturesque account of himself. Dr. Blair had been presented to him by Dr. James Fordyce. At this time the controversy concerning the pieces published by Mr. James Macpherson, as translations of Ossian, was at its height. Johnson had all along denied their authenticity; and, what was still more provoking to their admirers, maintained that they had no merit. The subject having been introduced by Dr. Fordyce, Dr. Blair, relying on the internal evidence of their antiquity, asked Dr. Johnson whether he thought any 80 man of a modern age could have written such poems? Johnson replied, "Yes, Sir, many men, many women, and many children." Johnson at this time, did not know that Dr. Blair had just published a Dissertation, not only defending their authenticity, but seriously ranking them with the poems of Homer and Virgil; and when he was afterwards informed of this circumstance, he expressed some displeasure at Dr. Fordyce's having suggested the topic, and said, "I am not sorry that they got thus much for their pains. Sir, 90 it was like leading one to talk of a book, when the author is concealed behind the door."

He received me very courteously; but, it must be confessed that his apartment, and furniture, and morning dress, were sufficiently uncouth. His brown suit of clothes looked very rusty; he had on a little old shrivelled unpowdered wig, which was too small for his head; his shirt-neck and knees of his breeches were loose; his black worsted stockings ill drawn up;

20. **Garrick,** David Garrick (1717–1779), the leading actor of his age. 21. **Miss Williams,** Anna Williams, a woman of rare talents, Johnson's friend and companion for many years. Up to this point in Boswell's *Life of Johnson,* she was mentioned as Mrs. Williams, "Mrs." being a common form of address for both married and unmarried women during the seventeenth and eighteenth centuries. Johnson uses both forms of address to her in his letters. Miss Williams was a woman with considerable interest in literature, and did some writing which Johnson tried without much success to publicize. 29. **Perhaps . . . pupil.** Boswell's own note follows: "That this was a momentary sally against Garrick there can be

no doubt; for at Johnson's desire he had, some years before, given a benefit-night at his theater to this very person, by which she had got two hundred pounds. Johnson, indeed, upon all other occasions, when I was in his company, praised the very liberal charity of Garrick. I once mentioned to him: 'It is observed, Sir, that you attack Garrick yourself but will suffer nobody else to do it.' *Johnson* (smiling): 'Why, Sir, that is true.' " 61. **Thornton . . . Lloyd.** All those mentioned here were literary wits and writers of the time: Bonnell Thornton (1727–1768); John Wilkes (1727–1797), champion of the rights of free representation in the government and friendly to the American cause in the Revolution

100 and he had a pair of unbuckled shoes by way of slippers. But all these slovenly particularities were forgotten the moment that he began to talk. Some gentlemen, whom I do not recollect, were sitting with him; and when they went away, I also rose; but he said to me, "Nay, don't go."—"Sir," said I, "I am afraid that I intrude upon you. It is benevolent to allow me to sit and hear you." He seemed pleased with this compliment, which I sincerely paid him, and answered, "Sir, I am obliged to any man who visits me."
110 —I have preserved the following short minute of what passed this day.

"Madness frequently discovers itself merely by unnecessary deviation from the usual modes of the world. My poor friend Smart showed the disturbance of his mind, by falling upon his knees, and saying his prayers in the street, or in any other unusual place. Now although, rationally speaking, it is greater madness not to pray at all, than to pray as Smart did, I am afraid there are so many who do not
120 pray, that their understanding is not called in question."

Concerning this unfortunate poet, Christopher Smart, who was confined in a mad-house, he had, at another time, the following conversation with Dr. Burney.—BURNEY. "How does poor Smart do, Sir; is he likely to recover?" JOHNSON. "It seems as if his mind had ceased to struggle with the disease; for he grows fat upon it." BURNEY. "Perhaps, Sir, that may be from want of exercise." JOHNSON. "No, Sir; he has partly as
130 much exercise as he used to have, for he digs in the garden. Indeed, before his confinement, he used for exercise to walk to the alehouse; but he was *carried* back again. I did not think he ought to be shut up. His infirmities were not noxious to society. He insisted on people praying with him; and I'd as lief pray with Kit Smart as anyone else. Another charge was, that he did not love clean linen; and I have no passion for it."

Johnson continued. "Mankind have a great aver-
140 sion to intellectual labor; but even supposing knowledge to be easily attainable, more people would be content to be ignorant than would take even a little trouble to acquire it.

"The morality of an action depends on the motive from which we act. If I fling half a crown to a beggar with intention to break his head, and he picks it up and buys victuals with it, the physical effect is good; but, with respect to me, the action is very wrong. So, religious exercises, if not performed with an inten-
150 tion to please God, avail us nothing. As our Savior says of those who perform them from other motives, 'Verily they have their reward.' " . . .

Talking of Garrick, he said, "He is the first man in the world for sprightly conversation."

When I rose a second time, he again pressed me to stay, which I did.

He told me that he generally went abroad at four in the afternoon, and seldom came home till two in the morning. I took the liberty to ask if he did not 160 think it wrong to live thus, and not make more use of his great talents. He owned it was a bad habit. On reviewing, at the distance of many years, my journal of this period, I wonder how, at my first visit, I ventured to talk to him so freely, and that he bore it with so much indulgence.

Before we parted, he was so good as to promise to favor me with his company one evening at my lodgings; and, as I took my leave, shook me cordially by the hand. It is almost needless to add, that I felt no little elation at having now so happily established an 170 acquaintance of which I had been so long ambitious. . . .

Oliver Goldsmith

As Dr. Oliver Goldsmith will frequently appear in this narrative, I shall endeavor to make my readers in some degree acquainted with his singular character. He was a native of Ireland, and a contemporary with Mr. Burke, at Trinity College, Dublin, but did not then give much promise of future celebrity. He, however, observed to Mr. Malone, that "though he made no great figure in mathematics, which was a 180 study in much repute there, he could turn an Ode of Horace into English better than any of them." He afterwards studied physic at Edinburgh, and upon the Continent; and I have been informed, was enabled to pursue his travels on foot, partly by demanding at universities to enter the lists as a disputant, by which, according to the custom of many of them, he was entitled to the premium of a crown, when luckily for him his challenge was not accepted; so that, as I once observed to Dr. Johnson, he *disputed* his passage 190 through Europe. He then came to England, and was employed successively in the capacities of an usher to an academy, a corrector of the press, a reviewer, and a writer for a newspaper. He had sagacity enough to cultivate assiduously the acquaintance of Johnson, and his faculties were gradually enlarged by the contemplation of such a model. To me and many others

of 1775, a rake and a political stormy petrel; Charles Churchill (1731–1764), author of the satiric poem *The Rosciad;* and Robert Lloyd (1733–1764). 66. **Blair.** Hugh Blair (1718–1800) was a noted preacher and critic, professor of rhetoric and belles-lettres at the University of Edinburgh. 72. **James Fordyce,** was another popular preacher and a poet as well (1720–1796). 74. **Macpherson . . . Ossian.** For Johnson's position on the question of the Ossianic poems, see his letter to Macpherson, p. 580. 114. **Smart.** Christopher Smart (1722–1771) was a minor poet of the day, chiefly famous because of Johnson's friendship for him. 125. **Burney.** Charles Burney (1726–1814), was a musician as well as an author, but is known to posterity as the father of Frances Burney (Madame d'Arblay), a brilliant woman novelist (1752–1840), whose *Evelina* (1778) and *Cecilia* (1782), to mention no other of her works, are excellent specimens of the novel of manners in the later eighteenth century. 152. **Verily . . . reward,** from Matthew 6:2. 173. **Dr. Oliver Goldsmith;** cf. p. 562. 177. **Mr. Burke,** Edmund Burke (1729–1797), the great statesman of the period. 179. **Mr. Malone,** Edmund Malone (1741–1812), editor of Shakespeare and a later reviser of Boswell's *Life of Johnson.*

it appeared that he studiously copied the manner of Johnson, though, indeed, upon a smaller scale.

At this time I think he had published nothing with his name, though it was pretty generally known that one Dr. Goldsmith was the author of *An Enquiry into the Present State of Polite Learning in Europe*, and of *The Citizen of the World*, a series of letters supposed to be written from London by a Chinese. No man had the art of displaying with more advantage as
10 a writer, whatever literary acquisitions he made. *"Nihil quod tetigit non ornavit."* His mind resembled a fertile, but thin soil. There was a quick, but not a strong vegetation, of whatever chanced to be thrown upon it. No deep root could be struck. The oak of the forest did not grow there: but the elegant shrubbery and the fragrant parterre appeared in gay succession. It has been generally circulated and believed that he was a mere fool in conversation; but, in truth, this has been greatly exaggerated. He had, no doubt, a
20 more than common share of that hurry of ideas which we often find in his countrymen, and which sometimes produces a laughable confusion in expressing them. He was very much what the French call *un étourdi*, and from vanity and an eager desire of being conspicuous wherever he was, he frequently talked carelessly without knowledge of the subject, or even without thought. His person was short, his countenance coarse and vulgar, his deportment that of a scholar awkwardly affecting the easy gentleman.
30 Those who were in any way distinguished, excited envy in him to so ridiculous an excess, that the instances of it are hardly credible. When accompanying two beautiful young ladies with their mother on a tour in France, he was seriously angry that more attention was paid to them than to him; and once at the exhibition of the *Fantoccini* in London, when those who sat next him observed with what dexterity a puppet was made to toss a pike, he could not bear that it should have such praise, and exclaimed with
40 some warmth, "Pshaw! I can do it better myself."

He, I am afraid, had no settled system of any sort, so that his conduct must not be strictly scrutinized; but his affections were social and generous, and when he had money he gave it away very liberally. His desire of imaginary consequence predominated over his attention to truth. When he began to rise into notice, he said he had a brother who was Dean of Durham, a fiction so easily detected, that it is wonderful how he should have been so inconsiderate as
50 to hazard it. He boasted to me at this time of the power of his pen in commanding money, which I believe was true in a certain degree, though in the instance he gave he was by no means correct. He told me that he had sold a novel for four hundred pounds. This was his *Vicar of Wakefield*. But Johnson informed me, that he had made the bargain for Goldsmith, and the price was sixty pounds. "And, Sir," said he, "a sufficient price too, when it was sold; for then the fame of Goldsmith had not been elevated, as it afterwards was, by his *Traveler*; and the bookseller 60 had such faint hopes of profit by his bargain, that he kept the manuscript by him a long time, and did not publish it till after the *Traveler* had appeared. Then, to be sure, it was accidentally worth more money."

Mrs. Piozzi and Sir John Hawkins have strangely misstated the history of Goldsmith's situation and Johnson's friendly interference, when this novel was sold. I shall give it authentically from Johnson's own exact narration:

"I received one morning a message from poor 70 Goldsmith that he was in great distress, and as it was not in his power to come to me, begging that I would come to him as soon as possible. I sent him a guinea, and promised to come to him directly. I accordingly went as soon as I was dressed, and found that his landlady had arrested him for his rent, at which he was in a violent passion. I perceived that he had already changed my guinea, and had got a bottle of Madeira and a glass before him. I put the cork into the bottle, desired he would be calm, and began to 80 talk to him of the means by which he might be extricated. He then told me that he had a novel ready for the press, which he produced to me. I looked into it, and saw its merit; told the landlady I should soon return, and having gone to a bookseller, sold it for sixty pounds. I brought Goldsmith the money, and he discharged his rent, not without rating his landlady in a high tone for having used him so ill."

My next meeting with Johnson was on Friday the 1st of July, when he and I and Dr. Goldsmith supped 90 together at the Mitre. I was before this time pretty well acquainted with Goldsmith, who was one of the brightest ornaments of the Johnsonian school. Goldsmith's respectful attachment to Johnson was then at its height; for his own literary reputation had not yet distinguished him so much as to excite a vain desire of competition with his great Master. He had increased my admiration of the goodness of Johnson's heart, by incidental remarks in the course of conversation, such as, when I mentioned Mr. Levet, 100

5. *An Enquiry . . . Europe*, a critical work by Oliver Goldsmith (p. 562), appearing in 1759. Its general thesis was that literary criticism and literary decadence go hand in hand. 7. *The Citizen of the World*, a series of letters contributed by Goldsmith to a newspaper called *The Public Ledger*, supposedly written by a Chinese traveler in London, impartially critical of English life and manners. The essays were later collected and published under the title *Letters from the Citizen of the World* (1762). 11. *Nihil . . . ornavit*, "He touched nothing that he did not adorn," from Johnson's epitaph on Goldsmith. 23. *un étourdi*, a rattle-brained blunderer. 33. **young ladies**, the Horneck sisters. 36. *Fantoccini*, a famous puppet show. 47. **Dean of Durham**.

Goldsmith's near relative Dr. Isaac Goldsmith was Dean of Cloyne, Ireland, in 1747. 60. *Traveler*, a didactic poem by Goldsmith (1764), attempting a survey of European culture. The poem brought Goldsmith both fame and money. 65. **Mrs. Piozzi**, formerly Mrs. Henry Thrale, who after the death of her husband married Signor Gabriele Piozzi, an Italian music master. The Thrales were intimate friends of Johnson, as the pathetic letter which Johnson wrote Mrs. Thrale at the time of her marriage to Piozzi (p. 581) well attests. Mrs. Piozzi's account of the Goldsmith matter is given in her *Anecdotes of Johnson*. **Sir John Hawkins**, a London attorney (1719–1789), relates the incident in his *Life of Johnson*. 88. **used him so ill**. Boswell's own note should be given

who he entertained under his roof, "He is poor and honest, which is recommendation enough to Johnson"; and when I wondered that he was very kind to a man of whom I had heard a very bad character, "He is now become miserable, and that insures the protection of Johnson." ...

He [Johnson] talked very contemptuously of Churchill's poetry, observing, that "it had a temporary currency, only from its audacity of abuse, and being filled with living names, and that it would sink into oblivion." I ventured to hint that he was not quite a fair judge, as Churchill had attacked him violently. JOHNSON. "Nay, Sir, I am a very fair judge. He did not attack me violently till he found I did not like his poetry; and his attack on me shall not prevent me from continuing to say what I think of him, from an apprehension that it may be ascribed to resentment. No, Sir, I called the fellow a blockhead at first, and I will call him a blockhead still. However, I will acknowledge that I have a better opinion of him now, than I once had; for he has shown more fertility than I expected. To be sure, he is a tree that cannot produce good fruit: he only bears crabs. But, Sir, a tree that produces a great many crabs is better than a tree which produces only a few." ...

Boswell's Apology

Let me here apologize for the imperfect manner in which I am obliged to exhibit Johnson's conversation at this period. In the early part of my acquaintance with him, I was so wrapt in admiration of his extraordinary colloquial talents, and so little accustomed to his peculiar mode of expression, that I found it extremely difficult to recollect and record his conversation with its genuine vigor and vivacity. In progress of time, when my mind was, as it were, *strongly impregnated with the Johnsonian aether*, I could with much more facility and exactness, carry in my memory and commit to paper the exuberant variety of his wisdom and wit.

Boswell's Party at the Mitre

On Wednesday, July 6, he was engaged to sup with me at my lodgings in Downing Street, Westminster. But on the preceding night my landlord having behaved very rudely to me and some company who were with me, I had resolved not to remain another night in his house. I was exceedingly uneasy at the awkward appearance I supposed I should make to Johnson and the other gentleman whom I had invited, not being able to receive them at home, and being obliged to order supper at the Mitre. I went to Johnson in the morning, and talked of it as of a serious distress. He laughed, and said, "Consider, Sir, how insignificant this will appear a twelve-month hence." —Were this consideration to be applied to most of the little vexatious incidents of life, by which our quiet is too often disturbed, it would prevent many painful sensations. I have tried it frequently with good effect. "There is nothing," continued he, "in this mighty misfortune; nay, we shall be better at the Mitre." I told him that I had been at Sir John Fielding's office, complaining of my landlord, and had been informed that though I had taken my lodgings for a year, I might, upon proof of his bad behavior, quit them when I pleased, without being under an obligation to pay rent for any longer time than while I possessed them. The fertility of Johnson's mind could show itself even upon so small a matter as this. "Why, Sir," said he, "I suppose this must be the law, since you have been told so in Bow Street. But, if your landlord could hold you to your bargain, and the lodgings should be yours for a year, you may certainly use them as you think fit. So, Sir, you may quarter two life-guardmen upon him; or you may send the greatest scoundrel you can find into your apartments; or you may say that you want to make some experiments in natural philosophy, and may burn a large quantity of assafoetida in his house."

Johnson and Boswell walking up the High Street, Edinburgh; a caricature by Thomas Rowlandson.

here: "It may not be improper to annex here Mrs. Piozzi's account of this transaction, in her own words, as a specimen of the extreme inaccuracy with which all her anecdotes of Dr. Johnson are related, or rather discolored and distorted. 'I have forgotten the year, but it could scarcely, I think, be later than 1765 or 1766, that he [Johnson] was *called abruptly from our house after dinner*, and returning *in about three hours*, said he had been with an enraged author, whose landlady pressed him for payment within doors, while the bailiffs beset him without; that he was *drinking himself drunk with Madeira*, to drown care, and fretting over a novel, which, when *finished*, was to be his *whole fortune*, but he *could not get it done for distraction*, nor could he step out of doors to offer it for sale. Mr. Johnson, therefore, sent away the bottle, and went to the bookseller, recommending the performance, and desiring some *immediate relief*, which when he brought back to the writer, *he called the woman of the house directly to partake of punch and pass their time in merriment.*'" 100. **Mr. Levet**, Robert Levett, a destitute surgeon who was one of Johnson's dependents, and lived in his house. 108. **Churchill** (1731–1764), a satirist, author of *The Rosciad*. 139. **July 6**. The year is 1763. 158. **Sir John Fielding**, a London magistrate (d. 1780). He was a half brother of the novelist Henry Fielding.

I had as my guests this evening at the Mitre tavern, Dr. Johnson, Dr. Goldsmith, Mr. Thomas Davies, Mr. Eccles, an Irish gentleman, for whose agreeable company I was obliged to Mr. Davies, and the Reverend Mr. John Ogilvie, who was desirous of being in company with my illustrious friend, while I in my turn, was proud to have the honor of showing one of my countrymen upon what easy terms Johnson permitted me to live with him.

10 Goldsmith, as usual, endeavored, with too much eagerness, to *shine*, and disputed very warmly with Johnson against the well known maxim of the British constitution, "the King can do no wrong"; affirming, that, "what was morally false could not be politically true; and as the King might, in the exercise of his regal power, command and cause the doing of what was wrong, it certainly might be said, in sense and in reason, that he could do wrong." JOHNSON. "Sir, you are to consider, that in our constitution, according 20 to its true principles, the King is the head, he is supreme: he is above everything, and there is no power by which he can be tried. Therefore, it is, Sir, that we hold the King can do no wrong; that whatever may happen to be wrong in government may not be above our reach, by being ascribed to Majesty. Redress is always to be had against oppression, by punishing the immediate agents. The King, though he should command, cannot force a judge to condemn a man unjustly; therefore it is the judge whom 30 we prosecute and punish. Political institutions are formed upon the consideration of what will most frequently tend to the good of the whole, although now and then exceptions may occur. Thus it is better in general that a nation should have a supreme legislative power, although it may at times be abused. And then, Sir, there is this consideration, that *if the abuse be enormous, Nature will rise up, and claiming her original rights, overturn a corrupt political system."* I mark this animated sentence with peculiar pleasure, 40 as a noble instance of that truly dignified spirit of freedom which ever glowed in his heart, though he was charged with slavish tenets by superficial observers; because he was at all times indignant against that false patriotism, that pretended love of freedom, that unruly restlessness which is inconsistent with the stable authority of any good government.

This generous sentiment, which he uttered with great fervor, struck me exceedingly, and stirred my blood to that pitch of fancied resistance, the possi- 50 bility of which I am glad to keep in mind, but to which I trust I never shall be forced.

"Great abilities," said he, "are not requisite for an historian; for in historical composition, all the greatest powers of the human mind are quiescent. He has facts ready to his hand, so there is no exercise of invention. Imagination is not required in any high degree; only about as much as is used in the lower kinds of poetry. Some penetration, accuracy, and coloring, will fit a man for the task, if he can give the application which is necessary." 60

"Bayle's *Dictionary* is a very useful work for those to consult who love the biographical part of literature, which is what I love most."

Talking of the eminent writers in Queen Anne's reign, he observed, "I think Dr. Arbuthnot the first man among them. He was the most universal genius, being an excellent physician, a man of deep learning, and a man of much humor. Mr. Addison was, to be sure, a great man; his learning was not profound; but his morality, his humor, and his ele- 70 gance of writing, set him very high."

Mr. Ogilvie was unlucky enough to choose for the topic of his conversation the praises of his native country. He began with saying, that there was very rich land around Edinburgh. Goldsmith, who had studied physic there, contradicted this, very untruly, with a sneering laugh. Disconcerted a little by this, Mr. Ogilvie then took a new ground, where, I suppose, he thought himself perfectly safe; for he observed that Scotland had a great many noble wild prospects. 80 JOHNSON. "I believe, Sir, you have a great many. Norway, too, has noble wild prospects; and Lapland is remarkable for prodigious noble wild prospects. But, Sir, let me tell you, the noblest prospect which a Scotchman ever sees, is the high road that leads him to England!" This unexpected and pointed sally produced a roar of applause. After all, however, those who admire the rude grandeur of nature, cannot deny it to Caledonia.

Rime and Blank Verse

He enlarged very convincingly upon the excellence 90 of rime over blank verse in English poetry. I mentioned to him that Dr. Adam Smith, in his lectures upon composition, when I studied under him in the College of Glasgow, had maintained the same opinion strenuously, and I repeated some of his arguments. JOHNSON. "Sir, I was once in company with Smith, and we did not take to each other; but had I known that he loved rime as much as you tell me he does, I should have *hugged* him." . . .

---

1. **Mitre tavern . . . Ogilvie.** The people mentioned have been met with before, except for Mr. Eccles, "an Irish gentleman." Mr. Thomas Davies was the actor at whose home Boswell first met Johnson (p. 587). l. 156); Mr. John Ogilvie was a Scotch minister with poetic pretensions. Boswell remarks in a note: "When I asked Dr. Johnson's permission to introduce him [Ogilvie], he obligingly agreed; adding, however, with a sly pleasantry, 'but he must give us none of his poetry.' " 61. **Bayle's**

Dictionary, the *Dictionnaire historique et critique* by Pierre Bayle (1647–1706), which is as much a résumé of the learning of the time as a dictionary. 65. **Dr. Arbuthnot,** John Arbuthnot (1665?–1735), friend of Addison, Steele, Swift, and Pope. See Pope's *Epistle to Dr. Arbuthnot,* p. 556. 68. **Mr. Addison,** Joseph Addison (1672–1719), the essayist, journalist, and man of affairs in the reign of Queen Anne (cf. p. 473). 92. **Dr. Adam Smith,** the noted political economist

100 Rousseau's treatise on the inequality of mankind was at this time a fashionable topic. It gave rise to an observation by Mr. Dempster, that the advantages of fortune and rank were nothing to a wise man, who ought to value only merit. JOHNSON. "If man were a savage, living in the woods by himself, this might be true; but in civilized society we all depend upon each other, and our happiness is very much owing to the good opinion of mankind. Now, Sir, in civilized society, external advantages make us more respected.
110 A man with a good coat upon his back meets with a better reception than he who has a bad one. Sir, you may analyze this, and say, 'What is there in it?' But that will avail you nothing, for it is a part of a general system. Pound St. Paul's church into atoms, and consider any single atom; it is, to be sure, good for nothing: but, put all these atoms together, and you have St. Paul's church. So it is with human felicity, which is made up of many ingredients, each of which may be shown to be very insignificant. In civilized
120 society, personal merit will not serve you so much as money will. Sir, you may make the experiment. Go into the street, and give one man a lecture on morality, and another a shilling, and see which will respect you most. If you wish only to support nature, Sir William Petty fixed your allowance at three pounds a year; but as times are much altered, let us call it six pounds. This sum will fill your belly, shelter you from the weather, and even get you a strong lasting coat, supposing it to be made of good bull's hide. Now,
130 Sir, all beyond this is artificial, and is desired in order to obtain a greater degree of respect from our fellow-creatures. And, Sir, if six hundred pounds a year procure a man more consequence, and, of course, more happiness than six pounds a year, the same proportion will hold as to six thousand, and so on, as far as opulence can be carried. Perhaps he who has a large fortune may not be so happy as he who has a small one; but that must proceed from other causes than from his having the large fortune: for, *caeteris*
140 *paribus,* he who is rich in a civilized society, must be happier than he who is poor; as riches, if properly used (and it is a man's own fault if they are not) must be productive of the highest advantages. Money, to be sure, of itself is of no use; for its only use is to part with it. Rousseau, and all those who deal in paradoxes, are led away by a childish desire of novelty. When I was a boy, I used always to choose the wrong side of a debate, because most ingenious things, that is to say, most new things, could be said upon it. Sir, there is nothing for which you may not muster up 150 more plausible arguments than those which are urged against wealth and other external advantages. Why, now, there is stealing; why should it be thought a crime? When we consider by what unjust methods property has been often acquired, and that what was unjustly got it must be unjust to keep, where is the harm in one man's taking the property of another from him? Besides, Sir, when we consider the bad use that many people make of their property, and how much better use the thief may make of it, it may 160 be defended as a very allowable practice. Yet, Sir, the experience of mankind has discovered stealing to be so very bad a thing, that they make no scruple to hang a man for it. When I was running about this town a very poor fellow, I was a great arguer for the advantages of poverty; but I was, at the same time, very sorry to be poor. Sir, all the arguments which are brought to represent poverty as no evil, show it to be evidently a great evil. You never find people laboring to convince you that you may live very happily 170 upon a plentiful fortune.—So you hear people talking how miserable a king must be; and yet they all wish to be in his place." . . .

Johnson's Melancholy

He mentioned to me now, for the first time, that he had been distressed by melancholy, and for that reason had been obliged to fly from study and meditation, to the dissipating variety of life. Against melancholy he recommended constant occupation of mind, a great deal of exercise, moderation in eating and drinking, and especially to shun drinking at night. 180 He said melancholy people were apt to fly to intemperance for relief, but that it sunk them much deeper in misery. He observed that laboring men who work hard, and live sparingly, are seldom or never troubled with low spirits. . . .

Relish for Good Eating

At supper this night he talked of good eating with uncommon satisfaction. "Some people," said he, "have a foolish way of not minding, or pretending not to mind, what they eat. For my part, I mind my belly very studiously, and very carefully; for I look upon it, 190 that he who does not mind his belly, will hardly mind anything else." He now appeared to me *Jean Bull philosophe,* and he was for the moment, not

(1723–1790). His *Wealth of Nations,* (1776) is a landmark in the history of economic thought. 100. **Rousseau's . . . topic.** The figure of Rousseau (1712–1778), poet, musician, vagabond, social reformer, and revolutionist, and his importance in the age of revolution will be commented upon later. The "treatise" referred to here is his *Contrat social (The Social Contract),* published in 1762. 102. **Mr. Dempster,** George Dempster (1732–1818), agriculturist and politician, who inherited a very large fortune from his father. 124. **Sir William Petty,** a political economist (1623–1687), whose chief title to fame rests upon his analysis of the origin of wealth. 136. **Perhaps, etc.** The rest of this paragraph has been quoted by many as an illustration of Johnson's "massive common sense." 139. *caeteris paribus,* other things being equal. 192. *Jean Bull philosophe,* John Bull, the typical Englishman, as philosopher.

only serious, but vehement. Yet I have heard him, upon other occasions, talk with great contempt of people who were anxious to gratify their palates; and the 206th number of his *Rambler* is a masterly essay against gulosity. His practice, indeed, I must acknowledge, may be considered as casting the balance of his different opinions upon this subject; for I never knew any man who relished good eating more than he did. When at table, he was totally absorbed in the business of the moment; his looks seemed riveted to his plate; nor would he, unless when in very high company, say one word, or even pay the least attention to what was said by others, till he had satisfied his appetite; which was so fierce, and indulged with such intenseness, that while in the act of eating, the veins of his forehead swelled, and generally a strong perspiration was visible. To those whose sensations were delicate, this could not but be disgusting; and it was doubtless not very suitable to the character of a philosopher, who should be distinguished by self-command. But it must be owned that Johnson, though he could be rigidly *abstemious*, was not a *temperate* man either in eating or drinking. He could refrain, but he could not use moderately. He told me that he had fasted two days without inconvenience, and that he had never been hungry but once. They who beheld with wonder how much he eat upon all occasions, when his dinner was to his taste, could not easily conceive what he must have meant by hunger; and not only was he remarkable for the extraordinary quantity which he eat, but he was, or affected to be, a man of very nice discernment in the science of cookery. He used to descant critically on the dishes which had been at table where he had dined or supped, and to recollect very minutely what he had liked. I remember when he was in Scotland, his praising "Gordon's palates" (a dish of palates at the Honorable Alexander Gordon's), with a warmth of expression which might have done honor to more important subjects. "As for Maclaurin's imitation of a *made dish*, it was a wretched attempt." He about the same time was so much displeased with the performances of a nobleman's French cook, that he exclaimed with vehemence, "I'd throw such a rascal into the river"; and he then proceeded to alarm a lady at whose house he was to sup, by the following manifesto of his skill: "I, Madam, who live at a variety of good tables, am a much better judge of cookery than any person who has a very tolerable cook, but lives much at home; for his palate is gradually adapted to the taste of his cook; whereas, Madam, in trying

by a wider range, I can more exquisitely judge." When invited to dine, even with an intimate friend, he was not pleased if something better than a plain dinner was not prepared for him. I have heard him say on such an occasion, "This was a good dinner enough, to be sure; but it was not a dinner to *ask* a man to." On the other hand, he was wont to express, with great glee, his satisfaction when he had been entertained quite to his mind. One day when he had dined with his neighbor and landlord, in Bolt Court, Mr. Allen, the printer, whose old housekeeper had studied his taste in everything, he pronounced this eulogy: "Sir, we could not have had a better dinner, had there been a *Synod of Cooks*."

While we were left by ourselves, after the Dutchman had gone to bed, Dr. Johnson talked of that studied behavior which many have recommended and practiced. He disapproved of it; and said, "I never considered whether I should be a grave man, or a merry man, but just let inclination, for the time, have its course."

He flattered me with some hopes that he would, in the course of the following summer, come over to Holland, and accompany me in a tour through the Netherlands.

I teased him with fanciful apprehensions of unhappiness. A moth having fluttered round the candle, and burnt itself, he laid hold of this little incident to admonish me; saying, with a sly look, and in a solemn but a quiet tone, "That creature was its own tormentor, and I believe its name was BOSWELL."

Next day we got to Harwich, to dinner; and my passage in the packet-boat to Helvoetsluys being secured, and my baggage put on board, we dined at our inn by ourselves. I happened to say it would be terrible if he should not find a speedy opportunity of returning to London, and be confined in so dull a place. JOHNSON. "Don't, Sir, accustom yourself to use big words for little matters. It would *not* be *terrible*, though I *were* to be detained some time here." The practice of using words of disproportionate magnitude, is, no doubt, too frequent everywhere; but, I think, most remarkable among the French, of which, all who have traveled in France must have been struck with innumerable instances.

We went and looked at the church, and having gone into it, and walked up to the altar, Johnson, whose piety was constant and fervent, sent me to my knees, saying, "Now that you are going to leave your native country, recommend yourself to the protection of your CREATOR and REDEEMER."

5. **gulosity**, excessive appetite, gluttony. 37. *palates*, things tasty or palatable. Johnson was in Scotland from August to November 1773. Alexander Gordon was a wealthy Scotchman of the age, afterwards Lord Rockville. 40. **Maclaurin's imitation, etc.** This is an allusion to the effort of John Maclaurin (1734–1796), a Scottish judge, afterwards Lord Dreghorn, to imitate the style of Johnson in Johnson's *Journey to the Western Islands* (1775). Of the imitation Johnson said, "I could caricature my own style much better myself." 66. **the Dutchman,** a fellow passenger in the stagecoach to Harwich. 84. **Helvoetsluys,** a seaport in The Netherlands. 104. **Berkeley's . . . matter.** Bishop George Berkeley (1685–1753), churchman and metaphysician, author of *Principles of Human Knowledge* (1710), which is based upon the "idealistic" philosophy that nothing exists except in so far as it is perceived by the senses. 112. *Père Bouffier.* Claude Bouffier (1661–1737), notable French writer on grammar and history, published in 1724 a *Traité des vérités premières*, which had for its purpose the discovery of the principles upon

After we came out of the church, we stood talking for some time together of Bishop Berkeley's ingenious sophistry to prove the non-existence of matter, and that everything in the universe is merely ideal. I observed that though we are satisfied his doctrine is not true, it is impossible to refute it. I never shall forget the alacrity with which Johnson answered, striking his foot with mighty force against a large stone, till he rebounded from it, "I refute it *thus*." This was a stout exemplification of the *first truths of Père Bouffier*, or the *original principles* of Reid and of Beattie; without admitting which, we can no more argue in metaphysics, than we can argue in mathematics without axioms. To me it is not conceivable how Berkeley can be answered by pure reasoning; but I know that the nice and difficult task was to have been undertaken by one of the most luminous minds of the present age, had not politics "turned him from calm philosophy aside." What an admirable display of subtilty, united with brilliance, might his contending with Berkeley have afforded us! How must we, when we reflect on the loss of such an intellectual feast, regret that he should be characterized as the man,

Who, born for the universe, narrowed his mind,
And to party gave up what was meant for mankind?

My revered friend walked down with me to the beach, where we embraced and parted with tenderness, and engaged to correspond by letters. I said, "I hope, Sir, you will not forget me in my absence." JOHNSON. "Nay, Sir, it is more likely you should forget me, than that I should forget you." As the vessel put out to sea, I kept my eyes upon him for a considerable time, while he remained rolling his majestic frame in his usual manner; and at last I perceived him walk back into the town, and he disappeared.

Johnson's Peculiarities (1764)

About this time he was afflicted with a very severe return of the hypochondriac disorder which was ever lurking about him. He was so ill as, notwithstanding his remarkable love of company, to be entirely averse to society, the most fatal symptom of that malady. Dr. Adams told me that as an old friend he was admitted to visit him, and that he found him in a deplorable state, sighing, groaning, talking to himself, and restlessly walking from room to room. He then used

this emphatical expression of the misery which he felt: "I would consent to have a limb amputated to recover my spirits."

Talking to himself was, indeed, one of his singularities ever since I knew him. I was certain that he was frequently uttering pious ejaculations; for fragments of the Lord's Prayer have been distinctly overheard. His friend Mr. Thomas Davies, of whom Churchill says, "That Davies hath a very pretty wife," when Dr. Johnson muttered "lead us not into temptation," used with waggish and gallant humor to whisper Mrs. Davies, "You, my dear, are the cause of this."

He had another particularity, of which none of his friends ever ventured to ask an explanation. It appeared to me some superstitious habit which he had contracted early, and from which he had never called upon his reason to disentangle him. This was his anxious care to go out or in at a door or passage by a certain number of steps from a certain point, or at least so as that either his right or his left foot (I am not certain which) should constantly make the first actual movement when he came close to the door or passage. Thus I conjecture: for I have upon innumerable occasions observed him suddenly stop, and then seem to count his steps with a deep earnestness; and when he had neglected or gone wrong in this sort of magical movement, I have seen him go back again, put himself in a proper posture to begin the ceremony, and, having gone through it, break from his abstraction, walk briskly on, and join his companion. A strange instance of something of this nature, even when on horseback, happened when he was in the Isle of Skye. Sir Joshua Reynolds has observed him to go a good way about rather than cross a particular alley in Leicester Fields; but this Sir Joshua imputed to his having had some disagreeable recollection associated with it.

That the most minute singularities which belonged to him, and made very observable parts of his appearance and manner, may not be omitted, it is requisite to mention that while talking or even musing as he sat in his chair, he commonly held his head to one side towards his right shoulder, and shook it in a tremulous manner, moving his body backwards and forwards, and rubbing his left knee in the same direction with the palm of his hand. In the intervals of articulating he made various sounds with his mouth, sometimes as if ruminating, or what is called chewing the cud, sometimes giving a half whistle, sometimes making his tongue play backwards from the roof of his mouth, as if clucking like a hen, and sometimes protruding it against his upper gums in front, as if pronouncing

which all human knowledge is based. The core of his philosophy is that of Descartes, a rational basis, but he partakes of some of the views of Berkeley (l. 104 and note)—the basis of all human knowledge and the foundation of every other truth lie in the sense we have of our own existence and of what we feel within ourselves. 113. **Reid . . . Beattie.** Professor Thomas Reid (1710–1796), a Scottish philosopher. Dr. James Beattie (1735–1803), a poet and professor of moral philosophy at Aberdeen University. 119. **luminous minds . . . age,** Edmund Burke (1729–

1797), famous statesman and orator. 127. **Who . . . mankind,** quoted from Goldsmith's poem *Retaliation* (1774). 143. **Dr. Adams,** Dr. William Adams, schoolfellow of Johnson's at Pembroke College, afterwards Master of Pembroke. 177. **strange instance . . . Skye.** The incident is related at length in Boswell's *Journal of a Tour to the Hebrides*, third edition, p. 316. *Skye* is the Isle of Skye, the large island off the northwest coast of Scotland.

quickly under his breath *too, too, too;* all this accompanied sometimes with a thoughtful look, but more frequently with a smile. Generally when he had concluded a period in the course of a dispute, by which time he was a good deal exhausted by violence and vociferation, he used to blow out his breath like a whale. This I supposed was a relief to his lungs; and seemed in him to be a contemptuous mode of expression, as if he had made the arguments of his opponent
10 fly like chaff before the wind.

I am fully aware how very obvious an occasion I here give for the sneering jocularity of such as have no relish of an exact likeness; which to render complete, he who draws it must not disdain the slightest strokes. But if witlings should be inclined to attack on this account, let them have the candor to quote what I have offered in my defense. . . .

The Fear of Death (1769)

When we were alone, I introduced the subject of death, and endeavored to maintain that the fear of it
20 might be got over. I told him that David Hume said to me he was no more uneasy to think he should *not be* after this life than that he *had not been* before he began to exist. JOHNSON. "Sir, if he really thinks so, his perceptions are disturbed; he is mad. If he does not think so, he lies. He may tell you he holds his finger in the flame of a candle without feeling pain; would you believe him? When he dies, he at least gives up all he has." BOSWELL. "Foote, Sir, told me that when he was very ill he was not afraid to die." JOHNSON. "It is not
30 true, Sir. Hold a pistol to Foote's breast, or to Hume's breast and threaten to kill them, and you'll see how they behave." BOSWELL. "But may we not fortify our minds for the approach of death?" Here I am sensible I was in the wrong, to bring before his view what he ever looked upon with horror; for although when in a celestial frame, in his *Vanity of Human Wishes,* he has supposed death to be "kind nature's signal for retreat," from this state of being to "a happier seat," his thoughts upon this awful change were in general full of dismal
40 apprehensions. His mind resembled the vast amphitheater, the Coliseum at Rome. In the center stood his judgment, which, like a mighty gladiator, combated those apprehensions that, like the wild beasts of the arena, were all around in cells, ready to be let out upon him. After a conflict, he drives them back into their dens; but not killing them, they were still assailing him. To my question, whether we might not fortify our minds for the approach of death, he answered in a

passion, "No, Sir, let it alone. It matters not how a man dies, but how he lives. The act of dying is not of 50 importance; it lasts so short a time." He added, with an earnest look, "A man knows it must be so, and submits. It will do him no good to whine."

I attempted to continue the conversation. He was so provoked that he said, "Give us no more of this," and was thrown into such a state of agitation that he expressed himself in a way that alarmed and distressed me; showed an impatience that I should leave him, and when I was going away, called to me sternly, "Don't let us meet tomorrow." 60

I went home exceedingly uneasy. All the harsh observations which I had ever heard made upon his character crowded into my mind; and I seemed to myself like the man who had put his head into the lion's mouth a great many times with perfect safety, but at last had it bit off.

Next morning I sent him a note stating that I might have been in the wrong, but it was not intentionally; he was therefore, I could not help thinking, too severe upon me. That notwithstanding our agreement not to 70 meet that day, I would call on him in my way to the city, and stay five minutes by my watch. "You are," said I, "in my mind, since last night, surrounded with cloud and storm. Let me have a glimpse of sunshine and go about my affairs in serenity and cheerfulness."

Upon entering his study, I was glad that he was not alone, which would have made our meeting more awkward. There were with him, Mr. Steevens and Mr. Tyers, both of whom I now saw for the first time. My note had, on his own reflection, softened him, for he 80 received me very complacently; so that I unexpectedly found myself at ease, and joined in the conversation. . . .

Johnson spoke unfavorably of a certain pretty voluminous author, saying, "He used to write anonymous books, and then other books commending those books, in which there was something of rascality."

I whispered him, "Well, Sir, you are now in good humor." JOHNSON. "Yes, Sir." I was going to leave him, and had got as far as the staircase. He stopped me, 90 and smiling, said, "Get you gone *in*"; a curious mode of inviting me to stay, which I accordingly did for some time longer.

This little incidental quarrel and reconciliation, which, perhaps, I may be thought to have detailed too minutely, must be esteemed as one of many proofs which his friends had, that though he might be charged with bad humor at times, he was always a good-natured man; and I have heard Sir Joshua Reynolds, a nice and delicate observer of manners, 100

20. **David Hume,** a Scottish historian and philosopher (1711–1776). 28. **Foote,** Samuel Foote (1720–1777), an English comedian and playwright. 37. **kind . . . seat,** from Johnson's philosophic poem, *The Vanity of Human Wishes* (1749), ll. 363 ff. 78. **Mr. Steevens,** George Steevens (1736–1800), editor of Shakespeare. **Mr. Tyers,** Thomas Tyers

(1726–1787), a dilettante author, who published a biographical sketch of Johnson. 127. **Rabelais,** Francois Rabelais (1490?–1553), noted French philosopher, satirist, and humorist; creator of the mighty hero Gargantua. 151. *pars magna fui,* in which I played a large part. Quoted from the *Aeneid,* II, 5. 156. **John Wilkes,** a liberal, radical, and free-

particularly remark that when upon any occasion Johnson had been rough to any person in company, he took the first opportunity of reconciliation, by drinking to him or addressing his discourse to him; but if he found his dignified indirect overtures sullenly neglected, he was quite indifferent, and considered himself as having done all that he ought to do, and the other as now in the wrong.

Goldsmith's Wit (1773)

He said, "Goldsmith should not be forever attempt-
110 ing to shine in conversation; he has not temper for it, he is so much mortified when he fails. Sir, a game of jokes is composed partly of skill, partly of chance. A man may be beat at times by one who has not the tenth part of his wit. Now Goldsmith's putting himself against another is like a man laying a hundred to one who cannot spare the hundred. It is not worth a man's while. A man should not lay a hundred to one unless he can easily spare it, though he has a hundred chances for him; he can get but a guinea,
120 and he may lose a hundred. Goldsmith is in this state. When he contends, if he gets the better, it is a very little addition to a man of his literary reputation; if he does not get the better, he is miserably vexed."

Johnson's own superlative powers of wit set him above any risk of such uneasiness. Garrick had remarked to me of him, a few days before, "Rabelais and all other wits are nothing compared with him. You may be diverted by them; but Johnson gives you a
130 forcible hug and shakes laughter out of you, whether you will or no."

Goldsmith, however, was often very fortunate in his witty contests, even when he entered the lists with Johnson himself. Sir Joshua Reynolds was in company with them one day when Goldsmith said that he thought he could write a good fable, mentioned the simplicity which that kind of composition requires, and observed that in most fables the animals introduced seldom talk in character. "For instance," said he, "the
140 fable of the little fishes who saw birds fly over their heads, and envying them, petitioned Jupiter to be changed into birds. The skill," continued he, "consists in making them talk like little fishes." While he indulged himself in this fanciful reverie, he observed Johnson shaking his sides and laughing. Upon which he smartly proceeded, "Why, Dr. Johnson, this is not so easy as you seem to think; for if you were to make little fishes talk, they would talk like WHALES." . . .

How Dr. Johnson and Mr. Wilkes Dined Together (1776)

I am now to record a very curious incident in Dr. Johnson's life, which fell under my own observation; 150 of which *pars magna fui*, and which I am persuaded will, with the liberal-minded, be much to his credit.

My desire of being acquainted with celebrated men of every description, had made me, much about the same time, obtain an introduction to Dr. Samuel Johnson and to John Wilkes, Esq. Two men more different could perhaps not be selected out of all mankind. They had even attacked one another with some asperity in their writings; yet I lived in habits of friendship with both. I could fully relish the ex- 160 cellence of each; for I have ever delighted in that intellectual chemistry, which can separate good qualities from evil in the same person.

Sir John Pringle, "mine own friend and my Father's friend," between whom and Dr. Johnson I in vain wished to establish an acquaintance, as I respected and lived in intimacy with both of them, observed to me once, very ingeniously, "It is not in friendship as in mathematics, where two things, each equal to a third, are equal between themselves. You agree with 170 Johnson as a middle quality, and you agree with me as a middle quality; but Johnson and I should not agree." Sir John was not sufficiently flexible; so I desisted; knowing, indeed, that the repulsion was equally strong on the part of Johnson; who, I know not from what cause, unless his being a Scotchman, had formed a very erroneous opinion of Sir John. But I conceived an irresistible wish, if possible, to bring Dr. Johnson and Mr. Wilkes together. How to manage it, was a nice and difficult matter. 180

My worthy booksellers and friends, Messieurs Dilly in the Poultry, at whose hospitable and well-covered table I have seen a greater number of literary men, than at any other, except that of Sir Joshua Reynolds, had invited me to meet Mr. Wilkes and some more gentlemen, on Wednesday, May 15. "Pray (said I,) let us have Dr. Johnson."—"What with Mr. Wilkes? not for the world, (said Mr. Edward Dilly;) Dr. Johnson would never forgive me."—"Come, (said I,) if you'll let me negotiate for you, I will be answerable 190 that all shall go well." DILLY. "Nay, if you will take it upon you, I am sure I shall be very happy to see them both here."

Notwithstanding the high veneration which I entertained for Dr. Johnson, I was sensible that he was sometimes a little actuated by the spirit of contradiction, and by means of that I hoped I should gain

living Whig. Johnson was a conservative, respectable Tory. 164. Sir John Pringle, a Scottish physician and Boswell's godfather (1707–1782). 176. Scotchman, Dr. Johnson made fun of Scots on all occasions, much to Boswell's discomfort. 182. Poultry, a district east of Cheapside where poultry was sold in medieval and Elizabethan times.

184. Sir Joshua Reynolds, famous portrait painter and member of the Johnson circle (1723–1792).

my point. I was persuaded that if I had come upon him with a direct proposal, "Sir, will you dine in company with Jack Wilkes?" he would have flown into a passion, and would probably have answered, "Dine with Jack Wilkes, Sir! I'd as soon dine with Jack Ketch." I therefore, while we were sitting quietly by ourselves at his house in an evening, took occasion to open my plan thus:—"Mr. Dilly, Sir, sends his respectful compliments to you, and would be happy

10 if you would do him the honor to dine with him on Wednesday next along with me, as I must soon go to Scotland." JOHNSON. "Sir, I am obliged to Mr. Dilly. I will wait upon him—" BOSWELL. "Provided, Sir, I suppose, that the company which he is to have, is agreeable to you." JOHNSON. "What do you mean, Sir? What do you take me for? Do you think I am so ignorant of the world, as to imagine that I am to prescribe to a gentleman what company he is to have at his table?" BOSWELL. "I beg your pardon, Sir, for

20 wishing to prevent you from meeting people whom you might not like. Perhaps he may have some of what he calls his patriotic friends with him." JOHNSON. "Well, Sir, and what then? What care I for his *patriotic friends*? Poh!" BOSWELL. "I should not be surprised to find Jack Wilkes there." JOHNSON. "And if Jack Wilkes *should* be there, what is that to *me*, Sir? My dear friend, let us have no more of this. I am sorry to be angry with you; but really it is treating me strangely to talk to me as if I could not meet any

30 company whatever, occasionally." BOSWELL. "Pray, forgive me, Sir: I meant well. But you shall meet whoever comes, for me." Thus I secured him, and told Dilly that he would find him very well pleased to be one of his guests on the day appointed.

Upon the much expected Wednesday, I called on him about half an hour before dinner, as I often did when we were to dine out together, to see that he was ready in time, and to accompany him. I found him buffeting his books, as upon a former occasion,

40 covered with dust, and making no preparation for going abroad. "How is this, Sir? (said I). Don't you recollect that you are to dine at Mr. Dilly's?" JOHNSON. "Sir, I did not think of going to Dilly's: it went out of my head. I have ordered dinner at home with Mrs. Williams." BOSWELL. "But, my dear Sir, you know you were engaged to Mr. Dilly, and I told him so. He will expect you, and will be much disappointed if you don't come." JOHNSON. "You must talk to Mrs. Williams about this."

50 Here was a sad dilemma. I feared that what I was so confident I had secured, would yet be frustrated.

He had accustomed himself to show Mrs. Williams such a degree of humane attention, as frequently imposed some restraint upon him; and I knew that if she should be obstinate, he would not stir. I hastened downstairs to the blind lady's room, and told her I was in great uneasiness, for Dr. Johnson had engaged to me to dine this day at Mr. Dilly's, but that he had told me he had forgotten his engagement, and had ordered dinner at home. "Yes, Sir, (said she, 60 pretty peevishly,) Dr. Johnson is to dine at home."— "Madam, (said I,) his respect for you is such, that I know he will not leave you, unless you absolutely desire it. But as you have so much of his company, I hope you will be good enough to forego it for a day: as Mr. Dilly is a very worthy man, has frequently had agreeable parties at his house for Dr. Johnson, and will be vexed if the Doctor neglects him today. And then, Madam, be pleased to consider my situation; I carried the message, and I assured Mr. Dilly that 70 Dr. Johnson was to come; and no doubt he has made a dinner, and invited a company, and boasted of the honor he expected to have. I shall be quite disgraced if the Doctor is not there." She gradually softened to my solicitations, which were certainly as earnest as most entreaties to ladies upon any occasion, and was graciously pleased to empower me to tell Dr. Johnson, "That all things considered, she thought he should certainly go." I flew back to him, still in dust, and careless of what should be the 80 event, "indifferent in his choice to go or stay;" but as soon as I had announced to him Mrs. Williams's consent, he roared, "Frank, a clean shirt," and was very soon drest. When I had him fairly seated in a hackney-coach with me, I exulted as much as a fortune-hunter who has got an heiress into a post-chaise with him to set out for Gretna-Green.

When we entered Mr. Dilly's drawing-room, he found himself in the midst of a company he did not know. I kept myself snug and silent, watching how 90 he would conduct himself. I observed him whispering to Mr. Dilly, "Who is that gentleman, sir?"—"Mr. Arthur Lee."—JOHNSON. "Too, too, too," (under his breath,) which was one of his habitual mutterings. Mr. Arthur Lee could not but be very obnoxious to Johnson, for he was not only a *patriot*, but an *American*. He was afterwards minister from the United States at the court of Madrid. "And who is the gentleman in lace?"—"Mr. Wilkes, Sir." This information confounded him still more; he had some 100 difficulty to restrain himself, and taking up a book, sat down upon a window-seat and read, or at least

6. **Jack Ketch,** the public executioner, who died in 1686. His successors inherited the name in popular slang. Of the imagined remark Boswell's note says: "This has been circulated as if actually said by Johnson, when the truth is, it was only *supposed* by me." 24. **patriotic friends.** Those Whigs who were most violently opposed to the autocracy of George III and his minister Lord North styled themselves patriots. Johnson, as a staunch Tory, disliked them heartily. 48. **Mrs. Williams,** a blind friend

of Mrs. Johnson's who lived in Johnson's house as a dependent. Every evening Johnson drank tea with her, and it was a signal favor to be invited by Johnson to attend. 83. **Frank,** Johnson's Negro servant. 87. **Gretna-Green,** a village just over the border in Scotland to which couples went to get married because of the lax Scottish marriage laws. 93. **Arthur Lee,** an American lawyer and English agent for the Massachusetts colony (1740–1792). He was an assistant to Benjamin Franklin

kept his eye upon it intently for some time, till he composed himself. His feelings, I dare way, were awkward enough. But he no doubt recollected his having rated me for supposing that he could be at all disconcerted by any company, and he, therefore, resolutely set himself to behave quite as an easy man of the world, who could adapt himself at once to the disposition and manners of those whom he might chance to meet.

The cheering sound of "Dinner is upon the table," dissolved his reverie, and we *all* sat down without any symptom of ill humor. There were present, beside Mr. Wilkes, and Mr. Arthur Lee, who was an old companion of mine when he studied physic at Edinburgh, Mr. (now Sir John) Miller, Dr. Lettsom, and Mr. Slater, the druggist. Mr. Wilkes placed himself next to Dr. Johnson, and behaved to him with so much attention and politeness, that he gained upon him insensibly. No man eat more heartily than Johnson, or loved better what was nice and delicate. Mr. Wilkes was very assiduous in helping him to some fine veal. "Pray give me leave, Sir;—It is better here—A little of the brown—Some fat, Sir—A little of the stuffing—Some gravy—Let me have the pleasure of giving you some butter—Allow me to recommend a squeeze of this orange;—or the lemon, perhaps, may have more zest."—"Sir, Sir, I am obliged to you, Sir," cried Johnson, bowing, and turning his head to him with a look for some time of "surly virtue," but, in a short while, of complacency.

Foote being mentioned, Johnson said, "He is not a good mimic." One of the company added, "A merry Andrew, a buffoon." JOHNSON. "But he has wit too, and is not deficient in ideas, or in fertility and variety of imagery, and not empty of reading; he has knowledge enough to fill up his part. One species of wit he has in an eminent degree, that of escape. You drive him into a corner with both hands; but he's gone, Sir, when you think you have got him—like an animal that jumps over your head. Then he has a great range for wit; he never lets truth stand between him and a jest, and he is sometimes mighty coarse. Garrick is under many restraints from which Foote is free." WILKES. "Garrick's wit is more like Lord Chesterfield's." JOHNSON. "The first time I was in company with Foote was at Fitzherbert's. Having no good opinion of the fellow, I was resolved not to be pleased; and it is very difficult to please a man against his will. I went on eating my dinner pretty sullenly, affecting not to mind him. But the dog was so very comical, that I was obliged to lay down my knife and fork, throw myself back upon my chair, and fairly laugh it out. No, Sir, he was irresistible. He upon one occasion experienced, in an extraordinary degree, the efficacy of his powers of entertaining. Amongst the many and various modes which he tried of getting money, he became a partner with a small-beer brewer, and he was to have a share of the profits for procuring customers amongst his numerous acquaintance. Fitzherbert was one who took his small-beer; but it was so bad that the servants resolved not to drink it. They were at some loss how to notify their resolution, being afraid of offending their master, who they knew liked Foote much as a companion. At last they fixed upon a little black boy, who was rather a favorite, to be their deputy, and deliver their remonstrance; and having invested him with the whole authority of the kitchen, he was to inform Mr. Fitzherbert, in all their names, upon a certain day, that they would drink Foote's small-beer no longer. On that day Foote happened to dine at Fitzherbert's, and this boy served at table; he was so delighted with Foote's stories, and merriment, and grimace, that when he went down stairs, he told them, 'This is the finest man I have ever seen. I will not deliver your message. I will drink his small-beer.'"

Somebody observed that Garrick could not have done this. WILKES. "Garrick would have made the small-beer still smaller. He is now leaving the stage; but he will play *Scrub* all his life." I knew that Johnson would let nobody attack Garrick but himself, as Garrick said to me, and I had heard him praise his liberality; so to bring out his commendation of his celebrated pupil, I said, loudly, "I have heard Garrick is liberal." JOHNSON. "Yes, Sir, I know that Garrick has given away more money than any man in England that I am acquainted with, and that not from ostentatious views. Garrick was very poor when he began life; so when he came to have money, he probably was very unskillful in giving away, and saved when he should not. But Garrick began to be liberal as soon as he could; and I am of opinion, the reputation of avarice which he has had, has been very lucky for him, and prevented his having many enemies. You despise a man for avarice, but do not hate him. Garrick might have been much better attacked for living with more splendor than is suitable to a player: if they had had the wit to have assaulted him in that quarter, they might have galled him more. But they have kept clamoring about his avarice, which has rescued him from much obloquy and envy."

Talking of the great difficulty of obtaining authen-

and afterwards his successor. He helped to negotiate the treaty between France and America (1778). 131. **"surly virtue,"** from Johnson's *London, a Poem,* V, 145—Boswell's note. 133. **Foote,** Samuel Foote (1720–1777), a popular comedian and dramatist. 147. **Lord Chesterfield,** an English earl who was both statesman and author (1694–1773). His manners were elegant, his ethics cynical. 148. **Fitzherbert's,** William Fitzherbert, a friend of Johnson's. 155. **irresistible,** "Foote told me that Johnson said of him 'For loud obstreperous broad-faced mirth, I know not his equal'"—Boswell's note. 160. **small-beer,** weak beer. 182. *Scrub,* a country servant in George Farquhar's *The Beaux' Stratagem* (1707).

tic information for biography, Johnson told us, "When I was a young fellow I wanted to write the 'Life of Dryden,' and in order to get materials, I applied to the only two persons then alive who had seen him; these were old Swinney, and old Cibber. Swinney's information was no more than this, 'That at Will's coffee-house Dryden had a particular chair for himself, which was set by the fire in winter, and was then called his winter-chair; and that it was carried out for him to the balcony in summer, and was then called his summer-chair.' Cibber could tell no more but 'That he remembered him a decent old man, arbiter of critical disputes at Will's.' You are to consider that Cibber was then at a great distance from Dryden, had perhaps one leg only in the room, and durst not draw in the other." BOSWELL. "Yet Cibber was a man of observation?" JOHNSON. "I think not." BOSWELL. "You will allow his 'Apology' to be well done." JOHNSON. "Very well done, to be sure, Sir. That book is a striking proof of the justice of Pope's remark:

'Each might his several province well command, Would all but stoop to what they understand.' "

BOSWELL. "And his plays are good." JOHNSON. "Yes; but that was his trade; l'esprit du corps; he had been all his life among players and play-writers. I wondered that he had so little to say in conversation, for he had kept the best company, and learnt all that can be got by the ear. He abused Pindar to me, and then showed me an ode of his own, with an absurd couplet, making a linnet soar on an eagle's wing. I told him that when the ancients made a simile, they always made it like something real."

Mr. Wilkes remarked, that "among all the bold flights of Shakespeare's imagination, the boldest was making Birnamwood march to Dunsinane; creating a wood where there never was a shrub; a wood in Scotland! ha! ha! ha!" And he also observed, that "the clannish slavery of the Highlands of Scotland was the single exception to Milton's remark of 'The Mountain Nymph, sweet Liberty,' being worshiped in all hilly countries."—"When I was at Inverary (said he,) on a visit to my old friend Archibald, Duke of Argyle, his dependents congratulated me on being such a favorite of his Grace. I said, 'It is then, gentlemen, truly lucky for me; for if I had displeased the Duke, and he had wished it, there is not a Campbell

among you but would have been ready to bring John Wilkes's head to him in a charger. It would have been only

'Off with his head! so much for Aylesbury.'

I was then member for Aylesbury."

Dr. Johnson and Mr. Wilkes talked of the contested passage in Horace's Art of Poetry, "Difficile est propriè communia dicere." Mr. Wilkes, according to my note, gave the interpretation thus: "It is difficult to speak with propriety of common things; as, if a poet had to speak of Queen Caroline drinking tea, he must endeavor to avoid the vulgarity of cups and saucers." But upon reading my note, he tells me that he meant to say, that "the word communia, being a Roman law-term, signifies here things communis juris, that is to say, what have never yet been treated by any body; and this appears clearly from what followed,

'————————Tuque
Rectiùs Iliacum carmen deducis in actus
Quàm si proferres ignota indictaque primus.'

You will easier make a tragedy out of the Iliad than on any subject not handled before." JOHNSON. "He means that it is difficult to appropriate to particular persons qualities which are common to all mankind, as Homer has done."

WILKES. "We have no City-Poet now: that is an office which has gone into disuse. The last was Elkanah Settle. There is something in names which one cannot help feeling. Now Elkanah Settle sounds so queer, who can expect much from that name? We should have no hesitation to give it for John Dryden, in preference to Elkanah Settle, from the names only, without knowing their different merits." JOHNSON. "I suppose Sir, Settle did as well for Aldermen in his time, as John Home could do now. Where did Beckford, and Trecothick learn English?"

Mr. Arthur Lee mentioned some Scotch who had taken possession of a barren part of America, and wondered why they should choose it. JOHNSON. "Why, Sir, all barrenness is comparative. The Scotch would not know it to be barren." BOSWELL. "Come, come, he is flattering the English. You have now been in Scotland, Sir, and say if you did not see meat and drink enough there." JOHNSON. "Why yes, Sir; meat and drink enough to give the inhabitants sufficient strength to run away from home." All these quick and lively sallies

5. **Swinney,** Owen M'Swinney, former manager of Drury Lane, who died in 1754. **Cibber,** Colley Cibber (1671–1757), a popular actor dramatist of the early eighteenth century. *The Apology for the Life of Mr. Colley Cibber* (1740), is his autobiography. 29. **Pindar** (522?–443? B.C.), a Greek lyric poet famous for his odes which he composed for the victors in athletic contests. 30. **showed me.** Johnson had alluded to this episode in a conversation with Boswell at the Mitre Tavern, June 25, 1763. Pindar created superb word pictures, but Cibber's imitations were bombastic. 47. **Campbell,** the Duke of Argylle, head of the

Campbell clan. 51. *Aylesbury.* Wilkes was elected Member of Parliament from Aylesbury in 1757 and 1761. The quotation is a parody of a line in Cibber's adaptation of Shakespeare's *Richard III.* 55. note. Boswell frequently kept notes of Johnson's conversations. 74. **Elkanah Settle,** a poet and dramatist of only average attainments (1648–1724) who became City Poet of London in 1691 through political influence. When an old man he became a pensioner in Charterhouse, where he died. 81. **John Home,** a Scottish dramatist (1722–1808), author of a very popular play, *Douglas* (1756). 82. **Beckford and Trecothick.**

were said sportively, quite in jest, and with a smile, which showed that he meant only wit. Upon this topic he and Mr. Wilkes could perfectly assimilate; here was a bond of union between them, and I was conscious that as both of them had visited Caledonia, both were fully satisfied of the strange narrow igno-
100 rance of those who imagine that it is a land of famine. But they amused themselves with persevering in the old jokes. When I claimed a superiority for Scotland over England in one respect, that no man can be arrested there for a debt merely because another swears it against him; but there must first be the judgment of a court of law ascertaining its justice; and that a seizure of the person, before judgment is obtained, can take place only, if his creditor should swear that he is about to fly from the country, or,
110 as it is technically expressed, is *in meditatione fugæ*: WILKES. "That, I should think, may be safely sworn of all the Scotch nation." JOHNSON. (To Mr. Wilkes) "You must know, Sir, I lately took my friend Boswell, and showed him genuine civilized life in an English provincial town. I turned him loose at Lichfield, my native city, that he might see for once real civility: for you know he lives among savages in Scotland, and among rakes in London." WILKES. "Except when he is with grave, sober, decent people, like
120 you and me." JOHNSON. (smiling) "And we ashamed of him."

Second Meeting with Wilkes (1781)

On Tuesday, May 8 [1781], I had the pleasure of again dining with him and Mr. Wilkes, at Mr. Dilly's. No *negotiation* was now required to bring them together; for Johnson was so well satisfied with the former interview, that he was very glad to meet Wilkes again, who was this day seated between Dr. Beattie and Dr. Johnson; (between *Truth* and *Reason*, as General Paoli said, when I told him of it.)
130 WILKES. "I have been thinking, Dr. Johnson, that there should be a bill brought into parliament that the controverted elections for Scotland should be tried in that country, at their own Abbey of Holy-Rood House, and not here; for the consequence of trying them here is, that we have an inundation of Scotchmen, who come up and never go back again. Now here is Boswell, who is come upon the election for his own county, which will not last a fortnight." JOHNSON. "Nay, Sir, I see no reason why they should
140 be tried at all; for, you know, one Scotchman is as good as another." WILKES. "Pray, Boswell, how much may be got in a year by an Advocate at the Scotch bar?" BOSWELL. "I believe, two thousand pounds." WILKES. "How can it be possible to spend that money in Scotland?" JOHNSON. "Why, Sir, the money may be spent in England; but there is a harder question. If one man in Scotland gets possession of two thousand pounds, what remains for all the rest of the nation?" WILKES. "You know, in the last war, the immense booty which Thurot carried off by the complete 150 plunder of seven Scotch isles; he re-embarked with *three and six-pence*." Here again Johnson and Wilkes joined in extravagant sportive raillery upon the supposed poverty of Scotland, which Dr. Beattie and I did not think it worth our while to dispute.

The subject of quotation being introduced, Mr. Wilkes censured it as pedantry. JOHNSON. "No, Sir, it is a good thing; there is a community of mind in it. Classical quotation is the *parole* of literary men all over the world." WILKES. "Upon the continent they all 160 quote the vulgate Bible. Shakespeare is chiefly quoted here; and we quote also Pope, Prior, Butler, Waller, and sometimes Cowley."

We talked of letter-writing. JOHNSON. "It is now become so much the fashion to publish letters, that, in order to avoid it, I put as little into mine as I can." BOSWELL. "Do what you will, Sir, you cannot avoid it. Should you even write as ill as you can, your letters would be published as curiosities:

'Behold a miracle! instead of wit, 170
See two dull lines with Stanhope's pencil writ.'"

He gave us an entertaining account of *Bet Flint*, a woman of the town, who, with some eccentric talents and much effrontery, forced herself upon his acquaintance. "Bet (said he) wrote her own life in verse, which she brought to me, wishing that I would furnish her with a preface to it. (Laughing.) I used to say of her, that she was generally slut and drunkard;—occasionally, whore and thief. She had, however, genteel lodgings, a spinnet on which she played, and a boy that 180 walked before her chair. Poor Bet was taken up on a charge of stealing a counterpane, and tried at the Old Bailey. Chief Justice ——, who loved a wench, summed up favorably, and she was acquitted. After which, Bet said, with a gay and satisfied air, 'Now that the counterpane is *my own*, I shall make a petticoat of it.'"

Talking of oratory, Mr. Wilkes described it as accompanied with all the charms of poetical expression.

William Beckford (1709–1770), one of the supporters of Wilkes, was Alderman of London and twice Lord Mayor (1762, 1769). Trecothick was another Alderman. Johnson is retorting to Wilkes' criticism of Settle by reminding him that some of his followers rose from very modest beginnings. 98. **Caledonia**, Scotland. 128. **Dr. Beattie**, James Beattie (1735–1803), professor of moral philosophy at Aberdeen, and a poet, author of *The Minstrel* (1771–1774). 129. **General Paoli**, Pasquale Paoli (1725–1807), Corsican general, friend of Boswell. 175. **verse**. Johnson, whose memory was wonderfully retentive, remembered the first four lines of this curious production, which have been communicated to me by a young lady of his acquaintance:
When first I drew my vital breath,
A little minikin I came upon earth;
And then I came from a dark abode,
Into this gay and gaudy world."
—Boswells' note.

JOHNSON. "No, Sir; oratory is the power of beating down your adversary's arguments, and putting better in their place." WILKES. "But this does not move the passions." JOHNSON. "He must be a weak man, who is to be so moved." WILKES. (naming a celebrated orator). "Amidst all the brilliancy of ——'s imagination, and the exuberance of his wit, there is a strange want of *taste*. It was observed of Apelles's Venus, that her flesh seemed as if she had been nourished by roses: 10 his oratory would sometimes make one suspect that he eats potatoes and drinks whisky."

Mr. Wilkes observed, how tenacious we are of forms in this country; and gave as an instance, the vote of the House of Commons for remitting money to pay the army in America *in Portugal pieces*, when, in reality, the remittance is made not in Portugal money, but in our specie. JOHNSON. "Is there not a law, Sir, against exporting the current coin of the realm?" WILKES. "Yes, Sir; but might not the House of Com-
20 mons, in case of real evident necessity, order our own current coin to be sent into our own colonies?"—Here Johnson, with that quickness of recollection which distinguished him so eminently, gave the *Middlesex Patriot* an admirable retort upon his own ground. "Sure, Sir, *you* don't think a *resolution of the House of Commons* equal to the *law of the land*." WILKES. (at once perceiving the application) "GOD forbid, Sir." —To hear what had been treated with such violence in *The False Alarm*, now turned into pleasant repartee,
30 was extremely agreeable. Johnson went on:—"Locke observes well, that a prohibition to export the current coin is impolitic; for when the balance of trade happens to be against a state, the current coin *must* be exported."

Mr. Beauclerk's great library was this season sold in London by auction. Mr. Wilkes said, he wondered to find in it such a numerous collection of sermons: seeming to think it strange that a gentleman of Mr. Beauclerk's character in the gay world, should have
40 chosen to have many compositions of that kind. JOHNSON. "Why, Sir, you are to consider that sermons make a considerable branch of English literature; so that a library must be very imperfect if it has not a numerous collection of sermons: and in all collections, Sir, the desire of augmenting them grows stronger in proportion to the advance in acquisition; as motion is accelerated by the continuance of the *impetus*. Besides, Sir, (looking at Mr. Wilkes with a placid but significant smile,) a man may collect sermons with intention of
50 making himself better by them. I hope Mr. Beauclerk intended that some time or other that should be the case with him."

Mr. Wilkes said to me, loud enough for Dr. Johnson to hear, "Dr. Johnson should make me a present of his *Lives of the Poets*, as I am a poor patriot, who cannot afford to buy them." Johnson seemed to take no notice of this hint; but in a little while, he called to Mr. Dilly, "Pray, Sir, be so good as to send a set of my *Lives* to Mr. Wilkes, with my compliments." This was accordingly done; and Mr. Wilkes 60 paid Dr. Johnson a visit, was courteously received, and sat with him a long time.

The company gradually dropped away. Mr. Dilly himself was called downstairs upon business; I left the room for some time; when I returned, I was struck with observing Dr. Samuel Johnson and John Wilkes, Esq. literally *tête-à-tête*; for they were reclined upon their chairs, with their heads leaning almost close to each other, and talking earnestly, in a kind of confidential whisper, of the personal quarrel between George 70 the Second and the King of Prussia. Such a scene of perfectly easy sociality between two such opponents in the war of political controversy, as that which I now beheld, would have been an excellent subject for a picture. It presented to my mind the happy days which are foretold in Scripture, when the lion shall lie down with the kid.

The Art of Conversation (1783)

Talking of conversation, he said, "There must, in the first place, be knowledge, there must be materials; in the second place, there must be a command of 80 words; in the third place, there must be imagination, to place things in such views as they are not commonly seen in; and in the fourth place, there must be presence of mind, and a resolution that is not to be overcome by failures. This last is an essential requisite; for want of it many people do not excel in conversation. Now I want it; I throw up the game upon losing a trick." I wondered to hear him talk thus of himself, and said, "I don't know, Sir, how this may be; but I am sure you beat other people's cards 90 out of their hands." I doubt whether he heard this remark. While he went on talking triumphantly, I was fixed in admiration, and said to Mrs. Thrale, "Oh, for shorthand to take this down!" "You'll carry it all in your head," said she; "a long head is as good as shorthand."

It has been observed and wondered at, that Mr. Charles Fox never talked with any freedom in the presence of Dr. Johnson, though it is well known, and I myself can witness, that his conversation is 100 various, fluent, and exceedingly agreeable. Johnson's own experience, however, of that gentleman's reserve was a sufficient reason for his going on thus: "Fox never talks in private company; not from any determination not to talk, but because he has not the

29. *The False Alarm*, a political pamphlet written by Johnson in 1770.
35. **Beauclerk**, Topham Beauclerk (1739–1780), a friend of Johnson.

97. **Mr. Charles Fox**, an eminent English statesman and orator (1749–1806). 114. **discovered**, uncovered, revealed. 160. "In . . . Ho-

first motion. A man who is used to the applause of the House of Commons has no wish for that of a private company. A man accustomed to throw for a thousand pounds, if set down to throw for six-pence, would not be at the pains to count his dice. Burke's talk is the ebullition of his mind; he does not talk from a desire of distinction, but because his mind is full." . . .

Kindness (1783)

Johnson's love of little children, which he dis-covered upon all occasions, calling them "pretty dears," and giving them sweetmeats, was an un-doubted proof of the real humanity and gentleness of his disposition.

His uncommon kindness to his servants, and serious concern, not only for their comfort in this world, but their happiness in the next, was another unquestionable evidence of what all who were inti-mately acquainted with him knew to be true.

Nor would it be just, under this head, to omit the fondness which he showed for animals which he had taken under his protection. I never shall forget the indulgence with which he treated Hodge, his cat; for whom he himself used to go out and buy oysters, lest the servants having that trouble should take a dislike to the poor creature. I am, unluckily, one of those who have an antipathy to a cat, so that I am uneasy when in the room with one; and I own, I frequently suffered a good deal from the presence of this same Hodge. I recollect him one day scrambling up Dr. Johnson's breast, apparently with much satis-faction, while my friend smiling and half-whistling, rubbed down his back, and pulled him by the tail; and when I observed he was a fine cat, saying, "Why yes, Sir, but I have had cats whom I liked better than this"; and then as if perceiving Hodge to be out of countenance, adding, "but he is a very fine cat, a very fine cat indeed."

This reminds me of the ludicrous account which he gave Mr. Langton, of the despicable state of a young gentleman of good family. "Sir, when I heard of him last, he was running about town shooting cats." And then in a sort of kindly reverie, he bethought him-self of his own favorite cat, and said, "But Hodge shan't be shot; no, no, Hodge shall not be shot." . . .

Intuition and Sagacity (1784)

He entered upon a curious discussion of the dif-ference between intuition and sagacity; one being immediate in its effect, the other requiring a cir-cuitous process; one he observed was the *eye* of the mind, the other the *nose* of the mind.

A young gentleman present took up the argument against him, and maintained that no man ever thinks of the *nose of the mind*, not adverting that though that figurative sense seems strange to us, as very unusual, it is truly not more forced than Hamlet's "In my *mind's eye*, Horatio." He persisted much too long, and appeared to Johnson as putting himself forward as his antagonist with too much presump-tion; upon which he called to him in a loud tone, "What is it you are contending for, if you *be* con-tending?" And afterwards imagining that the gentle-man retorted upon him with a kind of smart drollery, he said, "Mr. ——, it does not become you to talk so to me. Besides, ridicule is not your talent; you have *there* neither intuition nor sagacity." The gentleman protested that he had intended no improper freedom, but had the greatest respect for Dr. Johnson. After a short pause, during which we were somewhat un-easy, JOHNSON. "Give me your hand, Sir. You were too tedious, and I was too short." MR. ——. "Sir, I am honored by your attention in any way." JOHNSON. "Come, Sir, let's have no more of it. We offended one another by our contention; let us not offend the com-pany by our compliments." . . .

Johnson's Funeral (1784)

A few days before his death, he had asked Sir John Hawkins, as one of his executors, where he should be buried; and on being answered, "Doubt-less, in Westminster Abbey," seemed to feel a satis-faction, very natural to a poet; and indeed in my opinion very natural to every man of any imagination, who has no family sepulcher in which he can be laid with his fathers. Accordingly, upon Monday, De-cember 20, his remains were deposited in that noble and renowned edifice; and over his grave was placed a large blue flag-stone, with this inscription:

SAMUEL JOHNSON, LL.D.
Obiit XIII *die Decembris,*
Anno Domini
M.DCC.LXXXIV.
Aetatis suae LXXV.

His funeral was attended by a respectable number of his friends, particularly such of the members of the Literary Club as were then in town; and was also

---

ratio," spoken by Hamlet in *Hamlet,* I, ii, 185, when he has a vision of his father, who had been murdered some time before. 197. **Literary**

Club, Johnson's famous Circle, which included among others Reynolds, Burke, Garrick, Goldsmith, Boswell, and Gibbon, the historian.

honored with the presence of several of the Reverend Chapter of Westminster. Mr. Burke, Sir Joseph Banks, Mr. Windham, Mr. Langton, Sir Charles Bunbury, and. Mr. Colman, bore his pall. His school-fellow, Dr. Taylor, performed the mournful office of reading the burial service.

I trust, I shall not be accused of affectation, when I declare, that I find myself unable to express all that I felt upon the loss of such a "guide, philosopher,

and friend." I shall, therefore, not say one word of 10 my own, but adopt those of an eminent friend, which he uttered with an abrupt felicity, superior to all studied compositions: "He has made a chasm, which not only nothing can fill up, but which nothing has a tendency to fill up.—Johnson is dead.—Let us go to the next best:—there is nobody; no man can be said to put you in mind of Johnson." . . . (1791)

4. **Dr. Taylor,** Dr. John Taylor, the Prebend of Westminster. 9. **"guide . . . friend."** Cf. Pope's *Essay on Man,* IV, 390 ff.: Shall then this verse to future age pretend

Thou wert my guide, philosopher, and friend?
That, urged by thee, I turned the tuneful art
From sounds to things, from fancy to the heart . . .

Rustic Amusement, c. 1780, by Thomas Gainsborough. Twenty years before Wordsworth, Thomas Gainsborough, in his landscapes and genre paintings, was treating nature and simple life in the Wordsworthian manner.

REVOLUTION AND ROMANCE

From the Death of Samuel Johnson to the Accession

of Queen Victoria, 1784-1837

Chapter Four

Ullswater in the Lake District of northwestern England.

The Age of Revolution

Romanticism has provoked many famous definitions, among them "the renascence of wonder" and "the addition of strangeness to beauty." Such capsule definitions are arresting and useful in that they are memorable, but they must be employed with caution. Romanticism is a perennial way of looking at life; the "romantic period" in English literature is so designated because this particular "world-view" gained a new and revolutionary dominance. Romanticism is inimical to the severely rational; it has warmth where logic has not; it is not restrained by bare fact or scornful of intuition; large, sweeping, and passionate, it is as necessary a part of the human experience as is the purely rational.

Specifically, the romantic urges with intensity that mankind is a vast brotherhood; it stands in awe of man's immense possibilities for both good and evil; it sees the essential beauty as well as the savagery of nature. It praises beauty in all forms; it delights in the comeliness of the body and of the soul alike; it demands the sensuous and the sensitive. It can feel an unrestrained joy in living, or it can grow melancholy at the thought of the inevitable decay and death of all beauty and life. It honors the glories of the past, but it looks to the future with hope and enthusiasm. It resists what it considers arbitrary restraint and tyranny; it rebels against the unfriendly and remorseless logic of facts that oppose it. It brings softness, color, and warmth to life, and a freedom in the range of human feelings, imagination, and expression. It represents, in a word, the triumph of what man would like to be; it can be mankind's escape from unpleasant reality, but it can be also his inspiration to mighty deeds.

In English literature the romantic "movement," which began about 1740 and triumphed at the end of the eighteenth century, is in reality but a return to normal English currents of thought and expression. The neo-classical literature of eighteenth-century England was, in fact, unusual for English literature as a whole. The mind of the Englishman, from the time of the Anglo-Saxon invasions of Britain to the present, has always been given more to emotion and imagination, and less to intellectual balance, logical neatness, and mannered convention, than the arbiters of eighteenth-century taste would have allowed. It is true that for the space of almost a century and a half certain artistic and literary fashions were imposed upon the Englishman, and a distinctive literary style was produced for him to follow, in some cases wholeheartedly, in some cases reluctantly. For almost the first time, he was enabled to write a prose consistently clear, simple, and straightforward; and if his natural predilection for emotional lyrical utterance was temporarily stifled during this period, still he could find compensation in his strengthened grasp upon realities in his writing—in his novel, in his drama of manners, in his penetrating satire, in his discursive essay.

The neo-classical period unquestionably contributed much to the mind of the Englishman. But given the introspective quality, the energy, and the adventurousness of the Anglo-Saxons, the dash and audacity of the Normans, and the quick wit and fancy of the Celts, it is inconceivable that the literary formalities of the neo-classical age could have prevailed for long. A reaction was inevitable, and the seeds of it are to be found implanted within the soil of the neo-classical age itself, in the importance attached by that age to reason and demonstrable truth. *Cogito ergo sum* ("I

James Pollard's "The Liverpool Umpire," c. 1820.

A lady of fashion, from a contemporary fashion plate.

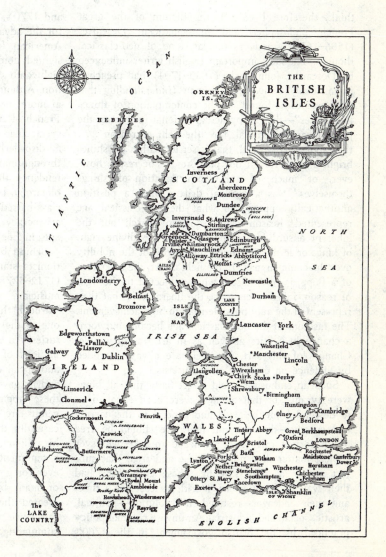

Nature Unimproved and Nature Improved, a contrast between a romantic and a classical treatment of the same landscape. The drawings are by T. Hearne for The Landscape, A Didactic Poem, *by Richard Payne Knight, 1794.*

think, therefore I exist"), the dictum of the great French philosopher and mathematician Descartes (1596–1650), stands as the keystone of neo-classical thought. The most important English writer influenced by Descartes, John Locke (1632–1704), had preached in his *Essay Concerning Human Understanding* that truth was to be found "in the contemplation of things themselves"—that is, by actual rational insight on the part of each individual, for "the light of reason . . . the candle of the Lord, that is set up within us, shines bright enough for all our purposes." The result, however, of much of this "contemplation of things themselves" was a gradual drift toward a position antithetically opposed to what the neo-classical age represented. Reason came soon to search out the inherent absurdities of the belief in the divine right of kings or in the pretended superiority of the nobility over the common man. In the field of art, the assertions of a Pope or an Addison, when subjected to the light of reason, failed to convince the liberal man that they represented the only possible road to high achievement. The fashions of the neo-classical age became outworn; a change in politics as well as in art was inevitable. Changes of this sort, however, are always attended by violence on the part of enthusiasts.

Such an enthusiast could assert flatly that all kings were tyrants, or that all men were born equal, or—to descend from the wide and general to the narrow and specific—that art and literature should be free of all formal rules and privileged to take whatever subject matter they might choose and treat that subject matter as they saw fit. These enthusiasts had their way in the Western World, at least for a time, and their endeavors resulted in revolution—political, artistic, social, and industrial. An unwise colonial policy practiced by the British government in the 1760's

and 1770's, based on the exploitation of the colonies for the advancement of the mother country, led to the American Revolution. Just as inevitably, the short-sighted domination of the French aristocracy in the eighteenth century brought about the French Revolution. Although the American Revolution was ultimately a more nearly complete political overturning, the French Revolution of the 1790's was far more spectacular and violent; it began as the outburst of a disorderly, blindly rebellious mob, and passed through many shapes of blood and fire, with a distinct tendency throughout to the rule of an unscrupulous oligarchy. It had come from a more primitive source— class hatred engendered by a tactless and often brutal aristocracy; it had a deeper emotional effect on the age, in England as well as in France.

Behind both the American and the French revolutionists stands the figure of Jean Jacques Rousseau (1712–1778), at various times churchman, vagabond, musician, social theorist, essayist, and novelist. Through the influence of his ideas, Rousseau became one of the most important men of the last three centuries. An erratic and emotional thinker, he convinced millions of the soundness of his religious, political, and social doctrines. He bred revolution in the state, and he gave a powerful impulse to lyrical poetry; but these apparently unrelated products of Rousseau's genius are not difficult to reconcile if one examines carefully the theories behind all of his writings. In his religion, Rousseau is what can be called technically a sentimental deist. To him, God is a spirit working ever for good—not a supernatural being in the image of man, but a beneficent, paternal force that has created the world and man. Any contemplation of this spirit must necessarily be inspiring, emotionally stimulating, and exalting. Since this creating spirit is manifest in nature and in man, it must follow that man in a natural setting, as free as possible from artificial restraints imposed by the demands of society, is in his happiest possible state. Hence the contemplation of nature, of natural landscape and natural phenomena, was the surest way in which man could approach God; the more primitive man's environment, the closer he was to perfection, which Rousseau and his followers thought by no means impossible of attainment because man, they maintained, was essentially good.

In politics, Rousseau was clearly and instinctively a republican. He was naturally predisposed to insistence on political equality, and although the arguments of his anti-monarchical tract *Contrat social* (1762) were weak, his largely emotional appeal to the masses of sympathetic readers was compelling and for the moment irresistible. Rousseau was not an original thinker or a great formal writer. His novels *La Nouvelle Héloise* (1761) and *Émile* (1762) are mainly valuable for their primitivistic ideas. But he was supreme as a portrayer of the passions of the human heart and of the beauties of nature. No European of the era was a more influential spokesman for the emotional forces underlying the Age of Revolution.

One cannot say how much of the content of Rousseau's work was really original and how much was derived from the ideas of others. It is seldom that one can have such a good subject for the ancient dispute as to whether the man produces the age or the age the man. The nature worship which Rousseau made famous was widespread among the intelligentsia of Europe. Moreover, other intellectual forces besides those of Rousseau were behind the theories of revolu-

tion. There was a group of philosophers, natural scientists, and mathematicians, known as the Encyclopedists (from their part in the production of the great French *Encyclopédie ou Dictionnaire Raisonné des Sciences, des Artes, des Métiers*, 1751-1776), which included the versatile Diderot (1713-1784), the famous critic, philosopher, and man of letters Voltaire (1694–1778), and the mathematician D'Alembert (1717–1783). There was also the German philosopher Immanuel Kant (1724–1804), who, in his *Critique of Pure Reason* (1781), taught that reason has its limitations; when it fails, one must fall back on intuition and instinct. Such men as the Encyclopedists typified the very spirit of the eighteenth century in their preoccupation with natural science and with deistic philosophy, and in their essential grasp of material things. But by their very hold upon realities they encouraged the feeling against royalty, against the social order then existing, against the narrowness of city life; they stimulated the conception of vastness in the cosmic order, and all this helped to produce a new era in thought and feeling.

Along with political revolution and its antecedent philosophical upheaval, another chain of events created a second revolution, purely social and economic, known generally as the Industrial Revolution. Its net effect was to change England from a primarily agricultural nation to one that was primarily industrial and mercantile. During the eighteenth century one man invented the steam engine; another man, the spinning jenny; still another, the power loom. Machines replaced hand labor, and there came the usual problem of unemployment. The factory

The pedestrian hobby-horse, c. 1820.

The romantic fondness for things past is shown in this archway, one of the "Views of Ruins, after the old Roman manner, for the Termination of Walks, Avenues &c." from Batty Langley, New Principles of Gardening, *1728. Such artificial ruins were sometimes called "follies," by the unromantic.*

system was introduced—in itself a complete revolution—and in the hands of self-seeking employers this system brought evils such as excessive, arduous labor by women and children, starvation wages, and sweat shops. Ultimately legislation began to catch up with these inhuman practices, but for a long time the lot of the submerged portion of society was the business of every political economist and critic of society. Although the aristocracy and the middle class as a whole remained inert, if not indifferent, still the agitation for legislative reform to take care of the vast and depressing social problems brought in by the Industrial Revolution was so much fuel for the fire of political dispute. The cry for equality, for the rights of man, for human brotherhood arose in the land; many reformers worked long and hard to bring to reality their desire for the betterment of the condition of mankind. The slave trade in the English colonies was abolished (1807); the penal code was reformed; a more just parliamentary representation was debated and finally enacted (1832). So came the first manifestations of England's awakening humanitarian instinct. Of all the revolutions to be observed in these years, the Industrial Revolution was perhaps ultimately the most important, the most far-reaching. Its effects are still to be felt, and many of the problems it raised have not yet been solved.

In spite of all the political agitation, England herself experienced rather quiet years between 1760 and 1830. Napoleon (1769–1821), of course, posed a constant threat to England from 1800 to 1815. But the country was prosperous and worldly, still ruled by the masculine portion of the landed gentry. Among the upper and middle classes women were sheltered; they were politically negligible everywhere. Education for the majority was poor, but business was good; England

was well on her way to becoming a "nation of shop-keepers." Yet the English, for all their native political conservatism, could not avoid the revolutionary ideas that were in the air. These ideas might be repellent to the prevailing majority, but there were always some to listen and to break the way for a new order. Excluding the more militant advocates of reform, there still remained the critics of society, in both prose and verse, the political and economic theorists, and the occasional revolutionary journalists to keep the ideas of social change current. It is an extremely complicated literary and intellectual product that this age of revolution ultimately brought forth, with many paradoxes and cross-currents of thought and emotion, but the general trend of ideas is toward the liberal and the experimental. The enthusiasm, and the imaginative vigor shown in the literature of the age, if not always in its life, bespeak the dominance of the romantic.

The Approach to Romanticism

The last of several revolutions produced by the eighteenth century was a revolution in literature. For nearly half a century, between 1740 and 1780, neoclassicism in England was dying a lingering death, while romanticism grew stronger and stronger.

Romantic Grief, from Baculard D'Arnaud, Epreuves du Sentiment, *1770.*

Shortly after the appearance of characteristically neo-classical works like the important comedies of the Restoration or the works of Dryden, Swift, or Pope, there can be seen the inception of revolts against the prevailing standards of the neo-classical age in regard to both the subject matter of literature and its forms. The revolt affecting subject matter was for the time being the more considerable. Where the classicists spoke mostly of city life, and, if they mentioned country life at all, dwelt on it but feebly and artificially, the Scotsman James Thomson (p. 629) attempted in *The Seasons* (1726–1730) to describe nature, the outdoors, in its grand, impressive aspects. Thomson's break with neo-classical standards is rather timid; he resorts to many neo-classical clichés, he moralizes at length, but his spirit is that of a man seeking inspiration of soul in Nature the goddess, not as one in city pent, but as one who can ramble in the fields for delight and worship. Thomson's other important contribution was *The Castle of Indolence* (1748), the most famous of many imitations of Spenser, imaginative and sensuous.

This tendency to sensuousness in poetry—a direct appeal to any of the five senses—deepens in the work of such a poet as William Collins (p. 646), whose beautiful *Ode to Evening* represents the gentle, the idyllic side of nature, the fleeting mood evoked by a sylvan scene at sunset.

During the 1740's and 1750's this cultivation of the pensive grew into a cult of the melancholy in nature which contemplated death, the inevitable end, and brooded upon the grave, the final home. The quality of melancholy, one of the most frequent moods entertained by the romantic mind, is found in the work of Collins; it is darkened and heightened into the characteristic "graveyard" poetry of the period in works like the *Night Thoughts* of Edward Young (1683–1765) and Gray's *Elegy Written in a Country Churchyard* (1751); it reached the macabre in *The Grave* by Robert Blair (1699–1746). Grim Nature and Melancholy soon came to walk hand in hand. At the same time there appeared another cult, that of the supernatural in literature; its chief effect, however, was restricted to the novel (p. 624) until the time of Coleridge.

Thomson's *Castle of Indolence* illustrates still another trend of the romantic mind—a reaching out for the glories, either real or imagined, of a past other than that of Greece and Rome, and a clothing of the past in the rosy color of a mystical glamor. Anything old—particularly if it had the additional attraction of primitivism—came to have emotional and imaginative appeal. Not only were Spenser and Milton imitated, but there was also a renewal of interest in popular ballads and medieval romances, the first collection of which was made by Bishop Thomas Percy in his noted *Reliques of Ancient English Poetry* (1765). Other antiquarians, like Thomas Warton (1728–1790) and his brother Joseph (1722–1800), Bishop Richard Hurd (1720–1808), and Thomas Tyrwhitt (1730–1786), by their studies of medieval poetry, chivalry, and romance, laid the foundations for further study, appreciation, and imitation and did much to dispel the eighteenth-century illusion that literate English poetry began with Dryden. Among the imitators of romance and ballad two names particularly deserve mention— James Macpherson (1736–1796) and Thomas Chatterton (1752–1770). In 1760 Macpherson astonished a receptive world with his *Fragments of Ancient Poetry Collected in the Highlands of Scotland,* and followed his success with two epics, *Fingal* (1762) and *Temora* (1763), which he ascribed to a third-century Gaelic bard named Ossian, and which he pretended he had translated from the Gaelic or Erse language. More gifted than Macpherson, Chatterton, "the marvelous boy," produced an amazing collection of ballads and romances which he ascribed to an imaginary fifteenth-century Bristol priest named Thomas Rowley. After failing to impress London, Chatterton committed suicide, at the age of seventeen. Macpherson (or "Ossian") and Chatterton were literary frauds, but they should not be dismissed lightly. Even in their hoaxes is contained important evidence of a persistent romantic return to the past.

Still another manifestation of the romantic in the subject matter of eighteenth-century English literature was the appearance of an interest in individual man, particularly the downtrodden. This humanitarian interest with occasional sentimental and idyllic tones, appears in Oliver Goldsmith's *The Deserted Village* (p. 562), but the sincere and realistic George Crabbe (1754–1832), who in his heroic couplets and occasional formal phrases seems the last outpost of neo-classicism, had an interest in humble life which was romantic in its depth and intensity. A village doctor, Crabbe chose

> to paint the cot
> As Truth will paint it, and as bards will not.

The same humanitarian spirit is to be found in many of Burns' poems (p. 653), in Cowper's *The Task* (p. 648), and especially in the songs of Blake (p. 673). As in the case of antiquarianism, the truly significant humanitarian literature of the age appears in the novel.

Although love is one of the most important of emotions, there are no great love poets in the eighteenth century until we get to Robert Burns, the greatest in English literature. But both the verse of friendship—the easy table-chat of an intimate—and the poetry of an emotionally religious soul are represented in the work of William Cowper (p. 647), with

The Task (1785), and the famous *Olney Hymns* (1779). As for religious poetry, there was a steady trickle of hymns from the days of Nahum Tate in the Restoration down to the days of the unhappy Cowper, the "stricken deer" who was driven by his religious frenzy from the ordinary course of life. Indeed, hymn writing had come to stay throughout the nineteenth century. Its appearance and its rapid development in the middle of the eighteenth century can be traced to the inevitable reaction against the intellectual and comfortless concept of God as a spirit detached and indifferent—the deism of the neo-classical philosophy. The movement known as Methodism originated at Oxford in 1729, under the inspiration of John Wesley (1703–1791) and his brother Charles (1707–1788), and developed after 1738 into an emotional, evangelical type of religion which demanded that every believer be converted to a new life. The influence of the Wesleys upon English religious verse cannot be overestimated; their lyrics stand in sharp contrast to both the sacred verse of the Middle Ages and the metaphysical verse of the seventeenth century, chiefly because the Wesleyan hymn is a direct appeal to the feelings, not too mystical on the one hand and not too full of conceits on the other.

The new romantic tendencies in English poetry were carried to their highest level of achievement in the eighteenth century by three writers of extraordinary talent: Thomas Gray (1716–1771), Robert Burns (1759–1796), and William Blake (1757–1827).

Thomas Gray, whose *Elegy Written in a Country*

Two views of the royal pavilion at Brighton, one before and one after alterations, from John Nash, The Royal Pavilion at Brighton, *1825. The classical lines of the original (below) were altered and expanded in the romantic style (above) by Nash for George IV.*

Churchyard is easily one of the best-known poems in English, combined in his work an eye for nature, a sense of the past, and a keen awareness of the lot of humble men. He had been schooled in the traditions of neo-classicism, and the marks of neo-classicism are perceptible in all of his work; but he was also a poet of individual inspiration. He saw the world pictorially and pensively; and for his work he stands out "the scantiest and frailest of classics in our poetry," according to Matthew Arnold, "but still . . . a classic."

Robert Burns was the "people's poet" of the century. Of peasant stock, he understood the passions and deprivations and genuine accent of the poor; of sturdy stock, he gave no quarter to maudlin sentimentality. He had, both as a man and as a poet, a tremendous zest for life and an unswerving insight into the nature of truth and justice. Hence he could write supreme poetic statements of love and friendship on the one hand and scathing satires of hypocrisy, almost brutal in their relentlessness, on the other. No matter what the type, the stamp of originality is upon nearly every poem Burns wrote, especially those written in his own Scottish dialect on matters close to the daily life of Scotland.

William Blake is somewhat more difficult to understand and far more difficult to analyze. He is the thoroughgoing mystic; for him God and all the angels are immediate realities; he seems to live at times in another world and to speak in an unearthly voice. Although neglected in his day, Blake has grown steadily in stature since that time, and today many place him among the greatest of English poets.

To read with understanding the romantically inclined poets of the eighteenth century from Thomson to Burns and Blake is to appreciate at once the fact that they had at least touched all the important themes dear to the heart of the English romanticist and had freely developed many of them. They had expressed, with varying emphasis, the love of nature in all her aspects; the love of mankind and of country; the yearning for the remote in space and time, with particular reference to the medieval and the primitive; the passion of the poet's own inmost thoughts and feelings—restless, unsatisfied, ever changing; the contemplation of death and the awesome terror inspired by the thoughts of eventual dissolution, complicated by the revival of the age-old interest in the supernatural. This varied and spectacular subject matter had been treated with imaginative warmth and fire, and with different degrees of emotional intensity. But all the writers except Burns were intent—sporadically in the case of men like Thomson, permanently in the case of men like Blake—on creating a new kind of reality, a reality that neglected superficial fact for underlying truth. Such is the very essence of the romantic. All but Blake had been more or less hampered by the fraying bonds of neo-classicism, which were tending to slip away entirely with the passing of time, and none except Blake was completely free. Burns may have come nearest to ridding himself of the neo-classical tradition; but others who were romantic in affinity continued to use many of the conventions of neo-classical style.

The Romantic Triumph in Poetry

At the end of the century, a declaration of independence of the romantic writers remained to be written. Moreover, there had been as yet no important body of poetry running deliberately counter to the immediate past, except, perhaps, for that of Blake and a few poems by Burns. William Wordsworth and Samuel Taylor Coleridge were responsible for both parts of this necessary groundwork. Their verse at the beginning of their careers was largely complementary. Their volume of poems done in collaboration, the famous *Lyrical Ballads* (1798), is one of the most important landmarks in the history of English literature. Wordsworth's portion of the first edition was a group of balladlike poems, simple in diction, plain in style, given to rustic scenes and rustic characters, recurring to the tutelage of nature; and, in addition, the superb contemplative poem *Tintern Abbey*, proclaiming in magnificent blank verse the characteristic absorptions and worship of the

This English bedroom of the Georgian period (1760-1775) reflects the contemporary interest in the oriental, and the style of decoration is called "Chinese Chippendale." From the Thorne European Rooms in Miniature, by courtesy of The Art Institute of Chicago.

true romantic. Coleridge's contribution was the supernatural imaginative literary ballad *The Rime of the Ancient Mariner*, notable for its weird, unearthly atmosphere, and its inspired aptness of phrasing—a poem in its way unmatched in English literature. The *Lyrical Ballads* caused laughter in some quarters and indifference in others, but the authors' purpose justified a second edition in 1800, to which Wordsworth wrote a long preface (p. 703), the reading of which is indispensable for a knowledge of the work of the two men and for an appreciation of the distance which poetry had traveled since the days of Alexander Pope.

This *Preface* to the *Lyrical Ballads* contains two extremely important passages. One describes the characteristically romantic conception of the nature and origin of poetry. To quote Wordsworth, "poetry is the spontaneous overflow of powerful feelings: it takes its origin from emotion recollected in tranquillity; the emotion is contemplated till, by a species of reaction, the tranquillity gradually disappears, and an emotion, kindred to that which was before the subject of contemplation, is gradually produced, and does itself actually exist in the mind." The author then explains that the mind of the poet, whatever the emotion, will be "on the whole, in a state of enjoyment." The second passage of importance is the statement of the ideals underlying the composition of the *Lyrical Ballads*. "The principal object, then, proposed in these poems was to choose incidents and situations from common life, and to relate or describe them, throughout, as far as possible in a selection of language really used by men, and at the same time to throw over them a certain coloring of the imagination, whereby ordinary things should be presented to the mind in an unusual aspect; and, further, and above all, to make these incidents and situations interesting by tracing in them, truly though not ostentatiously, the primary laws of our nature. . . . Humble and rustic life was generally chosen, because, in that condition, the essential passions of the heart find a better soil in which they can attain their maturity, are less under restraint, and speak a plainer and more emphatic language." The truth of the language of common man and the life of that common man were to Wordsworth "more philosophical" matters than "that which is frequently substituted for it by poets," that is, the neo-classical poets.

Wordsworth was sincerely convinced that his theory would make for greater truth and would hence develop greater art. He therefore wrote a multitude of poems in conformity to that theory—some of them angular, homely, fatally unhumorous, even ridiculous.

His many failures should deservedly be allowed to die. On the other hand, poems such as *The Solitary Reaper*, *I Wandered Lonely as a Cloud*, and *My Heart Leaps Up* are not likely soon to pass away. Fully as striking are his longer poems—*Tintern Abbey*, *Ode on Intimations of Immortality*, and parts of his autobiographical poems, *The Prelude* and *The Excursion*. These, together with his many fine sonnets, are magnificent departures from his theory, for in them his poetic flights, unusual in their loftiness and strength, demand—and receive—an utterance beyond the ordinary.

Wordsworth and Coleridge had, as friends in Somersetshire, in Germany, and later in the Lake Country (cf. p. 679), been students of the German philosopher Immanuel Kant (1724–1804), whose *Critique of Pure Reason* has already been mentioned (p. 611). Both were familiar with Plato and his doctrine of the ideal, but the effect of Plato can be seen primarily in Wordsworth. Coleridge, who had much the better reasoning mind, was an insatiable student of philosophy, and his brain teemed with ideas on philosophical and religious questions. It was a remarkable intellect—the mind of Coleridge—and a highly poetic one. In sheer poetic imagination, Coleridge was the superior of Wordsworth; one can but deplore the unsteadiness and indolence of his temperament, which could, however, almost in spite of itself, produce fitful flashes of the highest kind of poetry, such as *Kubla Khan*, *Christabel*, and *The Rime of the Ancient Mariner* (pp. 730, 723, and 714). Romantic English literature

"Children Bathing," portraits of Hoppner's children, from a mezzotint by James Ward after Hoppner.

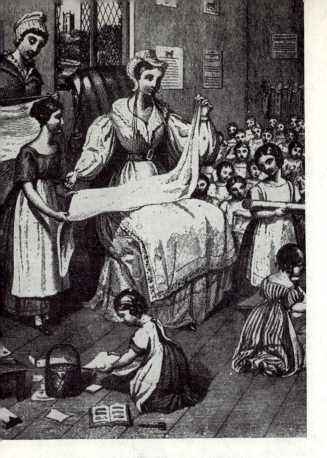

A dame school of the early nineteenth century.

rests more upon his novels than upon his poetry. And yet in his day he did a great service to romanticism in verse, both in his original narrative poems like *The Lay of the Last Minstrel* (1805) and in his revivals of ancient traditional Scottish songs and ballads. Although Scott did not reach the poetic heights of some of his contemporaries, on the whole his output was remarkably even, vigorous, and of a generally high level.

It was the misfortune of the older group of romantic poets—Wordsworth, Coleridge, and Scott—to be separated from the younger group of Byron, Shelley, and Keats by a yawning chasm, the chasm of the misunderstanding of older men by younger. Byron, in his first important work, the satirical *English Bards and Scotch Reviewers* (p. 741), pays his disrespects to all three. Wordsworth is to him a "mild apostate from poetic rule," simple, and inclined to the idiotic; Coleridge is obscure and "to turgid ode and tumid stanza dear"; Scott is a writer "of stale romance." These unflattering sentiments Byron repeated in his last work, *Don Juan,* with equal vehemence; it cannot, therefore, be urged that the insults hurled at the older romantics in *English Bards and Scotch Reviewers* spring from callow, impudent intolerance. Indeed, Byron expressed himself privately as dissatisfied with this new scheme of poetry on which the romantics were busy; he said that it "was not worth a damn in itself." It is easy to see that Byron is at least half a neo-classicist; his whiplash satire and his avowed admiration of Pope and Dryden make that clear. *Don Juan,* when viewed as a whole, is one of the great satires in English literature. Moreover, there is in Byron an eminently practical streak, earthy and coarse, that may lead at times to pedestrian poetry, but may also bring balance and critical acumen.

Nevertheless, the glamorous personality that is Byron can be almost wholly romantic. In his *Childe Harold* and in the series of oriental tales, he created the "Byronic hero," a type of young man who is moody, melodramatic, violent, tender, sinister, passionate, but restless and unsatisfied—a portrait of Byron himself. Furthermore, many of Byron's early poems are redolent of the sheer perfume of romanticism; such lines as

She walks in beauty, like the night
Of cloudless climes and starry skies

need no special interpreter to transmit their sensuous imagery and the emotional force of the pictures which they conjure up. As Byron developed, the satirical outlook in his poems became more and more prominent, but there is one romantic trait in his character that does not fade, a trait which is sincere to the very core—his love of human liberty, for which he never ceased to fight in his dashing, spectacular, half-posing manner. This love of liberty is the obverse of

owes Coleridge much for his achievements in supernatural and exotic poetry, fragmentary as those achievements too often are.

Both Wordsworth and Coleridge began as revolutionists, not only in literature but also in their philosophy of life. Coleridge at one time was even so carried away by the idea of a natural community free from restraints that he and Robert Southey conceived the idea of a "pantisocracy," or group of individuals living in a communistic and primitivistic way. But later he, like Wordsworth and the great mass of English citizenry, gradually became opposed to revolutionism because of the excesses of the French Revolution and its complete disavowal of God and the state. Wordsworth became virtually a recluse; Coleridge, the springs of his poetry dried up early through indolence and an unfortunate addiction to opium, settled in London, talked incessantly, and planned vast projects. These two men, and the other lesser lights of poetry like Southey, the poet laureate, withdrew within themselves. Having sounded the battle cry of new forms, new standards in poetry, they left the active warfare to younger men.

To that elder generation of romantic poets also belongs Sir Walter Scott (1771–1832). It is not customary to think of Scott as a great poet; his reputation

his hatred of tyranny, which he exaggerated into utter contempt for the English government of his day and into exceedingly faint praise for Napoleon, the terror of Europe. Even a casual reading of *Childe Harold* and *Don Juan*, the two great Byronic documents, will reveal the true revolutionism of Byron, which is a moderate republicanism. To put the matter in a different way, Byron greatly admired Washington and the type of revolution which he represented; he was suspicious of Rousseau, referring to him very accurately as a "self-torturing sophist," whose ardent frenzy against tyranny had made of France "a fearful monument." Exactly how much of this revolutionism of Byron was caused by his own personal misfortunes (p. 739) will never be known; but undoubtedly a great deal of it, for Byron was a tremendous egoist. He was the greatest individualist of the age, a world figure, whose influence outside England was greater than that of any other poet of his time. This influence originated partly from the magnetism of his personality and partly from the boldness of his strokes, his impetuousness, his emotional drive. The world might not learn much from Byron but could not fail to feel his presence. The careful critic might point out that Byron's workmanship left much to be desired, that his sense of the delicate in phrase and imagery was often sadly deficient, that he was earthy in spite of all his romance; but such criticism had no effect then and is not a great deterrent now. He is still admired because he possessed a tumultuous force, a sense of humor, and a devastating worldliness that the other great poets of the age lacked, even while they might surpass him in sheer poetic insight and technique.

Shelley, who loved Byron, was his opposite in almost every point except rebelliousness. No more passionate, self-convinced visionary exists in English literature; and it is doubtful that Shelley could be matched exactly in any other literature. Like every true Platonist, he had seen, once upon a time, Heaven open up before him; and the radiant vision was at once his ideal, the objective of his life and art—and his torment when he saw how far humanity fell short of Heaven. His childlike outlook, pathetically naïve, sublimely contemptuous of harsh realities, led Shelley to writhe at the mere suggestion of discipline, restraint, or law, which he considered tyrannous. This completely anti-social attitude came in part from his bringing up, in part from his school days, and in part from his association with Rousseauistic doctrines, particularly with those preached by William Godwin. Shelley's life was wrecked by the subversive forces in his philosophy, by his flouting of civil obligations, and most of all by his inability to let two and two equal four and live at peace with his neighbors.

Nevertheless, the doctrines of Shelley, however tragic their effect upon his personal life, gave him the vision sublime; it was in recapturing that vision, in seeking for the broken lights of that radiance and implanting it in man's soul that Shelley spent his life as a poet. No considerable piece of his poetry can fail to show his haunting, wistful quest. The *Hymn to Intellectual Beauty*, *The Sensitive Plant*, *The Cloud*, *To a Skylark* illustrate his refined sensitivity to beauty in nature, a beauty which transcends physical limitations and soars into the spiritual. Shelley regarded spiritual beauty, which is permanent and true, as the only real beauty. Only its shadow falls upon earth; the love of it is the light which illumines all worth while existence. His longer poems like *The Witch of Atlas*, *Prometheus Unbound*, or *Hellas* bring a violent revolutionary spirit, which demands political and social upheaval, into contact with this Platonic system of beauty; the harmonizing element here is poetically demonstrated in *Prometheus Unbound* to be love—the love of humanity, the New Testament conception of "charity." And so Shelley, to his generation a loathsome atheist, was in his teachings often more akin to Christ than was any other poet of his time.

In Shelley's shorter poems, the characteristic stamp of Platonic philosophy is evident, but here the poet's supreme lyric gifts are most important. Few English poets have been able to approach Shelley in melody, in finished harmony and sound effect, in fluency, fire, and intensity. A good reading of his *To Night* is virtually a demonstration of all the possibilities of the lyric. In all his poetry, Shelley is speaking directly for his poetic generation; nowhere could a better distillation of the essence of the romantic be found than in

The desire of the moth for the star,
Of the night for the morrow,
The devotion to something afar
From the sphere of our sorrow.

If this desire was too hopelessly visionary, and if he sank into moments of the most intense melancholy, still Shelley could rejoice, as in *Adonais*, that the soul seeking beauty could find it in the loveliness of nature, in the contemplation of poetry, and in the thought that

Life, like a dome of many-colored glass,
Stains the white radiance of Eternity.

A third member of the younger generation of romantic poets, and in some ways the greatest poet of the three, was John Keats (p. 784). Keats, like Shelley, had a profound love of abstract beauty, but he could also worship the warm, pulsing beauty of the earthly; both the physical charm of landscape and of humanity could inspire him to rare bursts of poetic passion. It is idle to seek in Keats for the element of revolt seen in Byron and Shelley. It is, of course, true that he was in complete opposition to the neo-classical stiffness of form and preciseness of thought that had characterized the preceding century. If he took the heroic couplet as a medium, he would unclose it, as in *Endymion* (p. 787). He poured upon the *Ode on a Grecian Urn* (p. 789) a luxuriant sensuousness that the neo-classical poet would scarcely have comprehended and would certainly have rejected. (It is ironic to note that this delight in color and sense appeal was far more Greek than anything the neo-classical age produced.) An avowed admirer of Spenser, Keats was one of the greatest pictorial poets in world literature, whose sense of color and imagery, of light and shade, and of sight and sound was almost unerringly right. Allowances must perhaps be made for his earlier work, such as *Endymion*, which exhibits a lack of restraint in the exercise of his almost prodigal powers of sensuous appeal, a fault which he himself recognized and sought successfully to rectify. Keats was the great exemplar of the pensive and the passive strains in English romanticism; he had no banner to unfurl, as did Shelley, no foes to crush, as did Byron; all he demanded was the opportunity to contemplate the beautiful and the significant, the meanings beneath mere externality and flux which were to him the ultimate reality. In the contemplation thus granted him he came to a philosophy both deep and fragile—fragile to the skeptic and the pragmatist, deep to the sympathetic student of beauty. Logic and cold reason have little place in any appraisal of Keats; instead there must be a surrender to imaginative participation, perhaps akin to what Coleridge once called the "willing suspension of disbelief."

Keats, indeed, has much in common with Coleridge. He has the same interest in the medieval, as *The Eve of St. Agnes* demonstrates; he has also the same witchery in ballad technique, as *La Belle Dame sans Merci* so brilliantly shows. His magnificent odes (*Ode to Melancholy, Ode on a Grecian Urn, Ode to a Nightingale, To Autumn*), like the short poems of Shelley and of Wordsworth, capture in masterful fashion the soul of romanticism. The song of the nightingale, the melancholy autumn days (touched here with a wholesomeness quite outside the traditional), the domain of unreality "in faery lands forlorn"—all are more significant to one seeking a definition of the romantic than many paragraphs of objective exposition. One of the most convincing proofs of Keats' genius is the fact that his works can bear repeated reading; his finest poems do not lead to surfeit or exhaustion, for they have an inevitableness of expression which only great poetry can possess. And so Keats, the youngest of the three younger romantic poets of importance, and the first of the three to die a premature and tragic death, comes in

A typical Regency house, on the Promenade in Cheltenham, c. 1825.

A Regency rotunda and library (1810-1820), from the Thorne European Rooms in Miniature, by courtesy of The Art Institute of Chicago.

his last years to represent a culmination of the English romantic poetry in the early nineteenth century. It is his influence that dominates the early days of the first great poet of the coming Victorian era, Alfred, Lord Tennyson (p. 841); it is Keats' decorativeness and sensuous artistry and Wordsworth's nature poetry that serve as the bridge between the romantic age and the next generation.

The entire period from the publication of the *Lyrical Ballads* (1798) until the appearance of Tennyson's first poems in 1832—the year that saw the death of Sir Walter Scott—was one of great poetic activity, especially in the field of lyric poetry. The drama in this period is on the whole negligible; the professional drama is beneath contempt. Yet many of the great poets of the period—Wordsworth, Coleridge, Byron, Shelley, and Keats—tried their hands at dramatic poetry. The many closet dramas that resulted were often beautiful in their poetry but technically unactable. Two brilliant exceptions should be noted: Byron's *Manfred* (1817) and Shelley's *The Cenci* (1820). Perhaps the romantic poets were too absorbed in psychological self-anatomy, too subjectively rooted, to be successful in a medium which depends on action and external representation.

The Waltz, a cartoon of 1812.

Romantic Prose—Imaginative, Critical, Revolutionary

Although it could hardly be expected that an age which was pre-eminent in lyric poetry would excel in prose, some remarkable prose writers flourished between 1795 and 1832, and several prose types came to maturity during this period. Excluding for the moment writers of the novel, one can find a body of prose essays impressive in bulk and often impressive in quality.

The background of these essays can be better understood if one pauses to consider briefly the rise of the periodical in the later years of the eighteenth century. The development of periodical writing was one of the greatest contributions of the neo-classical age. The appearance of newspaper-like periodicals, of which *The Tatler* and *The Spectator* were examples, was followed by the beginning of a few more varied and more casual prose collections that could be called magazines, such as *The Gentleman's Magazine*, starting in 1731. But it is rather difficult to think of these periodicals as magazines in the modern sense, for they usually were strongly political in their interests and hence catered to certain groups. As the eighteenth century rolled along, the newspapers increased in importance, while the "magazines" languished. With the first of the nineteenth century, however, came a group of periodicals which gave a real impetus to literature; they served as a means of publishing not only essays on all sorts of subjects, but a considerable amount of poetry, and even some fiction. In many ways, they bore a very close resemblance to the modern magazine.

At the head of the list of such enterprises stood *The Political Register* (1802), which was founded by William Cobbett (1762–1835) and dedicated chiefly to economic and social problems. Next came the famous *Edinburgh Review* (1802), an aggressive, hard-hitting periodical which was directed by Sidney Smith (1771–1845) and Francis Jeffrey (1773–1850). The policy of the editors of the *Edinburgh* in literary matters was very conservative; they could hardly be expected to hail with delight such a radical change in poetry as Wordsworth and Coleridge introduced, and they treated it with harshness. Next in time, and equal in importance, came the *Quarterly Review* (1809) the editor of which was William Gifford (1756–1826), a literary Tory and a vigorous opponent of romanticism. Paradoxically, Gifford numbered among his contributors Sir Walter Scott and Robert Southey. Leigh Hunt's *Examiner* (1808) by contrast had pronounced radical tendencies, but he himself trod upon the toes of royalty and was imprisoned for a time. *Blackwood's Magazine* (1817), directed by John Wilson, or "Christopher North" as he preferred to be

An Evening at Vauxhall, from Pierce Egan, Life in London, *1821, illustrated by J. R. and George Cruikshank.*

known (1785–1854), was another stronghold of Tory conservatism in literature. Its virulent attacks upon Keats have become notorious and have been ridiculously blamed by sentimentalists for Keats' death from tuberculosis. *Blackwood's* had a greater variety of offerings than its predecessors; it even began to include fiction.

Thus far, with the notable exception of Leigh Hunt's abortive *Examiner*, most of the magazines of the early 1800's were conservative, decrying the attempts of younger poets to break away from older tastes and literary habits. *The London Magazine* (1820), however, gave real encouragement to the finest romantic writers in the age. It came to bear the burden of developing a new creative spirit, an honor it later shared with *Fraser's Magazine* (1830). But both types of periodicals had their functions. The controversy in the older magazines formed the foundation for the finished product of the period's three outstanding prose writers: Lamb, Hazlitt, and De Quincey. Each was a critic of life as well as literature. Lamb, the book lover, the city-dweller by preference, wrote as a kind of avocation, for he earned his living in business. The casual nature of his literary activity does much to explain the abiding charm of his writings. The *Essays of Elia*, which appeared in *The London Magazine* between 1820 and 1823, to be published in book form later, are among the finest of English personal essays—whimsical, quaint, humorous, tender, dreamy, and sad. Comment on their romantic

quality is perhaps superfluous; one need only perceive their subjective nature to understand how thoroughly Lamb is a product of his romantic age. The very titles of his better-known essays are suggestive: *The Two Races of Men* (borrowers and lenders), *Old China, A Chapter on Ears, Valentine's Day, Poor Relations, Dream-Children.* Here is none of the formal preciseness, even primness, of an Addison; or the pithy penetration of a Lord Bacon. In his sentimentality, Lamb most nearly approaches Steele, but Steele was equipped with a neo-classical style. Lamb was not; he was a free, almost erratic writer of prose which can pause, leap, or linger at will. His content, viewed as a whole, is never so important as the way in which he treats it; he lends everlasting conviction to the statement that romance is never so much a material thing as an attitude or an approach.

The informal, personal essay in the hands of Hazlitt reveals the harsher, more acrid character of its writer. There is nothing of a lovable quality in Hazlitt; he is a vigorous and direct speaker, and one of varied interests. In his informal moments, Hazlitt is fully as self-revealing as Lamb; the difference between the two, apart from their personal divergences, is that Hazlitt is more bookish, more satirical, less ingratiating. His style is more formal than Lamb's; it could be called at times pedantic. Yet it shows strength and finish and feeling. A look at the titles of some of Hazlitt's better essays will give an idea of the nature of his subjects: *On Going a Journey, On the*

Pleasures of Hating, On the Fear of Death, On Reading New Books, On the Feeling of Immortality in Youth, The Fight. There is more love of adventure in Hazlitt than in most of his prose contemporaries outside of the novel; he is a lean, wiry kind of writer with intellectual and artistic sensibilities and acquisitiveness.

De Quincey's personal essays are markedly different from those of either Lamb or Hazlitt. He is, in effect, a poet in prose—he called himself a writer of "impassioned prose"—who must necessarily be romantic in his approach. Like Coleridge, De Quincey was for a time addicted to opium; he writes of the effect of the drug in his brilliant *Confessions of an English Opium Eater* (1821).

It is extremely difficult to make a synthesis of the creative work of these three fine writers; each is highly individualistic and must be read for his own sake to be fully appreciated. If one turns to the literary criticism that was written by these three, the task is easier, for there is common agreement among them as to their literary idols. They all owe much to Coleridge's able work in the fields of both literary criticism and philosophical writing.

Coleridge too was a prose writer of great importance. The most distinguished literary critic of his day, he was interested not only in the practice of criticism but in its theory as well. He was opposed to the rational, mechanistic, and materialistic philosophies which lay at the root of neo-classicism and was under the general spell of Kant and other German thinkers in professing certain idealistic convictions in ethics, politics, and literature. Hence his criticism tends to stress a work's spirituality, organicism, and generative faculty of the imagination much more than its material content or didactic value. In addition to his penetrating prose formulations on poetry and the creative process in *Biographia Literaria* and elsewhere, Coleridge was also a resuscitator of Shakespearean criticism. He was more responsible, probably, than any other single person for the change in Shakespeare's reputation. The object of rather reserved, sometimes condescending approval in the neo-classical age, the great Elizabethan poet and dramatist became the recipient of the whole-souled admiration of the nineteenth century. Coleridge's analyses of *Hamlet* and of Iago in *Othello* mark the high point of his Shakespearean criticism. His other literary lectures and the *Table Talk* of his later years show the acuity of his mind and his attractive loquaciousness. In sum, he set a fashion in criticism opposed both to the severe appraisals in which some of the neo-classical critics had indulged and to the shallow reviewing of many contemporary journalists.

One of Coleridge's major motivations as a critic was the result of his perception that a mechanical, literal, slavish approach to literary texts was inimical to the "magical power" of imaginative literature. In *Confessions of an Enquiring Spirit*, published posthumously in 1840, he applied the same critical values to the literature of the Bible. In this work, far ahead of its time when published and actually written more than two decades earlier, he sought to "save" the Bible from its literal advocates by advocating, in his turn, its moral relevance and imaginative profundity. Matthew Arnold, more than fifty years after Coleridge, carried the same approach further in *Literature and Dogma* (1873).

Coleridge's work was supplemented and expanded by the brilliant three—Lamb, Hazlitt, and De Quincey. Lamb, in his *Tales from Shakespeare* (1807), written in collaboration with his sister Mary, popularized the plays of the great dramatist; his annotated collection, *Specimens of English Dramatic Poets* (1808), did much for the fame of Marlowe, Heywood, Ben Jonson, and others from the spacious times of great Elizabeth. Furthermore, Lamb conceived a literary passion for the seventeenth-century prose writers like Thomas Browne, Thomas Fuller, and Jeremy Taylor; no doubt it was through his efforts that the elaborate, often strained, effects of these writers came to earn such exalted and even exaggerated praise during the rest of the century. Hazlitt's contributions in the Shakespearean field are comprised in *Characters of Shakespeare's Plays* (1817), notable for his fine study of Hamlet, and many lectures on Elizabethan literature that are terse and salty. His interests throughout the whole range of English literature were considerable; he was a remarkably well-read man, and not in the least backward about parading his command of his reading. In an essay like *On Familiar Style* (1821), he pleads for a freedom and informality of style which is at the same time to be kept free from vulgarity. As for De Quincey, his Shakespearean criticism is rather informal; the best-known piece is *On the Knocking at the Gate in Macbeth* (1823). A kind of critical writing of a more general sort is illustrated in his *The Poetry of Pope*, published in the *North British Review* as late as 1848; it contains the section, "The Literature of Knowledge and the Literature of Power," which sums up most convincingly the essential differences between the classical and the romantic minds. All three of these lieutenants of Coleridge in the army of literary critics had penetration, a persuasive style, and that most helpful asset for the convincing writer—entire sympathy with their subject.

The social critics are also numerous. Early in the era (1776) came Adam Smith's *Wealth of Nations*, a landmark in the history of economic thought, a kind of masterwork in the analysis of the capitalistic system of society. Thomas Malthus (1766–1834) believed that the population of the world would increase to the saturation point unless forces tending to check the spread of population, such as wars and disease, should be allowed to operate toward that end. Jeremy Bentham (1748–1832), with his doctrine of "the greatest good for the greatest number" and his constant testing of an idea or invention by the simple question, "What's the use of it?" (the "utilitarian" viewpoint), was perhaps the most practically democratic theorist of his time. William Cobbett (1762–1835) was the champion of the working man and of Parliamentary reform. Beside the work of Smith stands that of William Godwin and of his wife Mary Wollstonecraft (1759–1797). They were pioneer radicals, imbued

The North Front of Strawberry Hill.

The Gallery at Strawberry Hill. Horace Walpole's villa at Strawberry Hill is one of the best examples of romantic Gothicism; from A Description of the Villa of Mr. Horace Walpole at Strawberry Hill . . . , 1774.

A gentleman of fashion: Count Alfred D'Orsay, a drawing by Daniel Maclise (c. 1830).

with Rousseauism; they were intellectual and philosophical anarchists, who attacked all government and restraints upon human beings and advocated complete revolution, not by violence, but by the application of reason to all social problems. Their influence upon Wordsworth and Coleridge was profound, particularly through Godwin's *Enquiry Concerning Political Justice* (1793) and his *Caleb Williams* (1794). As for Shelley, later Godwin's son-in-law, a great many of his early views, revolutionary and socialistic, were derived from the Godwin circle.

The prose of this romantic age will probably never have the popular appeal of the poetry, notwithstanding the attractiveness to the general public of such a man as Lamb. The things that romanticism represents, the usually outspoken cravings of the human soul, are from their very nature more adapted to poetry than to prose. But it is well to remember that even the prose writers of the age have remarkable poetic insight; they have enthusiasm and charm, and when read in comfortable amounts, a considerable power of inspiration.

The Romantic Novel

Until some mention of the romantic novel has been made, the story of the romantic prose writers is only half told. Like all other types of literature written during this romantic age, the novel of emotional and imaginative appeal must be traced back to the middle of the eighteenth century. Richardson, in *Pamela* and his other novels, had set in motion the novel of character analysis; Fielding had brought the novel of incident and of character into equipoise; Smollett had given to the novel of incident a maritime and an international flavor; Sterne had introduced the whimsical and developed the sentimental. The work of these four men was imitated through the years from 1760 to 1800, and their individual contributions came to be merged into various combinations; a few new novel types were created. On the other hand, some of the types of the eighteenth-century novel, such as the sentimental and the picaresque, continued in the main unchanged. It is usual to divide the novels written after 1760 into the Gothic romance, the novel of purpose, the novel of manners, and the historical novel—always with the understanding that one type might touch any other at certain points.

The kind of fiction which most clearly portrays the drift toward the romantic, and the earliest to appear unmistakably, was the Gothic romance. The term "Gothic" suggested in the neo-classical environment that gave it its special meaning, the wild, the barbaric, and the primitive; specifically, it had reference to the medievalism of a Gothic cathedral, and so to the superstition of the Middle Ages, the mysterious, and the unknown. The Gothic novel represents the romantic return to the medieval, colored with the lurid hues of terror, the horror of the supernatural, the vaguely but monstrously sensational. Like the "graveyard" poetry of the period (p. 613), it is the result of a reaction against neo-classical rationalism. Probably the first striking instance of the Gothic element in an English novel occurs in Smollett's *Ferdinand Count Fathom* (1753), in one scene of which there is a visit to a graveyard in the blackness of midnight as the owls hoot and white figures appear. Smollett, indeed, had often made good use in his novels of the element of terror. A greater impetus was given to the Gothic romance by the appearance of *The Castle of Otranto* (1764) by Horace Walpole (1717–1797). Walpole, like a good many other neo-classicists of the mid-eigththeenth century, had a large country home near London, known as Strawberry Hill. Chiefly because of his personal eccentricity he had equipped the mansion with secret passages, grottoes, and dark staircases. In keeping with the atmosphere of the house, he wrote *The Castle of Otranto* as much for a joke as anything; but joke or not, the work had great influence. The age was ready for this romance and took it hungrily. The novel was a mad tale of a tyrant, Manfred, beautiful young women and a handsome prince, a haunted room, and ghosts.

Walpole's success was followed, though not immediately, by *Vathek* (1787), written by William Beckford (1759–1844), which is at once a Gothic romance and a pseudo-oriental tale; by such popular works as *The Mysteries of Udolpho* (1794) and *The Italian* (1797), by Mrs. Anne Radcliffe (1764–1823), who gave a rational explanation to her horrors; by the sensational *The Monk* (1795) of Matthew Gregory Lewis (1775–1818); by the vivid *Melmoth the Wanderer* (1820) by Charles Maturin (1782–1824), and by *Frankenstein* (1816), written by Mary Godwin Shelley (1797–1851). The latter has enjoyed a considerable revival in recent years because its terror is based upon monstrous possibilities of science—the artificial creation of human life. All are a mélange of melodramatic elements: haunted castles, terrible storms at night, secret footsteps, chastity in peril but eventually preserved, lost wills, forged documents, clanking chains, low moans, and piercing shrieks. There is the same moral justice that is to be found in most penny dreadfuls.

The Gothic romance, with its blood-and-thunder claptrap, might lead to the impression that romanticism had scored an early and sweeping victory over neo-classicism in the field of the novel. Such was not the case. There was a definite continuation of the eighteenth-century novel of manners—the satirical picture, often picaresque in structure, of English life and social customs. But where Defoe and Fielding and Smollett had been forthright, even brutal, in their portraiture, the later writers of the novels of manners were deft and quick in their thrusts, with a sly, gentle little malice that bespoke an amused detachment and a cool appraisal. This distinctly lighter touch may be explained by the fact that the most interesting writers of the genre were women. There was Frances Burney (Madam D'Arblay, 1752–1840), the friend of Dr. Johnson, who shows charm, narrative power, and shrewd portraiture in *Evelina* (1778), "the history of a young lady's entrance into the world," and *Cecilia* (1782), to mention but two of her works. There was Maria Edgeworth (1767–1849), a most capable novelist whose specialities were the delineation of life among the Irish tenants of absentee landlords and the exposition of Irish folk manners, as in *Castle Rackrent* (1800) and *The Absentee* (1809).

The greatest writer, however, among the novelists of manners in this age was Jane Austen (1775–1817). It is a mistake to attempt to make her in any essential way a romantic. She has all the instincts of a neo-classicist for the satirical; she is anti-enthusiastic, anti-extravagant, anti-sentimental. The remarkable clarity, the good sense, the humor, combined with the unusual detachment which she shows in all her works, belong to the preceding age—they are not to be matched again until the time of Thackeray, almost a half-century later—and even then there is a difference. Her purpose is clearly that of Fielding, and she accomplishes in feminine fashion what he did in his masculine muscularity and directness. *Pride and Prejudice* (1813) is one of the greatest of English novels. It is the story of a small-town family and its reactions to people from the outside, of the gossipings and schemings of the women and the futile defenses of the men. *Sense and Sensibility* (1811) is an attack, delivered from the stronghold of common sense, upon the sentimentality of many contemporary novels. *Northanger Abbey*, published posthumously in 1818, is a short but amusing burlesque of the Gothic romance. *Mansfield Park* (1814) is an able piece of realistic observation, but is looser in structure and not so crisp in style as its predecessors. The same defects are apparent in *Emma* (1816), but the satire on village life is so effective as to counterbalance any technical weaknesses. Much of the same can be said for *Persuasion*, published, like *Northanger Abbey*, after the author's death.

Jane Austen's brilliant achievement transmitted the novel of manners to subsequent writers like Thackeray (pp. 829-832), Mrs. Gaskell (p. 830), and George Eliot (pp. 830-832), who owe her so much.

In addition to the Gothic novel and the novel of manners, the age produced a number of characteristic works which clothed revolutionary ideas with the garments of fiction. This type, the so-called novel of purpose, was akin to the novel of manners; it was chiefly in the hands of second-rate writers, however, and consequently exhibited many of the weaknesses of the age—extreme sentimentality, turgidness, prolix characterizations and descriptions. None the less, it is an interesting reflection of the ideas prevalent during the time; it illustrates one side of the romantic temperament that is often overlooked—the missionary spirit, which attained its finest expression in Shelley. The novel of purpose falls roughly into two kinds— that which had a pedagogic aim, and that which advocated reform or revolution of social, political, or economic nature. Of the first kind, not one is of first rank. All stemmed in some way from Rousseau's *Emile* or *La Nouvelle Héloïse*; they preached the ideal of a natural environment for the growing child, and the inculcation of moral principles based upon the beneficent power of Nature herself. Henry Brooke's *The Fool of Quality* (1766-1770) and Thomas Day's *Sanford and Merton* (1783-1789) are perhaps the best known today. The social revolutionary novel received better treatment; William Godwin was responsible for at least two good narratives, *Caleb Williams* (1794), sometimes called the first English detective novel, and *St. Leon* (1799), a mixture of Gothicism and propaganda.

A millinery shop in the early nineteenth century, from a contemporary print.

Shop scenes of the early nineteenth century: Boot & Shoe Makers and Fishmongers.

West country mails at the Gloucester Coffee House, Piccadilly, by James Pollard, 1828.

Still one more important kind of romantic novel remains to be considered—the historical novel. The tendency to use real people as pegs on which to hang a story was strong in Defoe. With the growth of the antiquarian spirit during the eighteenth century and the inevitable subjective coloring given to fact by the romantic mind, the appearance of the historical novel would be only a question of time; but there was no great writer to blaze the trail. Instead, a long list of mediocre writers kept the type alive during the remainder of the eighteenth century, the most considerable of whom was Jane Porter (1776–1850). Her *Thaddeus of Warsaw* (1806) and *The Scottish Chiefs* (1809) achieved a great success in their time and are still readable.

The greatest of the historical novelists in English was Sir Walter Scott (1771–1832), who began his career as a poet, but turned to fiction with the publication of *Waverly* (1814), the first of a long line of nearly thirty novels written between that date and Scott's death in 1832. The Waverly novels are uneven, but at least nine are conspicuous: *Guy Mannering* (1815), a story of England and Scotland in the mid-eighteenth century; *The Antiquary* (1816), the scene of which is virtually contemporary with Scott, unusual in a Scott novel; *Old Mortality* (1816), the epic of the Scottish Covenanters of the seventeenth century; *Rob Roy* (1818), a novel of the Jacobite rebellion in the reign of George I; *The Heart of Midlothian* (1818), laid in the reign of George II; *The Bride of Lammermoor* (1819), Scott's most dramatic love story, and the basis of one of the most popular of modern

operas, Donizetti's *Lucia di Lammermoor*. These six novels are the best of the novels of Scottish history. The other three deal with England or the Continent: *Ivanhoe* (1820), Scott's most popular work, set in the days of Richard the Lion-Hearted and presenting a striking contrast of Norman and Anglo-Saxon; *Kenilworth* (1821), the best literary romance of the Elizabethan age, even if it does some violence to history; and *Quentin Durward* (1823), a dashing love story of a Scot at the court of Louis XI of France (fl. 1470).

Scott is unquestionably the greatest romantic novelist of his age. He has a splendid energy and manliness, a firm command of his characters, particularly of those from the middle class and the peasantry, and a vivid descriptive style shot through with brilliant poetic touches. To the modern reader his pace is overleisurely, his language seems at times stilted, and his lords and ladies are often pallid individuals—these are undoubtedly faults, perhaps concessions to the taste of his generation, but faults nevertheless. His cavalier adjusting of historical facts to suit his fancy sometimes causes the judicious to grieve. He falls below Jane Austen in intellectuality and humor; nor has he her ruthlessness. He fails, often lamentably, in his attempts to apply the delicate touch—something of which Jane Austen was mistress supreme. On the other hand, he excels in his varied subject matter, his breadth of interest, the warmth and sweep of his imagination, and in his ready acceptance of the noble possibilities in humankind. Perhaps it is enough to say that he is a romanticist and that

Jane Austen is not; his realism, effective though it often may be, does not seem to be so integral a part of Scott's character as his accounts of

> old, unhappy, far-off things,
And battles long ago.

Many writers all over Europe imitated Scott during his own lifetime and in the generation immediately following—De Vigny and Dumas in France; Freytag and Ebers in Germany; Manzoni in Italy; Cooper in America. But there is grandeur and solidity in Scott's work that his disciples did not fully possess; it remains the massive achievement in the history of early romantic fiction as well as an extraordinary contribution to the history of the English novel.

A Romantic Age in Review

It is extremely difficult to give the years from 1760 to 1832 an accurate characterizing title. The early decades of this period witnessed the gradual death of neo-classicism, it is true, but they witnessed also, even near the end of the period, an occasional resurrection of the neo-classical spirit in such a writer as Jane Austen or Lord Byron in his satirical mood. Nevertheless, the broad drift of the period was strikingly in a direction opposed to neo-classicism. The thoroughgoing liberation that it entailed in many areas of life, from literature to politics, was initiated in part by a strong reaction against the conservatism, the complacency, and the stasis of much eighteenth-century neo-classicism. The thoughts and actions of men in the latter half of the eighteenth century were increasingly the products of the emotions and the imagination—of that core of mind which has been termed the romantic. This is not to 'imply that the whole world suddenly lost all sense of fact and built up a cloud land of speculation, in which a new heaven and a new earth were to be established immediately upon the ruins of the old. The extreme, the fanatical, and the shortsighted dreamed such dreams, of course, and a few were actually brought to pass in certain parts of Europe. The early ideals of the French Revolution may have collapsed, as Coleridge mourned in his *France: An Ode,* yet the work of the political revolutionists had not been all in vain. "Liberty, equality, and fraternity," once uttered, was never again to be completely silenced. The phrase suggests the kind of adjustment that was necessary in the new industrial world that arose during the latter half of the eighteenth century. This adjustment was slow and painful and discouraging, and it has not yet been completed. But the chronicle of efforts made toward such adjustment is largely the history of the nineteenth century; it makes this age of revolution continuous with the modern age, overlapping it suggestively in aspiration and sensibility.

The expression of the period in the arts was highly charged with romanticism; it is represented by fine creators working in dissimilar media—Schumann, Schubert, Chopin, Corot, Turner, Keats, and Goethe. The list might be extended almost indefinitely, so rich was the profuse romantic product. Much of this romantic expression was intended by its originators as a practical remedy for the ills of humanity. So it was with those preaching human brotherhood, the beneficent force of nature, the hatred of tyranny and oppression.

The Bath steam carriage, c. 1820.

Winter in the Lake District: Derwentwater from Castle Head. The center peak is Catbells.

Part of the romanticism of the period, on the other hand, was a means of escaping reality or, perhaps, transcending it. Such was the effect of nympholeptic yearning after the beautiful, the good, and the sublime; the emotional intoxication coming from the glamour of the past or of the remote in space; the anesthetic absorption in an otherworldly religion—all this was the result of a pathetic regressive desire on the part of some romantics to build an ivory tower for habitation, where only the agreeable and entrancing could enter. It was in effect a facing away from reality as conventionally and externally apprehended to live in a new world or dimension of mind equally "real" to the romanticist. If it can be assumed that reality is something more than a mere amassing of facts, then this vein of romanticism, as well as the *ism* itself, constitutes a warming, expansive, liberalizing force, as necessary to life as air—or neo-classical logic.

Furthermore, it is difficult to say where, in the mind of the romanticist, practicality ends and romanticism begins. Rousseau and Shelley can be regarded as visionaries; nevertheless, they found themselves leaders, and many have followed them. Wordsworth prided himself on his desire to speak the language of common man and to share his inmost soul. Byron, the scoffer against the trend of his time in literature, usually the practical man, could dream of helping an enslaved people. The essential lesson to be learned here is the fact that the romantic mind, a highly individualized, subjective kind of mind, calls enticingly to its affinity and repels its opposite. To him who is severely rational and realistic, the romantic is either foolish or incomprehensible; to him who would be romantic, the romantic is the greatest of all forms of art. The true romanticist would make an even stronger statement; he would feel that this age, or any age approaching it (such as the Renaissance), was the only kind of literary age worth while. Let two great romanticists state their case. "The understanding heart," said De Quincey, "is the interchangeable formula for man in his highest state of capacity for the infinite. Tragedy, romance, fairy tale . . . all alike restore to man's mind the ideals of justice, of hope, of truth, of mercy, of retribution, which else (left to the support of daily life in its realities) would languish for want of sufficient illustration." One other element should be added to De Quincey's fine summary of truly romantic literature; that is the element of elusive beauty wedded to wonder, which, as Shelley expresses it in incomparable fashion,

> visits with inconstant glance
> Each human heart and countenance;
> Like hues and harmonies of evening—
> Like clouds in starlight widely spread—
> Like memory of music fled—
> Like aught that for its grace may be
> Dear, and yet dearer for its mystery.

EIGHTEENTH-CENTURY ROMANTICS

The full force of the romantic, as it manifests itself in the splendid blooming of the great writers of the early nineteenth century, did not make itself felt at once; the seeds of romanticism, however, had lain dormant in the English earth during the Restoration, and they took root and burgeoned slowly but surely during the middle of the eighteenth century. The beginnings of revolt affecting subject matter, mood, and form can be traced even in the age of Pope—the preference of country life to that of the city, an emphasis upon the grand, impressive aspects of nature, a contempla-tion of death and the grave, a new antiquarian prefer-ence for the Middle Ages rather than classical Greece and Rome. In mood there is a growth of humanitarian-ism, democracy, and a more personal and emotional religion. At the same time the younger poets, seeking freshness for their works, found it in the popular ballads, in the lush descriptions of Spenser, and in the harmonies of Milton, and discarded the closed couplet for blank verse and various stanzaic forms, including the sonnet, the Spenserian stanza, and forms of their own invention.

JAMES THOMSON 1700-1748

One of the earliest and most important of the pre-cursors to romanticism was James Thomson. He was a Scot, born in the little parish of Ednam, Roxburghshire, who scribbled verses at an early age, and was edu-cated at the University of Edinburgh. Like other of his countrymen in the eighteenth century, he drifted to London, where some ability and more self-assurance gained him a reputation in spite of a native indolence, which Thomson was not timid in acknowledging. Winter (below), his first important work, appeared in 1726, the year after his coming to London. Summer, Spring, and other poems soon followed, and an absurd bombastic tragedy Sophonisba was favorably received in 1728. Autumn, completing The Seasons, came in 1730, and was followed by a bulky poem on Liberty (1734), which Thomson considered his best work. Posterity has not concurred. A sinecure office as Sec-retary of the Briefs (1733) and a pension (1737) only pampered his indolence. But during the years from 1738 to 1744 came the world famous Rule, Britannia! (p. 634) and four plays, none of which received more than lukewarm approval. The Castle of Indolence, Thomson's last work (p. 634), had its beginnings in a little piece by Thomson joking at his laziness; it became, in the writing, a very extensive piece of poetry, and the finest of the many imitations of Spenser which were the fashion at the time.

His significance in the history of English literature is plain. Writing in an age that saw the publication of such thoroughly typical neo-classical works as those of Pope, Addison, and Steele, he turned in The Seasons to nature in her various moods, and described her in pictorially striking blank verse—not necessarily as a background against which moved that interesting crea-ture man, but largely for her own sake. These descrip-tions of nature Thomson often made rather timidly, relying upon many of the accepted neo-classical con-ventions of style and vocabulary. He still resorted to the clichés of the time, like "youthful swains" for "young men," "household feathery people" for "poul-try," "wanderers of heaven" for "birds," and "ethereal force" for "wind." But he did so with much poetic enjoyment of the spectacle and with a sincere appre-ciation for nature's wildness and beauty. Occasionally (p. 633) there is in his works a sympathy for the luckless human being—what was later called humani-tarianism—that is out of the ordinary for the age.

In The Castle of Indolence, Thomson returned to the Spenserian stanza of Elizabethan times, and de-scribed in sensuous and unconventional imagery a land of "pleasant drowsyhed" reminiscent of the medieval romance. Such striking departures from the usual neo-classical taste in subject matter, verse forms, and poetic interest are what have brought Thomson an honorable survival in the field of English letters.

from THE SEASONS

(from WINTER)

The four parts of The Seasons were first published separately in this order: Winter (1726), Summer (1727), Spring (1728), and Autumn (1730). They were later combined in logical order and republished several times with many additions and revisions. Thomson evidently was conscious that he was making

*an effort toward "the revival of poetry," as he shows
in his preface to the second edition of* Winter.

*Though written in a neo-classical period and re-
flecting the neo-classical modes of thought, as shown in
the regularity and orderliness of the verse, the moral
observations, compliments to patrons, conventional
diction, and stock elements of scenery, the poem nevertheless breaks with the temper of the day and marks
the real beginning of the nature worship so characteristic of later romantic poetry. Thomson was a keen and
sympathetic observer of the various aspects of nature,
particularly the sights and sounds associated with the
progress of the year, and he writes with much poetic
fervor. In his pictures of nature he follows the practice
of late seventeenth-century landscape painters in grouping "details in broad masses of color and striking contrasts of light and shadow" (cf.* The Castle of Indolence, *ll. 334 ff., p. 639).*

Thomson chose to write The Seasons *in blank verse
modeled after that of Milton rather than in the closed
couplets of Pope. He thus helped to reintroduce blank
verse as a favorite poetic medium, and in deliberately
imitating Milton in both style and vocabulary, he set
the fashion of a genuine Miltonic tradition in English
poetry.*

See, winter comes to rule the varied year,
Sullen and sad, with all his rising train—
Vapors, and clouds, and storms. Be these my theme;
These, that exalt the soul to solemn thought
And heavenly musing. Welcome, kindred glooms!
Cogenial horrors, hail! With frequent foot,
Pleased have I, in my cheerful morn of life,
When nursed by careless solitude I lived
And sung of nature with unceasing joy,
10 Pleased have I wandered through your rough domain;
Trod the pure virgin-snows, myself as pure;
Heard the winds roar, and the big torrent burst;
Or seen the deep-fermenting tempest brewed
In the grim evening-sky. Thus passed the time,
Till through the lucid chambers of the south
Looked out the joyous Spring—looked out and smiled.

To thee, the patron of this first essay,
The muse, O Wilmington! renews her song.
Since has she rounded the revolving year:
20 Skimmed the gay spring; on eagle-pinions borne,
Attempted through the summer-blaze to rise;
Then swept o'er autumn with the shadowy gale.
And now among the wintry clouds again,
Rolled in the doubling storm, she tries to soar,
To swell her note with all the rushing winds,

To suit her sounding cadence to the floods;
As is her theme, her numbers wildly great.
Thrice happy, could she fill thy judging ear
With bold description and with manly thought!
Nor art thou skilled in awful schemes alone, 30
And how to make a mighty people thrive;
But equal goodness, sound integrity,
A firm, unshaken, uncorrupted soul
Amid a sliding age, and burning strong,
Not vainly blazing, for thy country's weal,
A steady spirit, regularly free—
These, each exalting each, the statesman light
Into the patriot; these, the public hope
And eye to thee converting, bid the Muse
Record what envy dares not flattery call. 40

Now, when the cheerless empire of the sky
To Capricorn the Centaur-Archer yields,
And fierce Aquarius stains the inverted year—
Hung o'er that farthest verge of heaven, the sun
Scarce spreads o'er ether the dejected day.
Faint are his gleams, and ineffectual shoot
His struggling rays in horizontal lines
Through the thick air; as clothed in cloudy storm,
Weak, wan, and broad, he skirts the southern sky;
And, soon descending, to the long dark night, 50
Wide-shading all, the prostrate world resigns.
Nor is the night unwished; while vital heat,
Light, life, and joy the dubious day forsake.
Meantime, in sable cincture, shadows vast,
Deep-tinged and damp, and congregated clouds,
And all the vapory turbulence of heaven
Involve the face of things. Thus winter falls,
A heavy gloom oppressive o'er the world,
Through nature shedding influence malign,
And rouses up the seeds of dark disease. 60
The soul of man dies in him, loathing life,
And black with more than melancholy views.
The cattle droop; and o'er the furrowed land,
Fresh from the plow, the dun discolored flocks,
Untended spreading, crop the wholesome root.
Along the woods, along the moorish fens,
Sighs the sad genius of the coming storm;
And up among the loose disjointed cliffs
And fractured mountains wild, the brawling brook
And cave, presageful, send a hollow moan, 70
Resounding long in listening fancy's ear.

Then comes the father of the tempest forth,
Wrapped in black glooms. First, joyless rains obscure
Drive through the mingling skies with vapor foul,
Dash on the mountain's brow, and shake the woods

The Seasons. **6. Cogenial,** familiar from birth; some modern editors
have amended this to "congenial." The original reading, however, makes
much better sense. **18. Wilmington.** *Winter* was dedicated to Sir Spencer Compton (1673?-1743), Speaker of the House of Commons, and
made Earl of Wilmington in 1730. **42. Capricorn . . . Centaur-Archer,**
two constellations of the zodiac. When the sun passes from one constellation to the next, the first is said to "yield" to the second. Centaur-

Archer is the constellation of Sagittarius. The sun leaves the constellation Sagittarius about December 21, entering the sign of Capricorn
(the Goat); a month later it enters the sign of Aquarius (the Water-
bearer). **43. inverted year,** probably in the figurative sense of "upset"
or "overthrown"; possibly in the sense of "changed to the new (year)."
45. ether, in the general sense of "the heavens." **89. cottage-hind,**
peasant in a cottage; *hind* is from the Old English *hyne,* "servant,"

That grumbling wave below. The unsightly plain
Lies a brown deluge; as the low-bent clouds
Pour flood on flood, yet unexhausted still
Combine, and, deepening into night, shut up
80 The day's fair face. The wanderers of heaven,
Each to his home, retire; save those that love
To take their pastime in the troubled air,
Or skimming flutter round the dimply pool.
The cattle from the untasted fields return
And ask, with meaning low, their wonted stalls,
Or ruminate in the contiguous shade.
Thither the household feathery people crowd,
The crested cock, with all his female train,
Pensive and dripping; while the cottage-hind
90 Hangs o'er the enlivening blaze, and taleful there
Recounts his simple frolic: much he talks,
And much he laughs, nor recks the storm that blows
Without, and rattles on his humble roof.

Wide o'er the brim, with many a torrent swelled,
And the mixed ruin of its banks o'erspread,
At last the roused-up river pours along;
Resistless, roaring, dreadful, down it comes,
From the rude mountain and the mossy wild,
Tumbling through rocks abrupt, and sounding far;
100 Then o'er the sanded valley floating spreads,
Calm, sluggish, silent; till again, constrained
Between two meeting hills, it bursts a way
Where rocks and woods o'erhang the turbid stream;
There, gathering triple force, rapid and deep,
It boils, and wheels, and foams, and thunders through.

Nature! great parent! whose unceasing hand
Rolls round the seasons of the changeful year,
How mighty, how majestic are thy works!
With what a pleasing dread they swell the soul,
110 That sees astonished, and astonished sings!
Ye too, ye winds! that now begin to blow
With boisterous sweep, I raise my voice to you.
Where are your stores, ye powerful beings! say,
Where your aërial magazines reserved
To swell the brooding terrors of the storm?
In what far-distant region of the sky,
Hushed in deep silence, sleep you when 'tis calm?

When from the pallid sky the sun descends,
With many a spot, that o'er his glaring orb
120 Uncertain wanders, stained; red fiery streaks
Begin to flush around. The reeling clouds
Stagger with dizzy poise, as doubting yet
Which master to obey; while, rising slow,
Blank in the leaden-colored east, the moon
Wears a wan circle round her blunted horns.

Seen through the turbid, fluctuating air,
The stars obtuse emit a shivering ray;
Or frequent seem to shoot athwart the gloom,
And long behind them trail the whitening blaze.
130 Snatched in short eddies, plays the withered leaf;
And on the flood the dancing feather floats.
With broadened nostrils to the sky upturned,
The conscious heifer snuffs the stormy gale.
E'en as the matron, at her nightly task,
With pensive labor draws the flaxen thread,
The wasted taper and the crackling flame
Foretell the blast. But chief the plumy race,
The tenants of the sky, its changes speak.
Retiring from the downs, where all day long
140 They picked their scanty fare, a blackening train
Of clamorous rooks thick-urge their weary flight,
And seek the closing shelter of the grove.
Assiduous, in his bower, the wailing owl
Plies his sad song. The cormorant on high
Wheels from the deep, and screams along the land.
Loud shrieks the soaring hern; and with wild wing
The circling sea-fowl cleave the flaky clouds.
Ocean, unequal pressed, with broken tide
And blind commotion heaves; while from the shore,
150 Eat into caverns by the restless wave,
And forest-rustling mountain comes a voice
That, solemn-sounding, bids the world prepare.
Then issues forth the storm with sudden burst,
And hurls the whole precipitated air
Down in a torrent. On the passive main
Descends the ethereal force, and with strong gust
Turns from its bottom the discolored deep.
Through the black night that sits immense around,
Lashed into foam, the fierce-conflicting brine
160 Seems o'er a thousand raging waves to burn.
Meantime the mountain-billows, to the clouds
In dreadful tumult swelled, surge above surge,
Burst into chaos with tremendous roar,
And anchored navies from their stations drive
Wild as the winds, across the howling waste
Of mighty waters; now the inflated wave
Straining they scale, and now impetuous shoot
Into the secret chambers of the deep,
The wintry Baltic thundering o'er their head.
170 Emerging thence again, before the breath
Of full-exerted heaven they wing their course,
And dart on distant coasts—if some sharp rock
Or shoal insidious break not their career,
And in loose fragments fling them floating round.

Nor less at land the loosened tempest reigns.
The mountain thunders, and its sturdy sons

"retainer." 114. **magazines.** As in the case of *stores* (l. 113), *magazines* indicates a place for keeping something; specifically, a storehouse for the storms and thunders of heaven. This meaning of *magazine* is retained in "powder magazine." 127. **obtuse,** blunted, dulled in light. 139. **downs,** treeless chalk uplands, such as those along the southern coast of England. 146. **hern,** heron. 156. **ethereal,** from the heavens, from the sky. The phrase "ethereal force" for "wind" is a good illustration of Thomson's devotion to the neo-classical style which demands an abstract noun of vague force and of Latin derivations, qualified by a vague adjective or epithet. "Plumy race" (l. 137) for "birds" is another example. 173. **career,** wild flight.

Stoop to the bottom of the rocks they shade.
Lone on the midnight steep, and all aghast,
The dark wayfaring stranger breathless toils,
180 And, often falling, climbs against the blast.
Low waves the rooted forest, vexed, and sheds
What of its tarnished honors yet remain—
Dashed down and scattered, by the tearing wind's
Assiduous fury, its gigantic limbs.
Thus struggling through the dissipated grove,
The whirling tempest raves along the plain;
And, on the cottage thatched or lordly roof
Keen-fastening, shakes them to the solid base.
Sleep frighted flies; and round the rocking dome,
190 For entrance eager, howls the savage blast.
Then too, they say, through all the burdened air
Long groans are heard, shrill sounds, and distant sighs,
That, uttered by the demon of the night,
Warn the devoted wretch of woe and death.

Huge uproar lords it wide. The clouds, commixed
With stars swift-gliding, sweep along the sky.
All nature reels: till nature's king, who oft
Amid tempestuous darkness dwells alone,
And on the wings of the careering wind
200 Walks dreadfully serene, commands a calm;
Then straight air, sea, and earth are hushed at once.

As yet 'tis midnight deep. The weary clouds,
Slow-meeting, mingle into solid gloom.
Now, while the drowsy world lies lost in sleep,
Let me associate with the serious night,
And contemplation, her sedate compeer;
Let me shake off the intrusive cares of day,
And lay the meddling senses all aside.

Where now, ye lying vanities of life!
210 Ye ever-tempting, ever-cheating train!
Where are you now? and what is your amount?
Vexation, disappointment, and remorse.
Sad, sickening thought! and yet deluded man,
A scene of crude disjointed visions past,
And broken slumbers, rises still resolved,
With new-flushed hopes, to run the giddy round.

Father of light and life! thou Good Supreme!
O teach me what is good! teach me Thyself!
Save me from folly, vanity, and vice,
220 From every low pursuit; and feed my soul
With knowledge, conscious peace, and virtue pure—
Sacred, substantial, never-fading bliss!

The keener tempests come; and, fuming dun
From all the livid east or piercing north,
Thick clouds ascend, in whose capacious womb
A vapory deluge lies, to snow congealed.

Heavy they roll their fleecy world along,
And the sky saddens with the gathered storm.
Through the hushed air the whitening shower
    descends,
At first thin-wavering; till at last the flakes   230
Fall broad and wide and fast, dimming the day
With a continual flow. The cherished fields
Put on their winter-robe of purest white.
'Tis brightness all; save where the new snow melts
Along the mazy current. Low the woods
Bow their hoar head; and, ere the languid sun
Faint from the west emits his evening ray,
Earth's universal face, deep-hid and chill,
Is one wild dazzling waste, that buries wide
The works of man. Drooping, the laborer-ox   240
Stands covered o'er with snow, and then demands
The fruit of all his toil. The fowls of heaven,
Tamed by the cruel season, crowd around
The winnowing store, and claim the little boon
Which Providence assigns them. One alone,
The redbreast, sacred to the household gods,
Wisely regardful of the embroiling sky,
In joyless fields and thorny thickets leaves
His shivering mates, and pays to trusted man
His annual visit. Half afraid, he first   250
Against the window beats; then brisk alights
On the warm hearth; then, hopping o'er the floor,
Eyes all the smiling family askance,
And pecks, and starts, and wonders where he is—
Till, more familiar grown, the table-crumbs
Attract his slender feet. The foodless wilds
Pour forth their brown inhabitants. The hare,
Though timorous of heart, and hard beset
By death in various forms, dark snares, and dogs,
And more unpitying men, the garden seeks,   260
Urged on by fearless want. The bleating kind
Eye the bleak heaven, and next the glistening earth,
With looks of dumb despair; then, sad-dispersed,
Dig for the withered herb through heaps of snow.

Now, shepherds, to your helpless charge be kind;
Baffle the raging year, and fill their pens
With food at will; lodge them below the storm,
And watch them strict; for, from the bellowing east,
In this dire season, oft the whirlwind's wing
Sweeps up the burden of whole wintry plains   270
In one wide waft, and o'er the hapless flocks,
Hid in the hollow of two neighboring hills,
The billowy tempest whelms; till, upward urged,
The valley to a shining mountain swells,
Tipped with a wreath high-curling in the sky.

As thus the snows arise, and, foul and fierce,
All winter drives along the darkened air,
In his own loose-revolving fields the swain

<hr>

194. devoted, doomed. 228. saddens, grows dark and heavy. 261.
bleating kind, sheep. Cf. "plumy race" (l. 137) and "ethereal force"

(l. 156 and note). 311. officious, busy with duties. 359. generous
band, a committee appointed in 1729 to investigate the conditions of

Disastered stands; sees other hills ascend,
280 Of unknown joyless brow; and other scenes,
Of horrid prospect, shag the trackless plain;
Nor finds the river nor the forest hid
Beneath the formless wild; but wanders on
From hill to dale, still more and more astray—
Impatient flouncing through the drifted heaps,
Stung with the thoughts of home: the thoughts of home
Rust on his nerves and call their vigor forth
In many a vain attempt. How sinks his soul!
What black despair, what horror fills his heart,
290 When, for the dusky spot which fancy feigned
His tufted cottage rising through the snow,
He meets the roughness of the middle waste,
Far from the track and blest abode of man;
While round him night resistless closes fast,
And every tempest, howling o'er his head,
Renders the savage wilderness more wild.
Then throng the busy shapes into his mind
Of covered pits, unfathomably deep,
A dire descent! beyond the power of frost;
300 Of faithless bogs; of precipices huge,
Smoothed up with snow; and (what is land unknown,
What water) of the still unfrozen spring,
In the loose marsh or solitary lake,
Where the fresh fountain from the bottom boils.
These check his fearful steps; and down he sinks
Beneath the shelter of the shapeless drift,
Thinking o'er all the bitterness of death,
Mixed with the tender anguish nature shoots
Through the wrung bosom of the dying man—
310 His wife, his children, and his friends unseen.
In vain for him the officious wife prepares
The fire fair-blazing and the vestment warm;
In vain his little children, peeping out
Into the mingling storm, demand their sire
With tears of artless innocence. Alas!
Nor wife nor children more shall he behold,
Nor friends, nor sacred home. On every nerve
The deadly winter seizes, shuts up sense,
And, o'er his inmost vitals creeping cold,
320 Lays him along the snows a stiffened corse,
Stretched out, and bleaching in the northern blast.

   Ah! little think the gay licentious proud,
Whom pleasure, power, and affluence surround—
They, who their thoughtless hours in giddy
      mirth,
And wanton, often cruel, riot waste—
Ah! little think they, while they dance along,
How many feel, this very moment, death
And all the sad variety of pain;
How many sink in the devouring flood,
330 Or more devouring flame; how many bleed,
By shameful variance betwixt man and man;

How many pine in want, and dungeon-glooms,
Shut from the common air and common use
Of their own limbs; how many drink the cup
Of baleful grief, or eat the bitter bread
Of misery; sore pierced by wintry winds,
How many shrink into the sordid hut
Of cheerless poverty; how many shake
With all the fiercer tortures of the mind,
Unbounded passion, madness, guilt, remorse—   340
Whence, tumbled headlong from the height of
      life,
They furnish matter for the tragic muse;
Even in the vale, where wisdom loves to dwell,
With friendship, peace, and contemplation joined,
How many, racked with honest passions, droop
In deep retired distress; how many stand
Around the death-bed of their dearest friends,
And point the parting anguish! Thought fond man
Of these, and all the thousand nameless ills
That one incessant struggle render life,   350
One scene of toil, of suffering, and of fate,
Vice in his high career would stand appalled,
And heedless rambling impulse learn to think;
The conscious heart of charity would warm,
And her wide wish benevolence dilate;
The social tear would rise, the social sigh;
And, into clear perfection, gradual bliss,
Refining still, the social passions work.

   And here can I forget the generous band
Who, touched with human woe, redressive searched 360
Into the horrors of the gloomy jail?
Unpitied and unheard where misery moans,
Where sickness pines, where thirst and hunger
      burn,
And poor misfortune feels the lash of vice;
While in the land of liberty—the land
Whose every street and public meeting glow
With open freedom—little tyrants raged,
Snatched the lean morsel from the starving mouth,
Tore from cold wintry limbs the tattered weed,
E'en robbed them of the last of comforts, sleep,   370
The free-born Briton to the dungeon chained
Or, as the lust of cruelty prevailed,
At pleasure marked him with inglorious stripes,
And crushed out lives, by secret barbarous ways,
That for their country would have toiled or bled.
O great design! if executed well,
With patient care and wisdom-tempered zeal.
Ye sons of mercy! yet resume the search;
Drag forth the legal monsters into light,
Wrench from their hands oppression's iron rod,   380
And bid the cruel feel the pains they give.
Much still untouched remains; in this rank age,
Much is the patriot's weeding hand required.

jails and prisons. It discovered that the wardenships of prisons were bought by men who were accustomed to exact heavy fees from prisoners, on the penalty of severe treatment.

The toils of law—what dark insidious men
Have cumbrous added to perplex the truth
And lengthen simple justice into trade—
How glorious were the day that saw these broke,
And every man within the reach of right! . . .
(1726; 1730)

RULE, BRITANNIA!

This poem, first published in 1740 in Alfred: A
Masque, *neatly expresses Thomson's spirited nationalism.*

When Britain first, at Heaven's command,
  Arose from out the azure main,
This was the charter of the land,
  And guardian angels sung this strain—
    "Rule, Britannia, rule the waves;
    Britons never will be slaves."

The nations, not so blessed as thee,
  Must in their turns to tyrants fall;
While thou shalt flourish great and free,
10 The dread and envy of them all.
    "Rule, Britannia, rule the waves;
    Britons never will be slaves."

Still more majestic shalt thou rise,
  More dreadful from each foreign stroke;
As the loud blast that tears the skies
  Serves but to root thy native oak.
    "Rule," *etc.*

Thee haughty tyrants ne'er shall tame;
  All their attempts to bend thee down
20 Will but arouse thy generous flame,
  But work their woe and thy renown.
    "Rule," *etc.*

To thee belongs the rural reign;
  Thy cities shall with commerce shine;
All thine shall be the subject main,
  And every shore it circles thine.
    "Rule," *etc.*

The Muses, still with freedom found,
  Shall to thy happy coast repair;
30 Blessed isle! with matchless beauty crowned,
  And manly hearts to guard the fair.
    "Rule, Britannia, rule the waves;
    Britons never will be slaves."
(1740)

Rule, Britannia! 16. **oak.** The famous eighteenth-century British
men-of-war were made of oak, and this wood was also made the
symbol for the English seamen's bravery; cf. the phrase "hearts and

from THE CASTLE OF INDOLENCE

(*from* CANTO I)

The Castle of Indolence *is a romantic allegory written
in imitation of Spenser. It shows not only a deep admiration for that great poet's work but also some understanding of the qualities of his verse, his phrasing, and
his methods of description. A prefatory advertisement
by Thomson states that the "obsolete words and a
simplicity of diction" were necessary to perfect the
imitation. In the form and in the melody of the stanza;
in the intermingling of color, sound, and perfume; and
in the presentation of abstract qualities by means of
individuals like the "full-spread porter" (Laziness) and
his "little roguish page" (Idle Play) of lines 208 ff.,
the poem ranks as the best of the eighteenth-century
imitations of Spenser. In thus harking back to the Elizabethan period for material and for method,* The Castle
of Indolence *takes its place alongside* The Seasons *(p. 629) as an influential force in establishing
freer poetic traditions. Thomson's highest achievement is shown in the landscape with which the poem
opens.*

The castle hight of Indolence,
  And its false luxury;
Where for a little time, alas!
  We lived right jollily.

1

O mortal man! who livest here by toil,
Do not complain of this thy hard estate;
That like an emmet thou must ever moil,
Is a sad sentence of an ancient date;
And, certes, there is for it reason great;
For, though sometimes it makes thee weep and
    wail,
And curse thy star, and early drudge and late,
Withouten that would come an heavier bale,
Loose life, unruly passions, and diseases pale.

2

In lowly dale, fast by a river's side,   10
With woody hill o'er hill encompassed round,
A most enchanting wizard did abide,
Than whom a fiend more fell is nowhere found.
It was, I ween, a lovely spot of ground;
And there a season atween June and May,
Half prankt with spring, with summer half
    embrowned,

ships of oak."
Castle of Indolence. **hight,** was called. 3. **emmet,** ant. 5. **certes,**
surely, certainly. 16. **prankt,** dressed, decked. 18. **ne,** not. 32.

A listless climate made, where, sooth to say,
No living wight could work, ne caréd even for
    play.

3

  Was nought around but images of rest:
20 Sleep-soothing groves, and quiet lawns between;
And flowery beds that slumbrous influence kest
From poppies breathed; and beds of pleasant green,
Where never yet was creeping creature seen.
Meantime unnumbered glittering streamlets played,
And hurléd everywhere their waters sheen;
That, as they bickered through the sunny glade,
Though restless still themselves, a lulling murmur
    made.

4

  Joined to the prattle of the purling rills,
Were heard the lowing herds along the vale,
30 And flocks loud-bleating from the distant hills,
And vacant shepherds piping in the dale:
And now and then sweet Philomel would wail,
Or stock-doves plain amid the forest deep,
That drowsy rustled to the sighing gale;
And still a coil the grasshopper did keep;
Yet all these sounds yblent inclinéd all to sleep.

5

  Full in the passage of the vale, above,
A sable, silent, solemn forest stood;
Where nought but shadowy forms was seen to
    move,
40 As Idless fancied in her dreaming mood;
And up the hills, or either side, a wood
Of blackening pines, ay waving to and fro,
Sent forth a sleepy horror through the blood;
And where this valley winded out, below,
The murmuring main was heard, and scarcely heard,
    to flow.

6

  A pleasing land of drowsyhed it was:
Of dreams that wave before the half-shut eye;
And of gay castles in the clouds that pass,
Forever flushing round a summer sky;
50 There eke the soft delights, that witchingly
Instil a wanton sweetness through the breast,
And the calm pleasures, always hovered nigh;
But whate'er smacked of noyance, or unrest,
Was far, far off expelled from this delicious
    nest.

Philomel. In classical legend, Philomela, daughter of King Pandion of
Athens, was changed into a nightingale; hence, a nightingale. Cf.
Matthew Arnold's *Philomela*, p. 938. 35. **coil**, noise, tumult.

7

  The landskip such, inspiring perfect ease,
Where Indolence (for so the wizard hight)
Close hid his castle mid embowering trees,
That half shut out the beams of Phoebus bright,
And made a kind of checkered day and night;
Meanwhile, unceasing at the massy gate,   60
Beneath a spacious palm, the wicked wight
Was placed; and to his lute, of cruel fate,
And labor harsh, complained, lamenting man's estate.

8

  Thither continual pilgrims crowded still,
From all the roads of earth that pass there by;
For, as they chaunced to breathe on neighboring hill,
The freshness of this valley smote their eye,
And drew them ever and anon more nigh;
'Til clustering round th'enchanter false they hung,
Ymolten with his syren melody;   70
While o'er th'enfeebling lute his hand he flung,
And to the trembling chords these tempting verses
    sung:

9

  "Behold! ye pilgrims of this earth, behold!
See all but man with unearned pleasure gay.
See her bright robes the butterfly unfold,
Broke from her wintry tomb in prime of May!
What youthful bride can equal her array?
Who can with her for easy pleasure vie?
From mead to mead with gentle wing to stray,
From flower to flower on balmy gales to fly,   80
Is all she has to do beneath the radiant sky.

10

  "Behold the merry minstrels of the morn,
The swarming songsters of the careless grove,
Ten thousand throats! that, from the flowering thorn,
Hymn their good God, and carol sweet of love,
Such grateful kindly raptures them emove;
They neither plow, nor sow; ne, fit for flail,
E'er to the barn the nodding sheaves they drove;
Yet theirs each harvest dancing in the gale,
Whatever crowns the hill, or smiles along the vale. 90

11

  "Outcast of Nature, man! the wretched thrall
Of bitter-dropping sweat, of sweltry pain,
Of cares that eat away thy heart with gall,
And of the vices, an inhuman train,
That all proceed from savage thirst of gain:
For when hard-hearted interest first began

To poison earth, Astraea left the plain;
Guile, violence, and murder seized on man,
And, for soft milky streams, with blood the rivers
    ran.

12

100   "Come, ye, who still the cumbrous load of life
Push hard up hill; but as the farthest steep
You trust to gain, and put an end to strife,
Down thunders back the stone with mighty sweep,
And hurls your labors to the valley deep,
Forever vain; come, and, withouten fee,
I in oblivion will your sorrows steep,
Your cares, your toils, will steep you in a sea
Of full delight; O come, ye weary wights, to me!

13

   "With me, you need not rise at early dawn,
110 To pass the joyless day in various stounds;
Or, louting low, on upstart fortune fawn,
And sell fair honor for some paltry pounds;
Or through the city take your dirty rounds,
To cheat, and dun, and lie, and visit pay,
Now flattering base, now giving secret wounds;
Or prowl in courts of law for human prey,
In venal senate thieve, or rob on broad highway.

14

   "No cocks, with me, to rustic labor call,
From village on to village sounding clear;
120 To tardy swain no shrill-voiced matrons squall;
No dogs, no babes, no wives, to stun your ear;
No hammers thump; no horrid blacksmiths sear,
Ne noisy tradesmen your sweet slumbers start,
With sounds that are a misery to hear;
But all is calm, as would delight the heart
Of Sybarite of old, all nature, and all art.

15

   "Here nought but candor reigns, indulgent ease,
Good-natured lounging, sauntering up and down:
They who are pleased themselves must always please;
130 On others' ways they never squint a frown,
Nor heed what haps in hamlet or in town.
Thus, from the source of tender indolence,
With milky blood the heart is overflown,
Is soothed and sweetened by the social sense;
For interest, envy, pride, and strife, are banished
    hence.

16

   "What, what, is virtue, but repose of mind,
A pure ethereal calm, that knows no storm;
Above the reach of wild ambition's wind,
Above those passions that this world deform,
And torture man, a proud malignant worm!   140
But here, instead, soft gales of passion play
And gently stir the heart, thereby to form,
A quicker sense of joy; as breezes stray
Across th' enlivened skies, and make them still more
    gay.

17

   "The best of men have ever loved repose:
They hate to mingle in the filthy fray,
Where the soul sours, and gradual rancor grows,
Imbittered more from peevish day to day.
Even those whom fame has lent her fairest ray,
The most renowned of worthy wights of yore,   150
From a base world at last have stolen away:
So Scipio, to the soft Cumaean shore
Retiring, tasted joy he never knew before.

18

   "But if a little exercise you choose,
Some zest for ease, 'tis not forbidden here.
Amid the groves you may indulge the muse,
Or tend the blooms, and deck the vernal year;
Or, softly stealing, with your watery gear,
Along the brooks, the crimson-spotted fry
You may delude: the whilst, amused, you hear   160
Now the hoarse stream, and now the zephyr's sigh,
Attunéd to the birds, and woodland melody.

19

   "O grievous folly! to heap up estate,
Losing the days you see beneath the sun;
When, sudden, comes blind unrelenting fate,
And gives th' untasted portion you have won,
With ruthless toil, and many a wretch undone,
To those who mock you gone to Pluto's reign,
There with sad ghosts to pine, and shadows dun:
But sure it is of vanities most vain,   170
To toil for what you here untoiling may obtain."

20

He ceased. But still their trembling ears retained
The deep vibrations of his witching song;

97. **Astraea,** in classical mythology, the goddess of justice. 99. **milky streams,** an echo of the verse describing the Promised Land: "Unto whom the Lord sware that he would not show them the land which the Lord sware unto their fathers that he would give us, a land that floweth with milk and honey." (Joshua 5:6; cf. also Isaiah 55:1: "Ho, every one that thirsteth, come ye to the waters, and he that hath no money; come ye, buy, and eat; yea, come, buy wine and milk without money and without price.") 110. **stounds,** aches and sorrows. 126. **Sybarite,** an inhabitant of Sybaris, Italy, a city noted in ancient times for its luxurious living. 152. **Scipio,** Publius Scipio Africanus Major (234?–183 B.C.), famous Roman general, who after a life of warfare retired in 185 B.C. to his native seat near Cumae, a city in Campania,

That, by a kind of magic power, constrained
To enter in, pell-mell, the listening throng.
Heaps poured on heaps, and yet they slipped along,
In silent ease: as when beneath the beam
Of summer-moons, the distant woods among,
Or by some flood all silvered with the gleam,
180 The soft-embodied fays through airy portal stream.

21

By the smooth demon so it ordered was,
And here his baneful bounty first began;
Though some there were who would not further
    pass,
And his alluring baits suspected han.
The wise distrust the too fair-spoken man.
Yet through the gate they cast a wishful eye;
Not to move on, perdie, is all they can;
For, do their very best, they cannot fly,
But often each way look, and often sorely sigh.

22

190 When this the watchful, wicked wizard saw,
With sudden spring he leaped upon them strait;
And soon as touched by his unhallowed paw,
They found themselves within the cursèd gate;
Full hard to be repassed, like that of fate.
Not stronger were of old the giant-crew,
Who sought to pull high Jove from regal state;
Though feeble wretch he seemed, of sallow hue.
Certes, who bides his grasp, will that encounter rue.

23

For whomso'er the villain takes in hand,
200 Their joints unknit, their sinews melt apace;
As lithe they grow as any willow-wand,
And of their vanished force remains no trace;
So when a maiden fair, of modest grace,
In all her buxom, blooming May of charms,
Is seizèd in some losel's hot embrace,
She waxeth very weakly as she warms,
Then, sighing, yields her up to love's delicious harms.

24

Waked by the crowd, slow from his bench arose
A comely full-spread porter, swoln with sleep:
210 His calm, broad, thoughtless aspect breathed repose,
And in sweet torpor he was plungèd deep,
Ne could himself from ceaseless yawning keep;
While o'er his eyes the drowsy liquor ran,

Through which his half-waked soul would faintly
    peep.
Then taking his black staff, he called his man,
And roused himself as much as rouse himself he can.

25

The lad leaped lightly at his master's call;
He was, to weet, a little roguish page,
Save sleep and play who minded nought at all,
Like most the untaught striplings of his age.   220
This boy he kept each band to disengage,
Garters and buckles, task for him unfit,
But ill-becoming his grave personage,
And which his portly paunch would not permit,
So this same limber page to all performèd it.

26

Meantime the master-porter wide displayed
Great store of caps, of slippers, and of gowns,
Wherewith he those who entered in, arrayed,
Loose, as the breeze that plays along the downs,
And waves the summer-woods when evening frowns. 230
O fair undress, best dress! it checks no vein,
But every flowing limb in pleasure drowns,
And heightens ease with grace. This done, right fain
Sir Porter sat him down, and turned to sleep again.

27

Thus easy robed, they to the fountain sped,
That in the middle of the court up-threw
A stream, high-spouting from its liquid bed,
And falling back again in drizzly dew;
There each deep draughts, as deep he thirsted, drew.
It was a fountain of Nepenthe rare;   240
Whence, as Dan Homer sings, huge pleasaunce grew,
And sweet oblivion of vile earthly care,
Fair gladsome waking thoughts, and joyous dreams
    more fair.

28

This rite performed, all inly pleased and still,
Withouten trump was proclamation made;
"Ye sons of indolence, do what you will;
And wander where you list, through hall or glade!
Be no man's pleasure for another's stayed;
Let each as likes him best his hours employ,
And cursed be he who minds his neighbor's trade! 250
Here dwells kind ease and unreproving joy:
He little merits bliss who others can annoy."

Italy. 159. **fry,** young fishes. 168. **Pluto,** in classical mythology, the
god of the infernal regions. 184. **han,** have (cf. Chaucer's use of
the infinitive of the verb "to have," p. 111, l. 490). 187. **perdie,**
an oath formed from the French *par Dieu,* "by God!" 195. **giant-
crew,** in classical mythology, the Titans, who rebelled against Zeus
(Jove) and were defeated. 205. **losel,** rascal, worthless person. 218.

to **weet,** as far as one could tell. 240. **Nepenthe,** in classical lore,
a drug that caused forgetfulness of sorrow and pain. 241. **Dan
Homer,** Lord Homer. The reference here is to the *Odyssey,* IV, 220 ff.

29

Strait of these endless numbers, swarming round
As thick as idle motes in sunny ray,
Not one eftsoons in view was to be found,
But every man strolled off his own glad way.
Wide o'er this ample court's blank area,
With all the lodges that thereto pertained,
No living creature could be seen to stray;
260 While solitude and perfect silence reigned;
So that to think you dreamt you almost was con-
    strained.

30

As when a shepherd of the Hebrid Isles,
Placed far amid the melancholy main,
(Whether it be lone fancy him beguiles,
Or that aërial beings sometimes deign
To stand, embodied, to our senses plain)
Sees on the naked hill, or valley low,
The whilst in ocean Phoebus dips his wain,
A vast assembly moving to and fro;
270 Then all at once in air dissolves the wondrous show.

31

Ye gods of quiet, and of sleep profound!
Whose soft dominion o'er this castle sways,
And all the widely-silent places round,
Forgive me, if my trembling pen displays
What never yet was sung in mortal lays.
But how shall I attempt such arduous string,
I who have spent my nights and nightly days
In this soul-deadening place, loose-loitering?
• Ah! how shall I for this uprear my molted wing?

32

280   Come on, my muse, nor stoop to low despair,
Thou imp of Jove, touched by celestial fire!
Thou yet shalt sing of war, and actions fair,
Which the bold sons of Britain will inspire;
Of ancient bards thou yet shalt sweep the lyre;
Thou yet shalt tread in tragic pall the stage,
Paint love's enchanting woes, the hero's ire,
The sage's calm, the patriot's noble rage,
Dashing corruption down through every worthless age.

33

The doors, that knew no shrill alarming bell,
290 Ne cursèd knocker plied by villain's hand,

Self-opened into halls, where who can tell
What elegance and grandeur wide expand,
The pride of Turkey and of Persia land?
Soft quilts on quilts, on carpets carpets spread,
And couches stretch around in seemly band;
And endless pillows rise to prop the head,
So that each spacious room was one full-swelling bed.

34

And everywhere huge covered tables stood,
With wines high-flavored and rich viands crowned;
Whatever sprightly juice or tasteful food   300
On the green bosom of this earth are found,
And all old ocean genders in his round;
Some hand unseen these silently displayed,
Even undemanded by a sigh or sound;
You need but wish, and, instantly obeyed,
Fair-ranged the dishes rose, and thick the glasses
    played.

35

Here freedom reigned without the least alloy;
Nor gossip's tale, nor ancient maiden's gall,
Nor saintly spleen durst murmur at our joy,
And with envenomed tongue our pleasures pall.   310
For why? there was but one great rule for all;
To wit, that each should work his own desire,
And eat, drink, study, sleep, as it may fall,
Or melt the time in love, or wake the lyre,
And carol what, unbid, the Muses might inspire.

36

The rooms with costly tapestry were hung,
Where was inwoven many a gentle tale;
Such as of old the rural poets sung,
Or of Arcadian or Sicilian vale:
Reclining lovers, in the lonely dale,   320
Poured forth at large the sweetly-tortured heart;
Or, sighing tender passion, swelled the gale,
And taught charmed echo to resound their smart;
While flocks, woods, streams around, repose and peace
    impart.

37

Those pleased the most, where, by a cunning hand,
Depeinten was the patriarchal age;
What time Dan Abraham left the Chaldee land,
And pastured on from verdant stage to stage,

255. eftsoons, immediately. 261. was. Singular verbs with plural
subjects were not uncommon in earlier English literature. 262. Hebrid
Isles, the Hebrides, a group of islands to the west of Scotland. 318.
rural poets, those who wrote about pastoral subjects; notably Theocritus, Greek poet of the third century B.C. and Vergil (70-19 B.C.), one
of the great poets of ancient Rome. 326. Depeinten, painted, depicted.
327. Dan Abraham . . . Chaldee land. "Lord" Abraham's departure
from Chaldea is told in Genesis, Chapter 12. 331. silvan war, combat
in the woods. 333. golden age. In classical mythology, under the reign
of Saturn, one-time king of the gods, all nature was kindly; man knew
no want of any kind. This was the Golden Age, to be destroyed when
Zeus overcame his father Saturn and inaugurated the reign of the gods
of Olympus. 341. Lorrain, Claude Lorrain (1600–1682), a famous
French landscape painter. 342. Rosa, Salvator Rosa (1615–1673), a

Where fields and fountains fresh could best engage.
330 Toil was not then. Of nothing they took heed,
But with wild beasts the silvan war to wage,
And o'er vast plains their herds and flocks to feed;
Blest sons of nature they! true golden age indeed!

38

Sometimes the pencil, in cool airy halls,
Bade the gay gloom of vernal landskips rise,
Or autumn's varied shades imbrown the walls;
Now the black tempest strikes the astonished eyes;
Now down the steep the flashing torrent flies;
The trembling sun now plays o'er ocean blue,
340 And now rude mountains frown amid the skies;
Whate'er Lorrain light-touched with softening hue,
Or savage Rosa dashed, or learnéd Poussin drew.

39

Each sound, too, here to languishment inclined,
Lulled the weak bosom, and inducéd ease.
Aërial music in the warbling wind,
At distance rising oft, by small degrees,
Nearer and nearer came, till o'er the trees
It hung, and breathed such soul-dissolving airs
As did, alas! with soft perdition please;
350 Entangled deep in its enchanting snares,
The listening heart forgot all duties and all cares.

40

A certain music, never known before,
Here lulled the pensive melancholy mind;
Full easily obtained. Behooves no more,
But sidelong, to the gently-waving wind,
To lay the well-tuned instrument reclined;
From which with airy flying fingers light,
Beyond each mortal touch the most refined,
The god of winds drew sounds of deep delight;
360 Whence, with just cause, The Harp of Aeolus it hight.

41

Ah me! what hand can touch the string so fine?
Who up the lofty diapason roll
Such sweet, such sad, such solemn airs divine,
Then let them down again into the soul?
Now rising love they fanned; now pleasing dole
They breathed, in tender musings, through the heart;
And now a graver sacred strain they stole,
As when seraphic hands an hymn impart;
Wild warbling nature all, above the reach of art!

42

Such the gay splendor, the luxurious state,   370
Of Caliphs old, who on the Tygris' shore,
In mighty Bagdat, populous and great,
Held their bright court, where was of ladies store;
And verse, love, music still the garland wore;
When sleep was coy, the bard, in waiting there,
Cheered the lone midnight with the muse's lore;
Composing music bade his dreams be fair,
And music lent new gladness to the morning air.

43

Near the pavilions where we slept, still ran
Soft-tinkling streams, and dashing waters fell,   380
And sobbing breezes sighed, and oft began
(So worked the wizard) wintry storms to swell,
As heaven and earth they would together mell;
At doors and windows, threatening, seemed to call
The demons of the tempest, growling fell;
Yet the least entrance found they none at all;
Whence sweeter grew our sleep, secure in massy
    hall. . . .
(1748)

THOMAS GRAY 1716-1771

*To have written the most quoted poem in the
language is the distinction of Thomas Gray. Gray was
born in Cornhill, London, and was the only one of
a family of twelve children to survive infancy. His
father was a ne'er-do-well scrivener and from him
Gray received nothing but neglect. But his mother
gave him infinite care and a schooling at Eton, for
which she herself paid by keeping a shop. At Eton,
Gray became fast friends with two aristocrats, Horace
Walpole, son of the Prime Minister, and Richard
West, son of the Lord Chancellor of Ireland. The
association with West was broken off early by West's
death at the age of twenty-six (see Sonnet, p. 641);
that with Walpole lasted, with some interruption,
through Gray's lifetime.*

*After Eton came Cambridge, where Gray matricu-
lated in 1734. There he steeped himself in the classics,
and caused some comment by drinking tea instead of
beer for breakfast. After five years of college, he
accompanied Walpole on a "grand tour" of the Continent, where both young men were deeply impressed
by the beauty and grandeur of nature, particularly in
the Alps. Upon his return Gray retired to Cambridge,*

famous Italian painter of historical scenes, battles, and landscapes. **Poussin**, Nicolas Poussin (1594–1665), noted French landscape and historical painter. 360. **The Harp of Aeolus.** Aeolus was in classical
mythology the god of winds. The instrument referred to is the Aeolian
harp, consisting of a wooden frame strung with wires; the vibration
of the wires caused by the passing wind produces the tone. 372. **Bagdat**, Bagdad, the famous capital of the eastern division of the Mohammedan empire, called the Eastern Caliphate (the *caliphs* were the successors of Mohammed). The city was located on the Tigris River; it
was claimed by the Sultan of Turkey until 1924, and is now the
capital of Iraq. 383. **mell**, mingle.

became a bachelor of civil law, a college don, and professor of modern history. His literary output was not great—a score of short poems, a journal of a trip to the English Lake Country, and some of the most attractive letters that the age produced.

Gray's health, always fragile, prompted him in 1765 to go on a journey in Scotland, during which he kept a lively account of his impressions. He returned to Cambridge to accept a professorship in modern history, a post which he had solicited in vain a few years before, but in 1769, he was advised, because of his health, to go to the seashore in the south of England. He visited London once more, then returned to Cambridge in complete mental and physical exhaustion. Attacks of gout, which he had long suffered in milder form, now tortured him, and he died on July 3, 1771.

The small amount of verse Gray left behind tends to be reflective and passive, but it is highly important as one of the early manifestations of the growth of the English romantic school. Although Gray was academic and a classicist, he was also responsive to nature, given to a melancholy brooding inspired by a love of myth and the long-distant past. These traits of temperament were fatal to the integrity of his neo-classicism, but they enhanced his position as a romantic writer. By comparing Gray with Thomson (p. 629), one can see how Gray advanced the literature of introspection and imagination at the expense of the literature of reason and intellect. Gray was more complex as a person than most of his contemporaries and more gifted as a poet.

ODE ON A DISTANT PROSPECT OF ETON COLLEGE

Eton College, founded by King Henry VI in 1440, is situated in the valley of the Thames River, about twenty miles west of London. The royal castle of Windsor stands on an eminence in the city of Windsor on the opposite side of the river. The College is also near the village of Stoke Poges, where Gray was living when he wrote this poem. The poem was written shortly after the death of Richard West, Gray's most intimate friend. Two other friends of college days, Ashton and Walpole, were estranged from Gray at the time.

An example of Gray's early verse, the ode is conventional in its use of neo-classical poetic diction, personification, and moralizing, but it shows a few tendencies toward romanticism in its sensitiveness to nature and in its tone of melancholy.

Ye distant spires, ye antique towers,
  That crown the watery glade,

Where grateful Science still adores
  Her Henry's holy shade;
And ye, that from the stately brow
Of Windsor's heights the expanse below
  Of grove, of lawn, of mead survey,
Whose turf, whose shade, whose flowers among
Wanders the hoary Thames along
  His silver-winding way.   10

Ah, happy hills, ah, pleasing shade,
  Ah, fields beloved in vain,
Where once my careless childhood strayed,
  A stranger yet to pain!
I feel the gales, that from ye blow,
A momentary bliss bestow,
  As waving fresh their gladsome wing
My weary soul they seem to soothe,
And, redolent of joy and youth,
  To breathe a second spring.   20

Say, Father Thames, for thou hast seen
  Full many a sprightly race
Disporting on thy margent green
  The paths of pleasure trace,
Who foremost now delight to cleave
With pliant arm thy glassy wave?
  The captive linnet which enthral?
What idle progeny succeed
To chase the rolling circle's speed,
  Or urge the flying ball?   30

While some on earnest business bent
  Their murmuring labors ply
'Gainst graver hours, that bring constraint
  To sweeten liberty;
Some bold adventurers disdain
The limits of their little reign,
  And unknown regions dare descry;
Still as they run they look behind,
They hear a voice in every wind,
  And snatch a fearful joy.   40

Gay hope is theirs by fancy fed,
  Less pleasing when possessed;
The tear forgot as soon as shed,
  The sunshine of the breast;
Theirs buxom health of rosy hue,
Wild wit, invention ever-new,
  And lively cheer of vigor born;
The thoughtless day, the easy night,
The spirits pure, the slumbers light,
  That fly the approach of morn.   50

Alas, regardless of their doom,
  The little victims play!

Ode . . . Eton College. 3. Science, learning. 4. Her Henry, Henry VI, who founded Eton College in 1440. 23. margent, margin, bank. 29. rolling circle, etc. The rolling circle is the hoop used in the game of rolling hoops. The flying ball in the next line refers to the cricket ball.
Sonnet. Richard West (1716–1742) had been Gray's closest friend

No sense have they of ills to come,
  Nor care beyond today;
Yet see how all around 'em wait
The ministers of human Fate,
  And black Misfortune's baleful train!
Ah, show them where in ambush stand,
To seize their prey, the murtherous band!
60 Ah, tell them they are men!

These shall the fury Passions tear,
  The vultures of the mind,
Disdainful Anger, pallid Fear,
  And Shame that skulks behind;
Or pining Love shall waste their youth,
Or Jealousy with rankling tooth,
  That inly gnaws the secret heart,
And Envy wan, and faded Care,
Grim-visaged comfortless Despair,
70 And Sorrow's piercing dart.

Ambition this shall tempt to rise,
  Then whirl the wretch from high,
To bitter Scorn a sacrifice,
  And grinning Infamy.
The stings of Falsehood those shall try,
And hard Unkindness' altered eye,
  That mocks the tear it forced to flow;
And keen Remorse with blood defiled,
And moody Madness laughing wild
80 Amid severest woe.

Lo! in the vale of years beneath
  A grisly troop are seen,
The painful family of Death,
  More hideous than their queen.
This racks the joints, this fires the veins,
That every laboring sinew strains,
  Those in the deeper vitals rage;
Lo, Poverty, to fill the band,
That numbs the soul with icy hand,
90 And slow-consuming Age.

To each his sufferings; all are men,
  Condemned alike to groan,
The tender for another's pain,
  The unfeeling for his own.
Yet ah! why should they know their fate?
Since sorrow never comes too late,
  And happiness too swiftly flies,
Thought would destroy their paradise.
No more; where ignorance is bliss,
  Tis folly to be wise.
(1742; 1747)

at Eton. 3. descant, melody, song.
  Ode . . . Cat. 1. 'Twas . . . blow. The fish bowl was a large one made of Chinese porcelain. 16. Tyrian hue, the so-called Tyrian

SONNET

ON THE DEATH OF RICHARD WEST

In vain to me the smiling mornings shine,
And reddening Phoebus lifts his golden fire;
The birds in vain their amorous descant join;
Or cheerful fields resume their green attire;
These ears, alas! for other notes repine,
A different object do these eyes require;
My lonely anguish melts no heart but mine;
And in my breast the imperfect joys expire.
Yet morning smiles the busy race to cheer,
And new-born pleasure brings to happier men;   10
The fields to all their wonted tribute bear;
To warm their little loves the birds complain;
I fruitless mourn to him that cannot hear,
And weep the more because I weep in vain.
(1742; 1775)

ODE ON THE DEATH OF A FAVORITE CAT

DROWNED IN A TUB OF GOLD FISHES

Written with playful solemnity, this poem shows Gray in one of his lighter moods. The cat was a pet of Horace Walpole, Gray's friend.

Twas on a lofty vase's side,
Where China's gayest art had dyed
  The azure flowers, that blow;
Demurest of the tabby kind,
The pensive Selima reclined,
  Gazed on the lake below.

Her conscious tail her joy declared;
The fair round face, the snowy beard,
  The velvet of her paws,
Her coat, that with the tortoise vies,   10
Her ears of jet, and emerald eyes,
  She saw; and purred applause.

Still had she gazed; but 'midst the tide
Two angel forms were seen to glide,
  The genii of the stream;
Their scaly armor's Tyrian hue
Through richest purple to the view
  Betrayed a golden gleam.

The hapless nymph with wonder saw:
A whisker first and then a claw,   20
  With many an ardent wish,
She stretched in vain to reach the prize.
What female heart can gold despise?
  What cat's averse to fish?

purple, made by the ancient inhabitants of Tyre from the juice of a shellfish.

Presumptuous maid! with looks intent
Again she stretched, again she bent,
   Nor knew the gulf between.
(Malignant Fate sat by, and smiled)
The slippery verge her feet beguiled,
30 She tumbled headlong in.

Eight times emerging from the flood
She mewed to every watery god,
   Some speedy aid to send.
No dolphin came, no nereid stirred:
Nor cruel Tom, nor Susan heard.
   A favorite has no friend!

From hence, ye beauties, undeceived,
Know, one false step is ne'er retrieved,
   And be with caution bold.
40 Not all that tempts your wandering eyes
And heedless hearts, is lawful prize;
   Nor all, that glisters, gold.
(1747; 1748)

ELEGY WRITTEN IN A COUNTRY CHURCHYARD

*Gray's Elegy has long been one of the best known
and most popular pieces in the English language. As
Dr. Johnson says, it "abounds with images which
find a mirror in every mind, and with sentiments to
which every bosom returns an echo." The universality
of its appeal—thoughts on the ever-present facts of
life, death, and the transiency of human labor—combined with beauty and melody of phrase, explain the
enduring currency of the poem.*

*In its form, in the neatness and quotability of its
utterance, and in its aphoristic sentiments, Gray's
Elegy continues the neo-classical tradition; but it
points forward to the romantic movement in its delicate feeling for nature, its mood of reflective melancholy, and its exaltation of lowly folk. It is the
supreme example of the multitude of so-called "graveyard" poems (p. 613), that in the eighteenth century
followed Milton's Il Penseroso in expressing a somber
and thoughtful view of life.*

*If a definite scene for the Elegy was in Gray's mind,
it was doubtless that of the church and graveyard at
Stoke Poges, where the poet now lies buried.*

The curfew tolls the knell of parting day,
   The lowing herd wind slowly o'er the lea,
The plowman homeward plods his weary way,
   And leaves the world to darkness and to me.

An illustration for Gray's Elegy Written in a Country
Churchyard, *from* Designs by Mr. Bentley for Six Poems
by Mr. T. Gray, London, R. Dodsley, 1753.

Now fades the glimmering landscape on the sight,
   And all the air a solemn stillness holds,
Save where the beetle wheels his droning flight,
   And drowsy tinklings lull the distant folds;

Save that from yonder ivy-mantled tower
   The moping owl does to the moon complain   10
Of such as, wandering near her secret bower,
   Molest her ancient solitary reign.

Beneath those rugged elms, that yew-tree's shade,
   Where heaves the turf in many a moldering heap,
Each in his narrow cell forever laid,
   The rude forefathers of the hamlet sleep.

The breezy call of incense-breathing Morn,
   The swallow twittering from the straw-built shed,
The cock's shrill clarion, or the echoing horn,
   No more shall rouse them from their lowly bed.   20

For them no more the blazing hearth shall burn,
   Or busy housewife ply her evening care;

---

31. **Eight times,** alluding to a cat's nine lives. 34. **dolphin,** an allusion
to the legend that Arion, famous Greek musician, when forced from a
ship into the sea, was carried to shore on the back of a dolphin that
had been charmed by his music. **nereid,** in Greek mythology, a daughter
of Nereus, the Old Man of the Sea; hence, a nymph or water sprite.
Elegy . . . Churchyard. 19. **horn,** the huntsman's horn. 26. **glebe,**
the sod in cultivated ground. 41. **storied urn,** an urn inscribed with

pictures that tell a story; cf. Keats' *Ode on a Grecian Urn,* p. 789,
animated, lifelike. 57. **Some . . . Hampden,** some patriot who would
oppose unjust taxes as did John Hampden (1594–1643), noted English
statesman and member of the Puritan party, who resisted the unjust
levies of King Charles I in 1637 and 1638. 59. **Some . . . Milton,**
some great poet sprung from the lowly classes without technical training who could nevertheless, like Milton, lead a cause with poetic and

No children run to lisp their sire's return,
    Or climb his knees the envied kiss to share.

Oft did the harvest to their sickle yield,
    Their furrow oft the stubborn glebe has broke;
How jocund did they drive their team afield!
    How bowed the woods beneath their sturdy stroke!

Let not Ambition mock their useful toil,
30   Their homely joys, and destiny obscure;
Nor Grandeur hear, with a disdainful smile,
    The short and simple annals of the poor.

The boast of heraldry, the pomp of power,
    And all that beauty, all that wealth e'er gave,
Awaits alike the inevitable hour:
    The paths of glory lead but to the grave.

Nor you, ye proud, impute to these the fault,
    If Memory o'er their tomb no trophies raise,
Where through the long-drawn aisle and fretted vault
40   The pealing anthem swells the note of praise.

Can storied urn or animated bust
    Back to its mansion call the fleeting breath?
Can Honor's voice provoke the silent dust,
    Or Flattery soothe the dull cold ear of Death?

Perhaps in this neglected spot is laid
    Some heart once pregnant with celestial fire;
Hands that the rod of empire might have swayed,
    Or waked to ecstasy the living lyre.

But Knowledge to their eyes her ample page
50   Rich with the spoils of time did ne'er unroll;
Chill Penury repressed their noble rage,
    And froze the genial current of the soul.

Full many a gem of purest ray serene
    The dark unfathomed caves of ocean bear;
Full many a flower is born to blush unseen,
    And waste its sweetness on the desert air.

Some village Hampden that with dauntless breast
    The little tyrant of his fields withstood;
Some mute inglorious Milton here may rest,
60   Some Cromwell guiltless of his country's blood.

The applause of listening senates to command,
    The threats of pain and ruin to despise,
To scatter plenty o'er a smiling land,
    And read their history in a nation's eyes,

Their lot forbade; nor circumscribed alone
    Their growing virtues, but their crimes confined;
Forbade to wade through slaughter to a throne,
    And shut the gates of mercy on mankind,

The struggling pangs of conscious truth to hide,
    To quench the blushes of ingenuous shame,   70
Or heap the shrine of Luxury and Pride
    With incense kindled at the Muse's flame.

Far from the madding crowd's ignoble strife,
    Their sober wishes never learned to stray;
Along the cool sequestered vale of life
    They kept the noiseless tenor of their way.

Yet ev'n these bones from insult to protect
    Some frail memorial still erected nigh,
With uncouth rimes and shapeless sculpture decked,
    Implores the passing tribute of a sigh.   80

Their name, their years, spelt by the unlettered Muse,
    The place of fame and elegy supply;
And many a holy text around she strews,
    That teach the rustic moralist to die.

For who, to dumb Forgetfulness a prey,
    This pleasing anxious being e'er resigned,
Left the warm precincts of the cheerful day,
    Nor cast one longing, lingering look behind?

On some fond breast the parting soul relies,
    Some pious drops the closing eye requires;   90
Ev'n from the tomb the voice of Nature cries,
    Ev'n in our ashes live their wonted fires.

For thee, who mindful of the unhonored dead
    Dost in these lines their artless tale relate;
If chance, by lonely Contemplation led,
    Some kindred spirit shall inquire thy fate,

Haply some hoary-headed swain may say,
    "Oft have we seen him at the peep of dawn
Brushing with hasty steps the dews away
    To meet the sun upon the upland lawn.   100

"There at the foot of yonder nodding beech,
    That wreathes its old fantastic roots so high,
His listless length at noontide would he stretch,
    And pore upon the brook that babbles by.

"Hard by yon wood, now smiling as in scorn,
    Muttering his wayward fancies he would rove,

prophetic power. 60. **Some Cromwell,** someone as great as Cromwell, and as much of a leader, without his faults. Oliver Cromwell (1599–1658), the victorious leader of the Roundheads against the Royalists in the Civil War, and the Lord Protector of the Commonwealth, was regarded throughout the eighteenth century as one who had sacrificed his country to his ambition. In the original draft of this stanza, one of the most famous in the entire poem, Gray had Cato for Hampden, Tully

(Cicero) for Milton, and Caesar for Cromwell. The substitution of English names for classical illustrates Gray's romantic tendency, which was more fully expressed in his later poems. 79. **uncouth,** strange, odd. 93. **thee,** Gray himself.

Now drooping, woeful wan, like one forlorn,
   Or crazed with care, or crossed in hopeless love.

"One morn I missed him on the customed hill,
110   Along the heath, and near his favorite tree;
Another came; nor yet beside the rill,
   Nor up the lawn, nor at the wood was he;

"The next with dirges due in sad array
   Slow through the church-way path we saw him
      borne.
Approach and read (for thou canst read) the lay,
   Graved on the stone beneath yon aged thorn."

THE EPITAPH

Here rests his head upon the lap of Earth
   A youth to Fortune and to Fame unknown.
Fair Science frowned not on his humble birth,
120   And Melancholy marked him for her own.

Large was his bounty, and his soul sincere,
   Heaven did a recompense as largely send;
He gave to Misery all he had, a tear,
   He gained from Heaven ('twas all he wished)
      a friend.

No farther seek his merits to disclose,
   Or draw his frailties from their dread abode,
(There they alike in trembling hope repose),
   The bosom of his Father and his God.
(1750; 1751)

THE BARD

The Bard *is based upon a vague tradition that when King Edward I of England conquered Wales in 1276-1284 he ordered all the Welsh bards that fell into his hands to be put to death. Gray gives the following plan of the poem: "The army of Edward I, as they march through a deep valley, and approach Mount Snowdon, are suddenly stopped by the appearance of a venerable figure seated on the summit of an inaccessible rock, who, with a voice more than human, reproaches the king with all the desolation*

and misery which he had brought on his country, foretells the misfortunes of the Norman race, and with prophetic spirit declares that all his cruelty shall never extinguish the noble ardor of poetic genius in this island, and that men shall never be wanting to celebrate true virtue and valor in immortal strains, to expose vice and infamous pleasure, and boldly censure tyranny and oppression. His song ended, he precipitates himself from the mountain, and is swallowed up in the river that rolls at its foot."

As a piece of imaginative writing, this poem is both original and romantic. Thrilled by the picturesqueness of the medieval theme and of the wild mountain scenery of Wales, Gray writes with dramatic intensity free from all literary restrictions save those imposed by the structure and the manner of the odes of the Greek lyric poet Pindar (fifth century B.C.). Following Pindar's structural form, Gray composes his poem in three divisions, each of which consists of three sections corresponding to the strophe, the antistrophe, and the epode of the Greek model.

I. 1

"Ruin seize thee, ruthless King!
Confusion on thy banners wait,
   Though fanned by Conquest's crimson
      wing
They mock the air with idle state.
Helm, nor hauberk's twisted mail,
Nor even thy virtues, Tyrant, shall avail
To save thy secret soul from nightly fears,
   From Cambria's curse, from Cambria's tears!"
Such were the sounds, that o'er the crested pride
   Of the first Edward scattered wild dismay,   10
As down the steep of Snowdon's shaggy side
   He wound with toilsome march his long array.
Stout Glo'ster stood aghast in speechless trance;
"To arms!" cried Mortimer, and couched his quivering lance.

I. 2

On a rock, whose haughty brow
Frowns o'er old Conway's foaming flood,
   Robed in the sable garb of woe,
With haggard eyes the Poet stood;

The Bard. 8. **Cambria,** the old name for Wales. 11. **Snowdon,** a high mountain range and peak in northern Wales. 13. **Glo'ster,** the Earl of Gloucester, who was a leader in the army of King Edward I. 14. **Mortimer,** another important lieutenant of King Edward. 16. **Conway,** a small river in northern Wales, dividing Carnarvonshire from Denbighshire and emptying into the Irish Sea. 18. **Poet stood,** etc. Gray represents the old Welsh bard as composing spontaneously under the stress of great emotion. 28. **Hoel,** a prince and poet of north Wales in ancient days. **Llewellyn,** the leader of the Welsh revolt which Edward I was putting down. 29. **Cadwallo,** a common Welsh bardic name, as is also **Urien** (l. 31); but no bard by the name of *Modred* (l. 33) is known. 34. **Plinlimmon,** a mountain in Wales. 35. **Arvon's shore,** "the shores of Carnarvonshire opposite to the isle of Anglesey." —Gray's note. 38. **famished eagle screams,** a detail which will remind the reader of a common picture in Old English battle poetry (cf. *Beowulf,* p. 52, l. 2422). 44. **grisly band,** the whole band of murdered

bards, who join the sole survivor in prophesying the future of Edward's race. 49. **warp . . . woof.** The *warp* constitutes the threads extended lengthwise in the loom in weaving; the *woof* constitutes the threads that cross the warp. 51. **verge,** space. 54. **Severn . . . King.** The son of Edward I, later King Edward II, who reigned from 1307 to 1327, was cruelly murdered in Berkeley Castle, near the Severn River, in 1327. It has always been a legend that his wife Queen Isabella was present at the murder and perhaps participated (cf. l. 58). 57. **She-wolf of France.** Isabella, a French princess and Queen of England, wife of Edward II, notorious even during her husband's reign for her adulterous intrigue with Roger Mortimer, son of the leader mentioned in the note to l. 14. 63. **Mighty victor . . . lies,** King Edward III, grandson of Edward I, and son of Edward II, who reigned from 1327 to 1377. His death followed that of his popular eldest son Edward, the Black Prince, hero of the early years of the Hundred Years' War. 67. **sable Warrior fled,** an allusion to the death of Prince Edward

(Loose his beard, and hoary hair
20 Streamed, like a meteor, to the troubled air)
And with a master's hand and prophet's fire,
Struck the deep sorrows of his lyre.
"Hark, how each giant oak, and desert cave,
Sighs to the torrent's awful voice beneath!
O'er thee, oh King! their hundred arms they wave,
Revenge on thee in hoarser murmurs breathe;
Vocal no more, since Cambria's fatal day,
To high-born Hoel's harp, or soft Llewellyn's lay.

I. 3

"Cold is Cadwallo's tongue,
30 That hushed the stormy main;
Brave Urien sleeps upon his craggy bed;
Mountains, ye mourn in vain
Modred, whose magic song
Made huge Plinlimmon bow his cloud-topped
head.
On dreary Arvon's shore they lie,
Smeared with gore, and ghastly pale;
Far, far aloof the affrighted ravens sail;
The famished eagle screams, and passes by.
Dear lost companions of my tuneful art,
40 Dear, as the light that visits these sad eyes,
Dear, as the ruddy drops that warm my heart,
Ye died amidst your dying country's cries—
No more I weep. They do not sleep.
On yonder cliffs, a grisly band,
I see them sit, they linger yet,
Avengers of their native land;
With me in dreadful harmony they join,
And weave with bloody hands the tissue of thy line.

II. 1

"Weave the warp, and weave the woof,
50 The winding-sheet of Edward's race.
Give ample room, and verge enough
The characters of Hell to trace.
Mark the year, and mark the night,
When Severn shall re-echo with affright
The shrieks of death, through Berkley's roofs that
ring,
Shrieks of an agonizing King!
She-wolf of France, with unrelenting fangs,

That tear'st the bowels of thy mangled mate,
From thee be born, who o'er thy country hangs
The scourge of Heaven. What terrors round him
wait! 60
Amazement in his van, with Flight combined,
And Sorrow's faded form, and Solitude behind.

II. 2

"Mighty victor, mighty lord!
Low on his funeral couch he lies!
No pitying heart, no eye, afford
A tear to grace his obsequies.
Is the sable Warrior fled?
Thy son is gone. He rests among the dead.
The swarm, that in thy noon-tide beam were born?
Gone to salute the rising morn. 70
Fair laughs the morn, and soft the zephyr blows,
While proudly riding o'er the azure realm
In gallant trim the gilded vessel goes;
Youth on the prow, and Pleasure at the helm;
Regardless of the sweeping whirlwind's sway,
That, hushed in grim repose, expects his evening prey.

II. 3

"Fill high the sparkling bowl,
The rich repast prepare,
Reft of a crown, he yet may share the feast;
Close by the regal chair 80
Fell Thirst and Famine scowl
A baleful smile upon their baffled guest.
Heard ye the din of battle bray,
Lance to lance, and horse to horse?
Long years of havoc urge their destined course,
And through the kindred squadrons mow their
way.
Ye towers of Julius, London's lasting shame,
With many a foul and midnight murther fed,
Revere his consort's faith, his father's fame,
And spare the meek usurper's holy head. 90
Above, below, the rose of snow,
Twined with her blushing foe, we spread;
The bristled boar in infant gore
Wallows beneath the thorny shade.
Now, brothers, bending o'er the accursed loom
Stamp we our vengeance deep, and ratify his doom.

III. 1

"Edward, lo! to sudden fate
(Weave we the woof. The thread is spun.)
Half of thy heart we consecrate.
100 (The web is wove. The work is done.)
Stay, oh stay! nor thus forlorn,
Leave me unblessed, unpitied, here to mourn;
In yon bright track, that fires the western skies,
They melt, they vanish from my eyes.
But oh! what solemn scenes on Snowdon's height
Descending slow their glittering skirts unroll?
Visions of glory, spare my aching sight,
Ye unborn ages, crowd not on my soul!
No more our long-lost Arthur we bewail.
110 All hail, ye genuine kings, Britannia's issue, hail!

III. 2

"Girt with many a baron bold
Sublime their starry fronts they rear;
And gorgeous dames, and statesmen old
In bearded majesty, appear.
In the midst a form divine!
Her eye proclaims her of the Briton line;
Her lion-port, her awe commanding face,
Attempered sweet to virgin-grace.
What strings symphonious tremble in the air,
120 What strains of vocal transport round her play!
Hear from the grave, great Taliessin, hear;
They breathe a soul to animate thy clay.
Bright Rapture calls, and soaring, as she sings,
Waves in the eye of Heaven her many-colored wings

III. 3

"The verse adorn again
Fierce War, and faithful Love,
And Truth severe, by fairy fiction drest.
In buskined measures move
Pale Grief and pleasing Pain,
130 With Horror, tyrant of the throbbing breast.
A voice, as of the cherub-choir,
Gales from blooming Eden bear;
And distant warblings lessen on my ear,
That lost in long futurity expire.
Fond impious man, think'st thou, yon sanguine
cloud,
Raised by thy breath, has quenched the orb of
day?
Tomorrow he repairs the golden flood,
And warms the nations with redoubled ray.

Enough for me. With joy I see
The different doom our fates assign. 140
Be thine Despair and sceptered Care;
To triumph, and to die, are mine."
He spoke, and headlong from the mountain's
height
Deep in the roaring tide he plunged to endless night.
(1754; 1757)

WILLIAM COLLINS 1721-1759

William Collins from youth had an aptitude for verse. He was born in the cathedral town of Chichester, Sussex, was educated at Winchester and Magdalen College, Oxford, and, forsaking other professions, went to London as a "literary adventurer" with only a few pennies in his pocket, but with grandiose literary projects in his mind. Of his projects few materialized, and the quantity of his verse is small—he wrote less than 1500 lines—though some of his poems, like the Ode to Evening (below) have a rare vigor and a delightful sensuous appeal not only to the imagination but to the ear as well. The fitfulness of his talent can be accounted for partly by his unstable, nervous temperament, and by his improvident ways. Collins never knew a feeling of security. "A man doubtful of his dinner or trembling at a creditor is not much disposed to abstracted meditations or remote inquiries"—such was Dr. Johnson's apology for Collins. While still in his thirties, Collins failed mentally and physically, and for a time before his death was confined to a madhouse in Chelsea. He died at thirty-eight.

ODE TO EVENING

This ode, written in unrimed stanzas but revealing a most skillful and musical use of assonance and onomatopoeia, is one of the really great poems of the eighteenth century—perfect in form, exquisite in phrasing, and subtle in its power of suggestion. It belongs to the group of romantic poems that express enjoyment of nature in solitude and in the twilight hour.

If aught of oaten stop, or pastoral song,
May hope, chaste Eve, to soothe thy modest ear,
Like thy own solemn springs,
Thy springs, and dying gales,

---

99. **Half . . . consecrate.** The queen of Edward I, Eleanor of Castile, lost her life in 1290, after saving her husband's by sucking out the poison from a dagger wound. 104. **They . . . they,** the "grisly band" of murdered bards mentioned in l. 44. 109. **Arthur.** It was predicted and confidently believed by the Welsh people that King Arthur was still alive and that he would return to rule again over Britain. 110. **genuine kings,** the rule of the House of Tudor dates from the accession of Henry

VII in 1485 to the death of Elizabeth in 1603. The Tudor family descended from Owen Tudor the Welshman; Tudor was the second husband of Catharine, the widowed queen of King Henry V. 115. **form divine,** Elizabeth, queen of England from 1558 to 1603. 118. **virgin-grace.** Elizabeth is sometimes referred to as the Virgin Queen. 121. **Taliessin,** a famous Welsh bard of the sixth century. 125. **The verse . . . again,** an allusion to Spenser's *Faerie Queene* and its allegory.

O nymph reserved, while now the bright-haired sun
Sits in yon western tent, whose cloudy skirts,
　　With brede ethereal wove,
　　O'erhang his wavy bed:

Now air is hushed, save where the weak-eyed bat
10 With short, shrill shriek, flits by on leathern wing;
　　Or where the beetle winds
　　His small but sullen horn,

As oft he rises 'midst the twilight path,
Against the pilgrim borne in heedless hum:
　　Now teach me, maid composed,
　　To breathe some softened strain,

Whose numbers, stealing through thy darkening vale,
May, not unseemly, with its stillness suit,
　　As, musing slow, I hail
20 　　Thy genial loved return!

For when thy folding star arising shows
His paly circlet, at his warning lamp
　　The fragrant Hours, and elves
　　Who slept in flowers the day,

And many a nymph who wreathes her brows with
　　sedge,
And sheds the freshening dew, and, lovelier still,
　　The pensive Pleasures sweet
　　Prepare thy shadowy car.

Then lead, calm votaress, where some sheety lake
30 Cheers the lone heath, or some time-hallowed pile,
　　Or upland fallows gray
　　Reflect its last cool gleam.

But when chill blustering winds, or driving rain,
Forbid my willing feet, be mine the hut,
　　That from the mountain's side,
　　Views wilds, and swelling floods,

And hamlets brown, and dim-discovered spires;
And hears their simple bell, and marks o'er all
　　Thy dewy fingers draw
40 　　The gradual dusky veil.

While Spring shall pour his showers, as oft he wont,
And bathe thy breathing tresses, meekest Eve!
　　While Summer loves to sport
　　Beneath thy lingering light;

While sallow Autumn fills thy lap with leaves;
Or Winter, yelling through the troublous air,

Affrights thy shrinking train,
And rudely rends thy robes;

So long, sure-found beneath the sylvan shed,
Shall Fancy, Friendship, Science, rose-lipped Health, 50
　　Thy gentlest influence own,
　　And hymn thy favorite name!
(1746)

WILLIAM COWPER 1731-1800

The most attractive of the pre-romantics is William Cowper, the son of the rector of Great Berkhamstead in Herefordshire, whose mother, Anne Donne Cowper, could trace a relationship to John Donne the poet. She left the boy an orphan when he was only six, and the motherless lad evinced very early an abnormal sensitiveness and timidity. When he went to his first school, he was easy prey for the bullying of older boys, and the spiritual mark of this suffering was to stay with Cowper for the rest of his life. At fourteen he went to Westminster School in London. Later he studied law and was admitted to the bar in 1755, but he was apparently content to live in expectation of some legal sinecure from a well-to-do uncle, Ashley Cowper. This hope came to naught when Ashley Cowper objected to a growing love affair between Cowper and his cousin Theodora.

When he was twenty-four, Cowper suffered the first of several attacks of suicidal melancholy which took the form of an overwhelming consciousness of sin, and a belief that he had committed an unpardonable sin. In 1765, after his first recovery, Cowper took residence with the Unwins in Huntingdon to be near his younger brother, who was a fellow at Cambridge. In this acquaintance Cowper was fortunate; Morley Unwin was a clergyman and tutor; and Mrs. Unwin encouraged their boarder to write poetry. When Unwin was killed in a fall from his horse in 1767, Cowper remained as a boarder in Mrs. Unwin's house with her son and daughter, and moved with her to the nearby parish of Olney, where the evangelical John Newton was curate. Cowper became his assistant and collaborated with him on Olney Hymns (1779). But the religious environment at Olney was the worst kind for Cowper, and this new association was interrupted by another attack of insanity.

After Newton left Olney in 1780, Cowper enjoyed his happiest years. He occupied himself with gardening, carpentering, and raising domestic animals,

128. **buskined.** The buskin was the high shoe worn by actors of tragedy in the Greek theater; hence "buskined" is the equivalent of "tragic." 131. **A voice,** that of Milton. 133. **distant warblings,** of poets following Milton. 135. **Fond . . . man,** foolish man. 141. **Be thine Despair.** Edward I, who waged wars against the Welsh and the Scots, had a very troubled reign.
　Ode to Evening. 1. **If . . . stop.** If anything played upon the

shepherd's oat, or pipe. 7. **brede,** embroidery. 21. **folding star,** the evening star, which indicated that it was time for the sheep to be put into the fold. 30. **pile,** large building; here, a church. 47. **Affrights . . . train,** that is, "shortens the evening." Compare the remarks on winter here with those in Thomson's *Winter* (p. 629).

and the friendship of Mrs. Unwin and Lady Austen, a rich widow of the vicinity, brightened his social life. When Lady Austen challenged him to write a poem about a sofa, Cowper produced The Task (1785), which is his best work. In Miltonic blank verse it describes homely folk and working people. It is dedicated to the theme that "God made the country, and man made the town." It began as a kind of mock-heroic description of the sofa in Cowper's country home; it ended as a kind of spiritual autobiography that reminds one of the later work of Wordsworth, like The Prelude or The Excursion. When Lady Austen told him a funny story about a man who was at his horse's mercy, Cowper wrote The Diverting History of John Gilpin. This ballad, together with the affecting poem Upon the Receipt of My Mother's Picture, were printed with The Task. But the part Lady Austen had played in the production of Cowper's best poetry resulted in the end of their friendship. Sixty-year-old Mrs. Unwin was absurdly jealous of the friendship between a sophisticated society woman and a pathological poet, the least worldly of men. With the death of Mrs. Unwin in 1796, Cowper's mania returned, never to leave him till his death in 1800.

"I was a stricken deer that left the herd long since," wrote Cowper in one of those moments of frank self-revelation that showed his peculiar talents. No fair reader can possibly ignore the fragile personality of the poet, his moments of rare companionability, his shrinking timidity, and his morbid religiosity. His writings are uneven; he is never a great poet expressing great ideas in a grand manner, but rather a modest bard of nature and of rural village society, always with real devotion to the implacable figure that is his God. Like Blake (p. 671), Cowper is something of an isolated phenomenon, and a psychopathic one; but in that very individualism can be seen the strong current of the romantic which runs through his works. His talents as a nature poet are not considerable. He makes an important contribution to emotionally religious poetry; he is one of the most distinguished hymn writers of the century. Above all, he is a personality as much as a poet, for his letters and autobiographical writings are a frank and fascinating revelation of a tortured human soul.

from OLNEY HYMNS

WALKING WITH GOD

Oh! for a closer walk with God,
  A calm and heavenly frame;

A light to shine upon the road
  That leads me to the Lamb!

Where is the blessedness I knew
  When first I saw the Lord?
Where is the soul-refreshing view
  Of Jesus and His word?

What peaceful hours I once enjoyed!
  How sweet their memory still!   10
But they have left an aching void
  The world can never fill.

Return, O holy Dove, return,
  Sweet messenger of rest!
I hate the sins that made Thee mourn,
  And drove Thee from my breast.

The dearest idol I have known,
  Whate'er that idol be,
Help me to tear it from Thy throne,
  And worship only Thee.   20

So shall my walk be close with God,
  Calm and serene my frame;
So purer light shall mark the road
  That leads me to the Lamb.

(1779)

from THE TASK

The Task has been considered by many as Cowper's masterpiece. It takes its title from the fact that Cowper's friend, Lady Austen, asked the poet to write a poem in blank verse on the subject of the parlor sofa. In the "Advertisement" to the poem, Cowper says that he obeyed; "and, having much leisure, connected another subject with it; and, pursuing the train of thought to which my situation and turn of mind led me, brought forth at length, instead of the trifle which I at first intended, a serious affair—a volume!"

The purpose of the poem, as stated by Cowper in a letter to William Unwin (October 10, 1784), was "to discountenance the modern enthusiasm after a London life, and to recommend rural ease and leisure as friendly to the cause of piety and virtue." Burns calls the religion of The Task "the religion of God and nature, the religion that exalts, that ennobles man." And Coleridge, in speaking of "the divine chitchat" of Cowper, pays tribute to his lofty purpose and gracious manner.

In the six books of this poem is included a variety of themes—an interest in nature, in country life, in

---

The Sofa. 120. hips . . . haws. Hips are the ripe fruit of the rose-bush; haws, of the hawthorne. 121. crabs, crabapples. 122. sloes austere. The sloe is the fruit of the blackthorn; austere is used here in the sense of "sour." 144. companion . . . walks, Mary Unwin, from whom Cowper was never separated from 1765 until her death in 1796. 163. Ouse, a small river in Sussex. 180. those . . . describe, familiar

lowly people, in animals, and in social reform. A fore-runner of Wordsworth, Cowper recollects his earlier contacts with nature and gratefully records its healing influences upon his wounded and sensitive spirit. His scenes have actuality, and his minute descriptions, done with keen and sympathetic eye, confirm his faith in the poetic value of simple truth.

from BOOK I, THE SOFA

. . . For I have loved the rural walk through lanes
110 Of grassy swarth, close cropped by nibbling sheep,
And skirted thick with intertexture firm
Of thorny boughs; have loved the rural walk
O'er hills, through valleys, and by rivers' brink,
E'er since a truant boy I passed my bounds
To enjoy a ramble on the banks of Thames;
And still remember, nor without regret
Of hours that sorrow since has much endeared,
How oft, my slice of pocket store consumed,
Still hungering, penniless and far from home,
120 I fed on scarlet hips and stony haws,
Or blushing crabs, or berries, that emboss
The bramble, black as jet, or sloes austere.
Hard fare! but such as boyish appetite
Disdains not; nor the palate, undepraved
By culinary arts, unsavory deems.
No Sofa then awaited my return;
Nor Sofa then I needed. Youth repairs
His wasted spirits quickly, by long toil
Incurring short fatigue; and, though our years
130 As life declines speed rapidly away,
And not a year but pilfers as he goes
Some youthful grace that age would gladly keep;
A tooth or auburn lock, and by degrees
Their length and color from the locks they spare;
The elastic spring of an unwearied foot
That mounts the stile with ease, or leaps the fence,
That play of lungs, inhaling and again
Respiring freely the fresh air, that makes
Swift pace or steep ascent no toil to me,
140 Mine have not pilfered yet; nor yet impaired
My relish of fair prospect; scenes that soothed
Or charmed me young, no longer young, I find
Still soothing and of power to charm me still.
And witness, dear companion of my walks,
Whose arm this twentieth winter I perceive
Fast locked in mine, with pleasure such as love,
Confirmed by long experience of thy worth
And well-tried virtues, could alone inspire—
Witness a joy that thou hast doubled long.
150 Thou knowest my praise of nature most sincere,
And that my raptures are not conjured up
To serve occasions of poetic pomp,
But genuine, and art partner of them all.

How oft upon yon eminence our pace
Has slackened to a pause, and we have borne
The ruffling wind, scarce conscious that it blew,
While admiration, feeding at the eye,
And still unsated, dwelt upon the scene.
Thence with what pleasure have we just discerned
The distant plow slow moving, and beside   160
His laboring team, that swerved not from the track,
The sturdy swain diminished to a boy!
Here Ouse, slow winding through a level plain
Of spacious meads with cattle sprinkled o'er,
Conducts the eye along its sinuous course
Delighted. There, fast rooted in his bank,
Stand, never overlooked, our favorite elms,
That screen the herdsman's solitary hut;
While far beyond, and overthwart the stream
That, as with molten glass, inlays the vale,   170
The sloping land recedes into the clouds;
Displaying on its varied side the grace
Of hedge-row beauties numberless, square tower,
Tall spire, from which the sound of cheerful bells
Just undulates upon the listening ear,
Groves, heaths, and smoking villages remote.
Scenes must be beautiful, which daily viewed,
Please daily, and whose novelty survives
Long knowledge and the scrutiny of years—
Praise justly due to those that I describe.   180

Nor rural sights alone, but rural sounds
Exhilarate the spirit and restore
The tone of languid nature. Mighty winds,
That sweep the skirt of some far-spreading wood
Of ancient growth, make music not unlike
The wash of ocean on his winding shore,
And lull the spirit while they fill the mind;
Unnumbered branches waving in the blast,
And all their leaves fast fluttering, all at once.
Nor less composure waits upon the roar   190
Of distant floods, or on the softer voice
Of neighboring fountain, or of rills that slip
Through the cleft rock, and, chiming as they fall
Upon loose pebbles, lose themselves at length
In matted grass, that with a livelier green
Betrays the secret of their silent course.
Nature inanimate employs sweet sounds,
But animated nature sweeter still,
To soothe and satisfy the human ear.
Ten thousand warblers cheer the day, and one   200
The livelong night: nor these alone, whose notes
Nice-fingered art must emulate in vain,
But cawing rooks, and kites that swim sublime
In still repeated circles, screaming loud,
The jay, the pie, and e'en the boding owl
That hails the rising moon, have charms for me.
Sounds inharmonious in themselves and harsh,

---

scenes in the vicinity of Olney, Cowper's home. In a letter to the Reverend William Unwin, dated October 10, 1784, Cowper wrote: "My descriptions are all from nature; not one of them second hand. My

delineations of the heart are from my own experience; not one of them borrowed from books, or in the least degree conjectural."

Yet heard in scenes where peace forever reigns,
And only there, please highly for their sake. . . .

Where finds philosophy her eagle eye,
With which she gazes at yon burning disk
Undazzled, and detects and counts his spots?
In London. Where her implements exact,
With which she calculates, computes, and scans,
All distance, motion, magnitude, and now
Measures an atom, and now girds a world?
In London. Where has commerce such a mart,
720 So rich, so thronged, so drained, and so supplied,
As London—opulent, enlarged, and still
Increasing London? Babylon of old
Not more the glory of the earth than she,
A more accomplished world's chief glory now.

She has her praise. Now mark a spot or two,
That so much beauty would do well to purge;
And show this queen of cities that so fair
May yet be foul; so witty, yet not wise.
It is not seemly, nor of good report,
730 That she is slack in discipline; more prompt
To avenge than to prevent the breach of law:
That she is rigid in denouncing death
On petty robbers, and indulges life
And liberty, and oft-times honor too,
To peculators of the public gold:
That thieves at home must hang, but he that puts
Into his overgorged and bloated purse
The wealth of Indian provinces escapes.
Nor is it well, nor can it come to good,
740 That, through profane and infidel contempt
Of holy writ, she has presumed to annul
And abrogate, as roundly as she may,
The total ordinance and will of God;
Advancing fashion to the post of truth,
And centering all authority in modes
And customs of her own, till sabbath rites
Have dwindled into unrespected forms,
And knees and hassocks are well-nigh divorced.

God made the country, and man made the town.
750 What wonder then that health and virtue, gifts
That can alone make sweet the bitter draught
That life holds out to all, should most abound
And least be threatened in the fields and groves?
Possess ye, therefore, ye who, borne about
In chariots and sedans, know no fatigue
But that of idleness, and taste no scenes
But such as art contrives, possess ye still
Your element; there only can ye shine,
There only minds like yours can do no harm.

Our groves were planted to console at noon   760
The pensive wanderer in their shades. At eve
The moonbeam, sliding softly in between
The sleeping leaves, is all the light they wish,
Birds warbling all the music. We can spare
The splendor of your lamps; they but eclipse
Our softer satellite. Your songs confound
Our more harmonious notes; the thrush departs
Scared, and the offended nightingale is mute.
There is a public mischief in your mirth;
It plagues your country. Folly such as yours,   770
Graced with a sword, and worthier of a fan,
Has made, what enemies could ne'er have done,
Our arch of empire, steadfast but for you,
A mutilated structure, soon to fall.

from BOOK II. THE TIME-PIECE

Oh, for a lodge in some vast wilderness,
Some boundless contiguity of shade,
Where rumor of oppression and deceit,
Of unsuccessful or successful war,
Might never reach me more! My ear is pained,
My soul is sick, with every day's report
Of wrong and outrage with which earth is filled.
There is no flesh in man's obdurate heart,
It does not feel for man; the natural bond
Of brotherhood is severed as the flax   10
That falls asunder at the touch of fire.
He finds his fellow guilty of a skin
Not colored like his own; and, having power
To enforce the wrong, for such a worthy cause
Dooms and devotes him as his lawful prey.
Lands intersected by a narrow frith
Abhor each other. Mountains interposed
Make enemies of nations, who had else,
Like kindred drops, been mingled into one.
Thus man devotes his brother, and destroys;   20
And, worse than all, and most to be deplored,
As human nature's broadest, foulest blot,
Chains him, and tasks him, and exacts his sweat
With stripes, that Mercy, with a bleeding heart,
Weeps when she sees inflicted on a beast.
Then what is man? And what man, seeing this,
And having human feelings, does not blush,
And hang his head, to think himself a man?
I would not have a slave to till my ground,
To carry me, to fan me while I sleep,   30
And tremble when I wake, for all the wealth
That sinews bought and sold have ever earned.
No: dear as freedom is, and in my heart's
Just estimation prized above all price,
I had much rather be myself the slave,

727. **fair . . . foul**; cf. Shakespeare's *Macbeth*, I, iii, 38: "So foul and fair a day I have not seen." 732. **denouncing**, pronouncing. Petty crimes like shoplifting were at that time punishable by death. 735. **peculators**, embezzlers. 736. **he . . . escapes.** An allusion to the British policy of exploitation in India, carried out by Robert Clive (1725-1774) and Warren Hastings (1732-1818) through the period

from 1751 to 1785. Clive made a fortune for himself, and Hastings greatly increased the revenue for the British East India Company. 755. **sedans**, sedan chairs.
   The Time-Piece. 1. **lodge . . . wilderness**; cf. Jeremiah 9:2: "Oh that I had in the wilderness a lodging place of wayfaring men; that I might leave my people, and go from them!" 16. **frith**, a narrow arm

And wear the bonds, than fasten them on him.
We have no slaves at home.—Then why abroad?
And they themselves, once ferried o'er the wave
That parts us, are emancipate and loosed.
40 Slaves cannot breathe in England; if their lungs
Receive our air, that moment they are free;
They touch our country, and their shackles fall.
That's noble, and bespeaks a nation proud
And jealous of the blessing. Spread it then,
And let it circulate through every vein
Of all your empire; that where Britain's power
Is felt, mankind may feel her mercy too. . . .

from BOOK III. THE GARDEN

I was a stricken deer that left the herd
Long since; with many an arrow deep infixed
110 My panting side was charged, when I withdrew
To seek a tranquil death in distant shades.
There was I found by One Who had Himself
Been hurt by the archers. In His side He bore,
And in His hands and feet, the cruel scars.
With gentle force soliciting the darts,
He drew them forth, and healed, and bade me live.
Since then, with few associates, in remote
And silent woods I wander, far from those
My former partners of the peopled scene,
120 With few associates, and not wishing more.
Here much I ruminate, as much I may,
With other views of men and manners now
Than once, and others of a life to come.
I see that all are wanderers, gone astray
Each in his own delusions; they are lost
In chase of fancied happiness, still wooed
And never won; dream after dream ensues,
And still they dream that they shall still succeed,
And still are disappointed: rings the world
130 With the vain stir. I sum up half mankind,
And add two-thirds of the remainder half,
And find the total of their hopes and fears
Dreams, empty dreams. . . .
(1785)

ON THE RECEIPT OF MY MOTHER'S PICTURE OUT OF NORFOLK

THE GIFT OF MY COUSIN ANN BODHAM

Oh, that those lips had language! Life has passed
With me but roughly since I heard thee last.
Those lips are thine—thy own sweet smile I see,
The same that oft in childhood solaced me;
Voice only fails, else how distinct they say,
"Grieve not, my child, chase all thy fears away!"
The meek intelligence of those dear eyes
(Blest be the art that can immortalize,
The art that baffles Time's tyrannic claim
To quench it) here shines on me still the same.   10
Faithful remembrancer of one so dear,
O welcome guest, though unexpected here!
Who bidd'st me honor with an artless song,
Affectionate, a mother lost so long,
I will obey, not willingly alone,
But gladly, as the precept were her own:
And, while that face renews my filial grief,
Fancy shall weave a charm for my relief—
Shall steep me in Elysian reverie,
A momentary dream that thou art she.   20
My mother! when I learned that thou wast dead,
Say, wast thou conscious of the tears I shed?
Hovered thy spirit o'er thy sorrowing son,
Wretch even then, life's journey just begun?
Perhaps thou gavest me, though unfelt, a kiss,
Perhaps a tear, if souls can weep in bliss—
Ah, that maternal smile! It answers—Yes.
I heard the bell tolled on thy burial day,
I saw the hearse that bore thee slow away,
And turning from my nursery window, drew   30
A long, long sigh, and wept a last adieu!
But was it such?—It was.—Where thou art gone
Adieus and farewells are a sound unknown.
May I but meet thee on that peaceful shore,
The parting word shall pass my lips no more!
Thy maidens, grieved themselves at my concern,
Oft gave me promise of thy quick return.
What ardently I wished, I long believed,
And, disappointed still, was still deceived.
By expectation every day beguiled,   40
Dupe of *tomorrow* even from a child.
Thus many a sad tomorrow came and went,
Till, all my stock of infant sorrow spent,
I learned at last submission to my lot;
But, though I less deplored thee, ne'er forgot.
Where once we dwelt our name is heard no more,
Children not thine have trod my nursery floor;
And where the gardener Robin, day by day,
Drew me to school along the public way,
Delighted with my bauble coach, and wrapped   50
In scarlet mantle warm, and velvet capped,
'Tis now become a history little known,
That once we called the pastoral house our own.
Short-lived possession! but the record fair
That memory keeps of all thy kindness there,
Still outlives many a storm that has effaced
A thousand other themes less deeply traced.

of the sea. 20. **devotes,** gives over to destruction. 40. **Slaves . . .
England.** The court decision that "slaves cannot breathe in England"
was given by Lord Mansfield in 1772. The slave trade was not
abolished until 1807. Slavery in the British Colonies was abolished in
1833.
The Garden. 109. **Long since.** Cowper's first breakdown came in

1763. See headnote, p. 647.
On the Receipt of My Mother's Picture. 2. **heard thee last.**
Cowper was only six years old when his mother died in 1737. 53.
pastoral house, the rectory of Great Berkhampstead, Hertfordshire,
where Cowper was born.

Thy nightly visits to my chamber made,
That thou mightst know me safe and warmly laid;
60 Thy morning bounties ere I left my home,
The biscuit, or confectionary plum;
The fragrant waters on my cheeks bestowed
By thy own hand, till fresh they shone and glowed;
All this, and more endearing still than all,
Thy constant flow of love, that knew no fall,
Ne'er roughened by those cataracts and brakes
That humor interposed too often makes;
All this still legible in memory's page,
And still to be so to my latest age,
70 Adds joy to duty, makes me glad to pay
Such honors to thee as my numbers may;
Perhaps a frail memorial, but sincere,
Not scorned in heaven, though little noticed here.

    Could Time, his flight reversed, restore the hours,
When, playing with thy vesture's tissued flowers,
The violet, the pink, and jessamine,
I pricked them into paper with a pin
(And thou wast happier than myself the while,
Would softly speak, and stroke my head and smile),
80 Could those few pleasant days again appear,
Might one wish bring them, would I wish them here?
I would not trust my heart—the dear delight
Seems so to be desired, perhaps I might.—
But no—what here we call our life is such,
So little to be loved, and thou so much,
That I should ill requite thee to constrain
Thy unbound spirit into bonds again.

    Thou, as a gallant bark from Albion's coast
(The storms all weathered and the ocean crossed)
90 Shoots into port at some well-havened isle,
Where spices breathe, and brighter seasons smile,
There sits quiescent on the floods that show
Her beauteous form reflected clear below,
While airs impregnated with incense play
Around her, fanning light her streamers gay;
So thou, with sails how swift! hast reached the shore,
"Where tempests never beat nor billows roar."
And thy loved consort on the dangerous tide
Of life long since has anchored by thy side.
100 But me, scarce hoping to attain that rest,
Always from port withheld, always distressed—
Me howling blasts drive devious, tempest tossed,
Sails ripped, seams opening wide, and compass lost,
And day by day some current's thwarting force
Sets me more distant from a prosperous course.
Yet, oh, the thought that thou art safe, and he!
That thought is joy, arrive what may to me.
My boast is not that I deduce my birth
From loins enthroned and rulers of the earth;
110 But higher far my proud pretensions rise—
The son of parents passed into the skies!
And now, farewell—Time unrevoked has run

His wonted course, yet what I wished is done.
By contemplation's help, not sought in vain,
I seem to have lived my childhood o'er again;
To have renewed the joys that once were mine,
Without the sin of violating thine:
And, while the wings of Fancy still are free,
And I can view this mimic show of thee,
Time has but half succeeded in his theft—
120 Thyself removed, thy power to soothe me left.
(1790; 1798)

The Globe Tavern, Dumfries, Scotland, from a painting by George Thompson. Historical Pictures Service—Chicago.

67. **humor,** fancy, whim. 88. **Albion,** poetic for England. 97. **"Where . . . roar,"** incorrectly quoted from Garth's *Dispensary,* 3,226: "Where billows never break, nor tempests roar." 99. **long since.** Cowper's

father died in 1756. 109. **rulers of the earth.** On his mother's side Cowper was descended from Henry III.

ROBERT BURNS 1759-1796

The greatest poet that Scotland has produced was born in Ayrshire, the son of a hard-working farmer whose ambitious hopes for the upbringing of his children were blighted by poverty and discouragement. The childhood and boyhood of the poet consisted largely of a series of transient settlings and sudden uprootings on various unsuccessful farms—at Alloway, at Mt. Oliphant, at Lochlea, all little hamlets in the Lowlands of Scotland. On all of them young Burns labored as a plowboy. "This kind of life," he himself said, "the cheerless gloom of a hermit and the unceasing toil of a galley-slave, brought me to my sixteenth year." It is probable that much of Burns' later fragile health and his untimely death before he was forty can both be traced to this arduous life.

He went to school for a time at Kirkoswald, not far south of Ayr; there his uncertain and unformed ambitions became more definite. He learned something of the great works of literature, became fired with an enthusiasm for the songs and traditions of his native Scotland, and grew more and more sensitive to the beauties of nature as he saw them all about him in both graceful and severe guises. His immediate problem, however, was making a living. In 1781 he became a flax-dresser at Irvine, Ayrshire, and here he became familiar with the ways of the city. Here he fell in and out of love—there is more than one such episode in Burns' life—and found himself hailed as a boon companion.

In 1784 his father died, and Robert Burns, with his brother Gilbert, resumed the life of a poor farmer on land previously leased at Mossgiel. While at Mossgiel he entered on a liaison with Jean Armour, the daughter of a mason in the vicinity. This affair lasted intermittently for years, but the girl's father raised objections to their marriage, and Burns as a despised suitor was at one time about to sail away to America to try his fortunes. But the publication of his first volume of poems at Kilmarnock in 1786, a collection comprising some of his most famous poems, changed his plans completely. For the obscure young farmer became the literary rage; he was introduced to Edinburgh, the Athens of Scotland, where he was dined and wined but regarded as a rustic prodigy. Burns in the city was something of an anomaly, and his writing of verse in the manner of polite urban society has well been likened to a man's trying to dance the minuet with hobnailed shoes.

The second edition of the Poems (1787) brought him enough money for two brief tours: one through the northern counties of England and the other into the Highlands. In the next year Burns took another farm in Dumfriesshire, lost money, wrote more poems, and married Jean Armour. In 1789 he became the exciseman of the district and later took a similar position in the town of Dumfries.

Burns' last year of literary activity (1792) was spent largely in collecting and editing traditional songs and ballads of ancient Scotland; he was responsible for the publication not only of the traditional text of these ballads but of their melodies as well. Much of this editing resulted in virtually original compositions and added to his reputation as a great national poet. His growing sympathy with the ideas underlying the French Revolution lost him many friends; his health declined, and with that decline in health came irritability of temperament and defiance of conventions which led him to occasional excesses and ruined his good name for many decades to come.

He died in July 1796. The melancholy pulpiteers of the nineteenth century attributed his premature passing to dissipation, but the more considered view would account for his death as the result of heart disease incurred by his overwork in his early years and somewhat aggravated by his occasionally reckless living. But Burns was neither a sot nor a confirmed libertine; he is the poet of good fellowship, no doubt, and a stout-hearted and tender singer of the passion of love; yet the evidence does not show that he was an habitué of the tavern, and his involvement with three women—Mary Campbell, Elizabeth Paton, and Jean Armour—seems in each instance to have been based on sincere feeling. Perhaps the worst that can be said of Burns and his poetry is that both are earthy.

No doubt that very earthiness is one source of Burns' great popularity. But he has more spiritual achievements to his credit. He is sincere to the core, tender-hearted and impulsive as well, with the customary romantic individual's instinct to love and shelter the helpless. He is the romantic poet of nature and the sentimentalist at one and the same time; and it would be easy to quote the titles of a dozen poems by Burns—To a Mouse, To a Mountain Daisy, Sweet Afton are but three of the most famous—that would serve to illustrate these two cardinal traits of the romanticist. There is in Burns the national and the patriotic; he sings the glory of "auld Scotia," not only by the revival of old ballads, but also by the flaming expression of Scotch independence, as in Scots, Wha Hae. He is the poet of domestic felicity and the solid virtues of the humble folk in such poems as The Cotter's Saturday Night; he proclaims a triumphant democracy, even revolutionism, in A Man's a Man for A' That; he can play on the stops of young romantic love in To Jeanie or Bonnie Wee Thing and of tried and true devotion in John Anderson; he has touched the note of enduring friendship once and for all in Auld Lang Syne.

There is, however, another side to Burns which many have come to consider his greater talent, the expression of his satirical instinct. Burns was a lover of humanity—in its most erring as well as in its most endearing aspects. He has no patience with pretensions or hypocrisy; he rebels against the unyielding censoriousness of the "unco guid." When that satirical instinct coincides with his humanitarian promptings, the product is revolutionary poetry of a violent sort with raucous tone and sardonic wit, like Holy Willie's Prayer and The Jolly Beggars. Both poems, and particularly the latter, are harsh indictments of society which society must reject in self-defense.

There are times when Burns lapses into the didactic tone of the eighteenth-century moralist. Usually when he does so, he writes in a manner strongly suggestive of the English neo-classical poets. His satire, too, belongs by tradition to the foregoing age. But the great body of his poems, with their sweetness, warmth of emotion, lyric lilt, and spontaneous fervor, belong to Burns the Scotch romanticist. He is a transitional figure between the neo-classical and the romantic, but he has almost reached the romanticists' encampment. He belongs not to the drawing room but to the heaths and moorlands of his native Scotland.

MARY MORISON

The subject of this poem may have been Mary Campbell, Elison Begbie, or the Mary Morison, said to have been "as beautiful as amiable," who lived at Mauchline from 1784 till her death in 1791.

O Mary, at thy window be,
  It is the wish'd, the trysted hour!
Those smiles and glances let me see,
  That make the miser's treasure poor:
How blythely wad I bide the stoure,
  A weary slave frae sun to sun,
Could I the rich reward secure,
  The lovely Mary Morison.

Yestreen when to the trembling string
10 The dance gaed thro' the lighted ha',
To thee my fancy took its wing,
  I sat, but neither heard nor saw:
Tho' this was fair, and that was braw,
  And yon the toast of a' the town,
I sigh'd, and said amang them a',
  "Ye are na Mary Morison."

O Mary, canst thou wreck his peace,
  Wha for thy sake wad gladly die?
Or canst thou break that heart of his,
20 Whase only faut is loving thee?
If love for love thou wilt na gie
  At least be pity to me shown;
A thought ungentle canna be
  The thought o' Mary Morison.
(1781; 1800)

HOLY WILLIE'S PRAYER

"Holy Willie," the subject of this poem, was William Fisher, an elder in the parish church at Mauchline, in Ayrshire. He was later accused of embezzling church funds and ended in the gutter. The best introduction to the poem is to be found in Burns' own "argument":

"Holy Willie was a rather oldish bachelor elder, in the parish of Mauchline, and much and justly famed for that polemical chattering which ends in tippling orthodoxy, and for that spiritualized bawdry which refines to liquorish devotion. In a sessional process with a gentleman in Mauchline—a Mr. Gavin Hamilton—Holy Willie and his priest, Father Auld, after full hearing in the Presbytery of Ayr, came off but second best, owing partly to the oratorical powers of Mr. Robert Aiken, Mr. Hamilton's counsel; but chiefly to Mr. Hamilton's being one of the most irreproachable and truly respected characters in the country. On losing his process, the muse overheard him at his devotions as follows—" The poem then proceeds thus:

O Thou, wha in the Heavens dost dwell,
Wha, as it pleases best Thysel',
Sends ane to heaven an' ten to hell
    A' for Thy glory,
And no for onie guid or ill
    They've done bafore Thee!

I bless and praise Thy matchless might,
Whan thousands Thou hast left in night,
That I am here before Thy sight,

Mary Morison. 5. bide the stoure, endure the struggle. 9. Yestreen, last night. 10. gaed, went. 13. braw, fine, handsome. 20. faut, fault. 21. na gie, not give.

Holy Willie's Prayer. sessional process, a trial conducted before an ecclesiastical court that reproved evildoers. 38. fash'd, beset. 39. warldly, worldly. 49. maun, must. 51. fou, full, drunk. 54. steered,

For gifts an' grace,
A burning an' a shining light,
To a' this place.

What was I, or my generation,
That I should get sic exaltation?
I' wha deserv'd sic just damnation
For broken laws,
Five thousand years 'fore my creation,
Thro' Adam's cause!

When frae my mither's womb I fell,
20 Thou might hae plung'd me deep in hell,
To gnash my gums, to weep and wail,
In burnin' lake,
Where damnéd devils roar and yell,
Chain'd to a stake.

Yet I am here, a chosen sample,
To show Thy grace is great and ample;
I'm here a pillar in Thy temple,
Strong as a rock,
A guide, a buckler, an example
30 To a' Thy flock.

O Lord, Thou kens what zeal I bear,
When drinkers drink, and swearers swear,
And singin there and dancin here,
Wi' great an' sma':
For I am keepit by Thy fear,
Free frae them a'.

But yet, O Lord! confess I must:
At times I'm fash'd wi' fleshly lust;
An' sometimes, too, wi' warldly trust,
40 Vile self gets in;
But Thou remembers we are dust,
Defil'd in sin.

O Lord! yestreen, Thou kens, wi' Meg—
Thy pardon I sincerely beg,
O! may it ne'er be a livin plague
To my dishonor!
An' I'll ne'er lift a lawless leg
Again upon her.

Besides I farther maun allow,
50 Wi' Lizzie's lass, three times, I trow;
But, Lord, that Friday I was fou,
When I came near her,
Or else, Thou kens, Thy servant true
Wad ne'er hae steered her.

May be Thou lets this fleshly thorn
Beset Thy servant e'en and morn,

Lest he owre high and proud should turn,
'Cause he's sae gifted;
If sae, Thy hand maun e'en be borne,
Until Thou lift it.   60

Lord, bless Thy chosen in this place,
For here Thou hast a chosen race;
But God confound their stubborn face,
And blast their name,
Wha bring Thy elders to disgrace,
An' public shame!

Lord, mind Gau'n Hamilton's deserts:
He drinks, an' swears, an' plays at cartes,
Yet has sae monie takin arts
Wi' grit and sma',   70
Frae God's ain Priest the people's hearts
He steals awa'.

An' whan we chasten'd him therefore,
Thou kens how he bred sic a splore,
As set the warld in a roar
O' laughin at us;
Curse Thou his basket and his store,
Kail and potatoes!

Lord, hear my earnest cry an' pray'r
Against that Presbyt'ry o' Ayr!   80
Thy strong right hand, Lord, make it bare
Upo' their heads;
Lord, weigh it down, an' dinna spare,
For their misdeeds!

O Lord my God! that glib-tongu'd Aiken,
My very heart and flesh are quakin,
To think how we stood sweatin, shakin,
An' pish'd wi' dread,
While he, wi' hingin lip an' snakin,
Held up his head.   90

Lord, in the day of vengeance try him;
Lord, visit him wha did employ him,
And pass not in Thy mercy by 'em,
Nor hear their pray'r:
But, for Thy people's sake, destroy 'em,
An' dinna spare.

But, Lord, remember me and mine
Wi' mercies temp'ral and divine,
That I for gear and grace may shine,
Excelled by nane;   100
And a' the glory shall be Thine,
Amen, Amen.
(1785; 1808)

meddled with. 67. **Gau'n Hamilton,** Gavin Hamilton. See headnote.
68. **cartes,** cards. Card playing was against the rules of the church.
74. **sic a splore,** such a fuss. 88. **pish'd,** humiliated. 89. **hingin,**

hanging. **snakin,** sneering. 99. **gear,** wealth. 100. **nane,** none.

THE JOLLY BEGGARS

This, the most satirical, the most dramatic, and perhaps the most thoroughly revolutionary of Burns' poems, was not regarded highly by the family of the poet. It was not published until after his death, he himself in later years remarked to a friend who had heard of the existence of the poem: "I have forgot the cantata you allude to, as I kept no copy, and, indeed, did not know of its existence, however, I remember that none of the songs pleased myself except the last, something about

>   *Courts for cowards were erected,*
>   *Churches built to please the priest."*

The scene of The Jolly Beggars is Mauchline, Ayrshire; it is said that the poet actually visited the resort of Poosie Nansie. Such actual identification of place is doubtless interesting, but the piece has so much vigor and humanity that it transcends geographical limits. It portrays mankind in its most vagrant, vulgar, and earthy state, "wringing from Fate," as Carlyle has said, "another hour of wassail and good cheer." Perhaps the final criticism of The Jolly Beggars has been written by Matthew Arnold in his Study of Poetry (p. 965): "When the largeness and freedom of Burns get full sweep, as in . . . that puissant and splendid production, The Jolly Beggars, his world may be what it will, his poetic genius triumphs over it. In the world of The Jolly Beggars there is more than hideousness and squalor, there is bestiality, yet the piece is a superb poetic success. It has a breadth, truth, and power which make the famous scene in Auerbach's Cellar, of Goethe's Faust, seem artificial and tame beside it, and which are only matched by Shakespeare and Aristophanes."

A CANTATA

RECITATIVO

When lyart leaves bestrow the yird,
Or, wavering like the bauckie-bird,
  Bedim cauld Boreas' blast;
When hailstanes drive wi' bitter skyte,
And infant frosts begin to bite,
  In hoary cranreuch drest;
Ae night at e'en a merry core
  O' randie, gangrel bodies
In Poosie-Nansie's held the splore,
10 To drink their orra duddies:
    Wi' quaffing and laughing,

They ranted an' they sang;
  Wi' jumping an' thumping,
    The vera girdle rang.

First, niest the fire, in auld red rags,
Ane sat, weel brac'd wi' mealy bags,
  And knapsack a' in order;
His doxy lay within his arm;
Wi' usquebae an' blankets warm,
  She blinket on her sodger.   20
An' ay he gies the tozie drab
  The tither skelpin' kiss,
While she held up her greedy gab,
  Just like an aumous dish:
    Ilk smack still, did crack still,
      Just like a cadger's whup;
    Then, staggering and swaggering,
      He roar'd this ditty up—

AIR (Tune: *Soldier's Joy*)

I am a son of Mars, who have been in many wars,
  And show my cuts and scars wherever I come: 30
This here was for a wench, and that other in a trench
  When welcoming the French at the sound of the
    drum.

My 'prenticeship I past, where my leader breath'd his
    last,
  When the bloody die was cast on the heights of
    Abram;
And I serv'd out my trade when the gallant game was
    play'd,
  And the Moro low was laid at the sound of the drum.

I lastly was with Curtis among the floating batt'ries,
  And there I left for witness an arm and a limb:
Yet let my country need me, with Eliott to head me,
  I'd clatter on my stumps at the sound of the drum. 40

And now, tho' I must beg, with a wooden arm and leg,
  And many a tatter'd rag hanging over my bum,
I'm as happy with my wallet, my bottle, and my callet,
  As when I us'd in scarlet to follow a drum.

What tho' with hoary locks I must stand the winter
    shocks,
  Beneath the woods and rocks oftentimes for a home?
When the tother bag I sell, and the tother bottle tell,
  I could meet a troop of hell at the sound of a drum.

The Jolly Beggars. **1. lyart,** faded, gray. **yird,** earth. **2. bauckie-bird,** bat. **3. Boreas,** the north wind. **4. skyte,** dash. **6. cranreuch,** hoarfrost. **7. core,** company. **8. randie,** lawless. **gangrel,** vagrant. **9. splore,** carousal. **10. orra duddies,** spare rags or clothes. **12. ranted,** whooped. **14. girdle,** a round metal plate used as a frying pan. **15. niest,** next. **16. mealy bags,** bags that usually contained oatmeal, which could be used for food by the beggar or traded or

sold as need might arise. **18. doxy,** wench. **19. usquebae,** whiskey. **20. blinket,** smirked. **sodger,** soldier. **21. gies . . . drab,** gives the tipsy wench. **22. tither skelpin',** another smacking. **24. aumous,** alms. **25. Ilk,** each. **26. cadger's whup,** hawker's whip. **Tune:** *Soldier's Joy.* All the tunes mentioned in the poem were popular airs of the day. **34. heights of Abram,** at Quebec, in 1759, where Wolfe defeated Montcalm and assured the British possession of Canada. **36.**

50 He ended; and the kebars sheuk
Aboon the chorus roar;
While frighted rattons backward leuk,
And seek the benmost bore:
A fairy fiddler frae the neuk,
He skirled out *Encore!*
But up arose the martial chuck,
And laid the loud uproar.

AIR (Tune: *Soldier Laddie*)

I once was a maid, tho' I cannot tell when,
And still my delight is in proper young men.
Some one of a troop of dragoons was my daddie:
60 No wonder I'm fond of a sodger laddie!

The first of my loves was a swaggering blade:
To rattle the thundering drum was his trade;
His leg was so tight, and his cheek was so ruddy,
Transported I was with my sodger laddie.

But the godly old chaplain left him in the lurch;
The sword I forsook for the sake of the church;
He ventur'd the soul, and I risked the body:
'Twas then I prov'd false to my sodger laddie.

Full soon I grew sick of my sanctified sot;
70 The regiment at large for a husband I got;
From the gilded spontoon to the fife I was ready:
I asked no more but a sodger laddie.

But the peace it reduc'd me to beg in despair,
Till I met my old boy at Cunningham fair;
His rags regimental they flutter'd so gaudy:
My heart it rejoic'd at a sodger laddie.

And now I have liv'd—I know not how long!
But still I can join in a cup or a song;
But whilst with both hands I can hold the glass steady,
80 Here's to thee, my hero, my sodger laddie!

RECITATIVO

Poor Merry Andrew in the neuk
Sat guzzling wi' a tinkler hizzie;
They mind't na wha the chorus teuk,
Between themselves they were sae busy;
At length, wi' drink and courting dizzy,
He stoitered up an' made a face;
Then turn'd an' laid a smack on Grizzy,
Syne tun'd his pipes wi' grave grimace.

AIR (Tune: *Auld Syr Symon*)

Sir Wisdom's a fool when he's fou;
90 Sir Knave is a fool in a session:
He's there but a 'prentice I trow,
But I am a fool by profession.

My grannie she bought me a beuk,
And I held awa to the school;
I fear I my talent misteuk,
But what will ye hae of a fool?

For drink I wad venture my neck;
A hizzie's the half o' my craft:
But what could ye other expect
100 Of ane that's avowedly daft?

I ance was ty'd up like a stirk
For civilly swearing and quaffing;
I ance was abus'd i' the kirk
For towzling a lass i' my daffin.

Poor Andrew that tumbles for sport
Let naebody name wi' a jeer:
There's ev'n, I'm tauld, i' the Court
A tumbler ca'd the Premier.

Observ'd ye yon reverend lad
110 Maks faces to tickle the mob?
He rails at our mountebank squad—
It's rivalship just i' the job!

And now my conclusion I'll tell,
For faith! I'm confoundedly dry:
The chiel that's a fool for himsel',
Guid Lord! he's far dafter than I.

RECITATIVO

Then niest outspak a raucle carlin,
What kent fu' weel to cleek the sterlin,
For monie a pursie she had hooked,
120 And had in monie a well been douked.
Her love had been a Highland laddie,
But weary fa' the waefu' woodie!
Wi' sighs an' sabs she thus began
To wail her braw John Highlandman:

AIR (Tune: *O, An' Ye Were Dead, Guidman*)

A Highland lad my love was born,
The Lawlan' laws he held in scorn:

Moro . . . laid, at Santiago, Cuba, where the British attacked the fortress of El Moro in 1762. 37. with Curtis, at Gibraltar in 1782. 39. Eliott, Sir George Eliott, defender of Gibraltar against the French and the Spanish, 1779-1783. 43. callet, wench. 47. tell, count. 49. kebars sheuk, rafters shook. 50. Aboon, above. 51. rattons, rats. 52. benmost bore, inmost hole. 53. neuk, nook, corner. 54. skirled, yelled. 55. chuck, hen. 63. tight, trim, comely. 71. spontoon, a weapon carried by officers. 82. tinkler hizzie, tinker wench. 86. stoitered, staggered. 88. Syne, then. 89. fou, full, drunk. 90. session, court or church session. 101. stirk, young bull, i.e., he was made to wear a kind of iron collar. 104. daffin, fun. 115. chiel, young chap. 117. raucle carlin, a sturdy old woman. 118. cleek the sterlin, snatch the cash. 122. woodie, gallows, on which her lover had been hanged. 124. braw, handsome. 126. Lawlan', Lowland.

But he still was faithfu' to his clan,
My gallant braw John Highlandman.

Chorus

Sing hey, my braw John Highlandman!
130 Sing ho, my braw John Highlandman!
There's not a lad in a' the lan'
Was match for my John Highlandman!

With his philabeg, an' tartan plaid,
An' gude claymore down by his side,
The ladies' hearts he did trepan,
My gallant braw John Highlandman.

We rangéd a' from Tweed to Spey,
And liv'd like lords and ladies gay;
For a Lawlan' face he feared nane,
140 My gallant braw John Highlandman.

They banish'd him beyond the sea,
But ere the bud was on the tree,
Adown my cheeks the pearls ran,
Embracing my John Highlandman.

But, Oh! they catch'd him at the last,
And bound him in a dungeon fast.
My curse upon them every ane,
They've hang'd my braw John Highlandman!

And now a widow I must mourn
150 The pleasures that will ne'er return;
No comfort but a hearty can,
When I think on John Highlandman.

Chorus

Sing hey, my braw John Highlandman!
Sing ho, my braw John Highlandman!
There's not a lad in a' the lan'
Was match for my John Highlandman!

RECITATIVO

A pigmy scraper wi' his fiddle,
Wha us'd at trystes and fairs to driddle,
Her strappin limb an' gausy middle
160   (He reach'd nae higher),
Had hol't his heartie like a riddle,
         An' blawn 't on fire.

Wi' hand on haunch and upward ee,
He crooned his gamut, one, two, three,

Then, in an *arioso* key
         The wee Apollo
Set off wi' *allegretto* glee
         His *giga* solo.

AIR (Tune: *Whistle Owre the Lave O't*)

Let me ryke up to dight that tear;
An' go wi' me an' be my dear,
An' then your every care an' fear   170
         May whistle owre the lave o't.

Chorus

I am a fiddler to my trade,
And a' the tunes that e'er I played,
The sweetest still to wife or maid
         Was *Whistle Owre the Lave O't.*

At kirns an' weddings we'se be there,
And O, sae nicely 's we will fare!
We'll bowse about till Daddie Care
         Sing *Whistle Owre the Lave O't.*   180

Sae merrily the banes we'll pyke,
And sun oursels about the dyke;
And at our leisure, when ye like,
         We'll whistle owre the lave o't!

But bless me wi' your heav'n o' charms,
An' while I kittle hair on thairms,
Hunger, cauld, and a' sic harms
         May whistle owre the lave o't.

Chorus

I am a fiddler to my trade,
And a' the tunes that e'er I played,   190
The sweetest still to wife or maid
         Was *Whistle Owre the Lave O't.*

RECITATIVO

Her charms had struck a sturdy Caird
         As weel as poor Gut-scraper;
He taks the fiddler by the beard,
         An' draws a roosty rapier—
He swoor, by a' was swearing worth,
         To spit him like a pliver,
Unless he would from that time forth
         Relinquish her for ever.   200

---

133. **philabeg,** a short plaited skirt, or kilt. **tartan plaid,** shawl or
scarf. 134. **claymore,** broadsword. 135. **trepan,** ensnare. 137. **Tweed,
Spey,** rivers at opposite ends of Scotland; the *Tweed* is in the south,
the *Spey* in the north. 158. **trystes,** cattle markets. **fairs,** markets for
hiring servants and farm laborers. **driddle,** toddle. 159. **gausy,** buxom.
161. **hol't,** pierced. **riddle,** sieve. 164. **crooned,** hummed. 165.
arioso, smooth, melodious. 166. **Apollo,** god of music and poetry;
here, songster. 167. *allegretto,* quick, light. 168. *giga,* a lively

dance. Tune: *Lave,* remainder, rest. 169. **ryke . . . dight,** reach up
to wipe. 177. **kirns,** harvest homes. 179. **bowse,** booze. 181. **banes,**
bones. **pyke,** pick. 182. **dyke,** stone or turf fence. 186. **kittle . . .
thairms,** tickle hair on guts, i.e., play on the fiddle. 193. **Caird,**
tinker. 198. **pliver,** plover. 202. **hunkers,** hams. 207. **snirtle,**
snicker. Tune: *Clout,* mend. 220. **budget,** a tinker's bag of tools.
221. **stoup,** jug. 222. **Kilbagie,** a brand of whisky, named after a
noted distillery. 224. **weet my craigie,** wet my throat. 227. **sae sair,**

Wi' ghastly ee poor Tweedle-Dee
  Upon his hunkers bended,
And pray'd for grace wi' ruefu' face,
  And sae the quarrel ended.
But tho' his little heart did grieve
  When round the tinkler prest her,
He feigned to snirtle in his sleeve
  When thus the Caird address'd her:

AIR (Tune: *Clout the Cauldron*)

My bonie lass, I work in brass,
210 A tinkler is my station;
I've travell'd round all Christian ground
  In this my occupation;
I've ta'en the gold, I've been enrolled
  In many a noble squadron;
But vain they search'd when off I march'd
  To go and clout the cauldron.

Despise that shrimp, that wither'd imp,
  With a' his noise an' cap'rin',
And take a share wi' those that bear
220 The budget and the apron!
And by that stoup, my faith and houp!
  And by that dear Kilbagie!
If e'er ye want, or meet wi' scant,
  May I ne'er weet my craigie!

RECITATIVO

The Caird prevailed: th' unblushing fair
  In his embraces sunk,
Partly wi' love o'ercome sae sair,
  And partly she was drunk.
Sir Violino, with an air
230 That show'd a man o' spunk,
Wish'd unison between the pair,
  An' made the bottle clunk
    To their health that night.

But hurchin Cupid shot a shaft,
  That play'd a dame a shavie:
The fiddler rak'd her fore and aft
  Behint the chicken cavie.
Her lord, a wight o' Homer's craft,
  Tho' limpin' wi' the spavie,
240 He hirpled up, and lap like daft,
  And shored them "Dainty Davie,"
    O'boot that night.

He was a care-defying blade
  As ever Bacchus listed!

Tho' Fortune sair upon him laid,
  His heart, she ever miss'd it.
He had no wish but—to be glad,
  Nor want but—when he thirsted,
He hated nought but—to be sad;
  And thus the Muse suggested   250
    His sang that night.

AIR (Tune: *For A' That, An' A' That*)

I am a Bard, of no regard
  Wi' gentlefolks, an' a' that,
But Homer-like, the glowrin byke,
  Frae town to town I draw that.

Chorus

For a' that, an' a' that,
  And twice as meickle's a' that;
I've lost but ane, I've twa behin',
  I've wife eneugh for a' that.

I never drank the Muses' stank,   260
  Castalia's burn, an' a' that;
But there it streams, an' richly reams,
  My Helicon I ca' that.

Great love I bear to a' the fair,
  Their humble slave, an' a' that;
But lordly will, I hold it still
  A mortal sin to thraw that.

In raptures sweet this hour we meet
  Wi' mutual love, an' a' that;
But for how lang the flie may stang,   270
  Let inclination law that!

Their tricks an' craft hae put me daft,
  They've taen me in, an' a' that;
But clear your decks, an' here's the Sex!
  I like the jads for a' that.

Chorus

For a' that, an' a' that,
  An' twice as meickle's a' that,
My dearest bluid, to do them guid,
  They're welcome till 't, for a' that!

RECITATIVO

So sung the Bard—and Nansie's wa's   280
Shook with a thunder of applause,

---

so sorely. 232. **clunk**, gurgle. 234. **hurchin**, urchin. 235. **shavie**, trick. 237. **cavie**, coop. 238. **Homer's craft**, the poet's profession. Burns spoke of Homer as "the oldest ballad singer on record." 239. **spavie**, spavin (a disease). 240. **hirpled**, hobbled. **lap like daft**, leaped like mad. 241. **shored**, offered. **"Dainty Davie,"** name of a popular love song. 242. **O'boot**, to boot, gratis. 244. **Bacchus**, god of wine. **listed**, enrolled as a follower. 254. **glowrin byke**, staring crowd. 257. **meickle**, much. 260. **stank**, pool, ditch. 261. **Castalia**, a fountain on Mt. Parnassus, Greece, supposed to give inspiration to those who drank of it. **burn**, brook. 262. **reams**, foams; ale is his source of inspiration. 263. **Helicon**, a mountain range in Greece; it had two springs, sacred to the Muses. 267. **thraw**, thwart. 270. **stang**, sting, bite. 271. **law**, rule. 272. **hae put me daft**, have made me foolish. 279. **till 't**, to it.

Re-echo'd from each mouth!
They toom'd their pocks, and pawn'd their duds,
They scarcely left to co'er their fuds,
    To quench their lowan drouth.
Then owre again the jovial thrang
    The poet did request
To lowse his pack, an' wale a sang,
    A ballad o' the best:
290   He rising, rejoicing
        Between his twa Deborahs,
      Looks round him, an' found them
      Impatient for the chorus.

AIR (Tune: *Jolly Mortals, Fill Your Glasses*)

See the smoking bowl before us!
    Mark our jovial, ragged ring!
Round and round take up the chorus,
    And in raptures let us sing:

Chorus

A fig for those by law protected!
    Liberty's a glorious feast!
300 Courts for cowards were erected,
    Churches built to please the priest!

What is title? what is treasure?
    What is reputation's care?
If we lead a life of pleasure,
    'Tis no matter, how or where!

With the ready trick and fable
    Round we wander all the day;
And at night, in barn or stable,
    Hug our doxies on the hay.

310 Does the train-attended carriage
    Thro' the country lighter rove?
Does the sober bed of marriage
    Witness brighter scenes of love?

Life is all a variorum,
    We regard not how it goes;
Let them cant about decorum,
    Who have characters to lose.

Here's to budgets, bags, and wallets!
    Here's to all the wandering train!
320 Here's our ragged brats and callets!
    One and all, cry out, Amen!

Chorus

A fig for those by law protected!
    Liberty's a glorious feast,
Courts for cowards were erected,
    Churches built to please the priest!
(1785; 1799)

TO A MOUSE

ON TURNING UP HER NEST WITH THE PLOW,
NOVEMBER, 1785

Wee, sleekit, cowrin, tim'rous beastie,
O, what a panic's in thy breastie!
Thou need na start awa sae hasty
    Wi' bickering brattle!
I wad be laith to rin an' chase thee,
    Wi' murdering pattle!

I'm truly sorry man's dominion
Has broken Nature's social union,
An' justifies that ill opinion
    Which makes thee startle   10
At me, thy poor, earth-born companion
    An' fellow-mortal!

I doubt na whyles, but thou may thieve;
What then? poor beastie, thou maun live:
A daimen icker in a thrave
    'S a sma' request;
I'll get a blessin wi' the lave,
    An' never miss 't!

Thy wee-bit housie, too, in ruin!
Its silly wa's the win's are strewin!   20
An' naething, now, to big a new ane,
    O' foggage green!
An' bleak December's win's ensuin,
    Baith snell an' keen!

Thou saw the fields laid bare an' waste,
An' weary winter comin' fast,
An' cozie here, beneath the blast,
    Thou thought to dwell,
Till, crash! the cruel coulter passed
    Out through thy cell.   30

That wee bit heap o' leaves an' stibble,
Has cost thee monie a weary nibble!

283. toom'd their pocks, emptied their wallets. 284. co'er their fuds, cover their shirt tails. 285. lowan drouth, raging thirst. 288. lowse, open. wale, choose. 291. Deborah, Hebrew prophetess who celebrated the victory of the Israelites over the Canaanites in a famous song of triumph. See Judges, Chapters 4, 5.
    To a Mouse. 1. sleekit, sleek. 4. Wi' . . . brattle, with sudden scamper. 5. wad be laith, would be loath. 6. pattle, paddle, used for cleaning the plow. 13. whyles, sometimes. 15. daimen . . . thrave, an occasional ear or head of grain in a shock (of twenty-four sheaves).

17. lave, rest. 21. big, build. 22. foggage, coarse grass. 24. snell, sharp, bitter. 29. coulter, cutter attached to the beam of a plow to cut the sward. 34. But, without. hald, abode. 35. thole, endure. 36. cranreuch, hoarfrost. 37. no thy lane, not alone. 40. Gang aft agley, often go awry.
    Address to the Deil. O Prince, etc. From Paradise Lost, I, 128-129 (p. 389). The poem is, in part, a good-natured burlesque of the Miltonic conception of Satan. The first two lines of Burns' poem are imitated from Pope's Dunciad. 2. Clootie, little hoof. 5. Spairges,

Now thou's turned out, for a' thy trouble,
      But house or hald,
To thole the winter's sleety dribble,
      An' cranreuch cauld!

But Mousie, thou art no thy lane,
In proving foresight may be vain:
The best-laid schemes o' mice an' men
40   Gang aft agley,
An' lea'e us naught but grief an' pain,
      For promised joy!

Still thou art blest, compared wi' me!
The present only toucheth thee:
But och! I backward cast my e'e,
      On prospects drear!
An' forward, though I canna see,
      I guess an' fear!
(1785; 1786)

ADDRESS TO THE DEIL

O Prince, O Chief of many thronéd Powers
That led the embattled Seraphim to war!—MILTON.

O thou! whatever title suit thee—
Auld Hornie, Satan, Nick, or Clootie—
Wha in yon cavern grim an' sootie,
      Clos'd under hatches,
Spairges about the brunstane cootie,
      To scaud poor wretches!

Hear me, Auld Hangie, for a wee,
An' let poor damnéd bodies be;
I'm sure sma' pleasure it can gie,
10   Ev'n to a deil,
To skelp an' scaud poor dogs like me
      An' hear us squeel.

Great is thy pow'r an' great thy fame;
Far kend an' noted is thy name;
An' tho' yon lowin heugh's thy hame,
      Thou travels far;
An' faith! thou's neither lag, nor lame,
      Nor blate, nor scaur.

Whyles, ranging like a roarin lion,
20 For prey, a' holes an' corners trying;
Whyles, on the strong-wing'd tempest flyin,
      Tirlin the kirks;

Whyles, in the human bosom pryin,
      Unseen thou lurks.

I've heard my rev'rend graunie say,
In lanely glens ye like to stray;
Or, where auld ruin'd castles gray
      Nod to the moon,
Ye fright the nightly wand'rer's way
      Wi' eldritch croon.   30

When twilight did my graunie summon,
To say her pray'rs, douce, honest woman!
Aft yont the dyke she's heard you bummin,
      Wi' eerie drone;
Or, rustlin, thro' the boortrees comin,
      Wi' heavy groan.

Ae dreary, windy, winter night,
The stars shot down wi' sklentin light,
Wi' you mysel, I gat a fright:
      Ayont the lough,   40
Ye, like a rash-buss, stood in sight,
      Wi' waving sugh.

The cudgel in my nieve did shake,
Each bristl'd hair stood like a stake;
When wi' an eldritch, stoor "quaick, quaick,"
      Amang the springs,
Awa ye squatter'd like a drake,
      On whistling wings.

Let warlocks grim, an' wither'd hags,
Tell how wi' you, on ragweed nags,   50
They skim the muirs an' dizzy crags,
      Wi' wicked speed;
And in kirk-yards renew their leagues,
      Owre howkit dead.

Thence, countra wives, wi' toil an' pain,
May plunge an' plunge the kirn in vain;
For O! the yellow treasure's taen
      By witching skill;
An' dawtit, twal-pint hawkie 's gaen
      As yell's the bill.   60

Thence, mystic knots mak great abuse
On young guidmen, fond, keen an' croose;
When the best wark-lume i' the house,
      By cantraip wit,
Is instant made no worth a louse,
      Just at the bit.

splashes. **brunstane cootie,** brimstone ladle. 6. **scaud,** scald. 7. **Auld Hangie,** old hangman. **wee,** moment. 11. **skelp,** slap, smack. 15. **lowin heugh,** flaming cavern. 17. **lag,** slow. 18. **blate, nor scaur,** shy nor timid. 19. **Whyles,** sometimes. 22. **Tirlin the kirks,** unroofing the churches. 26. **lanely,** lonely. 30. **eldritch croon,** unearthly moan. 32. **douce,** grave, sober. 33. **Aft yont,** often beyond. **dyke,** wall. **bummin,** humming. 34. **eerie drone,** ghostly sound. 35. **boortrees,** elder bushes. 38. **sklentin,** slanting. 40. **Ayont the lough,** beyond the lake. 41. **rash-buss,** clump of rushes. 42. **sugh,** moan.

43. **nieve,** fist. 45. **eldritch,** unearthly. **stoor,** harsh. 47. **squatter'd,** fluttered on the water. 49. **warlocks,** wizards. 50. **ragweed nags,** ragweed stems used instead of broomsticks for horses. 51. **muirs,** moors. 53. **leagues,** covenants. 54. **Owre howkit,** over dug up. 56. **kirn,** churn. 57. **yellow . . . skill,** witchcraft prevents the butter from coming. 59. **dawtit . . . bill,** petted twelve-pint white-face has gone as dry as the bull. Ayrshire cattle have white markings. 62. **young guidmen,** newly-married men. **croose,** bold. 63. **wark-lume,** work loom, tool. 64. **cantraip,** magic. 66. **at the bit,** at the time most needed.

When thowes dissolve the snawy hoord,
An' float the jinglin icy-boord,
Then, water-kelpies haunt the foord,
70   By your direction,
An' nighted trav'llers are allur'd
        To their destruction.

And aft your moss-traversing spunkies
Decoy the wight that late an' drunk is:
The bleezin, curst, mischievous monkies
        Delude his eyes,
Till in some miry slough he sunk is,
        Ne'er mair to rise.

When Masons' mystic word an' grip
80 In storms an' tempests raise you up,
Some cock or cat your rage maun stop,
        Or, strange to tell!
The youngest brother ye wad whip
        Aff straught to hell.

Lang syne in Eden's bonie yard,
When youthfu' lovers first were pair'd,
An' all the soul of love they shar'd,
        The raptur'd hour,
Sweet on the fragrant flow'ry swaird,
90   In shady bow'r:

Then you, ye auld, snick-drawing dog!
Ye cam to Paradise incog,
An' play'd on man a cursed brogue
        (Black be your fa'!),
An' gied the infant warld a shog,
        'Maist ruin'd a'.

D' ye mind that day when in a bizz
Wi' reekit duds, an' reestit gizz,
Ye did present your smoutie phiz
100   'Mang better folk;
An' sklented on the man of Uzz
        Your spitefu' joke?

An' how ye gat him i' your thrall,
An' brak him out o' house an' hal',
While scabs an' botches did him gall,
        Wi' bitter claw;
An' lowsed his ill-tongu'd wicked scaul—
        Was warst ava?

But a' your doings to rehearse,
110 Your wily snares an' fechtin fierce,
Sin' that day Michael did you pierce

Down to this time,
Wad ding a Lallan tongue, or Erse,
        In prose or rhyme.

An' now, Auld Cloots, I ken ye're thinkin,
A certain Bardie's rantin, drinkin,
Some luckless hour will send him linkin,
        To your black Pit;
But, faith! he'll turn a corner jinkin,
        An' cheat you yet.   120

But fare-you-weel, Auld Nickie-Ben!
O, wad ye tak a thought an' men'!
Ye aiblins might—I dinna ken—
        Still hae a stake:
I'm wae to think upo' yon den,
        Ev'n for your sake!
(1785; 1786)

TO A MOUNTAIN DAISY

ON TURNING ONE DOWN WITH THE PLOW IN APRIL, 1786

Wee, modest, crimson-tippéd flow'r,
Thou's met me in an evil hour;
For I maun crush amang the stoure
        Thy slender stem:
To spare thee now is past my pow'r,
        Thou bonie gem.

Alas! it's no thy neebor sweet,
The bonie lark, companion meet,
Bending thee 'mang the dewy weet,
        Wi' spreckled breast!   10
When upward-springing, blythe, to greet
        The purpling east.

Cauld blew the bitter-biting north
Upon thy early, humble birth;
Yet cheerfully thou glinted forth
        Amid the storm,
Scarce reared above the parent-earth
        Thy tender form.

The flaunting flow'rs our gardens yield,
High shelt'ring woods and wa's maun shield: 20
But thou, beneath the random bield
        O' clod or stane,
Adorns the histie stibble-field,
        Unseen, alane.

67. thowes, thaws. 68. icy-boord, surface of ice. 69. water-kelpies, river demons, usually in the form of horses. 73. aft, often. spunkies, will-o'-the-wisps. 75. bleezin, blazing. 81. your rage maun stop, may stop your rage, by being offered as a sacrifice. 85. Lang syne, long since. 91. snick-drawing, latch-lifting, intruding. 93. brogue, trick. 94. fa', lot. 95. shog, shock. 97. bizz, flurry. 98. reekit, smoky. reestit gizz, singed wig. 101. sklented, directed, turned. man of Uzz, Job. See Job 1:1. 107. lowsed, let loose. scaul,

scold; Job's wife. 108. warst ava, worst of all. 110. fechtin, fighting. 111. Michael . . . pierce, as told in Paradise Lost, VI, 325 ff.; see also Revelation 12:7–10. 113. ding . . . Erse, outdo a Lowland tongue or Gaelic. Erse was the form of Gaelic spoken in the Scottish Highlands. 117. linkin, skipping. 119. jinkin, dodging. 123. aiblins, perhaps. 124. hae a stake, have a chance to gain something. 125. wae, sad.
To a Mountain Daisy. 3. maun, must. stoure, dust. 20. wa's,

There, in thy scanty mantle clad,
Thy snawie bosom sunward spread,
Thou lifts thy unassuming head
    In humble guise;
But now the share uptears thy bed,
30   And low thou lies!

Such is the fate of artless maid,
Sweet flow'ret of the rural shade!
By love's simplicity betrayed,
    And guileless trust;
Till she, like thee, all soiled, is laid
    Low i' the dust.

Such is the fate of simple Bard,
On Life's rough ocean luckless starred!
Unskilful he to note the card
40   Of prudent lore,
Till billows rage, and gales blow hard,
    And whelm him o'er!

Such fate to suffering Worth is giv'n,
Who long with wants and woes has striv'n,
By human pride or cunning driv'n
    To mis'ry's brink;
Till, wrenched of ev'ry stay but Heav'n,
    He, ruined, sink!

Ev'n thou who mourn'st the Daisy's fate,
50 That fate is thine—no distant date;
Stern Ruin's plowshare drives elate,
    Full on thy bloom,
Till crushed beneath the furrow's weight
    Shall be thy doom!

(1786)

TO A LOUSE

ON SEEING ONE ON A LADY'S BONNET AT CHURCH

Ha! wh'are ye gaun, ye crowlin ferlie?
Your impudence protects you sairly;
I canna say but ye strunt rarely,
    Owre gauze and lace,
Tho' faith! I fear ye dine but sparely
    On sic a place.

Ye ugly, creepin, blastit wonner,
Detested, shunned by saunt an' sinner,
How dare ye set your fit upon her,
10   Sae fine a lady?

Gae somewhere else, and seek your dinner
    On some poor body.

Swith, in some beggar's hauffet squattle;
There ye may creep, and sprawl, and sprattle
Wi' ither kindred jumping cattle,
    In shoals and nations;
Whare horn nor bane ne'er dare unsettle
    Your thick plantations.

Now haud you there! ye're out o' sight,
Below the fatt'rils, snug an' tight;   20
Na, faith ye yet! ye'll no be right
    Till ye've got on it,
The very tapmost tow'ring height
    O' Miss's bonnet.

My sooth! right bauld ye set your nose out,
As plump an' gray as onie grozet;
O for some rank mercurial rozet,
    Or fell red smeddum!
I'd gie you sic a hearty dose o't,
    Wad dress your droddum!   30

I wad na been surprised to spy
You on an auld wife's flainen toy;
Or aiblins some bit duddie boy,
    On's wyliecoat;
But Miss's fine Lunardi! fie,
    How daur ye do't?

O Jenny, dinna toss your head,
An' set your beauties a' abroad!
Ye little ken what curséd speed
    The blastie's makin!   40
Thae winks and finger-ends, I dread,
    Are notice takin!

O wad some Power the giftie gie us
To see oursels as ithers see us!
It wad frae monie a blunder free us,
    An' foolish notion:
What airs in dress an' gait wad lea'e us,
    An' ev'n devotion!

(1786)

KELLYBURN BRAES

There lived a carl in Kellyburn Braes,
    Hey, and the rue grows bonie wi' thyme;

walls. 21. **bield,** shelter. 23. **histie,** dry, bare. 39. **card,** compass card.
  To a Louse. 1. **crowlin ferlie,** crawling wonder. 2. **sairly,** greatly.
3. **strunt,** strut. 7. **blastit wonner,** blasted wonder. 9. **fit,** feet. 13.
Swith, quick. **hauffet,** temple, side of the head. **squattle,** settle, sprawl.
14. **sprattle,** scramble. 17. **horn nor bane,** horn comb, bone comb.
19. **haud,** hold. 20. **fatt'rils,** ribbon ends. 25. **bauld,** bold. 26.
grozet, gooseberry. 27. **rozet,** rosin. 28. **smeddum,** powder. 30.
droddum, breech. 32. **flainen toy,** flannel cap. 33. **aiblins,** perhaps.

bit duddie, small, ragged. 34. **wyliecoat,** undervest. 35. **Lunardi,**
balloon bonnet, named after Lunardi (1759–1806), a noted balloonist.
38. **abread,** abroad. 40. **blastie,** blasted creature. 43. **giftie,** small
gift.
  Kellyburn Braes, cf. *The Farmer's Curst Wife,* p. 66. 1. **carl,** old
man. **Kellyburn Braes,** the hills around Kelly Burn, or brook, which
forms the northern boundary of Ayrshire.

And he had a wife was the plague o' his days,
And the thyme it is withered, and rue is in prime.

Ae day as the carl gaed up the lang glen,
Hey, and the rue grows bonie wi' thyme;
He met wi' the Devil, says, "How do you fen?"
And the thyme it is withered, and rue is in prime.

"I've got a bad wife, sir; that's a' my complaint,"
10 Hey, and the rue grows bonie wi' thyme;
"For, saving your presence, to her ye're a saint,"
And the thyme it is withered, and rue is in prime.

"It's neither your stot nor your staig I shall crave,"
Hey, and the rue grows bonie wi' thyme;
"But gie me your wife, man, for her I must have,"
And the thyme it is withered, and rue is in prime.

"O welcome most kindly!" the blythe carl said,
Hey, and the rue grows bonie wi' thyme;
But if ye can match her ye're waur nor ye're ca'd,"
20 And the thyme it is withered, and rue is in prime.

The Devil has got the auld wife on his back,
Hey, and the rue grows bonie wi' thyme;
And, like a poor peddler, he's carried his pack,
And the thyme it is withered, and rue is in prime.

He's carried her hame to his ain hallandoor,
Hey, and the rue grows bonie wi' thyme;
Syne bade her gae in for a bitch and a whore,
And the thyme it is withered, and rue is in prime.

Then straight he makes fifty, the pick o' his band,
30 Hey, and the rue grows bonie wi' thyme,
Turn out on her guard in the clap o' a hand,
And the thyme it is withered, and rue is in prime.

The carlin gaed through them like ony wud bear,
Hey, and the rue grows bonie wi' thyme;
Whae'er she gat hands on cam near her nae mair,
And the thyme it is withered, and rue is in prime.

A reekit wee devil looks over the wa'
Hey, and the rue grows bonie wi' thyme;
"O help, maister, help, or she'll ruin us a'!"
40 And the thyme it is withered, and rue is in prime;

The Devil he swore by the edge o' his knife,
Hey, and the rue grows bonie wi' thyme;
He pitied the man that was tied to a wife,
And the thyme it is withered, and rue is in prime.

The Devil he swore by the kirk and the bell,
Hey, and the rue grows bonie wi' thyme;
He was not in wedlock, thank Heav'n, but in Hell,
And the thyme it is withered, and rue is in prime.

Then Satan has traveled again wi' his pack,
Hey, and the rue grows bonie wi' thyme;   50
And to her auld husband he's carried her back,
And the thyme it is withered, and rue is in prime.

"I hae been a Devil the feck o' my life,"
Hey, and the rue grows bonie wi' thyme;
"But ne'er was in Hell till I met wi' a wife,"
And the thyme it is withered, and rue is in prime.
(1787; 1792)

ADDRESS TO THE UNCO GUID,
OR THE RIGIDLY RIGHTEOUS

My son, these maxims make a rule,
And lump them ay thegither;
The Rigid Righteous is a fool,
The Rigid Wise another:
The cleanest corn that e'er was dight
May hae some pyles o' caff in;
So ne'er a fellow-creature slight
For random fits o' daffin.—SOLOMON,
Ecclesiastes 7:16.

O ye who are sae guid yoursel,
Sae pious and sae holy,
Ye've nought to do but mark and tell
Your neebour's fauts and folly;
Whase life is like a weel-gaun mill,
Supply'd wi' store o' water;
The heapet happer's ebbing still,
And still the clap plays clatter.

Hear me, ye venerable core,
As counsel for poor mortals   10
That frequent pass douce Wisdom's door
For glaikit Folly's portals:
I, for their thoughtless, careless sakes,
Would here propone defences—
Their donsie tricks, their black mistakes,
Their failings and mischances.

Ye see your state wi' theirs compar'd,
And shudder at the niffer;
But cast a moment's fair regard,
What makes the mighty differ?   20
Discount what scant occasion gave,
That purity ye pride in,

7. fen, make out, prosper. 13. stot, steer. staig, horse. 19. waur,
worse. 25. hallandoor, the door in the partition which divides a
Scot's cottage into the but (inside room) and the ben (outside room).
27. Syne, then. 33. carlin, old woman. wud, angry.
Address to the Unco Guid. caff, chaff. daffin, merriment, folly.
5. weel-gaun, well-going. 7. heapet, heaped. happer, hopper. 8. clap,

clapper of the mill. 11. douce, solemn, serious. 12. glaikit, thoughtless, flighty. 15. donsie, vicious. 18. niffer, exchange. 20. differ,
difference. 23. lave, rest. 32. unco, uncommon, mighty. 35. transmogrify'd, metamorphosed, transformed. 47. lug, ear. 48. aiblins,
perhaps. 51. kennin, a little bit.
Tam Glen. 1. tittie, sister. 5. sic, such. braw, brave, handsome,

And (what's aft mair than a' the lave)
　　Your better art o' hidin'.

Think, when your castigated pulse
　　Gies now and then a wallop,
What ragings must his veins convulse,
　　That still eternal gallop!
Wi' wind and tide fair i' your tail,
30　Right on ye scud your sea-way;
But in the teeth o' baith to sail,
　　It maks an unco leeway.

See Social-life and Glee sit down,
　　All joyous and unthinking,
Till, quite transmogrify'd, they're grown
　　Debauchery and Drinking:
O, would they stay to calculate
　　Th' eternal consequences;
Or—your more dreaded hell to state—
40　Damnation of expenses!

Ye high, exalted, virtuous dames,
　　Ty'd up in godly laces,
Before ye gie poor Frailty names,
　　Suppose a change o' cases:
A dear-lov'd lad, convenience snug,
　　A treacherous inclination—
But, let me whisper i' your lug,
　　Ye're aiblins nae temptation.

Then gently scan your brother man,
50　Still gentler sister woman;
Tho' they may gang a kennin wrang,
　　To step aside is human:
One point must still be greatly dark,
　　The moving *why* they do it;
And just as lamely can ye mark
　　How far perhaps they rue it.

Who made the heart, 'tis He alone
　　Decidedly can try us:
He knows each chord, its various tone,
60　Each spring, its various bias:
Then at the balance let's be mute,
　　We never can adjust it;
What's done we partly may compute,
　　But know not what's resisted.
(1787)

TAM GLEN

TUNE: *The Mucking O' Geordie's Byre*

My heart is a-breaking, dear tittie,
　　Some counsel unto me come len'.

To anger them a' is a pity;
　　But what will I do wi' Tam Glen?

I'm thinkin, wi' sic a braw fellow
　　In poortith I might mak a fen'.
What care I in riches to wallow,
　　If I mauna marry Tam Glen?

There's Lowrie the laird o' Dumeller:
　　'Guid-day to you'—brute! he comes ben.　　10
He brags and he blaws o' his siller,
　　But when will he dance like Tam Glen?

My minnie does constantly deave me,
　　And bids me beware o' young men.
They flatter, she says, to deceive me—
　　But wha can think sae o' Tam Glen?

My daddie says, gin I'll forsake him,
　　He'll gie me guid hunder marks ten.
But, if it's ordain'd I maun take him,
　　O wha will I get but Tam Glen?　　20

Yestreen at the valentines' dealing,
　　My heart to my mou gied a sten,
For thrice I drew ane without failing,
　　And thrice it was written 'Tam Glen'!

The last Halloween I was waukin
　　My droukit sark-sleeve, as ye ken—
His likeness cam up the house staukin,
　　And the very gray breeks o' Tam Glen!

Come, counsel, dear tittie, don't tarry!
　　I'll gie you my bonie black hen,　　30
Gif ye will advise me to marry
　　The lad I lo'e dearly, Tam Glen.
(1789)

AULD LANG SYNE

Should auld acquaintance be forgot,
　　And never brought to min'?
Should auld acquaintance be forgot,
　　And auld lang syne?

Chorus

For auld lang syne, my dear,
　　For auld lang syne,
We'll tak a cup o' kindness yet
　　For auld lang syne.

And surely ye'll be your pint-stowp,
10   And surely I'll be mine!
And we'll tak a cup o' kindness yet
    For auld lang syne.

We twa hae run about the braes,
    And pu'd the gowans fine;
But we've wandered monie a weary fit
    Sin' auld lang syne.

We twa hae paidled i' the burn,
    From mornin' sun till dine;
But seas between us braid hae roared
20   Sin' auld lang syne.

And there's a hand, my trusty fiere,
    And gie's a hand o' thine;
And we'll tak a right guid-willie waught
    For auld lang syne.
(1788; 1796)

JOHN ANDERSON, MY JO

John Anderson my jo, John,
    When we were first acquent,
Your locks were like the raven,
    Your bonie brow was brent;
But now your brow is beld, John,
    Your locks are like the snaw,
But blessings on your frosty pow,
    John Anderson my jo!

John Anderson my jo, John,
10   We clamb the hill thegither,
And monie a cantie day, John,
    We've had wi' ane anither;
Now we maun totter down, John,
    And hand in hand we'll go,
And sleep thegither at the foot,
    John Anderson my jo!
(1789; 1790)

WILLIE BREW'D A PECK O' MAUT

Burns has this to say of the following poem: "The air is Masterton's, the song mine. The occasion of it was this: Mr. William Nicol of the High School, Edinburgh, during the autumn vacation being at Moffat, honest Allan (who was at that time on a visit to Dalswinton) and I went to pay Nicol a visit. We had such a joyous visit, Mr. Masterton and I agreed, each in our own way, that we should celebrate the business." The Allan Masterton referred to was a teacher in the Edinburgh High School from 1789 to 1799.

O, Willie brew'd a peck o' maut,
And Rob an' Allan cam to see:
Three blyther hearts that lee-lang night
Ye wad na found in Christendie.

    Chorus

We are na fou, we're nae that fou,
But just a drappie in our ee;
The cock may craw, the day may daw,
And ay we'll taste the barley bree.

Here are we met, three merry boys,
Three merry boys, I trow, are we;   10
And monie a night we've merry been,
And monie mae we hope to be!

It is the moon, I ken her horn,
That's blinkin in the lift sae hie;
She shines sae bright to wyle us hame,
But, by my sooth, she'll wait a wee!

Wha first shall rise to gang awa',
A cuckold, coward loun is he!
Wha first beside his chair shall fa',
He is the king amang us three!   20

    Chorus

We are na fou, we're nae that fou,
But just a drappie in our ee;
The cock may craw, the day may daw,
And ay we'll taste the barley bree.
(1789; 1790)

TO MARY IN HEAVEN

The subject of the poem was Mary Campbell, one of the three women whose names have been most closely linked with that of Burns. "My 'Highland Lassie'," says the poet, "was as warm-hearted, charming a young creature as ever blessed a man with generous love. After a pretty long tract of the most ardent reciprocal attachment, we met by appointment on the second Sunday of May, in a sequestered spot by the banks of the Ayr, where we spent the day in taking farewell, before she should embark for the West Highlands to arrange matters for our projected change

9. ye'll . . . pint-stowp, you will pay for your pint measure of drink.
13. braes, hillsides. 14. pu'd, pulled. gowans, daisies. 15. fit, foot,
step. 17. paidled, paddled, dabbled. burn, brook. 18. dine, dinner
time. 19. braid, broad. 21. fiere, friend, comrade. 23. right . . .
waught, hearty good will draught.
    John Anderson, My Jo. 1. jo, sweetheart. 4. brent, smooth. 5.

beld, bald. 7. pow, head. 11. cantie, happy.
    Willie Brew'd a Peck o' Maut. 1. maut, malt. 3. lee-lang, live-
long. 5. fou, full, drunk. 6. drappie, small drop. 8. bree, brew. 12.
mae, more. 14. lift, sky. 15. wyle, entice. 16. wee, while.
    Tam o' Shanter. Brownyis . . . Bogillis, brownies and hobgoblins.
The line is quoted from Douglas' Prologue to a translation of Vergil's

of life. *At the close of the autumn following, she crossed the sea to meet me at Greenock, where she had scarce landed when she was seized with a malignant fever, which hurried my dear girl to the grave in a few days, before I could even hear of her illness." The poem was written on the anniversary of her death.*

Thou ling'ring star, with less'ning ray,
   That lov'st to greet the early morn,
Again thou usher'st in the day
   My Mary from my soul was torn.
O Mary! dear departed shade!
   Where is thy place of blissful rest?
See'st thou thy lover lowly laid?
   Hear'st thou the groans that rend his breast?

That sacred hour can I forget,
10 Can I forget the hallowed grove,
Where by the winding Ayr we met
   To live one day of parting love?
Eternity will not efface
   Those records dear of transports past,
Thy image at our last embrace—
   Ah! little thought we 'twas our last!

Ayr, gurgling, kiss'd his pebbl'd shore,
   O'erhung with wild woods, thick'ning green;
The fragrant birch and hawthorn hoar
20 Twin'd amorous round the raptur'd scene:
The flow'rs sprang wanton to be prest,
   The birds sang love on every spray,
Till too, too soon the glowing west
   Proclaim'd the speed of winged day.

Still o'er these scenes my mem'ry wakes,
   And fondly broods with miser care!
Time but th' impression stronger makes,
   As streams their channels deeper wear.
My Mary, dear departed shade!
30 Where is thy place of blissful rest?
See'st thou thy lover lowly laid?
   Hear'st thou the groans that rend his breast?
(1789; 1790)

TAM O' SHANTER

Burns' father was buried in the churchyard of Alloway Kirk. Burns asked an antiquarian friend of his to make a drawing of the church, partly because it was the burial place of his father and partly because Burns himself expected to be buried there. The request was accompanied by the statement that many witch legends had grown up about the vicinity of the kirk. The antiquarian friend, Francis Grose, agreed to supply the drawing provided Burns would write a witch tale to go with it. The narrative poem resulting was Tam o' Shanter, a fine example of a tale from Scotch folklore, with its hero drawn from real life in the person of Douglas Graham, a convivial soul of Alloway and adjacent parts. Burns himself always liked the poem for its energy and "roguish waggery."

A TALE

Of Brownyis and of Bogillis full is this Buke.
      —GAWIN DOUGLAS

   When chapman billies leave the street,
And drouthy neebors neebors meet,
As market-days are wearing late,
An' folk begin to take the gate;
While we sit bousing at the nappy,
An' gettin fou and unco happy,
We think na on the lang Scots miles,
The mosses, waters, slaps, and stiles,
That lie between us and our hame,
Whare sits our sulky, sullen dame,   10
Gathering her brows like gathering storm,
Nursing her wrath to keep it warm.

   This truth fand honest Tam o' Shanter,
As he frae Ayr ae night did canter:
(Auld Ayr, wham ne'er a town surpasses,
For honest men and bonie lasses.)

   O Tam! had'st thou but been sae wise
As taen thy ain wife Kate's advice!
She tauld thee weel thou was a skellum,
A bletherin, blusterin, drunken blellum;   20
That frae November till October,
Ae market-day thou was na sober;
That ilka melder wi' the miller,
Thou sat as lang as thou had siller;
That ev'ry naig was ca'd a shoe on,
The smith and thee gat roaring fou on;
That at the Lord's house, even on Sunday,
Thou drank wi' Kirkton Jean till Monday.
She prophesied, that, late or soon,
Thou would be found deep drowned in Doon;   30
Or catched wi' warlocks in the mirk,
By Alloway's auld haunted kirk.

   Ah, gentle dames! it gars me greet,
To think how monie counsels sweet,
How monie lengthened sage advices,
The husband frae the wife despises!

Aeneid. 1. **chapman billies**, peddler comrades. 2. **drouthy**, thirsty. 4. **take the gate**, take the way, i.e., go home. 5. **bousing at the nappy**, drinking ale or liquor. 6. **fou**, full, drunk. **unco**, very. 7. **lang . . . miles**. The old Scotch mile was 216 yards longer than the English mile. 8. **mosses**, bogs. **slaps**, fence gaps or gates. 13. **fand**, found. 16. **bonie**, winsome. 19. **skellum**, good-for-nothing. 20. **bletherin**,

idly talking. **blellum**, babbler, blowhard. 23. **ilka melder**, every grinding. 24. **siller**, silver, money. 25. **ca'd**, nailed. 28. **Kirkton**, any village near a church. 30. **Doon**, a small stream near Burns' birthplace. See Bonie Doon, p. 670. 31. **warlocks**, wizards or witches. **mirk**, dark. 33. **gars me greet**, makes me weep.

But to our tale:—Ae market night,
Tam had got planted unco right,
Fast by an ingle, bleezing finely,
40 Wi' reaming swats that drank divinely;
And at his elbow, Souter Johnie,
His ancient, trusty, drouthy cronie:
Tam loe'd him like a very brither;
They had been fou for weeks thegither.
The night drave on wi' sangs and clatter;
And ay the ale was growing better:
The landlady and Tam grew gracious
Wi' secret favors, sweet and precious:
The souter tauld his queerest stories;
50 The landlord's laugh was ready chorus:
The storm without might rair and rustle,
Tam did na mind the storm a whistle.

Care, mad to see a man sae happy,
E'en drowned himsel amang the nappy:
As bees flee hame wi' lades o' treasure,
The minutes winged their way wi' pleasure;
Kings may be blest, but Tam was glorious,
O'er a' the ills o' life victorious!

But pleasures are like poppies spread,
60 You seize the flow'r, its bloom is shed;
Or like the snow falls in the river,
A moment white—then melts forever;
Or like the borealis race,
That flit ere you can point their place;
Or like the rainbow's lovely form
Evanishing amid the storm.
Nae man can tether time nor tide:
The hour approaches Tam maun ride—
That hour, o' night's black arch the keystane,
70 That dreary hour Tam mounts his beast in;
And sic a night he taks the road in,
As ne'er poor sinner was abroad in.

The wind blew as 'twad blawn its last;
The rattling showers rose on the blast;
The speedy gleams the darkness swallowed;
Loud, deep, and lang the thunder bellowed:
That night, a child might understand,
The Deil had business on his hand.

Weel mounted on his gray mare, Meg—
80 A better never lifted leg—
Tam skelpit on thro' dub and mire,
Despising wind and rain and fire;
Whiles holding fast his guid blue bonnet,

Whiles crooning o'er some auld Scots sonnet,
Whiles glow'ring round wi' prudent cares,
Lest bogles catch him unawares.
Kirk-Alloway was drawing nigh,
Whare ghaists and houlets nightly cry.

By this time he was cross the ford,
Whare in the snaw the chapman smoored; 90
And past the birks and meikle stane,
Whare drunken Charlie brak's neck-bane;
And thro' the whins, and by the cairn,
Whare hunters fand the murdered bairn;
And near the thorn, aboon the well,
Whare Mungo's mither hanged hersel.
Before him Doon pours all his floods;
The doubling storm roars thro' the woods;
The lightnings flash from pole to pole,
Near and more near the thunders roll; 100
When, glimmering thro' the groaning trees
Kirk-Alloway seemed in a bleeze:
Thro' ilka bore the beams were glancing,
And loud resounded mirth and dancing.

Inspiring bold John Barleycorn!
What dangers thou canst make us scorn!
Wi' tippenny we fear nae evil;
Wi' usquebae we'll face the devil!
The swats sae reamed in Tammie's noddle,
Fair play, he cared na deils a boddle. 110
But Maggie stood right sair astonished,
Till, by the heel and hand admonished,
She ventured forward on the light;
And, wow! Tam saw an unco sight!

Warlocks and witches in a dance;
Nae cotillion brent-new frae France,
But hornpipes, jigs, strathspeys, and reels
Put life and mettle in their heels:
A winnock bunker in the east,
There sat Auld Nick in shape o' beast; 120
A towsie tyke, black, grim, and large,
To gie them music was his charge;
He screwed the pipes and gart them skirl,
Till roof and rafters a' did dirl.
Coffins stood round like open presses,
That shawed the dead in their last dresses;
And by some devilish cantraip sleight
Each in its cauld hand held a light,
By which heroic Tam was able
To note upon the haly table 130
A murderer's banes in gibbet airns;

38. unco, very, exactly. 39. ingle, fireplace. bleezing, blazing. 40.
reaming swats, foaming new ale. 41. Souter, cobbler. 42. drouthy,
thirsty. 68. maun, must. 69. hour . . . keystane, midnight. 81.
skelpit, clattered. dub, puddle. 83. Whiles, sometimes. 84. crooning,
humming. sonnet, song. 86. bogles, hobgoblins. 88. houlets, owls.
90. smoored, smothered. 91. birks, birches. meikle stane, great stone.
93. whins, furze. cairn, pile of stones. 94. bairn, child. 102. bleeze,
blaze. 103. ilka bore, every crevice. 107. tippenny, two-penny ale.
108. usquebae, whisky. 109. swats sae reamed, ale so foamed. 110.

deils a boddle, devil a farthing. 114. unco, strange. 116. brent-new,
brand-new. 117. hornpipes, etc., names of lively Scottish dances.
119. winnock bunker, window seat. 121. towsie tyke, shaggy cur.
123. gart them skirl, made them scream. 124. dirl, ring, tingle.
127. cantraip sleight, magic trick. 130. haly, holy. 131. banes in
gibbet airns, bones in gibbet irons. 132. unchristened, unbaptized,
and therefore lost. 133. rape, rope. 134. gab, mouth. 143. glowered,
stared. 147. cleekit, caught hold of each other. 148. ilka . . .
reekit, each hag sweat and steamed. 149. coost . . . wark, threw off

Twa span-lang, wee, unchristened bairns;
A thief, new-cutted frae a rape—
Wi' his last gasp his gab did gape;
Five tomahawks, wi' bluid red-rusted;
Five scymitars, wi' murder crusted;
A garter, which a babe had strangled;
A knife, a father's throat had mangled,
Whom his ain son o' life bereft—
140 The gray hairs yet stack to the heft;
Wi' mair o' horrible and awfu',
Which even to name wad be unlawfu'.

    As Tammie glowered, amazed and curious,
The mirth and fun grew fast and furious:
The piper loud and louder blew,
The dancers quick and quicker flew;
They reeled, they set, they crossed, they cleekit,
Till ilka carlin swat and reekit,
And coost her duddies to the wark
150 And linket at it in her sark!

    Now Tam, O Tam! had thae been queans,
A' plump and strapping in their teens!
Their sarks, instead o' creeshie flannen,
Been snaw-white seventeen hunder linen!—
Thir breeks o' mine, my only pair,
That ance were plush, o' guid blue hair,
I wad hae gien them aff my hurdies,
For ae blink o' the bonie burdies!

    But wither'd beldams, auld and droll,
160 Rigwoodie hags wad spean a foal,
Louping and flinging on a crummock,
I wonder didna turn thy stomach.

    But Tam kend what was what fu' brawlie;
There was ae winsome wench and wawlie,
That night enlisted in the core
Lang after kend on Carrick shore
(For monie a beast to dead she shot,
An' perished monie a bonie boat,
And shook baith meikle corn and bear,
170 And kept the countryside in fear).
Her cutty sark, o' Paisley harn,
That while a lassie she had worn,
In longitude tho' sorely scanty,
It was her best, and she was vauntie.
Ah! little kend thy reverend grannie,
That sark she coft for her wee Nannie,
Wi' twa pund Scots ('twas a' her riches),
Wad ever graced a dance o' witches!

    But here my Muse her wing maun cour,
Sic flights are far beyond her power;   180
To sing how Nannie lap and flang,
(A souple jade she was and strang,)
And how Tam stood like ane bewitched,
And thought his very een enriched;
Even Satan glowered and fidged fu' fain,
And hotched and blew wi' might and main:
Till first ae caper, syne anither,
Tam tint his reason a' thegither,
And roars out, "Weel done, Cutty-sark!"
And in an instant all was dark: 190
And scarcely had he Maggie rallied,
When out the hellish legion sallied.

    As bees bizz out wi' angry fyke,
When plundering herds assail their byke;
As open pussie's mortal foes,
When, pop! she starts before their nose;
As eager runs the market-crowd,
When "Catch the thief!" resounds aloud;
So Maggie runs, the witches follow,
Wi' monie an eldritch skriech and hollo.   200

    Ah, Tam! ah, Tam! thou'll get thy fairin!
In hell they'll roast thee like a herrin!
In vain thy Kate awaits thy comin!
Kate soon will be a woefu' woman!
Now, do thy speedy utmost, Meg,
And win the keystane of the brig:
There at them thou thy tail may toss,
A running stream they dare na cross.
But ere the keystane she could make,
The fient a tail she had to shake!   210
For Nannie, far before the rest,
Hard upon noble Maggie prest,
And flew at Tam wi' furious ettle;
But little wist she Maggie's mettle—
Ae spring brought aff her master hale,
But left behind her ain gray tail:
The carlin claught her by the rump,
And left poor Maggie scarce a stump.

    Now, wha this tale o' truth shall read,
Ilk man and mother's son, take heed,   220
Whene'er to drink you are inclined,
Or cutty-sarks run in your mind,
Think, ye may buy the joys o'er dear,
Remember Tam o' Shanter's Mare.
(1789; 1791)

her clothes for the work. 150. **linket . . . sark**, went at it in her shirt.
151. **queans**, young wenches. 153. **creeshie flannen**, greasy flannel.
154. **seventeen . . . linen**, fine linen, with 1700 threads to a width.
155. **Thir breeks**, these breeches. 157. **hurdies**, hips. 158. **burdies**,
lasses. 160. **Rigwoodie**, lean, withered. **spean**, wean (out of disgust).
161. **Louping . . . crummock**, leaping and capering on a crooked staff.
163. **kend**, knew. **fu' brawlie**, full well. 164. **wawlie**, buxom. 165.
core, company. 166. **Carrick**, the southern district of Ayrshire. 169.
corn and bear, wheat and barley. 171. **cutty sark**, short shirt. **Paisley**

harn, coarse linen made in the town of Paisley. 174. **vauntie**, proud.
176. **coft**, bought. 177. **twa pund Scots.** A pound Scots was worth
about forty cents. 179. **maun cour**, must lower. 181. **lap and flang**,
jumped and kicked. 185. **fidged fu' fain**, fidgeted with pleasure. 186.
hotched, jerked. 188. **tint**, lost. 193. **fyke**, fuss. 194. **herds**, herds-
men. **byke**, hive. 195. **open**, begin to bark. **pussie's**, the hare's. 200.
eldritch, unearthly. 201. **fairin**, reward, deserts; literally, a present
from a fair. 206. **brig**, bridge. 210. **fient**, devil. 213. **ettle**, aim,
intent. 214. **wist**, knew. 217. **claught**, seized.

BONIE DOON

Ye flowery banks o' bonie Doon,
   How can ye blume sae fair?
How can ye chant, ye little birds,
   And I sae fu' o' care?

Thou'll break my heart, thou bonie bird,
   That sings upon the bough;
Thou minds me o' the happy days,
   When my fause luve was true.

Thou'll break my heart, thou bonie bird,
10 That sings beside thy mate;
For sae I sat, and sae I sang,
   And wist na o' my fate.

Aft hae I roved by bonie Doon
   To see the woodbine twine,
And ilka bird sang o' its luve,
   And sae did I o' mine.

Wi' lightsome heart I pu'd a rose
   Frae aff its thorny tree;
And my fause luver staw my rose
20 But left the thorn wi' me.
(1791; 1808)

HIGHLAND MARY

*This song concerns Mary Campbell; Burns said that
it was in his happiest manner. See* To Mary in Heaven,
p. 666.

Ye banks, and braes, and streams around
   The castle o' Montgomery,
Green be your woods and fair your flowers,
   Your waters never drumlie!
There simmer first unfald her robes,
   And there the langest tarry;
For there I took the last fareweel,
   O' my sweet Highland Mary.

How sweetly bloom'd the gay green birk,
10 How rich the hawthorn's blossom,
As underneath their fragrant shade
   I clasp'd her to my bosom!
The golden hours on angel wings
   Flew o'er me and my dearie;
For dear to me as light and life,
   Was my sweet Highland Mary.

Wi' monie a vow and lock'd embrace
   Our parting was fu' tender;

And, pledging aft to meet again,
   We tore oursels asunder;   20
But O! fell Death's untimely frost,
   That nipt my flower sae early!
Now green's the sod, and cauld's the clay,
   That wraps my Highland Mary!

O pale, pale now, those rosy lips,
   I aft hae kiss'd sae fondly!
And clos'd for ay the sparkling glance,
   That dwalt on me sae kindly!
And moldering now in silent dust,
   That heart that lo'ed me dearly!   30
But still within my bosom's core
   Shall live my Highland Mary.
(1792; 1799)

SCOTS, WHA HAE

*In September 1793, Burns wrote to a friend: "There
is in many places of Scotland a tradition . . . that it
[the old air Hey tuttie taitie] was Robert Bruce's march
at the battle of Bannockburn. This thought in my yesternight's evening walk warmed me to a pitch of enthusiasm on the theme of Liberty and Independence,
which I threw into a kind of Scottish ode, fitted to the
air, that one might suppose to be the gallant royal
Scot's address to his heroic followers on that heroic
morning. So may God ever defend the cause of truth
and liberty as He did that day. Amen."*
*This victory of Bruce over Edward II at Bannockburn
(1314) made Scotland independent of England until
the two kingdoms were merged de facto in 1603 and
de iure in 1707 (cf. p. 423). The poem is an expression of Burns' patriotism, but it is impossible to avoid
the conclusion that he was powerfully affected in his
patriotic libertarianism by the French Revolution, then
at its most violent height.*

Scots, wha hae wi' Wallace bled,
Scots, wham Bruce has aften led,
Welcome to your gory bed
    Or to victorie!

Now's the day, and now's the hour:
See the front o' battle lour,
See approach proud Edward's power—
    Chains and slaverie!

Wha will be a traitor knave?
Wha can fill a coward's grave?   10
Wha sae base as be a slave?—
    Let him turn, and flee!

Bonie Doon. The Doon is a delightful small river near Burns' birthplace. 12. **wist na**, knew not. 15. **ilka**, every. 19. **staw**, stole.

Highland Mary. 1. **braes**, hillsides. 2. **castle o' Montgomery,**
Coilsfield House, near Tarbolton. 4. **drumlie**, muddy. 9. **birk**, birch.

Wha for Scotland's King and Law
Freedom's sword will strongly draw,
Freeman stand or freeman fa',
   Let him follow me!

By Oppression's woes and pains,
By your sons in servile chains,
We will drain our dearest veins.
20   But they shall be free!

Lay the proud usurpers low!
Tyrants fall in every foe!
Liberty's in every blow!
   Let us do, or die!
(1793; 1794)

A RED, RED ROSE

O, my luve is like a red, red rose,
 That's newly sprung in June.
O, my luve is like the melodie,
 That's sweetly played in tune.

As fair art thou, my bonie lass,
 So deep in luve am I,
And I will luve thee still, my dear,
 Till a' the seas gang dry.

Till a' the seas gang dry, my dear,
10 And the rocks melt wi' the sun!
And I will luve thee still, my dear,
 While the sands o' life shall run.

And fare thee weel, my only luve,
 And fare thee weel a while!
And I will come again, my luve,
 Tho' it were ten thousand mile!
(1794; 1796)

A MAN'S A MAN FOR A' THAT

Is there, for honest poverty,
 That hings his head, an' a' that?

A Man's a Man for A' That. 7. **guinea's stamp,** the imprint of the King's head on a coin as a statement of its value. 8. **gowd,** gold. 10. **hodden-gray,** coarse gray woolen cloth, undyed. 17. **birkie,** young

The coward slave, we pass him by,
 We dare be poor for a' that!
  For a' that, an' a' that,
   Our toils obscure, an' a' that;
  The rank is but the guinea's stamp;
  The man's the gowd for a' that.

What tho' on hamely fare we dine,
 Wear hodden-gray, an' a' that;   10
Gie fools their silks, and knaves their wine,
 A man's a man for a' that.
  For a' that, an' a' that,
   Their tinsel show, an' a' that;
  The honest man, tho' e'er sae poor,
  Is king o' men for a' that.

Ye see yon birkie, ca'd a lord,
 Wha struts, an' stares, an' a' that;
Tho' hundreds worship at his word,
 He's but a coof for a' that.   20
  For a' that, an' a' that,
   His riband, star, an' a' that
  The man o' independent mind,
  He looks and laughs at a' that.

A prince can mak a belted knight,
 A marquis, duke, an' a' that;
But an honest man's aboon his might,
 Guid faith he mauna fa' that!
  For a' that, an' a' that,
   Their dignities, an' a' that,   30
  The pith o' sense, an' pride o' worth,
  Are higher rank than a' that.

Then let us pray that come it may,
 As come it will for a' that,
That sense and worth, o'er a' the earth,
 May bear the gree, an' a' that.
  For a' that, an' a' that,
   It's coming yet, for a' that,
  That man to man, the warld o'er,
  Shall brothers be for a' that.   40
(1794; 1795)

fellow. 20. **coof,** fool. 27. **aboon,** above. 28. **mauna fa',** must not claim or get. 36. **bear the gree,** have the prize.

WILLIAM BLAKE 1757-1827

There are some writers—poets of the imagination and seers of mystic vision—who can tread with conviction and certainty the misty borderland between fact and fancy, who can behold God sitting in a tree with all his angels, and who can in the next moment turn to something as humble and human as a little lost child. Such a writer was William Blake. His life was in the main placid and uneventful. He was born in London in November 1757; his father, a hosier of limited means, could do little for the boy's education.

But it was soon apparent that young Blake had an unusual eye for design, and the wise father sent the lad to a drawing school and encouraged his visits to art exhibitions and sales rooms. In 1771 Blake was apprenticed to an engraver; the practice of engraving later became one of his most successful fields of artistic expression. At the end of this apprenticeship Blake went to school at the Royal Academy.

He cultivated his own talents assiduously, but his training does not appear to have been very academic. Nevertheless he met many of the prominent artists of his day, and with their help he embarked upon a career as an artist; his first picture was exhibited in 1780, and he continued to produce water colors until 1808. In the meantime he had married (1782) Catharine Boucher, who was an extremely wholesome and steadying influence upon his erratic genius, and a little later he had published a few poems under the title of Poetical Sketches (1783)—delicate, highly individual little works that showed unmistakable promise.

Blake next set himself up as a print seller and engraver (1784), first in partnership, and then alone (1787). It was while he was thus occupied that he produced Songs of Innocence (1789), a group of poems noteworthy for many reasons—first, because they show us a tender, romantic, thoroughly humanitarian poet in a complex but fascinating blend of the direct and simple with the symbolic; again, because the poems are completely divorced in matter and manner from the neo-classical tradition; and finally, because the production is a masterly combination of the two great arts of poetry and engraving. By a process all Blake's own, he had engraved upon copper both the text and the decorative designs of his poems and had tinted the whole by his own hand after printing. The entire performance bespoke genius.

In the same year (1789) appeared The Book of Thel, produced in the same manner as Songs of Innocence, but much more mystical and much less attuned to sense. This work was the first of a series of writings that have come to be called Blake's "prophetic books," which include among others The Marriage of Heaven and Hell (1790), The Gates of Paradise (1793), The Vision of the Daughters of Albion (1793), Jerusalem (1804), The Emanation of the Giant Albion (1804), and Milton (1804). Little in these books will interest the general reader; one must be a connoisseur of engraving and illustration, a zealot of Blake, and a devotee of ultra-symbolic poetry to understand and appreciate them. They

become increasingly obscure in text and thought, and increasingly clear and beautiful as specimens of the engraver's art.

Aside from the works already mentioned, the only other important contribution by Blake to literature was Songs of Experience (1794), richly symbolic, to be sure, but without the half-crazed atmosphere of the prophetic books. Songs of Experience and Songs of Innocence treat of similar subjects from the contrasting viewpoints of a mature man and of a child, as the titles of the two collections imply. They are short, arresting lyrics of clarity, skilled technique, impressive power and depth, and unforgettable phrase.

For a time Blake lived in the village of Felpham, Sussex (1801-1804), in the company of the obscure poet Hayley, who was writing a life of William Cowper and who wished Blake to illustrate his work. The enterprise was not successful, and Blake returned to London, where he lived until his death in 1827. He wrote nothing of any importance after his return, but his artistic work perhaps reached its peak in these later years. Particularly famous are his illustrations to an edition (1804-1805) of The Grave, a well-known "graveyard" poem by the eighteenth-century precursor of the romantic, Robert Blair (1699-1746); his representation of the Canterbury pilgrims (1809); and his magnificent illustrations to the Book of Job (c. 1825), in which his wild and untrammeled imagination had free play.

Today Blake has a steadily rising reputation, partly because of the historical circumstance that makes him the first major romantic poet and partly because of the modern triumph of symbolism and mythography. But Blake would have a unique position in literature regardless. In his mystically imaginative achievements in verse and art and in the emotional power of his lyric poetry, he can be classed as romantic. But his performance transcends ordinary academic labels: he remains a strangely unplaceable soul. He could see the angels of God about him; he could walk out on the heath and touch God with his finger; he could stand in awe of both the beneficent and baleful forces of nature, as in The Lamb and The Tiger. He could paint the beauty of the twilight in sheerest poetry in To the Evening Star; he could touch all the poignancy of human experience in such a brief poem as The Fly. He is a romantic in the sense that every great poet is, but it is perhaps safest to think of him as an extraordinarily gifted poet, painter, and visionary who could seize the pictorial element of an idea and transform it into the sensuous language of his religious, mystical genius.

TO THE EVENING STAR

Thou fair-haired angel of the evening,
Now, whilst the sun rests on the mountains, light
Thy bright torch of love; thy radiant crown
Put on, and smile upon our evening bed!
Smile on our loves, and while thou drawest the
Blue curtains of the sky, scatter thy silver dew
On every flower that shuts its sweet eyes
In timely sleep. Let thy west wind sleep on
The lake; speak silence with thy glimmering eyes,
10 And wash the dusk with silver. Soon, full soon,
Dost thou withdraw; then the wolf rages wide,
And the lion glares through the dun forest:
The fleeces of our flocks are covered with
Thy sacred dew; protect them with thine influence.

MY SILKS AND FINE ARRAY

My silks and fine array,
My smiles and languished air,
By love are driven away;
And mournful lean Despair
Brings me yew to deck my grave;
Such end true lovers have.

His face is fair as heaven
When springing buds unfold;
O why to him was't given,
10 Whose heart is wintry cold?
His breast is love's all-worshiped tomb,
Where all love's pilgrims come.

Bring me an ax and spade,
Bring me a winding-sheet;
When I my grave have made,
Let winds and tempests beat;
Then down I'll lie as cold as clay.
True love doth pass away!
(1783)

from SONGS OF INNOCENCE

INTRODUCTION

Piping down the valleys wild,
Piping songs of pleasant glee,
On a cloud I saw a child,
And he laughing said to me:

"Pipe a song about a Lamb!"
So I piped with merry cheer.
"Piper, pipe that song again";
So I piped: he wept to hear.

The title page for Songs of Innocence, 1789.

"Drop thy pipe, thy happy pipe;
Sing thy songs of happy cheer":
So I sang the same again,
While he wept with joy to hear.

"Piper, sit thee down and write
In a book, that all may read."
So he vanished from my sight,
And I plucked a hollow reed,

And I made a rural pen,
And I stained the water clear,
And I wrote my happy songs
Every child may joy to hear.

THE LAMB

Little Lamb, who made thee?
Dost thou know who made thee?
Gave thee life, and bid thee feed,
By the stream and o'er the mead;
Gave thee clothing of delight,
Softest clothing, woolly, bright;

William Blake   673

Gave thee such a tender voice,
Making all the vales rejoice?
  Little Lamb, who made thee?
10   Dost thou know who made thee?

  Little Lamb, I'll tell thee,
  Little Lamb, I'll tell thee:
He is calléd by thy name,
For He calls Himself a Lamb,
He is meek, and He is mild;
He became a little child.
I a child, and thou a lamb,
We are calléd by His name.
  Little Lamb, God bless thee!
  Little Lamb, God bless thee!

The Lamb

THE LITTLE BLACK BOY

My mother bore me in the southern wild,
And I am black, but O! my soul is white;
White as an angel is the English child,
But I am black, as if bereaved of light.

Holy Thursday. The Thursday of Holy Week, i.e., the week before
Easter. 4. **Paul's,** St. Paul's Cathedral, London.
  A Dream. 3. **emmet,** ant.

My mother taught me underneath a tree,
And, sitting down before the heat of day,
She took me on her lap and kisséd me,
And, pointing to the east, began to say:

"Look on the rising sun—there God does live,
And gives His light, and gives His heat away;   10
And flowers and trees and beasts and men receive
Comfort in morning, joy in the noonday.

"And we are put on earth a little space,
That we may learn to bear the beams of love;
And these black bodies and this sunburnt face
Is but a cloud, and like a shady grove.

"For when our souls have learned the heat to bear,
The cloud will vanish; we shall hear His voice,
Saying: 'Come out from the grove, My love and care,
And round My golden tent like lambs rejoice.' "   20

Thus did my mother say, and kisséd me;
And thus I say to little English boy.
When I from black and he from white cloud free,
And round the tent of God like lambs we joy,

I'll shade him from the heat, till he can bear
To lean in joy upon our Father's knee;
And then I'll stand and stroke his silver hair,
And be like him, and he will then love me.

HOLY THURSDAY

'Twas on a Holy Thursday, their innocent faces clean,
The children walking two and two, in red and blue
    and green;
Gray-headed beadles walked before, with wands as
    white as snow;
Till into the high dome of Paul's they like Thames'
    waters flow.

Oh, what a multitude they seemed, these flowers of
    London town!
Seated in companies, they sit with radiance all their
    own.
The hum of multitudes was there, but multitudes
    of lambs,
Thousands of little boys and girls raising their inno-
    cent hands.

Now like a mighty wind they raise to Heaven the
    voice of song,
Or like harmonious thunderings the seats of Heaven
    among.   10
Beneath them sit the agéd men, wise guardians of
    the poor;
Then cherish pity, lest you drive an angel from your
    door.

A CRADLE SONG

Sweet dreams, form a shade
O'er my lovely infant's head!
Sweet dreams of pleasant streams
By happy, silent, moony beams!

Sweet sleep, with soft down
Weave thy brows an infant crown.
Sweet sleep, Angel mild,
Hover o'er my happy child!

Sweet smiles, in the night
10 Hover over my delight;
Sweet smiles, mother's smile,
All the livelong night beguile.

Sweet moans, dovelike sighs,
Chase not slumber from thy eyes.
Sweet moans, sweeter smile,
All the dovelike moans beguile.

Sleep, sleep, happy child,
All creation slept and smiled;
Sleep, sleep, happy sleep,
20 While o'er thee thy mother weep.

Sweet babe, in thy face
Holy image I can trace.
Sweet babe, once like thee,
Thy Maker lay and wept for me:

Wept for me, for thee, for all,
When He was an infant small.
Thou His image ever see,
Heavenly face that smiles on thee!

Smiles on thee, on me, on all;
30 Who became an infant small.
Infant smiles are His own smiles;
Heaven and earth to peace beguiles.

THE DIVINE IMAGE

To Mercy, Pity, Peace, and Love
All pray in their distress;
And to these virtues of delight
Return their thankfulness.

For Mercy, Pity, Peace, and Love
Is God, our Father dear,
And Mercy, Pity, Peace, and Love
Is man, His child and care.

For Mercy has a human heart,
10 Pity a human face,
And Love, the human form divine,
And Peace, the human dress.

Then every man, of every clime,
That prays in his distress,
Prays to the human form divine,
Love, Mercy, Pity, Peace.

And all must love the human form,
In heathen, Turk, or Jew;
Where Mercy, Love, and Pity dwell   20
There God is dwelling too.

A DREAM

Once a dream did weave a shade
O'er my angel-guarded bed,
That an emmet lost its way
Where on grass methought I lay.

Troubled, 'wildered, and forlorn,
Dark, benighted, travel-worn,
Over many a tangled spray,
All heart-broke, I heard her say:

"Oh, my children! do they cry,
Do they hear their father sigh?   10
Now they look abroad to see;
Now return and weep for me."

Pitying, I dropped a tear;
But I saw a glow-worm near,
Who replied, "What wailing wight
Calls the watchman of the night?

"I am set to light the ground,
While the beetle goes his round;
Follow now the beetle's hum;
Little wanderer, hie thee home!"   20
(1789)

from SONGS OF EXPERIENCE

THE FLY

Little Fly,
Thy summer's play
My thoughtless hand
Has brushed away.

Am not I
A fly like thee?
Or art not thou
A man like me?

For I dance,
And drink, and sing,   10
Till some blind hand
Shall brush my wing.

On what wings dare he aspire?
What the hand dare seize the fire?

And what shoulder, and what art,
Could twist the sinews of thy heart?
And when thy heart began to beat,
What dread hand? and what dread feet?

What the hammer? what the chain?
In what furnace was thy brain?
What the anvil? what dread grasp
Dare its deadly terrors clasp?

When the stars threw down their spears,
And watered heaven with their tears,
Did he smile his work to see?
Did he who made the Lamb make thee?

The Tyger

The title page for Songs of Experience, 1794.

If thought is life
And strength and breath,
And the want
Of thought is death;

Then am I
A happy fly,
If I live
Or if I die.

THE TIGER

Tiger! Tiger! burning bright
In the forests of the night,
What immortal hand or eye
Could frame thy fearful symmetry?

In what distant deeps or skies
Burnt the fire of thine eyes?

Holy Thursday. Cf. this poem with one by the same title in *Songs of Innocence*, p. 674.

Tiger! Tiger! burning bright
In the forests of the night,
What immortal hand or eye
Dare frame thy fearful symmetry?

THE CLOD AND THE PEBBLE

"Love seeketh not itself to please,
Nor for itself hath any care,
But for another gives its ease,
And builds a Heaven in Hell's despair."

So sung a little Clod of Clay,
Trodden with the cattle's feet,
But a Pebble of the brook
Warbled out these meters meet:

"Love seeketh only Self to please,
10 To bind another to its delight,
Joys in another's loss of ease,
And builds a Hell in Heaven's despite."

HOLY THURSDAY

Is this a holy thing to see
In a rich and fruitful land—
Babes reduced to misery,
Fed with cold and usurous hand?

Is that trembling cry a song?
Can it be a song of joy?
And so many children poor?
It is a land of poverty!

And their sun does never shine,
10 And their fields are bleak and bare,
And their ways are filled with thorns:
It is eternal winter there.

For where'er the sun does shine,
And where'er the rain does fall,
Babe can never hunger there,
Nor poverty the mind appall.

A POISON TREE

I was angry with my friend:
I told my wrath, my wrath did end.
I was angry with my foe:
I told it not, my wrath did grow.

And I watered it in fears
Night and morning with my tears,
And I sunnéd it with smiles
And with soft deceitful wiles.

And it grew both day and night,
10 Till it bore an apple bright,

And my foe beheld it shine,
And he knew that it was mine—

And into my garden stole
When the night had veiled the pole;
In the morning, glad, I see
My foe outstretched beneath the tree.

THE GARDEN OF LOVE

I went to the Garden of Love,
And saw what I never had seen:
A chapel was built in the midst,
Where I used to play on the green.

And the gates of this chapel were shut,
And "Thou shalt not" writ over the door;
So I turned to the Garden of Love,
That so many sweet flowers bore:

And I saw it was filléd with graves,
And tombstones where flowers should be;   10

A Poison Tree

William Blake   677

And priests in black gowns were walking their rounds,
And binding with briars my joys and desires.

A LITTLE BOY LOST

"Nought loves another as itself,
Nor venerates another so,
Nor is it possible to Thought
A greater than itself to know:

"And, Father, how can I love you
Or any of my brothers more?
I love you like the little bird
That picks up crumbs around the door."

The Priest sat by and heard the child,
10 In trembling zeal he seized his hair:
He led him by his little coat,
And all admired the priestly care.

And standing on the altar high,
"Lo! what a fiend is here," said he,
"One who sets reason up for judge
Of our most holy Mystery."

The weeping child could not be heard,
The weeping parents wept in vain;
They stripped him to his little shirt,
20 And bound him in an iron chain;

And burned him in a holy place,
Where many had been burned before:
The weeping parents wept in vain.
Are such things done on Albion's shore?

LONDON

I wander through each chartered street,
Near where the chartered Thames does flow,
And mark in every face I meet
Marks of weakness, marks of woe.

In every cry of every man,
In every infant's cry of fear,
In every voice, in every ban,
The mind-forged manacles I hear:

How the chimney-sweeper's cry
Every blackening church appalls,
And the hapless soldier's sigh   10
Runs in blood down palace walls.

But most, through midnight streets I hear
How the youthful harlot's curse
Blasts the new-born infant's tear,
And blights with plagues the marriage hearse.

THE CHIMNEY-SWEEPER

A little black thing among the snow,
Crying "weep! weep!" in notes of woe!
"Where are thy father and mother? Say!"—
"They are both gone up to church to pray.

"Because I was happy upon the heath,
And smiled among the winter's snow,
They clothed me in the clothes of death,
And taught me to sing the notes of woe.

"And because I am happy, and dance and sing,
They think they have done me no injury,   10
And are gone to praise God and His priest and king,
Who make up a heaven of our misery."
(1794)

from AUGURIES OF INNOCENCE

To see a World in a grain of sand,
    And a Heaven in a wild flower;
Hold infinity in the palm of your hand,
    And eternity in an hour.
(1801-1803; 1863)

THEL'S MOTTO

Does the eagle know what is in the pit,
    Or wilt thou go ask the mole?
Can wisdom be put in a silver rod,
    Or love in a golden bowl?
(1789)

WILLIAM WORDSWORTH 1770-1850

William Wordsworth was born April 7, 1770, in the village of Cockermouth, Cumberland. His father was an attorney who belonged to the class of landed gentry; Wordsworth was therefore able to secure a university education, and entered Cambridge in 1787.

His course at the university was interrupted briefly by a tour of Switzerland and northern Italy. France was at that time in revolution, and to that country the young and enthusiastic Wordsworth departed after his graduation in 1791. His stay in France during the year 1792 coincided with some of the most turbulent days of the French Revolution; a new nation was in process of birth; law and order were secondary considerations. The whole picture left an impression upon the young Wordsworth that was years in the effacing; not the least important of his experiences was his affair with Annette Vallon and the birth of a child, Caroline.

Wordsworth returned to England shortly before the climax of the French Revolution—the execution of King Louis XVI in 1793—and his return found him still under the influence of the great Frenchman Rousseau and of Rousseau's English disciple William Godwin, whose Enquiry Concerning Political Justice (1793) was the authoritative work for the little group of English revolutionists with which Wordsworth affiliated himself. The years immediately following 1793 were restless years for the poet; he wandered about England in the absence of his devoted sister Dorothy, settling eventually at Racedown, Dorsetshire, in 1795, where he met Samuel Taylor Coleridge and developed into Coleridge's great friend and constant companion. When Coleridge moved into Somersetshire (1797), Wordsworth followed him, and in the next year the two men published jointly a collection of poems, known simply as Lyrical Ballads (1798). The poems illustrate the revolutionary theories of Wordsworth and Coleridge as applied to English poetry; their break with neoclassical ideals, to some of which Wordsworth had faintly subscribed in his very early verse like An Evening Walk (1793) or Descriptive Sketches (1793), was based in part upon Wordsworth's democratic and humanitarian leanings. The Lyrical Ballads was condemned by many as inadequate poetry, by others as revolutionary, a term which by 1798 had become anathema to the English. Even Coleridge himself was bothered by the whole-souled nature worship of Wordsworth's work in this collection, many of the poems seeming to him pagan and atheistical.

In spite of all the adverse judgments, however, the Lyrical Ballads survived; a second edition appeared in 1800, to which Wordsworth added a preface which stated formally the new ideals of sincerity, democracy, nature worship, and simple, unaffected diction to which he and Coleridge had dedicated themselves. This preface (p. 703) should be read by all who wish to understand thoroughly Wordsworth's contribution to the Romantic Movement and the Romantic Movement itself. Between the first and second editions of Lyrical Ballads, Wordsworth, his sister, and Coleridge took a trip to Germany; Coleridge to study at the University of Göttingen, Wordsworth to contemplate the new land and to wax nostalgic for the glories of his English countryside. Upon their return, Wordsworth and his sister settled in the superb Lake Country of northern England, taking a small cottage at Grasmere, which became their home for the next few years.

Wordsworth's ideas about the French Revolution, like those of many of the young English revolutionists, underwent a considerable change with the advent of Napoleon and the manifestation of the great Corsican's imperialistic ambitions. At first, however, Wordsworth remained sympathetic toward France. It is known that he had a meeting in France with Annette Vallon; but the decision of the two seems to have been to close the chapter, for shortly thereafter (1802) Wordsworth began to write sonnets against Napoleon, and married Mary Hutchinson, a friend of his sister. The final step in his conservative progress came in 1813, when he became distributor of stamps—an employee of the government—and so turned away from the young romantic and revolutionary group to become the "lost leader" (see Browning's poem of that name, p. 916). He remained by choice in the Lake Country, moving to Rydal Mount near Lake Windermere, where he spent the remainder of his long and peacefully idyllic life. In his seventies he became poet laureate (1843) in succession to Robert Southey, but his only important piece of laureate verse, addressed to Prince Albert, the consort of Queen Victoria, was completely uninspired and had better be forgotten. His death in 1850 came long after the ideas for which he labored had been not only accepted but in many ways superseded.

Wordsworth's significant work was all produced within a span of twenty-five years. In respect to subject matter, this work is a mixture of realistic humanitarianism, democratic liberalism, "the short and simple annals of the poor," and a pagan and thoroughly pantheistic worship of nature. These ingredients are to be found in Lyrical Ballads, particularly exemplified by such poems as Alice Fell, Michael, the "Lucy poems," and Tintern Abbey (p. 681). Indeed they can be found generally throughout most of Wordsworth's verse for the twenty-five years between 1798 and 1823; but whereas Wordsworth was a fairly complete radical in religion and politics about 1793-1795, as his letter to the Bishop of Llandaff will show, he seems to be striving more and more toward an orthodox religious outlook in his later work. That he ever achieves orthodoxy is questionable. But there is clearly discernible a somberer tone in his poetry after 1802, as can be seen in his Ode to Duty, his Resolution and Independence (p. 693), or his Elegiac Stanzas, sometimes known as Peele Castle. Certainly in his great Ode on Intimations of Immortality (p. 700), although it preaches the superiority of a childlike and instinctive perception over the more mature reflections prompted by experience, he is groping toward the accepted orthodox faith. On the other hand, there is always in Wordsworth a strong pagan love of natural beauty which no orthodoxy could possibly quench.

Fully as interesting to the student of literature as Wordsworth's philosophical change is his shifting treatment of his theory of poetic diction. In his famous Preface to the Lyrical Ballads (p. 703), Wordsworth proposed to write his poems "in a selection of language really used by men," which, so far as the type of mankind shown in the Lyrical Ballads is concerned, meant the language of humble and perhaps rustic men. In any case, it is clear that Wordsworth cherished the ideal of simple words to express great and essential truths. He wrote many of his best poems, such as I Wandered Lonely as a Cloud (p. 699) and The Solitary Reaper (p. 697), with just such simplicity of vocabulary. Nevertheless, he could depart from his principles and use elevated language, as in Tintern Abbey and in many of the sonnets, with magnificent results; indeed, there are many who would affirm that Wordsworth's important poetry was always that in which he departed from bare simplicity.

Both his friend Coleridge and Matthew Arnold, probably the best critics of the nineteenth century, placed Wordsworth second only to Shakespeare and Milton among the English poets. Time seems to have proved their bold early evaluation correct. Wordsworth does belong, by the quality and mass of his achievement, to the highest order of literary artists. With Coleridge, he was an important poetic revolutionary: he restored the Miltonic sonnet as a vehicle for noble lyrical utterance after a century and a half of nearly total neglect; he established himself in poems like The Solitary Reaper and his impressive Intimations ode, as one of the most versatile and individually distinctive practitioners in the shorter forms of English verse; and in his longer "philosophic" work, notably The Prelude, he attained what is so rare in the English language, an extended poem of unity, depth, and overall technical mastery, greatly conceived and greatly executed. While Arnold—and indeed the nineteenth century at large—prized Wordsworth's shorter poems, celebrating the "simple primary affections and duties," contemporary readers have viewed the last element of his canon, the "philosophic," with most interest and regard. Part of its appeal, of course, arises from the poet's unitary, affirmative vision of the universe, a Weltanschauung that has become increasingly enviable and elusive in modern times. But a work such as The Prelude is still more significant for the nature of its subject matter, its subjective location in the mind of man which Wordsworth called "My haunt, and the main region of my song." The province of all Wordsworth's philosophical or meditative poetry, then, is in fact the modern world, where the formulation and assimilation of human experience occurs, not within orthodoxies and inherited modes of thought, but, if ever, through a mighty act of individual perception. Accordingly, a larger selection than is perhaps usual from this latter realm of his poetry is offered here.

LINES WRITTEN IN EARLY SPRING

I heard a thousand blended notes,
While in a grove I sate reclined,
In that sweet mood when pleasant thoughts
Bring sad thoughts to the mind.

To her fair works did Nature link
The human soul that through me ran;
And much it grieved my heart to think
What man has made of man.

Through primrose tufts, in that green bower,
10 The periwinkle trailed its wreaths;

And 'tis my faith that every flower
Enjoys the air it breathes.

The birds around me hopped and played,
Their thoughts I cannot measure—
But the least motion which they made,
It seemed a thrill of pleasure.

The budding twigs spread out their fan,
To catch the breezy air;
And I must think, do all I can,
That there was pleasure there.

20

If this belief from heaven be sent,
If such be Nature's holy plan,

The Wye Valley at Symonds Yat. Note the hedgerows in the foreground.

Have I not reason to lament
What man has made of man?
(1798)

LINES

COMPOSED A FEW MILES ABOVE TINTERN ABBEY

Five years have past; five summers, with the
    length
Of five long winters! and again I hear
These waters, rolling from their mountain-
    springs
With a soft inland murmur.—Once again
Do I behold these steep and lofty cliffs,
That on a wild secluded scene impress

Thoughts of more deep seclusion; and connect
The landscape with the quiet of the sky.
The day is come when I again repose
Here, under this dark sycamore, and view   10
These plots of cottage-ground, these orchard-
    tufts,
Which at this season, with their unripe fruits,
Are clad in one green hue, and lose themselves
Mid groves and copses. Once again I see
These hedgerows, hardly hedgerows, little
    lines
Of sportive wood run wild: these pastoral farms,
Green to the very door; and wreaths of smoke
Sent up, in silence, from among the trees!
With some uncertain notice, as might seem
Of vagrant dwellers in the houseless woods,   20
Or of some Hermit's cave, where by his fire
The Hermit sits alone.
            These beauteous forms,

Lines. Tintern Abbey is a famous ruin in Monmouthshire. Wordsworth had visited the place in 1793.

William Wordsworth   681

Through a long absence, have not been to me
As is a landscape to a blind man's eye:
But oft, in lonely rooms, and 'mid the din
Of towns and cities, I have owed to them,
In hours of weariness, sensations sweet,
Felt in the blood, and felt along the heart;
And passing even into my purer mind,
30 With tranquil restoration—feelings too
Of unremembered pleasure: such, perhaps,
As have no slight or trivial influence
On that best portion of a good man's life,
His little, nameless, unremembered acts
Of kindness and of love. Nor less, I trust,
To them I may have owed another gift,
Of aspect more sublime; that blesséd mood,
In which the burthen of the mystery,
In which the heavy and the weary weight
40 Of all this unintelligible world,
Is lightened—that serene and blesséd mood,
In which the affections gently lead us on—
Until, the breath of this corporeal frame
And even the motion of our human blood
Almost suspended, we are laid asleep
In body, and become a living soul:
While with an eye made quiet by the power
Of harmony, and the deep power of joy,
We see into the life of things.
                              If this
50 Be but a vain belief, yet, oh! how oft—
In darkness and amid the many shapes
Of joyless daylight; when the fretful stir
Unprofitable, and the fever of the world,
Have hung upon the beatings of my heart—
How oft, in spirit, have I turned to thee,
O sylvan Wye! thou wanderer through the woods,
How often has my spirit turned to thee!
    And now, with gleams of half-extinguished
            thought,
With many recognitions dim and faint,
60 And somewhat of a sad perplexity,
The picture of the mind revives again:
While here I stand, not only with the sense
Of present pleasure, but with pleasing thoughts
That in this moment there is life and food
For future years. And so I dare to hope,
Though changed, no doubt, from what I was when
            first
I came among these hills; when like a roe
I bounded o'er the mountains, by the sides
Of the deep rivers, and the lonely streams,
70 Wherever nature led: more like a man
Flying from something that he dreads than one
Who sought the thing he loved. For nature
            then
(The coarser pleasures of my boyish days,

And their glad animal movements all gone by)
To me was all in all.—I cannot paint
What then I was. The sounding cataract
Haunted me like a passion: the tall rock,
The mountain, and the deep and gloomy wood,
Their colors and their forms, were then to me
An appetite; a feeling and a love,   80
That had no need of a remoter charm,
By thought supplied, nor any interest
Unborrowed from the eye.—That time is past,
And all its aching joys are now no more,
And all its dizzy raptures. Nor for this
Faint I, nor mourn nor murmur; other gifts
Have followed; for such loss, I would believe,
Abundant recompense. For I have learned
To look on nature, not as in the hour
Of thoughtless youth; but hearing oftentimes   90
The still, sad music of humanity,
Nor harsh nor grating, though of ample power
To chasten and subdue. And I have felt
A presence that disturbs me with the joy
Of elevated thoughts; a sense sublime
Of something far more deeply interfused,
Whose dwelling is the light of setting suns,
And the round ocean and the living air,
And the blue sky, and in the mind of man:
A motion and a spirit, that impels   100
All thinking things, all objects of all thought,
And rolls through all things. Therefore am I
            still
A lover of the meadows and the woods,
And mountains; and of all that we behold
From this green earth; of all the mighty world
Of eye, and ear—both what they half create,
And what perceive; well pleased to recognize
In nature and the language of the sense
The anchor of my purest thoughts, the nurse,
The guide, the guardian of my heart, and soul   110
Of all my moral being.
                      Nor perchance,
If I were not thus taught, should I the more
Suffer my genial spirits to decay:
For thou art with me here upon the banks
Of this fair river; thou my dearest Friend,
My dear, dear Friend; and in thy voice I catch
The language of my former heart, and read
My former pleasures in the shooting lights
Of thy wild eyes. Oh! yet a little while
May I behold in thee what I was once,   120
My dear, dear Sister! and this prayer I make,
Knowing that Nature never did betray
The heart that loved her; 'tis her privilege,
Through all the years of this our life, to
            lead
From joy to joy: for she can so inform

---

72. For nature, etc. With this passage (11.72–111), compare *Ode on Intimations of Immortality*, (p. 702), 11. 175–203. 97. Whose . . . suns, etc. Tennyson spoke of this line as giving the sense of "the permanent in the transitory." 115. Friend, Wordsworth's sister Dorothy. 125.

The mind that is within us, so impress
With quietness and beauty, and so feed
With lofty thoughts, that neither evil tongues,
Rash judgments, nor the sneers of selfish men,
130 Nor greetings where no kindness is, nor all
The dreary intercourse of daily life,
Shall e'er prevail against us, or disturb
Our cheerful faith, that all which we behold
Is full of blessings. Therefore let the moon
Shine on thee in thy solitary walk;
And let the misty mountain-winds be free
To blow against thee: and, in after years,
When these wild ecstasies shall be matured
Into a sober pleasure; when thy mind
140 Shall be a mansion for all lovely forms,
Thy memory be as a dwelling-place
For all sweet sounds and harmonies; oh! then,
If solitude, or fear, or pain, or grief,
Should be thy portion, with what healing
    thoughts
Of tender joy wilt thou remember me,
And these my exhortations! Nor, perchance—
If I should be where I no more can hear
Thy voice, nor catch from thy wild eyes these
    gleams
Of past existence—wilt thou then forget
150 That on the banks of this delightful stream
We stood together; and that I, so long
A worshiper of Nature, hither came
Unwearied in that service: rather say
With warmer love—oh! with far deeper
    zeal
Of holier love. Nor wilt thou then forget
That after many wanderings, many years
Of absence, these steep woods and lofty cliffs,
And this green pastoral landscape, were to me
More dear, both for themselves and for thy
    sake!
(1798)

STRANGE FITS OF PASSION HAVE I KNOWN

*This and the four following poems belong to the
so-called "Lucy poems," written in Germany in 1799.
Who Lucy was, if an actual person at all, is unknown.*

Strange fits of passion have I known:
And I will dare to tell,
But in the Lover's ear alone,
What once to me befell.

When she I loved looked every day
Fresh as a rose in June,

I to her cottage bent my way,
Beneath an evening-moon.

Upon the moon I fixed my eye,   10
All over the wide lea;
With quickening pace my horse drew nigh
Those paths so dear to me.

And now we reached the orchard-plot;
And, as we climbed the hill,
The sinking moon to Lucy's cot
Came near, and nearer still.

In one of those sweet dreams I slept,
Kind Nature's gentlest boon!
And all the while my eyes I kept
On the descending moon.   20

My horse moved on; hoof after hoof
He raised, and never stopped:
When down behind the cottage roof,
At once, the bright moon dropped.

What fond and wayward thoughts will slide
Into a Lover's head!
"O mercy!" to myself I cried,
"If Lucy should be dead!"
(1799; 1800)

SHE DWELT AMONG THE UNTRODDEN WAYS

She dwelt among the untrodden ways
    Beside the springs of Dove,
A Maid whom there were none to praise
    And very few to love:

A violet by a mossy stone
    Half hidden from the eye!
—Fair as a star, when only one
    Is shining in the sky.

She lived unknown, and few could know
    When Lucy ceased to be;   10
But she is in her grave, and, oh,
    The difference to me!
(1799; 1800)

I TRAVELED AMONG UNKNOWN MEN

I traveled among unknown men,
    In lands beyond the sea;
Nor, England! did I know till then
    What love I bore to thee.

inform, inspire. 149. **past existence**, the poet's past life.
She Dwelt Among the Untrodden Ways. 2. **Dove,** a river form-

ing part of the boundary between the counties of Derby and Stafford.

'Tis past, that melancholy dream!
    Nor will I quit thy shore
A second time; for still I seem
    To love thee more and more.

Among thy mountains did I feel
10   The joy of my desire;
And she I cherished turned her wheel
    Beside an English fire.

Thy mornings showed, thy nights concealed
    The bowers where Lucy played;
And thine too is the last green field
    That Lucy's eyes surveyed.
(1799; 1807)

THREE YEARS SHE GREW IN SUN AND SHOWER

Three years she grew in sun and shower,
Then Nature said, "A lovelier flower
On earth was never sown;
This Child I to myself will take;
She shall be mine, and I will make
A Lady of my own.

"Myself will to my darling be
Both law and impulse: and with me
The Girl, in rock and plain,
10 In earth and heaven, in glade and bower,
Shall feel an overseeing power
To kindle or restrain.

"She shall be sportive as the fawn
That wild with glee across the lawn,
Or up the mountains springs;
And hers shall be the breathing balm,
And hers the silence and the calm
Of mute insensate things.

"The floating clouds their state shall lend
20 To her; for her the willow bend;
Nor shall she fail to see
Even in the motions of the Storm
Grace that shall mold the Maiden's form
By silent sympathy.

"The stars of midnight shall be dear
To her; and she shall lean her ear
In many a secret place
Where rivulets dance their wayward round,
And beauty born of murmuring sound
30 Shall pass into her face.

"And vital feelings of delight
Shall rear her form to stately height,

Her virgin bosom swell;
Such thoughts to Lucy I will give
While she and I together live
Here in this happy dell."

Thus Nature spake.—The work was done.—
How soon my Lucy's race was run!
She died, and left to me
This heath, this calm, and quiet scene;   40
The memory of what has been,
And never more will be.
(1799; 1800)

A SLUMBER DID MY SPIRIT SEAL

A slumber did my spirit seal;
    I had no human fears:
She seemed a thing that could not feel
    The touch of earthly years.

No motion has she now, no force;
    She neither hears nor sees;
Rolled round in earth's diurnal course,
    With rocks, and stones, and trees.
(1799; 1800)

from THE PRELUDE

Wordsworth thus describes the occasion and the plan of The Prelude *in the preface to* The Excursion:

"Several years ago, when the author retired to his native mountains with the hope of being enabled to construct a literary work that might live, it was a reasonable thing that he should take a review of his own mind, and examine how far nature and education had qualified him for such an employment. As subsidiary to this preparation, he undertook to record, in verse, the origin and progress of his own powers, as far as he was acquainted with them. That work, addressed to a dear friend, most distinguished for his knowledge and genius, and to whom the author's intellect is deeply indebted, has been long finished; and the result of the investigation which gave rise to it, was a determination to compose a philosophical poem, containing views of man, nature, and society, and to be entitled The Recluse, *as having for its principal subject the sensations and opinions of a poet living in retirement.*

*"The preparatory poem [*The Prelude*] is biographical, and conducts the history of the author's mind to the point where he was emboldened to hope that his faculties were sufficiently matured for entering upon the arduous labor which he had proposed to*

The Prelude. 1. These lines (1–45) were written in September 1795 on the way from Bristol to Racedown, two and one-half years before

the idea of The Prelude was conceived. 7. **vast city,** London, where Wordsworth had lived from January to September 1795. 14. **earth . . .**

himself; and the two works [The Prelude and The Recluse] have the same kind of relation to each other, if he may so express himself, as the ante-chapel has to the body of a Gothic church. Continuing this allusion, he may be permitted to add, that his minor pieces, which have been long before the public, when they shall be properly arranged, will be found by the attentive reader to have such connection with the main work as may give them claim to be likened to the little cells, oratories, and sepulchral recesses, ordinarily included in those edifices."

The Prelude was to be the introduction to a larger work called The Recluse; in this larger work The Excursion was to be the second part. The project was not completed, but The Prelude and The Excursion remain as highly significant autobiographical poems. The "dear friend" to whom The Prelude was addressed was Coleridge. The poem was not published until 1850, the year of Wordsworth's death.

BOOK I. INTRODUCTION—CHILDHOOD AND SCHOOL-TIME

Oh, there is blessing in this gentle breeze,
A visitant that while it fans my cheek
Doth seem half-conscious of the joy it brings
From the green fields, and from yon azure sky.
Whate'er its mission, the soft breeze can come
To none more grateful than to me; escaped
From the vast city, where I long had pined
A discontented sojourner: now free,
Free as a bird to settle where I will.
10 What dwelling shall receive me? in what vale
Shall be my harbor? underneath what grove
Shall I take up my home? and what clear stream
Shall with its murmur lull me into rest?
The earth is all before me. With a heart
Joyous, nor scared at its own liberty,
I look about; and should the chosen guide
Be nothing better than a wandering cloud,
I cannot miss my way. I breathe again!
Trances of thought and mountings of the mind
20 Come fast upon me: it is shaken off,
That burthen of my own unnatural self,
The heavy weight of many a weary day
Not mine, and such as were not made for me.
Long months of peace (if such bold word accord
With any promises of human life),
Long months of ease and undisturbed delight
Are mine in prospect; whither shall I turn,
By road or pathway, or through trackless field,
Up-hill or down, or shall some floating thing
30 Upon the river point me out my course?

Dear Liberty! Yet what would it avail

But for a gift that consecrates the joy?
For I, methought, while the sweet breath of heaven
Was blowing on my body, felt within
A correspondent breeze, that gently moved
With quickening virtue, but is now become
A tempest, a redundant energy,
Vexing its own creation. Thanks to both,
And their congenial powers, that, while they join
In breaking up a long-continued frost,   40
Bring with them vernal promises, the hope
Of active days urged on by flying hours—
Days of sweet leisure, taxed with patient thought
Abstruse, nor wanting punctual service high,
Matins and vespers of harmonious verse!

Thus far, O Friend! did I, not used to make
A present joy the matter of a song,
Pour forth that day my soul in measured strains
That would not be forgotten, and are here
Recorded: to the open fields I told   50
A prophecy: poetic numbers came
Spontaneously to clothe in priestly robe
A renovated spirit singled out,
Such hope was mine, for holy services.
My own voice cheered me, and, far more, the mind's
Internal echo of the imperfect sound;
To both I listened, drawing from them both
A cheerful confidence in things to come.

Content and not unwilling now to give
A respite to this passion, I paced on   60
With brisk and eager steps; and came, at length,
To a green shady place, where down I sate
Beneath a tree, slackening my thoughts by choice,
And settling into gentler happiness.
'Twas autumn, and a clear and placid day,
With warmth, as much as needed, from a sun
Two hours declined toward the west; a day
With silver clouds, and sunshine on the grass,
And in the sheltered and the sheltering grove
A perfect stillness. Many were the thoughts   70
Encouraged and dismissed, till choice was made
Of a known Vale, whither my feet should turn,
Nor rest till they had reached the very door
Of the one cottage which methought I saw.
No picture of mere memory ever looked
So fair; and while upon the fancied scene
I gazed with growing love, a higher power
Than Fancy gave assurance of some work
Of glory there forthwith to be begun,
Perhaps too there performed. Thus long I mused, 80
Nor e'er lost sight of what I mused upon,
Save when, amid the stately grove of oaks,
Now here, now there, an acorn, from its cup
Dislodged, through sere leaves rustled, or at once

me, one of the many echoes of Milton in the poem. Cf. *Paradise Lost,* XII, 646: "The world was all before them, where to choose." 21. **That**

... for me. Cf. *Lines,* p. 682, ll. 37-41. 46. **Friend,** Samuel Taylor Coleridge. 72. **Vale,** Racedown

To the bare earth dropped with a startling sound.
From that soft couch I rose not, till the sun
Had almost touched the horizon; casting then
A backward glance upon the curling cloud
Of city smoke, by distance ruralized;
90 Keen as a Truant or a Fugitive,
But as a Pilgrim resolute, I took,
Even with the chance equipment of that hour,
The road that pointed toward the chosen Vale.
It was a splendid evening, and my soul
Once more made trial of her strength, nor lacked
Aeolian visitations; but the harp
Was soon defrauded, and the banded host
Of harmony dispersed in straggling sounds,
And lastly utter silence! "Be it so;
100 Why think of anything but present good?"
So, like a home-bound laborer, I pursued
My way beneath the mellowing sun, that shed
Mild influence; nor left in me one wish
Again to bend the Sabbath of that time
To a servile yoke. What need of many words?
A pleasant loitering journey, through three days
Continued, brought me to my hermitage.
I spare to tell of what ensued, the life
In common things—the endless store of things,
110 Rare, or at least so seeming, every day
Found all about me in one neighborhood—
The self-congratulation, and, from morn
To night, unbroken cheerfulness serene.
But speedily an earnest longing rose
To brace myself to some determined aim,
Reading or thinking; either to lay up
New stores, or rescue from decay the old
By timely interference: and therewith
Came hopes still higher, that with outward life
120 I might endue some airy phantasies
That had been floating loose about for years,
And to such beings temperately deal forth
The many feelings that oppressed my heart.
That hope hath been discouraged; welcome light
Dawns from the east, but dawns to disappear
And mock me with a sky that ripens not
Into a steady morning: if my mind,
Remembering the bold promise of the past,
Would gladly grapple with some noble theme,
130 Vain is her wish; where'er she turns she finds
Impediments from day to day renewed.

      And now it would content me to yield up
Those lofty hopes awhile, for present gifts
Of humbler industry. But, oh, dear Friend!

The Poet, gentle creature as he is,
Hath, like the Lover, his unruly times;
His fits when he is neither sick nor well,
Though no distress be near him but his own
Unmanageable thoughts: his mind, best pleased
While she as duteous as the mother dove   140
Sits brooding, lives not always to that end,
But like the innocent bird hath goadings on
That drive her as in trouble through the groves;
With me is now such passion to be blamed
No otherwise than as it lasts too long.

    When, as becomes a man who would prepare
For such an arduous work, I through myself
Make rigorous inquisition, the report
Is often cheering; for I neither seem
To lack that first great gift, the vital soul,   150
Nor general Truths, which are themselves a sort
Of Elements and Agents, Under-powers,
Subordinate helpers of the living mind:
Nor am I naked of external things,
Forms, images, nor numerous other aids
Of less regard, though won perhaps with toil
And needful to build up a Poet's praise.
Time, place, and manners do I seek, and these
Are found in plenteous store, but nowhere such
As may be singled out with steady choice;   160
No little band of yet remembered names
Whom I, in perfect confidence, might hope
To summon back from lonesome banishment,
And make them dwellers in the hearts of men
Now living, or to live in future years.
Sometimes the ambitious Power of choice, mistaking
Proud spring-tide swellings for a regular sea,
Will settle on some British theme, some old
Romantic tale by Milton left unsung;
More often turning to some gentle place   170
Within the groves of Chivalry, I pipe
To shepherd swains, or seated harp in hand,
Amid reposing knights by a river side
Or fountain, listen to the grave reports
Of dire enchantments faced and overcome
By the strong mind, and tales of warlike feats,
Where spear encountered spear, and sword with sword
Fought, as if conscious of the blazonry
That the shield bore, so glorious was the strife;
Whence inspiration for a song that winds   180
Through ever-changing scenes of votive quest
Wrongs to redress, harmonious tribute paid
To patient courage and unblemished truth,
To firm devotion, zeal unquenchable,

89. **city smoke,** from Bristol. 96. **Aeolian visitations,** thoughts that come and go with the breeze, as sounds are produced when the wind strikes the Aeolian harp, named after Aeolus, god of winds. 104. **Sabbath,** calm, restfulness. 168. **British theme . . . unsung.** Milton seriously considered writing an epic on the history of Britain before the Conquest and also a poem on King Arthur. 171. **groves of Chivalry,** an allusion to Spenser's *Faerie Queene,* Bk. VI. 187. **Mithridates,** king of Pontus, Asia Minor (120–63 B.C.); he was defeated by Pompey in 66 B.C. His identification with Odin, the supreme deity of

Scandinavian mythology, was suggested to Wordsworth by a passage in Gibbon's *Decline and Fall of the Roman Empire* (Chap. 10). Gibbon mentions Odin as chief of a tribe of barbarians who retreated to Sweden and laid the foundations for the overthrow of the Roman Empire by the Goths in the 3rd and 4th centuries. 191. **Sertorius,** a famous Roman general who resisted tyrannical rule for eight years, until he was assassinated in 72 B.C. On one of his journeys he landed in Spain, where he learned from sailors about the Fortunate Islands in the Atlantic, supposed to be the Canaries. Wordsworth read about him in Plutarch's

And Christian meekness hallowing faithful loves.
Sometimes, more sternly moved, I would relate
How vanquished Mithridates northward passed,
And, hidden in the cloud of years, became
Odin, the Father of a race by whom
190 Perished the Roman Empire: how the friends
And followers of Sertorius, out of Spain
Flying, found shelter in the Fortunate Isles,
And left their usages, their arts and laws,
To disappear by a slow gradual death,
To dwindle and to perish one by one,
Starved in those narrow bounds: but not the soul
Of Liberty, which fifteen hundred years
Survived, and, when the European came
With skill and power that might not be withstood,
200 Did, like a pestilence, maintain its hold
And wasted down by glorious death that race
Of natural heroes: or I would record
How, in tyrannic times, some high-souled man,
Unnamed among the chronicles of kings,
Suffered in silence for Truth's sake; or tell,
How that one Frenchman, through continued force
Of meditation on the inhuman deeds
Of those who conquered first the Indian Isles,
Went single in his ministry across
210 The Ocean; not to comfort the oppressed,
But, like a thirsty wind, to roam about
Withering the Oppressor: how Gustavus sought
Help at his need in Dalecarlia's mines:
How Wallace fought for Scotland; left the name
Of Wallace to be found, like a wild flower,
All over his dear Country; left the deeds
Of Wallace, like a family of Ghosts,
To people the steep rocks and river banks,
Her natural sanctuaries, with a local soul
220 Of independence and stern liberty.
Sometimes it suits me better to invent
A tale from my own heart, more near akin
To my own passions and habitual thoughts;
Some variegated story, in the main
Lofty, but the unsubstantial structure melts
Before the very sun that brightens it,
Mist into air dissolving! Then a wish,
My last and favorite aspiration, mounts
With yearning toward some philosophic song
230 Of Truth that cherishes our daily life;
With meditations passionate from deep
Recesses in man's heart, immortal verse
Thoughtfully fitted to the Orphean lyre;
But from this awful burthen I full soon
Take refuge and beguile myself with trust

That mellower years will bring a riper mind
And clearer insight. Thus my days are passed
In contradiction; with no skill to part
Vague longing, haply bred by want of power,
From paramount impulse not to be withstood, 240
A timorous capacity from prudence,
From circumspection, infinite delay.
Humility and modest awe themselves
Betray me, serving often for a cloak
To a more subtle selfishness; that now
Locks every function up in blank reserve,
Now dupes me, trusting to an anxious eye
That with intrusive restlessness beats off
Simplicity and self-presented truth.
Ah! better far than this, to stray about 250
Voluptuously through fields and rural walks,
And ask no record of the hours, resigned
To vacant musing, unreproved neglect
Of all things, and deliberate holiday.
Far better never to have heard the name
Of zeal and just ambition, than to live
Baffled and plagued by a mind that every hour
Turns recreant to her task; takes heart again,
Then feels immediately some hollow thought
Hang like an interdict upon her hopes. 260
This is my lot; for either still I find
Some imperfection in the chosen theme,
Or see of absolute accomplishment
Much wanting, so much wanting, in myself,
That I recoil and droop, and seek repose
In listlessness from vain perplexity,
Unprofitably traveling toward the grave,
Like a false steward who hath much received
And renders nothing back.
                           Was it for this
That one, the fairest of all rivers, loved 270
To blend his murmurs with my nurse's song,
And, from his alder shades and rocky falls,
And from his fords and shallows, sent a voice
That flowed along my dreams? For this, didst thou,
O Derwent! winding among grassy holms
Where I was looking on, a babe in arms,
Make ceaseless music that composed my thoughts
To more than infant softness, giving me
Amid the fretful dwellings of mankind
A foretaste, a dim earnest, of the calm 280
That Nature breathes among the hills and groves.

    When he had left the mountains and received
On his smooth breast the shadow of those towers
That yet survive, a shattered monument

Lives. **206. Frenchman,** Dominique de Gourges, who sailed to Florida in 1568 to avenge the massacre of French colonists by the Spaniards. **212. Gustavus,** Gustavus I of Sweden (1496-1560), who freed his country from the tyranny of Denmark. He worked out his plans in Dalecarlia, a mining district in the west midlands of Sweden, where he often disguised himself as a peasant or a miner to escape capture by the Danes. **215. Wallace,** William Wallace (d. 1305), celebrated Scottish hero and patriot. **233. Orphean lyre,** an allusion to the famous lyre of Orpheus, mythological poet and musician, whose music could charm beasts and move trees and stones. **268. false steward,** an allusion to the parable of the talents. Two of the three stewards were faithful to their trust, but the third was false. See Matthew 25:14-30. **270. fairest of all rivers,** Derwent. Wordsworth was born at Cockermouth situated at the junction of two rivers—Cocker and Derwent. **275. holms,** low flat lands. **283. those towers,** of Cockermouth Castle.

Of feudal sway, the bright blue river passed
Along the margin of our terrace walk;
A tempting playmate whom we dearly loved.
Oh, many a time have I, a five years' child,
In a small mill-race severed from his stream,
290 Made one long bathing of a summer's day;
Basked in the sun, and plunged and basked again
Alternate, all a summer's day, or scoured
The sandy fields, leaping through flowery groves
Of yellow ragwort; or when rock and hill,
The woods, and distant Skiddaw's lofty height,
Were bronzed with deepest radiance, stood alone
Beneath the sky, as if I had been born
On Indian plains, and from my mother's hut
Had run abroad in wantonness, to sport,
300 A naked savage, in the thunder-shower.

    Fair seed-time had my soul, and I grew up
Fostered alike by beauty and by fear:
Much favored in my birthplace, and no less
In that belovéd Vale to which erelong
We were transplanted—there were we let loose
For sports of wider range. Ere I had told
Ten birthdays, when among the mountain-slopes
Frost, and the breath of frosty wind, had snapped
The last autumnal crocus, 'twas my joy
310 With store of springes o'er my shoulder hung
To range the open heights where woodcocks run
Among the smooth green turf. Through half the night,
Scudding away from snare to snare, I plied
That anxious visitation;—moon and stars
Were shining o'er my head. I was alone,
And seemed to be a trouble to the peace
That dwelt among them. Sometimes it befell
In these night wanderings, that a strong desire
O'erpowered my better reason, and the bird
320 Which was the captive of another's toil
Became my prey; and when the deed was done,
I heard among the solitary hills
Low breathings coming after me, and sounds
Of undistinguishable motion, steps
Almost as silent as the turf they trod.

    Nor less when spring had warmed the cultured
      Vale,
Roved we as plunderers where the mother-bird
Had in high places built her lodge; though mean
Our object and inglorious, yet the end
330 Was not ignoble. Oh! when I have hung
Above the raven's nest, by knots of grass
And half-inch fissures in the slippery rock
But ill sustained, and almost (so it seemed)
Suspended by the blast that blew amain,
Shouldering the naked crag, oh, at that time
While on the perilous ridge I hung alone,

With what strange utterance did the loud dry wind
Blow through my ear! the sky seemed not a sky
Of earth—and with what motion moved the clouds!

    Dust as we are, the immortal spirit grows   340
Like harmony in music; there is a dark
Inscrutable workmanship that reconciles
Discordant elements, makes them cling together
In one society. How strange that all
The terrors, pains, and early miseries,
Regrets, vexations, lassitudes interfused
Within my mind, should e'er have borne a part,
And that a needful part, in making up
The calm existence that is mine when I
Am worthy of myself! Praise to the end!   350
Thanks to the means which Nature deigned to employ;
Whether her fearless visitings, or those
That came with soft alarm, like hurtless light
Opening the peaceful clouds; or she may use
Severer interventions, ministry
More palpable, as best might suit her aim.

    One summer evening (led by her) I found
A little boat tied to a willow tree
Within a rocky cave, its usual home.
Straight I unloosed her chain, and stepping in   360
Pushed from the shore. It was an act of stealth
And troubled pleasure, nor without the voice
Of mountain-echoes did my boat move on;
Leaving behind her still, on either side,
Small circles glittering idly in the moon,
Until they melted all into one track
Of sparkling light. But now, like one who rows,
Proud of his skill, to reach a chosen point
With an unswerving line, I fixed my view
Upon the summit of a craggy ridge,   370
The horizon's utmost boundary; for above
Was nothing but the stars and the gray sky.
She was an elfin pinnace; lustily
I dipped my oars into the silent lake,
And, as I rose upon the stroke, my boat
Went heaving through the water like a swan;
When, from behind that craggy steep till then
The horizon's bound, a huge peak, black and huge,
As if with voluntary power instinct
Upreared its head. I struck and struck again,   380
And growing still in stature the grim shape
Towered up between me and the stars, and still,
For so it seemed, with purpose of its own
And measured motion like a living thing,
Strode after me. With trembling oars I turned,
And through the silent water stole my way
Back to the covert of the willow tree;
There in her mooring-place I left my bark—
And through the meadows homeward went, in grave

---

294. **ragwort**, a common European weed. 295. **Skiddaw**, a mountain in Cumberlandshire. 304. **Vale**, Esthwaite, Lancashire, in which the village of Hawkshead, where Wordsworth attended school, is situated.

310. **springes**, snares, traps. 326. **Vale**, Yewdale, a valley near Hawkshead. 357. **her**, Nature. 373. **pinnace**, a light sailing vessel.

390 And serious mood; but after I had seen
   That spectacle, for many days, my brain
   Worked with a dim and undetermined sense
   Of unknown modes of being; o'er my thoughts
   There hung a darkness, call it solitude
   Or blank desertion. No familiar shapes
   Remained, no pleasant images of trees,
   Of sea or sky, no colors of green fields;
   But huge and mighty forms, that do not live
   Like living men, moved slowly through the mind
400 By day, and were a trouble to my dreams.

   Wisdom and Spirit of the universe!
   Thou Soul that art the eternity of thought,
   That givest to forms and images a breath
   And everlasting motion, not in vain
   By day or star-light thus from my first dawn
   Of childhood didst thou intertwine for me
   The passions that build up our human soul;
   Not with the mean and vulgar works of man,
   But with high objects, with enduring things—
410 With life and nature—purifying thus
   The elements of feeling and of thought,
   And sanctifying, by such discipline,
   Both pain and fear, until we recognize
   A grandeur in the beatings of the heart.
   Nor was this fellowship vouchsafed to me
   With stinted kindness. In November days,
   When vapors rolling down the valley made
   A lonely scene more lonesome, among woods,
   At noon and 'mid the calm of summer nights,
420 When, by the margin of the trembling lake,
   Beneath the gloomy hills homeward I went
   In solitude, such intercourse was mine;
   Mine was it in the fields both day and night,
   And by the waters, all the summer long.

   And in the frosty season, when the sun
   Was set, and visible for many a mile
   The cottage windows blazed through twilight gloom,
   I heeded not their summons: happy time
   It was indeed for all of us—for me
430 It was a time of rapture! Clear and loud
   The village clock tolled six—I wheeled about,
   Proud and exulting like an untired horse
   That cares not for his home. All shod with steel,
   We hissed along the polished ice in games
   Confederate, imitative of the chase
   And woodland pleasures—the resounding horn,
   The pack loud chiming, and the hunted hare.
   So through the darkness and the cold we flew,
   And not a voice was idle; with the din
440 Smitten, the precipices rang aloud;
   The leafless trees and every icy crag
   Tinkled like iron; while far distant hills
   Into the tumult sent an alien sound
   Of melancholy not unnoticed, while the stars

Eastward were sparkling clear, and in the west
The orange sky of evening died away.
Not seldom from the uproar I retired
Into a silent bay, or sportively
Glanced sideway, leaving the tumultuous throng,
To cut across the reflex of a star   450
That fled, and, flying still before me, gleamed
Upon the glassy plain; and oftentimes,
When we had given our bodies to the wind,
And all the shadowy banks on either side
Came sweeping through the darkness, spinning still
The rapid line of motion, then at once
Have I, reclining back upon my heels,
Stopped short; yet still the solitary cliffs
Wheeled by me—even as if the earth had rolled
With visible motion her diurnal round!   460
Behind me did they stretch in solemn train,
Feebler and feebler, and I stood and watched
Till all was tranquil as a dreamless sleep.

   Ye Presences of Nature in the sky
And on the earth! Ye Visions of the hills!
And Souls of lonely places! can I think
A vulgar hope was yours when ye employed
Such ministry, when ye through many a year
Haunting me thus among my boyish sports,
On caves and trees, upon the woods and hills,   470
Impressed upon all forms the characters
Of danger or desire; and thus did make
The surface of the universal earth
With triumph and delight, with hope and fear,
Work like a sea?
            Not uselessly employed,
Might I pursue this theme through every change
Of exercise and play, to which the year
Did summon us in his delightful round.

   We were a noisy crew; the sun in heaven
Beheld not vales more beautiful than ours;   480
Nor saw a band in happiness and joy
Richer, or worthier of the ground they trod.
I could record with no reluctant voice
The woods of autumn, and their hazel bowers
With milk-white clusters hung; the rod and line,
True symbol of hope's foolishness, whose strong
And unreproved enchantment led us on
By rocks and pools shut out from every star,
All the green summer, to forlorn cascades
Among the windings hid of mountain brooks.   490
—Unfading recollections! at this hour
The heart is almost mine with which I felt,
From some hill-top on sunny afternoons,
The paper kite high among fleecy clouds
Pull at her rein like an impetuous courser;
Or, from the meadows sent on gusty days,
Beheld her breast the wind, then suddenly
Dashed headlong, and rejected by the storm.

Ye lowly cottages wherein we dwelt,
500 A ministration of your own was yours;
Can I forget you, being as you were
So beautiful among the pleasant fields
In which ye stood? or can I here forget
The plain and seemly countenance with which
Ye dealt out your plain comforts? Yet had ye
Delights and exultations of your own.
Eager and never weary we pursued
Our home-amusements by the warm peat-fire
At evening, when with pencil, and smooth slate
510 In square divisions parceled out and all
With crosses and with ciphers scribbled o'er,
We schemed and puzzled, head opposed to head
In strife too humble to be named in verse;
Or round the naked table, snow-white deal,
Cherry or maple, sate in close array,
And to the combat, Loo or Whist, led on
A thick-ribbed army; not, as in the world,
Neglected and ungratefully thrown by
Even for the very service they had wrought,
520 But husbanded through many a long campaign.
Uncouth assemblage was it, where no few
Had changed their functions; some, plebeian cards
Which Fate, beyond the promise of their birth,
Had dignified, and called to represent
The persons of departed potentates.
Oh, with what echoes on the board they fell!
Ironic diamonds—clubs, hearts, diamonds, spades,
A congregation piteously akin!
Cheap matter offered they to boyish wit,
530 Those sooty knaves, precipitated down
With scoffs and taunts, like Vulcan out of heaven:
The paramount ace, a moon in her eclipse,
Queens gleaming through their splendor's last decay,
And monarchs surly at the wrongs sustained
By royal visages. Meanwhile abroad
Incessant rain was falling, or the frost
Raged bitterly, with keen and silent tooth;
And, interrupting oft that eager game,
From under Esthwaite's splitting fields of ice
540 The pent-up air, struggling to free itself,
Gave out to meadow-grounds and hills a loud
Protracted yelling, like the noise of wolves
Howling in troops along the Bothnic Main.

Nor, sedulous as I have been to trace
How Nature by extrinsic passion first
Peopled the mind with forms sublime or fair,
And made me love them, may I here omit
How other pleasures have been mine, and joys
Of subtler origin; how I have felt,
550 Not seldom even in that tempestuous time,
Those hallowed and pure emotions of the sense
Which seem, in their simplicity, to own

An intellectual charm; that calm delight
Which, if I err not, surely must belong
To those first-born affinities that fit
Our new existence to existing things,
And, in our dawn of being, constitute
The bond of union between life and joy.

Yes, I remember when the changeful earth,
And twice five summers on my mind had stamped 560
The faces of the moving year, even then
I held unconscious intercourse with beauty
Old as creation, drinking in a pure
Organic pleasure from the silver wreaths
Of curling mist, or from the level plain
Of waters colored by impending clouds.

The sands of Westmoreland, the creeks and bays
Of Cumbria's rocky limits, they can tell
How, when the Sea threw off his evening shade
And to the shepherd's hut on distant hills 570
Sent welcome notice of the rising moon,
How I have stood, to fancies such as these
A stranger, linking with the spectacle
No conscious memory of a kindred sight,
And bringing with me no peculiar sense
Of quietness or peace; yet have I stood,
Even while mine eye hath moved o'er many a league
Of shining water, gathering as it seemed,
Through every hair-breadth in that field of light,
New pleasure like a bee among the flowers. 580

Thus oft amid those fits of vulgar joy
Which, through all seasons, on a child's pursuits
Are prompt attendants, 'mid that giddy bliss
Which, like a tempest, works along the blood
And is forgotten; even then I felt
Gleams like the flashing of a shield; the earth
And common face of Nature spake to me
Rememberable things; sometimes, 'tis true,
By chance collisions and quaint accidents
(Like those ill-sorted unions, work supposed 590
Of evil-minded fairies), yet not vain
Nor profitless, if haply they impressed
Collateral objects and appearances,
Albeit lifeless then, and doomed to sleep
Until maturer seasons called them forth
To impregnate and to elevate the mind.
—And if the vulgar joy by its own weight
Wearied itself out of the memory,
The scenes which were a witness of that joy
Remained in their substantial lineaments 600
Depicted on the brain, and to the eye
Were visible, a daily sight; and thus
By the impressive discipline of fear,
By pleasure and repeated happiness,

---

514. **deal,** pine or fir wood. 516. **Loo,** a card game played for stakes.
Cf. the card game described in Pope's **The Rape of the Lock** (p. 542).
531. **Vulcan,** the blacksmith of the gods. 543. **Bothnic Main,** the
Baltic Sea, between Sweden and Finland. 556. **new...things.** Cf.
Ode on Intimations of Immortality, p. 700. 568. **Cumbria,** Cumberland-
shire, which made up most of the ancient British Kingdom of Cumbria.

So frequently repeated, and by force
Of obscure feelings representative
Of things forgotten, these same scenes so bright,
So beautiful, so majestic in themselves,
Though yet the day was distant, did become
610 Habitually dear, and all their forms
And changeful colors by invisible links
Were fastened to the affections.
                                        I began
My story early—not misled, I trust,
By an infirmity of love for days
Disowned by memory—ere the birth of spring
Planting my snowdrops among winter snows:
Nor will it seem to thee, O Friend! so prompt
In sympathy, that I have lengthened out
With fond and feeble tongue a tedious tale.
620 Meanwhile, my hope has been that I might fetch
Invigorating thoughts from former years;
Might fix the wavering balance of my mind,
And haply meet reproaches too, whose power
May spur me on, in manhood now mature,
To honorable toil. Yet should these hopes
Prove vain, and thus should neither I be taught
To understand myself, nor thou to know
With better knowledge how the heart was framed
Of him thou lovest; need I dread from thee
630 Harsh judgments, if the song be loath to quit
Those recollected hours that have the charm
Of visionary things, those lovely forms
And sweet sensations that throw back our life,
And almost make remotest infancy
A visible scene, on which the sun is shining?

    One end at least hath been attained; my mind
Hath been revived, and if this genial mood
Desert me not, forthwith shall be brought down
Through later years the story of my life.
640 The road lies plain before me;—'tis a theme
Single and of determined bounds; and hence
I choose it rather at this time, than work
Of ampler or more varied argument,
Where I might be discomfited and lost:
And certain hopes are with me, that to thee
This labor will be welcome, honored Friend!
(1795-1805; 1850)

from BOOK XII. IMAGINATION AND TASTE,
HOW IMPAIRED AND RESTORED

    There are in our existence spots of time,
That with distinct pre-eminence retain
210 A renovating virtue, whence—depressed
By false opinion and contentious thought,
Or aught of heavier or more deadly weight,

In trivial occupations, and the round
Of ordinary intercourse—our minds
Are nourished and invisibly repaired;
A virtue, by which pleasure is enhanced,
That penetrates, enables us to mount,
When high, more high, and lifts us up when fallen.
This efficacious spirit chiefly lurks
Among those passages of life that give   220
Profoundest knowledge to what point, and how,
The mind is lord and master—outward sense
The obedient servant of her will. Such moments
Are scattered everywhere, taking their date
From our first childhood. I remember well,
That once, while yet my inexperienced hand
Could scarcely hold a bridle, with proud hopes
I mounted, and we journeyed towards the hills:
An ancient servant of my father's house
Was with me, my encourager and guide;   230
We had not traveled long, ere some mischance
Disjoined me from my comrade; and, through fear
Dismounting, down the rough and stony moor
I led my horse, and, stumbling on, at length
Came to a bottom, where in former times
A murderer had been hung in iron chains.
The gibbet-mast had moldered down, the bones
And iron case were gone; but on the turf,
Hard by, soon after that fell deed was wrought,
Some unknown hand had carved the murderer's name.   240
The monumental letters were inscribed
In times long past; but still, from year to year
By superstition of the neighborhood,
The grass is cleared away, and to this hour
The characters are fresh and visible:
A casual glance had shown them, and I fled,
Faltering and faint, and ignorant of the road:
Then, reascending the bare common, saw
A naked pool that lay beneath the hills,
The beacon on the summit, and, more near,   250
A girl, who bore a pitcher on her head,
And seemed with difficult steps to force her way
Against the blowing wind. It was, in truth,
An ordinary sight; but I should need
Colours and words that are unknown to man,
To paint the visionary dreariness
Which, while I looked all round for my lost guide
Invested moorland waste and naked pool,
The beacon crowning the lone eminence,
The female and her garments vexed and tossed   260
By the strong wind. When, in the blessèd hours
Of early love, the loved one at my side,
I roamed, in daily presence of this scene,
Upon the naked pool and dreary crags,
And on the melancholy beacon, fell
A spirit of pleasure and youth's golden gleam;

Book XII. In this book Wordsworth reviews the "impairment" and gradual restoration of his creative sensibility in response to the natural world; its climax is the celebrated description of the "spots of time," ordinary moments of experience which become illuminated with a profound significance through the imaginative power of the beholder.

And think ye not with radiance more sublime
For these remembrances, and for the power
They had left behind? So feeling comes in aid
270 Of feeling, and diversity of strength
Attends us, if but once we have been strong.
Oh! mystery of man, from what a depth
Proceed thy honours. I am lost, but see
In simple childhood something of the base
On which thy greatness stands; but this I feel,
That from thyself it comes, that thou must give,
Else never canst receive. The days gone by
Return upon me almost from the dawn
Of life: the hiding-places of man's power
280 Open; I would approach them, but they close.
I see by glimpses now; when age comes on,
May scarcely see at all; and I would give,
While yet we may, as far as words can give,
Substance and life to what I feel, enshrining,
Such is my hope, the spirit of the Past
For future restoration.—Yet another
Of these memorials:—

              One Christmas-time,
On the glad eve of its dear holidays,
Feverish, and tired, and restless, I went forth
290 Into the fields, impatient for the sight
Of those led palfreys that should bear us home;
My brothers and myself. There rose a crag,
That, from the meeting-point of two highways
Ascending, overlooked them both, far stretched;
Thither, uncertain on which road to fix
My expectation, thither I repaired,
Scout-like, and gained the summit; 'twas a day
Tempestuous, dark, and wild, and on the grass
I sate half-sheltered by a naked wall;
300 Upon my right hand couched a single sheep,
Upon my left a blasted hawthorn stood;
With those companions at my side, I watched,
Straining my eyes intensely, as the mist
Gave intermitting prospect of the copse
And plain beneath. Ere we to school returned,—
That dreary time,—ere we had been ten days
Sojourners in my father's house, he died;
And I and my three brothers, orphans then,
Followed his body to the grave. The event,
310 With all the sorrow that it brought, appeared
A chastisement; and when I called to mind
That day so lately past, when from the crag
I looked in such anxiety of hope;
With trite reflections of morality,
Yet in the deepest passion, I bowed low
To God, Who thus corrected my desires;
And, afterwards, the wind and sleety rain,
And all the business of the elements,
The single sheep, and the one blasted tree,
320 And the bleak music from that old stone wall,
The noise of wood and water, and the mist
That on the line of each of those two roads

Advanced in such indisputable shapes;
All these were kindred spectacles and sounds
To which I oft repaired, and thence would drink,
As at a fountain; and on winter nights,
Down to this very time, when storm and rain
Beat on my roof, or, haply, at noon-day,
While in a grove I walk, whose lofty trees,
Laden with summer's thickest foliage, rock   330
In a strong wind, some working of the spirit,
Some inward agitations thence are brought,
Whate'er their office, whether to beguile
Thoughts over busy in the course they took,
Or animate an hour of vacant ease.

from BOOK XIII. IMAGINATION AND TASTE,
HOW IMPAIRED AND RESTORED (CONCLUDED)

    From Nature doth emotion come, and moods
Of calmness equally are Nature's gift;
This is her glory; these two attributes
Are sister horns that constitute her strength.
Hence Genius, born to thrive by interchange
Of peace and excitation, finds in her
His best and purest friend; from her receives
That energy by which he seeks the truth,
From her that happy stillness of the mind
Which fits him to receive it when unsought.   10

    Such benefit the humblest intellects
Partake of, each in their degree; 'tis mine
To speak, what I myself have known and felt;
Smooth task! for words find easy way, inspired
By gratitude, and confidence in truth.
Long time in search of knowledge did I range
The field of human life, in heart and mind
Benighted; but, the dawn beginning now
To reappear, 'twas proved that not in vain
I had been taught to reverence a power   20
That is the visible quality and shape
And image of right reason; that matures
Her processes by steadfast laws; gives birth
To no impatient or fallacious hopes,
No heat of passion or excessive zeal,
No vain conceits; provokes to no quick turns
Of self-applauding intellect; but trains
To meekness, and exalts by humble faith,
Holds up before the mind intoxicate
With present objects, and the busy dance   30
Of things that pass away, a temperate show
Of objects that endure; and by this course
Disposes her, when overfondly set
On throwing off incumbrances, to seek
In man, and in the frame of social life,
Whate'er there is desirable and good
Of kindred permanence, unchanged in form

And function, or, through strict vicissitude
Of life and death, revolving. Above all
40 Were re-established now those watchful thoughts
Which, seeing little worthy or sublime
In what the historian's pen so much delights
To blazon—power and energy detached
From moral purpose—early tutored me
To look with feelings of fraternal love
Upon the unassuming things that hold
A silent station in this beauteous world.

* * * * *

Here, calling up to mind what then I saw,
A youthful traveler, and see daily now
In the familiar circuit of my home,
Here might I pause, and bend in reverence
To Nature, and the power of human minds,
To men as they are men within themselves.
How oft high service is performed within,
When all the external man is rude in show—
Not like a temple rich with pomp and gold,
230 But a mere mountain chapel, that protects
Its simple worshipers from sun and shower.
Of these, said I, shall be my song; of these,
If future years mature me for the task,
Will I record the praises, making verse
Deal boldly with substantial things; in truth
And sanctity of passion, speak of these,
That justice may be done, obeisance paid
Where it is due: thus haply shall I teach,
Inspire; through unadulterated ears
240 Pour rapture, tenderness, and hope—my theme
No other than the very heart of man,
As found among the best of those who live,
Not unexalted by religious faith,
Nor uninformed by books, good books, though few,
In Nature's presence; thence may I select
Sorrow, that is not sorrow, but delight;
And miserable love, that is not pain
To hear of, for the glory that redounds
Therefrom to human kind, and what we are.
250 Be mine to follow with no timid step
Where knowledge leads me: it shall be my pride
That I have dared to tread this holy ground,
Speaking no dream, but things oracular;
Matter not lightly to be heard by those
Who to the letter of the outward promise
Do read the invisible soul; by men adroit
In speech, and for communion with the world
Accomplished; minds whose faculties are then
Most active when they are most eloquent,
260 And elevated most when most admired.
Men may be found of other mold than these,
Who are their own upholders, to themselves
Encouragement, and energy, and will,
Expressing liveliest thoughts in lively words
As native passion dictates.   (1799–1805; 1850)

MY HEART LEAPS UP WHEN I BEHOLD

My heart leaps up when I behold
    A rainbow in the sky:
So was it when my life began;
So is it now I am a man:
So be it when I shall grow old,
    Or let me die!
The Child is father of the Man;
And I could wish my days to be
Bound each to each by natural piety.   (1802; 1807)

RESOLUTION AND INDEPENDENCE

This poem is also known as The Leech-Gatherer.
*Dorothy Wordsworth tells us that the subject of the
poem was an old man that she and her brother met in
the course of one of their walks—a man pinched by
poverty and crippled. "He had been hurt in driving a
cart, his leg broken, his body driven over, his skull
fractured." Wordsworth evidently saw in him some
of the effects of the maleficent forces of nature; the
poem is therefore interesting as showing the attention
given by the poet to the possibility that nature was not
always kindly. This note of disillusionment appears
occasionally in his poems after 1800. Wordsworth
himself said, in a letter to some friends (June 14, 1802)
speaking of* Resolution and Independence: *"I describe
myself as having been exalted to the highest pitch of
delight by the joyousness and beauty of nature, and
then as depressed, even in the midst of those beautiful
objects, to the lowest dejection and despair. A young
poet in the midst of the happiness of nature is described as overwhelmed by the thoughts of the miserable reverses which have befallen the happiest of all
men...." Significant also is the last sentence in the
passage: "I cannot conceive a figure more impressive
than that of an old man like this... traveling alone
among the mountains and all lonely places, carrying
with him his own fortitude, and the necessities which
an unjust state of society has laid upon him."*

There was a roaring in the wind all night;
The rain came heavily and fell in floods;
But now the sun is rising calm and bright;
The birds are singing in the distant woods:
Over his own sweet voice the stock-dove broods;
The jay makes answer as the magpie chatters;
And all the air is filled with pleasant noise of waters.

All things that love the sun are out of doors;
The sky rejoices in the morning's birth;
The grass is bright with raindrops;—on the moors   10
The hare is running races in her mirth;
And with her feet she from the plashy earth
Raises a mist, that, glittering in the sun,
Runs with her all the way wherever she doth run.

My Heart Leaps Up. 9. **piety**, reverence, affection.
Resolution and Independence. 12. **plashy**, swampy, marshy.

I was a traveler then upon the moor;
I saw the hare that raced about with joy;
I heard the woods and distant waters roar,
Or heard them not, as happy as a boy:
The pleasant season did my heart employ:
20 My old remembrances went from me wholly;
And all the ways of men so vain and melancholy.

But, as it sometimes chanceth, from the might
Of joy in minds that can no further go,
As high as we have mounted in delight
In our dejection do we sink as low,
To me that morning did it happen so;
And fears, and fancies, thick upon me came;
Dim sadness—and blind thoughts, I knew not, nor
    could name.

I heard the skylark warbling in the sky;
30 And I bethought me of the playful hare:
Even such a happy child of earth am I;
Even as these blissful creatures do I fare;
Far from the world I walk, and from all care;
But there may come another day to me—
Solitude, pain of heart, distress, and poverty.

My whole life I have lived in pleasant thought,
As if life's business were a summer mood;
As if all needful things would come unsought
To genial faith, still rich in genial good;
40 But how can he expect that others should
Build for him, sow for him, and at his call
Love him, who for himself will take no heed at all?

I thought of Chatterton, the marvelous boy,
The sleepless soul that perished in his pride;
Of him who walked in glory and in joy
Following his plow, along the mountain side:
By our own spirits are we deified:
We poets in our youth begin in gladness;
But thereof come in the end despondency and madness.

50 Now, whether it were by peculiar grace,
A leading from above, a something given,
Yet it befell, that, in this lonely place,
When I with these untoward thoughts had striven,
Beside a pool bare to the eye of heaven
I saw a man before me unawares:
The oldest man he seemed that ever wore gray hairs.

As a huge stone is sometimes seen to lie
Couched on the bald top of an eminence;
Wonder to all who do the same espy,
60 By what means it could thither come, and whence;
So that it seems a thing endued with sense:
Like a sea-beast crawled forth, that on a shelf
Of rock or sand reposeth, there to sun itself;

Such seemed this man, not all alive nor dead,
Nor all asleep—in his extreme old age:
His body was bent double, feet and head
Coming together in life's pilgrimage;
As if some dire constraint of pain, or rage
Of sickness felt by him in times long past,
A more than human weight upon his frame had cast. 70

Himself he propped, limbs, body, and pale face,
Upon a long gray staff of shaven wood:
And, still as I drew near with gentle pace,
Upon the margin of that moorish flood
Motionless as a cloud the old man stood;
That heareth not the loud winds when they call,
And moveth altogether, if it move at all.

At length, himself unsettling, he the pond
Stirred with his staff and fixedly did look
Upon the muddy water, which he conned,   80
As if he had been reading in a book:
And now a stranger's privilege I took;
And, drawing to his side, to him did say,
"This morning gives us promise of a glorious day."

A gentle answer did the old man make,
In courteous speech which forth he slowly drew:
And him with further words I thus bespake:
"What occupation do you there pursue?
This is a lonesome place for one like you."
Ere he replied, a flash of mild surprise   90
Broke from the sable orbs of his yet vivid eyes.

His words came feebly, from a feeble chest,
But each in solemn order followed each,
With something of a lofty utterance dressed;
Choice word, and measured phrase, above the reach
Of ordinary men; a stately speech;
Such as grave Livers do in Scotland use,
Religious men, who give to God and man their dues.

He told, that to these waters he had come
To gather leeches, being old and poor: 100
Employment hazardous and wearisome!
And he had many hardships to endure:
From pond to pond he roamed, from moor to moor;
Housing, with God's good help, by choice or chance;
And in this way he gained an honest maintenance.

The old man still stood talking by my side;
But now his voice to me was like a stream
Scarce heard; nor word from word could I divide;
And the whole body of the man did seem
Like one whom I had met with in a dream;   110
Or like a man from some far region sent,
To give me human strength, by apt admonishment.

---

43. **Chatterton,** Thomas Chatterton (1752-1770), the youthful poet
who in despair and poverty took his own life. See p. 613.   45. **him...**

joy, Robert Burns. See p. 653.   74. **moorish,** marshy.
    It Is a Beauteous Evening.   9. **Dear Child,** Caroline, the daughter

My former thoughts returned: the fear that kills;
And hope that is unwilling to be fed;
Cold, pain and labor, and all fleshly ills;
And mighty poets in their misery dead.
Perplexed, and longing to be comforted,
My question eagerly did I renew,
"How is it that you live, and what is it you do?"

120 He with a smile did then his words repeat;
And said that, gathering leeches, far and wide
He traveled; stirring thus about his feet
The waters of the pools where they abide.
"Once I could meet with them on every side;
But they have dwindled long by slow decay;
Yet still I persevere, and find them where I may."

While he was talking thus, the lonely place,
The old man's shape, and speech, all troubled me:
In my mind's eye I seemed to see him pace
130 About the weary moors continually,
Wandering about alone and silently.
While I these thoughts within myself pursued,
He, having made a pause, the same discourse re-
newed.

And soon with this he other matter blended,
Cheerfully uttered, with demeanor kind,
But stately in the main; and when he ended,
I could have laughed myself to scorn to find
In that decrepit man so firm a mind.
"God," said I, "be my help and stay secure;
I'll think of the leech-gatherer on the lonely moor!"
(1802; 1807)

COMPOSED UPON WESTMINSTER BRIDGE

Earth has not anything to show more fair:
Dull would he be of soul who could pass by
A sight so touching in its majesty:
This City now doth like a garment wear
The beauty of the morning; silent, bare,
Ships, towers, domes, theaters, and temples lie
Open unto the fields, and to the sky;
All bright and glittering in the smokeless air.
Never did sun more beautifully steep
10 In his first splendor valley, rock, or hill;
Ne'er saw I, never felt, a calm so deep!
The river glideth at his own sweet will:
Dear God! the very houses seem asleep;
And all that mighty heart is lying still!
(1802; 1807)

COMPOSED BY THE SEASIDE, NEAR CALAIS

Fair Star of evening, Splendor of the west,
Star of my Country!—on the horizon's brink

Thou hangest, stooping, as might seem, to sink
On England's bosom, yet well pleased to rest,
Meanwhile, and be to her a glorious crest
Conspicuous to the Nations. Thou, I think,
Shouldst be my Country's emblem; and shouldst wink,
Bright Star! with laughter on her banners, dressed
In thy fresh beauty. There! that dusky spot
Beneath thee, that is England; there she lies.   10
Blessings be on you both! one hope, one lot,
One life, one glory!—I, with many a fear
For my dear Country, many heartfelt sighs,
Among men who do not love her, linger here.
(1802; 1807)

IT IS A BEAUTEOUS EVENING, CALM AND FREE

It is a beauteous evening, calm and free.
The holy time is quiet as a Nun,
Breathless with adoration: the broad sun
Is sinking down in its tranquillity;
The gentleness of heaven broods o'er the sea;
Listen! the mighty Being is awake,
And doth with his eternal motion make
A sound like thunder—everlastingly.
Dear Child! dear Girl! that walkest with me here,
If thou appear untouched by solemn thought,   10
Thy nature is not therefore less divine:
Thou liest in Abraham's bosom all the year,
And worship'st at the Temple's inner shrine,
God being with thee when we know it not.
(1802; 1807)

ON THE EXTINCTION OF THE
VENETIAN REPUBLIC

Venice was founded in the fifth century by refugees fleeing before the Huns under Attila. After conquering Constantinople in 1202, the new republic gained extensive possessions in the East and became a bulwark of western Europe against the Turks. In the sixteenth century her glory declined as the commercial power of England and Holland advanced. When Venice was conquered by Napoleon in 1797, her territory was divided between France and Austria.

Once did she hold the gorgeous East in fee;
And was the safeguard of the West: the worth
Of Venice did not fall below her birth,
Venice, the eldest Child of liberty.
She was a maiden City, bright and free;
No guile seduced, no force could violate;
And when she took unto herself a Mate,

of Wordsworth and Annette Vallon. here, on Calais beach, where the sonnet was composed. 12. in Abraham's bosom, in the presence of God's favor. See Luke 16:22.

She must espouse the everlasting Sea!
And what if she had seen those glories fade,
10 Those titles vanish, and that strength decay;
Yet shall some tribute of regret be paid
When her long life hath reached its final day:
Men are we, and must grieve when even the Shade
Of that which once was great is passed away.
(1802; 1807)

LONDON, 1802

Milton! thou shouldst be living at this hour:
England hath need of thee: she is a fen
Of stagnant waters: altar, sword, and pen,
Fireside, the heroic wealth of hall and bower,
Have forfeited their ancient English dower
Of inward happiness. We are selfish men:
Oh! raise us up, return to us again;
And give us manners, virtue, freedom, power.
Thy soul was like a Star, and dwelt apart:
10 Thou hadst a voice whose sound was like the sea,
Pure as the naked heavens, majestic, free;
So didst thou travel on life's common way
In cheerful godliness; and yet thy heart
The lowliest duties on herself did lay.
(1802; 1807)

TO THE DAISY

With little here to do or see
Of things that in the great world be,
Sweet Daisy! oft I talk to thee
    For thou art worthy,
Thou unassuming Commonplace
Of Nature, with that homely face,
And yet with something of a grace
    Which Love makes for thee!

Oft on the dappled turf at ease
10 I sit and play with similes,
Loose types of things through all degrees,
    Thoughts of thy raising;
And many a fond and idle name
I give to thee, for praise or blame
As is the humor of the game,
    While I am gazing.

A nun demure, of lowly port;
Or sprightly maiden, of Love's court,
In thy simplicity the sport
20   Of all temptations;
A queen in crown of rubies drest;

A starveling in a scanty vest;
Are all, as seems to suit thee best,
    Thy appellations.

A little Cyclops, with one eye
Staring to threaten and defy,
That thought comes next—and instantly
    The freak is over,
The shape will vanish, and behold!
A silver shield with boss of gold   30
That spreads itself, some faery bold
    In fight to cover.

I see thee glittering from afar—
And then thou art a pretty star,
Not quite so fair as many are
    In heaven above thee!
Yet like a star, with glittering crest,
Self-poised in air thou seem'st to rest;—
May peace come never to his nest
    Who shall reprove thee!   40

Sweet Flower! for by that name at last
When all my reveries are past
I call thee, and to that cleave fast,
    Sweet silent Creature!
That breath'st with me in sun and air,
Do thou, as thou art wont, repair
My heart with gladness, and a share
    Of thy meek nature!
(1802; 1807)

TO THE DAISY

Bright Flower! whose home is everywhere,
Bold in maternal Nature's care,
And all the long year through the heir
    Of joy and sorrow;
Methinks that there abides in thee
Some concord with humanity,
Given to no other flower I see
    The forest thorough!

Is it that Man is soon deprest?
A thoughtless Thing! who, once unblest,   10
Does little on his memory rest,
    Or on his reason,
And Thou wouldst teach him how to find
A shelter under every wind,
A hope for times that are unkind
    And every season?

Thou wander'st the wide world about,
Unchecked by pride or scrupulous doubt,

On the Extinction of the Venetian Republic. 8. She . . . Sea!
When the Venetians defeated the Germans in 1177 in defense of Pope
Alexander III, the Doge received from the Pope a ring with which he
was commanded to wed the Adriatic as a sign of the maritime power
of Venice. As a ceremony in token of this espousal, a ring was dropped
annually into the Adriatic by the Doge.

With friends to greet thee, or without,
20 Yet pleased and willing;
Meek, yielding to the occasion's call,
And all things suffering from all,
Thy function apostolical
    In peace fulfilling.
(1802; 1807)

TO A HIGHLAND GIRL

AT INVERSNEYDE, UPON LOCH LOMOND

Sweet Highland Girl, a very shower
Of beauty is thy earthly dower!
Twice seven consenting years have shed
Their utmost bounty on thy head:
And these gray rocks; that household lawn;
Those trees, a veil just half withdrawn;
This fall of water that doth make
A murmur near the silent lake;
This little bay; a quiet road
10 That holds in shelter thy Abode—
In truth together do ye seem
Like something fashioned in a dream;
Such Forms as from their covert peep
When earthly cares are laid asleep!
But, O fair Creature! in the light
Of common day, so heavenly bright,
I bless thee, Vision as thou art,
I bless thee with a human heart;
God shield thee to thy latest years!
20 Thee, neither know I, nor thy peers;
And yet my eyes are filled with tears.
    With earnest feeling I shall pray
For thee when I am far away:
For never saw I mien, or face,
In which more plainly I could trace
Benignity and home-bred sense
Ripening in perfect innocence.
Here scattered, like a random seed,
Remote from men, thou dost not need
30 The embarrassed look of shy distress,
And maidenly shamefacédness:
Thou wear'st upon thy forehead clear
The freedom of a Mountaineer:
A face with gladness overspread!
Soft smiles, by human kindness bred!
And seemliness complete, that sways
Thy courtesies, about thee plays;
With no restraint, but such as springs
From quick and eager visitings
40 Of thoughts that lie beyond the reach
Of thy few words of English speech:

A bondage sweetly brooked, a strife
That gives thy gestures grace and life!
So have I, not unmoved in mind,
Seen birds of tempest-loving kind—
Thus beating up against the wind.
    What hand but would a garland cull
For thee who art so beautiful?
O happy pleasure! here to dwell
Beside thee in some heathy dell;   50
Adopt your homely ways, and dress,
A Shepherd, thou a Shepherdess!
But I could frame a wish for thee
More like a grave reality:
Thou art to me but as a wave
Of the wild sea; and I would have
Some claim upon thee, if I could,
Though but of common neighborhood.
What joy to hear thee, and to see!
Thy elder Brother I would be,   60
Thy Father—anything to thee!
    Now thanks to Heaven! that of its grace
Hath led me to this lovely place.
Joy have I had; and going hence
I bear away my recompense.
In spots like these it is we prize
Our memory, feel that she hath eyes:
Then, why should I be loath to stir?
I feel this place was made for her;
To give new pleasure like the past,   70
Continued long as life shall last.
Nor am I loath, though pleased at heart,
Sweet Highland Girl! from thee to part:
For I, methinks, till I grow old,
As fair before me shall behold,
As I do now, the cabin small,
The lake, the bay, the waterfall;
And thee, the Spirit of them all!
(1803; 1807)

THE SOLITARY REAPER

This poem was suggested to Wordsworth by an actual experience in the Scottish Highlands, which he and his sister Dorothy visited in 1803, and also, as recorded in Dorothy Wordsworth's Recollections, by the following entry in Thomas Wilkinson's Tour in Scotland: "Passed a female who was reaping alone; she sung in Erse, as she bended over her sickle; the sweetest human voice I ever heard: her strains were tenderly melancholy, and felt delicious, long after she was heard no more."

Behold her, single in the field,
Yon solitary Highland lass!

London, 1802. 4. **hall and bower.** The hall was the public dwelling of the Teutonic chieftain, and the bower the private apartments.
To the Daisy. 25. **Cyclops,** in classical legend, one of a race of mythical giants having but one eye.
To a Highland Girl. Loch Lomond, the largest lake in Scotland, situated in the counties of Stirling and Dumbarton, noted for its scenery.

Reaping and singing by herself;
Stop here, or gently pass!
Alone she cuts and binds the grain,
And sings a melancholy strain;
O listen! for the vale profound
Is overflowing with the sound.

No nightingale did ever chaunt
10 More welcome notes to weary bands
Of travelers in some shady haunt,
Among Arabian sands:
A voice so thrilling ne'er was heard
In springtime from the cuckoo-bird,
Breaking the silence of the seas
Among the farthest Hebrides.

Will no one tell me what she sings?—
Perhaps the plaintive numbers flow
For old, unhappy, far-off things,
20 And battles long ago:
Or is it some more humble lay,
Familiar matter of today?
Some natural sorrow, loss, or pain,
That has been, and may be again?

Whate'er the theme, the maiden sang
As if her song could have no ending;
I saw her singing at her work,
And o'er the sickle bending;—
I listened, motionless and still;
30 And, as I mounted up the hill,
The music in my heart I bore,
Long after it was heard no more.
(1803; 1807)

TO THE CUCKOO

O blithe Newcomer! I have heard,
I hear thee and rejoice.
O Cuckoo! shall I call thee Bird,
Or but a wandering Voice?

While I am lying on the grass,
Thy twofold shout I hear;
From hill to hill it seems to pass,
At once far off, and near.

Though babbling only to the Vale,
Of sunshine and of flowers,   10
Thou bringest unto me a tale
Of visionary hours.

Thrice welcome, darling of the Spring!
Even yet thou art to me
No bird, but an invisible thing,
A voice, a mystery;

The same when in my schoolboy days
I listened to; that Cry
Which made me look a thousand ways
In bush, and tree, and sky.   20

To seek thee did I often rove
Through woods and on the green;
And thou wert still a hope, a love;
Still longed for, never seen.

And I can listen to thee yet;
Can lie upon the plain

*The daffodils
at Bassenthwaite.*

The Solitary Reaper. 16. **Hebrides,** a group of islands on the west coast of Scotland. 17. **what she sings.** She is singing in Gaelic (Erse), which the poet does not understand.

She Was a Phantom of Delight. 22. **machine,** body. *To a Skylark.* Cf. Shelley's *To a Skylark,* p. 773.

698   *Revolution and Romance*

And listen, till I do beget
That golden time again.

O blessèd Bird! the earth we pace
30 Again appears to be
An unsubstantial, faery place;
That is fit home for thee!
(1804; 1807)

SHE WAS A PHANTOM OF DELIGHT

*This poem is a tribute to Mary Hutchinson, whom
Wordsworth married in 1802.*

She was a phantom of delight
When first she gleamed upon my sight;
A lovely apparition, sent
To be a moment's ornament;
Her eyes as stars of twilight fair;
Like twilight's too, her dusky hair;
But all things else about her drawn
From May-time and the cheerful dawn;
A dancing shape, an Image gay,
10 To haunt, to startle, and waylay.

I saw her upon nearer view,
A spirit, yet a woman too!
Her household motions light and free,
And steps of virgin liberty;
A countenance in which did meet
Sweet records, promises as sweet;
A creature not too bright or good
For human nature's daily food:
For transient sorrows, simple wiles,
20 Praise, blame, love, kisses, tears, and smiles.

And now I see with eye serene
The very pulse of the machine;
A being breathing thoughtful breath,
A Traveler between life and death;
The reason firm, the temperate will,
Endurance, foresight, strength, and skill,
A perfect woman, nobly planned,
To warn, to comfort, and command;
And yet a spirit still, and bright
With something of angelic light.
(1804; 1807)

I WANDERED LONELY AS A CLOUD

I wandered lonely as a cloud
That floats on high o'er vales and hills,
When all at once I saw a crowd,
A host, of golden daffodils;
Beside the lake, beneath the trees,
Fluttering and dancing in the breeze.

Continuous as the stars that shine
And twinkle on the Milky Way,
They stretched in never-ending line
Along the margin of a bay: 10
Ten thousand saw I at a glance,
Tossing their heads in sprightly dance.

The waves beside them danced; but they
Outdid the sparkling waves in glee:
A poet could not but be gay,
In such a jocund company:
I gazed—and gazed—but little thought
What wealth the show to me had brought:

For oft, when on my couch I lie
In vacant or in pensive mood,   20
They flash upon that inward eye
Which is the bliss of solitude;
And then my heart with pleasure fills,
And dances with the daffodils.
(1804; 1807)

TO A SKYLARK

Up with me! up with me into the clouds!
   For thy song, Lark, is strong;
Up with me, up with me into the clouds!
   Singing, singing,
With clouds and sky about thee ringing,
   Lift me, guide me till I find
That spot which seems so to thy mind.

I have walked through wildernesses dreary,
And today my heart is weary;
Had I now the wings of a Faery   10
Up to thee would I fly.
There is madness about thee, and joy divine
In that song of thine;
Lift me, guide me, high and high
To thy banqueting-place in the sky!

   Joyous as morning,
Thou art laughing and scorning;
Thou hast a nest for thy love and thy rest,
And, though little troubled with sloth,
Drunken Lark! thou wouldst be loath   20
To be such a traveler as I.
Happy, happy Liver,
With a soul as strong as a mountain river
Pouring out praise to the almighty Giver,
   Joy and jollity be with us both!

   Alas! my journey, rugged and uneven,
Through prickly moors or dusty ways must wind;
But hearing thee, or others of thy kind,
   As full of gladness and as free of heaven,

30 I, with my fate contented, will plod on,
And hope for higher raptures, when life's day is done.
(1805; 1807)

NUNS FRET NOT AT THEIR CONVENT'S NARROW ROOM

Nuns fret not at their convent's narrow room;
And hermits are contented with their cells;
And students with their pensive citadels;
Maids at the wheel, the weaver at his loom,
Sit blithe and happy; bees that soar for bloom,
High as the highest Peak of Furness-fells,
Will murmur by the hour in foxglove bells:
In truth the prison, into which we doom
Ourselves, no prison is: and hence for me,
10 In sundry moods, 'twas pastime to be bound
Within the Sonnet's scanty plot of ground;
Pleased if some Souls (for such there needs must be)
Who have felt the weight of too much liberty,
Should find brief solace there, as I have found.
(1806; 1807)

THE WORLD IS TOO MUCH WITH US

The world is too much with us; late and soon,
Getting and spending, we lay waste our powers:
Little we see in Nature that is ours;
We have given our hearts away, a sordid boon!
The sea that bares her bosom to the moon;
The winds that will be howling at all hours,
And are up-gathered now like sleeping flowers;
For this, for everything, we are out of tune;
It moves us not.—Great God! I'd rather be
10 A Pagan suckled in a creed outworn;
So might I, standing on this pleasant lea,
Have glimpses that would make me less forlorn;
Have sight of Proteus rising from the sea;
Or hear old Triton blow his wreathéd horn.
(1806; 1807)

ODE

ON INTIMATIONS OF IMMORTALITY FROM RECOLLECTIONS OF EARLY CHILDHOOD

This ode is based upon a characteristically Words-worthian version of the Platonic doctrine that all knowledge is simply recollection. The following excerpts from Plato's Phaedo may be helpful: "Your favorite doctrine, Socrates, that knowledge is simply

recollection, if true, also necessarily implies a previous time in which we learned that which we now recollect. But this would be impossible unless our soul was in some place before existing in the human form; here then is another argument of the soul's immortality. . . . And if we acquired this knowledge before we were born and were born having it, then we also knew before we were born and at the instant of birth. . . . If, after having acquired, we have not forgotten that which we acquired, then we must always have been born with knowledge and shall always continue to know as long as life lasts—for knowledge is the acquiring and retaining knowledge and not forgetting. . . . But if the knowledge which we acquired before birth was lost by us at birth, and if afterwards by the use of the senses we recovered that which we previously knew, will not that which we call learning be a process of recovering our knowledge, and may not this be rightly termed recollection by us?" As Wordsworth says, the child knew the glory of his origin; the man has forgotten, but his vague instincts, based upon his knowledge as a child, can reassure him of his immortal beginnings.*

The Child is father of the Man;
And I could wish my days to be
Bound each to each by natural piety.

1

There was a time when meadow, grove, and stream,
 The earth, and every common sight,
  To me did seem
  Apparelled in celestial light,
The glory and the freshness of a dream.
It is not now as it hath been of yore;—
  Turn wheresoe'er I may,
   By night or day,
The things which I have seen I now can see no more.

2

  The Rainbow comes and goes,   10
  And lovely is the Rose;
  The Moon doth with delight
Look round her when the heavens are bare;
  Waters on a starry night
  Are beautiful and fair;
  The sunshine is a glorious birth;
  But yet I know, where'er I go,
That there hath passed away a glory from the earth.

3

Now, while the birds thus sing a joyous song,
  And while the young lambs bound 20

Nuns Fret Not. 3. **pensive citadels,** retreats suitable for quiet thought. 6. **Furness-fells,** upland tracts of Furness, on the coast of Lancashire. 13. **weight . . . liberty.** Writing sonnets was especially helpful to Wordsworth in overcoming his early discursive style.
The World Is Too Much with Us. 13. **Proteus,** a sea god in the service of Neptune, god of the sea. Triton (l. 14) is another sea god.

As to the tabor's sound,
To me alone there came a thought of grief:
A timely utterance gave that thought relief,
    And I again am strong:
The cataracts blow their trumpets from the steep;
No more shall grief of mine the season wrong;
I hear the Echoes through the mountains throng,
The Winds come to me from the fields of sleep,
    And all the earth is gay;
30   Land and sea
    Give themselves up to jollity,
        And with the heart of May
    Doth every Beast keep holiday;—
        Thou Child of Joy,
Shout round me, let me hear thy shouts, thou happy
    Shepherd-boy!

4

Ye blessèd Creatures, I have heard the call
    Ye to each other make; I see
The heavens laugh with you in your jubilee;
    My heart is at your festival,
40   My head hath its coronal,
The fulness of your bliss, I feel—I feel it all.
    Oh, evil day! if I were sullen
    While Earth herself is adorning,
        This sweet May-morning,
    And the Children are culling
        On every side,
    In a thousand valleys far and wide,
Fresh flowers; while the sun shines warm,
And the Babe leaps up on his Mother's arm—
50   I hear, I hear, with joy I hear!
    —But there's a Tree, of many, one,
A single Field which I have looked upon,
Both of them speak of something that is gone:
        The Pansy at my feet
        Doth the same tale repeat:
Whither is fled the visionary gleam?
Where is it now, the glory and the dream?

5

Our birth is but a sleep and a forgetting:
The Soul that rises with us, our life's Star,
60   Hath had elsewhere its setting,
        And cometh from afar:
    Not in entire forgetfulness,
    And not in utter nakedness,
But trailing clouds of glory do we come
        From God, who is our home:
Heaven lies about us in our infancy!
Shades of the prison-house begin to close
        Upon the growing Boy,

But he beholds the light, and whence it flows
        He sees it in his joy;   70
The Youth, who daily farther from the east
    Must travel, still is Nature's priest,
        And by the vision splendid
        Is on his way attended;
At length the Man perceives it die away,
And fade into the light of common day.

6

Earth fills her lap with pleasures of her own;
Yearnings she hath in her own natural kind,
And even with something of a Mother's mind,
        And no unworthy aim,   80
        The homely Nurse doth all she can
To make her Foster-child, her Inmate Man,
        Forget the glories he hath known,
And that imperial palace whence he came.

7

Behold the Child among his new-born blisses,
A six years' Darling of a pigmy size!
See, where 'mid work of his own hand he lies,
Fretted by sallies of his mother's kisses,
With light upon him from his father's eyes!
See, at his feet, some little plan or chart,   90
Some fragment from his dream of human life,
Shaped by himself with newly-learnèd art;
        A wedding or a festival,
        A mourning or a funeral,
            And this hath now his heart,
        And unto this he frames his song:
            Then will he fit his tongue
To dialogues of business, love, or strife;
        But it will not be long
        Ere this be thrown aside,   100
        And with new joy and pride
The little Actor cons another part;
Filling from time to time his "humorous stage"
With all the Persons, down to palsied Age,
That Life brings with her in her equipage;
        As if his whole vocation
        Were endless imitation.

8

Thou, whose exterior semblance doth belie
        Thy Soul's immensity;
Thou best Philosopher, who yet dost keep   110
Thy heritage, thou Eye among the blind,
That, deaf and silent, read'st the eternal deep,
Haunted forever by the eternal mind—
        Mighty Prophet! Seer blest!

Ode on Intimations of Immortality. The Child . . . piety, quoted from My Heart Leaps Up. p. 693. 21. tabor, a small drum. 26. No . . . wrong, due to lack of sympathy. 40. coronal, garland. 64. trail-

ing, bringing with us. 102. Actor . . . part, an allusion to Jaques' speech in As You Like It, II, vii, 139 ff.—"All the world's a stage," etc. 103. humorous, changeable, moody.

On whom those truths do rest,
Which we are toiling all our lives to find,
In darkness lost, the darkness of the grave;
Thou, over whom thy Immortality
Broods like the Day, a Master o'er a Slave,
120 A Presence which is not to be put by;
Thou little Child, yet glorious in the might
Of heaven-born freedom on thy being's height,
Why with such earnest pains dost thou provoke
The years to bring the inevitable yoke,
Thus blindly with thy blessedness at strife?
Full soon thy Soul shall have her earthly freight,
And custom lie upon thee with a weight,
Heavy as frost, and deep almost as life!

9

Oh, joy! that in our embers
130   Is something that doth live,
That nature yet remembers
What was so fugitive!
The thought of our past years in me doth breed
Perpetual benediction: not indeed
For that which is most worthy to be blest;
Delight and liberty, the simple creed
Of Childhood, whether busy or at rest,
With new-fledged hope still fluttering in his breast—
Not for these I raise
140   The song of thanks and praise;
But for those obstinate questionings
Of sense and outward things,
Fallings from us, vanishings;
Blank misgivings of a Creature
Moving about in worlds not realized,
High instincts before which our mortal nature
Did tremble like a guilty thing surprised:
But for those first affections,
Those shadowy recollections,
150   Which, be they what they may,
Are yet the fountain light of all our day,
Are yet a master light of all our seeing;
Uphold us, cherish, and have power to make
Our noisy years seem moments in the being
Of the eternal Silence: truths that wake,
To perish never;
Which neither listlessness, nor mad endeavor,
Nor Man nor Boy,
Nor all that is at enmity with joy,
160 Can utterly abolish or destroy!
Hence in a season of calm weather
Though inland far we be,
Our Souls have sight of that immortal sea
Which brought us hither,

Can in a moment travel thither,
And see the Children sport upon the shore,
And hear the mighty waters rolling evermore.

10

Then sing, ye Birds, sing, sing a joyous song!
And let the young Lambs bound
As to the tabor's sound!   170
We in thought will join your throng,
Ye that pipe and ye that play,
Ye that through your hearts today
Feel the gladness of the May!
What though the radiance which was once so bright
Be now forever taken from my sight,
Though nothing can bring back the hour
Of splendor in the grass, of glory in the flower;
We will grieve not, rather find
Strength in what remains behind;   180
In the primal sympathy
Which having been must ever be;
In the soothing thoughts that spring
Out of human suffering;
In the faith that looks through death,
In years that bring the philosophic mind.

11

And O, ye Fountains, Meadows, Hills, and Groves,
Forebode not any severing of our loves!
Yet in my heart of hearts I feel your might;
I only have relinquished one delight   190
To live beneath your more habitual sway.
I love the Brooks which down their channels fret,
Even more than when I tripped lightly as they;
The innocent brightness of a new-born Day
Is lovely yet;
The Clouds that gather round the setting sun
Do take a sober coloring from an eye
That hath kept watch o'er man's mortality.
Another race hath been, and other palms are won.
Thanks to the human heart by which we live,   200
Thanks to its tenderness, its joys, and fears,
To me the meanest flower that blows can give
Thoughts that do often lie too deep for tears.
(1803-06; 1807)

THOUGHT OF A BRITON ON THE SUBJUGATION OF SWITZERLAND

*Switzerland was conquered by the French in 1798.
By 1807, when this sonnet was written, Napoleon had
made himself master of Europe.*

175 ff. **What though,** etc. With this passage compare ll. 72-111 of
Lines, p. 682.
Thought of a Briton. 1. **Two Voices.** The voice of the sea is
England; that of the mountains is Switzerland.
Scorn Not the Sonnet. 3. **Shakespeare . . . heart.** This is poetic

exaggeration; many of Shakespeare's sonnets are conventional in subject
matter and in style. See p. 255. 4. **wound,** love for Laura, the inspiration for many sonnets by the Italian poet Petrarch (1304–1374).
5. **Tasso,** an Italian poet (1544–1595). 6. **Camoëns . . . grief.** Luiz
Vas de Camoëns (1524–1580) was a noted Portuguese poet who

Two Voices are there; one is of the sea,
One of the mountains; each a mighty Voice:
In both from age to age thou didst rejoice,
They were thy chosen music, Liberty!
There came a Tyrant, and with holy glee
Thou fought'st against him; but hast vainly striven:
Thou from thy Alpine holds at length art driven,
Where not a torrent murmurs heard by thee.
Of one deep bliss thine ear hath been bereft:
10 Then cleave, O cleave to that which still is left;
For, high-souled Maid, what sorrow would it be
That Mountain floods should thunder as before,
And Ocean bellow from his rocky shore,
And neither awful Voice be heard by thee!
(1807)

SCORN NOT THE SONNET

Scorn not the Sonnet; Critic, you have frowned,
Mindless of its just honors; with this key
Shakespeare unlocked his heart; the melody
Of this small lute gave ease to Petrarch's wound;
A thousand times this pipe did Tasso sound;
With it Camoëns soothed an exile's grief;
The Sonnet glittered a gay myrtle leaf
Amid the cypress with which Dante crowned
His visionary brow; a glowworm lamp,
10 It cheered mild Spenser, called from Faeryland
To struggle through dark ways; and when a damp
Fell round the path of Milton, in his hand
The Thing became a trumpet; whence he blew
Soul-animating strains—alas, too few!
(1827)

IF THOU INDEED DERIVE THY LIGHT
FROM HEAVEN

If thou indeed derive thy light from Heaven,
Then, to the measure of that heaven-born light,
Shine, Poet! in thy place, and be content—
The stars pre-eminent in magnitude,
And they that from the zenith dart their beams
(Visible though they be to half the earth,
Though half a sphere be conscious of their brightness)
Are yet of no diviner origin,
No purer essence, than the one that burns,
10 Like an untended watch-fire, on the ridge
Of some dark mountain; or than those which seem
Humbly to hang, like twinkling winter lamps,
Among the branches of the leafless trees;
All are the undying offspring of one sire:

Then, to the measure of the light vouchsafed,
Shine, Poet, in thy place, and be content.
(1832; 1836)

MOST SWEET IT IS WITH UNUPLIFTED EYES

Most sweet it is with unuplifted eyes
To pace the ground, if path be there or none,
While a fair region round the traveler lies
Which he forbears again to look upon;
Pleased rather with some soft ideal scene,
The work of Fancy, or some happy tone
Of meditation, slipping in between
The beauty coming and the beauty gone.
If Thought and Love desert us, from that day
Let us break off all commerce with the Muse: 10
With Thought and Love companions of our way,
Whate'er the senses take or may refuse,
The Mind's internal heaven shall shed her dews
Of inspiration on the humblest lay.
(1833; 1835)

from PREFACE TO LYRICAL BALLADS

This famous essay was published with the second edition of Lyrical Ballads *(1800). It should be compared with Chapter 14 of Coleridge's* Biographia Literaria *(p. 731).*

. . . The principal object, then, proposed in these poems was to choose incidents and situations from common life, and to relate or describe them, throughout, as far as was possible in a selection of language really used by men, and at the same time to throw over them a certain coloring of imagination, whereby ordinary things should be presented to the mind in an unusual aspect; and, further, and above all, to make these incidents and situations interesting by tracing in them, truly though not ostentatiously, the primary laws of 10 our nature: chiefly, as far as regards the manner in which we associate ideas in a state of excitement. Humble and rustic life was generally chosen, because, in that condition, the essential passions of the heart find a better soil in which they can attain their maturity, are less under restraint, and speak a plainer and more emphatic language; because in that condition of life our elementary feelings co-exist in a state of greater simplicity, and, consequently, may be more accurately contemplated, and more forcibly com- 20 municated; because the manners of rural life germinate from those elementary feelings, and, from the

necessary character of rural occupations, are more easily comprehended, and are more durable; and, lastly, because in that condition the passions of men are incorporated with the beautiful and permanent forms of nature. The language, too, of these men has been adopted (purified indeed from what appear to be its real defects, from all lasting and rational causes of dislike or disgust) because such men hourly communicate with the best objects from which the
10 best part of language is originally derived; and because, from their rank in society and the sameness and narrow circle of their intercourse, being less under the influence of social vanity, they convey their feelings and notions in simple and unelaborated expressions. Accordingly, such a language, arising out of repeated experience and regular feelings, is a more permanent and a far more philosophical language than that which is frequently substituted for it by poets, who think that they are conferring honor upon them-
20 selves and their art, in proportion as they separate themselves from the sympathies of men, and indulge in arbitrary and capricious habits of expression, in order to furnish food for fickle tastes and fickle appetites of their own creation.

I cannot, however, be insensible to the present outcry against the triviality and meanness, both of thought and language, which some of my contemporaries have occasionally introduced into their metrical compositions; and I acknowledge that this de-
30 fect, where it exists, is more dishonorable to the writer's own character than false refinement or arbitrary innovation, though I should contend at the same time that it is far less pernicious in the sum of its consequences. From such verses the poems in these volumes will be found distinguished at least by one mark of difference, that each of them has a worthy *purpose*. Not that I always began to write with a distinct purpose formally conceived; but habits of meditation have, I trust, so prompted and regulated
40 my feelings that my descriptions of such objects as strongly excite those feelings will be found to carry along with them a *purpose*. If this opinion be erroneous, I can have little right to the name of a poet. For all good poetry is the spontaneous overflow of powerful feelings: and though this be true, poems to which any value can be attached were never produced on any variety of subjects but by a man who, being possessed of more than usual organic sensibility, had also thought long and deeply. For
50 our continued influxes of feeling are modified and directed by our thoughts, which are indeed the representatives of all our past feelings; and, as by contemplating the relation of these general representatives to each other, we discover what is really important

to men, so, by the repetition and continuance of this act, our feelings will be connected with important subjects, till at length, if we be originally possessed of much sensibility, such habits of mind will be produced, that, by obeying blindly and mechanically the impulses of those habits, we shall describe objects 60 and utter sentiments, of such a nature, and in such connection with each other, that the understanding of the reader must necessarily be in some degree enlightened, and his affections strengthened and purified.

It has been said that each of these poems has a purpose. Another circumstance must be mentioned which distinguishes these poems from the popular poetry of the day; it is this, that the feeling therein developed gives importance to the action and situa- 70 tion, and not the action and situation to the feeling.

A sense of false modesty shall not prevent me from asserting that the reader's attention is pointed to this mark of distinction, far less for the sake of these particular poems than from the general importance of the subject. The subject is indeed important! For the human mind is capable of being excited without the application of gross and violent stimulants; and he must have a very faint perception of its beauty and dignity who does not know this, and who does not 80 further know that one being is elevated above another, in proportion as he possesses this capability. It has therefore appeared to me that to endeavor to produce or enlarge this capability is one of the best services in which, at any period, a writer can be engaged; but this service, excellent at all times, is especially so at the present day. For a multitude of causes, unknown to former times, are now acting with a combined force to blunt the discriminating powers of the mind, and, unfitting it for all 90 voluntary exertion, to reduce it to a state of almost savage torpor. The most effective of these causes are the great national events which are daily taking place, and the increasing accumulation of men in cities, where the uniformity of their occupations produces a craving for extraordinary incident, which the rapid communication of intelligence hourly gratifies. To this tendency of life and manners the literature and theatrical exhibitions of the country have conformed themselves. The invaluable works of our 100 elder writers—I had almost said the works of Shakespeare and Milton—are driven into neglect by frantic novels, sickly and stupid German tragedies, and deluges of idle and extravagant stories in verse.— When I think upon this degrading thirst after outrageous stimulation, I am almost ashamed to have spoken of the feeble endeavor made in these volumes to counteract it; and, reflecting upon the magnitude

27. **contemporaries.** Possibly a reference to Southey and Crabbe. 44. **all good poetry, etc.** Cf. Wordsworth's statements regarding poets and poetry with those of Coleridge (p. 733, l. 192, and p. 734, l. 39), and those of Arnold (p. 966, l. 88). 77. **human mind, etc.** Cf.

Ruskin's *The Relation of Art to Morals* (p. 1058). 93. **national events,** such as the war with France, the Irish Rebellion, and the passage of important labor laws. 102. **frantic novels,** like Mrs. Radcliffe's *Mysteries of Udolpho* (1794) and other Gothic romances. See p. 624.

of the general evil, I should be oppressed with no dishonorable melancholy, had I not a deep impression of certain inherent and indestructible qualities of the human mind, and likewise of certain powers in the great and permanent objects that act upon it, which are equally inherent and indestructible; and were there not added to this impression a belief that the time is approaching when the evil will be systematically opposed, by men of greater powers, and with far more distinguished success.

Having dwelt thus long on the subjects and aim of these poems, I shall request the reader's permission to apprise him of a few circumstances relating to their *style*, in order, among other reasons, that he may not censure me for not having performed what I never attempted. The reader will find that personifications of abstract ideas rarely occur in these volumes; and are utterly rejected, as an ordinary device, to elevate the style and raise it above prose. My purpose was to imitate, and, as far as possible, to adopt the very language of men; and assuredly such personifications do not make any natural or regular part of that language. They are, indeed, a figure of speech occasionally prompted by passion, and I have made use of them as such; but have endeavored utterly to reject them as a mechanical device of style, or as a family language which writers in meter seem to lay claim to by prescription. I have wished to keep the reader in the company of flesh and blood, persuaded that by so doing I shall interest him. Others who pursue a different track will interest him likewise; I do not interfere with their claim, but wish to prefer a claim of my own. There will also be found in these volumes little of what is usually called poetic diction; as much pains has been taken to avoid it as is ordinarily taken to produce it; this has been done for the reason already alleged, to bring my language near to the language of men, and further, because the pleasure which I have proposed to myself to impart, is of a kind very different from that which is supposed by many persons to be the proper object of poetry. Without being culpably particular, I do not know how to give my reader a more exact notion of the style in which it was my wish and intention to write than by informing him that I have at all times endeavored to look steadily at my subject; consequently, there is, I hope, in these poems little falsehood of description, and my ideas are expressed in language fitted to their respective importance. Something must have been gained by this practice, as it is friendly to one property of all good poetry, namely, good sense: but it has necessarily cut me off from a large portion of phrases and figures of speech which from father to son have long been regarded as the common inheri-

tance of poets. I have also thought it expedient to restrict myself still further, having abstained from the use of many expressions, in themselves proper and beautiful, but which have been foolishly repeated by bad poets, till such feelings of disgust are connected with them as it is scarcely possible by any art of association to overpower.

If in a poem there should be found a series of lines, or even a single line, in which the language, though naturally arranged and according to the strict laws of meter, does not differ from that of prose there is a numerous class of critics, who, when they stumble upon these prosaisms, as they call them, imagine that they have made a notable discovery, and exult over the poet as over a man ignorant of his own profession. Now these men would establish a canon of criticism which the reader will conclude he must utterly reject if he wishes to be pleased with these volumes. And it would be a most easy task to prove to him that not only the language of a large portion of every good poem, even of the most elevated character, must necessarily, except with reference to the meter, in no respect differ from that of good prose, but likewise that some of the most interesting parts of the best poems will be found to be strictly the language of prose when prose is well written. The truth of this assertion might be demonstrated by innumerable passages from almost all the poetical writings, even of Milton himself. To illustrate the subject in a general manner, I will here adduce a short composition of Gray, who was at the head of those who, by their reasonings, have attempted to widen the space of separation betwixt Prose and Metrical composition, and was more than any other man curiously elaborate in the structure of his own poetic diction.

In vain to me the smiling mornings shine,
And reddening Phoebus lifts his golden fire;
The birds in vain their amorous descant join,
Or cheerful fields resume their green attire.
These ears, alas! for other notes repine;
A different object do these eyes require;
My lonely anguish melts no heart but mine;
And in my breast the imperfect joys expire;
Yet morning smiles the busy race to cheer,
And new-born pleasure brings to happier men;
The fields to all their wonted tribute bear;
To warm their little loves the birds complain.
J fruitless mourn to him that cannot bear,
And weep the more because J weep in vain.

It will easily be perceived, that the only part of this Sonnet which is of any value is the lines printed in

103. stupid . . . tragedies, such as August Kotzebue's *Misanthropy and Repentance* (1790), known in England as *The Stranger.* 104. idle . . . verse, a probable reference to such poems as *Maviad* (1795) and *Baviad* (1794), two satires by William Gifford (1756–1826), editor

of *Quarterly Review;* Landor's *Gebir* (1798); and Scott's translations of Bürger's *Lenore.* 199. In vain, etc., Gray's *Sonnet on the Death of Richard West*, p. 641.

Italics; it is equally obvious that, except in the rime and in the use of the single word "fruitless" for "fruitlessly," which is so far a defect, the language of these lines does in no respect differ from that of prose.

By the foregoing quotation it has been shown that the language of Prose may yet be well adapted to Poetry; and it was previously asserted that a large portion of the language of every good poem can in
10 no respect differ from that of good Prose. We will go further. It may be safely affirmed that there neither is, nor can be, any *essential* difference between the language of prose and metrical composition. We are fond of tracing the resemblance between Poetry and Painting, and, accordingly, we call them Sisters; but where shall we find bonds of connection sufficiently strict to typify the affinity betwixt metrical and prose composition? They both speak by and to the same organs; the bodies in which both of them are clothed
20 may be said to be of the same substance, their affections are kindred, and almost identical, not necessarily differing even in degree; Poetry sheds no tears "such as Angels weep," but natural and human tears; she can boast of no celestial ichor that distinguishes her vital juices from those of Prose; the same human blood circulates through the veins of them both.

If it be affirmed that rime and metrical arrangement of themselves constitute a distinction which overturns what has just been said on the strict affinity of metrical
30 language with that of prose, and paves the way for other artificial distinctions which the mind voluntarily admits, I answer that the language of such poetry as is here recommended is, as far as is possible, a selection of the language really spoken by men; that this selection, wherever it is made with true taste and feeling, will of itself form a distinction far greater than would at first be imagined, and will entirely separate the composition from the vulgarity and meanness of ordinary life; and, if meter be superadded thereto, I
40 believe that a dissimilitude will be produced altogether sufficient for the gratification of a rational mind. What other distinction would we have? Whence is it to come? And where is it to exist? Not, surely, where the poet speaks through the mouths of his characters—it cannot be necessary here, either for elevation of style, or any of its supposed ornaments; for, if the poet's subject be judiciously chosen, it will naturally, and upon fit occasion, lead him to passions the language of which, if selected truly and judiciously, must
50 necessarily be dignified and variegated, and alive with metaphors and figures. I forbear to speak of an incongruity which would shock the intelligent reader, should the poet interweave any foreign splendor of

his own with that which the passion naturally suggests; it is sufficient to say that such addition is unnecessary. And, surely, it is more probable that those passages, which with propriety abound with metaphors and figures, will have their due effect, if, upon other occasions where the passions are of a milder character, the style also be subdued and temperate. 60

But, as the pleasure which I hope to give by the poems now presented to the reader must depend entirely on just notions upon this subject, and, as it is in itself of high importance to our taste and moral feelings, I cannot content myself with these detached remarks. And if, in what I am about to say, it shall appear to some that my labor is unnecessary, and that I am like a man fighting a battle without enemies, such persons may be reminded, that, whatever be the language outwardly holden by men, a 70 practical faith in the opinions which I am wishing to establish is almost unknown. If my conclusions are admitted and carried as far as they must be carried if admitted at all, our judgments concerning the works of the greatest poets both ancient and modern will be far different from what they are at present, both when we praise, and when we censure; and our moral feelings influencing and influenced by these judgments will, I believe, be corrected and purified.

Taking up the subject, then, upon general grounds, 80 let me ask, what is meant by the word poet? What is a poet? To whom does he address himself? And what language is to be expected from him?—He is a man speaking to men: a man, it is true, endowed with more lively sensibility, more enthusiasm and tenderness, who has a greater knowledge of human nature, and a more comprehensive soul than are supposed to be common among mankind; a man pleased with his own passions and volitions, and who rejoices more than other men in the spirit of life 90 that is in him; delighting to contemplate similar volitions and passions as manifested in the goings-on of the Universe, and habitually impelled to create them where he does not find them. To these qualities he has added a disposition to be affected more than other men by absent things as if they were present; an ability of conjuring up in himself passions which are indeed far from being the same as those produced by real events, yet (especially in those parts of the general sympathy which are pleasing 100 and delightful) do more nearly resemble the passions produced by real events, than anything which, from the motions of their own minds merely, other men are accustomed to feel in themselves—whence, and from practice, he has acquired a greater readiness and power in expressing what he thinks and feels,

22. **Poetry.** "I here use the word 'Poetry' (though against my own judgment) as opposed to the word 'Prose,' and synonymous with metrical composition. But such confusion has been introduced into criticism by this contradistinction of Poetry and Prose, instead of the more philosophical one of Poetry and Matter of Fact, or Science. The

only strict antithesis to Prose is Meter; nor is this, in truth, a *strict* antithesis, because lines and passages of meter so naturally occur in writing prose, that it would be scarcely possible to avoid them, even were it desirable."—Wordsworth's note. 24. **ichor,** an ethereal fluid that flowed in the veins of the gods. 25. **same . . . both.** It is pre-

and especially those thoughts and feelings which, by his own choice, or from the structure of his own mind, arise in him without immediate external excitement.

But whatever portion of this faculty we may suppose even the greatest poet to possess, there cannot be a doubt that the language which it will suggest to him must often, in liveliness and truth, fall short of that which is uttered by men in real life, under the actual pressure of those passions, certain shadows of which the poet thus produces, or feels to be produced, in himself.

However exalted a notion we would wish to cherish of the character of a poet, it is obvious that while he describes and imitates passions, his employment is in some degree mechanical, compared with the freedom and power of real and substantial action and suffering. So that it will be the wish of the poet to bring his feelings near to those of the persons whose feelings he describes, nay, for short spaces of time, perhaps, to let himself slip into an entire delusion, and even confound and identify his own feelings with theirs; modifying only the language which is thus suggested to him by a consideration that he describes for a particular purpose, that of giving pleasure. Here, then, he will apply the principle of selection which has been already insisted upon. He will depend upon this for removing what would otherwise be painful or disgusting in the passion; he will feel that there is no necessity to trick out or to elevate nature; and, the more industriously he applies this principle, the deeper will be his faith that no words, which *his* fancy or imagination can suggest, will be to be compared with those which are the emanations of reality and truth.

But it may be said by those who do not object to the general spirit of these remarks that, as it is impossible for the poet to produce upon all occasions language as exquisitely fitted for the passion as that which the real passion itself suggests, it is proper that he should consider himself as in the situation of a translator, who does not scruple to substitute excellencies of another kind for those which are unattainable by him; and endeavors occasionally to surpass his original, in order to make some amends for the general inferiority to which he feels that he must submit. But this would be to encourage idleness and unmanly despair. Further, it is the language of men who speak of what they do not understand; who talk of poetry as of a matter of amusement and idle pleasure; who will converse with us as gravely about a *taste* for poetry, as they express it, as if it were a thing as indifferent as a taste for rope-

dancing, or Frontiniac or Sherry. Aristotle, I have been told, has said that poetry is the most philosophic of all writing; it is so; its object is truth, not individual and local, but general and operative; not standing upon external testimony, but carried alive into the heart by passion; truth which is its own testimony, which gives competence and confidence to the tribunal to which it appeals, and receives them from the same tribunal. Poetry is the image of man and nature. The obstacles which stand in the way of the fidelity of the biographer and historian, and of their consequent utility, are incalculably greater than those which are to be encountered by the poet who comprehends the dignity of his art. The poet writes under one restriction only, namely, the necessity of giving immediate pleasure to a human being possessed of that information which may be expected from him, not as a lawyer, a physician, a mariner, an astronomer, or a natural philosopher, but as a man. Except this one restriction, there is no object standing between the poet and the image of things; between this, and the biographer and historian, there are a thousand.

Nor let this necessity of producing immediate pleasure be considered as a degradation of the poet's art. It is far otherwise. It is an acknowledgment of the beauty of the universe, an acknowledgment the more sincere, because not formal, but indirect; it is a task light and easy to him who looks at the world in the spirit of love; further, it is a homage paid to the native and naked dignity of man, to the grand elementary principle of pleasure, by which he knows, and feels, and lives, and moves. We have no sympathy but what is propagated by pleasure—I would not be misunderstood; but wherever we sympathize with pain, it will be found that the sympathy is produced and carried on by subtle combinations with pleasure. We have no knowledge, that is, no general principles drawn from the contemplation of particular facts, but what has been built up by pleasure, and exists in us by pleasure alone. The man of science, the chemist and mathematician, whatever difficulties and disgusts they may have had to struggle with, know and feel this. However painful may be the objects with which the anatomist's knowledge is connected, he feels that his knowledge is pleasure; and where he has no pleasure, he has no knowledge. What then does the poet? He considers man and the objects that surround him as acting and reacting upon each other, so as to produce an infinite complexity of pain and pleasure; he considers man in his own nature and in his ordinary life as contemplating this with a certain quantity of immediate

cisely this kind of statement that Byron derides in his *English Bards and Scotch Reviewers*, p. 743, 1. 242. 81. **What is a poet?** Cf. Wordsworth's *If Thou Indeed Derive Thy Light from Heaven*, p. 703. 160. **Frontiniac or Sherry**, kinds of wine; one French, the other Spanish. **Aristotle**, the most famous and influential of Greek philosophers (384–

322 B.C.). In his *Poetics*, 9, 3, he says, "Poetry is more philosophical and more serious than history."

knowledge, with certain convictions, intuitions, and deductions, which from habit acquire the quality of intuitions; he considers him as looking upon this complex scene of ideas and sensations, and finding everywhere objects that immediately excite in him sympathies which, from the necessities of his nature, are accompanied by an overbalance of enjoyment.

To this knowledge which all men carry about with them, and to these sympathies in which, without any other discipline than that of our daily life, we are fitted to take delight, the poet principally directs his attention. He considers man and nature as essentially adapted to each other, and the mind of man as naturally the mirror of the fairest and most interesting properties of nature. And thus the poet, prompted by this feeling of pleasure, which accompanies him through the whole course of his studies, converses with general nature, with affections akin to those, which, through labor and length of time, the man of science has raised up in himself by conversing with those particular parts of nature which are the objects of his studies. The knowledge both of the poet and the man of science is pleasure; but the knowledge of the one cleaves to us as a necessary part of our existence, our natural and unalienable inheritance; the other is a personal and individual acquisition, slow to come to us, and by no habitual and direct sympathy connecting us with our fellow-beings. The man of science seeks truth as a remote and unknown benefactor; he cherishes and loves it in his solitude; the poet, singing a song in which all human beings join with him, rejoices in the presence of truth as our visible friend and hourly companion. Poetry is the breath and finer spirit of all knowledge; it is the impassioned expression which is in the countenance of all science. Emphatically may it be said of the poet, as Shakespeare hath said of man, "that he looks before and after." He is the rock of defense for human nature; and upholder and preserver, carrying everywhere with him relationship and love. In spite of difference of soil and climate, of language and manners, of laws and customs, in spite of things silently gone out of mind and things violently destroyed; the poet binds together by passion and knowledge the vast empire of human society, as it is spread over the whole earth and over all time. The objects of the poet's thoughts are everywhere; though the eyes and senses of man are, it is true, his favorite guides, yet he will follow wheresoever he can find an atmosphere of sensation in which to move his wings. Poetry is the first and last of all knowledge—it is as immortal as the heart of man. If the labors of men of science should ever create any material revolution, direct or indirect, in our condition and in the impressions which we habitually receive, the poet will sleep then no more than at present; he will be ready to follow the steps of the man of science, not only in those general indirect effects, but he will be at his side, carrying sensation into the midst of the objects of science itself. The remotest discoveries of the chemist, the botanist, or mineralogist, will be as proper objects of the poet's art as any upon which it can be employed, if the time should ever come when these things shall be familiar to us, and the relations under which they are contemplated by the followers of these respective sciences shall be manifestly and palpably material to us as enjoying and suffering beings. If the time should ever come when what is now called science, thus familiarized to men, shall be ready to put on, as it were, a form of flesh and blood, the poet will lend his divine spirit to aid the transfiguration, and will welcome the being thus produced, as a dear and genuine inmate of the household of man.—It is not, then, to be supposed that anyone, who holds that sublime notion of poetry which I have attempted to convey, will break in upon the sanctity and truth of his pictures by transitory and accidental ornaments, and endeavor to excite admiration of himself by arts, the necessity of which must manifestly depend upon the assumed meanness of his subject.

What has been thus far said applies to poetry in general; but especially to those parts of composition where the poet speaks through the mouths of his characters; and upon this point it appears to authorize the conclusion that there are few persons of good sense, who would not allow that the dramatic parts of composition are defective, in proportion as they deviate from the real language of nature, and are colored by a diction of the poet's own, either peculiar to him as an individual poet or belonging simply to poets in general; to a body of men who, from the circumstance of their compositions being in meter, it is expected will employ a particular language.

It is not, then, in the dramatic parts of composition that we look for this distinction of language; but still it may be proper and necessary where the poet speaks to us in his own person and character. To this I answer by referring the reader to the description before given of a poet. Among the qualities there enumerated as principally conducing to form a poet is implied nothing differing in kind from other men, but only in degree. The sum of what was said is, that the poet is chiefly distinguished from other men by a greater promptness to think and feel without immediate external excitement and a greater power in expressing such thoughts and feelings as are produced in him in that manner. But these passions and thoughts and feelings are the general passions and thoughts and feelings of men. And with what are they connected? Undoubtedly with our moral sentiments and animal sensations, and with the causes

37. "that . . . after," *Hamlet*, IV, iv, 37. 181. **numbers,** the mechanics of verse, or verse itself. What Wordsworth says is part of the theory of free verse.

which excite these; with the operations of the elements and the appearances of the visible universe; with storm and sunshine, with the revolutions of the seasons, with cold and heat, with loss of friends and kindred, with injuries and resentments, gratitude and hope, with fear and sorrow. These, and the like, are the sensations and objects which the poet describes, as they are the sensations of other men, and the objects which interest them. The poet thinks and feels in the spirit of human passions. How, then, can his language differ in any material degree from that of all other men who feel vividly and see clearly? It might be *proved* that it is impossible. But supposing this were not the case, the poet might then be allowed to use a peculiar language when expressing his feelings for his own gratification, or that of men like himself. But poets do not write for poets alone, but for men. Unless therefore we are advocates for that admiration which subsists upon ignorance, and that pleasure which arises from hearing what we do not understand, the poet must descend from this supposed height; and, in order to excite rational sympathy, he must express himself as other men express themselves. To this it may be added, that while he is only selecting from the real language of men, or, which amounts to the same thing, composing accurately in the spirit of such selection, he is treading upon safe ground, and we know what we are to expect from him. Our feelings are the same with respect to meter; for, as it may be proper to remind the reader, the distinction of meter is regular and uniform, and not, like that which is produced by what is usually called POETIC DICTION, arbitrary and subject to infinite caprices upon which no calculation whatever can be made. In the one case, the reader is utterly at the mercy of the poet, respecting what imagery or diction he may choose to connect with the passion; whereas, in the other, the meter obeys certain laws to which the poet and reader both willingly submit because they are certain, and because no interference is made by them with the passion, but such as the concurring testimony of ages has shown to heighten and improve the pleasure which co-exists with it.

It will now be proper to answer an obvious question, namely: Why, professing these opinions, have I written in verse? To this, in addition to such answer as is included in what has been already said, I reply, in the first place: Because, however I may have restricted myself, there is still left open to me what confessedly constitutes the most valuable object of all writing, whether in prose or verse—the great and universal passions of men, the most general and interesting of their occupations, and the entire world of nature before me to supply endless combinations of forms and imagery. Now, supposing for a moment that whatever is interesting in these objects may be as vividly described in prose, why should I be condemned for

attempting to superadd to such description the charm which, by the consent of all nations, is acknowledged to exist in metrical language? To this, by such as are yet unconvinced, it may be answered that a very small part of the pleasure given by poetry depends upon the meter, and that it is injudicious to write in meter unless it be accompanied with the other artificial distinctions of style with which meter is usually accompanied, and that, by such deviation, more will be lost from the shock which will thereby be given to the reader's associations than will be counterbalanced by any pleasure which he can derive from the general power of numbers. In answer to those who still contend for the necessity of accompanying meter with certain appropriate colors of style in order to the accomplishment of its appropriate end, and who also, in my opinion, greatly underrate the power of meter in itself, it might, perhaps, as far as relates to these volumes, have been almost sufficient to observe, that poems are extant, written upon more humble subjects, and in a still more naked and simple style, which have continued to give pleasure from generation to generation. Now, if nakedness and simplicity be a defect, the fact here mentioned affords a strong presumption that poems somewhat less naked and simple are capable of affording pleasure at the present day; and, what I wished *chiefly* to attempt, at present, was to justify myself for having written under the impression of this belief. . . .

I have said that poetry is the spontaneous overflow of powerful feelings: it takes its origin from emotion recollected in tranquillity; the emotion is contemplated till, by a species of reaction, the tranquillity gradually disappears, and an emotion, kindred to that which was before the subject of contemplation, is gradually produced, and does itself actually exist in the mind. In this mood successful composition generally begins, and in a mood similar to this it is carried on; but the emotion, of whatever kind and in whatever degree, from various causes, is qualified by various pleasures, so that in describing any passions whatsoever which are voluntarily described, the mind will, upon the whole, be in a state of enjoyment. If nature be thus cautious to preserve in a state of enjoyment a being so employed, the poet ought to profit by the lesson held forth to him and ought especially to take care that, whatever passions he communicates to his reader, those passions, if his reader's mind be sound and vigorous, should always be accompanied with an overbalance of pleasure. Now the music of harmonious metrical language, the sense of difficulty overcome, and the blind association of pleasure which has been previously received from works of rime or meter of the same or similar construction, an indistinct perception perpetually renewed of language closely resembling that of real life, and yet, in the circumstance of meter, differing from it so widely —all these imperceptibly make up a complex feeling of delight which is of the most important use in tempering the painful feeling always found intermingled with powerful descriptions of the deeper passions. This effect is always produced in pathetic and impassioned poetry; while, in lighter compositions, the ease and gracefulness with which the poet manages his numbers are themselves confessedly a principal source of the gratification of the reader. All that it is *necessary* to say, however, upon this subject may be effected by affirming—what few persons will deny—that, of two descriptions, either of passions, manners, or characters, each of them equally well executed, the one in prose and the other in verse, the verse will be read a hundred times where the prose is read once.

Having thus explained a few of my reasons for writing in verse, and why I have chosen subjects from common life, and endeavored to bring my language near to the real language of men, if I have been too minute in pleading my own cause, I have at the same time been treating a subject of general interest; and for this reason a few words shall be added with reference solely to these particular poems and to some defects which will probably be found in them. I am sensible that my associations must have sometimes been particular instead of general, and that, consequently, giving to things a false importance, I may have sometimes written upon unworthy subjects; but I am less apprehensive on this account than that my language may frequently have suffered from those arbitrary connections of feelings and ideas with particular words and phrases from which no man can altogether protect himself. Hence I have no doubt, that, in some instances, feelings, even of the ludicrous, may be given to my readers by expressions which appeared to me tender and pathetic. Such faulty expressions, were I convinced they were faulty at present and that they must necessarily continue to be so, I would willingly take all reasonable pains to correct. But it is dangerous to make these alterations on the simple authority of a few individuals, or even of certain classes of men; for where the understanding of an author is not convinced, or his feelings altered, this cannot be done without great injury to himself: for his own feelings are his stay and support; and if he set them aside in one instance, he may be induced to repeat this act till his mind shall lose all confidence in itself, and become utterly debilitated. To this it may be added that the critic ought never to forget that he is himself exposed to the same errors as the poet, and, perhaps, in a much greater degree: for there can be no presumption in saying of most readers that it is not probable they will be so well acquainted with the various stages of meaning through which words have passed, or with the fickleness or stability of the relations of particular

ideas to each other; and, above all, since they are so much less interested in the subject, they may decide lightly and carelessly.

Long as the reader has been detained, I hope he will permit me to caution him against a mode of false criticism which has been applied to poetry, in which the language closely resembles that of life and nature. Such verses have been triumphed over in parodies, of which Dr. Johnson's stanza is a fair specimen:

I put my hat upon my head
And walked into the Strand,
And there I met another man
Whose hat was in his hand.

Immediately under these lines let us place one of the most justly-admired stanzas of the *Babes in the Wood*:

These pretty Babes with hand in hand
Went wandering up and down;
But never more they saw the Man
Approaching from the Town.

In both these stanzas the words and the order of the words in no respect differ from the most unimpassioned conversation. There are words in both, for example, "the Strand," and "the Town," connected with none but the most familiar ideas; yet the one stanza we admit as admirable and the other as a fair example of the superlatively contemptible. Whence arises this difference? Not from the meter, not from the language, not from the order of the words; but the *matter* expressed in Dr. Johnson's stanza is contemptible. The proper method of treating trivial and simple verses, to which Dr. Johnson's stanza would be a fair parallelism, is not to say, this is a bad kind of poetry, or, this is not poetry; but, this wants sense; it is neither interesting in itself nor can *lead* to anything interesting; the images neither originate in that sane state of feeling which arises out of thought nor can excite thought or feeling in the reader. This is the only sensible manner of dealing with such verses. Why trouble yourself about the species till you have previously decided upon the genus? Why take pains to prove that an ape is not a Newton when it is self-evident that he is not a man?

One request I must make of my reader, which is, that in judging these poems he would decide by his own feelings genuinely and not by reflection upon what will probably be the judgment of others. How common is it to hear a person say, I myself do not object to this style of composition, or this or that expression, but, to such and such classes of people it will appear mean or ludicrous! This mode of criticism, so destructive

64. **Dr. Johnson,** Samuel Johnson (p. 567), who had little interest in ballads, the style of which he parodied in the stanza quoted here. 66. **Strand,** a prominent street in London. 97. **Newton,** Sir Isaac Newton

(1642–1727), celebrated English mathematician, scientist, and natural philosopher.

of all sound unadulterated judgment, is almost universal; let the reader then abide, independently, by his own feelings, and, if he finds himself affected, let him not suffer such conjectures to interfere with his pleasure. . . .
(1800)

SAMUEL TAYLOR COLERIDGE 1772-1834

A man who does not make the most of his potentialities is always a tantalizing, provocative subject for discussion, but as far as Coleridge is concerned, any discussion must assume that he was a poet of the first rank, however incomplete his achievement. He was born at Ottery St. Mary, Devonshire, on October 21, 1772; his father, the village vicar, was a lovable and an utterly unworldly person. His death, when Samuel was only nine years of age, threw the boy very much on his own; but he was fortunate enough to secure an opportunity to enter Christ's Hospital, one of the best schools in England at the time. His stay at Christ's Hospital has been attractively described by Charles Lamb in one of his essays, Christ's Hospital Five-and-Thirty Years Ago. Lamb pictured the young Coleridge as lonely and friendless; Coleridge himself has told us the same in his Frost at Midnight. But his days at Christ's Hospital were not all drab; he fell in love and wrote juvenile poetry and showed great potential imaginative powers in his versifying, although none of his early verses deserved to survive.

In 1791 he matriculated at Jesus College, Cambridge, was a good student at first, but incurred some debts and, frightened, ran away to join the Light Dragoons under the incongruous name of Silas Tomkyn Comberbacke. It was with some difficulty that his friends purchased his discharge from the Dragoons. He returned to Cambridge, but left the university in 1794 without a degree, filled with revolutionary doctrines and a new religious radicalism called Unitarianism—ideas which he had apparently been nursing throughout his stay at Cambridge. About this time (1794) he met Robert Southey, and the two of them hatched the scheme of Pantisocracy. On the banks of the Susquehanna River in Pennsylvania the two, in company with some kindred spirits both male and female, intended to found an ideal community organized along lines suggested by Rousseau and Godwin. The scheme fell through, largely for financial reasons, but in the meantime Southey had married Edith Fricker, and Coleridge, fresh from a rejection by one young woman, had married Mrs. Southey's sister Sarah. The Fricker sisters, it may be interpolated, were the "two milliners of Bath" over whom Byron waxed superciliously merry in Don Juan (p.

763, l. 744). The truth of the matter is that the marriage of Coleridge and Sarah Fricker was not made in Heaven.

The rather ill-mated couple finally settled at Nether Stowey, Somersetshire; here it was that Coleridge met the Wordsworths, brother and sister. He was at that time trying to breathe a newspaper, The Watchman, into life, and was lecturing and preaching Unitarianism the while. The meeting of the two poets in 1797 came a year after Coleridge had published his first poems, the Juvenile Poems. These early efforts were of negligible value, but the contact of Coleridge and Wordsworth resulted in a splended burgeoning of both as poets. Indeed, the year 1797 was something of an annus mirabilis for Coleridge. The Rime of the Ancient Mariner (p. 714), that fine literary ballad of the supernatural, and Christabel (p. 723), that "magnificent torso," an uncompleted fragment that caught, even in its fragmentary state, all the magical glamour of medieval romance—these were both composed in 1797. In the next year were written the other great fragment looking out from "magic casements" and romantic witchery, Kubla Khan (p. 730), and the stirring France: An Ode, powerful in its highly charged emotion evoked by the beauties of nature and the tyrannies of governments. In 1798 came the Lyrical Ballads, the joint product of Coleridge and Wordsworth. The significance of this work has already been described (pp. 615 and 679). Coleridge's chief contribution to the collection was The Rime of the Ancient Mariner. It might be added that the dates of the composition and the printing of Coleridge's poetry are often far apart, such was the poet's procrastinating tendency.

Coleridge and the Wordsworths now took a trip to Germany, at the time a hotbed of romantic endeavor. Coleridge's purpose was to soak himself in this German romanticism, and with this end in view he attended the University of Göttingen, absorbed large doses of the philosophy of Immanuel Kant and mastered the German language so readily that he was able to translate Schiller's drama, Wallenstein, within six weeks on his arrival in Germany. The Wordsworths had meanwhile returned and settled at Grasmere. Thither Coleridge followed them in 1800 and settled down at Greta Hall, Keswick, twelve miles away, after a few desultory attempts to establish himself as a journalist with the London Morning Post. The coming of Coleridge to Keswick coincided with the ebbing of his creative power. Already inclined to be neurotic, he became the victim of opium, and although he was able eventually to free himself from the habit, his abilities were nevertheless stunted and his ambitions dissipated; he still retained his angelic potentialities, but as Lamb observed, his was the look of an "archangel a little damaged." His Dejection: an Ode (1802) and Youth and Age (1828-1832) reflect the disillusionment and bitterness which the realization of his waning abilities brought him.

In 1804, he became for a brief time secretary to the governor of Malta. Eventually he drifted back to London, where, at the home of Mr. Gilman at Highgate, he fought his opium habit and triumphed—only to spend the remaining years of his life in a state of creative exhaustion. He lectured extensively; to the very end of his days he was an accomplished conversationalist; and his interests were wide and varied. He did much to build up the romantic conception of Shakespeare; he gave his theories on education to all who would hear him; he planned a monumental work on Christianity; he dabbled in drama with passing success, as his tragedy Remorse (1813) shows. He supervised the publication of some of his ancient monuments of glory like Kubla Khan and added to the torso of Christabel; he gave vent to his political and social urgings, which were liberal views slowly congealing in a shell of growing conservatism, in his Lay Sermons (1816). And he constantly scattered little fragments of verse and began occasional longer projects in poetry, some of them personal, some melodramatic in the vein of the ballad or romance, some translations or adaptations, like his famous Hymn before Sunrise in the Vale of Chamouni. A very few satirical specimens can be found in Coleridge's work, but for the most part it is highly romantic, and all of the longer attempts, save one, unfinished; The Rime of the Ancient Mariner was the only long poem that Coleridge ever completed.

Coleridge had great poetic powers; it has been observed that he had every qualification of the great poet except the utterly commonplace virtues of perseverance and diligence. Had he possessed but a fraction of the industry of his friend Southey, he would have been one of the most noted figures in world literature. His great contribution is in the realm of the supernatural. He speaks with the voice of beauty wedded to imagination; no other poet has so thoroughly imbued his work with the spirit of mystery. It is easy enough to see that he owes something to the Gothic novel (p. 624) and the German tale of terror, but his originality challenges admiration in spite of his known obligations to other works and other poets' minds. As a prose critic of the romantic period, he is virtually supreme; his Biographia Literaria (1817, p. 731) is not only a most revealing description of his relations with Wordsworth; it is also an extremely penetrating exposition of the romantic ideals of art and life, and a spiritual autobiography to be ranked among the world's greatest. His studies of Shakespeare set a vogue that is still vital; his Table Talk of his last years ranks with the conversations of his great German contemporary Goethe. It is possible to view him as the pathetic man who fails to make the most of his capabilities; it is perhaps fairer to accept Shelley's glowing eulogy:

You will see Coleridge; he who sits obscure
In the exceeding luster and the pure
Intense irradiation of a mind
Which, with its own internal lightning blind,
Flags wearily through darkness and despair,
A cloud-encircled meteor of the air,
A hooded eagle among blinking owls.

THE EOLIAN HARP

Composed at Clevedon, Somersetshire

This is the first and, in Coleridge's opinion, the best of his graceful, meditative "conversation poems" (other examples of the type are This Lime-Tree Bower My Prison *and* Frost at Midnight*).*

My pensive Sara! thy soft cheek reclined
Thus on mine arm, most soothing sweet it is
To sit beside our cot, our cot o'ergrown
With white-flowered jasmin, and the broad-leaved
    myrtle,
(Meet emblems they of Innocence and Love!)
And watch the clouds, that late were rich with light,
Slow saddening round, and mark the star of eve
Serenely brilliant (such should Wisdom be)
Shine opposite! How exquisite the scents
10 Snatched from yon beanfield! and the world *so* hushed!
The stilly murmur of the distant sea
Tells us of silence.
            And that simplest lute,
Placed lengthways in the clasping casement, hark!
How by the desultory breeze caressed,
Like some coy maid half yielding to her lover,
It pours such sweet upbraiding, as must needs
Tempt to repeat the wrong! And now, its strings
Boldlier swept, the long sequacious notes
Over delicious surges sink and rise,
20 Such a soft floating witchery of sound
As twilight elfins make, when they at eve
Voyage on gentle gales from fairyland,
Where melodies round honey-dropping flowers,
Footless and wild, like birds of paradise,
Nor pause, nor perch, hovering on untamed wing!
O! the one life within us and abroad,
Which meets all motion and becomes its soul,
A light in sound, a sound-like power in light,
Rhythm in all thought, and joyance every where—
30 Methinks, it should have been impossible
Not to love all things in a world so filled;
Where the breeze warbles, and the mute still air
Is Music slumbering on her instrument.

And thus, my love! as on the midway slope
Of yonder hill I stretch my limbs at noon,
Whilst through my half-closed eyelids I behold
The sunbeams dance, like diamonds, on the main,
And tranquil muse upon tranquility;
Full many a thought uncalled and undetained,
40 And many idle flitting fantasies,
Traverse my indolent and passive brain,

As wild and various as the random gales
That swell and flutter on this subject lute!
    And what if all of animated nature
Be but organic harps diversely framed,
That tremble into thought, as o'er them sweeps
Plastic and vast, one intellectual breeze,
At once the soul of each, and God of all?
    But thy more serious eye a mild reproof
Darts, O beloved woman! nor such thoughts   50
Dim and unhallowed dost thou not reject,
And biddest me walk humbly with my God.
Meek daughter in the family of Christ!
Well hast thou said and holily dispraised
These shapings of the unregenerate mind;
Bubbles that glitter as they rise and break
On vain philosophy's aye-babbling spring.
For never guiltless may I speak of him,
The Incomprehensible! save when with awe
I praise him, and with faith that inly *feels*;   60
Who with his saving mercies healed me,
A sinful and most miserable man,
Wildered and dark, and gave me to possess
Peace, and this cot, and thee, heart-honored maid!
(1795; 1796)

THIS LIME-TREE BOWER MY PRISON

Addressed to Charles Lamb, of the India House, London

"In the June of 1797 some long-expected friends paid a visit to the author's cottage; and on the morning of their arrival, he met with an accident, which disabled him from walking during the whole time of their stay. One evening, when they had left him for a few hours, he composed the following lines in the garden-bower." —Coleridge's note

Well, they are gone, and here must I remain,
This lime-tree bower my prison! I have lost
Beauties and feelings, such as would have been
Most sweet to my remembrance even when age
Had dimmed mine eyes to blindness! They, meanwhile,
Friends, whom I never more may meet again,
On springy heath, along the hilltop edge,
Wander in gladness, and wind down, perchance,
To that still roaring dell of which I told;
The roaring dell, o'erwooded, narrow, deep,   10
And only speckled by the midday sun;
Where its slim trunk the ash from rock to rock
Flings arching like a bridge;—that branchless ash,

The Eolian Harp, crude ancient harp consisting of strings stretched over a box which is sounded by the wind. It was often used by the romantics as a symbol for the creative process. **Clevedon, Somersetshire,** village on the Bristol Channel where Coleridge spent his honeymoon in 1795. 1. **Sara,** Sara Fricker, Coleridge's wife. 3. **cot,** cottage. 12. **lute,** Eolian harp. 18. **sequacious,** successive. 24. **birds**

of paradise, legendary birds which, lacking feet, live on the wing and feed on air. 26-33. **O! the one life,** etc. These lines first appeared in the 1817 edition. *This Lime-Tree Bower My Prison.* **friends,** William and Dorothy Wordsworth and Charles Lamb. **accident.** Coleridge's wife Sara "emptied a skillet of boiling milk" on his foot.

Unsunned and damp, whose few poor yellow leaves
Ne'er tremble in the gale, yet tremble still,
Fanned by the waterfall! and there my friends
Behold the dark green file of long lank weeds,
That all at once (a most fantastic sight!)
Still nod and drip beneath the dripping edge
Of the blue clay stone.

20   Now my friends emerge
Beneath the wide wide heaven—and view again
The many-steepled tract magnificent
Of hilly fields and meadows, and the sea,
With some fair bark, perhaps, whose sails light up
The slip of smooth clear blue betwixt two isles
Of purple shadow! Yes! they wander on
In gladness all; but thou, methinks, most glad,
My gentle-hearted Charles! for thou hast pined
And hungered after nature, many a year,
30 In the great city pent, winning thy way
With sad yet patient soul, through evil and pain
And strange calamity! Ah! slowly sink
Behind the western ridge, thou glorious sun!
Shine in the slant beams of the sinking orb,
Ye purple heath flowers! richlier burn, ye clouds!
Live in the yellow light, ye distant groves!
And kindle, thou blue ocean! So my friend
Struck with deep joy may stand, as I have stood,
Silent with swimming sense; yea, gazing round
40 On the wide landscape, gaze till all doth seem
Less gross than bodily; and of such hues
As veil the Almighty Spirit, when yet he makes
Spirits perceive his presence.

        A delight
Comes sudden on my heart, and I am glad
As I myself were there! Nor in this bower,
This little lime-tree bower, have I not marked
Much that has soothed me. Pale beneath the blaze
Hung the transparent foliage; and I watched
Some broad and sunny leaf, and loved to see
50 The shadow of the leaf and stem above
Dappling its sunshine! And that walnut tree
Was richly tinged, and a deep radiance lay
Full on the ancient ivy which usurps
Those fronting elms, and now, with blackest mass
Makes their dark branches gleam a lighter hue
Through the late twilight: and though now the bat
Wheels silent by, and not a swallow twitters,
Yet still the solitary humblebee
Sings in the bean flower! Henceforth I shall know
60 That nature ne'er deserts the wise and pure;
No plot so narrow, be but nature there,

No waste so vacant, but may well employ
Each faculty of sense, and keep the heart
Awake to love and beauty! and sometimes
'Tis well to be bereft of promised good,
That we may lift the soul, and contemplate
With lively joy the joys we cannot share.
My gentle-hearted Charles! when the last rook
Beat its straight path along the dusky air
Homewards, I blest it! deeming its black wing 70
(Now a dim speck, now vanishing in light)
Had crossed the mighty orb's dilated glory,
While thou stood'st gazing; or, when all was still,
Flew creeking o'er thy head, and had a charm
For thee, my gentle-hearted Charles, to whom
No sound is dissonant which tells of life.

           (1797; 1800)

THE RIME OF THE ANCIENT MARINER

The first edition of Lyrical Ballads (1798) contained this poem anonymously; the second edition made some changes to eliminate a few archaisms which Coleridge had written in the original. It was not published separately under Coleridge's name until 1817; the marginal gloss first appeared at this time. The genesis of the poem has been described thoroughly by Coleridge in Biographia Literaria *(Chapter 14, page 731). Wordsworth states that it was he who suggested the shooting of the albatross, but the inspiration of the poem as a whole was probably given Coleridge by a pair of seventeenth-century voyage narratives, the* Letters of Saint Paulinus to Macarius *(1618) and Capt. J. James'* Strange and Dangerous Voyage *(1633). The idea of the albatross as a bird of good luck belongs to the folklore of the sea. The poem is Coleridge's most famous achievement and perhaps the greatest of all English literary ballads.*

In Seven Parts

ARGUMENT

How a Ship having passed the Line was driven by storms to the cold Country towards the South Pole, and how from thence she made her course to the tropical Latitude of the Great Pacific Ocean, and of

---

28. **gentle-hearted Charles.** The epithet displeased Lamb, who humorously replied, "For God's sake, don't make me ridiculous any more by terming me gentle-hearted in print."

32. **strange calamity,** the periodic attacks of insanity suffered by Lamb's sister Mary, who had killed their mother in 1796.
The Rime of the Ancient Mariner. 12. **Eftsoons,** at once. By the

the strange things that befell: and in what manner
the Ancyent Marinere came back to his own Country.

PART 1

It is an ancient Mariner,
And he stoppeth one of three.
"By thy long gray beard and glittering eye,
Now wherefore stopp'st thou me?

An ancient Mariner meeteth three Gallants bidden to a wedding-feast, and detaineth one.

"The Bridegroom's doors are opened wide,
And I am next of kin,
The guests are met, the feast is set:
May'st hear the merry din."

He holds him with his skinny hand,
10 "There was a ship," quoth he.
"Hold off! unhand me, gray-beard loon!"
Eftsoons his hand dropt he.

He holds him with his glittering eye—
The Wedding-Guest stood still,
And listens like a three years' child.
The Mariner hath his will.

The Wedding-Guest sat on a stone:
He cannot choose but hear;
And thus spake on that ancient man,
20 The bright-eyed Mariner.

The Wedding-Guest is spellbound by the eye of the old seafaring man and constrained to hear his tale.

"The ship was cheered, the harbor cleared,
Merrily did we drop
Below the kirk, below the hill,
Below the light-house top.

"The sun came up upon the left,
Out of the sea came he!
And he shone bright, and on the right
Went down into the sea.

The Mariner tells how the ship sailed southward with a good wind and fair weather, till it reached the Line.

"Higher and higher every day,
30 Till over the mast at noon—"
The Wedding-Guest here beat his breast,
For he heard the loud bassoon.

The bride hath paced into the hall,
Red as a rose is she;
Nodding their heads before her goes
The merry minstrelsy.

The Wedding-Guest heareth the bridal music; but the Mariner continueth his tale.

The Wedding-Guest he beat his breast,
Yet he cannot choose but hear;

And thus spake on that ancient man,
The bright-eyed Mariner.   40

"And now the Storm-blast came, and he
Was tyrannous and strong:
He struck with his o'ertaking wings,
And chased us south along.

The ship driven by a storm toward the south pole.

"With sloping masts and dipping prow,
As who pursued with yell and blow
Still treads the shadow of his foe,
And forward bends his head,
The ship drove fast, loud roared the blast,
And southward aye we fled.   50

"And now there came both mist and snow,
And it grew wondrous cold:
And ice, mast-high, came floating by,
As green as emerald.

"And through the drifts the snowy clifts
Did send a dismal sheen:
Nor shapes of men nor beasts we ken—
The ice was all between.

The land of ice, and of fearful sounds where no living thing was to be seen.

"The ice was here, the ice was there,
The ice was all around: 60
It cracked and growled, and roared and howled,
Like noises in a swound!

"At length did cross an Albatross,
Thorough the fog it came;
As if it had been a Christian soul,
We hailed it in God's name.

Till a great sea-bird, called the Albatross, came through the snow-fog, and was received with great joy and hospitality.

"It ate the food it ne'er had eat,
And round and round it flew.
The ice did split with a thunder-fit;
The helmsman steered us through!   70

"And a good south wind sprung up behind;
The Albatross did follow,
And every day, for food or play,
Came to the mariners' hollo!

And lo! the Albatross proveth a bird of good omen, and followeth the ship as it returned northward through fog and floating ice.

"In mist or cloud, on mast or shroud,
It perched for vespers nine;
Whiles all the night, through fog-smoke white,
Glimmered the white moon-shine."

"God save thee, ancient Mariner!
From the fiends, that plague thee thus!—

The ancient Mariner inhospitably killeth the pious bird of good omen.

80

use of such words, Coleridge reproduces something of the atmosphere of the old ballads. 13. **He . . . will.** Wordsworth states that he wrote this stanza. 30. **over . . . noon.** The ship is near the equator. 58. **between,** between the ship and the land. 62. **swound,** swoon, dream. 75. **shroud,** a rope running from the masthead to the side of the ship. 76. **vespers,** evenings.

Why look'st thou so?"—"With my
 cross-bow
I shot the Albatross!"

PART 2

"The Sun now rose upon the right:
Out of the sea came he,
Still hid in mist, and on the left
Went down into the sea.

"And the good south wind still blew behind,
But no sweet bird did follow,
Nor any day for food or play
90 Came to the mariners' hollo!

"And I had done a hellish thing,   His shipmates cry
And it would work 'em woe: out against the
                                          ancient Mariner, for
For all averred, I had killed the bird   killing the bird of
That made the breeze to blow.   good luck.
Ah, wretch! said they, the bird to slay,
That made the breeze to blow!

"Nor dim nor red, like God's own   But when the fog
 head,   cleared off they
                                          justify the same,
The glorious Sun uprist: and thus make them-
Then all averred, I had killed the   selves accomplices
 bird   in the crime.
100 That brought the fog and mist.
'Twas right, said they, such birds to slay,
That bring the fog and mist.

"The fair breeze blew, the white foam   The fair breeze con-
 flew,   tinues; the ship
                                          enters the Pacific
The furrow followed free;   Ocean, and sails
We were the first that ever burst   northward, even till
Into that silent sea.   it reaches the Line.

"Down dropt the breeze, the sails   The ship hath been
 dropt down,   suddenly becalmed.
'Twas sad as sad could be;
And we did speak only to break
110 The silence of the sea!

"All in a hot and copper sky,
The bloody Sun, at noon,
Right up above the mast did stand,
No bigger than the Moon.

"Day after day, day after day,
We stuck, nor breath nor motion;
As idle as a painted ship
Upon a painted ocean.

"Water, water, everywhere,   And the Albatross
120 And all the boards did shrink;   begins to be
                                          avenged.

Water, water, everywhere,
Nor any drop to drink.

"The very deep did rot: O Christ!
That ever this should be!
Yea, slimy things did crawl with legs
Upon the slimy sea.

"About, about, in reel and rout   A Spirit had fol-
The death-fires danced at night;   lowed them; one of
                                          the invisible inhab-
The water, like a witch's oils,   itants of this planet,
Burnt green, and blue and white.   neither departed
                                          souls nor angels;
"And some in dreams assured were   concerning whom   130
Of the Spirit that plagued us so;   the learned Jew,
                                          Josephus, and the
Nine fathom deep he had followed us   Platonic Constanti-
From the land of mist and snow.   nopolitan, Michael
                                          Psellus, may be con-
"And every tongue, through utter   sulted. They are
 drought,   very numerous, and
                                          there is no climate
Was withered at the root;   or element without
We could not speak, no more than if   one or more.
We had been choked with soot.
                                          The shipmates, in
                                          their sore distress,
                                          would fain throw
                                          the whole guilt on
                                          the ancient Mariner:
                                          in sign whereof they
                                          hang the dead sea-
                                          bird round his neck.

"Ah! well-a-day! what evil looks
Had I from old and young!   140
Instead of the cross, the Albatross
About my neck was hung.

PART 3

"There passed a weary time. Each throat
Was parched, and glazed each eye.
A weary time! a weary time!
How glazed each weary eye,
When looking westward, I beheld   The ancient Mariner
A something in the sky.   beholdeth a sign in
                                          the element afar off.

"At first it seemed a little speck,
And then it seemed a mist;   150
It moved and moved, and took at last
A certain shape, I wist.

"A speck, a mist, a shape, I wist!
And still it neared and neared:
As if it dodged a water-sprite,
It plunged and tacked and veered.

"With throats unslaked, with black   At its nearer ap-
 lips baked,   proach, it seemeth
                                          him to be a ship;
We could nor laugh nor wail;   and at a dear ransom
Through utter drought all dumb we   he freeth his speech
 stood!   from the bonds of
                                          thirst.
I bit my arm, I sucked the blood,   160
And cried, A sail! a sail!

83. Sun now rose. The ship has now gone around Cape Horn and is
headed north into the Pacific. 128. death-fires, phosphorescent lights,
considered omens of disaster. It is possible that Coleridge has in mind
the maritime will-o'-the-wisp phenomenon known as "St. Elmo's fire."
152. wist, thought, knew. 164. Gramercy, great thanks. 184. gossameres, fine spider webs.

An illustration
for Coleridge's
The Ancient Mariner
by Gustave Doré,
c. 1870.

"With throats unslaked, with black lips baked,
Agape they heard me call:
Gramercy! they for joy did grin,   *A flash of joy;*
And all at once their breath drew in,
As they were drinking all.

"See! see! (I cried) she tacks no   *And horror follows.*
    more!   *For can it be a ship*
                                     that comes onward
Hither to work us weal—   *without wind or*
                                     tide?
Without a breeze, without a tide,
170 She steadies with upright keel!

"The western wave was all aflame,
The day was well nigh done!
Almost upon the western wave
Rested the broad bright Sun;
When that strange shape drove suddenly
Betwixt us and the Sun.

"And straight the Sun was flecked   *It seemeth him but*
    with bars,   *the skeleton of a*
                                     ship.
(Heaven's Mother send us grace!)
As if through a dungeon-grate he peered
With broad and burning face.   180

"Alas! (thought I, and my heart beat loud)
How fast she nears and nears!
Are those her sails that glance in the
    Sun,
Like restless gossameres?

"Are those her ribs through which   *And its ribs are seen*
    the Sun   *as bars on the face*
                                     of the setting Sun.
Did peer, as through a grate?
And is that Woman all her crew?   *The Specter-Woman*
                                     and her Death-mate,
Is that a Death? and are there two?   *and no other on*
                                     board the skeleton
Is Death that woman's mate?   *ship.*

Samuel Taylor Coleridge   717

190 "Her lips were red, her looks were free,
Her locks were yellow as gold: *Like vessel,*
Her skin was as white as leprosy, *like crew!*
The Night-mare Life-in-Death was she,
Who thicks man's blood with cold.

"The naked hulk alongside came, *Death and Life-in-*
And the twain were casting dice; *Death have diced for*
'The game is done! I've won! I've *the ship's crew, and*
won!' *she (the latter)*
Quoth she, and whistles thrice. *winneth the ancient*
Mariner.

"The Sun's rim dips; the stars rush *No twilight within*
out: *the courts of the*
200 At one stride comes the dark; *Sun.*
With far-heard whisper, o'er the sea,
Off shot the specter-bark.

"We listened and looked sideways up! *At the rising of*
Fear at my heart, as at a cup, *the Moon.*
My life-blood seemed to sip!
The stars were dim, and thick the night,
The steersman's face by his lamp gleamed
white;
From the sails the dew did drip—
Till clomb above the eastern bar
210 The hornéd Moon, with one bright star
Within the nether tip.

"One after one, by the star-dogged *One after another.*
Moon,
Too quick for groan or sigh,
Each turned his face with a ghastly pang,
And cursed me with his eye.

"Four times fifty living men, *His shipmates drop*
(And I heard nor sigh nor groan) *down dead.*
With heavy thump, a lifeless lump,
They dropt down one by one.

220 "The souls did from their bodies fly— *But Life-in-Death*
They fled to bliss or woe! *begins her work on*
And every soul, it passed me by *the ancient Mariner.*
Like the whizz of my cross-bow!"

PART 4

"I fear thee, ancient Mariner! *The Wedding-Guest*
I fear thy skinny hand! *feareth that a Spirit*
And thou art long, and lank, and brown, *is talking to him;*
As is the ribbed sea-sand.

"I fear thee and thy glittering eye, *But the ancient*
And thy skinny hand, so brown."— *Mariner assureth*
him of his bodily

"Fear not, fear not, thou Wedding- *life, and proceedeth*
Guest! *to relate his horrible*
This body dropt not down. *penance.* 230

"Alone, alone, all, all alone,
Alone on a wide, wide sea!
And never a saint took pity on
My soul in agony.

"The many men, so beautiful! *He despiseth the*
And they all dead did lie: *creatures of the*
And a thousand thousand slimy things *calm.*
Lived on; and so did I.

"I looked upon the rotting sea, *And envieth that* 240
And drew my eyes away; *they should live, and*
I looked upon the rotting deck, *so many lie dead.*
And there the dead men lay.

"I looked to heaven, and tried to pray;
But or ever a prayer had gusht,
A wicked whisper came, and made
My heart as dry as dust.

"I closed my lids, and kept them close,
And the balls like pulses beat;
For the sky and the sea, and the sea and the sky 250
Lay like a load on my weary eye,
And the dead were at my feet.

"The cold sweat melted from their *But the curse liveth*
limbs, *for him in the eye*
Nor rot nor reek did they: *of the dead men.*
The look with which they looked on me
Had never passed away.

"An orphan's curse would drag to hell
A spirit from on high; *In his loneliness and*
But oh! more horrible than that *fixedness he yearneth*
Is a curse in a dead man's eye! *towards the journey-*
Seven days, seven nights, I saw that *ing Moon, and the*
curse, *stars that still* 260
And yet I could not die. *sojourn, yet still*
move onward; and
everywhere the blue
"The moving Moon went up the sky, *sky belongs to them,*
And nowhere did abide: *and is their ap-*
Softly she was going up, *pointed rest, and*
And a star or two beside— *their native country*
and their own
natural homes,
which they enter
unannounced, as
lords that are cer-
tainly expected, and
yet there is a silent
joy at their arrival.

"Her beams bemocked the sultry
main,
Like April hoar-frost spread;
But where the ship's huge shadow lay,
The charméd water burnt alway 270
A still and awful red.

210. **Moon . . . tip.** In a manuscript note Coleridge remarks that "it is a common superstition among sailors that something evil is about to happen whenever a star dogs the moon." It is impossible, however, for any star to appear between the horns of the crescent moon, for

the moon is the celestial object that is nearest the earth. 226. **And . . . sea-sand.** For these two lines Coleridge acknowledges indebtedness to Wordsworth. 228. **glittering eye.** It is a commonplace of European folklore that a person with evil attributes can do harm to another by

"Beyond the shadow of the ship,
I watched the water-snakes:
They moved in tracks of shining
    white,
And when they reared, the elfish light
Fell off in hoary flakes.

By the light of the Moon he beholdeth God's creatures of the great calm.

"Within the shadow of the ship
I watched their rich attire:
Blue, glossy green, and velvet black,
280 They coiled and swam; and every track
Was a flash of golden fire.

"O happy living things! no tongue
Their beauty might declare:
A spring of love gushed from my heart,
And I blessed them unaware;
Sure my kind saint took pity on me,
And I blessed them unaware.

Their beauty and their happiness.

He blesseth them in his heart.

The spell begins to break.

"The selfsame moment I could pray;
And from my neck so free
290 The Albatross fell off, and sank
Like lead into the sea."

PART 5

"Oh sleep! it is a gentle thing,
Beloved from pole to pole!
To Mary Queen the praise be given!
She sent the gentle sleep from Heaven,
That slid into my soul.

"The silly buckets on the deck,
That had so long remained,
I dreamt that they were filled with
    dew;
300 And when I awoke, it rained.

By grace of the holy Mother, the ancient Mariner is refreshed with rain.

"My lips were wet, my throat was cold,
My garments all were dank;
Sure I had drunken in my dreams,
And still my body drank.

"I moved, and could not feel my limbs:
I was so light—almost
I thought that I had died in sleep,
And was a blessed ghost.

"And soon I heard a roaring wind:
310 It did not come anear;
But with its sound it shook the sails,
That were so thin and sere.

He heareth sounds and seeth strange sights and commotions in the sky and the elements.

"The upper air burst into life!
And a hundred fire-flags sheen,
To and fro they were hurried about!
And to and fro, and in and out,
The wan stars danced between.

"And the coming wind did roar more loud,
And the sails did sigh like sedge;
And the rain poured down from one black cloud;   320
The Moon was at its edge.

"The thick black cloud was cleft, and still
The Moon was at its side:
Like waters shot from some high crag,
The lightning fell with never a jag,
A river steep and wide.

"The loud wind never reached the
    ship,
Yet now the ship moved on!
Beneath the lightning and the Moon
The dead men gave a groan.   330

The bodies of the ship's crew are inspired, and the ship moves on;

"They groaned, they stirred, they all uprose,
Nor spake, nor moved their eyes;
It had been strange, even in a dream,
To have seen those dead men rise.

"The helmsman steered, the ship moved on;
Yet never a breeze up blew;
The mariners all 'gan work the ropes,
Where they were wont to do;
They raised their limbs like lifeless tools—
We were a ghastly crew.   340

"The body of my brother's son
Stood by me, knee to knee:
The body and I pulled at one rope,
But he said nought to me."

"I fear thee, ancient Mariner!"
"Be calm, thou Wedding-Guest!
'Twas not those souls that fled in
    pain,
Which to their corses came again,
But a troop of spirits blest:

But not by the souls of the men, nor by demons of earth or middle air, but by a blessed troop of angelic spirits, sent down by the invocation of the guardian saint.

"For when it dawned—they dropped their arms,   350
And clustered round the mast;
Sweet sounds rose slowly through their mouths,
And from their bodies passed.

"Around, around, flew each sweet sound,
Then darted to the Sun;
Slowly the sounds came back again,
Now mixed, now one by one.

---

fixing him with his eye (the "evil eye" motif). 263. **The moving Moon, etc.** The atmosphere of this stanza might profitably be compared with that of the old popular ballad, *Sir Patrick Spens* (p. 58). 297. **silly,** literally, *innocent*; and by a poetic extension, *unused, empty.*

314. **fire-flags,** perhaps the northern lights. **sheen,** bright. 319. **sedge,** coarse marsh grass.

"Sometimes a-dropping from the sky
I heard the skylark sing;
360 Sometimes all little birds that are,
How they seemed to fill the sea and air
With their sweet jargoning!

"And now 'twas like all instruments,
Now like a lonely flute;
And now it is an angel's song,
That makes the heavens be mute.

"It ceased; yet still the sails made on
A pleasant noise till noon,
A noise like of a hidden brook
370 In the leafy month of June,
That to the sleeping woods all night
Singeth a quiet tune.

"Till noon we quietly sailed on,
Yet never a breeze did breathe:
Slowly and smoothly went the ship,
Moved onward from beneath.

"Under the keel nine fathom deep,
From the land of mist and snow,
The Spirit slid: and it was he
380 That made the ship to go.
The sails at noon left off their tune,
And the ship stood still also.

The lonesome Spirit from the South Pole carries on the ship as far as the Line, in obedience to the angelic troop, but still requireth vengeance.

"The Sun, right up above the mast,
Had fixed her to the ocean:
But in a minute she 'gan stir,
With a short uneasy motion—
Backwards and forwards half her length
With a short uneasy motion.

"Then like a pawing horse let go,
390 She made a sudden bound:
It flung the blood into my head,
And I fell down in a swound.

"How long in that same fit I lay,
I have not to declare;
But ere my living life returned,
I heard, and in my soul discerned,
Two voices in the air.

The Polar Spirit's fellow demons, the invisible inhabitants of the element, take part in his wrong; and two of them relate, one to the other that penance long and heavy for the ancient Mariner hath been accorded to the Polar Spirit, who returneth southward.

" 'Is it he?' quoth one, 'Is this the
man?
By Him who died on cross,
400 With his cruel bow he laid full low
The harmless Albatross.

" 'The Spirit who bideth by himself
In the land of mist and snow,

---

394. **have not,** have not the power or knowledge. 435. **charnel-dungeon,** a vault for bones of the dead. 489. **rood,** cross.

He loved the bird that loved the man
Who shot him with his bow.'

"The other was a softer voice,
As soft as honey-dew:
Quoth he, 'The man hath penance done,
And penance more will do.' "

PART 6

FIRST VOICE

" 'But tell me, tell me! speak again,
Thy soft response renewing—   410
What makes that ship drive on so fast?
What is the ocean doing?'

SECOND VOICE

" 'Still as a slave before his lord,
The ocean hath no blast;
His great bright eye most silently
Up to the Moon is cast—

" 'If he may know which way to go;
For she guides him smooth or grim.
See, brother, see! how graciously
She looketh down on him.'   420

FIRST VOICE

" 'But why drives on that ship so
fast,
Without or wave or wind?'

The Mariner hath been cast into a trance; for the angelic power causeth the vessel to drive northward faster than human life could endure.

SECOND VOICE

" 'The air is cut away before,
And closes from behind.'

" 'Fly, brother, fly! more high, more high!
Or we shall be belated:
For slow and slow that ship will go,
When the Mariner's trance is abated.'

"I woke, and we were sailing on
As in a gentle weather:
'Twas night, calm night, the moon
was high;
The dead men stood together.

The supernatural motion is retarded; the Mariner awakes, 430 and his penance begins anew.

"All stood together on the deck,
For a charnel-dungeon fitter:
All fixed on me their stony eyes,
That in the Moon did glitter.

"The pang, the curse, with which they died,
Had never passed away:

440 I could not draw my eyes from theirs,
Nor turn them up to pray.

"And now this spell was snapt: once   *The curse is finally*
      more   *expiated.*
I viewed the ocean green,
And looked far forth, yet little saw
Of what had else been seen—

"Like one, that on a lonesome road
Doth walk in fear and dread,
And having once turned round, walks on,
And turns no more his head;
450 Because he knows, a frightful fiend
Doth close behind him tread.

"But soon there breathed a wind on me,
Nor sound nor motion made:
Its path was not upon the sea,
In ripple or in shade.

"It raised my hair, it fanned my cheek
Like a meadow-gale of spring—
It mingled strangely with my fears,
Yet it felt like a welcoming.

460 "Swiftly, swiftly flew the ship,
Yet she sailed softly too:
Sweetly, sweetly blew the breeze—
On me alone it blew.

"Oh! dream of joy! is this indeed   *And the ancient*
The light-house top I see?   *Mariner beholdeth*
Is this the hill? is this the kirk? *his native country.*
Is this mine own countree?

"We drifted o'er the harbor-bar,
And I with sobs did pray—
470 O let me be awake, my God!
Or let me sleep alway.

"The harbor-bay was clear as glass,
So smoothly it was strewn!
And on the bay the moonlight lay,
And the shadow of the Moon.

"The rock shone bright, the kirk no less,
That stands above the rock:
The moonlight steeped in silentness
The steady weathercock.

480 "And the bay was white with silent light
Till, rising from the same,   *The angelic spirits*
Full many shapes, that shadows were, *leave the dead*
In crimson colors came.   *bodies.*

"A little distance from the prow
Those crimson shadows were:

I turned my eyes upon the deck—
Oh, Christ! what saw I there!

"Each corse lay flat, lifeless and flat,
And, by the holy rood!
A man all light, a seraph-man,   *And appear in their* 490
On every corse there stood.   *own forms of light.*

"This seraph-band, each waved his hand:
It was a heavenly sight!
They stood as signals to the land,
Each one a lovely light;

"This seraph-band, each waved his hand,
No voice did they impart—
No voice; but oh! the silence sank
Like music on my heart.

"But soon I heard the dash of oars,   500
I heard the Pilot's cheer;
My head was turned perforce away,
And I saw a boat appear.

"The Pilot and the Pilot's boy,
I heard them coming fast:
Dear Lord in Heaven! it was a joy
The dead men could not blast.

"I saw a third—I heard his voice:
It is the Hermit good!
He singeth loud his godly hymns   510
That he makes in the wood.
He'll shrieve my soul, he'll wash away
The Albatross's blood."

PART 7

"This Hermit good lives in that wood   *The Hermit of*
Which slopes down to the sea.   *the wood,*
How loudly his sweet voice he rears!
He loves to talk with marineres
That come from a far countree.

"He kneels at morn, and noon, and eve—
He hath a cushion plump: 520
It is the moss that wholly hides
The rotted old oak-stump.

"The skiff-boat neared: I heard them talk,
'Why, this is strange, I trow!
Where are those lights so many and fair,
That signal made but now?'

" 'Strange, by my faith!' the Hermit   *Approacheth the*
      said—   *ship with wonder.*
'And they answered not our cheer!
The planks looked warped! and see those sails,

530 How thin they are and sere!
I never saw aught like to them,
Unless perchance it were

" 'Brown skeletons of leaves that lag
My forest-brook along;
When the ivy-tod is heavy with snow,
And the owlet whoops to the wolf below,
That eats the she-wolf's young.'

" 'Dear Lord! it hath a fiendish look—
(The Pilot made reply)
540 I am a-feared'—'Push on, push on!'
Said the Hermit cheerily.

"The boat came closer to the ship,
But I nor spake nor stirred;
The boat came close beneath the ship,
And straight a sound was heard.

"Under the water it rumbled on, *The ship suddenly*
Still louder and more dread: *sinketh.*
It reached the ship, it split the bay;
The ship went down like lead.

"Stunned by that loud and dreadful *The ancient Mariner*
550 sound, *is saved in the*
Which sky and ocean smote, *Pilot's boat.*
Like one that hath been seven days drowned
My body lay afloat;
But swift as dreams, myself I found
Within the Pilot's boat.

"Upon the whirl, where sank the ship,
The boat spun round and round;
And all was still, save that the hill
Was telling of the sound.

560 "I moved my lips—the Pilot shrieked
And fell down in a fit;
The holy Hermit raised his eyes,
And prayed where he did sit.

"I took the oars: the Pilot's boy,
Who now doth crazy go,
Laughed loud and long, and all the while
His eyes went to and fro.
'Ha! ha!' quoth he, 'full plain I see,
The Devil knows how to row.'

570 "And now, all in my own countree,
I stood on the firm land!
The Hermit stepped forth from the boat,
And scarcely he could stand.

" 'O shrieve me, shrieve me, holy man!'
The Hermit crossed his brow. *The ancient Mariner*
'Say quick,' quoth he, 'I bid thee *earnestly entreateth*
say— *the Hermit to*
What manner of man art thou?' *shrieve him; and*
the penance of life
falls on him.

"Forthwith this frame of mine was wrenched
With a woful agony,
Which forced me to begin my tale; 580
And then it left me free.

"Since then, at an uncertain hour, *And ever and anon*
That agony returns; *throughout his*
And till my ghastly tale is told, *future life an agony*
This heart within me burns. *constraineth him to*
travel from land
to land.

"I pass, like night, from land to land;
I have strange power of speech;
That moment that his face I see,
I know the man that must hear me:
To him my tale I teach. 590

"What loud uproar bursts from that door!
The wedding-guests are there:
But in the garden-bower the bride
And bride-maids singing are:
And hark the little vesper bell,
Which biddeth me to prayer!

"O Wedding-Guest! this soul hath been
Alone on a wide, wide sea:
So lonely 'twas, that God himself
Scarce seemèd there to be. 600

"Oh sweeter than the marriage-feast,
'Tis sweeter far to me,
To walk together to the kirk
With a goodly company!—

"To walk together to the kirk,
And all together pray,
While each to his great Father bends,
Old men, and babes, and loving friends,
And youths and maidens gay!

"Farewell, farewell! but this I tell *And to teach by his* 610
To thee, thou Wedding-Guest! *own example love*
He prayeth well, who loveth well *and reverence to all*
Both man and bird and beast. *things that God*
made and loveth.

"He prayeth best, who loveth best
All things both great and small;
For the dear God who loveth us,
He made and loveth all."

535. ivy-tod, ivy bush. 558. hill . . . sound, referring to the echo
of the cataclysm. 575. crossed his brow, made the sign of the Cross
upon his forehead to avert evil. 623. of sense forlorn, deprived of
his senses.

The Mariner, whose eye is bright,
Whose beard with age is hoar,
620 Is gone: and now the Wedding-Guest
Turned from the bridegroom's door.

He went like one that hath been stunned,
And is of sense forlorn:
A sadder and a wiser man,
He rose the morrow morn.
(1797-1798; 1798)

CHRISTABEL

*Coleridge never finished this poem, never even car-
ried it much beyond the beginning of the story. The
first part was composed as early as 1797; the second
part, which has very little relation to the first, not
until 1800. Such portions of the poem as were completed were finally published in 1816. The reasons
for the unfinished state of Christabel are to be found
in Coleridge's own indolent and vacillating temperament, as he himself freely admitted as late as 1833:
"The reason of my not finishing Christabel is not
that I don't know how to do it—for I have, as I
always had, the whole plan entire from beginning to
end in my mind; but I fear I could not carry on
with equal success the execution of the idea, an extremely subtle and difficult one."*

*The meter of Christabel is an interesting revival by
Coleridge of the free four-stress line, divisible into two
half lines of two stresses each, that was an important
characteristic of Old English alliterative verse.*

PART 1

'Tis the middle of night by the castle clock,
And the owls have awakened the crowing cock,
Tu—whit!——Tu—whoo!
And hark, again! the crowing cock,
How drowsily it crew.

Sir Leoline, the Baron rich,
Hath a toothless mastiff bitch;
From her kennel beneath the rock
She maketh answer to the clock,
10 Four for the quarters, and twelve for the hour;
Ever and aye, by shine and shower,
Sixteen short howls, not over loud;
Some say, she sees my lady's shroud.

Is the night chilly and dark?
The night is chilly, but not dark.
The thin gray cloud is spread on high,
It covers but not hides the sky.
The moon is behind, and at the full;
And yet she looks both small and dull.

The night is chill, the cloud is gray: 20
'Tis a month before the month of May,
And the Spring comes slowly up this way.

The lovely lady, Christabel,
Whom her father loves so well,
What makes her in the wood so late,
A furlong from the castle gate?
She had dreams all yesternight
Of her own betrothéd knight;
And she in the midnight wood will pray
For the weal of her lover that's far away.   30

She stole along, she nothing spoke,
The sighs she heaved were soft and low,
And naught was green upon the oak
But moss and rarest mistletoe:
She kneels beneath the huge oak tree
And in silence prayeth she.

The lady sprang up suddenly,
The lovely lady, Christabel!
It moaned as near, as near can be,
But what it is she cannot tell.—   40
On the other side it seems to be,
Of the huge, broad-breasted, old oak tree.

The night is chill; the forest bare;
Is it the wind that moaneth bleak?
There is not wind enough in the air
To move away the ringlet curl
From the lovely lady's cheek—
There is not wind enough to twirl
The one red leaf, the last of its clan,
That dances as often as dance it can,   50
Hanging so light, and hanging so high,
On the topmost twig that looks up at the sky.

Hush, beating heart of Christabel!
Jesu Maria, shield her well!
She folded her arms beneath her cloak,
And stole to the other side of the oak.
    What sees she there?

There she sees a damsel bright,
Drest in a silken robe of white,
That shadowy in the moonlight shone: 60
The neck that made that white robe wan,
Her stately neck, and arms were bare;
Her blue-veined feet unsandalled were,
And wildly glittered here and there
The gems entangled in her hair.
I guess, 'twas frightful there to see
A lady so richly clad as she—
Beautiful exceedingly!

"Mary mother, save me now!"
(Said Christabel) "And who art thou?"   70

The lady strange made answer meet,
And her voice was faint and sweet:
"Have pity on my sore distress,
I scarce can speak for weariness":
"Stretch forth thy hand, and have no fear!"
Said Christabel, "How camest thou here?"
And the lady, whose voice was faint and sweet,
Did thus pursue her answer meet:

"My sire is of a noble line,
80 And my name is Geraldine:
Five warriors seized me yestermorn.
Me, even me, a maid forlorn:
They choked my cries with force and fright,
And tied me on a palfrey white.
The palfrey was as fleet as wind,
And they rode furiously behind.
They spurred amain, their steeds were white:
And once we crossed the shade of night.
As sure as Heaven shall rescue me,
90 I have no thought what men they be;
Nor do I know how long it is
(For I have lain entranced, I wis)
Since one, the tallest of the five,
Took me from the palfrey's back,
A weary woman, scarce alive.
Some muttered words his comrades spoke:
He placed me underneath this oak;
He swore they would return with haste;
Whither they went I cannot tell—
100 I thought I heard, some minutes past,
Sounds as of a castle bell.
Stretch forth thy hand (thus ended she),
And help a wretched maid to flee."

Then Christabel stretched forth her hand,
And comforted fair Geraldine:
"Oh well, bright dame! may you command
The service of Sir Leoline:
And gladly our stout chivalry
Will he send forth, and friends withal,
110 To guide and guard you safe and free
Home to your noble father's hall."

She rose: and forth with steps they passed
That strove to be, and were not, fast.
Her gracious stars the lady blest,
And thus spake on sweet Christabel:
"All our household are at rest,
The hall as silent as the cell;
Sir Leoline is weak in health,
And may not well awakened be,
120 But we will move as if in stealth,
And I beseech your courtesy,
This night, to share your couch with me."

They crossed the moat, and Christabel
Took the key that fitted well;
A little door she opened straight,
All in the middle of the gate;
The gate that was ironed within and without,
Where an army in battle array had marched out.
The lady sank, belike through pain,
And Christabel with might and main   130
Lifted her up, a weary weight,
Over the threshold of the gate:
Then the lady rose again,
And moved, as she were not in pain.

So free from danger, free from fear,
They crossed the court: right glad they were.
And Christabel devoutly cried
To the lady by her side:
"Praise we the Virgin all divine
Who hath rescued thee from thy distress!"   140
"Alas, alas!" said Geraldine,
"I cannot speak for weariness."
So free from danger, free from fear,
They crossed the court: right glad they were.

Outside her kennel the mastiff old
Lay fast asleep, in moonshine cold.
The mastiff old did not awake,
Yet she an angry moan did make!
And what can ail the mastiff bitch?
Never till now she uttered yell   150
Beneath the eye of Christabel.
Perhaps it is the owlet's scritch:
For what can ail the mastiff bitch?

They passed the hall, that echoes still,
Pass as lightly as you will!
The brands were flat, the brands were dying,
Amid their own white ashes lying;
But when the lady passed, there came
A tongue of light, a fit of flame;
And Christabel saw the lady's eye,   160
And nothing else saw she thereby,
Save the boss of the shield of Sir Leoline tall,
Which hung in a murky old niche in the wall.
"O softly tread," said Christabel,
"My father seldom sleepeth well."

Sweet Christabel her feet doth bare,
And jealous of the listening air,
They steal their way from stair to stair,
Now in glimmer, and now in gloom,
And now they pass the Baron's room,   170
As still as death, with stifled breath!
And now have reached her chamber door;
And now doth Geraldine press down
The rushes of the chamber floor.

Christabel. 129 ff. **The lady sank,** etc. These lines show Geraldine
to be an evil spirit. She was unable, without aid, to cross the threshold,
which had been blessed to keep evil spirits away; she refused to praise
the Virgin (1. 142); the dog had a premonition of the presence of evil

The moon shines dim in the open air,
And not a moonbeam enters here.
But they without its light can see
The chamber carved so curiously,
Carved with figures strange and sweet,
180 All made out of the carver's brain,
For a lady's chamber meet:
The lamp with twofold silver chain
Is fastened to an angel's feet.

The silver lamp burns dead and dim;
But Christabel the lamp will trim.
She trimmed the lamp, and made it bright,
And left it swinging to and fro,
While Geraldine, in wretched plight,
Sank down upon the floor below.

190 "O weary lady, Geraldine,
I pray you, drink this cordial wine!
It is a wine of virtuous powers;
My mother made it of wild flowers."

"And will your mother pity me,
Who am a maiden most forlorn?"
Christabel answered—"Woe is me!
She died the hour that I was born.
I have heard the gray-haired friar tell,
How on her death-bed she did say,
200 That she should hear the castle-bell
Strike twelve upon my wedding-day.
O mother dear! that thou wert here!"
"I would," said Geraldine, "she were!"

But soon with altered voice, said she—
"Off, wandering mother! Peak and pine!
I have power to bid thee flee."
Alas! what ails poor Geraldine?
Why stares she with unsettled eye?
Can she the bodiless dead espy?
210 And why with hollow voice cries she,
"Off, woman, off! this hour is mine—
Though thou her guardian spirit be,
Off, woman, off! 'tis given to me."

Then Christabel knelt by the lady's side,
And raised to heaven her eyes so blue—
"Alas!" said she, "this ghastly ride—
Dear lady! it hath wildered you!"
The lady wiped her moist cold brow,
And faintly said, " 'Tis over now!"

220 Again the wild-flower wine she drank:
Her fair large eyes 'gan glitter bright,
And from the floor whereon she sank,
The lofty lady stood upright;

She was most beautiful to see,
Like a lady of a far countree.

And thus the lofty lady spake—
"All they, who live in the upper sky,
Do love you, holy Christabel!
And you love them, and for their sake
And for the good which me befell,   230
Even I in my degree will try,
Fair maiden, to requite you well.
But now unrobe yourself; for I
Must pray, ere yet in bed I lie."

Quoth Christabel, "So let it be!"
And as the lady bade, did she.
Her gentle limbs did she undress,
And lay down in her loveliness.

But through her brain of weal and woe
So many thoughts moved to and fro,   240
That vain it were her lids to close:
So half-way from the bed she rose,
And on her elbow did recline
To look at the lady Geraldine.

Beneath the lamp the lady bowed,
And slowly rolled her eyes around;
Then drawing in her breath aloud,
Like one that shuddered, she unbound
The cincture from beneath her breast:
Her silken robe, and inner vest,   250
Dropt to her feet, and full in view,
Behold! her bosom and half her side—
A sight to dream of, not to tell!
Oh, shield her! shield sweet Christabel!

Yet Geraldine nor speaks nor stirs;
Ah! what a stricken look was hers!
Deep from within she seems half-way
To lift some weight with sick assay,
And eyes the maid and seeks delay;
Then suddenly, as one defied,   260
Collects herself in scorn and pride,
And lay down by the maiden's side!—
And in her arms the maid she took,
          Ah, well-a-day!
And with low voice and doleful look
          These words did say:
"In the touch of this bosom there worketh a spell,
Which is lord of thy utterance, Christabel!
Thou knowest tonight, and wilt know tomorrow,
This mark of my shame, this seal of my sorrow: 270
    But vainly thou warrest,
        For this is alone in
    Thy power to declare,

(l. 148); the action of the fire (ll. 156–159) was caused by the nearness of a supernatural being. 205. **Off . . . mother**. Geraldine has

power to drive away the beneficent spirit of Christabel's mother. 249.
cincture, girdle.

That in the dim forest
  Thou heard'st a low moaning,
And found'st a bright lady, surpassingly fair:
And didst bring her home with thee in love and in
    charity,
To shield her and shelter her from the damp air."

THE CONCLUSION TO PART 1

It was a lovely sight to see
280 The lady Christabel, when she
Was praying at the old oak tree.
    Amid the jagged shadows
    Of mossy leafless boughs,
    Kneeling in the moonlight,
    To make her gentle vows;
Her slender palms together prest,
Heaving sometimes on her breast;
Her face resigned to bliss or bale—
Her face, oh call it fair not pale,
290 And both blue eyes more bright than clear,
Each about to have a tear.

With open eyes (ah, woe is me!)
Asleep, and dreaming fearfully,
Fearfully dreaming, yet, I wis,
Dreaming that alone, which is—
O sorrow and shame! Can this be she,
The lady, who knelt at the old oak tree?
And lo! the worker of these harms,
That holds the maiden in her arms,
300 Seems to slumber still and mild,
As a mother with her child.

A star hath set, a star hath risen,
O Geraldine! since arms of thine
Have been the lovely lady's prison.
O Geraldine! one hour was thine—
Thou'st had thy will! By tairn and rill,
The night-birds all that hour were still.
But now they are jubilant anew,
From cliff and tower, tu—whoo! tu—whoo!
310 Tu—whoo! tu!—whoo! from wood and fell!

And see! the lady Christabel
Gathers herself from out her trance;
Her limbs relax, her countenance
Grows sad and soft; the smooth thin lids
Close o'er her eyes; and tears she sheds—
Large tears that leave the lashes bright!
And oft the while she seems to smile
As infants at a sudden light!

Yea, she doth smile, and she doth weep,
320 Like a youthful hermitess,

Beauteous in a wilderness,
Who, praying always, prays in sleep.
And, if she move unquietly,
Perchance, 'tis but the blood so free
Comes back and tingles in her feet.
No doubt she hath a vision sweet.
What if her guardian spirit 'twere?
What if she knew her mother near?
But this she knows, in joys and woes,
That saints will aid if men will call: 330
For the blue sky bends over all!

PART 2

Each matin bell, the Baron saith,
Knells us back to a world of death.
These words Sir Leoline first said,
When he rose and found his lady dead:
These words Sir Leoline will say,
Many a morn to his dying day!

And hence the custom and law began,
That still at dawn the sacristan,
Who duly pulls the heavy bell,   340
Five and forty beads must tell
Between each stroke—a warning knell,
Which not a soul can choose but hear
From Bratha Head to Wyndermere.

Saith Bracy the bard, "So let it knell!
And let the drowsy sacristan
Still count as slowly as he can!
There is no lack of such, I ween,
As well fill up the space between."
In Langdale Pike and Witch's lair,   350
And Dungeon-ghyll so foully rent,
With ropes of rock and bells of air
Three sinful sextons' ghosts are pent,
Who all give back, one after t' other,
The death-note to their living brother;
And oft too, by the knell offended,
Just as their one! two! three! is ended,
The devil mocks the doleful tale
With a merry peal from Borodale.

The air is still! through mist and cloud   360
That merry peal comes ringing loud;
And Geraldine shakes off her dread,
And rises lightly from the bed;
Puts on her silken vestments white,
And tricks her hair in lovely plight,
And nothing doubting of her spell
Awakens the lady Christabel.
"Sleep you, sweet lady Christabel?
I trust that you have rested well."

294. **wis,** think. 306. **tairn,** tarn, mountain pool. 344. **Bratha Head,** the source of the River Bratha, which flows through the county of Westmoreland into Lake Windermere. The other places named are in the beautiful and romantic Lake District, but the poem is not meant to be thus localized. 350. **Pike,** peak, hill. 351. **ghyll,** valley or ravine with a stream running through it. 365. **plight,** fold. 408 ff. **Alas!** etc.

370 And Christabel awoke and spied
The same who lay down by her side—
Oh, rather say, the same whom she
Raised up beneath the old oak tree!
Nay, fairer yet; and yet more fair!
For she belike hath drunken deep
Of all the blessedness of sleep!
And while she spake, her looks, her air,
Such gentle thankfulness declare,
That (so it seemed) her girded vests
380 Grew tight beneath her heaving breasts.
"Sure I have sinned!" said Christabel,
"Now heaven be praised if all be well!"
And in low faltering tones, yet sweet,
Did she the lofty lady greet,
With such perplexity of mind
As dreams too lively leave behind.

So quickly she rose, and quickly arrayed
Her maiden limbs, and having prayed
That He, who on the cross did groan,
390 Might wash away her sins unknown,
She forthwith led fair Geraldine
To meet her sire, Sir Leoline.

The lovely maid and lady tall
Are pacing both into the hall,
And pacing on through page and groom,
Enter the Baron's presence-room.

The Baron rose, and while he prest
His gentle daughter to his breast,
With cheerful wonder in his eyes
400 The lady Geraldine espies,
And gave such welcome to the same,
As might beseem so bright a dame!

But when he heard the lady's tale,
And when she told her father's name,
Why waxed Sir Leoline so pale,
Murmuring o'er the name again,
Lord Roland de Vaux of Tryermaine?

Alas! they had been friends in youth;
But whispering tongues can poison truth;
410 And constancy lives in realms above;
And life is thorny; and youth is vain;
And to be wroth with one we love
Doth work like madness in the brain.
And thus it chanced, as I divine,
With Roland and Sir Leoline.
Each spake words of high disdain
And insult to his heart's best brother:
They parted—ne'er to meet again!
But never either found another

Coleridge regarded these lines as "the best and sweetest passage" he
ever wrote. They may refer to his temporary estrangement from Southey.

To free the hollow heart from paining— 420
They stood aloof, the scars remaining,
Like cliffs which had been rent asunder;
A dreary sea now flows between—
But neither heat, nor frost, nor thunder,
Shall wholly do away, I ween,
The marks of that which once hath been.

Sir Leoline, a moment's space,
Stood gazing on the damsel's face:
And the youthful Lord of Tryermaine
Came back upon his heart again. 430

Oh then the Baron forgot his age,
His noble heart swelled high with rage;
He swore by the wounds in Jesu's side,
He would proclaim it far and wide,
With trump and solemn heraldry,
That they who thus had wronged the dame,
Were base as spotted infamy!
"And if they dare deny the same,
My herald shall appoint a week,
And let the recreant traitors seek 440
My tourney court—that there and then
I may dislodge their reptile souls
From the bodies and forms of men!"
He spake: his eye in lightning rolls!
For the lady was ruthlessly seized; and he kenned
In the beautiful lady the child of his friend!

And now the tears were on his face,
And fondly in his arms he took
Fair Geraldine, who met the embrace,
Prolonging it with joyous look. 450
Which when she viewed, a vision fell
Upon the soul of Christabel,
The vision of fear, the touch and pain!
She shrunk and shuddered, and saw again—
(Ah, woe is me! Was it for thee,
Thou gentle maid! such sights to see?)

Again she saw that bosom old,
Again she felt that bosom cold,
And drew in her breath with a hissing sound:
Whereat the Knight turned wildly round, 460
And nothing saw but his own sweet maid
With eyes upraised, as one that prayed.

The touch, the sight, had passed away,
And in its stead that vision blest,
Which comforted her after-rest
While in the lady's arms she lay,
Had put a rapture in her breast,
And on her lips and o'er her eyes
Spread smiles like light!
                        With new surprise,
"What ails then my belovèd child?" 470

Samuel Taylor Coleridge 727

The Baron said—His daughter mild
Made answer, "All will yet be well!"
I ween, she had no power to tell
Aught else: so mighty was the spell.

Yet he, who saw this Geraldine,
Had deemed her sure a thing divine.
Such sorrow with such grace she blended,
As if she feared she had offended
Sweet Christabel, that gentle maid!
480 And with such lowly tones she prayed,
She might be sent without delay
Home to her father's mansion.

                     "Nay!
Nay, by my soul!" said Leoline.
"Ho! Bracy, the bard, the charge be thine!
Go thou, with music sweet and loud,
And take two steeds with trappings proud,
And take the youth whom thou lov'st best
To bear thy harp, and learn thy song,
And clothe you both in solemn vest,
490 And over the mountains haste along,
Lest wandering folk, that are abroad,
Detain you on the valley road.
And when he has crossed the Irthing flood,
My merry bard! he hastes, he hastes
Up Knorren Moor, through Halegarth Wood,
And reaches soon that castle good
Which stands and threatens Scotland's wastes.

"Bard Bracy! bard Bracy! your horses are fleet
Ye must ride up the hall, your music so sweet
500 More loud than your horses' echoing feet!
And loud and loud to Lord Roland call,
Thy daughter is safe in Langdale hall!
Thy beautiful daughter is safe and free—
Sir Leoline greets thee thus through me.
He bids thee come without delay
With all thy numerous array;
And take thy lovely daughter home:
And he will meet thee on the way
With all his numerous array
510 White with their panting palfreys' foam:
And by mine honor! I will say,
That I repent me of the day
When I spake words of fierce disdain
To Roland de Vaux of Tryermaine!—
For since that evil hour hath flown,
Many a summer's sun hath shone;
Yet ne'er found I a friend again
Like Roland de Vaux of Tryermaine."

The lady fell, and clasped his knees,
520 Her face upraised, her eyes o'erflowing;

And Bracy replied, with faltering voice,
His gracious hail on all bestowing!—
"Thy words, thou sire of Christabel,
Are sweeter than my harp can tell;
Yet might I gain a boon of thee,
This day my journey should not be,
So strange a dream hath come to me;
That I had vowed with music loud
To clear yon wood from thing unblest,
Warned by a vision in my rest!   530
For in my sleep I saw that dove,
That gentle bird, whom thou dost love,
And call'st by thy own daughter's name—
Sir Leoline! I saw the same
Fluttering, and uttering fearful moan,
Among the green herbs in the forest alone.
Which when I saw and when I heard,
I wondered what might ail the bird
For nothing near it could I see,
Save the grass and green herbs underneath the old tree. 540

"And in my dream methought I went
To search out what might there be found;
And what the sweet bird's trouble meant,
That thus lay fluttering on the ground.
I went and peered, and could descry
No cause for her distressful cry;
But yet for her dear lady's sake
I stooped, methought, the dove to take,
When lo! I saw a bright green snake
Coiled around its wings and neck.   550
Green as the herbs on which it couched,
Close by the dove's its head it crouched;
And with the dove it heaves and stirs,
Swelling its neck as she swelled hers!
I woke; it was the midnight hour,
The clock was echoing in the tower;
But though my slumber was gone by,
This dream it would not pass away—
It seems to live upon my eye!
And thence I vowed this self-same day,   560
With music strong and saintly song
To wander through the forest bare,
Lest aught unholy loiter there."

Thus Bracy said: the Baron, the while
Half-listening heard him with a smile;
Then turned to Lady Geraldine,
His eyes made up of wonder and love;
And said in courtly accents fine,
"Sweet maid, Lord Roland's beauteous dove,
With arms more strong than harp or song,   570
Thy sire and I will crush the snake!"
He kissed her forehead as he spake,
And Geraldine, in maiden wise,

656. **A little child, etc.** These lines have little connection with the rest of the poem, and it is not likely that they were meant originally to be a part of it. They were sent to Southey in a letter dated May 6, 1801. They do not occur in any of the three extant manuscripts of the poem.

Casting down her large bright eyes,
With blushing cheek and courtesy fine
She turned her from Sir Leoline;
Softly gathering up her train,
That o'er her right arm fell again;
And folded her arms across her chest,
580 And couched her head upon her breast,
And looked askance at Christabel—
Jesu Maria, shield her well!

A snake's small eye blinks dull and shy,
And the lady's eyes they shrunk in her head,
Each shrunk up to a serpent's eye,
And with somewhat of malice, and more of dread,
At Christabel she looked askance!—
One moment—and the sight was fled!
But Christabel in dizzy trance
590 Stumbling on the unsteady ground
Shuddered aloud, with a hissing sound;
And Geraldine again turned round,
And like a thing that sought relief,
Full of wonder and full of grief,
She rolled her large bright eyes divine
Wildly on Sir Leoline.

The maid, alas! her thoughts are gone,
She nothing sees—no sight but one!
The maid, devoid of guile and sin,
600 I know not how, in fearful wise
So deeply had she drunken in
That look, those shrunken serpent eyes,
That all her features were resigned
To this sole image in her mind;
And passively did imitate
That look of dull and treacherous hate!
And thus she stood, in dizzy trance,
Still picturing that look askance
With forced unconscious sympathy
610 Full before her father's view—
As far as such a look could be
In eyes so innocent and blue!

And when the trance was o'er, the maid
Paused awhile, and inly prayed:
Then falling at the Baron's feet,
"By my mother's soul do I entreat
That thou this woman send away!"
She said: and more she could not say:
For what she knew she could not tell,
620 O'ermastered by the mighty spell.

Why is thy cheek so wan and wild,
Sir Leoline? Thy only child
Lies at thy feet, thy joy, thy pride,
So fair, so innocent, so mild;
The same, for whom thy lady died!
O, by the pangs of her dear mother

Think thou no evil of thy child!
For her, and thee, and for no other,
She prayed the moment ere she died:
Prayed that the babe for whom she died,   630
Might prove her dear lord's joy and pride!
That prayer her deadly pangs beguiled,
     Sir Leoline!
And wouldst thou wrong thy only child,
     Her child and thine?

Within the Baron's heart and brain
If thoughts, like these, had any share,
They only swelled his rage and pain,
And did but work confusion there.
His heart was cleft with pain and rage,   640
His cheeks they quivered, his eyes were wild,
Dishonored thus in his old age;
Dishonored by his only child,
And all his hospitality
To the insulted daughter of his friend
By more than woman's jealousy
Brought thus to a disgraceful end—
He rolled his eye with stern regard
Upon the gentle minstrel bard,
And said in tones abrupt, austere—   650
"Why, Bracy! dost thou loiter here?
I bade thee hence!" The bard obeyed;
And turning from his own sweet maid,
The aged knight, Sir Leoline,
Led forth the lady Geraldine!

THE CONCLUSION TO PART 2

A little child, a limber elf,
Singing, dancing to itself,
A fairy thing with red round cheeks,
That always finds, and never seeks,
Makes such a vision to the sight   660
As fills a father's eyes with light;
And pleasures flow in so thick and fast
Upon his heart, that he at last
Must needs express his love's excess
With words of unmeant bitterness.
Perhaps 'tis pretty to force together
Thoughts so all unlike each other;
To mutter and mock a broken charm,
To dally with wrong that does no harm.
Perhaps 'tis tender too and pretty   670
At each wild word to feel within
A sweet recoil of love and pity.
And what, if in a world of sin
(O sorrow and shame should this be true!)
Such giddiness of heart and brain
Comes seldom save from rage and pain,
So talks as it's most used to do.
(1797-1800; 1816)

According to Coleridge's friend Gilman, the outline of the rest of the Christabel story is this: "The following relation was to have occupied a third and fourth canto, and to have closed the tale. Over the mountains, the Bard, as directed by Sir Leoline, hastes with his disciple, but in consequence of one of those inundations supposed to be common to this country, the spot only where the castle once stood is discovered—the edifice itself being washed away. He determines to return. Geraldine, being acquainted with all that is passing, like the weird sisters in Macbeth, vanishes. Reappearing, however, she awaits the return of the Bard, exciting in the meantime, by her wily arts, all the anger she could rouse in the Baron's breast, as well as that jealousy of which he is described to have been susceptible. The old Bard and the youth at length arrive, and therefore she can no longer personate the character of Geraldine, the daughter of Lord Roland de Vaux, but changes her appearance to that of the accepted though absent lover of Christabel. Now ensues a courtship most distressing to Christabel, who feels, she knows not why, great disgust for her once favored knight. This coldness is very painful to the Baron, who has no more conception than herself of the supernatural transformation. She at last yields to her father's entreaties, and consents to approach the altar with the hated suitor. The real lover, returning, enters at this moment, and produces the ring which she had once given him in sign of her betrothment. Thus defeated, the supernatural being Geraldine disappears. As predicted, the castle bell tolls, the mother's voice is heard, and, to the exceeding great joy of the parties, the rightful marriage takes place, after which follows a reconciliation and explanation between the father and daughter."

KUBLA KHAN; OR, A VISION IN A DREAM

Kubla Khan, that most notable fragment, which breathes in every word and line the spirit of adventure, romance, and glamorous escape from reality, bore in its first printing (1816) a rather lengthy preface, of which the following is perhaps the most significant part:

"In the summer of the year 1797, the author, then in ill health, had retired to a lonely farmhouse between Porlock and Lynton, on the Exmoor confines of Somerset and Devonshire. In consequence of a slight indisposition, an anodyne had been prescribed, from the effects of which he fell asleep in his chair at the moment he was reading the following sentence, or words of the same substance, in Purchas's Pilgrimage: 'Here the Khan Kubla commanded a palace to be built, and a stately garden thereunto. And thus ten miles of fertile ground were inclosed with a wall.' The author continued for about three hours in a profound sleep, at least of the external senses, during which time he has the most vivid confidence that he could not have composed less than from two to three hundred lines, if that indeed can be called composition in which all the images rose up before him as things, with a parallel production of the correspondent expressions, without any sensation or consciousness of effort. On awaking he appeared to himself to have a distinct recollection of the whole, and taking his pen, ink, and paper, instantly and eagerly wrote down the lines that are here preserved. At this moment he was unfortunately called out by a person on business from Porlock, and detained by him above an hour, and on his return to his room, found, to his no small surprise and mortification, that though he still retained some vague and dim recollection of the general purport of the vision, yet, with the exception of some eight or ten scattered lines and images, all the rest had passed away like the images on the surface of a stream into which a stone had been cast, but alas! without the after restoration of the latter!" Coleridge's colorful account is now believed to be greatly exaggerated.

In Xanadu did Kubla Khan
A stately pleasure-dome decree:
Where Alph, the sacred river, ran
Through caverns measureless to man
   Down to a sunless sea.
So twice five miles of fertile ground
With walls and towers were girdled round:
And here were gardens bright with sinuous rills,
Where blossomed many an incense-bearing tree;
And here were forests ancient as the hills,   10
Enfolding sunny spots of greenery.
But oh! that deep romantic chasm which slanted
Down the green hill athwart a cedarn cover!
A savage place! as holy and enchanted
As e'er beneath a waning moon was haunted
By woman wailing for her demon-lover!
And from this chasm, with ceaseless turmoil seething,
As if this earth in fast thick pants were breathing,
A mighty fountain momently was forced;
Amid whose swift half-intermitted burst   20
Huge fragments vaulted like rebounding hail,
Or chaffy grain beneath the thresher's flail:
And 'mid these dancing rocks at once and ever
It flung up momently the sacred river.
Five miles meandering with a mazy motion
Through wood and dale the sacred river ran,
Then reached the caverns measureless to man,

Kubla Khan. 1. **Xanadu,** a region in Tartary. **Kubla Khan,** Cham or Emperor Kubla. He founded the Mogul dynasty in China in the thirteenth century. 14. **savage . . . lover.** These are three of the lines referred to by Kipling in his *Wireless:* "Remember that in all the millions permitted there are no more than five—five little lines—of which one can say, 'These are the magic. These are the vision. The rest is only poetry.'' The other two lines are in Keats' *Ode to a Nightingale,* p. 790, ll. 69-70. **Mount Abora,** a mountain of

And sank in tumult to a lifeless ocean:
And 'mid this tumult Kubla heard from far
30 Ancestral voices prophesying war!

The shadow of the dome of pleasure
Floated midway on the waves;
Where was heard the mingled measure
From the fountain and the caves.
It was a miracle of rare device,
A sunny pleasure-dome with caves of ice!
A damsel with a dulcimer
In a vision once I saw:
It was an Abyssinian maid,
40 And on her dulcimer she played,
Singing of Mount Abora.
Could I revive within me,
Her symphony and song,
To such a deep delight 'twould win me,
That with music loud and long,
I would build that dome in air,
That sunny dome! those caves of ice!
And all who heard should see them there,
And all should cry, Beware! Beware!
50 His flashing eyes, his floating hair!
Weave a circle round him thrice,
And close your eyes with holy dread,
For he on honey-dew hath fed,
And drunk the milk of Paradise.
(1797; 1816)

from BIOGRAPHIA LITERARIA

CHAPTER 14

During the first year that Mr. Wordsworth and I
were neighbors, our conversations turned frequently on
the two cardinal points of poetry: the power of exciting
the sympathy of the reader by a faithful adherence to
the truth of nature, and the power of giving the
interest of novelty by the modifying colors of imagination. The sudden charm, which accidents of light
and shade, which moonlight or sunset, diffused over
a known and familiar landscape, appeared to repre-
10 sent the practicability of combining both. These are
the poetry of nature. The thought suggested itself (to
which of us I do not recollect) that a series of poems
might be composed of two sorts. In the one, the
incidents and agents were to be, in part at least, supernatural; and the excellence aimed at was to consist
in the interesting of the affections by the dramatic
truth of such emotions as would naturally accompany such situations, supposing them real. And real
in this sense they have been to every human being

who, from whatever source of delusion, has at any 20
time believed himself under supernatural agency.
For the second class, subjects were to be chosen
from ordinary life; the characters and incidents were
to be such as will be found in every village and its
vicinity where there is a meditative and feeling mind
to seek after them or to notice them when they present
themselves.

In this idea originated the plan of the *Lyrical Ballads*, in which it was agreed that my endeavors should
be directed to persons and characters supernatural, or 30
at least romantic; yet so as to transfer from our inward
nature a human interest and a semblance of truth
sufficient to procure for these shadows of imagination
that willing suspension of disbelief for the moment
which constitutes poetic faith. Mr. Wordsworth, on
the other hand, was to propose to himself as his object,
to give the charm of novelty to things of every day,
and to excite a feeling analogous to the supernatural
by awakening the mind's attention from the lethargy
of custom and directing it to the loveliness and the 40
wonders of the world before us; an inexhaustible
treasure, but for which, in consequence of the film
of familiarity and selfish solicitude, we have eyes,
yet see not, ears that hear not, and hearts that neither
feel nor understand.

With this view I wrote the *Ancient Mariner*, and
was preparing, among other poems, the *Dark Ladie*
and the *Christabel*, in which I should have more
nearly realized my ideal than I had done in my first
attempt. But Mr. Wordsworth's industry had proved 50
so much more successful, and the number of his
poems so much greater that my compositions, instead of forming a balance, appeared rather an
interpolation of heterogeneous matter. Mr. Wordsworth added two or three poems written in his own
character, in the impassioned, lofty, and sustained
diction which is characteristic of his genius. In this
form the *Lyrical Ballads* were published; and were
presented by him, as an experiment, whether subjects, which from their nature rejected the usual 60
ornaments and extracolloquial style of poems in general, might not be so managed in the language of
ordinary life as to produce the pleasurable interest
which it is the peculiar business of poetry to impart. To the second edition he added a preface of
considerable length; in which, notwithstanding some
passages of apparently a contrary import, he was
understood to contend for the extension of this style
to poetry of all kinds, and to reject as vicious and
indefensible all phrases and forms of style that were 70
not included in what he (unfortunately, I think,
adopting an equivocal expression) called the language of real life. From this preface prefixed to poems

Coleridge's imagination; or, possibly, Mount Amara, the seat of a
terrestrial paradise in Abyssinia. The words suggest romantic remoteness.
Biographia Literaria. Cf. Wordsworth's *Preface to Lyrical Ballads*
(p. 703). 1. **first year,** 1797-1798. 43. **eyes . . . understand,** phrases

used many times in the Bible. See Psalms 115:5-7; Isaiah 6:9-10;
Matthew 13:13.

in which it was impossible to deny the presence of original genius, however mistaken its direction might be deemed, arose the whole long-continued controversy. For from the conjunction of perceived power with supposed heresy I explain the inveteracy and in some instances, I grieve to say, the acrimonious passions, with which the controversy has been conducted by the assailants.

Had Mr. Wordsworth's poems been the silly, the childish things which they were for a long time described as being; had they been really distinguished from the compositions of other poets merely by meanness of language and inanity of thought; had they indeed contained nothing more than what is found in the parodies and pretended imitations of them; they must have sunk at once, a dead weight, into the slough of oblivion, and have dragged the preface along with them. But year after year increased the number of Mr. Wordsworth's admirers. They were found, too, not in the lower classes of the reading public, but chiefly among young men of strong sensibility and meditative minds; and their admiration (inflamed perhaps in some degree by opposition) was distinguished by its intensity, I might almost say, by its religious fervor. These facts and the intellectual energy of the author, which was more or less consciously felt where it was outwardly and even boisterously denied, meeting with sentiments of aversion to his opinions, and of alarm at their consequences, produced an eddy of criticism, which would of itself have borne up the poems by the violence with which it whirled them round and round. With many parts of this preface, in the sense attributed to them, and which the words undoubtedly seem to authorize, I never concurred; but, on the contrary, objected to them as erroneous in principle and as contradictory (in appearance at least) both to other parts of the same preface and to the author's own practice in the greater number of the poems themselves. Mr. Wordsworth, in his recent collection, has, I find, degraded this prefatory disquisition to the end of his second volume, to be read or not at the reader's choice. But he has not, as far as I can discover, announced any change in his poetic creed. At all events, considering it as the source of a controversy, in which I have been honored more than I deserve by the frequent conjunction of my name with his, I think it expedient to declare, once for all, in what points I coincide with his opinions and in what points I altogether differ. But in order to render myself intelligible, I must previously, in as few words as possible, explain my ideas, first, of a poem; and secondly, of poetry itself, in kind and in essence.

The office of philosophical disquisition consists in just distinction; while it is the privilege of the philosopher to preserve himself constantly aware that distinction is not division. In order to obtain adequate notions of any truth, we must intellectually separate its distinguishable parts; and this is the technical process of philosophy. But having so done, we must then restore them in our conceptions to the unity in which they actually co-exist; and this is the result of philosophy. A poem contains the same elements as a prose composition; the difference, therefore, must consist in a different combination of them, in consequence of a different object proposed. According to the difference of the object will be the difference of the combination. It is possible that the object may be merely to facilitate the recollection of any given facts or observations by artificial arrangement; and the composition will be a poem, merely because it is distinguished from prose by meter, or by rime, or by both conjointly. In this, the lowest sense, a man might attribute the name of a poem to the well-known enumeration of the days in the several months:

Thirty days hath September,
April, June, and November, etc.

and others of the same class and purpose. And as a particular pleasure is found in anticipating the recurrence of sound and quantities, all compositions that have this charm superadded, whatever be their contents, *may* be entitled poems.

So much for the superficial form. A difference of object and contents supplies an additional ground of distinction. The immediate purpose may be the communication of truths: either of truth absolute and demonstrable, as in works of science; or of facts experienced and recorded, as in history. Pleasure, and that of the highest and most permanent kind, may result from the attainment of the end; but it is not itself the immediate end. In other works the communication of pleasure may be the immediate purpose; and though truth, either moral or intellectual, ought to be the ultimate end, yet this will distinguish the character of the author, not the class to which the work belongs. Blest indeed is that state of society, in which the immediate purpose would be baffled by the perversion of the proper ultimate end; in which no charm of diction or imagery could exempt the Bathyllus even of an Anacreon, or the Alexis of Virgil, from disgust and aversion!

But the communication of pleasure may be the immediate object of a work not metrically composed;

3. **whole . . . controversy,** that over Wordsworth's theory and practice of poetic art. 101. **Bathyllus,** a youth of Samos beloved by Anacreon, Greek lyric poet of the sixth century B.C.; *Ode* 17 is addressed to him. 102. **Alexis,** a youth beloved by the shepherd Corydon in the second *Eclogue* of Vergil (70-19 B.C.), famous Roman epic, didactic, and idyllic poet. 160. **Praecipitandus, etc.** The free spirit ought to be urged onward (from *Satyricon*, by Petronius Arbiter, a Roman satirist of the first century; he directed the imperial pleasures at the court of Nero). 167. **Plato,** celebrated Greek philosopher (427?-347 B.C.). **Bishop Taylor,** Jeremy Taylor (1613-1667), an English bishop and

and that object may have been in a high degree attained, as in novels and romances. Would then the mere superaddition of meter, with or without rime, entitle these to the name of poems? The answer is, that nothing can permanently please which does not contain in itself the reason why it is so, and not otherwise. If meter be superadded, all other parts must be made consonant with it. They must be such as to justify the perpetual and distinct attention to each part which an exact correspondent recurrence of accent and sound are calculated to excite. The final definition then, so deduced, may be thus worded. A poem is that species of composition which is opposed to works of science by proposing for its immediate object pleasure, not truth; and from all other species (having this object in common with it) it is discriminated by proposing to itself such delight from the whole as is compatible with a distinct gratification from each component part.

Controversy is not seldom excited in consequence of the disputants' attaching each a different meaning to the same word; and in few instances has this been more striking than in disputes concerning the present subject. If a man chooses to call every composition a poem which is rime, or measure, or both, I must leave his opinion uncontroverted. The distinction is at least competent to characterize the writer's intention. If it were subjoined, that the whole is likewise entertaining or affecting as a tale, or as a series of interesting reflections, I of course admit this as another fit ingredient of a poem and an additional merit. But if the definition sought for be that of a legitimate poem, I answer, it must be one the parts of which mutually support and explain each other; all in their proportion harmonizing with and supporting the purpose and known influences of metrical arrangement. The philosophic critics of all ages coincide with the ultimate judgment of all countries in equally denying the praises of a just poem, on the one hand, to a series of striking lines or distichs, each of which, absorbing the whole attention of the reader to itself, disjoins it from its context and makes it a separate whole, instead of a harmonizing part; and on the other hand, to an unsustained composition from which the reader collects rapidly the general result unattracted by the component parts. The reader should be carried forward, not merely or chiefly by the mechanical impulse of curiosity, or by a restless desire to arrive at the final solution; but by the pleasurable activity of mind excited by the attractions of the journey itself. Like the motion of a serpent, which the Egyptians made the emblem of intellectual power; or like the path of sound through the air, at every step he pauses and half recedes, and from the retrogressive movement collects the force which again carries him onward. *Praecipitandus est liber spiritus*, says Petronius Arbiter most happily. The epithet, *liber*, here balances the preceding verb; and it is not easy to conceive more meaning condensed in fewer words.

But if this should be admitted as a satisfactory character of a poem, we have still to seek for a definition of poetry. The writings of Plato and Bishop Taylor, and the *Theoria Sacra* of Burnet furnish undeniable proofs that poetry of the highest kind may exist without meter, and even without the contradistinguishing objects of a poem. The first chapter of *Isaiah* (indeed a very large proportion of the whole book) is poetry in the most emphatic sense; yet it would be not less irrational than strange to assert that pleasure, and not truth, was the immediate object of the prophet. In short, whatever specific import we attach to the word poetry, there will be found involved in it, as a necessary consequence, that a poem of any length neither can be, nor ought to be, all poetry. Yet if a harmonious whole is to be produced, the remaining parts must be preserved in keeping with the poetry; and this can be not otherwise effected than by such a studied selection and artificial arrangement as will partake of one, though not a peculiar property of poetry. And this again can be no other than the property of exciting a more continuous and equal attention than the language of prose aims at, whether colloquial or written.

My own conclusions of the nature of poetry, in the strictest use of the word, have been in part anticipated in the preceding disquisition on the fancy and imagination. What is poetry? is so nearly the same question with, what is a poet? that the answer to the one is involved in the solution of the other. For it is a distinction resulting from the poetic genius itself, which sustains and modifies the images, thoughts, and emotions of the poet's own mind. The poet, described in ideal perfection, brings the whole soul of man into activity, with the subordination of its faculties to each other, according to their relative worth and dignity. He diffuses a tone and spirit of unity that blends and (as it were) fuses each into each, by that synthetic and magical power to which we have exclusively appropriated the name of imagination. This power, first put in action by the will and understanding, and retained under their irremissive, though gentle and unnoticed, control (*laxis effertur habenis*) reveals itself in the balance or reconciliation of opposite or discordant qualities: of sameness, with difference; of the general, with the concrete; the

theological writer. **168. Burnet,** Thomas Burnet (1635?–1715), an English bishop, author of works notable for their vivid imagery and purity of style. In his *Sacred Theory of the Earth* he gives a fanciful hypothesis about the formation of the earth. **179. poem . . . poetry.** Cf. Poe's *Poetic Principle*, which sets forth the doctrine that there is no such thing as a long poem. **191. preceding disquisition,** Chapter 4 of *Biographia Literaria.* **207. laxis, etc.,** is borne along with loose reins.

idea, with the image; the individual, with the representative; the sense of novelty and freshness, with old and familiar objects; a more than usual state of emotion, with more than usual order; judgment ever awake and steady self-possession with enthusiasm and feeling profound or vehement; and while it blends and harmonizes the natural and the artificial, still subordinates art to nature; the manner to the matter; and our admiration of the poet to our sym-
10 pathy with the poetry. "Doubtless," as Sir John Davies observes of the soul (and his words may with slight alteration be applied, and even more appropriately, to the poetic imagination)—

Doubtless this could not be, but that she turns
Bodies to spirit by sublimation strange,
As fire converts to fire, the things it burns,
As we our food into our nature change.

From their gross matter she abstracts their forms,
And draws a kind of quintessence from things;
20 Which to her proper nature she transforms
To bear them light on her celestial wings.

Thus does she, when from individual states
She doth abstract the universal kinds;
Which then re-clothed in divers names and fates
Steal access through our senses to our minds.

Finally, good sense is the body of poetic genius, fancy its drapery, motion its life, and imagination the soul that is everywhere, and in each; and forms all into one graceful and intelligent whole.
(1815-16; 1817)

CHARACTERISTICS OF SHAKESPEARE'S DRAMAS

30   In lectures of which amusement forms a large part of the object, there are some peculiar difficulties. The architect places his foundation out of sight, and the musician tunes his instrument before he makes his appearance; but the lecturer has to try his chords in the presence of the assembly, an operation not likely, indeed, to produce much pleasure, but yet indispensably necessary to a right understanding of the subject to be developed.

   Poetry in essence is as familiar to barbarous as to
40 civilized nations. The Laplander and the savage Indian are cheered by it as well as the inhabitants of London and Paris; its spirit takes up and incorporates surrounding materials, as a plant clothes itself with soil and climate, whilst it exhibits the working

of a vital principle within, independent of all accidental circumstances. And to judge with fairness of an author's works, we ought to distinguish what is inward and essential from what is outward and circumstantial. It is essential to poetry that it be simple, and appeal to the elements and primary laws of our 50 nature; that it be sensuous, and by its imagery elicit truth at a flash; that it be impassioned, and be able to move our feelings and awaken our affections. In comparing different poets with each other, we should inquire which have brought into the fullest play our imagination and our reason, or have created the greatest excitement and produced the completest harmony. If we consider great exquisiteness of language and sweetness of meter alone, it is impossible to deny to Pope the character of a delightful writer; but 60 whether he be a poet must depend upon our definition of the word; and, doubtless, if everything that pleases be poetry, Pope's satires and epistles must be poetry. This I must say, that poetry, as distinguished from other modes of composition, does not rest in meter, and that it is not poetry if it make no appeal to our passions or our imagination. One character belongs to all true poets, that they write from a principle within, not originating in anything without; and that the true poet's work in its form, 70 its shapings, and its modifications, is distinguished from all other works that assume to belong to the class of poetry, as a natural from an artificial flower, or as the mimic garden of a child from an enameled meadow. In the former the flowers are broken from their stems and stuck into the ground; they are beautiful to the eye and fragrant to the sense, but their colors soon fade, and their odor is transient as the smile of the planter; while the meadow may be visited again and again with renewed delight; its beauty is 80 innate in the soil, and its bloom is of the freshness of nature.

   The next ground of critical judgment, and point of comparison, will be as to how far a given poet has been influenced by accidental circumstances. As a living poet must surely write, not for the ages past, but for that in which he lives, and those which are to follow, it is, on the one hand, natural that he should not violate, and on the other,. necessary that he should not depend on, the mere manners and 90 modes of his day. See how little does Shakespeare leave us to regret that he was born in his particular age! The great era in modern times was what is called the Restoration of Letters; the ages preceding it are called the dark ages; but it would be more wise, perhaps, to call them the ages in which we were in the dark. It is usually overlooked that the supposed

10. **Sir John Davies,** an English statesman and poet (1569-1626). The stanzas are quoted with slight alterations from his poem *Of the Soul of Man,* 4, 45-56. 20. **proper,** own.
Characteristics of Shakespeare's Dramas. Cf. the criticism of Shakespeare by De Quincy, p. 814. 49. **simple . . . impassioned.** Milton defined poetry as "simple, sensuous, passionate." See other definitions,

p. 704, l. 44 and note. 63. **Pope's . . . epistles.** See p. 556. 74. **enameled,** variegated, adorned as with flowers. 105. **enthusiasm for knowledge.** See p. 161. 107. **Erasmus,** Dutch classical scholar (1466?-1536). See p. 161. 116. **Dante,** the most famous of Italian poets (1265-1321). 117. **Virgil,** celebrated Roman epic, didactic, and idyllic poet (70-19 B.C.). **Ariosto,** a famous Italian poet (1474-1533).

dark period was not universal, but partial and successive, or alternate; that the dark age of England was not the dark age of Italy, but that one country was in its light and vigor, whilst another was in its gloom and bondage. But no sooner had the Reformation sounded through Europe like the blast of an archangel's trumpet, than from king to peasant there arose an enthusiasm for knowledge; the discovery of a manuscript became the subject of an embassy; Erasmus read by moonlight, because he could not afford a torch, and begged a penny, not for the love of charity, but for the love of learning. The three great points of attention were religion, morals, and taste; men of genius as well as men of learning, who in this age need to be so widely distinguished, then alike became copyists of the ancients; and this, indeed, was the only way by which the taste of mankind could be improved, or their understandings informed. Whilst Dante imagined himself a humble follower of Virgil, and Ariosto of Homer, they were both unconscious of that greater power working within them, which in many points carried them beyond their supposed originals. All great discoveries bear the stamp of the age in which they are made; hence we perceive the effects of the purer religion of the moderns, visible for the most part in their lives; and in reading their works we should not content ourselves with the mere narratives of events long since passed, but should learn to apply their maxims and conduct to ourselves.

Having intimated that times and manners lend their form and pressure to genius, let me once more draw a slight parallel between the ancient and modern stage, the stages of Greece and of England. The Greeks were polytheists; their religion was local; almost the only object of their knowledge, art, and taste was their gods; and, accordingly, their productions were, if the expression may be allowed, statuesque, whilst those of the moderns are picturesque. The Greeks reared a structure which in its parts, and as a whole, filled the mind with the calm and elevated impression of perfect beauty, and symmetrical proportions. The moderns also produced a whole, a more striking whole; but it was by blending materials and fusing the parts together. And as the Pantheon is to York Minster or Westminster Abbey, so is Sophocles compared with Shakespeare; in the one a completeness, a satisfaction, an excellence, on which the mind rests with complacency; in the other a multitude of interlaced materials, great and little, magnificent and mean, accompanied, indeed, with the sense of a falling short of perfection, and yet, at the same time, so promising of our social and individual progression that we would not, if we could, exchange it for that repose of the mind which swells on the forms of symmetry in the acquiescent admiration of grace. This general characteristic of the ancient and modern drama might be illustrated by a parallel of the ancient and modern music, the one consisting of melody arising from a succession only of pleasing sounds, the modern embracing harmony also, the result of combination and the effect of a whole.

I have said, and I say it again, that great as was the genius of Shakespeare, his judgment was at least equal to it. Of this anyone will be convinced, who attentively considers those points in which the dramas of Greece and England differ, from the dissimilitude of circumstances by which each was modified and influenced. The Greek stage had its origin in the ceremonies of a sacrifice, such as of the goat to Bacchus, whom we most erroneously regard as merely the jolly god of wine; for among the ancients he was venerable, as the symbol of that power which acts without our consciousness in the vital energies of nature—the *vinum mundi*—as Apollo was that of the conscious agency of our intellectual being. The heroes of old under the influences of this Bacchic enthusiasm performed more than human actions; hence tales of the favorite champions soon passed into dialogue. On the Greek stage the chorus was always before the audience; the curtain was never dropped, as we should say; and change of place being therefore, in general, impossible, the absurd notion of condemning it merely as improbable in itself was never entertained by anyone. If we can believe ourselves at Thebes in one act, we may believe ourselves at Athens in the next. If a story lasts twenty-four hours or twenty-four years, it is equally improbable. There seems to be no just boundary but what the feelings prescribe. But on the Greek stage where the same persons were perpetually before the audience, great judgment was necessary in venturing on any such change. The poets never, therefore, attempted to impose on the senses by bringing places to men, but they did bring men to places, as in the well known instance in the *Eumenides*, where, during an evident retirement of the chorus from the orchestra, the scene is changed to Athens, and Orestes is first introduced in the temple of Minerva, and the chorus of Furies come in afterwards in pursuit of him.

In the Greek drama there were no formal divisions into scenes and acts; there were no means, therefore, of allowing for the necessary lapse of time between one part of the dialogue and another, and unity of time in a strict sense was, of course, im-

---

Homer, ancient Greek poet, author of the *Iliad* and the *Odyssey*. 142. Pantheon, a circular temple at Rome, built 27 B.C. 144. Sophocles, one of the great tragic dramatists of Greece (fifth century B.C.). 168. goat . . . Bacchus. The goat was a common victim of sacrifice in the wild orgies of the devotees of Bacchus, god of wine and of luxuriant fertility. 173. *vinum mundi*, wine of the world. Apollo, god of poetry and music. 194. *Eumenides*, a tragedy by Aeschylus, great Greek dramatist (fifth century B.C.); the incident mentioned is in Act V, 230–239. The Eumenides are the Furies. 196. Orestes, a son of the Greek king Agamemnon and Clytemnestra; he slew his mother and her lover Aegisthus in revenge for their murder of Agamemnon. 197. Minerva, goddess of wisdom.

possible. To overcome that difficulty of accounting for time, which is effected on the modern stage by dropping a curtain, the judgment and great genius of the ancients supplied music and measured motion, and with the lyric ode filled up the vacuity. In the story of the *Agamemnon* of Aeschylus, the capture of Troy is supposed to be announced by a fire lighted on the Asiatic shore and the transmission of the signal by successive beacons to Mycenae. The signal is first seen at the 21st line, and the herald from Troy itself enters at the 486th, and Agamemnon himself at the 783rd line. But the practical absurdity of this was not felt by the audience, who, in imagination stretched the minutes into hours, while they listened to the lofty narrative odes of the chorus which almost entirely filled up the interspace. Another fact deserves attention here, namely, that regularly on the Greek stage a drama, or acted story, consisted in reality of three dramas, called together a trilogy, and performed consecutively in the course of one day. Now you may conceive a tragedy of Shakespeare's as a trilogy connected in one single representation. Divide *Lear* into three parts, and each would be a play with the ancients; or take the three Aeschylean dramas of *Agamemnon*, and divide them into, or call them, as many acts, and they together would be one play. The first act would comprise the usurpation of Aegisthus and the murder of Agamemnon; the second, the revenge of Orestes and the murder of his mother; and the third, the penance and absolution of Orestes;—occupying a period of twenty-two years.

The stage in Shakespeare's time was a naked room with a blanket for a curtain; but he made it a field for monarchs. That law of unity, which has its foundations, not in the factitious necessity of custom, but in nature itself, the unity of feeling, is everywhere and at all times observed by Shakespeare in his plays. Read *Romeo and Juliet*: all is youth and spring; youth with its follies, its virtues, its precipitancies; spring with its odors, its flowers, and its transciency. It is one and the same feeling that commences, goes through, and ends the play. The old men, the Capulets and the Montagues, are not common old men; they have an eagerness, a heartiness, a vehemence, the effect of spring; with Romeo, his change of passion, his sudden marriage, and his rash death, are all the effects of youth; whilst in Juliet, love has all that is tender and melancholy in the nightingale, all that is voluptuous in the rose, with whatever is sweet in the freshness of spring; but it ends with a long deep sigh like the last breeze of the Italian evening. This unity of feeling and character pervades every drama of Shakespeare.

It seems to me that his plays are distinguished from those of all other dramatic poets by the following characteristics:

1. Expectation in preference to surprise. It is like the true reading of the passage: "God said, Let there be light, and there was *light*"; not there *was* light. As the feeling with which we startle at a shooting star compared with that of watching the sunrise at the pre-established moment, such and so low is surprise compared with expectation.

2. Signal adherence to the great law of nature, that all opposites tend to attract and temper each other. Passion in Shakespeare generally displays libertinism, but involves morality; and if there are exceptions to this, they are, independently of their intrinsic value, all of them indicative of individual character, and, like the farewell admonitions of a parent, have an end beyond the parental relation. Thus the Countess's beautiful precepts to Bertram, by elevating her character, raise that of Helena her favorite, and soften down the point in her which Shakespeare does not mean us not to see, but to see and to forgive, and at length to justify. And so it is in Polonius, who is the personified memory of wisdom no longer actually possessed. This admirable character is always misrepresented on the stage. Shakespeare never intended to exhibit him as a buffoon; for although it was natural that Hamlet (a young man of fire and genius, detesting formality, and disliking Polonius on political grounds, as imagining that he had assisted his uncle in his usurpation) should express himself satirically; yet this must not be taken as exactly the poet's conception of him. In Polonius a certain induration of character had arisen from long habits of business; but take his advice to Laertes, and Ophelia's reverence for his memory, and we shall see that he was meant to be represented as a statesman somewhat past his faculties—his recollections of life all full of wisdom, and showing a knowledge of human nature, whilst what immediately takes place before him and escapes from him is indicative of weakness.

But as in Homer all the deities are in armor, even Venus, so in Shakespeare all the characters are strong. Hence real folly and dullness are made by him the vehicles of wisdom. There is no difficulty for one being a fool to imitate a fool; but to be, remain, and speak like a wise man and a great wit, and yet so as to give a vivid representation of a veritable fool—*hic labor, hoc opus est.* A drunken constable is not uncommon, nor hard to draw; but see and examine what goes to make up a Dogberry.

3. Keeping at all times in the high road of life. Shakespeare has no innocent adulteries, no interesting incests, no virtuous vice; he never renders that amiable which religion and reason alike teach us to detest,

9. **Mycenae,** an ancient city in Greece. 24. **three . . . dramas,** *Agamemnon, Choephorai,* and *Eumenides.* 58. **God . . . light,** quoted from Genesis 1:3. 72. **precepts to Bertram,** in *All's Well That Ends Well,* I, i. 76. **Polonius,** the king's chamberlain and the father of

Ophelia and Laertes in *Hamlet.* 88. **advice to Laertes,** in Act I, iii, 58–81. 96. **Venus,** goddess of love. 101. **hic . . . est,** this is the labor, this is the work (Aeneid, 6, 129). 104. **Dogberry,** a stupid constable in *Much Ado About Nothing.* 109. **Beaumont and Fletcher,**

or clothe impurity in the garb of virtue, like Beaumont and Fletcher, the Kotzebues of the day. Shakespeare's fathers are roused by ingratitude, his husbands stung by unfaithfulness; in him, in short, the
affections are wounded in those points in which all
may, nay, must, feel. Let the morality of Shakespeare
be contrasted with that of the writers of his own, or
the succeeding, age, or of those of the present day,
who boast their superiority in this respect. No one
can dispute that the result of such a comparison is
altogether in favor of Shakespeare; even the letters of
women of high rank in his age were often coarser
than his writings. If he occasionally disgusts a
keen sense of delicacy, he never injures the mind;
he neither excites nor flatters passion in order to
degrade the subject of it; he does not use the faulty
thing for a faulty purpose, nor carries on warfare
against virtue by causing wickedness to appear as no
wickedness through the medium of a morbid sympathy with the unfortunate. In Shakespeare vice
never walks as in twilight; nothing is purposely out
of its place; he inverts not the order of nature and
propriety, does not make every magistrate a drunkard or glutton, nor every poor man meek, humane,
and temperate; he has no benevolent butchers, nor
any sentimental rat-catchers.

4. Independence of the dramatic interest on the
plot. The interest in the plot is always in fact on
account of the characters, not *vice versa*, as in almost
all other writers; the plot is a mere canvass and no
more. Hence arises the true justification of the same
stratagem being used in regard to Benedict and
Beatrice, the vanity in each being alike. Take away
from the *Much Ado About Nothing* all that which is
not indispensable to the plot, either as having little
to do with it, or, at best, like Dogberry and his comrades, forced into the service when any other less
ingeniously absurd watchmen and night-constables
would have answered the mere necessities of the action; take away Benedict, Beatrice, Dogberry, and the
reaction of the former on the character of Hero, and
what will remain? In other writers the main agent of
the plot is always the prominent character; in Shakespeare it is so, or is not so, as the character is in
itself calculated, or not calculated, to form the plot.
Don John is the main-spring of the plot of this play;
but he is merely shown and then withdrawn.

5. Independence of the interest on the story as the
groundwork of the plot. Hence Shakespeare never
took the trouble of inventing stories. It was enough
for him to select from those that had been already
invented or recorded such as had one or other, or
both, of two recommendations, namely, suitableness
to his particular purpose, and their being parts of
popular tradition—names of which we had often
heard, and of their fortunes, and as to which all we
wanted was, to see the man himself. So it is just the
man himself, the Lear, the Shylock, the Richard, that
Shakespeare makes us for the first time acquainted
with. Omit the first scene in *Lear*, and yet everything
will remain; so the first and second scenes in *The
Merchant of Venice*. Indeed it is universally true.

6. Interfusion of the lyrical (that which in its very
essence is poetical) not only with the dramatic, as
in the plays of Metastasio, where at the end of the
scenes comes the *aria* as the *exit* speech of the character, but also in and through the dramatic. Songs
in Shakespeare are introduced as songs only, just as
songs are in real life, beautifully as some of them are
characteristic of the person who has sung or called
for them, as Desdemona's "Willow," and Ophelia's
wild snatches, and the sweet carollings in *As You
Like It*. But the whole of the *Midsummer-Night's
Dream* is one continued specimen of the dramatized
lyrical. And observe how exquisitely the dramatic of
Hotspur:

Marry and I'm glad on't with all my heart;
I'd rather be a kitten and cry mew, &c.

melts away into the lyric of Mortimer:

I understand thy looks: that pretty Welsh
Which thou pour'st down from these swelling heavens
I am too perfect in, &c.
                                    1 Henry IV, III, i

7. The characters of the *dramatis personae*, like
those in real life, are to be inferred by the reader;
they are not told to him. And it is well worth remarking that Shakespeare's characters, like those in
real life, are very commonly misunderstood, and almost always understood by different persons in different ways. The causes are the same in either case. If
you take only what the friends of the character say,
you may be deceived, and still more so, if that which
his enemies say; nay, even the character himself sees
through the medium of his character, and not exactly
as he is. Take all together, not omitting a shrewd hint
from the clown, or the fool, and perhaps your impression will be right; and you may know whether you
have in fact discovered the poet's own idea, by all
the speeches receiving light from it, and attesting
its reality by reflecting it.

Lastly, in Shakespeare the heterogeneous is united,
as it is in nature. You must not suppose a pressure
or passion always acting on or in the character.

prominent dramatists contemporary with Shakespeare; they did notable
work in tragicomedy and romance. 110. **Kotzebue**, August Kotzebue
(1761–1819), a prolific German writer of emotional plays for many
years popular in England. 173. **Metastasio**, an Italian lyric dramatist
(1698–1782). 174. *aria*, an elaborate melody sung by a single voice
in operas, cantatas, etc. 179. "Willow," in *Othello*, IV, iii, 41–57, a
song of forsaken love.

Samuel Taylor Coleridge   737

Passion in Shakespeare is that by which the individual is distinguished from others, not that which makes a different kind of him. Shakespeare followed the main march of the human affections. He entered into no analysis of the passions or faiths of men, but assured himself that such and such passions and faiths were grounded in our common nature, and not in the mere accidents of ignorance or disease. This is an important consideration and constitutes our Shakespeare the morning star, the guide and the 10 pioneer, of true philosophy.
(1818; 1836)

Drawings depict the Coleridge cottage at Clevedon (left) and the chamber of Samuel Taylor Coleridge (below). Culver Pictures, Inc.

GEORGE NOEL GORDON, LORD BYRON 1788-1824

Of the important English poets of the Romantic Movement, the one with the greatest international reputation is still Lord Byron, however much his countrymen have deprecated him, and even his countrymen have conceded that he had a more forceful personality than any of his English literary contemporaries. He was born in London, January 22, 1788; his father, "mad Jack Byron," was a rake from a decayed aristocratic family; his mother, an Aberdeen heiress and a woman of most erratic temperament. The father deserted his family while Byron was a mere child; the boy was sent to school in Aberdeen until the age of ten, then to Harrow, and eventually to Cambridge, where he remained from 1805 to 1808.

A moment's glance at Byron's ancestry is sufficient to account for the nervous instability, the rebelliousness, and the maladjustment that Byron showed not only as a schoolboy but as a man. His mother, in whose care he remained until his days at Harrow, was given to temper tantrums and to alternate fits of great tenderness and physical violence toward her son. A congenital lameness, painfully and ineffectively treated by various medical practitioners, rankled in the spirit of a morbidly proud, high-spirited boy. Byron tried to excel in every way; he became a good student, an excellent athlete, and—it must be confessed—a considerable playboy. The picture of Byron as a satyr-like debauchee is perhaps an unfair caricature, but even in his Harrow days we hear of love affairs—some harmless flirtations, some passing infatuations, some distinctly unpuritanical. His mother was upset by her son's wayward habits, and there was something of a break between the two, although Byron was sincerely grief-stricken at her death.

It was during his Cambridge days that Byron's first poems were published, the Hours of Idleness (1807). These were not very promising poems, and they were criticized unfavorably, particularly by the Edinburgh Review, under the editorship of the redoubtable Jeffrey. Byron's retort to the critics, with Jeffrey especially in mind—an inevitable retort, considering Byron's character—was well-considered and highly significant. It was English Bards and Scotch Reviewers (1809), a direct continuation of the tradition of neo-classical satire; it shows Byron's admiration for Pope and Dryden, and it illustrates amply the important satirical side of Byron's nature—one which cannot be ignored at any stage of Byron's career.

After the commotion caused by English Bards and Scotch Reviewers, Byron took the grand tour of the Continent and returned to tell of it in the first two cantos of Childe Harold (1812). He had nursed some political ambitions, but they were joyously cast aside in the sensational reception of Childe Harold, when Byron, to paraphrase himself, awoke and found himself famous. The reasons for the success of Childe Harold are not hard to give—it had great vigor and descriptive power, and it was extremely opportune, for it was a poetical guidebook of the Europe of Byron's own day, seen not through medieval lenses or through the imagination of a recluse but by an active, full-blooded young man with a soul that loved liberty and revolt and adventure. Moreover, there was an interestingly mysterious unhappiness which breathed through the lines, the hero was a melancholy young man with a melodramatic attitude, over whom hung the cloud of the sinister, perhaps of the evil. The romantic appeal of all this to the age was irresistible. In spite of Byron's denials, public opinion then, as now, insisted that the poem was autobiographical, the young poet was badly spoiled by society— by the feminine portion in particular—although he gained the reputation of being "mad, bad, and dangerous to know."

Having found a real outlet for his natural powers, Byron proceeded to follow it diligently. He launched upon a series of narrative poems, tales of adventure with scenes laid for the most part in the Near East or Mediterranean regions. They can be best described as excellent scenario material for an exotic motion picture. The Giaour (1813), The Bride of Abydos (1813), The Corsair (1814), Lara (1814), The Siege of Corinth (1816), Parisina (1816) are "Oriental tales"; each is good narrative poetry, although the vein is worked a trifle thin toward the end. Added to Childe Harold they made Byron distinctly the rage. Appearing in all these poems is what might be called a Byronic heroine as well as a Byronic hero.

Nothing remained in Byron's quest of worldly bliss, it seemed, but a steadying love and an advantageous marriage. Both were apparently forthcoming when, in

January 1815, Byron married Anne Milbanke, a rich, strict, beautiful, but unresponsive heiress. A daughter, Ada, was born to the couple in December; within a month the Byrons had separated. The controversy over the causes of this separation still rages. The explanation by Byron was that they were simply incompatible, as might well be true. A more sinister rumor was that Lady Byron had become aware of an incestuous relationship between Byron and his half sister Augusta Leigh. But the two women apparently continued on friendly terms after the separation of Lord and Lady Byron. Whatever the cause, the British public chose to believe the worst, and Byron, virtually ostracized, "shook the dust of England from his feet" in April 1816, and went to the Continent, never to return.

He traveled through Belgium, thence to Switzerland; the fruit of this journey was the third canto of Childe Harold (p. 745). The poetic drama of Manfred (1817), which was acted occasionally, paints anew the Byronic hero, this time under the spell of an ill-starred love. But Byron's advent in Italy resolved itself into a parade of the poet from one city to another attended by various light ladies. In Venice (1818-1819) he kept a virtual harem. He met Shelley for the second time, was friendly with him, and indulged in a liaison with a relative of Shelley's wife (p. 767). But all this debauchery did not stop a brilliant flow of poetry. When, at Ravenna, he saw the Countess Teresa Guiccioli, the young wife of an old Italian nobleman with revolutionary tendencies, an amicable arrangement was made with the young woman's family; her attachment for Byron was recognized and condoned, and when her family was forced to evacuate one Italian city, Byron moved along with them to the next. In 1819 he moved thus to Ravenna; in 1821 to Pisa; in 1822 to Genoa.

Teresa Guiccioli gave Byron a steadiness that he had never known before. His output of poetry, from the date of his arrival in Italy, mostly under the influence of the Countess Guiccioli, is astonishing. Childe Harold was completed (1817); the brilliant satirical fabliau, Beppo, appeared the same year; narrative poems like Mazeppa and The Prisoner of Chillon showed no diminution in his romantic story-telling powers; a few dramas, in the main unactable, like Cain (1821) or Marino Faliero (1820) were written; and the whiplash satire, The Vision of Judgment, blasted not only the poet laureate Robert Southey but the older school of romantic poets like Wordsworth and Coleridge and all that they represented—not to mention the crazed figure of King

Lord Byron's room in the Palazzo Moncenigo in Venice. Historical Pictures Service—Chicago.

George III and his fat, unlovely son, George IV. The crowning product of Byron's Italian days was **Don Juan** (p. 754), the various cantos of which were spread over the years from 1818 to Byron's death. Don Juan is Byron as a whole, his complex character blended into one romantic, cynical, satirical, amorous, adventurous, melodramatic, liberty-loving person who roams over Europe, tasting the joys of life, but ever searching, and ever unsatisfied. If it is possible to see any one phase of Byron's character uppermost in this poem, it is probably the satirical. Such are the shifting moods of the mad and bad Byron, however, that it is impossible to know in advance what type of poetry any given stanza of Don Juan will yield. Hence its enduring charm, for it can be witty as well as sentimental; warm and passionate as well as cold and sneering; farcical as well as tragic; trivial as well as powerful and solemnly impressive.

But Byron, though he may well be called his Don Juan incarnate, was not all theatricality and egotism. Neither was he purely a drawing-room revolutionist. He was asked to aid in the Greek war of liberation from the Turks and accepted. Before he could achieve anything of importance, however, he caught fever and died suddenly at Missolonghi, a town in western Greece, on April 19, 1824.

It is useless to moralize over this great personality, whose name was virtually a legend all over Europe. It is recognized now that Byron owes much of his fame to that same great personality, for his technique as a poet is uneven, as is his poetic taste. He can strike off a titanic line in one moment and lapse into the cheap or commonplace in the next. Some of this unevenness is deliberate, no doubt, and designed primarily to shock his reader in theatrical fashion. There is a coarser streak in Byron than is to be found in his great contemporaries—coarseness both as a man and as an artist. His nature poetry is chiefly a background for his powerful ego; unlike Wordsworth's it is highly dramatized and inclined to the tempestuous. As the trumpet of revolution he shares honors with Shelley. Patriotism is submerged in internationalism in his poetry, but his disgust for monarchy is genuine throughout, as the ill-fated venture in Greece bears witness. He is not so great a humanitarian as Shelley, for his was a more practical outlook on life. In many ways he was a great neo-classicist. But it is as a romanticist that Byron made his most powerful impression on the nineteenth century. Matthew Arnold's youthful reaction was:

He taught us little, but our soul
Had felt him like the thunder's roll.

WHEN WE TWO PARTED

This poem probably refers to Mary Chaworth, for whom Byron cherished a boyhood affection.

When we two parted
  In silence and tears,
Half broken-hearted
  To sever for years,
Pale grew thy cheek and cold,
  Colder thy kiss;
Truly that hour foretold
  Sorrow to this.

The dew of the morning
10 Sunk chill on my brow—
It felt like the warning
  Of what I feel now.
Thy vows are all broken,
  And light is thy fame;
I hear thy name spoken,
  And share in its shame.

They name thee before me,
  A knell to mine ear;
A shudder comes o'er me—
  Why wert thou so dear?   20
They know not I knew thee,
  Who knew thee too well—
Long, long shall I rue thee,
  Too deeply to tell.

In secret we met—
  In silence I grieve
That thy heart could forget,
  Thy spirit deceive,
If I should meet thee
  After long years,   30
How should I greet thee?—
  With silence and tears.
(1808; 1816)

from ENGLISH BARDS AND SCOTCH REVIEWERS

The immediate cause for this long satirical poem was a review of Byron's first work, Hours of Idleness,

*published in the Edinburgh Review for January 1808.
The review, written not by the editor Francis Jeffrey
but by Harry Brougham, was extremely harsh. Byron,
however, waited to hear from other reviews before
making answer. The significant part of this poem is
not the reply to the Edinburgh Review but rather the
lines on Wordsworth, Scott, Southey, and others. These
lines show how distinctly Byron was out of sympathy
with the older generation of English romantic poets.
The revolt of Byron is also seen in his other satirical
poetry—The Vision of Judgment and Don Juan; it is
clear that he did not change his opinions of Wordsworth and the others. As Byron said in a letter to
Murray, his publisher (September 15, 1817): "We
are upon a wrong revolutionary poetical system, or
systems, not worth a damn in itself. . . . I am the more
confirmed in this by having lately gone over some of
our classics, particularly Pope."*

. . . Behold! in various throngs the scribbling crew,
For notice eager, pass in long review:
Each spurs his jaded Pegasus apace,
And rime and blank maintain an equal race;
Sonnets on sonnets crowd, and ode on ode;
And tales of terror jostle on the road;
Immeasurable measures move along;
150 For simpering folly loves a varied song;
To strange mysterious dulness still the friend,
Admires the strain she cannot comprehend.
Thus Lays of Minstrels—may they be the last!—
On half-strung harps whine mournful to the blast.
While mountain spirits prate to river sprites,
That dames may listen to the sound at nights;
And goblin brats, of Gilpin Horner's brood,
Decoy young border-nobles through the wood,
And skip at every step, Lord knows how high,
160 And frighten foolish babes, the Lord knows why;
While high-born ladies in their magic cell,
Forbidding knights to read who cannot spell,
Dispatch a courier to a wizard's grave,
And fight with honest men to shield a knave.

Next view in state, proud prancing on his roan,
The golden-crested haughty Marmion,
Now forging scrolls, now foremost in the fight,
Not quite a felon, yet but half a knight,
The gibbet or the field prepared to grace;
170 A mighty mixture of the great and base.
And think'st thou, Scott! by vain conceit perchance,

On public taste to foist thy stale romance,
Though Murray with his Miller may combine
To yield thy muse just half-a-crown per line?
No! when the sons of song descend to trade,
Their bays are sear, their former laurels fade.
Let such forego the poet's sacred name,
Who rack their brains for lucre, not for fame:
Still for stern Mammon may they toil in vain!
And sadly gaze on gold they cannot gain!   180
Such be their meed, such still the just reward
Of prostituted muse and hireling bard!
For this we spurn Apollo's venal son,
And bid a long "good-night to Marmion."

These are the themes that claim our plaudits now;
These are the bards to whom the muse must bow;
While Milton, Dryden, Pope, alike forgot,
Resign their hallowed bays to Walter Scott.

The time has been, when yet the muse was young,
When Homer swept the lyre, and Maro sung,   190
An epic scarce ten centuries could claim,
While awe-struck nations hailed the magic name:
The work of each immortal bard appears
The single wonder of a thousand years.
Empires have moldered from the face of earth,
Tongues have expired with those who gave them birth,
Without the glory such a strain can give,
As even in ruin bids the language live.
Not so with us, though minor bards, content,
On one great work a life of labor spent: 200
With eagle pinion soaring to the skies,
Behold the ballad-monger Southey rise!
To him let Camoëns, Milton, Tasso yield,
Whose annual strains, like armies, take the field.
First in the ranks see Joan of Arc advance,
The scourge of England and the boast of France!
Though burnt by wicked Bedford for a witch,
Behold her statue placed in glory's niche;
Her fetters burst, and just released from prison,
A virgin phoenix from her ashes risen.   210
Next see tremendous Thalaba come on,
Arabia's monstrous, wild, and wondrous son;
Domdaniel's dread destroyer, who o'erthrew
More mad magicians than the world e'er knew.
Immortal hero! all thy foes o'ercome,
Forever reign—the rival of Tom Thumb!
Since startled meter fled before thy face,
Well wert thou doomed the last of all thy race!

English Bards and Scotch Reviewers. 145. **Pegasus,** a winged
horse associated with poetic inspiration. 148. **tales of terror,** an allusion to Lewis' *Tales of Terror* (1799) and *Tales of Wonder* (1800).
149. **Immeasurable . . . along,** a thrust at the new anapestic meters
introduced by Cowper (p. 647), Coleridge (p. 711), Southey, Moore,
and others. 153. **Lays . . . last,** a reference to Scott's *Lay of the
Last Minstrel,* which grew out of a suggestion for a ballad on
the Border legend of Gilpin Horner, a goblin; other allusions to this
poem follow. 173. **Murray . . . Miller,** John Murray and William
Miller, contemporary publishers. Murray was founder of the *Edinburgh Review.* See *Who Killed John Keats?* p. 765. 176. **bays,**
wreaths of honor made from leaves of the bay tree, a kind of laurel.

179. **Mammon,** god of riches, the personification of wealth. 183.
Apollo's venal son, Scott, who received £1000 for *Marmion.* Apollo
was the god of poetry and music. 190. **Homer,** Greek epic poet
assigned to the ninth century B.C. **Maro,** the family name of Vergil,
Latin epic poet (70–19 B.C.). 202. **Southey,** prolific writer of ballads
and epics. 203. **Camoëns,** noted Portuguese poet (1524–1580), author
of the *Lusiad,* the national epic. **Tasso,** celebrated Italian epic poet
(1544–1595). 205. **Joan of Arc.** Southey's *Joan of Arc, Thalaba,* and
Madoc, three ponderous epics, appeared in 1796, 1801, and 1805, respectively. 207. **Bedford,** Duke of Bedford (1389–1435), an English
general who abetted the execution of Joan of Arc in 1431. 210. **virgin
. . . risen,** an allusion to the ancient Oriental legend of the phoenix,

Well might triumphant genii bear thee hence,
220 Illustrious conqueror of common sense!
Now, last and greatest, Madoc spreads his sails,
Cacique in Mexico, and prince in Wales;
Tells us strange tales, as other travelers do,
More old than Mandeville's, and not so true.
Oh! Southey! Southey! cease thy varied song!
A bard may chant too often and too long:
As thou art strong in verse, in mercy, spare!
A fourth, alas! were more than we could bear.
But if, in spite of all the world can say,
230 Thou still wilt verseward plod thy weary way;
If still in Berkley ballads most uncivil,
Thou wilt devote old women to the devil,
The babe unborn thy dread intent may rue:
"God help thee," Southey, and thy readers too.

Next comes the dull disciple of thy school,
That mild apostate from poetic rule,
The simple Wordsworth, framer of a lay
As soft as evening in his favorite May,
Who warns his friend "to shake off toil and trouble,
240 And quit his books for fear of growing double";
Who, both by precept and example, shows
That prose is verse, and verse is merely prose;
Convincing all, by demonstration plain,
Poetic souls delight in prose insane;
And Christmas stories tortured into rime
Contain the essence of the true sublime.
Thus, when he tells the tale of Betty Foy,
The idiot mother of "an idiot boy";
A moon-struck, silly lad, who lost his way,
250 And, like his bard, confounded night with day;
So close on each pathetic part he dwells,
And each adventure so sublimely tells,
That all who view the "idiot in his glory"
Conceive the bard the hero of the story.

Shall gentle Coleridge pass unnoticed here,
To turgid ode and tumid stanza dear?
Though themes of innocence amuse him best,
Yet still obscurity's a welcome guest.
If Inspiration should her aid refuse
260 To him who takes a pixy for a muse,
Yet none in lofty numbers can surpass
The bard who soars to elegize an ass.
So well the subject suits his noble mind,
He brays, the laureate of the long-eared kind. . . .
(1809)

MAID OF ATHENS, ERE WE PART

Ζωή μου, σᾶς ἀγαπῶ.

The maiden eulogized in this poem is supposed to be Theresa Macri, who later married an Englishman named Black. The Greek phrase means, "My life, I love you."

Maid of Athens, ere we part,
Give, oh, give me back my heart!
Or, since that has left my breast,
Keep it now, and take the rest!
Hear my vow before I go,
Ζωή μου, σᾶς ἀγαπῶ.

By those tresses unconfined,
Wooed by each Aegean wind;
By those lids whose jetty fringe
Kiss thy soft cheeks' blooming tinge;   10
By those wild eyes like the roe,
Ζωή μου, σᾶς ἀγαπῶ.

By that lip I long to taste;
By that zone-encircled waist;
By all the token-flowers that tell
What words can never speak so well;
By love's alternate joy and woe,
Ζωή μου, σᾶς ἀγαπῶ.

Maid of Athens! I am gone:
Think of me, sweet! when alone.   20
Though I fly to Istanbul,
Athens holds my heart and soul:
Can I cease to love thee? No!
Ζωή μου, σᾶς ἀγαπῶ.
(1810; 1812)

SHE WALKS IN BEAUTY

This poem and the next are from Hebrew Melodies, a group of lyrics, many of which deal with incidents from the Old Testament; they were meant to be set to music. She Walks in Beauty refers to Lady Wilmot Horton, whom Byron had seen at a ball, attired in mourning with spangles on her dress.

She walks in beauty, like the night
Of cloudless climes and starry skies;

an immortal bird that, when consumed in fire, was resurrected from its ashes. 213. **Domdaniel**, in the *Arabian Nights* tales, a seminary for evil magicians and a resort of evil spirits. 216. **Tom Thumb**, a legendary diminutive personage celebrated in English literature. 222. **Cacique**, chief, petty king. 224. **Mandeville**, Sir John Mandeville, reputed author of a fourteenth-century book of travels. 230. **verseward . . . way.** Cf. Gray's *Elegy*, p. 642, l. 3. 231. **Berkley ballads.** One of Southey's ballads was entitled *The Old Woman of Berkeley*; in this the old woman is carried away by the devil. 234. **"God help thee,"** from a poem written by William Gifford (1756–1826) as a parody on Southey's dactylics. Southey had used the phrase in his *Soldier's Wife.* 236. **apostate . . . rule.** See Wordsworth's *Preface to Lyrical Ballads,*

p. 703, in which he argues that there is little difference between the language of prose and that of poetry. 239. **"to shake . . . double,"** from Wordsworth, *The Tables Turned.* 247. **tale of Betty Foy,** in *The Idiot Boy.* 256. **turgid . . . dear,** a characterization of some of Coleridge's odes but not of the one given in this book. 260. **pixy for a muse,** an allusion to Coleridge's *Songs of the Pixies* (Devonshire fairies.) 262. **an ass,** a reference to Coleridge's inane poem *To a Young Ass.*

Maid of Athens. 8. **Aegean,** the sea east of Greece. 14. **zone-encircled,** girdle-encircled. 21. **Istanbul,** Constantinople.

And all that's best of dark and bright
  Meet in her aspect and her eyes:
Thus mellowed to that tender light
  Which heaven to gaudy day denies.

One shade the more, one ray the less,
  Had half impaired the nameless grace
Which waves in every raven tress,
10 Or softly lightens o'er her face;
Where thoughts serenely sweet express
  How pure, how dear their dwelling-place.

And on that cheek, and o'er that brow,
  So soft, so calm, yet eloquent,
The smiles that win, the tints that glow,
  But tell of days in goodness spent,
A mind at peace with all below,
  A heart whose love is innocent!
(1814; 1815)

THE DESTRUCTION OF SENNACHERIB

The Assyrian came down like the wolf on the fold,
And his cohorts were gleaming in purple and gold;
And the sheen of their spears was like stars on the sea,
When the blue wave rolls nightly on deep Galilee.

Like the leaves of the forest when Summer is green,
That host with their banners at sunset were seen:
Like the leaves of the forest when Autumn hath blown,
That host on the morrow lay withered and strown.

For the Angel of Death spread his wings on the blast,
10 And breathed in the face of the foe as he passed;
And the eyes of the sleepers waxed deadly and chill,
And their hearts but once heaved, and forever grew
    still!

And there lay the steed with his nostril all wide,
But through it there rolled not the breath of his pride;
And the foam of his gasping lay white on the turf,
And cold as the spray of the rock-beating surf.

And there lay the rider distorted and pale,
With the dew on his brow, and the rust on his mail:
And the tents were all silent—the banners alone—
20 The lances unlifted—the trumpet unblown.

And the widows of Ashur are loud in their wail,
And the idols are broke in the temple of Baal;
And the might of the Gentile, unsmote by the sword,
Hath melted like snow in the glance of the Lord!
(1815)

STANZAS FOR MUSIC

*Here is an early but characteristic expression of one
of Byron's chief moods—romantic glorification of
youth and regret at its passing.*

There's not a joy the world can give like that it takes
  away,
When the glow of early thought declines in feeling's
  dull decay;
'Tis not on youth's smooth cheek the blush alone,
  which fades so fast,
But the tender bloom of heart is gone, ere youth itself
  be past.

Then the few whose spirits float above the wreck of
  happiness
Are driven o'er the shoals of guilt or ocean of excess:
The magnet of their course is gone, or only points in
  vain
The shore to which their shivered sail shall never
  stretch again.

Then the mortal coldness of the soul like death itself
  comes down;
It cannot feel for others' woes, it dare not dream its
  own   10
That heavy chill has frozen o'er the fountain of our
  tears,
And though the eye may sparkle still, 'tis where the
  ice appears.

Though wit may flash from fluent lips, and mirth distract the breast,
Through midnight hours that yield no more their
  former hope of rest;
'Tis but as ivy-leaves around the ruined turret wreath,
All green and wildly fresh without, but worn and gray
  beneath.

Oh, could I feel as I have felt—or be what I have been,
Or weep as I could once have wept, o'er many a vanished scene;
As springs, in deserts found, seem sweet, all brackish
  though they be,
So, midst the withered waste of life, those tears would
  flow to me.
(1815; 1816)

STANZAS FOR MUSIC

There be none of Beauty's daughters
  With a magic like thee;

The Destruction of Sennacherib. Sennacherib was a king of Assyria who invaded Palestine in the seventh century B.C. The story is told in 2 Kings, Chapters 18, 19. 21. **Ashur,** the highest god of the As-

syrians. 22. **Baal,** the supreme divinity of the ancient Syro-Phoenician nations.
Canto 3. 5. **with a hope.** Lady Byron left her husband in January

And like music on the waters
  Is thy sweet voice to me:
When, as if its sound were causing
The charméd ocean's pausing,
The waves lie still and gleaming,
And the lulled winds seem dreaming.

And the midnight moon is weaving
10 Her bright chain o'er the deep;
Whose breast is gently heaving,
  As an infant's asleep:
So the spirit bows before thee,
To listen and adore thee;
With a full but soft emotion,
Like the swell of Summer's ocean.
(1816)

SONNET ON CHILLON

The Castle of Chillon is situated at the eastern end of Lake Geneva, Switzerland. François de Bonnivard (1493-1570) was a Swiss patriot and religious reformer. For his participation in an effort to make Geneva a republic, free from the control of Charles III, Duke of Savoy, he was imprisoned in the Castle of Chillon from 1530 until he was released by his own party in 1536.

Eternal Spirit of the chainless Mind!
  Brightest in dungeons, Liberty! thou art:
  For there thy habitation is the heart—
The heart which love of thee alone can bind;
And when thy sons to fetters are consigned—
  To fetters, and the damp vault's dayless gloom,
  Their country conquers with their martyrdom,
And Freedom's fame finds wings on every wind.
Chillon! thy prison is a holy place,
10 And thy sad floor an altar—for 'twas trod,
Until his very steps have left a trace
  Worn, as if thy cold pavement were a sod,
By Bonnivard!—May none those marks efface!
  For they appeal from tyranny to God.
(1816)

CHILDE HAROLD'S PILGRIMAGE

The first two cantos of this poem appeared in 1812, the third and fourth after Byron's departure from England. But Byron's own remarks in the preface to the first two cantos hold good for the poem as a whole. "The following poem was written, for the most part, amidst the scenes which it attempts to describe. It was begun in Albania; and the parts relative to Spain and Portugal were composed from the author's obser-

vations in those countries. Thus much it may be necessary to state for the correctness of the descriptions. . . . A fictitious character is introduced for the sake of giving some connection to the piece, which, however, makes no pretension to regularity. It has been suggested to me by friends . . . that in this fictitious character, Childe Harold, I may incur the suspicion of having intended some real personage: this I beg leave, once for all, to disclaim—Harold is the child of imagination, for the purpose I have stated. In some very trivial particulars, and those merely local, there might be grounds for such a notion, but in the main points, I should hope, none whatever." Posterity, nevertheless, has felt that Childe Harold is Byron the romanticist, certainly in this poem, in Manfred, and in certain portions of Don Juan, Byron is at his romantic best. The figure of Childe Harold is an epitome of the "Byronic hero." The word Childe is used by Byron as in the old ballads and romances, signifying a youth of noble birth, usually one awaiting knighthood.

from CANTO 3

Is thy face like thy mother's, my fair child!
Ada! sole daughter of my house and heart?
When last I saw thy young blue eyes they smiled,
And then we parted—not as now we part,
But with a hope.—Awaking with a start,
The waters heave around me; and on high
The winds lift up their voices: I depart,
Whither I know not, but the hour's gone by,
When Albion's lessening shores could grieve or glad
  mine eye.

Once more upon the waters! yet once more!   10
And the waves bound beneath me as a steed
That knows his rider. Welcome to their roar!
Swift be their guidance, wheresoe'er it lead!
Though the strained mast should quiver as a reed,
And the rent canvas fluttering strew the gale,
Still must I on; for I am as a weed,
Flung from the rock, on Ocean's foam to sail
Where'er the surge may sweep, the tempest's breath
  prevail.

In my youth's summer I did sing of One,
The wandering outlaw of his own dark mind;   20
Again I seize the theme, then but begun,
And bear it with me, as the rushing wind
Bears the cloud onwards: in that Tale I find
The furrows of long thought, and dried-up tears,
Which, ebbing, leave a sterile track behind,
O'er which all heavily the journeying years
Plod the last sands of life—where not a flower appears.

of Childe Harold's Pilgrimage in 1809 at the age of twenty-one.

Since my young days of passion—joy, or pain,
Perchance my heart and harp have lost a string,
30 And both may jar: it may be, that in vain
I would essay as I have sung to sing.
Yet, though a dreary strain, to this I cling,
So that it wean me from the weary dream
Of selfish grief or gladness—so it fling
Forgetfulness around me—it shall seem
To me, though to none else, a not ungrateful theme.

He who, grown agéd in this world of woe,
In deeds, not years, piercing the depths of life,
So that no wonder waits him; nor below
40 Can love or sorrow, fame, ambition, strife,
Cut to his heart again with the keen knife
Of silent, sharp endurance: he can tell
Why thought seeks refuge in lone caves, yet rife
With airy images, and shapes which dwell
Still unimpaired, though old, in the soul's haunted
  cell.

'Tis to create, and in creating live
A being more intense that we endow
With form our fancy, gaining as we give
The life we image, even as I do now.
50 What am I? Nothing: but not so art thou,
Soul of my thought! with whom I traverse earth,
Invisible but gazing, as I glow
Mixed with thy spirit, blended with thy birth,
And feeling still with thee in my crushed feeling's
  dearth.

Yet must I think less wildly—I *have* thought
Too long and darkly, till my brain became,
In its own eddy boiling and o'er wrought,
A whirling gulf of phantasy and flame:
And thus, untaught in youth my heart to tame,
60 My springs of life were poisoned. 'Tis too late!
Yet am I changed; though still enough the same
In strength to bear what time cannot abate,
And feed on bitter fruits without accusing Fate.

Something too much of this—but now 'tis past,
And the spell closes with its silent seal.
Long absent HAROLD reappears at last;
He of the breast which fain no more would feel,
Wrung with the wounds which kill not, but ne'er heal;
Yet Time, who changes all, had altered him
70 In soul and aspect as in age: years steal
Fire from the mind as vigor from the limb;
And life's enchanted cup but sparkles near the brim.

His had been quaffed too quickly, and he found
The dregs were wormwood; but he filled again,

And from a purer fount, on holier ground,
And deemed its spring perpetual; but in vain!
Still round him clung invisibly a chain
Which galled forever, fettering though unseen,
And heavy though it clanked not; worn with pain,
Which pined although it spoke not, and grew keen, 80
Entering with every step he took through many a scene.

Secure in guarded coldness, he had mixed
Again in fancied safety with his kind,
And deemed his spirit now so firmly fixed
And sheathed with an invulnerable mind,
That, if no joy, no sorrow lurked behind;
And he, as one, might 'midst the many stand
Unheeded, searching through the crowd to find
Fit speculation; such as in strange land
He found in wonder-works of God and Nature's hand. 90

But who can view the ripened rose, nor seek
To wear it? who can curiously behold
The smoothness and the sheen of Beauty's cheek,
Nor feel the heart can never all grow old?
Who can contemplate Fame through clouds unfold
The star which rises o'er her steep, nor climb?
Harold, once more within the vortex, rolled
On with the giddy circle, chasing Time,
Yet with a nobler aim than in his youth's fond prime.

But soon he knew himself the most unfit   100
Of men to herd with Man; with whom he held
Little in common; untaught to submit
His thoughts to others, though his soul was quelled
In youth by his own thoughts; still uncompelled,
He would not yield dominion of his mind
To spirits against whom his own rebelled;
Proud though in desolation; which could find
A life within itself, to breathe without mankind.

Where rose the mountains, there to him were friends;
Where rolled the ocean, thereon was his home;   110
Where a blue sky, and glowing clime, extends,
He had the passion and the power to roam;
The desert, forest, cavern, breaker's foam,
Were unto him companionship; they spake
A mutual language, clearer than the tome
Of his land's tongue, which he would oft forsake
For Nature's pages glassed by sunbeams on the lake.

Like the Chaldean, he could watch the stars,
Till he had peopled them with beings bright
As their own beams; and earth, and earthborn jars, 120
And human frailties, were forgotten quite:
Could he have kept his spirit to that flight

---

64. **Something . . . this.** A phrase from *Hamlet*, III, ii, 79. 65. **spell
. . . seal.** The seal of silence is set upon the story of his personal
tragedy. 91. **nor,** and not. 99. **fond,** foolish. 118. **Chaldean.** The
Chaldeans were masters of astrology. 131. **came . . . again.** Cf. *Macbeth*, III, iv, 21: "Then comes my fit again." 153. **king-making.** The

battle of Waterloo gave security to the thrones of European kings. 158.
"**pride of place,**" a phrase from *Macbeth*, II, iv, 12. It is a term in
falconry meaning the highest point of flight. 168. **idol . . . days.** The
Holy Alliance, formed in 1815 by the emperors of Austria and Russia
and the king of Prussia, aimed at the restoration of pre-Revolutionary

He had been happy; but this clay will sink
Its spark immortal, envying it the light
To which it mounts, as if to break the link
That keeps us from yon heaven which woos us to its
brink.

But in Man's dwellings he became a thing
Restless and worn, and stern and wearisome,
Drooped as a wild-born falcon with clipped wing,
130 To whom the boundless air alone were home:
Then came his fit again, which to o'ercome,
As eagerly the barred-up bird will beat
His breast and beak against his wiry dome
Till the blood tinge his plumage, so the heat
Of his impeded soul would through his bosom eat.

Self-exiled Harold wanders forth again,
With nought of hope left, but with less of gloom,
The very knowledge that he lived in vain,
That all was over on this side the tomb,
140 Had made Despair a smilingness assume,
Which, though 'twere wild—as on the plundered wreck
When mariners would madly meet their doom
With draughts intemperate on the sinking deck—
Did yet inspire a cheer, which he forbore to check.

Stop!—for thy tread is on an Empire's dust!
An Earthquake's spoil is sepulchered below!
Is the spot marked with no colossal bust?
Nor column trophied for triumphal show?
None; but the moral's truth tells simpler so,
150 As the ground was before, thus let it be;—
How that red rain hath made the harvest grow!
And is this all the world has gained by thee,
Thou first and last of fields! king-making Victory?

And Harold stands upon this place of skulls,
The grave of France, the deadly Waterloo!
How in an hour the power which gave annuls
Its gifts, transferring fame as fleeting too!
In "pride of place" here last the eagle flew,
Then tore with bloody talon the rent plain,
160 Pierced by the shaft of banded nations through;
Ambition's life and labors all were vain;
He wears the shattered links of the world's broken
chain.

Fit retribution! Gaul may champ the bit
And foam in fetters;—but is Earth more free?
Did nations combat to make *One* submit;
Or league to teach all kings true sovereignty?
What! shall reviving Thralldom again be
The patched-up idol of enlightened days?

Shall we, who struck the Lion down, shall we
Pay the Wolf homage? proffering lowly gaze   170
And servile knees to thrones? No; *prove* before ye
praise!

If not, o'er one fallen despot boast no more!
In vain fair cheeks were furrowed with hot tears
For Europe's flowers long rooted up before
The trampler of her vineyards; in vain years
Of death, depopulation, bondage, fears,
Have all been borne, and broken by the accord
Of roused-up millions; all that most endears
Glory, is when the myrtle wreathes a sword
Such as Harmodious drew on Athens' tyrant lord. 180

There was a sound of revelry by night,
And Belgium's capital had gathered then
Her Beauty and her Chivalry, and bright
The lamps shone o'er fair women and brave men;
A thousand hearts beat happily; and when
Music arose with its voluptuous swell,
Soft eyes looked love to eyes which spake again,
And all went merry as a marriage bell;
But hush! hark! a deep sound strikes like a rising
knell!

Did ye not hear it?—No; 'twas but the wind,   190
Or the car rattling o'er the stony street;
On with the dance! let joy be unconfined;
No sleep till morn, when Youth and Pleasure meet
To chase the glowing Hours with flying feet—
But hark!—that heavy sound breaks in once more,
As if the clouds its echo would repeat;
And nearer, clearer, deadlier than before!
Arm! Arm! it is—it is—the cannon's opening roar!

Within a windowed niche of that high hall
Sat Brunswick's fated chieftain; he did hear   200
That sound the first amidst the festival,
And caught its tone with Death's prophetic ear;
And when they smiled because he deemed it near,
His heart more truly knew that peal too well
Which stretched his father on a bloody bier,
And roused the vengeance blood alone could quell;
He rushed into the field, and, foremost fighting, fell.

Ah! then and there was hurrying to and fro,
And gathering tears, and tremblings of distress,
And cheeks all pale, which but an hour ago   210
Blushed at the praise of their own loveliness;
And there were sudden partings, such as press
The life from our young hearts, and choking sighs
Which ne'er might be repeated; who could guess

conditions. 169. **Lion,** Napoleon. 170. **Wolf,** the imitation of imperial strength seen in the emperor of Austria and others. 180. **Harmodius . . . lord.** Harmodius and Aristogeiton were Athenian heroes who hid their swords under myrtle branches to aid in their attack upon Hipparchus, the tyrant of Athens, in 514 B.C. 181. **There . . . night.**

A ball was given at Brussels on the evening before the battle of Quatre-Bras, which occurred two days before the battle of Waterloo. 200. **Brunswick's . . . chieftain,** Frederick William, Duke of Brunswick. His father was killed in the battle of Auerstadt in 1806.

If ever more should meet those mutual eyes,
Since upon night so sweet such awful morn could
    rise!

And there was mounting in hot haste: the steed,
The mustering squadron, and the clattering car,
Went pouring forward with impetuous speed,
220 And swiftly forming in the ranks of war;
And the deep thunder peal on peal afar;
And near, the beat of the alarming drum
Roused up the soldier ere the morning star;
While thronged the citizens with terror dumb,
Or whispering, with white lips—"The foe! they come!
    they come!"

And wild and high the "Cameron's gathering" rose!
The war-note of Lochiel, which Albyn's hills
Have heard, and heard, too, have her Saxon foes—
How in the noon of night that pibroch thrills,
230 Savage and shrill! But with the breath which fills
Their mountain-pipe, so fill the mountaineers
With the fierce native daring which instills
The stirring memory of a thousand years,
And Evan's, Donald's fame rings in each clansman's
    ears!

And Ardennes waves above them her green leaves,
Dewy with nature's teardrops as they pass,
Grieving, if aught inanimate e'er grieves,
Over the unreturning brave—alas!
Ere evening to be trodden like the grass
240 Which now beneath them, but above shall grow
In its next verdure, when this fiery mass
Of living valor, rolling on the foe
And burning with high hope, shall molder cold and
    low.

Last noon beheld them full of lusty life,
Last eve in Beauty's circle proudly gay;
The midnight brought the signal-sound of strife,
The morn the marshaling in arms—the day
Battle's magnificently stern array!
The thunder-clouds close o'er it, which when rent
250 The earth is covered thick with other clay,
Which her own clay shall cover, heaped and pent,
Rider and horse—friend, foe—in one red burial
    blent! . . .

Lake Leman woos me with its crystal face,
The mirror where the stars and mountains view
The stillness of their aspect in each trace
Its clear depth yields of their far height and hue:
There is too much of man here, to look through

With a fit mind the might which I behold;
But soon in me shall Loneliness renew   650
Thoughts hid, but not less cherished than of old,
Ere mingling with the herd had penned me in their
    fold.

To fly from, need not be to hate, mankind:
All are not fit with them to stir and toil,
Nor is it discontent to keep the mind
Deep in its fountain, lest it overboil
In the hot throng, where we become the spoil
Of our infection, till too late and long
We may deplore and struggle with the coil,
In wretched interchange of wrong for wrong   660
Midst a contentious world, striving where none are
    strong.

There, in a moment we may plunge our years
In fatal penitence, and in the blight
Of our own soul turn all our blood to tears,
And color things to come with hues of Night;
The race of life becomes a hopeless flight
To those that walk in darkness: on the sea
The boldest steer but where their ports invite;
But there are wanderers o'er Eternity
Whose bark drives on and on, and anchored ne'er
    shall be.   670

Is it not better, then, to be alone,
And love Earth only for its earthly sake?
By the blue rushing of the arrowy Rhone,
Or the pure bosom of its nursing lake,
Which feeds it as a mother who doth make
A fair but froward infant her own care,
Kissing its cries away as these awake;—
Is it not better thus our lives to wear,
Than join the crushing crowd, doomed to inflict or
    bear?

I live not in myself, but I become   680
Portion of that around me; and to me
High mountains are a feeling, but the hum
Of human cities torture: I can see
Nothing to loathe in nature, save to be
A link reluctant in a fleshly chain,
Classed among creatures, when the soul can flee,
And with the sky, the peak, the heaving plain
Of ocean, or the stars, mingle, and not in vain.

And thus I am absorbed, and this is life:
I look upon the peopled desert past,   690
As on a place of agony and strife,
Where, for some sin, to sorrow I was cast,

---

226. **"Cameron's gathering,"** the war song that summoned the Cameron
clan. 227. **Lochiel,** the Cameron clan, from Lochiel, a district in the
counties of Argyll and Inverness, Scotland. **Albyn,** a poetic name for
Scotland. 228. **Saxon foes,** the English. 229. **pibroch,** a kind of
Highland bagpipe music. 234. **Evan, Donald,** Sir Evan Cameron

(1629–1719) and Donald Cameron (1695?–1748), Scottish Highland
chieftains; Donald Cameron was known as "Gentle Lochiel." They
were supporters of the Stuarts. 235. **Ardennes,** a large forest in
northern France, Belgium, and Luxembourg. 251. **pent,** closely confined. 644. **Lake Leman,** Lake Geneva, Switzerland. 669. **wanderers**

To act and suffer, but remount at last
With a fresh pinion; which I feel to spring,
Though young, yet waxing vigorous as the blast
Which it would cope with, on delighted wing,
Spurning the clay-cold bonds which round our being
    cling.

And when, at length, the mind shall be all free
From what it hates in this degraded form,
700 Reft of its carnal life, save what shall be
Existent happier in the fly and worm—
When elements to elements conform,
And dust is as it should be, shall I not
Feel all I see, less dazzling, but more warm?
The bodiless thought? the Spirit of each spot?
Of which, even now, I share at times the immortal lot?

Are not the mountains, waves, and skies a part
Of me and of my soul, as I of them?
Is not the love of these deep in my heart
710 With a pure passion? should I not contemn
All objects, if compared with these? and stem
A tide of suffering, rather than forgo
Such feelings for the hard and worldly phlegm
Of those whose eyes are only turned below,
Gazing upon the ground, with thoughts which dare
    not glow? . . .

Clear, placid Leman! thy contrasted lake,
With the wild world I dwelt in, is a thing
Which warns me, with its stillness, to forsake
800 Earth's troubled waters for a purer spring.
This quiet sail is as a noiseless wing
To waft me from distraction; once I loved
Torn ocean's roar, but thy soft murmuring
Sounds sweet as if a Sister's voice reproved,
That I with stern delights should e'er have been so
    moved.

It is the hush of night, and all between
Thy margin and the mountains, dusk, yet clear,
Mellowed and mingling, yet distinctly seen,
Save darkened Jura, whose capped heights appear
810 Precipitously steep; and drawing near,
There breathes a living fragrance from the shore,
Of flowers yet fresh with childhood; on the ear
Drops the light drip of the suspended oar,
Or chirps the grasshopper one good-night carol more.

He is an evening reveler, who makes
His life an infancy, and sings his fill;
At intervals, some bird from out the brakes
Starts into voice a moment, then is still.

There seems a floating whisper on the hill,
But that is fancy, for the starlight dews   820
All silently their tears of love instill,
Weeping themselves away, till they infuse
Deep into Nature's breast the spirit of her hues.

Ye stars! which are the poetry of heaven!
If in your bright leaves we would read the fate
Of men and empires—'tis to be forgiven,
That in our aspirations to be great,
Our destinies o'erleap their mortal state,
And claim a kindred with you; for ye are
A beauty and a mystery, and create   830
In us such love and reverence from afar,
That fortune, fame, power, life have named themselves
    a star.

All heaven and earth are still—though not in sleep,
But breathless, as we grow when feeling most;
And silent, as we stand in thoughts too deep—
All heaven and earth are still; from the high host
Of stars, to the lulled lake and mountain-coast,
All is concentered in a life intense,
Where not a beam, nor air, nor leaf is lost,
But hath a part of being, and a sense   840
Of that which is of all Creator and defense.

Then stirs the feeling infinite, so felt
In solitude, where we are *least* alone;
A truth, which through our being then doth melt,
And purifies from self: it is a tone,
The soul and source of music, which makes known
Eternal harmony, and sheds a charm
Like to the fabled Cytherea's zone,
Binding all things with beauty;—'twould disarm
The specter Death, had he substantial power to harm. 850

Not vainly did the early Persian make
His altar the high places, and the peak
Of earth-o'ergazing mountains, and thus take
A fit and unwalled temple, there to seek
The Spirit, in whose honor shrines are weak,
Upreared of human hands. Come, and compare
Columns and idol-dwellings, Goth or Greek,
With Nature's realms of worship, earth and air,
Nor fix on fond abodes to circumscribe thy prayer!

The sky is changed!—and such a change! Oh night, 860
And storm, and darkness, ye are wondrous strong,
Yet lovely in your strength, as is the light
Of a dark eye in woman! Far along,
From peak to peak, the rattling crags among
Leaps the live thunder! Not from one lone cloud,

o'er Eternity. See Shelley's *Adonais*, p. 779, l. 264. **682. High . . .
feeling.** Cf. Wordsworth's *Lines*, p. 682, ll. 76 ff. **683. cities torture,**
Cf. Keats' *To One Who Has Been Long in City Pent*, p. 785. **809.
Jura,** a chain of mountains in Switzerland and eastern France. **817.
brakes,** thickets. **833. All . . . still.** Cf. Wordsworth's *It Is a*

Beauteous Evening, p. 695. **848. Cytherea's zone,** the girdle of Venus,
goddess of love; it inspired love.

But every mountain now hath found a tongue
And Jura answers, through her misty shroud,
Back to the joyous Alps, who call to her aloud!

And this is in the night—most glorious night!
870 Thou wert not sent for slumber! let me be
A sharer in thy fierce and far delight—
A portion of the tempest and of thee!
How the lit lake shines, a phosphoric sea,
And the big rain comes dancing to the earth!
And now again 'tis black—and now, the glee
Of the loud hills shakes with its mountain-mirth,
As if they did rejoice o'er a young earthquake's
   birth. . . .

Thus far have I proceeded in a theme
Renewed with no kind auspices—to feel
We are not what we have been, and to deem
We are not what we should be, and to steel
The heart against itself; and to conceal,
With a proud caution, love, or hate, or aught—
Passion or feeling, purpose, grief or zeal—
Which is the tyrant spirit of our thought,
Is a stern task of soul—no matter—it is taught.

1040 And for these words, thus woven into song,
It may be that they are a harmless wile—
The coloring of the scenes which fleet along,
Which I would seize, in passing, to beguile
My breast, or that of others, for awhile.
Fame is the thirst of youth, but I am not
So young as to regard men's frown or smile,
As loss or guerdon of a glorious lot;
I stood and stand alone—remembered or forgot.

I have not loved the world, nor the world me;
1050 I have not flattered its rank breath, nor bowed
To its idolatries a patient knee,
Nor coined my cheek to smiles, nor cried aloud
In worship of an echo; in the crowd
They could not deem me one of such; I stood
Amongst them, but not of them; in a shroud
Of thoughts which were not their thoughts, and still
   could,
Had I not filed my mind, which thus itself subdued.

I have not loved the world, nor the world me—
But let us part fair foes; I do believe,
1060 Though I have found them not, that there may be
Words which are things, hopes which will not deceive,
And virtues which are merciful, nor weave
Snares for the failing; I would also deem
O'er others' griefs that some sincerely grieve;
That two, or one, are almost what they seem,
That goodness is no name, and happiness no dream.

My daughter! with thy name this song begun;
My daughter! with thy name thus much shall end;
I see thee not, I hear thee not, but none
Can be so wrapt in thee; thou art the friend   1070
To whom the shadows of far years extend:
Albeit my brow thou never shouldst behold,
My voice shall with thy future visions blend,
And reach into thy heart, when mine is cold,
A token and a tone, even from thy father's mold.

To aid thy mind's development, to watch
Thy dawn of little joys, to sit and see
Almost thy very growth, to view thee catch
Knowledge of objects—wonders yet to thee!
To hold thee lightly on a gentle knee,   1080
And print on thy soft cheek a parent's kiss—
This, it should seem, was not reserved for me;
Yet this was in my nature: as it is,
I know not what is there, yet something like to this.

Yet, though dull hate as duty should be taught,
I know that thou wilt love me, though my name
Should be shut from thee, as a spell still fraught
With desolation, and a broken claim:
Though the grave closed between us—'twere the same,
I know that thou wilt love me; though to drain   1090
My blood from out thy being were an aim,
And an attainment—all would be in vain—
Still thou wouldst love me, still that more than life
   retain.

The child of love, though born in bitterness,
And nurtured in convulsion—of thy sire
These were the elements, and thine no less.
As yet such are around thee, but thy fire
Shall be more tempered, and thy hope far higher.
Sweet be thy cradled slumbers! O'er the sea
And from the mountains where I now respire,   1100
Fain would I waft such blessing upon thee,
As, with a sigh, I deem thou might'st have been to me.

from CANTO 4

O Rome! my country! city of the soul!
The orphans of the heart must turn to thee,
Lone mother of dead empires! and control
In their shut breasts their petty misery.
What are our woes and sufferance? Come and see
The cypress, hear the owl, and plod your way
O'er steps of broken thrones and temples, Ye!   700
Whose agonies are evils of a day—
A world is at our feet as fragile as our clay.

The Niobe of nations! there she stands,
Childless and crownless, in her voiceless woe;

1057. **filed,** defiled. The phrase is from *Macbeth*, III, i, 65.
   Canto 4. 699. **cypress,** an emblem of mourning; it is a common
tree in graveyards. 703. **Niobe,** a mythological character, who in the

form of a rock wept continually over the loss of her twelve children.
707. **Scipios' tomb,** a group of ancient Roman tombs situated on the
Appian Way, near Rome. The Scipios were famous Roman generals,

An empty urn within her withered hands,
Whose holy dust was scattered long ago;
The Scipios' tomb contains no ashes now,
The very sepulchers lie tenantless
Of their heroic dwellers: dost thou flow,
710 Old Tiber! through a marble wilderness?
Rise, with thy yellow waves, and mantle her distress.

The Goth, the Christian, Time, War, Flood, and
    Fire,
Have dealt upon the seven-hilled city's pride;
She saw her glories star by star expire,
And up the steep barbarian monarchs ride
Where the car climbed the Capitol; far and wide
Temple and tower went down, nor left a site:
Chaos of ruins! who shall trace the void,
O'er the dim fragments cast a lunar light,
720 And say, "here was, or is," where all is doubly
    night? . . .

Arches on arches! as it were that Rome,
Collecting the chief trophies of her line,
Would build up all her triumphs in one dome,
Her Coliseum stands; the moonbeams shine
As 'twere its natural torches, for divine
Should be the light which streams here to illume
1150 This long-explored but still exhaustless mine
Of contemplation; and the azure gloom
Of an Italian night, where the deep skies assume

Hues which have words, and speak to ye of heaven,
Floats o'er this vast and wondrous monument,
And shadows forth its glory. There is given
Unto the things of earth, which Time hath bent,
A spirit's feeling, and where he hath leant
His hand, but broke his scythe, there is a power
And magic in the ruined battlement,
1160 For which the palace of the present hour
Must yield its pomp, and wait till ages are its
    dower.

O Time! the beautifier of the dead,
Adorner of the ruin, comforter
And only healer when the heart hath bled;
Time! the corrector where our judgments err,
The test of truth, love—sole philosopher,
For all beside are sophists—from thy thrift,
Which never loses though it doth defer—
Time, the avenger! unto thee I lift
My hands, and eyes, and heart, and crave of thee a
1170 gift:

Amidst this wreck, where thou hast made a shrine
And temple more divinely desolate,
Among thy mightier offerings here are mine,

Ruins of years, though few, yet full of fate:
If thou hast ever seen me too elate,
Hear me not; but if calmly I have borne
Good, and reserved my pride against the hate
Which shall not whelm me, let me not have worn
This iron in my soul in vain—shall *they* not mourn?

And thou, who never yet of human wrong   1180
Left the unbalanced scale, great Nemesis!
Here, where the ancient paid thee homage long—
Thou who didst call the Furies from the abyss,
And round Orestes bade them howl and hiss
For that unnatural retribution—just,
Had it but been from hands less near—in this
Thy former realm, I call thee from the dust!
Dost thou not hear my heart?—Awake! thou shalt,
    and must.

It is not that I may not have incurred
For my ancestral faults or mine the wound   1190
I bleed withal, and, had it been conferred
With a just weapon, it had flowed unbound;
But now my blood shall not sink in the ground;
To thee I do devote it—*thou* shalt take
The vengeance, which shall yet be sought and
    found,
Which if *I* have not taken for the sake——
But let that pass—I sleep, but thou shalt yet awake.

And if my voice break forth, 'tis not that now
I shrink from what is suffered: let him speak
Who hath beheld decline upon my brow,   1200
Or seen my mind's convulsion leave it weak;
But in this page a record will I seek.
Not in the air shall these my words disperse,
Though I be ashes; a far hour shall wreak
The deep prophetic fullness of this verse,
And pile on human heads the mountain of my
    curse!

That curse shall be Forgiveness.—Have I not—
Hear me, my mother Earth! behold it, Heaven!
Have I not had to wrestle with my lot?
Have I not suffered things to be forgiven?   1210
Have I not had my brain seared, my heart riven,
Hopes sapped, name blighted, Life's life lied away?
And only not to desperation driven,
Because not altogether of such clay
As rots into the souls of those whom I survey.

From mighty wrongs to petty perfidy
Have I not seen what human things could do?
From the loud roar of foaming calumny
To the small whisper of the as paltry few,
And subtler venom of the reptile crew,   1220

second century B.C. 710. **Tiber,** a river in central Italy; it flows through Rome. 716. **Capitol,** part of the Capitoline Hill in Rome. 1147. **Coliseum,** the celebrated amphitheater in Rome. 1181. **Nemesis,** the classical goddess of retributive justice. 1184. **Orestes,** son of the Greek king Agamemnon and Clytemnestra; he slew his mother and her lover Aegisthus in revenge for their murder of Agamemnon.

George Noel Gordon, Lord Byron   751

The Janus glance of whose significant eye,
Learning to lie with silence, would *seem* true,
And without utterance, save the shrug or sigh,
Deal round to happy fools its speechless obloquy.

But I have lived, and have not lived in vain:
My mind may lose its force, my blood its fire,
And my frame perish even in conquering pain;
But there is that within me which shall tire
Torture and Time, and breathe when I expire;
1230 Something unearthly, which they deem not of,
Like the remembered tone of a mute lyre,
Shall on their softened spirits sink, and move
In hearts all rocky now the late remorse of love.

The seal is set.—Now welcome, thou dread power!
Nameless, yet thus omnipotent, which here
Walk'st in the shadow of the midnight hour
With a deep awe, yet all distinct from fear;
Thy haunts are ever where the dead walls rear
Their ivy mantles, and the solemn scene
1240 Derives from thee a sense so deep and clear
That we become a part of what has been,
And grow unto the spot, all-seeing but unseen.

And here the buzz of eager nations ran,
In murmured pity, or loud-roared applause
As man was slaughtered by his fellow man.
And wherefore slaughtered? wherefore, but because
Such were the bloody Circus' genial laws,
And the imperial pleasure.—Wherefore not?
What matters where we fall to fill the maws
1250 Of worms—on battle-plains or listed spot?
Both are but theaters where the chief actors rot.

I see before me the Gladiator lie:
He leans upon his hand—his manly brow
Consents to death, but conquers agony,
And his drooped head sinks gradually low—
And through his side the last drops, ebbing slow
From the red gash, fall heavy, one by one,
Like the first of a thunder-shower; and now
The arena swims around him—he is gone,
Ere ceased the inhuman shout which hailed the
1260   wretch who won.

He heard it, but he heeded not—his eyes
Were with his heart, and that was far away;
He recked not of the life he lost nor prize,
But where his rude hut by the Danube lay,
There were his young barbarians all at play,
There was their Dacian mother—he, their sire,

Butchered to make a Roman holiday—
All this rushed with his blood—Shall he expire
And unavenged? Arise! ye Goths, and glut your ire!

But here, where Murder breathed her bloody steam; 1270
And here, where buzzing nations choked the ways,
And roared or murmured like a mountain stream
Dashing or winding as its torrent strays;
Here, where the Roman million's blame or praise
Was death or life, the playthings of a crowd,
My voice sounds much—and fall the stars' faint rays
On the arena void—seats crushed—walls bowed—
And galleries, where my steps seem echoes strangely
    loud.

A ruin—yet what ruin! from its mass
Walls, palaces, half-cities have been reared;   1280
Yet oft the enormous skeleton ye pass,
And marvel where the spoil could have appeared.
Hath it indeed been plundered, or but cleared?
Alas! developed, opens the decay,
When the colossal fabric's form is neared:
It will not bear the brightness of the day,
Which streams too much on all years, man, have reft
    away.

But when the rising moon begins to climb
Its topmost arch, and gently pauses there;
When the stars twinkle through the loops of time, 1290
And the low night-breeze waves along the air
The garland-forest, which the gray walls wear,
Like laurels on the bald first Caesar's head;
When the light shines serene but doth not glare,
Then in this magic circle raise the dead:
Heroes have trod this spot—'tis on their dust ye tread.

"While stands the Coliseum, Rome shall stand;
When falls the Coliseum, Rome shall fall;
And when Rome falls—the World." From our own
    land
Thus spake the pilgrims o'er this mighty wall   1300
In Saxon times, which we are wont to call
Ancient; and these three mortal things are still
On their foundations, and unaltered all;
Rome and her Ruin past Redemption's skill,
The World, the same wide den—of thieves, or what
    ye will. . . .

But I forget.—My Pilgrim's shrine is won,
And he and I must part—so let it be—
His task and mine alike are nearly done;
Yet once more let us look upon the sea;   1570

1221. **Janus,** an ancient Roman deity represented with two faces looking
in opposite directions. 1247. **Circus,** a large enclosure used frequently
for gladiatorial combats in Roman times. 1250. **listed spot,** field of
the list or tournament. 1252. **Gladiator,** a statue formerly called *The
Dying Gladiator,* but now thought to represent a wounded warrior, and
hence called *The Dying Gaul.* It is in the Museum of the Capitol.
1266. *There . . . holiday.* After Trajan had conquered the region
north of the Lower Danube and had made it into the Roman province
of Dacia (101 B.C.), he carried 10,000 captives to Rome and exhibited
them in combats for the amusement of the people. 1293. **laurels . . .
head.** In a note Byron quotes Suetonius, the Roman historian, as saying
that "Julius Caesar was particularly gratified by that decree of the senate
which enabled him to wear a wreath of laurel on all occasions. He was
anxious, not to show that he was the conqueror of the world, but to hide
that he was bald." 1297. **"While . . . World."** Byron cites Gibbon
(*Decline and Fall of the Roman Empire*) as quoting this passage from

The midland ocean breaks on him and me,
And from the Alban Mount we now behold
Our friend of youth, that Ocean, which when we
Beheld it last by Calpe's rock unfold
Those waves, we followed on till the dark Euxine
    rolled

Upon the blue Symplegades: long years—
Long, though not very many—since have done
Their work on both; some suffering and some tears
Have left us nearly where we had begun:
1580 Yet not in vain our mortal race hath run;
We have had our reward, and it is here—
That we can yet feel gladdened by the sun,
And reap from earth, sea, joy almost as dear
As if there were no man to trouble what is clear.

Oh! that the Desert were my dwelling-place,
With one fair Spirit for my minister,
That I might all forget the human race,
And, hating no one, love but only her!
Ye elements!—in whose ennobling stir
1590 I feel myself exalted—Can ye not
Accord me such a being? Do I err
In deeming such inhabit many a spot?
Though with them to converse can rarely be our lot.

There is a pleasure in the pathless woods,
There is a rapture on the lonely shore,
There is society, where none intrudes,
By the deep Sea, and music in its roar:
I love not Man the less, but Nature more,
From these our interviews, in which I steal
1600 From all I may be, or have been before,
To mingle with the Universe, and feel
What I can ne'er express, yet cannot all conceal.

Roll on, thou deep and dark blue Ocean—roll!
Ten thousand fleets sweep over thee in vain;
Man marks the earth with ruin—his control
Stops with the shore; upon the watery plain
The wrecks are all thy deed, nor doth remain
A shadow of man's ravage, save his own,
When for a moment, like a drop of rain,
1610 He sinks into thy depths with bubbling groan,
Without a grave, unknelled, uncoffined, and unknown.

His steps are not upon thy paths—thy fields
Are not a spoil for him—thou dost arise
And shake him from thee; the vile strength he wields
For earth's destruction thou dost all despise,
Spurning him from thy bosom to the skies,

And send'st him, shivering in thy playful spray
And howling, to his gods, where haply lies
His petty hope in some near port or bay,
And dashest him again to earth—there let him lay.   1620

The armaments which thunderstrike the walls
Of rock-built cities, bidding nations quake,
And monarchs tremble in their capitals,
The oak leviathans, whose huge ribs make
Their clay creator the vain title take
Of lord of thee, and arbiter of war—
These are thy toys, and, as the snowy flake,
They melt into thy yeast of waves, which mar
Alike the Armada's pride or spoils of Trafalgar.

Thy shores are empires, changed in all save thee—   1630
Assyria, Greece, Rome, Carthage, what are they?
Thy waters washed them power while they were free,
And many a tyrant since; their shores obey
The stranger, slave, or savage; their decay
Has dried up realms to deserts—not so thou;—
Unchangeable, save to thy wild waves' play,
Time writes no wrinkle on thine azure brow:
Such as creation's dawn beheld, thou rollest now.

Thou glorious mirror, where the Almighty's form
Glasses itself in tempests; in all time—   1640
Calm or convulsed, in breeze, or gale, or storm,
Icing the pole, or in the torrid clime
Dark-heaving—boundless, endless, and sublime,
The image of eternity, the throne
Of the Invisible; even from out thy slime
The monsters of the deep are made; each zone
Obeys thee; thou goest forth, dread, fathomless, alone.

And I have loved thee, Ocean! and my joy
Of youthful sports was on thy breast to be
Borne, like thy bubbles, onward: from a boy   1650
I wantoned with thy breakers—they to me
Were a delight; and if the freshening sea
Made them a terror—'twas a pleasing fear,
For I was as it were a child of thee,
And trusted to thy billows far and near,
And laid my hand upon thy mane—as I do here.

My task is done, my song hath ceased, my theme
Has died into an echo; it is fit
The spell should break of this protracted dream,
The torch shall be extinguished which hath lit   1660
My midnight lamp—and what is writ, is writ;
Would it were worthier! but I am not now
That which I have been—and my visions flit

Bede's *Glossarium* to prove that the Coliseum was entire when seen by
the Anglo-Saxon pilgrims in the seventh and eighth centuries. 1571.
midland ocean, the Mediterranean. 1572. **Alban Mount,** a mountain
near Rome. 1574. **Calpe's rock,** Gibraltar. Byron had last seen the
Mediterranean on his return journey to England in 1811. 1575. **Euxine,**
the Black Sea. 1576. **Symplegades,** two island rocks at the entrance of
the Bosporus into the Black Sea. 1586. **one fair Spirit,** Byron's half
sister Augusta. 1601. **mingle . . . Universe.** Cf. Canto 3, ll. 680–688.

1611. **unknelled, etc.** Cf. Scott's *The Lay of the Last Minstrel,* VI,
14–16,

>   . . . shall go down
> To the vile dust, from whence he sprung,
>   Unwept, unhonored, and unsung.

1629. **Alike . . . Trafalgar.** One-half of the Spanish Armada that sailed
against England in 1588 was destroyed in a storm, as were also most
of the French ships captured by Nelson at Trafalgar, in 1805.

Less palpably before me—and the glow
Which in my spirit dwelt is fluttering, faint, and low.

Farewell! a word that must be, and hath been—
A sound which makes us linger;—yet—farewell!
Ye! who have traced the Pilgrim to the scene
Which is his last, if in your memories dwell
1670 A thought which once was his, if on ye swell
A single recollection, not in vain
He wore his sandal-shoon and scallop-shell;
Farewell! with *him* alone may rest the pain,
If such there were—with *you*, the moral of his strain.
(1817; 1818)

TO THOMAS MOORE

*The first stanza of this poem was written in 1816 as
Byron was leaving England. He and Moore, to whom
the next poem was written from Venice, were boon
companions.*

My boat is on the shore,
  And my bark is on the sea;
But, before I go, Tom Moore,
  Here's a double health to thee!

Here's a sigh to those who love me,
  And a smile to those who hate;
And, whatever sky's above me,
  Here's a heart for every fate.

Though the Ocean roar around me,
10   Yet it still shall bear me on;
Though a desert should surround me,
  It hath springs that may be won.

Were't the last drop in the well,
  As I gasped upon the brink,
Ere my fainting spirit fell,
  'Tis to thee that I would drink.

With that water, as this wine,
  That libation I would pour
Should be—peace with thine and mine,
  And a health to thee, Tom Moore.
(1817; 1821)

SO WE'LL GO NO MORE A-ROVING

So we'll go no more a-roving
  So late into the night,

Though the heart be still as loving,
  And the moon be still as bright.

For the sword outwears its sheath,
  And the soul wears out the breast,
And the heart must pause to breathe,
  And love itself have rest.

Though the night was made for loving,
  And the day returns too soon,
10
Yet we'll go no more a-roving
  By the light of the moon.
(1817; 1830)

from DON JUAN

The poem Don Juan *owes its title and certain features
of the story to an old Spanish legend having the folklore theme of the universal lover. The legend had been
popular in Europe for centuries and had undergone a
revival during the neo-classical age; there had been a
play by Molière (1622-1673) and an opera,* Don Giovanni, *by Mozart (1756-1791). Byron's version, however, is highly original; it is decidedly autobiographical
in spirit; and although fragmentary, it is so wide in its
range of subject matter, incident, and character that
its incomplete design is immaterial. Byron said in a
letter to his friend Thomas Moore, dated September 19, 1818: "I have finished the first Canto (a
long one, of about 180 octaves) of a poem in the
style and manner of Beppo, encouraged by the good
success of the same. It is called* Don Juan, *and is meant
to be a little quietly facetious about everything. But I
doubt whether it is not—at least, as far as it has yet
gone—too free for these very modest days. However,
I shall try the experiment, anonymously; if it don't
take, it will be discontinued. It is dedicated to Southey
in good, simple, savage verse, upon the Laureate's
politics, and the way he got them." The experiment
was successful, and the sixteen cantos appeared in
steady succession between 1818 and March 1824, less
than a month before Byron's death. Byron's deliberate
facetiousness of attitude and his lack of plan make the
whole work most informal in tone; but common consent
makes it one of the greatest of English satires. The
narrative, which is episodic, is less important than the
digressions and the occasionally idyllic scenes, such as
the love passages of Juan and Haidée. The hero wanders
over Europe much in the manner of another Childe
Harold searching for, and experiencing, exciting adventures; the final canto, leaving him far from his native*

1672. **sandal . . . shell.** The sandals indicated travel by land; the scallop-shell, which was worn in the hat, travel by sea.
  Dedication. 1. **Southey.** Southey, like Wordsworth and Coleridge, was at one time an ardent Republican, but the excesses and the failures of the French Revolution led him to become a Tory. 6. **Lakers,** Wordsworth, Coleridge, and others, so called from their residence in the Lake District. 12. **Regent,** the Prince of Wales, afterwards George IV, who was appointed Regent when his father, George III, became insane in

1811. Southey was made poet laureate in 1813. 13. **Coleridge . . . wing,** a reference to his *Biographia Literaria* (p. 731), which appeared in 1817. 25. **"Excursion,"** the title of a long poem by Wordsworth. 32. **Tower of Babel,** a high tower described in Genesis 11:1–9. The audacious plan of the builders to make it reach heaven angered the Lord and resulted in the confusion of tongues. 35. **Keswick,** a town in the Lake District, where Southey joined Coleridge in 1803. 46. **the Excise.** Wordsworth was appointed Distributor of Stamps for Westmoreland in

Spain, concludes with Juan upon the threshold of a new adventure, still unsatisfied.

DEDICATION

Bob Southey! You're a poet—Poet laureate,
    And representative of all the race;
Although 'tis true that you turned out a Tory at
    Last—yours has lately been a common case;
And now, my Epic Renegade! what are ye at?
    With all the Lakers, in and out of place?
A nest of tuneful persons, to my eye
Like "four and twenty Blackbirds in a pye;

"Which pye being opened they began to sing"
10 (This old song and new simile holds good),
"A dainty dish to set before the King,"
    Or Regent, who admires such kind of food;—
And Coleridge, too, has lately taken wing,
    But like a hawk encumbered with his hood—
Explaining metaphysics to the nation—
I wish he would explain his Explanation.

You, Bob! are rather insolent, you know,
    At being disappointed in your wish
To supersede all warblers here below,
20   And be the only Blackbird in the dish;
And then you overstrain yourself, or so,
    And tumble downward like the flying fish
Gasping on deck, because you soar too high, Bob,
And fall for lack of moisture quite a-dry, Bob!

And Wordsworth, in a rather long "Excursion"
    (I think the quarto holds five hundred pages),
Has given a sample from the vasty version
    Of his new system to perplex the sages;
'Tis poetry—at least by his assertion,
30   And may appear so when the dog-star rages—
And he who understands it would be able
To add a story to the Tower of Babel.

You—Gentlemen! by dint of long seclusion
    From better company, have kept your own
At Keswick, and through still continued fusion
    Of one another's minds, at last have grown
To deem as a most logical conclusion,
    That poesy has wreaths for you alone;
There is a narrowness in such a notion,
Which makes me wish you'd change your lakes for
40   ocean.

I would not imitate the petty thought,
    Nor coin my self-love to so base a vice,

For all the glory your conversion brought,
    Since gold alone should not have been its price,
You have your salary; was't for that you wrought?
    And Wordsworth has his place in the Excise.
You're shabby fellows—true—but poets still,
And duly seated on the immortal hill.

Your bays may hide the baldness of your brows—
    Perhaps some virtuous blushes;—let them go— 50
To you I envy neither fruit nor boughs—
    And for the fame you would engross below,
The field is universal, and allows
    Scope to all such as feel the inherent glow;
Scott, Rogers, Campbell, Moore, and Crabbe will try
'Gainst you the question with posterity.

For me, who, wandering with pedestrian Muses,
    Contend not with you on the wingéd steed,
I wish your fate may yield ye, when she chooses,
    The fame you envy, and the skill you need; 60
And recollect a poet nothing loses
    In giving to his brethren their full meed
Of merit, and complaint of present days
Is not the certain path to future praise.

He that reserves his laurels for posterity
    (Who does not often claim the bright reversion)
Has generally no great crop to spare it, he
    Being only injured by his own assertion;
And although here and there some glorious rarity
    Arise like Titan from the sea's immersion, 70
The major part of such appellants go
To—God knows where—for no one else can know.

If, fallen in evil days on evil tongues,
    Milton appealed to the Avenger, Time,
If Time, the Avenger, execrates his wrongs,
    And makes the word *"Miltonic"* mean *"sublime,"*
He deigned not to belie his soul in songs,
    Nor turn his very talent to a crime;
He did not loathe the Sire to laud the Son,
But closed the tyrant-hater he begun. 80

Think'st thou, could he—the blind Old Man—arise,
    Like Samuel from the grave, to freeze once more
The blood of monarchs with his prophecies,
    Or be alive again—again all hoar
With time and trials, and those helpless eyes,
    And heartless daughters—worn—and pale—and
      poor;
Would *he* adore a sultan? *he* obey
The intellectual eunuch Castlereagh?

1813, but he never had any connection with the excise. **49. bays,** wreaths of honor made from leaves of the bay tree, a kind of laurel. **55. Scott...Crabbe.** See p. 742. Samuel Rogers (1763–1855), Thomas Campbell (1777–1844), Thomas Moore (1779–1852), and George Crabbe (1754–1832) were minor poets of the day. **58. wingéd steed,** Pegasus, associated with poetic inspiration. **70. Titan,** one of a mythological race of giants said to have piled mountain upon mountain to scale heaven. **73. fallen...tongues,** from *Paradise Lost,* VII, 26.

79. loathe . . . Son, as Southey did with reference to George III and his son. **82. Samuel.** See 1 Samuel, Chapter 28, **86. heartless daughters.** Milton is said to have received shameful treatment from his daughters. **88. Castlereagh,** Robert Stewart (1769–1822), Viscount Castlereagh, whose administration as Foreign Secretary was noted for its cruelty and contempt for all persons not of the aristocracy. At the time of the Irish rebellion in 1798, he was charged with encouraging inhuman punishments of the rebels.

George Noel Gordon, Lord Byron 755

Cold-blooded, smooth-faced, placid miscreant!
90 Dabbling its sleek young hands in Erin's gore
And thus for wider carnage taught to pant,
  Transferred to gorge upon a sister shore,
The vulgarest tool that Tyranny could want,
  With just enough of talent, and no more,
To lengthen fetters by another fixed,
And offer poison long already mixed.

An orator of such set trash of phrase
  Ineffably—legitimately vile,
That even its grossest flatterers dare not praise,
100 Nor foes—all nations—condescend to smile;
Not even a sprightly blunder's spark can blaze
  From that Ixion grindstone's ceaseless toil,
That turns and turns to give the world a notion
Of endless torments and perpetual motion.

A bungler even in its disgusting trade,
  And botching, patching, leaving still behind
Something of which its masters are afraid,
  States to be curbed, and thoughts to be confined,
Conspiracy or Congress to be made—
110 Cobbling at manacles for all mankind—
A tinkering slave-maker, who mends old chains,
With God and man's abhorrence for its gains.

If we may judge of matter by the mind,
  Emasculated to the marrow, *It*
Hath but two objects, how to serve, and bind,
  Deeming the chain it wears even men may fit,
Eutropius of its many masters—blind
  To worth as freedom, wisdom as to wit.
Fearless—because *no* feeling dwells in ice,
120 Its very courage stagnates to a vice.

Where shall I turn me not to *view* its bonds,
  For I will never *feel* them?—Italy!
Thy late reviving Roman soul desponds
  Beneath the lie this State-thing breathed o'er thee—
Thy clanking chain, and Erin's yet green wounds,
  Have voices—tongues to cry aloud for me.
Europe has slaves, allies, kings, armies still,
And Southey lives to sing them very ill.

Meantime, Sir Laureate, I proceed to dedicate,
130 In honest simple verse, this song to you.
And, if in flattering strains I do not predicate,
  'Tis that I still retain my "buff and blue";
My politics as yet are all to educate:
  Apostasy's so fashionable, too,

To keep *one* creed's a task grown quite Herculean:
Is it not so, my Tory, Ultra-Julian?

from CANTO 1

. . . My poem's epic and is meant to be
  Divided in twelve books; each book containing,
With love, and war, a heavy gale at sea,
  A list of ships, and captains, and kings reigning,
New characters; the episodes are three:
  A panoramic view of Hell's in training,
After the style of Virgil and of Homer,
So that my name of Epic's no misnomer.   1600

All these things will be specified in time,
  With strict regard to Aristotle's rules,
The *Vade Mecum* of the true sublime,
  Which makes so many poets, and some fools:
Prose poets like blank-verse, I'm fond of rime,
  Good workmen never quarrel with their tools;
I've got new mythological machinery,
And very handsome supernatural scenery.

There's only one slight difference between
  Me and my epic brethren gone before,   1610
And here the advantage is my own, I ween
  (Not that I have not several merits more,
But this will more peculiarly be seen);
  They so embellish, that 'tis quite a bore
Their labyrinth of fables to thread through,
Whereas this story's actually true.

If any person doubt it, I appeal
  To history, tradition, and to facts,
To newspapers, whose truth all know and feel,
  To plays in five, and operas in three acts;   1620
All these confirm my statement a good deal,
  But that which more completely faith exacts
Is, that myself, and several now in Seville,
Saw Juan's last elopement with the devil.

If ever I should condescend to prose,
  I'll write poetical commandments, which
Shall supersede beyond all doubt all those
  That went before; in these I shall enrich
My text with many things that no one knows,
  And carry precept to the highest pitch: 1630
I'll call the work "Longinus o'er a Bottle,
Or, Every Poet his *own* Aristotle."

Thou shalt believe in Milton, Dryden, Pope;
  Thou shalt not set up Wordsworth, Coleridge,
    Southey;

102. **Ixion,** a legendary king in Greece who for boasting of the favors of Hera, wife of Zeus, was bound to an endlessly revolving wheel in Hades. 117. **Eutropius,** a Byzantine statesman surnamed "The Eunuch," who served as a chamberlain in the household of Arcadius on his succession to the throne as emperor of the East in 395 A.D. 132. **"buff and blue,"** the colors of the uniform adopted by members of the Whig Club; hence the binding of the *Edinburgh Review,* the Whig organ. 136. **Ultra-Julian.** "I allude not to our friend Landor's hero, the

traitor Count Julian [in Landor's *Count Julian*], but to Gibbon's hero vulgarly yclept 'The Apostate.'"—Byron. Julian the Apostate was Roman emperor between 361 and 363.
  Canto 1. In the stanzas omitted Byron gives an account of the parents of Don Juan and their incompatibilities, of his early training, and of his escapades, one of which results in his being sent abroad to "mend his morals." 1602. **Aristotle's rules,** rules regarding epic and narrative poetry. 1603. *Vade Mecum,* handbook; literally, go with me.

Because the first is crazed beyond all hope,
   The second drunk, the third so quaint and mouthy:
With Crabbe it may be difficult to cope,
   And Campbell's Hippocrene is somewhat drouthy:
Thou shalt not steal from Samuel Rogers, nor
1640 Commit—flirtation with the muse of Moore.

Thou shalt not covet Mr. Sotheby's Muse,
   His Pegasus, nor anything that's his;
Thou shalt not bear false witness like "the Blues"—
   (There's one, at least, is very fond of this);
Thou shalt not write, in short, but what I
      choose;
   This is true criticism, and you may kiss—
Exactly as you please, or not—the rod;
   But if you don't, I'll lay it on, by G—d!

If any person should presume to assert
1650   This story is not moral, first I pray,
That they will not cry out before they're hurt,
   Then that they'll read it o'er again, and say
(But doubtless, nobody will be so pert),
   That this is not a moral tale, though gay;
Besides, in Canto Twelfth, I mean to show
The very place where wicked people go.

If, after all, there should be some so blind
   To their own good this warning to despise,
Led by some tortuosity of mind,
1660   Not to believe my verse and their own eyes,
And cry that they "the moral cannot find,"
   I tell him, if a clergyman, he lies;
Should captains the remark, or critics, make,
   They also lie too—under a mistake.

The public approbation I expect,
   And beg they'll take my word about the moral,
Which I with their amusement will connect
   (So children cutting teeth receive a coral);
Meantime they'll doubtless please to recollect
1670   My epical pretensions to the laurel:
For fear some prudish readers should grow skittish,
I've bribed my grandmother's review—the British.

I sent it in a letter to the Editor,
   Who thanked me duly by return of post—
I'm for a handsome article his creditor;
   Yet, if my gentle Muse he please to roast,
And break a promise after having made it her,
   Denying the receipt of what it cost,
And smear his page with gall instead of honey,
1680 All I can say is—that he had the money.

I think that with this holy new alliance
   I may ensure the public, and defy
All other magazines of art or science,
   Daily, or monthly, or three-monthly; I
Have not essayed to multiply their clients,
   Because they tell me 'twere in vain to try,
And that the *Edinburgh Review* and *Quarterly*
Treat a dissenting author very martyrly. . . .

from CANTO 2

Oh ye! who teach the ingenuous youth of nations,
   Holland, France, England, Germany, or Spain,
I pray ye flog them upon all occasions;
   It mends their morals, never mind the pain:
The best of mothers and of educations
   In Juan's case were but employed in vain,
Since, in a way that's rather of the oddest, he
Became divested of his native modesty.

Had he but been placed at a public school,
   In the third form, or even in the fourth,   10
His daily task had kept his fancy cool,
   At least, had he been nurtured in the north;
Spain may prove an exception to the rule,
   But then exceptions always prove its worth—
A lad of sixteen causing a divorce
Puzzled his tutors very much, of course.

I can't say that it puzzles me at all,
   If all things be considered; first, there was
His lady-mother, mathematical,
   A——never mind;—his tutor, an old ass;   20
A pretty woman—(that's quite natural,
   Or else the thing had hardly come to pass)
A husband rather old, not much in unity
With his young wife—a time, and opportunity.

Well—well; the world must turn upon its axis,
   And all mankind turn with it, heads or tails,
And live and die, make love and pay our taxes,
   And as the veering wind shifts, shift our sails;
The king commands us, and the doctor quacks us,
   The priest instructs, and so our life exhales,   30
A little breath, love, wine, ambition, fame,
Fighting, devotion, dust—perhaps a name.

I said that Juan had been sent to Cadiz—
   A pretty town, I recollect it well—
'Tis there the mart of the colonial trade is,
   (Or was, before Peru learned to rebel)
And such sweet girls—I mean, such graceful ladies,

1611. **ween,** think. 1623. **Seville,** a city in southwestern Spain. 1631. **Longinus,** a Greek Platonic philosopher and critic (third century A.D.). 1637. **Crabbe,** George Crabbe (1754–1832), a minor romantic poet. 1638. **Campbell,** Thomas Campbell (1777–1844), another minor romantic poet. **Hippocrene,** a fountain in Greece sacred to the Muses. 1639. **Samuel Rogers,** (1763–1855) a contemporary minor poet. 1640. **Moore,** Thomas Moore (1779–1852), another contemporary poet. 1641. **Sotheby,** William Sotheby (1757–1833), an English scholar and poet.

1642. **Pegasus,** a winged horse associated with poetic inspiration. 1643. **"the Blues,"** the Bluestockings, a name applied to a society of women affecting an interest in literature and politics. 1687. ***Edinburgh Review*** and ***Quarterly.*** Both magazines were hostile to Byron; he attacked them in his *English Bards and Scotch Reviewers* (p. 741).
   Canto 2. 9. **public school,** in England, a private school like Eton. 33. **Cadiz,** a city on the southwest coast of Spain.

Their very walk would make your bosom swell;
I can't describe it, though so much it strike,
40 Nor liken it—I never saw the like:

An Arab horse, a stately stag, a barb
    New broke, a cameleopard, a gazelle,
No—none of these will do—and then their garb,
    Their veil and petticoat—Alas! to dwell
Upon such things would very near absorb
    A canto—then their feet and ankles—well,
Thank Heaven I've got no metaphor quite ready,
(And so, my sober Muse—come, let's be steady—

Chaste Muse!—well, if you must, you must)—the veil
50   Thrown back a moment with the glancing hand,
While the o'erpowering eye, that turns you pale,
    Flashes into the heart—All sunny land
Of Love! when I forget you, may I fail
    To—say my prayers—but never was there planned
A dress through which the eyes give such a volley,
Excepting the Venetian Fazzioli.

But to our tale: the Donna Inez sent
    Her son to Cadiz only to embark;
To stay there had not answered her intent,
60   But why?—we leave the reader in the dark—
'Twas for a voyage the young man was meant,
    As if a Spanish ship were Noah's ark,
To wean him from the wickedness of earth,
And send him like a Dove of Promise forth.

Don Juan bade his valet pack his things
    According to directions, then received
A lecture and some money: for four springs
    He was to travel; and though Inez grieved
(As every kind of parting has its stings),
70   She hoped he would improve—perhaps believed:
A letter, too, she gave (he never read it)
Of good advice—and two or three of credit.

In the meantime, to pass her hours away,
    Brave Inez now set up a Sunday school
For naughty children, who would rather play
    (Like truant rogues) the devil, or the fool;
Infants of three years old were taught that day,
    Dunces were whipped, or set upon a stool:
The great success of Juan's education
80 Spurred her to teach another generation.

Juan embarked—the ship got under way,
    The wind was fair, the water passing rough;
A devil of a sea rolls in that bay,
    As I, who've crossed it oft, know well enough;
And, standing on the deck, the dashing spray

Flies in one's face, and makes it weather-tough:
And there he stood to take, and take again,
His first—perhaps his last—farewell of Spain.

I can't but say it is an awkward sight
    To see one's native land receding through   90
The growing waters; it unmans one quite,
    Especially when life is rather new:
I recollect Great Britain's coast looks white,
    But almost every other country's blue;
When gazing on them, mystified by distance,
We enter on our nautical existence.

So Juan stood, bewildered on the deck:
    The wind sung, cordage strained, and sailors swore,
And the ship creaked, the town became a speck,
    From which away so fair and fast they bore.   100
The best of remedies is a beefsteak
    Against seasickness: try it, Sir, before
You sneer, and I assure you this is true,
For I have found it answer—so may you.

Don Juan stood, and, gazing from the stern,
    Beheld his native Spain receding far:
First partings form a lesson hard to learn,
    Even nations feel this when they go to war;
There is a sort of unexpressed concern,
    A kind of shock that sets one's heart ajar,   110
At leaving even the most unpleasant people
And places—one keeps looking at the steeple.

But Juan had got many things to leave,
    His mother, and a mistress, and no wife,
So that he had much better cause to grieve
    Than many persons more advanced in life:
And if we now and then a sigh must heave
    At quitting even those we quit in strife,
No doubt we weep for those the heart endears—
That is, till deeper griefs congeal our tears.   120

So Juan wept, as wept the captive Jews
    By Babel's waters, still remembering Sion:
I'd weep—but mine is not a weeping Muse,
    And such light griefs are not a thing to die on;
Young men should travel, if but to amuse
    Themselves; and the next time their servants tie on
Behind their carriages their new portmanteau,
Perhaps it may be lined with this my canto.

And Juan wept, and much he sighed and thought,
    While his salt tears dropped into the salt sea,   130
"Sweets to the sweet"; (I like so much to quote;
    You must excuse this extract—'tis where she,
The Queen of Denmark, for Ophelia brought
    Flowers to the grave;) and, sobbing often, he

41. barb, a Barbary horse, noted for speed and endurance. 56. Fazzioli, "Literally, little handkerchiefs—the veils most availing of St.
Mark."—Byron. 64. Dove . . . forth, a reference to the dove sent

by Noah from the ark when he wanted to learn whether the waters were
receding. See Genesis 8:6–12. 121. So . . . Sion, from Psalms 137:1:
"By the rivers of Babylon, there we sat down, yea, we wept, when we

Reflected on his present situation,
And seriously resolved on reformation.

"Farewell, my Spain! a long farewell!" he cried,
    "Perhaps I may revisit thee no more,
But die, as many an exiled heart hath died,
140   Of its own thirst to see again thy shore:
Farewell, where Guadalquivir's waters glide!
    Farewell, my mother! and, since all is o'er,
Farewell, too, dearest Julia!—(here he drew
Her letter out again, and read it through.)

"And oh! if e'er I should forget, I swear—
    But that's impossible, and cannot be—
Sooner shall this blue ocean melt to air,
    Sooner shall earth resolve itself to sea,
Than I resign thine image, oh, my fair!
150   Or think of anything, excepting thee;
A mind diseased no remedy can physic—
(Here the ship gave a lurch, and he grew seasick.)

"Sooner shall Heaven kiss earth—(here he fell sicker)
    Oh, Julia! what is every other woe?—
(For God's sake let me have a glass of liquor;
    Pedro, Battista, help me down below.)
Julia, my love!—(you rascal, Pedro, quicker)—
    Oh, Julia!—(this curst vessel pitches so)—
Belovéd Julia, hear me still beseeching!"
160 (Here he grew inarticulate with retching.)

He felt that chilling heaviness of heart,
    Or rather stomach, which, alas! attends,
Beyond the best apothecary's art,
    The loss of Love, the treachery of friends,
Or death of those we dote on, when a part
    Of us dies with them as each fond hope ends:
No doubt he would have been much more pathetic,
But the sea acted as a strong emetic.

Love's a capricious power: I've known it hold
170   Out through a fever caused by its own heat,
But be much puzzled by a cough and cold,
    And find a quinsy very hard to treat;
Against all noble maladies he's bold,
    But vulgar illnesses don't like to meet,
Nor that a sneeze should interrupt his sigh,
Nor inflammation redden his blind eye.

But worst of all is nausea, or a pain
    About the lower region of the bowels;
Love, who heroically breathes a vein,
180   Shrinks from the applications of hot towels,
And purgatives are dangerous to his reign,
    Seasickness death: his love was perfect, how else
Could Juan's passion, while the billows roar,
Resist his stomach, ne'er at sea before?

The ship, called the most holy "Trinidada,"
    Was steering duly for the port Leghorn;
For there the Spanish family Moncada
    Were settled long ere Juan's sire was born:
They were relations, and for them he had a
    Letter of introduction, which the morn   190
Of his departure had been sent him by
His Spanish friends for those in Italy.

His suite consisted of three servants and
    A tutor, the licentiate Pedrillo,
Who several languages did understand,
    But now lay sick and speechless on his pillow,
And, rocking in his hammock, longed for land,
    His headache being increased by every billow;
And the waves oozing through the port-hole
        made
His berth a little damp, and him afraid.   200

'Twas not without some reason, for the wind
    Increased at night, until it blew a gale;
And though 't was not much to a naval mind,
    Some landsmen would have looked a little pale,
For sailors are, in fact, a different kind:
    At sunset they began to take in sail,
For the sky showed it would come on to blow,
And carry away, perhaps, a mast or so.

At one o'clock the wind with sudden shift
    Threw the ship right into the trough of the sea,   210
Which struck her aft, and made an awkward rift,
    Started the stern-post, also shattered the
Whole of her stern-frame, and, ere she could lift
    Herself from out her present jeopardy,
The rudder tore away; 'twas time to sound
The pumps, and there were four feet water found.

One gang of people instantly was put
    Upon the pumps, and the remainder set
To get up part of the cargo, and what not;
    But they could not come at the leak as yet;   220
At last they did get at it really, but
    Still their salvation was an even bet:
The water rushed through in a way quite puzzling,
While they thrust sheet, shirts, jackets, bales of muslin,

Into the opening; but all such ingredients
    Would have been vain, and they must have gone
        down,
Despite of all their efforts and expedients,
    But for the pumps; I'm glad to make them known
To all the brother tars who may have need hence,
    For fifty tons of water were upthrown   230
By them per hour, and they had all been undone,
But for the maker, Mr. Mann, of London.

remembered Zion." The reference is to the story of the Jews taken into
captivity by Nebuchadnezzar, king of Babylon. Cf. 2 Kings 24:10–16.
131. **"Sweets to the sweet,"** quoted from Gertrude's speech in *Hamlet*

(V, i, 266) at the burial of Ophelia. 186. **Leghorn,** a city in Tuscany,
on the west coast of Italy.

As day advanced the weather seemed to abate,
    And then the leak they reckoned to reduce,
And keep the ship afloat, though three feet yet
    Kept two hand- and one chain-pump still in use.
The wind blew fresh again: as it grew late
    A squall came on, and while some guns broke loose,
A gust—which all descriptive power transcends—
240 Laid with one blast the ship on her beam ends.

There she lay, motionless, and seemed upset;
    The water left the hold, and washed the decks,
And made a scene men do not soon forget;
    For they remember battles, fires, and wrecks,
Or any other thing that brings regret,
    Or breaks their hopes, or hearts, or heads, or necks:
Thus drownings are much talked of by the divers,
And swimmers, who may chance to be survivors.

Immediately the masts were cut away,
250   Both main and mizzen; first the mizzen went,
The main-mast followed: but the ship still lay
    Like a mere log, and baffled our intent.
Foremast and bowsprit were cut down, and they
    Eased her at last (although we never meant
To part with all till every hope was blighted),
And then with violence the old ship righted.

It may be easily supposed, while this
    Was going on, some people were unquiet,
That passengers would find it much amiss
260   To lose their lives, as well as spoil their diet;
That even the able seaman, deeming his
    Days nearly o'er, might be disposed to riot,
As upon such occasions tars will ask
For grog, and sometimes drink rum from the cask.

There's naught, no doubt, so much the spirit calms
    As rum and true religion: thus it was,
Some plundered, some drank spirits, some sung
      psalms,
    The high wind made the treble, and as bass
The hoarse harsh waves kept time; fright cured the
      qualms
270 Of all the luckless landsmen's seasick maws:
Strange sounds of wailing, blasphemy, devotion,
Clamored in chorus to the roaring Ocean.

Perhaps more mischief had been done, but for
    Our Juan, who, with sense beyond his years,
Got to the spirit-room, and stood before
    It with a pair of pistols; and their fears,
As if Death were more dreadful by his door
    Of fire than water, spite of oaths and tears,
Kept still aloof the crew, who, ere they sunk,
280 Thought it would be becoming to die drunk.

"Give us more grog," they cried, "for it will be
    All one an hour hence." Juan answered, "No!
'T is true that death awaits both you and me,
    But let us die like men, not sink below
Like brutes"—and thus his dangerous post kept he,
    And none liked to anticipate the blow;
And even Pedrillo, his most reverend tutor,
Was for some rum a disappointed suitor.

The good old gentleman was quite aghast,
    And made a loud and pious lamentation;   290
Repented all his sins, and made a last
    Irrevocable vow of reformation;
Nothing should tempt him more (this peril past)
    To quit his academic occupation,
In cloisters of the classic Salamanca,
To follow Juan's wake, like Sancho Panca.

But now there came a flash of hope once more;
    Day broke, and the wind lulled: the masts were gone;
The leak increased; shoals round her, but no shore,
    The vessel swam, yet still she held her own.   300
They tried the pumps again, and though, before,
    Their desperate efforts seemed all useless grown,
A glimpse of sunshine set some hands to bale—
The stronger pumped, the weaker thrummed a sail.

Under the vessel's keel the sail was passed,
    And for the moment it had some effect;
But with a leak, and not a stick of mast,
    Nor rag of canvas, what could they expect?
But still 'tis best to struggle to the last,
    'Tis never too late to be wholly wrecked: 310
And though 'tis true that man can only die once,
'Tis not so pleasant in the Gulf of Lyons.

There winds and waves had hurled them, and from
      thence,
    Without their will, they carried them away;
For they were forced with steering to dispense,
    And never had as yet a quiet day
On which they might repose, or even commence
    A jurymast or rudder, or could say
The ship would swim an hour, which, by good luck,
Still swam—though not exactly like a duck.   320

The wind, in fact, perhaps, was rather less,
    But the ship labored so, they scarce could hope
To weather out much longer; the distress
    Was also great with which they had to cope
For want of water, and their solid mess
    Was scant enough: in vain the telescope
Was used—nor sail nor shore appeared in sight,
Naught but the heavy sea, and coming night.

250. **mizzen,** the aftermost mast of a three-masted vessel. 253. **bow-sprit,** a large spar projecting forward from the stem of a ship to carry the sail forward and to support the masts by means of stays. 295. **Sala-** manca, a city in western Spain, the seat of a celebrated university. 296. **Sancho Panca,** Sancho Panza, the shrewd squire of the hero in *Don Quixote,* a burlesque Spanish romance by Cervantes (1547–1616). 304.

Again the weather threatened—again blew
330 A gale, and in the fore and after-hold
Water appeared; yet, though the people knew
All this, the most were patient, and some bold,
Until the chains and leathers were worn through
Of all our pumps—a wreck complete she rolled,
At mercy of the waves, whose mercies are
Like human beings during civil war.

Then came the carpenter, at last, with tears
In his rough eyes, and told the captain he
Could do no more: he was a man in years,
340 And long had voyaged through many a stormy sea,
And if he wept at length, they were not fears
That made his eyelids as a woman's be,
But he, poor fellow, had a wife and children,
Two things for dying people quite bewildering.

The ship was evidently settling now
Fast by the head; and, all distinction gone,
Some went to prayers again, and made a vow
Of candles to their saints—but there were none
To pay them with; and some looked o'er the bow;
350 Some hoisted out the boats; and there was one
That begged Pedrillo for an absolution,
Who told him to be damned—in his confusion.

Some lashed them in their hammocks; some put on
Their best clothes, as if going to a fair;
Some cursed the day on which they saw the sun,
And gnashed their teeth, and howling, tore their
hair;
And others went on as they had begun,
Getting the boats out, being well aware
That a tight boat will live in a rough sea,
360 Unless with breakers close beneath her lee.

The worst of all was, that in their condition,
Having been several days in great distress,
'Twas difficult to get out such provision
As now might render their long suffering less.
Men, even when dying, dislike inanition;
Their stock was damaged by the weather's stress.
Two casks of biscuit, and a keg of butter,
Were all that could be thrown into the cutter.

But in the long-boat they contrived to stow
370 Some pounds of bread, though injured by the wet;
Water, a twenty-gallon cask or so;
Six flasks of wine: and they contrived to get
A portion of their beef up from below,
And with a piece of pork, moreover, met,
But scarce enough to serve them for a luncheon—
Then there was rum, eight gallons in a puncheon.

The other boats, the yawl and pinnace, had
Been stove in the beginning of the gale;
And the long-boat's condition was but bad,
As there were but two blankets for a sail,   380
And one oar for a mast, which a young lad
Threw in by good luck over the ship's rail;
And two boats could not hold, far less be stored,
To save one half the people then on board.

'Twas twilight, and the sunless day went down
Over the waste of waters; like a veil,
Which, if withdrawn, would but disclose the frown
Of one whose hate is masked but to assail.
Thus to their hopeless eyes the night was shown,
And grimly darkled o'er the faces pale,   390
And the dim desolate deep: twelve days had Fear
Been their familiar, and now Death was here.

Some trial had been making at a raft,
With little hope in such a rolling sea,
A sort of thing at which one would have laughed,
If any laughter at such times could be,
Unless with people who too much have quaffed,
And have a kind of wild and horrid glee,
Half epileptical, and half hysterical—
Their preservation would have been a miracle.   400

At half-past eight o'clock, booms, hencoops, spars,
And all things, for a chance, had been cast loose
That still could keep afloat the struggling tars,
For yet they strove, although of no great use:
There was no light in heaven but a few stars,
The boats put off o'ercrowded with their crews;
She gave a heel, and then a lurch to port,
And, going down head foremost—sunk, in short.

Then rose from sea to sky the wild farewell—
Then shrieked the timid, and stood still the brave— 410
Then some leaped overboard with dreadful yell,
As eager to anticipate their grave;
And the sea yawned around her like a hell,
And down she sucked with her the whirling wave,
Like one who grapples with his enemy,
And strives to strangle him before he die.

And first one universal shriek there rushed,
Louder than the loud Ocean, like a crash
Of echoing thunder; and then all was hushed,
Save the wild wind and the remorseless dash   420
Of billows; but at intervals there gushed,
Accompanied by a convulsive splash,
A solitary shriek, the bubbling cry
Of some strong swimmer in his agony.
(1818-1819; 1821)

from CANTO 3

THE ISLES OF GREECE

The isles of Greece, the isles of Greece!
    Where burning Sappho loved and sung,
Where grew the arts of war and peace,
    Where Delos rose, and Phoebus sprung!
Eternal summer gilds them yet,
But all, except their sun, is set.

The Scian and the Teian muse,
    The hero's harp, the lover's lute,
Have found the fame your shores refuse:
10 Their place of birth alone is mute
To sounds which echo further west
Than your sires' "Islands of the Blest."

The mountains look on Marathon—
    And Marathon looks on the sea;
And musing there an hour alone,
    I dreamed that Greece might still be free;
For standing on the Persians' grave,
I could not deem myself a slave.

A king sat on the rocky brow
20 Which looks o'er sea-born Salamis;
And ships, by thousands, lay below,
    And men in nations;—all were his!
He counted them at break of day—
And when the sun set, where were they?

And where are they? and where art thou,
    My country? On thy voiceless shore
The heroic lay is tuneless now—
    The heroic bosom beats no more!
And must thy lyre, so long divine,
30 Degenerate into hands like mine?

'Tis something, in the dearth of fame,
    Though linked among a fettered race,
To feel at least a patriot's shame,
    Even as I sing, suffuse my face;
For what is left the poet here?
For Greeks a blush—for Greece a tear.

Must *we* but weep o'er days more blest?
Must *we* but blush?—Our fathers bled.

Earth! render back from out thy breast
    A remnant of our Spartan dead!   40
Of the three hundred grant but three,
To make a new Thermopylae!

What, silent still? and silent all?
    Ah! no;—the voices of the dead
Sound like a distant torrent's fall,
    And answer, "Let one living head,
But one arise—we come, we come!"
'Tis but the living who are dumb.

In vain—in vain: strike other chords;
    Fill high the cup with Samian wine!   50
Leave battles to the Turkish hordes,
    And shed the blood of Scio's vine!
Hark! rising to the ignoble call—
How answers each bold Bacchanal!

You have the Pyrrhic dance as yet;
    Where is the Pyrrhic phalanx gone?
Of two such lessons, why forget
    The nobler and the manlier one?
You have the letters Cadmus gave—
Think ye he meant them for a slave?   60

Fill high the bowl with Samian wine!
    We will not think of themes like these!
It made Anacreon's song divine:
    He served—but served Polycrates—
A tyrant; but our masters then
Were still, at least, our countrymen.

The tyrant of the Chersonese
    Was freedom's best and bravest friend;
That tyrant was Miltiades!
    Oh! that the present hour would lend   70
Another despot of the kind!
Such chains as his were sure to bind.

Fill high the bowl with Samian wine!
    On Suli's rock, and Parga's shore,
Exists the remnant of a line
    Such as the Doric mothers bore;
And there, perhaps, some seed is sown,
The Heracleidan blood might own.

Canto 3. Of nearly two hundred persons on the boat Juan is the only survivor of the wreck. He lands on one of the Cyclades, islands southeast of Greece, and is picked up unconscious by Haidée, the beautiful daughter of a pirate and smuggler, who is away from home. She hides Juan in a cave, secretly takes care of him, and soon the young people fall deeply in love. During the absence of her father the lovers hold a feast, at which the song given here is represented as being sung. 2. **Sappho,** a Greek lyric poetess (seventh century B.C.), known as the Tenth Muse. 4. **Delos,** an island off the coast of Greece. **Phoebus,** Apollo, god of music and poetry; he resided on Mt. Olympus, Greece, sacred to the gods. 7. **Scian . . . muse,** Homer, of the Island of Scio, east of Greece, and Anacreon, Greek lyric poet (fifth century B.C.), of Teos, Asia Minor. 12. **"Islands of the Blest,"** mythical islands said to lie in the Western Ocean, where the favorites of the gods dwelt after death. 13. **Marathon,** a plain in Attica, Greece, the scene of the famous Greek victory over the Persian army in 490 B.C. 19. **king,** Xerxes, king of Persia who ruled from 486 to 465 B.C. 20. **Salamis,** an island of Greece, west of Athens. It was the scene of the great naval battle of 480 B.C., in which the Greeks destroyed the Persian fleet of Xerxes (l. 24). 42. **Thermopylae,** a pass in northern Greece, celebrated for the valiant stand made there in 480 B.C. by Leonidas and his band of 300 Spartans against the Persian host of Xerxes. 50. **Samian,** from Samos, an island in the Aegean Sea. 52. **Scio,** an island in the Aegean Sea, once famous for its wines. 54. **Bacchanal,** devotee of Bacchus, god of wine. 55. **Pyrrhic dance,** an ancient war dance in quick time. 56. **Pyrrhic phalanx,** the heavily armed infantry used by Pyrrhus, the great Greek general (third century B.C.). 59. **Cadmus,** the reputed founder of Thebes. He brought the old Phoenician, or Cadmean, alphabet of sixteen letters to Greece. 63. **Anacreon,** a Greek lyric poet (563?–478? B.C.). 64. **Polycrates,** tyrant of Samos (who ruled from 535 to 522? B.C.), a patron of literature and art. 67. **Chersonese,** a peninsula of ancient Greece, the present-day Gallipoli. 69. **Miltiades,** a celebrated Athenian general (fifth century B.C.). 74. **Suli,** a mountainous district in European Turkey. **Parga,** a seaport in

Trust not for freedom to the Franks—
80   They have a king who buys and sells;
In native swords, and native ranks,
    The only hope of courage dwells:
But Turkish force, and Latin fraud,
Would break your shield, however broad.

Fill high the bowl with Samian wine!
    Our virgins dance beneath the shade—
I see their glorious black eyes shine;
    But gazing on each glowing maid,
My own the burning tear-drop laves,
90 To think such breasts must suckle slaves.

Place me on Sunium's marbled steep,
    Where nothing, save the waves and I,
May hear our mutual murmurs sweep;
    There, swan-like, let me sing and die:
A land of slaves shall ne'er be mine—
Dash down yon cup of Samian wine! . . .

Thus sung, or would, or could, or should have sung,
690   The modern Greek, in tolerable verse;
If not like Orpheus quite, when Greece was young,
    Yet in these times he might have done much worse:
His strain displayed some feeling—right or wrong;
    And feeling, in a poet, is the source
Of others' feeling; but they are such liars,
And take all colors—like the hands of dyers.

But words are things, and a small drop of ink,
    Falling like dew, upon a thought, produces
That which makes thousands, perhaps millions, think;
700   'Tis strange, the shortest letter which man uses
Instead of speech, may form a lasting link
    Of ages; to what straits old Time reduces
Frail man, when paper—even a rag like this,
Survives himself, his tomb, and all that's his!

And when his bones are dust, his grave a blank,
    His station, generation, even his nation,
Become a thing, or nothing, save to rank
    In chronological commemoration,
Some dull MS. oblivion long has sank,
710   Or graven stone found in a barrack's station
In digging the foundation of a closet,
May turn his name up, as a rare deposit.

And glory long has made the sages smile;
    'Tis something, nothing, words, illusion, wind—
Depending more upon the historian's style
    Than on the name a person leaves behind:
Troy owes to Homer what whist owes to Hoyle:
    The present century was growing blind
To the great Marlborough's skill in giving knocks,
Until his late Life by Archdeacon Coxe.   720

Milton's the prince of poets—so we say;
    A little heavy, but no less divine:
An independent being in his day—
    Learned, pious, temperate in love and wine;
But his life falling into Johnson's way,
    We're told this great high priest of all the Nine
Was whipped at college—a harsh sire—odd spouse,
For the first Mrs. Milton left his house.

All these are, certes, entertaining facts,
    Like Shakespeare's stealing deer, Lord Bacon's
        bribes;   730
Like Titus' youth, and Caesar's earliest acts;
    Like Burns (whom Doctor Currie well describes);
Like Cromwell's pranks;—but although truth exacts
    These amiable descriptions from the scribes,
As most essential to their hero's story,
They do not much contribute to his glory.

All are not moralists, like Southey, when
    He prated to the world of "Pantisocrasy";
Or Wordsworth unexcised, unhired, who then
    Seasoned his peddler poems with democracy;   740
Or Coleridge, long before his flighty pen
    Let to the Morning Post its aristocracy;
When he and Southey, following the same path,
Espoused two partners (milliners of Bath).

Such names at present cut a convict figure,
    The very Botany Bay in moral geography;
Their loyal treason, renegado rigor,
    Are good manure for their more bare biography;
Wordsworth's last quarto, by the way, is bigger
    Than any since the birthday of typography;   750
A drowsy, frowzy poem, called the "Excursion,"
Writ in a manner which is my aversion.

He there builds up a formidable dyke
    Between his own and others' intellect;

Turkey. **76. Doric,** from Doris, an ancient province in northern Greece. **78. Heracleidan,** tracing back to Hercules, i.e., ancient Greek. **91. Sunium,** in ancient geography the promontory at the southeastern extremity of Attica, Greece. **94. swan-like.** The swan was said to sing melodiously when about to die. **691. Orpheus,** a mythological poet and musician whose lyre could charm beasts and move trees and stones. **717. Troy . . . Homer.** Troy, an ancient city in Asia Minor, is the scene of Homer's *Iliad.* **Hoyle,** Edmund Hoyle (1672–1769), an English writer on whist and other card games. **719. Marlborough,** John Churchill (1650–1722), Duke of Marlborough, the famous English general who defeated the French in the battle of Blenheim, Bavaria, in 1704. **720. Coxe,** William Coxe (1747–1832), an English historian. His *Memoirs of the Duke of Marlborough* appeared in 1817–1819. **725. life . . . way.** Samuel Johnson wrote a life of Milton, published in his *Lives of the English Poets* (1779–1781). See p. 575. **726. the Nine,** the nine Muses. **730. stealing deer,** a fictitious anecdote popularly associated with Shakespeare's youth. **Bacon's bribes.** Bacon

was charged with accepting bribes and was therefore excluded from Parliament. See p. 317. **731. Titus' youth.** The youth of Titus Vespasianus, Roman emperor (79-81 A.D.), like that of Julius Caesar and that of Burns, p. 653, was noted for its voluptuousness. **732. Currie,** James Currie (1756-1805), a Scottish physician, who wrote a life of Burns for the benefit of the Burns family. **733. Cromwell's pranks.** The youthful Cromwell was noted for robbing orchards. **738. "Pantisocrasy,"** the name given to a scheme for an ideal community that Southey, Coleridge, and others planned in 1794 to establish in America. See p. 711. **739. unexcised.** See note on p. 755, l. 46. **740. peddler poems.** A reference to Wordsworth's *Peter Bell,* the hero of which is a peddler. **742. Morning Post.** Coleridge began his contributions to the *Morning Post* in 1798. **744. two partners.** Coleridge married Sarah Fricker, of Bath; Southey married her sister Edith; they were not milliners at the time of their marriages in 1795. **746. Botany Bay,** an inlet on the east coast of Australia, formerly used by the British as a convict station.

But Wordsworth's poem, and his followers, like
　　Joanna Southcote's Shiloh and her sect,
Are things which in this century don't strike
　　The public mind—so few are the elect;
And the new births of both their stale virginities
760 Have proved but dropsies, taken for divinities.

But let me to my story: I must own,
　　If I have any fault, it is digression,
Leaving my people to proceed alone,
　　While I soliloquize beyond expression:
But these are my addresses from the throne,
　　Which put off business to the ensuing session:
Forgetting each omission is a loss to
The world, not quite so great as Ariosto.

I know that what our neighbors call "longueurs,"
770 　(We've not so good a word, but have the thing,
In that complete perfection which insures
　　An epic from Bob Southey every spring—)
Form not the true temptation which allures
　　The reader; but 'twould not be hard to bring
Some fine examples of the épopée,
To prove its grand ingredient is ennui.

We learn from Horace, "Homer sometimes sleeps";
　　We feel without him, Wordsworth sometimes
　　　　wakes—
To show with what complacency he creeps,
780 　With his dear "Wagoners," around his lakes.
He wishes for "a boat" to sail the deeps—
　　Of ocean?—No, of air; and then he makes
Another outcry for "a little boat,"
And drivels seas to set it well afloat.

If he must fain sweep o'er the ethereal plain,
　　And Pegasus runs restive in his "Wagon,"
Could he not beg the loan of Charles's Wain?
　　Or pray Medea for a single dragon?
Or if, too classic for his vulgar brain,
790 　He feared his neck to venture such a nag on,
And he must needs mount nearer to the moon,
Could not the blockhead ask for a balloon?

"Peddlers," and "Boats," and "Wagons!" Oh! ye shades
　　Of Pope and Dryden, are we come to this?
That trash of such sort not alone evades
　　Contempt, but from the bathos' vast abyss
Floats scumlike uppermost, and these Jack Cades
　　Of sense and song above your graves may hiss—
The "little boatman" and his "Peter Bell"
800 Can sneer at him who drew "Achitophel"!

T' our tale.—The feast was over, the slaves gone,
　　The dwarfs and dancing girls had all retired;
The Arab lore and poet's song were done,
　　And every sound of revelry expired,
The lady and her lover, left alone,
　　The rosy flood of twilight's sky admired;—
Ave Maria o'er the earth and sea,
That heavenliest hour of Heaven is worthiest thee!

Ave Maria! blesséd be the hour
　　The time, the clime, the spot, where I so oft　　810
Have felt that moment in its fullest power
　　Sink o'er the earth so beautiful and soft,
While swung the deep bell in the distant tower,
　　Or the faint dying day-hymn stole aloft,
And not a breath crept through the rosy air,
And yet the forest leaves seemed stirred with prayer.

Ave Maria! 'tis the hour of prayer!
　　Ave Maria! 'tis the hour of love!
Ave Maria! may our spirits dare
　　Look up to thine and to thy Son's above!　　820
Ave Maria! oh that face so fair!
　　Those downcast eyes beneath the Almighty Dove—
What though 'tis but a pictured image?—strike—
That painting is no idol—'tis too like.

Some kinder casuists are pleased to say,
　　In nameless print—that I have no devotion;
But set those persons down with me to pray,
　　And you shall see who has the properest notion
Of getting into heaven the shortest way;
　　My altars are the mountains and the ocean,　　830
Earth, air, stars—all that springs from the great Whole,
Who hath produced, and will receive the soul.

Sweet hour of twilight!—in the solitude
　　Of the pine forest, and the silent shore
Which bounds Ravenna's immemorial wood,
　　Rooted where once the Adrian wave flowed o'er,
To where the last Caesarean fortress stood,
　　Evergreen forest! which Boccaccio's lore
And Dryden's lay made haunted ground to me,
How have I loved the twilight hour and thee!　　840

The shrill cicalas, people of the pine,
　　Making their summer lives one ceaseless song,
Were the sole echoes, save my steed's and mine,
　　And vesper bell's that rose the boughs along;
The specter huntsman of Onesti's line,
　　His hell-dogs, and their chase, and the fair
　　　　throng

756. **Joanna Southcote,** a visionary who prophesied that she would give birth to a second Shiloh, or Messiah, on October 19, 1814. When that time came, she fell into a trance and died ten days later. 768. **Ariosto,** a famous Italian poet (1474–1533). 769. **"longueurs,"** tedious passages. 775. **épopée,** epic. 776. **ennui,** languid weariness. 777. **Horace,** the famous Latin poet (first century B.C.). Cf. *Ars Poetica,* l. 359. 780. **"Wagoners."** One of Wordsworth's poems is entitled *The Wagoner.* 783. **"a little boat."** From Wordsworth's *Peter Bell,* stanza 1. 787. **Charles's Wain,** Charles' Wagon, a constellation known as the Big Dipper. 788. **Medea,** an enchantress, who aided her lover Jason to get the golden fleece. 797. **Jack Cades.** Jack Cade was the leader of "Cade's Rebellion," a political uprising in Kent in 1450. 800. **him,** Dryden, of whom Wordsworth was not fond. 830. **My altars ...stars.** Cf. *Childe Harold's Pilgrimage,* 3, 109 ff. (p. 746); 671 ff.

Which learned from this example not to fly
From a true lover—shadowed my mind's eye.

Oh, Hesperus! thou bringest all good things—
850   Home to the weary, to the hungry cheer,
To the young bird the parent's brooding wings,
   The welcome stall to the o'erlabored steer;
Whate'er of peace about our hearthstone clings,
   Whate'er our household goods protect of dear,
Are gathered round us by thy look of rest;
Thou bring'st the child, too, to the mother's breast.

Soft hour! which wakes the wish and melts the heart
   Of those who sail the seas, on the first day
When they from their sweet friends are torn apart;
860   Or fills with love the pilgrim on his way
As the far bell of vesper makes him start,
   Seeming to weep the dying day's decay;
Is this a fancy which our reason scorns?
Ah! surely nothing dies but something mourns! . . .
(1819-1820; 1821)

WHEN A MAN HATH NO FREEDOM

Byron sent this poem to Moore in November 1820, as a memorial chant for anyone who might be killed fighting for the cause of the Italian Revolution.

When a man hath no freedom to fight for at home,
   Let him combat for that of his neighbors;
Let him think of the glories of Greece and of Rome,
   And get knocked on the head for his labors.

To do good to mankind is the chivalrous plan,
   And is always as nobly requited;
Then battle for freedom wherever you can,
   And, if not shot or hanged, you'll get knighted.
(1820; 1824)

THE WORLD IS A BUNDLE OF HAY

The world is a bundle of hay,
   Mankind are the asses who pull;
Each tugs it a different way,
   And the greatest of all is John Bull.
(1820; 1830)

WHO KILLED JOHN KEATS?

These verses are in reference to the current belief that the death of Keats had been caused by a vitriolic attack on his Endymion, published in The Quarterly Review, *April 1818. See p. 784. In regard to these hostile attacks, Keats wrote his brother and his sister (October 1818): "This is a mere matter of the moment—I think I shall be among the English poets after my death." Henry Hart Milman, Robert Southey, and John Barrow were contemporary writers. Milman was also a clergyman.*

Who killed John Keats?
   "I," says the Quarterly,
   So savage and Tartarly;
" 'Twas one of my feats."

Who shot the arrow?
   "The poet-priest Milman
   (So ready to kill man),
Or Southey, or Barrow."
(1821; 1830)

STANZAS WRITTEN ON THE ROAD BETWEEN FLORENCE AND PISA

Oh, talk not to me of a name great in story;
The days of our youth are the days of our glory;
And the myrtle and ivy of sweet two-and-twenty
Are worth all your laurels, though ever so plenty.

What are garlands and crowns to the brow that is
   wrinkled?
'Tis but as a dead-flower with May-dew besprinkled.
Then away with all such from the head that is hoary!
What care I for the wreaths that can *only* give glory!

Oh Fame!—if I e'er took delight in thy praises,
'Twas less for the sake of thy high-sounding phrases, 10
Than to see the bright eyes of the dear one discover,
She thought that I was not unworthy to love her.

There chiefly I sought thee, *there* only I found thee;
Her glance was the best of the rays that surround
   thee;
When it sparkled o'er aught that was bright in my
   story,
I knew it was love, and I felt it was glory.
(1821; 1830)

ON THIS DAY I COMPLETE MY THIRTY-SIXTH YEAR

This is Byron's last poem, written at Missolonghi, Greece, just three months before his death.

(p. 748); 824 ff. (p. 749); and 4, 1594 ff. (p. 753). 835. **Ravenna,** a city and a province in Italy. 839. **Dryden's lay,** *Theodore and Honoria,* a tale of a specter huntsman who haunted the region of Ravenna; it is adapted from Boccaccio's *Decameron,* 5, 8. Boccaccio was a noted Italian writer of the fourteenth century. See Dryden's *Preface to the Fables* (p. 470). 841. **Cicalas,** locusts. 845. **Onesti,** the hero of Boccaccio's story; he becomes Dryden's Theodore. The specter merely appeared to Onesti; it was not of his line. 849. **Hesperus,** the evening star in Greek mythology.
The World . . . Hay. 4. John Bull, a personification of the typical Englishman.
Stanzas Written . . . Pisa. 3. myrtle and ivy. The myrtle was a symbol of love; ivy, of constancy in friendship.

'Tis time this heart should be unmoved,
   Since others it hath ceased to move;
Yet, though I cannot be beloved,
     Still let me love!

My days are in the yellow leaf;
   The flowers and fruits of love are gone;
The worm, the canker, and the grief
     Are mine alone!

The fire that on my bosom preys
10 Is lone as some volcanic isle;
No torch is kindled at its blaze—
     A funeral pile.

The hope, the fear, the jealous care,
   The exalted portion of the pain
And power of love, I cannot share,
     But wear the chain.

But 't is not *thus*—and 't is not *here*—
   Such thoughts should shake my soul, nor
     now,
Where glory decks the hero's bier,
20   Or binds his brow.

The sword, the banner, and the field,
   Glory and Greece, around me see!
The Spartan, borne upon his shield,
     Was not more free.

Awake! (not Greece—she *is* awake!)
   Awake, my spirit; Think through *whom*
Thy life-blood tracks its parent lake,
     And then strike home!

Tread those reviving passions down,
   Unworthy manhood!—unto thee   30
Indifferent should the smile or frown
     Of beauty be.

If thou regrett'st thy youth, *why live?*
   The land of honorable death
Is here—up to the field, and give
     Away thy breath!

Seek out—less often sought than found—
   A soldier's grave, for thee the best;
Then look around, and choose thy ground,
     And take thy rest.   40

(1824)

On This . . . Year. 5. **My . . . leaf,** from *Macbeth,* V, iii, 22— "My way of life is fall'n into the sear, the yellow leaf." 23. **Spartan . . . shield.** In ancient Sparta it was the custom to carry home a fallen warrior on his shield. 27. **life-blood . . . lake.** Byron's mother was a descendant of James I; his father traced his ancestry to heroes of the days of William the Conqueror. 38. **A soldier's grave.** Byron died of a complication of an illness while on a military expedition undertaken for the independence of Greece.

PERCY BYSSHE SHELLEY 1792-1822

Shelley was born on August 4, 1792, near the little village of Horsham, Sussex, where his father was a country squire of average means, but with expectations of a considerable income. From the beginning Shelley showed three strong traits of temperament that were to remain with him throughout his life and were to determine in great measure his achievement. He exhibited an extreme susceptibility to emotions and feelings both physical and spiritual—if he hurt himself, he would become hysterical; if he suffered any kind of mental anguish, his grief would be paroxysmal. He showed almost too lively an imagination; his soaring but uncertain fancy blotted out the essential importance of facts and blunted his common sense. Finally, the child Shelley—like the man Shelley later—was totally unable to accept any sign of authority, parental, scholastic, or religious.

With these moral peculiarities, which were fraught with disaster not only to Shelley himself but to those about him, the boy went to Eton at the age of twelve. A shy, sensitive lad, who at the sight of beauty might,

as he said, "shriek and clasp my hands with ecstasy," would naturally be fair game for the young barbarians of a thoroughly English school like Eton, particularly as the then headmaster, Dr. Goodall, was not a very good disciplinarian. Shelley was hectored, bullied, and subjected to hazing, or, as it was called, "fagging," which made every younger boy the virtual slave of an older boy. This treatment Shelley received with violent protest; his behavior at Eton was so distinctly nonconformist in so many ways that he became known as "Mad Shelley" and later as "Shelley the Atheist."

Eventually Shelley went up to Oxford, had as a particular friend Thomas Jefferson Hogg, later a biographer of the poet, and plunged into the study of poetry, philosophy, and the classics. But Hogg and he got into trouble with the college authorities over a little pamphlet entitled The Necessity of Atheism, and the pair were expelled in March 1811, after Shelley had been at Oxford but a bare five months. The whole incident was quite in keeping with Shelley's character.

He refused to answer any questions put to him by the authorities, and was probably dismissed as much for this breach of university discipline as for his ideas. From Oxford he went to London, and met there a friend of his sister's, Harriet Westbrook, daughter of a moderately successful retired hotel keeper. His missionary zeal for atheism had evidently remained with him, for he tried to convert Harriet. He succeeded, in any case, in getting her to fall in love with him, and finally to elope with him, or, as he put it, rebel against the tyranny of her father. A marriage ceremony was actually performed in Edinburgh, which, considering Shelley's publicly stated views on the tyranny of the institution of marriage—an idea which he possessed in common with William Godwin—was quite a concession on Shelley's part. The marriage took place in 1811.

The young couple then led a kind of wandering, semi-missionary existence for the next year and a half, they were supported by their two fathers. They covered most of the British Isles, including a trip to Ireland to fight for the Catholic emancipation. They returned to London early in 1813, where Shelley's first child was born and where Shelley's first poem of any importance, Queen Mab, was published. Extremely revolutionary toward church and state, it had to be printed privately. Shelley was not happy with Harriet, who was attractive but superficial; he was also bothered greatly by the constant presence of his sister-in-law, who hovered about with superfluous advice.

It happened that Shelley had begun a correspondence with William Godwin, the English disciple of Rousseau. They eventually met in London, and Shelley fell in love immediately with Godwin's daughter Mary. To a man of Shelley's character, the procedure to be followed was simple. He left Harriet and eloped (1814) to the Continent with Mary Godwin, not without much complaint from Godwin, who, in spite of his ideas about marriage, was greatly incensed. Shelley's alliance with Mary Godwin marks the true beginning of his poetic development, although the first fruit of the new Shelley, Alastor, did not appear until 1816. The truant couple were forgiven, after a fashion. In 1816 they took another trip to Switzerland, in company with Claire Clairmont, Mary's half sister, whose real purpose in accompanying them was to see Byron, for whom she had formed an attachment in London. The Clairmont episode is of no importance except to illustrate the naïve unconventionality of Shelley, who became innocently a kind of go-between. The return to London in the fall of 1816 brought tragedy to Shelley. Harriet, who had found consolation of a sort elsewhere, committed suicide in November; and although the way was thus left open for Shelley and Mary to marry, a court order in March 1817 took from Shelley his two children by Harriet and gave them into the custody of their grandfather. Crushed by the laws of England which he had flouted both in theory and in practice, Shelley, like Byron before him, left England in March 1818 for Italy, never to return.

The sojourn of the Shelleys in Italy, where they moved about from city to city, is most important in the intellectual and artistic life of the poet. For Shelley developed amazingly on Italian soil. Virtually all his remarkable poetic output appeared between 1818 and his death in 1822. In Italy he developed a friendship for Byron, and Platonic attachments to Emilia Viviani at Pisa and to Mrs. Williams ("Jane") at Leghorn. These associations are important chiefly for their effect upon Shelley's poetry. Shelley's death on July 8, 1822, was at least partially the result of his rash impracticality. A poor sailor and no swimmer at all, he went out with his friend Williams in a small boat off the west coast of Italy, and the two were drowned in a storm. Shelley's body was washed ashore, cremated, and buried in the Protestant cemetery at Rome under the not inappropriate inscription Cor Cordium! ("Heart of Hearts!")

Three principal qualities permeate Shelley's poetry. The first of these is revolutionism. Shelley had an iconoclastic spirit and a martyr's soul—unquestionably there was in him more than a spark of the fanatic and a great deal of the purely visionary. Queen Mab (1813) and The Revolt of Islam (1818) preach revolution, the first a violent, the second a bloodless one. Prometheus Unbound (1819) tells of Prometheus (man) chained to the rock by Zeus (tyranny) and freed by Asia (nature and love) and Demogorgon (the spirit of necessity.) Hellas is an elaborate allegory of revolution written in the form of a lyrical poetic drama, inspired by the Greek struggle for independence—the same struggle that cost Byron his life in 1824.

But Shelley's brand of revolutionism would lead to mere anarchy, as even he himself would admit, were it not for another quality, idealism. Shelley is the great lyric poet of the beautiful and sublime, of the ideals—eventually derived from Plato—of absolute goodness and truth. This idealism is at once Shelley's source of greatness and his most obvious defect. Too often it leads to vagueness, unreality, indistinct imagery, a cloudiness and mistiness, and an excess of the sensuous and the sentimental. So Matthew Arnold could apply to Shelley his noted phrase "a beautiful and ineffectual angel." The vagueness and its attendant evils can be seen in Alastor (1816), the epic of a poet's mind, and in The Witch of Atlas (1820), a long poem on the powers of the poet's fancy. But one need look only at the multitude of exquisite short lyrics, at the Hymn to Intellectual Beauty, at the choruses and lyrics from Prometheus Unbound, at The Sensitive Plant, and at the distinguished Adonais (1821) (p. 775), the elegy on John Keats, to see that this idealism has been unapproached elsewhere in English literature.

Finally there is in Shelley's poetry the undeniable quality of sheer music. Only Milton, Tennyson, and

Swinburne have had such a consummate command of rhythm, harmony, and clear-flowing melody. Again, the short lyrics are the best examples that could be named, The Indian Serenade (p. 771), To Night (p. 774), To— (p. 775), the songs from the plays, and portions of his more ambitious poems are excellent alike in their sensuous imagery and musical effect.

Shelley's own age passed a severe moral condemnation on him even though everyone who knew him well spoke of his character as noble; it was impossible to think of him and the earthy Byron in the same way. Shelley was generous and kindly and naive; one cannot call him, in all fairness, immoral, but simply unmoral. And still he was constructive enough in his criticism; the atheist Shelley could, in Prometheus Unbound, preach a gospel of love far closer to the teachings of Christ than the utterances of many devotional writers. None the less, he was essentially pagan, and a nature-worshiping pagan at that; for nature, even in its cruel forms, was to him a promise of immortality and beauty. The Ode to the West Wind (p. 770) and Adonais (p. 775) are sufficient illustration for the point. And physical nature, as seen in To a Skylark (p. 773), was merely symbolic of something beyond the physical, some ineffable abstraction which the eye and the ear of man have never perceived, but which, the poet assures us, in spite of doubt and despair, most certainly exists.

Of Shelley's prose little needs to be said. It is clear, direct, and has an exceedingly finished style. It is usually devoted to a defense of his revolutionary ideas. His powerful drama The Cenci (1819), eminently actable except for subject matter, is a tragedy of Renaissance Italy, founded on blood, incest, and horror, but with a poignant simplicity utterly unlike Shelley's usual cloud-like atmosphere. It has been called "the last great Elizabethan drama." It is, however, virtually isolated among Shelley's work. His satirical verse, like Peter Bell the Third, is negligible, for he lacked the requisite sense of humor. But his position as a lyric poet is secure; he is purely romantic, a great visionary, and a great singer of visions.

MUTABILITY

We are as clouds that veil the midnight moon;
  How restlessly they speed, and gleam, and quiver,
Streaking the darkness radiantly!—yet soon
  Night closes round, and they are lost forever:

Or like forgotten lyres, whose dissonant strings
  Give various response to each varying blast,
To whose frail frame no second motion brings
  One mood or modulation like the last.

We rest—a dream has power to poison sleep;
10 We rise—one wandering thought pollutes the day;
We feel, conceive or reason, laugh or weep;
  Embrace fond woe, or cast our cares away:

It is the same!—For, be it joy or sorrow,
  The path of its departure still is free:
Man's yesterday may ne'er be like his morrow;
  Naught may endure but Mutability.
(1815; 1816)

HYMN TO INTELLECTUAL BEAUTY

Shelley based this poem upon the Platonic idea of eternal beauty—in brief, a conception of absolute and perfect beauty, "simple, pure, uncontaminated with the intermixture of human flesh and colors, and all other idle and unreal shapes attendant upon mortality." This absolute beauty, which is of course immortal, pervades everything, although invisible, it can be perceived by him who has dedicated himself to the contemplation of the beautiful, the good, and the true, for "to him alone is accorded the prerogative of bringing forth, not images and shadows of virtue, for he is in contact not with a shadow, but reality, with virtue itself, in the production and nourishment of which he becomes dear to the gods, and, if such a privilege is conceded to any human being, himself immortal." The quotations are from Shelley's translation of Plato's Symposium. It may be added that Shelley takes the word "intellectual" in the general sense of "spiritual"; "intellectual beauty," which is immortal, must be distinguished from mere "physical beauty," the kind of beauty that Keats had in mind in his Ode on Melancholy (p. 788, l. 21), which is mortal.

The awful shadow of some unseen Power
  Floats though unseen among us—visiting
  This various world with as inconstant wing
As summer winds that creep from flower to flower—
Like moonbeams that behind some piny mountain
    shower,
  It visits with inconstant glance
  Each human heart and countenance;
Like hues and harmonies of evening—
  Like clouds in starlight widely spread—
  Like memory of music fled—
  Like aught that for its grace may be   10
Dear, and yet dearer for its mystery.

Hymn to Intellectual Beauty. 26. these responses, responses to these questions. 27. Demon, a supernatural being of Greek mythology, conceived as holding a position between gods and men.

Ozymandias. 8. hand . . . them, hand of the sculptor who imitated or reproduced them. heart, of Ozymandias, who nursed those passions.

Spirit of Beauty, that dost consecrate
  With thine own hues all thou dost shine upon
  Of human thought or form—where art thou gone?
Why dost thou pass away and leave our state,
This dim vast vale of tears, vacant and desolate?
    Ask why the sunlight not forever
    Weaves rainbows o'er yon mountain-river,
20 Why aught should fail and fade that once is shown,
    Why fear and dream and death and birth
    Cast on the daylight of this earth
    Such gloom—why man has such a scope
For love and hate, despondency and hope?

No voice from some sublimer world hath ever
  To sage or poet these responses given—
  Therefore the names of Demon, Ghost, and Heaven,
Remain the records of their vain endeavor,
Frail spells—whose uttered charm might not avail to
    sever,
30   From all we hear and all we see,
    Doubt, chance, and mutability.
Thy light alone—like mist o'er mountains driven,
    Or music by the night-wind sent
    Through strings of some still instrument,
    Or moonlight on a midnight stream,
Gives grace and truth to life's unquiet dream.

Love, Hope, and Self-Esteem, like clouds depart
  And come, for some uncertain moments lent.
  Man were immortal, and omnipotent,
40 Didst thou, unknown and awful as thou art,
Keep with thy glorious train firm state within his
    heart.
    Thou messenger of sympathies,
    That wax and wane in lovers' eyes—
Thou—that to human thought art nourishment,
    Like darkness to a dying flame!
    Depart not as thy shadow came,
    Depart not—lest the grave should be,
Like life and fear, a dark reality.

While yet a boy I sought for ghosts, and sped
50   Through many a listening chamber, cave and ruin,
  And starlight wood, with fearful steps pursuing
Hopes of high talk with the departed dead.
I called on poisonous names with which our youth
    is fed;
    I was not heard—I saw them not—
    When musing deeply on the lot
Of life, at that sweet time when winds are wooing
    All vital things that wake to bring
    News of birds and blossoming—
    Sudden, thy shadow fell on me;
60 I shrieked, and clasped my hands in ecstasy!

I vowed that I would dedicate my powers
  To thee and thine—have I not kept the vow?

With beating heart and streaming eyes, even now
I called the phantoms of a thousand hours
Each from his voiceless grave: they have in visioned
    bowers
    Of studious zeal or love's delight
    Outwatched with me the envious night—
They know that never joy illumed my brow
    Unlinked with hope that thou wouldst free
    This world from its dark slavery,   70
    That thou—O awful Loveliness,
Wouldst give whate'er these words cannot express.

The day becomes more solemn and serene
  When noon is past—there is a harmony
  In autumn, and a luster in its sky,
Which through the summer is not heard or seen,
As if it could not be, as if it had not been!
    Thus let thy power, which like the truth
    Of nature on my passive youth
Descended, to my onward life supply   80
    Its calm—to one who worships thee,
    And every form containing thee,
    Whom, Spirit fair, thy spells did bind
To fear himself, and love all human kind.
(1816; 1817)

OZYMANDIAS

According to the statement of the Greek historian Diodorus Siculus (first century B.C.), the statue of Ozymandias was reputed to be the largest in Egypt and to bear the following inscription: "I am Ozymandias, the King of Kings; if any man wishes to know what I am and where I am buried, let him surpass me in some of my achievements."

I met a traveler from an antique land
Who said: "Two vast and trunkless legs of stone
Stand in the desert. Near them, on the sand,
Half sunk, a shattered visage lies, whose frown,
And wrinkled lip, and sneer of cold command,
Tell that its sculptor well those passions read
Which yet survive, stamped on these lifeless things,
The hand that mocked them, and the heart that fed:
And on the pedestal these words appear:
'My name is Ozymandias, king of kings: 10
Look on my works, ye Mighty, and despair!'
Nothing beside remains. Round the decay
Of that colossal wreck, boundless and bare
The lone and level sands stretch far away."
(1817; 1818)

ENGLAND IN 1819

The poem was inspired by the Manchester (or Peterloo) Massacre, when soldiers engaged in keeping order fired into a crowd assembled in St. Peter's Field at Manchester, August 16, 1819, to petition Parliament for the redress of grievances regarding taxation and representation.

An old, mad, blind, despised, and dying king—
Princes, the dregs of their dull race, who flow
Through public scorn—mud from a muddy spring—
Rulers who neither see, nor feel, nor know,
But leech-like to their fainting country cling,
Till they drop, blind in blood, without a blow—
A people starved and stabbed in the untilled field—
An army, which liberticide and prey
Makes as a two-edged sword to all who wield—
10 Golden and sanguine laws which tempt and slay;
Religion, Christless, Godless—a book sealed;
A Senate—Time's worst statute unrepealed—
Are graves, from which a glorious Phantom may
Burst, to illumine our tempestuous day.
(1819; 1839)

ODE TO THE WEST WIND

This fine ode illustrates the myth-making faculty of Shelley and his power of identifying himself with the object described. The stanza form is adapted from the Italian terza rima.

1

O wild West Wind, thou breath of Autumn's being,
Thou, from whose unseen presence the leaves dead
Are driven, like ghosts from an enchanter fleeing,

Yellow, and black, and pale, and hectic red,
Pestilence-stricken multitudes: O thou,
Who chariotest to their dark wintry bed

The wingéd seeds, where they lie cold and low,
Each like a corpse within its grave, until
Thine azure sister of the Spring shall blow

Her clarion o'er the dreaming earth, and fill   10
(Driving sweet buds like flocks to feed in air)
With living hues and odors plain and hill:

Wild Spirit, which art moving everywhere;
Destroyer and preserver; hear, oh, hear!

2

Thou on whose stream, mid the steep sky's commotion,
Loose clouds like earth's decaying leaves are shed,
Shook from the tangled boughs of Heaven and Ocean,

Angels of rain and lightning: there are spread
On the blue surface of thine aëry surge,
Like the bright hair uplifted from the head   20

Of some fierce Maenad, even from the dim verge
Of the horizon to the zenith's height,
The locks of the approaching storm. Thou dirge

Of the dying year, to which this closing night
Will be the dome of a vast sepulcher,
Vaulted with all thy congregated might

Of vapors, from whose solid atmosphere
Black rain, and fire, and hail will burst: oh, hear!

The Manchester Massacre of 1819, from a contemporary print.

England in 1819. 1. **king**, George III, king of England (1760–1820). He became hopelessly insane in 1811. 12. **Time's . . . unrepealed**, the law that restricted the civil liberties of Roman Catholics; it was repealed in 1829. 13. **Phantom**, liberty.

Ode to the West Wind. 9. **sister of the Spring**, the south wind. 21. **Maenad**, a priestess or female votary of Bacchus, god of wine. 24. **closing night**, night sky closing down over the earth. 32. **pumice**, a light, porous volcanic substance. **Baiae**, a small seaport in Italy near

3

Thou who didst waken from his summer dreams
30 The blue Mediterranean, where he lay,
   Lulled by the coil of his crystalline streams,

Beside a pumice isle in Baiae's bay,
   And saw in sleep old palaces and towers
Quivering within the wave's intenser day,

All overgrown with azure moss and flowers
   So sweet, the sense faints picturing them! Thou
For whose path the Atlantic's level powers

Cleave themselves into chasms, while far below
   The sea-blooms and the oozy woods which wear
40 The sapless foliage of the ocean, know

Thy voice, and suddenly grow gray with fear,
   And tremble and despoil themselves: oh, hear!

4

If I were a dead leaf thou mightest bear,
   If I were a swift cloud to fly with thee;
A wave to pant beneath thy power, and share

The impulse of thy strength, only less free
   Than thou, O uncontrollable! If even
I were as in my boyhood, and could be

The comrade of thy wanderings over Heaven,
50 As then, when to outstrip thy skyey speed
Scarce seemed a vision; I would ne'er have striven

As thus with thee in prayer in my sore need.
   Oh, lift me as a wave, a leaf, a cloud!
I fall upon the thorns of life! I bleed!

A heavy weight of hours has chained and bowed
   One too like thee: tameless, and swift, and proud.

5

Make me thy lyre, even as the forest is:
   What if my leaves are falling like its own!
The tumult of thy mighty harmonies

60 Will take from both a deep, autumnal tone,
   Sweet though in sadness. Be thou, Spirit fierce,
My spirit! Be thou me, impetuous one!

Drive my dead thoughts over the universe
   Like withered leaves to quicken a new birth!
And, by the incantation of this verse,

Scatter, as from an unextinguished hearth
Ashes and sparks, my words among mankind!
Be through my lips to unawakened earth

The trumpet of a prophecy! O Wind,
If Winter comes, can Spring be far behind?
(1819; 1820)

THE INDIAN SERENADE

I arise from dreams of Thee
   In the first sweet sleep of night,
When the winds are breathing low
   And the stars are shining bright:
I arise from dreams of thee,
   And a spirit in my feet
Hath led me—who knows how?
   To thy chamber-window, Sweet!

The wandering airs, they faint
   On the dark, the silent stream—   10
The champak odors fail
   Like sweet thoughts in a dream;
The nightingale's complaint,
   It dies upon her heart,
As I must die on thine,
   O beloved as thou art!

Oh, lift me from the grass!
   I die, I faint, I fail!
Let thy love in kisses rain
   On my lips and eyelids pale.   20
My cheek is cold and white, alas!
   My heart beats loud and fast;
Oh! press it close to thine again,
   Where it will break at last.
(1819; 1822)

from PROMETHEUS UNBOUND

   The theme of Shelley's lyrical drama, Prometheus Unbound, has already been stated (p. 767). In discussing this work, John Addington Symonds remarked: "A genuine liking for Prometheus Unbound may be reckoned the touchstone of a man's capacity for understanding lyric poetry. The world in which the action [of the play] is supposed to move, rings with spirit voices; and what these spirits sing is melody more purged of mortal dross than any other poet's ear has caught, while listening to his own heart's song, or to the rhythms of this world. There are hymns in Prometheus, which seem to realize the miracle of making

---

Naples. 39. **sea-blooms . . . hear.** In a note on these lines Shelley states that "the vegetation at the bottom of the sea, of rivers, and of lakes, sympathizes with that of the land in the change of seasons, and is consequently influenced by the winds which announce it."

The Indian Serenade. 11. champak, an Indian tree of the magnolia family.

*words, detached from meaning, the substance of a new
ethereal music, and yet although their verbal harmony
is such, they are never devoid of definite significance
for those who understand."*

ASIA

My soul is an enchanted boat,
    Which, like a sleeping swan, doth float
Upon the silver waves of thy sweet singing;
    And thine doth like an angel sit
    Beside a helm conducting it,
Whilst all the winds with melody are ringing.
    It seems to float ever, forever,
    Upon that many-winding river,
    Between mountains, woods, abysses,
10 A paradise of wildernesses!
Till, like one in slumber bound,
Borne to the ocean, I float down, around,
Into a sea profound, of ever-spreading sound:

    Meanwhile thy spirit lifts its pinions
    In music's most serene dominions;
Catching the winds that fan that happy heaven.
    And we sail on, away, afar,
    Without a course, without a star,
But, by the instinct of sweet music driven;
20 Till through Elysian garden islets
    By thee, most beautiful of pilots,
    Where never mortal pinnace glided,
    The boat of my desire is guided:
Realms where the air we breathe is love,
Which in the winds and on the waves doth move,
Harmonizing this earth with what we feel above.

    We have passed Age's icy caves,
    And Manhood's dark and tossing waves,
And Youth's smooth ocean, smiling to betray:
30 Beyond the glassy gulfs we flee
    Of shadow-peopled Infancy,
Through Death and Birth, to a diviner day;
    A paradise of vaulted bowers,
    Lit by downward-gazing flowers,
    And watery paths that wind between
    Wildernesses calm and green,
Peopled by shapes too bright to see,
And rest, having beheld; somewhat like thee;
Which walk upon the sea, and chant melodiously!

DEMOGORGON

This is the day, which down the void abysm
At the Earth-born's spell yawns for Heaven's despot-
    ism,
    And Conquest is dragged captive through the deep:

Love, from its awful throne of patient power
In the wise heart, from the last giddy hour
    Of dead endurance, from the slippery, steep,
And narrow verge of crag-like agony, springs
And folds over the world its healing wings.

Gentleness, Virtue, Wisdom, and Endurance,
These are the seals of that most firm assurance   10
    Which bars the pit over Destruction's strength;
And if, with infirm hand, Eternity,
Mother of many acts and hours, should free
    The serpent that would clasp her with his length;
These are the spells by which to reassume
An empire o'er the disentangled doom.

To suffer woes which Hope thinks infinite;
To forgive wrongs darker than death or night;
    To defy Power, which seems omnipotent;
To love, and bear; to hope till Hope creates   20
From its own wreck the thing it contemplates;
    Neither to change, nor falter, nor repent;
This, like thy glory, Titan, is to be
Good, great and joyous, beautiful and free;
This is alone Life, Joy, Empire, and Victory.
(1818-19; 1820)

THE CLOUD

I bring fresh showers for the thirsting flowers,
    From the seas and the streams;
I bear light shade for the leaves when laid
    In their noonday dreams.
From my wings are shaken the dews that waken
    The sweet buds every one,
When rocked to rest on their mother's breast,
    As she dances about the sun.
I wield the flail of the lashing hail,
    And whiten the green plains under,   10
And then again I dissolve it in rain,
    And laugh as I pass in thunder.

I sift the snow on the mountains below,
    And their great pines groan aghast;
And all the night 'tis my pillow white,
    While I sleep in the arms of the blast.
Sublime on the towers of my skyey bowers,
    Lightning my pilot sits;
In a cavern under is fettered the thunder,
    It struggles and howls at fits;   20
Over earth and ocean, with gentle motion,
    This pilot is guiding me,
Lured by the love of the genii that move
    In the depths of the purple sea;
Over the rills, and the crags, and the hills,

Asia. 20. **Elysian,** of or pertaining to Elysium, the abode of the
blessed after death.

Demogorgon. (Cf. p. 767). 2. **Earth-born's spell,** the spell of
Prometheus, one of the Titans.

Over the lakes and the plains,
  Wherever he dream, under mountain or stream,
    The Spirit he loves remains;
  And I all the while bask in Heaven's blue smile,
30   Whilst he is dissolving in rains.

The sanguine Sunrise, with his meteor eyes,
  And his burning plumes outspread,
Leaps on the back of my sailing rack,
  When the morning star shines dead;
As on the jag of a mountain crag,
  Which an earthquake rocks and swings,
An eagle alit one moment may sit
  In the light of its golden wings.
And when Sunset may breathe, from the lit sea beneath,
40   Its ardors of rest and of love,
And the crimson pall of eve may fall
  From the depth of Heaven above,
With wings folded I rest, on mine airy nest,
  As still as a brooding dove.

That orbéd maiden with white fire laden,
  Whom mortals call the Moon,
Glides glimmering o'er my fleece-like floor,
  By the midnight breezes strewn;
And wherever the beat of her unseen feet,
50   Which only the angels hear,
May have broken the woof of my tent's thin roof,
  The stars peep behind her and peer;
And I laugh to see them whirl and flee,
  Like a swarm of golden bees,
When I widen the rent in my wind-built tent,
  Till the calm rivers, lakes, and seas,
Like strips of the sky fallen through me on high,
  Are each paved with the moon and these.

I bind the Sun's throne with a burning zone,
60   And the Moon's with a girdle of pearl;
The volcanoes are dim, and the stars reel and swim,
  When the whirlwinds my banner unfurl.
From cape to cape, with a bridge-like shape,
  Over a torrent sea,
Sunbeam-proof, I hang like a roof—
  The mountains its columns be.
The triumphal arch, through which I march,
  With hurricane, fire, and snow,
When the Powers of the air are chained to my chair,
70 Is the million-colored bow;
The sphere-fire above its soft colors wove,
  While the moist Earth was laughing below.

I am the daughter of Earth and Water,
  And the nursling of the Sky;
I pass through the pores of the ocean and shores,
  I change, but I cannot die.

For after the rain when with never a stain
  The pavilion of Heaven is bare,
And the winds and sunbeams with their convex gleams
  Build up the blue dome of air,   80
I silently laugh at my own cenotaph,
  And out of the caverns of rain,
Like a child from the womb, like a ghost from the tomb,
  I arise and unbuild it again.
(1820)

TO A SKYLARK

Hail to thee, blithe Spirit!
  Bird thou never wert,
That from Heaven, or near it,
  Pourest thy full heart
In profuse strains of unpremeditated art.

Higher still and higher
  From the earth thou springest
Like a cloud of fire;
  The blue deep thou wingest,
And singing still dost soar, and soaring ever singest. 10

In the golden lightning
  Of the sunken sun,
O'er which clouds are bright'ning,
  Thou dost float and run;
Like an unbodied joy whose race is just begun.

The pale purple even
  Melts around thy flight;
Like a star of Heaven,
  In the broad daylight
Thou art unseen, but yet I hear thy shrill delight, 20

Keen as are the arrows
  Of that silver sphere,
Whose intense lamp narrows
  In the white dawn clear
Until we hardly see—we feel that it is there.

All the earth and air
  With thy voice is loud,
As, when night is bare,
  From one lonely cloud
The moon rains out her beams, and Heaven is over-
    flowed. 30

What thou art we know not;
  What is most like thee?
From rainbow clouds there flow not
  Drops so bright to see
As from thy presence showers a rain of melody.

The Cloud. 33. rack, broken portion of a cloud. 58. these, the
stars. 59. zone, girdle. 81. cenotaph, an empty tomb that honors
someone lost or buried elsewhere; here, the blue dome of air.
To a Skylark. Cf. Wordsworth's To a Skylark, p. 699.

Like a Poet hidden
  In the light of thought,
Singing hymns unbidden,
  Till the world is wrought
40 To sympathy with hopes and fears it heeded not:

Like a high-born maiden
  In a palace tower,
Soothing her love-laden
  Soul in secret hour
With music sweet as love, which overflows her bower:

Like a glowworm golden
  In a dell of dew,
Scattering unbeholden
  Its aëreal hue
Among the flowers and grass, which screen it from the
50   view!

Like a rose embowered
  In its own green leaves,
By warm winds deflowered,
  Till the scent it gives
Makes faint with too much sweet those heavy-wingéd
    thieves:

Sound of vernal showers
  On the twinkling grass,
Rain-awakened flowers,
  All that ever was
60 Joyous, and clear, and fresh, thy music doth surpass:

Teach us, Sprite or Bird,
  What sweet thoughts are thine:
I have never heard
  Praise of love or wine
That panted forth a flood of rapture so divine.

Chorus Hymeneal,
  Or triumphal chant,
Matched with thine would be all
  But an empty vaunt,
A thing wherein we feel there is some hidden
70   want.

What objects are the fountains
  Of thy happy strain?
What fields, or waves, or mountains?
  What shapes of sky or plain?
What love of thine own kind? what ignorance of
    pain?

With thy clear keen joyance
  Languor cannot be:
Shadow of annoyance
  Never came near thee:
80 Thou lovest—but ne'er knew love's sad satiety.

Waking or asleep,
  Thou of death must deem
Things more true and deep
  Than we mortals dream,
Or how could thy notes flow in such a crystal stream?

We look before and after,
  And pine for what is not:
Our sincerest laughter
  With some pain is fraught;
Our sweetest songs are those that tell of saddest
    thought.   90

Yet if we could scorn
  Hate, and pride, and fear;
If we were things born
  Not to shed a tear,
I know not how thy joy we ever should come
    near.

Better than all measures
  Of delightful sound,
Better than all treasures
  That in books are found,
Thy skill to poet were, thou scorner of the ground!   100

Teach me half the gladness
  That thy brain must know,
Such harmonious madness
  From my lips would flow
The world should listen then—as I am listening now.
(1820)

TO NIGHT

Swiftly walk o'er the western wave,
        Spirit of Night!
Out of the misty eastern cave,
Where, all the long and lone daylight,
Thou wovest dreams of joy and fear,
Which make thee terrible and dear—
        Swift be thy flight!

Wrap thy form in a mantle gray,
        Star-inwrought!
Blind with thine hair the eyes of Day;   10
Kiss her until she be wearied out,
Then wander o'er city, and sea, and land,
Touching all with thine opiate wand—
        Come, long-sought!

When I arose and saw the dawn,
        I sighed for thee;
When light rode high, and the dew was gone,
And noon lay heavy on flower and tree,
And the weary Day turned to his rest,

20 Lingering like an unloved guest,
   I sighed for thee.

Thy brother Death came, and cried,
   "Wouldst thou me?"
Thy sweet child Sleep, the filmy-eyed,
Murmured like a noontide bee,
"Shall I nestle near thy side?
Wouldst thou me?"—And I replied,
   "No, not thee!"

Death will come when thou art dead,
30   Soon, too soon—
Sleep will come when thou art fled;
Of neither would I ask the boon
I ask of thee, belovéd Night—
Swift be thine approaching flight,
   Come soon, soon!
(1821; 1824)

TO——

Music, when soft voices die,
Vibrates in the memory—
Odors, when sweet violets sicken,
Live within the sense they quicken.

Rose leaves, when the rose is dead,
Are heaped for the belovéd's bed;
And so thy thoughts, when thou art gone,
Love itself shall slumber on.
(1821; 1824)

TIME

Unfathomable Sea! whose waves are years,
 Ocean of Time, whose waters of deep woe
Are brackish with the salt of human tears!
 Thou shoreless flood, which in thy ebb and flow
Claspest the limits of mortality,
And sick of prey, yet howling on for more,
Vomitest thy wrecks on its inhospitable shore;
 Treacherous in calm, and terrible in storm,
   Who shall put forth on thee,
   Unfathomable Sea?
(1821; 1824)

MUTABILITY

The flower that smiles today
   Tomorrow dies;
All that we wish to stay
   Tempts and then flies.
What is this world's delight?

Lightning that mocks the night,
   Brief even as bright.

Virtue, how frail it is!
   Friendship how rare!
Love, how it sells poor bliss   10
   For proud despair!
But we, though soon they fall,
Survive their joy, and all
   Which ours we call.

Whilst skies are blue and bright,
   Whilst flowers are gay,
Whilst eyes that change ere night
   Make glad the day;
Whilst yet the calm hours creep,
Dream thou—and from thy sleep   20
   Then wake to weep.
(1821; 1824)

A LAMENT

O world! O life! O time!
On whose last steps I climb,
 Trembling at that where I had stood before;
When will return the glory of your prime?
   No more—Oh, never more!

Out of the day and night
A joy has taken flight;
 Fresh spring, and summer, and winter hoar,
Move my faint heart with grief, but with delight
   No more—Oh, never more!
(1821; 1824)

ADONAIS

AN ELEGY ON THE DEATH OF JOHN KEATS

Keats' premature death (p. 784) from tuberculosis stirred many of the younger romantic poets, particularly Byron and Shelley. Some of them believed the melancholy event had been hastened, if not directly caused, by a harsh review of Keats' early poem En-dymion in the Quarterly Review for April 1818, three years before Keats' death. Such an idea was absurd, for Keats was made of sterner stuff than to allow himself to be killed by criticism. Even Byron admitted this likelihood:

 'Tis very strange the mind, that fiery particle,
 Should let itself be snuffed out by an article.
   (Don Juan, XI, stanza 60)

But to the emotional Shelley, Keats had been murdered by his critics, and Adonais, the beautiful elegy on the death of Keats, is partly an oblique attack upon his "murderers," who, as Shelley saw it, had forced him "to drink poison."

The title of the poem is an adaptation of the name of *Adonis*, the beautiful youth loved by Venus and killed by a boar. The immediate sources of the poem, particularly at the beginning, are the *Lament for Adonis* by the Greek poet Bion, and the *Lament for Bion* by the poet Moschus, who lived some time during the Alexandrian period of Greek literature (333-146 B.C.). Both Greek poets and Shelley follow the form of the memorial idyll by the Greek poet Theocritus (fl. 270 B.C.), which is poetry of a definitely pastoral nature. Milton had done the same in his *Lycidas* (p. 382). To be noted especially in Shelley's poem is the identification of the dead Keats with nature and the pantheism which underlies virtually all of the treatment of nature by the great romantic poets (cf. p. 780, ll. 370 ff.). It should not detract from the beauty and nobility of the poem, which, like every great elegy, transcends the individual who inspired it, to observe that Shelley knew Keats but slightly. The two had met at Leigh Hunt's home in London (1817), they never were intimate, and Keats appears not to have cared for Shelley. It is characteristic of Shelley that he made the principle more important than the mere fact. The poem is written in Spenserian stanzas.

I weep for Adonais—he is dead!
O, weep for Adonais! though our tears
Thaw not the frost which binds so dear a head!
And thou, sad Hour, selected from all years
To mourn our loss, rouse thy obscure compeers,
And teach them thine own sorrow, say: "With me
Died Adonais; till the Future dares
Forget the Past, his fate and fame shall be
An echo and a light unto eternity!"

10 Where wert thou, mighty Mother, when he lay,
When thy Son lay, pierced by the shaft which flies
In darkness? where was lorn Urania
When Adonais died? With veiléd eyes,
'Mid listening Echoes, in her Paradise
She sate, while one, with soft enamored breath,
Rekindled all the fading melodies,
With which, like flowers that mock the corse beneath,
He had adorned and hid the coming bulk of Death.

Oh, weep for Adonais—he is dead!
20 Wake, melancholy Mother, wake and weep!
Yet wherefore? Quench within their burning bed
Thy fiery tears, and let thy loud heart keep
Like his, a mute and uncomplaining sleep;

For he is gone, where all things wise and fair
Descend;—oh, dream not that the amorous Deep
Will yet restore him to the vital air;
Death feeds on his mute voice, and laughs at our despair.

Most musical of mourners, weep again!
Lament anew, Urania!—He died,
Who was the Sire of an immortal strain,   30
Blind, old, and lonely, when his country's pride,
The priest, the slave, and the liberticide,
Trampled and mocked with many a loathéd rite
Of lust and blood; he went, unterrified,
Into the gulf of death; but his clear Sprite
Yet reigns o'er the earth; the third among the sons of light.

Most musical of mourners, weep anew!
Not all to that bright station dared to climb;
And happier they their happiness who knew,
Whose tapers yet burn through that night of time 40
In which suns perished; others more sublime,
Struck by the envious wrath of man or god,
Have sunk, extinct in their refulgent prime;
And some yet live, treading the thorny road,
Which leads, through toil and hate, to Fame's serene abode.

But now, thy youngest, dearest one, has perished—
The nursling of thy widowhood, who grew,
Like a pale flower by some sad maiden cherished,
And fed with true-love tears, instead of dew;
Most musical of mourners, weep anew!   50
Thy extreme hope, the loveliest and the last,
The bloom, whose petals nipped before they blew
Died on the promise of the fruit, is waste;
The broken lily lies—the storm is overpast.

To that high Capital, where kingly Death
Keeps his pale court in beauty and decay,
He came; and bought, with price of purest breath,
A grave among the eternal.—Come away!
Haste, while the vault of blue Italian day
Is yet his fitting charnel-roof! while still   60
He lies, as if in dewy sleep he lay;
Awake him not! surely he takes his fill
Of deep and liquid rest, forgetful of all ill.

He will awake no more, oh, never more!—
Within the twilight chamber spreads apace
The shadow of white Death, and at the door
Invisible Corruption waits to trace

Adonais. 5. **thy . . . compeers,** the hours less memorable than the one that marked the death of Keats. 10. **Mother,** Urania, the muse of astronomy. Shelley here identifies her with Uranian Aphrodite, the spirit of lyrical poetry and heavenly love. 15. **one,** one echo. 30. **the Sire,** Milton, of whose *Lycidas* (p. 382) Shelley's poem is reminiscent. 31. **when . . . blood,** the Restoration period. See pp. 419 ff. 36. **third . . . light.** According to Shelley's *Defense of Poetry,* Homer and

Dante were the first and second epic poets. 44. **some yet live,** such as Wordsworth and Byron. 49. **tears . . . dew.** An allusion to Keats' *Isabella.* 51. **extreme,** last. 55. **Capital,** Rome, where Keats had gone for his health (see p. 784). 69. **Hunger,** the corruption of the grave. 80. **sweet pain,** birth pangs. 94. **anadem,** crown, chaplet. 107. **clips,** embraces. 127. **Echo,** in classical legend, a beautiful nymph who for love of Narcissus pined away into a mere voice. 133. **those,** of Nar-

His extreme way to her dim dwelling-place;
The eternal Hunger sits, but pity and awe
70 Soothe her pale rage, nor dares she to deface
So fair a prey, till darkness, and the law
Of change, shall o'er his sleep the mortal curtain draw.

Oh, weep for Adonais!—The quick Dreams,
The passion-wingéd Ministers of thought,
Who were his flocks, whom near the living streams
Of his young spirit he fed, and whom he taught
The love which was its music, wander not—
Wander no more, from kindling brain to brain,
But droop there, whence they sprung; and mourn their
  lot
80 Round the cold heart, where, after their sweet pain,
They ne'er will gather strength, or find a home again.

And one with trembling hands clasps his cold head,
And fans him with her moonlight wings, and cries;
"Our love, our hope, our sorrow, is not dead;
See, on the silken fringe of his faint eyes,
Like dew upon a sleeping flower, there lies
A tear some Dream has loosened from his brain."
Lost Angel of a ruined Paradise!
She knew not 'twas her own; as with no stain
90 She faded, like a cloud which had outwept its rain.

One from a lucid urn of starry dew
Washed his light limbs as if embalming them;
Another clipped her profuse locks, and threw
The wreath upon him, like an anadem,
Which frozen tears instead of pearls begem;
Another in her wilful grief would break
Her bow and wingéd reeds, as if to stem
A greater loss with one which was more weak;
And dull the barbéd fire against his frozen cheek.

100 Another Splendor on his mouth alit,
That mouth, whence it was wont to draw the breath
Which gave it strength to pierce the guarded wit,
And pass into the panting heart beneath
With lightning and with music: the damp death
Quenched its caress upon his icy lips;
And, as a dying meteor stains a wreath
Of moonlight vapor, which the cold night clips,
It flushed through his pale limbs, and passed to its
  eclipse.

And others came . . . Desires and Adorations,
110 Wingéd Persuasions and veiled Destinies,
Splendors, and Glooms, and glimmering Incarnations
Of hopes and fears, and twilight Phantasies;

And Sorrow, with her family of Sighs,
And Pleasure, blind with tears, led by the gleam
Of her own dying smile instead of eyes,
Came in slow pomp;—the moving pomp might seem
Like pageantry of mist on an autumnal stream.

All he had loved, and molded into thought,
From shape, and hue, and odor, and sweet sound,
Lamented Adonais. Morning sought   120
Her eastern watch-tower, and her hair unbound,
Wet with the tears which should adorn the ground,
Dimmed the aëreal eyes that kindle day;
Afar the melancholy thunder moaned,
Pale Ocean in unquiet slumber lay,
And the wild Winds flew round, sobbing in their dis-
  may.

Lost Echo sits amid the voiceless mountains,
And feeds her grief with his remembered lay,
And will no more reply to winds or fountains,
Or amorous birds perched on the young green spray, 130
Or herdsman's horn, or bell at closing day;
Since she can mimic not his lips, more dear
Than those for whose disdain she pined away
Into a shadow of all sounds—a drear
Murmur, between their songs, is all the woodmen
  hear.

Grief made the young Spring wild, and she threw down
Her kindling buds, as if she Autumn were,
Or they dead leaves; since her delight is flown,
For whom should she have waked the sullen year?
To Phoebus was not Hyacinth so dear   140
Nor to himself Narcissus, as to both
Thou, Adonais: wan they stand and sere
Amid the faint companions of their youth,
With dew all turned to tears; odor, to sighing ruth.

Thy spirit's sister, the lorn nightingale
Mourns not her mate with such melodious pain;
Not so the eagle, who like thee could scale
Heaven, and could nourish in the sun's domain
Her mighty youth with morning, doth complain,
Soaring and screaming round her empty nest,   150
As Albion wails for thee: the curse of Cain
Light on his head who pierced thy innocent breast,
And scared the angel soul that was its earthly guest!

Ah, woe is me! Winter is come and gone,
But grief returns with the revolving year;
The airs and streams renew their joyous tone;
The ants, the bees, the swallows reappear;

cissus. 140. **Phoebus,** Apollo, god of music and poetry. He loved a
beautiful youth named Hyacinthus, whom he accidentally killed with a
quoit. Upon his death Hyacinthus was changed into a flower. 141.
Narcissus. Narcissus fell in love with his own image as it was reflected
in a fountain. Upon his death he was changed into a flower because he
refused the love of Echo. 145. **nightingale.** An allusion to Keats
Ode to a Nightingale, p. 790, and to the melody of Keats' verse. 151.

Albion, poetic name for England. **curse of Cain.** For killing his brother
Abel (Genesis 4:1–15), Cain was condemned to be a homeless wanderer. 152. **his head,** the head of the critic. Shelley wrongly believed
that the death of Keats was caused by hostile attacks upon his poetry.
See Byron's *Who Killed John Keats?* and note, p. 765; also p. 784.

Fresh leaves and flowers deck the dead Seasons' bier;
The amorous birds now pair in every brake,
160 And build their mossy homes in field and brere;
And the green lizard, and the golden snake,
Like unimprisoned flames, out of their trance awake.

Through wood and stream and field and hill and Ocean
A quickening life from the Earth's heart has burst
As it has ever done, with change and motion,
From the great morning of the world when first
God dawned on Chaos; in its stream immersed,
The lamps of Heaven flash with a softer light;
All baser things pant with life's sacred thirst;
170 Diffuse themselves; and spend in love's delight,
The beauty and the joy of their renewéd might.

The leprous corpse, touched by this spirit tender,
Exhales itself in flowers of gentle breath;
Like incarnations of the stars, when splendor
Is changed to fragrance, they illumine death
And mock the merry worm that wakes beneath;
Nought we know, dies. Shall that alone which knows
Be as a sword consumed before the sheath
By sightless lightning?—the intense atom glows
180 A moment, then is quenched in a most cold repose.

Alas! that all we loved of him should be,
But for our grief, as if it had not been,
And grief itself be mortal! Woe is me!
Whence are we, and why are we? of what scene
The actors or spectators? Great and mean
Meet massed in death, who lends what life must borrow.
As long as skies are blue, and fields are green,
Evening must usher night, night urge the morrow,
Month follow month with woe, and year wake year to
    sorrow.

190 He will awake no more, oh, never more!
"Wake thou," cried Misery, "childless Mother, rise
Out of thy sleep, and slake, in thy heart's core,
A wound more fierce than his, with tears and sighs."
And all the Dreams that watched Urania's eyes,
And all the Echoes whom their sister's song
Had held in holy silence, cried: "Arise!"
Swift as a Thought by the snake Memory stung,
From her ambrosial rest the fading Splendor sprung.

She rose like an autumnal Night, that springs
200 Out of the East, and follows wild and drear
The golden Day, which, on eternal wings,
Even as a ghost abandoning a bier,

Had left the Earth a corpse. Sorrow and fear
So struck, so roused, so rapped Urania;
So saddened round her like an atmosphere
Of stormy mist; so swept her on her way
Even to the mournful place where Adonais lay.

Out of her secret Paradise she sped,
Through camps and cities rough with stone, and steel,
And human hearts, which to her aëry tread   210
Yielding not, wounded the invisible
Palms of her tender feet where'er they fell:
And barbéd tongues, and thoughts more sharp than
    they,
Rent the soft Form they never could repel,
Whose sacred blood, like the young tears of May,
Paved with eternal flowers that undeserving way.

In the death-chamber for a moment Death,
Shamed by the presence of that living Might,
Blushed to annihilation, and the breath
Revisited those lips, and Life's pale light   220
Flashed through those limbs, so late her dear delight.
"Leave me not wild and drear and comfortless,
As silent lightning leaves the starless night!
Leave me not!" cried Urania: her distress
Roused Death: Death rose and smiled, and met her
    vain caress.

"Stay yet awhile! speak to me once again;
Kiss me, so long but as a kiss may live;
And in my heartless breast and burning brain
That word, that kiss, shall all thoughts else survive,
With food of saddest memory kept alive,   230
Now thou art dead, as if it were a part
Of thee, my Adonais! I would give
All that I am to be as thou now art!
But I am chained to Time, and cannot thence depart!

"O gentle child, beautiful as thou wert,
Why didst thou leave the trodden paths of men
Too soon, and with weak hands though mighty heart
Dare the unpastured dragon in his den?
Defenseless as thou wert, oh, where was then
Wisdom the mirrored shield, or scorn the spear?   240
Or hadst thou waited the full cycle, when
Thy spirit should have filled its crescent sphere,
The monsters of life's waste had fled from thee like
    deer.

"The herded wolves, bold only to pursue;
The obscene ravens, clamorous o'er the dead;

---

159. **brake,** thicket. 160. **brere,** briar. 179. **sightless,** invisible. 228. **heartless breast.** Her breast was heartless because she had given her heart to Adonais. 238. **unpastured dragon,** the harsh and insatiable world. 240. **mirrored shield.** A reference to the shield that protected Perseus, famous mythological hero, from the fatal gaze of the demon Gorgons and that enabled him to cut off Medusa's head because he saw it only by reflection. 242. **filled . . . sphere,** attained maturity of power. 244. **herded wolves,** contemporary critics, who catered to the

political party in power. 250. **Pythian of the age,** Byron, who had "slain" the critics in his *English Bards and Scotch Reviewers* (see p. 741) as Apollo did the Python. 264. **Pilgrim of Eternity,** Byron, so called from his *Childe Harold's Pilgrimage,* 3, 669, p. 748. 268. **Ierne,** Ireland. The reference is to Thomas Moore (1779–1852) and his *Irish Melodies.* He sang the tragic death of the Irish patriot Robert Emmet in *Oh, Breathe Not His Name.* 271. **one frail Form,** Shelley himself. 276. **Actaeon-like.** Actaeon, the hunter, looked upon Diana

The vultures to the conqueror's banner true
Who feed where Desolation first has fed,
And whose wings rain contagion;—how they fled,
When, like Apollo, from this golden bow
250 The Pythian of the age one arrow sped
And smiled!—The spoilers tempt no second blow,
They fawn on the proud feet that spurn them lying
   low.

"The sun comes forth, and many reptiles spawn;
He sets, and each ephemeral insect then
Is gathered into death without a dawn,
And the immortal stars awake again;
So is it in the world of living men:
A godlike mind soars forth, in its delight
Making earth bare and veiling heaven, and when
260 It sinks, the swarms that dimmed or shared its light
Leave to its kindred lamps the spirit's awful night."

Thus ceased she: and the mountain shepherds came,
Their garlands sere, their magic mantles rent;
The Pilgrim of Eternity, whose fame
Over his living head like Heaven is bent,
An early but enduring monument,
Came, veiling all the lightnings of his song
In sorrow; from her wilds Ierne sent
The sweetest lyrist of her saddest wrong,
And Love taught Grief to fall like music from his
270   tongue.

Midst others of less note, came one frail Form,
A phantom among men; companionless
As the last cloud of an expiring storm
Whose thunder is its knell; he, as I guess,
Had gazed on Nature's naked loveliness,
Actaeon-like, and now he fled astray
With feeble steps o'er the world's wilderness,
And his own thoughts, along that rugged way,
Pursued, like raging hounds, their father and their
   prey.

280 A pardlike Spirit beautiful and swift—
A Love in desolation masked;—a Power
Girt around with weakness; it can scarce uplift
The weight of the superincumbent hour;
It is a dying lamp, a falling shower,
A breaking billow;—even whilst we speak
Is it not broken? On the withering flower
The killing sun smiles brightly: on a cheek
The life can burn in blood, even while the heart may
   break.

His head was bound with pansies overblown,
And faded violets, white, and pied, and blue;   290
And a light spear topped with a cypress cone,
Round whose rude shaft dark ivy-tresses grew
Yet dripping with the forest's noonday dew,
Vibrated, as the ever-beating heart
Shook the weak hand that grasped it; of that crew
He came the last, neglected and apart;
A herd-abandoned deer struck by the hunter's
   dart.

All stood aloof, and at his partial moan
Smiled through their tears; well knew that gentle
   band
Who in another's fate now wept his own,   300
As in the accents of an unknown land
He sung new sorrow; sad Urania scanned
The Stranger's mien, and murmured: "Who art thou?"
He answered not, but with a sudden hand
Made bare his branded and ensanguined brow,
Which was like Cain's or Christ's—oh! that it should
   be so!

What softer voice is hushed over the dead?
Athwart what brow is that dark mantle thrown?
What form leans sadly o'er the white deathbed,
In mockery of monumental stone,   310
The heavy heart heaving without a moan?
If it be He, who, gentlest of the wise,
Taught, soothed, loved, honored the departed one,
Let me not vex, with inharmonious sighs,
The silence of that heart's accepted sacrifice.

Our Adonais has drunk poison—oh!
What deaf and viperous murderer could crown
Life's early cup with such a draught of woe?
The nameless worm would now itself disown:
It felt, yet could escape, the magic tone   320
Whose prelude held all envy, hate, and wrong,
But what was howling in one breast alone,
Silent with expectation of the song,
Whose master's hand is cold, whose silver lyre
   unstrung.

Live thou, whose infamy is not thy fame!
Live! fear no heavier chastisement from me,
Thou noteless blot on a remembered name!
But be thyself, and know thyself to be!
And ever at thy season be thou free
To spill the venom when thy fangs o'erflow: 330
Remorse and Self-contempt shall cling to thee;

Hot Shame shall burn upon thy secret brow,
And like a beaten hound tremble thou shalt—as
    now.

Nor let us weep that our delight is fled
Far from these carrion kites that scream below;
He wakes or sleeps with the enduring dead;
Thou canst not soar where he is sitting now—
Dust to the dust! but the pure spirit shall flow
Back to the burning fountain whence it came,
340 A portion of the Eternal, which must glow
Through time and change, unquenchably the same,
Whilst thy cold embers choke the sordid hearth of
    shame.

Peace, peace! he is not dead, he doth not sleep—
He hath awakened from the dream of life—
'Tis we, who lost in stormy visions, keep
With phantoms an unprofitable strife,
And in mad trance, strike with our spirit's knife
Invulnerable nothings.—*We* decay
Like corpses in a charnel; fear and grief
350 Convulse us and consume us day by day,
And cold hopes swarm like worms within our living
    clay.

He has outsoared the shadow of our night;
Envy and calumny and hate and pain,
And that unrest which men miscall delight,
Can touch him not and torture not again;
From the contagion of the world's slow stain
He is secure, and now can never mourn
A heart grown cold, a head grown gray in vain;
Nor, when the spirit's self has ceased to burn,
360 With sparkless ashes load an unlamented urn.

He lives, he wakes—'tis Death is dead, not he;
Mourn not for Adonais.—Thou young Dawn,
Turn all thy dew to splendor, for from thee
The spirit thou lamentest is not gone;
Ye caverns and ye forests, cease to moan!
Cease, ye faint flowers and fountains, and thou Air,
Which like a mourning veil thy scarf hadst thrown
O'er the abandoned Earth, now leave it bare
Even to the joyous stars which smile on its despair!

370 He is made one with Nature: there is heard
His voice in all her music, from the moan
Of thunder, to the song of night's sweet bird;
He is a presence to be felt and known
In darkness and in light, from herb and stone,
Spreading itself where'er that Power may move

Which has withdrawn his being to its own;
Which wields the world with never-wearied love,
Sustains it from beneath, and kindles it above.

He is a portion of the loveliness
Which once he made more lovely: he doth bear   380
His part, while the one Spirit's plastic stress
Sweeps through the dull dense world, compelling there,
All new successions to the forms they wear;
Torturing th' unwilling dross that checks its flight
To its own likeness, as each mass may bear;
And bursting in its beauty and its might
From trees and beasts and men into the Heaven's
    light.

The splendors of the firmament of time
May be eclipsed, but are extinguished not;
Like stars to their appointed height they climb,   390
And death is a low mist which cannot blot
The brightness it may veil. When lofty thought
Lifts a young heart above its mortal lair,
And love and life contend in it, for what
Shall be its earthly doom, the dead live there
And move like winds of light on dark and stormy
    air.

The inheritors of unfulfilled renown
Rose from their thrones, built beyond mortal thought,
Far in the Unapparent. Chatterton
Rose pale—his solemn agony had not   400
Yet faded from him; Sidney, as he fought
And as he fell and as he lived and loved
Sublimely mild, a Spirit without spot,
Arose; and Lucan, by his death approved:
Oblivion as they rose shrank like a thing reproved.

And many more, whose names on Earth are dark,
But whose transmitted effluence cannot die
So long as fire outlives the parent spark,
Rose, robed in dazzling immortality.
"Thou art become as one of us," they cry,   410
"It was for thee yon kingless sphere has long
Swung blind in unascended majesty,
Silent alone amid an Heaven of Song.
Assume thy wingéd throne, thou Vesper of our throng!"

Who mourns for Adonais? Oh, come forth,
Fond wretch! and know thyself and him aright.
Clasp with thy panting soul the pendulous Earth;
As from a center, dart thy spirit's light
Beyond all worlds, until its spacious might
Satiate the void circumference: then shrink   420

Even to a point within our day and night;
And keep thy heart light lest it make thee sink
When hope has kindled hope, and lured thee to the
 brink.

Or go to Rome, which is the sepulcher,
Oh, not of him, but of our joy: 'tis nought
That ages, empires, and religions there
Lie buried in the ravage they have wrought;
For such as he can lend—they borrow not
Glory from those who made the world their prey;
430 And he is gathered to the kings of thought
Who waged contention with their time's decay,
And of the past are all that cannot pass away.

Go thou to Rome—at once the Paradise,
The grave, the city, and the wilderness;
And where its wrecks like shattered mountains
 rise,
And flowering weeds, and fragrant copses dress
The bones of Desolation's nakedness
Pass, till the spirit of the spot shall lead
Thy footsteps to a slope of green access
440 Where, like an infant's smile, over the dead
A light of laughing flowers along the grass is
 spread;

And gray walls molder round, on which dull Time
Feeds, like slow fire upon a hoary brand;
And one keen pyramid with wedge sublime,
Pavilioning the dust of him who planned
This refuge for his memory, doth stand
Like flame transformed to marble; and beneath,
A field is spread, on which a newer band
Have pitched in Heaven's smile their camp of death,
Welcoming him we lose with scarce extinguished
450   breath.

Here pause: these graves are all too young as yet
To have outgrown the sorrow which consigned
Its charge to each; and if the seal is set,
Here, on one fountain of a mourning mind,
Break it not thou! too surely shalt thou find
Thine own well full, if thou returnest home,
Of tears and gall. From the world's bitter wind
Seek shelter in the shadow of the tomb.
What Adonais is, why fear we to become?

460 The One remains, the many change and pass;
Heaven's light forever shines, Earth's shadows fly;
Life, like a dome of many-colored glass,
Stains the white radiance of Eternity,

Until Death tramples it to fragments.—Die,
If thou wouldst be with that which thou dost seek!
Follow where all is fled!—Rome's azure sky,
Flowers, ruins, statues, music, words are weak
The glory they transfuse with fitting truth to
 speak.

Why linger, why turn back, why shrink, my Heart?
Thy hopes are gone before: from all things here   470
They have departed; thou shouldst now depart!
A light is passed from the revolving year,
And man, and woman; and what still is dear
Attracts to crush, repels to make thee wither.
The soft sky smiles—the low wind whispers near:
'Tis Adonais calls! oh, hasten thither,
No more let Life divide what Death can join together.

That Light whose smile kindles the Universe,
That Beauty in which all things work and move,
That Benediction which the eclipsing Curse   480
Of birth can quench not, that sustaining Love
Which through the web of being blindly wove
By man and beast and earth and air and sea,
Burns bright or dim, as each are mirrors of
The fire for which all thirst; now beams on me,
Consuming the last clouds of cold mortality.

The breath whose might I have invoked in
 song
Descends on me; my spirit's bark is driven,
Far from the shore, far from the trembling throng
Whose sails were never to the tempest given;   490
The massy earth and spheréd skies are riven!
I am borne darkly, fearfully, afar;
Whilst, burning through the inmost veil of Heaven,
The soul of Adonais, like a star,
Beacons from the abode where the Eternal are.
(1821)

from HELLAS

   Hellas *is a lyrical drama inspired by the Greek war
for independence from Turkey, fought in 1821. Shelley
looked upon this struggle as the herald of a new golden
age of love and freedom.*

WORLDS ON WORLDS ARE ROLLING EVER

   Worlds on worlds are rolling ever
     From creation to decay,

to escape execution for taking part in a political conspiracy. 439. slope
. . . access, the Protestant cemetery, where Keats was buried. Shelley's
ashes were buried near Keats a short time after the writing of Adonais.
444. one . . . pyramid, the tomb of Caius Cestius, built in the time
of Augustus. 451. too young. Shelley's son William, who died in

June 1819, was buried there. The cemetery was new. 465. that . . .
seek, Absolute Beauty.

Like the bubbles on a river
  Sparkling, bursting, borne away.
But they are still immortal
  Who, through birth's orient portal
And death's dark chasm hurrying to and fro,
  Clothe their unceasing flight
  In the brief dust and light
10 Gathered around their chariots as they go;
  New shapes they still may weave,
  New gods, new laws receive,
Bright or dim are they as the robes they last
  On Death's bare ribs had cast.

  A power from the unknown God,
  A Promethean conqueror, came;
Like a triumphal path he trod
  The thorns of death and shame.
  A mortal shape to him
20   Was like the vapor dim
Which the orient planet animates with light;
  Hell, Sin, and Slavery came,
  Like bloodhounds mild and tame,
Nor preyed, until their lord had taken flight;
  The moon of Mahomet
  Arose, and it shall set:
While blazoned as on Heaven's immortal noon
  The cross leads generations on.

  Swift as the radiant shapes of sleep
30   From one whose dreams are Paradise,
Fly, when the fond wretch wakes to weep,
  And Day peers forth with her blank eyes;
  So fleet, so faint, so fair,
  The Powers of earth and air
Fled from the folding-star of Bethlehem:
  Apollo, Pan, and Love,
  And even Olympian Jove
Grew weak, for killing Truth had glared on them;
  Our hills and seas and streams,
40   Dispeopled of their dreams,
Their waters turned to blood, their dew to tears,
  Wailed for the golden years.

FINAL CHORUS

The world's great age begins anew,
  The golden years return,
The earth doth like a snake renew
  Her winter weeds outworn;
Heaven smiles, and faiths and empires gleam,
Like wrecks of a dissolving dream.

A brighter Hellas rears its mountains
  From waves serener far;
A new Peneus rolls his fountains
  Against the morning star.   130
Where fairer Tempes bloom, there sleep
Young Cyclads on a sunnier deep.

A loftier Argo cleaves the main,
  Fraught with a later prize;
Another Orpheus sings again,
  And loves, and weeps, and dies.
A new Ulysses leaves once more
Calypso for his native shore.

Oh, write no more the tale of Troy,
  If earth Death's scroll must be!   140
Nor mix with Laian rage the joy
  Which dawns upon the free;
Although a subtler Sphinx renew
Riddles of death Thebes never knew.

Another Athens shall arise,
  And to remoter time
Bequeath, like sunset to the skies,
  The splendor of its prime;
And leave, if nought so bright may live,
All earth can take or Heaven can give.   150

Saturn and Love their long repose
  Shall burst, more bright and good
Than all who fell, than One who rose,
  Than many unsubdued;
Not gold, not blood, their altar dowers,
But votive tears and symbol flowers.

Oh, cease! must hate and death return?
  Cease! must men kill and die?
Cease! drain not to its dregs the urn
  Of bitter prophecy.   160
The world is weary of the past,
Oh, might it die or rest at last!
(1821; 1822)

REMEMBRANCE

Swifter far than summer's flight—
Swifter far than youth's delight—
Swifter far than happy night,

Worlds on Worlds. 16. **Promethean,** pertaining to Prometheus, in Greek mythology, the founder of civilization and the benefactor of mankind. 25. **Mahomet,** Mohammed (570–632), founder of the Mohammedan religion. 35. **folding-star,** the evening star, which appears about the time the sheep are put into the fold. 36. **Apollo,** god of music and poetry. **Pan,** god of hills and woods, flocks and herds. 37. **Olympian Jove.** The gods were supposed to inhabit Olympus, a mountain in Thessaly, Greece.
Final Chorus. 121. **The world's great age.** At the end of the "great age" of the ancients, the sun, moon, and planets were to return to their original positions, and the history of the world would repeat itself; the Golden Age would return and be followed by ages of degradation and evil. Cf. Byron's *Don Juan,* 3, p. 762. 124. **weeds,** garments. 127. **Hellas,** Greece. 129. **Peneus,** a river in Thessaly, Greece. 131. **Tempe,** a beautiful valley through which the Peneus River flows. 132. **Cyclads,** the Cyclades, islands in the Aegean Sea. 133. **Argo,** the ship of the Argonauts, who accompanied Jason on his quest for the Golden Fleece. 135. **Orpheus,** mythological poet and musician, who went to the lower world to lead his wife Eurydice back to the upper world. He was given permission to do so on condition that he should not look

Art thou come and gone—
As the earth when leaves are dead,
As the night when sleep is sped,
As the heart when joy is fled,
    I am left lone, alone.

  The swallow summer comes again—
10 The owlet night resumes her reign—
But the wild-swan youth is fain
    To fly with thee, false as thou.—
My heart each day desires the morrow;
Sleep itself is turned to sorrow;
Vainly would my winter borrow
    Sunny leaves from any bough.

Lilies for a bridal bed—
Roses for a matron's head—
Violets for a maiden dead—
20   Pansies let *my* flowers be:
On the living grave I bear
Scatter them without a tear—
Let no friend, however dear,
    Waste one hope, one fear for me.
(1821; 1824)

TO ——

*This poem was addressed to Jane Williams, the wife
of Edward Williams; both were warm friends of Shelley
during his later years in Italy.*

One word is too often profaned
  For me to profane it,
One feeling too falsely disdained
  For thee to disdain it;
One hope is too like despair
  For prudence to smother,
And pity from thee more dear
    Than that from another.

I can give not what men call love,
10   But wilt thou accept not
The worship the heart lifts above
  And the Heavens reject not—
The desire of the moth for the star,
  Of the night for the morrow,
The devotion to something afar
    From the sphere of our sorrow?
(1821; 1824)

LINES

When the lamp is shattered,
The light in the dust lies dead—
  When the cloud is scattered,
The rainbow's glory is shed.
  When the lute is broken,
Sweet tones are remembered not;
  When the lips have spoken,
Loved accents are soon forgot.

  As music and splendor
Survive not the lamp and the lute,   10
  The heart's echoes render
No song when the spirit is mute—
  No song but sad dirges,
Like the wind through a ruined cell,
  Or the mournful surges
That ring the dead seaman's knell.

  When hearts have once mingled
Love first leaves the well-built nest;
  The weak one is singled
To endure what it once possessed.   20
  O Love! who bewailest
The frailty of all things here,
  Why choose you the frailest
For your cradle, your home, and your bier?

  Its passions will rock thee
As the storms rock the ravens on high;
  Bright reason will mock thee,
Like the sun from a wintry sky.
  From thy nest every rafter
Will rot, and thine eagle home   30
  Leave thee naked to laughter,
When leaves fall and cold winds come.
(1822; 1824)

A DIRGE

Rough wind, that moanest loud
  Grief too sad for song;
Wild wind, when sullen cloud
  Knells all the night long;
Sad storm, whose tears are vain,
Bare woods, whose branches strain,
Deep caves and dreary main—
  Wail, for the world's wrong!
(1822; 1824)

back at her until they reached the upper air. Orpheus broke the condition, and Eurydice vanished. 137. **Ulysses,** king of Ithaca, one of the
Greek heroes in the Trojan War. He is the hero of Homer's *Odyssey.*
When shipwrecked, he was detained on an island by the nymph Calypso,
who promised him immortal youth if he would remain with her, but
he refused. See Tennyson's *Ulysses,* p. 847. 141. **Laian rage.** Laius,
king of Thebes, upon learning from the oracle that he would be killed
by his son, left the infant Oedipus in an exposed place. The boy **was**
rescued and later slew his father unwittingly. 143. **Sphinx . . .
knew.** The Sphinx was a winged monster in Thebes that killed all **who**

could not solve her riddle. Oedipus solved it, and she cast herself down
from a rock and was killed. 151. **Saturn and Love,** supposed to have
ruled in the Golden Age of innocence and happiness. 153. **all who fell,**
the gods of Greece, Asia, and Egypt. **One who rose,** Christ. 154.
many unsubdued, objects of the idolatry of China, India, etc.
Remembrance. 10. **owlet night,** dim, uncanny night. 17. **Lilies,
etc.** The lily is a symbol of purity; the rose, of constancy; the violet,
of modesty; the pansy, of thought or remembrance. Cf. Shelley's *Adonais,*
p. 779, ll. 289-292.

JOHN KEATS 1795-1821

English literature has no more tragic story to offer than that of John Keats, if by tragedy we mean the death of a great personage before maturity. One of the most interesting subjects for speculation is the question as to what the three great young romantic poets of England—Byron, Shelley, and Keats—would have become if they had been allowed to complete the span of life usually allotted man. Byron, it is possible, would have followed the neo-classical bent that was certainly part of his make-up; concerning Shelley and Keats no answer is forthcoming. Both were young in years and in outlook; both were of the very essence of youth and romance, albeit in somewhat different ways. Would they ever have become middle-aged, and if so, how would their advancing years have dealt with them?

John Keats was born October 29, 1795. His father was a London livery-stable keeper. The boy's parents both died when he was young; the father when Keats was but nine, the mother when he was fifteen. He went to school at Enfield, and in 1810 was apprenticed to a surgeon at Edmonton—both towns near London. In school he was a sturdy, aggressive young fellow, athletically inclined. His friends all testified to his fine character and his general high-mindedness. He was a voracious reader and an honor student in school, but he left school as his uncles wanted to fit him for the medical profession. He finished his apprenticeship in 1815. Far more important than this event, however, was his discovery of Spenser's Faerie Queene, for the great Renaissance epic opened to him a new field of beauty. Although Keats spent a year or so in London hospitals, he finally abandoned the idea of a medical career to take up literature.

Through his friend Charles Cowden Clarke, who had shown him the Faerie Queene, Keats met Leigh Hunt, the tireless worker for revolutionary and romantic literature, and through Hunt he met Hazlitt and Shelley. He was able to publish a few sonnets in Leigh Hunt's periodical, The Examiner, and so make a start as a poet. He drifted into acquaintance with Wordsworth, Lamb, and Coleridge. He published (1817) a volume of poems, dedicated to Hunt, and followed this with Endymion in 1818. It happened that Hunt, for a variety of reasons, was persona non grata with the conservative critics of London, and Keats' friendship with Hunt doomed Endymion to harsh criticism, some of which it unquestionably deserved, for it was over-sensuous, with a kind of tropical lushness, and with many poor lines to offset the occasional noble ones.

The review in the Quarterly criticized the literary efforts of Keats, as did Blackwood's Magazine; but the latter also insulted Keats' humble beginnings and surgeon's profession beyond all bounds of good taste.

Keats was depressed by these reviews, of course, and even thought for a time of giving up literature. Yet there is certainly no cause to think that he suffered a broken heart, as Shelley had it in Adonais (p. 775). Indeed, Keats recognized the immaturity of Endymion. Family and personal cares, however, saddened him immeasurably. One brother left for America; another brother died of tuberculosis—apparently a family weakness, for Keats' mother had also died of it; financial troubles worried him; and he himself came to feel the ominous symptoms of the family disease. He took a trip through the north of England, but it yielded him no lasting relief. By the end of the year (1818) the suspicion of tuberculosis was confirmed. And, as a sort of tragic climax, he met and fell in love with Fanny Brawne—a hopeless passion, in view of his illness. None knew that better than John Keats.

He went to live for a time with a friend, Charles Brown, at a house near Hampstead Heath, London, but his illness progressed remorselessly to its fatal conclusion. As a last resort he tried the softer climate of Italy. But it was too late; in less than six months he was dead (February 23, 1821). He was buried in the Protestant cemetery at Rome under his own epitaph: "Here lies one whose name was writ in water."

Somewhere between 1816 and his early death five years later, John Keats underwent one of the most remarkable metamorphoses in English literary history. From the condition of what he called a "versifying pet lamb," Keats transformed himself into a poet of the highest order. Moreover, he earned the status of "major poet"; the evaluation is not a sentimental tribute to an unfulfilled potential for greatness. Although Keats bequeathed a limited canon, it is sufficiently varied, rich, and distinctive to win for him the immortality he sought:

> *O for ten years, that I may overwhelm*
> *Myself in poesy; so I may do the deed*
> *That my own soul has to itself decreed.*
> *—Sleep and Poetry (1816)*

Keats had only half of the time he asked, yet he succeeded. He was, next to Wordsworth, the outstanding sonneteer of the romantic period; his great odes are unsurpassed in English, and the minor pieces, such as La Belle Dame sans Merci (p. 789), and his magnificent fragment The Fall of Hyperion demonstrate the haunting, impressive mastery of form and subject which distinguishes all of his mature work.

In addition, as his letters show, Keats may deserve recognition also as a provocative literary theorist and critic of the romantic sensibility. The letters provide the best possible biography of Keats and greatly illuminate both his concept and his practice of poetry. Moreover, they offer a written record of the struggle toward personal equilibrium and philosophical self-integration which Keats often dramatized in his poems. The sureness of the vision projected in his ode To Autumn (p. 796) and The Fall of Hyperion suggests that the poet perhaps resolved these painful mental conflicts before his death. What Keats might have become and accomplished if he had lived a normal life span is beyond speculation, but when he stopped writing and lapsed into the "posthumous existence" of the last few months of his illness, he had achieved what no other major English poet can claim: secure greatness on the basis of work produced before the age of twenty-six.

ON FIRST LOOKING INTO CHAPMAN'S HOMER

A translation of Homer by George Chapman (c. 1559-1634), famous Elizabethan dramatist and translator of classics, which Keats and his friend Charles Cowden Clarke spent a night reading, was the inspiration of this notable sonnet.

Much have I traveled in the realms of gold,
And many goodly states and kingdoms seen;
Round many western islands have I been
Which bards in fealty to Apollo hold.
Oft of one wide expanse had I been told
That deep-browed Homer ruled as his demesne;
Yet did I never breathe its pure serene
Till I heard Chapman speak out loud and bold:
Then felt I like some watcher of the skies
10 When a new planet swims into his ken;
Or like stout Cortez when with eagle eyes
He stared at the Pacific—and all his men
Looked at each other with a wild surmise—
Silent, upon a peak in Darien.
(1815; 1816)

He mourns that day so soon has glided by:
E'en like the passage of an angel's tear
That falls through the clear ether silently.
(1816; 1817)

ADDRESSED TO HAYDON

Great spirits now on earth are sojourning;
He of the cloud, the cataract, the lake,
Who on Helvellyn's summit, wide awake,
Catches his freshness from Archangel's wing:
He of the rose, the violet, the spring,
The social smile, the chain for Freedom's sake:
And lo!—whose steadfastness would never take
A meaner sound than Raphael's whispering.
And other spirits there are standing apart
Upon the forehead of the age to come;   10
These, these will give the world another heart,
And other pulses. Hear ye not the hum
Of mighty workings in the human mart?
Listen awhile ye nations, and be dumb.
(1816; 1817)

TO ONE WHO HAS BEEN LONG IN CITY PENT

To one who has been long in city pent
'Tis very sweet to look into the fair
And open face of heaven—to breathe a prayer
Full in the smile of the blue firmament.
Who is more happy, when, with heart's content,
Fatigued he sinks into some pleasant lair
Of wavy grass, and reads a debonair
And gentle tale of love and languishment?
Returning home at evening, with an ear
10 Catching the notes of Philomel—an eye
Watching the sailing cloudlet's bright career,

ON SEEING THE ELGIN MARBLES

My spirit is too weak—mortality
Weighs heavily on me like unwilling sleep,
And each imagined pinnacle and steep
Of godlike hardship tells me I must die
Like a sick eagle looking at the sky.
Yet 'tis a gentle luxury to weep
That I have not the cloudy winds to keep,
Fresh for the opening of the morning's eye.
Such dim-conceivéd glories of the brain
Bring round the heart an undescribable feud;   10
So do these wonders a most dizzy pain,

On First . . . Homer. 4. **Apollo,** god of poetry and music. 11. **Cortez.** It was Balboa, not Cortez, who discovered the Pacific Ocean, in 1513. 14. **Darien,** a district forming the eastern part of the Isthmus of Panama.
To One . . . Pent. 10. **Philomel,** the nightingale.
Addressed to Haydon. Benjamin Robert Haydon (1786–1846) was a noted English historical painter and one of Keats' close friends. 2. **He . . . wing,** William Wordsworth. 3. **Helvellyn,** a mountain in Cumberlandshire, near Wordsworth's home. 5. **He . . . sake,** Leigh Hunt, to whom Keats dedicated his first volume of poems. 7. **whose . . . whispering,** Haydon. 8. **Raphael,** a noted Italian painter (1483–1520).
On Seeing the Elgin Marbles. Thomas Bruce (1766–1841), Earl of Elgin, was a British diplomat who collected the "Elgin Marbles," ancient Greek sculptures brought from the Parthenon in Athens, in 1803–1812, and placed them subsequently in the British Museum.

That mingles Grecian grandeur with the rude
Wasting of old Time—with a billowy main—
A sun—a shadow of a magnitude.
(1817)

ON THE SEA

It keeps eternal whisperings around
Desolate shores, and with its mighty swell
Gluts twice ten thousand caverns, till the spell
Of Hecate leaves them their old shadowy sound.
Often 'tis in such gentle temper found,
That scarcely will the very smallest shell
Be moved for days from whence it sometime fell,
When last the winds of heaven were unbound.
Oh ye! who have your eye-balls vexed and
    tired,
10 Feast them upon the wideness of the sea;
Oh ye! whose ears are dinned with uproar rude,
Or fed too much with cloying melody—
Sit ye near some old cavern's mouth, and brood
Until ye start, as if the sea-nymphs quired!
(1817; 1848)

WHEN I HAVE FEARS THAT
I MAY CEASE TO BE

When I have fears that I may cease to be
Before my pen has gleaned my teeming brain,
Before high piléd books, in charactry,
Hold like rich garners the full-ripened grain;
When I behold, upon the night's starred face,
Huge cloudy symbols of a high romance,
And think that I may never live to trace
Their shadows, with the magic hand of chance;
And when I feel, fair creature of an hour!
10 That I shall never look upon thee more,
Never have relish in the faery power
Of unreflecting love!—then on the shore
Of the wide world I stand alone, and think
Till Love and Fame to nothingness do sink.
(1818; 1848)

LINES ON THE MERMAID TAVERN

J. H. Reynolds (1796-1825), poet, critic, and lawyer, had sent Keats two sonnets on Robin Hood, this poem was sent to Reynolds by Keats in reply. The Mermaid Tavern was a famous London resort of Shakespeare, Ben Jonson, and other Elizabethan dramatists and men of letters. Keats was in full sympathy with the spirit of the Elizabethans.

On the Sea. 4. Hecate, an ancient goddess associated in part with the moon. The reference is to the moon's control of the tides.
When I Have Fears. 3. charactry, characters, letters.

Souls of Poets dead and gone,
What Elysium have ye known,
Happy field or mossy cavern,
Choicer than the Mermaid Tavern?
Have ye tippled drink more fine
Than mine host's Canary wine?
Or are fruits of Paradise
Sweeter than those dainty pies
Of venison? O generous food!
Drest as though bold Robin Hood   10
Would, with his maid Marian,
Sup and bowse from horn and can.

I have heard that on a day
Mine host's sign-board flew away,
Nobody knew whither, till
An astrologer's old quill
To a sheepskin gave the story,
Said he saw you in your glory,
Underneath a new old sign
Sipping beverage divine,   20
And pledging with contented smack
The Mermaid in the Zodiac.

Souls of Poets dead and gone,
What Elysium have ye known,
Happy field or mossy cavern,
Choicer than the Mermaid Tavern?
(1818; 1820)

IN A DREAR-NIGHTED DECEMBER

In a drear-nighted December,
Too happy, happy tree,
Thy branches ne'er remember
Their green felicity:
The north cannot undo them,
With a sleety whistle through them;
Nor frozen thawings glue them
From budding at the prime.

In a drear-nighted December,
Too happy, happy brook,   10
Thy bubblings ne'er remember
Apollo's summer look;
But with a sweet forgetting,
They stay their crystal fretting,
Never, never petting
About the frozen time.

Ah! would 'twere so with many
A gentle girl and boy!
But were there ever any
Writhed not at passéd joy?   20

Lines on . . . Tavern. 2. Elysium, abode of the blessed after death. 6. Canary wine, wine made in the Canary Islands; this was Elizabethan "sack." 10. Robin Hood, noted as a chivalrous and

To know the change and feel it,
When there is none to heal it,
Nor numbéd sense to steal it,
Was never said in rime.
(1818?; 1829)

from ENDYMION

Endymion was composed during the year 1817. Keats spent some time on the Isle of Wight in the spring of that year, and began the poem there. This, the first ambitious poem that Keats wrote, caused him much anxiety and self-dissatisfaction, for he was still a virtual neophyte in poetry but at the same time had a considerable amount of ability to criticize himself. The reception of the poem confirmed Keats' worst fears; the severe, unfavorable criticism accorded it has already been noted (pp. 775 and 784).

In the poem, Keats follows the general outline of the old classical myth of Endymion, the beautiful youth beloved of the moon goddess Diana. But, as he was to do again in Hyperion, he elaborates the story by giving it a luxuriant descriptive background, heightening the emotional effects wherever possible, and coloring it heavily with his own fervent imagination. In other words, he has romanticized the story, in greater degree than Wordsworth did the classical material in Laodamia, and in a manner that had a powerful influence upon Tennyson in such poems as Oenone and The Lotos Eaters (p. 845). To look at the poem from another point of view, Endymion is, along with the sonnet On First Looking into Chapman's Homer (p. 785), the first important manifestation by Keats of the interest in classical literature common among romantic writers. It may be remarked in passing that in their worship of beauty, the romantic writers like Keats and Shelley often came much closer to the ideals of ancient Greek art than did the neoclassical writers of the eighteenth century, however much the romantic quality of effusiveness ran against the old classical ideal of moderation. The opening passage in Endymion should be compared with the great Ode on a Grecian Urn (p. 789) for a complete expression of Keats' love of the classical ideal of beauty.

PROEM

A thing of beauty is a joy forever:
Its loveliness increases; it will never
Pass into nothingness; but still will keep
A bower quiet for us, and a sleep
Full of sweet dreams, and health, and quiet breathing.

Therefore, on every morrow, are we wreathing
A flowery band to bind us to the earth,
Spite of despondence, of the inhuman dearth
Of noble natures, of the gloomy days,
Of all the unhealthy and o'er-darkened ways   10
Made for our searching: yes, in spite of all,
Some shape of beauty moves away the pall
From our dark spirits. Such the sun, the moon,
Trees old, and young, sprouting a shady boon
For simple sheep; and such are daffodils
With the green world they live in; and clear rills
That for themselves a cooling covert make
'Gainst the hot season; the mid-forest brake,
Rich with a sprinkling of fair musk-rose blooms:
And such too is the grandeur of the dooms   20
We have imagined for the mighty dead;
All lovely tales that we have heard or read:
An endless fountain of immortal drink,
Pouring unto us from the heaven's brink.

Nor do we merely feel these essences
For one short hour; no, even as the trees
That whisper round a temple become soon
Dear as the temple's self, so does the moon,
The passion poesy, glories infinite,
Haunt us till they become a cheering light   30
Unto our souls, and bound to us so fast,
That, whether there be shine, or gloom o'ercast,
They always must be with us, or we die.

Therefore, 'tis with full happiness that I
Will trace the story of Endymion.
The very music of the name has gone
Into my being, and each pleasant scene
Is growing fresh before me as the green
Of our own valleys: so I will begin
Now while I cannot hear the city's din;   40
Now while the early budders are just new,
And run in mazes of the youngest hue
About old forests; while the willow trails
Its delicate amber; and the dairy pails
Bring home increase of milk. And, as the year
Grows lush in juicy stalks, I'll smoothly steer
My little boat, for many quiet hours,
With streams that deepen freshly into bowers.
Many and many a verse I hope to write,
Before the daisies, vermeil-rimmed and white,   50
Hide in deep herbage; and ere yet the bees
Hum about globes of clover and sweet peas,
I must be near the middle of my story.
O may no wintry season, bare and hoary,
See it half finished: but let Autumn bold,
With universal tinge of sober gold,
Be all about me when I make an end.
And now at once, adventuresome, I send

generous outlaw. Maid Marian was one of his associates. Keats was fond of this legendary medieval hero. For ballads of Robin Hood, see p. 61. **12. bowse,** drink. **22. Mermaid in the Zodiac,** the sign of the Virgin in the Zodiac.
In a Drear-Nighted December. 12. Apollo, god of poetry and music. 15. **petting,** complaining.

My herald thought into a wilderness:
60 There let its trumpet blow, and quickly dress
My uncertain path with green, that I may speed
Easily onward, thorough flowers and weed.
(1817-1818; 1818)

ODE

*This poem was addressed to Beaumont and Fletcher,
Elizabethan dramatists.*

Bards of Passion and of Mirth,
Ye have left your souls on earth!
Have ye souls in heaven too,
Double-lived in regions new?
Yes, and those of heaven commune
With the spheres of sun and moon;
With the noise of fountains wond'rous,
And the parle of voices thund'rous;
With the whisper of heaven's trees
10 And one another, in soft ease
Seated on Elysian lawns
Browsed by none but Dian's fawns;
Underneath large blue-bells tented,
Where the daisies are rose-scented,
And the rose herself has got
Perfume which on earth is not;
Where the nightingale doth sing
Not a senseless, trancéd thing,
But divine melodious truth;
20 Philosophic numbers smooth;
Tales and golden histories
Of heaven and its mysteries.

Thus ye live on high, and then
On the earth ye live again;
And the souls ye left behind you
Teach us, here, the way to find you,
Where your other souls are joying,
Never slumbered, never cloying.
Here, your earth-born souls still speak
30 To mortals, of their little week;
Of their sorrows and delights;
Of their passions and their spites;
Of their glory and their shame;
What doth strengthen and what maim.
Thus ye teach us, every day,
Wisdom, though fled far away.

Bards of Passion and of Mirth,
Ye have left your souls on earth!

Ye have souls in heaven too,
Double-lived in regions new!
(1819; 1820)

ODE ON MELANCHOLY

*The quality of melancholy, so common in romantic
literature, has never received more poetic treatment
than in this poem. The poem, although not published
until 1820, was written in 1819, after the disasters
which befell Keats in 1818 (p. 784). Keats wrote this
letter to his friend Haydon (p. 785 and note) at the
beginning of the year 1819: "I have been writing a
little now and then lately: but nothing to speak of—
being discontented and as it were moulting. Yet I do
not think I shall ever come to the rope or the pistol,
for after a day or two's melancholy, although I smoke
more and more my own insufficiency—I see by little
and little more of what is to be done, and how it is to
be done, should I ever be able to do it. On my soul,
there should be some reward for that continual agonie
ennuyeuse."*

No, No! go not to Lethe, neither twist
    Wolf's-bane, tight-rooted, for its poisonous wine;
Nor suffer thy pale forehead to be kissed
    By nightshade, ruby grape of Proserpine;
Make not your rosary of yew-berries,
    Nor let the beetle, nor the death-moth be
        Your mournful Psyche, nor the downy owl
A partner in your sorrow's mysteries;
    For shade to shade will come too drowsily,
        And drown the wakeful anguish of the soul.   10

But when the melancholy fit shall fall
    Sudden from heaven like a weeping cloud,
That fosters the droop-headed flowers all,
    And hides the green hill in an April shroud;
Then glut thy sorrow on a morning rose,
    Or on the rainbow of the salt sand-wave,
        Or on the wealth of globéd peonies;
Or if thy mistress some rich anger shows,
    Emprison her soft hand, and let her rave,
        And feed deep, deep upon her peerless eyes.   20

She dwells with Beauty—Beauty that must die;
    And Joy, whose hand is ever at his lips
Bidding adieu; and aching Pleasure nigh,
    Turning to poison while the bee-mouth sips:
Ay, in the very temple of Delight
    Veiled Melancholy has her sovran shrine,

Ode. 8. **parle,** talk, discourse. 11. **Elysian,** of Elysium, the home
of the blessed after death. 12. **Dian's fawns.** The fawn was the favorite
animal of Diana, goddess of the moon and the chase.
Ode on Melancholy. 1. **Lethe,** the river of forgetfulness in Hades.
2. **Wolf's-bane,** aconite, a poisonous plant. 4. **nightshade,** a poisonous
herb. **Proserpine.** Proserpina, whom Pluto, "the God of Torment,"

carried away as his bride to his realm in the lower world. 5. **yew-
berries.** The yew is an emblem of mourning. 6. **beetle.** The sacred
scarab of Egypt was regarded as a symbol of the resurrection of the
soul and hence was placed with the dead in coffins. **death-moth,** a moth
with markings resembling the human skull. 7. **Psyche,** in classical
mythology, the soul, symbolized by the butterfly.

Though seen of none save him whose strenuous tongue
Can burst Joy's grape against his palate fine;
His soul shall taste the sadness of her might,
And be among her cloudy trophies hung.
(1819; 1820)

ODE ON A GRECIAN URN

According to tradition, the urn that inspired this famous ode was one still preserved in the garden of Holland House, a noted mansion in Kensington, London. But there were many such marble treasures in the British Museum, decorated with figures carved in low relief (see ll. 41-42). The enduring beauty of any one of them would have been enough to confirm Keats in his characteristic belief that Beauty is the all-important element in human experience.

Thou still unravished bride of quietness,
    Thou foster-child of Silence and slow Time,
Sylvan historian, who canst thus express
    A flowery tale more sweetly than our rime:
What leaf-fringed legend haunts about thy shape
    Of deities or mortals, or of both,
        In Tempe or the dales of Arcady?
    What men or gods are these? What maidens loth?
What mad pursuit? What struggle to escape?
10   What pipes and timbrels? What wild ecstasy?

Heard melodies are sweet, but those unheard
    Are sweeter; therefore, ye soft pipes, play on;
Not to the sensual ear, but, more endeared,
    Pipe to the spirit ditties of no tone:
Fair youth, beneath the trees, thou canst not leave
    Thy song, nor ever can those trees be bare;
        Bold Lover, never, never canst thou kiss,
Though winning near the goal—yet, do not grieve;
    She cannot fade, though thou hast not thy bliss,
20   Forever wilt thou love, and she be fair!

Ah, happy, happy boughs! that cannot shed
    Your leaves, nor ever bid the Spring adieu;
And, happy melodist, unwearied,
    Forever piping songs forever new.
More happy love! more happy, happy love!
    Forever warm and still to be enjoyed,
        Forever panting, and forever young;
All breathing human passion far above,
    That leaves a heart high-sorrowful and cloyed,
30   A burning forehead, and a parching tongue.

Who are these coming to the sacrifice?
    To what green altar, O mysterious priest,
Lead'st thou that heifer lowing at the skies,
    And all her silken flanks with garlands dressed?
What little town by river or seashore,
    Or mountain-built with peaceful citadel,
        Is emptied of this folk, this pious morn?
And, little town, thy streets forevermore
    Will silent be; and not a soul to tell
        Why thou art desolate, can e'er return.   40

O Attic shape! Fair attitude! with brede
    Of marble men and maidens overwrought,
With forest branches and the trodden weed;
    Thou, silent form! dost tease us out of thought
As doth eternity: Cold Pastoral!
    When old age shall this generation waste,
        Thou shalt remain, in midst of other woe
Than ours, a friend to man, to whom thou say'st,
"Beauty is truth, truth beauty,—that is all
    Ye know on earth, and all ye need to know."
(1819; 1820)

LA BELLE DAME SANS MERCI

The ancient folklore theme of the fairy lover was illustrated in the old popular ballad Thomas Rymer *(p. 57). La Belle Dame sans Merci is Keats' highly romantic treatment of the same theme and a very distinguished literary ballad. The poem was printed by Leigh Hunt in* The Indicator *for May 10, 1820; the supposed source was a ballad by the French poet Alain Chartier (1392?-1436?), a translation of which was found by Keats in a volume of Chaucer's poetry.*

O what can ail thee, knight-at-arms!
    Alone and palely loitering!
The sedge has withered from the lake,
    And no birds sing.

O what can ail thee, knight-at-arms!
    So haggard and so woe-begone?
The squirrel's granary is full,
    And the harvest's done.

I see a lily on thy brow
    With anguish moist and fever dew,   10
And on thy cheeks a fading rose
    Fast withereth too.

"I met a lady in the meads,
    Full beautiful—a faery's child,

Her hair was long, her foot was light,
    And her eyes were wild.

"I made a garland for her head,
    And bracelets too, and fragrant zone;
She looked at me as she did love,
20   And made sweet moan.

"I set her on my pacing steed,
    And nothing else saw all day long.
For sidelong would she bend, and sing
    A faery's song.

"She found me roots of relish sweet,
    And honey wild and manna-dew;
And sure in language strange she said,
    'I love thee true.'

"She took me to her elfin grot,
30   And there she wept and sighed full sore;
And there I shut her wild, wild eyes
    With kisses four.

"And there she lulléd me asleep,
    And there I dreamed—ah! woe betide!—
The latest dream I ever dreamed
    On the cold hillside.

"I saw pale kings, and princes too,
    Pale warriors, death-pale were they all:
They cried—'La Belle Dame sans Merci
40   Hath thee in thrall!'

"I saw their starved lips in the gloam
    With horrid warning gapéd wide,
And I woke, and found me here
    On the cold hillside.

"And this is why I sojourn here
    Alone and palely loitering,
Though the sedge is withered from the lake,
    And no birds sing."
(1819; 1820)

ODE TO A NIGHTINGALE

*Many have seen in the last two stanzas of this
beautiful poem the very essence of romanticism. These
stanzas, added to the little lyric of Shelley's, To—
(p. 783), and the third stanza of Wordsworth's
Solitary Reaper (p. 697), make a very complete
and very satisfying composite picture of the roman-*
tic *poet. When Keats wrote this poem, he was already entering the valley of the shadow—a fact that
lends a peculiar poignancy to the entire ode.*

My heart aches, and a drowsy numbness pains
    My sense, as though of hemlock I had drunk,
Or emptied some dull opiate to the drains
    One minute past, and Lethe-wards had sunk:
'Tis not through envy of thy happy lot,
    But being too happy in thine happiness—
        That thou, light-wingéd Dryad of the trees,
            In some melodious plot
        Of beechen green, and shadows numberless,
    Singest of summer in full-throated ease.   10

O, for a draught of vintage! that hath been
    Cooled a long age in the deep-delvéd earth,
Tasting of Flora and the country green,
    Dance, and Provençal song, and sunburnt mirth!
O for a beaker full of the warm South,
    Full of the true, the blushful Hippocrene,
        With beaded bubbles winking at the brim,
            And purple-stainéd mouth;
    That I might drink, and leave the world unseen,
    And with thee fade away into the forest dim: 20

Fade far away, dissolve, and quite forget
    What thou among the leaves hast never known,
The weariness, the fever, and the fret
    Here, where men sit and hear each other groan;
Where palsy shakes a few, sad, last gray hairs,
    Where youth grows pale, and specter-thin, and dies;
        Where but to think is to be full of sorrow
            And leaden-eyed despairs,
    Where Beauty cannot keep her lustrous eyes,
    Or new Love pine at them beyond tomorrow.   30

Away! away! for I will fly to thee,
    Not charioted by Bacchus and his pards,
But on the viewless wings of Poesy,
    Though the dull brain perplexes and retards:
Already with thee! tender is the night,
    And haply the Queen-Moon is on her throne,
        Clustered around by all her starry Fays;
            But here there is no light,
    Save what from heaven is with the breezes blown
        Through verdurous glooms and winding mossy
        ways.   40

I cannot see what flowers are at my feet,
    Nor what soft incense hangs upon the boughs,
But, in embalméd darkness, guess each sweet
    Wherewith the seasonable month endows

The grass, the thicket, and the fruit-tree wild;
  White hawthorn, and the pastoral eglantine;
  Fast fading violets covered up in leaves;
    And mid-May's eldest child,
  The coming musk-rose, full of dewy wine,
50 The murmurous haunt of flies on summer eves.

Darkling I listen; and, for many a time,
  I have been half in love with easeful Death,
Called him soft names in many a musèd rime,
  To take into the air my quiet breath;
Now more than ever seems it rich to die,
  To cease upon the midnight with no pain,
    While thou art pouring forth thy soul abroad
      In such an ecstasy!
  Still wouldst thou sing, and I have ears in vain—
60   To thy high requiem become a sod.

Thou wast not born for death, immortal Bird!
  No hungry generations tread thee down;
The voice I hear this passing night was heard
  In ancient days by emperor and clown:
Perhaps the self-same song that found a path
  Through the sad heart of Ruth, when, sick for
    home,
    She stood in tears amid the alien corn;
      The same that oft-times hath
  Charmed magic casements, opening on the foam
70   Of perilous seas, in faery lands forlorn.

Forlorn! the very word is like a bell
  To toll me back from thee to my sole self,
Adieu! the fancy cannot cheat so well
  As she is famed to do, deceiving elf.
Adieu! adieu! thy plaintive anthem fades
  Past the near meadows, over the still stream,
    Up the hillside; and now 'tis buried deep
      In the next valley glades:
  Was it a vision, or a waking dream?
    Fled is that music—Do I wake or sleep?
(1819)

THE EVE OF ST. AGNES

*St. Agnes was a saint martyred in Rome about the
year 300. In the early days of the Catholic Church, on
St. Agnes' Day (January 21), the Agnus Dei (Lamb
of God) from the mass was chanted, and two lambs
were sacrificed, their wools to be woven later by nuns.
In the Middle Ages there grew up the legend that a
girl on St. Agnes' Eve (January 20) could find out
about her future husband; as she lay on her back, with*

*her hands beneath her head, he would appear before
her in a dream, kiss her, and feast with her.*

  *The Eve of St. Agnes is not only Keats' finest achieve-
ment in the field of the medieval; it can also demand
consideration as an almost perfect specimen of romantic art. Here are the "magic casements," "the far-
off things," the rich and fruitful warmth and color to
which Keats devoted himself. It is perhaps the only
poem by Keats of which the author was in any way
vain; he read aloud the supper picture in ll. 262-270
to Leigh Hunt "with manifest pleasure in his work;
the sole instance I can recall," says Palgrave in his
edition of Keats' Poetical Works (1884), where the
poet—modest in proportion to his greatness—yielded
even to so innocent an impulse of vanity."*

St. Agnes' Eve—Ah, bitter chill it was!
The owl, for all his feathers, was a-cold;
The hare limped trembling through the frozen grass,
And silent was the flock in woolly fold:
Numb were the Beadsman's fingers, while he told
His rosary, and while his frosted breath,
Like pious incense from a censer old,
Seemed taking flight for heaven, without a death,
Past the sweet Virgin's picture, while his prayer he
  saith.

His prayer he saith, this patient, holy man;   10
Then takes his lamp, and riseth from his knees,
And back returneth, meager, barefoot, wan,
Along the chapel aisle by slow degrees:
The sculptured dead, on each side, seem to freeze,
Emprisoned in black, purgatorial rails:
Knights, ladies, praying in dumb orat'ries,
He passeth by; and his weak spirit fails
To think how they may ache in icy hoods and mails.

Northward he turneth through a little door,
And scarce three steps, ere Music's golden tongue   20
Flattered to tears this aged man and poor;
But no—already had his death-bell rung:
The joys of all his life were said and sung:
His was harsh penance on St. Agnes' Eve:
Another way he went, and soon among
Rough ashes sat he for his soul's reprieve,
And all night kept awake, for sinners' sake to grieve.

That ancient Beadsman heard the prelude soft;
And so it chanced, for many a door was wide,
From hurry to and fro. Soon, up aloft,   30
The silver, snarling trumpets 'gan to chide:
The level chambers, ready with their pride,
Were glowing to receive a thousand guests:

corn, wheat. Cf. Book of Ruth. 69. **Charmed . . . forlorn.** See note
on *Kubla Khan*, p. 730, ll. 14-16.
  The Eve of St. Agnes. 1. **bitter chill.** St. Agnes' Eve, January 20,
is supposed to be the coldest night of the year. 5. **Beadsman,** a poor
man supported in an almshouse and required to pray for its founder.

told **His rosary,** numbered the beads on his rosary as he recited salutations to the Virgin Mary. 15. **rails,** garments. 16. **dumb orat'ries,**
small chapels for prayer, called "dumb" because they contain statues.

The carvéd angels, ever eager-eyed,
Stared, where upon their heads the cornice rests,
With hair blown back, and wings put cross-wise on
   their breasts.

At length burst in the argent revelry,
With plume, tiara, and all rich array,
Numerous as shadows haunting faerily
40 The brain, new-stuffed, in youth, with triumphs gay
Of old romance. These let us wish away,
And turn, sole-thoughted, to one Lady there,
Whose heart had brooded, all that wintry day,
On love, and winged St. Agnes' saintly care,
As she had heard old dames full many times declare.

They told her how, upon St. Agnes' Eve,
Young virgins might have visions of delight,
And soft adorings from their loves receive
Upon the honeyed middle of the night,
50 If ceremonies due they did aright;
As, supperless to bed they must retire,
And couch supine their beauties, lily white;
Nor look behind, nor sideways, but require
Of Heaven with upward eyes for all that they desire.

Full of this whim was thoughtful Madeline:
The music, yearning like a god in pain,
She scarcely heard: her maiden eyes divine,
Fixed on the floor, saw many a sweeping train
Pass by—she heeded not at all: in vain
60 Came many a tiptoe, amorous cavalier,
And back retired; not cooled by high disdain,
But she saw not: her heart was otherwhere:
She sighed for Agnes' dreams, the sweetest of the year.

She danced along with vague, regardless eyes,
Anxious her lips, her breathing quick and short:
The hallowed hour was near at hand: she sighs
Amid the timbrels, and the thronged resort
Of whisperers in anger, or in sport;
'Mid looks of love, defiance, hate, and scorn,
70 Hoodwinked with faery fancy; all amort,
Save to St. Agnes and her lambs unshorn,
And all the bliss to be before tomorrow morn.

So, purposing each moment to retire,
She lingered still. Meantime, across the moors,
Had come young Porphyro, with heart on fire
For Madeline. Beside the portal doors,
Buttressed from moonlight, stands he, and implores
All saints to give him sight of Madeline,
But for one moment in the tedious hours,
80 That he might gaze and worship all unseen;
Perchance speak, kneel, touch, kiss—in sooth such
   things have been.

He ventures in: let no buzzed whisper tell:
All eyes be muffled, or a hundred swords
Will storm his heart, Love's fev'rous citadel:
For him, those chambers held barbarian hordes,
Hyena foemen, and hot-blooded lords,
Whose very dogs would execrations howl
Against his lineage: not one breast affords
Him any mercy, in that mansion foul,
Save one old beldame, weak in body and in soul. 90

Ah, happy chance! the aged creature came,
Shuffling along with ivory-headed wand,
To where he stood, hid from the torch's flame,
Behind a broad hall-pillar, far beyond
The sound of merriment and chorus bland:
He startled her; but soon she knew his face,
And grasped his fingers in her palsied hand,
Saying, "Mercy, Porphyro! hie thee from this place;
They are all here tonight, the whole blood-thirsty race!

"Get hence! get hence! there's dwarfish Hildebrand; 100
He had a fever late, and in the fit
He curséd thee and thine, both house and land:
Then there's that old Lord Maurice, not a whit
More tame for his gray hairs—Alas me! flit!
Flit like a ghost away."—"Ah, Gossip dear,
We're safe enough; here in this armchair sit,
And tell me how"—"Good Saints not here, not here;
Follow me, child, or else these stones will be thy bier."

He followed through a lowly archéd way,
Brushing the cobwebs with his lofty plume; 110
And as she muttered, "Well-a—well-a-day!"
He found him in a little moonlight room,
Pale, latticed, chill, and silent as a tomb.
"Now tell me where is Madeline," said he,
"O tell me, Angela, by the holy loom
Which none but secret sisterhood may see,
When they St. Agnes' wool are weaving, piously."

"St. Agnes! Ah! it is St. Agnes' Eve—
Yet men will murder upon holy days:
Thou must hold water in a witch's sieve, 120
And be liege-lord of all the Elves and Fays,
To venture so: it fills me with amaze
To see thee, Porphyro!—St. Agnes' Eve!
God's help! my lady fair the conjuror plays
This very night: good angels her deceive!
But let me laugh awhile, I've mickle time to grieve."

Feebly she laugheth in the languid moon,
While Porphyro upon her face doth look,
Like puzzled urchin on an aged crone
Who keepeth closed a wond'rous riddle-book, 130
As spectacled she sits in chimney nook.

37. **argent**, shining. 38. **tiara**, a crownlike head ornament. 58. **sweeping train**, long trailing dress. 67. **timbrels**, small hand drums, or tam-
bourines. 70. **Hoodwinked**, blinded. **amort**, dead. 71. **lambs.** See

headnote. 105. **Gossip**, godmother; here, merely devoted friend. 120.
hold . . . sieve. This feat was regarded as a sign of supernatural power.
126. **mickle**, much, ample. 133. **brook**, restrain. 171. Merlin . . .

But soon his eyes grew brilliant, when she told
His lady's purpose; and he scarce could brook
Tears, at the thought of those enchantments cold,
And Madeline asleep in lap of legends old.

Sudden a thought came like a full-blown rose,
Flushing his brow, and in his painéd heart
Made purple riot: then doth he propose
A stratagem, that makes the beldame start:
140 "A cruel man and impious thou art:
Sweet lady, let her pray, and sleep, and dream
Alone with her good angels, far apart
From wicked men like thee. Go, go! I deem
Thou canst not surely be the same that thou didst seem."

"I will not harm her, by all saints I swear,"
Quoth Porphyro: "O may I ne'er find grace
When my weak voice shall whisper its last prayer,
If one of her soft ringlets I displace,
Or look with ruffian passion in her face:
150 Good Angela, believe me by these tears;
Or I will, even in a moment's space,
Awake, with horrid shout, my foemen's ears,
And beard them, though they be more fanged than
    wolves and bears."

"Ah! why wilt thou affright a feeble soul?
A poor, weak, palsy-stricken, churchyard thing,
Whose passing-bell may ere the midnight toll;
Whose prayers for thee, each morn and evening,
Were never missed." Thus plaining, doth she bring
A gentler speech from burning Porphyro;
160 So woeful, and of such deep sorrowing,
That Angela gives promise she will do
Whatever he shall wish, betide her weal or woe.

Which was, to lead him, in close secrecy,
Even to Madeline's chamber, and there hide
Him in a closet, of such privacy
That he might see her beauty unespied,
And win perhaps that night a peerless bride,
While legioned faeries paced the coverlet,
And pale enchantment held her sleepy-eyed.
170 Never on such a night have lovers met,
Since Merlin paid his Demon all the monstrous debt.

"It shall be as thou wishest," said the Dame:
"All cates and dainties shall be storéd there
Quickly on this feast-night: by the tambour frame
Her own lute thou wilt see: no time to spare,
For I am slow and feeble, and scarce dare
On such a catering trust my dizzy head.
Wait here, my child, with patience; kneel in prayer
The while: Ah! thou must needs the lady wed,
180 Or may I never leave my grave among the dead."

So saying, she hobbled off with busy fear.
The lover's endless minutes slowly passed;
The Dame returned, and whispered in his ear
To follow her—with agéd eyes aghast
From fright of dim espial. Safe at last,
Through many a dusky gallery, they gain
The maiden's chamber, silken, hushed, and chaste;
Where Porphyro took covert, pleased amain.
His poor guide hurried back with agues in her brain.

Her faltering hand upon the balustrade,   190
Old Angela was feeling for the stair,
When Madeline, St. Agnes' charméd maid,
Rose, like a missioned spirit, unaware:
With silver taper's light, and pious care,
She turned, and down the aged gossip led
To a safe level matting. Now prepare,
Young Porphyro, for gazing on that bed;
She comes, she comes again, like ring-dove frayed and
    fled.

Out went the taper as she hurried in;
Its little smoke, in pallid moonshine, died: 200
She closed the door, she panted, all akin
To spirits of the air, and visions wide:
No uttered syllable, or, woe betide!
But to her heart, her heart was voluble,
Paining with eloquence her balmy side;
As though a tongueless nightingale should swell
Her throat in vain, and die, heart-stifled in her dell.

A casement high and triple-arched there was,
All garlanded with carven imag'ries
Of fruits, and flowers, and bunches of knot-grass,   210
And diamonded with panes of quaint device,
Innumerable of stains and splendid dyes,
As are the tiger-moth's deep-damasked wings;
And in the midst, 'mong thousand heraldries,
And twilight saints, and dim emblazonings,
A shielded scutcheon blushed with blood of queens and
    kings.

Full on this casement shone the wintry moon,
And threw warm gules on Madeline's fair breast,
As down she knelt for heaven's grace and boon;
Rose-bloom fell on her hands, together pressed,   220
And on her silver cross soft amethyst,
And on her hair a glory, like a saint:
She seemed a splendid angel, newly dressed,
Save wings, for heaven—Porphyro grew faint:
She knelt, so pure a thing, so free from mortal taint.

Anon his heart revives: her vespers done,
Of all its wreathéd pearls her hair she frees;
Unclasps her warméd jewels one by one;

---

debt. According to one legend, Merlin, the magician of Arthurian
romance, was the son of a demon. He paid the "debt" for his existence
when he was killed by the enchantress Vivien, who used a magic spell

that he had taught her. 173. **cates,** delicacies. 174. **tambour frame,**
an embroidery frame in the shape of a drum. 188. **amain,** exceedingly.
198. **frayed,** frightened. 218. **gules,** red tinctures (a term in heraldry).

Loosens her fragrant bodice; by degrees
230 Her rich attire creeps rustling to her knees:
Half-hidden, like a mermaid in sea-weed,
Pensive awhile she dreams awake, and sees,
In fancy, fair St. Agnes in her bed,
But dares not look behind, or all the charm is fled.

Soon, trembling, in her soft and chilly nest,
In sort of wakeful swoon, perplexed she lay,
Until the poppied warmth of sleep oppressed
Her soothéd limbs, and soul fatigued away;
Flown, like a thought, until the morrow-day;
240 Blissfully havened both from joy and pain;
Clasped like a missal where swart Paynims pray;
Blinded alike from sunshine and from rain,
As though a rose should shut, and be a bud again.

Stol'n to this paradise, and so entranced,
Porphyro gazed upon her empty dress,
And listened to her breathing, if it chanced
To wake into a slumberous tenderness;
Which when he heard, that minute did he bless,
And breathed himself: then from the closet crept,
250 Noiseless as fear in a wide wilderness,
And over the hushed carpet, silent, stepped,
And 'tween the curtains peeped, where, lo!—how fast
she slept.

Then by the bedside, where the faded moon
Made a dim, silver twilight, soft he set
A table, and, half anguished, threw thereon
A cloth of woven crimson, gold, and jet—
O for some drowsy Morphean amulet!
The boisterous, midnight, festive clarion,
The kettle-drum, and far-heard clarionet,
260 Affray his ears, though but in dying tone—
The hall door shuts again, and all the noise is gone.

And still she slept an azure-lidded sleep,
In blanchéd linen, smooth, and lavendered,
While he from forth the closet brought a heap
Of candied apple, quince, and plum, and gourd;
With jellies soother than the creamy curd,
And lucent syrups, tinct with cinnamon;
Manna and dates, in argosy transferred
From Fez; and spicéd dainties, every one,
270 From silken Samarcand to cedared Lebanon.

These delicates he heaped with glowing hand
On golden dishes and in baskets bright
Of wreathéd silver: sumptuous they stand
In the retiréd quiet of the night,
Filling the chilly room with perfume light.—

"And now, my love, my seraph fair, awake!
Thou art my heaven, and I thine eremite:
Open thine eyes, for meek St. Agnes' sake,
Or I shall drowse beside thee, so my soul doth ache."

Thus whispering, his warm, unnervéd arm   280
Sank in her pillow. Shaded was her dream
By the dusk curtains—'twas a midnight charm
Impossible to melt as icéd stream:
The lustrous salvers in the moonlight gleam;
Broad golden fringe upon the carpet lies:
It seemed he never, never could redeem
From such a steadfast spell his lady's eyes;
So mused awhile, entoiled in wooféd phantasies.

Awakening up, he took her hollow lute—
Tumultuous—and, in chords that tenderest be,   290
He played an ancient ditty, long since mute,
In Provence called "La belle dame sans merci";
Close to her ear touching the melody;—
Wherewith disturbed, she uttered a soft moan:
He ceased—she panted quick—and suddenly
Her blue affrayéd eyes wide open shone:
Upon his knees he sank, pale as smooth-sculptured
stone.

Her eyes were open, but she still beheld,
Now wide awake, the vision of her sleep:
There was a painful change, that nigh expelled   300
The blisses of her dream so pure and deep
At which fair Madeline began to weep,
And moan forth witless words with many a sigh;
While still her gaze on Porphyro would keep;
Who knelt, with joinéd hands and piteous eye,
Fearing to move or speak, she looked so dreamingly.

"Ah, Porphyro!" said she, "but even now
Thy voice was at sweet tremble in mine ear,
Made tuneable with ever sweetest vow;
And those sad eyes were spiritual and clear: 310
How changed thou art! how pallid, chill, and drear!
Give me that voice again, my Porphyro,
Those looks immortal, those complainings dear!
Oh, leave me not in this eternal woe,
For if thou diest, my Love, I know not where to go."

Beyond a mortal man impassioned far
At these voluptuous accents, he arose,
Ethereal, flushed, and like a throbbing star
Seen mid the sapphire heaven's deep repose;
Into her dream he melted, as the rose   320
Blendeth its odor with the violet—
Solution sweet; meantime the frost-wind blows

---

241. **Clasped . . . pray,** closed like a Christian prayer book, which pagans would have no occasion to use. 250. **as fear,** as a person in fear. 257. **Morphean,** sleep-producing, from Morpheus, the son of Sleep and god of dreams. **amulet,** charm. 263. **lavendered,** perfumed with lavender, a European mint. 266. **soother,** softer, smoother. 267.

tinct, flavored. 268. **argosy,** a large merchant vessel. 269. **Fez,** an important commercial city in northern Morocco. 270. **Samarcand,** a city in Turkestan, Asiatic Russia, noted for its silks, pottery, silver and gold wares, etc. **Lebanon,** a mountain range in southern Syria, once famous for its forests of cedar. 277. **eremite,** hermit; here, devoted

A water color drawing for The Eve of Saint Agnes, *done by John Everett Millais, c. 1863. From the original in the Victoria and Albert Museum, and used by permission.*

Like Love's alarum pattering the sharp sleet
Against the window-panes; St. Agnes' moon hath set.

'Tis dark; quick pattereth the flaw-blown sleet;
"This is no dream, my bride, my Madeline!"
'Tis dark; the icéd gusts still rave and beat;
"No dream, alas! alas! and woe is mine!
Porphyro will leave me here to fade and pine.—
330 Cruel! what traitor could thee hither bring?
I curse not, for my heart is lost in thine.
Though thou forsakest a deceivéd thing;—
A dove forlorn and lost with sick unprunéd wing."

"My Madeline! sweet dreamer! lovely bride!
Say, may I be for aye thy vassal blest?
Thy beauty's shield, heart-shaped and vermeil-dyed?
Ah, silver shrine, here will I take my rest
After so many hours of toil and quest,
A famished pilgrim—saved by miracle.
340 Though I have found, I will not rob thy nest
Saving of thy sweet self; if thou think'st well
To trust, fair Madeline, to no rude infidel.

"Hark! 'tis an elfin storm from faery land,
Of haggard seeming, but a boon indeed:
Arise—arise! the morning is at hand—
The bloated wassailers will never heed—
Let us away, my love, with happy speed;
There are no ears to hear, or eyes to see—
Drowned all in Rhenish and the sleepy mead;

Awake! arise! my love, and fearless be,   350
For o'er the southern moors I have a home for thee."

She hurried at his words, beset with fears,
For there were sleeping dragons all around,
At glaring watch, perhaps, with ready spears—
Down the wide stairs a darkling way they found.—
In all the house was heard no human sound.
A chain-drooped lamp was flickering by each door;
The arras, rich with horseman, hawk, and hound,
Fluttered in the besieging wind's uproar;
And the long carpets rose along the gusty floor.   360

They glide, like phantoms, into the wide hall;
Like phantoms to the iron porch they glide,
Where lay the Porter, in uneasy sprawl,
With a huge empty flagon by his side;
The wakeful bloodhound rose, and shook his hide,
But his sagacious eye an inmate owns:
By one, and one, the bolts full easy slide—
The chains lie silent on the footworn stones;—
The key turns, and the door upon its hinges groans.

And they are gone: aye, ages long ago   370
These lovers fled away into the storm.
That night the Baron dreamt of many a woe,
And all his warrior-guests, with shade and form
Of witch, and demon, and large coffin-worm,
Were long be-nightmared. Angela the old
Died palsy-twitched, with meager face deform;

lover. **288. wooféd phantasies,** fancies woven together like threads.
292. "La belle ... merci," the beautiful lady without pity. See Keats'
poem of that title, p. 789. **344. haggard seeming,** wild appearance.
349. Rhenish, wine from the vineyards of the Rhine. **mead,** a fer-
mented drink made of honey, water, etc. **358. arras,** tapestry; the word

is derived from Arras, France, which was famous in the Middle Ages for such tapestries.

The Beadsman, after thousand aves told,
For aye unsought-for slept among his ashes cold.
(1819; 1820)

TO AUTUMN

*On September 22, 1819, Keats wrote to his friend
Reynolds: "How beautiful the season is now—how
fine the air. A temperate sharpness about it. Really,
without joking, chaste weather—Dian skies—I never
liked stubble-fields so much as now—Aye better than
the chilly green of the spring. Somehow, a stubble-
field looks warm—in the same way that some pictures look warm. This struck me so much in my Sunday's walk that I composed upon it." The composition
referred to is the following magnificent ode.*

Season of mists and mellow fruitfulness,
   Close bosom-friend of the maturing sun;
Conspiring with him how to load and bless
   With fruit the vines that round the thatch-eaves
      run;
To bend with apples the mossed cottage-trees,
   And fill all fruit with ripeness to the core;
     To swell the gourd, and plump the hazel shells
With a sweet kernel; to set budding more,
   And still more, later flowers for the bees,
10   Until they think warm days will never cease,
     For Summer has o'er-brimmed their clammy cells.

Who hath not seen thee oft amid thy store?
   Sometimes whoever seeks abroad may find
Thee sitting careless on a granary floor,
   Thy hair soft-lifted by the winnowing wind;
Or on a half-reaped furrow sound asleep,
   Drowsed with the fume of poppies, while thy hook
     Spares the next swath and all its twinéd flowers:
And sometime like a gleaner thou dost keep
20   Steady thy laden head across a brook;
   Or by a cider-press, with patient look,
     Thou watchest the last oozings, hours by hours.

377. **aves**, salutations to the Virgin Mary. The beads of a rosary are
counted as the Aves are uttered.

Where are the songs of Spring? Ay, where are they?
   Think not of them, thou hast thy music too—
While barréd clouds bloom the soft-dying day,
   And touch the stubble-plains with rosy hue;
Then in a wailful choir the small gnats mourn
   Among the river sallows, borne aloft
     Or sinking as the light wind lives or dies;
And full-grown lambs loud bleat from hilly bourn; 30
   Hedge-crickets sing; and now with treble soft
   The redbreast whistles from a garden-croft,
     And gathering swallows twitter in the skies.
(1819; 1820)

BRIGHT STAR! WOULD I WERE STEADFAST
AS THOU ART

*This sonnet in its final form was composed after
Keats embarked for Italy on September 30, 1820; a
preliminary draft had been made the previous year.
The sonnet was written in a copy of Shakespeare's
poems and given to his friend and companion Severn.
As Keats' death song, the sonnet should be compared
with Tennyson's* Crossing the Bar *(p. 910) and Browning's* Epilogue to Asolando *(p. 932).*

Bright star! would I were steadfast as thou art—
Not in lone splendor hung aloft the night,
And watching, with eternal lids apart,
Like Nature's patient sleepless Eremite,
The moving waters at their priestlike task
Of pure ablution round earth's human shores,
Or gazing on the new soft fallen mask
Of snow upon the mountains and the moors—
No—yet still steadfast, still unchangeable,
Pillowed upon my fair love's ripening breast,   10
To feel forever its soft fall and swell,
Awake forever in a sweet unrest,
Still, still to hear her tender-taken breath,
And so live ever—or else swoon to death.
(1820; 1846)

To Autumn. 28. **sallows**, willows. 31. **Hedge-crickets**, grass-
hoppers. 32. **garden-croft**, garden enclosure.

ROMANTIC ESSAYISTS

*As observed above (p. 620), the romantic period
was also an era of distinguished prose writers who
published their observations on men and manners in
reviews and magazines. Some of their work was social
and literary criticism—always with a strong personal
slant—but the most attractive prose writing of the age
was in the informal, familiar essay, a form characteristically romantic in its subjectivity and in its warm, intimate style. The selections which follow are typical of
the romantic essay at its best.*

CHARLES LAMB 1775-1834

Charles Lamb was born in London, February 10, 1775, the son of a scrivener in the service of one of the leading lawyers of the city. The boy's schooling was at Christ's Hospital, the same institution that trained Coleridge, indeed, Coleridge and Lamb were schoolmates, and Lamb has left us an interesting picture of the great poet in several essays written years afterwards. An impediment in Lamb's speech prevented him from taking examinations for honors, and he was therefore excluded from the opportunity of taking a college degree, he quit his schooling at the age of fourteen and began to earn his living. Three years later he entered the service of the East India House and became a most valuable accountant for the great commercial organization upon which rested the foundations of the British Empire in the Orient. Professionally his life was spent in this accountantship, he was finally pensioned off in 1825, an experience which he described whimsically in The Superannuated Man. After nine peaceful years of leisure living in the suburbs of London, he died in 1834.

Lamb was distinctly a Londoner. He loved the city in all its aspects—its crowds and its quaint districts alike, its bookshops and its taverns. "I often shed tears in the motley Strand," he once wrote, "for fulness of joy at so much life." Unlike Byron, the hum of cities was not torture to him, he throve upon the opportunity London offered him to meet the great literary men of his time, for his avocation from the very first was literature. He tried drama, with complete lack of success, he published a rather feeble prose tale called Rosamund Gray; he "obtruded upon the public," to use his own words, "sundry other poems and light prose matter, collected in two slight crown octavos and pompously christened his works, though in fact they were his recreations." Unfortunately Lamb's deprecatory tone about these literary efforts is near the truth—none of the works he produced in drama or poetry is of any special value. Two poems, Hester and The Old Familiar Faces, have a sentimental wistfulness that might be considered charming, their success depends upon the fact that some see in them a faint glimpse of the gracious, lovable personality of their author.

It is chiefly when Lamb reveals to us that personality that he becomes a significant writer. In a brief autobiographic sketch he remarks that he is "below the middle stature, cast of face slightly Jewish, with no Judaic tinge in his complexional religion, stammers abominably, and is therefore more apt to discharge his occasional conversation in a quaint aphorism, or a poor quibble, than in set and edifying speeches, has consequently been libeled as a person always aiming at wit, which as he told a dull fellow that charges him

with it, is at least as good as aiming at dullness, a small eater but not drinker, confesses a partiality for the product of the juniper berry, was a fiercer smoker of tobacco, but may be resembled to a volcano burnt out, emitting only now and then a casual puff." The light tone that Lamb here uses in speaking of himself is one part of his personality, the whimsical air with which he carries off his sayings is another. But there is another part, deep-seated and pathetic, even tragic, in Lamb's make-up. He was disappointed in love as a youth, probably because he recognized a trace of insanity in his family. He himself spent six weeks in an asylum (1795-1796), and the next year his only sister Mary killed her mother in a fit of mania. Lamb himself fully recovered, but his sister was subject to recurrent attacks, during which she had to be confined. Lamb took tender care of her, she became, during her sane intervals, his constant companion, and collaborated with him on some books for children, notably the Tales from Shakespeare (1807) and the Adventures of Ulysses (1808). The current of tragedy running throughout Lamb's life, the sadness and frustration which he met most heroically, go far to explain the coupling of pathos and poignant dreaminess with brave laughter to be found in his characteristic work.

That characteristic work is, first of all, the fine series of personal essays entitled the Essays of Elia, which appeared in The London Magazine (1820-1823) and later in book form (1823). A second series, running from 1824 to 1825, was collected and printed in 1833, a year before his death. Elia is Lamb himself. The pseudonym he chose was the name of an Italian previously in the service of the South Sea House, possibly a friend of his brother John—the subject of the first essay —who was at that time a clerk in that institution. The essays are written in an easy-flowing, informal style, now sprightly and whimsical in A Dissertation upon Roast Pig or A Chapter on Ears, now gently satirical in Mrs. Battle's Opinions on Whist, now quietly domestic in Mackery End, now delicately nostalgic in the exquisite reverie Dream-Children. Seldom has there been a more subtly touched portrait in literature than that of Mary Lamb (Bridget Elia) in Mackery End and in Old China. It is customary to underestimate Lamb's style, it is not so sharp as that of Hazlitt nor so impassioned as that of De Quincey, but even a first reading of such an essay as Poor Relations (p. 802) demonstrates Lamb's skillful incisiveness. The student of English literature can further thank Lamb for an excellent series of essays on Shakespeare, the other important Elizabethan writers, and the prose authors of the seventeenth century. His Letters, like his essays, bring to life a gentle, witty, lovable soul, tender in his sympathy for mankind, a man who, for all the darkness and disaster of life, could see and enjoy the world through the rose-tinted spectacles of courage and equanimity.

THE TWO RACES OF MEN

The human species, according to the best theory I can form of it, is composed of two distinct races, *the men who borrow*, and *the men who lend*. To these two original diversities may be reduced all those impertinent classifications of Gothic and Celtic tribes, white men, black men, red men. All the dwellers upon earth, "Parthians, and Medes, and Elamites," flock hither, and do naturally fall in with one or other of these primary distinctions. The infinite superiority of the former, which I choose to designate as the *great race*, is discernible in their figure, port, and a certain instinctive sovereignty. The latter are born degraded. "He shall serve his brethren." There is something in the air of one of this cast, lean and suspicious; contrasting with the open, trusting, generous manners of the other.

Observe who have been the greatest borrowers of all ages—Alcibiades—Falstaff—Sir Richard Steele—our late incomparable Brinsley—what a family likeness in all four!

What a careless, even deportment hath your borrower! what rosy gills! what a beautiful reliance on Providence doth he manifest—taking no more thought than lilies! What contempt for money—accounting it (yours and mine especially) no better than dross. What a liberal confounding of those pedantic distinctions of *meum* and *tuum*! or rather, what a noble simplification of language (beyond Tooke), resolving these supposed opposites into one clear, intelligible pronoun adjective! —What near approaches doth he make to the primitive *community*—to the extent of one half of the principle at least!

He is the true taxer who "calleth all the world up to be taxed"; and the distance is as vast between him and *one of us* as subsisted betwixt the Augustan Majesty and the poorest obolary Jew that paid it tribute-pittance at Jerusalem!—His exactions, too, have such a cheerful, voluntary air! So far removed from your sour parochial or state-gatherers—those ink-horn varlets, who carry their want of welcome in their faces! He cometh to you with a smile, and troubleth you with no receipt; confining himself to no set season. Every day is his Candlemas, or his Feast of Holy Michael. He applieth the *Lene tormentum* of a pleasant look to your

purse—which to that gentle warmth expands her silken leaves, as naturally as the cloak of the traveler, for which sun and wind contended! He is the true Propontic which never ebbeth! The sea which taketh handsomely at each man's hand. In vain the victim, whom he delighteth to honor, struggles with destiny; he is in the net. Lend therefore cheerfully, O man ordained to lend—that thou lose not in the end, with thy worldly penny, the reversion promised. Combine not preposterously in thine own person the penalties of Lazarus and of Dives!—but, when thou seest the proper authority coming, meet it smilingly, as it were half-way. Come, a handsome sacrifice! See how light *he* makes of it! Strain not courtesies with a noble enemy.

Reflections like the foregoing were forced upon my mind by the death of my old friend, Ralph Bigod, Esq., who departed this life on Wednesday evening, dying, as he had lived, without much trouble. He boasted himself a descendant from mighty ancestors of that name, who heretofore held ducal dignities in this realm. In his actions and sentiments he belied not the stock to which he pretended. Early in life he found himself invested with ample revenues, which, with that noble disinterestedness which I have noticed as inherent in men of the *great race*, he took almost immediate measures entirely to dissipate and bring to nothing: for there is something revolting in the idea of a king holding a private purse; and the thoughts of Bigod were all regal. Thus furnished, by the very act of disfurnishment; getting rid of the cumbersome luggage of riches, more apt (as one sings)

To slacken virtue, and abate her edge
Than prompt her to do aught may merit praise;

he set forth, like some Alexander, upon his great enterprise, "borrowing and to borrow"!

In his periegesis, or triumphant progress throughout this island, it has been calculated that he laid a tythe part of the inhabitants under contribution. I reject this estimate as greatly exaggerated:—but having had the honor of accompanying my friend, divers times, in his perambulations about this vast city, I own I was greatly struck at first with the prodigious number of faces we met who claimed a sort of respectful acquaintance with us. He was one day so obliging as to explain the

The Two Races of Men. 7. "Parthians . . . Elamites," quoted from Acts 2:9. 13. "He . . . brethren." See Genesis 9:25. 18. **Alcibiades . . . Brinsley.** Alcibiades was the famous Athenian general and politician (450–404 B.C.); Falstaff is the earthy character in Shakespeare's plays of *Henry IV* and *The Merry Wives of Windsor*; for Sir Richard Steele, see p. 473. Brinsley is Richard Brinsley Sheridan (1751–1816), the playwright. 23. **taking . . . lilies.** See Matthew 6:28–29: "And why take ye thought for raiment? Consider the lilies of the field, how they grow; they toil not, neither do they spin: And yet I say unto you, That even Solomon in all his glory was not arrayed like one of these." 27. *meum and tuum*, mine and thine. 28. **Tooke**, John Horne Tooke (1736–1812), an English politician and philologist. 33. "**calleth . . . taxed.**" Cf. Luke 2:1: "And it came to pass in those days, that there went out a decree from Caesar Augustus, that all the world should be taxed." 36. **obolary**, having only an obolus, a small silver coin of ancient Greece and Asia Minor, of extremely low monetary value. 43. **Candlemas . . . Michael.** Candlemas, or the feast of the candles, celebrates the presentation of Christ in the

Temple of Jerusalem, and is observed on Midwinter Day (February 2); the Feast of Holy Michael, or Michaelmas, is celebrated on September 29. 44. *Lene tormentum*, mild torture or gentle stimulus, quoted from Horace, *Odes*, Book III, No. 21, l. 13. 47. **Propontic . . . ebbeth.** See *Othello*, III, iii, 453. The Propontic, or Pontic, Sea is another name for the Black Sea. 55. **Lazarus . . . Dives.** The parable of Lazarus, the pauper, and Dives, the rich man, is told in Luke 16:19–31. Dives went to Hell and Lazarus to Heaven. 61. **Ralph Bigod.** It has not been established that Bigod represents any real person. 77. "**To . . . praise,**" quoted from Milton's *Paradise Regained*, Book II, 455–456. 80. "**borrowing . . . borrow,**" adapted from Revelation 6:2: "And I saw, and behold a white horse: and he that sat on him had a bow; and a crown was given unto him: and he went forth conquering, and to conquer." 82. **tythe,** tenth. 96. "**stocked . . . herd,**" quoted from Milton's *Comus*, l. 152. 110. **Hagar's . . . wilderness.** Hagar was the handmaid of Sarah, the wife of Abraham (cf. Genesis, Chapter 16). Abraham's relations with Hagar, suggested by Sarah (who was sterile), resulted in the son Ishmael. Sarah, reproved

90 phenomenon. It seems these were his tributaries; feeders of his exchequer; gentlemen, his good friends (as he was pleased to express himself), to whom he had occasionally been beholden for a loan. Their multitudes did no way disconcert him. He rather took a pride in numbering them; and, with Comus, seemed pleased to be "stocked with so fair a herd."

With such sources, it was a wonder how he contrived to keep his treasury always empty. He did it by force of an aphorism, which he had often in his mouth, that 100 "money kept longer than three days stinks." So he made use of it while it was fresh. A good part he drank away (for he was an excellent toss-pot), some he gave away, the rest he threw away, literally tossing and hurling it violently from him—as boys do burrs, or as if it had been infectious—into ponds, or ditches, or deep holes—inscrutable cavities of the earth;—or he would bury it (where he would never seek it again) by a river's side under some bank, which (he would face-tiously observe) paid no interest—but out away from 110 him it must go peremptorily, as Hagar's offspring into the wilderness, while it was sweet. He never missed it. The streams were perennial which fed his fisc. When new supplies became necessary, the first person that had the felicity to fall in with him, friend or stranger, was sure to contribute to the deficiency. For Bigod had an *undeniable* way with him. He had a cheerful, open exterior, a quick jovial eye, a bald forehead, just touched with gray (*cana fides*). He anticipated no excuse, and found none. And, waiving for awhile my 120 theory as to the *great race,* I would put it to the most untheorizing reader, who may at times have disposable coin in his pocket, whether it is not more repugnant to the kindliness of his nature to refuse such a one as I am describing, than to say *no* to a poor petitionary rogue (your bastard borrower) who, by his mumping visnomy, tells you that he expects nothing better, and, therefore, whose preconceived notions and expectations you do in reality so much less shock in the refusal.

When I think of this man; his fiery glow of heart; 130 his swell of feeling; how magnificent, how *ideal* he was; how great at the midnight hour; and when I compare with him the companions with whom I have associated since, I grudge the saving of a few idle ducats, and think that I am fallen into the society of *lenders,* and *little men.*

To one like Elia, whose treasures are rather cased in leather covers than closed in iron coffers, there is a class of alienators more formidable than that which I have touched upon; I mean your *borrowers of books*— those mutilators of collections, spoilers of the symmetry 140 of shelves, and creators of odd volumes. There is Comberbatch, matchless in his depredations!

That foul gap in the bottom shelf facing you, like a great eye-tooth knocked out (you are now with me in my little back study in Bloomsbury, reader!), with the huge Switzer-like tomes on each side (like the Guild-hall giants, in their reformed posture, guardant of nothing), once held the tallest of my folios, *Opera Bonaventurae,* choice and massy divinity, to which 150 its two supporters (school divinity also, but of a lesser calibre—Bellarmine, and Holy Thomas), showed but as dwarfs—itself an Ascapart—that Comberbatch abstracted upon the faith of a theory he holds, which is more easy, I confess, for me to suffer by than to refute, namely, that "the title to property in a book (my Bonaventure, for instance) is in exact ratio to the claimant's powers of understanding and appreciating the same." Should he go on acting upon this theory, which of our shelves is safe?

The slight vacuum in the left-hand case—two shelves 160 from the ceiling—scarcely distinguishable but by the quick eye of a loser—was whilom the commodious resting-place of Browne on *Urn Burial.* C. will hardly allege that he knows more about that treatise than I do, who introduced it to him, and was indeed the first (of the moderns) to discover its beauties—but so have I known a foolish lover to praise his mistress in the presence of a rival more qualified to carry her off than himself.—Just below, Dodsley's dramas want their fourth volume, where *Vittoria Corrombona* is! The 170 remainder nine are as distasteful as Priam's refuse sons, when the Fates *borrowed* Hector. Here stood *The Anatomy of Melancholy,* in sober state.—There loitered *The Complete Angler,* quiet as in life, by some stream side.—In yonder nook, *John Buncle,* a widower-volume, with "eyes closed," mourns his ravished mate.

One justice I must do my friend, that if he sometimes, like the sea, sweeps away a treasure, at another time, sea-like, he throws up as rich an equivalent to match it. I have a small under-collection of this nature (my 180 friend's gatherings in his various calls), picked up, he

by her conscience, turned upon Hagar, who was banished (with the Lord's approval) into the wilderness, where Ishmael grew to be "a wild man; his hand against every man, and every man's hand against him." 112. **fisc,** treasury. 118. **cana fides,** gray-haired fidelity; quoted from Vergil's *Aeneid,* I, 292. 125. **mumping visnomy,** mumbling physiognomy, or face. 141. **Comberbatch.** Coleridge at one time ran away from Cambridge and enlisted in the dragoons under the name of Silas Tomkyn Comberbacke. The reference here is undoubtedly to Coleridge, in spite of the slightly modified form of the pseudonym. 146. **Switzer-like,** huge, like the giant Swiss guards who protect the Pope. 146. **Guildhall giants,** referring to the colossal figures in the council hall at London, known as Gog and Magog. 148. *Opera Bonaventurae,* the works of St. Bonaventure, a famous medieval scholastic philosopher (1221–1274), who was later canonized. 151. **Bellarmine,** Robert Bellarmino (1542–1621), a Jesuit theologian and cardinal. **Holy Thomas,** St. Thomas Aquinas (c. 1225–1274), generally considered the greatest of medieval Catholic theologians and philosophers. 163. **Browne on *Urn Burial.*** See p. 359. **C.,** Comberbatch, or Cole-

ridge. 169. **Dodsley,** Robert Dodsley (1703–1764), an eminent bookseller and editor; his collection of English drama, the most famous of the time, was first printed in 1744. 170. *Vittoria Corrombona,* or *The White Devil,* now better known by the English title, a grim and bloody tragedy (1612) by the Elizabethan playwright John Webster. 171. **Priam . . . Hector.** In the Trojan War, Hector, the favorite son of King Priam of Troy and the most illustrious of Trojan champions, was slain by the Greek hero Achilles. With nine of his fifty sons still living, Priam begged Achilles for the body of Hector. The incident is told in the *Iliad,* Book XXIV, 486 ff. 172. **The . . . Melancholy,** an exhaustive treatise (1621) on the causes, nature, and cure of melancholy by Robert Burton (1577–1640). 174. **The Complete Angler.** See p. 363. 175. **John Buncle,** a novel (1756–1766) of the picaresque type by Thomas Amory (1691?–1788). The reference in this line is to the fact that John Buncle, the hero of the book, made the statement that when one of his wives died he remained four days with his eyes shut. In the course of the novel, he embarked upon no less than seven matrimonial adventures.

has forgotten at what odd places, and deposited with as little memory at mine. I take in these orphans, the twice-deserted. These proselytes of the gate are welcome as the true Hebrews. There the stand in conjunction; natives, and naturalized. The latter seem as little disposed to inquire out their true lineage as I am.—I charge no warehouse-room for these deodands, nor shall ever put myself to the ungentlemanly trouble of advertising a sale of them to pay expenses.

To lose a volume to C. carries some sense and meaning in it. You are sure that he will make one hearty meal on your viands, if he can give no account of the platter after it. But what moved thee, wayward, spiteful K., to be so importunate to carry off with thee, in spite of tears and adjurations to thee to forbear, the *Letters* of that princely woman, the thrice noble Margaret Newcastle?—knowing at the time, and knowing that I knew also, thou most assuredly wouldst never turn over one leaf of the illustrious folio:—what but the mere spirit of contradiction, and childish love of getting the better of thy friend?—Then, worst cut of all! to transport it with thee to the Gallican land—

Unworthy land to harbor such a sweetness,
A virtue in which all ennobling thoughts dwelt,
Pure thoughts, kind thoughts, high thoughts, her sex's
wonder!

—hadst thou not thy play-books, and books of jests and fancies, about thee, to keep thee merry, even as thou keepest all companies with thy quips and mirthful tales?—Child of the Green-room, it was unkindly done of thee. Thy wife, too, that part-French, betterpart Englishwoman!—that *she* could fix upon no other treatise to bear away, in kindly token of remembering us, than the works of Fulke Greville, Lord Brooke—of which no Frenchman, nor woman of France, Italy, or England, was ever by nature constituted to comprehend a tittle! *Was there not Zimmerman on Solitude?*

Reader, if haply thou art blessed with a moderate collection, be shy of showing it; or if thy heart overfloweth to lend them, lend thy books; but let it be to such a one as S.T.C.—he will return them (generally anticipating the time appointed) with usury; enriched with annotations, tripling their value. I have had experience. Many are these precious MSS. of his—(in *matter* oftentimes, and almost in *quantity* not unfrequently vying with the originals)—in no very clerkly hand—legible in my Daniel; in old Burton; in Sir Thomas Browne; and those abstruser cogitations of the Greville, now, alas! wandering in Pagan lands—

I counsel thee, shut not thy heart, nor thy library, against S.T.C.
(1820)

DREAM-CHILDREN: A REVERIE

This essay, a masterly combination of wistful melancholy and tender pathos, was prompted by the death of Lamb's brother John on October 26, 1821. The two men had never been very friendly, but the passing of John made Charles perhaps more aware of his loneliness in life. He had but one relative left, his sister Mary, and she was often away from him for months at a time recovering from fits of insanity. It is scarcely to be wondered at that Lamb should turn, in his hours of solitude, to the thoughts of what his life might have been had there been no such cloud over his family, and if he had been able to marry Alice Winterton, his old sweetheart.

Children love to listen to stories about their elders, when *they* were children; to stretch their imagination to the conception of a traditional great-uncle, or grandame, whom they never saw. It was in this spirit that my little ones crept about me the other evening to hear about their great-grandmother Field, who lived in a great house in Norfolk (a hundred times bigger than that in which they and papa lived) which had been the scene—so at least it was generally believed in that part of the country—of the tragic incidents which they had lately become familiar with from the ballad of the Children in the Wood. Certain it is that the whole story of the children and their cruel uncle was to be seen fairly carved out in wood upon the chimney-piece of the great hall, the whole story down to the Robin Redbreasts, till a foolish rich person pulled it down to set up a marble one of modern invention in its stead, with no story upon it. Here Alice put out one of her dear mother's looks, too tender to be called upbraiding. Then I went on to say how religious and how good their great-grandmother Field was, how beloved and respected by everybody, though she was not indeed the mistress of this great house, but had only the charge of it (and yet in some respects she might be said to be the mistress of it too) committed to her by the owner, who preferred living in a newer and more fashionable mansion which he had purchased somewhere in the adjoining county; but still she lived in it in a manner as if it had been her own, and kept up the dignity of the great house in a sort while she lived, which after-

7. deodands, in English law, things forfeited to the crown. 13. wayward, spiteful K., James Kenney (1780–1849), a minor dramatist of the time. 16. Letters . . . Newcastle, the *Sociable Letters* of Margaret Cavendish, Lady Newcastle (c. 1625–1673). 29. Green-room, originally the dressing-room of the theater; then applied to the stage as a whole. 33. Fulke Greville, first Lord Brooke (1554–1628), an Elizabethan poet, courtier, and statesman, friend of Queen Elizabeth and of

Sir Philip Sidney in particular; one of the most famous of Elizabethan gentlemen of the court. 36. Zimmerman, Johann Georg von Zimmerman (1728–1795), a Swiss physician and philosophical writer, best known for his monograph on solitude, which appeared in 1784–1785. 40. S.T.C., Samuel Taylor Coleridge. 46. Daniel, Samuel Daniel, the Elizabethan poet (see p. 209).
Dream-Children. 57. Norfolk, Lamb's grandmother lived at Blakes-

wards came to decay, and was nearly pulled down, and all its old ornaments stripped and carried away to the owner's other house, where they were set up, and looked as awkward as if someone were to carry away the old tombs they had seen lately at the Abbey, and stick them up in Lady C.'s tawdry gilt drawing-room. Here John smiled, as much as to say, "that would be foolish, indeed." And then I told
90 how, when she came to die, her funeral was attended by a concourse of all the poor, and some of the gentry too, of the neighborhood for many miles round, to show their respect for her memory, because she had been such a good and religious woman; so good indeed that she knew all the Psaltery by heart, ay, and a great part of the Testament besides. Here little Alice spread her hands. Then I told what a tall, upright, graceful person their great-grandmother Field once was; and how in her youth she was esteemed the
100 best dancer—here Alice's little right foot played an involuntary movement, till upon my looking grave, it desisted—the best dancer, I was saying, in the county, till a cruel disease, called a cancer, came, and bowed her down with pain; but it could never bend her good spirits, or make them stoop, but they were still upright, because she was so good and religious. Then I told how she was used to sleep by herself in a lone chamber of the great lone house; and how she believed that an apparition of two infants was to be
110 seen at midnight gliding up and down the great staircase near where she slept, but she said "those innocents would do her no harm"; and how frightened I used to be, though in those days I had my maid to sleep with me, because I was never half so good or religious as she—and yet I never saw the infants. Here John expanded all his eyebrows and tried to look courageous. Then I told how good she was to all her grandchildren, having us to the great house in the holidays, where I in particular used to
120 spend many hours by myself, in gazing upon the old busts of the twelve Caesars, that had been emperors of Rome, till the old marble heads would seem to live again, or I to be turned into marble with them; how I never could be tired with roaming about that huge mansion, with its vast empty rooms, with their worn-out hangings, fluttering tapestry, and carved oaken panels, with the gilding almost rubbed out—sometimes in the spacious old-fashioned gardens, which I had almost to myself, unless when now and then a
130 solitary gardening man would cross me—and how the nectarines and peaches hung upon the walls without my ever offering to pluck them, because they were forbidden fruit, unless now and then—and because I

had more pleasure in strolling about among the old melancholy-looking yew-trees, or the firs, and picking up the red berries, and the fir apples, which were good for nothing but to look at—or in lying about upon the fresh grass, with all the fine garden smells around me—or basking in the orangery, till I could almost fancy myself ripening too along with the or- 140 anges and the limes in that grateful warmth—or in watching the dace that darted to and fro in the fishpond, at the bottom of the garden, with here and there a great sulky pike hanging midway down the water in silent state, as if it mocked at their impertinent friskings—I had more pleasure in these busy-idle diversions than in all the sweet flavors of peaches, nectarines, oranges, and such-like common baits of children. Here John slyly deposited back upon the plate a bunch of grapes which, not unob- 150 served by Alice, he had meditated dividing with her, and both seemed willing to relinquish them for the present as irrelevant. Then in somewhat a more heightened tone, I told how, though their great-grandmother Field loved all her grandchildren, yet in an especial manner she might be said to love their uncle, John L—— because he was so handsome and spirited a youth, and a king to the rest of us; and, instead of moping about in solitary corners, like some of us, he would mount the most mettlesome horse he could 160 get, when but an imp no bigger than themselves, and make it carry him half over the county in a morning, and join the hunters when there were any out— and yet he loved the old great house and gardens too, but had too much spirit to be always pent up within their boundaries—and how their uncle grew up to man's estate as brave as he was handsome, to the admiration of everybody, but of their great-grandmother Field most especially; and how he used to carry me upon his back when I was a lame-footed 170 boy—for he was a good bit older than me—many a mile when I could not walk for pain;—and how in after-life he became lame-footed too, and I did not always (I fear) make allowances enough for him when he was impatient, and in pain, nor remember sufficiently how considerate he had been to me when I was lame-footed; and how when he died, though he had not been dead an hour, it seemed as if he had died a great while ago, such a distance there is betwixt life and death; and how I bore his death as 180 I thought pretty well at first, but afterwards it haunted and haunted me; and though I did not cry or take it to heart as some do, and as I think he would have done if I had died, yet I missed him all day long, and knew not till then how much I had loved

ware, Hertfordshire, not Norfolk. The county may have been changed by Lamb because William Plumer, also a resident of Hertfordshire, who had dismantled Blakesware, was still living when *Dream-Children* was published. 66. **Robin Redbreasts.** At the end of the ballad they cover the bodies of the murdered children with leaves. 95. **Psaltery,** the version of the Psalms in the Book of Common Prayer. 97. **spread her hands,** a sign of astonishment. 109. **apparition of two infants,** an old legend

of the Plumer family. 121. **busts . . . Caesars,** busts of Roman emperors from Julius Caesar to Domitian. These busts were among the things removed from Blakesware by Mr. Plumer. 131. **nectarine,** a kind of peach. 133. **forbidden fruit.** See Genesis 2:16–17; also the opening lines of *Paradise Lost* (p. 388). 136. **fir apples,** fir cones. 145. **impertinent friskings.** The pike feeds upon dace. 156. **John L—,** Lamb's brother John.

him. I missed his kindness, and I missed his crossness, and wished him to be alive again, to be quarreling with him (for we quarreled sometimes), rather than not have him again, and was as uneasy without him, as he, their poor uncle, must have been when the doctor took off his limb. Here the children fell a-crying, and asked if their little mourning which they had on was not for Uncle John, and they looked up, and prayed me not to go on about their uncle, but to tell them some stories about their pretty dead mother. Then I told how for seven long years, in hope sometimes, sometimes in despair, yet persisting ever, I courted the fair Alice W———n; and, as much as children could understand, I explained to them what coyness, and difficulty, and denial meant in maidens —when suddenly, turning to Alice, the soul of the first Alice looked out at her eyes with such a reality of represantment, that I became in doubt which of them stood there before me, or whose that bright hair was; and while I stood gazing, both the children gradually grew fainter to my view, receding, and still receding till nothing at last but two mournful features were seen in the uttermost distance, which without speech, strangely impressed upon me the effects of speech: "We are not of Alice, nor of thee, nor are we children at all. The children of Alice call Bartrum father. We are nothing; less than nothing, and dreams. We are only what might have been, and must wait upon the tedious shores of Lethe millions of ages before we have existence and a name"— and immediately awaking, I found myself quietly seated in my bachelor armchair, where I had fallen asleep, with the faithful Bridget unchanged by my side—but John L. (or James Elia) was gone forever. (1822)

POOR RELATIONS

A poor relation—is the most irrelevant thing in nature,—a piece of impertinent correspondency,—an odious approximation,—a haunting conscience,—a preposterous shadow, lengthening in the noontide of your prosperity,—an unwelcome remembrancer,—a perpetually recurring mortification,—a drain on your purse,—a more intolerable dun upon your pride,—a drawback upon success,—a rebuke to your rising,— a stain in your blood,—a blot on your scutcheon,—a rent in your garment,—a death's head at your banquet,—Agathocles' pot,—a Mordecai in your gate,—a Lazarus at your door,—a lion in your path,—a frog in your chamber,—a fly in your ointment,—a mote in your eye,—a triumph to your enemy, an apology to your friends,—the one thing not needful,—the hail in harvest,—the ounce of sour in a pound of sweet. 50

He is known by his knock. Your heart telleth you, "That is Mr. ———." A rap, between familiarity and respect, that demands, and at the same time seems to despair of, entertainment. He entereth smiling and —embarrassed. He holdeth out his hand to you to shake, and—draweth it back again. He casually looketh in about dinner-time—when the table is full. He offereth to go away, seeing you have company—but is induced to stay. He filleth a chair, and your visitor's two children are accommodated at a side table. He 60 never cometh upon open days, when your wife says with some complacency, "My dear, perhaps Mr. ——— will drop in today." He remembereth birthdays—and professeth he is fortunate to have stumbled upon one. He declareth against fish, the turbot being small—yet suffereth himself to be importuned into a slice, against his first resolution. He sticketh by the port—yet will be prevailed upon to empty the remainder glass of claret, if a stranger press it upon him. He is a puzzle to the servants, who are fearful of 70 being too obsequious, or not civil enough, to him. The guests think "they have seen him before." Everyone speculateth upon his condition; and the most part take him to be—a tide-waiter. He calleth you by your Christian name, to imply that his other is the same with your own. He is too familiar by half, yet you wish he had less diffidence. With half the familiarity, he might pass for a casual dependent; with more boldness, he would be in no danger of being taken for what he is. He is too humble for a 80 friend; yet taketh on him more state than befits a client. He is a worse guest than a country tenant, inasmuch as he bringeth up no rent—yet 'tis odds, from his garb and demeanor, that your guests take him for one. He is asked to make one at the whisttable; refuseth on the score of poverty, and—resents being left out. When the company break up, he proffereth to go for a coach—and lets the servant go. He recollects your grandfather; and will thrust in some mean and quite unimportant anecdote of—the 90 family. He knew it when it was not quite so flourishing as "he is blest in seeing it now." He reviveth past situations, to institute what he calleth—favorable comparisons. With a reflecting sort of congratulation, he will inquire the price of your furniture; and

6. **doctor . . . limb,** a detail of Lamb's imagination. 13. **Alice W——n.** Winterton, a feigned name. She was probably Ann Simmons, Lamb's boyhood sweetheart; she married a man named Bartrum. 15. **difficulty,** shyness. 18. **representment,** reincarnation. 19. **whose,** the first or the second Alice's. 29. **Lethe,** the river of forgetfulness in Hades. In the *Aeneid* (VI, 703–751) Vergil tells how the soul, after drinking of Lethe, will return many years to earth in a new body. 33. **Bridget . . . James Elia,** names given by Lamb to his sister Mary and his brother John in *My Relations.*
Poor Relations. Cf. the Character Writers, p. 356. 44. **death's head.** An allusion to the custom of the Egyptians of having a coffin containing a representation of a dead body carried through the banquet hall

during the course of a feast to remind the guests of their necessary end, and to suggest that they should drink and be merry. 45. **Agathocles' pot.** Agathocles, tyrant of Sicily, who ruled from 317–289 B.C., hated the sight of a pot because it reminded him that he was the son of a potter. **Mordecai . . . gate.** A reference to the vigils of Mordecai at the gates of King Ahasuerus. See Esther 3:1–2; 5:11–13. 46. **Lazarus . . . door.** Lazarus was the beggar who placed himself at the gate of a rich man to get the crumbs from his table. See Luke 16:20. **lion . . . path,** 1 Kings 13:24. **frog . . . chamber,** Exodus 8:3–4. 47. **fly . . . ointment,** Ecclesiastes 10:1. **mote . . . eye,** Matthew 7:3–5. 49. **one . . . needful,** Luke 10:42. **hail in harvest,** Proverbs 26:1. 50. **ounce . . . sweet,** Spenser's *Faerie Queene,* I, 3, 30. 73. **condition,** social rank.

insults you with a special commendation of your window-curtains. He is of opinion that the urn is the more elegant shape, but, after all, there was something more comfortable about the old tea-kettle—
100 which you must remember. He dare say you must find a great convenience in having a carriage of your own, and appealeth to your lady if it is not so. Inquireth if you have had your arms done on vellum yet; and did not know, till lately, that such-and-such had been the crest of the family. His memory is unseasonable; his compliments perverse; his talk a trouble; his stay pertinacious; and when he goeth away, you dismiss his chair into a corner, as precipitately as possible, and feel fairly rid of two nuisances.

110 There is a worse evil under the sun, and that is—a female Poor Relation. You may do something with the other; you may pass him off tolerably well; but your indigent she-relative is hopeless. "He is an old humorist," you may say, "and affects to go threadbare. His circumstances are better than folks would take them to be. You are fond of having a Character at your table, and truly he is one." But in the indications of female poverty there can be no disguise. No woman dresses below herself from caprice. The truth
120 must out without shuffling. "She is plainly related to the L——s; or what does she at their house?" She is, in all probability, your wife's cousin. Nine times out of ten, at least, this is the case. Her garb is something between a gentlewoman and a beggar, yet the former evidently predominates. She is most provokingly humble, and ostentatiously sensible to her inferiority. He may require to be repressed sometimes—*aliquando sufflaminandus erat*;—but there is no raising her. You send her soup at dinner, and she begs to
130 be helped—after the gentlemen. Mr. —— requests the honor of taking wine with her; she hesitates between port and Madeira, and chooses the former—because he does. She calls the servant "Sir"; and insists on not troubling him to hold her plate. The housekeeper patronizes her. The children's governess takes upon her to correct her when she has mistaken the piano for a harpsichord.

Richard Amlet, Esq., in the play, is a notable instance of the disadvantages to which this chimerical
140 notion of *affinity constituting a claim to acquaintance* may subject the spirit of a gentleman. A little foolish blood is all that is betwixt him and a lady of great estate. His stars are perpetually crossed by the malignant maternity of an old woman, who persists in calling him "her son Dick." But she has wherewithal

in the end to recompense his indignities, and float him again upon the brilliant surface, under which it had been her seeming business and pleasure all along to sink him. All men, besides, are not of Dick's temperament. I knew an Amlet in real life, who, want- 150 ing Dick's buoyancy, sank indeed. Poor W—— was of my own standing at Christ's, a fine classic, and a youth of promise. If he had a blemish, it was too much pride; but its quality was inoffensive; it was not of that sort which hardens the heart, and serves to keep inferiors at a distance; it only sought to ward off derogation from itself. It was the principle of self-respect carried as far as it could go without infringing upon that respect which he would have everyone else equally maintain for himself. He would have you 160 to think alike with him on this topic. Many a quarrel have I had with him, when we were rather older boys and our tallness made us more obnoxious to observation in the blue clothes, because I would not thread the alleys and blind ways of the town with him to elude notice, when we have been out together on a holiday in the streets of this sneering and prying metropolis. W—— went, sore with these notions, to Oxford, where the dignity and sweetness of a scholar's life, meeting with the alloy of a humble introduction, 170 wrought in him a passionate devotion to the place, with a profound aversion from the society. The servitor's gown (worse than his school array) clung to him with Nessian venom. He thought himself ridiculous in a garb under which Latimer must have walked erect, and in which Hooker, in his young days, possibly flaunted in a vein of no discommendable vanity. In the depth of college shades or in his lonely chamber, the poor student shrunk from observation. He found shelter among books, which insult 180 not; and studies, that ask no questions of a youth's finances. He was lord of his library, and seldom cared for looking out beyond his domains. The healing influence of studious pursuits was upon him, to soothe and to abstract. He was almost a healthy man; when the waywardness of his fate broke out against him with a second and worse malignity. The father of W—— had hitherto exercised the humble profession of house-painter at N——, near Oxford. A supposed interest with some of the heads of the colleges had 190 now induced him to take up his abode in that city, with the hope of being employed upon some public works which were talked of. From that moment I read in the countenance of the young man the determination which at length tore him from aca-

74. **tide-waiter**, literally, a minor customs official who waits for the arrival of ships and enforces the revenue laws; here, one, like Micawber in *David Copperfield*, who waits for something lucky to turn up. 82. **client**, dependent. 114. **humorist**, an eccentric person. **affects**, chooses. 128. *aliquando . . . erat*, sometimes he had to be checked. 132. **Madeira**, a kind of wine from the Portuguese island of Madeira northwest of Africa. 138. **the play**, *The Confederacy*, by Sir John Vanbrugh (1664–1726). 151. **Poor W——**. Lamb says elsewhere that W—— was his friend Favell, who "left Cambridge because he was ashamed of his father, who was a house painter there." See ll. 187 ff. 152. **Christ's**, Christ's Hospital. See p. 797. 163. **our tallness**. Lamb was really short of stature. 164. **blue clothes.** Boys at Christ's Hospital wore long blue coats and yellow stockings. 172. **servitor's gown**, the distinguishing dress of an undergraduate who was partly supported by college funds, and who waited table at the Commons. 174. **Nessian venom.** Hercules slew the centaur Nessus with a poisoned arrow and lost his own life by wearing a shirt dipped in the envenomed blood of Nessus. 175. **Latimer**, Hugh Latimer (1488?–1555), famous preacher and reformer, who had been a sizar (servitor) at Clare College, Cambridge. 176. **Hooker**, Richard Hooker (1553–1600), noted English divine, who had been a servitor at Oxford. 189. **N——**, a substitution for Cambridge. See note to l. 151.

demical pursuits forever. To a person unacquainted with our universities, the distance between the gownsmen and the townsmen, as they are called—the trading part of the latter especially—is carried to an excess that would appear harsh and incredible. The temperament of W——'s father was diametrically the reverse of his own. Old W—— was a little, busy, cringing tradesman, who, with his son upon his arm, would stand bowing and scraping, cap in hand, to anything that wore the semblance of a gown—insensible to the winks and opener remonstrances of the young man, to whose chamber-fellow or equal in standing, perhaps, he was thus obsequiously and gratuitously ducking. Such a state of things could not last. W—— must change the air of Oxford or be suffocated. He chose the former; and let the sturdy moralist, who strains the point of the filial duties as high as they can bear, censure the dereliction; he cannot estimate the struggle. I stood with W——, the last afternoon I ever saw him, under the eaves of his paternal dwelling. It was in the fine lane leading from the High-street to the back of —— College, where W—— kept his rooms. He seemed thoughtful and more reconciled. I ventured to rally him—finding him in a better mood—upon a representation of the artist Evangelist, which the old man, whose affairs were beginning to flourish, had caused to be set up in a splendid sort of frame over his really handsome shop, either as a token of prosperity or badge of gratitude to his saint. W—— looked up at the Luke, and, like Satan, "knew his mounted sign—and fled." A letter on his father's table the next morning announced that he had accepted a commission in a regiment about to embark for Portugal. He was among the first who perished before the walls of St. Sebastian.

I do not know how, upon a subject which I began with treating half seriously, I should have fallen upon a recital so eminently painful; but this theme of poor relationship is replete with so much matter for tragic as well as comic associations that it is difficult to keep the account distinct without blending. The earliest impressions which I received on this matter are certainly not attended with anything painful or very humiliating in the recalling. At my father's table (no very splendid one) was to be found, every Saturday, the mysterious figure of an aged gentleman, clothed in neat black, of a sad yet comely appearance. His deportment was of the essence of gravity; his words few or none; and I was not to make a noise in his presence. I had little inclination to have done so—for my cue was to admire in silence. A particular elbow-chair was appropriated to him, which was in no case to be violated. A peculiar sort of sweet pudding, which appeared on no other occasion, distin-

guished the days of his coming. I used to think him a prodigiously rich man. All I could make out of him was that he and my father had been schoolfellows a world ago at Lincoln, and that he came from the Mint. The Mint I knew to be a place where all the money was coined—and I thought he was the owner of all that money. Awful ideas of the Tower twined themselves about his presence. He seemed above human infirmities and passions. A sort of melancholy grandeur invested him. From some inexplicable doom I fancied him obliged to go about in an eternal suit of mourning; a captive, a stately being, let out of the Tower on Saturdays. Often have I wondered at the temerity of my father, who, in spite of an habitual general respect which we all in common manifested towards him, would venture now and then to stand up against him in some argument touching their youthful days. The houses of the ancient city of Lincoln are divided (as most of my readers know) between the dwellers on the hill and in the valley. This marked distinction formed an obvious division between the boys who lived above (however brought together in a common school) and the boys whose paternal residence was on the plain; a sufficient cause of hostility in the code of these young Grotiuses. My father had been a leading Mountaineer; and would still maintain the general superiority, in skill and hardihood, of the *Above Boys* (his own faction) over the *Below Boys* (so were they called), of which party his contemporary had been a chieftain. Many and hot were the skirmishes on this topic—the only one upon which the old gentleman was ever brought out—and bad blood bred; even sometimes almost to the recommencement (so I expected) of actual hostilities. But my father, who scorned to insist upon advantages, generally contrived to turn the conversation upon some adroit by-commendation of the old Minster; in the general preference of which before all other cathedrals in the island, the dweller on the hill and the plain-born could meet on a conciliating level, and lay down their less important differences. Once only I saw the old gentleman really ruffled, and I remembered with anguish the thought that came over me: "Perhaps he will never come here again." He had been pressed to take another plate of the viand which I have already mentioned as the indispensable concomitant of his visits. He had refused with a resistance amounting to rigor, when my aunt—an old Lincolnian, but who had something of this in common with my cousin Bridget, that she would sometimes press civility out of season—uttered the following memorable application: "Do take another slice, Mr. Billet, for you do not get pudding every day." The old gentleman said nothing at the

25. **artist Evangelist,** St. Luke, who by tradition was a painter as well as a physician. 31. **"knew . . . fled,"** *Paradise Lost,* IV, 1013, p. 415. 35. **St. Sebastian,** a seaport on the north coast of Spain; it was taken by Wellington in 1813. 58. **the Mint,** located near the Tower

(l. 61) of London, the historic state prison. 79. **young Grotiuses,** law students. Hugo Grotius (1583-1645) was the great Dutch authority on international law. 104. **Bridget.** See p. 802, and note to l. 33. *Old China.* 161. **the hays,** a country dance. 162. **couchant and**

time; but he took occasion in the course of the evening, when some argument had intervened between them, to utter with an emphasis which chilled the company, and which chills me now as I write it—"Woman, you are superannuated!" John Billet did not survive long after the digesting of this affront, but he survived long enough to assure me that peace was actually restored; and if I remember aright, another pudding was discreetly substituted in the place of that which had occasioned the offense. He died at the Mint (*anno 1781*), where he had long held what he accounted a comfortable independence; and with five pounds, fourteen shillings, and a penny, which were found in his *escritoire* after his decease, left the world, blessing God that he had enough to bury him and that he had never been obliged to any man for a sixpence. This was—a Poor Relation.

(1823)

OLD CHINA

I have an almost feminine partiality for old china. When I go to see any great house, I enquire for the china-closet, and next for the picture gallery. I cannot defend the order of preference, but by saying, that we have all some taste or other, of too ancient a date to admit of our remembering distinctly that it was an acquired one. I can call to mind the first play, and the first exhibition, that I was taken to; but I am not conscious of a time when china jars and saucers were introduced into my imagination.

I had no repugnance then—why should I now have?—to those little, lawless, azure-tinctured grotesques, that under the notion of men and women, float about, uncircumscribed by any element, in that world before perspective—a china tea-cup.

I like to see my old friends—whom distance cannot diminish—figuring up in the air (so they appear to our optics), yet on *terra firma* still—for so we must in courtesy interpret that speck of deeper blue,—which the decorous artist, to prevent absurdity, had made to spring up beneath their sandals.

I love the men with women's faces, and the women, if possible, with still more womanish expressions. Here is a young and courtly Mandarin, handing tea to a lady from a salver—two miles off. See how distance seems to set off respect! And here the same lady, or another—for likeness is identity on tea-cups—is stepping into a little fairy boat, moored on the hither side of this calm garden river, with a dainty mincing foot, which in a right angle of incidence (as angles go in our world) must infallibly land her in the midst of a flowery mead—a furlong off on the other side of the same strange stream!

Farther on—if far or near can be predicated of their world—see horses, trees, pagodas, dancing the hays.

Here—a cow and rabbit couchant, and co-extensive—so objects show, seen through the lucid atmosphere of fine Cathay.

I was pointing out to my cousin last evening, over our Hyson, (which we are old fashioned enough to drink unmixed still of an afternoon) some of these *speciosa miracula* upon a set of extraordinary old blue china (a recent purchase) which we were now for the first time using; and could not help remarking, how favourable circumstances had been to us of late years, that we could afford to please the eye sometimes with trifles of this sort—when a passing sentiment seemed to overshade the brows of my companion. I am quick at detecting these summer clouds in Bridget.

"I wish the good old times would come again," she said, "when we were not quite so rich. I do not mean, that I want to be poor; but there was a middle state"—so she was pleased to ramble on,—"in which I am sure we were a great deal happier. A purchase is but a purchase, now that you have money enough and to spare. Formerly it used to be a triumph. When we coveted a cheap luxury (and, O! how much ado I had to get you to consent in those times!)—we were used to have a debate two or three days before, and to weigh the *for* and *against*, and think what we might spare it out of, and what saving we could hit upon, that should be an equivalent. A thing was worth buying then, when we felt the money that we paid for it."

"Do you remember the brown suit, which you made to hang upon you, till all your friends cried shame upon you, it grew so thread-bare—and all because of that folio Beaumont and Fletcher, which you dragged home late at night from Barker's in Covent Garden? Do you remember how we eyed it for weeks before we could make up our minds to the purchase, and had not come to a determination till it was near ten o'clock of the Saturday night, when you set off from Islington, fearing you should be too late—and when the old bookseller with some grumbling opened his shop, and by the twinkling taper (for he was setting bedwards) lighted out the relic from his dusty treasures—and when you lugged it home, wishing it were twice as cumbersome—and when you presented it to me—and when we were exploring the perfectness of it (*collating* you called it)—and while I was repairing some of the loose leaves with paste, which your impatience would not suffer to be left till daybreak—was there no pleasure in being a poor man? or can those neat black clothes

coextensive, reclining and of the same size. 165. **cousin,** Lamb's sister Mary, referred to in the *Essays of Elia* as Bridgit Elia. 166. **Hyson,** a species of green tea from China. 168. *speciosa miracula,* brilliant wonders. 194. **folio Beaumont and Fletcher,** the first collected edition (1647) of these early seventeenth-century playwrights.

which you wear now, and are so careful to keep brushed, since we have become rich and finical, give you half the honest vanity, with which you flaunted it about in that overworn suit—your old corbeau—for four or five weeks longer than you should have done, to pacify your conscience for the mighty sum of fifteen—or sixteen shillings was it?—a great affair we thought it then—which you had lavished on the old folio. Now you can afford to buy any book that pleases you, but I do not see that you ever bring me home any nice old purchases now."

"When you came home with twenty apologies for laying out a less number of shillings upon that print after Lionardo, which we christened the 'Lady Blanch;' when you looked at the purchase, and thought of the money—and thought of the money, and looked again at the picture—was there no pleasure in being a poor man? Now, you have nothing to do but to walk into Colnaghi's, and buy a wilderness of Lionardos. Yet do you?"

"Then, do you remember our pleasant walks to Enfield, and Potter's Bar, and Waltham, when we had a holyday—holydays, and all other fun, are gone, now we are rich—and the little hand-basket in which I used to deposit our day's fare of savoury cold lamb and salad—and how you would pry about at noontide for some decent house, where we might go in, and produce our store—only paying for the ale that you must call for—and speculate upon the looks of the landlady, and whether she was likely to allow us a table-cloth—and wish for such another honest hostess, as Izaak Walton has described many a one· on the pleasant banks of the Lea, when he went a fishing—and sometimes they would prove obliging enough, and sometimes they would look grudgingly upon us—but we had cheerful looks still for one another, and would eat our plain food savorily, scarcely grudging Piscator his Trout Hall? Now,—when we go out a day's pleasuring, which is seldom moreover, we *ride* part of the way—and go into a fine inn, and order the best of dinners, never debating the expense—which, after all, never has half the relish of those chance country snaps, when we were at the mercy of uncertain usage, and a precarious welcome."

"You are too proud to see a play anywhere now but in the pit. Do you remember where it was we used to sit, when we saw the *Battle of Hexham,* and the *Surrender of Calais,* and Bannister and Mrs. Bland in the *Children in the Wood*—when we squeezed out our shillings a-piece to sit three or four times in a season in the one-shilling gallery—where you felt all the time that you ought not to have brought me—and more strongly I felt obligation to you for having brought me—and the pleasure was the better for a little shame—and when the curtain drew up, what cared we for our place in the house, or what mattered it where we were sitting, when our thoughts were with Rosalind in Arden, or with Viola at the Court of Illyria? You used to say, that the Gallery was the best place of all for enjoying a play socially— that the relish of such exhibitions must be in proportion to the infrequency of going—that the company we met there, not being in general readers of plays, were obliged to attend the more, and did attend, to what was going on, on the stage—because a word lost would have been a chasm, which it was impossible for them to fill up. With such reflections we consoled our pride then—and I appeal to you, whether, as a woman, I met generally with less attention and accommodation, than I have done since in more expensive situations in the house? The getting in indeed, and the crowding up those inconvenient staircases, was bad enough,—but there was still a law of civility to woman recognised to quite as great an extent as we ever found in the other passages—and how a little difficulty overcome heightened the snug seat, and the play, afterwards. Now we can only pay our money and walk in. You cannot see, you say, in the galleries now. I am sure we saw, and heard too, well enough then—but sight, and all, I think, is gone with our poverty."

"There was pleasure in eating strawberries, before they became quite common—in the first dish of peas, while they were yet dear—to have them for a nice supper, a treat. What treat can we have now? If we were to treat ourselves now—that is, to have dainties a little above our means, it would be selfish and wicked. It is very little more that we allow ourselves beyond what the actual poor can get at, that makes what I call a treat—when two people living together, as we have done, now and then indulge themselves in a cheap luxury, which both like; while each apologises, and is willing to take both halves of the blame to his single share. I see no harm in people making much of themselves in that sense of the word. It may give them a hint how to make much of others. But now—what I mean by the word—we never do make much of ourselves. None but the poor can do it. I do not mean the veriest poor of all, but persons as we were, just above poverty."

"I know what you were going to say, that it is mighty pleasant at the end of the year to make all meet,—and much ado we used to have every Thirty-first Night of December to account for our exceedings—many a long face did you make over your puzzled accounts, and in contriving to make it out how

4. corbeau, dark green cloth. 14. Lionardo, Leonardo da Vinci (1452–1519), an Italian painter. The picture alluded to is "Modesty and Vanity," on which Mary Lamb wrote a poem. 19. Colnaghi's, an art dealer in London. 27. house, tavern or inn. 32. Izaak Walton, author of The Complete Angler (p. 363). One of the speakers in these

dialogues is Piscator, the fisherman. His favorite inn was Trout Hall. 47. Battle of Hexham . . . Wood. The first two of these plays were written by George Colman the Younger (1762–1836); the third was by Thomas Morton (1764–1838). 48. Bannister . . . Mrs. Bland, John Bannister (c. 1760–1836), famous actor and one-time manager of

we had spent so much—or that we had not spent so much—or that it was impossible we should spend so much next year—and still we found our slender capital decreasing—but then, betwixt ways, and projects, and compromises of one sort or another, and talk of curtailing this charge, and doing without that for the future—and the hope that youth brings, and laughing spirits (in which you were never poor till now) we pocketed up our loss, and in conclusion, with 'lusty brimmers' (as you used to quote it out of *hearty cheerful Mr. Cotton*, as you called him), we used to welcome in the 'coming guest.' Now we have no reckoning at all at the end of the old year—no flattering promises about the new year doing better for us."

Bridget is so sparing of her speech on most occasions, that when she gets into a rhetorical vein, I am careful how I interrupt it. I could not help, however, smiling at the phantom of wealth which her dear imagination had conjured up out of a clear income of a poor—hundred pounds a year. "It is true we were happier when we were poorer, but we were also younger, my cousin. I am afraid we must put up with the excess, for if we were to shake the superflux into the sea, we should not much mend ourselves. That we had much to struggle with, as we grew up together, we have reason to be most thankful. It strengthened, and knit our compact closer. We could never have been what we have been to each other, if we had always had the sufficiency which you now complain of. The resisting power—those natural dilations of the youthful spirit, which circumstances cannot straighten—with us are long since passed away. Competence to age is supplementary youth, a sorry supplement indeed, but I fear the best that is to be had. We must ride, where we formerly walked: live better, and lie softer—and shall be wise to do so—than we had means to do in those good old days you speak of. Yet could those days return—could you and I once more walk our thirty miles a-day—could Bannister and Mrs. Bland again be young, and you and I be young to see them—could the good old one-shilling gallery days return—they are dreams, my cousin, now—but could you and I at this moment, instead of this quiet argument, by our well-carpeted fire-side, sitting on this luxurious sofa—be once more struggling up those inconvenient stair cases, pushed about, and squeezed, and elbowed by the poorest rabble or poor gallery scramblers—could I once more hear those anxious shrieks of yours—and the delicious *Thank God, we are safe*, which always followed when the topmost stair, conquered, let in the first light of the whole cheerful theatre down beneath us—I know not the fathom line that ever touched a descent so deep as I would be willing to bury more wealth in than Crœsus had, or the great Jew R—— is supposed to have, to purchase it. And now do just look at that merry little Chinese waiter holding an umbrella, big enough for a bed-tester, over the head of that pretty insipid half-Madonna-ish chit of a lady in that very blue summer house."
(1823)

WILLIAM HAZLITT 1778-1830

It is always ironically amusing to posterity when a man with pretensions in one field of human activity achieves whatever fame is to be his in something different. Such a man was William Hazlitt, the son of a Unitarian minister, born in Maidstone, April 10, 1778. His father lived for a time in America, but returned to England when the boy was nine years of age. Hazlitt was largely privately educated. Although his father would have liked to see his son in the ministry, the son was otherwise inclined. He was interested in philosophy of the speculative sort and in painting. Indeed, he finally decided (1802) not only to undertake painting as a career, but also to continue his study of metaphysics as a kind of second vocation. Hazlitt was neither an important philosopher nor an adequate painter, but the combination of the two interests apparently formed a third, and a very important one. His study of logic and metaphysics, combined with his eye for color and form, developed in Hazlitt an unusual critical ability, and when he applied this ability to literature and life, he had discovered his appointed path.

Hazlitt's first important piece of writing was the Essay on Principles of Human Action *(1807), but it is poor metaphysics and interesting now only because of the promise of style apparent in it. Resigned to his failure as a philosopher, Hazlitt turned to general critical writing, contributing to Hunt's* Examiner, *and grouping together a collection of essays known as* The Round Table. *His first solid achievement in literary criticism was* The Characters of Shakespeare's Plays *(1817); his most valuable miscellaneous collection of prose writings is* Table Talk *(1821). The years 1807 to 1821, easily the most active period of Hazlitt's life, saw the writing of the three prose collections just mentioned, and a considerable amount of lecturing, much of it on the Elizabethan playwrights, for whom Hazlitt shared the*

Drury Lane, and Maria Theresa Romanzini Bland (1769–1838), a well-known actress and ballad singer. They were friends of Lamb's. 117. **Cotton,** Charles Cotton (1630–1687), a miscellaneous writer who added a second part to Walton's *Complete Angler*. The quotations are from his poem *The New Year*. 162. **Crœsus,** king of Lydia and the richest man in the world. 162. **great Jew R——,** Nathan Meyer, Baron de Rothschild (1777–1836), a famous London banker. 165. **bed-tester,** a canopy for a four-poster bed.

enthusiasm shown by Coleridge (who had first interested him in metaphysics and literature), and by Hunt, Lamb, and De Quincey.

All his life Hazlitt was extremely liberal, not to say radical, in his tendencies. He had a lack of faith in Wordsworth and Southey, whom he regarded as turncoats; and he was constantly in hot water because of his relations with Hunt and the "extremists" of the age. His liberalism usually meant unfavorable criticisms of his work from the reviewers, particularly from those on the Quarterly Review. Nor did Hazlitt's private life help his isolated position. His first marriage was a dismal failure, although he put up with it for fourteen years. In 1823, however, he became involved with a servant girl; his wife and he separated; and he felt impelled to write Liber Amoris, an indiscreet account of the rather sordid affair, which won him little sympathy from anyone. He removed to the Continent, having contracted a rather casual second marriage in the meantime. Soon after (1825), he returned and published what may be called his critical farewell, The Spirit of the Age. This work exhibits Hazlitt's critical felicity, yet the complaint was raised that he was more happy in his analysis of writers of the past than in his evaluation of the writers of his own day. Such a complaint, however, is scarcely surprising, for in matters critical it takes a bold man to venture on a prophecy, and a lucky as well as a bold man to be right in his judgment. In the Life of Napoleon (1828-1830), Hazlitt clearly showed that he had passed his peak. His death occurred September 18, 1830.

Hazlitt was very much an individualist. He is an impressive combination of intellect and passion, a critic with a prose style vigorous but very bookish in manner and often very careless and inaccurate in details. He has charm, but not the essential warmth of Lamb nor the fine poetic sensibilities of De Quincey; yet he is an extremely good self-depicter, and his interests in life, for all his intellectuality, are clearly romantic. Probably his critical work in the history of English drama will keep him alive long after his personal opinions about life have become obsolete, for he was an honest and outspoken dramatic critic who was none the less keenly appreciative. In his more general criticisms of life, he is prejudiced, somewhat bitter and opinionated; but on the whole he had enough personal magnetism and literary influence to make Robert Louis Stevenson, himself an excellent essayist, remark once in a kind of jesting despair, "We are fine fellows, but we can't write like William Hazlitt."

My First . . . Poets. 1. W——m, Wem, a village near Shrewsbury. 3. "dreaded . . . Demogorgon," Paradise Lost, II, 964 (p. 405). Demogorgon was a mysterious infernal deity who controlled the fates of both gods and men. 21. "fluttering . . . dove-cote," Shakespeare, Coriolanus, V, vi, 115. Salopians are the inhabitants of Shropshire, from its old Latin name Salopia. 26. High-born . . . lay! Gray, The Bard, p. 645, l. 28. 31. siren, one of the sea nymphs said to inhabit an island near Italy and by their singing to lure mariners to destruction.

from MY FIRST ACQUAINTANCE WITH POETS

MEETING WITH COLERIDGE

My father was a Dissenting Minister at W——m in Shropshire; and in the year 1798 (the figures that compose that date are to me like the "dreaded name of Demogorgon") Mr. Coleridge came to Shrewsbury, to succeed Mr. Rowe in the spiritual charge of a Unitarian congregation there. He did not come till late on the Saturday afternoon before he was to preach; and Mr. Rowe, who himself went down to the coach in a state of anxiety and expectation to look for the arrival of his successor, could find no one at 10 all answering the description but a round-faced man in a short black coat (like a shooting jacket) which hardly seemed to have been made for him, but who seemed to be talking at a great rate to his fellow-passengers. Mr. Rowe had scarce returned to give an account of his disappointment, when the round-faced man in black entered, and dissipated all doubts on the subject, by beginning to talk. He did not cease while he stayed; nor has he since, that I know of. He held the good town of Shrewsbury in delightful sus- 20 pense for three weeks that he remained there, "fluttering the proud Salopians like an eagle in dove-cote"; and the Welsh mountains that skirt the horizon with their tempestuous confusion agree to have heard no such mystic sounds since the days of

High-born Hoel's harp or soft Llewellyn's lay!

As we passed along between W——m and Shrewsbury, and I eyed their blue tops seen through the wintry branches, or the red rustling leaves of the sturdy oak-trees by the roadside, a sound was in my ears as of a 30 siren's song; I was stunned, startled with it, as from deep sleep; but I had no notion then that I should ever be able to express my admiration to others in motley imagery or quaint allusion, till the light of his genius shone into my soul, like the sun's rays glittering in the puddles of the road. I was at that time dumb, inarticulate, helpless, like a worm by the wayside, crushed, bleeding, lifeless; but now, bursting from the deadly bands that bound them,

With Styx nine times round them, 40

my ideas float on winged words, and as they expand their plumes, catch the golden light of other years. My soul has indeed remained in its original bondage, dark, obscure, with longings infinite and unsatisfied;

The story of their attempts to lure Ulysses and his crew is told in Homer's Odyssey, Book XII. 40. With . . . them, Pope, Ode on St. Cecilia's Day, l. 90. 59. Agamemnon, a tragedy by Aeschylus, famous Greek dramatist (fifth century B.C.), in which fires are used to announce the fall of Troy. 76. Il y a des, etc. "There are impressions which neither time nor circumstances can efface. Were I enabled to live entire ages, the sweet days of my youth could not return for me, nor ever be obliterated from my memory."—Rousseau, Confessions, II, 7. 82.

my heart, shut up in the prison-house of this rude clay, has never found, nor will it ever find, a heart to speak to; but that my understanding also did not remain dumb and brutish, or at length found a language to express itself, I owe to Coleridge. But 50 this is not to my purpose.

My father lived ten miles from Shrewsbury, and was in the habit of exchanging visits with Mr. Rowe and with Mr. Jenkins of Whitchurch (nine miles farther on) according to the custom of Dissenting Ministers in each other's neighborhood. A line of communication is thus established, by which the flame of civil and religious liberty is kept alive, and nourishes its smoldering fire unquenchable, like the fires in the *Agamemnon* of Aeschylus, placed at dif- 60 ferent stations, that waited for ten long years to announce with their blazing pyramids the destruction of Troy. Coleridge had agreed to come over to see my father, according to the courtesy of the country, as Mr. Rowe's probable successor; but in the meantime I had gone to hear him preach the Sunday after his arrival. A poet and a philosopher getting up into a Unitarian pulpit to preach the Gospel was a romance in these degenerate days, a sort of revival of the primitive spirit of Christianity, which was not to be 70 resisted.

It was in January, 1798, that I rose one morning before daylight, to walk ten miles in the mud, and went to hear this celebrated person preach. Never, the longest day I have to live, shall I have such another walk as this cold, raw, comfortless one, in the winter of the year 1798. *Il y a des impressions que ni le temps ni les circonstances peuvent effacer. Dusse-je vivre des siècles entiers, le doux temps de ma jeunesse ne peut renaître pour moi, ni s'effacer jamais dans ma* 80 *mémoire.* When I got there, the organ was playing the 100th psalm, and, when it was done, Mr. Coleridge rose and gave out his text, "And he went up into the mountain to pray, HIMSELF, ALONE." As he gave out this text, his voice "rose like a steam of rich distilled perfumes," and when he came to the two last words, which he pronounced loud, deep, and distinct, it seemed to me, who was then young, as if the sounds had echoed from the bottom of the human heart, and as if that prayer might have floated in solemn silence 90 through the universe. The idea of St. John came into mind, "of one crying in the wilderness, who had his loins girt about, and whose food was locusts and wild honey." The preacher then launched into his subject, like an eagle dallying with the wind. The sermon was upon peace and war; upon church and state—not their alliance, but their separation—on the

spirit of the world and the spirit of Christianity, not as the same, but as opposed to one another. He talked of those who had "inscribed the cross of Christ on banners dripping with human gore." He 100 made a poetical and pastoral excursion—and to show the fatal effects of war, drew a striking contrast between the simple shepherd boy, driving his team afield, or sitting under the hawthorn, piping to his flock, "as though he should never be old," and the same poor country-lad, crimped, kidnaped, brought into town, made drunk at an ale-house, turned into a wretched drummer-boy, with his hair sticking on end with powder and pomatum, a long cue at his back, and tricked out in the loathsome finery of the 110 profession of blood.

Such were the notes our once-loved poet sung.

And for myself, I could not have been more delighted if I had heard the music of the spheres. Poetry and Philosophy had met together. Truth and Genius had embraced, under the eye and with the sanction of Religion. This was even beyond my hopes. I returned home well satisfied. The sun that was still laboring pale and wan through the sky, obscured by thick mists, seemed an emblem of the *good cause,* and 120 the cold dank drops of dew that hung half melted on the beard of the thistle had something genial and refreshing in them; for there was a spirit of hope and youth in all nature that turned everything into good. The face of nature had not then the brand of JUS DIVINUM on it:

Like to that sanguine flower inscribed with woe.

On the Tuesday following, the half-inspired speaker came. I was called down into the room where he was, and went half-hoping, half-afraid. He received me very 130 graciously, and I listened for a long time without uttering a word. I did not suffer in his opinion by my silence. "For those two hours," he afterwards was pleased to say, "he was conversing with W. H.'s forehead!" His appearance was different from what I had anticipated from seeing him before. At a distance, and in the dim light of the chapel, there was to me a strange wildness in his aspect, a dusky obscurity, and I thought him pitted with the small-pox. His complexion was at that time clear, and even bright— 140

As are the children of yon azure sheen.

His forehead was broad and high, light as if built of ivory, with large projecting eyebrows, and his eyes

"And . . . alone." Cf. Matthew 14:23; John 6:15. 84. "rose . . . perfumes," Milton, *Comus*, l. 556. 91. "of one . . . honey." Cf. Matthew 3:3–4. 105. "as . . . old," Sidney, *Arcadia*, l. 2. 109. pomatum, perfumed ointment for the hair. 112. Such . . . sung, Pope, *Epistle to Robert, Earl of Oxford*. 114. music . . . spheres. The ancients believed that the movement of the celestial planets produced music. 115. Truth . . . embraced. Cf. Psalms 85:10: "Mercy and truth are met together; righteousness and peace have kissed each

other." 120. *good cause,* Liberty; the phrase had been popular during the time of the French Revolution. 126. JUS DIVINUM, divine right, especially the divine right of kings. 127. Like . . . woe, *Lycidas*, p. 384, l. 106. The petals of the hyacinth (sanguine flower) were supposed to be marked with the exclamation Ai (alas) in lamentation for the Greek youth Hyacinthus, from whose blood the flower was said to have sprung. 141. As . . . sheen, Thomson, *The Castle of Indolence*, Canto 2, 295.

rolling beneath them like the sea with darkened luster. "A certain tender bloom his face o'erspread," a purple tinge as we see it in the pale thoughtful complexions of the Spanish portrait-painters, Murillo and Velasquez. His mouth was gross, voluptuous, open, eloquent; his chin good-humored and round; but his nose, the rudder of the face, the index of the will, was small, feeble, nothing—like what he has done. It might seem that the genius of his face as
10 from a height surveyed and projected him (with sufficient capacity and huge aspiration) into the world unknown of thought and imagination, with nothing to support or guide his veering purpose, as if Columbus had launched his adventurous course for the New World in a scallop, without oars or compass. So at least I comment on it after the event. Coleridge in his person was rather above the common size, inclining to the corpulent, or like Lord Hamlet, "somewhat fat and pursy." His hair (now, alas! gray) was
20 then black and glossy as the raven's, and fell in smooth masses over his forehead. This long pendulous hair is peculiar to enthusiasts, to those whose minds tend heavenward; and is traditionally inseparable (though of a different color) from the pictures of Christ. It ought to belong, as a character, to all who preach *Christ crucified,* and Coleridge was at that time one of those!

It was curious to observe the contrast between him and my father, who was a veteran in the cause and
30 then declining into the vale of years. He had been a poor Irish lad, carefully brought up by his parents, and sent to the University of Glasgow (where he studied under Adam Smith) to prepare him for his future destination. It was his mother's proudest wish to see her son a Dissenting Minister. So if we look back to past generations (as far as eye can reach) we see the same hopes, fears, wishes, followed by the same disappointments, throbbing in the human hearts; and so we may see them (if we look forward) rising up
40 forever, and disappearing, like vaporish bubbles, in the human breast! After being tossed about from congregation to congregation in the heats of the Unitarian controversy and squabbles about the American war, he had been relegated to an obscure village, where he was to spend the last thirty years of his life, far from the only converse that he loved, the talk about disputed texts of Scripture and the cause of civil and religious liberty. Here he passed his days, repining but resigned in the study of the Bible,
50 and the perusal of the Commentators—huge folios, not easily got through, one of which would outlast a winter! Why did he pore on these from morn to night (with the exception of a walk in the fields or a turn in the garden to gather broccoli plants or kidney-beans of his own rearing, with no small degree of pride and pleasure)? Here were "no figures nor no fantasies"—neither poetry nor philosophy—nothing to dazzle, nothing to excite modern curiosity; but to his lack-luster eyes there appeared, within the pages of the ponderous, unwieldy, neglected tomes, the sacred 60 name of JEHOVAH in Hebrew capitals: pressed down by the weight of the style, worn to the last fading thinness of the understanding, there were glimpses, glimmering notions of the patriarchal wanderings, with palm-trees hovering in the horizon, and processions of camels at the distance of three thousand years; there was Moses with the Burning Bush, the number of the Twelve Tribes, types, shadows, glosses on the law and the prophets; there were discussions (dull enough) on the age of Methuselah, a 70 mighty speculation! there were outlines, rude guesses at the shape of Noah's Ark and of the riches of Solomon's Temple; questions as to the date of the creation, predictions of the end of all things; the great lapses of time, the strange mutations of the globe were unfolded with the voluminous leaf, as it turned over; and though the soul might slumber with an hieroglyphic veil of inscrutable mysteries drawn over it, yet it was in a slumber ill-exchanged for all the sharpened realities of sense, wit, fancy, or reason. 80 My father's life was comparatively a dream; but it was a dream of infinity and eternity, of death, the resurrection, and a judgment to come!

No two individuals were ever more unlike than were the host and his guest. A poet was to my father a sort of nondescript: yet whatever added grace to the Unitarian cause was to him welcome. He could hardly have been more surprised or pleased if our visitor had worn wings. Indeed, his thoughts had wings; and as the silken sounds rustled round our 90 little wainscoted parlor, my father threw back his spectacles over his forehead, his white hairs mixing with its sanguine hue; and a smile of delight beamed across his rugged cordial face, to think that Truth had found a new ally in Fancy! Besides, Coleridge seemed to take considerable notice of me, and that of itself was enough. He talked very familiarly, but agreeably, and glanced over a variety of subjects. At dinner-time he grew more animated, and dilated in a very edifying manner on Mary Wollstonecraft and Mackintosh. The 100 last, he said, he considered (on my father's speaking of his *Vindiciae Gallicae* as a capital performance)

2. **"A . . . o'erspread,"** ibid., 1. 507. Thomson has *gloom* instead of *bloom.* 4. **Murillo and Velasquez,** Spanish painters of the seventeenth century. 15. **scallop,** a kind of sea-shell. 19. **pursy,** scant of breath. From *Hamlet,* V, ii, 298. 33. **Adam Smith,** a celebrated Scottish political economist (1723–1790). 56. **"no . . . fantasies,"** *Julius Caesar,* II, i, 231. 67. **Moses . . . Bush,** a reference to the angel of the Lord that appeared in a burning bush to Moses. Cf. Exodus 3:1–6. 68. **Twelve Tribes,** of Israel. See Genesis, Chapter 49. 70. **Methuselah,** a Hebrew patriarch said to have lived 969 years. See Genesis 5:27. 72.

Noah's Ark, described in Genesis 6:14–16. 72. **riches . . . Temple,** described in 1 Kings 6:20–35. 95. **ally in Fancy.** "My father was one of those who mistook his talent after all. He used to be very much dissatisfied that I preferred his Letters to his Sermons. The last were forced and dry; the first came naturally from him. For ease, half-plays on words, and a supine, monkish, indolent pleasantry, I have never seen them equaled."—Hazlitt. 100. **Mary Wollstonecraft,** a radical English author (1759–1797), wife of William Godwin, and mother of the second wife of Shelley. **Mackintosh,** Sir James Mackintosh (1765–

as a clever scholastic man—a master of the topics—or as the ready warehouseman of letters, who knew exactly where to lay his hand on what he wanted, though the goods were not his own. He thought him no match for Burke, either in style or matter. Burke was a metaphysician, Mackintosh a mere logician. Burke was an orator (almost a poet) who reasoned in figures, because he had an eye for nature: Mackintosh, on the other hand, was a rhetorician, who had only an eye to commonplaces. On this I ventured to say that I had always entertained a great opinion of Burke, and that (as far as I could find) the speaking of him with contempt might be made the test of a vulgar democratical mind. This was the first observation I ever made to Coleridge, and he said it was a very just and striking one. I remember the leg of Welsh mutton and the turnips on the table that day had the finest flavor imaginable. Coleridge added that Mackintosh and Tom Wedgwood (of whom, however, he spoke highly) had expressed a very indifferent opinion of his friend Mr. Wordsworth, on which he remarked to them—"He strides on so far before you that he dwindles in the distance!" Godwin had once boasted to him of having carried on an argument with Mackintosh for three hours with dubious success; Coleridge told him—"If there had been a man of genius in the room, he would have settled the question in five minutes." He asked me if I had ever seen Mary Wollstonecraft, and I said I had once for a few moments, and that she seemed to me to turn off Godwin's objections to something she advanced with quite a playful, easy air. He replied, that "this was only one instance of the ascendancy which people of imagination exercised over those of mere intellect." He did not rate Godwin very high (this was caprice or prejudice, real or affected) but he had a great idea of Mrs. Wollstonecraft's powers of conversation, none at all of her talent for book-making. We talked a little about Holcroft. He had been asked if he was not much struck *with* him, and he said he thought himself in more danger of being struck *by* him. I complained that he would not let me get on at all, for he required a definition of every commonest word, exclaiming, "What do you mean by a *sensation*, Sir? What do you mean by an *idea?*" This, Coleridge said, was barricadoing the road to truth—it was setting up a turnpike-gate at every step we took. I forgot a great number of things, many more than I remember; but the day passed off pleasantly, and the next morning Mr. Coleridge was to return to Shrewsbury. When I came down to breakfast, I found that he had just received a letter from his friend T. Wedgwood, making him an offer of £150 a year if he chose to waive his present pursuit, and devote himself entirely to the study of poetry and philosophy. Coleridge seemed to make up his mind to close with this proposal in the act of tying on one of his shoes. It threw an additional damp on his departure. It took the wayward enthusiast quite from us to cast him into Deva's winding vales, or by the shores of old romance. Instead of living at ten miles distance, of being the pastor of a Dissenting congregation at Shrewsbury, he was henceforth to inhabit the Hill of Parnassus, to be a Shepherd on the Delectable Mountains. Alas! I knew not the way thither, and felt very little gratitude for Mr. Wedgwood's bounty. I was presently relieved from the dilemma; for Mr. Coleridge, asking for a pen and ink, and going to a table to write something on a bit of card, advanced towards me with undulating step, and giving me the precious document, said that that was his address, *Mr. Coleridge, Nether Stowey, Somersetshire;* and that he should be glad to see me there in a few weeks' time, and, if I chose, would come half-way to meet me. I was not less surprised than the shepherd-boy (this simile is to be found in *Cassandra*) when he sees a thunder-bolt fall close at his feet. I stammered out my acknowledgments and acceptance of this offer (I thought Mr. Wedgwood's annuity a trifle to it) as well as I could; and this mighty business being settled, the poet-preacher took leave, and I accompanied him six miles on the road. It was a fine morning in the middle of winter, and he talked the whole way. The scholar in Chaucer is described as going

—sounding on his way.

So Coleridge went on his. In digressing, in dilating, in passing from subject to subject, he appeared to me to float in air, to slide on ice. He told me in confidence (going along) that he should have preached two sermons before he accepted the situation at Shrewsbury, one on Infant Baptism, the other on the Lord's supper; showing that he could not administer either, which would have effectually disqualified him for the object in view. I observed that he continually crossed me on the way by shifting from one side of the footpath to the other. This struck me as an odd movement; but I did not at that time connect it with any instability of purpose or involuntary change of principle, as I have done since. He seemed unable to keep on in a straight line. He spoke slightingly of

1832), a Scottish philosopher and historian in sympathy with the French Revolution; he published *Vindiciae Gallicae* (1791) in answer to Edmund Burke's *Reflections on the Revolution in France* (1790). 121. **Tom Wedgwood.** See ll. 155 ff. 141. **Holcroft,** Thomas Holcroft (1745–1809), an English dramatist, actor, and miscellaneous writer; also a prominent radical. 148. **barricadoing,** barricading. 161. **Deva,** the old Latin name for the River Dee, in North Wales. 162. **by . . . romance.** Cf. Wordsworth's *A Narrow Girdle of Rough Stones and Crags,* 38: "Sole-sitting by the shores of old romance." 165. **inhabit . . . Parnas-**

sus, become a poet. Parnassus is a mountain range in Greece, celebrated as the haunt of the Muses of poetry and music. 166. **Shepherd . . . Mountains.** In Bunyan's *Pilgrim's Progress,* Christian and Hopeful escape from Giant Despair and come to the Shepherds of the Delectable Mountains. 178. **Cassandra,** a French historical romance by La Calprenède (1610–1663). 187. **sounding . . . way.** From Chaucer's Prologue to the *Canterbury Tales,* p. 108, l. 307.

Hume (whose *Essay on Miracles* he said was stolen from an objection started in one of South's sermons— *Credat Judaeus Apella!*) I was not very much pleased at this account of Hume, for I had just been reading, with infinite relish, that completest of all metaphysical *choke-pears,* his *Treatise on Human Nature,* to which the *Essays,* in point of scholastic subtlety and close reasoning, are mere elegant trifling, light summer-read-
10 ing. Coleridge even denied the excellence of Hume's general style, which I think betrayed a want of taste or candor. He however made me amends by the manner in which he spoke of Berkeley. He dwelt particularly on his *Essay on Vision* as a masterpiece of analytical reasoning. So it undoubtedly is. He was exceedingly angry with Dr. Johnson for striking the stone with his foot, in allusion to this author's *Theory of Matter and Spirit,* and saying, "Thus I confute him, Sir." Coleridge drew a parallel (I don't know how he brought about the connection) between
20 Bishop Berkeley and Tom Paine. He said the one was an instance of a subtle, the other of an acute mind, than which no two things could be more distinct. The one was a shop-boy's quality, the other the characteristic of a philosopher. He considered Bishop Butler as a true philosopher, a profound and conscientious thinker, a genuine reader of nature and of his own mind. He did not speak of his *Analogy,* but of his *Sermons at the Rolls' Chapel,* of which I had never heard. Coleridge somehow always contrived to
30 prefer the *unknown* to the *known.* In this instance he was right. The *Analogy* is a tissue of sophistry, of wire-drawn, theological special-pleading; the *Sermons* (with the Preface to them) are in a fine vein of deep, matured reflection, a candid appeal to our observation of human nature, without pedantry and without bias. I told Coleridge I had written a few remarks, and was sometimes foolish enough to believe that I had made a discovery on the same subject (the *Natural Disinterestedness of the Human Mind*)—and I tried to
40 explain my view of it to Coleridge, who listened with great willingness, but I did not succeed in making myself understood. I sat down to the task shortly afterwards for the twentieth time, got new pens and paper, determined to make clear work of it, wrote a few meager sentences in the skeleton-style of a mathematical demonstration, stopped half way down the second page; and, after trying in vain to pump up any words, images, notions, apprehensions, facts, or observations, from that gulf of abstraction in which I
50 had plunged myself for four or five years preceding, gave up the attempt as labor in vain, and shed tears of helpless despondency on the blank unfinished paper. I can write fast enough now. Am I better than

I was then? Oh, no! One truth discovered, one pang of regret at not being able to express it, is better than all the fluency and flippancy in the world. Would that I could go back to what I then was! Why can we not revive past times as we can revisit old places? If I had the quaint Muse of Sir Philip Sidney to assist me, I would write a *Sonnet to the Road between W——m* 60 *and Shrewsbury,* and immortalize every step of it by some fond enigmatical conceit. I would swear that the very milestones had ears, and that Harmer-hill stooped with all its pines to listen to a poet as he passed! I remember but one other topic of discourse in this walk. He mentioned Paley, praised the naturalness and clearness of his style, but condemned his sentiments, thought him a mere time-serving casuist, and said that "the fact of his work on *Moral and Political Philosophy* being made a textbook in our 70 Universities was a disgrace to the national character." We parted at the six-mile stone; and I returned homeward, pensive but much pleased. I had met with unexpected notice from a person whom I believed to have been prejudiced against me. "Kind and affable to me had been his condescension, and should be honored ever with suitable regard." He was the first poet I had known, and he certainly answered to that inspired name. I had heard a great deal of his powers of conversation, and was not disappointed. In fact, 80 I never met with anything at all like them, either before or since. I could easily credit the accounts which were circulated of his holding forth to a large party of ladies and gentlemen, an evening or two before, on the Berkeleian Theory, when he made the whole material universe look like a transparency of fine words; and another story (which I believe he has somewhere told himself) of his being asked to a party at Birmingham, of his smoking tobacco and going to sleep after dinner on a sofa, where the 90 company found him to their no small surprise, which was increased to wonder when he started up of a sudden, and rubbing his eyes, looked about him, and launched into a three-hours' description of the third heaven, of which he had had a dream, very different from Mr. Southey's *Vision of Judgment,* and also from that other *Vision of Judgment,* which Mr. Murray, the Secretary of the Bridge-street Junto, has taken into his especial keeping!

On my way back I had a sound in my ears; it was 100 the voice of Fancy—I had a light before me; it was the face of Poetry. The one still lingers there; the other has not quitted my side! Coleridge in truth met me halfway on the ground of philosophy, or I should not have been won over to his imaginative creed. I had an uneasy, pleasurable sensation all the time, till

1. **Hume,** David Hume (1711–1776), famous Scottish philosopher. His *Essay on Miracles* shocked orthodox theologians of the period. 2. **South,** Robert South (1634–1716), a celebrated English divine. 3. *Credat . . . Apella!* Let the Jew Apella—i.e., a credulous person, believe it; I shall not (Horace, *Satires,* Book I, Satire V, 101). 12. **Berkeley,** George Berkeley (1685–1753), an Irish bishop and idealistic philosopher. 17.

"**Thus . . . Sir,**" Related in Boswell's *Life of Johnson* (see p. 595). 20. **Tom Paine,** Anglo-American liberal political writer (1737-1809). 24. **Bishop Butler,** Joseph Butler (1692-1752), an English theologian. 38. *Natural . . . Mind,* not published until 1805. 59. **Sidney,** see p. 206. 63. **Harmer-hill,** a prominent hill on the road between Wem and Shrewsbury. 66. **Paley,** William Paley (1743-1805), orthodox

I was to visit him. During those months the chill breath of winter gave me a welcoming; the vernal air was balm and inspiration to me. The golden sunsets, 110 the silver star of evening, lighted me on my way to new hopes and prospects. *I was to visit Coleridge in the spring.* This circumstance was never absent from my thoughts, and mingled with all my feelings. I wrote to him at the time proposed, and received an answer postponing my intended visit for a week or two, but very cordially urging me to complete my promise then. This delay did not damp, but rather increased my ardor. In the meantime I went to Llan-120 gollen Vale, by way of initiating myself in the mysteries of natural scenery; and I must say I was enchanted with it. I had been reading Coleridge's description of England, in his fine *Ode on the Departing Year*, and I applied it, *con amore*, to the objects before me. That valley was to me (in a manner) the cradle of a new existence: in the river that winds through it, my spirit was baptized in the waters of Helicon! . . .

(1823)

THOMAS DE QUINCEY 1785-1859

Thomas De Quincey was born near Manchester, the son of a rich merchant who died when the boy was young but who left a handsome patrimony, which seems to have endured through De Quincey's lifetime. The boy was unusually precocious and was educated in such a way as to encourage that precocity; he could write Greek fluently at the age of thirteen and could talk it with ease at fifteen. One of his teachers remarked that his pupil could have addressed a mob of Athenians with more effect than the teacher could have addressed a mob of Englishmen. In spite of his proficiency, De Quincey abhorred his early schooling, and on one occasion ran away to London, to be brought back and prepared for college only with the greatest difficulty. He went to Oxford, where his career was most irregular; he ran away again, and in the second year of his course became addicted to the opium habit, which was brought on through the use of the drug to alleviate the pain of an annoying illness. He left Oxford in 1808, having studied brilliantly but erratically, without a degree because he could not stand the necessary oral examination.

His interest in literature had been marked from the very first. It was not surprising, therefore, that De Quincey should be attracted to the company of the literary lights of the day, who in 1809 were assuredly

Wordsworth and Coleridge. He went to the Lake Country, took a home near Wordsworth at Grasmere (p. 679), and remained there for about ten years, studying the classics and cultivating Coleridge and Wordsworth. From Coleridge he got an interest in the Elizabethans and in German literature, at the time almost an unknown field. He married in 1816 and became the father of a large family. All this time there had been no significant work from his pen. But in 1820 he moved to London, where he renewed the acquaintance with Lamb which he had made in earlier days and learned from him much about the English prose writers of the seventeenth century, Browne, Fuller, and Taylor.

De Quincey's Confessions of an English Opium Eater appeared in 1821. He had taken enormous quantities of opium at one time (1813); but had greatly reduced the daily allowance before his marriage, although there had been some relapses. The book sold very well; it was authentically intimate in a sensational way; it was exciting and romantic in its account of De Quincey's early days when he had fled to London from school and college; and it was written in a beautiful prose style—rich, sensuous, imaginative, and pulsing with a singular driving power. The remainder of De Quincey's output was originally written for periodicals, particularly Blackwood's Magazine; it consists of essays on personal, political, social, critical, and historical subjects; some might even be called philosophical essays. Of these essays The English Mail Coach; Suspiria de Profundis, a sequel to the Confessions; The Flight of a Tartar Tribe; Murder Considered as One of the Fine Arts; and Joan of Arc are the best known.

De Quincey moved to Edinburgh in middle age, and remained there until his death on December 8, 1859. He was extremely quiet and secluded in his living, entertaining but rarely, though impressively. All this was in keeping with his gentle, scholarly, eccentric character. The desire for solitude amounted at times almost to a craze, for he would abandon his living quarters and go away to some other place, locking his study door behind him. Six such apartments, locked and stuffed with papers, were discovered after his death. Yet in spite of his eccentricity, all who met him were impressed by his courtesy, his generosity, his charm, and his tolerance.

De Quincey never became an extremist of any political party, but his drift was toward liberalism. More accurately, he went from liberal conservative to conservative liberal; never by any stretch of the imagination could he be called radical. He rather fancied himself as a political writer, and his historical writings have some permanence. His great contri-

theologian and philosopher.   75. **"Kind . . . regard,"** *Paradise Lost*, VIII, 648-650.   87. **he . . . himself.** In *Biographia Literaria*, 10.   89. **Birmingham,** a large manufacturing city in Warwickshire.   96. **Southey's Vision.** It describes the entrance of George III into heaven. The "other Vision" is Byron's ferocious satire of Southey's poem.   97. **Mr. Murray,** John Murray (1778-1843), Byron's publisher. He was publisher also of the Tory *Quarterly Review*. The Bridge-Street Association (called "Gang" by its enemies) was organized in 1821 to prevent seditious publications and acts.   118. **Llangollen Vale.** In Wales, about thirty-five miles from Wem.   123. *con amore*, with love.   127. **Helicon,** a mountain in Greece; it had two springs sacred to the Muses.

bution, however, lay in his general writings on personal topics; the more subjective De Quincey is, as a rule, the better he writes. That should be expected of the romanticist; and a romanticist De Quincey surely was. Give his imagination sea room, and his heart and pen do the rest.

De Quincey's style is his chief monument. Now it can be profuse and discursive; now the writing of a scholar, a wit, a man of the world. Always it is polished, and as De Quincey himself called it, "impassioned" prose. He was proud of his calling as a writer, for he regarded literature as the greatest of the arts. His own classification of his works is significant: "first, that class which proposes primarily to amuse the reader; second, papers which address themselves purely to the understanding as an insulated faculty, or do so primarily [in this group would fall his historical and political essays]; third, in virtue of their aim, as a far higher class of compositions, modes of impassioned prose ranging under no precedents that I am aware of in any literature." To this last group De Quincey's best work belongs. He errs in considering such impassioned prose original with him; but no one else has managed to maintain such a lofty flight in prose for so long a time.

"There is, first," said De Quincey, "the literature of knowledge, and, secondly, the literature of power. The function of the first is to teach; the function of the second is to move; the first is a rudder; the second, an oar or a sail." De Quincey's best work, like the best work of any great romanticist, belongs to the literature of power.

ON THE KNOCKING AT THE GATE IN MACBETH

From my boyish days I had always felt a great perplexity on one point in *Macbeth*. It was this: the knocking at the gate which succeeds to the murder of Duncan produced to my feelings an effect for which I never could account. The effect was that it reflected back upon the murderer a peculiar awfulness and a depth of solemnity; yet, however obstinately I endeavored with my understanding to comprehend this, for many years I never could see *why* it should
10 produce such an effect.

Here I pause for one moment to exhort the reader never to pay any attention to his understanding when it stands in opposition to any other faculty of his mind. The mere understanding, however useful and indispensable, is the meanest faculty in the human mind and the most to be distrusted; and yet the great majority of people trust to nothing else—

which may do for ordinary life, but not for philosophical purposes. Of this, out of ten thousand instances that I might produce, I will cite one. Ask of 20 any person whatsoever who is not previously prepared for the demand by a knowledge of perspective, to draw in the rudest way the commonest appearance which depends upon the laws of that science—as, for instance, to represent the effect of two walls standing at right angles to each other, or the appearance of the houses on each side of a street, as seen by a person looking down the street from one extremity. Now, in all cases, unless the person has happened to observe in pictures how it is that artists produce these 30 effects, he will be utterly unable to make the smallest approximation to it. Yet why? For he has actually seen the effect every day of his life. The reason is that he allows his understanding to overrule his eyes. His understanding, which includes no intuitive knowledge of the laws of vision, can furnish him with no reason why a line which is known and can be proved to be a horizontal line should not *appear* a horizontal line: a line that made any angle with the perpendicular less than a right angle would seem to him 40 to indicate that his houses were all tumbling down together. Accordingly he makes the line of his houses a horizontal line, and fails of course to produce the effect demanded. Here then is one instance out of many, in which not only the understanding is allowed to overrule the eyes, but where the understanding is positively allowed to obliterate the eyes, as it were; for not only does the man believe the evidence of his understanding in opposition to that of his eyes, but (what is monstrous) the idiot is not 50 aware that his eyes ever gave such evidence. He does not know that he has seen (and therefore *quoad* his consciousness has *not* seen) that which he *has* seen every day of his life.

But to return from this digression. My understanding could furnish no reason why the knocking at the gate in *Macbeth* should produce any effect, direct or reflected. In fact, my understanding said positively that it could *not* produce any effect. But I knew better; I felt that it did; and I waited and clung to 60 the problem until further knowledge should enable me to solve it. At length, in 1812, Mr. Williams made his *début* on the stage of Ratcliffe Highway, and executed those unparalleled murders which have procured for him such a brilliant and undying reputation. On which murders, by the way, I must observe, that in one respect they have had an ill effect, by making the connoisseur in murder very fastidious in his taste, and dissatisfied with anything that has been since done in that line. All other murders look 70

On the Knocking . . . Macbeth. 15. **meanest,** lowest. 52. *quoad his consciousness,* as far as his consciousness is concerned. 62. **in 1812.** It was in December 1811; two families were murdered—the Marrs and the Williamsons. **Mr. Williams,** John Williams, an English seaman and a notorious murderer of the early nineteenth century. 63. **Ratcliffe Highway,** a public thoroughfare in a disreputable quarter of the eastern wharf district of London. 71. **amateur,** here, one who makes a study of murders. 79. **knocking at the door,** by the servant of the Marrs, who had been sent out to buy oysters. 82. **dilettanti,** lovers of the art of murder; literally, lovers of art. 99. **"the . . . on,"** Shakespeare, *Measure for Measure,* III, i, 79. 103. **sympathy.** "It seems almost ludicrous to guard and explain my use of a word in a situation

pale by the deep crimson of his; and, as an amateur once said to me in a querulous tone, "There has been absolutely nothing *doing* since his time, or nothing that's worth speaking of." But this is wrong, for it is unreasonable to expect all men to be great artists, and born with the genius of Mr. Williams. Now it will be remembered that in the first of these murders (that of the Marrs) the same incident (of a knocking at the door soon after the work of extermi-80 nation was complete) did actually occur which the genius of Shakespeare has invented; and all good judges, and the most eminent dilettanti, acknowledged the felicity of Shakespeare's suggestion as soon as it was actually realized. Here, then, was a fresh proof that I had been right in relying on my own feeling in opposition to my understanding; and again I set myself to study the problem. At length I solved it to my own satisfaction; and my solution is this—Murder, in ordinary cases, where the sympathy is wholly 90 directed to the case of the murdered person, is an incident of coarse and vulgar horror; and for this reason—that it flings the interest exclusively upon the natural but ignoble instinct by which we cleave to life: an instinct which, as being indispensable to the primal law of self-preservation, is the same in kind (though different in degree) amongst all living creatures. This instinct, therefore, because it annihilates all distinctions, and degrades the greatest of men to the level of "the poor beetle that we tread on," ex-100 hibits human nature in its most abject and humiliating attitude. Such an attitude would little suit the purposes of the poet. What then must he do? He must throw the interest on the murderer. Our sympathy must be with *him* (of course I mean a sympathy of comprehension, a sympathy by which we enter into his feelings, and are made to understand them—not a sympathy of pity or approbation). In the murdered person all strife of thought, all flux and reflux of passion and of purpose, are crushed 110 by one overwhelming panic; the fear of instant death smites him "with its petrific mace." But in the murderer, such a murderer as a poet will condescend to, there must be raging some great storm of passion—jealousy, ambition, vengeance, hatred—which will create a hell within him; and into this hell we are to look.

In *Macbeth*, for the sake of gratifying his now enormous and teeming faculty of creation, Shakespeare has introduced two murderers: and, as usual in his hands, they are remarkably discriminated: but—though 120 in Macbeth the strife of mind is greater than in his wife, the tiger spirit not so awake, and his feelings caught chiefly by contagion from her—yet, as both were finally involved in the guilt of murder, the murderous mind of necessity is finally to be presumed in both. This was to be expressed; and on its own account, as well as to make it a more proportionable antagonist to the unoffending nature of their victim, "the gracious Duncan," and adequately to expound "the deep damnation of his taking off," this was to be expressed with peculiar energy. We 130 were to be made to feel that the human nature—i.e., the divine nature of love and mercy, spread through the hearts of all creatures, and seldom utterly withdrawn from man—was gone, vanished, extinct, and that the fiendish nature had taken its place. And, as this effect is marvelously accomplished in the *dialogues* and *soliloquies* themselves, so it is finally consummated by the expedient under consideration; and it is to this that I now solicit the reader's attention. If the reader has ever witnessed a wife, daughter, or 140 sister, in a fainting fit, he may chance to have observed that the most affecting moment in such a spectacle is *that* in which a sign and a stirring announce the recommencement of suspended life. Or, if the reader has ever been present in a vast metropolis on the day when some great national idol was carried in funeral pomp to his grave, and, chancing to walk near the course through which it passed, has felt powerfully, in the silence and desertion of the streets and in the stagnation of ordinary business, 150 the deep interest which at that moment was possessing the heart of man—if all at once he should hear the death-like stillness broken up by the sound of wheels rattling away from the scene, and making known that the transitory vision was dissolved, he will be aware that at no moment was his sense of the complete suspension and pause in ordinary human concerns so full and affecting as at that moment when the suspension ceases, and the goings-on of human life are suddenly resumed. All action in any 160 direction is best expounded, measured, and made apprehensible, by reaction. Now apply this to the case in *Macbeth*. Here, as I have said, the retiring of the human heart and the entrance of the fiendish heart was to be expressed and made sensible. Another world has stepped in; and the murderers are taken out of the region of human things, human purposes, human desires. They are transfigured: Lady Macbeth is "unsexed"; Macbeth has forgot that he was born of woman; both are conformed to the image 170 of devils; and the world of devils is suddenly revealed. But how shall this be conveyed and made palpable? In order that a new world may step in, this world must for a time disappear. The murderers, and the murder, must be insulated—cut off by an immeasurable gulf from the ordinary tide and suc-

where it would naturally explain itself. But it has become necessary to do so, in consequence of the unscholar-like use of the word *sympathy*, at present so general, by which, instead of taking it in its proper sense, as the act of reproducing in our minds the feelings of another, whether for hatred, indignation, love, pity, or approbation, it is made a mere synonym of the word pity; and hence, instead of saying 'sympathy *with* another,' many writers adopt the monstrous barbarism of 'sympathy *for* another'."—De Quincey. 111. **Petrific,** petrifying. The phrase is from *Paradise Lost*, X, 293. 128. **"the gracious Duncan,"** *Macbeth*, III, i, 66. 129. **"the deep . . . off,"** ibid., I, vii, 20. 169. **"unsexed,"** ibid., v, 42.

cession of human affairs—locked up and sequestered in some deep recess; we must be made sensible that the world of ordinary life is suddenly arrested—laid asleep—tranced—racked into a dread armistice; time must be annihilated; relation to things without abolished; and all must pass self-withdrawn into a deep syncope and suspension of earthly passion. Hence it is that, when the deed is done, when the work of darkness is perfect, then the world of darkness passes
10 away like a pageantry in the clouds: the knocking at the gate is heard, and it makes known audibly that the reaction has commenced; the human has made its reflux upon the fiendish: the pulses of life are beginning to beat again; and the re-establishment of the goings-on of the world in which we live first makes us profoundly sensible of the awful parenthesis that had suspended them.

O mighty poet! Thy works are not as those of other men, simply and merely great works of art, but are
20 also like the phenomena of nature, like the sun and the sea, the stars and the flowers, like frost and snow, rain and dew, hail-storm and thunder, which are to be studied with entire submission of our own faculties, and in the perfect faith that in them there can be no too much or too little, nothing useless or inert, but that, the farther we press in our discoveries, the more we shall see proofs of design and self-supporting arrangement where the careless eye had seen nothing but accident!
(1823)

from THE POETRY OF POPE

LITERATURE OF KNOWLEDGE AND
LITERATURE OF POWER

30 What is it that we mean by *literature*? Popularly, and amongst the thoughtless, it is held to include everything that is printed in a book. Little logic is required to disturb *that* definition. The most thoughtless person is easily made aware that in the idea of *literature* one essential element is—some relation to a general and common interest of man, so that what applies only to a local or professional or merely personal interest, even though presenting itself in the shape of a book, will not belong to literature. So far
40 the definition is easily narrowed; and it is as easily expanded. For not only is much that takes a station in books not literature, but, inversely, much that really *is* literature never reaches a station in books. The weekly sermons of Christendom, that vast pulpit literature which acts so extensively upon the popular

mind—to warn, to uphold, to renew, to comfort, to alarm—does not attain the sanctuary of libraries in the ten-thousandth part of its extent. The drama, again, as for instance the finest of Shakespeare's plays in England and all leading Athenian plays in the noon- 50 tide of the Attic stage, operated as a literature on the public mind, and were (according to the strictest letter of that term) *published* through the audiences that witnessed their representation, some time before they were published as things to be read; and they were published in this scenical mode of publication with much more effect than they could have had as books during ages of costly copying or of costly printing.

Books, therefore, do not suggest an idea co-extensive 60 and interchangeable with the idea of literature; since much literature, scenic, forensic, or didactic (as from lecturers and public orators), may never come into books, and much that does come into books may connect itself with no literary interest. But a far more important correction, applicable to the common vague idea of literature, is to be sought not so much in a better definition of literature as in a sharper distinction of the two functions which it fulfils. In that great social organ which, collectively, we call literature, there 70 may be distinguished two separate offices that may blend and often do so, but capable, severally, of a severe insulation, and naturally fitted for reciprocal repulsion. There is, first, the literature of *knowledge,* and secondly, the literature of *power.* The function of the first is to *teach;* the function of the second is to *move;* the first is a rudder, the second an oar or a sail. The first speaks to the mere discursive understanding; the second speaks ultimately, it may happen, to the higher understanding or reason, but 80 always through affections of pleasure and sympathy. Remotely, it may travel towards an object seated in what Lord Bacon calls *dry* light; but, proximately, it does and must operate—else it ceases to be a literature of *power*—on and through that *humid* light which clothes itself in the mists and glittering *iris* of human passions, desires, and genial emotions. Men have so little reflected on the higher functions of literature as to find it a paradox if one should describe it as a mean or subordinate purpose of books to give in- 90 formation. But this is a paradox only in the sense which makes it honorable to be paradoxical. Whenever we talk in ordinary language of seeking information or gaining knowledge, we understand the words as connected with something of absolute novelty. But it is the grandeur of all truth which *can* occupy a very high place in human interests that it is never absolutely novel to the meanest of minds:

---

7. syncope, cessation, swoon.
The Poetry of Pope. 50. noontide . . . stage, the time of Aeschylus, Sophocles, and Euripides, famous Greek dramatists of the fifth century B.C. 53. *published . . . audiences.* "Charles I, for example, when Prince of Wales, and many others in his father's court,

gained their known familiarity with Shakespeare—not through the original quartos, so slenderly diffused, nor through the first folio of 1623, but through the court representations of his chief dramas at Whitehall."—De Quincey. 83. Bacon . . . light. "Heraclitus the Obscure said: *The dry light was the best soul*—meaning, when the

it exists eternally by way of germ or latent principle in the lowest as in the highest, needing to be
developed, but never to be planted. To be capable
of transplantation is the immediate criterion of a
truth that ranges on a lower scale. Besides which,
there is a rarer thing than truth—namely, *power,* or
deep sympathy with truth. What is the effect, for
instance, upon society, of children? By the pity, by
the tenderness, and by the peculiar modes of admiration, which connect themselves with the helplessness,
with the innocence, and with the simplicity of children, not only are the primal affections strengthened
and continually renewed, but the qualities which are
dearest in the sight of heaven—the frailty, for instance, which appeals to forbearance, the innocence
which symbolizes the heavenly, and the simplicity
which is most alien from the worldly—are kept up
in perpetual remembrance, and their ideals are continually refreshed. A purpose of the same nature is
answered by the higher literature, viz., the literature
of power. What do you learn from *Paradise Lost?*
Nothing at all. What do you learn from a cookery-
book? Something new, something that you did not
know before, in every paragraph. But would you
therefore put the wretched cookery-book on a higher
level of estimation than the divine poem? What you
owe to Milton is not any knowledge, of which a
million separate items are still but a million of advancing steps on the same earthly level; what you owe
is *power*—that is, exercise and expansion to your
own latent capacity of sympathy with the infinite,
where every pulse and each separate influx is a step
upwards, a step ascending as upon a Jacob's ladder
from earth to mysterious altitudes above the earth.
All the steps of knowledge, from first to last, carry
you further on the same plane, but could never raise
you one foot above your ancient level of earth: whereas
the very *first* step in power is a flight—is an ascending
movement into another element where earth is forgotten.

Were it not that human sensibilities are ventilated
and continually called out into exercise by the great
phenomena of infancy, or of real life as it moves
through chance and change, or of literature as it
recombines these elements in the mimicries of poetry, romance, etc., it is certain that, like any animal
power or muscular energy falling into disuse, all such
sensibilities would gradually droop and dwindle. It
is in relation to these great *moral* capacities of man
that the literature of power, as contradistinguished
from that of knowledge, lives and has its field of
action. It is concerned with what is highest in man;
for the Scriptures themselves never condescended

to deal by suggestion or co-operation with the mere
discursive understanding: when speaking of man in
his intellectual capacity, the Scriptures speak not of
the understanding, but of *"the understanding heart"*
—making the heart, i.e., the great *intuitive* (or non-
discursive) organ, to be the interchangeable formula
for man in his highest state of capacity for the infinite. Tragedy, romance, fairy tale, or epopee, all
alike restore to man's mind the ideals of justice, of
hope, of truth, of mercy, of retribution, which else
(left to the support of daily life in its realities) would
languish for want of sufficient illustration.

What is meant, for instance, by *poetic justice?* It
does not mean a justice that differs by its object from
the ordinary justice of human jurisprudence, for then
it must be confessedly a very bad kind of justice; but
it means a justice that differs from common forensic
justice by the degree in which it attains its object—a
justice that is more omnipotent over its own ends,
as dealing, not with the refractory elements of
earthly life, but with the elements of its own creation, and with materials flexible to its own purest
preconceptions. It is certain that, were it not for the
literature of power, these ideals would often remain
amongst us as mere arid notional forms; whereas, by
the creative forces of man put forth in literature, they
gain a vernal life of restoration, and germinate into
vital activities. The commonest novel, by moving in
alliance with human fears and hopes, with human
instincts of wrong and right, sustains and quickens
those affections. Calling them into action, it rescues
them from torpor. And hence the pre-eminency over
all authors that merely *teach,* of the meanest that
moves, or that teaches, if at all, indirectly by moving.
The very highest work that has ever existed in the
literature of knowledge is but a provisional work—a
book upon trial and sufferance, and *quamdiu bene se
gesserit.* Let its teaching be even partially revised,
let it be but expanded—nay, even let its teaching be
but placed in a better order—and instantly it is superseded. Whereas the feeblest works in the literature
of power, surviving at all, survive as finished and
unalterable amongst men. For instance, the *Principia*
of Sir Isaac Newton was a book militant on earth from
the first. In all stages of its progress it would have
to fight for its existence: first, as regards absolute
truth; secondly, when that combat was over, as regards its form or mode of presenting the truth. And
as soon as a Laplace, or anybody else, builds higher
upon the foundations laid by this book, effectually
he throws it out of the sunshine into decay and
darkness; by weapons won from this book he super-
annuates and destroys this book, so that soon the

faculties intellectual are in vigor, not wet, nor, as it were, blooded by
the affections."—Bacon, *Apothegms New and Old,* 1. 268.   86. *Iris,*
rainbow; from Iris, goddess of the rainbow.   119. *Paradise Lost.* See
p. 386.   131. **Jacob's ladder.** In a dream Jacob beheld a ladder that
reached from earth to heaven. See Genesis 28:12.   155. **"the . . .**

heart," 1 Kings 3:9, "Give therefore thy servant an understanding
heart to judge thy people."   159. **epopee,** epic poem.   188. *quamdiu
. . . gesserit,* as long as it bore itself well.   194. *Principia,* The
Mathematical Principles of Natural Philosophy, published in 1687.   200.
Laplace, a French astronomer and mathematician (1749–1827).

name of Newton remains as a mere *nominis umbra*, but his book, as a living power, has transmigrated into other forms. Now, on the contrary, the *Iliad*, the *Prometheus* of Aeschylus, the *Othello* or *King Lear*, the *Hamlet* or *Macbeth*, and the *Paradise Lost*, are not militant, but triumphant forever, as long as the languages exist in which they speak or can be taught to speak. They never *can* transmigrate into new incarnations. To reproduce these in new forms, or varia-
10 tions, even if in some things they should be improved, would be to plagiarize. A good steam engine is properly superseded by a better. But one lovely pastoral valley is not superseded by another, nor a statue of Praxiteles by a statue of Michael Angelo. These things are separated not by imparity but by disparity. They are not thought of as unequal under the same standard, but as different in *kind*, and, if otherwise equal, as equal under a different standard. Human works of immortal beauty and works of
20 nature in one respect stand on the same footing: they never absolutely repeat each other, never approach so near as not to differ, and they differ not as better and worse, or simply by more and less—they differ by undecipherable and incommunicable differences, that cannot be caught by mimicries, that cannot be reflected in the mirror of copies, that cannot become ponderable in the scales of vulgar comparison.

Applying these principles to Pope as a representative of fine literature in general, we would wish to
30 remark the claim which he has, or which any equal writer has, to the attention and jealous winnowing of those critics in particular who watch over public morals. Clergymen, and all organs of public criticism put in motion by clergymen, are more especially concerned in the just appreciation of such writers, if the two canons are remembered which we have endeavored to illustrate, viz., that all works in this class, as opposed to those in the literature of knowledge, 1st, work by far deeper agencies, and 2dly, are
40 more permanent; in the strictest sense they are κτήματα ἐς ἀεί: and what evil they do, or what good they do, is commensurate with the national language, sometimes long after the nation has departed. At this hour, five hundred years since their creation, the tales of Chaucer, never equaled on this earth for their tenderness, and for life of picturesqueness, are read

familiarly by many in the charming language of their natal day, and by others in the modernisations of Dryden, of Pope, and Wordsworth. At this hour, one thousand eight hundred years since their creation, 50 the Pagan tales of Ovid, never equaled on this earth for the gayety of their movement and the capricious graces of their narrative, are read by all Christendom. This man's people and their monuments are dust; but *he* is alive: he has survived them, as he told us that he had it in his commission to do, by a thousand years "and *shall* a thousand more."

All the literature of knowledge builds only groundnests, that are swept away by floods, or confounded by the plow; but the literature of power builds nests in 60 aërial altitudes of temples sacred from violation, or of forests inaccessible to fraud. *This* is a great prerogative of the *power* literature; and it is a greater which lies in the mode of its influence. The *knowledge* literature, like the fashion of this world, passeth away. An Encyclopedia is its abstract; and, in this respect, it may be taken for its speaking symbol—that before one generation has passed, an Encyclopedia is superannuated; for it speaks through the dead memory and unimpassioned understanding, which have not 70 the repose of higher faculties, but are continually enlarging and varying their phylacteries. But all literature properly so called—literature κατ᾽ ἐξοχην—for the very same reason that it is so much more durable than the literature of knowledge, is (and by the very same proportion it is) more intense and electrically searching in its impressions. The directions in which the tragedy of this planet has trained our human feelings to play, and the combinations into which the poetry of this planet has thrown our human 80 passions of love and hatred, of admiration and contempt, exercise a power for bad or good over human life that cannot be contemplated, when stretching through many generations, without a sentiment allied to awe. And of this let everyone be assured—that he owes to the impassioned books which he has read many a thousand more of emotions than he can consciously trace back to them. Dim by their origination, these emotions yet arise in him and mold him through life, like forgotten incidents of his child- 90 hood.

(1848)

1. *nominis umbra*, shadow of a name. 3. *Iliad*, Homer's story of the Trojan War. 4. Aeschylus. See p. 816, note to l. 50. 14. **Praxiteles . . . Michael Angelo.** The work of the Greek sculptor Praxiteles (fourth century B.C.) is noted for its grace and naturalness; that of the Italian Michaelangelo (1475–1564) for its power. 41. κτήματα ἐς ἀεί, permanent possessions. 44. **tales of Chaucer.** See p. 116. 51. **Ovid,** Roman storyteller and poet (43 B.C.–17? A.D.). See Dryden's comparison of Ovid and Chaucer (pp. 470 ff.). 72. **phylacteries,** records; literally, an amulet consisting of boxes containing slips of parchment on which certain passages from the Pentateuch are written. They are bound on the forehead and left forearm by Jews at prayer to remind them to keep the law. Cf. Deuteronomy 6:8, 11:18. 73. κατ᾽ ἐξοχην, *par excellence.*

The interior of the Crystal Palace at the Great Exhibition of 1851, from Mighty London Illustrated, 1851. The Great Exhibition shows, better than any other single thing, the character of Victorian taste.

DEMOCRACY SCIENCE AND INDUSTRIALISM

From the Accession of Victoria to the First

World War, 1837-1914

Chapter Five

The Victorian Age Characterized

"Modern times," wrote Matthew Arnold in 1863, "find themselves with an immense system of institutions, established facts, accredited dogmas, customs, rules, which have come to them from times not modern. In this system their life has to be carried forward; yet they have a sense that this system is not of their own creation, that it by no means corresponds exactly with the wants of their actual life, that, for them, it is customary, not rational. The awakening of this sense is the awakening of the modern spirit. The modern spirit is now awake almost everywhere; the sense of want of correspondence between the forms of modern Europe and its spirit, between the new wine of the eighteenth and nineteenth centuries, and the old bottles of the eleventh and twelfth centuries, or even of the sixteenth and seventeenth, almost everyone now perceives; it is no longer dangerous to affirm that this want of correspondence exists; people are even beginning to be shy of denying it. To remove this want of correspondence is beginning to be the settled endeavour of most persons of good sense. Dissolvents of the old European system of dominant ideas and facts we must all be, all of us who have any power of working; what we have to study is that we may not be acrid dissolvents of it."

An example of Victorian taste, from the official illustrated catalogue of the Great Exhibition of 1851.

An ormolu clock, by Howell and James, from the Great Exhibition, 1851.

Matthew Arnold was the most acute analyst of the dominant characteristics of his age, and the student of Victorianism is well advised to read him carefully and to take him seriously. Born in 1822—a decade later than Browning, almost a generation later than Carlyle—he escaped the more enervating effects of an exhausted romanticism; preëminently a prose writer rather than a poet, he turned the floodlight of his cultivated intelligence upon the broad issues of his time—in literature, in politics and society, in philosophy and religion—and tried to see them as they really were and to call them by their right names; as earnest as any of his evangelistic contemporaries, he yet opposed reform for its own sake and urged upon his countrymen a return to first principles and to an idea of progress which was intellectual and spiritual rather than material.

Arnold was right: the chief work and burden of his age was the accommodation of the forms of modern life—educational, scientific, religious, economic, political, ethical, esthetic—to the ideas and facts of modern life. In 1830, illiteracy was the rule rather than the exception among the masses of Englishmen; by 1890, the foundations of free popular education had been firmly laid. In 1830, science was considered, save in the most exclusive coteries, a form of blasphemous speculation and witchcraft; by 1890, the friends of physical science stood in the "meridian radiance" of popular curiosity and approval. In 1830, England was deep in the throes of a fundamentalist religious revival; by 1890, God the Father had been seriously indicted, and God the Son had been dismissed as a myth. In 1830, it was assumed that poverty and plenty followed a pattern of "natural law"; by 1890, the fundamental assumptions of socialism and the welfare state had gained wide acceptance. In 1830, the House of Commons was peopled at the pleasure of the House of Lords; by 1890, England had become a modern democracy. In 1830, morality was a matter of Biblical law; by 1890, morality had become a matter of private judgment. In 1830, Tennyson declared: "The poetic word is mightier than the sword"; in 1890, Oscar Wilde declared: "All art is quite useless."

The Crystal Palace from the Serpentine, from Mighty London Illustrated, *1851. Here, The Great Exhibition of the Industry of All Nations—the first world's fair—was held in 1851.*

It is not surprising, then, to learn that Victorianism has been characterized in various and contradictory ways. Professor Jerome Buckley, in *The Victorian Temper*, has brought a representative number of these contradictions together as follows: "The Victorians . . . were 'a poor, blind, complacent people'; yet they were torn by doubt, spiritually bewildered, lost in a troubled universe. They were crass materialists, wholly absorbed in the present, quite unconcerned 'with abstract verities and eternal values'; but they were also excessively religious, lamentably idealistic, nostalgic for the past, and ready to forego present delights for the vision of a world beyond. Despite their slavish 'conformity,' their purblind respect for convention, they were, we learn, 'rugged individualists,' given to 'doing as one likes,' heedless of culture, careless of a great tradition; they were iconoclasts who worshipped the idols of authority. They were, besides, at once sentimental humanitarians and hard-boiled proponents of free enterprise. Politically, they were governed by narrow insular prejudice, but swayed by dark imperialistic designs. Intellectually and emotionally, they believed in progress, denied original sin, and affirmed the death of the Devil; yet by temperament they were patently Manichaeans to whom living was a desperate struggle between the force of good and the power of darkness. While they professed 'manliness,' they yielded to feminine standards; if they emancipated woman from age-old bondage, they also robbed her of a vital place in society. Though they were sexually inhibited and even failed to consider the existence of physical love, they begat incredibly large families and flaunted in their verses a morbidly overdeveloped erotic sensibility. Their art constitutes a shameless record of hypocrisy and ingenuousness. And their literature remains too purposeful, propagandistic, didactic, with too palpable a design upon the reader; yet it is clearly so romantic, aesthetic, 'escapist,' that it carries to posterity but a tale of little meaning."

Out of this chaos of conflicting attitudes one luminously self-evident truth emerges: it is futile to say that Victorianism means *this* or *that*. It was a vast age, a complex age, a fluid age. Aristocratic England was on the wane; proletarian England was on the move. And between them stood a middle-class England with responsibility in excess of experience, with more eagerness than insight, with an urgent will to reform the world but without any very clear notion of where, exactly, to begin. On the one hand, it was an age of "lost causes, and forsaken beliefs, and unpopular names, and impossible loyalties!" On the other hand, it was an age of rapid transformation of ideas and attitudes and values in which the premises of the Renaissance spirit were brought to their logical conclusions and through which the twentieth-century confrontation of life as it in fact is was made imperative.

Dating the Age

Obviously, that attractive young horsewoman who, at the age of eighteen, ascended the British throne in 1837 had nothing whatever to do with the exhausted romanticism or with the series of political, social, and personal crises which were to affect the shape and spiritual quality of a generation of literary men like Carlyle, Newman, Tennyson, Browning, and John Stuart Mill. Obviously, too, a whole generation had passed her by before she died in 1901. Except as a convenient tag, the ghost of Victoria should no longer be allowed to haunt the period.

Four dates can, if not taken too literally and seriously, provide a useful chronological structure for the period: 1832, 1859, 1870, 1914. In 1832, for example, Sir Walter Scott died, as did the German poet and commentator Goethe. In 1832, Tennyson published his second volume of poems, Browning was hard at work on his first long poem, and Carlyle was writing his principal critical essays and trying vainly to get *Sartor Resartus* published in England. In the same year, Newman was moving deeper and deeper into his antipathy to the rationalistic and liberal tendencies of the times, John Stuart Mill had passed through his mental crisis and was writing a series of articles which showed a new eclecticism, and, ironically, Macaulay was excluded from Parliament by the very bill he had advocated. That bill was, of course, the so-called Great Reform Bill of 1832, whereby the franchise was extended to all men owning property worth an annual rent of ten pounds or more. In other words, 1832 is the date on which the government of England was turned over to the middle classes and the date by which the older generation of Victorian writers had formulated their ruling ideas and had adopted their literary idiom.

The year 1859 is a watershed year, sometimes referred to as the "annus mirabilis" of the period because of the startling number of significant publications which appeared that year: Charles Darwin's *On the Origin of Species,* John Stuart Mill's *On Liberty,* Charles Dickens' *A Tale of Two Cities* and *All the Year Round,* the *Cornhill Magazine* under the editorship of William Makepeace Thackeray, Alfred, Lord Tennyson's *Idylls of the King,* Edward Fitzgerald's *Rubáiyát of Omar Khayyám,* George Eliot's first novel, *Adam Bede,* and George Meredith's first novel, *The Ordeal of Richard Feverel.* In 1859, Matthew Arnold began his career as a social

and political commentator with *England and the Italian Question,* and John Ruskin determined to turn from the pleasures of the few to the needs of the many—that is, from art to society. In 1859, De Quincey, Leigh Hunt, and Macaulay died, and France went to war with Austria. (The A&P and Rheingold Beer were also founded in 1859, and the first man crossed Niagara Falls on a tightrope.) In 1859, a new era of intellectual discussion was launched, and new voices were heard in literature.

The year 1870 is a significant one, not only because Charles Dickens died then but also because by that year the older generation of Victorian writers had had their say, had done the work upon which their *critical* reputations must ultimately rest. It is not, like 1859, a year in which a great many significant books were published; rather it is a convenient year around which to cluster the "last word" of the older Victorians: Tennyson's *The Holy Grail and Other Poems* (1869), Arnold's *Culture and Anarchy* (1869), Browning's *The Ring and the Book* (1868–1869), Mill's *On the Subjection of Women* (1869), Dante Gabriel Rossetti's *Poems* (1870), Newman's *Grammar of Assent* (1870), Herbert Spencer's *Principles of Psychology* (1870), George Eliot's *Middlemarch* (1871–1872), Darwin's *Descent of Man* (1871). After 1870, a new generation was in the ascendancy: Swinburne, Pater, Wilde, Hardy, Huxley, Samuel Butler, and Robert Louis Stevenson. The age of Carlyle and Tennyson had an intellectual center of gravity and an emotional texture quite different from those which characterize the age of Huxley, Pater, and Wilde. Their psychological orientation was different: they *cared* about different things in markedly different ways.

The year 1914 needs no explanation.

Some Characteristic Movements

Reform, radical or renovative, was in the air when the Victorian period began. Political justice, social and economic equity, esthetic and religious validity—indeed every area of modern thought was the object of fresh scrutiny; and, what is perhaps even more important for an understanding of the dynamics of the age, there was a prevailing determination to bring thought to action. Indeed, so persistent was the activist spirit in their contemporaries that John Henry Newman wrote *The Idea of a University* and Matthew Arnold wrote *Culture and Anarchy* in part at least as correctives to a tendency toward precipitate action, toward reform for its own sake, toward action which, however well-intentioned, was based on unsound or unexamined premises.

Out of this spirit of reform developed a series of more or less well-defined movements. Some of the movements which are traditionally associated with Victoria's reign acquired form, definition, and importance after the period of literature being dealt with here. For example, although the roots of estheticism, socialism, imperialism, and realism can be traced back through the 1840's, 1850's, and 1860's, they flourished rather in the 1880's and 1890's and carried the debate into the twentieth century. On the other hand, Chartism, Scientism, Tractarianism, and Pre-Raphaelitism do have a Victorian center of gravity.

Chartism

Chartism was a radical movement aimed at bringing political justice to the lower class and represents a significant break in its coalition with the middle class, which had received political satisfaction through passage of the Reform Bill of 1832. The People's Charter (or "Carta"),

A late Victorian house: Carlyle House, Chelsea Embankment, c. 1875.

The hansom cab — the "Gondola of London."

Young ladies of 1860.

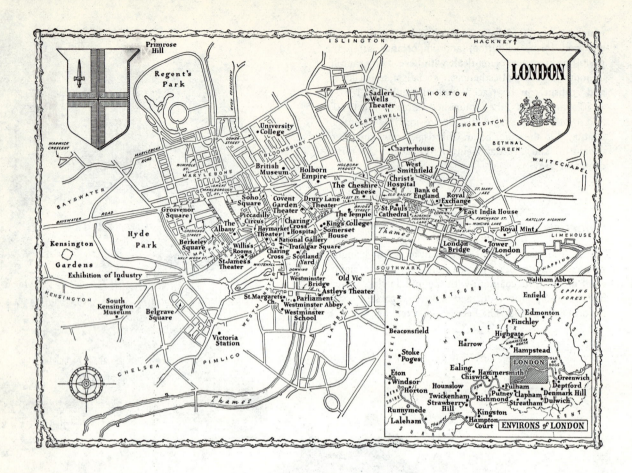

from which the movement got its name, contained "Six Points": (1) universal manhood suffrage, (2) vote by ballot, (3) annual Parliaments, (4) payment of members of Parliament, (5) abolition of property qualifications for membership in the House of Commons, and (6) equal electoral districts. The great political parties refused to adopt the program of the Chartists, and Parliament ignored their petitions as long as it could. The movement came to a dramatic climax in 1848 when the Chartist leader, Feargus O'Connor, gathered 500,000 men on the Kennington Common and threatened to march on Westminster. The government in turn rallied 200,000 special constables, augmented by troops, and effectively intimidated the Chartist movement out of existence. The point had been made, however, and most of the political claims of the Chartists were adopted by Parliament in 1867 and 1884. It was the first great move-

ment of the lonely crowd, leaderless and disenfranchised, to gain a voice in the shaping of public polity, and its members earned from Karl Marx the title of the real democrats of England.

Scientism

Science applied to industry did much ultimately to change English political and social philosophy. At the same time scientific thought in the fields of biology and geology created another revolution of a different sort. Against the ancient belief that man was created the center of the universe and was made in the image of God and endowed by his creator with authority over beast, bird, and fish, was advanced a new philosophy shocking beyond measure to many orthodox Victorians. The

Early nineteenth-century rolling stock.

theory of evolution claimed for man no such central position in the plan of creation; by slow growth and through a process of long development he ascended, rather, from earlier and lowlier forms. Thus his relation to God was not so scientifically demonstrable as was his kinship with the great apes and even with animals lower in the scale.

The new doctrine was the work of scientific philosophers. Of these the most notable were Charles Lyell (1797–1875), Alfred Russell Wallace (1823–1913), Charles Darwin (1809–1882), and Thomas Henry Huxley (1825–1895). The seeds of the doctrine lay in the early geological writings of Lyell, whose *Principles of Geology* deeply influenced *In Memoriam,* and Wallace; but the thinker who brought them to fruition was Darwin, and the scientist-educator who battled valiantly against "clerical minds" for their acceptance was Huxley. It was Darwin's *Origin of Species,* based on innumerable data which he had collected while naturalist on H. M. S. *Beagle,* that shocked Bishop Wilberforce and many other adherents of the older beliefs into coming vigorously to their defense. Darwin himself was a scientist too much absorbed in his own researches and thinking to fight for his hypotheses. In Huxley, however, who came to be popularly known as "Darwin's bull-dog," he found a tireless, clear-headed, and skillful supporter. Darwin's *Descent of Man* (1871) provided much ammunition for the scientists, and Huxley's *Man's Place in Nature* (1863) and *Lay Sermons* (1870) are popular and nontechnical expositions of both the biological theory and its geological counterpart. On the side of the conservatives were many clergymen and writers, including Bishop Samuel Wilberforce (1805–1873), who met Huxley on the debating platform, and Charles Kingsley, who attacked the biologists scathingly in *The Water Babies* (1863). Matthew Arnold, though characterizing Huxley as "the prince of debaters," could not agree with him that the scientific method of investigation should be made the staple of education. In *Dover Beach,* however, the melancholy poet expressed his belief that the "Sea of Faith" was ebbing; in the poems of Tennyson are many echoes of the suggestion that God and Nature are at strife, and that Nature cares not for the individual but only for the type.

If the new philosophy was disturbing to some minds, it was also stimulating. By removing man from his smug post at the center of the universe, it gave him a sounder view of the physical universe and a better sense of proportion. And the method of scientific investigation stiffened his system of thought; skepticism, as Huxley pointed out, was no longer a sin but a virtue, and knowledge based on human authority was replaced, at least in the empire of physical phenomena, by that rooted strongly in careful investigation, observation, and logical induction. So by seeing the world and by taking thought about it man increased his intellectual independence and his mental stature.

The penny black, the first adhesive postage stamp, 1840.

Tractarianism

The Victorian warfare between science and theology embraced a long series of skirmishes. To many of the contestants there seemed to be in general two ways out of the difficulties in which Victorian theological thinkers found themselves. One led forward with the scientists into atheism or agnosticism; the other led into the mystical region of divinely revealed truth. Before Darwin's disturbing *Origin of Species* had appeared, a definite change in the Church of England which took this second direction had already occurred. This was the Oxford Movement, named for its origin at Oxford University; it was also called Tractarianism, from the circumstance that the Oxford reformers published their doctrines in a series of *Tracts for the Times,* which began in September 1833 and ended with the famous Tract XC in 1841. The birthday of the movement was July 14, 1833, the date of a sermon by John Keble on national apostasy, delivered before the judges of assize at Oxford. The saintly author of *The Christian Year* was thus the founder of the Oxford Movement. The most powerful of the Oxford reformers, however, was John Henry Newman (p. 970), fellow of Oriel College and vicar of St. Mary's. Associated with him were Richard Hurrell Froude and Edward Bouverie Pusey, professor of Hebrew at Oxford. When the movement flamed into being in 1833, Newman and Froude were traveling in the Mediterranean. Filled with a sense that he had work to do in England, Newman turned back to the battle line. On his arrival at Oxford, he preached stirringly from his pulpit at St. Mary's and contributed to the *Tracts for the Times.* The publication of *The Literary Remains of Richard Hurrell Froude* in 1838 with its condemnation of the Protestant Reformation greatly alarmed the supporters of the Oxford Movement, and Matthew Arnold attacked "the Oxford malignants." Tract XC, written by Newman, was regarded as directed so definitely against the Church of England that the author could no longer continue to occupy his pulpit. He resigned in September 1843 and two years later was received into the Church of Rome. Some few followed him, but most of his disciples did not; and with his conversion the Oxford Movement came to an end as an acute controversy, although it lingered on in the form of ritualism.

There was about Tractarianism an element of romanticism—a return to the more picturesque religious observances of the Middle Ages. But more essentially it was an expression of Victorian idealism, born of disquiet over a flourishing utilitarianism and a growing materialism. The State had threatened to lay secular hands upon the Church; and the Tractarians, in a spirit of pain and emergency, appealed to the clergy to assert the sovereignty of God and the spiritual independence of the Church from the State.

Against the tide of rationalism and political liberalism it attempted to revitalize the Church and to reaffirm the values of tradition and of spiritual and moral excellence.

Pre-Raphaelitism

Against the conventional qualities of the Victorian poetic establishment, there were individual and group rebellions. The largest group of rebels were those who banded themselves together under the name of the Pre-Raphaelite Brotherhood. The leader of the group was Dante Gabriel Rossetti (p. 1090), and his associates were William Holman Hunt, John Everett Millais, Thomas Woolner, and—later—James Collinson, Fred-

erick George Stephens, Walter Deverell, and William Michael Rossetti (brother of Dante Gabriel), all young poets or artists. Several others were at one time or another associated with the Brotherhood or in sympathy with its ideas and objectives; among these were Christina Rossetti—sister of Dante Gabriel and William—William Morris (p. 1103), and John Ruskin (p. 1042), who came valiantly to their rescue when they were attacked by the conservatives. The P. R. B., as the Brotherhood signed itself, published from January to April 1850 four numbers of a little magazine called *The Germ: Thoughts towards Nature in Poetry, Literature, and Art.* This journal contained not only a statement of their artistic theories but specimens of their work in poetry and art. Eleven of the finest of D. G. Rossetti's lyrics appeared in *The Germ.*

The Pre-Raphaelite Brotherhood took its name from its objective, which was fidelity to nature as presented by the later medieval Italian painters before Raphael (1483–1520). In this medievalism the Pre-Raphaelite revolt was romantic; in their presentation of nature, however, there was an artistic sophistication which differentiated it sharply from the earlier romantics. Their work was, indeed, in both painting and poetry, a blending of the romantic, the realistic, and the supernatural. Because there was little in it of the conventionally spiritual and moral qualities of the Victorians, the P. R. B. was vigorously attacked for its sensuousness. The spirit-damsel of D. G. Rossetti's *Blessed Damozel* (p. 1091), who made the

The cry of the children: child labor; from a contemporary print.

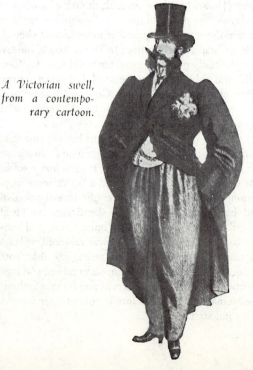

A Victorian swell, from a contemporary cartoon.

"*The Rights of Women, or the Effects of Female Enfranchisement*," a cartoon by George Cruikshank, from The Comic Almanac, 1853.

golden bar of heaven warm with the pressure of her bosom, seemed to most conservatives to be hardly disembodied and spiritual. This and similar "thoughts towards nature" and "adherences to the simplicity of art" led to the vitriolic attack of the critic Robert Buchanan upon the "fleshly" school of poetry in 1871–1872, in spite of Ruskin's earlier defense of the P. R. B. and its objectives. To most modern readers the poetry of the Brotherhood hardly seems shockingly pagan or even "fleshly"; it seems rather to be exotic, colorful, and romantic in its form and in its suggestion of the mystical and the remote from life. Even after the movement itself had passed, the principles and specimens of Pre-Raphaelitism continued to have a visible influence—for example, on the early poetry of William Butler Yeats and T. S. Eliot.

The Victorian Novel

The Victorian age was a reading age, and the readers were the people—not one special group. The Victorian novel, therefore, was democratic. The popular magazines did a valiant service in providing an outlet for literary products, and a great many Victorian novels were issued from month to month in sections. Because these installments usually appeared fresh from the pen of the author and often before he had completed his plan for the whole novel, the effect of this method of publication was not entirely good. It increased the likelihood of prolixity, and it had, moreover, a disintegrating effect upon the unity of the whole structure, for not infre-

quently—as, for example, with Dickens' *Pickwick Papers* (1836)—the plan for the book underwent considerable modification after several installments had been published. Novels published in this way tended, therefore, to be episodic and ill-proportioned with a story that was leisurely in development and with a unity that centered not so much in the plot as in the leading characters. Despite this publishing convention, the Victorian novel is one of the glories of English literature.

The Victorian novel took many forms, some inherited from the earlier decades of the nineteenth century, and some revealing the social pressures of the times. Three traditional forms are significant enough to mention: the sensational tale, the historical romance, and the novel of social life and manners. The first of these can be dismissed with a word, for the tale of terror was by no means as important in the Victorian period as in the preceding era; it appeared in some of the books of Bulwer-Lytton, who had a flair for the supernatural, but the major novelists made little use of it.

The historical romance is a more important Victorian form, but there was no Victorian novelist—excepting Thackeray in *Esmond*—who equaled Sir Walter Scott in this field of prose fiction. Bulwer-Lytton was melodramatic rather than romantic; his historical tales have, moreover, a lumbering self-conscious manner, quite foreign to the genius of Scott, and are stagey and artificial. *The Last Days of Pompeii* (1834), *Rienzi, the Last of the Tribunes* (1835), *The Last of the Barons* (1843), and *Harold, the Last of the Saxon Kings* (1848) reveal in their very titles this footlight quality, for the adjective *last* is suggestive of the popular-heroic and the melo-

A *Victorian drawing room (1810-1870), from the Thorne European Rooms in Miniature, by courtesy of The Art Institute of Chicago.*

dramatic. Another historical novelist with dramatic leanings was Charles Reade, whose *Cloister and the Hearth* (1861), an affecting story of the romance of the parents of Erasmus in the Europe of the fifteenth century, is one of the great historical novels that came out of the period. Charles Kingsley (1819–1875) turned his hand to many types of literature; his historical novels, *Hereward the Wake* (1865) and *Westward Ho!* (1855) —a tale of the days of the Spanish Armada—are entertaining but not so well balanced as Reade's tale. Finally, some of the major novelists tried their hand at this form of fiction. Thackeray's *Esmond* (1852) is one of the greatest historical novels in English literature. Dickens' two contributions to the genre, *Barnaby Rudge* (1841) and *A Tale of Two Cities* (1859), are more sensational and sentimental than historical. George Eliot's *Romola* (1863) is historically accurate but heavy with morality; it is, in fact, a problem novel stretched over a historical framework.

The novel of manners, made popular in the preceding era by Jane Austen, was a type to which the Victorians took eagerly, and many of the best of the Victorian novels belong in this class. In general, two essential elements enter into the making of these stories: (1) a realistic copy of contemporary life and (2) an interpretation of human foibles and human relationships. For some reason this is the type of prose fiction which women writers seem to have done best. Jane Austen was supreme in it, touching off social types with an accuracy and a delicacy that is yet to be surpassed. Her great successors were Elizabeth Cleghorn Gaskell (1810–1865), whose *Cranford* (1853) is a charming picture of English village life, and Charlotte Brontë (1816–1855), who drew out of the narrowness of her own experience materials for *The Professor* (1857), *Villette* (1853), and *Jane Eyre* (1847). A later novelist in the field of simple, democratic realism was Anthony Trollope (1815–

1882); his Barsetshire series of tales—*The Warden* (1855), *Barchester Towers* (1857), and *The Three Clerks* (1858)—were so popular in their delightful naturalness as to lead critics to believe that romance in prose fiction had been quite eclipsed by realism. It remained for Robert Louis Stevenson's romantic stories to explode this belief.

Not only did the Victorian novelists carry on the earlier fondness for historical and social tales, but they developed to a great height certain other types not so prominent in the preceding age. As might be expected, the novel of purpose made a very frequent appearance in Victorian England; and so, too, did what would now be called the psychological story. The first of these types was a vehicle which carried to English readers the social ideas of the authors. Such novels were sometimes propagandistic and sometimes merely expository; but since their center of interest was in a missionary purpose and not in either character or plot, they seldom belong among the best of Victorian tales. To this form nearly all Victorian novelists contributed at one time or another. Mrs. Gaskell's *Mary Barton* (1848) and *North and South* (1855) deal respectively with problems of capital and labor and the evils of the factory system. Charles Kingsley used the problems of agricultural labor as the basis for *Yeast* (1848) and those of industrial labor for *Alton Locke* (1850). Cardinal Newman's *Loss and Gain* (1848) interprets the Anglo-Catholic movement with which he was so intimately connected. Dickens devoted himself conscientiously and sometimes to the abandonment of plot interest to his theories of reform. *Oliver Twist* (1838) deals with the poor laws, *Nicholas Nickleby* (1839) with school reform, *Bleak House* (1853) with the red tape of the Court of Chancery, and *Hard Times* (1854) with the author's economic theories. But unlike most of the propagandist novelists Dickens did not give up the entire story to the presentation of his ideas of reform, but poured these elements into the complex literary mixture of his novels.

The psychological novel is often also the "problem" novel. That is, it frequently presents—even attempts to solve—some problem in human relationship, but in doing so, it must, perforce, analyze human nature. The greatest Victorian novelists in this field were George Eliot and George Meredith. As compared with Dickens, George Eliot is solid, profound, accurate in her analyses of human characters. She set aside the dominant emphasis on plot and stressed the development and interaction of characters. Thus her plots evolve from character and progress as slowly as her characters respond and change. Her successor, George Meredith (1828–1909), was not her equal in range and power, but he was one of the best of the Victorians in the realm of the problem novel and the human character study. He was a poet (p. 1074) and an essayist (his *Essay on Comedy*—1877—is one of the best analyses of the subject) as well as a novelist. His first novel, *The Ordeal of Richard Feverel* (1859), is typical of his work. It presents the psychological problem that arises out of a conflict between natural impulses in a youth and the educational system under which his father is trying to bring him up. The characters were taken—like most of Meredith's characters—from the upper classes; in this respect he differs from most of the earlier Victorian novelists. A few of the best of Meredith's other psychological studies are *Rhoda Fleming* (1865), *Beauchamp's Career* (1876), *The Egoist* (1879), which was perhaps his most famous novel, *Diana of the Crossways* (1885), and *The Amazing Marriage* (1895).

Three Victorian novelists stand out so distinctly above their fellow fiction writers that—like Tennyson and Browning among the poets—they deserve fuller treatment. They are Charles Dickens (1812–1870), William Makepeace Thackeray (1811–1863), and George Eliot (1819–1880).

Of the three major novelists Dickens was unquestionably the most popular. This was the natural result of his inclination to bring into his stories types familiar to the mass of readers and to display his men and women in familiar situations in which they were moved by what may be called "popular" emotions. He was essentially a realist in his art, but he romanticized his realism. To Dickens, moreover, more than to either of the other two more restrained novelists, may be applied the popular cliché, "He ran the gamut of human emotions." His great popularity lay partly in his melodramatic fondness for playing deliberately on his readers' feelings. Dickens was a literary caricaturist. His art included a capacity for effective exaggeration. Applied to characters this created unforgettable types so striking that the tag-names he gave them became common for the characteristics represented—Pecksniff for hypocrisy, Micawber for irresponsibility, Uriah Heep for false and vicious humility. Applied to comic situations his flair for exag-

geration resulted in broadly humorous episodes. Applied to pathetic situations, however, the result was often tawdry emotionalism. For this he has been criticized in his own time and since. Sorrow, say the critics, is most touching when restrained. But Dickens was a consciously popular writer and exaggerated all situations; and melodrama and sentimentalism are undeniably more popular than drama and sentiment. Dickens, finally, was popular because he was the novelist of the middle and lower classes. The aristocracy he did not know and could not interpret. His Sir Mulberry Hawks and Lady Dedlocks are lay figures; Sidney Carton was his only successful aristocrat. But among the middle class and the lowly he was completely at home—understanding and sympathetic. And the modern critic has found in Dickens a sustained symbolic density which several generations of readers either missed or ignored.

Dickens' literary ancestor among the early novelists was Tobias Smollett, the writer of picaresque tales; Thackeray's was Henry Fielding, moralist and satirist. The affinity of Thackeray and Fielding is not difficult to understand; their temperaments were much alike. Like Fielding, Thackeray was a moralist. He hated shams; he hated "man's inhumanity to man." With the essential kindliness in his writing is mingled a strain of cynicism. He disclaimed writing novels of purpose, and his material, indeed, was not always, as was that of Dickens, drawn from contemporary life. Unlike Dickens, again, he depicted the upper and middle classes. He called himself a snob, and perhaps he was one essentially, but he loathed snobs and snobbery and social pretense. The moral character of his works appears not only in his occasional invasion of his story in order to preach a sermon but in the high poetic justice of his climaxes. For example, his two most famous women characters, Becky Sharp (the nearest to a social vampire in Victorian literature) and Beatrix Esmond (the beauty whose selfishness cost an amorous prince his throne), both appear at the end of the story washed out and finished. In these and similar scenes Thackeray was never melodramatic and stagey; his characters who pay the price of sin are not picturesquely drowned, like Dickens' Quilp and Steerforth, but the effect of the lesson is probably greater because the treatment is more restrained. Thackeray was a critic of life and a good one. Unlike Dickens, however, he did not identify himself with his characters. He was a dissector of life, not an actor in it; he was the showman; his characters—to use his own figure from *Vanity Fair*—were puppets, and when the curtain went down, he put them back into the box.

Thackeray's list of novels is not nearly so long as that of Dickens, for he was a slow worker and a methodical one. But what he did was almost all first-class, whereas some of Dickens' novels, like some of Scott's, show the pressure that was forcing them to the level of journalistic hack work. *Vanity Fair* (1847–1848) is probably the best known of Thackeray's tales. Others are *Pendennis*

(1848–1850), *The Newcomes* (1853–1855), *The Virginians* (1857–1859), and—in some respects the best of all—*Henry Esmond* (1852), a story built upon the Jacobite plots to restore the Old Pretender to the throne of England.

To classify George Eliot (born Mary Ann Evans), as has sometimes been done, among the "women" novelists of the period is unfair, for it suggests an apology. She needs none; she is one of the great writers of the period and stands with Dickens and Thackeray secure of a high place in English literature. As a scholar and philosopher, indeed, and in sheer intellectual power she transcended both. In the two decades in which her novels were written the social-political novel was popular, and she lent her talents first to this type. *Adam Bede, The Mill on the Floss,* and *Silas Marner* are all tales of work and workers into which she wove her own vital experiences; in Adam there is much of her father, and in Tom and Maggie Tulliver she and her brother appear. In her later novels the trend was somewhat away from the social study and in the direction of problems of human relationships. *Middlemarch,* to illustrate, presents the problem of a young girl who is tricked by her admiration for scholarship into marriage with a desiccated old pedant; and

Romola is a study in consummate pride and selfishness, as well as a painstakingly complete and accurate historical picture of Italy in the days of Savonarola. The greatness of these and of her other novels lies in their penetration and power. Among Victorian novelists George Eliot is the representative of culture, sound philosophy, keen observation of men and women, and amazing ability to present life effectively. She is, it may be said, among Victorian novelists what Browning is among Victorian poets, and her place is as secure as his.

Postscript: Critical Cautions

It is true, as Arnold said, that a great work of literature is the product of the sympathetic concurrence of the power of a man with the power of a moment. A work of literary art, despite its qualities of universality, comes into being at a certain time, and the marks of that time are upon it. A truly great writer will certainly be concerned with "abstract verities and eternal values"; but he will use the facts of life around him and the idiom of his time to body them forth. Thus the serious student of literature has a responsibility to acquaint himself

Victorian hairdos—the heart-shaped face.

Full evening dress, 1870.

with the major facts and ideas among which an author had to work. But the sophisticated student will carefully distinguish between history and literature. History is a matter of fact; literature is a matter of form and idea. The major Victorian writers—for example, Tennyson, Browning, Arnold, Dickens, Thackeray, George Eliot, Carlyle, Newman, and Ruskin—were severe critics of modern life, attempting throughout their long literary careers to apply urgent correctives to many of its principal developments. From a historical point of view, then, they were "Victorians"; from a literary point of view, they were "anti-Victorians" in that they devoted their magnificent gifts of talent to a devastating anatomy of modern society and to the establishment of new spiritual bases for modern life.

That the Victorian writers were very earnest about their mission is evident: Oscar Wilde saw it and wrote a play about the unimportance of being earnest; Samuel Butler saw it and named the hero of *The Way of All Flesh* Ernest Pontifex. Indeed, the quarrel which the first three decades of the twentieth century had with Victorian literature was not primarily with its substance but with its tone: its seriousness seemed extravagant. A better understanding of the reasons for their earnestness has enabled the modern reader to put the Victorian writers into clearer critical perspective. They were not what they were because they wanted to be: *they had to be*. Thrown upon an era in which extremes had to be accommodated, they were a committed generation determined to make choices, determined, as Arnold said, to "introduce a little order into this chaos by establishing in any quarter a single sound rule of criticism, a single rule which clearly marks what is right as right, and what is wrong as wrong." And the compelling question which Victorian literature poses is not whether it was categorically right or wrong, but whether it was well conceived and well executed or poorly conceived and poorly executed.

Tennyson, George Eliot, and their contemporaries had, of course, to transmute the literary forms which they had inherited from writers as old as Homer and as recent as Sir Walter Scott; and they carried significantly further the experiments with form so brilliantly begun by the romantics. Until recently, however, their formal virtuosity has been obscured by their ideological intensity, and the Victorian writer has been generally confused with the speaker in a piece of Victorian writing. Thus one hears that *Browning* says:

> God's in his heaven—
> All's right with the world!

Or one hears that *Swinburne* says:

> Thou hast conquered, O pale Galilean;
> the world has grown gray from thy breath;

> We have drunken of things Lethean,
> and fed on the fullness of death.

The first of these is spoken by an Italian urchin, the second by the Emperor Julian, and the reader who ignores this distinction between writer and speaker is ignoring an essential characteristic of Victorian literature—namely, that it was essentially a literature, not of argument, but of experience. Victorian writers in general abided by Browning's resolution to present the world view of imaginary characters, not their own. Thus Tennyson created the *Idylls of the King*, in which the *dramatis personae* feel and act and think; thus Browning created *The Ring and the Book*, from which he as author "disappeared," while the poem itself became "all in all"; thus Arnold created *Empedocles on Etna*, a dramatic portrait of how a man of a certain type at a certain time in history responded to the fundamental questions of life; thus the novel became the dominant literary form. The Victorian writers had "views," of course—intense views; but between themselves and their readers they consistently imposed the distance of form because it was ultimately more important for them, *as writers*, to create than to believe.

The Break with Victorian Traditions

By about the year 1880 it is evident that many of the values in art and philosophy and literature which had been generally respected during the mid-Victorian age were becoming subtly altered. In spite of the fact that Queen Victoria was to reign for a score more years and that the effect of the way of life which she so clearly typified was to be felt for a long time thereafter, still the artist, the writer, and the thinking man of the 1880's and later, deviated considerably from their fathers of the 1840's and 1850's. As one looks back upon this later age, to be referred to hereafter as the post-Victorian era, the conclusion seems inescapable that it was an overture to a baffling kind of opera, the contemporary scene; and the final crashing chords of this overture are the cataclysmic events between August 1914 and November 1918, which are still spoken of, in grim realization of later developments, as the First World War.

The last two decades of the nineteenth century showed that England had become inextricably entangled in what some have called the besetting sin of an otherwise great century—the way of imperialism. The economic side of this imperialism, however, did not really come into the foreground much before the days of Cecil Rhodes of South Africa (1853–1902) or of Joseph Chamberlain (1836–1914), who as Colonial Secretary in 1896 proposed a commercial agreement binding together the many vast regions of the British Empire and caring for them by the imposition of a strong protective tariff. This idea cut completely across the long-established British tradition of free trade and was consequently met with great disfavor; but the conception was strongly prophetic of the concept of free dominions and colonies which is today associated with the British Empire.

In the meantime the dazzling dream of empire had been stimulated by the proclaiming of Victoria as Empress of India in 1876 and by the two Imperial Jubilees of 1887 and 1897, celebrating respectively the fiftieth and sixtieth anniversaries of Victoria's accession. The unparalleled greatness of the British rule "over palm and pine," symbolized most fittingly by the military pomp and pride on the one hand and the august, rock-ribbed respectability of the conventional Victoria on the other, could have received no greater popular tribute. As another chapter in the story of the expansion of Britain came the Boer War (1899–1902). It was, for the British government, an inefficiently conducted war which required the full resources of the Empire and troops from as far away as Canada and New Zealand, but which definitely marked the high-water level of the ascendancy of the British Empire.

Yet before the Boer War was over and the great new British Dominion of South Africa established, Queen Victoria had died, and with her went some considerable portion of the lives of millions of her subjects who had never known a time when she had not been the ruler of England. Her son, Edward VII, proved to be an unexpectedly good king, whose monument was his devotion to the task of insuring Britain against the tremendous expansive force of the new German Empire by concluding defensive treaties of alliance with other great powers of Europe in order to achieve a "balance of power." After many bickerings, retrogressions, and progressions, which constitute a fascinating chapter in the history of European diplomacy, Britain succeeded in establishing, with France and Russia, the Triple Entente (1907) to counterbalance the Triple Alliance of Germany, Austria-Hungary, and Italy which had been set up during the 1880's. But four years after the death of Edward VII (1910) and the accession of his son George V (1865–1936), the explosion that was the First World War reverberated around the world.

The nineteenth century had been a prosperous century for all but the poorer classes of British society, but they were very poor indeed. The situation in Britain was, however, the same as that to be noted all over the continent of Europe, and there had been many efforts to improve matters. There were movements toward the beautification of cities, slum clearance, and the founding of various settlement houses, although these were nearly always the result of the enterprise of some private citizen or civic group. Occasionally reformers tried to band together for political action; here the attempts were likely to beget socialistic associations like the Fabian Society, in which George Bernard Shaw and H. G. Wells were at one time interested. Old-age pensions, unemployment insurance, and housing projects were eventually instituted; the expense of carrying out all these plans had somehow to be met, and taxation seemed to be the best way to raise the money. The increase in taxation was felt chiefly by the landed gentry, and the consequent dissatisfaction produced a violent reaction in the House of Lords.

All through the nineteenth century there had been agitation for home rule in Ireland. But neither Daniel O'Connell (1775–1847) nor Charles Stewart Parnell (1846–1891) had succeeded, the first because he was probably too early, and the second largely for personal reasons. The House of Lords supported Protestant Northern Ireland and blocked repeated efforts to pass a Home Rule Bill. The agitation resulting from this impasse focused attention on the House of Lords, the ultra-conservative and decidedly obsolete house of Parliament, and this chamber's veto power was removed (1910). Although a Home Rule Bill was passed (1914) amid much turbulence, the outbreak of the First World War postponed the issue.

General Aspects of Post-Victorian Literature

Of considerable influence in the shaping of post-Victorian literature is the fact that English letters had become dependent, even more than before, upon foreign and international writers. There had been, of course, some such dependence in earlier eras: thus the Old English period owed a debt to Latin and Norse; the Middle English period had leaned upon the French; the Renaissance, upon the Italian, Spanish, and classical languages as well as the French; the neo-classical age upon the Greek, Latin, and French; the age of romanticism upon the classical literatures, French, and German. But in the post-Victorian age one can see in English letters the influences of the realism of the Frenchmen Balzac, Stendhal, Flaubert, and De Maupassant; the naturalism of the Frenchman Zola; the symbolism of the Frenchmen Baudelaire and Verlaine or of the Belgian Maeterlinck; the brilliant all-round achievements of the Russian writers Tolstoi, Dostoevsky, Chekhov, and Turgenev; the German Nietzsche's idea of a superman asserting his will to save mankind; the Frenchman Bergson's philosophy of creative evolution; the Austrian Freud's emphasis upon the subconscious mind; the American Mark Twain's pungent and often savage humor; the Norwegian Ibsen's or the Swedish Strindberg's severe indictments of conven-

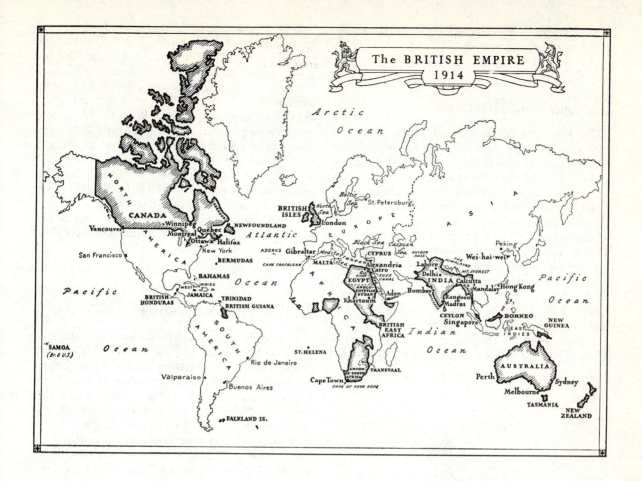

The BRITISH EMPIRE
1914

tional society. Moreover, in almost all of these influences there lie implicit and explicit revolts—revolts
against authority and the established order of things.

The Englishman in India, 1860, from a photograph.

Some Characteristic Post-Victorian Movements

For better or worse, the post-Victorian period lacked
a single titanic personality or craftsman *par excellence*
in any of the several literary genres to give it definition
and direction—lacked, for example, a Dickens or a
George Eliot in the novel, a Carlyle or an Arnold in
non-fictional prose, a Tennyson or a Browning in poetry.
It was a period rich as need be in writers of significant
talent in all the genres; but they tended to be isolated
and to work alone or to congregate in small clubs or
coteries devoted to a single literary thesis. The revolt
against Victorian premises and concerns produced a
non-cohesive, a fragmentary literary climate which can,
perhaps, be best understood through an awareness of

some of the points of view which drew together significant numbers of writers.

The "Aesthetic Movement"

The Pre-Raphaelite Brotherhood, in the 1850's and 1860's, had rejected the conventionality of Victorian art, especially as represented by the Royal Academy, and had asserted anew the responsibility of the artist to be true to nature. Combined with their dedication to pictorial realism was a somewhat ill-defined belief in the essential autonomy of art. "Art for art's sake," which had been a current creed in France during the 1830's, especially reflected in the theories of Théophile Gautier and in the practice of Flaubert, got its most explicit defense in England in the "Conclusion" to Walter Pater's *Studies in the History of the Renaissance* (1873). Pater was a very private sort of person, and it perplexed and pained him to see his meditative reflections about art clutched by the heavy hand of Oscar Wilde and made the banner of a public crusade:

The old love: riding on horseback.

The new love: the safety bicycle, 1896.

"All art is quite useless." Estheticism, dandyism, art for art's sake—all varying aspects of the same revolt against the over-use of art for moral, social, and religious edification—flourished extravagantly in the final quarter of the nineteenth century, although the esthetes felt, directly or by association, the severe rebuff of the law with the conviction of Oscar Wilde in 1895 of perverted sexual practices. And since the early 1890's, the stereotype of the esthete—precious, pained, posturing—has been fair game for satirists. Nonetheless, it should not be forgotten that the esthetic movement provided a concrete alternative to the traditional evaluation of the uses of art and accelerated the tendency of post-Victorian writers to concentrate with new vigor on the formal, as distinct from the thematic, aspects of their work.

Realism and Naturalism

To copy life exactly and vividly was one of the most common objectives of the authors of the post-Victorian period. The growth of realism had had a long, indigenous strain. The efforts of the eighteenth-century romantics to portray nature and the common man with a new particularity was an early tendency toward realism, a tendency which Wordsworth brought to a new level of visibility in his poetry and in his defense of common life and common language. The novelists of the 1840's—Dickens, Charlotte Brontë, Thackeray, Mrs. Gaskell—opened up new subjects for the novel, subjects often reflective of underprivileged sides of life, and this gave new impetus to English realism. The rise, throughout the century, of respect for the facts rather than the romance of history and the inductive method of the new science also served to create a climate conducive to realism.

The *theory* of realism and naturalism, however, was imported largely from France, especially from the prefaces and novels of Émile Zola. And it is somewhat ironic that, although the principal early tendencies toward realism were supported by romantic writers, in its ascendancy realism built upon its polar opposite, the romantic novelists of the 1880's and 1890's.

Realism and naturalism, although inseparable, are distinguishable. Both assume authorial responsibility for perceiving and representing the world as the world in fact is; both lay special emphasis on the usual rather than on the exceptional and the strange. Naturalism, however, carries realism beyond the limits of general practice onto a level of philosophy: it asserts that all consequences are the inevitable result of natural causes, and it instructs the writer to devote himself, like the scientist, to the credible portrayal of natural causes. It is true that naturalistic writers over-corrected the romantic tendencies of their fellow writers and dealt with the seamy side of life to the exclusion of other aspects of "nature" and "reality"—so much so that they have been characterized as indulging themselves in the "joy of stink." Such extremes are, however, more easily found in French than in English literature of the period.

The new realism runs throughout the fiction and the drama of the period in many different phases—in the harsh novels of George Gissing, in the somber stories and tragic ballads of Thomas Hardy, in John Millington Synge's powerful dramas of the Aran Islands, in the extraordinary but little-read works of Hugh Crackenthorpe and George Douglas Brown.

Ladies' and gentlemen's doubles, an illustrated paper, 1882.

Impressionism and Symbolism

Impressionism has been defined as the subjective presentation of a single aspect or point of view. The object of the impressionists in art and in literature was to escape entirely from the commonplace details of living and to express themselves in moods that were to be given as few words and as much simplicity as possible. Symbolism attempts to invest its material with some hidden spiritual or intellectual significance. The English writers of the post-Victorian period seem to have preferred the impressionistic to the symbolistic, though much of their inspiration came from French poets of symbolism, and there were actually a few English symbolists.

Many of the English poets of the last two decades of the nineteenth century who reacted against realism and who sought—after the manner of the French symbolists—to convey impressions by suggestion rather than by direct expression, belonged to the Rhymers' Club, which met in London at the Cheshire Cheese—Samuel Johnson's old meeting place—to discuss poetic theories and to read their poems: John Davidson (1857–1909), Lionel Johnson (1867–1902), Ernest Dowson (1867–1900), Arthur Symons (1865–1945), John Todhunter (1830–1916), and William Butler Yeats (p. 1196). The periodical which grew out of this association was the famous *Yellow Book,* an illustrated quarterly that ran for thirteen numbers from 1894 to 1897 and which was greatly aided by the support of the brilliant Oscar Wilde (1856–1900) and the talented artists and writers Aubrey Beardsley (1872–1898) and Max Beerbohm (1872–1956).

To many of the impressionists and symbolists the step to Catholic mysticism was easy; and there was in fact a rather considerable group of Catholic writers in the post-Victorian age, such as Gerard Manley Hopkins (p. 1172), Alice Meynell (1847–1922), Francis Thompson (p. 1081), Hilaire Belloc (1870–1953), and Gilbert Keith Chesterton (1874–1936), though none of these

can be considered a major writer on the strength of his expression of religious feeling.

The Irish Literary Renaissance

The efflorescence of Irish authors in the post-Victorian age was due to the conscious artistic and literary movement, coinciding with the agitation for Irish independence, which is known as the Irish Renaissance; its founder and leader was William Butler Yeats (p. 1196). Associated with Yeats, from about 1890 on, was an earnest group of poets, dramatists, essayists, and novelists whose purpose was to create a unity of spirit and national consciousness among the Irish people by reviving their romantic past and interpreting their modern life and character. Perhaps their greatest single achievement was the establishment of the Irish Theater (1901) and their building up of a good dramatic tradition. In most of these writers—too numerous to list here in their entirety—the romanticism and mysticism of the Celtic past and the realism of modern Ireland were, however, incongruously, thoroughly intermingled.

The most miscellaneous, powerful, and generally gifted of the group was, of course, Yeats himself. George Russell ("AE") (1867–1935) was a painter as well as a poet, and his scenes of the Donegal country have much of the haunting beauty of his verse. Lady Gregory published in 1902 an attractive retelling of the Celtic Legend of Cuchulain of Muirthemne; her one-act comedies, better known, are playful but sympathetic interpretations of the modern Irish scene. John Millington Synge's best plays, *The Shadow of the Glen* (1903), *Riders to the Sea* (1904), and *The Playboy of the Western World* (1907) are remarkable. The last-named of these three aroused fierce resentment among the Irish when it was first produced because of their objection to what they considered the author's maligning of the Irish people; it is now recognized as an amusing and effective drama, but it does not have the artistic compression and power of his one-act tragic masterpieces. As a matter of fact, the one-act plays produced at the Abbey Theatre established a new dramatic type, and of these plays Synge's are unquestionably the best in the years before the First World War.

The Post-Victorian Novel

The fact that post-Victorian novels tend to be shorter than those of the mid-Victorian age came partly from a quickening of the pace of living and partly from the influence of the compressed French fiction of Flaubert, De Maupassant, and others. In content and mood, too, there was a marked change. Many of the novels were realistic to the point of being sordid and depressing. The post-Victorian novelist tended to detach himself from his story instead of invading it, as did Thackeray and others of his generation.

But there survived a strong romantic streak in the novel, just the same. In the case of the excellent romantic novelist, Robert Louis Stevenson (p. 1120), his love of living, of travel, of action, of adventure on land and sea suffuses his stories. They are crowded with exciting individuals—pirates, wreckers, cabin boys, Highland warriors, and innumerable others—and the action is at times so brisk as to be breathless, with storms at sea, hunts for buried treasure, and plenty of vicious fighting. English literature produced a fictional character so famous that many still think of him as a historical personage—Sherlock Holmes, the creation of Sir Arthur Conan Doyle

An early motor car, 1895.

(1859–1930), appearing first in *A Study in Scarlet* (1887); then in *The Sign of the Four* (1889); *The Adventures of Sherlock Holmes* (1891), a series of short stories; and several others, including *The Hound of the Baskervilles* (1902), one of the greatest of detective novels. The tales of Sherlock Holmes quite eclipsed Doyle's historical romances, but his *Micah Clarke* (1888), a tale of Monmouth's Rebellion in the reign of Charles II, and *The White Company* (1891), a stirring yarn of a free-lance company of mercenaries in England and France during the Hundred Years' War, are spirited and well written.

Of the post-Victorian satirists the earliest and in some respects the most remarkable was Samuel Butler (1835–1902). Butler was a Nottingham man who, after graduating from Cambridge and spending some years in New Zealand as a sheep rancher, returned to England to settle down as a journalist and miscellaneous writer. His Utopian satire, *Erehwon* (*nowhere* spelled backwards) was written as early as 1872; it is a Swift-like attack on contemporary England, in which Butler assails not any one body of manners and morals but what he conceives to be the universal stagnation of thought that had settled like a blight on mid-Victorian England. His other novel, *The Way of All Flesh*, published posthumously in 1903, is a bitter attack on Victorian worship of the family as an institution.

The mordant realism and sharp satire of *The Way of All Flesh* gives it a kinship with the stories of a famous contemporary French novelist, who died in the same year as Butler and whose influence upon English fiction writers of the time was profound. Émile Zola (1840–1902) was the leader of the naturalistic school in France, and his brilliantly accurate expositions of the rawness of life made him in his day both celebrated and notorious. In his *Rougon-Macquart* series of novels he accomplished with great success what Butler later did in *The Way of All Flesh* and John Galsworthy in *The Forsyte Saga*. Another English Zolaist was the unhappy and disturbed George Gissing (1857–1903), who infused into his novels much of the pessimism that he acquired from experience and from his study of the German philosopher Schopenhauer (1788–1860). One of his earliest novels was *Workers of the Dawn* (1880); this was followed by *Demos* (1886) and *The Nether World* (1889). Gissing has been known, however, not so much for his studies of the industrial poor as for his more or less autobiographical works—*The New Grub Street* (1891) and *The Private Papers of Henry Ryecroft* (1903).

If we omit from consideration the novels of Henry James, on the grounds that he was an American by birth and became a British subject only in the last year of his life, then the most patrician novelist of the post-Victorian realists was John Galsworthy (1867–1933), who drew his materials from a narrower range of society than did Zola. He preferred to analyze and depict the propertied man of the Victorian period and later, as his two fine novel series, *The Forsyte Saga* (1906–1921) and *A Modern Comedy* (1929) most admirably attest. But all things considered, Thomas Hardy is the greatest of the English realists produced by the entire Victorian age. His picture of men and women is more tragic than Galsworthy's, for he shows them as crushed between the forces of nature and of social environment, with the fault not in themselves but in the system of the universe. Since, however, Hardy's spirit emerges in his poetry as clearly as in his prose fiction, a discussion of his novels may be included in the comment on his verse that appears below (p. 1181).

There are three novelists of altogether different natures that achieved great celebrity in their day, yet whose final position in the history of English literature it is still exceedingly difficult to determine. Herbert George Wells (1866–1946) began with what are the most original of his novels—fantastic romances like *The Time Machine* (1895) and *The War of the Worlds* (1898), in which he created imaginary worlds and then, playing the part of a god, studied the human beings with whom he had peopled them. His social novels, such as *The History of Mr. Polly* (1910) and *Tono-Bungay* (1909), show a good deal of insight, but it is clear now that Wells spread himself too widely as visionary, scientist, socialist, reformer, critic, and general literary factotum. The second of these novelists was in a way unique. That a man born in Poland and unacquainted with the English language until he was past twenty should nevertheless become a master of style is remarkable. From 1873 to 1895 Joseph Conrad (1857–1924) was a sailor in the British merchant marine; after 1895 he devoted himself to the writing of novels which he considered to be romantic like Stevenson's, but which were actually naturalistic, particularly in their treatment of the life of the sailor. That he was also a profound psychologist is demonstrated in *Almayer's Folly* (1895), *The Nigger of the Narcissus* (1897), *Lord Jim* (1900), *Nostromo* (1904), and his last novel—a truly moving performance, *Victory* (1915). Although the individual episodes in Conrad's novels give them a flavor of the Stevensonian romance, his probing into the motives and impulses of his characters brings him closer to George Eliot, Henry James, Galsworthy, and Masefield. The last of the three, Arnold Bennett (1867–1931), was an enormously prolific writer who often fell into pot-boiling mediocrity; but at his best, as in *The Old Wives' Tale* (1908), he showed a remarkable fidelity to detail and a bravura kind of journalistic genius. This powerful novel is certainly a parable of the times—it is the story of two sisters, daughters of a small shopkeeper in a suburban town, who have two fundamentally different temperaments, a realistic and a romantic. Of his other novels the *Clayhanger* trilogy (1910–1916) is easily the best.

The development of the short story was slower in England than in America, and the type did not become particularly significant until near the end of the nineteenth century, with the advent of Stevenson, Kipling, and Conan Doyle. Then other important writers took up the type, including Hardy, Wells, Chesterton, James, and the members of the Irish Renaissance.

The New Drama

When the drama is free to reflect life, as it was not during the mid-Victorian age, it employs ordinarily the themes, moods, and objectives of other literary types. For example, the characteristic mysticism of Yeats appears in both his poetry and his plays, and

A drawing by Aubrey Beardsley for the title page of The Yellow Book, *1894. The Yellow Book edited by Henry Harland from 1894-1897, and* The Savoy, *edited by Arthur Symons in 1896, were advanced organs of the fin de siècle literary movement. "Nothing like* The Yellow Book *had been seen before. It was newness in excelsis: novelty naked and unashamed. People were puzzled and shocked and delighted, and yellow became the colour of the hour, the symbol of the time-spirit." (Holbrook Jackson)*

the social sympathies of Galsworthy are revealed in both his novels and his dramas. All that is necessary here, therefore, is a general consideration of the post-Victorian theater and a more particular discussion of three or four of the most significant dramatists.

Just as the English impressionists derived their inspiration and technique from the French symbolists, and the English naturalists derived theirs from Zola, so in the drama a Continental writer exercised upon English playwrights in the last two decades of the nineteenth century a deep influence. Henrik Ibsen's *A Doll's House* (1879) showed how a woman had to leave her egoistic husband in order to preserve her integrity and self-respect; again, in *Ghosts* (1881) Ibsen replied to those who asserted that man and wife must remain inseparable with a drama in which hideous tragedy sprang from a wife's conventional and lying loyalty to a worthless husband. "Ibsenism" was long unpopular in England, but the direct and frank treatment of human relationships in the home and in the social group had become common in the English novel, and so it was inevitable that the same themes and the same treatment should eventually invade the theater.

Always with the exception of George Bernard Shaw, Sir Henry Arthur Jones (1851–1929) and Sir Arthur Wing Pinero (1855–1934) were the leading society dramatists in the two decades between 1890 and 1910. For the most part they dealt, like Ibsen, with social relationships and social problems. Of the two, Pinero was much the stronger dramatist; the most celebrated of his dramas are *The Second Mrs. Tanqueray* (1893), which decides in the negative, and very pathetically, the question whether a woman with a past can be admitted to polite society; *The Gay Lord Quex* (1899); and *Mid-Channel* (1909). Oscar Wilde, of course, went his own way; with the possible exception of *Lady Windermere's Fan* (1892) and *A Woman of No Importance* (1893), which skirt a social "situation," his plays are not problem plays, for the author preferred to be sparkling rather than serious. *An Ideal Husband* (1895) and *The Impor-*

tance of Being Earnest (1895) are satirical comedies, highly sophisticated, artificial but witty; they scintillate with comic epigrams, inverted commonplaces, and flippant but pungent phrases, based on the paradox supreme.

Two other great satirists in the theater—George Bernard Shaw and John Galsworthy—utterly different in temperament, purpose, and attainments—are more conveniently discussed in the next chapter, for their works have a certain timelessness which transcends the fact that they did most of their best work in the years before the great World Wars.

The Post-Victorian Period in Review

The confusing variety of forms, methods, moods, and movements that emerged out of the rebellion against Victorianism at the end of the nineteenth century and spread into the first two decades of the twentieth makes it difficult to bring the literature of the post-Victorian period into any clear focus, especially since it has not even yet been thoroughly winnowed by time. One element, the general spirit of reaction against Victorian restraint and conventionality, recurs consistently as a matter of course. On the whole, the post-Victorian age is freer, more outspoken, more "shocking" (even at the risk of being artistically and morally decadent) than the Victorian. The most urgent artistic and literary force of the post-Victorian age was the new type of realism which manifested itself not only in Zolaesque invasions of the lower strata of society but also in brilliantly objective and unsentimental analyses of family and social groups as well as individuals. These materials and methods are general in the novels of the period and also in dramas that broke away from the emptiness and artificiality of Victorian plays and made successful interpretations of contemporary life. The element of satire, finally, pervades in various degrees most of the writing of the time, whence it is obvious that the literature of these decades is haunted by a critical, corrective spirit.

ALFRED, LORD TENNYSON 1809-1892

From 1842 until his death, Tennyson was generally accepted as the first poet of his generation. Some critics lamented the uses to which he put his talents; and a limited number of readers preferred another poet —Browning, for example, or Matthew Arnold. But the typical Victorian reader accorded Tennyson the laurel.

It is not artificial to divide Tennyson's life into two halves with the year 1850. Not only is it the midpoint chronologically; in that year he married Emily Sellwood, published In Memoriam, and was named Poet Laureate. The early half of Tennyson's life was characterized by personal insecurity and poetic uncertainty. His family was gifted but neurotic; Cambridge yielded him little more than an opportunity to meet some intense young men with whom to debate the broad issues of the day—he left without a degree; the reviews of his early volumes of poems (Poems, Chiefly Lyrical, 1830, and Poems, 1832) were mostly hostile; his great friend and most favorable critic, Arthur Henry Hallam, died suddenly while traveling abroad in 1833. After Hallam's death, Tennyson withdrew into a period of silence, in which he worked through his intellectual dilemmas and perfected his craft. His publication, in 1842, of two volumes of Poems proved that he had spent his time well. In Memoriam, too, was largely the product of this period. ·

Before undertaking The Idylls of the King (1859-1885), Tennyson wrote two long experimental narrative poems—The Princess (1847) and Maud: A Monodrama (1855). His attention to poetry was deflected somewhat between 1875 and 1884 by his efforts to restore the Elizabethan tradition of poetic drama to the modern stage, efforts which earned him only the most modest degree of success. In 1883, he became Baron Tennyson of Aldworth and Farringford.

There is hardly another subject among the complex wealth of Victorian literature so fascinating as the unquiet mind and heart of Alfred Tennyson. Tennyson was, quite simply, a great poet. His struggle to establish his identity as a poet was painful and prolonged; and his reputation has had to bear the hardship of a singular shift in poetic idiom. Had he been born two hundred years earlier, he might have challenged Milton; had he been born half a century later, he might have challenged Yeats. A poet with epic propensities,

he yet inherited the conviction of his generation that the age of the epic as a practicable literary form had passed. Though he was sensitive to the poetic uses of a bare, colloquial style, he could hardly be expected to overleap a century and write poems "as cold and passionate as the dawn." Yet Tennyson was an individually distinctive poet who wrote "to the multitude and the happy few alike."

From his sixteenth to his sixtieth year—that is, from Armageddon (Timbuctoo) to The Holy Grail—Tennyson pursued his spiritual and esthetic quest with sincerity and a graduating complexity not generally appreciated. Fascinated, as a youthful rhymer, by such opposite models as Byron and Keats; torn, until the age of twenty-four, between an unrelenting drift toward poetry and a basic distrust of his own poetic powers; lonely, haunted by the specter of hereditary insanity, never entirely free of the death wish; engendered in an age of Evangelical fundamentalism and reared by an embittered clergyman subject to fits of the deepest melancholia; impressed as early as late adolescence with the antipoetic and antireligious implications of the new science—working both against and with such overwhelming psychic pressures, Tennyson evolved a poetic craft and a unique way with ideas.

Certain broad characteristics of Tennyson's poetry are evident to one who reads it in its length and breadth. (1) There is a recurrent motif of individual isolation, coupled with a habitual use of voyage or odyssey. (2) Tennyson frequently used an essentially dramatic technique within a lyrical frame—hence, internal dialogue, especially dialogue of the mind with itself. (3) He attempted to achieve a carefully controlled equilibrium between the public and the private obligations of the poet—most significantly in his two chief works, In Memoriam and The Idylls of the King. (4) There is in Tennyson's poetry an unusual quality of boldness. The whole body of his work testifies to his continual experimentation with form in all its multiple phases: Maud and The Princess, in completely different modes, are extraordinary examples. (5) Tennyson determined, for himself at least, to resolve the persistent war between the ancients and the moderns (the terms of which war can be seen clearly in the prefaces of Elizabeth Barrett Browning in the mid-forties and of Matthew Arnold in the mid-fifties) by extensively employing antique fables as vehicles of modern exploration—a determination unequivocally expressed even in his earliest poem of thematic significance, Timbuctoo. Finally (6), there is Tennyson's persistent dedication to the deeply poetic principle that sound is the major vehicle of sense—from Claribel and The Lady of Shalott to the Morte d'Arthur, from Come down, O Maid to Crossing the Bar—a dedication persisted in even though Tennyson knew that few besides himself would truly hear the sound or surmise its significance.

The central questions upon which, with endless variations, Tennyson's poetry turns are these: What is reality? What seems to be real, but is not? What is truth? How is one to take truth's measure? What is fact, what fable? What are the uses of fable? What is a poet? What are the uses of poetry? Am I a poet? In an age which is antipoetic in its rejection of both fable and religion, what are the poet's responsibilities? Reduced to the two essential issues, Tennyson's questions are the questions of his age: Who am I? What can I believe? Like Matthew Arnold and Robert Browning, Tennyson believed intensely in the spiritual role that poetry and poet must play in the modern world.

This introductory comment on Tennyson cannot end without a suggestion as to how a group of the earlier poems can most profitably be read. From the late twenties to the early forties—from Timbuctoo to Locksley Hall—one of the major questions which Tennyson's poetry posits concerns the poet himself—his power, his diffidence in the face of certain grossly antipoetic developments in modern life, his moral responsibility.

Throughout these poems, Tennyson revealed "the indecision of [his] present mind," often in the form of a dialogue of the mind with itself. The contenders for his commitment were the active versus the contemplative life, myth versus science, the past versus the present, self-indulgence versus service—indeed, withdrawal versus commitment itself. Through poem after poem— Timbuctoo, The Poet, The Lady of Shalott, Oenone, The Lotos-Eaters, Ulysses, Tithonus, to mention only a few examples given below—Tennyson turned the question round and round. Even The Palace of Art, written expressly on the thesis that the poet cannot live in art alone, cannot "love beauty only," ends equivocally: the "soul" portrayed there, though guilty of an Olympian pride and gone mad with feeding on itself, is merely rusticated in the valley for a time to undergo a spiritual renovation and regain the common touch. (The poet's very inability to resolve the issue easily shows that it was intensely real and deeply personal and refutes automatically the notion that he was a facile poet who hung foregone conclusions on ready-made myths.)

Tennyson did finally reach a definite statement in lines 153-173 of Locksley Hall (p. 853). There he gives explosive expression to the romantic primitivism which had for years seemed to be one of the legitimate alternatives of the modern poet, and finally rejects it as a fanciful dream: "but [now] I know my words are wild." He then chants in a few couplets his new commitment to the modern world. Thus Locksley Hall becomes one of the major "periods" in the poetry of Tennyson as, in different ways, do In Memoriam and The Idylls of the King.

THE LADY OF SHALOTT

The Lady of Shalott is a significant example of the two basic levels on which Tennyson worked. The poem tells a fascinating story framed in an extraordinary melody of carefully wrought sounds, but it also provides a serious allegorical commentary on art and life. The clue to the allegory, according to Tennyson himself, is in the closing lines of Part 2: "the new-born love for something, for someone in the wide world from which she has been so long excluded, takes her out of the region of shadows into that of realities." The exact meaning of the allegory still provokes fruitful discussion, but it is generally held that the lady is a poet or artist, the castle an ivory tower, the tapestry and the mirror metaphors for the creative imagination.

PART 1

On either side the river lie
Long fields of barley and of rye,
That clothe the wold and meet the sky;

And through the field the road runs by
    To many-towered Camelot;
And up and down the people go,
Gazing where the lilies blow
Round an island there below,
    The island of Shalott.

Willows whiten, aspens quiver,
Little breezes dusk and shiver
Through the wave that runs forever
By the island in the river

The Lady of Shalott. 3. **wold,** a plain. 5. **Camelot,** the city of King Arthur's court which may have been in Cornwall. 7. **blow,**

bloom. 10. **Willows whiten.** The wind turns up the white underside of the leaves. 22. **shallop,** a light open boat. 46. **mirror.** It is used

Flowing down to Camelot.
Four gray walls, and four gray towers,
Overlook a space of flowers,
And the silent isle embowers
    The Lady of Shalott.

By the margin, willow-veiled,
20 Slide the heavy barges trailed
By slow horses; and unhailed
The shallop flitteth silken-sailed
    Skimming down to Camelot:
But who hath seen her wave her hand?
Or at the casement seen her stand?
Or is she known in all the land,
    The Lady of Shalott?

Only reapers, reaping early
In among the bearded barley,
30 Hear a song that echoes cheerly
From the river winding clearly,
    Down to towered Camelot;
And by the moon the reaper weary,
Piling sheaves in uplands airy,
Listening, whispers, " 'Tis the fairy
    Lady of Shalott."

PART 2

There she weaves by night and day
A magic web with colors gay.
She has heard a whisper say,
40 A curse is on her if she stay
    To look down to Camelot.
She knows not what the curse may be,
And so she weaveth steadily,
And little other care hath she,
    The Lady of Shalott.

And moving through a mirror clear
That hangs before her all the year,
Shadows of the world appear.
There she sees the highway near
50   Winding down to Camelot;
There the river eddy whirls,
And there the surly village-churls,
And the red cloaks of market girls,
    Pass onward from Shalott.

Sometimes a troop of damsels glad,
An abbot on an ambling pad,
Sometimes a curly shepherd-lad,
Or long-haired page in crimson clad,
    Goes by to towered Camelot;
60 And sometimes through the mirror blue
The knights come riding two and two;

She hath no loyal knight and true,
    The Lady of Shalott.

But in her web she still delights
To weave the mirror's magic sights,
For often through the silent nights
A funeral, with plumes and lights
    And music, went to Camelot;
Or when the moon was overhead,
Came two young lovers lately wed;   70
"I am half sick of shadows," said
    The Lady of Shalott.

PART 3

A bow-shot from her bower eaves,
He rode between the barley sheaves;
The sun came dazzling through the leaves,
And flamed upon the brazen greaves
    Of bold Sir Lancelot.
A red-cross knight forever kneeled
To a lady in his shield,
That sparkled on the yellow field,   80
    Beside remote Shalott.

The gemmy bridle glittered free,
Like to some branch of stars we see
Hung in the golden Galaxy.
The bridle bells rang merrily
    As he rode down to Camelot;
And from his blazoned baldric slung
A mighty silver bugle hung,
And as he rode his armor rung,
    Beside remote Shalott.   90

All in the blue unclouded weather
Thick-jeweled shone the saddle-leather,
The helmet and the helmet-feather
Burned like one burning flame together
    As he rode down to Camelot;
As often through the purple night,
Below the starry clusters bright,
Some bearded meteor, trailing light,
    Moves over still Shalott.

His broad clear brow in sunlight glowed;   100
On burnished hooves his war horse trode;
From underneath his helmet flowed
His coal-black curls as on he rode,
    As he rode down to Camelot.
From the bank and from the river
He flashed into the crystal mirror,
"Tirra lirra," by the river
    Sang Sir Lancelot.

in weaving to reflect the pattern hanging behind her and the finished tapestry on the loom. **56. pad,** an easy-gaited horse. **76. greaves,** armor for the legs. **84. Galaxy,** the Milky Way. **87. baldric,** a belt worn over the shoulder to support a sword or bugle.

She left the web, she left the loom,
110 She made three paces through the room,
She saw the water lily bloom,
She saw the helmet and the plume,
    She looked down to Camelot.
Out flew the web and floated wide;
The mirror cracked from side to side;
"The curse is come upon me," cried
    The Lady of Shalott.

PART 4

In the stormy east wind straining,
The pale yellow woods were waning,
120 The broad stream in his banks complaining,
Heavily the low sky raining
    Over towered Camelot;
Down she came and found a boat
Beneath a willow left afloat,
And round about the prow she wrote
    The Lady of Shalott.

And down the river's dim expanse
Like some bold seër in a trance,
Seeing all his own mischance—
130 With a glassy countenance
    Did she look to Camelot.
And at the closing of the day
She loosed the chain, and down she lay;
The broad stream bore her far away,
    The Lady of Shalott.

Lying, robed in snowy white
That loosely flew to left and right—
The leaves upon her falling light—
Through the noises of the night
140   She floated down to Camelot;
And as the boat-head wound along
The willowy hills and fields among,
They heard her singing her last song,
    The Lady of Shalott.

Heard a carol, mournful, holy,
Chanted loudly, chanted lowly,
Till her blood was frozen slowly,
And her eyes were darkened wholly,
    Turned to towered Camelot.
150 For ere she reached upon the tide
The first house by the waterside,
Singing in her song she died,
    The Lady of Shalott.

Under tower and balcony,
By garden wall and gallery,
A gleaming shape she floated by,
Dead-pale between the houses high,
    Silent into Camelot.
Out upon the wharfs they came,
Knight and burgher, lord and dame, 160
And round the prow they read her name,
    The Lady of Shalott.

Who is this? And what is here?
And in the lighted palace near
Died the sound of royal cheer;
And they crossed themselves for fear,
    All the knights at Camelot.
But Lancelot mused a little space;
He said, "She has a lovely face;
God in his mercy lend her grace, 170
    The Lady of Shalott."

(1832; 1842)

In 1857, Edward Moxon published his famous illustrated edition of Tennyson's Poems. This illustration (by Dante Gabriel Rossetti) and those that follow were made especially for Moxon by well-known artists of the time.

THE LOTOS-EATERS

The story of the lotos-eaters Tennyson took from a brief episode in Book IX of the Odyssey, which narrates how the sailors who ate of "the lotos' boneyed fruit" wished "never to leave the place but with lotos-eaters there to stay, to feed on lotos and forget going home." The poem is obviously built on a contrast between "labor in the deep mid-ocean" and languid rest, "propped on beds of amaranth and moly", and although Ulysses calls for courage, there is nothing here of determination "to strive, to seek, to find, and not to yield." The underlying idea of the poem is the moral wrong of trying to escape human duties and responsibilities: weary though the mariners may be, they cannot subdue their own feelings of guilt.

"Courage!" he said, and pointed toward the land,
"This mounting wave will roll us shoreward soon."
In the afternoon they came unto a land
In which it seeméd always afternoon.
All round the coast the languid air did swoon,
Breathing like one that hath a weary dream.
Full-faced above the valley stood the moon;
And, like a downward smoke, the slender stream
Along the cliff to fall and pause and fall did seem.

A land of streams! some, like a downward smoke,
Slow-dropping veils of thinnest lawn, did go;
And some through wavering lights and shadows broke,
Rolling a slumbrous sheet of foam below.
They saw the gleaming river seaward flow
From the inner land; far off, three mountain-tops,
Three silent pinnacles of aged snow,
Stood sunset-flushed; and, dewed with showery drops,
Up-clomb the shadowy pine above the woven copse.

The charméd sunset lingered low adown
In the red West; through mountain clefts the dale
Was seen far inland, and the yellow down
Bordered with palm, and many a winding vale
And meadow, set with slender galingale;
A land where all things always seemed the same!
And round about the keel with faces pale,
Dark faces pale against that rosy flame,
The mild-eyed melancholy Lotos-eaters came.

Branches they bore of that enchanted stem,
Laden with flower and fruit, whereof they gave
To each, but whoso did receive of them

And taste, to him the gushing of the wave
Far far away did seem to mourn and rave
On alien shores; and if his fellow spake,
His voice was thin, as voices from the grave;
And deep-asleep he seemed, yet all awake,
And music in his ears his beating heart did make.

They sat them down upon the yellow sand
Between the sun and moon upon the shore;
And sweet it was to dream of Fatherland,
Of child, and wife, and slave; but evermore   40
Most weary seemed the sea, weary the oar,
Weary the wandering fields of barren foam.
Then someone said, "we will return no more";
And all at once they sang, "Our island home
Is far beyond the wave; we will no longer roam."

CHORIC SONG

There is sweet music here that softer falls
Than petals from blown roses on the grass,
Or night-dews on still waters between walls
Of shadowy granite, in a gleaming pass;
Music that gentlier on the spirit lies,   50
Than tired eyelids upon tired eyes;
Music that brings sweet sleep down from the blissful
    skies.
Here are cool mosses deep,
And through the moss the ivies creep,
And in the stream the long-leaved flowers weep,
And from the craggy ledge the poppy hangs in
    sleep.

Why are we weighed upon with heaviness,
And utterly consumed with sharp distress,
While all things else have rest from weariness?
All things have rest; why should we toil alone,   60
We only toil, who are the first of things,
And make perpetual moan,
Still from one sorrow to another thrown;
Nor ever fold our wings,
And cease from wanderings,
Nor steep our brows in slumber's holy balm;
Nor harken what the inner spirit sings,
"There is no joy but calm!"—
Why should we only toil, the roof and crown of
    things?

Lo! in the middle of the wood,   70
The folded leaf is wooed from out the bud
With winds upon the branch, and there
Grows green and broad, and takes no care,
Sun-steeped at noon, and in the moon
Nightly dew-fed; and turning yellow
Falls, and floats adown the air.
Lo! sweetened with the summer light,
The full-juiced apple, waxing over-mellow,

Drops in a silent autumn night.
80 All its allotted length of days
The flower ripens in its place,
Ripens and fades, and falls, and hath no toil,
Fast-rooted in the fruitful soil.

Hateful is the dark-blue sky,
Vaulted o'er the dark-blue sea.
Death is the end of life; ah, why
Should life all labor be?
Let us alone. Time driveth onward fast,
And in a little while our lips are dumb.
90 Let us alone. What is it that will last?
All things are taken from us, and become
Portions and parcels of the dreadful past.
Let us alone. What pleasure can we have
To war with evil? Is there any peace
In ever climbing up the climbing wave?
All things have rest, and ripen toward the grave
In silence—ripen, fall, and cease;
Give us long rest or death, dark death, or dreamful
    ease.

How sweet it were, hearing the downward stream
100 With half-shut eyes ever to seem
Falling asleep in a half-dream!
To dream and dream, like yonder amber light,
Which will not leave the myrrh-bush on the height;
To hear each other's whispered speech;
Eating the Lotos day by day,
To watch the crisping ripples on the beach,
And tender curving lines of creamy spray;
To lend our hearts and spirits wholly
To the influence of mild-minded melancholy;
110 To muse and brood and live again in memory,
With those old faces of our infancy
Heaped over with a mound of grass,
Two handfuls of white dust, shut in an urn of brass!

Dear is the memory of our wedded lives,
And dear the last embraces of our wives
And their warm tears; but all hath suffered change;
For surely now our household hearths are cold,
Our sons inherit us, our looks are strange,
And we should come like ghosts to trouble joy.
120 Or else the island princes over-bold
Have eat our substance, and the minstrel sings
Before them of the ten years' war in Troy,
And our great deeds, as half-forgotten things.
Is there confusion in the little isle?
Let what is broken so remain.
The gods are hard to reconcile;
'Tis hard to settle order once again.
There is confusion worse than death,

Trouble on trouble, pain on pain,
Long labor unto aged breath,   130
Sore task to hearts worn out by many wars
And eyes grown dim with gazing on the pilot-stars.

But, propped on beds of amaranth and moly,
How sweet—while warm airs lull us, blowing lowly—
With half-dropped eyelid still,
Beneath a heaven dark and holy,
To watch the long bright river drawing slowly
His waters from the purple hill—
To hear the dewy echoes calling
From cave to cave through the thick-twined vine— 140
To watch the emerald-colored water falling
Through many a woven acanthus-wreath divine!
Only to hear and see the far-off sparkling brine,
Only to hear were sweet, stretched out beneath the
    pine.

The Lotos blooms below the barren peak,
The Lotos blows by every winding creek;
All day the wind breathes low with mellower tone;
Through every hollow cave and alley lone
Round and round the spicy downs the yellow Lotos-
    dust is blown.
We have had enough of action, and of motion we, 150
Rolled to starboard, rolled to larboard, when the surge
    was seething free,
Where the wallowing monster spouted his foam-foun-
    tains in the sea.
Let us swear an oath, and keep it with an equal mind,
In the hollow Lotos-land to live and lie reclined
On the hills like gods together, careless of mankind.
For they lie beside their nectar, and the bolts are
    hurled
Far below them in the valleys, and the clouds are
    lightly curled
Round their golden houses, girdled with the gleaming
    world;
Where they smile in secret, looking over wasted lands,
Blight and famine, plague and earthquake, roaring
    deeps and fiery sands,   160
Clanging fights, and flaming towns, and sinking ships,
    and praying hands.
But they smile, they find a music centered in a dole-
    ful song
Steaming up, a lamentation and an ancient tale of
    wrong,
Like a tale of little meaning though the words are
    strong;
Chanted from an ill-used race of men that cleave the
    soil,
Sow the seed, and reap the harvest with enduring
    toil,

---

120. **island princes,** princes from other islands near Greece; these men were courting Odysseus' wife, Penelope, in his absence, and living in his palace. See *Ulysses*, p. 847. 132. **pilot-stars,** stars used as guides by sailors; they had no compass then. 133. **amaranth,** an imaginary

flower supposed never to fade. **moly,** a fabulous herb of magic power. It was given by Hermes, messenger of the gods, to Odysseus as a protection against the enchantress Circe. 142. **acanthus,** a plant sacred to the gods. 156. **bolts,** thunderbolts. 169. **Elysian . . . asphodel.**

Storing yearly little dues of wheat, and wine and oil;
Till they perish and they suffer—some, 'tis whispered
　　—down in hell
Suffer endless anguish, others in Elysian valleys dwell,
170 Resting weary limbs at last on beds of asphodel.
Surely, surely, slumber is more sweet than toil, the
　　shore
Than labor in the deep mid-ocean, wind and wave
　　and oar;
O rest ye, brother mariners, we will not wander more.
(1832; 1842)

YOU ASK ME, WHY, THOUGH ILL AT EASE

Tennyson here combines a conservative's anxiety over rapid political and social change, focused principally in the passage of the Reform Bill of 1832, with a persistent esthetic yearning after the "palms and temples of the South" and "the purple seas." It is instructive to note that Tennyson here uses the In Memoriam stanza and speaks of "spirits falter[ing] in the mist."

You ask me, why, though ill at ease,
　　Within this region I subsist,
　　Whose spirits falter in the mist,
And languish for the purple seas.

It is the land that freemen till,
　　That sober-suited Freedom chose,
　　The land where, girt with friends or foes,
A man may speak the thing he will;

A land of settled government,
10　A land of just and old renown,
　　Where Freedom slowly broadens down
From precedent to precedent;

Where faction seldom gathers head,
　　But, by degrees to fullness wrought,
　　The strength of some diffusive thought
Hath time and space to work and spread.

Should banded unions persecute
　　Opinion, and induce a time
　　When single thought is civil crime,
20 And individual freedom mute,

Though power should make from land to land
　　The name of Britain trebly great—
　　Though every channel of the State
Should fill and choke with golden sand—

Yet waft me from the harbor-mouth,
　　Wild wind! I seek a warmer sky,

Homer described the Elysian fields, the paradise of the Greeks, as being covered with asphodels, or daffodils.

And I will see before I die
The palms and temples of the South.
(c. 1833; 1842)

OF OLD SAT FREEDOM ON THE HEIGHTS

Of old sat Freedom on the heights,
　　The thunders breaking at her feet;
Above her shook the starry lights;
　　She heard the torrents meet.

There in her place she did rejoice,
　　Self-gathered in her prophet-mind,
But fragments of her mighty voice
　　Came rolling on the wind.

Then stepped she down through town and field
　　To mingle with the human race,　　　　　　10
And part by part to men revealed
　　The fullness of her face—

Grave mother of majestic works,
　　From her isle-altar gazing down,
Who, godlike, grasps the triple forks,
　　And, king-like, wears the crown.

Her open eyes desire the truth.
　　The wisdom of a thousand years
Is in them. May perpetual youth
　　Keep dry their light from tears;　　　　　20

That her fair form may stand and shine,
　　Make bright our days and light our dreams,
Turning to scorn with lips divine
　　The falsehood of extremes!
(c. 1833; 1842)

ULYSSES

Ulysses is one of Tennyson's most widely appreciated poems but it is frequently misread. The poem, it is said, "symbolizes the Victorian conception of the ideal heroic spirit" and "exalts the eternally restless aspiration." That the poem is calculated to exhilarate the multitude anyone reading the last fifteen lines can hardly doubt. But the central theme and tension of the poem lie elsewhere, and one must agree that there is in Tennyson's dramatic picture of the ancient mariner a significant portion of the peevish and the proud. The basic moral concept is taken from Canto XXVI of The Inferno, where Ulysses is condemned as an Evil Counselor, a spiritual thief. Between Ulysses as heroic and unyielding and Ulysses as tragic and condemned lies the central tension of the poem and the subtle question which it poses.

It little profits that an idle king,
By this still hearth, among these barren crags,
Matched with an aged wife, I mete and dole
Unequal laws unto a savage race,
That hoard, and sleep, and feed, and know not me.
I cannot rest from travel; I will drink
Life to the lees. All times I have enjoyed
Greatly, have suffered greatly, both with those
That loved me, and alone; on shore, and when
10 Through scudding drifts the rainy Hyades
Vexed the dim sea. I am become a name;
For always roaming with a hungry heart
Much have I seen and known—cities of men
And manners, climates, councils, governments,
Myself not least, but honored of them all—
And drunk delight of battle with my peers,
Far on the ringing plains of windy Troy.
I am a part of all that I have met;
Yet all experience is an arch wherethrough
20 Gleams that untraveled world whose margin fades
Forever and forever when I move.
How dull it is to pause, to make an end,
To rust unburnished, not to shine in use!
As though to breathe were life! Life piled on life
Were all too little, and of one to me
Little remains; but every hour is saved
From that eternal silence, something more,
A bringer of new things; and vile it were
For some three suns to store and hoard myself,
30 And this gray spirit yearning in desire
To follow knowledge like a sinking star,
Beyond the utmost bound of human thought.

   This is my son, mine own Telemachus,
To whom I leave the scepter and the isle—
Well-loved of me, discerning to fulfill
This labor, by slow prudence to make mild
A rugged people, and through soft degrees
Subdue them to the useful and the good.
Most blameless is he, centered in the sphere
40 Of common duties, decent not to fail
In offices of tenderness, and pay
Meet adoration to my household gods,
When I am gone. He works his work, I mine.

   There lies the port; the vessel puffs her sail;
There gloom the dark, broad seas. My mariners,
Souls that have toiled, and wrought, and thought
   with me—
That ever with a frolic welcome took
The thunder and the sunshine, and opposed
Free hearts, free foreheads—you and I are old;
50 Old age hath yet his honor and his toil.
Death closes all; but something ere the end,
Some work of noble note, may yet be done,

Not unbecoming men that strove with gods.
The lights begin to twinkle from the rocks;
The long day wanes; the slow moon climbs; the deep
Moans round with many voices. Come, my friends.
'Tis not too late to seek a newer world.
Push off, and sitting well in order smite
The sounding furrows; for my purpose holds
To sail beyond the sunset, and the baths   60
Of all the western stars, until I die.
It may be that the gulfs will wash us down;
It may be we shall touch the Happy Isles,
And see the great Achilles, whom we knew.
Though much is taken, much abides; and though
We are not now that strength which in old days
Moved earth and heaven, that which we are, we are—
One equal temper of heroic hearts,
Made weak by time and fate, but strong in will
To strive, to seek, to find, and not to yield.
(1842)

LOCKSLEY HALL

*"Locksley Hall," Tennyson said, "represents young
life, its good side, its deficiencies, and its yearnings."
Tennyson's statement provides an indispensable key
to a right reading of the poem: it is an expression of
the Byronic self-consciousness of a disillusioned young
idealist who, in his hurt and with the exaggerated
frenzy of youth, berates his age for its materialism, its
rationalism, its prudentialism, and its faithlessness. The
disagreeable tone of the speaker is consciously emphasized by the poet through the heavily stressed and
unfamiliar trochaic meter.*

Comrades, leave me here a little, while as yet 'tis
   early morn;
Leave me here, and when you want me, sound upon
   the bugle horn.

'Tis the place, and all around it, as of old, the
   curlews call,
Dreary gleams about the moorland flying over Locksley Hall;

Locksley Hall, that in the distance overlooks the
   sandy tracts,
And the hollow ocean-ridges roaring into cataracts.

Many a night from yonder ivied casement, ere I went
   to rest,
Did I look on great Orion sloping slowly to the west.

Many a night I saw the Pleiads, rising through the
   mellow shade,

Ulysses. 2. crags. On the bleak island of Ithaca, the home of
Ulysses. 3. aged wife, Penelope. 10. Hyades, a group of seven stars
in the constellation Taurus. They were associated with the rainy season.
27. eternal silence, a euphemism for death. 49. you, Ulysses' companions. The attitude expressed here is modern. 63. Happy Isles, the

Islands of the Blest, identified with the Elysian fields as the abode of just
men after death. 64. Achilles, the most famous of the Greek heroes in
the Trojan War. After slaying Hector and dragging his body three
times around the walls, Achilles was finally killed by Paris, wounded
with a poisoned arrow in the heel, his only vulnerable spot. The weapons

Glitter like a swarm of fireflies tangled in a silver
10   braid.

Here about the beach I wandered, nourishing a youth
  sublime
With the fairy tales of science, and the long result
  of time;

When the centuries behind me like a fruitful land
  reposed;
When I clung to all the present for the promise
  that it closed;

When I dipped into the future far as human eye
  could see,
Saw the vision of the world and all the wonder that
  would be.—

In the spring a fuller crimson comes upon the robin's
  breast;
In the spring the wanton lapwing gets himself another
  crest;

In the spring a livelier iris changes on the burnished
  dove;

By John Everett Millais.

Then her cheek was pale and thinner than should be
  for one so young,
And her eyes on all my motions with a mute observance hung

And I said, "My cousin Amy, speak and speak the
  truth to me;
Trust me, cousin, all the current of my being sets to
  thee."

On her pallid cheek and forehead came a color and
  a light,
As I have seen the rosy red flushing in the northern
  night.

And she turned—her bosom shaken with a sudden
  storm of sighs—
All the spirit deeply dawning in the dark of hazel
  eyes—

Saying, "I have hid my feelings, fearing they should
  do me wrong";
Saying, "Dost thou love me, cousin?" weeping, "I
  have loved thee long."   30

Love took up the glass of Time, and turned it in his
  glowing hands;
Every moment, lightly shaken, ran itself in golden
  sands.

Love took up the harp of Life, and smote on all the
  chords with might;
Smote the chord of Self, that, trembling, passed in
  music out of sight.

Many a morning on the moorland did we hear the
  copses ring,
And her whisper thronged my pulses with the fullness
  of the spring.

Many an evening by the waters did we watch the
  stately ships,
And our spirits rushed together at the touching of
  the lips.

O my cousin, shallow-hearted! O my Amy, mine no
  more!
O the dreary, dreary moorland! O the barren, barren
  shore!   40

Falser than all fancy fathoms, falser than all songs have sung,
Puppet to a father's threat, and servile to a shrewish tongue!

Is it well to wish thee happy?—having known me—to decline
On a range of lower feelings and a narrower heart than mine!

Yet it shall be; thou shalt lower to his level day by day,
What is fine within thee growing coarse to sympathize with clay.

As the husband is, the wife is; thou art mated with a clown,
And the grossness of his nature will have weight to drag thee down.

He will hold thee, when his passion shall have spent its novel force,
Something better than his dog, a little dearer than his
50   horse.

What is this? his eyes are heavy; think not they are glazed with wine.
Go to him, it is thy duty; kiss him, take his hand in thine.

It may be my lord is weary, that his brain is overwrought;
Soothe him with thy finer fancies, touch him with thy lighter thought.

He will answer to the purpose, easy things to understand—
Better thou wert dead before me, though I slew thee with my hand!

Better thou and I were lying, hidden from the heart's disgrace,
Rolled in one another's arms, and silent in a last embrace.

Cursèd be the social wants that sin against the strength of youth!
Cursèd be the social lies that warp us from the living
60   truth!

Cursèd be the sickly forms that err from honest Nature's rule!
Cursèd be the gold that gilds the straitened forehead of the fool!

Well—'tis well that I should bluster!—Hadst thou less unworthy proved—

Would to God—for I had loved thee more than ever wife was loved.

Am I mad, that I should cherish that which bears but bitter fruit?
I will pluck it from my bosom, though my heart be at the root.

Never—though my mortal summers to such length of years should come
As the many-wintered crow that leads the clanging rookery home.

Where is comfort? in division of the records of the mind?
Can I part her from herself, and love her, as I knew her, kind?   70

I remember one that perished; sweetly did she speak and move;
Such a one do I remember, whom to look at was to love.

Can I think of her as dead, and love her for the love she bore?
No—she never loved me truly; love is love for evermore.

Comfort? comfort scorned of devils! this is truth the poet sings,
That a sorrow's crown of sorrow is remembering happier things.

Drug thy memories, lest thou learn it, lest thy heart be put to proof,
In the dead unhappy night, and when the rain is on the roof.

Like a dog, he hunts in dreams, and thou art staring at the wall,
Where the dying night-lamp flickers, and the shadows rise and fall.   80

Then a hand shall pass before thee, pointing to his drunken sleep,
To thy widowed marriage-pillows, to the tears that thou wilt weep.

Thou shalt hear the "Never, never," whispered by the phantom years,
And a song from out the distance in the ringing of thine ears;

And an eye shall vex thee looking ancient kindness on thy pain.

41. all fancy fathoms, everything the imagination comprehends. 42. Puppet . . . tongue. Her father and mother forced her to marry another—a man of coarser nature. 68. crow, rook. 75. comfort . . . devils, as in *Paradise Lost*, I and II (pp. 387 ff.). 76. That . . . things. A favorite idea of the poets. Dante says in his *Inferno*, V, 121, "There is no greater sorrow than to remember happy times when one

Turn thee, turn thee on thy pillow; get thee to thy
rest again.

Nay, but Nature brings thee solace; for a tender
voice will cry.
'Tis a purer life than thine, a lip to drain thy trouble
dry.

Baby lips will laugh me down; my latest rival brings
thee rest.
90 Baby fingers, waxen touches, press me from the
mother's breast.

Oh, the child too clothes the father with a dearness
not his due.
Half is thine and half is his; it will be worthy of the
two.

Oh, I see thee old and formal, fitted to thy petty part,
With a little hoard of maxims preaching down a
daughter's heart.

"They were dangerous guides, the feelings—she herself was not exempt—
Truly, she herself had suffered"—Perish in thy self-
contempt!

Overlive it—lower yet—be happy! wherefore should
I care?

By John Everett Millais.

is in misery." 79. he, Amy's husband, a fox-hunting squire. 104.
winds are laid. It was an old belief that the discharge of cannon during
a battle stilled the winds.

I myself must mix with action, lest I wither by despair.

What is that which I should turn to, lighting upon
days like these?
Every door is barred with gold, and opens but to
golden keys.   100

Every gate is thronged with suitors, all the markets
overflow.
I have but an angry fancy; what is that which I should
do?

I had been content to perish, falling on the foeman's
ground,
When the ranks are rolled in vapor, and the winds
are laid with sound.

But the jingling of the guinea helps the hurt that
Honor feels,
And the nations do but murmur, snarling at each
other's heels.

Can I but relive in sadness? I will turn that earlier
page.
Hide me from my deep emotion, O thou wondrous
Mother-Age!

Make me feel the wild pulsation that I felt before the
strife,
When I heard my days before me, and the tumult
of my life;   110

Yearning for the large excitement that the coming
years would yield,
Eager-hearted as a boy when first he leaves his father's
field,

And at night along the dusky highway near and
nearer drawn,
Sees in heaven the light of London flaring like a
dreary dawn;

And his spirit leaps within him to be gone before
him then,
Underneath the light he looks at, in among the
throngs of men;

Men, my brothers, men the workers, ever reaping
something new;
That which they have done but earnest of the things
that they shall do.

For I dipped into the future, far as human eye
could see,
Saw the Vision of the world, and all the wonder
that would be;   120

Saw the heavens fill with commerce, argosies of magic sails,
Pilots of the purple twilight, dropping down with costly bales;

Heard the heavens fill with shouting, and there rained a ghastly dew
From the nations' airy navies grappling in the central blue;

Far along the world-wide whisper of the south wind rushing warm,
With the standards of the peoples plunging through the thunder-storm;

Till the war drum throbbed no longer, and the battle-flags were furled
In the Parliament of man, the Federation of the world.

There the common sense of most shall hold a fretful realm in awe,
130 And the kindly earth shall slumber, lapped in universal law.

So I triumphed ere my passion sweeping through me left me dry,
Left me with the palsied heart, and left me with the jaundiced eye;

Eye, to which all order festers, all things here are out of joint.
Science moves, but slowly, slowly, creeping on from point to point;

Slowly comes a hungry people, as a lion, creeping nigher,
Glares at one that nods and winks behind a slowly dying fire.

Yet I doubt not through the ages one increasing purpose runs,
And the thoughts of men are widened with the process of the suns.

What is that to him that reaps not harvest of his youthful joys,
140 Though the deep heart of existence beat forever like a boy's?

Knowledge comes, but wisdom lingers, and I linger on the shore,
And the individual withers, and the world is more and more.

Knowledge comes, but wisdom lingers, and he bears a laden breast,
Full of sad experience, moving toward the stillness of his rest.

Hark, my merry comrades call me, sounding on the bugle horn,
They to whom my foolish passion were a target for their scorn.

Shall it not be scorn to me to harp on such a moldered string?
I am shamed through all my nature to have loved so slight a thing.

Weakness to be wroth with weakness! woman's pleasure, woman's pain—
Nature made them blinder motions bounded in a shallower brain.
150

Woman is the lesser man, and all thy passions, matched with mine,
Are as moonlight unto sunlight, and as water unto wine—

Here at least, where nature sickens, nothing. Ah, for some retreat
Deep in yonder shining Orient, where my life began to beat,

Where in wild Mahratta-battle fell my father evil-starred—
I was left a trampled orphan, and a selfish uncle's ward.

Or to burst all links of habit—there to wander far away,
On from island unto island at the gateways of the day—

Larger constellations burning, mellow moons and happy skies,
Breadths of tropic shade and palms in cluster, knots of Paradise;
160

Never comes the trader, never floats an European flag,
Slides the bird o'er lustrous woodland, swings the trailer from the crag;

Droops the heavy-blossomed bower, hangs the heavy-fruited tree—
Summer isles of Eden lying in dark-purple spheres of sea.

132. jaundiced, prejudiced. 135. a hungry people. An allusion to the "dangerous" advance of democracy felt in the discontent preceding the revolutions in Europe in 1848—in France, in Germany, in Italy, in Austria-Hungary, and in Ireland. 138. process of the suns, the passing of the years. 141. Knowledge . . . more, new facts of life crowd in upon us, but fundamental truths are constant; science and evolution show us that the mass of humanity is more important than the individual. Cf. In Memoriam, ll. 1015-1016, p. 876. 150. motions, impulses. 155. fell my father. The hero is represented as having been born in India, the son of a British soldier who fell in battle against the Mahrattas, a people living in central and western India. 162. trailer, a trailing vine. 180. Joshua's moon in Ajalon. From Joshua 10:12—

There methinks would be enjoyment more than in this
    march of mind,
In the steamship, in the railway, in the thoughts that
    shake mankind.

There the passions cramped no longer shall have
    scope and breathing space;
I will take some savage woman, she shall rear my
    dusky race.

Iron-jointed, supple-sinewed, they shall dive, and
    they shall run,
Catch the wild goat by the hair, and hurl their lances
170   in the sun;

Whistle back the parrot's call, and leap the rainbows
    of the brooks,
Not with blinded eyesight poring over miserable
    books—

Fool, again the dream, the fancy! but I *know* my
    words are wild,
But I count the gray barbarian lower than the Christian
    child.

I, to herd with narrow foreheads, vacant of our
    glorious gains,
Like a beast with lower pleasures, like a beast with
    lower pains!

Mated with a squalid savage—what to me were sun
    or clime?
I the heir of all the ages, in the foremost files of time—

I that rather held it better men should perish one by
    one,
Than that earth should stand at gaze like Joshua's
180   moon in Ajalon!

Not in vain the distance beacons. Forward, forward
    let us range,
Let the great worlds spin forever down the ringing
    grooves of change.

Through the shadow of the globe we sweep into the
    younger day;
Better fifty years of Europe than a cycle of Cathay.

Mother-Age—for mine I knew not—help me as when
    life begun;
Rift the hills, and roll the waters, flash the lightnings,
    weigh the sun.

Oh, I see the crescent promise of my spirit hath not
    set.
Ancient founts of inspiration well through all my
    fancy yet.

Howsoever these things be, a long farewell to Locks-
    ley Hall!
Now for me the woods may wither, now for me the
    roof-tree fall.   190

Comes a vapor from the margin, blackening over heath
    and holt,
Cramming all the blast before it, in its breast a
    thunderbolt.

Let it fall on Locksley Hall, with rain or hail, or fire or
    snow;
For the mighty wind arises, roaring seaward, and I go.
(1842)

LOCKSLEY HALL SIXTY YEARS AFTER

This is a companion poem to the earlier Locksley
Hall. *The "sixty years after" reinforce the imaginary
character of the speaker, since they refer to his age,
not to the lapse of time between the two poems. Again,
the language and sentiments must be associated with
those of a disillusioned old man, not with the poet
himself.*

Late, my grandson! half the morning have I paced
    these sandy tracts,
Watched again the hollow ridges roaring into cata-
    racts,

Wandered back to living boyhood while I heard the
    curlews call,
I myself so close on death, and death itself in Locksley
    Hall.

So—your happy suit was blasted—she the faultless, the
    divine;
And you liken—boyish babble—this boy-love of yours
    with mine.

I myself have often babbled doubtless of a foolish
    past;
Babble, babble; our old England may go down in
    babble at last.

"Curse him!" curse your fellow-victim? call him dotard
    in your rage?
Eyes that lured a doting boyhood well might fool a
    dotard's age.   10

Jilted for a wealthier! wealthier? yet perhaps she was
    not wise;

13: "Then spake Joshua . . . in the sight of Israel, Sun, stand thou
still upon Gibeon; and thou, Moon, in the valley of Ajalon. And the
sun stood still, and the moon stayed, until the people had avenged
themselves upon their enemies." 181. **beacons,** lights a signal for
advance. 182. **grooves.** When Tennyson first rode on a railroad train
in 1830, he thought that the wheels ran in a groove. He states that he

composed this line at that time (*Memoir,* I, 195). 184. **a cycle of
Cathay,** a very long period spent in China. This is an illustration of
Tennyson's worship of Western culture. 186. **Rift the hills, etc.** This
line probably refers to Francis Baily's experiments (1838–1842) for
determining the mean density of the earth and the weight of the sun.
190. **for me,** as far as I am concerned.

I remember how you kissed the miniature with those sweet eyes.

In the hall there hangs a painting—Amy's arms about my neck—
Happy children in a sunbeam sitting on the ribs of wreck.

In my life there was a picture, she that clasped my neck had flown;
I was left within the shadow sitting on the wreck alone.

Yours has been a slighter ailment; will you sicken for her sake?
You, not you! your modern amorist is of easier, earthlier make.

Amy loved me, Amy failed me, Amy was a timid child;
But your Judith—but your wordling—*she* had never driven me wild.

She that holds the diamond necklace dearer than the golden ring,
She that finds a winter sunset fairer than a morn of spring.

She that in her heart is brooding on his briefer lease of life,
While she vows "till death shall part us," she, the would-be-widow wife.

She the wordling born of worldlings—father, mother —be content,
Even the homely farm can teach us there is something in descent.

Yonder in that chapel, slowly sinking now into the ground,
Lies the warrior, my forefather, with his feet upon the hound.

Crossed! for once he sailed the sea to crush the Moslem in his pride;
Dead the warrior, dead his glory, dead the cause in which he died.

Yet how often I and Amy in the moldering aisle have stood,
Gazing for one pensive moment on that founder of our blood.

There again I stood today, and where of old we knelt in prayer,

Close beneath the casement crimson with the shield of Locksley—there,

All in white Italian marble, looking still as if she smiled,
Lies my Amy dead in childbirth, dead the mother, dead the child.

Dead—and sixty years ago, and dead her aged husband now—
I, this old white-headed dreamer, stooped and kissed her marble brow.

Gone the fires of youth, the follies, furies, curses, passionate tears,
Gone like fires and floods and earthquakes of the planet's dawning years—

Fires that shook me once, but now to silent ashes fallen away.
Cold upon the dead volcano sleeps the gleam of dying day.

Gone the tyrant of my youth, and mute below the chancel stones,
All his virtues—I forgive them—black in white above his bones.

Gone the comrades of my bivouac, some in fight against the foe,
Some through age and slow diseases, gone as all on earth will go.

Gone with whom for forty years my life in golden sequence ran,
She with all the charm of woman, she with all the breadth of man,

Strong in will and rich in wisdom, Edith, yet so lowly-sweet,
Woman to her inmost heart, and woman to her tender feet,

Very woman of very woman, nurse of ailing body and mind,
She that linked again the broken chain that bound me to my kind.

Here today was Amy with me, while I wandered down the coast,
Near us Edith's holy shadow, smiling at the slighter ghost.

Gone our sailor son thy father, Leonard early lost at sea;

Locksley Hall Sixty Years After. 29. **Crossed**, with his feet crossed to indicate that he had been a crusader against the Turk, or Moslem. 79. **flay Captives.** The Assyrian kings were noted for their cruelty to captives. 82. **Timur**, Tamerlane, the famous Mongolian conqueror, notorious for his atrocities. In 1398 he sacked Delhi, India, and is said to have put to death 100,000 prisoners. 83. **here . . .**

flames. A reference to the religious persecutions in England perpetrated by the sovereigns immediately following Henry VIII. Edward VI was crowned in 1547. 85. **Love . . . great.** A reference to Christ's saying, "But I say unto you, Love your enemies, bless them that curse you, do good to them that hate you, and pray for them that despitefully use you, and persecute you."—Matthew 5:44. 88. **Rome of Caesar.** Dur-

Thou alone, my boy, of Amy's kin and mine art left to me.

Gone thy tender-natured mother, wearying to be left alone,
Pining for the stronger heart that once had beat beside her own.

Truth, for truth is truth, he worshiped, being true as he was brave;
60   Good, for good is good, he followed, yet he looked beyond the grave,

Wiser there than you, that crowning barren Death as lord of all,
Deem this over-tragic drama's closing curtain is the pall!

Beautiful was death in him, who saw the death, but kept the deck,
Saving women and their babes, and sinking with the sinking wreck,

Gone forever! Ever? No—for since our dying race began,
Ever, ever, and forever was the leading light of man.

Those that in barbarian burials killed the slave, and slew the wife,
Felt within themselves the sacred passion of the second life.

Indian warriors dream of ampler hunting grounds beyond the night;
70   Even the black Australian dying hopes he shall return, a white.

Truth for truth, and good for good! The good, the true, the pure, the just—
Take the charm "Forever" from them, and they crumble into dust.

Gone the cry of "Forward, forward," lost within a growing gloom;
Lost, or only heard in silence from the silence of a tomb.

Half the marvels of my morning, triumphs over time and space,
Staled by frequence, shrunk by usage into commonest commonplace!

"Forward" rang the voices then, and of the many mine was one.

Let us hush this cry of "Forward" till ten thousand years have gone.

Far among the vanished races, old Assyrian kings would flay
Captives whom they caught in battle—iron-hearted victors they.   80

Ages after, while in Asia, he that led the wild Moguls,
Timur built his ghastly tower of eighty thousand human skulls;

Then, and here in Edward's time, an age of noblest English names,
Christian conquerors took and flung the conquered Christian into flames.

Love your enemy, bless your haters, said the Greatest of the great;
Christian love among the Churches looked the twin of heathen hate.

From the golden alms of Blessing man had coined himself a curse:
Rome of Caesar, Rome of Peter, which was crueler? which was worse?

France had shown a light to all men, preached a Gospel, all men's good;
Celtic Demos rose a Demon, shrieked and slaked the light with blood.   90

Hope was ever on her mountain, watching till the day begun—
Crowned with sunlight—over darkness—from the still unrisen sun.

Have we grown at last beyond the passions of the primal clan?
"Kill your enemy, for you hate him," still, "your enemy" was a man.

Have we sunk below them? Peasants maim the helpless horse, and drive
Innocent cattle under thatch, and burn the kindlier brutes alive.

Brutes, the brutes are not your wrongers—burned at midnight, found at morn,
Twisted hard in mortal agony with their offspring, born-unborn,

Clinging to the silent mother! Are we devils? are we men?

ing the first century Rome, especially under Nero, persecuted and killed great numbers of Christians. **Rome of Peter,** the see of St. Peter, at Rome. Religious persecutions were common among all medieval peoples. Tennyson, the Protestant, here refers to the treatment of heretics by Roman Catholics. 89. **France . . . blood.** During the French Revolution and the Reign of Terror, 1793–1794, hundreds were sent to the guillotine. The doctrine of the Revolution was "Liberty, Equality, Fraternity." 90. **Demos,** a Greek word meaning people. 95. **Peasants . . . alive.** A reference to incidents of the agricultural disturbances of the time.

Sweet Saint Francis of Assisi, would that he were here
100   again,

He that in his Catholic wholeness used to call the
   very flowers
Sisters, brothers—and the beast—whose pains are
   hardly less than ours!

Chaos, Cosmos! Cosmos, Chaos! who can tell how all
   will end?
Read the wide world's annals, you, and take their
   wisdom for your friend.

Hope the best, but hold the Present fatal daughter of
   the Past,
Shape your heart to front the hour, but dream not
   that the hour will last.

Aye, if dynamite and revolver leave you courage to be
   wise—
When was age so crammed with menace? madness?
   written, spoken lies?

Envy wears the mask of Love, and, laughing sober fact
   to scorn,
Cries to weakest as to strongest, "Ye are equals, equal-
110   born."

Equal-born? Oh, yes, if yonder hill be level with the
   flat.
Charm us, orator, till the lion look no larger than
   the cat,

Till the cat through that mirage of overheated language loom
Larger than the lion—Demos end in working its own
   doom.

Russia bursts our Indian barrier; shall we fight her?
   shall we yield?
Pause! before you sound the trumpet, hear the voices
   from the field.

Those three hundred millions under one Imperial
   scepter now,
Shall we hold them? shall we loose them? take the
   suffrage of the plow.

Nay, but these would feel and follow Truth if only
   you and you,
Rivals of realm-ruining party, when you speak were
120   wholly true.

Plowmen, shepherds, have I found, and more than
   once, and still could find,

Sons of God, and kings of men in utter nobleness
   of mind,

Truthful, trustful, looking upward to the practiced
   hustings-liar;
So the higher wields the lower, while the lower is the
   higher.

Here and there a cotter's babe is royal-born by right
   divine;
Here and there my lord is lower than his oxen or
   his swine.

Chaos, Cosmos! Cosmos, Chaos! once again the sickening game;
Freedom, free to slay herself, and dying while they
   shout her name.

Step by step we gained a freedom known to Europe,
   known to all;
Step by step we rose to greatness—through the tongue-
   sters we may fall.   130

You that woo the Voices—tell them "old experience
   is a fool,"
Teach your flattered kings that only those who cannot
   read can rule.

Pluck the mighty from their seat, but set no meek
   ones in their place;
Pillory Wisdom in your markets, pelt your offal at
   her face.

Tumble Nature heel o'er head, and, yelling with the
   yelling street,
Set the feet above the brain and swear the brain is in
   the feet.

Bring the old dark ages back without the faith, without the hope,
Break the State, the Church, the Throne, and roll their
   ruins down the slope.

Authors—essayist, atheist, novelist, realist, rimester,
   play your part,
Paint the mortal shame of nature with the living
   hues of art.   140

Rip your brothers' vices open, strip your own foul
   passions bare;
Down with Reticence, down with Reverence—forward
   —naked—let them stare.

Feed the budding rose of boyhood with the drainage
   of your sewer;

---

100. **Saint Francis,** an Italian friar (1182–1226) noted for his gentleness and nobility of character. 103. **Chaos, Cosmos.** Tennyson refers
to the conflict between those who see no meaning in life and those
who see an ordered purpose in it. 115. **Russia . . . yield.** A reference
to Russia's persistent efforts during the nineteenth century to gain con-

trol of Afghanistan, the "Indian barrier." In 1877–1378 Russia sent an
expedition through the Balkans to Constantinople, and England promptly
sent a fleet in opposition. 116. **voices . . . field,** the votes of the
laboring classes. 123. **hustings,** the platform from which the candidates
for Parliament addressed the voters. 131. **the Voices,** the approval of

Send the drain into the fountain, lest the stream
    should issue pure.

Set the maiden fancies wallowing in the troughs of
    Zolaism—
Forward, forward, aye, and backward, downward too
    into the abysm!

Do your best to charm the worst, to lower the rising
    race of men;
Have we risen from out the beast, then back into
    the beast again?

Only "dust to dust" for me that sicken at your
    lawless din,
150 Dust in wholesome old-world dust before the newer
    world begin.

Heated am I? you—you wonder—well, it scarce be-
    comes mine age—
Patience! let the dying actor mouth his last upon
    the stage.

Cries of unprogressive dotage ere the dotard fall
    asleep?
Noises of a current narrowing, not the music of a
    deep?

Aye, for doubtless I am old, and think gray thoughts,
    for I am gray;
After all the stormy changes shall we find a change-
    less May?

After madness, after massacre, Jacobinism and Jac-
    querie,
Some diviner force to guide us through the days I
    shall not see?

When the schemes and all the systems, kingdoms
    and republics fall,
Something kindlier, higher, holier—all for each and
160   each for all?

All the full-brain, half-brain races, led by Justice,
    Love, and Truth;
All the millions one at length with all the visions of
    my youth?

All diseases quenched by Science, no man halt, or
    deaf, or blind;
Stronger ever born of weaker, lustier body, larger
    mind?

Earth at last a warless world, a single race, a single
    tongue—

I have seen her far away—for is not Earth as yet
    so young?—

Every tiger madness muzzled, every serpent passion
    killed,
Every grim ravine a garden, every blazing desert tilled,

Robed in universal harvest up to either pole she
    smiles,
Universal ocean softly washing all her warless isles. 170

Warless? when her tens are thousands, and her thou-
    sands millions, then—
All her harvest all too narrow—who can fancy warless
    men?

Warless? war will die out late then. Will it ever? late
    or soon?
Can it, till this outworn earth be dead as yon dead
    world the moon?

Dead the new astronomy calls her.—On this day and
    at this hour,
In this gap between the sand hills, whence you see
    the Locksley tower,

Here we met, our latest meeting—Amy—sixty years
    ago—
She and I—the moon was falling greenish through a
    rosy glow,

Just above the gateway tower, and even where you
    see her now—
Here we stood and clasped each other, swore the
    seeming-deathless vow.—   180

Dead, but how her living glory lights the hall, the
    dune, the grass!
Yet the moonlight is the sunlight, and the sun him-
    self will pass.

Venus near her! smiling downward at this earthlier
    earth of ours,
Closer on the sun, perhaps a world of never fading
    flowers.

Hesper, whom the poet called the bringer home of
    all good things—
All good things may move in Hesper, perfect peoples,
    perfect kings.

Hesper—Venus—were we native to that splendor or
    in Mars,

the masses. 139 ff. These lines show Tennyson's dislike of the realistic novels of the period. Emile Zola (l. 145) was a contemporary French realist. 157. Jacobinism, mad opposition to regular government. The Jacobins were a society of violent radicals in France during the Revolution of 1789. Jacquerie, the French peasant revolt of 1358. 182. sun

. . . pass. It is believed that the sun is slowly diminishing. 185. Hesper, Venus, the evening star. the poet, Sappho, a Greek lyric poetess (fl. 600 B.C.) The Greek passage is paraphrased by Byron in Don Juan, 3, 107.

Alfred, Lord Tennyson 857

We should see the globe we groan in, fairest of their
　　evening stars.

Could we dream of wars and carnage, craft and mad-
　　ness, lust and spite,
Roaring London, raving Paris, in that point of peaceful
190　　light?

Might we not in glancing heavenward on a star so
　　silver-fair,
Yearn, and clasp the hands and murmur, "Would to
　　God that we were there"?

Forward, backward, backward, forward, in the im-
　　measurable sea,
Swayed by vaster ebbs and flows than can be known
　　to you or me.

All the suns—are these but symbols of innumerable
　　man,
Man or Mind that sees a shadow of the planner or
　　the plan?

Is there evil but on earth? or pain in every peopled
　　sphere?
Well, be grateful for the sounding watchword "Evo-
　　lution" here,

Evolution ever climbing after some ideal good,
200 And Reversion ever dragging Evolution in the mud.

What are men that He should heed us? cried the king
　　of sacred song;
Insects of an hour, that hourly work their brother
　　insect wrong,

While the silent heavens roll, and suns along their
　　fiery way,
All their planets whirling round them, flash a million
　　miles a day.

Many an aeon molded earth before her highest, man,
　　was born,
Many an aeon too may pass when earth is manless
　　and forlorn,

Earth so huge, and yet so bounded—pools of salt,
　　and plots of land—
Shallow skin of green and azure—chains of mountain,
　　grains of sand!

Only That which made us meant us to be mightier
　　by and by,
Set the sphere of all the boundless heavens within
210　　the human eye,

Sent the shadow of Himself, the boundless, through
　　the human soul;
Boundless inward in the atom, boundless outward
　　in the Whole. . . .

Here is Locksley Hall, my grandson, here the lion-
　　guarded gate.
Not tonight in Locksley Hall—tomorrow—you, you
　　come so late.

Wrecked—your train—or all but wrecked? a shattered
　　wheel? a vicious boy!
Good, this forward, you that preach it, is it well to
　　wish you joy?

Is it well that while we range with Science, glorying
　　in the Time,
City children soak and blacken soul and sense in
　　city slime?

There among the glooming alleys Progress halts on
　　palsied feet,
Crime and hunger cast our maidens by the thousand
　　on the street.　　　　　　　　　　　　　　　　220

There the master scrimps his haggard sempstress of
　　her daily bread,
There a single sordid attic holds the living and the
　　dead.

There the smoldering fire of fever creeps across the
　　rotted floor,
And the crowded couch of incest in the warrens of the
　　poor.

Nay, your pardon, cry your "Forward," yours are
　　hope and youth, but I—
Eighty winters leave the dog too lame to follow with
　　the cry,

Lame and old, and past his time, and passing now into
　　the night;
Yet I would the rising race were half as eager for the
　　light.

Light the fading gleam of even? light the glimmer of
　　the dawn?
Aged eyes may take the growing glimmer for the
　　gleam withdrawn.　　　　　　　　　　　　　230

Far away beyond her myriad coming changes earth
　　will be
Something other than the wildest modern guess of
　　you and me.

Earth may reach her earthly worst, or if she gain her
　　earthly best,

201. **What . . . us,** from Psalms 8:4: "What is man, that thou art
mindful of him?" **king . . . song,** David. 224. **in . . . poor.** A
reference to the crowded conditions of poor families. A warren is a
protected piece of ground for the breeding of rabbits. 238. **the master,**

Would she find her human offspring this ideal man at rest?

Forward then, but still remember how the course of Time will swerve,
Crook and turn upon itself in many a backward streaming curve.

Not the Hall tonight, my grandson! Death and Silence hold their own.
Leave the master in the first dark hour of his last sleep alone.

Worthier soul was he than I am, sound and honest, rustic squire,
240 Kindly landlord, boon companion—youthful jealousy is a liar.

Cast the poison from your bosom, oust the madness from your brain.
Let the trampled serpent show you that you have not lived in vain.

Youthful! youth and age are scholars yet but in the lower school,
Nor is he the wisest man who never proved himself a fool.

Yonder lies our young sea-village—Art and Grace are less and less;
Science grows and Beauty dwindles—roofs of slated hideousness!

There is one old hostel left us where they swing the Locksley shield,
Till the peasant cow shall butt the "lion passant" from his field.

Poor old Heraldry, poor old History, poor old Poetry, passing hence,
250 In the common deluge drowning old political common sense!

Poor old voice of eighty crying after voices that have fled!
All I loved are vanished voices, all my steps are on the dead.

All the world is ghost to me, and as the phantom disappears,
Forward far and far from here is all the hope of eighty years. . . .

In this hostel—I remember—I repent it o'er his grave—

Like a clown—by chance he met me—I refused the hand he gave.

From that casement where the trailer mantles all the moldering bricks—
I was then in early boyhood, Edith but a child of six—

While I sheltered in this archway from a day of driving showers—
Peeped the winsome face of Edith like a flower among the flowers.   260

Here tonight! the Hall tomorrow, when they toll the chapel bell!
Shall I hear in one dark room a wailing, "I have loved thee well"?

Then a peal that shakes the portal—one has come to claim his bride,
Her that shrank, and put me from her, shrieked, and started from my side—

Silent echoes! You, my Leonard, use and not abuse your day,
Move among your people, know them, follow him who led the way,

Strove for sixty widowed years to help his homelier brother men,
Served the poor, and built the cottage, raised the school, and drained the fen.

Hears he now the voice that wronged him? who shall swear it cannot be?
Earth would never touch her worst, were one in fifty such as he.   270

Ere she gain her heavenly best, a god must mingle with the game.
Nay, there may be those about us whom we neither see nor name,

Felt within us as ourselves, the Powers of Good, the Powers of Ill,
Strowing balm, or shedding poison in the fountains of the will.

Follow you the star that lights a desert pathway, yours or mine.
Forward, till you see the Highest Human Nature is divine.

Follow Light, and do the Right—for man can half-control his doom—

Amy's husband, the dead master of Locksley Hall. See l. 37. 248. "lion passant," lion walking, a term in heraldry describing the figure of a lion on a shield. 266. him, the dead master of Locksley Hall. See l. 238.

Alfred, Lord Tennyson   859

Till you find the deathless Angel seated in the vacant
tomb.

Forward, let the stormy moment fly and mingle with
the past.
I that loathed have come to love him. Love will
280　conquer at the last.

Gone at eighty, mine own age, and I and you will
bear the pall;
Then I leave thee lord and master, latest lord of
Locksley Hall.

(1886)

BREAK, BREAK, BREAK

*This is one of the poems inspired by the death
of Tennyson's intimate friend, Arthur Hallam.*

Break, break, break,
　On thy cold gray stones, O Sea!
And I would that my tongue could utter
　The thoughts that arise in me.

O well for the fisherman's boy,
　That he shouts with his sister at play!
O well for the sailor lad,
　That he sings in his boat on the bay!

And the stately ships go on
10　To their haven under the hill;
But O for the touch of a vanished hand,
　And the sound of a voice that is still!

Break, break, break,
　At the foot of thy crags, O Sea!
But the tender grace of a day that is dead
　Will never come back to me.

(1842)

from THE PRINCESS

*It was Tennyson's belief that normal human affec-
tions should not be repressed by social patterns.
The Princess, a semi-burlesque narrative poem, recounts the failure of a princess to carry out her plan
of establishing a college for women alone. A young
prince gains admission to the college, disguised as a
girl, but is discovered, and finds himself ultimately
fighting in battle against warriors who have come to
the aid of the princess. He is defeated, but his
very defeat brings him victory because the sympathy of*
*the princess for the wounded hero leads to her falling
in love with him and marrying him. The symbol of the
triumph of natural affections over artificial ideas is a
child whom the princess loves and fondles even when
she seems most adamant in carrying on her plans for
the college. The songs in the poem suggest the moods
of the action. Some of these were inserted in the
second edition of 1850. They are among the finest of
Tennyson's lyrics, and some have been set to music.*

SWEET AND LOW

Sweet and low, sweet and low,
　Wind of the western sea,
Low, low, breathe and blow,
　Wind of the western sea!
Over the rolling waters go,
Come from the dying moon, and blow,
　Blow him again to me;
While my little one, while my pretty one, sleeps.

Sleep and rest, sleep and rest,
　Father will come to thee soon;　　　　　　　　10
Rest, rest, on mother's breast,
　Father will come to thee soon;
Father will come to his babe in the nest,
Silver sails all out of the west
　Under the silver moon;
Sleep, my little one, sleep, my pretty one,
　sleep.

THE SPLENDOR FALLS ON CASTLE WALLS

The splendor falls on castle walls
　And snowy summits old in story;
The long light shakes across the lakes,
　And the wild cataract leaps in glory.
Blow, bugle, blow, set the wild echoes flying,
Blow, bugle; answer, echoes, dying, dying, dying.

O hark, O hear! how thin and clear,
　And thinner, clearer, farther going!
O sweet and far from cliff and scar
　The horns of Elfland faintly blowing!　　　　10
Blow, let us hear the purple glens replying,
Blow, bugle; answer, echoes, dying, dying, dying.

O love, they die in yon rich sky,
　They faint on hill or field or river;
Our echoes roll from soul to soul,
　And grow forever and forever.
Blow, bugle, blow, set the wild echoes flying,
And answer, echoes, answer, dying, dying,
　dying.

---

278. **deathless . . . tomb.** An allusion to the angel seated at the tomb
of the risen Christ. See Matthew, Chapter 28.
Break, Break, Break. 11. **vanished hand,** Hallam's.

Now Sleeps the Crimson Petal. 7. **Now . . . stars.** The earth is
compared to Danaë, the princess whom Zeus, in the form of a shower
of gold, visited in a brass tower in which her father had imprisoned her.

TEARS, IDLE TEARS

Tears, idle tears, I know not what they mean;
Tears from the depth of some divine despair
Rise in the heart, and gather to the eyes,
In looking on the happy autumn fields,
And thinking of the days that are no more.

Fresh as the first beam glittering on a sail,
That brings our friends up from the underworld,
Sad as the last which reddens over one
That sinks with all we love below the verge;
10 So sad, so fresh, the days that are no more.

Ah, sad and strange as in dark summer dawns
The earliest pipe of half-awakened birds
To dying ears, when unto dying eyes
The casement slowly grows a glimmering square;
So sad, so strange, the days that are no more.

Dear as remembered kisses after death,
And sweet as those by hopeless fancy feigned
On lips that are for others; deep as love,
Deep as first love, and wild with all regret;
O Death in Life, the days that are no more!

HOME THEY BROUGHT HER WARRIOR DEAD

Home they brought her warrior dead,
    She nor swooned nor uttered cry.
All her maidens, watching, said,
    "She must weep or she will die."

Then they praised him, soft and low,
    Called him worthy to be loved,
Truest friend and noblest foe;
    Yet she neither spoke nor moved.

Stole a maiden from her place,
10 Lightly to the warrior stepped,
Took the face-cloth from the face;
    Yet she neither moved nor wept.

Rose a nurse of ninety years,
    Set his child upon her knee—
Like summer tempest came her tears—
    "Sweet my child, I live for thee."

ASK ME NO MORE

Ask me no more—the moon may draw the sea;
    The cloud may stoop from heaven and take the
        shape,
    With fold to fold, of mountain or of cape;

But O too fond, when have I answered thee?
        Ask me no more.

Ask me no more—what answer should I give?
    I love not hollow cheek or faded eye;
    Yet, O my friend, I will not have thee die!
Ask me no more, lest I should bid thee live;
        Ask me no more.   10

Ask me no more—thy fate and mine are sealed;
    I strove against the stream and all in vain;
    Let the great river take me to the main.
No more, dear love, for at a touch I yield;
        Ask me no more.

NOW SLEEPS THE CRIMSON PETAL

Now sleeps the crimson petal, now the white;
    Nor waves the cypress in the palace walk;
    Nor winks the gold fin in the porphyry font.
The firefly wakens; waken thou with me.

Now droops the milk-white peacock like a ghost,
And like a ghost she glimmers on to me.

Now lies the Earth all Danaë to the stars,
And all thy heart lies open unto me.

Now slides the silent meteor on, and leaves
A shining furrow, as thy thoughts in me.   10

Now folds the lily all her sweetness up,
And slips into the bosom of the lake.
So fold thyself, my dearest, thou, and slip
Into my bosom and be lost in me.

COME DOWN, O MAID

Come down, O maid, from yonder mountain height.
What pleasure lives in height (the shepherd sang),
In height and cold, the splendor of the hills?
But cease to move so near the heavens, and cease
To glide a sunbeam by the blasted pine.
To sit a star upon the sparkling spire;
And come, for Love is of the valley, come,
For Love is of the valley, come thou down
And find him; by the happy threshold, he,
Or hand in hand with Plenty in the maize,   10
Or red with spirted purple of the vats,
Or foxlike in the vine, nor cares to walk
With Death and Morning on the Silver Horns,
Nor wilt thou snare him in the white ravine,
Nor find him dropped upon the firths of ice;
That huddling slant in furrow-cloven falls

Come Down, O Maid. 12. **foxlike in the vine.** Cf. The Song of Solomon, 2:15: "Take us the foxes, the little foxes, that spoil the vines: for our vines have tender grapes." 13. **Silver Horns,** peaks of the mountains. The Silverhorn is a spur of the Jungfrau, in the Alps. 15. **firths of ice,** glaciers. 16. **furrow-cloven,** split by crevasses.

To roll the torrent out of dusky doors.
But follow; let the torrent dance thee down
To find him in the valley; let the wild
20 Lean-headed eagles yelp alone, and leave
The monstrous ledges there to slope, and spill
Their thousand wreaths of dangling water-smoke,
That like a broken purpose waste in air.
So waste not thou, but come; for all the vales
Await thee; azure pillars of the hearth
Arise to thee; the children call, and I,
Thy shepherd, pipe, and sweet is every sound,
Sweeter thy voice, but every sound is sweet;
Myriads of rivulets hurrying through the lawn,
30 The moan of doves in immemorial elms,
And murmuring of innumerable bees.
(1850)

IN MEMORIAM A. H. H.

In Memoriam is the watershed poem in the Tennyson
canon and one of the hallmarks of Victorianism. In it,
Tennyson renders a climactic statement on perhaps the
major question posited by his poetry from the late
twenties: namely, what are the foundations for hope—
other than legislative and dogmatic hope—in a world in
which "all things will die"? In it, further, Tennyson
not only reviews in a searching way representative
ideas and arguments but also relates those ideas and
arguments to personality.

It is difficult for the modern student to read In
Memoriam aright and to assign it a just value. In the
first place, the student tends to evaluate the poem according to its commentary on certain general ideas—the
tangled web of good and evil, evolutionary conclusions,
the seeming insignificance of the individual on a comparatively insignificant planet, the insufficiency of human reason, the token of material advance and its final
inadequacy, the apparent futility of human pursuits
and human values; and when these ideas appear to be
less original and provocative than they were when the
poem first appeared, the poem itself seems less original
and provocative. Secondly, commentators have pressed
the student to read the poem on a literal autobiographical level—stressing its verbal craftsmanship rather than
its qualities of esthetic distance and imaginative formulation; thus to be out of sympathy with the poet is to
disregard the poem. Finally, the poem evolves its distinctive form on an inner, psychological level; and a
generation habituated to poetic structures derived from
classical, public myths fails to see, immediately and
sympathetically, its universality.

The traditional view of In Memoriam as essentially
autobiographical can be seriously challenged. Throughout Tennyson's early poems—e.g., A Dirge, Love and
Death, Nothing Will Die, All Things Will Die, the
three-sonnet sequence entitled Love—the poet sheds
"no tears of love, but tears that Love can die." In 1830,
Tennyson published his Supposed Confessions of a
Second-Rate Sensitive Mind, in which he had asked the
question upon which, rationally, In Memoriam rests:

> Shall we not look into the laws
> Of life and death, and things that seem,
> And things that be, and analyze
> Our double nature, and compare
> All creeds till we have found the one,
> If one there be?

And quite explicitly these confessions are only "supposed." In 1833, Tennyson wrote The Two Voices, a
poem which bears such striking resemblances to In
Memoriam that it is often referred to as a "little
In Memoriam." In 1833, also, Tennyson wrote Ulysses.
Of it, Tennyson is reported to have said, while thinking
of In Memoriam: "There is more about myself in
'Ulysses,' which was written under the sense of loss
and that all had gone by, but that still life must be
fought out to the end."

On the basis of this and other evidence, then, one
can conclude that, although Tennyson used an autobiographical framework for In Memoriam, it is not an
autobiographical poem; and that the "I" of In Memoriam is an imaginary poet-narrator, not Alfred Tennyson.

The "religious" theme of In Memoriam has dominated commentary on the poem. But interwoven with its
religious theme is an indispensable esthetic theme. To
recognize this fact immediately and unequivocally, the
student needs only to study carefully the second climax
of reunion in Section CIII (the first occurs in Section
XCV). The extraordinary revelation in Section CIII is
implicit in the fact that, at the very moment in In
Memoriam which divides the poem between doubt and
"anxiety of heart," on the one hand, and "perfect peace
and contentment," on the other—at that very moment
the poet reaches into that other thought-stream of his
poetry and through allegorical situation and verbal
imagery merges his religious with his esthetic theme.
The "hall" of Section CIII holds kinship with the Lady
of Shalott's tower and with the soul's palace in The
Palace of Art: the maidens, according to Tennyson
himself, are "the muses, arts—all that makes life beautiful here." And the "river sliding by the wall," the
"rills," the "shallop," the "mead," and the "iris and
the golden reed" are verbal echoes of such poems as
Oenone, The Lotos-Eaters, and The Lady of Shalott.
Tennyson confirms the association of the two themes in
Section CVIII with such lines as "I will not shut me
from my kind" and "What find I in the highest place,/
But mine own phantom chanting hymns?"

17. **dusky doors,** the piled-up mass of refuse through which the stream
emerges at the foot of the glacier. 25. **azure . . . hearth,** columns of
blue smoke.

Throwing the searchlight of this revelation back through the earlier sections of In Memoriam, somewhat more than a neglected minor theme begins to emerge. Every reader knows that there are dozens of references throughout the poem, in single lines or in whole sections, to the relationship of the poet-narrator to the deep questions of life—why he writes, when he can write, how he writes, what he does and does not intend. Sections V, VIII, XIX, XXI, XXIII, XXXVII, XXXVIII, and XLVIII – XLIX are especially relevant. Some commentators have seen in these references apologies, partly of a conventional, partly of a personally diffident sort. Viewed from the vantage point of Section CIII, they suggest, perhaps, an oblique, muted Tennysonian Dichtung und Wahrheit, in which the poet is seriously, if tentatively, exploring the uses of poetry in man's search for spiritual values.

Tennyson has left a number of directives which provide the student some assistance in understanding the character of In Memoriam: (a) it is "a kind of Divina Commedia, ending in happiness"; (b) in it, the poet tried to portray "different moods of sorrow as in a drama"; (c) the poem expresses the poet's conviction that "anxieties of heart" rising out of fear, doubt, and suffering will find relief "only through Faith in a God of Love"; (d) the poem is divided according to the Christmas sections: XXVIII, LXXVIII, CIV; and (e) the poem falls into "nine natural groups" marking the stages of his grief and his thought: (1) I – VIII, (2) IX – XIX, (3) XX – XXVII, (4) XXVIII – XLIX, (5) L – LVIII, (6) LIX – LXXI, (7) LXXII – XCVIII, (8) XCIX – CIII, (9) CIV – CXXXI.

Finally, the thoughtful student will want to consider the distinctive characteristics of the In Memoriam stanza, which Tennyson mistakenly thought that he had invented. A useful point of departure for such consideration might be a careful comparison and contrast of it with that most popular of all elegies, Gray's Elegy Written in a Country Churchyard *(p. 642).*

Obiit MDCCCXXXIII

Strong Son of God, immortal Love,
    Whom we, that have not seen thy face,
    By faith, and faith alone, embrace,
Believing where we cannot prove;

Thine are these orbs of light and shade;
    Thou madest Life in man and brute;
    Thou madest Death; and lo, thy foot
Is on the skull which thou hast made.

Thou wilt not leave us in the dust:
10   Thou madest man, he knows not why,

He thinks he was not made to die;
And thou hast made him: thou art just.

Thou seemest human and divine,
    The highest, holiest manhood, thou.
    Our wills are ours, we know not how;
Our wills are ours, to make them thine.

Our little systems have their day;
    They have their day and cease to be;
    They are but broken lights of thee,
And thou, O Lord, art more than they.   20

We have but faith: we cannot know,
    For knowledge is of things we see;
    And yet we trust it comes from thee,
A beam in darkness: let it grow.

Let knowledge grow from more to more,
    But more of reverence in us dwell;
    That mind and soul, according well,
May make one music as before,

But vaster. We are fools and slight;   30
    We mock thee when we do not fear:
    But help thy foolish ones to bear;
Help thy vain worlds to bear thy light.

Forgive what seem'd my sin in me,
    What seem'd my worth since I began;
    For merit lives from man to man,
And not from man, O Lord, to thee.

Forgive my grief for one removed,
    Thy creature, whom I found so fair.
    I trust he lives in thee, and there
I find him worthier to be loved.   40

Forgive these wild and wandering cries,
    Confusions of a wasted youth;
    Forgive them where they fail in truth,
And in thy wisdom make me wise.
(1849; 1850)

I

I held it truth, with him who sings
    To one clear harp in divers tones,
    That men may rise on stepping-stones
Of their dead selves to higher things.

But who shall so forecast the years
    And find in loss a gain to match?
    Or reach a hand thro' time to catch
The far-off interest of tears?

---

5. **orbs,** planets. 17. **systems,** of theology and philosophy. 28. **as before,** before mind and soul were separated by modern skepticism. 42. wasted, desolated. 1. **him who sings,** Goethe, greatly admired by Tennyson for his ability to work in many different styles.

Let Love clasp Grief lest both be drown'd,
10   Let darkness keep her raven gloss.
    Ah, sweeter to be drunk with loss,
To dance with Death, to beat the ground,

Than that the victor Hours should scorn
    The long result of love, and boast,
    "Behold the man that loved and lost,
But all he was is overworn."

II

Old yew, which graspest at the stones
    That name the underlying dead,
    Thy fibres net the dreamless head,
20 Thy roots are wrapt about the bones.

The seasons bring the flower again,
    And bring the firstling to the flock;
    And in the dusk of thee the clock
Beats out the little lives of men.

O, not for thee the glow, the bloom,
    Who changest not in any gale,
    Nor branding summer suns avail
To touch thy thousand years of gloom;

And gazing on thee, sullen tree,
30   Sick for thy stubborn hardihood,
    I seem to fail from out my blood
And grow incorporate into thee.

III

O Sorrow, cruel fellowship,
    O Priestess in the vaults of Death,
    O sweet and bitter in a breath,
What whispers from thy lying lip?

"The stars," she whispers, "blindly run;
    A web is woven across the sky;
    From out waste places comes a cry,
40 And murmurs from the dying sun;

"And all the phantom, Nature, stands—
    With all the music in her tone,
    A hollow echo of my own,—
A hollow form with empty hands."

And shall I take a thing so blind,
    Embrace her as my natural good;
    Or crush her, like a vice of blood,
Upon the threshold of the mind?

IV

To Sleep I give my powers away;
50   My will is bondsman to the dark;

I sit within a helmless bark,
And with my heart I muse and say:

O heart, how fares it with thee now,
    That thou shouldst fail from thy desire,
    Who scarcely darest to inquire,
"What is it makes me beat so low?"

Something it is which thou hast lost,
    Some pleasure from thine early years.
    Break, thou deep vase of chilling tears,
That grief hath shaken into frost!   60

Such clouds of nameless trouble cross
    All night below the darken'd eyes;
    With morning wakes the will, and cries,
"Thou shalt not be the fool of loss."

V

I sometimes hold it half a sin
    To put in words the grief I feel;
    For words, like Nature, half reveal
And half conceal the Soul within.

But, for the unquiet heart and brain,
    A use in measured language lies;   70
    The sad mechanic exercise,
Like dull narcotics, numbing pain.

In words, like weeds, I'll wrap me o'er,
    Like coarsest clothes against the cold;
    But that large grief which these enfold
Is given in outline and no more.

VI

One writes, that "other friends remain,"
    That "loss is common to the race"—
    And common is the commonplace,
And vacant chaff well meant for grain.   80

That loss is common would not make
    My own less bitter, rather more.
    Too common! Never morning wore
To evening, but some heart did break.

O father, wheresoe'er thou be,
    Who pledgest now thy gallant son,
    A shot, ere half thy draught be done,
Hath still'd the life that beat from thee.

O mother, praying God will save
    Thy sailor,—while thy head is bow'd,   90

---

30. **Sick for,** yearning for. 73. **weeds,** mourning garments. 121. **Dark house,** 67 Wimpole Street, London, where Hallam had lived. 157. **Fair**

His heavy-shotted hammock-shroud
Drops in his vast and wandering grave.

Ye know no more than I who wrought
    At that last hour to please him well;
    Who mused on all I had to tell,
And something written, something thought;

Expecting still his advent home;
    And ever met him on his way
    With wishes, thinking, "here to-day,"
100 Or "here to-morrow will he come."

O, somewhere, meek, unconscious dove,
    That sittest ranging golden hair;
    And glad to find thyself so fair,
Poor child, that waitest for thy love!

For now her father's chimney glows
    In expectation of a guest;
    And thinking "this will please him best,"
She takes a riband or a rose;

For he will see them on to-night;
110   And with the thought her color burns;
    And having left the glass, she turns
Once more to set a ringlet right;

And, even when she turn'd, the curse
    Had fallen, and her future lord
    Was drown'd in passing thro' the ford,
Or kill'd in falling from his horse.

O, what to her shall be the end?
    And what to me remains of good?
    To her perpetual maidenhood,
120 And unto me no second friend.

VII

Dark house, by which once more I stand
    Here in the long unlovely street,
    Doors, where my heart was used to beat
So quickly, waiting for a hand,

A hand that can be clasp'd no more—
    Behold me, for I cannot sleep,
    And like a guilty thing I creep
At earliest morning to the door.

He is not here; but far away
130   The noise of life begins again,
    And ghastly thro' the drizzling rain
On the bald street breaks the blank day.

VIII

A happy lover who has come
    To look on her that loves him well,
    Who 'lights and rings the gateway bell,
And learns her gone and far from home;

He saddens, all the magic light
    Dies off at once from bower and hall,
    And all the place is dark, and all
The chambers emptied of delight: 140

So find I every pleasant spot
    In which we two were wont to meet,
    The field, the chamber, and the street,
For all is dark where thou art not.

Yet as that other, wandering there
    In those deserted walks, may find
    A flower beat with rain and wind,
Which once she foster'd up with care;

So seems it in my deep regret,
    O my forsaken heart, with thee   150
    And this poor flower of poesy
Which, little cared for, fades not yet.

But since it pleased a vanish'd eye,
    I go to plant it on his tomb,
    That if it can it there may bloom,
Or, dying, there at least may die.

IX

Fair ship, that from the Italian shore
    Sailest the placid ocean-plains
    With my lost Arthur's loved remains,
Spread thy full wings, and waft him o'er.   160

So draw him home to those that mourn
    In vain; a favorable speed
    Ruffle thy mirror'd mast, and lead
Thro' prosperous floods his holy urn.

All night no ruder air perplex
    Thy sliding keel, till Phosphor, bright
    As our pure love, thro' early light
Shall glimmer on the dewy decks.

Sphere all your lights around, above;
    Sleep, gentle heavens, before the prow;   170
    Sleep, gentle winds, as he sleeps now,
My friend, the brother of my love;

My Arthur, whom I shall not see
    Till all my widow'd race be run;

ship, the ship carrying Hallam's body back to England. The *thy* and the *thou* of Sections IX-XVII are addressed to the ship. 166. **Phosphor,** the morning star.

Dear as the mother to the son,
More than my brothers are to me.

X

I hear the noise about thy keel;
  I hear the bell struck in the night;
  I see the cabin-window bright;
180 I see the sailor at the wheel.

Thou bring'st the sailor to his wife,
  And travell'd men from foreign lands;
  And letters unto trembling hands;
And, thy dark freight, a vanish'd life.

So bring him; we have idle dreams;
  This look of quiet flatters thus
  Our home-bred fancies. O, to us,
The fools of habit, sweeter seems

To rest beneath the clover sod,
190   That takes the sunshine and the rains,
  Or where the kneeling hamlet drains
The chalice of the grapes of God;

Than if with thee the roaring wells
  Should gulf him fathom-deep in brine,
  And hands so often clasp'd in mine,
Should toss with tangle and with shells.

XI

Calm is the morn without a sound,
  Calm as to suit a calmer grief,
  And only thro' the faded leaf
200 The chestnut pattering to the ground;

Calm and deep peace on this high wold,
  And on these dews that drench the furze,
  And all the silvery gossamers
That twinkle into green and gold;

Calm and still light on yon great plain
  That sweeps with all its autumn bowers,
  And crowded farms and lessening towers,
To mingle with the bounding main;

Calm and deep peace in this wide air,
210   These leaves that redden to the fall,
  And in my heart, if calm at all,
If any calm, a calm despair;

Calm on the seas, and silver sleep,
  And waves that sway themselves in rest,

And dead calm in that noble breast
Which heaves but with the heaving deep.

XII

Lo, as a dove when up she springs
  To bear thro' heaven a tale of woe,
  Some dolorous message knit below
The wild pulsation of her wings;   220

Like her I go, I cannot stay;
  I leave this mortal ark behind,
  A weight of nerves without a mind,
And leave the cliffs, and haste away

O'er ocean-mirrors rounded large,
  And reach the glow of southern skies,
  And see the sails at distance rise,
And linger weeping on the marge,

And saying, "Comes he thus, my friend?
  Is this the end of all my care?"   230
  And circle moaning in the air,
"Is this the end? Is this the end?"

And forward dart again, and play
  About the prow, and back return
  To where the body sits, and learn
That I have been an hour away.

XIII

Tears of the widower, when he sees
  A late-lost form that sleep reveals,
  And moves his doubtful arms, and feels
Her place is empty, fall like these;   240

Which weep a loss for ever new,
  A void where heart on heart reposed;
  And, where warm hands have prest and closed,
Silence, till I be silent too;

Which weep the comrade of my choice,
  An awful thought, a life removed,
  The human-hearted man I loved,
A Spirit, not a breathing voice.

Come, Time, and teach me, many years,
  I do not suffer in a dream;   250
  For now so strange do these things seem,
Mine eyes have leisure for their tears,

My fancies time to rise on wing,
  And glance about the approaching sails,
  As tho' they brought but merchants' bales,
And not the burthen that they bring.

189-192. **To rest,** etc., i.e., to be buried in the churchyard or in the village church. 196. **tangle,** the tangle of seaweed. 201. **wold,** an upland plain, characteristic of Lincolnshire.

XIV

If one should bring me this report,
    That thou hadst touch'd the land to-day,
    And I went down unto the quay,
260 And found thee lying in the port;

And standing, muffled round with woe,
    Should see thy passengers in rank
    Come stepping lightly down the plank
And beckoning unto those they know;

And if along with these should come
    The man I held as half-divine,
    Should strike a sudden hand in mine,
And ask a thousand things of home;

And I should tell him all my pain,
270   And how my life had droop'd of late,
    And he should sorrow o'er my state
And marvel what possess'd my brain;

And I perceived no touch of change,
    No hint of death in all his frame,
    But found him all in all the same,
I should not feel it to be strange.

XV

To-night the winds begin to rise
    And roar from yonder dropping day;
    The last red leaf is whirl'd away,
280 The rooks are blown about the skies;

The forest crack'd, the waters curl'd,
    The cattle huddled on the lea;
    And wildly dash'd on tower and tree
The sunbeam strikes along the world:

And but for fancies, which aver
    That all thy motions gently pass
    Athwart a plane of molten glass,
I scarce could brook the strain and stir

That makes the barren branches loud;
290   And but for fear it is not so,
    The wild unrest that lives in woe
Would dote and pore on yonder cloud

That rises upward always higher,
    And onward drags a laboring breast,
    And topples round the dreary west,
A looming bastion fringed with fire.

XVI

What words are these have fallen from me?
    Can calm despair and wild unrest
Be tenants of a single breast,
Or Sorrow such a changeling be?   300

Or doth she only seem to take
    The touch of change in calm or storm,
    But knows no more of transient form
In her deep self, than some dead lake

That holds the shadow of a lark
    Hung in the shadow of a heaven?
    Or has the shock, so harshly given,
Confused me like the unhappy bark

That strikes by night a craggy shelf,
    And staggers blindly ere she sink?   310
    And stunn'd me from my power to think
And all my knowledge of myself;

And made me that delirious man
    Whose fancy fuses old and new,
    And flashes into false and true,
And mingles all without a plan?

XVII

Thou comest, much wept for; such a breeze
    Compell'd thy canvas, and my prayer
    Was as the whisper of an air
To breathe thee over lonely seas.   320

For I in spirit saw thee move
    Thro' circles of the bounding sky,
    Week after week; the days go by;
Come quick, thou bringest all I love.

Henceforth, wherever thou mayst roam,
    My blessing, like a line of light,
    Is on the waters day and night,
And like a beacon guards thee home.

So may whatever tempest mars
    Mid-ocean spare thee, sacred bark,   330
    And balmy drops in summer dark
Slide from the bosom of the stars;

So kind an office hath been done,
    Such precious relics brought by thee,
    The dust of him I shall not see
Till all my widow'd race be run.

XVIII

'T is well; 't is something; we may stand
    Where he in English earth is laid,
    And from his ashes may be made
The violet of his native land.   340

'T is little; but it looks in truth
  As if the quiet bones were blest
  Among familiar names to rest
And in the places of his youth.

Come then, pure hands, and bear the head
  That sleeps or wears the mask of sleep,
  And come, whatever loves to weep,
And hear the ritual of the dead.

Ah yet, even yet, if this might be,
350 I, falling on his faithful heart,
  Would breathing thro' his lips impart
The life that almost dies in me;

That dies not, but endures with pain,
  And slowly forms the firmer mind,
  Treasuring the look it cannot find,
The words that are not heard again.

XIX

The Danube to the Severn gave
  The darken'd heart that beat no more;
  They laid him by the pleasant shore,
360 And in the hearing of the wave.

There twice a day the Severn fills;
  The salt sea-water passes by,
  And hushes half the babbling Wye,
And makes a silence in the hills.

The Wye is hush'd nor moved along,
  And hush'd my deepest grief of all,
  When fill'd with tears that cannot fall,
I brim with sorrow drowning song.

The tide flows down, the wave again
370 Is vocal in its wooded walls;
  My deeper anguish also falls,
And I can speak a little then.

XX

The lesser griefs that may be said,
  That breathe a thousand tender vows,
  Are but as servants in a house
Where lies the master newly dead;

Who speak their feeling as it is,
  And weep the fulness from the mind.
  "It will be hard," they say, "to find
380 Another service such as this."

My lighter moods are like to these,
  That out of words a comfort win;

But there are other griefs within,
  And tears that at their fountain freeze;

For by the hearth the children sit
  Cold in that atmosphere of death,
  And scarce endure to draw the breath,
Or like to noiseless phantoms flit;

But open converse is there none,
  So much the vital spirits sink   390
  To see the vacant chair, and think,
"How good! how kind! and he is gone."

XXI

I sing to him that rests below,
  And, since the grasses round me wave,
  I take the grasses of the grave,
And make them pipes whereon to blow.

The traveller hears me now and then,
  And sometimes harshly will he speak:
  "This fellow would make weakness weak,
And melt the waxen hearts of men."   400

Another answers: "Let him be,
  He loves to make parade of pain,
  That with his piping he may gain
The praise that comes to constancy."

A third is wroth: "Is this an hour
  For private sorrow's barren song,
  When more and more the people throng
The chairs and thrones of civil power?

"A time to sicken and to swoon,
  When Science reaches forth her arms   410
  To feel from world to world, and charms
Her secret from the latest moon?"

Behold, ye speak an idle thing;
  Ye never knew the sacred dust.
  I do but sing because I must,
And pipe but as the linnets sing;

And one is glad; her note is gay,
  For now her little ones have ranged;
  And one is sad; her note is changed,
Because her brood is stolen away.   420

XXII

The path by which we twain did go,
  Which led by tracts that pleased us well,

357. **The Danube ... Severn.** Hallam died in Vienna on the Danube; he was buried on the banks of the Severn in southwest England. 363. **Wye,** a tributary of the Severn and partly tidal. It becomes silent when the tide flows in and "vocal" as it flows out. 452. **Pan,** god of nature.

Thro' four sweet years arose and fell,
From flower to flower, from snow to snow;

And we with singing cheer'd the way,
And, crown'd with all the season lent,
From April on to April went,
And glad at heart from May to May.

But where the path we walk'd began
430   To slant the fifth autumnal slope,
As we descended following Hope,
There sat the Shadow fear'd of man;

Who broke our fair companionship,
And spread his mantle dark and cold,
And wrapt thee formless in the fold,
And dull'd the murmur on thy lip,

And bore thee where I could not see
Nor follow, tho' I walk in haste,
And think that somewhere in the waste
440 The Shadow sits and waits for me.

XXIII

Now, sometimes in my sorrow shut,
Or breaking into song by fits,
Alone, alone, to where he sits,
The Shadow cloak'd from head to foot,

Who keeps the keys of all the creeds,
I wander, often falling lame,
And looking back to whence I came,
Or on to where the pathway leads;

And crying, How changed from where it ran
450   Thro' lands where not a leaf was dumb,
But all the lavish hills would hum
The murmur of a happy Pan;

When each by turns was guide to each,
And Fancy light from Fancy caught,
And Thought leapt out to wed with Thought
Ere Thought could wed itself with Speech;

And all we met was fair and good,
And all was good that Time could bring,
And all the secret of the Spring
460 Moved in the chambers of the blood;

And many an old philosophy
On Argive heights divinely sang,
And round us all the thicket rang
To many a flute of Arcady.

462. **Argive,** Greek. 464. **Arcady,** Arcadia, home of the shepherd poets.
Such references as this and the above carry on the pastoral conventions of

XXIV

And was the day of my delight
As pure and perfect as I say?
The very source and fount of day
Is dash'd with wandering isles of night.

If all was good and fair we met,
This earth had been the Paradise   470
It never look'd to human eyes
Since our first sun arose and set.

And is it that the haze of grief
Makes former gladness loom so great?
The lowness of the present state,
That sets the past in this relief?

Or that the past will always win
A glory from its being far,
And orb into the perfect star
We saw not when we moved therein?   480

XXV

I know that this was Life,—the track
Whereon with equal feet we fared;
And then, as now, the day prepared
The daily burden for the back.

But this it was that made me move
As light as carrier-birds in air;
I loved the weight I had to bear,
Because it needed help of Love;

Nor could I weary, heart or limb,
When mighty Love would cleave in twain   490
The lading of a single pain,
And part it, giving half to him.

XXVI

Still onward winds the dreary way;
I with it, for I long to prove
No lapse of moons can canker Love,
Whatever fickle tongues may say.

And if that eye which watches guilt
And goodness, and hath power to see
Within the green the moulder'd tree,
And towers fallen as soon as built—   500

O, if indeed that eye foresee
Or see—in Him is no before—
In more of life true life no more
And Love the indifference to be,

the elegy.

Alfred, Lord Tennyson   869

Then might I find, ere yet the morn
  Breaks hither over Indian seas,
  That Shadow waiting with the keys,
To shroud me from my proper scorn.

XXVII

I envy not in any moods
510   The captive void of noble rage,
  The linnet born within the cage,
That never knew the summer woods;

I envy not the beast that takes
  His license in the field of time,
  Unfetter'd by the sense of crime,
To whom a conscience never wakes;

Nor, what may count itself as blest,
  The heart that never plighted troth
  But stagnates in the weeds of sloth;
520 Nor any want-begotten rest.

I hold it true, whate'er befall;
  I feel it, when I sorrow most;
  'T is better to have loved and lost
Than never to have loved at all.

XXVIII

The time draws near the birth of Christ.
  The moon is hid, the night is still;
  The Christmas bells from hill to hill
Answer each other in the mist.

Four voices of four hamlets round,
530   From far and near, on mead and moor,
  Swell out and fail, as if a door
Were shut between me and the sound;

Each voice four changes on the wind,
  That now dilate, and now decrease,
  Peace and goodwill, goodwill and peace,
Peace and goodwill, to all mankind.

This year I slept and woke with pain,
  I almost wish'd no more to wake,
  And that my hold on life would break
540 Before I heard those bells again;

But they my troubled spirit rule,
  For they controll'd me when a boy;
  They bring me sorrow touch'd with joy,
The merry, merry bells of Yule.

XXIX

With such compelling cause to grieve
  As daily vexes household peace,

And chains regret to his decease,
How dare we keep our Christmas-eve,

Which brings no more a welcome guest
  To enrich the threshold of the night   550
  With shower'd largess of delight
In dance and song and game and jest?

Yet go, and while the holly boughs
  Entwine the cold baptismal font,
  Make one wreath more for Use and Wont,
That guard the portals of the house;

Old sisters of a day gone by,
  Gray nurses, loving nothing new—
  Why should they miss their yearly due
Before their time? They too will die.   560

XXX

With trembling fingers did we weave
  The holly round the Christmas hearth;
  A rainy cloud possess'd the earth,
And sadly fell our Christmas-eve.

At our old pastimes in the hall
  We gamboll'd, making vain pretence
  Of gladness, with an awful sense
Of one mute Shadow watching all.

We paused: the winds were in the beech;
  We heard them sweep the winter land;   570
  And in a circle hand-in-hand
Sat silent, looking each at each.

Then echo-like our voices rang;
  We sung, tho' every eye was dim,
  A merry song we sang with him
Last year; impetuously we sang.

We ceased; a gentler feeling crept
  Upon us: surely rest is meet.
  "They rest," we said, "their sleep is sweet,"
And silence follow'd, and we wept.   580

Our voices took a higher range;
  Once more we sang: "They do not die
  Nor lose their mortal sympathy,
Nor change to us, although they change;

"Rapt from the fickle and the frail
  With gather'd power, yet the same,
  Pierces the keen seraphic flame
From orb to orb, from veil to veil."

Rise, happy morn, rise, holy morn,
  Draw forth the cheerful day from night: 590

O Father, touch the east, and light
The light that shone when Hope was born.

XXXI

When Lazarus left his charnel-cave,
   And home to Mary's house return'd,
   Was this demanded—if he yearn'd
To hear her weeping by his grave?

"Where wert thou, brother, those four days?"
   There lives no record of reply,
   Which telling what it is to die
600 Had surely added praise to praise.

From every house the neighbors met,
   The streets were fill'd with joyful sound,
   A solemn gladness even crown'd
The purple brows of Olivet.

Behold a man raised up by Christ!
   The rest remaineth unreveal'd;
   He told it not, or something seal'd
The lips of that Evangelist.

XXXII

Her eyes are homes of silent prayer,
610   Nor other thought her mind admits
   But, he was dead, and there he sits,
And he that brought him back is there.

Then one deep love doth supersede
   All other, when her ardent gaze
   Roves from the living brother's face,
And rests upon the Life indeed.

All subtle thought, all curious fears,
   Borne down by gladness so complete,
   She bows, she bathes the Saviour's feet
620 With costly spikenard and with tears.

Thrice blest whose lives are faithful prayers,
   Whose loves in higher love endure;
   What souls possess themselves so pure,
Or is there blessedness like theirs?

XXXIII

O thou that after toil and storm
   Mayst seem to have reach'd a purer air,
   Whose faith has centre everywhere,
Nor cares to fix itself to form,

Leave thou thy sister when she prays
   Her early heaven, her happy views;   630
   Nor thou with shadow'd hint confuse
A life that leads melodious days.

Her faith thro' form is pure as thine,
   Her hands are quicker unto good.
   O, sacred be the flesh and blood
To which she links a truth divine!

See thou, that countest reason ripe
   In holding by the law within,
   Thou fail not in a world of sin,
And even for want of such a type.   640

XXXIV

My own dim life should teach me this,
   That life shall live for evermore,
   Else earth is darkness at the core,
And dust and ashes all that is;

This round of green, this orb of flame,
   Fantastic beauty; such as lurks
   In some wild poet, when he works
Without a conscience or an aim.

What then were God to such as I?
   'T were hardly worth my while to choose   650
   Of things all mortal, or to use
A little patience ere I die;

'T were best at once to sink to peace,
   Like birds the charming serpent draws,
   To drop head-foremost in the jaws
Of vacant darkness and to cease.

XXXV

Yet if some voice that man could trust
   Should murmur from the narrow house,
   "The cheeks drop in, the body bows;
Man dies, nor is there hope in dust;"   660

Might I not say? "Yet even here,
   But for one hour, O Love, I strive
   To keep so sweet a thing alive."
But I should turn mine ears and hear

The moanings of the homeless sea,
   The sound of streams that swift or slow
   Draw down Æonian hills, and sow
The dust of continents to be;

625-640. **O thou,** etc. These words are addressed to rationalistic liberals
who have put aside a dogmatic and ritualistic form of religion. 657-680.
Yet if, etc. The dialogue in this section poses the central question: Is not
Love a mockery if physical death closes all? The poet is identifying Love
with Christ; hence, the pagan imagery of lines 677-680. 667. **Aeonian,**
eons old.

And Love would answer with a sigh,
670 "The sound of that forgetful shore
   Will change my sweetness more and more,
   Half-dead to know that I shall die."

O me, what profits it to put
   An idle case? If Death were seen
   At first as Death, Love had not been,
   Or been in narrowest working shut,

Mere fellowship of sluggish moods,
   Or in his coarsest Satyr-shape
   Had bruised the herb and crush'd the grape,
680 And bask'd and batten'd in the woods.

XXXVI

Tho' truths in manhood darkly join,
   Deep-seated in our mystic frame,
   We yield all blessing to the name
Of Him that made them current coin;

For Wisdom dealt with mortal powers,
   Where truth in closest words shall fail,
   When truth embodied in a tale
Shall enter in at lowly doors.

And so the Word had breath, and wrought
690 With human hands the creed of creeds
   In loveliness of perfect deeds,
   More strong than all poetic thought;

Which he may read that binds the sheaf,
   Or builds the house, or digs the grave,
   And those wild eyes that watch the wave
In roarings round the coral reef.

XXXVII

Urania speaks with darken'd brow:
   "Thou pratest here where thou art least;
   This faith has many a purer priest,
700 And many an abler voice than thou.

"Go down beside thy native rill,
   On thy Parnassus set thy feet,
   And hear thy laurel whisper sweet
About the ledges of the hill."

And my Melpomene replies,
   A touch of shame upon her cheek:
   "I am not worthy even to speak
Of thy prevailing mysteries;

"For I am but an earthly Muse,
710 And owning but a little art

To lull with song an aching heart,
And render human love his dues;

"But brooding on the dear one dead,
   And all he said of things divine,—
   And dear to me as sacred wine
To dying lips is all he said,—

"I murmur'd, as I came along,
   Of comfort clasp'd in truth reveal'd,
   And loiter'd in the master's field,
And darken'd sanctities with song." 720

XXXVIII

With weary steps I loiter on,
   Tho' always under alter'd skies
   The purple from the distance dies,
My prospect and horizon gone.

No joy the blowing season gives,
   The herald melodies of spring,
   But in the songs I love to sing
A doubtful gleam of solace lives.

If any care for what is here
   Survive in spirits render'd free, 730
   Then are these songs I sing of thee
Not all ungrateful to thine ear.

XXXIX

Old warder of these buried bones,
   And answering now my random stroke
   With fruitful cloud and living smoke,
Dark yew, that graspest at the stones

And dippest toward the dreamless head,
   To thee too comes the golden hour
   When flower is feeling after flower;
But Sorrow,—fixt upon the dead, 740

And darkening the dark graves of men,—
   What whisper'd from her lying lips?
   Thy gloom is kindled at the tips,
And passes into gloom again.

XL

Could we forget the widow'd hour
   And look on Spirits breathed away,
   As on a maiden in the day
When first she wears her orange-flower!

When crown'd with blessing she doth rise
   To take her latest leave of home, 750

697-720. **Urania speaks, etc.** Urania is the Muse of astronomy, of the harmony of the spheres; Melpomene is the Muse of tragedy; Parnassus was the dwelling place of the Muses.

And hopes and light regrets that come
Make April of her tender eyes;

And doubtful joys the father move,
   And tears are on the mother's face,
   As parting with a long embrace
She enters other realms of love;

Her office there to rear, to teach,
   Becoming as is meet and fit
   A link among the days, to knit
760 The generations each with each;

And, doubtless, unto thee is given
   A life that bears immortal fruit
   In those great offices that suit
The full-grown energies of heaven.

Ay me, the difference I discern!
   How often shall her old fireside
   Be cheer'd with tidings of the bride,
How often she herself return,

And tell them all they would have told,
770   And bring her babe, and make her boast,
   Till even those that miss'd her most
Shall count new things as dear as old;

But thou and I have shaken hands,
   Till growing winters lay me low;
   My paths are in the fields I know,
And thine in undiscover'd lands.

XLI

Thy spirit ere our fatal loss
   Did ever rise from high to higher,
   As mounts the heavenward altar-fire,
780 As flies the lighter thro' the gross.

But thou art turn'd to something strange,
   And I have lost the links that bound
   Thy changes; here upon the ground,
No more partaker of thy change.

Deep folly! yet that this could be—
   That I could wing my will with might
   To leap the grades of life and light,
And flash at once, my friend, to thee!

For tho' my nature rarely yields
790   To that vague fear implied in death,
   Nor shudders at the gulfs beneath,
The howlings from forgotten fields;

Yet oft when sundown skirts the moor
   An inner trouble I behold,

A spectral doubt which makes me cold,
That I shall be thy mate no more,

Tho' following with an upward mind
   The wonders that have come to thee,
   Thro' all the secular to-be,
But evermore a life behind.   800

XLII

I vex my heart with fancies dim.
   He still outstript me in the race;
   It was but unity of place
That made me dream I rank'd with him.

And so may Place retain us still,
   And he the much-beloved again,
   A lord of large experience, train
To riper growth the mind and will;

And what delights can equal those
   That stir the spirit's inner deeps,   810
   When one that loves, but knows not, reaps
A truth from one that loves and knows?

XLIII

If Sleep and Death be truly one,
   And every spirit's folded bloom
   Thro' all its intervital gloom
In some long trance should slumber on;

Unconscious of the sliding hour,
   Bare of the body, might it last,
   And silent traces of the past
Be all the color of the flower: 820

So then were nothing lost to man;
   So that still garden of the souls
   In many a figured leaf enrolls
The total world since life began;

And love will last as pure and whole
   As when he loved me here in Time,
   And at the spiritual prime
Rewaken with the dawning soul.

XLIV

How fares it with the happy dead?
   For here the man is more and more;   830
   But he forgets the days before
God shut the doorways of his head.

The days have vanish'd, tone and tint,
   And yet perhaps the hoarding sense

Gives out at times—he knows not whence—
A little flash, a mystic hint;

And in the long harmonious years—
    If Death so taste Lethean springs—
    May some dim touch of earthly things
840 Surprise thee ranging with thy peers.

If such a dreamy touch should fall,
    O, turn thee round, resolve the doubt;
    My guardian angel will speak out
In that high place, and tell thee all.

XLV

The baby new to earth and sky,
    What time his tender palm is prest
    Against the circle of the breast,
Has never thought that "this is I";

But as he grows he gathers much,
850   And learns the use of "I" and "me,"
    And finds "I am not what I see,
And other than the things I touch."

So rounds he to a separate mind
    From whence clear memory may begin,
    As thro' the frame that binds him in
His isolation grows defined.

This use may lie in blood and breath,
    Which else were fruitless of their due,
    Had man to learn himself anew
860 Beyond the second birth of death.

XLVI

We ranging down this lower track,
    The path we came by, thorn and flower,
    Is shadow'd by the growing hour,
Lest life should fail in looking back.

So be it: there no shade can last
    In that deep dawn behind the tomb,
    But clear from marge to marge shall bloom
The eternal landscape of the past;

A lifelong tract of time reveal'd,
870   The fruitful hours of still increase;
    Days order'd in a wealthy peace,
And those five years its richest field.

O Love, thy province were not large,
    A bounded field, nor stretching far;
    Look also, Love, a brooding star,
A rosy warmth from marge to marge.

XLVII

That each, who seems a separate whole,
    Should move his rounds, and fusing all
    The skirts of self again, should fall
Remerging in the general Soul,   880

Is faith as vague as all unsweet.
    Eternal form shall still divide
    The eternal soul from all beside;
And I shall know him when we meet;

And we shall sit at endless feast,
    Enjoying each the other's good.
    What vaster dream can hit the mood
Of Love on earth? He seeks at least

Upon the last and sharpest height,
    Before the spirits fade away,   890
    Some landing-place, to clasp and say,
"Farewell! We lose ourselves in light."

XLVIII

If these brief lays, of Sorrow born,
    Were taken to be such as closed
    Grave doubts and answers here proposed,
Then these were such as men might scorn.

Her care is not to part and prove;
    She takes, when harsher moods remit,
    What slender shade of doubt may flit,
And makes it vassal unto love;   900

And hence, indeed, she sports with words,
    But better serves a wholesome law,
    And holds it sin and shame to draw
The deepest measure from the chords;

Nor dare she trust a larger lay,
    But rather loosens from the lip
    Short swallow-flights of song, that dip
Their wings in tears, and skim away.

XLIX

From art, from nature, from the schools,
    Let random influences glance,   910
    Like light in many a shiver'd lance
That breaks about the dappled pools.

The lightest wave of thought shall lisp,
    The fancy's tenderest eddy wreathe,
    The slightest air of song shall breathe
To make the sullen surface crisp.

893-908. **If these . . . lays, etc.** This section puts a severe limitation on the poem's intention and should be taken seriously.

And look thy look, and go thy way,
But blame not thou the winds that make
The seeming-wanton ripple break,
920 The tender-pencill'd shadow play.

Beneath all fancied hopes and fears
Ay me, the sorrow deepens down,
Whose muffled motions blindly drown
The bases of my life in tears.

L

Be near me when my light is low,
When the blood creeps, and the nerves prick
And tingle; and the heart is sick,
And all the wheels of being slow.

Be near me when the sensuous frame
930 Is rack'd with pangs that conquer trust;
And Time, a maniac scattering dust,
And Life, a Fury slinging flame.

Be near me when my faith is dry,
And men the flies of latter spring,
That lay their eggs, and sting and sing
And weave their petty cells and die.

Be near me when I fade away,
To point the term of human strife,
And on the low dark verge of life
940 The twilight of eternal day.

LI

Do we indeed desire the dead
Should still be near us at our side?
Is there no baseness we would hide?
No inner vileness that we dread?

Shall he for whose applause I strove,
I had such reverence for his blame,
See with clear eye some hidden shame
And I be lessen'd in his love?

I wrong the grave with fears untrue.
950 Shall love be blamed for want of faith?
There must be wisdom with great Death;
The dead shall look me thro' and thro'.

Be near us when we climb or fall;
Ye watch, like God, the rolling hours
With larger other eyes than ours,
To make allowance for us all.

LII

I cannot love thee as I ought,
For love reflects the thing beloved;

My words are only words, and moved
Upon the topmost froth of thought.   960

"Yet blame not thou thy plaintive song,"
The Spirit of true love replied;
"Thou canst not move me from thy side,
Nor human frailty do me wrong.

"What keeps a spirit wholly true
To that ideal which he bears?
What record? not the sinless years
That breathed beneath the Syrian blue;

"So fret not, like an idle girl,
That life is dash'd with flecks of sin.   970
Abide; thy wealth is gather'd in,
When Time hath sunder'd shell from pearl."

LIII

How many a father have I seen,
A sober man, among his boys,
Whose youth was full of foolish noise,
Who wears his manhood hale and green;

And dare we to this fancy give,
That had the wild oat not been sown,
The soil, left barren, scarce had grown
The grain by which a man may live?   980

Or, if we held the doctrine sound
For life outliving heats of youth,
Yet who would preach it as a truth
To those that eddy round and round?

Hold thou the good, define it well;
For fear divine Philosophy
Should push beyond her mark, and be
Procuress to the Lords of Hell.

LIV

O, yet we trust that somehow good
Will be the final goal of ill,   990
To pangs of nature, sins of will,
Deflects of doubt, and taints of blood;

That nothing walks with aimless feet;
That not one life shall be destroy'd,
Or cast as rubbish to the void,
When God hath made the pile complete;

That not a worm is cloven in vain;
That not a moth with vain desire
Is shrivell'd in a fruitless fire,
Or but subserves another's gain.   1000

967. **sinless years,** Christ's life upon earth.

Behold, we know not anything;
   I can but trust that good shall fall
   At last—far off—at last, to all,
And every winter change to spring.

So runs my dream; but what am I?
   An infant crying in the night;
   An infant crying for the light,
And with no language but a cry.

LV

The wish, that of the living whole
1010   No life may fail beyond the grave,
   Derives it not from what we have
The likest God within the soul?

Are God and Nature then at strife,
   That Nature lends such evil dreams?
   So careful of the type she seems,
So careless of the single life,

That I, considering everywhere
   Her secret meaning in her deeds,
   And finding that of fifty seeds
1020 She often brings but one to bear.

I falter where I firmly trod,
   And falling with my weight of cares
   Upon the great world's altar-stairs
That slope thro' darkness up to God,

I stretch lame hands of faith, and grope,
   And gather dust and chaff, and call
   To what I feel is Lord of all,
And faintly trust the larger hope.

LVI

"So careful of the type?" but no.
1030   From scarped cliff and quarried stone
   She cries, "A thousand types are gone;
I care for nothing, all shall go.

"Thou makest thine appeal to me.
   I bring to life, I bring to death;
   The spirit does but mean the breath:
I know no more." And he, shall he,

Man, her last work, who seem'd so fair,
   Such splendid purpose in his eyes,
   Who roll'd the psalm to wintry skies,
1040 Who built him fanes of fruitless prayer,

Who trusted God was love indeed
   And love Creation's final law—
   Tho' Nature, red in tooth and claw
With ravine, shriek'd against his creed—

Who loved, who suffer'd countless ills,
   Who battled for the True, the Just,
   Be blown about the desert dust,
Or seal'd within the iron hills?

No more? A monster then, a dream,
   A discord. Dragons of the prime,   1050
   That tare each other in their slime,
Were mellow music match'd with him.

O life as futile, then, as frail!
   O for thy voice to soothe and bless!
   What hope of answer, or redress?
Behind the veil, behind the veil.

LVII

Peace; come away: the song of woe
   Is after all an earthly song.
   Peace; come away: we do him wrong
To sing so wildly: let us go.   1060

Come; let us go: your cheeks are pale;
   But half my life I leave behind.
   Methinks my friend is richly shrined;
But I shall pass, my work will fail.

Yet in these ears, till hearing dies,
   One set slow bell will seem to toll
   The passing of the sweetest soul
That ever look'd with human eyes.

I hear it now, and o'er and o'er,
   Eternal greetings to the dead;   1070
   And "Ave, Ave, Ave," said,
"Adieu, adieu," for evermore.

LVIII

In those sad words I took farewell.
   Like echoes in sepulchral halls,
   As drop by drop the water falls
In vaults and catacombs, they fell;

And, falling, idly broke the peace
   Of hearts that beat from day to day,
   Half-conscious of their dying clay,
And those cold crypts where they shall cease.   1080

1029-1056. **So careful, etc.** This section contains the famous "Darwinian" lines in the poem. Actually, it was written some twenty years before the publication of *Origin of Species* (1859). Tennyson is reflecting the earlier evolutionary theories of geologists like Sir Charles Lyell; and, like Darwin himself, Tennyson could have found the concept of the struggle for existence in Thomas Robert Malthus. 1057-1072. **Peace, etc.** Some students

The high Muse answer'd: "Wherefore grieve
   Thy brethren with a fruitless tear?
   Abide a little longer here,
And thou shalt take a nobler leave."

LIX

O Sorrow, wilt thou live with me
   No casual mistress, but a wife,
   My bosom-friend and half of life;
As I confess it needs must be?

O Sorrow, wilt thou rule my blood,
1090   Be sometimes lovely like a bride,
   And put thy harsher moods aside,
If thou wilt have me wise and good?

My centred passion cannot move,
   Nor will it lessen from to-day;
   But I'll have leave at times to play
As with the creature of my love;

And set thee forth, for thou art mine,
   With so much hope for years to come,
   That, howsoe'er I know thee, some
1100 Could hardly tell what name were thine.

LX

He past, a soul of nobler tone;
   My spirit loved and loves him yet,
   Like some poor girl whose heart is set
On one whose rank exceeds her own.

He mixing with his proper sphere,
   She finds the baseness of her lot,
   Half jealous of she knows not what,
And envying all that meet him there.

The little village looks forlorn;
1110   She sighs amid her narrow days,
   Moving about the household ways,
In that dark house where she was born.

The foolish neighbors come and go,
   And tease her till the day draws by;
   At night she weeps, "How vain am I!
How should he love a thing so low?"

LXI

If, in thy second state sublime,
   Thy ransom'd reason change replied

<hr>

of Tennyson have read this section as addressed to Emily Tennyson,
Hallam's fiancee. It can also be read as addressed by the speaker to himself.

   With all the circle of the wise,
The perfect flower of human time;   1120

And if thou cast thine eyes below,
   How dimly character'd and slight,
   How dwarf'd a growth of cold and night,
How blanch'd with darkness must I grow!

Yet turn thee to the doubtful shore,
   Where thy first form was made a man;
   I loved thee, Spirit, and love, nor can
The soul of Shakespeare love thee more.

LXII

Tho' if an eye that's downward cast
   Could make thee somewhat blench or fail,   1130
   Then be my love an idle tale
And fading legend of the past;

And thou, as one that once declined,
   When he was little more than boy,
   On some unworthy heart with joy,
But lives to wed an equal mind,

And breathes a novel world, the while
   His other passion wholly dies,
   Or in the light of deeper eyes
Is matter for a flying smile.   1140

LXIII

Yet pity for a horse o'er-driven,
   And love in which my hound has part
   Can hang no weight upon my heart
In its assumptions up to heaven;

And I am so much more than these,
   As thou, perchance, art more than I,
   And yet I spare them sympathy,
And I would set their pains at ease.

So mayst thou watch me where I weep,
   As, unto vaster motions bound,   1150
   The circuits of thine orbit round
A higher height, a deeper deep.

LXIV

Dost thou look back on what hath been,
   As some divinely gifted man,
   Whose life in low estate began
And on a simple village green;

Who breaks his birth's invidious bar,
   And grasps the skirts of happy chance,

And breasts the blows of circumstance,
1160 And grapples with his evil star;

Who makes by force his merit known
    And lives to clutch the golden keys,
    To mould a mighty state's decrees,
And shape the whisper of the throne;

And moving up from high to higher,
    Becomes on Fortune's crowning slope
    The pillar of a people's hope,
The centre of a world's desire;

Yet feels, as in a pensive dream,
1170   When all his active powers are still,
    A distant dearness in the hill,
A secret sweetness in the stream,

The limit of his narrower fate,
    While yet beside its vocal springs
    He play'd at counsellors and kings,
With one that was his earliest mate;

Who ploughs with pain his native lea
    And reaps the labor of his hands,
    Or in the furrow musing stands:
1180 "Does my old friend remember me?"

LXV

Sweet soul, do with me as thou wilt;
    I lull a fancy trouble-tost
    With "Love's too precious to be lost,
A little grain shall not be spilt."

And in that solace can I sing,
    Till out of painful phases wrought
    There flutters up a happy thought,
Self-balanced on a lightsome wing;

Since we deserved the name of friends,
1190   And thine effect so lives in me,
    A part of mine may live in thee
And move thee on to noble ends.

LXVI

You thought my heart too far diseased;
    You wonder when my fancies play
    To find me gay among the gay,
Like one with any trifle pleased.

The shade by which my life was crost,
    Which makes a desert in the mind,
    Has made me kindly with my kind,
1200 And like to him whose sight is lost;

Whose feet are guided thro' the land,
    Whose jest among his friends is free,
    Who takes the children on his knee,
And winds their curls about his hand.

He plays with threads, he beats his chair
    For pastime, dreaming of the sky;
    His inner day can never die,
His night of loss is always there.

LXVII

When on my bed the moonlight falls,
    I know that in thy place of rest   1210
    By that broad water of the west
There comes a glory on the walls:

Thy marble bright in dark appears,
    As slowly steals a silver flame
    Along the letters of thy name,
And o'er the number of thy years.

The mystic glory swims away,
    From off my bed the moonlight dies;
    And closing eaves of wearied eyes
I sleep till dusk is dipt in gray;   1220

And then I know the mist is drawn
    A lucid veil from coast to coast,
    And in the dark church like a ghost
Thy tablet glimmers in the dawn.

LXVIII

When in the down I sink my head,
    Sleep, Death's twin-brother, times my breath;
    Sleep, Death's twin-brother, knows not Death,
Nor can I dream of thee as dead.

I walk as ere I walk'd forlorn,
    When all our path was fresh with dew,   1230
    And all the bugle breezes blew
Reveillée to the breaking morn.

But what is this? I turn about,
    I find a trouble in thine eye,
    Which makes me sad I know not why,
Nor can my dream resolve the doubt;

But ere the lark hath left the lea
    I wake, and I discern the truth;
    It is the trouble of my youth
That foolish sleep transfers to thee.   1240

1211. **that broad water,** the Severn River. 1280. **summer France.**

LXIX

I dream'd there would be Spring no more,
  That Nature's ancient power was lost;
  The streets were black with smoke and frost,
They chatter'd trifles at the door;

I wander'd from the noisy town,
  I found a wood with thorny boughs;
  I took the thorns to bind my brows,
I wore them like a civic crown;

I met with scoffs, I met with scorns
1250 From youth and babe and hoary hairs:
  They call'd me in the public squares
The fool that wears a crown of thorns.

They call'd me fool, they call'd me child:
  I found an angel of the night;
  The voice was low, the look was bright;
He look'd upon my crown and smiled.

He reach'd the glory of a hand,
  That seem'd to touch it into leaf;
  The voice was not the voice of grief,
1260 The words were hard to understand.

LXX

I cannot see the features right,
  When on the gloom I strive to paint
  The face I know; the hues are faint
And mix with hollow masks of night;

Cloud-towers by ghostly masons wrought,
  A gulf that ever shuts and gapes,
  A hand that points, and palled shapes
In shadowy thoroughfares of thought;

And crowds that stream from yawning doors,
1270 And shoals of pucker'd faces drive;
  Dark bulks that tumble half alive,
And lazy lengths on boundless shores;

Till all at once beyond the will
  I hear a wizard music roll,
  And thro' a lattice on the soul
Looks thy fair face and makes it still.

LXXI

Sleep, kinsman thou to death and trance
  And madness, thou hast forged at last
  A night-long present of the past
1280 In which we went thro' summer France.

Hadst thou such credit with the soul?
  Then bring an opiate trebly strong,
  Drug down the blindfold sense of wrong,
That so my pleasure may be whole;

While now we talk as once we talk'd
  Of men and minds, the dust of change,
  The days that grow to something strange,
In walking as of old we walk'd

Beside the river's wooded reach,
  The fortress, and the mountain ridge,   1290
  The cataract flashing from the bridge,
The breaker breaking on the beach.

LXXII

Risest thou thus, dim dawn, again,
  And howlest, issuing out of night,
  With blasts that blow the poplar white,
And lash with storm the streaming pane?

Day, when my crown'd estate begun
  To pine in that reverse of doom,
  Which sicken'd every living bloom,
And blurr'd the splendor of the sun;   1300

Who usherest in the dolorous hour
  With thy quick tears that make the rose
  Pull sideways, and the daisy close
Her crimson fringes to the shower;

Who mightst have heaved a windless flame
  Up the deep East, or, whispering, play'd
  A chequer-work of beam and shade
Along the hills, yet look'd the same,

As wan, as chill, as wild as now;
  Day, mark'd as with some hideous crime,   1310
  When the dark hand struck down thro' time,
And cancell'd nature's best: but thou,

Lift as thou mayst thy burthen'd brows
  Thro' clouds that drench the morning star,
  And whirl the ungarner'd sheaf afar,
And sow the sky with flying boughs,

And up thy vault with roaring sound
  Climb thy thick noon, disastrous day;
  Touch thy dull goal of joyless gray,
And hide thy shame beneath the ground.   1320

LXXIII

So many worlds, so much to do,
  So little done, such things to be,

Tennyson and Hallam had visited the French Pyrenees in the summer of 1830. 1293. **dim dawn,** the first anniversary of Hallam's death, September 15, 1834.

How know I what had need of thee,
For thou wert strong as thou wert true?

The fame is quench'd that I foresaw,
    The head hath miss'd an earthly wreath:
    I curse not Nature, no, nor Death;
For nothing is that errs from law.

We pass; the path that each man trod
1330   Is dim, or will be dim, with weeds.
    What fame is left for human deeds
In endless age? It rests with God.

O hollow wraith of dying fame,
    Fade wholly, while the soul exults,
    And self-infolds the large results
Of force that would have forged a name.

LXXIV

As sometimes in a dead man's face,
    To those that watch it more and more,
    A likeness, hardly seen before,
1340 Comes out—to some one of his race;

So, dearest, now thy brows are cold,
    I see thee what thou art, and know
    Thy likeness to the wise below,
Thy kindred with the great of old.

But there is more than I can see,
    And what I see I leave unsaid,
    Nor speak it, knowing Death has made
His darkness beautiful with thee.

LXXV

I leave thy praises unexpress'd
1350   In verse that brings myself relief,
    And by the measure of my grief
I leave thy greatness to be guess'd.

What practice howsoe'er expert
    In fitting aptest words to things,
    Or voice the richest-toned that sings,
Hath power to give thee as thou wert?

I care not in these fading days
    To raise a cry that lasts not long,
    And round thee with the breeze of song
1360 To stir a little dust of praise.

Thy leaf has perish'd in the green,
    And, while we breathe beneath the sun,
    The world which credits what is done
Is cold to all that might have been.

So here shall silence guard thy fame;
    But somewhere, out of human view,
    Whate'er thy hands are set to do
Is wrought with tumult of acclaim.

LXXVI

Take wings of fancy, and ascend,
    And in a moment set thy face   1370
    Where all the starry heavens of space
Are sharpen'd to a needle's end;

Take wings of foresight; lighten thro'
    The secular abyss to come,
    And lo, thy deepest lays are dumb
Before the mouldering of a yew;

And if the matin songs, that woke
    The darkness of our planet, last,
    Thine own shall wither in the vast,
Ere half the lifetime of an oak.   1380

Ere these have clothed their branchy bowers
    With fifty Mays, thy songs are vain;
    And what are they when these remain
The ruin'd shells of hollow towers?

LXXVII

What hope is here for modern rhyme
    To him who turns a musing eye
    On songs, and deeds, and lives, that lie
Foreshorten'd in the tract of time?

These mortal lullabies of pain
    May bind a book, may line a box,   1390
    May serve to curl a maiden's locks;
Or when a thousand moons shall wane

A man upon a stall may find,
    And, passing, turn the page that tells
    A grief, then changed to something else,
Sung by a long-forgotten mind.

But what of that? My darken'd ways
    Shall ring with music all the same;
    To breathe my loss is more than fame,
To utter love more sweet than praise.   1400

LXXVIII

Again at Christmas did we weave
    The holly round the Christmas hearth;
    The silent snow possess'd the earth,
And calmly fell our Christmas-eve.

The yule-clog sparkled keen with frost,
    No wing of wind the region swept,

But over all things brooding slept
The quiet sense of something lost.

As in the winters left behind,
1410   Again our ancient games had place,
   The mimic picture's breathing grace,
And dance and song and hoodman-blind.

Who show'd a token of distress?
   No single tear, no mark of pain—
   O sorrow, then can sorrow wane?
O grief, can grief be changed to less?

O last regret, regret can die!
   No—mixt with all this mystic frame,
   Her deep relations are the same,
1420 But with long use her tears are dry.

LXXIX

"More than my brothers are to me,"—
   Let this not vex thee, noble heart!
   I know thee of what force thou art
To hold the costliest love in fee.

But thou and I are one in kind,
   As moulded like in Nature's mint;
   And hill and wood and field did print
The same sweet forms in either mind.

For us the same cold streamlet curl'd
1430   Thro' all his eddying coves, the same
   All winds that roam the twilight came
In whispers of the beauteous world.

At one dear knee we proffer'd vows,
   One lesson from one book we learn'd,
   Ere childhood's flaxen ringlet turn'd
To black and brown on kindred brows.

And so my wealth resembles thine,
   But he was rich where I was poor,
   And he supplied my want the more
1440 As his unlikeness fitted mine.

LXXX

If any vague desire should rise,
   That holy Death ere Arthur died
   Had moved me kindly from his side,
And dropt the dust on tearless eyes;

Then fancy shapes, as fancy can,
   The grief my loss in him had wrought,

A grief as deep as life or thought,
But stay'd in peace with God and man.

I make a picture in the brain;
   I hear the sentence that he speaks;   1450
   He bears the burthen of the weeks,
But turns his burthen into gain.

His credit thus shall set me free;
   And, influence-rich to soothe and save,
   Unused example from the grave
Reach out dead hands to comfort me.

LXXXI

Could I have said while he was here,
   "My love shall now no further range;
   There cannot come a mellower change,
For now is love mature in ear"?   1460

Love, then, had hope of richer store:
   What end is here to my complaint?
   This haunting whisper makes me faint,
"More years had made me love thee more."

But Death returns an answer sweet:
   "My sudden frost was sudden gain,
   And gave all ripeness to the grain
It might have drawn from after-heat."

LXXXII

I wage not any feud with Death
   For changes wrought on form and face;   1470
   No lower life that earth's embrace
May breed with him can fright my faith.

Eternal process moving on,
   From state to state the spirit walks;
   And these are but the shatter'd stalks,
Or ruin'd chrysalis of one.

Nor blame I Death, because he bare
   The use of virtue out of earth;
   I know transplanted human worth
Will bloom to profit, otherwhere.   1480

For this alone on Death I wreak
   The wrath that garners in my heart:
   He put our lives so far apart
We cannot hear each other speak.

LXXXIII

Dip down upon the northern shore,
   O sweet new-year delaying long;

1411. **mimic picture's,** a form of charade. 1421-1440. **More ... brothers,** etc. The "brother" addressed in this section is Charles, with whom

Tennyson had collaborated in an early volume of poems.

Thou doest expectant Nature wrong;
  Delaying long, delay no more.

What stays thee from the clouded noons,
1490   Thy sweetness from its proper place?
    Can trouble live with April days,
Or sadness in the summer moons?

Bring orchis, bring the foxglove spire,
  The little speedwell's darling blue,
  Deep tulips dash'd with fiery dew,
Laburnums, dropping-wells of fire.

O thou, new-year, delaying long,
  Delayest the sorrow in my blood,
  That longs to burst a frozen bud
1500 And flood a fresher throat with song.

LXXXIV

When I contemplate all alone
  The life that had been thine below,
  And fix my thoughts on all the glow
To which thy crescent would have grown,

I see thee sitting crown'd with good,
  A central warmth diffusing bliss
  In glance and smile, and clasp and kiss,
On all the branches of thy blood;

Thy blood, my friend, and partly mine;
1510   For now the day was drawing on,
    When thou shouldst link thy life with one
Of mine own house, and boys of thine

Had babbled "Uncle" on my knee;
  But that remorseless iron hour
  Made cypress of her orange flower,
Despair of hope, and earth of thee.

I seem to meet their least desire,
  To clap their cheeks, to call them mine.
  I see their unborn faces shine
1520 Beside the never-lighted fire.

I see myself an honor'd guest,
  Thy partner in the flowery walk
  Of letters, genial table-talk,
Or deep dispute, and graceful jest;

While now thy prosperous labor fills
  The lips of men with honest praise,
  And sun by sun the happy days
Descend below the golden hills

1511. **one ... house.** Hallam had been engaged to Tennyson's sister.

With promise of a morn as fair;
  And all the train of bounteous hours   1530
  Conduct, by paths of growing powers,
To reverence and the silver hair;

Till slowly worn her earthly robe,
  Her lavish mission richly wrought,
  Leaving great legacies of thought,
Thy spirit should fail from off the globe;

What time mine own might also flee,
  As link'd with thine in love and fate,
  And, hovering o'er the dolorous strait
To the other shore, involved in thee,   1540

Arrive at last the blessed goal,
  And He that died in Holy Land
  Would reach us out the shining hand,
And take us as a single soul.

What reed was that on which I leant?
  Ah, backward fancy, wherefore wake
  The old bitterness again, and break
The low beginnings of content?

LXXXV

This truth came borne with bier and pall,
  I felt it, when I sorrow'd most,   1550
  'T is better to have loved and lost,
Than never to have loved at all—

O true in word, and tried in deed,
  Demanding, so to bring relief
  To this which is our common grief,
What kind of life is that I lead;

And whether trust in things above
  Be dimm'd of sorrow, or sustain'd;
  And whether love for him have drain'd
My capabilities of love;   1560

Your words have virtue such as draws
  A faithful answer from the breast,
  Thro' light reproaches, half exprest,
And loyal unto kindly laws.

My blood an even tenor kept,
  Till on mine ear this message falls,
  That in Vienna's fatal walls
God's finger touch'd him, and he slept.

The great Intelligences fair
  That range above our mortal state,   1570
  In circle round the blessed gate,
Received and gave him welcome there;

And led him thro' the blissful climes,
   And show'd him in the fountain fresh
   All knowledge that the sons of flesh
Shall gather in the cycled times.

But I remain'd, whose hopes were dim,
   Whose life, whose thoughts were little worth,
   To wander on a darken'd earth,
1580 Where all things round me breathed of him.

O friendship, equal-poised control,
   O heart, with kindliest motion warm,
   O sacred essence, other form,
O solemn ghost, O crowned soul!

Yet none could better know than I,
   How much of act at human hands
   The sense of human will demands
By which we dare to live or die.

Whatever way my days decline,
1590   I felt and feel, tho' left alone,
   His being working in mine own,
The footsteps of his life in mine;

A life that all the Muses deck'd
   With gifts of grace, that might express
   All-comprehensive tenderness,
All-subtilizing intellect:

And so my passion hath not swerved
   To works of weakness, but I find
   An image comforting the mind,
1600 And in my grief a strength reserved.

Likewise the imaginative woe,
   That loved to handle spiritual strife,
   Diffused the shock thro' all my life,
But in the present broke the blow.

My pulses therefore beat again
   For other friends that once I met;
   Nor can it suit me to forget
The mighty hopes that make us men.

I woo your love: I count it crime
1610   To mourn for any overmuch;
   I, the divided half of such
A friendship as had master'd Time;

Which masters Time indeed, and is
   Eternal, separate from fears.
   The all-assuming months and years
Can take no part away from this;

But Summer on the steaming floods,
   And Spring that swells the narrow brooks,

And Autumn, with a noise of rooks,
That gather in the waning woods,   1620

And every pulse of wind and wave
   Recalls, in change of light or gloom,
   My old affection of the tomb,
And my prime passion in the grave.

My old affection of the tomb,
   A part of stillness, yearns to speak:
   "Arise, and get thee forth and seek
A friendship for the years to come.

"I watch thee from the quiet shore;
   Thy spirit up to mine can reach;   1630
   But in dear words of human speech
We two communicate no more."

And I, "Can clouds of nature stain
   The starry clearness of the free?
   How is it? Canst thou feel for me
Some painless sympathy with pain?"

And lightly does the whisper fall:
   " 'T is hard for thee to fathom this;
   I triumph in conclusive bliss,
And that serene result of all."   1640

So hold I commerce with the dead;
   Or so methinks the dead would say;
   O so shall grief with symbols play
And pining life be fancy-fed.

Now looking to some settled end,
   That these things pass, and I shall prove
   A meeting somewhere, love with love,
I crave your pardon, O my friend;

If not so fresh, with love as true,
   I, clasping brother-hands, aver   1650
   I could not, if I would, transfer
The whole I felt for him to you.

For which be they that hold apart
   The promise of the golden hours?
   First love, first friendship, equal powers,
That marry with the virgin heart.

Still mine, that cannot but deplore,
   That beats within a lonely place,
   That yet remembers his embrace,
But at his footstep leaps no more,   1660

My heart, tho' widow'd, may not rest
   Quite in the love of what is gone,
   But seeks to beat in time with one
That warms another living breast.

Ah, take the imperfect gift I bring,
   Knowing the primrose yet is dear,
   The primrose of the later year,
As not unlike to that of Spring.

LXXXVI

Sweet after showers, ambrosial air,
1670 That rollest from the gorgeous gloom
   Of evening over brake and bloom
And meadow, slowly breathing bare

The round of space, and rapt below
   Thro' all the dewy tassell'd wood,
   And shadowing down the horned flood
In ripples, fan my brows and blow

The fever from my cheek, and sigh
   The full new life that feeds thy breath
   Throughout my frame, till Doubt and Death,
1680 Ill brethren, let the fancy fly

From belt to belt of crimson seas
   On leagues of odor streaming far,
   To where in yonder orient star
A hundred spirits whisper "Peace."

LXXXVII

I past beside the reverend walls
   In which of old I wore the gown;
   I roved at random thro' the town,
And saw the tumult of the halls;

And heard once more in college fanes
1690 The storm their high-built organs make,
   And thunder-music, rolling, shake
The prophet blazon'd on the panes;

And caught once more the distant shout,
   The measured pulse of racing oars
   Among the willows; paced the shores
And many a bridge, and all about

The same gray flats again, and felt
   The same, but not the same; and last
   Up that long walk of limes I past
1700 To see the rooms in which he dwelt.

Another name was on the door.
   I linger'd; all within was noise
   Of songs, and clapping hands, and boys
That crash'd the glass and beat the floor;

Where once we held debate, a band
   Of youthful friends, on mind and art,

And labor, and the changing mart,
And all the framework of the land;

When one would aim an arrow fair,
   But send it slackly from the string;   1710
   And one would pierce an outer ring,
And one an inner, here and there;

And last the master-bowman, he,
   Would cleave the mark. A willing ear
   We lent him. Who but hung to hear
The rapt oration flowing free

From point to point, with power and grace
   And music in the bounds of law,
   To those conclusions when we saw
The God within him light his face,   1720

And seem to lift the form, and glow
   In azure orbits heavenly-wise;
   And over those ethereal eyes
The bar of Michael Angelo?

LXXXVIII

Wild bird, whose warble, liquid sweet,
   Rings Eden thro' the budded quicks,
   O, tell me where the senses mix,
O, tell me where the passions meet,

Whence radiate: fierce extremes employ
   Thy spirits in the darkening leaf,   1730
   And in the midmost heart of grief
Thy passion clasps a secret joy;

And I—my harp would prelude woe—
   I cannot all command the strings;
   The glory of the sum of things
Will flash along the chords and go.

LXXXIX

Witch-elms that counterchange the floor
   Of this flat lawn with dusk and bright;
   And thou, with all thy breadth and height
Of foliage, towering sycamore;   1740

How often, hither wandering down,
   My Arthur found your shadows fair,
   And shook to all the liberal air
The dust and din and steam of town!

He brought an eye for all he saw;
   He mixt in all our simple sports;

1685. reverend walls, Trinity College, Cambridge.　1705. debate. Tennyson and Hallam had belonged to a group called the "Apostles."　1724.

bar, a prominent ridge of bone above the eyes.　1725. Wild bird, the nightingale.

They pleased him, fresh from brawling courts
And dusty purlieus of the law.

O joy to him in this retreat,
1750   Immantled in ambrosial dark,
    To drink the cooler air, and mark
The landscape winking thro' the heat!

O sound to rout the brood of cares,
    The sweep of scythe in morning dew,
    The gust that round the garden flew,
And tumbled half the mellowing pears!

O bliss, when all in circle drawn
    About him, heart and ear were fed
    To hear him, as he lay and read
1760 The Tuscan poets on the lawn!

Or in the all-golden afternoon
    A guest, or happy sister, sung,
    Or here she brought the harp and flung
A ballad to the brightening moon.

Nor less it pleased in livelier moods,
    Beyond the bounding hill to stray,
    And break the livelong summer day
With banquet in the distant woods;

Whereat we glanced from theme to theme,
1770   Discuss'd the books to love or hate,
    Or touch'd the changes of the state,
Or threaded some Socratic dream;

But if I praised the busy town,
    He loved to rail against it still,
    For "ground in yonder social mill
We rub each other's angles down,

"And merge," he said, "in form and gloss
    The picturesque of man and man."
    We talk'd: the stream beneath us ran,
1780 The wine-flask lying couch'd in moss,

Or cool'd within the glooming wave;
    And last, returning from afar,
    Before the crimson-circled star
Had fallen into her father's grave,

And brushing ankle-deep in flowers,
    We heard behind the woodbine veil
    The milk that bubbled in the pail,
And buzzings of the honeyed hours.

XC

He tasted love with half his mind,
1790   Nor ever drank the inviolate spring

Where nighest heaven, who first could fling
This bitter seed among mankind:

That could the dead, whose dying eyes
    Were closed with wail, resume their life,
    They would but find in child and wife
An iron welcome when they rise.

'T was well, indeed, when warm with wine,
    To pledge them with a kindly tear,
    To talk them o'er, to wish them here,
To count their memories half divine;   1800

But if they came who past away,
    Behold their brides in other hands;
    The hard heir strides about their lands,
And will not yield them for a day.

Yea, tho' their sons were none of these,
    Not less the yet-loved sire would make
    Confusion worse than death, and shake
The pillars of domestic peace.

Ah, dear, but come thou back to me!
    Whatever change the years have wrought,   1810
    I find not yet one lonely thought
That cries against my wish for thee.

XCI

When rosy plumelets tuft the larch,
    And rarely pipes the mounted thrush,
    Or underneath the barren bush
Flits by the sea-blue bird of March;

Come, wear the form by which I know
    Thy spirit in time among thy peers;
    The hope of unaccomplish'd years
Be large and lucid round thy brow.   1820

When summer's hourly-mellowing change
    May breathe, with many roses sweet,
    Upon the thousand waves of wheat
That ripple round the lowly grange,

Come; not in watches of the night,
    But where the sunbeam broodeth warm,
    Come, beauteous in thine after form,
And like a finer light in light.

XCII

If any vision should reveal
    Thy likeness, I might count it vain   1830
    As but the canker of the brain;
Yea, tho' it spake and made appeal

To chances where our lots were cast
    Together in the days behind,
    I might but say, I hear a wind
Of memory murmuring the past.

Yea, tho' it spake and bared to view
    A fact within the coming year;
    And tho' the months, revolving near,
1840 Should prove the phantom-warning true,

They might not seem thy prophecies,
    But spiritual presentiments,
    And such refraction of events
As often rises ere they rise.

XCIII

I shall not see thee. Dare I say
    No spirit ever brake the band
    That stays him from the native land
Where first he walked when claspt in clay?

No visual shade of some one lost,
1850   But he, the Spirit himself, may come
    Where all the nerve of sense is numb,
Spirit to Spirit, Ghost to Ghost.

O, therefore from thy sightless range
    With gods in unconjectured bliss,
    O, from the distance of the abyss
Of tenfold-complicated change,

Descend, and touch, and enter; hear
    The wish too strong for words to name,
    That in this blindness of the frame
1860 My Ghost may feel that thine is near.

XCIV

How pure at heart and sound in head,
    With what divine affections bold
    Should be the man whose thought would hold
An hour's communion with the dead.

In vain shalt thou, or any, call
    The spirits from their golden day,
    Except, like them, thou too canst say,
My spirit is at peace with all.

They haunt the silence of the breast,
1870   Imaginations calm and fair,
    The memory like a cloudless air,
The conscience as a sea at rest;

But when the heart is full of din,
    And doubt beside the portal waits,

They can but listen at the gates,
And hear the household jar within.

XCV

By night we linger'd on the lawn,
    For underfoot the herb was dry;
    And genial warmth; and o'er the sky
The silvery haze of summer drawn;   1880

And calm that let the tapers burn
    Unwavering: not a cricket chirr'd;
    The brook alone far-off was heard,
And on the board the fluttering urn.

And bats went round in fragrant skies,
    And wheel'd or lit the filmy shapes
    That haunt the dusk, with ermine capes
And woolly breasts and beaded eyes;

While now we sang old songs that peal'd
    From knoll to knoll, where, couch'd at ease,   1890
    The white kine glimmer'd, and the trees
Laid their dark arms about the field.

But when those others, one by one,
    Withdrew themselves from me and night,
    And in the house light after light
Went out, and I was all alone,

A hunger seized my heart; I read
    Of that glad year which once had been,
    In those fallen leaves which kept their green,
The noble letters of the dead.   1900

And strangely on the silence broke
    The silent-speaking words, and strange
    Was love's dumb cry defying change
To test his worth; and strangely spoke

The faith, the vigor, bold to dwell
    On doubts that drive the coward back,
    And keen thro' wordy snares to track
Suggestion to her inmost cell.

So word by word, and line by line,
    The dead man touch'd me from the past,   1910
    And all at once it seem'd at last
The living soul was flash'd on mine,

And mine in this was wound, and whirl'd
    About empyreal heights of thought,
    And came on that which is, and caught
The deep pulsations of the world,

1877-1940. **By night, etc.** This section contains the first climax of reunion
in the poem. The experience is mystical, but Tennyson very carefully pre-

Æonian music measuring out
    The steps of Time—the shocks of Chance—
    The blows of Death. At length my trance
1920 Was cancell'd, stricken thro' with doubt.

Vague words! but ah, how hard to frame
    In matter-moulded forms of speech,
    Or even for intellect to reach
Thro' memory that which I became;

Till now the doubtful dusk reveal'd
    The knolls once more where, couch'd at ease,
    The white kine glimmer'd, and the trees
Laid their dark arms about the field;

And suck'd from out the distant gloom
1930   A breeze began to tremble o'er
    The large leaves of the sycamore,
And fluctuate all the still perfume,

And gathering freshlier overhead,
    Rock'd the full-foliaged elms, and swung
    The heavy-folded rose, and flung
The lilies to and fro, and said,

"The dawn, the dawn," and died away;
    And East and West, without a breath,
    Mixt their dim lights, like life and death,
1940 To broaden into boundless day.

    XCVI

You say, but with no touch of scorn,
    Sweet-hearted, you, whose light-blue eyes
    Are tender over drowning flies,
You tell me, doubt is Devil-born.

I know not: one indeed I knew
    In many a subtle question versed,
    Who touch'd a jarring lyre at first,
But ever strove to make it true;

Perplext in faith, but pure in deeds,
1950   At last he beat his music out.
    There lives more faith in honest doubt,
Believe me, than in half the creeds.

He fought his doubts and gather'd strength,
    He would not make his judgment blind,
    He faced the spectres of the mind
And laid them; thus he came at length

To find a stronger faith his own,
    And Power was with him in the night,

Which makes the darkness and the light,
    And dwells not in the light alone,   1960

But in the darkness and the cloud,
    As over Sinai's peaks of old,
    While Israel made their gods of gold,
Altho' the trumpet blew so loud.

XCVII

My love has talk'd with rocks and trees;
    He finds on misty mountain-ground
    His own vast shadow glory-crown'd;
He sees himself in all he sees.

Two partners of a married life—
    I look'd on these and thought of thee   1970
    In vastness and in mystery,
And of my spirit as of a wife.

These two—they dwelt with eye on eye,
    Their hearts of old have beat in tune,
    Their meetings made December June,
Their every parting was to die.

Their love has never past away;
    The days she never can forget
    Are earnest that he loves her yet,
Whate'er the faithless people say.   1980

Her life is lone, he sits apart;
    He loves her yet, she will not weep,
    Tho' rapt in matters dark and deep
He seems to slight her simple heart.

He thrids the labyrinth of the mind,
    He reads the secret of the star,
    He seems so near and yet so far,
He looks so cold: she thinks him kind.

She keeps the gift of years before,
    A wither'd violet is her bliss;   1990
    She knows not what his greatness is,
For that, for all, she loves him more.

For him she plays, to him she sings
    Of early faith and plighted vows;
    She knows but matters of the house,
And he, he knows a thousand things.

Her faith is fixt and cannot move,
    She darkly feels him great and wise,
    She dwells on him with faithful eyes,
"I cannot understand; I love."   2000

pares the setting to achieve psychological truth.   1963. **While Israel, etc.**
The Israelites made a golden calf to worship while God was revealing the

Commandments to Moses.

XCVIII

You leave us: you will see the Rhine,
    And those fair hills I sail'd below,
    When I was there with him; and go
By summer belts of wheat and vine

To where he breathed his latest breath,
    That city. All her splendor seems
    No livelier than the wisp that gleams
On Lethe in the eyes of Death.

Let her great Danube rolling fair
2010   Enwind her isles, unmark'd of me;
    I have not seen, I will not see
Vienna; rather dream that there,

A treble darkness, Evil haunts
    The birth, the bridal; friend from friend
    Is oftener parted, fathers bend
Above more graves, a thousand wants

Gnarr at the heels of men, and prey
    By each cold hearth, and sadness flings
    Her shadow on the blaze of kings.
2020 And yet myself have heard him say,

That not in any mother town
    With statelier progress to and fro
    The double tides of chariots flow
By park and suburb under brown

Of lustier leaves; nor more content,
    He told me, lives in any crowd,
    When all is gay with lamps, and loud
With sport and song, in booth and tent,

Imperial halls, or open plain;
2030   And wheels the circled dance, and breaks
    The rocket molten into flakes
Of crimson or in emerald rain.

XCIX

Risest thou thus, dim dawn, again,
    So loud with voices of the birds,
    So thick with lowings of the herds,
Day, when I lost the flower of men;

Who tremblest thro' thy darkling red
    On yon swollen brook that bubbles fast
    By meadows breathing of the past,
2040 And woodlands holy to the dead;

Who murmurest in the foliaged eaves
    A song that slights the coming care,
    And Autumn laying here and there
A fiery finger on the leaves;

Who wakenest with thy balmy breath
    To myriads on the genial earth,
    Memories of bridal, or of birth,
And unto myriads more, of death.

O, wheresoever those may be,
    Betwixt the slumber of the poles,   2050
    To-day they count as kindred souls;
They know me not, but mourn with me.

C

I climb the hill: from end to end
    Of all the landscape underneath,
    I find no place that does not breathe
Some gracious memory of my friend;

No gray old grange, or lonely fold,
    Or low morass and whispering reed,
    Or simple stile from mead to mead,
Or sheepwalk up the windy wold;   2060

Nor hoary knoll of ash and haw
    That hears the latest linnet trill,
    Nor quarry trench'd along the hill
And haunted by the wrangling daw;

Nor runlet tinkling from the rock;
    Nor pastoral rivulet that swerves
    To left and right thro' meadowy curves,
That feed the mothers of the flock;

But each has pleased a kindred eye,
    And each reflects a kindlier day;   2070
    And, leaving these, to pass away,
I think once more he seems to die.

CI

Unwatch'd, the garden bough shall sway,
    The tender blossom flutter down,
    Unloved, that beech will gather brown,
This maple burn itself away;

Unloved, the sunflower, shining fair,
    Ray round with flames her disk of seed,
    And many a rose-carnation feed
With summer spice the humming air;   2080

2001-2032. **You leave us, etc.** Tennyson's brother Charles was going to
Vienna and the Rhine Valley on his honeymoon.   2053. **I climb the hill.**
In 1837, the Tennysons left Lincolnshire and moved close to London.

2083. **Lesser Wain,** the constellation Ursa Minor, the Little Dipper.
2121-2176. **On that last night, etc.** This section contains the second
climax of reunion in the poem, in the form of an allegorical dream-vision.

Unloved, by many a sandy bar,
  The brook shall babble down the plain,
  At noon or when the Lesser Wain
Is twisting round the polar star;

Uncared for, gird the windy grove,
  And flood the haunts of hern and crake,
  Or into silver arrows break
The sailing moon in creek and cove;

Till from the garden and the wild
2090 A fresh association blow,
  And year by year the landscape grow
Familiar to the stranger's child;

As year by year the laborer tills
  His wonted glebe, or lops the glades,
  And year by year our memory fades
From all the circle of the hills.

CII

We leave the well-beloved place
  Where first we gazed upon the sky;
  The roofs that heard our earliest cry
2100 Will shelter one of stranger race.

We go, but ere we go from home,
  As down the garden-walks I move,
  Two spirits of a diverse love
Contend for loving masterdom.

One whispers, "Here thy boyhood sung
  Long since its matin song, and heard
  The low love-language of the bird
In native hazels tassel-hung."

The other answers, "Yea, but here
2110 Thy feet have stray'd in after hours
  With thy lost friend among the bowers,
And this hath made them trebly dear."

These two have striven half the day,
  And each prefers his separate claim,
  Poor rivals in a losing game,
That will not yield each other way.

I turn to go; my feet are set
  To leave the pleasant fields and farms;
  They mix in one another's arms
2120 To one pure image of regret.

CIII

On that last night before we went
  From out the doors where I was bred,
  I dream'd a vision of the dead,
Which left my after-morn content.

Methought I dwelt within a hall,
  And maidens with me; distant hills
  From hidden summits fed with rills
A river sliding by the wall.

The hall with harp and carol rang.
  They sang of what is wise and good   2130
  And graceful. In the centre stood
A statue veil'd, to which they sang;

And which, tho' veil'd, was known to me,
  The shape of him I loved, and love
  For ever. Then flew in a dove
And brought a summons from the sea;

And when they learnt that I must go,
  They wept and wail'd, but led the way
  To where a little shallop lay
At anchor in the flood below;   2140

And on by many a level mead,
  And shadowing bluff that made the banks,
  We glided winding under ranks
Of iris and the golden reed;

And still as vaster grew the shore
  And roll'd the floods in grander space,
  The maidens gather'd strength and grace
And presence, lordlier than before;

And I myself, who sat apart
  And watch'd them, wax'd in every limb;   2150
  I felt the thews of Anakim,
The pulses of a Titan's heart;

As one would sing the death of war,
  And one would chant the history
  Of that great race which is to be,
And one the shaping of a star;

Until the forward-creeping tides
  Began to foam, and we to draw
  From deep to deep, to where we saw
A great ship lift her shining sides.   2160

The man we loved was there on deck,
  But thrice as large as man he bent

To greet us. Up the side I went,
And fell in silence on his neck;

Whereat those maidens with one mind
    Bewail'd their lot; I did them wrong:
    "We served thee here," they said, "so long,
And wilt thou leave us now behind?"

So rapt I was, they could not win
2170   An answer from my lips, but he
    Replying, "Enter likewise ye
And go with us": they enter'd in.

And while the wind began to sweep
    A music out of sheet and shroud,
    We steer'd her toward a crimson cloud
That landlike slept along the deep.

CIV

The time draws near the birth of Christ;
    The moon is hid, the night is still;
    A single church below the hill
2180 Is pealing, folded in the mist.

A single peal of bells below,
    That wakens at this hour of rest
    A single murmur in the breast,
That these are not the bells I know.

Like strangers' voices here they sound,
    In lands where not a memory strays,
    Nor landmark breathes of other days,
But all is new unhallow'd ground.

CV

To-night ungather'd let us leave
2190   This laurel, let this holly stand:
    We live within the stranger's land,
And strangely falls our Christmas-eve.

Our father's dust is left alone
    And silent under other snows:
    There in due time the woodbine blows,
The violet comes, but we are gone.

No more shall wayward grief abuse
    The genial hour with mask and mime;
    For change of place, like growth of time,
2200 Has broke the bond of dying use.

Let cares that petty shadows cast,
    By which our lives are chiefly proved,
    A little spare the night I loved,
And hold it solemn to the past.

But let no footstep beat the floor,
    Nor bowl of wassail mantle warm;
    For who would keep an ancient form
Thro' which the spirit breathes no more?

Be neither song, nor game, nor feast;
    Nor harp be touch'd, nor flute be blown;   2210
    No dance, no motion, save alone
What lightens in the lucid East

Of rising worlds by yonder wood.
    Long sleeps the summer in the seed;
    Run out your measured arcs, and lead
The closing cycle rich in good.

CVI

Ring out, wild bells, to the wild sky,
    The flying cloud, the frosty light:
    The year is dying in the night;
Ring out, wild bells, and let him die.   2220

Ring out the old, ring in the new,
    Ring, happy bells, across the snow:
    The year is going, let him go;
Ring out the false, ring in the true.

Ring out the grief that saps the mind,
    For those that here we see no more;
    Ring out the feud of rich and poor,
Ring in redress to all mankind.

Ring out a slowly dying cause,
    And ancient forms of party strife;   2230
    Ring in the nobler modes of life,
With sweeter manners, purer laws.

Ring out the want, the care, the sin,
    The faithless coldness of the times;
    Ring out, ring out my mournful rhymes,
But ring the fuller minstrel in.

Ring out false pride in place and blood,
    The civic slander and the spite;
    Ring in the love of truth and right,
Ring in the common love of good.   2240

Ring out old shapes of foul disease;
    Ring out the narrowing lust of gold;
    Ring out the thousand wars of old,
Ring in the thousand years of peace.

Ring in the valiant man and free,
    The larger heart, the kindlier hand;
    Ring out the darkness of the land,
Ring in the Christ that is to be.

It is the day when he was born,
2250   A bitter day that early sank
    Behind a purple-frosty bank
Of vapor, leaving night forlorn.

The time admits not flowers or leaves
    To deck the banquet. Fiercely flies
    The blast of North and East, and ice
Makes daggers at the sharpen'd eaves,

And bristles all the brakes and thorns
    To yon hard crescent, as she hangs
    Above the wood which grides and clangs
2260 Its leafless ribs and iron horns

Together, in the drifts that pass
    To darken on the rolling brine
    That breaks the coast. But fetch the wine,
Arrange the board and brim the glass;

Bring in great logs and let them lie,
    To make a solid core of heat;
    Be cheerful-minded, talk and treat
Of all things even as he were by;

We keep the day. With festal cheer,
2270   With books and music, surely we
    Will drink to him, whate'er he be,
And sing the songs he loved to hear.

CVIII

I will not shut me from my kind,
    And, lest I stiffen into stone,
    I will not eat my heart alone,
Nor feed with sighs a passing wind:

What profit lies in barren faith,
    And vacant yearning, tho' with might
    To scale the heaven's highest height,
2280 Or dive below the wells of death?

What find I in the highest place,
    But mine own phantom chanting hymns?
    And on the depths of death there swims
The reflex of a human face.

I'll rather take what fruit may be
    Of sorrow under human skies:
    'T is held that sorrow makes us wise,
Whatever wisdom sleep with thee.

2249. **day,** February 1.

Heart-affluence in discursive talk
    From household fountains never dry;   2290
    The critic clearness of an eye
That saw thro' all the Muses' walk:

Seraphic intellect and force
    To seize and throw the doubts of man;
    Impassion'd logic, which outran
The hearer in its fiery course;

High nature amorous of the good,
    But touch'd with no ascetic gloom;
    And passion pure in snowy bloom
Thro' all the years of April blood;   2300

A love of freedom rarely felt,
    Of freedom in her regal seat
    Of England; not the schoolboy heat,
The blind hysterics of the Celt;

And manhood fused with female grace
    In such a sort, the child would twine
    A trustful hand, unask'd, in thine,
And find his comfort in thy face;

All these have been, and thee mine eyes
    Have look'd on: if they look'd in vain,   2310
    My shame is greater who remain,
Nor let thy wisdom make me wise.

CX

Thy converse drew us with delight,
    The men of rathe and riper years;
    The feeble soul, a haunt of fears,
Forgot his weakness in thy sight.

On thee the loyal-hearted hung,
    The proud was half disarm'd of pride,
    Nor cared the serpent at thy side
To flicker with his double tongue.   2320

The stern were mild when thou wert by,
    The flippant put himself to school
    And heard thee, and the brazen fool
Was soften'd, and he knew not why;

While I, thy nearest, sat apart,
    And felt thy triumph was as mine;
    And loved them more, that they were thine,
The graceful tact, the Christian art;

Nor mine the sweetness or the skill,
    But mine the love that will not tire,   2330

And, born of love, the vague desire
That spurs an imitative will.

CXI

The churl in spirit, up or down
  Along the scale of ranks, thro' all,
  To him who grasps a golden ball,
By blood a king, at heart a clown,—

The churl in spirit, howe'er he veil
  His want in forms for fashion's sake,
  Will let his coltish nature break
2340 At seasons thro' the gilded pale;

For who can always act? but he,
  To whom a thousand memories call,
  Not being less but more than all
The gentleness he seem'd to be,

Best seem'd the thing he was, and join'd
  Each office of the social hour
  To noble manners, as the flower
And native growth of noble mind;

Nor ever narrowness or spite,
2350   Or villain fancy fleeting by,
  Drew in the expression of an eye
Where God and Nature met in light;

And thus he bore without abuse
  The grand old name of gentleman,
  Defamed by every charlatan,
And soil'd with all ignoble use.

CXII

High wisdom holds my wisdom less,
  That I, who gaze with temperate eyes
  On glorious insufficiencies,
2360 Set light by narrower perfectness.

But thou, that fillest all the room
  Of all my love, art reason why
  I seem to cast a careless eye
On souls, the lesser lords of doom.

For what wert thou? some novel power
  Sprang up for ever at a touch,
  And hope could never hope too much,
In watching thee from hour to hour,

Large elements in order brought,
2370   And tracts of calm from tempest made,
  And world-wide fluctuation sway'd
In vassal tides that follow'd thought.

CXIII

'T is held that sorrow makes us wise;
  Yet how much wisdom sleeps with thee
  Which not alone had guided me,
But served the seasons that may rise;

For can I doubt, who knew thee keen
  In intellect, with force and skill
  To strive, to fashion, to fulfil—
I doubt not what thou wouldst have been: 2380

A life in civic action warm,
  A soul on highest mission sent,
  A potent voice of Parliament,
A pillar steadfast in the storm,

Should licensed boldness gather force,
  Becoming, when the time has birth,
  A lever to uplift the earth
And roll it in another course,

With thousand shocks that come and go,
  With agonies, with energies,   2390
  With overthrowings, and with cries,
And undulations to and fro.

CXIV

Who loves not Knowledge? Who shall rail
  Against her beauty? May she mix
  With men and prosper! Who shall fix
Her pillars? Let her work prevail.

But on her forehead sits a fire;
  She sets her forward countenance
  And leaps into the future chance,
Submitting all things to desire.   2400

Half-grown as yet, a child, and vain—
  She cannot fight the fear of death.
  What is she, cut from love and faith,
But some wild Pallas from the brain

Of demons? fiery-hot to burst
  All barriers in her onward race
  For power. Let her know her place;
She is the second, not the first.

A higher hand must make her mild,
  If all be not in vain, and guide   2410
  Her footsteps, moving side by side
With Wisdom, like the younger child;

For she is earthly of the mind,
  But Wisdom heavenly of the soul.

O friend, who camest to thy goal
So early, leaving me behind,

I would the great world grew like thee,
    Who grewest not alone in power
    And knowledge, but by year and hour
2420 In reverence and in charity.

CXV

Now fades the last long streak of snow,
    Now burgeons every maze of quick
    About the flowering squares, and thick
By ashen roots the violets blow.

Now rings the woodland loud and long,
    The distance takes a lovelier hue,
    And drown'd in yonder living blue
The lark becomes a sightless song.

Now dance the lights on lawn and lea,
2430   The flocks are whiter down the vale,
    And milkier every milky sail
On winding stream or distant sea;

Where now the seamew pipes, or dives
    In yonder greening gleam, and fly
    The happy birds, that change their sky
To build and brood, that live their lives

From land to land; and in my breast
    Spring wakens too, and my regret
    Becomes an April violet,
2440 And buds and blossoms like the rest.

CXVI

Is it, then, regret for buried time
    That keenlier in sweet April wakes,
    And meets the year, and gives and takes
The colors of the crescent prime?

Not all: the songs, the stirring air,
    The life re-orient out of dust,
    Cry thro' the sense to hearten trust
In that which made the world so fair.

Not all regret: the face will shine
2450   Upon me, while I muse alone,
    And that dear voice, I once have known,
Still speak to me of me and mine.

Yet less of sorrow lives in me
    For days of happy commune dead,

Less yearning for the friendship fled
Than some strong bond which is to be.

CXVII

O days and hours, your work is this,
    To hold me from my proper place,
    A little while from his embrace,
For fuller gain of after bliss;   2460

That out of distance might ensue
    Desire of nearness doubly sweet,
    And unto meeting, when we meet,
Delight a hundredfold accrue,

For every grain of sand that runs,
    And every span of shade that steals,
    And every kiss of toothed wheels,
And all the courses of the suns.

CXVIII

Contemplate all this work of Time,
    The giant laboring in his youth;   2470
    Nor dream of human love and truth,
As dying Nature's earth and lime;

But trust that those we call the dead
    Are breathers of an ampler day
    For ever nobler ends. They say,
The solid earth whereon we tread

In tracts of fluent heat began,
    And grew to seeming-random forms,
    The seeming prey of cyclic storms,
Till at the last arose the man;   2480

Who throve and branch'd from clime to clime,
    The herald of a higher race,
    And of himself in higher place,
If so he type this work of time

Within himself, from more to more;
    Or, crown'd with attributes of woe
    Like glories, move his course, and show
That life is not as idle ore,

But iron dug from central gloom,
    And heated hot with burning fears,   2490
    And dipt in baths of hissing tears,
And batter'd with the shocks of doom

To shape and use. Arise and fly
    The reeling Faun, the sensual feast;

2404. **Pallas.** Pallas Athena, Greek goddess of wisdom, sprang from the forehead of Zeus. 2422. **quick,** hawthorn hedges. 2475. **They,** geologists and astronomers.

Move upward, working out the beast,
And let the ape and tiger die.

CXIX

Doors, where my heart was used to beat
    So quickly, not as one that weeps
    I come once more; the city sleeps;
2500 I smell the meadow in the street;

I hear a chirp of birds; I see
    Betwixt the black fronts long-withdrawn
    A light-blue lane of early dawn,
And think of early days and thee,

And bless thee, for thy lips are bland,
    And bright the friendship of thine eye;
    And in my thoughts with scarce a sigh
I take the pressure of thine hand.

CXX

I trust I have not wasted breath:
2510   I think we are not wholly brain,
    Magnetic mockeries; not in vain,
Like Paul with beasts, I fought with Death;

Not only cunning casts in clay:
    Let Science prove we are, and then
    What matters Science unto men,
At least to me? I would not stay.

Let him, the wiser man who springs
    Hereafter, up from childhood shape
    His action like the greater ape,
2520 But I was *born* to other things.

CXXI

Sad Hesper o'er the buried sun
    And ready, thou, to die with him,
    Thou watchest all things ever dim
And dimmer, and a glory done.

The team is loosen'd from the wain,
    The boat is drawn upon the shore;
    Thou listenest to the closing door,
And life is darken'd in the brain.

Bright Phosphor, fresher for the night,
2530   By thee the world's great work is heard
    Beginning, and the wakeful bird;
Behind thee comes the greater light.

The market boat is on the stream,
    And voices hail it from the brink;
    Thou hear'st the village hammer clink,
And see'st the moving of the team.

Sweet Hesper-Phosphor, double name
    For what is one, the first, the last,
    Thou, like my present and my past,
Thy place is changed; thou art the same.   2540

CXXII

O, wast thou with me, dearest, then,
    While I rose up against my doom,
    And yearn'd to burst the folded gloom,
To bare the eternal heavens again,

To feel once more, in placid awe,
    The strong imagination roll
    A sphere of stars about my soul,
In all her motion one with law?

If thou wert with me, and the grave
    Divide us not, be with me now,   2550
    And enter in at breast and brow,
Till all my blood, a fuller wave,

Be quicken'd with a livelier breath,
    And like an inconsiderate boy,
    As in the former flash of joy,
I slip the thoughts of life and death;

And all the breeze of Fancy blows,
    And every dewdrop paints a bow,
    The wizard lightnings deeply glow,
And every thought breaks out a rose.   2560

CXXIII

There rolls the deep where grew the tree.
    O earth, what changes hast thou seen!
    There where the long street roars hath been
The stillness of the central sea.

The hills are shadows, and they flow
    From form to form, and nothing stands;
    They melt like mist, the solid lands,
Like clouds they shape themselves and go.

But in my spirit will I dwell,
    And dream my dream, and hold it true;   2570
    For tho' my lips may breathe adieu,
I cannot think the thing farewell.

2521-2540. **Sad Hesper, etc.** In this section, Tennyson makes a twin image of the morning (Phosphor) and the evening (Hesper) stars, twin aspects of Venus, planet of love. This is in curious contrast to the East-West dichotomy of such early poems as *Timbuctoo*. 2525. **wain,** wagon.

CXXIV

That which we dare invoke to bless;
　　Our dearest faith; our ghastliest doubt;
　　He, They, One, All; within, without;
The Power in darkness whom we guess,—

I found Him not in world or sun,
　　Or eagle's wing, or insect's eye,
　　Nor thro' the questions men may try,
2580 The petty cobwebs we have spun.

If e'er when faith had fallen asleep,
　　I heard a voice, "believe no more,"
　　And heard an ever-breaking shore
That tumbled in the Godless deep,

A warmth within the breast would melt
　　The freezing reason's colder part,
　　And like a man in wrath the heart
Stood up and answer'd, "I have felt."

No, like a child in doubt and fear:
2590 But that blind clamor made me wise;
　　Then was I as a child that cries,
But, crying, knows his father near;

And what I am beheld again
　　What is, and no man understands;
　　And out of darkness came the hands
That reach thro' nature, moulding men.

CXXV

Whatever I have said or sung,
　　Some bitter notes my harp would give,
　　Yea, tho' there often seem'd to live
2600 A contradiction on the tongue,

Yet Hope had never lost her youth,
　　She did but look through dimmer eyes;
　　Or Love but play'd with gracious lies,
Because he felt so fix'd in truth;

And if the song were full of care,
　　He breathed the spirit of the song;
　　And if the words were sweet and strong
He set his royal signet there;

Abiding with me till I sail
2610 To seek thee on the mystic deeps,
　　And this electric force, that keeps
A thousand pulses dancing, fail.

CXXVI

Love is and was my lord and king,
　　And in his presence I attend

To hear the tidings of my friend,
　　Which every hour his couriers bring.

Love is and was my king and lord,
　　And will be, tho' as yet I keep
　　Within the court on earth, and sleep
Encompass'd by his faithful guard,　　　2620

And hear at times a sentinel
　　Who moves about from place to place,
　　And whispers to the worlds of space,
In the deep night, that all is well.

CXXVII

And all is well, tho' faith and form
　　Be sunder'd in the night of fear;
　　Well roars the storm to those that hear
A deeper voice across the storm,

Proclaiming social truth shall spread,
　　And justice, even tho' thrice again　　　2630
　　The red fool-fury of the Seine
Should pile her barricades with dead.

But ill for him that wears a crown,
　　And him, the lazar, in his rags!
　　They tremble, the sustaining crags;
The spires of ice are toppled down,

And molten up, and roar in flood;
　　The fortress crashes from on high,
　　The brute earth lightens to the sky,
And the great Æon sinks in blood,　　　2640

And compass'd by the fires of hell;
　　While thou, dear spirit, happy star,
　　O'erlook'st the tumult from afar,
And smilest, knowing all is well.

CXXVIII

The love that rose on stronger wings,
　　Unpalsied when he met with Death,
　　Is comrade of the lesser faith
That sees the course of human things.

No doubt vast eddies in the flood
　　Of onward time shall yet be made,　　　2650
　　And throned races may degrade;
Yet, O ye mysteries of good,

Wild Hours that fly with Hope and Fear,
　　If all your office had to do

2631. **Seine,** reference to periodic revolutionary disorders in France, more specifically to the revolution of 1830.

Alfred, Lord Tennyson 895

With old results that look like new—
If this were all your mission here,

To draw, to sheathe a useless sword,
    To fool the crowd with glorious lies,
    To cleave a creed in sects and cries,
2660 To change the bearing of a word,

To shift an arbitrary power,
    To cramp the student at his desk,
    To make old bareness picturesque
And tuft with grass a feudal tower,

Why, then my scorn might well descend
    On you and yours. I see in part
    That all, as in some piece of art,
Is toil coöperant to an end.

CXXIX

Dear friend, far off, my lost desire,
2670   So far, so near in woe and weal,
    O loved the most, when most I feel
There is a lower and a higher;

Known and unknown, human, divine;
    Sweet human hand and lips and eye;
    Dear heavenly friend that canst not die,
Mine, mine, for ever, ever mine;

Strange friend, past, present, and to be;
    Loved deeplier, darklier understood;
    Behold, I dream a dream of good,
2680 And mingle all the world with thee.

CXXX

Thy voice is on the rolling air;
    I hear thee where the waters run;
    Thou standest in the rising sun,
And in the setting thou art fair.

What are thou then? I cannot guess;
    But tho' I seem in star and flower
    To feel thee some diffusive power,
I do not therefore love thee less.

My love involves the love before;
2690   My love is vaster passion now;
    Tho' mix'd with God and Nature thou,
I seem to love thee more and more.

Far off thou art, but ever nigh;
    I have thee still, and I rejoice;

I prosper, circled with thy voice;
I shall not lose thee tho' I die.

CXXXI

O living will that shalt endure
    When all that seems shall suffer shock,
    Rise in the spiritual rock,
Flow thro' our deeds and make them pure,   2700

That we may lift from out of dust
    A voice as unto him that hears,
    A cry above the conquer'd years
To one that with us works, and trust,

With faith that comes of self-control,
    The truths that never can be proved
    Until we close with all we loved,
And all we flow from, soul in soul.

EPILOGUE

O true and tried, so well and long,
    Demand not thou a marriage lay;   2710
    In that it is thy marriage day
Is music more than any song.

Nor have I felt so much of bliss
    Since first he told me that he loved
    A daughter of our house, nor proved
Since that dark day a day like this;

Tho' I since then have number'd o'er
    Some thrice three years; they went and came,
    Remade the blood and changed the frame,
And yet is love not less, but more;   2720

No longer caring to embalm
    In dying songs a dead regret,
    But like a statue solid-set,
And moulded in colossal calm.

Regret is dead, but love is more
    Than in the summers that are flown,
    For I myself with these have grown
To something greater than before;

Which makes appear the songs I made
    As echoes out of weaker times,   2730
    As half but idle brawling rhymes,
The sport of random sun and shade.

But where is she, the bridal flower,
    That must be made a wife ere noon?

2709-2852. **O true and tried,** etc. The epilogue is addressed to Edward Lushington and is an epithalamium, or marriage hymn. Tennyson is fol- lowing elegiac tradition here, but he is also confirming his faith in human love.

She enters, glowing like the moon
Of Eden on its bridal bower.

On me she bends her blissful eyes
  And then on thee; they meet thy look
  And brighten like the star that shook
2740 Betwixt the palms of Paradise.

O, when her life was yet in bud,
  He too foretold the perfect rose.
  For thee she grew, for thee she grows
For ever, and as fair as good.

And thou art worthy, full of power;
  As gentle; liberal-minded, great,
  Consistent; wearing all that weight
Of learning lightly like a flower.

But now set out: the noon is near,
2750 And I must give away the bride;
  She fears not, or with thee beside
And me behind her, will not fear.

For I that danced her on my knee,
  That watch'd her on her nurse's arm,
  That shielded all her life from harm,
At last must part with her to thee;

Now waiting to be made a wife,
  Her feet, my darling, on the dead;
  Their pensive tablets round her head,
2760 And the most living words of life

Breathed in her ear. The ring is on,
  The "Wilt thou?" answer'd, and again
  The "Wilt thou?" ask'd, till out of twain
Her sweet "I will" has made you one.

Now sign your names, which shall be read,
  Mute symbols of a joyful morn,
  By village eyes as yet unborn.
The names are sign'd, and overhead

Begins the clash and clang that tells
2770 The joy to every wandering breeze;
  The blind wall rocks, and on the trees
The dead leaf trembles to the bells.

O happy hour, and happier hours
  Await them. Many a merry face
  Salutes them—maidens of the place,
That pelt us in the porch with flowers.

O happy hour, behold the bride
  With him to whom her hand I gave.
  They leave the porch, they pass the grave
2780 That has to-day its sunny side.

To-day the grave is bright for me,
  For them the light of life increased,
  Who stay to share the morning feast,
Who rest to-night beside the sea.

Let all my genial spirits advance
  To meet and greet a whiter sun;
  My drooping memory will not shun
The foaming grape of eastern France.

It circles round, and fancy plays,
  And hearts are warm'd and faces bloom,   2790
  As drinking health to bride and groom
We wish them store of happy days.

Nor count me all to blame if I
  Conjecture of a stiller guest,
  Perchance, perchance, among the rest,
And, tho' in silence, wishing joy.

But they must go, the time draws on,
  And those white-favor'd horses wait;
  They rise, but linger; it is late;
Farewell, we kiss, and they are gone.   2800

A shade falls on us like the dark
  From little cloudlets on the grass,
  But sweeps away as out we pass
To range the woods, to roam the park,

Discussing how their courtship grew,
  And talk of others that are wed,
  And how she look'd, and what he said,
And back we come at fall of dew.

Again the feast, the speech, the glee,
  The shade of passing thought, the wealth   2810
  Of words and wit, the double health,
The crowning cup, the three-times-three,

And last the dance;—till I retire.
  Dumb is that tower which spake so loud,
  And high in heaven the streaming cloud,
And on the downs a rising fire:

And rise, O moon, from yonder down,
  Till over down and over dale
  All night the shining vapor sail
And pass the silent-lighted town,   2820

The white-faced halls, the glancing rills,
  And catch at every mountain head,
  And o'er the friths that branch and spread
Their sleeping silver thro' the hills;

And touch with shade the bridal doors,
  With tender gloom the roof, the wall;

And breaking let the splendor fall
To spangle all the happy shores

By which they rest, and ocean sounds,
2830   And, star and system rolling past,
A soul shall draw from out the vast
And strike his being into bounds,

And, moved thro' life of lower phase,
Result in man, be born and think,
And act and love, a closer link
Betwixt us and the crowning race

Of those that, eye to eye, shall look
On knowledge; under whose command
Is Earth and Earth's, and in their hand
2840 Is Nature like an open book;

No longer half-akin to brute,
For all we thought and loved and did,
And hoped, and suffer'd, is but seed
Of what in them is flower and fruit;

Whereof the man that with me trod
This planet was a noble type
Appearing ere the times were ripe,
That friend of mine who lives in God,

That God, which ever lives and loves,
2850   One God, one law, one element,
And one far-off divine event,
To which the whole creation moves.

(1850)

THE CHARGE OF THE LIGHT BRIGADE

Tennyson's strong patriotism is revealed in this account of the famous charge of the Light Cavalry under Lord Cardigan at Balaclava near Sebastopol, on September 26, 1854, during the Crimean War. Through an error in orders the intrepid troop was thrown into the teeth of the entire Russian army of twelve thousand, supported by artillery, of 673 officers and men who participated, 247 were either killed or wounded.

Half a league, half a league,
Half a league, onward,
All in the valley of Death
  Rode the six hundred.
"Forward the Light Brigade!
Charge for the guns!" he said.

Into the valley of Death
  Rode the six hundred.

"Forward, the Light Brigade!"
Was there a man dismayed?   10
Not though the soldier knew
  Someone had blundered.
Theirs not to make reply,
Theirs not to reason why,
Theirs but to do and die.
Into the valley of Death
  Rode the six hundred.

Cannon to right of them,
Cannon to left of them,
Cannon in front of them   20
  Volleyed and thundered;
Stormed at with shot and shell,
Boldly they rode and well,
Into the jaws of Death,
Into the mouth of hell
  Rode the six hundred.

Flashed all their sabers bare,
Flashed as they turned in air
Sabering the gunners there,
Charging an army, while   30
  All the world wondered.
Plunged in the battery smoke
Right through the line they broke;
Cossack and Russian
Reeled from the saber stroke
  Shattered and sundered.
Then they rode back, but not,
  Not the six hundred.

Cannon to right of them,
Cannon to left of them,   40
Cannon behind them
  Volleyed and thundered;
Stormed at with shot and shell,
While horse and hero fell,
They that had fought so well
Came through the jaws of Death,
Back from the mouth of hell,
All that was left of them,
  Left of six hundred.

When can their glory fade?   50
O the wild charge they made!
  All the world wondered.
Honor the charge they made!
Honor the Light Brigade,
  Noble six hundred!

(1854; 1854)

from MAUD

These lyrics were part of a long poetical romance in which a morbid youth tells the story of his tragic love for Maud, the playmate of his youth, of the loss of his reason, and of his restoration under the emotions aroused by the Crimean War. The poem is filled with Tennyson's reflections on conflict and sorrow.

COME INTO THE GARDEN, MAUD

Come into the garden, Maud,
  For the black bat, night, has flown,
Come into the garden, Maud,
  I am here at the gate alone;
And the woodbine spices are wafted abroad,
  And the musk of the rose is blown.

For a breeze of morning moves,
  And the planet of Love is on high,
Beginning to faint in the light that she loves
10 On a bed of daffodil sky,
To faint in the light of the sun she loves,
  To faint in his light, and to die.

All night have the roses heard
  The flute, violin, bassoon;
All night has the casement jessamine stirred
  To the dancers dancing in tune;
Till a silence fell with the waking bird,
  And a hush with the setting moon.

I said to the lily, "There is but one,
20 With whom she has heart to be gay.
When will the dancers leave her alone?
  She is weary of dance and play."
Now half to the setting moon are gone,
  And half to the rising day;
Low on the sand and loud on the stone
  The last wheel echoes away.

I said to the rose, "The brief night goes
  In babble and revel and wine.
O young lord-lover, what sighs are those,
30 For one that will never be thine?
But mine, but mine," so I sware to the rose,
  "Forever and ever, mine."

And the soul of the rose went into my blood,
  As the music clashed in the hall;
And long by the garden lake I stood,
  For I heard your rivulet fall
From the lake to the meadow and on to the wood,
  Our wood, that is dearer than all;

From the meadow your walks have left so sweet
  That whenever a March wind sighs   40
He sets the jewel-print of your feet
  In violets blue as your eyes,
To the woody hollows in which we meet
  And the valleys of Paradise.

The slender acacia would not shake
  One long milk-bloom on the tree;
The white lake-blossom fell into the lake
  As the pimpernel dozed on the lea;
But the rose was awake all night for your sake,
  Knowing your promise to me;   50
The lilies and roses were all awake,
  They sighed for the dawn and thee.

Queen rose of the rosebud garden of girls,
  Come hither, the dances are done,
In gloss of satin and glimmer of pearls,
  Queen lily and rose in one;
Shine out, little head, sunning over with curls,
  To the flowers, and be their sun.

There has fallen a splendid tear
  From the passion-flower at the gate.   60
She is coming, my dove, my dear;
  She is coming, my life, my fate.
The red rose cries, "She is near, she is near";
  And the white rose weeps, "She is late";
The larkspur listens, "I hear, I hear";
  And the lily whispers, "I wait."

She is coming, my own, my sweet;
  Were it ever so airy a tread,
My heart would hear her and beat,
  Were it earth in an earthy bed;   70
My dust would hear her and beat,
  Had I lain for a century dead,
Would start and tremble under her feet,
  And blossom in purple and red.

O THAT 'TWERE POSSIBLE

Tennyson regarded this lyric as "the most touching of his works." Swinburne called it "the poem of deepest charm and fullest delight of pathos and melody ever written by Mr. Tennyson." It suggests his grief for his lost friend Hallam.

O that 'twere possible
After long grief and pain
To find the arms of my true love
Round me once again!

When I was wont to meet her
In the silent woody places
By the home that gave me birth,

Come into the Garden, Maud. Cf. *Now Sleeps the Crimson Petal* (p. 861). In that song the flowers sleep in sympathy. 8. **planet of Love,** Venus.

Alfred, Lord Tennyson   899

We stood tranced in long embraces
Mixed with kisses sweeter, sweeter
10 Than anything on earth.

A shadow flits before me,
Not thou, but like to thee.
Ah, Christ, that it were possible
For one short hour to see
The souls we loved, that they might tell us
What and where they be!

It leads me forth at evening,
It lightly winds and steals
In a cold white robe before me,
20 When all my spirit reels
At the shouts, the leagues of lights,
And the roaring of the wheels.

Half the night I waste in sighs,
Half in dreams I sorrow after
The delight of early skies;
In a wakeful doze I sorrow
For the hand, the lips, the eyes,
For the meeting of the morrow,
The delight of happy laughter,
30 The delight of low replies.

'Tis a morning pure and sweet,
And a dewy splendor falls
On the little flower that clings
To the turrets and the walls;
'Tis a morning pure and sweet,
And the light and shadow fleet.
She is walking in the meadow,
And the woodland echo rings;
In a moment we shall meet.
40 She is singing in the meadow,
And the rivulet at her feet
Ripples on in light and shadow
To the ballad that she sings.

Do I hear her sing as of old,
My bird with the shining head,
My own dove with the tender eye?
But there rings on a sudden a passionate cry,
There is someone dying or dead,
And a sullen thunder is rolled;
50 For a tumult shakes the city,
And I wake, my dream is fled.
In the shuddering dawn, behold,
Without knowledge, without pity,
By the curtains of my bed
That abiding phantom cold!

Get thee hence, nor come again,
Mix not memory with doubt,
Pass, thou deathlike type of pain,

Pass and cease to move about!
'Tis the blot upon the brain
60 That *will* show itself without.

Then I rise, the eave-drops fall,
And the yellow vapors choke
The great city sounding wide;
The day comes, a dull red ball
Wrapped in drifts of lurid smoke
On the misty river-tide.

Through the hubbub of the market
I steal, a wasted frame;
It crosses here, it crosses there,
70 Through all that crowd confused and loud,
The shadow still the same;
And on my heavy eyelids
My anguish hangs like shame.

Alas for her that met me,
That heard me softly call,
Came glimmering through the laurels
At the quiet evenfall,
In the garden by the turrets
Of the old manorial hall!
80

Would the happy spirit descend
From the realms of light and song,
In the chamber or the street,
As she looks among the blest,
Should I fear to greet my friend
Or to say, "Forgive the wrong,"
Or to ask her, "Take me, sweet,
To the regions of thy rest"?

But the broad light glares and beats,
And the shadow flits and fleets
90
And will not let me be;
And I loathe the squares and streets,
And the faces that one meets,
Hearts with no love for me.
Always I long to creep
Into some still cavern deep,
There to weep, and weep, and weep
My whole soul out to thee.

OH, LET THE SOLID GROUND

Oh, let the solid ground
   Not fail beneath my feet
Before my life has found
   What some have found so sweet!
Then let come what come may,
What matter if I go mad,
I shall have had my day.

Let the sweet heavens endure,
   Not close and darken above me

10 Before I am quite, quite sure
    That there is one to love me!
Then let come what come may
To a life that has been so sad—
I shall have had my day.
(1854; 1857)

FLOWER IN THE CRANNIED WALL

Flower in the crannied wall,
I pluck you out of the crannies,
I hold you here, root and all, in my hand,
Little flower—but *if* I could understand
What you are, root and all, and all in all,
I should know what God and man is.
(1869)

from IDYLLS OF THE KING

*Tennyson published the twelve narratives which con-
stitute his major single work between 1859 and 1885.
His principal source was Malory's* Morte Darthur, *but
he also drew upon other documents, such as the Welsh*
Mabinogion, *and freely invented and adapted.*

*"The Holy Grail," Tennyson said, "is one of the
most imaginative of my poems. I have expressed there
my strong feeling as to the Reality of the Unseen. The
end, when the king speaks of his work and of his visions,
is intended to be the summing up of all in the highest
note by the highest of human men. These three lines
in Arthur's speech are the (spiritually) central lines of
the* Idylls:*

    In moments when he feels he cannot die,
    And knows himself no vision to himself,
    Nor the High God a vision.*

*The general English view of God is as an immeasurable
clergyman; and some mistake the devil for God." This
is the most significant directive available for a right
reading of Tennyson's intention in his* Idylls: *it suggests that Tennyson's primary theme was spiritual
rather than moral and that it was not until he came to
a working out of* The Holy Grail *that he identified that
theme clearly and at the deepest level.*

*In general, Tennyson preferred the term parable to
the term allegory to describe the oblique method of the*
Idylls. *But in* The Holy Grail, *at least, he rose to a
Spenserian level of symbolic narrative requiring of the
reader the most sustained attention. Even the point of
view is carefully controlled: the story is told to the
cloistered "old badger" Ambrosius by Percivale "the
Pure," who in the end confesses that he himself does
not fully comprehend the experiences related or
Arthur's gloss upon them.*

THE HOLY GRAIL

From noiseful arms, and acts of prowess done
In tournament or tilt, Sir Percivale,
Whom Arthur and his knighthood call'd the Pure,
Had past into the silent life of prayer,
Praise, fast, and alms; and leaving for the cowl
The helmet in an abbey far away
From Camelot, there, and not long after, died.

And one, a fellow-monk among the rest,
Ambrosius, loved him much beyond the rest,
And honor'd him, and wrought into his heart   10
A way by love that waken'd love within,
To answer that which came; and as they sat
Beneath a world-old yew-tree, darkening half
The cloisters, on a gustful April morn
That puff'd the swaying branches into smoke
Above them, ere the summer when he died,
The monk Ambrosius question'd Percivale:

"O brother, I have seen this yew-tree smoke,
Spring after spring, for half a hundred years;
For never have I known the world without,   20
Nor ever stray'd beyond the pale. But thee,
When first thou camest—such a courtesy
Spake thro' the limbs and in the voice—I knew
For one of those who eat in Arthur's hall;
For good ye are and bad, and like to coins,
Some true, some light, but every one of you
Stamp'd with the image of the King; and now
Tell me, what drove thee from the Table Round,
My brother? was it earthly passion crost?"

"Nay," said the knight; "for no such passion mine.   30
But the sweet vision of the Holy Grail
Drove me from all vainglories, rivalries,
And earthly heats that spring and sparkle out
Among us in the jousts, while women watch
Who wins, who falls, and waste the spiritual strength
Within us, better offer'd up to heaven."

To whom the monk: "The Holy Grail!—I trust
We are green in Heaven's eyes; but here too much
We moulder—as to things without I mean—
Yet one of your own knights, a guest of ours,   40
Told us of this in our refectory,
But spake with such a sadness and so low
We heard not half of what he said. What is it?
The phantom of a cup that comes and goes?"

"Nay, monk! what phantom?" answer'd Percivale.
"The cup, the cup itself, from which our Lord
Drank at the last sad supper with his own.
This, from the blessed land of Aromat—

15. puff'd . . . smoke, blew the pollen of the yew. 48. **Aromat,**
Arimathea, in Palestine.

After the day of darkness, when the dead
50 Went wandering o'er Moriah—the good saint
Arimathæan Joseph, journeying brought
To Glastonbury, where the winter thorn
Blossoms at Christmas, mindful of our Lord.
And there awhile it bode; and if a man
Could touch or see it, he was heal'd at once,
By faith, of all his ills. But then the times
Grew to such evil that the holy cup
Was caught away to heaven, and disappear'd."

To whom the monk: "From our old books I know
60 That Joseph came of old to Glastonbury,
And there the heathen Prince, Arviragus,
Gave him an isle of marsh whereon to build;
And there he built with wattles from the marsh
A little lonely church in days of yore,
For so they say, these books of ours, but seem
Mute of this miracle, far as I have read.
But who first saw the holy thing to-day?"

"A woman," answer'd Percivale, "a nun,
And one no further off in blood from me
70 Than sister; and if ever holy maid
With knees of adoration wore the stone,
A holy maid; tho' never maiden glow'd,
But that was in her earlier maidenhood,
With such a fervent flame of human love,
Which, being rudely blunted, glanced and shot
Only to holy things; to prayer and praise
She gave herself, to fast and alms. And yet,
Nun as she was, the scandal of the Court,
Sin against Arthur and the Table Round,
80 And the strange sound of an adulterous race,
Across the iron grating of her cell
Beat, and she pray'd and fasted all the more.

"And he to whom she told her sins, or what
Her all but utter whiteness held for sin,
A man wellnigh a hundred winters old,
Spake often with her of the Holy Grail,
A legend handed down thro' five or six,
And each of these a hundred winters old,
From our Lord's time. And when King Arthur made
90 His Table Round, and all men's hearts became
Clean for a season, surely he had thought
That now the Holy Grail would come again;
But sin broke out. Ah, Christ, that it would come,
And heal the world of all their wickedness!
'O Father!' ask'd the maiden, 'might it come
To me by prayer and fasting?' 'Nay,' said he,
'I know not, for thy heart is pure as snow.'
And so she pray'd and fasted, till the sun

Shone, and the wind blew, thro' her, and I thought
She might have risen and floated when I saw her. 100

"For on a day she sent to speak with me.
And when she came to speak, behold her eyes
Beyond my knowing of them, beautiful,
Beyond all knowing of them, wonderful,
Beautiful in the light of holiness!
And 'O my brother Percivale,' she said,
'Sweet brother, I have seen the Holy Grail;
For, waked at dead of night, I heard a sound
As of a silver horn from o'er the hills
Blown, and I thought, "It is not Arthur's use 110
To hunt by moonlight." And the slender sound
As from a distance beyond distance grew
Coming upon me—O never harp nor horn,
Nor aught we blow with breath, or touch with hand,
Was like that music as it came; and then
Stream'd thro' my cell a cold and silver beam,
And down the long beam stole the Holy Grail,
Rose-red with beatings in it, as if alive,
Till all the white walls of my cell were dyed
With rosy colors leaping on the wall; 120
And then the music faded, and the Grail
Past, and the beam decay'd, and from the walls
The rosy quiverings died into the night.
So now the Holy Thing is here again
Among us, brother, fast thou too and pray,
And tell thy brother knights to fast and pray,
That so perchance the vision may be seen
By thee and those, and all the world be heal'd.'

"Then leaving the pale nun, I spake of this
To all men; and myself fasted and pray'd 130
Always, and many among us many a week
Fasted and pray'd even to the uttermost,
Expectant of the wonder that would be.

"And one there was among us, ever moved
Among us in white armor, Galahad.
'God make thee good as thou art beautiful!'
Said Arthur, when he dubb'd him knight, and none
In so young youth was ever made a knight
Till Galahad; and this Galahad, when he heard
My sister's vision, fill'd me with amaze; 140
His eyes became so like her own, they seem'd
Hers, and himself her brother more than I.

"Sister or brother none had he; but some
Call'd him a son of Lancelot, and some said
Begotten by enchantment—chatterers they,
Like birds of passage piping up and down,
That gape for flies—we know not whence they come;
For when was Lancelot wanderingly lewd?

"But she, the wan sweet maiden, shore away
150 Clean from her forehead all that wealth of hair
Which made a silken mat-work for her feet;
And out of this she plaited broad and long
A strong sword-belt, and wove with silver thread
And crimson in the belt a strange device,
A crimson grail within a silver beam;
And saw the bright boy-knight, and bound it on him,
Saying: 'My knight, my love, my knight of heaven,
O thou, my love, whose love is one with mine,
I, maiden, round thee, maiden, bind my belt.
160 Go forth, for thou shalt see what I have seen,
And break thro' all, till one will crown thee king
Far in the spiritual city;' and as she spake
She sent the deathless passion in her eyes
Thro' him, and made him hers, and laid her mind
On him, and he believed in her belief.

"Then came a year of miracle, O brother,
In our great hall there stood a vacant chair,
Fashion'd by Merlin ere he past away,
And carven with strange figures; and in and out
170 The figures, like a serpent, ran a scroll
Of letters in a tongue no man could read.
And Merlin call'd it 'the Siege Perilous,'
Perilous for good and ill; 'for there,' he said,
'No man could sit but he should lose himself.'
And once by misadventure Merlin sat
In his own chair, and so was lost; but he,
Galahad, when he heard of Merlin's doom,
Cried, 'If I lose myself, I save myself!'

"Then on a summer night it came to pass,
180 While the great banquet lay along the hall,
That Galahad would sit down in Merlin's chair.

"And all at once, as there we sat, we heard
A cracking and a riving of the roofs,
And rending, and a blast, and overhead
Thunder, and in the thunder was a cry.
And in the blast there smote along the hall
A beam of light seven times more clear than day;
And down the long beam stole the Holy Grail
All over cover'd with a luminous cloud,
190 And none might see who bare it, and it past.
But every knight beheld his fellow's face
As in a glory, and all the knights arose,
And staring each at other like dumb men
Stood, till I found a voice and sware a vow.

"I sware a vow before them all, that I,
Because I had not seen the Grail, would ride
A twelvemonth and a day in quest of it,
Until I found and saw it, as the nun

My sister saw it; and Galahad sware the vow,
And good Sir Bors, our Lancelot's cousin, sware,   200
And Lancelot sware, and many among the knights,
And Gawain sware, and louder than the rest."

Then spake the monk Ambrosius, asking him,
"What said the King? Did Arthur take the vow?"

"Nay, for my lord," said Percivale, "the King,
Was not in hall; for early that same day,
Scaped thro' a cavern from a bandit hold,
An outraged maiden sprang into the hall
Crying on help; for all her shining hair
Was smear'd with earth, and either milky arm   210
Red-rent with hooks of bramble, and all she wore
Torn as a sail that leaves the rope is torn
In tempest. So the King arose and went
To smoke the scandalous hive of those wild bees
That made such honey in his realm. Howbeit
Some little of this marvel he too saw,
Returning o'er the plain that then began
To darken under Camelot; whence the King
Look'd up, calling aloud, 'Lo, there! the roofs
Of our great hall are roll'd in thunder-smoke!   220
Pray heaven, they be not smitten by the bolt!'
For dear to Arthur was that hall of ours,
As having there so oft with all his knights
Feasted, and as the stateliest under heaven.

"O brother, had you known our mighty hall,
Which Merlin built for Arthur long ago!
For all the sacred mount of Camelot,
And all the dim rich city, roof by roof,
Tower after tower, spire beyond spire,
By grove, and garden-lawn, and rushing brook,   230
Climbs to the mighty hall that Merlin built.
And four great zones of sculpture, set betwixt
With many a mystic symbol, gird the hall;
And in the lowest beasts are slaying men,
And in the second men are slaying beasts,
And on the third are warriors, perfect men,
And on the fourth are men with growing wings,
And over all one statue in the mould
Of Arthur, made by Merlin, with a crown,
And peak'd wings pointed to the Northern Star.   240
And eastward fronts the statue, and the crown
And both the wings are made of gold, and flame
At sunrise till the people in far fields,
Wasted so often by the heathen hordes,
Behold it, crying, 'We have still a king.'

"And, brother, had you known our hall within,
Broader and higher than any in all the lands!

the metaphor to cover all forms of self-deception parading in the disguise of self-fulfillment. 232. **four great zones.** The significance of the "zones" has been variously interpreted—from stages in the quest to human progress in general. It seems more meaningful to interpret them as the preceding stages in the story of the *Idylls*: (1) before Arthur's coming; (2) the Arthurian conquest; (3) the Round Table in its pristine perfection; (4) the ominous moment of "The Holy Grail" itself, when Arthur's "paradise" is about to be lost through spiritual pride.

Where twelve great windows blazon Arthur's wars,
And all the light that falls upon the board
Streams thro' the twelve great battles of our King.
Nay, one there is, and at the eastern end,
Wealthy with wandering lines of mount and mere,
Where Arthur finds the brand Excalibur.
And also one to the west, and counter to it,
And blank; and who shall blazon it? when and how?—
O, there, perchance, when all our wars are done,
The brand Excalibur will be cast away!

"So to this hall full quickly rode the King,
In horror lest the work by Merlin wrought,
260 Dreamlike, should on the sudden vanish, wrapt
In unremorseful folds of rolling fire.
And in he rode, and up I glanced, and saw
The golden dragon sparkling over all;
And many of those who burnt the hold, their arms
Hack'd, and their foreheads grimed with smoke and
    sear'd,
Follow'd, and in among bright faces, ours,
Full of the vision, prest; and then the King
Spake to me, being nearest, 'Percivale,'—
Because the hall was all in tumult—some
270 Vowing, and some protesting,—'what is this?'

"O brother, when I told him what had chanced,
My sister's vision and the rest, his face
Darken'd, as I have seen it more than once,
When some brave deed seem'd to be done in vain,
Darken; and 'Woe is me, my knights,' he cried,
'Had I been here, ye had not sworn the vow.'
Bold was mine answer, 'Had thyself been here,
My King, thou wouldst have sworn.' 'Yea, yea,' said he,
'Art thou so bold and hast not seen the Grail?'

280 "'Nay, lord, I heard the sound, I saw the light,
But since I did not see the holy thing,
I sware a vow to follow it till I saw.'

"Then when he ask'd us, knight by knight, if any
Had seen it, all their answers were as one:
'Nay, lord, and therefore have we sworn our vows.'

"'Lo, now,' said Arthur, 'have ye seen a cloud?
What go ye into the wilderness to see?'

"Then Galahad on the sudden, and in a voice
Shrilling along the hall to Arthur, call'd,
290 'But I, Sir Arthur, saw the Holy Grail,
I saw the Holy Grail and heard a cry—
"O Galahad, and O Galahad, follow me!"'

"'Ah, Galahad, Galahad,' said the King, 'for such
As thou art is the vision, not for these.
Thy holy nun and thou have seen a sign—
Holier is none, my Percivale, than she—
A sign to maim this Order which I made.
But ye that follow but the leader's bell,'—
Brother, the King was hard upon his knights,—
'Taliessin is our fullest throat of song,   300
And one hath sung and all the dumb will sing.
Lancelot is Lancelot, and hath overborne
Five knights at once, and every younger knight,
Unproven, holds himself as Lancelot,
Till overborne by one, he learns—and ye,
What are ye? Galahads?—no, nor Percivales'—
For thus it pleased the King to range me close
After Sir Galahad;—'nay,' said he, 'but men
With strength and will to right the wrong'd, of power
To lay the sudden heads of violence flat,   310
Knights that in twelve great battles splash'd and dyed
The strong White Horse in his own heathen blood—
But one hath seen, and all the blind will see.
Go, since your vows are sacred, being made.
Yet—for ye know the cries of all my realm
Pass thro' this hall—how often, O my knights,
Your places being vacant at my side,
This chance of noble deeds will come and go
Unchallenged, while ye follow wandering fires
Lost in the quagmire! Many of you, yea most,   320
Return no more. Ye think I show myself
Too dark a prophet. Come now, let us meet
The morrow morn once more in one full field
Of gracious pastime, that once more the King,
Before ye leave him for this quest, may count
The yet-unbroken strength of all his knights,
Rejoicing in that Order which he made.'

"So when the sun broke next from underground,
All the great Table of our Arthur closed
And clash'd in such a tourney and so full,   330
So many lances broken—never yet
Had Camelot seen the like since Arthur came;
And I myself and Galahad, for a strength
Was in us from the vision, overthrew
So many knights that all the people cried,
And almost burst the barriers in their heat,
Shouting, 'Sir Galahad and Sir Percivale!'

"But when the next day brake from underground—
O brother, had you known our Camelot,
Built by old kings, age after age, so old   340
The King himself had fears that it would fall,
So strange, and rich, and dim; for where the roofs
Totter'd toward each other in the sky,

---

250. **twelve great battles,** by which Arthur drove the heathens out.
253. **Excalibur,** Arthur's sword. 263. **golden dragon,** symbol of
Arthur and of sovereignty among the British. 300-327. **Taliessin, etc.**
Arthur here explains, by analogy with the Welsh poet Taliessin and

Lancelot the Strong, why the quest will fail: vowing, however sacred
an act, will not make one be what he is not or do what he cannot. In
the meantime, the nobility of the possible is sacrificed. 312. **White
Horse,** emblem of the Saxons, regarded as heathen. 346. **necks of**

Met foreheads all along the street of those
Who watch'd us pass; and lower, and where the long
Rich galleries, lady-laden, weigh'd the necks
Of dragons clinging to the crazy walls,
Thicker than drops from thunder, showers of flowers
Fell as we past; and men and boys astride
350 On wyvern, lion, dragon, griffin, swan,
At all the corners, named us each by name,
Calling 'God speed!' but in the ways below
The knights and ladies wept, and rich and poor
Wept, and the King himself could hardly speak
For grief, and all in middle street the Queen,
Who rode by Lancelot, wail'd and shriek'd aloud,
'This madness has come on us for our sins.'
So to the Gate of the Three Queens we came,
Where Arthur's wars are render'd mystically,
360 And thence departed every one his way.

"And I was lifted up in heart, and thought
Of all my late-shown prowess in the lists,
How my strong lance had beaten down the knights,
So many and famous names; and never yet
Had heaven appear'd so blue, nor earth so green,
For all my blood danced in me, and I knew
That I should light upon the Holy Grail.

"Thereafter, the dark warning of our King,
That most of us would follow wandering fires,
370 Came like a driving gloom across my mind.
Then every evil word I had spoken once,
And every evil thought I had thought of old,
And every evil deed I ever did,
Awoke and cried, 'This quest is not for thee.'
And lifting up mine eyes, I found myself
Alone, and in a land of sand and thorns,
And I was thirsty even unto death;
And I, too, cried, 'This quest is not for thee.'

"And on I rode, and when I thought my thirst
380 Would slay me, saw deep lawns, and then a brook,
With one sharp rapid, where the crisping white
Play'd ever back upon the sloping wave
And took both ear and eye; and o'er the brook
Were apple-trees, and apples by the brook
Fallen, and on the lawns. 'I will rest here,'
I said, 'I am not worthy of the quest;'
But even while I drank the brook, and ate
The goodly apples, all these things at once
Fell into dust, and I was left alone
390 And thirsting in a land of sand and thorns.

"And then behold a woman at a door
Spinning; and fair the house whereby she sat,

And kind the woman's eyes and innocent,
And all her bearing gracious; and she rose
Opening her arms to meet me, as who should say,
'Rest here;' but when I touch'd her, lo! she, too,
Fell into dust and nothing, and the house
Became no better than a broken shed,
And in it a dead babe; and also this
Fell into dust, and I was left alone.   400

"And on I rode, and greater was my thirst.
Then flash'd a yellow gleam across the world,
And where it smote the plowshare in the field
The plowman left his plowing and fell down
Before it; where it glitter'd on her pail
The milkmaid left her milking and fell down
Before it, and I knew not why, but thought
'The sun is rising,' tho' the sun had risen.
Then was I ware of one that on me moved
In golden armor with a crown of gold   410
About a casque all jewels, and his horse
In golden armor jewelled everywhere;
And on the splendor came, flashing me blind,
And seem'd to me the lord of all the world,
Being so huge. But when I thought he meant
To crush me, moving on me, lo! he, too,
Open'd his arms to embrace me as he came,
And up I went and touch'd him, and he, too,
Fell into dust, and I was left alone
And wearying in a land of sand and thorns.   420

"And I rode on and found a mighty hill,
And on the top a city wall'd; the spires
Prick'd with incredible pinnacles into heaven.
And by the gateway stirr'd a crowd; and these
Cried to me climbing, 'Welcome, Percivale!
Thou mightiest and thou purest among men!'
And glad was I and clomb, but found at top
No man, nor any voice. And thence I past
Far thro' a ruinous city, and I saw
That man had once dwelt there; but there I found   430
Only one man of an exceeding age.
'Where is that goodly company,' said I,
'That so cried out upon me?' and he had
Scarce any voice to answer, and yet gasp'd,
'Whence and what art thou?' and even as he spoke
Fell into dust and disappear'd, and I
Was left alone once more and cried in grief,
'Lo, if I find the Holy Grail itself
And touch it, it will crumble into dust!'

"And thence I dropt into a lowly vale,   440
Low as the hill was high, and where the vale
Was lowest found a chapel, and thereby

---

dragons, figured supports. 350. wyvern . . . griffin, heraldic devices.
A wyvern is a two-legged dragon; a griffin is half lion, half eagle.
358. Gate of the Three Queens, a gate built to the three queens who
will help Arthur in his need. 361-437. And I was lifted, etc. The
various episodes in Percivale's quest are densely allegorical. The "holy
hermit" (445 ff.) is the internal interpreter.

A holy hermit in a hermitage,
To whom I told my phantoms, and he said:

"'O son, thou hast not true humility,
The highest virtue, mother of them all;
For when the Lord of all things made Himself
Naked of glory for His mortal change,
"Take thou my robe," she said, "for all is thine,"
450 And all her form shone forth with sudden light
So that the angels were amazed, and she
Follow'd Him down, and like a flying star
Led on the gray-hair'd wisdom of the east.
But her thou hast not known; for what is this
Thou thoughtest of thy prowess and thy sins?
Thou hast not lost thyself to save thyself
As Galahad.' When the hermit made an end,
In silver armor suddenly Galahad shone
Before us, and against the chapel door
460 Laid lance and enter'd, and we knelt in prayer.
And there the hermit slaked my burning thirst,
And at the sacring of the mass I saw
The holy elements alone; but he,
'Saw ye no more? I, Galahad, saw the Grail,
The Holy Grail, descend upon the shrine.
I saw the fiery face as of a child
That smote itself into the bread and went;
And hither am I come; and never yet
Hath what thy sister taught me first to see,
470 This holy thing, fail'd from my side, nor come
Cover'd, but moving with me night and day,
Fainter by day, but always in the night
Blood-red, and sliding down the blacken'd marsh
Blood-red, and on the naked mountain top
Blood-red, and in the sleeping mere below
Blood-red. And in the strength of this I rode,
Shattering all evil customs everywhere,
And past thro' Pagan realms, and made them mine,
And clash'd with Pagan hordes, and bore them down,
480 And broke thro' all, and in the strength of this
Come victor. But my time is hard at hand,
And hence I go, and one will crown me king
Far in the spiritual city; and come thou, too,
For thou shalt see the vision when I go.'

"While thus he spake, his eye, dwelling on mine,
Drew me, with power upon me, till I grew
One with him, to believe as he believed.
Then, when the day began to wane, we went.

"There rose a hill that none but man could climb,
490 Scarr'd with a hundred wintry watercourses—
Storm at the top, and when we gain'd it, storm
Round us and death; for every moment glanced
His silver arms and gloom'd, so quick and thick

The lightnings here and there to left and right
Struck, till the dry old trunks about us, dead,
Yea, rotten with a hundred years of death,
Sprang into fire. And at the base we found
On either hand, as far as eye could see,
A great black swamp and of an evil smell,
Part black, part whiten'd with the bones of men,   500
Not to be crost, save that some ancient king
Had built a way, where, link'd with many a bridge,
A thousand piers ran into the great Sea.
And Galahad fled along them bridge by bridge,
And every bridge as quickly as he crost
Sprang into fire and vanish'd, tho' I yearn'd
To follow; and thrice above him all the heavens
Open'd and blazed with thunder such as seem'd
Shoutings of all the sons of God. And first
At once I saw him far on the great Sea,   510
In silver-shining armor starry-clear;
And o'er his head the Holy Vessel hung
Clothed in white samite or a luminous cloud.
And with exceeding swiftness ran the boat,
If boat it were—I saw not whence it came.
And when the heavens open'd and blazed again
Roaring, I saw him like a silver star—
And had he set the sail, or had the boat
Become a living creature clad with wings?
And o'er his head the Holy Vessel hung   520
Redder than any rose, a joy to me,
For now I knew the veil had been withdrawn.
Then in a moment when they blazed again
Opening, I saw the least of little stars
Down on the waste, and straight beyond the star
I saw the spiritual city and all her spires
And gateways in a glory like one pearl—
No larger, tho' the goal of all the saints—
Strike from the sea; and from the star there shot
A rose-red sparkle to the city, and there   530
Dwelt, and I knew it was the Holy Grail,
Which never eyes on earth again shall see.
Then fell the floods of heaven drowning the deep.
And how my feet recrost the deathful ridge
No memory in me lives; but that I touch'd
The chapel-doors at dawn I know, and thence
Taking my war-horse from the holy man,
Glad that no phantom vext me more, return'd
To whence I came, the gate of Arthur's wars."

"O brother," ask'd Ambrosius,—"for in sooth   540
These ancient books—and they would win thee—teem,
Only I find not there this Holy Grail,
With miracles and marvels like to these,
Not all unlike; which oftentime I read,
Who read but on my breviary with ease,
Till my head swims, and then go forth and pass

---

449. she, humility. 452. star. Humility is compared to the Star of
Bethlehem. 462. sacring, consecrating. 526. spiritual city, the new
Jerusalem of Revelation. 539. gate of Arthur's wars, a gate to
Camelot on which the story of Arthur's wars was "done in weird de-

906   Democracy, Science, and Industrialism

Down to the little thorpe that lies so close,
And almost plaster'd like a martin's nest
To these old walls—and mingle with our folk;
550 And knowing every honest face of theirs
As well as ever shepherd knew his sheep,
And every homely secret in their hearts,
Delight myself with gossip and old wives,
And ills and aches, and teethings, lyings-in,
And mirthful sayings, children of the place,
That have no meaning half a league away;
Or lulling random squabbles when they rise,
Chafferings and chatterings at the market-cross,
Rejoice, small man, in this small world of mine,
560 Yea, even in their hens and in their eggs—
O brother, saving this Sir Galahad,
Came ye on none but phantoms in your quest,
No man, no woman?"

Then Sir Percivale:
"All men, to one so bound by such a vow,
And women were as phantoms. O, my brother,
Why wilt thou shame me to confess to thee
How far I falter'd from my quest and vow?
For after I had lain so many nights,
A bed-mate of the snail and eft and snake,
570 In grass and burdock, I was changed to wan
And meagre, and the vision had not come;
And then I chanced upon a goodly town
With one great dwelling in the middle of it.
Thither I made, and there was I disarm'd
By maidens each as fair as any flower;
But when they led me into hall, behold,
The princess of that castle was the one,
Brother, and that one only, who had ever
Made my heart leap; for when I moved of old
580 A slender page about her father's hall,
And she a slender maiden, all my heart
Went after her with longing, yet we twain
Had never kiss'd a kiss or vow'd a vow.
And now I came upon her once again,
And one had wedded her, and he was dead,
And all his land and wealth and state were hers.
And while I tarried, every day she set
A banquet richer than the day before
By me, for all her longing and her will
590 Was toward me as of old; till one fair morn,
I walking to and fro beside a stream
That flash'd across her orchard underneath
Her castle-walls, she stole upon my walk,
And calling me the greatest of all knights,
Embraced me, and so kiss'd me the first time,
And gave herself and all her wealth to me.
Then I remember'd Arthur's warning word,
That most of us would follow wandering fires,

And the quest faded in my heart. Anon,
The heads of all her people drew to me,   600
With supplication both of knees and tongue:
'We have heard of thee; thou art our greatest knight,
Our Lady says it, and we well believe.
Wed thou our Lady, and rule over us,
And thou shalt be as Arthur in our land.'
O me, my brother! but one night my vow
Burnt me within, so that I rose and fled,
But wail'd and wept, and hated mine own self,
And even the holy quest, and all but her;
Then after I was join'd with Galahad   610
Cared not for her nor anything upon earth."

Then said the monk: "Poor men, when yule is cold,
Must be content to sit by little fires.
And this am I, so that ye care for me
Ever so little; yea, and blest be heaven
That brought thee here to this poor house of ours
Where all the brethren are so hard, to warm
My cold heart with a friend; but O the pity
To find thine own first love once more—to hold,
Hold her a wealthy bride within thine arms,   620
Or all but hold, and then—cast her aside,
Foregoing all her sweetness, like a weed!
For we that want the warmth of double life,
We that are plagued with dreams of something sweet
Beyond all sweetness in a life so rich.—
Ah, blessed Lord, I speak too earthly-wise,
Seeing I never stray'd beyond the cell,
But live like an old badger in his earth,
With earth about him everywhere, despite
All fast and penance. Saw ye none beside,   630
None of your knights?"

"Yea, so," said Percivale:
"One night my pathway swerving east, I saw
The pelican on the casque of our Sir Bors
All in the middle of the rising moon,
And toward him spurr'd, and hail'd him, and he me,
And each made joy of either. Then he ask'd:
'Where is he? hast thou seen him—Lancelot?—Once,'
Said good Sir Bors, 'he dash'd across me—mad,
And maddening what he rode; and when I cried,
"Ridest thou then so hotly on a quest   640
So holy?" Lancelot shouted, "Stay me not!
I have been the sluggard, and I ride apace,
For now there is a lion in the way!"
So vanish'd.'

"Then Sir Bors had ridden on
Softly, and sorrowing for our Lancelot,
Because his former madness, once the talk
And scandal of our table, had return'd;

vices." 558. market-cross, a cross in the middle of the market, center of local gossip. 612. yule is cold. The festive Christmas log is burned out. 643. lion, perhaps a symbol of Lancelot's guilty love for Guinevere. 646. his former madness, from Guinevere's jealous anger.

Alfred, Lord Tennyson 907

For Lancelot's kith and kin so worship him
That ill to him is ill to them, to Bors
650 Beyond the rest. He well had been content
Not to have seen, so Lancelot might have seen,
The Holy Cup of healing; and, indeed,
Being so clouded with his grief and love,
Small heart was his after the holy quest.
If God would send the vision, well; if not,
The quest and he were in the hands of Heaven.

"And then, with small adventure met, Sir Bors
Rode to the lonest tract of all the realm,
And found a people there among their crags,
660 Our race and blood, a remnant that were left
Paynim amid their circles, and the stones
They pitch up straight to heaven; and their wise men
Were strong in that old magic which can trace
The wandering of the stars, and scoff'd at him
And this high quest as at a simple thing,
Told him he follow'd—almost Arthur's words—
A mocking fire: 'what other fire than he
Whereby the blood beats, and the blossom blows,
And the sea rolls, and all the world is warm'd?'
670 And when his answer chafed them, the rough crowd,
Hearing he had a difference with their priests,
Seized him, and bound and plunged him into a cell
Of great piled stones; and lying bounden there
In darkness thro' innumerable hours
He heard the hollow-ringing heavens sweep
Over him till by miracle—what else?—
Heavy as it was, a great stone slipt and fell,
Such as no wind could move; and thro' the gap
Glimmer'd the streaming scud. Then came a night
680 Still as the day was loud, and thro' the gap
The seven clear stars of Arthur's Table Round—
For, brother, so one night, because they roll
Thro' such a round in heaven, we named the stars,
Rejoicing in ourselves and in our King—
And these, like bright eyes of familiar friends,
In on him shone: 'And then to me, to me,'
Said good Sir Bors, 'beyond all hopes of mine,
Who scarce had pray'd or ask'd it for myself—
Across the seven clear stars—O grace to me!—
690 In color like the fingers of a hand
Before a burning taper, the sweet Grail
Glided and past, and close upon it peal'd
A sharp quick thunder.' Afterwards, a maid,
Who kept our holy faith among her kin
In secret, entering, loosed and let him go."

To whom the monk: "And I remember now
That pelican on the casque. Sir Bors it was
Who spake so low and sadly at our board,
And mighty reverent at our grace was he;

A square-set man and honest, and his eyes, 700
An outdoor sign of all the warmth within,
Smiled with his lips—a smile beneath a cloud,
But heaven had meant it for a sunny one.
Ay, ay, Sir Bors, who else? But when ye reach'd
The city, found ye all your knights return'd,
Or was there sooth in Arthur's prophecy,
Tell me, and what said each, and what the King?"

Then answer'd Percivale: "And that can I,
Brother, and truly; since the living words
Of so great men as Lancelot and our King 710
Pass not from door to door and out again,
But sit within the house. O, when we reach'd
The city, our horses stumbling as they trode
On heaps of ruin, hornless unicorns,
Crack'd basilisks, and splinter'd cockatrices,
And shatter'd talbots, which had left the stones
Raw that they fell from, brought us to the hall.

"And there sat Arthur on the dais-throne,
And those that had gone out upon the quest,
Wasted and worn, and but a tithe of them, 720
And those that had not, stood before the King,
Who, when he saw me, rose and bade me hail,
Saying: 'A welfare in thine eyes reproves
Our fear of some disastrous chance for thee
On hill or plain, at sea or flooding ford.
So fierce a gale made havoc here of late
Among the strange devices of our kings,
Yea, shook this newer, stronger hall of ours,
And from the statue Merlin moulded for us
Half-wrench'd a golden wing; but now—the quest, 730
This vision—hast thou seen the Holy Cup
That Joseph brought of old to Glastonbury?'

"So when I told him all thyself hast heard,
Ambrosius, and my fresh but fixt resolve
To pass away into the quiet life,
He answer'd not, but, sharply turning, ask'd
Of Gawain, 'Gawain, was this quest for thee?'

" 'Nay, lord,' said Gawain, 'not for such as I.
Therefore I communed with a saintly man,
Who made me sure the quest was not for me; 740
For I was much a-wearied of the quest,
But found a silk pavilion in a field,
And merry maidens in it; and then this gale
Tore my pavilion from the tenting-pin,
And blew my merry maidens all about
With all discomfort; yea, and but for this,
My twelvemonth and a day were pleasant to me.'

"He ceased; and Arthur turn'd to whom at first
He saw not, for Sir Bors, on entering, push'd

661. Paynim, pagan. They erected circles of stone as their temples. 667.
he, the sun. 681. seven clear stars, the Great Bear. 713-717. The

city, etc. This description of broken heraldic ornaments forebodes the
destruction of Camelot and the dissolution of Arthur's Order. 759.

750 Athwart the throng to Lancelot, caught his hand,
Held it, and there, half-hidden by him, stood,
Until the King espied him, saying to him,
'Hail, Bors! if ever loyal man and true
Could see it, thou hast seen the Grail;' and Bors,
'Ask me not, for I may not speak of it;
I saw it;' and the tears were in his eyes.

"Then there remain'd but Lancelot, for the rest
Spake but of sundry perils in the storm.
Perhaps, like him of Cana in Holy Writ,
760 Our Arthur kept his best until the last;
'Thou, too, my Lancelot,' ask'd the King, 'my friend,
Our mightiest, hath this quest avail'd for thee?'

" 'Our mightiest!' answer'd Lancelot, with a groan;
'O King!'—and when he paused methought I spied
A dying fire of madness in his eyes—
'O King, my friend, if friend of thine I be,
Happier are those that welter in their sin,
Swine in the mud, that cannot see for slime,
Slime of the ditch; but in me lived a sin
770 So strange, of such a kind, that all of pure,
Noble, and knightly in me twined and clung
Round that one sin, until the wholesome flower
And poisonous grew together, each as each,
Not to be pluck'd asunder; and when thy knights
Sware, I sware with them only in the hope
That could I touch or see the Holy Grail
They might be pluck'd asunder. Then I spake
To one most holy saint, who wept and said
That, save they could be pluck'd asunder, all
780 My quest were but in vain; to whom I vow'd
That I would work according as he will'd.
And forth I went, and while I yearn'd and strove
To tear the twain asunder in my heart,
My madness came upon me as of old,
And whipt me into waste fields far away.
There was I beaten down by little men,
Mean knights, to whom the moving of my sword
And shadow of my spear had been enow
To scare them from me once; and then I came
790 All in my folly to the naked shore,
Wide flats, where nothing but coarse grasses grew;
But such a blast, my King, began to blow,
So loud a blast along the shore and sea,
Ye could not hear the waters for the blast,
Tho' heapt in mounds and ridges all the sea
Drove like a cataract, and all the sand
Swept like a river, and the clouded heavens
Were shaken with the motion and the sound.
And blackening in the sea-foam sway'd a boat,
800 Half-swallow'd in it, anchor'd with a chain;
And in my madness to myself I said,

"I will embark and I will lose myself,
And in the great sea wash away my sin."
I burst the chain, I sprang into the boat.
Seven days I drove along the dreary deep,
And with me drove the moon and all the stars;
And the wind fell, and on the seventh night
I heard the shingle grinding in the surge,
And felt the boat shock earth, and looking up,
Behold, the enchanted towers of Carbonek, 810
A castle like a rock upon a rock,
With chasm-like portals open to the sea,
And steps that met the breaker! There was none
Stood near it but a lion on each side
That kept the entry, and the moon was full.
Then from the boat I leapt, and up the stairs,
There drew my sword. With sudden-flaring manes
Those two great beasts rose upright like a man,
Each gript a shoulder, and I stood between,
And, when I would have smitten them, heard a voice, 820
"Doubt not, go forward; if thou doubt, the beasts
Will tear thee piecemeal." Then with violence
The sword was dash'd from out my hand, and fell.
And up into the sounding hall I past;
But nothing in the sounding hall I saw,
No bench nor table, painting on the wall
Or shield of knight, only the rounded moon
Thro' the tall oriel on the rolling sea.
But always in the quiet house I heard,
Clear as a lark, high o'er me as a lark, 830
A sweet voice singing in the topmost tower
To the eastward. Up I climb'd a thousand steps
With pain; as in a dream I seem'd to climb
For ever; at the last I reach'd a door,
A light was in the crannies, and I heard,
"Glory and joy and honor to our Lord
And to the Holy Vessel of the Grail!"
Then in my madness I essay'd the door;
It gave, and thro' a stormy glare, a heat
As from a seven-times-heated furnace, I, 840
Blasted and burnt, and blinded as I was,
With such a fierceness that I swoon'd away—
O, yet methought I saw the Holy Grail,
All pall'd in crimson samite, and around
Great angels, awful shapes, and wings and eyes!
And but for all my madness and my sin,
And then my swooning, I had sworn I saw
That which I saw; but what I saw was veil'd
And covered, and this quest was not for me.'

"So speaking, and here ceasing, Lancelot left 850
The hall long silent, till Sir Gawain—nay,
Brother, I need not tell thee foolish words,—
A reckless and irreverent knight was he,
Now bolden'd by the silence of his King,—

---

him of Cana, the marriage feast at Cana, where the bridegroom was
accused of having kept the good wine until after the inferior wine had
been drunk. The accuser did not know that Christ had changed the water
into wine. 810. Carbonek, the castle built to house the Holy Grail.

Well, I will tell thee: 'O King, my liege,' he said,
'Hath Gawain fail'd in any quest of thine?
When have I stinted stroke in foughten field?
But as for thine, my good friend Percivale,
Thy holy nun and thou have driven men mad,
860 Yea, made our mightiest madder than our least.
But by mine eyes and by mine ears I swear,
I will be deafer than the blue-eyed cat,
And thrice as blind as any noonday owl,
To holy virgins in their ecstasies,
Henceforward.'

        " 'Deafer,' said the blameless King,
'Gawain, and blinder unto holy things,
Hope not to make thyself by idle vows,
Being too blind to have desire to see.
But if indeed there came a sign from heaven,
870 Blessed are Bors, Lancelot, and Percivale,
For these have seen according to their sight.
For every fiery prophet in old times,
And all the sacred madness of the bard,
When God made music thro' them, could but speak
His music by the framework and the chord;
And as ye saw it ye have spoken truth.

     " 'Nay—but thou errest, Lancelot; never yet
Could all of true and noble in knight and man
Twine round one sin, whatever it might be,
880 With such a closeness but apart there grew,
Save that he were the swine thou spakest of,
Some root of knighthood and pure nobleness;
Whereto see thou, that it may bear its flower.

     " 'And spake I not too truly, O my knights?
Was I too dark a prophet when I said
To those who went upon the Holy Quest,
That most of them would follow wandering fires,
Lost in the quagmire?—lost to me and gone,
And left me gazing at a barren board,
890 And a lean Order—scarce return'd a tithe—
And out of those to whom the vision came
My greatest hardly will believe he saw.
Another hath beheld it afar off,
And, leaving human wrongs to right themselves,
Cares but to pass into the silent life.
And one hath had the vision face to face,
And now his chair desires him here in vain,
However they may crown him otherwhere.

" 'And some among you held that if the King
Had seen the sight he would have sworn the vow.   900
Not easily, seeing that the King must guard
That which he rules, and is but as the hind
To whom a space of land is given to plow,
Who may not wander from the allotted field
Before his work be done, but, being done,
Let visions of the night or of the day
Come as they will; and many a time they come,
Until this earth he walks on seems not earth,
This light that strikes his eyeball is not light,
This air that smites his forehead is not air   910
But vision—yea, his very hand and foot—
In moments when he feels he cannot die,
And knows himself no vision to himself,
Nor the high God a vision, nor that One
Who rose again. Ye have seen what ye have seen.'

    "So spake the King; I knew not all he meant."
(1869)

CROSSING THE BAR

A few days before he died, Tennyson gave instructions that this lyric should be put at the end of all editions of his poems. Cf. Keats' Bright Star! Would I Were Steadfast As Thou Art, p. 796, and Browning's Epilogue to Asolando, p. 932.

Sunset and evening star,
   And one clear call for me!
And may there be no moaning of the bar,
   When I put out to sea,

But such a tide as moving seems asleep,
   Too full for sound and foam,
When that which drew from out the boundless deep
   Turns again home.

Twilight and evening bell,
   And after that the dark!
And may there be no sadness of farewell,   10
   When I embark;

For though from out our bourne of Time and Place
   The flood may bear me far,
I hope to see my Pilot face to face
   When I have crossed the bar.
(1889)

ROBERT BROWNING 1812-1889

Browning was the son of a wealthy clerk in the Bank of England and apparently enjoyed a secure, intellectually liberal childhood. He did not follow the traditional patterns of education, but acquired his massive information through private instruction and an ambitious reading program. If we overlook a volume of juvenilia entitled Incondita, Browning's first publication was Pauline (1833), an overheated, sentimentalized love story in which the influence of Shelley was especially noticeable. After travel in Italy and Russia, Browning next wrote Paracelsus (1835), a marked advance over his previous work. It was the first of his poems to exhibit his passionate love of the Renaissance and its ideals of art and life. His next venture was a drama for theatrical production—Strafford (1836)—which ran for only five nights. His succeeding plays —Pippa Passes (1841), King Victor and King Charles (1842), The Return of the Druses (1843), and A Blot in the 'Scutcheon (1843)—were also failures, although they contained many beautiful lines.

Browning continued with Sordello (1840), a long narrative poem on the life of an Italian poet. This work was so savagely reviewed that it led to a considerable amount of self-correction on Browning's part. His circle of readers being still ridiculously small, his publishers hit upon the device of issuing his poems and dramas written between 1841 and 1846 in cheap little pamphlets, under the title of Bells and Pomegranates.

A literary correspondence between Browning and Elizabeth Barrett, begun in 1845, climaxed in their marriage and removal to Italy in September 1846, partly for the sake of Mrs. Browning's health and chiefly to get away from the tyrannical influence of her father's domineering and unwholesome personality. After some traveling about, they settled at Casa Guidi in Florence, where they lived until the death of Mrs Browning in 1861. Browning became somewhat imbued with the current Italian spirit of independence and nationalism, but his ability to insulate himself from the important events of the age was remarkable. A great value of his Italian sojourn lay in the opportunity it offered him to soak himself in the traditions of Italian art, particularly those of the Renaissance.

The "dramatic monologue" had special formal characteristics for Browning: (1) like the soliloquy, it had to be spoken by one person; (2) unlike the soliloquy, it required the presence of an audience of at least one; (3) the progress of the monologue was fundamentally controlled by the personal dynamics between speaker and listener.

The first of Browning's dramatic monologues might be Christmas Eve and Easter Day (1850), although this should more properly be called a long religious poem spiritualizing his love for his wife. But Men and Women (2 volumes, 1855) contains some of his best known and most typical performances. Mrs. Browning's death led him to return to England; he did not come back to Italy again until 1878. When, in 1885, he was unsuccessful in finding a suitable residence abroad, he nevertheless resumed his visits, dying in Venice in 1889. His first work published after his return to England was another series of monologues, Dramatis Personae (1864), which contained such fine pieces as Rabbi Ben Ezra and Caliban upon Setebos.

Critics generally hold Men and Women, Dramatis Personae, and The Ring and the Book (4 installments, 1868-1869) to contain the finest concentration of Browning's work.

Space prevents the inclusion of any significant part of The Ring and the Book in this volume. This is the analysis in a series of dramatic monologues of a central event—the murder in Rome, during the Renaissance, of a young wife, Pompilia, by her arrogant, worthless, rat-like husband, Guido Franceschini, in spite of the attempt by a young priest, Caponsacchi, to save her. In all, there are twelve versions of the incident, in dramatic monologues by Pompilia, Caponsacchi, Guido at his trial, Guido before his execution, the lawyers concerned, two "halves" of Rome who have made up their minds about the case pro and con, a disinterested critic, and the Pope, who sits in final judgment. There is also a lyrical poem (p. 931) dedicated to Elizabeth Browning, a prologue in which Browning philosophizes about the whole case, and an epilogue which narrates the concluding event of the tragedy—Guido's execution.

Thereafter he published half-a-dozen long poems and a volume of shorter pieces, all of which have great merit, but none of which continues to be so attractive as the writings of his middle period.

Impalpable elements may deeply affect both the popular and the critical reputation of a poet—the changing climate of critical opinion, the emergence of a new generation of poets, the rise of altered educational assumptions in schools and colleges. Still, certain broad characteristics of Browning's poetry would seem to have played a considerable part in determining his acceptability to modern readers. In the first place, Browning did more to transmute the dominant tradition of English poetry than did any other major poet of his century. In his diction, formal structures, and assumptions about poetry, he has more in common with John Donne, T. S. Eliot, and Ezra Pound than with Spenser, Milton, Keats, and Tennyson: he abandoned the "sweet and lovely language" of the past. Secondly, Browning very early adopted the "technique of indirection" which has been one of the necessities of twentieth-century poets. It is this technique which he explained and defended at the end of The Ring and the Book:

> ...it is the glory and good of Art,
> That Art remains the one way possible
> Of speaking truth, to mouths like mine at least.

> ...Art may tell a truth
> Obliquely, do the thing shall breed the thought,
> Nor wrong the thought, missing the mediate word.
> So may you paint your picture, twice show truth,
> Beyond mere imagery on the wall,—...
> So write a book shall mean beyond the facts.

His principal formal device for achieving this "obliquity" was, of course, the dramatic monologue. Further, Browning was one of the most erudite of English poets, though his erudition was more idio-syncratic than conventional. Thus his knowledge, found mostly outside the establishment, contributed to his poetry a quality of surprise and intellectual challenge. Also, Browning's command of unusual subject matter, combined with his technique of indirection, produced a quality of resistance to easy understanding and facile appreciation which twentieth-century criticism has tended to require.

Another quality of Browning's poetry which has provoked a sympathetic response from twentieth-century readers, as in general it did not from his own contemporaries, is a generous portion of the grotesque, a quality which has been succinctly described as follows: "Its proper province would seem to be the exhibition of fanciful power by the artist, not beauty or truth in the literal sense at all, but inventive affluence of unreal yet absurdly comic forms, with just a flavour of the terrible added, to give a grim dignity, and save from the triviality of caricature." Thus, when one speaks of the grotesque element in Browning's poetry, he uses a specific esthetic term, not a general descriptive epithet; and it is clear from Browning's use of the word in his own poetry that he was aware of the specific meaning of the term and consciously working in the grotesque tradition. Finally, Browning's poetry is full of energy and exploration.

The characteristics outlined above more appropriately explain, perhaps, Browning's critical rather than

Robert Browning, taking tea with the Browning Society, a cartoon from The Poet's Corner, by Sir Max Beerbohm.

his popular acceptance. For the latter one can find less formal reasons. For example, Robert Browning was partner to one of the most romantic literary love affairs of all times; further, Browning's poems contain the greatest cast of characters of any poet in English: he has men, women, and children from most walks of life, ethnic groups, and historical epochs. Also, there is in most of Browning's well-known poems a genuinely dramatic situation, sensational in the sense that it is exceptional enough to be exciting—a friar taken in a frolic, an outraged husband wreaking his wrath, a duke ordering his bride, or a bishop ordering his tomb. Finally, to those who go to poetry for moral edification and spiritual nourishment, Browning offered a simple philosophy of life based on a set of secure principles: love gives meaning to life; spontaneity is a symptom of moral health as calculated prudence is a symbol of moral disease; failure is often the best token of success, as human imperfection is the best token of Divine perfection; a man should be judged by what he would do rather than by what he actually does; "trust God, see all, nor be afraid!"

PORPHYRIA'S LOVER

This poem is a soliloquy, as distinct from a dramatic monologue. It was first grouped with another poem under the title Madhouse Cells. The mind of the speaker, though deranged, yet has its own simple logic. His childlike manner is underscored by the directness and verbal economy with which he speaks; and the movement of his mind by association corresponds to the interlaced rhyme scheme. The last line is teasingly ambiguous.

The rain set early in tonight,
   The sullen wind was soon awake,
It tore the elm-tops down for spite,
   And did its worst to vex the lake:
   I listened with heart fit to break.
When glided in Porphyria; straight
   She shut the cold out and the storm,
And kneeled and made the cheerless grate
   Blaze up, and all the cottage warm;
10   Which done, she rose, and from her form
Withdrew the dripping cloak and shawl,
   And laid her soiled gloves by, untied
Her hat and let the damp hair fall,
   And, last, she sat down by my side
   And called me. When no voice replied,
She put my arm about her waist,
   And made her smooth white shoulder bare,
And all her yellow hair displaced,
   And, stooping, made my cheek lie there,
20   And spread, o'er all, her yellow hair,
Murmuring how she loved me—she
   Too weak, for all her heart's endeavor,
To set its struggling passion free
   From pride, and vainer ties dissever,
   And give herself to me forever.
But passion sometimes would prevail,
   Nor could tonight's gay feast restrain
A sudden thought of one so pale
   For love of her, and all in vain:

So, she was come through wind and rain.   30
Be sure I looked up at her eyes
   Happy and proud; at last I knew
Porphyria worshiped me: surprise
   Made my heart swell, and still it grew
   While I debated what to do.
That moment she was mine, mine, fair,
   Perfectly pure and good: I found
A thing to do, and all her hair
   In one long yellow string I wound
   Three times her little throat around,   40
And strangled her. No pain felt she;
   I am quite sure she felt no pain.
As a shut bud that holds a bee,
   I warily oped her lids: again
   Laughed the blue eyes without a stain.
And I untightened next the tress
   About her neck; her cheek once more
Blushed bright beneath my burning kiss:
   I propped her head up as before,
   Only, this time my shoulder bore   50
Her head, which droops upon it still:
   The smiling rosy little head,
So glad it has its utmost will,
   That all it scorned at once is fled,
   And I, its love, am gained instead!
Porphyria's love: she guessed not how
   Her darling one wish would be heard.
And thus we sit together now,
   And all night long we have not stirred,
   And yet God has not said a word!   60
(1834; 1836)

SOLILOQUY OF THE SPANISH CLOISTER

This poem, though a soliloquy rather than a dramatic monologue, is like My Last Duchess in that the person spoken about emerges as an innocent, flower-loving friar, while the speaker reveals himself as mean and venomous, completely unsuited to the religious life.

1

Gr-r-r—there go, my heart's abhorrence!
　Water your damned flowerpots, do!
If hate killed men, Brother Lawrence,
　God's blood, would not mine kill you!
What? your myrtle bush wants trimming?
　Oh, that rose has prior claims—
Needs its leaden vase filled brimming?
　Hell dry you up with its flames!

2

At the meal we sit together:
10　*Salve tibi!* I must hear
Wise talk of the kind of weather,
　Sort of season, time of year:
Not a plenteous cork crop: scarcely
　Dare we hope oak-galls, I doubt:
What's the Latin name for "parsley"?
　What's the Greek name for Swine's Snout?

3

Whew! We'll have our platter burnished,
　Laid with care on our own shelf!
With a fire-new spoon we're furnished,
20　And a goblet for ourself,
Rinsed like something sacrificial
　Ere 'tis fit to touch our chaps—
Marked with L. for our initial!
　(He-he! There his lily snaps!)

4

Saint, forsooth! While brown Dolores
　Squats outside the Convent bank
With Sanchicha, telling stories,
　Steeping tresses in the tank,
Blue-black, lustrous, thick like horsehairs,
30　—Can't I see his dead eye glow,
Bright as 'twere a Barbary corsair's?
　(That is, if he'd let it show!)

5

When he finishes refection,
　Knife and fork he never lays
Cross-wise, to my recollection,
　As do I, in Jesu's praise.
I the Trinity illustrate,
　Drinking watered orange pulp—
In three sips the Arian frustrate;
40　While he drains his at one gulp.

6

Oh, those melons? If he's able
　We're to have a feast! so nice!
One goes to the Abbot's table,
　All of us get each a slice.
How go on your flowers? None double?
　Not one fruit-sort can you spy?
Strange!—And I, too, at such trouble,
　Keep them close-nipped on the sly!

7

There's a great text in Galatians,
　Once you trip on it, entails　　　　　　50
Twenty-nine distinct damnations,
　One sure, if another fails:
If I trip him just a-dying,
　Sure of heaven as sure can be,
Spin him round and send him flying
　Off to hell, a Manichee?

8

Or, my scrofulous French novel
　On gray paper with blunt type!
Simply glance at it, you grovel
　Hand and foot in Belial's gripe:　　　60
If I double down its pages
　At the woeful sixteenth print,
When he gathers his greengages,
　Ope a sieve and slip it in't?

9

Or, there's Satan!—one might venture
　Pledge one's soul to him, yet leave
Such a flaw in the indenture
　As he'd miss till, past retrieve,
Blasted lay that rose-acacia
　We're so proud of! Hy, Zy, Hine . . .　　70
'St, there's Vespers! *Plena gratiá*
　Ave, Virgo! Gr-r-r—you swine!
(1842)

MY LAST DUCHESS

FERRARA

This poem is universally conceded to be one of Browning's finest dramatic monologues. The poem is

---

4. **God's blood,** by the blood of Christ, an especially blasphemous oath. 10. **Salve tibi,** hail to you. 14. **oak-galls,** form of tree fungus. 31. **corsair,** fierce, lecherous pirate. The speaker is, of course, accusing Lawrence of his own perverseness, as l. 29 proves. 33. **refection,** meal. 39. **Arian,** heretic who denied the doctrine of the Trinity, three persons in one God.
My Last Duchess. 3. **Frà Pandolf,** an imaginary artist-monk. 45.

based on incidents in the life of Alfonso II, Duke of Ferrara, who is the speaker; the person spoken to (or audience) is the envoy of the Count of Tyrol, for the hand of whose daughter the Duke is negotiating. The dramatic tension of the poem derives from several sources: the deft revelation of the relentless if cultivated arrogance of the Duke; the equally impressive and deeply ironic unveiling of the late Duchess as a beautiful, childlike creature; the subtle hints (ll. 5, 13, 47-48, 53-54) of the envoy's recognition of the innocence of the Duchess and of his disgust at the evil nature of the Duke.

That's my last Duchess painted on the wall,
Looking as if she were alive. I call
That piece a wonder, now; Frà Pandolf's hands
Worked busily a day, and there she stands.
Will 't please you sit and look at her? I said
"Frà Pandolf" by design, for never read
Strangers like you that pictured countenance,
The depth and passion of its earnest glance,
But to myself they turned (since none puts by
10 The curtain I have drawn for you, but I)
And seemed as they would ask me, if they durst,
How such a glance came there; so, not the first
Are you to turn and ask thus. Sir, 'twas not
Her husband's presence only, called that spot
Of joy into the Duchess' cheek; perhaps
Fra Pandolf chanced to say, "Her mantle laps
Over my lady's wrist too much," or "Paint
Must never hope to reproduce the faint
Half-flush that dies along her throat." Such stuff
20 Was courtesy, she thought, and cause enough
For calling up that spot of joy. She had
A heart—how shall I say?—too soon made glad,
Too easily impressed; she liked whate'er
She looked on, and her looks went everywhere.
Sir, 'twas all one! My favor at her breast,
The dropping of the daylight in the West,
The bough of cherries some officious fool
Broke in the orchard for her, the white mule
She rode with round the terrace—all and each
30 Would draw from her alike the approving speech,
Or blush, at least. She thanked men—good! but thanked
Somehow—I know not how—as if she ranked
My gift of a nine-hundred-years-old name
With anybody's gift. Who'd stoop to blame
This sort of trifling? Even had you skill
In speech—which I have not—to make your will
Quite clear to such an one, and say, "Just this
Or that in you disgusts me; here you miss,
Or there exceed the mark"—and if she let
40 Herself be lessoned so, nor plainly set

Her wits to yours, forsooth, and made excuse—
E'en then would be some stooping; and I choose
Never to stoop. Oh, sir, she smiled, no doubt,
Whene'er I passed her; but who passed without
Much the same smile? This grew; I gave commands;
Then all smiles stopped together. There she stands
As if alive. Will 't please you rise? We'll meet
The company below, then. I repeat,
The Count your master's known munificence
Is ample warrant that no just pretense   50
Of mine for dowry will be disallowed;
Though his fair daughter's self, as I avowed
At starting, is my object. Nay, we'll go
Together down, sir. Notice Neptune, though,
Taming a sea-horse, thought a rarity,
Which Claus of Innsbruck cast in bronze for me!
(1842)

THE LABORATORY

ANCIENT REGIME

The phrase Ancient Régime (Old Order), *originally used to designate the period before the French Revolution, suggests that the incident here recorded is characteristic of former days. During the sixteenth and seventeenth centuries poisoning was a favorite means of getting rid of rivals and other objectionable persons, and regular schools of poisoners for this purpose flourished in Italy. The first water color painted by D. G. Rossetti illustrated this poem and was labeled "Which is the poison to poison her, prithee?"*

Now that I, tying thy glass mask tightly,
May gaze through these faint smokes curling whitely,
As thou pliest thy trade in this devil's-smithy—
Which is the poison to poison her, prithee?

He is with her, and they know that I know
Where they are, what they do; they believe my tears
   flow
While they laugh, laugh at me, at me fled to the drear
Empty church, to pray God in, for them!—I am here.

Grind away, moisten and mash up thy paste,
Pound at thy powder—I am not in haste!   10
Better sit thus, and observe thy strange things,
Than go where men wait me and dance at the King's.

That in the mortar—you call it a gum?
Ah, the brave tree whence such gold oozings come!

commands . . . together. Browning said that he meant that "the commands were that she should be put to death, or he might have had her shut up in a convent." 54. Neptune, god of the sea. 56. Claus of

Innsbruck, an imaginary sculptor. Innsbruck, the capital of Tyrol in Austria, is noted for its bronze work on the tomb of the Emperor Maximilian (1459-1519).

And yonder soft phial, the exquisite blue,
Sure to taste sweetly—is that poison too?

Had I but all of them, thee and thy treasures,
What a wild crowd of invisible pleasures!
To carry pure death in an earring, a casket,
20 A signet, a fan-mount, a filigree basket!

Soon, at the King's, a mere lozenge to give,
And Pauline should have just thirty minutes to live!
But to light a pastile, and Elise, with her head
And her breast and her arms and her hands, should
    drop dead!

Quick—is it finished? The color's too grim!
Why not soft like the phial's, enticing and dim?
Let it brighten her drink, let her turn it and stir,
And try it and taste, ere she fix and prefer!

What a drop! She's not little, no minion like me!
30 That's why she ensnared him; this never will free
The soul from those masculine eyes—say "no!"
To that pulse's magnificent come-and-go.

For only last night, as they whispered, I brought
My own eyes to bear on her so, that I thought
Could I keep them one half minute fixed, she would
    fall
Shriveled; she fell not; yet this does it all!

Not that I bid you spare her the pain;
Let death be felt and the proof remain;
Brand, burn up, bite into its grace—
40 He is sure to remember her dying face!

Is it done? Take my mask off! Nay, be not morose;
It kills her, and this prevents seeing it close:
The delicate droplet, my whole fortune's fee!
If it hurts her, beside, can it ever hurt me?

Now, take all my jewels, gorge gold to your fill,
You may kiss me, old man, on my mouth if you will!
But brush this dust off me, lest horror it brings
Ere I know it—next moment I dance at the King's!
(1844)

THE LOST LEADER

*Browning stated that the idea of this poem was sug-
gested by Wordsworth's change of politics from liberalism to conservatism, but he emphatically denied that
any detailed identification was intended.*

Just for a handful of silver he left us,
    Just for a riband to stick in his coat—
Found the one gift of which fortune bereft us,
    Lost all the others she lets us devote;
They, with the gold to give, doled him out silver,
    So much was theirs who so little allowed;
How all our copper had gone for his service!
    Rags—were they purple, his heart had been proud!

We that had loved him so, followed him, honored him,
    Lived in his mild and magnificent eye,   10
Learned his great language, caught his clear accents,
    Made him our pattern to live and to die!
Shakespeare was of us, Milton was for us,
    Burns, Shelley, were with us—they watch from their
        graves!
He alone breaks from the van and the freemen—
    He alone sinks to the rear and the slaves!

We shall march prospering—not through his presence;
    Songs may inspirit us—not from his lyre;
Deeds will be done—while he boasts his quiescence,
    Still bidding crouch whom the rest bade aspire;   20
Blot out his name, then, record one lost soul more,
    One task more declined, one more footpath untrod,
One more devils'-triumph and sorrow for angels,
    One wrong more to man, one more insult to God!
Life's night begins; let him never come back to us!
    There would be doubt, hesitation, and pain,
Forced praise on our part—the glimmer of twilight,
    Never glad confident morning again!
Best fight on well, for we taught him—strike gallantly,
    Menace our heart ere we master his own;   30
Then let him receive the new knowledge and wait us,
    Pardoned in heaven, the first by the throne!
(1845)

MEETING AT NIGHT

The gray sea and the long black land;
And the yellow half-moon large and low;
And the startled little waves that leap
In fiery ringlets from their sleep,
As I gain the cove with pushing prow,
And quench its speed i' the slushy sand.

Then a mile of warm sea-scented beach;
Three fields to cross till a farm appears;
A tap at the pane, the quick sharp scratch
And blue spurt of a lighted match,   10
And a voice less loud, through its joys and fears,
Than the two hearts beating each to each!
(1845)

The Laboratory. 29. minion, a tiny and dainty person.
The Lost Leader. 29. Best fight, it were best for him to fight.
Parting at Morning. 3. him, the sun.
Home-Thoughts, from Abroad. 6. bole, trunk. 20. melon-flower,
blossom on the melon vine.

Home-Thoughts, from the Sea. 1. Cape Saint Vincent, the south-
western point of Portugal, near which England won a naval victory over
Spain in 1797. 2. Cadiz Bay, on the southern coast of Spain, east of
Cape St. Vincent, where an English fleet destroyed the second Spanish
Armada in 1596. 3. Trafalgar, a cape east of Cádiz Bay, off which

PARTING AT MORNING

Round the cape of a sudden came the sea,
And the sun looked over the mountain's rim:
And straight was a path of gold for him,
And the need of a world of men for me.
(1845)

HOME-THOUGHTS, FROM ABROAD

Oh, to be in England
Now that April's there,
And whoever wakes in England
Sees, some morning, unaware,
That the lowest boughs and the brushwood sheaf
Round the elm-tree bole are in tiny leaf,
While the chaffinch sings on the orchard bough
In England—now!

And after April, when May follows,
10 And the whitethroat builds, and all the swallows!
Hark, where my blossomed pear-tree in the hedge
Leans to the field and scatters on the clover
Blossoms and dewdrops—at the bent spray's
    edge—
That's the wise thrush; he sings each song twice
    over,
Lest you should think he never could recapture
The first fine careless rapture!
And though the fields look rough with hoary dew,
All will be gay when noontide wakes anew
The buttercups, the little children's dower—
Far brighter than this gaudy melon-flower!
(1845)

HOME-THOUGHTS, FROM THE SEA

Browning wrote this poem one evening in April while on shipboard off the northwest coast of Africa on a voyage to Italy, probably his first in 1838, or his second, in 1844.

Nobly, nobly Cape Saint Vincent to the Northwest
    died away;
Sunset ran, one glorious blood-red, reeking into Cadiz
    Bay;
Bluish 'mid the burning water, full in face Trafalgar lay;
In the dimmest northeast distance dawned Gibraltar
    grand and gray;
"Here and here did England help me; how can I help
    England?"—say,

Whoso turns as I, this evening, turn to God to praise
    and pray,
While Jove's planet rises yonder, silent over Africa.
(1845)

THE BISHOP ORDERS HIS TOMB AT SAINT PRAXED'S CHURCH

Ruskin's high tribute to this dramatic monologue in which Browning has interpreted the spirit of the Renaissance is colored by the critic's dislike of the whole period (see p. 1043) but contains, nevertheless, an admirable list of the traits that the Bishop revealed in his last orders. "I know no other piece of modern English, prose or poetry, in which there is so much told, as in these lines of the Renaissance spirit—its worldliness, inconsistency, pride, hypocrisy, ignorance of itself, love of art, of luxury, and of good Latin." The monologue is full of irony: a Bishop speaks from his deathbed to his illegitimate sons, whom he politely calls nephews; he wishes to be buried in the church of St. Praxedes, a holy virgin who distributed her wealth among the poor, while he hopes to cling to his possessions even in death; he offers to pray to the holy virgin that his sons will find good mistresses.

ROME, 15—

Vanity, saith the preacher, vanity!
Draw round my bed; is Anselm keeping back?
Nephews—sons mine . . . ah, God, I know not! Well—
She, men would have to be your mother once,
Old Gandolf envied me, so fair she was!
What's done is done, and she is dead beside,
Dead long ago, and I am Bishop since,
And as she died so must we die ourselves,
And thence ye may perceive the world's a dream.
Life, how and what is it? As here I lie   10
In this state-chamber, dying by degrees,
Hours and long hours in the dead night, I ask,
"Do I live, am I dead?" Peace, peace seems all.
Saint Praxed's ever was the church for peace;
And so, about this tomb of mine. I fought
With tooth and nail to save my niche, ye know—
Old Gandolf cozened me, despite my care;
Shrewd was that snatch from out the corner South
He graced his carrion with, God curse the same!
Yet still my niche is not so cramped but thence   20
One sees the pulpit o' the epistle-side,
And somewhat of the choir, those silent seats,
And up into the aëry dome where live
The angels, and a sunbeam's sure to lurk;
And I shall fill my slab of basalt there,

Lord Nelson won his greatest victory over the French and Spanish fleets in 1805.
  The Bishop Orders His Tomb. The church is named after the virgin St. Praxed, or Praxedes, a Christian saint of the first century. Both the Bishop and the tomb are imaginary. 1. **Vanity, etc.** From

Ecclesiastes 1:2: "Vanity of vanities, saith the Preacher, vanity of vanities; all is vanity." 5. **Gandolf,** the Bishop's predecessor and rival. 21. **the epistle-side,** the side of an altar from which the Epistle is read; the right-hand side as one faces the altar. The left is the gospel-side. 25. **basalt,** a hard rock of dark color.

And 'neath my tabernacle take my rest,
With those nine columns round me, two and two,
The odd one at my feet where Anselm stands:
Peach-blossom marble all, the rare, the ripe
30 As fresh-poured red wine of a mighty pulse.
—Old Gandolf with his paltry onion-stone,
Put me where I may look at him! True peach,
Rosy and flawless; how I earned the prize!
Draw close; that conflagration of my church—
What then? So much was saved if aught were missed!
My sons, ye would not be my death? Go dig
The white-grape vineyard where the oil-press stood,
Drop water gently till the surface sink,
And if ye find . . . Ah, God, I know not, I! . . .
40 Bedded in store of rotten fig-leaves soft,
And corded up in a tight olive-frail,
Some lump, ah, God, of *lapis lazuli*,
Big as a Jew's head cut off at the nape,
Blue as a vein o'er the Madonna's breast . . .
Sons, all have I bequeathed you, villas, all,
That brave Frascati villa with its bath,
So, let the blue lump poise between my knees,
Like God the Father's globe on both his hands
Ye worship in the Jesu Church so gay,
50 For Gandolf shall not choose but see and burst!
Swift as a weaver's shuttle fleet our years;
Man goeth to the grave, and where is he?
Did I say basalt for my slab, sons? Black—
'Twas ever antique-black I meant! How else
Shall ye contrast my frieze to come beneath?
The bas-relief in bronze ye promised me,
Those Pans and Nymphs ye wot of, and perchance
Some tripod, thyrsus, with a vase or so,
The Savior at his sermon on the mount,
60 Saint Praxed in a glory, and one Pan
Ready to twitch the Nymph's last garment off,
And Moses with the tables . . . but I know
Ye mark me not! What do they whisper thee,
Child of my bowels, Anselm? Ah, ye hope
To revel down my villas while I gasp
Bricked o'er with beggar's moldy travertine
Which Gandolf from his tomb-top chuckles at!
Nay, boys, ye love me—all of jasper, then!
'Tis jasper ye stand pledged to, lest I grieve.
70 My bath must needs be left behind, alas!
One block, pure green as a pistachio-nut,
There's plenty jasper somewhere in the world—
And have I not Saint Praxed's ear to pray
Horses for ye, and brown Greek manuscripts,
And mistresses with great smooth marbly limbs?
—That's if ye carve my epitaph aright

Choice Latin, picked phrase, Tully's every word,
No gaudy ware like Gandolf's second line—
Tully, my masters? Ulpian serves his need!
And then how I shall lie through centuries,   80
And hear the blessed mutter of the Mass,
And see God made and eaten all day long,
And feel the steady candle-flame, and taste
Good strong thick stupefying incense-smoke!
For as I lie here, hours of the dead night,
Dying in state and by such slow degrees,
I fold my arms as if they clasped a crook,
And stretch my feet forth straight as stone can point,
And let the bedclothes, for a mortcloth, drop
Into great laps and folds of sculptor's work;   90
And as yon tapers dwindle, and strange thoughts
Grow, with a certain humming in my ears
About the life before I lived this life,
And this life too, popes, cardinals, and priests,
Saint Praxed at his sermon on the mount,
Your tall pale mother with her talking eyes,
And new-found agate urns as fresh as day,
And marble's language, Latin pure, discreet—
Aha, ELUCESCEBAT quoth our friend?
No Tully, said I, Ulpian at the best!   100
Evil and brief hath been my pilgrimage.
All *lapis*, all, sons! Else I give the Pope
My villas! Will ye ever eat my heart?
Ever your eyes were as a lizard's quick,
They glitter like your mother's for my soul,
Or ye would heighten my impoverished frieze,
Piece out its starved design, and fill my vase
With grapes, and add a visor and a term,
And to the tripod ye would tie a lynx
That in his struggle throws the thyrsus down.   110
To comfort me on my entablature
Whereon I am to lie till I must ask,
"Do I live, am I dead?" There, leave me, there!
For ye have stabbed me with ingratitude
To death—ye wish it—God, ye wish it! Stone—
Gritstone, a-crumble! Clammy squares which sweat
As if the corpse they keep were oozing through—
And no more *lapis* to delight the world!
Well, go! I bless ye. Fewer tapers there,
But in a row; and, going, turn your backs—   120
Aye, like departing altar-ministrants,
And leave me in my church, the church for peace,
That I may watch at leisure if he leers—
Old Gandolf—at me, from his onion-stone,
As still he envied me, so fair she was!
(1845)

26. **tabernacle,** a protecting canopy. 29. **Peach-blossom marble,** exceptionally fine marble of a pinkish hue. 30. **of . . . pulse,** of great strength. 31. **onion-stone,** an inferior greenish marble that splits easily into thin layers like those of the onion. 41. **olive-frail,** a basket for holding olives. 42. *lapis lazuli*, a valuable blue stone, stolen by the Bishop from his own church. 46. **Frascati,** a wealthy resort near Rome. 49. **Jesu Church,** Il Gesu, the church of the Jesuits in Rome; it contains an image of God holding a globe made of lapis lazuli. 51. **Swift . . . years.** From Job 7:6: "My days are swifter than a weaver's shuttle, and are spent without hope." 54. **antique-black,** nero-antico, a beautiful black marble. 57. **Pans.** Pan was the god of flocks and pastures. The bas-relief was to contain a curious mixture of pagan and Christian symbols. 58. **tripod,** the three-legged stool on which the priestess of Apollo sat when giving responses to persons consulting the oracle at Delphi. **thyrsus,** the staff used by followers of Bacchus, god of wine. 59. **sermon on the mount.** Found in Matthew, Chapters 5–7. 62. **Moses . . . tables.** The account is found in Exodus, Chapters 24–34. 66. **travertine,** a kind of white limestone. 68. **jasper,** a dark green smooth stone. 74. **brown,** brown with age. 77. **Tully's . . . word,** in the style of Cicero (106–43 B.C.), i.e., the purest classic

A TOCCATA OF GALUPPI'S

*Baldassare Galuppi (1706-1785) was a noted popu-
lar Italian musician and composer. During his last years
he was organist at St. Mark's Cathedral in Venice.
Browning was very fond of playing his music. A toccata
(Italian toccare, to touch) is a musical composition
characterized by lightness of tone and freedom of movement. A Toccata is regarded as one of the finest of
Browning's music poems.*

O Galuppi, Baldassare, this is very sad to find!
I can hardly misconceive you; it would prove me deaf
and blind;
But although I take your meaning, 'tis with such a
heavy mind!

Here you come with your old music, and here's all the
good it brings.
What, they lived once thus at Venice where the merchants were the kings,
Where St. Mark's is, where the Doges used to wed the
sea with rings?

Aye, because the sea's the street there; and 'tis arched
by—what you call—
Shylock's bridge with houses on it, where they kept
the carnival.
I was never out of England—it's as if I saw it all.

Did young people take their pleasure when the sea
10 was warm in May?
Balls and masks begun at midnight, burning ever to
mid-day,
When they made up fresh adventures for the morrow,
do you say?

Was a lady such a lady, cheeks so round and lips so
red—
On her neck the small face buoyant, like a bell-flower
on its bed,
O'er the breast's superb abundance where a man might
base his head?

Well, and it was graceful of them—they'd break talk
off and afford—
She, to bite her mask's black velvet—he, to finger on
his sword,
While you sat and played toccatas, stately at the
clavichord?

What? Those lesser thirds so plaintive, sixths diminished, sigh on sigh,
Told them something? Those suspensions, those solutions—"Must we die?"   20
Those commiserating sevenths—"Life might last! we
can but try!"

"Were you happy?"—"Yes."—"And are you still as
happy?"—"Yes. And you?"
—"Then, more kisses!"—"Did I stop them, when a
million seemed so few?"
Hark, the dominant's persistence till it must be answered to!

So, an octave struck the answer. Oh, they praised you,
I dare say!
"Brave Galuppi! that was music! good alike at grave
and gay!
I can always leave off talking when I hear a master
play!"

Then they left you for their pleasure; till in due time,
one by one,
Some with lives that came to nothing, some with deeds
as well undone,
Death stepped tacitly and took them where they
never see the sun.   30

But when I sit down to reason, think to take my stand
nor swerve,
While I triumph o'er a secret wrung from nature's close
reserve,
In you come with your cold music till I creep through
every nerve.

Yes, you, like a ghostly cricket, creaking where a house
was burned:
"Dust and ashes, dead and done with, Venice spent
what Venice earned.
The soul, doubtless, is immortal—where a soul can
be discerned.

"Yours, for instance: you know physics, something of
geology,
Mathematics are your pastime; souls shall rise in their
degree;
Butterflies may dread extinction—you'll not die, it
cannot be!

"As for Venice and her people, merely born to bloom
and drop,   40

Latin. **79. Ulpian,** a noted Roman jurist (170–228), whose Latin style
was inferior to that of Cicero. **82. God . . . long,** in the sacrament of
the Mass. **87. crook,** a crozier, the pastoral staff of a bishop; it is the
symbol of his office as shepherd of the flock. **89. mortcloth,** a funeral
pall. **95. his.** The Bishop's mind is confused: St. Praxed was a woman.
99. ELUCESCEBAT, he was famous. The Bishop hates the form of
the word, the classic form being *elucebat.* **108. visor,** mask. **term,**
combined bust and pedestal. **116. Gritstone,** a kind of coarse sandstone.

A Toccata of Galuppi. **6. Doges.** The Doge was the chief magistrate of the city. **wed . . . rings.** See Wordsworth's *On the Extinction
of the Venetian Republic,* and notes, p. 695. **8. Shylock's bridge,**
the Rialto, a bridge over the Grand Canal. **18. clavichord,** an old-
fashioned instrument with keys and strings, the predecessor of the
modern piano. **19.** The technical musical terms in these lines (19–24)
are made clear by accompanying phrases. **35 ff.** The quotation is
what the music says to the speaker in the monologue concerning the
men and the women for whom life meant merely a butterfly pleasure.

Here on earth they bore their fruitage, mirth and folly
   were the crop;
What of soul was left, I wonder, when the kissing had
   to stop?

"Dust and ashes!" So you creak it, and I want the
   heart to scold.
Dear dead women, with such hair, too—what's become
   of all the gold
Used to hang and brush their bosoms? I feel chilly
   and grown old.

(1855)

MY STAR

*This lyric is supposed to refer to Mrs. Browning.
Cf. Prospice, p. 931.*

All that I know
   Of a certain star
Is, it can throw
   (Like the angled spar)
Now a dart of red,
   Now a dart of blue;
Till my friends have said
   They would fain see, too,
My star that dartles the red and the blue!
10 Then it stops like a bird; like a flower, hangs furled.
   They must solace themselves with the Saturn above
      it.
What matter to me if their star is a world?
   Mine has opened its soul to me; therefore I love
      it.

(1855)

MEMORABILIA

The title means Things Worth Remembering. *Browning first became acquainted with Shelley's poetry about
1825 and instantly fell under its spell. The poem was
inspired by Browning's overhearing a stranger remark one day in a London bookshop that he had
seen and talked with Shelley.*

Ah, did you once see Shelley plain,
   And did he stop and speak to you,
And did you speak to him again?
   How strange it seems and new!

But you were living before that,
   And also you are living after;

And the memory I started at—
   My starting moves your laughter!

I crossed a moor, with a name of its own
   And a certain use in the world, no doubt,   10
Yet a hand's-breadth of it shines alone
   'Mid the blank miles round about;

For there I picked up on the heather,
   And there I put inside my breast
A molted feather, an eagle-feather!
   Well, I forget the rest.

(1855)

A GRAMMARIAN'S FUNERAL

SHORTLY AFTER THE REVIVAL OF LEARNING IN EUROPE

*The speaker of the poem is a disciple of a dead
scholar of the early Renaissance who is noted for his
inexhaustible passion for knowledge. The speaker leads
other disciples as they bear the body of their master
to the top of a lofty mountain for burial at sunrise.
Cf. Pater's* Renaissance, *p. 1069.*

Let us begin and carry up this corpse,
   Singing together.
Leave we the common crofts, the vulgar thorpes,
   Each in its tether
Sleeping safe on the bosom of the plain,
   Cared for till cock-crow;
Look out if yonder be not day again
   Rimming the rock-row!
That's the appropriate country; there, man's thought,
   Rarer, intenser,   10
Self-gathered for an outbreak, as it ought,
   Chafes in the censer.
Leave we the unlettered plain its herd and crop;
   Seek we sepulture
On a tall mountain, citied to the top,
   Crowded with culture!
All the peaks soar, but one the rest excels;
   Clouds overcome it;
No! yonder sparkle is the citadel's
   Circling its summit.   20
Thither our path lies; wind we up the heights;
   Wait ye the warning?
Our low life was the level's and the night's;
   He's for the morning.
Step to a tune, square chests, erect each head,
   'Ware the beholders!

My Star. 4. **Like . . . spar,** like a prism, which reflects different
colors from different angles.
A Grammarian's Funeral. 3. **crofts,** enclosed farm lands. **thorpes,**
hamlets. 7. **day . . . rock-row.** The sun's rays are just striking the
rocky tops of the mountains. 12. **in the censer.** The figure of speech

likens man's seething brain to the censer or ecclesiastical vessel which
holds the burning incense. 18. **overcome,** conceal. 25. These lines
are directions to the bearers, as are also the passages in parentheses in
lines 41, 73, 76, 90. 26. **'Ware the beholders,** i.e., reveal our pride
to the onlookers. 34. **Apollo,** the Greek god of manly beauty and of

This is our master, famous, calm, and dead,
   Borne on our shoulders.

Sleep, crop and herd! sleep, darkling thorpe and croft,
30   Safe from the weather!
He whom we convoy to his grave aloft,
   Singing together,
He was a man born with thy face and throat,
   Lyric Apollo!
Long he lived nameless; how should Spring take note
   Winter would follow?
Till lo, the little touch, and youth was gone!
   Cramped and diminished,
Moaned he, "New measures, other feet anon!
40   My dance is finished"?
No, that's the world's way (keep the mountain-side,
   Make for the city!);
He knew the signal, and stepped on with pride
   Over men's pity;
Left play for work, and grappled with the world
   Bent on escaping;
"What's in the scroll," quoth he, "thou keepest furled?
   Show me their shaping,
Theirs who most studied man, the bard and sage—
50   Give!"—So, he gowned him,
Straight got by heart that book to its last page;
   Learned, we found him.
Yea, but we found him bald too, eyes like lead,
   Accents uncertain;
"Time to taste life," another would have said,
   "Up with the curtain!"
This man said rather, "Actual life comes next?
   Patience a moment!
Grant I have mastered learning's crabbed text,
60   Still there's the comment.
Let me know all! Prate not of most or least,
   Painful or easy!
Even to the crumbs I'd fain eat up the feast,
   Aye, nor feel queasy."
Oh, such a life as he resolved to live,
   When he had learned it,
When he had gathered all books had to give!
   Sooner, he spurned it.
Image the whole, then execute the parts—
70   Fancy the fabric
Quite, ere you build, ere steel strike fire from quartz,
   Ere mortar dab brick!

(Here's the town-gate reached; there's the market-
   place
   Gaping before us.)
Yea, this in him was the peculiar grace

(Hearten our chorus!)
That before living he'd learn how to live—
   No end to learning;
Earn the means first—God surely will contrive
   Use for our earning.   80
Others mistrust and say, "But time escapes;
   Live now or never!"
He said, "What's time? Leave Now for dogs and
   apes!
   Man has Forever."
Back to his book then; deeper drooped his head;
   Calculus racked him;
Leaden before, his eyes grew dross of lead;
   Tussis attacked him.
"Now, master, take a little rest!"—not he!
   (Caution redoubled,   90
Step two abreast, the way winds narrowly!)
   Not a whit troubled,
Back to his studies, fresher than at first,
   Fierce as a dragon
He (soul-hydroptic with a sacred thirst)
   Sucked at the flagon.
Oh, if we draw a circle premature,
   Heedless of far gain,
Greedy for quick returns of profit, sure
   Bad is our bargain!   100
Was it not great? did not he throw on God
   (He loves the burthen)—
God's task to make the heavenly period
   Perfect the earthen?
Did not he magnify the mind, show clear
   Just what it all meant?
He would not discount life, as fools do here,
   Paid by instalment.
He ventured neck or nothing—heaven's success
   Found, or earth's failure: 110
"Wilt thou trust death or not?" He answered "Yes!
   Hence with life's pale lure!"
That low man seeks a little thing to do,
   Sees it and does it;
This high man, with a great thing to pursue,
   Dies ere he knows it.
That low man goes on adding one to one,
   His hundred's soon hit;
This high man, aiming at a million,
   Misses an unit.   120
That, has the world here—should he need the next,
   Let the world mind him!
This, throws himself on God, and unperplexed
   Seeking shall find him.
So, with the throttling hands of death at strife,
   Ground he at grammar;
Still, through the rattle, parts of speech were rife;

music. 47. **scroll,** manuscript; this was before the time of books. 50.
he gowned him, he put on the scholastic gown. 86. *Calculus,* the
disease called the stone. 88. *Tussis,* a bronchial cough. 95. **soul-
hydroptic,** soul-thirsty. 113. These lines (113-124) express a favorite
doctrine with Browning. Cf. *Andrea del Sarto,* p. 927, ll. 97-98, and

Rabbi Ben Ezra, p. 929, ll. 40-41. 127. *the rattle,* the death rattle
in his throat.

While he could stammer
He settled *Hoti's* business—let it be!—
130 Properly based *Oun*—
Gave us the doctrine of the enclitic *De*,
Dead from the waist down.
Well, here's the platform, here's the proper place;
Hail to your purlieus,
All ye highfliers of the feathered race,
Swallows and curlews!
Here's the top-peak; the multitude below
Live, for they can, there;
This man decided not to Live but Know—
140 Bury this man there?
Here—here's his place, where meteors shoot, clouds form,
Lightnings are loosened,
Stars come and go! Let joy break with the storm,
Peace let the dew send!
Lofty designs must close in like effects;
Loftily lying,
Leave him—still loftier than the world suspects,
Living and dying.

(1855)

FRA LIPPO LIPPI

Fra Lippo Lippi (1406-1469)—Filippo Lippi—was a famous Florentine painter. The account upon which Browning based his interpretation of Lippi's life and art was found in Vasari's Lives of the Painters. Lippi is talking to Florentine guards who have caught him in a nocturnal frolic. Browning uses Lippo to enunciate one of his most important esthetic statements.

I am poor brother Lippo, by your leave!
You need not clap your torches to my face.
Zooks, what's to blame? you think you see a monk!
What, 'tis past midnight, and you go the rounds,
And here you catch me at an alley's end
Where sportive ladies leave their doors ajar?
The Carmine's my cloister; hunt it up,
Do—harry out, if you must show your zeal,
Whatever rat, there, haps on his wrong hole,
10 And nip each softling of a wee white mouse,
Weke, weke, that's crept to keep him company!
Aha, you know your betters! Then, you'll take
Your hand away that's fiddling on my throat,
And please to know me likewise. Who am I?
Why, one, sir, who is lodging with a friend
Three streets off—he's a certain . . . how d' ye call?
Master—a . . . Cosimo of the Medici,
I' the house that caps the corner. Boh! you were best!
Remember and tell me, the day you're hanged,
How you affected such a gullet's gripe! 20
But you, sir, it concerns you that your knaves
Pick up a manner nor discredit you;
Zooks, are we pilchards, that they sweep the streets
And count fair prize what comes into their net?
He's Judas to a tittle, that man is!
Just such a face! Why, sir, you make amends.
Lord, I'm not angry! Bid your hangdogs go
Drink out this quarter-florin to the health
Of the munificent House that harbors me
(And many more beside, lads! more beside!) 30
And all's come square again! I'd like his face—
His, elbowing on his comrade in the door
With the pike and lantern—for the slave that holds
John Baptist's head a-dangle by the hair
With one hand ("Look you, now," as who should say)
And his weapon in the other, yet unwiped!
It's not your chance to have a bit of chalk,
A wood-coal or the like? or you should see!
Yes, I'm the painter, since you style me so.
What, brother Lippo's doings, up and down, 40
You know them and they take you? like enough!
I saw the proper twinkle in your eye—
'Tell you, I liked your looks at very first.
Let's sit and set things straight now, hip to haunch.
Here's spring come, and the nights one makes up bands
To roam the town and sing out carnival,
And I've been three weeks shut within my mew,
A-painting for the great man, saints and saints
And saints again. I could not paint all night—
Ouf! I leaned out of window for fresh air. 50
There came a hurry of feet and little feet,
A sweep of lute strings, laughs, and whiffs of song—
Flower o' the broom,
Take away love, and our earth is a tomb!
Flower o' the quince,
I let Lisa go, and what good in life since?
Flower o' the thyme—and so on. Round they went.
Scarce had they turned the corner when a titter
Like the skipping of rabbits by moonlight—three slim shapes,
And a face that looked up . . . zooks, sir, flesh and blood, 60
That's all I'm made of! Into shreds it went,
Curtain and counterpane and coverlet,

---

129. **Hoti, Oun,** and **De** are Greek particles meaning respectively *that, therefore,* and *toward;* they provide critical points of syntax. 134. **purlieus,** haunts.
Fra Lippo Lippi. 3. **Zooks,** an oath shortened from *Gadzooks,* or *Godzooks,* possibly meaning "God's looks" or "God's hooks." 7. **The Carmine's.** Lippo entered the monastery of the Carmelite friars of the Carmine in Florence in 1420. 17. **Cosimo of the Medici,** Cosimo de' Medici (1389-1464), a rich Florentine banker, statesman, and patron of art and literature; the Medici palace, now known as the Palazzo Riccardi, is on the corner of Via Cavour and Via Gori. 23. **pilchards,** a kind of cheap common fish. 28. **quarter-florin.** The florin was a small gold coin first issued in Florence in 1252. It was probably worth about two dollars. 33. **the slave . . . hair,** an imaginary picture; in Lippo's real picture of the beheading of John the Baptist, the head is carried on a great platter by Salome, the daughter of Herodias. See Matthew 14:1-12. 46. **carnival,** a period of gaiety preceding Lent. 47. **mew,** coop, pen. (Lippo had been engaged to paint pictures in the palace and had been locked in a room until the work should be done.) 52. **song.** The song that follows is a *stornello,* a kind of short folk song of the Italians, usually improvised on the name of a flower or some other familiar object. 67. **Saint Laurence,** the Church of San Lorenzo. 73. **Jerome . . . breast.** Saint Jerome (340?-420) was the most learned

All the bed furniture—a dozen knots,
There was a ladder! Down I let myself,
Hands and feet, scrambling somehow, and so dropped,
And after them. I came up with the fun
Hard by Saint Laurence, hail fellow, well met—
Flower o' the rose,
If I've been merry, what matter who knows?
70 And so as I was stealing back again
To get to bed and have a bit of sleep
Ere I rise up tomorrow and go work
On Jerome knocking at his poor old breast
With his great round stone to subdue the flesh,
You snap me of a sudden. Ah, I see!
Though your eye twinkles still, you shake your head—
Mine's shaved—a monk, you say—the sting's in that!
If Master Cosimo announced himself,
Mum's the word naturally; but a monk!
80 Come, what am I a beast for? tell us, now!
I was a baby when my mother died
And father died and left me in the street.
I starved there, God knows how, a year or two
On fig skins, melon parings, rinds, and shucks,
Refuse and rubbish. One fine frosty day,
My stomach being empty as your hat,
The wind doubled me up, and down I went.
Old Aunt Lapaccia trussed me with one hand
(Its fellow was a stinger as I knew),
90 And so along the wall, over the bridge,
By the straight cut to the convent. Six words there,
While I stood munching my first bread that month:
"So, boy, you're minded," quoth the good fat father,
Wiping his own mouth—'twas refection time—
"To quit this very miserable world?
Will you renounce" . . . "the mouthful of bread?"
    thought I;
By no means! Brief, they made a monk of me;
I did renounce the world, its pride and greed,
Palace, farm, villa, shop, and banking house,
100 Trash, such as these poor devils of Medici
Have given their hearts to—all at eight years old.
Well, sir, I found in time, you may be sure,
'Twas not for nothing—the good bellyful,
The warm serge, and the rope that goes all round,
And day-long blessed idleness beside!
"Let's see what the urchin's fit for"—that came next.
Not overmuch their way, I must confess.
Such a to-do! They tried me with their books;
Lord, they'd have taught me Latin in pure waste!
110 *Flower o' the clove,*
All the Latin I construe is "amo," I love!

But, mind you, when a boy starves in the streets
Eight years together, as my fortune was,
Watching folk's faces to know who will fling
The bit of half-stripped grape-bunch he desires,
And who will curse or kick him for his pains—
Which gentleman processional and fine,
Holding a candle to the Sacrament,
Will wink and let him lift a plate and catch
The droppings of the wax to sell again,   120
Or holla for the Eight and have him whipped—
How say I?—nay, which dog bites, which lets
    drop
His bone from the heap of offal in the street—
Why, soul and sense of him grow sharp alike;
He learns the look of things, and none the less
For admonition from the hunger pinch.
I had a store of such remarks, be sure,
Which, after I found leisure, turned to use.
I drew men's faces on my copy books,
Scrawled them within the antiphonary's marge,   130
Joined legs and arms to the long music-notes,
Found eyes and nose and chin for A's and B's,
And made a string of pictures of the world
Betwixt the ins and outs of verb and noun,
On the wall, the bench, the door. The monks looked
    black.
"Nay," quoth the Prior, "turn him out, d'ye say?
In no wise. Lose a crow and catch a lark.
What if at last we get our man of parts,
We Carmelites, like those Camaldolese
And Preaching Friars, to do our church up fine   140
And put the front on it that ought to be!"
And hereupon he bade me daub away.
Thank you! my head being crammed, the walls a
    blank,
Never was such prompt disemburdening.
First, every sort of monk, the black and white,
I drew them, fat and lean; then, folk at church,
From good old gossips waiting to confess
Their cribs of barrel droppings, candle ends—
To the breathless fellow at the altar foot,
Fresh from his murder, safe and sitting there   150
With the little children round him in a row
Of admiration, half for his beard and half
For that white anger of his victim's son
Shaking a fist at him with one fierce arm,
Signing himself with the other because of Christ
(Whose sad face on the cross sees only this
After the passion of a thousand years),
Till some poor girl, her apron o'er her head

of the early Fathers of the Latin Church. He lived in the desert for
several years as a penance for his youthful sins. Early Christian art
depicted him on his knees before a crucifix, beating his breast with a
stone. 88. **Aunt Lapaccia,** Mona Lapaccia, his father's sister. **trussed
me,** lifted me up. 94. **refection time,** lunch time. 117. **gentleman
processional, etc.,** gentlemen wearing fine robes and walking in the
religious procession. 121. **the Eight,** the magistrates who governed
Florence. **antiphonary's marge,** the margins of the books used
by the choir. 131. **long music-notes.** The medieval music notes were
square or oblong with long stems. 139. **Carmelites, etc.** The Carmelites were monks of the order of Mount Carmel, in Syria; the

Camaldolese belonged to the convent of Camaldoli, near Florence; the
Preaching Friars are the Dominicans, named after St. Dominic—they
were called Brothers Preachers by Pope Innocent III in 1215. These
orders owned various monasteries and churches and were eager to possess
the greatest religious paintings. 141. **the front, etc.** The façade of
the Church of the Medici in Florence (San Lorenzo), designed by
Michelangelo, has never been finished but presents ragged brickwork,
waiting for its marble veneer. 148. **Their cribs, etc.,** small thefts of
wine, wax, etc. 150. **safe,** because he is in a sacred place, which by
law protected him from arrest. 154. **Shaking . . . Christ.** Revenge
and religion are at war in him. 157. **passion,** suffering.

(Which the intense eyes looked through), came at eve
160 On tiptoe, said a word, dropped in a loaf,
Her pair of earrings, and a bunch of flowers
(The brute took growling), prayed, and so was gone.
I painted all, then cried, " 'Tis ask and have;
Choose, for more's ready!"—laid the ladder flat,
And showed my covered bit of cloister wall.
The monks closed in a circle and praised loud
Till checked, taught what to see and not to see,
Being simple bodies—"That's the very man!
Look at the boy who stoops to pat the dog!
170 That woman's like the Prior's niece who comes
To care about his asthma; it's the life!"
But there my triumph's straw-fire flared and funked;
Their betters took their turn to see and say;
The Prior and the learned pulled a face
And stopped all that in no time. "How? what's here?
Quite from the mark of painting, bless us all!
Faces, arms, legs, and bodies like the true
As much as pea and pea! It's devil's game!
Your business is not to catch men with show,
180 With homage to the perishable clay,
But lift them over it, ignore it all,
Make them forget there's such a thing as flesh.
Your business is to paint the souls of men—
Man's soul, and it's a fire, smoke . . . no, it's not . . .
It's vapor done up like a new-born babe
(In that shape when you die it leaves your mouth)—
It's . . . well, what matters talking, it's the soul!
Give us no more of body than shows soul!
Here's Giotto, with his Saint a-praising God,
190 That sets us praising—why not stop with him?
Why put all thoughts of praise out of our head
With wonder at lines, colors, and what not?
Paint the soul, never mind the legs and arms!
Rub all out, try at it a second time.
Oh, that white smallish female with the breasts,
She's just my niece . . . Herodias, I would say—
Who went and danced and got men's heads cut off!
Have it all out!" Now, is this sense, I ask?
A fine way to paint soul, by painting body
200 So ill the eye can't stop there, must go further
And can't fare worse! Thus, yellow does for white
When what you put for yellow's simply black,
And any sort of meaning looks intense
When all beside itself means and looks naught.
Why can't a painter lift each foot in turn,
Left foot and right foot, go a double step,
Make his flesh liker and his soul more like,
Both in their order? Take the prettiest face,
The Prior's niece . . . patron saint—is it so pretty

You can't discover if it means hope, fear, 210
Sorrow, or joy? won't beauty go with these?
Suppose I've made her eyes all right and blue,
Can't I take breath and try to add life's flash,
And then add soul and heighten them threefold?
Or say there's beauty with no soul at all
(I never saw it—put the case the same);
If you get simple beauty and naught else,
You get about the best thing God invents—
That's somewhat; and you'll find the soul you have missed,
Within yourself, when you return him thanks. 220
"Rub all out!" Well, well, there's my life, in short,
And so the thing has gone on ever since.
I'm grown a man no doubt, I've broken bounds;
You should not take a fellow eight years old
And make him swear to never kiss the girls.
I'm my own master, paint now as I please—
Having a friend, you see, in the Corner-house!
Lord, it's fast holding by the rings in front—
Those great rings serve more purposes than just
To plant a flag in, or tie up a horse! 230
And yet the old schooling sticks, the old grave eyes
Are peeping o'er my shoulder as I work,
The heads shake still—"It's art's decline, my son!
You're not of the true painters, great and old;
Brother Angelico's the man, you'll find;
Brother Lorenzo stands his single peer—
Fag on at flesh, you'll never make the third!"
Flower o' the pine,
You keep your mistr . . . manners, and I'll stick to mine!
I'm not the third, then; bless us, they must know! 240
Don't you think they're the likeliest to know,
They with their Latin? So, I swallow my rage,
Clench my teeth, suck my lips in tight, and paint
To please them—sometimes do and sometimes don't;
For, doing most, there's pretty sure to come
A turn, some warm eve finds me at my saints—
A laugh, a cry, the business of the world
(*Flower o' the peach,*
Death for us all, and his own life for each!)—
And my whole soul revolves, the cup runs over, 250
The world and life's too big to pass for a dream,
And I do these wild things in sheer despite,
And play the fooleries you catch me at,
In pure rage! The old mill-horse, out at grass
After hard years, throws up his stiff heels so,
Although the miller does not preach to him
The only good of grass is to make chaff.
What would men have? Do they like grass or no—
May they or mayn't they? All I want's the thing

172. funked, smoked. 189. Giotto, Giotto di Bondone (1266?–1337), a famous Florentine painter, architect, and sculptor. He expressed the soul in his paintings and cared nothing for realistic art. Lippo and Guidi (l. 276) introduced realism, which Lippo here defends. 196. Herodias. See note on ll. 33. 228. the rings in front, large iron rings on the front of the palace. Lippo used them in climbing in and out of his window. 235. Brother Angelico, Fra Angelico, Giovanni da Fiesole (1387–1455), the greatest of the medieval school of religious artists who "painted souls." 236. Brother Lorenzo, Lorenzo Monaco, a painter of the Order of the Camaldolese, who also "painted souls." 276. Guidi, Tommaso Guidi, or Masaccio (1401–1428), nicknamed Hulking Tom. He is said to have been the first Italian artist to paint a nude figure. He was Lippo's master, not his disciple. 307. cullion, a low fellow. 323. a Saint Laurence, a picture of St. Laurence, who

260 Settled forever one way. As it is,
You tell too many lies and hurt yourself;
You don't like what you only like too much,
You do like what, if given you at your word,
You find abundantly detestable.
For me, I think I speak as I was taught;
I always see the garden and God there
A-making man's wife; and, my lesson learned—
The value and significance of flesh—
I can't unlearn ten minutes afterwards.

270   You understand me; I'm a beast, I know.
But see, now—why, I see as certainly
As that the morning star's about to shine,
What will hap some day. We've a youngster here
Comes to our convent, studies what I do,
Slouches and stares and lets no atom drop.
His name is Guidi—he'll not mind the monks—
They call him Hulking Tom; he lets them talk;
He picks my practice up—he'll paint apace,
I hope so—though I never live so long,
280 I know what's sure to follow. You be judge!
You speak no Latin more than I, belike;
However, you're my man, you've seen the world—
The beauty and the wonder and the power,
The shapes of things, their colors, lights, and shades,
Changes, surprises—and God made it all!
—For what? Do you feel thankful, aye or no,
For this fair town's face, yonder river's line,
The mountain round it and the sky above,
Much more the figures of man, woman, child,
290 These are the frame to? What's it all about?
To be passed over, despised? or dwelt upon,
Wondered at? Oh, this last of course!—you say.
But why not do as well as say—paint these
Just as they are, careless what comes of it?
God's works—paint any one, and count it crime
To let a truth slip. Don't object, "His works
Are here already; nature is complete:
Suppose you reproduce her—which you can't—
There's no advantage! you must beat her, then."
300 For, don't you mark? we're made so that we love
First when we see them painted, things we have passed
Perhaps a hundred times nor cared to see;
And so they are better, painted—better to us,
Which is the same thing. Art was given for that;
God uses us to help each other so,
Lending our minds out. Have you noticed, now,
Your cullion's hanging face? A bit of chalk,
And trust me but you should, though! How much more,
If I drew higher things with the same truth!
310 That were to take the Prior's pulpit-place,

Interpret God to all of you! Oh, oh,
It makes me mad to see what men shall do
And we in our graves! This world's no blot for us,
Nor blank; it means intensely, and means good—
To find its meaning is my meat and drink.
"Aye, but you don't so instigate to prayer!"
Strikes in the Prior; "when your meaning's plain,
It does not say to folk—remember matins,
Or, mind you fast next Friday!" Why, for this
What need of art at all? A skull and bones,   320
Two bits of stick nailed crosswise, or, what's best,
A bell to chime the hour with does as well.
I painted a Saint Laurence six months since
At Prato, splashed the fresco in fine style;
"How looks my painting, now the scaffold's down?"
I ask a brother. "Hugely," he returns—
"Already not one phiz of your three slaves
Who turn the Deacon off his toasted side,
But's scratched and prodded to our heart's content,
The pious people have so eased their own   330
With coming to say prayers there in a rage;
We get on fast to see the bricks beneath.
Expect another job this time next year,
For pity and religion grow i' the crowd—
Your painting serves its purpose!" Hang the fools!

  —That is—you'll not mistake an idle word
Spoke in a huff by a poor monk, God wot,
Tasting the air this spicy night, which turns
The unaccustomed head like Chianti wine!
Oh, the church knows! don't misreport me, now!   340
It's natural a poor monk out of bounds
Should have his apt word to excuse himself;
And hearken how I plot to make amends.
I have bethought me: I shall paint a piece
. . . There's for you! Give me six months, then go, see
Something in Sant' Ambrogio's! Bless the nuns!
They want a cast o' my office. I shall paint
God in the midst, Madonna and her babe,
Ringed by a bowery, flowery angel brood,
Lilies and vestments and white faces, sweet   350
As puff on puff of grated orris root
When ladies crowd to Church at midsummer.
And then i' the front, of course a saint or two—
Saint John, because he saves the Florentines,
Saint Ambrose, who puts down in black and white
The convent's friends and gives them a long day,
And Job, I must have him there past mistake,
The man of Uz (and Us without the z,
Painters who need his patience). Well, all these
Secured at their devotion, up shall come   360
Out of a corner when you least expect,

---

was martyred in 258 by being burned to death on a gridiron. 324.
At Prato. Some of Lippo's most important work is in the Cathedral
at Prato, a town near Florence. 339. **Chianti wine,** wine from Chianti,
a region south of Florence. 346. **Sant' Ambrogio's,** Saint Ambrose's
Church in Florence. St. Ambrose was a famous Church leader during
the fourth century. He became Bishop of Milan in 374. 347. **I shall
paint,** etc. The picture described is *The Coronation of the Virgin,* now

in the Academy of Fine Arts, Florence. The model for the Virgin was
Lucrezia Buti, Lippo's mistress. 354. **Saint John,** St. John the Baptist,
the patron saint of Florence. 357. **Job.** Cf. Job 1:1: "There was a man
in the land of Uz, whose name was Job." 361. **Out of a corner . . .
I.** Lippo's head appears in the lower right-hand corner of the picture.

As one by a dark stair into a great light,
Music and talking, who but Lippo! I!—
Mazed, motionless, and moonstruck—I'm the man!
Back I shrink—what is this I see and hear?
I, caught up with my monk's-things by mistake,
My old serge gown and rope that goes all round,
I, in this presence, this pure company!
Where's a hole, where's a corner for escape?
370 Then steps a sweet angelic slip of a thing
Forward, puts out a soft palm: "Not so fast!"
—Addresses the celestial presence, "Nay,
He made you and devised you, after all,
Though he's none of you! Could Saint John there
    draw—
His camel-hair make up a painting-brush?
We come to brother Lippo for all that,
Iste perfecit opus!" So, all smile—
I shuffle sideways with my blushing face
Under the cover of a hundred wings
380 Thrown like a spread of kirtles when you're gay
And play hot cockles, all the doors being shut,
Till, wholly unexpected, in there pops
The hothead husband! Thus I scuttle off
To some safe bench behind, not letting go
The palm of her, the little lily thing
That spoke the good word for me in the nick,
Like the Prior's niece . . . Saint Lucy, I would say.
And so all's saved for me, and for the church
A pretty picture gained. Go, six months hence!
390 Your hand, sir, and good-by; no lights, no lights!
The street's hushed, and I know my own way back,
Don't fear me! There's the gray beginning. Zooks!
(1855)

ANDREA DEL SARTO

CALLED "THE FAULTLESS PAINTER"

*Andrea d'Agnolo di Francesco (1486-1531) was
called "del Sarto" because he was the son of a tailor
(sarto). The perfection of his frescoes in the Church of
the Annunziata in Florence won him the title of "The
Faultless Painter." In 1512 he married Lucrezia del
Fede, whose influence led Andrea to neglect his art
work. The poem is based upon the account of Andrea
found in Vasari's Lives of the Painters.*

But do not let us quarrel any more,
No, my Lucrezia; bear with me for once.
Sit down and all shall happen as you wish.
You turn your face, but does it bring your heart?
I'll work then for your friend's friend, never fear,
Treat his own subject after his own way,
Fix his own time, accept too his own price,
And shut the money into this small hand
When next it takes mine. Will it? tenderly?
Oh, I'll content him—but tomorrow, Love!   10
I often am much wearier than you think,
This evening more than usual, and it seems
As if—forgive now—should you let me sit
Here by the window with your hand in mine
And look a half-hour forth on Fiesole,
Both of one mind, as married people use,
Quietly, quietly the evening through,
I might get up tomorrow to my work
Cheerful and fresh as ever. Let us try.
Tomorrow, how you shall be glad for this!   20
Your soft hand is a woman of itself,
And mine the man's bared breast she curls inside.
Don't count the time lost, neither; you must serve
For each of the five pictures we require—
It saves a model. So! keep looking so—
My serpentining beauty, rounds on rounds!
—How could you ever prick those perfect ears,
Even to put the pearl there! oh, so sweet—
My face, my moon, my everybody's moon,
Which everybody looks on and calls his,   30
And, I suppose, is looked on by in turn,
While she looks—no one's: very dear, no less.
You smile? why, there's my picture ready made,
There's what we painters call our harmony!
A common grayness silvers everything—
All in a twilight, you and I alike—
You, at the point of your first pride in me
(That's gone, you know), but I, at every point;
My youth, my hope, my art, being all toned down
To yonder sober pleasant Fiesole.   40
There's the bell clinking from the chapel-top;
That length of convent-wall across the way
Holds the trees safer, huddled more inside;
The last monk leaves the garden; days decrease,
And autumn grows, autumn in everything.
Eh? the whole seems to fall into a shape
As if I saw alike my work and self
And all that I was born to be and do,
A twilight-piece. Love, we are in God's hand.
How strange now looks the life he makes us lead;   50
So free we seem, so fettered fast we are!
I feel he laid the fetter; let it lie!
This chamber, for example—turn your head—
All that's behind us! You don't understand,
Nor care to understand, about my art,
But you can hear at least when people speak;
And that cartoon, the second from the door—
It is the thing, Love! so such thing should be—

374. **Saint John . . . camel-hair.** Cf. Mark 1:6: "And John was clothed with camel's hair." 377. *Iste . . . opus*, this one did the work. The inscription is on a scroll in the picture. 380. **kirtles,** tunics, coats. 381. **hot cockles,** an old English game in which a blindfolded player tries to guess who strikes him.
Andrea Del Sarto. 15. **Fiesole,** a suburb of Florence. 23. **you . . .**

model. Lucrezia is discernible in nearly all the women of Andrea's pictures. 65. **the Legate's talk.** The Legate was the representative of the Pope. 82. **forthright,** unswerving. 93. **Morello,** a high peak of the Apennines, north of Florence. 97. **Ah . . . for?** Cf. *A Grammarian's Funeral,* p. 921, ll. 113-120, and *Rabbi Ben Ezra,* p. 929, ll. 40-41 105. **The Urbinate,** Raphael Sanzio (1483-1520), one of

Behold Madonna!—I am bold to say.
60 I can do with my pencil what I know,
What I see, what at bottom of my heart
I wish for, if I ever wish so deep—
Do easily, too—when I say perfectly,
I do not boast, perhaps; yourself are judge,
Who listened to the Legate's talk last week,
And just as much they used to say in France.
At any rate, 'tis easy, all of it!
No sketches first, no studies—that's long past;
I do what many dream of all their lives—
70 Dream? strive to do, and agonize to do,
And fail in doing. I could count twenty such
On twice your fingers, and not leave this town,
Who strive—you don't know how the others strive
To paint a little thing like that you smeared
Carelessly passing with your robes afloat—
Yet do much less, so much less, Someone says
(I know his name, no matter)—so much less!
Well, less is more, Lucrezia; I am judged.
There burns a truer light of God in them,
80 In their vexed, beating, stuffed, and stopped-up brain,
Heart, or whate'er else, than goes on to prompt
This low-pulsed forthright craftsman's hand of mine.
Their works drop groundward, but themselves, I
    know,
Reach many a time a heaven that's shut to me,
Enter and take their place there sure enough,
Though they come back and cannot tell the world.
My works are nearer heaven, but I sit here.
The sudden blood of these men! at a word—
Praise them, it boils; or blame them, it boils too.
90 I, painting from myself and to myself,
Know what I do, am unmoved by men's blame
Or their praise either. Somebody remarks
Morello's outline there is wrongly traced,
His hue mistaken; what of that? or else,
Rightly traced and well ordered; what of that?
Speak as they please, what does the mountain care?
Ah, but a man's reach should exceed his grasp,
Or what's a heaven for? All is silver-gray,
Placid and perfect with my art: the worse!
100 I know both what I want and what might gain,
And yet how profitless to know, to sigh,
"Had I been two, another and myself,
Our head would have o'erlooked the world!" No doubt.
Yonder's a work now, of that famous youth,
The Urbinate, who died five years ago.
('Tis copied; George Vasari sent it me.)
Well, I can fancy how he did it all,
Pouring his soul, with kings and popes to see,
Reaching, that heaven might so replenish him,
110 Above and through his art—for it gives way:

That arm is wrongly put—and there again—
A fault to pardon in the drawing's lines,
Its body, so to speak: its soul is right,
He means right—that, a child may understand.
Still, what an arm! and I could alter it;
But all the play, the insight, and the stretch—
Out of me, out of me! And wherefore out?
Had you enjoined them on me, given me soul,
We might have risen to Rafael, I and you!
Nay, Love, you did give all I asked, I think— 120
More than I merit, yes, by many times.
But had you—oh, with the same perfect brow,
And perfect eyes, and more than perfect mouth,
And the low voice my soul hears, as a bird
The fowler's pipe, and follows to the snare—
Had you, with these the same, but brought a mind!
Some women do so. Had the mouth there urged,
"God and the glory! never care for gain.
The present by the future, what is that?
Live for fame, side by side with Agnolo! 130
Rafael is waiting; up to God, all three!"
I might have done it for you. So it seems;
Perhaps not. All is as God overrules.
Beside, incentives come from the soul's self;
The rest avail not. Why do I need you?
What wife had Rafael, or has Agnolo?
In this world, who can do a thing, will not;
And who would do it, cannot, I perceive;
Yet the will's somewhat—somewhat, too, the power—
And thus we half-men struggle. At the end, 140
God, I conclude, compensates, punishes.
'Tis safer for me, if the award be strict,
That I am something underrated here,
Poor this long while, despised, to speak the truth.
I dared not, do you know, leave home all day,
For fear of chancing on the Paris lords.
The best is when they pass and look aside;
But they speak sometimes; I must bear it all.
Well may they speak! That Francis, that first time,
And that long festal year at Fontainebleau! 150
I surely then could sometimes leave the ground,
Put on the glory, Rafael's daily wear,
In that humane great monarch's golden look—
One finger in his beard or twisted curl
Over his mouth's good mark that made the smile,
One arm about my shoulder, round my neck;
The jingle of his gold chain in my ear—
I painting proudly with his breath on me,
All his Court round him, seeing with his eyes,
Such frank French eyes, and such a fire of souls 160
Profuse, my hand kept plying by those hearts;
And, best of all, this, this, this face beyond,
This in the background, waiting on my work,

the greatest of Italian painters; he was born in the city of Urbino. 106. **George Vasari** (1512–1574), a pupil of Andrea and author of *The Lives of the Most Eminent Painters, Sculptors, and Architects.* 130. **Agnolo,** Michelangelo (1475–1564), celebrated as painter, sculptor, architect, and poet. 149. **That Francis,** Francis I, king of France (1515–1547). He had invited Andrea to come to Fontainebleau, the

seat of the richest of the royal palaces. While engaged upon important work there, Andrea was suddenly called home by Lucrezia. He was given money with which to secure works of art for the French King, but he purchased a house with it for Lucrezia.

Robert Browning 927

To crown the issue with a last reward!
A good time, was it not, my kingly days?
And had you not grown restless . . . but I know—
'Tis done and past; 'twas right, my instinct said;
Too live the life grew, golden and not gray,
And I'm the weak-eyed bat no sun should tempt
170 Out of the grange whose four walls make his world.
How could it end in any other way?
You called me, and I came home to your heart.
The triumph was—to reach and stay there; since
I reached it ere the triumph, what is lost?
Let my hands frame your face in your hair's gold,
You beautiful Lucrezia that are mine!
"Rafael did this, Andrea painted that;
The Roman's is the better when you pray,
But still the other's Virgin was his wife"—
180 Men will excuse me. I am glad to judge
Both pictures in your presence; clearer grows
My better fortune, I resolve to think.
For, do you know, Lucrezia, as God lives,
Said one day Agnolo, his very self,
To Rafael . . . I have known it all these years . . .
(When the young man was flaming out his thoughts
Upon a palace-wall for Rome to see,
Too lifted up in heart because of it),
"Friend, there's a certain sorry little scrub
190 Goes up and down our Florence, none cares how,
Who, were he set to plan and execute
As you are, pricked on by your popes and kings,
Would bring the sweat into that brow of yours!"
To Rafael's!—And indeed the arm is wrong.
I hardly dare . . . yet, only you to see,
Give the chalk here—quick, thus the line should go!
Ay, but the soul! he's Rafael! rub it out!
Still, all I care for, if he spoke the truth
(What he? why, who but Michel Agnolo?
200 Do you forget already words like those?),
If really there was such a chance, so lost—
Is, whether you're—not grateful—but more pleased.
Well, let me think so. And you smile indeed!
This hour has been an hour! Another smile?
If you would sit thus by me every night,
I should work better, do you comprehend?
I mean that I should earn more, give you more.
See, it is settled dusk now; there's a star;
Morello's gone, the watch-lights show the wall,
210 The cue-owls speak the name we call them by.
Come from the window, love—come in, at last,
Inside the melancholy little house
We built to be so gay with. God is just.
King Francis may forgive me; oft at nights
When I look up from painting, eyes tired out,
The walls become illumined, brick from brick
Distinct, instead of mortar, fierce bright gold,

That gold of his I did cement them with!
Let us but love each other. Must you go?
That Cousin here again? he waits outside?   220
Must see you—you, and not with me? Those loans?
More gaming debts to pay? you smiled for that?
Well, let smiles buy me! have you more to spend?
While hand and eye and something of a heart
Are left me, work's my ware, and what's it worth?
I'll pay my fancy. Only let me sit
The gray remainder of the evening out,
Idle, you call it, and muse perfectly
How I could paint, were I but back in France,
One picture, just one more—the Virgin's face,   230
Not yours this time! I want you at my side
To hear them—that is, Michel Agnolo—
Judge all I do and tell you of its worth.
Will you? Tomorrow, satisfy your friend.
I take the subjects for his corridor,
Finish the portrait out of hand—there, there,
And throw him in another thing or two
If he demurs; the whole should prove enough
To pay for this same Cousin's freak. Beside—
What's better and what's all I care about—   240
Get you the thirteen scudi for the ruff!
Love, does that please you? Ah, but what does he,
The Cousin! what does he to please you more?

I am grown peaceful as old age tonight.
I regret little, I would change still less.
Since there my past life lies, why alter it?
The very wrong to Francis!—it is true
I took his coin, was tempted, and complied,
And built this house and sinned, and all is
        said.
My father and my mother died of want.   250
Well, had I riches of my own? you see
How one gets rich! Let each one bear his lot.
They were born poor, lived poor, and poor they died;
And I have labored somewhat in my time
And not been paid profusely. Some good son
Paint my two hundred pictures—let him try!
No doubt, there's something strikes a balance. Yes,
You loved me quite enough, it seems tonight.
This must suffice me here. What would one have?
In heaven, perhaps, new chances, one more chance—   260
Four great walls in the New Jerusalem,
Meted on each side by the angel's reed,
For Leonard, Rafael, Agnolo, and me
To cover—the three first without a wife,
While I have mine! So—still they overcome
Because there's still Lucrezia—as I choose.

Again the Cousin's whistle! Go, my Love.
(1855)

178. The Roman's, Raphael's. 186. When . . . it, probably a
reference to Raphael's decorations made in certain rooms of the Vatican
under Julius II (1443–1513). 210. cue-owls, small European owls.
220. Cousin, a euphemism for lover. Cf. ll. 29–32. 241. scudi, plural
of scudo, an Italian coin worth about one dollar. 261. the New
Jerusalem. For a description of the New Jerusalem and its walls, see
Revelation 21:10–21. 263. Leonard, Leonardo da Vinci (1452–1519),
one of the greatest of Italian painters.

RABBI BEN EZRA

Rabbi Ben Ezra was a distinguished Jewish philosopher, physician, astronomer, and poet of the twelfth century. Although the ideas in the poem are drawn largely from his writings, the poem is one of the best expressions of Browning's own philosophy of life.

Grow old along with me!
The best is yet to be,
The last of life, for which the first was made.
Our times are in his hand
Who saith, "A whole I planned;
Youth shows but half. Trust God; see all, nor be afraid!"

Not that, amassing flowers,
Youth sighed, "Which rose make ours,
Which lily leave and then as best recall?"
10 Not that, admiring stars,
It yearned, "Nor Jove, nor Mars;
Mine be some figured flame which blends, transcends them all!"

Not for such hopes and fears
Annulling youth's brief years,
Do I remonstrate—folly wide the mark!
Rather I prize the doubt
Low kinds exist without,
Finished and finite clods, untroubled by a spark.

Poor vaunt of life indeed,
20 Were man but formed to feed
On joy, to solely seek and find and feast.
Such feasting ended, then
As sure an end to men;
Irks care the crop-full bird? Frets doubt the maw-crammed beast?

Rejoice we are allied
To that which doth provide
And not partake, effect and not receive!
A spark disturbs our clod;
Nearer we hold of God
30 Who gives, than of his tribes that take, I must believe.

Then, welcome each rebuff
That turns earth's smoothness rough,
Each sting that bids nor sit nor stand but go!
Be our joys three parts pain!
Strive, and hold cheap the strain;
Learn, nor account the pang; dare, never grudge the throe!

For thence—a paradox
Which comforts while it mocks—

Shall life succeed in that it seems to fail:
What I aspired to be,   40
And was not, comforts me;
A brute I might have been, but would not sink i' the scale.

What is he but a brute
Whose flesh has soul to suit,
Whose spirit works lest arms and legs want play?
To man, propose this test—
Thy body at its best,
How far can that project thy soul on its lone way?

Yet gifts should prove their use:
I own the Past profuse   50
Of power each side, perfection every turn;
Eyes, ears took in their dole,
Brain treasured up the whole;
Should not the heart beat once, "How good to live and learn"?

Not once beat, "Praise be thine!
I see the whole design,
I, who saw power, see now Love perfect too;
Perfect I call thy plan.
Thanks that I was a man!
Maker, remake, complete—I trust what thou shalt do!"   60

For pleasant is this flesh;
Our soul, in its rose-mesh
Pulled ever to the earth, still yearns for rest.
Would we some prize might hold
To match those manifold
Possessions of the brute—gain most, as we did best!

Let us not always say,
"Spite of this flesh today
I strove, made head, gained ground upon the whole!"
As the bird wings and sings,   70
Let us cry, "All good things
Are ours, nor soul helps flesh more, now, than flesh helps soul!"

Therefore I summon age
To grant youth's heritage,
Life's struggle having so far reached its term.
Thence shall I pass, approved
A man, for aye removed
From the developed brute—a god, though in the germ.

And I shall thereupon
Take rest, ere I be gone   80
Once more on my adventure brave and new;

Rabbi Ben Ezra. 7. **Not that.** *Not that* of ll. 7 and 10 and *Not for* of l. 13 go with *Do I remonstrate* of l. 15. 24. **Irks . . . bird,** does care irk the crop-full bird? 40. **What . . . me.** Cf. *A Grammarian's Funeral,* p. 921, ll. 113-120, and *Andrea del Sarto,* p. 927, ll. 97-98.

61. Cf. *Fra Lippo Lippi,* p. 924, ll. 205-214. 81. **adventure . . . new,** the life of an old person after the passions and problems of youth are left behind.

Fearless and unperplexed,
When I wage battle next,
What weapons to select, what armor to indue.

Youth ended, I shall try
My gain or loss thereby;
Leave the fire ashes, what survives is gold.
And I shall weigh the same,
Give life its praise or blame.
90 Young, all lay in dispute; I shall know, being old.

For note, when evening shuts,
A certain moment cuts
The deed off, calls the glory from the gray;
A whisper from the west
Shoots—"Add this to the rest,
Take it and try its worth. Here dies another day."

So, still within this life,
Though lifted o'er its strife,
Let me discern, compare, pronounce at last,
100 "This rage was right i' the main,
That acquiescence vain;
The Future I may face, now I have proved the Past."

For more is not reserved
To man, with soul just nerved
To act tomorrow what he learns today;
Here, work enough to watch
The Master work, and catch
Hints of the proper craft, tricks of the tool's true play.

As it was better, youth
110 Should strive, through acts uncouth,
Toward making, than repose on aught found made;
So, better, age, exempt
From strife, should know, than tempt
Further. Thou waitedst age; wait death nor be afraid!

Enough now, if the Right
And Good and Infinite
Be named here, as thou callest thy hand thine own,
With knowledge absolute,
Subject to no dispute
120 From fools that crowded youth, nor let thee feel alone.

Be there, for once and all,
Severed great minds from small,
Announced to each his station in the Past!
Was I, the world arraigned,
Were they, my soul disdained,
Right? Let age speak the truth and give us peace at
    last!

Now, who shall arbitrate?
Ten men love what I hate,

Shun what I follow, slight what I receive;
Ten, who in ears and eyes   130
Match me. We all surmise,
They this thing, and I that; whom shall my soul
    believe?

Not on the vulgar mass
Called "work," must sentence pass—
Things done, that took the eye and had the price;
O'er which, from level stand,
The low world laid its hand,
Found straightway to its mind, could value in a trice:

But all, the world's coarse thumb
And finger failed to plumb,   140
So passed in making up the main account;
All instincts immature,
All purposes unsure,
That weighed not as his work, yet swelled the man's
    amount:

Thoughts hardly to be packed
Into a narrow act,
Fancies that broke through language and escaped;
All I could never be,
All, men ignored in me,
This, I was worth to God, whose wheel the pitcher
    shaped.   150

Aye, note that Potter's wheel,
That metaphor! and feel
Why time spins fast, why passive lies our clay—
Thou, to whom fools propound,
When the wine makes its round,
"Since life fleets, all is change; the Past gone, seize
    today!"

Fool! All that is, at all,
Lasts ever, past recall;
Earth changes, but thy soul and God stand sure.
What entered into thee,   160
That was, is, and shall be.
Time's wheel runs back or stops; Potter and clay en-
    dure.

He fixed thee 'mid this dance
Of plastic circumstance,
This Present, thou, forsooth, would fain arrest—
Machinery just meant
To give thy soul its bent,
Try thee and turn thee forth, sufficiently impressed.

What though the earlier grooves,
Which ran the laughing loves   170
Around thy base, no longer pause and press?

84. to indue, to put on. 87. Leave . . . ashes, if the fire leaves
ashes. 124. Was I. Supply *whom* after *I* and also after *they*, l. 125.
151. Potter's wheel. Cf. Isaiah 64:8: "But now, O Lord, thou art

our father; we are the clay, and thou our potter; and we all are the
work of thy hand." Cf. also Fitzgerald's *Rubáiyát*, p. 1089, ll. 325-360.
The Ring and the Book. 23. **so blessing back, etc.** My eyes yearn

What though, about thy rim,
Skull-things in order grim
Grow out, in graver mood, obey the sterner stress?

Look not thou down but up!
To uses of a cup,
The festal board, lamp's flash, and trumpet's peal,
The new wine's foaming flow,
The Master's lips aglow!
Thou, heaven's consummate cup, what needst thou
180 with earth's wheel?

But I need, now as then,
Thee, God, who moldest men;
And since, not even while the whirl was worst,
Did I—to the wheel of life
With shapes and colors rife,
Bound dizzily—mistake my end, to slake Thy thirst.

So, take and use Thy work;
Amend what flaws may lurk,
What strain o' the stuff, what warpings past the aim!
190 My times be in Thy hand!
Perfect the cup as planned!
Let age approve of youth, and death complete the same!
(1864)

PROSPICE

   The title means Look Forward. *The poem was written shortly after the death of Mrs. Browning; it is a
triumphant statement of Browning's faith in personal
immortality.*

Fear death?—to feel the fog in my throat,
  The mist in my face,
When the snows begin, and the blasts denote
  I am nearing the place,
The power of the night, the press of the storm,
  The post of the foe;
Where he stands, the Arch Fear in a visible form,
  Yet the strong man must go.
For the journey is done and the summit attained,
10 And the barriers fall,
Though a battle's to fight ere the guerdon be gained,
  The reward of it all.
I was ever a fighter, so—one fight more,
  The best and the last!
I would hate that death bandaged my eyes, and fore-
    bore,
  And bade me creep past.
No! let me taste the whole of it, fare like my peers,
  The heroes of old,
Bear the brunt, in a minute pay glad life's arrears
20 Of pain, darkness, and cold.

For sudden the worst turns the best to the brave,
  The black minute's at end,
And the elements' rage, the fiend-voices that rave,
  Shall dwindle, shall blend,
Shall change, shall become first a peace out of pain,
  Then a light, then thy breast,
O thou soul of my soul! I shall clasp thee again,
  And with God be the rest!
(1861; 1864)

from THE RING AND THE BOOK

   *Browning's greatest triumph in the dramatic mono-
logue, his* Ring and the Book, *has been already outlined and characterized (see p. 911). The amazing
study of human nature which resulted from his imaginative reconstruction of the murder case recounted in*
The Old Yellow Book *is his longest and perhaps his
greatest poem.*
   *The ring is the symbol of Browning's attempted
achievement of a perfect circle of truth through the telling of the story from all possible points of view. The
selection given here is the closing passage of Book I;
it was intended as a memorial to Mrs. Browning,
who died in 1861.*

PROEM

O lyric Love, half angel and half bird,
And all a wonder and a wild desire—
Boldest of hearts that ever braved the sun,
Took sanctuary within the holier blue,
And sang a kindred soul out to his face—
Yet human at the red-ripe of the heart—
When the first summons from the darkling earth
Reached thee amid thy chambers, blanched their blue,
And bared them of the glory—to drop down,
To toil for man, to suffer or to die—   10
This is the same voice: can thy soul know change?
Hail then, and hearken from the realms of help!
Never may I commence my song, my due
To God who best taught song by gift of thee,
Except with bent head and beseeching hand—
That still, despite the distance and the dark,
What was, again may be; some interchange
Of grace, some splendor once thy very thought,
Some benediction anciently thy smile:
—Never conclude, but raising hand and head   20
Thither where eyes, that cannot reach, yet yearn
For all hope, all sustainment, all reward,
Their utmost up and on—so blessing back
In those thy realms of help, that heaven thy home,
Some whiteness which, I judge, thy face makes proud,
Some wanness where, I think, thy foot may fall!
(1869)

for reward from you in heaven—a glimpse of some whiteness glorified
by your presence, of some wanness reflected wherever you walk, which
will be evidence of your blessing to me. *Blessing* is a participle modifying *whiteness* and *wanness;* both nouns are parallel in construction with
hope and *reward* (l. 22).

WHY I AM A LIBERAL

"Why?" Because all I haply can and do,
All that I am now, all I hope to be—
Whence comes it save from fortune setting free
Body and soul the purpose to pursue,
God traced for both? If fetters not a few,
Of prejudice, convention, fall from me,
These shall I bid men—each in his degree
Also God-guided—bear, and gayly, too?

But little do or can the best of us;
10 That little is achieved through Liberty.
Who then, dares hold, emancipated thus,
His fellow shall continue bound? Not I,
Who live, love, labor freely, nor discuss
A brother's right to freedom. That is "Why."
(1885)

EPILOGUE TO ASOLANDO

This is Browning's last poem; it appears at the end of a collection of miscellaneous poems published under the title Asolando, *from* Asolo, Italy, *where Browning lived during his last summer. The poem should be compared with Keats'* Bright Star, p. 796, *and Tennyson's* Crossing the Bar, p. 910.

Why I am a Liberal. Cf. *The Lost Leader,* p. 916.
Epilogue to Asolando. 11. **One . . . forward.** With the idea

At the midnight in the silence of the sleeptime,
    When you set your fancies free,
Will they pass to where—by death, fools think, im-
        prisoned—
Low he lies who once so loved you, whom you loved
        so,
        —Pity me?

Oh, to love so, be so loved, yet so mistaken!
    What had I on earth to do
With the slothful, with the mawkish, the unmanly?
Like the aimless, helpless, hopeless, did I drivel—
        Being—who?
                                                    10

One who never turned his back but marched breast
        forward,
    Never doubted clouds would break,
Never dreamed, though right were worsted, wrong
        would triumph,
Held we fall to rise, are baffled to fight better,
        Sleep to wake.

No! At noonday, in the bustle of man's worktime,
    Greet the unseen with a cheer!
Bid him forward, breast and back as either should be,
"Strive and thrive!" cry, "Speed—fight on, fare ever
        There as here!"
(1889)

expressed here may be compared the philosophy contained in *Prospice,*
p. 931.

MATTHEW ARNOLD 1822-1888

Matthew Arnold was born in Laleham, Middlesex, England, the eldest son of Thomas Arnold (1795-1842), the distinguished headmaster of Rugby School and the leading educator of his generation in England. After his graduation from Oxford, Matthew became secretary to Lord Lansdowne (1847) and shortly thereafter accepted a government position as Inspector of Schools, which he held for almost all of the rest of his life. Although he found much of the work to be sheer drudgery, his natural instincts for teaching and preaching, as well as his almost puritan sense of duty, allowed him to transcend distasteful details; in fact, he extended his study of schools to those of the Continent and published his findings in a series of monographs between 1861 and 1868. Oxford honored him by appointing him Professor of Poetry in 1857; he was the first layman to occupy the chair. Meanwhile he worked

away at his inspectorship with the greatest energy, also writing both poetry and essays from time to time. After the expiration of his professorship (1867) only a lecture tour in the United States in 1883 broke his working pattern. These lectures were published under the title of Discourses in America. *In 1886 he retired, dying in Liverpool two years later.*

Arnold recognized his limitations as a poet. As he wrote to his sister in 1853: "Fret not yourself to make my poems square in all their parts, but like what you can, my darling. The true reason why parts suit you while others do not is that my poems are fragments—i.e. that I am fragments, while you are whole; the whole effect of my poems is quite vague and indeterminate—this is their weakness...a person who has any inward completeness can at best only like parts of them; in fact such a person stands firmly and knows what he is about while the poems stagger weakly and are at their wits end. I shall do better some day, I hope—meanwhile…do not plague yourself to find a consistent meaning for these last; which in fact they do not possess through my weakness." The judgment is not too harsh, and Arnold deserves great credit for having passed it on himself. He was a distinctly minor poet who occasionally wrote a truly distinguished poem—The Forsaken Merman, To Marguerite—Continued, Philomela, Sohrab and Rustum, Dover Beach, and perhaps two or three others. His other poems are often felicitous in their use of language and imagery, and the underlying thought is almost always fresh and apt.

The major motif of Arnold's poetry is that of modern man's exile, isolation, or alienation. The characters in Arnold's poems are exiles, "mindful how the past was glad," but themselves born "in an alien planet." We find this persistent theme not only in the lyrics, the short narratives, and the dramatic poems, but also in objective, epical episodes written in imitation of Homer. In Sohrab and Rustum, Sohrab is unknown even to his own father, is a soldier in an alien army, is searching for his own identity, and Rustum, himself out of harmony with man and nature and far from home, appears upon the field of battle in disguise. And the grand irony of the situation is that Sohrab is unwittingly fighting his father that he may find his father; and Rustum is battling his son, his fury half-inspired by the belief that he has no son. The scene in the end is a tremendous symbol of isolation:

> So, on the bloody sand, Sohrab lay dead,
> And the great Rustum drew his horseman's cloak
> Down o'er his face, and sate by his dead son.

The critic in prose spoke with a firmer voice than the critic in poetry. The resolute tone audible in the preface of 1853 persisted throughout Arnold's life as a literary critic. Two basic principles guided Arnold's literary criticism: his immense faith in poetry and his determination to introduce "a little order into this [modern] chaos by establishing in any quarter a single sound rule of criticism, a single rule which clearly marks what is right as right and what is wrong as wrong." To achieve this, Arnold relied on three essential qualities: on intellectual curiosity—the "disinterested love of a free play of the mind on all subjects for its own sake"; on literary conscience—that quality which asks, not whether one is amused or pleased or moved "by a work of art or mind," but whether one is "right in being amused with it, and in applauding it, and in being moved by it"; and on faith in the qualitative distinction—"Of this quality the world is impatient; it chafes against it, rails at it, hates it,—it ends by receiving its influence, and by undergoing its law. This quality at last inexorably corrects the world's blunders, and fixes the world's ideals."

QUIET WORK

One lesson, Nature, let me learn of thee,
One lesson which in every wind is blown,
One lesson of two duties kept at one
Though the loud world proclaim their enmity—
Of toil unsevered from tranquillity!
Of labor, that in lasting fruit outgrows
Far noisier schemes, accomplished in repose,
Too great for haste, too high for rivalry!
Yes, while on earth a thousand discords ring,
10 Man's fitful uproar mingling with his toil,
Still do thy sleepless ministers move on,
Their glorious tasks in silence perfecting;
Still working, blaming still our vain turmoil,
Laborers that shall not fail, when man is gone.
(1849)

SHAKESPEARE

Others abide our question. Thou art free.
We ask and ask—thou smilest and art still,

Out-topping knowledge. For the loftiest hill,
Who to the stars uncrowns his majesty,
Planting his steadfast footsteps in the sea,
Making the heaven of heavens his dwelling-place,
Spares but the cloudy border of his base
To the foiled searching of mortality;
And thou, who didst the stars and sunbeams know,
Self-schooled, self-scanned, self-honored, self-secure,   10
Didst tread on earth unguessed at.—Better so!
All pains the immortal spirit must endure,
All weakness which impairs, all griefs which bow,
Find their sole speech in that victorious brow.
(1849)

IN HARMONY WITH NATURE

The poem is addressed to a preacher who had urged his audience to live in harmony with nature.

TO A PREACHER

"In harmony with Nature?" Restless fool,
Who with such heat dost preach what were to thee,
When true, the last impossibility—

Shakespeare. 1. **Others . . . free,** other **poets** are easily understood. Thou art too deep for our understanding.

To be like Nature strong, like Nature cool!
Know, man hath all which Nature hath, but more,
And in that *more* lie all his hopes of good.
Nature is cruel, man is sick of blood;
Nature is stubborn, man would fain adore;
Nature is fickle, man hath need of rest;
10 Nature forgives no debt, and fears no grave;
Man would be mild, and with safe conscience blest.
Man must begin, know this, where Nature ends;
Nature and man can never be fast friends.
Fool, if thou canst not pass her, rest her slave!
(1849)

MEMORIAL VERSES

*Goethe died in 1832 and was buried in Weimar,
Germany. Byron died in 1824 while aiding the Greeks
in their fight for independence. Wordsworth died in
1850. Arnold gave high place to all three poets; he was
influenced especially by the poetry of Wordsworth.*

APRIL 1850

Goethe in Weimar sleeps, and Greece,
Long since, saw Byron's struggle cease.
But one such death remained to come;
The last poetic voice is dumb—
We stand today by Wordsworth's tomb.

When Byron's eyes were shut in death,
We bowed our head and held our breath.
He taught us little; but our soul
Had *felt* him like the thunder's roll.
10 With shivering heart the strife we saw
Of passion with eternal law;
And yet with reverential awe
We watched the fount of fiery life
Which served for that Titanic strife.

When Goethe's death was told, we said:
Sunk, then, is Europe's sagest head.
Physician of the iron age,
Goethe has done his pilgrimage.
He took the suffering human race,
20 He read each wound, each weakness clear;
And struck his finger on the place,
And said: *Thou ailest here, and here!*
He looked on Europe's dying hour
Of fitful dream and feverish power;
His eye plunged down the weltering strife,
The turmoil of expiring life—
He said: *The end is everywhere,
Art still has truth, take refuge there!*
And he was happy, if to know

Causes of things, and far below   30
His feet to see the lurid flow
Of terror, and insane distress,
And headlong fate, be happiness.

And Wordsworth!—Ah, pale ghosts, rejoice!
For never has such soothing voice
Been to your shadowy world conveyed,
Since erst, at morn, some wandering shade
Heard the clear song of Orpheus come
Through Hades, and the mournful gloom.
Wordsworth has gone from us—and ye,   40
Ah, may ye feel his voice as we!
He too upon a wintry clime
Had fallen—on this iron time
Of doubts, disputes, distractions, fears.
He found us when the age had bound
Our souls in its benumbing round;
He spoke, and loosed our heart in tears.
He laid us, as we lay at birth,
On the cool flowery lap of earth;
Smiles broke from us, and we had ease;   50
The hills were round us, and the breeze
Went o'er the sun-lit fields again;
Our foreheads felt the wind and rain.
Our youth returned; for there was shed
On spirits that had long been dead,
Spirits dried up and closely furled,
The freshness of the early world.

Ah! since dark days still bring to light
Man's prudence and man's fiery might,
Time may restore us in his course   60
Goethe's sage mind and Byron's force;
But where will Europe's latter hour
Again find Wordsworth's healing power?
Others will teach us how to dare,
And against fear our breast to steel;
Others will strengthen us to bear—
But who, ah! who, will make us feel?
The cloud of mortal destiny,
Others will front it fearlessly—
But who, like him, will put it by?   70

Keep fresh the grass upon his grave,
O Rotha, with thy living wave!
Sing him thy best! for few or none
Hears thy voice right, now he is gone.
(1850)

ISOLATION. TO MARGUERITE

*This poem and the next are from a group of six
love poems entitled Switzerland. The two poems given
here were originally published independently.*

Memorial Verses. 14. **Titanic strife.** Byron was noted for his fiery,
passionate nature, and the word *Titanic* is fittingly applied to him (see
p. 739). The Titans were superhuman beings of great size who rebelled
against the gods. 17. **iron age,** so called because of the terrible years
of the French Revolution and the period following. To Goethe they
seemed to portend the destruction of Europe. 29. **And he . . .**

We were apart; yet, day by day,
I bade my heart more constant be.
I bade it keep the world away,
And grow a home for only thee;
Nor feared but thy love likewise grew,
Like mine, each day, more tried, more true.

The fault was grave! I might have known,
What far too soon, alas! I learned—
The heart can bind itself alone,
10 And faith may oft be unreturned.
Self-swayed our feelings ebb and swell—
Thou lov'st no more;—Farewell! Farewell!

Farewell!—and thou, thou lonely heart,
Which never yet without remorse
Even for a moment didst depart
From thy remote and spheréd course
To haunt the place where passions reign—
Back to thy solitude again!

Back! with the conscious thrill of shame
20 Which Luna felt, that summer-night,
Flash through her pure immortal frame,
When she forsook the starry height
To hang over Endymion's sleep
Upon the pine-grown Latmian steep.

Yet she, chaste queen, had never proved
How vain a thing is mortal love,
Wandering in heaven, far removed.
But thou hast long had place to prove
This truth—to prove, and make thine own:
30 "Thou hast been, shalt be, art alone."

Or, if not quite alone, yet they
Which touch thee are unmating things—
Ocean and clouds and night and day;
Lorn autumns and triumphant springs;
And life, and others' joy and pain,
And love, if love, of happier men.

Of happier men—for they, at least,
Have *dreamed* two human hearts might blend
In one, and were through faith released
40 From isolation without end
Prolonged; nor knew, although not less
Alone than thou, their loneliness.
(1855)

TO MARGUERITE—CONTINUED

Yes! in the sea of life enisled,
With echoing straits between us thrown,
Dotting the shoreless watery wild,

We mortal millions live *alone*.
The islands feel the enclasping flow,
And then their endless bounds they know.

But when the moon their hollows lights,
And they are swept by balms of spring,
And in their glens, on starry nights,
The nightingales divinely sing;   10
And lovely notes, from shore to shore,
Across the sounds and channels pour—

Oh! then a longing like despair
Is to their farthest caverns sent;
For surely once, they feel, we were
Parts of a single continent!
Now round us spreads the watery plain—
Oh, might our marges meet again!

Who ordered that their longing's fire
Should be, as soon as kindled, cooled?   20
Who renders vain their deep desire?—
A god, a god their severance ruled!
And bade betwixt their shores to be
The unplumbed, salt, estranging sea.
(1852)

SELF-DEPENDENCE

Weary of myself, and sick of asking
What I am, and what I ought to be,
At this vessel's prow I stand, which bears me
Forwards, forwards o'er the starlit sea.

And a look of passionate desire
O'er the sea and to the stars I send:
"Ye who from my childhood up have calmed me,
Calm me, ah, compose me to the end!

"Ah, once more," I cried, "ye stars, ye waters,
On my heart your mighty charm renew;   10
Still, still let me, as I gaze upon you,
Feel my soul becoming vast like you!"

From the intense, clear, star-sown vault of heaven,
Over the lit sea's unquiet way,
In the rustling night-air came the answer:
"Wouldst thou *be* as these are? *Live* as they.

"Unaffrighted by the silence round them,
Undistracted by the sights they see,
These demand not that the things without them
Yield them love, amusement, sympathy.   20

"And with joy the stars perform their shining,
And the sea its long moon-silvered roll;

happiness. These lines are translated from Vergil's *Georgics*, II, 490-492. 38. **Orpheus.** See p. 763, note to l. 691. 72. **Rotha**, a small stream near Grasmere, Westmoreland, where Wordsworth is buried.

Isolation. 20. **Luna**, Diana, goddess of the moon and of chastity. She fell in love with Endymion, the shepherd boy whom she found sleeping on Mt. Latmos, in Asia Minor.

For self-poised they live, nor pine with noting
All the fever of some differing soul.

"Bounded by themselves, and unregardful
In what state God's other works may be,
In their own tasks all their powers pouring,
These attain the mighty life you see."

O air-born voice! long since, severely clear,
30 A cry like thine in mine own heart I hear:
"Resolve to be thyself; and know that he
Who finds himself loses his misery!"
(1852)

THE BURIED LIFE

*The title of this poem refers to man's hidden self
—the source of his thought and his feeling.*

Light flows our war of mocking words, and yet,
Behold, with tears mine eyes are wet!
I feel a nameless sadness o'er me roll.
Yes, yes, we know that we can jest,
We know, we know that we can smile!
But there's a something in this breast,
To which thy light words bring no rest,
And thy gay smiles no anodyne;
Give me thy hand, and hush awhile,
10 And turn those limpid eyes on mine,
And let me read there, love! thy inmost soul.

Alas! is even love too weak
To unlock the heart, and let it speak?
Are even lovers powerless to reveal
To one another what indeed they feel?
I knew the mass of men concealed
Their thoughts, for fear that if revealed
They would by other men be met
With blank indifference, or with blame reproved;
20 I knew they lived and moved
Tricked in disguises, alien to the rest
Of men, and alien to themselves—and yet
The same heart beats in every human breast!
But we, my love!—doth a like spell benumb
Our hearts, our voices?—must we too be dumb?
Ah! well for us, if even we,
Even for a moment, can get free
Our heart, and have our lips unchained;
For that which seals them hath been deep-
ordained!
30 Fate, which foresaw
How frivolous a baby man would be—
By what distractions he would be possessed,

How he would pour himself in every strife,
And well-nigh change his own identity—
That it might keep from his capricious play
His genuine self, and force him to obey
Even in his own despite his being's law,
Bade through the deep recesses of our breast
The unregarded river of our life
Pursue with indiscernible flow its way;   40
And that we should not see
The buried stream, and seem to be
Eddying at large in blind uncertainty,
Though driving on with it eternally.

But often, in the world's most crowded streets,
But often, in the din of strife,
There rises an unspeakable desire
After the knowledge of our buried life;
A thirst to spend our fire and restless force
In tracking out our true, original course;   50
A longing to inquire
Into the mystery of this heart which beats
So wild, so deep in us—to know
Whence our lives come and where they go.
And many a man in his own breast then delves,
But deep enough, alas! none ever mines.
And we have been on many thousand lines,
And we have shown, on each, spirit and power;
But hardly have we, for one little hour,
Been on our own line, have we been ourselves—   60
Hardly had skill to utter one of all
The nameless feelings that course through our
          breast,
But they course on forever unexpressed.
And long we try in vain to speak and act
Our hidden self, and what we say and do
Is eloquent, is well—but 'tis not true!
And then we will no more be racked
With inward striving, and demand
Of all the thousand nothings of the hour
Their stupefying power;   70
Ah yes, and they benumb us at our call!
Yet still, from time to time, vague and forlorn,
From the soul's subterranean depth upborne
As from an infinitely distant land,
Come airs, and floating echoes, and convey
A melancholy into all our day.

Only—but this is rare—
When a belovéd hand is laid in ours,
When, jaded with the rush and glare
Of the interminable hours,   80
Our eyes can in another's eyes read clear,
When our world-deafened ear
Is by the tones of a loved voice caressed—
A bolt is shot back somewhere in our breast,

The Buried Life. 77. *Only...goes.* Cf. *Dover Beach*, p. 944,
ll. 29-37.
   Lines. 4. *red-boled*, having reddish trunks. 18. **angler.** Arnold

was an enthusiastic fisherman. 24. **Pan,** god of shepherds and of the
country. Arnold was born at Laleham, a country village in Middlesex.

And a lost pulse of feeling stirs again;
The eye sinks inward, and the heart lies plain,
And what we mean, we say, and what we would, we
   know.
A man becomes aware of his life's flow,
And hears its winding murmur; and he sees
90 The meadows where it glides, the sun, the breeze.

And there arrives a lull in the hot race
Wherein he doth forever chase
That flying and elusive shadow, rest.
An air of coolness plays upon his face,
And an unwonted calm pervades his breast.
And then he thinks he knows
The hills where his life rose,
And the sea where it goes.
(1852)

LINES

WRITTEN IN KENSINGTON GARDENS

   *Kensington is a borough in the western part of
London; the Gardens are surrounded by busy streets.
This poem is regarded as one of the most Words-
worthian that Arnold wrote.*

In this lone, open glade I lie,
Screened by deep boughs on either hand;
And at its end, to stay the eye,
Those black-crowned, red-boled pine trees stand!

Birds here make song, each bird has his,
Across the girdling city's hum.
How green under the boughs it is!
How thick the tremulous sheep-cries come!

Sometimes a child will cross the glade
10 To take his nurse his broken toy;
Sometimes a thrush flits overhead
Deep in her unknown day's employ.

Here at my feet what wonders pass,
What endless, active life is here!
What blowing daisies, fragrant grass!
An air-stirred forest, fresh and clear.

Scarce fresher is the mountain-sod
Where the tired angler lies, stretched out,
And, eased of basket and of rod,
20 Counts his day's spoil, the spotted trout.

In the huge world, which roars hard by,
Be others happy if they can!
But in my helpless cradle I
Was breathed on by the rural Pan.

I, on men's impious uproar hurled,
Think often, as I hear them rave,
That peace has left the upper world
And now keeps only in the grave.

Yet here is peace forever new!
When I who watch them am away,   30
Still all things in this glade go through
The changes of their quiet day.

Then to their happy rest they pass!
The flowers upclose, the birds are fed,
The night comes down upon the grass,
The child sleeps warmly in his bed.

Calm soul of all things! make it mine
To feel, amid the city's jar,
That there abides a peace of thine,
Man did not make, and cannot mar.   40

The will to neither strive nor cry,
The power to feel with others give!
Calm, calm me more! nor let me die
Before I have begun to live.
(1852)

MORALITY

We cannot kindle when we will
The fire which in the heart resides;
The spirit bloweth and is still,
In mystery our soul abides.
   But tasks in hours of insight willed
   Can be through hours of gloom fulfilled.

With aching hands and bleeding feet
We dig and heap, lay stone on stone;
We bear the burden and the heat
Of the long day, and wish 'twere done.   10
   Not till the hours of light return,
   All we have built do we discern.

Then, when the clouds are off the soul,
When thou dost bask in Nature's eye,
Ask, how *she* viewed thy self-control,
Thy struggling, tasked morality—
   Nature, whose free, light, cheerful air,
   Oft made thee, in thy gloom, despair.

And she, whose censure thou dost dread,
Whose eye thou wast afraid to seek,   20
See, on her face a glow is spread,
A strong emotion on her cheek!
   "Ah, child!" she cries, "that strife divine,
   Whence was it, for it is not mine?

"There is no effort on *my* brow—
I do not strive, I do not weep;
I rush with the swift spheres and glow
In joy, and when I will, I sleep.
　　Yet that severe, that earnest air,
30　I saw, I felt it once—but where?

"I knew not yet the gauge of time,
Nor wore the manacles of space;
I felt it in some other clime,
I saw it in some other place.
　　'Twas when the heavenly house I trod,
　　And lay upon the breast of God."
(1852)

PHILOMELA

*Philomela and Procne were daughters of Pandion,
King of Athens. Procne was the wife of Tereus, King
of Thrace. Tereus dishonored Philomela and then cut
out her tongue that she might not betray him; but
Philomela wove the story in a piece of tapestry, which
she gave to her sister. Procne then killed her son
Itys (Itylus), served him as food to his father, and
fled with Philomela. On being pursued by Tereus, the
sisters prayed for deliverance and were changed into
birds—Philomela into a nightingale and Procne into
a swallow. In the poem Arnold has reversed the
positions of the sisters (see l. 21).*

Hark! ah, the nightingale—
The tawny-throated!
Hark, from that moonlit cedar what a burst!
What triumph! hark!—what pain!

O wanderer from a Grecian shore,
Still, after many years, in distant lands,
Still nourishing in thy bewildered brain
That wild, unquenched, deep-sunken, old-world pain—
Say, will it never heal?
10 And can this fragrant lawn
With its cool trees, and night,
And the sweet, tranquil Thames,
And moonshine, and the dew,
To thy racked heart and brain
Afford no balm?

Dost thou tonight behold,
Here, through the moonlight on this English grass,
The unfriendly palace in the Thracian wild?
Dost thou again peruse
20 With hot cheeks and seared eyes

The too clear web, and thy dumb sister's shame?
Dost thou once more assay
Thy flight, and feel come over thee,
Poor fugitive, the feathery change
Once more, and once more seem to make resound
With love and hate, triumph and agony,
Lone Daulis, and the high Cephissian vale?
Listen, Eugenia—
How thick the bursts come crowding through the
　　leaves?
Again—thou hearest?　　　　　　　　　　　　　30
Eternal passion!
Eternal pain!
(1853)

REQUIESCAT

Strew on her roses, roses,
　　And never a spray of yew!
In quiet she reposes;
　　Ah, would that I did too!

Her mirth the world required;
　　She bathed it in smiles of glee.
But her heart was tired, tired,
　　And now they let her be.

Her life was turning, turning,
　　In mazes of heat and sound.　　　　　　　　　10
But for peace her soul was yearning,
　　And now peace laps her round.

Her cabined, ample spirit,
　　It fluttered and failed for breath.
Tonight it doth inherit
　　The vasty hall of death.
(1853)

THE SCHOLAR-GYPSY

Arnold drew the story for this poem from The
Vanity of Dogmatizing *(1661), an attack on scholastic
philosophy written by Joseph Glanvil (1636-1680). Into
the tale Arnold wove a praise of the country life and
a condemnation of "the strange disease of modern
life."*

Go, for they call you, shepherd, from the hill;
　　Go, shepherd, and untie the wattled cotes!
　　No longer leave thy wistful flock unfed,
　　Nor let thy bawling fellows rack their throats,

Philomela. 27. **Daulis,** the scene of the tragedy, in Phocis, Greece.
The Cephissus was the chief river of Phocis. 28. **Eugenia,** an imaginary person.
　Requiescat. The title means *May She Rest.* 2. **yew,** a common tree
in graveyards. 13. **cabined,** confined, shut up as in a cabin.
　The Scholar-Gypsy. 2. **wattled cotes,** sheepfolds built of wattles,
interwoven twigs. 10. **the quest,** the search for the Scholar-Gypsy,
who is still supposed to haunt the vicinity. 19. **corn,** wheat, grain. 25.
convolvulus, a kind of morning-glory. 31. **Glanvil's book.** See headnote. 34. **pregnant parts,** inventive faculties. 57. **Hurst,** Cumner
Hurst, a prominent hill in the parish of Cumner, southwest of Oxford.
58. **Berkshire,** a county south of Oxford. 59. **ingle-bench,** bench in

Nor the cropped herbage shoot another head.
But when the fields are still,
And the tired men and dogs all gone to rest,
And only the white sheep are sometimes seen
Cross and recross the strips of moon-blanched
green,
10 Come, shepherd, and again begin the quest!

Here, where the reaper was at work of late—
In this high field's dark corner, where he leaves
His coat, his basket, and his earthen cruse,
And in the sun all morning binds the sheaves,
Then here, at noon, comes back his stores to use—
Here will I sit and wait,
While to my ear from uplands far away
The bleating of the folded flocks is borne,
With distant cries of reapers in the corn—
20 All the live murmur of a summer's day.

Screened is this nook o'er the high, half-reaped field,
And here till sun-down, shepherd! will I be.
Through the thick corn the scarlet poppies peep
And round green roots and yellowing stalks I see
Pale pink convolvulus in tendrils creep;
And air-swept lindens yield
Their scent, and rustle down their perfumed
showers
Of bloom on the bent grass where I am laid,
And bower me from the August sun with shade;
30 And the eye travels down to Oxford's towers.

And near me on the grass lies Glanvil's book—
Come let me read the oft-read tale again!
The story of the Oxford scholar poor,
Of pregnant parts and quick inventive brain,
Who, tired of knocking at preferment's door,
One summer-morn forsook
His friends, and went to learn the gypsy-lore,
And roamed the world with that wild brotherhood,
And came, as most men deemed, to little good,
40 But came to Oxford and his friends no more.

But once, years after, in the country-lanes,
Two scholars, whom at college erst he knew,
Met him, and of his way of life inquired;
Whereat he answered that the gypsy-crew,
His mates, had arts to rule as they desired
The workings of men's brains,
And they can bind them to what thoughts they
will.
"And I," he said, "the secret of their art,
When fully learned, will to the world impart;
50 But it needs heaven-sent moments for this skill."

This said, he left them, and returned no more.—
But rumors hung about the country-side,
That the lost scholar long was seen to stray,
Seen by rare glimpses, pensive and tongue-tied
In hat of antique shape, and cloak of gray,
The same the gypsies wore.
Shepherds had met him on the Hurst in spring;
At some lone alehouse in the Berkshire moors,
On the warm ingle-bench, the smock-frocked
boors
Had found him seated at their entering. 60

But 'mid their drink and clatter, he would fly.
And I myself seem half to know thy looks,
And put the shepherds, wanderer! on thy trace;
And boys who in lone wheatfields scare the rooks
I ask if thou hast passed their quiet place;
Or in my boat I lie
Moored to the cool bank in the summer-heats,
'Mid wide grass meadows which the sunshine
fills,
And watch the warm, green-muffled Cumner hills,
And wonder if thou haunt'st their shy retreats. 70

For most, I know, thou lov'st retired ground!
Thee at the ferry Oxford riders blithe,
Returning home on summer nights, have met
Crossing the stripling Thames at Bab-lock-hithe,
Trailing in the cool stream thy fingers wet,
As the punt's rope chops round;
And leaning backward in a pensive dream,
And fostering in thy lap a heap of flowers
Plucked in shy fields and distant Wychwood
bowers,
And thine eyes resting on the moonlit stream. 80

And then they land, and thou art seen no more!—
Maidens, who from the distant hamlets come
To dance around the Fyfield elm in May,
Oft through the darkening fields have seen thee
roam,
Or cross a stile into the public way.
Oft thou hast given them store
Of flowers—the frail-leafed, white anemone,
Dark bluebells drenched with dews of summer
eves,
And purple orchises with spotted leaves—
But none hath words she can report of thee. 90

And, above Godstow Bridge, when hay-time's here
In June, and many a scythe in sunshine flames,
Men who through those wide fields of breezy
grass

the chimney corner. **74. Bab-lock-hithe,** a ferry over the Thames about two miles west of the village of Cumner. **76. punt's . . . round.** The Scholar-Gypsy is seen reposing in a boat moored to the bank. The punt, or ferryboat, is pulled across the stream by a rope, and the boat moves in a kind of curve. The rope "chops" or suddenly shifts with the wind or the current. **79. Wychwood,** a forest ten miles north-

west of Oxford. **83. Fyfield . . . May,** a reference to the maypole dance at Fyfield, a village six miles southwest of Oxford. The large elm was a landmark for all the countryside. **91. Godstow Bridge,** about two miles up the Thames River from Oxford.

Where black-winged swallows haunt the glittering
   Thames,
   To bathe in the abandoned lasher pass,
      Have often passed thee near
Sitting upon the river bank o'ergrown;
   Marked thine outlandish garb, thy figure spare,
   Thy dark vague eyes, and soft abstracted air—
But, when they came from bathing, thou wast
100   gone!

At some lone homestead in the Cumner hills,
   Where at her open door the housewife darns,
   Thou hast been seen, or hanging on a gate
To watch the threshers in the mossy barns.
   Children, who early range these slopes and late
      For cresses from the rills,
   Have known thee eying, all an April-day,
   The springing pastures and the feeding kine;
   And marked thee, when the stars come out and
      shine,
110 Through the long dewy grass move slow away.

In autumn, on the skirts of Bagley Wood—
   Where most the gypsies by the turf-edged way
   Pitch their smoked tents, and every bush you see
With scarlet patches tagged and shreds of gray,
   Above the forest-ground called Thessaly—
      The blackbird, picking food,
   Sees thee, nor stops his meal, nor fears at all;
   So often has he known thee past him stray,
   Rapt, twirling in thy hand a withered spray,
120 And waiting for the spark from heaven to fall.

And once, in winter, on the causeway chill
   Where home through flooded fields foot-travelers
      go,
      Have I not passed thee on the wooden bridge,
   Wrapped in thy cloak and battling with the snow,
      Thy face tow'rd Hinksey and its wintry ridge?
      And thou hast climbed the hill,
   And gained the white brow of the Cumner range;
   Turned once to watch, while thick the snowflakes
      fall,
      The line of festal light in Christ-Church hall—
130 Then sought thy straw in some sequestered grange.

But what—I dream! Two hundred years are flown
   Since first thy story ran through Oxford halls,
   And the grave Glanvil did the tale inscribe
That thou wert wandered from the studious walls
   To learn strange arts, and join a gypsy tribe;
      And thou from earth art gone

Long since, and in some quiet churchyard laid—
   Some country-nook, where o'er thy unknown
      grave
   Tall grasses and white flowering nettles wave,
Under a dark, red-fruited yew-tree's shade.   140

—No, no, thou hast not felt the lapse of hours!
For what wears out the life of mortal men?
   'Tis that from change to change their being rolls;
   'Tis that repeated shocks, again, again,
      Exhaust the energy of strongest souls
      And numb the elastic powers,
   Till having used our nerves with bliss and teen,
      And tired upon a thousand schemes our wit,
      To the just-pausing Genius we remit
   Our worn-out life, and are—what we have been. 150

Thou hast not lived, why should'st thou perish, so?
   Thou hadst one aim, one business, one desire;
      Else wert thou long since numbered with the
         dead!
   Else hadst thou spent, like other men, thy fire!
      The generations of thy peers are fled,
         And we ourselves shall go;
   But thou possessest an immortal lot,
      And we imagine thee exempt from age
      And living as thou liv'st on Glanvil's page,
   Because thou hadst—what we, alas! have not.   160

For early didst thou leave the world, with powers
   Fresh undiverted to the world without,
      Firm to their mark, not spent on other things;
   Free from the sick fatigue, the languid doubt,
      Which much to have tried, in much been baffled,
         brings.
         O life unlike to ours!
   Who fluctuate idly without term or scope,
      Of whom each strives nor knows for what he
         strives,
      And each half lives a hundred different lives;
   Who wait like thee, but not, like thee, in hope.   170

Thou waitest for the spark from heaven! and we,
   Light half-believers of our casual creeds,
      Who never deeply felt, nor clearly willed,
   Whose insight never has borne fruit in deeds,
      Whose vague resolves never have been fulfilled;
         For whom each year we see
   Breeds new beginnings, disappointments new;
      Who hesitate and falter life away,
      And lose tomorrow the ground won today—
   Ah! do not we, wanderer! await it too?   180

95. **lasher,** pool below a dam.   111. **Bagley Wood,** southwest of Oxford; it was a favorite place of Arnold's father.   114. **scarlet patches . . . gray.** The bright-colored tattered garments of the gypsies were hung on the bushes.   115. **Thessaly,** a piece of forest ground near Bagley Wood.   125. **Hinksey,** a village south of Oxford.   129. **Christ-Church hall,** the dining hall in Christ Church College, Oxford.   147. **teen,** sorrow.   149. **just-pausing Genius.** According to the ancients the

Genius of a man was his spirit or guardian angel. The phrase may mean that the Genius pauses just for a moment before departing, or that the even-handed Spirit of the world impartially ends individual lives.   182. **one . . . suffered, etc.** These lines have been applied to Carlyle or Tennyson.   190. **anodynes,** pain-soothing drugs.   208. **Dido . . . turn.** Dido, queen of Carthage, killed herself because she was deserted by Aeneas. On his journey through Hades Aeneas met the shade of Dido,

Yes, we await it!—but it still delays,
　And then we suffer! and amongst us one,
　　Who most hast suffered, takes dejectedly
　　His seat upon the intellectual throne;
　　　And all his store of sad experience he
　　　　Lays bare of wretched days;
　　Tells us his misery's birth and growth and signs,
　　　And how the dying spark of hope was fed,
　　　And how the breast was soothed, and how the
　　　　head,
190　And all his hourly varied anodynes.

　This for our wisest! and we others pine,
　　And wish the long unhappy dream would end,
　　　And waive all claim to bliss, and try to bear;
　　With close-lipped patience for our only friend,
　　　Sad patience, too near neighbor to despair—
　　　　But none has hope like thine!
　　Thou through the fields and through the woods
　　　　dost stray,
　　　Roaming the country-side, a truant boy,
　　　Nursing thy project in unclouded joy,
200　And every doubt long blown by time away.

　O born in days when wits were fresh and clear,
　　And life ran gayly as the sparkling Thames;
　　　Before this strange disease of modern life,
　　With its sick hurry, its divided aims,
　　　Its heads o'ertaxed, its palsied hearts, was rife—
　　　　Fly hence, our contact fear!
　　Still fly, plunge deeper in the bowering wood!
　　　Averse, as Dido did with gesture stern
　　　From her false friend's approach in Hades turn,
210　Wave us away, and keep thy solitude!

　Still nursing the unconquerable hope,
　　Still clutching the inviolable shade,
　　　With a free, onward impulse brushing through,
　　By night, the silvered branches of the glade—
　　　Far on the forest-skirts, where none pursue,
　　　　On some mild pastoral slope
　　Emerge, and resting on the moonlit pales
　　　Freshen thy flowers as in former years
　　　With dew, or listen with enchanted ears,
220　From the dark dingles, to the nightingales!

　But fly our paths, our feverish contact fly!
　　For strong the infection of our mental strife,
　　　Which, though it gives no bliss, yet spoils for
　　　　rest;
　　And we should win thee from thy own fair life,
　　　Like us distracted, and like us unblest.

Soon, soon thy cheer would die,
　Thy hopes grow timorous, and unfixed thy powers,
　　And thy clear aims be cross and shifting made;
　　And then thy glad perennial youth would fade,
Fade, and grow old at last, and die like ours.　　230

Then fly our greetings, fly our speech and smiles!
　—As some grave Tyrian trader, from the sea,
　　Descried at sunrise an emerging prow
　Lifting the cool-haired creepers stealthily,
　　The fringes of a southward-facing brow
　　　Among the Aegean isles;
　And saw the merry Grecian coaster come,
　　Freighted with amber grapes, and Chian wine,
　　Green, bursting figs, and tunnies steeped in
　　　brine—
　And knew the intruders on his ancient home,　　240

The young light-hearted masters of the waves—
　And snatched his rudder, and shook out more sail;
　　And day and night held on indignantly
　O'er the blue Midland waters with the gale,
　　Betwixt the Syrtes and soft Sicily,
　　　To where the Atlantic raves
　Outside the western straits; and unbent sails
　　There, where down cloudy cliffs, through sheets
　　　of foam,
　　Shy traffickers, the dark Iberians come;
　And on the beach undid his corded bales.
(1853)

THYRSIS

A MONODY, TO COMMEMORATE THE AUTHOR'S FRIEND,
ARTHUR HUGH CLOUGH, WHO DIED AT FLORENCE, 1861

*Arnold's poetical memorial to his dead friend,
Arthur Hugh Clough, is written in the pastoral form
and mood employed in such tributes; see Milton's
Lycidas (p. 382). In the poem Arnold speaks of himself as Corydon and of Clough as Thyrsis. The elegy
is filled with reminiscences of the days which Arnold
and Clough spent together in Oxford and its neighborhood.*

How changed is here each spot man makes or fills!
　In the two Hinkseys nothing keeps the same;
　　The village street its haunted mansion lacks,
　And from the sign is gone Sibylla's name
　　And from the roofs the twisted chimney-stacks—
　　　Are ye too changed, ye hills?

but she turned scornfully away from him (*Aeneid*, VI, 450–471). 220.
dingles, wooded dells. 232. **Tyrian trader.** The Phoenicians of the
city of Tyre were the chief traders in the Mediterranean from 900 to
700 B.C. They were gradually displaced by the Greeks. 234. **cool-
haired creepers,** foliage overhanging the entrance to some cavern or
inlet. 236. **Aegean isles,** islands in the Aegean Sea, between Greece
and Asia Minor. 238. **Chian wine,** wine from Chios, an island in the
Aegean Sea. 239. **tunnies,** a kind of large fish. 244. **Midland waters,**
Mediterranean Sea. 245. **Syrtes,** the Gulf of Sidra, on the northeast
coast of Africa. 247. **western straits,** Strait of Gibraltar. 249. **Iberians,**
early inhabitants of Spain and Portugal.
　　Thyrsis. 2. **two Hinkseys,** villages southwest of Oxford across the
river. 4. **Sibylla's name.** Sibylla was the name of a woman who kept a
lodging house near Oxford. 5. **twisted,** set at an angle.

See, 'tis no foot of unfamiliar men
        Tonight from Oxford up your pathway strays!
        Here came I often, often, in old days—
10   Thyrsis and I; we still had Thyrsis then.

Runs it not here, the track by Childsworth Farm,
        Past the high wood, to where the elm-tree
                crowns
        The hill behind whose ridge the sunset flames?
        The signal-elm, that looks on Ilsley Downs,
        The Vale, the three lone weirs, the youthful
                Thames?—
                This winter's eve is warm,
        Humid the air! leafless, yet soft as spring,
        The tender purple spray on copse and briers!
        And that sweet city with her dreaming spires,
20   She needs not June for beauty's heightening,

Lovely all times she lies, lovely tonight!—
        Only, methinks, some loss of habit's power
        Befalls me wandering through this upland dim;
        Once passed I blindfold here, at any hour;
        Now seldom come I, since I came with him.
                That single elm tree bright
        Against the west—I miss it! it is gone?
        We prized it dearly; while it stood, we said,
        Our friend, the gypsy-scholar, was not dead;
30   While the tree lived, he in these fields lived on.

Too rare, too rare, grow now my visits here,
        But once I knew each field, each flower, each stick;
        And with the country folk acquaintance made
        By barn in threshing-time, by new-built rick.
                Here, too, our shepherd-pipes we first assayed.
                Ah me! this many a year
        My pipe is lost, my shepherd's holiday!
        Needs must I lose them, needs with heavy heart
        Into the world and wave of men depart;
40   But Thyrsis of his own will went away.

It irked him to be here; he could not rest.
        He loved each simple joy the country yields,
        He loved his mates; but yet he could not keep,
        For that a shadow lowered on the fields,
        Here with the shepherds and the silly sheep.
                Some life of men unblest
        He knew, which made him droop, and filled his
                head.
        He went; his piping took a troubled sound
        Of storms that rage outside our happy ground;
50   He could not wait their passing, he is dead.

So, some tempestuous morn in early June,
        When the year's primal burst of bloom is o'er,
        Before the roses and the longest day—
        When garden-walks and all the grassy floor
        With blossoms red and white of fallen May
                And chestnut flowers are strewn—
        So have I heard the cuckoo's parting cry,
        From the wet field, through the vexed garden-
                trees,
        Come with the volleying rain and tossing breeze:
        The bloom is gone, and with the bloom go I!   60

Too quick despairer, wherefore wilt thou go?
        Soon will the high midsummer pomps come on.
        Soon will the musk carnations break and swell,
        Soon shall we have gold-dusted snapdragon,
                Sweet-William with his homely cottage-smell,
                And stocks in fragrant blow;
        Roses that down the alleys shine afar,
        And open, jasmine-muffled lattices,
        And groups under the dreaming garden-trees,
        And the full moon, and the white evening-star.   70

He hearkens not! light comer, he is flown!
        What matters it? next year he will return,
        And we shall have him in the sweet spring days,
        With whitening hedges, and uncrumpling fern,
        And bluebells trembling by the forest-ways,
                And scent of hay new-mown.
        But Thyrsis never more we swains shall see;
        See him come back, and cut a smoother reed,
        And blow a strain the world at last shall heed—
        For Time, not Corydon, hath conquered thee!   80

Alack, for Corydon no rival now!—
        But when Sicilian shepherds lost a mate,
        Some good survivor with his flute would go,
        Piping a ditty sad for Bion's fate;
                And cross the unpermitted ferry's flow,
                And relax Pluto's brow,
        And make leap up with joy the beauteous head
                Of Proserpine, among whose crownéd hair
                Are flowers first opened on Sicilian air,
        And flute his friend, like Orpheus, from the dead. 90

O easy access to the hearer's grace
        When Dorian shepherds sang to Proserpine!
        For she herself had trod Sicilian fields,
        She knew the Dorian water's gush divine,
        She knew each lily white which Enna yields,
                Each rose with blushing face;

11. **Childsworth Farm,** modern Chilswel Farm, three miles from Oxford. 14. **signal-elm.** This famous tree has frequently been identified with an oak tree standing at the top of the knoll on the Oxford side of the ridge; but a large elm a short distance below the summit of the ridge fits the description better. **Ilsley Downs.** Ilsley is a parish in West Berkshire. 15. **weirs,** dams. **youthful Thames.** The Thames River is about fifty yards wide at Oxford. 19. **sweet city,** Oxford. 29. **gypsy-scholar.** See *The Scholar-Gypsy* and headnote, p. 938. 35. **shepherd-pipes,** the usual pastoral symbol for poetry. 36. **many a year . . . lost.** Arnold had not published any poetry for nine years. 40. **Thyrsis**

. . . **away.** Clough resigned his fellowship in Oriel College, Oxford, in 1848, partly on religious grounds. 45. **silly,** simple. 49. **storms that rage.** Much of the poetry of Clough reflects his spiritual struggles. 62. **pomps,** shows, displays. 66. **stocks,** gillyflowers. 82. **Sicilian shepherds,** pastoral poets of Sicily; a reference to the lament for Bion, a Sicilian pastoral poet, written by his friend Moschus, second century B.C. 85. **unpermitted . . . flow,** the River Styx, over which only the dead were permitted to pass. 86. **Pluto,** the god of the underworld. He carried off Proserpine to be his wife, finding her in the vale of Enna (l. 95), in Sicily, where she was gathering lilies and violets. 90.

She loved the Dorian pipe, the Dorian strain.
  But, ah, of our poor Thames she never heard!
  Her foot the Cumner cowslips never stirred;
100 And we should tease her with our plaint in vain!

Well! wind-dispersed and vain the words will be,
  Yet, Thyrsis, let me give my grief its hour
  In the old haunt, and find our tree-topped
    hill!
  Who, if not I, for questing here hath power?
  I know the wood which hides the daffodil,
    I know the Fyfield tree,
  I know what white, what purple fritillaries
  The grassy harvest of the river-fields,
  Above by Ensham, down by Sandford, yields,
110 And what sedged brooks are Thames's tributaries;

I know these slopes; who knows them if not I?—
  But many a dingle on the loved hillside,
  With thorns once studded, old, white-blossomed
    trees,
  Where thick the cowslips grew, and far descried
  High towered the spikes of purple orchises,
    Hath since our day put by
  The coronals of that forgotten time;
  Down each green bank hath gone the plowboy's
    team,
  And only in the hidden brookside gleam
120 Primroses, orphans of the flowery prime.

Where is the girl, who by the boatman's door,
  Above the locks, above the boating throng,
  Unmoored our skiff when through the Wytham
    flats,
  Red loosestrife and blond meadow-sweet among
  And darting swallows and light water-gnats,
    We tracked the shy Thames shore?
  Where are the mowers, who, as the tiny swell
  Of our boat passing heaved the river-grass,
  Stood with suspended scythe to see us pass?—
130 They are all gone, and thou art gone as well!

Yes, thou art gone! and round me too the night
  In ever-nearing circle weaves her shade.
  I see her veil draw soft across the day,
  I feel her slowly chilling breath invade
  The cheek grown thin, the brown hair sprent
    with gray;
    I feel her finger light
  Laid pausefully upon life's headlong train—
  The foot less prompt to meet the morning dew,

The heart less bounding at emotion new,
  And hope, once crushed, less quick to spring again. 140

And long the way appears, which seemed so short
  To the less practiced eye of sanguine youth;
  And high the mountain-tops, in cloudy air,
  The mountain-tops, where is the throne of Truth,
    Tops in life's morning-sun so bright and bare!
    Unbreachable the fort
  Of the long-battered world uplifts its wall;
  And strange and vain the earthly turmoil grows,
  And near and real the charm of thy repose,
  And night as welcome as a friend would fall.   150

But hush! the upland hath a sudden loss
  Of quiet!—Look, adown the dusk hillside,
  A troop of Oxford hunters going home,
  As in old days, jovial and talking, ride!
    From hunting with the Berkshire hounds they
      come.
    Quick! let me fly, and cross
  Into yon farther field;—'Tis done; and see,
  Backed by the sunset, which doth glorify
  The orange and pale violet evening sky,
  Bare on its lonely ridge, the Tree! the Tree!   160

I take the omen! Eve lets down her veil,
  The white fog creeps from bush to bush about,
    The west unflushes, the high stars grow bright,
  And in the scattered farms the lights come out.
    I cannot reach the signal-tree tonight,
      Yet, happy omen, hail!
  Hear it from thy broad lucent Arno-vale
  (For there thine earth-forgetting eyelids keep
  The morningless and unawakening sleep
  Under the flowery oleanders, pale),   170

Hear it, O Thyrsis, still our tree is there!—
  Ah, vain! These English fields, this upland dim,
  These brambles pale with mist engarlanded,
  That lone, sky-pointing tree, are not for him;
    To a boon southern country he is fled,
      And now in happier air,
  Wandering with the great Mother's train divine
  (And purer or more subtle soul than thee,
  I trow, the mighty Mother doth not see)
  Within a folding of the Apennine,   180

Thou hearest the immortal chants of old!—
  Putting his sickle to the perilous grain
    In the hot cornfield of the Phrygian king,

Orpheus. See note to p. 763, l. 691. 92. **Dorian,** Sicilian. 99. **Cumner,** hills near Oxford. 106. **Fyfield tree,** a giant elm near the village of Fyfield, six miles southwest of Oxford. 107. **fritillaries,** lily-like flowers. 109. **Ensham,** Eynsham, a village northwest of Oxford. Sandford is south of Oxford. 112. **dingle,** wooded dell. 123. **Wytham flats,** about two miles northwest of Oxford, between the village of Wytham and the Thames. 135. **sprent,** sprinkled. 137. **pausefully,** so as to make it pause. 155. **Berkshire,** a county south of Oxford. 160. **the Tree.** See ll. 12–14. 167. **Arno.** Clough died in Italy and was buried in Florence by the Arno River. 175. **boon,** rich, benign.

177. **great Mother,** Cybele, the goddess of nature, and the mother of the gods. 183. **Phrygian king,** Lityerses, who made strangers enter into a contest with him in reaping grain; if he defeated them, he put them to death. The Sicilian shepherd Daphnis (l. 185), son of Hermes, engaged in such a contest in order to release his mistress, who was in the King's power. Hercules reaped the grain for Daphnis and killed Lityerses. The Lityerses-song connected with the tradition used to be sung by Greek grain reapers. Another tradition represented Daphnis as having been blinded by a nymph whose love he slighted. Hermes raised Daphnis to Olympus and marked the place of his ascent by a fountain.

Matthew Arnold 943

For thee the Lityerses-song again
    Young Daphnis with his silver voice doth sing;
      Sings his Sicilian fold,
  His sheep, his hapless love, his blinded eyes—
  And how a call celestial round him rang,
  And heavenward from the fountain-brink he
      sprang,
190   And all the marvel of the golden skies.

There thou art gone, and me thou leavest here
  Sole in these fields! yet will I not despair.
    Despair I will not, while I yet descry
    'Neath the mild canopy of English air
      That lonely tree against the western sky.
      Still, still these slopes, 'tis clear,
  Our gypsy-scholar haunts, outliving thee!
    Fields where soft sheep from cages pull the
      hay,
    Woods with anemones in flower till May,
200   Know him a wanderer still; then why not me?

A fugitive and gracious light he seeks,
  Shy to illumine; and I seek it too.
    This does not come with houses or with gold,
  With place, with honor, and a flattering crew;
    'Tis not in the world's market bought and sold—
      But the smooth-slipping weeks
  Drop by, and leave its seeker still untired;
    Out of the heed of mortals he is gone,
    He wends unfollowed, he must house alone;
210   Yet on he fares, by his own heart inspired.

Thou too, O Thyrsis, on like quest wast bound;
  Thou wanderedst with me for a little hour!
    Men gave thee nothing; but this happy quest,
  If men esteemed thee feeble, gave thee power,
    If men procured thee trouble, gave thee rest.
      And this rude Cumner ground,
  Its fir-topped Hurst, its farms, its quiet fields,
    Here cam'st thou in thy jocund youthful time,
    Here was thine height of strength, thy golden
      prime!
220   And still the haunt beloved a virtue yields.

What though the music of thy rustic flute
  Kept not for long its happy, country tone;
    Lost it too soon, and learned a stormy note
  Of men contention-tossed, of men who groan,
    Which tasked thy pipe too sore, and tired thy
      throat—
      It failed, and thou wast mute!
  Yet hadst thou alway visions of our light,
    And long with men of care thou couldst not stay,
    And soon thy foot resumed its wandering way,
230   Left human haunt, and on alone till night.

Too rare, too rare, grow now my visits here!
  'Mid city-noise, not, as with thee of yore,
    Thyrsis! in reach of sheep-bells is my home.
  —Then through the great town's harsh, heart-weary-
      ing roar,
    Let in thy voice a whisper often come,
      To chase fatigue and fear:
Why faintest thou? I wandered till I died.
  Roam on! The light we sought is shining still.
  Dost thou ask proof? Our tree yet crowns the
    hill,
Our scholar travels yet the loved hillside.
(1866)

DOVER BEACH

The sea is calm tonight,
The tide is full, the moon lies fair
Upon the straits;—on the French coast the light
Gleams and is gone; the cliffs of England stand,
Glimmering and vast, out in the tranquil bay.
Come to the window, sweet is the night-air!

Only, from the long line of spray
Where the sea meets the moon-blanched land,
Listen! you hear the grating roar
Of pebbles which the waves draw back, and fling,   10
At their return, up the high strand,
Begin, and cease, and then again begin,
With tremulous cadence slow, and bring
The eternal note of sadness in.

Sophocles long ago
Heard it on the Aegean, and it brought
Into his mind the turbid ebb and flow
Of human misery; we
Find also in the sound a thought,
Hearing it by this distant northern sea.   20

The Sea of Faith
Was once, too, at the full, and round earth's shore
Lay like the folds of a bright girdle furled.
But now I only hear
Its melancholy, long, withdrawing roar,
Retreating, to the breath
Of the night-wind, down the vast edges drear
And naked shingles of the world.

Ah, love, let us be true
To one another! for the world, which seems   30
To lie before us like a land of dreams,
So various, so beautiful, so new,
Hath really neither joy, nor love, nor light,
Nor certitude, nor peace, nor help for pain;

---

202. **Shy to illumine,** reluctant to shine forth. 217. **Hurst,** a prominent hill in the parish of Cumner.

Dover Beach. 15. **Sophocles,** famous Greek tragic dramatist of the
fifth century B.C. The reference is to a passage in *Antigone,* 583 ff.

And we are here as on a darkling plain
Swept with confused alarms of struggle and flight,
Where ignorant armies clash by night.
(1867)

THE LAST WORD

Creep into thy narrow bed,
Creep, and let no more be said!
Vain thy onset! all stands fast.
Thou thyself must break at last.

Let the long contention cease!
Geese are swans, and swans are geese.
Let them have it how they will!
Thou art tired; best be still.

They out-talked thee, hissed thee, tore thee?
10 Better men fared thus before thee;
Fired their ringing shot and passed,
Hotly charged—and sank at last.

Charge once more, then, and be dumb!
Let the victors, when they come,
When the forts of folly fall,
Find thy body by the wall!
(1867)

RUGBY CHAPEL

This poem was written in memory of the poet's father, Dr. Thomas Arnold, the celebrated headmaster of Rugby School. He died suddenly in June 1842, and was buried in the school chapel.

NOVEMBER, 1857

Coldly, sadly descends
The autumn evening. The field
Strewn with its dank yellow drifts
Of withered leaves, and the elms,
Fade into dimness apace,
Silent—hardly a shout
From a few boys late at their play!
The lights come out in the street,
In the schoolroom windows;—but cold,
10 Solemn, unlighted, austere,
Through the gathering darkness, arise
The chapel walls, in whose bound
Thou, my father! art laid.

There thou dost lie, in the gloom
Of the autumn evening. But ah!

That word, *gloom,* to my mind
Brings thee back, in the light
Of thy radiant vigor, again;
In the gloom of November we passed
Days not dark at thy side;   20
Seasons impaired not the ray
Of thy buoyant cheerfulness clear.
Such thou wast! and I stand
In the autumn evening, and think
Of by-gone autumns with thee.

Fifteen years have gone round
Since thou arosest to tread,
In the summer morning, the road
Of death, at a call unforeseen,
Sudden. For fifteen years,   30
We who till then in thy shade
Rested as under the boughs
Of a mighty oak, have endured
Sunshine and rain as we might,
Bare, unshaded, alone,
Lacking the shelter of thee.

O strong soul, by what shore
Tarriest thou now? For that force,
Surely, has not been left vain!
Somewhere, surely, afar,   40
In the sounding labor-house vast
Of being, is practiced that strength,
Zealous, beneficent, firm!

Yes, in some far-shining sphere,
Conscious or not of the past,
Still thou performest the word
Of the Spirit in whom thou dost live—
Prompt, unwearied, as here!
Still thou upraisest with zeal
The humble good from the ground,   50
Sternly repressest the bad!
Still, like a trumpet, dost rouse
Those who with half-open eyes
Tread the border-land dim
'Twixt vice and virtue; revivest,
Succorest!—this was thy work,
This was thy life upon earth.

What is the course of the life
Of mortal men on the earth?—
Most men eddy about   60
Here and there—eat and drink,
Chatter and love and hate,
Gather and squander, are raised
Aloft, are hurled in the dust,
Striving blindly, achieving

---

28. **shingles,** beaches covered with shingles, large stones. 29. **Ah, love . . . night.** Cf. *The Buried Life,* p. 936, ll. 77 ff.

The Last Word. 16. body . . . wall, where it fell in attacking the forts of folly.

Nothing; and then they die—
Perish;—and no one asks
Who or what they have been,
More than he asks what waves,
70 In the moonlit solitudes mild
Of the midmost Ocean, have swelled,
Foamed for a moment, and gone.

And there are some, whom a thirst
Ardent, unquenchable, fires,
Not with the crowd to be spent,
Not without aim to go round
In an eddy of purposeless dust,
Effort unmeaning and vain.
Ah, yes! some of us strive
80 Not without action to die
Fruitless, but something to snatch
From dull oblivion, nor all
Glut the devouring grave!
We, we have chosen our path—
Path to a clear-purposed goal,
Path of advance!—but it leads
A long, steep journey, through sunk
Gorges, o'er mountains in snow.
Cheerful, with friends, we set forth—
90 Then, on the height, comes the storm.
Thunder crashes from rock
To rock, the cataracts reply,
Lightnings dazzle our eyes.
Roaring torrents have breached
The track, the stream-bed descends
In the place where the wayfarer once
Planted his footstep—the spray
Boils o'er its borders! aloft
The unseen snow-beds dislodge
100 Their hanging ruin; alas,
Havoc is made in our train!
Friends, who set forth at our side,
Falter, are lost in the storm.
We, we only are left!
With frowning foreheads, with lips
Sternly compressed, we strain on,
On—and at nightfall at last
Come to the end of our way,
To the lonely inn 'mid the rocks;
110 Where the gaunt and taciturn host
Stands on the threshold, the wind
Shaking his thin white hairs—
Holds his lantern to scan
Our storm-beat figures, and asks:
Whom in our party we bring?
Whom we have left in the snow?

Sadly we answer: We bring
Only ourselves! we lost

Sight of the rest in the storm.
Hardly ourselves we fought through,   120
Stripped, without friends, as we are.
Friends, companions, and train,
The avalanche swept from our side.

But thou would'st not *alone*
Be saved, my father! *alone*
Conquer and come to thy goal,
Leaving the rest in the wild.
We were weary, and we
Fearful, and we in our march
Fain to drop down and to die.   130
Still thou turnedst, and still
Beckonedst the trembler, and still
Gavest the weary thy hand.

If, in the paths of the world,
Stones might have wounded thy feet,
Toil or dejection have tried
Thy spirit, of that we saw
Nothing—to us thou wast still
Cheerful, and helpful, and firm!
Therefore to thee it was given   140
Many to save with thyself;
And, at the end of thy day,
O faithful shepherd! to come,
Bringing thy sheep in thy hand.
And through thee I believe
In the noble and great who are gone;
Pure souls honored and blessed
By former ages, who else—
Such, so soulless, so poor,
Is the race of men whom I see—   150
Seemed but a dream of the heart,
Seemed but a cry of desire.
Yes! I believe that there lived
Others like thee in the past,
Not like the men of the crowd
Who all round me today
Bluster or cringe, and make life
Hideous, and arid, and vile;
But souls tempered with fire,
Fervent, heroic, and good,   60
Helpers and friends of mankind.

Servants of God!—or sons
Shall I not call you? because
Not as servants ye knew
Your Father's innermost mind,
His, who unwillingly sees
One of his little ones lost—
Yours is the praise, if mankind
Hath not as yet in its march
Fainted, and fallen, and died!   170

Rugby Chapel. 110. **host,** probably Time, or Death. 148. **who else,** etc., who, but for what I have known of thee, would have seemed a dream. 162. **Servants . . . sons.** Cf. John 1:12: "But as many as received him, to them gave he power to become the sons of God." 190.

See! In the rocks of the world
Marches the host of mankind,
A feeble, wavering line.
Where are they tending?—A God
Marshaled them, gave them their goal.
Ah, but the way is so long!
Years they have been in the wild!
Sore thirst plagues them, the rocks,
Rising all round, overawe;
180 Factions divide them, their host
Threatens to break, to dissolve.
—Ah, keep, keep them combined!
Else, of the myriads who fill
That army, not one shall arrive;
Sole they shall stray; in the rocks
Stagger forever in vain,
Die one by one in the waste.

Then, in such hour of need
Of your fainting, dispirited race,
190 Ye, like angels, appear,
Radiant with ardor divine!
Beacons of hope, ye appear!
Languor is not in your heart,
Weakness is not in your word,
Weariness not on your brow.
Ye alight in our van! at your voice,
Panic, despair, flee away.
Ye move through the ranks, recall
The stragglers, refresh the outworn,
200 Praise, re-inspire the brave!
Order, courage, return.
Eyes rekindling, and prayers,
Follow your steps as ye go.
Ye fill up the gaps in our files,
Strengthen the wavering line,
Stablish, continue our march,
On, to the bound of the waste,
On, to the City of God.
(1867)

GEIST'S GRAVE

Geist was a dachshund much loved by the Arnold family.

Four years!—and didst thou stay above
The ground, which hides thee now, but four?
And all that life, and all that love,
Were crowded, Geist! into no more?

Only four years those winning ways,
Which make me for thy presence yearn,
Called us to pet thee or to praise,
Dear little friend! at every turn?

That loving heart, that patient soul,
Had they indeed no longer span,   10
To run their course, and reach their goal,
And read their homily to man?

That liquid, melancholy eye,
From whose pathetic, soul-fed springs
Seemed surging the Virgilian cry,
The sense of tears in mortal things—

That steadfast, mournful strain, consoled
By spirits gloriously gay,
And temper of heroic mold—
What, was four years their whole short day?   20

Yes, only four!—and not the course
Of all the centuries yet to come,
And not the infinite resource
Of Nature, with her countless sum

Of figures, with her fullness vast
Of new creation evermore,
Can ever quite repeat the past,
Or just thy little self restore.

Stern law of every mortal lot!
Which man, proud man, finds hard to bear,   30
And builds himself I know not what
Of second life I know not where.

But thou, when struck thine hour to go,
On us, who stood despondent by,
A meek last glance of love didst throw,
And humbly lay thee down to die.

Yet would we keep thee in our heart—
Would fix our favorite on the scene,
Nor let thee utterly depart
And be as if thou ne'er hadst been.   40

And so there rise these lines of verse
On lips that rarely form them now;
While to each other we rehearse:
*Such ways, such arts, such looks hadst
   thou!*

We stroke thy broad brown paws again,
We bid thee to thy vacant chair,
We greet thee by the window-pane,
We hear thy scuffle on the stair.

We see the flaps of thy large ears
Quick raised to ask which way we go;   50
Crossing the frozen lake, appears
Thy small black figure on the snow.

Ye, the servants of God of l. 162.
 Geist's Grave. 15. **Virgilian cry,** *Sunt lacrimae rerum*—There is

sadness in human affairs (*Aeneid,* I, 462).

Nor to us only art thou dear
Who mourn thee in thine English home;
Thou hast thine absent master's tear,
Dropped by the far Australian foam.

Thy memory lasts both here and there,
And thou shalt live as long as we.
And after that—thou dost not care!
60 In us was all the world to thee.

Yet, fondly zealous for thy fame,
Even to a date beyond our own
We strive to carry down thy name,
By mounted turf and graven stone.

We lay thee, close within our reach,
Here, where the grass is smooth and warm,
Between the holly and the beech,
Where oft we watched thy couchant form,

Asleep, yet lending half an ear
70 To travelers on the Portsmouth road—
There build we thee, O guardian dear,
Marked with a stone, thy last abode!

Then some, who through this garden pass,
When we too, like thyself, are clay,
Shall see thy grave upon the grass,
And stop before the stone, and say:

People who lived here long ago
Did by this stone, it seems, intend
To name for future times to know
80 *The dachshund, Geist, their little friend.*
(1881)

from ESSAYS IN CRITICISM

The essay printed first in Essays in Criticism, and
reprinted here, was actually written last; it shows the
principles toward which Arnold had been somewhat
inductively working. It contains, moreover, a sign of
the many directions, other than the purely literary, in
which Arnold's critical thinking was to lead him: social
conditions, science, philosophy, religion. Arnold used
the term essays *in the sense of "attempts" or "speci-*
mens."

55. **absent master,** Arnold's son, Richard, was in Australia when the dog died. 70. **Portsmouth road.** Arnold lived in the parish of Cobham,

THE FUNCTION OF CRITICISM AT THE PRESENT TIME

Many objections have been made to a proposition which, in some remarks of mine on translating Homer, I ventured to put forth; a proposition about criticism. and its importance at the present day. I said: "Of the literature of France and Germany, as of the intellect of Europe in general, the main effort, for now many years, has been a critical effort; the endeavour, in all branches of knowledge, theology, philosophy, history, art, science, to see the object as in itself it really is." I added, that owing to the operation in English litera- 10 ture of certain causes, "almost the last thing for which one would come to English literature is just that very thing which now Europe most desires,—criticism"; and that the power and value of English literature was thereby impaired. More than one rejoinder declared that the importance I here assigned to criticism was excessive, and asserted the inherent superiority of the creative effort of the human spirit over its critical effort. And the other day, having been led by a Mr. Shairp's excellent notice of Wordsworth to turn again 20 to his biography, I found, in the words of this great man, whom I, for one, must always listen to with the profoundest respect, a sentence passed on the critic's business, which seems to justify every possible disparagement of it. Wordsworth says in one of his letters:—

"The writers in these publications" (the Reviews), "while they prosecute their inglorious employment, cannot be supposed to be in a state of mind very favourable for being affected by the finer influences of 30 a thing so pure as genuine poetry."

And a trustworthy reporter of his conversation quotes a more elaborate judgment to the same effect:—

"Wordsworth holds the critical power very low, infinitely lower than the inventive; and he said to-day that if the quantity of time consumed in writing critiques on the works of others were given to original composition, of whatever kind it might be, it would be much better employed; it would make a man find out sooner his own level, and it would do infinitely less 40 mischief. A false or malicious criticism may do much injury to the minds of others; a stupid invention, either in prose or verse, is quite harmless."

It is almost too much to expect of poor human nature, that a man capable of producing some effect in one line of literature, should, for the greater good of society, voluntarily doom himself to impotence and obscurity in another. Still less is this to be expected from men addicted to the composition of the "false or malicious criticism" of which Wordsworth speaks. 50

Surrey, on the road from London to Portsmouth. *The Function of Criticism at the Present Time.* 20. **Shairp,** John Campbell Shairp

However, everybody would admit that a false or malicious criticism had better never have been written. Everybody, too, would be willing to admit, as a general proposition, that the critical faculty is lower than the inventive. But is it true that criticism is really, in itself, a baneful and injurious employment; is it true that all time given to writing critiques on the works of others would be much better employed if it were given to original composition, of whatever kind this may be? Is it true that Johnson had better have gone on producing more *Irenes* instead of writing his *Lives of the Poets,* nay, is it certain that Wordsworth himself was better employed in making his Ecclesiastical Sonnets than when he made his celebrated Preface, so full of criticism, and criticism of the works of others? Wordsworth was himself a great critic, and it is to be sincerely regretted that he has not left us more criticism; Goethe was one of the greatest of critics, and we may sincerely congratulate ourselves that he has left us so much criticism. Without wasting time over the exaggeration which Wordsworth's judgment on criticism clearly contains, or over an attempt to trace the causes,—not difficult, I think, to be traced, —which may have led Wordsworth to this exaggeration, a critic may with advantage seize an occasion for trying his own conscience, and for asking himself of what real service, at any given moment, the practice of criticism either is or may be made to his own mind and spirit, and to the minds and spirits of others.

The critical power is of lower rank than the creative. True; but in assenting to this proposition, one or two things are to be kept in mind. It is undeniable that the exercise of a creative power, that a free creative activity, is the highest function of man; it is proved to be so by man's finding in it his true happiness. But it is undeniable, also, that men may have the sense of exercising this free creative activity in other ways than in producing great works of literature or art; if it were not so, all but a very few men would be shut out from the true happiness of all men. They may have it in well-doing, they may have it in learning, they may have it even in criticising. This is one thing to be kept in mind. Another is, that the exercise of the creative power in the production of great works of literature or art, however high this exercise of it may rank, is not at all epochs and under all conditions possible; and that therefore labour may be vainly spent in attempting it, which might with more fruit be used in preparing for it, in rendering it possible. This creative power works with elements, with materials; what if it has not those materials, those elements, ready for its use? In that case it must surely wait till they are ready. Now, in literature,—I will limit myself to litera-

ture, for it is about literature that the question arises, —the elements with which the creative power works are ideas; the best ideas on every matter which literature touches, current at the time. At any rate we may lay it down as certain that in modern literature no manifestation of the creative power not working with these can be very important or fruitful. And I say *current* at the time, not merely accessible at the time; for creative literary genius does not principally show itself in discovering new ideas, that is rather the business of the philosopher. The grand work of literary genius is a work of synthesis and exposition, not of analysis and discovery; its gift lies in the faculty of being happily inspired by a certain intellectual and spiritual atmosphere, by a certain order of ideas, when it finds itself in them; of dealing divinely with these ideas, presenting them in the most effective and attractive combinations,—making beautiful works with them, in short. But it must have the atmosphere, it must find itself amidst the order of ideas, in order to work freely; and these it is not so easy to command. This is why great creative epochs in literature are so rare, this is why there is so much that is unsatisfactory in the productions of many men of real genius; because, for the creation of a masterwork of literature two powers must concur, the power of the man and the power of the moment, and the man is not enough without the moment; the creative power has, for its happy exercise, appointed elements, and those elements are not in its own control.

Nay, they are more within the control of the critical power. It is the business of the critical power, as I said in the words already quoted, "in all branches of knowledge, theology, philosophy, history, art, science, to see the object as in itself it really is." Thus it tends, at last, to make an intellectual situation of which the creative power can profitably avail itself. It tends to establish an order of ideas, if not absolutely true, yet true by comparison with that which it displaces; to make the best ideas prevail. Presently these new ideas reach society, the touch of truth is the touch of life, and there is a stir and growth everywhere; out of this stir and growth come the creative epochs of literature.

Or, to narrow our range, and quit these considerations of the general march of genius and of society,— considerations which are apt to become too abstract and impalpable,—every one can see that a poet, for instance, ought to know life and the world before dealing with them in poetry; and life and the world being in modern times very complex things, the creation of a modern poet, to be worth much, implies a great critical effort behind it; else it must be a compara-

(1819-1885), critic and professor of poetry at Oxford (1877-1884), whose notice—"Wordsworth: The Man and the Poet"—had appeared in the *North British Review* for August 1864. 64. **celebrated Preface,** Preface to the second edition (1800) of *Lyrical Ballads.*

tively poor, barren, and short-lived affair. This is why Byron's poetry had so little endurance in it, and Goethe's so much; both Byron and Goethe had a great productive power, but Goethe's was nourished by a great critical effort providing the true materials for it, and Byron's was not; Goethe knew life and the world, the poet's necessary subjects, much more comprehensively and thoroughly than Byron. He knew a great deal more of them, and he knew them much
10 more as they really are.

It has long seemed to me that the burst of creative activity in our literature, through the first quarter of this century, had about it in fact something premature; and that from this cause its productions are doomed, most of them, in spite of the sanguine hopes which accompanied and do still accompany them, to prove hardly more lasting than the productions of far less splendid epochs. And this prematureness comes from its having proceeded without having its proper
20 data, without sufficient materials to work with. In other words, the English poetry of the first quarter of this century, with plenty of energy, plenty of creative force, did not know enough. This makes Byron so empty of matter, Shelley so incoherent, Wordsworth even, profound as he is, yet so wanting in completeness and variety. Wordsworth cared little for books, and disparaged Goethe. I admire Wordsworth, as he is, so much that I cannot wish him different; and it is vain, no doubt, to imagine such a man different from
30 what he is, to suppose that he *could* have been different. But surely the one thing wanting to make Wordsworth an even greater poet than he is,—his thought richer, and his influence of wider application,—was that he should have read more books, among them, no doubt, those of that Goethe whom he disparaged without reading him.

But to speak of books and reading may easily lead to a misunderstanding here. It was not really books and reading that lacked to our poetry at this epoch:
40 Shelley had plenty of reading, Coleridge had immense reading. Pindar and Sophocles,—as we all say so glibly, and often with so little discernment of the real import of what we are saying,—had not many books; Shakespeare was no deep reader. True; but in the Greece of Pindar and Sophocles, in the England of Shakespeare, the poet lived in a current of ideas in the highest degree animating and nourishing to the creative power; society was, in the fullest measure, permeated by fresh thought, intelligent and alive. And
50 this state of things is the true basis for the creative power's exercise, in this it finds its data, its materials, truly ready for its hand; all the books and reading in

the world are only valuable as they are helps to this. Even when this does not actually exist, books and reading may enable a man to construct a kind of semblance of it in his own mind, a world of knowledge and intelligence in which he may live and work. This is by no means an equivalent to the artist for the nationally diffused life and thought of the epochs of Sophocles or Shakespeare; but, besides that it may be a means of 60 preparation for such epochs, it does really constitute, if many share in it, a quickening and sustaining atmosphere of great value. Such an atmosphere the many-sided learning and the long and widely combined critical effort of Germany formed for Goethe, when he lived and worked. There was no national glow of life and thought there as in the Athens of Pericles or the England of Elizabeth. That was the poet's weakness. But there was a sort of equivalent for it in the complete culture and unfettered thinking 70 of a large body of Germans. That was his strength. In the England of the first quarter of this century there was neither a national glow of life and thought, such as we had in the age of Elizabeth, nor yet a culture and a force of learning and criticism such as were to be found in Germany. Therefore the creative power of poetry wanted, for success in the highest sense, materials and a basis; a thorough interpretation of the world was necessarily denied to it.

At first sight it seems strange that out of the im- 80 mense stir of the French Revolution and its age should not have come a crop of works of genius equal to that which came out of the stir of the great productive time of Greece, or out of that of the Renascence, with its powerful episode the Reformation. But the truth is that the stir of the French Revolution took a character which essentially distinguished it from such movements as these. These were, in the main, disinterestedly intellectual and spiritual movements; movements in which the human spirit looked for its satisfaction in 90 itself and in the increased play of its own activity. The French Revolution took a political, practical character. The movement, which went on in France under the old *régime,* from 1700 to 1789, was far more really akin than that of the Revolution itself to the movement of the Renascence; the France of Voltaire and Rousseau told far more powerfully upon the mind of Europe than the France of the Revolution. Goethe reproached this last expressly with having "thrown quiet culture back." Nay, and the true key to how 100 much in our Byron, even in our Wordsworth, is this! —that they had their source in a great movement of feeling, not in a great movement of mind. The French Revolution, however,—that object of so much blind

41. **Pindar and Sophocles,** Greek writers. Pindar (522-448? b.c.) is noted for his odes, Sophocles (496?-406 b.c.), for his dramas. 68. **Pericles,** political leader of the era (495?-429 b.c.). 96-97. **France**

. . . **Rousseau,** that is, pre-Revolutionary France. 108. **English . . . time,** that is, the second quarter of the seventeenth century. 122-126. **old woman . . . strangers,** Jenny, or Janet, Geddes, protesting the

love and so much blind hatred,—found undoubtedly its motive-power in the intelligence of men, and not in their practical sense; this is what distinguishes it from the English Revolution of Charles the First's time. This is what makes it a more spiritual event than our
110 Revolution, an event of much more powerful and world-wide interest, though practically less successful; it appeals to an order of ideas which are universal, certain, permanent. 1789 asked of a thing, Is it rational? 1642 asked of a thing, Is it legal? or, when it went furthest, Is it according to conscience? This is the English fashion, a fashion to be treated, within its own sphere, with the highest respect; for its success, within its own sphere, has been prodigious. But what is law in one place is not law in another; what is
120 law here today is not law even here tomorrow; and as for conscience, what is binding on one man's conscience is not binding on another's. The old woman who threw her stool at the head of the surpliced minister in St. Giles' Church at Edinburgh obeyed an impulse to which millions of the human race may be permitted to remain strangers. But the prescriptions of reason are absolute, unchanging, of universal validity; *to count by tens is the easiest way of counting*—that is a proposition of which every one, from here to the
130 Antipodes, feels the force; at least I should say so if we did not live in a country where it is not impossible that any morning we may find a letter in the *Times* declaring that a decimal coinage is an absurdity. That a whole nation should have been penetrated with an enthusiasm for pure reason, and with an ardent zeal for making its prescriptions triumph, is a very remarkable thing, when we consider how little of mind, or anything so worthy and quickening as mind, comes into the motives which alone, in general, impel great
140 masses of men. In spite of the extravagant direction given to this enthusiasm, in spite of the crimes and follies in which it lost itself, the French Revolution derives from the force, truth, and universality of the ideas which it took for its law, and from the passion with which it could inspire a multitude for these ideas, a unique and still living power; it is,—it will probably long remain,—the greatest, the most animating event in history. And as no sincere passion for the things of the mind, even though it turn out in many respects an
150 unfortunate passion, is ever quite thrown away and quite barren of good, France has reaped from hers one fruit—the natural and legitimate fruit though not precisely the grand fruit she expected: she is the country in Europe where *the people* is most alive.

But the mania for giving an immediate political and practical application to all these fine ideas of the reason was fatal. Here an Englishman is in his element: on this theme we can all go on for hours. And all we are in the habit of saying on it has undoubtedly a great deal of truth. Ideas cannot be too much prized in and 160 for themselves, cannot be too much lived with; but to transport them abruptly into the world of politics and practice, violently to revolutionise this world to their bidding,—that is quite another thing. There is the world of ideas and there is the world of practice; the French are often for suppressing the one and the English the other; but neither is to be suppressed. A member of the House of Commons said to me the other day: "That a thing is an anomaly, I consider to be no objection to it whatever." I venture to think he was 170 wrong; that a thing is an anomaly *is* an objection to it, but absolutely and in the sphere of ideas: it is not necessarily, under such and such circumstances, or at such and such a moment, an objection to it in the sphere of politics and practice. Joubert has said beautifully: "C'est la force et le droit qui règlent toutes choses dans le monde; la force en attendant le droit." (Force and right are the governors of this world; force till right is ready.) *Force till right is ready*, and till right is ready, force, the existing order of things, is 180 justified, is the legitimate ruler. But right is something moral, and implies inward recognition, free assent of the will; we are not ready for right,—*right*, so far as we are concerned, *is not ready*,—until we have attained this sense of seeing it and willing it. The way in which for us it may change and transform force, the existing order of things, and become, in its turn, the legitimate ruler of the world, should depend on the way in which, when our time comes, we see it and will it. Therefore for other people enamoured of their own newly 190 discerned right, to attempt to impose it upon us as ours, and violently to substitute their right for our force, is an act of tyranny, and to be resisted. It sets at nought the second great half of our maxim, *force till right is ready*. This was the grand error of the French Revolution; and its movement of ideas, by quitting the intellectual sphere and rushing furiously into the political sphere, ran, indeed, a prodigious and memorable course, but produced no such intellectual fruit as the movement of ideas of the Renascence, and 200 created, in opposition to itself, what I may call an *epoch of concentration*. The great force of that epoch of concentration was England; and the great voice of that epoch of concentration was Burke. It is the fashion to treat Burke's writings on the French Revolution as superannuated and conquered by the event; as the eloquent but unphilosophical tirades of bigotry and prejudice. I will not deny that they are often disfig-

---

new church service prescribed by Charles I for Scotland. 175. **Joubert**, Joseph Joubert (1754-1824), French aphorist and author of *Pensées de J. Joubert*. 204. **Burke**, Edmund Burke (1729-1797), English states-

man and man of letters. Burke, born in Ireland, was an active member of the House of Commons from 1765 until just before his death.

ured by the violence and passion of the moment, and that in some directions Burke's view was bounded, and his observation therefore at fault. But on the whole, and for those who can make the needful corrections, what distinguishes these writings is their profound, permanent, fruitful, philosophical truth. They contain the true philosophy of an epoch of concentration, dissipate the heavy atmosphere which its own nature is apt to engender round it, and make its resistance rational in-
10 stead of mechanical.

But Burke is so great because, almost alone in England, he brings thought to bear upon politics, he saturates politics with thought. It is his accident that his ideas were at the service of an epoch of concentration, not of an epoch of expansion; it is his characteristic that he so lived by ideas, and had such a source of them welling up within him, that he could float even an epoch of concentration and English Tory politics with them. It does not hurt him that Dr. Price and the
20 Liberals were enraged with him; it does not even hurt him that George the Third and the Tories were enchanted with him. His greatness is that he lived in a world which neither English Liberalism nor English Toryism is apt to enter;—the world of ideas, not the world of catchwords and party habits. So far is it from being really true of him that he "to party gave up what was meant for mankind," that at the very end of his fierce struggle with the French Revolution, after all his invectives against its false pretensions, hollow-
30 ness, and madness, with his sincere convictions of its mischievousness, he can close a memorandum on the best means of combating it, some of the last pages he ever wrote,—the *Thoughts on French Affairs*, in December 1791,—with these striking words:—

"The evil is stated, in my opinion, as it exists. The remedy must be where power, wisdom, and information, I hope, are more united with good intentions than they can be with me. I have done with this subject, I believe, for ever. It has given me many anxious mo-
40 ments for the last two years. *If a great change is to be made in human affairs, the minds of men will be fitted to it; the general opinions and feelings will draw that way. Every fear, every hope will forward it; and then they who persist in opposing this mighty current in human affairs, will appear rather to resist the decrees of Providence itself, than the mere designs of men. They will not be resolute and firm, but perverse and obstinate."*

That return of Burke upon himself has always
50 seemed to me one of the finest things in English literature, or indeed in any literature. That is what I call living by ideas: when one side of a question has long

had your earnest support, when all your feelings are engaged, when you hear all round you no language but one, when your party talks this language like a steam-engine and can imagine no other,—still to be able to think, still to be irresistibly carried, if so it be, by the current of thought to the opposite side of the question, and, like Balaam, to be unable to speak anything *but what the Lord has put in your mouth.* I know 60 nothing more striking, and I must add that I know nothing more un-English.

For the Englishman in general is like my friend the Member of Parliament, and believes, point-blank, that for a thing to be an anomaly is absolutely no objection to it whatever. He is like the Lord Auckland of Burke's day, who, in a memorandum on the French Revolution, talks of certain "miscreants, assuming the name of philosophers, who have presumed themselves capable of establishing a new system of society." The 70 Englishman has been called a political animal, and he values what is political and practical so much that ideas easily become objects of dislike in his eyes, and thinkers, "miscreants," because ideas and thinkers have rashly meddled with politics and practice. This would be all very well if the dislike and neglect confined themselves to ideas transported out of their own sphere, and meddling rashly with practice; but they are inevitably extended to ideas as such, and to the whole life of intelligence; practice is everything, a free 80 play of the mind is nothing. The notion of the free play of the mind upon all subjects being a pleasure in itself, being an object of desire, being an essential provider of elements without which a nation's spirit, whatever compensations it may have for them, must, in the long run, die of inanition, hardly enters into an Englishman's thoughts. It is noticeable that the word *curiosity*, which in other languages is used in a good sense, to mean, as a high and fine quality of man's nature, just this disinterested love of a free play of 90 the mind on all subjects, for its own sake,—it is noticeable, I say, that this word has in our language no sense of the kind, no sense but a rather bad and disparaging one. But criticism, real criticism, is essentially the exercise of this very quality. It obeys an instinct prompting it to try to know the best that is known and thought in the world, irrespectively of practice, politics, and everything of the kind; and to value knowledge and thought as they approach this best, without the intrusion of any other considerations whatever. This is an 100 instinct for which there is, I think, little original sympathy in the practical English nature, and what there was of it has undergone a long benumbing period of blight and suppression in the epoch of concentration which followed the French Revolution.

19. **Dr. Price,** Richard Price (1723-1791), nonconformist minister and liberal commentator on morals, politics, and economics. 59.

Balaam, diviner who was rebuked by the ass he rode and blessed the Israelites when he had been commanded to curse them. 66. **Lord**

But epochs of concentration cannot well endure for ever; epochs of expansion, in the due course of things, follow them. Such an epoch of expansion seems to be opening in this country. In the first place all danger of a hostile forcible pressure of foreign ideas upon our practice has long disappeared; like the traveller in the fable, therefore, we begin to wear our cloak a little more loosely. Then, with a long peace, the ideas of Europe steal gradually and amicably in, and mingle, though in infinitesimally small quantities at a time, with our own notions. Then, too, in spite of all that is said about the absorbing and brutalising influence of our passionate material progress, it seems to me indisputable that this progress is likely, though not certain, to lead in the end to an apparition of intellectual life; and that man, after he has made himself perfectly comfortable and has now to determine what to do with himself next, may begin to remember that he has a mind, and that the mind may be made the source of great pleasure. I grant it is mainly the privilege of faith, at present, to discern this end to our railways, our business, and our fortune-making; but we shall see if, here as elsewhere, faith is not in the end the true prophet. Our ease, our travelling, and our unbounded liberty to hold just as hard and securely as we please to the practice to which our notions have given birth, all tend to beget an inclination to deal a little more freely with these notions themselves, to canvass them a little, to penetrate a little into their real nature. Flutterings of curiosity, in the foreign sense of the word, appear amongst us, and it is in these that criticism must look to find its account. Criticism first; a time of true creative activity, perhaps,—which, as I have said, must inevitably be preceded amongst us by a time of criticism,—hereafter, when criticism has done its work.

It is of the last importance that English criticism should clearly discern what rule for its course, in order to avail itself of the field now opening to it, and to produce fruit for the future, it ought to take. The rule may be summed up in one word,—*disinterestedness*. And how is criticism to show disinterestedness? By keeping aloof from what is called "the practical view of things"; by resolutely following the law of its own nature, which is to be a free play of the mind on all subjects which it touches. By steadily refusing to lend itself to any of those ulterior, political, practical considerations about ideas, which plenty of people will be sure to attach to them, which perhaps ought often to be attached to them, which in this country at any rate are certain to be attached to them quite sufficiently, but which criticism has really nothing to do with. Its business is, as I have said, simply to know the best that is known and thought in the world, and by in its turn making this known, to create a current of true and fresh ideas. Its business is to do this with inflexible honesty, with due ability; but its business is to do no more, and to leave alone all questions of practical consequences and applications, questions which will never fail to have due prominence given to them. Else criticism, besides being really false to its own nature, merely continues in the old rut which it has hitherto followed in this country, and will certainly miss the chance now given to it. For what is at present the bane of criticism in this country? It is that practical considerations cling to it and stifle it. It subserves interests not its own. Our organs of criticism are organs of men and parties having practical ends to serve, and with them those practical ends are the first thing and the play of mind the second; so much play of mind as is compatible with the prosecution of those practical ends is all that is wanted. An organ like the *Revue des Deux Mondes*, having for its main function to understand and utter the best that is known and thought in the world, existing, it may be said, as just an organ for a free play of the mind, we have not. But we have the *Edinburgh Review*, existing as an organ of the old Whigs, and for as much play of mind as may suit its being that; we have the *Quarterly Review*, existing as an organ of the Tories, and for as much play of mind as may suit its being that; we have the *British Quarterly Review*, existing as an organ of the political Dissenters, and for as much play of mind as may suit its being that; we have the *Times*, existing as an organ of the common, satisfied, well-to-do Englishman, and for as much play of mind as may suit its being that. And so on through all the various fractions, political and religious, of our society; every fraction has, as such, its organ of criticism, but the notion of combining all fractions in the common pleasure of a free disinterested play of mind meets with no favour. Directly this play of mind wants to have more scope, and to forget the pressure of practical considerations a little, it is checked, it is made to feel the chain. We saw this the other day in the extinction, so much to be regretted, of the *Home and Foreign Review*. Perhaps in no organ of criticism in this country was there so much knowledge, so much play of mind; but these could not save it. The *Dublin Review* subordinates play of mind to the practical business of English and Irish Catholicism, and lives. It must needs be that men should act in sects and parties, that each of these sects and parties should have its organ, and should make this organ subserve the interests of its action; but it would be well, too, that there should be a criticism, not the minister of these interests, not

Auckland. William Eden, first Baron Auckland (1744-1814), author and diplomat.   111. **traveller . . . fable,** that is, in Aesop's fable of the wind and the sun.

their enemy, but absolutely and entirely independent of them. No other criticism will ever attain any real authority or make any real way towards its end,—the creating a current of true and fresh ideas.

It is because criticism has so little kept in the pure intellectual sphere, has so little detached itself from practice, has been so directly polemical and controversial, that it has so ill accomplished, in this country, its best spiritual work; which is to keep man from a self-satisfaction which is retarding and vulgarising, to lead him towards perfection, by making his mind dwell upon what is excellent in itself, and the absolute beauty and fitness of things. A polemical practical criticism makes men blind even to the ideal imperfection of their practice, makes them willingly assert its ideal perfection, in order the better to secure it against attack; and clearly this is narrowing and baneful for them. If they were reassured on the practical side, speculative considerations of ideal perfection they might be brought to entertain, and their spiritual horizon would thus gradually widen. Sir Charles Adderley says to the Warwickshire farmers:—

"Talk of the improvement of breed! Why, the race we ourselves represent, the men and women, the old Anglo-Saxon race, are the best breed in the whole world . . . The absence of a too enervating climate, too unclouded skies, and a too luxurious nature, has produced so vigorous a race of people, and has rendered us so superior to all the world."

Mr. Roebuck says to the Sheffield cutlers:—

"I look around me and ask what is the state of England? Is not property safe? Is not every man able to say what he likes? Can you not walk from one end of England to the other in perfect security? I ask you whether, the world over or in past history, there is anything like it? Nothing. I pray that our unrivalled happiness may last."

Now obviously there is a peril for poor human nature in words and thoughts of such exuberant self-satisfaction, until we find ourselves safe in the streets of the Celestial City.

"Das wenige verschwindet leicht dem Blicke,
Der vorwärts sieht, wie viel noch übrig bleibt—"

says Goethe; "the little that is done seems nothing when we look forward and see how much we have yet to do." Clearly this is a better line of reflection for weak humanity, so long as it remains on this earthly field of labour and trial.

But neither Sir Charles Adderley nor Mr. Roebuck is by nature inaccessible to considerations of this sort.

They only lose sight of them owing to the controversial life we all lead, and the practical form which all speculation takes with us. They have in view opponents whose aim is not ideal, but practical; and in their zeal to uphold their own practice against these innovators, they go so far as even to attribute to this practice an ideal perfection. Somebody has been wanting to introduce a six-pound franchise, or to abolish church-rates, or to collect agricultural statistics by force, or to diminish local self-government. How natural, in reply to such proposals, very likely improper or ill-timed, to go a little beyond the mark and to say stoutly, "Such a race of people as we stand, so superior to all the world! The old Anglo-Saxon race, the best breed in the whole world! I pray that our unrivalled happiness may last! I ask you whether, the world over or in past history, there is anything like it?" And so long as criticism answers this dithyramb by insisting that the old Anglo-Saxon race would be still more superior to all others if it had no church-rates, or that our unrivalled happiness would last yet longer with a six-pound franchise, so long will the strain, "The best breed in the whole world!" swell louder and louder, everything ideal and refining will be lost out of sight, and both the assailed and their critics will remain in a sphere, to say the truth, perfectly unvital, a sphere in which spiritual progression is impossible. But let criticism leave church-rates and the franchise alone, and in the most candid spirit, without a single lurking thought of practical innovation, confront with our dithyramb this paragraph on which I stumbled in a newspaper immediately after reading Mr. Roebuck:—

"A shocking child murder has just been committed at Nottingham. A girl named Wragg left the workhouse there on Saturday morning with her young illegitimate child. The child was soon afterwards found dead on Mapperly Hills, having been strangled. Wragg is in custody."

Nothing but that; but, in juxtaposition with the absolute eulogies of Sir Charles Adderley and Mr. Roebuck, how eloquent, how suggestive are those few lines! "Our old Anglo-Saxon breed, the best in the whole world!"—how much that is harsh and ill-favoured there is in this best! Wragg! If we are to talk of ideal perfection, of "the best in the whole world," has any one reflected what a touch of grossness in our race, what an original shortcoming in the more delicate spiritual perceptions, is shown by the natural growth amongst us of such hideous names,—Higginbottom, Stiggins, Bugg! In Ionia and Attica they were luckier in this respect than "the best race in the world"; by the Ilissus there was no Wragg, poor thing!

21. **Charles Adderley,** first Baron Norton (1814-1905), Conservative politician. 30. **Roebuck,** John Arthur Roebuck (1801-1879), prominent radical reformer. 100. **Ionia and Attica,** districts in classical Greece. 102. **Ilissus,** a river near Athens. 181. **Lord Somers,** John Somers, Baron Somers (1651-1716), great champion of the English Constitution. 182. **Cobbett,** William Cobbett (1762-1835), violent

And "our unrivalled happiness";—what an element of grimness, bareness, and hideousness mixes with it and blurs it; the workhouse, the dismal Mapperly Hills, —how dismal those who have seen them will remember;—the gloom, the smoke, the cold, the strangled illegitimate child! "I ask you whether, the world over or in past history, there is anything like it?" Perhaps not, one is inclined to answer; but at any rate, in that case, the world is very much to be pitied. And the final touch,—short, bleak and inhuman: *Wragg is in custody.* The sex lost in the confusion of our unrivalled happiness; or (shall I say?) the superfluous Christian name lopped off by the straightforward vigour of our Anglo-Saxon breed! There is profit for the spirit in such contrasts as this; criticism serves the cause of perfection by establishing them. By eluding sterile conflict, by refusing to remain in the sphere where alone narrow and relative conceptions have any worth and validity, criticism may diminish its momentary importance, but only in this way has it a chance of gaining admittance for those wider and more perfect conceptions to which all its duty is really owed. Mr. Roebuck will have a poor opinion of an adversary who replies to his defiant songs of triumph only by murmuring under his breath, *Wragg is in custody,* but in no other way will these songs of triumph be induced gradually to moderate themselves, to get rid of what in them is excessive and offensive, and to fall into a softer and truer key.

It will be said that it is a very subtle and indirect action which I am thus prescribing for criticism, and that, by embracing in this manner the Indian virtue of detachment and abandoning the sphere of practical life, it condemns itself to a slow and obscure work. Slow and obscure it may be, but it is the only proper work of criticism. The mass of mankind will never have any ardent zeal for seeing things as they are; very inadequate ideas will always satisfy them. On these inadequate ideas reposes, and must repose, the general practice of the world. That is as much as saying that whoever sets himself to see things as they are will find himself one of a very small circle; but it is only by this small circle resolutely doing its own work that adequate ideas will ever get current at all. The rush and roar of practical life will always have a dizzying and attracting effect upon the most collected spectator, and tend to draw him into its vortex; most of all will this be the case where that life is so powerful as it is in England. But it is only by remaining collected, and refusing to lend himself to the point of view of the practical man, that the critic can do the practical man any service; and it is only by the greatest sincerity in pursuing his own course, and by at last convincing even the practical man of his sincerity, that he can escape misunderstandings which perpetually threaten him.

For the practical man is not apt for fine distinctions, and yet in these distinctions truth and the highest culture greatly find their account. But it is not easy to lead a practical man,—unless you reassure him as to your practical intentions, you have no chance of leading him,—to see that a thing which he has always been used to look at from one side only, which he greatly values, and which, looked at from that side, quite deserves, perhaps, all the prizing and admiring which he bestows upon it,—that this thing, looked at from another side, may appear much less beneficent and beautiful, and yet retain all its claims to our practical allegiance. Where shall we find language innocent enough, how shall we make the spotless purity of our intentions evident enough, to enable us to say to the political Englishman that the British Constitution itself, which, seen from the practical side, looks such a magnificent organ of progress and virtue, seen from the speculative side,—with its compromises, its love of facts, its horror of theory, its studied avoidance of clear thoughts,—that, seen from this side, our august Constitution sometimes looks,—forgive me, shade of Lord Somers!—a colossal machine for the manufacture of Philistines? How is Cobbett to say this and not be misunderstood, blackened as he is with the smoke of a lifelong conflict in the field of political practice? how is Mr. Carlyle to say it and not be misunderstood, after his furious raid into this field with his *Latter-day Pamphlets?* how is Mr. Ruskin, after his pugnacious political economy? I say, the critic must keep out of the region of immediate practice in the political, social, humanitarian sphere if he wants to make a beginning for that more free speculative treatment of things, which may perhaps one day make its benefits felt even in this sphere, but in a natural and thence irresistible manner.

Do what he will, however, the critic will still remain exposed to frequent misunderstandings, and nowhere so much as in this country. For here people are particularly indisposed even to comprehend that without this free disinterested treatment of things, truth and the highest culture are out of the question. So immersed are they in practical life, so accustomed to take all their notions from this life and its processes, that they are apt to think that truth and culture themselves can be reached by the processes of this life, and that it is an impertinent singularity to think of reaching them in any other. "We are all *terræ filii*," cries

democratic writer. 186. **Latter-day Pamphlets,** pamphlets by Thomas Carlyle of an extremely conservative bent published in 1850. 187.

Ruskin . . . **economy,** that is, in *Unto This Last.* 206. **terrae filii,** sons of the earth.

their eloquent advocate; "all Philistines together. Away with the notion of proceeding by any other course than the course dear to the Philistines; let us have a social movement, let us organise and combine a party to pursue truth and new thought, let us call it *the liberal party*, and let us all stick to each other, and back each other up. Let us have no nonsense about independent criticism, and intellectual delicacy, and the few and the many. Don't let us trouble ourselves about foreign 10 thought; we shall invent the whole thing for ourselves as we go along. If one of us speaks well, applaud him; if one of us speaks ill, applaud him too; we are all in the same movement, we are all liberals, we are all in pursuit of truth." In this way the pursuit of truth becomes really a social, practical, pleasurable affair, almost requiring a chairman, a secretary, and advertisements; with the excitement of an occasional scandal, with a little resistance to give the happy sense of difficulty overcome; but, in general, plenty of bustle 20 and very little thought. To act is so easy, as Goethe says; to think is so hard! It is true that the critic has many temptations to go with the stream, to make one of the party movement, one of these *terræ filii*; it seems ungracious to refuse to be a *terræ filius* when so many excellent people are; but the critic's duty is to refuse, or, if resistance is vain, at least to cry with Obermann: *Périssons en résistant*.

How serious a matter it is to try and resist, I had ample opportunity of experiencing when I ventured 30 some time ago to criticise the celebrated first volume of Bishop Colenso. The echoes of the storm which was then raised I still, from time to time, hear grumbling round me. That storm arose out of a misunderstanding almost inevitable. It is a result of no little culture to attain to a clear perception that science and religion are two wholly different things. The multitude will for ever confuse them; but happily that is of no great real importance, for while the multitude imagines itself to live by its false science, it does really live by its true 40 religion. Dr. Colenso, however, in his first volume did all he could to strengthen the confusion, and to make it dangerous. He did this with the best intentions, I freely admit, and with the most candid ignorance that this was the natural effect of what he was doing; but, says Joubert, "Ignorance, which in matters of morals extenuates the crime, is itself, in intellectual matters, a crime of the first order." I criticised Bishop Colenso's speculative confusion. Immediately there was a cry raised: "What is this? here is a liberal attacking a 50 liberal. Do not you belong to the movement? are you not a friend of truth? Is not Bishop Colenso in pursuit

of truth? then speak with proper respect of his book. Dr. Stanley is another friend of truth, and you speak with proper respect of his book; why make these invidious differences? both books are excellent, admirable, liberal; Bishop Colenso's perhaps the most so, because it is the boldest, and will have the best practical consequences for the liberal cause. Do you want to encourage to the attack of a brother liberal his, and your, and our implacable enemies, the *Church and* 60 *State Review* or the *Record*,—the High Church rhinoceros and the Evangelical hyena? Be silent, therefore; or rather speak, speak as loud as ever you can! and go into ecstasies over the eighty and odd pigeons."

But criticism cannot follow this coarse and indiscriminate method. It is unfortunately possible for a man in pursuit of truth to write a book which reposes upon a false conception. Even the practical consequences of a book are to genuine criticism no recommendation of it, if the book is, in the highest sense, 70 blundering. I see that a lady who herself, too, is in pursuit of truth, and who writes with great ability, but a little too much, perhaps, under the influence of the practical spirit of the English liberal movement, classes Bishop Colenso's book and M. Renan's together, in her survey of the religious state of Europe, as facts of the same order, works, both of them, of "great importance"; "great ability, power, and skill"; Bishop Colenso's, perhaps, the most powerful; at least, Miss Cobbe gives special expression to her gratitude that to 80 Bishop Colenso "has been given the strength to grasp, and the courage to teach, truths of such deep import." In the same way, more than one popular writer has compared him to Luther. Now it is just this kind of false estimate which the critical spirit is, it seems to me, bound to resist. It is really the strongest possible proof of the low ebb at which, in England, the critical spirit is, that while the critical hit in the religious literature of Germany is Dr. Strauss's book, in that of France M. Renan's book, the book of Bishop Colenso is the criti- 90 cal hit in the religious literature of England. Bishop Colenso's book reposes on a total misconception of the essential elements of the religious problem, as that problem is now presented for solution. To criticism, therefore, which seeks to have the best that is known and thought on this problem, it is, however well meant, of no importance whatever. M. Renan's book attempts a new synthesis of the elements furnished to us by the Four Gospels. It attempts, in my opinion, a synthesis, perhaps premature, perhaps impossible, certainly not 100 successful. Up to the present time, at any rate, we must acquiesce in Fleury's sentence on such recastings of

27. *Périssons en résistant.* "Let us die resisting." E. P. de Senancour (1770-1846), author of *Obermann*, was a major influence on Arnold. 31. Colenso, John William Colenso (1814-1883), Bishop of Natal, author of *The Pentateuch and Book of Joshua Critically Examined* (1862), a work in historical criticism of the Bible which caused much

religious furor. 53. Stanley, Arthur Penrhyn Stanley (1815-1881), Dean of Westminster and great friend of Arnold's father. 71. a lady, Frances Power Cobbe (1822-1904), writer on religious and moral subjects. 75. Renan, Ernest Renan (1823-1892), French philologist and historian, author of *Vie de Jésus* (1863). 89. Strauss, David Friedrich

the Gospel story: *Quiconque s'imagine la pouvoir mieux écrire, ne l'entend pas.* M. Renan had himself passed by anticipation a like sentence on his own work, when he said: "If a new presentation of the character of Jesus were offered to me, I would not have it; its very clearness would be, in my opinion, the best proof of its insufficiency." His friends may with perfect jus-110 tice rejoin that at the sight of the Holy Land, and of the actual scene of the Gospel-story, all the current of M. Renan's thoughts may have naturally changed, and a new casting of that story irresistibly suggested itself to him; and that this is just a case for applying Cicero's maxim: Change of mind is not inconsistency—*nemo doctus unquam mutationem consilii inconstantiam dixit esse.* Nevertheless, for criticism, M. Renan's first thought must still be the truer one, as long as his new casting so fails more fully to commend itself, more 120 fully (to use Coleridge's happy phrase about the Bible) to *find* us. Still M. Renan's attempt is, for criticism, of the most real interest and importance, since, with all its difficulty, a fresh synthesis of the New Testament *data*—not a making war on them, in Voltaire's fashion, not a leaving them out of mind, in the world's fashion, but the putting a new construction upon them, the taking them from under the old, traditional, conventional point of view and placing them under a new one,—is the very essence of the religious problem, as 130 now presented; and only by efforts in this direction can it receive a solution.

Again, in the same spirit in which she judges Bishop Colenso, Miss Cobbe, like so many earnest liberals of our practical race, both here and in America, herself sets vigorously about a positive reconstruction of religion, about making a religion of the future out of hand, or at least setting about making it. We must not rest, she and they are always thinking and saying, in negative criticism, we must be creative and construc-140 tive; hence we have such works as her recent *Religious Duty,* and works still more considerable, perhaps, by others, which will be in every one's mind. These works often have much ability; they often spring out of sincere convictions, and a sincere wish to do good; and they sometimes, perhaps, do good. Their fault is (if I may be permitted to say so) one which they have in common with the British College of Health, in the New Road. Every one knows the British College of Health; it is that building with the lion and the statue 150 of the Goddess Hygeia before it; at least I am sure about the lion, though I am not absolutely certain about the Goddess Hygeia. This building does credit, perhaps, to the resources of Dr. Morrison and his disciples; but it falls a good deal short of one's idea of what a British College of Health ought to be. In England, where we hate public interference and love individual enterprise, we have a whole crop of places like the British College of Health; the grand name without the grand thing. Unluckily, creditable to indi-160 vidual enterprise as they are, they tend to impair our taste by making us forget what more grandiose, noble, or beautiful character properly belongs to a public institution. The same may be said of the religions of the future of Miss Cobbe and others. Creditable, like the British College of Health, to the resources of their authors, they yet tend to make us forget what more grandiose, noble, or beautiful character properly belongs to religious constructions. The historic religions, with all their faults, have had this; it certainly belongs 170 to the religious sentiment, when it truly flowers, to have this; and we impoverish our spirit if we allow a religion of the future without it. What then is the duty of criticism here? To take the practical point of view, to applaud the liberal movement and all its works,—its New Road religions of the future into the bargain,— for their general utility's sake? By no means; but to be perpetually dissatisfied with these works, while they perpetually fall short of a high and perfect ideal.

For criticism, these are elementary laws; but they never can be popular, and in this country they have 180 been very little followed, and one meets with immense obstacles in following them. That is a reason for asserting them again and again. Criticism must maintain its independence of the practical spirit and its aims. Even with well-meant efforts of the practical spirit it must express dissatisfaction, if in the sphere of the ideal they seem impoverishing and limiting. It must not hurry on to the goal because of its practical importance. It must be patient, and know how to wait; and flexible, and know how to attach itself to things 190 and how to withdraw from them. It must be apt to study and praise elements that for the fulness of spiritual perfection are wanted, even though they belong to a power which in the practical sphere may be maleficent. It must be apt to discern the spiritual shortcomings or illusions of powers that in the practical sphere may be beneficent. And this without any notion of favouring or injuring, in the practical sphere, one power or the other; without any notion of playing off, in this sphere, one power against the other. When 200 one looks, for instance, at the English Divorce Court,— an institution which perhaps has its practical conveniences, but which in the ideal sphere is so hideous; an institution which neither makes divorce impossible

Strauss (1808-1874); the book alluded to is *Das Leben Jesu* (1835). 103-104. *Quiconque . . . pas.* "Whoever thinks he can write it better does not understand it"; from Claude Fleury (1640-1723), *Discours sur l'histoire ecclésiastique.* 115-117. *nemo . . . esse.* No learned person has ever said that change of mind is inconsistency (*Letters to Atticus*). 153. **Morrison,** James Morrison (1770-1840), seller of Morrison's Pills as universal cure-alls.

nor makes it decent, which allows a man to get rid of his wife, or a wife of her husband, but makes them drag one another first, for the public edification, through a mire of unutterable infamy,—when one looks at this charming institution, I say, with its crowded trials, its newspaper reports, and its money compensations, this institution in which the gross unregenerate British Philistine has indeed stamped an image of himself,—one may be permitted to find the marriage theory of Catholicism refreshing and elevating. Or when Protestantism, in virtue of its supposed rational and intellectual origin, gives the law to criticism too magisterially, criticism may and must remind it that its pretensions, in this respect, are illusive and do it harm; that the Reformation was a moral rather than an intellectual event; that Luther's theory of grace no more exactly reflects the mind of the spirit than Bossuet's philosophy of history reflects it; and that there is no more antecedent probability of the Bishop of Durham's stock of ideas being agreeable to perfect reason than of Pope Pius the Ninth's. But criticism will not on that account forget the achievements of Protestantism in the practical and moral sphere; nor that, even in the intellectual sphere, Protestantism, though in a blind and stumbling manner, carried forward the Renascence, while Catholicism threw itself violently across its path.

I lately heard a man of thought and energy contrasting the want of ardour and movement which he now found amongst young men in this country with what he remembered in his own youth, twenty years ago. "What reformers we were then!" he exclaimed; "What a zeal we had! how we canvassed every institution in Church and State, and were prepared to remodel them all on first principles!" He was inclined to regret, as a spiritual flagging, the lull which he saw. I am disposed rather to regard it as a pause in which the turn to a new mode of spiritual progress is being accomplished. Everything was long seen, by the young and ardent amongst us, in inseparable connection with politics and practical life. We have pretty well exhausted the benefits of seeing things in this connection, we have got all that can be got by so seeing them. Let us try a more disinterested mode of seeing them; let us betake ourselves more to the serener life of the mind and spirit. This life, too, may have its excesses and dangers; but they are not for us at present. Let us think of quietly enlarging our stock of true and fresh ideas, and not, as soon as we get an idea or half an idea, be running out with it into the street, and trying to make it rule there. Our ideas will, in the end, shape the world all the better for maturing a little. Perhaps in fifty years' time it will in the English House of Commons be an objection to an institution that it is an anomaly, and my friend the Member of Parliament will shudder in his grave. But let us in the meanwhile rather endeavour that in twenty years' time it may, in English literature, be an objection to a proposition that it is absurd. That will be a change so vast, that the imagination almost fails to grasp it. *Ab integro sæclorum nascitur ordo.*

If I have insisted so much on the course which criticism must take where politics and religion are concerned, it is because, where these burning matters are in question, it is more likely to go astray. I have wished, above all, to insist on the attitude which criticism should adopt towards things in general; on its right tone and temper of mind. But then comes another question as to the subject-matter which literary criticisms should most seek. Here, in general, its course is determined for it by the idea which is the law of its being; the idea of a disinterested endeavour to learn and propagate the best that is known and thought in the world, and thus to establish a current of fresh and true ideas. By the very nature of things, as England is not all the world, much of the best that is known and thought in the world cannot be of English growth, must be foreign; by the nature of things, again, it is just this that we are least likely to know, while English thought is streaming in upon us from all sides, and takes excellent care that we shall not be ignorant of its existence. The English critic of literature, therefore, must dwell much on foreign thought, and with particular heed on any part of it, which, while significant and fruitful in itself, is for any reason specially likely to escape him. Again, judging is often spoken of as the critic's one business, and so in some sense it is; but the judgment which almost insensibly forms itself in a fair and clear mind, along with fresh knowledge, is the valuable one; and thus knowledge, and ever fresh knowledge, must be the critic's great concern for himself. And it is by communicating fresh knowledge, and letting his own judgment pass along with it,—but insensibly, and in the second place, not the first, as a sort of companion and clue, not as an abstract lawgiver,—that the critic will generally do most good to his readers. Sometimes, no doubt, for the sake of establishing an author's place in literature, and his relation to a central standard (and if this is not done, how are we to get at our *best in the world?*), criticism may have to deal with a subject-matter so familiar that fresh knowledge is out of the question, and then it must be all judgment; an enunciation and detailed application of principles. Here the great safeguard is never to let

---

18. **Bossuet,** Jacques Bénigne Bosseut (1627-1704), French bishop and author who believed that all of history demonstrated that God had ordered events for the good of Christianity. 20. **Bishop of Durham,** Charles Thomas Baring (1807-1879). 60-61. *Ab . . . ordo.* Order is born from the renewal of the ages (Vergil, *Fourth Eclogue*).

oneself become abstract, always to retain an intimate and lively consciousness of the truth of what one is saying, and, the moment this fails us, to be sure that something is wrong. Still under all circumstances, this mere judgment and application of principles is, in itself, not the most satisfactory work to the critic; like mathematics, it is tautological, and cannot well give us, like fresh learning, the sense of creative activity.

But stop, some one will say; all this talk is of no practical use to us whatever; this criticism of yours is not what we have in our minds when we speak of criticism; when we speak of critics and criticism, we mean critics and criticism of the current English literature of the day; when you offer to tell criticism its function, it is to this criticism that we expect you to address yourself. I am sorry for it, for I am afraid I must disappoint these expectations. I am bound by my own definition of criticism: *a disinterested endeavour to learn and propagate the best that is known and thought in the world.* How much of current English literature comes into this "best that is known and thought in the world"? Not very much, I fear; certainly less, at this moment, than of the current literature of France or Germany. Well, then, am I to alter my definition of criticism, in order to meet the requirements of a number of practising English critics, who, after all, are free in their choice of a business? That would be making criticism lend itself just to one of those alien practical considerations, which, I have said, are so fatal to it. One may say, indeed, to those who have to deal with the mass—so much better disregarded—of current English literature, that they may at all events endeavour, in dealing with this, to try it, so far as they can, by the standard of the best that is known and thought in the world; one may say, that to get anywhere near this standard, every critic should try and possess one great literature, at least, besides his own; and the more unlike his own, the better. But, after all, the criticism I am really concerned with,—the criticism which alone can much help us for the future, the criticism which, throughout Europe, is at the present day meant, when so much stress is laid on the importance of criticism and the critical spirit,—is a criticism which regards Europe as being, for intellectual and spiritual purposes, one great confederation, bound to a joint action and working to a common re-

sult; and whose members have, for their proper outfit, a knowledge of Greek, Roman, and Eastern antiquity, and of one another. Special, local, and temporary advantages being put out of account, that modern nation will in the intellectual and spiritual sphere make most progress, which most thoroughly carries out this program. And what is that but saying that we too, all of us, as individuals, the more thoroughly we carry it out, shall make the more progress?

There is so much inviting us!—what are we to take? what will nourish us in growth towards perfection? That is the question which, with the immense field of life and of literature lying before him, the critic has to answer; for himself first, and afterwards for others. In this idea of the critic's business the essays brought together in the following pages have had their origin; in this idea, widely different as are their subjects, they have, perhaps, their unity.

I conclude with what I said at the beginning: to have the sense of creative activity is the great happiness and the great proof of being alive, and it is not denied to criticism to have it; but then criticism must be sincere, simple, flexible, ardent, ever widening its knowledge. Then it may have, in no contemptible measure, a joyful sense of creative activity; a sense which a man of insight and conscience will prefer to what he might derive from a poor, starved, fragmentary, inadequate creation. And at some epochs no other creation is possible.

Still, in full measure, the sense of creative activity belongs only to genuine creation; in literature we must never forget that. But what true man of letters ever can forget it? It is no such common matter for a gifted nature to come into possession of a current of true and living ideas, and to produce amidst the inspiration of them, that we are likely to underrate it. The epochs of Æschylus and Shakespeare make us feel their preeminence. In an epoch like those is, no doubt, the true life of literature; there is the promised land, towards which criticism can only beckon. That promised land it will not be ours to enter, and we shall die in the wilderness: but to have desired to enter it, to have saluted it from afar, is already, perhaps, the best distinction among contemporaries; it will certainly be the best title to esteem with posterity.
(1865)

*Matthew Arnold lectured in America in 1883 and 1884.
Historical Pictures Service—Chicago.*

from CULTURE AND ANARCHY

*Some of the utterances that earned for Arnold the
name of "elegant Jeremiah" appear in the series of
essays on political and social conditions and problems
which he issued in 1869 under the title* Culture and
Anarchy. *Of these* Hebraism and Hellenism, *an analysis of opposing cultures, forms Chapter IV. Arnold
derived his idea of culture most fully from Goethe,
and he found the Hebraic-Hellenic dichotomy in the
writings of Heinrich Heine.*

HEBRAISM AND HELLENISM

This fundamental ground is our preference of doing
to thinking. Now, this preference is a main element
in our nature, and as we study it we find ourselves
opening up a number of large questions on every side.

Let me go back for a moment to Bishop Wilson, who
says, "First, never go against the best light you
have; secondly, take care that your light be not darkness." We show, as a nation, laudable energy and
persistence in walking according to the best light
we have, but are not quite careful enough, perhaps, 10
to see that our light be not darkness. This is only
another version of the old story that energy is our
strong point and favorable characteristic, rather than
intelligence. But we may give to this idea a more
general form still, in which it will have a yet larger
range of application. We may regard this energy driving at practice, this paramount sense of the obligation
of duty, self-control, and work, this earnestness in
going manfully with the best light we have, as one
force. And we may regard the intelligence driving at 20
those ideas which are, after all, the basis of right
practice, the ardent sense for all the new and changing combinations of them which man's development
brings with it, the indomitable impulse to know and
adjust them perfectly, as another force. And these
two forces we may regard as in some sense rivals—
rivals, not by the necessity of their own nature, but
as exhibited in man and his history; and rivals dividing the empire of the world between them. And
to give these forces names from the two races of 30
men who have supplied the most signal and splendid
manifestations of them, we may call them respectively
the forces of Hebraism and Hellenism. Hebraism and
Hellenism—between these two points of influence
moves our world. At one time it feels more powerfully the attraction of one of them, at another time of
the other; and it ought to be, though it never is,
evenly and happily balanced between them.

The final aim of both Hellenism and Hebraism, as
of all great spiritual disciplines, is no doubt the 40
same: man's perfection, or salvation. The very language which they both of them use in schooling us
to reach this aim is often identical. Even when their
language indicates by variation—sometimes a broad
variation, often a but slight and subtle variation—
the different courses of thought which are uppermost
in each discipline, even then the unity of the final end
and aim is still apparent. To employ the actual words
of that discipline with which we ourselves are all of
us most familiar, and the words of which, therefore, 50
come most home to us, that final end and aim is
"that we might be partakers of the divine nature."
These are the words of a Hebrew apostle; but of Hellenism and Hebraism alike this is, I say, the aim.
When the two are confronted, as they very often are
confronted, it is nearly always with what I may call

Culture and Anarchy. 1. **This . . . ground.** A reference to the
concluding paragraph of the preceding chapter: "We see, then, how indispensable to that human perfection which we seek is, in the opinion of
good judges, some public recognition and establishment of our best self,
or right reason. We see how our habits and practice oppose themselves
to such a recognition, and the many inconveniences which we therefore
suffer. But now let us try to go a little deeper, and to find, beneath

our actual habits and practice, the very ground and cause out of which
they spring." 5. **Bishop Wilson,** Thomas Wilson (1663-1755), Bishop
of Sodor and Man. His *Maxims* and other writings appealed strongly to
Arnold. 52. **"that . . . nature,"** words of the Apostle Paul, 2 Peter
1:4. 64. **Frederick Robertson,** a brilliant Anglican clergyman (1816-
1853), whose sermon "The Grecian" (1849) expressed a rather liberal
point of view. 70. **Heinrich Heine,** a German lyric poet (1797-1856).

a rhetorical purpose: the speaker's whole design is to exalt and enthrone one of the two, and he uses the other only as a foil and to enable him the better to
60 give effect to his purpose. Obviously, with us, it is usually Hellenism which is thus reduced to minister to the triumph of Hebraism. There is a sermon on Greece and the Greek spirit by a man never to be mentioned without interest and respect, Frederick Robertson, in which this rhetorical use of Greece and the Greek spirit, and the inadequate exhibition of them necessarily consequent upon this, is almost ludicrous, and would be censurable if it were not to be explained by the exigencies of a sermon. On the
70 other hand, Heinrich Heine and other writers of his sort give us the spectacle of the tables completely turned, and of Hebraism brought in just as a foil and contrast to Hellenism and to make the superiority of Hellenism more manifest. In both these cases there is injustice and misrepresentation. The aim and end of both Hebraism and Hellenism is, as I have said, one and the same, and this aim and end is august and admirable.

Still, they pursue this aim by very different courses.
80 The uppermost idea with Hellenism is to see things as they really are; the uppermost idea with Hebraism is conduct and obedience. Nothing can do away with this ineffaceable difference. The Greek quarrel with the body and its desires is that they hinder right thinking; the Hebrew quarrel with them is that they hinder right acting. "He that keepeth the law, happy is he"; "Blessed is the man that feareth the Eternal, that delighteth greatly in His commandments";—that is the Hebrew notion of felicity; and, pursued with
90 passion and tenacity, this notion would not let the Hebrew rest till, as is well known, he had at last got out of the law a network of prescriptions to enwrap his whole life, to govern every moment of it, every impulse, every action. The Greek notion of felicity, on the other hand, is perfectly conveyed in these words of a great French moralist: *"C'est le bonheur des hommes"*—when? when they abhor that which is evil? no;—when they exercise themselves in the law of the Lord day and night? no;—when they
100 die daily? no;—when they walk about the New Jerusalem with palms in their hands? no;—but when they think aright, when their thought hits: *"quand ils pensent juste."* At the bottom of both the Greek and the Hebrew notion is the desire, native in man, for reason and the will of God, the feeling after the universal order—in a word, the love of God. But while Hebraism seizes upon certain plain, capital intimations of the universal order, and rivets itself, one

may say, with unequaled grandeur of earnestness and intensity on the study and observance of them, the 110 bent of Hellenism is to follow, with flexible activity, the whole play of the universal order, to be apprehensive of missing any part of it, of sacrificing one part to another, to slip away from resting in this or that intimation of it, however capital. An unclouded clearness of mind, an unimpeded play of thought, is what this bent drives at. The governing idea of Hellenism is *spontaneity of consciousness;* that of Hebraism, *strictness of conscience.*

Christianity changed nothing in this essential bent 120 of Hebraism to set doing above knowing. Self-conquest, self-devotion, the following not our own individual will but the will of God, *obedience,* is the fundamental idea of this form, also, of the discipline to which we have attached the general name of Hebraism. Only, as the old law and the network of prescriptions with which it enveloped human life were evidently a motive-power not driving and searching enough to produce the result aimed at—patient continuance in well-doing, self-conquest—Christianity 130 substituted for them boundless devotion to that inspiring and affecting pattern of self-conquest offered by Jesus Christ; and by the new motive-power, of which the essence was this, though the love and admiration of Christian churches have for centuries been employed in varying, amplifying, and adorning the plain description of it, Christianity, as St. Paul truly says, "establishes the law," and, in the strength of the ampler power which she has thus supplied to fulfill it, has accomplished the miracles, which we all see, of 140 her history.

So long as we do not forget that both Hellenism and Hebraism are profound and admirable manifestations of man's life, tendencies, and powers, and that both of them aim at a like final result, we can hardly insist too strongly on the divergence of line and of operation with which they proceed. It is a divergence so great that it most truly, as the prophet Zechariah says, "has raised up thy sons, O Zion, against thy sons, O Greece!" The difference whether 150 it is by doing or by knowing that we set most store, and the practical consequences which follow from this difference, leave their mark on all the history of our race and of its development. Language may be abundantly quoted from both Hellenism and Hebraism to make it seem that one follows the same current as the other towards the same goal. They are, truly, borne towards the same goal; but the currents which bear them are infinitely different. It is true, Solomon will praise knowing: "Understanding is a well-spring

He says, "All men are either Jews or Hellenes, men ascetic in their instincts, hostile to culture, spiritual fanatics, or men of vigorous good cheer, full of the pride of life, Naturalists."—*Ueber Ludwig Börne.* 86. "He that . . . he." From Proverbs 29:18. 87. "Blessed . . . commandments." From Psalms 112:1. 96. "*C'est . . . hommes,*" it is the good fortune of men. 97. abhor . . . evil, etc. Phrases from Romans 12:9; Psalms 1:2; 1 Corinthians 15:31; Revelation 3:12; 7:9.

107. capital, important (from L. *caput*, head). 129. patient . . . well-doing. From Romans 2:7. 138. "establishes the law." From Romans 3:31. 149. "has . . . Greece!" From Zechariah 9:13. 160. "Understanding . . . it." From Proverbs 16:22.

of life unto him that hath it." And in the New Testament, again, Jesus Christ is a "light," and "truth makes us free." It is true, Aristotle will undervalue knowing: "In what concerns virtue," says he, "three things are necessary—knowledge, deliberate will, and perseverance; but whereas the two last are all-important, the first is a matter of little importance." It is true that with the same impatience with which St. James enjoins a man to be not a forgetful hearer
10 but a *doer of the word*, Epictetus exhorts us to *do* what we have demonstrated to ourselves we ought to do; or he taunts us with futility, for being armed at all points to prove that lying is wrong, yet all the time continuing to lie. It is true, Plato, in words which are almost the words of the New Testament or the *Imitation*, calls life a learning to die. But underneath the superficial agreement the fundamental divergence still subsists. The "understanding" of Solomon is "the walking in the way of the commandments"; this is
20 "the way of peace," and it is of this that blessedness comes. In the New Testament, the truth which gives us the peace of God and makes us free is the love of Christ constraining us to crucify, as he did, and with a like purpose of moral regeneration, the flesh with its affections and lusts, and thus establishing, as we have seen, the law. The moral virtues, on the other hand, are with Aristotle but the porch and access to the intellectual, and with these last is blessedness. That partaking of the divine life, which both Hellenism and
30 Hebraism, as we have said, fix as their crowning aim, Plato expressly denies to the man of practical virtue merely, of self-conquest with any other motive than that of perfect intellectual vision. He reserves it for the lover of pure knowledge, of seeing things as they really are—the φιλομαθής.

Both Hellenism and Hebraism arise out of the wants of human nature, and address themselves to satisfying those wants. But their methods are so different, they lay stress on such different points, and
40 call into being by their respective disciplines such different activities, that the face which human nature presents when it passes from the hands of one of them to those of the other is no longer the same. To get rid of one's ignorance, to see things as they are, and by seeing them as they are to see them in their beauty, is the simple and attractive ideal which Hellenism holds out before human nature; and from the simplicity and charm of this ideal, Hellenism, and human life in the hands of Hellenism, is invested
50 with a kind of aërial ease, clearness, and radiancy;

they are full of what we call sweetness and light. Difficulties are kept out of view, and the beauty and rationalness of the ideal have all our thoughts. "The best man is he who most tries to perfect himself, and the happiest man is he who most feels that he *is* perfecting himself"—this account of the matter by Socrates, the true Socrates of the *Memorabilia,* has something so simple, spontaneous, and unsophisticated about it that it seems to fill us with clearness and hope when we hear it. But there is a saying 60 which I have heard attributed to Mr. Carlyle about Socrates—a very happy saying, whether it is really Mr. Carlyle's or not—which excellently marks the essential point in which Hebraism differs from Hellenism. "Socrates," this saying goes, "is terribly *at ease in Zion.*" Hebraism—and here is the source of its wonderful strength—has always been severely preoccupied with an awful sense of the impossibility of being at ease in Zion; of the difficulties which oppose themselves to man's pursuit or attainment of that 70 perfection of which Socrates talks so hopefully, and, as from this point of view one might almost say, so glibly. It is all very well to talk of getting rid of one's ignorance, of seeing things in their reality, seeing them in their beauty; but how is this to be done when there is something which thwarts and spoils all our efforts?

This something is *sin;* and the space which sin fills in Hebraism, as compared with Hellenism, is indeed prodigious. This obstacle to perfection fills the whole 80 scene, and perfection appears remote and rising away from earth, in the background. Under the name of sin, the difficulties of knowing oneself and conquering oneself which impede man's passage to perfection become, for Hebraism, a positive, active entity hostile to man, a mysterious power which I heard Dr. Pusey the other day, in one of his impressive sermons, compare to a hideous hunchback seated on our shoulders, and which it is the main business of our lives to hate and oppose. The discipline of the Old Testament may be 90 summed up as a discipline teaching us to abhor and flee from sin; the discipline of the New Testament, as a discipline teaching us to die to it. As Hellenism speaks of thinking clearly, seeing things in their essence and beauty, as a grand and precious feat for man to achieve, so Hebraism speaks of becoming conscious of sin, of awakening to a sense of sin, as a feat of this kind. It is obvious to what wide divergence these differing tendencies, actively followed, must lead. As one passes and repasses from Hellenism to Hebraism, from Plato 100

2. **"light . . . free."** Cf. John 8:12, 32: "I am the light of the world." "And ye shall know the truth, and the truth shall make you free." See also John 1:1–12. 3. **Aristotle,** a famous Greek philosopher (384–322 B.C.). The quotation is from his *Nicomachean Ethics,* 2, 3. 9. **St. James.** In James 1:25. 10. **Epictetus,** a noted Stoic philosopher (first century A.D.). The reference is to his *Discourses,* 2, 19. 14. **Plato,** a famous Greek philosopher (427–347 B.C.). The reference is to his *Gorgias.* 15. **the *Imitation,*** *Imitation of Christ,* an important devotional manual attributed to Thomas à Kempis (c. 1380–1471), a German religious writer. It traces the development of the soul toward Christian perfection through detachment from the world and union with God. 18. **"the walking . . . commandments."** From Psalms 119:32–35. 20. **"the way of peace."** From Isaiah 59:8. 21. **truth . . . law,** phrases from 2 Corinthians 5:14 and Galatians 5:24. 35. φιλομαθής, a lover of learning. 51. **sweetness and light,** a phrase that Arnold acknowledged he borrowed from Swift's *Battle of the Books;* it means beauty and intelligence. In the episode of the Spider and the Bee, Swift summarizes the superiority of the ancient writers over the modern, and says: "Instead of dirt and poison we have rather chose to fill our hives with honey and wax, thus furnishing mankind with the two noblest of things, which are sweetness and light." 57. **Socrates,** a famous Greek philosopher (fifth century B.C.); *the true Socrates* as portrayed by his

to St. Paul, one feels inclined to rub one's eyes and ask oneself whether man is indeed a gentle and simple being, showing the traces of a noble and divine nature, or an unhappy chained captive, laboring with groanings that cannot be uttered to free himself from the body of this death.

Apparently it was the Hellenic conception of human nature which was unsound, for the world could not live by it. Absolutely to call it unsound, however, is to fall 110 into the common error of its Hebraizing enemies; but it was unsound at that particular moment of man's development, it was premature. The indispensable basis of conduct and self-control, the platform upon which alone the perfection aimed at by Greece can come into bloom, was not to be reached by our race so easily; centuries of probation and discipline were needed to bring us to it. Therefore the bright promise of Hellenism faded, and Hebraism ruled the world. Then was seen that astonishing spectacle, so well marked by the often-120 quoted words of the prophet Zechariah, when men of all languages and nations took hold of the skirt of him that was a Jew, saying, "We will go with you, for we have heard that God is with you." And the Hebraism which thus received and ruled a world all gone out of the way, and altogether become unprofitable, was and could not but be the later, the more spiritual, the more attractive development of Hebraism. It was Christianity; that is to say, Hebraism aiming at self-conquest and rescue from the thrall of vile affections, not by 130 obedience to the letter of a law, but by conformity to the image of a self-sacrificing example. To a world stricken with moral enervation Christianity offered its spectacle of an inspired self-sacrifice; to men who refused themselves nothing, it showed one who refused himself everything;—"my Savior banished joy!" says George Herbert. When the *alma Venus*, the life-giving and joy-giving power of nature, so fondly cherished by the pagan world, could not save her followers from self-dissatisfaction and *ennui*, the severe words of the 140 apostle came bracingly and refreshingly: "Let no man deceive you with vain words, for because of these things cometh the wrath of God upon the children of disobedience." Through age after age and generation after generation, our race, or all that part of our race which was most living and progressive, was *baptized into a death*, and endeavored, by suffering in the flesh, to cease from sin. Of this endeavor, the animating labors and afflictions of early Christianity, the touching asceticism of medieval Christianity, are the great his-150 torical manifestations. Literary monuments of it, each in

its own way incomparable, remain in the *Epistles* of St. Paul, in St. Augustine's *Confessions*, and in the two original and simplest books of the *Imitation*.

Of two disciplines laying their main stress, the one on clear intelligence, the other on firm obedience; the one on comprehensively knowing the grounds of one's duty, the other on diligently practicing it; the one on taking all possible care (to use Bishop Wilson's words again) that the light we have be not darkness, the other that according to the best light we have we diligently 160 walk, the priority naturally belongs to that discipline which braces all man's moral powers and founds for him an indispensable basis of character. And, therefore, it is justly said of the Jewish people, who were charged with setting powerfully forth that side of the divine order to which the words "conscience" and "self-conquest" point, that they were "entrusted with the oracles of God"; as it is justly said of Christianity, which followed Judaism and which set forth this side with a much deeper effectiveness and a much 170 wider influence, that the wisdom of the old pagan world was foolishness compared to it. No words of devotion and admiration can be too strong to render thanks to these beneficent forces which have so borne forward humanity in its appointed work of coming to the knowledge and possession of itself; above all, in those great moments when their action was the wholesomest and the most necessary.

But the evolution of these forces, separately and in themselves, is not the whole evolution of humanity, 180 their single history is not the whole history of man; whereas their admirers are always apt to make it stand for the whole history. Hebraism and Hellenism are, neither of them, the *law* of human development, as their admirers are prone to make them; they are, each of them, *contributions* to human development, august contributions, invaluable contributions, and each showing itself to us more august, more invaluable, more preponderant over the other, according to the moment in which we take them and the relation in which we stand 190 to them. The nations of our modern world, children of that immense and salutary movement which broke up the pagan world, inevitably stand to Hellenism in a relation which dwarfs it and to Hebraism in a relation which magnifies it. They are inevitably prone to take Hebraism as the law of human development, and not as simply a contribution to it, however precious. And yet the lesson must perforce be learned, that the human spirit is wider than the most priceless of the forces which bear it onward, and that to the whole develop-

disciple Xenophon in *Memorabilia of Socrates*, rather than the Socrates of the *Dialogues* of Plato, in which he appears in part as the spokesman for Plato himself. The quotation is from *Memorabilia*, 4, 8. **61. Mr. Carlyle.** See p. 992. **65. at ease in Zion.** Cf. Amos 6:1: "Woe to them that are at ease in Zion." **83. knowing oneself.** See Carlyle's *Everlasting No*, p. 995, note to l. 159. **86. Dr. Pusey**, Edward B. Pusey (1800-1882), an outstanding scholar of the Anglican Church and a leader, with Newman, in the Tractarian movement at Oxford University; see p. 827. **104. chained captive**, etc. Cf. Romans 8:26: "The Spirit itself maketh intercession for us with groanings which cannot be uttered"; and 7:24: "O wretched man that I am! who shall deliver me

from the body of this death?" **117. the bright . . . Hellenism.** The flowering time of Greek culture was the fifth century B.C. **122. "We . . . you."** From Zechariah 8:23. **136. George Herbert**, poet and clergyman (1593-1633). See p. 336. The quotation is from his *The Size*, 5. **140. "Let . . . disobedience,"** words of Paul in Ephesians 5:6. **145. baptized . . . death.** From Romans 6:3. **152. St. Augustine**, one of the celebrated Fathers of the Roman Church (354-430). **167. "entrusted . . . God."** From Romans 3:2. **171. wisdom . . . foolishness.** Cf. 1 Corinthians 3:19: "For the wisdom of this world is foolishness with God."

ment of man Hebraism itself is, like Hellenism, but a contribution.

Perhaps we may help ourselves to see this clearer by an illustration drawn from the treatment of a single great idea which has profoundly engaged the human spirit, and has given it eminent opportunities for showing its nobleness and energy. It surely must be perceived that the idea of immortality, as this idea rises in its generality before the human spirit, is something grander, truer, and more satisfying than it is in the particular forms by which St. Paul, in the famous fifteenth chapter of the *Epistle to the Corinthians,* and Plato, in the *Phaedo,* endeavor to develop and establish it. Surely we cannot but feel that the argumentation with which the Hebrew apostle goes about to expound this great idea is, after all, confused and inconclusive; and that the reasoning, drawn from analogies of likeness and equality, which is employed upon it by the Greek philosopher, is over-subtle and sterile. Above and beyond the inadequate solutions which Hebraism and Hellenism here attempt, extends the immense and august problem itself, and the human spirit which gave birth to it. And this single illustration may suggest to us how the same thing happens in other cases also.

But meanwhile, by alternations of Hebraism and Hellenism, of a man's intellectual and moral impulses, of the effort to see things as they really are and the effort to win peace by self-conquest, the human spirit proceeds; and each of these two forces has its appointed hours of culmination and seasons of rule. As the great movement of Christianity was a triumph of Hebraism and man's moral impulses, so the great movement which goes by the name of the Renascence was an uprising and reinstatement of man's intellectual impulses and of Hellenism. We in England, the devoted children of Protestantism, chiefly know the Renascence by its subordinate and secondary side of the Reformation. The Reformation has been often called a Hebraizing revival, a return to the ardor and sincereness of primitive Christianity. No one, however, can study the development of Protestantism and of Protestant churches without feeling that into the Reformation too—Hebraizing child of the Renascence, and offspring of its fervor rather than its intelligence, as it undoubtedly was—the subtle Hellenic leaven of the Renascence found its way, and that the exact respective parts, in the Reformation, of Hebraism and of Hellenism are not easy to separate. But what we may with truth say is that all which Protestantism was to itself clearly conscious of, all which it succeeded in clearly setting forth in words, had the characters of Hebraism rather than of Hellenism. The Reformation was strong in that it was an earnest return to the Bible and to doing from the heart the will of God as there written. It was weak in

that it never consciously grasped or applied the central idea of the Renascence—the Hellenic idea of pursuing, in all lines of activity, the law and science, to use Plato's words, of things as they really are. Whatever direct superiority, therefore, Protestantism had over Catholicism was a moral superiority, a superiority arising out of its greater sincerity and earnestness—at the moment of its apparition, at any rate—in dealing with the heart and conscience. Its pretensions to an intellectual superiority are in general quite illusory. For Hellenism, for the thinking side in man as distinguished from the acting side, the attitude of **mind** of Protestantism towards the Bible in no respect differs from the attitude of mind of Catholicism towards the Church. The mental habit of him who imagines that Balaam's ass spoke in no respect differs from the mental habit of him who imagines that a Madonna of wood or stone winked; and the one, who says that God's Church makes him **believe** what he believes, and the other, who says that God's Word makes him believe what he believes, are for the philosopher perfectly alike in not really and truly knowing, when they say "God's Church" and "God's Word," what it is they say or whereof they affirm.

In the sixteenth century, therefore, Hellenism reëntered the world, and again stood in presence of Hebraism—a Hebraism renewed and purged. Now, it has not been enough observed, how, in the seventeenth century, a fate befell Hellenism in some respects analogous to that which befell it at the commencement of our era. The Renascence, that great reawakening of Hellenism, that irresistible return of humanity to nature and to seeing things as they are, which in art, in literature, and in physics produced such splendid fruits, had, like the anterior Hellenism of the pagan world, a side of moral weakness and of relaxation or insensibility of the moral fiber, which in Italy showed itself with the most startling plainness, but which in France, England, and other countries was very apparent too. Again this loss of spiritual balance, this exclusive preponderance given to man's perceiving and knowing side, this unnatural defect of his feeling and acting side, provoked a reaction. Let us trace that reaction where it most nearly concerns us.

Science has now made visible to everybody the great and pregnant elements of difference which lie in race, and in how signal a manner they make the genius and history of an Indo-European people vary from those of a Semitic people. Hellenism is of Indo-European growth, Hebraism is of Semitic growth; and we English, a nation of Indo-European stock, seem to belong naturally to the movement of Hellenism. But nothing more strongly marks the essential unity of man than the affinities we can percieve, in this point or that, between members of one family of peoples

11. **forms . . . it.** St. Paul rests his belief in immortality upon the spiritual appearance of Christ after his death; that appearance was observed by a number of persons including himself. In *Phaedo* (l. 65)

Plato argues for a belief in immortality on the assumption of the eternity of mind and knowledge. Opposite states, he says, come from their opposites, and because such a process is reciprocal, it follows that life

and members of another. And no affinity of this kind is more strongly marked than that likeness in the strength and prominence of the moral fiber, which, notwithstanding immense elements of difference, knits in some special sort the genius and history of us English, and our American descendants across the Atlantic, to the genius and history of the Hebrew people. Puritanism, which has been so great a power in the English nation, and in the strongest part of the English nation, was originally the reaction in the seventeenth century of the conscience and moral sense of our race against the moral indifference and lax rule of conduct which in the sixteenth century came in with the Renascence. It was a reaction of Hebraism against Hellenism; and it powerfully manifested itself, as was natural, in a people with much of what we call a Hebraizing turn, with a signal affinity for the bent which was the master-bent of Hebrew life. Eminently Indo-European by its *humor*, by the power it shows, through this gift, of imaginatively acknowledging the multiform aspects of the problem of life and of thus getting itself unfixed from its own over-certainty, of smiling at its own over-tenacity, our race has yet (and a great part of its strength lies here), in matters of practical life and moral conduct, a strong share of the assuredness, the tenacity, the intensity of the Hebrews. This turn manifested itself in Puritanism, and has had a great part in shaping our history for the last two hundred years. Undoubtedly it checked and changed amongst us that movement of the Renascence which we see producing in the reign of Elizabeth such wonderful fruits. Undoubtedly it stopped the prominent rule and direct development of that order of ideas which we call by the name of Hellenism, and gave the first rank to a different order of ideas. Apparently, too, as we said of the former defeat of Hellenism, if Hellenism was defeated this shows that Hellenism was imperfect and that its ascendency at that moment would not have been for the world's good.

Yet there is a very important difference between the defeat inflicted on Hellenism by Christianity eighteen hundred years ago, and the check given to the Renascence by Puritanism. The greatness of the difference is well measured by the difference in force, beauty, significance, and usefulness between primitive Christianity and Protestantism. Eighteen hundred years ago it was altogether the hour of Hebraism. Primitive Christianity was legitimately and truly the ascendant force in the world at that time, and the way of mankind's progress lay through its full development. Another hour in man's development began in the fifteenth century, and the main road of his progress then lay for a time through Hellenism. Puritanism was no longer the central current of the world's progress; it was a side stream crossing the central current and checking it. The cross and the check may have been necessary and salutary, but that does not do away with the essential difference between the main stream of man's advance and a cross or side stream. For more than two hundred years the main stream of man's advance has moved towards knowing himself and the world, seeing things as they are, spontaneity of consciousness; the main impulse of a great part, and that the strongest part, of our nation has been towards strictness of conscience. They have made the secondary the principal at the wrong moment, and the principal they have at the wrong moment treated as secondary. This contravention of the natural order has produced, as such contravention always must produce, a certain confusion and false movement, of which we are now beginning to feel, in almost every direction, the inconvenience. In all directions our habitual causes of action seem to be losing efficaciousness, credit, and control, both with others and even with ourselves. Everywhere we see the beginnings of confusion, and we want a clue to some sound order and authority. This we can only get by going back upon the actual instincts and forces which rule our life, seeing them as they really are, connecting them with other instincts and forces, and enlarging our whole view and rule of life.

(1867-1868)

from THE STUDY OF POETRY

The Study of Poetry appeared as the introductory essay to The English Poets, an anthology of poetry edited in 1880 by J. H. Ward. In his introduction Arnold sets forth very clearly his own theory of the meaning and function of poetry in phrases which are still quoted, gives some very practical suggestions for acquiring a taste for verse, and comments, finally, on the work of great poets in England and elsewhere. He warns the reader who would acquire a true estimate of the best in poetry to avoid the discolorations of his judgment that come from the "historic estimate" and the "personal estimate," and to seek the detachment and freedom from bias that will enable him to secure "a sense for the best, the really excellent" in poetry. The part of this concluding review which concerns English writers has been omitted in the following reprint of the essay.

"The future of poetry is immense, because in poetry, where it is worthy of its high destinies, our race, as time goes on, will find an ever surer and surer stay. There is not a creed which is not shaken, not an accredited dogma which is not shown to be ques-

---

must succeed death, since death certainly succeeds life. Cf. Wordsworth's *Ode on Immortality*, and headnote, p. 700. 69. **Balaam's ass spoke.** As related in Numbers 22:21-35. 127. ***humor,*** predominating mood or trait. 158. **Another . . . Hellenism.** The allusion is to the Renaissance. The ultimate source of the Renaissance was Greek culture.

tionable, not a received tradition which does not threaten to dissolve. Our religion has materialized itself in the fact, in the supposed fact; it has attached its emotion to the fact, and now the fact is failing it. But for poetry the idea is everything; the rest is a world of illusion, of divine illusion. Poetry attaches its emotion to the idea; the idea *is* the fact. The strongest part of our religion today is its unconscious poetry."

10 Let me be permitted to quote these words of my own, as uttering the thought which should, in my opinion, go with us and govern us in all our study of poetry. In the present work it is the course of one great contributory stream to the world-river of poetry that we are invited to follow. We are here invited to trace the stream of English poetry. But whether we set ourselves, as here, to follow only one of the several streams that make the mighty river of poetry, or whether we seek to know them all, our governing 20 thought should be the same. We should conceive of poetry worthily, and more highly than it has been the custom to conceive of it. We should conceive of it as capable of higher uses, and called to higher destinies, than those which in general men have assigned to it hitherto. More and more mankind will discover that we have to turn to poetry to interpret life for us, to console us, to sustain us. Without poetry, our science will appear incomplete; and most of what now passes with us for religion and philosophy will be replaced 30 by poetry. Science, I say, will appear incomplete without it. For finely and truly does Wordsworth call poetry "the impassioned expression which is in the countenance of all science"; and what is a countenance without its expression? Again, Wordsworth finely and truly calls poetry "the breath and finer spirit of all knowledge": our religion, parading evidences such as those on which the popular mind relies now; our philosophy, pluming itself on its reasonings about causation and finite and infinite being; what are they 40 but the shadows and dreams and false shows of knowledge? The day will come when we shall wonder at ourselves for having trusted to them, for having taken them seriously; and the more we perceive their hollowness, the more we shall prize "the breath and finer spirit of knowledge" offered to us by poetry.

But if we conceive thus highly of the destinies of poetry, we must also set our standard for poetry high, since poetry, to be capable of fulfilling such high 50 destinies, must be poetry of a high order of excellence. We must accustom ourselves to a high standard and to a strict judgment. Sainte-Beuve relates that Napoleon one day said, when somebody

was spoken of in his presence as a charlatan: "Charlatan as much as you please; but where is there *not* charlatanism?"—"Yes," answers Sainte-Beuve, "in politics, in the art of governing mankind, that is perhaps true. But in the order of thought, in art, the glory, the eternal honor is that charlatanism shall find no entrance; herein lies the inviolableness of that noble 60 portion of man's being." It is admirably said, and let us hold fast to it. In poetry, which is thought and art in one, it is the glory, the eternal honor, that charlatanism shall find no entrance; that this noble sphere be kept inviolate and inviolable. Charlatanism is for confusing or obliterating the distinctions between excellent and inferior, sound and unsound or only half-sound, true and untrue or only half-true. It is charlatanism, conscious or unconscious, whenever we confuse or obliterate these. And in poetry, more 70 than anywhere else, it is unpermissible to confuse or obliterate them. For in poetry the distinction between excellent and inferior, sound and unsound or only half-sound, true and untrue or only half-true, is of paramount importance. It is of paramount importance because of the high destinies of poetry. In poetry, as a criticism of life under the conditions fixed for such a criticism by the laws of poetic truth and poetic beauty, the spirit of our race will find, we have said, as time goes on and as other helps fail, 80 its consolation and stay. But the consolation and stay will be of power in proportion to the power of the criticism of life. And the criticism of life will be of power in proportion as the poetry conveying it is excellent rather than inferior, sound rather than unsound or half-sound, true rather than untrue or half-true.

The best poetry is what we want; the best poetry will be found to have a power of forming, sustaining, and delighting us, as nothing else can. A clearer, 90 deeper sense of the best in poetry, and of the strength and joy to be drawn from it, is the most precious benefit which we can gather from a poetical collection such as the present. And yet in the very nature and conduct of such a collection there is inevitably something which tends to obscure in us the consciousness of what our benefit should be, and to distract us from the pursuit of it. We should therefore steadily set it before our minds at the outset, and should compel ourselves to revert constantly to the thought 100 of it as we proceed.

Yes; constantly in reading poetry, a sense for the best, the really excellent, and of the strength and joy to be drawn from it, should be present in our minds and should govern our estimate of what we read. But this real estimate, the only true one, is liable to

The Study of Poetry. 2. **religion . . . fact.** An allusion to the growth of scientific knowledge and its influence on religious faith during the nineteenth century. See p. 827. 10. **these words.** Quoted with slight changes from Arnold's Introduction to *The Hundred Greatest Men* (1879). 31. **Wordsworth.** The quotations are from the *Preface to the*

Lyrical Ballads, p. 708, ll. 34 ff. 56. **Sainte-Beuve**, Charles Augustin Sainte-Beuve (1804-1869), a distinguished French literary critic, who influenced Arnold's critical theories. 93. **collection . . . present.** See headnote, p. 965. 144. **their . . . poetry**, that of the Old French period of the eleventh and twelfth centuries. The "so-called classical

be superseded, if we are not watchful, by two other kinds of estimate, the historic estimate and the personal estimate, both of which are fallacious. A poet or a poem may count to us historically, they may count to us on grounds personal to ourselves, and they may count to us really. They may count to us historically. The course of development of a nation's language, thought, and poetry is profoundly interesting; and by regarding a poet's work as a stage in this course of development we may easily bring ourselves to make it of more importance as poetry than in itself it really is, we may come to use a language of quite exaggerated praise in criticizing it; in short, to overrate it. So arises in our poetic judgments the fallacy caused by the estimate which we may call historic. Then, again, a poet or a poem may count to us on grounds personal to ourselves. Our personal affinities, liking, and circumstances have great power to sway our estimate of this or that poet's work, and to make us attach more importance to it as poetry than in itself it really possesses, because to us it is, or has been, of high importance. Here also we overrate the object of our interest, and apply to it a language of praise which is quite exaggerated. And thus we get the source of a second fallacy in our poetic judgments—the fallacy caused by an estimate which we may call personal.

Both fallacies are natural. It is evident how naturally the study of the history and development of a poetry may incline a man to pause over reputations and works once conspicuous but now obscure, and to quarrel with a careless public for skipping, in obedience to mere tradition and habit, from one famous name or work in its national poetry to another, ignorant of what it misses, and of the reason for keeping what it keeps, and of the whole process of growth in its poetry. The French have become diligent students of their own early poetry, which they long neglected; the study makes many of them dissatisfied with their so-called classical poetry, the court-tragedy of the seventeenth century, a poetry which Pellisson long ago reproached with its want of the true poetic stamp, with its *politesse stérile et rampante*, but which nevertheless has reigned in France as absolutely as if it had been the perfection of classical poetry indeed. The dissatisfaction is natural; yet a lively and accomplished critic, M. Charles d'Héricault, the editor of Clément Marot, goes too far when he says that "the cloud of glory playing round a classic is a mist as dangerous to the future of a literature as it is intolerable for the purposes of history." "It hinders," he goes on, "it hinders us from seeing more than one single point, the culminating and exceptional point; the summary, fictitious and arbitrary, of a thought and of a work. It substitutes a halo for a physiognomy, it puts a statue where there was once a man, and hiding from us all trace of the labor, the attempts, the weaknesses, the failures, it claims not study but veneration; it does not show us how the thing is done, it imposes upon us a model. Above all, for the historian this creation of classic personages is inadmissible; for it withdraws the poet from his time, from his proper life, it breaks historical relationships, it blinds criticism by conventional admiration, and renders the investigation of literary origins unacceptable. It gives us a human personage no longer, but a God seated immovable amidst His perfect work, like Jupiter on Olympus; and hardly will it be possible for the young student, to whom such work is exhibited at such a distance from him, to believe that it did not issue ready made from that divine head."

All this is brilliantly and tellingly said, but we must plead for a distinction. Everything depends on the reality of a poet's classic character. If he is a dubious classic, let us sift him; if he is a false classic, let us explode him. But if he is a real classic, if his work belongs to the class of the very best (for this is the true and right meaning of the word *classic, classical*), then the great thing for us is to feel and enjoy his work as deeply as ever we can, and to appreciate the wide difference between it and all work which has not the same high character. This is what is salutary, this is what is formative; this is the great benefit to be got from the study of poetry. Everything which interferes with it, which hinders it, is injurious. True, we must read our classic with open eyes, and not with eyes blinded with superstition; we must perceive when his work comes short, when it drops out of the class of the very best, and we must rate it, in such cases, at its proper value. But the use of this negative criticism is not in itself, it is entirely in its enabling us to have a clearer sense and a deeper enjoyment of what is truly excellent. To trace the labor, the attempts, the weaknesses, the failures of a genuine classic, to acquaint oneself with his time and his life and his historical relationship, is mere literary dilettantism unless it has that clear sense and deeper enjoyment for its end. It may be said that the more we know about a classic the better we shall enjoy him; and, if we lived as long as Methuselah and had all of us heads of perfect clearness and wills of perfect steadfastness, this might be true in fact as it is plausible in theory. But the case here is much the same as the case with the Greek and Latin studies of our schoolboys. The elaborate philo-

poetry" of the seventeenth century was noted for its emphasis upon set rules of form and correctness. 148. **Pellisson**, Paul Pellisson (1624–1693), a French writer and politician. 149. *politesse . . . rampante*, barren and inflated courtesy. 153. **d'Héricault**, a French novelist, critic, and historian of the nineteenth century. 154. **Marot**, a noted French lyric poet (*c.* 1495–1544), with a decided modern flavor. 174. **Olympus**, a mountain in Greece, the reputed home of Jupiter and the other gods. 207. **Methuselah**, one of the Hebrew patriarchs, who according to Genesis 5:27, lived 969 years.

logical groundwork which we require them to lay is in theory an admirable preparation for appreciating the Greek and Latin authors worthily. The more thoroughly we lay the groundwork, the better we shall be able, it may be said, to enjoy the authors. True, if time were not so short, and schoolboys' wits not so soon tired and their power of attention exhausted; only, as it is, the elaborate philological preparation goes on, but the authors are little known and less enjoyed. So with the investigator of "historic origins" in poetry. He ought to enjoy the true classic all the better for his investigations; he often is distracted from the enjoyment of the best, and with the less good he overbusies himself, and is prone to overrate it in proportion to the trouble which it has cost him.

The idea of tracing historic origins and historical relationships cannot be absent from a compilation like the present. And naturally the poets to be exhibited in it will be assigned to those persons for exhibition who are known to prize them highly, rather than to those who have no special inclination towards them. Moreover the very occupation with an author, and the business of exhibiting him, disposes us to affirm and amplify his importance. In the present work, therefore, we are sure of frequent temptation to adopt the historic estimate, or the personal estimate, and to forget the real estimate; which latter, nevertheless, we must employ if we are to make poetry yield us its full benefit. So high is that benefit, the benefit of clearly feeling and of deeply enjoying the really excellent, the truly classic in poetry, that we do well, I say, to set it fixedly before our minds as our object in studying poets and poetry, and to make the desire of attaining it the one principle to which, as the *Imitation* says, whatever we may read or come to know, we always return. *Cum multa legeris et cognoveris, ad unum semper oportet redire principium.*

The historic estimate is likely in especial to affect our judgment and our language when we are dealing with ancient poets; the personal estimate when we are dealing with poets our contemporaries, or at any rate modern. The exaggerations due to the historic estimate are not in themselves, perhaps, of very much gravity. Their report hardly enters the general ear; probably they do not always impose even on the literary men who adopt them. But they lead to a dangerous abuse of language. So we hear Caedmon, amongst our own poets, compared to Milton. I have already noticed the enthusiasm of one accomplished French critic for "his-

toric origins." Another eminent French critic, M. Vitet, comments upon that famous document of the early poetry of his nation, the *Chanson de Roland*. It is indeed a most interesting document. The *joculator* or *jongleur* Taillefer, who was with William the Conqueror's army at Hastings, marched before the Norman troops, so said the tradition, singing "of Charlemagne and of Roland and of Oliver, and of the vassals who died at Roncevaux"; and it is suggested that in the *Chanson de Roland* by one Turoldus or Théroulde, a poem preserved in a manuscript of the twelfth century in the Bodleian Library at Oxford, we have certainly the matter, perhaps even some of the words, of the chant which Taillefer sang. The poem has vigor and freshness; it is not without pathos. But M. Vitet is not satisfied with seeing in it a document of some poetic value, and of very high historic and linguistic value; he sees in it a grand and beautiful work, a monument of epic genius. In its general design he finds the grandiose conception, in its details he finds the constant union of simplicity with greatness, which are the marks, he truly says, of the genuine epic, and distinguish it from the artificial epic of literary ages. One thinks of Homer; this is the sort of praise which is given to Homer, and justly given. Higher praise there cannot well be, and it is the praise due to epic poetry of the highest order only, and to no other. Let us try, then, the *Chanson de Roland* at its best. Roland, mortally wounded, lays himself down under a pine-tree, with his face turned towards Spain and the enemy—

De plusurs choses à remembrer li prist,
De tantes teres cume li bers cunquist,
De dulce France, des humes de sun lign,
De Carlemagne sun seignor ki l'nurrit.

That is primitive work, I repeat, with an undeniable poetic quality of its own. It deserves such praise, and such praise is sufficient for it. But now turn to Homer—

Ὣς φάτο, τοὺς δ' ἤδη κατέχεν φυσίζοος αἶα
ἐν Λακεδαίμονι αὖθι, φίλη ἐν πατρίδι γαίη

We are here in another world, another order of poetry altogether; here is rightly due such supreme praise as that which M. Vitet gives to the *Chanson de Roland*. If our words are to have any meaning, if our judgments are to have any solidity, we must not heap

34. *Imitation.* See p. 962, note 1. 15. 36. *Cum ... principium*, although you have read and known many things, you must always return to one principle (3, 43, 2). 47. *Caedmon*, an Anglo-Saxon religious poet. See p. 8 ff. 50. *Vitet*, Ludovic Vitet (1802–1873), a French critic, dramatist, and politician. 52. *Chanson de Roland*, the Song of Roland, French national epic of the eleventh century. Roland, the hero of the poem, is a brave warrior of Charlemagne (742–814), the celebrated king of the Franks. Oliver is Roland's companion in arms. 53. *joculator or jongleur*, minstrel. 55. *Hastings*, the battle of Hastings in 1066. See p. 11 ff. 56. *Charlemagne*, Charles the Great, emperor of the West (800–814) and king of the Franks (768–814). 58. *Roncevaux*, a pass in the Pyrenees, between Spain and France, the scene of events narrated in the *Chanson*. 59. *Turoldus.* The Oxford

manuscript of the epic closes with the line, "Here ends the geste that Turoldus tells." He may have been the author of the poem, the minstrel who sang it, or the scribe who copied it. 81. *De plusurs, etc.*, "Then began he to call many things to remembrance—all the lands which his valor conquered, and pleasant France, and the men of his lineage, and Charlemagne his liege lord who nourished him"—*Chanson de Roland*, III, 939–942. 88. Ὣς φάτο, *etc.*

So said she; they long since in Earth's soft arms
    were reposing.
There in their own dear land, their fatherland,
    Lacedaemon.—*Iliad*, III, 243–244. Hawtrey's translation.
112. *brothers*, the twins Castor and Pollux, horsemen and patrons of games. 113. Ἀ δειλώ, *etc.*, "Ah, unhappy pair, why gave we you to

that supreme praise upon poetry of an order immeasurably inferior.

Indeed there can be no more useful help for discovering what poetry belongs to the class of the truly excellent, and can therefore do us most good, than to have always in one's mind lines and expressions of the great masters, and to apply them as a touchstone to other poetry. Of course we are not to require this other poetry to resemble them; it may be very dissimilar. But if we have any tact we shall find them, when we have lodged them well in our minds, an infallible touchstone for detecting the presence or absence of high poetic quality, and also the degree of this quality, in all other poetry which we may place beside them. Short passages, even single lines, will serve our turn quite sufficiently. Take the two lines which I have just quoted from Homer, the poet's comment on Helen's mention of her brothers;—or take his

Ἀ δειλώ, τί σφῶι δόμεν Πηλῆι ἄνακτι
θνητῷ; ὑμεῖς δ' ἐστὸν ἀγήρω τ' ἀθανάτω τε.
ἦ ἵνα δυστήνοισι μετ' ἀνδράσιν ἄλγε' ἔχητον;

the address of Zeus to the horses of Peleus;—or take finally his

Καὶ σέ, γέρον, τὸ πρὶν μὲν ἀκούομεν ὄλβιον εἶναι

the words of Achilles to Priam, a suppliant before him. Take that incomparable line and a half of Dante, Ugolino's tremendous words:

Io no piangeva; sì dentro impietrai.
Piangevan elli . . .

take the lovely words of Beatrice to Virgil:

Io son fatta da Dio, sua mercè, tale,
Che la vostra miseria non mi tange,
Nè fiamma d'esto incendio non m'assale . . .

take the simple, but perfect, single line:

In la sua volontade è nostra pace.

Take of Shakespeare a line or two of Henry the Fourth's expostulation with sleep:

Wilt thou upon the high and giddy mast

Seal up the ship-boy's eyes, and rock his brains
In cradle of the rude imperious surge . . .

and take, as well, Hamlet's dying request to Horatio:

If thou didst ever hold me in thy heart,
Absent thee from felicity awhile,
And in this harsh world draw thy breath in pain,
To tell my story . . .

Take of Milton that Miltonic passage:

Darkened so, yet shone
Above them all the archangel; but his face
Deep scars of thunder had intrenched, and care
Sat on his faded cheek . . .

add two such lines as:

And courage never to submit or yield
And what is else not to be overcome . . .

and finish with the exquisite close to the loss of Proserpine, the loss

. . . which cost Ceres all that pain
To seek her through the world.

These few lines, if we have tact and can use them, are enough even of themselves to keep clear and sound our judgments about poetry, to save us from fallacious estimates of it, to conduct us to a real estimate.

The specimens I have quoted differ widely from one another, but they have in common this: the possession of the very highest poetical quality. If we are thoroughly penetrated by their power, we shall find that we have acquired a sense enabling us, whatever poetry may be laid before us, to feel the degree in which a high poetical quality is present or wanting there. Critics give themselves great labor to draw out what in the abstract constitutes the characters of a high quality of poetry. It is much better simply to have recourse to concrete examples;— to take specimens of poetry of the high, the very highest quality, and to say: The characters of a high quality poetry are what is expressed *there*. They are far better recognized by being felt in the verse of the master, than by being perused in the prose of the critic. Nevertheless if we are urgently pressed to

King Peleus, to a mortal? but ye are without old age, and immortal. Was it that with men born to misery ye might have sorrow?''—*Iliad*, XVII, 443-445. 116. **Peleus**, king of Thessaly and father of Achilles, a principal character in the *Iliad*. 118. **Καὶ σέ**, etc., "Nay, and thou too, old man, in former days wast, as we hear, happy''—*Iliad*, XXIV, 543. 119. **Priam**, king of Troy at the time of the Trojan War. 120. **Dante**, the greatest of the Italian poets (1265-1321) and author of *The Divine Comedy*, written in three parts—Hell, Purgatory, and Paradise. **Ugolino**, an Italian political leader (thirteenth century) who, with his two nephews, was starved to death in prison at Pisa in 1288. Dante represents him as gnawing the head of his enemy in Hell, where both are frozen together in a lake of ice. 122. **Io no piangeva**, etc., "I wailed not; so of stone grew I within; *they* wailed''—*Inferno*,

XXXIII, 39-40. 124. **Beatrice to Virgil**. Beatrice Portinari (1266-1290) was the beautiful Italian lady celebrated in the poetry of Dante. In *The Divine Comedy*, Vergil guided Dante through Hell and Purgatory, but Beatrice guided him through Paradise. 125. **Io son fatta**, etc., "Of such sort hath God, thanked be His mercy, made me, that your misery toucheth me not, neither doth the flame of this fire strike me''—*Inferno*, II, 91-93. 129. **In . . . pace**, "In His will is our peace''—*Paradiso*, III, 851. 132. **Wilt thou**, etc. From *2 Henry IV*, III, i, 18-20. 136. **If thou didst**, etc. From *Hamlet*, V, ii, 358-360. 141. **Darkened so**, etc. From *Paradise Lost*, I, 599-602. 146. **And courage**, etc., ibid., I, 108-109. 149. **Proserpine**. See Swinburne's *The Garden of Proserpine* and headnote, p. 1113. 150. **which cost**, etc. From *Paradise Lost*, IV, 271-272.

give some critical account of them, we may safely, perhaps, venture on laying down, not indeed how and why the characters arise, but where and in what they arise. They are in the matter and substance of the poetry, and they are in its manner and style. Both of these, the substance and matter on the one hand, the style and manner on the other, have a mark, an accent of high beauty, worth, and power. But if we are asked to define this mark and accent in the abstract, our answer must be: No, for we should thereby be darkening the question, not clearing it. The mark and accent are given by the substance and matter of that poetry, by the style and manner of that poetry, and of all other poetry which is akin to it in quality.

Only one thing we may add as to the substance and matter of poetry, guiding ourselves by Aristotle's profound observation that the superiority of poetry over history consists in its possessing a higher truth and a higher seriousness (φιλοσοφώτερον καὶ σπουδαιότερον). Let us add, therefore, to what we have said, this: that the substance and matter of the best poetry acquire their special character from possessing, in an eminent degree, truth and seriousness. We may add yet further, what is in itself evident, that to the style and manner of the best poetry their special character, their accent, is given by their diction, and, even yet more, by their movement. And though we distinguish between the two characters, the two accents, of superiority, yet they are nevertheless vitally connected one with the other. The superior character of truth and seriousness, in the matter and substance of the best poetry, is inseparable from the superiority of diction and movement marking its style and manner. The two superiorities are closely related, and are in steadfast proportion one to the other. So far as high poetic truth and seriousness are wanting to a poet's matter and substance, so far also, we may be sure, will a high poetic stamp of diction and movement be wanting to his style and manner. In proportion as this high stamp of diction and movement, again, is absent from a poet's style and manner, we shall find, also, that high poetic truth and seriousness are absent from his substance and matter.

[In the rest of the essay Arnold traces the history of poetry in France and in England.]
(1880)

16. **Aristotle**, a famous Greek philosopher (384–322 B.C.). 19. φιλοσοφώτερον, **etc.,** ''more philosophic and more serious''—*Poetics*, 9.

PROPHETS IN PROSE

JOHN HENRY NEWMAN 1801-1890

It would not be difficult to build a case for the proposition that John Henry Newman was the finest prose stylist among the Victorians; and it would not be foolhardy, at least, to go a step further and say that he was not only their best prose stylist, but also their clearest, most honest, and most subtle thinker. He was as critical of slipshod logic as was Bentham, but this did not drive him into Bentham's over-wary and limited understanding of human nature—its motives and its possibilities. He was as much a master of the architectonics of ''the grand style'' as was Macaulay, but an understanding of Macaulay's stylistic blemishes practically provides one with a catalogue of Newman's stylistic merits. He was as humane as was John Stuart Mill, but he never deserted his premises to avoid a harsh or unwanted conclusion. He understood the value and importance of the Hellenic ideal as well as Arnold and Pater understood it; but he knew, too, that the difference between moral and intellectual excellence was a difference, not of degree, but of kind. Like Browning, he recognized that the cultured or educated man was not the infallible tribunal that some would make him. Since he had searched his beliefs more carefully than had Carlyle, personal disappointment did not drive him from his philosophical principles as it did Carlyle. Carlyle lived by a kind of desperate hope;

Newman's intellectual equanimity rested on a faith whose logic had been austerely analyzed.

Newman was born in London and educated at Oxford; after graduation he became a Fellow of Oriel College, Oxford, and later vicar of St. Mary's Church. He visited Italy in 1833, returning to England just as the theological war began; he contributed much to the series of prose tracts known as Tracts for the Times, which, with the pulpits of England, were the chief outlets for the ideas of these Oxford reformers. Gradually coming to believe that there were only two alternatives before him—the road to Rome or the road to atheism—Newman ultimately chose the former, not without great spiritual struggle. He left Oxford, resigned his charge, and was received into the Roman Catholic Church (1845); ordained in Rome the following year, he thenceforth became one of the most prominent English Catholic clergymen of the century.

Four of Newman's books continue, by their content and style, to assert their importance to and influence on modern thought. The Apologia pro Vita Sua (1864) is the greatest autobiography of an age of great autobiographies. It is a document in revelation, not only of the whole personality of Newman, but also of the age in which he lived. The Idea of a University (1873) contains, in full exposition or by implication, a considered statement on all of the intellectual issues still facing higher education. By virtue of its subject matter, its admirable reasoning, its rhythmic control, and its euphony, The Idea of a University is the most compelling of Newman's books for the general reader. In it, Newman faces every issue boldly in a style that combines simplicity with elaboration and regularity with infinite variety. His modulated voice comes from the printed page quite as audibly as it came from his mouth in the drab lecture-room in Dublin when the discourses were originally delivered. A Grammar of Assent (1870) and The Development of Christian Doctrine (1845) are more specialized, but they continue to be widely respected; the latter, for example, was frequently and favorably quoted in the proceedings of Vatican Council II.

Newman's art cost him heavily. "I write," he said, "I write again: I write a third time in the course of six months. Then I take the third: I literally fill the paper with corrections, so that another person could not read it. I then write it out fair for the printer. I put it by; I take it up; I begin to correct again: it will not do. Alterations multiply, pages are re-written, little lines sneak in and crawl about. The whole page is disfigured; I write again; I cannot count how many times this process is repeated." Nor was he compensated for his labor with the "keen and constant pleasure" which some writers claim: "It is one of my sayings, (so continually do I feel it) that the composition of a volume is like gestation and birth. I do not think that I ever thought out a question, or wrote my thoughts, without great pain, pain reaching to the body as well as to the mind. It has made me feel practically, that labour 'in sudore vultus sui' ['in the sweat of his brow'], is the lot of man, and that ignorance is truly one of his four wounds."

From May 10 to June 7, 1852, Newman delivered nine lectures to the Catholics of Dublin. In the same year these lectures were published as Discourses on the Scope and Nature of a University Education. Afterwards they were republished with some alterations, together with a series of "Occasional Lectures and Essays on University Subjects," as The Idea of a University (1873). Newman's principal concern was lest the Liberals substitute the subtle fault for the gross fault. To make knowledge the test of admirable men was to destroy the place of good and evil in admiration. Rationalism, the philosophical basis of Liberalism, was more concerned, said Newman, with concluding rightly than with right conclusions. Thus his purpose was not to attack secular knowledge but to expose the fallacy and resist the pretense that secular knowledge was more than it was or could do more than it could.

from THE IDEA OF A UNIVERSITY

In 1854 Newman was appointed rector of the newly established Catholic University of Dublin. Two years before his formal appointment he delivered a series of lectures on The Scope and Nature of University Education. In 1859 appeared another series, Lectures on Universities. Both series were published in 1873 under the title The Idea of a University. In these discourses Newman opposed the doctrine that university instruction should diffuse useful knowledge and argued, among other things, that the function of the university should be to discipline the mind very much as exercise disciplines the body. He also insisted—quite naturally—that religious training should be a part of this discipline. His educational definitions are so logical and clear that they have been accepted widely by educators who have faith in the value of a training in the liberal arts.

DISCOURSE V

KNOWLEDGE ITS OWN END

A university may be considered with reference either to its Students or to its Studies; and the principle, that all Knowledge is a whole and the separate Sciences parts of one, which I have hitherto been using in behalf of its studies, is equally important when we direct our attention to its students. Now then I turn to the students, and shall consider the education which, by virtue of this principle, a University will give them; and thus I shall be introduced, Gentlemen, to the second question, which I proposed to discuss, viz., whether and 10 in what sense its teaching, viewed relatively to the taught, carries the attribute of Utility along with it.

1.

I have said that all branches of knowledge are connected together, because the subject-matter of knowledge is intimately united in itself, as being the acts and the work of the Creator. Hence it is that the Sciences, into which our knowledge may be said to be cast, have multiplied bearings one on another, and an internal sympathy, and admit, or rather demand, comparison and adjustment. They complete, correct, balance each 20 other. This consideration, if well-founded, must be taken into account, not only as regards the attainment of truth, which is their common end, but as regards the influence which they exercise upon those whose education consists in the study of them. I have said already, that to give undue prominence to one is to be unjust to another; to neglect or supersede these is to divert those from their proper object. It is to unsettle the boundary lines between science and science, to disturb their action, to destroy the harmony which 30 binds them together. Such a proceeding will have a corresponding effect when introduced into a place of education. There is no science but tells a different tale, when viewed as a portion of a whole, from what it is likely to suggest when taken by itself, without the safeguard, as I may call it, of others.

Knowledge Its Own End. 4. hitherto, in earlier lectures in the series; see headnote. 9. second question. The first was whether theology has a place in university teaching.

Let me make use of an illustration. In the combination of colors, very different effects are produced by a difference in their selection and juxtaposition; red, green, and white change their shades, according to the contrast to which they are submitted. And, in like manner, the drift and meaning of a branch of knowledge varies with the company in which it is introduced to the student. If his reading is confined simply to one subject, however such division of labor may favor the
10 advancement of a particular pursuit, a point into which I do not here enter, certainly it has a tendency to contract his mind. If it is incorporated with others, it depends on those others as to the kind of influence which it exerts upon him. Thus the Classics, which in England are the means of refining the taste, have in France subserved the spread of revolutionary and deistical doctrines. In Metaphysics, again, Butler's *Analogy of Religion* which has had so much to do with the conversion of members of the University of Oxford,
20 appeared to Pitt and others, who had received a different training, to operate only in the direction of infidelity. And so again, Watson, Bishop of Llandaff, as I think he tells us in the narrative of his life, felt the science of Mathematics to indispose the mind to religious belief, while others see in its investigations the best defense of the Christian Mysteries. In like manner, I suppose, Arcesilaus would not have handled logic as Aristotle, nor Aristotle have criticized poets as Plato; yet reasoning and poetry are subject to
30 scientific rules.

It is a great point then to enlarge the range of studies which a University professes, even for the sake of the students; and, though they cannot pursue every subject which is open to them, they will be the gainers by living among those and under those who represent the whole circle. This I conceive to be the advantage of a seat of universal learning, considered as a place of education. An assemblage of learned men, zealous for their own sciences, and rivals of each other, are
40 brought, by familiar intercourse and for the sake of intellectual peace, to adjust together the claims and relations of their respective subjects of investigation. They learn to respect, to consult, to aid each other. Thus is created a pure and clear atmosphere of thought, which the student also breathes, though in his own case he only pursues a few sciences out of the multitude. He profits by an intellectual tradition, which is independent of particular teachers, which guides him in his choice of subjects, and duly inter-
50 prets for him those which he chooses. He apprehends the great outlines of knowledge, the principles on which it rests, the scale of its parts, its lights and its shades, its great points and its little, as he

otherwise cannot apprehend them. Hence it is that his education is called "Liberal." A habit of mind is formed which lasts through life, of which the attributes are, freedom, equitableness, calmness, moderation, and wisdom; or what in a former Discourse I have ventured to call a philosophical habit. This then I would assign as the special fruit of the educa- 60 tion furnished at a University, as contrasted with other places of teaching or modes of teaching. This is the main purpose of a University in its treatment of its students.

And now the question is asked me, What is the *use* of it? And my answer will constitute the main subject of the Discourses which are to follow.

2.

Cautious and practical thinkers, I say, will ask of me, what, after all, is the gain of this Philosophy, of which I make such account, and from which I promise 70 so much. Even supposing it to enable us to give the degree of confidence exactly due to every science respectively, and to estimate precisely the value of every truth which is anywhere to be found, how are we better for this master view of things, which I have been extolling? Does it not reverse the principle of the division of labor? will practical objects be obtained better or worse by its cultivation? to what then does it lead? where does it end? what does it do? how does it profit? what does it promise? Particular sciences 80 are respectively the basis of definite arts, which carry on to results tangible and beneficial the truths which are the subjects of the knowledge attained; what is the Art of this science of sciences? what is the fruit of such a Philosophy? what are we proposing to effect, what inducements do we hold out to the Catholic community, when we set about the enterprise of founding a University?

I am asked what is the end of University Education, and of the Liberal or Philosophical Knowledge which I 90 conceive it to impart: I answer, that what I have already said has been sufficient to show that it has a very tangible, real, and sufficient end, though the end cannot be divided from that knowledge itself. Knowledge is capable of being its own end. Such is the constitution of the human mind, that any kind of knowledge, if it be really such, is its own reward. And if this is true of all knowledge, it is true also of that special Philosophy, which I have made to consist in a comprehensive view of truth in all its branches, of the 100 relations of science to science, of their mutual bearings, and their respective values. What the worth of such an acquirement is, compared with other objects which

14. **Classics . . . doctrines.** From the beginning of the Renaissance the classics gave a cultural impetus to English life and thought; but in France, the Catholic University of Paris objected to that type of learning. Greek was regarded as the language of the devil. Hence the study of the classics forced many devotees of learning into the camp at war with Rome. 17. **Butler,** Joseph Butler (1692–1752), an English prelate

and theologian. His *Analogy of Religion,* published in 1736, was written to counteract the influence of deists and other freethinkers of the day. As an effective exposition of revealed or supernatural religion, it won many followers. 20. **Pitt,** William Pitt (1708–1778), a famous Whig statesman and orator. 22. **Watson,** Richard Watson (1737–1816), an English prelate, theological writer, and chemist. 27. **Arcesilaus,** a

we seek—wealth or power or honor or the conveniences and comforts of life—I do not profess here to discuss; but I would maintain, and mean to show, that it is an object, in its own nature so really and undeniably good, as to be the compensation of a great deal of thought in the compassing, and a great deal of trouble in the attaining.

Now, when I say that Knowledge is, not merely a means to something beyond it, or the preliminary of certain arts into which it naturally resolves, but an end sufficient to rest in and to pursue for its own sake, surely I am uttering no paradox, for I am stating what is both intelligible in itself, and has ever been the common judgment of philosophers and the ordinary feeling of mankind. I am saying what at least the public opinion of this day ought to be slow to deny, considering how much we have heard of late years, in opposition to Religion, of entertaining, curious, and various knowledge. I am but saying what whole volumes have been written to illustrate, by a "selection from the records of Philosophy, Literature, and Art, in all ages and countries, of a body of examples, to show how the most unpropitious circumstances have been unable to conquer an ardent desire for the acquisition of knowledge." That further advantages accrue to us and redound to others by its possession, over and above what it is in itself, I am very far indeed from denying; but, independent of these, we are satisfying a direct need of our nature in its very acquisition; and, whereas our nature, unlike that of the inferior creation, does not at once reach its perfection, but depends, in order to it, on a number of external aids and appliances, Knowledge, as one of the principal gifts or accessories by which it is completed, is valuable for what its very presence in us does for us after the manner of a habit, even though it be turned to no further account, nor subserve any direct end.

3.

Hence it is that Cicero, in enumerating the various heads of mental excellence, lays down the pursuit of Knowledge for its own sake, as the first of them. "This pertains most of all to human nature," he says, "for we are all of us drawn to the pursuit of Knowledge; in which to excel we consider excellent, whereas to mistake, to err, to be ignorant, to be deceived, is both an evil and a disgrace." And he considers Knowledge the very first object to which we are attracted, after the supply of our physical wants. After the calls and duties of our animal existence, as they may be termed, as regards ourselves, our family, and our neighbors, follows, he tells us, "the search after truth. Accordingly, as soon as we escape from the pressure of necessary cares, forthwith we desire to see, to hear, to learn; and consider the knowledge of what is hidden or is wonderful a condition of our happiness."

This passage, though it is but one of many similar passages in a multitude of authors, I take for the very reason that it is so familiarly known to us; and I wish you to observe, Gentlemen, how distinctly it separates the pursuit of Knowledge from those ulterior objects to which certainly it can be made to conduce, and which are, I suppose, solely contemplated by the persons who would ask of me the use of a University or Liberal Education. So far from dreaming of the cultivation of Knowledge directly and mainly in order to our physical comfort and enjoyment, for the sake of life and person, of health, of the conjugal and family union, of the social tie and civil security, the great Orator implies, that it is only after our physical and political needs are supplied, and when we are "free from necessary duties and cares," that we are in a condition for "desiring to see, to hear, and to learn." Nor does he contemplate in the least degree the reflex or subsequent action of Knowledge, when acquired, upon those material goods which we set out by securing before we seek it; on the contrary, he expressly denies its bearing upon social life altogether, strange as such a procedure is to those who live after the rise of the Baconian philosophy, and he cautions us against such a cultivation of it as will interfere with our duties to our fellow-creatures. "All these methods," he says, "are engaged in the investigation of truth; by the pursuit of which to be carried off from public occupations is a transgression of duty. For the praise of virtue lies altogether in action; yet intermissions often occur, and then we recur to such pursuits; not to say that the incessant activity of the mind is vigorous enough to carry us on in the pursuit of knowledge, even without any exertion of our own." The idea of benefiting society by means of "the pursuit of science and knowledge," did not enter at all into the motives which he would assign for their cultivation.

This was the ground of the opposition which the elder Cato made to the introduction of Greek Philosophy among his countrymen, when Carneades and his companions, on occasion of their embassy, were charming the Roman youth with their eloquent expositions of it. The fit representative of a practical people, Cato estimated everything by what it produced; whereas the Pursuit of Knowledge promised nothing beyond Knowledge itself. He despised that refinement or enlargement of mind of which he had no experience.

Greek skeptical philosopher (316?–241? B.C.). 58. **former Discourse,** Discourse IV, 3. 120. **much . . . knowledge.** This was an age of conflict between science and religion. 123. **"selection from,"** etc., from *The Pursuit of Knowledge under Difficulties,* by George Lillie Craik (1798–1866). 143. **"This pertains,"** etc., from Cicero's *De Officio, Initium.* 180: **Baconian philosophy,** Francis Bacon (p. 317) believed that man should be supreme over nature because of the practical benefits that would result. 196. **elder Cato,** Marcus Porcius Cato (234–149 B.C.), a Roman patriot. 197. **Carneades . . . companions.** Carneades was a Greek skeptical philosopher and rhetorician (c. 213–129 B.C.). With Diogenes the Stoic and Critolaüs, he was sent as ambassador to Rome in 155 B.C.

4.

Things, which can bear to be cut off from everything else and yet persist in living, must have life in themselves; pursuits, which issue in nothing, and still maintain their ground for ages, which are regarded as admirable, though they have not as yet proved themselves to be useful, must have their sufficient end in themselves, whatever it turn out to be. And we are brought to the same conclusion by considering the force of the epithet, by which the knowledge under consideration is popularly designated. It is common to speak of *"liberal* knowledge," of the *"liberal* arts and studies," and of a *"liberal* education," as the especial characteristic or property of a University and of a gentleman; what is really meant by the word? Now, first, in its grammatical sense it is opposed to *servile;* and by "servile work" is understood, as our catechisms inform us, bodily labor, mechanical employment, and the like, in which the mind has little or no part. Parallel to such works are those arts, if they deserve the name of which the poet speaks, which owe their origin and their method to hazard, not to skill; as, for instance, the practice and operations of an empiric. As far as this contrast may be considered as a guide into the meaning of the word, liberal knowledge and liberal pursuits are exercises of mind, of reason, of reflection.

But we want something more for its explanation, for there are bodily exercises which are liberal, and mental exercises which are not so. For instance, in ancient times the practitioners in medicine were commonly slaves; yet it was an art as intellectual in its nature, in spite of the pretense, fraud, and quackery with which it might then, as now, be debased, as it was heavenly in its aim. And so in like manner, we contrast a liberal education with a commercial education or a professional; yet no one can deny that commerce and the professions afford scope for the highest and most diversified powers of mind. There is then a great variety of intellectual exercises, which are not technically called "liberal"; on the other hand, I say, there are exercises of the body which do receive that appellation. Such, for instance, was the palaestra, in ancient times; such the Olympic games, in which strength and dexterity of body as well as of mind gained the prize. In Xenophon we read of the young Persian nobility being taught to ride on horseback and to speak the truth—both being among the accomplishments of a gentleman. War, too, however rough a profession, has ever been accounted liberal, unless in cases when it becomes heroic, which would introduce us to another subject.

Now comparing these instances together, we shall have no difficulty in determining the principle of this apparent variation in the application of the term which I am examining. Manly games, or games of skill, or military prowess, though bodily, are, it seems, accounted liberal; on the other hand, what is merely professional, though highly intellectual, nay, though liberal in comparison of trade and manual labor, is not simply called liberal, and mercantile occupations are not liberal at all. Why this distinction? because that alone is liberal knowledge, which stands on its own pretentions, which is independent of sequel, expects no complement, refuses to be *informed* (as it is called) by any end, or absorbed into any art, in order duly to present itself to our contemplation. The most ordinary pursuits have this specific character, if they are self-sufficient and complete; the highest lose it, when they minister to something beyond them. It is absurd to balance, in point of worth and importance, a treatise on reducing fractures with a game of cricket or a fox-chase; yet of the two the bodily exercise has that quality which we call "liberal," and the intellectual has it not. And so of the learned professions altogether, considered merely as professions; although one of them be the most popularly beneficial, and another the most politically important, and the third the most intimately divine of all human pursuits, yet the very greatness of their end, the health of the body, or of the commonwealth, or of the soul, diminishes, not increases, their claim to the appellation "liberal," and that still more, if they are cut down to the strict exigencies of that end. If, for instance, Theology, instead of being cultivated as a contemplation, be limited to the purposes of the pulpit or be represented by the catechism, it loses—not its usefulness, not its divine character, not its meritoriousness (rather it increases these qualities by such charitable condescension)—but it does lose the particular attribute which I am illustrating; just as a face worn by tears and fasting loses its beauty, or a laborer's hand loses its delicateness;—for Theology thus exercised is not simple knowledge, but rather is an art or a business making use of Theology. And thus it appears that even what is supernatural need not be liberal, nor need a hero be a gentleman, for the plain reason that one idea is not another idea. And in like manner the Baconian Philosophy, by using its physical sciences in the service of man, does thereby transfer them from the order of Liberal Pursuits to, I do not say the inferior, but the distinct class of the Useful. And, to take a different instance, hence again, as is evident, whenever personal gain is the motive, still more distinctive an effect has it upon the character of a given pursuit; thus racing, which was a liberal exercise in Greece, forfeits its rank in times like these, so far as it is made the occasion of gambling.

All that I have been now saying is summed up in a

19. name . . . speaks. In a note Newman cites Aristotle, *Nichomachean Ethics,* 6: "Art loves fate and fate loves art." **22. empiric,** one who forms judgments upon the basis of practical experience. **41. palaestra,** a place for athletic exercises, especially wrestling. **42. Olympic games,** a famous Greek festival held every four years in which contests were held in various athletic games. **44. Xenophon,** an Athenian historian and general (434?–355? B.C.). **63. informed,** endowed with form. **73. learned professions,** medicine, law, and theology. **107. the great**

few characteristic words of the great Philosopher. "Of possessions," he says, "those rather are useful, which bear fruit; those *liberal, which tend to enjoyment*. By 110 fruitful, I mean, which yield revenue; by enjoyable, where *nothing accrues of consequence beyond the use*."

5.

Do not suppose, Gentlemen, that in thus appealing to the ancients, I am throwing back the world two thousand years, and fettering Philosophy with the reasonings of paganism. While the world lasts, will Aristotle's doctrine on these matters last, for he is the oracle of nature and of truth. While we are men, we cannot help, to a great extent, being Aristotelians, for the great Master does but analyze the 120 thoughts, feelings, views, and opinions of human kind. He has told us the meaning of our own words and ideas, before we were born. In many subject-matters, to think correctly, is to think like Aristotle; and we are his disciples whether we will or no, though we may not know it. Now, as to the particular instance before us, the word "liberal" as applied to Knowledge and Education, expresses a specific idea, which ever has been, and ever will be, while the nature of man is the same, just as the idea of the 130 Beautiful is specific, or of the Sublime, or of the Ridiculous, or of the Sordid. It is in the world now, it was in the world then; and, as in the case of the dogmas of faith, it is illustrated by a continuous historical tradition, and never was out of the world, from the time it came into it. There have indeed been differences of opinion from time to time, as to what pursuits and what arts came under that idea, but such differences are but an additional evidence of its reality. That idea must have a substance in it, which has 140 maintained its ground amid these conflicts and changes, which has ever served as a standard to measure things withal, which has passed from mind to mind unchanged, when there was so much to color, so much to influence any notion or thought whatever, which was not founded in our very nature. Were it a mere generalization, it would have varied with the subjects from which it was generalized; but though its subjects vary with the age, it varies not itself. The palaestra may seem a liberal exercise 150 to Lycurgus, and illiberal to Seneca; coach-driving and prize-fighting may be recognized in Elis, and be condemned in England; music may be despicable in the eyes of certain moderns, and be in the highest place with Aristotle and Plato—(and the case is the same in the particular application of the idea of Beauty, or of Goodness, or of Moral Virtue, there is a difference of tastes, a difference of judgments)—still these varia-

tions imply, instead of discrediting, the archetypal idea, which is but a previous hypothesis or condition, by means of which issue is joined between contend- 160 ing opinions, and without which there would be nothing to dispute about.

I consider, then, that I am chargeable with no paradox, when I speak of a Knowledge which is its own end, when I call it liberal knowledge, or a gentleman's knowledge, when I educate for it, and make it the scope of a University. And still less am I incurring such a charge, when I make this acquisition consist, not in Knowledge in a vague and ordinary sense, but in that Knowledge which I have especially 170 called Philosophy or, in an extended sense of the word, Science; for whatever claims Knowledge has to be considered as a good, these it has in a higher degree when it is viewed not vaguely, not popularly, but precisely and transcendently as Philosophy. Knowledge, I say, is then especially liberal or sufficient for itself, apart from every external and ulterior object, when and so far as it is philosophical, and this I proceed to show.

6.

Now bear with me, Gentlemen, if what I am about 180 to say, has at first sight a fanciful appearance. Philosophy, then, or Science, is related to Knowledge in this way: Knowledge is called by the name of Science or Philosophy, when it is acted upon, informed, or if I may use a strong figure, impregnated by Reason. Reason is the principle of that intrinsic fecundity of Knowledge, which, to those who possess it, is its especial value, and which dispenses with the necessity of their looking abroad for any end to rest upon external to itself. Knowledge, indeed, when thus 190 exalted into a scientific form, is also power; not only is it excellent in itself, but whatever such excellence may be, it is something more, it has a result beyond itself. Doubtless; but that is a further consideration, with which I am not concerned. I only say that, prior to its being a power, it is a good; that it is, not only an instrument, but an end. I know well it may resolve itself into an art, and terminate in a mechanical process, and in tangible fruit; but it also may fall back upon that Reason, which informs 200 it, and resolve itself into Philosophy. In one case it is called Useful Knowledge, in the other Liberal. The same person may cultivate it in both ways at once; but this again is a matter foreign to my subject; here I do but say that there are two ways of using Knowledge, and in matter of fact those who use it in one way are not likely to use it in the other, or at least in a very limited measure. You see, then, here are two

---

Philosopher, Aristotle. The quotation is from his *Rhetoric*, I, 5. 115. While . . . truth. Newman was one of the numerous worshipers of Aristotle; indeed, many of the greatest systems of philosophy owe to Aristotle their chief ideas and methods. 150. Lycurgus, a Spartan lawgiver (ninth century B.C.). Seneca, a Roman Stoic philosopher and author (first century A.D.). 151. Elis, an ancient division of Greece. 158. archetypal, constituting a model.

methods of Education; the end of the one is to be philosophical, of the other to be mechanical; the one rises towards general ideas, the other is exhausted upon what is particular and external. Let me not be thought to deny the necessity, or to decry the benefit, of such attention to what is particular and practical, as belongs to the useful or mechanical arts; life could not go on without them; we owe our daily welfare to them; their exercise is the duty of the many, and we owe to the many a debt of gratitude for fulfilling that duty. I only say that Knowledge, in proportion as it tends more and more to be particular, ceases to be Knowledge. It is a question whether Knowledge can in any proper sense be predicated of the brute creation; without pretending to metaphysical exactness of phraseology, which would be unsuitable to an occasion like this, I say, it seems to me improper to call that passive sensation, or perception of things, which brutes seem to possess, by the name of Knowledge. When I speak of Knowledge, I mean something intellectual, something which grasps what it perceives through the senses; something which takes a view of things; which sees more than the senses convey; which reasons upon what it sees, and while it sees; which invests it with an idea. It expresses itself, not in a mere enunciation, but by an enthymeme: it is of the nature of science from the first, and in this consists its dignity. The principle of real dignity in Knowledge, its worth, its desirableness, considered irrespectively of its results, is this germ within it of a scientific or a philosophical process. This is how it comes to be an end in itself; this is why it admits of being called Liberal. Not to know the relative disposition of things is the state of slaves or children; to have mapped out the Universe is the boast, or at least the ambition, of Philosophy.

Moreover, such knowledge is not a mere extrinsic or accidental advantage, which is ours today and another's tomorrow, which may be got up from a book, and easily forgotten again, which we can command or communicate at our pleasure, which we can borrow for the occasion, carry about in our hand, and take into the market; it is an acquired illumination, it is a habit, a personal possession, and an inward endowment. And this is the reason, why it is more correct, as well as more usual, to speak of a University as a place of education, than of instruction, though, when knowledge is concerned, instruction would at first sight have seemed the more appropriate word. We are instructed, for instance, in manual exercises, in the fine and useful arts, in trades, and in ways of business; for these are methods, which have little or no effect upon the mind itself, are contained in rules committed to memory, to tradition, or to use, and bear upon an end external to themselves. But education is a higher word; it implies an action upon our mental nature, and the formation of a character; it is something individual and permanent, and is commonly spoken of in connection with religion and virtue. When, then, we speak of the communication of Knowledge as being Education, we thereby really imply that that Knowledge is a state or condition of mind; and since cultivation of mind is surely worth seeking for its own sake, we are thus brought once more to the conclusion, which the word "Liberal" and the word "Philosophy" have already suggested, that there is a Knowledge, which is desirable, though nothing come of it, as being of itself a treasure, and a sufficient remuneration of years of labor.

7.

This, then, is the answer which I am prepared to give to the question with which I opened this Discourse. Before going on to speak of the object of the Church in taking up Philosophy, and the uses to which she puts it, I am prepared to maintain that Philosophy is its own end, and, as I conceive, I have now begun proving it. I am prepared to maintain that there is a knowledge worth possessing for what it is, and not merely for what it does; and what minutes remain to me today I shall devote to the removal of some portion of the indistinctness and confusion with which the subject may in some minds be surrounded.

It may be objected then, that, when we profess to seek Knowledge for some end or other beyond itself, whatever it be, we speak intelligibly; but that, whatever men may have said, however obstinately the idea may have kept its ground from age to age, still it is simply unmeaning to say that we seek Knowledge for its own sake, and for nothing else; for that it ever leads to something beyond itself, which therefore is its end, and the cause why it is desirable;—moreover, that this end is twofold, either of this world or of the next; that all knowledge is cultivated either for secular objects or for eternal; that if it is directed to secular objects, it is called Useful Knowledge, if to eternal, Religious or Christian Knowledge;—in consequence, that if, as I have allowed, this Liberal Knowledge does not benefit the body or estate, it ought to benefit the soul; but if the fact be really so, that it is neither a physical or a secular good on the

26. **enthymeme,** a process of logical reasoning. 121. **time . . . world,** the fifth century B.C., the period of the great philosophers, dramatists, and orators. 133. **Cicero.** He was assassinated in 43 B.C. because of his attack upon Antony. 134. **Seneca . . . tyrant.** Because he was charged with having a share in the conspiracy against the tyrant Nero in 65 A.D., Seneca was forced to commit suicide. 135. **Brutus,** Marcus Junius Brutus (85–42 B.C.), one of the assassins of Julius Caesar. Defeated in battle by Octavius, Brutus committed suicide. 137. **Cato,**

Marcus Cato, the Younger (95–46 B.C.), who upon hearing of Ceasar's victory at Thapsus, committed suicide at Utica, North Africa, rather than be conquered. Cato had several panegyrists. The Roman poet Lucan, in his epic *Pharsalia,* spoke of Cato as "the noblest Roman of them all"; and Addison (p. 473) exalted Cato in his classical tragedy *Cato.* 139. **Polemo,** an Athenian Platonic philosopher, a man of great wealth and political distinction (d. 273 B.C.). In his youth he was extremely profligate, but upon hearing a discourse on temperance in

one hand, nor a moral good on the other, it cannot be a good at all, and is not worth the trouble which is necessary for its acquisition.

And then I may be reminded that the professors of this Liberal or Philosophical Knowledge have themselves, in every age, recognized this exposition of the matter, and have submitted to the issue in which it terminates; for they have ever been attempting to make men virtuous; or, if not, at least have assumed that refinement of mind was virtue, and that they themselves were the virtuous portion of mankind. This they have professed on the one hand; and on the other, they have utterly failed in their professions, so as ever to make themselves a proverb among men, and a laughing stock both to the grave and the dissipated portion of mankind, in consequence of them. Thus they have furnished against themselves both the ground and the means of their own exposure, without any trouble at all to anyone else. In a word, from the time that Athens was the University of the world, what has Philosophy taught men, but to promise without practicing, and to aspire without attaining? What has the deep and lofty thought of its disciples ended in but eloquent words? Nay, what has its teaching ever meditated, when it was boldest in its remedies for human ill, beyond charming us to sleep by its lessons, that we might feel nothing at all? like some melodious air, or rather like those strong and transporting perfumes, which at first spread their sweetness over everything they touch, but in a little while do but offend in proportion as they once pleased us. Did Philosophy support Cicero under the disfavor of the fickle populace, or nerve Seneca to oppose an imperial tyrant? It abandoned Brutus, as he sorrowfully confessed, in his greatest need, and it forced Cato, as his panegyrist strangely boasts, into the false position of defying heaven. How few can be counted among its professors, who, like Polemo, were thereby converted from a profligate course, or like Anaxagoras, thought the world well lost in exchange for its possession? The philosopher in *Rasselas* taught a superhuman doctrine, and then succumbed without an effort to a trial of human affection.

"He discoursed," we are told, "with great energy on the government of the passions. His look was venerable, his action graceful, his pronunciation clear, and his diction elegant. He showed, with great strength of sentiment and variety of illustration, that human nature is degraded and debased, when the lower faculties predominate over the higher. He communicated the various precepts given, from time to time, for the conquest of passion, and displayed the happiness of those who had obtained the important victory, after which man is no longer the slave of fear, nor the fool of hope. . . . He enumerated many examples of heroes immovable by pain or pleasure, who looked with indifference on those modes or accidents to which the vulgar give the names of good and evil."

Rasselas in a few days found the philosopher in a room half darkened, with his eyes misty, and his face pale. "Sir," said he, "you have come at a time when all human friendship is useless; what I suffer cannot be remedied, what I have lost cannot be supplied. My daughter, my only daughter, from whose tenderness I expected all the comforts of my age, died last night of a fever." "Sir," said the prince, "mortality is an event by which a wise man can never be surprised; we know that death is always near, and it should therefore always be expected." "Young man," answered the philosopher, "you speak like one who has never felt the pangs of separation." "Have you, then, forgot the precept," said Rasselas, "which you so powerfully enforced? . . . consider that external things are naturally variable, but truth and reason are always the same." "What comfort," said the mourner, "can truth and reason afford me? Of what effect are they now, but to tell me that my daughter will not be restored?"

8.

Better, far better, to make no professions, you will say, than to cheat others with what we are not, and to scandalize them with what we are. The sensualist, or the man of the world, at any rate is not the victim of fine words, but pursues a reality and gains it. The Philosophy of Utility, you will say, Gentlemen, has at least done its work; and I grant it—it aimed low, but it has fulfilled its aim. If that man of great intellect who has been its Prophet in the conduct of life played false to his own professions, he was not bound by his philosophy to be true to his friend or faithful in his trust. Moral virtue was not the line in which he undertook to instruct men; and though, as the poet calls him, he were the "meanest" of mankind, he was so in what may be called his private capacity, and without any prejudice to the theory of induction. He had a right to be so, if he chose, for anything that the Idols of the den or the theater had to say to the contrary. His mission was the increase of physical enjoyment and social comfort; and most wonderfully, most awfully has he fulfilled his conception and his design. Almost day by day have we fresh and fresh

the school of Xenocrates, he reformed, and later became head of the school. 140. **Anaxagoras,** a famous Greek philosopher and teacher (fifth century B.C.); because he advanced new theories of the order of the universe and presented scientific accounts of rainbows, eclipses, etc., he was arrested and exiled on the charge of contravening religious dogma. 142. *Rasselas,* a philosophical romance by Samuel Johnson (p. 567). 186. **Philosophy of Utility,** the doctrine that the useful is the good, and that any conduct is to be adjudged good if its consequences are useful. 188. **man . . . intellect,** Francis Bacon. He was convicted of bribery in 1621. He proved faithless to his early patron, the Earl of Essex, who was convicted and executed for treason. At the Queen's request Bacon drew up the charges against Essex and conducted the case. 193. **the poet,** Pope, who calls Bacon, "the wisest, brightest, meanest of mankind," in *An Essay on Man,* IV, 282. 198. **Idols . . . theater.** Cf. Bacon's *Novum Organum.*

shoots, and buds, and blossoms, which are to ripen into fruit, on that magical tree of Knowledge which he planted, and to which none of us perhaps, except the very poor, but owes, if not his present life, at least his daily food, his health, and general well-being. He was the divinely provided minister of temporal benefits to all of us so great, that, whatever I am forced to think of him as a man, I have not the heart, from mere gratitude, to speak of him severely. And
10 in spite of the tendencies of his philosophy, which are, as we see at this day, to depreciate, or to trample on Theology, he has himself, in his writings, gone out of his way, as if with a prophetic misgiving of those tendencies, to insist on it as the instrument of that beneficent Father, who, when He came on earth in visible form, took on Him first and most prominently the office of assuaging the bodily wounds of human nature. And truly, like the old mediciner in the tale, "he sat diligently at his work, and hummed, with
20 cheerful countenance, a pious song"; and then in turn "went out singing into the meadows so gayly, that those who had seen him from afar might well have thought it was a youth gathering flowers for his beloved, instead of an old physician gathering healing herbs in the morning dew."

Alas, that men, in the action of life or in their heart of hearts, are not what they seem to be in their moments of excitement, or in their trances or intoxications of genius—so good, so noble, so serene! Alas,
30 that Bacon too in his own way should after all be but the fellow of those heathen philosophers who in their disadvantages had some excuse for their inconsistency, and who surprise us rather in what they did say than in what they did not do! Alas, that he too, like Socrates or Seneca, must be stripped of his holy-day coat, which looks so fair, and should be but a mockery amid his most majestic gravity of phrase; and, for all his vast abilities, should, in the littleness of his own moral being, but typify the intellectual narrow-
40 ness of his school! However, granting all this, heroism after all was not his philosophy: I cannot deny he has abundantly achieved what he proposed. His is simply a Method whereby bodily discomforts and temporal wants are to be most effectually removed from the greatest number; and already, before it has shown any signs of exhaustion, the gifts of nature, in their most artificial shapes and luxurious profusion and diversity, from all quarters of the earth, are, it is undeniable, by its means brought even to our doors, and
50 we rejoice in them.

9.

Useful Knowledge then, I grant, has done its work; and Liberal Knowledge as certainly has not done its

work—supposing, that is, as the objectors assume, its direct end, like Religious Knowledge, is to make men better; but this I will not for an instant allow, and unless I allow it, those objectors have said nothing to the purpose. I admit, rather I maintain, what they have been urging, for I consider Knowledge to have its end in itself. For all its friends, or its enemies, may say, I insist upon it, that it is as real a mistake to 60 burden it with virtue or religion as with the mechanical arts. Its direct business is not to steel the soul against temptation, or to console it in affliction, any more than to set the loom in motion, or to direct the steam carriage; be it ever so much the means or the condition of both material and moral advancement, still, taken by and in itself, it as little mends our hearts as it improves our temporal circumstances. And if its eulogists claim for it such a power, they commit the very same kind of encroachment on 70 a province not their own as the political economist who should maintain that his science educated him for casuistry or diplomacy. Knowledge is one thing, virtue is another; good sense is not conscience, refinement is not humility, nor is largeness and justness of view faith. Philosophy, however enlightened, however profound, gives no command over the passions, no influential motives, no vivifying principles. Liberal Education makes not the Christian, not the Catholic, but the gentleman. It is well to be a gentle- 80 man, it is well to have a cultivated intellect, a delicate taste, a candid, equitable, dispassionate mind, a noble and courteous bearing in the conduct of life;— these are the connatural qualities of a large knowledge; they are the objects of a University; I am advocating, I shall illustrate and insist upon them; but still, I repeat, they are no guarantee for sanctity or even for conscientiousness they may attach to the man of the world, to the profligate, to the heartless— pleasant, alas, and attractive as he shows when 90 decked out in them. Taken by themselves, they do but seem to be what they are not; they look like virtue at a distance, but they are detected by close observers, and on the long run; and hence it is that they are popularly accused of pretense and hypocrisy, not, I repeat, from their own fault, but because their professors and their admirers persist in taking them for what they are not, and are officious in arrogating for them a praise to which they have no claim. Quarry the granite rock with razors, or moor the vessel 100 with a thread of silk; then may you hope with such keen and delicate instruments as human knowledge and human reason to contend against these giants, the passion and the pride of man.

Surely we are not driven to theories of this kind in order to vindicate the value and dignity of Liberal Knowledge. Surely the real grounds on which its pre-

14. insist . . . Father. In Bacon's *De Augmentis Scientiarum,* IV, 2. 19. "he sat," etc. From *The Unknown Patient,* by Friedrich Fouqué (1777–1843), a German poet and author. 35. Socrates, a famous

Greek philosopher (fifth century B.C.); accused of impiety and of corrupting the youth, he drank hemlock rather than compromise with his opinions. He was criticized for not adequately supporting his

tensions rest are not so very subtle or abstruse, so very strange or improbable. Surely it is very intelligible to say, and that is what I say here, that Liberal Education, viewed in itself, is simply the cultivation of the intellect as such, and its object is nothing more or less than intellectual excellence. Every thing has its own perfection, be it higher or lower in the scale of things; and the perfection of one is not the perfection of another. Things animate, inanimate, visible, invisible, all are good in their kind, and have a *best* of themselves, which is an object of pursuit. Why do you take such pains with your garden or your park? You see to your walks and turf and shrubberies; to your trees and drives; not as if you meant to make an orchard of the one, or corn or pasture land of the other, but because there is a special beauty in all that is goodly in wood, water, plain, and slope, brought all together by art into one shape, and grouped into one whole. Your cities are beautiful, your palaces, your public buildings, your territorial mansions, your churches; and their beauty leads to nothing beyond itself. There is a physical beauty and a moral: there is a beauty of person, there is a beauty of our moral being, which is natural virtue; and in like manner there is a beauty, there is a perfection, of the intellect. There is an ideal perfection in these various subject-matters, towards which individual instances are seen to rise, and which are the standards for all instances whatever. The Greek divinities and demigods, as the statuary has molded them, with their symmetry of figure, and their high forehead and their regular features, are the perfection of physical beauty. The heroes, of whom history tells, Alexander, or Caesar, or Scipio, or Saladin, are the representatives of that magnanimity or self-mastery which is the greatness of human nature. Christianity too has its heroes, and in the supernatural order, and we call them saints. The artist puts before him beauty of feature and form; the poet, beauty of mind; the preacher, the beauty of grace: then intellect too, I repeat, has its beauty, and it has those who aim at it. To open the mind, to correct it, to refine it, to enable it to know, and to digest, master, rule, and use its knowledge, to give it power over its own faculties, application, flexibility, method, critical exactness, sagacity, resource, address, eloquent expression, is an object as intelligible (for here we are inquiring, not what the object of a Liberal Education is worth, nor what use the Church makes of it, but what it is in itself), I say, an object as intelligible as the cultivation of virtue, while, at the same time, it is absolutely distinct from it.

10.

This indeed is but a temporal object, and a transitory possession; but so are other things in themselves which we make much of and pursue. The moralist will tell us that man, in all his functions, is but a flower which blossoms and fades, except so far as a higher principle breathes upon him, and makes him and what he is immortal. Body and mind are carried on into an eternal state of being by the gifts of Divine Munificence; but at first they do but fail in a failing world; and if the powers of intellect decay, the powers of the body have decayed before them, and, as an Hospital or an Almshouse, though its end be ephemeral, may be sanctified to the service of religion, so surely may a University, even were it nothing more than I have as yet described it. We attain to heaven by using this world well, though it is to pass away; we perfect our nature, not by undoing it, but by adding to it what is more than nature, and directing it towards aims higher than its own.

(1852)

from APOLOGIA PRO VITA SUA

Newman's "apology for," or defense of, his life was written as a reply to the Reverend Charles Kingsley, who had called Newman's intellectual honesty into question and had, through Newman, attacked the verity of the Catholic clergy. The work was written under great physical and emotional strain and at great speed in the early months of 1864, appearing as a series of pamphlets between April 21 and June 2. (Contrast this with Newman's usual method of composition.) The work was revised for book publication (1864), with much of the polemic against Kingsley stripped away. The selection below was the first chapter of the book publication. Newman's statement in the Preface to the 1864 edition about his perception of what he must ultimately do is instructive: "Yes, I said to myself, his very question is about my meaning: 'What does Dr. Newman mean?' It pointed in the very same direction as that into which my musings had turned me already. He asks what I mean; not about my words, not about my arguments, not about my actions, as his ultimate point, but about that living intelligence, by which I write, and argue, and act. He asks about my Mind and its Beliefs and its sentiments, and he shall be answered."

Newman's is perhaps the best-known religious pilgrimage of modern times. Between 1816 and 1845, when he became a Roman Catholic, he passed from individualism to institutionalism, from a self-regarding emotionalism to a self-abnegating authoritarianism. Thus he was a spokesman, not just for Roman Catholics, but for those of his contemporaries who, against the rising tide of Liberalism, held to the values of faith.

family. **Seneca,** a very wealthy man, voiced high ethical sentiments and spoke against riches; many persons thought that he did not live up to his utterances. 84. **connatural,** inherent, connected by nature. 140.

Scipio, the family name of two noted Roman generals who fought against the Carthaginians in the second century B.C. **Saladin,** a celebrated sultan of Egypt and Syria (1137–1193).

Many orthodox believers sought to combat Liberalism by vehement reiteration of traditional arguments or to flee from it into ritualism. Newman entered into the psychology of his age and offered, not the ever-disputable evidences, but the indisputable fact of his own acceptance of them.

HISTORY OF MY RELIGIOUS OPINIONS TO THE YEAR 1833

It may easily be conceived how great a trial it is to me to write the following history of myself; but I must not shrink from the task. The words "Secretum meum mihi," keep ringing in my ears; but as men draw towards their end, they care less for disclosures. Nor is it the least part of my trial, to anticipate that my friends may, upon first reading what I have written, consider much in it irrelevant to my purpose; yet I cannot help thinking that, viewed as a whole, it will
10 effect what I wish it to do.

I was brought up from a child to take great delight in reading the Bible; but I had no formal religious convictions till I was fifteen. Of course I had perfect knowledge of my Catechism.

After I was grown up, I put on paper such recollections as I had of my thoughts and feelings on religious subjects, at the time that I was a child and a boy. Out of these I select two, which are at once the most definite among them, and also have a bearing on
20 my later convictions.

In the paper to which I have referred, written either in the long vacation of 1820, or in October 1823, the following notices of my school days were sufficiently prominent in my memory for me to consider them worth recording:—"I used to wish the Arabian Tales were true: my imagination ran on unknown influences, on magical powers, and talismans.... I thought life might be a dream, or I an Angel, and all this world a deception, my fellow-angels by a playful device con-
30 cealing themselves from me, and deceiving me with the semblance of a material world."

Again, "Reading in the Spring of 1816 a sentence from [Dr. Watt's] *Remnants of Time*, entitled 'the Saints unknown to the world,' to the effect, that 'there is nothing in their figure or countenance to distinguish them,' etc., etc., I supposed he spoke of Angels who lived in the world, as it were disguised."

The other remark is this: "I was very superstitious, and for some time previous to my conversion" [when
40 I was fifteen] "used constantly to cross myself on going into the dark."

Of course I must have got this practice from some external source or other; but I can make no sort of conjecture whence; and certainly no one had ever spoken to me on the subject of the Catholic religion, which I only knew by name. The French master was an *emigré* priest, but he was simply made a butt, as French masters too commonly were in that day, and spoke English very imperfectly. There was a Catholic family in the village, old maiden ladies we used to 50 think; but I knew nothing but their name. I have of late years heard that there were one or two Catholic boys in the school; but either we were carefully kept from knowing this, or the knowledge of it made simply no impression on our minds. My brother will bear witness how free the school was from Catholic ideas.

I had once been into Warwick Street Chapel, with my father, who, I believe, wanted to hear some piece of music; all that I bore away from it was the recollection of a pulpit and a preacher and a boy swinging 60 a censer.

When I was at Littlemore, I was looking over old copybooks of my school days, and I found among them my first Latin verse-book; and in the first page of it there was a device which almost took my breath away with surprise. I have the book before me now, and have just been showing it to others. I have written in the first page, in my schoolboy hand, "John H. Newman, February 11th, 1811, Verse Book"; then follow my first verses. Between "Verse" and "Book" I 70 have drawn the figure of a solid cross upright, and next to it is, what may indeed be meant for a necklace, but what I cannot make out to be anything else than a set of beads suspended, with a little cross attached. At this time I was not quite ten years old. I suppose I got the idea from some romance, Mrs. Radcliffe's or Miss Porter's; or from some religious picture; but the strange thing is, how, among the thousand objects which meet a boy's eyes, these in particular should so have fixed themselves in my mind, that I 80 made them thus practically my own. I am certain there was nothing in the churches I attended, or the prayer books I read, to suggest them. It must be recollected that churches and prayer books were not decorated in those days as I believe they are now.

When I was fourteen, I read Paine's tracts against the Old Testament, and found pleasure in thinking of the objections which were contained in them. Also, I read some of Hume's essays; and perhaps that on Miracles. So at least I gave my father to understand; 90 but perhaps it was a brag. Also, I recollect copying out some French verses, perhaps Voltaire's, against the immortality of the soul, and saying to myself something like "How dreadful, but how plausible!"

3. **Secretum meum mihi,** my private life is my own affair. 14. **Catechism,** the Anglican Catechism, contained in the *Book of Common Prayer.* 33. **Dr. Watt,** Isaac Watt (1674-1748), popular theologian and hymn writer. 47. émigré, a Royalist fugitive from the French Revolution. 76. **Mrs. Radcliffe, Miss Porter,** Ann Radcliffe (1764-

1823) and Jane Porter (1776-1850), authors of Gothic and other romances. 86-87. **Paine's tracts . . . Old Testament,** Thomas Paine (1737-1809), in *The Age of Reason.* 89. **Hume's essays, etc.,** David Hume (1711-1776), historian and philosopher. "Of Miracles" appeared in *Enquiry Concerning Human Understanding* (1748). 92. **Voltaire,**

When I was fifteen (in the autumn of 1816) a great change of thought took place in me. I fell under the influences of a definite creed, and received into my intellect impressions of dogma, which, through God's mercy, have never been effaced or obscured. Above and beyond the conversations and sermons of the excellent man, long dead, who was the human means of this beginning of divine faith in me, was the effect of the books which he put into my hands, all of the school of Calvin. One of the first books I read was a work of Romaine's; I neither recollect the title nor the contents, except one doctrine, which of course I do not include among those which I believe to have come from a divine source, viz. the doctrine of final perseverance. I received it at once, and believed that the inward conversion of which I was conscious (and of which I still am more certain than that I have hands and feet) would last into the next life, and that I was elected to eternal glory. I have no consciousness that this belief had any tendency whatever to lead me to be careless about pleasing God. I retained it till the age of twenty-one, when it gradually faded away; but I believe that it had some influence on my opinions, in the direction of those childish imaginations which I have already mentioned, viz. in isolating me from the objects which surrounded me, in confirming me in my mistrust of the reality of material phenomena, and making me rest in the thought of two and two only supreme and luminously self-evident beings, myself and my Creator;—for while I considered myself predestined to salvation, I thought others simply passed over, not predestined to eternal death. I only thought of the mercy to myself.

The detestable doctrine last mentioned is simply denied and abjured, unless my memory strangely deceives me, by the writer who made a deeper impression on my mind than any other, and to whom (humanly speaking) I almost owe my soul—Thomas Scott of Aston Sandford. I so admired and delighted in his writings, that, when I was an undergraduate, I thought of making a visit to his parsonage, in order to see a man whom I so deeply revered. I hardly think I could have given up the idea of this expedition, even after I had taken my degree; for the news of his death in 1821 came upon me as a disappointment as well as a sorrow. I hung upon the lips of Daniel Wilson, afterwards Bishop of Calcutta, as in two sermons at St. John's Chapel he gave the history of Scott's life and death. I had been possessed of his essays from a boy; his commentary I bought when I was an undergraduate.

What, I suppose, will strike any reader of Scott's history and writings, is his bold unworldliness and vigorous independence of mind. He followed truth wherever it led him, beginning with Unitarianism, and ending in a zealous faith in the Holy Trinity. It was he who first planted deep in my mind that fundamental truth of religion. With the assistance of Scott's essays, and the admirable work of Jones of Nayland, I made a collection of Scripture texts in proof of the doctrine, with remarks (I think) of my own upon them, before I was sixteen; and a few months later I drew up a series of texts in support of each verse of the Athanasian Creed. These papers I have still.

Besides his unworldliness, what I also admired in Scott was his resolute opposition to Antinomianism, and the minutely practical character of his writings. They show him to be a true Englishman, and I deeply felt his influence; and for years I used almost as proverbs what I considered to be the scope and issue of his doctrine, "Holiness before peace," and "Growth is the only evidence of life."

Calvinists make a sharp separation between the elect and the world; there is much in this that is parallel or cognate to the Catholic doctrine; but they go on to say, as I understand them, very differently from Catholicism,—that the converted and the unconverted can be discriminated by man, that the justified are conscious of their state of justification, and that the regenerate cannot fall away. Catholics on the other hand shade and soften the awful antagonism between good and evil, which is one of their dogmas, by holding that there are different degrees of justification, that there is a great difference in point of gravity between sin and sin, that there is the possibility and the danger of falling away, and that there is no certain knowledge given to any one that he is simply in a state of grace, and much less that he is to persevere to the end:—of the Calvinistic tenets the only one which took root in my mind was the fact of heaven and hell, divine favour and divine wrath, of the justified and the unjustified. The notion that the regenerate and the justified were one and the same, and that the regenerate, as such, had the gift of perseverance, remained with me not many years, as I have said already.

This main Catholic doctrine of the warfare between the city of God and the powers of darkness was also deeply impressed upon my mind by a work of a very opposite character, Law's *Serious Call*.

From this time I have given a full inward assent and belief to the doctrine of eternal punishment, as delivered by our Lord Himself, in as true a sense as I hold that of eternal happiness; though I have tried in various ways to make that truth less terrible to the reason.

Now I come to two other works, which produced a deep impression on me in the same autumn of 1816,

French critic and skeptic (1694-1778). 105. **Romaine,** William Romaine (1714-1795), religious writer. 132. **Thomas Scott.** Scott (1747-1821) was the author of a serial commentary on the Bible. 140. **Daniel Wilson,** Evangelical preacher (1778-1858). 153. **Jones of Nayland,** William Jones, of Nayland, Suffolk (1726-1800), author of *The Catholic Doctrine of the Trinity.* 160. **Antinomianism,** the belief that faith alone is necessary for salvation, with its corollary that good works are not effective or obligatory. 193. **Law,** William Law (1686-1761), author of *Serious Call to a Devout and Holy Life* (1728).

when I was fifteen years old, each contrary to each, and planting in me the seeds of an intellectual inconsistency which disabled me for a long course of years. I read Joseph Milner's *Church History*, and was nothing short of enamoured of the long extracts from St. Augustine and the other Fathers which I found there. I read them as being the religion of the primitive Christians: but simultaneously with Milner I read Newton on the *Prophecies*, and in consequence became 10 most firmly convinced that the Pope was the Antichrist predicted by Daniel, St. Paul, and St. John. My imagination was stained by the effects of this doctrine up to the year 1843; it had been obliterated from my reason and judgment at an earlier date; but the thought remained upon me as a sort of false conscience. Hence came that conflict of mind, which so many have felt besides myself;—leading some men to make a compromise between two ideas, so inconsistent with each other—driving others to beat out the one idea or the 20 other from their minds—and ending in my own case, after many years of intellectual unrest, in the gradual decay and extinction of one of them—I do not say in its violent death, for why should I not have murdered it sooner, if I murdered it at all?

I am obliged to mention, though I do it with great reluctance, another deep imagination, which at this time, the autumn of 1816, took possession of me—there can be no mistake about the fact;—viz. that it was the will of God that I should lead a single life. This antici-30 pation, which has held its ground almost continuously ever since—with the break of a month now and a month then, up to 1829, and, after that date, without any break at all—was more or less connected, in my mind, with the notion that my calling in life would require such a sacrifice as celibacy involved; as, for instance, missionary work among the heathen, to which I had a great drawing for some years. It also strengthened my feeling of separation from the visible world, of which I have spoken above.

40 In 1822 I came under very different influences from those to which I had hitherto been subjected. At that time, Mr. Whately, as he was then, afterwards Archbishop of Dublin, for the few months he remained in Oxford, which he was leaving for good, showed great kindness to me. He renewed it in 1825, when he became Principal of Alban Hall, making me his vice-principal and tutor. Of Dr. Whately I will speak presently, for from 1822 to 1825 I saw most of the present Provost of Oriel, Dr. Hawkins, at that time 50 Vicar of St. Mary's; and, when I took orders in 1824 and had a curacy at Oxford, then, during the long vacations, I was especially thrown into his company. I can say with a full heart that I love him, and have never ceased to love him; and I thus preface what otherwise might sound rude, that in the course of the many years in which we were together afterwards, he provoked me very much from time to time, though I am perfectly certain that I have provoked him a great deal more. Moreover, in me such provocation was unbecoming, both because he was the head of my college, 60 and because in the first years that I knew him, he had been in many ways of great service to my mind.

He was the first who taught me to weigh my words, and to be cautious in my statements. He led me to that mode of limiting and clearing my sense in discussion and in controversy, and of distinguishing between cognate ideas, and of obviating mistakes by anticipation, which to my surprise has been since considered, even in quarters friendly to me, to savour of the polemics of Rome. He is a man of most exact mind 70 himself, and he used to snub me severely, on reading, as he was kind enough to do, the first sermons that I wrote, and other compositions which I was engaged upon.

Then as to doctrine, he was the means of great additions to my belief. As I have noticed elsewhere, he gave me the *Treatise on Apostolical Preaching*, by Sumner, afterwards Archbishop of Canterbury, from which I learned to give up my remaining Calvinism, and to receive the doctrine of Baptismal Regeneration. 80 In many other ways too he was of use to me, on subjects semi-religious and semi-scholastic.

It was Dr. Hawkins too who taught me to anticipate that, before many years were over, there would be an attack made upon the books and the canon of Scripture. I was brought to the same belief by the conversation of Mr. Blanco White, who also led me to have freer views on the subject of inspiration than were usual in the Church of England at the time.

There is one other principle, which I gained from 90 Dr. Hawkins, more directly bearing upon Catholicism, than any that I have mentioned; and that is the doctrine of Tradition. When I was an undergraduate, I heard him preach in the University pulpit his celebrated sermon on the subject, and recollect how long it appeared to me, though he was at that time a very striking preacher; but, when I read it and studied it as his gift, it made a most serious impression upon me. He does not go one step, I think, beyond the high Anglican doctrine, nay he does not reach it; but he 100 does his work thoroughly, and his view was original with him, and his subject was a novel one at the time. He lays down a proposition, self-evident as soon as stated, to those who have at all examined the structure of Scripture, viz. that the sacred text was never intended to teach doctrine, but only to prove it, and

4. **Joseph Milner,** Evangelical divine (1744-1797), author of *History of the Church of Christ* (1794-1797). 9. **Newton,** Thomas Newton (1704-1782), Bishop of Bristol, author of a *Dissertation on the Prophecies* (1754). 42. **Mr. Whately,** Richard Whately (1787-1863), critic of religious dogma and supporter of Broad Church views. 49. **Dr. Hawkins,** Edward Hawkins (1789-1882). 78. **Sumner,** John Bird Sumner (1780-1862). 87. **Mr. Blanco White,** Joseph Blanco White (1775-1841), theological writer. 127. **Bishop Butler,** Joseph Butler

that, if we would learn doctrine, we must have recourse to the formularies of the Church; for instance to the Catechism, and to the Creeds. He considers, that, after learning from them the doctrines of Christianity, the inquirer must verify them by Scripture. This view, most true in its outline, most fruitful in its consequences, opened upon me a large field of thought. Dr. Whately held it too. One of its effects was to strike at the root of the principle on which the Bible Society was set up. I belonged to its Oxford Association; it became a matter of time when I should withdraw my name from its subscription-list, though I did not do so at once.

It is with pleasure that I pay here a tribute to the memory of the Rev. William James, then Fellow of Oriel; who, about the year 1823, taught me the doctrine of Apostolical Succession, in the course of a walk, I think, round Christ Church meadow: I recollect being somewhat impatient on the subject at the time.

It was at about this date, I suppose, that I read Bishop Butler's *Analogy*; the study of which has been to so many, as it was to me, an era in their religious opinions. Its inculcation of a visible church, the oracle of truth and a pattern of sanctity, of the duties of external religion, and of the historical character of revelation, are characteristics of this great work which strike the reader at once; for myself, if I may attempt to determine what I most gained from it, it lay in two points, which I shall have an opportunity of dwelling on in the sequel; they are the underlying principles of a great portion of my teaching. First, the very idea of an analogy between the separate works of God leads to the conclusion that the system which is of less importance is economically or sacramentally connected with the more momentous system, and of this conclusion the theory, to which I was inclined as a boy, viz. the unreality of material phenomena, is an ultimate resolution. At this time I did not make the distinction between matter itself and its phenomena, which is so necessary and so obvious in discussing the subject. Secondly, Butler's doctrine that probability is the guide of life, led me, at least under the teaching to which a few years later I was introduced, to the question of the logical cogency of faith, on which I have written so much. Thus to Butler I trace those two principles of my teaching, which have led to a charge against me both of fancifulness and of scepticism.

And now as to Dr. Whately. I owe him a great deal. He was a man of generous and warm heart. He was particularly loyal to his friends, and to use the common phrase, "all his geese were swans." While I was still awkward and timid in 1822, he took me by the hand, and acted the part to me of a gentle and encouraging instructor. He, emphatically, opened my mind, and taught me to think and to use my reason. After being first noticed by him in 1822, I became very intimate with him in 1825, when I was his vice-principal at Alban Hall. I gave up that office in 1826, when I became tutor of my college, and his hold upon me gradually relaxed. He had done his work towards me or nearly so, when he had taught me to see with my own eyes and to walk with my own feet. Not that I had not a good deal to learn from others still, but I influenced them as well as they me, and co-operated rather than merely concurred with them. As to Dr. Whately, his mind was too different from mine for us to remain long on one line. I recollect how dissatisfied he was with an article of mine in the *London Review*, which Blanco White, good-humouredly, only called platonic. When I was diverging from him (which he did not like), I thought of dedicating my first book to him, in words to the effect that he had not only taught me to think, but to think for myself. He left Oxford in 1831; after that, as far as I can recollect, I never saw him but twice—when he visited the University; once in the street, once in a room. From the time that he left, I have always felt a real affection for what I must call his memory; for thenceforward he made himself dead to me. My reason told me that it was impossible that we could have got on together longer; yet I loved him too much to bid him farewell without pain. After a few years had passed, I began to believe that his influence on me in a higher respect than intellectual advance (I will not say through his fault) had not been satisfactory. I believe that he has inserted sharp things in his later works about me. They have never come in my way, and I have not thought it necessary to seek out what would pain me so much in the reading.

What he did for me in point of religious opinion, was first to teach me the existence of the Church, as a substantive body or corporation; next to fix in me those anti-Erastian views of Church polity, which were one of the most prominent features of the Tractarian Movement. On this point, and, as far as I know, on this point alone, he and Hurrell Froude intimately sympathised, though Froude's development of opinion here was of a later date. In the year 1826, in the course of a walk he said much to me about a work then just published, called *Letters on the Church by an Episcopalian*. He said that it would make my blood boil. It was certainly a most powerful composition. One of our common friends told me, that, after reading it, he could not keep still, but went on walking up and down his room. It was ascribed at once to Whately; I gave eager expression to the contrary opinion; but I found the belief of Oxford in the affirmative to be too strong

(1692-1752), author of *Analogy of Religion* (1736). **174. article ...London Review,** "Poetry, with Reference to Aristotle's Poetics," in the *London Review* (1829). **198. anti-Erastian,** from Thomas Erastus, sixteenth-century theologian who held that the state was supreme in ecclesiastical affairs. **201. Hurrell Froude,** Richard Hurrell Froude (1803-1836), brother of James Anthony Froude (editor of *Fraser's Magazine*, 1860-1874).

for me; rightly or wrongly I yielded to the general voice; and I have never heard, then or since, of any disclaimer of authorship on the part of Dr. Whately.

The main positions of this able essay are these; first that Church and State should be independent of each other:—he speaks of the duty of protesting "against the profanation of Christ's kingdom, by that *double usurpation*, the interference of the Church in temporals, of the State in spirituals" (p. 191); and, secondly, that the Church may justly and by right retain its property, though separated from the State. "The clergy," he says, p. 133, "though they ought not to be the hired servants of the Civil Magistrate, may justly retain their revenues; and the State, though it has no right of interference in spiritual concerns, not only is justly entitled to support from the ministers of religion, and from all other Christians, but would, under the system I am recommending, obtain it much more effectually." The author of this work, whoever he may be, argues out both these points with great force and ingenuity, and with a thorough-going vehemence, which perhaps we may refer to the circumstance, that he wrote, not *in propriâ personâ*, but in the professed character of a Scotch Episcopalian. His work had a gradual, but a deep effect on my mind.

I am not aware of any other religious opinion which I owe to Dr. Whately. For his special theological tenets I had no sympathy. In the next year, 1827, he told me he considered that I was Arianising. The case was this: though at that time I had not read Bishop Bull's *Defensio* nor the Fathers, I was just then very strong for that ante-Nicene view of the Trinitarian doctrine, which some writers, both Catholic and non-Catholic, have accused of wearing a sort of Arian exterior. This is the meaning of a passage in Froude's *Remains*, in which he seems to accuse me of speaking against the Athanasian Creed. I had contrasted the two aspects of the Trinitarian doctrine, which are respectively presented by the Athanasian Creed and the Nicene. My criticisms were to the effect that some of the verses of the former Creed were unnecessarily scientific. This is a specimen of a certain disdain for antiquity which had been growing on me now for several years. It showed itself in some flippant language against the Fathers in the *Encyclopædia Metropolitana*, about whom I knew little at the time, except what I had learnt as a boy from Joseph Milner. In writing on the Scripture Miracles in 1825-6, I had read Middleton on the *Miracles* of the early Church, and had imbibed a portion of his spirit.

The truth is, I was beginning to prefer intellectual excellence to moral; I was drifting in the direction of liberalism. I was rudely awakened from my dream at the end of 1827 by two great blows—illness and bereavement.

In the beginning of 1829, came the formal break between Dr. Whately and me; Mr. Peel's attempted re-election was the occasion of it. I think in 1828 or 1827 I had voted in the minority, when the petition to Parliament against the Catholic claims was brought into Convocation. I did so mainly on the views suggested to me by the theory of the *Letters of an Episcopalian*. Also I disliked the bigoted "two bottle orthodox," as they were invidiously called. I took part against Mr. Peel, on a simple academical, not at all an ecclesiastical or a political ground; and this I professed at the time. I considered that Mr. Peel had taken the University by surprise, that he had no right to call upon us to turn round on a sudden, and to expose ourselves to the imputation of time-serving, and that a great university ought not to be bullied even by a great Duke of Wellington. Also by this time I was under the influence of Keble and Froude; who, in addition to the reasons I have given, disliked the duke's change of policy as dictated by liberalism.

Whately was considerably annoyed at me, and he took a humorous revenge, of which he had given me due notice beforehand. As head of a house, he had duties of hospitality to men of all parties; he asked a set of the least intellectual men in Oxford to dinner, and men most fond of port; he made me one of the party; placed me between Provost this, and Principal that, and then asked me if I was proud of my friends. However, he had a serious meaning in his act; he saw, more clearly than I could do, that I was separating from his own friends for good and all.

Dr. Whately attributed my leaving his *clientela* to a wish on my part to be the head of a party myself. I do not think that it was deserved. My habitual feeling then and since has been, that it was not I who sought friends, but friends who sought me. Never man had kinder or more indulgent friends than I have had, but I expressed my own feeling as to the mode in which I gained them, in this very year 1829, in the course of a copy of verses. Speaking of my blessings, I said, "Blessings of friends, which to my door, *unasked, unhoped*, have come." They have come, they have gone; they came to my great joy, they went to my great grief. He who gave, took away. Dr. Whately's impression about me, however, admits of this explanation:—

During the first years of my residence at Oriel, though proud of my college, I was not at home there. I was very much alone, and I used often to take my daily walk by myself. I recollect once meeting Dr.

23. *in propriâ personâ*, in his own person. 29. **Arianising**, that is, tending to deny the divinity of Christ. 30. **Bishop Bull**, George Bull (1634-1710), author of *Defensio Fidei Nicænae* (1685). 32. **ante-Nicene view**, etc. The Nicene Creed, adopted by the Council of Nicæa in 325 and confirmed by the second ecumenical council at Constantinople in 381, is a summary of the Christian faith, including the

doctrine of three equal persons in one God. 35. **Froude's *Remains***, published in 1837-1839, included strictures on the Reformation and aroused hostility toward the Tractarian Movement. 45. *Encyclopædia Metropolitana*. Newman wrote a few articles for this encyclopedia in 1824. 48. **Middleton**, Conyers Middleton (1683-1750), author of a liberal treatise, *Miracles* (1748), which maintained that post-apostolic

Copleston, then provost, with one of the fellows. He turned round, and with the kind courteousness which sat so well on him, made me a bow and said "Nunquam minus solus, quàm cùm solus." At that time indeed (from 1823) I had the intimacy of my dear and true friend Dr. Pusey, and could not fail to admire and revere a soul so devoted to the cause of religion, so full of good works, so faithful in his affections; but he left residence when I was getting to know him well. As to Dr. Whately himself, he was too much my superior to allow of my being at my ease with him; and to no one in Oxford at this time did I open my heart fully and familiarly. But things changed in 1826. At that time I became one of the tutors of my college, and this gave me position; besides, I had written one or two essays which had been well received. I began to be known. I preached my first University sermon. Next year I was one of the public examiners for the B.A. degree. It was to me like the feeling of spring weather after winter; and, if I may so speak, I came out of my shell; I remained out of it till 1841.

The two persons who knew me best at that time are still alive, beneficed clergymen; no longer my friends. They could tell better than any one else what I was in those years. From this time my tongue was, as it were, loosened, and I spoke spontaneously and without effort. A shrewd man, who knew me at this time, said, "Here is a man who, when he is silent, will never begin to speak; and when he once begins to speak, will never stop." It was at this time that I began to have influence, which steadily increased for a course of years. I gained upon my pupils, and was in particular intimate and affectionate with two of our probationer fellows, Robert I. Wilberforce (afterwards archdeacon) and Richard Hurrell Froude. Whately then, an acute man, perhaps saw around me the signs of an incipient party of which I was not conscious myself. And thus we discern the first elements of that movement afterwards called Tractarian.

The true and primary author of it, however, as is usual with great motive-powers, was out of sight. Having carried off as a mere boy the highest honours of the university, he had turned from the admiration which haunted his steps, and sought for a better and holier satisfaction in pastoral work in the country. Need I say that I am speaking of John Keble? The first time that I was in a room with him was on occasion of my election to a fellowship at Oriel, when I was sent for into the tower, to shake hands with the provost and fellows. How is that hour fixed in my memory after the changes of forty-two years, forty-two this very day on which I write! I have lately had a letter in my

hands, which I sent at the time to my great friend, John Bowden, with whom I passed almost exclusively my undergraduate years. "I had to hasten to the tower," I say to him, "to receive the congratulations of all the fellows. I bore it till Keble took my hand, and then felt so abashed and unworthy of the honour done me, that I seemed desirous of quite sinking into the ground." His had been the first name which I had heard spoken of, with reverence rather than admiration, when I came up to Oxford. When one day I was walking in High Street with my dear earliest friend just mentioned, with what eagerness did he cry out, "There's Keble!" and with what awe did I look at him! Then at another time I heard a master of arts of my college give an account how he had just then had occasion to introduce himself on some business to Keble, and how gentle, courteous, and unaffected Keble had been, so as almost to put him out of countenance. Then too it was reported, truly or falsely, how a rising man of brilliant reputation, the present Dean of St. Paul's, Dr. Milman, admired and loved him, adding, that somehow he was unlike any one else. However, at the time when I was elected Fellow of Oriel he was not in residence, and he was shy of me for years in consequence of the marks which I bore upon me of the evangelical and liberal schools. At least so I have ever thought. Hurrell Froude brought us together about 1828: it is one of the sayings preserved in his *Remains,* —"Do you know the story of the murderer who had done one good thing in his life? Well; if I was ever asked what good deed I had ever done, I should say that I had brought Keble and Newman to understand each other."

The *Christian Year* made its appearance in 1827. It is not necessary, and scarcely becoming, to praise a book which has already become one of the classics of the language. When the general tone of religious literature was so nerveless and impotent, as it was at that time, Keble struck an original note and woke up in the hearts of thousands a new music, the music of a school, long unknown in England. Nor can I pretend to analyse, in my own instance, the effect of religious teaching so deep, so pure, so beautiful. I have never till now tried to do so; yet I think I am not wrong in saying, that the two main intellectual truths which it brought home to me, were the same two, which I had learned from Butler, though recast in the creative mind of my new master. The first of these was what may be called, in a large sense of the word, the sacramental system; that is, the doctrine that material phenomena are both the types and the instruments of real things unseen,—a doctrine, which embraces, not only what

miracles were unreal. 60. **Catholic claims,** that is, for political emancipation, which was passed in 1829. 63. **two bottle orthodox,** that is, as orthodox in politics and religion as in their taste for wine at table. 73. **Keble,** John Keble (1792-1866), founder of the Oxford (or Tractarian) Movement. 104. **Dr. Copleston,** Edward Copleston (1776-1849), prelate and pamphleteer. 107. **Nunquam . . . solus,** never less

alone than when alone. 138. **Robert I. Wilberforce.** Wilberforce (1802-1857), the son of a leading Evangelical, joined the Roman Catholic Church. 158. **John Bowden.** Bowden (1798-1844) was the author of *Life of Gregory VII.*

Anglicans, as well as Catholics, believe about sacraments properly so called; but also the article of "the Communion of Saints" in its fullness; and likewise the mysteries of the faith. The connection of this philosophy of religion with what is sometimes called "Berkeleyism" has been mentioned above; I knew little of Berkeley at this time except by name; nor have I ever studied him.

On the second intellectual principle which I gained from Mr. Keble, I could say a great deal; if this were the place for it. It runs through very much that I have written, and has gained for me many hard names. Butler teaches us that probability is the guide of life. The danger of this doctrine, in the case of many minds, is, its tendency to destroy in them absolute certainty, leading them to consider every conclusion as doubtful, and resolving truth into an opinion, which it is safe to obey or to profess, but not possible to embrace with full internal assent. If this were to be allowed, then the celebrated saying, "O God, if there be a God, save my soul, if I have a soul!" would be the highest measure of devotion:—but who can really pray to a being, about whose existence he is seriously in doubt?

I considered that Mr. Keble met this difficulty by ascribing the firmness of assent which we give to religious doctrine, not to the probabilities which introduced it, but to the living power of faith and love which accepted it. In matters of religion, he seemed to say, it is not merely probability which makes us intellectually certain, but probability as it is put to account by faith and love. It is faith and love which give to probability a force which it has not in itself. Faith and love are directed towards an object; in the vision of that object they live; it is that object, received in faith and love, which renders it reasonable to take probability as sufficient for internal conviction. Thus the argument about probability, in the matter of religion, became an argument from personality, which in fact is one form of the argument from authority.

In illustration, Mr. Keble used to quote the words of the psalm: "I will guide thee with mine *eye*. Be ye not like to horse and mule, which have no understanding; whose mouths must be held with bit and bridle, lest they fall upon thee." This is the very difference, he used to say, between slaves, and friends or children. Friends do not ask for literal commands; but, from their knowledge of the speaker, they understand his half-words, and from love of him they anticipate his wishes. Hence it is, that in his poem for St. Bartholomew's Day, he speaks of the "Eye of God's word"; and in the note quotes Mr. Miller, of Worcester College, who remarks, in his Bampton lectures, on the special power of Scripture, as having "this eye, like

that of a portrait, uniformly fixed upon us, turn where we will." The view thus suggested by Mr. Keble, is brought forward in one of the earliest of the *Tracts for the Times*. In No. 8 I say, "The Gospel is a Law of Liberty. We are treated as sons, not as servants; not subjected to a code of formal commandments, but addressed as those who love God, and wish to please Him."

I did not at all dispute this view of the matter, for I made use of it myself; but I was dissatisfied, because it did not go to the root of the difficulty. It was beautiful and religious, but it did not even profess to be logical; and accordingly I tried to complete it by considerations of my own, which are implied in my University sermons, *Essay on Ecclesiastical Miracles*, and *Essay on Development of Doctrine*. My argument is in outline as follows: that that absolute certitude which we were able to possess, whether as to the truths of natural theology, or as to the fact of a revelation, was the result of an *assemblage* of concurring and converging probabilities, and that, both according to the constitution of the human mind and the will of its Maker; that certitude was a habit of mind, that certainty was a quality of propositions; that probabilities which did not reach to logical certainty, might create a mental certitude; that the certitude thus created might equal in measure and strength the certitude which was created by the strictest scientific demonstration; and that to have such certitude might in given cases and to given individuals be a plain duty, though not to others in other circumstances:—

Moreover, that as there were probabilities which sufficed to create certitude, so there were other probabilities which were legitimately adapted to create opinion; that it might be quite as much a matter of duty in given cases and to given persons to have about a fact an opinion of a definite strength and consistency, as in the case of greater or of more numerous probabilities it was a duty to have a certitude; that accordingly we were bound to be more or less sure, on a sort of (as it were) graduated scale of assent, viz. according as the probabilities attaching to a professed fact were brought home to us, and, as the case might be, to entertain about it a pious belief, or a pious opinion, or a religious conjecture, or at least a tolerance of such belief, or opinion, or conjecture in others; that on the other hand, as it was a duty to have a belief, of more or less strong texture, in given cases, so in other cases it was a duty not to believe, not to opine, not to conjecture, not even to tolerate the notion that a professed fact was true, inasmuch as it would be credulity or superstition, or some other moral fault, to do so. This was the region of private judgment in religion; that is, of a private judgment, not formed arbitrarily and ac-

---

5. **Berkeleyism,** after George Berkeley (1685-1753), author of *Treatise Concerning Human Knowledge,* in which he maintained that it was im-

possible to have knowledge of an object beyond what is learned through the senses. 157. *ipse dixit.* He himself has said it.

cording to one's fancy or liking, but conscientiously, and under a sense of duty.

Considerations such as these throw a new light on the subject of Miracles, and they seem to have led me to reconsider the view which I took of them in my essay in 1825–6. I do not know what was the date of this change in me, nor of the train of ideas on which it was founded. That there had been already great miracles, as those of Scripture, as the Resurrection, was a fact establishing the principle that the laws of nature had sometimes been suspended by their Divine Author; and since what had happened once might happen again, a certain probability, at least no kind of improbability, was attached to the idea, taken in itself, of miraculous intervention in later times, and miraculous accounts were to be regarded in connection with the verisimilitude, scope, instrument, character, testimony, and circumstances, with which they presented themselves to us; and, according to the final result of those various considerations, it was our duty to be sure, or to believe, or to opine, or to surmise, or to tolerate, or to reject, or to denounce. The main difference between my essay on Miracles in 1826 and my essay in 1842 is this: that in 1826 I considered that miracles were sharply divided into two classes, those which were to be received, and those which were to be rejected; whereas in 1842 I saw that they were to be regarded according to their greater or less probability, which was in some cases sufficient to create certitude about them, in other cases only belief or opinion.

Moreover, the argument from analogy, on which this view of the question was founded, suggested to me something besides, in recommendation of the ecclesiastical miracles. It fastened itself upon the theory of church history which I had learned as a boy from Joseph Milner. It is Milner's doctrine, that upon the visible Church come down from above, from time to time, large and temporary *Effusions* of divine grace. This is the leading idea of his work. He begins by speaking of the Day of Pentecost, as marking "the first of those *Effusions* of the Spirit of God, which from age to age have visited the earth since the coming of Christ" (vol. i. p. 3). In a note he adds that "in the term 'Effusion' there is not here included the idea of the miraculous or extraordinary operations of the Spirit of God"; but still it was natural for me, admitting Milner's general theory, and applying to it the principle of analogy, not to stop short at his abrupt *ipse dixit*, but boldly to pass forward to the conclusion, on other grounds plausible, that, as miracles accompanied the first effusion of grace, so they might accompany the later. It is surely a natural and on the whole, a true anticipation (though of course there are exceptions in particular cases), that gifts and graces go together; now, according to the ancient Catholic doctrine, the gift of miracles was viewed as the attendant and shadow of transcendent sanctity: and more-

over, as such sanctity was not of every day's occurrence, nay further, as one period of church history differed widely from another, and, as Joseph Milner would say, there had been generations or centuries of degeneracy or disorder, and times of revival, and as one region might be in the mid-day of religious fervour, and another in twilight or gloom, there was no force in the popular argument, that, because we did not see miracles with our own eyes, miracles had not happened in former times, or were not now at this very time taking place in distant places:— but I must not dwell longer on a subject, to which in a few words it is impossible to do justice.

Hurrell Froude was a pupil of Keble's, formed by him, and in turn reacting upon him. I knew him first in 1826, and was in the closest and most affectionate friendship with him from about 1829 till his death in 1836. He was a man of the highest gifts—so truly many-sided, that it would be presumptuous in me to attempt to describe him, except under those aspects, in which he came before me. Nor have I here to speak of the gentleness and tenderness of nature, the playfulness, the free elastic force and graceful versatility of mind, and the patient winning considerateness in discussion, which endeared him to those to whom he opened his heart; for I am all along engaged upon matters of belief and opinion, and am introducing others into my narrative, not for their own sake, or because I love and have loved them, so much as because, and so far as, they have influenced my theological views. In this respect then, I speak of Hurrell Froude—in his intellectual aspect—as a man of high genius, brimful and overflowing with ideas and views, in him original, which were too many and strong even for his bodily strength, and which crowded and jostled against each other in their effort after distinct shape and expression. And he had an intellect as critical and logical as it was speculative and bold. Dying prematurely, as he did, and in the conflict and transition-state of opinion, his religious views never reached their ultimate conclusion, by the very reason of their multitude and their depth. His opinions arrested and influenced me, even when they did not gain my assent. He professed openly his admiration of the Church of Rome, and his hatred of the reformers. He delighted in the notion of an hierarchical system, of sacerdotal power and of full ecclesiastical liberty. He felt scorn of the maxim, "The Bible and the Bible only is the religion of Protestants"; and he gloried in accepting tradition as a main instrument of religious teaching. He had a high severe idea of the intrinsic excellence of virginity; and he considered the Blessed Virgin its great pattern. He delighted in thinking of the saints; he had a keen appreciation of the idea of sanctity, its possibility and its heights; and he was more than inclined to believe a large amount of miraculous interference as occurring in the early and middle ages. He embraced the principle of penance and mortification. He had a deep devotion to the Real Presence, in which he had a firm faith. He was powerfully drawn to the medieval church, but not to the primitive.

He had a keen insight into abstract truth; but he was an Englishman to the backbone in his severe adherence to the real and the concrete. He had a most classical taste, and a genius for philosophy and art;
10 and he was fond of historical inquiry, and the politics of religion. He had no turn for theology as such. He had no appreciation of the writings of the Fathers, of the detail or development of doctrine, of the definite traditions of the Church viewed in their matter, of the teaching of the ecumenical councils, or of the controversies out of which they arose. He took an eager, courageous view of things on the whole. I should say that his power of entering into the minds of others did not equal his other gifts; he could not believe, for
20 instance, that I really held the Roman Church to be Antichristian. On many points he would not believe but that I agreed with him, when I did not. He seemed not to understand my difficulties. His were of a different kind, the contrariety between theory and fact. He was a high Tory of the cavalier stamp, and was disgusted with the Toryism of the opponents of the Reform Bill. He was smitten with the love of the theocratic church; he went abroad and was shocked by the degeneracy which he thought he saw in the Catholics
30 of Italy.

It is difficult to enumerate the precise additions to my theological creed which I derived from a friend to whom I owe so much. He made me look with admiration towards the Church of Rome, and in the same degree to dislike the Reformation. He fixed deep in me the idea of devotion to the Blessed Virgin, and he led me gradually to believe in the Real Presence.

There is one remaining source of my opinions to be mentioned, and that far from the least important.
40 In proportion as I moved out of the shadow of liberalism which had hung over my course, my early devotion towards the fathers returned; and in the long vacation of 1828 I set about to read them chronologically, beginning with St. Ignatius and St. Justin. About 1830 a proposal was made to me by Mr. Hugh Rose, who with Mr. Lyall (afterwards Dean of Canterbury) was providing writers for a theological library, to furnish them with a history of the principal councils. I accepted it, and at once set to work on the Council of
50 Nicæa. It was launching myself on an ocean with currents innumerable; and I was drifted back first to the

ante-Nicene history, and then to the Church of Alexandria. The work at last appeared under the title of *The Arians of the Fourth Century*, and of its 422 pages, the first 117 consisted of introductory matter, and the Council of Nicæa did not appear till the 254th, and then occupied at most twenty pages.

I do not know when I first learnt to consider that antiquity was the true exponent of the doctrines of Christianity and the basis of the Church of England; 60 but I take it for granted that Bishop Bull, whose works at this time I read, was my chief introduction to this principle. The course of reading which I pursued in the composition of my work was directly adapted to develop it in my mind. What principally attracted me in the ante-Nicene period was the great Church of Alexandria, the historical centre of teaching in those times. Of Rome for some centuries comparatively little is known. The battle of Arianism was first fought in Alexandria; Athanasius, the champion of the truth, 70 was Bishop of Alexandria; and in his writings he refers to the great religious names of an earlier date, to Origen, Dionysius, and others who were the glory of its see, or of its school. The broad philosophy of Clement and Origen carried me away; the philosophy, not the theological doctrine; and I have drawn out some features of it in my volume, with the zeal and freshness, but with the partiality of a neophyte. Some portions of their teaching, magnificent in themselves, came like music to my inward ear, as if the response 80 to ideas, which, with little external to encourage them, I had cherished so long. These were based on the mystical or sacramental principle, and spoke of the various economies or dispensations of the eternal. I understood them to mean that the exterior world, physical and historical, was but the outward manifestation of realities greater than itself. Nature was a parable: Scripture was an allegory: pagan literature, philosophy, and mythology, properly understood, were but a preparation for the Gospel. The Greek poets and 90 sages were in a certain sense prophets; for "thoughts beyond their thought to those high bards were given." There had been a divine dispensation granted to the Jews; there had been in some sense a dispensation carried on in favour of the Gentiles. He who had taken the seed of Jacob for His elect people, had not therefore cast the rest of mankind out of His sight. In the fullness of time both Judaism and Paganism had come to nought; the outward framework, which concealed yet suggested the living truth, had never been 100 intended to last, and it was dissolving under the beams of the sun of justice behind it and through it. The process of change had been slow; it had been

26. **Reform Bill.** See the general introduction to Chapter 5, p. 824. 37. **the Real Presence,** that is, the actual presence of Christ in the bread and wine of the Eucharistic sacrament. 44. **St. Ignatius and St. Justin.** Ignatius (c. 50?-107 or 116) was Bishop of Antioch and a Father of the Church; Justin was a Christian apologist contemporaneous

with Ignatius. 45-46. **Mr. Hugh Rose . . . Mr. Lyall.** Hugh James Rose (1795-1838) and William Rowe Lyall (1788-1857) were a theologian connected with the beginnings of Tractarianism and the editor of the *Theological Library*, respectively. 49. **Council of Nicæa.** See p. 984, note 32. 70. **Athanasius,** St. Athanasius (296?-373), opponent

done not rashly, but by rule, and measure, "at sundry times and in divers manners," first one disclosure and then another, till the whole was brought into full manifestation. And thus room was made for the anticipation of further and deeper disclosures, of truths still under the veil of the letter, and in their season to be revealed. The visible world still remains without its divine interpretation; Holy Church in her sacraments and her hierarchical appointments, will remain even to the end of the world, only a symbol of those heavenly facts which fill eternity. Her mysteries are but the expressions in human language of truths to which the human mind is unequal. It is evident how much there was in all this in correspondence with the thoughts which had attracted me when I was young, and with the doctrine which I have already connected with the *Analogy* and the *Christian Year*.

I suppose it was to the Alexandrian school and to the early church that I owe in particular what I definitely held about the angels. I viewed them, not only as the ministers employed by the Creator in the Jewish and Christian dispensations, as we find on the face of Scripture, but as carrying on, as Scripture also implies, the economy of the visible world. I considered them as the real causes of motion, light, and life, and of those elementary principles of the physical universe, which, when offered in their developments to our senses, suggest to us the notion of cause and effect, and of what are called the laws of nature. I have drawn out this doctrine in my sermon for Michaelmas day, written not later than 1834. I say of the angels, "Every breath of air and ray of light and heat, every beautiful prospect is, as it were, the skirts of their garments, the waving of the robes of those whose faces see God." Again, I ask what would be the thoughts of a man who, "when examining a flower, or a herb, or a pebble, or a ray of light, which he treats as something so beneath him in the scale of existence, suddenly discovered that he was in the presence of some powerful being who was hidden behind the visible things he was inspecting, who, though concealing his wise hand, was giving them their beauty, grace, and perfection, as being God's instrument for the purpose, nay, whose robe and ornaments those objects were, which he was so eager to analyse?" and I therefore remark that "we may say with grateful and simple hearts with the Three Holy Children, 'O all ye works of the Lord, etc., etc., bless ye the Lord, praise Him, and magnify Him for ever.'"

Also, besides the hosts of evil spirits, I considered there was a middle race, δαιμόνια, neither in heaven, nor hell: partially fallen, capricious, wayward; noble or crafty, benevolent or malicious, as the case might be. They gave a sort of inspiration or intelligence to races, nations, and classes of men. Hence the action of bodies politic and associations, which is so different often from that of the individuals who compose them. Hence the character and the instinct of states and governments, of religious communities and communions. I thought they were inhabited by unseen intelligences. My preference of the personal to the abstract would naturally lead me to this view. I thought it countenanced by the mention of "the Prince of Persia" in the Prophet Daniel, and I think I considered that it was of such intermediate beings that the Apocalypse spoke, when it introduced "the Angels of the Seven Churches."

In 1837 I made a further development of this doctrine. I said to my great friend, Samuel Francis Wood, in a letter which came into my hands on his death, "I have an idea. The mass of the Fathers (Justin, Athenagoras, Irenæus, Clement, Tertullian, Origen, Lactantius, Sulpicius, Ambrose, Nazianzen), hold that, though Satan fell from the beginning, the Angels fell before the deluge, falling in love with the daughters of men. This has lately come across me as a remarkable solution of a notion which I cannot help holding. Daniel speaks as if each nation had its guardian Angel. I cannot but think that there are beings with a great deal of good in them, yet with great defects, who are the animating principles of certain institutions, etc., etc. . . . Take England, with many high virtues, and yet a low Catholicism. It seems to me that John Bull is a spirit neither of heaven nor hell. . . . Has not the Christian Church, in its parts, surrendered itself to one or other of these simulations of the truth? . . . How are we to avoid Scylla and Charybdis and go straight on to the very image of Christ?" etc., etc.

I am aware that what I have been saying will, with many men, be doing credit to my imagination at the expense of my judgment—"Hippoclides doesn't care"; I am not setting myself up as a pattern of good sense or of anything else: I am but vindicating myself from the charge of dishonesty.—There is indeed another view of the economy brought out, in the course of the same dissertation on the subject, in my History of the Arians, which has afforded matter for the latter imputation; but I reserve it for the concluding portion of my reply.

While I was engaged in writing my work upon the Arians, great events were happening at home and abroad, which brought out into form and passionate expression the various beliefs which had so gradually been winning their way into my mind. Shortly before,

---

of Arianism. 73. **Origen,** Christian theologian in Alexandria (c. 185-c. 254). **Dionysius,** the Great (c. 190-265), Bishop of Alexandria, student of Origen. 75. **Clement,** of Alexandria (c. 150-c. 215), Greek Christian theologian. 166. **Prince of Persia.** See Daniel, 10:13. 168. **Apocalypse, etc.** See Revelation 1. 194. **Hippoclides doesn't**

care. According to Herodotus, this is what Hippoclides said when his would-be father-in-law told him that his foolishness had lost him his bride.

there had been a revolution in France; the Bourbons had been dismissed: and I believed that it was unchristian for nations to cast off their governors, and, much more, sovereigns who had the divine right of inheritance. Again, the great Reform agitation was going around me as I wrote. The Whigs had come into power; Lord Grey had told the bishops to set their house in order, and some of the prelates had been insulted and threatened in the streets of London. The vital question was how were we to keep the Church from being liberalised? there was such apathy on the subject in some quarters, such imbecile alarm in others; the true principles of churchmanship seemed so radically decayed, and there was such distraction in the councils of the clergy. The Bishop of London of the day, an active and openhearted man, had been for years engaged in diluting the high orthodoxy of the Church by the introduction of the Evangelical body into places of influence and trust. He had deeply offended men who agreed with myself, by an off-hand saying (as it was reported) to the effect that belief in the Apostolical succession had gone out with the non-jurors. "We can count you," he said to some of the gravest and most venerated persons of the old school. And the Evangelical party itself seemed, with their late success, to have lost that simplicity and unworldliness which I admired so much in Milner and Scott. It was not that I did not venerate such men as the then Bishop of Lichfield, and others of similar sentiments, who were not yet promoted out of the ranks of the clergy, but I thought little of them as a class. I thought they played into the hands of the Liberals. With the establishment thus divided and threatened, thus ignorant of its true strength, I compared that fresh vigorous power of which I was reading in the first centuries. In her triumphant zeal on behalf of that primeval mystery, to which I had had so great a devotion from my youth, I recognised the movement of my Spiritual Mother. "Incessu patuit Dea." The self-conquest of her ascetics, the patience of her martyrs, the irresistible determination of her bishops, the joyous swing of her advance, both exalted and abashed me. I said to myself, "Look on this picture and on that;" I felt affection for my own Church, but not tenderness; I felt dismay at her prospects, anger and scorn at her do-nothing perplexity. I thought that if Liberalism once got a footing within her, it was sure of the victory in the event. I saw that Reformation principles were powerless to rescue her. As to leaving her, the thought never crossed my imagination; still I ever kept before me that there was something greater than the Established Church, and that that was

the Church Catholic and Apostolic, set up from the beginning, of which she was but the local presence and organ. She was nothing, unless she was this. She must be dealt with strongly, or she would be lost. There was need of a second Reformation.

At this time I was disengaged from college duties, and my health had suffered from the labour involved in the composition of my volume. It was ready for the press in July 1832, though not published till the end of 1833. I was easily persuaded to join Hurrell Froude and his father, who were going to the south of Europe for the health of the former.

We set out in December 1832. It was during this expedition that my verses which are in the *Lyra Apostolica* were written;— a few indeed before it, but not more than one or two of them after it. Exchanging, as I was, definite tutorial labours, and the literary quiet and pleasant friendships of the last six years, for foreign countries and an unknown future, I naturally was led to think that some inward changes, as well as some larger course of action, was coming upon me. At Whitchurch, while waiting for the down mail to Falmouth, I wrote the verses about my Guardian Angel, which begin with these words: "Are these the tracks of some unearthly Friend?" and go on to speak of "the vision" which haunted me:—that vision is more or less brought out in the whole series of these compositions.

I went to various coasts of the Mediterranean, parted with my friends at Rome; went down for the second time to Sicily, at the end of April, and got back to England by Palermo in the early part of July. The strangeness of foreign life threw me back into myself; I found pleasure in historical sites and beautiful scenes, not in men and manners. We kept clear of Catholics throughout our tour. I had a conversation with the Dean of Malta, a most pleasant man, lately dead; but it was about the fathers, and the library of the great church. I knew the Abbate Santini, at Rome, who did no more than copy for me the Gregorian tones. Froude and I made two calls upon Monsignore (now Cardinal) Wiseman at the Collegio Inglese, shortly before we left Rome. I do not recollect being in a room with any other ecclesiastics, except a priest at Castro-Giovanni in Sicily, who called on me when I was ill, and with whom I wished to hold a controversy. As to church services, we attended the Tenebræ, at the Sestine, for the sake of the Miserere; and that was all. My general feeling was, "All, save the spirit of man, is divine." I saw nothing but what was external; of the hidden life of Catholics I knew nothing. I was still more driven back into myself, and felt my

1-2. **Bourbons . . . dismissed.** Charles X was dethroned in the Revolution in France of July 27-29, 1830. 7. **Lord Grey,** Earl Grey (1764-1845), British Prime Minister, 1830-1834. 22. **Apostolical succession,** the doctrine of uninterrupted succession of bishops from the Apostles to the present time. 23. **non-jurors,** English and Scottish

clergymen with benefices who refused to take the oath of allegiance to William and Mary and their successors. 39. **Incessu . . . Dea.** The goddess stood revealed by her walk. 94. **Wiseman,** Nicholas Patrick Stephen Wiseman (1802-1865), Catholic Cardinal Primate of England in 1850. 99. **Tenebrae,** special Holy Week services commemorating

isolation. England was in my thoughts solely, and the news from England came rarely and imperfectly. The Bill for the Suppression of the Irish Sees was in progress, and filled my mind. I had fierce thoughts against the Liberals.

110 It was the success of the Liberal cause which fretted me inwardly. I became fierce against its instruments and its manifestations. A French vessel was at Algiers; I would not even look at the tricolour. On my return, though forced to stop a day in Paris, I kept indoors the whole time, and all that I saw of that beautiful city, was what I saw from the diligence. The Bishop of London had already sounded me as to my filling one of the Whitehall preacherships, which he had just then put on a new footing; but I was indignant at the 120 line which he was taking, and from my steamer I sent home a letter declining the appointment by anticipation, should it be offered to me. At this time I was specially annoyed with Dr. Arnold, though it did not last into later years. Some one, I think, asked in conversation at Rome, whether a certain interpretation of Scripture was Christian? it was answered that Dr. Arnold took it; I interposed, "But is *he* a Christian?" The subject went out of my head at once; when afterwards I was taxed with it I could say no more in ex-130 planation, than that I thought I must have been alluding to some free views of Dr. Arnold about the Old Testament:—I thought I must have meant, "But who is to answer for Arnold?" It was at Rome too that we began the *Lyra Apostolica* which appeared monthly in the *British Magazine*. The motto shows the feeling of both Froude and myself at the time: we borrowed from M. Bunsen a Homer, and Froude chose the words in which Achilles, on returning to the battle, says, "You shall know the difference, now that I am back again."

140 Especially when I was left by myself, the thought came upon me that deliverance is wrought, not by the many but by the few, not by bodies but by persons. Now it was, I think, that I repeated to myself the words, which had ever been dear to me from my school days, "Exoriare aliquis!"—now too, that Southey's beautiful poem of *Thalaba*, for which I had an immense liking, came forcibly to my mind. I began to think that I had a mission. There are sentences of my letters to my friends to this effect, if they are not de-150 stroyed. When we took leave of Monsignore Wiseman, he had courteously expressed a wish that we might make a second visit to Rome; I said with great gravity, "We have a work to do in England." I went down at once to Sicily, and the presentiment grew stronger. I struck into the middle of the island, and fell ill of a fever at Leonforte. My servant thought that I was dying and begged for my last directions. I gave them, as he wished; but I said, "I shall not die." I repeated, "I shall not die, for I have not sinned against light, I have not sinned against light." I never have been able 160 to make out at all what I meant.

I got to Castro-Giovanni, and was laid up there for nearly three weeks. Towards the end of May I set off for Palermo, taking three days for the journey. Before starting from my inn in the morning of May 26th or 27th, I sat down on my bed, and began to sob bitterly. My servant, who had acted as my nurse, asked what ailed me. I could only answer, "I have a work to do in England."

I was aching to get home; yet for want of a vessel 170 I was kept at Palermo for three weeks. I began to visit the churches, and they calmed my impatience, though I did not attend any services. I knew nothing of the presence of the Blessed Sacrament there. At last I got off in an orange boat, bound for Marseilles. We were becalmed a whole week in the Straits of Bonifacio. Then it was that I wrote the lines, "Lead, kindly light," which have since become well known. I was writing verses the whole time of my passage. At length I got to Marseilles, and set off for England. The fatigue of 180 traveling was too much for me, and I was laid up for several days at Lyons. At last I got off again, and did not stop night or day till I reached England, and my mother's house. My brother had arrived from Persia only a few hours before. This was on the Tuesday. The following Sunday, July 14th, Mr. Keble preached the assize sermon in the University pulpit. It was published under the title of *National Apostasy*. I have ever considered and kept the day as the start of the religious movement of 1833. (1864) 190

THE PILLAR OF THE CLOUD

The Pillar of the Cloud *became better known as* Lead, Kindly Light; *it was written on shipboard when Newman was returning to England from Italy, sick with doubts and fears, to take up the struggle for reform. The title as here given refers to God's leadership of the children of Israel as recounted in Exodus* 13:21: *"And the Lord went before them by day in a pillar of a cloud, to lead them the way, and by night in a pillar of fire, to give them light."*

Lead, Kindly Light, amid the encircling gloom,
    Lead Thou me on!
The night is dark, and I am far from home—
    Lead Thou me on!

---

the suffering of Christ. 100. **Sestine,** the Sistine Chapel in the Vatican. **Miserere,** musical setting of the Fifteenth Psalm (Vulgate). 123. **Dr. Arnold,** Thomas Arnold (1795-1842), Master of Rugby School, father of Matthew Arnold, and liberal student of Scripture.

137. **M. Bunsen,** Christian Charles Josias, Baron von Bunsen (1791-1860), envoy to the Papal court. 145. **Exoriare aliquis.** May someone arise.

Keep Thou my feet; I do not ask to see
The distant scene—one step enough for me.

I was not ever thus, nor prayed that Thou
   Shouldst lead me on.
I loved to choose and see my path; but now
10   Lead Thou me on!
I loved the garish day, and, spite of fears,
Pride ruled my will; remember not past years.

So long Thy power hath blessed me, sure it still
   Will lead me on,
O'er moor and fen, o'er crag and torrent, till
   The night is gone;
And with the morn those angel faces smile
Which I have loved long since, and lost awhile.
(1833; 1836)

from THE DREAM OF GERONTIUS

SOUL

Take me away, and in the lowest deep
   There let me be,
And there in hope the lone night-watches keep,
   Told out for me.
There, motionless and happy in my pain,
   Lone, not forlorn—
There will I sing my sad perpetual strain,
   Until the morn.
There will I sing, and soothe my stricken breast,
10   Which ne'er can cease
To throb and pine, and languish, till possessed
   Of its Sole Peace.
There will I sing my absent Lord and Love—
   Take me away,
That sooner I may rise, and go above,
   And see Him in the truth of everlasting day.

ANGEL

Now let the golden prison ope its gates,
Making sweet music, as each fold revolves
Upon its ready hinge. And ye great powers,
20 Angels of Purgatory, receive from me
My charge, a precious soul, until the day,
When, from all bond and forfeiture released,
I shall reclaim it for the courts of light. . . .

Softly and gently, dearly-ransomed soul,
   In my most loving arms I now enfold thee,
And, o'er the penal waters, as they roll,
   I poise thee, and I lower thee, and hold thee.

And carefully I dip thee in the lake,
   And thou, without a sob or a resistance,

Dost through the flood thy rapid passage take,
   Sinking deep, deeper into the dim distance.

Angels, to whom the willing task is given,
   Shall tend, and nurse, and lull thee, as thou liest;
And Masses on the earth, and prayers in heaven,
   Shall aid thee at the Throne of the Most Highest.

Farewell, but not forever! brother dear,
   Be brave and patient on thy bed of sorrow;
Swiftly shall pass thy night of trial here,
   And I will come and wake thee on the morrow.
(1865; 1865)

THOMAS CARLYLE 1795-1881

Thomas Carlyle was the patriarch of Victorianism. Born in the same year as John Keats, he outlived Dickens and Thackeray and John Stuart Mill. He attended the University of Edinburgh for a time because his parents wished him to take a course in divinity and become a minister in the Scottish Church, but his independence of spirit made such a career impossible, and in 1817 he definitely abandoned the idea. Similarly he gave up school-teaching after a year's trial (1816). Indeed, he seems at this time to have gone through a serious struggle with doubt and despondency.

Carlyle's first literary work reveals clearly his admiration for German thought and philosophy, and especially for the two great German poets Schiller and Goethe; he wrote an effective biographical study of the former (1823-1824). This work was followed by a translation of a portion of Goethe's novel Wilhelm Meister (1824) and by a series of essays on German literature which appeared during 1827 in The Edinburgh Review, The Foreign Review, and The Foreign Quarterly Review. The style of these early writings is strikingly different from the verbal explosions which characterize his later manner; it is clear, simple, direct, and comparatively free from exaggerated metaphors.

Two years after his marriage to Jane Welsh (1826), Carlyle retired to her farm at Craigenputtock for six years, a period which was to him what the Horton period was to Milton (p. 378). He went to Craigenputtock an obscure writer of essays and translations; he emerged in 1834 as one of the foremost figures of literature in England, what with his excellent essay on Burns, and Sartor Resartus, the grim, apocalyptic story of his spiritual struggles.

When the Carlyles emerged from their retirement, they took up residence at 5 Cheyne Row, Chelsea, London. Here "the Sage of Chelsea" lived and wrote for the remainder of his long life. The first of the many distinguished books to appear from Cheyne

Row was his History of the French Revolution. The manuscript of the first volume was completed in 1835, but its accidental destruction delayed the publication of the three volumes until two years later. Its success of esteem but not of money induced Carlyle to give four series of public lectures. Of these the most famous were those on Heroes, Hero-Worship, and the Heroic in History, delivered in 1840 and published in 1841; they express admirably Carlyle's creed of individualism and of the importance of a strong personality. Chartism (1839), Past and Present (1843), and the Latter-Day Pamphlets (1850) give his economic and social-political theories; The Letters and Speeches of Oliver Cromwell (1845), The Life of John Sterling (1851), and the huge History of Frederick II of Prussia Called Frederick the Great (1858-1865) are obviously biographical. To prepare himself for his Frederick the Great he went to Germany to study the battlefields of Frederick's campaigns—one of the very few journeys he ever took from London; this was his last important work. The honor which came to him in being made Lord Rector of Edinburgh in 1865 turned to bitterness with the sudden death of Jane Carlyle shortly afterwards.

Carlyle's literary work falls naturally into four major divisions: biography, history, literary comment, and economic and social criticism. He has been accused of inconsistencies in his work, and minor inconsistencies no doubt appear, as might be expected in half a century of furious writing. Essentially, however, his creed is a unit and may be traced in all his work. Its roots lie in his insistence on the ascendancy of the spiritual values over the material and on the importance of the individual as compared with the mass of mankind. He preached, furiously and tirelessly, that principles are superior to rules, that cant is hollow and sincerity sound, that love of labor is to be preferred to love of pleasure, that duty and not indulgence is the true guide of life. In the revolutionary doctrine of human equality he had no faith whatever. Men, he believed, are created unequal; some are born to be heroes and leaders, and some to be followers. "Big, black democracy" he loathed and feared; and the American Civil War for the freedom of the slaves he alluded to sneeringly. Similarly, the French Revolution was to him far from glorious; it provided simply a horrible example which should serve as a warning to the English. His success as a biographer and his distinction as a historian spring from his faith in the power of the individual. History he believed to be "the essence of innumerable biographies"; and his French Revolution thus bristles with personalities. His sermons for his own time were also molded by his creed of individualism. He looked for the strong, just man to slay the dragons of materialism and greed. Political economy was a "dismal science" that he hated; the doctrine of laissez faire was anathema to him, but he

had no faith in the value of social and industrial legislation. He subscribed to no current creed; he belonged to no political group. He was an individualist, an advocate of the supreme value of innate nobility.

The stormy quality of Carlyle's preaching finds a natural reflection in the style of his writing. He was himself a vitriolic Jeremiah and his ideas were dynamic; his style is—as John Stuart Mill said—"an insane rhapsody." Some of the obvious typographical characteristics of it come, no doubt, from his familiarity with German. But Carlyle's style goes beyond such superficial characteristics. It has an echo of the utterances of the Old Testament prophets. It abounds in vigorous figures which give it a savage, dour roughness. Not a restful style, it reflects the writer's fierce indignation and passionate love of truth. Like its creator it is profound, harsh, and grim with earnestness.

from SARTOR RESARTUS

Sartor Resartus was the product of Carlyle's formative years. It is his spiritual autobiography and contains the essence of his social philosophy and his prose style. The title means "The Tailor Retailored," and the "clothes philosophy" of the first part Carlyle took from Swift's similar ideas in A Tale of a Tub. Sartor Resartus is not a narrative in the ordinary sense of the word; it is a philosophical romance. The first part sets forth the idea that the universe is to be considered as "a large suit of clothes which invests everything"; the second is an autobiographical romance in which Carlyle, under the figure of a philosophical German named Diogenes Teufelsdröckh (God-begotten devil's dung), Professor of Things in General at the University of Weissnichtwo (I know not where), sets forth his own spiritual strains and stresses. It is in this second part that the author presents the episode of his denial of kinship with the Devil (the Everlasting No), his theory of The Center of Indifference, and his Everlasting Yea. The material and the style of this astonishing production kept some publishers from considering it; ultimately it appeared in Fraser's Magazine in 1833-1834. It nearly wrecked the magazine; subscriptions fell off, and critics damned it, one writer summarizing it as "a heap of clotted nonsense." It survived this storm of adverse criticism, however, and appeared in book form in New York in 1836 and in London in 1838. The "cracked and crazed" style, an "insane rhapsody" of figures, Germanisms, unusual words and phrases, helped to increase its unpopularity. Carlyle declared, however, that the style was natural, that he had, indeed, adapted it from the usual aggressive and chaotic vigor of his father's normal expression. Certainly it fits his personality and his subject matter as no smoothly bromidic style could possibly do.

Under the strange nebulous envelopment, wherein our Professor has now shrouded himself, no doubt but his spiritual nature is nevertheless progressive, and growing for how can the "Son of Time," in any case, stand still? We behold him, through those dim years, in a state of crisis, of transition: his mad Pilgrimings, and general solution into aimless Discontinuity, what is all this but a mad Fermentation; wherefrom, the fiercer it is, the clearer product will one day 10 evolve itself?

Such transitions are ever full of pain: thus the Eagle when he molts is sickly; and, to attain his new beak, must harshly dash-off the old one upon rocks. What Stoicism soever our Wanderer, in his individual acts and motions, may affect, it is clear that there is a hot fever of anarchy and misery raging within; coruscations of which flash out: as, indeed, how could there be other? Have we not seen him disappointed, bemocked of Destiny, through long 20 years? All that the young heart might desire and pray for has been denied; nay, as in the last worst instance, offered and then snatched away. Ever an "excellent Passivity"; but of useful, reasonable Activity, essential to the former as Food to Hunger, nothing granted: till at length, in this wild Pilgrimage, he must forcibly seize for himself an Activity, though useless, unreasonable. Alas, his cup of bitterness, which had been filling drop by drop, ever since that first "ruddy morning" in the Hinterschlag Gym- 30 nasium, was at the very lip; and then with that poison-drop, of the Towgood-and-Blumine business, it runs over, and even hisses over in a deluge of foam.

He himself says once, with more justice than originality: "Man is, properly speaking, based upon Hope; he has no other possession but Hope; this world of his is emphatically the 'Place of Hope.'" What, then, was our Professor's possession? We see him, for the present, quite shut-out from Hope; looking not into the golden orient, but vaguely all round into a dim 40 copper firmament, pregnant with earthquake and tornado.

Alas, shut-out from Hope, in a deeper sense than we yet dream of! For, as he wanders wearisomely through this world, he has now lost all tidings of another and higher. Full of religion, or at least of religiosity, as our Friend has since exhibited himself, he hides not that, in those days, he was wholly irreligious: "Doubt had darkened into Unbelief," says he; "shade after shade goes grimly over your soul, till you have the fixed, starless, Tartarean black." To such 50 readers as have reflected, what can be called reflecting, on man's life, and happily discovered, in contradiction to much Profit-and-Loss Philosophy, speculative and practical, that Soul is not synonymous with Stomach; who understands, therefore, in our Friend's words, "that, for man's well-being, Faith is properly the one thing needful; how, with it, Martyrs, otherwise weak, can cheerfully endure the shame and the cross; and without it, Worldlings puke-up their sick existence, by suicide, in the midst of luxury": to such it 60 will be clear that, for a pure moral nature, the loss of his religious Belief was the loss of everything. Unhappy young man! All wounds, the crush of long-continued Destitution, the stab of false Friendship and of false Love, all wounds in thy so genial heart, would have healed again, had not its life-warmth been withdrawn. Well might he exclaim, in his wild way: "Is there no God, then; but at best an absentee God, sitting idle, ever since the first Sabbath, at the outside of his Universe, and seeing it go? Has the word Duty no 70 meaning; is what we call Duty no divine Messenger and Guide, but a false earthly Fantasm, made-up of Desire and Fear, of emanations from the Gallows and from Doctor Graham's Celestial-Bed? Happiness of an approving Conscience! Did not Paul of Tarsus, whom admiring men have since named Saint, feel that he was 'the chief of sinners'; and Nero of Rome, jocund in spirit (wohlgemuth), spend much of his time in fiddling? Foolish Wordmonger and Motive-grinder, who in thy Logic-mill hast an earthly 80 mechanism for the Godlike itself, and wouldst fain grind me out Virtue from the husks of Pleasure— I tell thee, Nay! To the unregenerate Prometheus Vinctus of a man, it is ever the bitterest aggravation of his wretchedness that he is conscious of Virtue, that he feels himself the victim not of suffering only, but of injustice. What then? Is the heroic inspiration we name Virtue but some Passion; some bubble of the blood, bubbling in the direction others profit by? I know not: only this I know, If what thou 90 namest Happiness be our true aim, then are we all astray. With Stupidity and sound Digestion man may

Sartor Resartus. **1. nebulous envelopment.** Frustrated in love and consumed by inward misery, Teufelsdröckh, calling himself a "Son of Time," becomes a despairing wanderer over the earth. **12. Eagle . . . rocks.** A London book, *Domestic Habits of Birds* (1833), quotes St. Augustine as saying that "when the eagle becomes very old, the upper mandible of the beak grows so long that the bird can no longer feed, in which case it betakes itself to a rock or rough stone, and rubs its beak till the overgrown part is ground down into proper proportion." Carlyle's figure of speech, however, is not sound; the eagle molts its feathers but not its beak. **21. last worst instance,** the refusal of the young lady, Blumine, to return Teufelsdröckh's love, after first appearing to do so. **24. former,** passivity. **29. Hinterschlag Gymnasium,** literally, the Strike-behind Academy; it represents the Annan Grammar School, Dumfries, Scotland, which Carlyle entered at the age of ten. **31. Towgood . . . business.** Towgood was Teufelsdröckh's most intimate friend; Blumine his ladylove. After his painful last meeting with Blumine and his rejection by her, Teufelsdröckh wandered to the mountains, where he saw Towgood and Blumine drive past him on their wedding journey. (See p. 995, and note 173.) **50. Tartarean,** of Tartarus, the lowest portion of hell. **51. what . . . reflecting.** This sentence is a good example of the broken syntax frequently found in Carlyle. **53. Profit-and-Loss Philosophy,** the doctrine of utilitarianism, which held that conduct was morally good if it promoted the greatest good of the greatest number. This doctrine was supported by Jeremy Bentham (1748-1832) and John Stuart Mill (1806-1873); Carlyle and Ruskin were among its vigorous opponents (see p. 1042). **56. one thing needful.** Cf. Luke 10:42: "But one thing is needful: and Mary hath chosen that good part, which shall not be taken away from her." Mary "sat at Jesus' feet, and heard his word" while her sister Martha was "cumbered about much serving." **74. Doctor . . . Bed.** James Graham (1745-1794) was a notorious quack doctor whose famous "Celestial-Bed" was guaranteed, for fifty pounds, to cure sterility in those who slept upon it. Carlyle refers to the bed as a symbol of false hopes. **77. chief of sinners.** Paul so labels him-

front much. But what, in these dull unimaginative days, are the terrors of Conscience to the diseases of the Liver! Not on Morality, but on Cookery, let us build our stronghold: there brandishing our frying-pan, as censer, let us offer sweet incense to the Devil, and live at ease on the fat things *he* has provided for his Elect!"

100 Thus has the bewildered Wanderer to stand, as so many have done, shouting question after question into the Sibyl-cave of Destiny, and receive no Answer but an echo. It is all a grim Desert, this once-fair world of his; wherein is heard only the howling of wild-beasts, or the shrieks of despairing, hate-filled men; and no Pillar of Cloud by day, and no Pillar of Fire by night, any longer guides the Pilgrim. To such length has the spirit of Inquiry carried him. "But what boots it *(was thut's)*?" cries he: "it is but the 110 common lot in this era. Not having come to spiritual majority prior to the *Siècle de Louis Quinze,* and not being born purely a Loghead *(Dummkopf),* thou hadst no other outlook. The whole world is, like thee, sold to Unbelief; their old Temples of the Godhead, which for long have not been rainproof, crumble down; and men ask now: where is the Godhead; our eyes never saw him?"

Pitiful enough were it, for all these wild utterances, to call our Diogenes wicked. Unprofitable servants as 120 we all are, perhaps at no era of his life was he more decisively the Servant of Goodness, the Servant of God, than even now when doubting God's existence. "One circumstance I note," says he: "after all the nameless woe that Inquiry, which for me, what it is not always, was genuine Love of Truth, had wrought me, I nevertheless still loved Truth, and would bate no jot of my allegiance to her. 'Truth!' I cried, 'though the Heavens crush me for following her: no Falsehood! though a whole celestial Lubberland were the price of Apostasy.' 130 In conduct it was the same. Had a divine Messenger from the clouds, or miraculous Handwriting on the wall, convincingly proclaimed to me *This thou shalt do,* with what passionate readiness, as I often thought, would I have done it, had it been leaping into the infernal Fire. Thus, in spite of all Motive-grinders, and Mechanical Profit-and-Loss Philosophies, with the sick ophthalmia and hallucination they had brought on, was the Infinite nature of Duty still dimly present to me: living without God in the world, of God's light I

was not utterly bereft; if my as yet sealed eyes with 140 their unspeakable longing, could nowhere see Him, nevertheless in my heart He was present, and His heaven-written Law still stood legible and sacred there."

Meanwhile, under all these tribulations, and temporal and spiritual destitutions, what must the Wanderer, in his silent soul, have endured! "The painfullest feeling," writes he, "is that of your own Feebleness *(Unkraft),* ever, as the English Milton says, to be weak is the true misery. And yet of your 150 Strength there is and can be no clear feeling, save by what you have prospered in, by what you have done. Between vague wavering Capability and fixed indubitable Performance, what a difference! A certain inarticulate Self-consciousness dwells dimly in us; which only our Works can render articulate and decisively discernible. Our Works are the mirror wherein the spirit first sees its natural lineaments. Hence, too, the folly of that impossible Precept, *Know thyself;* till it be translated into this partially possible one, 160 *Know what thou canst work at.*

"But for me, so strangely unprosperous had I been, the net-result of my Workings amounted as yet simply to—Nothing. How then could I believe in my Strength, when there was as yet no mirror to see it in? Ever did this agitating, yet, as I now perceive, quite frivolous question, remain to me insoluble: Hast thou a certain Faculty, a certain Worth, such even as the most have not; or art thou the completest Dullard of these modern times? Alas, the fearful Unbelief is 170 unbelief in yourself; and how could I believe? Had not my first, last Faith in myself, when even to me the Heavens seemed laid open, and I dared to love, been all-too cruelly belied? The speculative Mystery of Life grew ever more mysterious to me: neither in the practical Mystery had I made the slightest progress, but been everywhere buffeted, foiled, and contemptuously cast out. A feeble unit in the middle of a threatening Infinitude, I seemed to have nothing given me but eyes, whereby to discern my own wretchedness. In- 180 visible yet impenetrable walls, as of Enchantment, divided me from all living: was there, in the wide world, any true bosom I could press trustfully to mine? O Heaven, No, there was none! I kept a lock upon my lips: why should I speak much with that shifting variety of so-called Friends, in whose withered, vain

self in 1 Timothy 1:15. **Nero . . . fiddling.** Emperor Nero (37–68 A.D.) is said to have played the fiddle while Rome was burning. 83. **unregenerate . . . man,** the man who, like Prometheus, refuses to recognize a supreme being. Because Prometheus stole fire from heaven for man, he was conquered (Vinctus) and chained to a rock by order of Zeus. 102. **Sibyl-cave of Destiny.** An allusion to the visit of Aeneas to the Sibyl, a prophetess, to learn his future, (Aeneid, VI, 36 ff.). 106. **Pillar . . . night.** From Exodus 13:21: "And the Lord went before them by day in a pillar of a cloud, to lead them the way; and by night in a pillar of fire, to give them light." 111. *Siècle . . . Quinze,* the age of Louis XV, the eighteenth century, noted for its rationalism and skepticism. 119. **Diogenes,** God-begotten, the first name of Teufelsdröckh. **Unprofitable servants,** a phrase from Luke 17:10. 121. **Servant . . . existence.** Cf. Tennyson's *In Memoriam,* ll. 1943–1944, p. 887. 131. **Handwriting on the wall.** Daniel interpreted the handwriting on the wall, which appeared to King Belshazzar at a feast, to mean the loss of his kingdom. See Daniel, Chapter 5. 150. **to**

be . . . misery. In Satan's speech to Beelzebub—"To be weak is miserable."—*Paradise Lost,* I, 157 (p. 389). 157. **Our Works.** Here is a suggestion of Carlyle's gospel of work, which he speaks of as noble and sacred. See *Past and Present,* p. 1005. 159. *Know thyself,* the famous maxim of the Greek lawgiver Solon (c. 638–559 B.C.); it is inscribed over the entrance to the temple of Apollo at Delphi. 162. **"But for me,"** etc. This passage is highly autobiographical. From 1819 to 1822 Carlyle suffered from insomnia and dyspepsia, which he called "a rat gnawing at the pit of his stomach." He was also sorely perplexed by mental and spiritual conflicts. 173. **I . . . love.** A reference to the love affair with Blumine (see p. 994, note to l. 31); perhaps Carlyle is thinking of his boyhood love for Margaret Gordon, or of his great love for Jane Welsh, which at first was fraught with misunderstanding and many obstacles. 176. **Mystery,** trade, occupation.

and too-hungry souls Friendship was but an incredible tradition? In such cases, your resource is to talk little, and that little mostly from the Newspapers. Now when I look back, it was a strange isolation I then lived in. The men and women around me, even speaking with me, were but Figures; I had, practically, forgotten that they were alive, that they were not merely automatic. In the midst of their crowded streets and assemblages, I walked solitary; and (ex-10 cept as it was my own heart, not another's, that I kept devouring) savage also, as the tiger in his jungle. Some comfort it would have been, could I, like a Faust, have fancied myself tempted and tormented of the Devil; for a Hell, as I imagine, without Life, though only diabolic Life, were more frightful: but in our age of Down-pulling and Disbelief, the very Devil has been pulled down, you cannot so much as believe in a Devil. To me the Universe was all void of Life, of Purpose, of Volition, even of Hostility: it was one 20 huge dead, immeasurable Steam-engine, rolling on, in its dead indifference, to grind me limb from limb. O, the vast, gloomy, solitary Golgotha, and Mill of Death! Why was the Living banished thither companionless, conscious? Why, if there is no Devil; nay, unless the Devil is your God?"

A prey incessantly to such corrosions, might not, moreover, as the worst aggravation to them, the iron constitution even of a Teufelsdröckh threaten to fail? We conjecture that he has known sickness; and, in 30 spite of his locomotive habits, perhaps sickness of the chronic sort. Hear this, for example: "How beautiful to die of broken-heart, on Paper! Quite another thing in practice; every window of your Feeling, even of your intellect, as it were, begrimed and mud-bespattered, so that no pure ray can enter; a whole Drugshop in your inwards; the fordone soul drowning slowly in quagmires of Disgust!"

Putting all which external and internal miseries together, may we not find in the following sentences, 40 quite in our Professor's still vein, significance enough? "From Suicide a certain aftershine (Nachschein) of Christianity withheld me: perhaps also a certain indolence of character; for, was not that a remedy I had at any time within reach? Often, however, was there a question present to me: Should some one now, at the turning of that corner, blow thee suddenly out of Space, into the other World, or other No-world, by pistol-shot—how were it? On which ground, too, I often, in sea-storms and sieged cities and other 50 death-scenes, exhibited an imperturbability, which passed, falsely enough, for courage."

"So had it lasted," concludes the Wanderer, "so had

it lasted as in bitter protracted Death-agony, through long years. The heart within me, unvisited by any heavenly dewdrop, was smoldering in sulphurous, slow-consuming fire. Almost since earliest memory I had shed no tear; or once only when I, murmuring half-audibly, recited Faust's Death-song, that wild *Selig der den er im Siegesglanze findet* (Happy whom he finds in Battle's splendor), and thought that of this 60 last Friend even I was not forsaken, that Destiny itself could not doom me not to die. Having no hope, neither had I any definite fear, were it of Man or of Devil: nay, I often felt as if it might be solacing, could the Arch-Devil himself, though in Tartarean terrors, but rise to me, that I might tell him a little of my mind. And yet, strangely enough, I lived in a continual, indefinite, pining fear; tremulous, pusillanimous, apprehensive of I knew not what; it seemed as if all things in the Heavens above and the Earth beneath 70 would hurt me; as if the Heavens and the Earth were but boundless jaws of a devouring monster, wherein I, palpitating, waited, to be devoured.

"Full of such humor, and perhaps the miserablest man in the whole French Capital or Suburbs, was I, one sultry Dogday, after much perambulation, toiling along the dirty little *Rue Saint-Thomas de l'Enfer*, among civic rubbish enough, in a close atmosphere, and over pavements hot as Nebuchadnezzar's Furnace; whereby doubtless my spirits were little cheered; 80 when, all at once, there rose a Thought in me, and I asked myself: 'What *art* thou afraid of? Wherefore, like a coward, dost thou forever pip and whimper, and go cowering and trembling? Despicable biped! what is the sum-total of the worst that lies before thee? Death? Well, Death; and say the pangs of Tophet too, and all that the Devil and Man may, will, or can do against thee! Hast thou not a heart; canst thou not suffer whatsoever it be; and, as a Child of Freedom, though outcast, trample Tophet itself under thy feet, 90 while it consumes thee? Let it come, then; I will meet it and defy it!' And as I so thought, there rushed like a stream of fire over my whole soul; and I shook base Fear away from me forever. I was strong, of unknown strength; a spirit, almost a god. Ever from that time, the temper of my misery was changed: not Fear or whining Sorrow was it, but Indignation and grim fire-eyed Defiance.

"Thus had the EVERLASTING NO (*das ewige Nein*) pealed authoritatively through all the recesses of my 100 Being, of my ME; and then was it that my whole ME stood up, in native God-created majesty, and with emphasis recorded its Protest. Such a Protest, the most important transaction in Life, may that same Indigna-

12. **Faust,** a medieval scholar and magician, reputed to have sold his soul to the devil. He is the hero of Goethe's *Faust*, and of Marlowe's *Dr. Faustus*. 15. **in our age.** Carlyle's age was a time of conflicting attitudes in religious and social spheres. See p. 822. 22. **Golgotha, the** place of the crucifixion of Christ; see Matthew 27:33; the word means "the place of the skull." 41. **Suicide.** During his years of misery Carlyle had contemplated suicide. 58. **Faust's Death-song.** In Goethe's *Faust*, IV, 1572–1576. 76. **one sultry Dogday, etc.** This incident

actually happened to Carlyle in Leith Walk, Edinburgh, in June 1821. The *Rue de l'Enfer* may be translated *Hell Street*. The term *dog days* is applied to the sultry period of July and August when Sirius, the Dog Star, *is* in the ascendant. 79. **Nebuchadnezzar's Furnace,** the fiery furnace into which King Nebuchadnezzar cast Shadrach, Meshach, and Abednego on their refusal to worship the image that he had set up (Daniel, Chapter 3). 86. **Tophet,** hell; also the name of a furnace in the Valley of Hinnom, near Jerusalem, where human sacrifices by

tion and Defiance, in a psychological point of view, be fitly called. The Everlasting No had said: 'Behold, thou art fatherless, outcast, and the Universe is mine (the Devil's)'; to which my whole ME now made answer: 'I am not thine, but Free, and forever hate thee!'

"It is from this hour that I incline to date my Spiritual New-birth, or Baphometic Fire-baptism; perhaps I directly thereupon began to be a Man." (II, 7)

CENTER OF INDIFFERENCE

Though, after this "Baphometic Fire-baptism" of his, our Wanderer signifies that his Unrest was but increased; as, indeed, "Indignation and Defiance," especially against things in general, are not the most peaceable inmates; yet can the Psychologist surmise that it was no longer a quite hopeless Unrest; that henceforth it had at least a fixed center to revolve round. For the fire-baptized soul, long so scathed and thunder-riven, here feels its own Freedom, which feeling is its Baphometic Baptism: the citadel of its whole kingdom it has thus gained by assault, and will keep inexpugnable; outwards from which the remaining dominions, not indeed without hard battling, will doubtless by degrees be conquered and pacificated. Under another figure, we might say, if in that great moment, in the *Rue Saint-Thomas de l'Enfer*, the old inward Satanic School was not yet thrown out of doors, it received peremptory judicial notice to quit;—whereby, for the rest, its howl-chantings, Ernulphus-cursings, and rebellious gnashings of teeth, might, in the meanwhile, become only the more tumultuous, and difficult to keep secret.

Accordingly, if we scrutinize these Pilgrimings well, there is perhaps discernible henceforth a certain incipient method in their madness. Not wholly as a Specter does Teufelsdröckh now storm through the world; at worst as a specter-fighting Man, nay who will one day be a Specter-queller. If pilgriming restlessly to so many "Saints' Wells," and ever without quenching of his thirst, he nevertheless finds little secular wells, whereby from time to time some alleviation is ministered. In a word, he is now, if not ceasing, yet intermitting to "eat his own heart"; and clutches round him outwardly on the NOT-ME for wholesomer food. Does not the following glimpse exhibit him in a much more natural state?

"Towns also and Cities, especially the ancient, I failed not to look upon with interest. How beautiful to see thereby, as through a long vista, into the remote Time! to have, as it were, an actual section of almost the earliest Past brought safe into the Present, and set before your eyes! There, in that old City, was a live ember of Culinary Fire put down, say only two thousand years ago; and there, burning more or less triumphantly, with such fuel as the region yielded, it has burnt, and still burns, and thou thyself seest the very smoke thereof. Ah! and the far more mysterious live ember of Vital Fire was then also put down there; and still miraculously burns and spreads; and the smoke and ashes thereof (in these Judgment-Halls and Churchyards), and its bellows-engines (in these Churches), thou still seest; and its flame, looking out from every kind countenance, and every hateful one, still warms thee or scorches thee.

"Of Man's Activity and Attainment the chief results are aeriform, mystic, and preserved in Tradition only: such are his Forms of Government, with the Authority they rest on; his Customs, or Fashions both of Cloth-habits and of Soul-habits; much more his collective stock of Handicrafts, the whole Faculty he has acquired of manipulating Nature: all these things, as indispensable and priceless as they are, cannot in any way be fixed under lock and key, but must flit, spiritlike, on impalpable vehicles, from Father to Son; if you demand sight of them, they are nowhere to be met with. Visible Ploughmen and Hammermen there have been, ever from Cain and Tubalcain downwards: but where does your accumulated Agricultural, Metallurgic, and other Manufacturing SKILL lie warehoused? It transmits itself on the atmospheric air, on the sun's rays (by Hearing and by Vision); it is a thing aeriform, impalpable, of quite spiritual sort. In like manner, ask me not, Where are the LAWS; where is the GOVERNMENT? In vain wilt thou go to Schönbrunn, to Downing Street, to the Palais Bourbon: thou findest nothing there but brick or stone houses, and some bundles of Papers tied with tape. Where, then, is that same cunningly-devised almighty GOVERNMENT of theirs to be laid hands on? Everywhere, yet nowhere: seen only in its works, this too is a thing aeriform, invisible; or if you will, mystic and miraculous. So spiritual (*geistig*) is our whole daily Life: all that we do springs out of Mystery, Spirit, invisible Force; only like a little Cloud-image, or Armida's Palace, airbuilt, does the Actual body itself forth from the great mystic Deep.

"Visible and tangible products of the Past, again, I reckon-up to the extent of three: Cities, with their Cabinets and Arsenals; then tilled Fields, to either or to both of which divisions Roads with their Bridges may belong; and thirdly——Books. In which third truly, the last invented, lies a worth far surpassing that

fire were performed. See 2 Kings 23:10. **112. Baphometic.** Baphomet, a medieval corruption of the word *Mahomet*, was an idol that the Knights Templar were accused of worshiping. In the story of the Fallen Master, Baffometus fails to build a temple at the Lord's command, and the Lord anoints his chin, brow, cheeks, and heart with hot fluid gold and sets a burning crown of gold upon his head. The entire phrase suggests sudden deliverance through spiritual illumination. **132. Ernulphus-cursings,** the excommunication curse of Ernulf, Bishop of Rochester

(1040–1124), which is repeated by Dr. Slop in Sterne's *Tristram Shandy*. **180. Cain and Tubalcain.** See Genesis 4:2, 22; Cain was the first "tiller of the soil," and Tubalcain was "an instructor of every artificer in brass and iron." **187. Schönbrunn, Downing Street, Palais Bourbon,** government centers of Austria, England, and France. **197. Armida's Palace,** in Tasso's *Jerusalem Delivered*, Book XVI, the palace with its enchanted garden to which the sorceress Armida lured the Christian knights from their siege of Jerusalem.

of the two others. Wondrous indeed is the virtue of a true Book. Not like a dead city of stones, yearly crumbling, yearly needing repair; more like a tilled field, but then a spiritual field: like a spiritual tree, let me rather say, it stands from year to year, and from age to age (we have Books that already number some hundred-and-fifty human ages); and yearly comes its new produce of leaves (Commentaries, Deductions, Philosophical, Political Systems; or were it only Sermons, Pamphlets, Journalistic Essays), every one of which is talismanic and thaumaturgic, for it can persuade men. O thou who art able to write a Book, which once in the two centuries or oftener there is a man gifted to do, envy not him whom they name City-builder, and inexpressibly pity him whom they name Conqueror or City-burner! Thou too art a Conqueror and Victor: but of the true sort, namely over the Devil: thou too hast built what will outlast all marble and metal, and be a wonder-bringing City of the Mind, a Temple and Seminary and Prophetic Mount, whereto all kindreds of the Earth will pilgrim.—Fool! why journeyest thou wearisomely, in thy antiquarian fervor, to gaze on the stone pyramids of Geeza, or the clay ones of Sacchara? These stand there, as I can tell thee, idle and inert, looking over the Desert, foolishly enough, for the last three-thousand years: but canst thou not open thy Hebrew Bible, then, or even Luther's Version thereof?"

No less satisfactory is his sudden appearance not in Battle, yet on some Battle-field; which, we soon gather, must be that of Wagram; so that here, for once, is a certain approximation to distinctness of date. Omitting much, let us impart what follows:

"Horrible enough! A whole Marchfeld strewed with shell-splinters, cannon-shot, ruined tumbrils, and dead men and horses; stragglers still remaining not so much as buried. And those red mould heaps: ay, there lie the Shells of Men, out of which all the Life and Virtue has been blown; and now are they swept together, and crammed-down out of sight, like blown Egg-shells!—Did Nature, when she bade the Donau bring down his mould-cargoes from the Carinthian and Carpathian Heights, and spread them out here into the softest, richest level—intend thee, O Marchfeld, for a corn-bearing Nursery, whereon her children might be nursed; or for a Cockpit, wherein they might the more commodiously be throttled and tattered? Were thy three broad Highways, meeting here from the ends of Europe, made for Ammunition-wagons, then? Were thy Wagrams and Stillfrieds but so many ready-built Casemates, wherein the house of Hapsburg might batter with artillery, and with

artillery be battered? König Ottokar, amid yonder hillocks, dies under Rodolf's truncheon; here Kaiser Franz falls a-swoon under Napoleon's: within which five centuries, to omit the others, how has thy breast, fair Plain, been defaced and defiled! The greensward is torn-up and trampled-down; man's fond care of it, his fruit-trees, hedge-rows, and pleasant dwellings, blown away with gun powder; and the kind seedfield lies a desolate, hideous Place of Skulls.—Nevertheless, Nature is at work; neither shall these Powder-Devilkins with their utmost devilry gainsay here: but all that gore and carnage will be shrouded-in, absorbed into manure; and next year the Marchfeld will be green, nay greener. Thrifty unwearied Nature, ever out of our great waste educing some little profit of thy own—how dost thou, from the very carcass of the Killer, bring Life for the Living!

"What, speaking in quite unofficial language, is the net-purport and upshot of war? To my own knowledge, for example, there dwell and toil, in the British village of Dumdrudge, usually some five-hundred souls. From these, by certain "Natural Enemies" of the French, there are successively selected, during the French war, say thirty able-bodied men. Dumdrudge, at her own expense, has suckled and nursed them: she has, not without difficulty and sorrow, fed them up to manhood, and even trained them to crafts, so that one can weave, another build, another hammer, and the weakest can stand under thirty stone avoirdupois. Nevertheless, amid much weeping and swearing, they are selected; all dressed in red; and shipped away, at the public charges, some two thousand miles, or say only to the south of Spain; and fed there till wanted. And now to that same spot, in the south of Spain, are thirty similar French artisans, from a French Dumdrudge, in like manner wending, till at length, after infinite effort, the two parties come into actual juxtaposition; and Thirty stands fronting Thirty, each with a gun in his hand. Straightway the word "Fire!" is given, and they blow the souls out of one another; and in place of sixty brisk useful craftsmen, the world has sixty dead carcasses, which it must bury, and anew shed tears for. Had these men any quarrel? Busy as the Devil is, not the smallest! They lived far enough apart; were the entirest strangers; nay, in so wide a Universe, there was even, unconsciously, by Commerce, some mutual helpfulness between them. How then? Simpleton! their Governors had fallen out; and, instead of shooting one another, had the cunning to make these poor blockheads shoot.—Alas, so is it in Deutschland, and hitherto in all other lands; still as of old, 'what

11. **thaumaturgic,** magical. 23. **stone pyramids of Geeza,** the trio of royal monuments at Gizeh near Cairo. 24. **Sacchara,** Saqqara, inferior brick tombs of an earlier dynasty than those at Gizeh. 28. **Luther's Version,** the translation of the Bible into German in 1534 by the Protestant reformer Martin Luther (1483–1546). 31. **Wagram,** an Austrian village in the plain of the Marchfeld (see l. 34), which gave its name to a battle fought there on July 5 and 6, 1809, between the French army under Napoleon and the Austrian army under the Arch-

duke Charles; the Austrians were defeated, but the casualties on both sides were unusually severe. 42. **Donau,** German form of "Danube." 50. **Stillfried,** a battle fought, like Wagram, on the banks of the March River in Austria, August 26, 1278, between Rudolph I of the House of Hapsburg and Ottokar II, king of Bohemia; Ottokar was defeated and killed. In his earlier allusion to Marchfeld "strewed with shell-splinters, cannon shot, ruined tumbrils" it is evident that Carlyle had in mind Wagram and not the thirteenth-century battle, in which

devilry soever Kings do, the Greeks must pay the piper!'—In that fiction of the English Smollett, it is true, the final Cessation of War is perhaps prophetically shadowed forth; where the two Natural Enemies, in person, take each a Tobacco-pipe, filled
110 with Brimstone; light the same, and smoke in one another's faces, till the weaker gives in: but from such predicted Peace-Era, what blood-filled trenches, and contentious centuries, may still divide us!"

Thus can the Professor, at least in lucid intervals, look away from his own sorrows, over the many-colored world, and pertinently enough note what is passing there. We may remark, indeed, that for the matter of spiritual culture, if for nothing else, perhaps few periods of his life were richer than this.
120 Internally, there is the most momentous instructive Course of Practical Philosophy, with Experiments, going on; towards the right comprehension of which his Peripatetic habits, favorable to Meditation, might help him rather than hinder. Externally, again, as he wanders to and fro, there are, if for the longing heart little substance, yet for the seeing eye sights enough: in these so boundless Travels of his, granting that the Satanic School was even partially kept down, what an incredible knowledge of our Planet, and
130 its Inhabitants and their Works, that is to say, of all knowable things, might not Teufelsdröckh acquire!

"I have read in most Public Libraries," says he, "including those of Constantinople and Samarcand: in most Colleges, except the Chinese Mandarin ones, I have studied, or seen that there was no studying. Unknown Languages have I oftenest gathered from their natural repertory, the Air, by my organ of Hearing; Statistics, Geographics, Topographics came, through the Eye, almost of their own accord. The
140 ways of Man, how he seeks food, and warmth, and protection for himself, in most regions, are ocularly known to me. Like the great Hadrian, I meted out much of the terraqueous Globe with a pair of Compasses that belonged to myself only.

"Of great Scenes why speak? Three summer days, I lingered reflecting, and even composing (*dichtete*), by the Pine-chasms of Vaucluse; and in that clear Lakelet moistened my bread. I have sat under the Palm-trees of Tadmor; smoked a pipe among the ruins
150 of Babylon. The great Wall of China I have seen; and can testify that it is of gray brick, coped and covered with granite, and shows only second-rate masonry.—Great Events, also, have not I witnessed? Kings sweated-down (*ausgemergelt*) into Berlin-and-Milan Customhouse-Officers; the World well won, and the World well lost; oftener than once a hundred

thousand individuals shot (by each other) in one day. All kindreds and peoples and nations dashed together and shifted and shoveled into heaps that they might ferment there, and in time unite. The birth-pangs of 160 Democracy, wherewith convulsed Europe was groaning in cries that reached Heaven, could not escape me.

"For great Men I have ever had the warmest predilection; and can perhaps boast that few such in this era have wholly escaped me. Great Men are the inspired (speaking and acting) Texts of that divine BOOK OF REVELATIONS, whereof a Chapter is completed from epoch to epoch, and by some named HISTORY; to which inspired Texts your numerous talented men, and your innumerable untalented men, 170 are the better or worse exegetic Commentaries, and wagonload of too-stupid, heretical or orthodox, weekly Sermons. For my study the inspired Texts themselves! Thus did not I, in very early days, having disguised me as tavern-waiter, stand behind the field-chairs, under that shady Tree at Treisnitz by the Jena Highway; waiting upon the great Schiller and greater Goethe; and hearing what I have not forgotten. For——"

——But at this point the Editor recalls his prin- 180 ciple of caution, some time ago laid down, and must suppress much. Let not the sacredness of Laureled, still more, of Crowned Heads, be tampered with. Should we, at a future day, find circumstances altered, and the time come for Publication, then may these glimpses into the privacy of the Illustrious be conceded; which for the present were little better than treacherous, perhaps traitorous Eavesdroppings. Of Lord Byron, therefore, of Pope Pius, Emperor Tarakwang, and the "White Water-roses" (Chinese 190 Carbonari) with their mysteries, no notice here! Of Napoleon himself we shall only, glancing from afar, remark that Teufelsdröckh's relation to him seems to have been of very varied character. At first we find our poor Professor on the point of being shot as a spy; then taken into private conversation, even pinched on the ear, yet presented with no money; at last indignantly dismissed, almost thrown out of doors, as an "Ideologist." "He himself," says the Professor, "was among the completest Ideologists, at 200 least Ideopraxists: in the Idea (*in der Idee*) he lived, moved, and fought. The man was a Divine Missionary, though unconscious of it; and preached, through the cannon's throat, that great doctrine, *La carrière ouverte aux talens* (The Tools to him that can handle them), which is our ultimate Political Evangel, wherein alone can liberty lie. Madly enough he preached, it is true, as Enthusiasts and first Missionaries are wont,

gunpowder was, of course, not used. 51. **Casemates,** bombproof chambers. 54. **Kaiser Franz,** the popular name for Francis I (1768–1835), emperor of Austria. 61. **Place of Skulls,** an allusion to Calvary, or Golgotha ("the place of a skull"); see John 19:17. 73. **Dumdrudge,** Carlyle's coined name for any typical British village. 81. **stone,** an English measure of weight, fourteen pounds. 106. **Smollett,** Tobias Smollett (1721–1771), English novelist. 133. **Samarcand,** a city of Russian Turkestan, once a great center of learning. 142.

Hadrian, Roman emperor who ruled from 117–138 A.D. 147. **Vaucluse,** a village in southeastern France. 149. **Tadmor,** Palmyra, an ancient city in an oasis of the Syrian desert. 176. **Jena,** a town in Germany, rich in memories of Goethe and Schiller. 189. **Emperor Tarakwang,** contemporary emperor of China. 191. **Carbonari,** a secret Italian political association; Carlyle applies the name to a similar group in China. 201. **Ideopraxist,** one who puts ideas into practice.

with imperfect utterance, amid much frothy rant; yet as articulately perhaps as the case admitted. Or call him, if you will, an American Backwoodsman, who had to fell unpenetrated forests, and battle with innumerable wolves, and did not entirely forbear strong liquor, rioting, and even theft; whom, notwithstanding, the peaceful Sower will follow, and, as he cuts the boundless harvest, bless."

More legitimate and decisively authentic is Teu10felsdröckh's appearance and emergence (we know not well whence) in the solitude of the North Cape, on that June Midnight. He has "a light-blue Spanish cloak" hanging round him, as his "most commodious, principal, indeed sole upper garment"; and stands there, on the World-promontory, looking over the infinite Brine, like a little blue Belfry (as we figure), now motionless indeed, yet ready, if stirred, to ring quaintest changes.

"Silence as of death," writes he; "for Midnight, 20even in the Arctic latitudes, has its character: nothing but the granite cliffs ruddy-tinged, the peaceable gurgle of that slow-heaving Polar Ocean, over which in the utmost North the great Sun hangs low and lazy, as if he too were slumbering. Yet is his cloud-couch wrought of crimson and cloth-of-gold; yet does his light stream over the mirror of waters, like a tremulous fire-pillar, shooting downwards to the abyss, and hide itself under my feet. In such moments, Solitude also is invaluable; for who would speak, or be looked 30on, when behind him lies all Europe and Africa, fast asleep, except the watchmen; and before him the silent Immensity, and Palace of the Eternal, whereof our Sun is but a porch-lamp?

"Nevertheless, in this solemn moment comes a man, or monster, scrambling from among the rock-hollows; and, shaggy, huge as the Hyperborean Bear, hails me in Russian speech: most probably, therefore, a Russian Smuggler. With courteous brevity, I signify my indifference to contraband trade, my humane in40tentions, yet strong wish to be private. In vain: the monster, counting doubtless on his superior stature, and minded to make sport for himself, or perhaps profit, were it with murder, continues to advance, ever assailing me with his importunate train-oil breath, and now has advanced, till we stand both on the verge of the rock, the deep Sea rippling greedily down below. What argument will avail? On the thick Hyperborean, cherubic reasoning, seraphic eloquence were lost. Prepared for such extremity, I, deftly 50enough, whisk aside one step; draw out, from my interior reservoirs, a sufficient Birmingham Horsepistol, and say, "Be so obliging as retire, Friend (*Er ziehe sich zurück, Freund*), and with promptitude!"

This logic even the Hyperborean understands; fast enough, with apologetic, petitionary growl, he sidles off; and, except for suicidal as well as homicidal purposes, need not return.

"Such I hold to be the genuine use of Gunpowder: that it makes all men alike tall. Nay, if thou be cooler, cleverer than I, if thou have more *Mind*, 60though all but no Body whatever, then canst thou kill me first, and art the taller. Hereby, at last, is the Goliath powerless, and the David resistless; savage Animalism is nothing, inventive Spiritualism is all.

"With respect to Duels, indeed, I have my own ideas. Few things, in this so surprising world, strike me with more surprise. Two little visual Spectra of men, hovering with insecure enough cohesion in the midst of the UNFATHOMABLE, and to dissolve therein, at any rate, very soon—make pause at the distance 70of twelve paces asunder; whirl round; and, simultaneously by the cunningest mechanism, explode one another into Dissolution; and off-hand become Air, and Non-extant! Deuce on it (*verdammt*), the little spitfires!—Nay, I think with old Hugo von Trimberg: 'God must needs laugh outright, could such a thing be, to see his wondrous Manikins here below.'"

But amid these specialties, let us not forget the great generality, which is our chief quest here: How prospered the inner man of Teufelsdröckh under so 80much outward shifting? Does Legion still lurk in him, though repressed; or has he exorcised that Devil's Brood? We can answer that the symptoms continue promising. Experience is the grand spiritual Doctor; and with him Teufelsdröckh has now been long a patient, swallowing many a bitter bolus. Unless our poor Friend belong to the numerous class of Incurables, which seems not likely, some cure will doubtless be effected. We should rather say that Legion, or the Satanic School, was now pretty well ex-90tirpated and cast out, but next to nothing introduced in its room; whereby the heart remains, for the while, in a quiet but no comfortable state.

"At length, after so much roasting," thus writes our Autobiographer, "I was what you might name calcined. Pray only that it be not rather, as is the more frequent issue, reduced to a *caput mortuum!* But in any case, by mere dint of practice, I had grown familiar with many things. Wretchedness was still wretched; but I could now partly see through it, 100and despise it. Which highest mortal, in this inane Existence, had I not found a Shadow-hunter, or Shadow-hunted; and, when I looked through his brave garnitures, miserable enough? Thy wishes have all been sniffed aside, thought I: but what, had they even

36. **Hyperborean**, from the extreme north, a region inhabited by a mythological race. 63. **Goliath**. For the story of David and Goliath, see 1 Samuel, Chapter 17. 75. **Hugo von Trimberg**, a German moral writer of the thirteenth century. 81. **Legion**. See Mark 5:9, where the "unclean spirit" replies to Jesus, "My name is Legion: for we are many." 86. **bolus**, pill. 90. **Satanic School**. Carlyle may

have had in mind the epithet given by Southey in his *Vision of Judgment* to Byron, Shelley, and other romantic poets of their period. 97. **caput mortuum**, a death's head, or skull; Carlyle's allusions to "roasting" and "calcining" indicate that he may have had in mind the term applied by chemists to the worthless residue after distillation. 115. **Arcturus, etc.**, stars and constellations. 117. **Shepherd . . . Shinar**.

been all granted! Did not the Boy Alexander weep because he had not two Planets to conquer; or a whole Solar System; or after that, a whole Universe? *Ach Gott,* when I gazed into these Stars, have they not looked down on me as if with pity, from their serene spaces, like Eyes glistening with heavenly tears over the little lot of man! Thousands of human generations, all as noisy as our own, have been swallowed-up of Time, and there remains no wreck of them any more; and Arcturus and Orion and Sirius and the Pleiades are still shining in their courses, clear and young, as when the Shepherd first noted them in the plain of Shinar. Pshaw! what is this paltry little Dog-cage of an Earth; what art thou that sittest whining there? Thou art still Nothing, Nobody; true; but who, then, is Something, Somebody? For thee the Family of Man has no use; it rejects thee; thou art wholly as a dissevered limb; so be it; perhaps it is better so!"

Too-heavy-laden Teufelsdröckh! Yet surely his bands are loosening; one day he will hurl the burden far from him, and bound forth free and with a second youth.

"This," says our Professor, "was the CENTER OF INDIFFERENCE I had now reached; through which whoso travels from the Negative Pole to the Positive must necessarily pass." (II, 8)

THE EVERLASTING YEA

"Temptations in the Wilderness!" exclaims Teufelsdröckh. "Have we not all to be tried with such? Not so easily can the old Adam, lodged in us by birth, be dispossessed. Our Life is compassed round with Necessity; yet is the meaning of Life itself no other than Freedom, than Voluntary Force: thus have we a warfare; in the beginning, especially, a hard-fought battle. For the God-given mandate, *Work thou in Well-doing,* lies mysteriously written, in Promethean Prophetic Characters, in our hearts; and leaves us no rest, night or day, till it be deciphered and obeyed; till it burn forth, in our conduct, a visible, acted Gospel of Freedom. And as the clay-given mandate, *Eat thou and be filled,* at the same time persuasively proclaims itself through every nerve—must not there be a confusion, a contest, before the better Influence can become the upper?

"To me nothing seems more natural than that the Son of Man, when such God-given mandate first prophetically stirs within him, and the Clay must now be vanquished, or vanquish—should be carried of the spirit into grim Solitudes, and there fronting the Tempter do grimmest battle with him; defiantly setting him at naught, till he yield and fly. Name it

as we choose: with or without visible Devil, whether in the natural Desert of rocks and sands, or in the populous moral Desert of selfishness and baseness—to such Temptation are we all called. Unhappy if we are not! Unhappy if we are but Half-men, in whom that divine handwriting has never blazed forth, all-subduing, in true sun-splendor; but quivers dubiously amid meaner lights or smolders, in dull pain, in darkness, under earthly vapors!—Our Wilderness is the wide World in an Atheistic Century; our Forty Days are long years of suffering and fasting: nevertheless, to these also comes an end. Yes, to me also was given, if not Victory, yet the consciousness of Battle, and the resolve to persevere therein while life or faculty is left. To me also, entangled in the enchanted forests, demon-peopled, doleful of sight and of sound, it was given, after weariest wanderings, to work out my way into the higher sunlit slopes—of that Mountain which has no summit, or whose summit is in Heaven only!"

He says elsewhere, under a less ambitious figure, as figures are, once for all, natural to him: "Has not thy Life been that of most sufficient men (*tüchtigen Männer*) thou hast known in this generation? An out-flush of foolish young Enthusiasm, like the first fallow crop, wherein are as many weeds as valuable herbs: this all parched away, under the Droughts of practical and spiritual Unbelief, as Disappointment, in thought and act, often-repeated gave rise to Doubt, and Doubt gradually settled into Denial! If I have had a second-crop, and now see the perennial greensward, and sit under umbrageous cedars, which defy all Drought (and Doubt); herein, too, be the Heavens praised, I am not without examples, and even exemplars."

So that, for Teufelsdröckh also, there has been a "glorious revolution": these mad shadow-hunting and shadow-hunted Pilgrimings of his were but some purifying "Temptation in the Wilderness," before his Apostolic work (such as it was) could begin; which Temptation is now happily over, and the Devil once more worsted! Was "that high moment in the *Rue de l'Enfer,*" then, properly the turning-point of the battle; when the Fiend said, *Worship me or be torn in shreds,* and was answered valiantly with an *Apage Satana?*—Singular Teufelsdröckh, would thou hadst told thy singular story in plain words! But it is fruitless to look there, in those Paper-bags, for such. Nothing but innuendoes, figurative crochets: a typical Shadow, fitfully wavering, prophetico-satiric; no clear logical Picture. "How paint to the sensual eye," asks he once, "what passes in the Holy-of-Holies of Man's Soul; in what words, known to these profane times, speak even afar-off of the unspeakable?" We ask in

See Genesis 15:5, where Abraham is told by the Lord to "Look now toward heaven and tell [i.e., count] the stars"; Abraham's ancestral home was in the plain of Shinar in Babylonia. 132. **"Temptations in the Wilderness."** See Matthew, Chapter 4, which contains an account of the forty days of Jesus' fasting, followed by his temptation by Satan. 134. **old Adam,** human frailty inherited by all from Adam. 140. **Prome-**

thean. In Greek myth Prometheus was a Titan who was punished by Zeus for giving to man the gift of fire; Promethean Characters are, therefore, letters written in divine fire. 145. *Eat . . . filled.* See Matthew 4:3; a "clay-given" mandate is an appeal to the flesh. 187. **umbrageous,** shady. 196. **"that . . . l'Enfer."** Cf. p. 996, ll. 74 ff. 199. *Apage Satana.* See Matthew 4:10, "Get thee hence, Satan."

turn: Why perplex these times, profane as they are, with needless obscurity, by omission and by commission? Not mystical only is our Professor, but whimsical; and involves himself, now more than ever, in eye-bewildering *chiaroscuro*. Successive glimpses, here faithfully imparted, our more gifted readers must endeavor to combine for their own behoof.

He says: "The hot Harmattan wind had raged itself out; its howl went silent within me; and the
10 long-deafened soul could now hear. I paused in my wild wanderings; and sat me down to wait, and consider; for it was as if the hour of change drew nigh. I seemed to surrender, to renounce utterly, and say: Fly, then, false shadows of Hope; I will chase you no more, I will believe you no more. And ye too, haggard specters of Fear, I care not for you; ye too are all shadows and a lie. Let me rest here: for I am way-weary and life-weary; I will rest here, were it but to die: to die or to live is alike to me; alike
20 insignificant."—And again: "Here, then, as I lay in that CENTER OF INDIFFERENCE; cast, doubtless by benignant upper Influence, into a healing sleep, the heavy dreams rolled gradually away, and I awoke to a new Heaven and a new Earth. The first preliminary moral Act, Annihilation of Self (*Selbsttödtung*), had been happily accomplished; and my mind's eyes were now unsealed, and its hands ungyved."

Might we not also conjecture that the following passage refers to his Locality, during this same
30 "healing sleep"; that his Pilgrimstaff lies cast aside here, on "the high table-land"; and indeed that the repose is already taking wholesome effect on him? If it were not that the tone, in some parts, has more of riancy, even of levity, than we could have expected! However, in Teufelsdröckh, there is always the strangest Dualism: light dancing, with guitar-music, will be going on in the fore-court, while by fits from within comes the faint whimpering of woe and wail. We transcribe the piece entire:

40 "Beautiful it was to sit there, as in my skyey Tent, musing and meditating; on the high table-land, in front of the Mountains; over me, as roof, the azure Dome, and around me, for walls, four azure-flowing curtains—namely, of the Four azure winds, on whose bottom-fringes also I have seen gilding. And then to fancy the fair Castles that stood sheltered in these Mountain hollows; with their green flower-lawns, and white dames and damosels, lovely enough: or better still, the straw-roofed Cottages, wherein stood many
50 a Mother baking bread, with her children round her:—all hidden and protectingly folded-up in the valley-folds; yet there and alive, as sure as if I beheld them. Or to see, as well as fancy, the nine Towns and Villages, that lay round my mountain-seat, which, in still weather, were wont to speak to me (by their

steeple-bells) with metal tongue; and, in almost all weather, proclaimed their vitality by repeated Smoke-clouds; whereon, as on a culinary horologe, I might read the hour of the day. For it was the smoke of cookery, as kind housewives at morning, midday, 60 eventide were boiling their husbands' kettles; and ever a blue pillar rose up into the air, successively or simultaneously, from each of the nine, saying, as plainly as smoke could say: Such and such a meal is getting ready here. Not uninteresting! For you have the whole Borough, with all its love-makings and scandal-mongeries, contentions and contentments, as in miniature, and could cover it all with your hat.— If, in my wide Wayfarings, I had learned to look into the business of the World in its details, here 70 perhaps was the place for combining it into general propositions, and deducing inferences therefrom.

"Often also could I see the black Tempest marching in anger through the Distance: round some Schreckhorn, as yet grim-blue, would the eddying vapor gather, and there tumultuously eddy, and flow down like a mad witch's hair; till, after a space, it vanished, and, in the clear sunbeam, your Schreckhorn stood smiling grim-white, for the vapor had held snow. How thou fer- 80 mentest and elaboratest, in thy great fermenting-vat and laboratory of an Atmosphere, of a World, O Nature!—Or what is Nature? Ha! why do I not name thee GOD? Art not thou the "Living Garment of God"? O Heavens, is it, in very deed, HE, then, that ever speaks through thee; that lives and loves in thee, that lives and loves in me?

"Fore-shadows, call them rather fore-splendors, of that Truth, and Beginning of Truths, fell mysteriously over my soul. Sweeter than Dayspring to the Ship- 90 wrecked in Nova Zembla; ah, like the mother's voice to her little child that strays bewildered, weeping, in unknown tumults; like soft streamings of celestial music to my too-exasperated heart, came that Evangel. The Universe is not dead and demoniacal, a charnel-house with specters; but godlike, and my Father's!

"With other eyes, too, could I now look upon my fellow man; with an infinite Love, an infinite Pity. Poor, wandering, wayward man! Art thou not tired, and beaten with stripes, even as I am? Ever, whether thou 100 bear the royal mantle or the beggar's gabardine, art thou not so weary, so heavy-laden; and thy Bed of Rest is but a Grave. O my Brother, my Brother, why cannot I shelter thee in my bosom, and wipe away all tears from thy eyes! Truly, the din of many-voiced Life, which, in this solitude, with the mind's organ, I could hear, was no longer a maddening discord, but a melting one; like inarticulate cries, and sobbings of a dumb creature, which in the ear of Heaven are prayers. The poor Earth, with her poor joys, was now my 110

---

5. *chiaroscuro*, pictorial art in black and white. 8. **Harmattan**, a dry wind that blows at certain seasons westward from the interior of Africa toward the Atlantic coast. 23. **new . . . Earth**, from Revelation 21:1.

34. **riancy**, gaiety. 75. **Schreckhorn**, a high mountain in the Bernese Oberland, Switzerland; the name means "peak of terror." 150. **Hochheimer**, a superior wine from the Rheingau district of Germany.

needy Mother, not my cruel Stepdame. Man, with his so mad Wants and so mean Endeavors, had become the dearer to me; and even for his sufferings and his sins, I now first named him Brother. Thus was I standing in the porch of that 'Sanctuary of Sorrow'; by strange, steep ways had I too been guided thither; and ere long its sacred gates would open, and the 'Divine Depth of Sorrow' lie disclosed to me."

The Professor says he here first got eye on the Knot that had been strangling him, and straightway could unfasten it, and was free. "A vain interminable controversy," writes he, "touching what is at present called Origin of Evil, or some such thing, arises in every soul, since the beginning of the world; and in every soul, that would pass from idle Suffering into actual Endeavoring, must first be put an end to. The most, in our time, have to go content with a simple, incomplete enough Suppression of this controversy; to a few some Solution of it is indispensable. In every new era, too, such Solution comes-out in different terms; and ever the Solution of the last era has become obsolete, and is found unserviceable. For it is man's nature to change his Dialect from century to century; he cannot help it though he would. The authentic *Church-Catechism* of our present century has not yet fallen into my hands: meanwhile, for my own private behoof, I attempt to elucidate the matter so. Man's Unhappiness, as I construe, comes of his Greatness; it is because there is an Infinite in him, which with all his cunning he cannot quite bury under the Finite. Will the whole Finance Ministers and Upholsterers and Confectioners of modern Europe undertake, in jointstock company, to make one Shoeblack HAPPY? They cannot accomplish it, above an hour or two; for the Shoeblack also has a Soul quite other than his Stomach; and would require, if you consider it, for his permanent satisfaction and saturation, simply this allotment, no more, and no less: *God's infinite Universe altogether to himself*, therein to enjoy infinitely, and fill every wish as fast as it rose. Oceans of Hochheimer, a Throat like that of Ophiuchus: speak not of them; to the infinite Shoeblack they are as nothing. No sooner is your ocean filled than he grumbles that it might have been of better vintage. Try him with half of a Universe, of an Omnipotence, he sets to quarreling with the proprietor of the other half and declares himself the most maltreated of men.—Always there is a black spot in our sunshine: it is even as I said, the *Shadow of Ourselves*.

"But the whim we have of Happiness is somewhat thus. By certain valuations, and averages, of our own striking, we come upon some sort of average terrestrial lot; this we fancy belongs to us by nature, and of indefeasible right. It is simple payment of our wages, of our deserts; requires neither thanks nor complaint; only such *overplus* as there may be do we account

Happiness; any *deficit* again is Misery. Now consider that we have the valuation of our own deserts ourselves, and what a fund of Self-conceit there is in each of us— do you wonder that the balance should so often dip the wrong way, and many a Blockhead cry: See there, what a payment; was ever worthy gentleman so used! —I tell thee, Blockhead, it all comes of thy Vanity; of what thou *fanciest* those same deserts of thine to be. Fancy that thou deservest to be hanged (as is most likely), thou wilt feel it happiness to be only shot: fancy that thou deservest to be hanged in a hair-halter, it will be a luxury to die in hemp.

"So true is it, what I then say, that *the Fraction of Life can be increased in value not so much by increasing your Numerator as by lessening your Denominator.* Nay, unless my Algebra deceive me, *Unity* itself divided by *Zero* will give *Infinity*. Make thy claim of wages a zero, then; thou hast the world under thy feet. Well did the Wisest of our time write: 'It is only with Renunciation (*Entsagen*) that Life, properly speaking, can be said to begin.'

"I asked myself: What is this that, ever since earliest years, thou hast been fretting and fuming, and lamenting and self-tormenting, on account of? Say it in a word: is it not because thou art not HAPPY? Because the THOU (sweet gentleman) is not sufficiently honored, nourished, soft-bedded, and lovingly cared for? Foolish soul! What Act of Legislature was there that *thou* shouldst be Happy? A little while ago thou hadst no right to *be* at all. What if thou wert born and predestined not to be Happy, but to be Unhappy! Art thou nothing other than a Vulture, then, that fliest through the Universe seeking after somewhat to *eat*, and shrieking dolefully because carrion enough is not given thee? Close thy *Byron*, open thy *Goethe*."

"*Es leuchtet mir ein*, I see a glimpse of it!" cries he elsewhere: "there is in man a HIGHER than Love of Happiness: he can do without Happiness, and instead thereof find Blessedness! Was it not to preach forth this same HIGHER that sages and martyrs, the Poet and the Priest, in all times, have spoken and suffered; bearing testimony, through life and through death, of the Godlike that is in Man, and how in the Godlike only has he Strength and Freedom? Which God-inspired Doctrine art thou also honored to be taught; O Heavens! and broken with manifold merciful Afflictions, even till thou become contrite, and learn it! O, thank thy Destiny for these; thankfully bear what yet remain: thou hadst need of them; the Self in thee needed to be annihilated. By benignant fever-paroxysms is Life rooting out the deep-seated chronic Disease, and triumphs over Death. On the roaring billows of Time, thou art not engulfed, but borne aloft into the azure of Eternity. Love not Pleasure; love God. This is the EVERLASTING YEA, wherein all contra-

Ophiuchus, in astronomy a northern constellation that is represented on charts as a man holding a serpent. 176. hair-halter, a noose made of hair. 184. the Wisest . . . time, Johann Wolfgang von Goethe

(1749–1832), German author whom Carlyle admired greatly.

diction is solved: wherein whoso walks and works, it is well with him."

And again: "Small is it that thou canst trample the Earth with its injuries under thy feet, as old Greek Zeno trained thee: thou canst love the Earth while it injures thee, and even because it injures thee; for this a Greater than Zeno was needed, and he too was sent. Knowest thou that 'Worship of Sorrow'? The Temple thereof, founded some eighteen centuries ago, now lies in ruins, 10 overgrown with jungle, the habitation of doleful creatures: nevertheless, venture forward; in a low crypt, arched out of falling fragments, thou findest the Altar still there, and its sacred Lamp perennially burning."

Without pretending to comment on which strange utterances, the Editor will only remark that there lies beside them much of a still more questionable character; unsuited to the general apprehension; nay wherein he himself does not see his way. Nebulous disquisitions on Religion, yet not without bursts of splendor; on the 20 "perennial continuance of Inspiration"; on Prophecy; that there are "true Priests, as well as Baal-Priests, in our own day": with more of the like sort. We select some fractions, by way of finish to this farrago.

"Cease, my much-respected Herr von Voltaire," thus apostrophizes the Professor: "shut thy sweet voice; for the task appointed thee seems finished. Sufficiently hast thou demonstrated this proposition, considerable or otherwise: That the Mythus of the Christian Religion looks not in the eighteenth century as it 30 did in the eighth. Alas, were thy six-and-thirty quartos, and the six-and-thirty thousand other quartos and folios, and flying sheets or reams, printed before and since on the same subject, all needed to convince us of so little! But what next? Wilt thou help us to embody the divine Spirit of that Religion in a new Mythus, in a new vehicle and vesture, that our Souls, otherwise too like perishing, may live? What! thou hast no faculty in that kind? Only a torch for burning, no hammer for building? Take our thanks, then, and——thyself away. 40 "Meanwhile what are antiquated Mythuses to me? Or is the God present, felt in my own heart, a thing which Herr von Voltaire will dispute out of me; or dispute into me? To the 'Worship of Sorrow' ascribe what origin and genesis thou pleasest, has not that Worship originated, and been generated; is it not here? Feel it in thy heart, and then say whether it is of God! This is Belief; all else is Opinion—for which latter whoso will let him worry and be worried."

"Neither," observes he elsewhere, "shall ye tear-out 50 one another's eyes, struggling over 'Plenary Inspiration,' and suchlike: try rather to get a little even Partial Inspiration, each of you for himself. One BIBLE I know, of whose Plenary Inspiration doubt is not so much as possible; nay with my own eyes I saw the God's-Hand writing it: thereof all other Bibles are but leaves—say, in Picture-Writing to assist the weaker faculty."

Or, to give the wearied reader relief, and bring it to an end, let him take the following perhaps more intelligible passage: 60

"To me, in this our life," says the Professor, "which is an internecine warfare with the Time-spirit, other warfare seems questionable. Hast thou in any way a Contention with thy brother, I advise thee, think well what the meaning thereof is. If thou gauge it to the bottom, it is simply this: 'Fellow, see! thou art taking more than thy share of Happiness in the world, something from my share: which, by the Heavens, thou shalt not; nay I will fight thee rather.'—Alas, and the whole lot to be divided is such a beggarly matter, truly 70 a 'feast of shells,' for the substance has been spilled out: not enough to quench one Appetite; and the collective human species clutching at them!—Can we not, in all such cases, rather say: 'Take it, thou too-ravenous individual; take that pitiful additional fraction of a share, which I reckoned mine, but which thou so wantest; take it with a blessing: would to Heaven I had enough for thee!'—If Fichte's Wissenschaftslehre be, 'to a certain extent, Applied Christianity,' surely to a still greater extent, so is this. We have here not 80 a Whole Duty of Man, yet a Half Duty, namely the Passive half: could we but do it, as we can demonstrate it!

"But indeed Conviction, were it never so excellent, is worthless till it convert itself into Conduct. Nay properly Conviction is not possible till then; inasmuch as all Speculation is by nature endless, formless, a vortex amid vortices: only by a felt indubitable certainty of Experience does it find any center to revolve round, and so fashion itself into a system. 90 Most true is it, as a wise man teaches us, that 'Doubt of any sort cannot be removed except by Action.' On which ground, too, let him who gropes painfully in darkness or uncertain light, and prays vehemently that the dawn may ripen into day, lay this other precept well to heart, which to me was of invaluable service: 'Do the Duty which lies nearest thee,' which thou knowest to be a Duty! Thy second Duty will already have become clearer.

"May we not say, however, that the hour of Spirit- 100 ual Enfranchisement is even this: When your Ideal World, wherein the whole man has been dimly struggling and inexpressibly languishing to work, becomes revealed, and thrown open; and you discover, with amazement enough, like the Lothario in Wilhelm Meister, that your 'America is here or nowhere'? The Situa-

4. Zeno, Greek philosopher (336?–264? B.C.), founder of the stoic school of philosophy. 8. Temple . . . ago. The allusion is, of course, to the founding of Christianity. 21. Baal-Priests, priests who serve the altars of false gods; cf. 1 Kings 18:17–40. 24. Voltaire, French philosopher and author (1694–1778); Carlyle alludes here to his skepticism. 78. Fichte's Wissenschaftslehre, the Theory of the Sciences by Johann Gottlieb Fichte (1762–1814), German philosopher. 81. Whole . . . Man, an anonymous devotional book published in 1658 and long popular. 105. Wilhelm Meister, Goethe's Wilhelm Meister's Travels. 125. Let . . . light, God's first command of creation; cf. Genesis 1:3. 137. World . . . Worldkin, i.e., a macrocosm, or great world, or a microcosm, or man. 143. Night . . . work, quoted

tion that has not its Duty, its Ideal, was never yet occupied by man. Yes, here, in this poor, miserable, hampered, despicable Actual, wherein thou even now
110 standest, here or nowhere is thy Ideal: work it out therefrom; and working, believe, live, be free. Fool! the Ideal is in thyself, the impediment too is in thyself: thy Condition is but the stuff thou art to shape that same Ideal out of: what matters whether such stuff be of this sort or that, so the Form thou give it be heroic, be poetic? O thou that pinest in the imprisonment of the Actual, and criest bitterly to the gods for a kingdom wherein to rule and create, know this of a truth: the thing thou seekest is already
120 with thee, 'here or nowhere,' couldst thou only see!

"But it is with man's Soul as it was with Nature: the beginning of Creation is—Light. Till the eye have vision, the whole members are in bonds. Divine moment, when over the tempest-tossed Soul, as once over the wild-weltering Chaos, it is spoken: Let there be Light! Ever to the greatest that has felt such moment, is it not miraculous and God-announcing; even as, under simpler figures, to the simplest and least. The mad primeval Discord is hushed; the rudely
130 jumbled conflicting elements bind themselves into separate Firmaments: deep silent rock-foundations are built beneath; and the skyey vault with its everlasting Luminaries above: instead of a dark wasteful Chaos, we have a blooming, fertile, heaven-encompassed World.

"I too could now say to myself: Be no longer a Chaos, but a World, or even Worldkin. Produce! Produce! Were it but the pitifullest infinitesimal fraction of a Product, produce it, in God's name! 'Tis
140 the utmost thou hast in thee: out with it, then. Up, up! Whatsoever thy hand findeth to do, do it with thy whole might. Work while it is called Today; for the Night cometh, wherein no man can work." (II, 9)
(1833-1834)

from PAST AND PRESENT

Past and Present was first published in 1843. It belongs to the economic-social group of Carlyle's writings, and is remarkable, among other things, for the fact that it was written in seven weeks, such ease of composition the author seldom commanded. As the title implies, Carlyle attempted in this series of essays to gather from the past some good lessons for the present. To personalize the material in his usual manner, he compared Victorian conditions to those recorded in the ancient chronicle written by Jocelyn of Brakelond, English monk of Bury St. Edmunds, at the beginning of the thirteenth century. Jocelyn's Latin narrative of the fortunes of his own monastery contains a glowing account of the work of Abbot Samson, whom Carlyle admired greatly. Carlyle's comparison of past and present is almost entirely in favor of the past, the advantages of which are highly, but very artistically, exaggerated. Carlyle's direct comment on contemporary conditions includes attacks on his radical, legislating friends, and a setting forth of his own theories of duty, responsibility, work, reward, capital, and labor—all presented vigorously in terms of abstract principle rather than concrete practicality.

LABOR

For there is a perennial nobleness, and even sacredness, in Work. Were he never so benighted, forgetful of his high calling, there is always hope in a man that actually and earnestly works: in Idleness alone is there perpetual despair. Work, never so Mammonish, mean, *is* in communication with Nature; the real desire to get Work done will itself lead one more and 150 more to truth, to Nature's appointments and regulations, which are truth.

The latest Gospel in this world is, Know thy work and do it. "Know thyself": long enough has that poor "self" of thine tormented thee; thou wilt never get to "know" it, I believe! Think it not thy business, this of knowing thyself; thou art an unknowable individual: know what thou canst work at; and work at it, like a Hercules! That will be thy better plan. 160

It has been written, "an endless significance lies in Work"; a man perfects himself by working. Foul jungles are cleared away, fair seedfields rise instead, and stately cities; and withal the man himself first ceases to be a jungle and foul unwholesome desert thereby. Consider how, even in the meanest sorts of Labor, the whole soul of a man is composed into a kind of real harmony, the instant he sets himself to work! Doubt, Desire, Sorrow, Remorse, Indignation, Despair itself, all these like helldogs lie beleaguering 170 the soul of the poor dayworker, as of every man: but he bends himself with free valor against his task, and all these are stilled, all these shrink murmuring far off into their caves. The man is now a man. The blessed glow of Labor in him, is it not as purifying fire, wherein all poison is burnt up, and of sour smoke itself there is made bright blessed flame!

Destiny, on the whole, has no other way of cultivating us. A formless Chaos, once set it *revolving*, grows round and ever rounder; ranges itself, by mere 180 force of gravity, into strata, spherical courses; is no

from John 9:4; this expresses in brief Carlyle's doctrine of labor, which he amplified in *Past and Present*, Book III, Chapter XI (1843).

Past and Present. 148. **Mammonish,** devoted merely to gaining money. Cf. Matthew 6:24: "Ye cannot serve God and mammon." In *Paradise Lost* Mammon is the fallen angel who advocates the getting of wealth. There is an earlier chapter on the Gospel of Mammonism in

Past and Present. 154. **"Know thyself."** See p. 995, note to l. 159. 159. **Hercules,** in classical mythology the son of Jupiter; he was noted for his great strength and for achieving the twelve "impossible labors" imposed upon him as a result of the hatred of Juno, wife of Jupiter. 161. **"an . . . Work."** Apparently Carlyle is quoting himself. The idea is the center of *Sartor Resartus.* See the chapter on Helotage.

longer a Chaos, but a round compacted World. What would become of the Earth, did she cease to revolve? In the poor old Earth, so long as she revolves, all inequalities, irregularities disperse themselves; all irregularities are incessantly becoming regular. Hast thou looked on the Potter's wheel—one of the venerablest objects; old as the Prophet Ezekiel and far older? Rude lumps of clay, how they spin themselves up, by mere quick whirling, into beautiful circular 10 dishes. And fancy the most assiduous Potter, but without his wheel; reduced to make dishes or rather amorphous botches, by mere kneading and baking! Even such a Potter were Destiny, with a human soul that would rest and lie at ease, that would not work and spin! Of an idle unrevolving man the kindest Destiny, like the most assiduous Potter without wheel, can bake and knead nothing other than a botch; let her spend on him what expensive coloring, what gilding and enameling she will, he is but a botch. Not a 20 dish; no, a bulging, kneaded, crooked, shambling, squint-cornered, amorphous botch—a mere enameled vessel of dishonor! Let the idle think of this.

Blessed is he who has found his work; let him ask no other blessedness. He has a work, a life-purpose; he has found it, and will follow it! How, as a free-flowing channel, dug and torn by noble force through the sour mud-swamp of one's existence, like an ever-deepening river there, it runs and flows;—draining-off the sour festering water, gradually from the root 30 of the remotest grass-blade; making, instead of pestilential swamp, a green fruitful meadow with its clear-flowing stream. How blessed for the meadow itself, let the stream and its value be great or small! Labor is Life: from the inmost heart of the Worker rises his god-given Force, the sacred celestial Life-essence breathed into him by Almighty God; from his inmost heart awakens him to all nobleness—to all knowledge, "self-knowledge" and much else, so soon as Work fitly begins. Knowledge? The knowledge that 40 will hold good in working, cleave thou to that; for Nature herself accredits that, says Yea to that. Properly thou hast no other knowledge but what thou hast got by working: the rest is yet all a hypothesis of knowledge; a thing to be argued of in schools, a thing floating in the clouds, in endless logic-vortices, till we try it and fix it. "Doubt, of whatever kind, can be ended by Action alone."

And again, hast thou valued Patience, Courage, Perseverance, Openness to light; readiness to own thyself 50 mistaken, to do better next time? All these, all virtues

in wrestling with the dim brute Powers of Fact, in ordering of thy fellows in such wrestle, there and elsewhere not at all, thou wilt continually learn. Set down a brave Sir Christopher in the middle of black ruined Stone-heaps, of foolish unarchitectural Bishops, redtape Officials, idle Nell-Gwyn Defenders of the Faith; and see whether he will ever raise a Paul's Cathedral out of all that, yea or no! Rough, rude, contradictory are all things and persons, from the mutinous masons and Irish hodmen, up to the idle 60 Nell-Gwyn Defenders, to blustering redtape Officials, foolish unarchitectural Bishops. All these things and persons are there not for Christopher's sake and his Cathedral's; they are there for their own sake mainly! Christopher will have to conquer and constrain all these—if he be able. All these are against him. Equitable Nature herself, who carries her mathematics and architectonics not on the face of her, but deep in the hidden heart of her—Nature herself is but partially for him; will be wholly against him, if he constrain 70 her not! His very money, where is it to come from? The pious munificence of England lies far-scattered, distant, unable to speak, and say, "I am here";—must be spoken to before it can speak. Pious munificence, and all help, is so silent, invisible like the gods; impediment, contradictions manifold are so loud and near! O brave Sir Christopher, trust thou in those notwithstanding, and front all these; understand all these; by valiant patience, noble effort, insight, by man's-strength, vanquish and compel all these—and, 80 on the whole, strike down victoriously the last topstone of that Paul's Edifice; thy monument for certain centuries, the stamp "Great Man" impressed very legibly on Portland-stone there!—

Yes, all manner of help, and pious response from Men or Nature, is always what we call silent; cannot speak or come to light, till it be seen, till it be spoken to. Every noble work is at first "impossible." In very truth, for every noble work the possibilities will lie diffused through Immensity; inarticulate, un- 90 discoverable except to faith. Like Gideon thou shalt spread out thy fleece at the door of thy tent; see whether under the wide arch of Heaven there be any bounteous moisture, or none. Thy heart and life-purpose shall be as a miraculous Gideon's fleece, spread out in silent appeal to Heaven: and from the kind Immensities, what from the poor unkind Localities and town and country Parishes there never could, blessed dew-moisture to suffice thee shall have fallen!
100

Work is of a religious nature—work is of a *brave*

6. **Potter's wheel.** The incident of the potter and the wheel is found in Jeremiah 18:1-6, not in Ezekiel. There is a "Vision of the Wheels" however, in Ezekiel 1:15-21. Cf. Browning's *Rabbi Ben Ezra*, p. 930. ll. 148 ff. 21. **squint-cornered**, irregular. 22. **vessel of dishonor.** Cf. Romans 9:21: "Hath not the potter power over the clay, of the same lump to make one vessel unto honor and another unto dishonor?" 44. **schools,** schools of philosophy. 46. **"Doubt . . . alone."** A profound saying of Goethe. 54. **Sir Christopher,** Sir Christopher Wren (1632-1723), a great English architect, designer of St. Paul's Cathedral and conspicuous in the rebuilding of London after the Great Fire

of 1666. (See Pepys' *Diary*, p. 443.) 56. **Nell-Gwyn,** a popular actress of the Restoration period and a mistress of Charles II. The title "Defender of the Faith" was bestowed by the Pope upon Henry VIII (1491-1547) for his *Defense of the Seven Sacraments* (1521), a book against Martin Luther, and the title has been retained by subsequent English sovereigns. 82. **monument.** Wren's monument in St. Paul's bears the inscription, "If you would seek his monument, look around you." 84. **Portland-stone,** a light-colored building stone from the Isle of Portland, on the coast of Dorset, England. 91. **Gideon . . . tent.** Gideon (Judges 6:36-38) was assured through two miracles that

nature; which it is the aim of all religion to be. All work of man is as the swimmer's: a waste ocean threatens to devour him; if he front it not bravely, it will keep its word. By incessant wise defiance of it, lusty rebuke and buffet of it, behold how it loyally supports him, bears him as its conqueror along. "It is so," says Goethe, "with all things that man undertakes in this world."

110   Brave Sea-captain, Norse Sea-king—Columbus, my hero, royalest Sea-king of all! it is no friendly environment this of thine, in the waste deep waters; around thee mutinous discouraged souls, behind thee disgrace and ruin, before thee the unpenetrated veil of Night. Brother, these wild water-mountains, bounding from their deep bases (ten miles deep, I am told), are not entirely there on thy behalf! Meseems *they* have other work than floating thee forward—and the huge Winds, that sweep from Ursa Major to the Tropics and
120 Equators, dancing their giant-waltz through the kingdoms of Chaos and Immensity, they care little about filling rightly or filling wrongly the small shoulder-of-mutton sails in this cockle-skiff of thine! Thou art not among articulate-speaking friends, my brother; thou art among immeasurable dumb monsters, tumbling, howling wide as the world here. Secret, far off, invisible to all hearts but thine, there lies a help in them: see how thou wilt get at that. Patiently thou wilt wait till the mad Southwester spend itself,
130 saving thyself by dextrous science of defense, the while: valiantly, with swift decision, wilt thou strike in, when the favoring East, the Possible, springs up. Mutiny of men thou wilt sternly repress; weakness, despondency, thou wilt cheerily encourage: thou wilt swallow down complaint, unreason, weariness, weakness of others and thyself;—how much wilt thou swallow down! There shall be a depth of Silence in thee, deeper than this Sea, which is but ten miles deep: a Silence unsoundable; known to God only. Thou shalt
140 be a Great Man. Yes, my World-Soldier, thou of the World Marine-service—thou wilt have to be *greater* than this tumultuous unmeasured World here round thee is; thou, in thy strong soul, as with wrestler's arms, shalt embrace it, harness it down; and make it bear thee on—to new Americas, or whither God wills!

                                     (III, 11)

ARISTOCRACIES

   To predict the Future, to manage the Present, would not be so impossible, had not the Past been so sacrilegiously mishandled; effaced, and what is worse,

defaced! The Past cannot be seen; the Past, looked at through the medium of "Philosophical History" in 150 these times, cannot even be *not* seen: it is misseen; affirmed to have existed—and to have been a godless impossibility. Your Norman Conquerors, true royal souls, crowned kings as such, were vulturous irrational tyrants: your Becket was a noisy egoist and hypocrite; getting his brains spilt on the floor of Canterbury Cathedral, to secure the main chance—somewhat uncertain how! "Policy, Fanaticism"; or say "Enthusiasm," even "honest-Enthusiasm"—ah yes, of course: 160

The Dog, to gain his private ends,
Went mad, and bit the Man!—

   For in truth, the eye sees in all things "what it brought with it the means of seeing." A godless century, looking back on centuries that were godly, produces portraitures more miraculous than any other. All was inane discord in the Past; brute Force bore rule everywhere; Stupidity, savage Unreason, fitter for Bedlam than for a human World! Whereby indeed it becomes sufficiently natural that the like qualities, in 170 new sleeker habiliments, should continue in our time to rule. Millions enchanted in Bastille Workhouses; Irish Widows proving their relationship by typhus-fever: what would you have? It was ever so, or worse. Man's History, was it not always even this: the cookery and eating-up of imbecile Dupedom by successful Quackhood; the battle, with various weapons, of vulturous Quack and Tyrant against vulturous Tyrant and Quack? No God was in the Past Time; nothing but Mechanisms and Chaotic Brute-Gods: how shall the 180 poor "Philosophic Historian," to whom his own century is all godless, see any God in other centuries?

   Men believe in Bibles, and disbelieve in them: but of all Bibles the frightfulest to disbelieve in is this "Bible of Universal History." This is the Eternal Bible and God's Book, "which every born man," till once the soul and eyesight are extinguished in him, "can and must, with his own eyes, see the God's-Finger writing!" To discredit this, is an *infidelity* like no other. Such infidelity you would punish, if not by fire and 190 faggot, which are difficult to manage in our times, yet by the most peremptory order, To hold its peace till it got something wiser to say. Why should the blessed Silence be broken into noises, to communicate only the like of this? If the Past have no God's-Reason in it, nothing but Devil's-Unreason, let the Past be eternally

God would favor Israel. In the first, a fleece of wool left on the floor became wet with dew while the ground about it was dry; in the second, the fleece remained dry while the ground was wet. 119. **Ursa Major,** the Great Bear, or Dipper, a constellation over the North Pole. 123. **cockle-skiff,** a flimsy boat. 150. **"Philosophical History."** In his essay *On History* Carlyle denies that history is philosophy teaching by experience. He holds a moral conception of history, in which he sees the laws of God made manifest in fact. He is aiming primarily at David Hume (1711–1776) and William Robertson (1721–1793), both Scottish historians. 155. **Becket,** Thomas à Becket (1118–1170), Arch-

bishop of Canterbury, who defended the Church against King Henry II, and was slain in Canterbury Cathedral by knights who had overheard the King's prayer "to be rid of this turbulent priest." Becket's shrine was the objective of Chaucer's pilgrims (p. 102). 161. **The Dog . . . Man,** Goldsmith, *An Elegy on the Death of a Mad Dog.* 169. **Bedlam,** name of a well-known hospital for the insane in London. 172. **Bastille Workhouses,** poorhouses, so called from the Bastille, the infamous French prison in Paris. **Irish . . . typhus-fever.** An allusion to the epidemics in Ireland caused by impoverishment of the people.

forgotten: mention it no more;—we whose ancestors were all hanged, why should we talk of ropes!

It is, in brief, not true that men ever lived by Delirium, Hypocrisy, Injustice, or any form of Unreason, since they came to inhabit this Planet. It is not true that they ever did, or ever will, live except by the reverse of these. Men will again be taught this. Their acted History will then again be a Heroism; their written History, what it once was, an Epic. Nay, for-
10 ever it is either such, or else it virtually is—Nothing. Were it written in a thousand volumes, the Unheroic of such volumes hastens incessantly to be forgotten: the net content of an Alexandrian Library of Unheroics is, and will ultimately show itself to be, zero. What man is interested to remember it, have not all men, at all times, the liveliest interest to forget it?—"Revelations," if not celestial, then infernal, will teach us that God is; we shall then, if needful, discern without difficulty that He has always been! The Dryasdust Philosophisms
20 and enlightened Skepticisms of the Eighteenth Century, historical and other, will have to survive for a while with the Physiologists, as a memorable Nightmare-Dream. All this haggard epoch, with its ghastly Doctrines, and death's-head Philosophies "teaching by example" or otherwise, will one day have become, what to our Moslem friends their godless ages are, "the Period of Ignorance."

If the convulsive struggles of the last Half-Century have taught poor struggling convulsed Europe any
30 truth, it may perhaps be this as the essence of innumerable others: That Europe requires a real Aristocracy, a real Priesthood, or it cannot continue to exist. Huge French Revolutions, Napoleonisms, then Bourbonisms with their corollary of Three Days, finishing in very unfinal Louis-Philippisms: all this ought to be didactic! All this may have taught us: That False Aristocracies are insupportable; that No-Aristocracies, Liberty-and-Equalities are impossible; that True Aristocracies are at once, indispensable and not easily at-
40 tained.

Aristocracy and Priesthood, a Governing Class and a Teaching Class: these two, sometimes separate, and endeavoring to harmonize themselves, sometimes conjoined as one, and the King a Pontiff-King: there did no Society exist without these two vital elements, there will none exist. It lies in the very nature of man: you will visit no remotest village in the most republican country of the world, where virtually or actually you do not find these two powers at work. Man, little as

he may suppose it, is necessitated to obey superiors. 50 He is a social being in virtue of this necessity; nay he could not be gregarious otherwise. He obeys those whom he esteems better than himself, wiser, braver; and will forever obey such; and even be ready and delighted to do it.

The Wiser, Braver: these, a Virtual Aristocracy everywhere and everywhen, do in all Societies that reach any articulate shape, develop themselves in a ruling class, an Actual Aristocracy, with settled modes of operating, what are called laws and even private- 60 laws or privileges, and so forth; very notable to look upon in this world.—Aristocracy and Priesthood, we say, are sometimes united. For indeed the Wiser and the Braver are properly but one class; no wise man but needed first of all to be a brave man, or he never had been wise. The noble Priest was always a noble Aristos to begin with, and something more to end with. Your Luther, your Knox, your Anselm, Becket, Abbot Samson, Samuel Johnson, if they had not been brave enough, by what possibility could 70 they ever have been wise?—If, from accident and forethought, this your Actual Aristocracy have got discriminated into Two Classes, there can be no doubt but the Priest Class is the more dignified; supreme over the other, as governing head is over active hand. And yet in practice again, it is likeliest the reverse will be found arranged;—a sign that the arrangement is already vitiated; that a split is introduced into it, which will widen and widen till the whole be rent asunder. 80

In England, in Europe generally, we may say that these two Virtualities have unfolded themselves into Actualities, in by far the noblest and richest manner any region of the world ever saw. A spiritual Guideship, a practical Governorship, fruit of the grand conscious endeavors, say rather of the immeasurable unconscious instincts and necessities of men, have established themselves; very strange to behold. Everywhere, while so much has been forgotten, you find the King's Palace, and the Viceking's Castle, Mansion, 90 Manorhouse; till there is not an inch of ground from sea to sea but has both its King and Viceking, long due series of Vicekings, its Squire, Earl, Duke or whatever the title of him—to whom you have given the land, that he may govern you in it.

More touching still, there is not a hamlet where poor peasants congregate, but, by one means and another, a Church-Apparatus has been got together—

13. **Alexandrian Library.** A famous library formed at Alexandria in the third and fourth centuries B.C. and partially destroyed by fire in the siege of the city by Julius Caesar in the first century B.C. 19. **Dryasdust Philosophisms,** subtle sophistries uttered by a type of dreary historian given to mere facts and details. 20. **enlightened . . . Century.** A reference to the rationalistic philosophy of such men in France as Rousseau and Voltaire, and in England as William Godwin (see p. 623). 22. **Physiologists,** the new mechanists, who reduced bodily functions to principles of physics and chemistry contrary to the old idea of God-given vitalism. The group included such men as Albrecht von Haller (1708–1777) and Johannes Müller (1801–1858) in Germany and Georges Cuvier (1769–1832), Etienne Geoffroy Saint-Hilaire (1772–1844), and Jean Lamarck (1744–1829) in France. 26. **Moslem friends,** followers of the Mohammedan religion. 33. **Bour-**

bonisms, obstinate conservatisms, characteristic of the Bourbon dynasty in France. 34. **Three Days,** the revolution of July 1830, which drove Charles X from the French throne. 35. **Louis-Philippisms.** A reference to the unstable career of Louis Philippe (1773–1850), king of France (1830–1848). He was in and out of political favor most of his life. He was deposed by the Revolution of 1848. 67. *Aristos,* aristocrat; it is a Greek word for "the best." 68. **Luther,** Martin Luther (1483–1546), the leader of the German Reformation. **Knox,** John Knox (1505–1572), a Scottish Protestant reformer and partisan. **Anselm,** Saint Anselm (1033–1109), Archbishop of Canterbury. He was an uncompromising defender of the Church against both William II and Henry I. 69. **Abbot Samson,** Abbot of St. Edmunds (1182–1211), a valiant economic and political reformer interested in the welfare of the people. He rebuffed Richard I while protecting a wealthy ward

roofed edifice, with revenues and belfries; pulpit, read-
100 ing-desk, with Books and Methods: possibility, in
short, and strict prescription: That a man stand there
and speak of spiritual things to men. It is beautiful;—
even in its great obscuration and decadence, it is
among the beautifulest, most touching objects one
sees on the Earth. This Speaking Man has indeed,
in these times, wandered terribly from the point; has,
alas, as it were, totally lost sight of the point: yet, at
bottom, whom have we to compare with him? Of
all public functionaries boarded and lodged on the
110 Industry of Modern Europe, is there one worthier of
the board he has? A man even professing, and
never so languidly making still some endeavor, to
save the souls of men: contrast him with a man
professing to do little but shoot the partridges of
men! I wish he could find the point again, this
Speaking One; and stick to it with tenacity, with deadly
energy; for there is need of him yet! The Speaking
Function, this of Truth coming to us with a living
voice, nay in a living shape, and as a concrete
120 practical exemplar: this, with all our Writing and
Printing Functions, has a perennial place. Could he
but find the point again—take the old spectacles off
his nose, and looking up discover, almost in contact
with him, what the *real* Satanas, and soul-devouring,
world-devouring *Devil,* now is! Original Sin and such-
like are bad enough, I doubt not: but distilled Gin,
dark Ignorance, Stupidity, dark Corn-Law, Bastille and
Company, what are they! *Will* he discover our new
real Satan, whom he has to fight; or go on droning
130 through his old nose-spectacles about old extinct
Satans; and never see the real one, till he *feel* him
at his own throat and ours? That is a question, for
the world! Let us not intermeddle with it here.

Sorrowful, phantasmal as this same Double Aristocracy of Teachers and Governors now looks, it is
worth all men's while to know that the purport of it
is and remains noble and most real. Dryasdust, looking merely at the surface, is greatly in error as to
those ancient Kings. William Conqueror, William
140 Rufus or Redbeard, Stephen Curthose himself much
more Henry Beauclerc and our brave Plantagenet
Henry: the life of these men was not a vulturous
Fighting; it was a valorous Governing—to which occasionally Fighting did, and alas must yet, though far
seldomer now, superadd itself as an accident, a distressing impedimental adjunct. The fighting too was
indispensable, for ascertaining who had the might

over whom, the right over whom. By much hard fighting, as we once said, "the unrealities, beaten into
dust, flew gradually off"; and left the plain reality 150
and fact, "Thou stronger than I; thou wiser than I;
thou king, and subject I," in a somewhat clearer
condition.

Truly we cannot enough admire, in those Abbot-Sam-
son and William Conqueror times, the arrangement
they had made of their Governing Classes. Highly
interesting to observe how the sincere insight, on
their part, into what did, of primary necessity, behove
to be accomplished, had led them to the way of ac-
complishing it, and in the course of time to get it 160
accomplished! No imaginary Aristocracy would serve
their turn; and accordingly they attained a real one.
The Bravest men, who, it is ever to be repeated and
remembered, are also on the whole the Wisest, Strongest, everyway Best, had here, with a respectable degree
of accuracy, been got selected; seated each on his
piece of territory, which was lent him, then gradually
given him, that he might govern it. These Vickings,
each on his portion of the common soil of England,
with a Head King over all, were a "Virtuality perfected 170
into an Actuality" really to an astonishing extent.

For those were rugged stalwart ages; full of earnestness, of a rude God's-truth—nay, at any rate, their
quilting was so unspeakably *thinner* than ours; Fact
came swiftly on them, if at any time they had
yielded to Phantasm! "The Knaves and Dastards" had
to be "arrested" in some measure; or the world, almost
within year and day, found that it could not live. The
Knaves and Dastards accordingly were got arrested.
Dastards upon the very throne had to be got arrested, 180
and taken off the throne—by such methods as there
were; by the roughest method, if there chanced to be
no smoother one! Doubtless there was much harshness of operation, much severity; as indeed government and surgery are often somewhat severe. Gurth,
born thrall of Cedric, it is like, got cuffs as often as
pork-parings, if he misdemeaned himself; but Gurth
did belong to Cedric: no human creature then went
about connected with nobody; left to go his way into
Bastilles or worse, under *Laissez-faire,* reduced to 190
prove his relationship by dying of typhus-fever!—Days
come when there is no King in Israel, but every man
is his own king, doing that which is right in his
own eyes;—and tarbarrels are burnt to "Liberty,"
"Ten-pound Franchise," and the like, with considerable effect in various ways!—

left in his care. **Samuel Johnson.** See p. 567. 90. **Vicking,** the
governor of a county or province who rules as the representative of his
sovereign. Under the feudal system in England the land, which
theoretically belonged to the king, was administered in practice by
barons, or vickings. 124. *real* **Satanas.** For the ancient Satan, the
incarnation of Sin, modern man had to resist the other devils which
Carlyle enumerates in the next sentence. 125. **Original Sin,** that supposed to have been inherited by all persons from Adam. 127. **Corn-
Law.** In 1815 laws were passed imposing a tariff on the export and
import of grain; they worked a hardship on the poor by raising the
price of flour, grain, etc. Carlyle was among those who were violently
opposed to the laws, which were finally repealed in 1846. 139. **William
Conqueror,** king of England (1066–1087). **William Rufus,** king
of England (1087–1100). 140. **Stephen Curthose,** king of England

(1135–1154); his uncle Robert was also surnamed *Curthose* (short
hose). 141. **Henry Beauclerc,** Henry I, king of England (1100–1135);
he gained the surname *Beauclerc* on account of his scholarship. **Plantagenet Henry,** Henry II, king of England (1154–1189). 185. **Gurth,**
the swineherd of Cedric the Saxon in Scott's *Ivanhoe;* in the chapter
on democracy Carlyle refers to Gurth "with the brass collar round his
neck." 190. *Laissez-faire,* a doctrine that favored unrestricted competition and stoutly opposed governmental intervention for regulating
conditions of industry and helping the laborer. 192. **no King . . .
eyes.** Cf. Judges 17:6: "In those days there was no king in Israel, but
every man did that which was right in his own eyes." 195. "**Ten-
pound Franchise.**" In the Reform Bill of 1832 the franchise was
limited to persons paying an annual house rent of ten pounds or more.

That Feudal Aristocracy, I say, was no imaginary one. To a respectable degree, its *Jarls*, what we now call Earls, were *Strong-Ones* in fact as well as etymology; its Dukes *Leaders*, its Lords *Law-wards*. They did all the Soldiering and Police of the country, all the Judging, Law-making, even the Church-Extension; whatsoever in the way of Governing, of Guiding and Protecting could be done. It was a Land Aristocracy; it managed the Governing of this English People, and
10 had the reaping of the Soil of England in return. It is, in many senses, the Law of Nature, this same Law of Feudalism;—no right Aristocracy but a Land one! The curious are invited to meditate upon it in these days. Soldiering, Police, and Judging, Church-Extension, nay real Government and Guidance, all this was actually *done* by the Holders of the Land in return for their Land. How much of it is now done by them; done by anybody? Good Heavens, "*Laissez-faire,* Do ye nothing, eat your wages and sleep" is everywhere
20 the passionate half-wise cry of this time; and they will not so much as do nothing, but must do mere Corn-Laws! We raise Fifty-two millions, from the general mass of us, to get our Governing done—or, alas, to get ourselves persuaded that it is done: and the "peculiar burden of the Land" is to pay, not all this, but to pay, as I learn, one twenty-fourth part of all this. Our first Chartist Parliament, or Oliver *Redivivus,* you would say, will know where to lay the new taxes of England!—Or, alas, taxes? If we made the Holders
30 of the Land pay every shilling still of the expense of Governing the Land, what were all that? The Land, by mere hired Governors, cannot be got governed. You cannot hire men to govern the Land; it is by mission not contracted for in the Stock-Exchange, but felt in their own hearts as coming out of Heaven, that men can govern a Land. The mission of a Land Aristocracy is a *sacred* one, in both the senses of that old word. The footing it stands on, at present, might give rise to thoughts other than of Corn-Laws!—
40 But truly a "Splendor of God," as in William Conqueror's rough oath, did dwell in those old rude veracious ages; did inform, more and more, with a heavenly nobleness, all departments of their work and life. Phantasms could not yet walk abroad in mere Cloth Tailorage; they were at least Phantasms "on the rim of the horizon," penciled there by an eternal Lightbeam from within. A most "practical" Hero-worship went on, unconsciously or half-consciously, everywhere. A Monk Samson, with a maxi-
50 mum of two shillings in his pocket, could, without

a ballot-box, be made a Viceking of, being seen to be worthy. The difference between a good man and a bad man was as yet felt to be, what it forever is, an immeasurable one. Who *durst* have elected a Pandarus Dogdraught, in those days, to any office, Carlton Club, Senatorship, or place whatsoever? It was felt that the arch Satanas and no other had a clear right of property in Pandarus; that it were better for you to have no hand in Pandarus, to keep out of Pandarus his neighborhood! Which is, to this hour, the mere 60 fact; though for the present, alas, the forgotten fact. I think they were comparatively blessed times those, in their way! "Violence," "war," "disorder": well, what is war, and death itself, to such a perpetual life-in-death, and "peace, peace, where there is no peace"! Unless some Hero-worship, in its new appropriate form, can return, this world does not promise to be very habitable long.

Old Anselm, exiled Archbishop of Canterbury, one of the purest-minded "men of genius," was traveling 70 to make his appeal to Rome against King Rufus—a man of rough ways, in whom the "inner Lightbeam" shone very fitfully. It is beautiful to read, in Monk Eadmer, how the continental populations welcomed and venerated this Anselm, as no French population now venerates Jean-Jacques or giant-killing Voltaire; as not even an American population now venerates a Schnüspel the distinguished Novelist! They had, by phantasy and true insight, the intensest conviction that a God's-Blessing dwelt in this Anselm—as is my 80 conviction too. They crowded round, with bent knees and enkindled hearts, to receive his blessing, to hear his voice, to see the light of his face. My blessings on them and on him!—but the notablest was a certain necessitous or covetous Duke of Burgundy, in straitened circumstances we shall hope—who reflected that in all likelihood this English Archbishop, going towards Rome to appeal, must have taken store of cash with him to bribe the Cardinals. Wherefore he of Burgundy, for his part, decided to lie in wait and 90 rob him. "In an open space of a wood," some "wood" then green and growing, eight centuries ago, in Burgundian Land—this fierce Duke, with fierce steel followers, shaggy, savage, as the Russian bear, dashes out on the weak old Anselm; who is riding along there, on his small quiet-going pony; escorted only by Eadmer and another poor Monk on ponies; and, except small modicum of roadmoney, not a gold coin in his possession. The steel-clad Russian bear emerges, glaring: the old white-bearded man starts not—paces on 100

3. *Strong-Ones.* Carlyle is usually not accurate in his etymologies. Anglo-Saxon *eorl* means nobleman. 27. **first . . . Parliament,** the one held after the adoption of reforms advocated by the Chartists, political agitators who voiced their demands in what was called "the people's charter. See p. 825. **Oliver** *Redivivus,* Oliver Restored. A reference to Oliver Cromwell, as a symbol of the Chartist movement. 40. **"Splendor of God,"** the favorite oath of William the Conqueror. 54. **Pandarus Dogdraught.** A name invented by Carlyle to describe the unscrupulous politician who buys his way into office. Pandarus was a go-between for the lovers Troilus and Cressida, in medieval story. 55. **Carlton Club,** a conservative political club established in London in

1832. 59. **Pandarus his.** An old form of the possessive. 65. **"peace . . . peace."** Jeremiah 6:14. 73. **Monk Eadmer,** a twelfth-century monk of Canterbury, companion and friend of Anselm, whose *Life* he wrote. 76. **Jean-Jacques,** Rousseau (1712-1778), the noted French philosopher and writer (see p. 610) who interpreted "Liberty, Fraternity, and Equality" to the French people. **Voltaire,** François Marie de Arouet (1694-1778), a famous French philosopher noted for his fearless skepticism. 78. **Schnüspel . . . Novelist.** An allusion to Dickens, under a coined German pseudonym; Dickens returned from a popular lecture tour in America shortly before *Past and Present* was composed. 115. *Per os Dei,* by the bones of God, another oath of William the Conqueror.

unmoved, looking into him with those clear old earnest eyes, with that venerable sorrowful time-worn face; of whom no man or thing need be afraid, and who also is afraid of no created man or thing. The fire-eyes of his Burgundian Grace meet these clear eye-glances, convey them swift to his heart: he bethinks him that probably this feeble, fearless, hoary Figure has in it something of the Most High God; that probably he shall be damned if he meddle with it—that, on the 110 whole, he had better not. He plunges, the rough savage, from his war-horse, down to his knees; embraces the feet of old Anselm: he too begs his blessing; orders men to escort him, guard him from being robbed, and under dread penalties see him safe on his way. *Per os Dei*, as his Majesty was wont to ejaculate!

Neither is this quarrel of Rufus and Anselm, of Henry and Becket uninstructive to us. It was, at bottom, a great quarrel. For, admitting that Anselm was full of 120 divine blessing, he by no means included in him all forms of divine blessing—there were far other forms withal, which he little dreamed of; and William Redbeard was unconsciously the representative and spokesman of these. In truth, could your divine Anselm, your divine Pope Gregory have had their way, the results had been very notable. Our Western World had all become a European Thibet, with one Grand Lama sitting at Rome; our one honorable business that of singing mass, all day and all night. Which would not in 130 the least have suited us. The Supreme Powers willed it not so.

It was as if King Redbeard unconsciously, addressing Anselm, Becket, and the others, had said: "Right Reverend, your Theory of the Universe is indisputable by man or devil. To the core of our heart we feel that this divine thing, which you call Mother Church, does fill the whole world hitherto known, and is and shall be all our salvation and all our desire. And yet—and yet —Behold, though it is an unspoken secret, the world 140 is *wider* than any of us think, Right Reverend! Behold, there are yet other immeasurable Sacrednesses in this that you call Heathenism, Secularity! On the whole, I, in an obscure but most rooted manner, feel that I cannot comply with you. Western Thibet and perpetual mass-chanting—No. I am, so to speak, in the family-way; with child, of I know not what—certainly of something far different from this! I have—*Per os Dei*, I have Manchester Cotton-trades, Bromwicham Iron-trades, American Commonwealths, Indian Empires, 150 Steam Mechanisms, and Shakespeare Dramas, in my

belly; and cannot do it, Right Reverend!"—So accordingly it was decided: and Saxon Becket spilt his life in Canterbury Cathedral, as Scottish Wallace did on Tower-hill, and as generally a noble man and martyr has to do—not for nothing; no, but for a divine something other than *he* had altogether calculated. We will now quit this of the hard, organic, but limited Feudal Ages; and glance timidly into the immense Industrial Ages, as yet all inorganic, and in a quite pulpy condition, requiring desperately to harden themselves into 160 some organism!

Our Epic having now become *Tools and the Man*, it is more than usually impossible to prophesy the Future. The boundless Future does lie there, predestined, nay already extant though unseen; hiding, in its Continents of Darkness, "gladness and sorrow"; but the supremest intelligence of man cannot prefigure much of it —the united intelligence and effort of All Men in all coming generations, this alone will gradually prefigure it, and figure and form it into a seen fact! Straining our 170 eyes hitherto, the utmost effort of intelligence sheds but some most glimmering dawn, a little way into its dark enormous Deeps: only huge outlines loom uncertain on the sight; and the ray of prophecy, at a short distance, expires. But may we not say, here as always, Sufficient for the day is the evil thereof! To shape the whole Future is not our problem; but only to shape faithfully a small part of it, according to rules already known. It is perhaps possible for each of us, who will with due earnestness inquire, to ascertain 180 clearly what he, for his own part, ought to do: this let him, with true heart, do, and continue doing. The general issue will, as it has always done, rest well with a Higher Intelligence than ours.

One grand "outline," or even two, many earnest readers may perhaps, at this stage of the business, be able to prefigure for themselves—and draw some guidance from. One prediction, or even two, are already possible. For the Life-Tree Igdrasil, in all its new developments, is the selfsame world-old Life-Tree: having 190 found an element or elements there, running from the very roots of it in Hela's Realms, in the Well of Mimer and of the Three Nornas or TIMES, up to this present hour of it in our own hearts, we conclude that such will have to continue. A man has, in his own soul, an Eternal; can read something of the Eternal there, if he will look! He already knows what will continue; what cannot, by any means or appliance whatsoever, be made to continue!

One wide and widest "outline" ought really, in all

125. **Pope Gregory,** Gregory the Great, Pope from 590 to 604. He was a zealous promoter of the Church; in 597 he sent St. Augustine and forty monks to Ethelbert, king of Kent. See p. 5. 127. **Thibet,** a land in central Asia. The Buddhism of Thibet and Mongolia was directed by two high priests known as Grand Lamas, each supreme in his own sphere. Carlyle means that if Anselm and Gregory had had their way, England would have been overreligious and of course subject to the Pope. 148. **Manchester,** a city noted for its many factories. **Bromwicham,** from West Bromwich, a town in Staffordshire. 153. **Wallace,** William Wallace, a thirteenth-century Scottish hero and patriot. He was captured by the English and executed for treason. 154. **Tower-hill,** a hill of execution in London. 162. *Tools and the Man.* Contrast with *Arms and the Man,* the opening words of the *Aeneid.* 176. **Sufficient . . . thereof!** From Matthew 6:34. 189. **Igdrasil,** in Norse mythology the great ash tree symbolizing the universe. 192. **Hela,** the Norse goddess of earth who presided over Niflheim, the underworld of Scandinavian mythology. **Well of Mimer,** a well at the roots of Igdrasil presided over by Mimer, a giant water demon; it was the source of wisdom. 193. **Nornas,** the Scandinavian Norns or Fates: Urth, Verthandi, and Skuld, representing the past, the present, and the future.

ways, to be becoming clear to us; this namely: That a "Splendor of God," in one form or other, will have to unfold itself from the heart of these our Industrial Ages too; or they will never get themselves "organized"; but continue chaotic, distressed, distracted evermore, and have to perish in frantic suicidal dissolution. A second "outline" or prophecy, narrower, but also wide enough, seems not less certain: That there will again *be* a King in Israel; a system of Order and Government; and every man shall, in some measure, see himself constrained to do that which is right in the King's eyes. This too we may call a sure element of the Future; for this too is of the Eternal;—this too is of the Present, though hidden from most; and without it no fiber of the Past ever was. An actual new Sovereignty, Industrial Aristocracy, real not imaginary Aristocracy, is indispensable and indubitable for us.

But what an Aristocracy; on what new, far more complex and cunningly devised conditions than that old Feudal fighting one! For we are to bethink us that the Epic verily is not *Arms and the Man,* but *Tools and the Man*—an infinitely wider kind of Epic. And again we are to bethink us that men cannot now be bound to men by *brass-collars*—not at all: that this brass-collar method, in all figures of it, has vanished out of Europe forevermore! Huge Democracy, walking the streets everywhere in its Sack Coat, has asserted so much; irrevocably, brooking no reply! True enough, man *is* forever the "born thrall" of certain men, born master of certain other men, born equal of certain others, let him acknowledge the fact or not. It is unblessed for him when he cannot acknowledge this fact; he is in the chaotic state, ready to perish, till he do get the fact acknowledged. But no man is, or can henceforth be, the brass-collar thrall of any man; you will have to bind him by other, far nobler and cunninger methods. Once for all, he is to be loose of the brass-collar, to have a scope *as* wide as his faculties now are—will he not be all the usefuler to you in that new state? Let him go abroad as a trusted one, as a free one; and return home to you with rich earnings at night! Gurth could only tend pigs; this one will build cities, conquer waste worlds.—How, in conjunction with inevitable Democracy, indispensable Sovereignty is to exist: certainly it is the hugest question ever heretofore propounded to Mankind! The solution of which is work for long years and centuries. Years and centuries, of one knows not what complexion;—blessed or unblessed, according as they shall, with earnest valiant effort, make progress therein, or, in slothful unveracity and dilettantism, only talk of making progress. For either progress therein, or swift and ever swifter progress towards dissolution, is henceforth a necessity.

It is of importance that this grand reformation were begun; that Corn-Law Debatings and other jargon, little less than delirious in such a time, had fled far away, and left us room to begin! For the evil has grown practical, extremely conspicuous; if it be not seen and provided for, the blindest fool will have to feel it ere long. There is much that can wait; but there is something also that cannot wait. With millions of eager Working Men imprisoned in "Impossibility" and Poor-Law Bastilles, it is time that some means of dealing with them were trying to become "possible"! Of the Government of England, of all articulate-speaking functionaries, real and imaginary Aristocracies, of me and of thee, it is imperatively demanded, "How do you mean to manage these men? Where are they to find a supportable existence? What is to become of them— and of you!"   (IV, 1)
(1843)

Thomas Carlyle, from The Maclise Portrait-Gallery of "Illustrious Literary Characters" *with Memoirs, London, William Bates, 1883.*

8. there will . . . Israel. Cf. 1 Samuel 8:19: "Nevertheless, the people refused to obey the voice of Samuel: and they said Nay; but we will have a king over us." 51. dilettantism, superficial dabbling.

62. millions . . . Men. "*The Return of the Paupers for England and Wales* at Ladyday, 1843, is 'Indoor, 221, 687. Outdoor, 1,207,402; Official Report.' "—Carlyle.

from ON HEROES, HERO-WORSHIP, AND THE HEROIC IN HISTORY

Carlyle delivered his six lectures On Heroes *in 1840: I. "The Hero as Divinity. Odin. Paganism: Scandinavian Mythology"; II. "The Hero as Prophet. Mahomet: Islam"; III. "The Hero as Poet. Dante; Shakspeare"; IV. "The Hero as Priest. Luther; Reformation: Knox; Puritanism"; V. "The Hero as Man of Letters. Johnson, Rousseau, Burns"; VI. "The Hero as King. Cromwell, Napoleon: Modern Revolutionism." "The History of the world," Carlyle said in the first lecture, "is but the Biography of great men. . . . Could we see them, we should get some glimpses into the very marrow of the world's history."*

from THE HERO AS POET. DANTE; SHAKSPEARE

The Hero as Divinity, the Hero as Prophet, are productions of old ages; not to be repeated in the new. They presuppose a certain rudeness of conception, which the progress of mere scientific knowledge puts an end to. There needs to be, as it were, a world vacant, or almost vacant of scientific forms, if men in their loving wonder are to fancy their fellow-man either a god or one speaking with the voice of a god.
80 Divinity and Prophet are past. We are now to see our Hero in the less ambitious, but also less questionable, character of Poet; a character which does not pass. The Poet is a heroic figure belonging to all ages; whom all ages possess, when once he is produced, whom the newest age as the oldest may produce;—and will produce, always when Nature pleases. Let Nature send a Hero-soul; in no age is it other than possible that he may be shaped into a Poet.

Hero, Prophet, Poet,—many different names, in
90 different times and places, do we give to Great Men; according to varieties we note in them, according to the sphere in which they have displayed themselves! We might give many more names, on this same principle. I will remark again, however, as a fact not unimportant to be understood, that the different *sphere* constitutes the grand origin of such distinction; that the Hero can be Poet, Prophet, King, Priest or what you will, according to the kind of world he finds himself born into. I confess, I have no notion of a
100 truly great man that could not be *all* sorts of men. The Poet who could merely sit on a chair, and compose stanzas, would never make a stanza worth much. He could not sing the Heroic warrior, unless he himself were at least a Heroic warrior too. I fancy there is in him the Politician, the Thinker, Legislator, Philosopher;—in one or the other degree, he could have been, he is all these. So too I cannot understand how a

Mirabeau, with that great glowing heart, with the fire that was in it, with the bursting tears that were in it, could not have written verses, tragedies, poems, 110 and touched all hearts in that way, had his course of life and education led him thitherward. The grand fundamental character is that of Great Man; that the man be great. Napoleon has words in him which are like Austerlitz Battles. Louis Fourteenth's Marshals are a kind of poetical men withal; the things Turenne says are full of sagacity and geniality, like sayings of Samuel Johnson. The great heart, the clear deep-seeing eye: there it lies; no man whatever, in what province soever, can prosper at all without these. Petrarch and 120 Boccaccio did diplomatic messages, it seems, quite well: one can easily believe it; they had done things a little harder than these! Burns, a gifted songwriter, might have made a still better Mirabeau. Shakspeare, —one knows not what *he* could not have made, in the supreme degree.

True, there are aptitudes of Nature, too. Nature does not make all great men, more than all other men, in the self-same mould. Varieties of aptitude doubtless; but infinitely more of circumstance; and far oftenest 130 it is the *latter* only that are looked to. But it is as with common men in the learning of trades. You take any man, as yet a vague capability of a man, who could be any kind of craftsman; and make him into a smith, a carpenter, a mason: he is then and thenceforth that and nothing else. And if, as Addison complains, you sometimes see a street-porter staggering under his load on spindle-shanks, and near at hand a tailor with the frame of a Samson handling a bit of cloth and small Whitechapel needle,—it cannot be considered that apti- 140 tude of Nature alone has been consulted here either!— The Great Man also, to what shall he be bound apprentice? Given your Hero, is he to become Conqueror, King, Philosopher, Poet? It is an inexplicably complex controversial-calculation between the world and him! He will read the world and its laws; the world with its laws will be there to be read. What the world, on *this* matter, shall permit and bid is, as we said, the most important fact about the world.—

Poet and Prophet differ greatly in our loose modern 150 notions of them. In some old languages, again, the titles are synonymous; *Vates* means both Prophet and Poet: and indeed at all times, Prophet and Poet, well understood, have much kindred of meaning. Fundamentally indeed they are still the same; in this most important respect especially, That they have penetrated both of them into the sacred mystery of the Universe; what Goethe calls "the open secret." "Which is the great secret?" asks one.—"The *open* secret,"—open to all, seen by almost none! That divine mystery, which lies 160 everywhere in all Beings, "the Divine Idea of the

---

108. **Mirabeau,** Honore Riqueti, Comte de Mirabeau (1749-1791), French Revolutionary leader. 116. **Turenne,** Henri de La Tour d'Auvergne, Vicomte de Turenne (1611-1675), Marshal of France dur-ing the age of Louis XIV. 140. **Whitechapel,** a largely Jewish section of London. 158. **the open secret,** from Goethe's *Maxims and Reflections.*

World, that which lies at the bottom of Appearance," as Fichte styles it; of which all Appearance, from the starry sky to the grass of the field, but especially the Appearance of Man and his work, is but the *vesture,* the embodiment that renders it visible. This divine mystery *is* in all times and in all places; veritably is. In most times and places it is greatly overlooked; and the Universe, definable always in one or the other dialect, as the realised Thought of God, is considered 10 a trivial, inert, commonplace matter,—as if, says the Satirist, it were a dead thing, which some upholsterer had put together! It could do no good, at present, to *speak* much about this; but it is a pity for every one of us if we do not know it, live ever in the knowledge of it. Really a most mournful pity;—a failure to live at all, if we live otherwise!

But now, I say, whoever may forget this divine mystery, the *Vates,* whether Prophet or Poet, has penetrated into it; is a man sent hither to make it 20 more impressively known to us. That always is his message; he is to reveal that to us,—that sacred mystery which he more than others lives ever present with. While others forget it, he knows it;—I might say, he has been driven to know it; without consent asked of *him,* he finds himself living in it, bound to live in it. Once more, here is no Hearsay, but a direct Insight and Belief; this man too could not help being a sincere man! Whosoever may live in the shows of things, it is for him a necessity of nature to live in the very fact of 30 things. A man once more, in earnest with the Universe, though all others were but toying with it. He is a *Vates,* first of all, in virtue of being sincere. So far Poet and Prophet, participators in the "open secret," are one.

With respect to their distinction again: the *Vates* Prophet, we might say, has seized that sacred mystery rather on the moral side, as Good and Evil, Duty and Prohibition; the *Vates* Poet on what the Germans call the aesthetic side, as Beautiful, and the like. The one we may call a revealer of what we are to do, the 40 other of what we are to love. But indeed these two provinces run into one another, and cannot be disjoined. The Prophet too has his eye on what we are to love: how else shall he know what it is we are to do? The highest Voice ever heard on this earth said withal, "Consider the lilies of the field; they toil not, neither do they spin: yet Solomon in all his glory was not arrayed like one of these." A glance, that, into the deepest deep of Beauty. "The lilies of the field,"— dressed finer than earthly princes, springing-up there 50 in the humble furrow-field; a beautiful *eye* looking-out on you, from the great inner Sea of Beauty! How could the rude Earth make these if her Essence, rugged as she looks and is, were not inwardly Beauty? In this point of view, too, a saying of Goethe's, which has

staggered several, may have meaning: "The Beautiful," he intimates, "is higher than the Good; the Beautiful includes in it the Good." The *true* Beautiful; which however, I have said somewhere, "differs from the *false* as Heaven does from Vauxhall!" So much for the distinction and identity of Poet and Prophet.— 60

In ancient and also in modern periods we find a few Poets who are accounted perfect; whom it were a kind of treason to find fault with. This is noteworthy; this is right: yet in strictness it is only an illusion. At bottom, clearly enough, there is no perfect Poet! A vein of Poetry exists in the hearts of all men; no man is made altogether of Poetry. We are all poets when we *read* a poem well. The "imagination that shudders at the Hell of Dante," is not that the same faculty, weaker in degree, as Dante's own? No one but 70 Shakspeare can embody, out of *Saxo Grammaticus,* the story of *Hamlet* as Shakspeare did: but every one models some kind of story out of it; every one embodies it better or worse. We need not spend time in defining. Where there is no specific difference, as between round and square, all definition must be more or less arbitrary. A man that has *so* much more of the poetic element developed in him as to have become noticeable, will be called Poet by his neighbours. World-Poets too, those whom we are to take for per- 80 fect Poets, are settled by critics in the same way. One who rises *so* far above the general level of Poets will, to such and such critics, seem a Universal Poet; as he ought to do. And yet it is, and must be, an arbitrary distinction. All Poets, all men, have some touches of the Universal; no man is wholly made of that. Most Poets are very soon forgotten: but not the noblest Shakspeare or Homer of them can be remembered *forever,*—a day comes when he too is not!

Nevertheless, you will say, there must be a difference 90 between true Poetry and true speech not poetical: what is the difference? On this point many things have been written, especially by late German Critics, some of which are not very intelligible at first. They say, for example, that the Poet has an *infinitude* in him; communicates an *Unendlichkeit,* a certain character of "infinitude," to whatsoever he delineates. This, though not very precise, yet on so vague a matter is worth remembering: if well meditated, some meaning will gradually be found in it. For my own part, I find con- 100 siderable meaning in the old vulgar distinction of Poetry being *metrical,* having music in it, being a Song. Truly, if pressed to give a definition, one might say this as soon as anything else: If your delineation be authentically *musical,* musical not in word only, but in heart and substance, in all the thoughts and utterances of it, in the whole conception of it, then it will be poetical; if not, not.—Musical: how much

2. **as Fichte styles it,** in *On the Nature of the Scholar* (1806). 11. **Satirist,** Carlyle himself. 44-47. **highest Voice . . . one of these.** See Matthew 6:28-29. 55-57. **The Beautiful . . . Good,** from Carlyle's journal, October 28, 1830. 58. **I have said somewhere,** in his essay *Diderot.* 59. **Vauxhall,** a pleasure spot on the bank of the Thames. 68-69. **imagination . . . Dante,** from Carlyle's essay on Burns. 71.

lies in that! A *musical* thought is one spoken by a mind that has penetrated into the inmost heart of the thing; detected the inmost mystery of it, namely the *melody* that lies hidden in it; the inward harmony of coherence which is its soul, whereby it exists, and has a right to be, here in this world. All inmost things, we may say, are melodious; naturally utter themselves in Song. The meaning of Song goes deep. Who is there that, in logical words, can express the effect music has on us? A kind of inarticulate unfathomable speech, which leads us to the edge of the Infinite, and lets us for moments gaze into that!

Nay all speech, even the commonest speech, has something of song in it: not a parish in the world but has its parish-accent;—the rhythm or *tune* to which the people there *sing* what they have to say! Accent is a kind of chanting; all men have accent of their own,—though they only *notice* that of others. Observe too how all passionate language does of itself become musical,—with a finer music than the mere accent; the speech of a man even in zealous anger becomes a chant, a song. All deep things are Song. It seems somehow the very central essence of us, Song; as if all the rest were but wrappages and hulls! The primal element of us; of us, and of all things. The Greeks fabled of Sphere-Harmonies: it was the feeling they had of the inner structure of Nature: that the soul of all her voices and utterances was perfect music. Poetry, therefore, we will call *musical Thought.* The Poet is he who *thinks* in that manner. At bottom, it turns still on power of intellect; it is a man's sincerity and depth of vision that makes him a Poet. See deep enough, and you see musically; the heart of Nature *being* everywhere music, if you can only reach it. . . .

Nay here in these ages, such as they are, have we not two mere Poets, if not deified, yet we may say beatified? Shakspeare and Dante are Saints of Poetry; really, if we will think of it, *canonised,* so that it is impiety to meddle with them. The unguided instinct of the world, working across all these perverse impediments, has arrived at such result. Dante and Shakspeare are a peculiar Two. They dwell apart, in a kind of royal solitude; none equal, none second to them: in the general feeling of the world, a certain transcendentalism, a glory as of complete perfection, invests these two. They *are* canonised, though no Pope or Cardinals took hand in doing it! Such, in spite of every perverting influence, in the most unheroic times, is still our indestructible reverence for heroism.—We will look a little at these Two, the Poet Dante and the Poet Shakspeare: what little it is permitted us to say here of the Hero as Poet will most fitly arrange itself in that fashion.

Many volumes have been written by way of commentary on Dante and his Book; yet, on the whole, with no great result. His Biography is, as it were, irrecoverably lost for us. An unimportant, wandering, sorrow-stricken man, not much note was taken of him while he lived; and the most of that has vanished, in the long space that now intervenes. It is five centuries since he ceased writing and living here. After all commentaries, the Book itself is mainly what we know of him. The Book;—and one might add that Portrait commonly attributed to Giotto, which, looking on it, you cannot help inclining to think genuine, whoever did it. To me it is a most touching face; perhaps of all faces that I know, the most so. Lonely there, painted as on vacancy, with the simple laurel wound round it; the deathless sorrow and pain, the known victory which is also deathless;—significant of the whole history of Dante! I think it is the mournfulest face that ever was painted from reality; an altogether tragic, heart-affecting face. There is in it, as a foundation of it, the softness, tenderness, gentle affection as of a child; but all this is as if congealed into sharp contradiction, into abnegation, isolation, proud hopeless pain. A soft ethereal soul looking-out so stern, implacable, grim-trenchant, as from imprisonment of thick-ribbed ice! Withal it is a silent pain too, a silent scornful one: the lip is curled in a kind of godlike disdain of the thing that is eating-out his heart,—as if it were withal a mean insignificant thing, as if he whom it had power to torture and strangle were greater than it. The face of one wholly in protest, and life-long unsurrendering battle, against the world. Affection all converted into indignation: an implacable indignation; slow, equable, silent, like that of a god! The eye too, it looks-out as in a kind of *surprise,* a kind of inquiry, Why the world was of such a sort? This is Dante: so he looks, this "voice of ten silent centuries," and sings us "his mystic unfathomable song."

The little that we know of Dante's Life corresponds well enough with this Portrait and this Book. He was born at Florence, in the upper class of society, in the year 1265. His education was the best then going; much school-divinity, Aristotelian logic, some Latin classics,—no inconsiderable insight into certain provinces of things: and Dante, with his earnest intelligent nature, we need not doubt, learned better than most all that was learnable. He has a clear cultivated understanding, and of great subtlety; this best fruit of education he had contrived to realise from these scholastics. He knows accurately and well what lies close to him; but, in such a time, without printed books or free intercourse, he could not know well what was distant: the small clear light, most luminous for what is near, breaks itself into singular *chiaroscuro*

Saxo Grammaticus, Danish historian of the thirteenth century. 172. *Giotto,* most famous painter of his era (c. 1267-1337), a friend of Dante's. 198-199. **voice of . . . song,** from Carlyle's *Essays.* 215. **chiaroscuro,** light and shadow.

striking on what is far off. This was Dante's learning from the schools. In life, he had gone through the usual destinies; been twice out campaigning as a soldier for the Florentine State, been on embassy; had in his thirty-fifth year, by natural gradation of talent and service, become one of the Chief Magistrates of Florence. He had met in boyhood a certain Beatrice Portinari, a beautiful little girl of his own age and rank, and grown-up thenceforth in partial sight of her, in some distant intercourse with her. All readers know his graceful affecting account of this; and then of their being parted; of her being wedded to another, and of her death soon after. She makes a great figure in Dante's Poem; seems to have made a great figure in his life. Of all beings it might seem as if she, held apart from him, far apart at last in the dim Eternity, were the only one he had ever with his whole strength of affection loved. She died: Dante himself was wedded; but it seems not happily, far from happily. I fancy, the rigorous earnest man, with his keen excitabilities, was not altogether easy to make happy. . . .

I said, Dante's Poem was a Song: it is Tieck who calls it "a mystic unfathomable Song"; and such is literally the character of it. Coleridge remarks very pertinently somewhere, that wherever you find a sentence musically worded, of true rhythm and melody in the words, there is something deep and good in the meaning too. For body and soul, word and idea, go strangely together here as everywhere. Song: we said before, it was the Heroic of Speech! All *old* Poems, Homer's and the rest, are authentically Songs. I would say, in strictness, that all right Poems are; that whatsoever is not *sung* is properly no Poem, but a piece of Prose cramped into jingling lines,—to the great injury of the grammar, to the great grief of the reader, for most part! What we want to get at is the *thought* the man had, if he had any: why should he twist it into jingle, if he *could* speak it out plainly? It is only when the heart of him is rapt into true passion of melody, and the very tones of him, according to Coleridge's remark, become musical by the greatness, depth and music of his thoughts, that we can give him right to rhyme and sing; that we call him a Poet, and listen to him as the Heroic of Speakers,—whose speech *is* Song. Pretenders to this are many; and to an earnest reader, I doubt, it is for most part a very melancholy, not to say an insupportable business, that of reading rhyme! Rhyme that had no inward necessity to be rhymed:—it ought to have told us plainly, without any jingle, what it was aiming at. I would advise all men who *can* speak their thought, not to sing it; to understand that, in a serious time, among serious men, there is no vocation in them for singing it. Precisely as we love the true song, and

are charmed by it as by something divine, so shall we hate the false song, and account it a mere wooden noise, a thing hollow, superfluous, altogether an insincere and offensive thing.

I give Dante my highest praise when I say of his *Divine Comedy* that it is, in all senses, genuinely a Song. In the very sound of it there is a *canto fermo*, it proceeds as by a chant. The language, his simple *terza rima*, doubtless helped him in this. One reads along naturally with a sort of *lilt*. But I add, that it could not be otherwise; for the essence and material of the work are themselves rhythmic. Its depth, and rapt passion and sincerity, makes it musical;—go *deep* enough, there is music everywhere. A true inward symmetry, what one calls an architectural harmony, reigns in it, proportionates it all: architectural; which also partakes of the character of music. The three kingdoms, *Inferno, Purgatorio, Paradiso,* look-out on one another like compartments of a great edifice; a great supernatural world-cathedral, piled-up there, stern, solemn, awful; Dante's World of Souls! It is, at bottom, the *sincerest* of all Poems; sincerity, here too, we find to be the measure of worth. It came deep out of the author's heart of hearts; and it goes deep, and through long generations, into ours. The people of Verona, when they saw him on the streets, used to say, "*Eccovi l' uom ch' è stato all' Inferno,* See, there is the man that was in Hell!" Ah yes, he had been in Hell;—in Hell enough, in long severe sorrow and struggle; as the like of him is pretty sure to have been. Commedias that come-out *divine* are not accomplished otherwise. Thought, true labour of any kind, highest virtue itself, is it not the daughter of Pain? Born as out of the black whirlwind;—true *effort*, in fact, as of a captive struggling to free himself: that is Thought. In all ways we are "to become perfect through *suffering*."—But, as I say, no work known to me is so elaborated as this of Dante's. It has all been as if molten, in the hottest furnace of his soul. It had made him "lean" for many years. Not the general whole only; every compartment of it is worked-out, with intense earnestness, into truth, into clear visuality. Each answers to the other; each fits in its place, like a marble stone accurately hewn and polished. It is the soul of Dante, and in this the soul of the middle ages, rendered forever rhythmically visible there. No light task; a right intense one: but a task which is *done*.

Perhaps one would say, *intensity*, with the much that depends on it, is the prevailing character of Dante's genius. Dante does not come before us as a large catholic mind, rather a narrow, and even sectarian mind: it is partly the fruit of his age and position, but partly too of his own nature. His greatness has, in all senses, concentered itself into fiery emphasis and depth. He is world-great not because he

22. **Tieck**, Ludwig Tieck, German poet, novelist, and critic (1773-1853), translated by Carlyle.   61. **canto fermo**, a plain Gregorian chant.   62. *terza rima*, third or triple rhyme—stanzas of three lines, the middle line of one stanza rhyming with the first and third lines of the following

110 is world-wide, but because he is world-deep. Through all objects he pierces as it were down into the heart of Being. I know nothing so intense as Dante. Consider, for example, to begin with the outermost development of his intensity, consider how he paints. He has a great power of vision; seizes the very type of a thing; presents that and nothing more. You remember that first view he gets of the Hall of Dite: *red pinnacle, redhot cone of iron glowing through the dim immensity of gloom,—so vivid, so distinct, visible at 120 once and forever!* It is as an emblem of the whole genius of Dante. There is a brevity, an abrupt precision in him: Tacitus is not briefer, more condensed; and then in Dante it seems a natural condensation, spontaneous to the man. One smiting word; and then there is silence, nothing more said. His silence is more eloquent than words. It is strange with what a sharp decisive grace he snatches the true likness of a matter: cuts into the matter as with a pen of fire. Plutus, the blustering giant, collapses at Virgil's rebuke; it is "as 130 the sails sink, the mast being suddenly broken." Or that poor Brunetto Latini, with the *cotto aspetto*, "face baked," parched brown and lean; and the "fiery snow" that falls on them there, a "fiery snow without wind," slow, deliberate, never-ending! Or the lids of those Tombs; square sarcophaguses, in that silent dim-burning Hall, each with its Soul in torment; the lids laid open there; they are to be shut at the Day of Judgment, through Eternity. And how Farinata rises; and how Cavalcante falls—at hearing of his Son, and 140 the past tense "*fue*"! The very movements in Dante have something brief; swift, decisive, almost military. It is of the inmost essence of his genius, this sort of painting. The fiery, swift Italian nature of the man, so silent, passionate, with its quick abrupt movements, its silent "pale rages," speaks itself in these things. . . .

Dante's Hell, Purgatory, Paradise, are a symbol withal, an emblematic representation of his Belief about this Universe:—some Critic in a future age, like those Scandinavian ones the other day, who has 150 ceased altogether to think as Dante did, may find this too all an "Allegory," perhaps an idle Allegory! It is a sublime embodiment, or sublimest, of the soul of Christianity. It expresses, as in huge worldwide architectural emblems, how the Christian Dante felt Good and Evil to be the two polar elements of this Creation, on which it all turns; that these two differ not by *preferability* of one to the other, but by incompatibility absolute and infinite; that the one is excellent and high as light and Heaven, the other hideous, black as Ge-160 henna and the Pit of Hell! Everlasting Justice, yet with Penitence, with everlasting Pity,—all Christianism, as Dante and the Middle Ages had it, is emblemed here. Emblemed: and yet, as I urged the other day,

with what entire truth of purpose; how unconscious of any embleming! Hell, Purgatory, Paradise: these things were not fashioned as emblems; was there, in our Modern European Mind, any thought at all of their being emblems! Were they not indubitable awful facts; the whole heart of man taking them for practically true, all Nature everywhere confirming them? 170 So is it always in these things. Men do not believe an Allegory. The future Critic, whatever his new thought may be, who considers this of Dante to have been all got-up as an Allegory, will commit one sore mistake!— Paganism we recognised as a veracious expression of the earnest awe-struck feeling of man towards the Universe; veracious, true once, and still not without worth for us. But mark here the difference of Paganism and Christianism; one great difference. Paganism emblemed chiefly the Operations of Nature; the des- 180 tinies, efforts, combinations, vicissitudes of things and men in this world; Christianism emblemed the Law of Human Duty, the Moral Law of Man. One was for the sensuous nature: a rude helpless utterance of the *first* Thought of men,—the chief recognised virtue, Courage, Superiority to Fear. The other was not for the sensuous nature, but for the moral. What a progress is here, if in that one respect only!—

And so in this Dante, as we said, had ten silent centuries, in a very strange way, found a voice. The 190 *Divina Commedia* is of Dante's writing; yet in truth it belongs to ten Christian centuries, only the finishing of it is Dante's. So always. The craftsman there, the smith with that metal of his, with these tools, with these cunning methods,—how little of all he does is properly *his* work! All past inventive men work there with him;—as indeed with all of us, in all things. Dante is the spokesman of the Middle Ages; the Thought they lived by stands here, in everlasting music. These sublime ideas of his, terrible and beauti- 200 ful, are the fruit of the Christian Meditation of all the good men who had gone before him. Precious they; but also is not he precious? Much, had not he spoken, would have been dumb; not dead, yet living voiceless. . . .

As Dante, the Italian man, was sent into our world to embody musically the Religion of the Middle Ages, the Religion of our Modern Europe, its Inner Life; so Shakspeare, we may say, embodies for us the Outer Life of our Europe as developed then, its chivalries, 210 courtesies, humours, ambitions, what practical way of thinking, acting, looking at the world, men then had. As in Homer we may still construe Old Greece; so in Shakspeare and Dante, after thousands of years, what our modern Europe was, in Faith and in Practice, will still be legible. Dante has given us the Faith or Soul;

stanza. 90. **to become . . . suffering.** See Hebrews 2:10. 117. **Hall of Dite,** in the *Inferno*, viii, 70-73. 122. **Tacitus,** Roman historian (c. 57-c. 117). 128. **Plutus,** god of wealth. 131. **Brunetto Latini,** an ardent member of the papal party in medieval Italy (c. 1210-1294).

Shakspeare, in a not less noble way, has given us the Practice or body. This latter also we were to have; a man was sent for it, the man Shakspeare. Just when that chivalry way of life had reached its last finish, and was on the point of breaking down into slow or swift dissolution, as we now see it everywhere, this other sovereign Poet, with his seeing eye, with his perennial singing voice, was sent to take note of it, to give long-enduring record of it. Two fit men: Dante, 10 deep, fierce as the central fire of the world; Shakspeare, wide, placid, far-seeing, as the Sun, the upper light of the world. Italy produced the one world-voice; we English had the honour of producing the other.

Curious enough how, as it were by mere accident, this man came to us. I think always, so great, quiet, complete and self-sufficing is this Shakspeare, had the Warwickshire Squire not prosecuted him for deer-stealing, we had perhaps never heard of him as a Poet! The woods and skies, the rustic Life of Man in Strat- 20 ford there, had been enough for this man! But indeed that strange outbudding of our whole English Ex- istence, which we call the Elizabethan Era, did not it too come as of its own accord? The "Tree Igdrasil" buds and withers by its own laws,—too deep for our scanning. Yet it does bud and wither, and every bough and leaf of it is there, by fixed eternal laws; not a Sir Thomas Lucy but comes at the hour fit for him. Curious, I say, and not sufficiently considered: how everything does coöperate with all; not a leaf rotting 30 on the highway but is indissoluble portion of solar and stellar systems; no thought, word or act of man but has sprung withal out of all men, and works sooner or later, recognisably or irrecognisably, on all men! It is all a Tree: circulation of sap and influences, mutual communication of every minutest leaf with the lowest talon of a root, with every other greatest and minutest portion of the whole. The Tree Igdrasil, that has its roots down in the Kingdoms of Hela and Death, and whose boughs overspread the highest Heaven!—

40 In some sense it may be said that this glorious Elizabethan Era with its Shakspeare, as the outcome and flowerage of all which had preceded it, is itself attributable to the Catholicism of the Middle Ages. The Christian Faith, which was the theme of Dante's Song, had produced this Practical Life which Shak- speare was to sing. For Religion then, as it now and always is, was the soul of Practice; the primary vital fact in men's life. And remark here, as rather curious, that Middle-Age Catholicism was abolished, so far as 50 Acts of Parliament could abolish it, before Shakspeare, the noblest product of it, made his appearance. He did make his appearance nevertheless. Nature at her own time, with Catholicism or what else might be necessary, sent him forth; taking small thought of Acts of Parlia-

ment. King-Henrys, Queen-Elizabeths go their way; and Nature too goes hers. Acts of Parliament, on the whole, are small, notwithstanding the noise they make. What Act of Parliament, debate at St. Stephen's, on the hustings or elsewhere, was it that brought this Shakspeare into being? No dining at Freemasons' 60 Tavern, opening subscription-lists, selling of shares, and infinite other jangling and true or false endeavour- ing! This Elizabethan Era, and all its nobleness and blessedness, came without proclamation, preparation of ours. Priceless Shakspeare was the free gift of Nature; given altogether silently;—received altogether silently, as if it had been a thing of little account. And yet, very literally, it is a priceless thing. One should look at that side of matters too.

Of this Shakspeare of ours, perhaps the opinion one 70 sometimes hears a little idolatrously expressed is, in fact, the right one; I think the best judgment not of this country only, but of Europe at large, is slowly pointing to the conclusion, That Shakspeare is the chief of all Poets hitherto; the greatest intellect who, in our recorded world, has left record of himself in the way of Literature. On the whole, I know not such a power of vision, such a faculty of thought, if we take all the characters of it, in any other man. Such a calmness of depth; placid joyous strength; all things imaged in that 80 great soul of his so true and clear, as in a tranquil unfathomable sea! It has been said, that in the con- structing of Shakspeare's Dramas there is, apart from all other "faculties" as they are called, an understand- ing manifested, equal to that in Bacon's *Novum Organum*. That is true; and it is not a truth that strikes every one. It would become more apparent if we tried, any of us for himself, how, out of Shak- speare's dramatic materials, *we* could fashion such a result! The built house seems all so fit,—everyway as it 90 should be, as if it came there by its own law and the nature of things,—we forget the rude disorderly quarry it was shaped from. The very perfection of the house, as if Nature herself had made it, hides the builder's merit. Perfect, more perfect than any other man, we may call Shakspeare in this: he discerns, knows as by instinct, what condition he works under, what his materials are, what his own force and its relation to them is. It is not a transitory glance of insight that will suffice; it is deliberate illumination of the whole 100 matter; it is a calmly *seeing* eye; a great intellect, in short. How a man, of some wide thing that he has witnessed, will construct a narrative, what kind of picture and delineation he will give of it,—is the best measure you could get of what intellect is in the man. Which circumstance is vital and shall stand prominent; which unessential, fit to be suppressed; where is the true *beginning*, the true sequence and ending? To find

---

17. **Warwickshire Squire,** Sir Thomas Lucy (1522-1600), said to have prosecuted Shakespeare for deer-stealing. 55. **King-Henrys, etc.,** that is, the anti-Catholic Tudor monarchs. 58. **St. Stephen's,** chapel at

Westminster, where the House of Commons sat. 59. **hustings,** elec- tions. 60. **Freemasons' Tavern,** where Carlyle and others met to found the London Library. 82. **It has been said,** by Carlyle himself. 85.

out this, you task the whole force of insight that is in the man. He must *understand* the thing; according to the depth of his understanding, will the fitness of his answer be. You will try him so. Does like join itself to like; does the spirit of method stir in that confusion, so that its embroilment become order? Can the man say, *Fiat lux,* Let there be light; and out of chaos make a world? Precisely as there is *light* in himself, will he accomplish this.

Or indeed we may say again, it is in what I called Portrait-painting, delineating of men and things, especially of men, that Shakspeare is great. All the greatness of the man comes out decisively here. It is unexampled, I think, that calm creative perspicacity of Shakspeare. The thing he looks at reveals not this or that face of it, but its inmost heart, and generic secret: it dissolves itself as in light before him, so that he discerns the perfect structure of it. Creative, we said: poetic creation, what is this too but *seeing* the thing sufficiently? The *word* that will describe the thing, follows of itself from such clear intense sight of the thing. And is not Shakspeare's *morality,* his valour, candour, tolerance, truthfulness; his whole victorious strength and greatness, which can triumph over such obstructions, visible there too? Great as the world! No *twisted,* poor convex-concave mirror, reflecting all objects with its own convexities and concavities; a perfectly *level* mirror;—that is to say withal, if we will understand it, a man justly related to all things and men, a good man. It it truly a lordly spectacle how this great soul takes-in all kinds of men and objects, a Falstaff, an Othello, a Juliet, a Coriolanus; sets them all forth to us in their round completeness; loving, just, the equal brother of all. *Novum Organum,* and all the intellect you will find in Bacon, is of a quite secondary order; early, material, poor in comparison with this. Among modern men, one finds, in strictness, almost nothing of the same rank. Goethe alone, since the days of Shakspeare, reminds me of it. Of him too you say that he *saw* the object; you may say what he himself says of Shakspeare: "His characters are like watches with dial-plates of transparent crystal; they show you the hour like others, and the inward mechanism also is all visible."

The seeing eye! It is this that discloses the inner harmony of things; what Nature meant, what musical idea Nature has wrapped-up in these often rough embodiments. Something she did mean. To the seeing eye that something were discernible. Are they base, miserable things? You can laugh over them, you can weep over them; you can in some way or other genially relate yourself to them;—you can, at lowest, hold your peace about them, turn away your own and others' face from them, till the hour come for practically ex-

terminating and extinguishing them! At bottom, it is the Poet's first gift, as it is all men's, that he have intellect enough. He will be a Poet if he have: a Poet in word; or failing that, perhaps still better, a Poet in act. Whether he write at all; and if so, whether in prose or in verse, will depend on accidents: who knows on what extremely trivial accidents,—perhaps on his having had a singing-master, on his being taught to sing in his boyhood! But the faculty which enables him to discern the inner heart of things, and the harmony that dwells there (for whatsoever exists has a harmony in the heart of it, or it would not hold together and exist), is not the result of habits or accidents, but the gift of Nature herself; the primary outfit for a Heroic Man in what sort soever. To the Poet, as to every other, we say first of all, *See.* If you cannot do that, it is of no use to keep stringing rhymes together, jingling sensibilities against each other, and *name* yourself a Poet; there is no hope for you. If you can, there is, in prose or verse, in action or speculation, all manner of hope. The crabbed old Schoolmaster used to ask, when they brought him a new pupil, "But are ye sure he's *not a dunce?*" Why, really one might ask the same thing, in regard to every man proposed for whatsoever function; and consider it as the one inquiry needful: Are ye sure he's not a dunce? There is, in this world, no other entirely fatal person. . . .

If I say, therefore, that Shakspeare is the greatest of Intellects, I have said all concerning him. But there is more in Shakspeare's intellect than we have yet seen. It is what I call an unconscious intellect; there is more virtue in it than he himself is aware of. Novalis beautifully remarks of him, that those Dramas of his are Products of Nature too, deep as Nature herself. I find a great truth in this saying. Shakspeare's Art is not Artifice; the noblest worth of it is not there by plan or precontrivance. It grows-up from the deeps of Nature, through this noble sincere soul, who is a voice of Nature. The latest generations of men will find new meanings in Shakspeare, new elucidations of their own human being; "new harmonies with the infinite structure of the Universe; concurrences with later ideas, affinities with the higher powers and senses of man." This well deserves meditating. It is Nature's highest reward to a true simple great soul, that he get thus to be *a part of herself.* Such a man's works, whatsoever he with utmost conscious exertion and forethought shall accomplish, grow up withal *unconsciously,* from the unknown deeps in him;—as the oak-tree grows from the Earth's bosom, as the mountains and waters shape themselves; with a symmetry grounded on Nature's own laws, conformable to all Truth whatsoever. How much in Shakspeare lies hid; his sorrows, his silent

Novum Organum, Francis Bacon's principal philosophical treatise (1620). 115. **Let there be light.** See Genesis 1:3. 183. **Schoolmaster,** one of Carlyle's early Scottish teachers. 194. **Novalis,** pen name of Friedrich von Hardenberg (1772-1801), German romantic poet and novelist whom Carlyle studied closely.

struggles known to himself; much that was not known at all, not speakable at all: like *roots*, like sap and forces working underground! Speech is great; but Silence is greater.

Withal the joyful tranquillity of this man is notable. I will not blame Dante for his misery: it is as battle without victory; but true battle,—the first, indispensable thing. Yet I call Shakspeare greater than Dante, in that he fought truly, and did conquer. Doubt it not, he had his own sorrows: those *Sonnets* of his will even testify expressly in what deep waters he had waded, and swum struggling for his life;—as what man like him ever failed to have to do? It seems to me a heedless notion, our common one, that he sat like a bird on the bough; and sang forth, free and off-hand, never knowing the troubles of other men. Not so; with no man is it so. How could a man travel forward from rustic deer-poaching to such tragedy-writing, and not fall-in with sorrows by the way? Or, still better, how could a man delineate a Hamlet, a Coriolanus, a Macbeth, so many suffering heroic hearts, if his own heroic heart had never suffered?—And now, in contrast with all this, observe his mirthfulness, his genuine overflowing love of laughter! You would say, in no point does he *exaggerate* but only in laughter. Fiery objurgations, words that pierce and burn, are to be found in Shakspeare; yet he is always in measure here; never what Johnson would remark as a specially "good hater." But his laughter seems to pour from him in floods; he heaps all manner of ridiculous nicknames on the butt he is bantering, tumbles and tosses him in all sorts of horse-play; you would say, with his whole heart laughs. And then, if not always the finest, it is always a genial laughter. Not at mere weakness, at misery or poverty; never. No man who *can* laugh, what we call laughing, will laugh at these things. It is some poor character only *desiring* to laugh, and have the credit of wit, that does so. Laughter means sympathy; good laughter is not "the crackling of thorns under the pot." Even at stupidity and pretension this Shakspeare does not laugh otherwise than genially. Dogberry and Verges tickle our very hearts; and we dismiss them covered with explosions of laughter: but we like the poor fellows only the better for our laughing; and hope they will get on well there, and continue Presidents of the City-watch. Such laughter, like sunshine on the deep sea, is very beautiful to me. . . .

Shakspeare's works . . . are so many windows, through which we see a glimpse of the world that was in him. All his works seem, comparatively speaking, cursory, imperfect, written under cramping circumstances; giving only here and there a note of the full utterance of the man. Passages there are that come upon you like splendour out of Heaven; bursts of radiance, illuminating the very heart of the thing: you say, "That is *true*, spoken once and forever; wheresoever and whensoever there is an open human soul, that will be recognised as true!" Such bursts, however, make us feel that the surrounding matter is not radiant; that it is, in part, temporary, conventional. Alas, Shakspeare had to write for the Globe Playhouse: his great soul had to crush itself, as it could, into that and no other mould. It was with him, then, as it is with us all. No man works save under conditions. The sculptor cannot set his own free Thought before us; but his Thought as he could translate it into the stone that was given, with the tools that were given. *Disjecta membra* are all that we find of any Poet, or of any man.

Whoever looks intelligently at this Shakspeare may recognise that he too was a *Prophet*, in his way; of an insight analogous to the Prophetic, though he took it up in another strain. Nature seemed to this man also divine; *unspeakable*, deep as Tophet, high as Heaven: "We are such stuff as Dreams are made of!" That scroll in Westminster Abbey, which few read with understanding, is of the depth of any seer. But the man sang; did not preach, except musically. We called Dante the melodious Priest of Middle-Age Catholicism. May we not call Shakspeare the still more melodious Priest of a *true* Catholicism, the "Universal Church" of the Future and of all times? No narrow superstition, harsh asceticism, intolerance, fanatical fierceness or perversion: a Revelation, so far as it goes, that such a thousandfold hidden beauty and divineness dwells in all Nature; which let all men worship as they can! We may say without offence, that there rises a kind of universal Psalm out of this Shakspeare too; not unfit to make itself heard among the still more sacred Psalms. Not in disharmony with these, if we understood them, but in harmony!—I cannot call this Shakspeare a "Sceptic," as some do; his indifference to the creeds and theological quarrels of his time misleading them. No: neither unpatriotic, though he says little about his Patriotism; nor sceptic, though he says little about his Faith. Such "indifference" was the fruit of his greatness withal: his whole heart was in his own grand sphere of worship (we may call it such); these other controversies, vitally important to other men, were not vital to him.

But call it worship, call it what you will, is it not a right glorious thing, and set of things, this that Shakspeare has brought us? For myself, I feel that there is actually a kind of sacredness in the fact of such a man being sent into this Earth. Is he not an eye to us all; a blessed heaven-sent Bringer of Light?—And, at bottom, was it not perhaps far better that this

3-4. **Speech is . . . greater,** an adaptation from Goethe's *Wilhelm Meister.* 28. **Johnson . . . good hater,** according to Mrs. Thrale's *Anecdotes of the Late Samuel Johnson* (1786). 39. **the crackling . . .** pot. See *Ecclesiastes* 7:6. 45-46. **Presidents of the City-watch,** in *Much Ado About Nothing,* III. iii. 67. *Disjecta membra,* scattered parts. 74. **Tophet,** hell. 75. **We are . . . made of,** from *The Tempest.*

Shakspeare, everyway an unconscious man, was *conscious* of no Heavenly message? He did not feel, like Mahomet, because he saw into those internal Splendours, that he specially was the "Prophet of God": and was he not greater than Mahomet in that? Greater; and also, if we compute strictly, as we did in Dante's case, more successful. It was intrinsically an error that notion of Mahomet's, of his supreme Prophethood; and has come down to us inextricably involved in error to this day; dragging along with it such a coil of fables, impurities, intolerances, as makes it a questionable step for me here and now to say, as I have done, that Mahomet was a true Speaker at all, and not rather an ambitious charlatan, perversity and simulacrum; no Speaker, but a Babbler! Even in Arabia, as I compute, Mahomet will have exhausted himself and become obsolete, while this Shakspeare, this Dante may still be young;—while this Shakspeare may still pretend to be a Priest of Mankind, of Arabia as of other places, for unlimited periods to come!

Compared with any speaker or singer one knows, even with Æschylus or Homer, why should he not, for veracity and universality, last like them? He is *sincere* as they; reaches deep down like them, to the universal and perennial. But as for Mahomet, I think it had been better for him *not* to be so conscious! Alas, poor Mahomet; all that he was *conscious* of was a mere error; a futility and triviality,—as indeed such ever is. The truly great in him too was the unconscious: that he was a wild Arab lion of the desert, and did speak-out with that great thunder-voice of his, not by words which he *thought* to be great, but by actions, by feelings, by a history which *were* great! His Koran has become a stupid piece of prolix absurdity; we do not believe, like him, that God wrote that! The Great Man here too, as always, is a Force of Nature: whatsoever is truly great in him springs up from the *inarticulate* deeps.

Well: this is our poor Warwickshire Peasant, who rose to be Manager of a Playhouse, so that he could live without begging; whom the Earl of Southampton cast some kind glances on; whom Sir Thomas Lucy, many thanks to him, was for sending to the Treadmill! We did not account him a god, like Odin, while he dwelt with us;—on which point there were much to be said. But I will say rather, or repeat: In spite of the sad state Hero-worship now lies in, consider what this Shakspeare has actually become among us. Which Englishman we ever made, in this land of ours, which million of Englishmen, would we not give-up rather than the Stratford Peasant? There is no regiment of highest Dignitaries that we would sell him for. He is the grandest thing we have yet done. For our honour among foreign nations, as an ornament to our English Household, what item is there that we would not surrender rather than him? Consider now, if they asked us, Will you give-up your Indian Empire or your Shakspeare, you English; never have had any Indian Empire, or never have had any Shakspeare? Really it were a grave question. Official persons would answer doubtless in official language; but we, for our part too, should not we be forced to answer: Indian Empire, or no Indian Empire; we cannot do without Shakspeare! Indian Empire will go, at any rate, some day; but this Shakspeare does not go, he lasts forever with us; we cannot give-up our Shakspeare!...

Yes, truly, it is a great thing for a Nation that it get an articulate voice; that it produce a man who will speak-forth melodiously what the heart of it means! Italy, for example, poor Italy lies dismembered, scattered asunder, not appearing in any protocol or treaty as a unity at all; yet the noble Italy is actually *one*: Italy produced its Dante; Italy can speak! The Czar of all the Russias, he is strong with so many bayonets, Cossacks and cannons; and does a great feat in keeping such a tract of Earth politically together; but he cannot yet speak. Something great in him, but it is a dumb greatness. He has had no voice of genius, to be heard of all men and times. He must learn to speak. He is a great dumb monster hitherto. His cannons and Cossacks will all have rusted into nonentity, while that Dante's voice is still audible. The Nation that has a Dante is bound together as no dumb Russia can be. —We must here end what we had to say of the Hero-Poet.

(1841)

JOHN STUART MILL 1806-1873

John Stuart Mill has been called the most enlightened man of his age, and the assessment is defensible if one accepts a speculative, eighteenth-century definition of "enlightenment." He was the "saint of rationalism," and his most famous disciples were among the articulate rationalists of the second half of the nineteenth century: Herbert Spencer, Thomas Henry Huxley, John Morley, and Leslie Stephen. His major sympathies, because of the temper of his mind and the austerity of his training, lay with utilitarianism; but he was the least rigid and the most effective of all the social commentators in the utilitarian-Liberal tradition. He was a literary critic of

IV, i, 157. 76. **scroll**, that is, the scroll containing the above passage.
129. **Æschylus**, Greek tragic poet (525-456 B.C.). 141. **Koran**, sacred book of the Moslems. 148. **Earl of Southampton**, Henry Wriothesley (1573-1624), Shakespeare's patron.

much sensitivity: his unpublished notes on Robert Browning's poem Pauline are said to have driven the young poet to recast his whole approach to poetry, and his review of Tennyson's poems in the mid-thirties did much to rehabilitate Tennyson's literary reputation.

Mill was the son of James Mill, a leader of the Utilitarians, and he was educated exclusively at home in London under his father's direction. As a boy, he read Latin and Greek with ease and could discourse intelligently on mathematics, philosophy, and economics. So intensive was his education that he felt that when he started his career, he had "an advantage of a quarter of a century" over his contemporaries. He worked for many years for the East India House, rising to the position of chief examiner, and served in Parliament from 1865 to 1868. But mainly he devoted himself to writing.

All of Mill's books were important in his day, and most of them still persist as significant primary documents in political and economic discussions. But the foundation of his reputation as a thinker in the nineteenth century was set by three books: his System of Logic (1843) became "the textbook of the Empirical School and the guide of all 'Radical' thinkers of the day"; his Principles of Political Economy (1848) became "the handbook of Victorian progressives who . . . thought that the 'state of polemical discussion' had now passed and that a great constructive era had dawned"; his On Liberty (1859) became, and remains, the great popular statement of utilitarianism which, according to Thomas Hardy, the students of the 1860's knew almost by heart. For later students of Mill, the Autobiography (1873) has taken on increasing importance as one of the principal documents, along with Carlyle's Sartor Resartus, Newman's Apologia, and Ruskin's Praeterita, for reviewing the forces which shaped the Victorian mind.

Mill was not a strict Benthamite, but after a short period of eclecticism resulting from the mental crisis described in Chapter V of the Autobiography, printed below, he returned fundamentally to utilitarian principles. He did, however, modify and liberalize the more dogged form of Benthamism as follows: (1) he admitted altruism into ethics, recognizing that the feelings must be cultivated if the finer forms of conduct are to be achieved; (2) like Carlyle, he made the pursuit of happiness the indirect rather than the direct object of thought and action; (3) he discarded Bentham's purely quantitative esthetic (for example, that a taste for pushpin was just as good as a taste

for poetry) and insisted upon the qualitative dimension of pleasure; (4) he urged "a perpetual and standing Opposition to the will of the majority," while Bentham, in reaction against the aristocratic abuses of the eighteenth century, had placed man under "the despotism of Public Opinion."

John Stuart Mill was a rationalist, and therefore one expects to find his prose style characterized by precise statement and simple clarity. By his own statement, he wrote all of his books twice. It is the style of mind speaking to mind, and, in contrast to Carlyle, Mill does not depend upon color or energy to accomplish his purposes.

from ON LIBERTY

In the first chapter of On Liberty, Mill stated that his object was "to assert one very simple principle, as entitled to govern absolutely the dealings of society with the individual in the way of compulsion and control, whether the means used be physical force in the form of legal penalties, or the moral coercion of public opinion. That principle is, that the sole end for which mankind are warranted, individually or collectively, in interfering with the liberty of action of any of their number, is self-protection. That the only purpose for which power can be rightfully exercised over any member of a civilized community, against his will, is to prevent harm to others." Thus Mill carries John Milton's classic argument, stated in Areopagitica, for freedom of speech and publication one step further—to freedom of action.

The immediate predecessors of On Liberty in the late eighteenth and early nineteenth centuries were Jeremy Bentham's Introduction to the Principles of Morals and Legislation (1789) and the writings of Claude Henri Saint-Simon (1760-1825) and Auguste Comte (1798-1857). In the longer western tradition, the book invites association with Plato's Republic, Aristotle's Politics, Machiavelli's Prince, Hobbes' Leviathan, and Rousseau's Social Contract. Further, it is suggestive to place the book in the frame of various ideological labels: culturally, it favors bohemianism over conformism; politically, it supports utilitarian Liberalism over governmental paternalism; it prefers free enterprise in economics to national collectivism and rationalism to traditional authoritarianism in philosophy.

18. **propriety.** "These words had scarcely been written, when, as if to give them an emphatic contradiction, occurred the Government Press Prosecutions of 1858. That ill-judged interference with the liberty of public discussion has not, however, induced me to alter a single word in the text, nor has it at all weakened my conviction that, moments of panic excepted, the era of pains and penalties for political discussion has, in our own country, passed away. For, in the first place, the prosecutions were not persisted in; and, in the second, they were never, properly speaking, political prosecutions. The offence charged was not that of criticizing institutions, or the acts or persons of rulers, but of circulating what was deemed an immoral doctrine, the lawfulness of Tyrannicide.

If the arguments of the present chapter are of any validity, there ought to exist the fullest liberty of professing and discussing, as a matter of ethical conviction, any doctrine, however immoral it may be considered. It would, therefore, be irrelevant and out of place to examine

The time, it is to be hoped, is gone by, when any defence would be necessary of the "liberty of the press" as one of the securities against corrupt or tyrannical government. No argument, we may suppose, can now be needed, against permitting a legislature or an executive, not identified in interest with the people, to prescribe opinions to them, and determine what doctrines or what arguments they shall be allowed to hear. This aspect of the question, besides,
10 has been so often and so triumphantly enforced by preceding writers, that it needs not be specially insisted on in this place. Though the law of England, on the subject of the press, is as servile to this day as it was in the time of the Tudors, there is little danger of its being actually put in force against political discussion, except during some temporary panic, when fear of insurrection drives ministers and judges from their propriety; and, speaking generally, it is not, in constitutional countries, to be apprehended,
20 that the government, whether completely responsible to the people or not, will often attempt to control the expression of opinion, except when in doing so it makes itself the organ of the general intolerance of the public. Let us suppose, therefore, that the government is entirely at one with the people, and never thinks of exerting any power of coercion unless in agreement with what it conceives to be their voice. But I deny the right of the people to exercise such coercion, either by themselves or by their government.
30 The power itself is illegitimate. The best government has no more title to it than the worst. It is as noxious, or more noxious, when exerted in accordance with public opinion, than when in opposition to it. If all mankind minus one, were of one opinion, and only one person were of the contrary opinion, mankind would be no more justified in silencing that one person, than he, if he had the power, would be justified in silencing mankind. Were an opinion a personal possession of no value except to the owner; if to be
40 obstructed in the enjoyment of it were simply a private injury, it would make some difference whether the injury was inflicted only on a few persons or on many. But the peculiar evil of silencing the expression of an opinion is, that it is robbing the human race; posterity as well as the existing generation; those who dissent from the opinion, still more than those who hold it. If the opinion is right, they are deprived of the opportunity of exchanging error for truth: if

wrong, they lose, what is almost as great a benefit, the clearer perception and livelier impression of truth, 50 produced by its collision with error.

It is necessary to consider separately these two hypotheses, each of which has a distinct branch of the argument corresponding to it. We can never be sure that the opinion we are endeavouring to stifle is a false opinion; and if we were sure, stifling it would be an evil still.

First: the opinion which it is attempted to suppress by authority may possibly be true. Those who desire to suppress it, of course deny its truth; but they are 60 not infallible. They have no authority to decide the question for all mankind, and exclude every other person from the means of judging. To refuse a hearing to an opinion, because they are sure that it is false, is to assume that *their* certainty is the same thing as *absolute* certainty. All silencing of discussion is an assumption of infallibility. Its condemnation may be allowed to rest on this common argument, not the worse for being common.

Unfortunately for the good sense of mankind, the 70 fact of their fallibility is far from carrying the weight in their practical judgement, which is always allowed to it in theory; for while every one well knows himself to be fallible, few think it necessary to take any precautions against their own fallibility, or admit the supposition that any opinion, of which they feel very certain, may be one of the examples of the error to which they acknowledge themselves to be liable. Absolute princes, or others who are accustomed to unlimited deference, usually feel this complete confidence 80 in their own opinions on nearly all subjects. People more happily situated, who sometimes hear their opinions disputed, and are not wholly unused to be set right when they are wrong, place the same unbounded reliance only on such of their opinions as are shared by all who surround them, or to whom they habitually defer: for in proportion to a man's want of confidence in his own solitary judgement, does he usually repose, with implicit trust, on the infallibility of "the world" in general. And the world, to each individual, 90 means the part of it with which he comes in contact; his party, his sect, his church, his class of society: the man may be called, by comparison, almost liberal and large-minded to whom it means anything so comprehensive as his own country or his own age. Nor is his faith in this collective authority at all shaken by his being aware that other ages, countries, sects, churches, classes, and parties have thought, and even

here, whether the doctrine of Tyrannicide deserves that title. I shall content myself with saying that the subject has been at all times one of the open questions of morals; that the act of a private citizen in striking down a criminal, who, by raising himself above the law, has placed himself beyond the reach of legal punishment or control, has been accounted by whole nations, and by some of the best and wisest of men, not a crime, but an act of exalted virtue; and that, right or wrong, it is

not of the nature of assassination, but of civil war. As such, I hold that the instigation to it, in a specific case, may be a proper subject of punishment, but only if an overt act has followed, and at least a probable connexion can be established between the act and the instigation. Even then, it is not a foreign government, but the very government assailed, which alone, in the exercise of self-defence, can legitimately punish attacks directed against its own existence."—Mill's note.

now think, the exact reverse. He devolves upon his own world the responsibility of being in the right against the dissentient worlds of other people; and it never troubles him that mere accident has decided which of these numerous worlds is the object of his reliance, and that the same causes which make him a Churchman in London, would have made him a Buddhist or a Confucian in Pekin. Yet it is as evident in itself, as any amount of argument can make it, that ages are no more infallible than individuals; every age having held many opinions which subsequent ages have deemed not only false but absurd; and it is as certain that many opinions, now general, will be rejected by future ages, as it is that many, once general, are rejected by the present.

The objection likely to be made to this argument would probably take some such form as the following. There is no greater assumption of infallibility in forbidding the propagation of error, than in any other thing which is done by public authority on its own judgement and responsibility. Judgement is given to men that they may use it. Because it may be used erroneously, are men to be told that they ought not to use it at all? To prohibit what they think pernicious, is not claiming exemption from error, but fulfilling the duty incumbent on them, although fallible, of acting on their conscientious conviction. If we were never to act on our opinions, because those opinions may be wrong, we should leave all our interests uncared for, and all our duties unperformed. An objection which applies to all conduct, can be no valid objection to any conduct in particular. It is the duty of governments, and of individuals, to form the truest opinions they can; to form them carefully, and never impose them upon others unless they are quite sure of being right. But when they are sure (such reasoners may say), it is not conscientiousness but cowardice to shrink from acting on their opinions, and allow doctrines which they honestly think dangerous to the welfare of mankind, either in this life or in another, to be scattered abroad without restraint, because other people, in less enlightened times, have persecuted opinions now believed to be true. Let us take care, it may be said, not to make the same mistake: but governments and nations have made mistakes in other things, which are not denied to be fit subjects for the exercise of authority: they have laid on bad taxes, made unjust wars. Ought we therefore to lay on no taxes, and, under whatever provocation, make no wars? Men, and governments, must act to the best of their ability. There is no such thing as absolute certainty, but there is assurance sufficient for the purposes of human life. We may, and must, assume our opinion to be true for the guidance of our own conduct: and it is assuming no more when we forbid bad men to pervert society by the propagation of opinions which we regard as false and pernicious.

I answer, that it is assuming very much more. There is the greatest difference between presuming an opinion to be true, because, with every opportunity for contesting it, it has not been refuted, and assuming its truth for the purpose of not permitting its refutation. Complete liberty of contradicting and disproving our opinion, is the very condition which justifies us in assuming its truth for purposes of action; and on no other terms can a being with human faculties have any rational assurance of being right.

When we consider either the history of opinion, or the ordinary conduct of human life, to what is it to be ascribed that the one and the other are no worse than they are? Not certainly to the inherent force of the human understanding; for, on any matter not self-evident, there are ninety-nine persons totally incapable of judging of it, for one who is capable; and the capacity of the hundredth person is only comparative; for the majority of the eminent men of every past generation held many opinions now known to be erroneous, and did or approved numerous things which no one will now justify. Why is it, then, that there is on the whole a preponderance among mankind of rational opinions and rational conduct? If there really is this preponderance—which there must be unless human affairs are, and have always been, in an almost desperate state—it is owing to a quality of the human mind, the source of everything respectable in man either as an intellectual or as a moral being, namely, that his errors are corrigible. He is capable of rectifying his mistakes, by discussion and experience. Not by experience alone. There must be discussion, to show how experience is to be interpreted. Wrong opinions and practices gradually yield to fact and argument: but facts and arguments, to produce any effect on the mind, must be brought before it. Very few facts are able to tell their own story, without comments to bring out their meaning. The whole strength and value, then, of human judgement, depending on the one property, that it can be set right when it is wrong, reliance can be placed on it only when the means of setting it right are kept constantly at hand. In the case of any person whose judgement is really deserving of confidence, how has it become so? Because he has kept his mind open to criticism of his opinions and conduct. Because it has been his practice to listen to all that could be said against him; to profit by as much of it as was just, and expound to himself, and upon occasion to others, the fallacy of what was fallacious. Because he has felt, that the only way in which a human being can make some approach to knowing the whole of a subject, is by hearing what can be said about it by persons of every variety of opinion, and studying all modes in which it can be looked at by every character of mind. No wise man ever acquired his wisdom in any mode but this; nor is it in the nature of human intellect to become wise in any other manner.

The steady habit of correcting and completing his own opinion by collating it with those of others, so far from causing doubt and hesitation in carrying it into practice, is the only stable foundation for a just reliance on it: for, being cognisant of all that can, at least obviously, be said against him, and having taken up his position against all gainsayers—knowing that he has sought for objections and difficulties, instead of avoiding them, and has shut out no light which can be thrown upon the subject from any quarter—he has a right to think his judgement better than that of any person, or any multitude, who have not gone through a similar process.

It is not too much to require that what the wisest of mankind, those who are best entitled to trust their own judgement, find necessary to warrant their relying on it, should be submitted to by that miscellaneous collection of a few wise and many foolish individuals, called the public. The most intolerant of churches, the Roman Catholic Church, even at the canonization of a saint, admits, and listens patiently to, a "devil's advocate." The holiest of men, it appears, cannot be admitted to posthumous honours, until all that the devil could say against him is known and weighed. If even the Newtonian philosophy were not permitted to be questioned, mankind could not feel as complete assurance of its truth as they now do. The beliefs which we have most warrant for, have no safeguard to rest on, but a standing invitation to the whole world to prove them unfounded. If the challenge is not accepted, or is accepted and the attempt fails, we are far enough from certainty still; but we have done the best that the existing state of human reason admits of; we have neglected nothing that could give the truth a chance of reaching us: if the lists are kept open, we may hope that if there be a better truth, it will be found when the human mind is capable of receiving it; and in the meantime we may rely on having attained such approach to truth, as is possible in our own day. This is the amount of certainty attainable by a fallible being, and this the sole way of attaining it.

Strange it is, that men should admit the validity of the arguments for free discussion, but object to their being "pushed to an extreme"; not seeing that unless the reasons are good for an extreme case, they are not good for any case. Strange that they should imagine that they are not assuming infallibility, when they acknowledge that there should be free discussion on all subjects which can possibly be *doubtful*, but think that some particular principle or doctrine should be forbidden to be questioned because it is so *certain*, that is, because *they are certain* that it is certain. To call any proposition certain, while there is any one who would deny its certainty if permitted, but who is not permitted, is to assume that we ourselves, and those who agree with us, are the judges of certainty, and judges without hearing the other side.

In the present age—which has been described as "destitute of faith, but terrified at scepticism"—in which people feel sure, not so much that their opinions are true, as that they should not know what to do without them—the claims of an opinion to be protected from public attack are rested not so much on its truth, as on its importance to society. There are, it is alleged, certain beliefs, so useful, not to say indispensable to well-being, that it is as much the duty of governments to uphold those beliefs, as to protect any other of the interests of society. In a case of such necessity, and so directly in the line of their duty, something less than infallibility may, it is maintained, warrant, and even bind, governments, to act on their own opinion, confirmed by the general opinion of mankind. It is also often argued, and still oftener thought, that none but bad men would desire to weaken these salutary beliefs; and there can be nothing wrong, it is thought, in restraining bad men, and prohibiting what only such men would wish to practise. This mode of thinking makes the justification of restraints on discussion not a question of the truth of doctrines, but of their usefulness; and flatters itself by that means to escape the responsibility of claiming to be an infallible judge of opinions. But those who thus satisfy themselves, do not perceive that the assumption of infallibility is merely shifted from one point to another. The usefulness of an opinion is itself matter of opinion: as disputable, as open to discussion, and requiring discussion as much, as the opinion itself. There is the same need of an infallible judge of opinions to decide an opinion to be noxious, as to decide it to be false, unless the opinion condemned has full opportunity of defending itself. And it will not do to say that the heretic may be allowed to maintain the utility or harmlessness of his opinion, though forbidden to maintain its truth. The truth of an opinion is part of its utility. If we would know whether or not it is desirable that a proposition should be believed, is it possible to exclude the consideration of whether or not it is true? In the opinion, not of bad men, but of the best men, no belief which is contrary to truth can be really useful: and can you prevent such men from urging that plea, when they are charged with culpability for denying some doctrine which they are told is useful, but which they believe to be false? Those who are on the side of received opinions, never fail to take all possible advantage of this plea; you do not find *them* handling the question of utility as if it could be completely abstracted from that of truth: on the contrary, it is, above all, because their doctrine is the "truth," that the knowledge or the belief of it is held to be so indispensable. There can be no fair discussion of the question of usefulness, when an argument so vital may be employed on one side, but not on the other. And in point of fact, when law or public feeling do not permit the truth of an opinion to be disputed, they are just as little tolerant of a denial of its usefulness. The utmost they allow is an extenuation of its absolute necessity, or of the positive guilt of rejecting it. . . .

To pass from this to the only other instance of judicial iniquity, the mention of which, after the condemnation of Socrates, would not be an anti-climax: the event which took place on Calvary rather more than eighteen hundred years ago. The man who left
10 on the memory of those who witnessed his life and conversation, such an impression of his moral grandeur, that eighteen subsequent centuries have done homage to him as the Almighty in person, was ignominiously put to death, as what? As a blasphemer. Men did not merely mistake their benefactor; they mistook him for the exact contrary of what he was, and treated him as that prodigy of impiety, which they themselves are now held to be, for their treatment of him. The feelings with which mankind now
20 regard these lamentable transactions, especially the later of the two, render them extremely unjust in their judgement of the unhappy actors. These were, to all appearance, not bad men—not worse than men commonly are, but rather the contrary; men who possessed in a full, or somewhat more than a full measure, the religious, moral and patriotic feelings of their time and people: the very kind of men who, in all times, our own included, have every chance of passing through life blameless and respected. The high-priest
30 who rent his garments when the words were pronounced, which, according to all the ideas of his country, constituted the blackest guilt, was in all probability quite as sincere in his horror and indignation, as the generality of respectable and pious men now are in the religious and moral sentiments they profess; and most of those who now shudder at his conduct, if they had lived in his time, and been born Jews, would have acted precisely as he did. Orthodox Christians who are tempted to think that those who
40 stoned to death the first martyrs must have been worse men than they themselves are, ought to remember that one of those persecutors was Saint Paul.

Let us add one more example, the most striking of all, if the impressiveness of an error is measured by the wisdom and virtue of him who falls into it. If ever any one, possessed of power, had grounds for thinking himself the best and most enlightened among his contemporaries, it was the Emperor Marcus Aurelius. Absolute monarch of the whole civilized world, he
50 preserved through life not only the most unblemished justice, but what was less to be expected from his Stoical breeding, the tenderest heart. The few failings which are attributed to him, were all on the side of indulgence: while his writings, the highest ethical product of the ancient mind, differ scarcely perceptibly, if they differ at all, from the most characteristic teachings of Christ. This man, a better Christian in all but the dogmatic sense of the word, than almost any of the ostensibly Christian sovereigns who have since reigned, persecuted Christianity. Placed at the 60 summit of all the previous attainments of humanity, with an open, unfettered intellect, and a character which led him of himself to embody in his moral writings the Christian ideal, he yet failed to see that Christianity was to be a good and not an evil to the world, with his duties to which he was so deeply penetrated. Existing society he knew to be in a deplorable state. But such as it was, he saw, or thought he saw, that it was held together, and prevented from being worse, by belief and reverence of the received 70 divinities. As a ruler of mankind, he deemed it his duty not to suffer society to fall in pieces; and saw not how, if its existing ties were removed, any others could be formed which could again knit it together. The new religion openly aimed at dissolving these ties: unless, therefore, it was his duty to adopt that religion, it seemed to be his duty to put it down. Inasmuch then as the theology of Christianity did not appear to him true or of divine origin; inasmuch as this strange history of a crucified God was not credible to him, 80 and a system which purported to rest entirely upon a foundation to him so wholly unbelievable, could not be foreseen by him to be that renovating agency which, after all abatements, it has in fact proved to be; the gentlest and most amiable of philosophers and rulers, under a solemn sense of duty, authorized the persecution of Christianity. To my mind this is one of the most tragical facts in all history. It is a bitter thought, how different a thing the Christianity of the world might have been, if the Christian faith had been 90 adopted as the religion of the empire under the auspices of Marcus Aurelius instead of those of Constantine. But it would be equally unjust to him and false to truth, to deny, that no one plea which can be urged for punishing anti-Christian teaching, was wanting to Marcus Aurelius for punishing, as he did, the propagation of Christianity. No Christian more firmly believes that Atheism is false, and tends to the dissolution of society, than Marcus Aurelius believed the same things of Christianity; he who, of all men then living, 100 might have been thought the most capable of appreciating it. Unless any one who approves of punishment for the promulgation of opinions, flatters himself that he is a wiser and better man than Marcus Aurelius—more deeply versed in the wisdom of his time, more elevated

6. **judicial iniquity.** In the portion here omitted, Mill had discussed the execution of Socrates as another example of judicial iniquity. 48. **Marcus Aurelius,** Marcus Aurelius Antoninus (121-180), Roman emperor and author of *Meditations,* expressive of the Stoical philosophy that man should keep himself free of passion, joyful or sorrowful, and submit to unavoidable necessity. 92. **Constantine.** Constantine (272-

in his intellect above it—more earnest in his search for truth, or more single-minded in his devotion to it when found;—let him abstain from that assumption of the joint infallibility of himself and the multitude, which the great Antoninus made with so unfortunate a result. . . .

Let us now pass to the second division of the argument, and dismissing the supposition that any of the received opinions may be false, let us assume them to be true, and examine into the worth of the manner in which they are likely to be held, when their truth is not freely and openly canvassed. However unwillingly a person who has a strong opinion may admit the possibility that his opinion may be false, he ought to be moved by the consideration that however true it may be, if it is not fully, frequently, and fearlessly discussed, it will be held as a dead dogma, not a living truth.

There is a class of persons (happily not quite so numerous as formerly) who think it enough if a person assents undoubtingly to what they think true, though he has no knowledge whatever of the grounds of the opinion, and could not make a tenable defence of it against the most superficial objections. Such persons, if they can once get their creed taught from authority, naturally think that no good, and some harm, comes of its being allowed to be questioned. Where their influence prevails, they make it nearly impossible for the received opinion to be rejected wisely and considerately, though it may still be rejected rashly and ignorantly; for to shut out discussion entirely is seldom possible, and when it once gets in, beliefs not grounded on conviction are apt to give way before the slightest semblance of an argument. Waiving, however, this possibility—assuming that the true opinion abides in the mind, but abides as a prejudice, a belief independent of, and proof against, argument—this is not the way in which truth ought to be held by a rational being. This is not knowing the truth. Truth, thus held, is but one superstition the more, accidentally clinging to the words which enunciate a truth.

If the intellect and judgement of mankind ought to be cultivated, a thing which Protestants at least do not deny, on what can these faculties be more appropriately exercised by any one, than on the things which concern him so much that it is considered necessary for him to hold opinions on them? If the cultivation of the understanding consists in one thing more than in another, it is surely in learning the grounds of one's own opinions. Whatever people believe, on subjects on which it is of the first importance to believe rightly, they ought to be able to defend against at least the common objections. But, some one may say, "Let them be *taught* the grounds of their opinions. It does not follow that opinions must be merely parroted because they are never heard controverted. Persons who learn geometry do not simply commit the theorems to memory, but understand and learn likewise the demonstrations; and it would be absurd to say that they remain ignorant of the grounds of geometrical truths, because they never hear any one deny, and attempt to disprove them." Undoubtedly: and such teaching suffices on a subject like mathematics, where there is nothing at all to be said on the wrong side of the question. The peculiarity of the evidence of mathematical truths is, that all the argument is on one side. There are no objections, and no answers to objections. But on every subject on which difference of opinion is possible, the truth depends on a balance to be struck between two sets of conflicting reasons. Even in natural philosophy, there is always some other explanation possible of the same facts; some geocentric theory instead of heliocentric, some phlogiston instead of oxygen; and it has to be shown why that other theory cannot be the true one: and until this is shown, and until we know how it is shown, we do not understand the grounds of our opinion. But when we turn to subjects infinitely more complicated, to morals, religion, politics, social relations, and the business of life, three-fourths of the arguments for every disputed opinion consist in dispelling the appearances which favour some opinion different from it. The greatest orator, save one, of antiquity, has left it on record that he always studied his adversary's case with as great, if not with still greater, intensity than even his own. What Cicero practised as the means of forensic success, requires to be imitated by all who study any subject in order to arrive at the truth. He who knows only his own side of the case, knows little of that. His reasons may be good, and no one may have been able to refute them. But if he is equally unable to refute the reasons on the opposite side; if he does not so much as know what they are, he has no ground for preferring either opinion. The rational position for him would be suspension of judgement, and unless he contents himself with that, he is either led by authority, or adopts, like the generality of the world, the side to which he feels most inclination. Nor is it enough that he should hear the arguments of adversaries from his own teachers, presented as they state them, and accompanied by what they offer as refutations. That is not the way to do justice to the arguments, or bring them into real contact with his own mind. He must be able to hear them from persons who actually believe them; who defend them in earnest, and do their very

337) was the Roman emperor who made Christianity the official religion in 330 and who enunciated a doctrine of despotic authority. 111. **result.** In the portion here omitted Mill attacks the notion that "persecution is an ordeal through which truth ought to pass."

utmost for them. He must know them in their most plausible and persuasive form; he must feel the whole force of the difficulty which the true view of the subject has to encounter and dispose of; else he will never really possess himself of the portion of truth which meets and removes that difficulty. Ninety-nine in a hundred of what are called educated men are in this condition; even of those who can argue fluently for their opinions. Their conclusion may be true, but it might be false for anything they know: they have never thrown themselves into the mental position of those who think differently from them, and considered what such persons may have to say; and consequently they do not, in any proper sense of the word, know the doctrine which they themselves profess. They do not know those parts of it which explain and justify the remainder; the considerations which show that a fact which seemingly conflicts with another is reconcilable with it, or that, of two apparently strong reasons, one and not the other ought to be preferred. All that part of the truth which turns the scale, and decides the judgement of a completely informed mind, they are strangers to; nor is it ever really known, but to those who have attended equally and impartially to both sides, and endeavoured to see the reasons of both in the strongest light. So essential is this discipline to a real understanding of moral and human subjects, that if opponents of all important truths do not exist, it is indispensable to imagine them, and supply them with the strongest arguments which the most skilful devil's advocate can conjure up.

To abate the force of these considerations, an enemy of free discussion may be supposed to say, that there is no necessity for mankind in general to know and understand all that can be said against or for their opinions by philosophers and theologians. That it is not needful for common men to be able to expose all the misstatements or fallacies of an ingenious opponent. That it is enough if there is always somebody capable of answering them, so that nothing likely to mislead uninstructed persons remains unrefuted. That simple minds, having been taught the obvious grounds of the truths inculcated on them, may trust to authority for the rest, and being aware that they have neither knowledge nor talent to resolve every difficulty which can be raised, may repose in the assurance that all those which have been raised have been or can be answered, by those who are specially trained to the task.

Conceding to this view of the subject the utmost that can be claimed for it by those most easily satisfied with the amount of understanding of truth which ought to accompany the belief of it; even so, the argument for free discussion is no way weakened. For even this doctrine acknowledges that mankind ought to have a rational assurance that all objections have been satisfactorily answered; and how are they to be answered if that which requires to be answered is not spoken? or how can the answer be known to be satisfactory, if the objectors have no opportunity of showing that it is unsatisfactory? If not the public, at least the philosophers and theologians who are to resolve the difficulties, must make themselves familiar with those difficulties in their most puzzling form; and this cannot be accomplished unless they are freely stated, and placed in the most advantageous light which they admit of. The Catholic Church has its own way of dealing with this embarrassing problem. It makes a broad separation between those who can be permitted to receive its doctrines on conviction, and those who must accept them on trust. Neither, indeed, are allowed any choice as to what they will accept; but the clergy, such at least as can be fully confided in, may admissibly and meritoriously make themselves acquainted with the arguments of opponents, in order to answer them, and may, therefore, read heretical books; the laity, not unless by special permission, hard to be obtained. This discipline recognizes a knowledge of the enemy's case as beneficial to the teachers, but finds means, consistent with this, of denying it to the rest of the world: thus giving to the *élite* more mental culture, though not more mental freedom, than it allows to the mass. By this device it succeeds in obtaining the kind of mental superiority which its purposes require; for though culture without freedom never made a large and liberal mind, it can make a clever *nisi prius* advocate of a cause. But in countries professing Protestantism, this resource is denied; since Protestants hold, at least in theory, that the responsibility for the choice of a religion must be borne by each for himself, and cannot be thrown off upon teachers. Besides, in the present state of the world, it is practically impossible that writings which are read by the instructed can be kept from the uninstructed. If the teachers of mankind are to be cognizant of all that they ought to know, everything must be free to be written and published without restraint.

If, however, the mischievous operation of the absence of free discussion, when the received opinions are true, were confined to leaving men ignorant of the grounds of those opinions, it might be thought that this, if an intellectual, is no moral evil, and does not affect the worth of the opinions, regarded in their influence on the character. The fact, however, is, that not only the grounds of the opinion are forgotten in the absence of discussion, but too often the meaning of the opinion itself. The words which convey it cease to suggest ideas, or suggest only a small portion of those they were originally employed to communicate. Instead of a vivid conception and a living belief, there remain only a few phrases retained by rote; or, if any part, the shell and husk only of the meaning is re-

87. *nisi prius*, unless before, a legal expression.

tained, the finer essence being lost. The great chapter in human history which this fact occupies and fills, cannot be too earnestly studied and meditated on.

It is illustrated in the experience of almost all ethical doctrines and religious creeds. They are all full of meaning and vitality to those who originate them, and to the direct disciples of the originators. Their meaning continues to be felt in undiminished strength, and is perhaps brought out into even fuller consciousness, so long as the struggle lasts to give the doctrine or creed an ascendancy over other creeds. At last it either prevails, and becomes the general opinion, or its progress stops; it keeps possession of the ground it has gained, but ceases to spread further. When either of these results has become apparent, controversy on the subject flags, and gradually dies away. The doctrine has taken its place, if not as a received opinion, as one of the admitted sects or divisions of opinion: those who hold it have generally inherited, not adopted it; and conversion from one of these doctrines to another, being now an exceptional fact, occupies little place in the thoughts of their professors. Instead of being, as at first, constantly on the alert either to defend themselves against the world, or to bring the world over to them, they have subsided into acquiescence, and neither listen, when they can help it, to arguments against their creed, nor trouble dissentients (if there be such) with arguments in its favour. From this time may usually be dated the decline in the living power of the doctrine. We often hear the teachers of all creeds lamenting the difficulty of keeping up in the minds of believers a lively apprehension of the truth which they nominally recognize, so that it may penetrate the feelings, and acquire a real mastery over the conduct. No such difficulty is complained of while the creed is still fighting for its existence: even the weaker combatants then know and feel what they are fighting for, and the difference between it and other doctrines; and in that period of every creed's existence, not a few persons may be found, who have realized its fundamental principles in all the forms of thought, have weighed and considered them in all their important bearings, and have experienced the full effect on the character, which belief in that creed ought to produce in a mind thoroughly imbued with it. But when it has come to be an hereditary creed, and to be received passively, not actively—when the mind is no longer compelled, in the same degree as at first, to exercise its vital powers on the questions which its belief presents to it, there is a progressive tendency to forget all of the belief except the formularies, or to give it a dull and torpid assent, as if accepting it on trust dispensed with the necessity of realizing it in consciousness, or testing it by personal experience; until it almost ceases to connect itself at all with the inner life of the human being. Then are seen the cases, so frequent in this age of the world as almost to form the majority, in which the creed remains as it were outside the mind, encrusting and petrifying it against all other influences addressed to the higher parts of our nature; manifesting its power by not suffering any fresh and living conviction to get in, but itself doing nothing for the mind or heart, except standing sentinel over them to keep them vacant.

To what an extent doctrines intrinsically fitted to make the deepest impression upon the mind may remain in it as dead beliefs, without being ever realized in the imagination, the feelings, or the understanding, is exemplified by the manner in which the majority of believers hold the doctrines of Christianity. By Christianity I here mean what is accounted such by all churches and sects—the maxims and precepts contained in the New Testament. These are considered sacred, and accepted as laws, by all professing Christians. Yet it is scarcely too much to say that not one Christian in a thousand guides or tests his individual conduct by reference to those laws. The standard to which he does refer it, is the custom of his nation, his class, or his religious profession. He has thus, on the one hand, a collection of ethical maxims, which he believes to have been vouchsafed to him by infallible wisdom as rules for his government; and on the other, a set of everyday judgements and practices, which go a certain length with some of those maxims, not so great a length with others, stand in direct opposition to some, and are, on the whole, a compromise between the Christian creed and the interests and suggestions of worldly life. To the first of these standards he gives his homage; to the other his real allegiance. All Christians believe that the blessed are the poor and humble, and those who are ill-used by the world; that it is easier for a camel to pass through the eye of a needle than for a rich man to enter the kingdom of heaven; that they should judge not, lest they be judged; that they should swear not at all; that they should love their neighbour as themselves; that if one take their cloak, they should give him their coat also; that they should take no thought for the morrow; that if they would be perfect, they should sell all that they have and give it to the poor. They are not insincere when they say that they believe these things. They do believe them, as people believe what they have always heard lauded and never discussed. But in the sense of that living belief which regulates conduct, they believe these doctrines just up to the point to which it is usual to act upon them. The doctrines in their integrity are serviceable to pelt adversaries with; and it is understood that they are to be put forward (when possible) as the reasons for whatever people do that they think laudable. But any one who reminded them that the maxims require an infinity of things which they never even think of doing, would gain nothing but to be classed among those very unpopular characters who affect to be better than other people. The doctrines have no hold on ordinary believers—are not a power in their minds. They have an habitual respect for the sound of them, but no feeling which spreads from the words to the things signified, and forces the mind to take *them* in, and make them conform to the formula. Whenever conduct is concerned, they look round for Mr. A and B to direct them how far to go in obeying Christ. . . .

It still remains to speak of one of the principal causes which make diversity of opinion advantageous, and will continue to do so until mankind shall have entered a stage of intellectual advancement which at present seems at an incalculable distance. We have hitherto considered only two possibilities: that the received opinion may be false, and some other opinion, consequently, true; or that, the received opinion being true, a conflict with the opposite error is essential to a clear apprehension and deep feeling of its truth. But there is a commoner case than either of these; when the conflicting doctrines, instead of being one true and the other false, share the truth between them; and the nonconforming opinion is needed to supply the remainder of the truth, of which the received doctrine embodies only a part. Popular opinions, on subjects not palpable to sense, are often true, but seldom or never the whole truth. They are a part of the truth; sometimes a greater, sometimes a smaller part, but exaggerated, distorted, and disjoined from the truths by which they ought to be accompanied and limited. Heretical opinions, on the other hand, are generally some of these suppressed and neglected truths, bursting the bonds which kept them down, and either seeking reconciliation with the truth contained in the common opinion, or fronting it as enemies, and setting themselves up, with similar exclusiveness, as the whole truth. The latter case is hitherto the most frequent, as, in the human mind, one-sidedness has always been the rule, and many-sidedness the exception. Hence, even in revolutions of opinion, one part of the truth usually sets while another rises. Even progress, which ought to superadd, for the most part only substitutes, one partial and incomplete truth for another; improvement consisting chiefly in this, that the new fragment of truth is more wanted, more adapted to the needs of the time, than that which it displaces. Such being the partial character of prevailing opinions, even when resting on a true foundation, every opinion which embodies somewhat of the portion of truth which the common opinion omits, ought to be considered precious, with whatever amount of error and confusion that truth may be blended. No sober judge of human affairs will feel bound to be indignant because those who force on our notice truths which we should otherwise have overlooked, overlook some of those which we see. Rather, he will think that so long as popular truth is one-sided, it is more desirable than otherwise that unpopular truth should have one-sided asserters too; such being usually the most energetic, and the most likely to compel reluctant attention to the fragment of wisdom which they proclaim as if it were the whole.

Thus, in the eighteenth century, when nearly all the instructed, and all those of the uninstructed who were led by them, were lost in admiration of what is called civilization, and of the marvels of modern science, literature, and philosophy, and while greatly overrating the amount of unlikeness between the men of modern and those of ancient times, indulged the belief that the whole of the difference was in their own favour; with what a salutary shock did the paradoxes of Rousseau explode like bombshells in the midst, dislocating the compact mass of one-sided opinion, and forcing its elements to recombine in a better form and with additional ingredients. Not that the current opinions were on the whole farther from the truth than Rousseau's were; on the contrary, they were nearer to it; they contained more of positive truth, and very much less of error. Nevertheless there lay in Rousseau's doctrine, and has floated down the stream of opinion along with it, a considerable amount of exactly those truths which the popular opinion wanted; and these are the deposit which was left behind when the flood subsided. The superior worth of simplicity of life, the enervating and demoralizing effect of the trammels and hypocrisies of artificial society, are ideas which have never been entirely absent from cultivated minds since Rousseau wrote; and they will in time produce their due effect, though at present needing to be asserted as much as ever, and to be asserted by deeds, for words, on this subject, have nearly exhausted their power.

In politics, again, it is almost a commonplace, that a party of order or stability, and a party of progress or reform, are both necessary elements of a healthy state of political life; until the one or the other shall have so enlarged its mental grasp as to be a party equally of order and of progress, knowing and distinguishing what is fit to be preserved from what ought to be swept away. Each of these modes of thinking derives its utility from the deficiencies of the other; but it is in a great measure the opposition of the other that keeps each within the limits of reason and sanity. Unless opinions favourable to democracy and to aristocracy, to property and to equality, to co-operation and to competition, to luxury and to abstinence, to sociality and individuality, to liberty and discipline, and all the other standing antagonisms of practical

71. **Rousseau,** Jean Jacques Rousseau (1712-1778), French social philosopher who believed in natural, primitive states of society and whose theory of the social contract prepared the way for the French Revolution and the romantic movement.

life, are expressed with equal freedom, and enforced and defended with equal talent and energy, there is no chance of both elements obtaining their due; one scale is sure to go up, and the other down. Truth, in the great practical concerns of life, is so much a question of the reconciling and combining of opposites, that very few have minds sufficiently capacious and impartial to make the adjustment with an approach to correctness, and it has to be made by the rough process of a struggle between combatants fighting under hostile banners. On any of the great open questions just enumerated, if either of the two opinions has a better claim than the other, not merely to be tolerated, but to be encouraged and countenanced, it is the one which happens at the particular time and place to be in a minority. That is the opinion which, for the time being, represents the neglected interests, the side of human well-being which is in danger of obtaining less than its share. I am aware that there is not, in this country, any intolerance of differences of opinion on most of these topics. They are adduced to show, by admitted and multiplied examples, the universality of the fact, that only through diversity of opinion is there, in the existing state of human intellect, a chance of fair play to all sides of the truth. When there are persons to be found, who form an exception to the apparent unanimity of the world on any subject, even if the world is in the right, it is always probable that dissentients have something worth hearing to say for themselves, and that truth would lose something by their silence.

It may be objected, "But *some* received principles, especially on the highest and most vital subjects, are more than half-truths. The Christian morality, for instance, is the whole truth on that subject, and if any one teaches a morality which varies from it, he is wholly in error." As this is of all cases the most important in practice, none can be fitter to test the general maxim. But before pronouncing what Christian morality is or is not, it would be desirable to decide what is meant by Christian morality. If it means the morality of the New Testament, I wonder that any one who derives his knowledge of this from the book itself, can suppose that it was announced, or intended, as a complete doctrine of morals. The Gospel always refers to a pre-existing morality, and confines its precepts to the particulars in which that morality was to be corrected, or superseded by a wider and higher; expressing itself, moreover, in terms most general, often impossible to be interpreted literally, and possessing rather the impressiveness of poetry or eloquence than the precision of legislation. To extract from it a body of ethical doctrine, has never been possible without eking it out from the Old Testament, that is, from a system elaborate indeed, but in many respects barbarous, and intended only for a barbarous people. St. Paul, a declared enemy to this Judaical

mode of interpreting the doctrine and filling up the scheme of his Master, equally assumes a pre-existing morality, namely that of the Greeks and Romans; and his advice to Christians is in a great measure a system of accommodation to that; even to the extent of giving an apparent sanction to slavery. What is called Christian, but should rather be termed theological, morality, was not the work of Christ or the Apostles, but is of much later origin, having been gradually built up by the Catholic church of the first five centuries, and though not implicitly adopted by moderns and Protestants, has been much less modified by them than might have been expected. For the most part, indeed, they have contented themselves with cutting off the additions which had been made to it in the middle ages, each sect supplying the place by fresh additions, adapted to its own character and tendencies. That mankind owe a great debt to this morality, and to its early teachers, I should be the last person to deny; but I do not scruple to say of it, that it is, in many important points, incomplete and one-sided, and that unless ideas and feelings, not sanctioned by it, had contributed to the formation of European life and character, human affairs would have been in a worse condition than they now are. Christian morality (so called) has all the characters of a reaction; it is, in great part, a protest against Paganism. Its ideal is negative rather than positive; passive rather than active; Innocence rather than Nobleness; Abstinence from Evil, rather than energetic Pursuit of Good: in its precepts (as has been well said) "thou shalt not" predominates unduly over "thou shalt." In its horror of sensuality, it made an idol of asceticism, which has been gradually compromised away into one of legality. It holds out the hope of heaven and the threat of hell, as the appointed and appropriate motives to a virtuous life: in this falling far below the best of the ancients, and doing what lies in it to give to human morality an essentially selfish character, by disconnecting each man's feelings of duty from the interests of his fellow-creatures, except so far as a self-interested inducement is offered to him for consulting them. It is essentially a doctrine of passive obedience; it inculcates submission to all authorities found established; who indeed are not to be actively obeyed when they command what religion forbids, but who are not to be resisted, far less rebelled against, for any amount of wrong to ourselves. And while, in the morality of the best Pagan nations, duty to the State holds even a disproportionate place, infringing on the just liberty of the individual; in purely Christian ethics, that grand department of duty is scarcely noticed or acknowledged. It is in the Koran, not the New Testament, that we read the maxim—"A ruler who appoints any man to an office, when there is in his dominions another man better qualified for it, sins against God and against the State." What little recognition the idea of obligation to the public obtains in modern morality, is derived from Greek and Roman sources, not from Christian; as, even in the morality of private life, whatever exists of magnanimity, high-mindedness, personal dignity, even the sense of honour, is derived from the purely human, not the religious part of our education, and never could have grown out of a standard of ethics in which the only worth, professedly recognized, is that of obedience.

10 I am as far as any one from pretending that these defects are necessarily inherent in the Christian ethics, in every manner in which it can be conceived, or that the many requisites of a complete moral doctrine which it does not contain, do not admit of being reconciled with it. Far less would I insinuate this of the doctrines and precepts of Christ himself. I believe that the sayings of Christ are all, that I can see any evidence of their having been intended to be; that they are irreconcilable with nothing which a comprehensive morality 20 requires; that everything which is excellent in ethics may be brought within them, with no greater violence to their language than has been done to it by all who have attempted to deduce from them any practical system of conduct whatever. But it is quite consistent with this, to believe that they contain, and were meant to contain, only a part of the truth; that many essential elements of the highest morality are among the things which are not provided for, nor intended to be provided for, in the recorded deliverances of the 30 Founder of Christianity, and which have been entirely thrown aside in the system of ethics erected on the basis of those deliverances by the Christian Church. And this being so, I think it a great error to persist in attempting to find in the Christian doctrine that complete rule for our guidance, which its author intended it to sanction and enforce, but only partially to provide. I believe, too, that this narrow theory is becoming a grave practical evil, detracting greatly from the value of the moral training and instruction, 40 which so many well-meaning persons are now at length exerting themselves to promote. I much fear that by attempting to form the mind and feelings on an exclusively religious type, and discarding those secular standards (as for want of a better name they may be called) which heretofore co-existed with and supplemented the Christian ethics, receiving some of its spirit, and infusing into it some of theirs, there will result, and is even now resulting, a low, abject, servile type of character, which, submit itself as it 50 may to what it deems the Supreme Will, is incapable of rising to or sympathizing in the conception of Supreme Goodness. I believe that other ethics than any which can be evolved from exclusively Christian sources, must exist side by side with Christian ethics to produce the moral regeneration of mankind; and that the Christian system is no exception to the rule,

that in an imperfect state of the human mind, the interests of truth require a diversity of opinions. It is not necessary that in ceasing to ignore the moral truths not contained in Christianity, men should ig- 60 nore any of those which it does contain. Such prejudice, or oversight, when it occurs, is altogether an evil; but it is one from which we cannot hope to be always exempt, and must be regarded as the price paid for an inestimable good. The exclusive pretension made by a part of the truth to be the whole, must and ought to be protested against; and if a reactionary impulse should make the protestors unjust in their turn, this one-sidedness, like the other, may be lamented, but must be tolerated. If Christians would 70 teach infidels to be just to Christianity, they should themselves be just to infidelity. It can do truth no service to blink the fact, known to all who have the most ordinary acquaintance with literary history, that a large portion of the noblest and most valuable moral teaching has been the work, not only of men who did not know, but of men who knew and rejected, the Christian faith.

I do not pretend that the most unlimited use of the freedom of enunciating all possible opinions would 80 put an end to the evils of religious or philosophical sectarianism. Every truth which men of narrow capacity are in earnest about, is sure to be asserted, inculcated, and in many ways even acted on, as if no other truth existed in the world, or at all events none that could limit or qualify the first. I acknowledge that the tendency of all opinions to become sectarian is not cured by the freest discussion, but is often heightened and exacerbated thereby; the truth which ought to have been, but was not, seen, being rejected all 90 the more violently because proclaimed by persons regarded as opponents. But it is not on the impassioned partisan, it is on the calmer and more disinterested bystander, that this collision of opinions works its salutary effect. Not the violent conflict between parts of the truth, but the quiet suppression of half of it, is the formidable evil; there is always hope when people are forced to listen to both sides; it is when they attend only to one that errors harden into prejudices, and truth itself ceases to have the effect 100 of truth, by being exaggerated into falsehood. And since there are few mental attributes more rare than that judicial faculty which can sit in intelligent judgement between two sides of a question, of which only one is represented by an advocate before it, truth has no chance but in proportion as every side of it, every opinion which embodies any fraction of the truth, not only finds advocates, but is so advocated as to be listened to.

We have now recognized the necessity to the 110 mental well-being of mankind (on which all their other well-being depends) of freedom of opinion, and freedom of the expression of opinion, on four distinct grounds; which we will now briefly recapitulate.

First, if any opinion is compelled to silence, that opinion may, for aught we can certainly know, be true. To deny this is to assume our own infallibility.

Secondly, though the silenced opinion be an error, it may, and very commonly does, contain a portion of truth; and since the general or prevailing opinion on any subject is rarely or never the whole truth, it is only by the collision of adverse opinions that the remainder of the truth has any chance of being supplied.

Thirdly, even if the received opinion be not only true, but the whole truth; unless it is suffered to be, and actually is, vigorously and earnestly contested, it will, by most of those who receive it, be held in the manner of a prejudice, with little comprehension or feeling of its rational grounds. And not only this, but, fourthly, the meaning of the doctrine itself will be in danger of being lost, or enfeebled, and deprived of its vital effect on the character and conduct: the dogma becoming a mere formal profession, inefficacious for good, but cumbering the ground, and preventing the growth of any real and heartfelt conviction, from reason or personal experience.

Before quitting the subject of freedom of opinion, it is fit to take some notice of those who say, that the free expression of all opinions should be permitted, on condition that the manner be temperate, and do not pass the bounds of fair discussion. Much might be said on the impossibility of fixing where these supposed bounds are to be placed; for if the test be offence to those whose opinion is attacked, I think experience testifies that this offence is given whenever the attack is telling and powerful, and that every opponent who pushes them hard, and whom they find it difficult to answer, appears to them, if he shows any strong feeling on the subject, an intemperate opponent. But this, though an important consideration in a practical point of view, merges in a more fundamental objection. Undoubtedly the manner of asserting an opinion, even though it be a true one, may be very objectionable, and may justly incur severe censure. But the principal offences of the kind are such as it is mostly impossible, unless by accidental self-betrayal, to bring home to conviction. The gravest of them is, to argue sophistically, to suppress facts or arguments, to misstate the elements of the case, or misrepresent the opposite opinion. But all this, even to the most aggravated degree, is so continually done in perfect good faith, by persons who are not considered, and in many other respects may not deserve to be considered, ignorant or incompetent, that it is rarely possible on adequate grounds conscientiously to stamp the misrepresentation as morally culpable; and still less could law presume to interfere with this kind of controversial misconduct. With regard to what is commonly meant by intemperate discussion, namely invective, sarcasm, personality, and the like, the denunciation of these weapons would deserve more sympathy if it were ever proposed to interdict them equally to both sides; but it is only desired to restrain the employment of them against the prevailing opinion: against the unprevailing they may not only be used without general disapproval, but will be likely to obtain for him who uses them the praise of honest zeal and righteous indignation. Yet whatever mischief arises from their use, is greatest when they are employed against the comparatively defenceless; and whatever unfair advantage can be derived by any opinion from this mode of asserting it, accrues almost exclusively to received opinions. The worst offence of this kind which can be committed by a polemic, is to stigmatize those who hold the contrary opinion as bad and immoral men. To calumny of this sort, those who hold any unpopular opinion are peculiarly exposed, because they are in general few and uninfluential, and nobody but themselves feels much interested in seeing justice done them; but this weapon is, from the nature of the case, denied to those who attack a prevailing opinion: they can neither use it with safety to themselves, nor, if they could, would it do anything but recoil on their own cause. In general, opinions contrary to those commonly received can only obtain a hearing by studied moderation of language, and the most cautious avoidance of unnecessary offence, from which they hardly ever deviate even in a slight degree without losing ground: while unmeasured vituperation employed on the side of the prevailing opinion, really does deter people from professing contrary opinions, and from listening to those who profess them. For the interest, therefore, of truth and justice, it is far more important to restrain this employment of vituperative language than the other; and, for example, if it were necessary to choose, there would be much more need to discourage offensive attacks on infidelity, than on religion. It is, however, obvious that law and authority have no business with restraining either, while opinion ought, in every instance, to determine its verdict by the circumstances of the individual case; condemning every one, on whichever side of the argument he places himself, in whose mode of advocacy either want of candour, or malignity, bigotry, or intolerance of feeling manifest themselves; but not inferring these vices from the side which a person takes, though it be the contrary side of the question to our own: and giving merited honour to every one, whatever opinion he may hold, who has calmness to see and honesty to state what his opponents and their opinions really are, exaggerating nothing to their discredit, keeping nothing back which tells, or can be supposed to tell, in their favour. This is the real morality of public discussion:

and if often violated, I am happy to think that there are many controversialists who to a great extent observe it, and a still greater number who conscientiously strive towards it.

OF INDIVIDUALITY, AS ONE OF THE ELEMENTS OF WELL-BEING

Such being the reasons which make it imperative that human beings should be free to form opinions, and to express their opinions without reserve; and such the baneful consequences to the intellectual, and through that to the moral nature of man, unless this 10 liberty is either conceded, or asserted in spite of prohibition; let us next examine whether the same reasons do not require that men should be free to act upon their opinions—to carry these out in their lives, without hindrance, either physical or moral, from their fellow men, so long as it is at their own risk and peril. This last proviso is of course indispensable. No one pretends that actions should be as free as opinions. On the contrary, even opinions lose their immunity, when the circumstances in which they are expressed are such as 20 to constitute their expression a positive instigation to some mischievous act. An opinion that corn-dealers are starvers of the poor, or that private property is robbery, ought to be unmolested when simply circulated through the press, but may justly incur punishment when delivered orally to an excited mob assembled before the house of a corn-dealer, or when handed about among the same mob in the form of a placard. Acts, of whatever kind, which, without justifiable cause, do harm to others, may be, and in the more 30 important cases absolutely require to be, controlled by the unfavourable sentiments, and, when needful, by the active interference of mankind. The liberty of the individual must be thus far limited; he must not make himself a nuisance to other people. But if he refrains from molesting others in what concerns them, and merely acts according to his own inclination and judgement in things which concern himself, the same reasons which show that opinion should be free, prove also that he should be allowed, without molestation, to 40 carry his opinions into practice at his own cost. That mankind are not infallible; that their truths, for the most part, are only half-truths; that unity of opinion, unless resulting from the fullest and freest comparison of opposite opinions, is not desirable, and diversity not an evil, but a good, until mankind are much more capable than at present of recognizing all sides of the truth, are principles applicable to men's modes of action, not less than to their opinions. As it is useful

that while mankind are imperfect there should be different opinions, so is it that there should be dif- 50 ferent experiments of living; that free scope should be given to varieties of character, short of injury to others; and that the worth of different modes of life should be proved practically, when any one thinks fit to try them. It is desirable, in short, that in things which do not primarily concern others, individuality should assert itself. Where, not the person's own character, but the traditions or customs of other people are the rule of conduct, there is wanting one of the principal ingredients of human happiness, and quite 60 the chief ingredient of individual and social progress.

In maintaining this principle, the greatest difficulty to be encountered does not lie in the appreciation of means towards an acknowledged end, but in the indifference of persons in general to the end itself. If it were felt that the free development of individuality is one of the leading essentials of well-being; that it is not only a co-ordinate element with all that is designated by the terms civilization, instruction, education, culture, but is itself a necessary part and condition of 70 all those things; there would be no danger that liberty should be undervalued, and the adjustment of the boundaries between it and social control would present no extraordinary difficulty. But the evil is, that individual spontaneity is hardly recognized by the common modes of thinking, as having any intrinsic worth, or deserving any regard on its own account. The majority, being satisfied with the ways of mankind as they now are (for it is they who make them what they are), cannot comprehend why those ways should not be 80 good enough for everybody; and what is more, spontaneity forms no part of the ideal of the majority of moral and social reformers, but is rather looked on with jealousy, as a troublesome and perhaps rebellious obstruction to the general acceptance of what these reformers, in their own judgement, think would be best for mankind. Few persons, out of Germany, even comprehend the meaning of the doctrine which Wilhelm von Humboldt, so eminent both as a savant and as a politician, made the text of a treatise—that 90 "the end of man, or that which is prescribed by the eternal or immutable dictates of reason, and not suggested by vague and transient desires, is the highest and most harmonious development of his powers to a complete and consistent whole"; that, therefore, the object "towards which every human being must ceaselessly direct his efforts, and on which especially those who design to influence their fellow men must ever keep their eyes, is the individuality of power and development"; that for this there are two requisites, 100 "freedom, and variety of situations"; and that from the union of these arise "individual vigour and mani-

88-104. **Wilhelm von Humboldt . . . originality,** identified by Mill himself as being from *The Sphere and Duties of Government,* by Baron Wilhelm von Humboldt (1767-1835), Prussian statesman and political theorist.

fold diversity," which combine themselves in "originality."

Little, however, as people are accustomed to a doctrine like that of Von Humboldt, and surprising as it may be to them to find so high a value attached to individuality, the question, one must nevertheless think, can only be one of degree. No one's idea of excellence in conduct is that people should do absolutely nothing but copy one another. No one would assert that people ought not to put into their mode of life, and into the conduct of their concerns, any impress whatever of their own judgement, or of their own individual character. On the other hand, it would be absurd to pretend that people ought to live as if nothing whatever had been known in the world before they came into it; as if experience had as yet done nothing towards showing that one mode of existence, or of conduct, is preferable to another. Nobody denies that people should be so taught and trained in youth, as to know and benefit by the ascertained results of human experience. But it is the privilege and proper condition of a human being, arrived at the maturity of his faculties, to use and interpret experience in his own way. It is for him to find out what part of recorded experience is properly applicable to his own circumstances and character. The traditions and customs of other people are, to a certain extent, evidence of what their experience has taught *them*; presumptive evidence, and as such, have a claim to his deference: but, in the first place, their experience may be too narrow; or they may not have interpreted it rightly. Secondly, their interpretation of experience may be correct, but unsuitable to him. Customs are made for customary circumstances, and customary characters; and his circumstances or his character may be uncustomary. Thirdly, though the customs be both good as customs, and suitable to him, yet to conform to custom, merely *as* custom, does not educate or develop in him any of the qualities which are the distinctive endowment of a human being. The human faculties of perception, judgement, discriminative feeling, mental activity, and even moral preference, are exercised only in making a choice. He who does anything because it is the custom makes no choice. He gains no practice either in discerning or in desiring what is best. The mental and moral, like the muscular powers, are improved only by being used. The faculties are called into no exercise by doing a thing merely because others do it, no more than by believing a thing only because others believe it. If the grounds of an opinion are not conclusive to the person's own reason, his reason cannot be strengthened, but is likely to be weakened, by his adopting it: and if the inducements to an act are not such as are consentaneous to his own feelings and character (where affection, or the rights of others, are not concerned) it is so much done towards rendering his feelings and character inert and torpid, instead of active and energetic.

He who lets the world, or his own portion of it, choose his plan of life for him, has no need of any other faculty than the ape-like one of imitation. He who chooses his plan for himself, employs all his faculties. He must use observation to see, reasoning and judgement to foresee, activity to gather materials for decision, discrimination to decide, and when he has decided, firmness and self-control to hold to his deliberate decision. And these qualities he requires and exercises exactly in proportion as the part of his conduct which he determines according to his own judgement and feelings is a large one. It is possible that he might be guided in some good path, and kept out of harm's way, without any of these things. But what will be his comparative worth as a human being? It really is of importance, not only what men do, but also what manner of men they are that do it. Among the works of man, which human life is rightly employed in perfecting and beautifying, the first in importance surely is man himself. Supposing it were possible to get houses built, corn grown, battles fought, causes tried, and even churches erected and prayers said, by machinery—by automatons in human form— it would be a considerable loss to exchange for these automatons even the men and women who at present inhabit the more civilized parts of the world, and who assuredly are but starved specimens of what nature can and will produce. Human nature is not a machine to be built after a model, and set to do exactly the work prescribed for it, but a tree, which requires to grow and develop itself on all sides, according to the tendency of the inward forces which make it a living thing.

It will probably be conceded that it is desirable people should exercise their understandings, and that an intelligent following of custom, or even occasionally an intelligent deviation from custom, is better than a blind and simply mechanical adhesion to it. To a certain extent it is admitted, that our understanding should be our own: but there is not the same willingness to admit that our desires and impulses should be our own likewise; or that to possess impulses of our own, and of any strength, is anything but a peril and a snare. Yet desires and impulses are as much a part of a perfect human being, as beliefs and restraints: and strong impulses are only perilous when not properly balanced; when one set of aims and inclinations is developed into strength, while others, which ought to co-exist with them, remain weak and inactive. It is not because men's desires are strong that they act ill; it is because their consciences are weak. There is no natural connexion between strong impulses and a weak conscience. The natural connexion is the other way. To say that one person's desires and feelings are stronger and more various than those of another, is merely to say that he has more of the raw material of human nature, and is therefore capable, perhaps of more evil, but certainly of more good. Strong impulses are but another name for energy. Energy may be turned to bad uses; but more good may always be made of an energetic nature, than of an indolent and impassive one. Those who have most natural feeling, are always those whose cultivated feelings may be made the strongest. The same strong susceptibilities which make the personal impulses vivid and powerful, are also the source from whence are generated the most passionate love of virtue, and the sternest self-control. It is through the cultivation of these, that society both does its duty and protects its interests: not by rejecting the stuff of which heroes are made, because it knows not how to make them. A person whose desires and impulses are his own—are the expression of his own nature, as it has been developed and modified by his own culture—is said to have a character. One whose desires and impulses are not his own, has no character, no more than a steam-engine has a character. If, in addition to being his own, his impulses are strong, and are under the government of a strong will, he has an energetic character. Whoever thinks that individuality of desires and impulses should not be encouraged to unfold itself, must maintain that society has no need of strong natures—is not the better for containing many persons who have much character—and that a high general average of energy is not desirable.

In some early states of society, these forces might be, and were, too much ahead of the power which society then possessed of disciplining and controlling them. There has been a time when the element of spontaneity and individuality was in excess, and the social principle had a hard struggle with it. The difficulty then was, to induce men of strong bodies or minds to pay obedience to any rules which required them to control their impulses. To overcome this difficulty, law and discipline, like the Popes struggling against the Emperors, asserted a power over the whole man, claiming to control all his life in order to control his character—which society had not found any other sufficient means of binding. But society has now fairly got the better of individuality; and the danger which threatens human nature is not the excess, but the deficiency, of personal impulses and preferences. Things are vastly changed, since the passions of those who were strong by station or by personal endowment were in a state of habitual rebellion against laws and ordinances, and required to be rigorously chained up to enable the persons within their reach to enjoy any particle of security. In our times, from the highest class of society down to the lowest, every one lives under the eye of a hostile and dreaded censorship. Not only in what concerns others, but in what concerns only themselves, the individual or the family do not ask themselves—what do I prefer? or, what would suit my character and disposition? or, what would allow the best and highest in me to have fair play, and enable it to grow and thrive? They ask themselves, what is suitable to my position? what is usually done by persons of my station and pecuniary circumstances? or (worse still) what is usually done by persons of a station and circumstances superior to mine? I do not mean that they choose what is customary, in preference to what suits their own inclination. It does not occur to them to have any inclination, except for what is customary. Thus the mind itself is bowed to the yoke: even in what people do for pleasure, conformity is the first thing thought of; they like in crowds; they exercise choice only among things commonly done: peculiarity of taste, eccentricity of conduct, are shunned equally with crimes: until by dint of not following their own nature, they have no nature to follow: their human capacities are withered and starved: they become incapable of any strong wishes or native pleasures, and are generally without either opinions or feelings of home growth, or properly their own. Now is this, or is it not, the desirable condition of human nature?

It is so, on the Calvinistic theory. According to that, the one great offence of man is self-will. All the good of which humanity is capable is comprised in obedience. You have no choice; thus you must do, and no otherwise: "whatever is not a duty, is a sin." Human nature being radically corrupt, there is no redemption for any one until human nature is killed within him. To one holding this theory of life, crushing out any of the human faculties, capacities, and susceptibilities, is no evil: man needs no capacity, but that of surrendering himself to the will of God: and if he uses any of his faculties for any other purpose but to do that supposed will more effectually, he is better without them. This is the theory of Calvinism; and it is held, in a mitigated form, by many who do not consider themselves Calvinists; the mitigation consisting in giving a less ascetic interpretation to the alleged will of God; asserting it to be his will that mankind should gratify some of their inclinations; of course not in the manner they themselves prefer, but in the way of obedience, that is, in a way prescribed to them by authority; and, therefore, by the necessary conditions of the case, the same for all.

In some such insidious form there is at present a strong tendency to this narrow theory of life, and to

---

112. **pollards,** trees cut back nearly to the trunk to produce a dense mass of branches. 125. **Pagan self-assertion . . . self-denial,** identified by Mill as from the *Essays* (1848) of John Sterling, minor social commentator and friend of Thomas Carlyle's, who wrote his biography.

the pinched and hidebound type of human character which it patronises. Many persons, no doubt, sincerely think that human beings thus cramped and dwarfed, are as their Maker designed them to be; just as many have thought that trees are a much finer thing when clipped into pollards, or cut out into figures of animals, than as nature made them. But if it be any part of religion to believe that man was made by a good Being, it is more consistent with that faith to believe, that this Being gave all human faculties that they might be cultivated and unfolded, not rooted out and consumed, and that he takes delight in every nearer approach made by his creatures to the ideal conception embodied in them, every increase in any of their capabilities of comprehension, of action, or of enjoyment. There is a different type of human excellence from the Calvinistic; a conception of humanity as having its nature bestowed on it for other purposes than merely to be abnegated. "Pagan self-assertion" is one of the elements of human worth, as well as "Christian self-denial." There is a Greek ideal of self-development, which the Platonic and Christian ideal of self-government blends with, but does not supersede. It may be better to be a John Knox than an Alcibiades, but it is better to be a Pericles than either; nor would a Pericles, if we had one in these days, be without anything good which belonged to John Knox.

It is not by wearing down into uniformity all that is individual in themselves, but by cultivating it and calling it forth, within the limits imposed by the rights and interests of others, that human beings become a noble and beautiful object of contemplation; and as the works partake the character of those who do them, by the same process human life also becomes rich, diversified, and animating, furnishing more abundant aliment to high thoughts and elevating feelings, and strengthening the tie which binds every individual to the race, by making the race infinitely better worth belonging to. In proportion to the development of his individuality, each person becomes more valuable to himself, and is therefore capable of being more valuable to others. There is a greater fullness of life about his own existence, and when there is more life in the units there is more in the mass which is composed of them. As much compression as is necessary to prevent the stronger specimens of human nature from encroaching on the rights of others, cannot be dispensed with; but for this there is ample compensation even in the point of view of human development. The means of development which the individual loses by being prevented from gratifying his inclinations to the injury of others, are chiefly obtained at the expense of the development of other people. And even to himself there is a full equivalent in the better development of the social part of his nature, rendered possible by the restraint put upon the selfish part. To be held to rigid rules of justice for the sake of others, develops the feelings and capacities which have the good of others for their object. But to be restrained in things not affecting their good, by their mere displeasure, develops nothing valuable, except such force of character as may unfold itself in resisting the restraint. If acquiesced in, it dulls and blunts the whole nature. To give any fair play to the nature of each, it is essential that different persons should be allowed to lead different lives. In proportion as this latitude has been exercised in any age, has that age been noteworthy to posterity. Even despotism does not produce its worst effects, so long as individuality exists under it; and whatever crushes individuality is despotism, by whatever name it may be called, and whether it professes to be enforcing the will of God or the injunctions of men.

Having said that Individuality is the same thing with development, and that it is only the cultivation of individuality which produces, or can produce, well-developed human beings, I might here close the argument: for what more or better can be said of any condition of human affairs, than that it brings human beings themselves nearer to the best thing they can be? or what worse can be said of any obstruction to good, than that it prevents this? Doubtless, however, these considerations will not suffice to convince those who most need convincing; and it is necessary further to show, that these developed human beings are of some use to the undeveloped—to point out to those who do not desire liberty, and would not avail themselves of it, that they may be in some intelligible manner rewarded for allowing other people to make use of it without hindrance.

In the first place, then, I would suggest that they might possibly learn something from them. It will not be denied by anybody, that originality is a valuable element in human affairs. There is always need of persons not only to discover new truths, and point out when what were once truths are true no longer, but also to commence new practices, and set the example of more enlightened conduct, and better taste and sense in human life. This cannot well be gainsaid by anybody who does not believe that the world has already attained perfection in all its ways and practices. It is true that this benefit is not capable of being rendered by everybody alike: there are but few persons, in comparison with the whole of mankind, whose experiments, if adopted by others, would be likely to be any improvement on established practice. But these few are the salt of the earth; without them, human life

---

130-131. **John Knox . . . Pericles.** John Knox (1505-1572) was a Scottish Calvinistic reformer; Alcibiades (450?-404 B.C.), an Athenian politician and general; Pericles (c. 490-429 B.C.), an Athenian statesman who gave the age his name.

would become a stagnant pool. Not only is it they who introduce good things which did not before exist; it is they who keep the life in those which already existed. If there were nothing new to be done, would human intellect cease to be necessary? Would it be a reason why those who do the old things should forget why they are done, and do them like cattle, not like human beings? There is only too great a tendency in the best beliefs and practices to degenerate into the 10 mechanical; and unless there were a succession of persons whose ever-recurring originality prevents the grounds of those beliefs and practices from becoming merely traditional, such dead matter would not resist the smallest shock from anything really alive, and there would be no reason why civilisation should not die out, as in the Byzantine Empire. Persons of genius, it is true, are, and are always likely to be, a small minority; but in order to have them, it is necessary to preserve the soil in which they grow. Genius can only 20 breathe freely in an *atmosphere* of freedom. Persons of genius are, *ex vi termini, more* individual than any other people—less capable, consequently, of fitting themselves, without hurtful compression, into any of the small number of moulds which society provides in order to save its members the trouble of forming their own character. If from timidity they consent to be forced into one of these moulds, and to let all that part of themselves which cannot expand under the pressure remain unexpanded, society will be little 30 the better for their genius. If they are of a strong character, and break their fetters, they become a mark for the society which has not succeeded in reducing them to commonplace, to point at with solemn warning as "wild," "erratic," and the like; much as if one should complain of the Niagara river for not flowing smoothly between its banks like a Dutch canal.

I insist thus emphatically on the importance of genius, and the necessity of allowing it to unfold 40 itself freely both in thought and in practice, being well aware that no one will deny the position in theory, but knowing also that almost every one, in reality, is totally indifferent to it. People think genius a fine thing if it enables a man to write an exciting poem, or paint a picture. But in its true sense, that of originality in thought and action, though no one says that it is not a thing to be admired, nearly all, at heart, think that they can do very well without it. Unhappily this is too natural to be wondered at. 50 Originality is the one thing which unoriginal minds cannot feel the use of. They cannot see what it is

to do for them: how should they? If they could see what it would do for them, it would not be originality. The first service which originality has to render them, is that of opening their eyes: which being once fully done, they would have a chance of being themselves original. Meanwhile, recollecting that nothing was ever yet done which some one was not the first to do, and that all good things which exist are the fruits of originality, let them be modest enough to believe that 60 there is something still left for it to accomplish, and assure themselves that they are more in need of originality, the less they are conscious of the want.

In sober truth, whatever homage may be professed, or even paid, to real or supposed mental superiority, the general tendency of things throughout the world is to render mediocrity the ascendant power among mankind. In ancient history, in the middle ages, and in a diminishing degree through the long transition from feudality to the present time, the individual was a 70 power in himself; and if he had either great talents or a high social position, he was a considerable power. At present individuals are lost in the crowd. In politics it is almost a triviality to say that public opinion now rules the world. The only power deserving the name is that of masses, and of governments while they make themselves the organ of the tendencies and instincts of masses. This is as true in the moral and social relations of private life as in public transactions. Those whose opinions go by the name of public opinion are 80 not always the same sort of public: in America they are the whole white population; in England, chiefly the middle class. But they are always a mass, that is to say, collective mediocrity. And what is a still greater novelty, the mass do not now take their opinions from dignitaries in Church or State, from ostensible leaders, or from books. Their thinking is done for them by men much like themselves, addressing them or speaking in their name, on the spur of the moment, through the newspapers. I am not complaining of all this. I do 90 not assert that anything better is compatible, as a general rule, with the present low state of the human mind. But that does not hinder the government of mediocrity from being mediocre government. No government by a democracy or a numerous aristocracy, either in its political acts or in the opinions, qualities, and tone of mind which it fosters, ever did or could rise above mediocrity, except in so far as the sovereign. Many have let themselves be guided (which in their best times they always have done) by 100 the counsels and influence of a more highly gifted and instructed One or Few. The initiation of all wise

16. **Byzantine Empire,** the Eastern Empire after the fall of the Western Roman Empire in 476, with Constantinople as its capital. 21. **ex vi termini,** by force of the term or by definition. 202-204. **de lunatico ...relations.** "There is something both contemptible and frightful in the sort of evidence on which, of late years, any person can be judicially declared unfit for the management of his affairs; and after his death, his disposal of his property can be set aside, if there is enough of it

to pay the expenses of litigation—which are charged on the property itself. All the minute details of his daily life are pried into, and whatever is found which, seen through the medium of the perceiving and describing faculties of the lowest of the low, bears an appearance unlike absolute commonplace, is laid before the jury as evidence of insanity, and often with success; the jurors being little, if at all, less vulgar and ignorant than the witnesses; while the judges, with that extraordinary

or noble things comes and must come from individuals; generally at first from some one individual. The honour and glory of the average man is that he is capable of following that initiative; that he can respond internally to wise and noble things, and be led to them with his eyes open. I am not countenancing the sort of "hero-worship" which applauds the strong man of genius for forcibly seizing on the government of the world and making it do his bidding in spite of itself. All he can claim is, freedom to point out the way. The power of compelling others into it, is not only inconsistent with the freedom and development of all the rest, but corrupting to the strong man himself. It does seem, however, that when the opinions of masses of merely average men are everywhere become or becoming the dominant power, the counterpoise and corrective to that tendency would be, the more and more pronounced individuality of those who stand on the higher eminences of thought. It is in these circumstances most especially, that exceptional individuals, instead of being deterred, should be encouraged in acting differently from the mass. In other times there was no advantage in their doing so, unless they acted not only differently, but better. In this age, the mere example of nonconformity, the mere refusal to bend the knee to custom, is itself a service. Precisely because the tyranny of opinion is such as to make eccentricity a reproach, it is desirable, in order to break through that tyranny, that people should be eccentric. Eccentricity has always abounded when and where strength of character has abounded; and the amount of eccentricity in a society has generally been proportional to the amount of genius, mental vigour, and moral courage it contained. That so few now dare to be eccentric marks the chief danger of the time.

I have said that it is important to give the freest scope possible to uncustomary things, in order that it may in time appear which of these are fit to be converted into customs. But independence of action, and disregard of custom, are not solely deserving of encouragement for the chance they afford that better modes of action, and customs more worthy of general adoption, may be struck out; nor is it only persons of decided mental superiority who have a just claim to carry on their lives in their own way. There is no reason that all human existence should be constructed on some one or some small number of patterns. If a person possesses any tolerable amount of common sense and experience, his own mode of laying out his existence is the best, not because it is the best in itself, but because it is his own mode. Human beings are not like sheep; and even sheep are not undistinguishably alike. A man cannot get a coat or a pair of boots to fit him, unless they are either made to his measure, or he has a whole warehouseful to choose from: and is it easier to fit him with a life than with a coat, or are human beings more like one another in their whole physical and spiritual conformation than in the shape of their feet? If it were only that people have diversities of taste, that is reason enough for not attempting to shape them all after one model. But different persons also require different conditions for their spiritual development; and can no more exist healthily in the same moral, than all the variety of plants can in the same physical, atmosphere and climate. The same things which are helps to one person towards the cultivation of his higher nature, are hindrances to another. The same mode of life is a healthy excitement to one, keeping all his faculties of action and enjoyment in their best order, while to another it is a distracting burthen, which suspends or crushes all internal life. Such are the differences among human beings in their sources of pleasure, their susceptibilities of pain, and the operation on them of different physical and moral agencies, that unless there is a corresponding diversity in their modes of life, they neither obtain their fair share of happiness, nor grow up to the mental, moral, and aesthetic stature of which their nature is capable. Why then should tolerance, as far as the public sentiment is concerned, extend only to tastes and modes of life which extort acquiescence by the multitude of their adherents? Nowhere (except in some monastic institutions) is diversity of taste entirely unrecognized; a person may, without blame, either like or dislike rowing, or smoking, or music, or athletic exercises, or chess, or cards, or study, because both those who like each of these things, and those who dislike them, are too numerous to be put down. But the man, and still more the woman, who can be accused either of doing "what nobody does," or of not doing "what everybody does," is the subject of as much depreciatory remark as if he or she had committed some grave moral delinquency. Persons require to possess a title, or some other badge of rank, or of the consideration of people of rank, to be able to indulge somewhat in the luxury of doing as they like without detriment to their estimation. To indulge somewhat, I repeat: for whoever allow themselves much of that indulgence, incur the risk of something worse than disparaging speeches—they are in peril of a commission *de lunatico,* and of having their property taken from them and given to their relations.

want of knowledge of human nature and life which continually astonishes us in English lawyers, often help to mislead them. These trials speak volumes as to the state of feeling and opinion among the vulgar with regard to human liberty. So far from setting any value on individuality—so far from respecting the right of each individual to act in things indifferent, as seems good to his own judgment and inclinations, judges and juries cannot even conceive that a person in a state of sanity can desire such freedom. In former days, when it was proposed to burn atheists, charitable people used to suggest putting them in a mad-house instead; it would be nothing surprising now-a-days were we to see this done, and the doers applauding themselves, because, instead of persecuting for religion, they had adopted so humane and Christian a mode of treating these unfortunates, not without a silent satisfaction at their having thereby obtained their deserts."—Mill's note.

There is one characteristic of the present direction of public opinion, peculiarly calculated to make it intolerant of any marked demonstration of individuality. The general average of mankind are not only moderate in intellect, but also moderate in inclinations: they have no tastes or wishes strong enough to incline them to do anything unusual, and they consequently do not understand those who have, and class all such with the wild and intemperate whom they are accustomed to
10 look down upon. Now, in addition to this fact which is general, we have only to suppose that a strong movement has set in towards the improvement of morals, and it is evident what we have to expect. In these days such a movement has set in; much has actually been effected in the way of increased regularity of conduct, and discouragement of excesses; and there is a philanthropic spirit abroad, for the exercise of which there is no more inviting field than the moral and prudential improvement of our fellow creatures. These tendencies
20 of the times cause the public to be more disposed than at most former periods to prescribe general rules of conduct, and endeavour to make every one conform to the approved standard. And that standard, express or tacit, is to desire nothing strongly. Its ideal of character is to be without any marked character; to maim by compression, like a Chinese lady's foot, every part of human nature which stands out prominently, and tends to make the person markedly dissimilar in outline to commonplace humanity.

30 As is usually the case with ideals which exclude one-half of what is desirable, the present standard of approbation produces only an inferior imitation of the other half. Instead of great energies guided by vigorous reason, and strong feelings strongly controlled by a conscientious will, its result is weak feelings and weak energies, which therefore can be kept in outward conformity to rule without any strength either of will or of reason. Already energetic characters on any large scale are becoming merely traditional. There is now scarce-
40 ly any outlet for energy in this country except business. The energy expended in this may still be regarded as considerable. What little is left from that employment, is expended on some hobby; which may be a useful, even a philanthropic hobby, but is always some one thing, and generally a thing of small dimensions. The greatness of England is now all collective: individually small, we only appear capable of anything great by our habit of combining; and with this our moral and religious philanthropists are perfectly con-
50 tented. But it was men of another stamp than this that made England what it has been; and men of another stamp will be needed to prevent its decline.

The despotism of custom is everywhere the standing hindrance to human advancement, being in unceasing antagonism to that disposition to aim at something better than customary, which is called, according to circumstances, the spirit of liberty, or that of progress or improvement. The spirit of improvement is not always a spirit of liberty, for it may aim at forcing improvements on an unwilling people; and the spirit 60 of liberty, in so far as it resists such attempts, may ally itself locally and temporarily with the opponents of improvement; but the only unfailing and permanent source of improvement is liberty, since by it there are as many possible independent centres of improvement as there are individuals. The progressive principle, however, in either shape, whether as the love of liberty or of improvement, is antagonistic to the sway of Custom, involving at least emancipation from that yoke; and the contest between the two constitutes the 70 chief interest of the history of mankind. The greater part of the world has, properly speaking, no history, because the despotism of Custom is complete. This is the case over the whole East. Custom is there, in all things, the final appeal; justice and right mean conformity to custom; the argument of custom no one, unless some tyrant intoxicated with power, thinks of resisting. And we see the result. Those nations must once have had originality; they did not start out of the ground populous, lettered, and versed in many of 80 the arts of life; they made themselves all this, and were then the greatest and most powerful nations of the world. What are they now? The subjects or dependents of tribes whose forefathers wandered in the forests when theirs had magnificent palaces and gorgeous temples, but over whom custom exercised only a divided rule with liberty and progress. A people, it appears, may be progressive for a certain length of time, and then stop: when does it stop? When it ceases to possess individuality. If a similar change 90 should befall the nations of Europe, it will not be in exactly the same shape: the despotism of custom with which these nations are threatened is not precisely stationariness. It proscribes singularity, but it does not preclude change, provided all change together. We have discarded the fixed costumes of our forefathers; every one must still dress like other people, but the fashion may change once or twice a year. We thus take care that when there is change it shall be for change's sake, and not from any idea of beauty or 100 convenience; for the same idea of beauty or convenience would not strike all the world at the same moment, and be simultaneously thrown aside by all at another moment. But we are progressive as well as changeable: we continually make new inventions in mechanical things, and keep them until they are again superseded by better; we are eager for improvement in politics, in education, even in morals, though in this last our idea of improvement chiefly consists in persuading or forcing other people to be as good as our- 110 selves. It is not progress that we object to; on the contrary, we flatter ourselves that we are the most progressive people who ever lived. It is individuality that we war against: we should think we had done wonders if we had made ourselves all alike; forgetting that the unlikeness of one person to another is generally the first thing which draws the attention of either to the imperfection of his own type, and the superiority of another, or the possibility, by combining the advantages of both, of producing something better than either. We have a warning example in China—a nation of much talent, and, in some respects, even wisdom, owing to the rare good fortune of having been provided at an early period with a particularly good set of customs, the work, in some measure, of men to whom even the most enlightened European must accord, under certain limitations, the title of sages and philosophers. They are remarkable, too, in the excellence of their apparatus for impressing, as far as possible, the best wisdom they possess upon every mind in the community, and securing that those who have appropriated most of it shall occupy the posts of honour and power. Surely the people who did this have discovered the secret of human progressiveness, and must have kept themselves steadily at the head of the movement of the world. On the contrary, they have become stationary—have remained so for thousands of years; and if they are ever to be farther improved, it must be by foreigners. They have succeeded beyond all hope in what English philanthropists are so industriously working at—in making a people all alike, all governing their thoughts and conduct by the same maxims and rules; and these are the fruits. The modern *régime* of public opinion is, in an unorganized form, what the Chinese educational and political systems are in an organized; and unless individuality shall be able successfully to assert itself against this yoke, Europe, notwithstanding its noble antecedents and its professed Christianity, will tend to become another China.

What is it that has hitherto preserved Europe from this lot? What has made the European family of nations an improving, instead of a stationary portion of mankind? Not any superior excellence in them, which, when it exists, exists as the effect, not as the cause; but their remarkable diversity of character and culture. Individuals, classes, nations, have been extremely unlike one another: they have struck out a great variety of paths, each leading to something valuable; and although at every period those who travelled in different paths have been intolerant of one another, and each would have thought it an excellent thing if all the rest could have been compelled to travel his road, their attempts to thwart each other's development have rarely had any permanent success, and each has in time en-

dured to receive the good which the others have offered. Europe is, in my judgement, wholly indebted to this plurality of paths for its progressive and many-sided development. But it already begins to possess this benefit in a considerably less degree. It is decidedly advancing towards the Chinese ideal of making all people alike. M. de Tocqueville, in his last important work, remarks how much more the Frenchmen of the present day resemble one another, than did those even of the last generation. The same remark might be made of Englishmen in a far greater degree. In a passage already quoted from Wilhelm von Humboldt, he points out two things as necessary conditions of human development, because necessary to render people unlike one another; namely, freedom, and variety of situations. The second of these two conditions is in this country every day diminishing. The circumstances which surround different classes and individuals, and shape their characters, are daily becoming more assimilated. Formerly, different ranks, different neighbourhoods, different trades and professions, lived in what might be called different worlds; at present, to a great degree in the same. Comparatively speaking, they now read the same things, listen to the same things, see the same things, go to the same places, have their hopes and fears directed to the same objects, have the same rights and liberties, and the same means of asserting them. Great as are the differences of position which remain, they are nothing to those which have ceased. And the assimilation is still proceeding. All the political changes of the age promote it, since they all tend to raise the low and to lower the high. Every extension of education promotes it, because education brings people under common influences, and gives them access to the general stock of facts and sentiments. Improvements in the means of communication promote it, by bringing the inhabitants of distant places into personal contact, and keeping up a rapid flow of changes of residence between one place and another. The increase of commerce and manufactures promotes it, by diffusing more widely the advantages of easy circumstances, and opening all objects of ambition, even the highest, to general competition, whereby the desire of rising becomes no longer the character of a particular class, but of all classes. A more powerful agency than even all these, in bringing about a general similarity among mankind, is the complete establishment, in this and other free countries, of the ascendancy of public opinion in the State. As the various social eminences which enabled persons entrenched on them to disregard the opinion of the multitude gradually become levelled; as the very idea of resisting the will of the public, when it is positively

172. **M. de Tocqueville, etc.,** Alexis de Tocqueville (1805-1859), French political theorist and historian, author of *Democracy in America* (1835-1839) and *L'Ancien Régime et la Révolution* (1850); to which Mill refers.

known that they have a will, disappears more and more from the minds of practical politicians; there ceases to be any social support for nonconformity—any substantive power in society, which, itself opposed to the ascendancy of numbers, is interested in taking under its protection opinions and tendencies at variance with those of the public.

The combination of all these causes forms so great a mass of influences hostile to Individuality, that it is 10 not easy to see how it can stand its ground. It will do so with increasing difficulty, unless the intelligent part of the public can be made to feel its value—to see that it is good there should be differences, even though not for the better, even though, as it may appear to them, some should be for the worse. If the claims of Individuality are ever to be asserted, the time is now, while much is still wanting to complete the enforced assimilation. It is only in the earlier stages that any stand can be successfully made against the encroach- 20 ment. The demand that all other people shall resemble ourselves grows by what it feeds on. If resistance waits till life is reduced *nearly* to one uniform type, all deviations from that type will come to be considered impious, immoral, even monstrous and contrary to nature. Mankind speedily become unable to conceive diversity, when they have been for some time unaccustomed to see it.

(1859)

JOHN RUSKIN 1819-1900

John Ruskin liked to consider himself a disciple of Thomas Carlyle, and in certain important aspects their characters are similar. Both, as rebels against many ideas prevailing in their time, disliked materialism, utilitarianism, crass and brutalized industrial objectives. Both, moreover, had a marked self-confidence and a persistent ruthlessness in controversy.

In Praeterita, the story of Ruskin's early life which he published in sections between 1885 and 1889, he attributes much of his adult philosophy to his loneliness as an only child and to the lack of independence that resulted from parental pampering and protection. He was the son of a wealthy London wine merchant and a sternly pietistic, Calvinistic mother. His father engaged private tutors for the boy and took him on long cultural trips through the British Isles and Europe; his mother did great harm to her son by developing in him an overwhelming mother-fixation. She forced him to read the Bible aloud to her from Genesis to Revelation not once but many times, and this disci-

Ruskin as he appeared in a cartoon in the late nineteenth-century English magazine, Vanity Fair. Historical Pictures Service—Chicago.

pline he characterized later as the one really essential part of his boyhood training. In addition, she imparted to him the conviction that no other woman could possibly take her place.

In 1836 Ruskin entered Christ Church College, Oxford, from which he graduated in 1843. His acquaintance with J. M. W. Turner (1775-1851), a distinguished English romantic painter, led him to move to the artist's defense when his water colors were severely criticized. The result was the first volume of Modern Painters, published in 1843 under the anonymity of "a Graduate of Oxford." The success of this led him into four more volumes of comments on painters and painting, the last of which appeared in 1860.

The first volume of Modern Painters had been written at Herne Hill, the home of Ruskin's parents outside London. Soon thereafter (1849) he married Euphemia Gray, but the marriage was annulled five years later. After the death of his mother (1871), Ruskin divided his time between Brantwood, in Westmoreland, and Oxford, where, from 1870 to 1879, and again in 1883-1884, he delivered lectures on art as Slade Professor. A mental breakdown forced his resignation, and he spent the last two decades of his long life at Brantwood, doing some writing during his better moments but undergoing a gradual decline in power until his death in 1900.

Ruskin's writing is divided by the year 1862, the date of publication of Unto This Last, a series of essays on wealth. Before that year his work had been primarily esthetic and ethical commentary. Those who read and disapproved of Unto This Last were convinced that the earlier Ruskin had been somehow eclipsed by a new, uncomfortably didactic writer. But Ruskin's very theory of esthetics had always been ethical, for throughout his life he conceived of art as related to morals, and considered a stone building or a painting chiefly in terms of the character of its creator. So Gothic architecture was noble, and Renaissance architecture ignoble, and a painting of gamblers throwing dice could not be a good painting, because the painter had chosen an immoral subject.

The books that belong to what may be called the early phase of his work are stylistically the best. After the second volume of Modern Painters he issued, in 1849, his Seven Lamps of Architecture. The "seven lamps" are what he conceived to be the seven leading principles of the art: Sacrifice, Truth, Power, Beauty, Life, Memory, and Obedience. The Stones of Venice, published in three volumes between 1851 and 1853, was written, as the author said, to glorify Gothic art and to attack "the pestilent art of the Renaissance." With Unto This Last, as has been said, he seemed to his friends completely to have abandoned art for economic theory. When the four essays which comprise the volume appeared in the Cornhill Magazine, they aroused such opposition that the projected series was abruptly discontinued by the novelist Thackeray (1811-1863), who was the editor of the magazine; a similar fate overtook another series, published in 1872 as Munera Pulveris. Sesame and Lilies (1865) is, in spite of its name, three lectures on the reading, education, and duties of women, and "The Mystery of Life and Its Arts." The Crown of Wild Olive (1866) is a collection of four lectures, given at various places, on War, The Future of England, Work, and Traffic; all lean to social and economic interpretation, as does the collection of letters to

workingmen, Fors Clavigera, which came out between 1871 and 1884.

In spite of his dictatorial and somewhat arrogantly condescending nature, Ruskin's eagerness to help others was genuine throughout his life. This eagerness was apparent in 1843, when he broke a lance in defense of Turner, and it appeared again in 1851 when he came to the rescue of the Pre-Raphaelite Brotherhood (p. 828) in a series of letters to The London Times. St. George's Guild was the most celebrated result of Ruskin's attempts to combine industry, art, and science, but the Hinksey Diggers, the handmade-linen workers' association of Langdale, and similar groups all derived their inspiration and their resources from him. On the theoretical and moral side Ruskin tried to do what Morris (p. 1103) did on the practical and material.

Like Carlyle, Ruskin had an earlier and a later literary style, but the distinction between the two styles is not so marked as with Carlyle. His earlier style, smooth, ornate, almost overelaborate and rhetorical—impassioned prose, if there ever was any—Ruskin believed he acquired from his reading of Wordsworth and other English poets and, more especially, from that thorough saturation in the Bible for which his mother was responsible. This idea is doubtful: the influences cited undoubtedly helped to shape his style, but to them should certainly be added that which came from his training as a critic of painting. For there is in Ruskin—even when in his later style he tried to emulate Carlyle—a romantic, almost rhapsodic, quality. His Modern Painters and The Stones of Venice contain some of the finest illustrations of the "grand style" in the whole library of Victorian prose.

from MODERN PAINTERS

The first volume of Ruskin's five-volume treatise on painters and painting was published in 1843 when the author was only twenty-four and had but recently graduated from Oxford. Its original inspiration has already been mentioned. Besides praising Turner in the first volume, he set forth there his own views of the principles of art. The second volume appeared in 1846; it continues the exposition of the author's theories of art and especially his ideas concerning the function of the imagination in art. Volume three (1856) deals with the Grand Style and Idealism and outlines the development of appreciation of landscape throughout the history of the civilized world. The fourth volume (1856) contains chapters on color, illumination, and natural landscape—clouds, water, leaves, etc. The fifth and last volume (1860) continues the discussion of natural landscape and then comments on the four orders of landscape painters:

Heroic, Classical, Pastoral, and Contemplative. Modern Painters *and* The Stones of Venice *contain the essence of Ruskin's theories of art.*

THE GRAND STYLE

. . . It seems to me, and may seem to the reader, strange that we should need to ask the question, "What is poetry?" Here is a word we have been using all our lives, and I suppose, with a very distinct idea attached to it; and when I am now called upon to give a definition of this idea, I find myself at a pause. What is more singular, I do not at present recollect hearing the question often asked, though surely it is a very natural one; and I never recollect hearing it answered, or
10 even attempted to be answered. In general, people shelter themselves under metaphors, and while we hear poetry described as an utterance of the soul, an effusion of Divinity, or voice of nature, or in other terms equally elevated and obscure, we never attain anything like a definite explanation of the character which actually distinguishes it from prose.

I come, after some embarrassment, to the conclusion, that poetry is "the suggestion by the imagination, of noble grounds for the noble emotions." I mean, by the
20 noble emotions, those four principal sacred passions— Love, Veneration, Admiration, and Joy (this latter especially, if unselfish); and their opposites—Hatred, Indignation (or Scorn), Horror, and Grief, this last when unselfish, becoming Compassion. These passions in their various combinations constitute what is called "poetical feeling" when they are felt on noble grounds, that is, on great and true grounds. Indignation, for instance, is a poetical feeling, if excited by serious injury; but it is not a poetical feeling if entertained on
30 being cheated out of a small sum of money. It is very possible the manner of the cheat may have been such as to justify considerable indignation; but the feeling is nevertheless not poetical unless the grounds of it be large as well as just. In like manner, energetic admiration may be excited in certain minds by a display of fireworks, or a street of handsome shops; but the feeling is not poetical, because the grounds of it are false, and therefore ignoble. There is in reality nothing to deserve admiration either in the firing of packets of
40 gunpowder, or in the display of the stocks of warehouses. But admiration excited by the budding of a flower is a poetical feeling, because it is impossible that this manifestation of spiritual power and vital beauty can ever be enough admired.

Farther, it is necessary to the existence of poetry that the grounds of these feelings should be *furnished by the imagination.* Poetical feeling, that is to say, mere noble emotion, is not poetry. It is happily inherent in all human nature deserving the name, and is found

often to be purest in the least sophisticated. But the 50 power of assembling, by *the help of the imagination,* such images as will excite these feelings, is the power of the poet or literally of the "Maker."

Now this power of exciting the emotions depends of course on the richness of the imagination, and on its choice of those images which, in combination, will be most effective, or, for the particular work to be done, most fit. And it is altogether impossible for a writer not endowed with invention to conceive what tools a true poet will make use of, or in what way he will 60 apply them, or what unexpected results he will bring out by them; so that it is vain to say that the details of poetry ought to possess, or ever do possess, any *definite* character. Generally speaking, poetry runs into finer and more delicate details than prose; but the details are not poetical because they are more delicate, but because they are employed so as to bring out an affecting result. For instance, no one but a true poet would have thought of exciting our pity for a bereaved father by describing his way of locking 70 the door of his house:

Perhaps to himself at that moment he said,
"The key I must take, for my Ellen is dead";
But of this in my ears not a word did he speak;
And he went to the chase with a tear on his cheek.

In like manner, in painting, it is altogether impossible to say beforehand what details a great painter may make poetical by his use of them to excite noble emotions; and we shall, therefore, find presently that a painting is to be classed in the great or inferior 80 schools, not according to the kind of details which it represents, but according to the uses for which it employs them.

It is only farther to be noticed, that infinite confusion has been introduced into this subject by the careless and illogical custom of opposing painting to poetry, instead of regarding poetry as consisting in a noble use, whether of colors or words. Painting is properly to be opposed to *speaking or writing,* but not to *poetry.* Both painting and speaking are methods of expression. 90 Poetry is the employment of either for the noblest purposes.

This question being thus far determined, we may proceed with our paper in the *Idler.*

"It is very difficult to determine the exact degree of enthusiasm that the arts of Painting and Poetry may admit. There may, perhaps, be too great indulgence as well as too great a restraint of imagination; if the one produces incoherent monsters, the other produces what is full as bad, lifeless insipidity. An intimate knowl- 100 edge of the passions, and good sense, but not common sense, must at last determine its limits. It has been

---

Modern Painters. 18. **"the suggestion . . . emotions."** Ruskin later stated that the definition should include rhythm. 53. **"Maker,"** an old word, for poet. 72. **Perhaps . . . cheek,** Wordsworth, *The*

Childless Father, ll. 20 ff. 94. **our . . . Idler.** The *Idler* was a publication by Samuel Johnson (p. 573). Sir Joshua Reynolds (1723-1792), noted English portrait painter, wrote the essay from which Ruskin

thought, and I believe with reason, that Michael Angelo sometimes transgressed those limits; and, I think, I have seen figures of him of which it was very difficult to determine whether they were in the highest degree sublime or extremely ridiculous. Such faults may be said to be the ebullitions of genius; but at least he had this merit, that he never was insipid; and whatever passion his works may excite, they will always escape contempt.

"What I have had under consideration is the sublimest style, particularly that of Michael Angelo, the Homer of painting. Other kinds may admit of this naturalness, which of the lowest kind is the chief merit; but in painting, as in poetry, the highest style has the least of common nature."

From this passage we gather three important indications of the supposed nature of the Great Style. That it is the work of men in a state of enthusiasm. That it is like the writing of Homer; and that it has as little as possible of "common nature" in it.

First, it is produced by men in a state of enthusiasm. That is, by men who feel *strongly* and *nobly*; for we do not call a strong feeling of envy, jealousy, or ambition, enthusiasm. That is, therefore, by men who feel poetically. This much we may admit, I think, with perfect safety. Great art is produced by men who feel acutely and nobly; and it is in some sort an expression of this personal feeling. We can easily conceive that there may be a sufficiently marked distinction between such art, and that which is produced by men who do not feel at all, but who reproduce, though ever so accurately, yet coldly, like human mirrors, the scenes which pass before their eyes.

Secondly, Great Art is like the writing of Homer, and this chiefly because it has little of "common nature" in it. We are not clearly informed what is meant by common nature in this passage. Homer seems to describe a great deal of what is common—cookery, for instance, very carefully in all its processes. I suppose the passage in the *Iliad* which, on the whole, has excited most admiration, is that which describes a wife's sorrow at parting from her husband, and a child's fright at its father's helmet; and I hope, at least, the former feeling may be considered "common nature." But the true greatness of Homer's style is, doubtless, held by our author to consist in his imaginations of things not only uncommon but impossible (such as spirits in brazen armor, or monsters with heads of men and bodies of beasts), and in his occasional delineations of the human character and form in their utmost, or heroic, strength and beauty. We gather then on the whole, that a painter in the Great Style must be enthusiastic, or full of emotion, and must paint the human form in its utmost strength and beauty, and perhaps certain impossible forms besides, liable by persons not

in an equally enthusiastic state of mind to be looked upon as in some degree absurd. This I presume to be Reynolds's meaning, and to be all that he intends us to gather from his comparisons of the Great Style with the writings of Homer. But if that comparison be a just one in all respects, surely two other corollaries ought to be drawn from it, namely, first, that these Heroic or Impossible images are to be mingled with others very unheroic and very possible; and, secondly, that in the representation of the Heroic or Impossible forms, the greatest care must be taken in *finishing the details,* so that a painter must not be satisfied with painting well the countenance and the body of his hero, but ought to spend the greatest part of his time (as Homer the greatest number of verses) in elaborating the sculptured pattern on his shield.   (III, 4, 1, 12-18)

THE PATHETIC FALLACY

German dullness, and English affectation, have of late much multiplied among us the use of two of the most objectionable words that were ever coined by the troublesomeness of metaphysicians—namely, "Objective" and "Subjective."

No words can be more exquisitely, and in all points, useless; and I merely speak of them that I may, at once and forever, get them out of my way, and out of my reader's. But to get that done, they must be explained.

The word "Blue," say certain philosophers, means the sensation of color which the human eye receives in looking at the open sky, or at a bell gentian.

Now, say they farther, as this sensation can only be felt when the eye is turned to the object, and as, therefore, no such sensation is produced by the object when nobody looks at it, therefore the thing, when it is not looked at, is not blue; and thus (say they) there are many qualities of things which depend as much on something else as on themselves. To be sweet, a thing must have a taster; it is only sweet while it is being tasted, and if the tongue had not the capacity of taste, then the sugar would not have the quality of sweetness.

And then they agree that the qualities of things which thus depend upon our perception of them, and upon our human nature as affected by them, shall be called Subjective; and the qualities of things which they always have, irrespective of any other nature, as roundness or squareness, shall be called Objective.

From these ingenious views the step is very easy to a farther opinion, that it does not much matter what things are in themselves, but only what they are to us; and that the only real truth of them is their appearance to, or effect upon, us. From which position, with a hearty desire for mystification, and much egotism,

quotes. 103. **Michael Angelo.** See p. 927, note 130. 114. **Homer of painting.** Michelangelo is to painting what Homer is to epic poetry. 140. **cookery.** See the *Iliad*, I, 463 ff. 144. **wife's sorrow . . .**

helmet. See the *Iliad*, VI, 390–502. The allusion is to the description of Hector's parting with Andromache and his infant son Astyanax.

selfishness, shallowness, and impertinence, a philosopher may easily go so far as to believe, and say, that everything in the world depends upon his seeing or thinking of it, and that nothing, therefore, exists, but what he sees or thinks of.

Now, to get rid of all these ambiguities and troublesome words at once, be it observed that the word "Blue" does *not* mean the *sensation* caused by a gentian on the human eye; but it means the *power*
10 of producing that sensation; and this power is always there, in the thing, whether we are there to experience it or not, and would remain there though there were not left a man on the face of the earth. Precisely in the same way gunpowder has a power of exploding. It will not explode if you put no match to it. But it has always the power of so exploding, and is therefore called an explosive compound, which it very positively and assuredly is, whatever philosophy may say to the contrary.

20 In like manner, a gentian does not produce the sensation of blueness if you don't look at it. But it has always the power of doing so; its particles being everlastingly so arranged by its Maker. And, therefore, the gentian and the sky are always verily blue, whatever philosophy may say to the contrary; and if you do not see them blue when you look at them, it is not their fault but yours.

Hence I would say to these philosophers: If, instead of using the sonorous phrase, "It is objectively
30 so," you will use the plain old phrase, "It *is* so," and if instead of the sonorous phrase, "It is subjectively so," you will say, in plain old English, "It *does* so," or "It seems so to me"; you will, on the whole, be more intelligible to your fellow-creatures; and besides, if you find that a thing which generally "does so" to other people (as a gentian looks blue to most men), does *not* so to you, on any particular occasion, you will not fall into the impertinence of saying that the thing is not so, or did not so, but you will say
40 simply (what you will be all the better for speedily finding out) that something is the matter with you. If you find that you cannot explode the gunpowder, you will not declare that all gunpowder is subjective and all explosion imaginary, but you will simply suspect and declare yourself to be an ill-made match. Which, on the whole, though there may be a distant chance of a mistake about it, is, nevertheless, the wisest conclusion you can come to until farther experiment.

Now, therefore, putting these tiresome and absurd 50 words quite out of our way, we may go on at our ease to examine the point in question—namely, the difference between the ordinary, proper, and true appearances of things to us; and the extraordinary, or false appearances, when we are under the influence of emotion, or contemplative fancy; false appearances, I say, as being entirely unconnected with any real power or character in the object, and only imputed to it by us.

For instance— 60

"The spendthrift crocus, bursting through the mold
Naked and shivering, with his cup of gold."

This is very beautiful, and yet very untrue. The crocus is not a spendthrift, but a hardy plant; its yellow is not gold, but saffron. How is it that we enjoy so much the having it put into our heads that it is anything else than a plain crocus?

It is an important question. For, throughout our past reasonings about art, we have always found that nothing could be good or useful, or ultimately pleas- 70 urable, which was untrue. But here is something pleasurable in written poetry which is nevertheless *untrue*. And what is more, if we think over our favorite poetry, we shall find it full of this kind of fallacy, and that we like it all the more for being so.

It will appear also, on consideration of the matter, that this fallacy is of two principal kinds. Either, as in this case of the crocus, it is the fallacy of willful fancy, which involves no real expectation that it will be believed; or else it is a fallacy caused by an excited 80 state of the feelings, making us, for the time, more or less irrational. Of the cheating of the fancy we shall have to speak presently; but, in this chapter, I want to examine the nature of the other error, that which the mind admits when affected strongly by emotion. Thus, for instance, in *Alton Locke*—

"They rowed her in across the rolling foam—
The cruel, crawling foam."

The foam is not cruel, neither does it crawl. The state of mind which attributes to it these characters of 90

24. **blue . . . yours.** "It is quite true that in all qualities involving sensation there may be a doubt whether different people receive the same sensation from the same thing (cf. Part II, Sec. I, Chap. V, 6); but, though this makes such facts not distinctly explicable, it does not alter the facts themselves. I derive a certain sensation, which I call sweetness, from sugar. That is a fact. Another person feels a sensation, which *he* also calls sweetness, from sugar. That is also a fact. The sugar's power to produce these two sensations, which we suppose to be, and which are, in all probability, very nearly the same in both of us, and, on the whole, in the human race, is its sweetness."—Ruskin. 48. **farther experiment.** At this point Ruskin added a footnote on *subness* and *obness*, in which he parodied the metaphysical style of the German philosophers. 61. **"The . . . gold."** "Holmes [Oliver Wendell], quoted by Miss Mitford in her *Recollections of a Literary Life*."—Ruskin. 86. **Alton Locke,** a novel (published 1850) by Charles Kingsley (1819–1875), English novelist. 102. **the second . . . it.** "I admit two orders of poets, but no third; and by these two orders I mean the Creative (Shakespeare, Homer, Dante), and Reflective or Perceptive (Wordsworth, Keats, Tennyson). But both of these must be *first-rate* in their range, though their range is different; and with poetry second-rate in *quality* no one ought to be allowed to trouble mankind. There is quite enough of the best—much more than we can ever read or enjoy in the length of a life; and it is a literal wrong or sin in any person to encumber us with inferior work. I have no patience with apologies made by young pseudo-poets, 'that they believe there is *some* good in what they have written: that they hope to do better in time,' etc. *Some* good! If there is not *all* good, there is no good. If they ever hope to do better, why do they trouble us now? Let them rather courageously burn all they have done and wait for the better days. There are few men, ordinarily educated, who in moments of strong feeling could not strike out a poetical thought and afterwards polish it so as to be presentable. But men of sense know better than so to waste their time; and those who sincerely love poetry know the touch of the master's hands on the chords too well to fumble among them after

a living creature is one in which the reason is unhinged by grief. All violent feelings have the same effect. They produce in us a falseness in all our impressions of external things, which I would generally characterize as the "Pathetic fallacy."

Now we are in the habit of considering this fallacy as eminently a character of poetical description, and the temper of mind in which we allow it, as one eminently poetical, because passionate. But, I believe, if we look well into the matter, that we shall find the greatest poets do not often admit this kind of falseness—that it is only the second order of poets who much delight in it.

Thus, when Dante describes the spirits falling from the bank of Acheron "as dead leaves flutter from a bough," he gives the most perfect image possible of their utter lightness, feebleness, passiveness, and scattering agony of despair, without, however, for an instant losing his own clear perception that *these* are souls, and *those* are leaves: he makes no confusion of one with the other. But when Coleridge speaks of

"The one red leaf, the last of its clan,
That dances as often as dance it can,"

he has a morbid, that is to say, a so far false, idea about the leaf: he fancies a life in it, and will, which there are not; confuses its powerlessness with choice, its fading death with merriment, and the wind that shakes it with music. Here, however, there is some beauty, even in the morbid passage; but take an instance in Homer and Pope. Without the knowledge of Ulysses, Elpenor, his youngest follower, has fallen from an upper chamber in the Circean palace, and has been left dead, unmissed by his leader, or companions, in the haste of their departure. They cross the sea to the Cimmerian land; and Ulysses summons the shades from Tartarus. The first which appears is that of the lost Elpenor. Ulysses, amazed, and in exactly the spirit of bitter and terrified lightness which is seen in Hamlet, addresses the spirit with the simple, startled words:

"Elpenor? How camest thou under the shadowy darkness? Hast thou come faster on foot than I in my black ship?"

Which Pope renders thus:

"O, say, what angry power Elpenor led
To glide in shades, and wander with the dead?
How could thy soul, by realms and seas disjoined,
Outfly the nimble sail, and leave the lagging wind?"

I sincerely hope the reader finds no pleasure here, either in the nimbleness of the sail, or the laziness of the wind! And yet how is it that these conceits are so painful now, when they have been pleasant to us in the other instances?

For a very simple reason. They are not a *pathetic* fallacy at all, for they are put into the mouth of the wrong passion—a passion which never could possibly have spoken them—agonized curiosity. Ulysses wants to know the facts of the matter; and the very last thing his mind could do at the moment would be to pause, or suggest in anywise what was *not* a fact. The delay in the first three lines, and conceit in the last, jar upon us instantly, like the most frightful discord in music. No poet of true imaginative power could possibly have written the passage.

Therefore, we see that the spirit of truth must guide us in some sort, even in our enjoyment of fallacy. Coleridge's fallacy has no discord in it, but Pope's has set our teeth on edge. Without farther questioning, I will endeavor to state the main bearings of this matter.

The temperament which admits the pathetic fallacy is, as I said above, that of a mind and body in some sort too weak to deal fully with what is before them or upon them; borne away, or over-clouded, or over-dazzled by emotion; and it is a more or less noble state, according to the force of the emotion which has induced it. For it is no credit to a man that he is not morbid or inaccurate in his perceptions, when he has no strength of feeling to warp them; and it is in general a sign of higher capacity and stand in the ranks of being that the emotions should be strong enough to vanquish, partly, the intellect, and make it believe what they choose. But it is still a grander condition when the intellect also rises, till it is strong enough to assert its rule against, or together with, the utmost efforts of the passions; and the whole man stands in an iron glow, white hot, perhaps, but still strong, and in no wise evaporating; even if he melts, losing none of his weight.

So, then, we have the three ranks: the man who perceives rightly, because he does not feel, and to whom

him. Nay, more than this; all inferior poetry is an injury to the good, inasmuch as it takes away the freshness of rimes, blunders upon and gives a wretched commonalty to good thoughts; and, in general, adds to the weight of human weariness in a most woeful and culpable manner. There are few thoughts likely to come across ordinary men, which have not already been expressed by greater men in the best possible way; and it is a wiser, more generous, more noble thing to remember and point out the perfect words than to invent poorer ones wherewith to encumber temporarily the world."—Ruskin. 104. **Dante . . . spirits,** in the *Inferno* of *Divina Commedia*. 111. **Coleridge.** See *Christabel,* p. 723, ll. 49–50. 119. **Homer,** from *The Odyssey,* beginning of Book XI. 128. **seen in Hamlet.** "Well said, old mole! can'st work i' the ground so fast?"—Ruskin's note, a quotation from *Hamlet,* I, v, 162; Hamlet thus addresses the ghost of his father that moves beneath the platform. 140. **conceits,** affected conceptions. 153. **passage.** "It is worth while comparing the way a similar question is put by the exquisite sincerity of Keats:

" 'He wept, and his bright tears
Went trickling down the golden bow he held.
Thus, with half-shut, suffused eyes, he stood;
While from beneath some cumb'rous boughs hard by,
With solemn step, an awful goddess came.
And there was purport in her looks for him,
Which he with eager guess began to read:
Perplexed the while, melodiously he said,
" ' 'How can'st thou over the unfooted sea?' '
           Hyperion, 3, 42."—Ruskin.
179. **to whom the primrose, etc.** The allusion is to Wordsworth's *Peter Bell,* Part I, Stanza 12:
    A primrose by a river's brim
    A yellow primrose was to him,
    And it was nothing more.

the primrose is very accurately the primrose, because he does not love it. Then, secondly, the man who perceives wrongly, because he feels, and to whom the primrose is anything else than a primrose—a star, or a sun, or a fairy's shield, or a forsaken maiden. And then, lastly, there is the man who perceives rightly in spite of his feelings, and to whom the primrose is forever nothing else than itself—a little flower, apprehended in the very plain and leafy fact of it, whatever
10 and how many soever the associations and passions may be, that crowd around it. And, in general, these three classes may be rated in comparative order, as the men who are not poets at all, and the poets of the second order, and the poets of the first; only however great a man may be, there are always some subjects which *ought* to throw him off his balance; some, by which his poor human capacity of thought should be conquered, and brought into the inaccurate and vague state of perception, so that the language of the highest
20 inspiration becomes broken, obscure, and wild in metaphor, resembling that of the weaker man, overborne by weaker things.

And thus, in full, there are four classes: the men who feel nothing, and therefore see truly; the men who feel strongly, think weakly, and see untruly (second order of poets); the men who feel strongly, think strongly, and see truly (first order of poets); and the men who, strong as human creatures can be, are yet submitted to influences stronger than they, and see in a
30 sort untruly, because what they see is inconceivably above them. This last is the usual condition of prophetic inspiration.

I separate these classes, in order that their character may be clearly understood; but of course they are united each to the other by imperceptible transitions, and the same mind, according to the influences to which it is subjected, passes at different times into the various states. Still, the difference between the great and less man is, on the whole, chiefly in this point of *altera-*
40 *bility*. That is to say, the one knows too much, and perceives and feels too much of the past and future, and of all things beside and around that which immediately affects him, to be in anywise shaken by it. His mind is made up; his thoughts have an accustomed current; his ways are steadfast; it is not this or that new sight which will at once unbalance him. He is tender to impression at the surface, like a rock with deep moss upon it; but there is too much mass of him to be moved. The smaller man, with the same degree of sensi-
50 bility, is at once carried off his feet; he wants to do something he did not want to do before; he views all the universe in a new light through his tears; he is gay or enthusiastic, melancholy or passionate, as things come and go to him. Therefore the high creative poet might even be thought, to a great extent, impassive

(as shallow people think Dante stern), receiving indeed all feelings to the full, but having a great center of reflection and knowledge in which he stands serene, and watches the feeling, as it were, from far off.

Dante, in his most intense moods, has entire com- 60 mand of himself, and can look around calmly, at all moments, for the image or the word that will best tell what he sees to the upper or lower world. But Keats and Tennyson, and the poets of the second order are generally themselves subdued by the feelings under which they write, or, at least, write as choosing to be so, and therefore admit certain expressions and modes of thought which are in some sort diseased or false.

Now so long as we see that the *feeling* is true, we 70 pardon, or are even pleased by, the confessed fallacy of sight which it induces: we are pleased, for instance, with those lines of Kingsley's, above quoted, not because they fallaciously describe foam, but because they faithfully describe sorrow. But the moment the mind of the speaker becomes cold, that moment every such expression becomes untrue, as being for ever untrue in the external facts. And there is no greater baseness in literature than the habit of using these metaphorical expressions in cold blood. 80 An inspired writer, in full impetuosity of passion, may speak wisely and truly of "raging waves of the sea, foaming out their own shame"; but it is only the basest writer who cannot speak of the sea without talking of "raging waves," "remorseless floods," "ravenous billows," etc.; and it is one of the signs of the highest power in a writer to check all such habits of thought, and to keep his eyes fixed firmly on the *pure fact*, out of which if any feeling comes to him or his reader, he knows it must be a true one.   90

To keep to the waves, I forget who it is who represents a man in despair, desiring that his body may be cast into the sea,

"Whose changing mound, and foam that passed away,
Might mock the eye that questioned where I lay."

Observe, there is not a single false, or even overcharged, expression. "Mound" of the sea wave is perfectly simple and true; "changing" is as familiar as may be; "foam that passed away," strictly literal; and the whole line descriptive of the reality with a 100 degree of accuracy which I know not any other verse, in the range of poetry, that altogether equals. For most people have not a distinct idea of the clumsiness and massiveness of a large wave. The word "wave" is used too generally of ripples and breakers, and bendings in light drapery or grass: it does not by itself convey a perfect image. But the word "mound" is heavy, large, dark, definite; there is no mistaking

146. *Iliad.* The passage is from Book III. 168. **Casimir de la Vigne,** Jean François Casimir Delavigne (1793–1843), French poet and drama-

tist, famous for his patriotic poems and very popular in his own time. *Constance's Toilette* is the tragedy of a gay young girl who, having

the kind of wave meant, nor missing the sight of it. Then the term "changing" has a peculiar force also. Most people think of waves as rising and falling. But if they look at the sea carefully, they will perceive that the waves do not rise and fall. They change. Change both place and form, but they do not fall; one wave goes on, and on, and still on; now lower, now higher, now tossing its mane like a horse, now building itself together like a wall, now shaking, now steady, but still the same wave, till at last it seems struck by something, and changes, one knows not how,—becomes another wave.

The close of the line insists on this image, and paints it still more perfectly—"foam that passed away." Not merely melting, disappearing, but passing on, out of sight, on the career of the wave. Then, having put the absolute ocean fact as far as he may before our eyes, the poet leaves us to feel about it as we may, and to trace for ourselves the opposite fact— the image of the green mounds that do not change, and the white and written stones that do not pass away; and thence to follow out also the associated images of the calm life with the quiet grave, and the despairing life with the fading foam:

"Let no man move his bones."
"As for Samaria, her king is cut off like the foam upon the water."

But nothing of this is actually told or pointed out, and the expressions, as they stand, are perfectly severe and accurate, utterly uninfluenced by the firmly governed emotion of the writer. Even the word "mock" is hardly an exception, as it may stand merely for "deceive" or "defeat," without implying any impersonation of the waves.

It may be well, perhaps, to give one or two more instances to show the peculiar dignity possessed by all passages which thus limit their expression to the pure fact, and leave the hearer to gather what he can from it. Here is a notable one from the *Iliad*. Helen, looking from the Scaean gate of Troy over the Grecian host, and telling Priam the names of its captains, says at last:

"I see all the other dark-eyed Greeks; but two I cannot see—Castor and Pollux—whom one mother bore with me. Have they not followed from fair Lacedaemon, or have they indeed come in their sea-wandering ships, but now will not enter into the battle of men, fearing the shame and the scorn that is in Me?"

Then Homer:

"So she spoke. But them, already, the life-giving earth possessed, there in Lacedaemon, in the dear fatherland."

Note, here, the high poetical truth carried to the extreme. The poet has to speak of the earth in sadness, but he will not let that sadness affect or change his thoughts of it. No; though Castor and Pollux be dead, yet the earth is our mother still, fruitful, life-giving. These are the facts of the thing. I see nothing else than these. Make what you will of them.

Take another very notable instance from Casimir de la Vigne's terrible ballad, "La Toilette de Constance." I must quote a few lines out of it here and there, to enable the reader who has not the book by him to understand its close.

"Vite, Anna, vite; au miroir
   Plus vite, Anna. L'heure s'avance
Et je vais au bal ce soir
   Chez l'ambassadeur de France.

Y pensez-vous, ils sont fanés, ces noeuds,
   Ils sont d'hier, mon Dieu, comme tout passe!
Que du réseau qui retient mes cheveux
   Les glands d'azur retombent avec grace.
Plus haut! Plus bas! Vous ne comprenez rien!
   Que sur mon front ce saphir étincelle:
Vous me piquez, mal-adroite. Ah, c'est bien,
   Bien—chère Anna! Je t'aime, je suis belle.

Celui qu'en vain je voudrais oublier
   (Anna, ma robe) il y sera, j'espère.
(Ah, fi, profane, est-ce la mon collier?
   Quoi! ces grains d'or bénits par le Saint-Père!)
Il y sera; Dieu, s'il pressait ma main,
   En y pensant, a peine je respire;
Père Anselmo doit m'entendre demain,
   Comment ferai-je, Anna, pour tout lui dire?

   Vite un coup d'oeil au miroir,
      Le dernier. ——J'ai l'assurance
   Qu'on va m'adorer ce soir
      Chez l'ambassadeur de France.

Près du foyer, Constance s'admirait.
   Dieu! sur sa robe il vole une étincelle!
Au feu. Courez; Quand l'espoir l'enivrait,
   Tout perdre ainsi! Quoi! Mourir—et si belle!
L'horrible feu rong avec volupté
   Ses bras, son sein, et l'entoure, et s'élève,
Et sans pitié dévore sa beauté,
   Ses dix-huit ans, hélas, et son doux rêve!

   Adieu, bal, plaisir, amour!
      On disait, Pauvre Constance!

dressed for the ambassador's ball, was burned to death when her robe caught fire; for her it was "farewell ball, pleasure, love"—but at the ambassador's, after a "Poor Constance," the dance went on.

Et on dansait, jusqu'au jour,
    Chez l'ambassadeur de France."

Yes, that is the fact of it. Right or wrong, the poet does not say. What you may think about it, he does not know. He has nothing to do with that. There lie the ashes of the dead girl in her chamber. There they danced, till the morning, at the Ambassador's of France. Make what you will of it.

If the reader will look through the ballad, of which
10 I have quoted only about the third part, he will find that there is not, from beginning to end of it, a single poetical (so-called) expression, except in one stanza. The girl speaks as simple prose as may be; there is not a word she would not have actually used as she was dressing. The poet stands by, impassive as a statue, recording her words just as they come. At last the doom seizes her, and in the very presence of death, for an instant, his own emotions conquer him. He records no longer the facts only, but the facts as
20 they seem to him. The fire gnaws with *voluptuousness—without pity*. It is soon past. The fate is fixed for ever; and he retires into his pale and crystalline atmosphere of truth. He closes all with the calm veracity,

"They said, 'Poor Constance!' "

Now in this there is the exact type of the consummate poetical temperament. For, be it clearly and constantly remembered that the greatness of a poet depends upon the two faculties, acuteness of feeling
30 and command of it. A poet is great, first in proportion to the strength of his passion, and then, that strength being granted, in proportion to his government of it; there being, however, always a point beyond which it would be inhuman and monstrous if he pushed this government, and, therefore, a point at which all feverish and wild fancy becomes just and true. Thus the destruction of the kingdom of Assyria cannot be contemplated firmly by a prophet of Israel. The fact is too great, too wonderful. It overthrows him, dashes
40 him into a confused element of dreams. All the world is, to his stunned thought, full of strange voices. "Yea, the fir-trees rejoice at thee, and the cedars of Lebanon, saying, 'Since thou art gone down to the grave, no feller is come up against us.' " So, still more, the thought of the presence of Deity cannot be borne without this great astonishment. "The mountains and the hills shall break forth before you into singing, and all the trees of the field shall clap their hands."
50 But by how much this feeling is noble when it is

justified by the strength of its cause, by so much it is ignoble when there is not cause enough for it; and beyond all other ignobleness is the mere affectation of it, in hardness of heart. Simply bad writing may almost always, as above noticed, be known by its adoption of these fanciful metaphorical expressions, as a sort of current coin; yet there is even a worse, at least a more harmful, condition of writing than this, in which such expressions are not ignorantly and feelinglessly caught up, but, by some master, skilful in handling, 60 yet insincere, deliberately wrought out with chill and studied fancy; as if we should try to make an old lava stream look red-hot again, by covering it with dead leaves, or white-hot, with hoar-frost.

When Young is lost in veneration, as he dwells on the character of a truly good and holy man, he permits himself for a moment to be overborne by the feeling so far as to exclaim—

"Where shall I find him? angels, tell me where.
You know him; he is near you; point him out. 70
Shall I see glories beaming from his brow,
Or trace his footsteps by the rising flowers?"

This emotion has a worthy cause, and is thus true and right. But now hear the cold-hearted Pope say to a shepherd girl—

"Where'er you walk, cool gales shall fan the glade;
Trees, where you sit, shall crowd into a shade;
Your praise the birds shall chant in every grove,
And winds shall waft it to the powers above.
But would you sing, and rival Orpheus' strain, 80
The wondering forests soon should dance again;
The moving mountains hear the powerful call,
And headlong streams hang, listening, in their fall."

This is not, nor could it for a moment be mistaken for, the language of passion. It is simple falsehood, uttered by hypocrisy; definite absurdity, rooted in affectation, and coldly asserted in the teeth of nature and fact. Passion will indeed go far in deceiving itself; but it must be a strong passion, not the simple wish of a lover to tempt his mistress to sing. Com- 90 pare a very closely parallel passage in Wordsworth, in which the lover has lost his mistress:

"Three years had Barbara in her grave been laid,
When thus his moan he made:

'Oh, move, thou cottage, from behind yon oak,
    Or let the ancient tree uprooted lie,
That in some other way yon smoke

38. **a prophet of Israel.** See Isaiah 14:8. 46. **"The mountains, etc."** See Isaiah 55:12. 65. **Young,** Edward Young (1683-1765), a pre-romantic poet. 74. **Pope,** Alexander Pope. See p. 532. 80. **Orpheus,** famous musician of Greek mythology. 93. **"Three years, etc.,"** from *'Tis Said That Some Have Died for Love,* 11-16, 33-36. 135. **"If through, etc.,"** from *Describing the Sorrow of an Ingenuous Mind,*

61-64, by William Shenstone (1714-1763), English poet. 140. **" 'Ah, why, etc.,"** from *The Excursion,* VI, 869 ff. 177. **strength.** "I cannot quit this subject without giving two more instances, both exquisite, of the pathetic fallacy, which I have just come upon in *Maud:*
     " 'For a great speculation had failed;
    And ever he muttered and maddened, and ever wanned with despair;

May mount into the sky.
If still behind yon pine-tree's ragged bough,
100 Headlong, the waterfall must come,
Oh, let it, then, be dumb—
Be anything, sweet stream, but that which thou art
now.' "

Here is a cottage to be moved, if not a mountain,
and a waterfall to be silent, if it is not to hang listening: but with what different relation to the mind
that contemplates them! Here, in the extremity of its
agony, the soul cries out wildly for relief, which at
the same moment it partly knows to be impossible,
but partly believes possible, in a vague impression
110 that a miracle *might* be wrought to give relief even
to a less sore distress—that nature is kind, and God
is kind, and that grief is strong; it knows not well
what *is* possible to such grief. To silence a stream, to
move a cottage wall—one might think it could do as
much as that!

I believe these instances are enough to illustrate
the main point I insist upon respecting the pathetic
fallacy—that so far as it *is* a fallacy, it is always the
sign of a morbid state of mind, and comparatively of
120 a weak one. Even in the most inspired prophet it is a
sign of the incapacity of his human sight or thought
to bear what has been revealed to it. In ordinary
poetry, if it is found in the thoughts of the poet himself, it is at once a sign of his belonging to the
inferior school; if in the thoughts of the characters
imagined by him, it is right or wrong according to
the genuineness of the emotion from which it springs;
always, however, implying necessarily *some* degree of
weakness in the character.

130 Take two most exquisite instances from master
hands. The Jessy of Shenstone, and the Ellen of
Wordsworth, have both been betrayed and deserted.
Jessy, in the course of her most touching complaint,
says:

"If through the garden's flowery tribes I stray,
    Where bloom the jasmines that could once allure,
'Hope not to find delight in us,' they say,
    'For we are spotless, Jessy; we are pure.' "

Compare with this some of the words of Ellen:

140 " 'Ah, why,' said Ellen, sighing to herself,
'Why do not words, and kiss, and solemn pledge,
And nature, that is kind in woman's breast,
And reason, that in man is wise and good,
And fear of Him who is a righteous Judge—

Why do not these prevail for human life,
To keep two hearts together, that began
Their springtime with one love, and that have need
Of mutual pity and forgiveness, sweet
To grant, or be received; while that poor bird—
O, come and hear him! Thou who hast to me   150
Been faithless, hear him;—though a lowly creature,
One of God's simple children, that yet know not
The Universal Parent, *how* he sings!
As if he wished the firmament of heaven
Should listen, and give back to him the voice
Of his triumphant constancy and love.
The proclamation that he makes, how far
His darkness doth transcend our fickle light.' "

The perfection of both these passages, as far as
regards truth and tenderness of imagination in the 160
two poets, is quite insuperable. But, of the two characters imagined, Jessy is weaker than Ellen, exactly
in so far as something appears to her to be in
nature which is not. The flowers do not really reproach her. God meant them to comfort her, not to
taunt her; they would do so if she saw them rightly.

Ellen, on the other hand, is quite above the slightest
erring emotion. There is not the barest film of fallacy
in all her thoughts. She reasons as calmly as if she
did not feel. And, although the singing of the bird 170
suggests to her the idea of its desiring to be heard
in heaven, she does not for an instant admit any
veracity in the thought. "As if," she says,—"I know
he means nothing of the kind; but it does verily
seem as if." The reader will find, by examining the
rest of the poem, that Ellen's character is throughout
consistent in this clear though passionate strength.

It then being, I hope, now made clear to the reader
in all respects that the pathetic fallacy is powerful
only so far as it is pathetic, feeble so far as it is 180
fallacious, and, therefore, that the dominion of Truth
is entire, over this, as over every other natural and
just state of the human mind, we may go on to the
subject for the dealing with which this prefatory inquiry became necessary; and why necessary, we shall
see forthwith.   (III, 4, 11, 1-16)
(1843-1860)

from UNTO THIS LAST

*"From 1845 to 1860," wrote Ruskin, "I went on
with more or less of public applause, and then in
1860 people saw a change come over me which they
highly disapproved, and I went on from 1860 to 1875*

And out he walked, when the wind like a broken worldling wailed,
    And the flying gold of the ruined woodlands drove thro'
        the air.
" 'There has fallen a splendid tear
    From the passion-flower at the gate.
    The red rose cries, " ' "She is near, she is near!"

And the white rose weeps, " ' "She is late."
    The larkspur listens, " ' "I hear, I hear!"
    And the lily whispers, " ' "I wait."'
        From Tennyson's *Maud* (1855), Part I, 1, 3, and XXII,
        10 (with ll. 3 and 4 omitted)."—Ruskin.

under the weight of continuously increasing public recusancy and reprobation." The immediate cause of the shift in popular favor of which Ruskin was so conscious was the publication in 1860-1862 of four essays on economics called Unto This Last. *These appeared in the Cornhill Magazine and were intended as the first of a greater number; such an outcry was raised against the series, however, that it was abruptly discontinued. The four published articles deal with employment, wages, legislative control of industry, true wealth, and other economic and social topics. Of all who read these papers at the time only Carlyle praised the author; others regarded him as a warped and impractical visionary and could not foresee that many of the reforms which he advocated would come, in time, to be generally accepted.*

ESSAY I

THE ROOTS OF HONOR

1. Among the delusions which at different periods have possessed themselves of the minds of large masses of the human race, perhaps the most curious —certainly the least creditable—is the modern *soidisant* science of political economy, based on the idea that an advantageous code of social action may be determined irrespectively of the influence of social affection.

Of course, as in the instances of alchemy, astrology,
10 witchcraft, and other such popular creeds, political economy has a plausible idea at the root of it. "The social affections," says the economist, "are accidental and disturbing elements in human nature; but avarice and the desire of progress are constant elements. Let us eliminate the inconstants, and, considering the human being merely as a covetous machine, examine by what laws of labor, purchase, and sale, the greatest accumulative result in wealth is attainable. Those laws once determined, it will be for each individual
20 afterwards to introduce as much of the disturbing affectionate element as he chooses, and to determine for himself the result on the new conditions supposed."

2. This would be a perfectly logical and successful method of analysis, if the accidentals afterwards to be introduced were of the same nature as the powers first examined. Supposing a body in motion to be influenced by constant and inconstant forces, it is usually the simplest way of examining its course to trace it
30 first under the persistent conditions, and afterwards introduce the causes of variation. But the disturbing elements in the social problem are not of the same nature as the constant ones; they alter the essence of the creature under examination the moment they

are added; they operate, not mathematically, but chemically, introducing conditions which render all our previous knowledge unavailable. We made learned experiments upon pure nitrogen, and have convinced ourselves that it is a very manageable gas: but behold! the thing which we have practically to deal with is its 40 chloride; and this, the moment we touch it on our established principles, sends us and our apparatus through the ceiling.

3. Observe, I neither impugn nor doubt the conclusions of the science, if its terms are accepted. I am simply uninterested in them, as I should be in those of a science of gymnastics which assumed that men had no skeletons. It might be shown, on that supposition, that it would be advantageous to roll the students up into pellets, flatten them into cakes, or 50 stretch them into cables; and that when these results were effected, the re-insertion of the skeleton would be attended with various inconveniences to their constitution. The reasoning might be admirable, the conclusions true, and the science deficient only in applicability. Modern political economy stands on a precisely similar basis. Assuming, not that the human being has no skeleton, but that is all skeleton, it founds an ossifiant theory of progress on this negation of a soul; and having shown the utmost that may be 60 made of bones, and constructed a number of interesting geometrical figures with death's-heads and humeri, successfully proves the inconvenience of the reappearance of a soul among these corpuscular structures. I do not deny the truth of this theory: I simply deny its applicability to the present phase of the world.

4. This inapplicability has been curiously manifested during the embarrassment caused by the late strikes of our workmen. Here occurs one of the 70 simplest cases, in a pertinent and positive form, of the first vital problem which political economy has to deal with (the relation between employer and employed); and at a severe crisis, when lives in multitudes, and wealth in masses, are at stake, the political economists are helpless—practically mute; no demonstrable solution of the difficulty can be given by them, such as may convince or calm the opposing parties. Obstinately the masters take one view of the matter; obstinately the operatives another; and no 80 political science can set them at one.

5. It would be strange if it could, it being not by "science" of any kind that men were ever intended to be set at one. Disputant after disputant vainly strives to show that the interests of the masters are, or are not, antagonistic to those of the men: none of the pleaders ever seeming to remember that it does not absolutely or always follow that the persons must be antagonistic because their interests are. If there

Unto This Last. **4. soi-disant,** self-named, so-called. **59. ossifiant,** hardening, turning to bone. **62. death's-heads and humeri,** skulls and crossbones. **69. late strikes,** the builders' strikes in the fall of 1859.

90 is only a crust of bread in the house, and mother and children are starving, their interests are not the same. If the mother eats it, the children want it; if the children eat it, the mother must go hungry to her work. Yet it does not necessarily follow that there will be "antagonism" between them, that they will fight for the crust, and that the mother, being strongest, will get it, and eat it. Neither, in any other case, whatever the relations of the persons may be, can it be assumed for certain that, because their interests 100 are diverse, they must necessarily regard each other with hostility, and use violence or cunning to obtain the advantage.

6. Even if this were so, and it were as just as it is convenient to consider men as actuated by no other moral influences than those which affect rats or swine, the logical conditions of the question are still indeterminable. It can never be shown generally either that the interests of master and laborer are alike, or that they are opposed; for, according to circumstances, 110 they may be either. It is, indeed, always the interest of both that the work should be rightly done, and a just price obtained for it; but, in the division of profits, the gain of the one may or may not be the loss of the other. It is not the master's interest to pay wages so low as to leave the men sickly and depressed, nor the workman's interest to be paid high wages if the smallness of the master's profit hinders him from enlarging his business, or conducting it in a safe and liberal way. A stoker ought not 120 to desire high pay if the company is too poor to keep the engine wheels in repair.

7. And the varieties of circumstances which influence these reciprocal interests are so endless, that all endeavor to deduce rules of action from balance of expediency is in vain. And it is meant to be in vain. For no human actions ever were intended by the Maker of men to be guided by balances of expediency, but by balances of justice. He has therefore rendered all endeavors to determine expediency 130 futile for evermore. No man ever knew, or can know, what will be the ultimate result to himself, or the others, of any given line of conduct. But every man may know, and most of us do know, what is a just and unjust act. And all of us may know also, that the consequences of justice will be ultimately the best possible, both to others and ourselves, though we can neither say what *is* best, nor how it is likely to come to pass.

I have said balances of justice, meaning, in the 140 term justice, to include affection—such affection as one man *owes* to another. All right relations between master and operative, and all their best interests, ultimately depend on these.

8. We shall find the best and simplest illustration of the relations of master and operative in the position of domestic servants.

We will suppose that the master of a household desires only to get as much work out of his servants as he can, at the rate of wages he gives. He never allows them to be idle; feeds them as poorly and 150 lodges them as ill as they will endure, and in all things pushes his requirements to the exact point beyond which he cannot go without forcing the servant to leave him. In doing this, there is no violation on his part of what is commonly called "justice." He agrees with the domestic for his whole time and service, and takes them;—the limits of hardship in treatment being fixed by the practice of other masters in his neighborhood; that is to say, by the current rate of wages for domestic labor. If the servant can 160 get a better place, he is free to take one, and the master can only tell what is the real market value of his labor, by requiring as much as he will give.

This is the politico-economical view of the case, according to the doctors of that science; who assert that by this procedure the greatest average of work will be obtained from the servant, and therefore, the greatest benefit to the community, and through the community, by reversion, to the servant himself.

That, however, is not so. It would be so if the 170 servant were an engine of which the motive power was steam, magnetism, gravitation, or any other agent of calculable force. But he being, on the contrary, an engine whose motive power is a Soul, the force of this very peculiar agent, as an unknown quantity, enters into all the political economist's equations, without his knowledge, and falsifies every one of their results. The largest quantity of work will not be done by this curious engine for pay, or under pressure, or by help of any kind of fuel which may 180 be supplied by the chaldron. It will be done only when the motive force, that is to say, the will or spirit of the creature, is brought to its greatest strength by its own proper fuel; namely, by the affections.

9. It may indeed happen, and does happen often, that if the master is a man of sense and energy, a large quantity of material work may be done under mechanical pressure, enforced by strong will and guided by wise method; also it may happen, and does happen often, that if the master is indolent and weak 190 (however good-natured), a very small quantity of work, and that bad, may be produced by the servant's undirected strength, and contemptuous gratitude. But the universal law of the matter is that, assuming any given quantity of energy and sense in master and servant, the greatest material result obtainable by them will be, not through antagonism to each other, but through affection for each other; and that if the master, instead of endeavoring to get as much work as possible from the servant, seeks rather to render 200 his appointed and necessary work beneficial to him, and to forward his interests in all just and wholesome ways, the real amount of work ultimately done, or

of good rendered, by the person so cared for, will indeed be the greatest possible.

Observe, I say, "of good rendered," for a servant's work is not necessarily or always the best thing he can give his master. But good of all kinds, whether in material service, in protective watchfulness of his master's interest and credit, or in joyful readiness to seize unexpected and irregular occasions of help.

Nor is this one whit less generally true because indulgence will be frequently abused, and kindness met with ingratitude. For the servant who, gently treated, is ungrateful, treated ungently, will be revengeful; and the man who is dishonest to a liberal master will be injurious to an unjust one.

10. In any case, and with any person, this unselfish treatment will produce the most effective return. Observe, I am here considering the affections wholly as a motive power; not at all as things in themselves desirable or noble, or in any other way abstractedly good. I look at them simply as an anomalous force, rendering every one of the ordinary political economist's calculations nugatory; while, even if he desired to introduce this new element into his estimates, he has no power of dealing with it; for the affections only become a true motive power when they ignore every other motive and condition of political economy. Treat the servant kindly, with the idea of turning his gratitude to account, and you will get, as you deserve, no gratitude, nor any value for your kindness; but treat him kindly without any economical purpose, and all economical purposes will be answered; in this, as in all other matters, whosoever will save his life shall lose it, whoso loses it shall find it.

11. The next clearest and simplest example of relation between master and operative is that which exists between the commander of a regiment and his men.

Supposing the officer only desires to apply the rules of discipline so as, with least trouble to himself, to make the regiment most effective, he will not be able, by any rules, or administration of rules, on this selfish principle, to develop the full strength of his subordinates. If a man of sense and firmness, he may, as in the former instance, produce a better result than would be obtained by the irregular kindness of a weak officer; but let the sense and firmness be the same in both cases, and assuredly the officer who has the most direct personal relations with his men, the most care for their interests, and the most value for their lives, will develop their effective strength, through their affection for his own person,

and trust in his character, to a degree wholly unattainable by other means. The law applies still more stringently as the numbers concerned are larger; a charge may often be successful, though the men dislike their officers; a battle has rarely been won, unless they loved their general.

12. Passing from these simple examples to the more complicated relations existing between a manufacturer and his workmen, we are met first by certain curious difficulties, resulting, apparently, from a harder and colder state of moral elements. It is easy to imagine an enthusiastic affection existing among soldiers for the colonel. Not so easy to imagine an enthusiastic affection among cotton-spinners for the proprietor of the mill. A body of men associated for purposes of robbery (as a Highland clan in ancient times) shall be animated by perfect affection, and every member of it be ready to lay down his life for the life of his chief. But a band of men associated for purposes of legal production and accumulation is usually animated, it appears, by no such emotions, and none of them are in anywise willing to give his life for the life of his chief. Not only are we met by this apparent anomaly, in moral matters, but by others connected with it, in administration of system. For a servant or a soldier is engaged at a definite rate of wages, for a definite period; but a workman at a rate of wages variable according to the demand for labor, and with the risk of being at any time thrown out of his situation by chances of trade. Now, as, under these contingencies, no action of the affections can take place, but only an explosive action of *disaffections*, two points offer themselves for consideration in the matter.

The first—How far the rate of wages may be so regulated as not to vary with the demand for labor.

The second—How far it is possible that bodies of workmen may be engaged and maintained at such fixed rate of wages (whatever the state of trade may be), without enlarging or diminishing their number, so as to give them permanent interest in the establishment with which they are connected, like that of the domestic servants in an old family, or an *esprit de corps*, like that of the soldiers in a crack regiment.

13. The first question is, I say, how far it may be possible to fix the rate of wages irrespectively of the demand for labor.

Perhaps one of the most curious facts in the history of human error is the denial by the common political economist of the possibility of thus regulating wages; while, for all the important, and much of the unimportant, labor on the earth, wages are already so regulated. We do not sell our prime-ministership by Dutch

---

32. **whosoever . . . it.** From Matthew 16:25. "The difference between the two modes of treatment, and between their effective material results, may be seen very accurately by a comparison of the relations of Esther and Charlie in *Bleak House*, with those of Miss Brass and the Marchioness in *Master Humphrey's Clock*. The essential value and truth of Dickens's writings have been unwisely lost sight of by many thoughtful persons, merely because he presents his truth with some color of caricature. Unwisely, because Dickens's caricature, though often gross, is never mistaken. Allowing for his manner of telling them, the things

he tells us are always true. I wish that he could think it right to limit his brilliant exaggeration to works written only for public amusement; and when he takes up a subject of high national importance, such as that which he handled in *Hard Times*, that he would use severer and more accurate analysis. The usefulness of that work (to my mind, in several respects, the greatest he has written) is with many persons seriously diminished because Mr. Bounderby is a dramatic monster, instead of a characteristic example of a worldly master; and Stephen Blackpool a dramatic perfection, instead of a characteristic example of

auction; nor, on the decease of a bishop, whatever may be the general advantages of simony, do we (yet) offer his diocese to the clergyman who will take the episcopacy at the lowest contract. We (with exquisite sagacity of political economy!) do indeed sell commissions, but not openly, generalships: sick, we do not inquire for a physician who takes less than a guinea; litigious, we never think of reducing six-and-eightpence to four-and-sixpence; caught in a shower, we do not canvass the cabmen, to find one who values his driving at less than sixpence a mile.

It is true that in all these cases there is, and in every conceivable case there must be, ultimate reference to the presumed difficulty of the work, or number of candidates for the office. If it were thought that the labor necessary to make a good physician would be gone through by a sufficient number of students with the prospect of only half-guinea fees, public consent would soon withdraw the unnecessary half-guinea. In this ultimate sense, the price of labor is indeed always regulated by the demand for it; but so far as the practical and immediate administration of the matter is regarded, the best labor always has been, and is, as *all* labor ought to be, paid by an invariable standard.

14. "What!" the reader perhaps answers amazedly: "pay good and bad workmen alike?"

Certainly. The difference between one prelate's sermons and his successor's—or between one physician's opinion and another's—is far greater, as respects the qualities of mind involved, and far more important in result to you personally, than the difference between good and bad laying of bricks (though that is greater than most people suppose). Yet you pay with equal fee, contentedly, the good and bad workmen upon your soul, and the good and bad workmen upon your body; much more may you pay, contentedly, with equal fees, the good and bad workmen upon your house. "Nay, but I choose my physician and (?) my clergyman, thus indicating my sense of the quality of their work." By all means, also, choose your bricklayer; that is the proper reward of the good workman, to be "chosen." The natural and right system respecting all labor is, that it should be paid at a fixed rate, but the good workman employed, and the bad workman unemployed. The false, unnatural, and destructive system is when the bad workman is allowed to offer his work at half-price, and either take the place of the good, or force him by his competition to work for an inadequate sum.

15. This equality of wages, then, being the first object towards which we have to discover the directest

available road; the second is, as above stated, that of maintaining constant numbers of workmen in employment, whatever may be the accidental demand for the article they produce.

I believe the sudden and extensive inequalities of demand which necessarily arise in the mercantile operations of an active nation, constitute the only essential difficulty which has to be overcome in a just organization of labor. The subject opens into too many branches to admit of being investigated in a paper of this kind; but the following general facts bearing on it may be noted.

The wages which enable any workman to live are necessarily higher, if his work is liable to intermission, than if it is assured and continuous; and however severe the struggle for work may become, the general law will always hold, that men must get more daily pay if, on the average, they can only calculate on work three days a week, than they would require if they were sure of work six days a week. Supposing that a man cannot live on less than a shilling a day, his seven shillings he must get, either for three days' violent work, or six days' deliberate work. The tendency of all modern mercantile operations is to throw both wages and trade into the form of a lottery, and to make the workman's pay depend on intermittent exertion, and the principal's profit on dexterously used chance.

16. In what partial degree, I repeat, this may be necessary, in consequence of the activities of modern trade, I do not here investigate; contenting myself with the fact, that in its fatalest aspects it is assuredly unnecessary, and results merely from love of gambling on the part of the masters, and from ignorance and sensuality in the men. The masters cannot bear to let any opportunity of gain escape them, and frantically rush at every gap and breach in the walls of Fortune, raging to be rich, and affronting, with impatient covetousness, every risk of ruin; while the men prefer three days of violent labor, and three days of drunkenness, to six days of moderate work and wise rest. There is no way in which a principal, who really desires to help his workmen, may do it more effectually than by checking these disorderly habits both in himself and them; keeping his own business operations on a scale which will enable him to pursue them securely, not yielding to temptations of precarious gain; and, at the same time, leading his workmen into regular habits of labor and life, either by inducing them rather to take low wages in the form of a fixed salary, than high wages, subject to the chance of their being thrown out of work; or, if this be impossible, by discouraging the system of

an honest workman. But let us no lose the use of Dickens's wit and insight, because he chooses to speak in a circle of stage fire. He is entirely right in his main drift and purpose in every book he has written; and all of them, but especially *Hard Times*, should be studied with close and earnest care by persons interested in social questions. They will find much that is partial, and, because partial, apparently unjust; but if they examine all the evidence on the other side, which Dickens seems to overlook, it will appear, after all their trouble, that his view was the finally right one, grossly and sharply told."—Ruskin.

67. **Highland clan.** Cf. the Robin Hood ballads (pp. 61 ff.). 102. **Dutch auction,** the public offer of property at a price above its value and the subsequent lowering of the price until a purchaser is found. 104. **simony,** buying or selling ecclesiastical preferment. 109. **litigious . . . four-and-sixpence,** if involved in a lawsuit, we do not quibble over the fee asked by a good lawyer. 128. "**pay . . . alike?**" This condition has resulted from the establishment of labor unions. 140. **and (?).** Ruskin is doubtful about choosing a clergyman.

violent exertion for nominally high day wages, and leading the men to take lower pay for more regular labor.

In effecting any radical changes of this kind, doubtless there would be great inconvenience and loss incurred by all the originators of movement. That which can be done with perfect convenience and without loss, is not always the thing that most needs to be done, or which we are most imperatively required to do.

17. I have already alluded to the difference hitherto existing between regiments of men associated for purposes of violence, and for purposes of manufacture; in that the former appear capable of self-sacrifice—the latter, not; which singular fact is the real reason of the general lowness of estimate in which the profession of commerce is held, as compared with that of arms. Philosophically, it does not, at first sight, appear reasonable (many writers have endeavored to prove it unreasonable) that a peaceable and rational person, whose trade is buying and selling, should be held in less honor than an unpeaceable and often irrational person, whose trade is slaying. Nevertheless, the consent of mankind has always, in spite of the philosophers, given precedence to the soldier.

And this is right.

For the soldier's trade, verily and essentially, is not slaying, but being slain. This, without well knowing its own meaning, the world honors it for. A bravo's trade is slaying; but the world has never respected bravos more than merchants: the reason it honors the soldier is, because he holds his life at the service of the State. Reckless he may be—fond of pleasure or of adventure—all kinds of by-motives and mean impulses may have determined the choice of his profession, and may affect (to all appearance exclusively) his daily conduct in it; but our estimate of him is based on this ultimate fact—of which we are well assured—that, put him in a fortress breach, with all the pleasures of the world behind him, and only death and his duty in front of him, he will keep his face to the front; and he knows that this choice may be put to him at any moment, and has beforehand taken his part—virtually takes such part continually—does, in reality, die daily.

18. Not less is the respect we pay to the lawyer and physician, founded ultimately on their self-sacrifice. Whatever the learning or acuteness of a great lawyer, our chief respect for him depends on our belief that, set in a judge's seat, he will strive to judge justly, come of it what may. Could we suppose that he would take bribes, and use his acuteness and legal knowledge to give plausibility to iniquitous decisions, no degree of intellect would win for him our respect. Nothing will win it, short of our tacit conviction, that in all important acts of his life justice is first with him; his own interest, second.

In the case of a physician, the ground of the honor we render him is clearer still. Whatever his science, we should shrink from him in horror if we found him regard his patients merely as subjects to experiment upon; much more, if we found that, receiving bribes from persons interested in their deaths, he was using his best skill to give poison in the mask of medicine.

Finally, the principle holds with utmost clearness as it respects clergymen. No goodness of disposition will excuse want of science in a physician or of shrewdness in an advocate; but a clergyman, even though his power of intellect be small, is respected on the presumed ground of his unselfishness and serviceableness.

19. Now there can be no question but that the tact, foresight, decision, and other mental powers, required for the successful management of a large mercantile concern, if not such as could be compared with those of a great lawyer, general, or divine, would at least match the general conditions of mind required in the subordinate officers of a ship, or of a regiment, or in the curate of a country parish. If, therefore, all the efficient members of the so-called liberal professions are still, somehow, in public estimate of honor, preferred before the head of a commercial firm, the reason must lie deeper than in the measurement of their several powers of mind.

And the essential reason for such preference will be found to lie in the fact that the merchant is presumed to act always selfishly. His work may be very necessary to the community; but the motive of it is understood to be wholly personal. The merchant's first object in all his dealings must be (the public believe) to get as much for himself, and leave as little to his neighbor (or customer) as possible. Enforcing this upon him, by political statute, as the necessary principle of his action; recommending it to him on all occasions, and themselves reciprocally adopting it; proclaiming vociferously, for law of the universe, that a buyer's function is to cheapen, and a seller's to cheat—the public, nevertheless, involuntarily condemn the man of commerce for his compliance with their own statement, and stamp him forever as belonging to an inferior grade of human personality.

20. This they will find, eventually, they must give up doing. They must not cease to condemn selfishness; but they will have to discover a kind of commerce which is not exclusively selfish. Or, rather, they will have to discover that there never was, or can be, any other kind of commerce; that this which they have called commerce was not commerce at all, but cozening; and that a true merchant differs as much from a merchant according to laws of modern political economy, as the hero of the *Excursion* from Autolycus. They will find that commerce is an occupation which gentlemen will every day see more need to

---

43. **die daily.** A phrase St. Paul applies to himself in 1 Corinthians 15:31. 108. **hero . . . Autolycus.** The hero of Wordsworth's *Excursion* is a mild and pious recluse; Autolycus, in Shakespeare's *Winter's Tale,* is a thieving rogue.

engage in, rather than in the businesses of talking to men, or slaying them: that, in true commerce, as in true preaching, or true fighting, it is necessary to admit the idea of occasional voluntary loss;—that sixpences have to be lost, as well as lives, under a sense of duty; that the market may have its martyrdoms as well as the pulpit; and trade its heroisms, as well as war.

May have—in the final issue, must have—and only 120 has not had yet, because men of heroic temper have always been misguided in their youth into other fields, not recognizing what is in our days, perhaps, the most important of all fields; so that, while many a zealous person loses his life in trying to teach the form of a gospel, very few will lose a hundred pounds in showing the practice of one.

21. The fact is, that people never have had clearly explained to them the true functions of a merchant with respect to other people. I should like the reader 130 to be very clear about this.

Five great intellectual professions, relating to daily necessities of life, have hitherto existed—three exist necessarily, in every civilized nation:

The Soldier's profession is to *defend* it.

The Pastor's, to *teach* it.

The Physician's, to *keep it in health.*

The Lawyer's, to *enforce justice* in it.

The Merchant's, to *provide* for it.

And the duty of all these men is, on due occasion, 140 to *die* for it.

"On due occasion," namely:

The Soldier, rather than leave his post in battle.

The Physician, rather than leave his post in plague.

The Pastor, rather than teach Falsehood.

The Lawyer, rather than countenance Injustice.

The Merchant—What is *his* "due occasion" of death?

22. It is the main question for the merchant, as for all of us. For, truly, the man who does not know 150 when to die, does not know how to live.

Observe, the merchant's function (or manufacturer's, for in the broad sense in which it is here used the word must be understood to include both) is to provide for the nation. It is no more his function to get profit for himself out of that provision than it is a clergyman's function to get his stipend. The stipend is a due and necessary adjunct, but not the object, of his life, if he be a true clergyman, any more than his fee (or *honorarium*) is the object of 160 life to a true physician. Neither is his fee the object of life to a true merchant. All three, if true men, have a work to be done irrespective of fee—to be done even at any cost, or for quite the contrary of fee; the pastor's function being to teach, the physician's to heal, and the merchant's, as I have said, to provide. That is to say, he has to understand to their very root the qualities of the thing he deals in, and the means of

obtaining or producing it; and he has to apply all his sagacity and energy to the producing or obtaining it in perfect state, and distributing it at the cheapest pos- 170 sible price where it is most needed.

And because the production or obtaining of any commodity involves necessarily the agency of many lives and hands, the merchant becomes in the course of his business the master and governor of large masses of men in a more direct, though less confessed way, than a military officer or pastor; so that on him falls, in great part, the responsibility for the kind of life they lead: and it becomes his duty, not only to be always considering how to produce what 180 he sells in the purest and cheapest forms, but how to make the various employments involved in the production, or transference of it, most beneficial to the men employed.

23. And as into these two functions, requiring for their right exercise the highest intelligence, as well as patience, kindness, and tact, the merchant is bound to put all his energy, so for their just discharge he is bound, as soldier or physician is bound, to give up, if need be, his life, in such way as it may be demanded 190 of him. Two main points he has in his providing function to maintain: first, his engagements (faithfulness to engagements being the real root of all possibilities in commerce); and, secondly, the perfectness and purity of the thing provided; so that, rather than fail in any engagement, or consent to any deterioration, adulteration, or unjust and exorbitant price of that which he provides, he is bound to meet fearlessly any form of distress, poverty, or labor, which may, through maintenance of these points, 200 come upon him.

24. Again: in his office as governor of the men employed by him, the merchant or manufacturer is invested with a distinctly paternal authority and responsibility. In most cases, a youth entering a commercial establishment is withdrawn altogether from home influence; his master must become his father, else he has, for practical and constant help, no father at hand: in all cases the master's authority, together with the general tone and atmosphere of his busi- 210 ness, and the character of the men with whom the youth is compelled in the course of it to associate, have more immediate and pressing weight than the home influence, and will usually neutralize it either for good or evil; so that the only means which the master has of doing justice to the men employed by him is to ask himself sternly whether he is dealing with such subordinate as he would with his own son, if compelled by circumstances to take such a position. 220

Supposing the captain of a frigate saw it right, or were by any chance obliged, to place his own son in the position of a common sailor; as he would then treat his son, he is bound always to treat every one of the men under him. So, also, supposing the master of a manufactory saw it right, or were by any chance obliged, to place his own son in the position of an ordinary workman; as he would then treat his son, he is bound always to treat every one of his men. This is the only effective, true, or practical RULE which can be given on this point of political economy.

And as the captain of a ship is bound to be the last man to leave his ship in case of wreck, and to
10 share his last crust with the sailors in case of famine, so the manufacturer, in any commercial crisis or distress, is bound to take the suffering of it with his men, and even to take more of it for himself than he allows his men to feel; as a father would in a famine, shipwreck, or battle, sacrifice himself for his son.

25. All which sounds very strange: the only real strangeness in the matter being, nevertheless, that it should so sound. For all this is true, and that
20 not partially nor theoretically, but everlastingly and practically: all other doctrine than this respecting matters political being false in premises, absurd in deduction, and impossible in practice, consistently with any progressive state of national life; all the life which we now possess as a nation showing itself in the resolute denial and scorn, by a few strong minds and faithful hearts, of the economic principles taught to our multitudes, which principles, so far as accepted, lead straight to national destruction. Re-
30 specting the modes and forms of destruction to which they lead, and, on the other hand, respecting the farther practical working of true polity, I hope to reason further in a following paper.
(1860)

from THE RELATION OF ART TO MORALS

From 1870 until his breakdown in 1878 and for a second period in 1883-1884 Ruskin was at Oxford University as Slade Professor of Art. His lectures were so pungent, informative, and vigorous that great crowds often attended them, and Ruskin was frequently forced to repeat his discourses. In recognition of his notable success he was elected honorary fellow of Corpus Christi College. Out of his appointment at Oxford came eight volumes of lectures, many of which—like the following—contain repetitions or elaborations of theories which he expressed earlier in Modern Painters, The Stones of Venice, *and other publications. To Ruskin great art was inseparable from a sound life in the individual, nation, and race, and this belief provided the channel that connected his conceptions of art and his theories of economics.*

. . . And now I pass to the arts with which I have special concern, in which, though the facts are exactly the same, I shall have more difficulty in proving my assertion, because very few of us are as cognizant of the merit of painting as we are of that of language; and I can only show you whence that merit springs, after having thoroughly shown you in what it consists. But 40 in the meantime, I have simply to tell you, that the manual arts are as accurate exponents of ethical state, as other modes of expression; first, with absolute precision, of that of the workman; and then with precision, disguised by many distorting influences, of that of the nation to which it belongs.

And, first, they are a perfect exponent of the mind of the workman: but, being so, remember, if the mind be great or complex, the art is not an easy book to read; for we must ourselves possess all the mental characters 50 of which we are to read the signs. No man can read the evidence of labor who is not himself laborious, for he does not know what the work cost: nor can he read the evidence of true passion if he is not passionate; nor of gentleness if he is not gentle: and the most subtle signs of fault and weakness of character he can only judge by having had the same faults to fight with. I myself, for instance, know impatient work, and tired work, better than most critics, because I am myself always impatient, and often tired: so also, the patient 60 and indefatigable touch of a mighty master becomes more wonderful to me than to others. Yet, wonderful in no mean measure it will be to you all, when I make it manifest;—and as soon as we begin our real work, and you have learned what it is to draw a true line, I shall be able to make manifest to you—and undisputably so—that the day's work of a man like Mantegna or Paul Veronese consists of an unfaltering, uninterrupted, succession of movements of the hand more precise than those of the finest fencer: the pencil 70 leaving one point and arriving at another, not only with unerring precision at the extremity of the line, but with an unerring and yet varied course—sometimes over spaces a foot or more in extent—yet a course so determined everywhere that either of these men could, and Veronese often does, draw a finished profile, or any other portion of the contour of the face with one line, not afterwards changed. Try, first, to realize to yourselves the muscular precision of that action, and the intellectual strain of it; for the movement of a fencer 80 is perfect in practiced monotony; but the movement of the hand of a great painter is at every instant governed by direct and new intention. Then imagine that muscular firmness and subtlety, and the instantaneously selective and ordinant energy of the brain, sustained all day long, not only without fatigue, but with a visible

The Relation of Art to Morals. 36. **my assertion.** That fine art has three functions—"the enforcing of the religious sentiments of men, the perfecting of their ethical state, and the doing them material service." 44. **the workman,** the artist. 67. **Mantegna,** Andrea Mantegna (1431–1506), an Italian painter and engraver; his work is noted for
its precision of outline. 68. **Paul Veronese** (1528–1588), a well-known painter of the Venetian School. 85. **ordinant,** commanding, placing in order. 111. **skill . . . North.** Ruskin refers to Dutch art, for which he had a strong dislike; he preferred the art of Italy. 114. **Assisi,** a district in central Italy. **Cadore,** a town in northern Italy. 115.

joy in the exertion, like that which an eagle seems to take in the wave of his wings, and this all life long, and through long life, not only without failure of power, but with visible increase of it, until the actually organic changes of old age. And then consider, so far as you know anything of physiology, what sort of an ethical state of body and mind that means!—ethic through ages past! what fineness of race there must be to get it, what exquisite balance and symmetry of the vital powers! And then, finally, determine for yourselves whether a manhood like that is consistent with any viciousness of soul, with any mean anxiety, any gnawing lust, any wretchedness of spite or remorse, any consciousness of rebellion against law of God or man, or any actual, though unconscious violation of even the least law to which obedience is essential for the glory of life, and the pleasing of its Giver.

It is, of course, true that many of the strong masters had deep faults of character, but their faults always show in their work. It is true that some could not govern their passions; if so, they died young, or they painted ill when old. But the greater part of our misapprehension in the whole matter is from our not having well known who the great painters were, and taking delight in the petty skill that was bred in the fumes of the taverns of the North, instead of theirs who breathed empyreal air, sons of the morning, under the woods of Assisi and the crags of Cadore.

It is true, however, also, as I have pointed out long ago, that the strong masters fall into two great divisions, one leading simple and natural lives, the other restrained in a Puritanism of the worship of beauty; and these two manners of life you may recognize in a moment by their work. Generally the naturalists are the strongest; but there are two of the Puritans, whose work if I can succeed in making clearly understandable to you during my three years here, it is all I need care to do. But of these two Puritans one I cannot name to you, and the other I at present will not. One I cannot, for no one knows his name, except the baptismal one, Bernard, or "dear little Bernard"—Bernardino, called from his birthplace (Luino, on the Lago Magiore), Bernard of Luino. The other is a Venetian, of whom many of you probably have never heard, and of whom, through me, you shall not hear, until I have tried to get some picture by him over to England. . . .

Finally, you must remember that great obscurity has been brought upon the truth in this matter by the want of integrity and simplicity in our modern life. I mean integrity in the Latin sense, wholeness. Everything is broken up, and mingled in confusion, both in our habits and thoughts; besides being in great part imitative:

so that you not only cannot tell what a man is, but sometimes you cannot tell whether he *is* at all!—whether you have indeed to do with a spirit, or only with an echo. And thus the same inconsistencies appear now, between the work of artists of merit and their personal characters, as those which you find continually disappointing expectation in the lives of men of modern literary power;—the same conditions of society having obscured or misdirected the best qualities of the imagination, both in our literature and art. Thus there is no serious question with any of us as to the personal character of Dante and Giotto, of Shakespeare and Holbein; but we pause timidly in the attempt to analyze the moral laws of the art skill in recent poets, novelists, and painters.

Let me assure you once for all, that as you grow older, if you enable yourselves to distinguish by the truth of your own lives, what is true in those of other men, you will gradually perceive that all good has its origin in good, never in evil; that the fact of either literature or painting being truly fine of their kind, whatever their mistaken aim, or partial error, is proof of their noble origin: and that, if there is indeed sterling value in the thing done, it has come of a sterling worth in the soul that did it, however alloyed or defiled by conditions of sin which are sometimes more appalling or more strange than those which all may detect in their own hearts, because they are part of a personality altogether larger than ours, and as far beyond our judgment in its darkness as beyond our following in its light. And it is sufficient warning against what some might dread as the probable effect of such a conviction on your own minds, namely, that you might permit yourselves in the weakness which you imagined to be allied to genius, when they took the form of personal temptations;—it is surely, I say, sufficient warning against so mean a folly, to discern, as you may with little pains, that, of all human existences, the lives of men of that distorted and tainted nobility of intellect are probably the most miserable.

I pass to the second, and for us the more practically important question, What is the effect of noble art upon other men; what has it done for national morality in time past: and what effect is the extended knowledge or possession of it likely to have upon us now? And here we are at once met by the facts, which are as gloomy as indisputable, that while many peasant populations, among whom scarcely the rudest practice of art has ever been attempted, have lived in comparative innocence, honor, and happiness, the worst foulness and cruelty of savage tribes have been frequently associated with fine ingenuities of decorative design; also, that no people has ever attained the higher

pointed out. In *The Stones of Venice*, II, 10 (1853). 123. **three years here,** at Oxford University; see headnote. 128. **Bernardino,** a noted Italian painter of the sixteenth century; a pupil of Leonardo da Vinci. 130. **The other,** Vittorio Carpaccio (1450?–1522?). The National Gallery, London, purchased one of his pictures in 1865 for £3400. 151. **Giotto,** a celebrated Florentine painter (1266?–1337?), sculptor, and architect. When asked by a messenger of the Pope for a specimen of his work, Giotto sent a perfect circle drawn freehand. 152. **Holbein,** Hans Holbein (c. 1460–1524), an eminent German painter.

stages of art skill, except at a period of its civilization which was sullied by frequent, violent, and even monstrous crime; and, lastly, that the attaining of perfection in art power, has been hitherto, in every nation, the accurate signal of the beginning of its ruin.

Respecting which phenomena, observe first, that although good never springs out of evil, it is developed to its highest by contention with evil. There are some groups of peasantry, in far-away nooks of Christian countries, who are nearly as innocent as lambs; but the morality which gives power to art is the morality of men, not of cattle.

Secondly, the virtues of the inhabitants of many country districts are apparent, not real; their lives are indeed artless, but not innocent; and it is only the monotony of circumstances, and the absence of temptation, which prevent the exhibition of evil passions not less real because often dormant, nor less foul because shown only in petty faults, or inactive malignities.

But you will observe also that *absolute* artlessness, to men in any kind of moral health, is impossible; they have always, at least, the art by which they live— agriculture or seamanship; and in these industries, skilfully practiced, you will find the law of their moral training; while, whatever the adversity of circumstances, every rightly-minded peasantry, such as that of Sweden, Denmark, Bavaria, or Switzerland, has associated with its needful industry a quite studied school of pleasurable art in dress; and generally also in song, and simple domestic architecture.

Again, I need not repeat to you here what I endeavored to explain in the first lecture in the book I called *The Two Paths*, respecting the arts of savage races: but I may now note briefly that such arts are the result of an intellectual activity which has found no room to expand, and which the tyranny of nature or of man has condemned to disease through arrested growth. And where neither Christianity, nor any other religion conveying some moral help, has reached, the animal energy of such races necessarily flames into ghastly conditions of evil, and the grotesque or frightful forms assumed by their art are precisely indicative of their distorted moral nature.

But the truly great nations nearly always begin from a race possessing this imaginative power; and for some time their progress is very slow, and their state not one of innocence, but of feverish and faultful animal energy. This is gradually subdued and exalted into bright human life; the art instinct purifying itself with the rest of the nature, until social perfectness is nearly reached; and then comes the period when conscience and intellect are so highly developed, that new forms of error begin in the inability to fulfill the demands of the one, or to answer the doubts of the other. Then the

wholeness of the people is lost; all kinds of hypocrisies and oppositions of science develop themselves; their faith is questioned on one side, and compromised with on the other; wealth commonly increases at the same period to a destructive extent; luxury follows; and the ruin of the nation is then certain: while the arts, all this time, are simply, as I said at first, the exponents of each phase of its moral state, and no more control it in its political career than the gleam of the firefly guides its oscillation. It is true that their most splendid results are usually obtained in the swiftness of the power which is hurrying to the precipice; but to lay the charge of the catastrophe to the art by which it is illumined is to find a cause for the cataract in the hues of its iris. It is true that the colossal vices belonging to periods of great national wealth (for wealth, you will find, is the real root of all evil) can turn every good gift and skill of nature or of man to evil purpose. If, in such times, fair pictures have been misused, how much more fair realities? And if Miranda is immoral to Caliban, is that Miranda's fault? . . .
(1870)

THOMAS HENRY HUXLEY 1825-1895

The best portrait of Huxley, which presents him at a lecture table with a human skull in his hand, suggests at once his life interest. He was a brilliant biologist and a skillful and an eager teacher. His life was devoted to the acquiring of biological and other scientific truth and to its earnest dissemination in language which the layman could understand.

Huxley was the seventh child of George Huxley, master of a school at Ealing, a suburb of London. In due time he became a medical student at the Charing Cross Hospital and took his degree there in 1845. The following year he was given an appointment as assistant surgeon on H.M.S. Rattlesnake, and for four years he traveled the seven seas, acquiring immense quantities of information and sending scientific articles by the dozen to technical journals in England, without learning until his return whether or not any had been accepted. But his reputation had already begun to grow from the fact that many of them were. In 1854 he was appointed Lecturer on Natural History at the School of Science and Naturalist to the Geographical Survey. This double appointment enabled him to settle down in London to a life of intense scientific and educational activity.

It was Huxley's aim, as he himself put it, "to smite all humbugs, however great; to set an example of abstinence from petty personal controversies, and

34. **The Two Paths,** two lectures delivered in 1858–1859 and published in 1859. 70. **iris,** rainbow effect produced by spray from the cataract or waterfall. 72. **wealth . . . evil.** Cf. 1 Timothy 6:10: "For the love of money is the root of all evil." 76. **Miranda,** the daughter of Prospero in Shakespeare's *Tempest.* **Caliban,** a brutal and degraded slave of Prospero.

of toleration for everything but lying, to be indifferent as to whether the work is recognized as mine or not, so long as it is done." His most prolonged and vigorous battle was his defense of Darwin's theory of evolution against the attacks of men with "clerical" minds like Richard Owen (1804-1892) and Bishop Wilberforce (1805-1873). Huxley, a much better anatomist than Darwin, was better able to demonstrate the soundness of the theory of evolution by making those keen studies in comparative anatomy for which he became famous. He was, moreover, a true popularizer of science as well as an industrious professional scholar. He has asserted modestly that he was not a natural writer or public speaker, and that he had to discipline himself severely in the art of composition. However true this may have been, it is clear that he was for years one of the most brilliant of popular expositors of scientific facts and theories, a great missionary of science.

Huxley's sense of anatomical structure seems to have stood him in good stead in the organization of his lectures and essays, for whatever he said or wrote was not only clear but luminous. Moreover, he always made courteous allowances for audiences not trained in scientific methods. He was, in brief, one of the most skillful and industrious of the Victorian group who had faith in their own times and who were eager to see England advance in the path which seemed to them to be the way of truth and light.

The books by which Huxley is best known are Man's Place in Nature (1863), The Physical Basis of Life (1868), Lay Sermons (1870), Science and Morals (1886), Essays upon Some Controverted Questions (1892), Evolution and Ethics (1893). Scattered articles in contemporary magazines include those which grew out of a fascinating controversy between "Darwin's Bulldog"—as Huxley was often nicknamed—and the staunch old statesman Gladstone on the matter of the Gadarene swine (cf. Mark, Chapter 5), a discussion that seems strangely like the tilts between William Jennings Bryan and the men of science many decades later in America.

ON THE ADVISABLENESS OF IMPROVING NATURAL KNOWLEDGE

This essay was delivered as an address in St. Martin's Hall, London, on January 7, 1866. It is one of the numerous contributions which Huxley, as scientist-educator, made to the cause of popular education, especially in the biological sciences.

This time two hundred years ago—in the beginning of January, 1666—those of our forefathers who inhabited this great and ancient city, took breath between the shocks of two fearful calamities, one not quite past, although its fury had abated; the other to come.

Within a few yards of the very spot on which we are assembled, so the tradition runs, that painful and deadly malady, the plague, appeared in the latter months of 1664; and, though no new visitor, smote the people of England, and especially of her capital, with a violence unknown before, in the course of the following year. The hand of a master has pictured what happened in those dismal months; and in that truest of fictions, The History of the Plague Year, Defoe shows death, with every accompaniment of pain and terror, stalking through the narrow streets of old London, and changing their busy hum into a silence broken only by the wailing of the mourners of fifty thousand dead; by the woeful denunciations and mad prayers of fanatics; and by the madder yells of despairing profligates.

But, about this time in 1666, the death rate had sunk to nearly its ordinary amount; a case of plague occurred only here and there, and the richer citizens who had flown from the pest had returned to their dwellings. The remnant of the people began to toil at the accustomed round of duty, or of pleasure; and the stream of city life bid fair to flow back along its old bed, with renewed and uninterrupted vigor.

The newly kindled hope was deceitful. The great plague, indeed, returned no more; but what it had done for the Londoners, the great fire, which broke out in the autumn of 1666, did for London; and, in September of that year, a heap of ashes and the indestructible energy of the people were all that remained of the glory of five-sixths of the city within the walls.

Our forefathers had their own ways of accounting for each of these calamities. They submitted to the plague in humility and in penitence, for they believed it to be the judgment of God. But towards the fire they were furiously indignant, interpreting it as the effect of the malice of man—as the work of the Republicans, or of the Papists, according as their prepossessions ran in favor of loyalty or of Puritanism.

It would, I fancy, have fared but ill with one who, standing where I now stand, in what was then a thickly-peopled and fashionable part of London, should have broached to our ancestors the doctrine which I now propound to you—that all their hypotheses were alike wrong; that the plague was no more, in their sense, a Divine judgment, than the fire was the work of any political, or of any religious, sect; but that they were themselves the authors of both plague and fire, and that they must look to themselves to pre-

On the Advisableness . . . Knowledge. 81. calamities, the London plague and the London fire. See Pepys' Diary (p. 446). 121. the Republicans, the supporters of Cromwell's party and the republican form of government as opposed to the monarchical.

vent the recurrence of calamities, to all appearance so peculiarly beyond the reach of human control— so evidently the result of the wrath of God, or of the craft and subtlety of an enemy.

And one may picture to oneself how harmoniously the holy cursing of the Puritan of that day would have chimed in with the unholy cursing and the crackling wit of the Rochesters and Sedleys, and with the revilings of the political fanatics, if my imagi-nary plain dealer had gone on to say that, if the return of such misfortunes were ever rendered impos-sible, it would not be in virtue of the victory of the faith of Laud, or of that of Milton; and, as little, by the triumph of republicanism, as by that of mon-archy. But that the one thing needful for compassing this end was that the people of England should second the efforts of an insignificant corporation, the establishment of which, a few years before the epoch of the great plague and the great fire, had been as little noticed, as they were conspicuous.

Some twenty years before the outbreak of the plague a few calm and thoughtful students banded themselves together for the purpose, as they phrased it, of "improving natural knowledge." The ends they proposed to attain cannot be stated more clearly than in the words of one of the founders of the organiza-tion:

"Our business was (precluding matters of theology and state affairs) to discourse and consider of philo-sophical inquiries, and such as related thereunto: as Physick, Anatomy, Geometry, Astronomy, Navigation, Staticks, Magneticks, Chymicks, Mechanicks, and Natural Experiments; with the state of these studies and their cultivation at home and abroad. We then discoursed of the circulation of the blood, the valves in the veins, the venae lacteae, the lymphatic vessels, the Copernican hypothesis, the nature of comets and new stars, the satellites of Jupiter, the oval shape (as it then appeared) of Saturn, the spots on the sun and its turning on its own axis, the inequalities and selenog-raphy of the moon, the several phases of Venus and Mercury, the improvement of telescopes and grinding of glasses for that purpose, the weight of air, the possibility or impossibility of vacuities and nature's abhorrence thereof, the Torricellian experiment in quicksilver, the descent of heavy bodies and the degree of acceleration therein, with divers other things of like nature, some of which were then but new dis-coveries, and others not so generally known and embraced as now they are; with other things apper-taining to what hath been called the New Philosophy, which from the times of Galileo at Florence, and Sir Francis Bacon (Lord Verulam) in England, hath been much cultivated in Italy, France, Germany, and other parts abroad, as well as with us in England."

The learned Dr. Wallis, writing in 1696, narrates in these words, what happened half a century before, or about 1645. The associates met at Oxford, in the rooms of Dr. Wilkins, who was destined to become a bishop; and subsequently coming together in London, they attracted the notice of the king. And it is a strange evi-dence of the taste for knowledge which the most obviously worthless of the Stuarts shared with his father and grandfather, that Charles the Second was not content with saying witty things about his philosophers, but did wise things with regard to them. For he not only bestowed upon them such attention as he could spare from his poodles and his mistresses, but, being in his usual state of impecuniosity, begged for them of the Duke of Ormond; and, that step being without effect, gave them Chelsea College, a charter, and a mace: crowning his favors in the best way they could be crowned, by burdening them no further with royal patronage or state interference.

Thus it was that the half-dozen young men, studious of the "New Philosophy," who met in one another's lodgings in Oxford or in London, in the middle of the seventeenth century, grew in numerical and in real strength, until, in its latter part, the "Royal Society for the Improvement of Natural Knowledge" had already become famous, and had acquired a claim upon the veneration of Englishmen, which it has ever since retained, as the principal focus of scientific activity in our islands, and the chief champion of the cause it was formed to support.

It was by the aid of the Royal Society that Newton published his *Principia*. If all the books in the world, except the *Philosophical Transactions*, were destroyed, it is safe to say that the foundations of physical science would remain unshaken, and that the vast intellectual progress of the last two centuries would be largely, though incompletely, recorded. Nor have any signs of halting or of decrepitude manifested themselves in our own times. As in Dr. Wallis's days, so in these, "our business is, precluding theology and state affairs, to dis-course and consider of philosophical inquiries." But our

8. **Rochesters and Sedleys.** John Wilmot (1647–1680), Earl of Roches-ter, and Sir Charles Sedley (1639?–1701) were friends of Charles II. They were court dramatists and poets noted for their sharp wit and dis-solute living. 13. **Laud,** William Laud (1573–1645), Archbishop of Canterbury, a violent opponent of Puritanism; he was executed by order of Parliament. 17. **corporation,** the Royal Society for the Improvement of Natural Knowledge; it was chartered by Charles II in 1662. 32. **Sta-ticks,** that branch of mechanics which deals with the condition of rest or the equilibrium of forces. **Chymicks,** chemistry. 36. **venae lacteae,** lacteal veins. 37. **Copernican hypothesis,** that established by Coper-nicus (1473–1543), a Polish astronomer—that the earth rotates daily on its axis, and that the planets revolve in orbits around the sun. 40. **selenography,** the science of the physical features of the moon. 45. **Torricellian experiment.** In 1643 Torricelli, an Italian physicist, had discovered the principle of the barometer. 51. **New Philosophy,** the ideas on science and philosophy set forth in the writings of Francis Bacon (p. 317). 52. **Galileo,** a noted Italian astronomer and physicist (1564–1642). His best-known work was the construction of a telescope and a thermometer; he made important discoveries regarding the pendu-lum, the satellites of Jupiter, the motion of the moon, and the law of gravitation. 56. **Dr. Wallis,** John Wallis (1616–1703), Professor of Mathematics at Oxford. 59. **Dr. Wilkins,** John Wilkins (1614–1672), Warden of Wadham College and Bishop of Chester. 61. **the king,** Charles II, who ruled from 1660 to 1685. 64. **father and grandfather,** Charles I and James I. 70. **Duke of Ormond,** James Butler (1610–1688), an influential Irish statesman and soldier, who was very active in support of Charles II. After the Restoration in 1660, Ormond re-gained his enormous estates in Ireland (lost during the war), received

"Mathematick" is one which Newton would have to go to school to learn; our "Staticks, Mechanicks, Magneticks, Chymicks, and Natural Experiments" constitute a mass of physical and chemical knowledge, a glimpse at which would compensate Galileo for the doings of a score of inquisitorial cardinals; our "Physick" and "Anatomy" have embraced such infinite varieties of being, have laid open such new worlds in time and space, have grappled, not unsuccessfully, with such complex problems, that the eyes of Vesalius and of Harvey might be dazzled by the sight of the tree that has grown out of their grain of mustard seed.

The fact is perhaps rather too much, than too little, forced upon one's notice, nowadays, that all this marvelous intellectual growth has a no less wonderful expression in practical life; and that, in this respect, if in no other, the movement symbolized by the progress of the Royal Society stands without a parallel in the history of mankind.

A series of volumes as bulky as the *Transactions* of the Royal Society might possibly be filled with the subtle speculations of the schoolmen; not improbably, the obtaining a mastery over the products of medieval thought might necessitate an even greater expenditure of time and of energy than the acquirement of the "New Philosophy"; but though such work engrossed the best intellects of Europe for a longer time than has elapsed since the great fire, its effects were "writ in water," so far as our social state is concerned.

On the other hand, if the noble first President of the Royal Society could revisit the upper air and once more gladden his eyes with a sight of the familiar mace, he would find himself in the midst of a material civilization more different from that of his day than that of the seventeenth was from that of the first century. And if Lord Brouncker's native sagacity had not deserted his ghost, he would need no long reflection to discover that all these ships, these railways, these telegraphs, these factories, these printing presses, without which the whole fabric of modern English society would collapse into a mass of stagnant and starving pauperism— that all these pillars of our State are but the ripples and the bubbles upon the surface of that great spiritual stream, the springs of which, only, he and his fellows were privileged to see; and seeing, to recognize as that which it behoved them above all things to keep pure and undefiled.

It may not be too great a flight of imagination to conceive our noble *revenant* not forgetful of the great troubles of his own day, and anxious to know how often London had been burned down since his time, and how often the plague had carried off its thousands. He would have to learn that, although London contains tenfold the inflammable matter that it did in 1666; though, not content with filling our rooms with woodwork and light draperies, we must needs lead inflammable and explosive gases into every corner of our streets and houses, we never allow even a street to burn down. And if he asked how this had come about, we should have to explain that the improvement of natural knowledge had furnished us with dozens of machines for throwing water upon fires, any one of which would have furnished the ingenious Mr. Hooke, the first "curator and experimenter" of the Royal Society, with ample materials for discourse before half a dozen meetings of that body; and that, to say truth, except for the progress of natural knowledge, we should not have been able to make even the tools by which these machines are constructed. And, further, it would be necessary to add that, although severe fires sometimes occur and inflict great damage, the loss is very generally compensated by societies, the operations of which have been rendered possible only by the progress of natural knowledge in the direction of mathematics, and the accumulation of wealth in virtue of other natural knowledge.

But the plague? My Lord Brouncker's observation would not, I fear, lead him to think that Englishmen of the nineteenth century are purer in life, or more fervent in religious faith, than the generation which could produce a Boyle, an Evelyn, and a Milton. He might find the mud of society at the bottom instead of at the top, but I fear that the sum total would be as deserving of swift judgment as at the time of the Restoration. And it would be our duty to explain once more, and this time not without shame, that we have no reason to believe that it is the improvement of our faith, nor that of our morals, which keeps the plague from our city; but, again, that it is the improvement of our natural knowledge.

We have learned that pestilences will only take up their abode among those who have prepared unswept and ungarnished residences for them. Their cities must have narrow, unwatered streets, foul with accumulated garbage. Their houses must be ill-drained, ill-

large grants of money from the King, and was made Lord High Steward of England. **71. Chelsea College,** Chelsea Royal Hospital, for invalid soldiers, initiated by Charles II but not opened until 1694. **a mace,** a staff carried as an emblem of authority. **86. Newton,** Sir Isaac Newton (1642–1727), a great mathematician and natural philosopher, who published his theory about gravitation in his *Principia* in 1687. **88.** *Philosophical Transactions,* one of the regular publications of the Royal Society. **102. inquisitorial cardinals.** Galileo was forced by the Inquisition in 1633 to renounce the Copernican theory of astronomy. **106. Vesalius,** Andreas Vesalius (1514–1564), a noted Belgian anatomist. **107. Harvey,** William Harvey (1578–1657), a celebrated English physician, who discovered the circulation of the blood. **tree . . . seed.** Cf. Luke 13:19: The kingdom of heaven "is like a grain of mustard seed, which a man took and cast into his garden; and

it grew, and waxed a great tree." **118. the schoolmen,** philosophers of the Middle Ages who engaged in fine-spun arguments. **124. "writ in water,"** a part of the inscription on the tomb of Keats in the Protestant Cemetery at Rome. **126. first President,** William Viscount Brouncker (1620?–1684). **145.** *revenant,* ghost. **159. Mr. Hooke,** Robert Hooke (1635–1703), an experimental philosopher. **168. societies,** insurance companies. **177. Boyle,** Robert Boyle, (1627–1691), an English chemist, the discoverer of the law of the elasticity of the air. He was noted for his piety. See headnote to Swift's *Meditation upon a Broomstick* p. 495. **Evelyn,** John Evelyn (1620–1706), a famous English diarist and a man of wide scientific interest. Like Boyle he was unusually pious.

lighted, ill-ventilated. Their subjects must be ill-washed, ill-fed, ill-clothed. The London of 1665 was such a city. The cities of the East, where plague has an enduring dwelling, are such cities. We, in later times, have learned somewhat of nature, and partly obey her. Because of this partial improvement of our natural knowledge and of that fractional obedience, we have no plague; because that knowledge is still very imperfect and that obedience yet incomplete, typhus is our companion and· cholera our visitor; but it is not presumptuous to express the belief that, when our knowledge is more complete and our obedience the expression of our knowledge, London will count her centuries of freedom from typhus and cholera, as she now gratefully reckons her two hundred years of ignorance of that plague, which swooped upon her thrice in the first half of the seventeenth century.

Surely, there is nothing in these explanations which is not fully borne out by the facts? Surely, the principles involved in them are now admitted among the fixed beliefs of all thinking men? Surely, it is true that our countrymen are less subject to fire, famine, pestilence, and all the evils which result from a want of command over and due anticipation of the course of nature, than were the countrymen of Milton; and health, wealth, and well-being are more abundant with us than with them? But no less certainly is the difference due to the improvement of our knowledge of nature, and the extent to which that improved knowledge has been incorporated with the household words of men, and has supplied the springs of their daily actions.

Granting for a moment, then, the truth of that which the depreciators of natural knowledge are so fond of urging, that its improvement can only add to the resources of our material civilization; admitting it to be possible that the founders of the Royal Society themselves looked for no other reward than this, I cannot confess that I was guilty of exaggeration when I hinted, that to him who had the gift of distinguishing between prominent events and important events, the origin of a combined effort on the part of mankind to improve natural knowledge might have loomed larger than the Plague and have outshone the glare of the Fire; as a something fraught with a wealth of beneficence to mankind, in comparison with which the damage done by those ghastly evils would shrink into insignificance.

It is very certain that for every victim slain by the plague, hundreds of mankind exist and find a fair share of happiness in the world by the aid of the spinning jenny. And the great fire, at its worst, could not have burned the supply of coal, the daily working

of which, in the bowels of the earth, made possible by the steam pump, gives rise to an amount of wealth to which the millions lost in old London are but as an old song.

But spinning jenny and steam pump are, after all, but toys, possessing an accidental value; and natural knowledge creates multitudes of more subtle contrivances, the praises of which do not happen to be sung because they are not directly convertible into instruments for creating wealth. When I contemplate natural knowledge squandering such gifts among men, the only appropriate comparison I can find for her is, to liken her to such a peasant woman as one sees in the Alps, striding ever upward, heavily burdened, and with mind bent only on her home; but yet, without effort and without thought, knitting for her children. Now stockings are good and comfortable things, and the children will undoubtedly be much the better for them; but surely it would be short-sighted, to say the least of it, to depreciate this toiling mother as a mere stocking-machine—a mere provider of physical comforts?

However, there are blind leaders of the blind, and not a few of them, who take this view of natural knowledge, and can see nothing in the bountiful mother of humanity but a sort of comfort-grinding machine. According to them, the improvement of natural knowledge always has been, and always must be, synonymous with no more than the improvement of the material resources and the increase of the gratifications of men.

Natural knowledge is, in their eyes, no real mother of mankind, bringing them up with kindness, and, if need be, with sternness in the way they should go, and instructing them in all things needful for their welfare; but a sort of fairy godmother, ready to furnish her pets with shoes of swiftness, swords of sharpness, and omnipotent Aladdin's lamps, so that they may have telegraphs to Saturn, and see the other side of the moon, and thank God they are better than their benighted ancestors.

If this talk were true, I, for one, should not greatly care to toil in the service of natural knowledge. I think I would just as soon be quietly chipping my own flint ax, after the manner of my forefathers a few thousand years back, as be troubled with the endless malady of thought which now infests us all, for such reward. But I venture to say that such views are contrary alike to reason and to fact. Those who discourse in such fashion seem to me to be so intent upon trying to see what is above nature, or what is behind her, that they are blind to what stares them in the face, in her.

I should not venture to speak thus strongly if my

53. **spinning jenny,** a machine for spinning wool and cotton by means of many spindles. 77. **blind . . . blind.** Cf. Matthew 15:14: "Let them alone: they be blind leaders of the blind. And if the blind lead the blind, both shall fall into the ditch." 87. **bringing . . . go.** Cf.

Proverbs 22:6: "Train up a child in the way he should go; and when he is old, he will not depart from it." 91. **shoes . . . sharpness,** magic objects of folklore. 92. **Aladdin,** a youth in the *Arabian Nights* who possessed a magic lamp and a ring that when rubbed brought genii

justification were not to be found in the simplest and most obvious facts—if it needed more than an appeal to the most notorious truths to justify my assertion, that the improvement of natural knowledge, whatever direction it has taken, and however low the aims of those who may have commenced it—has not only conferred practical benefits on men, but, in so doing, has effected a revolution in their conceptions of the universe and of themselves, and has profoundly altered their modes of thinking and their views of right and wrong. I say that natural knowledge, seeking to satisfy natural wants, has found the ideas which can alone still spiritual cravings. I say that natural knowledge, in desiring to ascertain the laws of comfort, has been driven to discover those of conduct, and to lay the foundations of a new morality.

Let us take these points separately; and, first, what great ideas has natural knowledge introduced into men's minds?

I cannot but think that the foundations of all natural knowledge were laid when the reason of man first came face to face with the facts of nature; when the savage first learned that the fingers of one hand are fewer than those of both; that it is shorter to cross a stream than to head it; that a stone stops where it is unless it be moved, and that it drops from the hand which lets it go; that light and heat come and go with the sun; that sticks burn away in a fire; that plants and animals grow and die; that if he struck his fellow savage a blow he would make him angry, and perhaps get a blow in return; while if he offered him a fruit he would please him, and perhaps receive a fish in exchange. When men had acquired this much knowledge, the outlines, rude though they were, of mathematics, of physics, of chemistry, of biology, of moral, economical, and political science, were sketched. Nor did the germ of religion fail when science began to bud. Listen to words which, though new, are yet three thousand years old:

. . . When in heaven the stars about the moon
Look beautiful, when all the winds are laid,
And every height comes out, and jutting peak
And valley, and the immeasurable heavens
Break open to their highest, and all the stars
Shine, and the shepherd gladdens in his heart.

But if the half-savage Greek could share our feelings thus far, it is irrational to doubt that he went further, to find, as we do, that upon that brief gladness there follows a certain sorrow—the little light of awakened human intelligence shines so mere a spark amidst the abyss of the unknown and unknowable; seems so insufficient to do more than illuminate the

imperfections that cannot be remedied, the aspirations that cannot be realized, of man's own nature. But in this sadness, this consciousness of the limitation of man, this sense of an open secret which he cannot penetrate, lies the essence of all religion; and the attempt to embody it in the forms furnished by the intellect is the origin of the higher theologies.

Thus it seems impossible to imagine but that the foundations of all knowledge—secular or sacred— were laid when intelligence dawned, though the superstructure remained for long ages so slight and feeble as to be compatible with the existence of almost any general view respecting the mode of governance of the universe. No doubt, from the first, there were certain phenomena which, to the rudest mind, presented a constancy of occurrence, and suggested that a fixed order ruled, among them at any rate. I doubt if the grossest of fetish worshipers ever imagined that a stone must have a god within it to make it fall, or that a fruit had a god within it to make it taste sweet. With regard to such matters as these, it is hardly questionable that mankind from the first took strictly positive and scientific views.

But, with respect to all the less familiar occurrences which present themselves, uncultured man, no doubt, has always taken himself as a standard of comparison, as the center and measure of the world; nor could he well avoid doing so. And finding that his apparently uncaused will has a powerful effect in giving rise to many occurrences, he naturally enough ascribed other and greater events to other and greater volitions, and came to look upon the world and all that therein is, as the product of the volitions of persons like himself, but stronger, and capable of being appeased or angered, as he himself might be soothed or irritated. Through such conceptions of the plan and working of the universe all mankind have passed, or are passing. And we may now consider what has been the effect of the improvement of natural knowledge on the views of men who have reached this stage, and who have begun to cultivate natural knowledge with no desire but that of "increasing God's honor and bettering man's estate."

For example: what could seem wiser, from a mere material point of view, more innocent from a theological one, to an ancient people, than that they should learn the exact succession of the seasons, as warnings for their husbandmen; or the position of the stars, as guides to their rude navigators? But what has grown out of this search for natural knowledge of so merely useful a character? You all know the reply. Astronomy —which of all sciences has filled men's minds with

<hr />

to do his bidding. **148. When in, etc.** "Need it be said that this is Tennyson's English for Homer's Greek?"—Huxley. The lines are from Tennyson's *Specimens of a Translation of the Iliad in Blank Verse* (*Iliad*, VIII, 555–559). **179. fetish worshipers,** worshipers of charms or objects of supposed magical power. **194. product . . . himself.** Cf. Browning's *Caliban upon Setebos*. **204. "increasing . . . estate,"** Bacon's statement of his purpose in writing *Of the Advancement of Learning*.

general ideas of a character most foreign to their daily experience, and has, more than any other, rendered it impossible for them to accept the beliefs of their fathers. Astronomy—which tells them that this so vast and seemingly solid earth is but an atom among atoms, whirling, no man knows whither, through illimitable space; which demonstrates that what we call the peaceful heaven above us, is but that space, filled by an infinitely subtle matter whose particles are seething
10 and surging, like the waves of an angry sea; which opens up to us infinite regions where nothing is known, or ever seems to have been known, but matter and force, operating according to rigid rules; which leads us to contemplate phenomena the very nature of which demonstrates that they must have had a beginning, and that they must have an end, but the very nature of which also proves that the beginning was, to our conceptions of time, infinitely remote, and that the end is as immeasurably distant.
20 But it is not alone those who pursue astronomy who ask for bread and receive ideas. What more harmless than the attempt to lift and distribute water by pumping it; what more absolutely and grossly utilitarian? But out of pumps grew the discussions about nature's abhorrence of a vacuum; and then it was discovered that nature does not abhor a vacuum, but that air has weight; and that notion paved the way for the doctrine that all matter has weight, and that the force which produces weight is co-extensive with the uni-
30 verse—in short, to the theory of universal gravitation and endless force. And learning how to handle gases led to the discovery of oxygen and to modern chemistry, and to the notion of the indestructibility of matter.

Again, what simpler, or more absolutely practical, than the attempt to keep the axle of a wheel from heating when the wheel turns round very fast? How useful for carters and gig drivers to know something about this; and how good were it, if any ingenious person would find out the cause of such phenomena, and
40 thence educe a general remedy for them. Such an ingenious person was Count Rumford; and he and his successors have landed us in the theory of the persistence or indestructibility of force. And in the infinitely minute, as in the infinitely great, the seekers after natural knowledge of the kinds called physical and chemical, have everywhere found a definite order and succession of events which seem never to be infringed.

And how has it fared with "Physick" and Anatomy?
50 Have the anatomist, the physiologist, or the physician, whose business it has been to devote themselves assiduously to that eminently practical and direct end, the alleviation of the sufferings of mankind—have they been able to confine their vision more absolutely to the strictly useful? I fear they are the worst offenders of

all. For if the astronomer has set before us the infinite magnitude of space, and the practical eternity of the duration of the universe; if the physical and chemical philosophers have demonstrated the infinite minuteness of its constituent parts, and the practical eternity of 60 matter and of force; and if both have alike proclaimed the universality of a definite and predicable order and succession of events, the workers in biology have not only accepted all these, but have added more startling theses of their own. For, as the astronomers discover in the earth no center of the universe, but an eccentric speck, so the naturalists find man to be no center of the living world, but one amidst endless modifications of life; and as the astronomer observes the mark of practically endless time set upon the arrangements of 70 the solar system, so the student of life finds the records of ancient forms of existence peopling the world for ages which, in relation to human experience, are infinite.

Furthermore, the physiologist finds life to be as dependent for its manifestation on particular molecular arrangements as any physical or chemical phenomenon; and, wherever he extends his researches, fixed order and unchanging causation reveal themselves, as plainly as in the rest of nature. 80

Nor can I find that any other fate has awaited the germ of Religion. Arising, like all other kinds of knowledge, out of the action and interaction of man's mind, with that which is not man's mind, it has taken the intellectual coverings of Fetishism or Polytheism; of Theism or Atheism; of Superstition or Rationalism. With these, and their relative merits and demerits, I have nothing to do; but this it is needful for my purpose to say, that if the religion of the present differs from that of the past, it is because the theology of the present has 90 become more scientific than that of the past; because it has not only renounced idols of wood and idols of stone, but begins to see the necessity of breaking in pieces the idols built up of books and traditions and fine-spun ecclesiastical cobwebs: and of cherishing the noblest and most human of man's emotions, by worship "for the most part of the silent sort" at the altar of the Unknown and Unknowable.

Such are a few of the new conceptions implanted in our minds by the improvement of natural knowledge. 100 Men have acquired the ideas of the practically infinite extent of the universe and of its practical eternity; they are familiar with the conception that our earth is but an infinitesimal fragment of that part of the universe which can be seen; and that, nevertheless, its duration is, as compared with our standards of time, infinite. They have further acquired the idea that man is but one of innumerable forms of life now existing on the globe, and that the present existences are but the last of an immeasurable series of predecessors. Furthermore, 110

21. **ask . . . ideas.** Cf. Matthew 7:9: "Or what man is there of you, whom if his son ask bread, will he give him a stone?" 41. **Count Rumford,** Benjamin Thompson (1753–1814), a scientist and

an inventor, American by birth. 66. **eccentric,** not located at the center. 97. **"for . . . sort,"** from Carlyle. **altar . . . Unknown.** Cf. Acts 17:23: "I found an altar with this inscription, TO THE

every step they have made in natural knowledge has tended to extend and rivet in their minds the conception of a definite order of the universe—which is embodied in what are called, by an unhappy metaphor, the laws of nature—and to narrow the range and loosen the force of men's belief in spontaneity, or in changes other than such as arise out of that definite order itself.

Whether these ideas are well or ill founded is not the question. No one can deny that they exist, and have 120 been the inevitable outgrowth of the improvement of natural knowledge. And if so, it cannot be doubted that they are changing the form of men's most cherished and most important convictions.

And as regards the second point—the extent to which the improvement of natural knowledge has remodeled and altered what may be termed the intellectual ethics of men—what are among the moral convictions most fondly held by barbarous and semibarbarous people?

130 They are the convictions that authority is the soundest basis of belief; that merit attaches to a readiness to believe; that the doubting disposition is a bad one, and skepticism a sin; that when good authority has pronounced what is to be believed, and faith has accepted it, reason has no further duty. There are many excellent persons who yet hold by these principles, and it is not my present business, or intention, to discuss their views. All I wish to bring clearly before your minds is the unquestionable fact that the improvement 140 of natural knowledge is affected by methods which directly give the lie to all these convictions, and assume the exact reverse of each to be true.

The improver of natural knowledge absolutely refuses to acknowledge authority, as such. For him, skepticism is the highest of duties; blind faith the one unpardonable sin. And it cannot be otherwise, for every great advance in natural knowledge has involved the absolute rejection of authority, the cherishing of the keenest skepticism, the annihilation of the spirit of blind 150 faith; and the most ardent votary of science holds his firmest convictions, not because the men he most venerates hold them; not because their verity is testified by portents and wonders; but because his experience teaches him that whenever he chooses to bring these convictions into contact with their primary source, nature—whenever he thinks fit to test them by appealing to experiment and to observation—nature will confirm them. The man of science has learned to believe in justification, not by faith, but by verification.

160 Thus, without for a moment pretending to despise the practical results of the improvement of natural knowledge, and its beneficial influence on material civilization, it must, I think, be admitted that the great ideas, some of which I have indicated, and the ethical spirit which I have endeavored to sketch, in the few moments

which remained at my disposal, constitute the real and permanent significance of natural knowledge.

If these ideas be destined, as I believe they are, to be more and more firmly established as the world grows older; if that spirit be fated, as I believe it is, to extend 170 itself into all departments of human thought, and to become co-extensive with the range of knowledge; if, as our race approaches its maturity, it discovers, as I believe it will, that there is but one kind of knowledge and but one method of acquiring it; then we, who are still children, may justly feel it our highest duty to recognize the advisableness of improving natural knowledge, and so to aid ourselves and our successors in our course towards the noble goal which lies before mankind.

(1866; 1870)

WALTER HORATIO PATER 1839-1894

Macaulay, Arnold, Ruskin, Huxley, and Morris were active participants in the social, intellectual, and artistic life of Victorian England. Walter Horatio Pater, on the other hand, lived the life of an esthetic recluse who looked at existence shyly through the windows of his palace of art and did not desire closer contact. Pater was the second son of a physician in the East End of London. He was born in the suburb of Shadwell, but on the early death of his father, his family moved to Chase Side, Enfield—another suburb. He attended Queen's College, Oxford, and in 1862 became a private tutor in the university community; in 1868 he was made a Fellow of Brasenose College, Oxford. He remained in Oxford until 1885; he then moved, with his sisters (who had been keeping house for him) to London, retaining, however, rooms in the university city that was always the center of his intellectual life. He returned to Oxford to finish his last work there.

Pater's self-absorption and extreme fastidiousness resulted in his being very slow to complete any writing; he was almost a Thomas Gray in prose. Nothing came from his pen until he was twenty-eight; then, in 1867, the Westminster Review published his essay on the German art critic and historian Winckelmann (1717-1768). Studies in the History of the Renaissance appeared in 1873; then followed an interval of twelve years before the publication of Marius the Epicurean, a philosophical romance of a young Roman drawn against the background of the early Roman Empire. In 1887 was printed his Imaginary Portraits—four in number—and in 1889 the collection of critical essays called Appreciations, studies of Shakespeare, Wordsworth, and others. The Child in the House (1894) is an exquisite and imaginative treatment of the sensitive boy who was Walter

UNKNOWN GOD. Whom therefore ye ignorantly worship, him declare I unto you." 159. **justification.** Cf. Romans 3:28: "Therefore we conclude that a man is justified by faith without the deeds of the law."

Pater himself. Greek Studies and Gaston de Latour—left unfinished—were published after his death in 1894.

Pater's philosophy of life led him to believe that the highest wisdom lay in extracting from literature and art a quickened sense of life, an ecstasy of beauty. This concept was undeniably hedonistic, or pleasure-seeking, but the hedonism was of a refined, noble type. His philosophy was, in short, Epicurean, but the term Epicurean was popularly understood to be the philosophy of physical self-indulgence only, and many read Pater's essays with the condescension and disapproval that accompany any suspicion of soft decadence. Pater's literary style undoubtedly increased the popular misconception of his philosophy of life and art. There was about his writing a luminous, phosphorescent beauty that annoyed the Philistines greatly. His writing was subjective and highly artificial and suggested, therefore, an unnaturalness that it did not actually possess, for it was undeniably the expression of the author's highly esthetic personality. Nevertheless, Pater's essays remain "caviar to the general" and are likely to stand as literature for the lovers of artistic finish rather than as reading for the multitude.

Pater's criticism has its roots in his philosophy of life. He began his intellectual career with philosophy, and Plato and Goethe were probably the greatest literary influences in his life. But from philosophy his interest narrowed down to esthetics, to a study of the principles of beauty in art and literature. Thus he became, in a sense, a connoisseur of beauty, and a high priest of art. His criticisms took the form of discovering the best in literature and art and of revealing these master strokes in appreciations of the craftsmen. His vision was thus upward; he praised the best rather than condemned the worst. And incidentally this continued contemplation of the best gave him a soundness and quickness of judgment that made possible such discriminating definitions as the lucid distinction between the classical and the romantic, where, without prejudice, he penetrates to the core of both moods and makes clear the beauty of each. To Pater the realms of art and literature probably owe more than they have yet been ready to acknowledge.

from LEONARDO DA VINCI

The best of several descriptions of Leonardo da Vinci's masterpiece, the famous Mona Lisa, is that of Walter Pater; it appeared in the essay on Leonardo da Vinci which forms one of his Studies in the History of the Renaissance (1873). The romantic, subtle, and enigmatic qualities of this portrait inspired in Pater the mood of the painting. Leonardo da Vinci—Italian painter, architect, musician, scientist, engineer—painted the portrait between 1503 and 1506 in Florence. His subject was the beautiful Mona (or Madonna) Lisa, "the young third wife of Francesco del Giocondo," a Florentine nobleman. La Gioconda's rapt expression, Leonardo explained, came from the effect of soft music which was played while he painted her. The king of France, François I, bought the portrait not long after it was finished, and took it to Paris, where it ultimately became one of the glories of the Louvre.

LA GIOCONDA

La Gioconda is, in the truest sense, Leonardo's masterpiece, the revealing instance of his mode of thought and work. In suggestiveness, only the Melancholia of Dürer is comparable to it; and no crude symbolism disturbs the effect of its subdued and graceful mystery. We all know the face and hands of the figure, set in its marble chair, in that circle of fantastic rocks, as in some faint light under sea. Perhaps of all ancient pictures time has chilled it least. As often happens with works in which invention seems to 10 reach its limit, there is an element in it given to, not invented by, the master. In that inestimable folio of drawings, once in the possession of Vasari, were certain designs by Verrocchio, faces of such impressive beauty that Leonardo in his boyhood copied them many times. It is hard not to connect with these designs of the elder, by-past master, as with its germinal principle, the unfathomable smile, always with a touch of something sinister in it, which plays over all Leonardo's work. Besides, the picture is a 20 portrait. From childhood we see this image defining itself on the fabric of his dreams, and but for express historical testimony, we might fancy that this was but his ideal lady, embodied and beheld at last. What was the relationship of a living Florentine to this creature of his thought? By what strange affinities had the dream and the person grown up thus apart, and yet so closely together? Present from the first incorporeally in Leonardo's brain, dimly traced in the designs of Verrocchio, she is found present at 30 last in Il Gioconda's house. That there is much of mere portraiture in the picture is attested by the legend that by artificial means, the presence of mimes and flute-players, that subtle expression was pro-

Leonardo da Vinci. 4. Dürer, Albrecht Dürer (1471–1528), the greatest artist of the Renaissance in Germany; he was a painter, an engraver, a sculptor, and an architect. His Melancholia is an intricate copperplate engraving. 7. circle, a kind of natural amphitheater. 13. Vasari, Giorgio Vasari (1511–1574), an Italian architect, painter, and writer on art. 14. Verrocchio, Andrea Verrocchio (1435–1488), another Italian Renaissance sculptor and painter. 33. mimes, jesters, clowns. 42. "the ends . . . come," quoted from 1 Corinthians 10:11. 53. animalism, the doctrine that men are animals; the worship of physical form. 56. the return . . . world. Near the end of the Middle Ages, Christianity lost much of its influence over the lives of the people. Borgias, a fifteenth-century family in Italy notorious for its violence, treachery, vices, and crimes. Leonardo served them in numerous ways. 58. vampire, in folklore, the reanimated body of a dead person,

tracted on the face. Again, was it in four years and by renewed labor never really completed, or in four months and as by stroke of magic, that the image was projected?

The presence that rose so strangely beside the waters, is expressive of what in the ways of a thousand years men had come to desire. Hers is the head upon which all "the ends of the world are come," and the eyelids are a little weary. It is a beauty wrought out from within upon the flesh, the deposit, little cell by cell, of strange thoughts and fantastic reveries and exquisite passions. Set it for a moment beside one of those white Greek goddesses or beautiful women of antiquity, and how would they be troubled by this beauty, into which the soul with all its maladies has passed! All the thoughts and experience of the world have etched and molded there, in that which they have of power to refine and make expressive the outward form, the animalism of Greece, the lust of Rome, the mysticism of the middle age with its spiritual ambition and imaginative loves, the return of the Pagan world, the sins of the Borgias. She is older than the rocks among which she sits; like the vampire, she has been dead many times, and learned the secrets of the grave; and has been a diver in deep seas, and keeps their fallen day about her; and trafficked for strange webs with Eastern merchants, and, as Leda, was the mother of Helen of Troy, and, as Saint Anne, the mother of Mary; and all this has been to her but as the sound of lyres and flutes, and lives only in the delicacy with which it has molded the changing lineaments, and tinged the eyelids and the hands. The fancy of a perpetual life, sweeping together ten thousand experiences, is an old one; and modern philosophy has conceived the idea of humanity as wrought upon by, and summing up in itself, all modes of thought and life. Certainly Lady Lisa might stand as the embodiment of the old fancy, the symbol of the modern idea.

(1873)

from STUDIES IN THE HISTORY OF THE RENAISSANCE

This chapter from Pater's Studies in the History of the Renaissance, which expresses so much of his theory of life and art, was printed in the first edition of 1873, omitted from the second edition of 1877, and finally restored in 1888 with the following explanation by Pater: "This brief 'Conclusion' was omitted in the

second edition of this book, as I conceived it might possibly mislead some of those young men into whose hands it might fall. On the whole, I have thought best to reprint it here, with some slight changes which bring it closer to my original meaning. I have dealt more fully in Marius the Epicurean *with the thoughts suggested by it."*

CONCLUSION

Λέγει που Ἡράκλειτος ὅτι πάντα Χωρει καὶ οὐδὲν μένει.

To regard all things and principles of things as inconstant modes or fashions has more and more become the tendency of modern thought. Let us begin with that which is without—our physical life. Fix upon it in one of its more exquisite intervals—the moment, for instance, of delicious recoil from the flood of water in summer heat. What is the whole physical life in that moment but a combination of natural elements to which science gives their names? But these elements, phosphorus and lime and delicate fibers, are present not in the human body alone: we detect them in places most remote from it. Our physical life is a perpetual motion of them—the passage of the blood, the wasting and repairing of the lenses of the eye, the modification of the tissues of the brain by every ray of light and sound—processes which science reduces to simpler and more elementary forces. Like the elements of which we are composed, the action of these forces extends beyond us; it rusts iron and ripens corn. Far out on every side of us those elements are broadcast, driven by many forces; and birth and gesture and death and the springing of violets from the grave are but a few out of ten thousand resultant combinations. That clear, perpetual outline of face and limb is but an image of ours, under which we group them—a design in a web, the actual threads of which pass out beyond it. This at least of flame-like our life has, that it is but the concurrence, renewed from moment to moment, of forces parting sooner or later on their ways.

Or if we begin with the inward whirl of thought and feeling, the whirlpool is still more rapid, the flame more eager and devouring. There it is no longer the gradual darkening of the eye and fading of color from the wall—the movement of the shoreside, where the water flows down indeed, though in apparent rest—but the race of the mid-stream, a drift of momentary acts of sight and passion and thought. At first sight experience seems to bury us under a flood of external objects, pressing upon us with a sharp and importunate

supposed to come from the grave and to wander about at night sucking the blood of persons asleep, thus causing their death and gaining a horrible immortality for itself. 60. **their fallen day,** the gloom that prevails at great depths in the sea. 62. **Leda,** in Greek mythology, the wife of the Spartan king Tyndareus and mistress of the god Zeus. Helen of Troy, daughter of Leda and Zeus, regarded as the most beautiful woman of her time, was faithless to her husband Menelaus. Thus, in

its relation to Leda and Helen and to St. Anne and Mary, the face of La Gioconda reveals elements of the beautiful, wanton wife and the saintly mother.

Studies in . . . Renaissance. Λέγει, etc., "Heraclitus says somewhere that everything flows and nothing remains"—Plato's *Cratylus.* 94. **corn,** grain of any kind. 96. **gesture,** behavior, bearing.

reality, calling us out of ourselves in a thousand forms of action. But when reflection begins to act upon those objects they are dissipated under its influence; the cohesive force seems suspended like a trick of magic; each object is loosed into a group of impressions—color, odor, texture—in the mind of the observer. And if we continue to dwell in thought on this world, not of objects in the solidity with which language invests them, but of impressions unstable, flickering, inconsistent, which burn and are extinguished with our consciousness of them, it contracts still further; the whole scope of observation is dwarfed to the narrow chamber of the individual mind. Experience, already reduced to a swarm of impressions, is ringed round for each one of us by that thick wall of personality through which no real voice has ever pierced on its way to us, or from us to that which we can only conjecture to be without. Every one of those impressions is the impression of the individual in his isolation, each mind keeping as a solitary prisoner its own dream of a world.

Analysis goes a step farther still, and assures us that those impressions of the individual mind to which, for each one of us, experience dwindles down, are in perpetual flight; that each of them is limited by time, and that as time is infinitely divisible, each of them is infinitely divisible also; all that is actual in it being a single moment, gone while we try to apprehend it, of which it may ever be more truly said that it has ceased to be than that it is. To such a tremulous wisp constantly reforming itself on the stream, to a single sharp impression, with a sense in it—a relic more or less fleeting—of such moments gone by, what is real in our life fines itself down. It is with this movement, with the passage and dissolution of impressions, images, sensations, that analysis leaves off—that continual vanishing away, that strange, perpetual weaving and unweaving of ourselves.

Philosophiren, says Novalis, *ist dephlegmatisiren, vivificiren.* The service of philosophy, of speculative culture, toward the human spirit is to rouse, to startle it into sharp and eager observation. Every moment some form grows perfect in hand or face; some tone on the hills or the sea is choicer than the rest; some mood of passion or insight or intellectual excitement is irresistibly real and attractive for us—but for that moment only. Not the fruit of experience, but experience itself, is the end. A counted number of pulses only is given to us of a variegated, dramatic life. How may we see in them all that is to be seen in them by the finest senses?

How shall we pass most swiftly from point to point, and be present always at the focus where the greatest number of vital forces unite in their purest energy?

To burn always with this hard, gemlike flame, to maintain this ecstasy, is success in life. In a sense it might even be said that our failure is to form habits: for, after all, habit is relative to a stereotyped world, and meantime it is only the roughness of the eye that makes any two persons, things, situations, seem alike. While all melts under our feet, we may well catch at any exquisite passion, or any contribution to knowledge that seems by a lifted horizon to set the spirit free for a moment, or any stirring of the senses, strange dyes, strange colors, and curious odors, or work of the artist's hands, or the face of one's friend. Not to discriminate every moment some passionate attitude in those about us, and in the brilliancy of their gifts some tragic dividing of forces on their ways, is, on this short day of frost and sun, to sleep before evening. With this sense of the splendor of our experience and of its awful brevity, gathering all we are into one desperate effort to see and touch, we shall hardly have time to make theories about the things we see and touch. What we have to do is to be forever curiously testing new opinions and courting new impressions, never acquiescing in a facile orthodoxy of Comte, or of Hegel, or of our own. Philosophical theories or ideas, as points of view, instruments of criticism, may help us to gather up what might otherwise pass unregarded by us. "Philosophy is the microscope of thought." The theory or idea or system which requires of us the sacrifice of any part of this experience, in consideration of some interest into which we cannot enter, or some abstract theory we have not identified with ourselves, or what is only conventional, has no real claim upon us.

One of the most beautiful passages in the writings of Rousseau is that in the sixth book of the *Confessions*, where he describes the awakening in him of the literary sense. An undefinable taint of death had always clung about him, and now in early manhood he believed himself smitten by mortal disease. He asked himself how he might make as much as possible of the interval that remained; and he was not biased by anything in his previous life when he decided that it must be by intellectual excitement, which he found just then in the clear, fresh writings of Voltaire. Well! we are all *condamnés*, as Victor Hugo says: we are all under sentence of death but with a sort of indefinite reprieve —*les hommes sont tous condamnés à mort avec des*

39. Philosophiren . . . vivificiren, "to be a philosopher is to rid oneself of apathy and to become alive." **Novalis**, the pseudonym of Friedrich von Hardenberg (1772–1801), a German romantic poet and novelist. **57. habit . . . world**, habit becomes fixed as man becomes stereotyped in his world. **76. Comte**, a celebrated French philosopher (1798–1857), who in his philosophy of positivism held that science is the key to the temple of truth because it abides rigorously by positive fact. **Hegel**, a celebrated German philosopher (1770–1831), in whom idealistic philosophy found its peak of intellectual acceptance. **88. Rousseau**, Jean Jacques Rousseau (1712–1778), the famous Swiss-French philosopher, sociologist, novelist, and musician. His was a remarkable and unfortunate genius; his life was a constant struggle marked by

periods of dissipation and virtue; he was unstable in love and friendship. Exiled from France because of the daring and frankness of his writings, he sought refuge in his native Switzerland. In his *Confessions*, one of the world's great autobiographies, he gave a candid and passionate revelation of his emotional life. **97. Voltaire**, the great French neo-classical philosopher and skeptic (1694–1778). **98. condamnés**, condemned. **Victor Hugo**, the celebrated French poet and novelist (1802–1885), the recognized leader of the romantic school of the nineteenth century in France. The quotation immediately below, which Pater translates in the text, comes from his best-known novel, *Les Misérables* (1862).

sursis indéfinis, we have an interval, and then our place knows us no more. Some spend this interval in listlessness, some in high passions, the wisest—at least among "the children of this world"—in art and song. For our one chance lies in expanding that interval, in getting as many pulsations as possible into the given time. Great passions may give us this quickened sense of life, ecstasy and sorrow of love, the various forms of enthusiastic activity, disinterested or otherwise, which come naturally to many of us. Only be sure it is passion—that it does yield you this fruit of a quickened, multiplied consciousness. Of this wisdom, the poetic passion, the desire of beauty, the love of art for art's sake, has most; for art comes to you professing frankly to give nothing but the highest quality to your moments as they pass, and simply for those moments' sake.

(1873)

LYRICAL AND PHILOSOPHICAL POETS

ELIZABETH BARRETT BROWNING
1806-1861

The most important date in the life of Elizabeth Barrett was September 12, 1846. On that day, by a clandestine marriage, she was wedded to Robert Browning, and a week later she left her dark and unhappy home at 50 Wimpole Street, London, where she had been dominated by an ogre-like father, for the light and sunshine of Casa Guidi in Florence, Italy, there she was for the rest of her life—at least so far as the world was to know—the "Lyric Love, half-angel and half-bird" of one of the greatest of English poets.

An injury to her spine when she was fifteen, the shock of her brother Edward's death by drowning in 1840, and the insane insistence of a neurotic father that none of his daughters should marry had made Elizabeth Barrett's life dark indeed. Confined in her gloomy home by her invalidism, she read and wrote, publishing some poems in 1844. With her ample time to study, she read Greek and Hebrew until, as she said, she got fairly dizzy. Before Browning, then an obscure poet, came to know her, she was already popularly thought of as a rival of Tennyson—incredible as such a judgment may seem now. She had translated in verse Aeschylus' Prometheus Bound (1833) and had written a turgid poem, Essay On Mind, published in the same year. In The Seraphim and Other Poems (1838), it is Byron's influence which is dominating. But in the Poems of 1844 her deep, almost painful, social sympathy—certainly not a characteristic of Byron—is fully expressed, notably in The Cry of the Children and Cry of the Human.

During Browning's courtship of Elizabeth, she had written some sonnets on love, after her marriage she added to these, and in 1850 gave them as a gift to her husband, under the title Sonnets from the Portuguese. *The intimate nature of these love poems is revealed in the title, for Browning had playfully called her his "little Portuguese" in reference to her dark complexion.*

Mrs. Browning's human sympathies resulted in an interest in Italian political affairs, which her husband shared. Casa Guidi Windows (1851) and Poems before Congress (1860) reflect this interest. Her remaining work of importance is Aurora Leigh (1857), her longest poem, which is a romance in blank verse, under the guise of an orphan's tale of love and life, it gave Mrs. Browning an opportunity not only to introduce many reflections on her own romantic career but also to give expression to her ideas on social, political, and economic subjects. The two volumes on Italy and this long romance were the last books that she saw through the press, her Last Poems (1862) appeared posthumously.

Elizabeth Barrett Browning's contemporary popularity was due largely to her indulgence in that humanitarian sentiment—and sentimentality—which was one of the most marked of Victorian characteristics. But she is something more than an emotional priestess. Some of her social poems seem written in blood, and they could not but move those who felt as she did. However, now that the conditions which gave them birth have been improved and forgotten, and her poems are read in the cold light of posterity, they sometimes seem more convulsive than powerful and lachrymose rather than moving. If art, as Aristotle says, is the elimination of the superfluous, then Mrs. Browning never attained high art—except in her sonnets, where the restricted form checked her natural and incorrigible fault of prolixity. Yet in spite of her faults of taste and technique and her lamentable lack of concentration, much of her poetry is genuine and some of it of high quality.

1

I thought once how Theocritus had sung
Of the sweet years, the dear and wished-for years,
Who each one in a gracious hand appears
To bear a gift for mortals, old or young;
And, as I mused it in his antique tongue,
I saw, in gradual vision through my tears,
The sweet, sad years, the melancholy years,
Those of my own life, who by turns had flung
A shadow across me. Straightway I was 'ware,
10 So weeping, how a mystic Shape did move
Behind me, and drew me backward by the hair;
And a voice said in mastery, while I strove—
"Guess now who holds thee?"—"Death," I said. But,
      there,
The silver answer rang—"Not Death, but Love."

3

Unlike are we, unlike, O princely Heart!
Unlike our uses and our destinies.
Our ministering two angels look surprise
On one another, as they strike athwart
Their wings in passing. Thou, bethink thee, art
A guest for queens to social pageantries,
With gages from a hundred brighter eyes
Than tears even can make mine, to play thy part
Of chief musician. What hast *thou* to do
10 With looking from the lattice-lights at me,
A poor, tired, wandering singer, singing through
The dark, and leaning up a cypress tree?
The chrism is on thine head—on mine, the dew—
And Death must dig the level where these agree.

6

Go from me. Yet I feel that I shall stand
Henceforward in thy shadow. Nevermore
Alone upon the threshhold of my door
Of individual life, I shall command
The uses of my soul, nor lift my hand
Serenely in the sunshine as before,
Without the sense of that which I forbore—
Thy touch upon the palm. The widest land
Doom takes to part us, leaves thy heart in
      mine
10 With pulses that beat double. What I do
And what I dream include thee, as the wine
Must taste of its own grapes. And when I sue
God for myself, He hears that name of thine,
And sees within my eyes the tears of two.

7

The face of all the world is changed, I think,
Since first I heard the footsteps of thy soul
Move still, oh, still, beside me, as the stole
Betwixt me and the dreadful outer brink
Of obvious death, where I, who thought to sink,
Was caught up into love, and taught the whole
Of life in a new rhythm. The cup of dole
God gave for baptism, I am fain to drink,
And praise its sweetness, Sweet, with thee anear.
The names of country, heaven, are changed away   10
For where thou art or shalt be, there or here;
And this . . . this lute and song . . . loved yesterday
(The singing angels know), are only dear
Because thy name moves right in what they say.

8

What can I give thee back, O liberal
And princely giver, who hast brought the gold
And purple of thine heart, unstained, untold,
And laid them on the outside of the wall
For such as I to take or leave withal,
In unexpected largesse? Am I cold,
Ungrateful, that for these most manifold
High gifts, I render nothing back at all?
Not so; not cold—but very poor instead.
Ask God, who knows. For frequent tears have run   10
The colors from my life, and left so dead
And pale a stuff, it were not fitly done
To give the same as pillow to thy head.
Go farther! let it serve to trample on.

10

Yet, love, mere love, is beautiful indeed
And worthy of acceptation. Fire is bright,
Let temple burn, or flax; an equal light
Leaps in the flame from cedar-plank or weed:
And love is fire. And when I say at need
I love thee . . . mark! . . . *I love thee*—in thy sight
I stand transfigured, glorified aright,
With conscience of the new rays that proceed
Out of my face toward thine. There's nothing low
In love, when love the lowest: meanest creatures 10
Who love God, God accepts while loving so.
And what I *feel*, across the inferior features
Of what I *am*, doth flash itself, and show
How that great work of Love enhances Nature's.

14

If thou must love me, let it be for naught
Except for love's sake only. Do not say

Sonnet 1. 1. **Theocritus,** a famous Greek pastoral poet of the third
century B.C. 13. **Death.** Mrs. Browning had been an invalid for years.
Sonnet 3. 7. **gages,** pledges. 12. **cypress tree,** a traditional
funereal symbol; see *Sonnet 1,* and note to l. 13.
Sonnet 7. 3. **stole,** a long, loose garment; hence, any protection.
Sonnet 35. 1. **leave all for thee.** Because of the hostile attitude of

"I love her for her smile—her look—her way
Of speaking gently—for a trick of thought
That falls in well with mine, and certes brought
A sense of pleasant ease on such a day"—
For these things in themselves, Beloved, may
Be changed, or change for thee—and love, so wrought,
May be unwrought so. Neither love me for
10 Thine own dear pity's wiping my cheeks dry—
A creature might forget to weep, who bore
Thy comfort long, and lose thy love thereby!
But love me for love's sake, that evermore
Thou mayst love on, through love's eternity.

20

Belovéd, my Belovéd, when I think
That thou wast in the world a year ago,
What time I sat alone here in the snow
And saw no footprint, heard the silence sink
No moment at thy voice, but, link by link,
Went counting all my chains as if that so
They never could fall off at any blow
Struck by thy possible hand,—why, thus I drink
Of life's great cup of wonder! Wonderful,
10 Never to feel thee thrill the day or night
With personal act or speech,—nor ever cull
Some prescience of thee with the blossoms white
Thou sawest growing! Atheists are as dull,
Who cannot guess God's presence out of sight.

26

I lived with visions for my company
Instead of men and women, years ago,
And found them gentle mates, nor thought to know
A sweeter music than they played to me.
But soon their trailing purple was not free
Of this world's dust, their lutes did silent grow,
And I myself grew faint and blind below
Their vanishing eyes. Then THOU didst come—to be,
Belovéd, what they seemed. Their shining fronts,
10 Their songs, their splendors (better, yet the same,
As river-water hallowed into fonts),
Met in thee, and from out thee overcame
My soul with satisfaction of all wants:
Because God's gifts put man's best dreams to shame.

35

If I leave all for thee, wilt thou exchange
And be all to me? Shall I never miss
Home-talk and blessing and the common kiss
That comes to each in turn, nor count it strange,
When I look up, to drop on a new range

Of walls and floors, another home than this?
Nay, wilt thou fill that place by me which is
Filled by dead eyes too tender to know change?
That's hardest. If to conquer love, has tried,
To conquer grief, tries more, as all things prove;   10
For grief indeed is love and grief beside.
Alas, I have grieved so I am hard to love.
Yet love me—wilt thou? Open thine heart wide,
And fold within the wet wings of thy dove.

41

I thank all who have loved me in their hearts,
With thanks and love from mine. Deep thanks to all
Who paused a little near the prison wall
To hear my music in its louder parts
Ere they went onward, each one to the mart's
Or temple's occupation, beyond call.
But thou, who, in my voice's sink and fall
When the sob took it, thy divinest Art's
Own instrument didst drop down at thy foot
To hearken what I said between my tears . . .   10
Instruct me how to thank thee! Oh, to shoot
My soul's full meaning into future years,
That *they* should lend it utterance, and salute
Love that endures, from Life that disappears!

43

How do I love thee? Let me count the ways.
I love thee to the depth and breadth and height
My soul can reach, when feeling out of sight
For the ends of Being and ideal Grace.
I love thee to the level of everyday's
Most quiet need, by sun and candle-light.
I love thee freely, as men strive for Right;
I love thee purely, as they turn from Praise.
I love thee with the passion put to use
In my old griefs, and with my childhood's faith.   10
I love thee with a love I seemed to lose
With my lost saints—I love thee with the breath,
Smiles, tears, of all my life!—and, if God choose,
I shall but love thee better after death.
(1845-1846; 1850)

Elizabeth Barrett's father, her marriage meant severing all home ties.
   Sonnet 43. 14. **I . . . death**. Compare Browning's *Prospice* (p. 931).

GEORGE MEREDITH 1828-1909

George Meredith's extremely significant novels have already been commented upon (p. 831). But it is often forgotten that he was also a poet of a high order. He was born in Portsmouth, the son of a tailor who was apparently not in a position to do much for the boy. After one year in a German school (1843-1844), Meredith was apprenticed to a London lawyer, but he dropped his study to enter journalism (1848) and to write. His wife, a daughter of the satirical poet and novelist Thomas Love Peacock (1785-1866), was an extremely difficult, temperamental woman, and after ten years of mutual disagreement, they finally separated—this losing struggle toward matrimonial adjustment formed the basis of the magnificent collection of fifty connected poems which he called Modern Love (1862). Shortly thereafter he settled in Surrey, where he spent the remainder of his long life, the final years darkened by serious ill health.

Meredith's poetry has been called difficult and obscure. Yet the difficulty lies almost wholly in its remarkable compression of phrase, few poets indeed have been able to concentrate so much thought into so few words. "Solid" and "intellectual" would be far sounder terms to apply to his poetry. As a novelist he was a penetrating interpreter of human nature and social problems, and as a poet he showed the same concern for man, but he also revealed an all-embracing love of nature and its deep spiritual implications. He had a towering as well as a fertile imagination, yet his descriptive details are at the same time unerringly accurate. For a correct reproduction of nature, Meredith's Lark Ascending (p. 1076) is superior to the famous skylark poems of Wordsworth (p. 699) and Shelley (p. 773), neither of these romantic poets could have approached the skill of Meredith's actual resinging of the bird's song.

The terminal dates of publication of Meredith's poetry are indicated by Poems (1851) and A Reading of Life, with Other Poems (1901). During these fifty years Modern Love appeared, with other poems, in 1862, Poems and Lyrics of the Joy of Earth in 1883, Ballads and Poems of Tragic Life (1887), A Reading of Earth in 1888, The Empty Purse and Other Poems in 1892, and Odes in Contribution to the Song of French History in 1898.

from MODERN LOVE

This is a series of sixteen-line poems recording the thoughts and feelings of a husband and a wife who loved each other once, but whose love has long been dying. The husband sometimes speaks in his own person as "I."

The poems of George Meredith are reprinted from his *Poems*, Vols. xxiv–xxvi in *The Works of George Meredith*, Memorial ed. (New York: Charles Scribner's Sons, 1910).

1

By this he knew she wept with waking eyes:
That, at his hand's light quiver by her head,
The strange low sobs that shook their common bed
Were called into her with a sharp surprise,
And strangled mute, like little gaping snakes,
Dreadfully venomous to him. She lay
Stone-still, and the long darkness flowed away
With muffled pulses. Then, as midnight makes
Her giant heart of Memory and Tears
Drink the pale drug of silence, and so beat   10
Sleep's heavy measure, they from head to feet
Were moveless, looking through their dead black years,
By vain regret scrawled over the blank wall.
Like sculptured effigies they might be seen
Upon their marriage-tomb, the sword between;
Each wishing for the sword that severs all.

13

"I play for Seasons, not Eternities!"
Says Nature, laughing on her way. "So must
All those whose stake is nothing more than dust!"
And lo, she wins, and of her harmonies
She is full sure! Upon her dying rose
She drops a look of fondness, and goes by,
Scarce any retrospection in her eye;
For she the laws of growth most deeply knows,
Whose hands bear, here, a seed-bag—there, an urn.
Pledged she herself to aught, 'twould mark her end!   10
This lesson of our only visible friend
Can we not teach our foolish hearts to learn?
Yes! yes!—but, oh, our human rose is fair
Surpassingly! Lose calmly Love's great bliss,
When the renewed forever of a kiss
Whirls life within the shower of loosened hair!

16

In our old shipwrecked days there was an hour,
When in the firelight steadily aglow,
Joined slackly, we beheld the red chasm grow
Among the clicking coals. Our library-bower
That eve was left to us; and hushed we sat
As lovers to whom Time is whispering.
From sudden-opened doors we heard them sing;
The nodding elders mixed good wine with chat.
Well knew we that Life's greatest treasure lay
With us, and of it was our talk. "Ah, yes!   10
Love dies!" I said (I never thought it less).
She yearned to me that sentence to unsay.

Then when the fire domed blackening, I found
Her cheek was salt against my kiss, and swift
Up the sharp scale of sobs her breast did lift.—
Now am I haunted by that taste! that sound!

29

Am I failing? For no longer can I cast
A glory round about this head of gold.
Glory she wears, but springing from the mold;
Not like the consecration of the Past!
Is my soul beggared? Something more than earth
I cry for still; I cannot be at peace
In having Love upon a mortal lease.
I cannot take the woman at her worth!
Where is the ancient wealth wherewith I clothed
10 Our human nakedness, and could endow
With a spiritual splendor a white brow
That else had grinned at me the fact I loathed?
A kiss is but a kiss now! and no wave
Of a great flood that whirls me to the sea.
But, as you will! we'll sit contentedly,
And eat our pot of honey on the grave.

43

Mark where the pressing wind shoots javelin-like
Its skeleton shadow on the broad-backed wave!
Here is a fitting spot to dig Love's grave;
Here where the ponderous breakers plunge and strike,
And dart their hissing tongues high up the sand:
In hearing of the ocean, and in sight
Of those ribbed wind-streaks running into white.
If I the death of Love had deeply planned,
I never could have made it half so sure,
10 As by the unblest kisses which upbraid
The full-waked sense; or failing that, degrade!
'Tis morning; but no morning can restore
What we have forfeited. I see no sin;
The wrong is mixed. In tragic life, God wot,
No villain need be! Passions spin the plot;
We are betrayed by what is false within.

44

They say that Pity in Love's service dwells,
A porter at the rosy temple's gate.
I missed him going: but it is my fate
To come upon him now beside his wells;
Whereby I know that I Love's temple leave,
And that the purple doors have closed behind.
Poor soul! if, in those early days unkind,
Thy power to sting had been but power to grieve,
We now might with an equal spirit meet,
10 And not be matched like innocence and vice.
She for the Temple's worship has paid price,
And takes the coin of Pity as a cheat.
She sees through simulation to the bone:

What's best in her impels her to the worst:
Never, she cries, shall Pity soothe Love's thirst,
Or foul hypocrisy for truth atone.

47

We saw the swallows gathering in the sky,
And in the osier-isle we heard them noise.
We had not to look back on summer joys,
Or forward to a summer of bright dye;
But in the largeness of the evening earth
Our spirits grew as we went side by side.
The hour became her husband and my bride.
Love, that had robbed us so, thus blessed our dearth!
The pilgrims of the year waxed very loud
In multitudinous chatterings, as the flood   10
Full brown came from the West, and like pale blood
Expanded to the upper crimson cloud.
Love, that had robbed us of immortal things,
This little moment mercifully gave,
Where I have seen across the twilight wave
The swan sail with her young beneath her wings.

48

Their sense is with their senses all mixed in,
Destroyed by subtleties these women are!
More brain, O Lord, more brain! or we shall mar
Utterly this fair garden we might win.
Behold! I looked for peace, and thought it near.
Our inmost hearts had opened, each to each
We drank the pure daylight of honest speech.
Alas! that was the fatal draft, I fear.
For when of my lost Lady came the word,
This woman, O this agony of flesh!   10
Jealous devotion bade her break the mesh,
That I might seek that other like a bird.
I do adore the nobleness! despise
The act! She has gone forth, I know not where.
Will the hard world my sentience of her share?
I feel the truth; so let the world surmise.

50

Thus piteously Love closed what he begat:
The union of this ever-diverse pair!
These two were rapid falcons in a snare,
Condemned to do the flitting of the bat.
Lovers beneath the singing sky of May,
They wandered once, clear as the dew on flowers.
But they fed not on the advancing hours;
Their hearts held cravings for the buried day.
Then each applied to each that fatal knife,
Deep questioning, which probes to endless dole.   10
Ah, what a dusty answer gets the soul
When hot for certainties in this our life!—

47.   2. *osier-isle*, island overgrown with osiers—i.e., willows.

In tragic hints here see what evermore
Moves dark as yonder midnight ocean's force,
Thundering like ramping hosts of warrior horse,
To throw that faint thin line upon the shore!
(1862)

THE LARK ASCENDING

He rises and begins to round;
He drops the silver chain of sound,
Of many links without a break,
In chirrup, whistle, slur, and shake—
All intervolved and spreading wide,
Like water-dimples down a tide
Where ripple ripple overcurls
And eddy into eddy whirls;
A press of hurried notes that run
10 So fleet they scarce are more than one,
Yet changingly the trills repeat
And linger ringing while they fleet—
Sweet to the quick o' the ear, and dear
To her beyond the handmaid ear,
Who sits beside our inner springs,
Too often dry for this he brings,
Which seems the very jet of earth
At sight of sun, her music's mirth,
As up he wings the spiral stair,
20 A song of light, and pierces air
With fountain ardor, fountain play,
To reach the shining tops of day,
And drink in everything discerned,
An ecstasy to music turned—
Impelled by what his happy bill
Disperses; drinking, showering still,
Unthinking save that he may give
His voice the outlet, there to live
Renewed in endless notes of glee,
30 So thirsty of his voice is he,
For all to hear and all to know
That he is joy, awake, aglow—
The tumult of the heart to hear
Through pureness filtered crystal-clear—
And know the pleasure sprinkled bright
By simple singing of delight,
Shrill, irreflective, unrestrained,
Rapt, ringing, on the jet sustained
Without a break, without a fall,
40 Sweet-silvery, sheer lyrical,
Perennial, quavering up the chord
Like myriad dews of sunny sward
That trembling into fullness shine,
And sparkle dropping argentine;
Such wooing as the ear receives
From zephyr caught in choric leaves
Of aspens when their chattering net

Is flushed to white with shivers wet;
And such the water-spirit's chime
On mountain heights in mornings prime, 50
Too freshly sweet to seem excess,
Too animate to need a stress;
But wider over many heads
The starry voice ascending spreads,
Awakening, as it waxes thin,
The best in us to him akin;
And every face to watch him raised
Puts on the light of children praised—
So rich our human pleasure ripes
When sweetness on sincereness pipes, 60
Though naught be promised from the seas—
But only a soft-ruffling breeze
Sweep glittering on a still content,
Serenity in ravishment.

For singing till his heaven fills,
'Tis love of earth that he instills,
And ever winging up and up,
Our valley is his golden cup,
And he the wine which overflows
To lift us with him as he goes— 70
But not from earth is he divorced,
He joyfully to fly enforced.
The woods and brooks, the sheep and kine,
He is, the hills, the human line,
The meadows green, the fallows brown,
The dreams of labor in the town;
He sings the sap, the quickened veins;
The wedding song of sun and rains
He is, the dance of children, thanks
Of sowers, shout of primrose-banks, 80
And eye of violets while they breathe;
All these the circling song will wreathe,
And you shall hear the herb and tree,
The better heart of men shall see,
Shall feel celestially—as long
As you crave nothing save the song.

Was never voice of ours could say
Our inmost in the sweetest way,
Like yonder voice aloft, and link
All hearers in the song they drink. 90
Our wisdom speaks from failing blood,
Our passion is too full in flood;
We want the key of his wild note
Of truthful in a tuneful throat,
The song seraphically free
Of taint of personality—
So pure that it salutes the suns,
The voice of one for millions,
In whom the millions rejoice
For giving their one spirit voice. 100

The Lark Ascending. Cf. the skylark odes of Wordsworth and
Shelley, pp. 699 and 773. 14. **her,** the spirit of earth or nature
within us. 44. **argentine,** silver-like substance. 96. **taint of person-**
ality, egotism. 112. **pass,** do without. 114. **brain's reflex,** mind's reflection or interpretation. 122. **More . . . home,** extending our habitat.
Lucifer in Starlight. 2. **his dark dominion,** hell. 9. **scars,** those

Yet men have we, whom we revere,
Now names—and men still housing here—
Whose lives, by many a battle-dint
Defaced, and grinding wheels on flint,
Yield substance, though they sing not, sweet
For song our highest heaven to greet;
Whom heavenly singing gives us new,
Enspheres them brilliant in our blue,
From firmest base to farthest leap,
110 Because their love of Earth is deep,
And they are warriors in accord
With life to serve, and pass reward—
So touching purest and so heard
In the brain's reflex of yon bird.
Wherefore their soul in me—or mine,
Through self-forgetfulness divine,
In them—that song aloft maintains,
To fill the sky and thrill the plains
With showerings drawn from human stores,
120 As he to silence nearer soars,
Extends the world at wings and dome,
More spacious making more our home,
Till lost on his aërial rings
In light—and then the fancy sings.
(1881)

LUCIFER IN STARLIGHT

On a starred night Prince Lucifer uprose.
Tired of his dark dominion, swung the fiend
Above the rolling ball, in cloud part screened,
Where sinners hugged their specter of repose.
Poor prey to his hot fit of pride were those.
And now upon his western wing he leaned,
Now his huge bulk o'er Afric's sands careened,
Now the black planet shadowed Arctic snows.
Soaring through wider zones that pricked his scars
10 With memory of the old revolt from Awe,
He reached a middle height, and at the stars,
Which are the brain of heaven, he looked, and sank.
Around the ancient track marched, rank on rank,
The army of unalterable law.
(1883)

MEDITATION UNDER STARS

What links are ours with orbs that are
    So resolutely far?—
The solitary asks, and they
Give radiance as from a shield:
    Still at the death of day,
    The seen, the unrevealed.
Implacable they shine

To us who would of Life obtain
An answer for the life we strain,
    To nourish with one sign.   10
Nor can imagination throw
The penetrative shaft: we pass
The breath of thought, who would divine
    If haply they may grow
As Earth; have our desire to know;
If life comes there to grain from grass,
And flowers like ours of toil and pain;
    Has passion to beat bar,
    Win space from cleaving brain;
    The mystic link attain,   20
    Whereby star holds on star.

Those visible immortals beam
    Allurement to the dream:
Ireful at human hungers brook
    No question in the look.
    Forever virgin to our sense,
    Remote they wane to gaze intense:
Prolong it, and in ruthlessness they smite
The beating heart behind the ball of sight:
    Till we conceive their heavens hoar,   30
    Those lights they raise but sparkles frore,
And Earth, our blood-warm Earth, a shuddering
        prey
To that frigidity of brainless ray.
Yet space is given for breath of thought
Beyond our bounds when musing: more
When to that musing love is brought,
And love is asked of love's wherefore.
'Tis Earth's, her gift; else have we naught:
Her gift, her secret, here our tie.
And not with her and yonder sky?   40
Bethink you: were it Earth alone
Breeds love, would not her region be
    The sole delight and throne
    Of generous Deity?

    To deeper than this ball of sight
Appeal the lustrous people of the night.
Fronting yon shoreless, sown with fiery sails,
    It is our ravenous that quails,
Flesh by its craven thirsts and fears distraught.
        The spirit leaps alight,   50
        Doubts not in them is he,
The binder of his sheaves, the same, the right:
Of magnitude to magnitude is wrought,
To feel it large of the great life they hold:
In them to come, or vaster intervolved,
The issues known in us, our unsolved solved:
That there with toil Life climbs the selfsame
        Tree,
Whose roots enrichment have from ripeness dropped.

received in his battle with the angels and in his fall through the
regions of air with the rebel hosts. See *Paradise Lost*, II (pp. 396 ff.).
    Meditation under Stars. 31. frore, frozen. 48. **our ravenous**, the
ravenous part of us: egoism.

Lyrical and Philosophical Poets 1077

So may we read and little find them cold:
60 Let it but be the lord of Mind to guide
Our eyes; no branch of Reason's growing lopped;
Nor dreaming on a dream; but fortified
By day to penetrate black midnight; see,
Hear, feel, outside the senses; even that we,
The specks of dust upon a mound of mold,
We who reflect those rays, though low our place,
    To them are lastingly allied.

So may we read, and little find them cold:
Not frosty lamps illuming dead space,
70 Not distant aliens, not senseless Powers.
The fire is in them whereof we are born;
The music of their motion may be ours.
Spirit shall deem them beckoning Earth and voiced
Sisterly to her, in her beams rejoiced.
Of love, the grand impulsion, we behold
    The love that lends her grace
    Among the starry fold.
Then at new flood of customary morn,
    Look at her through her showers,
80   Her mists, her streaming gold,
A wonder edges the familiar face:
She wears no more that robe of printed hours;
Half strange seems Earth, and sweeter than her
    flowers.
(1888)

SONG IN THE SONGLESS

They have no song, the sedges dry,
    And still they sing.
It is within my breast they sing,
    As I pass by.
Within my breast they touch a string,
    They wake a sigh.
There is but sound of sedges dry;
    In me they sing.
(1900)

YOUTH IN AGE

Once I was part of the music I heard
    On the boughs or sweet between earth and sky;
    For joy of the beating of wings on high
My heart shot into the breast of the bird.

I hear it now and I see it fly,
    And a life in wrinkles again is stirred;
    My heart shoots into the breast of the bird,
As it will for sheer love till the last long sigh.
(1908)

72. **music . . . ours.** Cf. Job 38:4–7: "Where wast thou . . . When the morning stars sang together, and all the sons of God shouted for joy?" The ancients believed that the stars made music as they

CHRISTINA ROSSETTI 1830-1894

The spirit of Italy which influenced so notably the poetry of the Brownings during their long sojourn in Florence was born in the blood of another remarkable couple of English poets, the Rossettis, a brother and a sister who were Italian by parentage and English in environment. Their father, Gabriele Rossetti, was an Italian patriot and scholar who was obliged to flee from Naples in 1822 because of his opposition to Austrian oppression; he settled in London in 1825 and married Frances Polidoro; there his four children were born. Of the first-born and most celebrated member of the family more will be said later (p.1090). The gentle and extremely gifted sister was somewhat eclipsed in her own time by her brilliant brother and the group of painters and poets with whom she associated.

As a child Christina remained quietly at her London home and never received any education beyond what she acquired from her mother and from her own habit of diligent reading. But her girlhood was far from drab; to the home of the noted Italian refugee came Italian painters, musicians, and writers; and the contacts with literature and art thus afforded the Rossetti children were unusual. For the Pre-Raphaelite painters she was an excellent model, with the pale, sensitive, rather anemic features and dark hair that they believed to be necessary for ideal female beauty. Most of the group wrote poetry, and this provided for her another link with them. Her first lyrics came out in The Germ (p. 828) in 1850; after their publication she maintained a long silence, shyly permitting her brother and his friends to eclipse her, until in 1862 she issued in one volume the poems which she had been writing since 1848. The book was entitled Goblin Market and Other Poems and contains not only the title poem—her longest effort—but also some of the very best of her lyrics. Between 1861 and 1865 she traveled in Europe; the year after her return from Italy, where, she said, "all was music," she published The Prince's Progress (1866). In 1871 an almost fatal illness turned her into a cloistered invalid, and from then until her death in 1894 she saw few people and scarcely ventured out except to attend the Anglican services in a neighboring church. Sing-Song, a little collection of verse for children, appeared in 1872. But Annus Domini (1874) was distinctly religious, and A Pageant (1881) chiefly so. Time Flies (1885)—a mixture of prose and verse—and her last publication, The Face of the Deep (1892), revealed her preoccupation with the deeply mystical emotions of her last years.

But in spite of her overserious attitude toward

revolved in their spheres.

Song. **4. cypress tree.** The cypress is a symbol of mourning; it is a common tree in graveyards.

life, Christina Rossetti shared her poet-brother's profound love of beauty. If Dante Gabriel's art was richly sensuous, Christina, in spite of her natural shyness and innate reserve, possessed much of the same instinct for loveliness of outward form, nor was it incompatible with her deep religious sense. An admixture of vivid detail and abstract mysticism appears throughout her best lyrics. Most of these have a filigree delicacy and a moving restraint that give them great charm—it is possible to maintain that, within her rather circumscribed range, Christina Rossetti is the best woman poet of nineteenth-century English literature.

SONG

When I am dead, my dearest,
  Sing no sad songs for me;
Plant thou no roses at my head,
  Nor shady cypress tree.
Be the green grass above me
  With showers and dewdrops wet;
And if thou wilt, remember,
  And if thou wilt, forget.

I shall not see the shadows,
10 I shall not feel the rain;
I shall not hear the nightingale
  Sing on as if in pain.
And dreaming through the twilight
  That doth not rise nor set,
Haply I may remember,
  And haply may forget.
(1848; 1862)

THE HEART KNOWETH ITS OWN BITTERNESS

    Weep yet awhile—
Weep till that day shall dawn when thou shalt
    smile:
    Watch till the day
When all save only love shall pass away.

    Weep, sick and lonely,
    Bow thy heart to tears,
    For none shall guess the secret
    Of thy griefs and fears.
    Weep, till the day dawn,
10   Refreshing dew:
    Weep till the spring:
    For genial showers

    Bring up the flowers,
    And thou shalt sing
In summertime of blossoming.

    Heart-sick and silent,
  Weep and watch in pain.
    Weep for hope perished,
  Not to live again:
    Weep for love's hope and fear   20
    And passion vain.
    Watch till the day
When all save only love shall pass away.

    Then love rejoicing
  Shall forget to weep:
  Shall hope or fear no more,
    Or watch, or sleep,
  But only love and cease not,
    Deep beyond deep.
  Now we sow love in tears,   30
    But then shall reap.
Have patience as the Lord's own flock of sheep:
  Have patience with His love
Who died below, who lives for thee above.
(1852)

A BETTER RESURRECTION

I have no wit, no words, no tears;
  My heart within me like a stone
Is numbed too much for hopes or fears.
  Look right, look left, I dwell alone;
I lift mine eyes, but dimmed with grief
  No everlasting hills I see.
My life is in the falling leaf;
  O Jesus, quicken me.

My life is like a faded leaf,
  My harvest dwindled to a husk;   10
Truly my life is void and brief
  And tedious in the barren dusk;
My life is like a frozen thing,
  No bud nor greenness can I see;
Yet rise it shall—the sap of Spring;
  O Jesus, rise in me.

My life is like a broken bowl,
  A broken bowl that cannot hold
One drop of water for my soul
  Or cordial in the searching cold;   20
Cast in the fire the perished thing;
  Melt and remold it, till it be

A Better Resurrection. 5. **lift . . . hills.** Cf. Psalms 121:1: "I will lift up mine eyes unto the hills, from whence cometh my help." 7. **life . . . leaf.** Cf. *Macbeth*, V, iii, 22–23:

My way of life
Is fall'n into the sear, the yellow leaf.

A royal cup for Him, my King;
   O Jesus, drink of me.
(1857; 1862)

ADVENT

This Advent moon shines cold and clear,
   These Advent nights are long;
Our lamps have burned year after year,
   And still their flame is strong.
"Watchman, what of the night?" we cry,
   Heart-sick with hope deferred;
"No speaking signs are in the sky,"
   Is still the watchman's word.

The Porter watches at the gate,
10   The servants watch within;
The watch is long betimes and late,
   The prize is slow to win.
"Watchman, what of the night?" But still
   His answer sounds the same:
"No daybreak tops the utmost hill,
   Nor pale our lamps of flame."

One to another hear them speak
   The patient virgins wise:
"Surely He is not far to seek"—
20   "All night we watch and rise."
"The days are evil looking back,
   The coming days are dim;
Yet count we not His promise slack,
   But watch and wait for Him."

One with another, soul with soul,
   They kindle fire from fire:
"Friends watch us who have touched the goal."
   "They urge us, come up higher."
"With them shall rest our waysore feet,
30   With them is built our home,
With Christ."—"They sweet, but He most
     sweet,
   Sweeter than honeycomb."

There no more parting, no more pain,
   The distant ones brought near,
The lost so long are found again,
   Long lost but longer dear;
Eye hath not seen, ear hath not heard,
   Nor heart conceived that rest,
With them our good things long deferred,
40   With Jesus Christ our Best.

We weep because the night is long,
   We laugh for day shall rise,
We sing a slow contented song
   And knock at Paradise.
Weeping we hold Him fast Who wept
   For us, we hold Him fast;
And will not let Him go except
   He bless us first or last.

Weeping we hold Him fast tonight;
   We will not let Him go   50
Till daybreak smite our wearied sight
   And summer smite the snow.
Then figs shall bud, and dove with dove
   Shall coo the livelong day;
Then He shall say, "Arise, My love,
   My fair one, come away."
(1858; 1862)

UPHILL

Does the road wind uphill all the way?
   Yes, to the very end.
Will the day's journey take the whole long day?
   From morn to night, my friend.

But is there for the night a resting-place?
   A roof for when the slow dark hours begin.
May not the darkness hide it from my face?
   You cannot miss that inn.

Shall I meet other wayfarers at night?
   Those who have gone before.
Then must I knock, or call when just in sight?   10
   They will not keep you standing at that door.

Shall I find comfort, travel-sore and weak?
   Of labor you shall find the sum.
Will there be beds for me and all who seek?
   Yea, beds for all who come.
(1858; 1861)

from SING-SONG

   Sing-Song *is the title of a collection of lyrics for* children.

IF I WERE A QUEEN

"If I were a queen,
   What would I do?

Advent. Advent is the period including the four Sundays preceding Christmas. **5. Watchman . . . night,** from Isaiah 21:11. **6. Heart-sick . . . deferred,** from Proverbs 13:12: "Hope deferred maketh the heart sick." **18. virgins, etc.** See the parable of the ten virgins, Matthew 25:1–13. **32. Sweeter than honeycomb,** from Psalms 19:10. **33. no . . . pain.** Cf. Revelation 21:4: "And God shall wipe away all tears from their eyes; and there shall be no more death, neither sorrow, nor crying, neither shall there be any more pain." **37. Eye . . .**

rest, from I Corinthians 2:9: "Eye hath not seen, nor ear heard, neither have entered into the heart of man, the things which God hath prepared for them that love him." **47. will . . . us.** Cf. Genesis 32:26: "And he said, I will not let thee go, except thou bless me." **55. "Arise . . . away,"** from The Song of Solomon 2:13.
   Uphill. **11. knock . . . door,** from Revelation 3:20: "Behold, I stand at the door and knock."

I'd make you king,
　And I'd wait on you."

"If I were a king,
　What would I do?
I'd make you queen,
　For I'd marry you."

MOTHER SHAKE THE CHERRY-TREE

Mother shake the cherry-tree,
　Susan catch a cherry;
Oh, how funny that will be—
　Let's be merry!

One for brother, one for sister,
　Two for mother more,
Six for father, hot and tired,
　Knocking at the door.

THE WIND HAS SUCH A RAINY SOUND

The wind has such a rainy sound
　Moaning through the town,
The sea has such a windy sound—
　Will the ships go down?

The apples in the orchard
　Tumble from their tree.
Oh, will the ships go down, go down,
　In the windy sea?

FLY AWAY, FLY AWAY

Fly away, fly away over the sea,
　Sun-loving swallow, for summer is done;
Come again, come again, come back to me,
　Bringing the summer and bringing the sun.

WHO HAS SEEN THE WIND?

Who has seen the wind?
　Neither I nor you;
But when the leaves hang trembling
　The wind is passing through.

Who has seen the wind?
　Neither you nor I;
But when the trees bow down their heads
　The wind is passing by.

BOATS SAIL ON THE RIVERS

Boats sail on the rivers,
　And ships sail on the seas;
But clouds that sail across the sky
　Are prettier far than these.

There are bridges on the rivers,
　As pretty as you please;
But the bow that bridges heaven,
　And overtops the trees,
And builds a road from earth to sky,
　Is prettier far than these.
(1872)

FRANCIS THOMPSON 1859-1907

Near the end of the nineteenth century, in a decade made colorful by cultists, individualists, and numerous rebels against the restraint of the Victorian fashion, there appeared in English poetry a shy and childlike mystic who had more in common with the metaphysical poets of the seventeenth century (p. 325) than with his contemporaries.

This was the Catholic poet Francis Thompson. He was the son of a Lancashire doctor who had become converted to Roman Catholicism. He was educated at the Catholic college of Ushaw, near Durham, and later studied medicine at Owens College, Manchester. But he never took a degree in medicine, withdrawing instead from life and living both friendless and solitary. Destitute and ill, he went to London but failed to secure work because of his utter incapability of answering the practical and persistent demands of any sort of labor. By chance, however, some of his verses and an essay on paganism came to the notice of the editor of Merry England, Wilfrid Meynell, whose wife Alice (1850-1922) had modest but pleasant talents as a poet. Meynell sought out the writer, after some difficulty found him in extremely sordid surroundings, and took him into his home. The notable aid which the Meynells gave to the lonely and impoverished poet was much like that which the Unwins gave to Cowper (p. 647). With their help, Thompson overcame the habit of taking laudanum, which he had been using to deaden his misery; he moved into a good London lodging house; above all he received friendship and encouragement. In 1893 he published his first volume of poetry, to be followed by Sister Songs (1895) and New Poems (1897). To these he added in 1905 a prose treatise entitled Health and Holiness. But much of the time Thompson, stricken with tuberculosis, was too ill to write. His essay on Shelley, a poet who had always exercised an influence over him, was published two years after his rather premature death in 1907.

Thompson, always an ardent Catholic, occupies an unusual position among the poets of his day. He owed much in substance to Crashaw (p. 337), but in his color, imagery, and exalted imaginative power he owes more to Keats and Shelley. His greatest poem, The Hound of Heaven, from his first volume of poetry, is inspired by an almost apocalyptic mood, it is marked by a radiant splendor of vision and by a depth of tone sharply at variance with the occasional sounding brass and tinkling cymbals of some of the more mundane poetry of the period.

THE HOUND OF HEAVEN

In his Study of Francis Thompson's "Hound of Heaven" (1912), Mr. J. F. O'Connor says: "As the hound follows the hare, never ceasing in its running, ever drawing nearer to the chase . . . so does God follow the fleeing soul by his Divine grace."

I fled Him, down the nights and down the days;
  I fled Him, down the arches of the years;
I fled Him, down the labyrinthine ways
  Of my own mind; and in the mist of tears
I hid from Him, and under running laughter.
    Up vistaed hopes I sped;
    And shot, precipitated,
Adown Titanic glooms of chasméd fears,
  From those strong Feet that followed, followed after.
10   But with unhurrying chase,
    And unperturbéd pace,
  Deliberate speed, majestic instancy,
    They beat—and a Voice beat
    More instant than the Feet—
  "All things betray thee, who betrayest Me."

    I pleaded, outlaw-wise,
By many a hearted casement, curtained red,
  Trellised with intertwining charities
(For, though I knew His love Who followed,
20   Yet was I sore adread
Lest, having Him, I must have naught beside);
But, if one little casement parted wide,
  The gust of His approach would clash it to.
Fear wist not to evade, as Love wist to pursue.
Across the margent of the world I fled,
  And troubled the gold gateways of the stars,
  Smiting for shelter on their clangéd bars;
    Fretted to dulcet jars
And silvern chatter the pale ports o' the moon.
30 I said to dawn, Be sudden; to eve, Be soon;
  With thy young skyey blossoms heap me over
    From this tremendous Lover!
Float thy vague veil about me, lest He see!
  I tempted all His servitors, but to find
My own betrayal in their constancy,
In faith to Him their fickleness to me,
  Their traitorous trueness, and their loyal deceit.

To all swift things for swiftness did I sue;
  Clung to the whistling mane of every wind.
    But whether they swept, smoothly fleet,   40
  The long savannahs of the blue;
    Or whether, Thunder-driven,
    They clanged his chariot 'thwart a heaven
Plashy with flying lightnings round the spurn o' their feet—
  Fear wist not to evade as Love wist to pursue.
    Still with unhurrying chase,
    And unperturbéd pace,
  Deliberate speed, majestic instancy,
    Came on the following Feet,
    And a Voice above their beat—   50
  "Naught shelters thee, who wilt not shelter Me."

I sought no more that after which I strayed
  In face of man or maid;
But still within the little children's eyes
  Seems something, something that replies;
They at least are for me, surely for me!
I turned me to them very wistfully;
But, just as their young eyes grew sudden fair
  With dawning answers there,
Their angel plucked them from me by the hair.   60
"Come then, ye other children, Nature's—share
With me" (said I) "your delicate fellowship;
    Let me greet you lip to lip,
    Let me twine with you caresses,
      Wantoning
    With our Lady-Mother's vagrant tresses,
      Banqueting
    With her in her wind-walled palace,
    Underneath her azured daïs,
    Quaffing, as your taintless way is,   70
      From a chalice
Lucent-weeping out of the dayspring."
      So it was done;
I in their delicate fellowship was one—
Drew the bolt of Nature's secrecies.
I knew all the swift importings
    On the willful face of skies;
  I knew how the clouds arise
  Spuméd of the wild sea-snortings;
    All that's born or dies   80
    Rose and drooped with—made them shapers
Of mine own moods, or wailful or divine—
  With them joyed and was bereaven.
  I was heavy with the even,
  When she lit her glimmering tapers
  Round the day's dead sanctities.
  I laughed in the morning's eyes.
I triumphed and I saddened with all weather,

The Hound of Heaven. **8. Titanic,** enormous, resembling the Titans, an ancient race of giants in Greek mythology. **12. instancy,** insistency. **17. hearted,** heart-shaped. **24. wist,** knew. **25. margent,** edge, boundary. **28. Fretted . . . moon,** troubled the doors of the moon until they vibrated with sweet sounds. **41. savannahs,** open, level regions. **44. Plashy,** speckled, sparkling. **66. Lady-Mother,** Nature. **72. Lucent-weeping,** dripping with luminous drops.

Heaven and I wept together,
90 And its sweet tears were salt with mortal mine;
Against the red throb of its sunset-heart
    I laid my own to beat,
      And share commingling heat;
But not by that, by that, was eased my human smart.
In vain my tears were wet on Heaven's gray cheek.
For ah! we know not what each other says,
    These things and I; in sound *I* speak—
Their sound is but their stir, they speak by silences.
Nature, poor stepdame, cannot slake my drouth;
100   Let her, if she would owe me,
Drop yon blue bosom-veil of sky, and show me
    The breasts o' her tenderness;
Never did any milk of hers once bless
    My thirsting mouth.
      Nigh and nigh draws the chase,
      With unperturbéd pace,
    Deliberate speed, majestic instancy;
      And past those noiséd Feet
      A voice comes yet more fleet—
110 "Lo! naught contents thee, who content'st not Me."

Naked I wait Thy love's uplifted stroke!
My harness piece by piece Thou hast hewn from me,
    And smitten me to my knee;
    I am defenseless utterly.
    I slept, methinks, and woke,
And, slowly gazing, find me stripped in sleep.
In the rash lustihead of my young powers,
    I shook the pillaring hours
And pulled my life upon me; grimed with smears,
120 I stand amid the dust o' the mounded years—
My mangled youth lies dead beneath the heap.
My days have crackled and gone up in smoke,
Have puffed and burst as sun-starts on a stream.
    Yea, faileth now even dream
The dreamer, and the lute the lutanist;
Even the linked fantasies, in whose blossomy
    twist
I swung the earth a trinket at my wrist,
Are yielding; cords of all too weak account
For earth with heavy griefs so overplussed.
130   Ah! is Thy love indeed
A weed, albeit an amaranthine weed,
Suffering no flowers except its own to mount?
    Ah! must—
    Designer infinite!—
Ah! must Thou char the wood ere Thou canst limn
    with it?

My freshness spent its wavering shower i' the dust;
And now my heart is as a broken fount,
Wherein tear-drippings stagnate, spilt down ever
    From the dank thoughts that shiver
Upon the sighful branches of my mind.   140
    Such is; what is to be?
The pulp so bitter, how shall taste the rind?
I dimly guess what Time in mists confounds;
Yet ever and anon a trumpet sounds
From the hid battlements of Eternity;
Those shaken mists a space unsettle, then
Round the half-glimpséd turrets slowly wash again.
    But not ere him who summoneth
    I first have seen, enwound
With glooming robes purpureal, cypress-crowned;   150
His name I know, and what his trumpet saith.
Whether man's heart or life it be which yields
    Thee harvest, must Thy harvest fields
    Be dunged with rotten death?
      Now of that long pursuit
      Comes on at hand the bruit;
    That Voice is round me like a bursting sea:
      "And is thy earth so marred,
      Shattered in shard on shard?
    Lo, all things fly thee, for thou fliest Me!   160
    Strange, piteous, futile thing,
Wherefore should any set thee love apart?
Seeing none but I makes much of naught"
    (He said),
"And human love needs human meriting,
    How hast thou merited—
Of all man's clotted clay the dingiest clot?
    Alack, thou knowest not
How little worthy of any love thou art!
Whom wilt thou find to love ignoble thee   170
    Save Me, save only Me?
All which I took from thee I did but take,
    Not for thy harms,
But just that thou might'st seek it in My arms.
    All which thy child's mistake
Fancies as lost, I have stored for thee at home;
    Rise, clasp My hand, and come!"

      Halts by me that footfall;
      Is my gloom, after all,
    Shade of His hand, outstretched caressingly?   180
      "Ah, fondest, blindest, weakest,
      I am He Whom thou seekest!
Thou dravest love from thee, who dravest Me."
(1891; 1893)

---

100. **owe**, own. 118. **shook . . . me**, as Samson shook the pillars of the temple at Gaza and pulled down the roof on his head. See Judges 16:29–30. 131. **amaranthine**, immortal, like the amaranth, which grows in the fields of Heaven. 135. **limn**, draw, as with charcoal. 150. **purpureal**, purple, as of royalty. **cypress-crowned**, as a symbol of sorrow and death. 156. **bruit**, noise, clamor. 159. **shard**, fragment.

POETS AESTHETIC AND PAGAN

EDWARD FITZGERALD 1809-1883

Edward Fitzgerald spent his childhood in Suffolk; he went to school at Bury St. Edmunds in metropolitan London and attended Trinity College, Cambridge. Here he became acquainted with both Thackeray and Tennyson. After his graduation his life became that of the country gentleman who dabbled in learning with special emphasis upon languages, such as Greek, Spanish, and Persian. His grasp of Persian brought forth his version of Omar Khayyám's Rubáiyát in 1859 (the same year as that which saw the publication of Darwin's Origin of Species); after publication of the Rubáiyát Fitzgerald bought a yacht and spent much time cruising about the North Sea. The easygoing amateur-gentleman's life of this shy scholar and littérateur came to an end in 1883.

We may pass over a Platonic dialogue by Fitzgerald called Euphranor and note that in 1856 he published Six Dramas of Calderón, a testimonial to his thorough mastery of Spanish. The versions of these plays by the eminent Spanish dramatist and poet (1600-1681) were not accurate translations, but they exemplified well Fitzgerald's peculiar ability to catch the spirit of an original and couch it in memorable English. The same thing is true also of his paraphrases of plays by Aeschylus and Sophocles, but it has been only his Rubáiyát that has brought Fitzgerald deserving fame.

When this famous poem appeared early in 1859, Fitzgerald had been studying Persian for six years under Professor Cowell of Cambridge; if he had cared to do so, he could undoubtedly have made an accurate literal translation of Omar's great poem. But he preferred to make a "transmutation" in which the soul of the old Persian astronomer and poet of the early twelfth century underwent a beautiful reincarnation in the form of a gentle, retiring Suffolk epicure-scholar, who, like his original, loved life ardently in all its delightful aspects of wine, women, song, friends, music, and poetry. The poem, therefore, is at least as much Victorian English as twelfth-century Persian. As Fitzgerald wrote to Cowell, "It is most ingeniously tesselated into a sort of Epicurean Eclogue in a Persian Garden." It is frankly and unabashedly pagan,

and it exerted an enormous influence on the popular mind which was becoming a little tired of uplift and straight-lacedness, because it was rendered in a beautiful, trenchant phraseology which has outlived any number of contemporaneous moral strictures.

THE RUBÁIYÁT OF OMAR KHAYYÁM

The aforementioned impact of the poetry of Omar Khayyám ("the tent-maker") upon the English-speaking peoples, thanks to Fitzgerald's gifted translation and adaptation, has tended to obscure the fact that Omar was a celebrated mathematician. He was born, probably in the sixth or seventh decade of the eleventh century (although the exact year is not known), at Nishapur, then one of the principal towns of the province of Khorasan in Persia. Here, as Astronomer Royal, he worked upon a reform of the calendar. He was noted also for a brilliant treatise on algebra, but his avocation during his lifetime was the composition of nearly five hundred quatrains, or rubáiyát, and, as so frequently happens, posterity remembers him for his avocational rather than his professional interest.

There is no accepted text of these quatrains; indeed, it is debatable whether all of them are to be accredited to Omar Khayyám, but there is no doubt about most of them. In substance these rubáiyát comprise: (1) complaints against Fate or the spirit of necessity; (2) satires on the pious, the learned, and the reputedly good people of the times; (3) love lyrics on the sorrows of separation and the joys of reunion; (4) poems in praise of gardens, flowers, and the springtime; (5) poems of rebellion against the prevailing conceptions of God, Heaven, and Hell, balancing their promise of an afterlife against the certainty or reality of the joys of the moment; and (6) addresses to the Deity, of a strongly mystical nature.

Evidently Omar's avowed liberalism made it hard for him at Nishapur. At all events, however, it remains a question whether the epicurean nature of some of the rubáiyát is to be taken literally. Omar believes that there are spiritual and intellectual joys as well as physical ones; yet he cannot be considered a pure mystic, for his scientific turn of mind would naturally counteract such a tendency. It is more likely that he, as a man who adopted the life of the observer and the spectator, was moved to poetic expression of his skepticism, his cynicism, and his regrets at the contemplation of that which is beautiful but which either does not last or is tainted with the commonplace and frustrated by the thwarting of the ideal.

This cartoon illustrating the famous stanza from the Rubáiyát of Omar Khayyám beginning "A book of verses underneath the bough" is from The Poet's Corner, by Sir Max Beerbohm.

Fitzgerald's translation of Omar's poetry is admittedly selective; it emphasizes the sybaritic and the rebellious more than did the original, and it passes rather quickly over the devotional quatrains. Yet no reader of Omar Khayyám in the original could well deny that Fitzgerald has caught the essence of Omar—his world-weariness, his love of ease and comfort, his skepticism and sophistication, his romantic yearning and passionate regret, his fatalism, his inquisitiveness, and his love of beauty—all expressed in phrases that, for all the popular overuse to which they have been put, come close to the immortal.

Wake! For the Sun, who scattered into flight
The Stars before him from the Field of Night,
    Drives Night along with them from Heav'n and
      strikes
The Sultán's Turret with a Shaft of Light.

Before the phantom of False morning died,
Methought a Voice within the Tavern cried,
    "When all the Temple is prepared within,
Why nods the drowsy Worshiper outside?"

And, as the Cock crew, those who stood before
The Tavern shouted—"Open, then, the Door!   10
    You know how little while we have to stay,
And, once departed, may return no more."

Now the New Year reviving old Desires,
The thoughtful Soul to Solitude retires,
    Where the WHITE HAND OF MOSES on the Bough
Puts out, and Jesus from the Ground suspires.

Iram indeed is gone with all his Rose,
And Jamshyd's Sev'n-ringed Cup where no one
      knows;
    But still a Ruby kindles in the Vine,
And many a Garden by the Water blows.   20

And David's lips are locked; but in divine
High-piping Pehleví, with "Wine! Wine! Wine!
    Red Wine!"—the Nightingale cries to the Rose
That sallow cheek of hers to incarnadine.

The Rubáiyát of Omar Khayyám. 5. **phantom . . . morning,** "a transient light on the horizon about an hour before the true dawn —a common phenomenon in the East"—Fitzgerald. 13. **New Year.** The Persian year begins with the vernal equinox. 15. **WHITE . . . Bough.** At the command of the Lord, Moses put his hand into his bosom and "when he took it out, behold, his hand was leprous as snow" (Exodus 4:6). The metaphor is applied to the blooming of the flowers. 16. **Jesus . . . suspires.** The Persians believed that the healing power of Jesus resided in his breath. 17. **Iram,** an ancient Persian garden, now obliterated. 18. **Jamshyd,** a legendary king of Persia. His seven-ringed cup symbolized the seven heavens, the seven planets, the seven seats, etc. 21. **David . . . Pehleví.** David's tongue is forgotten, but the nightingale still cries in Pehleví, the ancient literary language of Persia.

Come, fill the Cup, and in the fire of Spring
Your Winter-garment of Repentance fling;
  The Bird of Time has but a little way
To flutter—and the Bird is on the Wing.

Whether at Naishápúr or Babylon,
30 Whether the Cup with sweet or bitter run,
  The Wine of Life keeps oozing drop by drop,
The Leaves of Life keep falling one by one.

Each Morn a thousand Roses brings, you say;
Yes, but where leaves the Rose of Yesterday?
  And this first Summer month that brings the Rose
Shall take Jamshyd and Kaikobád away.

Well, let it take them! What have we to do
With Kaikobád the Great, or Kaikhosrú!
  Let Zál and Rustum bluster as they will,
40 Or Hátim call to Supper—heed not you.

With me along the strip of Herbage strown
That just divides the desert from the sown,
  Where name of Slave and Sultán is forgot—
And Peace to Mahmúd on his golden Throne!

A Book of Verses underneath the Bough,
A Jug of Wine, a Loaf of Bread—and Thou
  Beside me singing in the Wilderness—
Oh, Wilderness were Paradise enow!

Some for the Glories of This World; and some
50 Sigh for the Prophet's Paradise to come;
  Ah, take the Cash, and let the Credit go,
Nor heed the rumble of a distant Drum!

Look to the blowing Rose about us—"Lo,
Laughing," she says, "into the world I blow,
  At once the silken tassel of my Purse
Tear, and its Treasure on the Garden throw."

And those who husbanded the Golden Grain,
And those who flung it to the winds like Rain,
  Alike to no such aureate Earth are turned
60 As, buried once, Men want dug up again.

The Worldly Hope men set their Hearts upon
Turns Ashes—or it prospers; and anon,
  Like Snow upon the Desert's dusty Face,
Lighting a little hour or two—is gone.

Think, in this battered Caravanserai
Whose Portals are alternate Night and Day,

How Sultán after Sultán with his Pomp
Abode his destined Hour, and went his way.

They say the Lion and the Lizard keep
The Courts where Jamshyd gloried and drank
    deep;   70
  And Bahrám, that great hunter—the Wild Ass
Stamps o'er his Head, but cannot break his Sleep.

I sometimes think that never blows so red
The Rose as where some buried Caesar bled;
  That every Hyacinth the Garden wears
Dropped in her Lap from some once lovely Head.

And this reviving Herb whose tender Green
Fledges the River-Lip on which we lean—
  Ah, lean upon it lightly! for who knows
From what once lovely Lip it springs unseen!   80

Ah, my Belovéd, fill the Cup that clears
TODAY of past Regrets and future Fears:
  Tomorrow!—Why, Tomorrow I may be
Myself with Yesterday's Sev'n Thousand Years.

For some we loved, the loveliest and the best
That from his Vintage rolling Time hath prest,
  Have drunk their Cup a Round or two before,
And one by one crept silently to rest.

And we, that now make merry in the Room
They left, and Summer dresses in new bloom,   90
  Ourselves must we beneath the Couch of Earth
Descend—ourselves to make a Couch—for whom?

Ah, make the most of what we yet may spend,
Before we too into the Dust descend;
  Dust into Dust, and under Dust, to lie,
Sans Wine, sans Song, sans Singer, and—sans End!

Alike for those who for TODAY prepare,
And those that after some TOMORROW stare,
  A Muezzín from the Tower of Darkness cries,
"Fools, your Reward is neither Here nor There."   100

Why, all the Saints and Sages who discussed
Of the Two Worlds so wisely—they are thrust
Like foolish Prophets forth; their Words to Scorn
Are scattered, and their Mouths are stopped with
    Dust.

Myself when young did eagerly frequent
Doctor and Saint, and heard great argument

29. **Naishápúr**, a village in Persia; Omar's native place. 36. **Kaikobád**, the founder of the most celebrated of the dynasties of ancient Persia. 38. **Kaikhosrú**, a famous Persian hero, identified with Cyrus the Great (sixth century B.C.), founder of the Persian Empire. 39. **Zál and Rustum**, noted Persian heroes; Zál was the father of Rustum. 40. **Hátim**, "a type of Oriental Generosity"—Fitzgerald. 44. **Mahmúd**, the Sultan. Mahmud the Great (c. 970–1030)

was the famous Mohammedan conqueror of India; he was sultan of Ghazni, the city of his birth in Afghanistan. 50. **the Prophet**, Mohammed. 57. **Golden Grain**, wealth. 65. **Caravanserai**, an Oriental inn, where caravans rest at night. 70. **Courts**. Jamshyd's capital was Persepolis. 71. **Bahrám**, a Persian ruler who lost his life in a swamp while hunting a wild ass. 75. **Hyacinth**, a flower named after Hyacinthus, a youth accidentally killed by his friend, Apollo, god of the sun.

About it and about; but evermore
Came out by the same door where in I went.

With them the seed of Wisdom did I sow,
110 And with mine own hand wrought to make it grow;
    And this was all the Harvest that I reaped—
"I came like Water, and like Wind I go."

Into this Universe, and *Why* not knowing
Nor *Whence*, like Water willy-nilly flowing;
    And out of it, as Wind along the Waste,
I know not *Whither*, willy-nilly blowing.

What, without asking, hither hurried *Whence?*
And, without asking, *Whither* hurried hence!
    Oh, many a Cup of this forbidden Wine
120 Must drown the memory of that insolence!

Up from the Earth's Center through the Seventh Gate
I rose, and on the Throne of Saturn sate,
    And many a Knot unraveled by the Road;
But not the Master-knot of Human Fate.

There was the Door to which I found no Key;
There was the Veil through which I might not
    see;
    Some little talk awhile of ME and THEE
There was—and then no more of THEE and ME.

Earth could not answer; nor the Seas that mourn
130 In flowing Purple, of their Lord forlorn;
    Nor rolling Heaven, with all his Signs revealed
And hidden by the sleeve of Night and Morn.

Then of the THEE IN ME who works behind
The Veil, I lifted up my hands to find
    A lamp amid the Darkness; and I heard,
As from Without—"THE ME WITHIN THEE BLIND!"

Then to the Lip of this poor earthen Urn
I leaned, the Secret of my Life to learn;
    And Lip to Lip it murmured—"While you live,
140 Drink!—for, once dead, you never shall return."

I think the Vessel, that with fugitive
Articulation answered, once did live,
    And drink; and Ah! the passive Lip I kissed,
How many Kisses might it take—and give!

For I remember stopping by the way
To watch a Potter thumping his wet Clay;
    And with its all-obliterated Tongue
It murmured—"Gently, Brother, gently, pray!"

And has not such a Story from of Old
Down Man's successive generations rolled   150
    Of such a clod of saturated Earth
Cast by the Maker into Human mold?

And not a drop that from our Cups we throw
For Earth to drink of, but may steal below
    To quench the fire of Anguish in some Eye
There hidden—far beneath, and long ago.

As then the Tulip, for her morning sup
Of Heav'nly Vintage, from the soil looks up,
    Do you devoutly do the like, till Heav'n
To Earth invert you—like an empty Cup.   160

Perplexed no more with Human or Divine,
Tomorrow's tangle to the winds resign,
    And lose your fingers in the tresses of
The Cypress-slender Minister of Wine.

And if the Wine you drink, the Lip you press,
End in what All begins and ends in—Yes;
    Think that you are TODAY what YESTERDAY
You were—TOMORROW you shall not be less.

So when that Angel of the darker Drink
At last shall find you by the river-brink,   170
    And offering his Cup, invite your Soul
Forth to your Lips to quaff—you shall not shrink.

Why, if the Soul can fling the Dust aside,
And naked on the Air of Heaven ride,
    Were't not a Shame—were't not a Shame for him
In this clay carcass crippled to abide?

'Tis but a Tent where takes his one day's rest
A Sultan to the realm of Death addrest;
    The Sultán rises, and the dark Ferrásh
Strikes, and prepares it for another Guest.   180

And fear not lest Existence closing your
Account, and mine, should know the like no more;
    The Eternal Sákí from that Bowl has poured
Millions of Bubbles like us, and will pour.

When You and I behind the Veil are past,
Oh, but the long, long while the World shall
    last,
    Which of our Coming and Departure heeds
As the Sea's self should heed a pebble-cast.

A Moment's Halt—a momentary taste
Of BEING from the Well amid the Waste—   190

The flower sprang up where the blood of Hyacinthus flowed upon the ground. **84. Sev'n Thousand Years**, a thousand years to each planet. **96. Sans**, without. **99. Muezzín**, the officer who summons the faithful to prayer in Mohammedan countries. **119. forbidden Wine**. Orthodox Mohammedanism regards the use of wine as one of the twelve capital sins. **122. Saturn**, the lord of the seventh heaven, one of the concentric spheres into which, according to the ancients, the space around the earth was divided. **131. Signs**, the signs of the zodiac. **153. drop . . . Earth.** It was an old custom to throw a little wine on the ground before drinking; it refreshed some wine drinker who had gone before. **164. Cypress-slender . . . Wine**, the maiden who passes the wine; she is as slender as a cypress tree. **165. And if, etc.** This stanza stresses the joy of wine mingled with the joy of love. **179. Ferrásh**, a servant, a camp follower. **183. Sákí**, wine bearer.

And Lo!—the phantom Caravan has reached
The NOTHING it set out from—Oh, make haste!

Would you that spangle of Existence spend
About THE SECRET—quick about it, Friend!
   A Hair perhaps divides the False and True—
And upon what, prithee, does life depend?

A Hair perhaps divides the False and True—
Yes; and a single Alif were the clue—
   Could you but find it—to the Treasure-house,
200 And peradventure to THE MASTER too;

Whose secret Presence, through Creation's veins
Running Quicksilver-like, eludes your pains;
   Taking all shapes from Máh to Máhi; and
They change and perish all—but He remains;

A moment guessed—then back behind the Fold
Immersed of Darkness round the Drama rolled
   Which, for the Pastime of Eternity,
He doth Himself contrive, enact, behold.

But if in vain, down on the stubborn floor
210 Of Earth, and up to Heav'n's unopening Door,
   You gaze TODAY, while You are You—how then
TOMORROW, when You shall be You no more?

Waste not your Hour, nor in the vain pursuit
Of This and That endeavor and dispute;
   Better be jocund with the fruitful Grape
Than sadden after none, or bitter, Fruit.

You know, my Friends, with what a brave Carouse
I made a Second Marriage in my house;
   Divorced old barren Reason from my Bed,
220 And took the Daughter of the Vine to Spouse.

For "Is" and "IS-NOT" though with Rule and
   Line,
And "UP-AND-DOWN" by Logic, I define,
   Of all that one should care to fathom, I
Was never deep in anything but—Wine.

Ah, but my Computations, People say,
Reduced the Year to better reckoning?—Nay,
   'Twas only striking from the Calendar
Unborn Tomorrow, and dead Yesterday.

And lately, by the Tavern Door agape,
230 Came shining through the Dusk an Angel Shape
   Bearing a Vessel on his Shoulder; and
He bid me taste of it; and 'twas—the Grape!

The Grape that can with Logic absolute
The Two-and-Seventy jarring Sects confute;
   The sovereign Alchemist that in a trice
Life's leaden metal into Gold transmute;

The mighty Mahmúd, Allah-breathing Lord,
That all the misbelieving and black Horde
   Of fears and Sorrows that infest the Soul
Scatters before him with his whirlwind Sword.   240

Why, be this Juice the growth of God, who dare
Blaspheme the twisted tendril as a Snare?
   A Blessing, we should use it, should we not?
And if a Curse—why, then, Who set it there?

I must abjure the Balm of Life, I must,
Scared by some After-reckoning ta'en on trust
   Or lured with Hope of some Diviner Drink,
To fill the Cup—when crumbled into Dust!

Oh threats of Hell and Hopes of Paradise!
One thing at least is certain—*This* Life flies;   250
   One thing is certain and the rest is Lies—
The Flower that once has blown forever dies.

Strange, is it not? that of the myriads who
Before us passed the door of Darkness through,
   Not one returns to tell us of the Road,
Which to discover we must travel too.

The Revelations of Devout and Learned
Who rose before us, and as Prophets burned,
   Are all but Stories, which, awoke from Sleep,
They told their comrades, and to Sleep returned.   260

I sent my Soul through the Invisible,
Some letter of that After-life to spell;
   And by and by my Soul returned to me,
And answered, "I Myself am Heav'n and Hell"—

Heav'n but the Vision of fulfilled Desire,
And Hell the Shadow from a Soul on fire
   Cast on the Darkness into which Ourselves,
So late emerged from, shall so soon expire.

We are no other than a moving row
Of Magic Shadow-shapes that come and go   270
   Round with the Sun-illumined Lantern
      held
In Midnight by the Master of the Show;

But helpless Pieces of the Game He plays
Upon this Checker-board of Nights and Days;

198. **Alif,** the first letter of some ancient alphabets. 203. **from Máh to Máhi,** from fish to moon. 225. **Computations.** Omar was a learned astronomer, one of eight men employed to reform the calendar. 234. **Two-and-Seventy,** the number of religions supposed to be in the world. 237. **Allah-breathing.** The sultan worshiped Allah, the Mohammedan deity, and forced others to do likewise. 252. **blown,** bloomed. 277. **The Ball,** etc. An allusion to the game of polo, of ancient Persian origin. 298. **Foal Of Heav'n,** an equatorial constellation known as Equuleus (the Little Horse). 299. **Parwín and Mushtarí,** the Pleiades and Jupiter. 302. **Dervish,** a Mohammedan devotee. 317. **gin,** trap.

Hither and thither moves, and checks, and
    slays,
And one by one back in the Closet lays.

The Ball no question makes of Ayes and Noes,
But Here or There as strikes the Player goes;
    And He that tossed you down into the Field,
280 He knows about it all—HE knows—HE knows!

The Moving Finger writes, and, having writ,
Moves on; nor all your Piety nor Wit
    Shall lure it back to cancel half a Line,
Nor all your Tears wash out a Word of it.

And that inverted Bowl they call the Sky,
Whereunder crawling cooped we live and die,
    Lift not your hands to It for help—for It
As impotently moves as you or I.

With Earth's first Clay They did the Last Man
    knead,
290 And there of the Last Harvest sowed the Seed;
    And the first Morning of Creation wrote
What the Last Dawn of Reckoning shall read.

YESTERDAY This Day's Madness did prepare;
TOMORROW'S Silence, Triumph, or Despair.
    Drink! for you know not whence you came, nor
        why;
Drink, for you know not why you go, nor where.

I tell you this—When, started from the Goal,
Over the flaming shoulders of the Foal
    Of Heav'n Parwín and Mushtarí they flung,
300 In my predestined Plot of Dust and Soul

The Vine had struck a fiber; which about
If clings my Being—let the Dervish flout;
    Of my Base metal may be filed a Key,
That shall unlock the Door he howls without.

And this I know: whether the one True Light
Kindle to Love, or Wrath—consume me quite,
    One Flash of It within the Tavern caught
Better than in the Temple lost outright.

What! out of senseless Nothing to provoke
310 A conscious Something to resent the yoke
    Of unpermitted Pleasure, under pain
Of Everlasting Penalties, if broke!

What! from his helpless Creature be repaid
Pure Gold for what he lent him dross-allayed—
    Sue for a Debt he never did contract,
And cannot answer—Oh, the sorry trade!

Oh Thou, who didst with pitfall and with gin
Beset the Road I was to wander in,
    Thou wilt not with Predestined Evil round
Enmesh, and then impute my Fall to Sin!   320

Oh Thou, who Man of Baser Earth didst make,
And ev'n with Paradise devise the Snake,
    For all the Sin wherewith the Face of Man
Is blackened—Man's forgiveness give—and take!

As under cover of departing Day
Slunk hunger-stricken Ramazán away,
    Once more within the Potter's house alone
I stood, surrounded by the Shapes of Clay—

Shapes of all Sorts and Sizes, great and small,
That stood along the floor and by the wall;   330
    And some loquacious Vessels were; and some
Listened perhaps, but never talked at all.

Said one among them—"Surely not in vain
My substance of the common Earth was ta'en
    And to this Figure molded, to be broke,
Or trampled back to shapeless Earth again."

Then said a Second—"Ne'er a peevish Boy
Would break the Bowl from which he drank in joy;
    And He that with his hand the Vessel made
Will surely not in after Wrath destroy."   340

After a momentary silence spake
Some Vessel of a more ungainly Make:
    "They sneer at me for leaning all awry;
What! did the Hand, then, of the Potter shake?"

Whereat someone of the loquacious Lot—
I think a Súfi pipkin—waxing hot—
    "All this of Pot and Potter—Tell me then,
Who is the Potter, pray, and who the Pot?"

"Why," said another, "Some there are who tell
Of one who threatens he will toss to Hell   350
    The luckless Pots he marred in making—Pish!
He's a Good Fellow, and 'twill all be well."

"Well," murmured one, "Let whoso make or
    buy,
My Clay with long Oblivion is gone dry;
    But fill me with the old familiar Juice,
Methinks I might recover by and by."

So while the Vessels one by one were speaking
The little Moon looked in that all were seeking;
    And then they jogged each other, "Brother! Brother!
Now for the Porter's shoulder-knot a-creaking!"   360

---

326. **Ramazán**, the fasting month of the Mohammedans, during which they ate no food between sunrise and sunset. 346. **Súfi**, a member of a Persian sect whose purpose was to gain insight into the Divine Being through contemplation. 358. **Moon . . . seeking**, the new moon, which would mark the end of the fasting period. 360. **shoulder-knot**

a-creaking, with the load of wine he was carrying. The shoulder-knot was a strap on which the jars were hung.

Ah, with the Grape my fading Life provide,
And wash the Body whence the Life has died,
   And lay me, shrouded in the living Leaf,
By some not unfrequented Garden-side—

That ev'n my buried Ashes such a snare
Of Vintage shall fling up into the Air
   As not a True-believer passing by
But shall be overtaken unaware.

Indeed the Idols I have loved so long
370 Have done my credit in this World much wrong,
   Have drowned my Glory in a shallow Cup,
And sold my Reputation for a Song.

Indeed, indeed, Repentance oft before
I swore—but was I sober when I swore?
   And then and then came Spring, and Rose-in-hand
My thread-bare Penitence apieces tore.

And much as Wine has played the Infidel,
And robbed me of my Robe of Honor—Well,
   I wonder often what the Vintners buy
380 One-half so precious as the stuff they sell.

Yet Ah, that Spring should vanish with the Rose!
That Youth's sweet-scented manuscript should close!
   The Nightingale that in the branches sang,
Ah whence, and whither flown again, who knows!

Would but the Desert of the Fountain yield
One glimpse—if dimly, yet indeed, revealed,
   To which the fainting Traveler might spring,
As springs the trampled herbage of the field!

Would but some wingéd Angel ere too late
390 Arrest the yet unfolded Roll of Fate,
   And make the stern Recorder otherwise
Enregister, or quite obliterate!

Ah, Love! could you and I with Him conspire
To grasp this sorry Scheme of Things entire,
   Would not we shatter it to bits—and then
Remold it nearer to the Heart's Desire!

Yon rising Moon that looks for us again—
How oft hereafter will she wax and wane;
   How oft hereafter rising look for us
400 Through this same Garden—and for *one* in vain

And when like her, O Sákí, you shall pass
Among the Guests Star-scattered on the Grass,
   And in your joyous errand reach the spot
Where I made One—turn down an empty Glass!
(1859, 1868, 1872, 1879)

369. **Idols,** wine and wine poetry.

DANTE GABRIEL ROSSETTI 1828-1882

Dante Gabriel Rossetti was the leader of the first important rebellion against the artistic canons of the Victorians—the Pre-Raphaelite Brotherhood (p. 828). Like his "brothers," Rossetti was a poet and painter whose sympathies lay more with Greek and Continental habits of thought and feeling than with the Protestant, Hebraic, Anglo-Saxon tradition; like his "brothers," Rossetti was prone to "a dreamy or indeed morbid mood of desolation." The growing industrialism of a country of shopkeepers, with all of its consequent social, economic, and political problems, repelled him; so he decamped, in spirit and object of mind, to more congenial times and climes—to the moral and social and esthetic stability of the Middle Ages, to the simple, straightforward hedonism of the ancients.

Born in London of partly Italian extraction, Rossetti attended King's College School, studied art at the Royal Academy, and painted for a short time in the studio of the artist Ford Madox Brown (1821-1893). To The Germ—that unfortunately named little magazine that served as organ for the Pre-Raphaelite Brotherhood—Rossetti in 1850 contributed nearly a dozen of his best lyrics. In this same year he became acquainted with Elizabeth Siddall, the daughter of a London tradesman. Before and after their marriage ten years later (1860), Elizabeth sat as the model for Rossetti's paintings and served as the muse of his poetry. No doubt her interest in Rossetti's work was increased by the fact that she herself was a water colorist. She was too frail, however, to "serve as human nature's daily food," and died in 1862 of an obscure disease, probably tubercular. In her coffin Rossetti placed a bundle of poems in manuscript; seven years later these were recovered through the exhumation of Elizabeth's body and were published (1870) under the noncommittal title of Poems. In this volume appears Rossetti's distinguished sonnet sequence, The House of Life (an intensely personal cycle dedicated to his wife), and other lyrics. The poet, tending to be neurotic, began to suffer from failing eyesight, which prevented him from painting, and turned to poetry for consolation. To cure insomnia he fell into the habit of taking chloral, and the last years of his life were spent in seclusion; a last volume of poems was published in 1881.

Rossetti was primarily a painter, secondarily a poet, and the mark of the painter is upon his poems. The Blessed Damozel provides a revealing example. In the first two stanzas, the reader sees the blessed damozel leaning against the bar of heaven, clothed in simple white; he sees her hair "lying down her back" "yellow like ripe corn"; he sees three lilies in her hand and seven stars in her hair; his special attention is drawn to her dark, liquid eyes, and in the third stanza he is given an indication of their shape and of their importance as the index to the ambiguous state of her soul. In precision of detail, in love of sensuous beauty, in vague symbolism—all used to present a frozen image of a lady in an attitude—the reader sees the Pre-Raphaelite painter turned Pre-Raphaelite poet.

One of Rossetti's most famous and controversial ballads was not medieval, but modern; not tragic, but pathetic. This is the poem Jenny. The reviewers singled out this poem for abuse, an abuse which Rossetti himself had predicted. In a letter to Charles Eliot Norton, Rossetti had written: "there are a few things—and notably a poem called Jenny—which will raise objection in some quarters. I only know that they have been written neither recklessly nor aggressively (moods which I think are sure to result in the ruin of Art), but from a true impulse to deal with subjects which seem to me capable of being brought rightly within Art's province. Of my own position I feel sure, and so wait the final result without apprehension." Jenny is the furthest Rossetti ever went in the poetry of social criticism. In it, he suggests that sensuousness is a valid anti-intellectual protest. He condemns modern industrial society in figures less conventional but no less positive than Arnold's; where Fitzgerald dealt in terms of metaphysics, Rossetti dealt in terms of the mystery of fleshly evil—and both, significantly, used the potter metaphor. Jenny became to him a symbol of the Mammonism of modern life, of the impenetrable darkness disguising appearance as reality, of the mystery of God's ways to man and of man's inhumanity to his fellows.

In The Blessed Damozel Rossetti humanized heaven; in Jenny he spiritualized flesh. In The House of Life, one of the three most famous sonnet sequences since Shakespeare, he revealed the philosophical inclinations of his mind.

THE BLESSED DAMOZEL

The poet designed this poem as a complement to Poe's The Raven (1845).

The blessed damozel leaned out
   From the gold bar of heaven;
Her eyes were deeper than the depth
   Of waters stilled at even;
She had three lilies in her hand,
   And the stars in her hair were seven.

Her robe, ungirth from clasp to hem,
   No wrought flowers did adorn,
But a white rose of Mary's gift,
10   For service meetly worn;

Her hair that lay along her back
   Was yellow like ripe corn.

Herseemed she scarce had been a day
   One of God's choristers;
The wonder was not yet quite gone
   From that still look of hers;
Albeit, to them she left, her day
   Had counted as ten years.

(To *one* it is ten years of years.
   . . . Yet now, and in this place,   20
Surely she leaned o'er me—her hair
   Fell all about my face. . . .
Nothing: the autumn fall of leaves.
   The whole year sets apace.)

It was the rampart of God's house
   That she was standing on;
By God built over the sheer depth
   The which is Space begun;
So high, that looking downward thence
   She scarce could see the sun.   30

It lies in heaven, across the flood
   Of ether, as a bridge.
Beneath, the tides of day and night
   With flame and darkness ridge
The void, as low as where this earth
   Spins like a fretful midge.

Around her, lovers, newly met
   'Mid deathless love's acclaims,
Spoke evermore among themselves
   Their heart-remembered names;   40
And the souls mounting up to God
   Went by her like thin flames.

And still she bowed herself and stooped
   Out of the circling charm;
Until her bosom must have made
   The bar she leaned on warm,
And the lilies lay as if asleep
   Along her bended arm.

From the fixed place of heaven she saw
   Time like a pulse shake fierce   50
Through all the worlds. Her gaze still strove
   Within the gulf to pierce
Its path; and now she spoke as when
   The stars sang in their spheres.

The sun was gone now; the curled moon
   Was like a little feather
Fluttering far down the gulf; and now

The Blessed Damozel. 10. For . . . worn, fittingly worn in the service of the Virgin Mary. 13. Herseemed, it seemed to her. 36. midge, a kind of small gnat.

She spoke through the still weather.
Her voice was like the voice the stars
60   Had when they sang together.

(Ah, sweet! Even now, in that bird's song,
    Strove not her accents there,
Fain to be harkened? When those bells
    Possessed the midday air,
Strove not her steps to reach my side
    Down all the echoing stair?)

"I wish that he were come to me,
    For he will come," she said.
"Have I not prayed in heaven?—on earth,
70   Lord, Lord, has he not prayed?
Are not two prayers a perfect strength?
    And shall I feel afraid?

"When round his head the aureole clings,
    And he is clothed in white,
I'll take his hand and go with him
    To the deep wells of light;
As unto a stream we will step down,
    And bathe there in God's sight.

"We two will stand beside that shrine,
80   Occult, withheld, untrod,
Whose lamps are stirred continually
    With prayers sent up to God;
And see our old prayers, granted, melt
    Each like a little cloud.

"We two will lie i' the shadow of
    That living mystic tree
Within whose secret growth the Dove
    Is sometimes felt to be,
While every leaf that His plumes touch
90   Saith His Name audibly.

"And I myself will teach to him,
    I myself, lying so,
The songs I sing here; which his voice
    Shall pause in, hushed and slow,
And find some knowledge at each pause,
    Or some new thing to know."

(Alas! We two, we two, thou say'st!
    Yea, one wast thou with me
That once of old. But shall God lift
100   To endless unity
The soul whose likeness with thy soul
    Was but its love for thee?)

"We two," she said, "will seek the groves
    Where the lady Mary is,

With her five handmaidens, whose names
    Are five sweet symphonies,
Cecily, Gertrude, Magdalen,
    Margaret, and Rosalys.

"Circlewise sit they, with bound locks
    And foreheads garlanded;   110
Into the fine cloth white like flame
    Weaving the golden thread,
To fashion the birth-robes for them
    Who are just born, being dead.

"He shall fear, haply, and be dumb;
    Then will I lay my cheek
To his, and tell about our love,
    Not once abashed or weak;
And the dear Mother will approve
    My pride, and let me speak.   120

"Herself shall bring us, hand in hand,
    To Him round whom all souls
Kneel, the clear-ranged unnumbered heads
    Bowed with their aureoles;
And angels meeting us shall sing
    To their citherns and citoles.

"There will I ask of Christ the Lord
    Thus much for him and me—
Only to live as once on earth
    With Love, only to be,   130
As then awhile, forever now,
    Together, I and he."

She gazed and listened and then said,
    Less sad of speech than mild—
"All this is when he comes." She ceased.
    The light thrilled toward her, filled
With angels in strong, level flight.
    Her eyes prayed, and she smiled.

(I saw her smile.) But soon their path
    Was vague in distant spheres;   140
And then she cast her arms along
    The golden barriers,
And laid her face between her hands,
    And wept. (I heard her tears.)
(1847; 1850, 1856, 1870)

JENNY

*Vengeance of Jenny's case! Fie on her! Never name
her, child!*—(Mrs. Quickly.)

    Lazy laughing languid Jenny,
Fond of a kiss and fond of a guinea,

86. **living . . . tree,** the tree of life (see Revelation 22:2, 14). 87.
Dove, a symbol of the Holy Spirit, the third member of the Trinity;
cf. Luke 3:22. 107. **Cecily . . . Rosalys.** These are names of famous
Christian saints. St. Cecilia is the patron saint of the blind and

of musicians (see Dryden's *A Song for St. Cecilia's Day*); St. Gertrude is the patron saint of travelers; St. Mary Magdalen is the patron
saint of penitents; St. Margaret is the chosen type of female innocence
and meekness; St. Rosalie is the patron saint of the city of Palermo,

Whose head upon my knee to-night
Rests for a while, as if grown light
With all our dances and the sound
To which the wild tunes spun you round:
Fair Jenny mine, the thoughtless queen
Of kisses which the blush between
Could hardly make much daintier;
10 Whose eyes are as blue skies, whose hair
Is countless gold incomparable:
Fresh flower, scarce touched with signs that tell
Of Love's exuberant hotbed:—Nay,
Poor flower left torn since yesterday
Until to-morrow leave you bare;
Poor handful of bright spring-water
Flung in the whirlpool's shrieking face;
Poor shameful Jenny, full of grace
Thus with your head upon my knee;—
20 Whose person or whose purse may be
The lodestar of your reverie?

This room of yours, my Jenny, looks
A change from mine so full of books,
Whose serried ranks hold fast, forsooth,
So many captive hours of youth,—
The hours they thieve from day and night
To make one's cherished work come right,
And leave it wrong for all their theft,
Even as to-night my work was left:
30 Until I vowed that since my brain
And eyes of dancing seemed so fain,
My feet should have some dancing too:—
And thus it was I met with you.
Well, I suppose 'twas hard to part,
For here I am. And now, sweetheart,
You seem too tired to get to bed.

It was a careless life I led
When rooms like this were scarce so strange
Not long ago. What breeds the change,—
40 The many aims or the few years?
Because to-night it all appears
Something I do not know again.

The cloud's not danced out of my brain,—
The cloud that made it turn and swim
While hour by hour the books grew dim.
Why, Jenny, as I watch you there,—
For all your wealth of loosened hair,
Your silk ungirdled and unlac'd
And warm sweets open to the waist,
50 All golden in the lamplight's gleam,—
You know not what a book you seem,
Half-read by lightning in a dream!
How should you know, my Jenny? Nay,

And I should be ashamed to say:—
Poor beauty, so well worth a kiss!
But while my thought runs on like this
With wasteful whims more than enough,
I wonder what you're thinking of.

If of myself you think at all,
What is the thought?—conjectural   60
On sorry matters best unsolved?—
Or inly is each grace revolved
To fit me with a lure?—or (sad
To think!) perhaps you're merely glad
That I'm not drunk or ruffianly
And let you rest upon my knee.

For sometimes, were the truth confess'd,
You're thankful for a little rest,—
Glad from the crush to rest within,
From the heart-sickness and the din   70
Where envy's voice at virtue's pitch
Mocks you because your gown is rich;
And from the pale girl's dumb rebuke,
Whose ill-clad grace and toil-worn look
Proclaim the strength that keeps her weak,
And other nights than yours bespeak;
And from the wise unchildish elf,
To schoolmate lesser than himself
Pointing you out, what thing you are:—
Yes, from the daily jeer and jar,   80
From shame and shame's outbraving too,
Is rest not sometimes sweet to you?—
But most from the hatefulness of man,
Who spares not to end what he began,
Whose acts are ill and his speech ill,
Who, having used you at his will,
Thrusts you aside, as when I dine
I serve the dishes and the wine.

Well, handsome Jenny mine, sit up:
I've filled our glasses, let us sup,   90
And do not let me think of you,
Lest shame of yours suffice for two.
What, still so tired? Well, well then, keep
Your head there, so you do not sleep;
But that the weariness may pass
And leave you merry, take this glass,
Ah! lazy lily hand, more bless'd
If ne'er in rings it had been dress'd
Nor ever by a glove conceal'd!

Behold the lilies of the field,   100
They toil not neither do they spin;
(So doth the ancient text begin,—
Not of such rest as one of these

Sicily.   126. **citherns and citoles,** medieval stringed musical instruments.
    Jenny. Vengeance . . . **child.** See *The Merry Wives of Windsor,*
IV, i, 61.   17. **whirlpool,** of vice.   30. **brain . . . dancing,** i.e., from
overwork.   49. **sweets,** breasts.   75. **strength . . . weak.** Her strength

(virtue) restricts her to a life of hard work and poor food, which keeps
her weak.   102. **ancient text,** Matthew 6:28–29.

Can share.) Another rest and ease
Along each summer-sated path
From its new lord the garden hath,
Than that whose spring in blessings ran
Which praised the bounteous husbandman,
Ere yet, in days of hankering breath,
110 The lilies sickened unto death.

What, Jenny, are your lilies dead?
Aye, and the snow-white leaves are spread
Like winter on the garden-bed.
But you had roses left in May,—
They were not gone too. Jenny, nay,
But must your roses die, and those
Their purfled buds that should unclose?
Even so; the leaves are curled apart,
Still red as from the broken heart,
120 And here's the naked stem of thorns.

Nay, nay, mere words. Here nothing warns
As yet of winter. Sickness here
Or want alone could waken fear,—
Nothing but passion wrings a tear.
Except when there may rise unsought
Haply at times a passing thought
Of the old days which seem to be
Much older than any history
That is written in any book;
130 When she would lie in fields and look
Along the ground through the blown grass,
And wonder where the city was,
Far out of sight, whose broil and bale
They told her then for a child's tale.

Jenny, you know the city now.
A child can tell the tale there, how
Some things which are not yet enroll'd
In market-lists are bought and sold
Even till the early Sunday light,
140 When Saturday night is market-night
Everywhere, be it dry or wet,
And market-night in the Haymarket.
Our learned London children know,
Poor Jenny, all your pride and woe;
Have seen your lifted silken skirt
Advertise dainties through the dirt;
Have seen your coach-wheels splash rebuke
On virtue; and have learned your look
When, wealth and health slipped past, you stare
150 Along the streets alone, and there,
Round the long park, across the bridge,

The cold lamps at the pavement's edge
Wind on together and apart,
A fiery serpent for your heart.

Let the thoughts pass, an empty cloud!
Suppose I were to think aloud,—
What if to her all this were said?
Why, as a volume seldom read
Being opened halfway shuts again,
So might the pages of her brain   160
Be parted at such words, and thence
Close back upon the dusty sense.
For is there hue or shape defin'd
In Jenny's desecrated mind,
Where all contagious currents meet,
A Lethe of the middle street?
Nay, it reflects not any face,
Nor sound is in its sluggish pace,
But as they coil those eddies clot,
And night and day remember not.   170

Why, Jenny, you're asleep at last!
Asleep, poor Jenny, hard and fast,—
So young and soft and tired; so fair,
With chin thus nestled in your hair,
Mouth quiet, eyelids almost blue
As if some sky of dreams shone through!

Just as another woman sleeps!
Enough to throw one's thoughts in heaps
Of doubt and horror,—what to say
Or think,—this awful secret sway,   180
The potter's power over the clay!
Of the same lump (it has been said)
For honour and dishonour made,
Two sister vessels. Here is one.

My cousin Nell is fond of fun,
And fond of dress, and change, and praise,
So mere a woman in her ways:
And if her sweet eyes rich in youth
Are like her lips that tell the truth,
My cousin Nell is fond of love.   190
And she's the girl I'm proudest of.
Who does not prize her, guard her well?
The love of change, in cousin Nell,
Shall find the best and hold it dear:
The unconquered mirth turn quieter
Not through her own, through others' woe:
The conscious pride of beauty glow
Beside another's pride in her,

---

142. **Haymarket,** theater district of London.   166. **Lethe . . . street,**
a river of oblivion running down the middle of the street; some older
cities had gutters in the middle of the road.   258. **Psyche-wings,** moth
wings, but also an allusion to the soul.   282. **toad . . . stone,** fossil.

One little part of all they share.
For Love himself shall ripen these
In a kind soil to just increase
Through years of fertilising peace.

Of the same lump (as it is said)
For honour and dishonour made,
Two sister vessels. Here is one.

It makes a goblin of the sun.

So pure,—so fall'n! How dare to think
Of the first common kindred link?
Yet, Jenny, till the world shall burn
It seems that all things take their turn;
And who shall say but this fair tree
May need, in changes that may be,
Your children's children's charity?
Scorned then, no doubt, as you are scorn'd!
Shall no man hold his pride forewarn'd
Till in the end, the Day of Days,
At Judgment, one of his own race,
As frail and lost as you, shall rise,—
His daughter, with his mother's eyes?

How Jenny's clock ticks on the shelf!
Might not the dial scorn itself
That has such hours to register?
Yet as to me, even so to her
Are golden sun and silver moon,
In daily largesse of earth's boon,
Counted for life-coins to one tune.
And if, as blindfold fates are toss'd,
Through some one man this life be lost,
Shall soul not somehow pay for soul?

Fair shines the gilded aureole
In which our highest painters place
Some living woman's simple face.
And the stilled features thus descried
As Jenny's long throat droops aside,—
The shadows where the cheeks are thin,
And pure wide curve from ear to chin,—
With Raffael's, Leonardo's hand
To show them to men's souls, might stand,
Whole ages long, the whole world through,
For preachings of what God can do.
What has man done here? How atone,
Great God, for this which man has done?
And for the body and soul which by
Man's pitiless doom must now comply
With lifelong hell, what lullaby
Of sweet forgetful second birth
Remains? All dark. No sign on earth

What measure of God's rest endows
The many mansions of His house.

If but a woman's heart might see
Such erring heart unerringly
For once! But that can never be.

Like a rose shut in a book
In which pure women may not look,
For its base pages claim control
To crush the flower within the soul;
Where through each dead rose-leaf that clings,
Pale as transparent Psyche-wings,
To the vile text, are traced such things
As might make lady's cheek indeed
More than a living rose to read;
So nought save foolish foulness may
Watch with hard eyes the sure decay;
And so the life-blood of this rose,
Puddled with shameful knowledge, flows
Through leaves no chaste hand may unclose:
Yet still it keeps such faded show
Of when 't was gathered long ago,
That the crushed petals' lovely grain,
The sweetness of the sanguine stain,
Seen of a woman's eyes, must make
Her pitiful heart, so prone to ache,
Love roses better for its sake:—
Only that this can never be:—
Even so unto her sex is she.

Yet, Jenny, looking long at you,
The woman almost fades from view.
A cipher of man's changeless sum
Of lust, past, present, and to come,
Is left. A riddle that one shrinks
To challenge from the scornful sphinx.

Like a toad within a stone
Seated while Time crumbles on;
Which sits there since the earth was curs'd
For Man's transgression at the first;
Which, living through all centuries,
Not once has seen the sun arise;
Whose life, to its cold circle charmed,
The earth's whole summers have not warmed;
Which always—whitherso the stone
Be flung—sits there, dead, blind, alone;—
Aye, and shall not be driven out
Till that which shuts him round about
Break at the very Master's stroke,
And the dust thereof vanish as smoke,
And the seed of Man vanish as dust:—
Even so within this world is Lust.

Come, come, what use in thoughts like this?
Poor little Jenny, good to kiss,—
300 You'd not believe by what strange roads
Thought travels, when your beauty goads
A man to-night to think of toads!
Jenny, wake up . . . Why, there's the dawn!

And there's an early waggon drawn
To market, and some sheep that jog
Bleating before a barking dog;
And the old streets come peering through
Another night that London knew;
And all as ghostlike as the lamps.

310 So on the wings of day decamps
My last night's frolic. Glooms begin
To shiver off as lights creep in
Past the gauze curtains half drawn-to,
And the lamp's doubled shade grows blue,—
Your lamp, my Jenny, kept alight,
Like a wise virgin's, all one night!
And in the alcove coolly spread
Glimmers with dawn your empty bed;
And yonder your fair face I see
320 Reflected lying on my knee,
Where teems with first foreshadowings
Your pier-glass scrawled with diamond rings:
And on your bosom all night worn
Yesterday's rose now droops forlorn,
But dies not yet this summer morn.

And now without, as if some word
Had called upon them that they heard,
The London sparrows far and nigh
Clamour together suddenly;
330 And Jenny's cage-bird grown awake
Here in their song his part must take,
Because here too the day doth break.

And somehow in myself the dawn
Among stirred clouds and veils withdrawn
Strikes greyly on her. Let her sleep.
But will it wake her if I heap
These cushions thus beneath her head
Where my knee was? No,—there's your bed,
My Jenny, while you dream. And there
340 I lay among your golden hair
Perhaps the subject of your dreams,
These golden coins.
                For still one deems
That Jenny's flattering sleep confers
New magic on the magic purse,—
Grim web, how clogged with shrivelled flies!

Between the threads fine fumes arise
And shape their pictures in the brain.
There roll no streets in glare and rain,
Nor flagrant man-swine whets his tusk;
But delicately sighs in musk   350
The homage of the dim boudoir;
Or like a palpitating star
Thrilled into song, the opera-night
Breathes faint in the quick pulse of light;
Or at the carriage-window shine
Rich wares for choice; or, free to dine,
Whirls through its hour of health (divine
For her) the concourse of the Park.
And though in the discounted dark
Her functions there and here are one,   360
Beneath the lamps and in the sun
There reigns at least the acknowledged belle
Apparelled beyond parallel.
Ah Jenny, yes, we know your dreams.

For even the Paphian Venus seems
A goddess o'er the realms of love,
When silver-shrined in shadowy grove:
Aye, or let offerings nicely plac'd
But hide Priapus to the waist,
And whoso looks on him shall see   370
An eligible deity.

Why, Jenny, waking here alone
May help you to remember one,
Though all the memory's long outworn
Of many a double-pillowed morn.
I think I see you when you wake,
And rub your eyes for me, and shake
My gold, in rising, from your hair,
A Danaë for a moment there.

Jenny, my love rang true! for still   380
Love at first sight is vague, until
That tinkling makes him audible.

And must I mock you to the last,
Ashamed of my own shame,—aghast
Because some thoughts not born amiss
Rose at a poor fair face like this?
Well, of such thoughts so much I know:
In my life, as in hers, they show,
By a far gleam which I may near,
A dark path I can strive to clear.   390

Only one kiss. Good-bye, my dear.
(1848; 1870)

322. **scrawled . . . rings.** Her lovers scratched their names on her mirror.
365. **Paphian Venus.** Venus was said to have appeared from the foam at Paphos on the island of Crete, where she reigned over erotic rites.
369. **Priapus,** personification of lust.   379. **Danaë,** the daughter of the king of Argos who was seduced by Zeus; he appeared to her in a golden shower.
Sister Helen. 64. **Boyne Bar,** a famous sand bar at the mouth of the Boyne River, Leinster, Ireland.

SISTER HELEN

The basis of this poem is the old superstition that melting a waxen image of a person will bring suffering and death upon him. The false lover whom Helen is punishing is Keith of Ewern (l. 87). The refrain is a characteristic of the so-called Pre-Raphaelite ballads of the period.

"Why did you melt your waxen man,
          Sister Helen?
Today is the third since you began."
"The time was long, yet the time ran,
          Little brother."
       (O Mother, Mary Mother,
Three days today, between Hell and Heaven!)

"But if you have done your work aright,
          Sister Helen,
10 You'll let me play, for you said I might."
"Be very still in your play tonight,
          Little brother."
       (O Mother, Mary Mother,
Third night, tonight, between Hell and Heaven!)

"You said it must melt ere vesper-bell,
          Sister Helen;
If now it be molten, all is well."
"Even so—nay, peace! you cannot tell,
          Little brother."
20   *(O Mother, Mary Mother,*
Oh, what is this, between Hell and Heaven?)

"Oh, the waxen knave was plump today,
          Sister Helen;
How like dead folk he has dropped away!"
"Nay now, of the dead what can you say,
          Little brother?"
       (O Mother, Mary Mother,
What of the dead, between Hell and Heaven?)

"See, see, the sunken pile of wood,
30   Sister Helen,
Shines through the thinned wax red as blood!"
"Nay now, when looked you yet on blood,
          Little brother?"
       (O Mother, Mary Mother,
How pale she is, between Hell and Heaven!)

"Now close your eyes, for they're sick and sore,
          Sister Helen,
And I'll play without the gallery door."
"Aye, let me rest—I'll lie on the floor,
40   Little brother."
       (O Mother, Mary Mother,
What rest tonight, between Hell and Heaven?)

"Here high up in the balcony,
          Sister Helen,
The moon flies face to face with me."
"Aye, look and say whatever you see,
          Little brother."
       (O Mother, Mary Mother,
What sight tonight, between Hell and Heaven?)

"Outside it's merry in the wind's wake,   50
          Sister Helen;
In the shaken trees the chill stars shake."
"Hush, heard you a horse-tread as you spake,
          Little brother?"
       (O Mother, Mary Mother,
What sound tonight, between Hell and Heaven?)

"I hear a horse-tread, and I see,
          Sister Helen,
Three horsemen that ride terribly."
"Little brother, whence come the three,   60
          Little brother?"
       (O Mother, Mary Mother,
Whence should they come, between Hell and Heaven?)

"They come by the hill-verge from Boyne Bar,
          Sister Helen,
And one draws nigh, but two are afar."
"Look, look, do you know them who they are,
          Little brother?"
       (O Mother, Mary Mother,
Who should they be, between Hell and Heaven?) 70

"Oh, it's Keith of Eastholm rides so fast,
          Sister Helen,
For I know the white mane on the blast."
"The hour has come, has come at last,
          Little brother!"
       (O Mother, Mary Mother,
Her hour at last, between Hell and Heaven!)

"He has made a sign and called Halloo!
          Sister Helen,
And he says that he would speak with you."   80
"Oh, tell him I fear the frozen dew,
          Little brother."
       (O Mother, Mary Mother,
Why laughs she thus, between Hell and Heaven?)

"The wind is loud, but I hear him cry,
          Sister Helen,
That Keith of Ewern's like to die."
"And he and thou, and thou and I,
          Little brother."
       (O Mother, Mary Mother,   90
And they and we, between Hell and Heaven!)

"Three days ago, on his marriage-morn,
          Sister Helen,

He sickened, and lies since then forlorn."
"For bridegroom's side is the bride a thorn,
  Little brother?"
    (O Mother, Mary Mother,
Cold bridal cheer, between Hell and Heaven!)

"Three days and nights now he has lain abed,
  Sister Helen,
And he prays in torment to be dead."
"The thing may chance, if he have prayed,
  Little brother!"
    (O Mother, Mary Mother,
If he have prayed, between Hell and Heaven!)

"But he has not ceased to cry today,
  Sister Helen,
That you should take your curse away."
"My prayer was heard—he need but pray,
  Little brother!"
    (O Mother, Mary Mother,
Shall God not hear, between Hell and Heaven?)

"But he says, till you take back your ban,
  Sister Helen,
His soul would pass, yet never can."
"Nay then, shall I slay a living man,
  Little brother?"
    (O Mother, Mary Mother,
A living soul, between Hell and Heaven!)

"But he calls forever on your name,
  Sister Helen,
And says that he melts before a flame."
"My heart for his pleasure fared the same,
  Little brother."
    (O Mother, Mary Mother,
Fire at the heart, between Hell and Heaven!)

"Here's Keith of Westholm riding fast,
  Sister Helen,
For I know the white plume on the blast."
"The hour, the sweet hour I forecast,
  Little brother!"
    (O Mother, Mary Mother,
Is the hour sweet, between Hell and Heaven!)

"He stops to speak, and he stills his horse,
  Sister Helen;
But his words are drowned in the wind's course."
"Nay hear, nay hear, you must hear perforce,
  Little brother!"
    (O Mother, Mary Mother,
What word now heard, between Hell and Heaven!)

"Oh, he says that Keith of Ewern's cry,
  Sister Helen,

Is ever to see you ere he die."
"In all that his soul sees, there am I,
  Little brother!"
    (O Mother, Mary Mother,
The soul's one sight, between Hell and Heaven!)

"He sends a ring and a broken coin,
  Sister Helen,
And bids you mind the banks of Boyne."
"What else he broke will he ever join,
  Little brother?"
    (O Mother, Mary Mother,
No, never joined, between Hell and Heaven!)

"He yields you these and craves full fain,
  Sister Helen,
You pardon him in his mortal pain."
"What else he took will he give again,
  Little brother?"
    (O Mother, Mary Mother,
Not twice to give, between Hell and Heaven!)

"He calls your name in an agony,
  Sister Helen,
That even dead Love must weep to see."
"Hate, born of Love, is blind as he,
  Little brother!"
    (O Mother, Mary Mother,
Love turned to hate, between Hell and Heaven!)

"Oh, it's Keith of Keith now that rides fast,
  Sister Helen,
For I know the white hair on the blast."
"The short, short hour will soon be past,
  Little brother!"
    (O Mother, Mary Mother,
Will soon be past, between Hell and Heaven!)

"He looks at me and he tries to speak,
  Sister Helen,
But oh! his voice is sad and weak!"
"What here should the mighty Baron seek,
  Little brother?"
    (O Mother, Mary Mother,
Is this the end, between Hell and Heaven?)

"Oh! his son still cries, if you forgive,
  Sister Helen,
The body dies, but the soul shall live."
"Fire shall forgive me as I forgive,
  Little Brother!"
    (O Mother, Mary Mother,
As she forgives, between Hell and Heaven!)

"Oh, he prays you, as his heart would rive,
  Sister Helen,
To save his dear son's soul alive."

148. **broken coin.** The two had broken a coin, and each had kept half as a pledge.

"Fire cannot slay it; it shall thrive,
        Little brother!"
    (O Mother, Mary Mother,
Alas, alas, between Hell and Heaven!)

"He cries to you, kneeling in the road,
        Sister Helen,
To go with him for the love of God!"
200 "The way is long to his son's abode,
        Little brother."
    (O Mother, Mary Mother,
The way is long, between Hell and Heaven!)

"A lady's here, by a dark steed brought,
        Sister Helen,
So darkly clad, I saw her not."
"See her now or never see aught,
        Little brother!"
210 (O Mother, Mary Mother,
What more to see, between Hell and Heaven!)

"Her hood falls back, and the moon shines fair,
        Sister Helen,
On the Lady of Ewern's golden hair."
"Blest hour of my power and her despair,
        Little brother!"
    (O Mother, Mary Mother,
Hour blest and banned, between Hell and Heaven!)

"Pale, pale her cheeks, that in pride did glow,
        Sister Helen,
220 'Neath the bridal-wreath three days ago."
"One morn for pride and three days for woe,
        Little brother!"
    (O Mother, Mary Mother,
Three days, three nights, between Hell and Heaven!)

"Her clasped hands stretch from her bending head,
        Sister Helen;
With the loud wind's wail her sobs are wed."
"What wedding-strains hath her bridal-bed,
        Little brother?"
230 (O Mother, Mary Mother,
What strain but death's, between Hell and Heaven!)

"She may not speak, she sinks in a swoon,
        Sister Helen—
She lifts her lips and gasps on the moon."
"Oh! might I but hear her soul's blithe tune,
        Little brother!"
    (O Mother, Mary Mother,
Her woe's dumb cry, between Hell and Heaven!)

"They've caught her to Westholm's saddle-bow,
240 Sister Helen,
And her moonlit hair gleams white in its flow."
"Let it turn whiter than winter snow,

Little brother!"
    (O Mother, Mary Mother,
Woe-withered gold, between Hell and Heaven!)

"O Sister Helen, you heard the bell,
        Sister Helen!
More loud than the vesper-chime it fell."
"No vesper-chime, but a dying knell,
        Little brother!"   250
    (O Mother, Mary Mother,
His dying knell, between Hell and Heaven!)

"Alas! but I fear the heavy sound,
        Sister Helen;
Is it in the sky or in the ground?"
"Say, have they turned their horses round,
        Little brother?"
    (O Mother, Mary Mother,
What would she more, between Hell and Heaven?)

"They have raised the old man from his knee,   260
        Sister Helen,
And they ride in silence hastily."
"More fast the naked soul doth flee,
        Little brother!"
    (O Mother, Mary Mother,
The naked soul, between Hell and Heaven!)

"Flank to flank are the three steeds gone,
        Sister Helen,
But the lady's dark steed goes alone."
"And lonely her bridegroom's soul hath flown,   270
        Little brother."
    (O Mother, Mary Mother,
The lonely ghost, between Hell and Heaven!)

"Oh, the wind is sad in the iron chill,
        Sister Helen,
And weary sad they look by the hill."
"But Keith of Ewern's sadder still,
        Little brother!"
    (O Mother, Mary Mother,
Most sad of all, between Hell and Heaven!)   280

"See, see, the wax has dropped from its place,
        Sister Helen,
And the flames are winning up apace!"
"Yet here they burn but for a space,
        Little brother!"
    (O Mother, Mary Mother,
Here for a space, between Hell and Heaven!)

"Ah! what white thing at the door has crossed,
        Sister Helen?
Ah! what is this that sighs in the frost?"   290
"A soul that's lost as mine is lost,
        Little brother!"

(O Mother, Mary Mother,
Lost, lost, all lost, between Hell and Heaven!)
(1851-1852; 1853, 1870)

THE BALLAD OF DEAD LADIES

(from François Villon)

The Ballad of Dead Ladies *is a translation of* Ballade des Dames du Temp Jadis, *by François Villon, the greatest of the French medieval poets. (See Swinburne's* A Ballad of Francois Villon, *p. 1119.)*

Tell me now in what hidden way is
  Lady Flora the lovely Roman?
Where's Hipparchia, and where is Thaïs,
  Neither of them the fairer woman?
  Where is Echo, beheld of no man,
Only heard on river and mere—
  She whose beauty was more than human? . . .
But where are the snows of yester-year?

Where's Héloïse, the learned nun,
10 For whose sake Abeillard, I ween,
Lost manhood and put priesthood on?
  (From Love he won such dule and teen!)
  And where, I pray you, is the Queen
Who willed that Buridan should steer
  Sewed in a sack's mouth down the Seine? . . .
But where are the snows of yester-year?

White Queen Blanche, like a queen of lilies,
  With a voice like any mermaiden—
Bertha Broadfoot, Beatrice, Alice,
  And Ermengarde the lady of Maine—
  And that good Joan whom Englishmen
At Rouen doomed and burned her there—
  Mother of God, where are they then? . . .
But where are the snows of yester-year?

Nay, never ask this week, fair lord,
  Where they are gone, nor yet this year,
Except with this for an overword—
  But where are the snows of yester-year?
(1869; 1869)

from THE HOUSE OF LIFE

These sonnets were written during a period of thirty-three years—1848-1881. Although they do not form an organic whole, they fulfill the mission indicated in the introductory sonnet. The title came from Rossetti's interest in astrology, according to which the heavens were regarded as divided into "houses," the most important of which was the "house of human life." The sonnets are largely autobiographical. They were mainly inspired by Elizabeth Siddall, with whom Rossetti fell deeply in love in 1850 and whom he married in 1860.

Rossetti's own decoration for The Sonnet.

The Ballad of Dead Ladies. 2. Lady Flora, perhaps the Roman goddess of flowers and spring; other identifications made her a wealthy and beautiful woman, or any one of several famous courtesans of Rome, named Flora. **3. Hipparchia,** the wife of Crates, the famous Cynic philosopher of Thebes, Greece (third century B.C.). **Thaïs,** perhaps the celebrated Athenian courtesan who accompanied Alexander the Great on his expedition into Asia, 331 B.C. Another Thaïs was the noted Egyptian courtesan who became a saint. **5. Echo,** a beautiful nymph who for love of Narcissus pined away until nothing was left of her but her voice. **9. Héloïse,** the beautiful niece of Canon Fulbert, of Paris. She fell in love with her teacher, Pierre Abélard (1079-1142), a scholastic philosopher and theologian. After they eloped and were married, she returned to her uncle's house and denied the marriage, in order that her love might not be a hindrance to Abélard's advancement in the church. Fulbert was so enraged at this move that he caused Abélard to be emasculated in order to make him canonically incapable of ecclesiastical preferment. Abélard then became a monk in the abbey of St. Denis, in Paris, and induced Héloïse to become a nun. **10. ween,** think. **12. dule and teen,** grief and pain. **13. the Queen,** Marguerite de Bourgogne, wife of Louis le Hutin (fourteenth century). She is the heroine of the legend of the Tour de Nesle, according to which she had her numerous lovers killed and thrown into the Seine; one of them, *Jean Buridan,* rector of the University of Paris, escaped this fate. **17. Queen Blanche,** probably Blanche of Castille,

THE SONNET

A sonnet is a moment's monument—
Memorial from the Soul's eternity
To one dead deathless hour. Look that it be,
Whether for lustral rite or dire portent,
Of its own arduous fullness reverent.
Carve it in ivory or in ebony,
As Day or Night may rule; and let Time see
Its flowering crest impearled and orient.
A sonnet is a coin, its face reveals
10 *The Soul—its converse, to what Power 'tis due:—*
Whether for tribute to the august appeals
Of Life, or dower in Love's high retinue,
It serve, or 'mid the dark wharf's cavernous breath,
In Charon's palm it pay the toll to Death.
(1880; 1881)

18. GENIUS IN BEAUTY

Beauty like hers is genius. Not the call
Of Homer's or of Dante's heart sublime—
Not Michael's hand furrowing the zones of time—
Is more with compassed mysteries musical;
Nay, not in Spring's or Summer's sweet footfall
More gathered gifts exuberant Life bequeathes
Than doth this sovereign face, whose love-spell breathes
Even from its shadowed contour on the wall.
As many men are poets in their youth,
10 But for one sweet-strung soul the wires prolong
Even through all change the indomitable song;
So in like wise the envenomed years, whose tooth
Rends shallower grace with ruin void of ruth,
Upon this beauty's power shall wreak no wrong.
(1881)

19. SILENT NOON

Your hands lie open in the long, fresh grass—
The finger-points look through like rosy blooms;
Your eyes smile peace. The pasture gleams and glooms
'Neath billowing skies that scatter and amass.
All round our nest, far as the eye can pass,
Are golden kingcup-fields with silver edge
Where the cow-parsley skirts the hawthorn hedge.
'Tis visible silence, still as the hour-glass.
Deep in the sun-searched growths the dragon-fly
10 Hangs like a blue thread loosened from the sky—

So this winged hour is dropped to us from above.
Oh! clasp we to our hearts, for deathless dower,
This close-companioned inarticulate hour
When twofold silence was the song of love.
(1881)

24. PRIDE OF YOUTH

Even as a child, of sorrow that we give
The dead, but little in his heart can find,
Since without need of thought to his clear mind
Their turn it is to die and his to live—
Even so the winged New Love smiles to receive
Along his eddying plumes the auroral wind,
Nor, forward glorying, casts one look behind
Where night-rack shrouds the Old Love fugitive.
There is a change in every hour's recall,
And the last cowslip in the fields we see   10
On the same day with the first corn-poppy.
Alas for hourly change! Alas for all
The loves that from his hand proud Youth lets fall,
Even as the beads of a told rosary!
(1881)

48. DEATH-IN-LOVE

There came an image in Life's retinue
That had Love's wings and bore his gonfalon;
Fair was the web, and nobly wrought thereon,
O soul-sequestered face, thy form and hue!
Bewildering sounds, such as spring wakens to,
Shook in its folds; and through my heart its power
Sped trackless as the immemorable hour
When birth's dark portal groaned and all was new.
But a veiled woman followed, and she caught
The banner round its staff, to furl and cling—   10
Then plucked a feather from the bearer's wing,
And held it to his lips that stirred it not,
And said to me, "Behold, there is no breath;
I and this Love are one, and I am Death."
(1870)

53. WITHOUT HER

What of her glass without her? The blank gray
There where the pool is blind of the moon's face.
Her dress without her? The tossed empty space
Of cloud-rack whence the moon has passed away.
Her paths without her? Day's appointed sway
Usurped by desolate night. Her pillowed place

mother of Louis IX, king of France (1226–1270). 19. **Bertha Broadfoot**, the mother of Charlemagne (742–814), king of the Franks and emperor of the West. She is a prominent character in medieval romances dealing with Charlemagne and his court. **Beatrice, Alice.** These were names of various well-known women of the Middle Ages, and it is impossible to tell the exact persons meant. Beatrice might be Dante's Beatrice or Béatrix de Provence, wife of Charles, son of Louis VIII, king of France (1223–1226). Alice may be Aelis, one of the characters in the romance *Aliscans*, or Alix de Champagne, wife of Louis le Jeune (twelfth century). 20. **Ermengarde**, the daughter of d'Hélie, Count of Maine, an old province in northwestern France. She was the wife of Foulques V, Count of Anjou. She died in 1126. 21. **Joan**, Joan of

Arc (1412–1431), who saved France from conquest, but who later was imprisoned at Rouen, France, by the English, convicted of witchcraft and heresy, and burned at the stake. She was made a saint in 1920.
  The Sonnet. 4. **lustral rite,** ceremony of purification. 14. **Charon's . . . Death.** Charon was the boatman who ferried the souls of the dead over the Styx, one of the rivers of Hades. His pay was a coin found in the mouth of the passenger.
  Sonnet 18. 3. **Michael,** Michelangelo (1475–1564), a celebrated Italian painter, sculptor, and architect. The reference is to his figures of "Day," "Evening," "Night," etc.
  Sonnet 24. 14. **told,** counted.
  Sonnet 48. 2. **gonfalon,** banner.

Without her? Tears, ah me! for love's good grace,
And cold forgetfulness of night or day.
What of the heart without her? Nay, poor heart,
10 Of thee what word remains ere speech be still?
A wayfarer by barren ways and chill,
Steep ways and weary, without her thou art,
Where the long cloud, the long wood's counterpart,
Sheds doubled darkness up the laboring hill.
(1881)

55. STILLBORN LOVE

The hour which might have been yet might not be,
Which man's and woman's heart conceived and bore
Yet whereof life was barren—on what shore
Bides it the breaking of Time's weary sea?
Bondchild of all consummate joys set free,
It somewhere sighs and serves, and mute before
The house of Love, hears through the echoing door
His hours 'elect in choral consonancy.
But lo! what wedded souls now hand in hand
10 Together tread at last the immortal strand
With eyes where burning memory lights love home?
Lo! how the little outcast hour has turned
And leaped to them and in their faces yearned—
"I am your child; O parents, ye have come!"
(1869; 1870)

69. AUTUMN IDLENESS

This sunlight shames November where he
    grieves
In dead red leaves, and will not let him shun
The day, though bough with bough be overrun.
But with a blessing every glade receives
High salutation; while from hillock-eaves
The deer gaze calling, dappled white and dun,
As if, being foresters of old, the sun
Had marked them with the shade of forest-leaves.
Here dawn today unveiled her magic glass;
Here noon now gives the thirst and takes the
10   dew;
Till eve bring rest when other good things pass.
And here the lost hours the lost hours renew
While I still lead my shadow o'er the grass,
Nor know, for longing, that which I should do.
(1870)

77. SOUL'S BEAUTY

(Sibylla Palmifera)

The original title of this sonnet was Sibylla Palmi-
fera, *and it was written for a painting so named. In
the picture, Sibyl, the ancient prophetess, bears a
palm branch and is seated on a throne beneath a
canopy of stone overlooking the court of a temple.*

Under the arch of Life, where love and death,
Terror and mystery, guard her shrine I saw
Beauty enthroned; and though her gaze struck awe,
I drew it in as simply as my breath.
Hers are the eyes which, over and beneath,
The sky and sea bend on thee—which can draw,
By sea or sky or woman, to one law,
The allotted bondman of her palm and wreath.
This is that Lady Beauty, in whose praise
Thy voice and hand shake still;—long known to thee 10
By flying hair and fluttering hem—the beat
Following her daily of thy heart and feet,
How passionately and irretrievably,
In what fond flight, how many ways and days!
(1866; 1870)

78. BODY'S BEAUTY

(Lilith)

*Originally called Lilith, this sonnet was written for
a painting entitled Lady Lilith. Lilith was the traditional first wife of Adam. In both the painting and
the sonnet she represents fleshly beauty and passion.*

Of Adam's first wife, Lilith, it is told
(The witch he loved before the gift of Eve)
That, ere the snake's, her sweet tongue could deceive,
And her enchanted hair was the first gold.
And still she sits, young while the earth is old,
And, subtly of herself contemplative,
Draws men to watch the bright web she can weave,
Till heart and body and life are in its hold.
The rose and poppy are her flowers; for where
Is he not found, O Lilith, whom shed scent   10
And soft-shed kisses and soft sleep shall snare?
Lo! as that youth's eyes burned at thine, so went
Thy spell through him, and left his straight neck bent
And round his heart one strangling golden hair.
(1864; 1870)

86. LOST DAYS

The lost days of my life until today,
What were they, could I see them on the street
Lie as they fell? Would they be ears of wheat
Sown once for food but trodden into clay?
Or golden coins squandered and still to pay?
Or drops of blood dabbling the guilty feet?
Or such spilt water as in dreams must cheat
The undying throats of hell, athirst alway?
I do not see them here; but after death
God knows I know the faces I shall see,   10
Each one a murdered self, with low last breath.
"I am thyself—what hast thou done to me?"
"And I—and I—thyself" (lo! each one saith),
"And thou thyself to all eternity!"
(1858; 1869)

WILLIAM MORRIS 1834-1896

William Morris was a remarkable contrast to Rossetti, although his spiritual affinities were also with the Pre-Raphaelite Brotherhood. Like Rossetti he was one of the most assiduous and able interpreters of medieval beauty to nineteenth-century England, but unlike him he was an extremely rational artist. His contribution to English literature and life was therefore not only a philosophy of art, it included a real transformation of Victorian commonplaceness and stuffy ugliness in the physical environment of living into the rare and beautiful, whether it be in poetry, stained glass, interior decoration, printing and bookbinding, or furniture. We have all at one time or another been comfortable in a Morris chair.

Morris was the son of a wealthy broker of Walthamstow. At Exeter College, Oxford, his interest in architecture and painting was developed through his friendship with the eminent painter Edward Burne-Jones (1833-1898). Burne-Jones' influence was so strong that for a time Morris planned to devote his life to art. He eventually decided on a more practical

A view of Kelmscott Manor, the home of William Morris, the engraving is opposite the first page of Morris' News from Nowhere, printed at the Kelmscott Press, 1892.

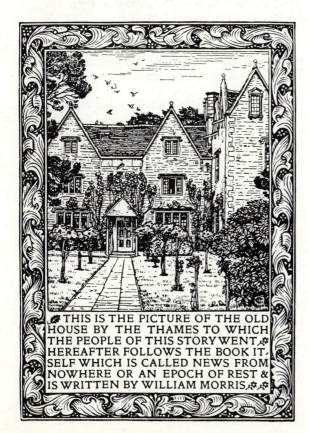

career, a further acquaintance with D. G. Rossetti and the poets and painters of the Pre-Raphaelite Brotherhood enabled him to crystallize his ideas about art, with the result that he established a firm which sought to correct and improve English artistic taste by bringing art into English homes. Burne-Jones and Madox Brown assisted him, but he eventually took over the business himself. His firm became known for the beauty of its tapestries, carpets, and furniture. In 1891 he founded the famous Kelmscott Press at his country estate at Hammersmith on the Thames, and in the five years left before his death he printed fifty-three books remarkable for their beauty of paper, typography, and binding. Among these the masterpieces were the Kelmscott Chaucer and Malory's Morte Darthur.

Morris followed Ruskin in allowing his hatred of the ugly and unjust in life to express itself in attacks on the existing order, but, unlike Ruskin, he embraced the cause of socialism. For several years he was so ardent in his beliefs that he almost deserted his art and poetry for the cause. He became treasurer of the National Liberal League in 1879, and, seceding with others of the extreme left wing four years later, he helped to form the Social Democrat Federation and soon became the leader of this organization although he turned out to be disillusioned to such an extent that he dropped from the leadership in 1889. His Dream of John Ball (1888) and News from Nowhere (1891), a Utopian vision, are the important literary products of this episode in Morris' life, but he wrote also a number of effective "marching songs" for his socialistic companions.

Morris' early poems are unquestionably Pre-Raphaelite in nature, his later technique, however, shows a strong influence by Chaucer in that it prefers narrative poetry to other types and in its details shows both some of the fluency of the great Middle English poet and a grasp of realistic details as well. But Morris does not possess either Chaucer's great incisiveness or his power of portraiture and characterization, for he was not the reporter of contemporary life that Chaucer was. The tempo of Morris' stories in verse is slow—almost static, the tone is one of sadness, the descriptions are numerous, the characters are medieval or classical types of faint beauty but as lacking in flesh and blood as figures on a vase. Except for the propagandistic romances of the years of his socialistic activity, Morris' poems had one main purpose—to express in the melody of words the same beauty that he expressed in his woodwork, glass, and textiles.

The first of Morris' publications was The Defense of Guenevere and Other Poems (1858), the title poem is written in Dantesque terza rima, and, like The Life and Death of Jason (1867)—a romantic treatment of the Greek legend of Jason and Medea—it illustrates supremely well the Pre-Raphaelite style of his early poetry. In The Earthly Paradise (1868-1870) he combined in a prologue, epilogue, and twenty-four tales an equal number of Greek and Norse tales. The framework of this poem suggests the influence of Chaucer's Canterbury Tales, although the division of the stories according to months of the year, with appropriate lyrics for each month, resembles the plan of Spenser's Shepheardes Calender. In any event, the antiquarian flavor is evident. Morris' most important long poem is probably his translation of Sigurd the Volsung (1876), a fine version of the great Norse saga. After his adventure in socialism he undertook a remarkable series of light prose romances, embellished with lyrics, that are most unusual in the Victorian period. These comprise The House of the Wolfings (1889), The Story of the Glittering Plain (1890), The Roots of the Mountains (1890), The Wood Beyond the World (1894), Child Christopher (1895), The Well at the World's End (1896), The Water of the Wondrous Isles (1897), and The Story of the Sundering Flood (1898). The last two of these were published after Morris' death.

THE DEFENSE OF GUENEVERE

An instinct for the picturesque and the dramatic led Morris to select from classical and medieval legends those episodes and situations which are most vivid and tense. In The Defense of Guenevere he represents King Arthur's queen as defending herself against the charge of adultery with Sir Launcelot which was brought against her by Sir Gauwaine. This was her second trial on the same charge; at the first she was saved by Launcelot, who slew her accuser, Sir Mellyagraunce, in a trial by combat (see ll. 166-219). In her defense at the second trial she accuses Sir Gauwaine of plotting and of perjury, but her infatuation for Sir Launcelot is so great that she seems more intent on praising him than on attempting to establish her own innocence (ll. 132-141). Morris drew the general material for his poem from Malory's Morte Darthur (p. 144 ff.), but changed many of the details. Furthermore, he brings into his account of the relations of Launcelot and Guenevere none of the morality which appears in Tennyson's Idylls of the King (p. 901), where the sin of the knight and the queen destroyed the virtue of the Table Round.

But, knowing now that they would have her speak,
She threw her wet hair backward from her brow,
Her hand close to her mouth touching her cheek,

As though she had had there a shameful blow,
And feeling it shameful to feel aught but shame
All through her heart, yet felt her cheek burned so,

She must a little touch it; like one lame
She walked away from Gauwaine, with her head
Still lifted up; and on her cheek of flame

The tears dried quick; she stopped at last and said: 10
"O knights and lords, it seems but little skill
To talk of well-known things past now and dead.

"God wot I ought to say, I have done ill,
And pray you all forgiveness heartily!
Because you must be right, such great lords; still

"Listen—suppose your time were come to die,
And you were quite alone and very weak;
Yea, laid a-dying, while very mightily

"The wind was ruffling up the narrow streak
Of river through your broad lands running well;   20
Suppose a hush should come, then someone speak:

"'One of these cloths is heaven, and one is hell;
Now choose one cloth forever—which they be,
I will not tell you; you must somehow tell

"'Of your own strength and mightiness; here, see!'
Yea, yea, my lord, and you to ope your eyes,
At foot of your familiar bed to see

"A great God's angel standing, with such dyes,
Not known on earth, on his great wings, and hands,
Held out two ways, light from the inner skies   30

"Showing him well, and making his commands
Seem to be God's commands, moreover, too,
Holding within his hands the cloths on wands;

"And one of these strange choosing cloths was blue,
Wavy and long, and one cut short and red;
No man could tell the better of the two.

"After a shivering half-hour you said:
'God help! heaven's color, the blue'; and he said,
  'hell.'
Perhaps you would then roll upon your bed,

"And cry to all good men that loved you well,   40
'Ah, Christ! if only I had known, known, known';
Launcelot went away, then I could tell,

"Like wisest man how all things would be, moan,
And roll and hurt myself, and long to die,
And yet fear much to die for what was sown.

The Defense of Guenevere. 11. **skill,** reason, wisdom. 13. **wot,** knows. 46. **you . . . lie.** Gauwaine is here presented as an accuser.

See headnote. 80. **the cloths.** See ll. 21 ff. 126. **yellow . . . singers,** thrushes (l. 106).

"Nevertheless, you, O Sir Gauwaine, lie;
Whatever may have happened through these years,
God knows I speak truth, saying that you lie."

Her voice was low at first, being full of tears,
50 But as it cleared, it grew full loud and shrill,
Growing a windy shriek in all men's ears,

A ringing in their startled brains, until
She said that Gauwaine lied, then her voice sunk,
And her great eyes began again to fill,

Though still she stood right up, and never shrunk,
But spoke on bravely, glorious lady fair!
Whatever tears her full lips may have drunk,

She stood, and seemed to think, and wrung her
     hair,
Spoke out at last with no more trace of shame,
60 With passionate twisting of her body there:

"It chanced upon a day that Launcelot came
To dwell at Arthur's court—at Christmas-time
This happened; when the heralds sung his name,

"Son of King Ban of Benwick, seemed to chime
Along with all the bells that rang that day,
O'er the white roofs, with little change of rime.

"Christmas and whitened winter passed away,
And over me the April sunshine came,
Made very awful with black hail-clouds; yea,

70 "And in the summer I grew white with flame,
And bowed my head down; autumn, and the sick
Sure knowledge things would never be the same,

"However often spring might be most thick
Of blossoms and buds, smote on me, and I grew
Careless of most things, let the clock tick, tick,

"To my unhappy pulse, that beat right through
My eager body; while I laughed out loud,
And let my lips curl up at false or true,

"Seemed cold and shallow without any cloud.
80 Behold, my judges, then the cloths were brought;
While I was dizzied thus, old thoughts would crowd,

"Belonging to the time ere I was bought
By Arthur's great name and his little love;
Must I give up forever then, I thought,

"That which I deemed would ever round me
     move
Glorifying all things; for a little word,
Scarce ever meant at all, must I now prove

"Stone-cold forever? Pray you, does the Lord
Will that all folks should be quite happy and good?
I love God now a little, if this cord   90

"Were broken, once for all what striving could
Make me love anything in earth or heaven?
So day by day it grew, as if one should

"Slip slowly down some path worn smooth and even,
Down to a cool sea on a summer day;
Yet still in slipping there was some small leaven

"Of stretched hands catching small stones by the way,
Until one surely reached the sea at last,
And felt strange new joy as the worn head lay

"Back, with the hair like sea-weed; yea, all past   100
Sweat of the forehead, dryness of the lips,
Washed utterly out by the dear waves o'ercast,

"In the lone sea, far off from any ships!
Do I not know now of a day in spring?
No minute of that wild day ever slips

"From out my memory; I hear thrushes sing,
And wheresoever I may be, straightway
Thoughts of it all come up with most fresh
     sting.

"I was half mad with beauty on that day,
And went, without my ladies, all alone,   110
In a quiet garden walled round every way;

"I was right joyful of that wall of stone,
That shut the flowers and trees up with the sky,
And trebled all the beauty; to the bone—

"Yea, right through to my heart, grown very shy
With wary thoughts—it pierced, and made me
     glad,
Exceedingly glad, and I knew verily,

"A little thing just then had made me mad;
I dared not think, as I was wont to do,
Sometimes, upon my beauty; if I had   120

"Held out my long hand up against the blue,
And, looking on the tenderly darkened fingers,
Thought that by rights one ought to see quite through,

"There, see you, where the soft still light yet lingers,
Round by the edges; what should I have done,
If this had joined with yellow spotted singers,

"And startling green drawn upward by the sun?
But shouting, loosed out, see now! all my hair,
And trancedly stood watching the west wind run

"With faithful half-heard breathing sound—why
130   there
I lose my head e'en now in doing this.
But shortly listen: In that garden fair

"Came Launcelot walking; this is true, the kiss
Wherewith we kissed in meeting that spring day,
I scarce dare talk of the remembered bliss,

"When both our mouths went wandering in one way,
And aching sorely, met among the leaves;
Our hands, being left behind, strained far away.

"Never within a yard of my bright sleeves
140 Had Launcelot come before—and now so nigh!
After that day why is it Guenevere grieves?

This colophon and the one on the opposite page show the ornamentation typical of the books published by the Kelmscott Press. The colophon above is from News from Nowhere, 1892.

"Nevertheless, you, O Sir Gauwaine, lie,
Whatever happened on through all those years—
God knows I speak truth, saying that you lie.

"Being such a lady, could I weep these tears
If this were true? A great queen such as I,
Having sinned this way, straight her conscience
   sears;

"And afterwards she liveth hatefully,
Slaying and poisoning—certes never weeps;
150 Gauwaine, be friends now, speak me lovingly.

"Do I not see how God's dear pity creeps
All through your frame, and trembles in your mouth?
Remember in what grave your mother sleeps,

"Buried in some place far down in the south,
Men are forgetting as I speak to you;
By her head, severed in that awful drouth

"Of pity that drew Agravaine's fell blow,
I pray your pity! let me not scream out
Forever after, when the shrill winds blow

"Through half your castle-locks! let me not shout 160
Forever after in the winter night
When you ride out alone! in battle-rout

"Let not my rusting tears make your sword light!
Ah! God of mercy, how he turns away!
So, ever must I dress me to the fight,

"So—let God's justice work! Gauwaine, I say,
See me hew down your proofs; yea, all men know,
Even as you said, how Mellyagraunce one day,

"One bitter day in *la Fausse Garde*, for so
All good knights held it after, saw—   170
Yea, sirs, by cursed unknightly outrage, though

"You, Gauwaine, held his word without a flaw,
This Mellyagraunce saw blood upon my bed—
Whose blood then pray you? is there any law

"To make a queen say why some spots of red
Lie on her coverlet? or will you say,
'Your hands are white, lady, as when you wed,

"'Where did you bleed?' and must I stammer out—
   'Nay,
I blush indeed, fair lord, only to rend
My sleeve up to my shoulder, where there lay 180

"'A knife-point last night': so must I defend
The honor of the Lady Guenevere?
Not so, fair lords, even if the world should end

"This very day, and you were judges here
Instead of God. Did you see Mellyagraunce
When Launcelot stood by him?—what white fear

"Curdled his blood, and how his teeth did dance,
His side sink in? as my knight cried and said:
'Slayer of unarmed men, here is a chance!

"'Setter of traps, I pray you guard your head; 190
By God, I am so glad to fight with you,
Stripper of ladies, that my hand feels lead

"'For driving weight; hurrah now! draw and ·do,
For all my wounds are moving in my breast,
And I am getting mad with waiting so.'

"He struck his hands together o'er the beast,
Who fell down flat, and groveled at his feet,
And groaned at being slain so young. 'At least,'

---

153. **your mother.** According to Malory she was Morgawse, Arthur's sister. She was slain by her son Sir Gaheris (not Agravaine) when he found her faithless to her husband, King Lot, in Orkney (*Morte*

Darthur, X, 24). 168. **Mellyagraunce.** See headnote. 169. *la Fausse Garde,* the false prison in which Mellyagraunce had held her. 171. **unknightly outrage.** Mellyagraunce had entered the chamber of

"My knight said, 'Rise you, sir, who are so fleet
200 At catching ladies; half-armed will I fight,
My left side all uncovered!' Then, I weet,

"Up sprang Sir Mellyagraunce with great delight
Upon his knave's face; not until just then
Did I quite hate him, as I saw my knight

"Along the lists look to my stake and pen
With such a joyous smile, it made me sigh
From agony beneath my waist-chain, when

"The fight began, and to me they drew nigh;
Ever Sir Launcelot kept him on the right,
210 And traversed warily, and ever high

"And fast leapt caitiff's sword, until my knight
Sudden threw up his sword to his left hand,
Caught it, and swung it; that was all the fight,

"Except a spout of blood on the hot land;
For it was hottest summer; and I know
I wondered how the fire, while I should stand,

"And burn, against the heat, would quiver so,
Yards above my head; thus these matters went;
Which things were only warnings of the woe

220 "That fell on me. Yet Mellyagraunce was shent,
For Mellyagraunce had fought against the Lord;
Therefore, my lords, take heed lest you be blent

"With all his wickedness—say no rash word
Against me, being so beautiful; my eyes,
Wept all away to gray, may bring some sword

"To drown you in your blood; see my breast rise,
Like waves of purple sea, as here I stand;
And how my arms are moved in wonderful wise;

"Yea, also at my full heart's strong command,
230 See through my long throat how the words go up
In ripples to my mouth; how in my hand

"The shadow lies like wine within a cup
Of marvelously colored gold; yea, now
This little wind is rising, look you up,

"And wonder how the light is falling so
Within my moving tresses. Will you dare
When you have looked a little on my brow,

"To say this thing is vile? or will you care
For any plausible lies of cunning woof,
240 When you can see my face with no lie there

"Forever? Am I not a gracious proof?—
'But in your chamber Launcelot was found'—
Is there a good knight then would stand aloof,

"When a queen says with gentle queenly sound,
'O true as steel, come now and talk with me;
I love to see your step upon the ground

" 'Unwavering; also well I love to see
That gracious smile light up your face, and hear
Your wonderful words, that all mean verily

" 'The thing they seem to mean. Good friend, so   250
dear
To me in everything, come here tonight,
Or else the hours will pass most dull and drear.

The colophon from the Kelmscott edition of Swinburne's
Atalanta in Calydon, 1894.

" 'If you come not, I fear this time I might
Get thinking overmuch of times gone by,
When I was young, and green hope was in sight;

" 'For no man cares now to know why I sigh;
And no man comes to sing me pleasant songs,
Nor any brings me the sweet flowers that lie

" 'So thick in the gardens; therefore one so
longs
To see you, Launcelot, that we may be   260
Like children once again, free from all wrongs

" 'Just for one night.' Did he not come to me?
What thing could keep true Launcelot away
If I said, 'Come'? There was one less than three

"In my quiet room that night, and we were
gay;
Till sudden I rose up, weak, pale, and sick,
Because a bawling broke our dream up; yea,

Guenevere before she was up. 190. **Setter of traps.** Mellyagraunce
had trapped Launcelot. 201. **weet,** observed, knew. 216. **while . . .**
burn. Upon the testimony of Mellyagraunce she was sentenced to be
burned, but Launcelot's victory saved her. 220. **shent,** destroyed. 222.
blent, blinded. 242. **'But . . . found.'** For the story of the fight in
Guenevere's chamber, see Malory's *Morte Darthur,* XX, 4.

"I looked at Launcelot's face and could not speak,
For he looked helpless, too, for a little while;
270 Then I remember how I tried to shriek,

"And could not, but fell down; from tile to tile
The stones they threw up rattled o'er my head
And made me dizzier; till within a while

"My maids were all about me, and my head
On Launcelot's breast was being soothed away
From its white chattering, until Launcelot said . . .

"By God! I will not tell you more today—
Judge any way you will; what matters it?
You know quite well the story of that fray,

280 "How Launcelot stilled their bawling, the mad fit
That caught up Gauwaine, all, all, verily,
But just that which would save me; these things flit.

"Nevertheless, you, O Sir Gauwaine, lie;
Whatever may have happened these long years,
God knows I speak truth, saying that you lie!

"All I have said is truth, by Christ's dear tears."
She would not speak another word, but stood
Turned sideways, listening, like a man who hears

His brother's trumpet sounding through the wood
290 Of his foes' lances. She leaned eagerly,
And gave a slight spring sometimes, as she could

At last hear something really; joyfully
Her cheek grew crimson, as the headlong speed
Of the roan charger drew all men to see
The knight who came was Launcelot at good need.
(1858)

from THE EARTHLY PARADISE

In The Earthly Paradise Morris employed the familiar medieval device of a framework to bind together a series of tales. The enveloping action has to do with a band of medieval mariners, who set out from Europe to find a country in which they can be happy. They chance upon an island, the "Earthly Paradise," where live the descendants of Greeks who had colonized the country centuries before. At each of a series of banquets, which occur twice a month, the mariners relate some medieval romance, or the hosts tell an ancient Greek legend. Thus the cycle of tales runs two a month throughout the year—twelve medieval and twelve Greek legends being retold. Each set of two stories is preceded by a lyric appropriate to the month of the

year in which the tales are recited. The following Apology introduces the whole series.

AN APOLOGY

Of Heaven or Hell I have no power to sing;
I cannot ease the burden of your fears,
Or make quick-coming death a little thing,
Or bring again the pleasure of past years;
Nor for my words shall ye forget your tears,
Or hope again for aught that I can say—
The idle singer of an empty day.

But rather, when aweary of your mirth,
From full hearts still unsatisfied ye sigh,
And, feeling kindly unto all the earth,   10
Grudge every minute as it passes by,
Made the more mindful that the sweet days die—
Remember me a little then, I pray,
The idle singer of an empty day.

The heavy trouble, the bewildering care
That weighs us down who live and earn our
        bread,
These idle verses have no power to bear;
So let me sing of names rememberéd,
Because they, living not, can ne'er be dead,
Or long time take their memory quite away   20
From us poor singers of an empty day.

Dreamer of dreams, born out of my due time,
Why should I strive to set the crooked straight?
Let it suffice me that my murmuring rime,
Beats with light wing against the ivory gate,
Telling a tale not too importunate
To those who in the sleepy region stay,
Lulled by the singer of an empty day.

Folk say, a wizard to a northern king
At Christmas-tide such wondrous things did
        show,   30
That through one window men beheld the spring,
And through another saw the summer glow,
And through a third the fruited vines a-row,
While still, unheard, but in its wonted way,
Piped the drear wind of that December day.

So with this Earthly Paradise it is,
If ye will read aright, and pardon me,
Who strive to build a shadowy isle of bliss
Midmost the beating of the steely sea,
Where tossed about all hearts of men must be;   40
Whose ravening monsters mighty men shall slay—
Not the poor singer of an empty day.
(1868-1870)

---

280. **mad fit.** Gauwaine was not present. 282. **that . . . me,** her innocence. 291. **as,** as if. 295. **knight . . . need.** Launcelot and his

kinsmen rescued the Queen from the fire.
The Earthly Paradise. 1. **Of Heaven or Hell.** Morris disclaims

THE DAY IS COMING

Late in the seventies Morris became interested in politics and joined the Socialist party. Virtually all his time in the years 1883-1885 was given to the cause. This poem expresses his interest in the welfare of the lower classes. It was published with other poems in a pamphlet entitled Chants for Socialists.

Come hither, lads, and harken, for a tale there is to tell,
Of the wonderful days a-coming, when all shall be better than well.

And the tale shall be told of a country, a land in the midst of the sea,
And folk shall call it England in the days that are going to be.

There more than one in a thousand in the days that are yet to come,
Shall have some hope of the morrow, some joy of the ancient home.

For then—laugh not, but listen to this strange tale of mine—
All folk that are in England shall be better lodged than swine.

Then a man shall work and bethink him, and rejoice in the deeds of his hand,
Nor yet come home in the even too faint and weary to
10   stand.

Men in that time a-coming shall work and have no fear
For tomorrow's lack of earning and the hunger-wolf anear.

I tell you this for a wonder, that no man then shall be glad
Of his fellow's fall and mishap to snatch at the work he had,

For that which the worker winneth shall then be his indeed,
Nor shall half be reaped for nothing by him that sowed no seed.

O strange new wonderful justice! But for whom shall we gather the gain?
For ourselves and for each of our fellows, and no hand shall labor in vain.

Then all Mine and all Thine shall be Ours, and no more shall any man crave
For riches that serve for nothing but to fetter a friend
20   for a slave.

And what wealth then shall be left us when none shall gather gold
To buy his friend in the market, and pinch and pine the sold?

Nay, what save the lovely city, and the little house on the hill,
And the wastes and the woodland beauty, and the happy fields we till;

And the homes of ancient stories, the tombs of the mighty dead;
And the wise men seeking out marvels, and the poet's teeming head;

And the painter's hand of wonder; and the marvelous fiddle-bow,
And the banded choirs of music—all those that do and know.

For all these shall be ours and all men's; nor shall any lack a share
Of the toil and the gain of living in the days when the world grows fair.   30

Ah! such are the days that shall be! But what are the deeds of today,
In the days of the years we dwell in, that wear our lives away?

Why, then, and for what are we waiting? There are three words to speak—
WE WILL IT—and what is the foeman but the dream-strong wakened and weak?

O why and for what are we waiting? while our brothers droop and die,
And on every wind of the heavens a wasted life goes by.

How long shall they reproach us where crowd on crowd they dwell,
Poor ghosts of the wicked city, the gold-crushed, hungry hell?

Through squalid life they labored, in sordid grief they died,
Those sons of a mighty mother, those props of England's pride.   40

They are gone; there is none can undo it, nor save our souls from the curse;
But many a million cometh, and shall they be better or worse?

equality with earlier poets who used these themes—Vergil, Dante, Milton. 25. **the ivory gate.** The house of Morpheus, god of sleep, had two gates through which dreams issued. True dreams passed through a gate of horn; false dreams, through a gate of ivory.

It is we must answer and hasten, and open wide the
door
For the rich man's hurrying terror, and the slow-foot
hope of the poor.

Yea, the voiceless wrath of the wretched, and their
unlearned discontent,
We must give it voice and wisdom till the waiting-tide
be spent.

Come, then, since all things call us, the living and the
dead,
And o'er the weltering tangle a glimmering light is
shed.

Come, then, let us cast off fooling, and put by ease and
rest,
For the Cause alone is worthy till the good days bring
the best.

Come, join in the only battle wherein no man can
fail,
Where whoso fadeth and dieth, yet his deed shall still
prevail.

Ah! come cast off all fooling, for this, at least, we
know:
That the Dawn and the Day is coming, and forth the
Banners go.
(1884)

ALGERNON CHARLES SWINBURNE
1837-1909

*Algernon Charles Swinburne, undoubtedly the great-
est of these "poets aesthetic and pagan," was born
in London but spent most of his youth on the Isle of
Wight, where his father, Admiral Charles Swinburne, had his estate, or in Northumberland, where
his grandfather lived. Thus his effective environmental
influences were the sea and the moorlands. During
his days at Balliol College, Oxford, and for a time
afterwards, Swinburne was intensely sympathetic toward the aims and ideals of the Pre-Raphaelite group,
but he was never a member of this fraternity, although
he had an artistic kinship with any and all lovers of
the medieval and of sensuous beauty. With Rossetti
and his circle Swinburne shared a love of the rich
and varied romance of the Middle Ages, but he was
also a brilliant classical scholar, and his interpretations of Greek legend often captured much of the
spirit of the classics. His mastery of French was also
sufficient to enable him to write acceptable French
verse. Nor was his interest in English literature restricted to any one period. He was inspired by the*
old romances, but he was thoroughly at home with
the Elizabethan dramatists, and turned often from
his poetry-making to praise the powers of the Elizabethans in critical essays that are stirring if too
unrestrained and effusive. Swinburne's name, indeed,
belongs with those of aristocratic young rebels like
Byron and Shelley—both of whom he admired intensely—whose love of liberty and aggressive resistance to authority fascinated society but also alarmed
its conservative members. Swinburne, as a matter of
record, was more than once referred to as the "Victorian Byron."

*His first publication revealed his regard for the Pre-
Raphaelites, inasmuch as it was dedicated to Rossetti.
The Queen Mother, Rosamond—Two Plays (1860)
contained two romantic dramas in blank verse with
occasional lyrics in both French and English. These
were of little moment, but the same cannot be said of
Atalanta in Calydon (1865). This was a drama in the
classical Greek form based on the ancient legend
of the Calydonian boar hunt. It is probable that the
hymn to Artemis, sung as the opening chorus by a
group of Aetolian maidens, is Swinburne's most famous
poem. Certainly it is one of his most melodious, and
it is doubtful whether any other comparable lyric
in the English language conveys so magnificently in
words the sounds of nature—"the lisp of leaves and
ripple of rain" and the "noise of winds and many
rivers." If it had not been that the paganism of the
drama is in harmony with its remote story, the shock
that Swinburne gave to Victorian conventionalities
would have come in Atalanta in Calydon rather than
in the Poems and Ballads of the following year
(1866), for not only is the "hoofed heel of a
satyr" stamped upon the choruses, but the entire
drama also is permeated with a rebellion against
the tyranny of creeds and against the gods with their
instruments of death and decay.*

*Also in 1865 appeared Chastelard, the first of three
romantic dramas dealing with the story of Mary
Stuart. In this play and its successors—Bothwell (1874)
and Mary Stuart (1881)—the swiftness of action, the
penetrating delineation of character, and the general
dramatic power show that Swinburne had profited
much by his study of the great Elizabethan writers
of tragedy.*

*But Poems and Ballads caused a sensation in the
Victorian literary world. Swinburne suddenly became
famous—not to say notorious—for his outspoken unconventionality, but all true lovers of poetry were
fascinated by the sheer music of his verses. These
lyrics, revealing as they did that Swinburne was an
unashamedly pagan poet, were followed by a second
series in 1878 and a third in 1889. But there were other
sources of inspiration in his poetry besides the pagan
—his enthusiasm for Italian liberty was one, as it
was evinced in A Song of Italy (1867) and Songs*

before Sunrise (1871), and his love of the sea was another, as he shows in Songs of Springtides and Studies in Song, both published in 1880. His early contacts with the Pre-Raphaelite Brotherhood bore rather late fruit in Tristram of Lyonesse (1882), a romantic poem on the famous Arthurian love story which displays, in its rimed couplets, Swinburne's lyrical warmth, color, and metrical skill, but lacks the overall effectiveness of Morris' poetic narratives. The work, written in the last twenty years or so of his productive life, when he was living in ill health at the home of his friend Theodore Watts-Dunton (1832-1914), a noted literary critic, shows a considerable decline in power. The best is probably the tragedy, Marino Faliero (1885), in which he tried to surpass Byron, who also had written a poetic drama on the same subject. It cannot be said that Swinburne succeeded.

With Swinburne began, suddenly and sensationally, the revolt against Victorian assumptions and Victorian concerns. He promulgated not merely the criticism of the main drift of his age (every major literary figure does as much) but also a rebellion against both the realities and the proffered literary remedies. His outlook, from as early as 1865, was deeply antagonistic to the notions of even such comparatively enlightened "believers" as Tennyson and Browning:

And most things are so wrong
That all things must be right.
This satisfies our Browning,
And that delights our Tennyson:
And soothed Britannia simpers in serene applause.

Thus Swinburne rejected the thought-burden of the poetry of his older and greater contemporaries: their assumptions about life and art were simply no longer acceptable to him and his most original associates. He was not a Pre-Raphaelite, however, though he came for a time under the strong influence of Rossetti, and he was not an esthete, though he helped prepare the way for the art-for-art's-sake movement. He was a neopagan who attacked Christianity for its doctrine of death, for its social and political tyranny, and for its depressing effect upon the creative imagination; and more than any other poet of his time, he secularized the Victorian esthetic.

Swinburne was one of the most individually distinctive poets in English, and a thoughtful exploration of the source of that distinctiveness beyond the level of rhythmic virtuosity is a sober critical exercise.

The poems from Atalanta in Calydon are from Collected Poetical Works by Algernon Charles Swinburne. Used by permission of William Heinemann, Ltd., London.

from ATALANTA IN CALYDON

In this drama Swinburne attempted, he said, "to do something original in English which might in some degree reproduce for English readers the likeness of a Greek tragedy with something of its true poetic life and charm." The play concerns the famous hunt for the wild boar which was sent, according to legend, by Artemis, revengeful goddess of the moon, to ravage Calydon, a province in ancient Greece. Meleager killed the beast and presented the spoils of victory to Atalanta, a beautiful Arcadian huntress with whom he had fallen in love. When Toxeus and Plexippus, brothers of Queen Althaea, Meleager's mother, attempted to rob the huntress of her prize, their nephew slew them. On hearing of the tragedy, Meleager's mother burned to ashes the fagot upon which her son's life depended, and which she had carefully preserved up to that time. The poem which follows here is the opening chorus of the drama, sung by a group of maidens from Aetolia, an ancient Greek province.

WHEN THE HOUNDS OF SPRING

When the hounds of spring are on winter's traces,
  The mother of months in meadow or plain
Fills the shadows and windy places
  With lisp of leaves and ripple of rain;
And the brown bright nightingale amorous
Is half assuaged for Itylus,
For the Thracian ships and the foreign faces,
  The tongueless vigil, and all the pain.

Come with bows bent and with emptying of quivers,
  Maiden most perfect, lady of light,   10
With a noise of winds and many rivers,
  With a clamor of waters, and with might;
Bind on thy sandals, O thou most fleet,
Over the splendor and speed of thy feet;
For the faint east quickens, the wan west shivers,
  Round the feet of the day and the feet of the night.

Where shall we find her, how shall we sing to her,
  Fold our hands round her knees, and cling?
Oh, that man's heart were as fire and could spring to her,
  Fire, or the strength of the streams that spring!   20
For the stars and the winds are unto her
As raiment, as songs of the harp-player;

When the Hounds of Spring. 2. mother of months, Artemis, goddess of the moon. 6. Itylus. See Arnold's Philomela, and headnote, p. 938.

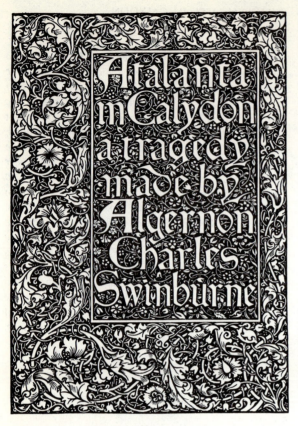
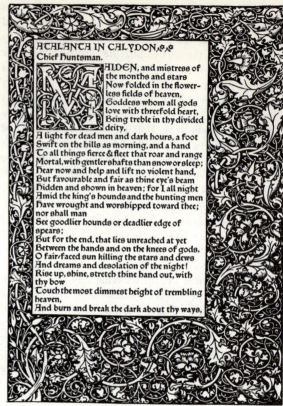

The opening pages of Swinburne's Atalanta in Calydon, *printed by William Morris at the Kelmscott Press, 1894.*

For the risen stars and the fallen cling to her,
    And the southwest wind and the west wind
        sing.

For winter's rains and ruins are over,
    And all the season of snows and sins;
The days dividing lover and lover,
    The light that loses, the night that wins;
And time remembered is grief forgotten,
30 And frosts are slain and flowers begotten,
And in green underwood and cover
    Blossom by blossom the spring begins.

The full streams feed on flower of rushes,
    Ripe grasses trammel a traveling foot,
The faint fresh flame of the young year
        flushes
    From leaf to flower and flower to fruit;
And fruit and leaf are as gold and fire,
And the oat is heard above the lyre,
And the hoofèd heel of a satyr crushes
40   The chestnut-husk at the chestnut-root.

And Pan by noon and Bacchus by night,
    Fleeter of foot than the fleet-foot kid,
Follows with dancing and fills with delight
    The Maenad and the Bassarid;
And soft as lips that laugh and hide
The laughing leaves of the trees divide,
And screen from seeing and leave in sight
    The god pursuing, the maiden hid.

The ivy falls with the Bacchanal's hair
    Over her eyebrows hiding her eyes;   50
The wild vine slipping down leaves bare
    Her bright breast shortening into sighs;
The wild vine slips with the weight of its leaves,
But the berried ivy catches and cleaves
To the limbs that glitter, the feet that scare
    The wolf that follows, the fawn that flies.
(1865)

BEFORE THE BEGINNING OF YEARS

This song is sung by the chorus after Althaea has

---

28. **light . . . wins,** a reference to the short days and long nights of winter. 38. **oat,** the shepherd's pipe of oaten straw. 39. **satyr,** a sylvan demigod, half man and half goat. 41. **Pan,** the god of flocks and pastures. **Bacchus,** the god of wine. 44. **Maenad,** a female worshiper of Bacchus. The name is derived from a Greek word meaning *to be*

frenzied. **Bassarid,** a Thracian worshiper of Bacchus. The celebrations of the Bassarids included licentious excesses and a sacrifice of some animal on the altar of the god. The participants ate the flesh raw. 47. **screen . . . hid.** As the god and the maiden slip through the forest, they are alternately concealed and revealed by the wind-swayed foliage.

departed to prepare her son Meleager for the hunt,
"lest love or some man's anger work him harm."

Before the beginning of years
    There came to the making of man
Time, with a gift of tears;
    Grief, with a glass that ran;
Pleasure, with pain for leaven;
    Summer, with flowers that fell;
Remembrance fallen from heaven,
    And madness risen from hell;
Strength without hands to smite;
10 Love that endures for a breath;
Night, the shadow of light,
    And life, the shadow of death.

And the high gods took in hand
    Fire, and the falling of tears,
And a measure of sliding sand
    From under the feet of the years;
And froth and drift of the sea;
    And dust of the laboring earth;
And bodies of things to be
20 In the houses of death and of birth;
And wrought with weeping and laughter,
    And fashioned with loathing and love,
With life before and after
    And death beneath and above,
For a day and a night and a morrow,
    That his strength might endure for a
      span
With travail and heavy sorrow,
    The holy spirit of man.

From the winds of the north and the
    south
30 They gathered as unto strife;
They breathed upon his mouth,
    They filled his body with life;
Eyesight and speech they wrought
    For the veils of the soul therein,
A time for labor and thought,
    A time to serve and to sin;
They gave him light in his ways,
    And love, and a space for delight,
And beauty and length of days,
40 And night, and sleep in the night.
His speech is a burning fire;
    With his lips he travaileth;
In his heart is a blind desire,
    In his eyes foreknowledge of death;
He weaves, and is clothed with derision;
    Sows, and he shall not reap;

His life is a watch or a vision
    Between a sleep and a sleep.
(1865)

THE GARDEN OF PROSERPINE

In Greek mythology Proserpine was the goddess
and queen of the lower world. She was the daughter
of Zeus and Demeter, or Ceres, goddess of the harvest,
and was carried off by Pluto, god of the lower world,
while she was gathering flowers in the Vale of Enna in
Sicily. Her mother wandered over the whole earth in
search of her. On Demeter's prayer to Zeus that Pro-
serpine be allowed to return to the upper world, he
permitted her to spend six months of the year on earth;
her alternate periods on earth and in Hades symbolize
the changes of the seasons.

This poem Swinburne represents as spoken by a
Roman pagan.

Here, where the world is quiet;
    Here, where all trouble seems
Dead winds' and spent waves' riot
    In doubtful dreams of dreams;
I watch the green field growing
For reaping folk and sowing,
For harvest-time and mowing,
    A sleepy world of streams.

I am tired of tears and laughter,
    And men that laugh and weep;   10
Of what may come hereafter
    For men that sow to reap;
I am weary of days and hours,
Blown buds of barren flowers,
Desires and dreams and powers
    And everything but sleep.

Here life has death for neighbor,
    And far from eye or ear
Wan waves and wet winds labor,
    Weak ships and spirits steer;   20
They drive adrift, and whither
They wot not who make thither;
But no such winds blow hither,
    And no such things grow here.

No growth of moor or coppice,
    No heather-flower or vine,
But bloomless buds of poppies,
    Green grapes of Proserpine,
Pale beds of blowing rushes

Before the Beginning of Years. 35. time . . . sin. Cf. Ecclesiastes
3:1–8.
    The Garden of Proserpine. 14. Blown . . . flowers, blossoming
flowers that will produce no fruit. They are used as a symbol of
unfulfilled desires and dreams. 22. wot, know. 27. poppies, the

flowers of oblivion, sacred to Proserpine, who was often represented
with a crown of them on her head (l. 50).
    The Garden of Proserpine is from *Collected Poetical Works* by Alger-
non Charles Swinburne. Used by permission of William Heinemann,
Ltd., London.

30 Where no leaf blooms or blushes
　　Save this whereout she crushes
　　　For dead men deadly wine.

　　Pale, without name or number,
　　　In fruitless fields of corn,
　　They bow themselves and slumber
　　　All night till light is born;
　　And like a soul belated,
　　In hell and heaven unmated,
　　By cloud and mist abated
40 　Comes out of darkness morn.

　　Though one were strong as seven,
　　　He too with death shall dwell,
　　Nor wake with wings in heaven,
　　　Nor weep for pains in hell;
　　Though one were fair as roses,
　　His beauty clouds and closes;
　　And well though love reposes,
　　　In the end it is not well.

　　Pale, beyond porch and portal,
50 　Crowned with calm leaves, she stands
　　Who gathers all things mortal
　　　With cold immortal hands;
　　Her languid lips are sweeter
　　Than love's who fears to greet her
　　To men that mix and meet her
　　　From many times and lands.

　　She waits for each and other,
　　　She waits for all men born;
　　Forgets the earth her mother,
60 　The life of fruits and corn;
　　And spring and seed and swallow
　　Take wing for her and follow
　　Where summer song rings hollow
　　　And flowers are put to scorn.

　　There go the loves that wither,
　　　The old loves with wearier wings;
　　And all dead years draw thither,
　　　And all disastrous things;
　　Dead dreams of days forsaken,
70 Blind buds that snows have shaken,
　　Wild leaves that winds have taken,
　　　Red strays of ruined springs.

　　We are not sure of sorrow,
　　　And joy was never sure;
　　Today will die tomorrow;
　　　Time stoops to no man's lure;
　　And love, grown faint and fretful,

With lips but half regretful
Sighs, and with eyes forgetful
　Weeps that no loves endure.　　　　　　　　80

From too much love of living,
　From hope and fear set free,
We thank with brief thanksgiving
　Whatever gods may be
That no life lives forever;
That dead men rise up never;
That even the weariest river
　Winds somewhere safe to sea.

Then star nor sun shall waken,
　Nor any change of light;　　　　　　　　　　90
Nor sound of waters shaken,
　Nor any sound or sight;
Nor wintry leaves nor vernal,
Nor days nor things diurnal;
Only the sleep eternal
　In an eternal night.
(1866)

DEDICATION TO POEMS AND BALLADS

Swinburne dedicated the first series of his Poems and
Ballads *(1866) to Sir Edward Burne-Jones (1833-
1898), an English painter, who was a member of the
Pre-Raphaelite group of artists and poets, a pupil of
Rossetti's, and a friend of Swinburne's.*

The sea gives her shells to the shingle,
　The earth gives her streams to the sea;
They are many, but my gift is single,
　My verses, the first fruits of me.
Let the wind take the green and the gray leaf,
　Cast forth without fruit upon air;
Take rose-leaf and vine-leaf and bay-leaf
　Blown loose from the hair.

The night shakes them round me in legions,
　Dawn drives them before her like dreams;　　10
Time sheds them like snows on strange regions,
　Swept shoreward on infinite streams;
Leaves pallid and somber and ruddy,
　Dead fruits of the fugitive years;
Some stained as with wine and made bloody,
　And some as with tears.

Some scattered in seven years' traces,
　As they fell from the boy that was then;
Long left among idle green places,
　Or gathered but now among men;　　　　　　20

---

94. **diurnal,** belonging to the daylight.
Dedication to Poems and Ballads is from *Collected Poetical Works* by
Algernon Charles Swinburne. Used by permission of William Heine-

mann, Ltd., London.
Dedication to Poems and Ballads. 1. **shingle,** coarse rounded
stones on the seashore. 7. **bay-leaf,** laurel leaf, sacred to the gods. 17.

On seas full of wonder and peril,
  Blown white round the capes of the north;
Or in islands where myrtles are sterile
  And loves bring not forth.

O daughters of dreams and of stories
  That life is not wearied of yet,
Faustine, Fragoletta, Dolores,
  Félise and Yolande and Juliette,
Shall I find you not still, shall I miss you,
30 When sleep, that is true or that seems,
Comes back to me hopeless to kiss you,
  O daughters of dreams?

They are past as a slumber that passes
  As the dew of a dawn of old time;
More frail than the shadows on glasses,
  More fleet than a wave or a rime.
As the waves after ebb drawing seaward,
  When their hollows are full of the night,
So the birds that flew singing to me-ward
40 Recede out of sight.

The songs of dead seasons, that wander
  On wings of articulate words;
Lost leaves that the shore-wind may squander,
  Light flocks of untameable birds;
Some sang to me dreaming in class time
  And truant in hand as in tongue;
For the youngest were born of boy's pastime,
  The eldest are young.

Is there shelter while life in them lingers,
50 Is there hearing for songs that recede,
Tunes touched from a harp with man's fingers
  Or blown with boy's mouth in a reed?
Is there place in the land of your labor,
  Is there room in your world of delight,
Where change has not sorrow for neighbor
  And day has not night?

In their wings though the sea-wind yet quivers,
  Will you spare not a space for them there
Made green with the running of rivers
60 And gracious with temperate air;
In the fields and the turreted cities,
  That cover from sunshine and rain
Fair passions and bountiful pities
  And loves without stain?

In a land of clear colors and stories,
  In a region of shadowless hours,
Where earth has a garment of glories
  And a murmur of musical flowers;

In woods where the spring half uncovers
  The flush of her amorous face,   70
By the waters that listen for lovers,
  For these is there place?

For the song-birds of sorrow, that muffle
  Their music as clouds do their fire;
For the storm-birds of passion, that ruffle
  Wild wings in a wind of desire;
In the stream of the storm as it settles
  Blown seaward, borne far from the sun,
Shaken loose on the darkness like petals
  Dropped one after one?   80

Though the world of your hands be more gracious
  And lovelier in lordship of things
Clothed round by sweet art with the spacious
  Warm heaven of her imminent wings,
Let them enter, unfledged and nigh fainting,
  For the love of old loves and lost times;
And receive in your palace of painting
  This revel of rimes.

Though the seasons of man full of losses
  Make empty the years full of youth,   90
If but one thing be constant in crosses,
  Change lays not her hand upon truth;
Hopes die, and their tombs are for token
  That the grief as the joy of them ends
Ere time that breaks all men has broken
  The faith between friends.

Though the many lights dwindle to one light,
  There is help if the heaven has one;
Though the skies be discrowned of the sunlight
  And the earth dispossessed of the sun,   100
They have moonlight and sleep for repayment,
  When, refreshed as a bride and set free,
With stars and sea-winds in her raiment,
  Night sinks on the sea.
(1866)

HERTHA

In Germanic mythology Hertha was goddess of the earth and of fertility and growth; Swinburne conceived of her as the personification of the world-soul. Of this poem he wrote in a letter to Stedman (February 21, 1875): "Of all I have done I rate Hertha highest as a single piece, finding in it the most lyric force and music combined with the most of condensed and clarified thought."

seven years' traces. The poems in the volume were apparently written between 1859 and 1866. 23. myrtles. Poets were crowned with wreaths of myrtle, sacred to the gods. 27. Faustine . . . Juliette, names of women appearing in the poems of the 1866 volume. 45. in class time, while he was at Eton, 1849-1853. 81. the world . . . hands, the paintings of Burne-Jones.

I am that which began;
    Out of me the years roll;
Out of me God and man;
    I am equal and whole;
God changes, and man, and the form of them bodily;
    I am the soul.

    Before ever land was,
        Before ever the sea,
    Or soft hair of the grass,
        Or fair limbs of the tree,
Or the flesh-colored fruit of my branches, I was, and
10   thy soul was in me.

    First life on my sources
        First drifted and swam;
    Out of me are the forces
        That save it or damn;
Out of me man and woman, and wild-beast and bird;
    before God was, I am.

    Beside or above me
        Naught is there to go;
Love or unlove me,
        Unknow me or know,
I am that which unloves me and loves; I am stricken,
20   and I am the blow.

    I the mark that is missed
        And the arrows that miss,
    I the mouth that is kissed
        And the breath in the kiss,
The search, and the sought, and the seeker, the soul
    and the body that is.

    I am that thing which blesses
        My spirit elate;
That which caresses
        With hands uncreate
My limbs unbegotten that measure the length of the
30   measure of fate.

    But what thing dost thou now,
        Looking Godward, to cry,
"I am I, thou art thou,
        I am low, thou art high"?
I am thou, whom thou seekest to find him; find thou
    but thyself, thou art I.

    I the grain and the furrow,
        The plow-cloven clod
And the plowshare drawn thorough,
        The germ and the sod,

The deed and the doer, the seed and the sower, the
    dust which is God.   40

    Hast thou known how I fashioned thee,
        Child, underground?
Fire that impassioned thee,
        Iron that bound,
Dim changes of water, what thing of all these hast thou
    known of or found?

    Canst thou say in thine heart
        Thou hast seen with thine eyes
With what cunning of art
        Thou wast wrought in what wise,
By what force of what stuff thou wast shapen, and
    shown on my breast to the skies?   50

    Who hath given, who hath sold it thee,
        Knowledge of me?
Hath the wilderness told it thee?
        Hast thou learnt of the sea?
Hast thou communed in spirit with night? Have the
    winds taken counsel with thee?

    Have I set such a star
        To show light on thy brow
That thou sawest from afar
        What I show to thee now?
Have ye spoken as brethren together, the sun and the
    mountains and thou?   60

    What is here, dost thou know it?
        What was, hast thou known?
Prophet nor poet
        Nor tripod nor throne
Nor spirit nor flesh can make answer, but only thy
    mother alone.

    Mother, not maker,
        Born, and not made;
Though her children forsake her,
        Allured or afraid,
Praying prayers to the God of their fashion, she stirs
    not for all that have prayed.   70

    A creed is a rod,
        And a crown is of night;
But this thing is God,
        To be man with thy might,
To grow straight in the strength of thy spirit, and live
    out thy life as the light.

    I am in thee to save thee,
        As my soul in thee saith;

    Hertha. 15. **before . . . am.** Cf. Exodus 3:14: "And God said unto Moses, I am that I am"; also John 8:58: "Jesus said unto them, Verily, verily, I say unto you, Before Abraham was, I am." 20. **I am that,** etc. The thought of these lines (ll. 20–40) is suggestive of

Emerson's *Brahma*, especially ll. 10–12:
        When me they fly, I am the wings;
        I am the doubter and the doubt,
        And I the hymn the Brahmin sings.
41. **Hast thou known,** etc. With these questions compare the words spoken to Job by the Lord out of the whirlwind (Job, Chapters 38–39).

Give thou as I gave thee,
       Thy life-blood and breath,
Green leaves of thy labor, white flowers of thy thought,
80   and red fruit of thy death.

       Be the ways of thy giving
           As mine were to thee;
       The free life of thy living,
           Be the gift of it free;
Not as servant to lord, nor as master to slave, shalt
       thou give thee to me.

       O children of banishment,
           Souls overcast,
       Were the lights ye see vanish meant
           Alway to last,
Ye would know not the sun overshining the shadows
90   and stars overpast.

       I that saw where ye trod
           The dim paths of the night
       Set the shadow called God
           In your skies to give light;
But the morning of manhood is risen, and the shadow-
       less soul is in sight.

       The tree many-rooted
           That swells to the sky
       With frondage red-fruited,
           The life-tree am I;
In the buds of your lives is the sap of my leaves; ye shall
100   live and not die.

       But the gods of your fashion
           That take and that give,
       In their pity and passion
           That scourge and forgive,
They are worms that are bred in the bark that falls
       off; they shall die and not live.

       My own blood is what stanches
           The wounds in my bark;
       Stars caught in my branches
           Make day of the dark,
And are worshiped as suns till the sunrise shall tread
110   out their fires as a spark.

       Where dead ages hide under
           The live roots of the tree,
       In my darkness the thunder
           Makes utterance of me;
In the clash of my boughs with each other ye hear the
       waves sound of the sea.

       That noise is of Time,
           As his feathers are spread
       And his feet set to climb
           Through the boughs overhead,
And my foliage rings round him and rustles, and
       branches are bent with his tread.   120

       The storm-winds of ages
           Blow through me and cease,
       The war-wind that rages,
           The spring-wind of peace,
Ere the breath of them roughen my tresses, ere one
       of my blossoms increase.

       All sounds of all changes,
           All shadows and lights
       On the world's mountain-ranges
           And stream-riven heights,
Whose tongue is the wind's tongue and language of
       storm-clouds on earth-shaking nights;   130

       All forms of all faces,
           All works of all hands
       In unsearchable places
           Of time-stricken lands,
All death and all life, and all reigns and all ruins,
       drop through me as sands.

       Though sore be my burden
           And more than ye know,
       And my growth have no guerdon
           But only to grow,
Yet I fail not of growing for lightnings above me or
       deathworms below.   140

       These too have their part in me,
           As I too in these;
       Such fire is at heart in me,
           Such sap is this tree's,
Which hath in it all sounds and all secrets of infinite
       lands and of seas.

       In the spring-colored hours
           When my mind was as May's,
       There brake forth of me flowers
           By centuries of days,
Strong blossoms with perfume of manhood shot out
       from my spirit as rays.   150

       And the sound of them springing
           And smell of their shoots
       Were as warmth and sweet singing
           And strength to my roots;

64. **Nor . . . throne**, neither priest nor king. The tripod was the altar, supported on three legs, on which the priestesses of Apollo at Delphi sat when they delivered their oracles. 67. **Born . . . made.** These lines are a protest against the idea of a single act of creation. Swinburne conceives nature as a continuous process of evolution. 88. **lights**, religious creeds and dogmas. 96. **The tree many-rooted**, the mighty ash tree

Igdrasil, supposed, in Norse mythology, to support the entire universe. It represents the whole of the universe, for its roots are in hell, its trunk is in earth, and its branches are in heaven.

And the lives of my children made perfect with freedom of soul were my fruits.

I bid you but be;
I have need not of prayer;
I have need of you free
As your mouths of mine air;
That my heart may be greater within me, beholding
160   the fruits of me fair.

More fair than strange fruit is
Of faiths ye espouse;
In me only the root is
That blooms in your boughs;
Behold now your God that ye made you, to feed him
with faith of your vows.

In the darkening and whitening
Abysses adored,
With dayspring and lightning
For lamp and for sword,
God thunders in heaven, and his angels are red with
170   the wrath of the Lord.

O my sons, O too dutiful
Toward gods not of me,
Was not I enough beautiful?
Was it hard to be free?
For behold, I am with you, am in you and of you;
look forth now and see.

Lo, winged with world's wonders,
With miracles shod,
With the fires of his thunders
For raiment and rod,
God trembles in heaven, and his angels are white
180   with the terror of God.

For his twilight is come on him,
His anguish is here;
And his spirits gaze dumb on him,
Grown gray from his fear;
And his hour taketh hold on him stricken, the last
of his infinite year.

Thought made him and breaks him,
Truth slays and forgives;
But to you, as time takes him,
This new thing it gives,
Even love, the beloved Republic, that feeds' upon
190   freedom and lives.

For truth only is living,
Truth only is whole,

And the love of his giving
Man's polestar and pole;
Man, pulse of my center, and fruit of my body, and
seed of my soul;

One birth of my bosom;
One beam of mine eye;
One topmost blossom
That scales the sky;
Man, equal and one with me, man that is made of me,
man that is I.

(1871)

A FORSAKEN GARDEN

*The scene is East Dene, on the Isle of Wight, where
Swinburne spent much of his youth.*

In a coign of the cliff between lowland and highland,
    At the sea-down's edge between windward and lee,
Walled round with rocks as an inland island,
    The ghost of a garden fronts the sea.
A girdle of brushwood and thorn encloses
    The steep square slope of the blossomless bed
Where the weeds that grew green from the graves of its
      roses
    Now lie dead.

The fields fall southward, abrupt and broken,
    To the low last edge of the long lone land.   10
If a step should sound or a word be spoken,
    Would a ghost not rise at the strange guest's hand?
So long have the gray bare walks lain guestless,
    Through branches and briars if a man make way,
He shall find no life, but the sea-wind's, restless
    Night and day.

The dense hard passage is blind and stifled
    That crawls by a track none turn to climb
To the strait waste place that the years have rifled
    Of all but the thorns that are touched not of time. 20
The thorns he spares when the rose is taken;
    The rocks are left when he wastes the plain.
The wind that wanders, the weeds wind-shaken,
    These remain.

Not a flower to be pressed of the foot that falls not;
    As the heart of a dead man the seed-plots are dry;
From the thicket of thorns whence the nightingale
    calls not,
    Could she call, there were never a rose to reply.
Over the meadows that blossom and wither

A *Forsaken Garden* is from *Collected Poetical Works* by Algernon
Charles Swinburne. Used by permission of William Heinemann, Ltd.,
London.

181. **his twilight.** The idea of the twilight of the gods is derived
from Norse mythology. This is a period, known as Ragnarök, which
involves the destruction of the universe. After this period a new heaven

and a new earth will arise out of the sea.
    A Forsaken Garden. 1. **coign,** corner, projection.
    A Ballad of François Villon. 1. **golden morn,** the Renaissance,
which succeeded the "dusk" of the Middle Ages. 6. **song new-born.**
Villon is regarded as the first and as one of the greatest of the French
lyric poets of the modern school. His verse, characterized by polish,

Wings but the note of a sea-bird's song;
Only the sun and the rain come hither
   All year long.

The sun burns sear and the rain dishevels
   One gaunt bleak blossom of scentless breath.
Only the wind here hovers and revels
   In a round where life seems barren as death.
Here there was laughing of old, there was weeping,
   Haply, of lovers none ever will know,
Whose eyes went seaward a hundred sleeping Years
40   ago.

Heart handfast in heart as they stood, "Look thither,"
   Did he whisper? "look forth from the flowers to the
      sea;
For the foam-flowers endure when the rose-blossoms
     wither,
   And men that love lightly may die—but we?"
And the same wind sang and the same waves whitened,
   And or ever the garden's last petals were shed,
In the lips that had whispered, the eyes that had
    lightened,
   Love was dead.

Or they loved their life through, and then went
    whither?
50   And were one to the end—but what end who knows?
Love deep as the sea as a rose must wither,
   As the rose-red seaweed that mocks the rose.
Shall the dead take thought for the dead to love them?
   What love was ever as deep as a grave?
They are loveless now as the grass above them
   Or the wave.

All are at one now, roses and lovers,
   Not known of the cliffs and the fields and the sea.
Not a breath of the time that has been hovers
60   In the air now soft with a summer to be.
Not a breath shall there sweeten the seasons here-
    after
   Of the flowers or the lovers that laugh now or
    weep,
When as they that are free now of weeping and
    laughter
   We shall sleep.

Here death may deal not again forever;
   Here change may come not till all change end.
From the graves they have made they shall rise up
    never,
   Who have left naught living to ravage and rend.
Earth, stones, and thorns of the wild ground growing,

While the sun and the rain live, these shall be; 70
Till a last wind's breath upon all these blowing
   Roll the sea.

Till the slow sea rise and the sheer cliff crumble,
   Till terrace and meadow the deep gulfs drink,
Till the strength of the waves of the high tides
    humble
   The fields that lessen, the rocks that shrink,
Here now in his triumph where all things falter,
   Stretched out on the spoils that his own hand
    spread,
As a god self-slain on his own strange altar,
   Death lies dead.

(1876)

A BALLAD OF FRANCOIS VILLON

PRINCE OF ALL BALLAD-MAKERS

*François Villon (1431-1463?) was a French poet
and vagabond, famous for his ballades. See Rossetti's
Ballad of Dead Ladies, and headnote, p. 1100.*

Bird of the bitter bright gray golden morn
   Scarce risen upon the dusk of dolorous years,
First of us all and sweetest singer born
   Whose far shrill note the world of new men hears
   Cleave the cold shuddering shade as twilight clears;
When song new-born put off the old world's attire
And felt its tune on her changed lips expire,
   Writ foremost on the roll of them that came
Fresh girt for service of the latter lyre,
   Villon, our sad bad glad mad brother's name!   10

Alas the joy, the sorrow, and the scorn,
   That clothed thy life with hopes and sins and fears,
And gave thee stones for bread and tares for corn
   And plume-plucked gaol-birds for thy starveling
    peers
   Till death clipped close their flight with shameful
    shears;
Till shifts came short and loves were hard to hire,
When lilt of song nor twitch of twangling wire
   Could buy thee bread or kisses; when light fame
Spurned like a ball and haled through brake and
    briar,
   Villon, our sad bad glad mad brother's name!   20

Poor splendid wings so frayed and soiled and torn!
   Poor kind wild eyes so dashed with light quick
    tears!

raciness, and intense subjectivity, had great influence. 13. **stones for
bread.** From Christ's Sermon on the Mount, Matthew 7:9: "Or what
man is there of you, whom if his son ask bread, will he give him a
stone?" **tares for corn.** An allusion to the parable of the tares sown
among the wheat (Matthew 13:25-40). 14. **gaol-birds . . . peers.**
For a number of years Villon was the leader of a band of vagabonds

and thieves that infested the streets of Paris. He was arrested and
imprisoned several times for robbery. 16. **shifts came short,** his
expedients for a livelihood were exhausted.
   A Ballad of François Villon is from *Collected Poetical Works* by
Algernon Charles Swinburne. Used by permission of William Heinemann, Ltd., London.

Poor perfect voice, most blithe when most forlorn,
    That rings athwart the sea whence no man steers
    Like joy-bells crossed with death-bells in our ears!
What far delight has cooled the fierce desire
That like some ravenous bird was strong to tire
    On that frail flesh and soul consumed with flame,
But left more sweet than roses to respire,
30 Villon, our sad bad glad mad brother's name?

29. **respire,** breathe. 32. **harlot . . . sire.** Many poets have sprung from humble origin, but Villon is unique in his startling combination of artistic fineness and baseness of life.

ENVOI

Prince of sweet songs made out of tears and fire,
A harlot was thy nurse, a god thy sire;
    Shame soiled thy song, and song assoiled thy shame.
But from thy feet now death has washed the
    mire,
Love reads out first at head of all our quire,
    Villon, our sad bad glad mad brother's name.
(1877)

POST-VICTORIAN ROMANTICISTS

ROBERT LOUIS STEVENSON 1850-1894

Robert Louis Stevenson, thin-legged, thin-chested, a mixture of Ariel, Puck, Antony, Hamlet, and the Calvinist preachers—so his friend Henley described him—was born in Edinburgh in 1850. He had a love of the sea which was born in his blood. Both his father and his grandfather were celebrated engineers and builders of lighthouses on the Scottish coast. Bad health and restlessness turned Louis away from the study of engineering at the University of Edinburgh to the life of a gay vagabond scribbler, and even the study of law could not interrupt his career as author. Few writers of the period took to their writing with such genuine enjoyment mingled with such seriousness. Stevenson read extensively and discriminatingly and "played the sedulous ape," as he said, to Hazlitt and other finished prose writers whom he admired. The excellence of style which he thus

Robert Louis Stevenson, from a drawing by J. W. Alexander. The Samoans acknowledged Stevenson with the name Tusitala which means "teller of tales." Historical Pictures Service—Chicago.

acquired was notable in his first volume of essays, Virginibus Puerisque ("For Girls and Boys") (1881), and in two highly romantic short stories, A Lodging for the Night and The Sire de Maletroit's Door.

From a canoe trip in Belgium and France and a walking tour through the mountains of Southern France, Stevenson brought back a written record in romantic prose which treated the adventure picturesquely and imaginatively—An Inland Voyage (1878) and Travels with a Donkey in the Cévennes (1879). Both books, especially the second, are charmingly touched with idyllic and even pastoral moods. In 1879 he followed to her home in California an American widow whom he had met in France, Mrs. Fanny Osbourne; he tells of this journey in The Amateur Immigrant. Mrs. Osbourne nursed him through a dangerous illness, and they were married in 1880. Their experiences together at Calistoga, a crude California mining town, he recorded in The Silverado Squatters (1883). Familiar Studies of Men and Books (1882) and the New Arabian Nights (1882), a series of romantic and fantastic tales, had already contributed to Stevenson's growing reputation, and the appearance in book form of Treasure Island in 1883 made him definitely famous. He returned to Scotland for a time, but subsequently had to travel for his health—to the Swiss Alps, to Southern France, to the Channel coast, and finally to Saranac Lake in New York. During these next few trying years he wrote tirelessly. In the remarkable short-novel "parable," The Strange Case of Dr. Jekyll and Mr. Hyde (1886), he struck a highly popular note of romance and pseudo-scientific mystery, and in Kidnapped (1886) he added to his tales of adventure. At Saranac he wrote what many consider his best novel, The Master of Ballantrae (1888), and a series of twelve essays in Scribner's Magazine. Among these is Pulvis et Umbra ("Dust and Shadow"), which he once characterized as "a Darwinian sermon," and which contains the eloquent and moving expression of his philosophy of life. Two volumes of poetry, A Child's Garden of Verses (1885)—like Treasure Island, an imperishable children's classic—and Underwoods (1887), had already appeared, as had the first of three unsuccessful dramas which he wrote in collaboration with Henley.

In 1888 Stevenson sailed from California in the schooner Casco for a long cruise among the islands of the South Pacific. He visited the leper colony in the Hawaiian Islands and wrote a defense of its then maligned director, Father Damien. In Australia he was again seriously sick and nearly died. At Samoa in the following year he found at last a climate and an environment which suited his health and his romantic spirit; and here he spent in happiness and comparative good health and peace the last four years of his life, writing in the quiet of his mountain home Vailima, directing the work about his plantation, acting as a sort of chieftain to what he called "a kind of feudal clan of servants and retainers," and mixing both benevolently and effectively in the political affairs of the Samoans, who loved him as Tusitala, the teller of tales. Three novels—The Wreckers; Catriona (called in the American edition David Balfour), the sequel to Kidnapped; and the unfinished Weir of Hermiston, in some respects his most promising work—all belong to the Samoan period; so also do his sparkling Vailima Letters, published by Sidney Colvin in 1895. Stevenson died almost literally, as he indicated in Aes Triplex he would like to die, with his pen in his hand, hard at work on his unfinished story St. Ives, and lies buried in Samoa.

This gifted author's attitude toward life shows a highly individual mixture of traits not often found in the same man. He had a moral earnestness in a high degree. Yet he upset many a theological apple cart in his frank espousal of the worth of vital existence. And he constantly threw over life the glow and glamor which romanticism requires. His fundamentally romantic quality as a teller of tales is not in the least impaired by the fact that from the realists he had learned the tricks of style that make the impossible seem to be the expected. Like Kipling he may be called a realist-romanticist, but in both cases the realism is only a surface realism.

In the essay Stevenson's romantic spirit gave him a kinship with Lamb, Hazlitt, and other romantic essayists of the early nineteenth century, and his talents made him the best essayist in England in the latter part of the century. He had the same disposition and technique as his predecessors just mentioned. He had, moreover, much of Lamb's charm, subjectivism, and occasional affectation; and his easy accounts of his boyhood experiences in Edinburgh, with their warmth and nostalgic feeling, resemble the essays that Lamb based upon his early life. In his essays as in his stories and novels, there is evidence of the master craftsman, for Stevenson was highly conscientious about all his work.

AES TRIPLEX

The title, meaning "Triple Bronze," is taken from Horace's Odes (1, 3, 9)—

> Ille robur et aes triplex
> Circa pectus erat qui fragilem truci
> Commisit pelago ratem
> Primus.

"Oak and triple brass encompassed the breast of him who first entrusted his frail craft to the wild sea." Stevenson uses the phrase as a symbol of courage. The essay appeared first in The Cornhill Magazine *for April 1878, and afterwards in* Virginibus Puerisque.

The changes wrought by death are in themselves so sharp and final, and so terrible and melancholy in their consequences, that the thing stands alone in man's experience, and has no parallel upon earth. It outdoes all other accidents because it is the last of them. Sometimes it leaps suddenly upon its victims, like a Thug; sometimes it lays a regular siege and creeps upon their citadel during a score of years. And when the business is done, there is sore havoc
10 made in other people's lives, and a pin knocked out by which many subsidiary friendships hung together. There are empty chairs, solitary walks, and single beds at night. Again, in taking away our friends, death does not take them away utterly, but leaves behind a mocking, tragical, and soon intolerable residue, which must be hurriedly concealed. Hence a whole chapter of sights and customs striking to the mind, from the pyramids of Egypt to the gibbets and dule trees of medieval Europe. The poorest persons have a bit of
20 pageant going towards the tomb; memorial stones are set up over the least memorable; and, in order to preserve some show of respect for what remains of our old loves and friendships, we must accompany it with much grimly ludicrous ceremonial, and the hired undertaker parades before the door. All this, and much more of the same sort, accompanied by the eloquence of poets, has gone a great way to put humanity in error; nay, in many philosophies the error has been embodied and laid down with every
30 circumstance of logic; although in real life the bustle and swiftness, in leaving people little time to think, have not left them time enough to go dangerously wrong in practice.

As a matter of fact, although few things are spoken of with more fearful whisperings than this prospect of death, few have less influence on conduct under healthy circumstances. We have all heard of cities in South America built upon the side of fiery mountains, and how, even in this tremendous neighborhood, the
40 inhabitants are not a jot more impressed by the solemnity of mortal conditions than if they were delving gardens in the greenest corner of England.

There are serenades and suppers and much gallantry among the myrtles overhead; and meanwhile the foundation shudders underfoot, the bowels of the mountain growl, and at any moment living ruin may leap sky-high into the moonlight, and tumble man and his merry-making in the dust. In the eyes of very young people, and very dull old ones, there is something indescribably reckless and desperate in such a 50 picture. It seems not credible that respectable married people, with umbrellas, should find appetite for a bit of supper within quite a long distance of a fiery mountain; ordinary life begins to smell of highhanded debauch when it is carried on so close to a catastrophe; and even cheese and salad, it seems, could hardly be relished in such circumstances without something like a defiance of the Creator. It should be a place for nobody but hermits dwelling in prayer and maceration, or mere born-devils drowning care 60 in a perpetual carouse.

And yet, when one comes to think upon it calmly, the situation of these South American citizens forms only a very pale figure for the state of ordinary mankind. This world itself, traveling blindly and swiftly in overcrowded space, among a million other worlds traveling blindly and swiftly in contrary directions, may very well come by a knock that would set it into explosion like a penny squib. And what, pathologically looked at, is the human body with all its organs, but 70 a mere bagful of petards? The least of these is as dangerous to the whole economy as the ship's powdermagazine to the ship; and with every breath we breathe, and every meal we eat, we are putting one or more of them in peril. If we clung as devotedly as some philosophers pretend we do to the abstract idea of life, or were half as frightened as they make out we are, for the subversive accident that ends it all, the trumpets might sound by the hour and no one would follow them into battle—the blue-peter 80 might fly at the truck, but who would climb into a seagoing ship? Think (if these philosophers were right) with what a preparation of spirit we should affront the daily peril of the dinner-table: a deadlier spot than any battlefield in history, where the far greater proportion of our ancestors have miserably left their bones! What woman would ever be lured into marriage, so much more dangerous than the wildest sea? And what would it be to grow old? For, after certain distance, every step we take in life we find the ice 90 growing thinner below our feet, and all around us and behind us we see our contemporaries going through. By the time a man gets well into the seventies, his continued existence is a mere miracle; and when

Aes Triplex. 7. **Thug,** originally a member of a religious brotherhood of robbers and murderers in northern India. 18. **dule trees,** hanging-trees, gallows. 60. **maceration,** mortification of the flesh. 69. **penny squib,** a cheap firecracker, bought for a penny. 71. **petards,** bombs used in the early modern period to blow up besieged walls. 80. **blue-peter,** a blue flag with a white square in the center; it is displayed as a signal when a vessel is ready to leave port. 81. **truck,** a small wooden cap at the top of a mast or flagstaff, having holes for ropes. 108. **Balaclava.** See Tennyson's *Charge of the Light Brigade,* p. 898. 112. **Curtius,** Mettus Curtius, a patriotic youth of Roman legend, who sacrificed his life and saved the city in 362 b.c. by plunging into a gulf that suddenly opened in the Forum at Rome. A soothsayer had declared the act necessary to appease the wrath of the gods. 117. **Valley . . . Death,** a phrase from Psalm 23. 121. **the Derby,** the famous

he lays his old bones in bed for the night, there is an overwhelming probability that he will never see the day. Do the old men mind it, as a matter of fact? Why, no. They were never merrier; they have their grog at night, and tell the raciest stories; 100 they hear of the death of people about their own age, or even younger, not as if it was a grisly warning, but with a simple childlike pleasure at having outlived some one else; and when a draught might puff them out like a guttering candle, or a bit of a stumble shatter them like so much glass, their old hearts keep sound and unaffrighted, and they go on, bubbling with laughter, through years of man's age compared to which the valley at Balaclava was as safe and peaceful as a village cricket-green on Sun- 110 day. It may fairly be questioned (if we look to the peril only) whether it was a much more daring feat for Curtius to plunge into the gulf, than for any old gentleman of ninety to doff his clothes and clamber into bed.

Indeed, it is a memorable subject for consideration, with what unconcern and gayety mankind pricks on along the Valley of the Shadow of Death. The whole is one wilderness of snares, and the end of it, for those who fear the last pinch, is irrevocable 120 ruin. And yet we go spinning through it all, like a party for the Derby. Perhaps the reader remembers one of the humorous devices of the deified Caligula: how he encouraged a vast concourse of holiday-makers on to his bridge over the Baiae bay; and when they were in the height of their enjoyment, turned loose the Praetorian guards among the company, and had them tossed into the sea. This is no bad miniature of the dealings of nature with the transitory race of man. Only, what a chequered picnic we have of it, 130 even while it lasts! and into what great waters, not to be crossed by any swimmer, God's pale Praetorian throws us over in the end!

We live the time that a match flickers; we pop the cork of a ginger-beer bottle, and the earthquake swallows us on the instant. Is it not odd, is it not incongruous, is it not, in the highest sense of human speech, incredible, that we should think so highly of the ginger-beer, and regard so little the devouring earthquake? The love of Life and the fear of Death 140 are two famous phrases that grow harder to understand the more we think about them. It is a well-known fact that an immense proportion of boat accidents would never happen if people held the sheet in their hands instead of making it fast; and yet, unless it be some martinet of a professional mariner or some landsman with shattered nerves, every one of

God's creatures makes it fast. A strange instance of man's unconcern and brazen boldness in the face of death!

We confound ourselves with metaphysical phrases, 150 which we import into daily talk with noble inappropriateness. We have no idea of what death is, apart from its circumstances and some of its consequences to others; and although we have some experience of living there is not a man on earth who has flown so high into abstraction as to have any practical guess at the meaning of the word *life*. All literature, from Job and Omar Khayyám to Thomas Carlyle or Walt Whitman, is but an attempt to look upon the human state with such largeness of view as shall enable us 160 to rise from the consideration of living to the Definition of Life. And our sages give us about the best satisfaction in their power when they say that it is a vapor, or a show, or made out of the same stuff with dreams. Philosophy, in its more rigid sense, has been at the same work for ages; and after a myriad bald heads have wagged over the problem, and piles of words have been heaped one upon another into dry and cloudy volumes without end, philosophy has the honor of laying before us, with modest pride, her 170 contribution towards the subject: that life is a Permanent Possibility of Sensation. Truly a fine result! A man may very well love beef, or hunting, or a woman; but surely, surely, not a Permanent Possibility of Sensation! He may be afraid of a precipice, or a dentist, or a large enemy with a club, or even an undertaker's man; but not certainly of abstract death. We may trick with the word *life* in its dozen senses until we are weary of tricking; we may argue in terms of all the philosophies on earth, but one fact remains 180 true throughout—that we do not love life, in the sense that we are greatly preoccupied about its conservation; that we do not, properly speaking, love life at all, but living. Into the views of the least careful there will enter some degree of providence; no man's eyes are fixed entirely on the passing hour; but although we have some anticipation of good health, good weather, wine, active employment, love, and self-approval, the sum of these anticipations does not amount to anything like a general view of life's possi- 190 bilities and issues; nor are those who cherish them most vividly, at all the most scrupulous of their personal safety. To be deeply interested in the accidents of our existence, to enjoy keenly the mixed texture of human experience, rather leads a man to disregard precautions, and risk his neck against a straw. For surely the love of living is stronger in an Alpine climber roping over a peril, or a hunter riding merrily

horse race at Epsom Downs, England, established in 1780 by the Earl of Derby. 122. **deified Caligula.** Caligula, the third emperor of Rome (ruled from 37–41) proclaimed himself a god. 124. **Baiae Bay,** a fashionable seaside resort of the Romans near the city of Naples. 126. **Praetorian guards,** the bodyguard of the Roman emperors, so called because they were originally the bodyguard of the *praetor,* a magistrate next to the consul in republican Rome. 158. **Job,** the hero of one of the great Poetic Books of the Old Testament. **Walt Whitman,** the distinguished American poet (1819–1892) noted for his individualism of themes and forms. 164. **vapor, or a show.** See Psalms 39:6—"Surely every man walketh in a vain show." **stuff with dreams;** cf. the famous lines in Shakespeare's *The Tempest,* IV, i, 156–158. 171. **Permanent . . . Sensation,** the definition of matter by John Stuart Mill (1806–1873), an English philosopher and political economist.

at a stiff fence, than in a creature who lives upon a diet and walks a measured distance in the interest of his constitution.

There is a great deal of very vile nonsense talked upon both sides of the matter; tearing divines reducing life to the dimensions of a mere funeral procession, so short as to be hardly decent; and melancholy unbelievers yearning for the tomb as if it were a world too far away. Both sides must feel 10 a little ashamed of their performances now and again when they draw in their chairs to dinner. Indeed, a good meal and a bottle of wine is an answer to most standard works upon the question. When a man's heart warms to his viands, he forgets a great deal of sophistry, and soars into a rosy zone of contemplation. Death may be knocking at the door, like the Commander's statue; we have something else in hand, thank God, and let him knock. Passing bells are ringing all the world over. All the world over, and 20 every hour, some one is parting company with all his aches and ecstasies. For us also the trap is laid. But we are so fond of life that we have no leisure to entertain the terror of death. It is a honeymoon with us all through, and none of the longest. Small blame to us if we give our whole hearts to this glowing bride of ours, to the appetites, to honor, to the hungry curiosity of the mind, to the pleasure of the eyes in nature, and the pride of our own nimble bodies.

30 We all of us appreciate the sensations; but as for caring about the Permanence of the Possibility, a man's head is generally very bald, and his senses very dull, before he comes to that. Whether we regard life as a lane leading to a dead wall—a mere bag's end, as the French say—or whether we think of it as a vestibule or gymnasium where we wait our turn and prepare our faculties for some more noble destiny; whether we thunder in a pulpit, or pule in little atheistic poetry-books, about its vanity and brevity; 40 whether we look justly for years of health and vigor, or are about to mount into a Bath-chair, as a step towards the hearse; in each and all of these views and situations there is but one conclusion possible: that a man should stop his ears against paralyzing terror, and run the race that is set before him with a single mind. No one surely could have recoiled with more heartache and terror from the thought of death than our respected lexicographer; and yet we know how little it affected his conduct, how wisely and 50 boldly he walked, and in what a fresh and lively vein he spoke of life. Already an old man, he ven-

tured on his Highland tour; and his heart, bound with triple brass, did not recoil before twenty-seven individual cups of tea. As courage and intelligence are the two qualities best worth a good man's cultivation, so it is the first part of intelligence to recognize our precarious estate in life, and the first part of courage to be not at all abashed before the fact. A frank and somewhat headlong carriage, not looking too anxiously before, not dallying in maudlin regret over 60 the past, stamps the man who is well armored for this world.

And not only well armored for himself, but a good friend and a good citizen to boot. We do not go to cowards for tender dealing; there is nothing so cruel as panic; the man who has least fear for his own carcass, has most time to consider others. That eminent chemist who took his walks abroad in tin shoes, and subsisted wholly upon tepid milk, had all his work cut out for him in considerate dealings 70 with his own digestion. So soon as prudence has begun to grow up in the brain, like a dismal fungus, it finds its first expression in a paralysis of generous acts. The victim begins to shrink spiritually; he develops a fancy for parlors with a regulated temperature, and takes his morality on the principle of tin shoes and tepid milk. The care of one important body or soul becomes so engrossing, that all the noises of the outer world begin to come thin and faint into the parlor with the regulated temperature; and the 80 tin shoes go equably forward over blood and rain. To be otherwise is to ossify; and the scruple-monger ends by standing stock-still. Now the man who has his heart on his sleeve, and a good whirling weathercock of a brain, who reckons his life as a thing to be dashingly used and cheerfully hazarded, makes a very different acquaintance of the world, keeps all his pulses going true and fast, and gathers impetus as he runs, until, if he be running towards anything better than wildfire, he may shoot up and become a 90 constellation in the end. Lord look after his health, Lord have a care of his soul, says he; and he has at the key of the position, and swashes through incongruity and peril towards his aim. Death is on all sides of him with pointed batteries, as he is on all sides of all of us; unfortunate surprises gird him round; mim-mouthed friends and relations hold up their hands in quite a little elegiacal synod about his path: and what cares he for all this? Being a true lover of living, a fellow with something pushing and 100 spontaneous in his inside, he must, like any other soldier, in any other stirring, deadly warfare, push on

---

16. **the Commander's statue.** In the Spanish legend of Don Juan, Don Juan kills the governor of the city and then holds a banquet at his tomb. Invited to join the feast, the statue of the dead man appears and carries Don Juan off to hell.   34. **a mere bag's end,** a translation of the French *cul de sac,* a blind alley, a dead end.   41. **Bath-chair,** an invalid's chair on wheels, so called from the city of Bath, an English health resort where such chairs were in common use.   45. **run . . . mind.** See Hebrews 12:1: ". . . let us run with patience the race that is set before us.   48. **our . . . lexicographer,** Samuel Johnson (p. 567), noted as a heavy tea drinker. See the account of his fear of death

as related in Boswell's *Life of Johnson,* p. 596.   59. **looking . . . before.** See Shelley's *To a Skylark,* p. 774, l. 86.   68. **eminent chemist,** Joseph Black (1728–1799), a Scottish chemist and physicist who discovered what is called "latent heat." He was in feeble health most of his life.   84. **heart on his sleeve.** See *Othello,* I, i, 63–65:

'tis not long after
But I will wear my heart upon my sleeve
For daws to peck at.

97. **mim-mouthed,** prudishly reticent, or affectedly proper in speech.   98. **elegiacal synod,** a glum group that pessimistically looks for the

1124   *Democracy, Science, and Industrialism*

at his best pace until he touch the goal. "A peerage or Westminster Abbey!" cried Nelson in his bright, boyish, heroic manner. These are great incentives; not for any of these, but for the plain satisfaction of living, of being about their business in some sort or other, do the brave, serviceable men of every nation tread down the nettle danger, and pass flyingly over
110 all the stumbling-blocks of prudence. Think of the heroism of Johnson, think of that superb indifference to mortal limitation that set him upon his dictionary, and carried him through triumphantly until the end! Who, if he were wisely considerate of things at large, would ever embark upon any work much more considerable than a half-penny post card? Who would project a serial novel, after Thackeray and Dickens had each fallen in mid-course? Who would find heart enough to begin to live, if he dallied with the con-
120 sideration of death?

And, after all, what sorry and pitiful quibbling all this is! To forego all the issues of living in a parlor with a regulated temperature—as if that were not to die a hundred times over, and for ten years at a stretch! As if it were not to die in one's own lifetime, and without even the sad immunities of death! As if it were not to die, and yet be the patient spectators of our own pitiable change! The Permanent Possibility is preserved, but the sensations carefully held at
130 arm's length, as if one kept a photographic plate in a dark chamber. It is better to lose health like a spendthrift than to waste it like a miser. It is better to live and be done with it, than to die daily in the sickroom. By all means begin your folio; even if the doctor does not give you a year, even if he hesitates about a month, make one brave push and see what can be accomplished in a week. It is not only in finished undertakings that we ought to honor useful labor. A spirit goes out of the man who means
140 execution, which outlives the most untimely ending. All who have meant good work with their whole hearts, have done good work, although they may die before they have the time to sign it. Every heart that has beat strong and cheerfully has left a hopeful impulse behind it in the world, and bettered the tradition of mankind. And even if death catch people, like an open pitfall, and in mid-career, laying out vast projects, and planning monstrous foundations, flushed with hope, and their mouths full of boastful
150 language, they should be at once tripped up and silenced: is there not something brave and spirited in such a termination? and does not life go down with a better grace, foaming in full body over a preci-pice, than miserably straggling to an end in sandy deltas? When the Greeks made their fine saying that those whom the gods love die young, I cannot help believing they had this sort of death also in their eye. For surely, at whatever age it overtake the man, this is to die young. Death has not been suffered to take so much as an illusion from his heart. In the 160 hot-fit of life, a-tiptoe on the highest point of being, he passes at a bound on to the other side. The noise of the mallet and chisel is scarcely quenched, the trumpets are hardly done blowing, when, trailing with him clouds of glory, this happy-starred, full-blooded spirit shoots into the spiritual land.
(1878)

PULVIS ET UMBRA

Stevenson took the title of this essay from one of Horace's Odes (4,7): "pulvis et umbra sumus"—"we become dust and a shade."

In April 1888, while at Saranac Lake, New York, for his health, Stevenson said in a letter to Miss Adelaide Boodle: "I wrote a paper the other day—Pulvis et Umbra;—I wrote it with great feeling and conviction; to me it seemed bracing and heathful; it is in such a world (so seen by me) that I am very glad to fight out my battle, and see some fine sunsets, and hear some excellent jests between whiles round the camp fire. . . . If my view be everything but the nonsense that it may be—to me it seems self-evident and blinding truth—surely of all things it makes this world holier. There is nothing in it but the moral side—but the great battle and the breathing times with their refreshments. I see no more and no less. And if you look again, it is not ugly, and it is filled with promise." The thought expressed in the essay should be compared with Pater's thought in the conclusion to Studies in the History of the Renaissance (p. 1069). The essay was first published in Scribner's Magazine for April 1888 and reprinted in Across the Plains (1892).

We look for some reward of our endeavors and are disappointed; not success, not happiness, not even peace of conscience, crowns our ineffectual efforts to do well. Our frailties are invincible, our virtues 170 barren; the battle goes sore against us to the going down of the sun. The canting moralist tells us of right and wrong; and we look abroad, even on the face of our small earth, and find them change with every climate, and no country where some action is not

---

worst. **104. Nelson,** Lord Nelson (1758–1805), England's greatest naval commander; he made this remark just before the battle of the Nile (1798). **109. tread . . . danger,** from Shakespeare's *I Henry IV,* II, iii, 10. **111. heroism of Johnson.** Samuel Johnson produced his celebrated *Dictionary* under great difficulties (see p. 567 ff.) and began his most ambitious work, *The Lives of the Poets,* at the age of sixty-seven. **117. Thackeray and Dickens.** Both, like Stevenson, died with unfinished novels on their hands. **135. doctor . . . year,** as in Stevenson's own case. **141. all who . . . work.** Compare Browning's *Rabbi Ben Ezra,* p. 930, ll. 133 ff. **156. whom . . . young,** a statement of the Greek poet Menander, in his *Dis Exapaton,* Fragment 4. It is quoted by Byron in his *Don Juan,* IV, l. 89. **164. trailing . . . glory.** Cf. Wordsworth's *Ode on Immortality,* p. 701, l. 64.

Pulvis et Umbra. **171. battle . . . sun.** See 1 Samuel 31:3: "And the battle went sore against Saul"; also *The Iliad,* XIX: "For no man fasting from food shall be able to fight with the foe all day till the going down of the sun.

honored for a virtue and none where it is not branded for a vice; and we look in our experience, and find no vital congruity in the wisest rules, but at the best a municipal fitness. It is not strange if we are tempted to despair of good. We ask too much. Our religions and moralities have been trimmed to flatter us, till they are all emasculate and sentimentalized, and only please and weaken. Truth is of a rougher strain. In the harsh face of life, faith can read a
10 bracing gospel. The human race is a thing more ancient than the ten commandments; and the bones and revolutions of the Kosmos, in whose joints we are but moss and fungus, more ancient still.

1

Of the Kosmos in the last resort, science reports many doubtful things and all of them appalling. There seems no substance on this solid globe on which we stamp: nothing but symbols and ratios. Symbols and ratios carry us and bring us forth and beat us down; gravity that swings the incommensur-
20 able suns and worlds through space, is but a figment varying inversely as the squares of distances; and the suns and worlds themselves, imponderable figures of abstractions, NH_3 and H_2O. Consideration dares not dwell upon this view; that way madness lies; science carries us into zones of speculation, where there is no habitable city for the mind of man.

But take the Kosmos with a grosser faith, as our senses give it us. We behold space sown with rotary islands, suns and worlds and the shards and wrecks
30 of systems: some, like the sun, still blazing; some rotting, like the earth; others, like the moon, stable in desolation. All of these we take to be made of something we call matter: a thing no analysis can help us to conceive; to whose incredible properties no familiarities can reconcile our minds. This stuff, when not purified by the lustration of fire, rots uncleanly into something we call life; seized through all its atoms with a pediculous malady; swelling in tumors that become independent, sometimes even (by an
40 abhorrent prodigy) locomotory; one splitting into millions, millions cohering into one, as the malady proceeds through varying stages. This vital putrescence of the dust, used as we are to it, yet strikes us with occasional disgust, and the profusion of worms in a piece of ancient turf, or the air of a marsh darkened with insects, will sometimes check our breathing so that we aspire for cleaner places. But none is clean: the moving sand is infected with lice; the pure spring, where it bursts out of the
50 mountain, is a mere issue of worms; even in the hard rock the crystal is forming.

In two main shapes this eruption covers the countenance of the earth: the animal and the vegetable: one in some degree the inversion of the other: the second rooted to the spot; the first coming detached out of its natal mud, and scurrying abroad with the myriad feet of insects or towering into the heavens on the wings of birds: a thing so inconceivable that, if it be well considered, the heart stops. To
60 what passes with the anchored vermin, we have little clue: doubtless they have their joys and sorrows, their delights and killing agonies: it appears not how. But of the locomotory, to which we ourselves belong, we can tell more. These share with us a thousand miracles: the miracles of sight, of hearing, of the projection of sound, things that bridge space; the miracles of memory and reason, by which the present is conceived, and when it is gone, its image kept living in the brains of man and brute; the miracle of reproduction, with its imperious desires and stag-
70 gering consequences. And to put the last touch upon this mountain mass of the revolting and the inconceivable, all these prey upon each other, lives tearing other lives in pieces, cramming them inside themselves, and by that summary process, growing fat: the vegetarian, the whale, perhaps the tree, not less than the lion of the desert; for the vegetarian is only the eater of the dumb.

Meanwhile our rotary island loaded with predatory life, and more drenched with blood, both animal
80 and vegetable, than ever mutinied ship, scuds through space with unimaginable speed, and turns alternate cheeks to the reverberation of a blazing world, ninety million miles away.

2

What a monstrous specter is this man, the disease of agglutinated dust, lifting alternate feet or lying drugged with slumber; killing, feeding, growing, bringing forth small copies of himself; grown upon with hair like grass, fitted with eyes that move and glitter in his face; a thing to set children screaming;—and yet
90 looked at nearlier, known as his fellows know him, how surprising are his attributes! Poor soul, here for so little, cast among so many hardships, filled with desires so incommensurate and so inconsistent, savagely surrounded, savagely descended, irremediably condemned to prey upon his fellow lives: who should have blamed him had he been of a piece with his destiny and a being merely barbarous? And we look and behold him instead filled with imperfect virtues: infinitely childish, often admirably valiant, often
100 touchingly kind; sitting down, amidst his momentary life, to debate of right and wrong and the attributes

4. **municipal,** pertaining to internal affairs. 12. **Kosmos,** the universe regarded as an orderly system. 23. **NH_3 and H_2O,** chemical symbols for ammonia and water respectively. 24. **that way madness lies,** from *King Lear,* III, iv, 21. King Lear, suffering in the storm, shuns the thought of his daughters' ingratitude by saying, "O, that way madness lies." 36. **lustration,** a ceremony of purification on entering a holy

place. 38. **pediculous,** covered with lice. 107. **heart . . . mystery.** Cf. *Hamlet,* III, ii, 382: "You would pluck out the heart of my mystery" (secret). 151. **Assiniboia,** a town in Saskatchewan, Canada. 153. **calumet,** the pipe of peace passed around by North American Indians when making treaties. 168. **drowns . . . river.** Before India came under British control, it was a common practice for children to

of the deity; rising up to do battle for an egg or die for an idea; singling out his friends and his mate with cordial affection; bringing forth in pain, rearing with long-suffering solicitude, his young. To touch the heart of his mystery, we find in him one thought, strange to the point of lunacy: the thought of duty; the thought of something owing to himself, to his neighbor, to his God: an ideal of decency, to which he would rise if it were possible; a limit of shame, below which, if it be possible, he will not stoop. The design in most men is one of conformity; here and there, in picked natures, it transcends itself and soars on the other side, arming martyrs with independence; but in all, in their degrees, it is a bosom thought:— Not in man alone, for we trace it in dogs and cats whom we know fairly well, and doubtless some similar point of honor sways the elephant, the oyster, and the louse, of whom we know so little:—But in man, at least, it sways with so complete an empire that merely selfish things come second, even with the selfish: that appetites are starved, fears are conquered, pains supported; that almost the dullest shrinks from the reproof of a glance, although it were a child's; and all but the most cowardly stand amid the risks of war; and the more noble, having strongly conceived an act as due to their ideal, affront and embrace death. Strange enough if, with their singular origin and perverted practice, they think they are to be rewarded in some future life: stranger still, if they are persuaded of the contrary, and think this blow, which they solicit, will strike them senseless for eternity. I shall be reminded what a tragedy of misconception and misconduct man at large presents: of organized injustice, cowardly violence, and treacherous crime; and of the damning imperfections of the best. They cannot be too darkly drawn. Man is indeed marked for failure in his efforts to do right. But where the best consistently miscarry, how tenfold more remarkable that all should continue to strive; and surely we should find it both touching and inspiriting, that in a field from which success is banished, our race should not cease to labor.

If the first view of this creature, stalking in his rotatory isle, be a thing to shake the courage of the stoutest, on this nearer sight, he startles us with an admiring wonder. It matters not where we look, under what climate we observe him, in what stage of society, in what depth of ignorance, burthened with what erroneous morality; by camp fires in Assiniboia, the snow powdering his shoulders, the wind plucking his blanket, as he sits, passing ceremonial calumet and uttering his grave opinions like a Roman senator; in ships at sea, a man inured to hardship and vile pleasures, his brightest hope a fiddle in a tavern and a bedizened trull who sells herself to rob him, and he for all that simple, innocent, cheerful, kindly like a child, constant to toil, brave to drown, for others; in the slums of cities, moving among indifferent millions to mechanical employments, without hope of change in the future, with scarce a pleasure in the present, and yet true to his virtues, honest up to his lights, kind to his neighbors, tempted perhaps in vain by the bright gin-palace, perhaps long-suffering with the drunken wife that ruins him; in India (a woman this time) kneeling with broken cries and streaming tears, as she drowns her child in the sacred river; in the brothel, the discard of society, living mainly on strong drink, fed with affronts, a fool, a thief, the comrade of thieves, and even here keeping the point of honor and the touch of pity, often repaying the world's scorn with service, often standing firm upon a scruple, and at a certain cost, rejecting riches:—everywhere some virtue cherished or affected, everywhere some decency of thought and carriage, everywhere the ensign of man's ineffectual goodness:—ah! if I could show you this! if I could show you these men and women, all the world over, in every stage of history, under every abuse of error, under every circumstance of failure without hope, without help, without thanks, still obscurely fighting the lost fight of virtue, still clinging, in the brothel or on the scaffold, to some rag of honor, the poor jewel of their souls! They may seek to escape, and yet they cannot; it is not alone their privilege and glory, but their doom; they are condemned to some nobility; all their lives long, the desire of good is at their heels, the implacable hunter.

Of all earth's meteors, here at least is the most strange and consoling: That this ennobled lemur, this hair-crowned bubble of the dust, this inheritor of a few years and sorrows, should yet deny himself his rare delights, and add to his frequent pains, and live for an ideal, however misconceived. Nor can we stop with man. A new doctrine, received with screams a little while ago by canting moralists, and still not properly worked into the body of our thoughts, lights us a step farther into the heart of this rough but noble universe. For nowadays the pride of man denies in vain his kinship with the original dust. He stands no longer like a thing apart. Close at his heels we see the dog, prince of another genus: and in him too, we see dumbly testified the same cultus of an unattainable ideal, the same constancy in failure. Does it stop with the dog? We look at our feet where the ground is blackened with the swarming ant: a creature so small, so far from us in the hierarchy of brutes, that

be drowned in the Ganges, the sacred river, as sacrifices to appease an angry god. 172. **point of honor.** Cf. the old proverb, "There is honor among thieves." **touch of pity.** See *Richard III*, I, ii, 71: "No beast so fierce but knows some touch of pity." 185. **jewel . . . souls.** Cf. *Othello*, III, iii, 156:
Good name in man and woman, dear my lord,
Is the immediate jewel of their souls.
191. **lemur,** a nocturnal animal resembling a monkey. 196. **A new doctrine,** the doctrine of evolution. 204. **cultus,** worship; a favorite word with Stevenson.

we can scarce trace and scarce comprehend his doings; and here also, in his ordered polities and rigorous justice, we see confessed the law of duty and the fact of individual sin. Does it stop, then, with the ant? Rather this desire of well-doing and this doom of frailty run through all the grades of life: rather is this earth, from the frosty top of Everest to the next margin of the internal fire, one stage of ineffectual virtues and one temple of pious tears and persever-¹⁰ance. The whole creation groaneth and travaileth together. It is the common and the god-like law of life. The browsers, the biters, the barkers, the hairy coats of field and forest, the squirrel in the oak, the thousand-footed creeper in the dust, as they share with us the gift of life, share with us the love of an ideal: strive like us—like us are tempted to grow weary of the struggle—to do well; like us receive at times unmerited refreshment, visitings of support, returns of courage; and are condemned like us to ²⁰be crucified between that double law of the members and the will. Are they like us, I wonder, in the timid hope of some reward, some sugar with the drug? do they, too, stand aghast at unrewarded virtues, at the sufferings of those whom, in our partiality, we take to be just, and the prosperity of such as, in our blindness we call wicked? It may be, and yet God knows what they should look for. Even while they look, even while they repent, the foot of man treads them by thousands in the dust, the yelping hounds ³⁰burst upon their trail, the bullet speeds, the knives are heating in the den of the vivisectionist; or the dew falls, and the generation of a day is blotted out. For these are creatures, compared with whom our weakness is strength, our ignorance wisdom, our brief span eternity.

And as we dwell, we living things, in our isle of terror and under the imminent hand of death, God forbid it should be man the erected, the reasoner, the wise in his own eyes—God forbid it should ⁴⁰be man that wearies in well-doing, that despairs of unrewarded effort, or utters the language of complaint. Let it be enough for faith, that the whole creation groans in mortal frailty, strives with unconquerable constancy: surely not all in vain. (1888)

RUDYARD KIPLING 1865-1936

Rudyard Kipling, the great literary exponent of imperialism, who claimed for the white man in general

and for the Englishman in particular virtues not possessed by "lesser breeds without the law," came by his attitude naturally. He was born in Bombay, India, where his father was professor of architectural sculpture in the British School of Art and also a painter and verse writer. When Kipling was six years of age, his parents took him to England, where he later became a student in the United Services College at Westward Ho in North Devon—an ungrateful and lonely experience which gave him ample material for the rather harsh boy's book, Stalky & Co. (1899). *His parents' plan was to have him trained for a government position in India; his very bad eyesight, however, made such a program impossible for him, and so he turned soon to writing and began sending poems to the London journals. No doubt his physical handicap suggested to him his touching novel of growing blindness,* The Light that Failed (1890).

By 1882 Kipling was back at Lahore, India, serving as subeditor on the Civil and Military Gazette. *To this magazine he contributed a number of poems and stories that were collected under the titles, respectively, of* Departmental Ditties (1886) *and* Plain Tales from the Hills (1887). *Some of his best short stories appeared in* Wheeler's Railway Library, *all of this work before he was twenty-four years old. An appointment to the editorial staff of the* Pioneer *at Allahabad (1887) gave him an opportunity to journey all over India, and to see some actual fighting on the Afghanistan border. A journey around the world to Australia, America, England, and back to India confirmed his sense of Anglo-Saxon supremacy. His world-famous Barrack-Room Ballads appeared in* The National Observer, *edited by W. E. Henley, in 1892. In the same year he married Caroline Balestier, an American, and settled down for a fairly long residence near Brattleboro, Vermont. A serio-comic family quarrel drove him back to England in 1896, but not before he had written much characteristic work, especially the effective* Jungle Books *(1894 and 1895). After further traveling to South Africa and America he bought an estate in Sussex and adopted the quiet life of a country gentleman. With the exception of* Kim (1901), *that amazing tale of a boy's odyssey through India, the best of Kipling's work was probably done before the turn of the century, but he was capable of a beautiful effort occasionally thereafter.* Puck of Pook's Hill (1906) *and* Rewards and Fairies (1910) *are two volumes of most effective short stories, interspersed with some of Kipling's best verse, designed to illustrate the progress of English history. In 1907 Kipling was awarded the Nobel Prize for literature. His last volumes of short stories are obscured*

---

7. **Everest,** the highest mountain in the world (29,141 feet), in the Himalayas. 10. **whole . . . travaileth.** Cf. Romans 8:22: "For we know that the whole creation groaneth and travaileth in pain together until now." 20. **double . . . will.** See Romans 7:23: "But I see another law in my members, warring against the law of my mind, and bringing me into captivity to the law of sin which is in my members." 31. **vivisectionist.** In his *Life of Robert Louis Stevenson,* Graham Balfour says: "It must be laid to the credit of his reason and the firm

balance of his judgment that although vivisection was a subject he could not endure even to have mentioned, yet, with all his imagination and sensibility, he never ranged himself among the opponents of this method of inquiry, provided, of course, it was limited, as in England, with the utmost rigor possible." 39. **wise . . . eyes.** See Isaiah 5:21: "Woe unto *them that are* wise in their own eyes, and prudent in their own sight!" 40. **wearies in well-doing.** Cf. Galatians 6:9: "And let us not be weary in well doing: for in due season we shall reap, if

by masonic arcana, and in addition he developed some bizarre stylistic effects. Certainly in the last quarter century of his life he never reached the literary heights he had scaled so easily as a young man in India.

Kipling had all the elements required of a popular writer. He had a keen sense of the dramatic, a remarkable power for observing characters and episodes, and a style with a strong and individual personality. Essentially he was a romanticist of adventurous persuasion, well able to turn to the supernatural or the horror story and to revel in the exotic charm of "old, unhappy, far-off" things. Moreover, in common with all writers of fiction at the end of the century, he had learned from the realists to value accuracy of detail and the revealing truth of phrase. He could, if he chose, be mystic, as well as nostalgic—so it is in many stories from Rewards and Fairies or in the beautiful They and The Brushwood

A self-caricature by Rudyard Kipling, "after the manner of Aubrey Beardsley."

Boy. But he seldom chose to be so; he was, in the main, a man's author. He is the interpreter of imperial Britain, and the bringer of romance into the world of commerce, colonization, and steam engines; yet he portrayed in indelible colors and with great fidelity of detail the psychology of the white colonial in India during the 1870's and 1880's. He was in this respect a true re-creator of an age and a society that has passed.

TOMMY

I went into a public-'ouse to get a pint o' beer,
The publican 'e up an' sez, "We serve no red-coats here."
The girls be'ind the bar they laughed an' giggled fit to die,
I outs into the street again an' to myself sez I:
    O it's Tommy this, an' Tommy that, an' "Tommy, go away";
    But it's "Thank you, Mister Atkins," when the band begins to play,
    The band begins to play, my boys, the band begins to play—
    O it's "Thank you, Mister Atkins," when the band begins to play.

I went into a theater as sober as could be,
They gave a drunk civilian room, but 'adn't none for me;   10
They sent me to the gallery or round the music-'alls,
But when it comes to fightin', Lord! they'll shove me in the stalls!
    For it's Tommy this, an' Tommy that, an' "Tommy, wait outside";
    But it's "Special train for Atkins" when the trooper's on the tide—
    The troopship's on the tide, my boys, the troopship's on the tide,
    O it's "Special train for Atkins" when the trooper's on the tide.

Yes, makin' mock o' uniforms that guard you while you sleep
Is cheaper than them uniforms, an' they're starvation cheap;
An' hustlin' drunken soldiers when they're goin' large a bit
Is five times better business than paradin' in full kit.   20
    Then it's Tommy this, an' Tommy that, an' "Tommy, 'ow's yer soul?"

we faint not."
    Tommy. 1. **public-'ouse,** a house where intoxicating liquors are sold to be consumed on the premises (a "pub"). During the reign of Queen Victoria, British soldiers were not welcome in such places. 2. **publican,** the owner of the public house. Kipling's soldier poems are written in the dialect of the lower-class Londoner, who always drops his initial h's. 5. **Tommy,** Thomas, or Tommy Atkins, the conventional nickname for a British private. It was the hypothetical name used in

instructing soldiers how to fill out blanks, reports, etc. 6. **band . . . play,** i.e., when the soldiers are marching off to war, to the music of the regimental band. 11. **music-'alls,** public halls for vaudeville performances. 12. **stalls,** orchestra seats; in other words, the front ranks.
    Tommy is from *Barrack-Room Ballads,* and from *Rudyard Kipling's Verse: Definitive Edition.* Reprinted by permission of Mrs. George Bambridge, Doubleday & Company, Inc., and the Macmillan Co. of Canada.

But it's "Thin red line of 'eroes" when the drums
    begin to roll—
The drums begin to roll, my boys, the drums begin
    to roll,
O it's "Thin red line of 'eroes" when the drums begin
    to roll.

We aren't no thin red 'eroes, nor we aren't no black-
    guards too,
But single men in barricks, most remarkable like you;
An' if sometimes our conduck isn't all your fancy
    paints,
Why, single men in barricks don't grow into plaster
    saints;
    While it's Tommy this, an' Tommy that, an'
      "Tommy, fall be'ind,"
    But it's "Please to walk in front, sir," when there's
30   trouble in the wind—
There's trouble in the wind, my boys, there's trouble
    in the wind,
O it's "Please to walk in front, sir," when there's
    trouble in the wind.

You talk o' better food for us, an' schools, an' fires,
    an' all:
We'll wait for extry rations if you treat us rational.
Don't mess about the cook-room slops, but prove it to
    our face
The Widow's Uniform is not the soldierman's disgrace.
    For it's Tommy this, an' Tommy that, an' "Chuck
      him out, the brute!"
    But it's "Savior of 'is country" when the guns begin
      to shoot;
    An' it's Tommy this, an' Tommy that, an' anything
      you please;
    An' Tommy ain't a bloomin' fool—you bet that
      Tommy sees!
(1890)

DANNY DEEVER

"What are the bugles blowin' for?" said Files-on-
    Parade.
"To turn you out, to turn you out," the Color-
    Sergeant said.
"What makes you look so white, so white?" said
    Files-on-Parade.
"I'm dreadin' what I've got to watch," the Color-
    Sergeant said.

For they're hangin' Danny Deever, you can hear the
    Dead March play,
The regiment's in 'ollow square—they're hangin'
    him today;
They've taken of his buttons off an' cut his stripes
    away,
An' they're hangin' Danny Deever in the mornin'.

"What makes the rear-rank breathe so 'ard?" said
    Files-on-Parade.
"It's bitter cold, it's bitter cold," the Color-Sergeant
    said.   10
"What makes that front-rank man fall down?" said
    Files-on-Parade.
"A touch o' sun, a touch o' sun," the Color-Sergeant
    said.
    They are hangin' Danny Deever, they are marchin'
      of 'im round,
    They 'ave 'alted Danny Deever by 'is coffin on the
      ground;
    An' 'e'll swing in 'arf a minute for a sneakin'
      shootin' hound—
    O they're hangin' Danny Deever in the mornin'!

"'Is cot was right-'and cot to mine," said Files-on-
    Parade.
"'E's sleepin' out an' far tonight," the Color-Sergeant
    said.
"I've drunk 'is beer a score o' times," said Files-on-
    Parade.
"'E's drinkin' bitter beer alone," the Color-Sergeant
    said.   20
    They are hangin' Danny Deever, you must mark
      'im to 'is place,
    For 'e shot a comrade sleepin'—you must look 'im
      in the face;
    Nine 'undred of 'is county an' the Regiment's dis-
      grace,
    While they're hangin' Danny Deever in the mornin'.

"What's that so black agin the sun?" said Files-on-
    Parade.
"It's Danny fightin' 'ard for life," the Color-Sergeant
    said.
"What's that that whimpers over'ead?" said Files-
    on-Parade.
"It's Danny's soul that's passin' now," the Color-Ser-
    geant said.
    For they're done with Danny Deever, you can 'ear
      the quickstep play,

Danny Deever is from *Barrack-Room Ballads*, and from *Rudyard Kipling's Verse: Definitive Edition*. Reprinted by permission of Mrs. George Bambridge, Doubleday & Company, Inc., and the Macmillan Co. of Canada.
22. **"Thin . . . 'eroes,"** a phrase used by a war correspondent in describing a company of soldiers in action during the Crimean War. Cf. Tennyson's *Charge of the Light Brigade*, p. 898. 35. **cook-room slops,** weak, unappetizing food. 36. **Widow,** a nickname, affectionate or otherwise, for Queen Victoria; the Prince Consort, Albert, had been dead since 1861.
Danny Deever. 1. **Files-on-Parade,** a term applied to a soldier assigned to close up the files or ranks. 2. **Color-Sergeant,** the non-commissioned officer who carried the regimental colors. 6. **regiment's . . . square.** The soldiers form the four sides of a square facing inwards. This is the formation used on ceremonial occasions, or when a soldier is to be publicly executed. 7. **taken . . . away,** a custom applied to a degraded soldier. 29. **quickstep,** a lively air played after the funeral march.
"Fuzzy-Wuzzy." 5. **ha'porth's change,** halfpenny's worth of change —i.e., we never got any advantage over him. 6. **'ocked our 'orses,** disabled our horses by cutting the tendons of the hock. 7. **Suakim,** a seaport on the Red Sea; headquarters of the British and Egyptian

The regiment's in column, an' they're marchin' us
30   away;
  Ho! the young recruits are shakin', an' they'll want
    their beer today,
After hangin' Danny Deever in the mornin'.

(1890)

"FUZZY-WUZZY"

(SUDAN EXPEDITIONARY FORCE)

*In 1884 a British army under General Gerald Graham
was sent on an expedition against the Sudanese. Although British forces had conducted successful campaigns against the Paythans (Afghans) in the mountains on the Indian frontier, the Zulus of southeast
Africa, and the Burmese—all exceedingly warlike—they
met new methods in the Sudan and were defeated in
the engagement commemorated in the poem.*

We've fought with many men acrost the seas,
  An' some of 'em was brave an' some was not:
The Paythan an' the Zulu an' Burmese;
  But the Fuzzy was the finest o' the lot.
We never got a ha'porth's change of 'im:
  'E squatted in the scrub an' 'ocked our 'orses,
'E cut our sentries up at Suakim,
  An' 'e played the cat an' banjo with our forces.
    So 'ere's *to* you, Fuzzy-Wuzzy, at your 'ome in the
      Sudan;
    You're a pore benighted 'eathen but a first-class
10   fightin' man;
    We gives you your certificate, an' if you want it
      signed,
    We'll come 'an 'ave a romp with you whenever
      you're inclined.

We took our chanst among the Kyber 'ills,
  The Boers knocked us silly at a mile,
The Burman give us Irriwaddy chills,
  An' a Zulu *impi* dished us up in style:
But all we ever got from such as they
  Was pop to what the Fuzzy made us swaller;
We 'eld our bloomin' own, the papers say,
20   But man for man the Fuzzy knocked us 'oller.

forces. 13. **Kyber 'ills,** the mountains between Afghanistan and British
India, the home of the Paythans and the scene of much fighting. 14.
Boers, Dutch settlers in South Africa, noted for their accuracy of gun-
fire at long range. They defeated the British forces in the Battle of
Majuba Hill (1881); this poem was written before the outbreak of the
Boer War. 15. **Irriwaddy chills.** The Irriwaddy is the chief river of
Burma. The malarial climate along the river made the Burmese campaign
very difficult for the British. 16. **Zulu impi,** a section of the Zulu
army, in southeastern Africa. In 1879 a Zulu force completely routed
a British regiment. 23. **Martinis,** Martini-Henry rifles, used from
1876 to 1886 by the British Army, named after Frederick Martini

Then 'ere's *to* you, Fuzzy-Wuzzy, an' the missis
  and the kid;
Our orders was to break you, an' of course we
  went an' did.
We sloshed you with Martinis, an' it wasn't
  'ardly fair;
But for all the odds agin' you, Fuzzy-Wuz, you
  broke the square.

'E 'asn't got no papers of 'is own,
  'E 'asn't got no medals nor rewards,
So *we* must certify the skill 'e's shown
  In usin' of 'is long two-'anded swords:
When 'e's 'oppin' in an' out among the bush
  With 'is coffin-'eaded shield an' shovel-spear,   30
An 'appy day with Fuzzy on the rush
  Will last an 'ealthy Tommy for a year.
    So 'ere's to you, Fuzzy-Wuzzy, an' your friends
      which are no more,
    If we 'adn't lost some messmates, we would 'elp
      you to deplore.
    But give an' take's the gospel, an' we'll call the
      bargain fair,
    For if you 'ave lost more than us, you crumpled
      up the square!

'E rushes at the smoke when we let drive,
  An', before we know, 'e's 'ackin' at our 'ead;
'E's all 'ot sand an' ginger when alive,
  An' 'e's generally shammin' when 'e's dead.   40
'E's a daisy, 'e's a ducky, 'e's a lamb!
  'E's a injia-rubber idiot on the spree,
'E's the on'y thing that doesn't give a damn
  For a Regiment o' British Infantree!
    So 'ere's *to* you, Fuzzy-Wuzzy, at your 'ome in the
      Sudan;
    You're a poor benighted 'eathen but a first-class
      fightin' man;
    An' 'ere's *to* you, Fuzzy-Wuzzy, with your 'ayrick
      'ead of 'air—
    You big black boundin' beggar—for you broke a
      British square!

(1890)

GUNGA DIN

You may talk o' gin and beer
When you're quartered safe out 'ere,
An' you're sent to penny-fights an' Aldershot it;

(1832–1897), a Swiss inventor, and a Scottish gunmaker named Henry
(d. 1894). 24. **the square,** the hollow square, a British defensive
fighting formation.
  Gunga Din. 2. **out 'ere,** in India. 3. **Aldershot it,** to live in
Aldershot, a military camp in Hampshire.
  "Fuzzy-Wuzzy" and *Gunga Din* are from *Barrack-Room Ballads,* and
from *Rudyard Kipling's Verse: Definitive Edition.* Reprinted by permission of Mrs. George Bambridge, Doubleday & Company, Inc., and the
Macmillan Co. of Canada.

But when it comes to slaughter
You will do your work on water,
An' you'll lick the bloomin' boots of 'im that's got
    it.
Now in Injia's sunny clime,
Where I used to spend my time
A-servin' of 'Er Majesty the Queen,
10 Of all them black-faced crew
The finest man I knew
Was our regimental bhisti, Gunga Din.
      He was "Din! Din! Din!
    "You limpin' lump o' brick-dust, Gunga Din!
      "Hi! *Slippy hitherao!*
      "Water, get it! *Panee lao!*
    "You squidgy-nosed old idol, Gunga Din!"

The uniform 'e wore
Was nothin' much before,
20 An' rather less than 'arf o' that be'ind,
For a piece o' twisty rag
An' a goatskin water-bag
Was all the field-equipment 'e could find.
When the sweatin' troop-train lay
In a sidin' through the · day,
Where the 'eat would make your bloomin' eyebrows
    crawl,
We shouted "Harry By!"
Till our throats were bricky-dry,
Then we wopped 'im 'cause 'e couldn't serve us all.
30   It was "Din! Din! Din!
    "You 'eathen, where the mischief 'ave you been?
      "You put some *juldee* in it
      "Or I'll *marrow* you this minute
    "If you don't fill up my helmet, Gunga Din!"

'E would dot an' carry one
Till the longest day was done;
An' 'e didn't seem to know the use o' fear.
If we charged or broke or cut,
You could bet your bloomin' nut,
40 'E'd be waitin' fifty paces right flank rear.
With 'is mussick on 'is back,
'E would skip with our attack,
An' watch us till the bugles made "Retire,"
An' for all 'is dirty 'ide
'E was white, clear white, inside
When 'e went to tend the wounded under fire!
      It was "Din! Din! Din!"
    With the bullets kickin' dust-spots on the green.
    When the cartridges ran out,
50   You could 'ear the front-ranks shout,
    "Hi! ammunition-mules an' Gunga Din!"

I sha'n't forgit the night
When I dropped be'ind the fight
With a bullet where my belt-plate should 'a' been.
I was chokin' mad with thirst,
An' the man that spied me first
Was our good old grinnin', gruntin' Gunga Din.
'E lifted up my 'ead,
An' 'e plugged me where I bled,
An' 'e guv me 'arf-a-pint o' water green. 60
It was crawlin' and it stunk,
But of all the drinks I've drunk,
I'm gratefullest to one from Gunga Din.
      It was "Din! Din! Din!
    "'Ere's a beggar with a bullet through 'is spleen;
      "'E's chawin' up the ground,
      "An' 'e's kickin' all around:
    "For Gawd's sake, git the water, Gunga Din!"

'E carried me away
To where a dooli lay, 70
An' a bullet come an' drilled the beggar clean.
'E put me safe inside,
An' just before 'e died,
"I 'ope you liked your drink," sez Gunga Din.
So I'll meet 'im later on
In the place where 'e is gone—
Where it's always double drill and no canteen.
'E'll be squattin' on the coals
Givin' drink to poor damned souls,
An' I'll get a swig in hell from Gunga Din! 80
      Yes, Din! Din! Din!
    You Lazarushian-leather Gunga Din!
      Though I've belted you an' flayed you,
      By the livin' God that made you,
    You're a better man than I am, Gunga Din!
(1890)

MANDALAY

Mandalay is one of the chief cities of Burma. A British force of occupation was stationed there after 1885, when the country was annexed.

By the old Moulmein Pagoda, lookin' eastward to the
    sea,
There's a Burma girl a-settin', and I know she thinks
    o' me;
For the wind is in the palm-trees, and the temple
    bells they say:
"Come you back, you British soldier; come you back
    to Mandalay!"

Mandalay is from *Barrack-Room Ballads*, and from *Rudyard Kipling's Verse: Definitive Edition.* Reprinted by permission of Mrs. George Bambridge, Doubleday & Company, Inc., and the Macmillan Co. of Canada.
12. **bhisti,** water-carrier; literally, heavenly one. 15. *Slippy hitherao,* mock dialect for "slip here." 16. *Panee lao,* bring water in a hurry. 27. **"Harry By,"** O Brother. 29. **wopped,** struck. 32. *juldee,* speed.

33. *marrow,* wallop. 41. **mussick,** leather water bag, made of goat-skin. 70. **dooli,** stretcher. 82. **Lazarushian-leather,** army slang for dark-skinned.
    Mandalay. 1. **Moulmein Pagoda,** a Buddhist temple in the city of Moulmein across the Gulf of Martaban from Rangoon, another chief city of Burma 375 miles south of Mandalay. 6. **old Flotilla,** steamers of the Flotilla Company plying between Rangoon and Mandalay, on the

Come you back to Mandalay,
Where the old Flotilla lay:
Can't you 'ear their paddles chunkin' from Rangoon
    to Mandalay?
On the road to Mandalay,
Where the flyin'-fishes play,
An' the dawn comes up like thunder outer China
10   'crost the Bay!

'Er petticoat was yaller an' 'er little cap was green,
An' 'er name was Supi-yaw-lat—jes' the same as Thee-
    baw's Queen,
An' I seed her first a-smokin' of a whackin' white che-
    root,
An' a-wastin' Christian kisses on an 'eathen idol's foot:

    Bloomin' idol made o' mud—
    Wot they called the Great Gawd Budd—
    Plucky lot she cared for idols when I kissed 'er where
      she stud!
    On the road to Mandalay . . .

When the mist was on the rice-fields an' the sun was
    droppin' slow,
20 She'd git 'er little banjo an' she'd sing "Kulla-lo-lo!"
With 'er arm upon my shoulder an' 'er cheek agin my
    cheek
We useter watch the steamers an' the hathis pilin'
    teak.

    Elephints a-pilin' teak
    In the sludgy, squdgy creek,
    Where the silence 'ung that 'eavy you was 'arf afraid
      to speak!
    On the road to Mandalay . . .

But that's all shove be'ind me—long ago an' fur away,
An' there ain't no 'busses runnin' from the Bank to
    Mandalay;
An' I'm learnin' 'ere in London what the ten-year
    soldier tells:
"If you've 'eard the East a-callin', you won't never 'eed
30   naught else."

    No! you won't 'eed nothin' else
    But them spicy garlic smells,
    An' the sunshine an' the palm-trees an' the tinkly
      temple bells;
    On the road to Mandalay . . .

I am sick o' wastin' leather on these gritty pavin'-
    stones,

An' the blasted Henglish drizzle wakes the fever in my
    bones;
Tho' I walks with fifty 'ousemaids outer Chelsea to the
    Strand,
An' they talks a lot o' lovin', but wot do they under-
    stand?

    Beefy face an' grubby 'and—
    Law! wot do they understand?   40
    I've a neater, sweeter maiden in a cleaner, greener
      land!
    On the road to Mandalay . . .

Ship me somewheres east of Suez, where the best is
    like the worst,
Where there aren't no Ten Commandments an' a
    man can raise a thirst;
For the temple bells are callin', an' it's there that I
    would be—
By the old Moulmein Pagoda, looking lazy at the sea;

    On the road to Mandalay,
    Where the old Flotilla lay,
    With our sick beneath the awnings when we went
      to Mandalay!

    On the road to Mandalay!   50
    Where the flyin'-fishes play,
    An' the dawn comes up like thunder outer China
      'crost the Bay!
(1890)

THE KING

"Farewell, Romance!" the Cave-men said;
    "With bone well carved he went away,
"Flint arms the ignoble arrowhead,
    "And jasper tips the spear today.
"Changed are the Gods of Hunt and Dance,
"And he with these. Farewell, Romance!"

"Farewell, Romance!" the Lake-folk sighed;
    "We lift the weight of flatling years;
"The caverns of the mountain-side
    "Hold Him who scorns our hutted piers.   10
"Lost hills whereby we dare not dwell,
"Guard ye his rest. Romance, farewell!"

"Farewell, Romance!" the Soldier spoke;
    "By sleight of sword we may not win,
"But scuffle 'mid uncleanly smoke

Irrawaddy River. 10. **dawn comes up,** as observed by one on the
road to Mandalay. 12. **Theebaw,** the last king of Burma (1876–1885).
His wife, Supaīyah Lat, was notoriously cruel. 16. **Budd,** Buddha,
worshiped by most Burmese. 22. **hathis,** elephants. **teak,** a valuable
hard wood. 28. **Bank,** the Bank of England, where several London bus
routes meet. 37. **Chelsea,** a district of London on the Thames River.
Strand, one of the main thoroughfares of London.

The King. 7. **the Lake-folk,** prehistoric inhabitants of Switzerland,
who lived in villages built on piers or piles near the shores of lakes.
    The King is from *The Seven Seas,* and from *Rudyard Kipling's Verse:
Definitive Edition.* Reprinted by permission of Mrs. George Bambridge,
Doubleday & Company, Inc., and the Macmillan Co. of Canada.

"Of arquebus and culverin.
"Honor is lost, and none may tell
"Who paid good blows. Romance, farewell!"

"Farewell, Romance!" the Traders cried;
20   "Our keels have lain with every sea;
"The dull-returning wind and tide
"Heave up the wharf where we would be;
"The known and noted breezes swell
"Our trudging sail. Romance, farewell!"

"Good-by, Romance!" the Skipper said;
"He vanished with the coal we burn.
"Our dial marks full-steam ahead,
"Our speed is timed to half a turn.
"Sure as the ferried barge we ply
30 " 'Twixt port and port. Romance, good-by!"

"Romance!" the season-tickets mourn,
"He never ran to catch his train,
"But passed with coach and guard and horn—
"And left the local—late again!"
Confound Romance! . . . And all unseen
Romance brought up the nine-fifteen.

His hand was on the lever laid,
His oil can soothed the worrying cranks,
His whistle waked the snowbound grade,
40   His fog-horn cut the reeking Banks;
By dock and deep and mine and mill
The Boy-god reckless labored still!

Robed, crowned, and throned, He wove his spell,
Where heart-blood beat or hearth-smoke curled,
With unconsidered miracle,
Hedged in a backward-gazing world:
Then taught his chosen bard to say:
"Our King was with us—yesterday!"
(1894)

RECESSIONAL

A recessional is a hymn sung as the choir leaves the church service. The poem was published in the London Times *in July 1897, near the close of the celebration of the sixtieth anniversary of the reign of Queen Victoria. High government officials and troops from all the colonies of the Empire, and nearly two hundred vessels of the Royal Navy, were assembled for the ceremonies. Thus it was an appropriate time for Kipling to sound a warning to the nation dazzled by the pomp and splendor of the occasion.*

Recessional *and* The White Man's Burden *are from* The Five Nations, *and from* Rudyard Kipling's Verse: Definitive Edition. *Reprinted by permission of Mrs. George Bambridge, Doubleday & Company, Inc., and the Macmillan Co. of Canada.*

16. **arquebus and culverin,** early kinds of firearms. 23. **known . . . breezes.** Records of prevailing winds were not kept before the nineteenth century. 40. **reeking Banks,** fog banks that the train runs through.

God of our fathers, known of old,
Lord of our far-flung battle-line,
Beneath whose awful Hand we hold
Dominion over palm and pine—
Lord God of Hosts, be with us yet,
Lest we forget—lest we forget!

The tumult and the shouting dies;
The Captains and the Kings depart:
Still stands Thine ancient sacrifice,
An humble and a contrite heart.   10
Lord God of Hosts, be with us yet,
Lest we forget—lest we forget!

Far-called, our navies melt away;
On dune and headland sinks the fire:
Lo, all our pomp of yesterday
Is one with Nineveh and Tyre!
Judge of the Nations, spare us yet,
Lest we forget—lest we forget!

If, drunk with sight of power, we loose
Wild tongues that have not Thee in awe,   20
Such boastings as the Gentiles use,
Or lesser breeds without the Law—
Lord God of Hosts, be with us yet,
Lest we forget—lest we forget!

For heathen heart that puts her trust
In reeking tube and iron shard,
All valiant dust that builds on dust,
And guarding, calls not Thee to guard,
For frantic boast and foolish word—
Thy Mercy on Thy People, Lord!
(1897)

THE WHITE MAN'S BURDEN

Published in McClure's Magazine, *shortly after the conclusion of peace between the United States and Spain, December 10, 1898, this poem describes the duty, as Kipling saw it, of the United States toward Cuba and the Philippines. Both poem and title coincide with a definite attitude of Kipling and of conservative England toward imperialism.*

Take up the White Man's burden—
Send forth the best ye breed—
Go bind your sons to exile
To serve your captives' need;
To wait in heavy harness,

Recessional. 4. **palm and pine,** an indication of the extent of the British Empire. 5. **Lord . . . Hosts,** a very common phrase in the Bible. Cf. Psalms 84:8—"O Lord God of Hosts, hear my prayer." 6. **Lest we forget.** Cf. Deuteronomy 6:12—"Then beware lest thou forget the Lord." 7. **tumult . . . dies.** Note Job 39:25—"He smelleth the battle afar off, the thunder of the captains and the shouting." 9. **sacrifice . . . heart.** Cf. Psalms 51:17—"The sacrifices of God are a broken spirit: a broken and a contrite heart, O God, thou wilt not

1134   Democracy, Science, and Industrialism

On fluttered folk and wild—
Your new-caught, sullen peoples,
   Half-devil and half-child.

Take up the White Man's burden—
10 In patience to abide,
To veil the threat of terror
   And check the show of pride;
By open speech and simple,
   An hundred times made plain,
To seek another's profit,
   And work another's gain.

Take up the White Man's burden—
   The savage wars of peace—
Fill full the mouth of Famine
20 And bid the sickness cease;
And when your goal is nearest
   The end for others sought,
Watch Sloth and heathen Folly
   Bring all your hope to nought.

Take up the White Man's burden—
   No tawdry rule of kings,
But toil of serf and sweeper—
   The tale of common things.
The ports ye shall not enter,
30 The roads ye shall not tread,
Go make them with your living,
   And mark them with your dead.

Take up the White Man's burden—
   And reap his old reward:
The blame of those ye better,
   The hate of those ye guard—
The cry of hosts ye humor
   (Ah, slowly!) toward the light:—
"Why brought ye us from bondage,
40 "Our loved Egyptian night?"

Take up the White Man's burden—
   Ye dare not stoop to less—
Nor call too loud on Freedom
   To cloak your weariness;
By all ye cry or whisper,
   By all ye leave or do,
The silent sullen peoples
   Shall weigh your Gods and you.

Take up the White Man's burden—
50 Have done with childish days—
The lightly proffered laurel,

The easy, ungrudged praise.
Comes now, to search your manhood
   Through all the thankless years,
Cold, edged with dear-bought wisdom,
   The judgment of your peers!
(1899)

SUSSEX

God gave all men all earth to love,
   But since our hearts are small,
Ordained for each one spot should prove
   Belovéd over all;
That, as He watched Creation's birth,
   So we, in godlike mood,
May of our love create our earth
   And see that it is good.

So one shall Baltic pines content,
   As one some Surrey's glade,   10
Or one the palm-grove's droned lament
   Before Levuka's Trade.
Each to his choice, and I rejoice
   The lot has fallen to me
In a fair ground—in a fair ground—
   Yea, Sussex by the sea!

No tender-hearted garden crowns,
   No bosomed woods adorn
Our blunt, bow-headed, whale-backed Downs,
   But gnarled and writhen thorn—   20
Bare slopes where chasing shadows skim,
   And, through the gaps revealed
Belt upon belt, the wooded, dim
   Blue goodness of the Weald.

Clean of officious fence or hedge,
   Half-wild and wholly tame,
The wise turf cloaks the white cliff edge
   As when the Romans came.
What sign of those that fought and died
   At shift of sword and sword?   30
The barrow and the camp abide,
   The sunlight and the sward.

Here leaps ashore the full Sou'west
   All heavy-winged with brine,
Here lies above the folded crest
   The Channel's leaden line;
And here the sea-fogs lap and cling,
   And here, each warning each,

despise." 16. **Nineveh and Tyre.** Nineveh was the ancient capital of Assyria; it is now buried under sand. Tyre, now an unimportant seaport, was once a great city of Phoenicia. 21. **Gentiles . . . Law.** Cf. Romans 2:14—"For when the Gentiles which have not the law, do by nature the things contained in the law, these, having not the law, are a law unto themselves." A Gentile is here thought of by Kipling as anyone not English.
  The White Man's Burden. 39. **"Why brought . . . night?"** On

their journey from Egypt, the Israelites complained because they had no food. They exclaimed: "Would to God we had died by the hand of the Lord in the land of Egypt, where we sat by the flesh pots, and when we did eat bread to the full." (Exodus 16:2–3).
  Sussex is from *The Five Nations,* and from *Rudyard Kipling's Verse: Definitive Edition.* Reprinted by permission of Mrs. George Bambridge, Doubleday & Company, Inc., and the Macmillan Co. of Canada.

The sheep-bells and the ship-bells ring
40   Along the hidden beach.

We have no waters to delight
   Our broad and brookless vales—
Only the dewpond on the height
   Unfed, that never fails—
Whereby no tattered herbage tells
   Which way the season flies—
Only our close-bit thyme that smells
   Like dawn in Paradise.

Here through the strong and shadeless days
50   The tinkling silence thrills;
Or little, lost Down churches praise
   The Lord who made the hills:
But here the Old Gods guard their round,
   And, in her secret heart,
The heathen kingdom Wilfrid found
   Dreams, as she dwells, apart.

Though all the rest were all my share,
   With equal soul I'd see
Her nine-and-thirty sisters fair,
60   Yet none more fair than she.
Choose ye your need from Thames to Tweed,
   And I will choose instead
Such lands as lie 'twixt Rake and Rye,
   Black Down and Beachy Head.

I will go out against the sun
   Where the rolled scarp retires,
And the Long Man of Wilmington
   Looks naked toward the shires;
And east till doubling Rother crawls
70   To find the fickle tide,
By dry and sea-forgotten walls,
   Our ports of stranded pride.

I will go north about the shaws
   And the deep ghylls that breed
Huge oaks and old, the which we hold
   No more than Sussex weed;
Or south where windy Piddinghoe's
   Begilded dolphin veers
And black beside wide-bankéd Ouse
80   Lie down our Sussex steers.

So to the land our hearts we give
   Till the sure magic strike,
And Memory, Use, and Love make live
   Us and our fields alike—
That deeper than our speech and thought,
   Beyond our reason's sway,
Clay of the pit whence we were wrought
   Yearns to its fellow-clay.

God gives all men all earth to love,
*   But since man's heart is small,*
90
Ordains for each one spot shall prove
*   Belovéd over all.*
Each to his choice, and I rejoice
*   The lot has fallen to me*
In a fair ground—in a fair ground—
*   Yea, Sussex by the sea!*

(1903)

A ST. HELENA LULLABY

How far is St. Helena from a little child at play?
   What makes you want to wander there with all the
      world between?
Oh, Mother, call your son again or else he'll run away.
   (No one thinks of winter when the grass is green!)

How far is St. Helena from a fight in Paris street?
   I haven't time to answer now—the men are falling
      fast.
The guns begin to thunder, and the drums begin to
      beat.
   (If you take the first step, you will take the last!)

How far is St. Helena from the field of Austerlitz?
   You couldn't hear me if I told—so loud the cannon
      roar.
   10
But not so far for people who are living by their wits.
   ("Gay go up" means "Gay go down" the wide
      world o'er!)

How far is St. Helena from an Emperor of France?
   I cannot see—I cannot tell—the Crowns they dazzle
      so.
The Kings sit down to dinner, and the Queens stand up
      to dance.
   (After open weather you may look for snow!)

How far is St. Helena from the Capes of Trafalgar?
   A longish way—a longish way—with ten years more
      to run.
It's South across the water underneath a setting star.
   (What you cannot finish you must leave undone!)   20

How far is St. Helena from the Beresina ice?
   An ill way—a chill way—the ice begins to crack.
But not so far for gentlemen who never took advice.
   (When you can't go forward you must e'en come
      back!)

How far is St. Helena from the field of Waterloo?
   A near way—a clear way—the ship will take you
      soon.
A pleasant place for gentlemen with little left to do.
   (Morning never tries you till the afternoon!)

Sussex. 55. **Wilfrid,** an Anglo-Saxon cleric and saint (634-709), who was an Archbishop of York in the early days of the archbishopric. In the course of his career he was a celebrated missionary among the South Saxons, who had founded the kingdom of Sussex. 59. **nine-and-thirty sisters.** There are forty shires in Britain.
A St. Helena Lullaby is from *Rewards and Fairies,* and from *Rudyard*

Kipling's Verse: Definitive Edition. Reprinted by permission of Mrs. George Bambridge, Doubleday & Company, Inc., and the Macmillan Co. of Canada.
   A St. Helena Lullaby. 5. **a fight . . . street,** an allusion to the disturbances leading up to the storming of the Bastille in the early days of the French Revolution (July 1789). 9. **Austerlitz,** a town in

How far from St. Helena to the Gate of Heaven's
    Grace?
    That no one knows—that no one knows—and no one
30   ever will.
But fold your hands across your heart and cover up
    your face,
And after all your trapesings, child, lie still! (1911)

WITHOUT BENEFIT OF CLERGY

1

"But if it be a girl?"

"Lord of my life, it cannot be. I have prayed for so
many nights, and sent gifts to Sheikh Badl's shrine so
often, that I know God will give us a son—a man-child
that shall grow into a man. Think of this and be glad.
My mother shall be his mother till I can take him
again, and the mullah of the Pattan Mosque shall cast
his nativity—God send he be born in an auspicious
hour!—and then, and then thou wilt never weary of
10 me, thy slave."

"Since when hast thou been a slave, my queen?"

"Since the beginning—till this mercy came to me.
How could I be sure of thy love when I knew that
I had been bought with silver?"

"Nay, that was the dowry. I paid it to thy mother."

"And she has buried it, and sits upon it all day long
like a hen. What talk is yours of dower! I was bought
as though I had been a Lucknow dancing-girl instead
of a child."

20   "Art thou sorry for the sale?"

"I have sorrowed; but to-day I am glad. Thou wilt
never cease to love me now?—Answer, my king."

"Never—never. No."

"Not even though the *mem-log*—the white women
of thy own blood—love thee? And remember, I have
watched them driving in the evening; they are very
fair."

"I have seen fire-balloons by the hundred, I have
seen the moon, and—then I saw no more fire-balloons."

30   Ameera clapped her hands and laughed. "Very good
talk," she said. Then with an assumption of great
stateliness, "It is enough. Thou hast my permission to
depart—if thou wilt."

The man did not move. He was sitting on a low red-
lacquered couch in a room furnished only with a blue
and white floor-cloth, some rugs, and a very complete
collection of native cushions. At his feet sat a woman
of sixteen, and she was all but all the world in his eyes.
By every rule and law she should have been otherwise,
40 for he was an Englishman and she a Mussulman's
daughter bought two years before from her mother,
who, being left without money, would have sold

Ameera, shrieking, to the Prince of Darkness, if the
price had been sufficient.

It was a contract entered into with a light heart; but
even before the girl had reached her bloom, she came
to fill the greater portion of John Holden's life. For her,
and the withered hag her mother, he had taken a
little house overlooking the great red-walled city,
and found,—when the marigolds had sprung up by the 50
wall in the courtyard, and Ameera had established herself according to her own ideas of comfort, and her
mother had ceased grumbling at the inadequacy of the
cooking-places, the distance from the daily market, and
at matters of housekeeping in general, that the house
was to him his home. Any one could enter his bachelor's
bungalow by day or night, and the life that he led
there was an unlovely one. In the house in the city his
feet only could pass beyond the outer courtyard to the
women's rooms; and when the big wooden gate was 60
bolted behind him, he was king in his own territory,
with Ameera for queen. And there was going to be
added to this kingdom a third person whose arrival
Holden felt inclined to resent. It interfered with his
perfect happiness. It disarranged the orderly peace of
the house that was his own. But Ameera was wild with
delight at the thought of it, and her mother not less
so. The love of a man, and particularly a white man,
was at the best an inconstant affair, but it might, both
women argued, be held fast by a baby's hands. "And 70
then," Ameera would always say—"then he will never
care for the white *mem-log*. I hate them all—I hate
them all."

"He will go back to his own people in time," said the
mother; "but by the blessing of God that time is yet
afar off."

Holden sat silent on the couch thinking of the future,
and his thoughts were not pleasant. The drawbacks of
a double life are manifold. The government, with singular care, had ordered him out of the station for a fort- 80
night on special duty in the place of a man who was
watching by the bedside of a sick wife. The verbal
notification of the transfer had been edged by a cheerful remark that Holden ought to think himself lucky
in being a bachelor and a free man. He came to break
the news to Ameera.

"It is not good," she said slowly, "but it is not all
bad. There is my mother here, and no harm will come
to me—unless indeed I die of pure joy. Go thou to thy
work and think no troublesome thoughts. When the 90
days are done I believe . . . nay, I am sure. And—and
then I shall lay *him* in thy arms, and thou wilt love
me forever. The train goes to-night, at midnight is it
not? Go now, and do not let thy heart be heavy by
cause of me. But thou wilt not delay in returning? Thou

Moravia (Bohemia), at that time a province of the Austrian Empire.
Here, in December 1805, Napoleon gained a great victory over the
Russians and Austrians, an important milestone in his career of empire.
    Without Benefit of Clergy. 7. mullah, a Mohammedan teacher
and expounder of the law of Islam. 18. **Lucknow,** a city of the United
Provinces in India.

Without Benefit of Clergy is from *Life's Handicap,* by Rudyard
Kipling. Reprinted by permission of Mrs. George Bambridge, Doubleday
& Company, Inc., and the Macmillan Co. of Canada.

wilt not stay on the road to talk to the bold white *mem-log*. Come back to me swiftly, my life."

As he left the courtyard to reach his horse that was tethered to the gate-post, Holden spoke to the white-haired old watchman who guarded the house, and bade him under certain contingencies dispatch the filled-up telegraph form that Holden gave him. It was all that could be done, and with the sensations of a man who has attended his own funeral Holden went away by the
10 night mail to his exile. Every hour of the day he dreaded the arrival of the telegram, and every hour of the night he pictured to himself the death of Ameera. In consequence his work for the state was not of first-rate quality, nor was his temper toward his colleagues of the most amiable. The fortnight ended without a sign from his home, and, torn to pieces by his anxieties, Holden returned to be swallowed up for two precious hours by a dinner at the club, wherein he heard, as a man hears in a swoon, voices telling him how execrably
20 he had performed the other man's duties, and how he had endeared himself to all his associates. Then he fled on horseback through the night with his heart in his mouth. There was no answer at first to his blows on the gate, and he had just wheeled his horse round to kick it in, when Pir Khan appeared with a lantern and held his stirrup.

"Has aught occurred?" said Holden.

"The news does not come from my mouth, Protector of the Poor, but—" He held out his shaking hand as
30 befitted the bearer of good news who is entitled to a reward.

Holden hurried through the courtyard. A light burned in the upper room. His horse neighed in the gateway, and he heard a shrill little wail that sent all the blood into the apple of his throat. It was a new voice, but it did not prove that Ameera was alive.

"Who is there?" he called up the narrow brick staircase.

There was a cry of delight from Ameera, and then
40 the voice of the mother, tremulous with old age and pride—"We be two women and—the—man—thy—son."

On the threshold of the room Holden stepped on a naked dagger, that was laid there to avert ill-luck, and it broke at the hilt under his impatient heel.

"God is great!" cooed Ameera in the half-light. "Thou hast taken his misfortunes on thy head."

"Ay, but how is it with thee, life of my life? Old woman, how is it with her?"

50 "She has forgotten her sufferings for joy that the child is born. There is no harm; but speak softly," said the mother.

"It only needed thy presence to make me all well," said Ameera. "My king, thou hast been very long away.

What gifts hast thou for me? Ah, ah! It is I that bring gifts this time. Look, my life, look. Was there ever such a babe? Nay, I am too weak even to clear my arm from him."

"Rest then, and do not talk. I am here, *bachari*, [little woman]." 60

"Well said, for there is a bond and a heel-rope [*pee-charee*] between us now that nothing can break. Look—canst thou see in this light? He is without spot or blemish. Never was such a man-child. *Ya illah!* he shall be a pundit—no, a trooper of the Queen. And, my life, dost thou love me as well as ever, though I am faint and sick and worn? Answer truly."

"Yea. I love as I have loved, with all my soul. Lie still, pearl, and rest."

"Then do not go. Sit by my side here—so. Mother, 70 the lord of this house needs a cushion. Bring it." There was an almost imperceptible movement on the part of the new life that lay in the hollow of Ameera's arm. "Aho!" she said, her voice breaking with love. "The babe is a champion from his birth. He is kicking me in the side with mighty kicks. Was there ever such a babe! And he is ours to us—thine and mine. Put thy hand on his head, but carefully, for he is very young, and men are unskilled in such matters."

Very cautiously Holden touched with the tips of his 80 fingers the downy head.

"He is of the Faith," said Ameera; "for lying here in the night-watches I whispered the call to prayer and the profession of faith into his ears. And it is most marvelous that he was born upon a Friday, as I was born. Be careful of him, my life; but he can almost grip with his hands."

Holden found one helpless little hand that closed feebly on his finger. And the clutch ran through his body till it settled about his heart. Till then his sole 90 thought had been for Ameera. He began to realize that there was some one else in the world, but he could not feel that it was a veritable son with a soul. He sat down to think, and Ameera dozed lightly.

"Get hence, *sahib*," said her mother under her breath. "It is not good that she should find you here on waking. She must be still."

"I go," said Holden submissively. "Here be rupees. See that my *baba* gets fat and finds all that he needs."

The chink of the silver roused Ameera. "I am his 100 mother, and no hireling," she said weakly. "Shall I look to him more or less for the sake of money? Mother, give it back. I have borne my lord a son."

The deep sleep of weakness came upon her almost before the sentence was completed. Holden went down to the courtyard very softly, with his heart at ease. Pir Khan, the old watchman, was chuckling with delight.

"This house is now complete," he said, and without further comment thrust into Holden's hands the hilt of 110 a saber worn many years ago, when Pir Khan served

65. pundit, a learned man, a scholar. 82. the Faith, i.e., the Mohammedan faith. 155. In Baltimore, etc., an old British sea ballad; in different versions many places other than Baltimore are mentioned.

the Queen in the police. The bleat of a tethered goat came from the well-kerb.

"There be two," said Pir Khan, "two goats of the best. I bought them, and they cost much money; and since there is no birth-party assembled their flesh will be all mine. Strike craftily, *sahib!* 'Tis an ill-balanced saber at the best. Wait till they raise their heads from cropping the marigolds."

120 "And why?" said Holden, bewildered.

"For the birth-sacrifice. What else? Otherwise the child being unguarded from fate may die. The Protector of the Poor knows the fitting words to be said."

Holden had learned them once with little thought that he would ever speak them in earnest. The touch of the cold saber-hilt in his palm turned suddenly to the clinging grip of the child upstairs—the child that was his own son—and a dread of loss filled him.

"Strike!" said Pir Khan. "Never life came into the 130 world but life was paid for it. See, the goats have raised their heads. Now. With a drawing cut!"

Hardly knowing what he did Holden cut twice as he muttered the Mohammedan prayer that runs: "Almighty! In place of this my son I offer life for life, blood for blood, head for head, bone for bone, hair for hair, skin for skin." The waiting horse snorted and bounded in his pickets at the smell of the raw blood that spurted over Holden's riding-boots.

"Well smitten!" said Pir Khan, wiping the saber. 140 "A swordsman was lost in thee. Go with a light heart, heaven-born. I am thy servant, and the servant of thy son. May the Presence live a thousand years and . . . the flesh of the goats is all mine?" Pir Khan drew back richer by a month's pay. Holden swung himself into the saddle and rode off through the low-hanging wood-smoke of the evening. He was full of riotous exultation, alternating with a vast vague tenderness directed toward no particular object, that made him choke as he bent over the neck of his uneasy horse. "I never felt like 150 this in my life," he thought. "I'll go to the club and pull myself together."

A game of pool was beginning, and the room was full of men. Holden entered, eager to get to the light and the company of his fellows, singing at the top of his voice—

In Baltimore a-walking, a lady I did meet!

"Did you?" said the club-secretary from his corner. "Did she happen to tell you that your boots were wringing wet? Great goodness, man, it's blood!"

"Bosh!" said Holden, picking his cue from the rack. 160 "May I cut in? It's dew. I've been riding through high crops. My faith! my boots are in a mess though!

And if it be a girl she shall wear a wedding-ring,
And if it be a boy he shall fight for his king,
With his dirk, and his cap, and his little jacket blue,
He shall walk the quarter-deck——

"Yellow and blue—green next player," said the marker monotonously.

"He shall walk the quarter-deck,—Am I green, marker? He shall walk the quarter-deck,—eh! that's a bad shot,—As his daddy used to do!" 170

"I don't see that you have anything to crow about," said a zealous junior civilian acidly. "The Government is not exactly pleased with your work when you relieved Sanders."

"Does that mean a wigging from headquarters?" said Holden with an abstracted smile. "I think I can stand it."

The talk beat up round the ever-fresh subject of each man's work, and steadied Holden till it was time to go to his dark empty bungalow, where his butler re- 180 ceived him as one who knew all his affairs. Holden remained awake for the greater part of the night, and his dreams were pleasant ones.

2

"How old is he now?"

"Ya illah! What a man's question! He is all but six weeks old; and on this night I go up to the housetop with thee, my life, to count the stars. For that is auspicious. And he was born on a Friday under the sign of the Sun, and it has been told to me that he will out-live us both and get wealth. Can we wish for aught bet- 190 ter, beloved?"

"There is nothing better. Let us go up to the roof, and thou shalt count the stars—but a few only, for the sky is heavy with cloud."

"The winter rains are late, and maybe they come out of season. Come, before all the stars are hid. I have put on my richest jewels."

"Thou hast forgotten the best of all."

"Ai! Ours. He comes also. He has never yet seen the skies." 200

Ameera climbed the narrow staircase that led to the flat roof. The child, placid and unwinking, lay in the hollow of her right arm, gorgeous in silver-fringed muslin with a small skull-cap on his head. Ameera wore all that she valued most. The diamond nose-stud that takes the place of the Western patch in drawing attention to the curve of the nostril, the gold ornament in the center of the forehead studded with tallow-drop emeralds and flawed rubies, the heavy circlet of beaten gold that was fastened round her neck by the softness of 210 the pure metal, and the chinking curb-patterned silver anklets hanging low over the rosy ankle-bone. She was dressed in jade-green muslin as befitted a daughter of the Faith, and from shoulder to elbow and elbow to wrist ran bracelets of silver tied with floss silk, frail glass bangles slipped over the wrist in proof of the slenderness of the hand, and certain heavy gold brace-lets that had no part in her country's ornaments but, since they were Holden's gift and fastened with a cunning European snap, delighted her immensely.

They sat down by the low white parapet of the roof, overlooking the city and its lights.

"They are happy down there," said Ameera. "But I do not think that they are as happy as we. Nor do I think the white *mem-log* are as happy. And thou?"

"I know they are not."

"How dost thou know?"

"They give their children over to the nurses."

"I have never seen that," said Ameera, with a sigh, "nor do I wish to see. *Ahi!*"—she dropped her head on Holden's shoulder,—"I have counted forty stars, and I am tired. Look at the child, love of my life. He is counting, too."

The baby was staring with round eyes at the dark of the heavens. Ameera placed him in Holden's arms, and he lay there without a cry.

"What shall we call him among ourselves?" she said. "Look! Art thou ever tired of looking? He carries thy very eyes. But the mouth——"

"Is thine, most dear. Who should know better than I?"

" 'Tis such a feeble mouth. Oh, so small! And yet it holds my heart between its lips. Give him to me now. He has been too long away."

"Nay, let him lie; he has not yet begun to cry."

"When he cries thou wilt give him back—eh? What a man of mankind thou art! If he cried he were only the dearer to me. But, my life, what little name shall we give him?"

The small body lay close to Holden's heart. It was utterly helpless and very soft. He scarcely dared to breathe for fear of crushing it. The caged green parrot that is regarded as a sort of guardian-spirit in most native households moved on its perch and fluttered a drowsy wing.

"There is the answer," said Holden. "Mian Mittu has spoken. He shall be the parrot. When he is ready he will talk mightily and run about. Mian Mittu is the parrot in thy—in the Mussulman tongue, is it not?"

"Why put me so far off?" said Ameera, fretfully. "Let it be like unto some English name—but not wholly. For he is mine."

"Then call him Tota, for that is likest English."

"Ay, Tota, and that is still the parrot. Forgive me, my lord, for a minute ago, but in truth he is too little to wear all the weight of Mian Mittu for name. He shall be Tota—our Tota to us. Hearest thou, O small one? Littlest, thou art Tota." She touched the child's cheek, and he waking wailed, and it was necessary to return him to his mother, who soothed him with the wonderful rime of *Aré koko, Jaré koko!* which says:

Oh crow! Go crow! Baby's sleeping sound,
And the wild plums grow in the jungle, only a penny a pound.

71. **Beebee Miriam**, the Virgin Mary. 166. **Suleiman and Aflatoun**, King Solomon and Plato.

Only a penny a pound, *baba*—only a penny a pound.

Reassured many times as to the price of those plums, Tota cuddled himself down to sleep. The two sleek, white well-bullocks in the courtyard were steadily chewing the cud of their evening meal; old Pir Khan squatted at the head of Holden's horse, his police saber across his knees, pulling drowsily at a big water-pipe that croaked like a bull-frog in a pond. Ameera's mother sat spinning in the lower veranda, and the wooden gate was shut and barred. The music of a marriage-procession came to the roof above the gentle hum of the city, and a string of flying-foxes crossed the face of the low moon.

"I have prayed," said Ameera after a long pause, "I have prayed for two things. First, that I may die in thy stead if thy death is demanded, and in the second that I may die in the place of the child. I have prayed to the Prophet and to Beebee Miriam. Thinkest thou either will hear?"

"From thy lips who would not hear the lightest word?"

"I asked for straight talk, and thou hast given me sweet talk. Will my prayers be heard?"

"How can I say? God is very good."

"Of that I am not sure. Listen now. When I die, or the child dies, what is thy fate? Living, thou wilt return to the bold white *mem-log*, for kind calls to kind."

"Not always."

"With a woman, no; with a man it is otherwise. Thou wilt in this life, later on, go back to thine own folk. That I could almost endure, for I should be dead. But in thy very death thou wilt be taken away to a strange place and a paradise that I do not know."

"Will it be paradise?"

"Surely, for who would harm thee? But we two—I and the child—shall be elsewhere, and we cannot come to thee, nor canst thou come to us. In the old days, before the child was born, I did not think of these things; but now I think of them always. It is very hard talk."

"It will fall as it will fall. To-morrow we do not know, but to-day and love we know well. Surely we are happy now."

"So happy that it were well to make our happiness assured. And thy Beebee Miriam should listen to me; for she is also a woman. But then she would envy me! It is not seemly for men to worship a woman."

Holden laughed aloud at Ameera's little spasm of jealousy.

"Is it not seemly? Why didst thou not turn me from worship of thee, then?"

"Thou a worshipper! And of me? My king, for all thy sweet words, well I know that I am thy servant and thy slave, and the dust under thy feet. And I would not have it otherwise. See!"

Before Holden could prevent her she stooped forward and touched his feet; recovering herself with a little laugh she hugged Tota closer to her bosom. Then, almost savagely—

"Is it true that the bold white *mem-log* live for three times the length of my life? Is it true that they make their marriages not before they are old women?"

"They marry as do others—when they are women."

"That I know, but they wed when they are twenty-five. Is that true?"

"That is true."

"*Ya illah!* At twenty-five! Who would of his own will take a wife even of eighteen? She is a woman—aging every hour. Twenty-five! I shall be an old woman at that age, and——Those *mem-log* remain young forever. How I hate them!"

"What have they to do with us?"

"I cannot tell. I know only that there may now be alive on this earth a woman ten years older than I who may come to thee and take thy love ten years after I am an old woman, gray-headed, and the nurse of Tota's son. That is unjust and evil. They should die too."

"Now, for all thy years thou art a child, and shalt be picked up and carried down the staircase."

"Tota! Have a care for Tota, my lord! Thou at least art as foolish as any babe!" Ameera tucked Tota out of harm's way in the hollow in her neck, and was carried downstairs laughing in Holden's arms, while Tota opened his eyes and smiled after the manner of the lesser angels.

He was a silent infant, and, almost before Holden could realize that he was in the world, developed into a small gold-colored little god and unquestioned despot of the house overlooking the city. Those were months of absolute happiness to Holden and Ameera—happiness withdrawn from the world, shut in behind the wooden gate that Pir Khan guarded. By day Holden did his work with an immense pity for such as were not so fortunate as himself, and a sympathy for small children that amazed and amused many mothers at the little station-gatherings. At nightfall he returned to Ameera—Ameera full of the wondrous doings of Tota; how he had been seen to clap his hands together and move his fingers with intention and purpose—which was manifestly a miracle—how later, he had of his own initiative crawled out of his low bedstead on to the floor and swayed on both feet for the space of three breaths.

"And they were long breaths, for my heart stood still with delight," said Ameera.

Then Tota took the beasts into his councils—the well-bullocks, the little gray squirrels, the mongoose that lived in a hole near the well, and especially Mian Mittu, the parrot, whose tail he grievously pulled, and Mian Mittu screamed till Ameera and Holden arrived.

"O villain! Child of strength! This to thy brother on the housetop! *Tobah, tobah!* Fie! Fie! But I know a charm to make him wise as Suleiman and Aflatoun.

Now look," said Ameera. She drew from an embroidered bag a handful of almonds. "See! we count seven. In the name of God!" She placed Mian Mittu, very angry and rumpled, on the top of his cage, and seating herself between the babe and the bird she cracked and peeled an almond less white than her teeth. "This is a true charm, my life, and do not laugh. See! I give the parrot one half and Tota the other." Mian Mittu with careful beak took his share from between Ameera's lips, and she kissed the other half into the mouth of the child, who ate it slowly with wondering eyes. "This I will do each day of seven, and without doubt he who is ours will be a bold speaker and wise. Eh, Tota, what wilt thou be when thou art a man and I am gray-headed?" Tota tucked his fat legs into adorable creases. He could crawl, but he was not going to waste the spring of his youth in idle speech. He wanted Mian Mittu's tail to tweak.

When he was advanced to the dignity of a silver belt—which, with a magic square engraved on silver and hung round his neck, made up the greater part of his clothing—he staggered on a perilous journey down the garden to Pir Khan and proffered him all his jewels in exchange for one little ride on Holden's horse, having seen his mother's mother chaffering with peddlers in the veranda. Pir Khan wept and set the untried feet on his own gray head in sign of fealty, and brought the bold adventurer to his mother's arms, vowing that Tota would be a leader of men ere his beard was grown.

One hot evening, while he sat on the roof between his father and mother watching the never-ending warfare of the kites that the city boys flew, he demanded a kite of his own with Pir Khan to fly it, because he had a fear of dealing with anything larger than himself, and when Holden called him a "spark," he rose to his feet and answered slowly in defense of his new-found individuality, "*Hum' park nahin hai. Hum admi hai.*" [I am no spark, but a man].

The protest made Holden choke, and devote himself very seriously to a consideration of Tota's future. He need hardly have taken the trouble. The delight of that life was too perfect to endure. Therefore it was taken away as many things are taken away in India—suddenly and without warning. The little lord of the house, as Pir Khan called him, grew sorrowful and complained of pains who had never known the meaning of pain. Ameera, wild with terror, watched him through the night, and in the dawning of the second day the life was shaken out of him by fever—the seasonal autumnal fever. It seemed altogether impossible that he could die, and neither Ameera nor Holden at first believed the evidence of the little body on the bedstead. Then Ameera beat her head against the wall and would have flung herself down the well in the garden had Holden not restrained her by main force.

One mercy only was granted to Holden. He rode to his office in broad daylight and found waiting him an unusually heavy mail that demanded concentrated attention and hard work. He was not, however, alive to this kindness of the gods.

3

The first shock of a bullet is no more than a brisk pinch. The wrecked body does not send in its protest to the soul till ten or fifteen seconds later. Then comes thirst, throbbing, and agony, and a ridiculous amount
10 of screaming. Holden realized his pain slowly, exactly as he had realized his happiness, and with the same imperious necessity for hiding all trace of it. In the beginning he only felt that there had been a loss, and that Ameera needed comforting, where she sat with her head on her knees shivering as Mian Mittu from the house-top called, *Tota! Tota! Tota!* Later all his world and the daily life of it rose up to hurt him. It was an outrage that any one of the children at the band-stand in the evening should be alive and clamorous,
20 when his own child lay dead. It was more than mere pain when one of them touched him, and stories told by over-fond fathers of their children's latest performances cut him to the quick. He could not declare his pain. He had neither help, comfort, nor sympathy; and Ameera at the end of each weary day would lead him through the hell of self-questioning reproach which is reserved for those who have lost a child, and believe that with a little—just a little—more care it might have been saved.

30 "Perhaps," Ameera would say, "I did not take sufficient heed. Did I, or did I not? The sun on the roof that day when he played so long alone and I was—*ahi!* braiding my hair—it may be that the sun then bred the fever. If I had warned him from the sun he might have lived. But, oh my life, say that I am guiltless! Thou knowest that I loved him as I love thee. Say that there is no blame on me, or I shall die—I shall die!"

"There is no blame,—before God, none. It was written and how could we do aught to save? What has been,
40 has been. Let it go, beloved."

"He was all my heart to me. How can I let the thought go when my arm tells me every night that he is not here? *Ahi! Ahi!* O Tota, come back to me—come back again, and let us be all together as it was before!"

"Peace, peace! For thine own sake, and for mine also, if thou lovest me—rest."

"By this I know thou dost not care; and how shouldst thou? The white men have hearts of stone and souls of
50 iron. Oh, that I had married a man of mine own people—though he beat me—and had never eaten the bread of an alien!"

"Am I an alien—mother of my son?"

"What else—*Sahib?*. . .Oh, forgive me—forgive! The death has driven me mad. Thou art the life of my heart, and the light of my eyes, and the breath of my life, and — and I have put thee from me, though it was but for a moment. If thou goest away, to whom shall I look for help? Do not be angry. Indeed, it was the pain that spoke and not thy slave."
60
"I know, I know. We be two who were three. The greater need therefore that we should be one."

They were sitting on the roof as of custom. The night was a warm one in early spring, and sheet-lightning was dancing on the horizon to a broken tune played by far-off thunder. Ameera settled herself in Holden's arms.

"The dry earth is lowing like a cow for the rain, and I—I am afraid. It was not like this when we counted the stars. But thou lovest me as much as before, though 70 a bond is taken away? Answer!"

"I love more because a new bond has come out of the sorrow that we have eaten together, and that thou knowest."

"Yea, I knew," said Ameera, in a very small whisper. "But it is good to hear thee say so, my life, who art so strong to help. I will be a child no more, but a woman and an aid to thee. Listen! Give me my *sitar*, and I will sing bravely."

She took the light silver-studded *sitar* and began a 80 song about the great hero Rajah Rasalu. The hand failed on the strings, the tune halted, checked, and at a low note turned off to the poor little nursery-rime about the wicked crow—

And the wild plums grow in the jungle, only a penny
    a pound.
Only a penny a pound, *baba*—only. . .

Then came the tears, and the piteous rebellion against fate till she slept, moaning a little in her sleep, with the right arm thrown clear of the body as though it protected something that was not there. It was after 90 this night that life became a little easier for Holden. The ever-present pain of loss drove him into his work, and the work repaid him by filling up his mind for nine or ten hours a day. Ameera sat alone in the house and brooded, but grew happier when she understood that Holden was more at ease, according to the custom of women. They touched happiness again, but this time with caution.

"It was because we loved 'Tota that he died. The jealousy of God was upon us," said Ameera. "I have 100 hung up a large black jar before our window to turn the evil eye from us, and we must make no protestations of delight, but go softly underneath the stars, lest God find us out. Is that not good talk, worthless one?"

She had shifted the accent on the word that means "beloved," in proof of the sincerity of her purpose. But the kiss that followed the new christening was a thing that any deity might have envied. They went about hence-forward saying, "It is naught, it is naught"; and hoping that all the Powers heard.

The Powers were busy on other things. They had allowed thirty million people four years of plenty wherein men fed well and the crops were certain, and the birthrate rose year by year; the districts reported a purely agricultural population varying from nine hundred to two thousand to the square mile of the over-burdened earth. It was time to make room. And the Member for Lower Tooting, wandering about India in top-hat and frock-coat, talked largely of the benefits of British rule and suggested as the one thing needful the establishment of a duly qualified electoral system and a general bestowal of the franchise. His long-suffering hosts smiled and made him welcome, and when he paused to admire, with pretty picked words, the blossom of the blood-red *dhak*-tree that had flowered untimely for a sign of the sickness that was coming, they smiled more than ever.

It was the Deputy Commissioner of Kot-Kumharsen, staying at the club for a day, who lightly told a tale that made Holden's blood run cold as he overheard the end.

"He won't bother any one any more. Never saw a man so astonished in my life. By Jove, I thought he meant to ask a question in the House about it. Fellow-passenger in his ship—dined next him—bowled over by cholera and died in eighteen hours. You needn't laugh, you fellows. The Member for Lower Tooting is awfully angry about it; but he's more scared. I think he's going to take his enlightened self out of India."

"I'd give a good deal if he were knocked over. It might keep a few countrymen of his kidney to their own parish. But what's this about cholera? It's full early for anything of that kind," said a warden of an unprofitable salt-lick.

"Dunno," said the Deputy Commissioner reflectively. "We've got locusts with us. There's sporadic cholera all along the north—at least we're calling it sporadic for decency's sake. The spring crops are short in five districts, and nobody seems to know where the winter rains are. It's nearly March now. I don't want to scare anybody, but it seems to me that Nature's going to audit her accounts with a big red pencil this summer."

"Just when I wanted to take leave, too!" said a voice across the room.

"There won't be much leave this year, but there ought to be a great deal of promotion. I've come in to persuade the Government to put my pet canal on the list of famine-relief works. It's an ill-wind that blows no good. I shall get that canal finished at last."

"Is it the old programme then," said Holden; "Famine, fever, and cholera?"

"Oh, no. Only local scarcity and an unusual prevalence of seasonal sickness. You'll find it all in the reports if you live till next year. You're a lucky chap. *You* haven't got a wife to send out of harm's way. The hill-stations ought to be full of women this year."

"I think you're inclined to exaggerate the talk in the bazaars," said a young civilian in the Secretariat. "Now I have observed——"

"I dare say you have," said the Deputy Commissioner, "but you've a great deal more to observe, my son. In the meantime, I wish to observe to you——" And he drew him aside to discuss the construction of the canal that was so dear to his heart.

Holden went to his bungalow and began to understand that he was not alone in the world, and also that he was afraid for the sake of another,—which is the most soul-satisfying fear known to man.

Two months later, as the Deputy had foretold, Nature began to audit her accounts with a red pencil. On the heels of the spring-reapings came a cry for bread, and the Government, which had decreed that no man should die for want, sent wheat. Then came the cholera from all four quarters of the compass. It struck a pilgrim-gathering of half a million at a sacred shrine. Many died at the feet of their god; the others broke and ran over the face of the land carrying the pestilence with them. It smote a walled city and killed two hundred a day. The people crowded the trains, hanging on to the footboards and squatting on the roofs of the carriages, and the cholera followed them, for at each station they dragged out the dead and the dying on the platforms reeking of lime-wash and carbolic acid. They died by the roadside, and the horses of the Englishmen shied at the corpses in the grass. The rains did not come, and the earth turned to iron lest men should escape by hiding in her. The English sent their wives away to the hills and went about their work, coming forward as they were bidden to fill the gaps in the fighting-line. Holden, sick with fear of losing his chiefest treasure on earth, had done his best to persuade Ameera to go away with her mother to the Himalayas.

"Why should I go?" said she one evening on the roof.

"There is sickness, and people are dying, and all the white *mem-log* have gone."

"All of them?"

"All—unless perhaps there remain some old scald-head who vexes her husband's heart by running risk of death."

"Nay; who stays is my sister, and thou must not abuse her, for I will be a scald-head too. I am glad all the bold *mem-log* are gone."

"Do I speak to a woman or a babe? Go to the hills and I will see to it that thou goest like a queen's daughter. Think, child. In a red-lacquered bullock-cart, veiled and curtained, with brass peacocks upon the pole and red cloth hangings. I will send two orderlies for guard, and——"

"Peace! Thou art the babe in speaking thus. What use are those toys to me? *He* would have patted the bullocks and played with the housings. For his sake, perhaps,—thou hast made me very English—I might have gone. Now, I will not. Let the *mem-log* run."

"Their husbands are sending them, beloved."

"Very good talk. Since when hast thou been my husband to tell me what to do? I have but borne thee a son. Thou art only all the desire of my soul to me. How shall I depart when I know that if evil befall thee by the breadth of so much as my littlest finger-nail—is that not small?—I should be aware of it though I were in paradise. And here, this summer thou mayest die—*ai, janee*, die!—and in dying they might call to tend thee a white woman, and she would rob me in the last of thy love!"

"But love is not born in a moment or on a death-bed!"

"What dost thou know of love, stoneheart? She would take thy thanks at least and, by God and the Prophet and Beebee Miriam, the mother of thy Prophet, that I will never endure. My lord and my love, let there be no more foolish talk of going away. Where thou art, I am. It is enough." She put an arm round his neck and a hand on his mouth.

There are not many happinesses so complete as those that are snatched under the shadow of the sword. They sat together and laughed, calling each other openly by every pet name that could move the wrath of the gods. The city below them was locked up in its own torments. Sulphur fires blazed in the streets; the conches in the Hindu temples screamed and bellowed, for the gods were inattentive in those days. There was a service in the great Mohammedan shrine, and the call to prayer from the minarets was almost unceasing. They heard the wailing in the houses of the dead, and once the shriek of a mother who had lost a child and was calling for its return. In the gray dawn they saw the dead borne out through the city gates, each litter with its own little knot of mourners. Wherefore they kissed each other and shivered.

It was a red and heavy audit, for the land was very sick and needed a little breathing-space ere the torrent of cheap life should flood it anew. The children of immature fathers and undeveloped mothers made no resistance. They were cowed and sat still, waiting till the sword should be sheathed in November, if it were so willed. There were gaps among the English, but the gaps were filled. The work of superintending famine-relief, cholera-sheds, medicine-distribution, and what little sanitation was possible, went forward because it was so ordered.

Holden had been told to keep himself in readiness to move to replace the next man who should fall. There were twelve hours in each day when he could not see Ameera, and she might die in three. He was considering what his pain would be if he could not see her for three months, or if she died out of his sight. He was absolutely certain that her death would be demanded—so certain that, when he looked up from the telegram and saw Pir Khan breathless in the doorway, he laughed aloud. "And?" said he——

"When there is a cry in the night and the spirit flutters into the throat, who has a charm that will restore? Come swiftly, Heaven-born. It is the black cholera."

Holden galloped to his home. The sky was heavy with clouds, for the long-deferred rains were near and the heat was stifling. Ameera's mother met him in the courtyard, whimpering, "She is dying. She is nursing herself into death. She is all but dead. What shall I do, *sahib?*"

Ameera was lying in the room in which Tota had been born. She made no sign when Holden entered, because the human soul is a very lonely thing, and when it is getting ready to go away, hides itself in a misty borderland where the living may not follow. The black cholera does its work quietly and without explanation. Ameera was being thrust out of life as though the Angel of Death had himself put his hand upon her. The quick breathing seemed to show that she was either afraid or in pain, but neither eyes nor mouth gave any answer to Holden's kisses. There was nothing to be said or done. Holden could only wait and suffer. The first drops of the rain began to fall on the roof, and he could hear shouts of joy in the parched city.

The soul came back a little and the lips moved. Holden bent down to listen. "Keep nothing of mine," said Ameera. "Take no hair from my head. *She* would make thee burn it later on. That flame I should feel. Lower! Stoop lower! Remember only that I was thine and bore thee a son. Though thou wed a white woman to-morrow, the pleasure of receiving in thy arms thy first son is taken from thee forever. Remember me when thy son is born—the one that shall carry thy name before all men. His misfortunes be on my head. I bear witness—I bear witness"—the lips were forming the words on his ear—"that there is no God but—thee, beloved!"

Then she died. Holden sat still, and all thought was taken from him,—till he heard Ameera's mother lift the curtain.

"Is she dead, *sahib?*"

"She is dead."

"Then I will mourn, and afterward take an inventory of the furniture in this house. For that will be mine. The *sahib* does not mean to resume it? It is so little, so very little, *sahib*, and I am an old woman. I would like to lie softly."

"For the mercy of God be silent awhile. Go out and mourn where I cannot hear."

"*Sahib*, she will be buried in four hours."

"I know the custom. I shall go ere she is taken away. That matter is in thy hands. Look to it, that the bed on which—on which she lies——"

"Aha! That beautiful red-lacquered bed. I have long desired——"

"That the bed is left here untouched for my disposal. All else in the house is thine. Hire a cart, take everything, go hence, and before sunrise let there be nothing in this house but that which I have ordered thee to respect."

"I am an old woman. I would stay at least for the days of mourning, and the rains have just broken. Whither shall I go?"

"What is that to me? My order is that there is a going. The house-gear is worth a thousand rupees and my orderly shall bring thee a hundred rupees to-night."

"That is very little. Think of the cart-hire."

"It shall be nothing unless thou goest, and with speed. O woman, get hence and leave me with my dead!"

The mother shuffled down the staircase, and in her anxiety to take stock of the house-fittings forgot to mourn. Holden stayed by Ameera's side, and the rain roared on the roof. He could not think connectedly by reason of the noise, though he made many attempts to do so. Then four sheeted ghosts glided dripping into the room and stared at him through their veils. They were the washers of the dead. Holden left the room and went out to his horse. He had come in a dead, stifling calm through ankle-deep dust. He found the courtyard a rain-lashed pond alive with frogs; a torrent of yellow water ran under the gate, and a roaring wind drove the bolts of the rain like buckshot against the mud-walls. Pir Khan was shivering in his little hut by the gate, and the horse was stamping uneasily in the water.

"I have been told the *sahib's* order," said Pir Khan. "It is well. This house is now desolate. I go also, for my monkey-face would be a reminder of that which has been. Concerning the bed, I will bring that to thy house yonder in the morning; but remember, *sahib*, it will be to thee as a knife turning in a green wound. I go upon a pilgrimage, and I will take no money. I have grown fat in the protection of the Presence whose sorrow is my sorrow. For the last time I hold his stirrup."

He touched Holden's foot with both hands and the horse sprang out into the road, where the creaking bamboos were whipping the sky and all the frogs were chuckling. Holden could not see for the rain in his face. He put his hands before his eyes and muttered—

"Oh you brute! You utter brute!"

The news of his trouble was already in his bungalow. He read the knowledge in his butler's eyes when Ahmed Khan brought in food, and for the first and last time in his life laid a hand upon his master's shoulder, saying, "Eat, *sahib*, eat. Meat is good against sorrow. I also have known. Moreover the shadows come and go, *sahib*; the shadows come and go. These be curried eggs."

Holden could neither eat nor sleep. The heavens sent down eight inches of rain in that night and scoured the earth clean. The waters tore down walls, broke roads, and washed open the shallow graves in the Mohammedan burying-ground. All next day it rained, and Holden sat still in his house considering his sorrow. On the morning of the third day he received a telegram which said only: "Ricketts, Myndonie. Dying. Holden relieve. Immediate." Then he thought that before he departed he would look at the house wherein he had been master and lord. There was a break in the weather, and the rank earth steamed with vapor, and Holden was vermilion from head to heel with the prickly-heat born of sultry moisture.

He found that the rains had torn down the mud pillars of the gateway, and the heavy wooden gate that had guarded his life hung drunkenly from one hinge. There was grass three inches high in the courtyard; Pir Khan's lodge was empty and the sodden thatch sagged between the beams. A gray squirrel was in possession of the veranda as if the house had been untenanted for thirty years instead of three days. Ameera's mother had removed everything except some mildewed matting. The *tick-tick* of the little scorpions as they hurried across the floor was the only sound in the house. Ameera's room and the other one where Tota had lived were heavy with mildew; and the narrow staircase leading to the roof was streaked and stained with rain-borne mud. Holden saw all these things, and came out again to meet in the road Durga Dass, his landlord,—portly, affable, clothed in white muslin, and driving a Cee-spring buggy. He was overlooking his property to see how the roofs withstood the stress of the first rains.

"I have heard," said he, "you will not take this place any more, *sahib*?"

"What are you going to do with it?"

"Perhaps I shall let it again."

"Then I will keep it on while I am away."

Durga Dass was silent for some time. "You shall not take it on, *sahib*," he said. "When I was a young man I also——,but to-day I am a member of the Municipality. Ho! Ho! No. When the birds have gone, what need to keep the nest? I will have it pulled down—the timber will sell for something always. It shall be pulled down, and the Municipality shall make a road across, as they desire, from the burning-ghat to the city wall, so that no man may say where this house stood."

(1890)

WILLIAM ERNEST HENLEY 1849-1903

Henley was born in the city of Gloucester, where he attended the Crypt Grammar School. His headmaster there was the Manx poet, T. E. Brown, who not only inspired the young pupil and directed his reading but encouraged him at a time when he was most in need of encouragement. A tuberculous infection necessitated the amputation of one of Henley's feet, and there was serious danger that he would lose the other. For twenty months he was in the Edinburgh Infirmary under the care of the great Joseph Lister (1827–1912), and the ravages of the disease were checked. The hospital experience was by no means unprofitable to him, for he managed to write some verses and have them published in The Cornhill Magazine. Furthermore, Leslie Stephen (1832-1904), then editor of the magazine, took to Henley's bedside another young contributor, and thus Henley developed with Robert Louis Stevenson a close friendship which lasted until an unhappy misunderstanding years later. Some of the most vivid and innovating of Henley's poems are those which grew out of his sojourn in the Edinburgh Infirmary, and which he collected in 1888 under the title In Hospital.

Discharged from the hospital, Henley did hack writing in Edinburgh for a short time and in 1877 went to London to become editor of London, a short-lived magazine in which appeared Stevenson's New Arabian Nights and a series of poems modeled on old French verse forms by Henley himself. From 1882 to 1886 he was editor of The Magazine of Art. Under Henley's later editorship, The National Observer became noted for its vigorous advocacy of British imperialism. True to this policy, it published, along with other imperialistic items, Kipling's Barrack-Room Ballads (p. 1129). Henley issued A Book of Verse in 1888 and a sheaf of his reviews and criticisms in 1890 under the title of Views and Reviews. Two years later three plays which he had written in collaboration with Stevenson—Beau Austin, Deacon Brodie, and Admiral Guinea—appeared and found their way to the stage but were not notably successful, nor was his own play Macaíre (1895). In 1893 another volume of poetry came out, The Song of the Sword (later titled London Voluntaries). Five years afterwards a collection of his verses appeared under the simple title Poems, and in 1901 another volume entitled Hawthorn and Lavender.

Henley's romantic individuality and independence of spirit emerge in all his poetry. He advocated all things new and had no fear of facing novelty himself.

This individuality of Henley's poetry comes from both its content and its form. Much of it is vividly impressionistic, for example, the startlingly modern poems from In Hospital, written some twenty-five years before the end of the nineteenth century. Henley was a master of the pictorial phrase, and the tempo of some of his poems is thoroughly modern. Finally, in his use of unrimed rhythms—a form of verse which he employed very often—he is clearly representative of the twentieth century, which he just barely lived to see.

from IN HOSPITAL

ENTER PATIENT

The morning mists still haunt the stony street;
The northern summer air is shrill and cold;
And, lo, the hospital, gray, quiet, old,
Where Life and Death like friendly chafferers
    meet.
Through the loud spaciousness and drafty gloom
A small, strange child—so agéd yet so young!—
Her little arm besplinted and beslung,
Precedes me gravely to the waiting-room.
I limp behind, my confidence all gone.
The gray-haired soldier-porter waves me on,   10
And on I crawl, and still my spirits fail;
A tragic meanness seems so to environ
These corridors and stairs of stone and iron.
Cold, naked, clean—half-workhouse and half-jail.

WAITING

A square, squat room (a cellar on promotion),
Drab to the soul, drab to the very daylight;
Plasters astray in unnatural-looking tinware;
Scissors and lint and apothecary's jars.
Here, on a bench a skeleton would writhe from,
Angry and sore, I wait to be admitted;
Wait till my heart is lead upon my stomach,
While at their ease two dressers do their chores.
One has a probe—it feels to me a crowbar.
A small boy sniffs and shudders after bluestone.   10
A poor old tramp explains his poor old ulcers.
Life is (I think) a blunder and a shame.

BEFORE

Behold me waiting—waiting for the knife.
A little while, and at a leap I storm

The poems of William Ernest Henley are reprinted from his *Poems* (New York: Charles Scribner's Sons, 1919).

Waiting. 10. **bluestone,** cupric sulfate, or blue vitriol, used as an emetic.

Before. 14. **You . . . fortunes,** Julius Caesar's words, quoted by Plutarch in his *Life of Caesar.* They were addressed, during the war with Pompey, to a boatman who had Caesar as his passenger.

Staff-Nurse: Old Style. 2. **REMBRANDT,** Rembrandt van Rijn, the famous Dutch painter (1606-1669). **SIR WALTER,** Sir Walter Scott, whose graphic word-paintings of Edinburgh characters, as in his novel *The Heart of Midlothian* (1818), were doubtless in Henley's mind. 10. **SYME,** James Syme (1799-1870), the greatest surgeon of his day. 14. **"The Chief,"** Dr. Joseph Lister, successor to Syme as Chief Surgeon at the Edinburgh Infirmary and a famous pioneer

The thick, sweet mystery of chloroform,
The drunken dark, the little death-in-life.
The gods are good to me—I have no wife,
No innocent child, to think of as I near
The fateful minute; nothing all-too dear
Unmans me for my bout of passive strife.
Yet I am tremulous and a trifle sick,
10 And, face to face with chance, I shrink a little;
My hopes are strong, my will is something weak.
Here comes the basket? Thank you. I am ready.
But, gentlemen my porters, life is brittle;
You carry Caesar and his fortunes—steady!

STAFF-NURSE: OLD STYLE

The great masters of the commonplace,
REMBRANDT and good SIR WALTER—only these
Could paint her all to you: experienced ease
And antique liveliness and ponderous grace;
The sweet old roses of her sunken face;
The depth and malice of her sly, gray eyes;
The broad Scots tongue that flatters, scolds, defies,
The thick Scots wit that fells you like a mace.
These thirty years has she been nursing here,
10 Some of them under SYME, her hero still.
Much is she worth, and even more is made of her.
Patients and students hold her very dear.
The doctors love her, tease her, use her skill.
They say "The Chief" himself is half-afraid of
    her.

STAFF-NURSE: NEW STYLE

Blue-eyed and bright of face but waning fast
Into the sear of virginal decay,
I view her as she enters, day by day,
As a sweet sunset almost overpast.
Kindly and calm, patrician to the last,
Superbly falls her gown of sober gray,
And on her chignon's elegant array
The plainest cap is somehow touched with caste.
She talks BEETHOVEN; frowns disapprobation
10 At BALZAC's name, sighs it at "poor GEORGE SAND'S":
Knows that she has exceeding pretty hands;
Speaks Latin with a right accentuation;
And gives at need (as one who understands)
Draft, counsel, diagnosis, exhortation.

MUSIC

Down the quiet eve,
Thro' my window with the sunset

Pipes to me a distant organ
Foolish ditties;

And, as when you change
Pictures in a magic lantern,
Books, beds, bottles, floors, and ceiling
Fade and vanish,

And I'm well once more . . .
August flares adust and torrid.   10
But my heart is full of April
Sap and sweetness.

In the quiet eve
I am loitering, longing, dreaming . . .
Dreaming, and a distant organ
Pipes me ditties.

I can see the shop,
I can smell the sprinkled pavement,
Where she serves—her chestnut chignon
Thrills my senses!   20

O, the sight and scent,
Wistful eve and perfumed pavement!
In the distance pipes an organ . . .
The sensation

Comes to me anew,
And my spirit for a moment
Thro' the music breathes the blessed
Airs of London.

APPARITION

This is an accurate sketch of Robert Louis Steven-
son (p. 1120), who visited Henley in the hospital in
1875 and became his close friend.

Thin-legged, thin-chested, slight unspeakably,
Neat-footed and weak-fingered; in his face—
Lean, large-boned, curved of beak, and touched with
    race,
Bold-lipped, rich-tinted, mutable as the sea,
The brown eyes radiant with vivacity—
There shines a brilliant and romantic grace,
A spirit intense and rare, with trace on trace
Of passion and impudence and energy.
Valiant in velvet, light in ragged luck,
Most vain, most generous, sternly critical,   10
Buffoon and poet, lover and sensualist;
A deal of Ariel, just a streak of Puck,

in the field of antisepsis.
    Staff-Nurse: New Style. **7. chignon,** a roll of hair worn on the
back of the head. **9. BEETHOVEN,** Ludwig van Beethoven (1770–
1827), the magnificent German composer; he was well established by
1872 as an old master. **10. BALZAC,** Honoré de Balzac (1799–1850),
the great French realistic writer of fiction. Conservative English women
of the 1870's found his frankness shocking. **GEORGE SAND,** the
pseudonym of Aurore Dudevant (1804–1876), a French novelist, celebrated for her romantic love affairs with the French author Alfred de
Musset (1810–1857) and the composer Frédéric Chopin (1809–1849).
    Apparition. **12. Ariel,** the airy spirit who executes Prospero's bid-
ding in Shakespeare's *The Tempest.* **Puck,** the mischievous spirit of
English folklore, most famous for the part he plays in Shakespeare's
A Midsummer-Night's Dream.

Much Antony, of Hamlet most of all,
And something of the Shorter-Catechist.

DISCHARGED

Carry me out
Into the wind and the sunshine,
Into the beautiful world.
O the wonder, the spell of the streets!
The stature and strength of the horses
The rustle and echo of footfalls,
The flat roar and rattle of wheels!
A swift tram floats huge on us . . .
It's a dream?
10 The smell of the mud in my nostrils
Blows brave—like a breath of the sea!

As of old,
Ambulant, undulant drapery,
Vaguely and strangely provocative,
Flutters and beckons. O yonder—
Is it?—the gleam of a stocking!
Sudden, a spire
Wedged in the mist! O the houses,
The long lines of lofty, gray houses,
20 Cross-hatched with shadow and light!
These are the streets . . .
Each is an avenue leading
Whither I will!

Free . . . !
Dizzy, hysterical, faint,
I sit, and the carriage rolls on with me
Into the wonderful world.
(1872-1875; 1888)

INVICTUS

Out of the night that covers me,
    Black as the Pit from pole to pole,
I thank whatever gods may be
    For my unconquerable soul.

In the fell clutch of circumstance
    I have not winced nor cried aloud.
Under the bludgeonings of chance
    My head is bloody, but unbowed.

Beyond this place of wrath and tears
10   Looms but the Horror of the shade,
And yet the menace of the years
    Finds, and shall find, me unafraid.

It matters not how strait the gate,
    How charged with punishments the scroll,
I am the master of my fate;
    I am the captain of my soul.
(1875; 1888)

I. M. MARGARITAE SORORI

Henley wrote this poem in memory of his wife's sister Margaret.

A late lark twitters from the quiet skies;
And from the west,
Where the sun, his day's work ended,
Lingers as in content,
There falls on the old, gray city
An influence luminous and serene,
A shining peace.

The smoke ascends
In a rosy-and-golden haze. The spires
Shine, and are changed. In the valley   10
Shadows rise. The lark sings on. The sun,
Closing his benediction,
Sinks, and the darkening air
Thrills with a sense of the triumphing night—
Night with her train of stars
And her great gift of sleep.

So be my passing!
My task accomplished and the long day done,
My wages taken, and in my heart
Some late lark singing,   20
Let me be gathered to the quiet west,
The sundown splendid and serene,
Death.
(1886; 1888)

WHAT IS TO COME

What is to come we know not. But we know
That what has been was good—was good to show,
Better to hide, and best of all to bear.
We are the masters of the days that were;
We have lived, we have loved, we have suffered . . .
    even so.

Shall we not take the ebb who had the flow?
Life was our friend. Now, if it be our foe—
Dear, though it spoil and break us!—need we care
        What is to come?

13. **Antony,** Marcus Antonius (83–30 B.C.), the fiery orator in Shakespeare's *Julius Caesar;* a sensualist and lover in Shakespeare's *Antony and Cleopatra.* **Hamlet,** the protagonist of Shakespeare's great play, is considered here as a melancholy man. 14. **Shorter-Catechist,** an adherent to strict Calvinistic religious and ethical principles as embodied in the Shorter Catechism, compiled by the Westminster Assembly in 1646–1647.
Invictus. 2. **the Pit,** Hell.

10 Let the great winds their worst and wildest blow,
Or the gold weather round us mellow slow;
We have fulfilled ourselves, and we can dare
And we can conquer, though we may not share
In the rich quiet of the afterglow
        What is to come.
(1888)

SPACE AND DREAD AND THE DARK

Space and dread and the dark—
Over a livid stretch of sky
Cloud-monsters crawling, like a funeral train
Of huge, primeval presences
Stooping beneath the weight

Of some enormous, rudimentary grief;
While in the haunting loneliness
The far sea waits and wanders with a sound
As of the trailing skirts of Destiny,
10 Passing unseen
To some immitigable end
With her gray henchman, Death.

What larve, what specter is this
Thrilling the wilderness to life
As with the bodily shape of Fear?
What but a desperate sense,
A strong foreboding of those dim
Interminable continents, forlorn
And many-silenced, in a dusk
20 Inviolable utterly, and dead
As the poor dead it huddles and swarms and styes
In hugger-mugger through eternity?

Life—life—let there be life!
Better a thousand times the roaring hours
When wave and wind,
Like the Arch-Murderer in flight
From the Avenger at his heel,
Storms through the desolate fastnesses
And wild waste places of the world!

Life—give me life until the end,
30 That at the very top of being,
The battle-spirit shouting in my blood,
Out of the reddest hell of the fight
I may be snatched and flung
Into the everlasting lull,
The immortal, incommunicable dream.
(1892)

Space and Dread and the Dark. 13. **larve,** ghost, specter.

ENGLAND, MY ENGLAND

What have I done for you,
  England, my England?
What is there I would not do,
  England, my own?
With your glorious eyes austere,
As the Lord were walking near,
Whispering terrible things and dear
  As the Song on your bugles blown, England—
  Round the world on your bugles blown!

Where shall the watchful Sun,   10
  England, my England,
Match the master-work you've done,
  England, my own?
When shall he rejoice again
Such a breed of mighty men
As come forward, one to ten,
  To the Song on your bugles blown, England—
  Down the years on your bugles blown?

Ever the faith endures,
  England, my England—   20
"Take and break us; we are yours,
  England, my own!
Life is good, and joy runs high
Between English earth and sky;
Death is death; but we shall die
  To the Song on your bugles blown, England—
  To the stars on your bugles blown!"

They call you proud and hard,
  England, my England;
You with worlds to watch and ward,   30
  England, my own!
You whose mailed hand keeps the keys
Of such teeming destinies
You could know nor dread nor ease
  Were the Song on your bugles blown,
    England—
  Round the Pit on your bugles blown!

Mother of Ships whose might,
  England, my England,
Is the fierce old Sea's delight,
  England, my own,   40
Chosen daughter of the Lord,
Spouse-in-Chief of the ancient Sword,
There's the menace of the Word
  In the Song on your bugles blown, England—
  Out of heaven on your bugles blown!
(1892)

A night view of the Festival of Britain, 1951, from the Architectural Review, August 1951. A comparison of this picture with that of the Great Exhibition of 1851 on p. 820 will show at a glance some of the differences in temper between the nineteenth and twentieth centuries.

THE STRUGGLE ON THE DARKLING PLAIN

A Time of Conflict and Change, 1914-1967

Militant suffragettes, from a photograph of a suffragist riot at Buckingham Palace, 1914.

The Crossroads

At eleven o'clock on the morning of November 11, 1918, the guns became silent in the war "to make the world safe for democracy." "Everything for which America fought has been accomplished," read the official announcement from President Woodrow Wilson —one of the most dramatically ironic public statements in history. For it soon became evident that the cessation of fighting established on that first Armistice Day was no more than an indefinite truce—if indeed it could be called that—which was to last only a little more than twenty years.

In the generation between 1918 and 1939, minor wars harassed all of the major quarters of the globe. Bolshevik Russia invaded Poland; Bolivia and Paraguay spilled blood in the Gran Chaco; France undertook punitive expeditions in Morocco and in Syria; Spain was bled in a civil conflict which served as the immediate prelude to the Second World War; Ethiopia was invaded by Italy; China was pillaged by Japan. In fact, scarcely a year in this critical span was free from either saber-rattling or outright bloodshed.

The two world wars, from 1914 to 1918 and from 1939 to 1945, together with the violence that lay between, must be considered as one struggle, a global Thirty Years' War of the twentieth century. In spite of the military victory of the antifascist forces in 1945, the world is still very much overcast; the conflict is now between communist and noncommunist, with Russia, China, and their satellites aligned against America and Western Europe. Now, however, the unleashing of the new forces of atomic energy has compelled men to recognize the absolute necessity for avoiding outright warfare, so the conflict is for the greater part a matter of propaganda, subversion, and diplomacy—the so-called Cold War. One cannot fail to be impressed by the extent to which, ever since the beginning of the twentieth century, the world has come to depend upon force or the threat of force.

The causes of this still critical state of the world are too complex for brief statement, but an outline of the main trends of events in Europe between 1918 and 1939 may help to clarify the situation to some extent, if it is kept in mind that political, sociological, and economic considerations are bound up inextricably. The Treaty of Versailles (1919) attempted to resolve the differences of the nations involved in the First World War, giving to Britain and France, as the countries which had suffered most, the economic leadership of Europe, restoring Alsace and Lorraine to France, "rectifying" the Austria-Italian, Austria-Serbian, and German-Polish borders, creating the smaller nations of Czechoslovakia, Yugoslavia, Poland, Finland, Lithuania, Latvia, Estonia, and Hungary, disposing of the German colonial empire, creating the League of Nations, and placing officially upon Germany the responsibility for having started the war.

This treaty was bitterly resented by Germany, of course; the staggering reparations demanded were a bar to its recovery and to the realization of its industrial potential. There were other flaws in the pact —Italy, for example, that had left the old Triple Alliance (Germany, Austria-Hungary, and Italy) and had fought on the side of the Allies, got little recognition of its interest in the Adriatic provinces. In the United States, Woodrow Wilson's plea that the treaty be accepted was rejected by Congress because it meant that the nation would have to join the League of Nations; not until 1921 did Congress pass a resolution which proclaimed the end of the war with Germany. Yet there was general satisfaction and optimism in Britain and France by the end of 1919.

Another source of worry for the Allies was Russia, which had been forced out of the war, a loser, during the winter of 1917–1918 and in the chaos of defeat had undergone the greatest political and social revolution of the last hundred years. Very disturbing to Western Europeans and Americans was the communist ideology of Russia's new regime and the extremely authoritarian measures sometimes taken to implement it. In accord with this social and political philosophy, a dictatorship, alleged to represent the proletariat, abolished private ownership of the means of production and carried on a reign of terror against all conservative or moderate opposition. Although until late in the 1920's severe economic shortages required the

leaders of the Communist Party to modify extreme state control over economic life, the party itself never lost its grip on political power. On the death of Lenin in 1924, the top Communists engaged in a struggle for power which ended in 1929 with the rout of Trotsky and the emergence of Stalin as dictator. Stalin immediately launched the first of his five-year plans for massive industrialization and for complete state control of all segments of the economy, including agriculture. Although most British subjects were totally unsympathetic to communist theory and to communist methods, Britain, because of her dependence on foreign trade, soon recognized the Soviet state. American recognition followed in the early 1930's, but Russia remained in the eyes of the West unpredictable, threatening, and dangerous.

Left as focal points for a new infection of the peace of the world were Germany, Italy, and Japan. Germany, in resources the greatest power on the Continent after Russia (and before 1939 much better organized than the Soviet state), eager to develop her great industrial potential; Italy, a nation whose political aspirations had been overlooked in the peace negotiations; and Japan, frustrated in her Asiatic ambitions by the presence in the Far East of colonial Britain, France, and the United States—all came to be called the "have-nots," as opposed to the "haves." There

Women's Land Army, 1918.

Fashion, 1914.

was at least enough truth in this distinction to give the leaders of the have-nots the excuse they wanted. It was easy to persuade sufficient segments of the population in Germany, Italy, and Japan—countries with little or no experience in democratic processes—to accept the rule of oligarchies and dictators who subjected the individual to the state through a system and philosophy of government which came to be known as fascism.

Regardless of the many aspects of power politics, the struggle for world markets and for a "place in the sun," all of which undoubtedly contributed greatly to the outbreak of the Second World War, the fact remains that this war was fought, and continues to be fought in the Cold War phase, as a struggle between the democratic and the totalitarian ways of life. Britain, France, and the United States, with their allies, represented the democratic way; Germany, Italy, and Japan represented the totalitarian way. In the middle stood Russia, also totalitarian, the subject of fierce debate but obviously far removed politically from the democratic traditions of individual liberty. Nevertheless, it is one of the ironies of history that the Soviet Union—out of sheer self-defense as well as out of real patriotism on the part of its people—should have fought vigorously on the side of democratic powers between 1941 and 1945, should have played an extremely important part in the defeat of Germany, and should then have loomed, with China, as the great enemy of democracy.

It is not necessary to relate here more than a mere outline of the Second World War. France actually went under in 1940, and England, taking a terrible

beating for a full year thereafter, barely managed to escape an invasion. The turning point came in 1941, with Germany's attack on Russia and with the assault by Japan upon all the Western powers in the Pacific, which forced the United States into open warfare and made available to the Allies the unparalleled technical and natural resources of an America geared to a full war economy. Italy, a military jackal to the Nazi military tiger, was knocked out of effective action in 1943, although bitter fighting between the Germans and the Allies continued in that country until the end of the war; Germany surrendered on May 8, 1945; the Japanese signed the papers of unconditional surrender aboard the American battleship *Missouri* in Tokyo Bay on September 2, 1945. Germany was partitioned into two sections, East and West, under Russian and Allied control respectively.

After victory, Russia and the Western powers—the United States, Britain, and France—gradually experienced a disintegration of their wartime partnership. The growing division between East and West was sharply accented in 1947 when the American Marshall Plan for the economic recovery of Europe was announced. Russia was invited to join in a general European alliance to foster this recovery but declined. From this point until the death of Stalin in 1953 and Khrushchev's assumption of power (which he held until 1964), America based its security on the economic and military rehabilitation of Western Europe and on the policy of "containment," whereas Russia based its security on the strengthening of its grasp upon its satellite nations and on a policy of creeping expansion, as well as on its mastery of nuclear power, which the United States had originally achieved in 1945. America's policy of containment of communism led to the support of a separate West German republic, the elimination of communist guerrillas in Greece, encouragement and aid to Yugoslavia in her successful break from Russian domination (1948), and open participation in the Korean War, which began on June 25, 1950. This invasion of South Korea came to an end, after protracted peace negotiations, in July 1953. With the emergence of Khrushchev, Soviet policy became somewhat less rigid, and brief periods of cultural and diplomatic thaws interrupted the usual posture of threat and bluster, which reached a dangerous climax in the Cuban crisis of 1962. By 1955 it was believed that a striking relaxation in international relations was taking place; this hope was climaxed by the Geneva meeting in July between the heads of state of Russia, the United States, Britain, and France. But in 1956 an aggressive Soviet policy in the Middle East following the Suez Canal crisis, and the brutal repression of a popular anticommunist revolt in Hungary during the same period, contributed greatly to a further deterioration of whatever concord had been

A street in Whitechapel.

The dole queue: unemployed in 1923.

established. Meanwhile, however, the mutual fear of nuclear warfare continued as a strong incentive to peaceful negotiations. The fear had been exacerbated when, in 1949, a unification of political elements in China under the banner of communism drove Chiang Kai-shek from the mainland of Asia and signified the emergence of a huge Communist nation, which in 1964 became something of a nuclear power. Unlike Russian communism, the Chinese brand has been utterly intransigent and belligerent.

One important agency in the prevention of world trouble has been the United Nations, founded in 1945; it has already had a longer life and exerted much greater influence than the League of Nations, which came with the Versailles Treaty and perished in the Second World War. The UN, an organization of more than one hundred sovereign states, has been of particular importance in the attempts it has made to settle local problems, some of them of particular danger, such as the Korean War and the civil strife in Cyprus, and the difficult warfare in Viet Nam; yet its power and resources are limited, and the major powers inevitably tend to dominate it.

During the turbulent postwar decades from 1946 to 1967, the Cold War between the Western powers and Russia has shared importance with the struggle for national independence of formerly colonial peoples in Asia and Africa. Often this has led to bitter contention and even open warfare of a limited nature, indicating that the world is in the throes of radical and global sociopolitical realignments, of which the North Atlantic Treaty Organization and the European Common Market are two more sophisticated and pacific examples. One needs only to mention the names of Israel, the United Arab Republic, Tunisia, Morocco, Algeria, Ghana, the Congo, Viet Nam, Laos, and Indonesia to comprehend the ferment going on. It is to be hoped that the world, further bewildered by awesome possibilities of space exploration, may accomplish the great revolution to bring about a better society, more international in scope and more attentive to the needs of all peoples.

English Chronicle, 1918-1967

When placed beside the garish, kaleidoscopic sequence of events which passed before American eyes in the years after 1918, conditions in Britain during that same period seem far more settled, at least until the very end of the 1930's. Many of the social reforms wrought during these decades in the United States, reforms which seemed to Americans so radical, already had been established in England. Britain spent the first few years after Armistice Day in a hopeful effort to pick up the fragments of the old way of life which the war had shattered. "A land fit for heroes to live in" became its immediate slogan. The unemployment incidental to the return of hundreds of thousands of veterans to civilian life was anticipated and relieved for a time by a dole of twenty-five shillings a week, but this measure proved to be only a helpful palliative. With a coalition government under David Lloyd George (1863–1945) in power, it was recognized that labor must be put back on its feet, for the dislocation of wartime prices following the Armistice had led to labor troubles. After a series of strikes an alliance of miners with railway and transport workers carried the Labour Party into power under the leadership of Ramsay MacDonald (1866–1937) in 1924.

One could hardly blame British statesmen, however, for being pessimistic in the political murk surrounding them. The United States, chief of the creditor nations, was demanding payment of Britain's war debts. Germany, formerly the major economic power on the Continent, went into a disastrous financial collapse in 1923 and 1924. To the Conservatives, the rise to power of Ramsay MacDonald seemed a calamity; it appeared to' them possible that England was headed toward communism. As it happened, however, the Labour Party of 1924 was far from radical; MacDonald himself was not politically stable, and his position became more and more that of a liberal seduced by conservatives. The Labour Party was based upon a combination of socialism of the nineteenth-century brand and present-day trade unionism, an anachronistic association that did not succeed in preventing strikes. Moreover, the Labour Government was unable to achieve a trade compact with Soviet Russia because its victory over the Conservatives had not been clear-cut. It was in power less than a year, but during this year it had to contend with the collapse of a temporary industrial boom caused by the French withdrawal from the Ruhr.

The Conservatives returned to power at the end of 1924 under Stanley Baldwin (1867–1947) and soon had to contend with a general strike, called in May 1926 in sympathy with striking miners. The country was paralyzed for ten days before the strike was broken. Nevertheless, the Baldwin ministry managed to weather the public storm raised by the general strike, and in spite of its colorless and reactionary nature was able to point to the granting of the vote to all adult women (1928). It was proud also of its part in the Locarno Pact (1925), which in the light of later developments appears to have been as quixotic as the Washington Disarmament Conference of a few years earlier in attempting to guarantee the peace of Europe in general and the boundaries of France, Germany, Belgium, Poland, and Czechoslovakia in particular. When, in addition, the United States signed the Kellogg-Briand Pact (1928), which repudiated all military aggression, it appeared to many idealists that the road to the millennium was becoming discernible in the jungle of international rivalries.

The failure of British business to make much progress during the 1920's, however, eventually brought Ramsay MacDonald back into power; but by this time he had lost touch with the leaders of the Labour Party

The tram, 1929.

Fashion, 1920.

and was more in political sympathy with the Liberals among the industrial class. The depression of 1929, which led to a coalition government, was a war emergency of a new kind. Britain went off the gold standard in 1931 and resorted to various governmental subsidies. Moreover, it was forced to pay attention to what was taking place on the Continent. Here Germany and Italy, self-proclaimed have-nots, were building up immense armaments and brandishing the sword and bayonet at every opportunity. The Japanese invaded Manchuria in 1931; the Italians marched into Ethiopia in 1935. The Germans, despite treaty obligations, in 1936 remilitarized their western border and launched upon a career of calculated Nazi aggression. Even so, Britain was slow to wake up to danger, and its endeavors to arm proved to be almost suicidally inadequate.

Obviously Britain did not understand any more than did the United States the true gravity of the state of the world; it was too pleasant to contemplate the present in terms of the past without much thought about the future. The Jubilee of the twenty-fifth anniversary of the accession of George V (1935) brought sentimental comfort. The Empire seemed as strong as ever; the depression had, indeed, brought about a certain unity among the people which had been lacking during the early 1920's.

If the domestic situation in the years between 1918 and 1923 was disturbed, the foreign situation was equally so. In Ireland, the nationalist party, the Sinn Fein, had caused great concern to Britain during the First World War by its sympathy for Germany and particularly by its role in the famous Easter Rebellion of 1916; it constantly agitated for an Irish Free State. The British government tried to suppress the agitation through a special Irish Constabulary Force, popularly known as the Black and Tans, which accomplished little beyond pointless violence and bloodshed. The Irish Free State, comprising the Catholic counties of Ireland, was set up late in 1921; at first under the administration of moderates and conservatives like William T. Cosgrave, it was later taken over by the fiery Eamon de Valera (1882–   ), whose every effort went toward the establishing of all Eire as an independent republic. Excluding the Protestant counties in the north, this republic was finally realized in the year 1947.

Trouble arose also in India, which in both world wars offered the Germans little comfort, although the British had great difficulty in saving India from Japan during the dark years of 1942 and 1943. The problem, again, lay in the nationalistic aspirations of the Indian people, and it was further complicated by their intransigent religious differences, which made the achievement of an integrated political state seem virtually impossible. The initially coercive policy of Britain collided here with the man who was the leader of his people throughout the generation—Mohandas K. Gandhi (1869–1948), the Mahatma, one of the great figures of this century. Gandhi's novel program of civil disobedience wrung concessions from reluctant Britain —permitting first a national Indian Congress Party (1920), then conferences in London (1929 and 1930), then missions to India during the emergencies of 1940– 1943, and finally outright independence to India (1945–1947). Out of the great diversity of religious, ethnic, and linguistic groups in the subcontinent, two new states were carved out roughly along religious lines and were proclaimed on August 15, 1947—India (for the Hindus) and Pakistan (for the Moslems).

Weakened by wars and economic problems and subjected to the pressures of a world-wide desire of colonial peoples for independence, the British Empire began to break up after the Second World War. In most instances, the British acted with their traditional common sense and guided the native peoples toward self-government in an orderly fashion. In other cases, dismayed by the impending dissolution, they resisted inevitable changes. The Near East saw the sharpest and most dramatic fall of British influence, for it was in this vitally important area that British diplomacy failed to react with flexibility.

Rolls-Royce, 1935.　　　　　*Sir Malcolm Campbell's Blue-Bird, 1935.*

Eventually faced, however, with a clearly forecast war between the Zionists and the Arabs in the old British mandate of Palestine, the British surrendered this mandate to the United Nations and withdrew their troops in May 1948. Open and bitter fighting over the United Nations' proposed partition promptly followed. Meanwhile, in Iran, popular feeling against the domination of the country's economy by the Anglo-Iranian Oil Company made it possible for Prime Minister Mossadegh to nationalize the oil fields. The British were obliged to evacuate the area in October 1951. Mossadegh was overthrown in August 1953, and foreign interests were permitted to return, but British influence in the country's affairs had all but disappeared.

The most decisive blow to British influence in the Near East, however, came in 1956, when the British and French, acting ostensibly to protect the Suez Canal from the fighting that had erupted between the Israelis and the Egyptians, invaded the canal area. Under the pressure of adverse world opinion and the threat of intervention by Russia, the British and the French withdrew after a few days without reaching their objectives, leaving Egypt's strong man, Nasser, in control of the canal and in a stronger position than ever. After this, British influence in the Near East was negligible, and the power vacuum thus created was filled by the conflicting interests of the Soviet Union and the United States. Meanwhile, in Africa the story turned out much the same. All over the world the traditional British colonial posture, romanticized by Kipling (p. 1128), has ceased to exist, and empire has been replaced by partnership in a loose commonwealth of nations and another partnership with the United States.

Stanley Baldwin retired in 1937 and handed over the leadership of the Conservative Party to Neville Chamberlain (1869–1940), son of Joseph Chamberlain of imperialistic fame. The new prime minister was a man of personal integrity and a true representative of the Church of England, the landed gentry, the peers of the realm, capitalists both of the middle class and of the aristocracy, and all those who preferred to do that which promised temporary security. As it happened, it was disastrous for Britain that its government should have been in the hands of such a man and such a party at this particular time, but in fairness to Chamberlain it must be pointed out that, in view of the state of unpreparedness his predecessors had allowed to develop, there is probably little that he could have done.

Germany and Italy, meanwhile, had intervened in the Spanish Civil War of 1936–1939 by sending aid to the fascistic Loyalists (Falangists) under Franco, while Russia had opposed them by giving aid to the Republicans. Neither England nor France, to say nothing of the United States, had ventured to interfere in any official way. Adolf Hitler (1889–1945), who had assumed the dictatorship in Germany in 1933,

marched into Austria (March 1938), and when Czechoslovakia refused to give up territory along its German border, he made the threat of a general European war so alarming and imminent that Chamberlain and Premier Daladier of France closed their eyes to their obligation to defend Czechoslovakia (according to the Locarno Pact of 1925) and handed over that country, created by the Treaty of Versailles, to be devoured shortly thereafter by Nazi Germany. Such was the true significance of the incredible Munich Conference in September 1938, when Chamberlain traveled to Germany and came back with an agreement which, he was certain, would bring "peace in our time."

And so a word in the English language came to have a new, pusillanimous significance. This was the word *appeasement*, which became synonymous with surrender. No longer was there any chance for Britain and France to make an alliance with Russia because Russia, afraid of Germany, also realized that Britain and France were relatively helpless. Hitler, during the summer of 1939, reapplied his now tried and true methods of pressure, this time on Poland; when Poland refused to appease him, he invaded it on September 1, and this time neither England nor France could afford to back down.

Britain and the Second World War

The war began slowly for the British people. It was not until April 1940 that anything significant happened in Western Europe. Hitler, who had immobilized the Russians by signing a remarkable nonaggression pact with the Soviets a week before he invaded Poland (a treaty blown to bits in June of 1941), overwhelmed Poland in three weeks. In April and May, Germany completed the occupation of Denmark and Norway; in the latter country, for the first time, the frightening inadequacies of Allied preparation for the war and the hopeless fumbling of the Chamberlain ministry were pitilessly exposed. On May 10, 1940, the Germans invaded Belgium and the Netherlands and began a brilliant flanking movement which by-passed the main defenses of the supposedly impregnable Maginot Line. The power of the onslaught, combined with ineffective Allied defenses, brought about the loss of the Low Countries to the Germans, the invasion of France, and the imperilment of the whole British Expeditionary Force. A skillful and heroic evacuation through Dunkirk saved most of the men but not the armament. At the same time, it brought into the premiership Winston Churchill (1874–1965), one of the most remarkable leaders in the history of Britain.

Shortly thereafter, on June 17, 1940, France was forced into ignominious capitulation. Britain spent the summer of 1940 in grim and desperate efforts to prepare for a German invasion of the island. Although that invasion never came, the country was pounded mercilessly from the air for months while the world marveled at its defensive fortitude. Now master of all continental Europe to the west of him, save for Spain and Portugal, Hitler even invaded northern Africa with the objective of seizing the Suez Canal, cutting off Britain from the Mediterranean and handicapping its communications with India and the Far East, while at the same time gaining the rich oil resources of the Arabian and Iranian sectors.

When Hitler invaded Russia (June 22, 1941), it was clear that Britain had been granted at least a breathing spell. American aid now became immediate; it became total when Japan struck at Pearl Harbor (December 7, 1941). Although the Germans reached almost to Moscow in 1941, and, farther south, actually reached Stalingrad on the Volga in 1942–1943, they never quite attained their objective in the east, and the Stalingrad campaign eventually proved to be disastrous. Meanwhile, the Japanese overran the Philippines, Malaya, and the entire southwestern Pacific as far as the northern coast of Australia. But eventually the balance gradually shifted, and the Allies moved from the defensive to the offensive. Slowly the Americans, assisted by the Australians and the New Zealanders, worked their way back through the Pacific—a rugged and brilliantly executed three-year campaign climaxed by the recovery of the Philippines in late 1944 and early 1945. The Allies, after clearing the Germans out of northern Africa (1942–1943), moved into Italy and forced the weakest of their enemies into surrender (July 25, 1943), although they were obliged to maintain a costly holding operation on the Italian peninsula for the better part of two years thereafter. They performed the greatest feat of invasion ever recorded when they landed in France (June 6, 1944) and penetrated into Germany by September. When the Anglo-American forces and the revivified Russians met in central Germany, it was all over; the Germans capitulated on May 8, 1945. Just three months later, the Japanese, then under constant attack by American air and sea forces and realizing that a total invasion of their home islands by American ground forces was only a matter of months, if not of weeks, surrendered without reservations. Their collapse was hastened by the dropping of atomic bombs on Hiroshima and Nagasaki (August 6 and 9, 1945), which presaged an entirely new era in technical science, and, to a lesser degree, by American naval assaults and the last-minute entry of Russia into the Pacific war. The final articles of surrender were signed exactly six years after Germany had invaded Poland.

Britain, however, was too preoccupied with the European and African theaters of war to take more than a nominal part in the overthrow of Japan. In the

Cricket.

elections of 1945, it surprised the world by ousting the war prime minister, Winston Churchill, as if recognizing that for all his inestimable services, he was more adapted to war than to reconstruction. The victory of the Labour Party under Clement Attlee (1883–   ) was not unexpected, for the trend of the times was antipathetic to a return of Conservative rule, and it was felt that a continuation of the coalition government which had guided the nation through the war was not desirable. The transition to a socialistic form of government proved to be relatively easy. The basic industries nationalized by the Labour Party had been under government control during the war; stockholders were compensated, and many of the old managers found positions side by side with union leaders on the new boards set up to control the industries.

The problem weighing more than any other upon the Attlee ministry was the discouraging one of putting back on its feet a nation bled to the point of anemia by six devastating years of frontline and home-front warfare—a nation, moreover, which had never made a full recovery from the First World War. *Austerity*, a word made current by Sir Stafford Cripps while he was Chancellor of the Exchequer (1947–1950), was the keyword during the first six postwar years. Rationing continued and in many instances became more stringent than during the war; a hard winter in 1947 resulted in a coal shortage, and there was a lack of sufficient dollar credits, a consequence of the end of lend-lease and of British losses in the export trade and overseas investments. Britain was saved from what looked like financial ruin by increased American aid under the Marshall Plan.

In 1951 the Conservatives were returned to power by a narrow margin, and Winston Churchill again became prime minister. Except for denationalizing the

Efficiency flats, 1933. "Highpoint," Highgate (Tecton Architects).

Fashion, 1930.

steel and trucking industries, the Conservatives left Labour legislation intact. A general recovery was strengthened by a growth of Western European prosperity. In April 1955, Churchill relinquished the premiership to Sir Anthony Eden (1897–   ). Eden's term in office was beset with international difficulties, and, at the height of the furor over the Anglo-French-Israeli invasion of Egypt, he resigned from office (1956). He was succeeded by Harold Macmillan (1894–   ), who was in turn succeeded (1963) by Alec Douglas-Home (1903–   ). Then, in a close election in 1964, the balance swung over again to the Labour Party under the leadership of Harold Wilson (1916–   ).

The Literature of the Age in General

It is customary to designate as "contemporary literature" only the literature of the last fifty years or so, although there are many whose memories of the period before the First World War are still fresh. This literature cannot be seen, of course, in the perspective and with the clarity possible in surveying the literature of an older period, for it is still too much a part of the present.

English literature since 1914 may be considered to fall into four phases. The first of these would run, in point of time, from the outbreak of the war to about 1923. Various literary currents appeared, but the most powerful was the desire of writers to hold on to the old, to preserve at least some of the traditional attitudes toward both form and substance that were to be found in the nineteenth century. A second period, between 1923 and 1929, was the famous "plateau of the 1920's," the fabulous Jazz Age, in which there was a tendency to jettison, deny, and ridicule the older morality and faith. It represented the extreme of anti-Victorianism. The years of the depression and of the prelude to the Second World War—from 1929 to 1939—make up a third period. Here the tendency was strongly toward the left in politics and toward collectivism in social outlook; the fashion was not to think of man any longer as a hopeless individual wandering in a howling wilderness but rather as a worthy part of a mass, though that mass might be more important than any one of its component parts. Finally, there is the period of the Second World War and its continuing aftermath, the Cold War—from 1939 to the present—a period singularly unproductive of outstanding literature, in which a powerful influence, the so-called existentialist philosophy, conceives of man as being strictly on his own and having significance only in terms of his individual actions. These four periods are admittedly makeshift designations and overlap one another at many points.

In view of the enormous output of contemporary writers and their multitudinous numbers and interests, to say nothing of the complex opportunities for outlet —books, magazines, newspapers, pamphlets, lectures, radio and television programs, the stage, the motion pictures, for example—it is impossible to define in a brief space the characteristics of contemporary literature. But certain attributes are noticeable. The literature written between 1914 and the present tends to be audacious in its reaction to traditional standards and perspectives. It is extremely self-conscious, often obscure and freakish. It can be sentimental, although the age obviously professes a horror of the sentimental. On the other hand, it seems to reflect the idea that this is more of a woman's world than it used to be. One is struck forcibly by its irreverence, by its emphasis upon the scientific, and by its preoccupation with sex, or rather with the physical manifestations thereof. It cannot shake off the eternal verities, of course, but it can be arrogant in its contemplation of them, and it is prone to insist that the greatest of all verities is change. It professes to know all the answers, but beneath this assumption of knowledge is a basic unsureness. It subscribes to realism, though it is often romantic; it has courage but not much steadiness; it has energy without much direction.

Some Traditionalists

Despite the fact that English literature since the romantic revolt of the late eighteenth century has been given to complaint, one might suppose that the findings of science should have shown man his place, where he could align himself with the order of things, as in the eighteenth century Alexander Pope urged in his *Essay on Man*. Such has not been the case, however; man of the twentieth century is not content, and this is one of his positive virtues.

A great many contemporary writers have adopted a pessimistic attitude. But there are some who still see beauty in life, and in the worship of this beauty they recover some of the faith which science has shattered. The finest poet among the latter was William Butler Yeats (p. 1196), who began as the presiding genius of the Irish Renaissance in the 1890's and developed during the twentieth century into one of the major poets of the age. The early phase of his poetry has already been touched upon, but it would be a manifest injustice to him if he were considered only as a Celtic romanticist. *Sailing to Byzantium* (p. 1201) is an expression of the often mystical experience that Yeats underwent in his attempts to fuse the romantic and idealistic with the stern exigencies of life. It is revealing to notice how often in his later poems, such as *The Second Coming* (p. 1201) and *Among School Children* (p. 1202), Yeats presents first an actual scene or fact, then his subjective reaction to that scene or fact, and then the mystical or symbolic interpretation of his reactions. He shows, therefore, that the mere process of living does not invalidate the "reality" of his dreams, for his intensely subjective poetry can still keep a firm hold upon actualities. What is really great about Yeats and his poetry, apart from his innate poetic genius, is that he was not static: he moved from one point to another in a positive development. He outgrew the Irish Renaissance, which he had helped to establish; when placed beside him, the other Celtic poets, with all their talents, seem either frail romantics or parochial interpreters of life.

Weaker though he may be in poetic capabilities, Walter de la Mare (1873–1956), for example, possesses an extremely delicate craftsmanship and a haunting, childlike imagination of melancholy cast wedded to a sensitive intuition which is not soon forgotten. He is much more wistful than Yeats; his eyes are turned much more unavertedly toward the past. Yet though he may be rooted in romanticism, he is no Stevenson with a specious hope that all will be well. *The Listeners* (1912) presents in less than forty lines a traveler in a forest, a traveler seeking spiritual values, who comes to a lonely house and knocks on the door, but only phantom listeners hear him, and they can give him no answer. *The Last Coachload* (1921) paints a coach—the world—bearing its many passengers —mankind—to their inevitable destination—death. In another poem, the poet is happy enough for the moment, but "life is a dread thing, too, dark with horror and fear."

Except for Yeats, however, the English poets of this traditionalist group have neither the vitality nor the challenging power of their American contemporaries. On the other hand, the English theater has contributed much, thanks particularly to the work of two or three men. The most striking playwright of the age has been George Bernard Shaw (1856–1950).

Shaw began his dramatic career as a disciple of Ibsen (p. 840); he was the first British writer to realize the true importance of the Norwegian playwright, whom he had tried to teach to the highly reluctant British public not only by his *Quintessence of Ibsenism* (1889) but by a series of plays beginning in the 1890's. He was too fiery an individualist, however, to be content as a disciple of anybody. In some of his more than twenty valuable plays—and in others less valuable—he showed that he belonged to the long line of Irish dramatic wits; his plays, often essays in dramatic form (and often furnished with brilliant and elaborate prefaces), always garrulous but penetrating in comment, were of immense importance in waking up the English-speaking audiences intellectually. Shaw had no single set of formulas, for his plays are on all kinds of subjects and situations. Like

Oscar Wilde, he enjoys paradox in dialogue and in thought; like the German philosophers Schopenhauer and Nietzsche, he detests the sentimental, the timid, and the weak; and he demonstrates a lavish wealth of dramatic imagination. Yet his plays are carried along as much by personality, humor, and shrewdly insulting observations as they are by any particular dramatic skill. At times Shaw can be genuinely moving, as a sympathetic listening to *Candida* (1898) and *Saint Joan* (1923) will prove, but most of the time he prefers the witty, and no man as a rule ever wrote worse love scenes. A sublime egoist, he never lost touch with reality and is at his best as a satirist. Probably, however, it would be more accurate to say that he was a law unto himself; and yet his liking for the honest man who tries to get somewhere even amid utter confusion, and his dislike for the pretentious, which is, after all, the true test of the satirist, are enough to keep Shaw in the camp of the traditionalists, however much he might have winced at the label and however much he might have derided the idea of his being classified at all.

Completely different were the plays of John Galsworthy (1867–1933). Yet, like Shaw, Galsworthy was nearly always in his dramas a social critic, especially interested in the class struggle, though he can scarcely be called a propagandist but rather an interested and sympathetic bystander. His favorite formula is the ironic presentation of a character crushed by some circumstances in themselves unimportant but magnified to irresistible significance by the importance which society places upon them. His picture of society is that of an impersonal, unscrupulous, unfeeling, and often ruthless power that batters down all who get in its way. In so far as he exhibits partiality toward his characters, Galsworthy is likely to bestow it upon the weak or unfortunate individual caught between the social and industrial scenes. The best plays in his canon are probably *Strife* (1909), on labor and capital in a small Welsh mining town; *Justice* (1910), on the inscrutable and unfair ways of the law; and *Loyalties* (1922), on social prejudice. He wrote more than twenty plays all told. Nor should we forget that Galsworthy's *The Forsyte Saga* (1906–1921), a multiple fictional panorama of about a dozen novels long and short, is one of the important landmarks of the modern English novel. Here the gallery of Forsytes and their descendants both direct and collateral extends from the mid-Victorian period well into the twentieth century—almost a hundred years; and the shifting tastes, moral standards, even the economic values of the succession of generations— the change from property owner to renter or buyer on the installment plan—are told with fidelity, sympathetic insight, beauty of style, and occasional high seriousness. Some critics have seen in this great work only "a manor-house hall hung with Rembrandts,"

but Galsworthy emerges obviously as more than a mere pictorial delineator. He has drawn his characters well and has thrown them in high relief against the background of modern industrial England, and he has made them live. He has the urbanity combined with the attention to form and style that characterized the nineteenth-century writer. But he was living in the twentieth century, and he was fully aware of the impact of the new order upon the old. More than that, he is the social commentator; and however much he is of the older generation born and bred, his value as a contemporary observer is none the less genuine. At times he is the mellow romanticist, and usually he is the sentimentalist; but his sense of human injustice is keen and real, as his sense of human character is broad. He never lapses from essential dignity in his account of men and women.

The tradition of the Irish theater, first made resplendent by Yeats and Synge, was ably carried on by Sean O'Casey (1880–1964), though his talent was uneven. His best works deal with the Irish revolutionary movement. *Juno and the Paycock* (1924) has superb characterization but violates almost every known principle of unity of action; still, the figures of old Boyle (the "Paycock") and of his wife are magnificent—the one because of his supreme typifying of the ne'er-do-well, the other because of her quiet courage in the face of the utter ruin of her family. In *The Plough and the Stars* (1926), a wife tries in vain, and quite disastrously, to keep her husband from taking part in the Easter Rebellion of 1916. But then in *The Silver Tassie* (1928), an antiwar play, O'Casey suddenly departed from his realistic manner and became allegorical; in *Within the Gates* (1933) he turned satirical critic of middle-class society and the Church and revived the old romantic motif of the joyous prostitute. Two later plays, *The Star Turns Red* (1940) and *Purple Dust* (1941), are in the first instance Marxist propaganda and in the second instance caricature. Beside O'Casey's powerful contribution to the Irish dramatic tradition, the whimsical, sentimental, and dainty plays of Sir James Barrie (1860–1937) and the fantastic dream-creations of Lord Dunsany (1878–1957) seem to belong to a vanished age.

On the whole, the fiction of the traditionalists has not weathered the storm of modernism in good condition, although many have tried to save the ship—too many to be named here. Katherine Mansfield (1888–1923) achieved success in the short story; her delicately wrought tales are dedicated primarily to mood, temperament, and atmosphere and are in many ways reminiscent of the stories of Anton Chekhov, for whom she revealed, in her journals and notebooks, a warm admiration. Her characters tend to react with the thought that life is—something; but words fail them. The interested reader will derive satisfaction from her *Journal*, for in it there is told the fascinating and pathetic story of a gifted woman's decline, her mercurial mind alive and quick until but a short time before her death. Inconsecutive and fragmentary as the *Journal* is, it represents the virtues as well as the limitations of its author's talents.

In the traditional fields of historiography and biography an arresting and typically satirical writer was Lytton Strachey (1880–1932), who in his excellent *Queen Victoria* (1921) painted a portrait with dramatic vividness and romantic nostalgia. Even his somewhat smug and condescending *Eminent Victorians* (1918) shows emotional drive. The same thing is true of such a work as the gripping *The Hundred Years* (1936) by Philip Guedalla (1889–1944). To be sure, the writers just named are two who happen to have become celebrated, but an exhaustive catalogue of other similar historians and biographers could be given, for such writing has been very much in vogue.

In brief, these traditionalist authors are those who may be said to have tried their best to maintain some hope, however illusory, that human life has value. They were formed by nineteenth-century thought, and it was not easy for science to tear them away from their mother. They could not believe that patriotism and honor and love could be anything but real. They rejected the mechanistic philosophy of life which a literal application of both biological and psychological science would impose upon them. They thought well, even if they could not push their thinking to any logical conclusions.

Disillusioned Truthseekers

Much has been said already about the impact of science upon the minds of the Victorian age, how this impact disillusioned some, cut the ground from under others, and forced almost everyone to some sort of readjustment. Yet in the modern age the findings of psychology seem to have caused more of a spiritual upheaval than the doctrine of evolution did among the Victorians; the theory of behaviorism put forth by John B. Watson or the analysis of the subconscious mind by Sigmund Freud have produced conclusions as disturbing as Darwin's were. When one realizes that his conscious mind may at any time be influenced by his unconscious mind, he questions the authority of the rational. If he thinks of himself as a set of conditioned reflexes, he must ultimately define himself as little more than a complicated machine.

To accept these revolutionary ideas is all very well, provided one understands that all such findings are tentative and that science is no more absolute than the humanities. As it happened, most intelligent persons who thought about the matter at all found that they must either swallow whole the teachings and implications of the new science or that they must accept them with reservations, always remembering that their knowledge was not and never could be complete. For there was no longer any likelihood that the new science could be rejected altogether. The writers of contemporary literature, few of whom knew much about science, although they all knew a great deal about living, were inclined to be too easily impressed by the negative aspects of the teachings of Watson, Freud, and others. The inference that man was a strange mixture of bone and tissue, mostly water, with sentient threads called nerves and some kind of quasi-electrical impulses called stimuli, a creature capable of being dissolved in the twinkling of an eye—to many this concept was so terrible that they abandoned hope. Unlike the brave whistling in the dark in which Stevenson indulged, in *Pulvis et Umbra* (p. 1125)—and Stevenson represents a way out of the predicament which the traditionalists are inclined to follow—there arose the cries of voices in the wilderness among a large number of writers, many of whom have come to be regarded as the most impressive in contemporary literature. To them life was sterile, decadent, unrewarding to virtue as well as to vice; there was no Celestial City

The Lambeth Walk, 1938.

A Blenheim bomber, 1940.

toward which man could strive, and no Inferno either; heaven and hell were alike on this earth; in this life the end came with death, which meant annihilation. All of this was far from new. It was only that the twentieth century, with its hyperaccelerated urban culture, shows "the strange disease of modern life" in aggravated form. Melancholy and pessimism have appeared before in English literature; they reached a morbid stage in the graveyard poetry of the allegedly rational eighteenth century. The twentieth century, however, with its skyscrapers and city battlements, its tumultuous means of transportation and supply, and its enormous technological equipment, has given man more room, more places, and at the same time, ironically enough, more opportunities to intensify his inherited miseries.

One type of disillusioned writer of the period may be referred to as the Wastelander, so named from the poem of epic disillusionment, *The Waste Land* (1922), by T. S. Eliot (p. 1236). Such a writer, more self-centered than usual, tends to be romantic in his outlook; in some instances he lives entirely in his own private world—the reduction to the absurd of the romanticist's subjective point of view—and builds up his own language, allowing his mental associations to race around until they produce a roaring stream of consciousness. Many of these writers are guilty of great obscurity, for the reasons just mentioned, yet so powerful is their impress upon the tastes and fashions of much contemporary literature that obscurity becomes something of a fetish, a talisman to ward off the danger that the writer may be too easily understood and his intellectual and emotional sterility exposed for what it is. Like his romantic ancestor of the nineteenth century, he is haunted by the thought that other times were better. Hence his natural inclination to-

The evacuation of Dunkirk, June 1940.
Combine Photos.

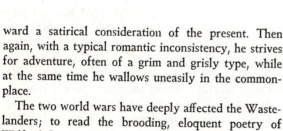

Spitfires.

El Alamein, 1942.

ward a satirical consideration of the present. Then again, with a typical romantic inconsistency, he strives for adventure, often of a grim and grisly type, while at the same time he wallows uneasily in the commonplace.

The two world wars have deeply affected the Wastelanders; to read the brooding, eloquent poetry of Wilfred Owen (1893–1918) is to understand the bitterness in the hearts of men whose friends and companions have been cut down in their youth and denied the promise that should be theirs. "No Man's Land," wrote Owen, "under snow is like the face of the moon, chaotic, crater-ridden, uninhabitable, awful, the abode of madness." Quite properly men like Owen could believe that they belonged to a lost generation, but whereas Owen died before the 1918 Armistice, others lived on in disillusionment.

In poetry, it is obvious that the most important single spokesman for the Wastelanders was T. S. Eliot in his earlier phase. This striking poet's *The Love Song of J. Alfred Prufrock* (p. 1237), *The Waste Land, The Hollow Men* (1925), and other poems composed in the 1920's catch the moods of vacillation, weakness, sordidness, and despair. Both as poet and as critic, Eliot long dominated the literary scene. He was born in the United States but lived abroad long enough to become first an internationalist and eventually a British subject. It is likely that the critics of the next century will consider Eliot and Yeats the most important English-speaking poets of the first half of this century. Like Yeats, Eliot progressed from his earlier work—a sure sign of the significant writer—for his poetry took on an increasingly religio-philosophical tone, culminating in such noble utterances as *Ash Wednesday* (p. 1240), *The Rock* (1934), and *Four Quartets* (1943).

Eliot's earlier work bristles with learned allusions and recondite imagery; much of it is derived from other poets, and many passages are tissues of quotations from or reminiscences of older writers. His affinity for the later Elizabethan and seventeenth-

century periods, both as poet and as critic, is marked. Even in his later poetry there is an undeniable bookishness. It is difficult to see the author of *The Waste Land* or *The Hollow Men* in the author of *Ash Wednesday* and *Four Quartets*, but the polarity of the moods of despair and desolation on the one hand and the stirrings of an orthodox, rather stable faith (laboriously attained, to be sure) on the other is typical of the age in which Eliot wrote; and the very fact that he could attain both poles of the sphere makes him a greater writer, highly representative of the paradox of his time.

The best dramatist of the Waste Land is the one best fitted to demonstrate that the Wastelander had his lighter side. Noel Coward (1899–   ) has always had the theater for his chief passion; he has attained success in comedy of manners, historical drama, domestic tragedy, operetta, and revue to such a marked degree that he remains one of the most versatile playwrights in the history of the English theater. Essentially an entertainer, he is in one way a twentieth-century Congreve (p. 430), except that, in keeping with the spirit of his time, he dares to discuss and attack things that Congreve would not have ventured to

Women fire-watchers on Salisbury Cathedral, 1940.

ing of Coward's sentimental and traditionalist streak. A true successor to the Oscar Wilde tradition, Coward's taste may sometimes be enough to make a Victorian wince, but that is only to be expected of a writer of the twentieth-century Waste Land.

Some of the novelists of the period have also tended toward disillusionment. Four noted representatives of this category are W. Somerset Maugham, Aldous Huxley, D. H. Lawrence, and James Joyce. It is generally agreed that Maugham was a gifted storyteller, a professional craftsman and entertainer in letters who was also a fine satirist; Huxley and Lawrence were basically preachers; and Joyce was the subjective artist going his own way.

W. Somerset Maugham (1874–1965) had his literary roots deep in the Continental soil of the nineteenth century. The first of his novels, *Liza of Lambeth* (1897), is a naturalistic novel, something of a rarity in English letters, showing an attitude toward life characteristic of a medical student, which Maugham once was. His masterpiece is the distinguished novel written as partial autobiography, *Of Human Bondage* (1915), but his many short stories and his plays are also notable as human documents. From his story *The Trembling of a Leaf* (1921) was adapted the once-sensational play *Rain*, one of the great dramatic successes of the 1920's. *Rain* deals with the old romantic situation of a prostitute who unintentionally and ironically brings about the moral ruin of a supposedly upright man, in this case a stiff-necked missionary, and at the same time manages to ennoble herself. In all of his work, Maugham reminds one of the French writer Guy de Maupassant (1850–1892). He is original in his treatment of old themes, economical in his style, subtle in his overtones, adventurous in his plots, and always dramatic.

It is ironic that the grandson of Thomas Henry Huxley (p. 1060) should have become perhaps the most brilliant critic of the triumph of modern science over the human soul. Aldous Huxley (p. 1248) began his work as an author by shattering the illusions of the conventional reading public. Though scintillating, his first novels, beginning with *Crome Yellow* (1921), are iconoclastic; they proceed, explicitly and implicitly, to demolish Victorianism in all its various manifestations and to lay man's whole life in intellectual and spiritual ruins. In referring to his novel *Antic Hay* (1923), Huxley asserted that it "dramatizes with relentless logic the necessary implications, in terms of life, of the skepticism of Thomas Huxley—skepticism battening on the vitals of animal faith." His two best novels, *Point Counter Point* (1928) and *Brave New World* (1932), are corrosive comments on the modern scene. Resounding through all these novels is a certain brooding undertone, an unsatisfied "Why?" which can have no final answer. *After Many a Summer Dies the Swan* (1939) sends man in quest of immortality by way of

lay hands on. Coward is at his best when he is presenting the unconventional, particularly the unorthodox in domestic relations. The son in *The Vortex* (1923) castigates his lecherous mother; the nagged husband in *Fumed Oak* (1936) turns violently on his unpleasant little family; in *Private Lives* (1930) a divorced couple, each of whom has remarried, meet on their respective new honeymoons and forget about their new marriages. In *Design for Living* (1933) there is established a delightful *ménage à trois*, involving a woman and two men, in which triangle each member loves the other two and cannot choose between them. Something of the same insouciance about marital relationships is obvious in *Blithe Spirit* (1941). In *Hands Across the Sea* (1936) a farcical situation is developed with keen satire. On the other hand, *Bitter Sweet* (1929), a charming operetta for which he composed both words and music, is Coward's most successful venture in the field of musical entertainment, but it is basically as lachrymose in its appeal as something out of the nineteenth century. Actually, the revue *Conversation Piece* (1934) is a trifle more typical. *Cavalcade* (1931) is the panorama of an English family from the Boer War to the end of the First World War; it contains memorable scenes and true power; but again, its appeal to the English people to recover their greatness and dignity is reveal-

science, and science turns up the answer that longevity can be attained through a diet of carp's intestines, but the horrible creatures that survive are worthy of comparison with Swift's Struldbrugs in *Gulliver's Travels*. *Time Must Have a Stop* (1944) reviews a man's life through the delirium attendant upon a fatal attack of coronary thrombosis.

Huxley, however, reached the limits in his study of man the animal. He therefore found it necessary to turn to man the thinker, or, as in *Ends and Means* (1937), to "an inquiry into the nature of ideals and into the methods employed for their realization." The eventual change in this author is as remarkable as the change in T. S. Eliot, to which it is analogous. Out of the Waste Land, which is too stifling to sustain life for long, man must seek the mountains of idealism and religion, and although he may grope blindly when he reaches them, he is at least on higher ground. In point of fact, Huxley came to repudiate the very intellect with which man has been endowed, the intellect which has given him his sharpest weapons. It is difficult to separate Huxley the novelist from Huxley the teacher and preacher—this in spite of the fact that, in his desire to be clever, a temptation which he found hard to resist, he frequently lapses into brittle and sophomoric utterances. His characters react in terms of their physical organisms, and their psychological entities are in consequence based on behaviorism.

The catalytic agent of Huxley's *Point Counter Point* is a character named Mark Rampion, who represents almost without disguise the philosophy of D. H. Lawrence (1885–1930). Each of Lawrence's best-known novels, *Sons and Lovers* (1913), *The Plumed Serpent* (1926), and *Lady Chatterley's Lover* (1928) caused a sensation when it appeared. The first, *Sons and Lovers*, is an autobiographical novel of a young boy in a mining town, beset by emotional family harassments. *The Plumed Serpent* is an esoteric novel involving an Englishwoman with the ancient pagan cults of Mexico; it questions the whole right of the decadent white race to survive. *Lady Chatterley's Lover*, a success of scandal, relates the passionate love affair of an English noblewoman and the gamekeeper of her invalid husband's estate. All three novels stress a new world of love, unhampered by caste, materialism, family ties, or notions of racial and religious superiority; and all three portray the frustrations bearing down on those who wish to enter this new world. Few can deny the warmth and color of *Sons and Lovers* or *The Plumed Serpent*; in these the author established himself as a distinguished romanticist. His ultimate success, however, particularly in *Lady Chatterley's Lover*, is questionable; the trouble lies in an essential naïveté and a strange humorlessness in dealing with matters of love and sex which paradoxically make him appear to some as amusing, even ridiculous. There is no greater enemy of romance than a guffaw.

St. Paul's, 1940.

Lawrence, a restless, tubercular man, spent his life wandering over the earth, but his wanderings in the spiritual realm caused him the greater anxiety, for he could never successfully harmonize the physical and spiritual sides of his characters, although such a reconciliation was essential to his philosophy. Perhaps he had puritanical tendencies, as some of his friends have said, although they do not lie on the surface. Yet he remains a skilled and sensitive craftsman, though over all his significant work there lowers a cloud of frustration and futility.

A notoriety akin to Lawrence's, now forgotten, was also the portion of James Joyce (p. 1203), but the two men were in most respects the absolute antitheses of each other. Since Joyce was born and educated in Ireland during the heyday of the Irish Renaissance, one might expect him to have shared in the efforts of that artistic movement, but he had little sympathy with it. His attack upon the Irish theater, the most valuable and at the same time the most sacrosanct institution of the Irish Renaissance, shows his particular individualism, an individualism which developed to such an extent that he became an expatriate on the Continent, and, what is more important, the greatest example in modern English literature of the subjective artist. *Dubliners* (1914), a collection of short stories, and his masterpiece, *Ulysses* (1922), exhibit his intimate knowledge not only of the Irish capital and the Irish temperament but of human nature. He was a learned individual with a marked interest in language and words, which he cultivated in his later work to such an extent that it interfered seriously with his line of communication with his readers. To his remarkable power of ob-

Painted relief, 1939, by Ben Nicholson. Collection of the Museum of Modern Art, New York. Gift of H. S. Ede and the artist.

Shelter scene, 1942, a drawing in water color, crayon, and pen and ink by Henry Moore, from the collection of Mr. and Mrs. George E. Dix. Reprinted by permission.

man in Bloom. In the meantime Bloom wanders all over Dublin. A great many other people appear in the pages of the novel, but they are all a part of Bloom's experience. Each section of the novel corresponds to a section of the *Odyssey*; even the minor characters and the city streets are analogous in name or quality to figures and localities in the great Homeric epic. Late at night Bloom returns with Stephen to find not a chaste Penelope but an adulterous Molly, whose uninhibited inner soliloquy at the end of the novel is a magnificent creation of feminine animality. *Ulysses* concludes on the affirmative chord of Molly's life-giving surrender. Yet in actuality this surrender is not for the giving of life but only for sensual pleasure, and the total effect of the novel is one of almost un-relieved human sterility and desolation.

Joyce's last novel, *Finnegans Wake* (1939), is a fourth-dimensional work, for all time and space are telescoped into Ireland and a character named Mr. H. C. Earwicker. The thesis seems to be that all life and all languages are one. Stylistically and linguisti-cally the novel is a freak. It is now universally recog-nized that certain objects in one's experience have associations, often a string of associations, peculiar to the individual—they conjure up sights, sounds, smells, tastes, and feelings. Joyce, however, in attempting to convey such associations, plays ducks and drakes with ordinary language and so does not deal fairly with the reader. A key is necessary. Even when the novel is understood, one is justified in asking whether it was worth the effort, whether the undeniable pyro-

servation and his expressiveness, then, he added erudi-tion and an irrepressible love for the symbolic.

Ulysses takes three people through one day in their lives—Leopold Bloom, a Jewish advertising solicitor of Dublin; Molly, his wife; and young Stephen Dedalus, the protagonist of Joyce's earlier novel, *A Portrait of the Artist As a Young Man* (1916), who has broken with his unloved family and is looking for some kind of spiritual father, a parallel with the search of Telemachus for Odysseus (Ulysses). He finds this

technics and ingenious wordmongering were in any way useful.

For all that, however, in his remarkable ability to portray the thoughts of more than one character, Joyce brought the writing of "stream of consciousness" literature to its highest peak in English letters. His influence upon many later writers has been immediate and direct. The general permanence of this influence is of course another question. Another somewhat similar influence at work on the writers of the age was that of Marcel Proust (1871–1922), whose multivolume *Remembrance of Things Past* is a remarkable reconstruction of a human being's life (conscious as well as subconscious) and a display of man's associational powers. As a matter of fact, the strangely forgotten Dorothy Richardson (1882–1957), in her massive *Pilgrimage* (1915–1938), was an earlier exponent of the type of writing to which she herself gave the name "interior monologue" instead of "stream of consciousness." Yet this author's talent is far less striking than that of another woman born, as were both Dorothy Richardson and James Joyce, in the year 1882.

Virginia Woolf, who committed suicide in 1941 and so put an end to a career which was in full flower, is by general consent the most important English woman writer of her generation. One critic put it well when he spoke of her as a priestess of psychological minutiae. For her, time, measured in hours, minutes, and seconds, is important chiefly because a lifetime can be covered in the writer's imagination during those same hours, minutes, and seconds.

Moreover, time in the abstract will continue long after the people affected by it have died; as in Proust's work, time is the greatest of villains. In *The Years* (1937), one of Virginia Woolf's most moving novels, it is Time that is the chief character. In *The Waves*, the lives of six characters are spread out, not in a consecutive chronicle, but through the way in which each character reacts to the sea, which is a kind of symbol for time. Time can triumph over persons and things, and even over sex, as in *Orlando* (1928); and yet there remains a curious residue of the permanent in the characters, as if Orlando, for example, were immortal, and all mankind were immortal, although subject to remorseless changes in which physical characteristics sink into nothingness. But this is never stated directly; rather it is presented in a style that has many of the characteristics of time itself. In *To the Lighthouse* (1927), a boy is promised an excursion to a lighthouse, but by the time he actually visits this lighthouse, a whole generation has passed. And the boy, eager to reach the lighthouse in Part I, is both unimpressed and bored by his final attainment of it as a man in Part III. The inner life, which is Virginia Woolf's preoccupation, as it is Joyce's, is revealed with consummate craft and loving attention.

It is not, however, the only life there is; and in that fact lies Virginia Woolf's greatest limitation.

The number of gifted novelists in the contemporary period is legion; each one of them commands a sufficient following to make the task of the critic in labeling them either major or minor a most distasteful and perhaps futile one. Besides, there remains always the possibility that any one of these "minor" writers may someday be hailed as "major." In an older group, however, one should place Frank Swinnerton (1884–   ), a penetrating realist in the manner of George Gissing, whose best work is probably *Nocturne* (1917). Of a different sort is Hugh Walpole (1884–1941), with his Trollopian *The Cathedral* (1922) and Stevensonian *Herries Chronicles* (1930–1934).

Much more incisive than either is E. M. Forster (1879–   ), whose *A Passage to India* (1924) is an ironic, almost cruel protest against material realism. Yet it is in keeping with this irony that he is likely to be most effective in his realistic portrayals, as in *Howard's End* (1910) or *A Room with a View* (1908), and this despite the fact that in his plots he can often be melodramatic to the point of implausibility. His apparent aim is the exposure of the insularity of liberal upper-class English society. In this aim he succeeds fitfully: he draws attention to the empty, the ignorant, and the ambivalent in a generally traditional way, but with mixed results, because it is difficult for him to see life as more than a series of inexplicable details and inexplicable people. Yet he is an artist capable of skillful presentation: his style is low-pitched and understated rather than overstated, and it is always readable. His outlook is usually rather pessimistic, but his irony, combined with some rather intellectual humor, does much to alleviate the pessimism.

Mention should be made also of Seán O'Faoláin (1900–   ), who in *A Nest of Simple Folk* (1933), like O'Casey in the drama, provides correctives to the over-romantic literary treatment of Ireland by earlier Irish writers; of James Hanley (1901–   ), who in *Stoker Bush* (1935) presents a sailor's life in such a way as to make the sea tales of John Masefield seem purely Victorian; and of Liam O'Flaherty (1896–   ), who in *The Informer* (1935) combined realism and melodrama with powerful effect. Graham Greene (1904–   ); Evelyn Waugh (1903–1966), and Wyndham Lewis (1884–1957) all made their reputations before the Second World War, but they continued to produce interesting works: Greene with *The End of the Affair* (1941) and *The Quiet American* (1955); Waugh with *Men at Arms* (1952), *Officers and Gentlemen* (1944), and *The Ordeal of Gilbert Pinfold* (1957); Lewis with *Self-Condemned* (1954), *Monstre Gai* (1955), and *Malign Fiesta* (1955). Particularly prominent since the Second World War have been William Golding (1911–   ), with *Lord of the Flies* (1954) and *The Spire* (1964); Kingsley Amis

Fashion, 1967. British designers created the mod look and the mini-skirt. In plaid tunic is Twiggy (Lesley Hornby).—UPI.

and in such poetic efforts as *On This Island* (1937) and *Letter to Lord Byron* (1937), he expresses his awareness of this social decadence. The resemblance between Auden and Byron in their satirical aspects is enhanced by Auden's imitation of the rambling, garrulous satire of the Byron of *Don Juan* or *Beppo*. But Byron had a romantic dream and put this dream into action by going off to fight for the independence of Greece, whereas Auden wandered about from England to Iceland to China to America, even during the years of the Second World War (although he drove an ambulance in Spain during the Spanish Civil War), dabbling in communism, then turning to the refuge of the Church of England, and later withdrawing from this refuge and becoming a naturalized citizen of the United States. In his earlier work he brooded over the fact that he and other young men of his generation were suspended between two worlds—the outworn world of an old Europe and the unknown world that must somehow be born out of all this violence and chaos if life is to have any meaning. In *The Age of Anxiety* (1947), he presents a conversation among four people of differing points of view, but the last word is given to the one who goes about his daily business with as much common sense as he can muster. Most of Auden's work, for all its occasional timeliness, has a curious kind of backward look. He sees the symbols of the old order receding but cannot catch a clear glimpse of what is coming to replace them. In two more recent works, *Nones* (1951) and *The Shield of Achilles* (1955), his scorn is tempered by high spirits and wit. Especially in *The Shield of Achilles* he puts aside some of his intellectual misgivings and, with his usual great prosodic skill, indulges in a vein of near-gaiety mixed with mockery.

The indeterminateness which appears in much of Auden's poetry is not so apparent in that of Stephen Spender (p. 1270). Spender's verse is most useful now for its indication of what has come over the point of view of the young revolutionary of the 1930's. In *World Within World* (1951), a sensitively written and self-critical autobiography, Spender provides a glimpse of the forming influence in his point of view. Obviously the art of Auden and Spender, and others, has social implications; indeed, these writers represent the general preoccupation with sociological interests characteristic of depression and post-depression literature, a preoccupation which, with different accents, is coming back into vogue during the 1960's.

For example, the disillusionment expressed by Spender in *What I Expected* (p. 1272) is most revealing. One can find a similar disillusionment in American literature of the same years. Some of the poets of the late 1930's and 1940's, like Thomas Hardy a half-century before, would prefer it to be otherwise and so call for a soul-searching on the part of the

(1922–   ), with *Lucky Jim* (1953) and *I Like It Here* (1958); Lawrence Durrell (1912–   ), who is also a poet of distinction, with *The Black Book* (1938; 1960) and *Alexandria Quartet* (1962); and Anthony Powell (1905–   ), with *A Question of Upbringing* (1951) and *The Valley of Bones* (1964). It would take a rash critic to say which among these will eventually come to be regarded as major writers, but meanwhile, one may take one's choice, for the work of these writers, seen as a whole, represents an extremely wide spectrum in both theme and technique.

The poetry of the present generation is the product of the restless iconoclasm of the 1920's, the socially motivated 1930's, the war-clouded 1940's, and the uncertain, perhaps timid, 1950's. Two poets, W. H. Auden and Stephen Spender, perhaps more than any others, have best reflected the changing climate. W. H. Auden (p. 1263), a satirist of rather uncertain touch, though sometimes extremely effective, was both irritated and disgusted by the decadence of the social order in Britain before the outbreak of the Second World War. In verse plays written in collaboration with his friend Christopher Isherwood (1904–   ),

present-day society, lest all be lost. Thus George Barker (1913–   ) pleads for a release from fear and sordidness. More violent and more cynical, though equally willing to share the responsibility for rebuilding the world, is Roy Campbell (1901–1957). A tendency to escape into the world of Yeats and Lawrence is unmistakable in the rich, sensuous, rhapsodic poetry of Dylan Thomas (p. 1273). After Thomas' death in 1953, critical interest in his poetry reached great proportions. It is difficult poetry, but thoroughly traditional in themes if not in treatment. In addition to the lesser poets of prewar reputation, such as Edwin Muir (1887–1959), and Dame Edith Sitwell (1887–1964), some of the postwar poets who have made names for themselves are Andrew Young (1885–   ), Louis MacNeice (1907–1963), Laurie Lee (1914–   ), and Robert Gittings (1911–   ).

General Characteristics

As one views the literature of England from a point seventeen years after midcentury, one gets the immediate impression that it is uncertain, even aimless. The loss of traditional values, of the social faith which animated many of the poets and novelists of the 1930's, the loss even of the conviction that the world of modern civilization will survive—all have contributed to a literary climate that is unclear and unsure. The momentous shadow of the atomic bomb, the titanic struggle between communist and noncommunist, the upheaval of nationalities throughout the world, the very scope and power of events themselves have obscured traditional vision.

The integrated thought of the Middle Ages and the confident spirit of the Renaissance are alike impossible for the twentieth century to accept, let alone attain, for the world today has neither the unity of the one nor the faith of the other. Nor could one expect it to be otherwise. The eighteenth-century deist might perhaps understand modern achievements in material accomplishments and thought, but he would insist that in other aspects of living men are still feeling out the path most uncertainly. The Middle Ages felt assured that its morality was the only one, but ever since that time mankind has been less and less sure about what constitutes true morality. On the whole, the twentieth century realizes that the clock cannot be turned back, but it still does not know what time it really is.

Yet contemporary literature is unafraid, and in its experimentation is bold and venturesome. The enormous output of the age, fostered by the creative urges of individual authors and by the demands of widely disseminated mass media, takes all human experience as legitimate grist for its mill; and where expression is uninhibited, as it is among the English-speaking peoples, it is capable of great forcefulness and great imaginative flights. Moreover, in all this generation of those who pry into matters that were once not supposed to be discussed, in all this playing and discarding of new cards, the English have held on steadfastly to their innate sense of artistic values. Even when they experiment, they do not go to the extremes reached by some of their American contemporaries.

This is to say that the British writers today often lack the raw impact of contemporaneous American authors; sometimes they are spinster-like in their ordered little island. But one gets the sense, in reading an important British writer, of correctness and ease of style, of plasticity and adaptability, of artistic finish and an appropriateness to artistic ends, of richness of vocabulary, of vividness and mastery of phrase, of strength and sinew and clarity of style, and above all of an overriding good taste. Where there is such a multiplicity of writers and writing, as there is in the present, there will here and there be examples of the crude, the flashy, the ineffective. But English literature at its best is still the magnificent fruit of a plant nurtured with loving care for nearly thirteen hundred years.

GERARD MANLEY HOPKINS 1844-1889

Hopkins had intended to enter the Church of England, but in 1866, while an undergraduate at Oxford, where he was popularly called "The Star of Balliol," he came under the influence of John Henry (later Cardinal) Newman, and underwent a spectacular conversion to Catholicism. When he was received into the Society of Jesus in 1868, he burned his early poems and abstained from writing for seven years. He later served as a Jesuit missionary in Liverpool and had a church at Oxford; but in 1884 he was appointed to the staff of the revived Catholic University of Dublin, Ireland, a post that he held until his death five years later.

In spite of their date of composition, the poems of Hopkins in their difficult imagery, great compression, and stylistic eccentricities are altogether twentieth-century in manner. Convinced that these startling innovations of Hopkins' verse, left in manuscript at the time of his death, would meet with indifference or ridicule if given too early to the literary world, Robert Bridges (1844-1930), his devoted friend (and poet laureate after 1913), delayed publication until 1918, thirty or more years after the poems were written. The slender volume at once won extravagant praise from some of the poets and critics who found in these tense and fervent poems an affinity with their own poetic manner; others called them purposely and perversely obscure.

The overwhelming vogue for Hopkins' poetry has now gone past its peak, for it is recognized that for all his religious devotion and mystic ecstasy wedded to fine imaginative power, his is essentially a limited human experience. But painstaking care to understand the method by which Hopkins combined thought and feeling in words and the rhythmical pattern he followed will yield rich rewards. Word-clusters are to him more important an outlet for his intense emotion than grammatical structure; alliteration is a favorite device, as are interior rhymes and repetitions and particularly assonance, but all these poetic instruments are used with surprising significance. Metrically he was much interested in medieval English forms, and although he was ostensibly imitating the verse form of Piers Plowman, his work more closely resembles Anglo-Saxon alliterative verse.

Some of the poems, so Hopkins avers, are written in what he calls "Sprung Rhythm," which is measured by feet of one to four syllables, with the stress always on the first syllable of the foot. "It is natural in Sprung Rhythm," he adds, "for the lines to be rove over, that is, for the scanning of each line immediately to take up that of the one before, so that if the first has one or more syllables at its end, the other must have so many the less at its beginning; and in fact the scanning runs on without break from the beginning, say, of a stanza to the end, and all the stanza is one long strain, though written in lines asunder." (Quoted by Bridges in the Preface to his edition of Hopkins' Poems, page 4.)

HEAVEN-HAVEN

(A NUN TAKES THE VEIL)

    I have desired to go
      Where springs not fail,
To fields where flies no sharp and sided
      hail,
      And a few lilies blow.

    And I have asked to be
      Where no storms come,
Where the green swell is in the haven
      dumb,
      And out of the swing of the sea.
(c. 1866; 1918)

THE HABIT OF PERFECTION

Elected Silence, sing to me
And beat upon my whorléd ear;
Pipe me to pastures still and be
The music that I care to hear.

Shape nothing, lips; be lovely-dumb—
It is the shut, the curfew sent
From there where all surrenders come
Which only makes you eloquent.

Be shelléd, eyes, with double dark
And find the uncreated light;   10
This ruck and reel which you remark
Coils, keeps, and teases simple sight.

The Habit of Perfection. 2. **whorléd,** having whorls. 11. **ruck and reel,** crowding and confusion. 27. **lily-colored . . . spun.** Cf. Matthew 6:28–29. "Consider the lilies of the field, how they grow; they toil not, neither do they spin: And yet I say unto you, That even Solomon in all his glory was not arrayed like one of these."

Palate, the hutch of tasty lust,
Desire not to be rinsed with wine;
The can must be so sweet, the crust
So fresh that come in fasts divine!

Nostrils, your careless breath that spend
Upon the stir and keep of pride,
What relish shall the censers send.
20 Along the sanctuary side!

O feel-of-primrose hands, O feet
That want the yield of plushy sward,
But you shall walk the golden street
And you unhouse and house the Lord.

And, Poverty, be thou the bride
And now the marriage feast begun,
And lily-colored clothes provide
Your spouse not labored-at nor spun.
(1866; 1918)

THE WRECK OF THE DEUTSCHLAND

*Disregarding at least for the moment Hopkins'
division of the poem into two parts, one may have
perhaps less difficulty in interpreting the outlines of
the work if one divides the poem into four sections:
the second and third sections deal with the actual
shipwreck of the Deutschland in the Thames estuary
in December 1875, while the first and last sections
emphasize the glory of God and the necessity for
accepting with faith his will. The following sketch
may be helpful.*

*The first section, lines 1-80, is a poetic essay on
the infiniteness of God, his omnipotence and his
sovereignty, and on the intuitive knowledge which
man, the dependent finite creature, acquires through
the contemplation of this omnipotence and awesome-
ness—a knowledge which leads him to grasp the
beauty and love of his Maker. For He can be comprehended through terror and grief as well as through
beauty and happiness. The Incarnation and the Passion, moreover, have taught the human heart and
mind the true significance of suffering and loss—a
paradox, no doubt, but an inescapable one. Therefore
adore Him! All men, however rebellious their first
thoughts, should bow to Him.*

*The second section, lines 81-136. The Deutschland,
with her emigrants and exiles bound for America, is
struck unexpectedly by a hurricane of wind and snow
and is driven onto a sandbank. For a whole night,
without any chance to seek help, the passengers and*
*crew of the crippled, sinking ship are pummeled by
the waves and the wind, and many perish.*

*The third section, lines 137-248. In the midst of
all this terror and confusion, a nun is heard calling
upon Christ to "come quickly" (l. 191). (She was one
of the five Franciscan exiles driven from Germany by
the discriminatory anti-Catholic Falk Laws of 1875.
The number five reminds the poet of the Five Wounds
of Christ, a symbol of sacrifice and heavenly reward.)
What did this nun mean? She represents all suffering
mankind. It is not so much danger from which man
seeks to escape—danger can be stimulating—but rather
the monotonous daily round of material toil and frustration. Such deliverance can come only from Christ,
whose failure and frustration meant victory; his Passion redeemed an otherwise "unshapeable" existence
(l. 227). The nun was right, the tragedy and pain in
life make clear and are in turn made clear by the
Redemption. This nun represents a second Virgin Birth
—a rebirth of the significance of Christ. The poet has
been touched by the finger of God (l. 8); so too has
been the nun who awoke hope and faith in those
who heard her.*

*The fourth section, lines 249-280. The poet returns
to the thoughts of the first section. He repeats his
adoration of the majesty and the unknowable wisdom
of God. May the dead nun, prophetess of faith unafraid and stable, intercede for the conversion of
"rare-dear Britain" (l. 278).*

To the happy memory of five
Franciscan Nuns exiles by the Falk Laws
drowned between midnight
and morning of Dec. 7th, 1875

PART THE FIRST

1

Thou mastering me
God! giver of breath and bread;
World's strand, sway of the sea;
Lord of living and dead;
Thou hast bound bones and veins in me, fastened me
flesh,
And after it almost unmade, what with dread,
Thy doing: and dost thou touch me afresh?
Over again I feel thy finger and find thee.

2

I did say yes
O at lightning and lashed rod;
Thou heardst me truer than tongue confess   10

The Wreck of the Deutschland. **Falk Laws.** Paul Falk (1827-
1898), as Minister of Worship and Instruction in Germany, closed all
monasteries in Prussia in May 1875 and expelled all members of religious orders from the country, except those who cared for the sick. The
act was part of a bitter conflict between the government and the Catholic
Church in Germany.

Thy terror, O Christ, O God;
Thou knowest the walls, altar and hour and night:
The swoon of a heart that the sweep and the hurl of
thee trod
Hard down with a horror of height:
And the midriff astrain with leaning of, laced with fire
of stress.

3

The frown of his face
Before me, the hurtle of hell
Behind, where, where was a, where was a place?
I whirled out wings that spell
And fled with a fling of the heart to the heart of the
Host.
My heart, but you were dovewinged, I can tell,
Carrier-witted, I am bold to boast,
To flash from the flame to the flame then, tower from
the grace to the grace.

4

I am soft sift
In an hourglass—at the wall
Fast, but mined with a motion, a drift,
And it crowds and it combs to the fall;
I steady as a water in a well, to a poise, to a pane,
But roped with, always, all the way down from the
tall
Fells or flanks of the voel, a vein
Of the gospel proffer, a pressure, a principle, Christ's
gift.

5

I kiss my hand
To the stars, lovely-asunder
Starlight, wafting him out of it; and
Glow, glory in thunder;
Kiss my hand to the dappled-with-damson west:
Since, tho' he is under the world's splendour and
wonder,
His mystery must be instressed, stressed;
For I greet him the days I meet him, and bless when I
understand.

6

Not out of his bliss
Springs the stress felt
Nor first from heaven (and few know this)
Swings the stroke dealt—
Stroke and a stress that stars and storms deliver,

That guilt is hushed by, hearts are flushed by and
melt—
But it rides time like riding a river
(And here the faithful waver, the faithless fable and
miss).

7

It dates from day
Of his going in Galilee;
Warm-laid grave of a womb-life grey;
Manger, maiden's knee;
The dense and the driven Passion, and frightful
sweat;
Thence the discharge of it, there its swelling to be,
Though felt before, though in high flood yet—
What none would have known of it, only the heart,
being hard at bay,

8

Is out with it! Oh,
We lash with the best or worst
Word last! How a lush-kept plush-capped sloe
Will, mouthed to flesh-burst,
Gush!—flush the man, the being with it, sour or
sweet,
Brim, in a flash, full!—Hither then, last or first,
To hero of Calvary, Christ,'s feet—
Never ask if meaning it, wanting it, warned of it—
men go.

9

Be adored among men,
God, three-numberèd form;
Wring thy rebel, dogged in den,
Man's malice, with wrecking and storm.
Beyond saying sweet, past telling of tongue,
Thou art lightning and love, I found it, a winter and
warm;
Father and fondler of heart thou hast wrung:
Hast thy dark descending and most art merciful then.

10

With an anvil-ding
And with fire in him forge thy will
Or rather, rather then, stealing as Spring
Through him, melt him but master him still:
Whether at once, as once at a crash Paul,
Or as Austin, a lingering-out swéet skíll,
Make mercy in all of us, out of us all
Mastery, but be adored, but be adored King.

11

'Some find me a sword; some
The flange and the rail; flame,
Fang, or flood' goes Death on drum,
And storms bugle his fame.
But wé dream we are rooted in earth—Dust!
Flesh falls within sight of us, we, though our flower
the same,
Wave with the meadow, forget that there must
The sour scythe cringe, and the blear share come.

12

On Saturday sailed from Bremen,
90   American-outward-bound,
Take settler and seamen, tell men with women,
Two hundred souls in the round—
O Father, not under thy feathers nor ever as guessing
The goal was a shoal, of a fourth the doom to be
drowned;
Yet did the dark side of the bay of thy blessing
Not vault them, the millions of rounds of thy mercy
not reeve even them in?

13

Into the snows she sweeps,
Hurling the haven behind,
The Deutschland, on Sunday; and so the sky
keeps,
100   For the infinite air is unkind,
And the sea flint-flake, black-backed in the regular
blow,
Sitting Eastnortheast, in cursed quarter, the wind;
Wiry and white-fiery and whirlwind-swivellèd
snow
Spins to the widow-making unchilding unfathering
deeps.

14

She drove in the dark to leeward,
She struck—not a reef or a rock
But the combs of a smother of sand: night drew her
Dead to the Kentish Knock;
And she beat the bank down with her bows and the
ride of her keel:
110   The breakers rolled on her beam with ruinous shock;
And canvas and compass, the whorl and the wheel
Idle for ever to waft her or wind her with, these she
endured.

15

Hope had grown grey hairs,
Hope had mourning on,
Trenched with tears, carved with cares,
Hope was twelve hours gone;
And frightful a nightfall folded rueful a day
Nor rescue, only rocket and lightship, shone,
And lives at last were washing away:
To the shrouds they took,—they shook in the hurling
and horrible airs.   120

16

One stirred from the rigging to save
The wild woman-kind below,
With a rope's end round the man, handy and
brave—
He was pitched to his death at a blow,
For all his dreadnought breast and braids of thew:
They could tell him for hours, dandled the to and fro
Through the cobbled foam-fleece, what could he do
With the burl of the fountains of air, buck and the
flood of the wave?

17

They fought with God's cold—
And they could not and fell to the deck   130
(Crushed them) or water (and drowned them) or
rolled
With the sea-romp over the wreck.
Night roared, with the heart-break hearing a
heart-broke rabble,
The woman's wailing, the crying of child without
check—
Till a lioness arose breasting the babble,
A prophetess towered in the tumult, a virginal tongue
told.

18

Ah, touched in your bower of bone
Are you! turned for an exquisite smart,
Have you! make words break from me here all
alone,
Do you!—mother of being in me, heart.   140
O unteachably after evil, but uttering truth;
Why, tears! is it? tears, such a melting, a madrigal
start!
Never-eldering revel and river of youth,
What can it be, this glee? the good you have there of
your own?

the ground at the bottom of the furrow. 91. **tell,** count. 96. **reeve,**
fasten them in, as with a rope. 107. **combs,** ridges. 108. **Kentish
Knock,** a sandbank near the mouth of the Thames River. 111. **whorl,**
propeller. 125. **thew,** muscle. 128. **burl,** fullness. **buck,** bucking,
plunging. 141. **after,** make after. 142. **madrigal,** used here with
reference to the joyous quality of most Elizabethan madrigals; hence,
joyful.

Gerard Manley Hopkins 1175

19

Sister, a sister calling
A master, her master and mine!—
And the inboard seas run swirling and hawling;
The rash smart sloggering brine
Blinds her; but she that weather sees one thing, one;
150 Has one fetch in her: she rears herself to divine
Ears, and the call of the tall nun
To the men in the tops and the tackle rode over the
storm's brawling.

20

She was first of a five and came
Of a coifèd sisterhood.
(O Deutschland, double a desperate name!
O world wide of its good!
But Gertrude, lily, and Luther, are two of a town,
Christ's lily and beast of the waste wood:
From life's dawn it is drawn down,
Abel is Cain's brother and breasts they have sucked
160 the same.)

21

Loathed for a love men knew in them,
Banned by the land of their birth,
Rhine refused them. Thames would ruin them;
Surf, snow, river, and earth
Gnashed: but thou art above, thou Orion of light;
Thy unchancelling poising palms were weighing the
worth,
Thou martyr-master: in thy sight
Storm flakes were scroll-leaved flowers, lily showers—
sweet heaven was astrew in them.

22

Five! the finding and sake
170 And cipher of suffering Christ,
Mark, the mark is of man's make
And the word of it Sacrificed.
But he scores it in scarlet himself on his own
bespoken,
Before-time-taken, dearest prizèd and priced—
Stigma, signal, cinquefoil token
For lettering of the lamb's fleece, ruddying of the
rose-flake.

23

Joy fall to thee, father Francis,
Drawn to the Life that died;
With the gnarls of the nails in thee, niche of the
lance, his
Lovescape crucified 180
And seal of his seraph-arrival! and these thy
daughters
And five-livèd and leavèd favour and pride,
Are sisterly sealed in wild waters,
To bathe in his fall-gold mercies, to breathe in his
all-fire glances.

24

Away in the loveable west,
On a pastoral forehead of Wales,
I was under a roof here, I was at rest,
And they the prey of the gales;
She to the black-about air, to the breaker, the
thickly
Falling flakes, to the throng that catches and quails 190
Was calling 'O Christ, Christ, come quickly':
The cross to her she calls Christ to her, christens her
wild-worst Best.

25

The majesty! what did she mean?
Breathe, arch and original Breath.
Is it love in her of the being as her lover had been?
Breathe, body of lovely Death.
They were else-minded then, altogether, the men
Woke thee with a *we are perishing* in the weather of
Gennesareth.
Or is it that she cried for the crown then,
The keener to come at the comfort for feeling the
combating keen? 200

26

For how to the heart's cheering
The down-dugged ground-hugged grey
Hovers off, the jay-blue heavens appearing
Of pied and peeled May!
Blue-beating and hoary-glow height; or night, still
higher,

---

147. **hawling,** an onomatopoetic coinage. 150. **fetch,** stratagem, device. 156. **wide . . . good,** unfriendly to what is good for it. 157. **Gertrude,** a German mystic and saint (1256?–1302?) who lived in a convent near Eisleben, birthplace of Martin Luther (1483–1546). Her visions are recorded in her *Insinuations,* published in 1662. Luther, the great Protestant leader ("beast of the waste wood," l. 158) was excommunicated in 1520 for denying the supremacy of the Pope. 160. **Abel . . . the same.** Abel and his brother and murderer Cain were both suckled by Eve; see Genesis 4:1-12. 161. **them,** the five nuns (ll. 153-154). 165. **Orion,** in classical mythology, a famous hunter of huge size; after his death he became perhaps the most famous of winter constellations in the northern hemisphere. The thought here seems to be that God, as a hunter, drove the nuns from their formerly safe place in Germany so that their bravery and devotion might be tested. 166. **unchan-** celling, not canceling, not revoking. 169. **finding,** mark or device. The poet calls attention to the fact that the number of nuns, five, corresponds to the Five Wounds of Christ. 175. **cinquefoil,** a decorative design having five points. 177. **Francis,** St. Francis of Assisi (1181?–1226), founder of the Franciscan order, to which the nuns belonged. 180. **Lovescape,** the pattern of the Five Wounds of Christ, which was the stigma on the body of St. Francis. 182. **five . . . leavèd,** a further reference to the cinquefoil (l. 175). 186. **pastoral forehead,** St. Bruno's College, located on a hill in the Vale of Clywd, in northern Wales. 192. **The cross to her.** She identifies her own suffering with that of Christ on the Cross. 194. **arch,** chief. 198. **weather of Gennesareth.** When the disciples in a ship on the Lake of Gennesareth were frightened by a heavy storm, Jesus astonished them by walking to them on the water and calming the waves and winds.

With belled fire and the moth-soft Milky Way,
What by your measure is the heaven of desire,
The treasure never eyesight got, nor was ever guessed
what for the hearing?

27

No, but it was not these.
210   The jading and jar of the cart,
Time's tasking, it is fathers that asking for ease
Of the sodden-with-its-sorrowing heart,
Not danger, electrical horror; then further it finds
The appealing of the Passion is tenderer in prayer
apart:
Other, I gather, in measure her mind's
Burden, in wind's burly and beat of endragonèd seas.

28

But how shall I . . . make me room there:
Reach me a . . . Fancy, come faster—
Strike you the sight of it? look at it loom there,
220   Thing that she . . . there then! the Master,
Ipse, the only one, Christ, King, Head:
He was to cure the extremity where he had cast her;
Do, deal, lord it with living and dead;
Let him ride, her pride, in his triumph, despatch and
have done with his doom there.

29

Ah! there was a heart right
There was single eye!
Read the unshapeable shock night
And knew the who and the why;
Wording it how but by him that present and past,
230   Heaven and earth are word of, worded by?—
The Simon Peter of a soul! to the blast
Tarpeian-fast, but a blown beacon of light.

30

Jesu, heart's light,
Jesu, maid's son,
What was the feast followed the night
Thou hadst glory of this nun?—
Feast of the one woman without stain.
For so conceivèd, so to conceive thee is done;

But here was heart-throe, birth of a brain,
Word, that heard and kept thee and uttered thee
outright.   240

31

Well, she has thee for the pain, for the
Patience; but pity of the rest of them!
Heart, go and bleed at a bitterer vein for the
Comfortless unconfessed of them—
No not uncomforted: lovely-felicitous Providence
Finger of a tender of, O of a feathery delicacy, the
breast of the
Maiden could obey so, be a bell to, ring of it, and
Startle the poor sheep back! is the shipwrack then a
harvest, does tempest carry the grain for thee?

32

I admire thee, master of the tides,
Of the Yore-flood, of the year's fall,   250
The recurb and the recovery of the gulf's sides,
The girth of it and the wharf of it and the wall;
Stanching, quenching ocean of a motionable mind;
Ground of being, and granite of it: past all
Grasp God, throned behind
Death with a sovereignty that heeds but hides, bodes
but abides;

33

With a mercy that outrides
The all of water, an ark
For the listener; for the lingerer with a love glides
Lower than death and the dark;   260
A vein for the visiting of the past-prayer, pent in
prison,
The-last-breath penitent spirits—the uttermost mark
Our passion-plungèd giant risen,
The Christ of the Father compassionate, fetched in the
storm of his strides.

34

Now burn, new born to the world,
Double-naturèd name,
The heaven-flung, heart-fleshed, maiden-furled
Miracle-in-Mary-of-flame,

The lake is better known as the Sea of Galilee. See Matthew, 14:22-34.
200. **come at**, attain, reach. 208. **treasure . . . hearing.** "Eye hath
not seen, nor ear heard, neither have entered into the heart of man, the
things which God hath prepared for them that love him"—1 Corinthians 2:9. 216. **burly**, bluster. 221. **Ipse**, Himself. 226. **single
eye.** "The light of the body is the eye; if therefore thine eye be single,
thy whole body shall be full of light"—Matthew 6:22. 231-232. **The
Simon . . . light.** The references here are to the personal qualities of
the nun—her steadfast devotion, her fear, and her surpassing example
to her doomed fellow passengers. Peter, one of Christ's twelve apostles,
was originally called Simon, but Jesus, having in mind his solid, steadfast character, changed his name to Peter ("rock"), saying: "Thou art
Peter, and upon this rock I will build my church"—Matthew 16:18.
Tarpeia is a famous peaklike rock on the Capitoline Hill in ancient
Rome, named after Tarpeia, who was hurled from it because she was
a traitor. 237. **Feast . . . stain**, the Feast of the Immaculate Conception of the Blessed Virgin Mary, which comes on December 8 (the day
following the disaster of the *Deutschland*). 238. **For so . . . done.**
The nun is also a virgin, like Mary. 250. **Yoreflood**, Noah's flood, the
Deluge; see Genesis 6-8. 251. **recurb . . . sides**, the stemming and
restemming of the waves and flood. "Or who shut up the sea with
doors, when it brake forth, as if it had issued out of the womb?"—Job
38:8. 252. **wharf . . . wall**, the restraining factors. 254. **granite.**
The restless human mind finds peace only in the granite of God. 256.
bodes, portends. 264. **fetched.** The subject is *giant* (l. 263).

Mid-numbered He in three of the thunder-throne!
Not a dooms-day dazzle in his coming nor dark as
270   he came;
    Kind, but royally reclaiming his own;
A released shower, let flash to the shire, not a lightning
    of fire hard-hurled.

35

    Dame, at our door
    Drowned, and among our shoals,
    Remember us in the roads, the heaven-haven of
        the Reward:
    Our King back, oh, upon English souls!
Let him easter in us, be a dayspring to the dimness
    of us, be a crimson-cresseted east,
More brightening her, rare-dear Britain, as his reign
    rolls,
    Pride, rose, prince, hero of us, high-priest,
280 Our hearts' charity's hearth's fire, our thoughts'
    chivalry's throng's Lord.
(1876–1889; 1918)

GOD'S GRANDEUR

The world is charged with the grandeur of God.
    It will flame out, like shining from shook foil;
    It gathers to a greatness, like the ooze of oil
Crushed. Why do men then now not reck his rod?
Generations have trod, have trod, have trod;
    And all is seared with trade; bleared, smeared with
        toil;
    And wears man's smudge and shares man's smell:
        the soil
Is bare now, nor can foot feel, being shod.

And for all this, nature is never spent;
10   There lives the dearest freshness deep down things;
And though the last lights off the black West went,
    Oh, morning, at the brown brink eastward, springs—
Because the Holy Ghost over the bent
    World broods with warm breast and with ah! bright
        wings.
(1877; 1918)

THE STARLIGHT NIGHT

Look at the stars! look, look up at the skies!
    O look at all the fire-folk sitting in the air!
    The bright boroughs, the circle-citadels there!
Down in dim woods the diamond delves! the elves'-
    eyes!
The gray lawns cold where gold, where quick-gold lies!

Wind-beat white-beam! airy abeles set on a flare!
Flake-doves sent floating forth at a farmyard scare!—
Ah well! it is all a purchase, all is a prize.
Buy then! bid then!—What?—Prayer, patience, alms,
    vows.
Look, look: a May-mess, like on orchard boughs!   10
    Look! March-bloom, like on mealed-with-yellow
        sallows!
These are indeed the barn; withindoors house
The shocks. This piece-bright paling shuts the Spouse
    Christ home, Christ and his mother and all his
        hallows.
(1877; 1918)

THE SEA AND THE SKYLARK

On ear and ear two noises too old to end
    Trench—right, the tide that ramps against the shore;
    With a flood or a fall, low lull-off or all roar,
Frequenting there while moon shall wear and wend.

Left hand, off land, I hear the lark ascend,
    His rash-fresh re-winded new-skeinèd score
    In crisps of curl off wild winch whirl, and pour
And pelt music, till none's to spill nor spend.

How these two shame this shallow and frail town!
    How ring right out our sordid turbid time,   10
Being pure! We, life's pride and cared-for crown,

    Have lost that cheer and charm of earth's past prime:
Our make and making break, are breaking, down
    To man's last dust, drain fast toward man's first
        slime.
(1877; 1918)

THE WINDHOVER

TO CHRIST OUR LORD

I caught this morning morning's minion, king-
    dom of daylight's dauphin, dapple-dawn-drawn
        Falcon, in his riding
    Of the rolling level underneath him steady air, and
        striding
High there, how he rung upon the rein of a wimpling
        wing
In his ecstasy! then off, off forth on a swing,
    As a skate's heel sweeps smooth on a bow-bend:
        the hurl and gliding
    Rebuffed the big wind. My heart in hiding
Stirred for a bird—the achieve of, the mastery of the
        thing!

269. **Mid-numbered He,** Christ, the second in the formula, "the Father, the Son, and the Holy Ghost." 272. **shire,** region.
  The Starlight Night. 5. **gold,** dewdrops. 6. **white-beam,** a small tree with leaves white on the underside. **abeles,** white poplars. 10. **May-mess,** medley of blossoms in May. 11. **mealed . . . sallows,** willows stained with yellow pollen. 13. **shocks,** leaves. 14. **hallows,** saints.

  The Windhover. The windhover is a kestrel, or sparrow hawk. Hopkins regarded this as his best poem, therefore he dedicated it to Christ; but this does not mean that the windhover is a symbol of Christ. 11. **sillion,** the ridge between two furrows of plowed land.
  Pied Beauty. 3. **stipple,** a method in painting of applying colors in dots. 4. **chestnut-falls,** chestnuts newly stripped of their husks. 5.

Brute beauty and valor and act, oh, air, pride, plume,
   here
    Buckle! AND the fire that breaks from thee then, a
    billion
10 Times told lovelier, more dangerous, O my chevalier!

    No wonder of it: shéer plód makes plow down
    sillion
Shine, and blue-bleak embers, ah, my dear,
   Fall, gall themselves, and gash gold-vermilion.
(1877; 1918)

PIED BEAUTY

Glory be to God for dappled things—
   For skies of couple-color as a brinded cow;
    For rose-moles all in stipple upon trout that swim;
Fresh-firecoal chestnut-falls; finches' wings;
   Landscape plotted and pieced—fold, fallow, and
    plow;
    And all trades, their gear and tackle and trim.

All things counter, original, spare, strange;
   Whatever is fickle, freckled (who knows how?)
    With swift, slow; sweet, sour; adazzle, dim;
10 He fathers-forth whose beauty is past change:
    Praise him.
(1877; 1918)

PEACE

When will you ever, Peace, wild wood-dove, shy wings
   shut,
Your round me roaming end, and under be my boughs?
When, when, Peace, will you, Peace? I'll not play
   hypocrite
To own my heart: I yield you do come sometimes; but
That piecemeal peace is poor peace. What pure peace
   allows
Alarms of wars, the daunting wars, the death of it?

O surely, reaving Peace, my Lord should leave in
   lieu
Some good! And so he does leave Patience exquisite,
That plumes to Peace thereafter. And when Peace here
   does house,
10 He comes with work to do, he does not come to coo,
   He comes to brood and sit.
(1879; 1918)

FELIX RANDAL

Felix Randal the farrier, O he is dead then? my duty
   all ended,
Who have watched his mold of man, big-boned and
   hardy-handsome
Pining, pining, till time when season rambled in it and
   some
Fatal four disorders, fleshed there, all contended?

Sickness broke him. Impatient he cursed at first, but
   mended
Being anointed and all; though a heavenlier heart began
   some
Months earlier, since I had our sweet reprieve and
   ransom
Tendered to him. Ah, well, God rest him all road ever
   he offended!

This seeing the sick endears them to us, us too it en-
   dears.
My tongue had taught thee comfort, touch had
   quenched thy tears,   10
Thy tears that touched my heart, child, Felix, poor
   Felix Randal;

How far from then forethought of, all thy more boisterous years,
When thou at the random grim forge, powerful amidst
   peers,
Didst fettle for the great gray drayhorse his bright and
   battering sandal!
(1880; 1918)

SPRING AND FALL

TO A YOUNG CHILD

Márgarét, are you gríeving
Over Goldengrove unleaving?
Leáves, líke the things of man, you
With your fresh thoughts care for, can you?
Ah! ás the heart grows older
It will come to such sights colder
By and by, nor spare a sigh
Though worlds of wanwood leafmeal lie;
And yet you wíll weep and know why.
Now no matter, child, the name: 10
Sórrow's spríngs áre the same,
Nor mouth had, no nor mind, expressed
What heart heard of, ghost guessed:

---

plotted and pieced, divided into fields. 6. trim, equipment. 7. counter, contrary to what is expected. spare, rare. 10. whose beauty . . .
change. Cf. James 1:17—"Every good gift and every perfect gift is
from above, and cometh down from the Father of lights, with whom is
no variableness, neither shadow of turning."
   Peace. 4. To own my heart, to my own heart. 7. reaving Peace,

when he takes peace away.
   Felix Randal. 1. farrier, blacksmith. 14. fettle, make ready.
   Spring and Fall. 8. leafmeal, powder covering the surface of leaves.

It ís the blight man was born for,
It is Margaret you mourn for.
(1880; 1918)

INVERSNAID

This darksome burn, horseback brown,
His rollrock highroad roaring down,
In coop and in comb the fleece of his foam
Flutes and low to the lake falls home.

A windpuff-bonnet of fáwn-fróth
Turns and twindles over the broth
Of a pool so pitchblack, féll-frówning,
It rounds and rounds Despair to drowning.

Degged with dew, dappled with dew
Are the groins of the braes that the brook treads
10   through,
Wiry heathpacks, flitches of fern,
And the beadbonny ash that sits over the burn.

What would the world be, once bereft
Of wet and of wildness? Let them be left,
Oh, let them be left, wildness and wet;
Long live the weeds and the wilderness yet.
(1881; 1918)

CARRION COMFORT

Not, I'll not, carrion comfort, Despair, not feast on
    thee;
Not untwist—slack they may be—these last strands of
    man
In me ór, most weary, cry *I can no more.* I can;
Can something, hope, wish day come, not choose not
    to be.
But ah, but O thou terrible, why wouldst thou rude on
    me
Thy wring-world right foot rock? lay a lion-limb
    against me? scan
With darksome devouring eyes my bruiséd bones? and
    fan,
O in turns of tempest, me heaped there; me frantic to
    avoid thee and flee?

    Why? That my chaff might fly; my grain lie, sheer
    and clear.
Nay in all that toil, that coil, since (seems) I kissed
10   the rod,

Hand rather, my heart lo! lapped strength, stole joy,
    would laugh, chéer.
Cheer whom though? the hero whose heaven-handling
    flung me, fóot tród
Me? or me that fought him? O which one? is it each
    one? That night, that year
Of now done darkness I wretch lay wrestling with (my
    God!) my God.
(c. 1886; 1918)

I WAKE AND FEEL THE FELL OF DARK

I wake and feel the fell of dark, not day.
What hours, O what black hoùrs we have spent
This night! what sights you, heart, saw; ways you
    went!
And more must, in yet longer light's delay.
    With witness I speak this. But where I say
Hours I mean years, mean life. And my lament
Is cries countless, cries like dead letters sent
To dearest him that lives alas! away.

    I am gall, I am heartburn. God's most deep decree
Bitter would have me taste: my taste was me;   10
Bones built in me, flesh filled, blood brimmed the
    curse.
    Selfyeast of spirit a dull dough sours. I see
The lost are like this, and their scourge to be
As I am mine, their sweating selves; but worse.
(c. 1886; 1918)

TO R. B.

The fine delight that fathers thought; the strong
Spur, live and lancing like the blowpipe flame,
Breathes once and, quenchéd faster than it came,
Leaves yet the mind a mother of immortal song.
Nine months she then, nay years, nine years she long
Within her wears, bears, cares, and molds the
    same:
The widow of an insight lost she lives, with aim
Now known and hand at work now never wrong.
    Sweet fire the sire of muse, my soul needs this;
I want the one rapture of an inspiration.   10
O then if in my lagging lines you miss
The roll, the rise, the carol, the creation,
My winter world, that scarcely breathes that
    bliss
Now, yields you, with some sighs, our explanation.
(1889; 1918)

Inversnaid. Inversnaid is a hamlet on the east shore of Loch Lomond, Scotland. Cf. Wordsworth's *To a Highland Girl* (p. 697). 1. **burn,** brook. 3. **coop,** hollow place between ridges of waves (combs). 4. **Flutes,** forms streaks or channels. 6. **twindles,** twists. 9. **Degged,** dampened. 10. **braes,** hillsides. 11. **heathpacks,** clumps of heather. **flitches,** patches.
To R.B. A poem addressed to Robert Bridges.

THOMAS HARDY 1840-1928

Thomas Hardy was born in Dorsetshire, in the southwest of England, the famous "Wessex" country which he used as the background for so much of his fiction and poetry. While apprenticed to a local architect, he put much of his spare time into the study of Latin and Greek and became acquainted with William Barnes (1800-1886), a local dialect poet of considerable merit, who stimulated in Hardy the love of literature. He actively followed the profession of architect as a junior assistant to Sir Arthur Blomfield in London, enjoying the opportunities of the city for art and literature, and at the same time winning two prizes for architectural design. He inaugurated his distinguished career with Desperate Remedies *(1871), the first of a series of fourteen novels which, over the next quarter-century, established Hardy as a front-rank writer of fiction and allowed him to give up architecture and rely on his pen. According to Hardy's own classification, three—* Desperate Remedies, The Hand of Ethelberta *(1876), and* A Laodicean *(1882)—were novels of ingenuity (with emphasis upon plot); four—* A Pair of Blue Eyes *(1873),* The Trumpet-Major *(1880),* Two on a Tower *(1882), and* The Well-Beloved *(an early tale not published until 1897)—were romances or fantasies; and the remaining seven, easily his best, were novels of character and environment—* Under the Greenwood Tree *(1872),* Far from the Madding Crowd *(1874),* The Return of the Native *(1878),* The Mayor of Casterbridge *(1886),* The Woodlanders *(1887),* Tess of the d'Urbervilles *(1891), and* Jude the Obscure *(1896).*

Hardy's novels of "character and environment" belong clearly to the realistic school; indeed, in the last of them, Jude the Obscure, *one of the most powerful novels in the English language, he attained a masterpiece of naturalism. The reception of this novel by the English and American public, which has never taken too kindly to naturalism, was so hostile that he completely abandoned the writing of novels and gave himself, during the remaining thirty years of his life, to the composition of poetry. All of his novels of major importance present the losing struggle of individuals against the twin pressures of nature and social forces, which gradually destroy them. Working behind these invincible forces is the vast and imponderable hand of Fate, achieving its effects cruelly and pitilessly, with results which, considering the ideals and ambitions of the human soul, are nothing less than cosmically ironical. More than that, this Fate (or Chance, or*

Hap, or Casualty, as he calls it) is a sinister force comparable in most respects to the Nemesis of Greek tragedy; and such is Hardy's power in his delineation of the operation of this force that he can awaken in the reader the same pity and terror evoked by a drama of Sophocles. There are in these novels, as well as in Hardy's poetry, a strong surface tendency toward melodrama and a "contriving" of incident, as well as a marvelous ability to describe the English peasant and country-dweller, in which last respect he is almost unequaled in English literature. On the whole, Hardy is impartial, although he is fascinated always by the way in which great effects grow from small causes. To him a second of time can make the whole difference in a human life.

Hardy actually took the novel for his medium because his earlier poetic writings were not readily published; then, after the success of his novels, he turned more and more to the writing of poetry. Wessex Poems *appeared in 1898;* Poems of the Past and Present *in 1902;* Time's Laughingstocks *in 1909;* Satires of Circumstance *in 1914;* Moments of Vision *in 1917; many miscellaneous small volumes along the way; and a final collection in 1928, the year of his death. There were also a few collections of short tales, notably* Wessex Tales *(1888) and* Life's Little Ironies *(1894). But, aside from his lyrical poetry, Hardy's greatest work in the latter half of his career—a most distinguished performance—is the enormous poetic drama,* The Dynasts *(1903-1908), on the subject of the Napoleonic Wars and their impact upon England. An interesting venture, successful in reading but not in dramaturgy, is the drama,* The Queen of Cornwall *(1923), based upon the medieval romance of Tristan and Isoude.*

It is still rather doubtful whether Hardy's reputation will rest ultimately upon his poetry or his novels, for both are remarkable contributions. They both contain the same philosophy and are couched in similar styles—plain, rather old-fashioned, with a wealth of attention to Anglo-Saxon words, phrases, and folklore, gritty and often rather awkward in expression, but inevitably strong. Much of his work in both prose and verse is satirical; and if not purely satirical, often inclined to point up the irony of a situation. In all of his works Hardy's general attitude may strike the reader as one of pessimism. He even tends to rub his characters' noses in the dirt; yet a closer reading reveals that he is what he says he is—a "meliorist," one who hoped that the world could be made better but was not confident. Even so, the optimist, the man with "robustious swaggering of optimism . . . at bottom cowardly and insincere," was his special enemy, for he believed that there could be no swing toward good without a full knowledge of what was evil.

HAP

If but some vengeful god would call to me
From up the sky, and laugh: "Thou suffering thing,
Know that thy sorrow is my ecstasy,
That thy love's loss is my hate's profiting!"

Then would I bear it, clench myself, and die,
Steeled by the sense of ire unmerited;
Half-eased in that a Powerfuller than I
Had willed and meted me the tears I shed.

But not so. How arrives it joy lies slain,
10 And why unblooms the best hope ever sown?—
Crass Casualty obstructs the sun and rain,
And dicing Time for gladness casts a moan. . . .
These purblind Doomsters had as readily strown
Blisses about my pilgrimage as pain.   (1866; 1898)

NEUTRAL TONES

We stood by a pond that winter day,
And the sun was white, as though chidden of God,
And a few leaves lay on the starving sod;
          —They had fallen from an ash, and were gray.

Your eyes on me were as eyes that rove
Over tedious riddles of years ago;
And some words played between us to and fro
          On which lost the more by our love.

The smile on your mouth was the deadest thing
10 Alive enough to have strength to die;
And a grin of bitterness swept thereby
          Like an ominous bird a-wing. . . .

Since then, keen lessons that love deceives
And wrings with wrong, have shaped to me
Your face, and the God-curst sun, and a tree,
          And a pond edged with grayish leaves.
(1867; 1898)

DRUMMER HODGE

The background of this poem is the Boer War, waged in South Africa in 1899-1902 between the British and the Dutch settlers.

They throw in Drummer Hodge, to rest
     Uncoffined—just as found:

His landmark is a kopje-crest
     That breaks the veldt around;
And foreign constellations west
     Each night above his mound.

Young Hodge the Drummer never knew—
     Fresh from his Wessex home—
The meaning of the broad Karoo,
     The Bush, the dusty loam,   10
And why uprose to nightly view
     Strange stars amid the gloam.

Yet portion of that unknown plain
     Will Hodge forever be;
His homely Northern breast and brain
     Grow to some Southern tree,
And strange-eyed constellations reign
     His stars eternally.
(1899; 1902)

THE DARKLING THRUSH

I leant upon a coppice gate
     When Frost was specter-gray,
And Winter's dregs made desolate
     The weakening eye of day.
The tangled bine-stems scored the sky
     Like strings of broken lyres,
And all mankind that haunted nigh
     Had sought their household fires.

The land's sharp features seemed to be
     The Century's corpse outleant,   10
His crypt the cloudy canopy,
     The wind his death lament.
The ancient pulse of germ and birth
     Was shrunken hard and dry,
And every spirit upon earth
     Seemed fervorless as I.

At once a voice arose among
     The bleak twigs overhead
In a full-hearted evensong
     Of joy illimited;   20
An aged thrush, frail, gaunt, and small,
     In blast-beruffled plume,

Hap, Neutral Tones, Drummer Hodge, and *The Darkling Thrush* are from *Collected Poems* by Thomas Hardy. Reprinted by permission of The Macmillan Company, the Hardy Estate, and The Macmillan Company of Canada, Limited.
Drummer Hodge. 3. **kopje-crest,** the top of a small hill. 4. **veldt,** pronounced *felt,* a tract of grassland; cf. the Modern English *field* and German *Feld.* 9. **Karoo,** a dry, elevated region in Cape Colony. 10. **Bush,** a vast area of scrub-covered country.
The Darkling Thrush. 1. **coppice gate,** a gate leading into a thicket. 5. **bine,** a kind of climbing plant. 10. **Century's corpse,** the dead body

Had chosen thus to fling his soul
   Upon the growing gloom.

So little cause for carolings
   Of such ecstatic sound
Was written on terrestrial things
   Afar or nigh around,
That I could think there trembled through
30 His happy good-night air
Some blessed Hope, whereof he knew
   And I was unaware.
(1900; 1900)

GOD-FORGOTTEN

I towered far, and lo! I stood within
The presence of the Lord Most High,
Sent thither by the sons of Earth, to win
   Some answer to their cry.

—"The Earth, sayest thou? The Human race?
By Me created? Sad its lot?
Nay: I have no remembrance of such place:
   Such world I fashioned not."—

—"O Lord, forgive me when I say
10 Thou spakest the word and made it all."—
"The Earth of men—let me bethink me . . . Yea!
   I dimly do recall

"Some tiny sphere I built long back
(Mid millions of such shapes of mine)
So named . . . It perished, surely—not a wrack
   Remaining, or a sign?

"It lost my interest from the first,
My aims therefore succeeding ill;
Haply it died of doing as it durst?"—
20 "Lord, it existeth still."—

"Dark, then, its life! For not a cry
Of aught it bears do I now hear;
Of its own act the threads were snapt whereby
   Its plaints had reached mine ear.

"It used to ask for gifts of good,
Till came its severance, self-entailed,
When sudden silence on that side ensued,
   And has till now prevailed.

"All other orbs have kept in touch;
30 Their voicings reach me speedily:

Thy people took upon them overmuch
   In sundering them from me!

"And it is strange—though sad enough—
Earth's race should think that one whose call
Frames, daily, shining spheres of flawless stuff
   Must heed their tainted ball! . . .

"But sayest it is by pangs distraught,
And strife, and silent suffering?—
Sore grieved am I that injury should be wrought
   Even on so poor a thing!   40

"Thou shouldst have learnt that *Not to Mend*
For Me could mean but *Not to Know:*
Hence, Messengers! and straightway put an end
   To what men undergo." . . .

Homing at dawn, I thought to see
One of the Messengers standing by.
—Oh, childish thought! . . . Yet often it comes to
   me
When trouble hovers nigh.
(1902)

THE TO-BE-FORGOTTEN

   I heard a small sad sound,
And stood awhile among the tombs around.
"Wherefore, old friends," said I, "are you distrest,
   Now, screened from life's unrest?"

   —"Oh, not at being here;
But that our future second death is near;
When, with the living, memory of us numbs,
   And blank oblivion comes!

   "These, our sped ancestry,
Lie here embraced by deeper death than we;   10
Nor shape nor thought of theirs can you descry
   With keenest backward eye.

   "They count as quite forgot;
They are as men who have existed not;
Theirs is a loss past loss of fitful breath;
   It is the second death.

   "We here, as yet, each day
Are blest with dear recall; as yet, can say
We hold in some soul loved continuance
   Of shape and voice and glance.   20

of the nineteenth century. Note that this poem was composed late in
1900, the final year of the nineteenth century, and is in effect an elegy
on the passing of that era.
   God-Forgotten. 45. Homing . . . thought. In this stanza and, indeed, in the entire poem, the audacity of Hardy's irony is apparent.

There is in man's dialogue with the Almighty a bleak hopelessness that
would have been unthinkable to some of the earlier religious poets.
   God-Forgotten and *The To-Be-Forgotten* are from *Collected Poems* by
Thomas Hardy. Reprinted by permission of The Macmillan Company,
the Hardy Estate, and The Macmillan Company of Canada, Limited.

"But what has been will be—
First memory, then oblivion's swallowing sea;
Like men foregone, shall we merge into those
  Whose story no one knows.

"For which of us could hope
To show in life that world-awakening scope
Granted the few whose memory none lets die,
  But all men magnify?

"We were but Fortune's sport;
30 Things true, things lovely, things of good report
We neither shunned nor sought . . . We see our bourne,
  And seeing it we mourn."
  (1902)

THE MAN HE KILLED

"Had he and I but met
  By some old ancient inn,
We should have sat us down to wet
  Right many a nipperkin!

"But ranged as infantry,
  And staring face to face,
I shot at him as he at me,
  And killed him in his place.

"I shot him dead because—
10 Because he was my foe,
Just so—my foe of course he was;
  That's clear enough; although

"He thought he'd 'list, perhaps,
  Off-hand like—just as I—
Was out of work—had sold his traps—
  No other reason why.

"Yes; quaint and curious war is!
  You shoot a fellow down
You'd treat if met where any bar is,
20 Or help to half-a-crown."
  (1909)

"AH, ARE YOU DIGGING ON MY GRAVE?"

"Ah, are you digging on my grave
  My loved one?—planting rue?"
—"No; yesterday he went to wed

One of the brightest wealth has bred.
'It cannot hurt her now,' he said,
  'That I should not be true.' "

"Then who is digging on my grave?
  My nearest dearest kin?"
—"Ah, no; they sit and think, 'What use!
What good will planting flowers produce?   10
No tendance of her mound can loose
  Her spirit from Death's gin.' "

"But some one digs upon my grave?
  My enemy?—prodding sly?"
—"Nay; when she heard you had passed the Gate
That shuts on all flesh soon or late,
She thought you no more worth her hate,
  And cares not where you lie."

"Then, who is digging on my grave?
  Say—since I have not guessed!"   20
—"O it is I, my mistress dear,
Your little dog, who still lives near,
And much I hope my movements here
  Have not disturbed your rest?"

"Ah, yes! *You* dig upon my grave . . .
  Why flashed it not on me
That one true heart was left behind!
What feeling do we ever find
To equal among human kind
  A dog's fidelity!"   30

"Mistress, I dug upon your grave
  To bury a bone, in case
I should be hungry near this spot
When passing on my daily trot.
I am sorry, but I quite forgot
  It was your resting-place."
  (1914)

IN TIME OF "THE BREAKING
OF NATIONS"

Only a man harrowing clods
  In a slow silent walk,
With an old horse that stumbles and nods
  Half asleep as they stalk.

The To-Be-Forgotten. 30. **Things . . . sought.** See Philippians
4:8—"Finally, brethren, whatsoever things are true, whatsoever things
are honest, whatsoever things are just, whatsoever things are pure, whatsoever things are lovely, whatsoever things are of good report; if there
be any virtue, and if there be any praise, think on these things."
  The Man He Killed; "Ah, Are You Digging on My Grave?"; and In

Time of "The Breaking of Nations" are from *Collected Poems* by Thomas
Hardy. Reprinted by permission of The Macmillan Company, the Hardy
Estate, and The Macmillan Company of Canada, Limited.
  The Man He Killed. 4. **nipperkin,** a half pint of ale. 13. **'list,** en-
list in the army. 20. **half-a-crown,** an English silver coin worth about
sixty-three cents in Hardy's time.

Only thin smoke without flame
 From the heaps of couch grass:
Yet this will go onward the same
 Though Dynasties pass.

Yonder a maid and her wight
10 Come whispering by;
War's annals will fade into night
 Ere their story die.
(1915; 1917)

THE OXEN

*This poem crystallizes the widespread folk belief
that cattle fall on their knees at midnight of Christmas
Eve, in the same way that the ox did in the stable of
Bethlehem when Christ was born.*

Christmas Eve, and twelve of the clock.
 "Now they are all on their knees,"
An elder said as we sat in a flock
 By the embers in hearthside ease.

We pictured the meek mild creatures where
 They dwelt in their strawy pen,
Nor did it occur to one of us there
 To doubt they were kneeling then.

So fair a fancy few would weave
10 In these years! Yet, I feel,
If someone said on Christmas Eve,
 "Come; see the oxen kneel,

"In the lonely barton by yonder coomb
 Our childhood used to know,"
I should go with him in the gloom,
 Hoping it might be so.
(1915; 1917)

FOR LIFE I HAD NEVER CARED GREATLY

For life I had never cared greatly,
 As worth a man's while;
 Peradventures unsought,
 Peradventures that finished in nought,
Had kept me from youth and through manhood till
 lately
 Unwon by its style.

In earliest years—why I know not—
 I viewed it askance;
 Conditions of doubt,
Conditions that leaked slowly out,   10
May haply have bent me to stand and to show not
 Much zest for its dance.

With symphonies soft and sweet color
 It courted me then,
 Till evasions seemed wrong,
Till evasions gave in to its song,
And I warmed, until living aloofly loomed duller
 Than life among men.

Anew I found nought to set eyes on,
 When, lifting its hand,   20
 It uncloaked a star,
Uncloaked it from fog-damps afar,
And showed its beams burning from pole to horizon
 As bright as a brand.

And so, the rough highway forgetting,
 I pace hill and dale
 Regarding the sky,
Regarding the vision on high,
And thus re-illumed have no humor for letting
 My pilgrimage fail.   30
(1917)

THE CONVERGENCE OF THE TWAIN

(LINES ON THE LOSS OF THE "TITANIC")

*Shortly before midnight on the evening of April 14,
1912, the White Star liner Titanic, at the time the
largest ship in the world and supposedly "unsinkable,"
on her maiden voyage to New York rammed into an
iceberg in mid-Atlantic. A little less than three hours
later she sank, carrying to their deaths more than 1500
persons. It is still the greatest peacetime marine catastrophe in history. Hardy's poem, written in 1913 and
included in the Satires of Circumstance (1914) is undoubtedly the best work to have been inspired by the
disaster; the circumstances of the event fit beautifully
into his fatalistic philosophy.*

1

 In a solitude of the sea
 Deep from human vanity,
And the Pride of Life that planned her, stilly couches
 she.

"*Ah, Are You Digging on My Grave?*" 2. **rue,** an herb with bitter leaves; the symbol of sorrow. 12. **gin,** trap.
 In Time of "The Breaking of Nations." See Jeremiah 51:20—
"Thou art my battle ax and weapons of war: for with thee will I break
in pieces the nations, and with thee will I destroy kingdoms." 6. **couch
grass,** a kind of grass with long creeping rootstocks.

The Oxen, For Life I Had Never Cared Greatly, and *The Convergence
of the Twain* are from *Collected Poems* by Thomas Hardy. Reprinted by
permission of The Macmillan Company, the Hardy Estate, and The
Macmillan Company of Canada, Limited.
 The Oxen. 13. **barton,** farmyard. **coomb,** a valley between steep hills.
 The Convergence of the Twain. 6. **thrid,** pass through.

2

Steel chambers, late the pyres
Of her salamandrine fires,
Cold currents thrid, and turn to rhythmic tidal lyres.

3

Over the mirrors meant
To glass the opulent
The sea-worm crawls—grotesque, slimed, dumb,
   indifferent.

4

10   Jewels in joy designed
To ravish the sensuous mind
Lie lightless, all their sparkles bleared and black and
   blind.

5

Dim moon-eyed fishes near
Gaze at the gilded gear
And query: "What does this vaingloriousness down
   here?" . . .

6

Well: while was fashioning
This creature of cleaving wing,
The Immanent Will that stirs and urges everything

7

Prepared a sinister mate
20   For her—so gaily great—
A Shape of Ice, for the time far and dissociate.

8

And as the smart ship grew
In stature, grace, and hue,
In shadowy silent distance grew the Iceberg too.

9

Alien they seemed to be;
No mortal eye could see

The intimate welding of their later history,

10

Or sign that they were bent
By paths coincident
On being anon twin halves of one august event,   30

11

Till the Spinner of the Years
Said "Now!" And each one hears,
And consummation comes, and jars two hemispheres.
(1913; 1914)

SNOW IN THE SUBURBS

Every branch big with it,
   Bent every twig with it;
Every fork like a white web-foot;
Every street and pavement mute;
Some flakes have lost their way, and grope back
         upward, when
Meeting those meandering down they turn and
         descend again.
   The palings are glued together like a wall,
   And there is no waft of wind with the fleecy fall.

A sparrow enters the tree,
   Whereon immediately   10
A snow-lump thrice his own slight size
Descends on him and showers his head and eyes,

And overturns him,
   And near inurns him,
And lights on a nether twig, when its brush
Starts off a volley of other lodging lumps with a rush.

The steps are a blanched slope,
   Up which, with feeble hope,
A black cat comes, wide-eyed and thin;
   And we take him in.   20
(1925)

ALFRED EDWARD HOUSMAN 1859-1936

Alfred Edward Housman was born in Worcestershire, but he said that he had "a sentimental feeling for Shropshire because its hills were our western horizon." At Oxford, from 1877 to 1881, he attained success in classical studies, but his more ardent love of poetry probably accounted for his failure to pass the final examination. In 1882 he went to London where for ten years he held a post in the Patent Office; during that period many long evenings were spent in reading Latin and Greek in the British Museum. Published studies in the minor Latin poets resulted in his appointment in 1892 to a professorship in Latin in University College, London, and to a similar position at Cambridge in 1911. Between 1886 and 1905 Housman lived in Highgate, London, and it was there that he wrote A Shropshire Lad. Most of the poems were composed in 1895, during a great burst of creative activity, just prior to publication. The title was suggested by a friend, A. W. Pollard, in place of the less attractive Poems by Terence Hearsay. In an autobiographical note, Housman says: "The Shropshire Lad is an imaginary figure, with something of my temper and view of life. Very little in the book is autobiographical." It was not until 1922 that Housman's next book, Last Poems, appeared. He died in 1936, and in the autumn of the same year his final work, More Poems, was issued by his brother Laurence.

Although Housman lists his chief sources as Shakespeare's songs, the Scottish Border ballads, and the German poet Heine, his verse shows distinctly the result of his saturation in the poetry of the Latin lyrists; there is about it a clean-limbed economy and directness with nothing of the unrestrained decoration of so much romantic verse. The quality of meagerness, in fact, suggests that the poet is speaking in silences rather than expressions. The mood is pagan and melancholy, not to say pessimistic. There is a classical element in the reiteration of the suggestion that youth and spring and all things beautiful must come to dust and decay. But this Latin material is made to settle down securely on the English countryside in verse that is notably easy, felicitous, and poignant. Like Fitzgerald, Housman has attained high rank among English poets despite the meagerness of his output.

---

from A SHROPSHIRE LAD

2

Loveliest of trees, the cherry now
Is hung with bloom along the bough,
And stands about the woodland ride
Wearing white for Eastertide.

Now, of my threescore years and ten,
Twenty will not come again,
And take from seventy springs a score,
It only leaves me fifty more.

And since to look at things in bloom
10 Fifty springs are little room,
About the woodlands I will go
To see the cherry hung with snow.

4. REVEILLE

Wake! The silver dusk returning
　Up the beach of darkness brims,
And the ship of sunrise burning
　Strands upon the eastern rims.

Wake! The vaulted shadow shatters,
　Trampled to the floor it spanned,
And the tent of night in tatters
　Straws the sky-pavilioned land.

Up, lad, up! 'Tis late for lying.
　Hear the drums of morning play;   10
Hark, the empty highways crying,
　"Who'll beyond the hills away?"

Towns and countries woo together,
　Forelands beacon, belfries call;
Never lad that trod on leather
　Lived to feast his heart with all.

Up, lad; thews that lie and cumber
　Sunlit pallets never thrive;
Morns abed and daylight slumber
　Were not meant for man alive.   20

Clay lies still, but blood's a rover;
　Breath's a ware that will not keep.
Up, lad; when the journey's over
　There'll be time enough to sleep.

Lyric 4. 8. **Straws,** is strewn across.

The town of Ludlow and the River Teme, as seen from Whitcliffe.

5

Oh, see how thick the goldcup flowers
  Are lying in field and lane,
With dandelions to tell the hours
  That never are told again.
Oh, may I squire you round the meads
  And pick you posies gay?
—'Twill do no harm to take my arm.
  "You may, young man, you may."

Ah, spring was sent for lass and lad,
10 'Tis now the blood runs gold,
And man and maid had best be glad
  Before the world is old.

What flowers today may flower tomorrow,
  But never as good as new.
—Suppose I wound my arm right round—
  " 'Tis true, young man, 'tis true."

Some lads there are, 'tis shame to say,
  That only court to thieve,
And once they bear the bloom away
  'Tis little enough they leave.
Then keep your heart for men like me
  And safe from trustless chaps.   20
My love is true and all for you.
  "Perhaps, young man, perhaps."

Oh, look in my eyes then, can you doubt?

Lyric 5. 1. **goldcup flowers,** marsh marigolds. 3. **dandelions . . . hours,** is an old children's game to "tell time" by blowing the dandelion that has gone to seed and counting the seeds that fly away.

Lyric 7. 1. **Ludlow,** a town in Shropshire, on the River Teme (l. 2).
Lyric 8. 19. **Lammastide,** August 1. 21. **rick,** a stack of grain, straw, or hay.

—Why, 'tis a mile from town.
How green the grass is all about!
We might as well sit down.
—Ah, life, what is it but a flower?
30   Why must true lovers sigh?
Be kind, have pity, my own, my pretty—
"Good-by, young man, good-by."

7

When smoke stood up from Ludlow,
    And mist blew off from Teme,
And blithe afield to plowing
    Against the morning beam
    I strode beside my team,

The blackbird in the coppice
    Looked out to see me stride,
And hearkened as I whistled
    The trampling team beside,
10   And fluted and replied:

"Lie down, lie down, young yeoman;
    What use to rise and rise?
Rise man a thousand mornings
    Yet down at last he lies,
    And then the man is wise."

I heard the tune he sang me,
    And spied his yellow bill;
I picked a stone and aimed it
    And threw it with a will.
20   Then the bird was still.

Then my soul within me
    Took up the blackbird's strain,
And still beside the horses
    Along the dewy lane
    It sang the song again:

"Lie down, lie down, young yeoman;
    The sun moves always west;
The road one treads to labor
    Will lead one home to rest,
    And that will be the best."

8

"Farewell to barn and stack and tree,
    Farewell to Severn shore.
Terence, look your last at me,
    For I come home no more.

"The sun burns on the half-mown hill,
    By now the blood is dried;

And Maurice amongst the hay lies still
    And my knife is in his side.

"My mother thinks us long away;
    'Tis time the field were mown.   10
She had two sons at rising day,
    Tonight she'll be alone.

"And here's a bloody hand to shake,
    And, oh, man, here's good-by;
We'll sweat no more on scythe and rake,
    My bloody hands and I.

"I wish you strength to bring you pride,
    And a love to keep you clean,
And I wish you luck, come Lammastide,
    At racing on the green.   20

"Long for me the rick will wait,
    And long will wait the fold,
And long will stand the empty plate,
    And dinner will be cold."

9

On moonlit heath and lonesome bank
    The sheep beside me graze,
And yon the gallows used to clank
    Fast by the four cross ways.

A careless shepherd once would keep
    The flocks by moonlight there,
And high amongst the glimmering sheep
    The dead man stood on air.

They hang us now in Shrewsbury jail;
    The whistles blow forlorn,   10
And trains all night groan on the rail
    To men that die at morn.

There sleeps in Shrewsbury jail tonight,
    Or wakes, as may betide,
A better lad, if things went right,
    Than most that sleep outside.

And naked to the hangman's noose
    The morning clocks will ring
A neck God made for other use
    Than strangling in a string.   20

And sharp the link of life will snap,
    And dead on air will stand
Heels that held up as straight a chap
    As treads upon the land.

So here I'll watch the night and wait
    To see the morning shine,

Alfred Edward Housman 1189

When he will hear the stroke of eight
  And not the stroke of nine;

And wish my friend as sound a sleep
30 As lads' I did not know,
That shepherded the moonlit sheep
  A hundred years ago.

13

When I was one-and-twenty
  I heard a wise man say,
"Give crowns and pounds and guineas,
  But not your heart, away;
Give pearls away and rubies,
  But keep your fancy free."
But I was one-and-twenty—
  No use to talk to me.

When I was one-and-twenty
10 I heard him say again,
"The heart out of the bosom
  Was never given in vain;
'Tis paid with sighs a plenty
  And sold for endless rue."
And I am two-and-twenty,
  And oh, 'tis true, 'tis true.

18

Oh, when I was in love with you,
  Then I was clean and brave,
And miles around the wonder grew
  How well did I behave.

And now the fancy passes by,
  And nothing will remain,
And miles around they'll say that I
  Am quite myself again.

19. TO AN ATHLETE DYING YOUNG

The time you won your town the race
We chaired you through the market-place;
Man and boy stood cheering by,
And home we brought you shoulder-high.

Today, the road all runners come,
Shoulder-high we bring you home,
And set you at your threshold down,
Townsman of a stiller town.

Smart lad, to slip betimes away
10 From fields where glory does not stay

And early though the laurel grows
It withers quicker than the rose.

Eyes the shady night has shut
Cannot see the record cut,
And silence sounds no worse than cheers
After earth has stopped the ears.

Now you will not swell the rout
Of lads that wore their honors out,
Runners whom renown outran
And the name died before the man.   20

So set, before its echoes fade,
The fleet foot on the sill of shade,
And hold to the low lintel up
The still-defended challenge-cup.

And round that early-laureled head
Will flock to gaze the strengthless dead,
And find unwithered on its curls
The garland briefer than a girl's.

21. BREDON HILL

In summertime on Bredon
  The bells they sound so clear;
Round both the shires they ring them
  In steeples far and near,
  A happy noise to hear.

Here of a Sunday morning
  My love and I would lie,
And see the colored counties,
  And hear the larks so high
  About us in the sky.   10

The bells would ring to call her
  In valleys miles away:
"Come all to church, good people;
  Good people, come and pray."
  But here my love would stay.

And I would turn and answer
  Among the springing thyme,
"Oh, peal upon our wedding,
  And we will hear the chime,
  And come to church in time."   20

But when the snows at Christmas
  On Bredon top were strown,
My love rose up so early
  And stole out unbeknown
  And went to church alone.

Lyric 13. 3. **crowns,** here the coin; at that time it was worth about $1.25.
  Lyric 21. 1. **Bredon,** Bredon Hill, a rounded elevation (960 feet high) near the border between Worcestershire and Gloucestershire. 8. **counties.** From Bredon Hill may be seen the variegated landscape of five shires—Worcester, Gloucester, Hereford, Warwick, and Oxford.

They tolled the one bell only,
  Groom there was none to see,
The mourners followed after,
  And so to church went she,
30 And would not wait for me.

The bells they sound on Bredon,
  And still the steeples hum,
"Come all to church, good people"—
  Oh, noisy bells, be dumb;
I hear you; I will come.

26

  Along the field as we came by
A year ago, my love and I,
The aspen over stile and stone
Was talking to itself alone.
"Oh, who are these that kiss and pass?
A country lover and his lass;
Two lovers looking to be wed;
And time shall put them both to bed,
But she shall lie with earth above,
10 And he beside another love."

  And sure enough beneath the tree
There walks another love with me,
And overhead the aspen heaves
Its rainy-sounding silver leaves;
And I spell nothing in their stir,
But now perhaps they speak to her,
And plain for her to understand
They talk about a time at hand
When I shall sleep with clover clad,
And she beside another lad.

27

"Is my team plowing,
  That I was used to drive
And hear the harness jingle
  When I was man alive?"

Aye, the horses trample,
  The harness jingles now;
No change though you lie under
  The land you used to plow.

"Is football playing
10 Along the river shore,
With lads to chase the leather,
  Now I stand up no more?"

Aye, the ball is flying,
  The lads play heart and soul;
The goal stands up, the keeper
  Stands up to keep the goal.

"Is my girl happy,
  That I thought hard to leave,
And has she tired of weeping
  As she lies down at eve?"   20

Aye, she lies down lightly,
  She lies not down to weep;
Your girl is well contented.
  Be still, my lad, and sleep.

"Is my friend hearty,
  Now I am thin and pine,
And has he found to sleep in
  A better bed than mine?"

Yes, lad, I lie easy,
  I lie as lads would choose;   30
I cheer a dead man's sweetheart—
  Never ask me whose.

40

Into my heart an air that kills
  From yon far country blows;
What are those blue remembered hills,
  What spires, what farms are those?

That is the land of lost content,
  I see it shining plain,
The happy highways where I went
  And cannot come again.

44

Shot? so quick, so clean an ending?
  Oh, that was right, lad, that was brave.
Yours was not an ill for mending;
  'Twas best to take it to the grave.

Oh, you had forethought, you could reason,
  And saw your road and where it led,
And early wise and brave in season
  Put the pistol to your head.

Oh, soon, and better so than later
  After long disgrace and scorn,   10
You shot dead the household traitor,
  The soul that should not have been born.

Right you guessed the rising morrow
  And scorned to tread the mire you
    must;
Dust's your wages, son of sorrow,
  But men may come to worse than dust.

Souls undone, undoing others—
  Long time since the tale began.

You would not live to wrong your brothers;
20   Oh, lad, you died as fits a man.

Now to your grave shall friend and stranger
      With ruth and some with envy come;
Undishonored, clear of danger,
      Clean of guilt, pass hence and home.

Turn safe to rest, no dreams, no waking;
      And here, man, here's the wreath I've made.
'Tis not a gift that's worth the taking,
      But wear it, and it will not fade.

45

If it chance your eye offend you,
      Pluck it out, lad, and be sound;
'Twill hurt, but here are salves to friend you,
      And many a balsam grows on ground.

And if your hand or foot offend you,
      Cut it off, lad, and be whole;
But play the man, stand up and end you,
      When your sickness is your soul.

48

Be still, my soul, be still; the arms you bear are brittle,
      Earth and high heaven are fixed of old and founded
         strong.
Think rather—call to thought, if now you grieve a
         little,
      The days when we had rest, O soul, for they were
         long.

Men loved unkindness then, but lightless in the
         quarry
      I slept and saw not; tears fell down, I did not mourn;
Sweat ran and blood sprang out and I was never
         sorry.
      Then it was well with me, in days ere I was born.

Now, and I muse for why and never find the reason,
10   I pace the earth, and drink the air, and feel the sun.
Be still, be still, my soul; it is but for a season;
      Let us endure an hour and see injustice done.

Aye, look—high heaven and earth ail from the prime
         foundation;
      All thoughts to rive the heart are here, and all are
         vain:
Horror and scorn and hate and fear and indignation—
      Oh, why did I awake? when shall I sleep again?

49

Think no more, lad; laugh, be jolly.
      Why should men make haste to die?
Empty heads and tongues a-talking
Make the rough road easy walking,
And the feather pate of folly
      Bears the falling sky.

Oh, 'tis jesting, dancing, drinking
      Spins the heavy world around.
If young hearts were not so clever,
Oh, they would be young forever.   10
Think no more; 'tis only thinking
      Lays lads underground.

54

With rue my heart is laden
      For golden friends I had,
For many a rose-lipped maiden
      And many a lightfoot lad.

By brooks too broad for leaping
      The lightfoot boys are laid;
The rose-lipped girls are sleeping
      In fields where roses fade.

62

"Terence, this is stupid stuff:
You eat your victuals fast enough;
There can't be much amiss, 'tis clear,
To see the rate you drink your beer.
But oh, good Lord, the verse you make,
It gives a chap the bellyache.
The cow, the old cow, she is dead;
It sleeps well, the horned head:
We poor lads, 'tis our turn now
To hear such tunes as killed the cow.   10
Pretty friendship 'tis to rhyme
Your friends to death before their time
Moping melancholy mad.
Come, pipe a tune to dance to, lad."

Why, if 'tis dancing you would be,
There's brisker pipes than poetry.
Say, for what were hop-yards meant,
Or why was Burton built on Trent?
Oh, many a peer of England brews
Livelier liquor than the Muse,   20
And malt does more than Milton can
To justify God's ways to man.

Lyric 45. 1. **eye . . . sound.** See Mark 9:47—"And if thine eye offend thee, pluck it out: it is better for thee to enter into the kingdom of
God with one eye, than having two eyes to be cast into hell fire." 5.
hand . . . off. See Mark 9:43–45—"And if thy hand offend thee, cut
it off . . . And if thy foot offend thee, cut it off. . . ."

Lyric 62. 18. **Burton . . . Trent.** Burton-upon-Trent, a city of
Staffordshire, is the metropolis of brewing in England. 22. **justify . . .
man.** See Milton's *Paradise Lost,* Book I, l. 26 (p. 388). 76. **Mithridates,** the "king" referred to in ll. 59 ff. He was king of Pontus, an
ancient country of Asia Minor located on the southern shores of the

Ale, man, ale's the stuff to drink
For fellows whom it hurts to think:
Look into the pewter pot
To see the world as the world's not.
And faith, 'tis pleasant till 'tis past:
The mischief is that 'twill not last.
Oh, I have been to Ludlow Fair
30 And left my necktie God knows where,
And carried half way home, or near,
Pints and quarts of Ludlow beer.
Then the world seemed none so bad,
And I myself a sterling lad;
And down in lovely muck I've lain,
Happy till I woke again.
Then I saw the morning sky—
Heigho, the tale was all a lie;
The world, it was the old world yet,
40 I was I, my things were wet,
And nothing now remained to do
But begin the game anew.

Therefore, since the world has still
Much good, but much less good than
    ill,
And while the sun and moon endure
Luck's a chance, but trouble's sure,
I'd face it as a wise man would,
And train for ill and not for good.
'Tis true, the stuff I bring for sale
50 Is not so brisk a brew as ale;
Out of a stem that scored the hand
I wrung it in a weary land.
But take it—if the smack is sour,
The better for the embittered hour;
It should do good to heart and head
When your soul is in my soul's stead;
And I will friend you, if I may,
In the dark and cloudy day.

There was a king reigned in the East;
60 There, when kings will sit to feast,
They get their fill before they think
With poisoned meat and poisoned drink.
He gathered all that springs to birth
From the many-venomed earth;
First a little, thence to more,
He sampled all her killing store;
And easy, smiling, seasoned sound,
Sate the king when healths went round.
They put arsenic in his meat
70 And stared aghast to watch him eat;
They poured strychnine in his cup
And shook to see him drink it up.

They shook, they stared as white's their shirt;
Them it was their poison hurt.
—I tell the tale that I heard told.
Mithridates, he died old.

63

I hoed and trenched and weeded,
    And took the flowers to fair.
I brought them home unheeded;
    The hue was not the wear.

So up and down I sow them
    For lads like me to find,
When I shall lie below them,
    A dead man out of mind.

Some seed the birds devour,
    And some the season mars,   10
But here and there will flower
    The solitary stars,

And fields will yearly bear them
    As light-leaved spring comes on,
And luckless lads will wear them
    When I am dead and gone.
(1896)

from LAST POEMS

2

As I gird on for fighting
    My sword upon my thigh,
I think on old ill fortunes
    Of better men than I.

Think I, the round world over,
    What golden lads are low
With hurts not mine to mourn for
    And shames I shall not know.

What evil luck soever
    For me remains in store,   10
'Tis sure much finer fellows
    Have fared much worse before.

So here are things to think on
    That ought to make me brave,
As I strap on for fighting
    My sword that will not save.

Black Sea. He lived from 132 to 63 B.C.
    Last Poems. Although these poems were not published until 1922,
Housman said that most of them were written between 1895 and 1910.
    Poems from *Last Poems,* from *The Collected Poems of A. E. Hous-
man.* Copyright 1922, 1936, 1950 by Barclays Bank Ltd. Copyright ©

1964 by Robert E. Symons. Reprinted by permission of Holt, Rinehart
and Winston, Inc., The Society of Authors as the literary representative
of the Estate of the late A. E. Housman, and Messrs. Jonathan Cape
Ltd., publishers of A. E. Housman's *Collected Poems.*

Alfred Edward Housman 1193

7

In valleys green and still
    Where lovers wander maying,
They hear from over hill
    A music playing.

Behind the drum and fife,
    Past hawthornwood and hollow,
Through earth and out of life
    The soldiers follow.

The soldier's is the trade:
10   In any wind or weather
He steals the heart of maid
    And man together.

The lover and his lass
    Beneath the hawthorn lying
Have heard the soldiers pass,
    And both are sighing.

And down the distance they
    With dying note and swelling
Walk the resounding way
    To the still dwelling.

9

The chestnut casts his flambeaux, and the flowers
    Stream from the hawthorn on the wind away,
The doors clap to, the pane is blind with showers.
    Pass me the can, lad; there's an end of May.

There's one spoilt spring to scant our mortal lot,
    One season ruined of our little store.
May will be fine next year as like as not:
    Oh ay, but then we shall be twenty-four.

We for a certainty are not the first
10   Have sat in taverns while the tempest hurled
Their hopeful plans to emptiness, and cursed
    Whatever brute and blackguard made the world.

It is in truth iniquity on high
    To cheat our sentenced souls of aught they crave,
And mar the merriment as you and I
    Fare on our long fool's-errand to the grave.

Iniquity it is; but pass the can.
    My lad, no pair of kings our mothers bore;
Our only portion is the estate of man:
20   We want the moon, but we shall get no more.

If here today the cloud of thunder lours,
    Tomorrow it will hie on far behests;

Lyric 9, 1. flambeaux, flaming torches.

The flesh will grieve on other bones than ours
    Soon, and the soul will mourn in other breasts.

The troubles of our proud and angry dust
    Are from eternity, and shall not fail.
Bear them we can, and if we can we must.
    Shoulder the sky, my lad, and drink your ale.

10

Could man be drunk forever
    With liquor, love, or fights,
Lief should I rouse at morning
    And lief lie down of nights.

But men at whiles are sober
    And think by fits and starts,
And if they think, they fasten
    Their hands upon their hearts.

11

Yonder see the morning blink:
    The sun is up, and up must I,
To wash and dress and eat and drink
And look at things and talk and think
    And work, and God knows why.

Oh often have I washed and dressed
    And what's to show for all my pain?
Let me lie abed and rest:
Ten thousand times I've done my best
    And all's to do again.
(1895)

12

    The laws of God, the laws of man,
He may keep that will and can;
Not I; let God and man decree
Laws for themselves and not for me;
And if my ways are not as theirs
Let them mind their own affairs.
Their deeds I judge and much condemn,
Yet when did I make laws for them?
Please yourselves, say I, and they
Need only look the other way.
But no, they will not; they must still   10
Wrest their neighbor to their will,
And make me dance as they desire
With jail and gallows and hell-fire.
And how am I to face the odds
Of man's bedevilment and God's?
I, a stranger and afraid
In a world I never made.
They will be master, right or wrong;
Though both are foolish, both are strong.   20

And since, my soul, we cannot fly
To Saturn nor to Mercury,
Keep we must, if keep we can,
These foreign laws of God and man.

14. THE CULPRIT

The night my father got me
    His mind was not on me;
He did not plague his fancy
    To muse if I should be
    The son you see.

The day my mother bore me
    She was a fool and glad,
For all the pain I cost her,
    That she had borne the lad
10   That borne she had.

My mother and my father
    Out of the light they lie;
The warrant would not find them,
    And here 'tis only I
    Shall hang so high.

Oh let not man remember
    The soul that God forgot,
But fetch the county kerchief
    And noose me in the knot,
20   And I will rot.

For so the game is ended
    That should not have begun.
My father and my mother
    They had a likely son,
    And I have none.

32

When I would muse in boyhood
    The wild green woods among,
And nurse resolves and fancies
    Because the world was young,
It was not foes to conquer,
    Nor sweethearts to be kind,
But it was friends to die for
    That I would seek and find.

I sought them far and found them,
10   The sure, the straight, the brave,

The hearts I lost my own to,
    The souls I could not save.
They braced their belts about them,
    They crossed in ships the sea,
They sought and found six feet of ground.
    And there they died for me.
(1922)

from MORE POEMS

THEY SAY MY VERSE IS SAD

They say my verse is sad: no wonder;
    Its narrow measure spans
Tears of eternity, and sorrow,
    Not mine, but man's.

This is for all ill-treated fellows
    Unborn and unbegot,
For them to read when they're in trouble
    And I am not.

27

To stand up straight and tread the turning mill,
To lie flat and know nothing and be still,
    Are the two trades of man; and which is worse
I know not, but I know that both are ill.

38

By shores and woods and steeples
    Rejoicing hearts receive
Poured on a hundred peoples
    The far-shed alms of eve.

Her hands are filled with slumber
    For world-wide laborers worn;
Yet those are more in number
    That know her not from morn.

Now who sees night forever,
    He sees no happier sight: 10
Night and no moon and never
    A star upon the night.
(1936)

Poems from *More Poems,* from *The Collected Poems* of A. E. Housman. Copyright 1922, 1936, 1950 by Barclays Bank Ltd. Copyright © 1964 by Robert E. Symons. Reprinted by permission of Holt, Rinehart and Winston, Inc., The Society of Authors as the literary representative of the Estate of the late A. E. Housman, and Messrs. Jonathan Cape Ltd., publishers of A. E. Housman's *Collected Poems.*

WILLIAM BUTLER YEATS 1865-1939

William Butler Yeats was born near Dublin of Anglo-Irish stock. His father was a distinguished portrait-painter and a member of the Royal Hibernian Academy. After attending schools in Hammersmith, London, and in Dublin, Yeats studied painting but soon turned to writing. His first poems and articles went to the Dublin University Review and other Irish periodicals. In 1888 he went to London and was welcomed into the Rhymers' Club. The next year he published his first volume of verse, The Wanderings of Oisin and Other Poems. His interest in both the ancient culture and the contemporary political and social problems of his native country was always intense and expressed itself in many ways. He helped to organize Irish literary societies in London and in Dublin and, in collaboration with the novelist George Moore (1852-1933) and others, established the Irish Literary Theater, which became in 1904 the Abbey Theater.

In 1897 he published The Secret Rose, a collection of Irish legends and tales in prose. Some of the best of his lyrics appeared in Poems (1895) and The Wind Among the Reeds (1899). His greatest eminence is probably as a lyric poet, but his most notable contributions to the Irish literary movement are in the field of the drama. His plays are Gaelic in content and spirit and are usually in verse. His first one, The Countess Cathleen, was a romantic drama written in 1892, but his best-known dramatic work is a one-act play-poem entitled The Land of Heart's Desire (1894). Then, breaking with his early attachment to the symbolist movement and experimenting continuously, he wrote numerous volumes of poetry and plays, among which are The Green Helmet and Other Poems (1910), Poems Written in Discouragement (1913), Responsibilities:

Poems and a Play (1914), and Reveries over Childhood and Youth (1915). It was the 1920's, however, that saw Yeats' most mature development, both in writing and in public affairs. In 1922 he was elected a senator in the new Irish Free State, and in 1923 he was awarded the Nobel Prize for literature. The pinnacle of his poetic achievement came in the collection The Tower (1928). In later years, he made a restless attempt to construct a philosophic justification for his beliefs in the reality of dreams and the life of the spirit. A Vision, published in 1925 in a private edition and revised in 1937, is a curious assortment of thoughts reflecting his interest in theosophy, magic, Swedenborgianism, and astrology. He had already given expression to some of these philosophic moods in a series of essays called Per Amica Silentia Lunae (1918), in which he categorizes humanity under various phases of the moon in a polarity of subjective and objective types. He died January 28, 1939, and was buried at Roquebrune, but his body was later brought back to Drumcliff Churchyard in Sligo.

Yeats represents the literary side of the Irish national movement. He introduced into the stream of modern English literature a romantic current, but he owed some of his inspiration to the Pre-Raphaelites, who influenced his father's painting, and also to Shelley and to Maeterlinck. He owed even more to the French symbolists and to Blake, the mystic (p. 671), but his work is, nevertheless, uniquely his own. It has an elusive, elfin charm and much Celtic melancholy. It suggests rather than expresses sorrow, and has something of the plaintive quality of a dirge. But in his later work, from about 1910 on, there is a resonant combination of the rhetorical and the lyrical.

THE STOLEN CHILD

Where dips the rocky highland
Of Sleuth Wood in the lake,
There lies a leafy island
Where flapping herons wake
The drowsy water rats;
There we've hid our faery vats,
Full of berries,
And of reddest stolen cherries.

Come away, O human child!
To the waters and the wild
With a faery, hand in hand,
For the world's more full of weeping than you can
    understand.

Where the wave of moonlight glosses
The dim gray sands with light,
Far off by furthest Rosses
We foot it all the night,

10

The Stolen Child. 2. Sleuth Wood in the lake. The lake of Glen-Car, surrounded by wooded hills, is in the county of Sligo, in north-western Ireland. 15. Rosses, stone headlands along the coast of Sligo. The vicinity was regarded as a favorite haunt of fairies.
The White Birds. 9. Danaän shore, the land of eternal happiness, the fairy world of Irish tradition, inhabited by the ancient race of the Tuatha Dé Danaän.

Weaving olden dances,
Mingling hands and mingling glances
Till the moon has taken flight;
20 To and fro we leap
And chase the frothy bubbles,
While the world is full of troubles
And is anxious in its sleep.
Come away, O human child!
To the waters and the wild
With a faery, hand in hand,
For the world's more full of weeping than you can
understand.

Where the wandering water gushes
From the hills above Glen-Car,
30 In pools among the rushes
That scarce could bathe a star,
We seek for slumbering trout
And whispering in their ears
Give them unquiet dreams;
Leaning softly out
From ferns that drop their tears
Over the young streams.
Come away, O human child!
To the waters and the wild
40 *With a faery, hand in hand,*
For the world's more full of weeping than you can
understand.

Away with us he's going,
The solemn-eyed;
He'll hear no more the lowing,
Of the calves on the warm hillside
Or the kettle on the hob
Sing peace into his breast,
Or see the brown mice bob
Round and round the oatmeal-chest.
50 *For he comes, the human child,*
To the waters and the wild
With a faery, hand in hand,
From a world more full of weeping than he can under-
stand.
(1889)

THE WHITE BIRDS

The white bird is a symbol of the soul.

I would that we were, my belovéd, white birds on the
  foam of the sea!
We tire of the flame of the meteor, before it can fade
  and flee;

And the flame of the blue star of twilight, hung low on
  the rim of the sky,
Has awaked in our hearts, my belovéd, a sadness that
  may not die.

A weariness comes from those dreamers, dew dabbled,
  the lily and rose;
Ah, dream not of them, my belovéd, the flame of the
  meteor that goes,
Or the flame of the blue star that lingers hung low in
  the fall of the dew:
For I would we were changed to white birds on the
  wandering foam: I and you!

I am haunted by numberless islands, and many a
  Danaän shore,
Where Time would surely forget us, and Sorrow come
  near us no more;   10
Soon far from the rose and the lily, and fret of the
  flames would we be,
Were we only white birds, my belovéd, buoyed out on
  the foam of the sea!
(1892)

THE ROSE OF THE WORLD

The rose is here regarded as the traditional symbol
of love. To Yeats the beauty of a woman sums up all
other beauties in the world. The woman in question may
be a real woman, such as Yeats' love, Maud Gonne, or
may represent Ireland itself.

Who dreamed that beauty passes like a dream?
For these red lips, with all their mournful pride,
Mournful that no new wonder may betide,
Troy passed away in one high funeral gleam,
And Usna's children died.

We and the laboring world are passing by;
Amid men's souls, that waver and give place,
Like the pale waters in their wintry race,
Under the passing stars, foam of the sky,
Lives on this lonely face.   10

Bow down, archangels, in your dim abode.
Before you were, or any hearts to beat,
Weary and kind, one lingered by His
  seat;
He made the world to be a grassy road
Before her wandering feet.
(1893)

The Rose of the World. **4. Troy . . . gleam.** It was the beauty of
Helen that occasioned the Trojan War and the burning of Troy, as related
in Homer's *Iliad.* **5. Usna's . . . died.** Naoise, a son of Usna, was in
love with Deirdre, the heroine of Irish legends. King Conchobar of Ulster
desired her for his wife, and Naoise and his two brothers carried her off
to Scotland. Lured back by Conchobar, the brothers were treacherously

slain, and Deirdre killed herself in sorrow. **14. He,** God.
  The White Birds and *The Rose of the World* are reprinted with per-
mission of The Macmillan Company, Mr. M. B. Yeats, and the Macmillan
Co. of Canada from *Collected Poems* by W. B. Yeats. Copyright 1906 by
The Macmillan Company, renewed 1934 by William Butler Yeats.

The Isle of Innisfree, in County Sligo.

THE LAKE ISLE OF INNISFREE

Innisfree is an island in Lough Gill, a lake in the county of Sligo, Ireland.

I will arise and go now, and go to Innisfree,
And a small cabin build there, of clay and wattles made;
Nine bean rows will I have there, a hive for the honey
    bee,
And live alone in the bee-loud glade.

And I shall have some peace there, for peace comes
    dropping slow,
Dropping from the veils of the morning to where the
    cricket sings;
There midnight's all a glimmer, and noon a purple glow,
And evening full of the linnet's wings.

I will arise and go now, for always night and day
I hear lake water lapping with low sounds by the
10 shore;

While I stand on the roadway, or on the pavements
    gray,
I hear it in the deep heart's core.
(1893)

WHEN YOU ARE OLD

When you are old and gray and full of sleep,
And nodding by the fire, take down this book,
And slowly read, and dream of the soft look
Your eyes had once, and of their shadows deep;

How many loved your moments of glad
    grace,
And loved your beauty with love false or true;
But one man loved the pilgrim soul in you,
And loved the sorrows of your changing face.

And bending down beside the glowing bars
Murmur, a little sadly, how love fled   **10**

The Lake Isle of Innisfree and *When You Are Old* are reprinted with permission of The Macmillan Company, Mr. M. B. Yeats, and the Macmillan Co. of Canada from *Collected Poems* by W. B. Yeats. Copyright 1906 by The Macmillan Company, renewed 1934 by William Butler Yeats.
The Lake Isle of Innisfree. 2. **wattles,** interwoven sticks and twigs.

3. **Nine bean rows.** The writers of the Irish Renaissance shared the Pre-Raphaelite fondness for definite numbers of mystic suggestion. Cf. Rossetti's *Blessed Damozel* (p. 1091, l. 6).
    Song. A lyric in Yeats' one-act drama, *The Land of Heart's Desire.*

And paced upon the mountains overhead
And hid his face amid a crowd of stars.
(1893)

SONG

The wind blows out of the gates of the day,
  The wind blows over the lonely of heart,
And the lonely of heart is withered away
  While the faeries dance in a place apart,
Shaking their milk-white feet in a ring,
  Tossing their milk-white arms in the air;
For they hear the wind laugh and murmur and sing
  Of a land where even the old are fair,
And even the wise are merry of tongue;
10 But I heard a reed of Coolaney say,
  "When the wind has laughed and murmured and sung,
  The lonely of heart is withered away."
(1894)

THE HOST OF THE AIR

The "Host of the Air" is an especially malignant branch of the fairy race. Yeats says that the poem "is founded on an old Gaelic ballad that was sung and translated for me by a woman at Ballisodare, in County Sligo."

O'Driscoll drove with a song
The wild duck and the drake
From the tall and the tufted reeds
Of the drear Hart Lake.

And he saw how the reeds grew dark
At the coming of night tide,
And dreamed of the long dim hair
Of Bridget his bride.

He heard while he sang and dreamed
10 A piper piping away,
And never was piping so sad,
And never was piping so gay.

And he saw young men and young girls
Who danced on a level place
And Bridget his bride among them,
With a sad and a gay face.

The dancers crowded about him,
And many a sweet thing said,
And a young man brought him red wine
20 And a young girl white bread.

But Bridget drew him by the sleeve,
Away from the merry bands,
To old men playing at cards
With a twinkling of ancient hands.

The bread and the wine had a doom,
For these were the host of the air;
He sat and played in a dream
Of her long dim hair.

He played with the merry old men
And thought not of evil chance,   30
Until one bore Bridget his bride
Away from the merry dance.

He bore her away in his arms,
The handsomest young man there,
And his neck and his breast and his arms
Were drowned in her long dim hair.

O'Driscoll scattered the cards
And out of his dream awoke:
Old men and young men and young girls
Were gone like a drifting smoke;   40

But he heard high up in the air
A piper piping away,
And never was piping so sad,
And never was piping so gay.
(1899)

INTO THE TWILIGHT

Out-worn heart, in a time out-worn,
Come clear of the nets of wrong and right;
Laugh, heart, again in the gray twilight,
Sigh, heart, again in the dew of the morn.

Your mother Eire is always young,
Dew ever shining and twilight gray;
Though hopes fall from you and love decay,
Burning in fires of a slanderous tongue.

Come, heart, where hill is heaped upon hill;
For there the mystical brotherhood   10
Of sun and moon and hollow and wood
And river and stream work out their will;

And God stands winding His lonely horn,
And time and the world are ever in flight;
And love is less kind than the gray twilight,
And hope is less dear than the dew of the morn.
(1899)

The Host of the Air. **4. Hart Lake,** a dreary pond bordered by trees, five miles south of Sligo. **25. doom,** curse.
Song, The Host of the Air, and *Into the Twilight* are reprinted with permission of The Macmillan Company, Mr. M. B. Yeats, and the Mac-
millan Co. of Canada from *Collected Poems* by W. B. Yeats. *Song,* copyright 1919 by The Macmillan Company, renewed 1946 by Bertha Georgie Yeats. *The Host of the Air* and *Into the Twilight,* copyright 1906 by The Macmillan Company, renewed 1934 by William Butler Yeats.

HE REMEMBERS FORGOTTEN BEAUTY

When my arms wrap you round I press
My heart upon the loveliness
That has long faded from the world;
The jeweled crowns that kings have hurled
In shadowy pools, when armies fled;
The love tales wrought with silken thread
By dreaming ladies upon cloth
That has made fat the murderous moth;
The roses that of old time were
10 Woven by ladies in their hair;
The dew-cold lilies ladies bore
Through many a sacred corridor
Where such gray clouds of incense rose
That only the gods' eyes did not close:
For that pale breast and lingering hand
Come from a more dream-heavy land,
A more dream-heavy hour than this;
And when you sigh from kiss to kiss
I hear white Beauty sighing, too,
20 For hours when all must fade like dew;
But flame on flame, deep under deep,
Throne over throne, where in half sleep
Their swords upon their iron knees
Brood her high lonely mysteries.
(1899)

THE SONG OF WANDERING AENGUS

*Aengus is the Celtic god of love, his kisses changed
to birds that constantly flew about his head.*

I went out to the hazel wood,
Because a fire was in my head,
And cut and peeled a hazel wand,
And hooked a berry to a thread;
And when white moths were on the wing,
And moth-like stars were flickering out,
I dropped the berry in a stream
And caught a little silver trout.

When I had laid it on the floor,
I went to blow the fire a-flame,
10 But something rustled on the floor,
And some one called me by my name:
It had become a glimmering girl
With apple blossom in her hair
Who called me by my name and ran
And faded through the brightening air.

Though I am old with wandering
Through hollow lands and hilly lands,

I will find out where she has gone,
And kiss her lips and take her hands;   20
And walk among long dappled grass,
And pluck till time and times are done
The silver apples of the moon,
The golden apples of the sun.
(1899)

THE FIDDLER OF DOONEY

When I play on my fiddle in Dooney,
Folk dance like a wave of the sea;
My cousin is priest in Kilvarnet,
My brother in Moharabuiee.

I passed my brother and cousin:
They read in their books of prayer;
I read in my book of songs
I bought at the Sligo fair.

When we come at the end of time,
To Peter sitting in state,   10
He will smile on the three old spirits,
But call me first through the gate;

For the good are always the merry,
Save by an evil chance,
And the merry love the fiddle
And the merry love to dance:

And when the folk there spy me,
They will all come up to me,
With "Here is the fiddler of Dooney!"
And dance like a wave of the sea.
(1899)

AN IRISH AIRMAN FORESEES HIS DEATH

I know that I shall meet my fate
Somewhere among the clouds above;
Those that I fight I do not hate,
Those that I guard I do not love;
My country is Kiltartan Cross,
My countrymen Kiltartan's poor,
No likely end could bring them loss
Or leave them happier than before.
Nor law, nor duty bade me fight,
Nor public men, nor cheering crowds,   10
A lonely impulse of delight
Drove to this tumult in the clouds;
I balanced all, brought all to mind,

He Remembers Forgotten Beauty, The Song of Wandering Aengus,
The Fiddler of Dooney, and *An Irish Airman Foresees His Death* are re-
printed with permission of The Macmillan Company, Mr. M. B. Yeats,
and the Macmillan Co. of Canada from *Collected Poems* by W. B. Yeats.
He Remembers Forgotten Beauty, The Song of Wandering Aengus, and
The Fiddler of Dooney, copyright 1906 by The Macmillan Company,
renewed 1934 by William Butler Yeats. *An Irish Airman Foresees His
Death,* copyright 1919 by The Macmillan Company, renewed 1946 by

Bertha Georgie Yeats.
The Fiddler of Dooney. 1. **Dooney.** Dooney and the other places
named are hamlets on the west coast of Ireland. *Sligo* (l. 8) was Yeats'
boyhood home. 2. **dance . . . sea.** Compare Florizel's speech to Perdita
in Shakespeare's *The Winter's Tale,* IV, iv, 140-141.
The Second Coming. 12. *Spiritus Mundi,* the soul of the world,
the organizing principle of the physical universe. Yeats uses this theo-
sophical phrase also to mean the Great Memory.

The years to come seemed waste of breath,
A waste of breath the years behind
In balance with this life, this death.
(1919)

THE SECOND COMING

*Various interpretations have been put upon the event
designated as the second coming of Christ. Although
the expression is not found in Scripture, synonyms of
the event and allusions to it have been identified. One
definition in the Dictionary of the Bible calls it "an
Advent at the end of the age to judge the world, to
destroy evil, to reward the saints, and to establish
the Kingdom of Glory." Yeats here is prophesying
disaster for our modern world, but he believes that
even this disaster has its place in a divine pattern.*

Turning and turning in the widening gyre
The falcon cannot hear the falconer;
Things fall apart: the center cannot hold;
Mere anarchy is loosed upon the world,
The blood-dimmed tide is loosed, and everywhere
The ceremony of innocence is drowned;
The best lack all conviction, while the worst
Are full of passionate intensity.

Surely some revelation is at hand;
10 Surely the Second Coming is at hand.
The Second Coming! Hardly are those words out
When a vast image out of *Spiritus Mundi*
Troubles my sight: somewhere in sands of the desert
A shape with lion body and the head of a man,
A gaze blank and pitiless as the sun,
Is moving its slow thighs, while all about it
Reel shadows of the indignant desert birds.
The darkness drops again; but now I know
That twenty centuries of stony sleep
20 Were vexed to nightmare by a rocking cradle,
And what rough beast, its hour come round at last,
Slouches towards Bethlehem to be born?
(1921)

LEDA AND THE SWAN

*The union of mortals and immortals always had a
strong symbolic value for Yeats. In classical mythology
Leda, wife of the Spartan king Tyndareus, was beloved
by Zeus, who visited her in the form of a swan. From
their mating was born the beautiful Helen of Troy. The
abduction of Helen from her husband, Menelaus, by*

*Paris, who fled with her to Troy, was the legendary
cause of the Trojan War. (According to another version
Leda brought forth two eggs, from one sprang Helen
and Pollux, and from the other Clytemnestra and Castor.) The poem appeared first in A Vision (1925)—an
exposition of Yeats' symbolical interpretation of history and civilization—as the opening section of Book
V, entitled "Dove or Swan."*

A sudden blow: the great wings beating still
Above the staggering girl, her thighs caressed
By the dark webs, her nape caught in his bill,
He holds her helpless breast upon his breast.

How can those terrified vague fingers push
The feathered glory from her loosening thighs?
And how can body, laid in that white rush,
But feel the strange heart beating where it lies?

A shudder in the loins engenders there
The broken wall, the burning roof and tower   10
And Agamemnon dead.
                              Being so caught up,
So mastered by the brute blood of the air,
Did she put on his knowledge with his power
Before the indifferent beak could let her drop?
(1925)

SAILING TO BYZANTIUM

*Grown old and weary in his own country, an old
man seeks repose for his soul in the more intellectual
and ideal environment symbolized by Byzantium. In
ancient geography Byzantium was a Greek city founded
in the seventh century B.C. In 330 A.D., Constantine
the Great made it the capital of the Roman Empire and
changed the name to Constantinople. From 395 A.D.
it was the famous capital of the Byzantine, or Eastern,
Empire and was noted, Yeats observes, for "an architecture that suggests the Sacred City in the Apocalypse
of St. John." The present name of the city is Istanbul.
In the poem the city is presented symbolically as the
ideal journey's end for the old, since it was the one
place in all the world in which the forces of body,
mind, and spirit existed in proper balance. In A Vision
Yeats expressed the belief that "in early Byzantium,
maybe never before nor since in recorded history, religious, aesthetic, and practical life were one." The
poem is symbolical of the change from life to death.*

That is no country for old men. The young
In one another's arms, birds in the trees

Leda and the Swan. 10. **broken wall . . . dead,** well-known incidents in the Greek attack upon Troy in the Trojan War. Agamemnon
was the brother of Menelaus and the commander-in-chief of the allied
Greek forces. While he was absent from home, his wife Clytemnestra,
another daughter of Leda and Zeus, fell in love with Aegisthus. Upon
his return from Troy, Agamemnon was killed either by his wife or
(according to Homer) by Aegisthus.
The Second Coming, Leda and the Swan, and Sailing to Byzantium are
reprinted with permission of The Macmillan Company, Mr. M. B. Yeats,
and the Macmillan Co. of Canada from *Collected Poems* by W. B. Yeats.
The Second Coming, copyright 1924 by The Macmillan Company, renewed
1952 by Georgie Yeats. *Leda and the Swan* and *Sailing to Byzantium*, copyright 1928 by The Macmillan Company, renewed 1956 by Georgie Yeats.

(Those dying generations) at their song,
The salmon-falls, the mackerel-crowded seas,
Fish, flesh, or fowl, commend all summer long
Whatever is begotten, born, and dies.
Caught in that sensual music, all neglect
Monuments of unaging intellect.

An aged man is but a paltry thing,
10 A tattered coat upon a stick, unless
Soul clap its hands and sing, and louder sing
For every tatter in its mortal dress;
Nor is there singing school but studying
Monuments of its own magnificence;
And therefore I have sailed the seas and come
To the holy city of Byzantium.

O sages, standing in God's holy fire
As in the gold mosaic of a wall,
Come from the holy fire, perne in a gyre,
20 And be the singing-masters of my soul.
Consume my heart away—sick with desire
And fastened to a dying animal
It knows not what it is—and gather me
Into the artifice of eternity.

Once out of nature I shall never take
My bodily form from any natural thing,
But such a form as Grecian goldsmiths make
Of hammered gold and gold enamelling
To keep a drowsy emperor awake;
30 Or set upon a golden bough to sing
To lords and ladies of Byzantium
Of what is past, or passing, or to come.
(1928)

AMONG SCHOOL CHILDREN

*Yeats was much interested in the educational system
in Ireland. He wrote to a friend regarding a tour
of inspection of the primary schools that he went "to
study a very remarkable convent school." In this
poem, he ponders the relation of the child to the adult,
as represented by his own experience, and raises in his
own mind certain questions—are the love and sacrifice
necessary to raise children, however unrewarded,
worth while? Can the images which people hold in
reverence be realized in actual life? The general con-*

*clusion reached is that, if the mind and body can be
brought into harmony, the real and the ideal become
the same thing—there can be no difference between
the image and the actuality.*

I walk through the long schoolroom questioning,
A kind old nun in a white hood replies;
The children learn to cipher and to sing,
To study reading-books and history,
To cut and sew, be neat in everything
In the best modern way—the children's eyes
In momentary wonder stare upon
A sixty year old smiling public man.

I dream of a Ledaean body, bent
Above a sinking fire, a tale that she   10
Told of a harsh reproof, or trivial event
That changed some childish day to tragedy—
Told, and it seemed that our two natures blent
Into a sphere from youthful sympathy,
Or else, to alter Plato's parable,
Into the yolk and white of the one shell.

And thinking of that fit of grief or rage
I look upon one child or t'other there
And wonder if she stood so at that age—
For even daughters of the swan can share   20
Something of every paddler's heritage—
And had that color upon cheek or hair;
And thereupon my heart is driven wild:
She stands before me as a living child.

Her present image floats into the mind—
Did quattrocento finger fashion it
Hollow of cheek as though it drank the wind
And took a mess of shadows for its meat?
And I though never of Ledaean kind
Had pretty plumage once—enough of that,   30
Better to smile on all that smile, and show
There is a comfortable kind of old scarecrow.

What youthful mother, a shape upon her lap
Honey of generation had betrayed,
And that must sleep, shriek, struggle to escape
As recollection or the drug decide,
Would think her son, did she but see that shape
With sixty or more winters on its head,

Among School Children is reprinted with permission of The Macmillan
Company, Mr. M. B. Yeats, and the Macmillan Co. of Canada from *Collected Poems* by W. B. Yeats. Copyright 1928 by The Macmillan Company, renewed 1956 by Georgie Yeats.
      Sailing to Byzantium. 4. **salmon-falls . . . seas,** a reference to the
spawning period of salmon, which are noted for jumping up waterfalls
at that time, and of mackerel, which crowd up streams. This whole
stanza is an expression of the fertility of nature contrasted to the sterility
of physical old age. 19. **perne in a gyre,** spool in a circular or spiral
motion—a good example of the "preciousness" of some of Yeats' language in his later verse. 30. **golden bough.** "I have read somewhere
that in the Emperor's palace in Byzantium was a tree made of gold and
silver, and artificial birds that sang."—Yeats' note.
      Among School Children. 9. **Ledaean,** like Leda, whose graceful
arched figure was a frequent subject of Renaissance art. See *Leda and the*

Swan, p. 1201. Some have thought that Yeats was thinking of his mother
—but more probably he was thinking of his beloved Maude Gonne, who
was for Yeats the perfect symbol of beauty throughout the greater part
of his life. 15. **Plato's parable.** Plato was a famous Greek philosopher
of the fourth century B.C. This is probably an allusion to the satirical
discourse on the nature of man as related by Plato in the *Symposium,*
189 ff. As there presented, the sexes were three in number—male, female, and androgynous (a union of the two). The last was a spherical
creature, who because of an attack upon the gods was "cut in two as you
might divide an egg with a hair." Plato frequently refers to the blending
of mutually sympathetic natures. Such a union is symbolized by Yeats in
the yolk and the white of an egg. 20. **daughters of the swan,** symbolical for children of high birth. 21. **paddler,** figurative for child of low
birth. 26. **quattrocento,** of the great fifteenth-century period of
Italian art.

A compensation for the pang of his birth,
40 Or the uncertainty of his setting forth?

Plato thought nature but a spume that plays
Upon a ghostly paradigm of things;
Solider Aristotle played the taws
Upon the bottom of a king of kings;
World-famous golden-thighed Pythagoras
Fingered upon a fiddle stick or strings
What a star sang and careless Muses heard:
Old clothes upon old sticks to scare a bird.

Both nuns and mothers worship images,
50 But those the candles light are not as those
That animate a mother's reveries,

But keep a marble or a bronze repose.
And yet they too break hearts—O Presences
That passion, piety or affection knows,
And that all heavenly glory symbolize—
O self-born mockers of man's enterprise;

Labor is blossoming or dancing where
The body is not bruised to pleasure soul,
Nor beauty born out of its own despair,
Nor blear-eyed wisdom out of midnight oil. 60
O chestnut tree, great rooted blossomer,
Are you the leaf, the blossom or the bole?
O body swayed to music, O brightening glance,
How can we know the dancer from the dance?
(1928)

42. **ghostly paradigm,** spiritual model or pattern. 43. **Aristotle,** with
Plato was the most celebrated and influential of the great Greek philosophers (384–322 B.C.). He is more objective and realistic than the
dreamer Plato. **played the taws,** plied the whip. Aristotle was practical
enough as a teacher of Alexander the Great (the King of Kings, 356–323
B.C.) to give the young prince the flogging that he needed. 45. **Pythagoras,** famous Greek philosopher and mathematician of the sixth century

B.C., said to have had a golden thigh. He is credited with the invention
of the lyre. He is an example of the mystic, with his creation of the
theory concerning the music of the spheres. All of these philosophies—
of Plato, of Aristotle, and of Pythagoras—are in contrast to the solid
reality of birth and death—"old clothes upon old sticks to scare a bird."
Cf. *Sailing to Byzantium,* ll. 9–10. 57. **Labor,** childbirth. 62. **bole,**
tree trunk.

JAMES JOYCE 1882-1941

The eldest son of a large middle-class family, James Joyce was born in a suburb of Dublin, Ireland, February 2, 1882. Originally intended for the priesthood, Joyce was given the best education available; after attending the Jesuit Clongowes Wood College, in Clane, he went to Belvedere College, Dublin, and finally to the Royal University, from which he received his bachelor's degree in October 1902.

During his years of study he showed marked originality and independence and displayed a special bent for creative writing and facility in a dozen or more languages. Joyce's first serious writing was a laudatory essay on Henrik Ibsen, published in 1900 in The Fortnightly Review. His interest in Ibsen and other non-Irish writers led Joyce to oppose the movement, begun in 1901, for the establishment of a national theater for Ireland.

In 1902 Joyce left Ireland on what proved to be a long self-imposed exile. He returned twice—in 1903, because of his mother's fatal illness, and in 1912, in the interest of publishing one of his books. In Paris in 1902, Joyce gave up the idea of studying medicine because he lacked the necessary funds, and also abandoned the notion of preparing for a career as a singer. In 1904, he served as a teacher in Clifton School, Dalkey, Ireland; then he taught in the Berlitz School in Trieste.

Joyce had done some writing of verse in the Elizabethan manner. After four London publishers had re-

jected the poems, the thin volume of lyrics, Chamber Music, was published in 1907. He had also left the manuscript for some short stories based upon Dublin life with a publisher in Dublin, who at first refused to risk publication, but finally published the stories under the title Dubliners in 1914. These masterly incidents, portraits, and dramatic episodes, of which The Dead, which follows, is an excellent example, in many ways foreshadow the longer and more individualistic prose works.

Joyce's first novel, A Portrait of the Artist As a Young Man, a thinly disguised account of the author's youthful years, first appeared serially in The Egoist, an English periodical, and was then published in book form in 1916, with the imprint "Dublin, 1904—Trieste, 1914." During the next few years Joyce suffered an eye ailment that frequently brought on nearly complete blindness. Nevertheless, he worked on a long sequel to A Portrait—his masterpiece, Ulysses, begun in Trieste in 1914 and finished in Paris in 1921. Expurgated portions were printed in The Egoist, and twenty-three installments appeared in the United States in The Little Review in 1918-1920. Three were confiscated by the United States Post Office, and the publishers were fined for sending allegedly immoral matter through the mails. In 1922 the novel was published in Paris. Five hundred copies were burned in New York by the United States Post Office, and a similar number were confiscated by the British Cus-

toms. These actions served only to stimulate the public interest in what was described by some as "an infamously obscene book" and by others as the "greatest fiction of the twentieth century." After the ban was removed by the United States Courts in 1933, the novel circulated freely.

Portions of Joyce's next novel, Finnegans Wake, appeared first in Paris in periodicals under the title Work in Progress. This ponderous volume, published in 1939, which occupied Joyce for fifteen years or more, employs the same individualistic style—but in greatly increased complexity—as that used in Ulysses.

With his family Joyce left Paris in 1940 following the outbreak of the Second World War. After a brief stay in southern France, he managed to get to Zurich, Switzerland, where he died, January 13, 1941.

Joyce, a bold experimentalist, wrote with unabashed frankness and made use of a new form of narrative writing, a new prose style, and a rather startling vocabulary. His most conspicuous innovation, the so-called stream of consciousness technique, tries to approximate the operation of the human mind, in a fluid precommunicative linguistic state, as it expresses a continuous flow of ideas, desires, or past experiences. It represents subjectivity carried to an extreme which occasionally makes communication between author and reader impossible. Critics have rightly spoken of Joyce, however, as a great creative artist, and the reader of modern fiction will note his marked influence upon many later writers.

THE DEAD

Lily, the caretaker's daughter, was literally run off her feet. Hardly had she brought one gentleman into the little pantry behind the office on the ground floor and helped him off with his overcoat than the wheezy hall-door bell clanged again and she had to scamper along the bare hallway to let in another guest. It was well for her she had not to attend to the ladies also. But Miss Kate and Miss Julia had thought of that and had converted the bathroom upstairs into a ladies'
10 dressing-room. Miss Kate and Miss Julia were there, gossiping and laughing and fussing, walking after each other to the head of the stairs, peering down over the banisters and calling down to Lily to ask her who had come.

It was always a great affair, the Misses Morkan's annual dance. Everybody who knew them came to it, members of the family, old friends of the family, the members of Julia's choir, any of Kate's pupils that were grown up enough, and even some of Mary Jane's
20 pupils too. Never once had it fallen flat. For years and years it had gone off in splendid style, as long as anyone could remember, ever since Kate and Julia, after the death of their brother Pat, had left the house in Stoney Batter and taken Mary Jane, their only niece, to live with them in the dark, gaunt house on Usher's Island, the upper part of which they had rented from Mr. Fulham, the corn-factor on the ground floor. That was a good thirty years ago if it was a day. Mary Jane, who was then a little girl in short clothes,
30 was now the main prop of the household, for she had the organ in Haddington Road. She had been through the Academy and gave a pupils' concert every year in the upper room of the Ancient Concert Rooms. Many of her pupils belonged to the better-class families on the Kingstown and Dalkey line. Old as they were, her aunts also did their share. Julia, though she was quite grey, was still the leading soprano in Adam and Eve's, and Kate, being too feeble to go about much, gave music lessons to beginners on the old square piano in the back room. Lily, the caretaker's daughter, did 40 housemaid's work for them. Though their life was modest, they believed in eating well; the best of everything: diamond-bone sirloins, three-shilling tea and the best bottled stout. But Lily seldom made a mistake in the orders, so that she got on well with her three mistresses. They were fussy, that was all. But the only thing they would not stand was back answers.

Of course, they had good reason to be fussy on such a night. And then it was long after ten o'clock and yet there was no sign of Gabriel and his wife. Besides 50 they were dreadfully afraid that Freddy Malins might turn up screwed. They would not wish for worlds that any of Mary Jane's pupils should see him under the influence; and when he was like that it was sometimes very hard to manage him. Freddy Malins always came late, but they wondered what could be keeping Gabriel: and that was what brought them every two minutes to the banisters to ask Lily had Gabriel or Freddy come.

"O, Mr. Conroy," said Lily to Gabriel when she 60 opened the door for him, "Miss Kate and Miss Julia thought you were never coming. Good-night, Mrs. Conroy."

"I'll engage they did," said Gabriel, "but they forget that my wife here takes three mortal hours to dress herself."

He stood on the mat, scraping the snow from his goloshes, while Lily led his wife to the foot of the stairs and called out:

"Miss Kate, here's Mrs. Conroy." 70

The Dead. 52. screwed, drunk. 151. Melodies, Irish Melodies, a collection of lyrics about Ireland and the Irish written by Thomas Moore (1779–1852) and adapted to well-known Irish folk-songs.

Kate and Julia came toddling down the dark stairs at once. Both of them kissed Gabriel's wife, said she must be perished alive, and asked was Gabriel with her.

"Here I am as right as the mail, Aunt Kate! Go on up. I'll follow," called out Gabriel from the dark.

He continued scraping his feet vigorously while the three women went upstairs, laughing, to the ladies' dressing-room. A light fringe of snow lay like a cape
80 on the shoulders of his overcoat and like toecaps on the toes of his goloshes; and, as the buttons of his overcoat slipped with a squeaking noise through the snow-stiffened frieze, a cold, fragrant air from out-of-doors escaped from crevices and folds.

"Is it snowing again, Mr. Conroy?" asked Lily.

She had preceded him into the pantry to help him off with his overcoat. Gabriel smiled at the three syllables she had given his surname and glanced at her. She was a slim, growing girl, pale in complexion
90 and with hay-coloured hair. The gas in the pantry made her look still paler. Gabriel had known her when she was a child and used to sit on the lowest step nursing a rag doll.

"Yes, Lily," he answered, "and I think we're in for a night of it."

He looked up at the pantry ceiling, which was shaking with the stamping and shuffling of feet on the floor above, listened for a moment to the piano and then glanced at the girl, who was folding his overcoat care-
100 fully at the end of a shelf.

"Tell me, Lily," he said in a friendly tone, "do you still go to school?"

"O no, sir," she answered. "I'm done schooling this year and more."

"O, then," said Gabriel gaily, "I suppose we'll be going to your wedding one of these fine days with your young man, eh?"

The girl glanced back at him over her shoulder and said with great bitterness:
110 "The men that is now is only all palaver and what they can get out of you."

Gabriel coloured, as if he felt he had made a mistake and, without looking at her, kicked off his go-loshes and flicked actively with his muffler at his patent-leather shoes.

He was a stout, tallish young man. The high colour of his cheeks pushed upwards even to his forehead, where it scattered itself in a few formless patches of pale red; and on his hairless face there scintillated
120 restlessly the polished lenses and the bright gilt rims of the glasses which screened his delicate and restless eyes. His glossy black hair was parted in the middle and brushed in a long curve behind his ears where it curled slightly beneath the groove left by his hat.

When he had flicked lustre into his shoes he stood up and pulled his waistcoat down more tightly on his plump body. Then he took a coin rapidly from his pocket.

"O Lily," he said, thrusting it into her hands, "it's Christmas-time, isn't it? Just . . . here's a little . . ." 130

He walked rapidly towards the door.

"O no, sir!" cried the girl, following him. "Really, sir, I wouldn't take it."

"Christmas-time! Christmas-time!" said Gabriel, almost trotting to the stairs and waving his hand to her in deprecation.

The girl, seeing that he had gained the stairs, called out after him:

"Well, thank you, sir."

He waited outside the drawing-room door until the 140 waltz should finish, listening to the skirts that swept against it and to the shuffling of feet. He was still discomposed by the girl's bitter and sudden retort. It had cast a gloom over him which he tried to dispel by arranging his cuffs and the bows of his tie. He then took from his waistcoat pocket a little paper and glanced at the headings he had made for his speech. He was undecided about the lines from Robert Browning, for he feared they would be above the heads of his hearers. Some quotation that they would recognise 150 from Shakespeare or from the Melodies would be better. The indelicate clacking of the men's heels and the shuffling of their soles reminded him that their grade of culture differed from his. He would only make himself ridiculous by quoting poetry to them which they could not understand. They would think that he was airing his superior education. He would fail with them just as he had failed with the girl in the pantry. He had taken up a wrong tone. His whole speech was a mistake from first to last, an utter failure. 160

Just then his aunts and his wife came out of the ladies' dressing-room. His aunts were two small, plainly dressed old women. Aunt Julia was an inch or so the taller. Her hair, drawn low over the tops of her ears, was grey; and grey also, with darker shadows, was her large flaccid face. Though she was stout in build and stood erect, her slow eyes and parted lips gave her the appearance of a woman who did not know where she was or where she was going. Aunt Kate was more vivacious. Her face, healthier 170 than her sister's, was all puckers and creases, like a shrivelled red apple, and her hair, braided in the same old-fashioned way, had not lost its ripe nut colour.

They both kissed Gabriel frankly. He was their favourite nephew, the son of their dead elder sister, Ellen, who had married T. J. Conroy of the Port and Docks.

"Gretta tells me you're not going to take a cab back to Monkstown tonight, Gabriel," said Aunt Kate.

"No," said Gabriel, turning to his wife, "we had 180 quite enough of that last year, hadn't we? Don't you remember, Aunt Kate, what a cold Gretta got out of it? Cab windows rattling all the way, and the east wind blowing in after we passed Merrion. Very jolly it was. Gretta caught a dreadful cold."

Aunt Kate frowned severely and nodded her head at every word.

"Quite right, Gabriel, quite right," she said. "You can't be too careful."

"But as for Gretta there," said Gabriel, "she'd walk home in the snow if she were let."

Mrs. Conroy laughed.

"Don't mind him, Aunt Kate," she said. "He's really an awful bother, what with green shades for Tom's eyes at night and making him do the dumb-bells, and forcing Eva to eat the stirabout. The poor child! And she simply hates the sight of it! . . . O, but you'll never guess what he makes me wear now!"

She broke out into a peal of laughter and glanced at her husband, whose admiring and happy eyes had been wandering from her dress to her face and hair. The two aunts laughed heartily, too, for Gabriel's solicitude was a standing joke with them.

"Goloshes!" said Mrs. Conroy. "That's the latest. Whenever it's wet underfoot I must put on my goloshes. Tonight even, he wanted me to put them on, but I wouldn't. The next thing he'll buy me will be a diving suit."

Gabriel laughed nervously and patted his tie reassuringly, while Aunt Kate nearly doubled herself, so heartily did she enjoy the joke. The smile soon faded from Aunt Julia's face and her mirthless eyes were directed towards her nephew's face. After a pause she asked:

"And what are goloshes, Gabriel?"

"Goloshes, Julia!" exclaimed her sister. "Goodness me, don't you know what goloshes are? You wear them over your . . . over your boots, Gretta, isn't it?"

"Yes," said Mrs. Conroy. "Guttapercha things. We both have a pair now. Gabriel says everyone wears them on the Continent."

"O, on the Continent," murmured Aunt Julia, nodding her head slowly.

Gabriel knitted his brows and said, as if he were slightly angered:

"It's nothing very wonderful, but Gretta thinks it very funny because she says the word reminds her of Christy Minstrels."

"But tell me, Gabriel," said Aunt Kate, with brisk tact. "Of course, you've seen about the room. Gretta was saying . . ."

"O, the room is all right," replied Gabriel. "I've taken one in the Gresham."

"To be sure," said Aunt Kate, "by far the best thing to do. And the children, Gretta, you're not anxious about them?"

"O, for one night," said Mrs. Conroy. "Besides, Bessie will look after them."

"To be sure," said Aunt Kate again. "What a comfort it is to have a girl like that, one you can depend on! There's that Lily, I'm sure I don't know what has come over her lately. She's not the girl she was at all."

Gabriel was about to ask his aunt some questions on this point, but she broke off suddenly to gaze after her sister, who had wandered down the stairs and was craning her neck over the banisters.

"Now, I ask you," she said almost testily, "where is Julia going? Julia! Julia! Where are you going?"

Julia, who had gone half way down one flight, came back and announced blandly: "Here's Freddy."

At the same moment a clapping of hands and a final flourish of the pianist told that the waltz had ended. The drawing-room door was opened from within and some couples came out. Aunt Kate drew Gabriel aside hurriedly and whispered into his ear.

"Slip down, Gabriel, like a good fellow and see if he's all right, and don't let him up if he's screwed. I'm sure he's screwed. I'm sure he is."

Gabriel went to the stairs and listened over the banisters. He could hear two persons talking in the pantry. Then he recognised Freddy Malins' laugh. He went down the stairs noisily.

"It's such a relief," said Aunt Kate to Mrs. Conroy, "that Gabriel is here. I always feel easier in my mind when he's here. . . . Julia, there's Miss Daly and Miss Power will take some refreshment. Thanks for your beautiful waltz, Miss Daly. It made lovely time."

A tall wizen-faced man, with a stiff grizzled moustache and swarthy skin, who was passing out with his partner, said:

"And may we have some refreshment, too, Miss Morkan?"

"Julia," said Aunt Kate summarily, "and here's Mr. Browne and Miss Furlong. Take them in, Julia, with Miss Daly and Miss Power."

"I'm the man for the ladies," said Mr. Browne, pursing his lips until his moustache bristled and smiling in all his wrinkles. "You know, Miss Morkan, the reason they are so fond of me is—"

He did not finish his sentence, but, seeing that Aunt Kate was out of earshot, at once led the three young ladies into the back room. The middle of the room was occupied by two square tables placed end to end, and on these Aunt Julia and the caretaker were straightening and smoothing a large cloth. On the sideboard were arrayed dishes and plates, and glasses and bundles of knives and forks and spoons. The top of the closed square piano served also as a sideboard for viands and sweets. At a smaller sideboard in one corner two young men were standing, drinking hop-bitters.

Mr. Browne led his charges thither and invited them all, in jest, to some ladies' punch, hot, strong and sweet. As they said they never took anything strong, he opened three bottles of lemonade for them. Then he asked one of the young men to move aside, and, taking hold of the decanter, filled out for himself a goodly measure of whisky. The young men eyed him respectfully while he took a trial sip.

"God help me," he said, smiling, "it's the doctor's orders."

His wizened face broke into a broader smile, and the three young ladies laughed in musical echo to his pleasantry, swaying their bodies to and fro, with nervous jerks of their shoulders. The boldest said:

"O, now, Mr. Browne, I'm sure the doctor never ordered anything of the kind."

Mr. Browne took another sip of his whisky and said, with sidling mimicry:

"Well, you see, I'm like the famous Mrs. Cassidy, who is reported to have said: 'Now, Mary Grimes, if I don't take it, make me take it, for I feel I want it.'"

His hot face had leaned forward a little too confidently and he had assumed a very low Dublin accent so that the young ladies, with one instinct, received his speech in silence. Miss Furlong, who was one of Mary Jane's pupils, asked Miss Daly what was the name of the pretty waltz she had played; and Mr. Browne, seeing that he was ignored, turned promptly to the two young men who were more appreciative.

A red-faced young woman, dressed in pansy, came into the room, excitedly clapping her hands and crying:

"Quadrilles! Quadrilles!"

Close on her heels came Aunt Kate, crying:

"Two gentlemen and three ladies, Mary Jane!"

"O, here's Mr. Bergin and Mr. Kerrigan," said Mary Jane. "Mr. Kerrigan, will you take Miss Power? Miss Furlong, may I get you a partner, Mr. Bergin. O, that'll just do now."

"Three ladies, Mary Jane," said Aunt Kate.

The two young gentlemen asked the ladies if they might have the pleasure, and Mary Jane turned to Miss Daly.

"O, Miss Daly, you're really awfully good, after playing for the last two dances, but really we're so short of ladies tonight."

"I don't mind in the least, Miss Morkan."

"But I've a nice partner for you, Mr. Bartell D'Arcy, the tenor. I'll get him to sing later on. All Dublin is raving about him."

"Lovely voice, lovely voice!" said Aunt Kate.

As the piano had twice begun the prelude to the first figure Mary Jane led her recruits quickly from the room. They had hardly gone when Aunt Julia wandered slowly into the room, looking behind her at something.

"What is the matter, Julia?" asked Aunt Kate anxiously. "Who is it?"

Julia, who was carrying in a column of tablenapkins, turned to her sister and said, simply, as if the question had surprised her:

"It's only Freddy, Kate, and Gabriel with him."

In fact right behind her Gabriel could be seen piloting Freddy Malins across the landing. The latter, a young man of about forty, was of Gabriel's size and build, with very round shoulders. His face was fleshy and pallid, touched with colour only at the thick hanging lobes of his ears and at the wide wings of his nose. He had coarse features, a blunt nose, a convex and receding brow, tumid and protruded lips. His heavy-lidded eyes and the disorder of his scanty hair made him look sleepy. He was laughing heartily in a high key at a story which he had been telling Gabriel on the stairs and at the same time rubbing the knuckles of his left fist backwards and forwards into his left eye.

"Good evening, Freddy," said Aunt Julia.

Freddy Malins bade the Misses Morkan goodevening in what seemed an offhand fashion by reason of the habitual catch in his voice and then, seeing that Mr. Browne was grinning at him from the sideboard, crossed the room on rather shaky legs and began to repeat in an undertone the story he had just told to Gabriel.

"He's not so bad, is he?" said Aunt Kate to Gabriel.

Gabriel's brows were dark, but he raised them quickly and answered:

"O, no, hardly noticeable."

"Now, isn't he a terrible fellow!" she said. "And his poor mother made him take the pledge on New Year's Eve. But come on, Gabriel, into the drawingroom."

Before leaving the room with Gabriel she signalled to Mr. Browne by frowning and shaking her forefinger in warning to and fro. Mr. Browne nodded in answer and, when she had gone, said to Freddy Malins:

"Now, then, Teddy, I'm going to fill you out a good glass of lemonade just to buck you up."

Freddy Malins, who was nearing the climax of his story, waved the offer aside impatiently but Mr. Browne, having first called Freddy Malins' attention to a disarray in his dress, filled out and handed him a full glass of lemonade. Freddy Malins' left hand accepted the glass mechanically, his right hand being engaged in the mechanical readjustment of his dress. Mr. Browne, whose face was once more wrinkling with mirth, poured out for himself a glass of whisky while Freddy Malins exploded, before he had well reached the climax of his story, in a kink of high-pitched bronchitic laughter and, setting down his untasted and overflowing glass, began to rub the knuckles of his left fist backwards and forwards into his left eye, repeating words of his last phrase as well as his fit of laughter would allow him.

Gabriel could not listen while Mary Jane was play-

ing her Academy piece, full of runs and difficult passages, to the hushed drawing-room. He liked music but the piece she was playing had no melody for him and he doubted whether it had any melody for the other listeners, though they had begged Mary Jane to play something. Four young men, who had come from the refreshment-room to stand in the doorway at the sound of the piano, had gone away quietly in couples after a few minutes. The only persons who seemed to
10 follow the music were Mary Jane herself, her hands racing along the keyboard or lifted from it at the pauses like those of a priestess in momentary imprecation, and Aunt Kate standing at her elbow to turn the page.

Gabriel's eyes, irritated by the floor, which glittered with beeswax under the heavy chandelier, wandered to the wall above the piano. A picture of the balcony scene in *Romeo and Juliet* hung there and beside it was a picture of the two murdered princes in the Tower
20 which Aunt Julia had worked in red, blue and brown wools when she was a girl. Probably in the school they had gone to as girls that kind of work had been taught for one year. His mother had worked for him as a birthday present a waistcoat of purple tabinet, with little foxes' heads upon it, lined with brown satin and having round mulberry buttons. It was strange that his mother had had no musical talent though Aunt Kate used to call her the brains carrier of the Morkan family. Both she and Julia had always seemed a little
30 proud of their serious and matronly sister. Her photograph stood before the pierglass. She held an open book on her knees and was pointing out something in it to Constantine who, dressed in a man-o'-war suit, lay at her feet. It was she who had chosen the names of her sons for she was very sensible of the dignity of family life. Thanks to her, Constantine was now senior curate in Balbriggan and, thanks to her, Gabriel himself had taken his degree in the Royal University. A shadow passed over his face as he remembered her
40 sullen opposition to his marriage. Some slighting phrases she had used still rankled in his memory; she had once spoken of Gretta as being country cute and that was not true of Gretta at all. It was Gretta who had nursed her during all her last long illness in their house at Monkstown.

He knew that Mary Jane must be near the end of her piece for she was playing again the opening melody with runs of scales after every bar and while he waited for the end the resentment died down in his heart.
50 The piece ended with a trill of octaves in the treble and a final deep octave in the bass. Great applause greeted Mary Jane as, blushing and rolling up her music nervously, she escaped from the room. The

most vigorous clapping came from the four young men in the doorway who had gone away to the refreshment-room at the beginning of the piece but had come back when the piano had stopped.

Lancers were arranged. Gabriel found himself partnered with Miss Ivors. She was a frank-mannered talkative young lady, with a freckled face and prom- 60 inent brown eyes. She did not wear a low-cut bodice and the large brooch which was fixed in the front of her collar bore on it an Irish device and motto.

When they had taken their places she said abruptly: "I have a crow to pluck with you."

"With me?" said Gabriel.

She nodded her head gravely.

"What is it?" asked Gabriel, smiling at her solemn manner.

"Who is G. C.?" answered Miss Ivors, turning her 70 eyes upon him.

Gabriel coloured and was about to knit his brows, as if he did not understand, when she said bluntly:

"O, innocent Amy! I have found out that you write for *The Daily Express.* Now, aren't you ashamed of yourself?"

"Why should I be ashamed of myself?" asked Gabriel, blinking his eyes and trying to smile.

"Well, I'm ashamed of you," said Miss Ivors frankly. "To say you'd write for a paper like that. 80 I didn't think you were a West Briton."

A look of perplexity appeared on Gabriel's face. It was true that he wrote a literary column every Wednesday in *The Daily Express,* for which he was paid fifteen shillings. But that did not make him a West Briton surely. The books he received for review were almost more welcome than the paltry cheque. He loved to feel the covers and turn over the pages of newly printed books. Nearly every day when his teaching in the college was ended he used to wander 90 down the quays to the second-hand booksellers, to Hickey's on Bachelor's Walk, to Webb's or Massey's on Aston's Quay, or to O'Clohissey's in the by-street. He did not know how to meet her charge. He wanted to say that literature was above politics. But they were friends of many years' standing and their careers had been parallel, first at the University and then as teachers: he could not risk a grandiose phrase with her. He continued blinking his eyes and trying to smile and murmured lamely that he saw nothing political in 100 writing reviews of books.

When their turn to cross had come he was still perplexed and inattentive. Miss Ivors promptly took his hand in a warm grasp and said in a soft friendly tone:

"Of course, I was only joking. Come, we cross now."

When they were together again she spoke of the University question and Gabriel felt more at ease. A friend of hers had shown her his review of Browning's poems. That was how she had found out the secret:

---

24. tabinet, a kind of poplin cloth. 81. **West Briton,** one not in sympathy with the Irish nationalist movement, although living in Ireland.

but she liked the review immensely. Then she said suddenly:

"O, Mr. Conroy, will you come for an excursion to the Aran Isles this summer? We're going to stay there a whole month. It will be splendid out in the Atlantic. You ought to come. Mr. Clancy is coming, and Mr. Kilkelly and Kathleen Kearney. It would be splendid for Gretta too if she'd come. She's from Connacht, isn't she?"

"Her people are," said Gabriel shortly.

"But you will come, won't you?" said Miss Ivors, laying her warm hand eagerly on his arm.

"The fact is," said Gabriel, "I have just arranged to go—"

"Go where?" asked Miss Ivors.

"Well, you know, every year I go for a cycling tour with some fellows and so—"

"But where?" asked Miss Ivors.

"Well, we usually go to France or Belgium or perhaps Germany," said Gabriel awkwardly.

"And why do you go to France and Belgium," said Miss Ivors, "instead of visiting your own land?"

"Well," said Gabriel, "it's partly to keep in touch with the languages and partly for a change."

"And haven't you your own language to keep in touch with—Irish?" asked Miss Ivors.

"Well," said Gabriel, "if it comes to that, you know, Irish is not my language."

Their neighbours had turned to listen to the cross-examination. Gabriel glanced right and left nervously and tried to keep his good humour under the ordeal which was making a blush invade his forehead.

"And haven't you your own land to visit," continued Miss Ivors, "that you know nothing of, your own people, and your own country?"

"O, to tell you the truth," retorted Gabriel suddenly, "I'm sick of my own country, sick of it!"

"Why?" asked Miss Ivors.

Gabriel did not answer for his retort had heated him.

"Why?" repeated Miss Ivors.

They had to go visiting together and, as he had not answered her, Miss Ivors said warmly:

"Of course, you've no answer."

Gabriel tried to cover his agitation by taking part in the dance with great energy. He avoided her eyes for he had seen a sour expression on her face. But when they met in the long chain he was surprised to feel his hand firmly pressed. She looked at him from under her brows for a moment quizzically until he smiled. Then, just as the chain was about to start again, she stood on tiptoe and whispered into his ear:

"West Briton!"

When the lancers were over Gabriel went away to a remote corner of the room where Freddy Malins' mother was sitting. She was a stout feeble old woman with white hair. Her voice had a catch in it like her son's and she stuttered slightly. She had been told that Freddy had come and that he was nearly all right. Gabriel asked her whether she had had a good crossing. She lived with her married daughter in Glasgow and came to Dublin on a visit once a year. She answered placidly that she had had a beautiful crossing and that the captain had been most attentive to her. She spoke also of the beautiful house her daughter kept in Glasgow, and of all the friends they had there. While her tongue rambled on Gabriel tried to banish from his mind all memory of the unpleasant incident with Miss Ivors. Of course the girl or woman, or whatever she was, was an enthusiast but there was a time for all things. Perhaps he ought not to have answered her like that. But she had no right to call him a West Briton before people, even in joke. She had tried to make him ridiculous before people, heckling him and staring at him with her rabbit's eyes.

He saw his wife making her way towards him through the waltzing couples. When she reached him she said into his ear:

"Gabriel, Aunt Kate wants to know won't you carve the goose as usual. Miss Daly will carve the ham and I'll do the pudding."

"All right," said Gabriel.

"She's sending in the younger ones first as soon as this waltz is over so that we'll have the table to ourselves."

"Were you dancing?" asked Gabriel.

"Of course I was. Didn't you see me? What row had you with Molly Ivors?"

"No row. Why? Did she say so?"

"Something like that. I'm trying to get that Mr. D'Arcy to sing. He's full of conceit, I think."

"There was no row," said Gabriel moodily, "only she wanted me to go for a trip to the west of Ireland and I said I wouldn't."

His wife clasped her hands excitedly and gave a little jump.

"O, do go, Gabriel," she cried. "I'd love to see Galway again."

"You can go if you like," said Gabriel coldly.

She looked at him for a moment, then turned to Mrs. Malins and said:

"There's a nice husband for you, Mrs. Malins."

While she was threading her way back across the room Mrs. Malins, without adverting to the interruption, went on to tell Gabriel what beautiful places there were in Scotland and beautiful scenery. Her son-in-law brought them every year to the lakes and they used to go fishing. Her son-in-law was a splendid fisher. One day he caught a beautiful big fish and the man in the hotel cooked it for their dinner.

Gabriel hardly heard what she said. Now that supper was coming near he began to think again about

his speech and about the quotation. When he saw
Freddy Malins coming across the room to visit his
mother Gabriel left the chair free for him and retired
into the embrasure of the window. The room had already cleared and from the back room came the clatter
of plates and knives. Those who still remained in the
drawing-room seemed tired of dancing and were conversing quietly in little groups. Gabriel's warm trembling fingers tapped the cold pane of the window. How
10 cool it must be outside! How pleasant it would be to
walk out alone, first along by the river and then
through the park! The snow would be lying on the
branches of the trees and forming a bright cap on the
top of the Wellington Monument. How much more
pleasant it would be there than at the supper-table!

He ran over the headings of his speech: Irish hospitality, sad memories, the Three Graces, Paris, the
quotation from Browning. He repeated to himself a
phrase he had written in his review: "One feels that
20 one is listening to a thought-tormented music." Miss
Ivors had praised the review. Was she sincere? Had
she really any life of her own behind all her propa-
gandism? There had never been any ill-feeling between them until that night. It unnerved him to think
that she would be at the supper-table, looking up at
him while he spoke with her critical quizzing eyes.
Perhaps she would not be sorry to see him fail in his
speech. An idea came into his mind and gave him
courage. He would say, alluding to Aunt Kate and
30 Aunt Julia: "Ladies and Gentlemen, the generation
which is now on the wane among us may have had its
faults but for my part I think it had certain qualities of
hospitality, of humour, of humanity, which the new
and very serious and hypereducated generation that
is growing up around us seems to me to lack." Very
good: that was one for Miss Ivors. What did he care
that his aunts were only two ignorant old women?

A murmur in the room attracted his attention. Mr.
Browne was advancing from the door, gallantly es-
40 corting Aunt Julia, who leaned upon his arm, smiling
and hanging her head. An irregular musketry of applause escorted her also as far as the piano and then,
as Mary Jane seated herself on the stool, and Aunt
Julia, no longer smiling, half turned so as to pitch her
voice fairly into the room, gradually ceased. Gabriel
recognised the prelude. It was that of an old song of
Aunt Julia's—*Arrayed for the Bridal*. Her voice, strong
and clear in tone, attacked with great spirit the runs
which embellish the air and though she sang very
50 rapidly she did not miss even the smallest of the grace
notes. To follow the voice, without looking at the
singer's face, was to feel and share the excitement of
swift and secure flight. Gabriel applauded loudly with
all the others at the close of the song and loud applause was borne in from the invisible supper-table.
It sounded so genuine that a little colour struggled into

Aunt Julia's face as she bent to replace in the music-
stand the old leather-bound songbook that had her
initials on the cover. Freddy Malins, who had listened
with his head perched sideways to hear her better, was 60
still applauding when everyone else had ceased and
talking animatedly to his mother who nodded her head
gravely and slowly in acquiescence. At last, when he
could clap no more, he stood up suddenly and hurried
across the room to Aunt Julia whose hand he seized
and held in both his hands, shaking it when words
failed him or the catch in his voice proved too much
for him.

"I was just telling my mother," he said, "I never
heard you sing so well, never. No. I never heard your 70
voice so good as it is tonight. Now! Would you believe
that now? That's the truth. Upon my word and honour
that's the truth. I never heard your voice sound so
fresh and so . . . so clear and fresh, never."

Aunt Julia smiled broadly and murmured something
about compliments as she released her hand from his
grasp. Mr. Browne extended his open hand towards
her and said to those who were near him in the manner
of a showman introducing a prodigy to an audience:

"Miss Julia Morkan, my latest discovery!" 80

He was laughing very heartily at this himself when
Freddy Malins turned to him and said:

"Well, Browne, if you're serious you might make a
worse discovery. All I can say is I never heard her
sing half so well as long as I am coming here. And
that's the honest truth."

"Neither did I," said Mr. Browne. "I think her
voice has greatly improved."

Aunt Julia shrugged her shoulders and said with
meek pride: 90

"Thirty years ago I hadn't a bad voice as voices go."

"I often told Julia," said Aunt Kate emphatically,
"that she was simply thrown away in that choir. But
she never would be said by me."

She turned as if to appeal to the good sense of
the others against a refractory child while Aunt Julia
gazed in front of her, a vague smile of reminiscence
playing on her face.

"No," continued Aunt Kate, "she wouldn't be said
or led by anyone, slaving there in that choir night 100
and day, night and day. Six o'clock on Christmas
morning! And all for what?"

"Well, isn't it for the honour of God, Aunt Kate?"
asked Mary Jane, twisting round on the piano stool
and smiling.

Aunt Kate turned fiercely on her niece and said:

"I know all about the honour of God, Mary Jane,
but I think it's not at all honourable for the pope to
turn out the women out of the choirs that have
slaved there all their lives and put little whipper- 110
snappers of boys over their heads. I suppose it is for
the good of the Church if the pope does it. But it's

not just, Mary Jane, and it's not right."

She had worked herself into a passion and would have continued in defence of her sister for it was a sore subject with her but Mary Jane, seeing that all the dancers had come back, intervened pacifically:

"Now, Aunt Kate, you're giving scandal to Mr. Browne who is of the other persuasion."

120 Aunt Kate turned to Mr. Browne, who was grinning at this allusion to his religion, and said hastily:

"O, I don't question the pope's being right. I'm only a stupid old woman and I wouldn't presume to do such a thing. But there's such a thing as common everyday politeness and gratitude. And if I were in Julia's place I'd tell that Father Healey straight up to his face . . ."

"And besides, Aunt Kate," said Mary Jane, "we really are all hungry and when we are hungry we 130 are all very quarrelsome."

"And when we are thirsty we are also quarrelsome," added Mr. Browne.

"So that we had better go to supper," said Mary Jane, "and finish the discussion afterwards."

On the landing outside the drawing-room Gabriel found his wife and Mary Jane trying to persuade Miss Ivors to stay for supper. But Miss Ivors, who had put on her hat and was buttoning her cloak, would not stay. She did not feel in the least hungry 140 and she had already overstayed her time.

"But only for ten minutes, Molly," said Mrs. Conroy. "That won't delay you."

"To take a pick itself," said Mary Jane, "after all your dancing."

"I really couldn't," said Miss Ivors.

"I am afraid you didn't enjoy yourself at all," said Mary Jane hopelessly.

"Ever so much, I assure you," said Miss Ivors, "but you really must let me run off now."

150 "But how can you get home?" asked Mrs. Conroy.

"O, it's only two steps up the quay."

Gabriel hesitated a moment and said:

"If you will allow me, Miss Ivors, I'll see you home if you are really obliged to go."

But Miss Ivors broke away from them.

"I won't hear of it," she cried. "For goodness' sake go in to your suppers and don't mind me. I'm quite well able to take care of myself."

"Well, you're the comical girl, Molly," said Mrs. 160 Conroy frankly.

"*Beannacht libh*," cried Miss Ivors, with a laugh, as she ran down the staircase.

Mary Jane gazed after her, a moody puzzled expression on her face, while Mrs. Conroy leaned over the banisters to listen for the hall-door. Gabriel asked himself was he the cause of her abrupt departure. But

she did not seem to be in ill humour: she had gone away laughing. He stared blankly down the staircase.

At the moment Aunt Kate came toddling out of the supper-room, almost wringing her hands in despair. 170

"Where is Gabriel?" she cried. "Where on earth is Gabriel? There's everyone waiting in there, stage to let, and nobody to carve the goose!"

"Here I am, Aunt Kate!" cried Gabriel, with sudden animation, "ready to carve a flock of geese, if necessary."

A fat brown goose lay at one end of the table and at the other end, on a bed of creased paper strewn with sprigs of parsley, lay a great ham, stripped of its outer skin and peppered over with crust crumbs, 180 a neat paper frill round its shin and beside this was a round of spiced beef. Between these rival ends ran parallel lines of side-dishes: two little minsters of jelly, red and yellow; a shallow dish full of blocks of blancmange and red jam, a large green leaf-shaped dish with a stalk-shaped handle, on which lay bunches of purple raisins and peeled almonds, a companion dish on which lay a solid rectangle of Smyrna figs, a dish of custard topped with grated nutmeg, a small bowl full of chocolates and sweets wrapped in gold 190 and silver papers and a glass vase in which stood some tall celery stalks. In the centre of the table there stood, as sentries to a fruit-stand which upheld a pyramid of oranges and American apples, two squat old-fashioned decanters of cut glass, one containing port and the other dark sherry. On the closed square piano a pudding in a huge yellow dish lay in waiting and behind it were three squads of bottles of stout and ale and minerals, drawn up according to the colours of their uniforms, the first two black, with 200 brown and red labels, the third and smallest squad white, with transverse green sashes.

Gabriel took his seat boldly at the head of the table and, having looked to the edge of the carver, plunged his fork firmly into the goose. He felt quite at ease now for he was an expert carver and liked nothing better than to find himself at the head of a well-laden table.

"Miss Furlong, what shall I send you?" he asked. "A wing or a slice of the breast?" 210

"Just a small slice of the breast."

"Miss Higgins, what for you?"

"O, anything at all, Mr. Conroy."

While Gabriel and Miss Daly exchanged plates of goose and plates of ham and spiced beef Lily went from guest to guest with a dish of hot floury potatoes wrapped in a white napkin. This was Mary Jane's idea and she had also suggested apple sauce for the goose but Aunt Kate had said that plain roast goose without any apple sauce had always been good enough 220 for her and she hoped she might never eat worse. Mary Jane waited on her pupils and saw that they

---

143. **take . . . itself**, to have a snack. 161. *Beannacht libh*, good-bye to you. 183. **minsters**, serving-dishes.

got the best slices and Aunt Kate and Aunt Julia opened and carried across from the piano bottles of stout and ale for the gentlemen and bottles of minerals for the ladies. There was a great deal of confusion and laughter and noise, the noise of orders and counter-orders, of knives and forks, of corks and glass-stoppers. Gabriel began to carve second helpings as soon as he had finished the first round without serving himself. Everyone protested loudly so that he compromised by taking a long draught of stout for he found the carving hot work. Mary Jane settled down quietly to her supper but Aunt Kate and Aunt Julia were still toddling round the table, walking on each other's heels, getting in each other's way and giving each other unheeded orders. Mr. Browne begged of them to sit down and eat their suppers and so did Gabriel but they said there was time enough, so that, at last, Freddy Malins stood up and, capturing Aunt Kate, plumped her down on her chair amid general laughter.

When everyone had been well served Gabriel said, smiling:

"Now, if anyone wants a little more of what vulgar people call stuffing let him or her speak."

A chorus of voices invited him to begin his own supper and Lily came forward with three potatoes which she had reserved for him.

"Very well," said Gabriel amiably, as he took another preparatory draught, "kindly forget my existence, ladies and gentlemen, for a few minutes."

He set to his supper and took no part in the conversation with which the table covered Lily's removal of the plates. The subject of talk was the opera company which was then at the Theatre Royal. Mr. Bartell D'Arcy, the tenor, a dark-complexioned young man with a smart moustache, praised very highly the leading contralto of the company but Miss Furlong thought she had a rather vulgar style of production. Freddy Malins said there was a Negro chieftain singing in the second part of the Gaiety pantomime who had one of the finest tenor voices he had ever heard.

"Have you heard him?" he asked Mr. Bartell D'Arcy across the table.

"No," answered Mr. Bartell D'Arcy carelessly.

"Because," Freddy Malins explained, "now I'd be curious to hear your opinion of him. I think he has a grand voice."

"It takes Teddy to find out the really good things," said Mr. Browne familiarly to the table.

"And why couldn't he have a voice too?" asked Freddy Malins sharply. "Is it because he's only a black?"

Nobody answered this question and Mary Jane led the table back to the legitimate opera. One of her pupils had given her a pass for *Mignon*. Of course it was very fine, she said, but it made her think of poor Georgina Burns. Mr. Browne could go back farther still, to the old Italian companies that used to come to Dublin—Tietjens, Ilma de Murzka, Campanini, the great Trebelli, Giuglini, Ravelli, Aramburo. Those were the days, he said, when there was something like singing to be heard in Dublin. He told too of how the top gallery of the old Royal used to be packed night after night, of how one night an Italian tenor had sung five encores to *Let me like a Soldier fall*, introducing a high C every time, and of how the gallery boys would sometimes in their enthusiasm unyoke the horses from the carriage of some great *prima donna* and pull her themselves through the streets to her hotel. Why did they never play the grand old operas now, he asked, *Dinorah*, *Lucrezia Borgia*? Because they could not get the voices to sing them: that was why.

"O, well," said Mr. Bartell D'Arcy, "I presume there are as good singers today as there were then."

"Where are they?" asked Mr. Browne defiantly.

"In London, Paris, Milan," said Mr. Bartell D'Arcy warmly. "I suppose Caruso, for example, is quite as good, if not better than any of the men you have mentioned."

"Maybe so," said Mr. Browne. "But I may tell you I doubt it strongly."

"O, I'd give anything to hear Caruso sing," said Mary Jane.

"For me," said Aunt Kate, who had been picking a bone, "there was only one tenor. To please me, I mean. But I suppose none of you ever heard of him."

"Who was he, Miss Morkan?" asked Mr. Bartell D'Arcy politely.

"His name," said Aunt Kate, "was Parkinson. I heard him when he was in his prime and I think he had then the purest tenor voice that was ever put into a man's throat."

"Strange," said Mr. Bartell D'Arcy. "I never even heard of him."

"Yes, yes, Miss Morkan is right," said Mr. Browne. "I remember hearing of old Parkinson but he's too far back for me."

"A beautiful, pure, sweet, mellow English tenor," said Aunt Kate with enthusiasm.

Gabriel having finished, the huge pudding was transferred to the table. The clatter of forks and spoons began again. Gabriel's wife served out spoonfuls of the pudding and passed the plates down the table. Midway down they were held up by Mary Jane, who replenished them with raspberry or orange jelly or with blancmange and jam. The pudding was

54. *Mignon*, a popular opera by Ambroise Thomas (1811–1896), first produced in 1866. 56. **Georgina Burns**, a fictitious singer in Dublin. 58-59. **Tietjens . . . Aramburo.** Some of the singers named here are historical; others can no longer be traced and may well be fictitious.

Therese Tietjens (1831–1877) was a German soprano; Ilma de Murska (Murzka) (1836–1889) was a Croatian soprano; Zelie Gilbert (pseud. Trebelli) (1838–1892) was a French mezzo-soprano; and Italo Campanini (1845–1896) and Antonio Giuglini (1827–1865) Italian operatic

of Aunt Julia's making and she received praises for it from all quarters. She herself said that it was not quite brown enough.

110 "Well, I hope, Miss Morkan," said Mr. Browne, "that I'm brown enough for you because, you know, I'm all brown."

All the gentlemen, except Gabriel, ate some of the pudding out of compliment to Aunt Julia. As Gabriel never ate sweets the celery had been left for him. Freddy Malins also took a stalk of celery and ate it with his pudding. He had been told that celery was a capital thing for the blood and he was just then under doctor's care. Mrs. Malins, who had been silent

120 all through the supper, said that her son was going down to Mount Melleray in a week or so. The table then spoke of Mount Melleray, how bracing the air was down there, how hospitable the monks were and how they never asked for a penny-piece from their guests.

"And do you mean to say," asked Mr. Browne incredulously, "that a chap can go down there and put up there as if it were a hotel and live on the fat of the land and then come away without paying any-

130 thing?"

"O, most people give some donation to the monastery when they leave," said Mary Jane.

"I wish we had an institution like that in our Church," said Mr. Browne candidly.

He was astonished to hear that the monks never spoke, got up at two in the morning and slept in their coffins. He asked what they did it for.

"That's the rule of the order," said Aunt Kate firmly.

140 "Yes, but why?" asked Mr. Browne.

Aunt Kate repeated that it was the rule, that was all. Mr. Browne still seemed not to understand. Freddy Malins explained to him, as best he could, that the monks were trying to make up for the sins committed by all the sinners in the outside world. The explanation was not very clear for Mr. Browne grinned and said:

"I like that idea very much but wouldn't a comfortable spring bed do them as well as a coffin?"

150 "The coffin," said Mary Jane, "is to remind them of their last end."

As the subject had grown lugubrious it was buried in a silence of the table during which Mrs. Malins could be heard saying to her neighbour in an indistinct undertone:

"They are very good men, the monks, very pious men."

The raisins and almonds and figs and apples and oranges and chocolates and sweets were now passed about the table and Aunt Julia invited all the guests 160 to have either port or sherry. At first Mr. Bartell D'Arcy refused to take either but one of his neighbours nudged him and whispered something to him upon which he allowed his glass to be filled. Gradually as the last glasses were being filled the conversation ceased. A pause followed, broken only by the noise of the wine and by unsettlings of chairs. The Misses Morkan, all three, looked down at the tablecloth. Someone coughed once or twice and then a few gentlemen patted the table gently as a signal for silence. The 170 silence came and Gabriel pushed back his chair and stood up.

The patting at once grew louder in encouragement and then ceased altogether. Gabriel leaned his ten trembling fingers on the tablecloth and smiled nervously at the company. Meeting a row of upturned faces he raised his eyes to the chandelier. The piano was playing a waltz tune and he could hear the skirts sweeping against the drawing-room door. People, perhaps, were standing in the snow on the quay outside, 180 gazing up at the lighted windows and listening to the waltz music. The air was pure there. In the distance lay the park where the trees were weighted with snow. The Wellington Monument wore a gleaming cap of snow that flashed westward over the white field of Fifteen Acres.

He began:

"Ladies and Gentlemen,

"It has fallen to my lot this evening, as in years past, to perform a very pleasing task but a task for 190 which I am afraid my poor powers as a speaker are all too inadequate."

"No, no!" said Mr. Browne.

"But, however that may be, I can only ask you tonight to take the will for the deed and to lend me your attention for a few moments while I endeavour to express to you in words what my feelings are on this occasion.

"Ladies and Gentlemen, it is not the first time that we have gathered together under this hospitable roof, 200 around this hospitable board. It is not the first time that we have been the recipients—or perhaps, I had better say, the victims—of the hospitality of certain good ladies."

He made a circle in the air with his arm and paused. Everyone laughed or smiled at Aunt Kate and Aunt Julia and Mary Jane who all turned crimson with pleasure. Gabriel went on more boldly:

"I feel more strongly with every recurring year that our country has no tradition which does it so 210 much honour and which it should guard so jealously as that of its hospitality. It is a tradition that is unique

tenors. Ravelli and Aramburo are no longer identifiable and Parkinson (ll. 89-96) is fictitious. 64. *Let . . . fall*, an extremely popular aria for tenor from the opera *Maritana* (1845) by William Vincent Wallace (1812–1865). 70. **Dinorah**, an opera (1859) by the German com-

poser Jakob Meyerbeer (1791–1864). *Lucrezia Borgia*, an opera (1833) by the Italian composer Gaetano Donizetti (1798–1848). 77. **Caruso**, Enrico Caruso (1873–1921), the most famous operatic tenor of his generation.

as far as my experience goes (and I have visited not a few places abroad) among the modern nations. Some would say, perhaps, that with us it is rather a failing than anything to be boasted of. But granted even that, it is, to my mind, a princely failing, and one that I trust will long be cultivated among us. Of one thing, at least, I am sure. As long as this one roof shelters the good ladies aforesaid—and I wish from my heart it may do so for many and many a long year to come 10 —the tradition of genuine warm-hearted courteous Irish hospitality, which our forefathers have handed down to us and which we in turn must hand down to our descendants, is still alive among us." ·

A hearty murmur of assent ran round the table. It shot through Gabriel's mind that Miss Ivors was not there and that she had gone away discourteously: and he said with confidence in himself:

"Ladies and Gentlemen,

"A new generation is growing up in our midst, 20 a generation actuated by new ideas and new principles. It is serious and enthusiastic for these new ideas and its enthusiasm, even when it is misdirected, is, I believe, in the main sincere. But we are living in a sceptical and, if I may use the phrase, a thought-tormented age: and sometimes I fear that this new generation, educated or hypereducated as it is, will lack those qualities of humanity, of hospitality, of kindly humour which belonged to an older day. Listening tonight to the names of all those great 30 singers of the past it seemed to me, I must confess, that we were living in a less spacious age. Those days might, without exaggeration, be called spacious days: and if they are gone beyond recall let us hope, at least, that in gatherings such as this we shall still speak of them with pride and affection, still cherish in our hearts the memory of those dead and gone great ones whose fame the world will not willingly let die."

"Hear, hear!" said Mr. Browne loudly.

"But yet," continued Gabriel, his voice falling into 40 a softer inflection, "there are always in gatherings such as this sadder thoughts that will recur to our minds: thoughts of the past, of youth, of changes, of absent faces that we miss here tonight. Our path through life is strewn with many such sad memories: and were we to brood upon them always we could not find the heart to go on bravely with our work among the living. We have all of us living duties and living affections which claim, and rightly claim, our strenuous endeavours.

50 "Therefore, I will not linger on the past. I will not let any gloomy moralising intrude upon us here tonight. Here we are gathered together for a brief moment from the bustle and rush of our everyday routine. We are met here as friends, in the spirit of good-fellowship, as colleagues, also to a certain extent, in the true spirit of *camaraderie*, and as the guest of—

what shall I call them?—the Three Graces of the Dublin musical world."

The table burst into applause and laughter at this allusion. Aunt Julia vainly asked each of her neigh- 60 bours in turn to tell her what Gabriel had said.

"He says we are the Three Graces, Aunt Julia," said Mary Jane.

Aunt Julia did not understand but she looked up, smiling, at Gabriel, who continued in the same vein:

"Ladies and Gentlemen,

"I will not attempt to play tonight the part that Paris played on another occasion. I will not attempt to choose between them. The task would be an invidious one and one beyond my poor powers. For 70 when I view them in turn, whether it be our chief hostess herself, whose good heart, whose too good heart, has become a byword with all who know her, or her sister, who seems to be gifted with perennial youth and whose singing must have been a surprise and a revelation to us all tonight, or, last but not least, when I consider our youngest hostess, talented, cheerful, hard-working and the best of nieces, I confess, Ladies and Gentlemen, that I do not know to which of them I should award the prize." 80

Gabriel glanced down at his aunts and, seeing the large smile on Aunt Julia's face and the tears which had risen to Aunt Kate's eyes, hastened to his close. He raised his glass of port gallantly, while every member of the company fingered a glass expectantly, and said loudly:

"Let us toast them all three together. Let us drink to their health, wealth, long life, happiness and prosperity and may they long continue to hold the proud and self-won position which they hold in their pro- 90 fession and the position of honour and affection which they hold in our hearts."

All the guests stood up, glass in hand, and turning towards the three seated ladies, sang in unison, with Mr. Browne as leader:

> For they are jolly gay fellows,
> For they are jolly gay fellows,
> For they are jolly gay fellows,
> Which nobody can deny.

Aunt Kate was making frank use of her handker- 100 chief and even Aunt Julia seemed moved. Freddy Malins beat time with his pudding-fork and the singers turned towards one another, as if in melodious conference, while they sang with emphasis:

> Unless he tells a lie,
> Unless he tells a lie,

68. **Paris,** a reference to the award for beauty given to the goddess Venus by Paris, prince of Troy; he was obliged to judge among Venus, Juno, and Minerva.

Then, turning once more towards their hostesses, they sang:

> For they are jolly gay fellows,
> For they are jolly gay fellows,
> For they are jolly gay fellows,
> Which nobody can deny.

The acclamation which followed was taken up beyond the door of the supper-room by many of the other guests and renewed time after time, Freddy Malins acting as officer with his fork on high.

The piercing morning air came into the hall where they were standing so that Aunt Kate said:

"Close the door, somebody. Mrs. Malins will get her death of cold."

"Browne is out there, Aunt Kate," said Mary Jane.

"Browne is everywhere," said Aunt Kate, lowering her voice.

Mary Jane laughed at her tone.

"Really," she said archly, "he is very attentive."

"He has been laid on here like the gas," said Aunt Kate in the same tone, "all during the Christmas."

She laughed herself this time good-humouredly and then added quickly:

"But tell him to come in, Mary Jane, and close the door. I hope to goodness he didn't hear me."

At that moment the hall-door was opened and Mr. Browne came in from the doorstep, laughing as if his heart would break. He was dressed in a long green overcoat with mock astrakhan cuffs and collar and wore on his head an oval fur cap. He pointed down the snow-covered quay from where the sound of shrill prolonged whistling was borne in.

"Teddy will have all the cabs in Dublin out," he said.

Gabriel advanced from the little pantry behind the office, struggling into his overcoat and, looking round the hall, said:

"Gretta not down yet?"

"She's getting on her things, Gabriel," said Aunt Kate.

"Who's playing up there?" asked Gabriel.

"Nobody. They're all gone."

"O no, Aunt Kate," said Mary Jane. "Bartell D'Arcy and Miss O'Callaghan aren't gone yet."

"Someone is fooling at the piano anyhow," said Gabriel.

Mary Jane glanced at Gabriel and Mr. Browne and said with a shiver:

"It makes me feel cold to look at you two gentlemen muffled up like that. I wouldn't like to face your journey home at this hour."

"I'd like nothing better this minute," said Mr. Browne stoutly, "than a rattling fine walk in the country or a fast drive with a good spanking goer between the shafts."

"We used to have a very good horse and trap at home," said Aunt Julia sadly.

"The never-to-be-forgotten Johnny," said Mary Jane, laughing.

Aunt Kate and Gabriel laughed too.

"Why, what was wonderful about Johnny?" asked Mr. Browne.

"The late lamented Patrick Morkan, our grandfather, that is," explained Gabriel, "commonly known in his later years as the old gentleman, was a glueboiler."

"O, now, Gabriel," said Aunt Kate, laughing, "he had a starch mill."

"Well, glue or starch," said Gabriel, "the old gentleman had a horse by the name of Johnny. And Johnny used to work in the old gentleman's mill, walking round and round in order to drive the mill. That was all very well; but now comes the tragic part about Johnny. One fine day the old gentleman thought he'd like to drive out with the quality to a military review in the park."

"The Lord have mercy on his soul," said Aunt Kate compassionately.

"Amen," said Gabriel. "So the old gentleman, as I said, harnessed Johnny and put on his very best tall hat and his very best stock collar and drove out in grand style from his ancestral mansion somewhere near Back Lane, I think."

Everyone laughed, even Mrs. Malins, at Gabriel's manner and Aunt Kate said:

"O, now, Gabriel, he didn't live in Back Lane, really. Only the mill was there."

"Out from the mansion of his forefathers," continued Gabriel, "he drove with Johnny. And everything went on beautifully until Johnny came in sight of King Billy's statue: and whether he fell in love with the horse King Billy sits on or whether he thought he was back again in the mill, anyhow he began to walk round the statue."

Gabriel paced in a circle round the hall in his goloshes amid the laughter of the others.

"Round and round he went," said Gabriel, "and the old gentleman, who was a very pompous old gentleman, was highly indignant. 'Go on, sir! What do you mean, sir? Johnny! Johnny! Most extraordinary conduct! Can't understand the horse!'"

The peal of laughter which followed Gabriel's imitation of the incident was interrupted by a resounding knock at the hall-door. Mary Jane ran to open it and let in Freddy Malins. Freddy Malins, with his hat well back on his head and his shoulders humped

---

197. **King Billy,** William III of England, who reigned from 1688 to 1702 and suppressed the Jacobite rebellion in Ireland at the Battle of the Boyne in 1690.

with cold, was puffing and steaming after his exertions.

"I could only get one cab," he said.

"O, we'll find another along the quay," said Gabriel.

"Yes," said Aunt Kate. "Better not keep Mrs. Malins standing in the draught."

Mrs. Malins was helped down the front steps by her son and Mr. Browne and, after many manoeuvres, hoisted into the cab. Freddy Malins clambered in after her and spent a long time settling her on the seat, Mr. Browne helping him with advice. At last she was settled comfortably and Freddy Malins invited Mr. Browne into the cab. There was a good deal of confused talk, and then Mr. Browne got into the cab. The cabman settled his rug over his knees, and bent down for the address. The confusion grew greater and the cabman was directed differently by Freddy Malins and Mr. Browne, each of whom had his head out through a window of the cab. The difficulty was to know where to drop Mr. Browne along the route, and Aunt Kate, Aunt Julia and Mary Jane helped the discussion from the doorstep with cross-directions and contradictions and abundance of laughter. As for Freddy Malins he was speechless with laughter. He popped his head in and out of the window every moment to the great danger of his hat, and told his mother how the discussion was progressing, till at last Mr. Browne shouted to the bewildered cabman above the din of everybody's laughter:

"Do you know Trinity College?"

"Yes, sir," said the cabman.

"Well, drive bang up against Trinity College gates," said Mr. Browne, "and then we'll tell you where to go. You understand now?"

"Yes, sir," said the cabman.

"Make like a bird for Trinity College."

"Right, sir," said the cabman.

The horse was whipped up and the cab rattled off along the quay amid a chorus of laughter and adieus.

Gabriel had not gone to the door with the others. He was in a dark part of the hall gazing up the staircase. A woman was standing near the top of the first flight, in the shadow also. He could not see her face but he could see the terra-cotta and salmon-pink panels of her skirt which the shadow made appear black and white. It was his wife. She was leaning on the banisters, listening to something. Gabriel was surprised at her stillness and strained his ear to listen also. But he could hear little save the noise of laughter and dispute on the front steps, a few chords struck on the piano and a few notes of a man's voice singing.

He stood still in the gloom of the hall, trying to catch the air that the voice was singing and gazing up at his wife. There was grace and mystery in her attitude as if she were a symbol of something. He asked himself what is a woman standing on the stairs in the shadow, listening to distant music, a symbol of. If he were a painter he would paint her in that attitude. Her blue felt hat would show off the bronze of her hair against the darkness and the dark panels of her skirt would show off the light ones. *Distant Music* he would call the picture if he were a painter.

The hall-door was closed; and Aunt Kate, Aunt Julia and Mary Jane came down the hall, still laughing.

"Well, isn't Freddy terrible?" said Mary Jane. "He's really terrible."

Gabriel said nothing but pointed up the stairs towards where his wife was standing. Now that the hall-door was closed the voice and the piano could be heard more clearly. Gabriel held up his hand for them to be silent. The song seemed to be in the old Irish tonality and the singer seemed uncertain both of his words and of his voice. The voice, made plaintive by distance and by the singer's hoarseness, faintly illuminated the cadence of the air with words expressing grief.

> O, the rain falls on my heavy locks
> And the dew wets my skin,
> My babe lies cold . . .

"O," exclaimed Mary Jane. "It's Bartell D'Arcy singing and he wouldn't sing all the night. O, I'll get him to sing a song before he goes."

"O, do, Mary Jane," said Aunt Kate.

Mary Jane brushed past the others and ran to the staircase, but before she reached it the singing stopped and the piano was closed abruptly.

"O, what a pity!" she cried. "Is he coming down, Gretta?"

Gabriel heard his wife answer yes and saw her come down towards them. A few steps behind her were Mr. Bartell D'Arcy and Miss O'Callaghan.

"O, Mr. D'Arcy," cried Mary Jane, "it's downright mean of you to break off like that when we were all in raptures listening to you."

"I have been at him all the evening," said Miss O'Callaghan, "and Mrs. Conroy, too, and he told us he had a dreadful cold and couldn't sing."

"O, Mr. D'Arcy," said Aunt Kate, "now that was a great fib to tell."

"Can't you see that I'm as hoarse as a crow?" said Mr. D'Arcy roughly.

He went into the pantry hastily and put on his overcoat. The others, taken aback by his rude speech, could find nothing to say. Aunt Kate wrinkled her brows and made signs to the others to drop the subject. Mr. D'Arcy stood swathing his neck carefully and frowning.

"It's the weather," said Aunt Julia, after a pause.

"Yes, everybody has colds," said Aunt Kate readily, "everybody."

"They say," said Mary Jane, "we haven't had snow like it for thirty years; and I read this morning in the newspapers that the snow is general all over Ireland."

"I love the look of snow," said Aunt Julia sadly.

"So do I," said Miss O'Callaghan. "I think Christmas is never really Christmas unless we have the snow on the ground."

"But poor Mr. D'Arcy doesn't like the snow," said Aunt Kate, smiling.

120 Mr. D'Arcy came from the pantry, fully swathed and buttoned, and in a repentant tone told them the history of his cold. Everyone gave him advice and said it was a great pity and urged him to be very careful of his throat in the night air. Gabriel watched his wife, who did not join in the conversation. She was standing right under the dusty fanlight and the flame of the gas lit up the rich bronze of her hair, which he had seen her drying at the fire a few days before. She was in the same attitude and seemed unaware of the 130 talk about her. At last she turned towards them and Gabriel saw that there was colour on her cheeks and that her eyes were shining. A sudden tide of joy went leaping out of his heart.

"Mr. D'Arcy," she said, "what is the name of that song you were singing?"

"It's called *The Lass of Aughrim*," said Mr. D'Arcy, "but I couldn't remember it properly. Why? Do you know it?"

"*The Lass of Aughrim*," she repeated. "I couldn't 140 think of the name."

"It's a very nice air," said Mary Jane. "I'm sorry you were not in voice tonight."

"Now, Mary Jane," said Aunt Kate, "don't annoy Mr. D'Arcy. I won't have him annoyed."

Seeing that all were ready to start she shepherded them to the door, where good-night was said:

"Well, good-night, Aunt Kate, and thanks for the pleasant evening."

"Good-night, Gabriel. Good-night Gretta!"

150 "Good-night, Aunt Kate, and thanks ever so much. Good-night, Aunt Julia."

"O, good-night, Gretta, I didn't see you."

"Good-night, Mr. D'Arcy. Good-night, Miss O'Callaghan."

"Good-night, Miss Morkan."

"Good-night, again."

"Good-night, all. Safe home."

"Good-night. Good-night."

The morning was still dark. A dull, yellow light 160 brooded over the houses and the river; and the sky seemed to be descending. It was slushy underfoot; and only streaks and patches of snow lay on the roofs, on the parapets of the quay and on the area railings. The lamps were still burning redly in the murky air and, across the river, the palace of the Four Courts stood out menacingly against the heavy sky.

She was walking on before him with Mr. Bartell D'Arcy, her shoes in a brown parcel tucked under one arm and her hands holding her skirt up from the slush. She had no longer any grace of attitude, but Gabriel's 170 eyes were still bright with happiness. The blood went bounding along his veins; and the thoughts went rioting through his brain, proud, joyful, tender, valorous.

She was walking on before him so lightly and so erect that he longed to run after her noiselessly, catch her by the shoulders and say something foolish and affectionate into her ear. She seemed to him so frail that he longed to defend her against something and then to be alone with her. Moments of their secret life together burst like stars upon his memory. A heliotrope 180 envelope was lying beside his breakfast-cup and he was caressing it with his hand. Birds were twittering in the ivy and the sunny web of the curtain was shimmering along the floor: he could not eat for happiness. They were standing on the crowded platform and he was placing a ticket inside the warm palm of her glove. He was standing with her in the cold, looking in through a grated window at a man making bottles in a roaring furnace. It was very cold. Her face, fragrant in the cold air, was quite close to his; and suddenly he 190 called out to the man at the furnace:

"Is the fire hot, sir?"

But the man could not hear with the noise of the furnace. It was just as well. He might have answered rudely.

A wave of yet more tender joy escaped from his heart and went coursing in warm flood along his arteries. Like the tender fire of stars moments of their life together, that no one knew of or would ever know of, broke upon and illumined memory. He longed 200 to recall to her those moments, to make her forget the years of their dull existence together and remember only their moments of ecstasy. For the years, he felt, had not quenched his soul or hers. Their children, his writing, her household cares had not quenched all their souls' tender fire. In one letter that he had written to her then he had said: "Why is it that words like these seem to me so dull and cold? Is it because there is no word tender enough to be your name?"

Like distant music these words that he had written 210 years before were borne towards him from the past. He longed to be alone with her. When the others had gone away, when he and she were in the room in the hotel, then they would be alone together. He would call her softly:

"Gretta!"

Perhaps she would not hear at once: she would be undressing. Then something in his voice would strike her. She would turn and look at him. . . .

At the corner of Winetavern Street they met a cab. 220 He was glad of its rattling noise as it saved him from conversation. She was looking out of the window and seemed tired. The others spoke only a few words, pointing out some building or street. The horse galloped along wearily under the murky morning sky, dragging his old rattling box after his heels, and Gabriel was again in a cab with her, galloping to catch the boat, galloping to their honeymoon.

As the cab drove across O'Connell Bridge Miss O'Callaghan said:

"They say you never cross O'Connell Bridge with-
10 out seeing a white horse."

"I see a white man this time," said Gabriel.

"Where?" asked Mr. Bartell D'Arcy.

Gabriel pointed to the statue, on which lay patches of snow. Then he nodded familiarly to it and waved his hand.

"Good-night, Dan," he said gaily.

When the cab drew up before the hotel, Gabriel jumped out and, in spite of Mr. Bartell D'Arcy's pro-test, paid the driver. He gave the man a shilling over
20 his fare. The man saluted and said:

"A prosperous New Year to you, sir."

"The same to you," said Gabriel cordially.

She leaned for a moment on his arm in getting out of the cab and while standing at the curbstone, bidding the others good-night. She leaned lightly on his arm, as lightly as when she had danced with him a few hours before. He had felt proud and happy then, happy that she was his, proud of her grace and wifely carriage. But now, after the kindling again of so many mem-
30 ories, the first touch of her body, musical and strange and perfumed, sent through him a keen pang of lust. Under cover of her silence he pressed her arm closely to his side; and, as they stood at the hotel door, he felt that they had escaped from their lives and duties, escaped from home and friends and run away together with wild and radiant hearts to a new adventure.

An old man was dozing in a great hooded chair in the hall. He lit a candle in the office and went before them to the stairs. They followed him in silence, their
40 feet falling in soft thuds on the thickly carpeted stairs. She mounted the stairs behind the porter, her head bowed in the ascent, her frail shoulders curved as with a burden, her skirt girt tightly about her. He could have flung his arms about her hips and held her still, for his arms were trembling with desire to seize her and only the stress of his nails against the palms of his hands held the wild impulse of his body in check. The porter halted on the stairs to settle his guttering candle. They halted, too, on the steps below
50 him. In the silence Gabriel could hear the falling of the molten wax into the tray and the thumping of his own heart against his ribs.

The porter led them along a corridor and opened a door. Then he set his unstable candle down on a toilet-table and asked at what hour they were to be called in the morning.

"Eight," said Gabriel.

The porter pointed to the tap of the electric-light and began a muttered apology, but Gabriel cut him short. 60

"We don't want any light. We have light enough from the street. And I say," he added, pointing to the candle, "you might remove that handsome article, like a good man."

The porter took up his candle again, but slowly, for he was surprised by such a novel idea. Then he mumbled good-night and went out. Gabriel shot the lock to.

A ghastly light from the street lamp lay in a long shaft from one window to the door. Gabriel threw his 70 overcoat and hat on a couch and crossed the room towards the window. He looked down into the street in order that his emotion might calm a little. Then he turned and leaned against a chest of drawers with his back to the light. She had taken off her hat and cloak and was standing before a large swinging mirror, un-hooking her waist. Gabriel paused for a few moments, watching her, and then said:

"Gretta!"

She turned away from the mirror slowly and walked 80 along the shaft of light towards him. Her face looked so serious and weary that the words would not pass Gabriel's lips. No, it was not the moment yet.

"You look tired," he said.

"I am a little," she answered.

"You don't feel ill or weak?"

"No, tired: that's all."

She went on to the window and stood there, look-ing out. Gabriel waited again and then, fearing that diffidence was about to conquer him, he said abruptly: 90

"By the way, Gretta!"

"What is it?"

"You know that poor fellow Malins?" he said quickly.

"Yes. What about him?"

"Well, poor fellow, he's a decent sort of chap, after all," continued Gabriel in a false voice. "He gave me back that sovereign I lent him, and I didn't expect it, really. It's a pity he wouldn't keep away from that Browne, because he's not a bad fellow, really." 100

He was trembling now with annoyance. Why did she seem so abstracted? He did not know how he could begin. Was she annoyed, too, about something? If she would only turn to him or come to him of her own accord! To take her as she was would be brutal. No, he must see some ardour in her eyes first. He longed to be master of her strange mood.

"When did you lend him the pound?" she asked, after a pause.

Gabriel strove to restrain himself from breaking 110 out into brutal language about the sottish Malins and his pound. He longed to cry to her from his soul, to crush her body against his, to overmaster her. But he said:

"O, at Christmas, when he opened that little Christmas-card shop in Henry Street."

He was in such a fever of rage and desire that he did not hear her come from the window. She stood before him for an instant, looking at him strangely. 120 Then, suddenly raising herself on tiptoe and resting her hands lightly on his shoulders, she kissed him.

"You are a very generous person, Gabriel," she said.

Gabriel, trembling with delight at her sudden kiss and at the quaintness of her phrase, put his hands on her hair and began smoothing it back, scarcely touching it with his fingers. The washing had made it fine and brilliant. His heart was brimming over with happiness. Just when he was wishing for it she had come to him of her own accord. Perhaps her thoughts 130 had been running with his. Perhaps she had felt the impetuous desire that was in him, and then the yielding mood had come upon her. Now that she had fallen to him so easily, he wondered why he had been so diffident.

He stood, holding her head between his hands. Then, slipping one arm swiftly about her body and drawing her towards him, he said softly:

"Gretta, dear, what are you thinking about?"

She did not answer nor yield wholly to his arm. 140 He said again, softly:

"Tell me what it is, Gretta. I think I know what is the matter. Do I know?"

She did not answer at once. Then she said in an outburst of tears:

"O, I am thinking about that song, *The Lass of Aughrim*."

She broke loose from him and ran to the bed and, throwing her arms across the bed-rail, hid her face. Gabriel stood stock-still for a moment in astonish- 150 ment and then followed her. As he passed in the way of the cheval-glass he caught sight of himself in full length, his broad, well-filled shirt-front, the face whose expression always puzzled him when he saw it in a mirror, and his glimmering gilt-rimmed eyeglasses. He halted a few paces from her and said:

"What about the song? Why does that make you cry?"

She raised her head from her arms and dried her eyes with the back of her hand like a child. A kinder 160 note than he had intended went into his voice.

"Why, Gretta?" he asked.

"I am thinking about a person long ago who used to sing that song."

"And who was the person long ago?" asked Gabriel, smiling.

"It was a person I used to know in Galway when I was living with my grandmother," she said.

The smile passed away from Gabriel's face. A dull anger began to gather again at the back of his mind and the dull fires of his lust began to glow angrily in 170 his veins.

"Someone you were in love with?" he asked ironically.

"It was a young boy I used to know," she answered, "named Michael Furey. He used to sing that song, *The Lass of Aughrim*. He was very delicate."

Gabriel was silent. He did not wish her to think that he was interested in this delicate boy.

"I can see him so plainly," she said, after a moment. "Such eyes as he had: big, dark eyes! And 180 such an expression in them—an expression!"

"O, then, you are in love with him?" said Gabriel.

"I used to go out walking with him," she said, "when I was in Galway."

A thought flew across Gabriel's mind.

"Perhaps that was why you wanted to go to Galway with that Ivors girl?" he said coldly.

She looked at him and asked in surprise:

"What for?"

Her eyes made Gabriel feel awkward. He shrugged 190 his shoulders and said:

"How do I know? To see him, perhaps."

She looked away from him along the shaft of light towards the window in silence.

"He is dead," she said at length. "He died when he was only seventeen. Isn't it a terrible thing to die so young as that?"

"What was he?" asked Gabriel, still ironically.

"He was in the gasworks," she said.

Gabriel felt humiliated by the failure of his irony 200 and by the evocation of this figure from the dead, a boy in the gasworks. While he had been full of memories of their secret life together, full of tenderness and joy and desire, she had been comparing him in her mind with another. A shameful consciousness of his own person assailed him. He saw himself as a ludicrous figure, acting as a pennyboy for his aunts, a nervous, well-meaning sentimentalist, orating to vulgarians and idealising his own clownish lusts, the pitiable fatuous fellow he had caught a glimpse of in the mirror. In- 210 stinctively he turned his back more to the light lest she might see the shame that burned upon his forehead.

He tried to keep up his tone of cold interrogation, but his voice when he spoke was humble and indifferent.

"I suppose you were in love with this Michael Furey, Gretta," he said.

"I was great with him at that time," she said.

Her voice was veiled and sad. Gabriel, feeling now how vain it would be to try to lead her whither he had 220 purposed, caressed one of her hands and said, also sadly:

"And what did he die of so young, Gretta? Consumption, was it?"

"I think he died for me," she answered.

A vague terror seized Gabriel at this answer, as if, at that hour when he had hoped to triumph, some impalpable and vindictive being was coming against him, gathering forces against him in its vague world. But he shook himself free of it with an effort of reason and continued to caress her hand. He did not question her again, for he felt that she would tell him of herself. Her hand was warm and moist: it did not respond to his touch, but he continued to caress it just as he had caressed her first letter to him that spring morning.

"It was in the winter," she said, "about the beginning of the winter when I was going to leave my grandmother's and come up here to the convent. And he was ill at the time in his lodgings in Galway and wouldn't be let out, and his people in Oughterard were written to. He was in decline, they said, or something like that. I never knew rightly."

She paused for a moment and sighed.

"Poor fellow," she said. "He was very fond of me and he was such a gentle boy. We used to go out together, walking, you know, Gabriel, like the way they do in the country. He was going to study singing only for his health. He had a very good voice, poor Michael Furey."

"Well; and then?" asked Gabriel.

"And then when it came to the time for me to leave Galway and come up to the convent he was much worse and I wouldn't be let see him so I wrote him a letter saying I was going up to Dublin and would be back in the summer, and hoping he would be better then."

She paused for a moment to get her voice under control, and then went on:

"Then the night before I left, I was in my grandmother's house in Nuns' Island, packing up, and I heard gravel thrown up against the window. The window was so wet I couldn't see, so I ran downstairs as I was and slipped out the back into the garden and there was the poor fellow at the end of the garden, shivering."

"And did you not tell him to go back?" asked Gabriel.

"I implored of him to go home at once and told him he would get his death in the rain. But he said he did not want to live. I can see his eyes as well as well! He was standing at the end of the wall where there was a tree."

"And did he go home?" asked Gabriel.

"Yes, he went home. And when I was only a week in the convent he died and he was buried in Oughterard, where his people came from. O, the day I heard that, that he was dead!"

She stopped, choking with sobs, and overcome by emotion, flung herself face downward on the bed, sobbing in the quilt. Gabriel held her hand for a moment longer, irresolutely, and then, shy of intruding on her grief, let it fall gently and walked quietly to the window.

She was fast asleep.

Gabriel, leaning on his elbow, looked for a few moments unresentfully on her tangled hair and half-open mouth, listening to her deep-drawn breath. So she had had that romance in her life: a man had died for her sake. It hardly pained him now to think how poor a part he, her husband, had played in her life. He watched her while she slept, as though he and she had never lived together as man and wife. His curious eyes rested long upon her face and on her hair: and, as he thought of what she must have been then, in that time of her first girlish beauty, a strange, friendly pity for her entered his soul. He did not like to say even to himself that her face was no longer beautiful, but he knew that it was no longer the face for which Michael Furey had braved death.

Perhaps she had not told him all the story. His eyes moved to the chair over which she had thrown some of her clothes. A petticoat string dangled to the floor. One boot stood upright, its limp upper fallen down: the fellow of it lay upon its side. He wondered at his riot of emotions of an hour before. From what had it proceeded? From his aunt's supper, from his own foolish speech, from the wine and dancing, the merrymaking when saying good-night in the hall, the pleasure of the walk along the river in the snow. Poor Aunt Julia! She, too, would soon be a shade with the shade of Patrick Morkan and his horse. He had caught that haggard look upon her face for a moment when she was singing *Arrayed for the Bridal*. Soon, perhaps, he would be sitting in that same drawing-room, dressed in black, his silk hat on his knees. The blinds would be drawn down and Aunt Kate would be sitting beside him, crying and blowing her nose and telling him how Julia had died. He would cast about in his mind for some words that might console her, and would find only lame and useless ones. Yes, yes: that would happen very soon.

The air of the room chilled his shoulders. He stretched himself cautiously along under the sheets and lay down beside his wife. One by one, they were all becoming shades. Better pass boldly into that other world, in the full glory of some passion, than fade and wither dismally with age. He thought of how she who lay beside him had locked in her heart for so many years that image of her lover's eyes when he had told her that he did not wish to live.

Generous tears filled Gabriel's eyes. He had never felt like that himself towards any woman, but he knew that such a feeling must be love. The tears gathered more thickly in his eyes and in the partial darkness he imagined he saw the form of a young man standing under a dripping tree. Other forms were near. His soul had approached that region where dwell the vast hosts of the dead. He was conscious of, but could not apprehend, their wayward and flickering existence. His own identity was fading out into a grey impalpable world: the solid world itself, which these dead had one time reared and lived in, was dissolving and dwindling.

A few light taps upon the pane made him turn to the window. It had begun to snow again. He watched sleepily the flakes, silver and dark, falling obliquely against the lamplight. The time had come for him to set out on his journey westward. Yes, the newspapers were right: snow was general all over Ireland. It was falling on every part of the dark central plain, on the treeless hills, falling softly upon the Bog of Allen and, farther westward, softly falling into the dark mutinous Shannon waves. It was falling, too, upon every part of the lonely churchyard on the hill where Michael Furey lay buried. It lay thickly drifted on the crooked crosses and headstones, on the spears of the little gate, on the barren thorns. His soul swooned slowly as he heard the snow falling faintly through the universe and faintly falling, like the descent of their last end, upon all the living and the dead.   (1914)

DAVID HERBERT LAWRENCE 1885-1930

D. H. Lawrence was born in Eastwood, Nottinghamshire, the son of a coal miner, who hated the boy, drank to excess, and beat his wife. The boy attended the Nottingham High School, was for a while a clerk, and taught in various places, finally coming to temporary rest at Croydon, a suburb of London (1908). His adolescent scribbling had been encouraged by a friendly neighbor girl (the "Miriam" of Sons and Lovers). Some of his poems were submitted to The English Review, and Ford Madox Ford, the editor, was so impressed that he arranged with young Lawrence for a novel, which was published in 1911 as The White Peacock. As first novels go, it was a most promising effort.

In the meantime he had fallen in love with Frieda von Richthofen Weekley, sister of the chief German ace during the First World War and wife of Ernest Weekley, the lexicographer. The two eloped from under the nose of the husband and went to the Continent, where Lawrence's second novel, The Trespasser (1912), was completed and where they spent the winter "penniless" in Italy. Eventually, following Frieda's divorce, they married and returned to England. In the meantime, Lawrence worked feverishly on his new novel, Sons and Lovers (1913), having published a volume of romantic poetry earlier the same year. Sons and Lovers was ultimately extremely successful, although it was rejected by the first publisher approached as "a dirty book." Actually, it is probably Lawrence's best work, intensely autobiographical and poignantly expressive. About this time Lawrence met J. Middleton Murry and his wife, Katherine Mansfield, both of whom encouraged him greatly in his literary endeavors. Lawrence spent the entire war at various places in England, wandering about in poor health—he was three times rejected for military service on account of tuberculosis—but always keeping away from the great cities, which he hated and dreaded.

But these war years were far from unproductive. The Rainbow (1915) caused a sensation; it was the first of Lawrence's novels to present sex situations in frank, unashamed language, and it dwelt far more than Sons and Lovers upon the problems of sex. In the following year Lawrence was in Cornwall, where Look! We Have Come Through (1917), a volume of poems on his life with Frieda, added fuel to the fire of controversy kindled by The Rainbow. Since he was regarded as "queer" and possibly a German spy by the people of the neighborhood, he found it wiser to move away from Cornwall. In 1918 he nearly died of influenza.

Never happy in England, Lawrence left the country after the Armistice and, except for a very few brief visits, never returned. Italy was his first resting place; he lived at Capri and in Sicily from 1920 to 1922, producing some short stories, an excellent novel—Women in Love (1920)—and a book on history—Movements in European History (1921)—under the rather transparent pseudonym of "Lawrence H. Davidson." Leaving Italy in 1922, he began a kind of vagabondage around the world. First he went to Ceylon, then to Australia, then to San Francisco via New Zealand and Tahiti, then to Taos, New Mexico. His general hope was that at Taos he might build a new social existence, a hope reminiscent of the idealistic dreams of Rousseau and Coleridge. "Let us all live together," he wrote, "and create a new world." But the terrestrial paradise at Taos was broken up by a devoted admirer, Mabel Dodge Luhan. She and Frieda Lawrence became jealous of each other, and Lawrence himself was greatly harassed by her presence. In the winter of 1923 he took refuge for a time at Chapala, near Guadalajara, Mexico. A flying trip to Europe followed, and a return to Taos bringing along another admirer, one Dorothy Brett, and again, conditions in the New Mexican retreat were far from harmonious. He wintered once more in Mexico, this time at Oaxaca.

Lawrence's final departure from the United States (1925) was an admission that his social dream had been dissipated, for he never returned. He went to Italy and the French Riviera, now that he was seriously ill; here he wrote, painted, and met Aldous Huxley. His writing during these last five years of life was chiefly miscellaneous, but he managed to create an international scandal with Lady Chatterley's Lover (1928)—a novel which he perversely yet characteristically insisted was "the best of all"—a novel recounting the love of an English lady for her lodge-keeper, told in the bluntest possible language, liberally powdered with all the four-letter Anglo-Saxon monosyllables which would make it unacceptable to the general public. It was immediately banned, and only in the 1950's was the ban lifted. Lawrence was disgusted, as Hardy had been with the reception of Jude the Obscure, and did little more writing before his death in March 1930.

Lawrence himself saw a three-stage development in his work; the first stage comprises those works written before he left England for his peregrinations abroad; the second is covered by those works he composed abroad with a foreign background; and the third embraces the books from his pen during his last years in Italy and on the French Riviera. But the differences among these three stages are more or less external. Lawrence preferred Sons and Lovers from the first stage; Women in Love from the second; and Lady Chatterley's Lover from the third. In retrospect, however, it seems that Sons and Lovers is likely to remain his masterpiece; it has greater balance, greater comprehensiveness, and greater universality than the others. Besides, he wrote many distinctive short stories, many beautiful poems and stimulating essays; he even attempted some plays. To give all one's attention to his novels is therefore a mistake.

Lawrence's experiences in Ceylon, in Australia, in the United States, and in Mexico gave him locales which he could describe in brilliant contrast to those of his stories of English life. But essentially he remained unchanged as to the theme of his stories, and was thus limited. The struggle of the human being in love caused by the sexual expression of his love on the one hand and its spiritual phase on the other is what lies at the core of his work. Sexual love he proceeded to exalt into a religio-philosophical belief; as one critic has observed, a complete acceptance of the logical consequences of Lawrence's sex-philosophy would banish the sexual joke from the face of the earth. The sociological leveling which Lawrence hoped for in his later novels is simply one step in the acceptance of his beliefs. But unfortunately for Lawrence's peace of mind and for the worth of his net achievement, he could never decide upon the philosophical viewpoint which his characters should adopt. The ideal state would come about through a frank and universal acceptance of sexual love, but there are all kinds of social, economic, and other practical pressures that thwart the ideal. Consequently Lawrence gropes and suffers, and his characters with him. In Lawrence's work there is usually the itch of an unsatisfied longing, partly physical and partly spiritual. His characters are harried by moral scruples, associations of guilt, and lust—"they would and they would not"—and like their creator are appallingly deficient in a sense of humor.

But, if this philosophical torment seems inevitable in Lawrence, and if he seems to be unable to escape from the waste land in which he finds himself—still, few can deny his power of expression, his passionate warmth, his vividness of language, and his sense of futility and tragedy. In the long run he may be a puritan; often, however, he gives the impression of being a naïve, and at the same time decadent, tilter against windmills and scatterer of sheep. This is not to say that he cannot be regarded as a fine artist.

THE LOVELY LADY

At seventy-two, Pauline Attenborough could still sometimes be mistaken, in the half-light, for thirty. She really was a wonderfully preserved woman, of perfect chic. Of course, it helps a great deal to have the right frame. She would be an exquisite skeleton, and her skull would be an exquisite skull, like that of some Etruscan woman, with feminine charm still in the swerve of the bone and the pretty naïve teeth.

Mrs. Attenborough's face was of the perfect oval and slightly flat type that wears best. There is no flesh to sag. Her nose rode serenely in its finely bridged curve. Only her big grey eyes were a tiny bit prominent on the surface of her face, and they gave her away most. The bluish lids were heavy, as if they ached sometimes with the strain of keeping the eyes beneath them arch and bright; and at the corners of the eyes were fine little wrinkles which would slacken with haggardness, then be pulled up tense again, to that bright, gay look, like a Leonardo woman who really could laugh outright.

Her niece Cecilia was perhaps the only person in the world who was aware of the invisible little wire which connected Pauline's eye-wrinkles with Pauline's will power. Only Cecilia consciously watched the eyes go haggard and old and tired, and remain so, for hours; until Robert came home. Then, ping!—the mysterious little wire that worked between Pauline's will and her face went taut; the weary, haggard, prominent eyes suddenly began to gleam; the eyelids arched; the queer curved eyebrows, which floated in such frail arches on Pauline's forehead, began to gather a mocking significance, and you had the real lovely lady, in all her charm.

She really had the secret of everlasting youth; that is to say, she could don her youth again like an eagle. But she was sparing of it. She was wise enough not to try being young for too many people. Her son Robert, in the evenings, and Sir Wilfred Knipe sometimes in the afternoon to tea; then occasional visitors on Sunday, when Robert was home; for these she was her lovely and changeless self, that age could not wither, nor custom stale; so bright and kindly and yet subtly mocking, like Mona Lisa who knew a thing or two. But Pauline knew more, so she needn't be smug at all, she could laugh that lovely mocking Bacchante laugh of hers, which was at the same time never malicious, always good-naturedly tolerant, both of vir-

The Lovely Lady is from The Complete Short Stories of D. H. Lawrence, Vol. III. Copyright 1933 by the Estate of D. H. Lawrence; 1961, by Angelo Ravagli and C. Montague Weekley, Executors of the Estate of Frieda Lawrence Ravagli. Reprinted by permission of The Viking Press, Inc.

tues and vices. The former, of course, taking much more tolerating. So she suggested, roguishly.

Only with her niece Cecilia she did not trouble to keep up the glamor. Ciss was not very observant, anyhow; and more than that, she was plain; more still, she was in love with Robert; and most of all, she was thirty, and dependent on her Aunt Pauline. Oh, Cecilia! Why make music for her?

Cecilia, called by her aunt and by her cousin Robert just Ciss, like a cat spitting, was a big dark-complexioned pug-faced young woman who very rarely spoke, and, when she did, couldn't get it out. She was the daughter of a poor Congregational minister who had been, while he lived, brother to Ronald, Aunt Pauline's husband. Ronald and the Congregational minister were both well dead, and Aunt Pauline had had charge of Ciss for the last five years.

They lived all together in a quite exquisite though rather small Queen Anne house some twenty-five miles out of town, secluded in a little dale, and surrounded by small but very quaint and pleasant grounds. It was an ideal place and an ideal life for Aunt Pauline, at the age of seventy-two. When the kingfishers flashed up the little stream in the garden, going under the alders, something still flashed in her heart. She was that kind of woman.

Robert, who was two years older than Ciss, went every day to town, to his chambers in one of the Inns. He was a barrister, and, to his secret but very deep mortification, he earned about a hundred pounds a year. He simply *couldn't* get above that figure, though it was rather easy to get below it. Of course, it didn't matter. Pauline had money. But then what was Pauline's was Pauline's, and, though she could give almost lavishly, still, one was always aware of having a *lovely* and *undeserved* present made to one: presents are so much nicer when they are undeserved, Aunt Pauline would say.

Robert too was plain, and almost speechless. He was medium-sized, rather broad and stout, though not fat. Only his creamy, clean-shaven face was rather fat and sometimes suggestive of an Italian priest, in its silence and its secrecy. But he had grey eyes like his mother but very shy and uneasy, not bold like hers. Perhaps Ciss was the only person who fathomed his awful shyness and *malaise*, his habitual feeling that he was in the wrong place: almost like a soul that has got into the wrong body. But he never did anything about it. He went up to his chambers, and read law. It was, however, all the weird old processes that interested him. He had, unknown to everybody but his mother, a quite extraordinary collection of old Mexican legal documents, reports of processes and trials, pleas, accusations, the weird and awful mixture of ecclesiastical law and common law in seventeenth-century Mexico. He had started a study in this direction through coming across a report of a trial of two English sailors, for murder, in Mexico in 1620, and he had gone on, when the next document was an accusation against a Don Miguel Estrada for seducing one of the nuns of the Sacred Heart Convent in Oaxaca in 1680.

Pauline and her son Robert had wonderful evenings with these old papers. The lovely lady knew a little Spanish. She even looked a trifle Spanish herself, with a high comb and a marvelous dark brown shawl embroidered in thick silvery silk embroidery. So she would sit at the perfect old table, soft as velvet in its deep brown surface, a high comb in her hair, earrings with dropping pendants in her ears, her arms bare and still beautiful, a few strings of pearls round her throat, a puce velvet dress on, and this or another beautiful shawl, and by candlelight she looked, yes, a Spanish high-bred beauty of thirty-two or three. She set the candles to give her face just the chiaroscuro she knew suited her; her high chair that rose behind her face was done in old green brocade, against which her face emerged like a Christmas rose.

They were always three at table; and they always drank a bottle of champagne: Pauline two glasses, Ciss two glasses, Robert the rest. The lovely lady sparkled and was radiant. Ciss, her black hair bobbed, her broad shoulders in a very nice and becoming dress that Aunt Pauline had helped her to make, stared from her aunt to her cousin and back again, with rather confused, mute, hazel eyes, and played the part of an audience suitably impressed. She *was* impressed, somewhere, all the time. And even rendered speechless by Pauline's brilliancy, even after five years. But at the bottom of her consciousness were the data of as weird a document as Robert ever studied: all the things she knew about her aunt and cousin.

Robert was always a gentleman, with an oldfashioned punctilious courtesy that covered his shyness quite completely. He was, and Ciss knew it, more confused than shy. He was worse than she was. Cecilia's own confusion dated from only five years back—Robert's must have started before he was born. In the lovely lady's womb he must have felt *very* confused.

He paid all his attention to his mother, drawn to her as a humble flower to the sun. And yet, priestlike, he was all the time aware, with the tail of his consciousness, that Ciss was there, and that she was a bit shut out of it, and that something wasn't right. He was aware of the third consciousness in the room. Whereas, to Pauline, her niece Cecilia was an appropriate part of her own setting, rather than a distinct consciousness.

Robert took coffee with his mother and Ciss in the warm drawing-room, where all the furniture was so lovely, all collectors' pieces—Mrs. Attenborough had made her own money, dealing privately in pictures and furniture and rare things from barbaric countries—and the three talked desultorily till about eight or half-past. It was very pleasant, very cosy, very homely even: Pauline made a real home cosiness out of so much elegant material. The chat was simple and nearly always bright. Pauline was her *real* self, emanating a friendly mockery and an odd, ironic gaiety. Till there came a little pause.

120 At which Ciss always rose and said good night and carried out the coffee tray, to prevent Burnett from intruding any more.

And then! Oh, then, the lovely glowing intimacy of the evening, between mother and son, when they deciphered manuscripts and discussed points, Pauline with that eagerness of a girl, for which she was famous. And it was quite genuine. In some mysterious way she had *saved up* her power for being thrilled, in connexion with a man. Robert, solid, rather quiet and sub-
130 dued, seemed like the elder of the two: almost like a priest with a young girl pupil. And that was rather how he felt.

Ciss had a flat for herself just across the courtyard, over the old coachhouse and stables. There were no horses. Robert kept his car in the coachhouse. Ciss had three very nice rooms up there, stretching along in a row one after another, and she had got used to the ticking of the stable clock.

But sometimes she did not go up to her rooms. In
140 the summer she would sit on the lawn, and from the open window of the drawing-room upstairs she would hear Pauline's wonderful heart-searching laugh. And in the winter the young woman would put on a thick coat and walk slowly to the little balustraded bridge over the stream, and then look back at the three lighted windows of that drawing-room where mother and son were so happy together.

Ciss loved Robert, and she believed that Pauline intended the two of them to marry: when she was dead.
150 But poor Robert, he was so convulsed with shyness already, with man or woman. What would he be when his mother was dead?—in a dozen more years. He would be just a shell, the shell of a man who had never lived.

The strange unspoken sympathy of the young with one another, when they are overshadowed by the old, was one of the bonds between Robert and Ciss. But another bond, which Ciss did not know how to draw tight, was the bond of passion. Poor Robert was by
160 nature a passionate man. His silence and his agonized, though hidden, shyness were both the result of a secret physical passionateness. And how Pauline could play on this! Ah, Ciss was not blind to the eyes which he fixed on his mother, eyes fascinated yet humiliated, full of shame. He was ashamed that he was not a man. And he did not love his mother. He was fascinated by her. Completely fascinated. And for the rest, paralyzed in a life-long confusion.

Ciss stayed in the garden till the lights leapt up in
170 Pauline's bedroom—about ten o'clock. The lovely lady had retired. Robert would now stay another hour

or so, alone. Then he too would retire. Ciss, in the dark outside, sometimes wished she could creep up to him and say: "Oh, Robert! It's all wrong!" But Aunt Pauline would hear. And anyhow, Ciss couldn't do it. She went off to her own rooms, once more, and so for ever.

In the morning, coffee was brought up on a tray to each of the three relatives. Ciss had to be at Sir Wilfred Knipe's at nine o'clock, to give two hours' lessons 180 to his little granddaughter. It was her sole serious occupation, except that she played the piano for the love of it. Robert set off to town about nine. And, as a rule, Aunt Pauline appeared to lunch, though sometimes not until tea-time. When she appeared, she looked fresh and young. But she was inclined to fade rather quickly, like a flower without water, in the daytime. Her hour was the candle hour.

So she always rested in the afternoon. When the sun shone, if possible she took a sun bath. This was 190 one of her secrets. Her lunch was very light, she could take her sun-and-air bath before noon or after, as it pleased her. Often it was in the afternoon, when the sun shone very warmly into a queer little yew-walled square just behind the stables. Here Ciss stretched out the lying-chair and rugs, and put the light parasol handy in the silent little enclosure of thick dark yew hedges beyond the red walls of the unused stables. And hither came the lovely lady with her book. Ciss then had to be on guard in one of her own rooms, should 200 her aunt, who was very keen-eared, hear a footstep.

One afternoon it occurred to Cecilia that she herself might while away this rather long afternoon by taking a sun bath. She was growing restive. The thought of the flat roof of the stable buildings, to which she could climb from a loft at the end, started her on a new adventure. She often went on to the roof: she had to, to wind up the stable clock, which was a job she had assumed to herself. Now she took a rug, climbed out under the heavens, looked at the sky and 210 the great elm-tops, looked at the sun, then took off her things and lay down perfectly serenely, in a corner of the roof under the parapet, full in the sun.

It was rather lovely, to bask all one's length like this in warm sun and air. Yes, it was very lovely! It even seemed to melt some of the hard bitterness of her heart, some of that core of unspoken resentment which never dissolved. Luxuriously, she spread herself, so that the sun should touch her limbs fully, fully. If she had no other lover, she should have the 220 sun! She rolled voluptuously. And suddenly, her heart stood still in her body, and her hair almost rose on end as a voice said very softly, musingly in her ear:

"No, Henry dear! It was not my fault you died instead of marrying that Claudia. No, darling. I was quite, quite willing for you to marry her, unsuitable though she was."

Cecilia sank down on her rug powerless and perspiring with dread. That awful voice, so soft, so musing, yet so unnatural. Not a human voice at all. Yet there must, there must be someone on the roof! Oh, how unspeakably awful!

She lifted her weak head and peeped across the sloping leads. Nobody! The chimneys were far too narrow to shelter anybody. There was nobody on the roof. Then it must be someone in the trees, in the elms. Either that, or terror unspeakable, a bodiless voice! She reared her head a little higher:

And as she did so, came the voice again:

"No, darling! I told you you would tire of her in six months. And you see, it was true, dear. It was true, true, true! I wanted to spare you that. So it wasn't I who made you feel weak and disabled, wanting that very silly Claudia; poor thing, she looked so woebegone afterwards! Wanting her and not wanting her, you got *yourself* into that perplexity, my dear. I only warned you. What else could I do? And you lost your spirit and died without ever knowing me again. It was bitter, bitter——"

The voice faded away. Cecilia subsided weakly on to her rug, after the anguished tension of listening. Oh, it was awful. The sun shone, the sky was blue, all seemed so lovely and afternoony and summery. And yet, oh, horror!—she was going to be forced to believe in the supernatural! And she loathed the supernatural, ghosts and voices and rappings and all the rest.

But that awful creepy bodiless voice, with its rusty sort of whisper of an overtone! It had something so fearfully familiar in it too! and yet was so utterly uncanny. Poor Cecilia could only lie there unclothed, and so all the more agonizingly helpless, inert, collapsed in sheer dread.

And then she heard the thing sigh! A deep sigh that seemed weirdly familiar, yet was not human. "Ah, well; ah, well, the heart must bleed! Better it should bleed than break. It is grief, grief! But it wasn't my fault, dear. And Robert could marry our poor dull Ciss tomorrow, if he wanted her. But he doesn't care about it, so why force him into anything!" The sounds were very uneven, sometimes only a husky sort of whisper. Listen! Listen!

Cecilia was about to give vent to loud and piercing screams of hysteria, when the last two sentences arrested her. All her caution and her cunning sprang alert. It was Aunt Pauline! It must be Aunt Pauline, practising ventriloquism or something like that! What a devil she was!

Where was she? She must be lying down there, right below where Cecilia herself was lying. And it was either some fiend's trick of ventriloquism, or else thought transference that conveyed itself like sound. The sounds were very uneven. Sometimes quite inaudible, sometimes only a brushing sort of noise. Ciss listened intently. No, it could not be ventriloquism. It was worse, some form of thought transference. Some horror of that sort. Cecilia still lay weak and inert, terrified to move, but she was growing calmer, with suspicion. It was some diabolic trick of that unnatural woman.

But *what a devil* of a woman! She even knew that she, Cecilia, had mentally accused her of killing her son Henry. Poor Henry was Robert's elder brother, twelve years older than Robert. He had died suddenly when he was twenty-two, after an awful struggle with himself, because he was passionately in love with a young and very good-looking actress, and his mother had humorously despised him for the attachment. So he had caught some sudden ordinary disease, but the poison had gone to his brain and killed him, before he ever regained consciousness. Ciss knew the few facts from her own father. And lately, she had been thinking that Pauline was going to kill Robert as she had killed Henry. It was clear murder: a mother murdering her sensitive sons, who were fascinated by her: the Circe!

"I suppose I may as well get up," murmured the dim unbreaking voice. "Too much sun is as bad as too little. Enough sun, enough love thrill, enough proper food, and not too much of any of them, and a woman might live for ever. I verily believe for ever. If she absorbs as much vitality as she expends! Or perhaps a trifle more!"

It was certainly Aunt Pauline! How, how horrible! She, Ciss, was hearing Aunt Pauline's thoughts. Oh, how ghastly! Aunt Pauline was sending out her thoughts in a sort of radio, and she, Ciss, had to *hear* what her aunt was thinking. How ghastly! How insufferable! One of them would surely have to die.

She twisted as she lay inert and crumpled, staring vacantly in front of her. Vacantly! Vacantly! And her eyes were staring almost into a hole. She was staring into it unseeing, a hole going down in the corner from the lead gutter. It meant nothing to her. Only it frightened her a little more.

When suddenly out of the hole came a sigh and a last whisper. "Ah, well! Pauline! Get up, it's enough for today!"—Good God! Out of the hole of the rainpipe! The rain-pipe was acting as a speaking-tube! Impossible! No, quite possible. She had read of it even in some book. And Aunt Pauline, like the old and guilty woman she was, talked aloud to herself. That was it!

A sullen exultance sprang into Ciss's breast. *That* was why she would never have anybody, not even Robert, in her bedroom. That was why she never dozed in a chair, never sat absent-minded anywhere, but went to her room, and kept to her room, except when she roused herself to be alert. When she slackened off, she talked to herself! She talked in a soft crazy little

The Lovely Lady. 139. Renoir, Pierre Auguste Renoir (1841–1919), one of the most distinguished French impressionistic painters. 140.

Rousseau, Pierre Etienne Theodore Rousseau (1812–1867), French painter of romantic persuasion.

voice, to herself. But she was not crazy. It was only her thoughts murmuring themselves aloud.

So she had qualms about poor Henry! Well, she might have! Ciss believed that Aunt Pauline had loved her big, handsome, brilliant first-born much more than she loved Robert, and that his death had been a terrible blow and a chagrin to her. Poor Robert had been only ten years old when Henry died. Since then he had been the substitute.

120 Ah, how awful!

But Aunt Pauline was a strange woman. She had left her husband when Henry was a small child, some years even before Robert was born. There was no quarrel. Sometimes she saw her husband again, quite amicably, but a little mockingly. And she even gave him money.

For Pauline earned all her own. Her father had been a Consul in the East and in Naples, and a devoted collector of beautiful and exotic things. When he died, 130 soon after his grandson Henry was born, he left his collection of treasures to his daughter. And Pauline, who had really a passion and a genius for loveliness, whether in texture or form or color, had laid the basis of her fortune on her father's collection. She had gone on collecting, buying where she could, and selling to collectors and to museums. She was one of the first to sell old, weird African wooden figures to the museums, and ivory carvings from New Guinea. She bought Renoir as soon as she saw his pictures. But 140 not Rousseau. And all by herself, she made a fortune.

After her husband died, she had not married again. She was not even *known* to have had lovers. If she did have lovers, it was not among the men who admired her most and paid her devout and open attendance. To these she was a "friend."

Cecilia slipped on her clothes and caught up her rug, hastening carefully down the ladder to the loft. As she descended she heard the ringing musical call: "All right, Ciss!" which meant that the lovely lady 150 was finished, and returning to the house. Even her voice was marvellously young and sonorous, beautifully balanced and self-possessed. So different from the little voice in which she talked to herself. *That* was much more the voice of an old woman.

Ciss hastened round to the yew enclosure, where lay the comfortable chaise-longue with the various delicate rugs. Everything Pauline had was choice, to the fine straw mat on the floor. The great yew walls were beginning to cast long shadows. Only in the 160 corner, where the rugs tumbled their delicate colors, was there hot, still sunshine.

The rugs folded up, the chair lifted away, Cecilia stooped to look at the mouth of the rain-pipe. There it was, in the corner, under a little hood of masonry and just projecting from the thick leaves of the creeper on the wall. If Pauline, lying there, turned her face towards the wall, she would speak into the very mouth

of the hole. Cecilia was reassured. She had heard her aunt's thoughts indeed, but by no uncanny agency.

That evening, as if aware of something, Pauline 170 was a little quicker than usual, though she looked her own serene, rather mysterious self. And after coffee she said to Robert and Ciss: "I'm so sleepy. The sun has made me so sleepy. I feel full of sunshine like a bee. I shall go to bed, if you don't mind. You two sit and have a talk."

Cecilia looked quickly at her cousin.

"Perhaps you would rather be alone," she said to him.

"No, no," he replied. "Do keep me company for a 180 while, if it doesn't bore you."

The windows were open, the scent of the honeysuckle wafted in, with the sound of an owl. Robert smoked in silence. There was a sort of despair in the motionless, rather squat body. He looked like a caryatid bearing a weight.

"Do you remember Cousin Henry?" Cecilia asked him suddenly.

He looked up in surprise.

"Yes, very well," he said. 190

"What did he look like?" she said, glancing into her cousin's big secret-troubled eyes, in which there was so much frustration.

"Oh, he was handsome; tall and fresh-colored, with mother's soft brown hair." As a matter of fact, Pauline's hair was gray. "The ladies admired him very much; he was at all the dances."

"And what kind of character had he?"

"Oh, very good-natured and jolly. He liked to be amused. He was rather quick and clever, like mother, 200 and very good company."

"And did he love your mother?"

"Very much. She loved him too—better than she does me, as a matter of fact. He was so much more nearly her idea of a man."

"Why was he more her idea of a man?"

"Tall—handsome—attractive, and very good company—and would, I believe, have been very successful at law. I'm afraid I am merely negative in all those respects." 210

Ciss looked at him attentively, with her slow-thinking hazel eyes. Under his impassive mask, she knew he suffered.

"Do you think you are so much more negative than he?" she said.

He did not lift his face. But after a few moments he replied:

"My life, certainly, is a negative affair."

She hesitated before she dared ask him:

"And do you mind?" 220

He did not answer her at all. Her heart sank.

"You see, I am afraid my life is as negative as yours is," she said. "And I'm beginning to mind bitterly. I'm thirty."

She saw his creamy, well-bred hand tremble.

"I suppose," he said, without looking at her, "one will rebel when it is too late."

That was queer, from him.

"Robert," she said, "do you like me at all?"

She saw his dusky creamy face, so changeless in its folds, go pale.

"I am very fond of you," he murmured.

"Won't you kiss me? Nobody ever kisses me," she
10 said pathetically.

He looked at her, his eyes strange with fear and a certain haughtiness. Then he rose and came softly over to her, and kissed her gently on the cheek.

"It's an awful shame, Ciss!" he said softly.

She caught his hand and pressed it to her breast.

"And sit with me sometime in the garden," she said, murmuring with difficulty. "Won't you?"

He looked at her anxiously and searchingly.

"What about mother?" he said.

20 Ciss smiled a funny little smile, and looked into his eyes. He suddenly flushed crimson, turning aside his face. It was a painful sight.

"I know," he said, "I am no lover of women."

He spoke with sarcastic stoicism against himself, but even she did not know the shame it was to him.

"You never try to be!" she said.

Again his eyes changed uncannily.

"Does one have to try?" he said.

"Why, yes! One never does anything if one doesn't
30 try."

He went pale again.

"Perhaps you are right," he said.

In a few minutes she left him, and went to her rooms. At least, she had tried to take off the everlasting lid from things.

The weather continued sunny, Pauline continued her sun baths, and Ciss lay on the roof eavesdropping in the literal sense of the word. But Pauline was not to be heard. No sound came up the pipe. She must be
40 lying with her face away into the open. Ciss listened with all her might. She could just detect the faintest, faintest murmur away below, but no audible syllable.

And at night, under the stars, Cecilia sat and waited in silence, on the seat which kept in view the drawing-room windows and the side door into the garden. She saw the light go up in her aunt's room. She saw the lights at last go out in the drawing-room. And she waited. But he did not come. She stayed on in the dark-
50 ness half the night, while the owl hooted. But she stayed alone.

Two days she heard nothing, her aunt's thoughts were not revealed, and at evening nothing happened. Then the second night, as she sat with heavy, helpless persistence in the garden, suddenly she started.

He had come out. She rose and went softly over the grass to him.

"Don't speak," he murmured.

And in silence, in the dark, they walked down the garden and over the little bridge to the paddock, 60 where the hay, cut very late, was in cock. There they stood disconsolate under the stars.

"You see," he said, "how can I ask for love, if I don't feel any love in myself. You know I have a real regard for you——"

"How can you feel any love, when you never feel anything?" she said.

"That is true," he replied.

And she waited for what next.

"And how can I marry?" he said. "I am a failure 70 even at making money. I can't ask my mother for money."

She sighed deeply.

"Then don't bother yet about marrying," she said. "Only love me a little. Won't you?"

He gave a short laugh.

"It sounds so atrocious, to say it is hard to begin," he said.

She sighed again. He was so stiff to move.

"Shall we sit down a minute?" she said. And then 80 as they sat on the hay, she added: "May I touch you? Do you mind?"

"Yes, I mind! But do as you wish," he replied, with that mixture of shyness and queer candor which made him a little ridiculous, as he knew quite well. But in his heart there was almost murder.

She touched his black, always tidy hair with her fingers.

"I suppose I shall rebel one day," he said again, suddenly.
90

They sat some time till it grew chilly. And he held her hand fast, but he never put his arms round her. At last she rose and went indoors, saying good night.

The next day, as Cecilia lay stunned and angry on the roof, taking her sunbath, and becoming hot and fierce with sunshine, suddenly she started. A terror seized her in spite of herself. It was the voice.

"Caro, caro, tu non l'hai visto!" it was murmuring away, in a language Cecilia did not understand. She 100 lay and writhed her limbs in the sun, listening intently to words she could not follow. Softly, whisperingly, with infinite caressiveness and yet with that subtle, insidious arrogance under its velvet, came the voice, murmuring in Italian: *"Bravo, si, molto bravo, poverino, ma uomo come te non lo sara mai, mai, mai!"* Oh, especially in Italian Cecilia heard the poisonous charm of the voice, so caressive, so soft and flexible, yet so utterly egoistic. She hated it with intensity as it sighed and whispered out of nowhere. Why, why 110

---

99. *"Caro . . . visto,"* "Beloved, you haven't seen him!" 105. *"Bravo . . . mai,"* "Beloved . . . yes, there is none like you . . . won-derful, yes, wonderful, poor sweetheart, there will never be a man like you, never, never." 121. *"Cara . . . umana,"* "Beloved, most beauti-

should it be so delicate, so subtle and flexible and beautifully controlled, while she herself was so clumsy! Oh, poor Cecilia, she writhed in the afternoon sun, knowing her own clownish clumsiness and lack of suavity, in comparison.

"No, Robert dear, you will never be the man your father was, though you have some of his looks. He was a marvellous lover, soft as a flower yet piercing as a humming-bird. No, Robert dear, you will never 120 know how to serve a woman as Monsignor Mauro did. *Cara, cara mia bellissima, ti ho aspettato come l'agoniz- zante aspetta la morte, morte deliziosa, quasi quasi troppo deliziosa per un' anima umana*—Soft as a flower, yet probing like a humming-bird. He gave himself to a woman as he gave himself to God. Mauro! Mauro! How you loved me!"

The voice ceased in reverie, and Cecilia knew what she had guessed before, that Robert was not the son of her Uncle Ronald, but of some Italian.

130 "I am disappointed in you, Robert. There is no poignancy in you. Your father was a Jesuit, but he was the most perfect and poignant lover in the world. You are a Jesuit like a fish in a tank. And that Ciss of yours is the cat fishing for you. It is less edifying even than poor Henry."

Cecilia suddenly bent her mouth down to the tube, and said in a deep voice:

"Leave Robert alone! Don't kill him as well."

There was a dead silence, in the hot July afternoon 140 that was lowering for thunder. Cecilia lay prostrate, her heart beating in great thumps. She was listening as if her whole soul were an ear. At last she caught the whisper:

"Did someone speak?"

She leaned again to the mouth of the tube.

"Don't kill Robert as you killed me," she said with a slow enunciation, and a deep but small voice.

"Ah!" came the sharp little cry. "Who is that speaking?"

150 "Henry!" said the deep voice.

There was dead silence. Poor Cecilia lay with all the use gone out of her. And there was dead silence. Till at last came the whisper:

"I didn't kill Henry. No, NO! Henry, surely you can't blame me! I loved you, dearest. I only wanted to help you."

"You killed me!" came the deep, artificial, accusing voice. "Now, let Robert live. Let him go! Let him marry!"

160 There was a pause.

"How very, very awful!" mused the whispering voice. "Is it possible, Henry, you are a spirit, and you condemn me?"

"Yes! I condemn you!"

Cecilia felt all her pent-up rage going down that

rain-pipe. At the same time, she almost laughed. It was awful.

She lay and listened and listened. No sound! As if time had ceased, she lay inert in the weakening sun. The sky was yellowing. Quickly she dressed herself, 170 went down, and out to the corner of the stables.

"Aunt Pauline!" she called discreetly. "Did you hear thunder?"

"Yes! I am going in. Don't wait," came a feeble voice.

Cecilia retired, and from the loft watched, spying, as the figure of the lovely lady, wrapped in a lovely wrap of old blue silk, went rather totteringly to the house.

The sky gradually darkened, Cecilia hastened in with 180 the rugs. Then the storm broke. Aunt Pauline did not appear to tea. She found the thunder trying. Robert also did not arrive till after tea, in the pouring rain. Cecilia went down the covered passage to her own house, and dressed carefully for dinner, putting some white columbines at her breast.

The drawing-room was lit with a softly shaded lamp. Robert, dressed, was waiting, listening to the rain. He too seemed strangely crackling and on edge. Cecilia came in, with the white flowers nodding at her breast. 190 Robert was watching her curiously, a new look on his face. Cecilia went to the bookshelves near the door and was peering for something, listening acutely. She heard a rustle, then the door softly opening. And as it opened, Ciss suddenly switched on the strong electric light by the door.

Her aunt, in a dress of black lace over ivory color, stood in the doorway. Her face was made up, but haggard with a look of unspeakable irritability, as if years of suppressed exasperation and dislike of her 200 fellow-men had suddenly crumpled her into an old witch.

"Oh, aunt!" cried Cecilia.

"Why, mother, you're a little old lady!" came the astounded voice of Robert; like an astonished boy; as if it were a joke.

"Have you only just found it out?" snapped the old woman venomously.

"Yes! Why, I thought——" his voice trailed out in misgiving. 210

The haggard, old Pauline, in a frenzy of exaspera- tion, said:

"Aren't we going down?"

She had never even noticed the excess of light, a thing she shunned. And she went downstairs almost tottering.

At table she sat with her face like a crumpled mask of unspeakable irritability. She looked old, very old, and like a witch. Robert and Cecilia fetched furtive glances at her. And Ciss, watching Robert, saw that he 220 was so astonished and repelled by his mother's looks, that he was another man.

ful . . . I have awaited you as the dying awaits death, delicious death . . . as if . . . as if it were almost too wonderful for a human being."

"What kind of a drive home did you have?" snapped Pauline, with an almost gibbering irritability.

"It rained, of course," he said.

"How clever of you to have found that out!" said his mother, with the grisly grin of malice that had succeeded her arch smirk.

"I don't understand," he said with quiet suavity.

"It's apparent," said his mother, rapidly and sloppily eating her food.

She rushed through the meal like a crazy dog, to the utter consternation of the servant. And the moment it was over, she darted in a queer, crab-like way upstairs. Robert and Cecilia followed her, thunderstruck, like two conspirators.

"You pour the coffee. I loathe it! I'm going! Good night!" said the old woman, in a succession of sharp shots. And she scrambled out of the room.

There was a dead silence. At last he said:

"I'm afraid mother isn't well. I must persuade her to see a doctor."

"Yes!" said Cecilia.

The evening passed in silence. Robert and Ciss stayed on in the drawing-room, having lit a fire. Outside was cold rain. Each pretended to read. They did not want to separate. The evening passed with ominous mysteriousness, yet quickly.

At about ten o'clock, the door suddenly opened, and Pauline appeared, in a blue wrap. She shut the door behind her and came to the fire. Then she looked at the two young people in hate, real hate.

"You two had better get married quickly," she said in an ugly voice. "It would look more decent; such a passionate pair of lovers!"

Robert looked up at her quietly.

"I thought you believed that cousins should not marry, mother," he said.

"I do! But you're not cousins. Your father was an Italian priest." Pauline held her daintily slippered foot to the fire, in an old coquettish gesture. Her body tried to repeat all the old graceful gestures. But the nerve had snapped, so it was a rather dreadful caricature.

"Is that really true, mother?" he asked.

"True! What do you think? He was a distinguished man, or he wouldn't have been my lover. He was far too distinguished a man to have had you for a son. But that joy fell to me."

"How unfortunate all round," he said slowly.

"Unfortunate for you? *You* were lucky. It was my misfortune," she said acidly to him.

She was really a dreadful sight, like a piece of lovely Venetian glass that had been dropped, and gathered up again in horrible, sharp-edged fragments.

Suddenly she left the room again.

For a week it went on. She did not recover. It was

as if every nerve in her body had suddenly started screaming in an insanity of discordance. The doctor came, and gave her sedatives, for she never slept. Without drugs, she never slept at all, only paced back and forth in her room, looking hideous and evil, reeking with malevolence. She could not bear to see either her son or her niece. Only when either of them came, she asked in pure malice:

"Well! When's the wedding? Have you celebrated the nuptials yet?"

At first Cecilia was stunned by what she had done. She realized vaguely that her aunt, once a definite thrust of condemnation had penetrated her beautiful armor, had just collapsed squirming inside her shell. It was too terrible. Ciss was almost terrified into repentance. Then she thought: This is what she always was. Now let her live the rest of her days in her true colors.

But Pauline would not live long. She was literally shrivelling away. She kept her room, and saw no one. She had her mirrors taken away.

Robert and Cecilia sat a good deal together. The jeering of the mad Pauline had not driven them apart, as she had hoped. But Cecilia dared not confess to him what she had done.

"Do you think your mother ever loved anybody?" Ciss asked him tentatively, rather wistfully, one evening.

He looked at her fixedly.

"Herself!" he said at last.

"She didn't even *love* herself," said Ciss. "It was something else—what was it?" She lifted a troubled, utterly puzzled face to him.

"Power!" he said curtly.

"But what power?" she asked. "I don't understand."

"Power to feed on other lives," he said bitterly. "She was beautiful, and she fed on life. She has fed on me as she fed on Henry. She put a sucker into one's soul, and sucked up one's essential life."

"And don't you forgive her?"

"No."

"Poor Aunt Pauline!"

But even Ciss did not mean it. She was only aghast.

"I *know* I've got a heart," he said, passionately striking his breast. "But it's almost sucked dry. I *know* people who want power over others."

Ciss was silent; what was there to say?

And two days later, Pauline was found dead in her bed, having taken too much veronal, for her heart was weakened. From the grave even she hit back at her son and her niece. She left Robert the noble sum of one thousand pounds; and Ciss one hundred. All the rest, with the nucleus of her valuable antiques, went to form the "Pauline Attenborough Museum."

(1933)

KATHERINE MANSFIELD 1888-1923

Kathleen Mansfield Beauchamp, who wrote under the name of Katherine Mansfield, showed signs of remarkable skill in writing while she was still at school in her native city of Wellington, New Zealand. In 1903 she was sent to London to "complete her education," as the colonial phrase went, in Queen's College, where she served as editor of the college magazine and developed a special interest in music. By 1908, after a visit to New Zealand and her return to London, she had chosen writing as a career, but her first efforts to get into print were not encouraging. Besides, her first marriage had ended quickly and unhappily, and she had serious financial worries. A brief turn with a traveling opera company undermined her health, which was already showing signs of fragility, she tried to recover it by visiting Germany. While in that country she wrote her first important stories, which were published in The New Age in 1910-1911 and collected in book form under the title In a German Pension (1911). Through her writings for this and other periodicals she became acquainted with the London critic John Middleton Murry, with whom she edited a short-lived literary review called Rhythm (later The Blue Review), and. with whom in 1912 she entered into a common-law marriage, this was legalized in 1918. Several of her stories which first appeared in Rhythm were later collected and published under the title Something Childish and Other Stories (in the United States, The Little Girl) (1924).

She traveled to France in 1914 to regain her health, but returned in that same year to Buckinghamshire, England, her ailment had been diagnosed as tuberculosis, and she was never again to find peace or comfort. During the remaining nine years of her life she hastened from one place to another in search of relief, writing when she could do so. A compelling incentive to her work was the death of her brother, Leslie Beauchamp, who was killed in action during the summer of 1915, she wrote stories as a "sacred debt" to him.

In November 1915, she went to Bandol, in southern France, where she wrote The Aloe, eventually condensed and published as Prelude (1918). A year spent in England (1916) was followed by another stay at Bandol in 1917, here she finished Bliss and Other Stories, her first genuine literary success, which was published in 1920. She returned once more to England in 1918 and contributed numerous reviews of current novels to the London Athenaeum, of which her husband had become editor, these reviews were published posthumously as Novels and Novelists. In Switzerland in 1920 she completed her best-known stories, those published in 1922 as The Garden Party and Other Stories. Now in desperate health, she became a follower of the Russian mystic Gurdjieff, and her last year was spent in Fontainebleau, near Paris, in the study of his teachings, here she died early in 1923.

Katherine Mansfield's work was incomplete, but it was always a most delicate blend of the poignant, the tender, and the cuttingly satirical. Her sensitiveness stemmed at least in part from the fact that she lived most of her artistic life in constant fear of death, there is no doubt, however, that she was gifted with rare psychological perceptions and an instinct for quiet nuances that is most rare. To her understanding, literature was essentially "an initiation into truth," and in her portrayal of everyday middle-class life, in feminine terms, she displayed an unusual talent, though her material was only too often thin and anemic. In all her best stories, however, atmosphere is always more important than incident, and her skill in building this atmosphere is obvious.

MARRIAGE A LA MODE

On his way to the station William remembered with a fresh pang of disappointment that he was taking nothing down to the kiddies. Poor little chaps! It was hard lines on them. Their first words always were as they ran to greet him, "What have you got for me, daddy?" and he had nothing. He would have to buy them some sweets at the station. But that was what he had done for the past four Saturdays; their faces had fallen last time when they saw the same old boxes produced again. 10

And Paddy had said, "I had red ribbing on mine bee-fore!"

And Johnny had said, "It's always pink on mine. I hate pink."

But what was William to do? The affair wasn't so easily settled. In the old days, of course, he would have taken a taxi off to a decent toyshop and chosen them something in five minutes. But nowadays they had Russian toys, French toys, Serbian toys—toys from God knows where. It was over a year since Isabel had scrapped the old donkeys and engines and so on because they were so "dreadfully sentimental" and "so appallingly bad for the babies' sense of form."

"It's so important," the new Isabel had explained, "that they should like the right things from the very 10 beginning. It saves so much time later on. Really, if the poor pets have to spend their infant years staring at these horrors, one can imagine them growing up and asking to be taken to the Royal Academy."

And she spoke as though a visit to the Royal Academy was certain immediate death to any one. . . .

"Well, I don't know," said William slowly. "When I was their age I used to go to bed hugging an old towel with a knot in it."

The new Isabel looked at him, her eyes narrowed, 20 her lips apart.

"*Dear* William! I'm sure you did!" She laughed in the new way.

Sweets it would have to be, however, thought William gloomily, fishing in his pocket for change for the taxi-man. And he saw the kiddies handing the boxes round—they were awfully generous little chaps—while Isabel's precious friends didn't hesitate to help themselves. . . .

What about fruit? William hovered before a stall just 30 inside the station. What about a melon each? Would they have to share that, too? Or a pineapple for Pad, and a melon for Johnny? Isabel's friends could hardly go sneaking up to the nursery at the children's meal-times. All the same, as he bought the melon William had a horrible vision of one of Isabel's young poets lapping up a slice, for some reason, behind the nursery door.

With his two very awkward parcels he strode off to his train. The platform was crowded, the train was in. 40 Doors banged open and shut. There came such a loud hissing from the engine that people looked dazed as they scurried to and fro. William made straight for a first-class smoker, stowed away his suitcase and parcels, and taking a huge wad of papers out of his inner pocket, he flung down in the corner and began to read.

"Our client moreover is positive. . . . We are inclined to reconsider . . . in the event of ——" Ah, that was better. William pressed back his flattened hair and stretched his legs across the carriage floor. The familiar 50 dull gnawing in his breast quietened down. "With re-gard to our decision——" He took out a blue pencil and scored a paragraph slowly.

Two men came in, stepped across him, and made for the farthest corner. A young fellow swung his golf clubs into the rack and sat down opposite. The train gave a gentle lurch, they were off. William glanced up and saw the hot, bright station slipping away. A red-faced girl raced along by the carriages, there was something strained and almost desperate in the way she waved and called. "Hysterical!" thought William dully. Then 60 a greasy, black-faced workman at the end of the plat-form grinned at the passing train. And William thought, "A filthy life!" and went back to his papers.

When he looked up again there were fields, and beasts standing for shelter under the dark trees. A wide river, with naked children splashing in the shallows, glided into sight and was gone again. The sky shone pale, and one bird drifted high like a dark fleck in a jewel.

"We have examined our client's correspondence 70 files. . . ." The last sentence he had read echoed in his mind. "We have examined. . ." William hung on to that sentence, but it was no good; it snapped in the middle, and the fields, the sky, the sailing bird, the water, all said, "Isabel." The same thing happened every Saturday afternoon. When he was on his way to meet Isabel there began those countless imaginary meetings. She was at the station, standing just a little apart from everybody else; she was sitting in the open taxi outside; she was at the garden gate; walking 80 across the parched grass; at the door, or just inside the hall.

And her clear, light voice said, "It's William," or "Hillo, William!" or "So William has come!" He touched her cool hand, her cool cheek.

The exquisite freshness of Isabel! When he had been a little boy, it was his delight to run into the garden after a shower of rain and shake the rose-bush over him. Isabel was that rose-bush, petal-soft, spark-ling and cool. And he was still that little boy. But there 90 was no running into the garden now, no laughing and shaking. The dull, persistent gnawing in his breast started again. He drew up his legs, tossed the papers aside, and shut his eyes.

"What is it, Isabel? What is it?" he said tenderly. They were in their bedroom in the new house. Isabel sat on a painted stool before the dressing-table that was strewn with little black and green boxes.

"What is what, William?" And she bent forward, and her fine light hair fell over her cheeks. 100

"Ah, you know!" He stood in the middle of the strange room and felt a stranger. At that Isabel wheeled round quickly, and faced him.

"Oh, William!" she cried imploringly, and she held up the hair-brush: "Please! Please don't be so dread-fully stuffy and—tragic. You're always saying or look-ing or hinting that I've changed. Just because I've got to know really congenial people, and go about more, and am frightfully keen on—on everything, you behave as though I'd——" Isabel tossed back her hair and 110 laughed—"killed our love or something. It's so awfully absurd"—she bit her lip—"and it's so maddening, William. Even this new house and the servants you grudge me."

"Isabel!"

"Yes, yes, it's true in a way," said Isabel quickly. "You think they are another bad sign. Oh, I know you do. I feel it," she said softly, "every time you come up the stairs. But we couldn't have gone on living in that other poky little hole, William. Be practical, at least! Why, there wasn't enough room for the babies even."

No, it was true. Every morning when he came back from chambers it was to find the babies with Isabel in the back drawing-room. They were having rides on the leopard skin thrown over the sofa back, or they were playing shops with Isabel's desk for a counter, or Pad was sitting on the hearthrug rowing away for dear life with a little brass fire shovel, while Johnny shot at pirates with the tongs. Every evening they each had a pick-a-back up the narrow stairs to their fat old Nanny.

Yes, he supposed it was a poky little house. A little white house with blue curtains and a window-box of petunias. William met their friends at the door with "Seen our petunias? Pretty terrific for London, don't you think?"

But the imbecile thing, the absolutely extraordinary thing was that he hadn't the slightest idea that Isabel wasn't as happy as he. God, what blindness! He hadn't the remotest notion in those days that she really hated that inconvenient little house, that she thought the fat Nanny was ruining the babies, that she was desperately lonely, pining for new people and new music and pictures and so on. If they hadn't gone to that studio party at Moira Morrison's—if Moira Morrison hadn't said as they were leaving "I'm going to rescue your wife, selfish man. She's like an exquisite little Titania"—if Isabel hadn't gone with Moira to Paris—if—if. . .

The train stopped at another station. Bettingford. Good heavens! They'd be there in ten minutes. William stuffed the papers back into his pockets; the young man opposite had long since disappeared. Now the other two got out. The late afternoon sun shone on women in cotton frocks and little sunburnt, barefoot children. It blazed on a silky yellow flower with coarse leaves which sprawled over a bank of rock. The air ruffling through the window smelled of the sea. Had Isabel the same crowd with her this week-end, wondered William?

And he remembered the holidays they used to have, the four of them, with a little farm girl, Rose, to look after the babies. Isabel wore a jersey and her hair in a plait; she looked about fourteen. Lord! how his nose used to peel! And the amount they ate, and the amount they slept in that immense feather bed with their feet locked together. . . . William couldn't help a grim smile as he thought of Isabel's horror if she knew the full extent of his sentimentality.

"Hillo, William!" She was at the station after all, standing just as he had imagined, apart from the others, and—William's heart leapt—she was alone.

"Hallo, Isabel!" William stared. He thought she looked so beautiful that he had to say something, "You look very cool."

"Do I?" said Isabel. "I don't feel very cool. Come along, your horrid old train is late. The taxi's outside." She put her hand lightly on his arm as they passed the ticket collector. "We've all come to meet you," she said. "But we've left Bobby Kane at the sweet shop, to be called for."

"Oh!" said William. It was all he could say for the moment.

There in the glare waited the taxi, with Bill Hunt and Dennis Green sprawling on one side, their hats tilted over their faces, while on the other, Moira Morrison, in a bonnet like a huge strawberry, jumped up and down.

"No ice! No ice! No ice!" she shouted gaily.

And Dennis chimed in from under his hat. "*Only* to be had from the fishmonger's."

And Bill Hunt, emerging, added, "With *whole* fish in it."

"Oh, what a bore!" wailed Isabel. And she explained to William how they had been chasing round the town for ice while she waited for him. "Simply everything is running down the steep cliffs into the sea, beginning with the butter."

"We shall have to anoint ourselves with the butter," said Dennis. "May thy head, William, lack not ointment."

"Look here," said William, "how are we going to sit? I'd better get up by the driver."

"No, Bobby Kane's by the driver," said Isabel. "You're to sit between Moira and me." The taxi started. "What have you got in those mysterious parcels?"

"De-cap-it-ated heads!" said Bill Hunt, shuddering beneath his hat.

"Oh, fruit!" Isabel sounded very pleased. "Wise William! A melon and a pineapple. How too nice!"

"No, wait a bit," said William, smiling. But he really was anxious. "I brought them down for the kiddies."

"Oh, my dear!" Isabel laughed, and slipped her hand through his arm. "They'd be rolling in agonies if they were to eat them. No"—she patted his hand—"you must bring them something next time. I refuse to part with my pineapple."

"Cruel Isabel! Do let me smell it!" said Moira. She flung her arms across William appealingly. "Oh!" The strawberry bonnet fell forward: she sounded quite faint.

"A Lady in Love with a Pineapple," said Dennis, as the taxi drew up before a little shop with a striped blind. Out came Bobby Kane, his arms full of little packets.

"I do hope they'll be good. I've chosen them because of the colours. There are some round things which really look too divine. And just look at this nougat," he cried ecstatically, "just look at it! It's a perfect little ballet."

But at that moment the shopman appeared. "Oh, I forgot. They're none of them paid for," said Bobby, looking frightened. Isabel gave the shopman a note, and Bobby was radiant again. "Hallo, William! I'm sitting by the driver." And bareheaded, all in white, with his sleeves rolled up to the shoulders, he leapt into his place. "*Avanti!*" he cried. . . .

After tea the others went off to bathe, while William stayed and made his peace with the kiddies. But Johnny and Paddy were asleep, the rose-red glow had paled, bats were flying, and still the bathers had not returned. As William wandered downstairs, the maid crossed the hall carrying a lamp. He followed her into the sitting-room. It was a long room, colored yellow. On the wall opposite William some one had painted a young man, over life-size, with very wobbly legs, offering a wide-eyed daisy to a young woman who had one very short arm and one very long, thin one. Over the chairs and sofa there hung strips of black material, covered with big splashes like broken eggs, and everywhere one looked there seemed to be an ashtray full of cigarette ends. William sat down in one of the arm-chairs. Nowadays, when one felt with one hand down the sides, it wasn't to come upon a sheep with three legs or a cow that had lost one horn, or a very fat dove out of the Noah's Ark. One fished up yet another little paper-covered book of smudged-looking poems. . . . He thought of the wad of papers in his pocket, but he was too hungry and tired to read. The door was open; sounds came from the kitchen. The servants were talking as if they were alone in the house. Suddenly there came a loud screech of laughter and an equally loud "Sh!" They had remembered him. William got up and went through the French windows into the garden, and as he stood there in the shadow he heard the bathers coming up the sandy road; their voices rang through the quiet.

"I think it's up to Moira to use her little arts and wiles."

A tragic moan from Moira.

"We ought to have a gramophone for the week-ends that played 'The Maid of the Mountains.' "

"Oh no! Oh no!" cried Isabel's voice. "That's not fair to William. Be nice to him, my children! He's only staying until to-morrow evening."

"Leave him to me," cried Bobby Kane. "I'm awfully good at looking after people."

The gate swung open and shut. William moved on the terrace; they had seen him. "Hallo, William!" And Bobby Kane, flapping his towel, began to leap and pirouette on the parched lawn. "Pity you didn't come, William. The water was divine. And we all went to a little pub afterwards and had sloe gin."

The others had reached the house. "I say, Isabel," called Bobby, "would you like me to wear my Nijinsky dress to-night?"

"No," said Isabel, "nobody's going to dress. We're all starving. William is starving, too. Come along, *mes amis*, let's begin with sardines."

"I've found the sardines," said Moira, and she ran into the hall, holding a box high in the air.

"A Lady with a Box of Sardines," said Dennis gravely.

"Well, William, and how's London?" asked Bill Hunt, drawing the cork out of a bottle of whisky.

"Oh, London's not much changed," answered William.

"Good old London," said Bobby, very hearty, spearing a sardine.

But a moment later William was forgotten. Moira Morrison began wondering what color one's legs really were under water.

"Mine are the palest, palest mushroom color."

Bill and Dennis ate enormously. And Isabel filled glasses, and changed plates, and found matches, smiling blissfully. At one moment she said, "I do wish, Bill, you'd paint it."

"Paint what?" said Bill loudly, stuffing his mouth with bread.

"Us," said Isabel, "round the table. It would be so fascinating in twenty years' time."

Bill screwed up his eyes and chewed. "Light's wrong," he said rudely, "far too much yellow"; and went on eating. And that seemed to charm Isabel, too.

But after supper they were all so tired they could do nothing but yawn until it was late enough to go to bed. . . .

It was not until William was waiting for his taxi the next afternoon that he found himself alone with Isabel. When he brought his suit-case down into the hall, Isabel left the others and went over to him. She stooped down and picked up the suit-case. "What a weight!" she said, and she gave a little awkward laugh. "Let me carry it! To the gate."

"No, why should you?" said William. "Of course, not. Give it to me."

"Oh, please do let me," said Isabel. "I want to, really." They walked together silently. William felt there was nothing to say now.

"There," said Isabel triumphantly, setting the suit-case down, and she looked anxiously along the sandy road. "I hardly seem to have seen you this time," she said breathlessly. "It's so short, isn't it? I feel you've only just come. Next time——" The taxi came into sight. "I hope they look after you properly in London. I'm so sorry the babies have been out all day, but Miss Neil had arranged it. They'll hate miss-

Marriage à la Mode. 12. *"Avanti!"* "Forward!" 60. **Nijinsky dress,** a costume of the type worn by Waslaw Nijinsky (1890–1950), generally considered the greatest male ballet dancer of his time. 63. *mes amis,* my friends. 217. **Titania,** queen of the fairies.

ing you. Poor William, going back to London." The taxi turned. "Good-bye!" She gave him a little hurried kiss; she was gone.

Fields, trees, hedges streamed by. They shook through the empty, blind-looking little town, ground up the steep pull to the station.

The train was in. William made straight for a first-class smoker, flung back into the corner, but this time he let the papers alone. He folded his arms against the dull, persistent gnawing, and began in his mind to write a letter to Isabel.

The post was late as usual. They sat outside the house in long chairs under coloured parasols. Only Bobby Kane lay on the turf at Isabel's feet. It was dull, stifling; the day drooped like a flag.

"Do you think there will be Mondays in Heaven?" asked Bobby childishly.

And Dennis murmured, "Heaven will be one long Monday."

But Isabel couldn't help wondering what had happened to the salmon they had for supper last night. She had meant to have fish mayonnaise for lunch and now. . .

Moira was asleep. Sleeping was her latest discovery. "It's so wonderful. One simply shuts one's eyes, that's all. It's so delicious."

When the old ruddy postman came beating along the sandy road on his tricycle one felt the handle-bars ought to have been oars.

Bill Hunt put down his book. "Letters," he said complacently, and they all waited. But, heartless postman —O malignant world! There was only one, a fat one for Isabel. Not even a paper.

"And mine's only from William," said Isabel mournfully.

"From William—already?"

"He's sending you back your marriage lines as a gentle reminder."

"Does everybody have marriage lines? I thought they were only for servants."

"Pages and pages! Look at her! A Lady reading a Letter," said Dennis.

My darling, precious Isabel. Pages and pages there were. As Isabel read on her feeling of astonishment changed to a stifled feeling. What on earth had induced William. . . ? How extraordinary it was. . . . What could have made him. . . ? She felt confused, more and more excited, even frightened. It was just like William. Was it? It was absurd, of course, it must be absurd, ridiculous. "Ha, ha, ha! Oh dear!" What was she to do? Isabel flung back in her chair and laughed till she couldn't stop laughing.

"Do, do tell us," said the others. "You must tell us."

"I'm longing to," gurgled Isabel. She sat up, gathered the letter, and waved it at them. "Gather round," she said. "Listen, it's too marvelous. A love-letter!"

"A love-letter! But how divine!" *Darling, precious Isabel.* But she had hardly begun before their laughter interrupted her.

"Go on, Isabel, it's perfect."

"It's the most marvelous find."

"Oh, do go on, Isabel!"

God forbid, my darling, that I should be a drag on your happiness.

"Oh! oh! oh!"

"Sh! sh! sh!"

And Isabel went on. When she reached the end they were hysterical: Bobby rolled on the turf and almost sobbed.

"You must let me have it just as it is, entire, for my new book," said Dennis firmly. "I shall give it a whole chapter."

"Oh, Isabel," moaned Moira, "that wonderful bit about holding you in his arms!"

"I always thought those letters in divorce cases were made up. But they pale before this."

"Let me hold it. Let me read it, mine own self," said Bobby Kane.

But, to their surprise, Isabel crushed the letter in her hand. She was laughing no longer. She glanced quickly at them all; she looked exhausted. "No, not just now. Not just now," she stammered.

And before they could recover she had run into the house, through the hall, up the stairs into her bedroom. Down she sat on the side of the bed. "How vile, odious, abominable, vulgar," muttered Isabel. She pressed her eyes with her knuckles and rocked to and fro. And again she saw them, but not four, more like forty, laughing, sneering, jeering, stretching out their hands while she read them William's letter. Oh, what a loathsome thing to have done. How could she have done it! *God forbid, my darling, that I should be a drag on your happiness.* William! Isabel pressed her face into the pillow. But she felt that even the grave bedroom knew her for what she was, shallow, tinkling, vain. . . .

Presently from the garden below there came voices.

"Isabel, we're all going for a bathe. Do come!"

"Come, thou wife of William!"

"Call her once before you go, call once yet!"

Isabel sat up. Now was the moment, now she must decide. Would she go with them, or stay here and write to William. Which, which should it be? "I must make up my mind." Oh, but how could there be any question? Of course she would stay here and write.

"Titania!" piped Moira.

"Isa-bel?"

No, it was too difficult. "I'll—I'll go with them, and write to William later. Some other time. Later. Not now. But I shall *certainly* write," thought Isabel hurriedly.

And, laughing in the new way, she ran down the stairs.

(1922)

THOMAS STEARNS ELIOT 1888-1965

One of the most significant poets and critics of the modern age was T. S. Eliot. He was born in St. Louis, Missouri, of a branch of a distinguished Boston family. He lived in St. Louis until he was eighteen and attended local schools, then, after a brief period at Milton Academy, near Boston, he matriculated at Harvard in 1906, received the bachelor's degree in 1910, and the master's degree a year later. He continued his graduate work, first at the Sorbonne in Paris, then back at Harvard, and finally at Merton College, Oxford, eventually settling in England. In London he taught briefly at the Highgate School and then became a clerk in the famous Lloyds Bank. His interest in literature, particularly in poetry and criticism, had always been marked. By 1917 he had attracted enough attention among poets and readers of poetry to be named an assistant editor of The Egoist, a periodical founded by Ezra Pound (1885-   ), who was a pioneer in the imagist school of contemporary poetry. Pound's encouragement and poetic discernment did much for Eliot; in fact, Eliot's first volume of prose studies, Ezra Pound, His Metric and Poetry (1917) is a sincere tribute to a poet whom Eliot always called his master.

In 1917 appeared also Eliot's first published poems of importance, Prufrock and Other Observations. The most famous of these today is The Love Song of J. Alfred Prufrock, a classic conception of a twentieth-century Hamlet, timid, blasé, mediocre, and defeatist. Another collection, Poems, was issued in 1919. Two more volumes, one from 1925 and another from 1936, are cumulative collections including pieces from as far back as Eliot's Harvard days. Three Critical Essays (1919) and The Sacred Wood (1920) firmly established Eliot's position as a literary critic. In The Sacred Wood he gave clear evidence that he was by taste and nature an antisentimental, antiromantic classicist dedicated to finish in form and to balance and symmetry in expression. His impact on modern criticism has been exceeded only by his impact on modern poetry. His interest in the seventeenth-century metaphysical poets did much to stimulate the popularity they enjoy today.

In 1922 he published The Waste Land, a poem which caught so aptly the spirit of disillusionment prevailing after the First World War that it gave its name to a whole tendency in the literature of the 1920's and early 1930's, and won for Eliot the Dial award. It is neither outright allegory nor plain narrative but rather a difficult though fascinating mixture of associations, tags of quotations, bursts of conversation, descriptions, and fragmentary interior monologues, held together very loosely within the framework of the Legend of the Holy Grail and its primitive analogues. There were objections to its obscure language and allusion, to the long and learned footnotes which were of no great help to the reader, to the mythology and the psychoanalysis—but even the dissidents appreciated that it was a landmark. Its subsequent influence, particularly upon Continental poets, has been great, although in England and America it has been somewhat overshadowed by Eliot's later work, cast in an entirely different, more nearly universal, mold.

Eliot founded his own magazine, The Criterion, in 1922. Until its discontinuation in 1939, it was not only an organ for his own views but also a bible for the rapidly growing Eliot cult. The poet's association with Faber and Faber, a major British publishing house, put him in a strong position as an encourager and discourager of literary talent. In The Criterion appeared many of his essays which were later gathered together in various volumes.

Eliot became a naturalized British subject in 1927, and in the foreword to For Lancelot Andrewes (1928) he declared himself to be "an Anglo-Catholic in religion, a classicist in literature, and a royalist in politics." This statement was in strong contrast to the pessimism of The Waste Land; the change, moreover, was a logical development. To one of his intellectual background and training, classical taste, and attachment to tradition and authority, there was no farther distance to go down the road of pessimism and disillusionment. He turned away, therefore, from the Lost Generation of the 1920's and looked to the mystical, as Ibsen and Strindberg, to take but two modern examples, had done before him.

This new Eliot made his position very plain in nearly all of his important works written during the 1930's. In 1930 itself was published Ash Wednesday, a poem

The Love Song of J. Alfred Prufrock. S'io . . . rispondo. "If I could believe that my answer might be to a person who should ever return into the world, this flame would stand without more quiverings;

of tortuous conflict between his poetic intelligence and his desire to attain the grace of God. Much more assured are the fine Choruses from The Rock (1934), where the call for a return to Christian spiritual values is sounded unmistakably and brilliantly. His absorbing drama on the story of Thomas à Becket, the Archbishop of Canterbury assassinated in 1170, entitled Murder in the Cathedral (1935), is further evidence that in Eliot the twentieth century had found a most articulate religious poet, though his spirit was still questing rather than attaining. Another play, The Family Reunion (1939), deals with the Holy Family but is far less incisive than Murder in the Cathedral.

Yet the ardent religious flame of the Choruses from The Rock cooled somewhat during the later 1930's. Four moving poems—East Coker (1940), Burnt Norton (1941), The Dry Salvages (1941), and Little Gidding (1942)—published together in 1943 as Four Quartets, are among Eliot's most beautiful and poignant expressions, but they vacillate between his desire for emotional security through religion and his still older pessimism. The same kind of uncertainty is to be observed in his philosophical play, The Cocktail Party (1950), where a rather vapid group of society people, who remind one of those in Eliot's earlier poetry, are influenced by a spiritual psychiatrist, and one of them undergoes Christian sacrifice and martyrdom. Unfortunately Eliot was not a good dramatist, and his message here, at least, strikes one as pretentious. The Confidential Clerk (1954), ostensibly a comedy in verse, actually leaves the reader with a sense of the isolation of each human being, the vanity of human wishes, and the importance of being able to live with things as they are rather than as they should be.

In 1948 Eliot received the Nobel Prize for literature, and after 1947 he occupied chairs of poetry at Harvard and Princeton and elsewhere. There is no doubt that he came to represent, better than any other important poet of the twentieth century, the intellectual, social, and philosophical moods of the decades between the First and Second World Wars; his consummate skill in treating traditional forms promises him longevity as a poet and spokesman for the whole first half of the twentieth century. He died on January 4, 1965.

THE LOVE SONG OF J. ALFRED PRUFROCK

J. Alfred Prufrock is the embodiment of a young man of modern times—blasé, intellectual, sensitive, but completely incapable of action or even of decision. The poem is Prufrock's fragmentary soliloquy, as he walks the streets in the evening, reluctant to come to a decision about love—or, for that matter, about anything. He imagines bits of conversation, typical drawing room scenes; he thinks of death. And with death in his mind, love and intellectual inquiry become empty. The epigraph indicates Eliot's view of life's futility, since death is final. Man no longer imagines that he can conquer death, no longer believes he can bend the universe to his will. He is mediocre, and his actions and decisions inconsequential.

S'io credesse che mia risposta fosse
A persona che mai tornasse al mondo,
Questa fiamma staria senza piu scosse.
Ma perciocche giammai di questo fondo
Non torno vivo alcun, s'i'odo il vero,
Senza tema d'infamia ti rispondo.

Let us go then, you and I,
When the evening is spread out against the sky
Like a patient etherised upon a table;

Let us go, through certain half-deserted streets,
The muttering retreats
Of restless nights in one-night cheap hotels
And sawdust restaurants with oyster-shells:
Streets that follow like a tedious argument
Of insidious intent
To lead you to an overwhelming question . . .   10
Oh, do not ask, "What is it?"
Let us go and make our visit.

In the room the women come and go
Talking of Michelangelo.

The yellow fog that rubs its back
    upon the window-panes,
The yellow smoke that rubs its muzzle
    on the window-panes
Licked its tongue into the corners of the evening,
Lingered upon the pools that stand in drains,
Let fall upon its back the soot that falls from chimneys,
Slipped by the terrace, made a sudden leap,   20
And seeing that it was a soft October night,
Curled once about the house, and fell asleep.

And indeed there will be time
For the yellow smoke that slides along the street,
Rubbing its back upon the window-panes;
There will be time, there will be time

To prepare a face to meet the faces that you meet;
There will be time to murder and create,
And time for all the works and days of hands
30 That lift and drop a question on your plate;
Time for you and time for me,
And time yet for a hundred indecisions,
And for a hundred visions and revisions,
Before the taking of a toast and tea.

In the room the women come and go
Talking of Michelangelo.

And indeed there will be time
To wonder, "Do I dare?" and, "Do I dare?"
Time to turn back and descend the stair,
40 With a bald spot in the middle of my hair—
[They will say: "How his hair is growing thin!"]
My morning coat, my collar mounting
        firmly to the chin,
My necktie rich and modest,
        but asserted by a simple pin—
[They will say: "But how his arms and legs are thin!"]
Do I dare
Disturb the universe?
In a minute there is time
For decisions and revisions which a minute will reverse.

For I have known them all already, known them all:—
50 Have known the evenings, mornings, afternoons,
I have measured out my life with coffee spoons;
I know the voices dying with a dying fall
Beneath the music from a farther room.
        So how should I presume?

And I have known the eyes already, known them all—
The eyes that fix you in a formulated phrase,
And when I am formulated, sprawling on a pin,
When I am pinned and wriggling on the wall,
Then how should I begin
60 To spit out all the butt-ends of my days and ways?
        And how should I presume?

And I have known the arms already, known them all—
Arms that are braceleted and white and bare
[But in the lamplight, downed with light brown hair!]
Is it perfume from a dress
That makes me so digress?
Arms that lie along a table, or wrap about a shawl.

And should I then presume?
And how should I begin?

Shall I say, I have gone at dusk through narrow streets   70
And watched the smoke that rises from the pipes
Of lonely men in shirt-sleeves,
        leaning out of windows? . . .

I should have been a pair of ragged claws
Scuttling across the floors of silent seas.

And the afternoon, the evening, sleeps so peacefully!
Smoothed by long fingers,
Asleep . . . tired . . . or it malingers,
Stretched on the floor, here beside you and me.
Should I, after tea and cakes and ices,
Have the strength to force the moment to its crisis?   80
But though I have wept and fasted, wept and prayed,
Though I have seen my head [grown slightly bald]
        brought in upon a platter,
I am no prophet—and here's no great matter;
I have seen the moment of my greatness flicker,
And I have seen the eternal Footman hold my coat,
        and snicker,
And in short, I was afraid.

And would it have been worth it, after all,
After the cups, the marmalade, the tea,
Among the porcelain, among some talk of you and me,
Would it have been worth while,   90
To have bitten off the matter with a smile,
To have squeezed the universe into a ball
To roll it toward some overwhelming question,
To say: "I am Lazarus, come from the dead,
Come back to tell you all, I shall tell you all"—
If one, settling a pillow by her head,
        Should say: "That is not what I meant at all.
        That is not it, at all."

And would it have been worth it, after all,
Would it have been worth while,   100
After the sunsets and the dooryards and
        the sprinkled streets,
After the novels, after the teacups, after the skirts
        that trail along the floor—
And this, and so much more?—
It is impossible to say just what I mean!
But as if a magic lantern threw the nerves
        in patterns on a screen:

82. **my head . . . platter,** a reference to the execution of St. John the Baptist at the importuning of Salome. Cf. Mark 6, especially verses 27 and 28.   94. **Lazarus,** the young man who was resurrected by Christ. Cf. John 11:1-46.   111. **Prince Hamlet, etc.,** a conscious renunciation by the young man of any true resemblance between himself and the principal figure in a tragedy.

Sweeney Among the Nightingales. ὤμοι . . . ἔσω. "Ay me! I am smitten with a mortal blow." The passage is quoted from Aeschylus' *Agamemnon.*   1. **Sweeney,** the primitive in man; note animal references to *apeneck* (l. 1), *zebra* (l. 3), *giraffe* (l. 4). He is in some kind

of peril.   4. **maculate,** spotted, striped.   6. **River Plate,** Rio de la Plata, dividing Argentina from Uruguay.   7. **Raven,** the small constellation Corvus, in the southern hemisphere. In this line the conjunction of Death and the Raven suggests the bird of death hovering above Sweeney.   8. **hornèd gate.** In classical legend, the gate of horn in Hades, through which unpleasant but true dreams came to the upper world. Cf. Vergil, *Aeneid,* VI, ll. 893-896. In this poem it is also perhaps the gate of death.   9. **Orion and the Dog,** the two great winter constellations of Orion and Canis Major, in the latter of which is located the brilliant star Sirius (the Dog Star). In classical myth,

Would it have been worth while
If one, settling a pillow or throwing off a shawl,
And turning toward the window, should say:
    "That is not it at all,
110   That is not what I meant, at all."

        .   .   .   .   .

No! I am not Prince Hamlet, nor was meant to be;
Am an attendant lord, one that will do
To swell a progress, start a scene or two,
Advise the prince; no doubt, an easy tool,
Deferential, glad to be of use,
Politic, cautious, and meticulous;
Full of high sentence, but a bit obtuse;
At times, indeed, almost ridiculous—
Almost, at times, the Fool.

120 I grow old . . . I grow old . . .
I shall wear the bottoms of my trousers rolled.

Shall I part my hair behind? Do I dare to eat a peach?
I shall wear white flannel trousers,
        and walk upon the beach.
I have heard the mermaids singing, each to each.

I do not think that they will sing to me.

I have seen them riding seaward on the waves
Combing the white hair of the waves blown back
When the wind blows the water white and black.

We have lingered in the chambers of the sea
130 By sea-girls wreathed with seaweed red and brown
Till human voices wake us, and we drown.
(1910-1911; 1915)

SWEENEY AMONG THE NIGHTINGALES

*This poem contrasts the vulgarity of the present age
to the passion of the heroic periods of history. Lust,
cruelty, and violence have always existed in the world,
but in heroic ages they were the result of grand passions, while in the present they are characterized by
unheroic action and lack of faith in anything.*

ὤμοι, πέπληγμαι καιρίαν πληγὴν ἔσω

Apeneck Sweeney spreads his knees
Letting his arms hang down to laugh,
The zebra stripes along his jaw
Swelling to maculate giraffe.

The circles of the stormy moon
Slide westward toward the River Plate,
Death and the Raven drift above
And Sweeney guards the hornéd gate.

    Gloomy Orion and the Dog
Are veiled; and hushed the shrunken seas;   10
The person in the Spanish cape
Tries to sit on Sweeney's knees

Slips and pulls the table cloth
Overturns a coffee-cup,
Reorganized upon the floor
She yawns and draws a stocking up;

The silent man in mocha brown
Sprawls at the window-sill and gapes;
The waiter brings in oranges
Bananas figs and hothouse grapes;   20

The silent vertebrate in brown
Contracts and concentrates, withdraws;
Rachel *née* Rabinovitch
Tears at the grapes with murderous paws;

She and the lady in the cape
Are suspect, thought to be in league;
Therefore the man with heavy eyes
Declines the gambit, shows fatigue,

Leaves the room and reappears
Outside the window, leaning in,   30
Branches of wistaria
Circumscribe a golden grin;

The host with someone indistinct
Converses at the door apart,
The nightingales are singing near
The Convent of the Sacred Heart,

And sang within the bloody wood
When Agamemnon cried aloud,
And let their liquid siftings fall
To stain the stiff dishonoured shroud.   40
(1920)

Orion, the famous hunter, was in love with Merope and tried to carry her off, but was slain by her father. The sun god Apollo restored him to life, but he was killed again by Diana, the moon goddess and goddess of chastity. He then became a constellation, but the moon daily kills him with Diana's darts. King Agamemnon (l. 38) once killed one of Diana's harts; she took revenge on him. 28. **gambit,** opening move in a chess game. 35-36. **nightingales . . . Heart.** Note the juxtaposition of the Christian and the pagan. The nightingales remind one of the legend of Philomela, who was turned into a nightingale after she was raped by her brother-in-law, Tereus. Violence and animality are every-where, even near the convent. 37. **bloody wood.** Agamemnon was actually murdered in a bath. However, there is a telescoping of sugges-tion here of Agamemnon's murder with the wood where Philomela was ravished and also with the wood of Nemi, where, according to the first chapter of Sir James Frazer's *The Golden Bough,* the old priest of the grove was killed by his young successor, who was in turn killed when he grew old.

T. S. Eliot, whose writings exerted a marked impact on twentieth-century criticism as well as twentieth-century poetry. Historical Pictures Service—Chicago.

ASH WEDNESDAY

Ash Wednesday is Eliot's first long analytical and personal poem concerned with his own religious conversion. It is in part a study of the way a highly poetic and intellectual mind attempts to shed mundane considerations and earthly doubts in order that the spirit may obtain salvation. Apparently that is what Eliot tried to do in his own case. But his honesty is so great that the poem is more a cry imploring grace, a plea for pardon and redemption through the church, showing both the skeptical mind, which Eliot demonstrated in his earlier poems, and his poetic sensitivity.

Eliot opens the poem with a statement of the change in his former attitude and of his decision not to return to the infirm glory of life; at the end of the first section he gives his prayer for mercy. He is convinced of his unworthiness and of his need for repentance.

The theme of the second section is "dust to dust"—the destruction of the body. The poet is willing to relinquish the human form if some greater sense of permanence can be reached. The third section deals with the ascent of three staircases, as one escapes the flesh. On the first stairs it is impossible to consider oneself except through human eyes and in human form; on the second stairs the image of old age makes it possible to leave behind the life of the flesh, and on the third stairs one abandons what is most dear—the sensual perceptions. The fourth section, more mystical throughout, tells how the poet was led away from the images of earthly life, away from the pagan images of poetic delight, in order that he might, after dismissing the flesh, know once more the fertile, the replenishing, and the spiritual. The fifth section is a development of the opposing ideas of reality: (1) the Word of God, the word from which all others derive, and (2) the *word of man unredeemed, who must seek the spiritual truth again, because he has walked in darkness and has denied the voice of truth and God. The poet is led to redemption by the veiled sister (ll. 168 and 177), the Madonna. He himself has found it difficult to lay aside his doubts; he himself has denied God between the rocks—the altars of primitive gods, now empty of all sacrifice. The sixth section repeats, with a slight but important variation, the theme of the first. The poet sees the images of the white sails of poetic exploration; he remembers the poetic delight of the senses, and the smell of all that is earthly. He is now at the critical moment which calls for dying and for birth, in the spiritual sense. And so again, the image of life (the Virgin, the spirit of water or of all fertility) is the image evoked. He must be spiritually reborn or he is indeed dead, and so he prays for grace that he may be forgiven and saved.*

The poem is, as a whole, a moving record of the struggle to relinquish the cherished weapon, a poetic intelligence of high order, to attain through the church (Anglo-Catholic) the grace of God. But it should be thought of throughout as a poem of conflict and repentance rather than of religious ecstasy.

I

Because I do not hope to turn again
Because I do not hope
Because I do not hope to turn
Desiring this man's gift and that man's scope
I no longer strive to strive towards such things
(Why should the agèd eagle stretch its wings?)
Why should I mourn
The vanished power of the usual reign?

Because I do not hope to know again
10 The infirm glory of the positive hour
Because I do not think

Because I know I shall not know
The one veritable transitory power
Because I cannot drink
There, where trees flower, and springs flow,
    for there is nothing again

Because I know that time is always time
And place is always and only place
And what is actual is actual only for one time
And only for one place
I rejoice that things are as they are and   20
I renounce the blessèd face
And renounce the voice
Because I cannot hope to turn again
Consequently I rejoice, having to construct something
Upon which to rejoice

And pray to God to have mercy upon us
And I pray that I may forget
These matters that with myself I too much discuss
Too much explain
Because I do not hope to turn again   30
Let these words answer
For what is done, not to be done again
May the judgement not be too heavy upon us

Because these wings are no longer wings to fly
But merely vans to beat the air
The air which is now thoroughly small and dry
Smaller and dryer than the will
Teach us to care and not to care
Teach us to sit still.

Pray for us sinners now and at the hour of our death   40
Pray for us now and at the hour of our death.

II

Lady, three white leopards sat under a juniper-tree
In the cool of the day, having fed to satiety

Ash Wednesday. **1. Because I . . . again, etc.** This is a direct translation of *Perch'io non spero di tornar gia mai,* from the writings of the Florentine poet and philosopher Guido Cavàlcanti (c. 1250-1300), a friend of Dante. But there is also some connection between these lines of Eliot and a sermon by the English divine Lancelot Andrewes (1555–1626), Bishop of Winchester. "Now at this time is the turning of the year. . . . Everything now turning that we also would make it our time to turn to God. . . . Upon this turning, *cardo vertitur,* the hinge turns, of our well and evil doing for ever. . . . Repentance itself is nothing but a kind of circling. . . . Which circle consists of two turnings. . . . First a turn wherein we look forward to God and with our whole heart resolve to turn to Him. Then a turn again wherein we look backward to our sins wherein we have turned from God. . . . The wheel turns apace, and if we turn not the rather these turnings may overtake us." **4. Desiring . . . scope.** Cf. Shakespeare, Sonnet 29, l. 7: "Desiring this man's art and that man's scope." **6. Why should . . . wings?** The eagle here is reminiscent of the image in *L'Albatros* by the French poet Baudelaire (1821–1867), about whom Eliot has written an essay; but the image is certainly religious in purpose here. The Psalmist (Psalms 103:5) says, "thy youth is renewed like the eagle's," and in the Middle Ages the eagle was always the symbol of baptismal grace. Connected with this is Dante's dream of the eagle, in *Purgatorio,* IX, and the legend in the medieval Bestiary that the agèd eagle flies into a circle of fire where his feathers are burned away and he falls into a fountain of water, to emerge with his youth again restored. **10. The infirm . . . hour.** It may be possible to oppose this to the last clause of the Lord's Prayer,

"For thine is the kingdom, and the power, and the glory for ever and ever," or to associate it as a subconscious echo of "the uncertain glory of an April day," from Shakespeare's *The Two Gentlemen of Verona,* I, iii, 85. **35. vans,** the fans of a winnowing-machine. **40. Pray for us,** "Ora pro nobis," best known in the *Ave Maria.* **42. Lady.** Cf. Eliot's essay on Dante: "In the Earthly Paradise Dante encounters a lady named Matilda, whose identity need not at first bother us." **three white leopards.** Again, cf. Eliot's essay on Dante: "I do not recommend, in first reading the first canto of the *Inferno,* worrying about the identity of the Leopard, the Lion, or the She-Wolf. It is really better, at the start, not to know or care what they do mean. What we should consider is not so much the meaning of the images, but the reverse process, that which led a man having an idea to express it in images. We have to consider the type of mind which by nature and *practice* tended to express itself in allegory; and for a competent poet, allegory means *clear visual images.*" Actually, Dante's animals derive from Jeremiah 5:6: "Wherefore a lion out of the forest shall slay them, and a wolf of the evenings shall spoil them, a leopard shall watch over their cities: every one that goeth out thence shall be torn in pieces: because their transgressions are many, and their back-slidings are increased." But Eliot's leopards are obviously instruments of good, whereas Dante's beasts are sinister. **a juniper-tree.** The prophet Elijah "came and sat down under a juniper tree" in the wilderness (1 Kings 19:4). But Eliot may also be thinking of Grimm's fairy tale, *The Juniper Tree,* in which Marlinchen buried a little boy's bones under a juniper tree.

On my legs my heart my liver and that
    which had been contained
In the hollow round of my skull. And God said
Shall these bones live? shall these
Bones live? And that which had been contained
In the bones (which were already dry) said chirping:
Because of the goodness of this Lady
50 And because of her loveliness, and because
She honours the Virgin in meditation,
We shine with brightness. And I who am here
    dissembled
Proffer my deeds to oblivion, and my love
To the posterity of the desert and the fruit of the gourd.
It is this which recovers
My guts the strings of my eyes and the
    indigestible portions
Which the leopards reject. The Lady is withdrawn
In a white gown, to contemplation, in a white gown.
Let the whiteness of bones atone to forgetfulness.
60 There is no life in them. As I am forgotten
And would be forgotten, so I would forget
Thus devoted, concentrated in purpose. And God said
Prophesy to the wind, to the wind only for only
The wind will listen. And the bones sang chirping
With the burden of the grasshopper, saying

Lady of silences
Calm and distressed
Torn and most whole
Rose of memory
70 Rose of forgetfulness
Exhausted and life-giving
Worried reposeful
The single Rose
Is now the Garden
Where all loves end
Terminate torment
Of love unsatisfied
The greater torment
Of love satisfied
80 End of the endless
Journey to no end
Conclusion of all that
Is inconclusible
Speech without word and

Word of no speech
Grace to the Mother
For the Garden
Where all love ends.

Under a juniper-tree the bones sang,
    scattered and shining
We are glad to be scattered, we did little good
    to each other,   90
Under a tree in the cool of the day, with the
    blessing of sand,
Forgetting themselves and each other, united
In the quiet of the desert. This is the land which ye
Shall divide by lot. And neither division nor unity
Matters. This is the land. We have our inheritance.

III

At the first turning of the second stair
I turned and saw below
The same shape twisted on the banister
Under the vapour in the fetid air
Struggling with the devil of the stairs who wears   100
The deceitful face of hope and of despair.

At the second turning of the second stair
I left them twisting, turning below;
There were no more faces and the stair was dark,
Damp, jaggèd, like an old man's mouth
    drivelling, beyond repair,
Or the toothed gullet of an agèd shark.

At the first turning of the third stair
Was a slotted window bellied like the fig's fruit
And beyond the hawthorn blossom and a pasture scene
The broadbacked figure drest in blue and green   110
Enchanted the maytime with an antique flute.
Blown hair is sweet, brown hair over the mouth blown,
Lilac and brown hair;
Distraction, music of the flute, stops and steps of
    the mind over the third stair,
Fading, fading; strength beyond hope and despair
Climbing the third stair.

Lord, I am not worthy

45. In the hollow . . . skull. For the passages dealing with the destruction of the body, Eliot is indebted to Baudelaire's poem *Voyage à Cythère*. 46. Shall . . . live? Cf. Ezekiel 37:3: "And he said unto me . . . can these bones live?" 54. the fruit of the gourd. Cf. Jonah 4:10: "Thou hast had pity on the gourd." 63. Prophesy to the wind. Cf. Ezekiel 37:9: "Prophesy unto the wind, prophesy, son of man." 65. With . . . grasshopper. Cf. Ecclesiastes 12:5: "and the grasshopper shall be a burden, and desire shall fail." 69. Rose of memory. One of the titles of the Virgin Mary is *Rosa Mystica*, and in Dante's *Paradiso* (XXIII, ll. 73-74) she is "the Rose wherein the Word Divine made itself flesh." 73. The single Rose, Christ, who is the Rose of Sharon. Dante saw the whole company of saints in Paradise as the petals of one white rose. See also *Church-Rents and Schisms* (ll. 1-4) by the English metaphysical poet George Herbert (1593-1633): "Brave rose, (alas!) where art thou? in the chair/ Where thou didst lately so triumph and shine/ A worm doth sit, whose many feet and hair/ Are the more foul, the more thou wert divine." 74. Is . . . Garden. No doubt this is a reference to the Garden of Gethsemane, where Christ prayed all through the night before his betrayal; cf. Matthew 26:36-46. 93-94. This . . . lot. See Ezekiel 48:29: "This is the land which ye shall divide by lot unto the tribes of Irsael for inheritance, and these are their portions, saith the Lord God." 96. the second stair. The conception of the stairs in section III may have been suggested by Dante's *Purgatorio*, XXVI, ll. 145-147: "I pray you by that Goodness which doth deign/ To guide you to the summit of this stair/ Bethink you in due season of my pain." But see also *The Song of Solomon*, 2:14: "O my dove, that art in the clefts of the rock, in the secret places of the stairs, let me see thy countenance." 117. Lord . . . worthy. See Matthew 8:8: "The centurion answered and said, Lord, I am not worthy that thou shouldest come under my roof: but speak the word only, and my servant shall be healed." 123. in Mary's colour, suggested by the paintings of the Italians and of the English Pre-Raphaelites, who always depicted the Virgin Mary in white and blue. 130. Sovegna vos, "bethink you"; see quotation from Dante in note to line 96. 134. White . . . sheathed.

Lord, I am not worthy

but speak the word only.

IV

120 Who walked between the violet and the violet
Who walked between
The various ranks of varied green
Going in white and blue, in Mary's colour,
Talking of trivial things
In ignorance and in knowledge of eternal dolour
Who moved among the others as they walked,
Who then made strong the fountains and made
    fresh the springs

Made cool the dry rock and made firm the sand
In blue of larkspur, blue of Mary's colour,
130 Sovegna vos

Here are the years that walk between, bearing
Away the fiddles and the flutes, restoring
One who moves in the time between sleep
    and waking, wearing

White light folded, sheathed about her, folded.
The new years walk, restoring
Through a bright cloud of tears, the years, restoring
With a new verse the ancient rhyme. Redeem
The time. Redeem
The unread vision in the higher dream
140 While jewelled unicorns draw by the gilded hearse.

The silent sister veiled in white and blue
Between the yews, behind the garden god,
Whose flute is breathless, bent her head and
    signed but spoke no word

But the fountain sprang up and the bird sang down
Redeem the time, redeem the dream
The token of the word unheard, unspoken

Till the wind shake a thousand whispers from the yew

And after this our exile

V

If the lost word is lost, if the spent word is spent
If the unheard, unspoken   150
Word is unspoken, unheard;
Still is the unspoken word, the Word unheard,
The Word without a word, the Word within
The world and for the world;
And the light shone in darkness and
Against the Word the unstilled world still whirled
About the centre of the silent Word.

O my people, what have I done unto thee.

Where shall the word be found, where will the word
Resound? Not here, there is not enough silence   160
Not on the sea or on the islands, not
On the mainland, in the desert or the rain land,
For those who walk in darkness
Both in the day time and in the night time
The right time and the right place are not here
No place of grace for those who avoid the face
No time to rejoice for those who walk among
    noise and deny the voice

Will the veiled sister pray for
Those who walk in darkness, who chose thee
    and oppose thee,
Those who are torn on the horn between season and
    season, time and time, between   170
Hour and hour, word and word, power and power,
    those who wait
In darkness? Will the veiled sister pray
For children at the gate
Who will not go away and cannot pray:
Pray for those who chose and oppose

O my people, what have I done unto thee.

Will the veiled sister between the slender
Yew trees pray for those who offend her
And are terrified and cannot surrender
And affirm before the world and deny between the
    rocks   180
In the last desert between the last blue rocks

Dante often used the image of a figure swathed or sheathed (*fasciato*) in light or joy. 140. **jewelled unicorns.** These unicorns may derive from Guido Cavalcanti (see note to l.1) or from one of the Florentine engravings of the Triumphs of the Italian poet Petrarch (1304–1374), where the car in the Triumph of Chastity is drawn by unicorns. By tradition, the legendary unicorn could be captured only by a virgin and was therefore the symbol of chastity. 142. **the yews.** The yew is by tradition the tree planted in English churchyards, being described as "an emblem of Resurrection from its perpetual verdure" by Sir Thomas Browne (1605-1682). 148. **And . . . exile,** from the prayer *Salve Regina*, which followed the celebration of the Catholic Mass: "To thee do we send up our sighs mourning and weeping in this valley of tears; turn, then, most gracious advocate, thine eyes of mercy towards us; and after this our exile, show unto us the blessed fruit of thy womb, Jesus." 149-154. **If the lost . . . for the world.** The whole of this passage is a variation on John 1:1-14 and on "the word within a word,

unable to speak a word," a phrase from "Lancelot Andrewes" in Eliot's essay *For Lancelot Andrewes* (see note to l. 1). 158. **O my . . . thee.** See Micah 6:3. 163. **those . . . darkness.** The Bible is full of allusions to those who walk in darkness: Job 29:3; Isaiah 9:2; Psalms 82:5 and 91:6; Ecclesiastes 2:14; Isaiah 59:9; John 8:12 and 12:35; 1 John 1:6 and 2:11. 167. **deny the voice,** probably an allusion to Peter's denial of Christ; see Matthew 26:34-35. 169. **chose . . . thee.** See Matthew 12:30: "He that is not with me is against me." 170. **torn on the horn,** as if by a bull. But perhaps the reference is to the horns of a dilemma, in which case those referred to are in the "agony of indecision." 180. **affirm . . . rocks,** probably a reference to *Madonna of the Rocks* by the Italian Renaissance painter Leonardo da Vinci (1452–1519), in which the artist affirmed in the painting of the rocks some of the geological theories he could not express in writing to the world, since it was heretical to oppose the Biblical and Aristotelian concepts of the Creation.

The desert in the garden the garden in the desert
Of drouth, spitting from the mouth the withered
    apple-seed.

    O my people.

VI

Although I do not hope to turn again
Although I do not hope
Although I do not hope to turn

Wavering between the profit and the loss
In this brief transit where the dreams cross
190 The dreamcrossed twilight between birth and dying
    (Bless me father) though I do not wish to wish these
        things
From the wide window towards the granite shore
The white sails still fly seaward, seaward flying
Unbroken wings

And the lost heart stiffens and rejoices
In the lost lilac and the lost sea voices
And the weak spirit quickens to rebel
For the bent golden-rod and the lost sea smell
Quickens to recover
200 The cry of quail and the whirling plover
And the blind eye creates
The empty forms between the ivory gates
And smell renews the salt savour of the sandy earth

This is the time of tension between dying and birth
The place of solitude where three dreams cross
Between blue rocks
But when the voices shaken from the yew-tree drift
    away
Let the other yew be shaken and reply.

Blessèd sister, holy mother, spirit of the fountain, spirit
    of the garden,
210 Suffer us not to mock ourselves with falsehood
Teach us to care and not to care
Teach us to sit still
Even among these rocks,
Our peace in His will
And even among these rocks
Sister, mother
And spirit of the river, spirit of the sea,

Suffer me not to be separated

And let my cry come unto Thee.
(1930)

from FOUR QUARTETS

LITTLE GIDDING

I

Midwinter spring is its own season
Sempiternal though sodden towards sundown,
Suspended in time, between pole and tropic.
When the short day is brightest, with frost and fire,
The brief sun flames the ice, on pond and ditches,
In windless cold that is the heart's heat,
Reflecting in a watery mirror
A glare that is blindness in the early afternoon.
And glow more intense than blaze of branch, or brazier,
Stirs the dumb spirit: no wind, but pentecostal fire   10
In the dark time of the year. Between melting and
    freezing
The soul's sap quivers. There is no earth smell
Or smell of living thing. This is the spring time
But not in time's covenant. Now the hedgerow
Is blanched for an hour with transitory blossom
Of snow, a bloom more sudden
Than that of summer, neither budding nor fading,
Not in the scheme of generation.
Where is the summer, the unimaginable
Zero summer?   20

        If you came this way,
Taking the route you would be likely to take
From the place you would be likely to come from,
If you came this way in may time, you would find the
    hedges
White again, in May, with voluptuary sweetness.
It would be the same at the end of the journey,
If you came at night like a broken king,
If you came by day not knowing what you came for,
It would be the same, when you leave the rough road
And turn behind the pig-sty to the dull façade   30
And the tombstone. And what you thought you came for
Is only a shell, a husk of meaning

---

182. **The desert in the garden.** See Isaiah 51:3: "he will make . . . her desert like the garden of the Lord." 183. **the withered apple-seed,** doubtless connected poetically with the fruit of the tree of knowledge of good and evil in the Garden of Eden, traditionally an apple. 191. **Bless me father,** the opening formula of the confession. 193. **seaward,** suggested by Dante's *Paradiso*, III, ll. 85-87: "and his will is our peace; it is that sea to which all moves that it createth and that nature maketh." 200. **cry . . . plover.** See Numbers 11:31. 214. **Our . . . will.** See note to l. 193. 218. **Suffer . . . separated,** the ancient prayer *Anima Christi* (Suffer me not to be separated from Thee). 219. **And let . . . Thee.** See Psalms 119:169: "Let my cry come near before thee, O Lord."

    Little Gidding is from *Four Quartets*, copyright, 1943, by T. S. Eliot. Reprinted by permission of Harcourt, Brace & World, Inc., and Faber and Faber Ltd.

    Four Quartets. The *Four Quartets* are four related poems (*Burnt Norton, East Coker, The Dry Salvages,* and *Little Gidding*), each named after a place Eliot visited, and each in the form of a musical

From which the purpose breaks only when it is fulfilled
If at all. Either you had no purpose
Or the purpose is beyond the end you figured
And is altered in fulfillment. There are other places
Which also are the world's end, some at the sea jaws,
Or over a dark lake, in a desert or a city—
But this is the nearest, in place and time,
40 Now and in England.

              If you came this way,
Taking any route, starting from anywhere,
At any time or at any season,
It would always be the same: you would have to put off
Sense and notion. You are not here to verify,
Instruct yourself, or inform curiosity
Or carry report. You are here to kneel
Where prayer has been valid. And prayer is more
Than an order of words, the conscious occupation
50 Of the praying mind, or the sound of the voice praying.
And what the dead had no speech for, when living,
They can tell you, being dead: the communication
Of the dead is tongued with fire beyond the language
    of the living.
Here, the intersection of the timeless moment
In England and nowhere. Never and always.

II

Ash on an old man's sleeve
Is all the ash the burnt roses leave.
Dust in the air suspended
Marks the place where a story ended.
60 Dust inbreathed was a house—
The wall, the wainscot and the mouse.
The death of hope and despair,
    This is the death of air.

    There are flood and drouth
Over the eyes and in the mouth,
Dead water and dead sand
Contending for the upper hand.
The parched eviscerate soil
Gapes at the vanity of toil,
70 Laughs without mirth.
    This is the death of earth.

    Water and fire succeed
The town, the pasture and the weed.
Water and fire deride

The sacrifice that we denied.
Water and fire shall rot
The marred foundations we forgot,
Of sanctuary and choir.
    This is the death of water and fire.

    In the uncertain hour before the morning   80
    Near the ending of interminable night
    At the recurrent end of the unending
After the dark dove with the flickering tongue
    Had passed below the horizon of his homing
    While the dead leaves still rattled on like tin
Over the asphalt where no other sound was
    Between three districts whence the smoke arose
    I met one walking, loitering and hurried
As if blown towards me like the metal leaves
    Before the urban dawn wind unresisting.   90
    And as I fixed upon the down-turned face
That pointed scrutiny with which we challenge
    The first-met stranger in the waning dusk
    I caught the sudden look of some dead master
Whom I had known, forgotten, half recalled
    Both one and many; in the brown baked features
    The eyes of a familiar compound ghost
Both intimate and unidentifiable.
    So I assumed a double part, and cried
    And heard another's voice cry: 'What! are *you* here?' 100
Although we were not. I was still the same,
    Knowing myself yet being someone other—
    And he a face still forming; yet the words sufficed
To compel the recognition they preceded.
    And so, compliant to the common wind,
    Too strange to each other for misunderstanding,
In concord at this intersection time
    Of meeting nowhere, no before and after,
    We trod the pavement in a dead patrol.
I said: 'The wonder that I feel is easy,   110
    Yet ease is cause of wonder. Therefore speak:
    I may not comprehend, may not remember.'
And he: 'I am not eager to rehearse
    My thought and theory which you have forgotten.
    These things have served their purpose: let them be.
So with your own, and pray they be forgiven
    By others, as I pray you to forgive
    Both bad and good. Last season's fruit is eaten
And the fullfed beast shall kick the empty pail.
    For last year's words belong to last year's language   120
    And next year's words await another voice.
But, as the passage now presents no hindrance

---

quartet or sonata. Each deals with some aspect of the relation between time and eternity, the meaning of history, and the moments of illumination in which the human spirit achieves the moment of timeless insight. **Little Gidding.** The title is derived from the name of a small Anglican religious community founded in 1625 and destroyed in 1647, in the course of the English Civil War. Many of the lines are made more comprehensible if one remembers that *Little Gidding* was written during the Second World War, the great fires of which in London undoubtedly reminded Eliot of the supremacy of fire as a destructive element. The "broken king" of l. 27 is Charles I, who stopped at Little Gidding following his defeat at the Battle of Naseby (1645). 2. **Sempiternal,** everlasting, eternal. 10. **pentecostal fire.** On the Pentecost day (seventh Sunday following Easter) after the death and resurrection of Christ, the apostles heard "a sound from heaven as of a rushing mighty wind. . . . And there appeared unto them cloven tongues like as of fire. . . . And they were all filled with the Holy Ghost." See Acts 2:2-4. 97. **ghost.** Cf. Shakespeare, *Sonnet 59,* l. 9: "that affable familiar ghost."

Thomas Stearns Eliot   1245

To the spirit unappeased and peregrine
Between two worlds become much like each other,
So I find words I never thought to speak
In streets I never thought I should revisit
When I left my body on a distant shore.
Since our concern was speech, and speech impelled us
To purify the dialect of the tribe
130 And urge the mind to aftersight and foresight,
Let me disclose the gifts reserved for age
To set a crown upon your lifetime's effort.
First, the cold friction of expiring sense
Without enchantment, offering no promise
But bitter tastelessness of shadow fruit
As body and soul begin to fall asunder.
Second, the conscious impotence of rage
At human folly, and the laceration
Of laughter at what ceases to amuse.
140 And last, the rending pain of re-enactment
Of all that you have done, and been; the shame
Of motives late revealed, and the awareness
Of things ill done and done to others' harm
Which once you took for exercise of virtue.
Then fools' approval stings, and honour stains.
From wrong to wrong the exasperated spirit
Proceeds, unless restored by that refining fire
Where you must move in measure, like a dancer.'
The day was breaking. In the disfigured street
150 He left me, with a kind of valediction,
And faded on the blowing of the horn.

III

There are three conditions which often look alike
Yet differ completely, flourish in the same hedgerow:
Attachment to self and to things and to persons,
     detachment
From self and from things and from persons; and,
     growing between them, indifference
Which resembles the others as death resembles life,
Being between two lives—unflowering, between

The live and the dead nettle. This is the use of memory:
For liberation—not less of love but expanding
Of love beyond desire, and so liberation   160
From the future as well as the past. Thus, love of a
     country
Begins as attachment to our own field of action
And comes to find that action of little importance
Though never indifferent. History may be servitude,
History may be freedom. See, now they vanish,
The faces and places, with the self which, as it could,
     loved them,
To become renewed, transfigured, in another pattern.

     Sin is Behovely, but
All shall be well, and
All manner of thing shall be well.   170
If I think, again, of this place,
And of people, not wholly commendable,
Of no immediate kin or kindness,
But some of peculiar genius,
All touched by a common genius,
United in the strife which divided them;
If I think of a king at nightfall,
Of three men, and more, on the scaffold
And a few who died forgotten
In other places, here and abroad,   180
And of one who died blind and quiet,
Why should we celebrate
These dead men more than the dying?
It is not to ring the bell backward
Nor is it an incantation
To summon the spectre of a Rose.
We cannot revive old factions
We cannot restore old policies
Or follow an antique drum.
These men, and those who opposed them   190
And those whom they opposed
Accept the constitution of silence
And are folded in a single party.
Whatever we inherit from the fortunate

---

123. **peregrine,** foreign. 129. **To purify . . . tribe,** from *The Tomb of Edgar Poe* by the contemporary French poet Stéphane Mallarmé. 151. **faded . . . horn.** Cf. *Hamlet*, I, i, 157: "It faded on the crowing of the cock." The horn is the all-clear signal after an air raid. 177. **king,** Charles I. He, along with his advisors Archbishop Laud and the Earl of Strafford (l. 178), were executed. 212. **shirt**

We have taken from the defeated
What they had to leave us—a symbol:
A symbol perfected in death.
And all shall be well and
All manner of thing shall be well
200 By the purification of the motive
In the ground of our beseeching.

IV

The dove descending breaks the air
With flame of incandescent terror
Of which the tongues declare
The one discharge from sin and error.
The only hope, or else despair
  Lies in the choice of pyre or pyre—
  To be redeemed from fire by fire.

  Who then devised the torment? Love.
210 Love is the unfamiliar Name
Behind the hands that wove
The intolerable shirt of flame
Which human power cannot remove.
  We only live, only suspire
  Consumed by either fire or fire.

V

What we call the beginning is often the end
And to make an end is to make a beginning.
The end is where we start from. And every phrase
And sentence that is right (where every word is at
    home,
220 Taking its place to support the others,
The word neither diffident nor ostentatious,
An easy commerce of the old and the new,
The common word exact without vulgarity,
The formal word precise but not pedantic,
The complete consort dancing together)

Every phrase and every sentence is an end and a
    beginning,
Every poem an epitaph. And any action
Is a step to the block, to the fire, down the sea's throat
Or to an illegible stone: and that is where we start.
We die with the dying: 230
See, they depart, and we go with them.
We are born with the dead:
See, they return, and bring us with them.
The moment of the rose and the moment of the
    yew-tree
Are of equal duration. A people without history
Is not redeemed from time, for history is a pattern
Of timeless moments. So, while the light fails
On a winter's afternoon, in a secluded chapel
History is now and England.
With the drawing of this Love and the voice of this
    Calling   240

  We shall not cease from exploration
And the end of all our exploring
Will be to arrive where we started
And know the place for the first time.
Through the unknown, remembered gate
When the last of earth left to discover
Is that which was the beginning;
At the source of the longest river
The voice of the hidden waterfall
And the children in the apple-tree   250
Not known, because not looked for
But heard, half-heard, in the stillness
Between two waves of the sea.
Quick now, here, now, always—
A condition of complete simplicity
(Costing not less than everything)
And all shall be well and
All manner of thing shall be well
When the tongues of flame are in-folded
Into the crowned knot of fire   260
And the fire and the rose are one.   (1942)

of flame. Deianira gave her husband Hercules the poisoned shirt of
Nessus with the mistaken belief that it would increase his love for her.
Instead, it corroded his flesh so agonizingly that he burned himself to
death. 225. consort. This word means both *company* and *harmony
of sounds*. Both meanings are to be taken here.

ALDOUS HUXLEY 1894-

Aldous Huxley's grandfather was Thomas Henry Huxley (p. 1060); his maternal great-uncle was Matthew Arnold (p. 932). At various times he was to write much about himself. His education at Eton, he said, was interrupted by a serious eye affliction that was annoying to him ever since, but this interruption was probably fortunate for him, he believed, because it prevented him from becoming the complete English public-school gentleman and particularly because it turned him aside from the paths of medicine which he had been expected to follow. Although he was at all times sympathetic to the scientific viewpoint, he became professionally an apostate of science. He went to Oxford, where he graduated (1916) with honors in English literature, and after some rather haphazard work in a government office and in teaching, he joined the editorial staff of the Athenaeum (1919) under the leadership of J. Middleton Murry, husband of the noted short-story writer Katherine Mansfield and intimate of the fiery novelist and poet D. H. Lawrence. He soon became a miscellaneous journalistic writer whose recreations and hobbies were all centered in the art of solitary reading, if we are to take his word for it. But he traveled as well as read, spending much of his time in Italy.

Huxley began his literary career by editing an anthology of Oxford poetry (1916), and subsequently wrote some poetry of his own, including The Burning Wheel *(1916),* Jonah *(1917), which contains verse in French as well as in English,* The Defeat of Youth *(1918),* Leda *(1920), and* Arabia Infelix *(1929). As might be expected from a reading of his better-known prose, Huxley's poetry is bitter and disillusioned, with a certain air of the unwholesome and the decadent. His grip upon fiction was much firmer. Among his volumes of short stories are* Limbo *(1920), seven characteristic narratives;* Mortal Coils *(1922),* The Little Mexican and Other Stories *(1924), published in the United States as* Young Archimedes and Other Sketches; Two or Three Graces *(1926); and* Brief Candles *(1930). The novels, which naturally made a much more forceful impact upon the reading public and which are much more garrulous and diffuse, are* Crome Yellow *(1921), written, so the author declares, in the mock-romantic style of Thomas Love Peacock (1785-1866), although the comparison is certainly not obvious;* Antic Hay *(1923), a novel which, Huxley stated, "dramatizes with relentless logic the necessary implications, in terms of life, of the skepticism of Thomas Huxley—skepticism battening at the vitals of animal faith"; and* Those Barren

Leaves (1925). *His masterpieces are* Point Counter Point *(1928), a heartless, loquacious, and brilliant satire on contemporary society, and the equally devastating and effective* A Brave New World *(1932). This cycle of mordant novels is more or less rounded out by* Eyeless in Gaza *(1936).* After Many a Summer Dies the Swan *(1940), a satire on certain aspects of southern California culture, gives over many pages to a discussion of man and his place in the scheme of things. This semi-religious questing is in keeping with Huxley's intellectual character throughout the 1930's, as evinced in his many essays, notably* Ends and Means *(1937).* Grey Eminence *(1941), a biography of Father Joseph, the seventeenth-century French mystic and statesman, confidant of the great Cardinal Richelieu (1585-1642), has many of the unmistakable traits of a religious novel. The same dichotomy between satire and mysticism is apparent in* Time Must Have a Stop *(1944), but his innate pessimism breaks through in* Ape and Essence *(1948), which predicts a shattering atomic war that reduces its survivors to the fearful worship of evil as the primal world force.*

To many critics, Huxley's contributions as a writer are more valuable in the field of the essay than in the field of prose fiction. Like T. S. Eliot, he has in this type turned from the Waste Land *into a realm of serious moral and religious purpose, although he cannot be content to drop anchor in any fixed creed. And in any event, there is at best great difficulty in distinguishing between Huxley the novelist and Huxley the didactic commentator. His essays date as far back as 1923, when* On the Margin *was published. Following this came the travel essays included under the bizarre title of* Jesting Pilate *(1923);* Do What You Will *(1929);* The Holy Face and Other Essays *(1929);* Vulgarity in Literature *(1930);* Music at Night *(1931);* Texts and Pretexts *(1932), an anthology of criticism;* Beyond the Mexique Bay *(1934);* The Olive Tree and Other Essays *(1936);* An Encyclopedia of Pacifism *(1937);* Ends and Means *(1937), perhaps the most revealing of all;* The Art of Seeing *(1942), born of his own painful experiences with eye trouble;* Science, Liberty, and Peace *(1944); and* The Perennial Philosophy *(1945).*

Huxley was learned but refreshingly witty and cynical; sometimes, however, his desire to be clever at all costs led him into painful lapses from good or even passable taste. Particularly significant is his preoccupation with the scientific in general and the medical in particular; his characters are virtually test-tube speci-

mens, and he watched them with the same degree of detachment as that with which any conscientious scientist observes his laboratory material. In his stories, therefore, human beings are behavioristic and completely without faith; in extreme moments they touch absolute negation, and most of them, even in their spiritual crises, leave the impression that it is solely their body chemistry, their endocrine glands, that drive them along. At least this was true of Huxley's work through the 1920's and early 1930's. But his later work has subdued this gaudy sophomoric brilliance to a search for values of a more spiritual nature; Ends and Means, in its subtitle, indicates the general trend of the later Huxley, for it is "the inquiry into the nature of ideals and into the methods employed for their realization." The eventual position which Huxley will occupy in the history of English literature, in spite of his topical brilliance, is not clear.

YOUNG ARCHIMEDES

"Young Archimedes" presents a dramatic episode in the tragedy of genius. Incidentally, it stresses the close relationship between music and mathematics. In its romantic descriptions of nature, its realistic characterization, its flashes of humor, and its genuine pathos, it reveals Huxley in one of his more sympathetic moods. The brilliant intellect and technical skill of the hero align him with Archimedes, the celebrated philosopher, mathematician, and physicist of the third century before Christ.

It was the view which finally made us take the place. True, the house had its disadvantages. It was a long way out of town and had no telephone. The rent was unduly high, the drainage system poor. On windy nights, when the ill-fitting panes were rattling so furiously in the window-frames that you could fancy yourself in an hotel omnibus, the electric light, for some mysterious reason, used invariably to go out and leave you in the noisy dark. There was a splendid
10 bathroom; but the electric pump, which was supposed to send up water from the rain-water tanks in the terrace, did not work. Punctually every autumn the drinking well ran dry. And our landlady was a liar and a cheat.

But these are the little disadvantages of every hired house, all over the world. For Italy they were not really at all serious. I have seen plenty of houses which had them all and a hundred others, without possessing the compensating advantages of ours—the southward
20 facing garden and terrace for the winter and spring, the large cool rooms against the midsummer heat, the hilltop air and freedom from mosquitoes, and finally the view.

And what a view it was! Or rather, what a succession of views. For it was different every day; and without stirring from the house one had the impression of an incessant change of scene: all the delights of travel without its fatigues. There were autumn days when all the valleys were filled with mist and the crests of the Apennines rose darkly out of a flat white lake. There 30 were days when the mist invaded even our hilltop and we were enveloped in a soft vapor in which the mist-colored olive trees, that sloped away below our windows towards the valley, disappeared as though into their own spiritual essence; and the only firm and definite things in the small, dim world within which we found ourselves confined were the two tall black cypresses growing on a little projecting terrace a hundred feet down the hill. Black, sharp, and solid, they stood there, twin pillars of Hercules at the 40 extremity of the known universe; and beyond them there was only pale cloud and round them only the cloudy olive trees.

These were the wintry days; but there were days of spring and autumn, days unchangingly cloudless, or —more lovely still—made various by the huge floating shapes of vapor that, snowy above the far-away snow-capped mountains, gradually unfolded, against the pale bright blue, enormous heroic gestures. And in the height of the sky the bellying draperies, the swans, 50 the aerial marbles, hewed and left unfinished by gods grown tired of creation almost before they had begun, drifted sleeping along the wind, changing form as they moved. And the sun would come and go behind them; and now the town in the valley would fade and almost vanish in the shadow, and now, like an immense fretted jewel between the hills, it would glow as though by its own light. And looking across the nearer tributary valley that wound from below our crest down towards the Arno, looking over the low dark 60 shoulder of hill on whose extreme promontory stood the towered church of San Miniato, one saw the huge dome airily hanging on its ribs of masonry, the square campanile, the sharp spire of Santa Croce, and the canopied tower of the Signoria, rising above the in-

Young Archimedes is from Young Archimedes and Other Stories, by Aldous Huxley. Copyright 1924, 1952 by Aldous Huxley. Reprinted by permission of Harper & Row, Publishers. Young Archimedes was published in England in Little Mexican, by Aldous Huxley, copyright 1924. Reprinted by permission of Chatto & Windus Ltd. and Mrs. Laura Huxley.

Young Archimedes. 30. Apennines, a mountain range north of Florence, in central Italy. 40. pillars of Hercules, two promontories in the Strait of Gibraltar, reputed in classical legend to have been set there by the mythological hero Hercules; they were supposed to mark the end of the known world. 60. Arno, a river in Tuscany which flows through the city of Florence. 62. San Miniato, a famous old church on a high elevation overlooking Florence; the elevation is known as the Piazzale Michelangelo. huge dome, of the massive Duomo, or Cathedral of Santa Maria del Fiore (St. Mary of the Flower). The dome is 350 feet high. 64. campanile, the magnificent bell-tower of the Cathedral; it was designed by Giotto, famous Florentine architect of the early fourteenth century. Santa Croce, the oldest and finest church of the Franciscans. Because many of the famous men of Italy are buried in this shrine, it is called the Westminster Abbey of Florence. 65. Signoria, the fortress-like town hall erected in the fourteenth century for the use of the city directors, who were members of a committee called Signoria. The structure is also known as the Palazzo del Vecchio.

tricate maze of houses, distinct and brilliant, like small treasures carved out of precious stones. For a moment only, and then their light would fade away once more, and the travelling beam would pick out, among the indigo hills beyond, a single golden crest.

There were days when the air was wet with passed or with approaching rain, and all the distances seemed miraculously near and clear. The olive trees detached themselves one from another on the distant slopes; the 10 far-away villages were lovely and pathetic like the most exquisite small toys. There were days in summer-time, days of impending thunder when, bright and sunlit against huge bellying masses of black and purple, the hills and the white houses shone as it were precariously, in a dying splendor, on the brink of some fearful calamity.

How the hills changed and varied! Every day and every hour of the day, almost, they were different. There would be moments when, looking across the plain 20 of Florence, one would see only a dark blue silhouette against the sky. The scene had no depth; there was only a hanging curtain painted flatly with the symbols of mountains. And then, suddenly almost, with the passing of a cloud, or when the sun had declined to a certain level in the sky, the flat scene transformed itself; and where there had been only a painted curtain, now there were ranges behind ranges of hills, graduated tone after tone from brown, or gray, or a green gold to far-away blue. Shapes that a moment before had been 30 fused together indiscriminately into a single mass, now came apart into their constituents. Fiesole, which had seemed only a spur of Monte Morello, now revealed itself as the jutting headland of another system of hills, divided from the nearest bastions of its greater neighbor by a steep and shadowy valley.

At noon, during the heats of summer, the landscape became dim, powdery, vague, and almost colorless under the midday sun; the hills disappeared into the trembling fringes of the sky. But as the afternoon wore 40 on the landscape emerged again, it dropped its anonymity, it climbed back out of nothingness into form and life. And its life, as the sun sank and slowly sank through the long afternoon, grew richer, grew more intense with every moment. The level light, with its attendant long, dark shadows, laid bare, so to speak, the anatomy of the land; the hills—each western escarpment shining, and each slope averted from the sunlight profoundly shadowed—became massive, jutty, and solid. Little folds and dimples in the seemingly even 50 ground revealed themselves. Eastward from our hilltop, across the plain of the Ema, a great bluff cast its ever-increasing shadow; in the surrounding brightness of the valley a whole town lay eclipsed within it. And as the sun expired on the horizon, the further hills flushed in its warm light, till their illumined flanks

were the color of tawny roses; but the valleys were already filled with the blue mist of evening. And it mounted, mounted; the fire went out of the western windows of the populous slopes; only the crests were still alight, and at last they too were all extinct. The 60 mountains faded and fused together again into a flat painting of mountains against the pale evening sky. In a little while it was night; and if the moon were full, a ghost of the dead scene still haunted the horizons.

Changeful in its beauty, this wide landscape always preserved a quality of humanness and domestication which made it, to my mind at any rate, the best of all landscapes to live with. Day by day one travelled through its different beauties; but the journey, like our ancestors' Grand Tour, was always a journey 70 through civilization. For all its mountains, its steep slopes and deep valleys, the Tuscan scene is dominated by its inhabitants. They have cultivated every rood of ground that can be cultivated; their houses are thickly scattered even over the hills, and the valleys are populous. Solitary on the hilltop, one is not alone in a wilderness. Man's traces are across the country, and already—one feels it with satisfaction as one looks out across it—for centuries, for thousands of years, it has been his, submissive, tamed, and humanized. The 80 wide, blank moorlands, the sands, the forests of innumerable trees—these are places for occasional visitation, healthful to the spirit which submits itself to them for not too long. But fiendish influences as well as divine haunt these total solitudes. The vegetative life of plants and things is alien and hostile to the human. Men cannot live at ease except where they have mastered their surroundings and where their accumulated lives outnumber and outweigh the vegetative lives about them. Stripped of its dark woods, planted, ter- 90 raced, and tilled almost to the mountains' tops, the Tuscan landscape is humanized and safe. Sometimes upon those who live in the midst of it there comes a longing for some place that is solitary, inhuman, lifeless, or peopled only with alien life. But the longing is soon satisfied, and one is glad to return to the civilized and submissive scene.

I found that house on the hilltop the ideal dwelling-place. For there, safe in the midst of a humanized landscape, one was yet alone; one could be as solitary 100 as one liked. Neighbors whom one never sees at close quarters are the ideal and perfect neighbors.

Our nearest neighbors, in terms of physical proximity, lived very near. We had two sets of them, as a matter of fact, almost in the same house with us. One was the peasant family, who lived in a long, low building, part dwelling-house, part stables, storerooms and cowsheds, adjoining the villa. Our other neighbors—intermittent neighbors, however, for they only ventured out of town every now and then, during the most 110

31. **Fiesole**, a town three miles northeast of Florence. 34. **bastions**, literally, outward projections from the main enclosure of a fortification; here applied to hills. 46. **escarpment**, literally, the very steep ground

above a fortified place, cut to prevent hostile attack; here a steep, expansive slope. 70. **Grand Tour**, an extended tour on the continent of Europe, commonly taken by aristocratic young men as a part of their

flawless weather—were the owners of the villa, who had reserved for themselves the smaller wing of the huge L-shaped house—a mere dozen rooms or so—leaving the remaining eighteen or twenty to us.

They were a curious couple, our proprietors. An old husband, gray, listless, tottering, seventy at least; and a signora of about forty, short, very plump, with tiny fat hands and feet and a pair of very large, very dark black eyes, which she used with all the skill of a born comedian. Her vitality, if you could have harnessed it and made it do some useful work, would have supplied a whole town with electric light. The physicists talk of deriving energy from the atom; they would be more profitably employed nearer home—in discovering some way of tapping those enormous stores of vital energy which accumulate in unemployed women of sanguine temperament and which, in the present imperfect state of social and scientific organization, vent themselves in ways that are generally so deplorable: in interfering with other people's affairs, in working up emotional scenes, in thinking about love and making it, and in bothering men till they cannot get on with their work.

Signora Bondi got rid of her superfluous energy, among other ways, by "doing in" her tenants. The old gentleman, who was a retired merchant with a reputation for the most perfect rectitude, was allowed to have no dealings with us. When we came to see the house, it was the wife who showed us round. It was she who, with a lavish display of charm, with irresistible rollings of the eyes, expatiated on the merits of the place, sang the praises of the electric pump, glorified the bathroom (considering which, she insisted, the rent was remarkably moderate), and when we suggested calling in a surveyor to look over the house, earnestly begged us, as though our well-being were her only consideration, not to waste our money unnecessarily in doing anything so superfluous. "After all," she said, "we are honest people. I wouldn't dream of letting you the house except in perfect condition. Have confidence." And she looked at me with an appealing, pained expression in her magnificent eyes, as though begging me not to insult her by my coarse suspiciousness. And leaving us no time to pursue the subject of surveyors any further, she began assuring us that our little boy was the most beautiful angel she had ever seen. By the time our interview with Signora Bondi was at an end, we had definitely decided to take the house.

"Charming woman," I said, as we left the house. But I think that Elizabeth was not quite so certain of it as I.

Then the pump episode began.

On the evening of our arrival in the house we switched on the electricity. The pump made a very professional whirring noise; but no water came out of the taps in the bathroom. We looked at one another doubtfully.

"Charming woman?" Elizabeth raised her eyebrows.

We asked for interviews; but somehow the old gentleman could never see us, and the Signora was invariably out or indisposed. We left notes; they were never answered. In the end, we found that the only method of communicating with our landlords, who were living in the same house with us, was to go down into Florence and send a registered express letter to them. For this they had to sign two separate receipts and even, if we chose to pay forty centimes more, a third incriminating document, which was then returned to us. There could be no pretending, as there always was with ordinary letters or notes, that the communication had never been received. We began at last to get answers to our complaints. The Signora, who wrote all the letters, started by telling us that, naturally, the pump didn't work, as the cisterns were empty, owing to the long drought. I had to walk three miles to the post office to register my letter reminding her that there had been a violent thunderstorm only last Wednesday, and that the tanks were consequently more than half full. The answer came back: bath water had not been guaranteed in the contract; and if I wanted it, why hadn't I had the pump looked at before I took the house? Another walk into town to ask the Signora next door whether she remembered her adjurations to us to have confidence in her, and to inform her that the existence in a house of a bathroom was in itself an implicit guarantee of bath water. The reply to that was that the Signora couldn't continue to have communications with people who wrote so rudely to her. After that I put the matter into the hands of a lawyer. Two months later the pump was actually replaced. But we had to serve a writ on the lady before she gave in. And the costs were considerable.

One day, towards the end of the episode, I met the old gentleman in the road, taking his big maremman dog for a walk—or being taken, rather, for a walk by the dog. For where the dog pulled the old gentleman had perforce to follow. And when it stopped to smell, or scratch the ground, or leave against a gatepost its visiting-card or an offensive challenge, patiently, at his end of the leash, the old man had to wait. I passed him standing at the side of the road, a few hundred yards below our house. The dog was sniffing at the roots of one of the twin cypresses which grew one on either side of the entry to a farm; I heard the beast growling indignantly to itself, as though it scented an intolerable insult. Old Signor Bondi, leashed to his dog, was waiting. The knees inside the tubular gray trousers were slightly bent. Leaning on his cane, he stood gazing mournfully and vacantly at the view. The whites of

cultural education. 135. **"doing in,"** British slang for *cheating* or *taking in.* 178. **centimes,** copper coins worth about one tenth of one cent each. 205. **maremman,** from Maremma, a low, marshy maritime region in Tuscany on the northwestern coast of Italy.

Aldous Huxley 1251

his old eyes were discolored, like ancient billiard balls. In the gray, deeply wrinkled face, his nose was dyspeptically red. His white moustache, ragged and yellowing at the fringes, drooped in a melancholy curve. In his black tie he wore a very large diamond; perhaps that was what Signora Bondi had found so attractive about him.

I took off my hat as I approached. The old man stared at me absently, and it was only when I was already almost past him that he recollected who I was.

"Wait," he called after me, "wait!" And he hastened down the road in pursuit. Taken utterly by surprise and at a disadvantage—for it was engaged in retorting to the affront imprinted on the cypress roots—the dog permitted itself to be jerked after him. Too much astonished to be anything but obedient, it followed its master. "Wait!"

I waited.

"My dear sir," said the old gentleman, catching me by the lapel of my coat and blowing most disagreeably in my face, "I want to apologize." He looked around him, as though afraid that even here he might be overheard. "I want to apologize," he went on, "about that wretched pump business. I assure you that, if it had been only my affair, I'd have put the thing right as soon as you asked. You were quite right: a bathroom is an implicit guarantee of bath water. I saw from the first that we should have no chance if it came to court. And besides, I think one ought to treat one's tenants as handsomely as one can afford to. But my wife"—he lowered his voice—"the fact is that she likes this sort of thing, even when she knows that she's in the wrong and must lose. And besides, she hoped, I dare say, that you'd get tired of asking and have the job done yourself. I told her from the first that we ought to give in; but she wouldn't listen. You see, she enjoys it. Still, now she sees that it must be done. In the course of the next two or three days you'll be having your bath water. But I thought I'd just like to tell you how . . ."

But the Maremmano, which had recovered by this time from its surprise of a moment since, suddenly bounded, growling, up the road. The old gentleman tried to hold the beast, strained at the leash, tottered unsteadily, then gave way and allowed himself to be dragged off. ". . . how sorry I am," he went on, as he receded from me, "that this little misunderstanding . . ." But it was no use. "Good-bye." He smiled politely, made a little deprecating gesture, as though he had suddenly remembered a pressing engagement, and had no time to explain what it was. "Good-bye." He took off his hat and abandoned himself completely to the dog.

A week later the water really did begin to flow, and the day after our first bath Signora Bondi, dressed in dove-gray satin and wearing all her pearls, came to call.

"Is it peace now?" she asked, with a charming frankness, as she shook hands.

We assured her that, so far as we were concerned, it certainly was.

"But why *did* you write me such dreadfully rude letters?" she said, turning on me a reproachful glance that ought to have moved the most ruthless malefactor to contrition. "And then that writ. How could you? To a lady . . ."

I mumbled something about the pump and our wanting baths.

"But how could you expect me to listen to you while you were in that mood? Why didn't you set about it differently—politely, charmingly?" She smiled at me and dropped her fluttering eyelids.

I thought it best to change the conversation. It is disagreeable, when one is in the right, to be made to appear in the wrong.

A few weeks later we had a letter—duly registered and by express messenger—in which the Signora asked us whether we proposed to renew our lease (which was only for six months), and notifying us that, if we did, the rent would be raised 25 per cent, in consideration of the improvements which had been carried out. We thought ourselves lucky, at the end of much bargaining, to get the lease renewed for a whole year with an increase in the rent of only 15 per cent.

It was chiefly for the sake of the view that we put up with these intolerable extortions. But we had found other reasons, after a few days' residence, for liking the house. Of these, the most cogent was that, in the peasant's youngest child, we had discovered what seemed the perfect playfellow for our own small boy. Between little Guido—for that was his name—and the youngest of his brothers and sisters there was a gap of six or seven years. His two elder brothers worked with their father in the fields; since the time of the mother's death, two or three years before we knew them, the eldest sister had ruled the house, and the younger, who had just left school, helped her and in betweenwhiles kept an eye on Guido, who by this time, however, needed very little looking after; for he was between six and seven years old and as precocious, self-assured, and responsible as the children of the poor, left as they are to themselves almost from the time they can walk, generally are.

Though fully two and a half years older than little Robin—and at that age thirty months are crammed with a half a life-time's experience—Guido took no undue advantage of his superior intelligence and strength. I have never seen a child more patient, tolerant, and untyrannical. He never laughed at Robin for his clumsy efforts to imitate his own prodigious feats; he did not tease or bully, but helped his small companion when he was in difficulties and ex-

148. **Lorenzo the Magnificent,** Michelangelo's statue of Lorenzo de Medici (1449–1492), his great benefactor and patron. It shows Lorenzo seated, his right hand on his knee, his head resting on his left hand, with his left elbow on the arm of the chair. 218. **Via Tornabuoni,** one of the principal streets of Florence.

plained when he could not understand. In return, Robin adored him, regarded him as the model and perfect Big Boy, and slavishly imitated him in every way he could.

These attempts of Robin's to imitate his companion were often exceedingly ludicrous. For by an obscure psychological law, words and actions in themselves quite serious become comic as soon as they are copied; and the more accurately, if the imitation is a deliberate
120 parody, the funnier—for an overloaded imitation of someone we know does not make us laugh so much as one that is almost indistinguishably like the original. The bad imitation is only ludicrous when it is a piece of sincere and earnest flattery which does not quite come off. Robin's imitations were mostly of this kind. His heroic and unsuccessful attempts to perform the feats of strength and skill, which Guido could do with ease, were exquisitely comic. And his careful, long-drawn imitations of Guido's habits and manner-
130 isms were no less amusing. Most ludicrous of all, because most earnestly undertaken and most incongruous in the imitator, were Robin's impersonations of Guido in the pensive mood. Guido was a thoughtful child, given to brooding and sudden abstractions. One would find him sitting in a corner by himself, chin in hand, elbow on knee, plunged, to all appearances, in the profoundest meditation. And sometimes, even in the midst of his play, he would suddenly break off, to stand, his hands behind his back, frowning and
140 staring at the ground. When this happened Robin became overawed and a little disquieted. In a puzzled silence he looked at his companion. "Guido," he would say softly, "Guido." But Guido was generally too much preoccupied to answer; and Robin, not venturing to insist, would creep near him, and throwing himself as nearly as possible into Guido's attitude—standing Napoleonically, his hands clasped behind him, or sitting in the posture of Michelangelo's Lorenzo the Magnificent—would try to meditate too. Every few
150 seconds he would turn his bright blue eyes towards the elder child to see whether he was doing it quite right. But at the end of a minute he began to grow impatient; meditation wasn't his strong point. "Guido," he called again and, louder, "Guido!" And he would take him by the hand and try to pull him away. Sometimes Guido roused himself from his reverie and went back to the interrupted game. Sometimes he paid no attention. Melancholy, perplexed, Robin had to take himself off to play by himself. And Guido would go on
160 sitting or standing there, quite still; and his eyes, if one looked into them, were beautiful in their grave and pensive calm.

They were large eyes, set far apart and, what was strange in a dark-haired Italian child, of a luminous pale blue-gray color. They were not always grave and calm, as in these pensive moments. When he was playing, when he talked or laughed, they lit up; and

the surface of those clear, pale lakes of thought seemed, as it were, to be shaken into brilliant sun-flashing ripples. Above those eyes was a beautiful 170 forehead, high and steep and domed in a curve that was like the subtle curve of a rose petal. The nose was straight, the chin small and rather pointed, the mouth drooped a little sadly at the corners.

I have a snapshot of the two children sitting together on the parapet of the terrace. Guido sits almost facing the camera, but looking a little to one side and downwards; his hands are crossed in his lap and his expression, his attitude are thoughtful, grave, and meditative. It is Guido in one of those moods of abstrac- 180 tion into which he would pass even at the height of laughter and play—quite suddenly and completely, as though he had all at once taken it into his head to go away and had left the silent and beautiful body behind, like an empty house, to wait for his return. And by his side sits little Robin, turning to look up at him, his face half averted from the camera, but the curve of his cheek showing that he is laughing; one little raised hand is caught at the top of a gesture, the other clutches at Guido's sleeve as though he were urging 190 him to come away and play. And the legs dangling from the parapet have been seen by the blinking instrument in the midst of an impatient wriggle; he is on the point of slipping down and running off to play hide-and-seek in the garden. All the essential characteristics of both the children are in that little snapshot.

"If Robin were not Robin," Elizabeth used to say, "I could almost wish he were Guido."

And even at that time, when I took no particular interest in the child, I agreed with her. Guido seemed to 200 me one of the most charming little boys I had ever seen.

We were not alone in admiring him. Signora Bondi when, in those cordial intervals between our quarrels, she came to call, was constantly speaking of him. "Such a beautiful, beautiful child!" she would exclaim with enthusiasm. "It's really a waste that he should belong to peasants who can't afford to dress him properly. If he were mine, I should put him into black velvet; or little white knickers and a white knitted silk jersey with a red line at the collar and cuffs! or perhaps a 210 white sailor suit would be pretty. And in winter a little fur coat, with a squirrel skin cap, and possibly Russian boots . . ." Her imagination was running away with her. "And I'd let his hair grow, like a page's, and have it just curled up a little at the tips. And a straight fringe across his forehead. Everyone would turn round and stare after us if I took him out with me in Via Tornabuoni."

What you want, I should have liked to tell her, is not a child; it's a clock-work doll or a performing 220 monkey. But I did not say so—partly because I could not think of the Italian for a clock-work doll and partly because I did not want to risk having the rent raised another 15 per cent.

"Ah, if only I had a little boy like that!" She sighed and modestly dropped her eyelids. "I adore children. I sometimes think of adopting one—that is, if my husband would allow it."

I thought of the poor old gentleman being dragged along at the heels of his big white dog and inwardly smiled.

"But I don't know if he would," the Signora was continuing, "I don't know if he would." She was 10 silent for a moment, as though considering a new idea.

A few days later, when we were sitting in the garden after luncheon, drinking our coffee, Guido's father, instead of passing with a nod and the usual cheerful good-day, halted in front of us and began to talk. He was a fine handsome man, not very tall, but well-proportioned, quick and elastic in his movements, and full of life. He had a thin brown face, featured like a Roman's and lit by a pair of the most intelligent-looking gray eyes I ever saw. They exhibited almost too much 20 intelligence when, as not infrequently happened, he was trying, with an assumption of perfect frankness and a childlike innocence, to take one in or get something out of one. Delighting in itself, the intelligence shone there mischievously. The face might be ingenuous, impassive, almost imbecile in its expression; but the eyes on these occasions gave him completely away. One knew, when they glittered like that, that one would have to be careful.

Today, however, there was no dangerous light in 30 them. He wanted nothing out of us, nothing of any value—only advice, which is a commodity, he knew, that most people are only too happy to part with. But he wanted advice on what was, for us, rather a delicate subject: on Signora Bondi. Carlo had often complained to us about her. The old man is good, he told us, very good and kind indeed. Which meant, I dare say, among other things, that he could easily be swindled. But his wife . . . Well, the woman was a beast. And he would tell us stories of her insatiable rapacity: she 40 was always claiming more than the half of the produce which, by the laws of the metayage system, was the proprietor's due. He complained of her suspiciousness: she was forever accusing him of sharp practices, of downright stealing—him, he struck his breast, the soul of honesty. He complained of her short-sighted avarice: she wouldn't spend enough on manure, wouldn't buy him another cow, wouldn't have electric light installed in the stables. And we had sympathized, but cautiously, without expressing too strong an opinion on the subject. 50 The Italians are wonderfully non-committal in their speech; they will give nothing away to an interested person until they are quite certain that it is right and necessary and, above all, safe to do so. We had lived long enough among them to imitate their caution. What we said to Carlo would be sure, sooner or later, to get back to Signora Bondi. There was nothing to be gained by unnecessarily embittering our relations with the lady—only another 15 per cent, very likely, to be lost.

Today he wasn't so much complaining as feeling 60 perplexed. The Signora had sent for him, it seemed, and asked him how he would like it if she were to make an offer—it was all very hypothetical in the cautious Italian style—to adopt little Guido. Carlo's first instinct had been to say that he wouldn't like it at all. But an answer like that would have been too coarsely committal. He had preferred to say that he would think about it. And now he was asking for our advice.

Do what you think best, was what in effect we replied. But we gave it distantly but distinctly to be un- 70 derstood that we didn't think that Signora Bondi would make a very good foster-mother for the child. And Carlo was inclined to agree. Besides, he was very fond of the boy.

"But the thing is," he concluded rather gloomily, "that if she has really set her heart on getting hold of the child, there's nothing she won't do to get him—nothing."

He too, I could see, would have liked the physicists to start on unemployed childless women of sanguine 80 temperament before they tried to tackle the atom. Still, I reflected, as I watched him striding away along the terrace, singing powerfully from a brazen gullet as he went, there was force there, there was life enough in those elastic limbs, behind those bright gray eyes, to put up a good fight even against the accumulated vital energies of Signora Bondi.

It was a few days after this that my gramophone and two or three boxes of records arrived from England. They were a great comfort to us on the hilltop, 90 providing as they did the only thing in which that spiritually fertile solitude—otherwise a perfect Swiss Family Robinson's island—was lacking: music. There is not much music to be heard nowadays in Florence. The times when Dr. Burney could tour through Italy, listening to an unending succession of new operas, symphonies, quartets, cantatas, are gone. Gone are the days when a learned musician, inferior only to the Reverend Father Martini of Bologna, could admire what the peasants sang and the strolling players thrummed and 100

41. metayage, a system of farming on shares. 92. **Swiss Family Robinson,** the family wrecked on a desert island in the romance written by the Swiss author Johann Wyss (1781–1830). 95. **Dr. Burney,** Charles Burney (1726–1814), English music critic and historian. He toured the Continent in 1770 and in 1772 to gather material for his four-volume History. 99. **Martini,** Giovanni Battista Martini (1706–1784), famous Italian composer, theorist, and teacher. He lived in Bologna, a prominent city in northern Italy. 103. **"Salome,"** the name of a popular song, probably not the celebrated opera by Richard Strauss (1864–1949). 116. **Benin,** a large town in western Africa. **Nuneaton,** a town in Warwickshire, England. **Tozeur,** a town in Tunis, in northern Africa. 117.

Mozart quartets, a group of musical compositions for four stringed instruments by the great composer Wolfgang Mozart (1756–1791). 118. **Well-Tempered Clavichord,** a set of forty-eight pieces of music for the clavichord (the immediate ancestor of the piano) in all major and minor keys, by Johann Sebastian Bach (1685–1750). **Fifth Symphony,** one of the best-known of the nine symphonies composed by Ludwig van Beethoven (1770–1827). 119. **Brahms clarinet quintet,** one of the last compositions of Johannes Brahms (1833–1897). **motets by Palestrina,** ecclesiastical choral compositions by Giovanni da Palestrina (1525–1594), early Italian composer of church music. 133. **Piedigrotta songs,** popular songs of Naples. 145. **lire,** plural of *lira,* the Italian unit of cur-

scraped on their instruments. I have travelled for weeks through the peninsula and hardly heard a note that was not "Salome" or the Fascists' song. Rich in nothing else that makes life agreeable or even supportable, the northern metropolises are rich in music. That is perhaps the only inducement that a reasonable man can find for living there. The other attractions—organized gaiety, people, miscellaneous conversation, the social pleasures —what are those, after all, but an expense of spirit 110 that buys nothing in return? And then the cold, the darkness, the moldering dirt, the damp and squalor. . . . No, where there is no necessity that retains, music can be the only inducement. And that, thanks to the ingenious Edison, can now be taken about in a box and unpacked in whatever solitude one chooses to visit. One can live at Benin, or Nuneaton, or Tozeur in the Sahara, and still hear Mozart quartets, and selections from the Well-Tempered Clavichord, and the Fifth Symphony, and the Brahms clarinet quintet, and motets 120 by Palestrina.

Carlo, who had gone down to the station with his mule and cart to fetch the packing-case, was vastly interested in the machine.

"One will hear some music again," he said, as he watched me unpacking the gramophone and the disks. "It is difficult to do much oneself."

Still, I reflected, he managed to do a good deal. On warm nights we used to hear him, where he sat at the door of his house, playing his guitar and softly 130 singing; the eldest boy shrilled out the melody on the mandolin, and sometimes the whole family would join in, and the darkness would be filled with their passionate, throaty singing. Piedigrotta songs they mostly sang; and the voices drooped slurringly from note to note, lazily climbed or jerked themselves with sudden sobbing emphases from one tone to another. At a distance and under the stars the effect was not unpleasing.

"Before the war," he went on, "in normal times" 140 (and Carlo had a hope, even a belief, that the normal times were coming back and that life would soon be as cheap and easy as it had been in the days before the flood), "I used to go and listen to the operas at the Politeama. Ah, they were magnificent. But it costs five lire now to get in."

"Too much," I agreed.

"Have you got *Trovatore?*" he asked.

I shook my head.

"*Rigoletto?*"

150 "I'm afraid not."

"Bohème? Fanciulla del West? Pagliacci?"

I had to go on disappointing him.

"Not even *Norma?* Or the *Barbiere?*"

I put on Battistini in "La ci darem" out of *Don Giovanni.* He agreed that the singing was good; but I could see that he didn't much like the music. Why not? He found it difficult to explain.

"It's not like *Pagliacci,*" he said at last.

"Not palpitating?" I suggested, using a word with which I was sure he would be familiar; for it occurs 160 in every Italian political speech and patriotic leading article.

"Not palpitating," he agreed.

And I reflected that it is precisely by the difference between *Pagliacci* and *Don Giovanni,* between the palpitating and the non-palpitating, that modern musical taste is separated from the old. The corruption of the best, I thought, is the worst. Beethoven taught music to palpitate with his intellectual and spiritual passion. It has gone on palpitating ever since, but with the 170 passion of inferior men. Indirectly, I thought, Beethoven is responsible for *Parsifal, Pagliacci,* and the *Poem of Fire,* still more indirectly for *Samson and Delilah* and "Ivy, cling to me." Mozart's melodies may be brilliant, memorable, infectious; but they don't palpitate, don't catch you between wind and water, don't send the listener off into erotic ecstasies.

Carlo and his elder children found my gramophone, I am afraid, rather a disappointment. They were too polite, however, to say so openly; they merely ceased, 180 after the first day or two, to take any interest in the machine and the music it played. They preferred the guitar and their own singing.

Guido, on the other hand, was immensely interested. And he liked, not the cheerful dance tunes, to whose sharp rhythms our little Robin loved to go stamping round and round the room, pretending that he was a whole regiment of soldiers, but the genuine stuff. The first record he heard, I remember, was that of the slow movement of Bach's Concerto in D Minor for two 190 violins. That was the disk I put on the turntable as soon as Carlo had left me. It seemed to me, so to speak, the most musical piece of music with which I could refresh my long-parched mind—the coolest and clearest of all draughts. The movement had just got under way and was beginning to unfold its pure and melancholy beauties in accordance with the laws of the most exacting intellectual logic, when the two children, Guido in front and little Robin breathlessly following, came clattering into the room from the loggia.

rency, normally worth about twenty cents. 147. *Trovatore*, Il Trovatore, a famous Italian opera composed by Giuseppe Verdi (1813-1901). 149. *Rigoletto*, another opera by Verdi. 151. *Bohème*, La Bohème, an opera by the Italian composer Giacomo Puccini (1858-1924). *Fanciulla del West*, The Girl of the Golden West, another opera by Puccini based upon a play of the same name by David Belasco (1854-1931), American dramatic manager and author. *Pagliacci*, a celebrated opera based on a melodramatic Italian tale of traveling players by Ruggiero Leoncavallo (1858-1919). 153. *Norma*, a popular Italian opera by Vincenzo Bellini (1801-1835). *Barbiere*, The Barber of Seville, an operatic masterpiece by Gioachino Rossini (1792-1868). 154. **Battistini**, Mattia Battistini (1857-1928), Italian operatic baritone. **"La ci darem."** The full title is "La ci darem la mano," "Give me thy little hand, love," a duet from *Don Giovanni*, perhaps the greatest of Mozart's operas. 172. *Parsifal*, the great religious music drama by Richard Wagner (1813-1883). *Poem of Fire*, the same as Prometheus, an orchestral tone poem by the Russian pianist and composer Alexander Scriabin (1872-1915). 173. *Samson and Delilah*, an effective opera by Charles Camille Saint-Saëns (1835-1921). 174. **"Ivy, cling to me,"** a current popular song of the London music halls. 190. **Bach's . . . Minor**, considered by many the greatest of Bach's multitudinous masterpieces.

Guido came to a halt in front of the gramophone and stood there, motionless, listening. His pale blue-gray eyes opened themselves wide; making a little nervous gesture that I had often noticed in him before, he plucked at his lower lip with his thumb and forefinger. He must have taken a deep breath; for I noticed that, after listening for a few seconds, he sharply expired and drew in a fresh gulp of air. For an instant he looked at me—a questioning, astonished, rapturous look—gave a little laugh that ended in a kind of nervous shudder, and turned back towards the source of the incredible sounds. Slavishly imitating his elder comrade, Robin had also taken up his stand in front of the gramophone, and in exactly the same position, glancing at Guido from time to time to make sure that he was doing everything, down to plucking at his lip, in the correct way. But after a minute or so he became bored.

"Soldiers," he said, turning to me; "I want soldiers. Like in London." He remembered the rag-time and the jolly marches round and round the room.

I put my fingers to my lips. "Afterwards," I whispered.

Robin managed to remain silent and still for perhaps another twenty seconds. Then he seized Guido by the arm, shouting, "Vieni, Guido! Soldiers. Soldati. Vieni giuocare soldati."

It was then, for the first time, that I saw Guido impatient. "Vai!" he whispered angrily, slapped at Robin's clutching hand and pushed him roughly away. And he leaned a little closer to the instrument, as though to make up by yet intenser listening for what the interruption had caused him to miss.

Robin looked at him, astonished. Such a thing had never happened before. Then he burst out crying and came to me for consolation.

When the quarrel was made up—and Guido was sincerely repentant, was as nice as he knew how to be when the music had stopped and his mind was free to think of Robin once more—I asked him how he liked the music. He said he thought it was beautiful. But *bello* in Italian is too vague a word, too easily and frequently uttered, to mean very much.

"What did you like best?" I insisted. For he had seemed to enjoy it so much that I was curious to find out what had really impressed him.

He was silent for a moment, pensively frowning. "Well," he said at last, "I liked the bit that went like this." And he hummed a long phrase. "And then there's the other thing singing at the same time—but what are those things," he interrupted himself, "that sing like that?"

"They're called violins," I said.

"Violins." He nodded. "Well, the other violin goes like this." He hummed again. "Why can't one sing both at once? And what is in that box? What makes it make that noise?" The child poured out his questions.

I answered him as best I could, showing him the little spirals on the disk, the needle, the diaphragm. I told him to remember how the string of the guitar trembled when one plucked it; sound is a shaking in the air, I told him, and I tried to explain how those shakings get printed on the black disk. Guido listened to me very gravely, nodding from time to time. I had the impression that he understood perfectly well everything I was saying.

By this time, however, poor Robin was so dreadfully bored that in pity for him I had to send the two children out into the garden to play. Guido went obediently; but I could see that he would have preferred to stay indoors and listen to more music. A little while later, when I looked out, he was hiding in the dark recesses of the big bay tree, roaring like a lion, and Robin, laughing, but a little nervously, as though he were afraid that the horrible noise might possibly turn out, after all, to be the roaring of a real lion, was beating the bush with a stick, and shouting, "Come out, come out! I want to shoot you."

After lunch, when Robin had gone upstairs for his afternoon sleep, he reappeared. "May I listen to the music now?" he asked. And for an hour he sat there in front of the instrument, his head cocked slightly on one side, listening while I put on one disk after another.

Thenceforward he came every afternoon. Very soon he knew all my library of records, had his preferences and dislikes, and could ask for what he wanted by humming the principal theme.

"I don't like that one," he said of Strauss's "Till Eulenspiegel." "It's like what we sing in our house. Not really like, you know. But somehow rather like, all the same. You understand?" He looked at us perplexedly and appealingly, as though begging us to understand what he meant and so save him from going on explaining. We nodded. Guido went on. "And then," he said, "the end doesn't seem to come properly out of the beginning. It's not like the one you played the first time." He hummed a bar or two from the slow movement of Bach's D Minor Concerto.

"It isn't," I suggested, "like saying: All little boys like playing. Guido is a little boy. Therefore Guido likes playing."

He frowned. "Yes, perhaps that's it," he said at last. "The one you played first is more like that.

26. **"Viene . . . soldati,"** come play soldiers. 29. **"Vai!"** Go (away). 42. *bello,* beautiful, fine; used freely in various expressions. 89. **"Till Eulenspiegel,"** "Till Owlglass," a symphonic poem by Richard Strauss (1864–1949), based on the life and adventures of a famous rogue of medieval German folklore. Till, the hero, is finally sentenced and hanged as an adventurous troublemaker. 107. **Debussy,** Claude Debussy (1862–1918), French composer; his *Arabesques* belong to the Impressionistic

school of music. 113. **"Après-Midi d'un Faune,"** "The Afternoon of a Faun," a celebrated musical tone poem by Debussy, based upon a poem of the same title by the French symbolist poet, Stéphane Mallarmé (1842–1898). 128. **"Deh . . . finestra,"** "Open Thy Window," a charming serenade from Mozart's opera, *Don Giovanni.* 129. **"Che soave zefiretto,"** "What a Soft Little Breeze," an aria from Mozart's opera, *The Marriage of Figaro.* 140. **Egmont overture,** from the inci-

But, you know," he added, with an excessive regard for truth, "I don't like playing as much as Robin does."

Wagner was among his dislikes; so was Debussy. When I played the record of one of Debussy's Arabesques, he said, "Why does he say the same thing over and over again? He ought to say something new, or go on, or make the thing grow. Can't he think of anything different?" But he was less censorious about the "Après-Midi d'un Faune." "The things have beautiful voices," he said.

Mozart overwhelmed him with delight. The duet from *Don Giovanni*, which his father had found insufficiently palpitating, enchanted Guido. But he preferred the quartets and the orchestral pieces.

"I like music," he said, "better than singing."

Most people, I reflected, like singing better than music; are more interested in the executant than in what he executes, and find the impersonal orchestra less moving than the soloist. The touch of the pianist is the human touch, and the soprano's high C is the personal note. It is for the sake of this touch, that note, that audiences fill the concert halls.

Guido, however, preferred music. True, he liked "La ci darem"; he liked "Deh vieni alla finestra"; he thought "Che soave zefiretto" so lovely that almost all our concerts had to begin with it. But he preferred the other things. The *Figaro* overture was one of his favorites. There is a passage not far from the beginning of the piece, where the first violins suddenly go rocketing up into the heights of loveliness; as the music approached that point, I used always to see a smile developing and gradually brightening on Guido's face, and when, punctually, the thing happened, he clapped his hands and laughed aloud with pleasure.

On the other side of the same disk, it happened, was recorded Beethoven's *Egmont* overture. He liked that almost better than *Figaro*.

"It has more voices," he explained. And I was delighted by the acuteness of the criticism; for it is precisely in the richness of its orchestration that *Egmont* goes beyond *Figaro*.

But what stirred him almost more than anything was the *Coriolan* overture. The third movement of the Fifth Symphony, the second movement of the Seventh, the slow movement of the Emperor Concerto—all these things ran it pretty close. But none excited him so much as *Coriolan*. One day he made me play it three or four times in succession; then he put it away.

"I don't think I want to hear that any more," he said.

"Why not?"

"It's too . . . too . . ." he hesitated, "too big," he said at last. "I don't really understand it. Play me the one that goes like this." He hummed the phrase from the D Minor Concerto.

"Do you like that one better?" I asked.

He shook his head. "No, it's not that exactly. But it's easier."

"Easier?" It seemed to me rather a queer word to apply to Bach.

"I understand it better."

One afternoon, while we were in the middle of our concert, Signora Bondi was ushered in. She began at once to be overwhelmingly affectionate towards the child; kissed him, patted his head, paid him the most outrageous compliments on his appearance. Guido edged away from her.

"And do you like music?" she asked.

The child nodded.

"I think he has a gift," I said. "At any rate, he has a wonderful ear and a power of listening and criticizing such as I've never met with in a child of that age. We're thinking of hiring a piano for him to learn on."

A moment later I was cursing myself for my undue frankness in praising the boy. For Signora Bondi began immediately to protest that, if she could have the upbringing of the child, she would give him the best masters, bring out his talent, make an accomplished maestro of him—and, on the way, an infant prodigy. And at that moment, I am sure, she saw herself sitting maternally, in pearls and black satin, in the lee of the huge Steinway, while an angelic Guido, dressed like little Lord Fauntleroy, rattled out Liszt and Chopin, to the loud delight of a thronged auditorium. She saw the bouquets and all the elaborate floral tributes, heard the clapping and the few well-chosen words with which the veteran maestri, touched almost to tears, would hail the coming of the little genius. It became more than ever important for her to acquire the child.

"You've sent her away fairly ravening," said Elizabeth, when Signora Bondi had gone. "Better tell her next time that you made a mistake, and that the boy's got no musical talent whatever."

In due course, the piano arrived. After giving him the minimum of preliminary instruction, I let Guido loose on it. He began by picking out for himself the melodies he had heard, reconstructing the harmonies in which they were embedded. After a few lessons, he understood the rudiments of musical notation and could read a simple passage at sight, albeit very slowly. The whole process of reading was still strange to him; he had picked up his letters somehow, but nobody had yet taught him to read whole words and sentences.

dental music which Beethoven wrote for Goethe's famous tragedy, *Egmont*. **147. Coriolan overture,** the Coriolanus Overture by Beethoven, based upon a tragedy of Heinrich Joseph von Collin (1771–1811), Austrian poet and playwright. **148. the Seventh,** by Beethoven, which the master considered the best of his nine. **149. Emperor Concerto,** the fifth and last of Beethoven's concertos for piano and orchestra. **188. Lord Fauntleroy,** title and child hero of a popular novel by Frances Hodgson Burnett (1849–1924). His conventional dress consisted of velvet trousers and Eton waist with large collar and black tie. He was also afflicted with long curls. **Liszt,** Franz Liszt (1811–1886), Hungarian pianist and composer, pioneer in the composition of the symphonic tone poem, and generally conceded to be the greatest piano virtuoso in history. **Chopin,** Frédéric Chopin (1810?–1849), French-Polish pianist and composer.

I took occasion, next time I saw Signora Bondi, to assure her that Guido had disappointed me. There was nothing in his musical talent, really. She professed to be very sorry to hear it; but I could see that she didn't for a moment believe me. Probably she thought that we were after the child too, and wanted to bag the infant prodigy for ourselves, before she could get in her claim, thus depriving her of what she regarded almost as her feudal right. For, after all, weren't they her peasants? If anyone was to profit by adopting the child it ought to be herself.

Tactfully, diplomatically, she renewed her negotiations with Carlo. The boy, she put it to him, had genius. It was the foreign gentleman who had told her so, and he was the sort of man, clearly, who knew about such things. If Carlo would let her adopt the child, she'd have him trained. He'd become a great maestro and get engagements in the Argentine and the United States, in Paris and London. He'd earn millions and millions. Think of Caruso, for example. Part of the millions, she explained, would of course come to Carlo. But before they began to roll in, those millions, the boy would have to be trained. But training was very expensive. In his own interest, as well as in that of his son, he ought to let her take charge of the child. Carlo said he would think it over, and again applied to us for advice. We suggested that it would be best in any case to wait a little and see what progress the boy made.

He made, in spite of my assertions to Signora Bondi, excellent progress. Every afternoon, while Robin was asleep, he came for his concert and his lesson. He was getting along famously with his reading; his small fingers were acquiring strength and agility. But what to me was more interesting was that he had begun to make up little pieces on his own account. A few of them I took down as he played them and I have them still. Most of them, strangely enough, as I thought then, are canons. He had a passion for canons. When I explained to him the principles of the form he was enchanted.

"It is beautiful," he said, with admiration. "Beautiful, beautiful. And so easy!"

Again the word surprised me. The canon is not, after all, so conspicuously simple. Thenceforward he spent most of his time at the piano in working out little canons for his own amusement. They were often remarkably ingenious. But in the invention of other kinds of music he did not show himself so fertile as I had hoped. He composed and harmonized one or two solemn little airs like hymn tunes, with a few sprightlier pieces in the spirit of the military march. They were extraordinary, of course, as being the inventions of a child. But a great many children can

do extraordinary things; we are all geniuses up to the age of ten. But I had hoped that Guido was a child who was going to be a genius at forty; in which case what was extraordinary for an ordinary child was not extraordinary enough for him. "He's hardly a Mozart," we agreed, as we played his little pieces over. I felt, it must be confessed, almost aggrieved. Anything less than a Mozart, it seemed to me, was hardly worth thinking about.

He was not a Mozart. No. But he was somebody, as I was to find out, quite as extraordinary. It was one morning in the early summer that I made the discovery. I was sitting in the warm shade of our westward-facing balcony, working. Guido and Robin were playing in the little enclosed garden below. Absorbed in my work, it was only, I suppose, after the silence had prolonged itself a considerable time that I became aware that the children were making remarkably little noise. There was no shouting, no running about; only a quiet talking. Knowing by experience that when children are quiet it generally means that they are absorbed in some delicious mischief, I got up from my chair and looked over the balustrade to see what they were doing. I expected to catch them dabbing in water, making a bonfire, covering themselves with tar. But what I actually saw was Guido, with a burnt stick in his hand, demonstrating on the smooth paving-stones of the path, that the square on the hypotenuse of a right-angled triangle is equal to the sum of the squares on the other two sides.

Kneeling on the floor, he was drawing with the point of his blackened stick on the flagstones. And Robin, kneeling imitatively beside him, was growing, I could see, rather impatient with this very slow game.

"Guido," he said. But Guido paid no attention. Pensively frowning, he went on with his diagram. "Guido!" The younger child bent down and then craned round his neck so as to look up into Guido's face. "Why don't you draw a train?"

"Afterwards," said Guido. "But I just want to show you this first. It's so beautiful," he added cajolingly.

"But I want a train," Robin persisted.

"In a moment. Do just wait a moment." The tone was almost imploring. Robin armed himself with renewed patience. A minute later Guido had finished both his diagrams.

"There!" he said triumphantly, and straightened himself up to look at them. "Now I'll explain."

And he proceeded to prove the theorem of Pythagoras—not in Euclid's way, but by the simpler and more satisfying method which was, in all probability, employed by Pythagoras himself. He had drawn a square and dissected it, by a pair of crossed perpendiculars, into two squares and two equal rectangles.

20. Caruso, Enrico Caruso (1873–1921), the greatest Italian tenor of his generation. 39. canon, a musical composition in two or more voice parts; it is based upon the principle of imitation, somewhat like a musical round. 103. Pythagoras, a Greek philosopher and mathematician of the

sixth century before Christ. 104. Euclid, a Greek geometrician of the third century before Christ. 145. "Cattivo Guido," "bad, naughty Guido!" 187. Bushman, one of an aboriginal race of nomadic hunters of South Africa, of low cranial capacity. The term is applied also to the

The equal rectangles he divided up by their diagonals into four equal right-angled triangles. The two squares are then seen to be the squares on the two sides of any one of these triangles other than the hypotenuse. So much for the first diagram. In the next he took the four right-angled triangles into which the rectangles had been divided and rearranged them round the original square so that their right angles filled the corners of the square, the hypotenuses looked inwards and the greater and less sides of the triangles were in continuation along the sides of the square (which are each equal to the sum of these sides). In this way the original square is redissected into four right-angled triangles and the square on the hypotenuse. The four triangles are equal to the two rectangles of the original dissection. Therefore the square on the hypotenuse is equal to the sum of the two squares—the squares on the other two sides—into which, with the rectangles, the original square was first dissected.

In very untechnical language, but clearly and with a relentless logic, Guido expounded his proof. Robin listened, with an expression on his bright, freckled face of perfect incomprehension.

"Treno," he repeated from time to time. "Treno. Make a train."

"In a moment," Guido implored. "Wait a moment. But do just look at this. Do." He coaxed and cajoled. "It's so beautiful. It's so easy."

So easy. . . . the theorem of Pythagoras seemed to explain for me Guido's musical predilections. It was not an infant Mozart we had been cherishing; it was a little Archimedes with, like most of his kind, an incidental musical twist.

"Treno, treno!" shouted Robin, growing more and more restless as the exposition went on. And when Guido insisted on going on with his proof, he lost his temper. "Cattivo Guido," he shouted, and began to hit out at him with his fists.

"All right," said Guido resignedly. "I'll make a train." And with his stick of charcoal he began to scribble on the stones.

I looked on for a moment in silence. It was not a very good train. Guido might be able to invent for himself and prove the theorem of Pythagoras; but he was not much of a draughtsman.

"Guido!" I called. The two children turned up. "Who taught you to draw those squares?" It was conceivable, of course, that somebody might have taught him.

"Nobody." He shook his head. Then, rather anxiously, as though he were afraid there might be something wrong about drawing squares, he went on to apologize and explain. "You see," he said, "it seemed to me so beautiful. Because those squares"—he pointed

at the two small squares in the first figure—"are just as big as this one." And, indicating the square on the hypotenuse in the second diagram, he looked up at me with a deprecating smile.

I nodded. "Yes, it's very beautiful," I said—"it's very beautiful indeed."

An expression of delighted relief appeared on his face; he laughed with pleasure. "You see, it's like this," he went on, eager to initiate me into the glorious secret he had discovered. "You cut these two long squares"—he meant the rectangles—"into two slices. And then there are four slices, all just the same, because, because—oh, I ought to have said that before—because these long squares are the same, because those lines, you see . . . ."

"But I want a train," protested Robin.

Leaning on the rail of the balcony, I watched the children below. I thought of the extraordinary thing I had just seen and of what it meant.

I thought of the vast differences between human beings. We classify men by the color of their eyes and hair, the shape of their skulls. Would it not be more sensible to divide them up into intellectual species? There would be even wider gulfs between the extreme mental types than between a Bushman and a Scandinavian. This child, I thought, when he grows up, will be to me, intellectually, what a man is to a dog. And there are other men and women who are, perhaps, almost as dogs to me.

Perhaps the men of genius are the only true men. In all the history of the race there have been only a few thousand real men. And the rest of us—what are we? Teachable animals. Without the help of the real men, we should have found out almost nothing at all. Almost all the ideas with which we are familiar could never have occurred to minds like ours. Plant the seeds there and they will grow; but our minds could never spontaneously have generated them.

There have been whole nations of dogs, I thought; whole epochs in which no Man was born. From the dull Egyptians the Greeks took crude experience and rules of thumb and made sciences. More than a thousand years passed before Archimedes had a comparable successor. There has been only one Buddha, one Jesus, only one Bach that we know of, one Michelangelo.

Is it by a mere chance, I wondered, that a Man is born from time to time? What causes a whole constellation of them to come contemporaneously into being and from out of a single people? Taine thought that Leonardo, Michelangelo, and Raphael were born when they were because the time was ripe for great painters and the Italian scene congenial. In the mouth of a rationalizing nineteenth-century Frenchman the doctrine is strangely mystical; it may be none the less

aborigines of Australia. The Scandinavian ranks among the most literate peoples of the earth. 206. **Buddha,** Indian philosopher and religious leader of the fifth century before Christ; he was the founder of Buddhism, one of the world's great religions. 211. **Taine,** Hippolyte Adolphe Taine (1828–1893), French historian and critic of literature who based his approach to literature on the overwhelming importance of race and environment.

Aldous Huxley 1259

true for that. But what of those born out of time? Blake, for example. What of those?

This child, I thought, has had the fortune to be born at a time when he will be able to make good use of his capacities. He will find the most elaborate analytical methods lying ready to his hand; he will have a prodigious experience behind him. Suppose him born while Stonehenge was building; he might have spent a lifetime discovering the rudiments, guessing darkly
10 where now he might have had a chance of proving. Born at the time of the Norman Conquest, he would have had to wrestle with all the preliminary difficulties created by an inadequate symbolism; it would have taken him long years, for example, to learn the art of dividing MMMCCCCLXXXVIII by MCMXIX. In five years, nowadays, he will learn what it took generations of Men to discover.

And I thought of the fate of all the Men born so hopelessly out of time that they could achieve little
20 or nothing of value. Beethoven born in Greece, I thought, would have had to be content to play thin melodies on the flute or lyre; in those intellectual surroundings it would hardly have been possible for him to imagine the nature of harmony.

From drawing trains, the children in the garden below had gone on to playing trains. They were trotting round and round; with blown round cheeks and pouting mouth, like the cherubic symbol of a wind, Robin puff-puffed, and Guido, holding the skirt of his
30 smock, shuffled behind him, tooting. They ran forward, backed, stopped at imaginary stations, shunted, roared over bridges, crashed through tunnels, met with occasional collisions and derailments. The young Archimedes seemed to be just as happy as the little towheaded barbarian. A few minutes ago he had been busy with the theorem of Pythagoras. Now, tooting indefatigably along imaginary rails, he was perfectly content to shuffle backwards and forwards among the flower-beds, between the pillars of the loggia, in and
40 out of the dark tunnels of the laurel tree. The fact that one is going to be Archimedes does not prevent one from being an ordinary cheerful child meanwhile. I thought of this strange talent distinct and separate from the rest of the mind, independent, almost, of experience. The typical child-prodigies are musical and mathematical; the other talents ripen slowly under the influence of emotional experience and growth. Till he was thirty Balzac gave proof of nothing but ineptitude; but at four the young Mozart
50 was already a musician, and some of Pascal's most brilliant work was done before he was out of his teens.

In the weeks that followed, I alternated the daily piano lessons with lessons in mathematics. Hints rather than lessons they were; for I only made suggestions, indicated methods, and left the child himself to work out the ideas in detail. Thus I introduced him to algebra by showing him another proof of the theorem of Pythagoras. In this proof one drops a perpendicular from the right angle on to the hypotenuse, and arguing 60 from the fact that the two triangles thus created are similar to one another and to the original triangle, and that the proportions which their corresponding sides bear to one another are therefore equal, one can show in algebraical form that $c^2 + d^2$ (the squares on the other two sides) are equal to $a^2 + b^2$ (the squares on the two segments of the hypotenuse) $+ 2ab$; which last, it is easy to show geometrically, is equal to $(a+b)^2$, or the square on the hypotenuse. Guido was as much enchanted by the rudiments of algebra as he would have 70 been if I had given him an engine worked by steam, with a methylated spirit lamp to heat the boiler; more enchanted, perhaps—for the engine would have got broken, and remaining always itself, would in any case have lost its charm, while the rudiments of algebra continued to grow and blossom in his mind with an unfailing luxuriance. Every day he made the discovery of something which seemed to him exquisitely beautiful; the new toy was inexhaustible in its potentialities.
80

In the intervals of applying algebra to the second book of Euclid, we experimented with circles; we stuck bamboos into the parched earth, measured their shadows at different hours of the day, and drew exciting conclusions from our observations. Sometimes, for fun, we cut and folded sheets of paper so as to make cubes and pyramids. One afternoon Guido arrived carrying carefully between his small and rather grubby hands a flimsy dodecahedron.

"E tanto bello!" he said, as he showed us his paper 90 crystal; and when I asked him how he managed to make it, he merely smiled and said it had been so easy. I looked at Elizabeth and laughed. But it would have been more symbolically to the point, I felt, if I had gone down on all fours, wagged the spiritual outgrowth of my os coccyx, and barked my astonished admiration.

It was an uncommonly hot summer. By the beginning of July our little Robin, unaccustomed to these high temperatures, began to look pale and tired; he 100 was listless, had lost his appetite and energy. The doctor advised mountain air. We decided to spend the next ten or twelve weeks in Switzerland. My parting gift to Guido was the first six books of Euclid in Italian. He turned over the pages, looked ecstatically at the figures.

2. **Blake,** William Blake (p. 671). 39. **loggia,** an open gallery with a roof. 48. **Balzac,** Honoré de Balzac (1799–1850), famous French novelist and pioneer of the realistic school of fiction. 50. **Pascal,** Blaise Pascal (1623–1662), French philosopher and mathematician. 72. **methylated spirit lamp,** a lamp that burns methyl alcohol. 89. **dodeca-** hedron, a box-shaped figure with twelve sides or faces. 90. **"E tanto bello!"** "It's so beautiful." 96. **os coccyx,** the end bone of the vertebrate column. 109. **Grindelwald,** a village in the canton of Berne, Switzerland. 110. **Alp-horns,** carved wooden horns about three feet long with a cupped mouthpiece and a bell. 111. **edelweiss,** famous flower

"If only I knew how to read properly," he said. "I'm so stupid. But now I shall really try to learn."

From our hotel near Grindelwald we sent the child, in Robin's name, various post cards of cows, Alphorns, Swiss chalets, edelweiss, and the like. We received no answers to these cards; but then we did not expect answers. Guido could not write, and there was no reason why his father or his sisters should take the trouble to write for him. No news, we took it, was good news. And then one day, early in September, there arrived at the hotel a strange letter. The manager had it stuck up on the glass-fronted notice-board in the hall, so that all the guests might see it, and whoever conscientiously thought that it belonged to him might claim it. Passing the board on the way in to lunch, Elizabeth stopped to look at it.

"But it must be from Guido," she said.

I came and looked at the envelope over her shoulder. It was unstamped and black with postmarks. Traced out in pencil, the big uncertain capital letters sprawled across its face. In the first line was written: AL BABBO DI ROBIN, and there followed a travestied version of the name of the hotel and the place. Round the address bewildered postal officials had scrawled suggested emendations. The letter had wandered for a fortnight at least, back and forth across the face of Europe.

"Al Babbo di Robin. To Robin's father." I laughed. "Pretty smart of the postmen to have got it here at all." I went to the manager's office, set forth the justice of my claim to the letter and, having paid the fifty-centime surcharge for the missing stamp, had the case unlocked and the letter given me. We went in to lunch.

"The writing's magnificent," we agreed, laughing, as we examined the address at close quarters. "Thanks to Euclid," I added. "That's what comes of pandering to the ruling passion."

But when I opened the envelope and looked at its contents I no longer laughed. The letter was brief and almost telegraphical in style. "SONO DALLA PADRONA," it ran, "NON MI PIACE HA RUBATO IL MIO LIBRO NON VOGLIO SUONARE PIU VOGLIO TORNARE A CASA VENGA SUBITO GUIDO."

"What is it?"

I handed Elizabeth the letter. "That blasted woman's got hold of him," I said.

Busts of men in Homburg hats, angels bathed in marble tears extinguishing torches, statues of little girls, cherubs, veiled figures, allegories and ruthless realisms—the strangest and most diverse idols beckoned and gesticulated as we passed. Printed indelibly on tin and embedded in the living rock, the brown photographs looked out, under glass, from the humbler crosses, headstones, and broken pillars. Dead ladies in the cubistic geometrical fashions of thirty years ago—two cones of black satin meeting point to point at the waist, and the arms: a sphere to the elbow, a polished cylinder below—smiled mournfully out of their marble frames; the smiling faces, the white hands, were the only recognizably human things that emerged from the solid geometry of their clothes. Men with black moustaches, men with white beards, young clean-shaven men, stared or averted their gaze to show a Roman profile. Children in their stiff best opened wide their eyes, smiled hopefully in anticipation of the little bird that was to issue from the camera's muzzle, smiled sceptically in the knowledge that it wouldn't, smiled laboriously and obediently because they had been told to. In spiky Gothic cottages of marble the richer dead privately reposed; through grilled doors one caught a glimpse of pale Inconsolables weeping, of distraught Geniuses guarding the secret of the tomb. The less prosperous sections of the majority slept in communities, close-crowded but elegantly housed under smooth continuous marble floors, whose every flagstone was the mouth of a separate grave.

These continental cemeteries, I thought, as Carlo and I made our way among the dead, are more frightful than ours, because these people pay more attention to their dead than we do. That primordial cult of corpses, that tender solicitude for their material wellbeing, which led the ancients to house their dead in stone, while they themselves lived between wattles and under thatch, still lingers here; persists, I thought, more vigorously than with us. There are a hundred gesticulating statues here for every one in an English graveyard. There are more family vaults, more "luxuriously appointed" (as they say of liners and hotels) than one would find at home. And embedded in every tombstone there are photographs to remind the powdered bones within what form they will have to resume on the Day of Judgment; beside each are little hanging lamps to burn optimistically on All Souls' Day. To the Man who built the Pyramids they are nearer, I thought, than we.

"If I had known," Carlo kept repeating, "if only I had known." His voice came to me through my reflections as though from a distance. "At the time he didn't mind at all. How should I have known that he would take it so much to heart afterwards? And she deceived me, she lied to me."

I assured him yet once more that it wasn't his fault. Though, of course, it was, in part. It was mine too, in part; I ought to have thought of the possibility and somehow guarded against it. And he shouldn't have

of Switzerland, growing high in the Alps. 146. "SONO . . . GUIDO,"
"I am at the Padrona's—I don't like it here—she has stolen my book—
I don't want to play [the piano] any more—I want to go back home—
come quickly—Guido." 153. Homburg hat, a man's soft felt hat with
dented crown, first worn in Homburg, a town and fashionable watering

place of Prussia, noted for the manufacture of hats and machines. 189.
wattles, long, flexible stalks or rods.

let the child go, even temporarily and on trial, even though the woman was bringing pressure to bear on him. And the pressure had been considerable. They had worked on the same holding for more than a hundred years, the men of Carlo's family; and now she had made the old man threaten to turn him out. It would be a dreadful thing to leave the place; and besides, another place wasn't so easy to find. It was made quite plain, however, that he could stay if he let her have the
10 child. Only for a little to begin with; just to see how he got on. There would be no compulsion whatever on him to stay if he didn't like it. And it would be all to Guido's advantage; and to his father's, too, in the end. All that the Englishman had said about his not being such a good musician as he had thought at first was obviously untrue—mere jealousy and little-mindedness: the man wanted to take credit for Guido himself, that was all. And the boy, it was obvious, would learn nothing from him. What he needed was a real good
20 professional master.

All the energy that, if the physicists had known their business, would have been driving dynamos, went into this campaign. It began the moment we were out of the house, intensively. She would have more chance of success, the Signora doubtless thought, if we weren't there. And besides, it was essential to take the opportunity when it offered itself and get hold of the child before we could make our bid—for it was obvious to her that we wanted Guido just as much as she did.
30 Day after day she renewed the assault. At the end of a week she sent her husband to complain about the state of the vines: they were in a shocking condition; he had decided, or very nearly decided, to give Carlo notice. Meekly, shamefacedly, in obedience to higher orders, the old gentleman uttered his threats. Next day Signora Bondi returned to the attack. The padrone, she declared, had been in a towering passion; but she'd do her best, her very best, to mollify him. And after a significant pause she went on to talk about Guido.
40 In the end Carlo gave in. The woman was too persistent and she held too many trump cards. The child could go and stay with her for a month or two on trial. After that, if he really expressed a desire to remain with her, she could formally adopt him.

At the idea of going for a holiday to the seaside— and it was to the seaside, Signora Bondi told him, that they were going—Guido was pleased and excited. He had heard a lot about the sea from Robin. "Tanta acqua!" It had sounded almost too good to be true.
50 And now he was actually to go and see this marvel. It was very cheerfully that he parted from his family.

But after the holiday by the sea was over, and Signora Bondi had brought him back to her town house in Florence, he began to be homesick. The Signora, it was true, treated him exceedingly kindly, bought him

36. **padrone,** the landlord, her husband. 48. **"Tanta acqua!"** "So much water!"

new clothes, took him out to tea in the Via Tornabuoni and filled him up with cakes, iced strawberryade, whipped cream, and chocolates. But she made him practice the piano more than he liked, and what was worse, she took away his Euclid, on the score that he 60 wasted too much time with it. And when he said that he wanted to go home, she put him off with promises and excuses and downright lies. She told him that she couldn't take him at once, but that next week, if he were good and worked hard at his piano meanwhile, next week. . . . And when the time came she told him that his father didn't want him back. And she redoubled her petting, gave him expensive presents, and stuffed him with yet unhealthier foods. To no purpose. Guido didn't like his new life, didn't want to practice scales, 70 pined for his book, and longed to be back with his brothers and sisters. Signora Bondi, meanwhile, continued to hope that time and chocolates would eventually make the child hers; and to keep his family at a distance, she wrote to Carlo every few days letters which still purported to come from the seaside (she took the trouble to send them to a friend, who posted them back again to Florence), and in which she painted the most charming picture of Guido's happiness.

It was then that Guido wrote his letter to me. Aban- 80 doned, as he supposed, by his family—for that they shouldn't take the trouble to come to see him when they were so near was only to be explained on the hypothesis that they really had given him up—he must have looked to me as his last and only hope. And the letter, with its fantastic address, had been nearly a fortnight on its way. A fortnight—it must have seemed hundreds of years; and as the centuries succeeded one another gradually, no doubt, the poor child became convinced that I too had abandoned him. There was no hope 90 left.

"Here we are," said Carlo.

I looked up and found myself confronted by an enormous monument. In a kind of grotto hollowed in the flanks of a monolith of gray sandstone, Sacred Love, in bronze, was embracing a funerary urn. And in bronze letters riveted into the stone was a long legend to the effect that the inconsolable Ernesto Bondi had raised this monument to the memory of his beloved wife, Annunziata, as a token of his undying love 100 for one whom, snatched from him by a premature death, he hoped very soon to join beneath this stone. The first Signora Bondi had died in 1912. I thought of the old man leased to his white dog; he must always, I reflected, have been a most uxorious husband.

"They buried him here."

We stood there for a long time in silence. I felt the tears coming into my eyes as I thought of the poor child lying there underground. I thought of those 110 luminous grave eyes, and the curve of that beautiful forehead, the droop of the melancholy mouth, of the expression of delight which illumined his face when he learned of some new idea that pleased him, when he heard a piece of music that he liked. And this beautiful small being was dead; and the spirit that inhabited this form, the amazing spirit, that too had been destroyed almost before it had begun to exist.

And the unhappiness that must have preceded the 120 final act, the child's despair, the conviction of his utter abandonment—those were terrible to think of, terrible.

"I think we had better come away now," I said at last, and touched Carlo on the arm. He was standing there like a blind man, his eyes shut, his face slightly lifted towards the light; from between his closed eyelids the tears welled out, hung for a moment, and trickled down his cheeks. His lips trembled and I could see that he was making an effort to keep them 130 still. "Come away," I repeated.

The face which had been still in its sorrow, was suddenly convulsed; he opened his eyes, and through the tears they were bright with a violent anger. "I shall kill her," he said, "I shall kill her. When I think of him throwing himself out, falling through the air. . . ." With his two hands he made a violent gesture, bringing them down from over his head and arresting them with a sudden jerk when they were on a level with his breast. "And then crash." He shud- 140 dered. "She's as much responsible as though she had pushed him down herself. I shall kill her." He clenched his teeth.

To be angry is easier than to be sad, less painful. It is comforting to think of revenge. "Don't talk like that," I said. "It's no good. It's stupid. And what would be the point?" He had had those fits before, when grief became too painful and he had tried to escape from it. Anger had been the easiest way of escape. I had had, before this, to persuade him back into the harder path of grief. "It's stupid to talk like 150 that," I repeated, and I led him away through the ghastly labyrinth of tombs, where death seemed more terrible even than it is.

By the time we had left the cemetery, and were walking down from San Miniato towards the Piazzale Michelangelo below, he had become calmer. His anger had subsided again into sorrow from which it had derived all its strength and its bitterness. In the Piazzale we halted for a moment to look down at the city in the valley below us. It was a day of floating clouds— 160 great shapes, white, golden, and gray; and between them patches of a thin, transparent blue. Its lantern level, almost, with our eyes, the dome of the cathedral revealed itself in all its grandiose lightness, its vastness and aerial strength. On the innumerable brown and rosy roofs of the city the afternoon sunlight lay softly, sumptuously, and the towers were as though varnished and enamelled with an old gold. I thought of all the Men who had lived here and left the visible traces of their spirit and conceived extraor- 170 dinary things, I thought of the dead child.

(1924)

WYSTAN HUGH AUDEN 1907-

The most significant and the most influential of the English poets of his generation is W. H. Auden, born in York on February 21, 1907. While at Christ Church College, Oxford, where he matriculated in 1925, he became interested in literature and in writing and attracted some attention as a poet. After graduation he devoted five years to teaching in schools for boys, first in Scotland and then near Malvern, in Worcestershire. During 1935 and 1936 he was employed by the General Post Office in making documentary films.

In the meantime Auden had published several books of verse: Poems (1930); a critical analysis of contemporary life, The Orators (1932); a satirical drama, The Dance of Death (1933); and in collaboration with Christopher Isherwood, English critic and novelist and a long-time personal friend, two satirical dramas—The Dog Beneath the Skin (1935) and The Ascent of F6 (1936); and a volume of miscellanea, Look, Stranger (1936), published in the United States as On This

Island (1937). His journey to Iceland with another literary figure, Louis MacNeice, resulted in another collaborative poetic work, Letters from Iceland (1937), which is actually verse and prose mingled. Similarly, Auden took a journey to China with Isherwood, which was the basis for a joint work, Journey to a War (1939).

Auden's work, for which he was awarded the King's Gold Medal in 1937, is witty, satirical, perceptive of the vacuity of the modern social pattern—qualities which persisted in another satirical drama, On the Frontier (1938). It was clear that Auden faced toward the left in politics, but he was not, strictly speaking, a Marxist; although he sympathized with the communist viewpoint for a time, he could not bring himself to embrace the Russian cause. He drove an ambulance for the Spanish Loyalists during the civil war. But it was clear that his period of political poetry was about over. With the coming of the Second World War to Europe, he came to the United States, where he taught and lectured at various institutions and is still in considerable demand as a public reader and lecturer. In due time he became a naturalized American citizen. The second period of his literary career began with Another Time (1940) and The Double Man (1941). The latter of these is an exhaustive examination of the dualism between good and evil, of the split between body and soul, expressed in a completely skeptical and individual manner. His Collected Poems appeared in 1945, as well as a new volume, For the Time Being, but his most important recent work is The Age of Anxiety (1947), which won for its author the Pulitzer Prize for Poetry.

Auden has often been compared with Byron, and it is true that he is an ardent individualist who demands freedom for himself perhaps more than for others, but the twentieth-century Auden has none of the faith that the nineteenth-century Byron possessed. He can see no new world coming, and so he falls back upon semi-philosophical, semi-religious inquiry. His poetry is disturbed constantly with fears and anxieties, and he catches admirably the tensions and misgivings and uncertainties of the years immediately before and immediately after the Second World War; he partakes, too, of the curiously passive reaction to new and urgent circumstances of life which characterizes the liberal intellectual of the 1930's and 1940's. But his creativeness as a satirical artist is unusually rich, and it is very likely that his position in English literature will be fixed as a satirist rather than as either a lyrical, dramatic, or philosophical poet.

The young Auden—from a 1938 photograph. Historical Pictures Service—Chicago.

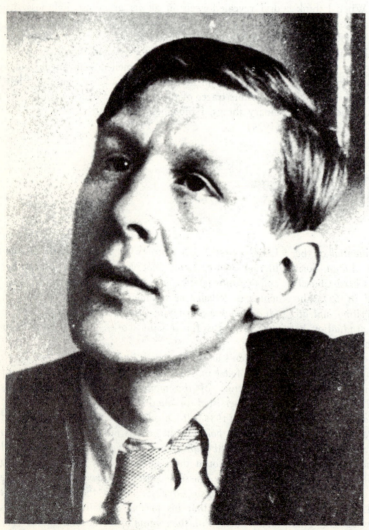

WATCH ANY DAY HIS NONCHALANT PAUSES

Watch any day his nonchalant pauses, see
His dextrous handling of a wrap as he
Steps after into cars, the beggar's envy.

"There is a free one," many say, but err.
He is not that returning conqueror,
Nor ever the poles' circumnavigator.

But poised between shocking falls on razoredge
Has taught himself this balancing subterfuge
Of the accosting profile, the erect carriage.

10 The song, the varied action of the blood
Would drown the warning from the iron
    wood
Would cancel the inertia of the buried:

Travelling by daylight on from house to
    house
The longest way to the intrinsic peace,
With love's fidelity and with love's weakness.
(1930)

THERE ARE SOME BIRDS IN THESE VALLEYS

There are some birds in these valleys
Who flutter round the careless
With intimate appeal,
By seeming kindness trained to snaring,
They feel no falseness.

Under the spell completely
They circle can serenely,
And in the tricky light
The masked hill has a purer greenness.
10 Their flight looks fleeter.

But fowlers, O, like foxes,
Lie ambushed in the rushes.
Along the harmless tracks
The madman keeper crawls through brush-
    wood,
Axe under oxter.

Alas, the signal given,
Fingers on trigger tighten.
The real unlucky dove
Must smarting fall away from brightness
Its love from living.
(1932)

EPILOGUE

This poem presents the age-old conflict between the instinct of self-preservation and the urge to risk adventure and danger. It resembles in structure an English folk-poem, "The Cutty Wren" (see The Oxford Book of Light Verse, p. 393).

"O where are you going?" said reader to rider,
"That valley is fatal when furnaces burn,
Yonder's the midden whose odors will madden,
That gap is the grave where the tall return."

"O do you imagine," said fearer to farer,
"That dusk will delay on your path to the pass,
Your diligent looking discover the lacking
Your footsteps feel from granite to grass?"

"O what was that bird," said horror to hearer,
"Did you see that shape in the twisted trees?   10
Behind you swiftly the figure comes softly,
The spot on your skin is a shocking disease?"

"Out of this house"—said rider to reader
"Yours never will"—said farer to fearer
"They're looking for you"—said hearer to horror
As he left them there, as he left them there.
(1932)

DOOM IS DARK AND DEEPER
THAN ANY SEA-DINGLE

Doom is dark and deeper than any sea-dingle.
Upon what man it fall
In spring, day-wishing flowers appearing,
Avalanche sliding, white snow from rock-face,
That he should leave his house,
No cloud-soft hand can hold him, restraint by
    women;
But ever that man goes
Through place-keepers, through forest trees,
A stranger to strangers over undried sea,
Houses for fishes, suffocating water,   10
Or lonely on fell as chat,
By pot-holed becks
A bird stone-haunting, an unquiet bird.

There head falls forward, fatigued at evening,
And dreams of home,
Waving from window, spread of welcome,
Kissing of wife under single sheet;
But waking sees

Watch Any Day His Nonchalant Pauses and *There Are Some Birds in These Valleys*, copyright 1934 and renewed 1961 by W. H. Auden. Reprinted from *Poems* by W. H. Auden (in England, *Collected Shorter Poems 1927–1957*) by permission of Random House, Inc., and Faber and Faber Ltd.
    Epilogue ("O Where Are You Going") and *Doom Is Dark and Deeper Than Any Sea-Dingle*, copyright 1934 and renewed 1961 by W. H. Auden. Reprinted from *The Collected Poetry of W. H. Auden* (in England, Col-
lected Shorter Poems 1927–1957) by permission of Random House, Inc., and Faber and Faber Ltd.
    There Are Some Birds in These Valleys. 15. oxter, the armpit or the arm.
    Epilogue. 3. midden, refuse.
    Doom Is Dark and Deeper Than Any Sea-Dingle. Note the resemblance of this poem in both style and manner of diction to the poetry of the Anglo-Saxon period. 11. chat, a kind of song sparrow.

Wystan Hugh Auden   1265

Bird-flocks nameless to him, through doorway
   voices
20 Of new men making another love.

Save him from hostile capture,
From sudden tiger's spring at corner;
Protect his house,
His anxious house where days are counted
From thunderbolt protect,
From gradual ruin spreading like a stain;
Converting number from vague to certain,
Bring joy, bring day of his returning,
Lucky with day approaching, with leaning dawn.
   (1934)

from ON THIS ISLAND

[HERE ON THE CROPPED GRASS]

Here on the cropped grass of the narrow ridge I stand,
A fathom of earth, alive in air,
Aloof as an admiral on the old rocks,
   England below me:
Eastward across the Midland plains
An express is leaving for a sailor's country;
   Westward is Wales
Where on clear evenings the retired and rich
From the french windows of their sheltered mansions
10 See the Sugarloaf standing, an upright sentinel
   Over Abergavenny.

When last I stood here I was not alone; happy
Each thought the other, thinking of a crime,
And England to our meditations seemed
   The perfect setting:
But now it has no innocence at all;
It is the isolation and the fear,
   The mood itself;
It is the body of the absent lover,
20 An image to the would-be hero of the soul,
The little area we are willing to forgive
   Upon conditions.

For private reasons I must have the truth, remember
These years have seen a boom in sorrow;
The presses of idleness issued more despair
   And it was honored,
Gross Hunger took on more hands every
   month,
Erecting here and everywhere his vast
   Unnecessary workshops;
30 Europe grew anxious about her health,

Combines tottered, credits froze,
And business shivered in a banker's winter
   While we were kissing.

Today, no longer occupied like that, I give
The children at the open swimming pool
Lithe in their first and little beauty
   A closer look;
Follow the cramped clerk crooked at his desk,
The guide in shorts pursuing flowers
   In their careers;   40
A digit of the crowd, would like to know
Them better whom the shops and trams are full of,
The little men and their mothers, not plain but
   Dreadfully ugly.

Deaf to the Welsh wind now, I hear arising
From lanterned gardens sloping to the river
Where saxophones are moaning for a comforter,
   From Gaumont theaters
Where fancy plays on hunger to produce
The noble robber, ideal of boys,   50
   And from cathedrals,
Luxury liners laden with souls,
Holding to the east their hulls of stone,
The high thin rare continuous worship
   Of the self-absorbed.

Here, which looked north before the Cambrian align-
   ment,
Like the cupped hand of the keen excavator
Busy with bones, the memory uncovers
   The hopes of time;
Of empires stiff in their brocaded glory,   60
The luscious lateral blossoming of woe
   Scented, profuse;
And of intercalary ages of disorder
When, as they prayed in antres, fell
Upon the noblest in the country night
   Angel assassins.

Small birds above me have the grace of those who
   founded
The civilization of the delicate olive,
Learning the laws of love and sailing
   On the calm Aegean;   70
The hawk is the symbol of the rule by thirst,
The central state controlling the canals;
   And the blank sky
Of the womb's utter peace before
The cell, dividing, multiplied desire,
And raised instead of death the image
   Of the reconciler.

[Here on the Cropped Grass], copyright 1937 and renewed 1964 by
W. H. Auden. Reprinted from On This Island (in England, Look, Stranger)
by W. H. Auden by permission of Random House, Inc., and Faber and
Faber Ltd.
   On This Island. 10. Sugarloaf, a mountain in western England near
Abergavenny, a small town in Monmouthshire. 23. the truth, the facts
about present conditions in England. 48. Gaumont, Léon Gaumont (d.

1946), a well-known producer of motion pictures and owner of theaters
in Britain and France. 56. Cambrian alignment, the earliest division
of the Paleozoic era in geology, so called from Cambria, or Wales, where
the system was first differentiated. The Cambrian formations indicate a
period of long duration. 63. intercalary . . . disorder, ages of disorder
interpolated among ages of order. 64. antres, caves. 66. Angel assassins, hostile bombers—winged killers. 67. Small . . . Aegean, a ref-

And over the Cotswolds now the thunder mutters:
"What little of the truth your seers saw
80 They dared not tell you plainly but combined
    Assertion and refuge
In the common language of collective lying,
In codes of a bureau, laboratory slang
    And diplomats' French.
The relations of your lovers were, alas, pictorial;
The treasure that you stole, you lost; bad luck
It brought you, but you cannot put it back
    Now with caresses.

"Already behind you your last evening hastens up
90 And all the customs your society has chosen
Harden themselves into the unbreakable
    Habits of death.
Has not your long affair with death
Of late become increasingly more serious;
    Do you not find
Him growing more attractive every day?
You shall go under and help him with the crops,
Be faithful to him, and to your friends
    Remain indifferent."

100 And out of the turf the bones of the war continue;
"Know then, cousin, the major cause of our collapse
Was a distortion in the human plastic by luxury pro-
    duced,

Never higher than in our time were the vital advantages;
To matter entire, to the unbounded vigors of the in-
    strument,
To all logical precision we were the rejoicing heirs.

But pompous, we assumed their power to be our own,
Believed machines to be our hearts' spontaneous fruit,
Taking our premises as shoppers take a tram.

While the disciplined love which alone could have em-
    ployed these engines
Seemed far too difficult and dull, and when hatred
110   promised
An immediate dividend, all of us hated.

Denying the liberty we knew quite well to be our
    destiny,
It dogged our steps with its accusing shadow
Until in every landscape we saw murder ambushed.

Unable to endure ourselves, we sought relief
In the insouciance of the soldier, the heroic sexual
    pose
Playing at fathers to impress the little ladies.

Call us not tragic; falseness made farcical our death:
Nor brave; ours was the will of the insane to suffer
By which since we could not live we gladly died: 120
And now we have gone for ever to our foolish graves."

The Priory clock chimes briefly and I recollect
I am expected to return alive
My will effective and my nerves in order
    To my situation.
"The poetry is in the pity," Wilfred said,
And Kathy in her journal, "To be rooted in life,
    That's what I want."
These moods give no permission to be idle,
For men are changed by what they do;   130
And through loss and anger the hands of the unlucky
    Love one another.
(1936)

---

from IN TIME OF WAR

1

So from the years the gifts were showered; each
Ran off with his at once into his life:
Bee took the politics that make a hive,
Fish swam as fish, peach settled into peach.

And were successful at the first endeavor;
The hour of birth their only time at college,
They were content with their precocious knowledge,
And knew their station and were good forever.

Till finally there came a childish creature
On whom the years could model any feature,   10
And fake with ease a leopard or a dove;

erence to the civilization of ancient Greece, which has perished. 71.
hawk . . . thirst, etc., a warning of the possible doom of England's
civilization. 78. **Cotswolds,** large hilly tracts in eastern Gloucestershire.
115. **Unable . . . ladies,** an allusion to the part played by capitalism in
fostering war and low morals. 122. **Priory,** monastic house. 126.
Wilfred, Wilfred Owen (1893–1918), perhaps the most gifted of the
English poets produced by World War I. 127. **Kathy,** Katherine Mans-

field (1888–1923), a gifted short story writer.
In Time of War. This poem consists of a group of sonnets written
when Auden was on a trip to China during the war.
Sonnets 1, 2, 4, 5, 6, 7 from In Time of War, copyright 1945 by
W. H. Auden. Reprinted from *The Collected Poetry of W. H. Auden* (in
England, *Collected Shorter Poems 1927–1957*) by permission of Random
House, Inc., and Faber and Faber Ltd.

Who by the lightest wind was changed and shaken,
And looked for truth and was continually mistaken,
And envied his few friends and chose his love.

2

They wondered why the fruit had been forbidden;
It taught them nothing new. They hid their pride,
But did not listen much when they were chidden;
They knew exactly what to do outside.

They left: immediately the memory faded
Of all they'd learnt; they could not understand
The dogs now who, before, had always aided;
The stream was dumb with whom they'd always
    planned.

They wept and quarreled: freedom was so wild.
10 In front, maturity, as he ascended,
Retired like a horizon from the child;

The dangers and the punishments grew greater:
And the way back by angels was defended
Against the poet and the legislator.

4

He stayed: and was imprisoned in possession.
The seasons stood like guards about his ways,
The mountains chose the mother of his children,
And like a conscience the sun ruled his days.

Beyond him his young cousins in the city
Pursued their rapid and unnatural course,
Believed in nothing but were easy-going,
And treated strangers like a favorite horse.

And he changed little,
10 But took his color from the earth,
And grew in likeness to his sheep and cattle.

The townsman thought him miserly and simple,
The poet wept and saw in him the truth,
And the oppressor held him up as an example.

5

His generous bearing was a new invention:
For life was slow; earth needed to be careless;
With horse and sword he drew the girls' attention;
He was the Rich, the Bountiful, the Fearless.

And to the young he came as a salvation;
They needed him to free them from their mothers,

In Memory of W. B. Yeats. See headnote, p. 1196. **1. He . . .
winter.** Yeats died on January 28, 1939. **25. Bourse,** the name of the
stock exchange in Paris.

And grew sharp-witted in the long migration,
And round his camp fires learnt all men are brothers.

But suddenly the earth was full: he was not wanted.
And he became the shabby and demented,   10
And took to drink to screw his nerves to murder;

Or sat in offices and stole,
And spoke approvingly of Law and Order,
And hated life with all his soul.

6

He watched the stars and noted birds in flight;
The rivers flooded or the Empire fell:
He made predictions and was sometimes right;
His lucky guesses were rewarded well.

And fell in love with Truth before he knew her,
And rode into imaginary lands,
With solitude and fasting hoped to woo her,
And mocked at those who served her with their hands.

But her he never wanted to despise,
But listened always for her voice; and when   10
She beckoned to him, he obeyed in meekness,

And followed her and looked into her eyes;
Saw there reflected every human weakness,
And saw himself as one of many men.

7

He was their servant—some say he was blind—
And moved among their faces and their things;
Their feeling gathered in him like a wind
And sang: they cried—"It is a God that sings"—

And worshiped him and set him up apart,
And made him vain, till he mistook for song
The little tremors of his mind and heart
At each domestic wrong.

Songs came no more: he had to make them.
With what precision was each strophe planned,   10
He hugged his sorrow like a plot of land,

And walked like an assassin through the town,
And looked at men and did not like them,
But trembled if one passed him with a frown.

IN MEMORY OF W. B. YEATS

1

He disappeared in the dead of winter:
The brooks were frozen, the air-ports almost deserted,

And snow disfigured the public statues;
The mercury sank in the mouth of the dying day.
O all the instruments agree
The day of his death was a dark cold day.

Far from his illness
The wolves ran on through the evergreen forests,
The peasant river was untempted by the fashionable
    quays;
10 By mourning tongues
The death of the poet was kept from his poems.

But for him it was his last afternoon as himself,
An afternoon of nurses and rumors;
The provinces of his body revolted,
The squares of his mind were empty,
Silence invaded the suburbs,
The current of his feeling failed: he became his
    admirers.

Now he is scattered among a hundred cities
And wholly given over to unfamiliar affections;
20 To find his happiness in another kind of wood
And be punished under a foreign code of conscience.
The words of a dead man
Are modified in the guts of the living.

But in the importance and noise of tomorrow
When the brokers are roaring like beasts on the floor
    of the Bourse,
And the poor have the sufferings to which they are
    fairly accustomed,
And each in the cell of himself is almost convinced of
    his freedom;
A few thousand will think of this day
As one thinks of a day when one did something
    slightly unusual.

30 O all the instruments agree
The day of his death was a dark cold day.

2

You were silly like us: your gift survived it all;
The parish of rich women, physical decay,
Yourself; mad Ireland hurt you into poetry.
Now Ireland has her madness and her weather still,
For poetry makes nothing happen: it survives
In the valley of its saying where executives
Would never want to tamper; it flows south
From ranches of isolation and the busy griefs,
40 Raw towns that we believe and die in; it survives,
A way of happening, a mouth.

3

Earth, receive an honored guest;
William Yeats is laid to rest:
Let the Irish vessel lie
Emptied of its poetry.

Time that is intolerant
Of the brave and innocent,
And indifferent in a week
To a beautiful physique,   50

Worships language and forgives
Everyone by whom it lives;
Pardons cowardice, conceit,
Lays its honors at their feet.

Time that with this strange excuse
Pardoned Kipling and his views,
And will pardon Paul Claudel,
Pardons him for writing well.

In the nightmare of the dark   60
All the dogs of Europe bark,
And the living nations wait,
Each sequestered in its hate;

Intellectual disgrace
Stares from every human face,
And the seas of pity lie
Locked and frozen in each eye.

Follow, poet, follow right
To the bottom of the night,
With your unconstraining voice
Still persuade us to rejoice;   70

With the farming of a verse
Make a vineyard of the curse,
Sing of human unsuccess
In a rapture of distress;

In the deserts of the heart
Let the healing fountain start,
In the prison of his days
Teach the free man how to praise.
(1940)

MUSÉE DES BEAUX ARTS

About suffering they were never wrong,
The Old Masters: how well they understood
Its human position; how it takes place

---

55. **Pardoned . . . views.** Rudyard Kipling (p. 1128) said some very sharp things about English conservatism and complacency. His views probably prevented him from being made poet laureate; see, for example, his *Recessional* (p. 1134). 56. **Claudel,** Paul Claudel (1868–1955), a French poet, playwright, and diplomat who occupied a high position in contemporary French poetry. 71. **vineyard . . . curse,** a reference to

Adam and Eve being driven out of the Garden of Eden. The meaning is, of course, to make good out of bad.
    In Memory of W. B. Yeats and *Musée des Beaux Arts,* copyright 1940 by W. H. Auden. Reprinted from *The Collected Poetry of W. H. Auden* (in England, *Collected Shorter Poems 1927–1957*) by permission of Random House, Inc., and Faber and Faber Ltd.

While someone else is eating or opening a window or
    just walking dully along;
How, when the aged are reverently, passionately
    waiting
For the miraculous birth, there always must be
Children who did not specially want it to happen,
    skating
On a pond at the edge of the wood:
They never forgot
10 That even the dreadful martyrdom must run its course
Anyhow in a corner, some untidy spot
Where the dogs go on with their doggy life and the
    torturer's horse
Scratches its innocent behind on a tree.

In Breughel's *Icarus*, for instance: how everything
    turns away
Quite leisurely from the disaster; the ploughman may
Have heard the splash, the forsaken cry,
But for him it was not an important failure; the sun
    shone
As it had to on the white legs disappearing into the
    green
Water; and the expensive delicate ship that must have
    seen
Something amazing, a boy falling out of the sky,   20
Had somewhere to get to and sailed calmly on.
(1940)

Musée des Beaux Arts. The title means *Museum of Fine Arts*, which is the name of the Brussels museum housing Breughel's *Icarus*. 14. **Breughel,** Pieter Breughel (1568–1625), a noted Flemish painter. **Icarus** was in Greek legend an Athenian youth who tried to escape from Crete with his father by the use of artificial wings. He flew too near the sun; the wax of the wings melted and he fell into the sea and was drowned.

STEPHEN SPENDER 1909-

The son of talented parents—his father, Edward H. Spender, was a novelist, journalist, and lecturer—Stephen Spender was born near London and attended University College, Oxford. While at the university, he served as one of the editors of the Oxford Poetry anthologies and published his first efforts at writing verse—Nine Experiments (1928) and Twenty Poems (1930). In a more significant volume, Poems (1933), he revealed genuine poetic gifts, shown both in technique and in purposefulness. He was, like many of the young poets of the 1930's, strongly stirred by left-wing ideas, as in Vienna (1934), a long didactic poem, and Trial of a Judge (1938). Since the Second World War, however, Spender has shown himself to be more and more of a romanticist; disillusioned by the harsh realities of modern power politics and social programs, he has turned to personal themes, as in The Still Centre (1939), Selected Poems (1940), Ruins and Visions (1941), and Poems of Dedication (1946). But he attracted much attention by a book of criticism, The Destructive Element (1935), and, along with other works in that field, has tried his hand at psychological fiction, political essays, and travel journals. Of late he has assumed the position of a miscellaneous writer and journalist. His autobiography World Within World was published in 1951.

ROLLED OVER ON EUROPE

Rolled over on Europe: the sharp dew frozen to
    stars
Below us: above our heads the night
Frozen again to stars: the stars
In pools between our coats, and that charmed
    moon:
Ah, what supports? What cross draws out our
    arms,
Heaves up our bodies towards the wind
And hammers us between the mirrored lights?

Only my body is real: which wolves
Are free to oppress and gnaw. Only this rose
My friend laid on my breast, and these few
10   lines
Written from home, are real.
(1933)

Rolled Over on Europe; Your Body Is Stars; Without That Once Clear Aim; I Think Continually of Those; The Pylons; Not Palaces, an Era's Crown; and What I Expected, copyright 1934 and renewed 1961 by Stephen Spender. Reprinted from *Collected Poems 1928–1953* (in England,

YOUR BODY IS STARS

Your body is stars whose million glitter here:
I am lost amongst the branches of this sky
Here near my breast, here in my nostrils, here
Where our vast arms like streams of fire lie.

How can this end? My healing fills the night
And hangs its flags in worlds I cannot near.
Our movements range through miles, and when we kiss
The moment widens to enclose long years. . . .

Beholders of the promised dawn of truth
The explorers of immense and simple lines,   10
Here is our goal, men cried, but it was lost
Amongst the mountain mists and mountain pines.

So with this face of love, whose breathings are
A mystery shadowed on the desert floor:

Collected Poems) by Stephen Spender by permission of Random House, Inc., and Faber and Faber Ltd.
The Pylons. A pylon is a steel or concrete tower used to support telegraph or electric power lines over a long span.

The promise hangs, this swarm of stars and flowers,
And then there comes the shutting of a door.
(1933)

WITHOUT THAT ONCE CLEAR AIM

Without that once clear aim, the path of flight
To follow for a life-time through white air,
This century chokes me under roots of night
I suffer like history in Dark Ages, where
Truth lies in dungeons, from which drifts no whisper:
We hear of towers long broken off from sight
And tortures and war, in dark and smoky rumor,
But on men's buried lives there falls no light.

Watch me who walk through coiling streets where
    rain
10 And fog drown every cry: at corners of day
Road drills explore new areas of pain,
Nor summer nor light may reach down here to play.
The city builds its horror in my brain,
This writing is my only wings away.
(1933)

I THINK CONTINUALLY OF THOSE

I think continually of those who were truly great.
Who, from the womb, remembered the soul's history
Through corridors of light where the hours are suns
Endless and singing. Whose lovely ambition
Was that their lips, still touched with fire,
Should tell of the Spirit clothed from head to foot in
    song.
And who hoarded from the Spring branches
The desires falling across their bodies like blossoms.

What is precious is never to forget
The essential delight of the blood drawn from ageless
10   springs
Breaking through rocks in worlds before our earth.
Never to deny its pleasure in the morning simple light
Nor its grave evening demand for love.
Never to allow gradually the traffic to smother
With noise and fog the flowering of the spirit.

Near the snow, near the sun, in the highest fields
See how these names are feted by the waving grass
And by the streamers of white cloud
And whispers of wind in the listening sky.
20 The names of those who in their lives fought for life
Who wore at their hearts the fire's center.
Born of the sun they travelled a short while towards
    the sun,
And left the vivid air signed with their honor.
(1933)

THE PYLONS

The secret of these hills was stone, and cottages
Of that stone made,
And crumbling roads
That turned on sudden hidden villages.

Now over these small hills they have built the concrete
That trails black wire:
Pylons, those pillars
Bare like nude, giant girls that have no secret.

The valley with its gilt and evening look
And the green chestnut   10
Of customary root
Are mocked dry like the parched bed of a brook.

But far above and far as sight endures
Like whips of anger
With lightning's danger
There runs the quick perspective of the future.

This dwarfs our emerald country by its trek
So tall with prophecy:
Dreaming of cities
Where often clouds shall lean their swan-white neck.
(1933)

NOT PALACES, AN ERA'S CROWN

Not palaces, an era's crown
Where the mind dwells, intrigues, rests;
The architectural gold-leaved flower
From people ordered like a single mind,
I build. This only what I tell:
It is too late for rare accumulation
For family pride, for beauty's filtered dusts;
I say, stamping the words with emphasis,
Drink from here energy and only energy,
As from the electric charge of a battery,   10
To will this Time's change.
Eye, gazelle, delicate wanderer,
Drinker of horizon's fluid line,
Ear that suspends on a chord
The spirit drinking timelessness;
Touch, love, all senses,
Leave your gardens, your singing feasts,
Your dreams of suns circling before our sun,
Of heaven after our world.
Instead, watch images of flashing brass   20
That strike the outward sense, the polished
    will,
Flag of our purpose which the wind engraves.
No spirit seek here rest. But this: No man
Shall hunger: Man shall spend equally.
Our goal which we compel: Man shall be man.

—That program of the antique Satan
Bristling with guns on the indented page
With battleship towering from hilly waves:
For what? Drive of a ruining purpose
30 Destroying all but its age-long exploiters.
Our program like this, yet opposite,
Death to the killers, bringing light to life.
(1933)

WHAT I EXPECTED

What I expected was
Thunder, fighting,
Long struggles with men
And climbing.
After continual straining
I should grow strong;
Then the rocks would shake
And I should rest long.

What I had not foreseen
10 Was the gradual day
Weakening the will
Leaking the brightness away,
The lack of good to touch
The fading of body and soul
Like smoke before wind
Corrupt, unsubstantial.

The wearing of Time,
And the watching of cripples pass
With limbs shaped like questions
20 In their odd twist,
The pulverous grief
Melting the bones with pity,
The sick falling from earth—
These, I could not foresee.

For I had expected always
Some brightness to hold in trust,

Some final innocence
To save from dust;
That, hanging solid,
Would dangle through all   30
Like the created poem
Or the dazzling crystal.
(1933)

THE BOMBED HAPPINESS

Children, who extend their smile of crystal,
And their leaping gold embrace,
And wear their happiness as a frank jewel,
Are forced in the mould of the groaning bull
And engraved with lines on the face.

Their harlequin-striped flesh,
Their blood twisted in rivers of song,
Their flashing, trustful emptiness,
Are trampled by an outer heart that pressed
From the sky right through the coral breast   10
And kissed the heart and burst.

This timed, exploding heart that breaks
The loved and little hearts, is also one
Splintered through the lungs and wombs
And fragments of squares in the sun,
And crushing the floating, sleeping babe
Into a deeper sleep.

Its victoried drumming enters
Above the limbs of bombed laughter
The body of an expanding State   20
And throbs there and makes it great,
But nothing nothing can recall
Gaiety buried under these dead years,
Sweet jester and young playing fool
Whose toy was human happiness.
(1939)

The Bombed Happiness, copyright 1942 by Stephen Spender. Reprinted from Poems 1934–1942 (in England, The Still Centre) by Stephen Spender by permission of Random House, Inc., and Faber and Faber Ltd.

The Bombed Happiness. 6. harlequin-striped, bearing marks or stripes like those on the parti-colored suit worn by the Harlequin, a character in popular Italian comedy.

DYLAN THOMAS 1914-1953

Dylan Thomas was born in Wales in 1914 and was educated at Swansea Grammar School, where his father taught English. He published Eighteen Poems in 1934 and Twenty-Five Poems in 1936, both volumes attracting less attention than they might have if the star of Auden had not been at the time so definitely in the ascendant. The Map of Love and The World I Breathe both appeared in 1939, New Poems in 1943, and Death and Entrances in 1946. During the Second World War Thomas was a documentary film editor for the British Broadcasting Company. He came to America in 1950 for a short visit and returned in January 1952 for an extended lecture tour. An extraordinary reader of poetry, he was enthusiastically received in dozens of American colleges and universities. He died on November 9, 1953 at St. Vincent's Hospital in New York.

In his first poems, Thomas showed an unquestionable affinity for the surrealistic, as well as a glut of imagery drawn from primitive Celtic rituals of rebirth and sacrifice, but in his later poems, without losing any of the typical Celtic "magic of words," he gained greater control of style and metaphor. Thomas, like Eliot, has been charged with willful obscurity, and if this is at times true, it is an obscurity that comes not from the use of far-fetched allusions to unfamiliar readings, but from a tremendous condensation of metaphor and syntax that sometimes seems impenetrable to rational analysis, a poetic density that creates a magic verbal world which is its own subject.

The sudden death of Thomas at the age of thirty-nine activated an unusually large number of critical and biographical studies, but it is still difficult to assess how much of this attention was due to the circumstances of his life and death and how much to the excellence of his work. The corpus of his work is quite small. There are only ninety-two poems in his Collected Poems (1953), all of them short lyrics. Two plays, The Doctor and the Devils (1953), a filmscript, and Under Milk Wood (1954), a verse play for broadcasting, three chapters of an uncompleted novel, Adventures in the Skin Trade (1941), seven tales in prose, included in The Map of Love (1939), a thinly veiled autobiography, Portrait of the Artist As a Young Dog (1940) comprehend the general scope of his creative output. There is no doubt, however, that at least a score of his short lyrics are among the finest that have been produced in this century. It remains for posterity to evaluate more fully whether he is entitled to the rank of a major poet. But few can remain unmoved by the richness of sound and metaphor, the startlingly fresh refurbishing of stale diction and syntax; many would agree with Sir Herbert Read's judgment of Thomas' poetry — "the most absolute poetry that has been written in our time."

THE FORCE THAT THROUGH THE GREEN FUSE DRIVES THE FLOWER

The force that through the green fuse drives the flower
Drives my green age; that blasts the roots of trees
Is my destroyer.
And I am dumb to tell the crooked rose
My youth is bent by the same wintry fever.

The force that drives the water through the rocks
Drives my red blood; that dries the mouthing streams
Turns mine to wax.
And I am dumb to mouth unto my veins
10 How at the mountain spring the same mouth sucks.

The hand that whirls the water in the pool
Stirs the quicksand; that ropes the blowing wind
Hauls my shroud sail.
And I am dumb to tell the hanging man
How of my clay is made the hangman's lime.

The lips of time leech to the fountain head;
Love drips and gathers, but the fallen blood
Shall calm her sores.
And I am dumb to tell a weather's wind
How time has ticked a heaven round the stars.   20

And I am dumb to tell the lover's tomb
How at my sheet goes the same crooked worm.
(1934; 1952)

TO-DAY, THIS INSECT, AND THE WORLD I BREATHE

Here, as in all of Thomas' poems, there is a reliance on words as the basis of images out of which an idea originates; the sound is even more important than the strict sense. In this poem Thomas is stating his creed that through the creation of poetry the poet can create also the magic of belief. No matter what the external symbols of disaster, Thomas insists that the poet should write of his "madman's love of man" and do what he can to bring this love to pass.

To-day, this insect, and the world I breathe,
Now that my symbols have outelbowed space,
Time at the city spectacles, and half
The dear, daft time I take to nudge the sentence,
In trust and tale have I divided sense,
Slapped down the guillotine, the blood-red double
Of head and tail made witnesses to this
Murder of Eden and green genesis.

The insect certain is the plague of fables.

10 This story's monster has a serpent caul,
Blind in the coil scrams round the blazing outline,
Measures his own length on the garden wall
And breaks his shell in the last shocked beginning;
A crocodile before the chrysalis,
Before the fall from love the flying heartbone,
Winged like a sabbath ass this children's piece
Uncredited blows Jericho on Eden.

The insect fable is the certain promise.

Death: death of Hamlet and the nightmare madmen,
20 An air-drawn windmill on a wooden horse,
John's beast, Job's patience, and the fibs of vision,
Greek in the Irish sea the ageless voice:

'Adam I love, my madmen's love is endless,
No tell-tale lover has an end more certain,
All legends' sweethearts on a tree of stories,
My cross of tales behind the fabulous curtain.'
(1936)

THE HAND THAT SIGNED THE PAPER FELLED A CITY

This poem was most probably inspired by the Munich crisis of 1938 (see p. 1158).

The hand that signed the paper felled a city;
Five sovereign fingers taxed the breath,
Doubled the globe of dead and halved a country;
These five kings did a king to death.

The mighty hand leads to a sloping shoulder,
The finger joints are cramped with chalk;
A goose's quill has put an end to murder
That put an end to talk.

The hand that signed the treaty bred a fever,
And famine grew, and locusts came;   10
Great is the hand that holds dominion over
Man by a scribbled name.

The five kings count the dead but do not soften
The crusted wound nor pat the brow;
A hand rules pity as a hand rules heaven;
Hands have no tears to flow.
(1936)

WHEN ALL MY FIVE AND COUNTRY SENSES SEE

This poem is a good example of Thomas' felicitous "word-madness." It is obviously an appeal for a return to the sensuous and sensual as the only way of creating and feeling.

When all my five and country senses see,
The fingers will forget green thumbs and mark
How, through the halfmoon's vegetable eye,
Husk of young stars and handfull zodiac,
Love in the frost is pared and wintered by,
The whispering ears will watch love drummed away
Down breeze and shell to a discordant beach,
And, lashed to syllables, the lynx tongue cry
That her fond wounds are mended bitterly.
My nostrils see her breath burn like a bush.   10

My one and noble heart has witnesses
In all love's countries, that will grope awake;
And when blind sleep drops on the spying senses,
The heart is sensual, though five eyes break.
(1939)

FERN HILL

This poem might well be compared with Wordsworth's Prelude in intent, though it is radically different in style and philosophy. But in both poems

---

To-day, This Insect. **8-21. Murder of Eden . . . vision.** These lines contain a series of metaphors and allusions to illustrate how violence and evil break in upon the ideal peaceful condition of life typified by the Garden of Eden. This violence and evil is "the insect"

of the poem. **Jericho,** the Old Testament city destroyed by Joshua (see the Biblical Book of Joshua), illustrates human destruction. (l. 17); the windmill and the horse (l. 20), as well as the "fibs of vision" (l. 21) illustrate the dangers of impractical or false visions or ideals, as

*there is the autobiographical account of the impression
made by nature upon the youthful poet.*

Now as I was young and easy under the apple boughs
About the lilting house and happy as the grass was
      green,
    The night above the dingle starry,
        Time let me hail and climb
    Golden in the heydays of his eyes,
And honoured among wagons I was prince of the apple
      towns
And once below a time I lordly had the trees and leaves
      Trail with daisies and barley
    Down the rivers of the windfall light.

And as I was green and carefree, famous among the
10   barns
About the happy yard and singing as the farm was
      home,
    In the sun that is young once only,
        Time let me play and be
    Golden in the mercy of his means,
And green and golden I was huntsman and herdsman,
      the calves
Sang to my horn, the foxes on the hills barked clear
      and cold,
        And the sabbath rang slowly
    In the pebbles of the holy streams.

All the sun long it was running, it was lovely, the hay
Fields high as the house, the tunes from the chimneys,
20   it was air,
    And playing, lovely and watery
        And fire green as grass.
    And nightly under the simple stars
As I rode to sleep the owls were bearing the farm away,
All the moon long I heard, blessed among stables, the
      nightjars
    Flying with the ricks, and the horses
        Flashing into the dark.

And then to awake, and the farm, like a wanderer white
With the dew, come back, the cock on his shoulder: it
      was all
30   Shining, it was Adam and maiden,
        The sky gathered again
    And the sun grew round that very day.
So it must have been after the birth of the simple light
In the first, spinning place, the spellbound horses
      walking warm
    Out of the whinnying green stable
        On to the fields of praise.

And honoured among foxes and pheasants by the gay
      house
Under the new made clouds and happy as the heart
      was long,
    In the sun born over and over,
        I ran my heedless ways,   40
    My wishes raced through the house high hay
And nothing I cared, at my sky blue trades, that time
      allows
In all his tuneful turning so few and such morning
      songs
    Before the children green and golden
        Follow him out of grace,

Nothing I cared, in the lamb white days, that time
      would take me
Up to the swallow thronged loft by the shadow of my
      hand,
    In the moon that is always rising,
        Nor that riding to sleep
I should hear him fly with the high fields   50
And wake to the farm forever fled from the childless
      land.
Oh as I was young and easy in the mercy of his
      means,
        Time held me green and dying
    Though I sang in my chains like the sea.
(1946)

HOLY SPRING

*This is a spring song in time of war, which may
well mean that it will be our last spring.*

        O
    Out of a bed of love
When that immortal hospital made one more move to
      soothe
      The cureless counted body,
        And ruin and his causes
Over the barbed and shooting sea assured an army
        And swept into our wounds and houses,
I climb to greet the war in which I have no heart but
      only
        That one dark I owe my light,
Call for confessor and wiser mirror but there is none
        To glow after the god stoning night   10
And I am struck as lonely as a holy maker by the sun.

        No
    Praise that the spring time is all
Gabriel and radiant shrubbery as the morning grows
      joyful

---

typified in Don Quixote's adventures. **21. John's beast,** the Beast
referred to in the Book of Revelation, the apocalyptic vision of St. John
the Evangelist.
    When All My Five and Country Senses See. **14. five eyes,** the

five senses.
    Holy Spring. **8. That one . . . light.** The poet, through this de-
liberately dark metaphor, explains that he does not have any real heart
for war but is trying in a groping manner to discover its purposes.

Out of the woebegone pyre
And the multitude's sultry tear turns cool on the
  weeping wall,
   My arising prodigal
Sun the father his quiver full of the infants of pure fire,
   But blessed be hail and upheaval
That uncalm still it is sure alone to stand and sing
20   Alone in the husk of man's home
And the mother and toppling house of the holy spring,
   If only for a last time.
(1946)

AMONG THOSE KILLED IN THE DAWN RAID WAS A MAN AGED A HUNDRED

When the morning was waking over the war
He put on his clothes and stepped out and he died,
The locks yawned loose and a blast blew them wide,
He dropped where he loved on the burst pavement stone
And the funeral grains of the slaughtered floor.
Tell his street on its back he stopped a sun
And the craters of his eyes grew springshoots and fire
When all the keys shot from the locks, and rang.

Dig no more for the chains of his grey-haired heart.
10 The heavenly ambulance drawn by a wound
Assembling waits for the spades' ring on the cage.
O keep his bones away from that common cart,
The morning is flying on the wings of his age
And a hundred storks perch on the sun's right hand.
(1943)

AND DEATH SHALL HAVE NO DOMINION

And death shall have no dominion.
Dead men naked they shall be one
With the man in the wind and the west moon;
When their bones are picked clean and the clean bones
  gone,
They shall have stars at elbow and foot;
Though they go mad they shall be sane,
Though they sink through the sea they shall rise
  again;
Though lovers be lost love shall not;
And death shall have no dominion.

And death shall have no dominion.   10
Under the windings of the sea
They lying long shall not die windily;
Twisting on racks when sinews give way,
Strapped to a wheel, yet they shall not break;
Faith in their hands shall snap in two,
And the unicorn evils run them through;
Split all ends up they shan't crack;
And death shall have no dominion.

And death shall have no dominion.
No more may gulls cry at their ears   20
Or waves break loud on the seashores;
Where blew a flower may a flower no more
Lift its head to the blows of the rain;
Though they be mad and dead as nails,
Heads of the characters hammer through daisies;
Break in the sun till the sun breaks down,
And death shall have no dominion.
(1936)

IN MY CRAFT OR SULLEN ART

In my craft or sullen art
Exercised in the still night
When only the moon rages
And the lovers lie abed
With all their griefs in their arms,
I labor by singing light
Not for ambition or bread
Or the strut and trade of charms
On the ivory stages
But for the common wages   10
Of their most secret heart.

Not for the proud man apart
From the raging moon I write
On these spindrift pages
Nor for the towering dead
With their nightingales and psalms
But for the lovers, their arms
Round the griefs of the ages,
Who pay no praise or wages
Nor heed my craft or art.   20
(1946)

Among Those Killed in the Dawn Raid. Note that this is a sonnet in form. 6. **sun,** a symbol of life ever returning. 14. **storks,** symbols of life reborn as the ancient die.

INDEX OF AUTHORS AND TITLES

INDEX OF FIRST LINES